IN SIX VOLUMES, CAREFULLY REVISED AND CORRECTED

MATTHEW HENRY'S COMMENTARY

ON THE WHOLE BIBLE

WHEREIN EACH CHAPTER IS SUMMED UP IN ITS CONTENTS: THE SACRED TEXT INSERTED AT LARGE IN DISTINCT PARAGRAPHS; EACH PARAGRAPH REDUCED TO ITS PROPER HEADS: THE SENSE GIVEN, AND LARGELY ILLUSTRATED

WITH

PRACTICAL REMARKS AND OBSERVATIONS

VOL. II.—JOSHUA TO ESTHER

MAC DONALD PUBLISHING COMPANY
MC LEAN, VIRGINIA 22102

ISBN 0-917006-21-6

PREFACE.

This second volume of methodized and practical expositions of the inspired writings ventures abroad with fear and trembling in the same plain and homely dress with the former on the Pentateuch. *Ornari res ipsa negat; contenta doceri—the subject requires no ornament; to have it apprehended is all.* But I trust, through grace, it proceeds from the same honest design to promote the knowledge of the scripture, in order to the reforming of men's hearts and lives. If I may but be instrumental to make my readers wise and good, wiser and better, more watchful against sin and more careful of their duty both to God and man, and, in order thereto, more in love with the word and law of God, I have all I desire, all I aim at. *May he that ministereth seed to the sower multiply the seed sown, by increasing the fruits of* our *righteousness*, 2 Cor. ix. 10. It is the history of the Jewish church and nation that fills this volume, from their first settlement in the promised land, after their 430 years' bondage in Egypt and their forty years' wandering in the wilderness, to their re-settlement there after their seventy years' captivity in Babylon—from Joshua to Nehemiah. The five books of Moses were taken up more with their laws, institutes, and charters; but all these books are purely historical, and in this way of writing a great deal of very valuable learning and wisdom has been conveyed from one generation to another. The chronology of this history, and the ascertaining of the times when the several events contained in it happened, would very much illustrate the history, and add to the brightness of it; it is therefore well worthy the search of the curious and ingenious, and they may find both pleasure and profit in perusing the labours of many learned men who have directed their studies that way. I confess I could willingly have entertained myself and reader, in this preface, with a calculation of the times through which this history passes; but I consider that such a babe in knowledge as I am could not pretend either to add to or correct what has been done by so many great writers, much less to decide the controversies that have been agitated among them. I had indeed some thoughts of consulting my worthy and ever-honoured friend Mr. Tallents of Shrewsbury, the learned author of the "View of Universal History," and of begging some advice and assistance from him in methodizing the contents of this history; but, in the very week in which I put my last hand to this part, it pleased God to put an end to his useful life (and useful it was to the last) and to call him to his rest, in the eighty-ninth year of his age: so that purpose was broken off, that thought of my heart. But that elaborate performance of his commonly called his "Chronological Tables" gives great light to this, as indeed to all other parts of history. And Dr. Lightfoot's "Chronology of the Old Testament," and Mr. Cradock's "History of the Old Testament Methodized," may also be of great use to such readers as I write for. As to the particular chronological difficulties which occur in the thread of this history, I have not been large upon them, because many times I could not satisfy myself, and how then could I satisfy my reader concerning them? I have not indeed met with any difficulties so great but that solutions might be given of them sufficient to silence the atheists and antiscripturists, and roll away from the sacred records all the reproach of contradiction and inconsistency with themselves; for, to do that, it is enough to show that the difference may be accommodated either this way or that, when at the same time one cannot satisfy one's self which way is the right. But it is well that these are things about which we may very safely and very comfortably be ignorant and unresolved. What concerns our salvation is plain enough, and we need not perplex ourselves about the niceties of chronology, genealogy, or chorography. At least my undertaking leads me not into those labyrinths. What is *profitable for doctrine, for reproof, for correction, and for instruction in righteousness*, is what I intend to observe, and I would endeavour to open what is dark and hard to be understood only in order to that. Every author must be taken in his way of writing; the sacred penmen, as they have not left us formal systems, so they have not left us formal annals, but useful narratives of things proper for our direction in the way of duty, which some great judges of common writers have thought to be the most pleasant and profitable histories, and most likely to answer the end. The word of God *manifestis pascit, obscuris exercet* (Aug. in Joh. Tract. 45), as one of the ancients expresses it, that is, *it has enough in it that is easy to nourish the meanest to life eternal, yet enough that is difficult to try the industry and humility of the greatest.* There are several things which should recommend this part of sacred writ to our diligent and constant search.

I. That it is *history*, and therefore entertaining and very pleasant, edifying and very serviceable to the conduct of human life. It gratifies the inquisitive with the knowledge of that which the most intense speculation could not discover any other way. By a retirement into ourselves, and a serious contemplation of the objects we are surrounded with, close reasoning may advance many excellent truths without being beholden to any other. But for the knowledge of past events we are entirely indebted (and must be so) to the reports and records of others. A notion or hypothesis of a man's own framing may gain him the reputation of a wit, but a history of a man's own framing will lay him under the reproach of a cheat any further than as it respects that which he himself is an eye or ear-witness of. How much are we indebted then to the divine wisdom and goodness for these writings, which have made things so long since past as familiar to us as any of the occurrences of the age and place we live in! History is so edifying that parables and apologues have been invented to make up the deficiencies of it for our instruction concerning good and evil; and, whatever may be said of other history, we are sure that in this history there is no matter of fact recorded but what has its use and will help either to expound God's providence or guide man's prudence.

II. That it is *true* history, and what we may rely upon the credit of, and need not fear being deceived in. That which the heathens reckoned *tempus* ἄδηλον *(which they knew nothing at all of)* and *tempus* μυθικὸν *(the account of which was wholly fabulous)* is to us *tempus* ἱστορικὸν, *what we have a most authentic account of*. The Greeks were with them the most celebrated historians, and yet their successors in learning and dominion, the Romans, put them into no good name for their credibility, witness that of the poet: *Et quicquid Græcia mendax audet in historia—All that lying Greece has dared to record*, Juv. Sat. 10. But the history which we have before us is of undoubted certainty, and no cunningly devised fable. To be well assured of this is a great satisfaction, especially since we meet with so many things in it truly miraculous, and many more great and marvellous.

III. That it is *ancient* history, far more ancient than was ever pretended to come from any other hand. Homer, the most ancient genuine heathen writer now entirely extant, is reckoned to have lived at the beginning of the Olympiads, near the time when it is computed that the city of Rome was founded by Romulus, which was but about the reign of Hezekiah king of Judah. And his writings pretend not to be historical, but poetical fiction all over: rhapsodies indeed they are, and the very Alcoran of paganism. The most ancient authentic historians now extant are Herodotus and Thucydides, who were contemporaries with the latest of our historians, Ezra and Nehemiah, and could not write with any certainty of events much before their own time. The obscurity, deficiency, and uncertainty of all ancient history, except that which we find in the scripture, is abundantly made out by the learned bishop Stillingfleet, in that most useful book, his *Origines Sacræ*, lib. i. Let the antiquity of this history not only recommend it to the curious, but recommend to us all that way of religion it directs us in, as the good old way, in which if we walk we *shall find rest for our souls*, Jer. vi. 16.

IV. That it is *church* history, the history of the Jewish church, that sacred society, incorporated for religion, and the custody of the oracles and ordinances of God, by a charter under the broad seal of heaven, a covenant confirmed by miracles. Many great and mighty nations there were at this time in the world, celebrated it is likely for wisdom, and learning, and valour, illustrious men and illustrious actions; yet the records of them are all lost, either in silence or fables, while that little inconsiderable people of the Jews that *dwelt alone*, and *was not reckoned among the nations* (Num. xxiii. 9), makes so great a figure in the best known, most ancient, and most lasting of all histories; and no notice is taken in it of the affairs of other nations, except only as they fall in with the affairs of the Jews: *for the Lord's portion is his people; Jacob is the lot of his inheritance*, Deut. xxxii. 8, 9. Such a concern has God for his church in every age, and so dear have its interests been to him. Let them therefore be so to us, that we may be *followers of him as dear children*.

V. That it is a *divine* history, given by inspiration of God, and a part of that blessed book which is to be the standing rule of our faith and practice. And we are not to think it a part of it which might have been spared, or which we may now pass over or cast a careless eye upon, as if it were indifferent whether we read it or no; but we are to read it as a sacred record, preserved for our benefit *on whom the ends of the world have come*. 1. This history is of great use for the understanding of some parts of the Old Testament. The account we have here of David's life and reign, and especially of his troubles, is a key to many of his Psalms; and much light is given to most of the prophecies by these histories. 2. Though we have not altogether so many types of Christ here as we had in the history and the law of Moses, yet even here we meet with many who were figures of him that was to come, such as Joshua, Samson, Solomon, Cyrus, but especially David, whose kingdom was typical of the kingdom of the Messiah and the covenant of royalty made with him, a dark representation of the covenant of redemption made with the eternal Word; nor know we how to call Christ the son of David unless we be acquainted with this history, nor how to *receive* the declaration that John Baptist was the *Elias that was to come*, Matt. xi. 14. 3. The state of the Jewish church which is here set before us was typical of the gospel church and the state of that in the days of the Messiah; and, as the prophecies which related to it looked further to the latter days, so did the histories of it; and still *these things happened to them for ensamples*, 1 Cor. x. 11. By the tenour of this history we are given to understand these three things concerning the church (for *the thing that hath been is that which shall be*, Eccl. i. 9):—(1.) That we are not to expect the perfect purity and unity of the church in this world, and therefore not to be stumbled, though we are grieved, at its corruptions, distempers, and divisions; we are not to think it strange concerning them, as though some strange thing happened, much less to think the worse of its laws and constitutions for the sake of them or to despair of its perpetuity. What wretched stains of idolatry, impiety, and immorality, appear on the Jewish church, and what a woeful breach was there between Judah and Ephraim! yet God took them (as I may say) with all their faults, and never wholly rejected them till they rejected the Messiah. *Israel hath not been forsaken, nor Judah, of their God, though their land was filled with sin against the Holy One of Israel*, Jer. li. 5. (2.) That we are not to expect the constant tranquillity and prosperity of the church. It was then often oppressed and afflicted from its youth, had its years of servitude as well as its days of triumph, was often obscured, diminished, impoverished, and brought low; and yet still God secured to himself a remnant, *a holy seed*, which was *the substance thereof*, Isa. vi. 13. Let us not then be surprised to see the gospel church sometimes under hatches, and driven into the wilderness, and the gates of hell prevailing far against it. (3.) That yet we need not fear the utter extirpation of it. The gospel church is called the *Israel of God* (Gal. vi. 16), and the *Jerusalem which is above* (Gal. iv. 26), the *heavenly Jerusalem;* for as *Israel after the flesh*, and the *Jerusalem that then was*, by the wonderful care of the divine Providence, outrode all the storms with which they were tossed and threatened, and continued in being till they were made to resign all their honours to the gospel church, which they were the figures of, so shall that also, notwithstanding all its shocks, be preserved, till the mystery of God shall be finished, and the kingdom of grace shall have its perfection in the kingdom of glory. 4. This history is of great use to us for our direction in the way of our duty; it was written for our learning, that we may see the evil we should avoid and be armed against it, and the good we should do and be quickened to it. Though they are generally judges, and kings, and great men, whose lives are here written, yet in them even those of the meanest rank may see the deformity of sin and hate it, and the beauty of holiness and be in love with it; nay, the greater the person is the more evident are both these; for, if the great be good, it is their goodness that makes their greatness honourable; if bad, their greatness does but make their badness the more shameful. The failings even of good people are also recorded here for our admonition, that he who thinks he stands may take heed lest he fall, and that he who has fallen may not despair of forgiveness if he recover himself by repentance. 5. This history, as it shows what God requires of us, so it shows what we may expect from his providence, especially concerning states and kingdoms. By the dealings of God with the Jewish nation it appears that, as nations are, so they must expect to fare—that while princes and people serve the interests of God's kingdom among men he will secure and advance their interests, but that when they shake off his government, and rebel against him, they can look for no other than an inundation of judgments. It was so all along with Israel; while they kept close to God they prospered; when they forsook him every thing went cross. That great man archbishop Tillotson (*Vol. I. Serm.* 3. on Prov. xiv. 34) suggests that though, as to particular persons, the providences of God are promiscuously administered in this world, because there is another world of rewards and punishments for them, yet it is not so with nations as such, but national virtues are ordinarily rewarded with temporal blessings and national sins punished with temporal judgments, because, as he says, public bodies and communities of men, as such, can be rewarded and punished only in this world, for in the next they will all be dissolved. So plainly are God's ways of disposing kingdoms laid before us in the glass of this history that I could wish Christian statesmen would think themselves as much concerned as preachers to acquaint themselves with it; they might fetch as good maxims of state and rules of policy from this as from the best of the Greek and Roman historians. We are blessed (as the Jews were) with a divine revelation, and make a national profession of religion and relation to God, and therefore are to look upon ourselves as in a peculiar manner under a divine regimen, so that the things which happened to them were designed for ensamples to us.

I cannot pretend to write for great ones. But if what is here done may be delightful to any in reading and helpful in understanding and improving this sacred history, and governing themselves by the dictates of it, let God have all the glory and let all the rivers return to the ocean whence they came. When I look back on what is done I see nothing to boast of, but a great deal to be ashamed of; and, when I look forward on what is to be done, I see nothing in myself to trust to for the doing of it. I have no sufficiency of my own; but *by the grace of God I am what I am*, and that grace will, I trust, be sufficient for me. *Surely in the Lord have I righteousness and strength.* That blessed ἐπιχορηγία which the apostle speaks of (Phil. i. 19), that continual supply or communication *of the Spirit of Jesus Christ*, is what we may in faith pray for, and depend upon, to furnish us for every good word and work. The pleasantness of the study has drawn me on to the writing of this, and the candour with which my friends have been pleased to receive my poor endeavours on the Pentateuch encourages me to publish it; it is done according to the best of my skill, not without some care and application of mind, in the same method and manner with that; I wish I could have done it in less compass, that it might have been more within reach of *the poor of the flock*. But then it would not have been so plain and full as I desire it may be for the benefit of the *lambs of the flock*. *Brevis esse laboro, obscurus fio—labouring to be concise I become obscure.* With a humble submission to the divine providence and its disposals, and a humble reliance on the divine grace and its guidance and operation, I purpose still to proceed, as I have time, in this work. Two volumes more will, if God permit, conclude the Old Testament; and then if my friends encourage me, and my God spare me and enable me for it, I intend to go on to the New Testament. For though *many have taken in hand to set forth in order a declaration of those* parts of scripture which are yet before us (Luke i. 1), whose works *praise them in the gates* and are likely to outlive mine, yet while the subject is really so copious as it is and the manner of handling it may possibly be so various, and while one book comes into the hands of some and another into the hands of others, and all concur in the same design to advance the common interests of Christ's kingdom, the *common faith* once delivered to the saints, and the *common salvation* of precious souls (Tit. i. 4, Jude 3), I hope store of this kind will be thought no sore. I make bold to mention my purpose to proceed thus publicly in hopes I may have the advice of my friends in it, and their prayers for me that I may be made more *ready and mighty in the scriptures*, that understanding and utterance may be given to me, and that I may *obtain mercy of the Lord Jesus to be found* his *faithful* servant, who am less than the least of all that call him *Master*.

M. H.

Chester,
June 2, 1708.

AN

EXPOSITION,

WITH PRACTICAL OBSERVATIONS,

OF THE BOOK OF

JOSHUA.

I. We have now before us the history of the Jewish nation in this book and those that follow it to the end of the book of Esther. These books, to the end of the books of the Kings, the Jewish writers call *the first book of the prophets*, to bring them within the distribution of the books of the *Old Testament*, into the Law, the Prophets, and the Chetubim, or Hagiographa, Luke xxiv. 44. The rest they make part of the Hagiographa. For, though history is their subject, it is justly supposed that prophets were their penmen. To those books that are purely and properly *prophetical* the name of the prophet is prefixed, because the credibility of the prophecies depended much upon the character of the prophets; but these historical books, it is probable, were collections of the authentic records of the nation, which some of the prophets (and the Jewish church was for many ages more or less continually blessed with such) were divinely directed and helped to put together for the service of the church to the end of the world; as their other officers, so their historiographers, had their authority *from heaven*.—It should seem that though the substance of the several histories was written when the events were fresh in memory, and written under a divine direction, yet, under the same direction, they were put into the form in which we now have them by some other hand, long afterwards, probably all by the same hand, or about the same time. The grounds of the conjecture are, 1. Because former writings are so often referred to, as the Book of Jasher (Josh. x. 13 and 2 Sam. i. 18), the Chronicles of the Kings of Israel and Judah, and the books of Gad, Nathan, and Iddo. 2. Because the days when the things were done are spoken of sometimes as days long since passed; as 1 Sam. ix. 9, *He that is now called a prophet was formerly called a seer*. And, 3. Because we so often read of things remaining *unto this day;* as stones (Josh. iv. 9; vii. 26; viii. 29; x. 27; 1 Sam. vi. 18), names of places (Josh. v. 9; vii. 26; Judg. i. 26; xv. 19; xviii. 12; 2 Kings xiv. 7), rights and possessions (Judg. i. 21; 1 Sam. xxvii. 6), customs and usages (1 Sam. v. 5; 2 Kings xvii. 41), which clauses have been since added to the history by the inspired collectors for the confirmation and illustration of it to those of their own age. And, if one may offer a mere conjecture, it is not unlikely that the historical books, to the end of the Kings, were put together by Jeremiah the prophet, a little before the captivity; for it is said of Ziklag (1 Sam. xxvii. 6) that it pertains to the *kings of Judah* (which style began after Solomon and ended in the captivity) *unto this day*. And it is still more probable that those which follow were put together by Ezra the scribe, some time after the captivity. However, though we are in the dark concerning their authors, we are in no doubt concerning their authority; they were a part of the oracles of God, which were committed to the Jews, and were so received and referred to by our Saviour and the apostles.

In the five books of Moses we had a very full account of the rise, advance, and constitution, of the Old-Testament church, the family out of which it was raised, the promise, that great charter by which it was incorporated, the miracles by which it was built up, and the laws and ordinances by which it was to be governed, from which one would conceive an expectation of its character and state very different from what we find in this history. A nation that had statutes and judgments so righteous, one would think, should have been very holy; and a nation that had promises so rich should have been very happy. But, alas! a great part of the history is a melancholy representation of their sins and miseries; for *the law made nothing perfect*, but this was to be done by the *bringing in of the better hope*. And yet, if we compare the history of the Christian church with its constitution, we shall find the same cause for wonder, so many have been its errors and corruptions; for neither does the *gospel make any thing perfect* in this world, but leaves us still in expectation of a *better hope* in the future state.

II. We have next before us the *book of Joshua*, so called, perhaps, not because it was written *by* him, for that is uncertain. Dr. Lightfoot thinks that Phinehas wrote it. Bishop Patrick is clear that Joshua wrote it himself. However that be, it is written *concerning* him, and, if any other wrote it, it was collected out of his journals or memoirs. It contains the history of Israel under the command and government of Joshua, how he presided as general of their armies, 1. In their entrance into Canaan, *ch.* i.—v. 2. In their conquest of Canaan, *ch.* vi.—xii. 3. In the distribution of the land of Canaan among the tribes of Israel, *ch.* xiii.—xxi. 4. In the settlement and establishment of religion among them, *ch.* xxii.—xxiv. In all which he was a great example of wisdom, courage, fidelity, and piety, to all that are in places of public trust.

But this is not all the use that is to be made of this history. We may see in it, 1. *Much of God* and *his providence*—his power in the kingdom of nature, his justice in punishing the Canaanites when the *measure of their iniquity was full,* his faithfulness to his covenant with the patriarchs, and his kindness to his people Israel, notwithstanding their provocations. We may see him as the Lord of Hosts *determining the issues of war*, and as the director of the lot, *determining the bounds of men's habitations.* 2. *Much of Christ* and *his grace.* Though Joshua is not expressly mentioned in the New Testament as a type of Christ, yet all agree that he was a very eminent one. He bore our Saviour's name, as did also another type of him, Joshua the high priest, Zech. vi. 11, 12. The LXX., giving the name of Joshua a Greek termination, call him all along Ἰησοῦς, *Jesus*, and so he is called Acts vii. 45, and Heb. iv. 8. Justin Martyr, one of the first writers of the Christian church (*Dialog. cum Tryph. p.* mihi 300), makes that promise in Exod. xxiii. 20, *My angel shall bring thee into the place I have prepared,* to point at Joshua; and these words, *My name is in him*, to refer to this, that his name should be the same with that of the Messiah. It signifies, *He shall save.* Joshua saves God's people from the Canaanites; our Lord Jesus saves them *from their sins.* Christ, as Joshua, is the *captain of our salvation*, a *leader and commander of the people*, to tread Satan under their feet, to put them in possession of the heavenly Canaan, and to *give them rest*, which (it is said, Heb. iv. 8) Joshua did not.

CHAP. I.

The book begins with the history, not of Joshua's life (many remarkable passages of that we had before in the books of Moses) but of his reign and government. In this chapter, I. God appoints him to the government in the stead of Moses, gives him an ample commission, full instructions, and great encouragements, ver. 1—9. II. He accepts the government, and addresses himself immediately to the business of it, giving orders to the officers of the people in general, ver. 10, 11, and particularly to the two tribes and a half, ver. 12—15. III. The people agree to it, and take an oath of fealty to him, ver. 16—18. A reign which thus began with God could not but be honourable to the prince and comfortable to the subject. The last words of Moses are still verified, "Happy art thou, O Israel! Who is like unto thee, O people?" Deut. xxxiii. 29.

NOW after the death of Moses the servant of the LORD it came to pass, that the LORD spake unto Joshua the son of Nun, Moses' minister, saying, 2 Moses my servant is dead; now therefore arise, go over this Jordan, thou, and all this people, unto the land which I do give to them, *even* to the children of Israel. 3 Every place that the sole of your foot shall tread upon, that have I given unto you, as I said unto Moses. 4 From the wilderness and this Lebanon even unto the great river, the river Euphrates, all the land of the Hittites, and unto the great sea toward the going down of the sun, shall be your coast. 5 There shall not any man be able to stand before thee all the days of thy life: as I was with Moses, *so* I will be with thee: I will not fail thee, nor forsake thee. 6 Be strong and of a good courage: for unto this people shalt thou divide for an inheritance the land, which I sware unto their fathers to give them. 7 Only be thou strong and very courageous, that thou mayest observe to do according to all the law, which Moses my servant commanded thee: turn not from it *to* the right hand or *to* the left, that thou mayest prosper whithersoever thou goest. 8 This book of the law shall not depart out of thy mouth; but thou shalt meditate therein day and night, that thou mayest observe to do according to all that is written therein: for then thou shalt make thy way prosperous, and then thou shalt have good success. 9 Have not I commanded thee? Be strong and of a good courage; be not afraid, neither be thou dismayed: for the LORD thy God *is* with thee whithersoever thou goest.

Honour is here put upon Joshua, and great power lodged in his hand, by him that is the fountain of honour and power, and by whom kings reign. Instructions are given him by Infinite Wisdom, and encouragements by the God of all consolation. God had before spoken to Moses concerning him (Num. xxvii. 18), but now he speaks to him (*v.* 1), probably as he spoke to Moses (Lev. i. 1) *out of the tabernacle of the congregation*, where Joshua had with Moses presented himself (Deut. xxxi. 14), to learn the way of attending there. Though Eleazar had the breast-plate of judgment, which Joshua was directed to consult as there was occasion (Num. xxvii. 21), yet, for his greater encouragement, God here speaks to him immediately, some think in a dream or vision (as Job xxxiii. 15); for though God has tied us to instituted ordinances, in them to attend him, yet he has not tied himself to them, but that he may without them make himself known to his people, and speak to their hearts otherwise than by their ears. Concerning Joshua's call to the government observe here,

I. The time when it was given him: *After the death of Moses.* As soon as ever Moses was dead, Joshua took upon him the administration, by virtue of his solemn ordination in Moses's life-time. An interregnum, though but for a few days, might have been of bad consequence; but it is probable that God did not speak to him to go forward towards Canaan till after the thirty days of mourning for Moses were ended; not, as the Jews say, because the sadness of his spirit during those days unfitted him for communion with God (he sorrowed not as one that had no hope), but by this solemn pause, and a month's adjournment of the public councils, even now when time was so very precious to them, God would put an honour upon the memory of Moses, and give time to the people not only to lament their loss of him, but to repent of their miscarriages towards him during the forty years of his government.

II. The place Joshua had been in before he was thus preferred. He was Moses's minister, that is, an immediate attendant upon his person and assistant in business. The LXX. translate it ὑπουργος, a workman under Moses, under his direction and command. Observe, 1. He that was here called to honour had been long bred to business. Our Lord Jesus himself took upon him the form of a servant, and then God highly exalted him. 2. He was trained up in subjection and under command. Those are fittest to rule that have learnt to obey. 3. He that was to succeed Moses was intimately acquainted with him, that he might *fully know his doctrine and manner of life, his purpose and long-suffering* (2 Tim. iii. 10), might take the same measures, walk in the same spirit, in the same steps, having to carry on the same work. 4. He was herein a type of Christ, who might therefore be called Moses's minister, because he was made under the law and fulfilled all the righteousness of it.

III. The call itself that God gave him, which is very full.

1. The consideration upon which he was called to the government: *Moses my servant is dead, v.* 2. All good men are God's servants; and it is no disparagement, but an honour, to the greatest of men to be so: angels themselves are his ministers. Moses was called to extraordinary work, was a steward in God's house, and in the discharge of the trusts reposed in him he served not himself but God who employed him; he was faithful as a servant, and with an eye to the Son, as is intimated, Heb. iii. 5, where what he did is said to be for a *testimony of the things that should be spoken after*. God will own his servants, will confess them in the great day. But Moses, though God's servant, and one that could ill be spared, is dead; for God will change hands, to show that whatever instruments he uses he is not tied to any. Moses, when he has done his work as a servant, dies and goes to *rest from his labours, and enters into the joy of his Lord.* Observe, God takes notice of the death of his servants. It is precious in his sight, Ps. cxvi. 15.

2. The call itself. *Now therefore arise.* (1.) "Though Moses is dead, the work must go on; therefore arise, and go about it." Let not weeping hinder sowing, nor the withering of the most useful hands be the weakening of ours; for, when God has work to do, he will either find or make instruments fit to carry it on. Moses the *servant* is dead, but God the *Master* is not: he lives for ever. (2.) "Because Moses is dead, therefore the work devolves upon thee as his successor, for hereunto thou wast appointed. Therefore there is need of thee to fill up his place; up, and be doing." Note, [1.] The removal of useful men should quicken survivers to be so much the more diligent in doing good. Such and such are dead, and we must die shortly, therefore let us work while it is day. [2.] It is a great mercy to a people, if, when useful men are taken away in the midst of their usefulness, others are raised up in their stead to go on where they broke off. Joshua must arise to finish what Moses began. Thus the latter generations enter into the labours of the former. And thus Christ, our Joshua, does that for us which could never be done by the law of Moses,—*justifies* (Acts xiii. 39), and *sanctifies*, Romans viii. 3. The life of Moses made way for Joshua, and prepared the people for what was to be done by him. Thus the law is a schoolmaster to bring us to Christ: and then the death of Moses made room for Joshua; thus we are dead to the law, our first husband, that we may be *married to Christ*, Rom. vii. 4.

3. The particular service he was now called out to: "*Arise, go over this Jordan*, this river which you have in view, and on the banks of which you lie encamped." This was a trial to the faith of Joshua, whether he would give orders to make preparation for passing the river when there was no visible way of getting over it, at least not at this place and at this time, when *all the banks were overflown, ch.* iii. 15. He had no pontons or bridge of boats by which to convey them over, and yet he must believe that God, who had ordered them over, would open a way for them. Going over Jordan was going into Canaan; thither Moses might not, could not, bring them, Deut. xxxi. 2. Thus the honour of bringing the many sons to glory is reserved for Christ the *captain of our salvation*, Heb. ii. 10.

4. The grant of the land of Canaan to the children of Israel is here repeated (*v.* 2—4): *I do give it them.* To the patriarchs it was promised, *I will give it;* but, now that the fourth generation had expired, the iniquity of the Amorites was full, and the time had come for the performance of the promise, it is actually conveyed, and they are put in possession of that which they had long been in expectation of: "I do give it, enter upon

it, it is all your own; nay (*v.* 3), *I have given it;* though it be yet unconquered, it is as sure to you as if it were in your hands." Observe, (1.) The persons to whom the conveyance is made: *To them, even to the children of Israel* (*v.* 2), because they are the seed of Jacob, who was called *Israel* at the time when this promise was made to him, Gen. xxxv. 10, 12. The children of Israel, though they had been very provoking in the wilderness, yet, for their fathers' sakes, should have the entail preserved. And it was the children of the murmurers that God said should enter Canaan, Num. xiv. 31. (2.) The land itself that is conveyed: From the river Euphrates eastward, to the Mediterranean Sea westward, *v.* 4. Though their sin cut them short of this large possession, and they never replenished all the country within the bounds here mentioned, yet, had they been obedient, God would have given them this and much more. Out of all these countries, and many others, there were in process of time proselytes to the Jewish religion, as appears, Acts ii. 5, &c. If their church was enlarged, though their nation was not multiplied, it cannot be said that the promise was of no effect. And, if this promise had not its full accomplishment in the letter, believers might thence infer that it had a further meaning, and was to be fulfilled in the kingdom of the Messiah, both that of grace and that of glory. (3.) The condition is here implied upon which this grant is made, in those words, *as I said unto Moses*, that is, "upon the terms that Moses told you of many a time, *if you will keep my statutes*, you shall go in and possess that good land. Take it under those provisos and limitations, and not otherwise." The precept and promise must not be separated. (4.) It is intimated with what ease they should gain the possession of this land, if it were not their own fault, in these words, "*Every place that the sole of your foot shall tread upon* (within the following bounds) shall be your own. Do but set your foot upon it and you have it."

5. The promises God here makes to Joshua for his encouragement. (1.) That he should be sure of the presence of God with him in this great work to which he was called (*v.* 5): "*As I was with Moses*, to direct and strengthen him, to own and prosper him, and give him success in bringing Israel out of Egypt and leading them through the wilderness, so I will be with thee to enable thee to settle them in Canaan." Joshua was sensible how far he came short of Moses in wisdom and grace; but what Moses did was done by virtue of the presence of God with him, and, though Joshua had not always the same presence of mind that Moses had, yet, if he had always the same presence of God, he would do well enough. Note, It is a great comfort to the rising generation of ministers and Christians that the same grace which was sufficient for those that went before them shall not be wanting to them if they be not wanting to themselves in the improvement of it. It is repeated here again (*v.* 9), "*The Lord thy God is with thee* as a God of power, and that power engaged for thee whithersoever thou goest." Note, Those that go where God sends them shall have him with them wherever they go, and they need desire no more to make them easy and prosperous. (2.) That the presence of God should never be withdrawn from him: *I will not fail thee, nor forsake thee, v.* 5. Moses had assured him of this (Deut. xxxi. 8), that, though he must now leave him, God never would: and here God himself confirms that word of his servant Moses (Isa. xliv. 26), and engages never to leave Joshua. We need the presence of God, not only when we are beginning our work to set us in, but in the progress of it to further us with a continual help. If that at any time fail us, we are gone; but of this we may be sure, that *the Lord is with us while we are with him.* This promise here made to Joshua is applied to all believers, and improved as an argument against covetousness, Heb. xiii. 5, *Be content with such things as you have, for he hath said, I will never leave thee.* (3.) That he should have victory over all the enemies of Israel (*v.* 5): *There shall not any man* that comes against thee *be able to stand before thee.* Note, There is no standing before those that have God on their side. *If he be for us, who can be against us?* God promises him clear success—the enemy should not make any head against him; and constant success—all the days of his life. However it might be with Israel when he was gone, all his reign should be graced with triumphs. What Joshua had himself encouraged the people with long ago (Num. xiv. 9) God here encourages him with. (4.) That he should himself have the dividing of this land among the people of Israel, *v.* 6. It was a great encouragement to him in beginning this work that he was sure to see it finished and his labour should not be in vain. Some make it a reason why he should arm himself with resolution, and be of good courage, because of the bad character of the people whom he must cause to inherit that land. He knew well what a froward discontented people they were, and how unmanageable they had been in his predecessor's time; let him therefore expect vexation from them and be of good courage.

6. The charge or command he gives to Joshua, which is,

(1.) That he conform himself in every thing to the law of God, and make this his rule, *v.* 7, 8. God does, as it were, put the book of the law into Joshua's hand; as, when Joash was crowned, they *gave him the testimony*, 2 Kings xi. 12. And concerning this book he is charged, [1.] To *meditate therein day and night*, that he might understand it and have it ready to him upon all occasions. If ever any man's business might have excused him from meditation, and other acts of devotion, one would think Joshua's might at this time. It was a great trust that was lodged in his hands; the care of it was enough to fill him, if he had had ten souls, and yet he must find time and thoughts for meditation. Whatever affairs of this world we have to mind, we must not neglect the one thing needful. [2.] Not to let it depart out of his mouth; that is, all his orders to the people, and his judgments upon appeals made to him, must be consonant to the law of God; upon all occasions he must *speak according to this rule,* Isa. viii. 20. Joshua was to maintain and carry on the work that Moses had begun, and therefore he must not only complete the salvation Moses had wrought for them, but must uphold the holy religion he had established among them. There was no occasion to make new laws; but *that good thing which was committed to him* he must carefully and faithfully keep, 2 Tim. i. 14. [3.] He must *observe to do according to all this law.* To this end he must meditate therein, not for contemplation-sake only, or to fill his head with notions, or that he might find something to puzzle the priests with, but that he might, both as a man and as a magistrate, observe to do *according to what was written* therein; and several things were written there which had particular reference to the business he had now before him, as the laws concerning their wars, the destroying of the Canaanites and the dividing of Canaan, &c.; these he must religiously observe. Joshua was a man of great power and authority, yet he must himself be under command and do as he is bidden. No man's dignity or dominion, how great soever, sets him above the law of God. Joshua must not only govern by law, and take care that the people observed the law, but he must observe it himself, and so by his own example maintain the honour and power of it. *First,* He must do what was written. It is not enough to hear and read the word, to commend and admire it, to know and remember it, to talk and discourse of it, but we must do it. *Secondly,* He must do according to what was written, exactly observing the law as his copy, and doing, not only that which was there required, but in all circumstances according to the appointment. *Thirdly,* He must do according to all that was written, without exception or reserve, having a *respect to all God's commandments,* even those which are most displeasing to flesh and blood. *Fourthly,* He must observe to do so, observe the checks of conscience, the hints of providence; and all the advantages of opportunity. Careful observance is necessary to universal obedience. *Fifthly,* He must *not turn from it,* either in his own practice or in any act of government, to the right hand or to the left, for there are errors on both hands, and virtue is in the mean. *Sixthly,* He must be *strong and courageous,* that he might do according to the law. So many discouragements there are in the way of duty that those who will proceed and persevere in it must put on resolution. And, *lastly,* to encourage him in his obedience, he assures him that then he shall *do wisely* (as it is in the margin) and *make his way prosperous, v.* 7, 8. Those that make the word of God their rule, and conscientiously walk by that rule, shall both do well and speed well; it will furnish them with the best maxims by which to order their conversation (Ps. cxi. 10); and it will entitle them to the best blessings: God shall *give them the desire of their heart.*

(2.) That he encourage himself herein with the promise and presence of God, and make these his stay (*v.* 6): *Be strong and of a good courage.* And again (*v.* 7), as if this was the one thing needful: *Only be strong and very courageous.* And he concludes with this (*v.* 9): *Be strong and of a good courage; be not afraid, neither be thou dismayed.* Joshua had long since signalized his valour, in the war with Amalek, and in his dissent from the report of the evil spies; and yet God sees fit thus to inculcate this precept upon him. Those that have grace have need to be called upon again and again to exercise grace and to improve in it. Joshua was humble and low in his own eyes, not distrustful of God, and his power, and promise, but diffident of himself, and of his own wisdom, and strength, and sufficiency for the work, especially coming after so great a man as Moses; and therefore God repeats this so often, "*Be strong and of a good courage;* let not the sense of thy own infirmities dishearten thee; God is all-sufficient. *Have not I commanded thee?* [1.] "I have commanded the work to be done, and therefore it shall be done, how invincible soever the difficulties may seem that lie in the way." Nay, [2.] "I have commanded, called, and commissioned, thee to do it, and therefore will be sure to own thee, and strengthen thee, and bear thee out in it." Note, When we are in the way of our duty we have reason to be strong and very courageous; and it will help very much to animate and embolden us if we keep our eye upon the divine warrant, and hear God saying, "*Have not I commanded thee?* I will therefore help thee, succeed thee, accept thee, reward thee." Our Lord Jesus, as Joshua here, was borne up under his sufferings by a regard to the will of God and the *commandment he had received from his Father,* John x. 18.

10 Then Joshua commanded the officers of the people, saying, 11 Pass through the host, and command the people, saying, Prepare you victuals; for within three days ye shall pass over this Jordan, to go in to possess the land, which the LORD

your God giveth you to possess it. 12 And to the Reubenites, and to the Gadites, and to half the tribe of Manasseh, spake Joshua, saying, 13 Remember the word which Moses the servant of the LORD commanded you, saying, The LORD your God hath given you rest, and hath given you this land. 14 Your wives, your little ones, and your cattle, shall remain in the land which Moses gave you on this side Jordan; but ye shall pass before your brethren armed, all the mighty men of valour, and help them; 15 Until the LORD have given your brethren rest, as *he hath given* you, and they also have possessed the land which the LORD your God giveth them: then ye shall return unto the land of your possession, and enjoy it, which Moses the LORD's servant gave you on this side Jordan toward the sunrising.

Joshua, being settled in the government, immediately applies himself to business; not to take state or to take his pleasure, but to further the work of God among the people over whom God had set him. As he that desires the office of a minister (1 Tim. iii. 1), so he that desires the office of a magistrate, desires a work, a good work; neither is preferred to be idle.

I. He issues out orders to the people to provide for a march; and they had been so long encamped in their present post that it would be a work of some difficulty to decamp. The officers of the people that commanded under Joshua in their respective tribes and families attended him for orders, which they were to transmit to the people. Inferior magistrates are as necessary and as serviceable to the public good in their places as the supreme magistrate in his. What could Joshua have done without officers? We are therefore required to be subject, not only to *the king as supreme, but to governors as to those that are sent by him,* 1 Pet. ii. 13, 14. By these officers, 1. Joshua gives public notice that they were *to pass over Jordan within three days.* These orders, I suppose, were not given till after the return of the spies that were sent to bring an account of Jericho, though the story of that affair follows, *ch.* ii. And perhaps that was such an instance of his jealousy, and excessive caution, as made it necessary that he should be so often bidden as he was to be strong and of a good courage. Observe with what assurance Joshua says to the people, because God had said it to him, *You shall pass over Jordan, and shall possess* the land. We greatly honour the truth of God when we stagger not at the promise of God. 2. He gives them directions to prepare victuals, not to prepare transport vessels. He that bore them out of Egypt upon eagles' wings would in like manner bear them into Canaan, to bring them to himself, Exod. xix. 4. But those that were desirous to have other victuals besides the manna, which had not yet ceased, must prepare it, and have it ready against the time appointed. Perhaps, though the manna did not quite cease till they came into Canaan (*ch.* v. 12), yet since they had come *into a land inhabited* (Exod. xvi. 35), where they might be furnished in part with other provisions, it did not fall so plentifully, nor did they gather so much as when they had it first given to them in the wilderness, but decreased gradually, and therefore they are ordered to provide other victuals, in which perhaps was included all other things necessary to their march. And some of the Jewish writers, considering that having manna they needed not to provide other victuals, understand it figuratively, that they must *repent of their sins,* and make their *peace with God,* and resolve to live a new life, that they might be ready to receive this great favour. See Exod. xix. 10, 11.

II. He reminds the two tribes and a half of the obligations they were under to go over Jordan with their brethren, though they left their possessions and families on this side. Interest would make the other tribes glad to go over Jordan, but in these it was an act of self-denial, and against the grain; therefore it was needful to produce the agreement which Moses had made with them, when he gave them their possession before their brethren (*v.* 13): *Remember the word which Moses commanded you.* Some of them perhaps were ready to think now that Moses was dead, who they thought was too hard upon them in this matter, they might find some excuse or other to release themselves from this engagement, or might prevail with Joshua to dispense with them; but he holds them to it, and lets them know that, though Moses was dead, his commands and their promises were still in full force. He reminds them, 1. Of the advantages they had received in being first settled: "*The Lord your God hath given you rest.* He has given your minds rest; you know what you have to trust to, and are not as the rest of the tribes waiting the issue of the war first and then of the lot. He has also given your families rest, your wives and children, whose settlement is your satisfaction. He has given you rest by giving you this land, this good land, of which you are in full and quiet possession." Note, When God by his providence has given us rest we ought to consider how we may honour him with the advantages of it, and what service we may do to our brethren who are unsettled, or not so well settled as we are. When God had given David rest (2 Sam. vii. 1), see how restless he was till he had *found out a habitation* for the ark, Ps. cxxxii. 4, 5. When God has given us rest, we must take heed of slothfulness and of settling upon our lees. 2. He reminds them of their agreement to help their brethren in the wars of Canaan till God had in like manner given them rest, *v.* 14, 15. This was, (1.) Reasonable in itself. So closely were all the tribes incorporated that they must needs look upon themselves as members one of another. (2.) It was enjoined them by Moses, the servant of the Lord; he commanded them to do this, and Joshua his successor would see his commands observed. (3.) It was the only expedient they had to save themselves from the guilt of a great sin in settling on that side Jordan, a sin which would one time or other find them out, Num. xxxii. 23. (4.) It was the condition of the grant Moses had made them of the land they were possessed of, so that they could not be sure of a good title to, or a comfortable enjoyment of, *the land of their possession,* as it is here called (*v.* 15), if they did not fulfil the condition. (5.) They themselves had covenanted and agreed thereunto (Num. xxxii. 25): *Thy servants will do as my Lord commandeth.* Thus we all lie under manifold obligations to strengthen the hands one of another, and not to seek our own welfare only, but one another's.

16 And they answered Joshua, saying, All that thou commandest us we will do, and whithersoever thou sendest us, we will go. 17 According as we hearkened unto Moses in all things, so will we hearken unto thee: only the LORD thy God be with thee, as he was with Moses. 18 Whosoever *he be* that doth rebel against thy commandment, and will not hearken unto thy words in all that thou commandest him, he shall be put to death: only be strong and of a good courage.

This answer was given not by the two tribes and a half only (though they are spoken of immediately before), but by the *officers of all the people* (*v.* 10), as their representatives, concurring with the divine appointment, by which Joshua was set over them, and they did it heartily, and with a great deal of cheerfulness and resolution.

I. They promise him obedience (*v.* 16), not only as subjects to their prince, but as soldiers to their general, of whose particular orders they are to be observant. He that hath *soldiers under him saith to this man, Go, and he goeth; and to another, Come, and he cometh,* Matt. viii. 9. Thus the people of Israel here engage themselves to Joshua: "*All that thou commandest us we will readily do,* without murmuring or disputing; and whithersoever thou sendest us, though upon the most difficult and perilous expedition, we will go." We must thus swear allegiance to our Lord Jesus, as the captain of our salvation, and bind ourselves to do what he commands us by his word, and to go where he sends us by his providence. And since Joshua, being humbly conscious to himself how far short he came of Moses, feared he should not have such an influence upon the people and such an interest in them as Moses had, they here promise that they will be as obedient to him as ever they had been to Moses, *v.* 17. To speak truth, they had no reason to boast of their obedience to Moses; he had found them a stiff-necked people, Deut. ix. 24. But they meant that they would be as observant of Joshua as they should have been, and as some of them were (and the generality of them at least sometimes) of Moses. Note, We must not so magnify those that are gone, how eminent soever they were, either in the magistracy or in the ministry, as to be wanting in the honour and duty we owe to those that survive and succeed them, though in gifts they may come short of them. Obedience for conscience' sake will continue, though Providence change the hands by which it rules and acts.

II. They pray for the presence of God with him (*v.* 17): "*Only the Lord thy God be with thee,* to bless and prosper thee, and give thee success, *as he was with Moses.*" Prayers and supplications are to be made for all in authority, 1 Tim. ii. 1, 2. And the best thing we can ask of God for our magistrates is that they may have the presence of God with them; this will make them blessings to us, so that in seeking this for them we consult our own interest. A reason is here intimated why they would obey him as they had obeyed Moses, because they believed (and in faith prayed) that God's presence would be with him as it was with Moses. Those that we have reason to think have favour from God should have honour and respect from us. Some understand it as a limitation of their obedience: "We will obey only as far as we perceive the Lord is with thee, but no further. While thou keepest close to God we will keep close to thee; hitherto shall our obedience come, but no further." But they were so far from having any suspicion of Joshua's deviating from the divine rule that there needed not such a proviso.

III. They pass an act to make it death for any Israelite to disobey Joshua's orders, or *rebel against his commandment, v.* 18. Perhaps if such a law had been made in Moses's time it might have prevented many of the rebellions that were formed against him; for most men fear the sword of the magistrate more than the justice of God. Yet there was a special reason for the making of this law now that they were entering upon the wars of Canaan; for in times of war the severity of military discipline is more necessary than at other times. Some think that in this statute they had an eye to that law concerning the prophet God would raise up like unto Moses, which they think, though it refer chiefly to Christ, yet takes in Joshua by the way as a type of him, that whosoever would not hearken to him should be *cut off from his people.* Deut. xviii. 19, *I will require it of him.*

IV. They animate him to go on with cheerfulness in the work to which God had called him; and, in desiring that he would be strong and of a good courage, they did in effect promise him that they would do all they could, by an exact, bold, and cheerful observance of all his orders, to encourage him. It very much heartens those that lead in a good work to see those that follow follow with a good will. Joshua, though of approved valour, did not take it as an affront, but as a great kindness, for the people to bid him be strong and of a good courage.

CHAP. II.

In this chaptor we have an account of the sconts that were employed to bring an account to Joshua of the posture of the city of Jericho. Observe here, I. How Joshua sent them, ver. 1. II. How Rahab received them, and protected them, and told a lie for them (ver. 2—7), so that they escaped out of the hands of the enemy. III. The account she gave them of the present posture of Jericho, and the panic-fear they were struck with upon the approach of Israel, ver. 8—11. IV. The bargain she made with them for the security of herself and her relations in the ruin she saw coming upon her city, ver. 12—21. V. Their safe return to Joshua, and the account they gave him of their expedition, ver. 22—24. And that which makes this story most remarkable is that Rahab, the person principally concerned in it, is twice celebrated in the New Testament as a great believer (Heb. xi. 31) and as one whose faith proved itself by good works, James ii. 25.

AND Joshua the son of Nun sent out of Shittim two men to spy secretly, saying, Go view the land, even Jericho. And they went, and came into a harlot's house, named Rahab, and lodged there. 2 And it was told the king of Jericho, saying, Behold, there came men in hither to night of the children of Israel to search out the country. 3 And the king of Jericho sent unto Rahab, saying, Bring forth the men that are come to thee, which are entered into thine house: for they be come to search out all the country. 4 And the woman took the two men, and hid them, and said thus, There came men unto me, but I wist not whence they *were:* 5 And it came to pass *about the time* of shutting of the gate, when it was dark, that the men went out: whither the men went I wot not: pursue after them quickly; for ye shall overtake them. 6 But she had brought them up to the roof of the house, and hid them with the stalks of flax, which she had laid in order upon the roof. 7 And the men pursued after them the way to Jordan unto the fords: and as soon as they which pursued after them were gone out, they shut the gate.

In these verses we have,

I. The prudence of Joshua, in sending spies to observe this important pass, which was likely to be disputed at the entrance of Israel into Canaan (*v.* 1). *Go view the land, even Jericho.* Moses had sent spies (Num. xiii.); Joshua himself was one of them; and it proved of ill consequence. Yet Joshua now sent spies, not, as the former were sent, to survey the whole land, but Jericho only; not to bring the account to the whole congregation, but to Joshua only, who, like a watchful general, was continually projecting for the public good, and was particularly careful to take the first step well and not to stumble at the threshold. It was not fit that Joshua should venture over Jordan, to make his remarks *incognito—in disguise;* but he sends two men (two young men, say the LXX.), to view the land, that from their report he might take his measures in attacking Jericho. Observe, 1. There is no remedy, but great men must see with other people's eyes, which makes it very necessary that they be cautious in the choice of those they employ, since so much often depends upon their fidelity. 2. Faith in God's promise ought not to supersede but encourage our diligence in the use of proper means. Joshua is sure he has God with him, and yet sends men before him. We do not trust God, but tempt him, if our expectations slacken our endeavours. 3. See how ready these men were to go upon this hazardous enterprise. Though they put their lives in their hands, yet they ventured in obedience to Joshua their general, in zeal for the service of the camp, and in dependence upon the power of that God who, being the keeper of Israel in general, is the protector of every particular Israelite in the way of his duty.

II. The providence of God directing the spies to the house of Rahab. How they got over Jordan we are not told; but into Jericho they came, which was about seven or eight miles from the river, and there seeking for a convenient inn were directed to the house of Rahab, here called a *harlot*, a woman that had formerly been of ill fame, the reproach of which stuck to her name, though of late she had repented and reformed. Simon the leper (Matt. xxvi. 6), though cleansed from his leprosy, wore the reproach of it in his name as long as he lived; so Rahab the harlot; and she is so called in the New Testament, where both her faith and her good works are praised, to teach us, 1. That the greatness of sin is no bar to pardoning mercy if it be truly repented of in time. We read of publicans and harlots entering into the kingdom of the Messiah, and being welcomed to all the privileges of that kingdom, Matt. xxi. 31. 2. That there are many who before their conversion were very wicked and vile, and yet afterwards come to great eminence in faith and holiness. 3. Even those that through grace have repented of the sins of their youth must expect to bear the reproach of them, and when they hear of their old faults must renew their repentance, and, as an evidence of that, hear of them patiently. God's Israel, for aught that appears, had but one friend, but one well-wisher in all Jericho, and that was Rahab a harlot. God has often served his own purposes and his church's interests by men of indifferent morals. Had these scouts gone to any other house than this they would certainly have been betrayed and put to death without mercy. But God knew where they had a friend that would be true to them, though they did not, and directed them thither. Thus that which seems to us most contingent and accidental is often over-ruled by the divine providence to serve its great ends. And those that faithfully acknowledge God in their ways he will *guide with his eye.* See Jer. xxxvi. 19, 26.

III The piety of Rahab in receiving and protecting these Israelites. Those that keep public-houses entertain all comers, and think themselves obliged to be civil to their guests. But Rahab showed her guests more than common civility, and went upon an uncommon principle in what she did; it was *by faith* that she received those with peace against whom her king and country had denounced war, Heb. xi. 31. 1. She bade them welcome to her house; they lodged there, though it appears by what she said to them (*v.* 9) she knew both whence they came and what their business was. 2. Perceiving that they were observed coming into the city, and that umbrage was taken at it, she hid them upon the roof of the house, which was flat, and covered them with stalks of flax (*v.* 6), so that, if the officers should come thither to search for them, there they might lie undiscovered. By these stalks of flax, which she herself had lain in order upon the roof to dry in the sun, in order to the beating of it and making it ready for the wheel, it appears she had one of the good characters of the virtuous woman, however in others of them she might be deficient, that she *sought wool and flax, and wrought willingly with her hands,* Prov. xxxi. 13. From this instance of her honest industry one would hope that, whatever she had been formerly, she was not now a harlot. 3. When she was examined concerning them, she denied they were in her house, turned off the officers that had a warrant to search for them with a sham, and so secured them. No marvel that the king of Jericho sent to enquire after them (*v.* 2, 3); he had cause to fear when the enemy was at his door, and his fear made him suspicious and jealous of all strangers. He had reason to demand from Rahab that she should *bring forth the men* to be dealt with as spies; but Rahab not only disowned that she knew them, or knew where they were, but, that no further search might be made for them in the city, told the pursuers they had gone away again, and in all probability might be overtaken, *v.* 4, 5. Now, (1.) We are sure this was a good work: it is canonized by the apostle (James ii. 25), where she is said to be *justified by works*, and this is specified, that *she received the messengers, and sent them out another way*, and she did it by faith, such a faith as set her above the fear of man, even of the wrath of the king. She believed, upon the report she had heard of the wonders wrought for Israel, that their God was the only true God, and that therefore their declared design upon Canaan would undoubtedly take effect, and in this faith she sided with them, protected them, and courted their favour. Had she said, "I believe God is yours and Canaan yours, but I dare not show you any kindness," her faith had been dead and inactive, and would not have justified her. But by this it appeared to be both alive and lively, that she exposed herself to the utmost peril, even of life, in obedience to her faith. Note, Those only are true believers that can find in their hearts to venture for God; and those that by faith take the Lord for their God take his people for their people, and cast in their lot among them. Those that have God for their refuge and hiding-place must testify their gratitude by their readiness to shelter his people when there is occasion. *Let my outcasts dwell with thee,* Isa. xvi. 3, 4. And we must be glad of an opportunity of testifying the sincerity and zeal of our love to God by hazardous services to his church and kingdom among men. But, (2.) There is that in it which it is not easy to justify, and yet it must be justified, or else it could not be so good a work as to justify her. [1.] It is plain that she betrayed her country by harbouring the enemies of it, and aiding those that were designing its destruction, which could not consist with her allegiance to her prince and her affection and duty to the community she was a member of. But that which justifies her in this is that *she knew the Lord had given Israel this land* (*v.* 9), knew it by the incontestable miracles God had wrought for them, which confirmed that grant; and her obligations to God were higher than her obligations to any other. If she knew *God had given them this land,* it would have been a sin to join with those that hindered them from possessing it. But, since no such grant of any land to any people can now be proved, this will by no means justify any such treacherous practices against the public welfare. [2.] It is plain that she deceived the officers that examined her with an untruth—That she knew not whence the men were, that they had gone out, that she knew not whither they had gone. What shall we say to this? If she had either told the truth or been silent, she would have betrayed the spies, and this would certainly have been a great sin; and it does not appear that she had any other way of concealing them than by this ironical direction to the officers to pursue them another way, which if they would suffer themselves to be deceived by, let them be deceived. None are bound to accuse themselves, or their friends, of that which, though enquired after as a crime, they know to be a virtue. This case was altogether extraordinary, and therefore cannot be drawn into a precedent; and that may be justified here which would be by no means lawful in a common case. Rahab knew, by what was already done on the other side Jordan, that no mercy was to be shown to the Canaanites, and thence inferred that, if mercy was not owing them, truth was not; those that might be destroyed might be deceived. Yet divines generally conceive that it was a sin, which however admitted of this extenuation, that being a Canaanite she was not better taught the evil of lying; but God accepted her faith and pardoned her infirmity. However it was in this case, we are sure it is our duty to speak every man the truth to his neighbour, to dread and detest lying, and never to *do evil, that* evil, *that good may come of it,* Rom. iii. 8. But God accepts what is sincerely and honestly intended, though there be a mixture of frailty and folly in it, and is not extreme to mark what we do amiss. Some suggest that what she said might possibly be true of some other men.

8 And before they were laid down, she came up unto them upon the roof; 9 And she said unto the men, I know that the LORD hath given you the land, and that your terror is fallen upon us, and that all the inhabitants of the land faint because of you. 10 For we have heard how the LORD dried up the water of the Red sea for you, when ye came out of Egypt; and what ye did unto the two kings of the Amorites, that *were* on the other side Jordan, Sihon and Og, whom ye utterly destroyed. 11 And as soon as we had heard *these things*, our hearts did melt, neither did there remain any more courage in any man, because of you: for the LORD your God, he *is* God in heaven above, and in earth beneath. 12 Now therefore, I pray you, swear unto me by the LORD, since I have showed you kindness, that ye will also show kindness unto my father's house, and give me a true token: 13 And *that* ye will save alive my father, and my mother, and my brethren, and my sisters, and all that they have, and deliver our lives from death. 14 And the men answered her, Our life for your's, if ye utter not this our business. And it shall be, when the LORD hath given us the land, that we will deal kindly and truly with thee. 15 Then she let them down by a cord through the window: for her house *was* upon the town wall, and she dwelt upon the wall. 16 And she said unto them, Get you to the mountain, lest the pursuers meet you; and hide yourselves there three days, until the pursuers be returned: and afterward may ye go your way. 17 And the men said unto her, We *will be* blameless of this thine oath which thou hast made us swear. 18 Behold, *when* we come into the land, thou shalt bind this line of scarlet thread in the window which thou didst let us down by: and thou shalt bring thy father, and thy mother, and thy brethren, and all thy father's household, home unto thee. 19 And it shall be, *that* whosoever shall go out of the doors of thy house into the street, his blood *shall be* upon his head, and we *will be* guiltless: and whosoever shall be with thee in the house, his blood *shall be* on our head, if *any* hand be upon him. 20 And if thou utter this our business, then we will be quit of thine oath which thou hast made us to swear. 21 And she said, According unto your words, so *be* it. And she sent them away, and they departed: and she bound the scarlet line in the window.

The matter is here settled between Rahab and the spies respecting the service she was now to do for them, and the favour they were afterwards to show to her. She secures them on condition that they should secure her.

I. She gives them, and by them sends to Joshua and Israel, all the encouragement that could be desired to make their intended descent upon Canaan. This was what they came for, and it was worth coming for. Having got clear of the officers, she comes up to them to the *roof of the house* where they lay hid, finds them perhaps somewhat dismayed at the peril they apprehended themselves in from the officers, and scarcely recovered from the fright, but has that to say to them which will give them abundant satisfaction. 1. She lets them know that the report of the great things God had done for them had come to Jericho (*v.* 10), not only that they had an account of their late victories obtained over the Amorites in the neighbouring country, on the other side of the river, but that their miraculous deliverance out of Egypt, and passage through the Red Sea, a great way off, and forty years ago, were remembered and talked of afresh in Jericho, to the amazement of every body. Thus *this* Joshua and his fellows were *men wondered at*, Zech. iii. 8. See how God *makes his wonderful works to be remembered* (Ps. cxi. 4), so that *men shall speak of the might of his terrible acts*, Ps. cxlv. 6. 2. She tells them what impressions the tidings of these things had made upon the Canaanites: Your *terror has fallen upon us* (*v.* 9); *our hearts did melt*, *v.* 11. If she kept a public house, this would give her an opportunity of understanding the sense of various companies and of travellers from other parts of the country, so that they could not know this any way better than by her information; and it would be of great use to Joshua and Israel to know it; it would put ccurage into the most cowardly Israelite to hear how their enemies were dispirited, and it was easy to conclude that those who now fainted before them would infallibly fall before them, especially because it was the accomplishment of a promise God had made them, that he would *lay the fear and dread of them upon all this land* (Deut. xi. 25), and so it would be an earnest of the accomplishment of all the other promises God had made to them. Let not the stout man glory in his courage, any more than the strong man in his strength; for God can weaken both mind and body. Let not God's Israel be afraid of their most powerful enemies; for their God can, when he pleases, make their most powerful enemies afraid of them. Let none think to harden their hearts against God and prosper; for he that made man's soul can at any time make the sword of his terrors approach to it. 3. She hereupon makes profession of her faith in God and his promise; and perhaps *there was not found so great faith* (all things considered), *no, not in Israel*, as in this woman of Canaan. (1.) She believes God's power and dominion over all the world (*v.* 11): "Jehovah your God, whom you worship and call upon, is so far above all gods that he is the only true God; for *he is God in heaven above and in earth beneath*, and is served by all the hosts of both." A vast distance there is between heaven and earth, yet both are equally under the inspection and government of the great Jehovah. Heaven is not above his power, nor is earth below his cognizance. (2.) She believes his promise to his people Israel (*v.* 9): *I know that the Lord hath given you the land.* The king of Jericho had heard as much as she had of the great things God had done for Israel, yet he cannot infer thence that the Lord had given them this land, but resolves to hold it out against them to the last extremity; for the most powerful means of conviction will not of themselves attain the end without divine grace, and by that grace Rahab the harlot, who had only heard of the wonders God had wrought, speaks with more assurance of the truth of the promise made to the fathers than all the elders of Israel had done who were eye-witnesses of those wonders, many of whom perished through unbelief of this promise. *Blessed are those that have not seen, and yet have believed;* so Rahab did. *O woman, great is thy faith!*

II. She engaged them to take her and her relations under their protection, that they might not perish in the destruction of Jericho, *v.* 12, 13. Now, 1. It was an evidence of the sincerity and strength of her faith concerning the approaching revolution in her country that she was so solicitous to make an interest for herself with the Israelites, and courted their kindness. She foresaw the conquest of her country, and in the belief of that bespoke in time the favour of the conquerors. Thus Noah, being *moved with fear, prepared an ark to the saving of his house, and the condemning of the world*, Heb. xi. 7. Those who truly believe the divine revelation concerning the ruin of sinners, and the grant of the heavenly land to God's Israel, will give diligence to flee from the wrath to come, and to lay hold on eternal life, by joining themselves to God and to his people. 2. The provision she made for the safety of her relations, as well as for her own, is a laudable instance of natural affection, and an intimation to us in like manner to do all we can for the salvation of the souls of those that are dear to us, and, with ourselves, to bring them, if possible, into the bond of the covenant. No mention is made of her husband and children, but only her parents, and brothers, and sisters, for whom, though she was herself a housekeeper, she retained a due concern. 3. Her request that they would swear unto her by Jehovah is an instance of her acquaintance with the only true God, and her faith in him and devotion towards him, one act of which is religiously to *swear by his name.* 4. Her petition is very just and reasonable, that, since she had protected them, they should protect her, and since her kindness to them extended to their people, for whom they were now negociating, their kindness to her should take in all hers. It was the least they could do for one that had saved their lives with the hazard of her own. Note, Those that show mercy may expect to find mercy. Observe, She does not demand any preferment by way of reward for her kindness to them, though they lay so much at her mercy that she might have made her own terms, but only indents for her life, which in a general destruction would be a singular favour. Thus God promised Ebed-Melech, in recompence for his kindness to Jeremiah, that in the worst of times he should have *his life for a prey*, Jer. xxxix. 18. Yet this Rahab was afterwards advanced to be a princess in Israel, the wife of Salmon, and one of the ancestors of Christ, Matt. i. 5. Those that faithfully serve Christ and suffer for him he will not only protect, but prefer, and will do for them *more than they are able to ask or think*.

III. They solemnly engaged for her preservation in the common destruction (*v.* 14): "*Our life for yours*. We will take as much care of your lives as of our own, and would as soon hurt ourselves as any of you." Nay, they imprecate God's judgments on themselves if they should violate their promise to her. She had pawned her life for theirs, and now they in requital pawn their lives for hers, and (as public persons) with them they pawn the public faith and the credit of their nation, for they plainly interest all Israel in the engagement in those words, *When the Lord has given us the land*, meaning not themselves only, but the people whose agents they were. No doubt they knew themselves sufficiently authorized to treat with Rahab concerning this matter, and were confident that Joshua would ratify what they did, else they had not dealt honestly; the general law that they should make no covenant with the Canaanites (Deut. vii. 2) did not forbid them to take under their protection a particular person, that had heartily come into their interests and had done them real kindnesses. The law of gratitude is one of the laws of nature. Now observe here, 1. The promises they made her. In general, "*We will deal kindly and truly with thee*, *v.* 14. We will not only be kind in promising now, but true in performing what we promise; and not only true in performing just what we promise, but kind in out-doing thy demands and expectations." The goodness of God is often expressed by his kindness and truth (Ps. cxvii. 2), and in both these we must be followers of him. In particular, "If a *hand be upon any in the house with thee*, his *blood shall be on our head*, *v.* 19. If hurt come through our carelessness to those whom we are obliged to protect, we thereby contract guilt, and blood will be found a heavy load. 2. The provisos and limitations of their promises. Though they were in haste, and it may be in some confusion, yet we find them very cautious in settling this agreement and the terms of it, not to bind themselves to more than was fit for them to perform. Note, Covenants must be made with care, and we must swear in judgment, lest we find ourselves perplexed and entangled when it is too late *after vows to make enquiry*. Those that will be conscientious in keeping their promises will be cautious in making them, and perhaps may insert conditions which others may think frivolous. Their promise is here accompanied with three provisos, and they were necessary ones. They will protect Rahab, and all her relations always, provided, (1.) That she tie the scarlet cord with which she was now about to let them down in the window of her house, *v.* 18. This was to be a mark upon the house, which the spies would take care to give notice of to the camp of Israel, that no soldier, how hot and eager soever he was in military executions, might offer any violence to the house that was thus distinguished. This was like the blood sprinkled upon the door-post, which secured the first-born from the destroying angel, and, being of the same colour, some allude to this also to represent the safety of believers, under the protection of the blood of Christ sprinkled on the conscience. The same cord that she made use of for the preservation of these Israelites was to be made use of for her preservation. What we serve and honour God with we may expect he will bless and make comfortable to us. (2.) That she should have all those whose safety she had desired in the house with her and keep them there, and that, at the time of taking the town, none of them should dare to stir out of doors, *v.* 18, 19. This was a *necessary* proviso, for Rahab's kindred could not be distinguished any other way than by being in her distinguished house; should they mingle with their neighbours, there was no remedy, but the sword would devour *one as well as another*. It was a *reasonable* proviso that, since they were saved purely for Rahab's sake, her house should have the honour of being their castle, and that, if they would not *perish with those that believed not*, they should thus far believe the certainty and severity of the ruin coming upon their city as to retire into a place made safe by promise, as Noah into the ark and Lot into Zoar, and should *save themselves from this untoward generation*, by separating from them. It was likewise a *significant* proviso, intimating to us that those who are added to the church that they may be saved must keep close to the society of the faithful, and, having *escaped the corruption that is in the world through lust*, must take heed of being again entangled therein. (3.) That she should keep counsel (*v.* 14, 20): *If thou utter this our business*, that is, "If thou betray us when we are gone, or if thou make this agreement public, so as that others tie scarlet lines in their windows and so confound us, then we will be clear of thy oath." Those are unworthy of *the secret of the Lord* that know not how to keep it to themselves when there is occasion.

IV. She then took effectual care to secure her new friends, and *sent them out another way*, James ii. 25. Having fully understood the bargain they made with her, and consented to it (*v.* 21), she then *let them down by a cord* over the city wall (*v.* 15), the situation of her house befriending them herein: thus Paul made his escape out of Damascus, 2 Cor. xi. 33. She also directed them which way to go for their own safety, being better acquainted with the country than they were, *v.* 16. She directs them to leave the high road, and abscond in the mountains till the pursuers returned, for till then they could not safely venture over Jordan. Those that are in the way of God and their duty may expect that Providence will protect them, but this will not excuse them from taking all prudent methods for their own safety. God will keep us, but then we must not wilfully expose ourselves. Providence must be trusted, but not tempted. Calvin thinks that their charge to Rahab to keep this matter secret, and not to utter it, was intended for her safety, lest she, boasting of her security from the sword of Israel, should, before they came to protect her, fall into the hands of the king of Jericho and be put to death for treason: thus do they prudently advise her for her safety, as she advised them for theirs. And it is good advice, which we should at any time be thankful for, to *take heed to ourselves.*

22 And they went, and came unto the mountain, and abode there three days, until the pursuers were returned: and the pursuers sought *them* throughout all the way, but found *them* not. 23 So the two men returned, and descended from the mountain, and passed over, and came to Joshua the son of Nun, and told him all *things* that befel them: 24 And they said unto Joshua, Truly the LORD hath delivered into our hands all the land; for even all the inhabitants of the country do faint because of us.

We have here the safe return of the spies Joshua had sent, and the great encouragement they brought with them to Israel to proceed in their descent upon Canaan. Had they been disposed to discourage the people, as the evil spies did that Moses sent, they might have told them what they had observed of the height and strength of the walls of Jericho, and the extraordinary vigilance of the king of Jericho, and how narrowly they escaped out of his hands; but they were of another spirit, and, depending themselves upon the divine promise, they animated Joshua likewise. 1. Their return in safety was itself an encouragement to Joshua, and a token for good. That God provided for them so good a friend as Rahab was in an enemy's country, and that notwithstanding the rage of the king of Jericho and the eagerness of the pursuers they had come back in peace, was such an instance of God's great care concerning them for Israel's sake as might assure the people of the divine guidance and care they were under, which would undoubtedly make the progress of their arms glorious. He that so wonderfully protected their scouts would preserve their men of war, and cover their heads in the day of battle. 2. The report they brought was much more encouraging (*v.* 24): "*All the inhabitants of the country,* though resolved to stand it out, yet *do faint because of us,* they have neither wisdom to yield nor courage to fight," whence they conclude, "*Truly the Lord has delivered into our hands all the land,* it is all our own; we have nothing to do, in effect, but to take possession." Sinners' frights are sometimes sure presages of their fall. If we resist our spiritual enemies they will flee before us, which will encourage us to hope that in due time we shall be more than conquerors.

CHAP. III.

This chapter, and that which follows it, give us the history of Israel's passing through Jordan into Canaan, and a very memorable history it is. Long afterwards, they are told to remember what God did for them between Shittim (whence they decamped, ver. 1) and Gilgal, where they next pitched, chap. iv. 19, Mic. vi. 5, that they might know the righteousness of the Lord. By Joshua's order they marched up to the river's side (ver. 1), and then almighty power led them through it. They passed through the Red Sea unexpectedly, and in their flight by night, but they have notice some time before of their passing through Jordan, and their expectations raised. I. The people are directed to follow the ark, ver. 2—4. II. They are commanded to sanctify themselves, ver. 5. III. The priests with the ark are ordered to lead the van, ver. 6. IV. Joshua is magnified and made commander in chief, ver. 7, 8. V. Public notice is given of what God is about to do for them, ver. 9—13. VI. The thing is done, Jordan is divided, and Israel brought safely through it, ver. 14—17. This was the Lord's doing, and it is marvellous in our eyes.

AND Joshua rose early in the morning; and they removed from Shittim, and came to Jordan, he and all the children of Israel, and lodged there before they passed over. 2 And it came to pass after three days, that the officers went through the host; 3 And they commanded the people, saying, When ye see the ark of the covenant of the LORD your God, and the priests the Levites bearing it, then ye shall remove from your place, and go after it. 4 Yet there shall be a space between you and it, about two thousand cubits by measure: come not near unto it, that ye may know the way by which ye must go: for ye have not passed *this* way heretofore. 5 And Joshua said unto the people, Sanctify yourselves: for to-morrow the LORD will do wonders among you. 6 And Joshua spake unto the priests, saying, Take up the ark of the covenant, and pass over before the people. And they took up the ark of the covenant, and went before the people.

Rahab, in mentioning to the spies the *drying up of the Red Sea* (*ch.* ii. 10), the report of which terrified the Canaanites more than any thing else, intimates that those on that side the water expected that Jordan, that great defence of their country, would in like manner give way to them. Whether the Israelites had any expectation of it does not appear. God often *did things for them which they looked not for*, Isa. lxiv. 3. Now here we are told,

I. That they *came to Jordan and lodged there, v.* 1. Though they were not yet told how they should pass the river, and were unprovided for the passing of it in any ordinary way, yet they went forward in faith, having been told (*ch.* i. 11) that they should pass it. We must go on in the way of our duty though we foresee difficulties, trusting God to help us through them when we come to them. Let us proceed as far as we can, and depend on divine sufficiency for that which we find ourselves not sufficient for. In this march Joshua led them, and particular notice is taken of his early rising, as there is afterwards upon other occasions (*ch.* vi. 12; vii. 16; viii. 10), which intimates how little he loved his ease, how much he loved his business, and what care and pains he was willing to take in it. Those that would bring great things to pass must rise early. *Love not sleep, lest thou come to poverty.* Joshua herein set a good example to the officers under him, and taught them to rise early, and to all that are in public stations especially to attend continually to the duty of their place.

II. That the people were directed to follow the ark. Officers were appointed to go through the host to give these directions (*v.* 2), that every Israelite might know both what to do and what to depend upon.

1. They might depend upon the ark to lead them; that is, upon God himself, of whose presence the ark was an instituted sign and token. It seems, the pillar of cloud and fire was removed, else that would have led them, unless we suppose that it now hovered over the ark, and so they had a double guide: honour was put upon the ark, and a defence upon that glory. It is called here the *ark of the covenant of the Lord their God.* What greater encouragement could they have than this, that the Lord was their God, a God in covenant with them? Here was the *ark of the covenant;* if God be ours, we need not fear any evil. He was nigh to them, present with them, went before them: what could come amiss to those that were thus guided, thus guarded? Formerly the ark was carried in the midst of the camp, but now it went before them to *search out a resting-place* for them (Num. x. 33), and, as it were, to give them livery and seisin of the promised land, and put them in possession of it. In the ark the tables of the law were, and over it the mercy-seat; for the divine law and grace reigning in the heart are the surest pledges of God's presence and favour, and those that would be led to the heavenly Canaan must take the law of God for their guide (*if thou wilt enter into life keep the commandments*) and have the great propitiation in their eye, *looking for the mercy of our Lord Jesus Christ unto eternal life.*

2. They might depend upon the priests and Levites, who were appointed for that purpose to carry the ark before them. The work of ministers is to hold forth the word of life, and to take care of the administration of those ordinances which are the tokens of God's presence and the instruments of his power and grace; and herein they must go before the people of God in their way to heaven.

3. The people must follow the ark: *Remove from your place and go after it,* (1.) As those that are resolved never to forsake it. Wherever God's ordinances are, there we must be; if they flit, we must remove and go after them. (2.) As those that are entirely satisfied in its guidance, that it will lead in the best way to the best end; and therefore, *Lord, I will follow thee whithersoever thou goest.* This must be all their care, to attend the motions of the ark, and follow it with an implicit faith. Thus must we walk after the rule of the word and the direction of the Spirit in every thing, so shall *peace be upon us,* as it now was upon the Israel of God. They must follow the priests as far as they carried the ark, but no further; so we must follow our ministers only as they follow Christ.

4. In following the ark, they must *keep their distance, v.* 4. They must none of them come within a thousand yards of the ark. (1.) They must thus express their awful and reverent regard to that token of God's presence, lest its familiarity with them should breed contempt. This charge to them not to come near was agreeable to that dispensation of darkness, bondage, and terror: but we now through Christ have access with boldness. (2.) Thus it was made to appear that the ark was able to protect itself, and needed not to be guarded by the men of war, but was itself a guard to them. With what a noble defiance of the enemy did it leave all its friends half a mile behind except the unarmed priests that carried it, as perfectly sufficient for its own safety and theirs that followed it! (3.) Thus it was the better seen by those that were to be led by it: *That you may know the way by which you must go,* seeing it, as it were, chalked out or tracked by the ark. Had they been allowed to come near it, they would have surrounded it, and none would have had the sight of it but those that were close to it; but, as it was put at such a distance before them, they would all have the satisfaction of seeing it, and would be animated by the sight. And it was with good reason that this provision was made for their encouragement: *For you have not passed this way heretofore.* This had been the character of all their way through the wilderness, it was an untrodden path, but this especially through Jordan. While we

are here we must expect and prepare for unusual events, to pass ways that we have not passed before, and much more when we go hence; our way through the *valley of the shadow of death* is a way we have not gone before, which makes it the more formidable. But, if we have the assurance of God's presence, we need not fear; that will furnish us with such strength as we never had when we come to do a work we never did.

III. They were commanded to sanctify themselves, that they might be prepared to attend the ark; and with good reason: For *to-morrow the Lord will do wonders among you, v.* 5. See how magnificently he speaks of God's works: he *doeth wonders,* and is therefore to be adored, admired, and trusted in. See how intimately acquainted Joshua was with the divine counsels: he could tell before-hand what God would do, and when. See what preparation we must make to receive the discoveries of God's glory and the communications of his grace: we must sanctify ourselves. This we must do when we are to attend the ark, and God by it is about to do wonders among us; we must separate ourselves from all other cares, devote ourselves to God's honour, and *cleanse ourselves from all filthiness of flesh and spirit.* The people of Israel were now entering into the holy land, and therefore must sanctify themselves. God was about to give them uncommon instances of his favour, which by meditation and prayer they must compose their minds to a very careful observation of, that they might give God the glory, and take to themselves the comfort, of these appearances.

IV. The priests were ordered to take up the ark and carry it *before the people, v.* 6. It was the Levites' work ordinarily to carry the ark, Num. iv. 15. But on this great occasion the priests were ordered to do it. And they did as they were commanded, *took up the ark,* and did not think themselves disparaged, *went before the people,* and did not think themselves exposed; the ark they carried was both their honour and their defence. And now we may suppose that prayer of Moses used, when the ark set forward (Num. x. 35), *Rise up, Lord, and let thy enemies be scattered.* Magistrates are here instructed to stir up ministers to their work, and to make use of their authority for the furtherance of religion. Ministers must likewise learn to go before in the way of God, and not to shrink nor draw back when dangers are before them. They must expect to be most struck at, but they *know whom they have trusted.*

7 And the LORD said unto Joshua, This day will I begin to magnify thee in the sight of all Israel, that they may know that, as I was with Moses, *so* I will be with thee. 8 And thou shalt command the priests that bear the ark of the covenant, saying, When ye are come to the brink of the water of Jordan, ye shall stand still in Jordan. 9 And Joshua said unto the children of Israel, Come hither, and hear the words of the LORD your God. 10 And Joshua said, Hereby ye shall know that the living God *is* among you, and *that* he will without fail drive out from before you the Canaanites, and the Hittites, and the Hivites, and the Perizzites, and the Girgashites, and the Amorites, and the Jebusites. 11 Behold, the ark of the covenant of the Lord of all the earth passeth over before you into Jordan. 12 Now therefore take you twelve men out of the tribes of Israel, out of every tribe a man. 13 And it shall come to pass, as soon as the soles of the feet of the priests that bear the ark of the LORD, the Lord of all the earth, shall rest in the waters of Jordan, *that* the waters of Jordan shall be cut off *from* the waters that come down from above; and they shall stand upon a heap.

We may observe here how God honours Joshua, and by this wondrous work he is about to do designs to make Israel know that he is their governor, and then how Joshua honours God and endeavours by it to make Israel know that he is their God. Thus those that honour God he will honour, and those whom he has advanced should do what they can in their places to exalt him.

I. God speaks to Joshua to put honour upon him, *v.* 7, 8. 1. It was a great honour God did him that he spoke to him, as he had done to Moses from off the mercy-seat, before the priests removed it with the ark. This would make Joshua easy in himself and great among the people, that God was pleased to speak so familiarly to him. 2. That he designed to *magnify him in the sight of all Israel.* He had told him before that he would be with him (*ch.* i. 5), and that comforted him, but now all Israel shall see it, and this would magnify him. Those are truly great with whom God is and whom he employs and owns in his service. God magnified him because he would have the people magnify him. Pious magistrates are to be highly honoured and esteemed as public blessings, and the more we see of God with them the more we should honour them. By the dividing of the Red Sea Israel was convinced that God was with Moses in bringing them out of Egypt; therefore they are said to be *baptized unto Moses in the sea,* 1 Cor. x. 2. And upon that occasion they *believed him,* Exod. xiv. 31. And now, by the dividing of Jordan, they shall be convinced that God is in like manner with Joshua in bringing them into Canaan. God had magnified Joshua before on several occasions, but now he began to magnify him as the successor of Moses in the government. Some have observed that it was at the banks of Jordan that God began to magnify Joshua, and at the same place he began to magnify our Lord Jesus as Mediator; for John was baptizing at Bethabara, *the house of passage*, and there it was that when our Saviour was baptized it was proclaimed concerning him, *This is my beloved Son*. 3. That by him he gave orders to the priests themselves, though they were his immediate attendants (*v.* 8): *Thou shalt command the priests*, that is, "thou shalt make known to them the divine command in this matter, and take care that they observe it, to stand still at the brink of Jordan while the waters part, that it may appear to be *at the presence of the Lord*, of the mighty God of Jacob, that Jordan is *driven back*," Ps. cxiv. 5, 7. God could have divided the river without the priests, but they could not without him. The priests must herein set a good example to the people, and teach them to do their utmost in the service of God, and trust him for help in time of need.

II. Joshua speaks to the people, and therein honours God.

1. He demands attention (*v.* 9): "*Come hither* to me, as many as can come within hearing, and, before you see the works, *hear the words of the Lord your God*, that you may compare them together and they may illustrate each other." He had commanded them to sanctify themselves, and therefore calls them to *hear the word of God*, for that is the ordinary means of sanctification, John xvii. 17.

2. He now tells them, at length, by what way they should pass over Jordan, by the stopping of its streams (*v.* 13): *The waters of Jordan shall be cut off*. God could by a sudden and miraculous frost have congealed the surface, so that they might all have gone over upon the ice; but that being a thing sometimes done even in that country, by the ordinary power of nature (Job. xxxviii. 30), it would not have been such an honour to Israel's God, nor such a terror to Israel's enemies; it must therefore be done in such a way as had no precedent but the dividing of the Red Sea: and that miracle is here repeated, to show that God has the same power to finish the salvation of his people that he had to begin it, for he is the *Alpha* and the *Omega*; and that *the word of the Lord* (as the Chaldee reads it, *v.* 7), the essential, eternal Word, was as truly with Joshua as he was with Moses. And by the dividing of the waters from the waters, and the making of the dry land to appear which had been covered, God would remind them of that in which Moses by revelation had instructed them concerning the work of creation (Gen. i. 6, 9), that by what they now saw their belief of that which they there read might be assisted, and they might know that the God whom they worshipped was the same God that made the world and that it was the same power that was engaged and employed for them.

3. The people having been directed before to follow the ark are here told that it should *pass before them into Jordan*, *v.* 11. Observe, (1.) The ark of the covenant must be their guide. During the reign of Moses, the cloud was their guide, but now, in Joshua's reign, the ark; both were visible signs of God's presence and presidency, but divine grace under the Mosaic dispensation was wrapt up as in a cloud and covered with a veil, while by Christ, our Joshua, it is revealed in the ark of the covenant unveiled. (2.) It is called *the ark of the covenant of the Lord of all the earth*. "He that is your God (*v.* 9), in covenant with you, is the *Lord of all the earth*, has both right and power to command, control, use, and dispose of all nations and of all creatures. He is the *Lord of all the earth*, therefore he needs not you, nor can he be benefited by you; therefore it is your honour and happiness to have him in covenant with you: if he be yours, all the creatures are at your service, and when he pleases shall be employed for you." When we are praising and worshipping God as Israel's God, and ours through Christ, we must remember that he is the *Lord of the whole earth*, and reverence him and trust in him accordingly. Some observe an accent in the original, which they think directs us to translate it somewhat more emphatically, *Behold the ark of the covenant, even the ark of the Lord*, or *even of the covenant of the Lord of all the earth*. (3.) They are told that the ark should *pass before them into Jordan*. God would not appoint them to go any where but where he himself would go before them and go with them; and they might safely venture, even into Jordan itself, if the ark of the covenant led them. While we make God's precepts our rule, his promises our stay, and his providence our guide, we need not dread the greatest difficulties we may meet with in the way of duty. That promise is sure to all the seed (Isa. xliii. 2), *When thou passest through the waters I will be with thee, and through the rivers they shall not overflow thee*.

4. From what God was now about to do for them he infers an assurance of what he would yet further do. This he mentions first, so much was his heart upon it, and so great a satisfaction did it give him (*v.* 10): "*Hereby you shall know that the living God* (the true God, and God of power, not one of the dead gods of the heathen) *is among you*, though you see him not, nor are to have any image of him, is among you to give you law, secure your welfare, and receive your homage,—is among you in this great undertaking now before you; and therefore you shall, nay, he himself *will, without fail, drive*

out from before you the Canaanites." So that the dividing of Jordan was intended to be to them, (1.) A sure token of God's presence with them. By this they could not but *know that God was among them*, unless their unbelief was as obstinate against the most convincing evidence as that of their fathers was, who, presently after God had divided the Red Sea before them, impudently asked, *Is the Lord among us, or is he not?* Exod. xvii. 7. (2.) A sure pledge of the conquest of Canaan. If the living God is among you, *expelling he will expel* (so the Hebrew phrase is) *from before you the Canaanites.*" He will do it certainly, and do it effectually. What should hinder him? What can stand in his way before whom rivers are divided and dried up? The forcing of the lines was a certain presage of the ruin of all their hosts: how could they stand their ground when Jordan itself was driven back? When they had not courage to dispute this pass, but trembled at the approach of the *mighty God of Jacob* (Ps. cxiv. 7), what opposition could they ever make after this? This assurance which Joshua here gives them was so well grounded that it would enable one Israelite to chase a thousand Canaanites, and two to put ten thousand to flight; and it would be abundantly strengthened by remembering the song of Moses, dictated forty years before, which plainly foretold the dividing of Jordan and the influence it would have upon the driving out of the Canaanites. Exod. xv. 15—17, "*The inhabitants of Canaan shall melt away*, and so be effectually driven out; they shall be as still as a stone till thy people pass over, and then thou shalt bring them in and plant them." Note, God's glorious appearances for his church and people ought to be improved by us for the encouragement of our faith and hope for the future. *As for God, his work is perfect.* If Jordan's flood cannot keep them out, Canaan's force cannot turn them out again.

5. He directs them to get twelve men ready, one of each tribe, who must be within call, to receive such orders as Joshua should afterwards give them, *v.* 12. It does not appear that they were to attend the priests, and walk with them when they carried the ark, that they might more immediately be witnesses of the wonders done by it, as some think; but they were to be at hand for the service they were called to, *ch.* iv. 4, &c.

14 And it came to pass, when the people removed from their tents, to pass over Jordan, and the priests bearing the ark of the covenant before the people; 15 And as they that bare the ark were come unto Jordan, and the feet of the priests that bare the ark were dipped in the brim of the water, (for Jordan overfloweth all his banks all the time of harvest,) 16 That the waters which came down from above stood *and* rose up upon a heap very far from the city Adam, that *is* beside Zaretan: and those that came down toward the sea of the plain, *even* the salt sea, failed, *and* were cut off: and the people passed over right against Jericho. 17 And the priests that bare the ark of the covenant of the LORD stood firm on dry ground in the midst of Jordan, and all the Israelites passed over on dry ground, until all the people were passed clean over Jordan.

Here we have a short and plain account of the dividing of the river Jordan, and the passage of the children of Israel through it. The story is not garnished with the flowers of rhetoric (gold needs not to be painted), but it tells us, in short, matter of fact.

I. That this river was now broader and deeper than usually it was at other times of the year, *v.* 15. The melting of the snow on the mountains of Lebanon, near which this river had its rise, was the occasion that at the time of harvest, barley-harvest, which was the spring of the year, Jordan overflowed all his banks. This great flood, just at that time (which Providence might have restrained for once, or which he might have ordered them to cross at another time of the year) very much magnified the power of God and his kindness to Israel. Note, Though the opposition given to the salvation of God's people have all imaginable advantages, yet God can and will conquer it. Let the banks of Jordan be filled to the brink, filled till they run over, it is as easy to Omnipotence to divide them, and dry them up, as if they were ever so narrow, ever so shallow; it is all one with the Lord.

II. That as soon as ever the feet of the priests dipped in the brim of the water the stream stopped immediately, as if a sluice had been let down to dam it up, *v.* 15, 16. So that the waters above swelled, stood on a heap, and ran back, and yet, as it should seem, did not spread, but congealed, which unaccountable rising of the river was observed with amazement by those that lived upward upon it many miles off, and the remembrance of it remained among them long after: the waters on the other side this invisible dam ran down of course, and left the bottom of the river dry as far downward, it is likely, as they swelled upward. When they passed through the Red Sea, the waters were a wall on either hand, here only on the right-hand. Note, The God of nature can, when he pleases, change the course of nature, and alter its properties, can turn fluids into solids, *waters into standing rocks*, as, on the contrary, *rocks into standing waters*, to serve his own purposes. See Ps. cxiv. 5, 8.

What cannot God do? What will he not do for the perfecting of his people's salvation? Sometimes he *cleaves the earth with rivers* (Hab. iii. 9), and sometimes, as here, cleaves the rivers without earth. It is easy to imagine how, when the course of this strong and rapid stream was arrested on a sudden, *the waters roared and were troubled,* so that the mountains seemed to *shake with the swelling thereof* (Ps. xlvi. 3), how *the floods lifted up their voice, the floods lifted up their waves,* while the Lord on high showed himself *mightier than the noise of* these *many waters,* Ps. xciii. 3, 4. With reference to this the prophet asks, *Was the Lord displeased against the rivers? was thine anger against the rivers?* Hab. iii. 8. No, *Thou wentest forth for the salvation of thy people, v.* 13. In allusion to this, it is foretold, among the great things God will do for the gospel church in the latter days, that the great river Euphrates shall be dried up, that *the way of the kings of the east may be prepared,* Rev. xvi. 12. When the time has come for Israel's entrance into the land of promise all difficulties shall be conquered, *mountains shall become plains* (Zech. iv. 7) and rivers become dry, for the *ransomed of the Lord to pass over.* When we have finished our pilgrimage through this wilderness, death will be like this Jordan between us and the heavenly Canaan, but the ark of the covenant has prepared us a way through it; it is the last enemy that shall be destroyed.

III. That *the people passed over right against Jericho,* which was, 1. An instance of their boldness, and a noble defiance of their enemies. Jericho was one of the strongest cities, and yet they dared to face it at their first entrance. 2. It was an encouragement to them to venture through Jordan, for Jericho was a goodly city and the country about it extremely pleasant; and, having that in view as their own, what difficulties could discourage them from taking possession? 3. It would increase the confusion and terror of their enemies, who no doubt strictly observed their motions, and were the amazed spectators of this work of wonders.

IV. That the priests *stood still in the midst of Jordan while all the people passed over, v.* 17. There the ark was appointed to be, to show that the same power that parted the waters kept them parted as long as there was occasion; and had not the divine presence, of which the ark was a token, been their security, the waters would have returned upon them and buried them. There the priests were appointed to stand still, 1. To try their faith, whether they could venture to take their post, when God assigned it to them, with mountains of water over their heads. As they made a bold step when they set the first foot into Jordan, so now they made a bold stand when they tarried longest in Jordan; but they knew they carried their own protection with them. Note, Ministers in times of peril should be examples of courage and confidence in the divine goodness. 2. It was to encourage the faith of the people, that they might go triumphantly into Canaan, and *fear no evil,* no, not in this *valley of the shadow of death* (for so the divided river was), being assured of God's presence, which interposed between them and the greatest danger, between them and the proud waters, which otherwise had gone over their souls. Thus in the greatest dangers the saints are *comforted* with *his rod and his staff,* Ps xxiii. 4.

CHAP. IV.

This chapter gives a further account of the miraculous passage of Israel through Jordan. I. The provision that was made at that time to preserve the memorial of it, by twelve stones set up in Jordan (ver. 9) and other twelve stones taken up out of Jordan, ver. 1—8. II. The march of the people through Jordan's channel, the two tribes first, then all the people, and the priests that bore the ark last, ver. 10—14. III. The closing of the waters again upon their coming up with the ark, ver. 15—19. IV. The erecting of the monument in Gilgal, to preserve the remembrance of this work of wonder to posterity, ver. 20—24.

AND it came to pass, when all the people were clean passed over Jordan, that the LORD spake unto Joshua, saying, 2 Take you twelve men out of the people, out of every tribe a man, 3 And command ye them, saying, Take you hence out of the midst of Jordan, out of the place where the priests' feet stood firm, twelve stones, and ye shall carry them over with you, and leave them in the lodging place, where ye shall lodge this night. 4 Then Joshua called the twelve men, whom he had prepared of the children of Israel, out of every tribe a man: 5 And Joshua said unto them, Pass over before the ark of the LORD your God into the midst of Jordan, and take you up every man of you a stone upon his shoulder, according unto the number of the tribes of the children of Israel: 6 That this may be a sign among you, *that* when your children ask *their fathers* in time to come, saying, What *mean* ye by these stones? 7 Then ye shall answer them, That the waters of Jordan were cut off before the ark of the covenant of the LORD; when it passed over Jordan, the waters of Jordan were cut off: and these stones shall be for a memorial unto the children of Israel for ever. 8 And the children of Israel did so as Joshua commanded, and took up twelve stones out of the midst of Jordan, as the LORD spake unto Joshua, according to the number of the tribes of the children of Israel, and carried them over with them unto the place where they lodged, and laid them down there. 9 And Joshua set up twelve stones in the midst of Jordan, in the place where the feet of the priests which bare the ark of the covenant stood: and they are there unto this day.

We may well imagine how busy Joshua and all the men of war were while they were passing over Jordan, when besides their own marching into an enemy's country, and in the face of the enemy, which could not but occasion them many thoughts of heart, they had their wives, and children, and families, their cattle, and tents, and all their effects, bag and baggage, to convey by this strange and untrodden path, which we must suppose either very muddy or very stony, troublesome to the weak and frightful to the timorous, the descent to the bottom of the river and the ascent out of it steep, so that every man must needs have his head full of care and his hands full of business, and Joshua more than any of them. And yet, in the midst of all his hurry, care must be taken to perpetuate the memorial of this wondrous work of God, and this care might not be adjourned to a time of greater leisure. Note, How much soever we have to do of business for ourselves and our families, we must not neglect nor omit what we have to do for the glory of God and the serving of his honour, for that is our best business. Now,

I. God gave orders for the preparing of this memorial. Had Joshua done it without divine direction, it might have looked like a design to perpetuate his own name and honour, nor would it have commanded so sacred and venerable a regard from posterity as now, when God himself appointed it. Note, God's works of wonder ought to be kept in everlasting remembrance, and means devised for the preserving of the memorial of them. Some of the Israelites that passed over Jordan perhaps were so stupid, and so little affected with this great favour of God to them, that they felt no concern to have it remembered; while others, it may be, were so much affected with it, and had such deep impressions made upon them by it, that they thought there needed no memorial of it to be erected, the heart and tongue of every Israelite in every age would be a living lasting monument of it. But God, knowing their frame, and how apt they had been soon to forget his works, ordered an expedient for the keeping of this in remembrance to all generations, that those who could not, or would not, read the record of it in the sacred history, might come to the knowledge of it by the monument set up in remembrance of it, of which the common tradition of the country would be an explication; it would likewise serve to corroborate the proof of the matter of fact, and would remain a standing evidence of it to those who in after-ages might question the truth of it. A monument is to be erected, and, 1. Joshua, as chief captain, must give directions about it (*v.* 1): *When all the people had clean passed over Jordan,* not even the feeble, that were the hindmost of them, left behind, so that God had done his work completely, and every Israelite got safe into Canaan, then God spoke unto Joshua to provide materials for this monument. It is the pious conjecture of the learned bishop Patrick that Joshua had gone into some place of retirement to return thanks immediately for this wonderful mercy, and then God met him, and spoke thus to him. Or, perhaps, it was by Eleazar the priest that God gave these and other instructions to Joshua; for, though he is not mentioned here, yet, when Joshua was ordained by the imposition of hands to this great trust, God appointed that Eleazar should *ask counsel for him after the judgment of Urim, and at his word Joshua and all the children of Israel must go out and come in,* Num. xxvii. 21. 2. One man out of each tribe, and he a chosen man, must be employed to prepare materials for this monument, that each tribe might have the story told them by one of themselves, and each tribe might contribute something to the glory of God thereby (*v.* 2, 4): *Out of every tribe a man.* Not the Levites only, but every Israelite must, in his place, help to *make known to the sons of men God's mighty acts,* Ps. cxlv. 12. The two tribes, though seated already in their possession, yet, sharing in the mercy, must lend a hand to the memorial of it. 3. The stones that must be set up for this memorial are ordered to be taken out of the midst of the channel (where, probably, there lay abundance of great stones), and as near as might be from the very place where the priests stood *with the ark, v.* 3, 5. This intended monument deserved to be made of stones curiously cut with the finest and most exquisite art, but these stones out of the bottom of the river were more natural and more apt indications of the miracle. Let posterity know by this that Jordan was driven back, for these very stones were then fetched out of it. In the institution of signs, God always chose that which was most proper and significant, rather than that which is pompous or curious; for *God hath chosen the foolish things of the world.* These twelve men, after they got over Jordan, must be sent back to the place where the ark stood, being permitted to come near it (which others might not) for this service: "*Pass over before the ark* (*v.* 5), that is, into the presence of the ark, which now stands in the midst of Jordan, and thence fetch these stones." 4. The use of these stones is here appointed for a sign (*v.* 6), a memorial, *v.* 7. They would give occasion to the children to ask their parents in time to come, *How came these stones hither?* (probably the land about not being stony), and then the parents would inform them, as they themselves had been informed, that in this place Jordan was divided by the almighty power of God, to give Israel passage into Canaan, as Joshua enlarges on this head, *v.* 22, &c.

II. According to these orders the thing was done. 1. Twelve stones were taken up out of the midst of Jordan, and carried in the sight of the people to the place where they had their head-quarters that night, *v.* 8. It is probable that the stones they took were as big as they could well carry, and as near as might be of a size and shape. But whether they went away with them immediately to the place, or whether they staid to attend the ark, and kept pace with the solemn procession of that, to grace its triumphant entry into Canaan, is not certain. By these stones which they were ordered to take up God did, as it were, give them livery and seisin of this good land; it is all their own, let them enter and take possession; therefore what these twelve did the children of Israel are said to do (*v.* 8), because they were the representatives of their respective tribes. In allusion to this, we may observe that when the Lord Jesus, our Joshua, having overcome the sharpness of death and dried up that Jordan, had opened the kingdom of heaven to all believers, he appointed his twelve apostles according to the number of the tribes of Israel, by the memorial of the gospel to transmit the knowledge of this to remote places and future ages. 2. Other twelve stones (probably much larger than the other, for we read not that they were each of them one man's load) were set up *in the midst of Jordan* (*v.* 9), piled up so high in a heap or pillar as that the top of it might be seen above water when the river was low, or seen in the water when it was clear, or at least the noise or commotion of the water passing over it would be observable, and the bargemen would avoid it, as they do a rock. Some way or other, it is likely, it was discernible, so as to notify the very place where the ark stood, and to serve for a duplicate to the other monument, which was to be set up on dry land in Gilgal, for the confirming of its testimony and the preserving of its tradition. The sign being doubled, no doubt the thing was certain.

10 For the priests which bare the ark stood in the midst of Jordan, until every thing was finished that the LORD commanded Joshua to speak unto the people, according to all that Moses commanded Joshua: and the people hasted and passed over. 11 And it came to pass, when all the people were clean passed over, that the ark of the LORD passed over, and the priests, in the presence of the people. 12 And the children of Reuben, and the children of Gad, and half the tribe of Manasseh, passed over armed before the children of Israel, as Moses spake unto them: 13 About forty thousand prepared for war passed over before the LORD unto battle, to the plains of Jericho. 14 On that day the LORD magnified Joshua in the sight of all Israel; and they feared him, as they feared Moses, all the days of his life. 15 And the LORD spake unto Joshua, saying, 16 Command the priests that bear the ark of the testimony, that they come up out of Jordan. 17 Joshua therefore commanded the priests, saying, Come ye up out of Jordan. 18 And it came to pass, when the priests that bare the ark of the covenant of the LORD were come up out of the midst of Jordan, *and* the soles of the priests' feet were lifted up unto the dry land, that the waters of Jordan returned unto their place, and flowed over all his banks, as *they did* before. 19 And the people came up out of Jordan on the tenth *day* of the first month, and encamped in Gilgal, in the east border of Jericho.

The inspired historian seems to be so well pleased with his subject here that he is loth to quit it, and is therefore very particular in his narrative, especially in observing how closely Joshua pursued the orders God gave him, and that he did nothing without divine direction, finishing all that *the Lord had commanded* him (*v.* 10), which is also said to be what *Moses commanded.* We read not of any particular commands that Moses gave to Joshua about this matter: the thing was altogether new to him. It must therefore be understood of the general instructions Moses had given him to follow the divine direction, to deliver that to the people which he had *received of the Lord,* and to take all occasions to remind them of their duty to God, as the best return for his favours to them. This which Moses, who was now dead and gone, had said to him, he had in mind at this time, and *did accordingly.* It is well for us to have the good instructions that have been given us ready to us when we have occasion for them.

I. *The people hasted and passed over,* *v.* 10. Some understand this of the twelve men that carried the stones, but it seems rather to be meant of the body of the people; for, though an account was given of their passing over (*v.* 1), yet here it is repeated for the sake of this circumstance, which was to be added, that they passed over *in haste,* either because Joshua by their officers ordered them to make haste, for it was to be but one day's work and they must not *leave a hoof behind,* or perhaps it was their own inclination that hastened them. 1. Some hasted because they were not able to trust God. They were afraid the waters should return upon them, being conscious of guilt, and diffident of the divine power and goodness. 2. Others because they were not willing to tempt God to continue the miracle longer than needs must, nor would they put the patience of the priests that bore the ark too much to the stretch by unnecessary delay. 3. Others because they were eager to be in Canaan, and would thus show how much they longed after that pleasant land. 4. Those that considered least, yet hasted because others did. He that believeth doth not make haste to *anticipate* God's counsels, but he makes haste to *attend* them, Isa. xxviii. 16.

II. The two tribes and a half led the van, *v.* 12, 13. So they had promised when they had their lot given them on that side Jordan, Num. xxxii. 27. And Joshua had lately reminded them of their promise, *ch.* i. 12—15. It was fit that those who had the first settlement should be the first in the encounter of difficulties, the rather because they had not the incumbrance of families with them as the other tribes had, and they were all chosen men, and fit for service, ready armed. It was a good providence that they had so strong a body to lead them on, and would be an encouragement to the rest. And the two tribes had no reason to complain: the post of danger is the post of honour.

III. When all the people had got clear to the other side, the priests with the ark came up out of Jordan. This, one would think, should have been done of course; their own reason would tell them that now there was no more occasion for them, and yet they did not stir a step till Joshua ordered them to move, and Joshua did not order them out of Jordan till God directed him to do so, *v.* 15—17. So observant were they of Joshua, and he of God, which was their praise, as it was their happiness to be under such good direction. How low a condition soever God may at any time bring his priests or people to, let them patiently wait, till by his providence he shall call them up out of it, as the priests here were called to come up out of Jordan, and let them not be weary of waiting, while they have the tokens of God's presence with them, even the ark of the covenant, in the depth of their adversity.

IV. As soon as ever the priests and the ark had come up out of Jordan, the waters of the river, which had stood on a heap, gradually flowed down according to their nature and usual course, and soon filled the channel again, *v.* 18. This makes it yet more evident that the stop which had now been given to the river was not from any secret natural cause, but purely from the power of God's presence, and for the sake of his Israel; for when Israel's turn was served, and the token of God's presence was removed, immediately the water went forward again; so that if it be asked, *What ailed thee, O Jordan! that thou wast driven back?* It must be answered, It was purely in obedience to the God of Israel, and in kindness to the Israel of God. There is therefore none *like unto the God of Jeshurun; happy also art thou, O Israel! who is like unto thee, O people?* Some observe here, by way of allusion, that when the ark, and the priests that bore it, are removed from any place, the flood-gates are drawn up, the defence has departed, and an inundation of judgments is to be expected shortly. Those that are unchurched will soon be undone. The glory has departed if the ark is taken.

V. Notice is taken of the honour put upon Joshua by all this (*v.* 14): *On that day the Lord magnified Joshua,* both by the fellowship he admitted him to with himself, speaking to him upon all occasions and being ready to be consulted by him, and by the authority he confirmed him in over both priests and people. Those that honour God he will honour, and when he will magnify a man, as he had said he would magnify Joshua (*ch.* iii. 7), he will do it effectually. Yet it was not for Joshua's sake only that he was thus magnified, but to put him in a capacity of doing so much the more service to Israel, for hereupon they feared him as they feared Moses. See here what is the best and surest way to command the respect of inferiors, and to gain their reverence and observance, not by blustering and threatening, and carrying it with a high hand, but by holiness and love, and all possible indications of a constant regard to their welfare, and to God's will and honour. Those are feared in the best manner, and to the best purpose, who make it to appear that God is with them, and that they set him before them. Those that are sanctified are truly magnified, and are worthy of double honour. Favourites of heaven should be looked on with awe.

VI. An account is kept of the time of this great event (*v.* 19): it was *on the tenth day of the first month,* just forty years since they came out of Egypt, wanting five days. God had said in his wrath that they should wander forty years in the wilderness, but, to make up that forty, we must take in the first year, which was then past, and had been a year of triumph in their deliverance out of Egypt, and this last, which had been a year of triumph likewise on the other side Jordan, so that all the forty were not years of sorrow; and at last he brought them into Canaan five days before the forty years were ended, to show how little pleasure God takes in punishing, how swift he is to show mercy, and that *for the elects' sake the days* of trouble *are shortened,* Matt. xxiv. 22. God ordered it so that they should enter Canaan four days before the annual solemnity of the passover, and on the very day when the preparation for it was to begin (Exod. xii. 3), because he would have their entrance into Canaan graced and sanctified with that religious feast, and would have them then to be reminded of their deliverance out of Egypt, that, comparing them together, God might be glorified as the *Alpha* and *Omega* of their bliss.

20 And those twelve stones, which they took out of Jordan, did Joshua pitch in Gilgal. 21 And he spake unto the children of Israel, saying, When your children shall ask their fathers in time to come, saying, What *mean* these stones? 22 Then ye shall let your children know, saying, Israel came over this Jordan on dry land. 23 For the LORD your God dried up the waters of Jordan from before you, until ye were passed over, as the LORD your God did to the Red sea, which he dried up from before us, until we were gone over: 24 That all the people of the earth might know the hand of the LORD, that it *is* mighty: that ye might fear the LORD your God for ever.

The twelve stones which were *laid down in Gilgal* (*v.* 8) are here set up either one upon another, yet so as that they might be distinctly counted, or one by another in rows; for after they were fixed they are not called *a heap of stones*, but *these stones*.

I. It is here taken for granted that posterity would enquire into the meaning of them, supposing them intended for a memorial: *Your children shall ask their fathers* (for who else should they ask?) *What mean these stones?* Note, Those that will be wise when they are old must be inquisitive when they are young. Our Lord Jesus, though he had in himself the fulness of knowledge, has by his example taught children and young people to hear and ask questions, Luke ii. 46. Perhaps when John was baptizing in Jordan at Bethabara (the house of passage, where the people passed over) he pointed at these very stones, while saying (Matt. iii. 9) *God is able of these stones* (which were at first set up by the twelve tribes) *to raise up children unto Abraham.* The stones being the memorial of the miracle, the children's question gave occasion for the improvement of it; but our Saviour says (Luke x. 40), *If the children should hold their peace, the stones would immediately cry out;* for one way or other the Lord will be glorified in his works of wonder.

II. The parents are here directed what answer to give to this enquiry (*v.* 22): "*You shall let your children know* that which you have yourselves learned from the written word and from your fathers." Note, It is the duty of parents to acquaint their children betimes with the word and works of God, that they may be trained up in the way they should go.

1. They must let their children know that Jordan was driven back before Israel, who *went through it upon dry land*, and that this was the very place where they passed over. They saw how deep and strong a stream Jordan now was, but the divine power put a stop to it, even when it overflowed all its banks—"and this for you, that live so long after." Note, God's mercies to our ancestors were mercies to us; and we should take all occasions to revive the remembrance of the great things God did for our fathers *in the days of old.* The place thus marked would be a memorandum to them: Israel came over this Jordan. A local memory would be of use to them, and the sight of the place remind them of that which was done there; and not only the inhabitants of that country, but strangers and travellers, would look upon these stones and receive instruction. Many, upon the sight of the stones, would go to their Bibles, and there read the history of this wondrous work; and some perhaps, upon reading the history, though living at a distance, would have the curiosity to go and see the stones.

2. They must take that occasion to tell their children of the drying up of the Red Sea forty years before: *As the Lord your God did to the Red Sea.* Note, (1.) It greatly magnifies later mercies to compare them with former mercies, for, by making the comparison, it appears that God is the same yesterday, to-day, and for ever. (2.) Later mercies should bring to remembrance former mercies, and revive our thankfulness for them.

3. They must put them in the way of making a good use of these works of wonder, the knowledge whereof was thus carefully transmitted to them, *v.* 24. (1.) The power of God was hereby magnified. All the world was or might be convinced that *the hand of the Lord is mighty*, that nothing is too hard for God to do; nor can any power, no, not that of nature itself, obstruct what God will effect. The deliverances of God's people are instructions to all people, and fair warnings not to contend with Omnipotence. (2.) The people of God were engaged and encouraged to persevere in his service "*That you might fear the Lord your God,* and consequently do your duty to him, and this for ever," or *all days (margin)*, "every day, all the days of your lives, and your seed throughout your generations." The remembrance of this wonderful work should effectually restrain them from the worship of other gods, and constrain them to abide and abound in the service of their own God. Note, In all the instructions and informations parents give their children, they should have this

chiefly in their eye, to teach and engage them to *fear God for ever.* Serious godliness is the best learning.

CHAP. V.

Israel have now got over Jordan, and the waters which had opened before them, to favour their march forward, are closed again behind them, to forbid their retreat backward. They have now got footing in Canaan, and must apply themselves to the conquest of it, in order to which this chapter tells us, I. How their enemies were dispirited, ver. 1. II. What was done at their first landing to assist and encourage them. 1. The covenant of circumcision was renewed, ver. 2—9. 2. The feast of the passover was celebrated, ver. 10. 3. Their camp was victualled with the corn of the land, whereupon the manna ceased, ver. 11, 12. 4. The captain of the Lord's host himself appeared to Joshua to animate and direct him, ver. 13—15.

AND it came to pass, when all the kings of the Amorites, which *were* on the side of Jordan westward, and all the kings of the Canaanites, which *were* by the sea, heard that the LORD had dried up the waters of Jordan from before the children of Israel, until we were passed over, that their heart melted, neither was there spirit in them any more, because of the children of Israel. 2 At that time the LORD said unto Joshua, Make thee sharp knives, and circumcise again the children of Israel the second time. 3 And Joshua made him sharp knives, and circumcised the children of Israel at the hill of the foreskins. 4 And this *is* the cause why Joshua did circumcise: All the people that came out of Egypt, *that were* males, *even* all the men of war, died in the wilderness by the way, after they came out of Egypt. 5 Now all the people that came out were circumcised: but all the people *that were* born in the wilderness by the way as they came forth out of Egypt, *them* they had not circumcised. 6 For the children of Israel walked forty years in the wilderness, till all the people *that were* men of war, which came out of Egypt, were consumed, because they obeyed not the voice of the LORD: unto whom the LORD sware that he would not show them the land, which the LORD sware unto their fathers that he would give us, a land that floweth with milk and honey. 7 And their children, *whom* he raised up in their stead, them Joshua circumcised: for they were uncircumcised, because they had not circumcised them by the way. 8 And it came to pass, when they had done circumcising all the people, that they abode in their places in the camp, till they were whole. 9 And the LORD said unto Joshua, This day have I rolled away the reproach of Egypt from off you. Wherefore the name of the place is called Gilgal unto this day.

A vast show, no doubt, the numerous camp of Israel made in the plains of Jericho, where now they had pitched their tents. *Who can count the dust of Jacob?* That which had long been the *church in the wilderness has now come up from the wilderness, leaning upon her beloved, and looks forth as the morning, fair as the moon, clear as the sun, and terrible as an army with banners.* How terrible she was in the eyes of her enemies we are here told, *v.* 1. How fair and clear she was made in the eyes of her friends, by the rolling away of the reproach of Egypt, we are told in the following verses.

I. Here is the fright which the Canaanites were put into by their miraculously passing over Jordan, *v.* 1. The news of it was soon dispersed all the country over, not only as a prodigy in itself, but as an alarm to all the kings and kingdoms of Canaan. Now, as when Babylon was taken, *One post runs to meet another, and one messenger to meet another,* to carry the amazing tidings to every corner of their land, Jer. li. 31. And here we are told what impressions the tidings made upon the kings of this land: *Their heart melted* like wax before the fire, *neither was there spirit in them any more.* This intimates that, though the heart of the people generally had fainted before (as Rahab owned, *ch.* ii. 9), yet the kings had till now kept up their spirits pretty well, had promised themselves that, being in possession, their country populous, and their cities fortified, they should be able to make their part good against the invaders; but when they heard not only that they had come over Jordan, and that this defence of their country was broken through, but that they had come over by a miracle, the God of nature manifestly fighting for them, *their hearts failed them* too, they gave up the cause for gone, and were now at their wits' end. And, 1. They had reason enough to be afraid; Israel itself was a formidable body, and much more so when God was its head, a God of almighty power. What can make head against them if Jordan be driven back before them? 2. God impressed these fears upon them, and dispirited them, as he had promised (Exod. xxiii. 27), *I will send my fear before thee.* God can make the wicked to fear *where no fear is* (Ps. liii. 5), much more where there is such cause for fear as was here. He that made the soul can, when he pleases, make his sword thus to approach to it and kill it with his terrors.

II. The opportunity which this gave to the Israelites to circumcise those among them that were uncircumcised: *At that time* (*v.* 2), when the country about them was in that great consternation, God ordered Joshua to circumcise the children of Israel, for at that time it might be done with safety even in an enemy's country; their hearts being melted, their hands were tied, that they could not take this advantage against them as Simeon and Levi did against the Shechemites, to come upon them *when they were sore.* Joshua could not be sure of this, and therefore, if he had ordered this general circumcision just at this time of his own head, he might justly have been censured as imprudent; for, how good soever the thing was in itself, in the eye of reason it was not seasonable at this time, and might have been of dangerous consequence; but, when God commanded him to do it, he must not *consult with flesh and blood:* he that bade them to do it would, no doubt, protect them and bear them out in it. Now observe,

1. The occasion there was for this general circumcision. (1.) All that came out of Egypt were circumcised, *v.* 5. While they had peace in Egypt doubtless they circumcised their children the eighth day according to the law. But after they began to be oppressed, especially when the edict was made for the destruction of their male infants, the administration of this ordinance was interrupted; many of them were uncircumcised, of whom there was a general circumcision, either during the time of the three days' darkness, as Dr. Lightfoot conjectures, or a year after, just before their eating the second passover at Mount Sinai, and in order to that solemnity (Num. ix. 2) as many think. And it is with reference to that general circumcision that this is called a *second, v.* 2. But the learned Masius thinks it refers to the general circumcision of Abraham's family when that ordinance was first instituted, Gen. xvii. 23. That first confirmed the promise of the land of Canaan, this second was a thankful celebration of the performance of that promise. But, (2.) All that were *born in the wilderness,* namely, after their walking in the wilderness, became by the divine sentence a judgment upon them for their disobedience, as is intimated by that repetition of the sentence, *v.* 6. All that were born since that fatal day on which God swore in his wrath that none of that generation should *enter into his rest* were uncircumcised. But what shall we say to this? Had not God enjoined it to Abraham, under a very severe penalty, that every man-child of his seed should be circumcised on the eighth day? Gen. xvii. 9—14. Was it not the seal of the everlasting covenant? Was not so great a stress laid upon it when they were coming out of Egypt that when, immediately after the first passover, the law concerning that feast was made perpetual, this was one clause of it, that no uncircumcised person should eat of it, but should be deemed as a stranger? and yet, under the government of Moses himself, to have all their children that were born for thirty-eight years together left uncircumcised is unaccountable. So great an omission could not be general but by divine direction. Now, [1.] Some think circumcision was omitted because it was needless: it was appointed to be a mark of distinction between the Israelites and other nations, and therefore in the wilderness, where they were so perfectly separated from all and mingled with none, there was no occasion for it. [2.] Others think that they did not look upon the precept of circumcision as obligatory till they came to settle in Canaan; for in the covenant made with them at Mount Sinai nothing was said about circumcision, neither was it of Moses but *of the fathers* (John vii. 22), and with particular reference to the grant of the land of Canaan, Gen. xvii. 8. [3.] Others think that God favourably dispensed with the observance of this ordinance in consideration of the unsettledness of their state, and their frequent removals while they were in the wilderness. It was requisite that children after they were circumcised should rest for some time while they were sore, and stirring them might be dangerous to them; God therefore would have mercy and not sacrifice. This reason is generally acquiesced in, but to me it is not satisfactory, for sometimes they staid a year in a place (Num. ix. 22), if not much longer, and in their removals the little children, though sore, might be wrapped so warm, and carried so easy, as to receive no damage, and might certainly be much better accommodated than the mothers in travail or while lying in. Therefore, [4.] To me it seems to have been a continued token of God's displeasure against them for their unbelief and murmuring. Circumcision was originally a seal of the promise of the land of Canaan, as we observed before. It was in the believing hope of that good land that the patriarchs circumcised their children; but when God had *sworn in his wrath* concerning the men of war who came out of Egypt that they should be consumed in the wilderness, and never enter Canaan, nor come within sight of it (as that sentence is here repeated, *v.* 6, reference being made to it), as a further ratification of that sentence, and to be a constant memorandum of it to them, all that fell under that sentence, and were to fall by it, were forbidden to circumcise their children, by which they were plainly told that, whatever others might, they should never have the benefit of that promise of which circumcision was the seal. And this was such a significant indication of God's wrath as the breaking of the tables of the covenant was when Israel had broken the covenant by making the golden calf. It is true that there is no express mention of this judicial prohibition in the account of that sentence; but an intimation of it in Num. xiv. 33, *Your children shall bear your whoredoms.* It is probable the children

of Caleb and Joshua were circumcised, for they were excepted out of that sentence, and of Caleb it is particularly said, *To him will I give the land, and to his children* (Deut. i. 36), which was the very promise that circumcision was the seal of: and Joshua is here told to circumcise the people, not his own family. Whatever the reason was, it seems that this great ordinance was omitted in Israel for almost forty years together, which is a plain indication that it was not of absolute necessity, nor was to be of perpetual obligation, but should in the fulness of time be abolished, as now it was for so long a time suspended.

2. The orders given to Joshua for this general circumcision (*v.* 2): *Circumcise again the children of Israel*, not the same persons, but the body of the people. Why was this ordered to be done now? Answ. (1.) Because now the promise of which circumcision was instituted to be the seal was performed. The seed of Israel was brought safely into the land of Canaan. "Let them therefore hereby own the truth of that promise which their fathers had disbelieved, and could not find in their hearts to trust to." (2.) Because now the threatening of which the suspending of circumcision for thirty-eight years was the ratification was fully executed by the expiring of the forty years. That *warfare is accomplished, that iniquity is pardoned* (Isa. xl. 2), and therefore now the seal of the covenant is revived again. But why was it not done sooner? why not while they were resting some months in the plains of Moab? why not during the thirty days of their mourning for Moses? Why was it not deferred longer, till they had made some progress in the conquest of Canaan, and had gained a settlement there, at least till they had entrenched themselves, and fortified their camp? Why must it be done the very next day after they had come over Jordan? Answ. Because divine Wisdom saw that to be the fittest time, just when the forty years were ended, and they had entered Canaan; and the reasons which human wisdom would have offered against it were easily overruled. [1.] God would hereby show that the camp of Israel was not governed by the ordinary rules and measures of war, but by immediate direction from God, who by thus exposing them, in the most dangerous moments, magnified his own power in protecting them even then. And this great instance of security, in disabling themselves for action just when they were entering upon action, proclaimed such confidence in the divine care for their safety as would increase their enemies' fears, much more when their scouts informed them not only of the thing itself that was done, but of the meaning of it, that it was a seal of the grant of this land to Israel. [2.] God would hereby animate his people Israel against the difficulties they were now to encounter, by confirming his covenant with them, which gave them unquestionable assurance of victory and success, and the full possession of the land of promise. [3.] God would hereby teach them, and us with them, in all great undertakings to *begin with God*, to make sure of his favour, by offering ourselves to him *a living sacrifice* (for that was signified by the blood of circumcision), and then we may expect to prosper in all we do. [4.] The reviving of circumcision, after it had been so long disused, was designed to revive the observance of other institutions, the omission of which had been connived at in the wilderness. This command to circumcise them was to remind them of that which Moses had told them (Deut. xii. 8), that when they should have come *over Jordan* they must not do as they had done *in the wilderness*, but must come under a stricter discipline. It was said concerning many of the laws God had given them that they must observe them *in the land* to which they were going, Deut. vi. 1; xii. 1. [5.] This *second* circumcision, as it is here called, was typical of the spiritual circumcision with which the Israel of God, when they enter into the gospel rest, are circumcised; it is the learned bishop Pierson's observation that this circumcision being performed under the direction of Joshua, Moses's successor, it points to *Jesus as the true circumciser*, the author of *another circumcision* than that *of the flesh*, commanded by the law, even the *circumcision of the heart* (Rom. ii. 29), called the *circumcision of Christ*, Col. ii. 11.

3. The people's obedience to these orders. Joshua *circumcised the children of Israel* (*v.* 3), not himself with his own hands, but he commanded that it should be done, and took care that it was done: it might soon be despatched, for it was not necessary that it should be done by a priest or Levite, but any one might be employed to do it. All those that were under twenty years old when the people were numbered at Mount Sinai, and not being numbered with them fell not by the fatal sentence, were circumcised, and by them all the rest might be circumcised in a little time. The people had promised to hearken to Joshua as they had hearkened to Moses (*ch.* i. 17), and here they gave an instance of their dutifulness by submitting to this painful institution, and not calling him for the sake of it a bloody governor, as Zipporah because of the circumcision called Moses a bloody husband.

4. The names given to the place where this was done, to perpetuate the memory of it. (1.) It was called *the hill of the foreskins*, *v.* 3. Probably the foreskins that were cut off were laid on a heap, and covered with earth, so that they made a little hillock. (2.) It was called *Gilgal*, from a word which signifies to take away, from that which God said to Joshua (*v.* 9), *This day have I rolled away the reproach of Egypt*. God is jealous for the honour of his people, his own honour

being so much interested in it; and, whatever reproach they may lie under for a time, first or last it will certainly be rolled away, and every tongue that riseth up against them he will condemn. [1.] Their circumcision rolled away the reproach of Egypt. They were hereby owned to be the free-born children of God, having the seal of the covenant in their flesh, and so the reproach of their bondage in Egypt was removed. They were tainted with the idolatry of Egypt, and that was their reproach; but now that they were circumcised it was to be hoped they would be so entirely devoted to God that the reproach of their affection to Egypt would be rolled away. [2.] Their coming safely to Canaan rolled away the reproach of Egypt, for it silenced that spiteful suggestion of the Egyptians, that *for mischief they were brought out, the wilderness had shut them in,* Exod. xiv. 3. Their wandering so long in the wilderness confirmed the reproach, but now that they had entered Canaan in triumph that reproach was done away. When God glorifies himself in perfecting the salvation of his people he not only silences the reproach of their enemies, but rolls it upon themselves.

10 And the children of Israel encamped in Gilgal, and kept the passover on the fourteenth day of the month at even in the plains of Jericho. 11 And they did eat of the old corn of the land on the morrow after the passover, unleavened cakes, and parched *corn* in the selfsame day. 12 And the manna ceased on the morrow after they had eaten of the old corn of the land; neither had the children of Israel manna any more; but they did eat of the fruit of the land of Canaan that year.

We may well imagine that the people of Canaan were astonished, and that when they observed the motions of the enemy they could not but think them very strange. When soldiers take the field they are apt to think themselves excused from religious exercises (they have not time nor thought to attend to them), yet Joshua opens the campaign with one act of devotion after another. What was afterwards said to another Joshua might truly be said to this, *Hear now, O Joshua! thou and thy fellows that sit before thee are men wondered at* (Zech. iii. 8), and yet indeed he took the right method. That is likely to end well which begins with God. Here is,

I. A solemn passover kept, at the time appointed by the law, *the fourteenth day of the first month,* and in the same place where they were circumcised, *v.* 10. While they were wandering in the wilderness they were denied the benefit and comfort of this ordinance, as a further token of God's displeasure; but now, in answer to the prayer of Moses upon the passing of that sentence Ps. xc. 15, God comforted them again, after the time that he had afflicted them, and therefore now that joyful ordinance is revived again. Now that they had entered into Canaan it was very seasonable to remember those wondrous works of divine power and goodness by which they were brought out of Egypt. The finishing of mercies should bring to mind the beginning of them; and when it is perfect day we must not forget how welcome the morning-light was when we had long waited for it. The solemn passover followed immediately after the solemn circumcision; thus, when those that received the word were baptized, immediately we find them *breaking bread,* Acts ii. 41, 42. They kept this passover in the plains of Jericho, as it were in defiance of the Canaanites that were round about them and enraged against them, and yet could not give them any disturbance. Thus God gave them an early instance of the performance of that promise that when they went up to keep the feasts their land should be taken under the special protection of the divine Providence. Exod. xxxiv. 24, *Neither shall any man desire thy land.* He now *prepared a table before them in the presence of their enemies,* Ps. xxiii. 5.

II. Provision made for their camp of the *corn of the land,* and the *ceasing of the manna* thereupon, *v.* 11, 12. Manna was a wonderful mercy to them when they needed it. But it was the mark of a wilderness state; it was the food of children; and therefore, though it was angel's food, and not to be complained of as light bread, yet it would be more acceptable to them to eat of the *corn of the land,* and this they are now furnished with.

1. The country people, having retired for safety into Jericho, had left their barns and fields, and all that was in them, which served for the subsistence of this great army. And the supply came very seasonably, for, (1.) After the passover they were to keep *the feast of unleavened bread,* which they could not do according to the appointment when they had nothing but manna to live upon; and perhaps this was one reason why it was intermitted in the wilderness. But now they found old corn enough in the barns of the Canaanites to supply them plentifully for that occasion; thus *the wealth of the sinner is laid up for the just,* and little did those who laid it up think *whose all these things should be which they had provided.* (2.) On the morrow after the passover-sabbath they were to *wave the sheaf of first-fruits before the Lord,* Lev. xxiii. 10, 11. And this they were particularly ordered to do when they *came into the land which God would give them:* and they were furnished for this with the *fruit of the land that year* (*v.* 12), which

was then growing and beginning to be ripe. Thus they were well provided for, both with *old and new corn, as good householders.* See Matt. xiii. 52. And as soon as ever the fruits of this good land came to their hands they had an opportunity of honouring God with them, and employing them in his service according to his appointment. And thus, *behold, all things were clean* and comfortable *to them.* Calvin is of opinion that they had kept the passover every year in its season during their wandering in the wilderness, though it is not mentioned, and that God dispensed with their being uncircumcised, as he did, notwithstanding that, admit them to offer other sacrifices. But some gather from Amos v. 25 that after the sentence passed upon them there were no sacrifices offered till they came to Canaan, and consequently no passover was kept. And it is observable that after that sentence (Num. xiv.) the law which follows (Num. xv.) concerning sacrifices begins thus: "*When you shall have come into the land of your habitations*" you shall do so and so.

2. Notice is taken of the ceasing of the manna as soon as ever they had eaten the *old corn of the land,* (1.) To show that it did not come by chance or common providence, as snow or hail does, but by the special designation of divine wisdom and goodness; for, as it came just when they needed it, so it continued as long as they had occasion for it and no longer. (2.) To teach us not to expect extraordinary supplies when supplies may be had in an ordinary way. If God had dealt with Israel according to their deserts, the manna would have ceased when they called it light bread; but as long as they needed it God continued it, though they despised it; and now that they needed it not God withdrew it, though perhaps some of them desired it. He is a wise Father, who knows the necessities of his children, and accommodates his gifts to *them,* not to their humours. The word and ordinances of God are spiritual manna, with which God nourishes his people in this wilderness, and, though often forfeited, yet they are continued while we are here; but when we come to the heavenly Canaan this manna will cease, for we shall no longer have need of it.

13 And it came to pass, when Joshua was by Jericho, that he lifted up his eyes and looked, and, behold, there stood a man over against him with his sword drawn in his hand: and Joshua went unto him, and said unto him, *Art* thou for us, or for our adversaries? 14 And he said, Nay; but *as* captain of the host of the LORD am I now come. And Joshua fell on his face to the earth, and did worship, and said unto him, What saith my lord unto his servant? 15 And the captain of the LORD's host said unto Joshua, Loose thy shoe from off thy foot; for the place whereon thou standest *is* holy. And Joshua did so.

We have hitherto found God often speaking to Joshua, but we read not till now of any appearance of God's glory to him; now that his difficulties increased his encouragements were increased in proportion. Observe,

I. The time when he was favoured with this vision. It was immediately after he had performed the great solemnities of circumcision and the passover; then God made himself known to him. Note, We may then expect the discoveries of the divine grace when we are found in the way of our duty and are diligent and sincere in our attendance on holy ordinances.

II. The place where he had this vision. It was *by Jericho; in Jericho,* so the word is; in it by faith and hope, though as yet he had not begun to lay siege to it; in it in thought and expectation; or in the fields of Jericho, hard by the city. There, it should seem, he was all alone, fearless of danger, because sure of the divine protection. There he was (some think) meditating and praying; and to those who are so employed God often graciously manifests himself. Or perhaps there he was to take a view of the city, to observe its fortifications, and contrive how to attack it; and perhaps he was at a loss within himself how to make his approaches, when God came and directed him. Note, God will *help those that help themselves. Vigilantibus non dormientibus succurrit lex—The law succours those who watch, not those who sleep.* Joshua was in his post as a general, when God came and made himself known as Generalissimo.

III. The appearance itself. Joshua, as is usual with those that are full of thought and care, was looking downwards, his eyes fixed on the ground, when of a sudden he was surprised with the appearance of a man who stood before him at some little distance, which obliged him to lift up his eyes, and gave a diversion to his musings, *v.* 13. He appeared to him as a man, but a considerable man, and one fit to be taken notice of. Now, 1. We have reason to think that this man was the Son of God, the eternal Word, who, before he assumed the human nature for a perpetuity, frequently appeared in a human shape. So bishop Patrick thinks, consonant to the judgment of the fathers. Joshua gave him divine honours, and he received them, which a created angel would not have done, and he is called *Jehovah, ch.* vi. 2. 2. He here appeared as a soldier, with *his sword drawn in his hand.* To Abraham in his tent he appeared as a traveller; to Joshua in the field as a man of war. Christ will be to his people what their faith expects and desires. Christ had his sword drawn, which served, (1.) To justify the war Joshua was engaging in, and to show him that it was of God, who gave him commission to kill and slay. If the sovereign draw the sword, this proclaims war, and authorizes the subject to do so too. The sword is then well drawn when Christ *draws it, and gives the banner to those that fear him, to be displayed because of the truth,* Ps. lx. 4. (2.) To encourage him to carry it on with vigour; for Christ's sword drawn in his hand denotes how ready he is for the defence and salvation of his people, who through him shall do valiantly. His sword turns every way.

IV. The bold question with which Joshua accosted him; he did not send a servant, but stepped up to him himself, and asked, *Art thou for us or for our adversaries?* which intimates his readiness to entertain him if he were for them, and to fight him if he were against them. This shows, 1. His great courage and resolution. He was not ruffled by the suddenness of the appearance, nor daunted with the majesty and bravery which no doubt appeared in the countenance of the person he saw; but, with a presence of mind that became so great a general, put this fair question to him. God had bidden Joshua be courageous, and by this it appears that he was so; for what God by his word requires of his people he does by his grace work in them. 2. His great concern for the people and their cause; so heartily has he embarked in the interests of Israel that none shall stand by him with the face of a man but he will know whether he be a friend or a foe. It should seem, he suspected him for an enemy, a Goliath that had come to *defy the armies of the living God,* and to give him a challenge. Thus apt are we to look upon that as against us which is most for us. The question plainly implies that the cause between the Israelites and the Canaanites, between Christ and Beelzebub, will not admit of a neutrality. *He that is not with us is against us.*

V. The account he gave of himself, *v.* 14. "Nay, not for your adversaries, you may be sure, but *as captain of the host of the Lord have I now come,* not only for you as a friend, but over you as commander in chief." Here were now, as of old (Gen. xxxii. 2), *Mahanaim, two hosts,* a host of Israelites ready to engage the Canaanites and a host of angels to protect them therein, and he, as captain of both, conducts the host of Israel and commands the host of angels to their assistance. Perhaps in allusion to this Christ is called the *captain of our salvation* (Heb. ii. 10), *and a leader and commander to the people,* Isa. lv. 4. Those cannot but be victorious that have such a captain. He now came as captain to review the troops, to animate them, and to give the necessary orders for the besieging of Jericho.

VI. The great respect Joshua paid him when he understood who he was; it is probable that he perceived, not only by what he said but by some other sensible indications, that he was a divine person, and not a man. 1. Joshua paid homage to him: He *fell on his face to the earth and did worship.* Joshua was himself general of the forces of Israel, and yet he was far from looking with jealousy upon this stranger, who produced a commission as captain of the Lord's host above him; he did not offer to dispute his claims, but cheerfully submitted to him as his commander. It will become the greatest of men to be humble and reverent in their addresses to God. 2. He begged to receive commands and directions from him: *What saith my Lord unto his servant?* His former question was not more bold and soldier-like than this was pious and saint-like; nor was it any disparagement to the greatness of Joshua's spirit thus to humble himself when he had to do with God: even crowned heads cannot bow too low before the throne of the Lord Jesus, who is *King of kings,* Ps. ii. 10, 11; lxxii. 10, 11; Rev. xix. 16. Observe, (1.) The relation he owns between himself and Christ, that Christ was his Lord and himself his servant and under his command, Christ his Captain and himself a soldier under him, to do as he is bidden, Matt. viii. 9. Note, The foundation of all acceptable obedience is laid in a sincere dedication of ourselves, as servants to Jesus Christ as *our Lord,* Ps. xvi. 2. (2.) The enquiry he makes pursuant to this relation: *What saith my Lord?* which implies an earnest desire to know the will of Christ, and a cheerful readiness and resolution to do it. Joshua owns himself an inferior officer, and stands to receive orders. This temper of mind shows him fit for the post he was in; for those know best how to command that know how to obey.

VII. The further expressions of reverence which this divine captain required from Joshua (*v.* 15): *Loose thy shoe from off thy foot,* in token of reverence and respect (which with us are signified by uncovering the head), and as an acknowledgment of a divine presence, which, while it continued there, did in a manner sanctify the place and dignify it. We are accustomed to say of a person for whom we have a great affection that we love the very ground he treads upon; thus Joshua must show his reverence for this divine person, he must not tread the ground he stood on with his dirty shoes, Eccl. v. 1. Outward expressions of inward reverence, and a religious awe of God, well become us, and are required of us, whenever we approach to him in solemn ordinances. Bishop Patrick well observes here that the very same orders that God gave to Moses at the bush, when he was sending him to bring Israel out of Egypt (Exod. iii. 5), he here gives to Joshua, for the confirming of his faith in the promise he had lately given him, that as he had been with Moses so he would be with him, *ch.* i. 5. Had Moses such a presence of God with him as, when it became sensible, sanctified the ground? So had Joshua.

And *(lastly)* Hereby he prepares him to receive the instructions he was about to give him concerning the siege of Jericho, which this captain of the Lord's host had now come to give Israel possession of.

CHAP. VI.

Joshua opened the campaign with the siege of Jericho, a city which could not trust so much to the courage of its people as to act offensively, and to send out its forces to oppose Israel's landing and encamping, but trusted so much to the strength of its walls as to stand upon its defence, and not to surrender, or desire conditions of peace. Now here we have the story of the taking of it, I. The directions and assurances which the captain of the Lord's host gave concerning it, ver. 1—5. II. The trial of the people's patient obedience in walking round the city six days, ver. 6—14. III. The wonderful delivery of it into their hands the seventh day, with a solemn charge to them to use it as a devoted thing, ver. 15—21, and ver. 24. IV. The preservation of Rahab and her relations, ver. 22, 23, 25. V. A curse pronounced upon the man that should dare to rebuild this city, ver. 26, 27. An abstract of this story we find among the trophies of faith, Heb. xi. 30. "By faith the walls of Jericho fell down, after they were compassed about seven days."

NOW Jericho was straitly shut up because of the children of Israel: none went out, and none came in. 2 And the LORD said unto Joshua, See, I have given into thine hand Jericho, and the king thereof, *and* the mighty men of valour. 3 And ye shall compass the city, all *ye* men of war, *and* go round about the city once. Thus shalt thou do six days. 4 And seven priests shall bear before the ark seven trumpets of rams' horns: and the seventh day ye shall compass the city seven times, and the priests shall blow with the trumpets. 5 And it shall come to pass, that when they make a long *blast* with the ram's horn, *and* when ye hear the sound of the trumpet, all the people shall shout with a great shout; and the wall of the city shall fall down flat, and the people shall ascend up every man straight before him.

We have here a contest between God and the men of Jericho, and their different resolutions, upon which it is easy to say whose word shall prevail.

I. Jericho resolves Israel shall *not* be its master, *v.* 1. It was *straitly shut up, because of the children of Israel.* It *did shut up, and it was shut up* (so it is in the margin); it *did shut up* itself, being strongly fortified both by art and nature, and it *was shut up* by the obstinacy and resolution of the inhabitants, who agreed never to surrender nor so much as sound a parley; none went out as deserters or to treat of peace, nor were any admitted in to offer peace. Thus were they infatuated, and their hearts hardened to their own destruction—the miserable case and character of all those that *strengthen themselves against the Almighty,* Job xv. 25.

II. God resolves Israel *shall* be its master, and that quickly. The captain of the Lord's host, here called *Jehovah,* taking notice how strongly Jericho was fortified and how strictly guarded, and knowing Joshua's thoughts and cares about reducing it, and perhaps his fears of a disgrace there and of stumbling at the threshold, gave him here all the assurance he could desire of success (*v.* 2): *See, I have given into thy hand Jericho.* Not, "*I will do it,* but, *I have done it;* it is all thy own, as sure as if it were already in thy possession." It was designed that this city, being the first-fruits of Canaan, should be entirely devoted to God, and that neither Joshua nor Israel should ever be one mite the richer for it, and yet it is here said to be *given into their hand;* for we must reckon that most our own which we have an opportunity of honouring God with and employing in his service. Now, 1. The captain of the Lord's host gives directions how the city should be besieged. No trenches are to be opened, no batteries erected, nor battering rams drawn up, nor any military preparations made; but the ark of God must be carried by the priests round the city once a day for six days together, and seven times the seventh day, attended by the men of war in silence, the priests all the while blowing with trumpets of rams' horns, *v.* 3, 4. This was all they were to do. 2. He assures them that on the seventh day before night they should, without fail, be masters of the town. Upon a signal given, they must all shout, and immediately the wall should fall down, which would not only expose the inhabitants, but so dispirit them that they would not be able to make any resistance, *v.* 5. God appointed this way, (1.) To magnify his own power, that he might be *exalted in his own strength* (Ps. xxi. 13), not in the strength of instruments. God would hereby yet further make bare his own almighty arm for the encouragement of Israel and the terror and confusion of the Canaanites. (2.) To put an honour upon his ark, the instituted token of his presence, and to give a reason for the laws by which the people were obliged to look upon it with the most profound veneration and respect. When, long after this, the ark was brought into the camp without orders from God, it was looked upon as a profanation of it, and the people paid dearly for their presumption, 1 Sam. iv. 3, &c. But now that it was done by the divine appointment it was an honour to the ark of God, and a great encouragement to the faith of Israel. (3.) It was likewise to put honour upon the priests, who were appointed upon this occasion to carry the ark and sound the trumpets. Ordinarily the priests were excused from war, but that this privilege, with other honours and powers that the law had given them, might not be grudged them, in this service they are principally employed, and so the people are made sensible what blessings they were to the public and how well worthy of all the advantages conferred upon them. (4.) It was to try the faith, obedience, and patience, of the people, to try whether they would observe a precept which to human policy seemed foolish to obey and believe a promise which in human probability seemed impossible to be performed. They were also proved whether they could patiently bear the reproaches of their enemies and patiently wait for the salvation of the Lord. Thus by faith, not by force, the walls of Jericho fell down. (5.) It was to encourage the hope of Israel with reference to the remaining difficulties that were before them. That suggestion of the evil spies that Canaan could never be conquered because the cities were *walled up to heaven* (Deut. i. 28) would by this be for ever silenced. The strongest and highest walls cannot hold out against Omnipotence; they needed not to fight, and therefore needed not to fear, because God fought for them.

6 And Joshua the son of Nun called the priests, and said unto them, Take up the ark of the covenant, and let seven priests bear seven trumpets of rams' horns before the ark of the LORD. 7 And he said unto the people, Pass on, and compass the city, and let him that is armed pass on before the ark of the LORD. 8 And it came to pass, when Joshua had spoken unto the people, that the seven priests bearing the seven trumpets of rams' horns passed on before the LORD, and blew with the trumpets: and the ark of the covenant of the LORD followed them. 9 And the armed men went before the priests that blew with the trumpets, and the rereward came after the ark, *the priests* going on, and blowing with the trumpets. 10 And Joshua had commanded the people, saying, Ye shall not shout, nor make any noise with your voice, neither shall *any* word proceed out of your mouth, until the day I bid you shout; then shall ye shout. 11 So the ark of the LORD compassed the city, going about *it* once: and they came into the camp, and lodged in the camp. 12 And Joshua rose early in the morning, and the priests took up the ark of the LORD. 13 And seven priests bearing seven trumpets of rams' horns before the ark of the LORD went on continually, and blew with the trumpets: and the armed men went before them; but the rereward came after the ark of the LORD, *the priests* going on, and blowing with the trumpets. 14 And the second day they compassed the city once, and returned unto the camp: so they did six days. 15 And it came to pass on the seventh day, that they rose early about the dawning of the day, and compassed the city after the same manner seven times: only on that day they compassed the city seven times. 16 And it came to pass at the seventh time, when the priests blew with the trumpets, Joshua said unto the people, Shout; for the LORD hath given you the city.

We have here an account of the cavalcade which Israel made about Jericho, the orders Joshua gave concerning it, as he had received them from the Lord and their punctual observance of these orders. We do not find that he gave the people the express assurances God had given him that he would deliver the city into their hands; but he tried whether they would obey orders with a general confidence that it would end well, and we find them very observant both of God and Joshua.

I. Wherever the ark went the people attended it, *v.* 9. The armed men went before it to clear the way, not thinking it any disparagement to them, though they were men of war, to be pioneers to the ark of God. If any obstacle should be found in crossing the roads that led to the city (which they must do in walking round it) they would remove it; if any opposition should be made by the enemy, they would encounter it, that the priests' march with the ark might be easy and safe. It is an honour to the greatest men to do any good office to the ark and to serve the interests of religion in their country. The *rereward,* either another body of armed men, or Dan's squadron, which marched last through the wilderness, or, as some think, the multitude of the people who were not armed or disciplined for war (as many of them as would) followed the ark, to testify their respect to it, to grace the solemnity, and to be witnesses of what was done. Every faithful zealous Israelite would be willing to undergo the same fatigues and run the same hazard with the priests that bore the ark.

II. Seven priests went immediately before the ark, having trumpets in their hands, with which they were continually sounding, *v.* 4, 5, 9, 13. The priests were God's ministers, and thus in his name, 1. They proclaimed war with the Canaanites, and so struck a terror upon them; for by terrors upon their spirits they were to be conquered and subdued. Thus God's ministers, by the solemn declarations of his wrath against all ungodliness and unrighteousness of men, must blow the trumpet in Zion, and sound an alarm in the holy mountain, that the sinners in Zion may be afraid. They are God's heralds to denounce war against all those that go on still in their trespasses, but say, "We shall have peace, though we go on." 2. They proclaimed God's gracious presence with Israel, and so put life and courage into them. It was appointed that when they went to war the priests should encourage them with the assurance of God's presence with them, Deut. xx. 2—4. And particularly their blowing with trumpets was to be a sign to the people that they should be remembered before the Lord their God in the day of battle, Num. x. 9. It encouraged Abijah, 2 Chron. xiii. 12. Thus God's ministers, by sounding the Jubilee trumpet of the everlasting gospel, which proclaims liberty and victory, must encourage the good soldiers of Jesus Christ in their spiritual warfare.

III. The trumpets they used were not those silver trumpets which were appointed to be made for their ordinary service, but trumpets of rams' horns, bored hollow for the purpose, as some think. These trumpets were of the basest matter, dullest sound, and least show, that the excellency of the power might be of God. Thus by the foolishness of preaching, fitly compared to the sounding of these rams' horns, the devil's kingdom is thrown down; and the *weapons of our warfare,* though they are not carnal nor seem to a carnal eye likely to bring any thing to pass, are yet *mighty through God to the pulling down of strong-holds,* 2 Cor. x. 4, 5. The word here is *trumpets of Jobel,* that is, such trumpets as they used to blow withal in the year of jubilee; so many interpreters understand it, as signifying the complete liberty to which Israel was now brought, and the bringing of the land of Canaan into the hands of its just and rightful owners.

IV. All the people were commanded to be silent, not to speak a word, nor make any noise (*v.* 10), that they might the more carefully attend to the sound of the sacred trumpets, which they were now to look upon as the voice of God among them; and it does not become us to speak when God is speaking. It likewise intimates their reverent expectation of the event. Zech. ii. 13, *Be silent, O all flesh, before the Lord.* Exod. xiv. 14, *God shall fight, and you shall hold your peace.*

V. They were to do this once a day for six days together and seven times the seventh day, and they did so, *v.* 14, 15. God could have caused the walls of Jericho to fall upon the first surrounding of them, but they must go round them thirteen times before they fall, that they might be kept waiting patiently for the Lord. Though they had lately come into Canaan, and their time was very precious (for they had a great deal of work before them), yet they must linger so many days about Jericho, seeming to do nothing, nor to make any progress in their business. As promised deliverances must be expected in God's way, so they must be expected in his time. *He that believes does not make haste,* not more haste than God would have him make. *Go yet seven times,* before any thing hopeful appears, 1 Kings xviii. 43.

VI. One of these days must needs be a sabbath day, and the Jews say that it was the last, but this is not certain; however, if he that appointed them to rest on the other sabbath days appointed them to walk on this, that was sufficient to justify them in it; he never intended to bind himself by his own laws, but that when he pleased he might dispense with them. The impotent man went upon this principle when he argued (John v. 11), *He that made me whole* (and therefore has a divine power) *said unto me, Take up thy bed.* And, in this case here, it was an honour to the sabbath day, by which our time is divided into weeks, that just seven days were to be spent in this work, and seven priests were employed to sound seven trumpets, this number being, on this occasion, as well as many others, made remarkable, in remembrance of the six days' work of creation and the seventh day's rest from it. And, besides, the law of the sabbath forbids our own work, which is servile and secular, but this which they did was a religious act. It is certainly no breach of the sabbath rest to do the sabbath work, for the sake of which the rest was instituted; and what is the sabbath work but to attend the ark in all its motions?

VII. They continued to do this during the time appointed, and seven times the seventh day, though they saw not any effect of it, believing that *at the end the vision would speak and not lie,* Hab. ii. 3. If we persevere in the way of duty, we shall lose nothing by it in the long run. It is probable they walked at such a distance from the walls as to be out of the reach of the enemies' arrows and out of the hearing of their scoffs. We may suppose the oddness of the thing did at first amuse the besieged, but by the seventh day they had grown secure, feeling no harm from that which perhaps they looked upon as an enchantment. Probably they bantered the besiegers, as those mentioned in Neh. iv. 2, "*What do these feeble Jews?* Is this the people we thought so formidable? Are these their methods of attack?" Thus they cried peace and safety, that the destruction might be the more terrible when it came. *Wicked men* (says bishop Hall) *think God in jest when he is preparing for their judgment;* but they will be convinced of their mistake when it is too late.

VIII. At last they were to give a shout, and did so, and immediately the walls fell, *v.* 16. This was a shout for mastery, a triumphant shout; the *shout of a king is among them,* Num. xxiii. 21. This was a shout of faith; they believed that the walls of Jericho would fall, and by this faith the walls were thrown down. It was a shout of prayer, an echo to the sound of the trumpets which proclaimed the promise that God would remember them; with one accord, as one man, they cry to heaven for help, and help comes in. Some allude to this to show that we must never expect a complete victory over our own corruptions till the very evening of our last day, and then we shall shout in triumph over them, *when we come to the number and measure of our perfection,* as bishop Hall expresses it. *A good heart* (says he) *groans under the sense of his infirmities, fain would be rid of them, and strives and prays, but, when all is done, until the end of the seventh day it cannot be;* then judgment shall be brought forth unto victory. And at the end of time, when our Lord shall descend from heaven with a shout, and the sound of a trumpet, Satan's kingdom shall be completely ruined, and not till then, when all opposing rule, principality, and power, shall be effectually and eternally put down.

17 And the city shall be accursed, *even* it, and all that *are* therein, to the LORD: only Rahab the harlot shall live, she and all that *are* with her in the house, because she hid the messengers that we sent. 18 And ye, in any wise keep *yourselves* from the accursed thing, lest ye make *yourselves* accursed, when ye take of the accursed thing, and make the camp of Israel a curse, and trouble it. 19 But all the silver, and gold, and vessels of brass and iron, *are* consecrated unto the LORD: they shall come into the treasury of the LORD. 20 So the people shouted when *the priests* blew with the trumpets: and it came to pass, when the people heard the sound of the trumpet, and the people shouted with a great shout, that the wall fell down flat, so that the people went up into the city, every man straight before him, and they took the city. 21 And they utterly destroyed all that *was* in the city, both man and woman, young and old, and ox, and sheep, and ass, with the edge of the sword. 22 But Joshua had said unto the two men that had spied out the country, Go into the harlot's house, and bring out thence the woman, and all that she hath, as ye sware unto her. 23 And the young men that were spies went in, and brought out Rahab, and her father, and her mother, and her brethren, and all that she had; and they brought out all her kindred, and left them without the camp of Israel. 24 And they burnt the city with fire, and all that *was* therein: only the silver, and the gold, and the vessels of brass and of iron, they put into the treasury of the house of the LORD. 25 And Joshua saved Rahab the harlot alive, and her father's household, and all that she had; and she dwelleth in Israel *even* unto this day; because she hid the messengers, which Joshua sent to spy out Jericho. 26 And Joshua adjured *them* at that time, saying, Cursed *be* the man before the LORD, that riseth up and buildeth this city Jericho: he shall lay the foundation thereof in his firstborn, and in his youngest *son* shall he set up the gates of it. 27 So the LORD was with Joshua; and his fame was *noised* throughout all the country.

The people had religiously observed the orders given them concerning the besieging of Jericho, and now at length Joshua had told them (*v.* 16), "*The Lord hath given you the city,* enter and take possession." Accordingly in these verses we have,

I. The rules they were to observe in taking possession. God gives it to them, and therefore may direct it to what uses and intents, and clog it with what provisos and limitations he thinks fit. It is given to them to be devoted to God, as the first and perhaps the worst of all the cities of Canaan. 1. The city must be burnt, and all the lives in it sacrificed without mercy to the justice of God. All this they knew was included in those words, *v.* 17. The city shall be a *cherem,* a devoted thing, it and all therein, to the Lord. No life in it might be ransomed upon any terms; they must all be surely *put to death,* Lev. xxvii. 29. So he appoints from whom as creatures they had received their lives, and to whom as sinners they had forfeited them; and who may dispute his sentence? *Is God unrighteous, who thus taketh vengeance?* God forbid we should entertain such a thought! There was more of God seen in the taking of Jericho than of any other of the cities of Canaan, and therefore that must be more than any other devoted to him. And the severe usage of this city would strike a terror upon all the rest and melt their hearts yet more before Israel. Only, when this severity is ordered, Rahab and her family are excepted: *She shall live and all that are with her.* She had distinguished herself from her neighbours by the kindness she showed to Israel, and therefore shall be distinguished from them by the speedy return of that kindness. 2. All the treasure of it, the money and plate and valuable goods, must be consecrated to the service of the tabernacle, and brought into the stock of dedicated things, the Jews say because the city was taken on the sabbath day. Thus God would be honoured by the beautifying and enriching of his tabernacle; thus preparation was made for the extraordinary expenses of his service; and thus the Israelites were taught not to set their hearts upon worldly wealth nor to aim at heaping up abundance of it for themselves. God had promised them a land *flowing with milk and honey,* not a land abounding with silver and gold; for he would have them live comfortably in it, that they might serve him cheerfully, but not covet either to trade with distant countries or to hoard for after times. He would likewise have them to reckon themselves enriched in the enriching of the tabernacle, and to think that which was laid up in God's house as truly their honour and wealth as if it had been laid up in their own. 3. A particular caution is given them to take heed of meddling with the forbidden spoil; for what was devoted to God, if they offered to appropriate it to their own use, would prove accursed to them; therefore (*v.* 18) "*In any wise keep yourselves from the accursed thing;* you will find yourselves inclined to reach towards it, but check yourselves, and frighten yourselves from having any thing to do with it." He speaks as if he foresaw the sin of Achan, which we have an account of in the next chapter, when he gives this reason for the caution, *lest you make the camp of Israel a curse and trouble it,* as it proved that Achan did.

II. The entrance that was opened to them into the city by the sudden fall of the walls, or at least that part of the wall over against which they then were when they gave the shout (*v.* 20): *The wall fell down flat,* and probably killed abundance of people, the guards that stood sentinel upon it, or others that crowded about it, to look at the Israelites that were walking round. We read of thousands killed by the fall of a wall, 1 Kings xx. 30. That which they trusted to for defence proved their destruction. The sudden fall of the wall, no doubt, put the inhabitants into such a consternation that they had no strength nor spirit to make any resistance, but they became an easy prey to the sword of Israel, and saw to how little purpose it was to shut their gates against a people that had *the Lord on the head of them,* Mic. ii. 13. Note, The God of heaven easily can, and certainly will, break down all the opposing power of his and his church's enemies. Gates of brass and bars of iron are, before him, but as straw and rotten wood, Isa. xlv. 1, 2. *Who will bring me into the strong city? Wilt not thou, O God?* Ps. lx. 9, 10. Thus shall Satan's kingdom fall, nor shall any prosper that harden themselves against God.

III. The execution of the orders given concerning this devoted city. All that breathed were put to the sword; not only the men that were found in arms, but the women, and children, and old people. Though they cried for quarter, and begged ever so earnestly for their lives, there was no room for compassion, pity must be forgotten: they *utterly destroyed all, v.* 21. If they had not had a divine warrant under the seal of miracles for this execution, it could not have been justified, nor can it justify the like now, when we are sure no such warrant can be produced. But, being appointed by the righteous Judge of heaven and earth to do it, who is not unrighteous in taking vengeance, they are to be applauded in doing it as the faithful ministers of his justice. Work for God was then bloody work; and *cursed was he that did it deceitfully, keeping back his sword from blood,* Jer. xlviii. 10. But the spirit of the gospel is very different, for Christ came not to destroy men's lives but to save them, Luke ix. 56. Christ's victories were of another nature. The cattle were put to death with the owners, as additional sacrifices to the divine justice. The cattle of the Israelites, when slain at the altar, were accepted as sacrifices *for* them, but the cattle of these Canaanites were required to be slain as sacrifices *with* them, for their iniquity was not to be purged with sacrifice and offering: both were for the glory of God. 2. The city was *burnt with fire, and all that was in it, v.* 24. The Israelites, perhaps, when they had taken Jericho, a large and well-built city, hoped they should have that for their head-quarters; but God will have them yet to dwell in tents, and therefore fires this nest, lest they should nestle in it. 3. All the silver and gold, and all those vessels which were capable of being purified by fire, were brought into the treasury of the house of the Lord; not that he needed it, but that he would be honoured by it, as the Lord of hosts, of their hosts in particular, the God that gave the victory and therefore might demand the spoil, either the whole, as here, or, as sometimes, a tenth, Heb. vii. 4.

IV. The preservation of Rahab the harlot, or inn-keeper, who *perished not with those that believed not,* Heb. xi. 31. The public faith was engaged for her safety by the two spies, who acted therein as public persons; and therefore, though the hurry they were in at the taking of the town was no doubt very great, yet Joshua took effectual care for her preservation. The same persons that she had secured were employed to secure her, *v.* 22, 23. They were best able to do it who knew her and her house, and they were fittest to do it, that it might appear it was for the sake of her kindness to them that she was thus distinguished and had her life given her for a prey. All her kindred were saved with her; like Noah she *believed to the saving of her house;* and thus faith in Christ *brings salvation to the house,* Acts xvi. 31. Some ask how her house, which is said to have been *upon the wall* (*ch.* ii. 15), escaped falling with the wall; we are sure it did escape, for she and her relations were safe in it, either though it joined so near to the wall as to be said to be *upon it,* yet it was so far off as not to fall either with the wall or under it; or, rather, that part of the wall on which her house stood fell not. Now being preserved alive, 1. She was left for some time without the camp to be purified from the Gentile superstition, which she was to renounce, and to be prepared for her admission as a proselyte. 2. She was in due time incorporated with the church of Israel, and she and her posterity dwelt in Israel, and her family was remarkable long after. We find her the wife of Salmon, prince of Judah, mother of Boaz, and named among the ancestors of our Saviour, Matt. i. 5. Having received Israelites in the name of Israelites, she had an Israelite's reward. Bishop Pierson observes that Joshua's saving Rahab the harlot, and admitting her into Israel, were a figure of Christ's receiving into his kingdom, and entertaining there, the publicans and the harlots, Matt. xxi. 31. Or it may be applied to the conversion of the Gentiles.

V. Jericho is condemned to a perpetual desolation, and a curse pronounced upon the man that at any time hereafter should offer to rebuild it (*v.* 26): *Joshua adjured them,* that is, the elders and people of Israel, not only by their own consent, obliging themselves and their posterity never to rebuild this city, but by the divine appointment, God himself having forbidden it under the severe penalty here annexed. 1. God would hereby show the weight of a divine curse; where it rests there is no contending with it nor getting from under it; it brings ruin without remedy or repair. 2. He would have it to remain in its ruins a standing monument of his wrath against the Canaanites when the measure of their iniquity was full, and of his mercy to his people when the time had come for their settlement in Canaan. The desolations of their enemies were witnesses of his favour to them, and would upbraid them with their ingratitude to that God who had done so much for them. The situation of the city was very pleasant, and probably its nearness to Jordan was an advantage to it, which would tempt men to build upon the same spot; but they are here told it is at their peril if they do it. Men build for their posterity, but he that builds Jericho shall have no posterity to enjoy what he builds; his eldest son shall die when he begins the work, and if he take not warning by that stroke to desist, but will go on presumptuously, the finishing of his work shall be attended with the funeral of his youngest, and we must suppose all the rest cut off between. This curse, not being a *curse causeless,* did come upon that man who long after rebuilded Jericho (1 Kings xvi. 34), but we are not to think it made the place ever the worse when it was built, or brought any hurt to those that inhabited it. We find Jericho afterwards graced with the presence, not only of those two great prophets Elijah and Elisha, but of our blessed Saviour himself, Luke xviii. 35; xix. 1; Matt. xx. 29. Note, It is a dangerous thing to attempt the building up of that which God will have to be destroyed. See Mal. i. 4.

Lastly, All this magnified Joshua and raised his reputation (*v.* 27); it made him not only acceptable to Israel, but formidable to the Canaanites, because it appeared that God was with him of a truth: the Word of the Lord was with him, so the Chaldee, even Christ himself, the same that was with Moses. Nothing can more raise a man's reputation, nor make him appear more truly great, than to have the evidences of God's presence with him.

CHAP. VII.

More than once we have found the affairs of Israel, even when they were in the happiest posture and gave the most hopeful prospects, perplexed and embarrassed by sin, and a stop thereby put to the most promising proceedings. The golden calf, the murmuring at Kadesh, and the iniquity of Peor, had broken their measures and given them great disturbance; and in this chapter we have such another instance of the interruption given to the progress of their arms by sin. But it being only the sin of one person or family, and soon expiated, the consequences were not so mischievous as of those other sins; however it served to let them know that they were still upon their good behaviour. We have here, I. The sin of Achan in meddling with the accursed thing, ver. 1. II. The defeat of Israel before Ai thereupon, ver. 2—5. III. Joshua's humiliation and prayer on occasion of that sad disaster, ver. 6—9. IV. The directions God gave him for the putting away of the guilt which had provoked God thus to contend with them, ver. 10—15. V. The discovery, trial, conviction, condemnation, and execution, of the criminal, by which the anger of God was turned away, ver. 16—26. And by this story it appears that, as the laws, so Canaan itself, "made nothing perfect," the perfection both of holiness and peace to God's Israel is to be expected in the heavenly Canaan only.

BUT the children of Israel committed a trespass in the accursed thing: for Achan, the son of Carmi, the son of Zabdi, the son of Zerah, of the tribe of Judah, took of the accursed thing: and the anger of the LORD was kindled against the children of Israel. 2 And Joshua sent men from Jericho to Ai, which *is* beside Beth-aven, on the east side of Beth-el, and spake unto them, saying, Go up and view the country. And the men went up and viewed Ai. 3 And they returned to Joshua, and said unto him, Let not all the people go up; but let about two or three thousand men go up and smite Ai; *and* make not all the people to labour thither; for they *are but* few. 4 So there went up thither of the people about three thousand men: and they fled before the men of Ai. 5 And the men of Ai smote of them about thirty and six men: for they chased them *from* before the gate *even* unto Shebarim, and smote them in the going down: wherefore the hearts of the people melted, and became as water.

The story of this chapter begins with a *but. The Lord was with Joshua, and his fame was noised through all that country,* so the foregoing chapter ends, and it left no room to doubt but that he would go on as he had begun *conquering and to conquer.* He did right, and observed his orders in every thing. *But the children of Israel committed a trespass,* and so set God against them; and then even Joshua's name and fame, his wisdom and courage, could do them no service. If we lose our God, we lose our friends, who cannot help us unless God be for us. Now here is,

I. Achan sinning, *v.* 1. Here is only a general mention made of the sin; we shall afterwards have a more particular account of it from his own mouth. The sin is here said to be *taking of the accursed thing,* in disobedience to the command and in defiance of the threatening, *ch.* vi. 18. In the sacking of Jericho orders were given that they should neither spare any lives nor take any treasure to themselves; we read not of the breach of the former prohibition (there were none to whom they showed any mercy), but of the latter: compassion was put off and yielded to the law, but covetousness was indulged. The love of the world is that root of bitterness which of all others is most hardly rooted up. Yet the history of Achan is a plain intimation that he of all the thousands of Israel was the only delinquent in this matter. Had there been more in like manner guilty, no doubt we should have heard of it; and it is strange there were no more. The temptation was strong. It was easy to suggest what a pity it was that so many things of value should be burnt; to what purpose is this waste? In plundering cities, every man reckons himself entitled to what he can lay his hands on. It was easy to promise themselves secresy and impunity. Yet by the grace of God such impressions were made upon the minds of the Israelites by the ordinances of God, circumcision and the passover, which they had lately been partakers of, and by the providences of God which had been concerning them, that they stood in awe of the divine precept and judgment, and generously denied themselves in obedience to their God. And yet, though it was a single person that sinned, the children of Israe. are said *to commit the trespass,* because one of their body did it, and he was not as yet separated from them, nor disowned by them. They did it, that is, by what Achan did guilt was brought upon the whole society of which he was a member. This should be a warning to us to take heed of sin ourselves, lest by it many be defiled or disquieted (Heb. xii. 15), and to take heed of having fellowship with sinners, and of being in league with them, lest we share in their guilt. Many a careful tradesman has been broken by a careless partner. And it concerns us to watch over one another for the preventing of sin, because others' sins may redound to our damage.

II. The camp of Israel suffering for the same: *The anger of the Lord was kindled against Israel;* he saw the offence, though they did not, and takes a course to make them see it; for one way or other, sooner or later, secret sins will be brought to light; and, if men enquire not after them, God will, and with his enquiries will awaken theirs. Many a community is under guilt and wrath and is not aware of it till the fire breaks out: here it broke out quickly. 1. Joshua sends a detachment to seize upon the next city that was in their way, and that was Ai. Only 3000 men were sent, advice being brought him by his spies that the place was inconsiderable, and needed no greater force for the reduction of it, *v.* 2, 3. Now perhaps it was a culpable assurance, or security rather that led them to send so small a party on this expedition; it might also be an indulgenceof the people in the love of ease, for they will not have all *the people to labour thither.* Perhaps the people were the less forward to go upon this expedition because they were denied the plunder of Jericho; and these spies were willing they should be gratified. Whereas when that town was to be taken, though God by his own power would throw down the walls, yet they must *all labour thither* and *labour there* too, in walking round it. It did not bode well at all that God's Israel began to think much of their labour, and contrived how to spare their pains. It is required that we *work out our salvation,* though it is *God that works in us.* It has likewise often proved of bad consequence to make too light of an enemy. *They are but few* (say the spies), but, as few as they were, they were too many for them. It will awaken our care and diligence in our Christian warfare to consider that *we wrestle with principalities and powers.* 2. The party he sent, in their first attack upon the town, were repulsed with some loss (*v.* 4, 5): *They fled before the men of Ai,* finding themselves unaccountably dispirited, and their enemies to sally out upon them with more vigour and resolution than they expected. In their retreat they had about thirty-six men cut off: no great loss indeed out of such a number, but a dreadful surprise to those who had no reason to expect any other in any attack than clear, cheap, and certain victory. And now, as it proves, it is well there were but 3000 that fell under this disgrace. Had the body of the army been there, they would have been no more able to keep their ground, now they were under guilt and wrath, than this small party, and to them the defeat would have been much more grievous and dishonourable. However, it was bad enough as it was, and served, (1.) To humble God's Israel, and to teach them always to *rejoice with trembling. Let not him that girdeth on the harness boast as he that putteth it off.* (2.) To harden the Canaanites, and to make them the more secure notwithstanding the terrors they had been struck with, that their ruin, when it came, might be the more dreadful. (3.) To be an evidence of God's displeasure against Israel, and a call to them to *purge out the old leaven.* And this was principally intended in their defeat. 3. The retreat of this party in disorder put the whole camp of Israel into a fright: *The hearts of the people melted,* not so much for the loss as for the disappointment. Joshua had assured them that *the living God would without fail drive out the Canaanites from before them, ch.* iii. 10. How can this event be reconciled to that promise? To every thinking man among them it appeared an indication of God's displeasure, and an omen of something worse, and therefore no marvel it put them into such a consternation; if *God turn to be their enemy and fight against them,* what will become of them? True Israelites tremble when God is angry.

6 And Joshua rent his clothes, and fell to the earth upon his face before the ark of the LORD until the eventide, he and the elders of Israel, and put dust upon their heads. 7 And Joshua said, Alas, O Lord GOD, wherefore hast thou at all brought this people over Jordan, to deliver us into the hand of the Amorites, to destroy us? would to God we had been content, and dwelt on the other side Jordan! 8 O Lord, what shall I say, when Israel turneth their backs before their enemies! 9 For the Canaanites and all the inhabitants of the land shall hear *of it,* and shall environ us round, and cut off our name from the earth: and what wilt thou do unto thy great name?

We have here an account of the deep concern Joshua was in upon this sad occasion. He, as a public person, interested himself more than any other in this public loss, and is therein an example to princes and great men, and teaches them to lay much to heart the calamities that befal their people: he is also a type of Christ, to whom the blood of his subjects is precious, Ps. lxxii. 14. Observe,

I. How he grieved: He *rent his clothes* (*v.* 6), in token of great sorrow for this public disaster, and especially a dread of God's displeasure, which was certainly the cause of it. Had it been but the common chance of war (as we are too apt to express it), it would not have become a general to droop thus under it; but, when God was angry, it was his duty and honour to feel thus. One of the bravest soldiers that ever was owned that his *flesh trembled for fear of God,* Ps. cxix. 120. As one *humbling himself under the mighty hand of God, he fell to the earth upon his face,* not thinking it any disparagement to him to lie thus low before the great God, to whom he directed this token of reverence, by keeping his eye towards *the ark of the Lord.* The elders of Israel, being interested in the cause and influenced by his example, prostrated themselves with him, and, in token of deep humiliation, *put dust upon their heads,* not only as mourners, but as penitents; not doubting but it was for some sin or other that God did thus contend with them (though they knew not what it was), they *humbled themselves* before God, and thus deprecated the progress of his wrath. This they continued *until even-tide,* to show that it was not the result of a sudden feeling, but proceeded from a deep conviction of their misery and danger if God were any way provoked to depart from them. Joshua did not fall foul upon his spies for their misinformation concerning the strength of the enemy, nor upon the soldiers for their cowardice, though perhaps both were blameworthy, but *his eye is up to God; for is there any evil in the camp and he has not done it?* His eye is upon God as displeased, and that troubles him

II. How he prayed, or pleaded rather, humbly expostulating the case with God, not sullen, as David when *the Lord had made a breach upon Uzzah,* but much affected; his spirit seemed to be somewhat ruffled and discomposed, yet not so as to be put out of frame for prayer; but, by giving vent to his trouble in a humble address to God, he keeps his temper and it ends well. 1. Now he wishes they had all taken up with the lot of the two tribes on the other side Jordan, *v.* 7. He thinks it would have been better to have staid there and been cut short than come hither to be cut off. This savours too much of discontent and distrust of God, and cannot be justified, though the surprise and disappointment to one deeply concerned for the public interest may in part excuse it. Those words, *wherefore hast thou brought us over Jordan to destroy us?* are too like what the murmurers often said (Exod. xiv. 11, 12; xvi. 3; xvii. 3; Num. xiv. 2, 3); but he that searches the heart knew they came from another spirit, and therefore was not extreme to mark what he said amiss. Had Joshua considered that this disorder which their affairs were put into no doubt proceeded from something amiss, which yet might easily be redressed, and all set to rights again (as often in his predecessor's time), he would not have spoken of it as a thing taken for granted that they were *delivered into the hands of the Amorites to be destroyed.* God knows what he does, though we do not; but this we may be sure of, he never did nor ever will do us any wrong. 2. He speaks as one quite at a loss concerning the meaning of this event (*v.* 8): "*What shall I say*, what construction can I put upon it, *when Israel,* thy own people, for whom thou hast lately done such great things and to whom thou hast promised the full possession of this land, when they *turn their backs before their enemies*" (their *necks*, so the word is), "when they not only flee before them, but fall before them, and become a prey to them? What shall we think of the divine power? Is the Lord's arm shortened? Of the divine promise? Is his word yea and nay? Of what God has done for us? Shall this be all undone again and prove in vain?" Note, The methods of Providence are often intricate and perplexing, and such as the wisest and best of men know not what to say to; but *they shall know hereafter*, John xiii. 7. 3. He pleads the danger Israel was now in of being ruined. He gives up all for lost: "*The Canaanites will environ us round,* concluding that now our defence having departed, and the scales being turned in their favour, we shall soon be as contemptible as ever we were formidable, and they will *cut off our name from the earth,*" *v.* 9. Thus even good men, when things go against them a little, are too apt to fear the worst, and make harder conclusions than there is reason for. But this comes in here as a plea: "Lord, let not Israel's name, which has been so dear to thee and so great in the world, be cut off." 4. He pleads the reproach that would be cast on God, and that if Israel were ruined his glory would suffer by it. They will *cut off our name,* says he, yet, as if he had corrected himself for insisting upon that, it is no great matter (thinks he) what becomes of our little name (the cutting off of that will be a small loss), but *what wilt thou do for thy great name?* This he looks upon and laments as the great aggravation of the calamity. He feared it would reflect on God, his wisdom and power, his goodness and faithfulness; what would the Egyptians say? Note, Nothing is more grievous to a gracious soul than dishonour done to God's name. This also he insists upon as a plea for the preventing of his fears and for a return of God's favour; it is the only word in all his address that has any encouragement in it, and he concludes with it, leaving it to this issue, *Father, glorify thy name.* The name of God is a great name, above every name; and, whatever happens, we ought to believe that he will, and pray that he would, work for his own name, that *this may not be polluted.* This should be our concern more than any thing else. On this we must fix our eye as the end of all our desires, and from this we must fetch our encouragement as the foundation of all our hopes. We cannot urge a better plea than this, Lord, *What wilt thou do for thy great name?* Let God in all be glorified, and then welcome his whole will.

10 And the LORD said unto Joshua, Get thee up; wherefore liest thou thus upon thy face? 11 Israel hath sinned, and they have also transgressed my covenant which I commanded them: for they have even taken of the accursed thing, and have also stolen, and dissembled also, and they have put *it* even among their own stuff. 12 Therefore the children of Israel could not stand before their enemies, *but* turned *their* backs before their enemies, because they were accursed: neither will I be with you any more, except ye destroy the accursed from among you. 13 Up, sanctify the people, and say, Sanctify yourselves against to-morrow: for thus saith the LORD God of Israel, *There is* an accursed thing in the midst of thee, O Israel: thou canst not stand before thine enemies, until ye take away the accursed thing from among you. 14 In the morning therefore ye shall be brought according to your tribes: and it shall be, *that* the tribe which the LORD taketh shall come according to the families *thereof;* and the family which the LORD shall take shall come by households; and the household which the LORD shall take shall come man by man. 15 And it shall be, *that* he that is taken with the accursed thing shall be burnt with fire, he and all that he hath: because he hath transgressed the covenant of the LORD, and because he hath wrought folly in Israel.

We have here God's answer to Joshua's address, which, we may suppose, came from the oracle over the ark, before which Joshua had prostrated himself, *v.* 6. Those that desire to know the will of God must attend with their desires upon the lively oracles, and wait at wisdom's gates for wisdom's dictates, Prov. viii. 34. And let those that find themselves under the tokens of God's displeasure never complain *of* him, but complain *to* him, and they shall receive an answer of peace. The answer came immediately, *while he was yet speaking* (Isa. lxv. 24), as that to Daniel, Dan. ix. 20, &c.

I. God encourages Joshua against his present despondencies, and the black and melancholy apprehensions he had of the present posture of Israel's affairs (*v.* 10): "*Get thee up*, suffer not thy spirits to droop and sink thus; *wherefore liest thou thus upon thy face?*" No doubt Joshua did well to humble himself before God, and mourn as he did, under the tokens of his displeasure; but now God told him it was enough, he would not have him continue any longer in that melancholy posture, for God delights not in the grief of penitents when they afflict their souls further than as it qualifies them for pardon and peace; the days even of that mourning must be ended. *Arise, shake thyself from the dust*, Isa. lii. 2. Joshua continued his mourning *till eventide* (*v.* 6), so late that they could do nothing that night towards the discovery of the criminal, but were forced to put it off till next morning. Daniel (Dan. ix. 21), and Ezra (Ezra ix. 5, 6), continued their mourning only *till the time of the evening sacrifice;* that revived them both: but Joshua went past that time, and therefore is thus roused: "*Get thee up*, do not lie all night there." Yet we find that Moses fell down before the Lord forty days and forty nights, to make intercession for Israel, Deut. ix. 18. Joshua must get up because he has other work to do than to lie there; the accursed thing must be discovered and cast out, and the sooner the better; Joshua is the man that must do it, and therefore it is time for him to lay aside his mourning weeds, and put on his judge's robes, and *clothe himself with zeal as a cloak.* Weeping must not hinder sowing, nor one duty of religion jostle out another. Every thing is beautiful in its season. Shechaniah perhaps had an eye to this in what he said to Ezra upon a like occasion. See Ezra x. 2—4.

II. He informs him of the true and only cause of this disaster, and shows him wherefore he contended with them (*v.* 11): *Israel hath sinned.* "Think not that God's mind is changed, his arm shortened, or his promise about to fail; no, it is sin, it is sin, that great mischief-maker, that has stopped the current of divine favours and has made this breach upon you." The sinner is not named, though the sin is described, but it is spoken of as the act of Israel in general, till they have fastened it upon the particular person, and their *godly sorrow* have so wrought a *clearing of themselves*, as theirs did, 2 Cor. vii. 11. Observe how the sin is here made to appear exceedingly sinful. 1. *They have transgressed my covenant*, an express precept with a penalty annexed to it. It was agreed that God should have all the spoil of Jericho, and they should have the spoil of the rest of the cities of Canaan; but, in robbing God of his part, they *transgressed this covenant.* 2. *They have even taken of the devoted thing*, in contempt of the curse which was so solemnly denounced against him that should dare to break in upon God's property, as if that curse had nothing in it formidable. 3. They *have also stolen;* they did it clandestinely, as if they could conceal it from the divine omniscience, and they were ready to say, *The Lord shall not see*, or will not miss so small a matter out of so great a spoil. Thus *thou thoughtest I was altogether such a one as thyself.* 4. They have *dissembled* also. Probably, when the action was over, Joshua called all the tribes, and asked them whether they had faithfully disposed of the spoil, according to the divine command, and charged them, if they knew of any transgression, that they should discover it, but Achan joined with the rest in a general protestation of innocency, and kept his countenance, like the adulterous woman that *eats and wipes her mouth, and says, I have done no wickedness.* Nay, 5. They have put the accursed thing *among their own goods*, as if they had as good a title to that as to any thing they have, never expecting to be called to an account, nor designing to make restitution. All this Joshua, though a wise and vigilant ruler, knew nothing of, till God told him, who knows all the secret wickedness that is in the world, which men know nothing of. God could at this time have told him who the person was that had done this thing, but he does not, (1.) To exercise the zeal of Joshua and Israel, in searching out the criminal. (2.) To give the sinner himself space to repent and make confession. Joshua no doubt proclaimed it immediately throughout the camp that there was such a transgression committed, upon which, if Achan had surrendered himself, and penitently owned his guilt, and prevented the scrutiny, who knows but he might have had the benefit of that law which accepted of a trespass-offering, with restitution, from those that had *sinned through ignorance in the holy things of the law?* Lev. v. 15, 16. But Achan never discovering himself till the lot discovered him evidenced the hardness of his heart, and therefore he found no mercy.

III. He awakens him to enquire further into it, by telling him, 1. That this was the only ground for the controversy God had with them, this, and nothing else; so that when this accursed thing was put away he needed not fear, all would be well, the stream of their successes, when this one obstruction was removed, would run as strong as ever. 2. That if this accursed thing were not destroyed they could not expect the return of God's gracious presence; in plain terms, *neither will I be with you any more* as I have been, *except you destroy the accursed*, that is, the accursed person, who is made so by the accursed thing. That which is accursed will be destroyed; and those whom God has entrusted to bear the sword bear it in vain if they make it not a terror to that wickedness which brings these judgments of God on a land. By personal repentance and reformation, we destroy the accursed thing in our own hearts, and, unless we do this, we must never expect the favour of the blessed God. Let all men know that it is nothing but sin that separates between them and God, and, if it be not sincerely repented of and forsaken, it will separate eternally.

IV. He directs him in what method to make this enquiry and prosecution. 1. He must *sanctify the people,* now over-night, that is, as it is explained, he must command them to *sanctify themselves, v.* 13. And what can either magistrates or ministers do more towards sanctification? They must put themselves into a suitable frame to appear before God and submit to the divine scrutiny, must examine themselves, now that God was coming to examine them, must *prepare to meet their God.* They were called to sanctify themselves when they were to *receive the divine law* (Exod. xix.), and now also when they were to *come under the divine judgment;* for in both God is to be attended with the utmost reverence. "There is *an accursed thing in the midst of you,* and therefore *sanctify yourselves,"* that is, Let all that are innocent be able to clear themselves, and be the more careful to cleanse themselves. The sin of others may be improved by us as furtherances of our sanctification, as the scandal of the incestuous Corinthian occasioned a blessed reformation in that church, 2 Cor. vii. 11. 2. He must bring them all under the scrutiny of the lot (*v.* 14); the tribe which the guilty person was of should first be discovered by lot, then the family, then the household, and last of all the person. The conviction came upon him thus gradually that he might have some space given him to come in and surrender himself; for God is *not willing that any should perish, but that all should come to repentance.* Observe, The Lord is said to take the tribe, and family, and household, on which the lot fell, because *the disposal of the lot is of the Lord,* and, however casual it seems, is under the direction of infinite wisdom and justice; and to show that when the sin of sinners finds them out God is to be acknowledged in it; it is he that seizes them, and the arrests are in his name. *God hath found out the iniquity of thy servants,* Gen. xliv. 16. It is also intimated with what a certain and unerring judgment the righteous God does and will distinguish between the innocent and the guilty, so that though for a time they seem involved in the same condemnation, as the whole tribe did when it was first taken by the lot, yet he who has his fan in his hand will effectually provide for the *taking out of the precious from the vile;* so that though the righteous be of the same tribe, and family, and household, with the wicked, yet they shall never be treated *as the wicked,* Gen. xviii. 25. 3. When the criminal was found out he must be put to death *without mercy* (Heb. x. 28), and with all the expressions of a holy detestation, *v.* 15. He and all that he has must be burnt with fire, that there might be no remainders of the accursed thing among them; and the reason given for this severe sentence is because the criminal has, (1.) Given a great affront to God: He has *transgressed the covenant of the Lord,* who is jealous particularly for the honour of the holy covenant. (2.) He has done a great injury to the church of God: He has *wrought folly in Israel,* has shamed that nation which is looked upon by all its neighbours to be a *wise and understanding people,* has infected that nation which is sanctified to God, and troubled that nation of which he is the protector. These being crimes so heinous in their nature, and of such pernicious consequence and example, the execution, which otherwise would have come under the imputation of cruelty, is to be applauded as a piece of necessary justice. It was *sacrilege;* it was invading God's rights, alienating his property, and converting to a private use that which was devoted to his glory and appropriated to the service of his sanctuary—this was the crime to be thus severely punished, for warning to all people in all ages to take heed how they rob God.

16 So Joshua rose up early in the morning, and brought Israel by their tribes; and the tribe of Judah was taken: 17 And he brought the family of Judah; and he took the family of the Zarhites: and he brought the family of the Zarhites man by man; and Zabdi was taken: 18 And he brought his household man by man; and Achan, the son of Carmi, the son of Zabdi, the son of Zerah, of the tribe of Judah, was taken. 19 And Joshua said unto Achan, My son, give, I pray thee, glory to the LORD God of Israel, and make confession unto him; and tell me now what thou hast done; hide *it* not from me. 20 And Achan answered Joshua, and said, Indeed I have sinned against the LORD God of Israel, and thus and thus have I done: 21 When I saw among the spoils a goodly Babylonish garment, and two hundred shekels of silver, and a wedge of gold of fifty shekels weight, then I coveted them, and took them; and, behold, they *are* hid in the earth in the midst

of my tent, and the silver under it. 22 So Joshua sent messengers, and they ran unto the tent: and, behold, *it was* hid in his tent, and the silver under it. 23 And they took them out of the midst of the tent, and brought them unto Joshua, and unto all the children of Israel, and laid them out before the LORD. 24 And Joshua, and all Israel with him, took Achan the son of Zerah, and the silver, and the garment, and the wedge of gold, and his sons, and his daughters, and his oxen, and his asses, and his sheep, and his tent, and all that he had: and they brought them unto the valley of Achor. 25 And Joshua said, Why hast thou troubled us? the LORD shall trouble thee this day. And all Israel stoned him with stones, and burned them with fire, after they had stoned them with stones. 26 And they raised over him a great heap of stones unto this day. So the LORD turned from the fierceness of his anger. Wherefore the name of that place was called, The valley of Achor, unto this day.

We have in these verses,

I. The discovery of Achan by the lot, which proved a perfect lot, though it proceeded gradually. Though we may suppose that Joshua slept the better, and with more ease and satisfaction, when he knew the worst of the disease of that body of which, under God, he was the head, and was put into a certain method of cure, yet *he rose up early in the morning* (*v.* 16), so much was his heart upon it, to put away the accursed thing. We have found Joshua upon other occasions an early riser; here it shows his zeal and vehement desire to see Israel restored to the divine favour. In the scrutiny observe, 1. That the guilty tribe was that of Judah, which was, and was to be, of all the tribes, the most honourable and illustrious; this was an alloy to their dignity, and might serve as a check to their pride: many there were who were its glories, but here was one that was its reproach. Let not the best families think it strange if there be those found in them, and descending from them, that prove their grief and shame. Judah was to have the first and largest lot in Canaan; the more inexcusable is one of that tribe if, not content to wait for his own share, he break in upon God's property. The Jews' tradition is that when the tribe of Judah was taken the valiant men of that tribe drew their swords, and professed they would not sheathe them again till they saw the criminal punished and themselves cleared who knew their own innocency. 2. That the guilty person was at length fastened upon, and the language of the lot was, *Thou art the man*, *v.* 18. It was strange that Achan, being conscious to himself of guilt, when he saw the lot come nearer and nearer to him, had not either the wit to make an escape or the grace to make a confession; but *his heart was hardened through the deceitfulness of sin*, and it proved to be *to his own destruction*. We may well imagine how his countenance changed, and what horror and confusion seized him when he was singled out as the delinquent, when the eyes of all Israel were fastened upon him, and every one was ready to say, *Have we found thee, O our enemy?* See here, (1.) The folly of those that promise themselves secresy in sin: the righteous God has many ways of bringing to light the hidden works of darkness, and so bringing to shame and ruin those that continue their fellowship with those unfruitful works. *A bird of the air*, when God pleases, shall *carry the voice*, Eccl. x. 20. See Ps. xciv. 7, &c. (2.) How much it is our concern, when God is contending with us, to find out what the cause of action is, what the particular sin is, that, like Achan, troubles our camp. We must thus examine ourselves and carefully review the records of conscience, that we may find out the accursed thing, and pray earnestly with holy Job, *Lord, show me wherefore thou contendest with me.* Discover the traitor and he shall be no longer harboured.

II. His arraignment and examination, *v.* 19. Joshua sits judge, and, though abundantly satisfied of his guilt by the determination of the lot, yet urges him to make a penitent confession, that his soul might be saved by it in the other world, though he could not give him any encouragement to hope that he should save his life by it. Observe, 1. How he accosts him with the greatest mildness and tenderness that could be, like a true disciple of Moses. He might justly have called him "thief," and "rebel," "Raca," and "thou fool," but he calls him "son;" he might have adjured him to confess, as the high priest did our blessed Saviour, or threatened him with the torture to extort a confession, but for love's sake he rather beseeches him: *I pray thee make confession.* This is an example to all not to insult over those that are in misery, though they have brought themselves into it by their own wickedness, but to treat even offenders with the spirit of meekness, not knowing what we ourselves should have been and done if God had put us into the hands of our own counsels. It is likewise an example to magistrates, in executing justice, to govern their own passions with a strict and prudent hand, and never suffer themselves to be transported by them into any indecencies of behaviour or language, no, not towards those that have given the greatest provocations. *The wrath of man worketh not the righteousness of God.* Let them remember *the judgment is God's, who is Lord of his anger.* This is the likeliest method of bringing offenders to repentance. 2. What he wishes him to do, to confess the fact, to confess it to God, the party offended by the crime; Joshua was to him in God's stead, so that in confessing to him he confessed to God. Hereby he would satisfy Joshua and the congregation concerning that which was laid to his charge; his confession would also be an evidence of his repentance, and a warning to others to take heed of sinning after the similitude of his transgression: but that which Joshua aims at herein is that God might be honoured by it, as the Lord, the God of infinite knowledge and power, from whom no secrets are hid; and as the God of Israel, who, as he does particularly resent affronts given to his Israel, so he does the affronts given him by Israel. Note, In confessing sin, as we take shame to ourselves, so we give glory to God as a righteous God, owning him justly displeased with us, and as a good God, who will not improve our confessions as evidences against us, but is faithful and just to forgive when we are brought to own that he would be faithful and just if he should punish. By sin we have injured God in his honour. Christ by his death has made satisfaction for the injury; but it is required that we by repentance show our good will to his honour, and, as far as in us lies, give glory to him. Bishop Patrick quotes the Samaritan chronicle, making Joshua to say here to Achan, *Lift up thy eyes to the king of heaven and earth, and acknowledge that nothing can be hidden from him who knoweth the greatest secrets.*

III. His confession, which now at last, when he saw it was to no purpose to conceal his crime, was free and ingenuous enough, *v.* 20, 21. Here is, 1. A penitent acknowledgment of the fault. "Indeed I have sinned; what I am charged with is too true to be denied and too bad to be excused. I own it, I lament it; the Lord is righteous in bringing it to light, for indeed I have sinned." This is the language of a penitent that is sick of his sin, and whose conscience is loaded with it. "I have nothing to accuse any one else of, but a great deal to say against myself; it is with me that the accursed thing is found; I am the man who has *perverted that which was right and it profited me not.*" And that wherewith he aggravates the sin is that it was committed *against the Lord God of Israel.* He was himself an Israelite, a sharer with the rest of that exalted nation in their privileges, so that, in offending *the God of Israel,* he offended his own God, which laid him under the guilt of the basest treachery and ingratitude imaginable. 2. A particular narrative of the fact: *Thus and thus have I done.* God had told Joshua in general that a part of the devoted things was alienated, but leaves it to him to draw from Achan an account of the particulars; for, one way or other, God will make sinners' *own tongues to fall upon them* (Ps. lxiv. 8); if ever he bring them to repentance, they will be their own accusers, and their awakened consciences will be instead of a thousand witnesses. Note, It becomes penitents, in the confession of their sins to God, to be very particular; not only, "I have sinned," but, "In this and that instance I have sinned," reflecting with regret upon all the steps that led to the sin and all the circumstances that aggravated it and made it exceedingly sinful: *thus and thus have I done.* He confesses, (1.) To the things taken. In plundering a house in Jericho he found a goodly Babylonish garment; the word signifies a robe, such as princes wore when they appeared in state, probably it belonged to the king of Jericho; it was far fetched, if fetched, as we translate it, from *Babylon.* A garment of divers colours, so some render it. Whatever it was, in his eyes it made a very glorious show. "A thousand pities" (thinks Achan) "that it should be burnt; then it will do nobody any good; if I take it for myself, it will serve me many a year for my best garment." Under these pretences, he makes bold with this first, and thinks it no harm to save it from the fire; but, his hand being thus in, he proceeds to take a bag of money, *two hundred shekels,* that is, one hundred ounces of silver, and a *wedge of gold* which weighed *fifty shekels,* that is, twenty-five ounces. He could not plead that, in taking these, he saved them *from the fire* (for the *silver and gold* were to be laid up in *the treasury);* but those that make a slight excuse to serve in daring to commit one sin will have their hearts so hardened by it that they will venture upon the next without such an excuse; for the way of sin is downhill. See what a poor prize it was for which Achan ran this desperate hazard, and what an unspeakable loser he was by the bargain. See Matt. xvi. 26. (2.) He confesses the manner of taking them. [1.] The sin began in the eye. He saw these fine things, as Eve saw the forbidden fruit, and was strangely charmed with the sight. See what comes of suffering the heart to walk after the eyes, and what need we have to make this covenant with our eyes, that if they wander they shall be sure to weep for it. *Look not thou upon the wine that is red,* upon the woman that is fair; close the right eye that thus offends thee, to prevent the necessity of plucking it out, and casting it from thee, Matt. v. 28, 29. [2.] It proceeded out of the heart. He owns, *I coveted them.* Thus lust conceived and brought forth this sin. Those that would be kept from sinful actions must mortify and check in themselves sinful desires, particularly the desire of worldly wealth, which we more particularly call *covetousness.* O what a world of evil is the love of money the root of! Had Achan looked upon these things with an eye of faith, he would have seen them accursed things, and would have dreaded them, but, looking upon them with an eye of sense only, he saw them goodly things, and coveted them. It was not the looking, but the lusting that ruined him. [3.] When he had committed it he was very industrious to conceal it. Having taken of the forbidden treasures, fearing lest any search should be made for prohibited goods, he *hid them in the earth,* as one that resolved to keep what he had gotten, and never to make restitution. Thus does Achan confess the whole matter, that God might be justified in the sentence passed upon him. See the *deceitfulness of sin;* that which is pleasing in the commission is bitter in the reflection; at the last it bites like a serpent. Particularly, see what comes of ill-gotten goods, and how those will be cheated that rob God. Job xx. 15, *He hath swallowed down riches, and he shall vomit them up again.*

IV. His conviction. God had convicted him by the lot; he had convicted himself by his own confession; but, that no room might be left for the most discontented Israelite to object against the process, Joshua has him further convicted by the searching of his tent, in which the goods were found which he confessed to. Particular notice is taken of the haste which the messengers made that were sent to search: They *ran to the tent* (*v.* 22), not only to show their readiness to obey Joshua's orders, but to show how uneasy they were till the camp was cleared of the accursed thing, that they might regain the divine favour. Those that feel themselves under wrath find themselves concerned not to defer the putting away of sin. Delays are dangerous, and it is no time to trifle. When the stolen goods were brought they were *laid out before the Lord* (*v.* 23), that all Israel might see how plain the evidence was against Achan, and might adore the strictness of God's judgments in punishing so severely the stealing of such small things, and yet the justice of his judgments in maintaining his right to devoted things, and might be afraid of ever offending in the like kind. In laying them out before the Lord they acknowledged his title to them, and waited to receive his directions concerning them. Note, Those that think to put a cheat upon God do but deceive themselves; what is taken from him he will recover (Hos. ii. 9) and he will be a loser by no man at last.

V. His condemnation. Joshua passes sentence upon him (*v.* 25): *Why hast thou troubled us?* There is the ground of the sentence. *O, how much hast thou troubled us!* so some read it. He refers to what was said when the warning was given not to meddle with the accursed thing (*ch.* vi. 18), *lest you make the camp of Israel a curse and trouble it.* Note, Sin is a very troublesome thing, not only to the sinner himself, but to all about him. *He that is greedy of gain,* as Achan was, *troubles his own house* (Prov. xv. 27) and all the communities he belongs to. Now (says Joshua) *God shall trouble thee.* See why Achan was so severely dealt with, not only because he had robbed God, but because he had troubled Israel; over his head he had (as it were) this accusation written, "Achan, *the troubler of Israel,*" as Ahab, 1 Kings xviii. 18. This therefore is his doom: *God shall trouble thee.* Note, The righteous God will certainly *recompense tribulation to those that trouble* his people, 2 Thess. i. 6. Those that are troublesome shall be troubled. Some of the Jewish doctors, from that word which determines the troubling of him to *this day,* infer that therefore he should not be troubled in the world to come; the flesh was destroyed that the spirit might be saved, and, if so, the dispensation was really less severe than it seemed. In the description both of his sin and of his punishment, by the trouble that was in both, there is a plain allusion to his name *Achan,* or, as he is called, 1 Chron. ii. 7, *Achar,* which signifies *trouble.* He did too much answer his name.

VI. His execution. No reprieve could be obtained; a gangrened member must be cut off immediately. When he is proved to be an anathema, and the troubler of the camp, we may suppose all the people cry out against him, *Away with him, away with him! Stone him, stone him!* Here is,

1. The place of execution. They brought him out of the camp, in token of their putting *far from them that wicked person,* 1 Cor. v. 13. When our Lord Jesus was made a curse for us, that by his trouble we might have peace, he suffered as an accursed thing *without the gate,* bearing our reproach, Heb. xiii. 12, 13. The execution was at a distance, that the camp which was disturbed by Achan's sin might not be defiled by his death.

2. The persons employed in his execution. It was the act of all Israel, *v.* 24, 25. They were all spectators of it, that they might see and fear. Public executions are public examples. Nay, they were all consenting to his death, and as many as could were active in it, in token of the universal detestation in which they held his sacrilegious attempt, and their dread of God's displeasure against them.

3. The partakers with him in the punishment; for *he perished not alone in his iniquity, ch.* xxii. 20. (1.) The stolen goods were destroyed with him, the garment burnt, as it should have been with the rest of the combustible things in Jericho, and the silver and gold defaced, melted, lost, and buried, in the ashes of the rest of his goods under *the heap of stones,* so as never to be put to any other use. (2.) All his other goods were destroyed likewise, not only his tent, and the furniture of that, but his *oxen, asses, and sheep,* to show that goods gotten unjustly, especially if they be gotten by sacrilege, will not only

turn to no account, but will blast and waste the rest of the possessions to which they are added. The eagle in the fable, that stole flesh from the altar, brought a coal of fire with it, which burnt her nest, Hab. ii. 9, 10; Zech. v. 3, 4. Those lose their own that grasp at more than their own. (3.) His sons and daughters were put to death with him. Some indeed think that they were *brought out* (*v.* 24) only to be the spectators of their father's punishment, but most conclude that they died with him, and that they must be meant *v.* 25, where it is said they *burned them with fire, after they had stoned them with stones.* God had expressly provided that magistrates should not put the children to death for the fathers' sins; but he did not intend to bind himself by that law, and in this case he had expressly ordered (*v.* 15) that the criminal, and all that he had, should be burnt. Perhaps his sons and daughters were aiders and abettors in the villany, had helped to carry off the accursed thing. It is very probable that they assisted in the concealment, and that he could not hide them in the midst of his tent but they must know and keep his counsel, and so they became accessaries *ex post facto—after the fact;* and, if they were ever so little partakers in the crime, it was so heinous that they were justly sharers in the punishment. However God was hereby glorified, and the judgment executed was thus made the more tremendous.

4. The punishment itself that was inflicted on him. He was stoned (some think as a sabbath breaker, supposing that the sacrilege was committed on the sabbath day), and then his dead body was burnt, as an accursed thing, of which there should be no remainder left. The concurrence of all the people in this execution teaches us how much it is the interest of a nation that all in it should contribute what they can, in their places, to the suppression of vice and profaneness, and the reformation of manners; *sin is a reproach to any people*, and therefore every Israelite indeed will have a stone to throw at it.

5. The pacifying of God's wrath hereby (*v.* 26): *The Lord turned from the fierceness of his anger.* The putting away of sin by true repentance and reformation, as it is the only way, so it is a sure and most effectual way, to recover the divine favour. Take away the cause, and the effect will cease.

VII. The record of his conviction and execution. Care was taken to preserve the remembrance of it, for warning and instruction to posterity. 1. A heap of stones was raised on the place where Achan was executed, every one perhaps of the congregation throwing a stone to the heap, in token of his detestation of the crime. 2. A new name was given to the place; it was called the *Valley of Achor,* or *trouble.* This was a perpetual brand of infamy upon Achan's name, and a perpetual warning to all people not to invade God's property. By this severity against Achan, the honour of Joshua's government, now in the infancy of it, was maintained, and Israel, at their entrance upon the promised Canaan, were reminded to observe, at their peril, the provisos and limitations of the grant by which they held it. The *Valley of Achor* is said to be given for a *door of hope,* because when we put away the accursed thing then there begins to be hope in Israel, Hos. ii. 15; Ezra x. 2.

CHAP. VIII.

The embarrassment which Achan's sin gave to the affairs of Israel being over, we have them here in a very good posture again, the affairs both of war and religion. Here is, I. The glorious progress of their arms in the taking of Ai, before which they had lately suffered disgrace. 1. God encourages Joshua to attack it, with the assurance of success, and directs him what method to take, ver. 1, 2. 2. Joshua gives orders accordingly to the men of war, ver. 3—8. 3. The stratagem is managed as it was projected, and succeeds as it was desired, ver. 9—22. 4. Joshua becomes master of this city, puts all the inhabitants to the sword, burns it, hangs the king, but gives the plunder to the soldiers, ver. 23—29. II. The great solemnity of writing and reading the law before a general assembly of all Israel, drawn up for that purpose upon the two mountains of Gerizim and Ebal, according to an order which Moses had received from the Lord, and delivered to them, ver. 30—35. Thus did they take their work before them, and make the business of their religion to keep pace with their secular business.

AND the LORD said unto Joshua, Fear not, neither be thou dismayed: take all the people of war with thee, and arise, go up to Ai: see, I have given into thy hand the king of Ai, and his people, and his city, and his land: 2 And thou shalt do to Ai and her king as thou didst unto Jericho and her king: only the spoil thereof, and the cattle thereof, shall ye take for a prey unto yourselves: lay thee an ambush for the city behind it.

Israel were very happy in having such a commander as Joshua, but Joshua was more happy in having such a director as God himself; when any difficulty occurred, he needed not to call a council of war who had *God so nigh unto him,* not only to answer, but even to anticipate, his enquiries. It should seem, Joshua was now at a stand, had scarcely recovered the discomposure he was put into by the trouble Achan gave them, and could not think, without fear and trembling, of pushing forward, lest there should be in the camp another Achan; then God spoke to him, either by vision, as before (*ch.* v.), as a man of war with his sword drawn, or by the breastplate of judgment. Note, When we have faithfully put away sin, that accursed thing, which *separates between us and God,* then, and not till then, we may expect to hear from God to our comfort; and God's directing us how to go on in our Christian work and warfare is a good evidence of his being reconciled to us. Observe here,

I. The encouragement God gives to Joshua to proceed: *Fear not, neither be thou dismayed, v.* 1. This intimates that the sin of Achan, and the consequences of it, had been a very great discouragement to Joshua, and made his heart almost ready to fail. Corruptions within the church weaken the hands, and damp the spirits, of her guides and helpers, more than oppositions from without; treacherous Israelites are to be dreaded more than malicious Canaanites. But God bids Joshua not be dismayed; the same power that keeps Israel from being ruined by their enemies shall keep them from ruining themselves. To animate him, 1. He assures him of success against Ai, tells him it is all his own; but he must take it as God's gift: *I have given it into thy hands,* which secured him both title and possession, and obliged him to give God the glory of both, Ps. xliv. 3. 2. He allows the people to take the spoil to themselves. Here the spoil was not consecrated to God as that of Jericho, and therefore there was no danger of the people's committing such a trespass as they had committed there. Observe, How Achan who caught at forbidden spoil lost that, and life, and all, but the rest of the people who had conscientiously refrained from the accursed thing were quickly recompensed for their obedience with the spoil of Ai. The way to have the comfort of what God allows us is to forbear what he forbids us. No man shall lose by his self-denial; let God have his dues first, and then all will be clean to us and sure. 1 Kings xvii. 13. God did not bring them to these *goodly cities,* and *houses filled with all good things,* to tantalize them with the sight of that which they might not touch; but, having received the first-fruits from Jericho, the spoil of Ai, and of all the cities which thenceforward came into their hands, they might take for a prey to themselves.

II. The direction he gives him in attacking Ai. It must not be such a work of time as the taking of Jericho was; this would have prolonged the war too much. Those that had patiently waited seven days for Jericho shall have Ai given them in one day. Nor was it, as that, to be taken by miracle, and purely by the act of God, but now their own conduct and courage must be exercised; having seen God work for them, they must now bestir themselves. God directs him, 1. To take all the people, that they might all be spectators of the action and sharers in the spoil. Hereby God gave him a tacit rebuke for sending so small a detachment against Ai in the former attempt upon it, *ch.* vii. 4. 2. To lay an ambush behind the city; this was a method which perhaps Joshua would not have thought of at this time, if God had not directed him to it; and though now we are not to expect direction, as here, by visions, voices, or oracles, yet, whenever those who are entrusted with public councils take prudent measures for the public good, it must be acknowledged that God puts it into their hearts; he that teaches the husbandman discretion no doubt teaches the statesman and general.

3 So Joshua arose, and all the people of war, to go up against Ai: and Joshua chose out thirty thousand mighty men of valour, and sent them away by night. 4 And he commanded them, saying, Behold, ye shall lie in wait against the city, *even* behind the city: go not very far from the city, but be ye all ready: 5 And I, and all the people that *are* with me, will approach unto the city: and it shall come to pass, when they come out against us, as at the first, that we will flee before them, 6 (For they will come out after us) till we have drawn them from the city; for they will say, They flee before us, as at the first: therefore we will flee before them. 7 Then ye shall rise up from the ambush, and seize upon the city: for the LORD your God will deliver it into your hand. 8 And it shall be, when ye have taken the city, *that* ye shall set the city on fire: according to the commandment of the LORD shall ye do. See, I have commanded you. 9 Joshua therefore sent them forth: and they went to lie in ambush, and abode between Beth-el and Ai, on the west side of Ai: but Joshua lodged that night among the people. 10 And Joshua rose up early in the morning, and numbered the people, and went up, he and the elders of Israel, before the people to Ai. 11 And all the people, *even the people* of war that *were* with him, went up, and drew nigh, and came before the city, and pitched on the north side of Ai: now *there was* a valley between them and Ai. 12 And he took about five thousand men, and set them to lie in ambush between Bethel and Ai, on the west side of the city. 13 And when they had set the people, *even* all the host that *was* on the north of the city, and their liers in wait on the west of the city, Joshua went that night into the midst of the valley. 14 And it came to pass, when the king of Ai saw *it,* that they hasted and rose up early, and the men of the city went out against Israel to battle, he and all his people, at a time appointed, before the plain; but he wist not that *there were* liers in ambush against him behind the city. 15 And Joshua and

all Israel made as if they were beaten before them, and fled by the way of the wilderness. 16 And all the people that *were* in Ai were called together to pursue after them: and they pursued after Joshua, and were drawn away from the city. 17 And there was not a man left in Ai or Beth-el, that went not out after Israel: and they left the city open, and pursued after Israel. 18 And the LORD said unto Joshua, Stretch out the spear that *is* in thy hand toward Ai; for I will give it into thine hand. And Joshua stretched out the spear that *he had* in his hand toward the city. 19 And the ambush arose quickly out of their place, and they ran as soon as he had stretched out his hand: and they entered into the city, and took it, and hasted and set the city on fire. 20 And when the men of Ai looked behind them, they saw, and, behold, the smoke of the city ascended up to heaven, and they had no power to flee this way or that way: and the people that fled to the wilderness turned back upon the pursuers. 21 And when Joshua and all Israel saw that the ambush had taken the city, and that the smoke of the city ascended, then they turned again, and slew the men of Ai. 22 And the other issued out of the city against them; so they were in the midst of Israel, some on this side, and some on that side: and they smote them, so that they let none of them remain or escape.

We have here an account of the taking of Ai by stratagem. The stratagem here used, we are sure, was lawful and good; God himself appointed it, and we have no reason to think but that the like is lawful and good in other wars. Here was no league broken, no oath or promise violated, nor any thing like it; it was not by the pretence of a parley, or treaty of peace, that the advantage was gained; no, these are sacred things, and not to be jested with, nor used to serve a turn; truth, when once it is plighted, becomes a debt even to the enemy. But in this stratagem here was no untruth told; nothing was concealed but their own counsels, which no enemy ever pretended a right to be entrusted with; nothing was dissembled, nothing counterfeited but a retreat, which was no natural or necessary indication at all of their inability to maintain their onset, or of any design not to renew it. The enemy ought to have been upon their guard, and to have kept within the defence of their own walls. Common prudence, had they been governed by it, would have directed them not to venture on the pursuit of an army which they saw was so far superior to them in numbers, and leave their city unguarded; but (*si populus vult decipi, decipiatur—if the people will be deceived, let them*) if the Canaanites will be so easily imposed upon, and in pursuit of God's Israel will break through all the laws of policy and good management, the Israelites are not at all to be blamed for taking advantage of their fury and thoughtlessness; nor is it any way inconsistent with the character God is pleased to give of them, that they are *children that will not lie.* Now in the account here given of this matter,

I. There is some difficulty in adjusting the numbers that were employed to effect it. Mention is made (*v.* 3) of 30,000 that were *chosen and sent away by night,* to whom the charge was given to surprise the city as soon as ever they perceived it was evacuated, *v.* 4, 7, 8. And yet afterwards (*v.* 12) it is said, Joshua *took* 5000 *men and set them to lie in ambush* behind the city, and that *ambush entered the city,* and *set it on fire, v.* 19. Now, 1. Some think there were two parties sent out to lie in ambush, 30,000 first, and afterwards 5000 to guard the roads, and to intercept those of the city that might think to save themselves by flight, or to strengthen those that were first sent out; and that Joshua made his open attack upon the city with all the thousands of Israel. So the learned bishop Patrick, insisting upon God's command (*v.* 1) to take *all the people of war with him.* But, 2. Others think that all the people were taken only to encamp before the city, and that out of them Joshua chose out 30,000 men to be employed in the action, out of which he sent out 5000 to lie in ambush, which were as many as could be supposed to march *incognito—without being discovered* (more would have been seen, and thus the design would have been broken), and that then with the other 25,000 he made the open attack, as Masius thinks, or with the 30,000, which, as Calvin thinks, he kept entire for that purpose, having, besides them, sent out 5000 for an ambuscade. And those 5000 (they think) must be meant by those (*v.* 3) whom he *sent away by night,* with orders to lie in wait behind the city, though the particular number is not specified till *v.* 12. If we admit such a seeming disturbance in the order of the narrative (of which, perhaps, similar instances might be cited from the other scripture histories), it seems most probable that there was but one ambushment, which consisted only of 5000, enough for such a purpose.

II. Yet the principal parts of the story are plain enough, that a detachment being secretly marched behind the city, on the other side to that on which the main body of the army lay (the situation of the country, it is probable, favouring their concealment), Joshua, and the forces with him, faced the city; the garrison made a vigorous sally out upon them, whereupon they withdrew, gave ground, and retreated in some seeming disorder towards the wilderness, which being perceived by the men of Ai, they drew out all the force they had to pursue them. This gave a fair opportunity for those that lay in ambush to make themselves masters of the city, whereof when they had given notice by a smoke to Joshua, he, with all his force, returned upon the pursuers, who now, when it was too late, were aware of the snare they were drawn into, and, their retreat being intercepted, they were every man of them cut off. The like artifice we find used, Judg. xx. 30, &c. Now in this story we may observe,

1. What a brave commander Joshua was. See, (1.) His conduct and prudence. God gave him the hint (*v.* 2) that he should lay an ambush behind the city, but left him to himself to order the particulars, which he did admirably well. Doubtless *wisdom strengthens the wise more than ten mighty men,* Eccl. vii. 19. (2.) His care and industry (*v.* 10): *He rose up early in the morning,* that he might lose no time, and to show how intent his mind was upon his business. Those that would maintain their spiritual conflicts must not love their ease. (3.) His courage and resolution; though an army of Israelites had been repulsed before Ai, yet he resolves to lead them on in person the second time, *v.* 5. Being himself also an elder, he took the elders of Israel with him to make this attack upon the city (*v.* 10), as if he were going rather to sit in judgment upon them as criminals than to fight them as enemies. (4.) His caution and consideration (*v.* 13): He *went that night into the midst of the valley,* to make the necessary dispositions for an attack, and to see that every thing was in good order. It is the pious conjecture of the learned bishop Patrick that he went into the valley alone, to pray to God for a blessing upon his enterprise, and he did not seek in vain. (5.) His constancy and perseverance; when he had stretched out his spear towards the city (*v.* 18, a spear almost as fatal and formidable to the enemies of Israel as the rod of Moses was) he never drew back his hand till the work was done. His hands in fighting, like Moses's in interceding, were steady till the going down of the sun. Those that have stretched out their hands against their spiritual enemies must never draw them back. *Lastly,* What Joshua did in the stratagem is applicable to our Lord Jesus, of whom he was a type. Joshua conquered by yielding, as if he had himself been conquered; so our Lord Jesus, when he bowed his head and gave up the ghost, seemed as if death had triumphed over him, and as if he and all his interests had been routed and ruined); but in his resurrection he rallied again and gave the powers of darkness a total defeat; he broke the serpent's head, by suffering him to bruise his heel. A glorious stratagem!

2. What an obedient people Israel was What *Joshua commanded them to do, according to the commandment of the Lord* (*v.* 8), they did it without murmuring or disputing. Those that were sent to lie in ambush between Beth-el and Ai (two cities confederate against them) were in a post of danger, and had they been discovered might all have been cut off, and yet they ventured; and, when the body of the army retreated and fled, it was both disgraceful and perilous, and yet, in obedience to Joshua, they did it.

3. What an infatuated enemy the king of Ai was, (1.) That he did not by his scouts discover those that lay in ambush behind the city, *v.* 14. Some observe it as a remarkable instance of the power of God in making men blind to their own interest, and the things that belong to their peace, that *he wist not that there were liers in wait against him.* Those are most in danger who are least aware that they are so. (2.) That when Israel seemed to fly he drew out all his forces to pursue them, and left none to guard his city and to secure his retreat, *v.* 17. Thus the church's enemies often run themselves into destruction by their own fury and the violence of their rage against the Israel of God. Pharaoh plunged himself into the Red Sea by the eagerness with which he pursued Israel. (3.) That from the killing of thirty-six men out of 3000, when Israel made the former attack upon his city, he should infer the total routing of so great an army as now he had to deal with (*v.* 6): *They flee before us as at the first.* See how the prosperity of fools destroys them and hardens them to their ruin. God had made use of the men of Ai as a scourge to chastise his people for meddling with the accursed thing, and this had puffed them up with a conceit that they must have the honour of delivering their country from these formidable invaders; but they were soon made to see their mistake, and that when the Israelites had reconciled themselves to their God they could have no power against them. God had made use of them only for the rebuking of Israel, with a purpose, when the correction was over, to throw the rod itself into the fire; *howbeit, they meant not so,* but *it was in their heart to destroy and cut off,* Isa. x. 5—7.

4. What a complete victory Israel obtained over them by the favour and blessing of God. Each did his part: the divided forces of Israel, by signals agreed on, understood one another, and every thing succeeded according to the project; so that the men of Ai, even when they were most confident of victory, found themselves surrounded, so that they had neither spirit to resist nor room to fly, but were under a fatal necessity of yield-

ing their lives to the destroyers. And now it is hard to say whether the shouts of the men of Israel, or the shrieks of the men of Ai, were the louder, but easy to imagine what terror and confusion they were filled with, when their highest assurances sunk so suddenly into the heaviest despair. Note, The triumphing of the wicked is short, Job xx. 5. They are *exalted for a little while*, that their fall and ruin may be the sorer, Job xxiv. 24. See how easily, how quickly, the scale turns against those that have not God on their side.

23 And the king of Ai they took alive, and brought him to Joshua. 24 And it came to pass, when Israel had made an end of slaying all the inhabitants of Ai in the field, in the wilderness wherein they chased them, and when they were all fallen on the edge of the sword, until they were consumed, that all the Israelites returned unto Ai, and smote it with the edge of the sword. 25 And *so* it was, *that* all that fell that day, both of men and women, *were* twelve thousand, *even* all the men of Ai. 26 For Joshua drew not his hand back, wherewith he stretched out the spear, until he had utterly destroyed all the inhabitants of Ai. 27 Only the cattle and the spoil of that city Israel took for a prey unto themselves, according unto the word of the LORD which he commanded Joshua. 28 And Joshua burnt Ai, and made it a heap for ever, *even* a desolation unto this day. 29 And the king of Ai he hanged on a tree until eventide: and as soon as the sun was down, Joshua commanded that they should take his carcase down from the tree, and cast it at the entering of the gate of the city, and raise thereon a great heap of stones, *that remaineth* unto this day.

We have here an account of the improvement which the Israelites made of their victory over Ai. 1. They put all to the sword, not only in the field, but in the city, man, woman, and child, none of them remained, *v.* 24. God, the righteous Judge, had passed this sentence upon them for their wickedness, so that the Israelites were only the ministers of his justice and the executioners of his doom. Once in this story, and but once, mention is made of the men of Beth-el, as confederates with the men of Ai, *v.* 17. Though they had a king of their own, and were not subjects to the king of Ai (for the king of Beth-el is reckoned among the thirty-one kings that Joshua destroyed, *ch.* xii. 16), yet Ai being a stronger place they threw themselves into that, for their own safety, and the strengthening of their neighbours' hands, and so (we may presume) were all cut off with them; thus that by which they hoped to prevent their own ruin hastened it. The whole number of the slain, it seems, was but 12,000, an inconsiderable body to make head against all the thousands of Israel; but those whom God will destroy he infatuates. Here it is said (*v.* 26) that *Joshua drew not his hand back wherewith he stretched out the spear* (*v.* 18) till the slaughter was completed. Some think the spear he stretched out was not to slay the enemies, but to animate and encourage his own soldiers, some flag or ensign being hung out at the end of this spear; and they observe it as an instance of his self-denial that though the fire of courage wherewith his breast was filled would have pushed him forward, sword in hand, into the hottest of the action, yet, in obedience to God, he kept the inferior post of a standard-bearer, and did not quit it till the work was done. By the spear stretched out, he directed the people to expect their help from God, and to him to give the praise. 2. They plundered the city and took all the spoil to themselves, *v.* 27. Thus the wealth of the sinner is laid up for the just; the spoil they brought out of Egypt, by borrowing of their neighbours, was much of it expended upon the tabernacle they had reared in the wilderness, for which they are now reimbursed with interest. The spoil here taken, it is probable, was all brought together, and distributed by Joshua in due proportions, as that of the Midianites was, Num. xxxi. 26, &c. It was not seized with irregularity or violence, for God is the God of order and equity, and not of confusion. 3. They laid the city in ashes, and left it to remain so, *v.* 28. Israel must yet dwell in tents, and therefore this city, as well as Jericho, must be burnt. And, though there was no curse entailed upon him that should rebuild it, yet, it seems, it was not rebuilt, unless it be the same with Aijah, which we read of, long after, Neh. xi. 31. Some think it was not rebuilt because Israel had received a defeat before it, the remembrance of which should be buried in the ruins of the city. 4. The king of Ai was taken prisoner and cut off, not by the sword of war as a soldier, but by the sword of justice as a malefactor. Joshua ordered him to be hanged, and his dead body thrown at the gate of his own city, *under a heap of stones*, *v.* 23, 29. Some particular reason, no doubt, there was for this severity against the king of Ai; it is likely he had been notoriously wicked and vile, and a blasphemer of the God of Israel, perhaps upon occasion of the repulse he had given to the forces of Israel in their first onset. Some observe that his dead body was thrown at the gate where he had been wont to sit in judgment that so much the greater contempt might thereby be poured upon the dignity he had been proud of, and he might be punished for the unrighteous decrees he had made in the very place where he had made them. Thus the Lord is known by the judgments which he executes.

30 Then Joshua built an altar unto the LORD God of Israel in mount Ebal, 31 As Moses the servant of the LORD commanded the children of Israel, as it is written in the book of the law of Moses, an altar of whole stones, over which no man hath lift up *any* iron: and they offered thereon burnt offerings unto the LORD, and sacrificed peace offerings. 32 And he wrote there upon the stones a copy of the law of Moses, which he wrote in the presence of the children of Israel. 33 And all Israel, and their elders, and officers, and their judges, stood on this side the ark and on that side before the priests the Levites, which bare the ark of the covenant of the LORD, as well the stranger, as he that was born among them; half of them over against mount Gerizim, and half of them over against mount Ebal; as Moses the servant of the LORD had commanded before, that they should bless the people of Israel. 34 And afterward he read all the words of the law, the blessings and cursings, according to all that is written in the book of the law. 35 There was not a word of all that Moses commanded, which Joshua read not before all the congregation of Israel, with the women, and the little ones, and the strangers that were conversant among them.

This religious solemnity of which we have here an account comes in somewhat surprisingly in the midst of the history of the wars of Canaan. After the taking of Jericho and Ai, we should have expected that the next news would be of their taking possession of the country, the pushing on of their victories in other cities, and the carrying of the war into the bowels of the nation, now that they had made themselves masters of these frontier towns. But here a scene opens of quite another nature; the camp of Israel is drawn out into the field, not to engage the enemy, but to offer sacrifice, to hear the law read, and to say *Amen* to the blessings and the curses. Some think this was not done till after some of the following victories were obtained which we read of, *ch.* x. and xi. But it should seem by the maps that Shechem (near to which these two mountains Gerizim and Ebal were) was not so far off from Ai but that when they had taken that they might penetrate into the country as far as those two mountains, and therefore I would not willingly admit a transposition of the story; and the rather because, as it comes in here, it is a remarkable instance, 1. Of the zeal of Israel for the service of God and for his honour. Though never was war more honourable, more pleasant, or more gainful, nor ever was war more sure of victory, or more necessary to a settlement (for they had neither houses nor lands of their own till they had won them by the sword, no, not Joshua himself), yet all the business of the war shall stand still, while they make a long march to the place appointed, and there attend this solemnity. God appointed them to do this when they should have got over Jordan, and they did it as soon as possibly they could, though they might have had a colourable pretence to put it off. Note, We must not think to defer our covenanting with God till we are settled in the world, nor must any business put us by from minding and pursuing the one thing needful. The way to prosper is to begin with God, Matt. vi. 33. 2. It is an instance of the care of God concerning his faithful servants and worshippers. Though they were in an enemy's country, as yet unconquered, yet in the service of God they were safe, as Jacob when in this very country he was going to Beth-el to pay his vows: *the terror of God was upon the cities round about,* Gen. xxxv. 5. Note, When we are in the way of duty God takes us under his special protection.

Twice Moses had given express orders for this solemnity; once Deut. xi. 29, 30, where he seems to have pointed to the very place where it was to be performed; and again Deut. xxvii. 2, &c. It was a federal transaction: the covenant was now renewed between God and Israel upon their taking possession of the land of promise, that they might be encouraged in the conquest of it, and might know upon what terms they held it, and come under fresh obligations to obedience. In token of the covenant,

I. They built an altar, and offered sacrifice to God (*v.* 30, 31), in token of their dedication of themselves to God, as living sacrifices to his honour, in and by a Mediator, who is the altar that sanctifies this gift. This altar was erected on Mount *Ebal,* the mount on which the curse was put (Deut. xi. 29), to signify that there, where by the law we had reason to expect a curse, by Christ's sacrifice of himself for us and his mediation we have peace with God; he has redeemed us from the curse of the law by being made a *curse for us,* Gal. iii. 13. Even where it was said, by the curse, *You are not my people,* there it is said, through Christ the altar, *You are the children of the living God,* Hos. i. 10. The curses pronounced on Mount Ebal would immediately have been executed if atonement had not been made by sacrifice. By the sacrifices offered on this altar they did likewise give God the glory of the victories they had already obtained, as Exod. xvii. 15. Now that they had had the comfort of them, in the spoils of Ai, it was fit that God should have the praise of them. And they also implored his favour for their future success; for supplications as well as thanksgivings were intended in their peace-offerings. The way to prosper in all that we put our hand to is to take God along with us, and in all our ways to acknowledge him by prayer, praise, and dependence. The altar they built was of rough unhewn stone, according to the law (Exod. xx. 25), for that which is most plain and natural, and least artful and affected, in the worship of God, he is best pleased with. Man's device can add no beauty to God's institutions.

II. They received the law from God; and this those must do that would find favour with him, and expect to have their offerings accepted; for, if we turn away our ear from hearing the law, our prayers will be an abomination. When God took Israel into covenant he gave them his law, and they, in token of their consent to the covenant, subjected themselves to the law. Now here,

1. The law of the ten commandments was written upon stones in the presence of all Israel, as an abridgment of the whole, *v.* 32. This copy was not graven in the stone, as that which was reserved in the ark: that was to be done only by the finger of God; it is his prerogative to write the law in the heart. But the stones were plastered, and it was written upon the plaster, Deut. xxvii. 4, 8. It was written, that all might see what it was that they consented to, and that it might be a standing remaining testimony to posterity of God's goodness in giving them such good laws, and a testimony against them if they were disobedient to them. It is a great mercy to any people to have the law of God in writing, and it is fit that the written law should be exposed to common view in a known tongue, that it may be seen and read of all men.

2. The blessings and the curses, the sanctions of the law, were publicly read, and the people (we may suppose), according to Moses's appointment, said *Amen* to them, *v.* 33, 34.

(1.) The auditory was very large. [1.] The greatest prince was not excused. The elders, officers, and judges, are not above the cognizance of the law, but will come under the blessing or the curse, according as they are or are not obedient to it, and therefore they must be present to consent to the covenant and to go before the people therein. [2.] The poorest stranger was not excluded. Here was a general naturalization of them: as well the stranger as he that was born among them was taken into covenant. This was an encouragement to proselytes, and a happy presage of the kindnesses intended for the poor Gentiles in the latter days.

(2.) The tribes were posted, as Moses directed, six towards Gerizim and six towards Ebal. And the ark in the midst of the valley was between them, for it was the *ark of the covenant;* and in it were shut up the close rolls of that law which was copied out and shown openly upon the stones. The covenant was commanded, and the command covenanted. The priests that attended the ark, or some of the Levites that attended them, after the people had all taken their places, and silence was proclaimed, pronounced distinctly the blessings and the curses, as Moses had drawn them up, to which the tribes said *Amen;* and yet it is here only said that they should *bless the people,* for the blessing was that which was first and chiefly intended, and which God designed in giving the law. If they fell under the curse, that was their own fault. And it was really a blessing to the people that they had this matter laid so plainly before them, *life and death, good and evil;* he *had not dealt so with other nations.*

3. The law itself also containing the precepts and prohibitions was read (*v.* 35), it should seem by Joshua himself, who did not think it below him to be a reader in the congregation of the Lord. In conformity to this example, the solemn reading of the law, which was appointed once in seven years (Deut. xxxi. 10, 11), was performed by their king or chief magistrate. It is here intimated what a general publication of the law this was. (1.) Every word was read; even the minutest precepts were not omitted, nor the most copious abridged; not one iota or tittle of the law shall pass away, and therefore none was, in reading, skipped over, under pretence of want of time, or that any part was needless or not proper to be read. It was not many weeks since Moses had preached the whole book of *Deuteronomy* to them, yet Joshua must now read it all over again; it is good to hear twice what God has spoken once (Ps. lxii. 11) and to review what has been delivered to us, or to have it repeated, that we may not let it slip. (2.) Every Israelite was present, even *the women and the little ones* that all might know and do their duty. Note, Masters of families should bring their wives and children with them to the solemn assemblies for religious worship. All that are capable of learning must come to be *taught out of the law.* The strangers also attended with them; for wherever we are, though but as strangers, we should improve every opportunity of acquainting ourselves with God and his holy will.

CHAP. IX.

Here is in this chapter, I. The impolitic confederacy of the kings of Canaan against Israel, ver. 1, 2. II. The politic confederacy of the inhabitants of Gibeon with Israel. 1. How it was subtly

proposed and petitioned for by the Gibeonites pretending to come from a far country, ver. 3—13. 2. How it was unwarily consented to by Joshua and the Israelites, to the disgust of the congregation when the fraud was discovered, ver. 14—18. 3. How the matter was adjusted to the satisfaction of all sides, by giving these Gibeonites their lives because they had covenanted with them, yet depriving them of their liberties because the covenant was not fairly obtained, ver. 19—27.

AND it came to pass, when all the kings which *were* on this side Jordan, in the hills, and in the valleys, and in all the coasts of the great sea over against Lebanon, the Hittite, and the Amorite, the Canaanite, the Perizzite, the Hivite, and the Jebusite, heard *thereof;* 2 That they gathered themselves together, to fight with Joshua and with Israel, with one accord.

Hitherto the Canaanites had acted defensively; the Israelites were the aggressors upon Jericho and Ai. But here the kings of Canaan are in consultation to attack Israel, and concert matters for a vigorous effort of their united forces to check the progress of their victorious arms. Now, 1. It was strange they did not do this sooner. They had notice long since of their approach; Israel's design upon Canaan was no secret; one would have expected that a prudent concern for their common safety would put them upon taking some measures to oppose their coming over Jordan, and maintain that pass against them, or to give them a warm reception as soon as they were over. It was strange they did not attempt to raise the siege of Jericho, or at least fall in with the men of Ai, when they had given them a defeat. But they were, either through presumption or despair, wonderfully infatuated and at their wits' end. Many know not the things that belong to their peace till they are hidden from their eyes. 2. It was more strange that they did it now. Now that the conquest of Jericho had given such a pregnant proof of God's power, and that of Ai of Israel's policy, one would have thought the end of their consultation should be, not to fight with Israel, but to make peace with them, and to gain the best terms they could for themselves. This would have been their wisdom (Luke xiv. 32), but their minds were blinded, and their hearts hardened to their destruction. Observe, (1.) What induced them now at last to enter upon this consultation. When they *heard thereof* (*v.* 1), not only of the conquest of Jericho and Ai, but of the convention of the states of Mount Ebal, of which we have an account immediately before,—when they heard that Joshua, as if he thought himself already completely master of the country, had had all his people together, and had read the laws to them by which they must be governed, and taken their promises to submit to those laws,—then they perceived the Israelites were in good earnest, and thought it was high time for them to bestir themselves. The pious devotion of God's people sometimes provokes and exasperates their enemies more than any thing else. (2.) How unanimous they were in their resolves. Though they were many kings of different nations, Hittites, Amorites, Perizzites, &c., doubtless of different interests, and that had often been at variance one with another, yet they determined, *nemine contradicente—unanimously,* to unite against Israel. O that Israel would learn this of Canaanites, to sacrifice private interests to the public welfare, and to lay aside all animosities among themselves, that they may cordially unite against the common enemies of God's kingdom among men!

3 And when the inhabitants of Gibeon heard what Joshua had done unto Jericho and to Ai, 4 They did work wilily, and went and made as if they had been ambassadors, and took old sacks upon their asses, and wine bottles, old, and rent, and bound up; 5 And old shoes and clouted upon their feet, and old garments upon them; and all the bread of their provision was dry *and* mouldy. 6 And they went to Joshua unto the camp at Gilgal, and said unto him, and to the men of Israel, We be come from a far country: now therefore make ye a league with us. 7 And the men of Israel said unto the Hivites, Peradventure ye dwell among us; and how shall we make a league with you? 8 And they said unto Joshua, We *are* thy servants. And Joshua said unto them, Who *are* ye? and from whence come ye? 9 And they said unto him, From a very far country thy servants are come because of the name of the LORD thy God: for we have heard the fame of him, and all that he did in Egypt, 10 And all that he did to the two kings of the Amorites, that *were* beyond Jordan, to Sihon king of Heshbon, and to Og king of Bashan, which *was* at Ashtaroth. 11 Wherefore our elders and all the inhabitants of our country spake to us, saying, Take victuals with you for the journey, and go to meet them, and say unto them, We *are* your servants: therefore now make ye a league with us. 12 This our bread we took hot *for* our provision out of our houses on the day

we came forth to go unto you; but now, behold, it is dry, and it is mouldy: 13 And these bottles of wine, which we filled, *were* new; and, behold, they be rent: and these our garments and our shoes are become old by reason of the very long journey. 14 And the men took of their victuals, and asked not *counsel* at the mouth of the LORD.

Here, I. The Gibeonites desire to make peace with Israel, being alarmed by the tidings they heard of the destruction of Jericho, *v.* 3. Other people heard those tidings, and were irritated thereby to make war upon Israel; but the Gibeonites heard them and were induced to make peace with them. Thus the discovery of the glory and grace of God in the gospel is to some a *savour of life unto life, but to others a savour of death unto death,* 2 Cor. ii. 16. The same sun softens wax and hardens clay. I do not remember that we read any where of a king of Gibeon. Had their government been at this time in a single person, perhaps his heart would have been too high to yield to Israel, and he would have joined with the rest of the kings against Israel. But these four united cities (mentioned *v.* 17) seem to have been governed by elders, or senators (*v.* 11), who consulted the common safety more than their own personal dignity. The inhabitants of Gibeon did well for themselves. We have,

II. The method they took to compass it. They knew that all the inhabitants of the land of Canaan were to be cut off; perhaps they had some spies in the congregation at Ebal, when the law was read, who observed and brought them notice of the command given to Israel (Deut. vii. 1—3), that they should *show no mercy* to the Canaanites, give them no quarter in battle, which made them afraid of fighting them, and that they should *make no covenant with them,* which made them despair of gaining any advantage by treating with them; and therefore there was no way of saving their lives from the sword of Israel unless they could, by disguising themselves, make Joshua believe that they came from some very far country, which the Israelites were not commanded to make war upon nor forbidden to *make peace with,* but were particularly appointed to *offer peace to,* Deut. xx. 10, 15. Unless they could be admitted under this notion, they saw there was but one way with them: they must submit to the fate of Jericho and Ai. Though the neighbouring princes *knew that all the men thereof were mighty* (*ch.* x. 2), and they knew it themselves, yet they durst not contend with Israel, who had an Almighty God on their side. This therefore is the only game they have to play, and observe,

1. They play it very artfully and successfully. Never was any such thing more craftily managed.

(1.) They come under the character of ambassadors from a foreign state, which they thought would please the princes of Israel, and make them proud of the honour of being courted by distant countries: we find Hezekiah fond of those that came to him from a far country (Isa. xxxix. 3); they were not used to be thus courted.

(2.) They pretended to have undergone the fatigues of a very long journey, and produced what passed for an ocular demonstration of it. It should seem it was then usual for those that undertook long journeys to take with them, as we do now for long voyages, all manner of provision in kind, the country not being furnished as ours is now with houses of entertainment, for the convenience of which, when we have occasion to make use of them, we have reason to be very thankful. Now they here pretended that their provision, when they brought it from home, was fresh and new, but now it appeared to be old and dry, whereas it might well be presumed they had not loitered, but made the best of their way; so that hence it must be inferred that they came, as they said they did, from a very far country: their sacks or portmanteaus were old; the wine was all drunk, and the bottles in which it had been were broken; their shoes and clothes were worse than those of the Israelites in forty years, and their bread was mouldy, *v.* 4, 5, and again, *v.* 12, 13. Thus God's Israel have often been deceived and imposed upon with a show of antiquity. But (as bishop Hall expresses it) *errors are never the older for being patched,* and so seeming old; but those that will be caught with this Gibeonitish stratagem prove they have not consulted with God. And thus there are those who make themselves poor with the badges of want and distress and yet have great riches (Prov. xiii. 7), or at least have no need of relief, by which fraud charity is misplaced and diverted from those that are real objects of it.

(3.) When they were suspected, and more strictly examined as to whence they came, they industriously declined telling the name of their country, till the agreement was settled. [1.] The men of Israel suspected a fraud (*v.* 7): "*Peradventure you dwell among us,* and then we may not, we must not, make any league with you." This might have discouraged the Gibeonites from urging the matter any further, concluding that if the peace were made the Israelites would not think themselves obliged to keep it, having thus solemnly protested against it in case they *dwelt among them;* but, knowing that there was no hope at all if they stood it out, they bravely ventured a submission. "Who knows but the people of Israel may save us alive, though thus inveigled into a promise; and if we tell them at last we shall but die." [2.] Joshua put the questions to them, *Who are you? and whence come you?* He finds himself concerned to stand upon his guard against secret fraud as well as against open force. We in our spiritual warfare must *stand against the wiles of the devil,* remembering he is a subtle serpent as well as a roaring lion. In all leagues of relation and friendship we must first try and then trust, lest we repent at leisure agreements made in haste. [3.] They would not tell whence they came; but still repeat the same thing: *We have come from a very far country, v.* 9. They will have it thought that it is a country Joshua knows nothing of nor ever heard of, and therefore would be never the wiser if they should tell him the name of it.

(4.) They profess a respect for the God of Israel, the more to ingratiate themselves with Joshua, and we charitably believe they were sincere in this profession: "*We have come because of the name of the Lord thy God* (*v.* 9), because of what we have heard of that name, which has convinced us that it is *above every name,* and because we have a desire towards that name and the remembrance of it, and would gladly come under its protection."

(5.) They fetch their inducements from what had been done some time before in Moses's reign, the tidings whereof might easily be supposed ere this to have reached distant regions, the plagues of Egypt and the destruction of Sihon and Og (*v.* 9, 10), but prudently say nothing of the destruction of Jericho and Ai (though this was the true inducement, *v.* 3), because they will have it supposed that they came from home long before those conquests were made. We need not be long to seek for reasons why we should submit to the God of Israel; we may be furnished either with new or old, which we will.

(6.) They make a general submission—*We are your servants;* and humbly sue for a general agreement—*Make a league with us, v.* 11. They insist not upon terms, but will be glad of peace upon any terms; nor will the case admit of delays, lest the fraud be discovered; they would fain have the bargain struck up immediately; if Joshua will but *make a league* with them, they have all they come for, and they hope their ragged clothes and clouted shoes will be no exception against them. God and Israel reject none for their poverty. But,

2. There is a mixture of good and evil in their conduct. (1.) Their falsehood cannot be justified, nor ought it to be drawn into a precedent. We must not do evil that good may come. Had they owned their country but renounced the idolatries of it, resigning the possession of it to Israel and themselves to the God of Israel, we have reason to think Joshua would have been directed by the oracle of God to spare their lives, and they needed not to have made these pretensions. It is observable that when they had once said, *We have come from a far country* (*v.* 6), they found themselves necessitated to say it again (*v.* 9), and to say what was utterly false concerning their bread, their bottles, and their clothes (*v.* 12, 13), for one lie is an inlet to another, and that to a third, and so on. The way of that sin is down-hill. But, (2.) Their faith and prudence are to be greatly commended. Our Lord commended even the unjust steward, because he had done wisely and well for himself, Luke xvi. 8. In submitting to Israel, they submitted to the God of Israel, which implied a renunciation of the god they had served, a resignation to the laws of the true religion. They had heard enough to convince them of the infinite power of the God of Israel, and thence might infer his other perfections of wisdom and goodness; and how can we do better for ourselves than surrender at discretion to infinite wisdom, and cast ourselves upon the mercy of a God of infinite goodness. The submission of these Gibeonites was the more laudable because it was, [1.] Singular. Their neighbours took another course, and expected they should join with them. [2.] Speedy. They did not stay till Israel had besieged their cities; then it would have been too late to capitulate; but when they were at some distance they desired conditions of peace. The way to avoid a judgment is to meet it by repentance. Let us imitate these Gibeonites, and make our peace with God in the rags of humiliation, godly sorrow, and mortification, so our iniquity shall not be our ruin. Let us be servants to Jesus, our blessed Joshua, and make a league with him and the Israel of God, and we shall live.

15 And Joshua made peace with them, and made a league with them, to let them live: and the princes of the congregation sware unto them. 16 And it came to pass at the end of three days after they had made a league with them, that they heard that they *were* their neighbours, and *that* they dwelt among them. 17 And the children of Israel journeyed, and came unto their cities on the third day. Now their cities *were* Gibeon, and Chephirah, and Beeroth, and Kirjath-jearim. 18 And the children of Israel smote them not, because the princes of the congregation had sworn unto them by the LORD God of Israel. And all the congregation murmured against the princes. 19 But all the princes said unto all the congregation, We have sworn unto them by the LORD God of Israel: now therefore we may not touch them. 20 This we will do to

them; we will even let them live, lest wrath be upon us, because of the oath which we sware unto them. 21 And the princes said unto them, Let them live; but let them be hewers of wood and drawers of water unto all the congregation; as the princes had promised them.

Here is, I. The treaty soon concluded with the Gibeonites, *v.* 15. The thing was not done with much formality, but in short, 1. They agreed to let them live, and more the Gibeonites did not ask. In a common war this would have been but a small matter to be granted; but in the wars of Canaan, which were to make a general destruction, it was a great favour to a Canaanite to have his *life given him for a prey,* Jer. xlv. 5. 2. This agreement was made not by Joshua only, but by the princes of the congregation in conjunction with him. Though Joshua had an extraordinary call to the government, and extraordinary qualifications for it, yet he would not act in an affair, of this nature without the counsel and concurrence of the princes, who were neither kept in the dark nor kept under foot, but were treated by him as sharers in the government. 3. It was ratified by an oath; they swore unto them, not by any of the gods of Canaan, but by the God of Israel only, *v.* 19. Those that mean honestly do not startle at assurances, but satisfy those with whom they treat, and glorify God by calling him to witness to the sincerity of their intentions. 4. Nothing appears to have been culpable in all this but that it was done rashly; they took of their victuals, by which they satisfied themselves that it was indeed old and dry, but did not consider that this was no proof of their bringing it fresh from home; so that, making use of their senses only, but not their reason, *they received the men* (as the margin reads it) *because of their victuals,* perceiving perhaps, upon the view and taste of their bread, not only that now it was old, but that it had been fine and very good at first, whence they inferred that they were persons of some quality, and therefore the friendship of their country was not to be despised. But *they asked not counsel at the mouth of the Lord.* They had the Urim and Thummim with them, which they might have advised with in this difficult case, and which would have told them no lie, would have led them into no error; but they relied so much on their own politics that they thought it needless to bring the matter to the oracle. Joshua himself was not altogether without blame herein. Note, We make more haste than good speed in any business when we stay not to take God along with us, and by the word and prayer to consult him. Many a time we see cause to reflect upon it with regret that such and such an affair miscarried, because we *asked not counsel at the mouth of the Lord;* would we acknowledge him in all our ways, we should find them more safe, easy, and successful.

II. The fraud soon discovered, by which this league was procured. *A lying tongue is but for a moment,* and truth will be the daughter of time. Within three days they found, to their great surprise, that the cities which these ambassadors had treated for were very near them, but one night's foot-march from the camp at Gilgal, *ch.* x. 9. Either their own scouts or the parties that sallied out to acquaint themselves with the country, or perhaps some deserters that came over to them from the enemy, informed them of the truth in this matter. Those that suffer themselves to be deceived by the wiles of Satan will soon be undeceived to their confusion, and will find that near, even at the door, which they imagined was very far off.

III. The disgust of the congregation at this. They did indeed submit to the restraints which this league laid upon them, and smote not the cities of the Gibeonites, neither slew the persons nor seized the prey; but it vexed them to have their hands thus tied, and they *murmured against the princes* (*v.* 18), it is to be feared, more from a jealousy for their own profit than from a zeal for the fulfilling of God's command, though some of them perhaps had a regard to that. Many are forward to arraign and censure the actions of princes while they are ignorant of the springs of those actions and are incompetent judges of the reasons of state that govern them. While therefore we are satisfied in general that those who are over us aim at nothing but the public good, and sincerely seek the welfare of their people, we ought to make the best of what they do and not exercise ourselves in things above us.

IV. The prudent endeavour of the princes to pacify the discontented congregation, and to accommodate the matter; herein all the princes concurred and were unanimous, which doubtless disposed the people to acquiesce.

1. They resolved to spare the lives of the Gibeonites, for so they had expressly sworn to do (*v.* 15), to let them live. (1.) The oath was lawful, else it had not bound them any more than Herod's oath bound him to cut off John Baptist's head; it is true God had appointed them to destroy all the Canaanites, but that law must be construed, *in favorem vitæ—with some tender allowance,* to mean those only that stood it out and would not surrender their country to them, and not to bind them so far to put off the sense of honour and humanity as to slay those who had never lifted up a hand against them nor ever would, but before they were reduced to any extremity, or ever attempted any act of hostility, with one consent humbled themselves; the *kings of Israel were certainly*

more merciful kings than to do so (1 Kings xx. 31), and the God of Israel a more merciful God than to order it so. *Satis est prostrâsse leoni—It is enough to have laid the lion prostrate.* And besides, the reason of the law is the law; the mischief designed to be prevented by that law was the infecting of the Israelites with their idolatry, Deut. vii. 4. But if the Gibeonites renounce their idolatry, and become friends and servants to the house of God, the danger is effectually prevented, the reason of the law ceases, and consequently the obligation of it, especially to a thing of this nature. The conversion of sinners shall prevent their ruin. (2.) The oath being lawful, both the princes and the people for whom they transacted were bound by it, bound in conscience, bound in honour to the God of Israel, by whom they had sworn, and whose name would have been blasphemed by the Canaanites if they had violated this oath. They speak as those that *feared an oath* (Eccl. ix. 2), when they argued thus: *We will let them live, lest wrath be upon us, because of the oath which we swore,* v. 20. He that ratifies a promise with an oath imprecates the divine vengeance if he wilfully break his promise, and has reason to expect that divine justice will take him at his word. God is not mocked, and therefore oaths are not to be jested with. The princes would keep their word, [1.] Though they lost by it. A citizen of Zion *swears to his own hurt and changes not,* Ps. xv. 4. Joshua and the princes, when they found it was to their prejudice that they had thus bound themselves, did not apply to Eleazar for a dispensation, much less did they pretend that no faith is to be kept with heretics, with Canaanites; no, they were strangers to the modern artifices of the Romish church to elude the most sacred bonds, and even to sanctify perjuries. [2.] Though the people were uneasy at it, and their discontent might have ended in a mutiny, yet the princes would not violate their engagement to the Gibeonites; we must never be over-awed, either by majesty or multitude, to do a sinful thing, and go against our consciences. [3.] Though they were drawn into this league by a wile, and might have had a very plausible pretence to declare it null and void, yet they adhered to it. They might have pleaded that though those were the men with whom they exchanged the ratifications, yet these were not the cities intended in the league; they had promised to spare certain cities, without names, that were very far off, and upon the express consideration of their being so; but these were very near, and therefore not the cities that they covenanted with. And many learned men have thought that they were so grossly imposed upon by the Gibeonites that it would have been lawful for them to have recalled their promise, but to preserve their reputation, and to keep up in Israel a veneration for an oath, they would stand to it; but it is plain that they thought themselves indispensably obliged by it, and were apprehensive that the wrath of God would fall upon them if they broke it. And, however their adherence to it might be displeasing to the congregation, it is plain that it was acceptable to God; for when, in pursuance of this league, they undertook the protection of the Gibeonites, God gave them the most glorious victory that ever they had in all their wars (*ch.* x.), and long afterwards severely avenged the wrong Saul did to the Gibeonites in violation of this league, 2 Sam. xxi. 1. Let this convince us all how religiously we ought to perform our promises, and make good our bargains; and what conscience we ought to make of our words when they are once given. If a covenant obtained by so many lies and deceits might not be broken, shall we think to evade the obligation of those that have been made with all possible honesty and fairness? If the fraud of others will not justify or excuse our falsehood, certainly the honesty of others in dealing with us will aggravate and condemn our dishonesty in dealing with them.

2. Though they spared their lives, yet they seized their liberties, and sentenced them to be *hewers of wood and drawers of water to the congregation, v.* 21. By this proposal the discontented congregation was pacified; for, (1.) Those who were angry that the Gibeonites lived might be content when they saw them condemned to that which, in the general apprehension, is worse than death, perpetual servitude. (2.) Those who were angry that they were not spoiled might be content when their serving the congregation would be more to the public advantage than their best effects could be; and, in short, the Israelites would be no losers either in honour or profit by this peace with the Gibeonites; convince them of this, and they will be satisfied.

22 And Joshua called for them, and he spake unto them, saying, Wherefore have ye beguiled us, saying, We *are* very far from you; when ye dwell among us? 23 Now therefore ye *are* cursed, and there shall none of you be freed from being bondmen, and hewers of wood and drawers of water for the house of my God. 24 And they answered Joshua, and said, Because it was certainly told thy servants, how that the LORD thy God commanded his servant Moses to give you all the land, and to destroy all the inhabitants of the land from before you, therefore we were sore afraid of our lives because of you, and have done this thing. 25 And now, behold, we *are* in thine

hand: as it seemeth good and right unto thee to do unto us, do. 26 And so did he unto them, and delivered them out of the hand of the children of Israel, that they slew them not. 27 And Joshua made them that day hewers of wood and drawers of water for the congregation, and for the altar of the LORD, even unto this day, in the place which he should choose.

The matter is here settled between Joshua and the Gibeonites, and an explanation of the league agreed upon. We may suppose that now, not the messengers who were first sent, but the elders of Gibeon, and of the cities that were dependent upon it, were themselves present and treated with, that the matter might be fully compromised.

I. Joshua reproves them for their fraud, *v.* 22. And they excuse it as well as they can, *v.* 24. 1. Joshua gives the reproof very mildly: *Wherefore have you beguiled us?* He does not load them with any ill names, does not give them any harsh provoking language, does not call them, as they deserved to be called, *base liars,* but only asks them, *Why have you beguiled us?* Under the greatest provocations, it is our wisdom and duty to keep our temper, and to bridle our passion; a just cause needs not anger to defend it, and a bad one is made never the better by it. 2. They make the best excuse for themselves, that the thing would bear, *v.* 24. They found by the word of God that sentence of death was passed upon them (the command was to *destroy all the inhabitants of the land,* without exception), and they found by the works of God already wrought that there was no opposing the execution of this sentence; they considered that God's sovereignty is incontestable, his justice inflexible, his power irresistible, and therefore resolved to try what his mercy was, and found it was not in vain to cast themselves upon it. They do not go about to justify their lie, but in effect beg pardon for it, pleading it was purely to save their lives that they did it, which every man that finds in himself the force of the law of self-preservation will therefore make great allowances for, especially in such a case as this, where the fear was not merely of the power of man (if that were all, one might flee from that to the divine protection), but of the power of God himself, which they saw engaged against them.

II. Joshua condemns them to servitude, as a punishment of their fraud (*v.* 23), and they submit to the sentence (*v.* 25), and for aught that appears both sides are pleased.

1. Joshua pronounces them perpetual bondmen. They had purchased their lives with a lie, but, that being no good consideration, he obliges them to hold their lives under the rent and reservation of their continual labours, in hewing wood and drawing water, the meanest and most toilsome employments. Thus their lie was punished; had they dealt fairly and plainly with Israel, perhaps they would have had more honourable conditions granted them, but now, since they gain their lives with ragged clothes and clouted shoes, the badges of servitude, they are condemned for ever to wear such, so must their doom be. And thus the ransom of their lives is paid; dominion is acquired by the preservation of a life that lies at mercy *(servus dicitur a servando—a servant is so called from the act of saving);* they owe their service to those to whom they owe their lives. Observe how the judgment is given against them. (1.) Their servitude is made a curse to them. "Now you are cursed with the ancient curse of Canaan," from whom these Hivites descended, *a servant of servants shalt thou be,* Gen. ix. 25. What shall be done to the false tongue but this? Cursed shall it be. (2.) Yet this curse is turned into a blessing; they must be servants, but it shall be for *the house of my God.* The princes would have them slaves *unto all the congregation* (*v.* 21), at least they chose to express themselves so, for the pacifying of the people that were discontented; but Joshua mitigates the sentence, both in honour to God and in favour to the Gibeonites: it would be too hard upon them to make them every man's drudge; if they must be *hewers of wood and drawers of water,* than which there cannot be a greater disparagement, especially to those who are citizens of a royal city, and *all mighty men* (*ch.* x. 2), yet they shall be so to *the house of my God,* than which there cannot be a greater preferment: David himself could have wished to be a door-keeper there. Even servile work becomes honourable when it is done for the house of our God and the offices thereof. [1.] They were hereby excluded from the liberties and privileges of true-born Israelites, and a remaining mark of distinction was put upon their posterity throughout all their generations. [2.] They were hereby employed in such services as required their personal attendance upon *the altar of God in the place which he should choose* (*v.* 27), which would bring them to the knowledge of the law of God, keep them strictly to that holy religion to which they were proselyted, and prevent their revolt to the idolatries of their fathers. [3.] This would be a great advantage to the priests and Levites to have so many, and those mighty men, constant attendants upon them, and engaged by office to do all the drudgery of the tabernacle. A great deal of wood must be hewed for fuel for God's house, not only to keep the fire burning continually upon the altar, but to boil the flesh of the peace-offerings, &c. And a great deal of water must be drawn for the divers wash-

ings which the law prescribed. These and other such servile works, such as washing the vessels, carrying out ashes, sweeping the courts, &c., which otherwise the Levites must have done themselves, these Gibeonites were appointed to do. [4.] They were herein servants to the congregation too; for whatever promotes and helps forward the worship of God is real service to the commonwealth. It is the interest of every Israelite that the altar of God be well attended. Hereby also the congregation was excused from much of that servile work which perhaps would otherwise have been expected from some of them. God had made a law that the Israelites should never make any of their brethren bondmen; if they had slaves, they must be of the heathen that were round about them, Lev. xxv. 44. Now in honour of this law, and of Israel that was honoured by it, God would not have the drudgery, no, not of the tabernacle itself, to be done by Israelites, but by Gibeonites, who were afterwards called *Nethinim,* men given to the Levites, as the Levites were to the priests (Num. iii. 9), to minister to them in the service of God. [5.] This may be looked upon as typifying the admission of the Gentiles into the gospel church. Now they were taken in upon their submission to be under-officers, but afterwards God promises that he will *take of them for priests and Levites,* Isa. lxvi. 21.

2. They submit to this condition, *v.* 25. Conscious of a fault in framing a lie whereby to deceive the Israelites, and sensible also how narrowly they escaped with their lives and what a kindness it was to have them spared, they acquiesce in the proposal: *Do as it seemeth right unto thee.* Better live in servitude, especially such servitude, than not live at all. Those of the very meanest and most despicable condition are described to be *hewers of wood and drawers of water,* Deut. xxix. 11. But skin for skin, liberty, and labour, and *all that a man has, will he give for his life,* and no ill bargain. Accordingly the matter was determined. (1.) Joshua delivered them out of the hands of the Israelites that they should not be slain, *v.* 26. It seems there were those who would have fallen upon them with the sword if Joshua had not interposed with his authority; but wise generals know when to sheathe the sword, as well as when to draw it. (2.) He then delivered them again into the hands of the Israelites to be enslaved, *v.* 27. They were not to keep possession of their cities, for we find afterwards that three of them fell to the lot of Benjamin and one to that of Judah; nor were they themselves to be at their own disposal, but, as bishop Patrick thinks, were dispersed into the cities of the priests and Levites, and came up with them in their courses to serve at the altar, out of the profits of which, it is probable, they were maintained. And thus Israel's bondmen became the Lord's freemen, for his service in the meanest office is liberty, and his work is its own wages. And this they got by their early submission. Let us, in like manner, submit to our Lord Jesus, and refer our lives to him, saying, "*We are in thy hand, do unto us as seemeth good and right unto thee;* only save our souls, and we shall not repent it:" if he appoint us to bear his cross, and draw in his yoke, and serve at his altar, this shall be afterwards neither shame nor grief to us, while the meanest office in God's service will entitle us to a *dwelling in the house of the Lord all the days of our life.*

CHAP. X.

We have in this chapter an account of the conquest of the kings and kingdoms of the southern part of the land of Canaan, as, in the next chapter, of the reduction of the northern parts, which together completed the glorious successes of the wars of Canaan. In this chapter we have an account, I. Of the routing of their forces in the field, in which observe, 1. Their confederacy against the Gibeonites, ver. 1—5. 2. The Gibeonites' request to Joshua to assist them, ver. 6. 3. Joshua's speedy march under divine encouragement for their relief, ver. 7—9. 4. The defeat of the armies of these confederate kings, ver. 10, 11. 5. The miraculous prolonging of the day by the standing still of the sun in favour of the conquerors, ver. 12—14. II. Of the execution of the kings that escaped out of the battle, ver. 15—27. III. Of the taking of the particular cities, and the total destruction of all that were found in them. Makkedah, ver. 28. Libnah, ver. 29, 30. Lachish, ver. 31, 32, and the king of Gezer that attempted its rescue, ver. 33. Eglon, ver. 34, 35. Hebron, ver. 36, 37. Debir, ver. 38, 39. And the bringing of all that country into the hands of Israel, ver. 40—42. And, lastly, the return of the army to their head-quarters, ver. 43.

NOW it came to pass, when Adoni-zedec king of Jerusalem had heard how Joshua had taken Ai, and had utterly destroyed it; as he had done to Jericho and her king, so he had done to Ai and her king; and how the inhabitants of Gibeon had made peace with Israel, and were among them; 2 That they feared greatly, because Gibeon *was* a great city, as one of the royal cities, and because it *was* greater than Ai, and all the men thereof *were* mighty. 3 Wherefore Adoni-zedec king of Jerusalem sent unto Hoham king of Hebron, and unto Piram king of Jarmuth, and unto Japhia king of Lachish, and unto Debir king of Eglon, saying, 4 Come up unto me, and help me, that we may smite Gibeon: for it hath made peace with Joshua and with the children of Israel. 5 Therefore the five kings of the Amorites, the king of Jerusalem, the king of Hebron, the king of Jarmuth, the king of Lachish, the king of Eglon, gathered themselves together, and went up, they and all their hosts, and encamped before Gibeon, and made war against it. 6 And the men of Gibeon sent unto Joshua to the camp to Gilgal, saying, Slack not thy hand from thy servants;

come up to us quickly, and save us, and help us: for all the kings of the Amorites that dwell in the mountains are gathered together against us.

Joshua and the hosts of Israel had now been a good while in the land of Canaan, and no great matters were effected; they were made masters of Jericho by a miracle, of Ai by stratagem, and of Gibeon by surrender, and that was all; hitherto the progress of their victories had not seemed proportionable to the magnificence of their entry and the glory of their beginnings. Those among them that were impatient of delays, it is probable, complained of Joshua's slowness, and asked why they did not immediately penetrate into the heart of the country, before the enemy could rally their forces to make head against them, why they stood trifling, while they were so confident both of their title and of their success. Thus Joshua's prudence, perhaps, was censured as slothfulness, cowardice, and want of spirit. But, 1. Canaan was not to be conquered in a day. God had said that *by little and little* he would drive out the Canaanites, Exod. xxiii. 30. He that believeth will not make haste, or conclude that the promise will never be performed because it is not performed so soon as he expected. 2. Joshua waited for the Canaanites to be the aggressors; let them first make an onset upon Israel, or the allies of Israel, and then their destruction will be, or at least will appear to be, the more just and the more justifiable. Joshua had warrant sufficient to set upon them, yet he stays till they strike the first stroke, that he might provide for honest things in the sight, not only of God, but of men; and they would be the more inexcusable in their resistance, now that they had seen what favour the Gibeonites found with Israel. 3. It was for the advantage of Israel to sit still awhile, that the forces of these little kings might unite in one body, and so might the more easily be cut off at one blow. This God had in his eye when he put it into their hearts to combine against Israel; though they designed thereby to strengthen one another, that which he intended was to gather them as sheaves into the floor, to fall together under the flail, Mic. iv. 12. Thus oftentimes that seeming paradox proves wholesome counsel, *Stay awhile, and we shall have done the sooner.*

After Israel had waited awhile for an occasion to make war upon the Canaanites, a fair one offers itself. 1. Five kings combine against the Gibeonites. Adoni-zedec king of Jerusalem was the first mover and ringleader of this confederacy. He had a good name (it signifies *lord of righteousness*), being a descendant perhaps from Melchizedek, *king of righteousness;* but, notwithstanding the goodness of his name and family, it seems he was a bad man, and an implacable enemy to the posterity of that Abraham to whom his predecessor, Melchizedek, was such a faithful friend. He called upon his neighbours to join against Israel either because he was the most honourable prince, and had the precedency among these kings (perhaps they had some dependence upon him, at least they paid a deference to him, as the most public, powerful, and active man they had among them), or because he was first or most apprehensive of the danger his country was in, not only by the conquest of Jericho and Ai, but the surrender of Gibeon, which, it seems, was the chief thing that alarmed him, it being one of the most considerable frontier towns they had. Against Gibeon therefore all the force he could raise must be levelled. *Come,* says he, *and help me, that we may smite Gibeon.* This he resolves to do, either, (1.) In policy, that he might retake the city, because it was a strong city, and of great consequence to his country in whose hands it was; or, (2.) In passion, that he might chastise the citizens for making peace with Joshua, pretending that they had perfidiously betrayed their country and strengthened the common enemy, whereas they had really done the greatest kindness imaginable to their country, by setting them a good example, if they would have followed it. Thus Satan and his instruments make war upon those that make peace with God. *Marvel not if the world hate you,* and treat those as deserters who are converts to Christ. 2. The Gibeonites send notice to Joshua of the distress and danger they are in, *v.* 6. Now they expect benefit from the league they had made with Israel, because, though it was obtained by deceit, it was afterwards confirmed when the truth came out. They think Joshua obliged to help them, (1.) In conscience, because they were his servants; not in compliment, as they had said in their first address (*ch.* ix. 8), *We are thy servants,* but in reality made servants to the congregation; and it is the duty of masters to take care of the poorest and meanest of their servants, and not to see them wronged when it is in the power of their hand to right them. Those that pay allegiance may reasonably expect protection. Thus David pleads with God (Ps. cxix. 94), *I am thine, save me;* and so may we, if indeed we be his. (2.) In honour, because the ground of their enemies' quarrel with them was the respect they had shown to Israel, and the confidence they had in a covenant with them. Joshua cannot refuse to help them when it is for their affection to him, and to the name of his God, that they are attacked. David thinks it a good plea with God (Ps. lxix. 7), *For thy sake I have borne reproach.* When our spiritual enemies set themselves in array against us, and threaten to swallow us up, let us, by faith and prayer, apply to Christ, our Joshua, for strength and succour, as Paul did, and we shall receive the same answer of peace, ***My grace is sufficient for thee,*** 2 Cor. xii. 8, 9.

7 So Joshua ascended from Gilgal, he, and all the people of war with him, and all the mighty men of valour. 8 And the LORD said unto Joshua, Fear them not: for I have delivered them into thine hand; there shall not a man of them stand before thee. 9 Joshua therefore came unto them suddenly, *and* went up from Gilgal all night. 10 And the LORD discomfited them before Israel, and slew them with a great slaughter at Gibeon, and chased them along the way that goeth up to Beth-horon, and smote them to Azekah, and unto Makkedah. 11 And it came to pass, as they fled from before Israel, *and* were in the going down to Beth-horon, that the LORD cast down great stones from heaven upon them unto Azekah, and they died: *they were* more which died with hailstones than *they* whom the children of Israel slew with the sword. 12 Then spake Joshua to the LORD in the day when the LORD delivered up the Amorites before the children of Israel, and he said in the sight of Israel, Sun, stand thou still upon Gibeon; and thou, Moon, in the valley of Ajalon. 13 And the sun stood still, and the moon stayed, until the people had avenged themselves upon their enemies. *Is* not this written in the book of Jasher? So the sun stood still in the midst of heaven, and hasted not to go down about a whole day. 14 And there was no day like that before it or after it, that the LORD hearkened unto the voice of a man: for the LORD fought for Israel.

Here, I. Joshua resolves to assist the Gibeonites, and God encourages him in this resolve. 1. He ascended from Gilgal (*v.* 7), that is, he designed, determined, and prepared for, this expedition to relieve Gibeon, for it is probable it was before he stirred a step that God spoke to him to encourage him. It was generous and just in Joshua to help his new allies, though perhaps the king of Jerusalem, when he attacked them, little thought that Joshua would be so ready to help them, but expected he would abandon them as Canaanites, the rather because they had obtained their league with him by fraud; therefore he speaks with assurance (*v.* 4) of smiting Gibeon. But Joshua knew that his promise to let them live obliged him, not only not to slay them himself, but not to stand by and see them slain when it was in the power of his hand to prevent it, Prov. xxiv. 11, 12. He knew that when they embraced the faith and worship of the God of Israel they came to trust under the shadow of his wings (Ruth ii. 12), and therefore, as his servants, he was bound to protect them. 2. God animated him for his undertaking, (*v.* 8): *Fear not*, that is, (1.) "Doubt not of the goodness of thy cause and the clearness of thy call; though it be to assist Gibeonites, thou art in the way of duty, and God is with thee of a truth." (2.) "Dread not the power of the enemy; though so many kings are confederate against thee, and are resolved to make their utmost efforts for the reduction of Gibeon, and it may be will fight desperately in a desperate cause, yet let not this discourage thee, *I have delivered them into thy hand;*" and those can make neither resistance nor escape whom God has marked for destruction.

II. Joshua applies himself to execute this resolve, and God assists him in the execution. Here we have,

1. The great industry of Joshua, and the power of God working with it for the defeat of the enemy. In this action, (1.) Joshua showed his good-will in the haste he made for the relief of Gibeon (*v.* 9): *He came unto them suddenly*, for the extremity was such as would not admit delay. If one of the tribes of Israel had been in danger, he could not have shown more care or zeal for its relief than here for Gibeon, remembering in this, as in other cases, there must be one law for the stranger that was proselyted and for him that was born in the land. Scarcely had the confederate princes got their forces together, and sat down before Gibeon, when Joshua was upon them, the surprise of which would put them into the greatest confusion. Now that the enemy were actually drawn up into a body, which had all as it were but one neck, despatch was as serviceable to his cause as before delay was, while he waited for this general rendezvous; and now that things were ripe for execution no man more expeditious than Joshua, who before had seemed slow. Now it shall never be said, *He left that to be done to-morrow which he could do to-day.* When Joshua found he could not reach Gibeon in a day, lest he should lose any real advantages against the enemy, or so much as seem to come short or to neglect his new allies, he marched all night, resolving not to give sleep to his eyes, nor slumber to his eye-lids, till he had accomplished this enterprise. It was well the forces he took with him were mighty men of valour, not only able-bodied men, but men of spirit and resolution, and hearty in the cause, else they neither could nor would have borne this fatigue, but would have murmured at their

leader, and would have asked, "Is this the rest we were promised in Canaan?" But they well considered that the present toil was in order to a happy settlement, and therefore were reconciled to it. Let the *good soldiers of Jesus Christ* learn hence to *endure hardness, in following the Lamb whithersoever he goes,* and not think themselves undone if their religion lose them now and then a night's sleep; it will be enough to rest when we come to heaven. But why needed Joshua to put himself and his men so much to the stretch? Had not God promised him that without fail he would *deliver the enemies into his hand?* It is true he had; but God's promises are intended, not to slacken and supersede, but to quicken and encourage our endeavours. He that believeth doth not make haste to anticipate providence, but doth make haste to attend it, with a diligent, not a distrustful, speed. (2.) God showed his great power in defeating the enemies whom Joshua so vigorously attacked, *v.* 10, 11. Joshua had a very numerous and powerful army with him, hands enough to despatch a dispirited enemy, so that the enemy might have been scattered by the ordinary fate of war; but God himself would appear in this great and decisive battle, and draw up the artillery of heaven against the Canaanites, to demonstrate to his people that they *got not this land in possession by their own sword, neither did their own arm save them, but God's right hand and his arm,* Ps. xliv. 3. *The Lord discomfited them before Israel.* Israel did what they could, and yet God did all. [1.] It must needs be a very great terror and confusion to the enemy to perceive that heaven itself fought against them; for who can contest with, flee from, or fence against, the powers of heaven? They had affronted the true God and robbed him of his honour by worshipping the host of heaven, giving that worship to the creature which is due to the Creator only; and now the host of heaven fights against them, and even that part of the creation which they had idolized is at war with them, aud even triumphs in their ruin, Jer. viii. 2. There is no way of making any creature propitious to us, no, not by sacrifice nor offering, but only by making our peace with God and keeping ourselves in his love. This had been enough to make them an easy prey to the victorious Israelites, yet this was not all. [2.] Besides the terror struck upon them, there was a great slaughter made of them by hail-stones, which were so large, and came down with such a force, that more were killed by the hail-stones than by the sword of the Israelites, though no doubt they were busy. God himself speaks to Job of treasures, or magazines, of snow and hail, which he has *reserved for the day of battle and war* (Job xxxviii. 22, 23), and here they are made use of to destroy the Canaanites. Here was hail, shot from God's great ordnance, that, against whomsoever it was directed, was sure to hit (and never glanced upon the Israelites mixed with them), and wherever it hit was sure to kill. See here how miserable those are that have God for their enemy, and how sure to perish; it is a fearful thing to fall into his hands, for there is no fleeing out of them. Some observe that Beth-horon lay north of Gibeon, Azekah and Makkedah lay south, so that they fled each way; but, which way soever they fled, the hail-stones pursued them, and met them at every turn.

2. The great faith of Joshua, and the power of God crowning it with the miraculous arrest of the sun, that the day of Israel's victories might be prolonged, and so the enemy totally defeated. The hail-stones had their rise no higher than the clouds, but, to show that Israel's help came from above the clouds, the sun itself, who by his constant motion serves the whole earth, by halting when there was occasion served the Israelites, and did them a kindness. *The sun and moon stood still in their habitation, at the light of thy arrows* which gave the signal, Hab. iii. 11.

(1.) Here is the prayer of Joshua that the sun might stand still. I call it his prayer, because it is said (*v.* 12) *he spoke to the Lord;* as Elijah, though we read (1 Kings xvii. 1) only of his prophesying of the drought, yet is said (James v. 17) to pray for it. Observe, [1.] An instance of Joshua's unwearied activity in the service of God and Israel, that though he had marched all night and fought all day, and, one might expect, would be inclined to repose himself and get a little sleep, and give his army some time to rest—that, like the hireling, he would earnestly desire the shadow, and bid the night welcome, when he had done such a good day's work—yet, instead of this, he wishes for nothing so much as the prolonging of the day. Note, Those that *wait on the Lord* and work for him *shall renew their strength, shall run and not be weary, shall walk and not faint,* Isa. xl. 31. [2.] An instance of his great faith in the almighty power of God, as above the power of nature, and able to control and alter the usual course of it. No doubt Joshua had an extraordinary impulse or impression upon his spirit, which he knew to be of divine origin, prompting him to desire that this miracle might be wrought upon this occasion, else it would have been presumption in him to desire or expect it; the prayer would not have been granted by the divine power, if it had not been dictated by the divine grace. God wrought this faith in him, and then said, "*According to thy faith,* and thy prayer of faith, *be it unto thee.*" It cannot be imagined, however, that such a thing as this should have entered into his mind if God had not put it there; a man would have had a thousand projects in his head for the completing of the victory before he would have thought of desiring the sun to stand still; but even in the Old-Testament saints *the Spirit made intercession according to the will of God.* What God will give he inclines the hearts of his praying people to ask, and for what he will do he will be enquired of, Ezek. xxxvi. 37. Now, *First,* It looked great for Joshua to say, *Sun, stand thou still.* His ancestor Joseph had indeed dreamed that the sun and moon did homage to him; but who would have thought that, after it had been fulfilled in the figure, it should be again fulfilled in the letter to one of his posterity? The prayer is thus expressed with authority, because it was not an ordinary prayer, such as is directed and supported only by God's common providence or promise, but the prayer of a prophet at this time divinely inspired for this purpose; and yet it intimates to us the prevalency of prayer in general, so far as it is regulated by the word of God, and may remind us of that honour put upon prayer (Isa. xlv. 11), *Concerning the work of my hands command you me.* He bids the sun stand still upon Gibeon, the place of action and the seat of war, intimating that what he designed in this request was the advantage of Israel against their enemies; it is probable that the sun was now declining, and that he did not call for the lengthening out of the day until he observed it hastening towards its period. He does likewise, in the name of the King of kings, arrest the moon, perhaps because it was requisite for the preserving of the harmony and good order of the spheres that the course of the rest of the heavenly bodies should be stayed likewise, otherwise, while the sun shone, he needed not the moon; and here he mentions the valley of Ajalon, which was near to Gibeon, because there he was at that time. *Secondly,* It was bold indeed to say so before Israel, and argues a very strong assurance of faith. If the event had not answered the demand, nothing could have been a greater slur upon him; the Israelites would have concluded he was certainly going mad, or he would never have talked so extravagantly. But he knew very well God would own and answer a petition which he himself directed to be drawn up and presented, and therefore was not afraid to say before all Israel, calling them to observe this work of wonder, *Sun, stand thou still,* for he was confident in him whom he had trusted. He believed the almighty power of God, else he could not have expected that the sun, going on in its strength, driving in a full career, and *rejoicing as a strong man to run a race,* should be stopped in an instant. He believed the sovereignty of God in the kingdom of nature, else he could not have expected that the established law and course of nature should be changed and interrupted, the ordinances of heaven, and the constant usage according to these ordinances, broken in upon. And he believed God's particular favour to Israel above all people under the sun, else he could not have expected that, to favour them upon an emergency with a double day, he should (which must follow of course) amaze and terrify so great a part of the terrestrial globe with a double night at the same time. It is true, he *causeth the sun to shine upon the just and the unjust;* but for this once the unjust shall wait for it beyond the usual time, while, in favour to righteous Israel, it stands still.

(2.) The wonderful answer to this prayer. No sooner said than done (*v.* 13): *The sun stood still, and the moon staid.* Notwithstanding the vast distance between the earth and the sun, at the word of Joshua the sun stopped immediately; for the same God that rules in heaven above rules at the same time on this earth, and, when he pleases, even *the heavens shall hear the earth,* as here. Concerning this great miracle it is here said, [1.] *That it continued a whole day,* that is, the sun continued as long again above the horizon as otherwise it would have done. It is commonly supposed to have been about the middle of summer that this happened, when, in that country, it was about fourteen hours between sun and sun, so that this day was about twenty-eight hours long; yet, if we suppose it to have been at that time of the year when the days are at the shortest, it will be the more probable that Joshua should desire and pray for the prolonging of the day. [2.] That hereby the people had full time to avenge themselves of their enemies, and to give them a total defeat. We often read in history of battles which the night put an end to, the shadows of which favoured the retreat of the conquered; to prevent this advantage to the enemy in their flight, the day was doubled, that the hand of Israel might *find out all their enemies;* but the eye and hand of God can find them out without the help of the sun's light, for to him *the night shineth as the day,* Ps. cxxxix. 12. Note, Sometimes God completes a great salvation in a little time, and makes but one day's work of it. Perhaps this miracle is alluded to Zech. xiv. 6, 7, where the day of God's fighting against the nations is said to be *one day,* and that *at evening time it shall be light,* as here. And, [3.] That there was *never any day like it,* before or since, in which God put such an honour upon faith and prayer, and upon Israel's cause; never did he so wonderfully comply with the request of a man, nor so wonderfully fight for his people. [4.] This is said to be written *in the book of Jasher,* a collection of state-poems, in which the poem made upon this occasion was preserved among the rest; probably the same with that *book of the wars of the Lord* (Num. xxi. 14), which afterwards was continued and carried on by one Jasher. Those words, *Sun, stand thou still upon Gibeon, and thou moon in the valley of Ajalon,* sounding metrical, are supposed to be taken from the narrative of this event as it was found in the book of Jasher. Not that the divine testimony of the book of Joshua needed confirmation from the book of Jasher, a human composition; but to those who had that book in their hands it would be of use to compare this history with it, which warrants the appeals the learned make to profane history for corroborating the proofs of the truth of sacred history. [5.] But surely this stupendous miracle of the standing still of the sun was intended for something more than merely to give Israel so much the more time to find out and kill their enemies, which, without this, might have been done the next day. *First,* God would hereby magnify Joshua (*ch.* iii .7), as a particular favourite, and one whom he did delight to honour, being a type of him who has all power both in heaven and in earth and whom the winds and the seas obey. *Secondly,* He would hereby notify to all the world what he was doing for his people Israel here in Canaan; the sun, the eye of the world, must be fixed for some hours upon Gibeon and the valley of Ajalon, as if to contemplate the great works of God there for Israel, and so to engage the children of men to look that way, and to *enquire of this wonder done in the land,* 2 Chron. xxxii. 31. Proclamation was hereby made to all the neighbouring nations. *Come, behold the works of the Lord* (Ps. xlvi. 8), and say, *What nation is there so great as Israel is, who has God so nigh unto them?* One would have supposed that this would bring such real ambassadors as the Gibeonites pretended to be from a very far country, to court the friendship of Israel because of the name of the Lord their God. *Thirdly,* He would hereby convince and confound those idolaters that worshipped the sun and moon and gave divine honours to them, by demonstrating that they were subject to the command of the God of Israel, and that, as high as they were, he was above them; and thus he would fortify his people against temptations to this idolatry, which he foresaw they would be addicted to (Deut. iv. 19), and which, notwithstanding this, they afterwards corrupted themselves with. *Fourthly,* This miracle signified (it is the learned bishop Pierson's notion) that in the latter days, when the light of the world was tending towards a night of darkness, the *Sun of righteousness,* even our Joshua, should arise (Mal. iv. 2), give check to the approaching night, and be the true light. To which let me add that when Christ conquered our spiritual enemies upon the cross the miracle wrought on the sun was the reverse of this; it was then darkened as if it had gone down at noon, for Christ needed not the light of the sun to carry on his victories: he then made darkness his pavilion. And, *Lastly,* The arresting of the sun and moon in this day of battle prefigured the turning of the sun into darkness, and the moon into blood, in the last great and terrible day of the Lord.

15 And Joshua returned, and all Israel with him, unto the camp to Gilgal. 16 But these five kings fled, and hid themselves in a cave at Makkedah. 17 And it was told Joshua, saying, The five kings are found hid in a cave at Makkedah. 18 And Joshua said, Roll great stones upon the mouth of the cave, and set men by it for to keep them: 19 And stay ye not, *but* pursue after your enemies, and smite the hindmost of them; suffer them not to enter into their cities: for the LORD your God hath delivered them into your hand. 20 And it came to pass, when Joshua and the children of Israel had made an end of slaying them with a very great slaughter, till they were consumed, that the rest *which* remained of them entered into fenced cities. 21 And all the people returned to the camp to Joshua at Makkedah in peace: none moved his tongue against any of the children of Israel. 22 Then said Joshua, Open the mouth of the cave, and bring out those five kings unto me out of the cave. 23 And they did so, and brought forth those five kings unto him out of the cave, the king of Jerusalem, the king of Hebron, the king of Jarmuth, the king of Lachish, *and* the king of Eglon. 24 And it came to pass, when they brought out those kings unto Joshua, that Joshua called for all the men of Israel, and said unto the captains of the men of war which went with him, Come near, put your feet upon the necks of these kings. And they came near, and put their feet upon the necks of them. 25 And Joshua said unto them, Fear not, nor be dismayed, be strong and of good courage: for thus shall the LORD do to all your enemies against whom ye fight. 26 And afterward Joshua smote them, and slew them, and hanged them on five trees: and they were hanging upon the trees until the evening. 27 And it came to pass at the time of the going down of the sun, *that* Joshua commanded, and they took them down off the trees, and cast them into the cave wherein they had been hid, and laid great

stones in the cave's mouth, *which remain* until this very day.

It was a brave appearance, no doubt, which the five kings made when they took the field for the reducing of Gibeon, and a brave army they had following them; but they were all routed, put into disorder first, and then brought to destruction by the hail-stones. And now Joshua thought, his work being done, he might go with his army into quarters of refreshment. Accordingly it was resolved, perhaps in a council of war, that they should presently return *to the camp at Gilgal* (*v.* 15), till they should receive orders from God to take possession of the country they had now conquered; but he soon finds he has more work cut out for him. The victory must be pursued, that the spoils might be divided. Accordingly he applies himself to it with renewed vigour.

I. The forces that had dispersed themselves must be followed and smitten. When tidings were brought to Joshua where the kings were he ordered a guard to be set upon them for the present (*v.* 18), *reserving them* for another *day of destruction*, and to be *brought forth to a day of wrath,* Job xxi. 30. He directs his men to pursue the common soldiers, as much as might be, to prevent their escaping to the garrisons, which would strengthen them, and make the reduction of them the more difficult, *v.* 19. Like a prudent general, he does that first which is most needful, and defers his triumphs till he has completed his conquests; nor was he in such haste to insult over the captive kings but that he would first prevent the rallying again of their scattered forces. The result of this vigorous pursuit was, 1. That a very great slaughter was made of the enemies of God and Israel. And, 2. The field was cleared of them, so that none remained but such as got into fenced cities, where they would not long be safe themselves, nor were they capable of doing any service to the cities that sheltered them, unless they could have left their fears behind them. 3. *None moved his tongue against any of the children of Israel, v.* 21. This expression intimates, (1.) Their perfect safety and tranquillity; some think it should be read (from Exod. xi. 7), *Against any of the children of Israel did not a dog move his tongue;* no, not against any one man of them. They were not threatened by any danger at all after their victory, no, not so much as the barking of a dog. Not one single Israelite (for the original makes it so particular) was brought into any distress, either in the battle or in the pursuit. (2.) Their honour and reputation; no man had any reproach to cast upon them, nor an ill word to give them. God not only tied the hands, but stopped the mouths, of their enraged enemies, and put lying lips to silence. (3.) The Chaldee paraphrase makes it an expression of their unalloyed joy for this victory, reading it, *There was no hurt nor loss to the children of Israel, for which any man should afflict his soul.* When the army came to be reviewed after the battle, there was none slain, none wounded, none missing. Not one Israelite had occasion to lament either the loss of a friend or the loss of a limb, so cheap, so easy, so glorious, was this victory.

II. The kings that had hidden themselves must now be called to an account, as rebels against the Israel of God, to whom, by the divine promise and grant, this land did of right belong and should have been surrendered upon demand. See here,

1. How they were secured. The cave which they fled to, and trusted in for a refuge, became their prison, in which they were clapped up, till Joshua sat in judgment on them, *v.* 18. It seems they all escaped both the hail-stones and the sword, God so ordering it, not in kindness to them, but that they might be reserved for a more solemn and terrible execution; as, for this cause, Pharaoh survived the plagues of Egypt, and was made to stand, that God might in him *show his power*, Exod. ix. 16. They all fled, and met at the same place, Providence directing them; and now those who were lately consulting against Israel were put upon new counsels to preserve themselves, and agreed to take shelter in the same cave. The information brought to Joshua of this is an evidence that there were those of the country, who knew the holes and fastnesses of it, that were in his interests. And the care Joshua took to keep them there when they were there, as it is an instance of his policy and presence of mind, even in the heat of action, so, in the result of their project, it shows how those not only deceive themselves, but destroy themselves, who think to hide themselves from God. Their refuge of lies will but bind them over to God's judgment.

2. How they were triumphed over. Joshua ordered them to be brought forth out of the cave, set before him as at the bar, and their names called over, *v.* 22, 23. And when they either were bound and cast upon the ground unable to help themselves, or threw themselves upon the ground, humbly to beg for their lives, he called for the general officers and great men, and commanded them to trample upon these kings, and set their feet upon their necks, not in sport and to make themselves and the company merry, but with the gravity and decorum that became the ministers of the divine justice, who were not herein to gratify any pride or passion of their own, but to give glory to the God of Israel as higher than the highest, who *treads upon princes as mortar* (Isa. xli. 25), and *is terrible to the kings of the earth,* Ps. lxxvi. 12. The thing does indeed look barbarous, thus to insult over men in misery, who had suddenly fallen from the highest pitch of honour into this disgrace. It was hard for crowned heads to be thus trodden upon, not by Joshua

himself (that might better have been borne), at least not by him only, but by all the captains of the army. Certainly it ought not to be drawn into a precedent, for the case was extraordinary, and we have reason to think it was by divine direction and impulse that Joshua did this. (1.) God would hereby punish the abominable wickedness of these kings, the measure of whose iniquity was now full. And, by this public act of justice done upon these ringleaders of the Canaanites in sin, he would possess his people with the greater dread and detestation of those sins of *the nations that God cast out from before them,* which they would be tempted to imitate. (2.) He would hereby have the promise by Moses made good (Deut. xxxiii. 29), *Thou shalt tread upon their high places,* that is, their great men, which should the rather be speedily fulfilled in the letter because they are the very last words of Moses that we find upon record. (3.) He would hereby encourage the faith and hope of his people Israel in reference to the wars that were yet before them. Therefore Joshua said (*v.* 25): *Fear not, nor be dismayed.* [1.] "Fear not these kings, nor any of theirs, as if there were any danger of having this affront now put upon them in after-time revenged upon yourselves, a consideration which keeps many from being insolent towards those they have at their mercy, because they know not how soon the uncertain fate of war may turn the same wheel upon themselves; but you need not fear that any should rise up ever to revenge this quarrel." [2.] "Fear not any other kings, who may at any time be in confederacy against you, for you see these brought down, whom you thought formidable. *Thus shall the Lord do to all your enemies;* now that they begin to fall, to fall so low that you may set your feet on their necks, you may be confident that they shall not prevail, but shall *surely fall before you,*" Esth. vi. 13. (4.) He would hereby give a type and figure of Christ's victories over the powers of darkness, and believers' victories through him. All the enemies of the Redeemer shall be *made his footstool,* Ps. cx. 1. And see Ps. xviii. 40. The *kings of the earth set themselves* against him (Ps. ii. 2), but sooner or later we shall see all things put under him (Heb. ii. 8), and *principalities and powers* made a show of, Col. ii. 15. And in these triumphs we are more than conquerors, may *tread upon the lion and adder* (Ps. xci. 13), may *ride on the high places of the earth* (Isa. lviii. 14), and may be confident that *the God of peace shall tread Satan under our feet,* shall do it shortly and do it effectually, Rom. xvi. 20. See Ps. cxlix. 8, 9.

3. How they were put to death. Perhaps, when they had undergone that terrible mortification of being trodden upon by the captains of Israel, they were ready to say, as Agag, *Surely the bitterness of death is past,* and that *sufficient unto them was this punishment which was inflicted by many;* but their honours cannot excuse their lives, their forfeited devoted lives. Joshua smote them with the sword, and then hanged up their bodies till evening, when they were taken down, and thrown *into the cave in which they had hidden themselves, v.* 26, 27. That which they thought would have been their shelter was made their prison first and then their grave; so shall we be disappointed in that which we flee to from God: yet to good people the grave is still *a hiding-place,* Job xiv. 13. If these five kings had humbled themselves in time, and had begged peace instead of waging war, they might have saved their lives; but now the decree had gone forth, and they *found no place for repentance,* or the reversal of the judgment; it was too late to expect it, though perhaps *they sought it carefully with tears.*

28 And that day Joshua took Makkedah, and smote it with the edge of the sword, and the king thereof he utterly destroyed, them, and all the souls that *were* therein; he let none remain: and he did to the king of Makkedah as he did unto the king of Jericho. 29 Then Joshua passed from Makkedah, and all Israel with him, unto Libnah, and fought against Libnah: 30 And the LORD delivered it also, and the king thereof, into the hand of Israel; and he smote it with the edge of the sword, and all the souls that *were* therein; he let none remain in it; but did unto the king thereof as he did unto the king of Jericho. 31 And Joshua passed from Libnah, and all Israel with him, unto Lachish, and encamped against it, and fought against it: 32 And the LORD delivered Lachish into the hand of Israel, which took it on the second day, and smote it with the edge of the sword, and all the souls that *were* therein, according to all that he had done to Libnah 33 Then Horam king of Gezer came up to help Lachish; and Joshua smote him and his people, until he had left him none remaining. 34 And from Lachish Joshua passed unto Eglon, and all Israel with him; and they encamped against it, and fought against it: 35 And they took it on that day, and smote it with the edge of the sword, and all the souls that *were* therein he utterly destroyed that day, accord-

ing to all that he had done to Lachish. 36 And Joshua went up from Eglon, and all Israel with him, unto Hebron; and they fought against it: 37 And they took it, and smote it with the edge of the sword, and the king thereof, and all the cities thereof, and all the souls that *were* therein; he left none remaining, according to all that he had done to Eglon; but destroyed it utterly, and all the souls that *were* therein. 38 And Joshua returned, and all Israel with him, to Debir; and fought against it: 39 And he took it, and the king thereof, and all the cities thereof; and they smote them with the edge of the sword, and utterly destroyed all the souls that *were* therein; he left none remaining: as he had done to Hebron, so he did to Debir, and to the king thereof; as he had done also to Libnah, and to her king. 40 So Joshua smote all the country of the hills, and of the south, and of the vale, and of the springs, and all their kings: he left none remaining, but utterly destroyed all that breathed, as the LORD God of Israel commanded. 41 And Joshua smote them from Kadesh-barnea even unto Gaza, and all the country of Goshen, even unto Gibeon. 42 And all these kings and their land did Joshua take at one time, because the LORD God of Israel fought for Israel. 43 And Joshua returned, and all Israel with him, unto the camp to Gilgal.

We are here informed how Joshua improved the late glorious victory he had obtained and the advantages he had gained by it, and to do this well is a general's praise.

I. Here is a particular account of the several cities which he immediately made himself master of. 1. The cities of three of the kings whom he had conquered in the field he went and took possession of, Lachish (*v.* 31, 32), Eglon (*v.* 34, 35), and Hebron, *v.* 36, 37. The other two, Jerusalem and Jarmuth, were not taken at this time; perhaps his forces were either so much fatigued with what they had done or so well content with what they had got that they had no mind to attack those places, and so they let slip the fairest opportunity they could ever expect of reducing them with ease, which afterwards was not done without difficulty, Judg. i. 8; 2 Sam. v. 6. 2. Three other cities, and royal cities too, he took: Makkedah, into the neighbourhood of which the five kings had fled, which brought Joshua and his forces thither in pursuit of them, and so hastened its ruin (*v.* 28), Libnah (*v.* 29, 30), and Debir, *v.* 38, 39. 3. One king that brought in his forces for the relief of Lachish, that had lost its king, proved to meddle to his own hurt; it was Horam king of Gezer, who, either in friendship to his neighbours or for his own security, offered to stop the progress of Joshua's arms, and was cut off with all his forces, *v.* 33. Thus wicked men are often snared in their counsels, and, by opposing God in the way of his judgments, bring them the sooner on their own heads.

II. A general account of the country which was hereby reduced and brought into Israel's hands (*v.* 40—42), that part of the land of Canaan of which they first got possession, which lay south of Jerusalem, and afterwards fell, for the most part, to the lot of the tribe of Judah. Observe in this narrative,

1. The great speed Joshua made in taking these cities, which, some think, is intimated in the manner of relating it, which is quick and concise. He flew like lightning from place to place; and though they all stood it out to the last extremity, and none of these cities opened their gates to him, yet in a little time he got them all into his hands, summoned them, and seized them, the same day (*v.* 28), or in two days, *v.* 32. Now that they were struck with fear, by the defeat of their armies and the death of their kings, Joshua prudently followed his blow. See what a great deal of work may be done in a little time, if we will but be busy and improve our opportunities.

2. The great severity Joshua used towards those he conquered. He gave no quarter to man, woman, nor child, put to the sword *all the souls* (*v.* 28, 30, 32, 35, &c.), *utterly destroyed all that breathed* (*v.* 40), and *left none remaining.* Nothing could justify this military execution but that herein they did *as the Lord God of Israel commanded* (*v.* 40), which was sufficient not only to bear them out, and save them from the imputation of cruelty, but to sanctify what they did, and make it an acceptable piece of service to his justice. God would hereby, (1.) Manifest his hatred of the idolatries and other abominations which the Canaanites had been guilty of, and leave us to judge how great the provocation was which they had given him by the greatness of the destruction which was brought upon them when the measure of their iniquity was full. (2.) He would hereby magnify his love to his people Israel, in giving so many men for them, and *people for their life,* Isa. xliii. 4. When the *heathen are to be cast out to make room for this vine* (Ps. lxxx. 8) divine justice appears more prodigal than ever of human blood, that the Israelites might find themselves for ever obliged to spend their lives to the glory of that God who had sacrificed so

many of the lives of his creatures to their interest. (3.) Hereby was typified the final and eternal destruction of all the impenitent implacable enemies of the Lord Jesus, who, having slighted the riches of his grace, must for ever feel the weight of his wrath, and shall *have judgment without mercy. Nations that forget God shall be turned into hell,* and no reproach at all to God's infinite goodness.

3. The great success of this expedition. The spoil of these cities was now divided among the men of war that plundered them; and the cities themselves, with the land about them, were shortly to be divided among the tribes, for the Lord *fought for Israel, v.* 42. They could not have gotten the victory if God had not undertaken the battle; then we conquer when God fights for us; and, *if he be for us, who can be against us?*

CHAP. XI.

This chapter continues and concludes the history of the conquest of Canaan; of the reduction of the southern parts we had an account in the foregoing chapter, after which we may suppose Joshua allowed his forces some breathing-time; now here we have the story of the war in the north, and the happy success of that war. I. The confederacy of the northern crowns against Israel, ver. 1—5. II. The encouragement which God gave to Joshua to engage them, ver. 6. III. His victory over them, ver. 7—9. IV. The taking of their cities, ver. 10—15. V. The destruction of the Anakim, ver. 21, 22. VI. The general conclusion of the story of this war, ver. 16—20, 23.

AND it came to pass, when Jabin king of Hazor had heard *those things,* that he sent to Jobab king of Madon, and to the king of Shimron, and to the king of Achshaph, 2 And to the kings that *were* on the north of the mountains, and of the plains south of Chinneroth, and in the valley, and in the borders of Dor on the west, 3 *And to* the Canaanite on the east and on the west, and *to* the Amorite, and the Hittite, and the Perizzite, and the Jebusite in the mountains, and *to* the Hivite under Hermon in the land of Mizpeh. 4 And they went out, they and all their hosts with them, much people, even as the sand that *is* upon the sea shore in multitude, with horses and chariots very many. 5 And when all these kings were met together, they came and pitched together at the waters of Merom, to fight against Israel. 6 And the LORD said unto Joshua, Be not afraid because of them: for to morrow about this time will I deliver them up all slain before Israel: thou shalt hough their horses, and burn their chariots with fire. 7 So Joshua came, and all the people of war with him, against them by the waters of Merom suddenly; and they fell upon them. 8 And the LORD delivered them into the hand of Israel, who smote them, and chased them unto great Zidon, and unto Misrephoth-maim, and unto the valley of Mizpeh eastward; and they smote them, until they left them none remaining. 9 And Joshua did unto them as the LORD bade him: he houghed their horses, and burnt their chariots with fire.

We are here entering upon the story of another campaign that Joshua made, and it was a glorious one, no less illustrious than the former in the success of it, though in respect of miracles it was inferior to it in glory. The wonders God then wrought for them were to animate and encourage them to act vigorously themselves. Thus the war carried on by the preaching of the gospel against Satan's kingdom was at first forwarded by miracles; but, the war being by them sufficiently proved to be of God, the managers of it are now left to the ordinary assistance of divine grace in the use of the sword of the Spirit, and must not expect hail-stones nor the standing still of the sun. In this story we have,

I. The Canaanites taking the field against Israel. They were the aggressors, God hardening their hearts to begin the war, that Israel might be justified beyond exception in destroying them. Joshua and all Israel had returned to the camp at Gilgal, and perhaps these kings knew no other than that they intended to sit down content with the conquest they had already made, and yet they prepare war against them. Note, Sinners bring ruin upon their own heads, so that *God will be justified when he speaks,* and they alone shall bear the blame for ever. Judah had now *couched as a lion gone up from the prey;* if the northern kings rouse him up, it is at their peril, Gen. xlix. 9. Now, 1. Several nations joined in this confederacy, some *in the mountains* and some *in the plains, v.* 2. Canaanites from east and west, Amorites, Hittites, Perizzites, &c. (*v.* 3), of different constitutions and divided interests among themselves, and yet they here unite against Israel as against a common enemy. Thus are *the children of this world* more unanimous, and therein *wiser, than the children of light.* The oneness of the church's enemies should shame the church's friends out of their discords and divisions, and engage them to be one. 2. The head of this confederacy was *Jabin king of Hazor* (*v.* 1), as Adoni-zedec was of the former; it is said (*v.* 10) Hazor had been the *head of all those kingdoms,* which could not have revolted without occasioning ill-will; but this was forgotten and laid aside upon this occasion, by consent of parties, Luke xxiii. 12. When they had all drawn up their forces together, every kingdom bringing in its quota, they were a very great army, much greater than the former, *as the sand on the sea-shore in multitude*, and upon this account much stronger and more formidable, that they had horses and chariots very many, which we do not find the southern kings had; hereby they had a great advantage against Israel, for their army consisted only of foot, and they never brought horses nor chariots into the field. Josephus tells us that the army of the Canaanites consisted of 300,000 foot, 10,000 horse, and 20,000 chariots. *Many there be that rise up* against God's Israel; doubtless their numbers made them very confident of success, but it proved that so much the greater slaughter was made of them.

II. The encouragement God gave to Joshua to give them the meeting, even upon the ground of their own choosing (*v.* 6): *Be not afraid because of them.* Joshua was remarkable for his courage—it was his master grace, and yet it seems he had need to be again and again cautioned not to be afraid. Fresh dangers and difficulties make it necessary to fetch in fresh supports and comforts from the word of God, which we have always nigh unto us, to be made use of in every time of need. Those that have God on their side need not be disturbed at the number and power of their enemies; *more are those that are with us than those that are against us;* those have the hosts of the Lord that have the Lord of hosts engaged for them. For his encouragement, 1. God assures him of success, and fixes the hour: *To-morrow about this time,* when an engagement (it is probable) was expected and designed on both sides, *I will deliver them up slain.* Though they were to be slain by the sword of Israel, yet it is spoken of as God's work, that he would deliver them up. 2. He appoints him to *hough their horses, hamstring* them, *lame* them, and *burn their chariots,* not only that Israel might not use them hereafter, but that they might not fear them now, their God designing this contempt to be put upon them. Let Israel look upon their chariots but as rotten wood designed for the fire, and their horses of war as disabled things, scarcely good enough for the cart. This encouragement which God here gave to Joshua no doubt he communicated to the people, who perhaps were under some apprehensions of danger from this vast army, notwithstanding the experience they had had of God's power engaged for them. And the wisdom and goodness of God are to be observed, (1.) In infatuating the counsels of the enemy, that all the kings of Canaan, who were not dispersed at such a distance from each other but that they might have got all together in a body, did not at first confederate against Israel, but were divided into the southern and northern combination, and so became the less formidable. And, (2.) In preparing his people to encounter the greater force, by breaking the less. They first engage with five kings together, and now with many more. God proportions our trials to our strength and our strength to our trials.

III. Joshua's march against these confederate forces, *v.* 7. He *came upon them suddenly,* and surprised them in their quarters. He made this haste, 1. That he might put them into the greater confusion, by giving them an alarm, when they little thought he was near them. 2. That he might be sure not to come short of the honour God had fixed, to give him the meeting at the enemies' camp, *to-morrow about this time.* It is fit we should keep time with God.

IV. His success, *v.* 8. He obtained the honour and advantage of a complete victory; he smote them and chased them, in the several ways they took in their flight; some fled towards Zidon, which lay to the north-west, others towards Mizpeh, eastward, but the parties Joshua sent out pursued them each way. So *the Lord delivered them into the hand of Israel;* they would not deliver themselves into the hands of Israel to be made proselytes and tributaries, and so offered up to God's grace (Rom. xv. 16), and therefore God delivered them into their hands to be made sacrifices to his justice; for God will be honoured by us or upon us.

V. His obedience to the orders given him, in destroying the horses and chariots (*v.* 9), which was an instance, 1. Of his subjection to the divine will, as one under authority, that must do as he is bidden. 2. Of his self-denial, and crossing his own genius and inclination in compliance with God's command. 3. Of his confidence in the power of God engaged for Israel, which enabled them to despise the chariots and horses which others trusted in, Ps. xx. 7; xxxiii. 17. 4. Of his care to keep up in the people the like confidence in God, by taking that from them which they would be tempted to trust too much to. This was *cutting off a right hand.*

10 And Joshua at that time turned back, and took Hazor, and smote the king thereof with the sword: for Hazor beforetime was the head of all those kingdoms. 11 And they smote all the souls that *were* therein with the edge of the sword, utterly destroying *them:* there was not any left to breathe: and he burnt Hazor with fire. 12 And all the cities of those kings, and all the kings of them, did Joshua take, and smote them with the edge of the sword, *and* he utterly destroyed them, as Moses the servant of the LORD commanded. 13 But *as for* the cities that stood still in their strength, Israel burned none of them, save Hazor only; *that*

did Joshua burn. 14 And all the spoil of these cities, and the cattle, the children of Israel took for a prey unto themselves; but every man they smote with the edge of the sword, until they had destroyed them, neither left they any to breathe.

We have here the same improvement made of this victory as was made of that in the foregoing chapter. 1. The destruction of Hazor is particularly recorded, because in it, and by the king thereof, this daring design against Israel was laid, *v.* 10, 11. The king of Hazor, it seems, escaped with his life out of the battle, and thought himself safe when he had got back into his own city, and Joshua had gone in pursuit of the scattered troops another way. But it proved that that which he thought would be for his welfare was his trap; in it *he was taken as in an evil net;* there he was slain, and his city, for his sake, burned. Yet we find that the remains of it being not well looked after by Israel the Canaanites rebuilt it, and settled there under another king of the same name, Judg. iv. 2. 2. The rest of the cities of that part of the country are spoken of only in general, that Joshua got them all into his hands, but did not burn them as he did Hazor, for Israel was to dwell in *great and goodly cities which they builded not* (Deut. vi. 10) and in these among the rest. And here we find Israel rolling in blood and treasure. (1.) In the blood of their enemies; *they smote all the souls* (*v.* 11), *neither left they any to breathe* (*v.* 14), that there might be none to infect them with the abominations of Canaan, and none to disturb them in the possession of it. The children were cut off, lest they should afterwards lay claim to any part of this land in the right of their parents. (2.) In the wealth of their enemies. The spoil, and the cattle, they *took for a prey to themselves*, *v.* 14. As they were enriched with the spoil of their oppressors when they came out of Egypt, wherewith to defray the charges of their apprenticeship in the wilderness, so they were now enriched with the spoil of their enemies for a stock wherewith to set up in the land of Canaan. Thus is the wealth of the sinner laid up for the just.

15 As the LORD commanded Moses his servant, so did Moses command Joshua, and so did Joshua; he left nothing undone of all that the LORD commanded Moses. 16 So Joshua took all that land, the hills, and all the south country, and all the land of Goshen, and the valley, and the plain, and the mountain of Israel, and the valley of the same; 17 *Even* from the mount Halak, that goeth up to Seir, even unto Baal-gad in the valley of Lebanon under mount Hermon: and all their kings he took, and smote them, and slew them. 18 Joshua made war a long time with all those kings. 19 There was not a city that made peace with the children of Israel, save the Hivites the inhabitants of Gibeon: all *other* they took in battle. 20 For it was of the LORD to harden their hearts, that they should come against Israel in battle, that he might destroy them utterly, *and* that they might have no favour, but that he might destroy them, as the LORD commanded Moses. 21 And at that time came Joshua, and cut off the Anakims from the mountains, from Hebron, from Debir, from Anab, and from all the mountains of Judah, and from all the mountains of Israel: Joshua destroyed them utterly with their cities. 22 There was none of the Anakims left in the land of the children of Israel: only in Gaza, in Gath, and in Ashdod, there remained. 23 So Joshua took the whole land, according to all that the LORD said unto Moses; and Joshua gave it for an inheritance unto Israel according to their divisions by their tribes. And the land rested from war.

We have here the conclusion of this whole matter.

I. A short account is here given of what was done in four things:—1. The obstinacy of the Canaanites in their opposition to the Israelites. It was strange that though it appeared so manifestly that God fought for Israel, and in every engagement the Canaanites had the worst of it, yet they stood it out to the last; not one city made peace with Israel, but the Gibeonites only, who understood the things that belonged to their peace better than their neighbours, *v.* 19. It is intimated that other cities might have made as good terms for themselves, without ragged clothes and clouted shoes, if they would have humbled themselves, but they never so much as *desired conditions of peace.* We here are told whence this unaccountable infatuation came: *It was of the Lord to harden their hearts*, *v.* 20. As Pharaoh's heart was hardened by his own pride and wilfulness first, and afterwards by the righteous judgment of God, to his destruction, so were the hearts of these Canaanites. To punish them for all their other follies, God left them to this, to make those their enemies whom they might have made their friends. This was it that ruined them: they *came against Israel in battle*, and gave the first blow, and therefore *might have no favour* shown them. Those know not what they do who give the provocation to divine justice, or the authorized instruments of it. *Are we stronger than God?* Observe here, That hardness of heart is the ruin of sinners. Those that are stupid and secure, and heedless of divine warnings, are already marked for destruction. What hope is there of those concerning whom God has said, *Go, make their hearts fat?* 2. The constancy of the Israelites in prosecuting this war (*v.* 18): *Joshua made war a long time;* some reckon it five years, others seven, that were spent in subduing this land: so long God would train up Israel to war, and give them repeated instances of his power and goodness in every new victory that he gave them. 3. The conquest of the Anakim at last, *v.* 21, 22. Either this was done as they met with them where they were dispersed, as some think, or rather it should seem the Anakim had retired to their fastnesses, and so were hunted out and cut off at last, after all the rest of Israel's enemies. The mountains of Judah and Israel were the habitations of those mountains of men; but not their height, nor the strength of their caves, nor the difficulty of the passes to them, could secure, no, not these mighty men, from the sword of Joshua. The cutting off of the sons of Anak is particularly mentioned because these had been such a terror to the spies forty years before, and their bulk and strength had been thought an insuperable difficulty in the way of the reducing of Canaan, Num. xiii. 28, 33. Even that opposition which seemed invincible was got over. Never let the sons of Anak be a terror to the Israel of God, for even their day will come to fall. Giants are dwarfs to Omnipotence; yet this struggle with the Anakim was reserved for the latter end of the war, when the Israelites had become more expert in the arts of war, and had had more experience of the power and goodness of God. Note, God sometimes reserves the sharpest trials of his people by affliction and temptation for the latter end of their days. Therefore *let not him that girds on the harness boast as he that puts it off.* Death, that tremendous son of Anak, is the last enemy that is to be encountered; but it is *to be destroyed*, 1 Cor. xv. 26. Thanks be to God, who will give us the victory. 4. The end and issue of this long war. The Canaanites were rooted out, not perfectly (as we shall find after in the book of Judges), but in a good measure; they were not able to make any head, either, (1.) So as to keep the Israelites out of possession of the land: *Joshua took all that land*, *v.* 16, 17. And we may suppose the people dispersed themselves and their families into the countries they had conquered, at least those that lay nearest to the head-quarters at Gilgal, until an orderly distribution should be made by lot, that every man might know his own. Or, (2.) So as to keep them in action, or give them any molestation (*v.* 23): *The land rested from war.* It ended not in a peace with the Canaanites (that was forbidden), but in a peace from them. There is a rest, a rest from war, remaining for the people of God, into which they shall enter when their warfare is accomplished.

II. That which was now done is here compared with that which had been said to Moses. God's word and his works, if viewed and considered together, will mutually illustrate each other. It is here observed in the close, 1. That all the precepts God had given to Moses relating to the conquest of Canaan were obeyed on the people's part, at least while Joshua lived. See how solemnly this is remarked (*v.* 15): *As the Lord commanded Moses his servant*, by whose hand the law was given, *so did Moses command Joshua*, for Moses was faithful, as a law-giver, to him that appointed him; he did his part, and then he died: but were the commands of Moses observed when he was in his grave? Yes, they were: *So did Joshua*, who was, in his place, as faithful as Moses in his. *He left nothing undone* (Heb. he *removed nothing) of all that the Lord commanded Moses.* Those that leave their duty undone do what they can to remove or make void the command of God, by which they are bound to do it; but Joshua, by performing the precept, *confirmed* it, as the expression is, Deut. xxvii. 26. Joshua was himself a great commander, and yet nothing was more his praise than his obedience. Those that rule others at their will must themselves be ruled by the divine will; then their power is indeed their honour, and not otherwise. The pious obedience for which Joshua is here commended respects especially the command to destroy the Canaanites, and to *break down their altars and burn their images*, Deut. vii. 2—5; Exod. xxiii. 24; xxxiv. 13. Joshua, in his zeal for the Lord of hosts, spared neither the idols nor the idolaters. Saul's disobedience, or rather his partial obedience, to the command of God, for the utter destruction of the Amalekites, cost him his kingdom. It should seem Joshua himself gives this account of his most careful and punctual observance of his orders in the execution of his commission, that in all respects he had done as Moses commanded him; and then it intimates that he had more pleasure and satisfaction in reflecting upon his obedience to the commands of God in all this war, and valued himself more upon that, than upon all the gains and triumphs with which he was enriched and advanced. 2. That all the promises God had given to Moses relating to this conquest were accomplished *on his part*, *v.* 23. Joshua *took the whole land*, conquered it, and took possession of it, *according to all that the*

Lord said unto Moses. God had promised to drive out the nations before them (Exod. xxxiii. 2; xxxiv. 11), and to *bring them down,* Deut. ix. 3. And now it was done. There failed not one word of the promise. Our successes and enjoyments are then doubly sweet and comfortable to us when we see them flowing to us from the promise (this is *according to what the Lord said),* as our obedience is then acceptable to God when it has an eye to the precept. And, if we make conscience of our duty, we need not question the performance of the promise.

CHAP. XII.

This chapter is a summary of Israel's conquests. I Their conquests under Moses, on the other side Jordan (for we now suppose ourselves in Canaan) eastward, which we had the history of, Num. xxi. 24, &c. And here the abridgment of that history, ver. 1—6. II. Their conquests under Joshua, on this side Jordan, westward. 1. The country they reduced, ver. 7, 8. 2. The kings they subdued, thirty-one in all, ver. 9—24. And this comes in here, not only as a conclusion of the history of the wars of Canaan (that we might at one view see what they had got), but as a preface to the history of the dividing of Canaan, that all that might be put together which they were now to make a distribution of.

NOW these *are* the kings of the land, which the children of Israel smote, and possessed their land on the other side Jordan toward the rising of the sun, from the river Arnon unto mount Hermon, and all the plain on the east: 2 Sihon king of the Amorites, who dwelt in Heshbon, *and* ruled from Aroer, which *is* upon the bank of the river Arnon, and from the middle of the river, and from half Gilead, even unto the river Jabbok, *which is* the border of the children of Ammon; 3 And from the plain to the sea of Chinneroth on the east, and unto the sea of the plain, *even* the salt sea on the east, the way to Beth-jeshimoth; and from the south, under Ashdoth-pisgah: 4 And the coast of Og king of Bashan, *which was* of the remnant of the giants, that dwelt at Ashtaroth and at Edrei, 5 And reigned in mount Hermon, and in Salcah, and in all Bashan, unto the border of the Geshurites and the Maachathites, and half Gilead, the border of Sihon king of Heshbon. 6 Them did Moses the servant of the LORD and the children of Israel smite: and Moses the servant of the LORD gave it *for* a possession unto the Reubenites, and the Gadites, and the half tribe of Manasseh.

Joshua, or whoever else is the historian, before he comes to sum up the new conquests Israel had made, in these verses recites their former conquests in Moses's time, under whom they became masters of the great and potent kingdoms of Sihon and Og. Note, Fresh mercies must not drown the remembrance of former mercies, nor must the glory of the present instruments of good to the church be suffered to eclipse and diminish the just honour of those who have gone before them, and who were the blessings and ornaments of their day. Joshua's services and achievements are confessedly great, but let not those under Moses be overlooked and forgotten, since God was the same who wrought both, and both put together proclaim him the Alpha and Omega of Israel's great salvation. Here is, 1. A description of this conquered country, the measure and bounds of it in general (*v.* 1): *From the river Arnon* in the south, to *Mount Hermon* in the north. In particular, here is a description of the kingdom of Sihon (*v.* 2, 3), and that of Og, *v.* 4, 5. Moses had described this country very particularly (Deut. ii. 36; iii. 4, &c.), and this description here agrees with his. King Og is said to dwell at Ashtaroth and Edrei (*v.* 4), probably because they were both his royal cities; he had palaces in both, and resided sometimes in one and sometimes in the other; one perhaps was his summer seat and the other his winter seat. But Israel took both from him, and made one grave to serve him that could not be content with one palace. 2. The distribution of this country. Moses assigned it to the two tribes and a half, at their request, and divided it among them (*v.* 6), of which we had the story at large, Num. xxxii. The dividing of it when it was conquered by Moses is here mentioned as an example to Joshua what he must do now that he had conquered the country on this side Jordan. Moses, in his time, gave to one part of Israel a very rich and fruitful country, but it was on the outside of Jordan; but Joshua gave to all Israel the holy land, the mountain of God's sanctuary, within Jordan: so the law conferred upon some few of God's spiritual Israel external temporal blessings, which were earnests of good things to come; but our Lord Jesus, the true Joshua, has provided for all the children of promise spiritual blessings—the privileges of the sanctuary, and the heavenly Canaan. The triumphs and grants of the law were glorious, but those of the gospel far exceed in glory.

7 And these *are* the kings of the country which Joshua and the children of Israel smote on this side Jordan on the west, from Baal-gad in the valley of Lebanon even unto the mount Halak, that goeth up to Seir; which Joshua gave unto the tribes of Israel *for* a possession according to their divisions; 8 In the mountains,

and in the valleys, and in the plains, and in the springs, and in the wilderness, and in the south country; the Hittites, the Amorites, and the Canaanites, the Perizzites, the Hivites, and the Jebusites: 9 The king of Jericho, one; the king of Ai, which *is* beside Beth-el, one; 10 The king of Jerusalem, one; the king of Hebron, one; 11 The king of Jarmuth, one; the king of Lachish, one; 12 The king of Eglon, one; the king of Gezer, one; 13 The king of Debir, one; the king of Geder, one; 14 The king of Hormah, one; the king of Arad, one; 15 The king of Libnah, one; the king of Adullam, one; 16 The king of Makkedah, one; the king of Beth-el, one; 17 The king of Tappuah, one; the king of Hepher, one; 18 The king of Aphek, one; the king of Lasharon, one; 19 The king of Madon, one; the king of Hazor, one; 20 The king of Shimron-meron, one; the king of Achshaph, one; 21 The king of Taanach, one; the king of Megiddo, one; 22 The king of Kedesh, one; the king of Jokneam of Carmel, one; 23 The king of Dor in the coast of Dor, one; the king of the nations of Gilgal, one; 24 The king of Tirzah, one: all the kings thirty and one.

We have here a breviate of Joshua's conquests.

I. The limits of the country he conquered. It lay between Jordan on the east and the Mediterranean Sea on the west, and extended from Baal-gad near Lebanon in the north to Halak, which lay upon the country of Edom in the south, *v.* 7. The boundaries are more largely described, Num. xxxiv. 2, &c. But what is here said is enough to show that God had been as good as his word, and had given them possession of all he had promised them by Moses, if they would but have kept it.

II. The various kinds of land that were found in this country, which contributed both to its pleasantness and to its fruitfulness, *v.* 8. There were mountains, not craggy, and rocky, and barren, which are frightful to the traveller and useless to the inhabitants, but fruitful hills, such as put forth *precious things* (Deut. xxxiii. 15), which charmed the spectator's eye and filled the owner's hand. And valleys, not mossy and boggy, but *covered with corn,* Ps. lxv. 13. There were plains, and springs to water them; and even in that rich land there were wildernesses too, or forests, which were not so thickly inhabited as other parts, yet had towns and houses in them, but served as foils to set off the more pleasant and fruitful countries.

III. The several nations that had been in possession of this country—Hittites, Amorites, Canaanites, &c., all of them descended from Canaan, the accursed son of Ham, Gen. x. 15—18. Seven nations they are called (Deut. vii. 1), and so many are there reckoned up, but here six only are mentioned, the Girgashites being either lost or left out, though we find them, Gen. x. 16 and xv. 21. Either they were incorporated with some other of these nations, or, as the tradition of the Jews is, upon the approach of Israel under Joshua they all withdrew and went into Africa, leaving their country to be possessed by Israel, with whom they saw it was to no purpose to contend, and therefore they are not named among the nations that Joshua subdued.

IV. A list of the kings that were conquered and subdued by the sword of Israel, some in the field, others in their own cities, thirty-one in all, and very particularly named and counted, it should seem, in the order in which they were conquered; for the catalogue begins with the kings of Jericho and Ai, then takes in the king of Jerusalem and the princes of the south that were in confederacy with him, and then proceeds to those of the northern association. Now, 1. This shows what a very fruitful country Canaan then was, which could support so many kingdoms, and in which so many kings chose to throng together rather than disperse themselves into other countries, which we may suppose not yet inhabited, but where, though they might find more room, they could not expect such plenty and pleasure: this was the land God spied out for Israel; and yet at this day it is one of the most barren, despicable, and unprofitable countries in the world: such is the effect of the curse it lies under, since its possessors rejected Christ and his gospel, as was foretold by Moses, Deut. xxix. 23. 2. It shows what narrow limits men's ambition was then confined to. These kings contented themselves with the government, each of them, of one city and the towns and villages that pertained to it; and no one of them, for aught that appears, aimed to make himself master of the rest, but, when there was occasion, all united for the common safety. Yet it should seem that what was wanting in the extent of their territories was made up in the absoluteness of their power, their subjects being all their tenants and vassals, and entirely at their command. 3. It shows how good God was to Israel, in giving them victory over all these kings, and possession of all these kingdoms, and what obligations he hereby laid upon them to *observe his statutes and to keep his laws,* Ps. cv. 44, 45.

Here were thirty-one kingdoms, or seigniories, to be divided among nine tribes and a half of Israel. Of these there fell to the lot of Judah the kingdoms of Hebron, Jarmuth, Lachish, Eglon, Debir, Arad, Libnah, and Adullam, eight in all, besides part of the kingdom of Jerusalem and part of Geder. Benjamin had the kingdoms of Jericho, Ai, Jerusalem, Makkedah, Beth-el, and the nations of Gilgal, six in all. Simeon had the kingdom of Hormah and part of Geder. Ephraim had the kingdoms of Gezer and Tirzah. Manasseh (that half-tribe) had the kingdoms of Tappuah and Hepher, Taanach and Megiddo. Asher had the kingdoms of Aphek and Achshaph. Zebulun had the kingdoms of Lasharon, Shimron-meron, and Jokneam. Naphtali had the kingdoms of Madon, Hazor, and Kedesh. And Issachar had that of Dor. These were some of the great and famous kings that God smote, *for his mercy endureth for ever; and gave their land for a heritage, even a heritage unto Israel his servant, for his mercy endureth for ever,* Ps. cxxxvi. 17, &c.

CHAP. XIII.

At this chapter begins the account of the dividing of the land of Canaan among the tribes of Israel by lot, a narrative not so entertaining and instructive as that of the conquest of it, and yet it is thought fit to be inserted in the sacred history, to illustrate the performance of the promise made to the fathers, that this land should be given to the seed of Jacob, to them and not to any other. The preserving of this distribution would be of great use to the Jewish nation, who were obliged by the law to keep up this first distribution, and not to transfer inheritances from tribe to tribe, Num. xxxvi. 9. It is likewise of use to us for the explaining of other scriptures: the learned know how much light the geographical description of a country gives to the history of it. And therefore we are not to skip over these chapters of hard names as useless and not to be regarded; where God has a mouth to speak and a hand to write we should find an ear to hear and an eye to read; and God give us a heart to profit! In this chapter, I. God informs Joshua what parts of the country that were intended in the grant to Israel yet remained unconquered, and not got in possession, ver. 1—6. II. He appoints him, notwithstanding, to make a distribution of what was conquered, ver. 7 III. To complete this account, here is a repetition of the distribution Moses had made of the land on the other side Jordan; in general (ver. 8—14), in particular, the lot of Reuben (ver. 15—23), of Gad (ver. 24—28), of the half tribe of Manasseh, ver. 29—33.

NOW Joshua was old *and* stricken in years; and the LORD said unto him, Thou art old *and* stricken in years, and there remaineth yet very much land to be possessed. 2 This *is* the land that yet remaineth: all the borders of the Philistines, and all Geshuri, 3 From Sihor, which *is* before Egypt, even unto the borders of Ekron northward, *which* is counted to the Canaanite: five lords of the Philistines; the Gazathites, and the Ashdothites, the Eshkalonites, the Gittites, and the Ekronites; also the Avites: 4 From the south, all the land of the Canaanites, and Mearah that *is* beside the Sidonians, unto Aphek, to the borders of the Amorites: 5 And the land of the Giblites, and all Lebanon, toward the sun-rising, from Baal-gad under mount Hermon unto the entering into Hamath. 6 All the inhabitants of the hill country from Lebanon unto Misrephoth-maim, *and* all the Sidonians, them will I drive out from before the children of Israel: only divide thou it by lot unto the Israelites for an inheritance, as I have commanded thee.

Here, I. God puts Joshua in mind of his old age, *v.* 1. 1. It is said that Joshua was *old and stricken in years,* and he and Caleb were at this time the only old men among the thousands of Israel, none except them of all those who were numbered at Mount Sinai being now alive. He had been a man of war from his youth (Exod. xvii. 10); but now he yielded to the infirmities of age, with which it is in vain for the stoutest to think of contesting. It should seem Joshua had not the same strength and vigour in his old age that Moses had; all that come to old age do not find it alike good; generally, the days of old age are evil days, and such as there is no pleasure in, nor expectation of service from. 2. God takes notice of it to him: *God said to him, Thou art old.* Note, It is good for those who are *old and stricken in years* to be put in remembrance of their being so. Some have *gray hairs here and there upon them, and perceive it not* (Hos. vii. 9); they do not care to think of it, and therefore need to be told of it, that they may be quickened to do the work of life, and make preparation for death, which is coming towards them apace. But God mentions Joshua's age and growing infirmities, (1.) As a reason why he should now lay by the thoughts of pursuing the war; he cannot expect to see an end of it quickly, for there remained much land, more perhaps than he thought, to be possessed, in several parts remote from each other: and it was not fit that at his age he should be put upon the fatigue of renewing the war, and carrying it to such distant places; no, it was enough for him that he had reduced the body of the country. "Let him be gathered to rest with honour and the thanks of his people for the good services he had done them, and let the conquering of the skirts of the country be left for those that shall come after." As he had entered into the labours of Moses, so let others enter into his, and bring forth the top-stone, the doing of which was reserved for David long after. Observe, God considers the frame of his people, and would not have them burdened with work above their strength. It cannot be expected that old people should do as they have done for God and their country. (2.) As a reason why he should speedily apply himself to the dividing of that which he had conquered. That work must be done, and done quickly; it was necessary that he should preside in the doing of it, and therefore, he being *old and stricken in years,* and not likely to continue long, let him make this his concluding piece of service to God and Israel. All people, but especially old people, should set themselves to do that quickly which must be done before they die, lest death prevent them, Eccl. ix. 10.

II. He gives him a particular account of the land that yet remained unconquered, which was intended for Israel, and which, in due time, they should be masters of if they did not put a bar in their own door. Divers places are here mentioned, some in the south, as the country of the Philistines, governed by five lords, and the land that lay towards Egypt (*v.* 2, 3), some westward, as that which lay towards the Sidonians (*v.* 4), some eastward, as all Lebanon (*v.* 5), some towards the north, as that in the entering in of Hamath, *v.* 5. Joshua is told this, and he made the people acquainted with it, 1. That they might be the more affected with God's goodness to them in giving them this good land, and might thereby be engaged to love and serve him; for, if this which they had was too little, God would moreover *give them such and such things,* 2 Sam. xii. 8. 2. That they might not be tempted to make any league, or contract any dangerous familiarity with these their neighbours so as to learn their way, but might rather be jealous of them, as a people that kept them from their right and that they had just cause of quarrel with. 3. That they might keep themselves in a posture for war, and not think of putting off the harness so long as there remained any land to be possessed. Nor must we lay aside our spiritual armour, nor be off our watch, till our victory be completed in the kingdom of glory.

III. He promises that he would make the Israelites masters of all those countries that were yet unsubdued, though Joshua was old and not able to do it, old and not likely to live to see it done. Whatever becomes of us, and however we may be laid aside as despised broken vessels, God will do his own work in his own time (*v.* 6): *I will drive them out.* The original is emphatic: "*It is I* that *will do it,* I that can do it when thou art dead and gone, and will do it if Israel be not wanting to themselves." "I will do it by my Word," so the Chaldee here, as in many other places, "by the eternal Word, the captain of the hosts of the Lord." This promise that he would drive them out from before the children of Israel plainly supposes it as the condition of the promise that the children of Israel must themselves attempt their extirpation, must go up against them, else they could not be said to be driven out before them; if afterwards Israel, through sloth, or cowardice, or affection to these idolaters, sit still and let them alone, they must blame themselves, and not God, if they be not driven out. We must work out our salvation, and then God will work in us and work with us; we must resist our spiritual enemies, and then God will tread them under our feet; we must go forth to our Christian work and warfare, and then God will go forth before us.

7 Now therefore divide this land for an inheritance unto the nine tribes, and the half tribe of Manasseh. 8 With whom the Reubenites and the Gadites have received their inheritance, which Moses gave them, beyond Jordan eastward, *even* as Moses the servant of the LORD gave them; 9 From Aroer, that *is* upon the bank of the river Arnon, and the city that *is* in the midst of the river, and all the plain of Medeba unto Dibon; 10 And all the cities of Sihon king of the Amorites, which reigned in Heshbon, unto the border of the children of Ammon; 11 And Gilead, and the border of the Geshurites and Maachathites, and all mount Hermon, and all Bashan unto Salcah; 12 All the kingdom of Og in Bashan, which reigned in Ashtaroth and in Edrei, who remained of the remnant of the giants: for these did Moses smite, and cast them out. 13 Nevertheless the children of Israel expelled not the Geshurites, nor the Maachathites: but the Geshurites and the Maachathites dwell among the Israelites until this day. 14 Only unto the tribe of Levi he gave none inheritance; the sacrifices of the LORD God of Israel made by fire *are* their inheritance, as he said unto them. 15 And Moses gave unto the tribe of the children of Reuben *inheritance* according to their families. 16 And their coast was from Aroer, that *is* on the bank of the river Arnon, and the city that *is* in the midst of the river, and all the plain by Medeba; 17 Heshbon, and all her cities that *are* in the plain; Dibon, and Bamoth-baal, and Beth-baal-meon, 18 And Jahaza, and Kedemoth, and Mephaath, 19 And Kirjathaim, and Sibmah, and Zarethshahar in the mount of the valley, 20 And Beth-peor, and Ashdoth-pisgah, and Beth-jeshimoth, 21 And all the cities of the plain, and all the kingdom of

Sihon king of the Amorites, which reigned in Heshbon, whom Moses smote with the princes of Midian, Evi, and Rekem, and Zur, and Hur, and Reba, *which were* dukes of Sihon, dwelling in the country. 22 Balaam also the son of Beor, the soothsayer, did the children of Israel slay with the sword among them that were slain by them. 23 And the border of the children of Reuben was Jordan, and the border *thereof*. This *was* the inheritance of the children of Reuben after their families, the cities and the villages thereof. 24 And Moses gave *inheritance* unto the tribe of Gad, *even* unto the children of Gad according to their families. 25 And their coast was Jazer, and all the cities of Gilead, and half the land of the children of Ammon, unto Aroer that *is* before Rabbah; 26 And from Heshbon unto Ramath-mizpeh, and Betonim; and from Mahanaim unto the border of Debir; 27 And in the valley, Beth-aram, and Beth-nimrah, and Succoth, and Zaphon, the rest of the kingdom of Sihon king of Heshbon, Jordan and *his* border, *even* unto the edge of the sea of Chinnereth on the other side Jordan eastward. 28 This *is* the inheritance of the children of Gad after their families, the cities, and their villages. 29 And Moses gave *inheritance* unto the half tribe of Manasseh: and *this* was *the possession* of the half tribe of the children of Manasseh by their families. 30 And their coast was from Mahanaim, all Bashan, all the kingdom of Og king of Bashan, and all the towns of Jair, which *are* in Bashan, threescore cities: 31 And half Gilead, and Ashtaroth, and Edrei, cities of the kingdom of Og in Bashan, *were pertaining* unto the children of Machir the son of Manasseh, *even* to the one half of the children of Machir by their families. 32 These *are the countries* which Moses did distribute for inheritance in the plains of Moab, on the other side Jordan, by Jericho, eastward. 33 But unto the tribe of Levi Moses gave not *any* inheritance: the LORD God of Israel *was* their inheritance, as he said unto them.

Here we have, I. Orders given to Joshua to assign to each tribe its portion of this land, including that which was yet unsubdued, which must be brought into the lot, in a believing confidence that it should be conquered when Israel was multiplied so as to have occasion for it (*v.* 7): *Now divide this land.* Joshua thought all must be conquered before any must be divided. "No," said God, "there is as much conquered as will serve your turn for the present; divide this, and make your best of it, and wait for the remainder hereafter." Note, We must take the comfort of what we have, though we cannot compass all we would have. Observe,

1. The land must be divided among the several tribes, and they must not always live in common, as now they did. Which way soever a just property is acquired, it is the will of that God who has given the earth to the children of men that there should be such a thing, and that every man should know his own, and not invade that which is another's. The world must be governed, not by force, but right, by the law of equity, not of arms.

2. That it must be divided for an inheritance, though they got it by conquest. (1.) The promise of it came to them as an inheritance from their fathers; the land of promise pertained to the children of promise, who were thus beloved for their fathers' sakes, and in performance of the covenant with them. (2.) The possession of it was to be transmitted by them, as an inheritance to their children. Frequently, what is got by force is soon lost again; but Israel, having an incontestable title to this land by the divine grant, might see it hereby secured as an inheritance to their seed after them, and that God kept this mercy for thousands.

3. That Joshua must not divide it by his own will. Though he was a very wise, just, and good man, it must not be left to him to give what he pleased to each tribe; but he must do it by lot, which referred the matter wholly to God, and to his determination, for he it is that appoints the bounds of our habitation, and every man's judgment must proceed from him. But Joshua must preside in this affair, must manage this solemn appeal to Providence, and see that the lot was drawn fairly and without fraud, and that every tribe did acquiesce in it. The lot indeed *causeth contention to cease*, Prov. xviii. 18. But, if upon this lot any controversy should arise, Joshua by his wisdom and authority must determine it, and prevent any ill consequences of it. Joshua must have the honour of dividing the land, (1.) Because he had undergone the fatigue of conquering it: and when, through his hand, each tribe received its allotment, they would

thereby be made the more sensible of their obligations to him. And what a pleasure must it needs be to a man of such a public spirit as Joshua was to see the people that were so dear to him eating of the labour of his hands! (2.) That he might be herein a type of Christ, who has not only conquered for us the gates of hell, but has opened to us the gates of heaven, and, having purchased the eternal inheritance for all believers, will in due time put them all in possession of it.

II. An account is here given of the distribution of the land on the other side Jordan among the Reubenites, and Gadites, and half the tribe of Manasseh. Observe,

1. How this account is introduced. It comes in, (1.) As the reason why this land within Jordan must be divided only to the nine tribes and a half, because the other two and a half were already provided for. (2.) As a pattern to Joshua in the work he had now to do. He had seen Moses distribute that land, which would give him some aid in distributing this, and thence he might take his measures; only this was to be done by lot, but it should seem Moses did that himself, according to the wisdom given unto him. (3.) As an inducement to Joshua to hasten the dividing of this land, that the nine tribes and a half might not be kept any longer than was necessary out of their possession, since their brethren of the two tribes and a half were so well settled in theirs; and God their common Father would not have such a difference made between his children.

2. The particulars of this account.

(1.) Here is a general description of the country that was given to the two tribes and a half, *which Moses gave them, even as Moses gave them*, *v.* 8. The repetition implies a ratification of the grant by Joshua. Moses settled this matter, and, as Moses settled it, so shall it rest; Joshua will not, under any pretence whatsoever, go about to alter it. And a reason is intimated why he would not, because Moses was the servant of the Lord, and acted in this matter by secret direction from him and was faithful as a servant. Here we have, [1.] The fixing of the boundaries of this country, by which they were divided from the neighbouring nations, *v.* 9, &c. Israel must know their own and keep to it, and may not, under pretence of their being God's peculiar people, encroach upon their neighbours, and invade their rights and properties, to which they had a good and firm title by providence, though not, as Israel, a title by promise. [2.] An exception of one part of this country from Israel's possession, though it was in their grant, namely, the Geshurites and the Maachathites, *v.* 13. They had not leisure to reduce all the remote and obscure corners of the country in Moses's time, and afterwards they had no mind to it, being easy with what they had. Thus those who are not straitened in God's promises are yet straitened in their own faith, and prayers, and endeavours.

(2.) A very particular account of the inheritances of these two tribes and a half, how they were separated from each other, and what cities, with the towns, villages, and fields, commonly known and reputed to be appurtenances to them, belonged to each tribe. This is very fully and exactly set down in order that posterity might, in reading this history, be the more affected with the goodness of God to their ancestors, when they found what a large and fruitful country, and what abundance of great and famous cities, he put them in possession of (God's grants look best when we descend to the particulars); and also that the limits of every tribe being punctually set down in this authentic record disputes might be prevented, and such contests between the tribes as commonly happen where boundaries have not been adjusted nor this matter brought to a certainty. And we have reason to think that the register here prescribed and published of the lot of each tribe was of great use to Israel in after-ages, was often appealed to, and always acquiesced in, for the determining of *meum* and *tuum*—*mine* and *thine.*

[1.] We have here the lot of the tribe of Reuben, Jacob's first-born, who, though he had lost the dignity and power which pertained to the birthright, yet, it seems, had the advantage of being first served. Perhaps those of that tribe had an eye to this in desiring to be seated on that side Jordan, that, since they could not expect the benefit of the best lot, they might have the credit of the first. Observe, *First*, In the account of the lot of this tribe mention is made of the slaughter, 1. Of Sihon, king of the Amorites, who reigned in this country, and might have kept it and his life if he would have been neighbourly, and have suffered Israel to pass through his territories, but, by attempting to oppose them, justly brought ruin upon himself, Num. xxi. 21, &c. 2. Of the princes of Midian, who were slain afterwards in another war (Num. xxxi. 8), and yet are here called *dukes of Sihon*, and are said to be *smitten with him*, because they were either tributaries to him, or, in his opposition to Israel, confederates with him, and hearty in his interests, and his fall made way for theirs not long after. 3. Of Balaam particularly, that would, if he could, have cursed Israel, and was soon after recompensed *according to the wickedness of his endeavour* (Ps. xxviii. 4), for he fell with those that set him on. This was recorded before (Num. xxxi. 8), and is here repeated, because the defeating of Balaam's purpose to curse Israel was the turning of that curse into a blessing, and was such an instance of the power and goodness of God as was fit to be had in everlasting remembrance. See Mic. vi. 5. *Secondly*, Within the lot of this tribe was that Mount Pisgah from the top of which Moses took his view of the earthly Canaan and his flight to the heavenly. And not far off thence Elijah was when he was fetched up to heaven in a chariot of fire. The separation of this tribe from the rest, by the river Jordan, was that which Deborah lamented; and the preference they gave to their private interests above the public was what she censured, Judg. v. 15, 16. In this tribe lay Heshbon and Sibmah, famed for their fruitful fields and vineyards. See Isa. xvi. 8, 9; Jer. xlviii. 32. This tribe, with that of Gad, was sorely shaken by Hazael king of Syria (2 Kings x. 33), and afterwards dislodged and carried into captivity, twenty years before the general captivity of the ten tribes by the king of Assyria, 1 Chron. v. 26.

[2.] The lot of the tribe of Gad, *v.* 24—28. This lay north of Reuben's lot; the country of Gilead lay in this tribe, so famous for its balm that it is thought strange indeed if there be no balm in Gilead, and the cities of Jabesh-Gilead and Ramoth-Gilead which we often read of in scripture. Succoth and Penuel, which we read of in the story of Gideon, were in this tribe; and that forest which is called the *wood of Ephraim* (from the slaughter Jephthah made there of the Ephraimites), in which Absalom's rebellious army was beaten, while his father David lay at Mahanaim, one of the frontier-cities of this tribe, *v.* 26. Sharon, famous for roses, was in this tribe. And within the limits of this tribe lived those Gadarenes that loved their swine better than their Saviour, fitter to be called *Girgashites* than *Israelites.*

[3.] The lot of the half-tribe of Manasseh, *v.* 29—31. Bashan, the kingdom of Og, was in this allotment, famous for the best timber, witness the oaks of Bashan—and the best breed of cattle, witness the bulls and rams of Bashan. This tribe lay north of Gad, reached to Mount Hermon, and had in it part of Gilead. Mizpeh was in this half-tribe, and Jephthah was one of its ornaments; so was Elijah, for in this tribe was Thisbe, whence he is called the Tishbite; and Jair was another. In the edge of the tribe stood Chorazin, honoured with Christ's wondrous works, but ruined by his righteous woe for not improving them.

[4.] Twice in this chapter it is taken notice of that to the tribe of Levi *Moses gave no inheritance* (*v.* 14, 33), for so God had appointed, Num. xviii. 20. If they had been appointed to a lot entire by themselves, Moses would have served them first, not because it was his own tribe, but because it was God's; but they must be provided for in another manner; their habitations must be scattered in all the tribes, and their maintenance brought out of all the tribes, and God himself was the portion both of their inheritance and of their cup, Deut. x. 9; xviii. 2.

CHAP. XIV.

Here is, I. The general method that was taken in dividing the land, ver. 1—5. II. The demand Caleb made of Hebron, as his by promise, and therefore not to be put into the lot with the rest, ver. 6—12. And Joshua's grant of that demand, ver. 13—15. This was done at Gilgal, which was as yet their head-quarters.

AND these *are the* countries which the children of Israel inherited in the land of Canaan, which Eleazar the priest, and Joshua the son of Nun, and the heads of the fathers of the tribes of the children of Israel, distributed for inheritance to them. 2 By lot *was* their inheritance, as the LORD commanded by the hand of Moses, for the nine tribes, and *for* the half tribe. 3 For Moses had given the inheritance of two tribes and a half tribe on the other side Jordan: but unto the Levites he gave none inheritance among them. 4 For the children of Joseph were two tribes, Manasseh and Ephraim: therefore they gave no part unto the Levites in the land, save cities to dwell *in*, with their suburbs for their cattle and for their substance. 5 As the LORD commanded Moses, so the children of Israel did, and they divided the land.

The historian, having in the foregoing chapter given an account of the disposal of the countries on the other side Jordan, now comes to tell us what they did with the countries in the land of Canaan. They were not conquered to be left desert, *a habitation for dragons, and a court for owls,* Isa. xxxiv. 13. No, the Israelites that had hitherto been closely encamped in a body, and the greatest part of them such as never knew any other way of living, must now disperse themselves to replenish these new conquests. It is said of the earth, *God created it not in vain; he formed it to be inhabited,* Isa. xlv. 18. Canaan would have been subdued in vain if it had not been inhabited. Yet every man might not go and settle where he pleased, but as there seems to have been in the days of Peleg an orderly and regular division of the habitable earth among the sons of Noah (Gen. x. 25, 32), so there was now such a division of the land of Canaan among the sons of Jacob. God had given Moses directions how this distribution should be made, and those directions are here punctually observed. See Num. xxvi. 53, &c.

I. The managers of this great affair were Joshua the chief magistrate, Eleazar the chief priest, and ten princes, one of each of the tribes that were now to have their inheritance, whom God himself had nominated (Num. xxxiv. 17, &c.) some years before; and, it should seem, they were all now in being, and attended this service, that every tribe, having a representative of its own, might be satisfied that there was fair dealing, and might the more contentedly sit down by its lot.

II. The tribes among whom this dividend was to be made were nine and a half. 1. Not the two and a half that were already seated (*v.* 3), though perhaps now that they saw what a good land Canaan was, and how effectually it was subdued, they might some of them repent their choice, and wish they had now been to have their lot with their brethren, upon which condition they would gladly have given up what they had on the other side Jordan; but it could not be admitted: they had made their election without power of revocation, and so must their doom be; they themselves have decided it, and they must adhere to their choice. 2. Not the tribe of Levi; this was to be otherwise provided for. God had distinguished them from, and dignified them above, the other tribes, and they must not now mingle themselves with them, nor cast in their lot among them, for this would entangle them in the affairs of this life, which would not consist with a due attendance on their sacred function. But, 3. Joseph made two tribes, Manasseh and Ephraim, pursuant to Jacob's adoption of Joseph's two sons, and so the number of the tribes was kept up to twelve, though Levi was taken out, which is intimated here (*v.* 4): *The children of Joseph were two tribes, therefore they gave no part to Levi,* they being twelve without them.

III. The rule by which they went was the lot, *v.* 2. *The disposal* of that is *of the Lord,* Prov. xvi. 33. It was here used in an affair of weight, and which could not otherwise be accommodated to universal satisfaction, and it was used in a solemn religious manner as an appeal to God, by consent of parties. In dividing by lot, 1. They referred themselves to God, and to his wisdom and sovereignty, believing him fitter to determine for them than they for themselves. Ps. xlvii. 4, *He shall choose our inheritance for us.* 2. They professed a willingness to abide by the determination of it; for every man must take what is his lot, and make the best of it. In allusion to this we are said to *obtain an inheritance in Christ* (Eph. i. 11), ἐκληρώθημεν—*we have obtained it by lot,* so the word signifies; for it is obtained by a divine designation. Christ, our Joshua, gives eternal life to *as many as were given him,* John xvii. 2.

6 Then the children of Judah came unto Joshua in Gilgal: and Caleb the son of Jephunneh the Kenezite said unto him, Thou knowest the thing that the LORD said unto Moses the man of God concerning me and thee in Kadesh-barnea. 7 Forty years old *was* I when Moses the servant of the LORD sent me from Kadesh-barnea to espy out the land; and I brought him word again as *it was* in mine heart. 8 Nevertheless my brethren that went up with me made the heart of the people melt: but I wholly followed the LORD my God. 9 And Moses sware on that day, saying, Surely the land whereon thy feet have trodden shall be thine inheritance, and thy children's for ever, because thou hast wholly followed the LORD my God. 10 And now, behold, the LORD hath kept me alive, as he said, these forty and five years, even since the LORD spake this word unto Moses, while *the children of* Israel wandered in the wilderness: and now, lo, I *am* this day fourscore and five years old. 11 As yet I *am as* strong this day as *I was* in the day that Moses sent me: as my strength *was* then, even so *is* my strength now, for war, both to go out, and to come in. 12 Now therefore give me this mountain, whereof the LORD spake in that day; for thou heardest in that day how the Anakims *were* there, and *that* the cities *were* great *and* fenced: if so be the LORD *will be* with me, then I shall be able to drive them out, as the LORD said. 13 And Joshua blessed him, and gave unto Caleb the son of Jephunneh Hebron for an inheritance. 14 Hebron therefore became the inheritance of Caleb the son of Jephunneh the Kenezite unto this day, because that he wholly followed the LORD God of Israel. 15 And the name of Hebron before *was* Kirjath-arba; *which Arba was* a great man among the Anakims. And the land had rest from war.

Before the lot was cast into the lap for the determining of the portions of the respective tribes, the particular portion of Caleb was assigned to him. He was now, except Joshua, not only the oldest man in all Israel, but was twenty years older than any of them, for all that were above twenty years old when he was forty were dead in the wilderness; it was fit therefore that this phœnix of his age should have some particular marks of honour put upon him in the dividing of the land. Now,

I. Caleb here presents his petition, or

rather makes his demand, to have Hebron given him for a possession (*this mountain* he calls it, *v.* 12), and not to have that put into the lot with the other parts of the country. To justify his demand, he shows that God had long since, by Moses, promised him *that very mountain;* so that God's mind being already made known in this matter it would be a vain and needless thing to consult it any further by casting lots, by which we are to appeal to God in those cases only which cannot otherwise be decided, not in those which, like this, are already determined. Caleb is here called the *Kenezite,* some think from some remarkable victory obtained by him over the Kenezites, as the Romans gave their great generals titles from the countries they conquered, as Africanus, Germanicus, &c. Observe,

1. To enforce his petition, (1.) He brings the children of Judah, that is, the heads and great men of that tribe, along with him, to present it, who were willing thus to pay their respects to that ornament of their tribe, and to testify their consent that he should be provided for by himself, and that they would not take it as any reflection upon the rest of this tribe. Caleb was the person whom God had chosen out of that tribe to be employed in dividing the land (Num. xxxiv. 19), and therefore, lest he should seem to improve his authority as a commissioner for his own private advantage and satisfaction, he brings his brethren along with him, and, waiving his own power, seems rather to rely upon their interest. (2.) He appeals to Joshua himself concerning the truth of the allegations upon which he grounded his petition: *Thou knowest the thing, v.* 6. (3.) He makes a very honourable mention of Moses, which he knew would not be at all unpleasing to Joshua: Moses the *man of God* (*v.* 6), and the *servant of the Lord, v.* 7. What Moses said he took as from God himself, because Moses was his mouth and his agent, and therefore he had reason both to desire and expect that it should be made good. What can be more earnestly desired than the tokens of God's favour? And what more confidently expected than the grants of his promise?

2. In his petition he sets forth,

(1.) The testimony of his conscience concerning his integrity in the management of that great affair on which it proved the fate of Israel turned, the spying out of the land. Caleb was one of the twelve that were sent out on that errand (*v.* 7), and he now reflected upon it with comfort, and mentioned it, not in pride, but as that which, being the consideration of the grant, was necessary to be inserted in the plea, [1.] That he made his report as it was in his heart, that is, he spoke as he thought when he spoke so honourably of the land of Canaan, so confidently of the power of God to put them in possession of it, and so contemptibly of the opposition that the Canaanites, even the Anakim themselves, could make against them, as we find he did, Num. xiii. 30; xiv. 7—9. He did not do it merely to please Moses, or to keep the people quiet, much less from a spirit of contradiction to his fellows, but from a full conviction of the truth of what he said and a firm belief of the divine promise. [2.] That herein he *wholly followed the Lord his God,* that is, he kept close to his duty, and sincerely aimed at the glory of God in it. He conformed himself to the divine will with an eye to the divine favour. He had obtained this testimony from God himself (Num. xiv. 24), and therefore it was not vain-glory in him to speak of it, any more than it is for those who have *God's Spirit witnessing with their spirits* that they are the children of God humbly and thankfully to tell others for their encouragement what God has done for their souls. Note, Those that follow God fully when they are young shall have both the credit and comfort of it when they are old, and the reward of it for ever in the heavenly Canaan. [3.] That he did this when all his brethren and companions in that service, except Joshua, did otherwise. They *made the heart of the people melt* (*v.* 8), and how pernicious the consequences of it were was very well known. It adds much to the praise of following God if we adhere to him when others desert and decline from him. Caleb needed not to mention particularly Joshua's conduct in this matter; it was sufficiently known, and he would not seem to flatter him; it was enough to say (*v.* 6), *Thou knowest what the Lord spoke concerning me and thee.*

(2.) The experience he had had of God's goodness to him ever since to this day. Though he had wandered with the rest in the wilderness, and had been kept thirty-eight years out of Canaan as they were, for that sin which he was so far from having a hand in that he had done his utmost to prevent it, yet, instead of complaining of this, he mentions, to the glory of God, his mercy to him in two things:—[1.] That he was kept alive in the wilderness, not only notwithstanding the common perils and fatigues of that tedious march, but though all that generation of Israelites, except himself and Joshua, were one way or other cut off by death. With what a grateful sense of God's goodness to him does he speak it! (*v.* 10). *Now behold* (behold and wonder) *the Lord hath kept me alive these forty and five years,* thirty-eight years in the wilderness, through the plagues of the desert, and seven years in Canaan through the perils of war! Note, *First,* While we live, it is God that keeps us alive; by his power he protects us from death, and by his bounty supplies us continually with the supports and comforts of life. He *holdeth our soul in life. Secondly,* The longer we live the more sensible we should be of God's goodness to us in keeping us alive, his care in prolonging our frail lives, his patience in prolonging our forfeited lives. Has he kept me alive these forty-five years? Is it about that time of life with us? Or is it more? Or is it less? We have reason to say, *It is of the Lord's mercies that we are not consumed.* How much are we indebted to the favour of God, and what shall we render? Let the life thus kept by the providence of God be devoted to his praise. *Thirdly*, The death of many others round about us should make us the more thankful to God for sparing us and keeping us alive. Thousands falling on our right hand and our left and yet ourselves spared. These distinguishing favours impose on us strong obligations to singular obedience. [2.] That he was fit for business, now that he was in Canaan. Though eighty-five years old, yet as hearty and lively as when he was forty (*v.* 11): *As my strength was then, so is it now.* This was the fruit of the promise, and out-did what was said; for God not only gives what he promises, but he gives more: life by promise shall be life, and health, and strength, and all that which will make the promised life a blessing and comfort. Moses had said in his prayer (Ps. xc. 10) that at *eighty years old* even their *strength is labour and sorrow*, and so it is most commonly. But Caleb was an exception to the rule; his strength at eighty-five was ease and joy: this he got by *following the Lord fully*. Caleb here takes notice of this to the glory of God, and as an excuse for his asking a portion which he must fetch out of the giants' hands. Let not Joshua tell him he *knew not what he asked;* could he get the possession of that which he begged for a title to? "Yes," says he, "why not? I am as fit for war now as ever I was."

(3.) The promise Moses had made him in God's name that he should have *this mountain*, *v.* 9. This promise is his chief plea, and that on which he relies. As we find it (Num. xiv. 24) it is general, *him will I bring into the land whereunto he went, and his seed shall possess it;* but it seems it was more particular, and Joshua knew it; both sides understood this mountain for which Caleb was now a suitor to be intended. This was the place from which, more than any other, the spies took their report, for here they met with the sons of Anak (Num. xiii. 22), the sight of whom made such an impression upon them, *v.* 33. We may suppose that Caleb, observing what stress they laid upon the difficulty of conquering Hebron, a city garrisoned by the giants, and how thence they inferred that the conquest of the whole land was utterly impracticable, in opposition to their suggestions, and to convince the people that he spoke as he thought, bravely desired to have that city which they called *invincible* assigned to himself for his own portion: "I will undertake to deal with that, and, if I cannot get it for my inheritance, I will be without." "Well," said Moses, "it shall be thy own then, win it and wear it." Such a noble heroic spirit Caleb had, and so desirous was he to inspire his brethren with it, that he chose this place only because it was the most difficult to be conquered. And, to show that his soul did not decay any more than his body, now forty-five years after he adheres to his choice and is still of the same mind.

(4.) The hopes he had of being master of it, though the sons of Anak were in possession of it (*v.* 12): *If the Lord will be with me, then I shall be able to drive them out.* The city of Hebron Joshua had already reduced (*ch.* x. 37), but the mountain which belonged to it, and which was inhabited by the sons of Anak, was yet unconquered; for though the cutting off of the Anakim from Hebron was mentioned *ch.* xi. 21, because the historian would relate all the military actions together, yet it seems it was not conquered till after they had begun to divide the land. Observe, He builds his hopes of driving out the sons of Anak upon the presence of God with him. He does not say, "Because I am now as strong for war as I was at forty, therefore I shall drive them out," depending upon his personal valour; nor does he depend upon his interest in the warlike tribe of Judah, who attended him now in making this address, and no doubt would assist him; nor does he court Joshua's aid, or put it upon that, "If thou wilt be with me I shall gain my point." But, *If the Lord will be with me.* Here, [1.] He seems to speak doubtfully of God's being with him, not from any distrust of his goodness or faithfulness. He had spoken without the least hesitation of God's presence with Israel in general (Num. xiv. 9); *the Lord is with us.* But for himself, from a humble sense of his own unworthiness of such a favour, he chooses to express himself thus, *If the Lord will be with me.* The Chaldee paraphrase reads it, *If the Word of the Lord be my helper*, that Word which is God, and in the fulness of time was made flesh, and is the captain of our salvation. [2.] But he expresses without the least doubt his assurance that if God were with him he should be able to dispossess the sons of Anak. "If God be with us, *If God be for us, who can be against us*, so as to prevail?" It is also intimated that if God were not with him, though all the forces of Israel should come in to his assistance, he should not be able to gain his point. Whatever we undertake, God's favourable presence with us is all in all to our success; this therefore we must earnestly pray for, and carefully make sure of, by keeping ourselves in the love of God; and on this we must depend, and from this take our encouragement against the greatest difficulties.

3. Upon the whole matter, Caleb's request is (*v.* 12), *Give me this mountain,* (1.)

Because it was formerly in God's promise, and he would let Israel know how much he valued the promise, insisting upon *this mountain, whereof the Lord spake in that day*, as most desirable, though perhaps as good a portion might have fallen to him by lot in common with the rest. Those that live by faith value that which is given by promise far above that which is given by providence only. (2.) Because it was now in the Anakim's possession, and he would let Israel know how little he feared the enemy, and would by his example animate them to push on their conquests. Herein Caleb answered his name, which signifies *all heart*.

II. Joshua grants his petition (*v.* 13): *Joshua blessed him*, commended his bravery, applauded his request, and gave him what he asked. He also prayed for him, and for his good success in his intended undertaking against the sons of Anak. Joshua was both a prince and a prophet, and upon both accounts it was proper for him to give Caleb his blessing, for *the less is blessed of the better*. Hebron was settled on Caleb and his heirs (*v.* 14), *because he wholly followed the Lord God of Israel*. And happy are we if we follow him. Note, Singular piety shall be crowned with singular favours. Now, 1. We are here told what Hebron had been, the city of Arba, a great man among the Anakim (*v.* 15); we find it called *Kirjath-arba* (Gen. xxiii. 2), as the place where Sarah died. Hereabouts Abraham, Isaac, and Jacob lived most of their time in Canaan, and near to it was the cave of Machpelah, where they were buried, which perhaps had led Caleb hither when he went to spy out the land, and had made him covet this rather than any other part for his inheritance. 2. We are afterwards told what Hebron was. (1.) It was one of the cities belonging to the priests (Josh. xxi. 13), and a *city of refuge*, Josh. xx. 7. When Caleb had it, he contented himself with the country about it, and cheerfully gave the city to the priests, the Lord's ministers, thinking it could not be better bestowed, no, not upon his own children, nor that it was the less his own for being thus devoted to God. (2.) It was a royal city, and, in the beginning of David's reign, the metropolis of the kingdom of Judah; thither the people resorted to him, and there he reigned seven years. Thus highly was Caleb's city honoured; it is a pity there should have been such a blemish upon his family long after as Nabal was, who was *of the house of Caleb*, 1 Sam. xxv. 3. But the best men cannot entail their virtues.

CHAP. XV.

Though the land was not completely conquered, yet being (as was said in the close of the foregoing chapter) at rest from war for the present, and their armies all drawn out of the field to a general rendezvous at Gilgal, there they began to divide the land, though the work was afterwards perfected at Shiloh, ch. xviii. 1, &c. In this chapter we have the lot of the tribe of Judah, which in this, as in other things, had the precedency. I. The borders or bounds of the inheritance of Judah, ver. 1—12. II. The particular assignment of Hebron and the country thereabout to Caleb and his family, ver. 13—19. III. The names of the several cities that fell within Judah's lot, ver. 20—63.

THIS then was the lot of the tribe of the children of Judah by their families; *even* to the border of Edom the wilderness of Zin southward *was* the uttermost part of the south coast. 2 And their south border was from the shore of the salt sea, from the bay that looketh southward: 3 And it went out to the south side to Maaleh-acrabbim, and passed along to Zin, and ascended up on the south side unto Kadesh-barnea, and passed along to Hezron, and went up to Adar, and fetched a compass to Karkaa: 4 *From thence* it passed toward Azmon, and went out unto the river of Egypt; and the goings out of that coast were at the sea: this shall be your south coast. 5 And the east border *was* the salt sea, *even* unto the end of Jordan. And *their* border in the north quarter *was* from the bay of the sea at the uttermost part of Jordan: 6 And the border went up to Beth-hogla, and passed along by the north of Beth-arabah; and the border went up to the stone of Bohan the son of Reuben: 7 And the border went up toward Debir from the valley of Achor, and so northward, looking toward Gilgal, that *is* before the going up to Adummim, which *is* on the south side of the river: and the border passed toward the waters of En-shemesh, and the goings out thereof were at En-rogel: 8 And the border went up by the valley of the son of Hinnom unto the south side of the Jebusite; the same *is* Jerusalem: and the border went up to the top of the mountain that *lieth* before the valley of Hinnom westward, which *is* at the end of the valley of the giants northward: 9 And the border was drawn from the top of the hill unto the fountain of the water of Nephtoah, and went out to the cities of mount Ephron; and the border was drawn to Baalah, which *is* Kirjath-jearim: 10 And the border compassed from Baalah westward unto mount Seir, and passed along unto the side of mount Jearim, which *is* Chesalon, on the north side, and went down to Beth-shemesh, and passed on to Timnah: 11 And the border went out unto the side of Ekron northward: and the border was drawn to Shicron, and passed along to mount Baalah, and went out unto Jabneel; and the goings out of the border were at the sea. 12 And the west border *was* to the great sea, and the coast *thereof*. This *is* the coast of the children of Judah round about according to their families.

Judah and Joseph were the two sons of Jacob on whom Reuben's forfeited birthright devolved. Judah had the dominion entailed on him, and Joseph the double portion, and therefore these two tribes were first seated, Judah in the southern part of the land of Canaan and Joseph in the northern part, and on them the other seven did attend, and had their respective lots as appurtenances to these two; the lots of Benjamin, Simeon, and Dan, were appendant to Judah, and those of Issachar and Zebulun, Naphtali and Asher, to Joseph. These two were first set up to be provided for, it should seem, before there was such an exact survey of the land as we find afterwards, *ch.* xviii. 9. It is probable that the most considerable parts of the northern and southern countries, and those that lay nearest to Gilgal, and which the people were best acquainted with, were first put into two portions, and the lot was cast upon them between these two principal tribes, of the one of which Joshua was, and of the other Caleb, who was the first commissioner in this writ of partition; and, by the decision of that lot, the southern country, of which we have an account in this chapter, fell to Judah, and the northern, of which we have an account in the two following chapters, to Joseph. And when this was done there was a more equal dividend (either in quantity or quality) of the remainder among the seven tribes. And this, probably, was intended in that general rule which was given concerning this partition (Num. xxxiii. 54), *to the more you shall give the more inheritance, and to the fewer you shall give the less*, and *every man's inheritance shall be where his lot falleth*; that is, "You shall appoint two greater portions which shall be determined by lot to those more numerous tribes of Judah and Joseph, and then the rest shall be less portions to be allotted to the less numerous tribes." The former was done in Gilgal, the latter in Shiloh.

In these verses, we have the borders of the lot of Judah, which, as the rest, is said to be *by their families*, that is, with an eye to the number of their families. And it intimates that Joshua and Eleazar, and the rest of the commissioners, when they had by lot given each tribe its portion, did afterwards (it is probable by lot likewise) subdivide those larger portions, and assign to each family its inheritance, and then to each household, which would be better done by this supreme authority, and be apt to give less disgust than if it had been left to the inferior magistrates of each tribe to make that distribution. The borders of this tribe are here largely fixed, yet not unalterably, for a good deal of that which lies within these bounds was afterwards assigned to the lots of Simeon and Dan. 1. The eastern border was all, and only, the Salt Sea, *v.* 5. Every sea is salt, but this was of an extraordinary and more than natural saltness, the effects of that fire and brimstone with which Sodom and Gomorrah were destroyed in Abraham's time, whose ruins lie buried in the bottom of this dead water, which never either was moved itself or had any living thing in it. 2. The southern border was that of the land of Canaan in general, as will appear by comparing *v.* 1—4 with Num. xxxiv. 3—5. So that this powerful and warlike tribe of Judah guarded the frontiers of the whole land, on that side which lay towards their old sworn enemies (though their two fathers were twin-brethren), the Edomites. Our Lord therefore, who *sprang out of Judah*, and whose *the kingdom is, shall judge the mount of Esau*, Obad. 21. 3. The northern border divided it from the lot of Benjamin. In this, mention is made of *the stone of Bohan* a Reubenite (*v.* 6), who probably was a great commander of those forces of Reuben that came over Jordan, and died in the camp at Gilgal, and was buried not far off under this stone. The valley of Achor likewise lies upon this border (*v.* 7), to remind the men of Judah of the trouble which Achan, one of their tribe, gave to the congregation of Israel, that they might not be too much lifted up with their services. This northern line touched closely upon Jerusalem (*v.* 8), so closely as to include in the lot of this tribe Mount Zion and Mount Moriah, though the greater part of the city lay in the lot of Benjamin. 4. The west border went near to the great sea at first (*v.* 12), but afterwards the lot of the tribe of Dan took off a good part of Judah's lot on that side; for the lot was only to determine between Judah and Joseph, which should have the north and which the south, and not immovably to fix the border of either. Judah's inheritance had its boundaries determined. Though it was a powerful warlike tribe, and had a great interest in the other tribes, yet they must not therefore be left to their own choice, to enlarge their possessions at pleasure, but must live so as that their neighbours might live by them. Those that are placed high yet must not think to be *placed alone in the midst of the earth*.

13 And unto Caleb the son of Jephunneh he gave a part among

the children of Judah, according to the commandment of the LORD to Joshua, *even* the city of Arba the father of Anak, which *city is* Hebron. 14 And Caleb drove thence the three sons of Anak, Sheshai, and Ahiman, and Talmai, the children of Anak. 15 And he went up thence to the inhabitants of Debir: and the name of Debir before *was* Kirjath-sepher. 16 And Caleb said, He that smiteth Kirjath-sepher, and taketh it, to him will I give Achsah my daughter to wife. 17 And Othniel the son of Kenaz, the brother of Caleb, took it: and he gave him Achsah his daughter to wife. 18 And it came to pass, as she came *unto him*, that she moved him to ask of her father a field: and she lighted off *her* ass; and Caleb said unto her, what wouldest thou? 19 Who answered, Give me a blessing; for thou hast given me a south land; give me also springs of water. And he gave her the upper springs, and the nether springs.

The historian seems pleased with every occasion to make mention of Caleb and to do him honour, because he had honoured God in following him fully. Observe,

I. The grant Joshua made him of the mountain of Hebron for his inheritance is here repeated (*v.* 13), and it is said to be given him, 1. *According to the commandment of the Lord to Joshua.* Though Caleb, in his petition, had made out a very good title to it by promise, yet, because God had ordered Joshua to divide the land by lot, he would not in this one single instance, no, not to gratify his old friend Caleb, do otherwise, without orders from God, whose oracle, it is probable, he consulted upon this occasion. In every doubtful case it is very desirable to know the mind of God, and to see the way of our duty plain. 2. It is said to be a part *among the children of Judah;* though it was assigned him before the lot of that tribe came up, yet it proved, God so directing the lot, to be in the heart of that tribe, which was graciously ordered in kindness to him, that he might not be as one separated from his brethren and surrounded by those of other tribes.

II. Caleb having obtained this grant, we are told,

1. How he signalized his own valour in the conquest of Hebron (*v.* 14): *He drove thence the three sons of Anak,* he and those that he engaged to assist him in this service. This is mentioned here to show that the confidence he had expressed of success in this affair, through the presence of God with him (*ch.* xiv. 12), did not deceive him, but the event answered his expectation. It is not said that he *slew these giants,* but he *drove them thence,* which intimates that they retired upon his approach and fled before him; the strength and stature of their bodies could not keep up the courage of their minds, but with the countenances of lions they had the hearts of trembling hares. Thus does God often *cut off the spirit of princes* (Ps. lxxvi. 12), *take away the heart of the chief of the people* (Job xii. 24), and so shame the confidence of the proud; and thus if we resist the devil, that roaring lion, though he fall not, yet he will flee.

2. How he encouraged the valour of those about him in the conquest of Debir, *v.* 15, &c. It seems, though Joshua had once made himself master of Debir (*ch.* x. 39), yet the Canaanites had regained the possession in the absence of the army, so that the work had to be done a second time; and when Caleb had completed the reduction of Hebron, which was for himself and his own family, to show his zeal for the public good, as much as for his own private interest, he pushes on his conquest to Debir, and will not lay down his arms till he sees that city also effectually reduced, which lay but ten miles southward from Hebron, though he had not any particular concern in it, but the reducing of it would be to the general advantage of his tribe. Let us learn hence not to seek and mind our own things only, but to concern and engage ourselves for the welfare of the community we are members of; we are not born for ourselves, nor must we *live to ourselves.*

(1.) Notice is taken of the name of this city. It had been called *Kirjath-sepher, the city of a book,* and *Kirjath-sannah* (*v.* 49), which some translate *the city of learning* (so the LXX. Πόλις γραμμάτων), whence some conjecture that it had been a university among the Canaanites, like Athens in Greece, in which their youth were educated; or perhaps the books of their chronicles or records, or the antiquities of the nation, were laid up there; and, it may be, this was it that made Caleb so desirous to see Israel master of this city, that they might get acquainted with the ancient learning of the Canaanites.

(2.) The proffer that Caleb made of his daughter, and a good portion with her, to any one that would undertake to reduce that city, and to command the forces that should be employed in that service, *v.* 16. Thus Saul promised a daughter to him that would kill Goliath (1 Sam. xvii. 25), neither of them intending to force his daughter to marry such as she could not love, but both of them presuming upon their daughters' obedience, and submission to their fathers' will, though it might perhaps be contrary to their own humour or inclination. Caleb's family was not only honourable and wealthy, but religious; he that himself *followed the Lord fully* no doubt taught his children to do so, and therefore it could not but be a desirable match to any young gentleman. Caleb, in making the proposal, aims, [1.] To do service to his country by the reducing of that important place; and, [2.] To marry a daughter well, to a man of learning, that would have a particular affection for *the city of books,* and a man of war, that would be likely to serve his country, and do worthily in his generation. Could he but marry his child to a man of such a character, he would think her well bestowed, whether the share in the lot of his tribe were more or less.

(3.) The place was bravely taken by Othniel, a nephew of Caleb, whom probably Caleb had thoughts of when he made the proffer, *v.* 17. This Othniel, who thus signalized himself when he was young, had long after, in his advanced years, the honour to be both a deliverer and a judge in Israel, the first single person that presided in their affairs after Joshua's death. It is good for those who are setting out in the world to begin betimes with that which is great and good, that, excelling in service when they are young, they may excel in honour when they grow old.

(4.) Hereupon (all parties being agreed) Othniel married his cousin-german Achsah, Caleb's daughter. It is probable that he had a kindness for her before, which put him upon this bold undertaking to obtain her. Love to his country, an ambition of honour, and a desire to find favour with the princes of his people, might not have engaged him in this great action, but his affection for Achsah did. This made it intolerable to him to think that any one should do more to win her favour than he would, and so inspired him with this generous fire. Thus is love strong as death, and jealousy cruel as the grave.

(5.) Because the historian is now upon the dividing of the land, he gives us an account of Achsah's portion, which was in land, as more valuable because enjoyed by virtue of the divine promise, though we may suppose the conquerors of Canaan, who had had the spoil of so many rich cities, were full of money too. [1.] Some land she obtained by Caleb's free grant, which was allowed while she married within her own tribe and family, as Zelophehad's daughters did. He *gave her a south land, v.* 19. Land indeed, but *a south land,* dry, and apt to be parched. [2.] She obtained more upon her request; she would have had her husband to ask for a field, probably some particular field, or champaign ground, which belonged to Caleb's lot, and joined to that south land which he had settled upon his daughter at marriage. She thought her husband had the best interest in her father, who, no doubt, was extremely pleased with his late glorious achievement, but he thought it was more proper for her to ask, and she would be more likely to prevail; accordingly she did, submitting to her husband's judgment, though contrary to her own; and she managed the undertaking with great address. *First,* She took the opportunity when her father brought her home to the house of her husband, when the satisfaction of having disposed of his daughter so well would make him think nothing too much to do for her. *Secondly,* She *lighted off her ass,* in token of respect and reverence to her father, whom she would honour still, as much as before her marriage. She *cried* or *sighed* from off her ass, so the LXX. and the vulgar Latin read it; she expressed some grief and concern, that she might give her father occasion to ask her what she wanted. *Thirdly,* She calls it *a blessing,* because it would add much to the comfort of her settlement; and she was sure that, since she married not only with her father's consent, but in obedience to his command, he would not deny her his blessing. *Fourthly,* She asks only for the *water,* without which the ground she had would be of little use either for tillage or pasture, but she means the field in which the springs of water were. The modesty and reasonableness of her request gave it a great advantage. Earth without water would be like a tree without sap, or the body of an animal without blood; therefore, when God *gathered the waters into one place,* he wisely and graciously left some in every place, that the earth might be enriched for the service of man. See Ps. civ. 10, &c. Well, Achsah gained her point; her father gave her what she asked, and perhaps more, for *he gave her the upper springs and the nether springs,* two fields so called from the springs that were in them, as we commonly distinguish between the higher field and the lower field. Those who understand it but of one field, watered both with the rain of heaven and the springs that issued out of the bowels of the earth, give countenance to the allusion we commonly make to this, when we pray for spiritual and heavenly blessings which relate to our souls as blessings of the upper springs, and those which relate to the body and the life that now is as blessings of the nether springs.

From this story we learn, 1. That it is no breach of the tenth commandment moderately to desire those comforts and conveniences of this life which we see attainable in a fair and regular way. 2. That husbands and wives should mutually advise, and jointly agree, about that which is for the common good of their family; and much more should they concur in asking of their heavenly Father the best blessings, those of the upper springs. 3. That parents must never think that lost which is bestowed upon their children for their real advantage, but must be free in giving them portions as well as maintenance, especially when they are dutiful. Caleb had sons (1 Chron. iv. 15), and yet gave thus liberally to his daughter. Those parents forget themselves and their relation who grudge their children what is convenient for them when they can conveniently part with it.

20 This *is* the inheritance of the tribe of the children of Judah according to their families. 21 And the uttermost cities of the tribe of the children of Judah toward the coast of Edom southward were Kabzeel, and Eder, and Jagur, 22 And Kinah, and Dimonah, and Adadah, 23 And Kedesh, and Hazor, and Ithnan, 24 Ziph, and Telem, and Bealoth, 25 And Hazor, Hadattah, and Kerioth, *and* Hezron, which *is* Hazor, 26 Amam, and Shema, and Moladah, 27 And Hazar-gaddah, and Heshmon, and Beth-palet, 28 And Hazar-shual, and Beer-sheba, and Bizjothjah, 29 Baalah, and Iim, and Azem, 30 And Eltolad, and Chesil, and Hormah, 31 And Ziklag, and Madmannah, and Sansannah, 32 And Lebaoth, and Shilhim, and Ain, and Rimmon: all the cities *are* twenty and nine, with their villages: 33 *And* in the valley, Eshtaol, and Zoreah, and Ashnah, 34 And Zanoah, and En-gannim, Tappuah, and Enam, 35 Jarmuth, and Adullam, Socoh, and Azekah, 36 And Sharaim, and Adithaim, and Gederah, and Gederothaim; fourteen cities with their villages: 37 Zenan, and Hadashah, and Migdal-gad, 38 And Dilean, and Mizpeh, and Joktheel, 39 Lachish, and Bozkath, and Eglon, 40 And Cabbon, and Lahmam, and Kithlish, 41 And Gederoth, Beth-dagon, and Naamah, and Makkedah; sixteen cities with their villages: 42 Libnah, and Ether, and Ashan, 43 And Jiphtah, and Ashnah, and Nezib, 44 And Keilah, and Achzib, and Mareshah; nine cities with their villages: 45 Ekron, with her towns and her villages: 46 From Ekron even unto the sea, all that *lay* near Ashdod, with their villages: 47 Ashdod with her towns and her villages, Gaza with her towns and her villages, unto the river of Egypt, and the great sea, and the border *thereof:* 48 And in the mountains, Shamir, and Jattir, and Socoh, 49 And Dannah, and Kirjath-sannah, which *is* Debir, 50 And Anab, and Eshtemoh, and Anim, 51 And Goshen, and Holon, and Giloh; eleven cities with their villages: 52 Arab, and Dumah, and Eshean, 53 And Janum, and Beth-tappuah, and Aphekah, 54 And Humtah, and Kirjath-arba, which *is* Hebron, and Zior; nine cities with their villages: 55 Maon, Carmel, and Ziph, and Juttah, 56 And Jezreel, and Jokdeam, and Zanoah, 57 Cain, Gibeah, and Timnah; ten cities with their villages: 58 Halhul, Beth-zur, and Gedor, 59 And Maarath, and Beth-anoth, and Eltekon; six cities with their villages: 60 Kirjath-baal, which *is* Kirjath-jearim, and Rabbah; two cities with their villages: 61 In the wilderness, Beth-arabah, Middin, and Secacah, 62 And Nibshan, and the city of Salt, and En-gedi; six cities with their villages. 63 As for the Jebusites the inhabitants of Jerusalem, the children of Judah could not drive them out: but the Jebusites dwell with the children of Judah at Jerusalem unto this day.

We have here a list of the several cities that fell within the lot of the tribe of Judah, which are mentioned by name, that they might know their own, and both keep it and keep to it, and might neither through cowardice nor sloth lose the possession of what was their own.

I. The cities are here named, and numbered in several classes, which they then could account for the reason of better than we can now. Here are, 1. Some that are said to be the uttermost cities *towards the coast of Edom, v.* 21—32. Here are thirty-eight named, and yet said to be *twenty-nine* (*v.* 32), because nine of these were afterwards transferred to the lot of Simeon, and are reckoned as belonging to that, as appears by comparing *ch.* xix. 2, &c.; therefore those only are counted (though the rest are named) which remained to Judah. 2. Others that are said to be *in the valley* (*v.* 33) are counted to be fourteen, yet fifteen are named; but it is probable that Gederah and Gederathaim were either two names or two parts of one and the same city. 3. Then sixteen are named without any head of distinction, *v.* 37—41, and nine more, *v.* 42—44. 4. Then the three Philistine-cities, Ekron, Ashdod, and Gaza, *v.* 45—47. 5. Cities *in the moun-*

tains, eleven in all (*v.* 48—51), nine more (*v.* 52—54), ten more (*v.* 55—57), six more (*v.* 58, 59), then two (*v.* 60), and six in the wilderness, a part of the country not so thick of inhabitants as some others were.

II. Now here, 1. We do not find Bethlehem, which was afterwards the city of David, and was ennobled by the birth of our Lord Jesus in it. But that city, which at the best was but *little among the thousands of Judah* (Mic. v. 2), except that it was thus dignified, was now so little as not to be accounted one of the cities, but perhaps was one of the villages not named. Christ came to give honour to the places he was related to, not to receive honour from them. 2. Jerusalem is said to continue in the hands of the Jebusites (*v.* 63), *for the children of Judah could not drive them out*, through their sluggishness, stupidity, and unbelief. Had they attempted it with vigour and resolution, we have reason to think God would not have been wanting to them to give them success; but they could not do it, because they would not. Jerusalem was afterwards to be the holy city, the royal city, the city of the great King, the brightest ornament of all the land of Israel. God had designed it should be so. It may therefore be justly looked upon as a punishment of their neglect to conquer other cities which God had given them that they were so long kept out of this. 3. Among the cities of Judah (in all 114) we meet with Libnah, which in Joram's days revolted, and probably set up for a free independent state (2 Kings viii. 22), and Lachish, where king Amaziah was slain (1 Kings xiv. 19); it led the dance in idolatry (Mic. i. 13); it was the *beginning of sin to the daughter of Zion.* Giloh, Ahithophel's town, is here mentioned, and Tekoa, of which the prophet Amos was, and near which Jehoshaphat obtained that glorious victory, 2 Chron. xx. 20, &c., and Maresha, where Asa was a conqueror. Many of the cities of this tribe occur in the history of David's troubles. Adullam, Ziph, Keilah, Maon, Engedi, Ziklag, here reckoned in this tribe, were places near which David had most of his haunts; for, though sometimes Saul drove him out from the inheritance of the Lord, yet he kept as close to it as he could. The wilderness of Judah he frequented much, and in it John Baptist preached, and there the kingdom of heaven commenced, Matt. iii. 1. The riches of this country no doubt answered Jacob's blessing of this tribe, that he should *wash his garments in wine*, Gen. xlix. 11. And, in general, *Judah, thou art he whom thy brethren shall praise*, not envy.

CHAP. XVI.

It is a pity that this and the following chapter should be separated, for both of them give us the lot of the children of Joseph, Ephraim and Manasseh, who, next to Judah, were to have the post of honour, and therefore had the first and best portion in the northern part of Canaan, as Judah now had in the southern part. In this chapter we have, I. A general account of the lot of these two tribes together, ver. 1—4. II. The borders of the lot of Ephraim in particular, ver. 5—10. That of Manasseh following in the next chapter.

AND the lot of the children of Joseph fell from Jordan by Jericho, unto the water of Jericho on the east, to the wilderness that goeth up from Jericho throughout mount Beth-el, 2 And goeth out from Beth-el to Luz, and passeth along unto the borders of Archi to Ataroth, 3 And goeth down westward to the coast of Japhleti, unto the coast of Beth-horon the nether, and to Gezer: and the goings out thereof are at the sea. 4 So the children of Joseph, Manasseh and Ephraim, took their inheritance.

Though Joseph was one of the younger sons of Jacob, yet he was his eldest by his most just and best beloved wife Rachel, was himself *his best beloved son*, and had been the greatest ornament and support of his family, kept it from perishing in a time of famine, and had been the *shepherd and stone of Israel*, and therefore his posterity were very much favoured by the lot. Their portion lay in the very heart of the land of Canaan. It extended from Jordan in the east (*v.* 1) to the sea, the Mediterranean Sea, in the west, so that it took up the whole breadth of Canaan from side to side; and no question the fruitfulness of the soil answered the blessings both of Jacob and Moses, Gen. xlix. 25, 26, and Deut. xxxiii. 13, &c. The portions allotted to Ephraim and Manasseh are not so particularly described as those of the other tribes; we have only the limits and boundaries of them, not the particular cities in them, as before we had the cities of Judah and afterwards those of the other tribes. For this no reason can be assigned, unless we may suppose that Joshua being himself of the children of Joseph they referred it to him alone to distribute among them the several cities that lay within their lot, and therefore did not bring in the names of their cities to the great council of their princes who sat upon this affair, by which means it came to pass that they were not inserted with the rest in the books.

5 And the border of the children of Ephraim according to their families was *thus:* even the border of their inheritance on the east side was Ataroth-addar, unto Beth-horon the upper; 6 And the border went out toward the sea to Michmethah on the north side; and the border went about eastward unto Taanath-shiloh, and passed by it on the east to Janohah; 7 And it went down from Janohah to Ataroth, and to Naarath, and came to

Jericho, and went out at Jordan. 8 The border went out from Tappuah westward unto the river Kanah; and the goings out thereof were at the sea. This *is* the inheritance of the tribe of the children of Ephraim by their families. 9 And the separate cities for the children of Ephraim *were* among the inheritance of the children of Manasseh, all the cities with their villages. 10 And they drave not out the Canaanites that dwelt in Gezer: but the Canaanites dwell among the Ephraimites unto this day, and serve under tribute.

Here, 1. The border of the lot of Ephraim is set down, by which it was divided on the south from Benjamin and Dan, who lay between it and Judah, and on the north from Manasseh; for east and west it reached from Jordan to the great sea. The learned, who aim to be exact in drawing the line according to the directions here, find themselves very much at a loss, the description being short and intricate. The report of those who in these latter ages have travelled those countries will not serve to clear the difficulties, so vastly unlike is it now to what it was then; not only cities have been so destroyed as that no mark nor footstep of them remains, but brooks are dried up, rivers alter their courses, and *even the mountain falling cometh to nought, and the rock is removed out of his place,* Job xiv. 18. Unless I could hope to solve the doubts that arise upon this draught of the border of Ephraim, it is to no purpose to mention them: no doubt it was then perfectly understood, so as that the first intention of recording it was effectually answered, which was to notify the ancient landmarks, which posterity must by no means remove. 2. Some separate cities are spoken of, that lay not within these borders, at least not if the line was drawn direct, but lay within the lot of Manasseh (*v.* 9), which might better be read, *and there were separate cities for the children of Ephraim among the inheritance of the children of Manasseh,* because it proved that Manasseh could spare them, and Ephraim had need of them, and it might be hoped that no inconvenience would arise from this mixture of these two tribes together, who were both the sons of Joseph, and should *love as brethren.* And by this it appears that though, when the tribes were numbered in the plains of Moab, Manasseh had got the start of Ephraim in number, for Manasseh was then 52,000, and Ephraim but 32,000 (Num. xxvi. 34, 37), yet by the time they were well settled in Canaan the hands were crossed again, and the blessing of Moses was verified, Deut. xxxiii. 17, *They are the ten thousands of Ephraim and they are the thousands of Manasseh.* Families and kingdoms are diminished and increased, increased and diminished again, as God pleases. 3. A brand is put upon the Ephraimites, that they did not drive out the Canaanites from Gezer (*v.* 10), either through carelessness or cowardice, either for want of faith in the promise of God, that he would give them success if they would make a vigorous effort, or for want of zeal for the command of God, which obliged them *utterly to drive out the Canaanites,* and to make no peace with them. And, though they hoped to satisfy the law by putting them under tribute, yet (as Calvin thinks) this made the matter worse, for it shows that they spared them out of covetousness, that they might be profited by their labours, and by dealing with them for their tribute they were in danger of being infected with their idolatry; yet some think that, when they brought them under tribute, they obliged them to renounce their idols, and to observe the seven precepts of the sons of Noah; and I should think so, but that we find in the sequel of the story that the Israelites were so far from restraining idolatry in others that they soon fell into it themselves. Many famous places were within this lot of the tribe of Ephraim, though not mentioned here. In it were Ramah, Samuel's city (called in the New Testament *Arimathea,* of which Joseph was, that took care of our Saviour's burial), and Shiloh, where the tabernacle was first set up. Tirzah also, the royal city of Jeroboam and his successors, and Deborah's palm-tree, under which she judged Israel, were in this tribe. Samaria, built by Omri after the burning of the royal palace of Tirzah, was in this tribe, and was long the royal city of the kingdom of the ten tribes; not far from it were Shechem, and the mountains Ebal and Gerizim, and Sychar, near which was Jacob's well, where Christ talked with the woman of Samaria. We read much of Mount Ephraim in the story of the Judges, and of a city called *Ephraim,* it is probable in this tribe, to which Christ retired, John xi. 54. The whole kingdom of the ten tribes is often, in the prophets, especially in Hosea, called *Ephraim.*

CHAP. XVII.

The half tribe of Manasseh comes next to be provided for; and here we have, I. The families of that tribe that were to be portioned, ver. 1—6. II. The country that fell to their lot, ver. 7—13. III. The joint request of the two tribes that descended from Joseph, for the enlargement of their lot, and Joshua's answer to that request, ver. 14—18.

THERE was also a lot for the tribe of Manasseh; for he *was* the firstborn of Joseph; *to wit,* for Machir the firstborn of Manasseh, the father of Gilead: because he was a man of war, therefore he had Gilead and Bashan. 2 There was also *a lot* for the rest of the children of Manasseh by their families; for the children of Abiezer, and for the children of Helek, and for the children of Asriel, and for the children of Shechem, and for the children of Hepher, and for the children of Shemida: these *were* the male children of Manasseh the son of Joseph by their families. 3 But Zelophehad, the son of Hepher, the son of Gilead, the son of Machir, the son of Manasseh, had no sons, but daughters: and these *are* the names of his daughters, Mahlah, and Noah, Hoglah, Milcah, and Tirzah. 4 And they came near before Eleazar the priest, and before Joshua the son of Nun, and before the princes, saying, The LORD commanded Moses to give us an inheritance among our brethren. Therefore according to the commandment of the LORD he gave them an inheritance among the brethren of their father. 5 And there fell ten portions to Manasseh, beside the land of Gilead and Bashan, which *were* on the other side Jordan; 6 Because the daughters of Manasseh had an inheritance among his sons: and the rest of Manasseh's sons had the land of Gilead.

Manasseh was itself but one half of the tribe of Joseph, and yet was divided and subdivided. 1. It was divided into two parts, one already settled on the other side Jordan, consisting of those who were the posterity of Machir, *v.* 1. This Machir was born to Manasseh in Egypt; there he had signalized himself as a man of war, probably in the contests between the Ephraimites and the men of Gath, 1 Chron. vii. 21. His warlike disposition descended to his posterity, and therefore Moses gave them Gilead and Bashan, on the other side Jordan, of which before, *ch.* xiii. 31. It is here said that the lot came to Manasseh, *for he was the first-born of* Joseph. Bishop Patrick thinks it should be translated, *though he was the first-born of* Joseph, and then the meaning is plain, that the second lot was for Manasseh, because, though he was the first-born, yet Jacob had preferred Ephraim before him. See the names of those heads of the families that settled on the other side Jordan, 1 Chron. v. 24. 2. That part on this side Jordan was subdivided into ten families, *v.* 5. There were six sons of Gilead here named (*v.* 2), the same that are recorded Num. xxvi. 30—32, only that he who is there called *Jezeer* is here called *Abiezer.* Five of these sons had each of them their portion; the sixth, which was Hepher, had his male line cut off in his son Zelophehad, who left daughters only, five in number, of whom we have often read, and these five had each of them a portion; though perhaps, they claiming under Hepher, all their five portions were but equal to one of the portions of the five sons. Or if Hepher had other sons besides Zelophehad, in whom the name of his family was kept up, their posterity married to the daughters of Zelophehad the elder brother, and in their right had these portions assigned them. See Num. xxxvi. 12. Here is, (1.) The claim which the daughters of Zelophehad made, grounded upon the command God gave to Moses concerning them, *v.* 4. They had themselves, when they were young, pleaded their own cause before Moses, and obtained the grant of an inheritance with their brethren, and now they would not lose the benefit of that grant for want of speaking to Joshua, but seasonably put in their demand themselves, as it should seem, and not their husbands for them.. (2.) The assignment of their portions according to their claim. Joshua knew very well what God had ordered in their case, and did not object that they having not served in the wars of Canaan there was no reason why they should share in the possessions of Canaan, but readily *gave them an inheritance among the brethren of their father.* And now they reaped the benefit of their own pious zeal and prudent forecast in this matter. Thus those who take care in the wilderness of this world to make sure to themselves a place in the inheritance of the saints in light will certainly have the comfort of it in the other world, while those that neglect it now will lose it for ever.

7 And the coast of Manasseh was from Asher to Michmethah, that *lieth* before Shechem; and the border went along on the right hand unto the inhabitants of En-tappuah. 8 *Now* Manasseh had the land of Tappuah: but Tappuah on the border of Manasseh *belonged* to the children of Ephraim; 9 And the coast descended unto the river Kanah, southward of the river: these cities of Ephraim *are* among the cities of Manasseh: the coast of Manasseh also *was* on the north side of the river, and the outgoings of it were at the sea: 10 Southward *it was* Ephraim's, and northward *it was* Manasseh's, and the sea is his border; and they met together in Asher on the north, and in Issachar on the east. 11 And Manasseh had in Issachar and in Asher Beth-shean and

her towns, and Ibleam and her towns, and the inhabitants of Dor and her towns, and the inhabitants of En-dor and her towns, and the inhabitants of Taanach and her towns, and the inhabitants of Megiddo and her towns, *even* three countries. 12 Yet the children of Manasseh could not drive out *the inhabitants of* those cities; but the Canaanites would dwell in that land. 13 Yet it came to pass, when the children of Israel were waxen strong, that they put the Canaanites to tribute; but did not utterly drive them out.

We have here a short account of the lot of this half tribe. It reached from Jordan on the east to the great sea on the west; on the south it lay all along contiguous to Ephraim, but on the north it abutted upon Asher and Issachar. Asher lay north-west, and Issachar north-east, which seems to be the meaning of that (*v.* 10), that they (that is, Manasseh and Ephraim, as related to it, both together making the tribe of Joseph) met in Asher on the north and Issachar on the east, for Ephraim itself reached not those tribes. Some things are particularly observed concerning this lot:—1. That there was great communication between this tribe and that of Ephraim. The city of Tappuah belonged to Ephraim, but the country adjoining to Manasseh (*v.* 8); there were likewise many cities of Ephraim that lay within the border of Manasseh (*v.* 9), of which before, *ch.* xvi. 9. 2. That Manasseh likewise had cities with their appurtenances in the tribes of Issachar and Asher (*v.* 11), God so ordering it, that though every tribe had its peculiar inheritance, which might not be alienated from it, yet they should thus intermix one with another, to keep up mutual acquaintance and correspondence among the tribes, and to give occasion for the doing of good offices one to another, as became those who, though of different tribes, were all one Israel, and were bound to love as brethren. 3. That they suffered the Canaanites to live among them, contrary to the command of God, serving their own ends by conniving at them, for they made them tributaries, *v.* 12, 13. The Ephraimites had done the same (*ch.* xvi. 10), and from them perhaps the Manassites learned it, and with their example excused themselves in it. The most remarkable person of this half tribe in after-time was Gideon, whose great actions were done within this lot. He was of the family of Abiezer; Cesarea was in this lot, and Antipatris, famed in the latter ages of the Jewish state.

14 And the children of Joseph spake unto Joshua, saying, Why hast thou given me *but* one lot and one portion to inherit, seeing I *am* a great people, forasmuch as the LORD hath blessed me hitherto? 15 And Joshua answered them, if thou *be* a great people, *then* get thee up to the wood *country,* and cut down for thyself there in the land of the Perizzites and of the giants, if mount Ephraim be too narrow for thee. 16 And the children of Joseph said, The hill is not enough for us: and all the Canaanites that dwell in the land of the valley have chariots of iron, *both they* who *are* of Beth-shean and her towns, and *they* who *are* of the valley of Jezreel. 17 And Joshua spake unto the house of Joseph, *even* to Ephraim and to Manasseh, saying, Thou *art* a great people, and hast great power: thou shalt not have one lot *only:* 18 But the mountain shall be thine; for it *is* a wood, and thou shalt cut it down: and the outgoings of it shall be thine: for thou shalt drive out the Canaanites, though they have iron chariots, *and* though they *be* strong.

Here, I. The children of Joseph quarrel with their lot; if they had had any just cause to quarrel with it, we have reason to think Joshua would have relieved them, by adding to it, or altering it, which it does not appear he did. It is probable, because Joshua was himself of the tribe of Ephraim, they promised themselves that they should have some particular favour shown them, and should not be confined to the decision of the lot so closely as the other tribes; but Joshua makes them know that in the discharge of his office, as a public person, he had no more regard to his own tribe than to any other, but would administer impartially, without favour or affection, wherein he has left an excellent example to all in public trusts. It was a very competent provision that was made for them, as much, for aught that appears, as they were able to manage, and yet they call it in disdain but *one lot,* as if that which was assigned to them both was scarcely sufficient for one. The word for *complainers* (Jude 16) is μεμψίμοιροι, blamers of their lot, like the children of Joseph, who would have that altered, the disposal whereof is from the Lord. Two things they suggest, to enforce their petition for an augmentation of their lot:—1. That they were very numerous, through the blessing of God upon them (*v.* 14): *I am a great people, for the Lord has blessed me;* and we have reason to hope that he that hath sent mouths will send meat. "*I am a great people,* and in so small a lot shall not have *room to thrive.*" Yet observe, when they speak thankfully of their present increase, they do not speak confidently of the continuance of it. "The Lord has blessed me hitherto, however he may see fit to deal with me for the future." The uncertainty of what may be must not make us unthankful for what has been and is done in kindness to us. 2. That a good part of that country which had now fallen to their lot was in the hands of the Canaanites, and that they were formidable enemies, who brought into the field of battle *chariots of iron* (*v.* 16), that is, chariots with long scythes fastened to the sides of them, or the axle-tree, which made great destruction of all that came in their way, mowing them down like corn. They urge that though they had a good portion assigned them, yet it was in bad hands, and they could not come to the possession of it, wishing to have their lot in those countries that were more thoroughly reduced than this was.

II. Joshua endeavours to reconcile them to their lot. He owns they were a *great people,* and being two tribes ought to have more than *one lot only* (*v.* 17), but tells them that what had fallen to their share would be a sufficient lot for them both, if they would but work and fight. They desired a lot in which they might indulge themselves in ease and luxury. "No," says Joshua, "you must not count upon that; *in the sweat of thy face shalt thou eat bread* is a sentence in force even in Canaan itself." He retorts their own argument, that they were a *great people.* "If so, you are the better able to help yourselves, and have the less reason to expect help from others. If thou hast many mouths to be filled, thou hast twice as many hands to be employed; earn, and then eat." 1. He bids them work for more (*v.* 15): "*Get thee up to the wood-country,* which is within thy own border, and let all hands be set to work to cut down the trees, rid the rough lands, and make them, with art and industry, good arable ground." Note, Many wish for larger possessions who do not cultivate and make the best of what they have, think they should have more talents given them who do not trade with those with which they are entrusted. Most people's poverty is the effect of their idleness; would they dig, they need not beg. 2. He bids them fight for more (*v.* 17, 18), when they pleaded that they could not come at the wood-lands he spoke of because in the valley between them and it there were Canaanites whom they durst not enter the lists with. "Never fear them," said Joshua; "thou hast God on thy side, and *thou shalt drive out the Canaanites,* if thou wilt set about it in good earnest, *though they have iron chariots.*" We straiten ourselves by apprehending the difficulties in the way of our enlargement to be greater than really they are. What can be insuperable to faith and holy resolution?

CHAP. XVIII.

In this chapter we have, I. The setting up of the tabernacle at Shiloh, ver. 1. II. The stirring up of the seven tribes that were yet unsettled to look after their lot, and the putting of them in a method for it, by Joshua, ver. 2—7. III. The distributing of the land into seven lots, by certain men employed for that purpose, ver. 8, 9. IV. The determining of these seven portions to the seven tribes yet unprovided for by lot, ver. 10. V. The particular lot of the tribe of Benjamin, the borders of it, ver. 11—20. And the cities contained in it, ver. 21—28. The other six tribes we shall find well provided for in the next chapter.

AND the whole congregation of the children of Israel assembled together at Shiloh, and set up the tabernacle of the congregation there. And the land was subdued before them.

In the midst of the story of the dividing of the land comes in this account of the setting up of the tabernacle, which had hitherto continued in its old place in the centre of their camp; but now that three of the four squadrons that used to surround it in the wilderness were broken and diminished, those of Judah, Ephraim, and Reuben, by the removal of those tribes to their respective possessions, and that of Dan only remained entire, it was time to think of removing the tabernacle itself into a city. Many a time the priests and Levites had taken it down, carried it, and set it up again in the wilderness, according to the directions given them (Num. iv. 5, &c.); but now they must do it for good and all, not one of the stakes thereof must any more be removed, nor any of the cords thereof broken, Isa. xxxiii. 20. Observe,

I. The place to which the tabernacle was removed, and in which it was set up. It was *Shiloh,* a city in the lot of Ephraim, but lying close upon the lot of Benjamin. Doubtless God himself did some way or other direct them to this place, for he had promised to *choose the place* where he would make *his name to dwell,* Deut. xii. 11. It is most probable God made known his mind in this matter by the judgment of Urim. This place was pitched upon, 1. Because it was in the heart of the country, nearer the centre than Jerusalem was, and therefore the more convenient for the meeting of all Israel there from the several parts of the country; it had been in the midst of their camp in the wilderness, and therefore must now be in the midst of their nation, as that which sanctified the whole, and was *the glory in the midst of them.* See Ps. xlvi. 5. 2. Because it was in the lot of that tribe of which Joshua was, who was now their chief magistrate, and it would be both for his honour and convenience and for the advantage of the country to have it near him. The testimony of Israel and the thrones of judgment do well together, Ps. cxxii. 4, 5. 3. Some think there was an eye to the name of the place, *Shiloh* being the name by which the Messiah was known in dying Jacob's prophecy (Gen. xlix. 10), which prophecy, no doubt, was well known among the Jews; the setting up of the tabernacle in Shiloh gave them a hint that in that Shiloh whom Jacob spoke of all the ordinances of this worldly sanctuary should have their accomplishment in a greater and more perfect tabernacle, Heb. ix. 1, 11. And Dr. Lightfoot thinks that the place where the tabernacle was set up was therefore called *Shiloh*, because of the peaceableness of the land at this time; as afterwards in Salem was his temple, which also signifies *peaceable*.

II. The solemn manner of doing it: *The whole congregation assembled together* to attend the solemnity, to do honour to the ark of God, as the token of his presence, and to bid it welcome to its settlement. Every Israelite was interested in it, and therefore all testified their joy and satisfaction upon this occasion. See 2 Sam. vi. 15. It is probable those tribes that were yet encamped when the tabernacle was removed to Shiloh decamped from Gilgal and pitched about Shiloh, for every true Israelite will desire to fix where God's tabernacle fixes. Mention is made, on this occasion, of the land being subdued before them, to intimate that the country, hereabouts at least, being thoroughly reduced, they met with no opposition, nor were they apprehensive of any danger, but thought it time to make this grateful acknowledgment of God's goodness to them in the constant series of successes with which he had blessed them. It was a good presage of a comfortable settlement to themselves in Canaan, when their first care was to see the ark well settled as soon as they had a safe place ready to settle it in. Here the ark continued about 300 years, till the sins of Eli's house forfeited the ark, lost it and ruined Shiloh, and its ruins were long after made use of as warnings to Jerusalem. *Go, see what I did to Shiloh*, Jer. vii. 12; Ps. lxxviii. 60.

2 And there remained among the children of Israel seven tribes, which had not yet received their inheritance. 3 And Joshua said unto the children of Israel, How long *are* ye slack to go to possess the land, which the LORD God of your fathers hath given you? 4 Give out from among you three men for *each* tribe: and I will send them, and they shall rise, and go through the land, and describe it according to the inheritance of them; and they shall come *again* to me. 5 And they shall divide it into seven parts: Judah shall abide in their coast on the south, and the house of Joseph shall abide in their coasts on the north. 6 Ye shall therefore describe the land *into* seven parts, and bring *the description* hither to me, that I may cast lots for you here before the LORD our God. 7 But the Levites have no part among you; for the priesthood of the LORD *is* their inheritance: and Gad, and Reuben, and half the tribe of Manasseh, have received their inheritance beyond Jordan on the east, which Moses the servant of the LORD gave them. 8 And the men arose, and went away: and Joshua charged them that went to describe the land, saying, Go and walk through the land, and describe it, and come again to me, that I may here cast lots for you before the LORD in Shiloh. 9 And the men went and passed through the land, and described it by cities into seven parts in a book, and came *again* to Joshua to the host at Shiloh. 10 And Joshua cast lots for them in Shiloh before the LORD: and there Joshua divided the land unto the children of Israel according to their divisions.

Here, I. Joshua reproves those tribes which were yet unsettled that they did not bestir themselves to gain a settlement in the land which God had given them. Seven tribes were yet unprovided for, though sure of an inheritance, yet uncertain where it should be, and it seems in no great care about it, *v.* 2. And with them Joshua reasons (*v.* 3): *How long are you slack?* 1. They were too well pleased with their present condition, liked well enough to live in a body together, the more the merrier, and, like the Babel-builders, had no mind to be scattered abroad and break good company. The spoil of the cities they had taken served them to live plentifully upon for the present, and they banished the thoughts of time to come. Perhaps the tribes of Judah and Joseph, who had already received their inheritance in the countries next adjoining, were generous in entertaining their brethren who were yet unprovided for, so that they went from one good house to another among their friends, with which, instead of grudging that they were postponed, they were so well pleased that they cared not for going to houses of their own. 2. They were slothful and dilatory. It may be they wished the thing done, but had not spirit to stir in it, or move towards the doing of it, though it was so much for their own advantage; like the sluggard, that *hides his hand in his bosom, and it grieves him to bring it to his mouth again.* The countries that remained to be divided lay at a distance, and some parts of them in the hands of the Canaanites. If they go to take possession of them, the cities must be rebuilt or repaired, they must drive their flocks and herds a great way, and carry their wives and children to strange places, and this will not be done without care and pains, and breaking through some hardships; thus *he that observes the wind shall not sow, and he that regards the clouds shall not reap*, Eccl. xi. 4. Note, Many are diverted from real duties, and debarred from real comforts, by seeming difficulties. God by his grace has given us a title to a good land, the heavenly Canaan, but we are *slack to take possession;* we enter not into that rest, as we might by faith, and hope, and holy joy; we live not in heaven, as we might by setting our affections on things above and having our conversation there. How long shall it be thus with us? How long shall we thus stand in our own light, and *forsake our own mercies* for lying vanities? Joshua was sensible of the inconveniences of this delay, that, while they neglected to take possession of the land that was conquered, the Canaanites were recovering strength and spirit, and fortifying themselves in the places that were yet in their hands, which would make the total expulsion of them the more difficult. They would lose their advantages by not following their blow; and therefore, *as an eagle stirreth up her nest*, so Joshua stirs them up to take possession of their lot. He is ready to do his part, if they will but do theirs.

II. He puts them in a way to settle themselves.

1. The land that remained must be surveyed, an account taken of the cities, and the territories belonging to them, *v.* 4. These must be divided into seven equal parts, as near as they could guess at their true value, which they must have an eye to, and not merely to the number of the cities and extent of the country. Judah is fixed on the south and Joseph on the north of Shiloh, to protect the tabernacle (*v.* 5), and therefore they need not describe their country, but those countries only that were yet undisposed of. He gives a reason (*v.* 7) why they must divide it into seven parts only, because the Levites were to have no temporal estate (as we say), but their benefices only, which were entailed upon their families: *The priesthood of the Lord is their inheritance*, and a very honourable, comfortable, plentiful inheritance it was. Gad and Reuben, with half of the tribe of Manasseh, were already fixed, and needed not to have any further care taken of them. Now, (1.) The surveyors were three men out of each of the seven tribes that were to be provided for (*v.* 4), one-and-twenty in all, who perhaps for greater expedition, because they had already lost time, divided themselves into three companies, one of each tribe in each company, and took each their district to survey. The matter was thus referred equally, that there might be neither any partiality used in making up the seven lots, nor any shadow of suspicion given, but all might be satisfied that they had right done them. (2.) The survey was accordingly made, and brought in to Joshua, *v.* 8, 9. Josephus says it was seven months in the doing. And we must in it observe, [1.] The faith and courage of the persons employed: abundance of Canaanites remained in the land, and all raging against Israel, *as a bear robbed of her whelps;* the business of these surveyors would soon be known, and what could they expect but to be way-laid, and have their brains knocked out by the fierce observers? But in obedience to Joshua's command, and in dependence upon God's power, they thus put their lives in their hands to serve their country. [2.] The good providence of God in protecting them from the many deaths they were exposed to, and bringing them all safely again to the host at Shiloh. When we are in the way of our duty we are under the special protection of the Almighty.

2. When it was surveyed, and reduced to seven lots, then Joshua would, by appeal to God, and direction from him, determine which of these lots should belong to each tribe (*v.* 6): *That I may cast lots for you here* at the tabernacle (because it was a sacred transaction) *before the Lord our God*, to whom each tribe must have an eye, with thankfulness for the conveniences and submission to the inconveniences of their allotment. What we have in the world we must acknowledge God's property in, and dispose of it as before him, with justice, and charity, and dependence upon Providence. The heavenly Canaan is described to us in a book, the book of the scriptures, and there are in it mansions and portions sufficient for all God's spiritual Israel. Christ is our Joshua that divides it to us. On him we must attend, and to him we must apply for an inheritance with the saints in light. See John xvii. 2, 3.

11 And the lot of the tribe of the children of Benjamin came up according to their families: and the coast of their lot came forth between the children of Judah and the children of Joseph. 12 And their border on the north side was from Jordan; and the border went up to the side of Jericho on the north side, and went up through the mountains westward; and the goings out thereof were at the wilderness of Beth-aven. 13 And the border went over from thence toward Luz, to the side of Luz, which *is* Beth-el, southward; and the border descended to Ataroth-adar, near the hill that *lieth* on the south side of the nether Beth-

horon. 14 And the border was drawn *thence*, and compassed the corner of the sea southward, from the hill that *lieth* before Beth-horon southward; and the goings out thereof were at Kirjath-baal, which *is* Kirjath-jearim, a city of the children of Judah: this *was* the west quarter. 15 And the south quarter *was* from the end of Kirjath-jearim, and the border went out on the west, and went out to the well of waters of Nephtoah: 16 And the border came down to the end of the mountain that *lieth* before the valley of the son of Hinnom, *and* which *is* in the valley of the giants on the north, and descended to the valley of Hinnom, to the side of Jebusi on the south, and descended to En-rogel, 17 And was drawn from the north, and went forth to En-shemesh, and went forth toward Geliloth, which *is* over against the going up of Adummim, and descended to the stone of Bohan the son of Reuben, 18 And passed along toward the side over against Arabah northward, and went down unto Arabah: 19 And the border passed along to the side of Beth-hoglah northward: and the outgoings of the border were at the north bay of the salt sea at the south end of Jordan: this *was* the south coast. 20 And Jordan was the border of it on the east side. This *was* the inheritance of the children of Benjamin, by the coasts thereof round about, according to their families. 21 Now the cities of the tribe of the children of Benjamin according to their families were Jericho, and Beth-hoglah, and the valley of Keziz, 22 And Beth-arabah, and Zemaraim, and Beth-el, 23 And Avim, and Parah, and Ophrah, 24 And Chephar-haammonai, and Ophni, and Gaba; twelve cities with their villages. 25 Gibeon, and Ramah, and Beeroth, 26 And Mizpeh, and Chephirah, and Mozah, 27 And Rekem, and Irpeel, and Taralah, 28 And Zelah, Eleph, and Jebusi, which *is* Jerusalem, Gibeath, *and* Kirjath; fourteen cities with their villages. This *is* the inheritance of the children of Benjamin according to their families.

We have here the lot of the tribe of Benjamin, which Providence cast next to Joseph on the one hand, because Benjamin was own and only brother to Joseph, and was little Benjamin (Ps. lxviii. 27), that needed the protection of great Joseph, and yet had a better protector, for *the Lord shall cover him all the day long,* Deut xxxiii. 12. And it was next to Judah on the other hand, that this tribe might hereafter unite with Judah in an adherence to the throne of David and the temple at Jerusalem. Here we have, 1. The exact borders and limits of this tribe, which we need not be exact in the explication of. As it had Judah on the south and Joseph on the north, so it had Jordan on the east and Dan on the west. The western border is said to *compass the corner of the sea southward* (*v.* 14), whereas no part of the lot of this tribe came near to the great sea. Bishop Patrick thinks the meaning is that it ran along in a parallel line to the great sea, though at a distance. Dr. Fuller suggests that since it is not called *the great sea,* but only *the sea,* which often signifies any lake or mere, it may be meant of the pool of Gibeon, which may be called *a corner* or *canton* of the sea; it is called the *great waters of Gibeon* (Jer. xli. 12), and it is compassed by the western border of this tribe. 2. The particular cities in this tribe, not all, but the most considerable. Twenty-six are here named. Jericho is put first, though dismantled, and forbidden to be rebuilt as a city with gates and walls, because it might be built and inhabited as a country village, and so was not useless to this tribe. Gilgal, where Israel first encamped when Saul was made king (1 Sam. xi. 15), was in this tribe. It was afterwards a very profane place. Hos. ix. 15, *All their wickedness is in Gilgal.* Beth-el was in this tribe, a famous place. Though Benjamin adhered to the house of David, yet Beth-el, it seems, was in the possession of the house of Joseph (Judg. i. 23—25), and there Jeroboam set up one of his calves. In this tribe was Gibeon, where the altar was in the beginning of Solomon's time, 2 Chron. i. 3. Gibeah likewise, that infamous place where the Levite's concubine was abused. Mizpeh, and near it Samuel's Ebenezer, and also Anathoth, Jeremiah's city, were in this tribe, as was the northern part of Jerusalem. Paul was the honour of this tribe (Rom. xi. 1; Phil. iii. 5); but where his land lay we know not: he sought the better country.

CHAP. XIX.

In the description of the lots of Judah and Benjamin we have an account both of the borders that surrounded them and of the cities contained in them. In that of Ephraim and Manasseh we have the borders, but not the cities; in this chapter Simeon and Dan are described by their cities only, and not their borders, because they lay very much within Judah, especially the former; the rest have both their borders described and their cities named, especially frontiers. Here is, I. The lot of Simeon, ver. 1—9. II. Of Zebulun, ver. 10—16. III. Of Issachar, ver. 17—23. IV. Of Asher, ver. 24—31. V. Of Naphtali, ver. 32—39. VI. Of Dan,

ver. 40—48. Lastly, The inheritance assigned to Joshua himself and his own family, ver. 49—51.

AND the second lot came forth to Simeon, *even* for the tribe of the children of Simeon according to their families: and their inheritance was within the inheritance of the children of Judah. 2 And they had in their inheritance Beer-sheba, and Sheba, and Moladah, 3 And Hazar-shual, and Balah, and Azem, 4 And Eltolad, and Bethul, and Hormah, 5 And Ziklag, and Beth-marcaboth, and Hazar-susah, 6 And Beth-lebaoth, and Sharuhen; thirteen cities and their villages: 7 Ain, Remmon, and Ether, and Ashan; four cities and their villages: 8 And all the villages that *were* round about these cities to Baalath-beer, Ramath of the south. This *is* the inheritance of the tribe of the children of Simeon according to their families. 9 Out of the portion of the children of Judah *was* the inheritance of the children of Simeon: for the part of the children of Judah was too much for them: therefore the children of Simeon had their inheritance within the inheritance of them.

Simeon's lot was drawn after Judah's, Joseph's, and Benjamin's, because Jacob had put that tribe under disgrace; yet it is put before the two younger sons of Leah and the three sons of the handmaids. Not one person of note, neither judge nor prophet, was of this tribe, that we know of.

I. The situation of their lot was within that of Judah (*v.* 1) and was taken from it, *v.* 9. It seems, those that first surveyed the land thought it larger than it was, and that it would have held out to give every tribe in proportion as large a share as they had carved out for Judah; but, upon a more strict enquiry, it was found that it would not reach (*v.* 9): *The part of the children of Judah was too much for them,* more than they needed, and more, as it proved, than fell to their share. Yet God did not by the lot lessen it, but left it to their prudence and care afterwards to discover and rectify the mistake, which when they did, 1. The men of Judah did not oppose the taking away of the cities again, which by the first distribution fell within their border, when they were convinced that they had more than their proportion. In all such cases errors must be excepted and a review admitted if there be occasion. Though, in strictness, what fell to their lot was their right against all the world, yet they would not insist upon it when it appeared that another tribe would want what they had to spare. Note, We must look on the things of others, and not on our own only. The abundance of some must supply the wants of others, that there may be somewhat of an equality, for which there may be equity where there is not law. 2. That which was thus taken off from Judah to be put into a new lot Providence directed to the tribe of Simeon, that Jacob's prophecy concerning this tribe might be fulfilled, *I will divide them in Jacob.* The cities of Simeon were scattered in Judah, with which tribe they were surrounded, except on that side towards the sea. This brought them into a confederacy with the tribe of Judah (Judg. i. 3), and afterwards was a happy occasion of the adherence of many of this tribe to the house of David, at the time of the revolt of the ten tribes to Jeroboam. 2 Chron. xv. 9, *out of Simeon they fell to* Asa *in abundance.* It is good being in a good neighbourhood.

II. The cities within their lot are here named. Beersheba, or Sheba, for these names seem to refer to the same place, is put first. Ziklag, which we read of in David's story, is one of them. What course they took to enlarge their borders and make room for themselves we find 1 Chron. iv. 39, &c.

10 And the third lot came up for the children of Zebulun according to their families: and the border of their inheritance was unto Sarid: 11 And their border went up toward the sea, and Maralah, and reached to Dabbasheth, and reached to the river that *is* before Jokneam; 12 And turned from Sarid eastward toward the sunrising unto the border of Chislothtabor, and then goeth out to Daberath, and goeth up to Japhia, 13 And from thence passeth on along on the east to Gittah-hepher, to Ittahkazin, and goeth out to Remmonmethoar to Neah; 14 And the border compasseth it on the north side to Hannathon: and the outgoings thereof are in the valley of Jiphthah-el: 15 And Kattath, and Nahallal, and Shimron, and Idalah, and Beth-lehem: twelve cities with their villages. 16 This *is* the inheritance of the children of Zebulun according to their families, these cities with their villages.

This is the lot of Zebulun, who, though born of Leah after Issachar, yet was blessed by Jacob and Moses before him; and therefore it was so ordered that his lot was drawn before that of Issachar, north of which it lay, and south of Asher. 1. The lot of this tribe was washed by the great sea on the west, and by the sea of Tiberias on the east, answering Jacob's prophecy (Gen. xlix. 13), *Zebulun shall be a haven of ships,* trading ships on the great sea and fishing ships on the sea of Galilee. 2. Though there were some places in this tribe which were made famous in the Old Testament, especially *Mount Carmel,* on which the famous trial was between God and Baal in Elijah's time, yet it was made much more illustrious in the New Testament; for within the lot of this tribe was Nazareth, where our blessed Saviour spent so much of his time on earth, and from which he was called *Jesus* of *Nazareth,* and *Mount Tabor* on which he was transfigured, and that coast of the sea of Galilee on which Christ preached so many sermons and wrought so many miracles.

17 *And* the fourth lot came out to Issachar, for the children of Issachar according to their families. 18 And their border was toward Jezreel, and Chesulloth, and Shunem, 19 And Haphraim, and Shihon, and Anaharath, 20 And Rabbith, and Kishion, and Abez, 21 And Remeth, and En-gannim, and En-haddah, and Beth-pazzez; 22 And the coast reacheth to Tabor, and Shahazimah, and Beth-shemesh; and the outgoings of their border were at Jordan: sixteen cities with their villages. 23 This *is* the inheritance of the tribe of the children of Issachar according to their families, the cities and their villages.

The lot of Issachar ran from Jordan in the east to the great sea in the west, Manasseh on the south, and Zebulun on the north. A numerous tribe, Num. xxvi. 25. Tola, one of the judges, was of this tribe, Judg. x. 1. So was Baasha, one of the kings of Israel, 1 Kings xv. 27. The most considerable places in this tribe were, 1. Jezreel, in which was Ahab's palace, and near it Naboth's vineyard. 2. Shunem, where lived the good Shunamite that entertained Elisha. 3. The river Kishon, on the banks of which, in this tribe, Sisera was beaten by Deborah and Barak. 4. The mountains of Gilboa, on which Saul and Jonathan were slain, which were not far from Endor, where Saul consulted the witch. 5. The valley of Megiddo, where Josiah was slain near Hadad-rimmon, 2 Kings xxiii. 29; Zech. xii. 11.

24 And the fifth lot came out for the tribe of the children of Asher according to their families. 25 And their border was Helkath, and Hali, and Beten, and Achshaph, 26 And Alammelech, and Amad, and Misheal; and reacheth to Carmel westward, and to Shihor-libnath; 27 And turneth toward the sunrising to Beth-dagon, and reacheth to Zebulun, and to the valley of Jiphthah-el toward the north side of Beth-emek, and Neiel, and goeth out to Cabul on the left hand, 28 And Hebron, and Rehob, and Hammon, and Kanah, *even* unto great Zidon; 29 And *then* the coast turneth to Ramah, and to the strong city Tyre; and the coast turneth to Hosah; and the outgoings thereof are at the sea from the coast to Achzib: 30 Ummah also, and Aphek, and Rehob: twenty and two cities with their villages. 31 This *is* the inheritance of the tribe of the children of Asher according to their families, these cities with their villages.

The lot of Asher lay upon the coast of the great sea. We read not of any famous person of this tribe but Anna the prophetess, who was a constant resident in the temple at the time of our Saviour's birth, Luke ii. 36. Nor were there many famous places in this tribe. Aphek (mentioned *v.* 30) was the place near which Benhadad was beaten by Ahab, 1 Kings xx. 30. But close adjoining to this tribe were the celebrated sea-port towns of Tyre and Sidon, which we read so much of. Tyre is called here *that strong city* (*v.* 29), but bishop Patrick thinks it was not the same Tyre that we read of afterwards, for that was built on an island; this old strong city was on the continent. And it is conjectured by some that into these two strong-holds, Sidon and Tzor, or Tyre, many of the people of Canaan fled and took shelter when Joshua invaded them.

32 The sixth lot came out to the children of Naphtali, *even* for the children of Naphtali according to their families. 33 And their coast was from Heleph, from Allon to Zaanannim, and Adami, Nekeb, and Jabneel, unto Lakum; and the outgoings thereof were at Jordan: 34 And *then* the coast turneth westward to Aznoth-tabor, and goeth out from thence to Hukkok, and reacheth to Zebulun on the south side, and reacheth to Asher on the west side, and to Judah upon Jordan toward the sunrising. 35 And the fenced cities *are* Ziddim, Zer, and Hammath,

Rakkath, and Chinnereth, 36 And Adamah, and Ramah, and Hazor, 37 And Kedesh, and Edrei, and En-hazor, 38 And Iron, and Migdal-el, Horem, and Beth-anath, and Beth-shemesh; nineteen cities with their villages. 39 This *is* the inheritance of the tribe of the children of Naphtali according to their families, the cities and their villages.

Naphtali lay furthest north of all the tribes, bordering on Mount Libanus. The city of Leshem, or Laish, lay on the utmost edge of it to the north, and therefore when the Danites had made themselves masters of it, and called it *Dan*, the length of Canaan from north to south was reckoned from Dan to Beersheba. It had Zebulun on the south, Asher on the west, and Judah upon Jordan, probably a city of that name, and so distinguished from the tribe of Judah on the east. It was in the lot of this tribe, near the waters of Merom, that Joshua fought and routed Jabin, *ch.* xi. 1. &c. In this tribe stood Capernaum and Bethsaida, on the north end of the sea of Tiberias, in which Christ did so many mighty works; and the mountain (as is supposed) on which Christ preached, Matt. v. 1.

40 *And* the seventh lot came out for the tribe of the children of Dan according to their families. 41 And the coast of their inheritance was Zorah, and Eshtaol, and Ir-shemesh, 42 And Shaalabbin, and Ajalon, and Jethlah, 43 And Elon, and Thimnathah, and Ekron, 44 And Eltekeh, and Gibbethon, and Baalath, 45 And Jehud, and Bene-berak, and Gath-rimmon, 46 And Me-jarkon, and Rakkon, with the border before Japho. 47 And the coast of the children of Dan went out *too little* for them: therefore the children of Dan went up to fight against Leshem, and took it, and smote it with the edge of the sword, and possessed it, and dwelt therein, and called Leshem, Dan, after the name of Dan their father. 48 This *is* the inheritance of the tribe of the children of Dan according to their families, these cities with their villages.

Dan, though commander of one of the four squadrons of the camp of Israel, in the wilderness, that which brought up the rear, yet was last provided for in Canaan, and his lot fell in the southern part of Canaan, between Judah on the east and the land of the Philistines on the west, Ephraim on the north and Simeon on the south. Providence ordered this numerous and powerful tribe into a post of danger, as best able to deal with those vexatious neighbours the Philistines, and so it was found in Samson. Here is an account, 1 Of what fell to this tribe by lot, Zorah, and Eshtaol, and the camp of Dan thereabouts, of which we read in the story of Samson. And near there was the valley of Eshcol, whence the spies brought the famous bunch of grapes. Japho, or Joppa was in this lot. 2. Of what they got by their own industry and valour, which is mentioned here (*v.* 47), but related at large, Judg. xviii. 7, &c.

49 When they had made an end of dividing the land for inheritance by their coasts, the children of Israel gave an inheritance to Joshua the son of Nun among them: 50 According to the word of the LORD they gave him the city which he asked, *even* Timnath-serah in mount Ephraim: and he built the city, and dwelt therein. 51 These *are* the inheritances, which Eleazar the priest, and Joshua the son of Nun, and the heads of the fathers of the tribes of the children of Israel, divided for an inheritance by lot in Shiloh before the LORD, at the door of the tabernacle of the congregation. So they made an end of dividing the country.

Before this account of the dividing of the land is solemnly closed up, in the last verse, which intimates that the thing was done to the satisfaction of all, here is an account of the particular inheritance assigned to Joshua. 1. He was last served, though the eldest and greatest man of all Israel, and who, having commanded in the conquest of Canaan, might have demanded the first settlement in it for himself and his family. But he would make it to appear that in all he did he sought the good of his country, and not any private interest of his own. He was content to be unfixed till he saw them all settled; and herein is a great example to all in public places to prefer the common welfare before their particular satisfaction. Let the public be first served. 2. He had his lot *according to the word of the Lord.* It is probable that, when God by Moses told Caleb what inheritance he should have (*ch.* xiv. 9), he gave the like promise to Joshua, which he had an eye to in making his election: this made his portion doubly pleasant, that he had it, not as the rest by common providence, but by special promise. 3. He chose it in Mount Ephraim, which belonged to his own tribe, with which he thereby put himself in common, when he might by prerogative have chosen his inheritance in some other tribe, as suppose that of Judah, and thereby have distinguished himself from them. Let no man's preferment or honour make him ashamed of his family or country, or estrange him from it. The tabernacle was set up in the lot of Ephraim, and Joshua would forecast not to be far from that. 4. The *children of Israel* are said to *give it to him* (*v.* 49), which bespeaks his humility, that he would not take it to himself without the people's consent and approbation, as if he would thereby own himself, though *major singulis—greater than any one*, yet *minor universis—less than the whole assemblage*, and would hold even the estate of his family, under God, by the grant of the people. 5. It was a city that must be built before it was fit to be dwelt in. While others dwelt in houses which they built not, Joshua must erect for himself (that he might be a pattern of industry and contentment with mean things) such buildings as he could hastily run up, without curiosity or magnificence. Our Lord Jesus thus came and dwelt among us, not in pomp but poverty, providing rest for us, yet himself not having where to lay his head. *Even Christ pleased not himself.*

CHAP. XX.

This short chapter is concerning the cities of refuge, which we often read of in the writings of Moses; but this is the last time that we find mention of them, for now that matter was thoroughly settled. Here is, I. The law God gave concerning them, ver. 1—6. II. The people's designation of the particular cities for that use, ver. 7—9. And this remedial law was a figure of good things to come.

THE LORD also spake unto Joshua, saying, 2 Speak to the children of Israel, saying, Appoint out for you cities of refuge, whereof I spake unto you by the hand of Moses: 3 That the slayer that killeth *any* person unawares *and* unwittingly may flee thither: and they shall be your refuge from the avenger of blood. 4 And when he that doth flee unto one of those cities shall stand at the entering of the gate of the city, and shall declare his cause in the ears of the elders of that city, they shall take him into the city unto them, and give him a place, that he may dwell among them. 5 And if the avenger of blood pursue after him, then they shall not deliver the slayer up into his hand; because he smote his neighbour unwittingly, and hated him not before time. 6 And he shall dwell in that city, until he stand before the congregation for judgment, *and* until the death of the high priest that shall be in those days: then shall the slayer return, and come unto his own city, and unto his own house, unto the city from whence he fled.

Many things were by the law of Moses ordered to be done when they came to Canaan and this among the rest, the appointing of sanctuaries for the protecting of those that were guilty of casual murder, which was a privilege to all Israel, since no man could be sure but some time or other it might be his own case; and it was for the interest of the land that the blood of an innocent person, whose hand only was guilty but not his heart, should not be shed, no, not by the avenger of blood: of this law, which was so much for their advantage, God here reminds them, that they might remind themselves of the other laws he had given them, which concerned his honour. 1. Orders are given for the appointing of these cities (*v.* 2), and very seasonably at this time when the land was newly surveyed, and so they were the better able to divide the coasts of it into three parts, as God had directed them, in order to the more convenient situation of these cities of refuge, Deut. xix. 3. Yet it is probable that it was not done till after the Levites had their portion assigned them in the next chapter, because the cities of refuge were all to be Levites' cities. As soon as ever God had given them cities of rest, he bade them appoint cities of refuge, to which none of them knew but they might be glad to escape. Thus God provided, not only for their ease at all times, but for their safety in times of danger, and such times we must expect and prepare for in this world. And it intimates what God's spiritual Israel have and shall have, in Christ and heaven, not only rest to repose themselves in, but refuge to secure themselves in. And we cannot think these cities of refuge would have been so often and so much spoken of in the law of Moses, and have had so much care taken about them (when the intention of them might have been effectually answered, as it is in our law, by authorizing the courts of judgment to protect and acquit the manslayer in all those cases wherein he was to have privilege of sanctuary), if they were not designed to typify the relief which the gospel provides for poor penitent sinners, and their protection from the curse of the law and the wrath of God, in our Lord Jesus, to whom believers flee for refuge (Heb. vi. 18), and in whom they are found (Phil. iii. 9) as in a sanctuary, where they are privileged from arrests, and *there is now no condemnation to them*, Rom. viii. 1. 2. Instructions are given for the using of these cities. The laws in this matter we had before, Num. xxxv. 10, &c., where they were opened at large. (1.) It is supposed that a man might possibly kill a person, it might be his own child or dearest friend, unawares and unwittingly (*v.* 3), not only whom he hated not, but whom he truly loved beforetime (*v.* 5);

for *the way of man is not in himself.* What reason have we to thank God who has kept us both from slaying and from being slain by accident! In this case, it is supposed that the relations of the person slain would demand the life of the slayer, as a satisfaction to that ancient law that *whoso sheds man's blood, by man shall his blood be shed.* (2.) It is provided that if upon trial it appeared that the murder was done purely by accident, and not by design, either upon an old grudge or a sudden passion, then the slayer should be sheltered from the avenger of blood in any one of these cities, *v.* 4—6. By this law he was entitled to a dwelling in that city, was taken into the care of the government of it, but was confined to it, as a prisoner at large; only, if he survived the high priest, then, and not till then, he might return to his own city. And the Jews say, "If he died before the high priest in the city of his refuge and exile, and was buried there, yet, at the death of the high priest, his bones should be removed with respect to the place of his fathers' sepulchres."

7 And they appointed Kedesh in Galilee in mount Naphtali, and Shechem in mount Ephraim, and Kirjath-arba, which *is* Hebron, in the mountain of Judah. 8 And on the other side Jordan by Jericho eastward, they assigned Bezer in the wilderness upon the plain out of the tribe of Reuben, and Ramoth in Gilead out of the tribe of Gad, and Golan in Bashan out of the tribe of Manasseh. 9 These were the cities appointed for all the children of Israel, and for the stranger that sojourneth among them, that whosoever killeth *any* person at unawares might flee thither, and not die by the hand of the avenger of blood, until he stood before the congregation.

We have here the nomination of the cities of refuge in the land of Canaan, which was made by the advice and authority of Joshua and the princes (*v.* 7); and upon occasion of the mention of this is repeated the nomination of the other three in the lot of the other two tribes and a half, which was made by Moses (Deut. iv. 43), but (as bishop Patrick thinks) they had not the privilege till now. 1. They are said to *sanctify* these cities, that is the original word for *appointed, v.* 7. Not that any ceremony was used to signify the consecration of them, only they did by a public act of court solemnly declare them cities of refuge, and as such sacred to the honour of God, as the protector of exposed innocency. If they were sanctuaries, it was proper to say they were *sanctified.* Christ, our refuge, was sanctified by his Father; nay, for our sakes he sanctified himself, John xvii. 19. 2. These cities (as those also on the other side Jordan) stood in the three several parts of the country, so conveniently that a man might (they say) in half a day reach some one of them from any corner of the country. Kedesh was in Naphtali, the most northern tribe, Hebron in Judah, the most southern, and Shechem in Ephraim, which lay in the middle, about equally distant from the other two. God is a refuge at hand. 3. They were all Levites' cities, which put an honour upon God's tribe, making them judges in those cases wherein divine Providence was so nearly concerned, and protectors to oppressed innocency. It was also a kindness to the poor refugee, that when he might not go up to the house of the Lord, nor tread his courts, yet he had the servants of God's house with him, to instruct him, and pray for him, and help to make up the want of public ordinances. If he must be confined, it shall be to a Levite-city, where he may, if he will, improve his time. 4. These cities were upon hills to be seen afar off, for a city on a hill cannot be hid; and this would both direct and encourage the poor distressed man that was making that way; and, though therefore his way at last was up-hill, yet this would comfort him, that he would be in his place of safety quickly, and if he could but get into the suburbs of the city he was well enough off. 5. Some observe a significancy in the names of these cities with application to Christ our refuge. I delight not in quibbling upon names, yet am willing to take notice of these. *Kedesh* signifies *holy,* and our refuge is the holy Jesus. *Shechem, a shoulder,* and the government is upon his shoulder. *Hebron, fellowship,* and believers are called into the fellowship of Christ Jesus our Lord. *Bezer, a fortification,* for he is a strong-hold to all those that trust in him. *Ramoth, high* or *exalted,* for him hath God exalted with his own right hand. *Golan, joy* or *exultation,* for in him all the saints are justified, and shall glory. *Lastly,* Besides all these, the horns of the altar, wherever it was, were a refuge to those who took hold of them, if the crime were such as that sanctuary allowed. This is implied in that law (Exod. xxi. 14), that a wilful murderer shall be taken from God's altar to be put to death. And we find the altar used for this purpose, 1 Kings i. 50; ii. 28. Christ is our altar, who not only *sanctifies the gift,* but protects the giver.

CHAP. XXI.

It had been often said that the tribe of Levi should have "no inheritance with their brethren," no particular part of the country assigned them, as the other tribes had, no, not the country about Shiloh, which one might have expected to be appropriated to them as the lands of the church; but, though they were not thus cast into a country by themselves, it appears, by the provision made for them in this chapter, that they were no losers, but the rest of the tribes were very much gainers, by their being dispersed. We have here, I. The motion they made to have their cities assigned them, according to God's appointment, ver. 1, 2. II. The nomination of the cities accordingly out of the several

tribes, and the distribution of them to the respective families of this tribe, ver. 3—8. III. A catalogue of the cities, forty-eight in all, ver. 9—42. IV. A receipt entered in full of all that God had promised to his people Israel, ver. 43—45.

THEN came near the heads of the fathers of the Levites unto Eleazar the priest, and unto Joshua the son of Nun, and unto the heads of the fathers of the tribes of the children of Israel; 2 And they spake unto them at Shiloh in the land of Canaan, saying, The LORD commanded by the hand of Moses to give us cities to dwell in, with the suburbs thereof for our cattle. 3 And the children of Israel gave unto the Levites out of their inheritance, at the commandment of the LORD, these cities and their suburbs. 4 And the lot came out for the families of the Kohathites: and the children of Aaron the priest, *which were* of the Levites, had by lot out of the tribe of Judah, and out of the tribe of Simeon, and out of the tribe of Benjamin, thirteen cities. 5 And the rest of the children of Kohath *had* by lot out of the families of the tribe of Ephraim, and out of the tribe of Dan, and out of the half tribe of Manasseh, ten cities. 6 And the children of Gershon *had* by lot out of the families of the tribe of Issachar, and out of the tribe of Asher, and out of the tribe of Naphtali, and out of the half tribe of Manasseh in Bashan, thirteen cities. 7 The children of Merari by their families *had* out of the tribe of Reuben, and out of the tribe of Gad, and out of the tribe of Zebulun, twelve cities. 8 And the children of Israel gave by lot unto the Levites these cities with their suburbs, as the LORD commanded by the hand of Moses.

Here is, I. The Levites' petition presented to this general convention of the states, now sitting at Shiloh, *v.* 1, 2. Observe, 1. They had not their lot assigned them till they made their claim. There is an inheritance provided for all the saints, that royal priesthood, but then they must petition for it. *Ask, and it shall be given you.* Joshua had quickened the rest of the tribes who were slack to put in their claims, but the Levites, it may be supposed, knew their duty and interest better than the rest, and were therefore forward in this matter, when it came to their turn, without being called upon. They build their claim upon a very good foundation, not their own merits nor services, but the divine precept: "*The Lord commanded by the hand of Moses to give us cities,* commanded you to grant them, which implied a command to us to ask them." Note, The maintenance of ministers is not an arbitrary thing, left purely to the good-will of the people, who may let them starve if they please; no, as the God of Israel commanded that the Levites should be well provided for, so has the Lord Jesus, the King of the Christian church, ordained, and a perpetual ordinance it is, that *those who preach the gospel should live of the gospel* (1 Cor. ix. 14), and should live comfortably. 2. They did not make their claim till all the rest of the tribes were provided for, and then they did it immediately. There was some reason for it; every tribe must first know their own, else they would not know what they gave the Levites, and so it could not be such a reasonable service as it ought to be. But it is also an instance of their humility, modesty, and patience (and Levites should be examples of these and other virtues), that they were willing to be served last, and they fared never the worse for it. Let not God's ministers complain if at any time they find themselves postponed in men's thoughts and cares, but let them make sure of the favour of God and the honour that comes from him, and then they may well enough afford to bear the slights and neglects of men.

II. The Levites' petition granted immediately, without any dispute, the princes of Israel being perhaps ashamed that they needed to be called upon in this matter, and that the motion had not been made among themselves for the settling of the Levites. 1. The children of Israel are said to give the cities for the Levites. God had appointed how many they should be in all, forty-eight. It is probable that Joshua and the princes, upon consideration of the extent and value of the lot of each tribe as it was laid before them, had appointed how many cities should be taken out of each; and then the fathers of the several tribes themselves agreed which they should be, and therefore are said to give them, as an offering, to the Lord; so God had appointed. Num. xxxv. 8, *Every one shall give of his cities to the Levites.* Here God tried their generosity, and it was found to praise and honour, for it appears by the following catalogue that the cities they gave to the Levites were generally some of the best and most considerable in each tribe. And it is probable that they had an eye to the situation of them, taking care they should be so dispersed as that no part of the country should be too far distant from a Levites' city. 2. They gave them *at the commandment of the Lord,* that is, with an eye to the command and in obedience to it, which was it that sanctified the grant. They gave the number that God commanded, and it was well this matter was settled, that the Levites might not ask more nor the Israelites offer less. They gave them also with their suburbs, or glebe-lands, belonging to them, so many cubits by measure from the walls of the city, as God had commanded (Num. xxxv. 4, 5), and did not go about to cut them short. 3. When the forty-eight cities were pitched upon, they were divided into four lots, as they lay next together, and then by lot were determined to the four several families of the tribe of Levi. When the Israelites had surrendered the cities into the hand of God, he would himself have the distributing of them among his servants. (1.) The family of Aaron, who were the only priests, had for their share the thirteen cities that were given by the tribes of Judah, Simeon, and Benjamin, *v.* 4. God in wisdom ordered it thus, that though Jerusalem itself was not one of their cities, it being as yet in the possession of the Jebusites (and those generous tribes would not mock the Levites, who had another warfare to mind, with a city that must be recovered by the sword before it could be enjoyed), yet the cities that fell to their lot were those which lay next to Jerusalem, because that was to be, in process of time, the holy city, where their business would chiefly lie. (2.) The Kohathite-Levites (among whom were the posterity of Moses, though never distinguished from them) had the cities that lay in the lot of Dan, which lay next to Judah, and in that of Ephraim, and the half-tribe of Manasseh, which lay next to Benjamin. So those who descended from Aaron's father joined nearest to Aaron's sons. (3.) Gershon was the eldest son of Levi, and therefore, though the younger house of the Kohathites was preferred before his, yet his children had the precedency of the other family of Merari, *v.* 6. (4.) The Merarites, the youngest house, had their lot last, and it lay furthest off, *v.* 7. The rest of the sons of Jacob had a lot for every tribe only, but Levi, God's tribe, had a lot for each of its families; for there is a particular providence directing and attending the removals and settlements of ministers, and appointing where those shall fix who are to be the lights of the world.

9 And they gave out of the tribe of the children of Judah, and out of the tribe of the children of Simeon, these cities which are *here* mentioned by name, 10 Which the children of Aaron, *being* of the families of the Kohathites, *who were* of the children of Levi, had: for their's was the first lot. 11 And they gave them the city of Arba the father of Anak, which *city is* Hebron, in the hill *country* of Judah, with the suburbs thereof round about it. 12 But the fields of the city, and the villages thereof, gave they to Caleb the son of Jephunneh for his possession. 13 Thus they gave to the children of Aaron the priest Hebron with her suburbs, *to be* a city of refuge for the slayer; and Libnah with her suburbs, 14 And Jattir with her suburbs, and Eshtemoa with her suburbs, 15 And Holon with her suburbs, and Debir with her suburbs, 16 And Ain with her suburbs, and Juttah with her suburbs, *and* Beth-shemesh with her suburbs; nine cities out of those two tribes. 17 And out of the tribe of Benjamin, Gibeon with her suburbs, Geba with her suburbs, 18 Anathoth with her suburbs, and Almon with her suburbs; four cities. 19 All the cities of the children of Aaron, the priests, *were* thirteen cities with their suburbs. 20 And the families of the children of Kohath, the Levites which remained of the children of Kohath, even they had the cities of their lot out of the tribe of Ephraim. 21 For they gave them Shechem with her suburbs in mount Ephraim, *to be* a city of refuge for the slayer; and Gezer with her suburbs, 22 And Kibzaim with her suburbs, and Beth-horon with her suburbs; four cities. 23 And out of the tribe of Dan, Eltekeh with her suburbs, Gibbethon with her suburbs, 24 Aijalon with her suburbs, Gath-rimmon with her suburbs; four cities. 25 And out of the half tribe of Manasseh, Tanach with her suburbs, and Gath-rimmon with her suburbs; two cities. 26 All the cities *were* ten with their suburbs for the families of the children of Kohath that remained. 27 And unto the children of Gershon, of the families of the Levites, out of the *other* half tribe of Manasseh *they gave* Golan in Bashan with her suburbs, *to be* a city of refuge for the slayer; and Beesh-terah with her suburbs; two cities. 28 And out of the tribe of Issachar, Kishon with her suburbs, Dabareh with her suburbs, 29 Jarmuth with her suburbs, En-gannim with her suburbs; four cities. 30 And out of the tribe of Asher, Mishal with her suburbs, Abdon with her suburbs, 31 Helkath with her suburbs, and Rehob with her suburbs; four cities. 32 And out of the tribe

of Naphtali, Kedesh in Galilee with her suburbs, *to be* a city of refuge for the slayer; and Hammoth-dor with her suburbs, and Kartan with her suburbs; three cities. 33 All the cities of the Gershonites according to their families *were* thirteen cities with their suburbs. 34 And unto the families of the children of Merari, the rest of the Levites, out of the tribe of Zebulun, Jokneam with her suburbs, and Kartah with her suburbs, 35 Dimnah with her suburbs, Nahalal with her suburbs; four cities. 36 And out of the tribe of Reuben, Bezer with her suburbs, and Jahazah with her suburbs, 37 Kedemoth with her suburbs, and Mephaath with her suburbs; four cities. 38 And out of the tribe of Gad, Ramoth in Gilead with her suburbs, *to be* a city of refuge for the slayer; and Mahanaim with her suburbs, 39 Heshbon with her suburbs, Jazer with her suburbs; four cities in all. 40 So all the cities for the children of Merari by their families, which were remaining of the families of the Levites, were *by* their lot twelve cities. 41 All the cities of the Levites within the possession of the children of Israel *were* forty and eight cities with their suburbs. 42 These cities were every one with their suburbs round about them: thus *were* all these cities.

We have here a particular account of the cities which were given to the children of Levi out of the several tribes, not only to be occupied and inhabited by them, as tenants to the several tribes in which they lay—no, their interest in them was not dependent and precarious, but to be owned and possessed by them as lords and proprietors, and as having the same title to them that the rest of the tribes had to their cities or lands, as appears by the law which preserved the houses in the Levites' cities from being alienated any longer than till the year of jubilee, Lev. xxv. 32, 33. Yet it is probable that the Levites having only the cities and suburbs, while the land about pertained to the tribes in which they lay, those of that tribe, for the convenience of occupying that land, might commonly rent houses of the Levites, as they could spare them in their cities, and so live among them as their tenants. Several things may be observed in this account, besides what was observed in the law concerning it, Num. xxxv.

I. That the Levites were dispersed into all the tribes, and not suffered to live all together in any one part of the country. This would find them all with work, and employ them all for the good of others; for ministers, of all people, must neither be idle nor live to themselves or to one another only. Christ left his twelve disciples together in a body, but left orders that they should in due time disperse themselves, that they might *preach the gospel to every creature*. The mixing of the Levites thus with the other tribes would be an obligation upon them to walk circumspectly, and as became their sacred function, and to avoid every thing that might disgrace it. Had they lived all together, they would have been tempted to wink at one another's faults, and to excuse one another when they did amiss; but by this means they were made to see the eyes of all Israel upon them, and therefore saw it their concern to walk so as that their ministry might in nothing be blamed nor their high character suffer by their ill carriage.

II. That every tribe of Israel was adorned and enriched with its share of Levites' cities in proportion to its compass, even those that lay most remote. They were all God's people, and therefore they all had Levites among them, 1. To show kindness to, as God appointed them, Deut. xii. 19; xiv. 29. They were God's receivers, to whom the people might give their grateful acknowledgments of God's goodness, as the occasion and disposition were. 2. To receive advice and instruction from; when they could not go up to the tabernacle, to consult those who attended there, they might go to a Levites' city, and be taught the good knowledge of the Lord. Thus God set up a candle in every room of his house, to give light to all his family; as those that attended the altar *kept the charge of the Lord*, to see that no divine appointment was neglected there, so those that were scattered in the country had their charge too, which was to see that no idolatrous superstitious usages were introduced at a distance and to watch for the souls of God's Israel. Thus did God graciously provide for the keeping up of religion among them, and that they might have the word nigh them; yet, blessed be God, we, under the gospel, have it yet nigher, not only Levites in every county, but Levites in every parish, whose office it is still to teach the people knowledge, and to go before them in the things of God.

III. That there were thirteen cities, and those some of the best, appointed for the priests, the sons of Aaron, *v.* 19. Aaron left but two sons, Eleazar and Ithamar, yet his family was now so much increased, and it was foreseen that it would in process of time grow so numerous, as to replenish all these cities, though a considerable number must of necessity be resident wherever the ark and the altar were. We read in both

Testaments of such numbers of priests that we may suppose none of all the families of Israel that came out of Egypt increased afterwards so much as that of Aaron did; and the promise afterwards to the house of Aaron is, *God shall increase you more and more, you and your children*, Ps. cxv. 12, 14. He will raise up a *seed to serve him.*

IV. That some of the Levites' cities were afterwards famous upon other accounts. Hebron was the city in which David began his reign, and in Mahanaim, another Levites' city (*v.* 38), he lay, and had his head-quarters when he fled from Absalom. The first Israelite that ever wore the title of king (namely, Abimelech, the son of Gideon) reigned in Shechem, another Levites' city, *v.* 21.

V. That the number of them in all was more than of most of the tribes, except Judah, though the tribe of Levi was one of the least of the tribes, to show how liberal God is, and his people should be, to his ministers; yet the disproportion will not appear so great as at first it seems, if we consider that the Levites had cities only with their suburbs to dwell in, but the rest of the tribes, besides their cities (and those perhaps were many more than are named in the account of their lot), had many unwalled towns and villages which they inhabited, besides country houses.

Upon the whole, it appears that effectual care was taken that the Levites should live both comfortably and usefully: and those, whether ministers or others, for whom Providence has done well, must look upon themselves as obliged thereby to do good, and, according as their capacity and opportunity are, to serve their generation.

43 And the LORD gave unto Israel all the land which he sware to give unto their fathers; and they possessed it, and dwelt therein. 44 And the LORD gave them rest round about, according to all that he sware unto their fathers: and there stood not a man of all their enemies before them; the LORD delivered all their enemies into their hand. 45 There failed not aught of any good thing which the LORD had spoken unto the house of Israel; all came to pass.

We have here the conclusion of this whole matter, the foregoing history summed up, and, to make it appear the more bright, compared with the promise of which it was the full accomplishment. God's word and his works mutually illustrate each other. The performance makes the promise appear very true and the promise makes the performance appear very kind.

I. God had promised to give the seed of Abraham the land of Canaan for a possession, and how at last he performed this promise (*v.* 43): *They possessed it, and dwelt therein* Though they had often forfeited the benefit of that promise, and God had long delayed the performance of it, yet at last all difficulties were conquered, and Canaan was their own. And the promise of the heavenly Canaan is as sure to all God's spiritual Israel, for it is the promise of him that cannot lie.

II. God had promised to give them rest in that land, and now they had rest round about, rest from the fatigues of their travel through the wilderness (which tedious march, perhaps, was long in their bones), rest from their wars in Canaan, and the insults which their enemies there had at first offered them. They now dwelt, not only in habitations of their own, but those quiet and peaceable ones; though there were Canaanites that remained, yet none that had either strength or spirit to attack them, nor so much as give them an alarm. This rest continued till they by their own sin and folly put thorns into their own beds and their own eyes.

III. God had promised to give them victory and success in their wars, and this promise likewise was fulfilled: *There stood not a man before them, v.* 44. They had the better in every battle, and which way soever they turned their forces they prospered. It is true there were Canaanites now remaining in many parts of the land, and such as afterwards made head against them, and became very formidable. But, 1. As to the present remains of the Canaanites, they were no contradiction to the promise, for God had said he would not drive them out all at once, but by *little and little*, Exod. xxiii. 30. They had now as much in their full possession as they had occasion for and as they had hands to manage, so that the Canaanites only kept possession of some of the less cultivated parts of the country against the beasts of the field, till Israel, in process of time, should become numerous enough to replenish them. 2. As to the after prevalency of the Canaanites, that was purely the effect of Israel's cowardice and slothfulness, and the punishment of their sinful inclination to the idolatries and other abominations of the heathen, whom the Lord would have cast out before them but that they harboured and indulged them. So that the foundation of God stands sure. Israel's experience of God's fidelity is here upon record, and is an acquittance under their hands to the honour of God, the vindication of his promise which had been so often distrusted, and the encouragement of all believers to the end of the world: *There failed not any good thing*, no, nor *aught* of any good thing (so full is it expressed), *which the Lord had spoken unto the house of Israel*, but in due time *all came to pass, v.* 45. Such an acknowledgment as this, here subscribed by Joshua in the name of all Israel, we afterwards find made by Solomon, and all Israel did in effect say *Amen* to it, 1 Kings viii. 56. The inviolable truth of God's promise, and the performance of it to the utmost, are what all the saints have been ready to bear their testimony to; and, if in any thing the performance has seemed to come short, they have been as ready to own that they themselves must bear all the blame.

CHAP. XXII.

Many particular things we have read concerning the two tribes and a half, though nothing separated them from the rest of the tribes except the river Jordan, and this chapter is wholly concerning them. I. Joshua's dismission of the militia of those tribes from the camp of Israel, in which they had served as auxiliaries, during all the wars of Canaan, and their return thereupon to their own country, ver. 1—9. II. The altar they built on the borders of Jordan, in token of their communion with the land of Israel, ver. 10. III. The offence which the rest of the tribes took at this altar, and the message they sent thereupon, ver. 11—20. IV. The apology which the two tribes and a half made for what they had done, ver. 21—29. V. The satisfaction which their apology gave to the rest of the tribes, ver. 30—34. And (which is strange), whereas in most differences that happen there is a fault on both sides, on this there was fault on no side; none (for aught that appears) were to be blamed, but all to be praised.

THEN Joshua called the Reubenites, and the Gadites, and the half tribe of Manasseh, 2 And said unto them, Ye have kept all that Moses the servant of the LORD commanded you, and have obeyed my voice in all that I commanded you: 3 Ye have not left your brethren these many days unto this day, but have kept the charge of the commandment of the LORD your God. 4 And now the LORD your God hath given rest unto your brethren, as he promised them: therefore now return ye, and get you unto your tents, *and* unto the land of your possession, which Moses the servant of the LORD gave you on the other side Jordan. 5 But take diligent heed to do the commandment and the law, which Moses the servant of the LORD charged you, to love the LORD your God, and to walk in all his ways, and to keep his commandments, and to cleave unto him, and to serve him with all your heart and with all your soul. 6 So Joshua blessed them, and sent them away: and they went unto their tents. 7 Now to the *one* half of the tribe of Manasseh Moses had given *possession* in Bashan: but unto the *other* half thereof gave Joshua among their brethren on this side Jordan westward. And when Joshua sent them away also unto their tents, then he blessed them, 8 And he spake unto them, saying, Return with much riches unto your tents, and with very much cattle, with silver, and with gold, and with brass, and with iron, and with very much raiment: divide the spoil of your enemies with your brethren. 9 And the children of Reuben and the children of Gad and the half tribe of Manasseh returned, and departed from the children of Israel out of Shiloh, which *is* in the land of Canaan, to go unto the country of Gilead, to the land of their possession, whereof they were possessed, according to the word of the LORD by the hand of Moses.

The war being ended, and ended gloriously, Joshua, as a prudent general, disbands his army, who never designed to make war their trade, and sends them home, to enjoy what they had conquered, and to beat their swords into plough-shares and their spears into pruning-hooks; and particularly the forces of these separate tribes, who had received their inheritance on the other side Jordan from Moses upon this condition, that their men of war should assist the other tribes in the conquest of Canaan, which they promised to do (Num. xxxii. 32), and renewed the promise to Joshua at the opening of the campaign, Josh. i. 16. And, now that they had performed their bargain, Joshua publicly and solemnly in Shiloh gives them their discharge. Whether this was done, as it was placed, not till after the land was divided, as some think, or whether after the war was ended, and before the division was made, as others think (because there was no need of their assistance in dividing the land, but only in conquering it, nor were there any of their tribes employed as commissioners in that affair, but only of the other ten, Num. xxxiv. 18, &c.), this is certain, it was not done till after Shiloh was made the head-quarters (*v.* 2), and the land was begun to be divided before they removed from Gilgal, *ch.* xiv. 6.

It is probable that this army of Reubenites and Gadites, which had led the van in all the wars of Canaan, had sometimes, in the intervals of action, and when the rest of the army retired into winter-quarters, some of them at least, made a step over Jordan, for it was not far, to visit their families, and to look after their private affairs, and perhaps tarried at home, and sent others in their room more serviceable; but still these two tribes and a half had their quota of troops ready, 40,000 in all, which, whenever there was occasion, presented themselves at their respective posts, and now attended in a body to receive their discharge. Though their affection to their families, and concern for their affairs, could not but make them, after so long an absence, very desirous to return, yet, like good soldiers, they would not move till they had orders from their general. So, though our heavenly Father's house above be ever so desirable (it is bishop Hall's allusion), yet must we stay on earth till our warfare be accomplished, wait for a due discharge, and not anticipate the time of our removal.

I. Joshua dismisses them to the *land of their possession, v.* 4. Those that were first in the assignment of their lot were last in the enjoyment of it; they got the start of their brethren in title, but their brethren were before them in full possession; so *the last shall be first, and the first last,* that there may be something of equality.

II. He dismisses them with their pay; for who goes a warfare at his own charge? *Return with much riches unto your tents, v.* 8. Though all the land they had helped to conquer was to go to the other tribes, yet they should have their share of the plunder, and had so, and this was all the pay that any of the soldiers expected; for the wars of Canaan bore their own charges. "Go," says Joshua, "go home to your tents," that is, "your houses," which he calls *tents,* because they had been so much used to tents in the wilderness; and indeed the strongest and stateliest houses in this world are to be looked upon but as tents, mean and movable in comparison with our house above. "Go home *with much riches,* not only cattle, the spoil of the country, but silver and gold, the plunder of the cities, and," 1. "Let your brethren whom you leave behind have your good word, who have allowed you your share in full, though the land is entirely theirs, and have not offered to make any drawback. Do not say that you are losers by us." 2. "Let your brethren whom you go to, who abode by the stuff, have some share of the spoil: *Divide the spoil with your brethren,* as that was divided which was taken in the war with Midian, Num. xxxi. 27. Let your brethren that have wanted you all this while be the better for you when you come home."

III. He dismisses them with a very honourable character. Though their service was a due debt, and the performance of a promise, and they had done no more than was their duty to do, yet he highly commends them; not only gives them up their bonds, as it were, now that they had fulfilled the condition, but applauds their good services. Though it was by the favour of God and his power that Israel got possession of this land, and he must have all the glory, yet Joshua thought there was a thankful acknowledgment due to their brethren who assisted them, and whose sword and bow were employed for them. God must be chiefly eyed in our praises, yet instruments must not be altogether overlooked. He here commends them, 1. For the readiness of their obedience to their commanders, *v.* 2. When Moses was gone, they remembered and observed the charge he had given them; and all the orders which Joshua, as general of the forces, had issued out, they had carefully obeyed, went, and came, and did, as he appointed, Matt. viii. 9. It is as much as any thing the soldier's praise to observe the word of command. 2. For the constancy of their affection and adherence to their brethren: *You have not left them these many days.* How many days he does not say, nor can we gather it with certainty from any other place. Calvisius and others of the best chronologers compute that the conquering and dividing of the land was the work of about six or seven years, and so long these separate tribes attended their camp, and did them the best service they could. Note, It will be the honour of those that have espoused the cause of God's Israel, and twisted interests with them, to adhere to them, and never to leave them till God has given them rest, and then they shall rest with them. 3. For the faithfulness of their obedience to the divine law. They had not only done their duty to Joshua and Israel, but, which was best of all, they had made conscience of their duty to God: *You have kept the charge,* or, as the word is, *You have kept the keeping,* that is, "You have carefully and circumspectly kept the *commandment of the Lord your God,* not only in this particular instance of continuing in the service of Israel to the end of the war, but, in general, you have kept up religion in your part of the camp, a rare and excellent thing among soldiers, and where it is worthy to be praised."

IV. He dismisses them with good counsel, not to cultivate their ground, fortify their cities, and, now that their hands were inured to war and victory, to invade their neighbours, and so enlarge their own territories, but to keep up serious godliness among them in the power of it. They were not political but pious instructions that he gave them, *v.* 5. 1. In general, to *take diligent heed to do the commandment and the law.* Those that have the commandment have it in vain unless they *do* the commandment; and it will not be done aright (so apt are we to turn aside, and so industrious are our spiritual enemies to turn us aside) unless we take heed, diligent heed. 2. In particular, to *love the Lord our God,* as the best of beings, and the best of friends; and as far as this principle rules in the heart, and is the spring of its pulses, there will be a constant care and sincere endeavour to *walk in his ways,* in all his ways, even those that are narrow and up-hill, in every particular instance, in all manner of conversation to *keep his commandments,* at all times and in all conditions with purpose of heart to *cleave unto him,* and to serve him and his honour, and the interest of his kingdom among men, *with all our heart and with all our soul.* What good counsel was here given to them is given to us all. God give us grace to take it!

V. He dismisses them with a blessing (*v.* 6), particularly the half tribe of Manasseh, to which Joshua, as an Ephraimite, was somewhat nearer akin than to the other two, and who perhaps were the more loth to depart because they left one half of their own tribe behind them, and therefore, bidding often farewell, and lingering behind, had a second dismission and blessing, *v.* 7. Joshua not only prayed for them as a friend, but blessed them as a father in the name of the Lord, recommending them, their families, and affairs, to the grace of God. Some by the blessing Joshua gave them understand the presents he made them, in recompence of their services; but Joshua being a prophet, and having given them one part of a prophet's reward in the instructions he gave them (*v.* 5), no doubt we must understand this of the other, even the prayers he made for them, as one having authority, and as God's vicegerent.

VI. Being thus dismissed, they returned to *the land of their possession* in a body (*v.* 9), ferry-boats being, it is likely, provided for their repassing Jordan. Though masters of families may sometimes have occasion to be absent, long absent, from their families, yet, when their business abroad is finished, they must remember home is their place, from which they ought not to wander as a bird from her nest.

10 And when they came unto the borders of Jordan, that *are* in the land of Canaan, the children of Reuben and the children of Gad and the half tribe of Manasseh built there an altar by Jordan, a great altar to see to. 11 And the children of Israel heard say, Behold, the children of Reuben and the children of Gad and the half tribe of Manasseh have built an altar over against the land of Canaan, in the borders of Jordan, at the passage of the children of Israel. 12 And when the children of Israel heard *of it*, the whole congregation of the children of Israel gathered themselves together at Shiloh, to go up to war against them. 13 And the children of Israel sent unto the children of Reuben, and to the children of Gad, and to the half tribe of Manasseh, into the land of Gilead, Phinehas the son of Eleazar the priest, 14 And with him ten princes, of each chief house a prince throughout all the tribes of Israel; and each one *was* a head of the house of their fathers among the thousands of Israel. 15 And they came unto the children of Reuben, and to the children of Gad, and to the half tribe of Manasseh, unto the land of Gilead, and they spake with them, saying, 16 Thus saith the whole congregation of the LORD, What trespass *is* this that ye have committed against the God of Israel, to turn away this day from following the LORD, in that ye have builded you an altar, that ye might rebel this day against the LORD? 17 *Is* the iniquity of Peor too little for us, from which we are not cleansed until this day, although there was a plague in the congregation of the LORD, 18 But that ye must turn away this day from following the LORD? and it will be, *seeing* ye rebel to day against the LORD, that to morrow he will be wroth with the whole congregation of Israel. 19 Notwithstanding, if the land of your possession *be* unclean, *then* pass ye over unto the land of the possession of the LORD, wherein the LORD's tabernacle dwelleth, and take possession among us: but rebel not against the LORD, nor rebel against us, in building you an altar beside the altar of the LORD our God. 20 Did not Achan the son of Zerah commit a trespass in the accursed thing, and wrath fell on all the congregation of Israel? and that man perished not alone in his iniquity.

Here is, I. The pious care of the separated tribes to keep their hold of Canaan's religion, even when they were leaving Canaan's land, that they might not be as the *sons of the stranger, utterly separated from God's people*, Isa. lvi. 3. In order to this, they built a great altar on the borders of Jordan, to be a witness for them that they were Israelites, and as such *partakers of the altar of* the Lord, 1 Cor. x. 18. When they came to Jordan (*v.* 10) they did not consult how to preserve the remembrance of their own exploits in the wars of Canaan, and the services they had done their brethren, by erecting a monument to the immortal honour of the two tribes and a half; but their relation to the church of God, together with their interest in the communion of saints, is that which they are solicitous to preserve and perpetuate the proofs and evidences of; and therefore without delay, when the thing was first proposed by some among them, who, though glad to think that they were going towards home, were sorry to think that they were going from the altar of God, immediately they erected this altar, which served as a bridge to keep up their fellowship with the other tribes in the things of God. Some think they built this altar on the Canaan-side of Jordan, in the lot of Benjamin, that, looking over the river, they might see the figure of the altar at Shiloh, when they could not conveniently go to it; but it is more likely that they built it on their own side of the water, for what had they to do to build on another man's land without his consent? And it is said to be *over-against* the land of Canaan; nor would there have been any cause of suspecting it designed for sacrifice if they had not built it among themselves. This altar was very innocently and honestly designed, but it would have been well if, since it had in it an appearance of evil, and might be an occasion of offence to their brethren, they had consulted the oracle of God about it before they did it, or at least acquainted their brethren with their purpose, and given them the same explication of their altar before, to prevent their jealousy, which they did afterwards, to remove it. Their zeal was commendable, but it ought to have been guided with discretion. There was no need to hasten the building of an altar for the purpose for which they intended this, but they might have taken time to consider and take advice; yet, when their sincerity was made to appear, we do not find that they were blamed for their rashness. God does, and men should, overlook the weakness of an honest zeal.

II. The holy jealousy of the other tribes for the honour of God and his altar at Shiloh. Notice was immediately brought to the princes of Israel of the setting up of this altar, *v.* 11. And they, knowing how strict and severe that law was which required them to offer all their sacrifices in the place which God should choose, and not elsewhere (Deut. xii. 5—7), were soon apprehensive that the setting up of another altar was an affront to the choice which God had lately made of a place to put his name in, and had a direct tendency to the worship of some other God. Now,

1. Their suspicion was very excusable, for it must be confessed the thing, *prima facie—at first sight,* looked ill, and seemed to imply a design to set up and maintain a competitor with the altar at Shiloh. It was no strained *innuendo* from the building of an altar to infer an intention to offer sacrifice upon it, and that might introduce idolatry and end in a total apostasy from the faith and worship of the God of Israel. So great a matter might this fire kindle. God is jealous for his own institutions, and therefore we should be so too, and afraid of every thing that looks like, or leads to, idolatry.

2. Their zeal, upon this suspicion, was very commendable, *v.* 12. When they apprehended that these tribes, which by the river Jordan were separated from them, were separating themselves from God, they took it as the greatest injury that could be done to themselves, and showed a readiness, if it were necessary, to put their lives in their hands in defence of the altar of God, and to take up arms for the chastising and reducing of these rebels, and to prevent the spreading of the infection, if no gentler methods would serve, by cutting off from their body the gangrened member. They all gathered together, and Shiloh was the place of their rendezvous, because it was in defence of the divine charter lately granted to that place that they now appeared; their resolution was as became a kingdom of priests, who, being devoted to God and his service, did not *acknowledge their brethren* nor *know their own children,* Deut. xxxiii. 9. They would immediately *go up to war against them* if it appeared they had revolted from God, and were in rebellion against him. Though they were *bone of their bone,* had been *companions with them in tribulation* in the wilderness, and serviceable to them in the wars of Canaan, yet, if they turn to *serve other gods,* they will treat them as enemies, not as sons of Israel, but as *children of whoredoms,* for so God had appointed, Deut. xiii. 12, &c. They had but lately sheathed their swords, and retired from the perils and fatigues of war to the rest God had given them, and yet they are willing to begin a new war rather than be any way wanting in their duty to restrain, repress, and revenge, idolatry, and every step towards it—a brave resolution, and which shows them hearty for their religion, and, we hope, careful and diligent in the practice of it themselves. Corruptions in religion are best dealt with at first, before they get head and plead prescription.

3. Their prudence in the prosecution of this zealous resolution is no less commendable. God had appointed them, in cases of this nature, to *enquire and make search* (Deut. xiii. 14), that they might not wrong their brethren under pretence of righting their religion; accordingly they resolve here not to send forth their armies, to wage war, till they had first sent their ambassadors to enquire into the merits of the cause, and these men of the first rank, one out of each tribe, and Phinehas at the head of them to be their spokesman, *v.* 13, 14. Thus was their zeal for God tempered, guided, and governed by the *meekness of wisdom.* He that knows all things, and hates all evil things, would not punish the worst of criminals but he would first *go down and see,* Gen. xviii. 21. Many an unhappy strife would be prevented, or soon healed by an impartial and favourable enquiry into that which is the matter of the offence. The rectifying of mistakes and misunderstandings, and the setting of misconstrued words and actions in a true light, would be the most effectual way to accommodate both private and public quarrels, and bring them to a happy period.

4. The ambassadors' management of this matter came fully up to the sense and spirit of the congregation concerning it, and bespeaks much both of zeal and prudence.

(1.) The charge they draw up against their brethren is indeed very high, and admits no other excuse than that it was in their zeal for the honour of God, and was now intended to justify the resentments of the congregation at Shiloh and to awaken the supposed delinquents to clear themselves, otherwise they might have suspended their judgment, or mollified it at least, and not have taken it for granted, as they do here (*v.* 16), that the building of this altar was *a trespass against the God of Israel,* and a trespass no less heinous than the revolt of soldiers from their captain *(you turn from following the Lord),* and the rebellion of subjects against their sovereign: *that you might rebel this day against the Lord.* Hard words. It is well they were not able to make good their charge. Let not innocency think it strange to be thus misrepresented and accused. *They laid to my charge things that I knew not.*

(2.) The aggravation of the crime charged upon their brethren is somewhat far-fetched: Is *the iniquity of Peor too little for us? v.* 17. Probably that is mentioned because Phinehas, the first commissioner in this treaty, had signalized himself in that matter (Num. xxv. 7), and because we may suppose they were now about the very place in which that iniquity was committed on the other side Jordan. It is good to recollect and improve those instances of the wrath of God, revealed from heaven *against the ungodliness and unrighteousness of men,* which have fallen out in our own time, and which we ourselves have been eye-witnesses of. He reminds them of the iniquity of Peor, [1.] As a very great sin, and very provoking to God. The building of this altar seemed but a small matter, but it might lead to an iniquity as bad as that of Peor, and therefore must be crushed in its first rise. Note, The remembrance of great sins committed formerly should engage us to stand upon our guard against the least occasions and beginnings of sin; for the way of sin is down-hill. [2.] As a sin that the whole congregation had smarted for: "*There was a plague in the congregation of the Lord,* of which, in one day, there died no fewer than 24,000; was not that enough for ever to warn you against idolatry? What! will you bring upon yourselves another plague? Are you so mad upon an idolatrous altar that you will run yourselves thus upon the sword's point of God's judgments? Does not our camp still feel from that sin and the punishment of it? We *are not cleansed from it unto this day;* there are remaining sparks," *First,* "Of the infection of that sin; some among us so inclined to idolatry that if you set up another altar they will soon take occasion from that, whether you intend it or no, to worship another God." *Secondly,* "Of the wrath of God against us for that sin. We have reason to fear that, if we provoke God by another sin *to visit,* he will remember against us the iniquity of Peor, as he threatened to do that of the golden calf, Exod. xxxii. 34. And dare you wake the sleeping lion of divine vengeance?" Note, It is a foolish and dangerous thing for people to think their former sins little, *too little for them,* as those do who add sin to sin, and so *treasure up wrath against the day of wrath.* Let therefore the time past suffice, 1 Pet. iv. 3.

(3.) The reason they give for their concerning themselves so warmly in this matter is very sufficient. They were obliged to it, in their own necessary defence, by the law of self-preservation: "For, if you revolt from God to-day, who knows but to-morrow his judgments may break in upon the *whole congregation* (*v.* 18), as in the case of Achan? *v.* 20. He sinned, and we all smarted for it, by which we should receive instruction, and from what God did then infer what he may do, and fear what he will do, if we do not witness against your sin, who are so many, and punish it." Note, The conservators of the public peace are obliged, in justice to the common safety, to use their power for the restraining and suppressing of vice and profaneness, lest, if it be connived at, the sin thereby become national, and bring God's judgments upon the community. Nay, we are all concerned to reprove our neighbour when he does amiss, lest we bear sin for him, Lev. xix. 17.

(4.) The offer they make is very fair and kind (*v.* 19), that if they thought the land of their possession unclean, for want of an altar, and therefore could not be easy without one, rather than they should set up another in competition with that at Shiloh they should be welcome to come back to the land *where the Lord's tabernacle was,* and settle there, and they would very willingly straiten themselves to make room for them. By this they showed a sincere and truly pious zeal against schism, that rather than their brethren should have any occasion to set up a separate altar, though their pretence for it, as here supposed, was very weak and grounded upon a great mistake, yet they were willing to part with a considerable share of the land which God himself had by the lot assigned them, to comprehend them and take them in among them. This was the spirit of Israelites indeed.

21 Then the children of Reuben and the children of Gad and the half tribe of Manasseh answered, and said unto the heads of the thousands of Israel, 22 The LORD God of gods, the LORD God of gods, he knoweth, and Israel he shall know; if *it be* in rebellion, or if in transgression against the LORD, (save us not this day,) 23 That we have built us an altar to turn from following the LORD, or if to offer thereon burnt offering or meat offering, or if to offer peace offerings thereon, let the LORD himself require *it;*

24 And if we have not *rather* done it for fear of *this* thing, saying, In time to come your children might speak unto our children, saying, What have ye to do with the LORD God of Israel? 25 For the LORD hath made Jordan a border between us and you, ye children of Reuben and children of Gad; ye have no part in the LORD: so shall your children make our children cease from fearing the LORD. 26 Therefore we said, Let us now prepare to build us an altar, not for burnt offering, nor for sacrifice: 27 But *that* it *may be* a witness between us, and you, and our generations after us, that we might do the service of the LORD before him with our burnt offerings, and with our sacrifices, and with our peace offerings; that your children may not say to our children in time to come, Ye have no part in the LORD. 28 Therefore said we, that it shall be, when they should *so* say to us or to our generations in time to come, that we may say *again*, Behold the pattern of the altar of the LORD, which our fathers made, not for burnt offerings, nor for sacrifices; but it *is* a witness between us and you. 29 God forbid that we should rebel against the LORD, and turn this day from following the LORD, to build an altar for burnt offerings, for meat offerings, or for sacrifices, beside the altar of the LORD our God that *is* before his tabernacle.

We may suppose there was a general convention called of the princes and great men of the separate tribes, to give audience to these ambassadors; or perhaps the army, as it came home, was still encamped in a body, and not yet dispersed; however it was, there were enough to represent the two tribes and a half, and to give their sense. Their reply to the warm remonstrance of the ten tribes is very fair and ingenuous. They do not retort their charge, upbraid them with the injustice and unkindness of their threatenings, nor reproach them for their rash and hasty censures, but give them a soft answer which turns away wrath, avoiding all those *grievous words which stir up anger;* they demur not to their jurisdiction, nor plead that they were not accountable to them for what they had done, nor bid them mind their own business, but, by a free and open declaration of their sincere intention in what they did, free themselves from the imputation they were under, and set themselves right in the opinion of their brethren, tc do which they only needed to state the case and put the matter in a true light.

I. They solemnly protest against any design to use this altar for sacrifice or offering, and therefore were far from setting it up in competition with the altar at Shiloh, or from entertaining the least thought of deserting that. They had indeed set up that which had the shape and fashion of an altar, but they had not dedicated it to a religious use, had had no solemnity of its consecration, and therefore ought not to be charged with a design to put it to any such use. To gain credit to this protestation here is,

1. A solemn appeal to God concerning it, with which they begin their defence, intending thereby to give glory to God first, and then to give satisfaction to their brethren, *v.* 22. (1.) A profound awe and reverence of God are expressed in the form of their appeal: *The Lord God of gods, the Lord God of gods, he knows.* Or, as it might be read somewhat closer to the original, *The God of gods, Jehovah, the God of gods, Jehovah, he knows,* which bespeaks his self-existence and self-sufficiency; he is Jehovah, and has sovereignty and supremacy over all beings and powers whatsoever, even those that are called *gods,* or that are worshipped. This brief confession of their faith would help to obviate and remove their brethren's suspicion of them, as if they intended to desert the God of Israel, and worship other gods: how could those entertain such a thought who believed him to be God over all? Let us learn hence always to speak of God with reverence and seriousness, and to mention his name with a solemn pause. Those who make their appeals to heaven with a slight, careless, "God knows," have reason to fear lest they take his name in vain, for it is very unlike this appeal. (2.) It is a great confidence of their own integrity which they express in the matter of their appeal. They refer the controversy to the God of gods, whose judgment, we are sure, is *according to truth,* such as the guilty have reason to dread and the upright to rejoice in. "*If* it be *in rebellion or transgression* that we have built this altar, to confront the altar of the Lord at Shiloh, to make a party, or to set up any new gods or worships," [1.] "*He knows it* (*v.* 22), for he is perfectly acquainted with the thoughts and intents of the heart, and particularly with all inclinations to idolatry (Ps. xliv. 20, 21); this is in a particular manner before him. We believe he knows it, and we cannot by any arts conceal it from him." [2.] "*Let him require it,* as we know he will, for he is a jealous God." Nothing but a clear conscience would have thus imprecated divine justice to avenge the rebellion if there had been any. Note, *First,* In every thing we do in religion, it highly concerns us to approve

ourselves to God in our integrity therein, remembering that he knows the heart. *Secondly,* When we fall under the censures of men, it is very comfortable to be able with a humble confidence to appeal to God concerning our sincerity. See 1 Cor. iv. 3, 4.

2. A sober apology presented to their brethren: *Israel, he shall know.* Though the record on high, and the witness in our bosoms, are principally to be made sure for us, yet there is a satisfaction besides which we owe to our brethren who doubt concerning our integrity, and which we should be ready to give with meekness and fear. If our sincerity be known to God, we should study likewise to let others know it by its fruits, especially those who, though they mistake us, yet show a zeal for the glory of God, as the ten tribes here did.

3. A serious abjuration or renunciation of the design which they were suspected to be guilty of. With this they conclude their defence (*v.* 29): "*God forbid that we should rebel against the Lord,* as we own we should if we had set up this altar for burnt-offerings; no, we abhor the thought of it. We have as great a value and veneration for the altar of the Lord at Shiloh as any of the tribes of Israel have, and are as firmly resolved to adhere to it and constantly to attend it; we have the same concern that you have for the purity of God's worship and the unity of his church; far be it, far be it from us, to think of turning away from following God."

II. They fully explain their true intent and meaning in building this altar; and we have all the reason in the world to believe that it is a true representation of their design, and not advanced now to palliate it afterwards, as we have reason to think that these same persons meant very honestly when they petitioned to have their lot on that side Jordan, though then also it was their unhappiness to be misunderstood even by Moses himself. In their vindication, they make it out that the building of this altar was so far from being a step towards a separation from their brethren, and from the altar of the Lord at Shiloh, that, on the contrary, it was really designed for a pledge and preservative of their communion with their brethren and with the altar of God, and a token of their resolution to *do the service of the Lord before him* (*v.* 27), and to continue to do so.

1. They gave an account of the fears they had lest, in process of time, their posterity, being seated at such a distance from the tabernacle, should be looked upon and treated as strangers to the commonwealth of Israel (*v.* 24); it was for fear of this thing, and the word signifies a great perplexity and solicitude of mind which they were in, until they eased themselves by this expedient. As they were returning home (and we may suppose it was not thought of before, else they would have made Joshua acquainted with their purpose), some of them in discourse started this matter, and the rest took the hint, and represented to themselves and one another a very melancholy prospect of what might probably happen in after-ages, that their children would be looked upon by the other tribes as having no interest in the altar of God and the sacrifices there offered. Now indeed they were owned as brethren, and were as welcome at the tabernacle as any other of the tribes; but what if their children after them should be disowned? They, by reason of their distance, and the interposition of Jordan, which it was not easy at all times to pass and repass, could not be so numerous and constant in their attendance on the three yearly feasts as the other tribes, to make a continual claim to the privileges of Israelites, and would therefore be looked upon as inconsiderable members of their church, and by degrees would be rejected as not members of it at all: *So shall your children* (who in their pride will be apt to monopolize the privileges of the altar) *make our children* (who perhaps will not be so careful as they ought to be to keep hold of those privileges) *cease from fearing the Lord.* Note, (1.) Those that are cut off from public ordinances are likely to lose all religion, and will by degrees cease from fearing the Lord. Though the form and profession of godliness are kept up by many without the life and power of it, yet the life and power of it will not long be kept up without the form and profession. You take away grace if you take away the means of grace. (2.) Those who have themselves found the comfort and benefit of God's ordinances cannot but desire to preserve and perpetuate the entail of them upon their seed, and use all possible precautions that their children after them may not be *made to cease from following the Lord,* or be looked upon as having no part in him.

2. The project they had to prevent this, *v.* 26—28. "Therefore, to secure an interest in the altar of God to those who shall come after us, and to prove their title to it, *we said, Let us build an altar, to be a witness between us and you,*" that, having this copy of the altar in their custody, it might be produced as an evidence of their right to the privileges of the original. Every one that saw this altar, and observed that it was never used for sacrifice and offering, would enquire what was the meaning of it, and this answer would be given to that enquiry, that it was built by those separate tribes, in token of their communion with their brethren and their joint-interest with them in the altar of the Lord. Christ is the great altar that sanctifies every gift; the best evidence of our interest in him will be the pattern of his Spirit in our hearts, and our conformity to him. If we can produce this it will be a testimony for us that we have *a part in the Lord,* and an earnest of our perseverance in following him.

30 And when Phinehas the priest, and the princes of the congregation and heads of the thousands of Israel which *were* with him, heard the words that the children of Reuben and the children of Gad and the children of Manasseh spake, it pleased them. 31 And Phinehas the son of Eleazar the priest said unto the children of Reuben, and to the children of Gad, and to the children of Manasseh, This day we perceive that the LORD *is* among us, because ye have not committed this trespass against the LORD: now ye have delivered the children of Israel out of the hand of the LORD. 32 And Phinehas the son of Eleazar the priest, and the princes, returned from the children of Reuben, and from the children of Gad, out of the land of Gilead, unto the land of Canaan, to the children of Israel, and brought them word again. 33 And the thing pleased the children of Israel; and the children of Israel blessed God, and did not intend to go up against them in battle, to destroy the land wherein the children of Reuben and Gad dwelt. 34 And the children of Reuben and the children of Gad called the altar *Ed:* for it *shall be* a witness between us that the LORD *is* God.

We have here the good issue of this controversy, which, if there had not been on both sides a disposition to peace, as there was on both sides a zeal for God, might have been of ill consequence; for quarrels about religion, for want of wisdom and love, often prove the most fierce and most difficult to be accomodated. But these contending parties, when the matter was fairly stated and argued, were so happy as to understand one another very well, and so the difference was presently compromised.

I. The .ambassadors were exceedingly pleased when the separate tribes had given in a protestation of the innocency of their intentions in building this altar. 1. The ambassadors did not call in question their sincerity in that protestation, did not say, "You tell us you design it not for sacrifice and offering, but who can believe you? What security will you give us that it shall never be so used?" No. *Charity believes all things, hopes all things,* believes and hopes the best, and is very loth to give the lie to any. 2. They did not upbraid them with the rashness and unadvisedness of this action, did not tell them, "If you would do such a thing, and with this good intention, yet you might have had so much respect for Joshua and Eleazar as to have advised with them, or at least have made them acquainted with it, and so have saved the trouble and expense of this embassy." But a little want of consideration and good manners should be excused and overlooked in those who, we have reason to think, mean honestly. 3. Much less did they go about to fish for evidence to make out their charge, because they had once exhibited it, but were glad to have their mistake rectified, and were not at all ashamed to own it. Proud and peevish spirits, when they have passed an unjust censure upon their brethren, though ever so much convincing evidence be brought of the injustice of it, will stand to it, and can by no means be persuaded to retract it. These ambassadors were not so prejudiced; their brethren's vindication pleased them, *v.* 30. They looked upon their innocency as a token of God's presence (*v.* 31), especially when they found that what was done was so far from being an indication of their growing cool to the altar of God that, on the contrary, it was a fruit of their zealous affection to it: *You have delivered the children of Israel out of the hand of the Lord,* that is, "You have not, as we feared, delivered them into the hand of the Lord, or exposed them to his judgments by the trespass we were jealous of."

II. The congregation was abundantly satisfied when their ambassadors reported to them their brethren's apology for what they had done. It should seem they staid together, at least by their representatives, until they heard the issue (*v.* 32); and when they understood the truth of the matter it pleased them (*v.* 33), and they *blessed God.* Note, Our brethren's constancy in religion, their zeal for the power of godliness, and their keeping the *unity of the Spirit* in faith and love, notwithstanding the jealousies conceived of them as breaking the unity of the church, are things which we should be very glad to be satisfied of, and should make the matter both of our rejoicing and of our thanksgiving; let God have the glory of it, and let us take the comfort of it. Being thus satisfied, they laid down their arms immediately, and were so far from any thoughts of prosecuting the war they had been meditating against their brethren that we may suppose them wishing for the next feast, when they should meet them at Shiloh.

III. The separate tribes were gratified, and, since they had a mind to preserve among them this pattern of the altar of God, though there was not likely to be that occasion for it which they fancied, yet Joshua and the princes let them have their humour, and did not give orders for the demolishing of it, though there was as much reason to fear that it might in process of time be an occasion of idolatry as there was to hope that ever it might be a preservation from idolatry. Thus did *the strong bear the infirmities of the weak.* Only care was taken that they having explained the meaning of their altar, that it was intended for no more than a testimony of their communion with the altar at Shiloh, this explanation should be recorded, which was done according to the usage of those times by giving a name to it signifying so much (*v.* 34); they called it *Ed, a witness* to that, and no more, a witness of the relation they stood in to God and Israel, and of their concurrence with the rest of the tribes in the same common faith, *that Jehovah he is God,* he and no other. It was a witness to posterity of their care to transmit their religion pure and entire to them, and would be a witness against them if ever they should forsake God and turn from following after him.

CHAP. XXIII.

In this and the following chapter we have two farewell sermons, which Joshua preached to the people of Israel a little before his death. Had he designed to gratify the curiosity of succeeding ages, he would rather have recorded the method of Israel's settlement in their new conquests, their husbandry, manufactures, trade, customs, courts of justice, and the constitutions of their infant commonwealth, which one would wish to be informed of; but that which he intended in the registers of this book was to entail on posterity a sense of religion and their duty to God; and therefore, overlooking these things which are the usual subjects of a common history, he here transmits to his reader the methods he took to persuade Israel to be faithful to their covenant with their God, which might have a good influence on the generations to come who should read those reasonings, as we may hope they had on that generation which then heard them. In this chapter we have, I. A convention of the states called (ver. 1, 2), probably to consult about the common concerns of their land, and to set in order that which, after some years' trial, being left to their prudence, was found wanting. II. Joshua's speech to them at the opening, or perhaps at the concluding, of the sessions, to hear which was the principal design of their coming together. In it, 1. Joshua reminds them of what God had done for them (ver. 3, 4, 9, 14), and what he was ready to do yet further, ver. 5, 10. 2. He exhorts them carefully and resolutely to persevere in their duty to God, ver. 6, 8, 11. III. He cautions them against all familiarity with their idolatrous neighbours, ver. 7. IV. He gives them fair warning of the fatal consequences of it, if they should revolt from God and turn to idols, ver. 12, 13, 15, 16. In all this he showed himself zealous for his God, and jealous over Israel with a godly jealousy.

AND it came to pass a long time after that the LORD had given rest unto Israel from all their enemies round about, that Joshua waxed old *and* stricken in age. 2 And Joshua called for all Israel, *and* for their elders, and for their heads, and for their judges, and for their officers, and said unto them, I am old *and* stricken in age: 3 And ye have seen all that the LORD your God hath done unto all these nations because of you; for the LORD your God *is* he that hath fought for you. 4 Behold, I have divided unto you by lot these nations that remain, to be an inheritance for your tribes, from Jordan, with all the nations that I have cut off, even unto the great sea westward. 5 And the LORD your God, he shall expel them from before you, and drive them from out of your sight; and ye shall possess their land, as the LORD your God hath promised unto you. 6 Be ye therefore very courageous to keep and to do all that is written in the book of the law of Moses, that ye turn not aside therefrom *to* the right hand or *to* the left; 7 That ye come not among these nations, these that remain among you; neither make mention of the name of their gods, nor cause to swear *by them,* neither serve them, nor bow yourselves unto them. 8 But cleave unto the LORD your God, as ye have done unto this day. 9 For the LORD hath driven out from before you great nations and strong: but *as for* you, no man hath been able to stand before you unto this day. 10 One man of you shall chase a thousand: for the LORD your God, he *it is* that fighteth for you, as he hath promised you.

As to the date of this edict of Joshua,

I. No mention at all is made of the place where this general assembly was held; some think it was at Timnath-serah, Joshua's own city, where he lived, and whence, being old, he could not well remove. But it does not appear that he took so much state upon him; therefore it is more probable this meeting was at Shiloh, where the tabernacle of meeting was, and to which place, perhaps, all the males that could had now come up to worship before the Lord, at one of the three great feasts, which Joshua took the opportunity of, for the delivering of this charge to them.

II. There is only a general mention of the time when this was done. It was *long after the Lord had given them rest,* but it is not said how long, *v.* 1. It was, 1. So long as that Israel had time to feel the comforts of their rest and possessions in Canaan, and to enjoy the advantages of that good land. 2. So long as that Joshua had time to observe which way their danger lay of being corrupted, namely, by their intimacy with the Canaanites that remained, against which he is therefore careful to arm them.

III. The persons to whom Joshua made this speech: *To all Israel, even their elders, &c.* So it might be read, *v.* 2. They could not all come within hearing, but he called for all the elders, that is, the privy-counsellors, which in later times constituted the great Sanhedrim, the heads of the tribes, that is, the noblemen and gentlemen of their respective countries, the judges learned in the laws, that tried criminals and causes, and gave judgment upon them, and, *lastly,* the officers or sheriffs, who were entrusted with the execution of those judgments. These Joshua called together, and to them he addressed himself, 1. That they might communicate what he said, or at least the sense and substance of it, to those under them in their respective countries, and so this charge might be dispersed through the whole nation. 2. Because, if they would be prevailed upon to serve God and cleave to him, they, by their influence on the common people, would keep them faithful. If great men be good men, they will help to make many good.

IV. Joshua's circumstances when he gave them this charge: He *was old and stricken in age* (*v.* 1), probably it was in the last year of his life, and he lived to be 110 years old, *ch.* xxiv. 29. And he himself takes notice of it, in the first words of his discourse, *v.* 2. When he began to be old, some years ago, God reminded him of it (*ch.* xiii. 1): *Thou art old.* But now he did himself feel so much of the decays of age that he needed not to be told of it, he readily speaks of it himself: *I am old and stricken in age.* He uses it, 1. As an argument with himself to give them this charge, because being old he could expect to be but a little while with them, to advise and instruct them, and therefore (as Peter speaks, 2 Pet. i. 13) *as long as he is in this tabernacle* he will take all opportunities to *put them in remembrance* of their duty, knowing by the increasing infirmities of age that he must shortly put off this tabernacle, and desiring that after his decease they might continue as good as they were now. When we see death hastening towards us, this should quicken us to do the work of life with all our might. 2. As an argument with them to give heed to what he said. He was old and experienced, and therefore to be the more regarded, for days should speak; he had grown old in their service, and had spent himself for their good, and therefore was to be the more regarded by them. He was old and dying; they would not have him long to preach to them; therefore let them observe what he said now, and lay it up in store for the time to come.

V. The discourse itself, the scope of which is to engage them if possible, them and their seed after them, to persevere in the true faith and worship of the God of Israel.

1. He puts them in mind of the great things God had done for them, now in his days, and under his administration, for here he goes no further back. And for the proof of this he appeals to their own eyes (*v.* 3): "*You have seen all that the Lord your God has done;* not what I have done, or what you have done (we were only instruments in God's hand), but what God himself has done by me and for you." (1.) Many great and mighty nations (as the rate of nations then went) were driven out from as fine a country as any was at that time upon the face of the earth, to make room for Israel. "You see *what he has done to these nations,* who were his creatures, the work of his hands, and whom he could have made new creatures and fit for his service; yet see what destruction he has made of them *because of you* (*v.* 2), how he has *driven them out from before you* (*v.* 9), as if they were of no account with him, though great and strong in comparison with you." (2.) They were not only driven out (this they might have been, and yet sent to some other country less rich to begin a new plantation there, suppose to that wilderness in which Israel had wandered so long, and so they would only have exchanged seats with them), but they were trodden down before them; though they held out against them with the greatest obstinacy that could be, yet they were subdued before them, which made the possessing of their land so much the more glorious to Israel and so much the more illustrious an instance of the power and goodness of the God of Israel (*v.* 3): "*The Lord your God* has not only led you, and fed you, and kept you, but he has fought for you as a man of war," by which title he was known among them when he first brought them out of Egypt, Exod. xv. 3. So clear and cheap were all their victories, during the course of this long war, that *no man had been able to stand before them* (*v.* 9), that is, to make head against them, so as to put them in fear, create them any difficulty, or give any check to the progress of their victorious arms. In every battle they carried the day, and in every siege they carried the city; their loss before Ai was upon a particular occasion, was inconsiderable, and only served to show them on what terms they stood with God; but, otherwise, never was army crowned with such a constant uninterrupted series of successes as the armies of Israel were in the wars of Canaan. (3.) They had not only conquered the Canaanites, but were put in full possession of their land (*v.* 4): "*I have divided to you by lot these nations,* both those which are cut off and those which remain, not only that you may spoil and plunder them, and live at discretion in their country for a time, but to be a sure and lasting inheritance for your tribes. You have it not only under your feet, but in your hands."

2. He assures them of God's readiness to carry on and complete this glorious work in due time. It is true some of the Canaanites did yet remain, and in some places were strong and daring, but this should be no disappointment to their expectations; when Israel was so multiplied as to be able to replenish this land God would expel the Canaanites to the last man, provided Israel would pursue their advantages and carry on the war against them with vigour (*v.* 5): "*The Lord your God will drive them from out of your sight,* so that there shall not be a Canaanite to be seen in the land; and even that part of the country which is yet in their hands you shall possess." If it were objected that the men of war of the several

tribes being dispersed to their respective countries, and the army disbanded, it would be difficult to get them together when there was occasion to renew the war upon the remainder of the Canaanites, in answer to this he tells them what little need they had to be in care about the numbers of their forces (*v.* 10): *One man of you shall chase a thousand,* as Jonathan did, 1 Sam. xiv. 13. "Each tribe may venture for itself, and for the recovery of its own lot, without fearing disadvantage by the disproportion of numbers; for the Lord your God, whose all power is, both to inspirit and to dispirit, and who has all the creatures at his beck, *he it is that fighteth for you;* and how many do you reckon him for?"

3. He hereupon most earnestly charges them to adhere to their duty, to go on and persevere in the good ways of the Lord wherein they had so well set out. He exhorts them,

(1.) To be very courageous (*v.* 6): "God fighteth for you against your enemies, do you therefore *behave yourselves valiantly* for him. Keep and do with a firm resolution *all that is written in the book of the law.*" He presses upon them no more than what they were already bound to. "Keep with care, do with diligence, and eye what is written with sincerity."

(2.) To be very cautious: "Take heed of missing it, either on the right hand or on the left, for there are errors and extremes on both hands. Take heed of running either into a profane neglect of any of God's institutions or into a superstitious addition of any of your own inventions." They must especially take heed of all approaches towards idolatry, the sin to which they were first inclined and would be most tempted, *v.* 7. [1.] They must not acquaint themselves with idolaters, nor come among them to visit them or be present at any of their feasts or entertainments, for they could not contract any intimacy nor keep up any conversation with them, without danger of infection. [2.] They must not show the least respect to any idol, nor *make mention of the name of their gods,* but endeavour to bury the remembrance of them in perpetual oblivion, that the worship of them may never be revived. "Let the very name of them be forgotten. Look upon idols as filthy detestable things, not to be named without the utmost loathing and detestation." The Jews would not suffer their children to name swine's flesh, because it was forbidden, lest the name of it should occasion their desiring it; but, if they had occasion to speak of it, they must call it *that strange thing.* It is a pity that among Christians the names of the heathen gods are so commonly used, and made so familiar as they are, especially in plays and poems: let those names which have been set up in rivalship with God be for ever loathed and lost. [3.] They must not countenance others in showing respect to them. They must not only not swear by them themselves, but they must not cause others to swear by them, which supposes that they must not make any covenants with idolaters, because they, in the confirming of their covenants, would swear by their idols; never let Israelites admit such an oath. [4.] They must take heed of these occasions of idolatry, lest by degrees they should arrive at the highest step of it, which was serving false gods, and bowing down to them, against the letter of the second commandment.

(3.) To be very constant (*v.* 8): *Cleave unto the Lord your God,* that is, "delight in him, depend upon him, devote yourselves to his glory, and continue to do so to the end, *as you have done unto this day,* ever since you came to Canaan;" for, being willing to make the best of them, he looks not so far back as the iniquity of Peor. There might be many things amiss among them, but they had not forsaken the Lord their God, and it is in order to insinuate his exhortation to perseverance with the more pleasing power that he praises them. "Go on and prosper, for the Lord is with you while you are with him." Those that command should commend; the way to make people better is to make the best of them. "You have cleaved to the Lord unto this day, therefore go on to do so, else you lose the praise and recompence of what you have wrought. Your righteousness will not be mentioned unto you if you turn from it."

11 Take good heed therefore unto yourselves, that ye love the LORD your God. 12 Else if ye do in any wise go back, and cleave unto the remnant of these nations, *even* these that remain among you, and shall make marriages with them, and go in unto them, and they to you: 13 Know for a certainty that the LORD your God will no more drive out *any of* these nations from before you; but they shall be snares and traps unto you, and scourges in your sides, and thorns in your eyes, until ye perish from off this good land which the LORD your God hath given you. 14 And, behold, this day I *am* going the way of all the earth: and ye know in all your hearts and in all your souls, that not one thing hath failed of all the good things which the LORD your God spake concerning you; all are come to pass unto you, *and* not one thing hath failed thereof. 15 Therefore it shall come to pass, *that* as all good things are

come upon you, which the LORD your God promised you; so shall the LORD bring upon you all evil things, until he have destroyed you from off this good land which the LORD your God hath given you. 16 When ye have transgressed the covenant of the LORD your God, which he commanded you, and have gone and served other gods, and bowed yourselves to them; then shall the anger of the LORD be kindled against you, and ye shall perish quickly from off the good land which he hath given unto you.

Here, I. Joshua directs them what to do, that they might persevere in religion, *v.* 11. Would we cleave to the Lord, and not forsake him, 1. We must always stand upon our guard, for many a precious soul is lost and ruined through carelessness: "Take heed therefore, *take good heed to yourselves,* to your *souls* (so the word is), that the inward man be kept clean from the pollutions of sin, and closely employed in the service of God." God has given us precious souls with this charge, "Take good heed to them, keep them with all diligence, above all keepings." 2. What we do in religion we must do from a principle of love, not by constraint or from a slavish fear of God, but of choice and with delight. "*Love the Lord your God,* and you will not leave him."

II. He urges God's fidelity to them as an argument why they should be faithful to him (*v.* 14): "*I am going the way of all the earth,* I am old and dying." To die is to go a journey, a journey to our long home; it is the way of all the earth, the way that all mankind must go, sooner or later. Joshua himself, though so great and good a man, and one that could so ill be spared, cannot be exempted from this common lot. He takes notice of it here that they might look upon these as his dying words, and regard them accordingly. Or thus: "*I am dying,* and leaving you. *Me you have not always;* but if you cleave to the Lord he will never leave you." Or thus, "Now that I am near my end it is proper to look back upon the years that are past; and, in the review, I find, and you *yourselves know it in all your hearts and in all your souls,* by a full conviction on the clearest evidence, and the thing has made an impression upon you"—(that knowledge does us good which is seated, not in the head only, but in the heart and soul, and with which we are duly affected)—"you know that *not one thing hath failed of all the good things which the Lord spoke concerning you*" (and he spoke a great many); see *ch.* xxi. 45. God had promised them victory, rest, plenty, his tabernacle among them, &c., and *not one thing had failed* of all he had promised. "Now," said he, "has God been thus true to you? Be not you false to him." It is the apostle's argument for perseverance (Heb. x. 23), *He is faithful that has promised.*

III. He gives them fair warning what would be the fatal consequences of apostasy (*v.* 12, 13, 15, 16): "If you go back, know for a certainty it will be your ruin." Observe,

1. How he describes the apostasy which he warns them against. The steps of it would be (*v.* 12) growing intimate with idolaters, who would craftily wheedle them, and insinuate themselves into their acquaintance, now that they had become lords of the country, to serve their own ends. The next step would be intermarrying with them, drawn to it by their artifices, who would be glad to bestow their children upon these wealthy Israelites. And the consequence of that would be (*v.* 16) *serving other gods* (which were pretended to be the ancient deities of the country) and bowing down to them. Thus the way of sin is down-hill, and those who have fellowship with sinners cannot avoid having fellowship with sin. This he represents, (1.) As a base and shameful desertion; "it is going back from what you have so well begun," *v.* 12. (2.) As a most perfidious breach of promise (*v.* 16): "It is a transgression of *the covenant of the Lord your God, which he commanded you,* and which you yourselves set your hand to." Other sins were transgressions of the law God commanded them, but this was a transgression of the covenant he commanded them, and amounted to a breach of the relation between God and them and a forfeiture of all the benefits of the covenant.

2. How he describes the destruction which he warns them of. He tells them, (1.) That these remainders of the Canaanites, if they should harbour them, and indulge them, and join in affinity with them, would be snares and traps to them, both to draw them to sin (not only to idolatry, but to all immoralities, which would be the ruin, not only of their virtue, but of their wisdom and sense, their spirit and honour), and also to draw them into foolish bargains, unprofitable projects, and all manner of inconveniences; and having thus by underhand practices decoyed them into one mischief or other, so as to gain advantages against them, they would then act more openly, and be *scourges in their sides* and *thorns in their eyes,* would perhaps kill or drive away their cattle, burn or steal their corn, alarm or plunder their houses, and would by all ways possible be vexatious to them; for, whatever pretences of friendship they might make, a Canaanite, unless proselyted to the faith and worship of the true God, would in every age hate the very name and sight of an Israelite. See how the punishment would be made to answer the sin, nay, how the sin itself would be the punishment. (2.) That the anger of the Lord would be kindled against them. Their making leagues with the Canaanites would

not only give those idolaters the opportunity of doing them a mischief, and be the fostering of snakes in their bosoms, but it would likewise provoke God to become their enemy, and would kindle the fire of his displeasure against them. (3.) That all the threatenings of the word would be fulfilled, as the promise had been, for the God of eternal truth is faithful to both (*v.* 15): "*As all good things have come upon you* according to the promise, so long as you have kept close to God, so all evil things will come upon you according to the threatening, if you forsake him." Moses had *set before them good and evil;* they had experienced the good, and were now in the enjoyment of it, and the evil would as certainly come if they were disobedient. As God's promises are not a fool's paradise, so his threatenings are not bugbears. (4.) That it would end in the utter ruin of their church and nation, as Moses had foretold. This is three times mentioned here. Your enemies will vex you *until you perish from off this good land, v.* 13. Again, "God will plague you *until he have destroyed you from off this good land, v.* 15. Heaven and earth will concur to root you out, so that (*v.* 16) *you shall perish from off the good land.*" It will aggravate their perdition that the land from which they shall perish is a good land, and a land which God himself had given them, and which therefore he would have secured to them if they by their wickedness had not thrown themselves out of it. Thus the goodness of the heavenly Canaan, and the free and sure grant God has made of it, will aggravate the misery of those that shall for ever be shut out and perish from it. Nothing will make them see how wretched they are so much as to see how happy they might have been. Joshua thus sets before them the fatal consequences of their apostasy, that, *knowing the terror of the Lord,* they might be persuaded *with purpose of heart to cleave to him.*

CHAP. XXIV.

This chapter concludes the life and reign of Joshua, in which we have, I. The great care and pains he took to confirm the people of Israel in the true faith and worship of God, that they might, after his death, persevere therein. In order to this he called another general assembly of the heads of the congregation of Israel (ver. 1) and dealt with them, 1. By way of narrative, recounting the great things God had done for them and their fathers, ver. 2—13. 2. By way of charge to them, in consideration thereof, to serve God, ver. 14. 3. By way of treaty with them, wherein he aims to bring them, (1.) To make religion their deliberate choice; and they did so, with reasons for their choice, ver. 15—18. (2.) To make it their determinate choice, and to resolve to adhere to it, ver. 19—24. 4. By way of covenant upon that treaty, ver. 25—28. II. The conclusion of this history, with, 1. The death and burial of Joshua (ver. 29, 30) and Eleazar (ver. 33), and the mention of the burial of Joseph's bones upon that occasion, ver. 32. 2. A general account of the state of Israel at that time, ver. 31.

AND Joshua gathered all the tribes of Israel to Shechem, and called for the elders of Israel, and for their heads, and for their judges, and for their officers; and they presented themselves before God. 2 And Joshua said unto all the people, Thus saith the LORD God of Israel, Your fathers dwelt on the other side of the flood in old time, *even* Terah the father of Abraham, and the father of Nachor: and they served other gods. 3 And I took your father Abraham from the other side of the flood, and led him throughout all the land of Canaan, and multiplied his seed, and gave him Isaac. 4 And I gave unto Isaac, Jacob, and Esau: and I gave unto Esau mount Seir, to possess it; but Jacob and his children went down into Egypt. 5 I sent Moses also and Aaron, and I plagued Egypt, according to that which I did among them: and afterward I brought you out. 6 And I brought your fathers out of Egypt: and ye came unto the sea; and the Egyptians pursued after your fathers with chariots and horsemen unto the Red sea. 7 And when they cried unto the LORD, he put darkness between you and the Egyptians, and brought the sea upon them, and covered them; and your eyes have seen what I have done in Egypt: and ye dwelt in the wilderness a long season. 8 And I brought you into the land of the Amorites, which dwelt on the other side Jordan; and they fought with you: and I gave them into your hand, that ye might possess their land; and I destroyed them from before you. 9 Then Balak the son of Zippor, king of Moab, arose and warred against Israel, and sent and called Balaam the son of Beor to curse you: 10 But I would not hearken unto Balaam; therefore he blessed you still: so I delivered you out of his hand. 11 And ye went over Jordan, and came unto Jericho: and the men of Jericho fought against you, the Amorites, and the Perizzites, and the Canaanites, and the Hittites, and the Girgashites, the Hivites, and the Jebusites; and I delivered them into your hand. 12 And I sent the hornet before you, which drave them out from before you, *even* the two kings of the Amorites; *but* not with thy sword, nor with thy bow. 13 And I have given you a land for which ye did not labour, and cities which ye built not, and ye dwell in them; of the vineyards and oliveyards which ye planted not do ye eat. 14 Now therefore fear the LORD, and serve him in sincerity and in truth: and put away the gods which your fathers served on the other side of the flood, and in Egypt; and serve ye the LORD.

Joshua thought he had taken his last farewell of Israel in the solemn charge he gave them in the foregoing chapter, when he said, *I go the way of all the earth;* but God graciously continuing his life longer than expected, and renewing his strength, he was desirous to improve it for the good of Israel. He did not say, "I have taken my leave of them once, and let that serve;" but, having yet a longer space given him, he summons them together again, that he might try what more he could do to engage them for God. Note, We must never think our work for God done till our life is done; and, if he lengthen out our days beyond what we thought, we must conclude it is because he has some further service for us to do.

The assembly is the same with that in the foregoing chapter, the *elders, heads, judges, and officers of Israel, v.* 1. But it is here made somewhat more solemn than it was there.

I. The place appointed for their meeting is *Shechem,* not only because that lay nearer to Joshua than Shiloh, and therefore more convenient now that he was infirm and unfit for travelling, but because it was the place where Abraham, the first trustee of God's covenant with this people, settled at his coming to Canaan, and where God appeared to him (Gen. xii. 6, 7), and near which stood mounts Gerizim and Ebal, where the people had renewed their covenant with God at their first coming into Canaan, Josh. viii. 30. Of the promises God had made to their fathers, and of the promises they themselves had made to God, this place might serve to put them in mind.

II. They presented themselves not only before Joshua, but before God, in this assembly, that is, they came together in a solemn religious manner, as into the special presence of God, and with an eye to his speaking to them by Joshua; and it is probable the service began with prayer. It is the conjecture of interpreters that upon this great occasion Joshua ordered the ark of God to be brought by the priests to Shechem, which, they say, was about ten miles from Shiloh, and to be set down in the place of their meeting, which is therefore called (*v.* 26) *the sanctuary of the Lord,* the presence of the ark making it so at that time; and this was done to grace the solemnity, and to strike an awe upon the people that attended. We have not now any such sensible tokens of the divine presence, but are to believe that *where two or three are gathered together* in Christ's name he is as really in the midst of them as God was where the ark was, and they are indeed presenting themselves before him.

III. Joshua spoke to them in God's name, and as from him, in the language of a prophet (*v.* 2): "*Thus saith the Lord,* Jehovah, the great God, and the God of Israel, your God in covenant, whom therefore you are bound to hear and give heed to." Note, The word of God is to be received by us as his, whoever is the messenger that brings it, whose greatness cannot add to it, nor his meanness diminish from it. His sermon consists of doctrine and application.

1. The doctrinal part is a history of the great things God had done for his people, and for their fathers before them. God by Joshua recounts the marvels of old: "I did so and so." They must know and consider, not only that such and such things were done, but that God did them. It is a series of wonders that is here recorded, and perhaps many more were mentioned by Joshua, which for brevity' sake are here omitted. See what God had wrought. (1.) He brought Abraham out of Ur of the Chaldees, *v.* 2, 3. He and his ancestors had served other gods there, for it was the country in which, though celebrated for learning, idolatry, as some think, had its rise; there *the world by wisdom knew not God.* Abraham, who afterwards was the friend of God and the great favourite of heaven, was bred up in idolatry, and lived long in it, till God by his grace snatched him as a brand out of that burning. Let them remember that rock out of which they were hewn, and not relapse into that sin from which their fathers by a miracle of free grace were delivered. "I took him," says God, "else he had never come out of that sinful state." Hence Abraham's justification is made by the apostle an instance of God's *justifying the ungodly,* Rom. iv. 5. (2.) He brought him to Canaan, and built up his family, led him through the land to Shechem, where they now were, multiplied his seed by Ishmael, who begat twelve princes, but at last gave him Isaac the promised son, and in him multiplied his seed. When Isaac had two sons, Jacob and Esau, God provided an inheritance for Esau elsewhere in Mount Seir, that the land of Canaan might be reserved entire for the seed of Jacob, and the posterity of Esau might not pretend to a share in it. (3.) He delivered the seed of Jacob out of Egypt with a high hand (*v.* 5, 6), and rescued them out of the hands of Pharaoh and his host at the Red Sea, *v.* 6, 7. The same waters were the Israelites' guard and the Egyptians' grave, and this in answer to prayer; for, though we find in the story that they in that distress murmured against God (Exod. xiv. 11, 12), notice is here taken of their *crying to God;* he graciously accepted those that prayed to him, and overlooked the folly of those that quarrelled with him. (4.)

He protected them in the wilderness, where they are here said, not to *wander*, but to *dwell for a long season*, v. 7. So wisely were all their motions directed, and so safely were they kept, that even there they had as certain a dwelling-place as if they had been in a walled city. (5.) He gave them the land of the Amorites, on the other side Jordan (*v.* 8), and there defeated the plot of Balak and Balaam against them, so that Balaam could not curse them as he desired, and therefore Balak durst not fight them as he designed, and as, because he designed it, he is here said to have done it. The turning of Balaam's tongue to bless Israel, when he intended to curse them, is often mentioned as an instance of the divine power put forth in Israel's favour as remarkable as any, because in it God proved (and does still, more than we are aware of) his dominion over the powers of darkness, and over the spirits of men. (6.) He brought them safely and triumphantly into Canaan, delivered the Canaanites into their hand (*v.* 11), *sent hornets before them*, when they were actually engaged in battle with the enemy, which with their stings tormented them and with their noise terrified them, so that they became a very easy prey to Israel. These dreadful swarms first appeared in their war with Sihon and Og, the two kings of the Amorites, and afterwards in their other battles, *v.* 12. God had promised to do this for them, Exod. xxiii. 27, 28. And here Joshua takes notice of the fulfilling of that promise. See Exod. xxiii. 27, 28; Deut. vii. 20. These hornets, it should seem, annoyed the enemy more than the artillery of Israel, and therefore he adds, *not with thy sword nor bow.* It was purely the Lord's doing. *Lastly,* They were now in the peaceable possession of a good land, and lived comfortably upon the fruit of other people's labours, *v.* 13.

2. The application of this history of God's mercies to them is by way of exhortation to fear and serve God, in gratitude for his favour, and that it might be continued to them, *v.* 14. Now therefore, in consideration of all this, (1.) "*Fear the Lord,* the Lord and his goodness, Hos. iii. 5. Reverence a God of such infinite power, fear to offend him and to forfeit his goodness, keep up an awe of his majesty, a deference to his authority, a dread of his displeasure, and a continual regard to his all-seeing eye upon you." (2.) Let your practice be consonant to this principle, and serve him both by the outward acts of religious worship and every instance of obedience in your whole conversation, and this *in sincerity and truth*, with a single eye and an upright heart, and inward impressions answerable to outward expressions." This is the *truth in the inward part,* which God requires, Ps. li. 6. For what good will it do us to dissemble with a God that searches the heart? (3.) *Put away the strange gods,* both Chaldean and Egyptian idols, for those they were most in danger of revolting to. It should seem by this charge, which is repeated (*v.* 23), that there were some among them that privately kept in their closets the images or pictures of these dunghill-deities, which came to their hands from their ancestors, as heir-looms of their families, though, it may be, they did not worship them; these Joshua earnestly urges them to throw away: "Deface them, destroy them, lest you be tempted to serve them." Jacob pressed his household to do this, and at this very place; for, when they gave him up the little images they had, he buried them *under the oak which was by Shechem*, Gen. xxxv. 2, 4. Perhaps the oak mentioned here (*v.* 26) was the same oak, or another in the same place, which might be well called *the oak of reformation,* as there were idolatrous oaks.

15 And if it seem evil unto you to serve the LORD, choose you this day whom ye will serve; whether the gods which your fathers served that *were* on the other side of the flood, or the gods of the Amorites, in whose land ye dwell: but as for me and my house, we will serve the LORD. 16 And the people answered and said, God forbid that we should forsake the LORD, to serve other gods; 17 For the LORD our God, he *it is* that brought us up and our fathers out of the land of Egypt, from the house of bondage, and which did those great signs in our sight, and preserved us in all the way wherein we went, and among all the people through whom we passed: 18 And the LORD drave out from before us all the people, even the Amorites which dwelt in the land: *therefore* will we also serve the LORD; for he *is* our God. 19 And Joshua said unto the people, Ye cannot serve the LORD: for he *is* a holy God; he *is* a jealous God; he will not forgive your transgressions nor your sins. 20 If ye forsake the LORD, and serve strange gods, then he will turn and do you hurt, and consume you, after that he hath done you good. 21 And the people said unto Joshua, Nay; but we will serve the LORD. 22 And Joshua said unto the people, Ye *are* witnesses against yourselves that ye have chosen you the LORD, to serve him. And they said, *We are* witnesses. 23 Now therefore put away, *said he,*

the strange gods which *are* among you, and incline your heart unto the LORD God of Israel. 24 And the people said unto Joshua, The LORD our God will we serve, and his voice will we obey. 25 So Joshua made a covenant with the people that day, and set them a statute and an ordinance in Shechem. 26 And Joshua wrote these words in the book of the law of God, and took a great stone, and set it up there under an oak, that *was* by the sanctuary of the LORD. 27 And Joshua said unto all the people, Behold, this stone shall be a witness unto us; for it hath heard all the words of the LORD which he spake unto us: it shall be therefore a witness unto you, lest ye deny your God. 28 So Joshua let the people depart, every man unto his inheritance.

Never was any treaty carried on with better management, nor brought to a better issue, than this of Joshua with the people, to engage them to serve God. The manner of his dealing with them shows him to have been in earnest, and that his heart was much upon it, to leave them under all possible obligations to cleave to him, particularly the obligation of a choice and of a covenant.

I. Would it be any obligation upon them if they made the service of God their choice?—he here puts them to their choice, not as if it were antecedently indifferent whether they served God or no, or as if they were at liberty to refuse his service, but because it would have a great influence upon their perseverance in religion if they embraced it with the reason of men and with the resolution of men. These two things he here brings them to.

1. He brings them to embrace their religion rationally and intelligently, for it is a reasonable service. The will of man is apt to glory in its native liberty, and, in a jealousy for the honour of this, adheres with most pleasure to that which is its own choice and is not imposed upon it; therefore it is God's will that this service should be, not our chance, or a force upon us, but our choice. Accordingly,

(1.) Joshua fairly puts the matter to their choice, *v.* 15. Here, [1.] He proposes the candidates that stand for the election. The Lord, Jehovah, on one side, and on the other side either the gods of their ancestors, which would pretend to recommend themselves to those that were fond of antiquity, and that which was received by tradition from their fathers, or the *gods of their neighbours,* the Amorites, in *whose land they dwelt,* which would insinuate themselves into the affections of those that were complaisant and fond of good fellowship. [2.] He supposes there were those to whom, upon some account or other, it would *seem evil to serve the Lord.* There are prejudices and objections which some people raise against religion, which, with those that are inclined to the world and the flesh, have great force. It seems evil to them, hard and unreasonable, to be obliged to deny themselves, mortify the flesh, take up their cross, &c. But, being in a state of probation, it is fit there should be some difficulties in the way, else there were no trial. [3.] He refers it to themselves: "*Choose you whom you will serve,* choose this day, now that the matter is laid thus plainly before you, speedily bring it to a head, and do not stand hesitating." Elijah, long after this, referred the decision of the controversy between Jehovah and Baal to the consciences of those with whom he was treating, 1 Kings xviii. 21. Joshua's putting the matter here to this issue plainly intimates two things:—*First,* That it is the will of God we should every one of us make religion our serious and deliberate choice. Let us state the matter impartially to ourselves, weigh things in an even balance, and then determine for that which we find to be really true and good. Let us resolve upon a life of serious godliness, not merely because we know no other way, but because really, upon search, we find no better. *Secondly,* That religion has so much self-evident reason and righteousness on its side that it may safely be referred to every man that allows himself a free thought either to choose or refuse it; for the merits of the cause are so plain that no considerate man can do otherwise but choose it. The case is so clear that it determines itself. Perhaps Joshua designed, by putting them to their choice, thus to try if there were any among them who, upon so fair an occasion given, would show a coolness and indifference towards the service of God, whether they would desire time to consider and consult their friends before they gave in an answer, and if any such should appear he might set a mark upon them, and warn the rest to avoid them. [4.] He directs their choice in this matter by an open declaration of his own resolutions: "*But as for me and my house,* whatever you do, *we will serve the Lord,* and I hope you will all be of the same mind." Here he resolves, *First,* For himself: *As for me, I will serve the Lord.* Note, The service of God is nothing below the greatest of men; it is so far from being a diminution and disparagement to princes and those of the first rank to be religious that it is their greatest honour, and adds the brightest crown of glory to them. Observe how positive he is: "I will serve God." It is no abridgment of our liberty to bind ourselves with a bond to God. *Secondly,* For *his house,* that is, his family, his children and servants, such as were immediately under his eye and care, his inspection and influence. Joshua was a ruler, a judge in Israel, yet he did not make his necessary application to public affairs an excuse for the neglect of family religion. Those that have the charge of many families, as magistrates and ministers, must take special care of their own (1 Tim. iii. 4, 5): *I and my house* will serve God. 1. "Not my house, without me." He would not engage them to that work which he would not set his own hand to. As some who would have their children and servants good, but will not be so themselves; that is, they would have them go to heaven, but intend to go to hell themselves. 2. "Not I, without my house." He supposes he might be forsaken by his people, but in his house, where his authority was greater and more immediate, there he would over-rule. Note, When we cannot bring as many as we would to the service of God we must bring as many as we can, and extend our endeavours to the utmost sphere of our activity; if we cannot reform the land, let us put away iniquity far from our own tabernacle. 3. "First I, and then my house." Note, Those that lead and rule in other things should be first in the service of God, and go before in the best things. *Thirdly,* He resolves to do this whatever others did. Though all the families of Israel should revolt from God, and serve idols, yet Joshua and his family will stedfastly adhere to the God of Israel. Note, Those that resolve to serve God must not mind being singular in it, nor be drawn by the crowd to forsake his service. Those that are bound for heaven must be willing to swim against the stream, and must not do as the most do, but as the best do.

(2.) The matter being thus put to their choice, they immediately determine it by a free, rational, and intelligent declaration, for the God of Israel, against all competitors whatsoever, *v.* 16—18. Here, [1.] They concur with Joshua in his resolution, being influenced by the example of so great a man, who had been so great a blessing to them (*v.* 18): *We also will serve the Lord.* See how much good great men might do, if they were but zealous in religion, by their influence on their inferiors. [2.] They startle at the thought of apostatizing from God (*v.* 16): *God forbid;* the word intimates the greatest dread and detestation imaginable. "Far be it, far be it from us, that we or ours should ever *forsake the Lord to serve other gods.* We must be perfectly lost to all sense of justice, gratitude, and honour, ere we can harbour the least thought of such a thing." Thus must our hearts rise against all temptations to desert the service of God. *Get thee behind me, Satan.* [3.] They give very substantial reasons for their choice, to show that they did not make it purely in compliance to Joshua, but from a full conviction of the reasonableness and equity of it. They make this choice for, and in consideration, *First,* Of the many great and very kind things God had done for them, bringing them out of Egypt through the wilderness into Canaan, *v.* 17, 18. Thus they repeat to themselves Joshua's sermon, and then express their sincere compliance with the intentions of it. *Secondly,* Of the relation they stood in to God, and his covenant with them: "We *will serve the Lord* (*v.* 18), *for he is our God,* who has graciously engaged himself by promise to us, and to whom we have by solemn vow engaged ourselves."

2. He brings them to embrace their religion resolutely, and to express a full purpose of heart to cleave to the Lord. Now that he has them in a good mind he follows his blow, and drives the nail to the head, that it might, if possible, be a nail in a sure place. Fast bind, fast find.

(1.) In order to this he sets before them the difficulties of religion, and that in it which might be thought discouraging (*v.* 19, 20): *You cannot serve the Lord, for he is a holy God,* or, as it is in the Hebrew, *he is the holy Gods,* intimating the mystery of the Trinity, three in one; *holy, holy, holy,* holy Father, holy Son, holy Spirit. *He will not forgive.* And, *if you forsake him, he will do you hurt.* Certainly Joshua does not intend hereby to deter them from the service of God as impracticable and dangerous. But, [1.] He perhaps intends to represent here the suggestions of seducers, who tempted Israel from their God, and from the service of him; with such insinuations as these, that he was a hard master, his work impossible to be done, and he not to be pleased, and, if displeased, implacable and revengeful,—that he would confine their respects to himself only, and would not suffer them to show the least kindness for any other,—and that herein he was very unlike the gods of the nations, which were easy, and neither holy nor jealous. It is probable that this was then commonly objected against the Jewish religion, as it has all along been the artifice of Satan ever since he tempted our first parents thus to misrepresent God and his laws, as harsh and severe; and Joshua by his tone and manner of speaking might make them perceive he intended it as an objection, and would put it to them how they would keep their ground against the force of it. Or, [2.] He thus expresses his godly jealousy over them, and his fear concerning them, that, notwithstanding the profession they now made of zeal for God and his service, they would afterwards draw back, and if they did they would find him just and jealous to avenge it. Or, [3.] He resolves to let them know the worst of it, and what strict terms they must expect to stand upon with God, that they might sit down and count the cost. "*You cannot serve the Lord,* except you put away all other gods for he is holy and jealous, and will by no means admit a rival, and therefore you must be very watchful and careful, for it is at your peril if you desert his service; better you had never known it." Thus, though our Master has assured us that *his yoke is easy*, yet lest, upon the presumption of this, we should grow remiss and careless, he has also told us that the gate is strait, and the way narrow, that leads to life, that we may therefore strive to enter, and not seek only. "*You cannot serve God and Mammon;* therefore, if you resolve to serve God, you must renounce all competitors with him. You cannot serve God in your own strength, nor will he forgive your transgressions for any righteousness of your own; but *all the seed of Israel must be justified and must glory in the Lord alone as their righteousness* and *strength*," Isa. xlv. 24, 25. They must therefore come off from all confidence in their own sufficiency, else their purposes would be to no purpose. Or, [4.] Joshua thus urges on them the seeming discouragements which lay in their way, that he might sharpen their resolutions, and draw from them a promise yet more express and solemn that they would continue faithful to God and their religion. He draws it from them that they might catch at it the more earnestly and hold it the faster.

(2.) Notwithstanding this statement of the difficulties of religion, they declare a firm and fixed resolution to continue and persevere therein (*v.* 21): "*Nay, but we will serve the Lord.* We will think never the worse of him for his being a holy and jealous God, nor for his confining his servants to worship himself only. Justly will he consume those that forsake him, but we never will forsake him; not only we have a good mind to serve him, and we hope we shall, but we are at a point, we cannot bear to hear any *entreaties to leave him or to turn from following after him* (Ruth i. 16); in the strength of divine grace we are resolved that we will serve the Lord." This resolution they repeat with an explication (*v.* 24): "*The Lord our God will we serve,* not only be called his servants and wear his livery, but our religion shall rule us in every thing, *and his voice will we obey.*" And in vain do we *call him Master and Lord, if we do not the things which he saith,* Luke vi. 46. This last promise they make in answer to the charge Joshua gave them (*v.* 23), that, in order to their perseverance, they should, [1.] Put away the images and relics of the strange gods, and not keep any of the tokens of those other lovers in their custody, if they resolved their *Maker should be their husband;* they promise, in this, to obey his voice. [2.] That they should *incline their hearts to the God of Israel,* use their authority over their own hearts to engage them for God, not only to set their affections upon him, but to settle them so. These terms they agree to, and thus, as Joshua explains the bargain, they strike it: *The Lord our God will we serve.*

II. The service of God being thus made their deliberate choice, Joshua binds them to it by a solemn covenant, *v.* 25. Moses had twice publicly ratified this covenant between God and Israel, at Mount Sinai (Exod. xxiv.) and in the plains of Moab, Deut. xxix. 1. Joshua had likewise done it once (*ch.* viii. 31, &c.) and now the second time. It is here called a *statute* and an *ordinance,* because of the strength and perpetuity of its obligation, and because even this covenant bound them to no more than what they were antecedently bound to by the divine command. Now, to give it the formalities of a covenant, 1. He calls witnesses, no other than themselves (*v.* 22): *You are witnesses that you have chosen the Lord.* He promises himself that they would never forget the solemnities of this day; but, if hereafter they should break this covenant, he assures them that the professions and promises they had now made would certainly rise up in judgment against them and condemn them; and they agreed to it: "*We are witnesses;* let us be judged out of our own mouths if ever we be false to our God." 2. He put it in writing, and inserted it, as we find it here, in the sacred canon: He *wrote it in the book of the law* (*v.* 26), in that original which was laid up in the side of the ark, and thence, probably, it was transcribed into the several copies which the princes had for the use of each tribe. There it was written, that their obligation to religion by the divine precept, and that by their own promise, might remain on record together. 3. He erected a memorandum of it, for the benefit of those who perhaps were not conversant with writings, *v.* 26, 27. He *set up a great stone under an oak,* as a monument of this covenant, and perhaps wrote an inscription upon it (by which stones are made to speak) signifying the intention of it. When he says, *It hath heard* what was past, he tacitly upbraids the people with the hardness of their hearts, as if this stone had heard to as good purpose as some of them; and, if they should forget what was now done, this stone would so far preserve the remembrance of it as to reproach them for their stupidity and carelessness, and be a witness against them.

The matter being thus settled, Joshua dismissed this assembly of the grandees of Israel (*v.* 28), and took his last leave of them, well satisfied in having done his part, by which he had delivered his soul; if they perished, their blood would be upon their own heads.

29 And it came to pass after these things, that Joshua the son of Nun, the servant of the LORD, died, *being* a hundred and ten years old. 30

And they buried him in the border of his inheritance in Timnath-serah, which is in mount Ephraim, on the north side of the hill of Gaash. 31 And Israel served the LORD all the days of Joshua, and all the days of the elders that overlived Joshua, and which had known all the works of the LORD, that he had done for Israel. 32 And the bones of Joseph, which the children of Israel brought up out of Egypt, buried they in Shechem, in a parcel of ground which Jacob bought of the sons of Hamor the father of Shechem for a hundred pieces of silver: and it became the inheritance of the children of Joseph. 33 And Eleazar the son of Aaron died; and they buried him in a hill *that pertained to* Phinehas his son, which was given him in mount Ephraim.

This book, which began with triumphs, here ends with funerals, by which all the glory of man is stained. We have here, 1. The burial of Joseph, *v.* 32. He died about 200 years before in Egypt, but *gave commandment concerning his bones,* that they should not rest in their grave until Israel had rest in the land of promise; now therefore the children of Israel, who had brought this coffin full of bones with them out of Egypt, carried it along with them in all their marches through the wilderness (the two tribes of Ephraim and Manasseh, it is probable, taking particular care of it), and kept it in their camp till Canaan was perfectly reduced, now at last they deposited it in that piece of ground which his father gave him near Shechem, Gen. xlviii. 22. Probably it was upon this occasion that Joshua called for all Israel to meet him at Shechem (*v.* 1), to attend Joseph's coffin to the grave there, so that the sermon in this chapter served both for Joseph's funeral sermon and his own farewell sermon; and if it was, as is supposed, in the last year of his life, the occasion might very well remind him of his own death being at hand, for he was now just at the same age that his illustrious ancestor Joseph had arrived at when he died, 110 *years old;* compare *v.* 29 with Gen. l. 26. 2. The death and burial of Joshua, *v.* 29, 30. We are not told how long he lived after the coming of Israel into Canaan. Dr. Lightfoot thinks it was about seventeen years; but the Jewish chronologers generally say it was about twenty-seven or twenty-eight years. He is here called the *servant of the Lord,* the same title that was given to Moses (*ch.* i. 1) when mention was made of his death; for, though Joshua was in many respects inferior to Moses, yet in this he was equal to him, that, according as his work was, he approved himself a diligent and faithful servant of God. And he that traded with his two talents had the same approbation that he had who traded with five. *Well done, good and faithful servant.* Joshua's burying-place is here said to be *on the north side of the hill Gaash,* or *the quaking hill;* the Jews say it was so called because it trembled at the burial of Joshua, to upbraid the people of Israel with their stupidity in that they did not lament the death of that great and good man as they ought to have done. Thus at the death of Christ, our Joshua, the earthquaked. The learned bishop Patrick observes that there is no mention of any days of mourning being observed for Joshua, as there were for Moses and Aaron, in which, he says, St. Hierom and others of the fathers think there is a mystery, namely, that under the law, when life and immortality were not brought to so clear a light as they are now, they had reason to mourn and weep for the death of their friends; but now that Jesus, our Joshua, has opened the kingdom of heaven, we may rather rejoice. 3. The death and burial of Eleazar the chief priest, who, it is probable, died about the same time that Joshua did, as Aaron in the same year with Moses, *v.* 33. The Jews say that Eleazar, a little before he died, called the elders together, and gave them a charge as Joshua had done. He was buried in a hill that pertained to Phinehas his son, which came to him, not by descent, for then it would have pertained to his father first, nor had the priests any cities in Mount Ephraim, but either it fell to him by marriage, as the Jews conjecture, or it was freely bestowed upon him, to build a country seat on, by some pious Israelite that was well-affected to the priesthood, for it is here said to have been *given him;* and there he buried his dear father. 4. A general idea given us of the state of Israel at this time, *v.* 31. While Joshua lived, religion was kept up among them under his care and influence; but soon after he and his contemporaries died it went to decay, so much oftentimes does one head hold up: how well is it for the gospel church that Christ, our Joshua, is still with it, by his Spirit, and will be always, even *unto the end of the world!*

AN

EXPOSITION,

WITH PRACTICAL OBSERVATIONS,

OF THE BOOK OF

JUDGES.

THIS is called in the Hebrew *Shepher Shophtim*, the *Book of Judges,* which the Syriac and Arabic versions enlarge upon, and call it, *The Book of the Judges of the Children of Israel;* the judgments of that nation being peculiar, so were their judges, whose office differed vastly from that of the judges of other nations. The LXX. entitle it only Κριταὶ, *Judges.* It is the history of the *commonwealth of Israel*, during the government of the judges from Othniel to Eli, so much of it as God saw fit to transmit to us. It contains the history (according to Dr. Lightfoot's computation) of 299 years, reckoning to Othniel of Judah forty years, to Ehud of Benjamin eighty years, to Barak of Naphtali forty years, to Gideon of Manasseh forty years, to Abimelech his son three years, to Tola of Issachar twenty-three, to Jair of Manasseh twenty-two, to Jephtha of Manasseh six, to Ibzan of Judah seven, to Elon of Zebulun ten, to Abdon of Ephraim eight, to Samson of Dan twenty, in all 299. As for the years of their servitude, as where Eglon is said to oppress them eighteen years and Jabin twenty years, and so some others, those must be reckoned to fall in with some or other of the years of the judges. The judges here appear to have been of eight several tribes; that honour was thus diffused, until at last it centred in Judah. Eli and Samuel, the two judges that fall not within this book, were of Levi. It seems, there was no judge of Reuben or Simeon, Gad or Asher. The history of these judges in their order we have in this book to the end of *ch.* xvi. And then in the last five chapters we have an account of some particular memorable events which happened, as the story of Ruth did (Ruth i. 1) *in the days when the judges ruled*, but it is not certain in which judge's days; but they are put together at the end of the book, that the thread of the general history might not be interrupted. Now as to the state of the commonwealth of Israel during this period, I. They do not appear here either so great or so good as one might have expected the character of such a peculiar people would be, that were governed by such laws and enriched by such promises. We find them wretchedly corrupted, and wretchedly oppressed by their neighbours about them, and nowhere in all the book, either in war or council, do they make any figure proportionable to their glorious entry into Canaan. What shall we say to it? God would hereby show us the lamentable imperfection of all persons and things under the sun, that we may look for complete holiness and happiness in the other world, and not in this. Yet, II. We may hope that though the historian in this book enlarges most upon their provocations and grievances, yet there was a face of religion upon the land; and, however there were those among them that were drawn aside to idolatry, yet the tabernacle-service, according to the law of Moses, was kept up, and there were many that attended it. Historians record not the common course of justice and commerce in a nation, taking that for granted, but only the wars and disturbances that happen; but the reader must consider the other, to balance the blackness of them. III. It should seem that in these times each tribe had very much its government in ordinary within itself, and acted separately, without one common head, or council, which occasioned many differences among themselves, and kept them from being or doing any thing considerable. IV. The government of the judges was not constant, but occasional; when it is said that after Ehud's victory *the land rested eighty years*, and after Barak's *forty*, it is not certain that they lived, much less that they governed, so long; but they and the rest were raised up and animated by the Spirit of God to do particular service to the public when there was occasion, to *avenge Israel of their enemies*, and to purge Israel of their idolatries, which are the two things principally meant by their judging Israel. Yet Deborah, as a prophetess, was attended for judgment by all Israel, before there was occasion for her agency in war, *ch.* iv. 4. V. During the government of the judges, God was in a more especial manner Israel's king; so Samuel tells them when they were resolved to throw off this form of government, 1 Sam. xii. 12. God would try what his own law and the constitutions of that would do to keep them in order, and it proved that when *there was no king in Israel every man did that which was right in his own eyes;* he therefore, towards the latter end of this time, made the government of the judges more constant and universal than it was at first, and at length gave them David, a king after his own heart; then, and not till then, Israel began to flourish, which should make us very thankful for magistrates both supreme and subordinate, for they are *ministers of God unto us for good.* Four of the judges of Israel are canonized (Heb. xi. 32), Gideon, Barak, Samson, and Jephtha. The learned bishop Patrick thinks the prophet Samuel was the penman of this Book.

CHAP. I.

This chapter gives us a particular account what sort of progress the several tribes of Israel made in the reducing of Canaan after the death of Joshua. He did (as we say) break the neck of that great work, and put it into such a posture that they might easily have perfected it in due time, if they had not been wanting to themselves; what they did in order hereunto, and wherein they came short, we are told. I. The united tribes of Judah and Simeon did bravely. 1. God appointed Judah to begin, ver. 1, 2. 2. Judah took Simeon to act in conjunction with him, ver. 3. 3. They succeeded in their enterprises against Bezek, (ver. 4—7) Jerusalem (ver. 8), Hebron and Debir (ver. 9—15), Hormah, Gaza, and other places, ver. 17—19. 4. Yet where there were chariots of iron their hearts failed them, ver. 19. Mention is made of the Kenites settling among them, ver. 16. II. The other tribes, in comparison with these, acted a cowardly part. 1. Benjamin failed, ver. 21. 2. The house of Joseph did well against Beth-el (ver. 22—26), but in other places did not improve their advantages, nor Manasseh (ver. 27, 28), nor Ephraim, ver. 29. 3. Zebulun spared the Canaanites, ver. 30. 4. Asher truckled worse than any of them to the Canaanites, ver. 31, 32. 5. Naphtali was kept out of the full possession of several of his cities, ver. 33. 6. Dan was straitened by the Amorites, ver. 34. No account is given of Issachar, nor of the two tribes and a half on the other side Jordan.

NOW after the death of Joshua it came to pass, that the children of Israel asked the LORD, saying, Who shall go up for us against the Canaanites first, to fight against them? 2 And the LORD said, Judah shall go up. behold, I have delivered the land into his hand. 3 And Judah said unto Simeon his brother, Come up with me into my lot, that we may fight against the Canaanites; and I likewise will go with thee into thy lot. So Simeon went with him. 4 And Judah went up; and the LORD delivered the Canaanites and the Perizzites into their hand: and they slew of them in Bezek ten thousand men. 5 And they found Adoni-bezek in Bezek: and they fought against him, and they slew the Canaanites and the Perizzites. 6 But Adoni-bezek fled; and they pursued after him, and caught him, and cut off his thumbs and his great toes. 7 And Adoni-bezek said, Threescore and ten kings, having their thumbs and their great toes cut off, gathered *their meat* under my table: as I have done, so God hath requited me. And they brought him to Jerusalem, and there he died. 8 Now the children of Judah had fought against Jerusalem, and had taken it, and smitten it with the edge of the sword, and set the city on fire.

Here, I. The children of Israel consult the oracle of God for direction which of all the tribes should first attempt to clear their country of the Canaanites, and to animate and encourage the rest. It was *after the death of Joshua.* While he lived he directed them, and all the tribes were obedient to him, but when he died he left no successor in the same authority that he had; but the people must consult the breast-plate of judgment, and thence receive the word of command; for God himself, as he was their King, so he was the Lord of their hosts. The question they ask is, *Who shall go up first? v.* 1. By this time, we may suppose, they were so multiplied that the places they were in possession of began to be too strait for them, and they must thrust out the enemy to make room; now they enquire who should first take up arms. Whether each tribe was ambitious of being first, and so strove for the honour of it, or whether each was afraid of being first, and so strove to decline it, does not appear; but by common consent the matter was referred to God himself, who is the fittest both to dispose of honours and to cut out work.

II. God appointed that Judah should go up first, and promised him success (*v.* 2): "*I have delivered the land into his hand,* to be possessed, and therefore will deliver the enemy into his hand, that keeps him out of possession, to be destroyed." And why must Judah be first in this undertaking? 1. Judah was the most numerous and powerful tribe, and therefore let Judah venture first. Note, God appoints service according to the strength he has given. Those that are most able, from them most work is expected. 2. Judah was first in dignity, and therefore must be first in duty. He it is whom *his brethren must praise,* and therefore he it is who must lead in perilous services. Let the burden of honour and the burden of work go together. 3. Judah was first served; the lot came up for Judah first, and therefore Judah must first fight. 4. Judah was the tribe out of which our Lord was to spring: so that in Judah, Christ, the Lion of the tribe of Judah, went before them. Christ engaged the powers of darkness first, and foiled them, which animates us for our conflicts; and it is in him that we are *more than conquerors.* Observe, The service and the success are put together: "Judah shall go up; let him do his part, and then he shall find that *I have delivered the land into his hand.*" His service will not avail unless God give the success; but God will not give the success unless he vigorously apply himself to the service.

III. Judah hereupon prepares to go up, but courts his brother and neighbour the tribe of Simeon (the lot of which tribe fell within that of Judah and was assigned out of it) to join forces with him, *v.* 3. Observe here, 1. That the strongest should not despise but desire the assistance even of those that are weaker. Judah was the most considerable of all the tribes, and Simeon the least considerable, and yet Judah begs Simeon's friendship, and prays an aid from him; the head cannot say to the foot, *I have no need of thee,* for we are *members one of another.* 2. Those that crave assistance must be ready to give assistance: *Come with me into my lot*, and then *I will go with thee into thine*. It becomes Israelites to help one another against Canaanites; and all Christians, even those of different tribes, should strengthen one another's hands against the common interests of Satan's kingdom. Those who thus help one another in love have reason to hope that God will graciously help them both.

IV. The confederate forces of Judah and Simeon take the field: *Judah went up* (*v.* 4), and Simeon with him, *v.* 3. Caleb, it is probable, was commander-in-chief of this expedition; for who so fit as he who had both an old man's head and a young man's hand, the experience of age and the vigour of youth? Josh. xiv. 10, 11. It should seem too, by what follows (*v.* 10, 11), that he was not yet in possession of his own allotment. It was happy for them that they had such a general as, according to his name, was all heart. Some think that the Canaanites had got together into a body, a formidable body, when Israel consulted who should go and *fight against them*, and that they then began to stir when they heard of the death of Joshua, whose name had been so dreadful to them; but, if so, it proved they did but meddle to their own hurt.

V. God gave them great success. Whether they invaded the enemy, or the enemy first gave them the alarm, *the Lord delivered them into their hand*, *v.* 4. Though the army of Judah was strong and bold, yet the victory is attributed to God: he *delivered the Canaanites into their hand;* having given them authority, he here gives them ability to destroy them—put it in their power, and so tried their obedience to his command, which was *utterly to cut them off*. Bishop Patrick observes upon this that we meet not with such religious expressions in the heathen writers, concerning the success of their arms, as we have here and elsewhere in this sacred history. I wish such pious acknowledgments of the divine providence had not grown into disuse at this time with many that are called Christians. Now, 1. We are told how the army of the Canaanites was routed in the field, in or near Bezek, the place where they drew up, which afterwards Saul made the place of a general rendezvous (1 Sam. xi. 8); they slew 10,000 men, which blow, if followed, could not but be a very great weakening to those that were already brought so very low. 2. How their king was taken and mortified. His name was Adoni-bezek, which signifies, *lord of Bezek*. There have been those that called their lands by *their own names* (Ps. xlix. 11), but here was one (and there has been many another) that called himself by his land's name. He was taken prisoner after the battle, and we are here told how they used him; they cut off his thumbs, to disfit him for fighting, and his great toes, that he might not be able to run away, *v.* 6. It had been barbarous thus to triumph over a man in misery, and that lay at their mercy, but that he was a devoted Canaanite, and one that had in like manner abused others, which probably they had heard of. Josephus says, "They cut off his hands and his feet," probably supposing those more likely to be mortal wounds than only the cutting off of his thumbs and his great toes. But this indignity which they did him extorted from him an acknowledgment of the righteousness of God, *v.* 7. Here observe, (1.) What a great man this Adoni-bezek had been, how great in the field, where armies fled before him, how great at home, where kings were *set with the dogs of his flock;* and yet now himself a prisoner, and reduced to the extremity of meanness and disgrace. See how changeable this world is, and how slippery its high places are. Let not the highest be proud, nor the strongest secure, for they know not how low they may be brought before they die. (2.) What desolations he had made among his neighbours: he had wholly subdued seventy kings, to such a degree as to have them his prisoners; he that was the chief person in a city was then called a *king*, and the greatness of their title did but aggravate their disgrace, and fired the pride of him that insulted over them. We cannot suppose that Adoni-bezek had seventy of these petty princes at once his slaves; but first and last, in the course of his reign, he had thus deposed and abused so many, who perhaps were many of them kings of the same cities that successively opposed him, and whom he thus treated to please his own imperious barbarous fancy, and for a terror to others. It seems the Canaanites had been wasted by civil wars, and those bloody ones, among themselves, which would very much facilitate the conquest of them by Israel. "Judah," says Dr. Lightfoot, "in conquering Adoni-bezek, did, in effect, conquer seventy kings." (3.) How justly he was treated as he had treated others. Thus the righteous God sometimes, in his providence, makes the punishment to answer the sin, and observes an equality in his judgments; the spoiler shall be spoiled, and the *treacherous dealer dealt treacherously* with, Isa. xxxiii. 1. And those that *showed no mercy* shall have *no mercy shown* them, Jam. ii. 13. See Rev. xiii. 10; xviii. 6. (4.) How honestly he owned the righteousness of God herein: *As I have done, so God has requited me.* See the power of conscience, when God by his judgments awakens it, how it brings sin to remembrance, and subscribes to the justice of God. He that in his pride had set God at defiance now yields to him, and reflects with as much regret upon the kings under his table as ever he had looked upon them with pleasure when he had them there. He seems to own that he was better dealt with than he had dealt with his prisoners; for though the Israelites maimed him (according to the law of retaliation, an *eye for an eye,* so a thumb for a thumb), yet they did not put him *under the table* to be fed with the crumbs there, because, though the other might well be looked upon as an act of justice, this would have savoured more of pride and haughtiness than did become an Israelite.

VI. Particular notice is taken of the conquest of Jerusalem, *v.* 8. Our translators judge it spoken of here as done formerly in Joshua's time, and only repeated on occasion of Adoni-bezek's dying there, and therefore read it, "they had fought against Jerusalem," and put this verse in a parenthesis; but the original speaks of it as a thing now done, and this seems most probable because it is said to be done by the children of Judah in particular, not by all Israel in general, whom Joshua commanded. Joshua indeed conquered and slew Adoni-zedec, king of Jerusalem (Josh. x.), but we read not there of his taking the city; probably, while he was pursuing his conquests elsewhere, this Adoni-bezek, a neighbouring prince, got possession of it, whom Israel having conquered in the field, the city fell into their hands, and they slew the inhabitants, except those who retreated into the castle and held out there till David's time, and they *set the city on fire,* in token of their detestation of the idolatry wherewith it had been deeply infected, yet probably not so utterly as to consume it, but to leave convenient habitations for as many as they had to put into the possession of it.

9 And afterward the children of Judah went down to fight against the Canaanites, that dwelt in the mountain, and in the south, and in the valley. 10 And Judah went against the Canaanites that dwelt in Hebron: (now the name of Hebron before *was* Kirjath-arba:) and they slew Sheshai, and Ahiman, and Talmai. 11 And from thence he went against the inhabitants of Debir: and the name of Debir before *was* Kirjath-sepher: 12 And Caleb said, He that smiteth Kirjath-sepher, and taketh it, to him will I give Achsah my daughter to wife. 13 And Othniel the son of Kenaz, Caleb's younger brother, took it: and he gave him Achsah his daughter to wife. 14 And it came to pass, when she came *to him,* that she moved him to ask of her father a field: and she lighted from off *her* ass; and Caleb said unto her, What wilt thou? 15 And she said unto him, Give me a blessing: for thou hast given me a south land; give me also springs of water. And Caleb gave her the upper springs and the nether springs. 16 And the children of the Kenite, Moses' father in law, went up out of the city of palm trees with the children of Judah into the wilderness of Judah, which *lieth* in the south of Arad; and they went and dwelt among the people. 17 And Judah went with Simeon his brother, and they slew the Canaanites that inhabited Zephath, and utterly destroyed it. And the name of the city was called Hormah. 18 Also Judah took Gaza with the coast thereof, and Askelon with the coast thereof, and Ekron with the coast thereof. 19 And the LORD was with Judah; and he drave out *the inhabitants of* the mountain; but could not drive out the inhabitants of the valley, because they had chariots of iron. 20 And they gave Hebron unto Caleb, as Moses said: and he expelled thence the three sons of Anak.

We have here a further account of that glorious and successful campaign which Judah and Simeon made. 1. The lot of Judah was pretty well cleared of the Canaanites, yet not thoroughly. Those that *dwelt in the mountain* (the mountains that were round about Jerusalem) were driven out (*v.* 9, 19), but those in the valley kept their ground against them, having *chariots of iron,* such as we read of, Josh. xvii. 16. Here the men of Judah failed, and thereby spoiled the influence which otherwise their example hitherto might have had on the rest of the tribes, who followed them in this instance of their cowardice, rather than in all the other instances of their courage. They had iron chariots, and therefore it was thought not safe to attack them: but had not Israel God on their side, *whose chariots are thousands of angels* (Ps. lxviii. 17), before whom these iron chariots would be but as stubble to the fire? Had not God expressly promised by the oracle (*v.* 2) to give them success against the Canaanites in this very expedition, without excepting those that had iron chariots? Yet they suffered their fears to prevail against their faith, they could not trust God under any disadvantages, and therefore durst not face the iron chariots, but meanly withdrew their forces, when with one bold stroke they might have completed their victories; and it proved of pernicious consequence. They did run well, what hindered them? Gal. v. 7. 2. Caleb was put in possession of Hebron, which, though given him by Joshua ten or twelve years before (as Dr. Lightfoot computes), yet being employed in public service, for the settling of the tribes, which he preferred before his own private interests, it seems he did not till now make himself master of; so well content was that good man to serve others, while he left himself to be served last; few are like-minded, for *all seek their own*, Phil. ii. 20, 21. Yet now the men of Judah all came in to his assistance for the reducing of Hebron (*v.* 10), slew the sons of Anak, and put him in possession of it, *v.* 20. They gave Hebron unto Caleb. And now Caleb, that he might return the kindness of his countrymen, is impatient to see Debir reduced and put into the hands of the men of Judah, to expedite which he proffers his daughter to the person that will undertake to command in the siege of that important place, *v.* 11, 12. Othniel bravely undertakes it, and wins the town and the lady (*v.* 13), and by his wife's interest and management with her father gains a very good inheritance for himself and his family, *v.* 14, 15. We had this passage before, Josh. xv. 16—19, where it was largely explained and improved. 3. Simeon got ground of the Canaanites in his border, *v.* 17, 18. In the eastern part of Simeon's lot, they destroyed the Canaanites in Zephath, and called it *Hormah—destruction,* adding this to some other devoted cities not far off, which they had some time ago, with good reason, called by that name, Num. xxi. 2, 3. And this perhaps was the complete performance of the vow they then made that they would utterly destroy these cities of the Canaanites in the south. In the western part they took Gaza, Askelon, and Ekron, cities of the Philistines; they gained present possession of the cities, but, not destroying the inhabitants, the Philistines in process of time recovered the cities, and proved inveterate enemies to the Israel of God, and no better could come of doing their work by the halves. 4. The Kenites gained a settlement in the tribe of Judah, choosing it there rather than in any other tribe, because it was the strongest, and there they hoped to be safe and quiet, *v.* 16. These were the posterity of Jethro, who either went with Israel when Moses invited them (Num. x. 29) or met them about the same place when they came up from their wanderings in the wilderness thirty-eight years after, and went with them then to Canaan, Moses having promised them that they should fare as Israel fared, Num. x. 32. They had at first seated themselves in the *city of palm-trees*, that is, Jericho, a city which never was to be rebuilt, and therefore the fitter for those who *dwelt in tents,* and did not mind building. But afterwards they removed into the wilderness of Judah, either out of their affection to that place, because solitary and retired, or out of their affection to that tribe, which perhaps had been in a particular manner kind to them. Yet we find the tent of Jael, who was of that family, far north, in the lot of Naphtali, when Sisera took shelter there, *ch.* iv. 17. This respect Israel showed them, to let them fix where they pleased, being a quiet people, who, wherever they were, were content with a little. Those that molested none were molested by none. *Blessed are the meek, for* thus *they shall inherit the earth.*

21 And the children of Benjamin did not drive out the Jebusites that inhabited Jerusalem; but the Jebusites dwell with the children of Benjamin in Jerusalem unto this day. 22 And the house of Joseph, they also went up against Beth-el: and the LORD *was* with them. 23 And the house of Joseph sent to descry Beth-el. (Now the name of the city before *was* Luz.) 24 And the spies saw a man come forth out of the city, and they said unto him, Show us, we pray thee, the entrance into the city, and we will show thee mercy. 25 And when he showed them the entrance into the city, they smote the city with the edge of the sword; but they let go the man and all his family. 26 And the man went into the land of the Hittites, and built a city, and called the name thereof Luz: which *is* the name thereof unto this day. 27 Neither did Manasseh drive out *the inhabitants of* Beth-shean and her towns, nor Taanach and her towns, nor the inhabitants of Dor and her towns, nor the inhabitants of Ibleam and her towns, nor the inhabitants of Megiddo and her towns: but the Canaanites would dwell in that land. 28 And it came to pass, when Israel was strong, that they put the Canaanites to tribute, and did not utterly drive them out. 29 Neither did Ephraim drive out the Canaanites that dwelt in Gezer; but the Canaanites dwelt in Gezer among them. 30 Neither did Zebulun drive out the inhabitants of Kitron, nor the inhabitants of Nahalol; but the Canaanites dwelt among them, and became tributaries. 31 Neither did Asher drive out the inhabitants of Accho, nor the inhabitants of Zidon, nor of Ahlab, nor of Achzib, nor of Helbah, nor of Aphik, nor of Rehob: 32 But the Asherites dwelt among the Canaanites, the inhabitants of the land: for they did not drive them out.

33 Neither did Naphtali drive out the inhabitants of Beth-shemesh, nor the inhabitants of Beth-anath; but he dwelt among the Canaanites, the inhabitants of the land: nevertheless the inhabitants of Beth-shemesh and of Beth-anath became tributaries unto them. 34 And the Amorites forced the children of Dan into the mountain: for they would not suffer them to come down to the valley: 35 But the Amorites would dwell in mount Heres in Aijalon, and in Shaalbim: yet the hand of the house of Joseph prevailed, so that they became tributaries. 36 And the coast of the Amorites *was* from the going up to Akrabbim, from the rock, and upward.

We are here told upon what terms the rest of the tribes stood with the Canaanites that remained.

I. Benjamin neglected to drive the Jebusites out of that part of the city of Jerusalem which fell to their lot, *v.* 21. Judah had set them a good example, and gained them great advantages by what they did (*v.* 9), but they did not follow the blow for want of resolution.

II. The house of Joseph,

1. Bestirred themselves a little to get possession of Beth-el, *v.* 22. That city is mentioned in the tribe of Benjamin, Josh. xviii. 22. Yet it is spoken of there (*v.* 13) as a city in the borders of that tribe, and, it should seem, the line went through it, so that one half of it only belonged to Benjamin, the other half to Ephraim; and perhaps the activity of the Ephraimites at this time, to recover it from the Canaanites, secured it entirely to them henceforward, or at least the greatest part of it, for afterwards we find it so much under the power of the ten tribes (and Benjamin was none of them) that Jeroboam set up one of his calves in it. In this account of the expedition of the Ephraimites against Beth-el observe,

(1.) Their interest in the divine favour: *The Lord was with them,* and would have been with the other tribes if they would have exerted their strength. The Chaldee reads it here, as in many other places, *The Word of the Lord was their helper,* namely, Christ himself, the captain of the Lord's host, now that they acted separately, as well as when they were all in one body.

(2.) The prudent measures they took to gain the city. They sent spies to observe what part of the city was weakest, or which way they might make their attack with most advantage, *v.* 23. These spies got very good information from a man they providentially met with, who showed them a private way into the town, which was left unguarded because, being not generally known, no danger was suspected on that side. And here, [1.] He is not to be blamed for giving them this intelligence if he did it from a conviction that *the Lord was with them,* and that by his donation the land was theirs of right, any more than Rahab was for entertaining those whom she knew to be enemies of her country, but friends of God. Nor, [2.] Are those to be blamed who *showed him mercy,* gave him and his family not only their lives, but liberty to go wherever they pleased: for one good turn requires another. But, it seems, he would not join himself to the people of Israel, he feared them rather than loved them, and therefore he removed after a colony of the Hittites, which, it should seem, had gone into Arabia and settled there upon Joshua's invasion of the country; with them this man chose to dwell, and among them he built a city, a small one, we may suppose, such as planters commonly build, and in the name of it preserved the ancient name of his native city, *Luz, an almond-tree,* preferring this before its new name, which carried religion in it, *Bethel—the house of God.*

(3.) Their success. The spies brought or sent notice of the intelligence they had gained to the army, which improved their advantages, surprised the city, and put them all to the sword, *v.* 25. But,

2. Besides this achievement, it seems, the children of Joseph did nothing remarkable (1.) Manasseh failed to drive out the Canaanites from several very considerable cities in their lot, and did not make any attempt upon them, *v.* 27. But the Canaanites, being in possession, were resolved not to quit it; they would dwell in that land, and Manasseh had not resolution enough to offer to dispossess them; as if there was no meddling with them unless they were willing to resign, which it was not to be expected they ever would be. Only as Israel got strength they got ground, and served themselves, both by their contributions and by their personal services, *v.* 28, 35. (2.) Ephraim likewise, though a powerful tribe, neglected Gezer a considerable city, and suffered the Canaanites to *dwell among them* (*v.* 29), which, some think, intimates their allowing them a quiet settlement, and indulging them with the privileges of an unconquered people, not so much as making them tributaries.

III. Zebulun, perhaps inclining to the sea-trade, for it was foretold that it should be a haven for ships, neglected to reduce Kitron and Nahalol (*v.* 30), and only made the inhabitants of those places tributaries to them.

IV. Asher quitted itself worse than any of the tribes (*v.* 31, 32), not only in leaving more towns than any of them in the hands of the Canaanites, but in submitting to the Canaanites instead of making them tributaries; for so the manner of expression intimates, that the Asherites dwelt among the

Canaanites, as if the Canaanites were the more numerous and the more powerful, would still be lords of the country, and the Israelites must be only upon sufferance among them.

V. Naphtali also permitted the Canaanites to live among them (*v.* 33), only by degrees they got them so far under as to exact contributions from them.

VI. Dan was so far from extending his conquests where his lot lay that, wanting spirit to make head against the Amorites, he was forced by them to retire into the mountains and inhabit the cities there, but durst not venture into the valley, where, it is probable, the chariots of iron were, *v.* 34. Nay, and some of the cities in the mountains were kept against them, *v.* 35. Thus were they straitened in their possessions, and forced to seek for more room at Laish, a great way off, *ch.* xviii. 1, &c. In Jacob's blessing Judah is compared to a lion, Dan to a serpent; now observe how Judah with his lion-like courage prospered and prevailed, but Dan with all his serpentine subtlety could get no ground; craft and artful management do not always effect the wonders they pretend to. What Dan came short of doing, it seems, his neighbours the Ephraimites in part did for him; they put the Amorites under tribute, *v.* 35.

Upon the whole matter it appears that the people of Israel were generally very careless both of their duty and interest in this thing; they did not what they might have done to expel the Canaanites and make room for themselves. And, 1. It was owing to their slothfulness and cowardice. They would not be at the pains to complete their conquests; like the sluggard, that dreamed of a lion in the way, a lion in the streets, they fancied insuperable difficulties, and frightened themselves with winds and clouds from sowing and reaping. 2. It was owing to their covetousness; the Canaanites' labour and money would do them more good (they thought) than their blood, and therefore they were willing to let them live among them, that they might make a hand of them. 3. They had not that dread and detestation of idolatry which they ought to have had; they thought it a pity to put these Canaanites to the sword, though the measure of their iniquity was full, thought it would be no harm to let them live among them, and that they should be in no danger from them. 4. The same thing that kept their fathers forty years out of Canaan kept them now out of the full possession of it, and that was unbelief. Distrust of the power and promise of God lost them their advantages, and ran them into a thousand mischiefs.

CHAP. II.

In this chapter we have, I. A particular message which God sent to Israel by an angel, and the impression it made upon them, ver. 1—5. II. A general idea of the state of Israel during the government of the judges, in which observe, 1. Their adherence to God while Joshua and the elders lived, ver. 6—10. 2. Their revolt afterwards to idolatry, ver. 11—13. 3. God's displeasure against them, and his judgments upon them for it, ver. 14, 15. 4. His pity towards them, shown in raising them up deliverers, ver. 16—18. 5. Their relapse into idolatry after the judgment was over, ver. 17—19. 6. The full stop God in anger put to their successes, ver. 20—23. These are the contents, not only of this chapter, but of the whole book.

AND an angel of the LORD came up from Gilgal to Bochim, and said, I made you to go up out of Egypt, and have brought you unto the land which I sware unto your fathers; and I said, I will never break my covenant with you. 2 And ye shall make no league with the inhabitants of this land; ye shall throw down their altars: but ye have not obeyed my voice: why have ye done this? 3 Wherefore I also said, I will not drive them out from before you; but they shall be *as thorns* in your sides, and their gods shall be a snare unto you. 4 And it came to pass when the angel of the LORD spake these words unto all the children of Israel, that the people lifted up their voice, and wept. 5 And they called the name of that place Bochim: and they sacrificed there unto the LORD.

It was the privilege of Israel that they had not only a law in general sent them from heaven, once for all, to direct them into and keep them in the way of happiness, but that they had particular messages sent them from heaven, as there was occasion, for reproof, for correction, and for instruction in righteousness, when at any time they turned aside out of that way. Besides the written word which they had before them to read, they often *heard a word behind them, saying, This is the way,* Isa. xxx. 21. Here begins that way of God's dealing with them. When they would not hear Moses, let it be tried whether they will hear the prophets. In these verses we have a very awakening sermon that was preached to them when they began to cool in their religion.

I. The preacher was an *angel of the Lord* (*v.* 1), not a prophet, not Phinehas, as the Jews conceit; gospel ministers are indeed called *angels of the churches,* but the Old-Testament prophets are never called angels of the Lord; no doubt this was a messenger from heaven. Such extraordinary messengers we sometimes find in this book employed in the raising up of the judges that delivered Israel, as Gideon and Samson; and now, to show how various are the good offices they do for God's Israel, here is one sent to preach to them, to prevent their falling into sin and trouble. This extraordinary messenger was sent to command, if possible, the greater regard to the message, and to affect the minds of a people whom nothing seemed to affect but what was sensible. The learned bishop Patrick is clearly of opinion that this was not a created angel, but the Angel of the covenant, the same that appeared to Joshua as *captain of the hosts of the Lord*, who was God himself. Christ himself, says Dr. Lightfoot; who but God and Christ could say, *I made you to go up out of Egypt?* Joshua had lately admonished them to take heed of entangling themselves with the Canaanites, but they regarded not the words of a dying man; the same warning therefore is here brought them by the living God himself, the Son of God appearing as an angel. If they slight his servants, surely they will reverence his Son. This angel of the Lord is said to come up from Gilgal, perhaps not walking on the earth, but flying swiftly, as the angel Gabriel did to Daniel, in the open firmament of heaven; but, whether walking or flying, he seemed to come from Gilgal for a particular reason. Gilgal was long their head-quarters after they came into Canaan, many signal favours they had there received from God, and there the covenant of circumcision was renewed (Mic. vi. 5), of all which it was designed they should be reminded by his coming from Gilgal. The remembrance of *what we have received and heard* will prepare us for a warning to hold fast, Rev. iii. 2, 3.

II. The persons to whom this sermon was preached were *all the children of Israel, v.* 4. A great congregation for a great preacher! They were assembled either for war, each tribe sending in its forces for some great expedition, or rather for worship, and then the place of their meeting must be Shiloh, where the tabernacle was, at which they were all to come together three times a year. When we attend upon God in instituted ordinances we may expect to hear from him, and to receive his gifts at his own gates. The place is called *Bochim* (*v.* 1), because it gained that name upon this occasion. All Israel needed the reproof and warning here given, and therefore it is spoken to them all.

III. The sermon itself is short, but very close. God here tells them plainly, 1. What he had done for them, *v.* 1. He had brought them out of Egypt, a land of slavery and toil, into Canaan, a land of rest, liberty, and plenty. The miseries of the one served as a foil to the felicities of the other. God had herein been kind to them, true to the oath sworn to their fathers, had given such proofs of his power as left them inexcusable if they distrusted it, and such engagements to his service as left them inexcusable if they deserted it. 2. What he had promised them: *I said, I will never break my covenant with you.* When he took them to be his peculiar people, it was not with any design to cast them off again, or to change them for another people at his pleasure; let them but be faithful to him, and they should find him unchangeably constant to them. He told them plainly that the covenant he entered into with them should never break, unless it broke on their side. 3. What were his just and reasonable expectations from them (*v.* 2): that being taken into covenant with God they should make no league with the Canaanites, who were both his enemies and theirs,—that having set up his altar they should throw down their altars, lest they should be a temptation to them to serve their gods. Could any thing be demanded more easy? 4. How they had in this very thing, which he had most insisted on, disobeyed him: "But you have not in so small a matter obeyed my voice." In contempt of their covenant with God, and their confederacy with each other in that covenant, they made leagues of friendship with the idolatrous devoted Canaanites, and connived at their altars, though they stood in competition with God's. *Why have you done this?* What account can you give of this perverseness of yours at the bar of right reason? What apology can you make for yourselves, or what excuse can you offer?" Those that throw off their communion with God, and have fellowship with the unfruitful works of darkness, know not what they do now, and will have nothing to say for themselves in the day of account shortly. 5. How they must expect to smart by and by for this their folly, *v.* 3. Their tolerating the Canaanites among them would, (1.) Put a period to their victories: "*You* will not drive them out," says God, "and therefore *I* will not;" thus their sin was made their punishment. Thus those who indulge their lusts and corruptions, which they should mortify, forfeit the grace of God, and it is justly withdrawn from them. If we will not resist the devil, we cannot expect that God should tread him under our feet. (2.) It would involve them in continual troubles. "They shall be thorns in your sides to gore you, which way soever you turn, always doing you one mischief or other." Those deceive themselves who expect advantage by friendship with those that are enemies to God. (3.) It would (which was worst of all) expose them to constant temptation and draw them to sin. "Their gods" (their *abominations*, so the Chaldee) "will be a snare to you; you will find yourselves wretchedly entangled in an affection to them, and it will be your ruin," so some read it. Those that approach sin are justly left to themselves to fall into sin and to perish in it. God often makes men's sin their punishment; and thorns and snares are *in the way of the froward*, who will walk contrary to God.

IV. The good success of this sermon is very remarkable: The people *lifted up their voice and wept, v.* 4. 1. The angel had told them of their sins, for which they thus expressed their sorrow: they lifted up their voice in confession of sin, crying out against their own folly and ingratitude, and wept, as those that were both ashamed of themselves and angry at themselves, as having acted so directly contrary both to their reason and to their interest. 2. The angel had threatened them with the judgments of God, of which they thus expressed their dread: they lifted up their voice in prayer to God to turn away his wrath from them, and wept for fear of that wrath. They relented upon this alarm, and their hearts melted within them, and trembled at the word, and not without cause. This was good, and a sign that the word they heard made an impression upon them: it is a wonder sinners can ever read their Bibles with dry eyes. But this was not enough; they wept, but we do not find that they reformed, that they went home and destroyed all the remains of idolatry and idolaters among them. Many are melted under the word that harden again before they are cast into a new mould. However, this general weeping, (1.) Gave a new name to the place (*v.* 5): they called it *Bochim, Weepers,* a good name for our religious assemblies to answer. Had they kept close to God and their duty, no voice but that of singing would have been heard in their congregation; but by their sin and folly they had made other work for themselves, and now nothing is to be heard but the voice of weeping. (2.) It gave occasion for a solemn sacrifice: They *sacrificed there unto the Lord,* having (as is supposed) met at Shiloh, where God's altar was. They offered sacrifice to turn away God's wrath, and to obtain his favour, and in token of their dedication of themselves to him, and to him only, making a covenant by this sacrifice. The disease being thus taken in time, and the physic administered working so well, one would have hoped a cure might be effected. But by the sequel of the story it appears to have been too deeply rooted to be wept out.

6 And when Joshua had let the people go, the children of Israel went every man unto his inheritance to possess the land. 7 And the people served the LORD all the days of Joshua, and all the days of the elders that outlived Joshua, who had seen all the great works of the LORD, that he did for Israel. 8 And Joshua the son of Nun, the servant of the LORD, died, *being* a hundred and ten years old. 9 And they buried him in the border of his inheritance in Timnath-heres, in the mount of Ephraim, on the north side of the hill Gaash. 10 And also all that generation were gathered unto their fathers: and there arose another generation after them, which knew not the LORD, nor yet the works which he had done for Israel. 11 And the children of Israel did evil in the sight of the LORD, and served Baalim: 12 And they forsook the LORD God of their fathers, which brought them out of the land of Egypt, and followed other gods, of the gods of the people that *were* round about them, and bowed themselves unto them, and provoked the LORD to anger. 13 And they forsook the LORD, and served Baal and Ashtaroth. 14 And the anger of the LORD was hot against Israel, and he delivered them into the hands of spoilers that spoiled them, and he sold them into the hands of their enemies round about, so that they could not any longer stand before their enemies. 15 Whithersoever they went out, the hand of the LORD was against them for evil, as the LORD had said, and as the LORD had sworn unto them: and they were greatly distressed. 16 Nevertheless the LORD raised up judges, which delivered them out of the hand of those that spoiled them. 17 And yet they would not hearken unto their judges, but they went a whoring after other gods, and bowed themselves unto them: they turned quickly out of the way which their fathers walked in, obeying the commandments of the LORD; *but* they did not so. 18 And when the LORD raised them up judges, then the LORD was with the judge, and delivered them out of the hand of their enemies all the days of the judge: for it repented the LORD because of their groanings by reason of them that oppressed them and vexed them. 19 And it came to pass, when the judge was dead, *that* they returned, and corrupted *themselves* more than their fathers, in following other gods to serve them, and to bow down unto them; they ceased not from their own doings, nor from their stubborn way. 20 And the anger of the LORD was hot against Israel; and he said, Because that this people hath transgressed my covenant which I commanded their fathers, and have not hearkened unto my voice; 21 I also will not henceforth drive out any from

before them of the nations which Joshua left when he died: 22 That through them I may prove Israel, whether they will keep the way of the LORD to walk therein, as their fathers did keep *it*, or not. 23 Therefore the LORD left those nations, without driving them out hastily; neither delivered he them into the hand of Joshua.

The beginning of this paragraph is only a repetition of what account we had before of the people's good character during the government of Joshua, and of his death and burial (Josh. xxiv. 29, 30), which comes in here again only to make way for the following account, which this chapter gives, of their degeneracy and apostasy. The angel had foretold that the Canaanites and their idols would be a snare to Israel; now the historian undertakes to show that they were so, and, that this may appear the more clear, he looks back a little, and takes notice, 1. Of their happy settlement in the land of Canaan. Joshua, having distributed this land among them, dismissed them to the quiet and comfortable possession of it (*v.* 6): *He sent them away*, not only every tribe, but *every man to his inheritance*, no doubt giving them his blessing. 2. Of their continuance in the faith and fear of God's holy name as long as Joshua lived, *v.* 7. As they went to their possessions with good resolutions to cleave to God, so they persisted for some time in these good resolutions, as long as they had good rulers that set them good examples, gave them good instructions, and reproved and restrained the corruptions that crept in among them, and as long as they had fresh in remembrance the great things God did for them when he brought them into Canaan: those that had seen these wonders had so much sense as to believe their own eyes, and so much reason as to serve that God who had appeared so gloriously on their behalf; but those that followed, because they had not seen, believed not. 3. Of the death and burial of Joshua, which gave a fatal stroke to the interests of religion among the people, *v.* 8, 9. Yet so much sense they had of their obligations to him that they did him honour at his death, and buried him in *Timnath-heres;* so it is called here, not, as in Joshua, *Timnath-serah. Heres* signifies the *sun*, a representation of which, some think, was set upon his sepulchre, and gave name to it, in remembrance of the sun's standing still at his word. So divers of the Jewish writers say; but I much question whether an image of the sun would be allowed to the honour of Joshua at that time, when, by reason of men's general proneness to worship the sun, it would be in danger of being abused to the dishonour of God. 4. Of the rising of a new generation, *v.* 10. All that generation in a few years wore off, their good instructions and examples died and were buried with them, and there arose another generation of Israelites who had so little sense of religion, and were in so little care about it, that, notwithstanding all the advantages of their education, one might truly say that they knew not the Lord, knew him not aright, knew him not as he had revealed himself, else they would not have forsaken him. They were so entirely devoted to the world, so intent upon the business of it or so indulgent of the flesh in ease and luxury, that they never minded the true God and his holy religion, and so were easily drawn aside to false gods and their abominable superstitions.

And so he comes to give us a general idea of the series of things in Israel during the time of the judges, the same repeated in the same order.

I. The people of Israel forsook the God of Israel, and gave that worship and honour to the dunghill deities of the Canaanites which was due to him alone. *Be astonished, O heavens! at this, and wonder, O earth! Hath a nation*, such a nation, so well fed, so well taught, *changed its God*, such a God, a God of infinite power, unspotted purity, inexhaustible goodness, and so very jealous of a competitor, for stocks and stones that could do neither good nor evil? Jer. ii. 11, 12. Never was there such an instance of folly, ingratitude, and perfidiousness. Observe how it is described here, *v.* 11—13. In general, *they did evil*, nothing could be more evil, that is, more provoking to God, nor more prejudicial to themselves, and it was *in the sight of the Lord;* all evil is before him, but he takes special notice of the sin of having any other god. In particular, 1. They *forsook the Lord* (*v.* 12, and again *v.* 13); this was one of the two great evils they were guilty of, Jer. ii. 13. They had been joined to the Lord in covenant, but now they forsook him, as a wife *treacherously departs from her husband.* "They forsook the worship of the Lord," so the Chaldee: for those that forsake the worship of God do in effect forsake God himself. It aggravated this that he was *the God of their fathers*, so that they were *born in his house*, and therefore bound to serve him; and that he *brought them out of the land of Egypt*, he *loosed their bonds*, and upon that account also they were obliged to serve him. 2. When they forsook the only true God they did not turn atheists, nor were they such fools as to say, *There is no God;* but they followed other gods: so much remained of pure nature as to own a God, yet so much appeared of corrupt nature as to multiply gods, and take up with any, and to follow the fashion, not the rule, in religious worship. Israel had the honour of being a peculiar people and dignified above all others, and yet so false were they to their own privileges that they were fond of the gods *of the people that were round about them.* Baal and Ashtaroth, he-gods and she-gods; they made their court to sun and moon, Jupiter and Juno. *Baalim* signifies *lords*, and *Ashtaroth blessed ones*, both plural, for when they forsook Jehovah, who is one, they had gods many and lords many, as a luxuriant fancy pleased to multiply them. Whatever they took for their gods, they served them and bowed down to them, gave honour to them and begged favours from them.

II. The God of Israel was hereby provoked to anger, and delivered them up into the hand of their enemies, *v.* 14, 15. He was wroth with them, for he is a jealous God and true to the honour of his own name; and the way he took to punish them for their apostasy was to make those their tormentors whom they yielded to as their tempters. They made themselves as mean and miserable by forsaking God as they would have been great and happy if they had continued faithful to him. 1. The scale of victory turned against them. After they forsook God, whenever they took the sword in hand they were as sure to be beaten as before they had been sure to conquer. Formerly their enemies could not stand before them, but, wherever they went, the hand of the Lord was for them; when they began to cool in their religion, God suspended his favour, stopped the progress of their successes, and would not drive out their enemies any more (*v.* 3), only suffered them to keep their ground; but now, when they had quite revolted to idolatry, the war turned directly against them, and they *could not any longer stand before their enemies.* God would rather give the success to those that had never known nor owned him than to those that had done both, but had now deserted him. Wherever they went, they might perceive that God himself had *turned to be their enemy, and fought against them,* Isa. lxiii. 10. 2. The balance of power then turned against them of course. Whoever would might spoil them, whoever would might oppress them. God sold them into the hands of their enemies; not only he delivered them up freely, as we do that which we have sold, but he did it upon a valuable consideration, that he might get himself honour as a jealous God, who would not spare even his own peculiar people when they provoked him. He sold them as insolvent debtors are sold (Matt. xviii. 25), by their sufferings to make some sort of reparation to his glory for the injury it sustained by their apostasy. Observe how their punishment, (1.) Answered what they had done. They served the gods of *the nations that were round about them,* even the meanest, and God made them serve the princes of the nations that were round about them, even the meanest. He that is company for every fool is justly made a fool of by every company. (2.) How it answered what God had spoken. The hand of heaven was thus turned against them, *as the Lord had said,* and *as the Lord had sworn* (*v.* 15), referring to the curse and death set before them in the covenant, with the blessing and life. Those that have found God true to his promises may thence infer that he will be as true to his threatenings.

III. The God of infinite mercy took pity on them in their distresses, though they had brought themselves into them by their own sin and folly, and wrought deliverance for them. Nevertheless, though their trouble was the punishment of their sin and the accomplishment of God's word, yet they were in process of time saved out of their trouble, *v.* 16—18. Here observe, 1. The inducement of their deliverance. It came purely from God's pity and tender compassion; the reason was fetched from within himself. It is not said, *It repented them because of their iniquities* (for it appears, *v.* 17, that many of them continued unreformed), but, *It repented the Lord because of their groanings;* though it is not so much the burden of sin as the burden of affliction that they are said to groan under. It is true they deserved to perish for ever under his curse, yet, this being the day of his patience and our probation, he does not stir up all his wrath. He might in justice have abandoned them, but he could not for pity do it. 2. The instruments of their deliverance. God did not send angels from heaven to rescue them, nor bring in any foreign power to their aid, but raised up judges from among themselves, as there was occasion, men to whom God gave extraordinary qualifications for, and calls to, that special service for which they were designed, which was to reform and deliver Israel, and whose great attempts he crowned with wonderful success: *The Lord was with the judges* when he raised them up, and so they became saviours. Observe, (1.) In the days of the greatest degeneracy and distress of the church there shall be some whom God will either find or make fit to redress its grievances and set things to rights. (2.) God must be acknowledged in the seasonable rising up of useful men for public service. He endues men with wisdom and courage, gives them hearts to act and venture. All that are in any way the blessings of their country must be looked upon as the gifts of God. (3.) Whom God calls he will own, and give them his presence; whom he raises up he will be with. (4.) The judges of a land are its saviours.

IV. The degenerate Israelites were not effectually and thoroughly reformed, no, not by their judges, *v.* 17—19. 1. Even while their judges were with them, and active in the work of reformation, there were those that *would not hearken to their judges,* but at that very time *went a whoring after other gods,* so mad were they upon their idols, and so obstinately *bent to backslide.* They had been espoused to God, but broke the marriage-covenant, and went a whoring after these gods. Idolatry is spiritual adultery, so vile, and base, and perfidious a thing is it, and so hardly are those reclaimed that are addicted to it. 2. Those that in the times of reformation began to amend *yet turned quickly out of the way* again, and became as bad as ever. The way they turned out of was that which their godly ancestors walked in, and set them out in; but they soon started from under the influence both of their fathers' good example and of their own good education. The wicked children of godly parents do so, and will therefore have a great deal to answer for. However, *when the judge was dead,* they looked upon the dam which checked the stream of their idolatry as removed, and then it flowed down again with so much the more fury, and the next age seemed to be rather the worse for the attempts that had been made towards reformation, *v.* 19. *They corrupted themselves more than their fathers,* strove to outdo them in multiplying strange gods and inventing profane and impious rites of worship, as it were in contradiction to their reformers. *They ceased not* from, or, as the word is, *they would not let fall,* any of their own doings, grew not ashamed of those idolatrous services that were most odious nor weary of those that were most barbarous, would not so much as diminish one step of their hard and stubborn way. Thus those that have forsaken the good ways of God, which they have once known and professed, commonly grow most daring and desperate in sin, and have their hearts most hardened.

V. God's just resolution hereupon was still to continue the rod over them, 1. Their sin was sparing the Canaanites, and this in contempt and violation of the covenant God had made with them and the commands he had given them, *v.* 20. 2. Their punishment was that the Canaanites were spared, and so they were beaten with their own rod. They were not all delivered into the hand of Joshua while he lived, *v.* 23. Our Lord Jesus, though he *spoiled principalities and powers,* yet did not complete his victory at first. *We see not yet all things put under him;* there are remains of Satan's interest in the church, as there were of the Canaanites in the land: but our Joshua lives for ever, and will in the great day perfect his conquest. After Joshua's death, little was done for a long time against the Canaanites: Israel indulged them, and grew familiar with them, and therefore God would not drive them out any more, *v.* 21. If they will have such inmates as these among them, let them take them, and see what will come of it. God chose their delusions, Isa. lxvi. 4. Thus men cherish and indulge their own corrupt appetites and passions, and, instead of mortifying them, make provision for them, and therefore God justly leaves them to themselves under the power of their sins, which will be their ruin. *So shall their doom be; they themselves have decided it.* These remnants of the Canaanites were left to prove Israel (*v.* 22), *whether they would keep the way of the Lord or not;* not that God might know them, but that they might know themselves. It was to try, (1.) Whether they could resist the temptations to idolatry which the Canaanites would lay before them. God had told them they could not, Deut. vii. 4. But they thought they could. "Well," said God, "I will try you;" and, upon trial, it was found that the tempters' charms were far too strong for them. God has told us how deceitful and desperately wicked our hearts are, but we are not willing to believe it till by making bold with temptation we find it too true by sad experience. (2.) Whether they would make a good use of the vexations which the remaining natives would give them, and the many troubles they would occasion them, and would thereby be convinced of sin and humbled for it, reformed, and driven to God and their duty, whether by continual alarms from them they would be kept in awe and made afraid of provoking God.

CHAP. III.

In this chapter, I. A general account of Israel's enemies is premised, and of the mischief they did them, ver. 1–7. II. A particular account of the brave exploits done by the first three of the judges. 1. Othniel, whom God raised up to fight Israel's battles, and plead their cause against the king of Mesopotamia, ver. 8–11. 2. Ehud, who was employed in rescuing Israel out of the hands of the Moabites, and did it by stabbing the king of Moab. ver. 12–30. 3. Shamgar, who signalized himself in an encounter with the Philistines, ver. 31.

NOW these *are* the nations which the LORD left to prove Israel by them, *even* as many *of Israel* as had not known all the wars of Canaan; 2 Only that the generations of the children of Israel might know, to teach them war, at the least such as before knew nothing thereof; 3 *Namely,* five lords of the Philistines, and all the Canaanites, and the Sidonians, and the Hivites that dwelt in mount Lebanon, from mount Baal-hermon unto the entering in of Hamath. 4 And they were to prove Israel by them, to know whether they would hearken unto the commandments of the LORD, which he commanded their fathers by the hand of Moses. 5 And the children of Israel dwelt among the Canaanites, Hittites, and Amorites, and Perizzites, and Hivites, and Jebusites: 6 And they took their daughters to be their wives, and gave their daughters to their sons, and served their gods. 7 And the children of Israel did evil in the sight of the LORD, and forgat the LORD their God, and served Baalim and the groves.

We are here told what remained of the old inhabitants of Canaan. 1. There were some of them that kept together in united bodies, unbroken (*v.* 3): *The five lords of the Philistines*, namely, Ashdod, Gaza, Askelon, Gath, and Ekron, 1 Sam. vi. 17. Three of these cities had been in part reduced (*ch.* i. 18), but it seems the Philistines (probably with the help of the other two, which strengthened their confederacy with each other thenceforward) recovered the possession of them. These gave the greatest disturbance to Israel of any of the natives, especially in the latter times of the judges, and they were never quite reduced until David's time. There was a particular nation called *Canaanites*, that kept their ground with the Sidonians, upon the coast of the great sea. And in the north the Hivites held much of Mount Lebanon, it being a remote corner, in which perhaps they were supported by some of the neighbouring states. But, besides these, 2. There were every where in all parts of the country some scatterings of the nations (*v.* 5), Hittites, Amorites, &c., which, by Israel's foolish connivance and indulgence, were so many, so easy, and so insolent, that the *children of Israel* are said to *dwell among them*, as if the right had still remained in the Canaanites, and the Israelites had been taken in by their permission and only as tenants at will.

Now concerning these remnants of the natives observe,

I. How wisely God permitted them to remain. It is mentioned in the close of the foregoing chapter as an act of God's justice, that he let them remain for Israel's correction. But here another construction is put upon it, and it appears to have been an act of God's *wisdom*, that he let them remain for Israel's real advantage, that those who *had not known the wars of Canaan* might *learn war*, *v.* 1, 2. It was the will of God that the people of Israel should be inured to war, 1. Because their country was *exceedingly rich and fruitful*, and abounded with dainties of all sorts, which, if they were not sometimes made to know hardship, would be in danger of sinking them into the utmost degree of luxury and effeminacy. They must sometimes wade in blood, and not always in milk and honey, lest even their men of war, by the long disuse of arms, should become as soft and as nice as the *tender and delicate woman, that would not set so much as the sole of her foot to the ground for tenderness and delicacy*, a temper as destructive to every thing that is good as it is to every thing that is great, and therefore to be carefully watched against by all God's Israel. 2. Because their country lay very much in the midst of enemies, by whom they must expect to be insulted; for God's heritage was as a *speckled bird; the birds round about were against her*, Jer. xii. 9. It was therefore necessary they should be well disciplined, that they might defend their coasts when invaded, and might hereafter enlarge their coast as God had promised them. The art of war is best learnt by experience, which not only acquaints men with martial discipline, but (which is no less necessary) inspires them with a martial disposition. It was for the interest of Israel to breed soldiers, as it is the interest of an island to breed seamen, and therefore God left Canaanites among them, that, by the less difficulties and hardships they met with in encountering them, they might be prepared for greater, and, by *running with the footmen*, might learn *to contend with horses*, Jer. xii. 5. Israel was a figure of the church militant, that must fight its way to a triumphant state. The soldiers of Christ must endure hardness, 2 Tim. ii. 3. Corruption is therefore left remaining in the hearts even of good Christians, that they may learn war, may keep on the *whole armour of God*, and stand continually upon their guard. The learned bishop Patrick offers another sense of *v.* 2: *That they might know to teach them war*, that is, they shall know what it is to be left to themselves. Their fathers fought by a divine power. God taught their hands to war and their fingers to fight; but now that they have forfeited his favour let them learn what it is to fight like other men.

II. How wickedly Israel mingled themselves with those that did remain. One thing God intended in leaving them among them was *to prove Israel* (*v.* 4), that those who were faithful to the God of Israel might have the honour of resisting the Canaanites' allurements to idolatry, and that those who were false and insincere might be discovered, and might fall under the shame of yielding to those allurements. Thus in the Christian churches there must needs be heresies, *that those who are perfect may be made manifest*, 1 Cor. xi. 19. Israel, upon trial, proved bad. 1. They joined in marriage with the Canaanites (*v.* 6), though they could not advance either their honour or their estate by marrying with them. They would mar their blood instead of mending it, and sink their estates instead of raising them, by such marriages. 2. Thus they were brought to join in worship with them; they served their *gods* (*v.* 6), *Baalim and the groves* (*v.* 7), that is, the images that were worshipped in groves of thick trees, which were a sort of natural temples. In such unequal matches there is more reason to fear that the bad will corrupt the good than to hope that the good will reform the bad, as there is in laying two pears together, the one rotten and the other sound. When they inclined to worship other gods they *forgot the Lord their God.* In complaisance to their new relations, they talked of nothing but Baalim and the groves, so that by degrees they lost the remembrance of the true God, and forgot there was such a Being, and what obligations they lay under to him. In nothing is the corrupt memory of man more treacherous than in this, that it is apt to forget God; because out of sight, he is out of mind; and here begins all the wickedness that is in the world: they *have perverted their way,* for they have *forgotten the Lord their God.*

8 Therefore the anger of the LORD was hot against Israel, and he sold them into the hand of Chushan-rishathaim king of Mesopotamia: and the children of Israel served Chushan-rishathaim eight years. 9 And when the children of Israel cried unto the LORD, the LORD raised up a deliverer to the children of Israel, who delivered them, *even* Othniel the son of Kenaz, Caleb's younger brother. 10 And the Spirit of the LORD came upon him, and he judged Israel, and went out to war: and the LORD delivered Chushan-rishathaim king of Mesopotamia into his hand; and his hand prevailed against Chushan-rishathaim. 11 And the land had rest forty years. And Othniel the son of Kenaz died.

We now come to the records of the government of the particular judges, the first of which was Othniel, in whom the story of this book is knit to that of Joshua, for even in Joshua's time Othniel began to be famous, by which it appears that it was not long after Israel's settlement in Canaan before their purity began to be corrupted and their peace (by consequence) disturbed. And those who have taken pains to enquire into the sacred chronology are generally agreed that the Danites' idolatry, and the war with the Benjamites for abusing the Levite's concubine, though related in the latter end of this book, happened about this time, under or before the government of Othniel, who, though a judge, was not such a king in Israel as would keep men from doing what was *right in their own eyes.* In this short narrative of Othniel's government we have,

I. The distress that Israel was brought into for their sin, *v.* 8. God being justly displeased with them for plucking up the hedge of their peculiarity, and laying themselves in common with the nations, plucked up the hedge of their protection and laid them open to the nations, set them to sale as goods he would part with, and the first that laid hands on them was Chushan-rishathaim, king of that Syria which lay between the two great rivers of Tigris and Euphrates, thence called *Mesopotamia,* which signifies *in the midst of rivers.* It is probable that this was a warlike prince, and, aiming to enlarge his dominions, he invaded the two tribes first on the other side Jordan that lay next him, and afterwards, perhaps by degrees, penetrated into the heart of the country, and as far as he went put them under contribution, exacting it with rigour, and perhaps quartering soldiers upon them. Laban, who oppressed Jacob with a hard service, was of this country; but it lay at such a distance that one could not have thought Israel's trouble would come from such a far country, which shows so much the more of the hand of God in it.

II. Their return to God in this distress: *When he slew them, then they sought him* whom before they had slighted. The *children of Israel,* even the generality of them, *cried unto the Lord, v.* 9. At first they made light of their trouble, and thought they could easily shake off the yoke of a prince at such a distance; but, when it continued eight years, they began to feel the smart of it, and then those cried under it who before had laughed at it. Those who in the day of their mirth had cried to Baalim and Ashtaroth now that they are in trouble cry to the Lord from whom they had revolted, whose justice brought them into this trouble, and whose power and favour could alone help them out of it. Affliction makes those cry to God with importunity who before would scarcely speak to him.

III. God's return in mercy to them for their deliverance. Though need drove them to him, he did not therefore reject their prayers, but graciously raised up a deliverer, or *saviour,* as the word is. Observe, 1. Who the deliverer was. It was Othniel, who married Caleb's daughter, one of the old stock that had *seen the works of the Lord,* and had himself, no question, kept his integrity, and secretly lamented the apostasy of his people, but waited for a divine call to appear publicly for the redress of their grievances. He was now, we may suppose, far advanced in years, when God raised him up to this honour, but the decays of age were no hindrance to his usefulness when God had work for him to do. 2. Whence he had his commission, not of man, nor by man; but *the Spirit of the Lord came upon him* (*v.* 10), the spirit of wisdom and courage to qualify him for the service, and a spirit of power to excite him to it, so as to give him and others full satisfaction that it was the will of God he should engage in it. The Chaldee says, *The spirit of prophecy remained on him.* 3. What method he took. He first judged Israel, reproved them, called them to an account for their sins, and reformed them, and then went out to war. This was the right method. Let sin at home be conquered, that worst of enemies, and then enemies abroad will be the more easily dealt with. Thus let Christ be our Judge and Law-giver, and then *he will save us,* and on no other terms, Isa. xxxiii. 22. 4. What good success he had. He prevailed to break the yoke of the oppression, and, as it should seem, to break the neck of the oppressor; for it is said, *The Lord delivered Chushan-rishathaim into his hand.* Now was Judah, of which tribe Othniel was, *as a lion's whelp gone up from the prey.* 5. The happy consequence of Othniel's good services. The land, though not getting ground, yet had rest, and some fruits of the reformation, forty years; and the benefit would have been perpetual if they had kept close to God and their duty.

12 And the children of Israel did evil again in the sight of the LORD: and the LORD strengthened Eglon the king of Moab against Israel, because they had done evil in the sight of the LORD. 13 And he gathered unto him the children of Ammon and Amalek, and went and smote Israel, and possessed the city of palm trees. 14 So the children of Israel served Eglon the king of Moab eighteen years. 15 But when the children of Israel cried unto the LORD, the LORD raised them up a deliverer, Ehud the son of Gera, a Benjamite, a man left-handed: and by him the children of Israel sent a present unto Eglon the king of Moab. 16 But Ehud made him a dagger which had two edges, of a cubit length; and he did gird it under his raiment upon his right thigh. 17 And he brought the present unto Eglon king of Moab: and Eglon *was* a very fat man. 18 And when he had made an end to offer the present, he sent away the people that bare the present. 19 But he himself turned again from the quarries that *were* by Gilgal, and said, I have a secret errand unto thee, O king: who said, Keep silence. And all that stood by him went out from him. 20 And Ehud came unto him; and he was sitting in a summer parlour, which he had for himself alone. And Ehud said, I have a message from God unto thee. And he arose out of *his* seat. 21 And Ehud put forth his left hand, and took the dagger from his right thigh, and thrust it into his belly: 22 And the haft also went in after the blade; and the fat closed upon the blade, so that he could not draw the dagger out of his belly; and the dirt came out. 23 Then Ehud went forth through the porch, and shut the doors of the parlour upon him, and locked them. 24 When he was gone out, his servants came; and when they saw that, behold, the doors of the parlour *were* locked, they said, Surely he covereth his feet in his summer chamber. 25 And they tarried till they were ashamed: and, behold, he opened not the doors of the parlour; therefore they took a key, and opened *them*: and, behold, their lord *was* fallen down dead on the earth. 26 And Ehud escaped while they tarried, and passed beyond the quarries, and escaped unto Seirath. 27 And it came to pass, when he was come, that he blew a trumpet in the mountain of Ephraim, and the children of Israel went down with him from the mount, and he before them. 28 And he said unto them, Follow after me: for the LORD hath delivered your enemies the Moabites into your hand. And they went down after him, and took the fords of Jordan toward Moab, and suffered not a man to pass over. 29 And they slew of Moab at that time about ten thousand men, all lusty, and all men of valour; and there escaped not a man. 30 So Moab was subdued that day under the hand of Israel. And the land had rest fourscore years.

Ehud is the next of the judges whose achievements are related in this history, and here is an account of his actions.

I. When Israel sins again God raises up a new oppressor, *v.* 12—14. It was an aggravation of their wickedness that they did evil again after they had smarted so long for their former iniquities, promised so fair when Othniel judged them, and received so much mercy from God in their deliverance. What, and after all this, again to break his commandments! Was the disease obstinate to all the methods of cure, both corrosives and lenitives? It seems it was. Perhaps they thought they might make the more bold with their old sins because they saw themselves in no danger from their old oppressor; the powers of that kingdom were weakened and brought low. But God made them know that he had variety of rods wherewith to chastise them: He *strengthened Eglon king of Moab against them.* This oppressor lay nearer to them than the former, and therefore would be the more mischievous to them; God's judgments thus approached them gradually, to bring them to repentance. When Israel dwelt in tents, but kept their integrity, Balak king of Moab, who would have strengthened himself against them, was baffled; but now that they had forsaken God, and worshipped the gods of the nations round about them (and perhaps those of the Moabites among the rest), here was another king of Moab, whom God strengthened against them, put power into his hands, though a wicked man, that he might be a scourge to Israel. The staff in his hand with which he beat Israel was God's indignation; *howbeit he meant not so, neither did his heart think so*, Isa. x. 6, 7. Israelites did ill, and, we may suppose, Moabites did worse; yet because God commonly punishes the sins of his own people in this world, that, the flesh being destroyed, the spirit may be saved, Israel are weakened and Moab strengthened against them. God would not suffer the Israelites, when they were the stronger, to distress the Moabites, nor give them any disturbance, though they were idolaters (Deut. ii. 9); yet now he suffered the Moabites to distress Israel, and strengthened them on purpose that they might: *Thy judgments, O God! are a great deep.* The king of Moab took to his assistance the Ammonites and Amalekites (*v.* 13), and this strengthened him; and we are here told how they prevailed. 1. They beat them in the field: They *went and smote Israel* (*v.* 13), not only those tribes that lay next them on the other side Jordan, who, though first settled, being frontier-tribes, were most disturbed; but those also within Jordan, for they made themselves masters of *the city of palm-trees*, which, it is probable, was a strong-hold erected near the place where Jericho had stood, for that was so called (Deut. xxxiv. 3), into which the Moabites put a garrison, to be a bridle upon Israel, and to secure the passes of Jordan, for the preservation of the communication with their own country. It was well for the Kenites that they had left this city (*ch.* i. 16) before it fell into the hands of the enemy. See how quickly the Israelites lost that by their own sin which they had gained by miracles of divine mercy. 2. They made them to serve (*v.* 14), that is, exacted tribute from them, either the fruits of the earth in kind or money in lieu of them. They neglected the service of God, and did not pay him his tribute; thus therefore did God recover from them that *wine and oil*, that silver and gold, which they prepared for Baal, Hos. ii. 8. What should have been paid to the divine grace, and was not, was distrained for, and paid to the divine justice. The former servitude (*v.* 8) lasted but eight years, this eighteen; for, if less troubles do not do the work, God will send greater.

II. When Israel prays again God raises up a new deliverer (*v.* 15), named *Ehud*. We are here told,

1. That he was a Benjamite. The city of palm-trees lay within the lot of this tribe, by which it is probable that they suffered most, and therefore stirred first to shake off the yoke. It is supposed by the chronologers that the Israelites' war with Benjamin for the wickedness of Gibeah, by which that whole tribe was reduced to 600 men, happened before this, so that we may well think that tribe to be now the weakest of all the tribes, yet out of it God raised up this deliverer, in token of his being perfectly reconciled to them, to manifest his own power in ordaining strength out of weakness, and that he might bestow *more abundant honour upon that part which lacked*, 1 Cor. xii. 24.

2. That he was left-handed, as it seems many of that tribe were, *ch.* xx. 16. Benjamin signifies *the son of the right hand*, and yet multitudes of them were left-handed; for men's natures do not always answer their names. The LXX. say he was an *ambi-dexter*, one that could use both hands alike, supposing that this was an advantage to him in the action he was called to; but the Hebrew phrase, that he was *shut of his right hand*, intimates that, either through disease or disuse, he made little or no use of that, but of his left hand only, and so was the less fit for war, because he must needs handle his sword but awkwardly; yet God chose this left-handed man to be the man of his right hand, whom he would *make strong for himself*, Ps. lxxx. 17. It was *God's right hand* that gained Israel the victory (Ps. xliv. 3), not the right hand of the instruments he employed.

3. We are here told what Ehud did for the deliverance of Israel out of the hands of the Moabites. He saved the oppressed by destroying the oppressors, when the measure of their iniquity was full and the set time to favour Israel had come.

(1.) He put to death Eglon the king of Moab; I say, *put him to death*, not murdered or assassinated him, but as a judge, or minister of divine justice, executed the judgments of God upon him, as an implacable enemy to God and Israel. This story is particularly related.

[1.] He had a fair occasion of access to him. Being an ingenious active man, and fit to stand before kings, his people chose him to carry a present in the name of all Israel, over and above their tribute, to their great lord the king of Moab, that they might find favour in his eyes, *v.* 15. The present is called *mincha* in the original, which is the word used in the law for the offerings that were presented to God to obtain his favour; these the children of Israel had not offered in their season to the God that loved them; and now, to punish them for their neglect, they are laid under a necessity of bringing their offerings to a heathen prince that hated them. Ehud went on his errand to Eglon, offered his present with the usual ceremony and expressions of dutiful respect, the better to colour what he intended and to prevent suspicion.

[2.] It should seem, from the first, he designed to be the death of him, God putting it into his heart, and letting him know also that the motion was from himself, by the

Spirit that came upon him, the impulses of which carried with them their own evidence, and so gave him full satisfaction both as to the lawfulness and the success of this daring attempt, of both which he would have had reason enough to doubt. If he be sure that God bids him do it, he is sure both that he may do it and that he shall do it; for a command from God is sufficient to bear us out, and bring us off, both against our consciences and against all the world. That he compassed and imagined the death of this tyrant appears by the preparation he made of a weapon for the purpose, a short dagger, but half a yard long, like a bayonet, which might easily be concealed under his clothes (*v.* 16), perhaps because none were suffered to come near the king with their swords by their sides. This he wore on his right thigh, that it might be the more ready to his left hand, and might be the less suspected.

[3.] He contrived how to be alone with him, which he might the more easily be now that he had not only made himself known to him, but ingratiated himself by the present, and the compliments which perhaps, on this occasion, he had passed upon him. Observe how he laid his plot. *First,* He concealed his design even from his own attendants, brought them part of the way, and then ordered them to go forward towards home, while he himself, as if he had forgotten something behind him, went back to the king of Moab's court, *v.* 18. There needed but one hand to do the execution; had more been engaged they could not so safely have kept counsel, nor so easily have made an escape. *Secondly,* He returned from the quarries by Gilgal (*v.* 19), from the *graven images* (so it is in the margin) which were with Gilgal, set up perhaps by the Moabites with the twelve stones which Joshua had set up there. Some suggest that the sight of these idols stirred up in him such an indignation against the king of Moab as put him upon the execution of that design which otherwise he had thought to let fall for the present. Or, perhaps, he came so far as to these images, that, telling from what place he returned, the king of Moab might be the more apt to believe he had a message from God. *Thirdly,* He begged a private audience, and obtained it in a withdrawing-room, here called a *summer parlour.* He told the king he had a secret errand to him, who thereupon ordered all his attendants to withdraw, *v.* 19. Whether he expected to receive some private instructions from an oracle, or some private informations concerning the present state of Israel, as if Ehud would betray his country, it was a very unwise thing for him to be all alone with a stranger and one whom he had reason to look upon as an enemy; but those that are marked for ruin are infatuated, and their *hearts hid from understanding;* God deprives them of discretion.

[4.] When he had him alone he soon dispatched him. His summer parlour, where he used to indulge himself in ease and luxury, was the place of his execution. *First,* Ehud demands his attention to *a message from God* (*v.* 20), and that message was a dagger. God sends to us by the judgments of his hand, as well as by the judgments of his mouth. *Secondly,* Eglon pays respect to a message from God. Though a king, though a heathen king, though rich and powerful, though now tyrannizing over the people of God, though a fat unwieldy man that could not easily rise nor stand long, though in private and what he did was not under observation, yet, when he expected to receive orders from heaven, he rose out of his seat; whether it was low and easy, or whether it was high and stately, he quitted it, and stood up when God was about to speak to him, thereby owning God his superior. This shames the irreverence of many who are called Christians, and yet, when a message from God is delivered to them, study to show, by all the marks of carelessness, how little they regard it. Ehud, in calling what he had to do *a message from God,* plainly avouches a divine commission for it; and God's inclining Eglon to stand up to it did both confirm the commission and facilitate the execution. *Thirdly,* The message was delivered, not to his ear, but immediately, and literally, to his heart, into which the fatal knife was thrust, and was left there, *v.* 21, 22. His extreme fatness made him unable to resist or to help himself; probably it was the effect of his luxury and excess; and, when *the fat closed up the blade,* God would by this circumstance show how those that pamper the body do but prepare for their own misery. However, it was an emblem of his carnal security and senselessness. His heart was as fat as grease, and in that he thought himself enclosed. See Ps. cxix. 70; xvii. 10. Eglon signifies a *calf,* and he fell like a fatted calf, by the knife, an acceptable sacrifice to divine justice. Notice is taken of the coming out of the dirt or dung, that the death of this proud tyrant may appear the more ignominious and shameful. He that had been so very nice and curious about his own body, to keep it easy and clean, shall now be found wallowing in his own blood and excrements. Thus does God pour contempt upon princes. Now this act of Ehud's may justify itself because he had special direction from God to do it, and it was agreeable to the usual method which, under that dispensation, God took to avenge his people of their enemies, and to manifest to the world his own justice. But it will by no means justify any now in doing the like. No such commissions are now given, and to pretend to them is to blaspheme God, and make him patronize the worst of villanies. Christ bade Peter sheathe the sword, and we find not that he bade him draw it again.

[5.] Providence wonderfully favoured his escape, when he had done the execution.

First, The tyrant fell silently, without any shriek or out-cry, which might have been overheard by his servants at a distance. How silently does he go down to the pit, choked up, it may be, with his own fat, which stifled his dying groans, though he had made so great a noise in the world, and had been *the terror of the mighty in the land of the living! Secondly,* The heroic executioner of this vengeance, with such a presence of mind as discovered not only no consciousness of guilt, but a strong confidence in the divine protection, shut the doors after him, took the key with him, and passed through the guards with such an air of innocence, and boldness, and unconcernedness, as made them not at all to suspect his having done any thing amiss. *Thirdly,* The servants that attended in the antechamber, coming to the door of the inner parlour, when Ehud had gone, to know their master's pleasure, and finding it locked and all quiet, concluded he had lain down to sleep, had covered his feet upon his couch, and gone to consult his pillow about the message he had received, and to dream upon it (*v.* 24), and therefore would not offer to open the door. Thus by their care not to disturb his sleep they lost the opportunity of revenging his death. See what comes of men's taking state too much, and obliging those about them to keep their distance; some time or other it may come against them more than they think of. *Fourthly,* The servants at length opened the door, and found their master had *slept indeed his long sleep, v.* 25. The horror of this tragical spectacle, and the confusion it must needs put them into, to reflect upon their own inconsideration in not opening the door sooner, quite put by the thoughts of sending pursuers after him that had done it, whom now they despaired of overtaking. *Lastly,* Ehud by this means made his escape to Sierath, *a thick wood;* so some, *v.* 26. It is not said any where in this story what was the place in which Eglon lived now; but, there being no mention of Ehud passing and repassing Jordan, I am inclined to think that Eglon had left his own country of Moab, on the other side Jordan, and made his principal residence at this time in the city of palm-trees, within the land of Canaan, a richer country than his own, and that there he was slain, and then the quarries by Gilgal were not far off him. There where he had settled himself, and thought he had sufficiently fortified himself to lord it over the people of God, there he was cut off, and proved to be fed for the slaughter *like a lamb in a large place.*

(2.) Ehud, having slain the king of Moab, gave a total rout to the forces of the Moabites that were among them, and so effectually shook off the yoke of their oppression. [1.] He raised an army immediately in Mount Ephraim, at some distance from the head-quarters of the Moabites, and headed them himself, *v.* 27. The trumpet he blew was indeed a jubilee-trumpet, proclaiming liberty, and a joyful sound it was to the oppressed Israelites, who for a long time had heard no other trumpets than those of their enemies. [2.] Like a pious man, and as one that did all this in faith, he took encouragement himself, and gave encouragement to his soldiers, from the power of God engaged for them (*v.* 28): "*Follow me, for the Lord hath delivered your enemies into your hands;* we are sure to have God with us, and therefore may go on boldly, and shall go on triumphantly." [3.] Like a politic general, he first secured the fords of Jordan, set strong guards upon all those passes, to cut off the communications between the Moabites that were in the land of Israel (for upon them only his design was) and their own country on the other side Jordan, that if, upon the alarm given them, they resolved to fly, they might not escape thither, and, if they resolved to fight, they might not have assistance thence. Thus he shut them up in that land as their prison in which they were pleasing themselves as their palace and paradise. [4.] He then fell upon them, and put them all to the sword, 10,000 of them, which it seems was the number appointed to keep Israel in subjection (*v.* 29): *There escaped not a man* of them. And they were the best and choicest of all the king of Moab's forces, all lusty men, men of bulk and stature, and not only able-bodied, but high spirited too, and men of valour, *v.* 29. But neither their strength nor their courage stood them in any stead when the set time had come for God to deliver them into the hand of Israel. [5.] The consequence of this victory was that the power of the Moabites was wholly broken in the land of Israel. The country was cleared of these oppressors, and *the land had rest eighty years, v.* 30. We may hope that there was likewise a reformation among them, and a check given to idolatry, by the influence of Ehud which continued a good part of this time. It was a great while for the land to rest, fourscore years; yet what is that to the saints' everlasting rest in the heavenly Canaan?

31 And after him was Shamgar the son of Anath, which slew of the Philistines six hundred men with an ox goad: and he also delivered Israel.

When it is said *the land had rest eighty years,* some think it is meant chiefly of that part of the land which lay eastward on the banks of Jordan, which had been oppressed by the Moabites; but it seems, by this passage here, that the other side of the country which lay south-west was in that time infested by the Philistines, against whom Shamgar made head. 1. It seems Israel needed deliverance, for *he delivered Israel;* how great the distress was Deborah afterwards related in her song (*ch.* v. 6.), that *in the days of Shamgar the highways were un-*

occupied, &c.; that part of the country which lay next to the Philistines was so infested with plunderers that people could not travel the roads in safety, but were in danger of being set upon and robbed, nor durst they dwell in the unguarded villages, but were forced to take shelter in the fortified cities. 2. God raised him up to deliver them, as it should seem, while Ehud was yet living, but superannuated. So inconsiderable were the enemies for number that it seems the killing of 600 of them amounted to a deliverance of Israel, and so many he slew with an ox-goad, or, as some read it, *a plough-share.* It is probable that he was himself following the plough when the Philistines made an inroad upon the country to ravage it, and God put it into his heart to oppose them; the impulse being sudden and strong, and having neither sword nor spear to do execution with, he took the instrument that was next at hand, some of the tools of his plough, and with that killed so many hundred men and came off unhurt. See here, (1.) That God can make those eminently serviceable to his glory and his church's good whose extraction, education, and employment, are very mean and obscure. He that has the residue of the Spirit could, when he pleased, make ploughmen judges and generals, and fishermen apostles. (2.) It is no matter how weak the weapon is if God direct and strengthen the arm. An ox-goad, when God pleases, shall do more than Goliath's sword. And sometimes he chooses to work by such unlikely means, that the excellency of the power may appear to be of God.

CHAP. IV.

The method of the history of Deborah and Barak (the heroes in this chapter) is the same with that before. Here is, I. Israel revolted from God, ver. 1. II. Israel oppressed by Jabin, ver. 2, 3. III. Israel judged by Deborah, ver. 4, 5. IV. Israel rescued out of the hands of Jabin. 1. Their deliverance is concerted between Deborah and Barak, ver. 6, 9. 2. It is accomplished by their joint-agency. Barak takes the field, ver. 10. Sisera, Jabin's general, meets him, ver. 12, 13. Deborah encourages him, ver. 14. And God gives him a complete victory. The army routed, ver. 15, 16. The general forced to flee, ver. 17. And where he expected shelter he had his life stolen from him by Jael while he was asleep (ver. 18—21), which completes Barak's triumph (ver. 22) and Israel's deliverance, ver. 23, 24.

AND the children of Israel again did evil in the sight of the LORD, when Ehud was dead. 2 And the LORD sold them into the hand of Jabin king of Canaan, that reigned in Hazor; the captain of whose host *was* Sisera, which dwelt in Harosheth of the Gentiles. 3 And the children of Israel cried unto the LORD: for he had nine hundred chariots of iron; and twenty years he mightily oppressed the children of Israel.

Here is, I. Israel backsliding from God: They again *did evil in his sight,* forsook his service, and worshipped idols; for this was the sin which now most easily beset them, *v.* 1. See in this, 1. The strange strength of corruption, which hurries men into sin notwithstanding the most frequent experience of its fatal consequences. The bent to backslide is with great difficulty restrained. 2. The common ill effects of a long peace. The land had rest eighty years, which should have confirmed them in their religion; but, on the contrary, it made them secure and wanton, and indulgent of those lusts which the worship of the false gods was calculated for the gratification of. Thus *the prosperity of fools destroys them. Jeshurun waxeth fat and kicketh.* 3. The great loss which a people sustains by the death of good governers. *They did evil, because Ehud was dead.* So it may be read. He kept a strict eye upon them, restrained and punished every thing that looked towards idolatry, and kept them close to God's service. But, when he was gone, they revolted, fearing him more than God.

II. Israel oppressed by their enemies. When they forsook God, he forsook them; and then they became an easy prey to every spoiler. They alienated themselves from God as if he were none of theirs; and then God alienated them as none of his. Those that threw themselves out of God's service threw themselves out of his protection. *What has my beloved to do in my house* when she has thus played the harlot? Jer. xi. 15. He *sold them into the hand of Jabin, v.* 2. This Jabin reigned in Hazor, as another of the same name, and perhaps his ancestor, had done before him, whom Joshua routed and slew, and burnt his city, Josh. xi. 1, 10. But it seems, in process of time, the city was rebuilt, the power regained, the loss retrieved, and, by degrees, the king of Hazor becomes able to tyrannize over Israel, who by sin had lost all their advantage against the Canaanites. This servitude was longer than either of the former, and much more grievous. Jabin, and his general Sisera, did mightily oppress Israel. That which aggravated the oppression was, 1. That this enemy was nearer to them than any of the former, in their borders, in their bowels, and by this means had the more opportunity to do them a mischief. 2. That they were the natives of the country, who bore an implacable enmity to them, for invading and dispossessing them, and when they had them in their power would be so much the more cruel and mischievous towards them in revenge of the old quarrel. 3. That these Canaanites had formerly been conquered and subdued by Israel, were of old sentenced to be their servants (Gen. ix. 25), and might now have been under their feet, and utterly incapable of giving them any disturbance, if their own slothfulness, cowardice, and unbelief, had not suffered them thus to get head. To be oppressed by those whom their fathers had conquered, and whom they themselves had foolishly spared, could not but be very grievous.

III. Israel returning to their God: They *cried unto the Lord,* when distress drove them to him, and they saw no other way of relief. Those that slight God in their prosperity will find themselves under a necessity of seeking him when they are in trouble.

4 And Deborah, a prophetess, the wife of Lapidoth, she judged Israel at that time. 5 And she dwelt under the palm tree of Deborah between Ramah and Beth-el in mount Ephraim: and the children of Israel came up to her for judgment. 6 And she sent and called Barak the son of Abinoam out of Kedesh-naphtali, and said unto him, Hath not the LORD God of Israel commanded, *saying,* Go and draw toward mount Tabor, and take with thee ten thousand men of the children of Naphtali and of the children of Zebulun? 7 And I will draw unto thee to the river Kishon Sisera, the captain of Jabin's army, with his chariots and his multitude; and I will deliver him into thine hand. 8 And Barak said unto her, If thou wilt go with me, then I will go: but if thou wilt not go with me, *then* I will not go. 9 And she said, I will surely go with thee: notwithstanding the journey that thou takest shall not be for thine honour; for the LORD shall sell Sisera into the hand of a woman. And Deborah arose, and went with Barak to Kedesh.

The year of the redeemed at length came, when Israel was to be delivered out of the hands of Jabin, and restored again to their liberty, which we may suppose the northern tribes, that lay nearest to the oppressors and felt most the effects of his fury, did in a particular manner cry to God for. *For the oppression of the poor, and the sighing of the needy, now will* God *arise* Now here we have,

I. The preparation of the people for their deliverance, by the prophetic conduct and government of Deborah, *v.* 4, 5. Her name signifies a *bee;* and she answered her name by her industry, sagacity, and great usefulness to the public, her sweetness to her friends and sharpness to her enemies. She is said to be *the wife of Lapidoth;* but, the termination not being commonly found in the name of a man, some make this the name of a place: she was *a woman of Lapidoth.* Others take it appellatively, Lapidoth signifies *lamps.* The Rabbin say she had employed herself in making wicks for the lamps of the tabernacle; and, having stooped to that mean office for God, she was afterwards thus preferred. Or she was a woman of *illuminations,* or of *splendours,* one that was extraordinarily knowing and wise, and so came to be very eminent and illustrious. Concerning her we are here told, 1. That she was intimately acquainted with God; she was *a prophetess,* one that was instructed in divine knowledge by the immediate inspiration of the Spirit of God, and had gifts of wisdom, to which she attained not in an ordinary way: she *heard the words of God,* and probably *saw the visions of the Almighty.* 2. That she was entirely devoted to the service of Israel. She judged Israel at the time that Jabin oppressed them; and perhaps, being a woman, she was the more easily permitted by the oppressor to do it. She judged, not as a princess, by any civil authority conferred upon her, but as a prophetess, and as God's mouth to them, correcting abuses and redressing grievances, especially those which related to the worship of God. The children of Israel came up to her from all parts for judgment, not so much for the deciding of controversies between man and man as for advice in the reformation of what was amiss in things pertaining to God. Those among them who before had secretly lamented the impieties and idolatries of their neighbours, but knew not where to apply for the restraining of them, now made their complaints to Deborah, who, by the sword of the Spirit, showing them the judgment of God, reduced and reclaimed many, and excited and animated the magistrates in their respective districts to put the laws in execution. It is said she *dwelt,* or, as some read it, she *sat* under a palm-tree, called ever after from her *the palm-tree of Deborah.* Either she had her house under that tree, a mean habitation which would couch under a tree, or she had her judgment-seat in the open air, under the shadow of that tree, which was an emblem of the justice she sat there to administer, which will thrive and grow against opposition, as palms under pressures. Josephus says that the children of Israel came to Deborah, to desire her to pray to God for them, that they might be delivered out of the hand of Jabin; and Samuel is said at one particular time to judge Israel in Mizpeh, that is, to bring them back again to God, when they made the same address to him upon a like occasion, 1 Sam. vii. 6, 8.

II. The project laid for their deliverance. When the children of Israel *came to her for judgment,* with her they found salvation. So those that seek to God for grace shall have grace and peace, grace and comfort, grace and glory. She was not herself fit to command an army in person, being a woman; but she nominated one that was fit, Barak of Naphtali, who, it is probable, had already signalized himself in some rencounters with the forces of the oppressor, living near him (for Hazor and Harosheth lay within the lot of that tribe), and thereby had gained a reputation and interest among his people. Some struggles, we may suppose, that brave man had made towards the shaking off of the yoke, but could not effect it till he had his commission and instructions from Deborah. He could do nothing without her head, nor she without his hands; but both together made a complete deliverer, and effected a complete deliverance. The greatest and best are not self-sufficient, but need one another.

1. By God's direction, she orders Barak to raise an army, and engage Jabin's forces, that were under Sisera's command, *v.* 6, 7. Barak, it may be, had been meditating some great attempt against the common enemy; a spark of generous fire was glowing in his breast, and he would fain do something to the purpose for his people and for the cities of his God. But two things discouraged him:

(1.) He wanted a commission to levy forces; this therefore Deborah here gives him under the broad seal of heaven, which, as a prophetess, she had a warrant to affix to it: "*Hath not the Lord God of Israel commanded it?* Yes, certainly he has; take my word for it." Some think she intends this as an appeal to Barak's own heart. "Has not God, by a secret whisper to thyself, given thee some intimation of his purpose to make use of thee as an instrument in his hands to save Israel? Hast not thou felt some impulse of this kind upon thy own spirit?" If so, the spirit of prophesy in Deborah confirms the spirit of a soldier in Barak: *Go and draw towards Mount Tabor.* [1.] She directs him what number of men to raise—10,000; and let him not fear that these will be too few, when God hath said he will by them save Israel. [2.] Whence he should raise them—only out of his own tribe, and that of Zebulun next adjoining. These two counties should furnish him with an army sufficient; he need not stay to go further. And, [3.] She orders him where to make his rendezvous—at Mount Tabor, in his own neighbourhood.

(2.) When he had an army raised, he knew not how he should have an opportunity of engaging the enemy, who perhaps declined fighting, having heard that Israel, if they had but courage enough to make head against an enemy, seldom failed of success. "Well," says Deborah, in the name of "God, *I will draw unto thee Sisera and his army.*" She assured him that the matter should be determined by one pitched battle, and should not be long in the doing. [1.] In mentioning the power of the enemy, Sisera, a celebrated general, bold and experienced, his chariots, his iron chariots, and his multitude of soldiers, she obliged Barak to fortify himself with the utmost degree of resolution; for the enemy he was to engage was a very formidable one. It is good to know the worst, that we may provide accordingly. But, [2.] In fixing the very place to which Sisera would draw his army, she gave him a sign, which might help to confirm his faith when he came to engage. It was a contingent thing, and depended upon Sisera's own will; but, when afterwards Barak should see the event falling out just as Deborah had foretold, he might thence infer that certainly in the rest she said she spoke under a divine direction, which would be a great encouragement to him, especially because with this, [3.] She gave him an express promise of success *I will* (that is, God will, in whose name I speak) *deliver them into thy hand;* so that when he saw them drawn up against him, according to Deborah's word, he might be confident that, according to her word, he should soon see them fallen before him. Observe, God *drew them to him* only that he might *deliver them into his hand.* When Sisera drew his forces together, he designed the destruction of Israel; but God *gathered them as sheaves into the floor,* for their own destruction, Mic. iv. 11, 12. *Assemble yourselves, and you shall be broken to pieces,* Isa. viii. 9. See Rev. xix. 17, 18.

2. At Barak's request, she promises to go along with him to the field of battle. (1.) Barak insisted much upon the necessity of her presence, which would be to him better than a council of war (*v.* 8): "*If thou wilt go with me* to direct and advise me, and in every difficult case to let me know God's mind, *then I will go* with all my heart, and not fear the chariots of iron; otherwise not." Some make this to be the language of a weak faith; he could not take her word unless he had her with him in pawn, as it were, for performance. It seems rather to arise from a conviction of the necessity of God's presence and continual direction, a pledge and earnest of which he would reckon Deborah's presence to be, and therefore begged thus earnestly for it. "*If thou go not up with me,* in token of God's going with me, *carry me not up hence.*" Nothing would be a greater satisfaction to him than to have the prophetess with him to animate the soldiers and to be consulted as an oracle upon all occasions. (2.) Deborah promised to go with him, *v.* 9. No toil nor peril shall discourage her from doing the utmost that becomes her to do for the service of her country. She would not send him where she would not go herself. Those that in God's name call others to their duty should be very ready to assist them in it. Deborah was the weaker vessel, yet had the stronger faith. But though she agrees to go with Barak, if he insists upon it, she gives him a hint proper enough to move a soldier not to insist upon it: *The journey thou undertakest* (so confident was she of the success that she called his engaging in war but the undertaking of a journey) *shall not be for thy honour;* not so much for thy honour as if thou hadst gone by thyself; for *the Lord shall sell Sisera* (now his turn comes to be sold as Israel was,

v. 2., by way of reprisal) *into the hands of a woman;*" that is, [1.] The world would ascribe the victory to the hand of Deborah: this he might himself foresee. [2.] God (to correct his weakness) would complete the victory by the hand of Jael, which would be some eclipse to his glory. But Barak values the satisfaction of his mind, and the good success of his enterprise, more than his honour; and therefore will by no means drop his request. He dares not fight unless he have Deborah with him, to direct him and pray for him. She therefore stood to her word with a masculine courage; this noble heroine *arose and went with Barak.*

10 And Barak called Zebulun and Naphtali to Kedesh; and he went up with ten thousand men at his feet: and Deborah went up with him. 11 Now Heber the Kenite, *which was* of the children of Hobab the father in law of Moses, had severed himself from the Kenites, and pitched his tent unto the plain of Zaanaim, which *is* by Kedesh. 12 And they showed Sisera that Barak the son of Abinoam was gone up to mount Tabor. 13 And Sisera gathered together all his chariots, *even* nine hundred chariots of iron, and all the people that *were* with him, from Harosheth of the Gentiles unto the river of Kishon. 14 And Deborah said unto Barak, Up; for this *is* the day in which the LORD hath delivered Sisera into thine hand: is not the LORD gone out before thee? So Barak went down from mount Tabor, and ten thousand men after him. 15 And the LORD discomfited Sisera, and all *his* chariots, and all *his* host, with the edge of the sword before Barak; so that Sisera lighted down off *his* chariot, and fled away on his feet. 16 But Barak pursued after the chariots, and after the host, unto Harosheth of the Gentiles: and all the host of Sisera fell upon the edge of the sword; *and* there was not a man left.

Here, I. Barak beats up for volunteers, and soon has his quota of men ready, *v.* 10. Deborah had appointed him to raise an army of 10,000 men (*v.* 6), and so many he has presently *at his feet,* following him, and subject to his command. God is said to call us *to his feet* (Isa. xli. 2), that is, into obedience to him. Some think it intimates that they were all footmen, and so the armies of the Jews generally were, which made the disproportion of strength between them and the enemy (who had horses and chariots) very great, and the victory the more illustrious; but the presence of God and his prophetess was abundantly sufficient to balance that disproportion. Barak had his men *at his feet,* which intimates their cheerfulness and readiness to attend him whithersoever he went, Rev. xiv. 4. Though the tribes of Zebulun and Naphtali were chiefly depended on, yet it appears by Deborah's song that some had come in to him from other tribes (Manasseh and Issachar), and more were expected that came not, from Reuben, Dan, and Asher, *ch.* v. 14—17. But these are overlooked here; and we are only told that to make his 10,000 men effective indeed *Deborah went up with him.* The 11th verse, concerning the removal of Heber, one of the families of the Kenites, out of the wilderness of Judah, in the south, where those families had fixed themselves (*ch.* i. 16), into the northern country, comes in for the sake of what was to follow concerning the exploit of Jael, a wife of that family.

II. Sisera, upon notice of Barak's motions, takes the field with a very numerous and powerful army (*v.* 12, 13): *They showed Sisera,* that is, it was shown to him. Yet some think it refers to the Kenites, mentioned immediately before, *v.* 11. They gave Sisera notice of Barak's rendezvous, there being peace at this time between Jabin and that family, *v.* 17. Whether they intended it as a kindness to him or no, it served to accomplish what God had said by Deborah (*v.* 7): *I will draw unto thee Sisera.* Sisera's confidence was chiefly in his chariots; therefore particular notice is taken of them, 900 *chariots of iron,* which, with the scythes fastened to their axle-trees, when they were driven into an army of footmen, did terrible execution. So ingenious have men been in inventing methods of destroying one another, to gratify those lusts *from which come wars and fightings.*

III. Deborah gives orders to engage the enemy, *v.* 14. Josephus says that when Barak saw Sisera's army drawn up, and attempting to surround the mountain on the top of which he and his forces lay encamped, his heart quite failed him, and he determined to retire to a place of greater safety; but Deborah animated him to make a descent upon Sisera, assuring him that this was the day marked out in the divine counsels for his defeat. "Now they appear most threatening they are ripe for ruin. The thing is as sure to be done as if it were done already: *The Lord hath delivered Sisera into thy hand.*" See how the work and honour of this great action are divided between Deborah and Barak; she, as the head, *gives the word,* he, as the hand, *does the work.* Thus does God dispense his gifts variously, 1 Cor. xii. 4, &c. But, though ordinarily *the head of the woman is the man* (1 Cor. xi. 3), he that has the residue of the Spirit was pleased to cross hands, and to put the head upon the woman's shoulders, choosing the weak things of the world to shame the mighty, that no flesh might glory in his presence. It was well for Barak that he had Deborah with him; for she made up what was defective, 1. In his conduct, by telling him, *This is the day.* 2. In his courage, by assuring him of God's presence: "*Has not the Lord gone out before thee?* Darest not thou follow when thou hast God himself for thy leader?" Note, (1.) In every undertaking it is good to be satisfied that God goes before us, that we are in the way of our duty and under his direction. (2.) If we have ground to hope that God goes before us, we ought to go on with courage and cheerfulness. Be not dismayed at the difficulties thou meetest with in resisting Satan, in serving God, or suffering for him; for *has not the Lord gone out before thee?* Follow him fully then.

IV. God himself routs the enemy's army, *v.* 15. Barak, in obedience to Deborah's orders, went down into the valley, though there upon the plain the iron chariots would have so much the more advantage against him, quitting his fastn esses upon the mountain in dependence upon the divine power; for *in vain is salvation hoped for from hills and mountains; in the Lord alone is the salvation of his people,* Jer. iii. 23. And he was not deceived in his confidence: *The Lord discomfited Sisera.* It was not so much the bold and surprising alarm which Barak gave their camp that dispirited and dispersed them, but God's terror seized their spirits and put them into an unaccountable confusion. *The stars,* it seems, fought against them, *ch.* v. 20. Josephus says that a violent storm of hail which beat in their faces gave them this rout, disabled them, and drove them back; so that they became a very easy prey to the army of Israel, and Deborah's words were made good: "*The Lord has delivered them into thy hand;* it is now in thy power to do what thou wilt with them."

V. Barak bravely improves his advantage, follows the blow with undaunted resolution and unwearied diligence, prosecutes the victory, pursues the scattered forces, even to their general's head-quarters at Harosheth (*v.* 16), and spares none whom God had delivered into his hand to be destroyed: *There was not a man left.* When God goes before us in our spiritual conflicts we must bestir ourselves; and, when by grace he gives us some success against the enemies of our souls, we must improve it by watchfulness and resolution, and carry on the holy war with vigour.

17 Howbeit Sisera fled away on his feet to the tent of Jael the wife of Heber the Kenite: for *there was* peace between Jabin the king of Hazor and the house of Heber the Kenite. 18 And Jael went out to meet Sisera, and said unto him, Turn in, my lord, turn in to me; fear not. And when he had turned in unto her into the tent, she covered him with a mantle. 19 And he said unto her, Give me, I pray thee, a little water to drink; for I am thirsty. And she opened a bottle of milk, and gave him drink, and covered him. 20 Again he said unto her, Stand in the door of the tent, and it shall be, when any man doth come and enquire of thee, and say, Is there any man here? that thou shalt say, No. 21 Then Jael Heber's wife took a nail of the tent, and took a hammer in her hand, and went softly unto him, and smote the nail into his temples, and fastened it into the ground: for he was fast asleep and weary. So he died. 22 And, behold, as Barak pursued Sisera, Jael came out to meet him, and said unto him, Come, and I will show thee the man whom thou seekest. And when he came into her *tent,* behold, Sisera lay dead, and the nail *was* in his temples. 23 So God subdued on that day Jabin the king of Canaan before the children of Israel. 24 And the hand of the children of Israel prospered, and prevailed against Jabin the king of Canaan, until they had destroyed Jabin king of Canaan.

We have seen the army of the Canaanites totally routed. It is said (Ps. lxxxiii. 9, 10, where the defeat of this army is pleaded as a precedent for God's doing the like in after times) that they became *as dung for the earth.* Now here we have,

I. The fall of their general, Sisera, captain of the host, in whom, it is likely, Jabin their king put an entire confidence, and therefore was not himself present in the action. Let us trace the steps of this mighty man's fall.

1. He quitted his chariot, and took to his feet, *v.* 15, 17. His chariots had been his pride and his confidence; and we may suppose he had therefore despised and defied the armies of the living God, because they were all on foot, and had neither chariot nor horse, as he had. Justly therefore is he thus made ashamed of his confidence, and forced to quit it, and thinks himself then most safe and easy when he has got clear of his chariot, though we may well suppose it the best made, and best drawn, of any of them. Thus are those disappointed who

rest on the creature; like a broken reed, it not only breaks under them, but runs into their hand, and pierceth them with many sorrows. The idol may quickly become a burden (Isa. xlvi. 1), and what we were sick for God can make us sick of. How miserable doth Sisera look now he is dismounted! It is hard to say whether he blusheth or trembleth more. Put not your trust in princes, if they may so soon be brought to this, if he who but lately trusted to his arms with so much assurance must now trust to his heels only with so little.

2. He fled for shelter to the tents of the Kenites, having no strong-hold, nor any place of his own in reach to retire to. The mean and solitary way of the Kenites' living, perhaps, he had formerly despised and ridiculed, and the more because religion was kept up among them; yet now he is glad to put himself under the protection of one of these tents: and he chooses the wife's tent or apartment, either because less suspected, or because it happened to be next to him, and the first he came to, *v.* 17. And that which encouraged him to go thither was that at this time there was peace between his master and the house of Heber: not that there was any league offensive and defensive between them, only at present there were no indications of hostility. Jabin did them no harm, did not oppress them as he did the Israelites, their plain, quiet, harmless way of living making them not suspected nor feared, and perhaps God so ordering it as a recompence for their constant adherence to the true religion. Sisera thought he might therefore be safe among them; not considering that, though they themselves suffered not by Jabin's power, they heartily sympathized with the Israel of God that did.

3. Jael invited him in, and bade him very welcome. Probably she stood at the tent door, to enquire what news from the army, and what was the success of the battle which was fought not far off. (1.) She invited him in. Perhaps she stood waiting for an opportunity to show kindness to any distressed Israelite, if there should be occasion for it; but seeing Sisera come in great haste, panting and out of breath, she invited him to come and repose himself in her tent, in which, while she seemed to design the relieving of his fatigue, perhaps she really intended the retarding of his flight, that he might fall into the hands of Barak, who was now in a hot chase after him (*v.* 18), and it may well be questioned whether she had at first any thought of taking away his life, but rather God afterwards put it into her heart. (2.) She made very much of him, and seemed mighty careful to have him easy, as her invited guest. Was he weary? she finds him a very convenient place to repose himself in, and recruit his strength. Was he thirsty? well he might. Did he want a little water to cool his tongue? the best liquor her tent afforded was at his service, and that was milk (*v.* 19), which, we may suppose, he drank heartily of, and, being refreshed with it, was the better disposed to sleep. Was he cold, or afraid of catching cold? or did he desire to be hid from the pursuers, if they should search that tent? she covered him with a mantle, *v.* 18. All expressions of care for his safety. Only when he desired her to tell a lie for him, and to say he was not there, she declined making any such promise, *v.* 20. We must not sin against God, no, not to oblige those we would show ourselves most observant of. *Lastly,* We must suppose she kept her tent as quiet as she could, and free from noise, that he might sleep the sooner and the faster. And now was Sisera least safe when he was most secure. How uncertain and precarious is human life! and what assurance can we have of it, when it may so easily be betrayed by those with whom it is trusted, and those may prove its destroyers who we hoped would be its protectors! It is best making God our friend, for he will not deceive us.

4. When he lay fast asleep she drove a long nail through his temples, so fastened his head to the ground, and killed him, *v.* 21. And, though this was enough to do the business, yet, to make sure work (if we translate it right, *ch.* v. 26), she cut off his head, and left it nailed there. Whether she designed this or no when she invited him into her tent does not appear; probably the thought was darted into her mind when she saw him lie so conveniently to receive such a fatal blow; and, doubtless, the thought brought with it evidence sufficient that it came not from Satan as a murderer and destroyer, but from God as a righteous judge and avenger, so much of brightness and heavenly light did she perceive in the inducements to it that offered themselves, the honour of God and the deliverance of Israel, and nothing of the blackness of malice, hatred, or personal revenge. (1.) It was a divine power that enabled her to do it, and inspired her with a more than manly courage. What if her hand should shake, and she should miss her blow? What if he should awake when she was attempting it? Or suppose some of his own attendants should follow him, and surprise her in the fact, how dearly would she and all hers be made to pay for it? Yet, obtaining help of God, she did it effectually. (2.) It was a divine warrant that justified her in the doing of it; and therefore, since no such extraordinary commissions can now be pretended, it ought not in any case to be imitated. The laws of friendship and hospitality must be religiously observed, and we must abhor the thought of betraying any whom we have invited and encouraged to put a confidence in us. And, as to this act of Jael (like that of Ehud in the chapter before), we have reason to think she was con-

scious of such a divine impulse upon her spirit to do it as did abundantly satisfy herself (and it ought therefore to satisfy us) that it was well done. God's judgments are a great deep. The instrument of this execution was a nail of the tent, that is, one of the great pins with which the tent, or the stakes of it, were fastened. They often removing their tents, she had been used to drive these nails, and therefore knew how to do it the more dexterously on this great occasion. He that thought to destroy Israel with his many iron chariots is himself destroyed with one iron nail. Thus do the weak things of the world confound the mighty. See here Jael's glory and Sisera's shame. The great commander dies, [1.] In his sleep, fast asleep, and weary. It comes in as a reason why he stirred not, to make resistance. So fettered was he in the chains of sleep that he could not find his hands. Thus *the stout-hearted are spoiled at thy rebuke, O God of Jacob! they are cast into a dead sleep,* and so are made to sleep their last, Ps. lxxvi. 5, 6. Let not the strong man then glory in his strength; for when he sleeps where is it? It is weak, and he can do nothing; a child may insult him then, and steal his life from him; and yet if he sleep not he is soon spent and weary, and can do nothing either. Those words which we here put in a parenthesis *(for he was weary)* all the ancient versions read otherwise: *he struggled* (or started, as we say) *and died,* so the Syriac and Arabic, *Exagitans sese mortuus est. He fainted and died,* so the Chaldee. *He was darkened and died,* so the LXX. *Consocians morte soporem,* so the vulgar Latin, joining sleep and death together, seeing they are so near akin. *He fainted and died.* He dies, [2.] With his head nailed to the ground, an emblem of his earthly-mindedness. *O curve in terram animæ!* His ear (says bishop Hall) was fastened close to the earth, as if his body had been listening what had become of his soul. He dies, [3.] By the hand of a woman. This added to the shame of his death before men; and had he but known it, as Abimelech (*ch.* ix. 54), we may well imagine how much it would have added to the vexation of his own heart.

II. The glory and joy of Israel hereupon. 1. Barak their leader finds his enemy dead, (*v.* 22), and no doubt, he was very well pleased to find his work done so well to his hand, and so much to the glory of God and the confusion of his enemies. Had he stood too nicely upon a point of honour, he would have resented it as an affront to have the general slain by any hand but his; but now he remembered that this diminution of his honour he was sentenced to undergo, for insisting upon Deborah's going with him *(the Lord shall sell Sisera into the hand of a woman),* though then it was little thought that the prediction would be fulfilled in such a way as this. 2. Israel is completely delivered out of the hands of Jabin king of Canaan, *v.* 23, 24. They not only shook off his yoke by this day's victory, but they afterwards prosecuted the war against him, till they had destroyed him, he and his nation being by the divine appointment devoted to ruin and not to be spared. The Israelites, having soundly smarted for their foolish pity in not doing it before, resolve now it is in their power to indulge them no longer, but to make a thorough riddance of them, as a people to whom to show mercy was as contrary to their own interest as it was to God's command; and probably it is with an eye to the sentence they were under that this enemy is named three times here in these last two verses, and called *king of Canaan;* for as such he was to be destroyed; and so thoroughly was he destroyed that I do not remember to read of the kings of Canaan any more after this. The children of Israel would have prevented a great deal of mischief if they had sooner destroyed these Canaanites, as God had both commanded and enabled them; but better be wise late, and buy wisdom by experience, than never wise.

CHAP. V.

This chapter contains the triumphal song which was composed and sung upon occasion of that glorious victory which Israel obtained over the forces of Jabin king of Canaan and the happy consequences of that victory. Probably it was usual then to publish poems upon such occasions, as now; but this only is preserved of all the poems of that age of the judges, because dictated by Deborah a prophetess, designed for a psalm of praise then, and a pattern of praise to after-ages, and it gives a great deal of light to the history of these times. I. It begins with praise to God, ver. 2, 3. II. The substance of this song transmits the memory of this great achievement. 1. Comparing God's appearances for them on this occasion with his appearances to them on Mount Sinai, ver. 4, 5. 2. Magnifying their deliverance from the consideration of the calamitous condition they had been in, ver. 6—8. 3. Calling those to join in praise that shared in the benefits of the success, ver. 9—13. 4. Reflecting honour upon those tribes that were forward and active in that war, and disgrace on those that declined the service, ver. 14—19, 23. 5. Taking notice how God himself fought for them, ver. 20—22. 6. Celebrating particularly the honour of Jael, that slew Sisera, on which head the song is very large, ver. 24—30. It concludes with a prayer to God, ver. 31.

THEN sang Deborah and Barak the son of Abinoam on that day, saying, 2 Praise ye the LORD for the avenging of Israel, when the people willingly offered themselves. 3 Hear, O ye kings; give ear, O ye princes; I, *even* I, will sing unto the LORD; I will sing *praise* to the LORD God of Israel. 4 LORD, when thou wentest out of Seir, when thou marchedst out of the field of Edom, the earth trembled, and the heavens dropped, the clouds also dropped water. 5 The mountains melted from before the LORD, *even* that Sinai from before the LORD God of Israel.

The former chapter let us know what great things God had done for Israel; in this we have the thankful returns they made to God, that all ages of the church might learn that work of heaven to praise God.

I. God is praised by a song, which is, 1.

A very natural expression of rejoicing. *Is any merry? Let him sing;* and holy joy is the very soul and root of praise and thanksgiving. God is pleased to reckon himself glorified by our joy in him, and in his wondrous works. His servants' joy is his delight, and their songs are melody to him. 2. A very proper expedient for spreading the knowledge and perpetuating the remembrance of great events. Neighbours would learn this song one of another and children of their parents; and by that means those who had not books, or could not read, yet would be made acquainted with these works of God; and *one generation* would thus *praise God's works to another,* and *declare his mighty acts,* Ps. cxlv. 4, &c.

II. Deborah herself penned this song, as appears by *v.* 7: *Till I Deborah arose.* And the first words should be rendered, *Then she sang, even Deborah.* 1. She used her gifts as a prophetess in composing the song, and the strain throughout is very fine and lofty, the images are lively, the expressions elegant, and an admirable mixture there is in it of sweetness and majesty. No poetry is comparable to the sacred poetry. And, 2. We may suppose she used her power as a princess, in obliging the conquering army of Israel to learn and sing this song. She expects not that they should, by their poems, celebrate her praises and magnify her, but requires that in this poem they should join with her in celebrating God's praises and magnifying him. She had been the first wheel in the action, and now is so in the thanksgiving.

III. It was sung on that day, not the very day that the fight was, but on that occasion, and soon after, as soon as a thanksgiving day could conveniently be appointed. When we have received mercy from God, we ought to be speedy in our returns of praise, while the impressions of the mercy are fresh. It is rent to be paid at the day.

1. She begins with a general Hallelujah: *Praise* (or *bless,* for that is the word) *you the Lord, v.* 2. The design of the song is to give glory to God; this therefore is put first, to explain and direct all that follows, like the first petition of the Lord's prayer, *Hallowed be thy name.* Two things God is here praised for:—(1.) The vengeance he took on Israel's enemies, for the avenging of Israel upon their proud and cruel oppressors, recompensing into their bosoms all the injuries they had done to his people. *The Lord is known* as a righteous God, and the God to whom vengeance belongs *by the judgments which he executeth.* (2.) The grace he gave to Israel's friends, *when the people willingly offered themselves* to serve in this war. God is to have the glory of all the good offices that are at any time done us; and the more willingly they are done the more is to be observed of that grace which gives both to will and to do. For these two things she resolves to leave this song upon record, to the honour of the everlasting God (*v.* 3): *I, even I, will sing unto the Lord,* Jehovah, that God of incontestable sovereignty and irresistible power, even to *the Lord God of Israel,* who governs all for the good of the church.

2. She calls to the great ones of the world, that sit at the upper end of its table, to attend to her song, and take notice of the subject of it: *Hear, O you kings! give ear, O you princes!* (1.) She would have them know that as great and as high as they were there was one above them with whom it is folly to contend, and to whom it was their interest to submit, that horses and chariots are vain things for safety. (2.) She would have them to join with her in praising the God of Israel, and no longer to praise their counterfeit deities, as Belshazzar did. Dan. v. 4, *He praised the gods of gold and silver.* She bespeaks them as the psalmist (Ps. ii. 10, 11), *Be wise now therefore, O you kings! serve the Lord with fear.* (3.) She would have them take warning by Sisera's fate, and not dare to offer any injury to the people of God, whose cause, sooner or later, God will plead with jealousy.

3. She looks back upon God's former appearances, and compares this with them, the more to magnify the glorious author of this great salvation. What God is doing should bring to our mind what he has done; for he is the same yesterday, to-day, and for ever (*v.* 4): *Lord, when thou wentest out of Seir.* This may be understood either, (1.) Of the appearances of God's power and justice against the enemies of Israel to subdue and conquer them; and so Hab. iii. 3, 4, &c., is parallel to it, where the destruction of the church's enemies is thus described. When God had led his people Israel from the country of Edom he brought down under their feet Sihon and Og, striking them and their armies with such terror and amazement that they seemed apprehensive heaven and earth were coming together. Their hearts melted, as if all the world had been melting round about them. Or it notes the glorious displays of the divine majesty, and the surprising effects of the divine power, enough to make the earth tremble, the heavens drop like snow before the sun, and the mountains to melt. Compare Ps. xviii. 7. God's counsels are so far from being hindered by any creature that, when the time of their accomplishment comes, that which seemed to stand in their way will not only yield before them, but be made to serve them. See Isa. lxiv. 1, 2. Or, (2.) It is meant of the appearances of God's glory and majesty to Israel, when he gave them his law at Mount Sinai. It was then literally true, *the earth trembled, and the heavens dropped,* &c. Compare Deut. xxxiii. 2; Ps. lxviii. 7, 8. Let all the kings and princes know that this is the God whom Deborah praises, and not such mean and impotent deities as they paid

their homage to. The Chaldee paraphrase applies it to the giving of the law, but has a strange descant on those words, *the mountains melted. Tabor, Hermon, and Carmel, contended among themselves: one said, Let the divine majesty dwell upon me; the other said, Let it dwell upon me; but God made it to dwell upon Mount Sinai, the meanest and least of all the mountains.* I suppose it means the least valuable, because barren and rocky.

6 In the days of Shamgar the son of Anath, in the days of Jael, the highways were unoccupied, and the travellers walked through byways. 7 *The inhabitants* of the villages ceased, they ceased in Israel, until that I Deborah arose, that I arose a mother in Israel. 8 They chose new gods; then *was* war in the gates: was there a shield or spear seen among forty thousand in Israel? 9 My heart *is* toward the governors of Israel, that offered themselves willingly among the people. Bless ye the LORD. 10 Speak, ye that ride on white asses, ye that sit in judgment, and walk by the way. 11 *They that are* delivered from the noise of archers in the places of drawing water, there shall they rehearse the righteous acts of the LORD, *even* the righteous acts *toward the inhabitants* of his villages in Israel: then shall the people of the LORD go down to the gates.

Here, I. Deborah describes the distressed state of Israel under the tyranny of Jabin, that the greatness of their trouble might make their salvation appear the more illustrious and the more gracious (*v.* 6): *From the days of Shamgar,* who did something towards the deliverance of Israel from the Philistines, to the days of Jael, the present day, in which Jael has so signalized herself, the country has been in a manner desolate. 1. No trade. For want of soldiers to protect men of business in their business from the incursions of the enemy, and for want of magistrates to restrain and punish thieves and robbers among them (men of broken fortunes and desperate spirits, that, having no employment, took to rob on the highroad), all commerce ceased, and the highways were unoccupied; no caravans of merchants, as formerly. 2. No travelling. Whereas in times when there was some order and government the travellers might be safe in the open roads, and the robbers were forced to lurk in the by-ways, now, on the contrary, the robbers insulted on the open roads without check, and the honest travellers were obliged to sculk and walk through by-ways, in continual frights. 3. No tillage. The fields must needs be laid waste and unoccupied when the inhabitants of the villages, the country farmers, ceased from their employment, quitted their houses which were continually alarmed and plundered by the banditti, and were obliged to take shelter for themselves and their families in walled and fenced cities. 4. No administration of justice. There was war in the gates where their courts were kept, *v.* 8. So that it was not till this salvation was wrought that *the people of the Lord* durst *go down to the gates, v.* 11. The continual incursions of the enemy deprived the magistrates of the dignity, and the people of the benefit, of their government. 5. No peace to him that went out nor to him that came in. The gates through which they passed and repassed were infested by the enemy; nay, the places of drawing water were alarmed by the archers—a mighty achievement to terrify the drawers of water. 6. Neither arms nor spirit to help themselves with, not a *shield nor spear seen among forty thousand, v.* 8. Either they were disarmed by their oppressors, or they themselves neglected the art of war; so that, though they had spears and shields, they were not to be seen, but were thrown by and suffered to rust, they having neither skill nor will to use them.

II. She shows in one word what it was that brought all this misery upon them: *They chose new gods, v.* 8. It was their idolatry that provoked God to give them up thus into the hands of their enemies. The Lord their God was one Lord, but this would not content them: they must have more, many more, still more. Their God was the Ancient of days, still the same, and therefore they grew weary of him, and must have new gods, which they were as fond of as children of new clothes, names newly invented, heroes newly canonized. Their fathers, when put to their choice, chose the Lord for their God (Josh. xxiv. 21), but they would not abide by that choice, they must have gods of their own choosing.

III. She takes notice of God's great goodness to Israel in raising up such as should redress these grievances. Herself first (*v.* 7): *Till that I Deborah arose,* to restrain and punish those who disturbed the public peace, and protect men in their business, and then the face of things was changed for the better quickly; those beasts of prey retired upon the breaking forth of this joyful light, and *man went forth again to his work and labour,* Ps. civ. 22, 23. Thus she became a mother in Israel, a nursing mother, such was the affection she bore to her people, and such the care and pains she took for the public welfare. Under her there were other governors of Israel (*v.* 9), who, like her, had done their part as governors to reform the people, and then, like her, offered themselves willingly to serve in the war, not insisting upon the exemption which their dignity and office entitled them to, when they had so fair an opportunity of appearing in their country's cause; and no doubt the example of the governors influenced the people in like manner *willingly to offer themselves, v.* 2. Of these governors she says, *My heart is towards them,* that is, "I truly love and honour them; they have won my heart for ever; I shall never forget them." Note, Those are worthy of double honour that recede voluntarily from the demands of their honour to serve God and his church.

IV. She calls upon those who had a particular share in the advantages of this great salvation to offer up particular thanks to God for it, *v.* 10, 11. Let every man speak as he found of the goodness of God in this happy change of the posture of public affairs. 1. *You that ride on white asses,* that is, the nobility and gentry. Horses were little used in that country; they had, it is probable, a much better breed of asses than we have; but persons of quality, it seems, were distinguished by the colour of the asses they rode on; the white being more rare were therefore more valued. Notice is taken of Abdon's sons and grandsons riding on ass-colts, as indicating them to be men of distinction, *ch.* xii. 14. Let such as are by this salvation restored, not only to their liberty as other Israelites, but to their dignity, speak God's praises. 2. Let those that *sit in judgment* be sensible of it, and thankful for it as a very great mercy, that they may sit safely there, that the sword of justice is not struck out of their hand by the sword of war. 3. Let those that *walk by the way,* and meet with none there to make them afraid, speak to themselves in pious meditations, and to their fellow-travellers in religious discourses, of the goodness of God in ridding the roads of those banditti that had so long infested them. 4. Let those that draw in peace, and have not their wells taken from them, or stopped up, nor are in danger of being caught by the enemy when they go forth to draw, there, where they find themselves so much more safe and easy than they have been, *there let them rehearse the acts of the Lord,* not Deborah's acts, nor Barak's, but the Lord's, taking notice of his hand making peace in their borders, and creating a defence upon all the glory. This *is the Lord's doing.* Observe in these acts of his, (1.) Justice executed on his daring enemies. They are the righteous acts of the Lord. See him pleading a righteous cause, and sitting in the throne judging aright, and give him glory as the Judge of all the earth. (2.) Kindness shown to his trembling people, *the inhabitants of the villages,* who lay most open to the enemy, had suffered most, and were most in danger, Ezek. xxxviii. 11. It is the glory of God to protect those that are most exposed, and to help the weakest. Let us all take notice of the share we in particular have in the public peace and tranquillity, the inhabitants of the villages especially, and give God the praise of it.

12 Awake, awake, Deborah: awake, awake, utter a song: arise, Barak, and lead thy captivity captive, thou son of Abinoam. 13 Then he made him that remaineth have dominion over the nobles among the people: the LORD made me have dominion over the mighty. 14 Out of Ephraim *was there* a root of them against Amalek; after thee, Benjamin, among thy people; out of Machir came down governors, and out of Zebulun they that handle the pen of the writer. 15 And the princes of Issachar *were* with Deborah; even Issachar, and also Barak: he was sent on foot into the valley. For the divisions of Reuben *there were* great thoughts of heart. 16 Why abodest thou among the sheepfolds, to hear the bleatings of the flocks? For the divisions of Reuben *there were* great searchings of heart. 17 Gilead abode beyond Jordan: and why did Dan remain in ships? Asher continued on the sea shore, and abode in his breaches. 18 Zebulun and Naphtali *were* a people *that* jeoparded their lives unto the death in the high places of the field. 19 The kings came *and* fought, then fought the kings of Canaan in Taanach by the waters of Megiddo; they took no gain of money. 20 They fought from heaven; the stars in their courses fought against Sisera. 21 The river of Kishon swept them away, that ancient river, the river Kishon. O my soul, thou hast trodden down strength. 22 Then were the horsehoofs broken by the means of the prancings, the prancings of their mighty ones. 23 Curse ye Meroz, said the angel of the LORD, curse ye bitterly the inhabitants thereof; because they came not to the help of the LORD, to the help of the LORD against the mighty.

Here, I. Deborah stirs up herself and Barak to celebrate this victory in the most solemn manner, to the glory of God and the honour of Israel, for the encouragement of their friends and the greater confusion of their enemies, *v.* 12. 1. Deborah, as a prophetess, must do it by a song, to compose and sing which she excites herself: *Awake, awake,* and again, *awake, awake,* which intimates the sense she had of the excellency and difficulty of the work; it needed and well deserved the utmost liveliness and vigour of soul in the performance of it; all the powers and faculties of the soul in their closest intensity and application ought to be employed in it. Thus too she expresses the sense she had of her own infirmity, and aptness to flag and remit in her zeal in this work. Note, Praising God is work that we should awake to, and awake ourselves to, Ps. cviii. 2. 2. Barak, as a general, must do it by a triumph: *Lead thy captivity captive.* Though the army of Sisera was cut off in the field, and no quarter given, yet we may suppose in the prosecution of the victory, when the war was carried into the enemy's country, many not found in arms were seized and made prisoners of war. These she would have led in chains after Barak, when he made his public entry into his own city, to grace his triumphs; not as if it should be any pleasure to him to trample upon his fellow-creatures, but thus he must give glory to God, and serve that great purpose of his government which is to *look upon those that are proud and to abase them.*

II. She gives good reason for this praise and triumph, *v.* 13. This glorious victory had made the remnant of Israel, and Deborah in particular, look very great, a circumstance which they owed entirely to God. 1. The Israelites had become few and inconsiderable, and yet to them God gave dominion over nobles. Many of them were cut off by the enemy, many died of grief, and perhaps some had removed their families and effects into foreign parts; yet those few that remained, by divine assistance, with one brave and generous effort, not only shook off the yoke of oppression from their own neck, but got power over their oppressors. As long as any of God's Israel remain (and a remnant God will have in the worst of times) there is hope, be it ever so small a remnant, for God can make him that remains, though it should be but one single person, triumph over the most proud and potent. 2. Deborah was herself of the weaker sex, and the sex that from the fall had been sentenced to subjection, and yet the Lord that is himself higher than the highest authorized her to rule over the mighty men of Israel, who willingly submitted to her direction, and enabled her to triumph over the mighty men of Canaan, who fell before the army she commanded; so wonderfully did he *advance the low estate of his handmaid.* "The Lord made me, a woman, to have dominion over mighty men." A despised stone is made *head of the corner. This is* indeed the *Lord's doing, and marvellous in our eyes.*

III. She makes particular remarks on the several parties concerned in this great action, taking notice who fought against them, who fought for them, and who stood neuter.

1. Who fought against them. The power of the enemy must be taken notice of, that the victory may appear the more glorious. Jabin and Sisera had been mentioned in the history, but here it appears further, (1.) That Amalek was in league with Jabin, and sent him in assistance, or endeavoured to do it. Ephraim is here said to act against Amalek (*v* 14), probably intercepting and cutting off some forces of the Amalekites that were upon their march to join Sisera. Amalek had helped Moab to oppress Israel (*ch.* iii. 13) and now had helped Jabin; they were inveterate enemies to God's people—their hand had always *been against the throne of the Lord* (Exod. xvii. 16); and therefore they were the more dangerous. (2.) That others of the kings of Canaan, who had somewhat recovered themselves since their defeat by Joshua, joined with Jabin, and strengthened his army with their forces, having the same implacable enmity to Israel that he had, and those kingdoms, when they were in their strength, having been subject to that of Hazor, Josh. xi. 10. These kings *came and fought, v.* 19. Israel had no king; their enemies had many, whose power and influence, especially acting in confederacy, made them very formidable; and yet Israel, having the Lord for their King, was too hard for them all. It is said of these kings that *they took no gain of money,* they were not mercenary troops hired into the service of Jabin (such often fail in an extremity), but they were volunteers, and hearty in the cause against Israel: they *desired not the riches of silver,* so the Chaldee, but only the satisfaction of helping to ruin Israel. Acting upon this principle, they were the more formidable, and would be the more cruel.

2. Who fought for them. The several tribes that assisted in this great exploit are here spoken of with honour; for, though God is chiefly to be glorified, instruments must have their due praise, for the encouragement of others: but, after all, it was heaven that turned the scale.

(1.) Ephraim and Benjamin, those tribes among whom Deborah herself lived, bestirred themselves, and did bravely, by her influence upon them; for her palm-tree was in the tribe of Ephraim, and very near to that of Benjamin (*v.* 14): *Out of Ephraim was there a root,* and life in the root, against Amalek. There was in Ephraim a mountain called *the mount of Amalek,* mentioned, *ch.* xii. 15, which, some think, is here meant, and some read it, *there was a root in Amalek,* that is, in that mountain, a strong resolution in the minds of that people to make head against the oppressors, which was the root of the matter. Herein Benjamin had set them a good example among his people. "Ephraim moved *after thee, Benjamin;*" though Benjamin was the junior tribe, and much inferior, especially at this time, to Ephraim, both in number and wealth, yet when they led Ephraim followed in appearing for the common cause. If we be not so bold as to lead, yet we must not be so proud and sullen as not to follow even our inferiors in a good work. Ephraim was at a distance from the place of action, and therefore could not send forth many of its boughs to the service; but Deborah, who was one of them, knew there was a root of them, that they were hearty well-wishers to the cause. Dr. Lightfoot gives quite another sense of this. Joshua, of Ephraim, had been a root of such victories against Amalek (Exod xvii.), and Ehud of Benjamin lately against Amalek and Moab.

(2.) The ice being broken by Ephraim and Benjamin, Machir (the half-tribe of Manasseh beyond Jordan) and Zebulun sent in men that were very serviceable to this great design. When an army is to be raised, especially under such disadvantages as Balak now experienced from the long disuse of arms and the dispiritedness of the people, it is of great consequence to be furnished, [1.] With men of courage for officers, and such the family of Machir furnished them with, for thence came down *governors.* The children of Machir were particularly famous for their valour in Moses's time (Num. xxxii. 39), and it seems it continued in their family, the more because they were seated in the frontiers. [2.] With men of learning and ingenuity for secretaries of war, and with such they were supplied out of Zebulun: thence came men *that handle the pen of the writer*, clerks that issued out orders, wrote circular letters, drew commissions, mustered their men, and kept their accounts. Thus must every man, *according as he has received the gift, minister the same,* for the public good (1 Pet. iv. 10); the eyes see, and the ears hear, for the whole body. I know it is generally understood of the forwardness even of the scholars of this tribe, who studied the law and expounded it, to take up arms in this cause, though they were better skilled in books than in the art of war. So Sir Richard Blackmore paraphrases it:—

The scribes of Zebulun and learned men,
To wield the sword, laid down the pen.

(3.) Issachar did good service too; though he *saw that rest was good,* and therefore *bowed his shoulder to bear,* which is the character of that tribe (Gen. xlix. 15), yet they disdained to bear the yoke of Jabin's tribute, and now preferred the generous toils of war to a servile rest. Though it should seem there were not many common soldiers enlisted out of that tribe, yet *the princes of Issachar were with Deborah and Barak* (*v.* 15), probably, as a great council of war to advise upon emergencies. And, it should seem, these princes of Issachar did in person accompany Barak into the field of battle. Did he go on foot? They footed it with him, not consulting their honour or ease. Did he go into the valley, the place of most danger? They exposed themselves with him, and were still at his right hand to advise him: for the men of Issachar were men that *had understanding of the times,* 1 Chron. xii. 32.

(4.) Zebulun and Naphtali were the most bold and active of all the tribes, not only out of a particular affection to Barak their countryman, but because, they lying nearest to Jabin, the yoke of oppression lay heavier on their necks than on those of any other tribe. Better die in honour than live in bondage; and therefore, in a pious zeal for God and their country, they *jeoparded their lives unto the death in the high places of the field, v.* 18. With what heroic bravery did they charge and push on even upon the chariots of iron, despising danger, and setting death itself at defiance in so good a cause!

(5.) The stars from heaven appeared, or acted at least, on Israel's side (*v.* 20): *The stars in their courses,* according to the order and direction of him who is the great Lord of their hosts, *fought against Sisera,* by their malignant influences, or by causing the storms of hail and thunder which contributed so much to the rout of Sisera's army. The Chaldee reads it, *from heaven, from the place where the stars go forth, war was waged against Sisera,* that is, the power of the God of heaven was engaged against him, making use of the ministration of the angels of heaven. Some way or other, the heavenly bodies (not arrested, as when the sun stood still at Joshua's word, but going on in their courses) fought against Sisera. Those whom God is an enemy to the whole creation is at war with. Perhaps the flashes of lightning by which the stars fought was that which frightened the horses, so as that they pranced till their very hoofs were broken (*v.* 22), and probably overturned the chariots of iron which they drew or turned them back upon their owners.

(6.) The river of Kishon fought against their enemies. It swept away multitudes of those that hoped to make their escape through it, *v.* 21. Ordinarily, it was but a shallow river, and, being in their own country, we may suppose they well knew its fords and safest passages, and yet now, probably by the great rain that fell, it was so swollen, and the stream so deep and strong, that those who attempted to pass it were drowned, being feeble and faint, and unable to make their way through it. And then were the horse-hoofs broken by means of the *plungings.* So it is in the margin, *v.* 22. The river of Kishon is called *that ancient river* because described or celebrated by ancient historians or poets, or rather because it was designed of old, in the counsel of God, to serve his purposes against Sisera at this time, and did so, as if it had been made on purpose; thus *the water of the old pool* God is said to have fashioned long ago for that use to which it was put, Isa. xxii. 11.

(7.) Deborah's own soul fought against

them; she speaks of it with a holy exultation (*v.* 21): *O, my soul, thou hast trodden down strength.* She did it by exciting others to do it, and assisting them, which she did with all her heart. Also by her prayers; as Moses conquered Amalek by lifting up his hand, so Deborah vanquished Sisera by lifting up her heart. And when the soul is employed in holy exercises, and heart-work is made of them, through the grace of God the strength of our spiritual enemies will be trodden down and will fall before us.

3. In this great engagement she observes who stood *neuter*, and did not side with Israel as might have been expected. It is strange to find how many, even of those who were called Israelites, basely deserted this glorious cause and declined to appear. No mention is made of Judah nor Simeon among the tribes concerned, because they, lying so very remote from the scene of action, had not an opportunity to appear, and therefore it was not expected from them; but for those that lay near, and yet would not venture, indelible marks of disgrace are here put upon them, as they deserved.

(1.) Reuben basely declined the service, *v.* 15, 16. Justly had he long ago been deprived of the privileges of the birth-right, and still does his dying father's doom stick by him: *unstable as water, he shall not excel.* Two things hindered them from engaging:—[1.] Their divisions. This jarring string she twice strikes upon to their shame: *For the divisions of Reuben* (or in these divisions) *there were great thoughts,* impressions, and searchings *of heart.* Not only for their division from Canaan by the river Jordan, which needed not to have hindered them had they been hearty in the cause, for Gilead abode beyond Jordan, and yet from Machir of Gilead came down governors; but it means either that they were divided among themselves, could not agree who should go or who should lead, each striving to gain the posts of honour and shun those of danger, some unhappy contests in their tribe kept them from uniting together, and with their brethren, for the common good, or that they were divided in their opinion of this war from the rest of the tribes, thought the attempt either not justifiable or not practicable, and therefore blamed those that engaged in it and did themselves decline it. This occasioned great searchings of heart among the rest, especially when they had reason to suspect that, whatever Reuben pretended, his sitting still now proceeded from a cooling of his affections to his brethren and an alienation of mind from them, which occasioned them many sad thoughts. It grieves us to see our mother's children angry with us for doing our duty and looking strange upon us when we most need their friendship and assistance. [2.] Their business in the world: *Reuben abode among the sheepfolds,* a warmer and safer place than the camp, pretending they could not conveniently leave the sheep they tended; he loved to *hear the bleatings of the flocks,* or, as some read it, the *whistlings* of the flocks, the music which the shepherds made with their oaten reeds or pipes, and the pastorals which they sung; these Reuben preferred before the martial drum and trumpet. Thus many are kept from doing their duty by the fear of trouble, the love of ease, and an inordinate affection to their worldly business and advantage. Narrow selfish spirits care not what becomes of the interests of God's church, so they can but get, keep, and save money. *All seek their own,* Phil. ii. 21.

(2.) Dan and Asher did the same, *v.* 17. These two lay on the sea-coast, and, [1.] Dan pretended he could not leave his ships but they would be exposed, and therefore *I pray thee have me excused.* Those of that tribe perhaps pleaded that their sea-trade disfitted them for land-service and diverted them from it; but Zebulun also was a haven for ships, a sea-faring tribe, and yet was forward and active in this expedition. There is no excuse we make to shift off duty but what some or other have broken through and set aside, whose courage and resolution will rise up against us and shame us. [2.] Asher pretended he must stay at home to repair the breaches which the sea had in some places made upon his land, and to fortify his works against the encroachments of it, or he abode in his creeks, or small havens, where his trading vessels lay to attend them. A little thing will serve those for a pretence to stay at home who have no mind to engage in the most necessary services because there are difficulty and danger in them.

(3.) But above all Meroz is condemned, and a curse pronounced upon the inhabitants of it, *Because they came not to the help of the Lord, v.* 23. Probably this was some city that lay near the scene of action, and therefore the inhabitants had a fair opportunity of showing their obedience to God and their concern for Israel, and of doing good service to the common cause; but they basely declined it, for fear of Jabin's iron chariots, being willing to sleep in a whole skin. The Lord needed not their help; he made it to appear he could do his work without them; but no thanks to them: for aught they knew the attempt might have miscarried for want of their hand, and therefore they are cursed for *not coming to the help of the Lord,* when it was in effect proclaimed, *Who is on the Lord's side?* The cause between God and the mighty (the principalities and powers of the kingdom of darkness) will not admit of neutrality. God looks upon those as against him that are not with him. This curse is pronounced by the *angel of the Lord,* our Lord Jesus, the captain of the Lord's host (and *those whom he curses are cursed indeed),* and further than we have warrant and authority from him we may not curse. He that will richly reward all his good soldiers will certainly and severely punish all cowards and deserters. This city of Meroz seems to have been at this time a considerable place, since something great was expected from it; but probably, after the angel of the Lord had pronounced this curse upon it, it dwindled, and, like the fig-tree which Christ cursed, withered away, so that we never read of it after this in scripture.

24 Blessed above women shall Jael the wife of Heber the Kenite be, blessed shall she be above women in the tent. 25 He asked water, *and* she gave *him* milk; she brought forth butter in a lordly dish. 26 She put her hand to the nail, and her right hand to the workmen's hammer; and with the hammer she smote Sisera, she smote off his head, when she had pierced and stricken through his temples. 27 At her feet he bowed, he fell, he lay down: at her feet he bowed, he fell: where he bowed, there he fell down dead. 28 The mother of Sisera looked out at a window, and cried through the lattice, Why is his chariot *so* long in coming? why tarry the wheels of his chariots? 29 Her wise ladies answered her, yea, she returned answer to herself, 30 Have they not sped? have they *not* divided the prey; to every man a damsel *or* two; to Sisera a prey of divers colours, a prey of divers colours of needlework, of divers colours of needlework on both sides, *meet* for the necks of *them that take* the spoil? 31 So let all thine enemies perish, O LORD: but *let* them that love him *be* as the sun when he goeth forth in his might. And the land had rest forty years.

Deborah here concludes this triumphant song,

I. With the praises of Jael, her sister-heroine, whose valiant act had completed and crowned the victory. She had mentioned her before (*v.* 6) as one that would have served her country if it had been in her power; now she applauds her as one that did serve it admirably well when it was in her power. Her poetry is finest and most florid here in the latter end of the song. How honourably does she speak of Jael (*v.* 24), who preferred her peace with the God of Israel before her peace with the king of Canaan, and though not a native of Israel (for aught that appears) yet heartily espoused the cause of Israel in this critical conjuncture, jeoparded her life as truly as if she had been in the high places of the field, and bravely fought for those whom she saw God fought for! *Blessed shall she be above women in the tent.* Note, Those whose lot is cast in the tent, in a very low and narrow sphere of activity, if they serve God in that according to their capacity, shall in no wise lose their reward. Jael in the tent wins as rich a blessing as Barak in the field. Nothing is more confounding, grievous, and shameful, than disappointment, and Deborah here does most elegantly describe two great disappointments, the shame of which was typical of sinners' everlasting shame.

1. Sisera found a fatal enemy where he expected a firm and faithful friend. (1.) Jael showed him the kindness of a friend, and perhaps at that time intended no other than kindness, until God, by an immediate impulse upon her mind (which impulses then were to be regarded, and carried so much of their own evidence with them that they might be relied upon, but cannot now be pretended to), directed her to do otherwise, *v.* 25. He asked only for fair water to quench his thirst, but she, not only to show her housewifery and good housekeeping, but to express her respect to him, *gave him milk* and *brought forth butter,* that is (say some interpreters), milk which had the butter taken from it; we call it butter-milk. No (say others), it was milk that had the butter still in it; we call it cream. Whichsoever it was, it was probably the best her house afforded; and, to set it off, she brought it *in a lordly dish,* such as she called so, the finest she had, and better than she ordinarily used at her own table. This confirmed Sisera's opinion of her friendship, and made him sleep the faster and the more secure. But, (2.) She proved his mortal enemy, gave him his death's stroke: it is curiously described, *v.* 26, 27. [1.] How great does Jael look, *hammering Sisera,* as it is in the margin, mauling that proud man who had been so long the terror of the mighty, and sending him down slain to the pit with *his iniquities upon his bones!* Ezek. xxxii. 27. She seems to have gone about it with no more terror nor concern than if she had been going to nail one of the boards or bars of her tent, so confident was she of divine aid and protection. We read it she *smote off his head,* probably with his own sword, which, now that his head was nailed through, she durst take from his side, but not before, for fear of waking him. But because there was no occasion for cutting off his head, nor was it mentioned in the history, many think it should be read, *she struck through his head.* That head which had been proudly lifted up against God and Israel, and in which had been forged bloody designs for the destruction of God's people, Jael finds a soft place in, and into that with a good will strikes her nail. [2.] How mean does Sisera look, fallen at Jael's feet! *v.* 27

At the feet of this female executioner he bowed, he fell; all his struggles for life availed not; she followed her blow until he fell down dead. There lies extended the deserted carcase of that proud man, not on the bed of honour, not in the high places of the field, not having any glorious wound to show from a glittering sword, or a bow of steel, but in the corner of a tent, at the feet of a woman, with a disgraceful wound by a sorry nail struck through his head Thus is shame the fate of proud men. And this is a very lively representation of the ruin of those sinners whose prosperity slays them; it flatters and caresses them with milk and butter in a lordly dish, as if it would make them easy and happy, but it nails their heads and hearts too to the ground in earthly-mindedness, and pierces them through with many sorrows; its flatteries are fatal, and sink them at last into destruction and perdition, 1 Tim. vi. 9, 10.

2. Sisera's mother had the tidings brought her of her son's fall and ruin when she was big with expectation of his glorious and triumphant return, *v.* 28—30, where we have, (1.) Her fond desire to see her son come back in triumph: *Why is his chariot so long in coming?* She speaks this, not so much out of a concern for his safety, or any jealousy of his having miscarried (she had no fear of that, so confident was she of his success), but out of a longing for his glory, which with a feminine weakness she was passionately impatient to see, chiding the lingering chariot, and expostulating concerning the delays of it, little thinking that her unhappy son had been, before this, forced to quit that chariot which they were so proud of, and which she thought came so slowly. *The chariots of his glory had now become the shame of his house,* Isa. xxii. 18. Let us take heed of indulging such desires as these towards any temporal good thing, particularly towards that which cherishes vain-glory, for this was what she here doted on. Eagerness and impatience in our desires do us a great deal of prejudice, and make it intolerable to us to be crossed. But towards the second coming of Jesus Christ, and the glories of that day, we should thus stand affected *(Come, Lord Jesus, come quickly)*, for here we cannot be disappointed. (2.) Her foolish hope and confidence that he would come at last in so much the greater pomp. Her wise ladies answered her, and thought they gave a very good account of the delay; yea, she *(in her wisdom,* says the Chaldee) tauntingly made answer to herself, "*Have they not sped?* No doubt they have, and that which delays them is that they are *dividing the prey*, which is so much that it is a work of time to make a distribution of it." In the spoil they pleased themselves with the thought of, observe, [1.] How impudently, and to the reproach and scandal of their sex, these ladies boast of the multitude of damsels which the soldiers would have the abusing of. [2.] How childishly they pleased themselves with the hope of seeing Sisera himself in a gaudy mantle of *divers colours;* how charmingly would it look! *of divers colours of needle-work,* plundered out of the wardrobe of some Israelitish lady; it is repeated again, as that which pleased their fancy above any thing, *of divers colours of needle-work on both sides,* and therefore very rich; such pieces of embroidery they hoped Sisera would have to present his mother and the ladies with. Thus apt are we to deceive ourselves with great expectations and confident hopes of honour, and pleasure, and wealth in this world, by which we prepare for ourselves the shame and grief of a disappointment. And thus does God often bring ruin on his enemies when they are most elevated.

II. She concludes all with a prayer to God, 1. For the destruction of all his foes: "*So,* so shamefully, so miserably, *let all thy enemies perish, O Lord;* let all that hope to triumph in Israel's ruin be thus disappointed and triumphed over. *Do to them all as unto Sisera,*" Ps. lxxxiii. 9. Though our enemies are to be prayed for, God's enemies, as such, are to be prayed against; and, when we see some of God's enemies remarkably humbled and brought down, this is an encouragement to us to pray for the downfal of all the rest. Deborah was a prophetess, and this prayer was a prediction that in due time all God's enemies shall perish, Ps. xcii. 9. None ever hardened his heart against God and prospered. 2. For the exaltation and comfort of all his friends. "But let those that love him, and heartily wish well to his kingdom among men, be *as the sun when he goeth forth in his strength;* let them shine so bright, appear so glorious in the eye of the world, cast such benign influences, be as much out of the reach of their enemies, who curse the rising sun because it scorches them; let them *rejoice as a strong man to run a race,* Ps. xix. 5. Let them, as burning and shining lights in their places, dispel the mists of darkness, and shine with more and more lustre and power *unto the perfect day,*" Prov. iv. 18. Such shall be the honour, and such the joy, of all that love God in sincerity, and for ever they shall *shine as the sun in the firmament of our Father.*

The victory here celebrated with this song was of such happy consequence to Israel that for the best part of one age they enjoyed the peace which it opened the way to: *The land had rest forty years,* that is, so long it was from this victory to the raising up of Gideon. And well would it have been if, when the churches and the tribes had rest, they had been edified, *and had walked in the fear of the Lord.*

CHAP. VI.

Nothing that occurred in the quiet and peaceable times of Israel is recorded; the forty years' rest after the conquest of Jabin is passed over in silence; and here begins the story of another distress and another deliverance, by Gideon, the fourth of the judges. Here is, I. The calamitous condition of Israel, by the inroads of

the Midianites, ver. 1—6. II. The message God sent them by a prophet, by convincing them of sin, to prepare them for deliverance, ver. 7—10. III. The raising up of Gideon to be their deliverer. 1. A commission which God sent him by the hand of an angel, and confirmed by a sign, ver. 11—24. 2. The first-fruits of his government in the reform of his father's house, ver. 25—32. 3. The preparations he made for a war with the Midianites, and the encouragement given him by a sign, ver. 33—40.

AND the children of Israel did evil in the sight of the LORD: and the LORD delivered them into the hand of Midian seven years. 2 And the hand of Midian prevailed against Israel: *and* because of the Midianites the children of Israel made them the dens which *are* in the mountains, and caves, and strong holds. 3 And *so* it was, when Israel had sown, that the Midianites came up, and the Amalekites, and the children of the east, even they came up against them; 4 And they encamped against them, and destroyed the increase of the earth, till thou come unto Gaza, and left no sustenance for Israel, neither sheep, nor ox, nor ass. 5 For they came up with their cattle and their tents, and they came as grasshoppers for multitude; *for* both they and their camels were without number: and they entered into the land to destroy it. 6 And Israel was greatly impoverished because of the Midianites; and the children of Israel cried unto the LORD.

We have here, I. Israel's sin renewed: *They did evil in the sight of the Lord, v.* 1. The burnt child dreads the fire; yet this perverse unthinking people, that had so often smarted sorely for their idolatry, upon a little respite of God's judgments return to it again. *This people hath a revolting rebellious heart,* not kept in awe by the terror of God's judgments, nor engaged in honour and gratitude by the great things he had done for them to keep themselves in his love. The providence of God will not change the hearts and lives of sinners.

II. Israel's troubles repeated. This would follow of course; let all that sin expect to suffer; let all that return to folly expect to return to misery. *With the froward God will show himself froward* (Ps. xviii. 26), and will walk contrary to those that walk contrary to him, Lev. xxvi. 21, 24. Now as to this trouble, 1. It arose from a very despicable enemy. God delivered them into the hand of Midian (*v.* 1), not Midian in the south where Jethro lived, but Midian in the east that joined to Moab (Num. xxii. 4), a people that all men despised as uncultivated and unintelligent; hence we read not here of any king, lord, or general, that they had, but the force with which they destroyed Israel was an undisciplined mob; and, which made it the more grievous, they were a people that Israel had formerly subdued, and in a manner destroyed (see Num. xxxi. 7), and yet by this time (nearly 200 years after) the poor remains of them were so multiplied, and so magnified, that they were capable of being made a very severe scourge to Israel. Thus *God moved them to jealousy with those who were not a people,* even a foolish nation, Deut. xxxii. 21. The meanest creature will serve to chastise those that have made the great Creator their enemy. And, when those we are authorized to rule prove rebellious and disobedient to us, it concerns us to enquire whether we have not been so to our sovereign Ruler. 2. It arose to a very formidable height (*v.* 2): *The hand of Midian prevailed,* purely by their multitude. God had promised to increase Israel as the sand on the sea shore; but their sin stopped their growth and diminished them, and then their enemies, though otherwise every way inferior to them, overpowered them with numbers. They came upon them as *grasshoppers for multitude* (*v.* 5), not in a regular army to engage them in the field, but in a confused swarm to plunder the country, quarter themselves upon it, and enrich themselves with its spoils—bands of robbers, and no better. And sinful Israel, being separated by sin from God, had not spirit to make head against them. Observe the wretched havoc that these Midianites made with their bands of plunderers in Israel. Here we have, (1.) The Israelites imprisoned, or rather imprisoning themselves, in dens and caves, *v.* 2. This was owing purely to their own timorousness and faint-heartedness, that they would rather fly than fight; it was the effect of a guilty conscience, which made them tremble at the shaking of a leaf, and the just punishment of their apostasy from God, who thus fought against them with those very terrors with which he would otherwise have fought for them. Had it not been for this, we cannot but think Israel a match for the Midianites, and able enough to make head against them; but the heart that departs from God is lost, not only to that which is good, but to that which is great. Sin dispirits men, and makes them sneak into dens and caves. The day will come when chief captains and mighty men will call in vain to rocks and mountains to hide them. (2.) The Israelites impoverished, greatly impoverished, *v.* 6. The Midianites and the other children of the east that joined with them to live by spoil and rapine (as long before the Sabeans and Chaldeans did that plundered Job, free-booters) made frequent incursions into the land of Canaan. This fruitful land was a great temptation to them; and the sloth and luxury into which the Israelites had sunk by forty years' rest made them and their substance an easy prey to them. They came up against them (*v.* 3), pitched their camps among them (*v.* 4), and brought their cattle with them, particularly camels innumerable (*v.* 5), not a flying party to make a sally upon them and be gone presently, but they resolved to force their way, and penetrated through the heart of the country as far as Gaza on the western side, *v.* 4. They let the Israelites alone to sow their ground, but towards harvest they came and seized all, and ate up and destroyed it, both grass and corn, and when they went away took with them the sheep and oxen, so that in short they left no sustenance for Israel, except what was privately taken by the rightful owners into the dens and caves. Now here we may see, [1.] The justice of God in the punishment of their sin. They had neglected to honour God with their substance in tithes and offerings, and had prepared that for Baal with which God should have been served, and now God justly sends an enemy to take it away *in the season thereof,* Hos. ii. 8, 9. [2.] The consequence of God's departure from a people; when he goes all good goes and all mischiefs break in. When Israel kept in with God, they reaped what others sowed (Josh. xxiv. 13; Ps. cv. 44); but now that God had forsaken them others reaped what they sowed. Let us take occasion from this to bless God for our national peace and tranquillity, that we *eat the labour of our hands.*

III. Israel's sense of God's hand revived at last. Seven years, year after year, did the Midianites make these inroads upon them, each we may suppose worse than the other (*v.* 1), until at last, all other succours failing, *Israel cried unto the Lord* (*v.* 6), for crying to Baal ruined them, and would not help them. When God judges he will overcome; and sinners shall be made either to bend or break before him.

7 And it came to pass, when the children of Israel cried unto the LORD because of the Midianites, 8 That the LORD sent a prophet unto the children of Israel, which said unto them, Thus saith the LORD God of Israel, I brought you up from Egypt, and brought you forth out of the house of bondage; 9 And I delivered you out of the hand of the Egyptians, and out of the hand of all that oppressed you, and drave them out from before you, and gave you their land; 10 And I said unto you, I *am* the LORD your God; fear not the gods of the Amorites, in whose land ye dwell: but ye have not obeyed my voice.

Observe here, I. The cognizance God took of the cries of Israel, when at length they were directed towards him. Though in their prosperity they had neglected him and made court to his rivals, and though they never looked towards him until they were driven to it by extremity, yet, upon their complaint and prayer, he intended relief for them. Thus would he show how ready he is to forgive, how swift he is to show mercy, and how inclinable to hear prayer, that sinners may be encouraged to return and repent, Ps. cxxx. 4.

II. The method God took of working deliverance for them.

1. Before he sent an angel to raise them up a saviour he sent a prophet to reprove them for sin, and to bring them to repentance, *v.* 8. This prophet is not named, but he was a man, a prophet, not an angel, as *ch.* ii. 1. Whether this prophet took an opportunity of delivering his message to the children of Israel when they had met together in a general assembly, at some solemn feast or other great occasion, or whether he went from city to city and from tribe to tribe, preaching to this purport, is not certain; but his errand was to convince them of sin, that, in their crying to the Lord, they might confess that with sorrow and shame, and not spend their breath in only complaining of their trouble. They cried to God for a deliverer, and God sent them a prophet to instruct them, and to make them ready for deliverance. Note, (1.) We have reason to hope God is designing mercy for us if we find he is by his grace preparing us for it. If to those that are sick he sends a messenger, an interpreter, by whom he *shows unto man his uprightness, then he is gracious,* and grants a recovery, Job xxxiii. 23, 24. (2.) The sending of prophets to a people, and the furnishing of a land with faithful ministers, is a token for good, and an evidence that God has mercy in store for them. He thus turns us to him, and then causes his face to shine, Ps. lxxx. 19.

2. We have here the heads of the message which this prophet delivered in to Israel, in the name of the Lord.

(1.) He sets before them the great things God had done for them (*v.* 8, 9): *Thus saith the Lord God of Israel;* they had worshipped the *gods of the nations,* as if they had had no God of their own to worship and therefore might choose whom they pleased; but they are here reminded of one whom they had forgotten, who was known by the title of *the God of Israel,* and to him they must return. They had turned to other gods, as if their own had been either incapable or unwilling to protect them, and therefore they are told what he did for their fathers, in whose loins they were, the benefit of which descended and still remained to this their ungrateful seed. [1.] He brought them out of Egypt, where otherwise they would have continued in perpetual poverty and slavery. [2.] He *delivered them out of the hands of all that oppressed them;* this is mentioned to intimate that the reason why they were not now delivered out of the hands of the oppressing

Midianites was not for want of any power or good-will in God, but because by their iniquity they had sold themselves, and God would not redeem them until they by repentance revoked the bargain. [3.] He put them in quiet possession of this good land; this not only aggravated their sin, and affixed the brand of base ingratitude to it, but it justified God, and cleared him from blame upon account of the trouble they were now in. They could not say he was unkind, for he had given all possible proofs of his designing well for them; if ill befel them notwithstanding, they must thank themselves.

(2.) He shows the easiness and equity of God's demands and expectations from them (*v.* 10): "*I am the Lord your God,* to whom you lie under the highest obligations, *fear not the gods of the Amorites,*" that is, "do not worship them, nor show any respect to them; do not worship them for fear of their doing you any hurt, for what hurt can they do you while I am your God? Fear God, and you need not fear them."

(3.) He charges them with rebellion against God, who had laid this injunction upon them: *But you have not obeyed my voice.* The charge is short, but very comprehensive; this was the malignity of all their sin, it was disobedience to God; and therefore it was this that brought those calamities upon them under which they were now groaning, pursuant to the threatenings annexed to his commands. He intends hereby to bring them to repentance; and our repentance is then right and genuine when the sinfulness of sin, as disobedience to God, is that in it which we chiefly lament.

11 And there came an angel of the LORD, and sat under an oak which *was* in Ophrah, that *pertained* unto Joash the Abi-ezrite: and his son Gideon threshed wheat by the winepress, to hide *it* from the Midianites. 12 And the angel of the LORD appeared unto him, and said unto him, The LORD *is* with thee, thou mighty man of valour. 13 And Gideon said unto him, Oh my Lord, if the LORD be with us, why then is all this befallen us? and where *be* all his miracles which our fathers told us of, saying, Did not the LORD bring us up from Egypt? but now the LORD hath forsaken us, and delivered us into the hands of the Midianites. 14 And the LORD looked upon him, and said, Go in this thy might, and thou shalt save Israel from the hand of the Midianites: have not I sent thee? 15 And he said unto him Oh my Lord, wherewith shall I save Israel? behold, my family *is* poor in Manasseh, and I *am* the least in my father's house. 16 And the LORD said unto him, Surely I will be with thee, and thou shalt smite the Midianites as one man. 17 And he said unto him, If now I have found grace in thy sight, then show me a sign that thou talkest with me. 18 Depart not hence, I pray thee, until I come unto thee, and bring forth my present, and set *it* before thee. And he said, I will tarry until thou come again. 19 And Gideon went in, and made ready a kid, and unleavened cakes of an ephah of flour: the flesh he put in a basket, and he put the broth in a pot, and brought *it* out unto him under the oak, and presented *it.* 20 And the angel of God said unto him, Take the flesh and the unleavened cakes, and lay *them* upon this rock, and pour out the broth. And he did so. 21 Then the angel of the LORD put forth the end of the staff that *was* in his hand, and touched the flesh and the unleavened cakes; and there rose up fire out of the rock, and consumed the flesh and the unleavened cakes. Then the angel of the LORD departed out of his sight. 22 And when Gideon perceived that he *was* an angel of the LORD, Gideon said, Alas, O Lord GOD! for because I have seen an angel of the LORD face to face. 23 And the LORD said unto him, Peace *be* unto thee; fear not: thou shalt not die. 24 Then Gideon built an altar there unto the LORD, and called it Jehovah-shalom: unto this day it *is* yet in Ophrah of the Abi-ezrites.

It is not said what effect the prophet's sermon had upon the people, but we may hope it had a good effect, and that some of them at least repented and reformed upon it; for here, immediately after, we have the dawning of the day of their deliverance, by the effectual calling of Gideon to take upon him the command of their forces against the Midianites.

I. The person to be commissioned for this service was Gideon, the son of Joash, *v.* 14. The father was now living, but he was passed by, and this honour put upon the son, for the father kept up in his own family the worship of Baal (*v.* 25), which we may suppose this son, as far as was in his power, witnessed against. He was of the half tribe of Manasseh that lay in Canaan, of the family of Abiezer; the eldest house of that tribe, Josh. xvii. 2. Hitherto the judges were raised up out of that tribe which suffered most by the oppression, and probably it was so here.

II. The person that gave him the commission was an *angel of the Lord;* it should seem not a created angel, but the Son of God himself, the eternal Word, the Lord of the angels, who then appeared upon some great occasions in human shape, as a prelude (says the learned bishop Patrick) to what he intended in the fulness of time, when he would take our nature upon him, as we say, for good and all. This angel is here called *Jehovah,* the incommunicable name of God (*v.* 14, 16), and he said, *I will be with thee.*

1. This divine person appeared here to Gideon, and it is observable how he found him, (1.) Retired—all alone. God often manifests himself to his people when they are out of the noise and hurry of this world. Silence and solitude befriend our communion with God. (2.) Employed in threshing wheat, with a *staff* or *rod* (so the word signifies), such as they used in beating out fitches and cummin (Isa. xxviii. 27), but now used for wheat, probably because he had but little to thresh, he needed not the oxen to tread it out. It was not then looked upon as any diminution to him, though he was a person of some account and a *mighty man of valour,* to lay his hand to the business of the husbandman. He had many servants (*v.* 27), and yet would not himself live in idleness. We put ourselves in the way of divine visits when we employ ourselves in honest business. Tidings of Christ's birth were brought to the shepherds when they were keeping their flocks. The work he was about was an emblem of that greater work to which he was now to be called, as the disciples' fishing was. From threshing corn he is fetched to thresh the Midianites, Isa. xli. 15. (3.) Distressed; he was threshing his wheat, not in the threshing-floor, the proper place, but *by the wine-press,* in some private unsuspected corner, for fear of the Midianites. He himself shared in the common calamity, and now the angel came to animate him against Midian when he himself could speak so feelingly of the heaviness of their yoke. The day of the greatest distress is God's time to appear for his people's relief.

2. Let us now see what passed between the angel and Gideon, who knew not with certainty, till after he was gone, that he was an angel, but supposed he was a prophet.

(1.) The angel accosted him with respect, and assured him of the presence of God with him, *v.* 12. He calls him a *mighty man of valour,* perhaps because he observed how he threshed his corn with all his might; and seest thou a man diligent in his business? whatever his business is, he shall *stand before kings.* He that is faithful in a few things shall be ruler over many. Gideon was a man of a brave active spirit, and yet buried alive in obscurity, through the iniquity of the times; but he is here animated to undertake something great, like himself, with that word, *the Lord is with thee,* or, as the Chaldee reads it, *the Word of the Lord is thy help.* It was very sure that the Lord was with him when this angel was with him. By this word, [1.] He gives him his commission. If we have God's presence with us, this will justify us and bear us out in our undertakings. [2.] He inspires him with all necessary qualifications for the execution of his commission. "The Lord is with thee to guide and strengthen thee, to animate and support thee." [3.] He assures him of success; for, *if God be for us, who can* prevail *against us?* If he be with us, nothing can be wanting to us. The presence of God with us is all in all to our prosperity, whatever we do. Gideon was a mighty man of valour, and yet he could bring nothing to pass without the presence of God, and that presence is enough to make any man mighty in valour and to give a man courage at any time.

(2.) Gideon gave a very melancholy answer to this joyful salutation (*v.* 13): *O my Lord! if the Lord be with us* (which the Chaldee reads, *Is the Shechinah of the Lord our help?* making that the same with *the Word of the Lord) why then has all this befallen us?* "all this trouble and distress from the Midianites' incursions, which force me to thresh wheat here by the wine-press—all this loss, and grief, and fright; and *where are all the miracles which our fathers told us of?*" Observe, In his reply he regards not the praise of his own valour, nor does this in the least elevate him or give him any encouragement, though it is probable the angel adapted what he said to that which Gideon was at the same time thinking of; while his labouring hands were employed about his wheat, his working head and daring heart were meditating Israel's rescue and Midian's ruin, with which thought he that knows the heart seasonably sets in, calls him a man of valour for his brave projects, and opens him a way to put them in execution; yet Gideon, as if not conscious to himself of any thing great or encouraging in his own spirit, fastens only on the assurance the angel had given him of God's presence, as that by which they held all their comfort. Observe, The angel spoke in particular to him: *The Lord is with thee;* but he expostulates for all: *If the Lord be with us,* herding himself with the thousands of Israel, and admitting no comfort but what they might be sharers in, so far is he from the thoughts of monopolizing it, though he had so fair an occasion given him. Note, Public spirits reckon that only an honour and joy to themselves which puts them in a capacity of serving the common interests of God's church. Gideon was a mighty man of valour, but as yet weak in faith, which makes it hard to him to reconcile to the assurances now given him of the presence of God, [1.] The distress to which Israel was reduced: *Why has all this* (and *all this* was no little) *befallen us?* Note, It is sometimes hard, but never impossible, to reconcile cross providences with the presence of God and his favour. [2.] The delay of their deliverance: "*Where are all the miracles which our fathers told us of?* Why does not the same power which delivered our fathers from the yoke of the Egyptians deliver us out of the hands of the Midianites?" As if because God did not immediately work miracles for their deliverance, though they had by their sins forfeited his favour and help, it must be questioned whether ever he had wrought the miracles which their fathers told them of, or, if he had, whether he had now the same wisdom, and power, and good-will to his people, that he had had formerly. This was his weakness. We must not expect that the miracles which were wrought when a church was in the forming, and some great truth in the settling, should be continued and repeated when the formation and settlement are completed: no, nor that the mercies God showed to our fathers that served him, and kept close to him, should be renewed to us, if we degenerate and revolt from him. Gideon ought not to have said either, *First,* That *God had delivered them into the hands of the Midianites,* for by their iniquities they had sold themselves, or, *Secondly,* That now they were in their hands he had forsaken them, for he had lately sent them a prophet (*v.* 8), which was a certain indication that he had not forsaken them.

(3.) The angel gave him a very effectual answer to his objections, by giving him a commission to deliver Israel out of the hands of the Midianites, and assuring him of success therein, *v.* 14. Now the angel is called *Jehovah,* for he speaks as one having authority, and not as a messenger. [1.] There was something extraordinary in the look he now gave to Gideon; it was a gracious favourable look, which revived his spirits that drooped, and silenced his fears, such a look as that with which God's *countenance beholds the upright,* Ps. xi. 7. He looked upon him, and smiled at the objections he made, which he gave him no direct answer to, but girded and clothed him with such power as would shortly enable him to answer them himself, and make him ashamed that ever he had made them. It was a speaking look, like Christ's upon Peter (Luke xxii. 61), a powerful look, a look that strangely darted new light and life into Gideon's breast, and inspired him with a generous heat, far above what he felt before. [2.] But there was much more in what he said to him. *First,* He commissioned him to appear and act as Israel's deliverer. Such a one the few thinking people in the nation, and Gideon among the rest, were now expecting to be raised up, according to God's former method, in answer to the cries of oppressed Israel; and now Gideon is told, "Thou art the man: *Go in this thy might,* this might wherewith thou art now threshing wheat; go and employ it to a nobler purpose; *I will make thee a thresher of men.*" Or, rather, "this might wherewith thou art now endued by this look." God gave him his commission by giving him all the qualifications that were necessary for the execution of it, which is more than the mightiest prince and potentate on earth can do for those to whom he gives commissions. God's fitting men for work is a sure and constant evidence of his calling them to it. "Go, not in thy might, that which is natural, and of thyself, depend not on thy own valour; but go in *this* thy might, this which thou hast now received, *go in the strength of the Lord God,* that is, the strength with which thou must strengthen thyself." *Secondly,* He assured him of success. This was enough to put courage into him; he might be confident he should not miscarry in the attempt; it should not turn either to his own disgrace or the damage of his people (as baffled enterprises do), but to his honour and their happiness: *Thou shalt save Israel from the hand of the Midianites,* and so shalt not only be an eye-witness, but a glorious instrument, of such wonders as thy *fathers told thee of.* Gideon, we may suppose, looked as one astonished at this strange and surprising power conferred upon him, and questions whether he may depend upon what he hears: the angel ratifies his commission with a *teste meipso—an appeal to his own authority;* there needed no more. "*Have not I commanded thee*—I that have all power in heaven and earth, and particular authority here as Israel's King, giving commissions immediately—*I* who *am that I am,* the same that sent Moses?" Exod. iii. 14.

(4.) Gideon made a very modest objection against this commission (*v.* 15): *O my Lord! wherewith shall I save Israel?* This question bespeaks him either, [1.] Distrustful of God and his power, as if, though God should be with him, yet it were impossible for him to save Israel. True faith is often weak, yet it shall not be rejected, but encouraged and strengthened. Or, [2.] Inquisitive concerning the methods he must take: "Lord, I labour under all imaginable disadvantages for it; if I must do it, thou must put me in the way." Note, Those who receive commissions from God must expect and seek for instructions from him. Or rather, [3.] Humble, self-diffident, and self-denying. The angel had honoured him, but see how meanly he speaks of himself: "My family is comparatively poor in Manasseh" (impoverished, it may be, more than other families by the Midianites), "and I am the least, that have the least honour and interest, *in my father's house;* what can I pretend to do? I am utterly unfit for the service, and unworthy of the honour." Note, God often chooses to do great things by those that are little, especially that are so in their own eyes. God delights to advance the humble.

(5.) This objection was soon answered by a repetition of the promise that God would be with him, *v.* 16. "Object not thy poverty and meanness; such things have indeed often hindered men in great enterprises, but what are they to a man that has the presence of God with him, which will make up all the deficiencies of honour and estate. *Surely I will be with thee,* to direct and strengthen thee, and put such a reputation upon thee that, how weak soever thy personal interest is, thou shalt have soldiers enough to follow thee, and be assured *thou shalt smite the Midianites as one man,* as easily as if they were but one man and as effectually. All the thousands of Midian shall be as if they had but one neck, and thou shalt have the cutting of it off."

(6.) Gideon desires to have his faith confirmed touching this commission; for he would not be over-credulous of that which tended so much to his own praise, would not venture upon an undertaking so far above him, and in which he must engage many more, but he would be well satisfied himself of his authority, and would be able to give satisfaction to others as to him who gave him that authority. He therefore humbly begs of this divine person, whoever he was, [1.] That he would give him a sign, *v.* 17. And, the commission being given him out of the common road of providence, he might reasonably expect it should be confirmed by some act of God out of the common course of nature: "Show me a sign to assure me of the truth of this concerning which thou talkest with me, that it is something more than talk, and that thou art in earnest." Now, under the dispensation of the Spirit, we are not to expect signs before our eyes, such as Gideon here desired, but must earnestly pray to God that, if *we have found grace in his sight,* he would show us a sign in our heart, by the powerful operations of his Spirit there, *fulfilling the work of faith,* and perfecting what is lacking in it. [2.] In order hereunto, that he would accept of a treat, and so give him a further and longer opportunity of conversation with him, *v.* 18. Those who know what it is to have communion with God desire the continuance of it, and are loth to part, praying with Gideon, *Depart not hence, I pray thee.* That which Gideon desired in courting his stay was that he might bring out some provision of meat for this stranger. He did not take him into the house to entertain him there, perhaps because his father's house were not well affected to him and his friends, or because he desired still to be in private with this stranger, and to converse with him alone (therefore he calls not for a servant to bring the provision, but fetches it himself), or because thus his father Abraham entertained angels unawares, not in his tent, but under a tree, Gen. xviii. 8. Upon the angel's promise to stay to dinner with him, he hastened to bring out a kid, which, it is likely, was ready boiled for his own dinner, so that in making it ready he had nothing to do but to put it in the basket (for here was no sauce to serve it up in, nor the dish garnished) and the broth in a vessel, and so he presented it, *v.* 19. Hereby he intended, *First,* To testify his grateful and generous respects to this stranger, and, in him, to God who sent him, as one that studied what he should render. He had pleaded the poverty of his family (*v.* 15) to excuse himself from being a general, but not here to excuse himself from being hospitable. Out of the little which the Midianites had left him he would gladly spare enough to entertain a friend, especially a messenger from heaven. *Secondly,* To try who and what this extraordinary person was. What he brought out is called his *present, v.* 18. It is the same word that is used for a meat-offering, and perhaps that word is used which signifies both because Gideon intended to leave it to this divine person to determine which it should be when he had it before him: whether a feast or a meat-offering, and accordingly he would be able to judge concerning him: if he ate of it as common meat, he would suppose him to be a man, a prophet; if otherwise, as it proved, he should know him to be an angel.

(7.) The angel gives him a sign in and by that which he had kindly prepared for his entertainment. For what we offer to God for his glory, and in token of our gratitude to him, will be made by the grace of God to turn to our own comfort and satisfaction. The angel ordered him to take the flesh and bread out of the basket, and lay it upon a hard and cold rock, and to pour out the broth upon it, which, if he brought it hot, would soon be cold there; and *Gideon did so* (*v.* 20), believing that the angel appointed it, not in contempt of his courtesy, but with an intention to give him a sign, which he did, abundantly to his satisfaction. For, [1.] He turned the *meat into an offering made by fire, of a sweet savour* unto himself, showing hereby that he was not a man who needed meat, but the Son of God who was to be served and honoured by sacrifice, and who in the fulness of time was to make himself a sacrifice. [2.] He brought fire *out of the rock,* to consume this sacrifice, summoning it, not by striking the rock, as we strike fire out of a flint, but by a gentle touch given to the offering with the end of his staff, *v.* 21. Hereby he gave him a sign that he had *found grace in his sight,* for God testified his acceptance of sacrifices by kindling them, if public, with fire from heaven, as those of Moses and Elias, if private, as this, with fire out of the earth, which was equivalent: both were the effect of divine power; and this acceptance of his sacrifice evidenced the acceptance of his person, confirmed his commission, and perhaps was intended to signify his success in the execution of it, that he and his army should be a surprising terror and consumption to the Midianites, like this fire out of the rock. [3.] He *departed out of his sight* immediately, did not walk off as a man, but vanished and disappeared as a spirit. Here was as much of a sign as he could wish.

(8.) Gideon, though no doubt he was confirmed in his faith by the indications given of the divinity of the person who had spoken to him, yet for the present was put into a great fright by it, till God graciously pacified him and removed his fears. [1.] Gideon speaks peril to himself (*v.* 22): *When he perceived that he was an angel* (which was not till he had departed, as the two disciples knew not it was Jesus they had been talking with till he was going, Luke xxiv. 31), then he cried out, *Alas! O Lord God!* be merciful to me, I am undone, for *I have seen an angel,* as Jacob, who wondered that his life was preserved when he had seen God, Gen. xxxii. 30. Ever since man has by sin exposed himself to God's wrath and curse an express from heaven has been a terror to him, as he scarcely dares to expect good tidings thence; at least, in this world of sense, it is a very awful thing to have any sensible conversation with that world of spirits to which we are so much strangers. Gideon's courage failed him now. [2.] God speaks peace to him, *v.* 23. It might have been fatal to him, but he assures him it should not. The Lord had *departed out of his sight, v.* 21. But though he must no longer walk by sight he might still live by faith, that faith which comes by hearing; for the Lord said to him, with an audible voice (as bishop Patrick thinks) these encouraging words, "*Peace be unto thee,* all is well, and be thou satisfied that it is so. Fear not; he that came to employ thee did not intend to slay thee; *thou shalt not die.*" See how ready God is to revive the hearts of those that tremble at his word and presence, and to give those that stand in awe of his majesty assurances of his mercy.

3. The memorial of this vision which Gideon set up was a monument in form of an altar, the rather because it was by a kind of sacrifice upon a rock, without the solemnity of an altar, that the angel manifested his acceptance of him; then an altar was unnecessary (the angel's staff was sufficient to sanctify the gift without an altar), but now it was of use to preserve the remembrance of the vision, which was done by the name Gideon gave to this memorial, *Jehovah-shalom* (*v.* 24)—*The Lord peace.* This is, (1.) The title of the Lord that spoke to him. Compare Gen. xvi. 13. The same that is the *Lord our righteousness* is *our peace* (Eph. ii. 14), our reconciler and so our Saviour. Or, (2.) The substance of what he said to him: "*The Lord spoke peace,* and created that fruit of the lips, bade me be easy when I was in that agitation." Or, (3.) A prayer grounded upon what he had said, so the margin understands it: *The Lord send peace,* that is, rest from the present trouble, for still the public welfare lay nearest his heart.

25 And it came to pass the same night, that the LORD said unto him, Take thy father's young bullock, even the second bullock of seven years old, and throw down the altar of Baal that thy father hath, and cut down the grove that *is* by it: 26 And build an altar unto the LORD thy God upon the top of this rock, in the ordered place, and take the second bullock, and offer a burnt sacrifice with the wood of the grove which thou shalt cut down. 27 Then Gideon took ten men of his servants, and did as the LORD had said unto him: and *so* it was, because he feared his father's household, and the men of the city, that he could not do *it* by day, that he did *it* by night. 28 And when the men of the city arose early in the morning, behold, the altar of Baal was cast down, and the grove was cut down that *was* by it, and the second bullock was offered upon the altar *that was* built. 29 And they said one to another, Who hath done this thing? And when they enquired and asked, they said, Gideon the son of Joash hath done this thing. 30 Then the men of the city said unto Joash, Bring out thy son, that he may die: because he hath cast down the altar of Baal, and because he hath cut down the grove that *was* by it. 31 And Joash said unto all that stood against him, Will ye plead for Baal? will ye save him? he that will plead for him, let him be put to death whilst *it is yet* morning: if he *be* a god, let him plead for himself, because *one* hath cast down his altar. 32 Therefore on that day he called him Jerubbaal, saying, Let Baal plead against him, because he hath thrown down his altar.

Here, I. Orders are given to Gideon to

begin his government with the reformation of his father's house, *v.* 25, 26. A correspondence being settled between God and Gideon, by the appearance of the angel to him, it was kept up in another way; the same night after he had seen God, when he was full of thoughts concerning what had passed, which probably he had not yet communicated to any, *the Lord said unto him* in a dream, *Do so and so.* Note, God's visits, if gratefully received, shall be graciously repeated. Bid God welcome, and he will come again. Gideon is appointed, 1. To throw down Baal's altar, which it seems his father had, either for his own house or perhaps for the whole town. See the power of God's grace, that he could raise up a reformer, and the condescensions of his grace, that he would raise up a deliverer, out of the family of one that was a ring-leader in idolatry. But Gideon must not now think it enough not to worship at that altar, which we charitably hope he had not done, but he must throw it down; not consecrate the same altar to God (it is bishop Hall's observation), but utterly demolish it. God first commands down the monuments of superstition, and then enjoins his own service. He must likewise *cut down the grove that was by it*, the plantation of young trees, designed to beautify the place. The learned bishop Patrick, by the grove, understands the image in the grove, probably the image of Ashtaroth (for the word for a grove is *Ashereh)*, which stood upon or close by the altar. 2. To erect an altar to God, *to Jehovah his God*, which probably was to be notified by an inscription upon the altar to that purport—to Jehovah, Gideon's God, or Israel's. It would have been an improper thing for him to build an altar, even to the God of Israel, especially for burnt-offering and sacrifice, and would have been construed into a contempt of the altar at Shiloh, if God, who has not tied up himself to his own laws, had not bidden him to do it. But now it was his duty and honour to be thus employed. God directs him to the place where he should build it, on the *top of the rock*, perhaps in the same place in which the angel had appeared to him, near to the altar he had already built: and he must not do it in a hurry, but with the decency that became a religious action *(in an orderly manner*, as it is in the margin), according to the ancient law for altars raised on particular occasions, that they must be of earth not of hewn stone. The word here used for the rock on which the altar was to be built signifies a fortress, or strong-hold, erected, some think, to secure them from the Midianites; if so, it was no security while the altar of Baal was so near it, but it was effectually fortified when an altar to the Lord was built on the top of it, for that is the best defence upon our glory. On this altar, (1.) He was to offer sacrifice. Two bullocks he must offer: his father's *young bullock, and the second bullock of seven years old*, so it should rather be read, not *even* the second as we read it. The former, we may suppose, he was to offer for himself, the latter *for the sins of the people* whom he was to deliver. It was requisite he should thus make peace with God, before he made war on Midian. Till sin be pardoned through the great sacrifice, no good is to be expected. These bullocks, it is supposed, were intended for sacrifices on the altar of Baal, but were now converted to a better use. Thus, when the *strong man armed* is overcome and dispossessed, the stronger than he divides the spoil, seizes that for himself *which was prepared for Baal.* Let him come *whose right it is*, and *give it to him.* (2.) Baal's grove, or image, or whatever it was that was the sanctity or beauty of his altar, must not only be burnt, but must be used as fuel for God's altar, to signify not only that whatever sets up itself in opposition to God shall be destroyed, but that the justice of God will be glorified in its destruction. God ordered Gideon to do this, [1.] To try his zeal for religion, which it was necessary he should give proofs of before he took the field, to give proof of his valour there. [2.] That some steps might hereby be taken towards Israel's reformation, which must prepare the way for their deliverance. Sin, the cause, must be taken away, else how should the trouble, which was but the effect, come to an end? And it might be hoped that this example of Gideon's, who was now shortly to appear so great a man, would be followed by the rest of the cities and tribes, and the destruction of this one altar of Baal would be the destruction of many.

II. Gideon was *obedient to the heavenly vision, v.* 27. He that was to command the Israel of God must be subject to the God of Israel, without disputing, and, as a type of Christ, must first *save his people from their sins*, and then save them from their enemies. 1. He had servants of his own, whom he could confide in, who, we may suppose, like him, had kept their integrity, and had *not bowed the knee to Baal*, and therefore were forward to assist him in destroying the altar of Baal. 2. He did not scruple taking his father's bullock and offering it to God without his father's consent, because God, who expressly commanded him to do so, had a better title to it than his father had, and it was the greatest real kindness he could do to his father to prevent his sin. 3. He expected to incur the displeasure of his father's household by it, and the ill-will of his neighbours, yet he did it, remembering how much it was Levi's praise that, in the cause of God, *he said to his father and mother, I have not seen him*, Deut xxxiii. 9. And, while he was sure of the favour of God, he feared not the anger of men; he that bade him do it would bear him out. Yet, 4.

Though he feared not their resentment when it was done, to prevent their resistance in the doing of it he prudently chose to do it by night, that he might not be disturbed in these sacred actions. And some think it was the same night in which God spoke to him to do it, and that, as soon as ever he had received the orders, he immediately applied himself to the execution of them, and finished before morning.

III. He was brought into peril of his life for doing it, *v.* 28—30. 1. It was soon discovered what was done. Gideon, when he had gone through with the business, did not desire the concealment of it, nor could it be hid, for the men of the city *rose early in the morning,* as it should seem, to say their matins at Baal's altar, and so to begin the day with their god, such a one as he was, a shame to those who say the true God is their God, and yet, in the morning, direct no prayer to him, nor look up. 2. It was soon discovered who had done it. Strict enquiry was made. Gideon was known to be disaffected to the worship of Baal, which brought him into suspicion, and positive proof immediately came against him: "Gideon, no doubt, *has done this thing.*" 3. Gideon being found guilty of the fact, to such a pitch of impiety had these degenerate Israelites arrived that they take it for law he must die for the same, and require his own father (who, by patronising their idolatry, had given them too much cause to expect he would comply with them herein) to deliver him up: *Bring out thy son, that he may die.* Be astonished, O heavens! at this, and tremble, O earth! By the law of God the worshippers of Baal were to die, but these wicked men impiously turn the penalty upon the worshippers of the God of Israel. How prodigiously mad were they upon their idols! Was it not enough to offer the choicest of their bullocks to Baal, but must the bravest youth of their city fall as a sacrifice to that dunghill-deity, when they pretended he was provoked? How soon will idolaters become persecutors!

IV. He was rescued out of the hands of his persecutors by his own father, *v.* 31.

1. There were those that stood against Gideon, that not only appeared at the first to make a demand, but insisted on it, and would have him put to death. Notwithstanding the heavy judgments they were at this time under for their idolatry, yet they hated to be reformed, and walked contrary to God even when he was walking contrary to them.

2. Yet then *Joash stood for him;* he was one of the chief men of the city. Those that have power may do a great deal for the protection of an honest man and an honest cause, and when they so use their power they are ministers of God for good.

(1.) This Joash had patronised Baal's altar, yet now protects him that had destroyed it, [1.] Out of natural affection to his son, and perhaps a particular esteem for him as a virtuous, valiant, valuable, young man, and never the worse for not joining with him in the worship of Baal. Many that have not courage enough to keep their integrity themselves yet have so much conscience left as makes them love and esteem those that do. If Joash had a kindness for Baal, yet he had a greater kindness for his son. Or, [2.] Out of a care for the public peace. The mob grew riotous, and, he feared, would grow more so, and therefore, as some think, he bestirred himself to repress the tumult: "Let it be left to the judges; it is not for you to pass sentence upon any man; he that offers it, *let him be put to death:* he means not as an idolater, but as a disturber of the peace, and the mover of sedition. Under this same colour Paul was rescued at Ephesus from those that were as zealous for Diana as these were for Baal, Acts xix. 40. Or, [3.] Out of a conviction that Gideon had done well. His son, perhaps, had reasoned with him, or God, who has all hearts in his hands, had secretly and effectually influenced him to appear thus against the advocates for Baal, though he had complied with them formerly in the worship of Baal. Note, It is good to appear for God when we are called to it, though there be few or none to second us, because God can incline the hearts of those to stand by us from whom we little expect assistance. Let us do our duty, and then trust God with our safety.

(2.) Two things Joash urges:—[1.] That it was absurd for them to plead for Baal. "Will you that are Israelites, the worshippers of the one only living and true God, plead for Baal, a false god? Will you be so sottish, so senseless? Those whose fathers' god Baal was, and who never knew any other, are more excusable in pleading for him than you are, that are in covenant with Jehovah, and have been trained up in the knowledge of him. You that have smarted so much for worshipping Baal, and have brought all this mischief and calamity upon yourselves by it, will you yet plead for Baal?" Note, It is bad to commit sin, but it is great wickedness indeed to plead for it, especially to plead for Baal, that idol, whatever it is, which possesses that room in the heart which God should have. [2.] That it was needless for them to plead for Baal. If he were not a god, as was pretended, they could have nothing to say for him; if he were, he was able to plead for himself, as the God of Israel had often done by fire from heaven, or some other judgment against those who put contempt upon him. Here is a fair challenge to Baal to *do either good or evil,* and the result convinced his worshippers of their folly in praying to one to help them that could not avenge himself; after this Gideon remarkably prospered, and thereby it appeared how unable Baal was to maintain his own cause.

(3.) Gideon's father hereupon gave him

a new name (*v.* 32); he called him *Jerubbaal:* "Let Baal plead; let him plead against him if he can; if he have any thing to say for himself against his destroyer, let him say it." This name was a standing defiance to Baal: "Now that Gideon is taking up arms against the Midianites that worship Baal, let him defend his worshippers if he can." It likewise gave honour to Gideon (a sworn enemy to that great usurper, and that had carried the day against him), and encouragement to his soldiers, that they fought under one that fought for God against this great competitor with him for the throne. It is the probable conjecture of the learned that that Jerombalus whom Sanchoniathon (one of the most ancient of all the heathen writers) speaks of as *a priest of the god Jao* (a corruption of the name *Jehovah),* and one to whom he was indebted for a great deal of knowledge, was this Jerubbaal. He is called *Jerubbesheth* (2 Sam. xi. 12), *Baal,* a *lord,* being fitly turned into *Besheth, shame.*

33 Then all the Midianites and the Amalekites and the children of the east were gathered together, and went over, and pitched in the valley of Jezreel. 34 But the Spirit of the LORD came upon Gideon, and he blew a trumpet; and Abi-ezer was gathered after him. 35 And he sent messengers throughout all Manasseh; who also was gathered after him: and he sent messengers unto Asher, and unto Zebulun, and unto Naphtali; and they came up to meet them. 36 And Gideon said unto God, If thou wilt save Israel by mine hand, as thou hast said, 37 Behold, I will put a fleece of wool in the floor; *and* if the dew be on the fleece only, and *it be* dry upon all the earth *beside,* then shall I know that thou wilt save Israel by mine hand, as thou hast said. 38 And it was so: for he rose up early on the morrow, and thrust the fleece together, and wringed the dew out of the fleece, a bowl full of water. 39 And Gideon said unto God, Let not thine anger be hot against me, and I will speak but this once: let me prove, I pray thee, but this once with the fleece; let it now be dry only upon the fleece, and upon all the ground let there be dew. 40 And God did so that night: for it was dry upon the fleece only, and there was dew on all the ground.

Here we have, I. The descent which the enemies of Israel made upon them, *v.* 33. A vast number of Midianites, Amalekites, and Arabians, got together, and came over Jordan, none either caring or daring to guard that important and advantageous pass against them, and they made their head-quarters in the valley of Jezreel, in the heart of Manasseh's tribe, not far from Gideon's city. Some think that the notice they had of Gideon's destroying Baal's altar brought them over, and that they came to plead for Baal and to make that a pretence for quarrelling with Israel; but it is more likely that it was now harvest-time, when they had been wont each year to make such a visit as this (*v.* 3), and that they were expected when Gideon was threshing, *v.* 11. God raised up Gideon to be ready against this terrible blow came. Their success so many years in these incursions, the little opposition they had met with and the great booty they had carried off, made them now both very eager and very confident. But it proved that *the measure of their iniquity was full* and the year of recompence had come; they must now *make an end to spoil* and *must be spoiled,* and they are *gathered as sheaves to the floor* (Mic. iv. 12, 13), for Gideon to thresh.

II. The preparation which Gideon makes to attack them in their camp, *v.* 34, 35. 1. God by his Spirit put life into Gideon: *The Spirit of the Lord clothed Gideon* (so the word is), clothed him as a robe, to put honour upon him, clothed him as a coat of mail, to put defence upon him. Those are well clad that are thus clothed. *A spirit of fortitude from before the Lord clothed Gideon;* so the Chaldee. He was of himself a mighty man of valour; yet personal strength and courage, though vigorously exerted, would not suffice for this great action; he must have the *armour of God* upon him, and this is what he must depend upon: *The Spirit of the Lord clothed him* in an extraordinary manner. Whom God calls to his work he will qualify and animate for it. 2. Gideon with his trumpet put life into his neighbours, God working with him; he *blew a trumpet,* to call in volunteers, and more came in than perhaps he expected. (1.) The men of Abiezer, though lately enraged against him for throwing down the altar of Baal, and though they had condemned him to death as a criminal, were now convinced of their error, bravely came in to his assistance, and submitted to him as their general: *Abiezer was gathered after him, v.* 34. So suddenly can God turn the hearts even of idolaters and persecutors. (2.) Distant tribes, even Asher and Naphtali, which lay most remote, though strangers to him, obeyed his summons, and sent him in the best of their forces, *v.* 35. Though they lay furthest from the danger, yet, considering that if their neighbours were over-run by the Midianites their own turn would be next, they were forward to join against a common enemy.

III. The signs which God gratified him with, for the confirming both of his own faith and that of his followers; and perhaps it was more for their sakes than for his own that he desired them. Or, perhaps, he desired by these to be satisfied whether this was the time of his conquering the Midianites, or whether he was to wait for some other opportunity. Observe, 1. His request for a sign (*v.* 36, 37): "Let me by this *know that thou wilt save Israel by my hand,* let *a fleece of wool,* spread in the open air, be *wet with the dew,* and let the ground about it be dry." The purport of this is, *Lord, I believe, help thou my unbelief.* He found his own faith weak and wavering, and therefore begged of God by this sign to perfect what was lacking in it. We may suppose that God, who intended to give him these signs, for the glorifying of his own power and goodness, put it into his heart to ask them. Yet, when he repeated his request for a second sign, the reverse of the former, he did it with a very humble apology, deprecating God's displeasure, because it looked so like a peevish humoursome distrust of God and dissatisfaction with the many assurances he had already given him (*v.* 39): *Let not thy anger be hot against me.* Though he took the boldness to ask another sign, yet he did it with such fear and trembling as showed that the familiarity God had graciously admitted him to did not breed any contempt of God's glory, nor presumption on God's goodness. Abraham had given him an example of this, when God gave him leave to be very free with him (Gen. xviii. 30, 32), *O let not the Lord be angry, and I will speak.* God's favour must be sought with great reverence, a due sense of our distance, and a religious fear of his wrath. 2. God's gracious grant of his request. See how tender God is of true believers though they be weak, and how ready to condescend to their infirmities, that the bruised reed may not be broken nor the smoking flax quenched. Gideon would have *the fleece wet* and the *ground dry;* but then, lest any should object, "It is natural for wool, if ever so little moisture fall, to drink it in and retain it, and therefore there was nothing extraordinary in this," though the quantity wrung out was sufficient to obviate such an objection, yet he desires that next night the ground might be wet and the fleece dry, and it is done, so willing is God to *give to the heirs of promise strong consolation* (Heb. vi. 17, 18), even by two immutable things. He suffers himself, not only to be prevailed with by their importunities, but even to be prescribed to by their doubts and dissatisfactions. These signs were, (1.) Truly miraculous, and therefore abundantly serving to confirm his commission. It is said of the dew that it is *from the Lord,* and *tarrieth not for man, nor waiteth for the sons of men* (Micah. v. 7); and yet God here in this matter *hearkened to the voice of a man;* as to Joshua, in directing the course of the sun, so to Gideon in directing that of the dew, by which it appears that it falls not by chance, but by providence. The latter sign inverted the former, and, to please Gideon, it was wrought backward and forward, whence Dr. Fuller observes that *heaven's real miracles will endure turning, being inside and outside both alike.* (2.) Very significant. He and his men were going to engage the Midianites; could God distinguish between a small fleece of Israel and the vast floor of Midian? Yes, by this he is made to know that he can. Is Gideon desirous that the dew of divine grace might descend upon himself in particular? He sees the fleece wet with dew to assure him of it. Does he desire that God will be as the dew to all Israel? Behold, all the ground is wet. Some make this fleece an emblem of the Jewish nation, which, when time was, was wet with the dew of God's word and ordinances, while the rest of the world was dry; but since the rejection of Christ and his gospel they are dry *as the heath in the wilderness,* while the nations about are *as a watered garden.*

CHAP. VII.

This chapter presents us with Gideon in the field, commanding the army of Israel, and routing the army of the Midianites, for which great exploit we found in the former chapter how he was prepared by his converse with God and his conquest of Baal. We are here told, I. What direction God gave to Gideon for the modelling of his army, by which it was reduced to 300 men, ver. 1, 8. II. What encouragement God gave to Gideon to attack the enemy, by sending him secretly into their camp to hear a Midianite tell his dream, ver. 9--15. III. How he formed his attack upon the enemy's camp with his 300 men, not to fight them, but to frighten them, ver. 16—20. IV. The success of this attack; it put them to flight, and gave them a total rout, the disbanded forces, and their other neighbours, then coming in to his assistance, ver. 21--25. It is a story that shines very brightly in the book of the wars of the Lord.

THEN Jerubbaal, who *is* Gideon, and all the people that *were* with him, rose up early, and pitched beside the well of Harod: so that the host of the Midianites were on the north side of them, by the hill of Moreh, in the valley. 2 And the LORD said unto Gideon, The people that *are* with thee *are* too many for me to give the Midianites into their hands, lest Israel vaunt themselves against me, saying, Mine own hand hath saved me. 3 Now therefore go to, proclaim in the ears of the people, saying, Whosoever *is* fearful and afraid, let him return and depart early from mount Gilead. And there returned of the people twenty and two thousand; and there remained ten thousand. 4 And the LORD said unto Gideon, The people *are* yet *too* many: bring them down unto the water, and I will try them for thee there: and it shall be, *that* of whom I say unto thee, This shall go with thee, the same shall go with thee; and of whomsoever I say unto thee, This shall not go with thee, the same shall not go. 5 So he brought down the people unto the water: and the LORD said unto Gideon, Every one that lappeth of the water with his tongue, as a dog lappeth, him shalt thou set by himself; likewise every one that boweth down upon his knees to drink. 6 And the number of them that lapped, *putting* their hand to their mouth, were three hundred men: but all the rest of the people bowed down upon their knees to drink water. 7 And the LORD said unto Gideon, By the three hundred men that lapped will I save you, and deliver the Midianites into thine hand: and let all the *other* people go every man unto his place. 8 So the people took victuals in their hand, and their trumpets: and he sent all *the rest of* Israel every man unto his tent, and retained those three hundred men: and the host of Midian was beneath him in the valley.

Here, I. Gideon applies himself with all possible care and industry to do the part of a good general, in leading on the hosts of Israel against the Midianites (*v.* 1): *He rose up early,* as one whose heart was upon his business, and who was afraid of losing time. Now that he is sure God is with him he is impatient of delay. He pitched near a famous well, that his army might not be distressed for want of water, and gained the higher ground, which possibly might be some advantage to him, for the Midianites *were beneath him in the valley.* Note, Faith in God's promises must not slacken, but rather quicken, our endeavours. When we are sure God goes before us, then we must bestir ourselves, 2 Sam. v. 24.

II. God provides that the praise of the intended victory may be reserved wholly to himself, by appointing 300 men only to be employed in this service.

1. The army consisted of 32,000 men, a small army in comparison with what Israel might have raised upon so great an occasion, and a very small one in comparison with what the Midianites had now brought into the field; Gideon was ready to think them too few, but God comes to him, and tells him they are *too many, v.* 2. Not but that those did well who offered themselves willingly to this expedition, but God saw fit not to make use of all that came. We often find God bringing great things to pass by a few hands, but this was the only time that he purposely made them fewer. Had Deborah lately blamed those who *came not to the help of the Lord,* and yet in the next great action must those be turned off that do come? Yes; (1.) God would hereby show that when he employed suitable instruments in his service he did not need them, but could do his work without them, so that he was not indebted to them for their service, but they to him for employing them. (2.) He would hereby put those to shame for their cowardice who had tamely submitted to the Midianites, and durst not make head against them, because of the disproportion of their numbers. They now saw that, if they had but made sure of the favour of God, one of them might have chased a thousand. (3.) He would hereby silence and exclude boasting. This is the reason here given by him who knows the pride that is in men's hearts: *Lest Israel vaunt themselves against me.* Justly were those denied the honour of the service who would not give God the honour of the success. *My own hand hath saved me* is a word that must never come out of the mouth of such as shall be saved. *He that glories must glory in the Lord,* and all flesh must be silent before him.

2. Two ways God took to lessen their numbers:—(1.) He ordered all that would own themselves timorous and faint-hearted to be dismissed, *v.* 3. They were now encamped on a mountain close to the enemy, called *Mount Gilead,* from Gilead, the common ancestor of these families of Manasseh, which were seated on this side Jordan (Num. xxvi. 30), and thence they might see perhaps the vast numbers of the enemy; those therefore who were disheartened at the sight were left to their liberty, to go back if they pleased. There was a law for making such a proclamation as this, Deut. xx. 8. But Gideon perhaps thought that concerned only those wars which were undertaken for the enlarging of their coast, not, as this, for their necessary defence against an invader; therefore Gideon would not have proclaimed this if God, who knew how his forces would hereby be diminished, had not commanded him. Cowards would be as likely as any, after the victory, to take the honour of it from God, and therefore God would not do them the honour to employ them in it. One would have thought there would be scarcely one Israelite to be found that against such an enemy as the Midianites, and under such a leader as Gideon, would own himself fearful; yet above two parts of three took advantage of this proclamation, and filed off, when they saw the strength of the enemy and their own weakness, not considering the assurances of the divine presence which their general had received of the Lord, and, it is likely, delivered unto them. Some think the op-

pression they had been under so long had broken their spirits, others, more probably, that consciousness of their own guilt had deprived them of their courage. Sin stared them in the face, and therefore they durst not look death in the face. Note, Fearful faint-hearted people are not fit to be employed for God; and, among those that are enlisted under the banner of Christ, there are more such than we think there are. (2.) He directed the cashiering of all that remained except 300 men, and he did it by a sign: *The people are yet too many* for me to make use off, *v.* 4. See how much God's thoughts and ways are above ours. Gideon himself, it is likely, thought they were too few, though they were as many as Barak encountered Sisera with (*ch.* iv. 14); and, had he not forced his way through the discouragement by dint of faith, he himself would have started back from so hazardous an enterprise, and have made the best of his own way back. But God saith, they are *too many,* and, when diminished to a third part, they are yet *too many,* which may help us to understand those providences which sometimes seem to weaken the church and its interests: its friends are too many, too mighty, too wise, for God to work deliverance by; God is taking a course to lessen them, that he may be *exalted in his own strength.* Gideon is ordered to bring his soldiers to the watering, probably to the well of Harod (*v.* 1) and the stream that ran from it; he, or some appointed by him, must observe how they drank. We must suppose they were all thirsty, and were inclined to drink; it is likely he told them they must prepare to enter upon action immediately, and therefore must refresh themselves accordingly, not expecting, after this, to drink any thing else but the blood of their enemies. Now some, and no doubt the most, would kneel down on their knees to drink, and put their mouths to the water as horses do, and so they might get their full draught. Others, it may be, would not make such a formal business of it, but as a dog laps with his tongue, a lap and away, so they would hastily take up a little water in their hands, and cool their mouths with that, and be gone. Three hundred and no more there were of this latter sort, that drank in haste, and by those God tells Gideon he would rout the Midianites, *v.* 7. By the former distinction none were retained but hearty men, that were resolved to do their utmost for retrieving the liberties of Israel; but by this further distinction it was provided that none should be made use of but, [1.] Men that were hardy, that could endure long fatigue, without complaining of thirst or weariness, that had not in them any dregs either of sloth or luxury. [2.] Men that were hasty, that thought it long till they were engaged with the enemy, preferring the service of God and their country before their necessary refreshment; such as these God chooses to employ, that are not only well affected, but zealously affected in a good thing. And also because these were the smaller number, and therefore the least likely to effect what they were designed for, God would by them save Israel. It was a great trial to the faith and courage of Gideon, when God bade him let all the rest of the people but these 300 *go every man to his place,* that is, go where they pleased out of his call, and from under his command; yet we may suppose those that were hearty in the cause, though now set aside, did not go so far out of hearing but that they were ready to follow the blow, when the 300 had broken the ice, though this does not appear. Thus strangely was Gideon's army purged, and modelled, and reduced, instead of being recruited, as one would think in so great an action it both needed and deserved to be. Now,

3. Let us see how this little despicable regiment, on which the stress of the action must lie, was accoutred and fitted out. Had these 300 been double-manned with servants and attendants, and double-armed with swords and spears, we should have thought them the more likely to bring something to pass. But, instead of making them more serviceable by their equipment, they are made less so. For, (1.) Every soldier turns sutler: They *took victuals in their hands* (*v.* 8), left their bag and baggage behind, and every man burdened himself with his own provision, which was a trial of their faith, whether they could trust God when they had no more provisions with them than they could carry, and a trial of their diligence, whether they would carry as much as they had occasion for. This was indeed living from hand to mouth. (2.) Every soldier turns trumpeter. The regiments that were cashiered left their trumpets behind them for the use of these 300 men, who were furnished with these instead of weapons of war, as if they had been going rather to a game than to a battle.

9 And it came to pass the same night, that the LORD said unto him, Arise, get thee down unto the host; for I have delivered it into thine hand. 10 But if thou fear to go down, go thou with Phurah thy servant down to the host: 11 And thou shalt hear what they say; and afterward shall thine hands be strengthened to go down unto the host. Then went he down with Phurah his servant unto the outside of the armed men that *were* in the host. 12 And the Midianites and the Amalekites and all the children of the east lay along in the valley like grasshoppers for multitude;

and their camels *were* without number, as the sand by the sea side for multitude. 13 And when Gideon was come, behold, *there was* a man that told a dream unto his fellow, and said, Behold, I dreamed a dream, and, lo, a cake of barley bread tumbled into the host of Midian, and came unto a tent, and smote it that it fell, and overturned it, that the tent lay along. 14 And his fellow answered and said, This *is* nothing else save the sword of Gideon the son of Joash, a man of Israel: *for* into his hand hath God delivered Midian, and all the host. 15 And it was *so*, when Gideon heard the telling of the dream, and the interpretation thereof, that he worshipped, and returned into the host of Israel, and said, Arise; for the LORD hath delivered into your hand the host of Midian.

Gideon's army being diminished as we have found it was, he must either fight by faith or not at all; God therefore here provides recruits for his faith, instead of recruits for his forces.

I. He furnishes him with a good foundation to build his faith upon. Nothing but a word from God will be a footing for faith. He has this as full and express as he can desire, *v.* 9. 1. A word of command to warrant the action, which otherwise seemed rash and indiscreet, and unbecoming a wise general: *Arise, get thee down* with this handful of men *unto the host.* 2. A word of promise to assure him of the success, which otherwise seemed very improbable : *I have delivered it into thy hand;* it is all thy own. This *word of the Lord* came to him the same night, when he was (we may suppose) greatly agitated and full of care how he should come off; *in the multitude of his thoughts within him these comforts did delight his soul.* Divine consolations are given in to believers not only strongly but seasonably.

II. He furnishes him with a good prop to support his faith with. 1. He orders him to be his own spy, and now in the dead of the night to go down privately into the host of Midian, and see what intelligence he could gain: "*If thou fear to go down* to fight, go first only with thy own servant (*v.* 10) and *hear what they say*" (*v.* 11); and it is intimated to him that he should hear that which would greatly strengthen his faith. God knows the infirmities of his people, and what great encouragement they may sometimes take from a small matter; and therefore, knowing beforehand what would occur to Gideon, in that very part of the camp to which he would go down, he orders him to go down and hearken to what they said, that he might the more firmly believe what God said. He must take with him *Phurah his servant,* one that he could confide in, probably one of the ten that had helped him to break down the altar of Baal. He must take him and no one else with him, must take him with him to be a witness of what he should hear the Midianites say, that out of the mouth of these two witnesses, when the matter came to be reported to Israel, the word might be established. He must take his servant with him, because two are better than one and a little help is better than none. 2. Being so, he orders him the sight of something that was discouraging. It was enough to frighten him to discern, perhaps by moon-light, the vast numbers of the enemy (*v.* 12), the men like grasshoppers for multitude, and they proved no better than grasshoppers for strength and courage; the camels one could not count, any more than the sand. But, 3. He causes him to hear that which was to him a very good omen; and when he had heard it he went back again immediately, supposing he now had what he was sent thither for. He overheard two soldiers of the enemy, that were comrades, talking; probably they were in bed together, waking in the night. (1.) One of them tells his dream, and as our dreams generally are, and therefore not worth telling again, it is a very foolish one. He dreamed that he saw a barley-cake come rolling down the hill into the camp of the Midianites, and "methought," says he (for so we speak in telling our dreams), "this rolling cake struck one of our tents" (perhaps one of the chief of their tents) "and with such violence that" (would you think it?) "it overturned the tent, forced down the stakes, and broke the cords at one blow, so that the tent lay along and buried its inhabitants," *v.* 13. *In multitudes of dreams there are divers vanities,* says Solomon, Eccl. v. 7. One would wonder what odd incoherent things are often put together by a ludicrous fancy in our dreams. (2.) The other, it may be between sleeping and waking, undertakes to interpret this dream, and the interpretation is very far-fetched: *This is nothing else save the sword of Gideon, v.* 14. Our expositors now can tell us how apt the resemblance was, that Gideon, who had threshed corn for his family, and made cakes for his friend (*ch.* vi. 11—19), was fitly represented by a cake,—that he and his army were as inconsiderable as a cake made of a little flour, as contemptible as a barley-cake, hastily got together as a cake suddenly baked upon the coals, and as unlikely to conquer this great army as a cake to overthrow a tent. But, after all, do *not interpretations belong to God?* He put it into the head of the one to dream and into the mouth of the other to give the sense of it; if Gideon had heard the dream only, and he and his servant had been left to interpret it themselves, it had so little significancy in it that it would have done him little service; but, having the interpretation from the mouth of an enemy, it not only appeared to come from God, who has all men's hearts and tongues in his hand, but it was likewise an evidence that the enemy was quite dispirited, and that the name of Gideon had become so formidable to them that it disturbed their sleep. The victory would easily be won which was already so tamely yielded: *Into his hand hath God delivered Midian.* Those were not likely to fight who saw God fighting against them.

Lastly, Gideon, observing the finger of God pointing him to this very place, at this very time, to hear this dream and the interpretation of it, was exceedingly encouraged by it against the melancholy apprehensions he had upon the reducing of his army. He was very well pleased to hear himself compared to a barley-cake, when it proved to effect such great things. Being hereby animated, we are told (*v.* 15), 1. How he gave God the glory of it; he worshipped immediately, bowed his head, or, it may be, lifted up his eyes and hands, and in a short ejaculation thanked God for the victory he was now sure of, and for this encouragement to expect it. Wherever we are, we may speak to God, and worship him, and find a way open heavenward. God must have the praise of that which is encouraging to our faith, and his providence must be acknowledged in those events which, though minute and seemingly accidental, prove serviceable to us. 2. How he gave his friends a share in the encouragements he had received: *Arise,* prepare to march presently; *the Lord has delivered Midian into your hand.*

16 And he divided the three hundred men *into* three companies, and he put a trumpet in every man's hand, with empty pitchers, and lamps within the pitchers. 17 And he said unto them, Look on me, and do likewise: and, behold, when I come to the outside of the camp, it shall be *that,* as I do, so shall ye do. 18 When I blow with a trumpet, I and all that *are* with me, then blow ye the trumpets also on every side of all the camp, and say, *The sword* of the LORD, and of Gideon. 19 So Gideon, and the hundred men that *were* with him, came unto the outside of the camp in the beginning of the middle watch; and they had but newly set the watch: and they blew the trumpets, and brake the pitchers that *were* in their hands. 20 And the three companies blew the trumpets, and brake the pitchers, and held the lamps in their left hands, and the trumpets in their right hands to blow *withal:* and they cried, The sword of the LORD, and of Gideon. 21 And they stood every man in his place round about the camp: and all the host ran, and cried, and fled. 22 And the three hundred blew the trumpets, and the LORD set every man's sword against his fellow, even throughout all the host: and the host fled to Beth-shittah in Zererath, *and* to the border of Abel-meholah, unto Tabbath.

Here is, I. The alarm which Gideon gave to the hosts of Midian in the dead time of the night; for it was intended that those who had so long been a terror to Israel, and had so often frightened them, should themselves be routed and ruined purely by terror.

1. The attack here made was, in many circumstances, like that which Abraham made upon the army that had taken Lot captive. The number of men was much the same: Abraham had 318, Gideon 300; they both divided their forces, both made their attack by night, and were both victorious under great disadvantages (Gen. xiv. 14, 15); and Gideon is not only a son of Abraham (so were the Midianites by Keturah) but an heir of his faith. Gideon, (1.) Divided his army, small as it was, into three battalions (*v* 16), one of which he himself commanded (*v.* 19), because great armies (and such a one he would make a show of) were usually divided into the right wing, and left wing, and the body of the army. (2.) He ordered them all to do as he did, *v.* 17. He told them now, it is very likely, what they must do, else the thing was so strange that they would scarcely have done it of a sudden, but he would, by doing it first, give notice to them when to do it, as officers exercise their soldiers with the word of command or by beat of drum: *Look on me, and do likewise.* Such is the word of command which our Lord Jesus, the captain of our salvation, gives his soldiers; for he has *left us an example,* with a charge to follow it: *As I do, so shall you do.* (3.) He made his descent in the night, when they were secure and least expected it, which would put them into great consternation, and when the smallness of his army would not be discovered. In the night all frights are most frightful, especially in the dead of the night, as this was, a little after midnight, when the middle watch began, and the alarm would wake them out of their sleep. We read of *terror by night* as very terrible (Ps. xci. 5), and *fear in the night,* Cant. iii. 8. (4.) That which Gideon aimed at was to frighten this huge host, to give them not only a fatal rout, but a very shameful one. He accoutred his army with every man a trumpet in his right hand, and an earthen pitcher, with a

torch in it, in his left, and he himself thought it no disparagement to him to march before them thus armed. He would make but a jest of conquering this army, and goes out against them rather as against a company of children than against a host of soldiers. *The virgin, the daughter of Zion, hath despised thee,* and *laughed thee to scorn,* Isa. xxxvii. 22. The fewness of his men favoured his design; for, being so few, they marched to the camp with the greater secresy and expedition, so that they were not discovered till they were close by the camp; and he contrived to give the alarm when they had just mounted the guards (*v.* 19), that the sentinels, being then wakeful, might the sooner disperse the alarm through the camp, which was the best service they could do him. Three ways Gideon contrived to strike a terror upon this army, and so put them into confusion. [1.] With a great noise. Every man must blow his trumpet in the most terrible manner he could and clatter an earthen pitcher to pieces at the same time; probably each dashed his pitcher to his next man's, and so they were broken both together, which would not only make a great crash, but was a figure of what would be the effects of the fright, even the Midianites' killing one another. [2.] With a great blaze. The lighted torches were hid in the pitchers, like *a candle under a bushel,* until they came to the camp, and then, being taken out all together of a sudden, would make a glaring show, and run through the camp like a flash of lightning. Perhaps with these they set some of the tents on the outside of the camp on fire, which would very much increase the confusion. [3.] With a great shout. Every man must cry, *For the Lord, and for Gideon,* so some think it should be read in *v.* 18, for there the sword is not in the original, but it is in *v.* 20, *The sword of the Lord, and of Gideon.* It should seem, he borrowed the word from the Midianite's dream (*v.* 14): it is *the sword of Gideon.* Finding his name was a terror to them, he thus improves it against them, but prefixes the name of Jehovah, as the figure without which his own was but an insignificant cypher. This would put life into his own men, who might well take courage when they had such a God as Jehovah, and such a man as Gideon, both to *fight for,* and to *fight for them;* well might those follow who had such leaders. It would likewise put their enemies into a fright, who had of old heard of Jehovah's great name, and of late of Gideon's. The sword of the Lord is all in all to the success of the sword of Gideon, yet the sword of Gideon must be employed. Men the instruments, and God the principal agent, must both be considered in their places, but men, the greatest and best, always in subserviency and subordination to God. This army was to be defeated purely by terrors, and these are especially the *sword of the Lord.* These soldiers, if they had swords by their sides, that was all, they had none in their hands, but they gained the victory by shouting "The sword." So the church's enemies are routed by *a sword out of the mouth,* Rev. xix. 21.

2. This method here taken of defeating the Midianites may be alluded to, (1.) As typifying the destruction of the devil's kingdom in the world by the preaching of the everlasting gospel, the sounding of that trumpet, and the holding forth of that light out of earthen vessels, for such the ministers of the gospel are, in whom the treasure of that light is deposited, 2 Cor. iv. 6, 7. Thus God chose the *foolish things of the world to confound the wise,* a barley-cake to overthrow the tents of Midian, that the *excellency of the power might be of God only;* the gospel is a sword, not in the hand, but in the mouth, the sword *of the Lord and of Gideon,* of God and Jesus Christ, him that sits on the throne and the Lamb. (2.) As representing the terrors of the great day. So the excellent bishop Hall applies it; if these pitchers, trumpets, and firebrands, did so daunt and dismay the proud troops of Midian and Amalek, who shall be able to stand before the last terror, when the trumpet of the archangel shall sound, the elements shall be on a flame, the heavens pass away with a great noise, and the Lord himself shall descend with a shout!

II. The wonderful success of this alarm. The Midianites were shouted out of their lives, as the walls of Jericho were shouted down, that Gideon might see what he lately despaired of ever seeing, the *wonders that their fathers told them of.* Gideon's soldiers observed their orders, and *stood every man in his place round about the camp* (*v.* 21), sounding his trumpet to excite them to fight one another, and holding out his torch to light them to their ruin. They did not rush into the host of Midian, as greedy either of blood or spoil, but patiently stood still to *see the salvation of the Lord,* a salvation purely of his own working. Observe how the design took effect. 1. They feared the Israelites. *All the host* immediately took the alarm; it flew like lightning through all their lines, and *they ran, and cried, and fled, v.* 21. There was something natural in this fright. We may suppose they had not had intelligence of the great diminution of Gideon's army, but rather concluded that since their last advices it had been growing greater and greater; and therefore they had reason to suspect, knowing how odious and grievous they had made themselves and what bold steps had been taken towards the throwing off of their yoke, that it was a very great army which was to be ushered in with all those trumpeters and torch-bearers. But there was more of a supernatural power impressing this terror upon them. God himself gave it the setting on, to show how that promise should have been fulfilled if they had not forfeited it, *One of you shall chase a thousand.* See the power of imagination, and how much it may become a terror at some times, as at other times it is a pleasure. 2. They fell foul upon one another: *The Lord set every man's sword against his fellow, v.* 22. In this confusion, observing the trumpeters and torch-bearers to stand still without their camp, they concluded the body of the army had already entered and was in the midst of them, and therefore every one ran at the next he met, though a friend, supposing him an enemy, and one such mistake as this would occasion many, for then he that slew him would certainly be taken for an enemy, and would be dispatched immediately. It is our interest to preserve such a command of our own spirits as never to *be afraid with any amazement,* for we cannot conceive what mischiefs we thereby plunge ourselves into. See also how God often makes the enemies of his church instruments to destroy one another; it is a pity the church's friends should ever be thus infatuated. 3. They fled for their lives. Perhaps when day-light came they were sensible of their mistake in fighting with one another, and concluded that by this fatal error they had so weakened themselves that now it was impossible to make any head against Israel, and therefore made the best of their way towards their own country, though, for aught that appears, the 300 men kept their ground. *The wicked flee when none pursueth,* Prov. xxviii. 1. *Terrors make him afraid on every side, and drive him to his feet,* Job xviii. 11.

23 And the men of Israel gathered themselves together out of Naphtali, and out of Asher, and out of all Manasseh, and pursued after the Midianites. 24 And Gideon sent messengers throughout all mount Ephraim, saying, Come down against the Midianites, and take before them the waters unto Beth-barah and Jordan. Then all the men of Ephraim gathered themselves together, and took the waters unto Beth-barah and Jordan. 25 And they took two princes of the Midianites, Oreb and Zeeb; and they slew Oreb upon the rock Oreb, and Zeeb they slew at the winepress of Zeeb, and pursued Midian, and brought the heads of Oreb and Zeeb to Gideon on the other side Jordan.

We have here the prosecution of this glorious victory. 1. Gideon's soldiers that had been dismissed, and perhaps had begun to disperse themselves, upon notice of the enemies' flight got together again, and vigorously pursued those whom they had not courage to face The men of Israel out of Naphtali and Asher who did this (*v.* 23) were not such as now came from those distant countries, but the same that had enlisted themselves (*ch.* vi. 35), but had been cashiered. Those who were fearful and afraid to fight (*v.* 3) now took heart, when the worst was over, and were ready enough to divide the spoil, though backward to make the onset. Those also that might not fight though they had a mind to it, and were disbanded by order from God, did not as those, 2 Chron. xxv. 10, 13, *return in great anger,* but waited for an opportunity of doing service in pursuing the victory, though they were denied the honour of helping to force the lines. 2. The Ephraimites, upon a summons from Gideon, came in unanimously, and secured the passes over Jordan, by the several fords, to cut off the enemies' retreat into their own country, that they might be entirely destroyed, to prevent the like mischief to Israel another time. Now that they had begun to fall, it was easy to say, Down with them, Esth. vi. 13. They *took the waters* (*v.* 24), that is, posted themselves along the river side, so that the Midianites, who fled from those who pursued them, fell into the hands of those that waited to intercept them. Here were *fear, and the pit, and the snare,* Isa. xxiv. 17. 3. Two of the chief commanders of the host of Midian were taken and slain by the Ephraimites on this side Jordan, *v.* 25. Their names perhaps signified their nature, *Oreb* signifies a *raven,* and *Zeeb* a *wolf (corvus* and *lupus).* These in their flight had taken shelter, one *in a rock* (Isa. ii. 21; Rev. vi. 15), the other by a *wine-press,* as Gideon for fear of them had lately hid his corn by a wine-press, *ch.* vi. 11. But the places of their shelter were made the places of their slaughter, and the memory of it was preserved to posterity in the names of the places, to their perpetual infamy: *Here fell the princes of Midian.*

CHAP. VIII.

This chapter gives us a further account of Gideon's victory over the Midianites, with the residue of the story of his life and government. I. Gideon prudently pacifies the offended Ephraimites, ver. 1—3. II. He bravely pursues the flying Midianites, ver. 4, 10—12. III. He justly chastises the insolence of the men of Succoth and Penuel, who basely abused him (ver. 5—9), and were reckoned with for it, ver. 13—17. IV. He honourably slays the two kings of Midian, ver. 18—21. V. After all this he modestly declines the government of Israel, ver. 22, 23. VI. He foolishly gratified the superstitious humour of his people, by setting up an ephod in his own city, which proved a great snare, ver. 24—27. VII. He kept the country quiet for forty years, ver. 28. VIII. He died in honour, and left a numerous family behind him, ver. 29—32. IX. Both he and his God were soon forgotten by ungrateful Israel, ver. 33—35.

AND the men of Ephraim said unto him, Why hast thou served us thus, that thou calledst us not, when thou wentest to fight with the Midianites? And they did chide with him sharply. 2 And he said unto them, What have I done now in comparison of you? *Is* not the gleaning of the grapes of Ephraim better than the vintage of Abi-ezer? 3 God

hath delivered into your hands the princes of Midian, Oreb and Zeeb: and what was I able to do in comparison of you? Then their anger was abated toward him, when he had said that.

No sooner were the Midianites, the common enemy, subdued, than, through the violence of some hot spirits, the children of Israel were ready to quarrel among themselves; an unhappy spark was struck, which, if Gideon had not with a great deal of wisdom and grace extinguished immediately, might have broken out into a flame of fatal consequence. The Ephraimites, when they brought the heads of Oreb and Zeeb to Gideon as general, instead of congratulating him upon his successes and addressing him with thanks for his great services, as they ought to have done, picked a quarrel with him and grew very hot upon it.

I. Their accusation was very peevish and unreasonable: *Why didst thou not call us when thou wentest to fight with the Midianites? v.* 1. Ephraim was brother to Manasseh, Gideon's tribe, and had the pre-eminence in Jacob's blessing and in Moses's, and therefore was very jealous of Manasseh, lest that tribe should at any time eclipse the honour of theirs. Hence we find Manasseh against Ephraim and Ephraim against Manasseh, Isa. ix. 21. *A brother offended is harder to be won than a strong city, and their contentions are as the bars of a castle,* Prov. xviii. 19. But how unjust was their quarrel with Gideon! They were angry that he did not send for them to begin the attack upon Midian, as well as to follow the blow. Why were they not called to lead the van? The post of honour, they thought, belonged to them. But, 1. Gideon was called of God, and must act as he directed; he neither took the honour to himself nor did he himself dispose of honours, but left it to God to do all. So that the Ephraimites, in this quarrel, reflected upon the divine conduct; and what was Gideon that they *murmured against him?* 2. Why did not the Ephraimites offer themselves willingly to the service? They knew the enemy was in their country, and had heard of the forces that were raising to oppose them, to which they ought to have joined themselves, in zeal for the common cause, though they had not a formal invitation. Those seek themselves more than God that stand upon a point of honour to excuse themselves from doing real service to God and their generation. In Deborah's time there was a root of Ephraim, *ch.* v. 14. Why did not this appear now? The case itself called them, they needed not wait for a call from Gideon. 3. Gideon had saved their credit in not calling them. If he had sent for them, no doubt many of them would have gone back with the faint-hearted, or been dismissed with the lazy, slothful, and intemperate; so that by not calling them he prevented the putting of those slurs upon them. Cowards will seem valiant when the danger is over, but those consult their reputation who try not their courage when danger is near.

II. Gideon's answer was very calm and peaceable, and was intended not so much to justify himself as to please and pacify them, *v.* 2, 3. He answers them, 1. With a great deal of meekness and temper. He did not resent the affront, nor answer anger with anger, but mildly reasoned the case with them, and he won as true honour by this command which he had over his own passion as by his victory over the Midianites. *He that is slow to anger is better than the mighty.* 2. With a great deal of modesty and humility, magnifying their performances above his own: *Is not the gleaning of the grapes of Ephraim,* who picked up the stragglers of the enemy, and cut off those of them that escaped, *better than the vintage of Abiezer*—a greater honour to them, and better service to the country, than the first attack Gideon made upon them? The destruction of the church's enemies is compared to a vintage, Rev. xiv. 18. In this he owns their gleanings better than his gatherings. The improving of a victory is often more honourable, and of greater consequence, than the winning of it; in this they had signalized themselves, and their own courage and conduct, or, rather, God had dignified them; for though, to magnify their achievements, he is willing to diminish his own performances, yet he will not take any flowers from God's crown to adorn theirs with: "*God has delivered into your hands the princes of Midian,* and a great slaughter has been made of the enemy by your numerous hosts, and *what was I able to do* with 300 men, *in comparison of you* and your brave exploits?" Gideon stands here a very great example of self-denial, and this instance shows us, (1.) That humility of deportment is the best way to remove envy. It is true even right works are often envied, Eccl. iv. 4. Yet they are not so apt to be so when those who do them appear not to be proud of them. Those are malignant indeed who seek to cast down from their excellency those that humble and abase themselves. (2.) It is likewise the surest method of ending strife, for *only by pride comes contention,* Prov. xiii. 10. (3.) Humility is most amiable and admirable in the midst of great attainments and advancements. Gideon's conquests did greatly set off his condescensions. (4.) It is the proper act of humility to *esteem others better than ourselves,* and *in honour to prefer one another.*

Now what was the issue of this controversy? The Ephraimites had *chidden with him sharply* (*v.* 1), forgetting the respect due to their general and one whom God had honoured, and giving vent to their passion in a very indecent liberty of speech, a certain sign of a weak and indefensible cause. Reason runs low when the chiding flies high. But Gideon's *soft answer turned away their wrath,* Prov. xv. 1. *Their anger was abated towards him, v.* 3. It is intimated that they retained some resentment, but he prudently overlooked it and let it cool by degrees. Very great and good men must expect to have their patience tried by the unkindnesses and follies even of those they serve and must not think it strange.

4 And Gideon came to Jordan, *and* passed over, he, and the three hundred men that *were* with him, faint, yet pursuing *them.* 5 And he said unto the men of Succoth, Give, I pray you, loaves of bread unto the people that follow me; for they *be* faint, and I am pursuing after Zebah and Zalmunna, kings of Midian. 6 And the princes of Succoth said, *Are* the hands of Zebah and Zalmunna now in thine hand, that we should give bread unto thine army? 7 And Gideon said, Therefore when the LORD hath delivered Zebah and Zalmunna into mine hand, then I will tear your flesh with the thorns of the wilderness and with briers. 8 And he went up thence to Penuel, and spake unto them likewise: and the men of Penuel answered him as the men of Succoth had answered *him.* 9 And he spake also unto the men of Penuel, saying, When I come again in peace, I will break down this tower. 10 Now Zebah and Zalmunna *were* in Karkor, and their hosts with them, about fifteen thousand *men,* all that were left of all the hosts of the children of the east: for there fell a hundred and twenty thousand men that drew sword. 11 And Gideon went up by the way of them that dwelt in tents on the east of Nobah and Jogbehah, and smote the host: for the host was secure. 12 And when Zebah and Zalmunna fled, he pursued after them, and took the two kings of Midian, Zebah and Zalmunna, and discomfited all the host. 13 And Gideon the son of Joash returned from battle before the sun *was up,* 14 And caught a young man of the men of Succoth, and enquired of him: and he described unto him the princes of Succoth, and the elders thereof, *even* threescore and seventeen men. 15 And he came unto the men of Succoth, and said, Behold Zebah and Zalmunna, with whom ye did upbraid me, saying, *Are* the hands of Zebah and Zalmunna now in thine hand, that we should give bread unto thy men *that are* weary? 16 And he took the elders of the city, and thorns of the wilderness and briers, and with them he taught the men of Succoth. 17 And he beat down the tower of Penuel, and slew the men of the city.

In these verses we have,

I. Gideon, as a valiant general, pursuing the remaining Midianites, and bravely following his blow. A very great slaughter was made of the enemy at first: 120,000 *men that drew the sword, v.* 10. Such a terrible execution did they make among themselves, and so easy a prey were they to Israel. But, it seems, the two kings of Midian, being better provided than the rest for an escape, with 15,000 men got over Jordan before the passes could be secured by the Ephraimites, and made towards their own country. Gideon thinks he does not fully execute his commission to save Israel if he let them escape. He is not content to chase them out of the country, but he will *chase them out of the world,* Job xviii. 18. This resolution is here pushed on with great firmness, and crowned with great success.

1. His firmness was very exemplary. He effected his purpose under the greatest disadvantages and discouragements that could be. (1.) He took none with him but his 300 men, who now laid aside their trumpets and torches, and betook themselves to their swords and spears. God had said, *By these* 300 *men will I save you* (*ch.* vii. 7); and, confiding in that promise, Gideon kept to them only, *v.* 4. He expected more from 300 men, supported by a particular promise, than from so many thousands supported only by their own valour. (2.) They were *faint, and yet pursuing,* much fatigued with what they had done, and yet eager to do more against the enemies of their country. Our spiritual warfare must thus be prosecuted with what strength we have, though we have but little; it is many a time the true Christian's case, fainting and yet pursuing. (3.) Though he met with discouragement from those of his own people, was jeered for what he was doing, as going about what he could never accomplish, yet he went on with it. If those that should be our helpers in the way of our duty prove hindrances to us, let not this drive us off from it. Those know not how to value God's acceptance that know not how to despise the reproaches and contempts of men. (4.) He

made a very long march by *the way of those that dwelt in tents* (*v.* 11), either because he hoped to find them kinder to him than the men of Succoth and Penuel, that dwelt in walled towns (sometimes there is more generosity and charity found in country tents than in city palaces), or because that was a road in which he would be least expected, and therefore that way it would be the greater surprise to them. It is evident he spared no pains to complete his victory. Now he found it an advantage to have his 300 men such as could bear hunger, and thirst, and toil. It should seem, he set upon the enemy by night, as he had done before, for *the host was secure.* The security of sinners often proves their ruin, and dangers are most fatal when least feared.

2. His success was very encouraging to resolution and industry in a good cause. He routed the army (*v.* 11), and took the two kings prisoners, *v.* 12. Note, The fear of the wicked shall come upon him. Those that think to run *from the sword of the Lord and of Gideon* do but run *upon* it. If he *flee from the iron weapon,* yet *the bow of steel shall strike him through;* for *evil pursueth sinners.*

II. Here is Gideon, as a righteous judge, chastising the insolence of the disaffected Israelites, the men of Succoth and the men of Penuel, both in the tribe of Gad, on the other side Jordan.

1. Their crime was great. Gideon, with a handful of feeble folk was pursuing the common enemy, to complete the deliverance of Israel. His way led him through the city of Succoth first and afterwards of Penuel. He expected not that the magistrates should meet him in their formalities, congratulate him upon his victory, present him with the keys of their city, and give him a treat, much less that they should send forces in to his assistance, though he was entitled to all this; but he only begs some necessary food for his soldiers that were ready to faint for want, and he does it very humbly and importunately: *Give, I pray you, loaves of bread unto the people that follow me, v.* 5. The request would have been reasonable if they had been but poor travellers in distress; but considering that they were soldiers, *called, and chosen, and faithful* (Rev. xvii.14), men whom God had greatly honoured and to whom Israel was highly obliged, who had done great service to their country and were now doing more,—that they were conquerors, and had power to put them under contribution,—and that they were fighting God's battles and Israel's,—nothing could be more just than that their brethren should furnish them with the best provisions their city afforded. But the princes of Succoth neither *feared God nor regarded man.* For, (1.) In contempt of God, they refused to answer the just demands of him whom God had raised up to save them, affronted him, bantered him, despised the success he had already been honoured with, despaired of the success of his present undertaking, did what they could to discourage him in prosecuting the war, and were very willing to believe that the remaining forces of Midian, which they had now seen march through their country, would be too hard for him: *Are the hands of Zebah and Zalmunna now in thy hand?* "No, nor ever will be," so they conclude, judging by the disproportion of numbers. (2.) The bowels of their compassion were shut up against their brethren; they were as destitute of love as they were of faith, would not give morsels of bread (so some read it) to those that were ready to perish. Were these princes? were these Israelites? unworthy either title, base and degenerate men! Surely they were worshippers of Baal, or in the interests of Midian. The men of Penuel gave the same answer to the same request, defying *the sword of the Lord and of Gideon, v.* 8.

2. The warning he gave them of the punishment of their crime was very fair. (1.) He did not punish it immediately, because he would not lose so much time from the pursuit of the enemy that were flying from him, because he would not seem to do it in a heat of passion, and because he would do it more to their shame and confusion when he had completed his undertaking, which they thought impracticable. But, (2.) He told them how he would punish it (*v.* 7, 9), to show the confidence he had of success in the strength of God, and that, if they had the least grain of grace and consideration left, they might upon second thoughts repent of their folly, humble themselves, and contrive how to atone for it, by sending after him succours and supplies, which if they had done, no doubt, Gideon would have pardoned them. God gives notice of danger, and space to repent, that sinners may *flee from the wrath to come.*

3. The warning being slighted, the punishment, though very severe, was really very just. (1.) The princes of Succoth were first made examples. Gideon got intelligence of their number, seventy-seven men, their names, and places of abode, which were described in writing to him, *v.* 14. And, to their great surprise, when they thought he had scarcely overtaken the Midianites, he returned a conqueror. His 300 men were now the ministers of his justice; they secured all these princes, and brought them before Gideon, who showed them his royal captives in chains. "These are the men you thought me an unequal match for, and would give me no assistance in the pursuit of," *v.* 15. And he punished them with thorns and briers, but, it should seem, not unto death. With these, [1.] He tormented their bodies, either by scourging or by rolling them in the thorns and briers; some way or other he *tore their flesh, v.* 7. Those shall have judgment without mercy that have shown no mercy. Perhaps he observed them to be soft and deli-

cate men, who despised him and his company for their roughness and hardiness, and therefore Gideon thus mortified them for their effeminacy. [2.] He instructed their minds: With these *he taught the men of Succoth*, *v.* 16. The correction he gave them was intended, not for destruction, but wholesome discipline, to make them wiser and better for the future. *He made them know* (so the word is), made them know themselves and their folly, God and their duty, made them know who Gideon was, since they would not know by the success wherewith God had crowned him. Note, Many are taught with the briers and thorns of affliction that would not learn otherwise. God gives *wisdom* by *the rod and reproof*, *chastens* and *teaches*, and by correction *opens the ear to discipline.* Our blessed Saviour, though he was a Son, yet *learnt obedience by the things which he suffered*, Heb. v. 8. Let every *pricking brier*, and *grieving thorn*, especially when it becomes a *thorn in the flesh*, be thus interpreted, thus improved. "By this God designs to teach me; what good lesson shall I learn?"

(2.) The doom of the men of Penuel comes next, and it should seem he used them more severely than the other, for good reason, no doubt, *v.* 17. [1.] He *beat down their tower*, of which they gloried, in which they trusted, perhaps scornfully advising Gideon and his men rather to secure themselves in that than to pursue the Midianites. What men make their pride is justly by its ruin made their shame. [2.] He *slew the men of the city*, not all, perhaps not the elders or princes, but those that had affronted him, and those only. He slew some of the men of the city that were most insolent and abusive, for terror to the rest, and *so he taught the men of Penuel.*

18 Then said he unto Zebah and Zalmunna, What manner of men *were they* whom ye slew at Tabor? And they answered, As thou *art*, so *were* they; each one resembled the children of a king. 19 And he said, They *were* my brethren, *even* the sons of my mother: *as* the LORD liveth, if ye had saved them alive, I would not slay you. 20 And he said unto Jether his firstborn, Up, *and* slay them. But the youth drew not his sword: for he feared, because he *was* yet a youth. 21 Then Zebah and Zalmunna said, Rise thou, and fall upon us: for as the man *is, so is* his strength. And Gideon arose, and slew Zebah and Zalmunna, and took away the ornaments that *were* on their camels' necks.

Judgment began *at the house of God*, in the just correction of the men of Succoth and Penuel, who were Israelites, but it did not end there. The kings of Midian, when they had served to demonstrate Gideon's victories, and grace his triumphs, must now be reckoned with. 1. They are indicted for the murder of Gideon's brethren some time ago at Mount Tabor. When the children of Israel, for fear of the Midianites, made themselves *dens in the mountains* (*ch.* vi. 2), those young men, it is likely, took shelter in that mountain, where they were found by these two kings, and most basely and barbarously slain in cold blood. When he asks them *what manner of men they were* (*v.* 18), it is not because he was uncertain of the thing, or wanted proof of it; he was not so little concerned for his brethren's blood as not to enquire it out before now, nor were these proud tyrants solicitous to conceal it. But he puts that question to them that by their acknowledgment of the more than ordinary comeliness of the persons they slew their crime might appear the more heinous, and consequently their punishment the more righteous. They could not but own that, though they were found in a mean and abject condition, yet they had an unusual greatness and majesty in their countenances, not unlike Gideon himself at this time: they *resembled the children of a king*, born for something great. 2. Being found guilty of this murder by their own confession, Gideon, though he might have put them to death as Israel's judge for the injuries done to that people in general, as Oreb and Zeeb (*ch.* vii. 25), yet chooses rather to put on the character of an *avenger of blood*, as next of kin to the persons slain: *They were my brethren*, *v.* 19. Their other crimes might have been forgiven, at least Gideon would not have slain them himself, let them have answered it to the people; but *the voice of his brethren's blood cries*, cries *to him*, now it is in the power of his hand to avenge it, and therefore there is no remedy—by him must *their blood be shed*, though they were kings. Little did they think to hear of this so long after; but murder seldom goes unpunished even in this life. 3. The execution is done by Gideon himself with his own hand, because he was the *avenger of blood;* he bade his son slay them, for he was a near relation to the persons murdered, and fittest to be his father's substitute and representative, and he would thus train him up to the acts of justice and boldness, *v.* 20. But, (1.) The young man himself desired to be excused; he feared, though they were bound and could make no resistance, *because he was yet a youth*, and not used to such work: courage does not always run in the blood. (2.) The prisoners themselves desired that Gideon would excuse it (*v.* 21), begged that, if they must die, they might die *by his own hand*, which would be somewhat more honourable to them, and more easy; for by his great strength they would sooner be dispatched and rid out of their pain. *As is the man, so is his strength.* Either they mean it of themselves (they were men of such strength as called for a better hand than that young man's to overpower quickly) or of Gideon, "Thou art at thy full strength; he has not yet come to it; therefore be thou the executioner." From those that are grown up to maturity, it is expected that what they do in any service be done with so much the more strength. Gideon dispatched them quickly, and seized the *ornaments that were on their camels' necks, ornaments like the moon,* so it is in the margin, either badges of their royalty or perhaps of their idolatry, for Ashteroth was represented by the moon, as Baal by the sun. With these he took all their other ornaments, as appears *v.* 26, where we find that he did not put them to so good a use as one would have wished. The destruction of these two kings, and that of the two princes (*ch.* vii. 25) is long afterwards pleaded as a precedent in prayer for the ruin of others of the church's enemies, Ps. lxxxiii. 11, *Make their nobles like Oreb and Zeeb, and all their princes as Zebah and Zalmunna,* let them all be cut off in like manner.

22 Then the men of Israel said unto Gideon, Rule thou over us, both thou, and thy son, and thy son's son also: for thou hast delivered us from the hand of Midian. 23 And Gideon said unto them, I will not rule over you, neither shall my son rule over you: the LORD shall rule over you. 24 And Gideon said unto them, I would desire a request of you, that ye would give me every man the earrings of his prey. (For they had golden earrings, because they *were* Ishmaelites.) 25 And they answered, We will willingly give *them.* And they spread a garment, and did cast therein every man the earrings of his prey. 26 And the weight of the golden earrings that he requested was a thousand and seven hundred *shekels* of gold; beside ornaments, and collars, and purple raiment that *was* on the kings of Midian, and beside the chains that *were* about their camels' necks. 27 And Gideon made an ephod thereof, and put it in his city, *even* in Ophrah: and all Israel went thither a whoring after it: which thing became a snare unto Gideon, and to his house. 28 Thus was Midian subdued before the children of Israel, so that they lifted up their heads no more. And the country was in quietness forty years in the days of Gideon.

Here is, I. Gideon's laudable modesty, after his great victory, in refusing the government which the people offered him. 1. It was honest in them to offer it: *Rule thou over us, for thou hast delivered us, v.* 22. They thought it very reasonable that he who had gone through the toils and perils of their deliverance should enjoy the honour and power of commanding them ever afterwards, and very desirable that he who in this great and critical juncture had had such manifest tokens of God's presence with him should ever afterwards preside in their affairs. Let us apply it to the Lord Jesus: he hath delivered us out of the hands of our enemies, our spiritual enemies, the worst and most dangerous, and therefore it is fit he should rule over us; for how can we be better ruled than by one that appears to have so great an interest in heaven and so great a kindness for this earth? We are delivered that we may *serve him without fear,* Luke i. 74, 75. 2. It was honourable in him to refuse it: *I will not rule over you, v.* 23. What he did was with a design to serve them, not to rule them—to make them safe, easy, and happy, not to make himself great or honourable. And, as he was not ambitious of grandeur himself, so he did not covet to entail it upon his family: "*My son shall not rule over you,* either while I live or when I am gone, *but the Lord shall* still *rule over you,* and constitute your judges by the special designation of his own Spirit, as he has done." This intimates, (1.) His modesty, and the mean opinion he had of himself and his own merits. He thought the honour of doing good was recompence enough for all his services, which needed not to be rewarded with the honour of bearing sway. *He that is greatest, let him be your minister.* (2.) His piety, and the great opinion he had of God's government. Perhaps he discerned in the people a dislike of the theocracy, or divine government, a desire of a king like the nations, and thought they availed themselves of his merits as a colourable pretence to move for this change of government. But Gideon would by no means admit it. No good man can be pleased with any honour done to himself which ought to be peculiar to God. *Were you baptized in the name of Paul?* 1 Cor. i. 13.

II. Gideon's irregular zeal to perpetuate the remembrance of this victory by an ephod made of the choicest of the spoils. 1. He asked the men of Israel to give him the earrings of their prey; for such ornaments they stripped the slain of in abundance. These he demanded, either because they were the finest gold, and therefore fittest for a religious use, or because they had had as ear-rings some superstitious signification, which he thought too well of. Aaron called for the ear-rings to make the golden calf of, Exod. xxxii. 2. These Gideon begged *v.* 24. And he had reason enough to think that those who offered him a crown, when he declined it, would not deny him their ear-rings, when he begged them, nor did they, *v.* 25. 2. He himself added the spoil he took from the kings of Midian, which, it should seem, had fallen to his share, *v.* 26. The generals had that part of the prey which was most splendid, the *prey of divers colours, ch.* v. 30. 3. Of this he made an ephod, *v.* 27. It was plausible enough, and might be well intended to preserve a memorial of so divine a victory in the judge's own city. But it was a very unadvised thing to make that memorial to be an ephod, a sacred garment. I would gladly put the best construction that can be upon the actions of good men, and such a one we are sure Gideon was. But we have reason to suspect that this ephod had, as usual, a teraphim annexed to it (Hos iii. 4), and that, having an altar already built by divine appointment (*ch.* vi. 26), which he erroneously imagined he might still use for sacrifice, he intended this for an oracle, to be consulted in doubtful cases. So the learned Dr. Spencer supposes. Each tribe having now very much its government within itself, they were too apt to covet their religion among themselves. We read very little of Shiloh, and the ark there, in all the story of the Judges. Sometimes by divine dispensation, and much oftener by the transgression of men, that law which obliged them to worship only at that one altar seems not to have been so religiously observed as one would have expected, any more than afterwards, when in the reigns even of very good kings *the high places were not taken away*, from which we may infer that that law had a further reach as a type of Christ, by whose mediation alone all our services are accepted. Gideon therefore, through ignorance or inconsideration, sinned in making this ephod, though he had a good intention in it. Shiloh, it is true, was not far off, but it was in Ephraim, and that tribe had lately disobliged him (*v.* 1), which made him perhaps not care to go so often among them as his occasions would lead him to consult the oracle, and therefore he would have one nearer home. However this might be honestly intended, and at first did little hurt, yet in process of time, (1.) *Israel went a whoring after it*, that is, they deserted God's altar and priesthood, being fond of change, and prone to idolatry, and having some excuse for paying respect to this ephod, because so good a man as Gideon had set it up, and by degrees their respect to it grew more and more superstitious. Note, Many are led into false ways by one false step of a good man. The beginning of sin, particularly of idolatry and will-worship, *is as the letting forth of water*, so it has been found in the fatal corruptions of the church of Rome; therefore *leave it off before it be meddled with.* (2.) It became a snare to Gideon himself, abating his zeal for the house of God in his old age, and much more to his house, who were drawn by it into sin, and it proved the ruin of the family.

III. Gideon's happy agency for the repose of Israel, *v.* 28. The Midianites that had been so vexatious gave them no more disturbance. Gideon, though he would not assume the honour and power of a king, governed as a judge, and did all the good offices he could for his people; so that *the country was in quietness forty years.* Hitherto the times of Israel had been reckoned by forties. Othniel judged forty years, Ehud eighty—just two forties, Barak forty, and now Gideon forty, providence so ordering it to bring in mind the forty years of their wandering in the wilderness. *Forty years long was I grieved with this generation.* And see Ezek. iv. 6. After these, Eli ruled forty years (1 Sam. iv. 18), Samuel and Saul forty (Acts xiii. 21), David forty, and Solomon forty. Forty years is about an age.

29 And Jerubbaal the son of Joash went and dwelt in his own house. 30 And Gideon had threescore and ten sons of his body begotten: for he had many wives. 31 And his concubine that *was* in Shechem, she also bare him a son, whose name he called Abimelech. 32 And Gideon the son of Joash died in a good old age, and was buried in the sepulchre of Joash his father, in Ophrah of the Abi-ezrites. 33 And it came to pass, as soon as Gideon was dead, that the children of Israel turned again, and went a whoring after Baalim, and made Baal-berith their god. 34 And the children of Israel remembered not the LORD their God, who had delivered them out of the hands of all their enemies on every side: 35 Neither showed they kindness to the house of Jerubbaal, *namely*, Gideon, according to all the goodness which he had showed unto Israel.

We have here the conclusion of the story of Gideon. 1. He lived privately, *v.* 29. He was not puffed up with his great honours, did not covet a palace or castle to dwell in, but retired to the house he had lived in before his elevation. Thus that brave Roman who was called from the plough upon a sudden occasion to command the army when the action was over returned to his plough again. 2. His family was multiplied. He had many wives (therein he transgressed the law); by them he had seventy sons (*v.* 30,) but by a concubine he had one whom he named *Abimelech* (which signifies, *my father a king),* that proved the ruin of his family, *v.* 31. 3. He died in honour, in a good old age, when he had lived as long as he was capable of serving God and his country; and who would desire to live any longer? And he was *buried in the sepulchre of his fathers.* 4. After his death the people corrupted themselves, and went all to naught. As soon as ever Gideon was dead, who had kept them close to the worship of the God of Israel, they found themselves under no restraint, and then they *went a whoring after Baalim, v.* 33. They went a whoring first after another ephod (*v.* 27), for which irregularity Gideon had himself given them too much occasion, and now they went a whoring after another god. False worships made way for false deities. They now chose a new god (*ch.* v. 8), a god of a new name, *Baal-berith* (a goddess, say some); Berith, some think, was Berytus, the place where the Phœnicians worshipped this idol. The name signifies *the Lord of a covenant.* Perhaps he was so called because his worshippers joined themselves by covenant to him, in imitation of Israel's covenanting with God; for the devil is God's ape. In this revolt of Israel to idolatry they showed, (1.) Great ingratitude to God (*v.* 34): *They remembered not the Lord,* not only who had delivered them into the hands of their enemies, to punish them for their idolatry, but who had also *delivered them out of the hands of their enemies,* to invite them back again into his service; both the judgments and the mercies were forgotten, and the impressions of them lost. (2.) Great ingratitude to Gideon, *v.* 35. A great deal of *goodness he had shown unto Israel,* as a father to his country, for which they ought to have been kind to his family when he was gone, for that is one way by which we ought to show ourselves grateful to our friends and benefactors, and may be returning their kindnesses when they are in their graves. But Israel showed not this kindness to Gideon's family, as we shall find in the next chapter. No wonder if those who forget their God forget their friends.

CHAP. IX.

The apostasy of Israel after the death of Gideon is punished, not as the former apostasies by a foreign invasion, or the oppressions of any neighbouring power, but by intestine broils among themselves, which in this chapter we have the story of; and it is hard to say whether their sin or their misery appears most in it. It is an account of the usurpation and tyranny of Abimelech, who was base son to Gideon; so we must call him, and not more modishly his natural son: he was so unlike him. We are here told, I. How he thrust himself into the government at Shechem, his own city, by subtlety and cruelty, particularly by the murder of all his brethren, ver. 1—6. II. How his doom was read in a parable by Jotham, Gideon's youngest son, ver. 7—21. III. What strifes there were between Abimelech and his friends the Shechemites, ver. 22--41. IV. How this ended in the ruin of the Shechemites (ver. 42—49), and of Abimelech himself, ver. 50—57. Of this meteor, this ignis fatuus of a prince, that was not a protector but a plague to his country, we may say, as once was said of a great tyrant, that he came in like a fox, ruled like a lion, and died like a dog. "For the transgression of a land, such are the princes thereof."

AND Abimelech the son of Jerubbaal went to Shechem unto his mother's brethren, and communed with them, and with all the family of the house of his mother's father, saying, 2 Speak, I pray you, in the ears of all the men of Shechem, Whether *is* better for you, either that all the sons of Jerubbaal, *which are* threescore and ten persons, reign over you, or that one reign over you? remember also that I *am* your bone and your flesh. 3 And his mother's brethren spake of him in the ears of all the men of Shechem all these words: and their hearts inclined to follow Abimelech; for they said, He *is* our brother. 4 And they gave him threescore and ten *pieces* of silver out of the house of Baal-berith, wherewith Abimelech hired vain and light persons, which followed him. 5 And he went unto his father's house at Ophrah, and slew his brethren the sons of Jerubbaal, *being* threescore and ten persons, upon one stone: notwithstanding yet Jotham the youngest son of Jerubbaal was left; for he hid himself. 6 And all the men of Shechem gathered together, and all the house of Millo, and went, and made Abimelech king, by the plain of the pillar that *was* in Shechem.

We are here told by what arts Abimelech got into authority, and made himself great. His mother perhaps had instilled into his mind some towering ambitious thoughts, and the name his father gave him, carrying royalty in it, might help to blow up these sparks; and now that he has buried his father nothing will serve his proud spirit but he will succeed him in the government of Israel, directly contrary to his father's will, for he had declared *no son of his should rule over them.* He had no call from God to this honour as his father had, nor was there any present occasion for a judge to deliver Israel as there was when his father was advanced; but his own ambition must be gratified, and its gratification is all he aims at. Now observe here,

I. How craftily he got his mother's relations into his interests. Shechem was a city in the tribe of Ephraim, of great note. Joshua had held his last assembly there. If that city would but appear for him, and set him up, he thought it would go far in his favour. There he had an interest in the family of which his mother was, and by them he made an interest in the leading men of the city. It does not appear that any of them had an eye to him as a man of merit, who had any thing to recommend him to such a choice, but the motion came first from himself. None would have dreamed of making such a one king, if he had not dreamed of it himself. And see here, 1. How he wheedled them into the choice, *v.* 2, 3. He basely suggested that Gideon having left seventy sons, who made a good figure and had a good interest, they were designing to keep the power which their father had in their hands, and by a joint-influence to reign over Israel. "Now," says he, "you had better have one king than more, than many, than so many. Affairs of state are best managed by a single person," *v.* 2. We have no reason to think that all or any of Gideon's sons had the least intention to reign over Israel (they were of their father's mind, that *the Lord should reign over them,* and they were not called of him), yet this he insinuates to pave the way to his own pretensions. Note, Those who design ill themselves are commonly most apt to suspect that others design ill. As for himself, he only puts them in mind of his relation to them *(verbum sapienti—A word to the wise is sufficient): Remember that I am your bone and your flesh.* The plot took wonderfully. The magistrates of Shechem were pleased to think of their city being a royal city and the metropolis of Israel, and therefore they *inclined to follow him; for they said, "He is our brother,* and his advancement will be our advantage." 2. How he got money from them to bear the charges of his pretensions (*v.* 4): *They gave him seventy pieces of silver;* it is not said what the value of these pieces was; so many shekels are less, and so many talents more, than we can well imagine; therefore it is supposed they were each a pound weight: but they gave this money out of the house of Baal-berith, that is, out of the public treasury, which, out of respect to their idol, they deposited in his temple to be protected by him; or out of the offerings that had been made to that idol, which they hoped would prosper the better in his hands for its having been consecrated to their god. How unfit was he to reign over Israel, because unlikely to defend them, who, instead of restraining and punishing idolatry, thus early made himself a pensioner to an idol! 3. What soldiers he enlisted. He hired into his service vain and light persons, the scum and scoundrels of the country, men of broken fortunes, giddy heads, and profligate lives; none but such would own him, and they were fittest to serve his purpose. Like leader like followers.

II. How cruelly he got his father's sons out of the way.

1. The first thing he did with the rabble he headed was to kill all his brethren at once, publicly and in cold blood, threescore and ten men, one only escaping, all slain upon one stone. See in this bloody tragedy, (1.) The power of ambition what beasts it will turn men into, how it will break through all the ties of natural affection and natural conscience, and sacrifice that which is most sacred, dear, and valuable, to its designs. Strange that ever it should enter into the heart of a man to be so very barbarous! (2.) The peril of honour and high birth. Their being the sons of so great a man as Gideon exposed them thus and made Abimelech jealous of them. We find just the same number of Ahab's sons slain together at Samaria, 2 Kings x. 1, 7. The grand seigniors have seldom thought themselves safe while any of their brethren have been unstrangled. Let none then envy those of high extraction, or complain of their own meanness and obscurity. The lower the safer.

2. Way being thus made for Abimelech's election, the men of Shechem proceeded to choose him king, *v.* 6. God was not consulted whether they should have any king at all, much less who it should be; here is no advising with the priest or with their brethren of any other city or tribe, though it was designed that he should reign over Israel, *v.* 22. But, (1.) The Shechemites, as if they were the people and wisdom must die with them, did all; they aided and abetted him in the murder of his brethren (*v.* 24), and then they *made him king.* The men of Shechem (that is, the great men, the chief magistrates of the city), and the house of Millo (that is, the common-council, the *full house* or *house of fulness,* as the word signifies), those that met in their guildhall (we read often of the house of Millo, or state-house in Jerusalem, or the city of David, 2 Sam. v. 9; 2 Kings xii. 20), these gathered together, not to prosecute and punish Abimelech for this barbarous murder, as they ought to have done, he being one of their citizens, but to *make him king. Pretium sceleris tulit hic diadema—His wickedness was rewarded with a diadem.* What could they promise themselves from a king that laid the foundation of his kingdom in blood? (2.) The rest of the Israelites were so very sottish as to sit by unconcerned. They took no care to give check to this usurpation, to protect the sons of Gideon, or to avenge their death, but tamely submitted to the bloody tyrant, as men who with their religion had lost their reason, and all sense of honour and liberty, justice and gratitude. How vigorously had their fathers appeared to avenge the death of the Levite's concubine, and yet so wretchedly degenerate are they now as not to attempt the avenging of the death of Gideon's sons; it is for this that they are charged with ingratitude (*ch.* viii. 35): *Neither showed they kindness to the house of Jerubbaal.*

7 And when they told *it* to Jotham, he went and stood in the top of mount Gerizim, and lifted up his voice, and cried, and said unto them, Hearken

unto me, ye men of Shechem, that God may hearken unto you. 8 The trees went forth *on a time* to anoint a king over them; and they said unto the olive tree, Reign thou over us. 9 But the olive tree said unto them, Should I leave my fatness, wherewith by me they honour God and man, and go to be promoted over the trees? 10 And the trees said to the fig tree, Come thou, *and* reign over us. 11 But the fig tree said unto them, Should I forsake my sweetness, and my good fruit, and go to be promoted over the trees? 12 Then said the trees unto the vine, Come thou, *and* reign over us. 13 And the vine said unto them, Should I leave my wine, which cheereth God and man, and go to be promoted over the trees? 14 Then said all the trees unto the bramble, Come thou, *and* reign over us. 15 And the bramble said unto the trees, If in truth ye anoint me king over you, *then* come *and* put your trust in my shadow: and if not, let fire come out of the bramble, and devour the cedars of Lebanon. 16 Now therefore, if ye have done truly and sincerely, in that ye have made Abimelech king, and if ye have dealt well with Jerubbaal and his house, and have done unto him according to the deserving of his hands; 17 (For my father fought for you, and adventured his life far, and delivered you out of the hand of Midian: 18 And ye are risen up against my father's house this day, and have slain his sons, threescore and ten persons, upon one stone, and have made Abimelech, the son of his maid-servant, king over the men of Shechem, because he *is* your brother;) 19 If ye then have dealt truly and sincerely with Jerubbaal and with his house this day, *then* rejoice ye in Abimelech, and let him also rejoice in you: 20 But if not, let fire come out from Abimelech, and devour the men of Shechem, and the house of Millo; and let fire come out from the men of Shechem, and from the house of Millo, and devour Abimelech. 21 And Jotham ran away, and fled, and went to Beer, and dwelt there, for fear of Abimelech his brother.

We have here the only testimony that appears to have been borne against the wicked confederacy of Abimelech and the men of Shechem. It was a sign they had provoked God to depart from them that neither any prophet was sent nor any remarkable judgment, to awaken this stupid people, and to stop the progress of this threatening mischief. Only Jotham, the youngest son of Gideon, who by a special providence escaped the common ruin of his family (*v.* 5), dealt plainly with the Shechemites, and his speech, which is here recorded, shows him to have been a man of such great ingenuity and wisdom, and really such an accomplished gentleman, that we cannot but the more lament the fall of Gideon's sons. Jotham did not go about to raise an army out of the other cities of Israel (in which, one would think, he might have made a good interest for his father's sake), to avenge his brethren's death, much less to set up himself in competition with Abimelech, so groundless was the usurper's suggestion that the sons of Gideon aimed at dominion (*v.* 2); but he contents himself with giving a faithful reproof to the Shechemites, and fair warning of the fatal consequences. He got an opportunity of speaking to them from the top of Mount Gerizim, the mount of blessings, at the foot of which probably the Shechemites were, upon some occasion or other, gathered together (Josephus says, solemnizing a festival), and it seems they were willing to hear what he had to say.

I. His preface is very serious: "*Hearken unto me, you men of Shechem, that God may hearken unto you, v.* 7. As ever you hope to obtain God's favour, and to be accepted of him, give me a patient and impartial hearing." Note, Those who expect God to hear their prayers must be willing to hear reason, to hear a faithful reproof, and to hear the complaints and appeals of wronged innocency. If we *turn away our ear from hearing the law, our prayer will be an abomination,* Prov. xxviii. 9.

II. His parable is very ingenious—that when the trees were disposed to choose a king the government was offered to those valuable trees the olive, the fig-tree, and the vine, but they refused it, choosing rather to serve than rule, to do good than bear sway. But the same tender being made to the bramble he accepted it with vain-glorious exultation. The way of instruction by parables is an ancient way, and very useful, especially to give reproofs by.

1. He hereby applauds the generous modesty of Gideon, and the other judges who were before him, and perhaps of the sons of Gideon, who had declined accepting the state and power of kings when they might have had them, and likewise shows that it is in ge-

neral the temper of all wise and good men to decline preferment and to choose rather to be useful than to be great. (1.) There was no occasion at all for the trees to choose a king; they are all the *trees of the Lord which he has planted* (Ps. civ. 16) and which therefore he will protect. Nor was there any occasion for Israel to talk of setting a king over them; for *the Lord was their king.* (2.) When they had it in their thoughts to choose a king they did not offer the government to the stately cedar, or the lofty pine, which are only for show and shade, and not otherwise useful till they are cut down, but to the fruit-trees, the vine and the olive. Those that bear fruit for the public good are justly respected and honoured by all that are wise more than those that affect to make a figure. For a good useful man some *would even dare to die.* (3.) The reason which all these fruit-trees gave for their refusal was much the same. The olive pleads (*v.* 9), *Should I leave my fatness?* And the vine (*v.* 13), *Should I leave my wine,* wherewith both God and man are served and honoured? for oil and wine were used both at God's altars and at men's tables. And *shall I leave my sweetness, saith the fig-tree, and my good fruit* (*v.* 11), *and go to be promoted over the trees?* or, as the margin reads it, *go up and down for the trees?* It is intimated, [1.] That government involves a man in a great deal both of toil and care; he that is promoted over the trees must go up and down for them, and make himself a perfect drudge to business. [2.] That those who are preferred to places of public trust and power must resolve to forego all their private interests and advantages, and sacrifice them to the good of the community. The fig-tree must lose its sweetness, its sweet retirement, sweet repose, and sweet conversation and contemplation, if it go to be *promoted over the trees,* and must undergo a constant fatigue. [3.] That those who are advanced to honour and dignity are in great danger of losing their fatness and fruitfulness. Preferment is apt to make men proud and slothful, and thus spoil their usefulness, with which in a lower sphere they honoured God and man, for which reason those that desire to do good are afraid of being too great.

2. He hereby exposes the ridiculous ambition of Abimelech, whom he compares to the bramble or thistle, *v.* 14. He supposes the trees to make their court to him: *Come thou and reign over us,* perhaps because he knew not that the first motion of Abimelech's preferment came from himself (as we found, *v.* 2), but thought the Shechemites had proposed it to him; however, supposing it so, his folly in accepting it deserved to be chastised. The bramble is a worthless plant, not to be numbered among the trees, useless and fruitless, nay, hurtful and vexatious, scratching and tearing, and doing mischief; it began with the curse, and its end is to be burned. Such a one was Abimelech, and yet chosen to the government *by the trees, by all the trees;* this election seems to have been more unanimous than any of the others. Let us not think it strange if we see *folly set in great dignity* (Eccl. x. 6), and the *vilest men exalted* (Ps. xii. 8), and men blind to their own interest in the choice of their guides. The bramble, being chosen to the government, takes no time to consider whether he should accept it or no, but immediately, as if he had been born and bred to dominion, hectors, and assures them they shall find him as he found them. See what *great swelling words of vanity* he speaks (*v.* 15), what promises he makes to his faithful subjects: *Let them come and trust in my shadow:* a goodly shadow to trust in! How unlike to *the shadow of a great rock in a weary land,* which a good magistrate is compared to! Isa. xxxii. 2. Trust in his shadow!—more likely to be scratched if they came near him—more likely to be injured by him than benefited. Thus men *boast of a false gift.* Yet he threatens with as much confidence as he promises: If you be not faithful, *let fire come out of the bramble* (a very unlikely thing to emit fire) and *devour the cedars of Lebanon*—more likely to catch fire, and be itself devoured.

III. His application is very close and plain. In it, 1. He reminds them of the many good services his father had done for them, *v.* 17. He fought their battles, at the hazard of his own life, and to their unspeakable advantage. It was a shame that they needed to be put in mind of this. 2. He aggravates their unkindness to his father's family. They had not *done to him according to the deserving of his hands*, *v.* 16. Great merits often meet with very ill returns, especially to posterity, when the benefactor is forgotten, as Joseph was among the Egyptians. Gideon had left many sons that were an honour to his name and family, and these they had barbarously murdered; one son he had left that was the blemish of his name and family, for he was *the son of his maid-servant,* whom all that had any respect to Gideon's honour would endeavour to conceal, yet him they made their king. In both they put the utmost contempt imaginable upon Gideon. 3. He leaves it to the event to determine whether they had done well, whereby he lodges the appeal with the divine providence. (1.) If they prospered long in this villany, he would give them leave to say they had done well, *v.* 19. "If your conduct towards the house of Gideon be such as can be justified at any bar of justice, honour, or conscience, much good may it do you with your new king." But, (2.) If they had, as he was sure they had, dealt basely and wickedly in this matter, let them never expect to prosper, *v.* 20. Abimelech and the Shechemites, that had strengthened one another's hands in this villany, would certainly be a plague and ruin one to another. Let none expect to do ill and fare well.

Jotham, having given them this admonition, made a shift to escape with his life, *v.* 21. Either they could not reach him or they were so far convinced that they would not add the guilt of his blood to all the rest. But, for fear of Abimelech, he lived in exile, in some remote obscure place. Those whose extraction and education are ever so high know not to what difficulties and straits they may be reduced.

22 When Abimelech had reigned three years over Israel, 23 Then God sent an evil spirit between Abimelech and the men of Shechem; and the men of Shechem dealt treacherously with Abimelech: 24 That the cruelty *done* to the threescore and ten sons of Jerubbaal might come, and their blood be laid upon Abimelech their brother, which slew them; and upon the men of Shechem, which aided him in the killing of his brethren. 25 And the men of Shechem set liers in wait for him in the top of the mountains, and they robbed all that came along that way by them: and it was told Abimelech. 26 And Gaal the son of Ebed came with his brethren, and went over to Shechem: and the men of Shechem put their confidence in him. 27 And they went out into the fields, and gathered their vineyards, and trode *the grapes*, and made merry, and went into the house of their god, and did eat and drink, and cursed Abimelech. 28 And Gaal the son of Ebed said, Who *is* Abimelech, and who *is* Shechem, that we should serve him? *is* not *he* the son of Jerubbaal? and Zebul his officer? serve the men of Hamor the father of Shechem: for why should we serve him? 29 And would to God this people were under my hand! then would I remove Abimelech. And he said to Abimelech, Increase thine army, and come out. 30 And when Zebul the ruler of the city heard the words of Gaal the son of Ebed, his anger was kindled. 31 And he sent messengers unto Abimelech privily, saying, Behold, Gaal the son of Ebed and his brethren be come to Shechem; and, behold, they fortify the city against thee. 32 Now therefore up by night, thou and the people that *is* with thee, and lie in wait in the field: 33 And it shall be, *that* in the morning, as soon as the sun is up, thou shalt rise early, and set upon the city: and, behold, *when* he and the people that *is* with him come out against thee, then mayest thou do to them as thou shalt find occasion. 34 And Abimelech rose up, and all the people that *were* with him, by night, and they laid wait against Shechem in four companies. 35 And Gaal the son of Ebed went out, and stood in the entering of the gate of the city: and Abimelech rose up, and the people that *were* with him, from lying in wait. 36 And when Gaal saw the people, he said to Zebul, Behold, there come people down from the top of the mountains. And Zebul said unto him, Thou seest the shadow of the mountains as *if they were* men. 37 And Gaal spake again and said, See there come people down by the middle of the land, and another company come along by the plain of Meonenim. 38 Then said Zebul unto him, Where *is* now thy mouth, wherewith thou saidst, Who *is* Abimelech, that we should serve him? *is* not this the people that thou hast despised? go out, I pray now, and fight with them. 39 And Gaal went out before the men of Shechem, and fought with Abimelech. 40 And Abimelech chased him, and he fled before him, and many were overthrown *and* wounded, *even* unto the entering of the gate. 41 And Abimelech dwelt at Arumah: and Zebul thrust out Gaal and his brethren, that they should not dwell in Shechem. 42 And it came to pass on the morrow, that the people went out into the field; and they told Abimelech. 43 And he took the people, and divided them into three companies, and laid wait in the field, and looked, and, behold, the people *were* come forth out of the city; and he rose up against them, and smote them. 44 And Abimelech, and the company that *was* with him, rushed forward, and stood in the entering of the gate of the city:

and the two *other* companies ran upon all *the people* that *were* in the fields, and slew them. 45 And Abimelech fought against the city all that day; and he took the city, and slew the people that *was* therein, and beat down the city, and sowed it with salt. 46 And when all the men of the tower of Shechem heard *that*, they entered into a hold of the house of the god Berith. 47 And it was told Abimelech, that all the men of the tower of Shechem were gathered together. 48 And Abimelech gat him up to mount Zalmon, he and all the people that *were* with him; and Abimelech took an axe in his hand, and cut down a bough from the trees, and took it, and laid *it* on his shoulder, and said unto the people that *were* with him, What ye have seen me do, make haste, *and* do as I *have done*. 49 And all the people likewise cut down every man his bough, and followed Abimelech, and put *them* to the hold, and set the hold on fire upon them; so that all the men of the tower of Shechem died also, about a thousand men and women.

Three years Abimelech reigned, after a sort, without any disturbance; it is not said, He judged Israel, or did any service at all to his country, but so long he enjoyed the title and dignity of a king; and not only the Shechemites, but many other places, paid him respect. They must have been fond of a king that could please themselves with such a one as this. But the triumphing of the wicked is short. *Within three years, as the years of a hireling, all this glory shall be contemned*, and laid in the dust, Isa. xvi. 14. The ruin of these confederates in wickedness was from the righteous hand of the God to whom vengeance belongs. *He sent an evil spirit between Abimelech and the Shechemites* (*v.* 23), that is, they grew jealous one of another and ill-affected one to another. He slighted those that set him up, and perhaps countenanced other cities which now began to come into his interests more than he did theirs; and then they grew uneasy at his government, blamed his conduct, and quarrelled at his impositions. This was from God. He permitted the devil, that great mischief-maker, to sow discord between them, and he is *an evil spirit*, whom God not only keeps under his check, but sometimes serves his own purposes by. Their own lusts were evil spirits; they are devils in men's own hearts; from them come wars and fightings. These God gave them up to, and so might be said to *send the evil spirits between them.* When men's sin is made their punishment, though God is not the author of the sin, yet the punishment is from him. The quarrel God had with Abimelech and the Shechemites was for the murder of the sons of Gideon (*v.* 24): *That the cruelty done to them might come and their blood be laid* as a burden *upon Abimelech that slew them, and the men of Shechem that helped him.* Note, 1. Sooner or later God will make inquisition for blood, innocent blood, and will return it on the heads of those that shed it, who shall have blood given them to drink, for they are worthy. 2. Accessaries shall be reckoned with, as well as principals, in that and other sins. The Shechemites that countenanced Abimelech's pretensions, aided and abetted him in his bloody project, and avowed the fact by making him king after he had done it, must fall with him, fall by him, and fall first. 3. Those that combine together to do wickedly are justly dashed in pieces one against another. Blood cannot be a lasting cement to any interest.

I. The Shechemites began to affront Abimelech, perhaps they scarcely knew why or wherefore, but they were given to change. 1. They *dealt treacherously with him, v.* 23. It is not said, They repented of their sin in owning him. Had they done so, it would have been laudable to disown him; but they did it only upon some particular pique conceived against him by their pride or envy. Those that set him up were the first that deserted him and endeavoured to dethrone him. It is not strange that those who were ungrateful to Gideon were unfaithful to Abimelech; for what will hold those that will not be held by the obligation of such merits as Gideon's? Note, It is just with God that those who tempt others to be once perfidious should afterwards be themselves betrayed by those whom they have taught to be perfidious. 2. They aimed to seize him when he was at Arumah (*v.* 41), his country-seat. Expecting him to come to town, they *set liers in wait for him* (*v.* 25), who should make him their prisoner whom they had lately made their prince. Those who were thus posted, he not coming, took the opportunity of robbing travellers, which would help to make the people more and more uneasy under Abimelech, when they saw he could not or would not protect them from highway-men. 3. They entertained one Gaal, and set him up as their head in opposition to Abimelech, *v.* 26. This Gaal is said to be the son of *Ebed*, which signifies *a servant*, perhaps denoting the meanness of his extraction. As Abimelech was by the mother's side, so he by the father's, the son of a servant. Here was one bramble contesting with another. We have reason to suspect that this Gaal was a native Canaanite, because he courts the Shechemites into subjection to the men of Hamor, who was the ancient lord of this city in Jacob's time. He was a bold ambitious man, served their purpose admirably well when they were disposed to quarrel with Abimelech, and they also served his purpose; so he went over to them to blow the coals, and they *put their confidence in him.* 4. They did all the despite they could to Abimelech's name, *v.* 27. They made themselves very merry in his absence, as those who were glad he was out of the way, and who, now that they had another to head them, were in hopes to get clear of him; nay, they *went into the house of their god,* to solemnize their feast of in-gathering, and there *they did eat, and drink, and cursed Abimelech,* not only said all the ill they could of him in their table-talk and the song of their drunkards, but wished all the ill they could to him over their sacrifices, praying to their idol to destroy him. They drank healths to his confusion, and with as loud huzzas as ever they had drunk them to his prosperity. That very temple whence they had fetched money to set him up with did they now meet in to curse him and contrive his ruin. Had they deserted their idol-god with their image-king, they might have hoped to prosper; but, while they still cleave to the former, the latter shall cleave to them to their ruin. How should Satan cast out Satan? 5. They pleased themselves with Gaal's vaunted defiance of Abimelech, *v.* 28, 29. They loved to hear that impudent upstart speak scornfully, (1.) Of Abimelech, though calling him in disdain *Shechem,* or *a Shechemite,* he reflected upon their own city. (2.) Of his good father likewise, Gideon: *Is not he the son of Jerubbaal?* So he calls him, perhaps in an impious indignation at his name and memory for throwing down the altar of Baal, turning that to his reproach which was his praise. (3.) Of his prime minister of state, *Zebul his officer, and ruler of the city.* "We may well be ashamed to serve them, and need not be afraid to oppose them." Men of turbulent ambitious spirits thus *despise dominion, and speak evil of dignities.* Gaal aimed not to recover Shechem's liberty, only to change their tyrant: "*O that this people were under my hand!* What I would do! I would challenge Abimelech to try titles for the crown;" and it should seem he desired his friends to send him word that he was ready to dispute it with him whenever he pleased: "*Increase thy army, and come out.* Do thy worst; let the point be determined by the sword." This pleased the Shechemites, who were now as sick of Abimelech as ever they had been fond of him. Men of no conscience will be men of no constancy.

II. Abimelech turned all his force upon them, and, in a little time, quite ruined them. Observe the steps of their overthrow.

1. The Shechemites' counsels were betrayed to Abimelech by Zebul his confidant, the ruler of the city, who continued hearty for him. *His anger was kindled* (*v.* 30), and the more because Gaal had spoken slightly of him (*v.* 28), for perhaps, if he had complimented and caressed him now that things were in this ferment, he might have gained him to his interest; but he, being disobliged, sends notice to Abimelech of all that was said and done in Shechem against him, *v.* 31. Betrayers are often betrayed by some among themselves, and the cursing of the king is sometimes strangely carried by a bird of the air. He prudently advises him to come against the city immediately, and lose no time, *v.* 32, 33. He thinks it best that he should march his forces by night into the neighbourhood, surprise the city in the morning, and then make the best of his advantages. How could the Shechemites hope to speed in their attempt when the ruler of their city was in the interests of their enemy? They knew it, and yet took no care to secure him.

2. Gaal, that headed their faction, having been betrayed by Zebul, Abimelech's confidant, was most wretchedly bantered by him. Abimelech, according to Zebul's advice, drew all his forces down upon Shechem by night, *v.* 34. Gaal, in the morning, went out *to the gate* (*v.* 35) to see what posture things were in, and to enquire, What news? Zebul, as a ruler of the city, met him there as a friend. Abimelech and his forces beginning to move towards the city, Gaal discovers them (*v.* 36), takes notice of their approach to Zebul that was standing with him, little thinking that he had sent for them and was now expecting them. "Look," says he, "do not I see a body of men coming down from the mountain towards us? Yonder they are," pointing to the place. "No, no," says Zebul; "thy eye-sight deceives thee; it is but *the shadow of the mountains* which thou takest to be an army." By this he intended, (1.) To ridicule him, as a man of no sense or spirit, and therefore very unfit for what he pretended to, as a man that might easily be imposed upon and made to believe any thing, and that was so silly and so cowardly that he apprehended danger where there was none, and was ready to fight with a shadow. (2.) To detain him, and hold him in talk, while the forces of Abimelech were coming up, that thereby they might gain advantage. But when Gaal, being content to believe those he now saw to be but the shadow of the mountains (perhaps the mountains of Ebal and Gerizim, which lay close by the city), was undeceived by the discovery of two other companies that marched apace towards the city, then Zebul took another way to banter him, upbraiding him with what he had said but a day or two before, in contempt of Abimelech (*v.* 38): *Where is now thy mouth,* that foul mouth of thine, *wherewith thou saidst, Who is Abimelech?* Note, Proud and haughty people are often made in a little time to change their note, and to dread those whom they had

most despised. Gaal had, in a bravado, challenged Abimelech to *increase his army and come out;* but now Zebul, in Abimelech's name, challenges him: *Go out, and fight with them,* if thou darest. Justly are the insolent thus insulted over.

3. Abimelech routed Gaal's forces that sallied out of the town, *v.* 39, 40. Gaal, disheartened no doubt by Zebul's hectoring him, and perceiving his interest weaker than he thought it was, though he marched out against Abimelech with what little force he had, was soon put to the worst, and obliged to retire into the city with great precipitation. In this action the Shechemites' loss was considerable: *Many were overthrown and wounded,* the common effect of popular tumults, in which the inconsiderate multitude are often drawn into fatal snares by those that promise them glorious success.

4. Zebul that night expelled Gaal, and the party he had brought with him into Shechem, out of the city (*v.* 41), sending him to the place whence he came. For though the generality of the city continued still averse to Abimelech, as appears by the sequel of the story, yet they were willing to part with Gaal, and did not oppose his expulsion, because, though he had talked big, both his skill and courage had failed him when there was occasion for them. Most people judge of men's fitness for business by their success, and he that does not speed well is concluded not to do well. Well, Gaal's interest in Shechem is soon at an end, and he that had talked of removing Abimelech is himself removed, nor do we ever hear of him any more. *Exit Gaal—Gaal retires.*

5. Abimelech, the next day, set upon the city, and quite destroyed it, for their treacherous dealings with him. Perhaps Abimelech had notice of their expelling Gaal, who had headed the faction, with which they thought he would have been satisfied, but the crime was too deep to be thus atoned for, and his resentments were too keen to be pacified by so small an instance of submission, besides that it was more Zebul's act than theirs; by it their hands were weakened, and therefore he resolved to follow his blow, and effectually to chastise their treachery. (1.) He had intelligence brought him that the people of Shechem had come out *into the field, v.* 42. Some think into the field of business to plough and sow (having lately gathered in their harvest), or to perfect their harvest, for it was only their vintage that they had made an end of (*v.* 27), and then it intimates that they were secure. And because Abimelech had retired (*v.* 41) they thought themselves in no danger from him, and then the issue of it is an instance of sudden destruction coming upon those that cry, Peace and safety. Others think they went out into the field of battle; though Gaal was driven out, they would not lay down their arms, but put themselves into a posture for another engagement with Abimelech, in which they hoped to retrieve what they had lost the day before. (2.) He himself, with a strong detachment, cut off the communication between them and the city, *stood in the entering of the gate* (*v.* 44), that they might neither make their retreat into the city nor receive any succours from the city, and then sent two companies of his men, who were too strong for them, and they put them all to the sword, *ran upon those that were in the fields and slew them.* When we go out about our business we are not sure that we shall come home again; there are deaths both in the city and in the field. (3.) He then fell upon the city itself, and, with a rage reaching up to heaven, though it was the place of his nativity, laid it in ruins, slew all the people, beat down all the buildings, and, in token of his desire that it might be a perpetual desolation, sowed it with salt, that it might remain a lasting monument of the punishment of perfidiousness. Yet Abimelech prevailed not to make its desolations perpetual; for it was afterwards rebuilt, and became so considerable a place that all Israel came thither to make Rehoboam king, 1 Kings xii. 1. And the place proved an ill omen. Abimelech intended hereby to punish the Shechemites for their slighting him now, but God intended to punish them for their serving him formerly in the murder of Gideon's sons. Thus, when God makes use of men as instruments in his hand to do his work, he means one thing and they another, Isa. x. 6, 7. They design to maintain their honour, but God to maintain his.

6. Those that retired into a strong-hold of their idol-temple were all destroyed there. These are called *the men of the tower of Shechem* (*v.* 46, 47), some castle that belonged to the city, but lay at some distance from it. They, hearing of the destruction of the city, withdrew into a hold of the temple, trusting, it is likely, not so much to its strength as to its sanctity; they put themselves under the protection of their idol: for thus *all people will walk in the name of their god,* and shall not we then choose to dwell in the house of the Lord all the days of our life? For *in the time of trouble he shall hide us in his pavilion,* Ps. xxvii. 5. The *name of the Lord is a strong tower,* Prov. xviii. 10. But that which they hoped would be for their welfare proved to them a snare and a trap, as those will certainly find that run to idols for shelter; it will prove a refuge of lies. When Abimelech had them altogether penned up in that hold he desired no more. That barbarous project immediately came into his head of setting fire to the strong-hold, and, so to speak, burning all the birds together in the nest. He kept the design to himself, but set all his men on work to expedite the execution of it, *v.* 48, 49. He ordered them all to follow him, and do as he did: as his father had said to his men (*ch.* vii. 17), *Look on me, and do likewise;* so saith he to his, as becomes a

general that will not be wanting to give both the plainest direction and the highest encouragement that can be to his soldiers: *What you have seen me do make haste to do, as I have done.* Not *Ite illuc—Go thither;* but *Venite huc—Come hither*. The officers in Christ's army should thus teach by their example, Phil. iv. 9. He and they fetched each of them a bough from a wood not far off, laid all their boughs together under the wall of this tower, which it is probable was of wood, set fire to their boughs, and so burnt down their hold and all that were in it, who were either burnt or stifled with the smoke What inventions men have to destroy one another! Whence come these cruel wars and fightings but from their lusts? Some think that the men of the tower of Shechem were the same with the house of Millo, and then Jotham's just imprecation was answered in the letter: *Let fire come out from* Abimelech, and devour not only in general the men of Shechem, but in particular the house of Millo, *v.* 20. About 1000 men and women perished in these flames, many of whom, it is probable, were no way concerned in the quarrel between Abimelech and the Shechemites, nor meddled with either side, yet, in this civil war, they came to this miserable end; for men of factious turbulent spirits *perish not alone in their iniquity*, but involve many more, that follow them in their simplicity, in the same calamity with them.

50 Then went Abimelech to Thebez, and encamped against Thebez, and took it. 51 But there was a strong tower within the city, and thither fled all the men and women, and all they of the city, and shut *it* to them, and gat them up to the top of the tower. 52 And Abimelech came unto the tower, and fought against it, and went hard unto the door of the tower to burn it with fire. 53 And a certain woman cast a piece of a millstone upon Abimelech's head, and all to brake his scull. 54 Then he called hastily unto the young man his armour bearer, and said unto him, Draw thy sword, and slay me, that men say not of me, A woman slew him. And his young man thrust him through, and he died. 55 And when the men of Israel saw that Abimelech was dead, they departed every man unto his place. 56 Thus God rendered the wickedness of Abimelech, which he did unto his father, in slaying his seventy brethren: 57 And all the evil of the men of Shechem did God render upon their heads: and upon them came the curse of Jotham the son of Jerubbaal.

We have seen the ruin of the Shechemites completed by the hand of Abimelech; and now it comes to his turn to be reckoned with who was their leader in villany. Thebez was a small city, probably not far from Shechem, dependent upon it, and in confederacy with it. Now,

I. Abimelech attempted the destruction of this city (*v.* 50), drove all the inhabitants of the town into the castle, or citadel, *v.* 51. When he had them there he did not doubt but he should do the same execution here that he had lately done at the strong-hold of the temple of Baal-berith, not considering that the tower of an idol-temple lay more exposed to divine vengeance than any other tower. He attempted to set fire to this tower, at least to burn down the door, and so force an entrance, *v.* 52. Those who have escaped and succeeded well in one desperate attempt are apt to think the like attempt another time not desperate. This instance was long after quoted to show how dangerous it is to come near the wall of a besieged city, 2 Sam. xi. 20, &c. But God infatuates those whom he will ruin.

II. In the attempt he was himself destroyed, having his brains knocked out with a piece of a millstone, *v.* 57. *No doubt this man was a murderer, whom, though he had escaped* the dangers of the war with Shechem, yet *vengeance suffered not to live,* Acts xxviii. 4. *Evil pursues sinners,* and sometimes overtakes them when they are not only secure, but triumphant. Thebez, we may suppose, was a weak inconsiderable place, compared with Shechem. Abimelech, having conquered the greater, makes no doubt of being master of the less without any difficulty, especially when he had taken the city, and had only the tower to deal with; yet he lays his bones by that, and there is all his honour buried. Thus are the *mighty things of the world* often confounded by the weakest and those things that are most made light of. See here what rebukes those are justly put under many times by the divine providence that are unreasonable in their demands of satisfaction for injuries received. Abimelech had some reason to chastise the Shechemites, and he had done it with a witness; but when he will carry his revenges further, and nothing will serve but that Thebez also must be sacrificed to his rage, he is not only disappointed there, but destroyed; *for verily there is a God that judges in the earth.* Three circumstances are worthy of observation in the death of Abimelech:—1. That he was slain with a stone, as he had slain his brethren all *upon one stone.* 2. That he had his skull broken. Vengeance aimed at that guilty head which had worn the usurped crown. 3. That the stone was cast upon him by a woman, *v.* 53. He saw the stone come;

it was therefore strange he did not avoid it, but, no doubt, this made it so much the greater mortification to him to see from what hand it came. Sisera died by a woman's hand and knew it not; but Abimelech not only fell by the hand of a woman but knew it, and, when he found himself ready to breathe his last, nothing troubled him so much as this, that it should be said, A woman slew him. See, (1.) His foolish pride, in laying so much to heart this little circumstance of his disgrace. Here was no care taken about his precious soul, no concern what would become of that, no prayer to God for his mercy; but very solicitous he is to patch up his shattered credit, when there is no patching his shattered skull. "O let it never be said that such a mighty man as Abimelech was killed by a woman!" The man was dying, but his pride was alive and strong, and the same vain-glorious humour that had governed him all along appears now at last. *Qualis vita, finis ita—As was his life, such was his death.* As God punished his cruelty by the manner of his death, so he punished his pride by the instrument of it. (2.) His foolish project to avoid this disgrace; nothing could be more ridiculous; his own servant must run him through, not to rid him the sooner out of his pain, but *that men say not, A woman slew him.* Could he think that this would conceal what the woman had done, and not rather proclaim it the more? Nay, it added to the infamy of his death, for hereby he became a self-murderer. Better have it said, *A woman slew him,* than that it should be said, His servant slew him by his own order; yet now both will be said of him to his everlasting reproach. And it is observable that this very thing which Abimelech was in such care to conceal appears to have been more particularly remembered by posterity than most passages of his history; for Joab speaks of it as that which he expected David would reproach him with, for coming so *nigh the wall,* 2 Sam. xi. 21. The ignominy we seek to avoid by sin we do but perpetuate the remembrance of.

III. The issue of all is that Abimelech being slain, 1. Israel's peace was restored, and an end was put to this civil war; for those that followed him *departed every man to his place, v.* 55. 2. God's justice was glorified (*v.* 56, 57): *Thus God* punished *the wickedness of Abimelech, and of the men of Shechem,* and fulfilled Jotham's curse, for it was not a *curse causeless.* Thus he preserved the honour of his government, and gave warning to all ages to expect blood for blood. *The Lord is known by the judgments which he executes,* when *the wicked is snared in the work of his own hands.* Though wickedness may prosper awhile, it will not prosper always.

CHAP. X.

In this chapter we have, I. The peaceable times Israel enjoyed under the government of two judges, Tola and Jair, ver. 1—5. II. The troublesome times that ensued. 1. Israel's sin that brought them into trouble, ver. 6. 2. The trouble itself they were in, ver. 7—9. III. Their repentance and humiliation for sin, their prayers and reformation, and the mercy they found with God thereupon, ver. 10—16. IV. Preparation made for their deliverance out of the hand of their oppressors, ver. 17, 18.

AND after Abimelech there arose to defend Israel Tola the son of Puah, the son of Dodo, a man of Issachar; and he dwelt in Shamir in mount Ephraim. 2 And he judged Israel twenty and three years, and died, and was buried in Shamir. 3 And after him arose Jair, a Gileadite, and judged Israel twenty and two years. 4 And he had thirty sons that rode on thirty ass colts, and they had thirty cities, which are called Havoth-jair unto this day, which *are* in the land of Gilead. 5 And Jair died, and was buried in Camon.

Quiet and peaceable reigns, though the best to live in, are the worst to write of, as yielding least variety of matter for the historian to entertain his reader with; such were the reigns of these two judges, Tola and Jair, who make but a small figure and take up but a very little room in this history. But no doubt they were both *raised up of God* to serve their country in the quality of judges, not pretending, as Abimelech had done, to the grandeur of kings, nor, like him, taking the honour they had to themselves, but being called of God to it. 1. Concerning Tola it is said that he arose after Abimelech to defend Israel, *v.* 1. After Abimelech had debauched Israel by his wickedness, disquieted and disturbed them by his restless ambition, and, by the mischiefs he brought on them, exposed them to enemies from abroad, God animated this good man to appear for the reforming of abuses, the putting down of idolatry, the appeasing of tumults, and the healing of the wounds given to the state by Abimelech's usurpation. Thus he saved them from themselves, and guarded them against their enemies. He was of the tribe of Issachar, a tribe disposed to serve, for he *bowed his shoulder to bear* (Gen. xlix. 14, 15), yet one of that tribe is here raised up to rule; for those that humble themselves shall be exalted. He bore the name of him that was ancestor to the first family of that tribe; of the sons of Issachar Tola was the first, Gen. xlvi. 13; Num. xxvi. 23. It signifies a *worm,* yet, being the name of his ancestor, he was not ashamed of it. Though he was of Issachar, yet, when he was raised up to the government, he came and dwelt in Mount Ephraim, which was more in the heart of the country, that the people might the more conveniently resort to him for judgment. He judged Israel twenty-three years (*v.* 2), kept things in good order, but did not any thing very memorable. 2. Jair was a Gileadite, so was his next successor

Jephthah, both of that half tribe of the tribe of Manasseh which lay on the other side Jordan; though they seemed separated from their brethren, yet God took care, while the honour of the government was shifted from tribe to tribe and before it settled in Judah, that those who lay remote should sometimes share in it, *putting more abundant honour on that part which lacked.* Jair bore the name of a very famous man of the same tribe who in Moses's time was very active in reducing this country, Num. xxxii. 41; Josh. xiii. 30. That which is chiefly remarkable concerning this Jair is the increase and honour of his family: *He had thirty sons, v.* 4. And, (1.) They had good preferments, for they *rode on thirty ass colts;* that is, they were judges itinerant, who, as deputies to their father, rode from place to place in their several circuits to administer justice. We find afterwards that Samuel made his sons judges, though he could not make them good ones, 1 Sam. viii. 1—3. (2.) They had good possessions, every one a city, out of those that were called, from their ancestor of the same name with their father, *Havoth-jair—the villages of Jair;* yet they are called *cities,* either because those young gentlemen to whom they were assigned enlarged and fortified them, and so improved them into cities, or because they were as well pleased with their lot in those country towns as if they had been cities compact together and fenced with gates and bars. Villages are cities to a contented mind.

6 And the children of Israel did evil again in the sight of the LORD, and served Baalim, and Ashtaroth, and the gods of Syria, and the gods of Zidon, and the gods of Moab, and the gods of the children of Ammon, and the gods of the Philistines, and forsook the LORD, and served not him. 7 And the anger of the LORD was hot against Israel, and he sold them into the hands of the Philistines, and into the hands of the children of Ammon. 8 And that year they vexed and oppressed the children of Israel eighteen years, all the children of Israel that *were* on the other side Jordan in the land of the Amorites, which *is* in Gilead. 9 Moreover the children of Ammon passed over Jordan to fight also against Judah, and against Benjamin, and against the house of Ephraim; so that Israel was sore distressed.

While those two judges, Tola and Jair, presided in the affairs of Israel, things went well, but afterwards,

I. Israel returned to their idolatry, that sin which did most easily beset them (*v.* 6): *They did evil again in the sight of the Lord,* from whom they were unaccountably bent to backslide, as a *foolish people and unwise.* 1. They worshipped many gods; not only their old demons Baalim and Ashtaroth, which the Canaanites had worshipped, but, as if they would proclaim their folly to all their neighbours, they served the gods of Syria, Zidon, Moab, Ammon, and the Philistines. It looks as if the chief trade of Israel had been to import deities from all countries. It is hard to say whether it was more impious or impolitic to do this. By introducing these foreign deities, they rendered themselves mean and despicable, for no nation that had any sense of honour changed their gods. Much of the wealth of Israel, we may suppose, was carried out, in offerings to the temples of the deities in the several countries whence they came, on which, as their mother-churches, their temples in Israel were expected to own their dependence; the priests and devotees of those sorry deities would follow their gods, no doubt, in crowds into the land of Israel, and, if they could not live in their own country, would take root there, and so *strangers would devour their strength.* If they did it in compliment to the neighbouring nations, and to ingratiate themselves with them, justly were they disappointed; for those nations which by their wicked arts they sought to make their friends by the righteous judgments of God became their enemies and oppressors. *In quo quis peccat, in eo punitur—Wherein a person offends, therein he shall be punished.* 2. They did not so much as admit the God of Israel to be one of those many deities they worshipped, but quite cast him off: They *forsook the Lord, and served not him* at all. Those that think to serve both God and Mammon will soon come entirely to forsake God, and to serve Mammon only. If God have not all the heart, he will soon have none of it.

II. God renewed his judgments upon them, bringing them under the power of oppressing enemies. Had they *fallen into the hands of the Lord* immediately, they might have found that *his mercies were great;* but God let them *fall into the hands of man,* whose tender mercies are cruel. He *sold them into the hands of the Philistines* that lay south-west of Canaan, and of the Ammonites that lay north-east, both at the same time; so that between those two millstones they were miserably *crushed,* as the original word is (*v.* 8) for *oppressed.* God had appointed that, if any of the cities of Israel should revolt to idolatry, the rest should make war upon them and cut them off, Deut. xiii. 12, &c. They had been jealous enough in this matter, almost to an extreme, in the case of the altar set up by the two tribes and a half (Josh. xxii.); but now they had grown so very bad that when one city was infected with idolatry the next took the infection and instead of punishing it, imitated and out-did it; and therefore, since those that should have been revengers to *execute wrath on those that did* this *evil* were themselves guilty, or *bore the sword in vain,* God brought the neighbouring nations upon them, to chastise them for their apostasy. The oppression of Israel by the Ammonites, the posterity of Lot, was, 1. Very long. It continued eighteen years. Some make those years to be part of the judgeship of Jair, who could not prevail to reform and deliver Israel as he would. Others make them to commence at the death of Jair, which seems the more probable because that part of Israel which was most infested by the Ammonites was Gilead, Jair's own country, which we cannot suppose to have suffered so much while he was living, but that part at least would be reformed and protected. 2. Very grievous. They vexed them and oppressed them. It was a great vexation to be oppressed by such a despicable people as the children of Ammon were. They began with those tribes that lay next them on the other side Jordan, here called *the land of the Amorites* (*v.* 8) because the Israelites had so wretchedly degenerated, and had made themselves so like the heathen, that they had become, in a manner, perfect Amorites (Ezek. xvi. 3), or because by their sin they forfeited their title to this land, so that it might justly be looked upon as *the land of the Amorites* again, from whom they took it. But by degrees they pushed forward, came over Jordan, and invaded Judah, and Benjamin, and Ephraim (*v.* 9), three of the most famous tribes of Israel, yet thus insulted when they had forsaken God, and unable to make head against the invader. Now the threatening was fulfilled that they should be *slain before their enemies,* and should have *no power to stand before them,* Lev. xxvi. 17, 37. Their *ways and their doings procure this to themselves;* they have sadly degenerated, and so they come to be sorely distressed.

10 And the children of Israel cried unto the LORD, saying, We have sinned against thee, both because we have forsaken our God, and also served Baalim. 11 And the LORD said unto the children of Israel, *Did* not *I deliver you* from the Egyptians, and from the Amorites, from the children of Ammon, and from the Philistines? 12 The Zidonians also, and the Amalekites, and the Maonites, did oppress you; and ye cried to me, and I delivered you out of their hand. 13 Yet ye have forsaken me, and served other gods: wherefore I will deliver you no more. 14 Go and cry unto the gods which ye have chosen; let them deliver you in the time of your tribulation. 15 And the children of Israel said unto the LORD, We have sinned: do thou unto us whatsoever seemeth good unto thee; deliver us only, we pray thee, this day. 16 And they put away the strange gods from among them, and served the LORD: and his soul was grieved for the misery of Israel. 17 Then the children of Ammon were gathered together, and encamped in Gilead. And the children of Israel assembled themselves together, and encamped in Mizpeh. 18 And the people *and* princes of Gilead said one to another, What man *is he* that will begin to fight against the children of Ammon? he shall be head over all the inhabitants of Gilead.

Here is, I. A humble confession which Israel make to God in their distress, *v.* 10. Now they own themselves guilty, like a malefactor upon the rack, and promise reformation, like a child under the rod. They not only complain of the distress, but acknowledge it is their own sin that has brought them into the distress; therefore God is righteous, and they have no reason to repine. They confess their omissions, for in them their sin began—"We have forsaken our God," and their commissions—"We have served Baalim, and herein have done foolishly, treacherously, and very wickedly."

II. A humbling message which God thereupon sends to Israel, whether by an angel (as *ch.* ii. 1) or by a prophet (as *ch.* vi. 8) is not certain. It was kind that God took notice of their cry, and did not turn a deaf ear to it and send them no answer at all; it was kind likewise that when they began to repent he sent them such a message as was proper to increase their repentance, that they might be qualified and prepared for deliverance. Now in this message, 1. He upbraids them with their great ingratitude, reminds them of the great things he had done for them, delivering them from such and such enemies, the Egyptians first, out of whose land they were rescued, the Amorites whom they conquered and into whose land they entered, and since their settlement there, when the Ammonites had joined with the Moabites to oppress them (*ch.* iii. 13), when the Philistines were vexatious in the days of Shamgar, and afterwards other enemies had given them trouble, upon their petition God had wrought many a great salvation for them, *v.* 11, 12. Of their being oppressed by the Zidonians and the Maonites we read not elsewhere. God had in justice corrected them, and in mercy delivered them, and therefore might reasonably expect that either through fear or through love they would adhere to him and his service. Well therefore might the word cut them to the heart (*v.* 13), "Yet *you have forsaken me* that have brought you out of your troubles and *served other gods* that brought you into your troubles." Thus did they *forsake their own mercies* for *their own delusions.* 2. He shows them how justly he might now abandon them to ruin, by abandoning them to the *gods that they had served.* To awaken them to a thorough repentance and reformation, he lets them see, (1.) Their folly in serving Baalim. They had been at a vast expense to obtain the favour of such gods as could not help them when they had most need of their help: "*Go, and cry unto the gods which you have chosen* (*v.* 14), try what they can do for you now. You have worshipped them as gods—try if they have now either a divine power or a divine goodness to be employed for you. You paid your homage to them as your kings and lords—try if they will now protect you. You brought your sacrifices of praise to their altars as your benefactors, imagining that they gave you your corn, and wine, and oil, but a friend indeed will be a friend in need; what stead will their favour stand you in now?" Note, It is necessary, in true repentance, that there be a full conviction of the utter insufficiency of all those things to help us and do us any kindness which we have idolized and set upon the throne in our hearts in competition with God. We must be convinced that the pleasures of sense on which we have doted cannot be our satisfaction, nor the wealth of the world which we have coveted be our portion, that we cannot be happy or easy any where but in God. (2.) Their misery and danger in forsaking God. "See what a pass you have brought yourselves to; now you can expect no other than that I should say, *I will deliver you no more*, and what will become of you then?" *v.* 13. This he tells them, not only as what he *might* do, but as what he *would* do if they rested in a confession of what they had done amiss, and did not put away their idols and amend for the future.

III. A humble submission which Israel hereupon made to God's justice, with a humble application to his mercy, *v.* 15. *The children of Israel met together*, probably in a solemn assembly at the door of the tabernacle, received the impressions of the message God had sent them, were not driven by it to despair, though it was very threatening, but resolve to lie at God's feet, and, if they perish, they will perish there. They not only repeat their confession, *We have sinned*, but, 1. They surrender themselves to God's justice: *Do thou unto us whatsoever seemeth good unto thee.* Hereby they own that they deserved the severest tokens of God's displeasure and were sure he could do them no wrong, whatever he laid upon them; they humbled themselves under his mighty and heavy hand, and *accepted of the punishment of their iniquity*, which Moses had made the condition of God's return in mercy to them, Lev. xxvi. 41. Note, True penitents dare and will refer themselves to God to correct them as he thinks fit, knowing that their sin is highly malignant in its deserts, and that God is not rigorous or extreme in his demands. 2. They supplicate for God's mercy: *Deliver us only, we pray thee, this day*, from this enemy. They acknowledge what they deserved, yet pray to God not to deal with them according to their deserts. Note, We must submit to God's justice with a hope in his mercy.

IV. A blessed reformation set on foot hereupon. They brought forth fruits meet for repentance (*v.* 16): *They put away the gods of strangers* (as the word is), strange gods, and worshipped by those nations that were strangers to the commonwealth of Israel and to the covenants of promise, and they *served the Lord.* Need drove them to him. They knew it was to no purpose to go to the gods whom they had served, and therefore returned to the God whom they had slighted. This is true repentance not only for sin, but from sin.

V. God's gracious return in mercy to them, which is expressed here very tenderly (*v.* 16): *His soul was grieved for the misery of Israel.* Not that there is any grief in God (he has infinite joy and happiness in himself, which cannot be broken in upon by either the sins or the miseries of his creatures), nor that there is any change in God: he *is in one mind, and who can turn him?* But his goodness is his glory. By it he proclaims his name, and magnifies it above all names; and, as he is pleased to put himself into the relation of a father to his people that are in covenant with him, so he is pleased to represent his goodness to them by the compassions of a father towards his children; for, as he is the Father of lights, so he is the Father of mercies. As the disobedience and misery of a child are a grief to a tender father, and make him feel very sensibly from his natural affection, so the provocations of God's people are a grief to him (Ps. xcv. 10), he is *broken with their whorish heart* (Ezek. vi. 9); their troubles also are a grief to him; so he is pleased to speak when he is pleased to appear for the deliverance of his people, changing his way and method of proceeding, as tender parents when they begin to relent towards their children with whom they have been displeased. Such are the tender mercies of our God, and so far is he from having any pleasure in the death of sinners.

VI. Things are now working towards their deliverance from the Ammonites' oppression, *v.* 17, 18. God had said, "I will deliver you no more;" but now they are not what they were, they are other men, they are new men, and now he will deliver them. That threatening was denounced to convince and humble them, and, now that it had taken its desired effect, it is revoked in order to their deliverance. 1. The Ammonites are hardened to their own ruin. They gathered together in one body, that they might be destroyed at one blow, Rev. xvi. 16. 2. The Israelites are animated to their own rescue. They assembled likewise, *v.* 17. During their eighteen years' oppression, as in their former servitudes, they were run down by their enemies, because they would not incorporate; each family, city, or tribe, would stand by itself, and act independently, and so they all became an easy prey to the oppressors, for want of a due sense of a common interest to cement them: but, whenever they got together, they did well; so they did here. When God's Israel become as one man to advance a common good and oppose a common enemy what difficulty can stand before them? The people and princes of Gilead, having met, consult first about a general that should command in chief against the Ammonites. Hitherto most of the deliverers of Israel had an extraordinary call to the office, as Ehud, Barak, Gideon; but the next is to be called in a more common way, by a convention of the states, who enquired out a fit man to command their army, found out one admirably well qualified for the purpose, and God owned their choice by putting his Spirit upon him (*ch.* xi. 29); so that this instance is of use for direction and encouragement in after-ages, when extraordinary calls are no longer to be expected. Let such be impartially chosen to public trust and power as God has qualified, and then God will graciously own those who are thus chosen.

CHAP. XI.

This chapter gives us the history of Jephthah, another of Israel's judges, and numbered among the worthies of the Old Testament, that by faith did great things (Heb. xi. 32), though he had not such an extraordinary call as the rest there mentioned had. Here we have, I. The disadvantages of his origin, ver. 1—3. II. The Gileadites' choice of him to be commander-in-chief against the Ammonites, and the terms he made with them, ver. 4—11. III. His treaty with the king of Ammon about the rights of the two nations, that the matter might be determined, if possible, without bloodshed, ver. 12—28. IV. His war with the Ammonites, which he enters upon with a solemn vow (ver. 29—31), prosecutes with bravery (ver. 32), and ends with a glorious victory, ver. 33. V. The straits he was brought into at his return to his own house by the vow he had made, ver. 34—40.

NOW Jephthah the Gileadite was a mighty man of valour, and he *was* the son of a harlot: and Gilead begat Jephthah. 2 And Gilead's wife bare him sons; and his wife's sons grew up, and they thrust out Jephthah, and said unto him, Thou shalt not inherit in our father's house; for thou *art* the son of a strange woman. 3 Then Jephthah fled from his brethren, and dwelt in the land of Tob: and there were gathered vain men to Jephthah, and went out with him.

The princes and people of Gilead we left, in the close of the foregoing chapter, consulting about the choice of a general, having come to this resolve, that whoever would undertake to lead their forces against the children of Ammon should by common consent be head over all the inhabitants of Gilead. The enterprise was difficult, and it was fit that so great an encouragement as this should be proposed to him that would undertake it. Now all agreed that Jephthah, the Gileadite, was a mighty man of valour, and very fit for that purpose, none so fit as he, but he lay under three disadvantages:—1. He was *the son of a harlot* (*v.* 1), of *a strange woman* (*v.* 2), one that was neither a wife nor a concubine; some think his mother was a Gentile; so Josephus, who calls him *a stranger by the mother's side.* An Ishmaelite, say the Jews. If his mother was a harlot, that was not his fault, however it was his disgrace. Men ought not to be reproached with any of the infelicities of their parentage or extraction, so long as they are endeavouring by their personal merits to roll away the reproach. The son of a harlot, if born again, born from above, shall be accepted of God, and be as welcome as any other to the glorious liberties of his children. Jephthah could not read in the law the brand there put on the Ammonites, the enemies he was to grapple with, that they should *not enter into the congregation of the Lord,* but in the same paragraph he met with that which looked black upon himself, that a bastard should be in like manner excluded, Deut. xxiii. 2, 3. But if that law means, as most probably it does, only those that are born of incest, not of fornication, he was not within the reach of it. 2. He had been driven from his country by his brethren. His father's legitimate children, insisting upon the rigour of the law, thrust him out from having any inheritance with them, without any consideration of his extraordinary qualifications, which merited a dispensation, and would have made him a mighty strength and ornament of their family, if they had overlooked his being illegitimate and admitted him to a child's part, *v.* 2. One would not have thought this abandoned youth was intended to be Israel's deliverer and judge, but God often humbles those whom he designs to exalt, and makes that *stone the head of the corner which the builders refused;* so Joseph, Moses, and David, the three most eminent of the shepherds of Israel, were all thrust out by men, before they were called of God to their great offices. 3. He had, in his exile, headed a rabble, *v.* 3. Being driven out by his brethren, his great soul would not suffer him either to dig or beg, but by his sword he must live; and, being soon noted for his bravery, those that were reduced to such straits, and animated by such a spirit, enlisted themselves under him. *Vain men* they are here called, that is, men that had run through their estates and had to seek for a livelihood. These went out with him, not to rob or plunder, but to hunt wild beasts, and perhaps to make incursions upon those countries which Israel was entitled to, but had not as yet come to the possession of, or were some way or other injured by. This is the man that must save Israel. That people had by their idolatry made themselves children of whoredoms, and aliens from God and his covenant, and therefore, though God upon their repentance will deliver them, yet, to mortify them and remind them of their sin, he chooses to do it by a bastard and an exile.

4 And it came to pass in process of time, that the children of Ammon made war against Israel. 5 And it was so, that when the children of Ammon made war against Israel, the elders of Gilead went to fetch Jephthah out of the land of Tob: 6 And they said unto Jephthah, Come, and be our captain, that we may fight with the children of Ammon. 7 And Jephthah said unto the elders of Gilead, Did not ye hate me, and expel me out of my father's house? and why are ye come unto me now when ye are in distress? 8 And the elders of Gilead said unto Jephthah, Therefore we turn again to thee now, that thou mayest go with us, and fight against the children of Ammon, and be our head over all the inhabitants of Gilead. 9 And Jephthah said unto the elders of Gilead, If ye bring me home again to fight against the children of Ammon, and the LORD deliver them before me, shall I be your head? 10 And the elders of Gilead said unto Jephthah, The LORD be witness between us, if we do not so according to thy words. 11 Then Jephthah went with the elders of Gilead, and the people made him head and captain over them: and Jephthah uttered all his words before the LORD in Mizpeh.

Here is, I. The distress which the children of Israel were in upon the Ammonites' invasion of their country, *v.* 4. Probably this was the same invasion with that mentioned, *ch.* x. 17, when *the children of Ammon* were *gathered together and encamped in or against Gilead.* And those words, *in process of time,* refer to what goes immediately before of the expulsion of Jephthah; many days after he had been thus thrust out in disgrace was he fetched back again with honour.

II. The court which the elders made to Jephthah hereupon to come and help them They did not write or send a messenger to him, but went themselves to fetch him, resolving to have no denial, and the exigence of the case was such as would admit no delay. Their errand to him was, *Come, and be our captain, v.* 6. They knew none among themselves that was able to undertake that great trust, but in effect confessed themselves unfit for it; they know him to be a bold man, and inured to the sword, and therefore he must be the man. See how God prepares men for the service he designs them for, and makes their troubles work for their advancement. If Jephthah had not been put to his shifts by his brethren's unkindness, he would not have had such occasion as this gave him to exercise and improve his martial genius, and so to signalize himself and become famous. *Out of the eater comes forth meat.* The children of Israel were assembled and encamped, *ch.* x. 17. But an army without a general is like a body without a head; therefore *Come,* say they, *and be our captain, that we may fight.* See the necessity of government; though they were hearty enough in the cause, yet they owned they could not fight without a captain to command them. So necessary is it to all societies that there be a *pars imperans* and a *pars subdita, some to rule* and *others to obey,* that any community would humbly beg the favour of being commanded rather than that every man should be his own master. Blessed be God for government, for a good government.

III. The objections Jephthah makes against accepting their offer: *Did you not hate me, and expel me? v.* 7. It should seem that his brethren were some of these elders, or these elders by suffering his brethren to abuse him, and not righting him as they ought to have done (for their business is to *defend the poor and fatherless,* Ps. lxxxii. 3, 4), had made themselves guilty of his expulsion, and he might justly charge them with it. Magistrates, that have power to protect those that are injured, if they neglect to redress their grievances are really guilty of inflicting them. "You hated me and expelled me, and therefore how can I believe that you are sincere in this proposal, and how can you expect that I should do you any service?" Not but that Jephthah was very willing to serve his country, but he thought fit to give them a hint of their former unkindness to him, that they might repent of their sin in using him so ill, and might for the future be the more sensible of their obligations. Thus Joseph humbled his brethren before he made himself known to them. The particular case between the Gileadites and Jephthah was a resemblance of the general state of the case between Israel and God at this time. They had thrust God out by their idolatries, yet in their distress begged his help; he told them how justly he might have rejected them, and yet graciously delivered them. So did Jephthah.

Many slight God and good men till they come to be in distress, and then they are desirous of God's mercy and good men's prayers.

IV. Their urgency with him to accept the government they offer him, *v.* 8. "Therefore because we formerly did thee that wrong, and to show thee that we repent of it and would gladly atone for it, we *turn again to thee now,* to put such an honour upon thee as shall balance that indignity." Let this instance be, 1. A caution to us not to despise or trample upon any because they are mean, nor to be injurious to any that we have advantage against, because, whatever we think of them now, the time may come when we may have need of them, and may be glad to be beholden to them. It is our wisdom to make no man our enemy, because we know not how soon our distresses may be such as that we may be highly concerned to make him our friend. 2. An encouragement to men of worth that are slighted or ill-treated. Let them bear it with meekness and cheerfulness, and leave it to God to make their light shine out of obscurity. Fuller's remark on this story, in his "Pisgah Sight," is this: "Virtue once in an age will work her own advancement, and, when such as hate it chance to need it, they will be forced to prefer it," and then the honour will appear the brighter.

V. The bargain he makes with them. He had mentioned the injuries they had formerly done him, but, perceiving their repentance, his spirit was too great and generous to mention them any more. God had forgiven Israel the affronts they had put upon him (*ch.* x. 16), and therefore Jephthah will forgive. Only he thinks it prudent to make his bargain wisely for the future, since he deals with men that he had reason to distrust. 1. He puts to them a fair question, *v.* 9. He speaks not with too much confidence of his success, knowing how justly God might suffer the Ammonites to prevail for the further punishment of Israel; but puts an *if* upon it. Nor does he speak with any confidence at all in himself; if he do succeed, it is *the Lord that delivers them into his hand,* intending hereby to remind his countrymen to look up to God, as arbitrator of the controversy and the giver of victory, for so *he* did. "Now if, by the blessing of God, I come home a conqueror, tell me plainly *shall I be your head?* If I deliver you, under God, shall I, under him, reform you?" The same question is put to those who desire salvation by Christ. "If he save you, will you be willing that he shall rule you? for on no other terms will he save you. If he make you happy, shall he make you holy? If he be your helper, shall he be your head?" 2. They immediately give him a positive answer (*v.* 10): "We will *do according to thy words;* command us in war, and thou shalt command us in peace." They do not take time to consider of it. The case was too plain to need a debate, and the necessity too pressing to admit a delay. They knew they had power to conclude a treaty for those whom they represented, and therefore bound it with an oath, *The Lord be witness between us.* They appeal to God's omniscience as the judge of their present sincerity, and to his justice as an avenger if afterwards they should prove false. *The Lord be a hearer,* so the word is. Whatever we speak, it concerns us to remember that God is a hearer, and to speak accordingly. Thus was the original contract ratified between Jephthah and the Gileadites, which all Israel, it should seem, agreed to afterwards, for it is said (*ch.* xii. 7), *he judged Israel.* He hereupon went with them (*v.* 11) to the place where they were all assembled (*ch.* x. 17), and there by common consent they *made him head and captain,* and so ratified the bargain their representatives had made with him, that he should be not only captain now, but head for life. Jephthah, to obtain this little honour, was willing to expose his life for them (*ch.* xii. 3), and shall we be discouraged in our Christian warfare by any of the difficulties we may meet with in it, when Christ himself has promised *a crown of life to him that overcometh?*

VI. Jephthah's pious acknowledgment of God in this great affair (*v.* 11): *He uttered all his words before the Lord in Mizpeh,* that is, upon his elevation, he immediately retired to his devotions, and in prayer spread the whole matter before God, both his choice to the office and his execution of the office, as one that had his eye ever towards the Lord, and would do nothing without him, that leaned not to his own understanding or courage, but depended on God and his favour. He utters before God all his thoughts and cares in this matter; for God gives us leave to be free with him. 1. "Lord, the people have made me their head; wilt thou confirm the choice, and own me as thy people's head under thee and for thee?" God justly complains of Israel (Hos. viii. 4), *they have set up kings, but not by me.* "Lord," said Jephthah, "I will be no head of their making without thee. I will not accept the government unless thou give me leave." Had Abimelech done this, he might have prospered. 2. "Lord, they have made me their captain, to go before them in this war with the Ammonites; shall I have thy presence? Wilt thou go before me? If not, carry me not up hence. Lord, satisfy me in the justice of the cause. Assure me of success in the enterprise." This is a rare example, to be imitated by all, particularly by great ones; in all our ways let us acknowledge God, seek his favour, ask counsel at his mouth, and take him along with us; so shall we make our way prosperous. Thus Jephthah opened the campaign with prayer. That was likely to end gloriously which began thus piously.

12 And Jephthah sent messengers unto the king of the children of Ammon, saying, What hast thou to do with me, that thou art come against me to fight in my land? 13 And the king of the children of Ammon answered unto the messengers of Jephthah, Because Israel took away my land, when they came up out of Egypt, from Arnon even unto Jabbok, and unto Jordan: now therefore restore those *lands* again peaceably. 14 And Jephthah sent messengers again unto the king of the children of Ammon: 15 And said unto him, Thus saith Jephthah, Israel took not away the land of Moab, nor the land of the children of Ammon: 16 But when Israel came up from Egypt, and walked through the wilderness unto the Red sea, and came to Kadesh; 17 Then Israel sent messengers unto the king of Edom, saying, Let me, I pray thee, pass through thy land: but the king of Edom would not hearken *thereto*. And in like manner they sent unto the king of Moab: but he would not *consent:* and Israel abode in Kadesh. 18 Then they went along through the wilderness, and compassed the land of Edom, and the land of Moab, and came by the east side of the land of Moab, and pitched on the other side of Arnon, but came not within the border of Moab: for Arnon *was* the border of Moab. 19 And Israel sent messengers unto Sihon king of the Amorites, the king of Heshbon; and Israel said unto him, Let us pass, we pray thee, through thy land into my place. 20 But Sihon trusted not Israel to pass through his coast: but Sihon gathered all his people together, and pitched in Jahaz, and fought against Israel. 21 And the LORD God of Israel delivered Sihon and all his people into the hand of Israel, and they smote them: so Israel possessed all the land of the Amorites, the inhabitants of that country. 22 And they possessed all the coasts of the Amorites, from Arnon even unto Jabbok, and from the wilderness even unto Jordan. 23 So now the LORD God of Israel hath dispossessed the Amorites from before his people Israel, and shouldest thou possess it? 24 Wilt not thou possess that which Chemosh thy god giveth thee to possess? So whomsoever the LORD our God shall drive out from before us, them will we possess. 25 And now *art* thou any thing better than Balak the son of Zippor, king of Moab? did he ever strive against Israel, or did he ever fight against them, 26 While Israel dwelt in Heshbon and her towns, and in Aroer and her towns, and in all the cities that *be* along by the coasts of Arnon, three hundred years? why therefore did ye not recover *them* within that time? 27 Wherefore I have not sinned against thee, but thou doest me wrong to war against me: the LORD the Judge be judge this day between the children of Israel and the children of Ammon. 28 Howbeit the king of the children of Ammon hearkened not unto the words of Jephthah which he sent him.

We have here the treaty between Jephthah, now judge of Israel, and the king of the Ammonites (who is not named), that the controversy between the two nations might, if possible, be accommodated without the effusion of blood.

I. Jephthah, as one having authority, sent to the king of Ammon, who in this war was the aggressor, to demand his reasons for invading the land of Israel: "*Why hast thou come to fight against me in my land? v.* 12. Had I come first into thy land to disturb thee in thy possession, this would have been reason enough for fighting against me, for how must force be repelled but by force? but what hast thou to do to come thus in a hostile manner into *my land?*" so he calls it, in the name both of God and Israel. Now this fair demand shows, 1. That Jephthah did not delight in war, though he was a mighty man of valour, but was willing to prevent it by a peaceable accommodation. If he could by reason persuade the invaders to retire, he would not compel them to do it by the sword. War should be the last remedy, not to be used till all other methods of ending matters in variance have been tried in vain, *ratio ultima regum—the last resource of kings*. This rule should be observed in going to law. The sword of justice, as well as the sword of war, must not be appealed to till the contending parties have first endeavoured by gentler means to understand one another, and to accommodate matters in variance, 1 Cor. vi. 1. 2. That Jephthah did delight in equity, and designed no other than to do justice. If the children of Ammon could convince him that Israel had done them wrong, he was ready to restore the rights of the Ammonites. If not, it was plain by their invasion that they did Israel wrong, and he was ready to maintain the rights of the Israelites. A sense of justice should guide and govern us in all our undertakings.

II. The king of the Ammonites now gives in his demand, which he should have published before he had invaded Israel, *v.* 13. His pretence is, "Israel took away my lands long since; now therefore restore those lands." We have reason to think the Ammonites, when they made this descent upon Israel, meant no other than to spoil and plunder the country, and enrich themselves with the prey, as they had done formerly under Eglon (*ch.* iii. 13) when no such demand as this was made, though the matter was then fresh; but when Jephthah demanded the cause of their quarrel, and they could not for shame own what was their true intent and meaning, some old musty records were searched, or some ancient traditions enquired into, and from them this reason was drawn to serve the present turn, for a colourable pretence of equity in the invasion. Even those that do the greatest wrong yet have such a conviction in their consciences of justice that they would seem to do right. *Restore those lands.* See upon what uncertain terms we hold our worldly possessions; what we think we have the surest hold of may be challenged from us, and wrested out of our hands. Those that have got to the heavenly Canaan need not fear having their titles questioned.

III. Jephthah gives in a very full and satisfactory answer to this demand, showing it to be altogether unjust and unreasonable, and that the Ammonites had no title to this country that lay between the rivers Arnon and Jabbok, now in the possession of the tribes of Reuben and Gad. As one very well versed in the history of his country, he shows,

1. That Israel never took any land away either from the Moabites or Ammonites. He puts them together because they were brethren, the children of Lot, near neighbours, and of united interests, having the same god, Chemosh, and perhaps sometimes the same king. The lands in question Israel took away, not from the Moabites or Ammonites (they had particular orders from God not to meddle with them nor any thing they had, Deut. ii. 9, 19, and religiously observed their orders), but they found them in the possession of Sihon king of the Amorites, and out of his hand they took them justly and honourably, as he will show afterwards. If the Amorites, before Israel came into that country, had taken these lands from the Moabites or Ammonites, as it should seem they had (Num. xxi. 26; Josh. xiii. 25), Israel was not concerned to enquire into that or answer for it. If the Ammonites had lost these lands and their title to them, the children of Israel were under no obligation to recover the possession for them. Their business was to conquer for themselves, not for other people. This is his first plea, "Not guilty of the trespass."

2. That they were so far from invading the property of any other nations than the devoted posterity of cursed Canaan (one of the branches of which the Amorites were, Gen. x. 16) that they would not so much as force a passage through the country either of the Edomites, the seed of Esau, or of the Moabites, the seed of Lot; but even after a very tedious march through the wilderness, with which they were sadly tired (*v.* 16), when the king of Edom first, and afterwards the king of Moab, denied them the courtesy of a way through their country (*v.* 17), rather than give them any offence or annoyance, weary as they were, they put themselves to the further fatigue of compassing both the land of Edom and that of Moab, and came not within the border of either, *v.* 18. Note, Those that behave themselves inoffensively may take the comfort of it, and plead it against those that charge them with injustice and wrong doing. Our *righteousness will answer for us in time to come* (Gen. xxx. 33) and will *put to silence the ignorance of foolish men*, 1 Pet. ii. 15.

3. That in that war in which they took this land out of the hands of Sihon king of the Amorites he was the aggressor, and not they, *v.* 19, 20. They sent a humble petition to him for leave to go through his land, willing to give him any security for their good behaviour in their march. "*Let us pass* (say they) *unto our place*, that is, to the land of Canaan, which is the only place we call ours, and to which we are pressing forward, not designing a settlement here." But Sihon not only denied them this courtesy, as Edom and Moab had done (had he only done so, who knows but Israel might have gone about some other way?) but he mustered all his forces, and fought against Israel (*v.* 20), not only shut them out of his own land, but would have cut them off from the face of the earth (Num. xxi. 23, 24), aimed at nothing less than their ruin, *v.* 20. Israel therefore, in their war with him, stood in their own just and necessary defence, and therefore, having routed his army, might justly, in further revenge of the injury, seize his country as forfeited. Thus Israel came to the possession of this country, and doubted not to make good their title to it; and it is very unreasonable for the Ammonites to question their title, for the Amorites were the inhabitants of that country, and it was purely their land and their coasts that the Israelites then made themselves masters of, *v.* 21, 22.

4. He pleads a grant from the crown, and claims under that, *v.* 23, 24. It was not

Israel (they were fatigued with their long march, and were not fit for action so soon), but it was the Lord God of Israel, who is King of nations, whose the earth is and the fulness thereof, he it was that dispossessed the Amorites and planted Israel in their room. God gave them the land by an express and particular conveyance, such as vested the title in them, which they might make good against all the world. Deut. ii. 24, *I have given into thy hand Sihon and his land;* he gave it to them, by giving them a complete victory over the present occupants, notwithstanding the great disadvantages they were under. "Can you think that God gave it to us in such an extraordinary manner with design that we should return it to the Moabites or Ammonites again? No, we put a higher value upon God's favours than to part with them so easily." To corroborate this plea, he urges an argument *ad hominem—directed to the man: Wilt not thou possess that which Chemosh thy god giveth thee?* He not only appeals to the common resolutions of men to hold their own against all the world, but to the common religion of the nations, which, they thought, obliged them to make much of that which their gods gave them. Not that Jephthah thought Chemosh a god, only he is *thy god,* and the worshippers even of those dunghill deities that could do neither good nor evil yet thought themselves beholden to them for all they had (Hos. ii. 12, *These are my rewards which my lovers have given me;* and see Judg. xvi. 24) and made this a reason why they would hold it fast, that their gods gave it to them. "This thou thinkest a good title, and shall not we?" The Ammonites had dispossessed those that dwelt in their land before them; they thought they did it by the help of Chemosh their god, but really it was Jehovah the God of Israel that did it for them, as is expressly said, Deut. ii. 19, 21. "Now," says Jephthah, "we have as good a title to our country as you have to yours." Note, One instance of the honour and respect we owe to God, as our God, is rightly to possess that which he gives us to possess, receive it from him, use it for him, keep it for his sake, and part with it when he calls for it. He has given it to us to possess, not to enjoy. He himself only must be enjoyed.

5. He pleads prescription. (1.) Their title had not been disputed when they first entered upon it, *v.* 25. "Balak who was then king of Moab, from whom the greatest part of these lands had been taken by the Amorites, and who was most concerned and best able to oppose us, if he had had any thing to object against our settlement there, yet sat still, and never offered to strive against Israel." He knew that for his own part he had fairly lost it to the Amorites and was not able to recover it, and could not but acknowledge that Israel had fairly won it of the Amorites, and therefore all his care was to secure what was left: he never pretended a title to what was lost. See Num. xxii. 2, 3. "He then acquiesced in God's way of disposing of kingdoms, and wilt not thou now?" (2.) Their possession had never yet been disturbed, *v.* 26. He pleads that they had kept this country as their own now about 300 years, and the Ammonites in all that time had never attempted to take it from them, no, not when they had it in their power to oppress them, *ch.* iii. 13, 14. So that, supposing their title had not been clear at the first (which yet he had proved it was), yet, no claim having been made for so many generations, the entry of the children of Ammon, without doubt, was barred for ever. A title so long unquestioned shall be presumed unquestionable.

6. By these arguments Jephthah justifies himself and his own cause ("I have not sinned against thee in taking or keeping what I have no right to; if I had, I would instantly make restitution"), and condemns the Ammonites: "*Thou doest me wrong to war against me,* and must expect to speed accordingly," *v.* 27. It seems to me an evidence that the children of Israel, in the days of their prosperity and power (for some such days they had in the times of the judges) had conducted themselves very inoffensively to all their neighbours and had not been vexatious or oppressing to them (either by way of reprisal or under colour of propagating their religion), that the king of the Ammonites, when he would seek an occasion of quarrelling with them, was forced to look 300 years back for a pretence. It becomes the people of God thus to be blameless and harmless, and without rebuke.

7. For the deciding of the controversy, he puts himself upon God and his sword, and the king of Ammon joins issue with him (*v.* 27, 28): *The Lord the Judge be judge this day.* With this solemn reference of the matter to the Judge of heaven and earth he designs either to deter the Ammonites from proceeding and oblige them to retire, when they saw the right of the cause was against them, or to justify himself in subduing them if they should go on. Note, War is an appeal to heaven, to God the Judge of all, to whom the issues of it belong. If doubtful rights be disputed, he is hereby requested to determine them. If manifest rights be invaded or denied, he is hereby applied to for the vindicating of what is just and the punishing of wrong. As the sword of justice was made for lawless and disobedient persons (1 Tim. i. 9), so was the sword of war made for lawless and disobedient princes and nations. In war therefore the eye must be ever up to God, and it must always be thought a dangerous thing to desire or expect that God should patronise unrighteousness.

Neither Jephthah's apology, nor his appeal, wrought upon the king of the children of Ammon; they had found the sweets of the spoil of Israel, in the eighteen years wherein they had oppressed them (*ch.* x. 8), and hoped now to make themselves masters of the tree with the fruit of which they had so often enriched themselves. He hearkened not to the words of Jephthah, his heart being hardened to his destruction.

29 Then the Spirit of the LORD came upon Jephthah, and he passed over Gilead, and Manasseh, and passed over Mizpeh of Gilead and from Mizpeh of Gilead he passed over *unto* the children of Ammon. 30 And Jephthah vowed a vow unto the LORD, and said, If thou shalt without fail deliver the children of Ammon into mine hands, 31 Then it shall be, that whatsoever cometh forth of the doors of my house to meet me, when I return in peace from the children of Ammon, shall surely be the LORD's, and I will offer it up for a burnt offering. 32 So Jephthah passed over unto the children of Ammon to fight against them; and the LORD delivered them into his hands. 33 And he smote them from Aroer, even till thou come to Minneth, *even* twenty cities, and unto the plain of the vineyards, with a very great slaughter. Thus the children of Ammon were subdued before the children of Israel. 34 And Jephthah came to Mizpeh unto his house, and, behold, his daughter came out to meet him with timbrels and with dances: and she *was his* only child; beside her he had neither son nor daughter. 35 And it came to pass, when he saw her, that he rent his clothes, and said, Alas, my daughter! thou hast brought me very low, and thou art one of them that trouble me: for I have opened my mouth unto the LORD, and I cannot go back. 36 And she said unto him, My father, *if* thou hast opened thy mouth unto the LORD, do to me according to that which hath proceeded out of thy mouth; forasmuch as the LORD hath taken vengeance for thee of thine enemies, *even* of the children of Ammon. 37 And she said unto her father, Let this thing be done for me: let me alone two months, that I may go up and down upon the mountains, and bewail my virginity, I and my fellows. 38 And he said, Go. And he sent her away *for* two months: and she went with her companions, and bewailed her virginity upon the mountains. 39 And it came to pass at the end of two months, that she returned unto her father, who did with her *according* to his vow which he had vowed: and she knew no man. And it was a custom in Israel, 40 *That* the daughters of Israel went yearly to lament the daughter of Jephthah the Gileadite four days in a year.

We have here Jephthah triumphing in a glorious victory, but, as an alloy to his joy, troubled and distressed by an unadvised vow.

I. Jephthah's victory was clear, and shines very brightly, both to his honour and to the honour of God, his in pleading and God's in owning a righteous cause. 1. God gave him an excellent spirit, and he improved it bravely, *v.* 29. When it appeared by the people's unanimous choice of him for their leader that he had so clear a call to engage, and by the obstinate deafness of the king of Ammon to the proposals of accommodation that he had so just a cause to engage in, then the Spirit of the Lord came upon him, and very much advanced his natural faculties, enduing him with power from on high, and making him more bold and more wise than ever he had been, and more fired with a holy zeal against the enemies of his people. Hereby God confirmed him in his office, and assured him of success in his undertaking. Thus animated, he loses no time, but with an undaunted resolution takes the field. Particular notice is taken of the way by which he advanced towards the enemy's camp, probably because the choice of it was an instance of that extraordinary discretion with which the Spirit of the Lord had furnished him; for those who sincerely walk after the Spirit shall be led forth the right way. 2. God gave him eminent success, and he bravely improved that too (*v.* 32): *The Lord delivered the Ammonites into his hand,* and so gave judgment upon the appeal in favour of the righteous cause, and made those feel the force of war that would not yield to the force of reason; for he *sits in the throne, judging right.* Jephthah lost not the advantages given him, but pursued and completed his victory. Having routed their forces in the field, he pursued them to their cities, where he put to the sword all he found in arms, so as utterly to disable them from giving Israel any molestation, *v.* 33. But it does not appear that he utterly destroyed the people, as Joshua had destroyed the devoted nations, nor that he offered to make himself master of the country, though their pretensions to the land of Israel might have given him colour to do so: only he took care that they should be effectually subdued. Though others' attempting wrong to us will justify us in the defence of our own right, yet it will not authorize us to do them wrong.

II. Jephthah's vow is dark, and much in the clouds. When he was going out from his own house upon this hazardous undertaking, in prayer to God for his presence with him he makes a secret but solemn vow or religious promise to God, that, if God would graciously bring him back a conqueror, whosoever or whatsoever should first come out of his house to meet him it should be devoted to God, and offered up for a burnt-offering. At his return, tidings of his victory coming home before him, his own and only daughter meets him with the seasonable expressions of joy. This puts him into a great confusion; but there was no remedy: after she had taken some time to lament her own infelicity, she cheerfully submitted to the performance of his vow. Now,

1. There are several good lessons to be learnt out of this story. (1.) That there may be remainders of distrust and doubting even in the hearts of true and great believers. Jephthah had reason enough to be confident of success, especially when he found *the Spirit of the Lord come upon him,* and yet, now that it comes to the settling, he seems to hesitate (*v.* 30): *If thou wilt without fail deliver them into my hand,* then I will do so and so. And perhaps the snare into which his vow brought him was designed to correct the weakness of his faith, and a fond conceit he had that he could not promise himself a victory unless he proffered something considerable to be given to God in lieu of it. (2.) That yet it is very good, when we are in the pursuit or expectation of any mercy, to make vows to God of some instance of acceptable service to him, not as a purchase of the favour we desire, but as an expression of our gratitude to him and the deep sense we have of our obligations to render according to the benefit done to us. The matter of such a singular vow (Lev. xxvii. 2) must be something that has a plain and direct tendency either to the advancement of God's glory, and the interests of his kingdom among men, or to the furtherance of ourselves in his service, and in that which is antecedently our duty. (3.) That we have great need to be very cautious and well advised in the making of such vows, lest, by indulging a present emotion even of pious zeal, we entangle our own consciences, involve ourselves in perplexities, and are forced at last to *say before the angel that it was an error,* Eccl. v. 2—6. *It is a snare to a man* hastily to *devour that which is holy,* without due consideration *quid valeant humeri, quid ferre recusent—what we are able or unable to effect,* and without inserting the needful provisos and limitations which might prevent the entanglement, and then after vows to make the enquiry which should have been made before, Prov. xx. 25. Let Jephthah's harm be our warning in this matter. See Deut. xxiii. 22. (4.) That what we have solemnly vowed to God we must conscientiously perform, if it be possible and lawful, though it be ever so difficult and grievous to us. Jephthah's sense of the powerful obligation of his vow must always be ours (*v.* 35): "*I have opened my mouth unto the Lord* in a solemn vow, *and I cannot go back,*" that is, "I cannot recal the vow myself, it is too late, nor can any power on earth dispense with it, or give me up my bond." The thing was my own, and *in my own power* (Acts v. 4), but now it is not. *Vow and pay,* Ps. lxxvi. 11. We deceive ourselves if we think to mock God. If we apply this to the consent we have solemnly given, in our sacramental vows, to the covenant of grace made with poor sinners in Christ, what a powerful argument will it be against the sins we have by those vows bound ourselves out from, what a strong inducement to the duties we have hereby bound ourselves up to, and what a ready answer to every temptation! "*I have opened my mouth to the Lord,* and *I cannot go back;* I must therefore go forward. I have sworn, and I must, I will, perform it. Let me not dare to play fast and loose with God." (5.) That it well becomes children obediently and cheerfully to submit to their parents in the Lord, and particularly to comply with their pious resolutions for the honour of God and the keeping up of religion in their families, though they be harsh and severe, as the Rechabites, who for many generations religiously observed the commands of Jonadab their father in forbearing wine, and Jephthah's daughter here, who, for the satisfying of her father's conscience, and for the honour of God and her country, yielded herself as one devoted (*v.* 36): "*Do to me according to that which hath proceeded out of thy mouth;* I know I am dear to thee, but am well content that God should be dearer." The father might disallow any vow made by the daughter (Num. xxx. 5), but the daughter could not disallow or disannul, no, not such a vow as this, made by the father. This magnifies the law of the fifth commandment. (6.) That our friends' grievances should be our griefs. Where she went to bewail her hard fate the virgins, her companions, joined with her in her lamentations, *v.* 38. With those of her own sex and age she used to associate, who no doubt, now that her father had on a sudden grown so great, expected, shortly after his return, to dance at her wedding, but were heavily disappointed when they were called to retire to the mountains with her and share in her griefs. Those are unworthy the name of friends that will only rejoice with us, and not weep with us. (7.) That heroic zeal for the honour of God and Israel, though alloyed with infirmity and indiscretion, is worthy to be had in perpetual remembrance. It well became the daughters of Israel by an annual solemnity to preserve the honourable memory of Jephthah's daughter, who made light even of her

own life like a noble heroine, when God had taken vengeance on Israel's enemies, *v.* 36. Such a rare instance of one that preferred the public interest before life itself was never to be forgotten. Her sex forbade her to follow to the war, and so to expose her life in battle, in lieu of which she hazards it much more (and perhaps apprehended that she did so, having some intimation of his vow, and did it designedly; for he tells her, *v.* 35, *Thou hast brought me very low)* to grace his triumphs. So transported was she with the victory as a common benefit that she was willing to be herself offered up as a thank-offering for it, and would think her life well bestowed when laid down on so great an occasion. She thinks it an honour to die, not as a sacrifice of atonement for the people's sins (that honour was reserved for Christ only), but as a sacrifice of acknowledgment for the people's mercies. (8.) From Jephthah's concern on this occasion, we must learn not to think it strange if the day of our triumphs in this world prove upon some account or other the day of our griefs, and therefore must always rejoice with trembling; we hope for a day of triumph hereafter which will have no alloy.

2. Yet there are some difficult questions that do arise upon this story which have very much employed the pens of learned men. I will say but little respecting them, because Mr. Poole has discussed them very fully in his English annotations.

(1.) It is hard to say what Jephthah did to his daughter in performance of his vow. [1.] Some think he only shut her up for a nun, and that it being unlawful, according to one part of his vow (for they make it disjunctive), to offer her up for a burnt-offering, he thus, according to the other part, engaged her to *be the Lord's,* that is, totally to sequester herself from all the affairs of this life, and consequently from marriage, and to employ herself wholly in the acts of devotion all her days. That which countenances this opinion is that she is *said to bewail her virginity* (*v.* 37, 38) and that *she knew no man, v.* 39. But, if he sacrificed her, it was proper enough for her to bewail, not her death, because that was intended to be for the honour of God, and she would undergo it cheerfully, but that unhappy circumstance of it which made it more grievous to her than any other, because she was her father's only child, in whom he hoped his name and family would be built up, that she was unmarried, and so left no issue to inherit her father's honour and estate; therefore it is particularly taken notice of (*v.* 34) that besides her he had neither son nor daughter. But that which makes me think Jephthah did not go about thus to satisfy his vow, or evade it rather, is that we do not find any law, usage, or custom, in all the Old Testament, which does in the least intimate that a single life was any branch or article of religion, or that any person, man or woman, was looked upon as the more holy, more the Lord's, or devoted to him, for living unmarried: it was no part of the law either of the priests or of the Nazarites. Deborah and Huldah, both prophetesses, are both of them particularly recorded to have been married women. Besides, had she only been confined to a single life, she needed not to have desired these two months to bewail it in: she had her whole life before her to do that, if she saw cause. Nor needed she to take such a sad leave of her companions; for those that are of that opinion understand what is said in *v.* 40 of their coming to *talk with her,* as our margin reads it, four days in a year. Therefore, [2.] It seems more probable that he offered her up for a sacrifice, according to the letter of his vow, misunderstanding that law which spoke of persons devoted by the curse of God as if it were to be applied to such as were devoted by men's vows (Lev. xxvii. 29, *None devoted shall be redeemed, but shall surely be put to death),* and wanting to be better informed of the power the law gave him in this case to redeem her. Abraham's attempt to offer up Isaac perhaps encouraged him, and made him think, if God would not accept this sacrifice which he had vowed, he would send an angel to stay his hand, as he did Abraham's. If she came out designedly to be made a sacrifice, as who knows but she might? perhaps he thought that would make the case the plainer. *Volenti non sit injuria—No injury is done to a person by that to which he himself consents.* He imagined, it may be, that where there was neither anger nor malice there was no murder, and that his good intention would sanctify this bad-action; and, since he had made such a vow, he thought better to kill his daughter than break his vow, and let Providence bear the blame, that brought her forth to meet him.

(2.) But, supposing that Jephthah did sacrifice his daughter, the question is whether he did well. [1.] Some justify him in it, and think he did well, and as became one that preferred the honour of God before that which was dearest to him in this world. He is mentioned among the eminent believers who by faith did great things, Heb. xi. 32. And this was one of the great things he did. It was done deliberately, and upon two months' consideration and consultation. He is never blamed for it by any inspired writer. Though it highly exalts the paternal authority, yet it cannot justify any in doing the like. He was an extraordinary person. *The Spirit of the Lord came upon him.* Many circumstances, now unknown to us, might make this altogether extraordinary, and justify it, yet not so as that it might justify the like. Some learned men have made this sacrifice a figure of Christ the great sacrifice: he was of unspotted purity and innocency, as she a chaste virgin; he was devoted to death by his Father, and so made a curse, or an anathema, for us; he submitted himself, as she did, to his Father's will: *Not as I will, but as thou wilt.* But, [2.] Most condemn Jephthah; he did ill to make so rash a vow, and worse to perform it. He could not be bound by his vow to that which God had forbidden by the letter of the sixth commandment: *Thou shalt not kill.* God had forbidden human sacrifices, so that it was (says Dr. Lightfoot) in effect a sacrifice to Moloch. And, probably, the reason why it is left dubious by the inspired penman whether he sacrificed her or no was that those who did afterwards offer their children might not take any encouragement from this instance. Concerning this and some other such passages in the sacred story, which learned men are in the dark, divided, and in doubt about, we need not much perplex ourselves; what is necessary to our salvation, thanks be to God, is plain enough.

CHAP. XII.

In this chapter we have, I. Jephthah's rencounter with the Ephraimites, and the blood shed on that unhappy occasion (ver. 1–6), and the conclusion of Jephthah's life and government, ver. 7. II. A short account of three other of the judges of Israel: Ibzan (ver. 8–10), Elon (ver. 11, 12), Abdon, ver. 13–15.

AND the men of Ephraim gathered themselves together, and went northward, and said unto Jephthah, Wherefore passedst thou over to fight against the children of Ammon, and didst not call us to go with thee? we will burn thine house upon thee with fire. 2 And Jephthah said unto them, I and my people were at great strife with the children of Ammon; and when I called you, ye delivered me not out of their hands. 3 And when I saw that ye delivered *me* not, I put my life in my hands, and passed over against the children of Ammon, and the LORD delivered them into my hand: wherefore then are ye come up unto me this day, to fight against me? 4 Then Jephthah gathered together all the men of Gilead, and fought with Ephraim: and the men of Gilead smote Ephraim, because they said, Ye Gileadites *are* fugitives of Ephraim among the Ephraimites, *and* among the Manassites. 5 And the Gileadites took the passages of Jordan before the Ephraimites: and it was *so*, that when those Ephraimites which were escaped said, Let me go over; that the men of Gilead said unto him, *Art* thou an Ephraimite? If he said, Nay; 6 Then said they unto him, Say now Shibboleth: and he said Sibboleth: for he could not frame to pronounce *it* right. Then they took him, and slew him at the passages of Jordan: and there fell at that time of the Ephraimites forty and two thousand. 7 And Jephthah judged Israel six years. Then died Jephthah the Gileadite, and was buried in *one of* the cities of Gilead.

Here is, I. The unreasonable displeasure of the men of Ephraim against Jephthah, because he had not called them in to his assistance against the Ammonites, that they might share in the triumphs and spoils, *v.* 1. Pride was at the bottom of the quarrel. Only by that comes contention. Proud men think all the honours lost that go beside themselves, and then *who can stand before envy?* The Ephraimites had the same quarrel with Gideon (*ch.* viii. 1), who was of Manasseh on their side Jordan, as Jephthah was of Manasseh on the other side Jordan. Ephraim and Manasseh were nearer akin than any other of the tribes, being both the sons of Joseph, and yet they were more jealous one of another than any other of the tribes. Jacob having crossed hands, and given Ephraim the preference, looking as far forward as the kingdom of the ten tribes, which Ephraim was the head of, after the revolt from the house of David, that tribe, not content with that honour in the promise, was displeased if Manasseh had any honour done it in the mean time. It is a pity that kindred or relationship, which should be an inducement to love and peace, should be ever an occasion (as it often proves) of strife and discord. *A brother offended is harder to be won, than a strong city, and contentions among brethren are as the bars of a castle.* The anger of the Ephraimites at Jephtha was, 1. Causeless and unjust. Why *didst thou not call us to go with thee?* For a good reason. Because it was the men of Gilead that had made him their captain, not the men of Ephraim, so that he had no authority to call them. Had his attempt miscarried for want of their help, they might justly have blamed him for not desiring it. But when the work was done, and done effectually, the Ammonites being subdued and Israel delivered, there was no harm done, though their hands were not employed in it. 2. It was cruel and outrageous. They get together in a tumultuous manner, pass over Jordan as far as Mizpeh in Gilead, where Jephthah lived, and no less will satisfy their fury but they will burn his house and him in it. *Cursed be their anger, for it was fierce.* Those resentments that have the least reason for them have commonly the most rage in them. Jephthah was now a conqueror over the common enemies of Israel, and they should have come to congratulate him, and return him the thanks of their tribe for the good services he had done; but we must not think it strange if we receive ill from those from whom we deserve well. Jephthah was now a mourner for the calamity of his family upon his daughter's account, and they should have come to condole with him and comfort him; but barbarous men take a pleasure in adding affliction to the afflicted. In this world, the end of one trouble often proves the beginning of another; nor must we ever *boast as though we had put off the harness.*

II. Jephthah's warm vindication of himself. He did not endeavour to pacify them, as Gideon had done in the like case; the Ephraimites were now more outrageous than they were then, and Jephthah had not so much of a meek and quiet spirit as Gideon had. Whether they would be pacified or no, Jephthah takes care,

1. To justify himself, *v.* 2, 3. He makes it out that they had no cause at all to quarrel with him, for, (1.) It was not in pursuit of glory that he had engaged in this war, but for the necessary defence of his country, with which the children of Ammon greatly strove. (2.) He had invited the Ephraimites to come and join with him, though he neither needed them nor was under any obligation to pay that respect to them, but they had declined the service: *I called you, and you delivered me not out of their hands.* Had that been true which they charged him with, yet it would not have been a just ground of quarrel; but it seems it was false, and, as the matter of fact now appears, he had more cause to quarrel with them for deserting the common interests of Israel in a time of need. It is no new thing for those who are themselves most culpable to be most clamorous in accusing the innocent. (3.) The enterprise was very hazardous, and they had more reason to pity him than to be angry with him: *I put my life in my hands*, that is, "exposed myself to the utmost peril in what I did, having so small an army." The honour they envied was bought dearly enough; they needed not to grudge it to him; few of them would have ventured so far for it. (4.) He does not take the glory of the success to himself (that would have been invidious), but gives it all to God: "*The Lord delivered them into my hands.* If God was pleased so far to make use of me for his glory, why should you be offended at that? Have you any reason to *fight against me?* Is not that in effect to fight against God, in whose hand I have been only an unworthy instrument?"

2. When this just answer (though not so soft an answer as Gideon's) did not prevail to turn away their wrath, he took care both to defend himself from their fury and to chastise their insolence with the sword, by virtue of his authority as Israel's judge. (1.) The Ephraimites had not only quarrelled with Jephthah, but, when his neighbours and friends appeared to take his part, they had abused them, and given them foul language; for I adhere to our translation, and so take it, *v.* 4. They said in scorn, "You Gileadites that dwell here on the other side Jordan are but fugitives of Ephraim, the scum and dregs of the tribes of Joseph, of which Ephraim is the chief, the refuse of the family, and are so accounted among the Ephraimites and among the Manassites. Who cares for you? All your neighbours know what you are, no better than fugitives and vagabonds, separated from your brethren, and driven hither into a corner." The Gileadites were as true Israelites as any other, and at this time had signalized themselves, both in the choice of Jephthah and in the war with Ammon, above all the families of Israel, and yet are most basely and unjustly called *fugitives.* It is an ill thing to fasten names or characters of reproach upon persons or countries, as is common, especially upon those that lie under outward disadvantages: it often occasions quarrels that prove of ill consequence, as it did here. See likewise what a mischievous thing an abusive tongue is, that calls ill names, and gives scurrilous language: it *sets on fire the course of nature, and is set on fire of hell* (Jam. iii. 6), and many a time cuts the throat of him that uses it, as it did here, Ps. lxiv. 8. If these Ephraimites could have denied themselves the poor satisfaction of calling the Gileadites *fugitives,* they might have prevented a great deal of bloodshed; for *grievous words stir up anger,* and who knows how great a matter a little of that fire may kindle? (2.) This affront raises the Gileadites' blood, and the indignity done to themselves, as well as to their captain, must be revenged. [1.] They routed them in the field, *v.* 4. They fought with Ephraim, and, Ephraim being but a rude unheaded rabble, smote Ephraim, and put them to flight. [2.] They cut off their retreat, and so completed their revenge, *v.* 5, 6. The Gileadites, who perhaps were better acquainted with the passages of Jordan than the Ephraimites were, secured them with strong guards, who were ordered to slay every Ephraimite that offered to pass the river. Here was, *First,* Cruelty enough in the destruction of them. Sufficient surely was *the punishment which was inflicted by many;* when they were routed in the field, there needed not this severity to cut off all that escaped. Shall the sword devour for ever? Whether Jephthah is to be praised for this I know not; perhaps he saw it to be a piece of necessary justice. *Secondly,* Cunning enough in the discovery of them. It seems the Ephraimites, though they spoke the same language with other Israelites, yet had got a custom in the dialect of their country to pronounce the Hebrew letter *Shin* like *Samech,* and they had so strangely used themselves to it that they could not do otherwise, no, not to save their lives. We learn to speak by imitation; those that first used *s* for *sh,* did it either because it was shorter or because it was finer, and their children learnt to speak like them, so that you might know an Ephraimite by it;

as in England we know a west-country man or a north-country man, nay, perhaps a Shropshire man, and a Cheshire man, by his pronunciation. *Thou art a Galilean, and thy speech betrays thee.* By this the Ephraimites were discovered. If they took a man that they suspected to be an Ephraimite, but he denied it, they bade him say *Shibboleth;* but either he *could not,* as our translation reads it, or he did not heed, or frame, or direct himself, as some read, to pronounce it aright, but said *Sibboleth,* and so was known to be an Ephraimite, and was slain immediately. *Shibboleth* signifies a *river or stream:* "Ask leave to go over Shibboleth, the river." Those that were thus cut off made up the whole number of slaughtered Ephraimites forty-two thousand, *v.* 6. Thus another mutiny of that angry tribe was prevented.

3. Now let us observe the righteousness of God in the punishment of these proud and passionate Ephraimites, which in several instances answered to their sin. (1.) They were proud of the honour of their tribe, gloried in this, that they were Ephraimites; but how soon were they brought to be ashamed or afraid to own their country! *Art thou an Ephraimite?* No, now rather of any tribe than that. (2.) They had gone in a rage over Jordan to burn Jephthah's house with fire, but now they came back to Jordan as sneakingly as they had passed it furiously, and were cut off from ever returning to their own houses. (3.) They had upbraided the Gileadites with the infelicity of their country, lying at such a distance, and now they suffered by an infirmity peculiar to their own country, in not being able to pronounce *Shibboleth.* (4.) They had called the Gileadites, unjustly, fugitives, and now they really and in good earnest became fugitives themselves; and in the Hebrew the same word (*v.* 5) is used of the Ephraimites that escaped, or that fled, which they had used in scorn of the Gileadites, calling them *fugitives.* He that rolls the stone of reproach unjustly upon another, let him expect that it will justly return upon himself.

III. Here is the end of Jephthah's government. He judged Israel but six years, and then died, *v.* 7. Perhaps the death of his daughter sunk him so that he never looked up afterwards, but it shortened his days, and he went to his grave mourning.

8 And after him Ibzan of Beth-lehem judged Israel. 9 And he had thirty sons, and thirty daughters, *whom* he sent abroad, and took in thirty daughters from abroad for his sons. And he judged Israel seven years. 10 Then died Ibzan, and was buried at Beth-lehem. 11 And after him Elon, a Zebulonite, judged Israel; and he judged Israel ten years. 12 And Elon the Zebulonite died, and was buried in Aijalon in the country of Zebulun. 13 And after him Abdon the son of Hillel, a Pirathonite, judged Israel. 14 And he had forty sons and thirty nephews, that rode on threescore and ten ass colts: and he judged Israel eight years. 15 And Abdon the son of Hillel the Pirathonite died, and was buried in Pirathon in the land of Ephraim, in the mount of the Amalekites.

We have here a short account of the short reigns of three more of the judges of Israel, the first of whom governed but seven years, the second ten, and the third eight. *For the transgression of a land, many are the princes thereof,* many in a short time, successively (Prov. xxviii. 2), good men being removed in the beginning of their usefulness and by the time that they have applied themselves to their business.

I. Ibzan of Bethlehem, most probably Bethlehem of Judah, David's city, not that in Zebulun, which is only mentioned once, Josh. xix. 15. He ruled but seven years, but by the number of his children, and his disposing of them all in marriage himself, it appears that he lived long; and probably the great increase of his family, and the numerous alliances he made, added to his personal merits, made him the more fit to be either chosen by the people as Jephthah was, or called of God immediately, as Gideon was, to be Israel's judge, to keep up and carry on the work of God among them. That which is remarkable concerning him is, 1. That he had many children, sixty in all, a quiver full of these arrows. Thus was Bethlehem of old famous for increase, the very city where *he* was to be born whose spiritual seed should be *as the stars of heaven.* 2. That he had an equal number of each sex, thirty sons and thirty daughters, a thing which does not often happen in the same family, yet, in the great family of mankind, he that at first made two, male and female, by his wise providence preserves a succession of both in some sort of equality as far as is requisite to the keeping up of the generations of men upon earth. 3. That he took care to marry them all. His daughters he sent abroad, *et maritis dedit,* so the vulgar Latin adds—*he provided husbands for them;* and, as it were in exchange, and both ways, strengthening his interest, he *took in thirty daughters from abroad for his sons.* The Jews say, Every father owes three things to his son: to teach him to read the law, give him a trade, and get him a wife. What a difference was there between Ibzan's family and that of his immediate predecessor Jephthah! Ibzan has sixty children and all married, Jephthah but one, a daughter, that dies or lives unmarried. Some are increased, others are diminished: both are the Lord's doing.

II. Elon of Zebulun, in the north of Canaan, was next raised up to preside in public affairs, to administer justice, and to reform abuses. Ten years he continued a blessing to Israel, and then died, *v.* 11, 12. Dr. Lightfoot computes that in the beginning of his time the forty years' oppression by the Philistines began (spoken of *ch.* xiii. 1), and about that time Samson was born. Probably, his residence being in the north, the Philistines who bordered upon the southern parts of Canaan took the opportunity of making incursions upon them.

III. Abdon, of the tribe of Ephraim, succeeded, and in him that illustrious tribe begins to recover its reputation, having not afforded any person of note since Joshua; for Abimelech the Shechemite was rather a scandal to it. This Abdon was famous for the multitude of his offspring (*v.* 14): he had forty sons and thirty grandsons, all of whom he lived to see grown up, and they rode on seventy ass-colts either as judges and officers or as gentlemen and persons of distinction. It was a satisfaction to him thus to see his children's children, but it is feared he did not see peace upon Israel, for by this time the Philistines had begun to break in upon them. Concerning this, and the rest of these judges that have ever so short an account given of them, yet notice is taken where they were buried (*v.* 7, 10, 12, 15), perhaps because the inscriptions upon their monuments (for such were anciently used, 2 Kings xxiii. 17) would serve for the confirmation and enlargement of their story, and might be consulted by such as desired further information concerning them. Peter, having occasion to speak of David, says, *His sepulchre is with us unto this day*, Acts ii. 29. Or it is intended for the honour of the places where they laid their bones, but may be improved for the lessening of our esteem of all worldly glory, of which death and the grave will stain the pride. These judges, that were as gods to Israel, died like men, and all their honour was laid in the dust.

It is very strange that in the history of all these judges, some of whose actions are very particularly related, there is not so much as once mention made of the high priest, or any other priest or Levite, appearing either for counsel or action in any public affair, from Phinehas (Judg. xx. 28) to Eli, which may well be computed 250 years; only the names of the high priests at that time are preserved, 1 Chron. vi. 4—7; and Ezra vii. 3—5. How can this strange obscurity of that priesthood for so long a time, now in the beginning of its days, agree with that mighty splendour with which it was introduced and the figure which the institution of it makes in the law of Moses? Surely it intimates that the institution was chiefly intended to be typical, and that the great benefits that seemed to be promised by it were to be chiefly looked for in its antitype, the everlasting priesthood of our Lord Jesus, in comparison of the superior glory of which that priesthood had no glory, 2 Cor. iii. 10.

CHAP. XIII.

At this chapter begins the story of Samson, the last of the judges of Israel whose story is recorded in this book, and next before Eli. The passages related concerning him are, from first to last, very surprising and uncommon. The figure he makes in this history is really great, and yet vastly different from that of his predecessors. We never find him at the head either of a court or of an army, never upon the throne of judgment nor in the field of battle, yet, in his own proper person, a great patriot of his country, and a terrible scourge and check to its enemies and oppressors; he was an eminent believer (Heb. xi. 32) and a glorious type of him who with his own arm wrought salvation. The history of the rest of the judges commences from their advancement to that station, but Samson's begins with his birth, nay, with his conception, and no less than an angel from heaven ushers him into the world, as a pattern of what should be afterwards done to John Baptist and to Christ. This is related in this chapter. I. The occasion of raising up this deliverer was the oppression of Israel by the Philistines, ver. 1. II. His birth is foretold by an angel to his mother, ver. 2—5. III. She relates the prediction to his father, ver. 6, 7. IV. They both together have it again from the angel (ver. 8—14), whom they treat with respect (ver. 15—18), and who, to their great amazement, discovers his dignity at parting, ver. 19—23. V. Samson is born, ver. 24, 25.

AND the children of Israel did evil again in the sight of the LORD; and the LORD delivered them into the hand of the Philistines forty years. 2 And there was a certain man of Zorah, of the family of the Danites, whose name *was* Manoah; and his wife *was* barren, and bare not. 3 And the angel of the LORD appeared unto the woman, and said unto her, Behold now, thou *art* barren, and bearest not: but thou shalt conceive, and bear a son. 4 Now therefore beware, I pray thee, and drink not wine nor strong drink, and eat not any unclean *thing*: 5 For, lo, thou shalt conceive, and bear a son; and no razor shall come on his head: for the child shall be a Nazarite unto God from the womb: and he shall begin to deliver Israel out of the hand of the Philistines. 6 Then the woman came and told her husband, saying, A man of God came unto me, and his countenance *was* like the countenance of an angel of God, very terrible: but I asked him not whence he *was*, neither told he me his name: 7 But he said unto me, Behold, thou shalt conceive, and bear a son; and now drink no wine nor strong drink, neither eat any unclean *thing*: for the child shall be a Nazarite to God from the womb to the day of his death.

The first verse gives us a short account,

such as we have too often met with already, of the great distress that Israel was in, which gave occasion for the raising up of a deliverer. They did evil, as they had done, *in the sight of the Lord,* and then God delivered them, as he had done, into the hands of their enemies. If there had been no sin, there would have needed no Saviour; but sin was suffered to abound, that grace might much more abound. The enemies God now sold them to were the Philistines, their next neighbours, that lay among them, the first and chief of the nations which were devoted to destruction, but which God *left to prove them* (*ch.* iii. 1, 3), *the five lords of the Philistines,* an inconsiderable people in comparison with Israel (they had but five cities of any note), and yet, when God made use of them as the staff in his hand, they were very oppressive and vexatious. And this trouble lasted longer than any yet: it continued forty years, though probably not always alike violent. When Israel was in this distress Samson was born; and here we have his birth foretold by an angel. Observe,

I. His extraction. He was of the tribe of Dan, *v.* 2. *Dan* signifies a *judge* or *judgment,* Gen. xxx. 6. And probably it was with an eye to Samson that dying Jacob foretold, *Dan shall judge his people,* that is, "he shall produce a judge for his people, though one of the sons of the handmaids, as one, as well as any one, of the tribes of Israel," Gen. xlix. 16. The lot of the tribe of Dan lay next to the country of the Philistines, and therefore one of that tribe was most fit to be made a bridle upon them. His parents had been long childless. Many eminent persons were born of mothers that had been kept a great while in the want of the blessing of children, as Isaac, Joseph, Samuel, and John Baptist, that the mercy might be the more acceptable when it did come. *Sing, O barren! thou that didst not bear,* Isa. liv. 1. Note, Mercies long waited for often prove signal mercies, and it is made to appear that they were worth waiting for, and by them others may be encouraged to continue their hope in God's mercy.

II. The glad tidings brought to his mother, that she should have a son. The messenger was an *angel of the Lord* (*v.* 3), yet appearing as a man, with the aspect and garb of a prophet, or man of God. And this angel (as the learned bishop Patrick supposes, on *v.* 18) was the Lord himself, that is, the *Word of the Lord,* who was to be the Messiah, for his name is called *Wonderful, v.* 18, and *Jehovah, v.* 19. The great Redeemer did in a particular manner concern himself about this typical redeemer. It was not so much for the sake of Manoah and his wife, obscure Danites, that this extraordinary message was sent, but for Israel's sake, whose deliverer he was to be, and not only so (his services to Israel not seeming to answer to the grandeur of his entry) but for the Messiah's sake, whose type he was to be, and whose birth must be foretold by an angel, as his was. The angel, in the message he delivers, 1. Takes notice of her affliction: *Behold now, thou art barren and bearest not.* Hence she might gather he was a prophet, that though a stranger to her, and one she had never seen before, yet he knew this to be her grievance. He tells her of it, not to upbraid her with it, but because perhaps at this time she was actually thinking of this affliction and bemoaning herself as one written childless. God often sends in comfort to his people very seasonably, when they feel most from their troubles. "*Now* thou art barren, but thou shalt not be always so," as she feared, "nor long so." 2. He assures her that she should *conceive and bear a son* (*v.* 3) and repeats the assurance, *v.* 5. To show the power of a divine word, the strongest man that ever was was a child of promise, as Isaac, born by force and virtue of a promise, and faith in that promise, Heb. xi. 11; Gal. iv. 23. Many a woman, after having been long barren, has borne a son by providence, but Samson was by promise, because a figure of the promised seed, so long expected by the faith of the Old-Testament saints. 3. He appoints that the child should be a Nazarite from his birth, and therefore that the mother should be subject to the law of the Nazarites (though not under the vow of a Nazarite) and should *drink no wine or strong drink* so long as this child was to have its nourishment from her, either in the womb or at the breast, *v.* 4, 5. Observe, This deliverer of Israel must be in the strictest manner devoted to God and an example of holiness. It is spoken of as a kindness to the people that God raised up of their young men for Nazarites, Amos ii. 11. Other judges had corrected their apostasies from God, but Samson must appear as one, more than any of them, consecrated to God; and, notwithstanding what we read of his faults, we have reason to think that being a Nazarite of God's making he did, in the course of his conversation, exemplify, not only the ceremony, but the substance of that *separation to the Lord* in which the Nazariteship did consist, Num. vi. 2. Those that would save others must by singular piety distinguish themselves. Samuel, who carried on Israel's deliverance from the Philistines, was a Nazarite by his mother's vow (1 Sam. i. 11), as Samson by the divine appointment. The mother of this deliverer must therefore deny herself, and not eat any unclean thing; what was lawful at another time was now to be forborne. As the promise tried her faith, so this precept tried her obedience; for God requires both from those on whom he will bestow his favours. Women with child ought conscientiously to avoid whatever they have reason to think will be any way prejudicial to the health or good constitution of the fruit of their body.

And perhaps Samson's mother was to refrain from wine and strong drink, not only because he was designed for a Nazarite, but because he was designed for a man of great strength, which his mother's temperance would contribute to. 4. He foretels the service which this child should do to his country: *He shall begin to deliver Israel.* Note, It is very desirable that our children may be not only devoted entirely to God themselves, but instrumental for the good of others, and the service of their generation—not recluses, candles *under a bushel,* but *on a candlestick.* Observe, *He shall begin* to deliver Israel. This intimated that the oppression of the Philistines should last long, for Israel's deliverance from it should not so much as begin, not one step be taken towards it, till this child, who was now unborn, should have grown up to a capacity of beginning it. And yet he must not complete the deliverance: he shall only *begin* to deliver Israel, which intimates that the trouble should still be prolonged. God chooses to carry on his work gradually and by several hands. One lays the foundation of a good work, another builds, and perhaps a third brings forth the top stone. Now herein Samson was a type of Christ, (1.) As a Nazarite to God, a Nazarite from the womb. For, though our Lord Jesus was not a Nazarite himself, yet he was typified by the Nazarites, as being perfectly pure from all sin, not so much as conceived in it, and entirely devoted to his Father's honour. Of the Jewish church, *as concerning the flesh, Christ came,* because to them pertained the promise of him, Rom. ix. 4, 5. By virtue of that promise, he long lay as it were in the womb of that church, which for many ages was pregnant of him, and therefore, like Samson's mother, during that pregnancy was made a holy nation and a peculiar people, and strictly forbidden to *touch any unclean thing for his sake,* who in the fulness of time was to come from them. (2.) As a deliverer of Israel; for he is Jesus a Saviour, who saves his people from their sins. But with this difference: Samson did only begin to deliver Israel (David was afterwards raised up to complete the destruction of the Philistines), but our Lord Jesus is both Samson and David too, both the *author and finisher of our faith.*

III. The report which Manoah's wife, in a transport of joy, brings in all haste to her husband, of this surprising message *v.* 6, 7. The glad tidings were brought her when she was alone, perhaps religiously employed in meditation or prayer; but she could not, she would not, conceal them from her husband, but gives him an account, 1. Of the messenger. It was a man of God, *v.* 6. His countenance she could describe; it was very awful: he had such a majesty in his looks, such a sparkling eye, such a shining face, so powerfully commanding reverence and respect, that according to the idea she had of an angel he had the very countenance of one. But his name she can give no account of, nor to what tribe or city of Israel he belonged, for he did not think fit to tell her, and, for her part, the very sight of him struck such an awe upon her that she durst not ask him. She was abundantly satisfied that he was a servant of God; his person and message she thought carried their own evidence along with them, and she enquired no further. 2. Of the message. She gives him a particular account both of the promise and of the precept (*v.* 7), that he also might believe the promise and might on all occasions be a monitor to her to observe the precept. Thus should yoke-fellows communicate to each other their experiences of communion with God, and their improvements in acquaintance with him, that they may be helpful to each other in *the way that is called holy.*

8 Then Manoah intreated the LORD, and said, O my Lord, let the man of God which thou didst send come again unto us, and teach us what we shall do unto the child that shall be born. 9 And God hearkened to the voice of Manoah; and the angel of God came again unto the woman as she sat in the field: but Manoah her husband *was* not with her. 10 And the woman made haste, and ran, and showed her husband, and said unto him, Behold, the man hath appeared unto me, that came unto me the *other* day. 11 And Manoah arose, and went after his wife, and came to the man, and said unto him, *Art* thou the man that spakest unto the woman? And he said, I *am.* 12 And Manoah said, Now let thy words come to pass. How shall we order the child, and *how* shall we do unto him? 13 And the angel of the LORD said unto Manoah, Of all that I said unto the woman let her beware. 14 She may not eat of any *thing* that cometh of the vine, neither let her drink wine or strong drink, nor eat any unclean *thing:* all that I commanded her let her observe.

We have here an account of a second visit which the angel of God made to Manoah and his wife.

I. Manoah earnestly prayed for it, *v.* 8. He was not incredulous of the story his wife told him; he knew she was a virtuous woman, and therefore the *heart of her husband did safely trust in her;* he knew she would not go about to impose upon him, much less was he, as Josephus unworthily represents him, jealous of his wife's conversation with this stranger; but, 1. He takes it for granted that this child of promise shall in due time be given them, and speaks without hesitation of *the child that shall be born.* There was *not found so great faith,* no, not in Zechariah, a priest, then in waiting at the altar of the Lord, and to whom the angel himself appeared, as was in this honest Danite. Things hidden from the wise and prudent, who value themselves upon the niceness of their enquiries, are often revealed unto babes, who know how to prize God's gifts and to take God's word. *Blessed are those that have not seen and yet,* as Manoah here, *have believed.* 2. All his care is *what they should do to the child* that should be born. Note, Good men are more solicitous and desirous to know the duty that is to be done by them than to know the events that shall occur concerning them; for duty is ours, events are God's. Solomon enquires concerning the good men should *do,* not the good they should *have,* Eccl. ii. 3. 3. He therefore prays to God to send the same blessed messenger again, to give them further instructions concerning the management of this Nazarite, fearing lest his wife's joy for the promise might have made her forget some part of the precept, in which he was desirous to be fully informed, and lie under no mistake: "*Lord, let the man of God come again unto us,* for we desire to be better acquainted with him." Note, Those that have heard from heaven cannot but wish to hear more thence, again and again to meet with the man of God. Observe, He does not go or send his servants abroad, to find out this man of God, but seeks him upon his knees, prays to God to send him, and, thus seeking, finds him. Would we have God's messengers, the ministers of his gospel, to bring a word proper for us, and for our instruction? *Entreat the Lord* to send them to us, to teach us, Rom. xv. 30, 32.

II. God graciously granted it: *God hearkened to the voice of Manoah, v.* 9. Note, God will not fail some way or other to guide those by his counsel that are sincerely desirous to know their duty, and apply themselves to him to teach them, Psal. xxv. 8, 9.

1. The angel appears the second time also to the wife, when she is sitting alone, probably tending the flocks, or otherwise well employed in the field where she has retired. Solitude is often a good opportunity of communion with God; good people have thought themselves never less alone than when alone, if God be with them.

2. She goes in all haste to call her husband, doubtless humbly beseeching the stay of this blessed messenger till she should return and her husband with her, *v.* 10, 11. She did not desire him to go with her to her husband, but would fetch her husband to him. Those that would meet with God must attend where he is pleased to manifest himself. "Oh," says she, overjoyed, "my dear love, thy prayers are answered — yonder is the man of God, come to make us another visit —he that came the other day," or, as some read it, *this* day, for *other* is not in the original, and it is probable enough that both these visits were on the same day, and at the same place, and that the second time she sat expecting him. The man of God is very willing she should call her husband, John iv. 16. Those that have an acquaintance with the things of God themselves should invite others to the same acquaintance, John i. 45, 46. Manoah is not disgusted that the angel did not this second time appear to him, but very willingly goes after his wife to the man of God. To atone (as it were) for the first fatal miscarriage, when Eve earnestly pressed Adam to that which was evil, and he too easily yielded to her, let yoke-fellows excite one another to love and good works; and, if the wife will lead, let not the husband think it any disparagement to him to follow her in that which is virtuous and praiseworthy.

3. Manoah having come to the angel, and being satisfied by him that he was the same that had appeared to his wife, does, with all humility, (1.) Welcome the promise (*v.* 12): *Now let thy words come to pass;* this was the language, not only of his desire, but of his faith, like that of the blessed Virgin, Luke i. 38. "*Be it according to thy word.* Lord, I lay hold on what thou hast said, and depend upon it; *let it come to pass.*" (2.) Beg that the prescriptions given might be repeated: *How shall we order the child?* The directions were given to his wife, but he looks upon himself as concerned to assist her in the careful management of this promised seed, according to order; for the utmost care of both the parents, and their constant joint endeavour, are little enough to be engaged for the good ordering of children that are devoted to God and to be brought up for him. Let not one devolve it on the other, but both do their best. Observe from Manoah's enquiry, [1.] In general, that, when God is pleased to bestow any mercy upon us, our great care must be how to use it well, and as we ought, because it is then only a mercy indeed when it is rightly managed. God has given us bodies, souls, estates; how shall we order them, that we may answer the intent of the donor, and give a good account of them? [2.] In particular, those to whom God has given children must be very careful how they order them, and what they do unto them, that they may drive out the foolishness that is *bound up in their hearts,* form their minds and manners well betimes, and *train them in the way wherein they should go.* Herein pious parents will beg divine assistance. "Lord, teach us how we may order our children, that they may be Nazarites, and living sacrifices to thee."

4. The angel repeats the directions he had before given (*v.* 13, 14): *Of all* that I forbad *let her beware;* and *all that I commanded her let her observe.* Note, There is need of a good deal both of caution and observation, for the right ordering both of ourselves and of our children. Beware and observe; take heed not only of drinking *wine* or *strong drink,* but of *eating any thing that cometh of the vine.* Those that would preserve themselves pure must keep at a distance from that which borders upon sin or leads to it. When she was with child of a Nazarite, she must not eat *any unclean thing;* so those *in whom Christ is formed* must carefully *cleanse themselves from all filthiness of flesh and spirit,* and do nothing to the prejudice of that new man.

15 And Manoah said unto the angel of the LORD, I pray thee, let us detain thee, until we shall have made ready a kid for thee. 16 And the angel of the LORD said unto Manoah, Though thou detain me, I will not eat of thy bread: and if thou wilt offer a burnt offering, thou must offer it unto the LORD. For Manoah knew not that he *was* an angel of the LORD. 17 And Manoah said unto the angel of the LORD, What *is* thy name, that when thy sayings come to pass we may do thee honour? 18 And the angel of the LORD said unto him, Why askest thou thus after my name, seeing it *is* secret? 19 So Manoah took a kid with a meat offering, and offered *it* upon a rock unto the LORD: and *the angel* did wondrously; and Manoah and his wife looked on. 20 For it came to pass, when the flame went up toward heaven from off the altar, that the angel of the LORD ascended in the flame of the altar. And Manoah and his wife looked on *it,* and fell on their faces to the ground. 21 But the angel of the LORD did no more appear to Manoah and to his wife. Then Manoah knew that he *was* an angel of the LORD. 22 And Manoah said unto his wife, We shall surely die, because we have seen God. 23 But his wife said unto him, If the LORD were pleased to kill us, he would not have received a burnt offering and a meat offering at our hands, neither would he have showed us all these *things,* nor would as at this time have told us *such things* as these.

We have here an account,

I. Of what further passed between Manoah and the angel at this interview. It was in kindness to him that while the angel was with him it was concealed from him that he was an angel; for, had he known it, it would have been such a terror to him that he durst not have conversed with him as he did (*v.* 16): *He knew not that he was an angel.* So Christ *was in the world, and the world knew him not. Verily thou art a God that hidest thyself.* We could not bear the sight of the divine glory unveiled. God having determined to speak to us by men like ourselves, prophets and ministers, even when he spoke by his angels, or by his Son, they appeared in the likeness of men, and were taken but for men of God. Now,

1. The angel declined to accept his treat, and appointed him to turn it into a sacrifice. Manoah, being desirous to show some token of respect and gratitude to this venerable stranger who had brought them these glad tidings, begged he would take some refreshment with him (*v.* 15): We will soon *make ready a kid for thee.* Those that welcome the message will be kind to the messengers for his sake that sends them, 1 Thess. v. 13. But the angel told him (*v.* 16) he would *not eat of his bread,* any more than he would of Gideon's, but, as there, directed him to offer it to God, *ch.* vi. 20, 21. Angels need not meat nor drink; but the glorifying of God is their meat and drink, and it was Christ's, John iv. 34. And we in some measure do the will of God as they do it if, though we cannot live without meat and drink, yet we eat and drink to the glory of God, and so turn even our common meals into sacrifices.

2. The angel declined telling him his name, and would not so far gratify his curiosity. Manoah desired to know his name (*v.* 17), and of what tribe he was, not as if he doubted the truth of his message, but that they might return his visit, and be better acquainted with him (it is good to increase and improve our acquaintance with good men and good ministers); and he has a further design: "*That when thy sayings come to pass, we may do thee honour,* celebrate thee as a true prophet, and recommend others to thee for divine instructions,—that we may call the child that shall be born after thy name, and so do thee honour,—or that we may send thee a present, honouring one whom God has honoured." But the angel denies his request with something of a check to his curiosity (*v.* 18): *Why askest thou thus after my name?* Jacob himself could not prevail for this favour, Gen. xxxii. 29. Note, We have not what we ask when we ask we know not what. Manoah's request was honestly meant and yet was denied. God told Moses his name (Exod. iii 13, 14), because there was a particular occasion for his knowing it, but here there was no occasion. What Manoah asked for instruction in his duty he

was readily told (*v.* 12, 13), but what he asked to gratify his curiosity was denied. God has in his word given us full directions concerning our duty, but never designed to answer all the enquiries of a speculative head. He gives him a reason for his refusal: *It is secret.* The names of angels were not as yet revealed, to prevent the idolizing of them. After the captivity, when the church was cured of idolatry, angels made themselves known to Daniel by their names, Michael and Gabriel; and to Zacharias the angel told his name unasked (Luke i. 19): *I am Gabriel.* But here it is *secret,* or it is *wonderful,* too wonderful for us. One of Christ's names is *Wonderful,* Isa. ix. 6. His name was long a secret, but by the gospel it is brought to light: *Jesus a Saviour.* Manoah must not ask because he must not know. Note, (1.) There are secret things which belong not to us, and which we must content ourselves to be in the dark about while we are here in this world. (2.) We must therefore never indulge a vain curiosity in our enquiries concerning these things, Col. ii. 18. *Nescire velle quæ Magister maximus docere non vult erudita inscitia est—To be willingly ignorant of those things which our great Master refuses to teach us is to be at once ignorant and wise.*

3. The angel assisted and owned their sacrifice, and, at parting, gave them to understand who he was. He had directed them to offer their burnt-offering to the Lord, *v.* 16. Praises offered up to God are the most acceptable entertainment of the angels; see Rev. xxii. 9, *worship God.* And Manoah, having so good a warrant, though he was no priest and had no altar, turned his meat into a meat offering, and *offered it upon a rock to the Lord* (*v.* 19), that is, he brought and laid it to be offered. "Lord, here it is, do what thou pleasest with it." Thus we must bring our hearts to God as living sacrifices, and submit them to the operation of his Spirit. All things being now ready, (1.) *The angel did wondrously,* for his name was *Wonderful.* Probably the wonder he did was the same with what he had done for Gideon, he made fire to come either down from heaven or up out of the rock to consume the sacrifice. (2.) He ascended up towards heaven *in the flame of the sacrifice, v.* 20. By this it appeared that he was not, as they thought, a mere man, but a messenger immediately from heaven. Thence certainly he descended, for thither he ascended, John iii. 13; vi. 62. This signified God's acceptance of the offering and intimates to what we owe the accept ice of all our offerings, even to the mediation of the angel of the covenant, that other angel, who puts *much incense to the prayers of saints* and *so offers them before the throne,* Rev. viii. 3. Prayer is the ascent of the soul to God. But it is Christ in the heart by faith that makes it an offering of a sweet-smelling savour: without him our services are offensive smoke, but, in him, acceptable flame. We may apply it to Christ's sacrifice of himself for us; he ascended in the flame of his own offering, for *by his own blood he entered in once into the holy place,* Heb. ix. 12. While the angel did this, it is twice said (*v.* 19, 20) *that Manoah and his wife looked on.* This is a proof of the miracle: the matter of fact was true, for out of the mouth of these two eye-witnesses the report of it is established. The angel did all that was done in the sacrifice; they did but look on; yet doubtless, when the angel ascended towards heaven, their hearts ascended with him in thanksgiving for the promise which came thence and in expectation of the performance to come thence too. Yet, when the angel has ascended, they dared not, as those that were the witnesses of Christ's ascension, stand gazing up into heaven, but in holy fear and reverence they fell on their faces to the ground. And now, [1.] They *knew that it was an angel, v.* 21. It was plain it was not the body of a man they saw, since it was not chained to the earth, nor prejudiced by fire; but ascended, and ascended in flame, and therefore with good reason they conclude it was an angel; for he *maketh his angels spirits, and his ministers a flame of fire.* [2.] But he did not any more appear to them; it was for a particular occasion, now over, that he was sent, not to settle a constant correspondence, as with prophets. They must remember and observe what the angel had said and not expect to hear more.

II. We have an account of the impressions which this vision made upon Manoah and his wife. While the angel did wondrously, they looked on, and said nothing (so it becomes us carefully to observe the wondrous works of God, and to be silent before him); but when he had gone, having finished his work, they had time to make their reflections. 1. In Manoah's reflection upon it there is *great fear, v.* 22. He had spoken with great assurance of the son they should shortly be the joyful parents of (*v.* 8, 12), and yet is now put into such a confusion by that very thing which should have strengthened and encouraged his faith that he counts upon nothing but their being both cut off immediately: *We shall surely die.* It was a vulgar opinion generally received among the ancient Jews that it was present death to see God or an angel; and this notion quite overcome his faith for the present, as it did Gideon's, *ch.* vi. 22. 2. In his wife's reflection upon it there is great faith, *v.* 23. Here the weaker vessel was the stronger believer, which perhaps was the reason why the angel chose once and again to appear to her. Manoah's heart began to fail him, but his wife, as a help meet for him, encouraged him. Two are better than one, for, if one fall into dejections and despondencies, the other will help to raise him up. Yoke-fellows should piously assist each other's faith and joy as there is occasion. None could argue better than Manoah's wife does here: *We shall surely die*, said her husband; "Nay," said she, "we need not fear that; let us never turn that against us which is really for us. We shall not die unless God be pleased to kill us: our death must come from his hand and his pleasure. Now the tokens of his favour which we have received forbid us to think that he designs our destruction. Had he thought fit to kill us, (1.) He would not have accepted our sacrifice, and signified to us his acceptance of it by *turning it to ashes*, Ps. xx. 3, *margin*. The sacrifice was the ransom of our lives, and the fire fastening upon that was a plain indication of the turning away of his wrath from us. The sacrifice of the wicked is an abomination, but you see ours is not so. (2.) He would not have shown us all these things, these strange sights, now at a time when there is little or no open vision (1 Sam. iii. 1), nor would he have given these exceedingly great and precious promises of a son that shall be a Nazarite and a deliverer of Israel—he would not have told us such things as these if he had been pleased to kill us. We need not fear the withering of those roots out of which such a branch is yet to spring." Note, Hereby it appears that God designs not the death of sinners that he has accepted the great sacrifice which Christ offered up for their salvation, has put them in a way of obtaining his favour, and has assured them of it upon their repentance. Had he been pleased to kill them, he would not have done so. And let those good Christians who have had communion with God in the word and prayer, to whom he has graciously manifested himself, and who have had reason to think God has accepted their works, take encouragement thence in a cloudy and dark day. "God would not have done what he has done for my soul if he had designed to forsake me, and leave me to perish at last; for his work is perfect, nor will he mock his people with his favours." Learn to reason as Manoah's wife did, "If God had designed me to perish under his wrath, he would not have given me such distinguishing tokens of his favour." *O woman! great is thy faith.*

24 And the woman bare a son, and called his name Samson: and the child grew, and the LORD blessed him. 25 And the Spirit of the LORD began to move him at times in the camp of Dan between Zorah and Eshtaol.

Here is, 1. Samson's birth. The woman that had been long barren bore a son, according to the promise; for no word of God shall fall to the ground. Hath he spoken, and shall he not make it good? 2. His name, *Samson*, has been derived by some, from *Shemesh, the sun*, turned into a diminutive, *sol exiguus—the sun in miniature*, perhaps because, being born like Moses to be a deliverer, he was like him exceedingly fair, his face shone like a little sun; or his parents so named him in remembrance of the shining countenance of that man of God who brought them the notice of him; though they knew not his name, yet thus, now that his sayings had come to pass, they did him honour. A little sun, because a Nazarite born (for the Nazarites were as *rubies* and *sapphires* (Lam. iv. 7), and because of his great strength. The sun is compared to a *strong man* Ps. xix. 5); why should not a strong man then be compared to the sun when he goes forth in his strength? A little sun, because the glory of, and a light to, his people Israel, a type of Christ, the Sun of righteousness. 3. His childhood. He grew more than is usual in strength and stature, far out-grew other children of his age; and not in that only, but in other instances, it appeared that the Lord blessed him, qualified him, both in body and mind, for something great and extraordinary. Children of promise shall have the blessing. 4. His youth. When he grew up a little *the Spirit of the Lord began to move him, v.* 25. This was an evidence that the Lord blessed him. Where God gives his blessing he gives his Spirit to qualify for the blessing. Those are blessed indeed in whom the Spirit of grace begins to work betimes, in the days of their childhood. If the *Spirit be poured out upon our offspring*, they will spring up as *willows by the water courses*, Isa. xliv. 3, 4. The Spirit of God moved Samson in the camp of Dan, that is, in the general muster of the trained bands of that tribe, who probably had formed a camp between Zorah and Eshtaol, near the place where he lived, to oppose the incursions of the Philistines; there Samson, when a child, appeared among them, and signalized himself by some very brave actions, excelling them all in manly exercises and trials of strength: and probably he showed himself more than ordinarily zealous against the enemies of his country, and discovered more of a public spirit than could be expected in a child. The Spirit moved him *at times*, not at all times, but as the wind blows, when he listed, to show that what he did was not from himself, for then he could have done it at any time. Strong men think themselves greatly animated by wine (Ps. lxxviii. 65), but Samson drank no wine, and yet excelled in strength and courage, and every thing that was bold and brave, for he had the Spirit of God moving him; therefore *be not drunk with wine, but be filled with the Spirit*, who will come to those that are sober and temperate.

CHAP. XIV.

The idea which this chapter gives us of Samson is not what one might have expected concerning one who, by the special designation of heaven, was a Nazarite to God and a deliverer of Israel; and yet really he was both. Here is, I. Samson's courtship of a daughter of the Philistines, and his marriage to her, ver. 1—5, 7, 8. II. His conquest of a lion, and the prize he found in the carcase of it, ver. 5, 6, 8, 9. III. Samson's riddle proposed to his companions (ver. 10—14) and unriddled by the treachery of his wife, ver. 15—18. IV. The occasion this gave him to kill thirty of the Philistines (ver. 19) and to break off his new alliance, ver. 20.

AND Samson went down to Timnath, and saw a woman in Timnath of the daughters of the Philistines. 2 And he came up, and told his father and his mother, and said, I have seen a woman in Timnath of the daughters of the Philistines: now therefore get her for me to wife. 3 Then his father and his mother said unto him, *Is there* never a woman among the daughters of thy brethren, or among all my people, that thou goest to take a wife of the uncircumcised Philistines? And Samson said unto his father, Get her for me; for she pleaseth me well. 4 But his father and his mother knew not that it *was* of the LORD, that he sought an occasion against the Philistines: for at that time the Philistines had dominion over Israel. 5 Then went Samson down, and his father and his mother, to Timnath, and came to the vineyards of Timnath: and, behold, a young lion roared against him. 6 And the Spirit of the LORD came mightily upon him, and he rent him as he would have rent a kid, and *he had* nothing in his hand: but he told not his father or his mother what he had done. 7 And he went down, and talked with the woman; and she pleased Samson well. 8 And after a time he returned to take her, and he turned aside to see the carcase of the lion: and, behold, *there was* a swarm of bees and honey in the carcase of the lion. 9 And he took thereof in his hands, and went on eating, and came to his father and mother, and he gave them, and they did eat: but he told not them that he had taken the honey out of the carcase of the lion.

Here, I. Samson, under the extraordinary guidance of Providence, seeks an occasion of quarrelling with the Philistines, by joining in affinity with them—a strange method, but the truth is Samson was himself a riddle, a paradox of a man, did that which was really great and good, by that which was seemingly weak and evil, because he was designed not to be a pattern to us (who must walk by rule, not by example), but a type of him who, though he knew no sin, was made sin for us, and appeared *in the likeness of sinful flesh,* that he might *condemn* and *destroy sin in the flesh,* Rom. viii. 3.

1. As the negociation of Samson's marriage was a common case, we may observe, (1.) That it was weakly and foolishly done of him to set his affections upon a daughter of the Philistines; the thing appeared very improper. Shall one that is not only an Israelite, but a Nazarite, devoted to the Lord, covet to become one with a worshipper of Dagon? Shall one marked for a patriot of his country match among those that are its sworn enemies? He saw this woman (*v.* 1), and she *pleased him well, v.* 3. It does not appear that he had any reason to think her wise or virtuous, or in any way likely to be a help-meet for him; but he saw something in her face that was very agreeable to his fancy, and therefore nothing will serve but she must be his wife. He that in the choice of a wife is guided only by his eye, and governed by his fancy, must afterwards thank himself if he find a Philistine in his arms. (2.) Yet it was wisely and well done not to proceed so much as to make his addresses to her till he had first made his parents acquainted with the matter. He told them, and desired them to *get her for him to wife, v.* 2. Herein he is an example to all children. Conformably to the law of the fifth commandment, children ought not to marry, nor to move towards marrying, without the advice and consent of their parents; those that do (as bishop Hall here expresses it) *wilfully unchild themselves, and exchange natural affections for violent.* Parents have a property in their children as parts of themselves. In marriage this property is transferred; for such is the law of the relation that *a man shall leave his father and his mother and cleave to his wife.* It is therefore not only unkind and ungrateful, but very unjust, to alienate this property without their concurrence; whoso thus *robbeth his father or mother,* stealing himself from them, who is nearer and dearer to them than their goods, *and* yet *saith, It is no transgression, the same is the companion of a destroyer,* Prov. xxviii. 24. (3.) His parents did well to dissuade him from yoking himself thus unequally with unbelievers. Let those who profess religion, but are courting an affinity with the profane and irreligious, matching into families where they have reason to think the fear of God is not, nor the worship of God, let them hear their reasoning, and apply it to themselves: "*Is there never a woman among the daughters of thy brethren,* or, if none of our tribe, *never a one among all thy people,* never an Israelite, that pleases thee, or that thou canst think worthy of thy affection, that thou shouldest marry a Philistine?" In the old world the sons of God corrupted and ruined themselves, their families, and that truly

primitive church, by marrying with the *daughters of men,* Gen. vi. 2. God had forbidden the people of Israel to marry with the devoted nations, one of which the Philistines were, Deut. vii. 3. (4.) If there had not been a special reason for it, it certainly would have been improper in him to insist upon his choice, and in them to agree to it at last. Yet their tender compliance with his affections may be observed as an example to parents not to be unreasonable in crossing their children's choices, nor to deny their consent, especially to those that have seasonably and dutifully asked it, without some very good cause. As children must *obey their parents in the Lord,* so parents must not *provoke their children to wrath, lest they be discouraged.* This Nazarite, in his subjection to his parents, asking their consent, and not proceeding till he had it, was not only an example to all children, but a type of the holy child Jesus, who *went down with his parents to Nazareth* (thence called a *Nazarene)* and was subject to them, Luke ii. 51.

2. But this treaty of marriage is expressly said to be *of the Lord, v.* 4. Not only that God afterwards overruled it to serve his designs against the Philistines, but that he put it into Samson's heart to make this choice, that he *might have occasion against the Philistines.* It was not a thing evil in itself for him to marry a Philistine. It was forbidden because of the danger of receiving hurt by idolaters; where there was not only no danger of that kind, but an opportunity hoped for of doing that hurt to them which would be good service to Israel, the law might well be dispensed with. It was said (*ch.* xiii. 25) that *the Spirit of the Lord began to move him at times,* and we have reason to think he himself perceived that Spirit to move him at this time, when he made this choice, and that otherwise he would have yielded to his parents' dissuasives, nor would they have consented at last if he had not satisfied them it was *of the Lord.* This would bring him into acquaintance and converse with the Philistines, by which he might have such opportunities of galling them as otherwise he could not have. It should seem, the way in which the Philistines oppressed Israel was, not by great armies, but by the clandestine incursions of their giants and small parties of their plunderers. In the same way therefore Samson must deal with them; let him but by this marriage get among them, and he would be a *thorn in their sides.* Jesus Christ, having to deliver us from this present evil world, and to cast out the prince of it, did himself visit it, though full of pollution and enmity, and, by assuming a body, did in some sense join in affinity with it, that he might destroy our spiritual enemies, and his own arm might work the salvation.

II. Samson, by a special providence, is animated and encouraged to attack the Philistines. That being the service for which he was designed, God, when he called him to it, prepared him for it by two occurrences:—

1. By enabling him, in one journey to Timnath, to *kill a lion, v.* 5, 6. Many decline doing the service they might do because they *know not their own strength.* God let Samson know what he could do in the strength of the *Spirit of the Lord,* that he might never be afraid to look the greatest difficulties in the face. David, who was to complete the destruction of the Philistines, must try his hand first upon *a lion and a bear,* that thence he might infer, as we may suppose Samson did, that the uncircumcised Philistine should be as one of them, 1 Sam. xvii. 36. (1.) Samson's encounter with the lion was hazardous. It was a young lion, one of the fiercest sort, that set upon him, roaring for his prey, and setting his eye particularly upon him; *he roared in meeting him,* so the word is. He was all alone in the vineyards, whither he had rambled from his father and mother (who kept the high road), probably to eat grapes. Children consider not how they expose themselves to the roaring lion that seeks to devour when, out of a foolish fondness for liberty, they wander from under the eye and wing of their prudent pious parents. Nor do young people consider what lions lurk in the vineyards, the vineyards of red wines, as dangerous as snakes under the green grass. Had Samson met with this lion in the way, he might have had more reason to expect help both from God and man than here in the solitary vineyards, out of his road. But there was a special providence in it, and the more hazardous the encounter was, (2.) The victory was so much the more illustrious. It was obtained without any difficulty: he strangled the lion, and tore his throat as easily as he would have strangled a kid, yet without any instrument, not only no sword nor bow, but not so much as a staff or knife; he had *nothing in his hand.* Christ engaged the roaring lion, and conquered him in the beginning of his public work (Matt. iv. 1, &c.), and afterwards spoiled principalities and powers, triumphing over them *in himself,* as some read it, not by any instrument. He was *exalted in his own strength.* That which added much to the glory of Samson's triumph over the lion was that when he had done this great exploit he did not boast of it, did *not so much as tell his father nor mother* that which many a one would soon have published through the whole country. Modesty and humility make up the brightest crown of great performances.

2. By providing him, the next journey, with honey in the carcase of this lion, *v.* 8, 9. When he came down the next time to solemnize his nuptials, and his parents with him, he had the curiosity to turn aside into the vineyard where he had killed the lion,

perhaps that with the sight of the place he might affect himself with the mercy of that great deliverance, and might there solemnly give thanks to God for it. It is good thus to *remind ourselves* of God's former favours to us. There he found the carcase of the lion; the birds or beasts of prey, it is likely, had eaten the flesh, and in the skeleton a swarm of bees had knit, and made a hive of it, and had not been idle, but had there laid up a good stock of honey, which was one of the staple commodities of Canaan; such plenty there was of it that the land is said to *flow with milk and honey*. Samson, having a better title than any man to the hive, seizes the honey with his hands. This supposes an encounter with the bees; but he that dreaded not the lion's paws had no reason to fear *their* stings. As by his victory over the lion he was emboldened to encounter the Philistine-giants, if there should be occasion, notwithstanding their strength and fierceness, so by dislodging the bees he was taught not to fear the multitude of the Philistines; though they *compassed him about like bees, yet in the name of the Lord he should destroy them*, Ps. cxviii. 12. Of the honey he here found, (1.) He ate himself, asking no questions for conscience' sake; for the dead bones of an unclean beast had not that ceremonial pollution in them that the bones of a man had. John Baptist, that Nazarite of the New Testament, lived upon wild honey. (2.) He gave to his parents, and they did eat; he did not eat all himself. *Hast thou found honey? eat so much as is sufficient for thee*, and no more, Prov. xxv. 16. He let his parents share with him. Children should be grateful to their parents with the fruits of their own industry, and so *show piety at home*, 1 Tim. v. 4. Let those that by the grace of God have found sweetness in religion themselves communicate their experience to their friends and relations, and invite them to come and share with them. He told not his parents whence he had it, lest they should scruple eating it. Bishop Hall observes here that *those are less wise and more scrupulous than Samson that decline the use of God's gifts because they find them in ill vessels.* Honey is honey still, though in a dead lion. Our Lord Jesus having conquered Satan, that roaring lion, believers find honey in the carcase, abundant strength and satisfaction, enough for themselves and for all their friends, from that victory.

10 So his father went down unto the woman: and Samson made there a feast; for so used the young men to do. 11 And it came to pass, when they saw him, that they brought thirty companions to be with him. 12 And Samson said unto them, I will now put forth a riddle unto you: if ye can certainly declare it me within the seven days of the feast, and find *it* out, then I will give you thirty sheets and thirty change of garments: 13 But if ye cannot declare *it* me, then shall ye give me thirty sheets and thirty change of garments. And they said unto him, Put forth thy riddle, that we may hear it. 14 And he said unto them, Out of the eater came forth meat, and out of the strong came forth sweetness. And they could not in three days expound the riddle. 15 And it came to pass on the seventh day, that they said unto Samson's wife, Entice thy husband, that he may declare unto us the riddle, lest we burn thee and thy father's house with fire: have ye called us to take that we have? *is it* not *so?* 16 And Samson's wife wept before him, and said, Thou dost but hate me, and lovest me not: thou hast put forth a riddle unto the children of my people, and hast not told *it* me. And he said unto her, Behold, I have not told *it* my father nor my mother, and shall I tell *it* thee? 17 And she wept before him the seven days, while their feast lasted: and it came to pass on the seventh day, that he told her, because she lay sore upon him: and she told the riddle to the children of her people. 18 And the men of the city said unto him on the seventh day before the sun went down, What *is* sweeter than honey? and what *is* stronger than a lion? And he said unto them, If ye had not ploughed said with my heifer, ye had not found out my riddle. 19 And the Spirit of the LORD came upon him, and he went down to Ashkelon, and slew thirty men of them, and took their spoil, and gave change of garments unto them which expounded the riddle. And his anger was kindled, and he went up to his father's house. 20 But Samson's wife was *given* to his companion, whom he had used as his friend.

We have here an account of Samson's wedding feast and the occasion it gave him to fall foul upon the Philistines.

I. Samson conformed to the custom of the country in making a festival of his nuptial solemnities, which continued seven days, *v.* 10. Though he was a Nazarite, he did not affect, in a thing of this nature, to be singular, but did *as the young men used to do* upon such occasions. It is no part of religion to go contrary to the innocent usages of the places where we live: nay, it is a reproach to religion when those who profess it give just occasion to others to call them covetous, sneaking, and morose. A good man should strive to make himself, in the best sense, a good companion.

II. His wife's relations paid him the accustomed respect of the place upon that occasion, and brought him thirty young men to keep him company during the solemnity, and to attend him as his grooms-men (*v.* 11): *When they saw him*, what a comely man he was, and what an ingenuous graceful look he had, they brought him these to do him honour, and to improve by his conversation while he staid among them. Or, rather, when they saw him, what a strong stout man he was, they brought these, seemingly to be his companions, but really to be a guard upon him, or spies to observe him. Jealous enough they were of him, but would have been more so had they known of his victory over the lion, which therefore he had industriously concealed. The favours of Philistines have often some mischief or other designed in them.

III. Samson, to entertain the company, propounds a riddle to them, and lays a wager with them that they cannot find it out in seven days, *v.* 12—14. The usage, it seems, was very ancient upon such occasions, when friends were together, to be innocently merry, not to spend all the time in dull eating and drinking, as bishop Patrick expresses it, or in other gratifications of sense, as music, dancing, or shows, but to propose questions, by which their learning and ingenuity might be tried and improved. This becomes men, wise men, that value themselves by their reason; but very unlike to it are the infamous and worse than brutish entertainments of this degenerate age, which send nothing round but the glass and the health, till reason is drowned, and wisdom sunk. Now, 1. Samson's riddle was his own invention, for it was his own achievement that gave occasion for it: *Out of the eater came forth meat, and out of the strong came forth sweetness.* Read my riddle, what is this? Beasts of prey do not yield meat for man, yet *food came from the devourer;* and those creatures that are strong when they are alive commonly smell strong and are every way offensive when they are dead, as horses, and yet *out of the strong*, or out of *the bitter*, so the Syriac and Arabic read it, *came sweetness.* If they had but so much sense as to consider what eater is most strong, and what meat is most sweet, they would have found out the riddle, and neither lions nor honey were such strangers to their country that the thoughts of them needed to be out of the way; and the solving of the riddle would have given him occasion to tell them the entertaining story on which it was founded. This riddle is applicable to many of the methods of divine providence and grace. When God, by an over-ruling providence, brings good out of evil to his church and people,—when that which threatened their ruin turns to their advantage,—when their enemies are made serviceable to them, and the wrath of men turns to God's praise,—then comes *meat out of the eater* and *sweetness out of the strong.* See Phil. i. 12. 2. His wager was more considerable to him than to them, because he was one against thirty partners. It was not a wager laid upon God's providence, or upon the chance of a die or a card, but upon their ingenuity, and amounted to no more than an honorary recompence of wit and a disgrace upon stupidity.

IV. His companions, when they could not expound the riddle themselves, obliged his wife to get from him the exposition of it, *v.* 15. Whether they were really of a dull capacity, or whether under a particular infatuation at this time, it was strange that none of the thirty could in all this time stumble upon so plain a thing as that, *What is sweeter than honey* and *what stronger than a lion?* It should seem that in wit, as well as manners, they were barbarous—barbarous indeed to threaten the bride that, if she would not use means with the bridegroom to let them into the meaning of it, they would *burn her and her father's house with fire.* Could any thing be more brutish? It was base enough to turn a jest into earnest, and those were unworthy of conversation that would grow so outrageous rather than confess their ignorance and lose so small a wager; nor would it save their credit at all to tell the riddle when they were told it. It was yet more villanous to engage Samson's wife to be a traitor to her own husband, and to pretend a greater interest in her than he had. Now that she was married she must *forget her own people.* Yet most inhuman of all was it to threaten, if she could not prevail, to burn her and all her relations with fire, and all for fear of losing each of them the value of a shirt and a coat: *Have you called us to take what we have?* Those must never lay wagers that cannot lose more tamely and easily than thus.

V. His wife, by unreasonable importunity, obtains from him a key to his riddle. It was *on the seventh day*, that is, the seventh day of the week (as Dr. Lightfoot conjectures), but the fourth day of the feast, that they solicited her to entice her husband (*v.* 15), and she did it, 1. With great art and management (*v.* 16), resolving not to believe he loved her, unless he would gratify her in this thing. She knew he could not bear to have his love questioned, and therefore, if any thing would work upon him, that would: "*Thou dost but hate me, and lovest me not,* if thou deniest me;" whereas he had much more reason to say, "Thou dost but *hate me,* and *lovest me not,* if thou insistest on it." And, that she might not make this the test of his affection, he assures her he had not told his own parents, notwithstanding the confidence he reposed in them. If this prevail not, she will try the powerful eloquence of tears: she *wept before him* the rest of *the days of the feast,* choosing rather to mar the mirth, as the bride's tears must needs do, than not gain her point, and oblige her countrymen, *v.* 17. 2. With great success. At last, being quite wearied with her importunity, he told her what was the meaning of his riddle, and though we may suppose she promised secresy, and that if he would but let her know she would tell nobody, she immediately told it to the *children of her people;* nor could he expect better from a Philistine, especially when the interests of her country were ever so little concerned. See Mic. vii. 5, 6. The riddle is at length *unriddled* (*v.* 18): *What is sweeter than honey,* or a better meat? Prov. xxiv. 13. *What is stronger than a lion,* or a greater devourer? Samson generously owns they had won the wager, though he had good reason to dispute it, because they had not declared the riddle, as the bargain was (*v.* 12), but it had been declared to them. But he only thought fit to tell them of it: *If you had not ploughed with my heifer,* made use of your interest with my wife, *you would not have found out my riddle.* Satan, in his temptations, could not do us the mischief he does if he did not plough with the heifer of our own corrupt nature.

VI. Samson pays his wager to these Philistines with the spoils of others of their countrymen, *v.* 19. He took this occasion to quarrel with the Philistines, went down to Ashkelon, one of their cities, where probably he knew there was some great festival observed at this time, to which many flocked, out of whom he picked out thirty, slew them, and took their clothes, and gave them to those that had expounded the riddle; so that, in balancing the account, it appeared that the Philistines were the losers, for one of the lives they lost was worth all the suits of clothes they won: the body is more than raiment. *The Spirit of the Lord came upon him,* both to authorize and to enable him to do this.

VII. This proves a good occasion of weaning Samson from his new relations. He found how his companions had abused him and how his wife had betrayed him, and therefore *his anger was kindled, v.* 19. Better be angry with Philistines than in love with them, because, when we join ourselves to them, we are most in danger of being ensnared by them. And, meeting with this ill usage among them, he *went up to his father's house.* It were well for us if the unkindnesses we meet with from the world, and our disappointments in it, had but this good effect upon us, to oblige us by faith and prayer to return to our heavenly Father's house and rest there. The inconveniences that occur in our way should make us love home and long to be there. No sooner had he gone than his wife was disposed of to another, *v.* 20. Instead of begging his pardon for the wrong she had done him, when he justly signified his resentment of it only by withdrawing in displeasure for a time, she immediately marries him that was the chief of the guests, the friend of the bridegroom, whom perhaps she loved too well, and was too willing to oblige, when she got her husband to tell her the riddle. See how little confidence is to be put in man, when those may prove our enemies whom we have used as our friends.

CHAP. XV.

Samson, when he courted an alliance with the Philistines, did but seek an occasion against them, ch. xiv. 4. Now here we have a further account of the occasions he took to weaken them, and to avenge, not his own, but Israel's quarrels, upon them. Every thing here is surprising; if any thing be thought incredible, because impossible, it must be remembered that with God nothing is impossible, and it was by the Spirit of the Lord coming upon him that he was both directed to and strengthened for those unusual ways of making war. I. From the perfidiousness of his wife and her father, he took occasion to burn their corn, ver. 1—5. II. From the Philistines' barbarous cruelty to his wife and her father, he took occasion to smite them with a great slaughter, ver 6—8. III. From the treachery of his countrymen, who delivered him bound to the Philistines, he took occasion to kill 1000 of them with the jaw-bone of an ass, ver. 9—17. IV. From the distress he was then in for want of water, God took occasion to show him favour in a seasonable supply, ver. 18—20.

BUT it came to pass within a while after, in the time of wheat harvest, that Samson visited his wife with a kid; and he said, I will go in to my wife into the chamber. But her father would not suffer him to go in. 2 And her father said, I verily thought that thou hadst utterly hated her; therefore I gave her to thy companion: *is* not her younger sister fairer than she? take her, I pray thee, instead of her. 3 And Samson said concerning them, Now shall I be more blameless than the Philistines, though I do them a displeasure. 4 And Samson went and caught three hundred foxes, and took firebrands, and turned tail to tail, and put a firebrand in the midst between two tails. 5 And when he had set the brands on fire, he let *them* go into the standing corn of the Philistines, and burnt up both the shocks, and also the standing corn, with the vineyards *and* olives. 6 Then the Philistines said,

Who hath done this? And they answered, Samson, the son in law of the Timnite, because he had taken his wife, and given her to his companion. And the Philistines came up, and burnt her and her father with fire. 7 And Samson said unto them, Though ye have done this, yet will I be avenged of you, and after that I will cease. 8 And he smote them hip and thigh with a great slaughter: and he went down and dwelt in the top of the rock Etam.

Here is, I. Samson's return to his wife, whom he had left in displeasure; not hearing perhaps that she was given to another, when time had a little cooled his resentments, he came back to her, *visited her with a kid, v.* 1. The value of the present was inconsiderable, but it was intended as a token of reconciliation, and perhaps was then so used, when those that had been at variance were brought together again; he sent this, that he might sup with her, in her apartments, and she with him, on his provision, and so they might be friends again. It was generously done of Samson, though he was the party offended and the superior relation, to whom therefore she was bound in duty to sue for peace and to make the first motion of reconciliation. When differences happen between near relations, let those be ever reckoned the wisest and the best that are most forward to forgive and forget injuries and most willing to stoop and yield for peace' sake.

II. The repulse he met with. Her father forbade him to come near her; for truly he had married her to another, *v.* 2. He endeavours, 1. To justify himself in this wrong: *I verily thought that thou hadst utterly hated her.* A very ill opinion he had of Samson, measuring that Nazarite by the common temper of the Philistines; could he think worse of him than to suspect that, because he was justly angry with his wife, he utterly hated her, and, because he had seen cause to return to his father's house for a while, therefore he had abandoned her for ever? Yet this is all he had to say in excuse of this injury. Thus he made the worst of jealousies to patronize the worst of robberies. But it will never bear us out in doing ill to say, "We thought others designed ill." 2. He endeavours to pacify Samson by offering him his younger daughter, whom, because the handsomer, he thought Samson might accept, in full recompence for the wrong. See what confusions those did admit and bring their families to that were not governed by the fear and law of God, marrying a daughter this week to one and next week to another, giving a man one daughter first and then another. Samson scorned his proposal; he knew better things than *to take a wife to her sister,* Lev. xviii. 18.

III. The revenge Samson took upon the Philistines for this abuse. Had he designed herein only to plead his own cause he would have challenged his rival, and would have chastised him and his father-in-law only. But he looks upon himself as a public person, and the affront as done to the whole nation of Israel, for probably they put this slight upon him because he was of that nation, and pleased themselves with it, that they had put such an abuse upon an Israelite; and therefore he resolves to do the Philistines a displeasure, and does not doubt but this treatment which he had met with among them would justify him in it (*v.* 3): *Now shall I be more blameless than the Philistines.* He had done what became him in offering to be reconciled to his wife, but, she having rendered it impracticable, now they could not blame him if he showed his just resentment. Note, When differences arise we ought to do our duty in order to the ending of them, and then, whatever the ill consequences of them may be, we shall be blameless. Now the way Samson took to be revenged on them was by setting their corn-fields on fire, which would be a great weakening and impoverishing to the country, *v.* 4, 5. 1. The method he took to do it was very strange. He sent 150 couple of foxes, tied tail to tail, into the corn-fields; every couple had a stick of fire between their tails, with which, being terrified, they ran into the corn for shelter, and so set fire to it; thus the fire would break out in many places at the same time, and therefore could not be conquered, especially if this was done, as it is probable it was, in the night. He might have employed men to do it, but perhaps he could not find Israelites enough that had courage to do it, and he himself could do it but in one place at a time, which would not effect his purpose. We never find Samson, in any of his exploits, making use of any person whatsoever, either servant or soldier, therefore, in this project, he chose to make use of foxes as his incendiaries. They had injured Samson by their subtlety and malice, and now Samson returns the injury by subtle foxes and mischievous fire-brands. By the meanness and weakness of the animals he employed, he designed to put contempt upon the enemies he fought against. This stratagem is often alluded to to show how the church's adversaries, that are of different interests and designs among themselves, that look and draw contrary ways in other things, yet have often united in a fire-brand, some cursed project or other, to waste the church of God, and particularly to kindle the fire of division in it. 2. The mischief he hereby did to the Philistines was very great. It was in the time of wheat harvest (*v.* 1), so that the straw being dry it soon burnt the shocks of corn that were cut, and *the standing corn, and the vineyards and olives.* This was a waste of the good creatures, but where other acts of hostility are lawful destroying the forage is justly reckoned to be so: if he might take away their lives, he might take away their livelihood. And God was righteous in it: the *corn, and the wine, and the oil,* which they had prepared for Dagon, to be a meat-offering to him, were thus, in the season thereof, made a burnt-offering to God's justice.

IV. The Philistines' outrage against Samson's treacherous wife and her father. Understanding that they had provoked Samson to do this mischief to the country, the rabble set upon them and burnt them with fire, perhaps in their own house, *v.* 6. Samson himself they durst not attack, and therefore, with more justice than perhaps they themselves designed in it, they wreak their vengeance upon those who, they could not but own, had given him cause to be angry. Instead of taking vengeance upon Samson, they took vengeance for him, when he, out of respect to the relation he had stood in to them, was not willing to do it for himself. See his hand in it *to whom vengeance belongs.* Those that deal treacherously shall be spoiled and dealt treacherously with; and *the Lord is known by these judgments which he executes,* especially when, as here, he makes use of his people's enemies as instruments for revenging one upon another his people's quarrels. When a barbarous Philistine sets fire to a treacherous one, the *righteous* may *rejoice to see the vengeance,* Ps. lviii. 10, 11. Thus shall *the wrath of man praise God,* Ps. lxxvi. 10. The Philistines had threatened Samson's wife that, if she would not get the riddle out of him, they would *burn her and her father's house with fire, ch.* xiv. 15. She, to save herself and oblige her countrymen, betrayed her husband; and what came of it? The very thing that she feared, and sought by sin to avoid, came upon her; she and her father's house were burnt with fire, and her countrymen, whom she sought to oblige by the wrong she did to her husband, brought this evil upon her. The mischief we seek to escape by any unlawful practices we often pull upon our own heads. *He that will* thus *save his life shall lose it.*

V. The occasion Samson took hence to do them a yet greater mischief, which touched their bone and their flesh, *v.* 7, 8. "*Though you have done this* to them, and thereby shown what you would do to me if you could, yet that shall not deter me from being further vexatious to you." Or, "Though you think, by doing this, you have made me satisfaction for the affront I received among you, yet I have Israel's cause to plead as a public person, and for the wrongs done to them *I will be avenged on you,* and, if you will then forbear your insults, I will cease, aiming at no more than the deliverance of Israel." So he *smote them hip and thigh with a great stroke,* so the word is. We suppose the wounds he gave them to have been mortal, as wounds in the hip or thigh often prove, and therefore translate it, *with a great slaughter.* Some think he only lamed them, disabled them for service, as horses were houghed or ham-strung. It seems to be a phrase used to express a desperate attack; he killed them pell-mell, or routed them horse and foot. He smote them with his hip upon thigh, that is, with the strength he had, not in his arms and hands, but in his hips and thighs, for he kicked and spurned at them, and so mortified them, *trod them in his anger,* and *trampled them in his fury,* Isa. lxiii. 3. And, when he had done, he retired to a natural fortress in the top of the rock Etam, where he waited to see whether the Philistines would be tamed by the correction he had given them.

9 Then the Philistines went up, and pitched in Judah, and spread themselves in Lehi. 10 And the men of Judah said, Why are ye come up against us? And they answered, To bind Samson are we come up, to do to him as he hath done to us. 11 Then three thousand men of Judah went to the top of the rock Etam, and said to Samson, Knowest thou not that the Philistines *are* rulers over us? what *is* this *that* thou hast done unto us? And he said unto them, As they did unto me, so have I done unto them. 12 And they said unto him, We are come down to bind thee, that we may deliver thee into the hand of the Philistines. And Samson said unto them, Swear unto me, that ye will not fall upon me yourselves. 13 And they spake unto him, saying, No; but we will bind thee fast, and deliver thee into their hand: but surely we will not kill thee. And they bound him with two new cords, and brought him up from the rock. 14 *And* when he came unto Lehi, the Philistines shouted against him: and the Spirit of the LORD came mightily upon him, and the cords that *were* upon his arms became as flax that was burnt with fire, and his bands loosed from off his hands. 15 And he found a new jawbone of an ass, and put forth his hand, and took it, and slew a thousand men therewith. 16 And

Samson said, With the jawbone of an ass, heaps upon heaps, with the jaw of an ass have I slain a thousand men. 17 And it came to pass, when he had made an end of speaking, that he cast away the jawbone out of his hand, and called that place Ramath-lehi.

Here is, I. Samson violently pursued by the Philistine They went up in a body, a more formidable force than they had together when Samson smote them hip and thigh; and they pitched in Judah, and spread themselves up and down the country, to find out Samson, who they heard had come this way, *v.* 9. When the men of Judah, who had tamely submitted to their yoke, pleaded that they had paid their tribute, and that none of their tribe had given them any offence, they freely own they designed nothing in this invasion but to seize Samson; they would fight *neither against small nor great,* but only that judge of Israel (*v.* 10), to *do to him as he has done to us,* that is, to smite his hip and thigh, as he did ours—*an eye for an eye.* Here was an army sent against one man, for indeed he was himself an army. Thus a whole band of men was sent to seize our Lord Jesus, that blessed Samson, though a tenth part would have served now that his hour had come, and ten times as many would have done nothing if he had not yielded.

II. Samson basely betrayed and delivered up by the men of Judah, *v.* 11. Of Judah were they? Degenerate branches of that valiant tribe! Utterly unworthy to carry in their standard *the lion of the tribe of Judah.* Perhaps they were disaffected to Samson because he was not of their tribe. Out of a foolish fondness for their forfeited precedency, they would rather be oppressed by Philistines than rescued by a Danite. Often has the church's deliverance been obstructed by such jealousies and pretended points of honour. Rather it was because they stood in awe of the Philistines, and were willing, at any rate, to get them out of their country. If their spirits had not been perfectly cowed and broken by their sins and troubles, and they had not been given up to a spirit of slumber, they would have taken this fair opportunity to shake off the Philistines' yoke. If they had had the least spark of ingenuousness and courage remaining in them, having so brave a man as Samson was to head them, they would now have made one bold struggle for the recovery of their liberty; but no marvel if those that had debased themselves to hell in the worship of their dung-hill gods (Isa. lvii. 9) thus debased themselves to the dust, in submission to their insulting oppressors. Sin dispirits men, nay, it infatuates them, and hides from their eyes the things that belong to their peace. Probably Samson went into the border of that country to offer his service, *supposing his brethren would have understood how that God by his hand would deliver them,* as Moses did, Acts vii. 25. But they thrust him from them, and very disingenuously, 1. Blamed him for what he had done against the Philistines, as if he had done them a great injury. Such ungrateful returns have those often received that have done the best service imaginable to their country. Thus our Lord Jesus did many good works, and for these they were ready to stone him. 2. They begged of him that he would suffer them to bind him, and deliver him up to the Philistines. Cowardly unthankful wretches! Fond of their fetters and in love with servitude! Thus the Jews delivered up our Saviour, under pretence of a fear lest the Romans should come and take away their place and nation. With what a sordid servile spirit do they argue, *Knowest thou not that the Philistines rule over us?* And whose fault was that? They knew they had no right to rule over them, nor would they have been sold into their hands if they had not first *sold themselves to work wickedness.*

III. Samson tamely yielding to be bound by his countrymen, and delivered into the hands of his enraged enemies, *v.* 12, 13. How easily could he have beaten them off, and kept the top of his rock against these 3000 men, and none of them all could, or durst, have laid hands on him; but he patiently submitted, 1. That he might give an example of great meekness, mixed with great strength and courage; as one that had rule over his own spirit, he knew how to yield as well as how to conquer. 2. That, by being delivered up to the Philistines, he might have an opportunity of making a slaughter among them. 3. That he might be a type of Christ, who, when he had shown what he could do, in striking those down that came to seize him, yielded to be bound and led as a *lamb to the slaughter.* Samson justified himself in what he had done against the Philistines: "*As they did to me, so I did to them;* it was a piece of necessary justice, and they ought not to retaliate it upon me, for they began." He covenants with the men of Judah that, if he put himself into their hands, they should not fall upon him themselves, because then he should be tempted to fall upon them, which he was very loth to do. This they promised him (*v.* 13), and then he surrendered. The men of Judah, being his betrayers, were in effect his murderers; they would not kill him themselves, but they did that which was worse, they delivered him into the hands of the uncircumcised Philistines, who they knew would do worse than kill him, would abuse and torment him to death. Perhaps they thought, as some think Judas did when he betrayed Christ, that he would by his great strength deliver himself out of their hands; but no thanks to them if he had delivered himself, and, if they thought he would do so, they might of themselves have thought this again, that he could and would deliver them too if they would adhere to him and make him their head. Justly is their misery prolonged who, to oblige their worst enemies, thus abuse their best friend. Never were men so infatuated except those who thus treated our blessed Saviour.

IV. Samson making his part good against the Philistines, even when he was delivered into their hands, fast pinioned with two new cords. The Philistines, when they had him among them, *shouted against him* (*v.* 14), so triumphing in their success, and insulting over him. If God had not tied their hands faster than the men of Judah had tied his, they would have shot at him (as their archers did at Saul) to dispatch him immediately, rather than have shouted at him, and given him time to help himself. But their security and joy were a presage of their ruin. When they shouted against him as a man run down, confident that all was their own, then the *Spirit of the Lord came upon him,* came mightily upon him, inspired him with more than ordinary strength and resolution. Thus fired, 1. He presently got clear of his bonds. The two new cords, upon the first struggle he gave, broke, and were *melted* (as the original word is) from off his hands, no doubt to the great amazement and terror of those that shouted against him, whose shouts were hereby turned into shrieks. Observe, When the *Spirit of the Lord came upon him, his cords were loosed. Where the Spirit of the Lord is there is liberty,* and those are free indeed who are thus freed. This typified the resurrection of Christ by the power of the Spirit of holiness. In it he loosed the bands of death, and its cords, the grave-clothes, fell from his hands without being loosed, as Lazarus's were, because it was impossible that the mighty Saviour should be holden of them; and thus he triumphed over the powers of darkness that shouted against him, as if they had him sure. 2. He made a great destruction among the Philistines, who all gathered about him to make sport with him, *v.* 15. See how poorly he was armed: he had no better weapon than the jaw-bone of an ass, and yet what execution he did with it! he never laid it out of his hand till he had with it laid 1000 Philistines dead upon the spot; and thus that promise was more than accomplished. *One of you shall chase a thousand,* Josh. xxiii. 10. A jaw-bone was an inconvenient thing to grasp, and, one would think, might easily be wrested out of his hand, and a few such blows as he gave with it might have crushed and broken it, and yet it held good to the last. Had it been the jaw-bone of a lion, especially that which he himself had slain, it might have helped to heighten his fancy and to make him think himself the more formidable; but to take the bone of that despicable animal was to do wonders by *the foolish things of the world,* that the *excellency of the power might be of God and not of man.* One of David's worthies slew 300 Philistines at once, but it was *with a spear,* 1 Chron. xi. 11. Another slew of them till his hand was weary and stuck to his sword, 2 Sam. xxiii. 10. But they all came short of Samson. What could be thought too hard, too much, for him to do, on whom the Spirit of the Lord came mightily! *Through God we shall do valiantly.* It was strange the men of Judah did not now come in to his aid: cowards can strike a falling enemy. But he was to be a type of him that *trod the wine-press alone.*

V. Samson celebrating his own victory, since the men of Judah would not do even that for him. He composed a short song, which he sang to himself, for the daughters of Israel did not meet him, as afterwards they did Saul, to sing, with more reason, *Samson hath slain his thousands.* The burden of this song was, *With the jaw-bone of an ass, heaps upon heaps, have I slain a thousand men, v.* 16. The same word in Hebrew *(chamor)* signifies both an *ass* and a *heap,* so that this is an elegant paronomasia, and represents the Philistines falling as tamely as asses. He also gave a name to the place, to perpetuate the Philistines' disgrace, *v.* 17. *Ramath-lehi,* the *lifting up of the jaw-bone.* Yet he did not vain-gloriously carry the bone about with him for a show, but threw it away when he had done with it. So little were relics valued then.

18 And he was sore athirst, and called on the LORD, and said, Thou hast given this great deliverance into the hand of thy servant: and now shall I die for thirst, and fall into the hand of the uncircumcised? 19 But God clave a hollow place that *was* in the jaw, and there came water thereout; and when he had drunk, his spirit came again, and he revived: wherefore he called the name thereof En-hakkore, which *is* in Lehi unto this day. 20 And he judged Israel in the days of the Philistines twenty years.

Here is, I. The distress which Samson was in after this great performance (*v.* 18): *He was sore athirst.* It was a natural effect of the great heat he had been in, and the great pains he had taken; his zeal consumed him, ate him up, and made him forget himself, till, when he had time to pause a little, he found himself reduced to the last extremity for want of water and ready to faint. Perhaps there was a special hand of God in it, as there was in the whole transaction; and God would hereby keep him from being proud of his great strength and great achievements, and let him know that he was but a man, and liable to the calamities that are common to men. And Josephus says, It was designed to chastise him for not making mention of God and his hand in his memorial of the victory he had obtained, but taking all the praise to himself: *I have slain a thousand men;* now that he is ready to die for thirst he is under a sensible conviction that his own arm could not have saved him, without God's right hand and arm. Samson had drunk largely of the blood of the Philistines, but blood will never quench any man's thirst. Providence so ordered it that there was no water near him, and he was so fatigued that he could not go far to seek it; the men of Judah, one would think, should have met him, now that he had come off a conqueror, *with bread and wine*, as Melchizedek did Abram, to atone for the injury they had done him; but so little notice did they take of their deliverer that he was ready to perish for want of a draught of water. Thus are the greatest slights often put upon those that do the greatest services. Christ, on the cross, said, *I thirst*.

II. His prayer to God in this distress. Those that forget to attend God with their praises may perhaps be compelled to attend him with their prayers. Afflictions are often sent to bring unthankful people to God. Two things he pleads with God in this prayer, 1. His having experienced the power and goodness of God in his late success: *Thou hast given this great deliverance into the hand of thy servant.* He owns himself God's servant in what he had been doing: "Lord, wilt thou not own a poor servant of thine, that has spent himself in thy service? *I am thine, save me.*" He calls his victory a *deliverance*, a *great* deliverance; for, if God had not helped him, he had not only not conquered the Philistines, but had been swallowed up by them. He owns it to come from God, and now corrects his former error in assuming it too much to himself; and this he pleads in his present strait. Note, Past experiences of God's power and goodness are excellent pleas in prayer for further mercy. "Lord, thou hast delivered often, wilt thou not deliver still? 2 Cor. i. 10. Thou hast begun, wilt thou not finish? Thou hast done the greater, wilt thou not do the less?" Ps. lvi. 13. 2. His being now exposed to his enemies: *Lest I fall into the hands of the uncircumcised*, and then they will triumph, will *tell it in Gath, and in the streets of Ashkelon;* and will it not redound to God's dishonour if his champion become so easy a prey to the uncircumcised?" The best pleas are those taken from God's glory.

III. The seasonable relief God sent him. God heard his prayer, and sent him water, either out of the bone or out of the earth through the bone, *v.* 19. That bone which he had made an instrument of God's service God, to recompense him, made an instrument of his supply. But I rather incline to our marginal reading: *God clave a hollow place that was in Lehi:* the place of this action was, from the jaw-bone, called *Lehi;* even before the action we find it so called, *v.* 9, 14. And there, in that field, or hill, or plain, or whatever it was, that was so called, God caused a fountain suddenly and seasonably to open just by him, and water to spring up out of it in abundance, which continued a well ever after. Of this fair water he drank, and his spirits revived. We should be more thankful for the mercy of water did we consider how ill we can spare it. And this instance of Samson's relief should encourage us to trust in God, and seek to him, for, when he pleases, he can *open rivers in high places.* See Isa. xli. 17, 18.

IV. The memorial of this, in the name Samson gave to this upstart fountain, *En-hakkore, the well of him that cried*, thereby keeping in remembrance both his own distress, which occasioned him to cry, and God's favour to him, in answer to his cry. Many a spring of comfort God opens to his people, which may fitly be called by this name; it is *the well of him that cried.* Samson had given a name to the place which denoted him great and triumphant—*Ramath-lehi*, the *lifting up of the jaw-bone;* but here he gives it another name, which denotes him needy and dependent.

V. The continuance of Samson's government after these achievements, *v.* 20. At length Israel submitted to him whom they had betrayed. Now it was past dispute that God was with him, so that henceforward they all owned him and were directed by him as their judge. *The stone which the builders refused became the head-stone.* It intimates the low condition of Israel that the government was dated by *the days of the Philistines;* yet it was a mercy to Israel that, though they were oppressed by a foreign enemy, yet they had a judge that preserved order and kept them from ruining one another. Twenty years his government continued, according to the usages of the judges' administration; but of the particulars we have no account, save of the beginning of his government in this chapter and the end of it in the next.

CHAP. XVI.

Samson's name (we have observed before) signifies a little sun (sol parvus); we have seen this sun rising very bright, and his morning ray strong and clear; and, nothing appearing to the contrary, we take it for granted that the middle of the day was proportionably illustrious, while he judged Israel twenty years; but the melancholy story of this chapter gives us such an account of his evening as did not commend his day. This little sun set under a cloud, and yet, just in the setting, darted forth one such strong and glorious beam as made him even then a type of Christ, conquering by death. Here is, I. Samson greatly endangered by his familiarity with one harlot, and hardly escaping, ver. 1—3. II. Samson quite ruined by his familiarity with another harlot, Delilah. Observe, 1. How he was betrayed to her by his own lusts, ver. 4. 2. How he was betrayed by her to his sworn enemies, the Philistines, who, (1.) By her means got it out of him at last where his great strength lay, ver. 5—17. (2.) Then robbed him of his strength, by taking from his head the crown of his separation, ver. 18—20. (3.) Then seized him, blinded him, imprisoned him, abused him, and, at a solemn festival, made a show of him, ver. 21—25. But, lastly, he avenged himself of them by pulling down the theatre upon their heads, and so dying with them, ver. 26—31.

THEN went Samson to Gaza, and saw there a harlot, and went in unto her. 2 *And it was told* the Gazites, saying, Samson is come hither. And they compassed *him* in, and laid wait for him all night in the gate of the city, and were quiet all the night, saying, In the morning, when it is day, we shall kill him. 3 And Samson lay till midnight, and arose at midnight, and took the doors of the gate of the city, and the two posts, and went away with them, bar and all, and put *them* upon his shoulders, and carried them up to the top of a hill that *is* before Hebron.

Here is, 1. Samson's sin, *v.* 1. His taking a Philistine to wife, in the beginning of his time, was in some degree excusable, but to join himself to a harlot that he accidentally saw among them was such a profanation of his honour as an Israelite, as a Nazarite, that we cannot but blush to read it. *Tell it not in Gath.* This vile impurity makes the graceful visage of this Nazarite *blacker than a coal,* Lam. iv. 7, 8. We find not that Samson had any business at Gaza; if he went thither in quest of a harlot it would make one willing to hope that, as bad as things were otherwise, there were no prostitutes among the daughters of Israel. Some think he went thither to observe what posture the Philistines were in, that he might get some advantages against them; if so, he forgot his business, neglected that, and so fell into this snare. His sin began in his eye, with which he should have made a covenant; he saw there one in the *attire of a harlot,* and the lust which conceived brought forth sin: he *went in unto her.* 2. Samson's danger. Notice was sent to the magistrates of Gaza, perhaps by the treacherous harlot herself, that Samson was in the town, *v.* 2. Probably he came in a disguise, or in the dusk of the evening, and went into an inn or public-house, which happened to be kept by this harlot. The gates of the city were hereupon shut, guards set, all kept quiet, that Samson might suspect no danger. Now they thought they had him in a prison, and doubted not but to be the death of him the next morning. O that all those who indulge their sensual appetites in drunkenness, uncleanness, or any fleshly lusts, would see themselves thus surrounded, waylaid, and marked for ruin, by their spiritual enemies! The faster they sleep, and the more secure they are, the greater is their danger. 3. Samson's escape, *v.* 3. He rose at midnight, perhaps roused by a dream, in slumberings upon the bed (Job xxxiii. 15), by his guardian angel, or rather by the checks of his own conscience. He arose with a penitent abhorrence (we hope) of the sin he was now committing, and of himself because of it, and with a pious resolution not to return to it,—rose under an apprehension of the danger he was in, that he was as one that slept upon the top of a mast,—rose with such thoughts as these: "Is this a bed fit for a Nazarite to sleep in? Shall a temple of the living God be thus polluted? Can I be safe under this guilt?" It was bad that he lay down without such checks; but it would have been worse if he had lain still under them. He makes immediately towards the gate of the city, probably finds the guards asleep, else he would have made them sleep their last, stays not to break open the gates, but plucks up the posts, takes them, gates and bar and all, all very large and strong and a vast weight, yet he carries them on his back several miles, *up to the top of a hill,* in disdain of their attempt to secure him with gates and bars, designing thus to render himself more formidable to the Philistines and more acceptable to his people, thus to give a proof of the great strength God had given him and a type of Christ's victory over death and the grave. He not only rolled away the stone from the door of the sepulchre, and so came forth himself, but carried away the gates of the grave, bar and all, and so left it, ever after, an open prison to all that are his; it shall not, it cannot, always detain them. *O death! where is thy sting?* Where are thy gates? Thanks be to him that not only gained a victory for himself, but giveth us the victory!

4 And it came to pass afterward, that he loved a woman in the valley of Sorek, whose name *was* Delilah. 5 And the lords of the Philistines came up unto her, and said unto her, Entice him, and see wherein his great strength *lieth,* and by what *means* we may prevail against him, that we may bind him to afflict him: and we will give thee every one of us eleven hundred *pieces* of silver. 6 And Delilah said to Samson, Tell me, I pray thee, wherein thy great strength *lieth,* and wherewith thou mightest be bound to afflict thee. 7 And Samson said unto her, If they bind me with seven green withs that were never dried, then shall I be weak, and be as another man. 8 Then the lords of the Philistines brought up to her seven green withs which had not been dried, and she bound him with them. 9 Now *there were* men lying in wait, abiding with her in the chamber. And she said unto him, The Philistines *be*

upon thee, Samson. And he brake the withs, as a thread of tow is broken when it toucheth the fire. So his strength was not known. 10 And Delilah said unto Samson, Behold, thou hast mocked me, and told me lies: now tell me, I pray thee, wherewith thou mightest be bound. 11 And he said unto her, If they bind me fast with new ropes that never were occupied, then shall I be weak, and be as another man. 12 Delilah therefore took new ropes, and bound him therewith, and said unto him, The Philistines *be* upon thee, Samson. And *there were* liers in wait abiding in the chamber. And he brake them from off his arms like a thread. 13 And Delilah said unto Samson, Hitherto thou hast mocked me, and told me lies: tell me wherewith thou mightest be bound. And he said unto her, If thou weavest the seven locks of my head with the web. 14 And she fastened *it* with the pin, and said unto him, The Philistines *be* upon thee, Samson. And he awaked out of his sleep, and went away with the pin of the beam, and with the web. 15 And she said unto him, How canst thou say, I love thee, when thine heart *is* not with me? thou hast mocked me these three times, and hast not told me wherein thy great strength *lieth*. 16 And it came to pass, when she pressed him daily with her words, and urged him, *so* that his soul was vexed unto death; 17 That he told her all his heart, and said unto her, There hath not come a razor upon mine head; for I *have been* a Nazarite unto God from my mother's womb: if I be shaven, then my strength will go from me, and I shall become weak, and be like any *other* man.

The burnt child dreads the fire; yet Samson, that has more than the strength of a man, in this comes short of the wisdom of a child; for, though he had been more than once brought into the highest degree of mischief and danger by the love of women and lusting after them, yet he would not take warning, but is here again taken in the same snare, and this third time pays for all. Solomon seems to refer especially to this story of Samson when, in his caution against uncleanness, he gives this account of a whorish woman (Prov. vii. 26), that *she hath cast down many wounded, yea, many strong men have been slain by her;* and (Prov. vi. 26) that *the adulteress will hunt for the precious life.* This bad woman, that brought Samson to ruin, is here named *Delilah,* an infamous name, and fitly used to express the person, or thing, that by flattery or falsehood brings mischief and destruction on those to whom kindness is pretended. See here,

I. The affection Samson had for Delilah: he loved her, *v.* 4. Some think she was his wife, but then he would have had her home to his own house; others that he courted her to make her his wife; but there is too much reason to suspect that it was a sinful affection he had for her, and that he lived in uncleanness with her. Whether she was an Israelite or a Philistine is not certain. If an Israelite, which is scarcely probable, yet she had the heart of a Philistine.

II. The interest which the lords of the Philistines made with her to betray Samson, *v.* 5. 1. That which they told her they designed was to humble him, or afflict him; they would promise not to do him any hurt, only they would disable him not to do them any. And so much conscience it should seem they made of this promise that even then, when he lay ever so much at their mercy, they would not kill him, no, not when the razor that cut his hair might sooner and more easily have cut his throat. 2. That which they desired, in order hereunto, was to know where his great strength lay, and by what means he might be bound. Perhaps they imagined he had some spell or charm which he carried about with him, by the force of which he did these great things, and doubted not but that, if they could get this from him, he would be manageable; and therefore, having had reason enough formerly to know which was his blind side, hoped to find out his riddle a second time by ploughing with his heifer. They engaged Delilah to get it out of him, telling her what a kindness it would be to them, and perhaps assuring her it should not be improved to any real mischief, either to him or her. 3. For this they bid high, promised to give her each of them 1100 pieces of silver, 5500 in all. So many shekels amounted to above 1000*l.* sterling; with this she was hired to betray one she pretended to love. See what horrid wickedness the love of money is the root of. Our blessed Saviour was thus betrayed by one whom he called *friend,* and with a kiss too, for filthy lucre. No marvel if those who are unchaste, as Delilah, be unjust; such as lose their honesty in one instance will in another.

III. The arts by which he put her off from time to time, and kept his own counsel a great while. She asked him *where his great strength lay,* and whether it were possible for him to be bound and afflicted (*v.* 6), pretending that she only desired he would satisfy her curiosity in that one thing, and that she thought it was impossible he should be bound otherwise than by her charms.

1. When she urged him very much, he told her, (1.) That he might be bound with *seven green withs, v.* 7. The experiment was tried (*v.* 8), but it would not do: he *broke the withs* as easily *as a thread of tow is broken when it toucheth the fire, v.* 9. (2.) When she still continued her importunity (*v.* 10) he told her that with two new ropes he might be so cramped and hampered that he might be as easily dealt with as any other man, *v.* 11. This experiment was tried too, but it failed: the *new ropes* broke from off his arm *like a thread, v.* 12. (3.) When she still pressed him to communicate the secret, and upbraided him with it as an unkindness that he had bantered her so long, he then told her that the weaving of the seven locks of his head would make a great alteration in him, *v.* 13. This came nearer the matter than any thing he had yet said, but it would not do: his strength appeared to be very much in his hair, when, upon the trial of this, purely by the strength of his hair, he carried away the *pin of the beam* and *the web.*

2. In the making of all these experiments, it is hard to say whether there appears more of Samson's weakness or Delilah's wickedness. (1.) Could any thing be more wicked than her restless and unreasonable importunity with him to discover a secret which she knew would endanger his life if ever it were lodged any where but in his own breast? What could be more base and disingenuous, more false and treacherous, than to lay his head in her lap, as one whom she loved, and at the same time to design the betraying of him to those by whom he was mortally hated? (2.) Could any thing be more weak than for him to continue a parley with one who, he so plainly saw, was aiming to do him a mischief,—that he should lend an ear so long to such an impudent request, that she might know how to do him a mischief,—that when he perceived liers in wait for him in the chamber, and that they were ready to apprehend him if they had been able, he did not immediately quit the chamber, with a resolution never to come into it any more,—nay, that he should again lay his head in that lap out of which he had been so often roused with that alarm, *The Philistines are upon thee, Samson?* One can hardly imagine a man so perfectly besotted, and void of all consideration, as Samson now was; but whoredom is one of those things that *take away the heart.* . It is hard to say what Samson meant in suffering her to try so often whether she could weaken and afflict him; some think he did not certainly know himself where his strength lay, but, it should seem, he did know, for, when he told her that which would disable him indeed, it is said, *He told her all his heart.* It seems, he designed to banter her, and to try if he could turn it off with a jest, and to baffle the *liers in wait,* and make fools of them; but it was very unwise in him that he did not quit the field as soon as ever he perceived that he was not able to keep the ground.

IV. The disclosure he at last made of this great secret; and, if the disclosure proved fatal to him, he must thank himself, who had not power to keep his own counsel from one that manifestly sought his ruin. *Surely in vain is the net spread in the sight of any bird,* but in Samson's sight is the net spread, and yet he is taken in it. If he had not been blind before the Philistines put out his eyes, he might have seen himself betrayed. Delilah signifies a *consumer;* she was so to him. Observe, 1. How she teazed him, telling him she would not believe he loved her, unless he would gratify her in this matter (*v.* 15): *How canst thou say, I love thee, when thy heart is not with me?* That is, "when thou canst not trust me with the counsels of thy heart?" Passionate lovers cannot bear to have their love called in question; they would do any thing rather than their sincerity should be suspected. Here therefore Delilah had this fond fool (excuse me that I call him so) at an advantage. This expostulation is indeed grounded upon a great truth, that those only have our love, not that have our good words or our good wishes, but that have our hearts. That is love without dissimulation; but it is falsehood and flattery in the highest degree to say we love those with whom our hearts are not. How can we say we love either our brother, whom we have seen, or God, whom we have not seen, if our hearts be not with him? She continued many days vexatious to him with her importunity, so that he had no pleasure of his life with her (*v.* 16); why then did he not leave her? It was because he was captivated to her by the power of love, falsely so called, but truly lust. This bewitched and perfectly intoxicated him, and by the force of it see, 2. How she conquered him (*v.* 17): He *told her all his heart.* God left him to himself to do this foolish thing, to punish him for indulging himself in the lusts of uncleanness. The angel that foretold his birth said nothing of his great strength, but only that he should be a Nazarite, and particularly that *no razor should come upon his head, ch.* xiii. 5. His consecration to God was to be his strength, for he was to be *strengthened according to the glorious power of that Spirit which wrought in him mightily,* that his strength, by promise, not by nature, might be a type and figure of the spiritual strength of believers, Col. i. 11, 29. Therefore the badge of his consecration was the pledge of his strength; if he lose the former, he knows he forfeits the latter. "If I be shaven, I shall no longer be a Nazarite, and then my strength will be lost." The making of his bodily strength to depend so much on his hair, which could have no natural influence upon it either one way or other, teaches us to magnify divine institutions, and to expect God's grace, and the continuance of it, only in the use of those means of grace wherein he has appointed us to attend upon him, the word, sacraments, and prayer. In these earthen vessels is this treasure.

18 And when Delilah saw that he had told her all his heart, she sent and called for the lords of the Philistines, saying, Come up this once, for he hath showed me all his heart. Then the lords of the Philistines came up unto her, and brought money in their hand. 19 And she made him sleep upon her knees; and she called for a man, and she caused him to shave off the seven locks of his head; and she began to afflict him, and his strength went from him. 20 And she said, The Philistines *be* upon thee, Samson. And he awoke out of his sleep, and said, I will go out as at other times before, and shake myself. And he wist not that the LORD was departed from him. 21 But the Philistines took him, and put out his eyes, and brought him down to Gaza, and bound him with fetters of brass; and he did grind in the prison house.

We have here the fatal consequences of Samson's folly in betraying his own strength; he soon paid dearly for it. A *whore is a deep ditch; he that is abhorred of the Lord shall fall therein.* In that pit Samson sinks. Observe, 1. What care Delilah took to make sure of the money for herself. She now perceived, by the manner of his speaking, that he had *told her all his heart*, and the lords of the Philistines that hired her to do this base thing are sent for; but they must be sure to bring *the money in their hands*, *v.* 18. The wages of unrighteousness are accordingly produced, unknown to Samson. It would have grieved one's heart to have seen one of the bravest men then in the world sold and bought, as a *sheep for the slaughter;* how does this instance sully all the glory of man, and forbid the strong man ever to boast of his strength! 2. What course she took to deliver him up to them according to the bargain. Many in the world would, for the hundredth part of what was here given Delilah, sell those that they pretend the greatest respect for. *Trust not in a friend then, put not confidence in a guide.* See what a treacherous method she took (*v.* 19): She *made him sleep upon her knees.* Josephus says, She gave him some intoxicating liquor, which laid him to sleep. What opiates she might steal into his cup we know not, but we cannot suppose that he knowingly drank wine or strong drink, for that would have been a forfeiture of his Nazariteship as much as the cutting off of his hair. She pretended the greatest kindness even when she designed the greatest mischief, which yet she could not have compassed if she had not made him sleep. See the fatal consequences of security. Satan ruins men by rocking them asleep, flattering them into a good opinion of their own safety, and so bringing them to mind nothing and fear nothing, and then he robs them of their strength and honour and leads them captive at his will. When we sleep our spiritual enemies do not. When he was asleep she had a person ready to cut off his hair, which he did so silently and so quickly that it did not awake him, but plainly afflicted him; even in his sleep, his spirit manifestly sunk upon it. I think we may suppose that if this ill turn had been done to him in his sleep by some spiteful body, without his being himself accessory to it, as he was here, it would not have had this strange effect upon him; but it was his own wickedness that corrected him. It was his iniquity, else it would not have been so much his infelicity. 3. What little concern he himself was in at it, *v.* 20. He could not but miss his hair as soon as he awoke, and yet said, "*I will shake myself as at other times* after sleep," or, "as at other times when the Philistines were upon me, to make my part good against them." Perhaps he thought to shake himself the more easily, and that his head would feel the lighter, now that his hair was cut, little thinking how much heavier the burden of guilt was than that of hair. He soon found in himself some change, we have reason to think so, and yet *wist not that the Lord had departed from him:* he did not consider that this was the reason of the change. Note, Many have lost the favourable presence of God and are not aware of it; they have provoked God to withdraw from them, but are not sensible of their loss, nor ever complain of it. Their souls languish and grow weak, their gifts wither, every thing goes cross with them; and yet they impute not this to the right cause: they are not aware that *God has departed from them,* nor are they in any care to reconcile themselves to him or to recover his favour. When God has departed we cannot do as at other times. 4. What improvement the Philistines soon made of their advantages against him, *v.* 21. The Philistines took him when God had departed from him. Those that have thrown themselves out of God's protection become an easy prey to their enemies. If we sleep in the lap of our lusts, we shall certainly wake in the hands of the Philistines. It is probable they had promised Delilah not to kill him, but they took an effectual course to disable him. The first thing they did, when they had him in their hands and found they could manage him, was to *put out his eyes,* by *applying fire to them,* says the Arabic version. They considered that his eyes would never come again, as perhaps his hair might, and that the strongest arms could do little without eyes to guide them, and therefore, if now they blind him, they for ever blind him. His eyes were the inlets of his sin: he saw the harlot at Gaza, and went in unto her (*v.* 1), and now his punishment began there. Now that the Philistines had blinded him he had time to remember how his own lust had blinded him. The best preservative of the eyes is to turn them away from beholding vanity. *They brought him down to Gaza,* that there he might appear in weakness where he had lately given such proofs of his strength (*v.* 3), and be a jest to those to whom he had been a terror. They *bound him with fetters of brass* who had before been held in the cords of his own iniquity, and he did *grind in the prison,* work in their bridewell, either for their profit or his punishment, or for both. The devil does thus by sinners, *blinds the minds of those who believe not,* and so enslaves them, and secures them in his interests. Poor Samson, how hast thou fallen! How is thy honour laid in the dust! How has the glory and defence of Israel become the drudge and triumph of the Philistines! *The crown has fallen from his head; woe unto him, for he hath sinned.* Let all take warning by his fall carefully to preserve their purity, and to watch against all fleshly lusts; for all our glory has gone, and our defence departed from us, when the covenant of our separation to God, as spiritual Nazarites, is profaned.

22 Howbeit the hair of his head began to grow again after he was shaven. 23 Then the lords of the Philistines gathered them together for to offer a great sacrifice unto Dagon their god, and to rejoice: for they said, Our god hath delivered Samson our enemy into our hand. 24 And when the people saw him, they praised their god: for they said, Our god hath delivered into our hands our enemy, and the destroyer of our country, which slew many of us. 25 And it came to pass, when their hearts were merry, that they said, Call for Samson, that he may make us sport. And they called for Samson out of the prison house; and he made them sport: and they set him between the pillars. 26 And Samson said unto the lad that held him by the hand, Suffer me that I may feel the pillars whereupon the house standeth, that I may lean upon them. 27 Now the house was full of men and women; and all the lords of the Philistines *were* there; and *there were* upon the roof about three thousand men and women, that beheld while Samson made sport. 28 And Samson called unto the LORD, and said, O Lord GOD, remember me, I pray thee, and strengthen me, I pray thee, only this once, O God, that I may be at once avenged of the Philistines for my two eyes. 29 And Samson took hold of the two middle pillars upon which the house stood, and on which it was borne up, of the one with his right hand, and of the other with his left. 30 And Samson said, Let me die with the Philistines. And he bowed himself with *all his* might; and the house fell upon the lords, and upon all the people that *were* therein. So the dead which he slew at his death were more than *they* which he slew in his life. 31 Then his brethren and all the house of his father came down, and took him, and brought *him* up, and buried him between Zorah and Eshtaol in the burying place of Manoah his father. And he judged Israel twenty years.

Though the last stage of Samson's life was inglorious, and one could wish there were a veil drawn over it, yet this account here given of his death may be allowed to lessen, though it does not quite roll away, the reproach of it; for there was honour in his death. No doubt he greatly repented of his sin, the dishonour he had by it done to God and his forfeiture of the honour God had put upon him; for that God was reconciled to him appears, 1. By the return of the sign of his Nazariteship (*v.* 22): *His hair began to grow again, as when he was shaven,* that is, to be as thick and as long as when it was cut off. It is probable that their general thanksgiving to Dagon was not long deferred, before which Samson's hair had thus grown, by which, and the particular notice taken of it, it seems to have been extraordinary, and designed for a special indication of the return of God's favour to him upon his repentance. For the growth of his hair was neither the cause nor the sign of the return of his strength further than as it was the badge of his consecration, and a token that God accepted him as a Nazarite again, after the interruption, without those ceremonies which were appointed for the restoration of a lapsed Nazarite, which he had not now the opportunity of performing, Num. vi. 9. It is strange that the Philistines in whose hands he was were not jealous of the growth of his hair again, and did not cut it; but perhaps they were willing his great strength should return to him, that they might have so much the more work out of him, and now that he was blind they were in no fear of any hurt from him. 2. By the use God made of him for the destruction of the enemies of his people, and that at a time when it would be most for the vindication of the honour of God, and not immediately for the defence and deliverance of Israel. Observe,

I. How insolently the Philistines affronted the God of Israel, 1. By the sacrifices they offered to Dagon, his rival. This Dagon they call their *god*, a god of their own making, represented by an image, the upper part of which was in the shape of a man, the lower part of a fish, purely the creature of fancy; yet it served them to set up in opposition to the true and living God. To this pretended deity they ascribe their success (*v.* 23, 24): *Our god has delivered Samson our enemy, and the destroyer of our country, into our hands.* So they dreamed, though he could do neither good nor evil. They knew Delilah had betrayed him, and they had paid her for doing it, yet they attribute it to their god, and are confirmed by it in their belief of his power to protect them. All people will thus walk in the name of their gods: they will give them the praise of their achievements; and shall not we pay this tribute to our God whose kingdom ruleth over all? Yet, considering what wicked arts they used to get Samson into their hands, it must be confessed it was only such a dunghill-deity as Dagon that was fit to be made a patron of the villany. Sacrifices were offered, and songs of praise sung, on the general thanksgiving day, for this victory obtained over one man; there were great expressions of joy, and all to the honour of Dagon. Much more reason have we to give the praise of all our successes to our God. *Thanks be to him who causeth us to triumph in Christ Jesus!* 2. By the sport they made with Samson, God's champion, they reflected on God himself. When they were merry with wine, to make them more merry Samson must be fetched to make sport for them (*v.* 25, 27), that is, for them to make sport with. Having sacrificed to their god, and eaten and drunk upon the sacrifice, they rose up to play, according to the usage of idolaters (1 Cor. x. 7), and Samson must be the fool in the play. They made themselves and one another laugh to see how, being blind, he stumbled and blundered. It is likely they *smote this judge of Israel upon the cheek* (Mic. v. 1), and said, *Prophesy who smote thee.* It was an instance of their barbarity to trample thus upon a man in misery, at the sight of whom awhile ago they would have trembled. It put Samson into the depth of misery, and as a sword in his bones were their reproaches, when they said, *Where is now thy God?* Nothing could be more grievous to so great a spirit; yet, being a penitent, his godly sorrow makes him patient, and he accepts the indignity as the punishment of his iniquity. How unrighteous soever the Philistines were, he could not but own that God was righteous. He had sported himself in his own deceivings and with his own deceivers, and justly are the Philistines let loose upon him to make sport with him. Uncleanness is a sin that makes men vile, and exposes them to contempt. *A wound and dishonour shall he get* whose heart is deceived by a woman, and *his reproach shall not be wiped away.* Everlasting shame and contempt will be the portion of those that are blinded and bound by their own lusts. The devil that deceived them will insult over them.

II. How justly the God of Israel brought sudden destruction upon them by the hands of Samson. Thousands of the Philistines had got together, to attend their lords in the sacrifices and joys of this day, and to be the spectators of this comedy; but it proved to them a fatal tragedy, for they were all slain, and buried in the ruins of the house: whether it was a temple or a theatre, or whether it was some slight building run up for the purpose, is uncertain. Observe,

1. Who were destroyed: All the *lords of the Philistines* (*v.* 27), who had by bribes corrupted Delilah to betray Samson to them. Evil pursued those sinners. Many of the people likewise, to the number of 3000, and among them a great many women, one of whom, it is likely, was that harlot of Gaza mentioned, *v.* 1. Samson had been drawn into sin by the Philistine women, and now a great slaughter is made among them, as was by Moses's order among the women of Midian, because it was they that *caused the children of Israel to trespass against the Lord in the matter of Peor,* Num. xxxi. 16.

2. When they were destroyed. (1.) When they were merry, secure, and jovial, and far from apprehending themselves in any danger. When they saw Samson lay hold of the pillars, we may suppose, his doing so served them for a jest, and they made sport with that too: *What will this feeble Jew do?* How are sinners brought to desolation in a moment! They are lifted up in pride and mirth, that their fall may be the more dreadful. Let us never envy the mirth of wicked people, but infer from this instance that their triumphing is short and their joy but for a moment. (2.) It was when they were praising Dagon their god, and giving that honour to him which is due to God only, which is no less than treason against the King of kings, his crown and dignity. Justly therefore is the blood of these traitors mingled with their sacrifices. Belshazzar was cut off when he was praising his man-made gods, Dan. v. 4. (3.) It was when they were making sport with an Israelite, a Nazarite, and insulting over him, persecuting him whom God had

smitten. Nothing fills the measure of the iniquity of any person or people faster than mocking and misusing the servants of God, yea, though it is by their own folly that they are brought low. Those know not what they do, nor whom they affront, that make sport with a good man.

3. How they were destroyed. Samson pulled the house down upon them, God no doubt putting it into his heart, as a public person, thus to avenge God's quarrel with them, Israel's, and his own. (1.) He gained strength to do it by prayer, *v.* 28. That strength which he had lost by sin he, like a true penitent, recovers by prayer; as David, who, when he had provoked the Spirit of grace to withdraw, prayed (Ps. li. 12), *Restore unto me the joy of thy salvation, and uphold me with thy free Spirit.* We may suppose that this was only a mental prayer, and that his voice was not heard (for it was made in a noisy clamorous crowd of Philistines); but, though his voice was not heard of men, yet his prayer was heard of God and graciously answered, and though he lived not to give an account himself of this his prayer, as Nehemiah did of his, yet God not only accepted it in heaven, but, by revealing it to the inspired penman, provided for the registering of it in his church. He prayed to God to remember him and strengthen him this once, thereby owning that his strength for what he had already done he had from God, and begged it might be afforded to him once more, to give them a parting blow. That it was not from a principle of passion or personal revenge, but from a holy zeal for the glory of God and Israel, that he desired to do this, appears from God's accepting and answering the prayer. Samson died praying, so did our blessed Saviour; but Samson prayed for vengeance, Christ for forgiveness. (2.) He gained opportunity to do it by leaning on the two pillars which were the chief supports of the building, and were, it seems, so near together that he could take hold of them both at one time, *v.* 26, 29. Having hold of them, he bore them down with all his might, crying aloud, *Let me die with the Philistines, v.* 30. *Animamque in vulnere ponit—While inflicting the wound he dies.* The vast concourse of people that were upon the roof looking down through it to see the sport, we may suppose, contributed to the fall of it. A weight so much greater than ever it was designed to carry might perhaps have sunk of itself, at least it made the fall more fatal to those within: and indeed few of either could escape being either stifled or crushed to death. This was done, not by any natural strength of Samson, but by the almighty power of God, and is not only marvellous, but miraculous, in our eyes. Now in this, [1.] The Philistines were greatly mortified. All their lords and great men were killed, and abundance of their people, and this in the midst of their triumph; the temple of Dagon (as many think the house was) was pulled down, and Dagon buried in it. This would give a great check to the insolence of the survivors, and, if Israel had but had so much sense and spirit left them as to improve the advantages of this juncture, they might now have thrown off the Philistines' yoke. [2.] Samson may very well be justified, and brought in not guilty of any sinful murder either of himself or the Philistines. He was a public person, a declared enemy to the Philistines, against whom he might therefore take all advantages. They were now in the most barbarous manner making war upon him; all present were aiding and abetting, and justly die with him. Nor was he *felo de se,* or *a self-murderer,* in it; for it was not his own life that he aimed at, though he had too much reason to be weary of it, but the lives of Israel's enemies, for the reaching of which he bravely resigned his own, *not counting it dear to him, so that he might finish his course* with honour. [3.] God was very much glorified in pardoning Samson's great transgressions, of which this was an evidence. It has been said that the prince's giving a commission to one convicted amounts to a pardon. Yet, *though he was a God that forgave him, he took vengeance of his inventions* (Ps. xcix. 8), and, by suffering his champion to die in fetters, warned all to take heed of those lusts which war against the soul. However, we have good reason to hope that though Samson died with the Philistines he had not his everlasting portion with them. *The Lord knows those that are his.* [4.] Christ was plainly typified. He pulled down the devil's kingdom, as Samson did Dagon's temple; and, when he died, he obtained the most glorious victory over the powers of darkness. Then when his arms were stretched out upon the cross, as Samson's to the two pillars, he gave a fatal shake to the gates of hell, and, *through death, destroyed him that had the power of death, that is, the devil* (Heb. ii. 14, 15), and herein exceeded Samson, that he not only died with the Philistines, but rose again to triumph over them.

Lastly, The story of Samson concludes, 1. With an account of his burial. His own relations, animated by the glories that attended his death, came and found out his body among the slain, brought it honourably to his own country, and buried it in the place of his fathers' sepulchres, the Philistines being in such a consternation that they durst not oppose it. 2. With the repetition of the account we had before of the continuance of his government: *He judged Israel twenty years;* and, if they had not been as mean and sneaking as he was brave and daring, he would have left them clear of the Philistines' yoke. They might have been easy, safe, and happy, if they would but have given God and their judges leave to make them so.

CHAP. XVII.

All agree that what is related in this and the rest of the chapters to the end of this book was not done, as the narrative occurs, after Samson, but long before, even soon after the death of Joshua, in the days of Phinehas the son of Eleazar, ch xx. 28. But it is cast here into the latter part of the book that it might not interrupt the history of the Judges. That it might appear how happy the nation was in the judges it is here shown how unhappy they were when there was none. I. Then idolatry began in the family of Micah, ch. xvii. II. Then it spread itself into the tribe of Dan, ch. xviii. III. Then villany was committed in Gibeah of Benjamin, ch. xix. IV. Then that whole tribe was destroyed for countenancing it, ch. xx. V. Then strange expedients were adopted to keep up that tribe, ch. xxi. Therefore blessed be God for the government we are under! In this chapter we are told how Micah an Ephraimite furnished himself, 1. With an image for his god, ver. 1—6. 2. With a Levite, such a one as he was, for his priest, ver. 7—13.

AND there was a man of mount Ephraim, whose name *was* Micah. 2 And he said unto his mother, The eleven hundred *shekels* of silver that were taken from thee, about which thou cursedst, and spakest of also in mine ears, behold, the silver *is* with me; I took it. And his mother said, Blessed *be thou* of the LORD, my son. 3 And when he had restored the eleven hundred *shekels* of silver to his mother, his mother said, I had wholly dedicated the silver unto the LORD from my hand for my son, to make a graven image and a molten image: now therefore I will restore it unto thee. 4 Yet he restored the money unto his mother, and his mother took two hundred *shekels* of silver, and gave them to the founder, who made thereof a graven image and a molten image: and they were in the house of Micah. 5 And the man Micah had a house of gods, and made an ephod, and teraphim, and consecrated one of his sons, who became his priest. 6 In those days *there was* no king in Israel, *but* every man did *that which was* right in his own eyes.

Here we have, I. Micah and his mother quarrelling. 1. The son robs the mother. The old woman had hoarded, with long scraping and saving, a great sum of money, 1100 pieces of silver. It is likely she intended, when she died, to leave it to her son: in the mean time it did her good to look upon it, and to count it over. The young man had a family of children grown up, for he had one of age to be a priest, *v.* 5. He knows where to find his mother's cash, thinks he has more need of it than she has, cannot stay till she dies, and so takes it away privately for his own use. Though it is a fault in parents to withhold from their children that which is meet, and lead them into temptation to wish them in their graves, yet even this will by no means excuse the wickedness of those children that steal from their parents, and think all their own that they can get from them, though by the most indirect methods. 2. The mother curses the son, or whoever had taken her money. It should seem she suspected her son; for, when she cursed, she spoke in his ears so loud, and with so much passion and vehemence, as made both his ears to tingle. See what mischief the love of money makes, how it destroys the duty and comfort of every relation. It was the love of money that made Micah so undutiful to his mother as to rob her, and made her so unkind and void of natural affection to her son as to curse him if he had it and concealed it. Outward losses drive good people to their prayers, but bad people to their curses. This woman's silver was her god before it was made either into a graven or a molten image, else the loss of it would not have put her into such a passion as caused her quite to forget and break through all the laws of decency and piety. It is a very foolish thing for those that are provoked to throw their curses about *as a madman that casteth fire-brands, arrows, and death,* since they know not but they may light upon those that are most dear to them.

II. Micah and his mother reconciled. 1. The son was so terrified with his mother's curses that he restored the money. Though he had so little grace as to take it, he had so much left as not to dare to keep it when his mother had sent a curse after it. He cannot believe his mother's money will do him any good without his mother's blessing, nor dares he deny the theft when he is charged with it, nor retain the money when it is demanded by the right owner. It is best not to do evil, but it is next best, when it is done, to undo it again by repentance, confession, and restitution. Let children be afraid of having the prayers of their parents against them; for, though the curse causeless shall not come, yet that which is justly deserved may be justly feared, even though it was passionately and indecently uttered. 2. The mother was so pleased with her son's repentance that she recalled her curses, and turned them into prayers for her son's welfare: *Blessed be thou of the Lord, my son.* When those that have been guilty of a fault appear to be free and ingenuous in owning it they ought to be commended for their repentance, rather than still be condemned and upbraided for their fault.

III. Micah and his mother agreeing to turn their money into a god, and set up idolatry in their family; and this seems to have been the first instance of the revolt of any Israelite from God and his instituted worship after the death of Joshua and the elders that out-lived him, and is therefore thus particularly related. And though this was only the worship of the true God by an image, against the *second* commandment, yet this opened the door to the worship of other gods, Baalim and the groves, against the *first and great* commandment. Observe,

1. The mother's contrivance of this matter. When the silver was restored she pretended she had *dedicated it to the Lord* (*v.* 3), either before it was stolen, and then she would have this thought to be the reason why she was so much grieved at the loss of it and imprecated evil on him that had taken it, because it was a dedicated and therefore an accursed thing, or after it was stolen she had made a vow that, if she could retrieve it, she would dedicate it to God, and then she would have the providence that had so far favoured her as to bring it back to her hands to be an owning of her vow. "Come," said she to her son, "the money is mine, but thou hast a mind to it; let it be neither mine nor thine, but let us both agree to make it into an image for a religious use." Had she put it to a use that was indeed for the service and honour of God, this would have been a good way of accommodating the matter between them; but, as it was, the project was wicked. Probably this old woman was one of those that came out of Egypt, and would have such images made as she had seen there; now that she began to dote she called to remembrance the follies of her youth, and perhaps told her son that this way of worshipping God by images was, to her knowledge, the old religion.

2. The son's compliance with her. It should seem, when she first proposed the thing he stumbled at it, knowing what the second commandment was; for, when she said (*v.* 3) she designed it for her son to make an image of, yet he restored it to his mother (being loth to have a hand in making the image), and she gave it to the founder and had the thing done, blaming him perhaps for scrupling at it, *v.* 4. But, when the images were made, Micah, by his mother's persuasion, was not only well reconciled to them, but greatly pleased and in love with them; so strangely bewitching was idolatry, and so much supported by *traditions received from their parents,* 1 Pet. i. 18; Jer. xliv. 17. But observe how the old woman's covetousness prevailed, in part, above her superstition. She had wholly dedicated the silver to make the graven and molten images (*v.* 3), all the 1100 pieces; but, when it came to be done, she made less than a fifth part serve, even 200 *shekels, v.* 4. She thought that enough, and indeed it was too much to give for an image that is a teacher of lies. Had it been devoted truly to the honour of God, he would not thus have been put off with part of the price, but would have signified his resentment of the affront, as he did in the case of Ananias and Sapphira. Now observe,

(1.) What was the corruption here introduced, *v.* 5. The man Micah had *a house of gods, a house of God,* so the LXX., for so he thought it, as good as that at Shiloh, and better, because his own, of his own inventing and at his own disposal; for people love to have their religion under their girdle, to manage it as they please. *A house of error,* so the Chaldee, for really it was so, a deviation from the way of truth and an inlet to all deceit. Idolatry is a great cheat, and one of the worst of errors. That which he aimed at in the progress of his idolatry, whether he designed it at first or no, was to mimic and rival both God's oracles and his ordinances. [1.] His oracles; for he made *teraphim,* little images which he might advise with as there was occasion, and receive informations, directions, and predictions from. What the *urim* and *thummim* were to the prince and people these *teraphim* should be to his family; yet he could not think that the true God would own them, or give answers by them, and therefore depended upon such demons as the heathen worshipped to inspire them and make them serviceable to him. Thus, while the honour of Jehovah was pretended (*v.* 3), yet, his institution being relinquished, these Israelites unavoidably lapsed into downright idolatry and demon-worship. [2.] His ordinances. Some room or apartment in the house of Micah was appointed for the temple or house of God; an ephod, or holy garment, was provided for his priest to officiate in, in imitation of those used at the tabernacle of God, and one of his sons he consecrated, probably the eldest, to be his priest. And, when he had set up a graven or molten image to represent the object of his worship, no marvel if a priest of his own getting and his own making served to be the manager of it. Here is no mention of any altar, sacrifice, or incense, in honour of these silver gods, but, having a priest, it is probable he had all these, unless we suppose that, at first, his gods were intended only to be advised with, not to be adored, like Laban's teraphim; but the beginning of idolatry, as of other sins, is *like the letting forth of water:* break the dam, and you bring a deluge. Here idolatry began, and it spread like a fretting leprosy. Dr. Lightfoot would have us observe that as 1100 pieces of silver were here devoted to the making of an idol, which ruined religion, especially in the tribe of Dan (as we shall presently find), which was Samson's tribe, so 1100 pieces of silver were given by each Philistine lord for the ruin of Samson.

(2.) What was the cause of this corruption (*v.* 6): *There was no king in Israel,* no judge or sovereign prince to take cognizance of the setting up of these images (which, doubtless, the country about soon resorted to), and to give orders for the destroying of them, none to convince Micah of his error and to restrain and punish him, to take this disease in time, by which the spreading of the infection might have been happily prevented. Every man did that which was *right in his own eyes,* and then they soon did that which was *evil in the sight of the Lord.* When they were without a king to keep good order among them, God's house was forsaken, his priests were neglected, and all went to ruin among them. See what a mercy government is, and what reason there is that not only *prayers and intercessions, but giving of thanks,* should *be made for kings and all in authority,* 1 Tim. ii. 1, 2. Nothing contributes more, under God, to the support of religion in the world, than the due administration of those two great ordinances, magistracy and ministry.

7 And there was a young man out of Beth-lehem-judah of the family of Judah, who *was* a Levite, and he sojourned there. 8 And the man departed out of the city from Beth-lehem-judah to sojourn where he could find *a place:* and he came to mount Ephraim to the house of Micah, as he journeyed. 9 And Micah said unto him, Whence comest thou? And he said unto him, I *am* a Levite of Beth-lehem judah, and I go to sojourn where I may find *a place.* 10 And Micah said unto him, Dwell with me, and be unto me a father and a priest, and I will give thee ten *shekels* of silver by the year, and a suit of apparel, and thy victuals. So the Levite went in. 11 And the Levite was content to dwell with the man; and the young man was unto him as one of his sons. 12 And Micah consecrated the Levite; and the young man became his priest, and was in the house of Micah. 13 Then said Micah, Now know I that the LORD will do me good, seeing I have a Levite to *my* priest.

We have here an account of Micah's furnishing himself with a Levite for his chaplain, either thinking his son, because the heir of his estate, too good to officiate, or rather, because not of God's tribe, not good enough. Observe,

I. What brought this Levite to Micah. By his mother's side he was of the family of Judah, and lived at Bethlehem among his mother's relations (for that was not a Levites' city), or, upon some other account, as a stranger or inmate, sojourned there, *v.* 7. Thence he went to *sojourn where he could find a place,* and in his travels came to the house of Micah in Mount Ephraim, *v.* 8. Now, 1. Some think it was his unhappiness that he was under a necessity of removing, either because he was persecuted and abused, or rather neglected and starved, at Bethlehem. God had made plentiful provision for the Levites, but the people withheld their dues, and did not help them into the possession of the cities assigned to them; so that they were reduced to straits, and no care was taken for their relief. Israel's forsaking God began with forsaking the Levites, which therefore they are warned against, Deut. xii. 19. It is a sign religion is going to decay when good ministers are neglected and at a loss for a livelihood. But, 2. It seems rather to have been his fault and folly, that he loved to wander, threw himself out where he was, and forfeited the respect of his friends, and, having a roving head, would go to seek his fortune, as we say. We cannot conceive that things had yet come to such a pass among them that a Levite should be poor, unless it was his own fault. As those are fit to be pitied that would fix but may not, so those are fit to be punished that might fix but will not. Unsettledness being, one would think, a constant uneasiness, it is strange that any Israelite, especially any Levite, should affect it.

II. What bargain Micah made with him. Had he not been well enough content with his son for his priest, he would have gone or sent abroad to enquire out a Levite, but now he only takes hold of one that drops into his hands, which showed that he had no great zeal in the matter. It is probable that this rambling Levite had heard, in the country, of Micah's house of *gods, his graven and molten image,* which, if he had had any thing of the spirit of a Levite in him, would have brought him thither to reprove Micah for his idolatry, to tell how directly contrary it was to the law of God, and how it would bring the judgments of God upon him; but instead of this, like a base and degenerate branch of that sacred tribe, thither he goes to offer his service, with, *Have you any work for a Levite?* for I am out of business, and *go to sojourn where I may find a place;* all he aimed at was to get bread, not to do good, *v.* 9. Micah courts him into his family (*v.* 10), and promises him, 1. Good preferment: *Be unto me a father and a priest.* Though a young man, and taken up at the door, yet, if he take him for a priest, he will respect him as a father, so far is he from setting him among his servants. He asks not for his credentials, takes no time to enquire how he behaved in the place of his last settlement, considers not whether, though he was a Levite, yet he might not be of such a bad character as to be a plague and scandal to his family, but thinks, though he should be ever so great a rake, he might serve for a priest to a graven image, like Jeroboam's priest of the *lowest of the people,* 1 Kings xii. 31. No marvel if those who can make any thing serve for a god can also make any thing serve for a priest. 2. A tolerable maintenance. He will allow him *meat, and drink, and clothes,* a *double suit,* so the word is in the margin, a better and a worse, one for every day's wear and one for holy days, and ten shekels, about twenty-five shillings, a year for spending money—a poor salary in comparison of what God provided for the Levites that behaved well; but those that forsake God's service will never better themselves, nor find a better master. The ministry is the best calling but the worst trade in the world.

III. The Levite's settlement with him (*v.* 11): He was *content to dwell with the man;* though his work was superstitious and his wages were scandalous, he objected against neither, but thought himself happy that he had lighted on so good a house. Micah, thinking himself holier than any of his neighbours, presumed to consecrate this Levite, *v.* 12. As if his building, furnishing, and endowing this chapel authorized him, not only to appoint the person that should officiate there, but to confer those orders upon him which he had no right to give nor the other to receive. And now he shows him respect as a father and tenderness as a son, and is willing thus to make up the deficiency of the coin he gave him.

IV. Micah's satisfaction in this (*v.* 13): *Now know I that the Lord will do me good* (that is, he hoped that his new establishment would gain reputation among his neighbours, which would turn to his advantage, for he would share in the profit of his altar; or, rather, he hoped that God would countenance and bless him in all he put his hand unto) *because I have a Levite to be my priest.* 1. He thought it was a sign of God's favour to him and his images that he had so opportunely sent a Levite to his door. Thus those who please themselves with their own delusions, if Providence unexpectedly bring any thing to their hands that furthers them in their evil way, are too apt to infer thence that God is pleased with them. 2. He thought now that the error of his priesthood was amended all was well, though he still retained his graven and molten image. Note, Many deceive themselves into a good opinion of their state by a partial reformation. They think they are as good as they should be, because, in some one particular instance, they are not so bad as they have been, as if the correcting of one fault would atone for their persisting in all the rest. 3. He thought the making of a Levite into a priest was a very meritorious act, which really was a presumptuous usurpation, and very provoking to God. Men's pride, and ignorance, and self-flattery, will undertake, not only to justify, but magnify and sanctify, the most daring impieties and invasions upon the divine prerogatives. With much reason might Micah have said, "Now may I fear that God will curse me, because I have debauched one of his own tribe, and drawn him into the worship of a graven image;" yet for this he hopes God will do him good. 4. He thought that having a Levite in the house with him would of course entitle him to the divine favour. Carnal hearts are apt to build too much upon their external privileges, and to conclude that God will certainly do them good because they are born of godly parents, dwell in praying families, are linked in society with those that are very good, and sit under a lively ministry; whereas all this is but like having a Levite to be their priest, which amounts to no security at all that God will do them good, unless they be good themselves, and make a good use of these advantages.

CHAP. XVIII.

How idolatry crept into the family of Micah we read in the preceding chapter, how it was translated thence into the tribe of Dan we have an account in this chapter, and how it gained a settlement in a city of note; for how great a matter does a little fire kindle! The tribe of Dan had their lot assigned them last of all the tribes, and, it happening to be too strait for them, a considerable city in the utmost corner of Canaan northward was added to it. "Let them get it, and take it;" it was called Laish or Leshem, Josh. xix. 47. Now here we are told, I. How they sent spies to bring them an account of the place, who, by the way, got acquainted with Micah's priest, ver. 1--6. II. What an encouraging report these spies brought back, ver. 7—10. III. What forces were sent to conquer Laish, ver. 11—13. IV. How they, by the way, plundered Micah of his gods, ver. 14—26. V. How easily they conquered Laish, ver. 27—29, and, when they had it, set up the graven image in it, ver. 30, 31.

IN those days *there was* no king in Israel: and in those days the tribe of the Danites sought them an inheritance to dwell in; for unto that day *all their* inheritance had not fallen unto them among the tribes of Israel. 2 And the children of Dan sent of their family five men from their coasts, men of valour, from Zorah, and from Eshtaol, to spy out the land, and to search it; and they said unto them, Go, search the land: who when they came to mount Ephraim, to the house of Micah, they lodged there. 3 When they *were* by the house of Micah, they knew the voice of the young man the Levite: and they turned in thither, and said unto him, Who brought thee hither? and what makest thou in this *place?* and what hast thou here? 4 And he said unto them, Thus and thus dealeth Micah with me, and hath hired me, and I am his priest. 5 And they said unto him, Ask counsel, we pray thee, of God, that we may know whether our way which we go shall be prosperous. 6 And the priest said unto them, Go in peace: before the LORD *is* your way wherein ye go.

Here is, 1. The eye which these Danites had upon Laish, not the whole tribe of Dan, but one family of them, to whose lot, in the subdivision of Canaan, that city fell. Hitherto this family had sojourned with their brethren, who had taken possession of their lot, which lay between Judah and the Philistines, and had declined going to their own city, because there was *no king in Israel* to rule over them, *v.* 1. It lay a great way off, separate from the rest of their tribe; it was entirely in the enemy's hand, and therefore they would sponge upon their brethren rather than go far to provide for themselves. But at length necessity forced them to arouse themselves, and they began to think of an inheritance to dwell in. It is better to have a little of one's own than always to hang upon others. 2. The enquiry which this family of the Danites made concerning Laish: They sent *five men to search the land* (*v.* 2), that they might know the character of the country, whether it was an inheritance worth going so far for, and the posture of the people, whether the making of themselves masters of it was a thing practicable, what force was necessary in order thereunto, and which was the best way of making an attack upon it. The men they sent were men of valour, who, if they fell into their enemies' hands, knew how to look danger in the face. It is prudent to look before we leap. Dan had the subtlety of *a serpent by the way* (Gen. xlix. 17), as well as the courage of a *lion's whelp, leaping from Bashan*, Deut. xxxiii. 22. 3. The acquaintance which their spies got with Micah's priest, and the use they made of that acquaintance. It seems, they had known this Levite formerly, he having in his rambles been sometimes in their country; and, though his countenance might be altered, they knew him again by his voice, *v.* 3. They were surprised to find him so far off, enquired what brought him thither, and he told them (*v.* 4) what business he had there, and what encouragement. They, understanding that he had an oracle in his custody, desired he would tell them whether they should prosper in their present undertaking, *v.* 5. See their carelessness and regardlessness of God and his providence; they would not have enquired of the Lord at all if this Levite's mentioning the teraphim he had with him had not put it into their heads. Many never think of religion but just when it falls in their way and they cannot avoid it, like chance customers. See their ignorance of the divine law, that they thought God, who had forbidden the religious use of graven images, would yet own them in consulting an image, and give them an answer of peace. *Should he be enquired of by them?* Ezek. xiv. 3. They seem to have had a greater opinion of Micah's teraphim than of God's urim; for they had passed by Shiloh, and, for aught that appears, had not enquired there of God's high priest, but Micah's shabby Levite shall be an oracle to them. He betakes himself to his usual method of consulting his teraphim; and, whether he himself believed it or no, he humoured the thing so well that he made them believe he had an answer from God encouraging them to go on, and assuring them of good success (*v.* 6): "*Go in peace*, you shall be safe, and may be easy, for *before the Lord is your way*," that is, "he approves it" (as the Lord is said to *know the way of the righteous* with acceptation), "and therefore he will make it prosperous, his eye will be upon you for good, he will direct your way, and preserve your *going out and coming in*." Note, Our great care should be that our way be such as God approves, and, if it be so, we may *go in peace*. If God care for us, on him let us cast our care, and be satisfied that we cannot miss our way if he *go before us*.

7 Then the five men departed, and came to Laish, and saw the people that *were* therein, how they dwelt careless, after the manner of the Zidonians, quiet and secure; and *there was* no magistrate in the land, that might put *them* to shame in *any* thing; and they *were* far from the Zidonians, and had no business with *any* man. 8 And they came unto their brethren to Zorah and Eshtaol: and their brethren said unto them, What *say* ye? 9 And they said, Arise, that we may go up against them: for we have seen the land, and, behold, it *is* very good: and *are* ye still? be not slothful to go, *and* to enter to possess the land. 10 When ye go, ye shall come unto a people secure, and to a large land: for God hath given it into your hands; a place where *there is* no want of any thing that *is* in the earth. 11 And there went from thence of the family of the Danites, out of Zorah and out of Eshtaol, six hundred men appointed with weapons of war. 12 And they went up, and pitched in Kirjath-jearim, in Judah: wherefore they called that place Mahaneh-dan unto this day: behold, *it is* behind Kirjath-jearim. 13 And they passed thence unto mount Ephraim, and came unto the house of Micah.

Here is, I. The observation which the spies made upon the city of Laish, and the posture of its inhabitants, *v.* 7. Never was place so ill governed and so ill guarded, which would make it a very easy prey to the invader.

1. It was ill governed, for every man might be as bad as he would, and there was

no magistrate, no *heir of restraint* (as the word is), that might so much as *put them to shame in any thing*, much less *put them to death*, so that by the most impudent immoralities they provoked God's wrath, and by all manner of mutual mischiefs weakened and consumed one another. See here, (1.) What the office of magistrates is. They are to be *heirs of restraint*, that is, to preserve a constant entail of power, as heirs to an inheritance, in the places where they are, for the restraining of that which is evil. They are *possessors of restraint*, entrusted with their authority for this end, that they may check and suppress every thing that is vicious and be *a terror to evil doers*. It is only God's grace that can renew men's depraved minds and turn their hearts; but the magistrate's power may restrain their bad practices and tie their hands, so that the wickedness of the wicked may not be either so injurious or so infectious as otherwise it would be. Though the sword of justice cannot cut up the root of bitterness, it may cut off its branches and hinder its growth and spreading, that vice may not go without a check, for then it becomes daring and dangerous, and the community shares in the guilt. (2.) See what method must be used for the restraint of wickedness. Sinners must be put to shame, that those who will not be restrained by the shamefulness of the sin before God and their own consciences may be restrained by the shamefulness of the punishment before men. All ways must be tried to dash sin out of countenance and cover it with contempt, to make people ashamed of their idleness, drunkenness, cheating, lying, and other sins, by making reputation always appear on virtue's side. (3.) See how miserable, and how near to ruin, those places are that either have no magistrates or none that bear the sword to any purpose; the wicked then *walk on every side*, Ps. xii. 8. And how happy we are in good laws and a good government.

2. It was ill guarded. The people of Laish were careless, quiet, and secure, their gates left open, their walls out of repair, because under no apprehension of danger in any way, though their wickedness was so great that they had reason to fear divine vengeance every day. It was a sign that the Israelites, through their sloth and cowardice, were not now such a terror to the Canaanites as they were when they first came among them, else the city of Laish, which probably knew itself to be assigned to them, would not have been so very secure. Though they were an open and inland town, they *lived secure, like the Zidonians* (who were surrounded with the sea and were well fortified both by art and nature), but were *far from the Zidonians*, who therefore could not come in to their assistance, nor help to defend them from the danger which, by debauching their manners, they had helped to bring them into. And, *lastly*, they had *no business with any man*, which bespeaks either the idleness they affected (they followed no trade, and so grew lazy and luxurious, and utterly unable to defend themselves) or the independency they affected: they scorned to be either in subjection to or alliance with any of their neighbours, and so they had none to protect them nor bring in any aid to them. They cared for nobody and therefore nobody cared for them. Such as these were the men of Laish.

II. The encouragement which they consequently gave to their countrymen that sent them to prosecute their design upon this city, *v.* 8—10. Probably the Danites had formed notions of the insuperable difficulties of the enterprise, thought it impossible ever to make themselves masters of Laish, and therefore had kept themselves so long out of the possession of it, perhaps suggesting likewise to one another, in their unbelief, that it was not a country worth going so far and running such a risk for, which jealousies the spies (and they were not, in this, evil spies) had an eye to in their report. 1. They represent the place as desirable: "If you will trust our judgments, *we have seen the land*, and we are agreed in our verdict upon the view, that, behold, *it is very good* (*v.* 9), better than this mountainous country into which we are here crowded by the Philistines. You need not doubt of living comfortably in it, for it is a place *where there is no want of any thing*," *v.* 10. See what a good land Canaan was, that this city which lay furthest of all northward, in the utmost corner of the country, stood on such a fruitful spot. 2. They represent it as attainable. They do not at all question but, with God's blessing, they may soon get possession of it; for *the people are secure*, *v.* 10. And the more secure always the less safe. "God *has given it into your hands*, and you may have it for the taking." They stir them up to the undertaking: "*Arise, that we may go up against them*, let us go about it speedily and resolutely." They expostulate with them for their delays, and chide them out of their sluggishness: *Are you still? Be not slothful to go*. Men need to be thus stirred up to mind even their interest. Heaven is *a very good land, where there is no want of any thing;* our God has, by the promise, *given it into our hands;* let us not then be slothful in making it sure, and *laying hold on eternal life*, but *strive to enter*.

III. The Danites' expedition against Laish. This particular family of them, to whose lot that city fell, now at length make towards it, *v.* 11—13. The military men were but 600 in all, not a hundredth part of that tribe, for when they entered Canaan the Danites were above 64,000, Num. xxvi. 43. It was strange that none of their brethren of their own tribe, much less of any other, came in to their assistance; but it was long after Israel came to Canaan before there appeared among them any thing of a public spirit, or concern for a common interest, which was the reason why they seldom united in a common head, and this kept them low and inconsiderable. It appears (by *v.* 21) that these 600 were the whole number that went to settle there, for they had their families and effects with them, their *little ones and cattle*, so confident were they of success. The other tribes gave them a free passage through their country. Their first day's march brought them to Kirjath-jearim (*v.* 12), and such rare things had military encampments now become in Israel that the place where they rested that night was thence called *Mahaneh-dan, the camp of Dan*, and probably the place whence they began their march between Zorah and Eshtaol was called by the same name, and is meant, *ch.* xiii. 25. The second day's march brought them to Mount Ephraim, near Micah's house (*v.* 13), and there we must pause awhile.

14 Then answered the five men that went to spy out the country of Laish, and said unto their brethren, Do ye know that there is in these houses an ephod, and teraphim, and a graven image, and a molten image? now therefore consider what ye have to do. 15 And they turned thitherward, and came to the house of the young man the Levite, *even* unto the house of Micah, and saluted him. 16 And the six hundred men appointed with their weapons of war, which *were* of the children of Dan, stood by the entering of the gate. 17 And the five men that went to spy out the land went up, *and* came in thither, *and* took the graven image, and the ephod, and the teraphim, and the molten image: and the priest stood in the entering of the gate with the six hundred men *that were* appointed with weapons of war. 18 And these went into Micah's house, and fetched the carved image, the ephod, and the teraphim, and the molten image. Then said the priest unto them, What do ye? 19 And they said unto him, Hold thy peace, lay thine hand upon thy mouth, and go with us, and be to us a father and a priest: *is it* better for thee to be a priest unto the house of one man, or that thou be a priest unto a tribe and a family in Israel? 20 And the priest's heart was glad, and he took the ephod, and the teraphim, and the graven image, and went in the midst of the people. 21 So they turned and departed, and put the little ones and the cattle and the carriage before them. 22 *And* when they were a good way from the house of Micah, the men that *were* in the houses near to Micah's house were gathered together, and overtook the children of Dan. 23 And they cried unto the children of Dan. And they turned their faces, and said unto Micah, What aileth thee, that thou comest with such a company? 24 And he said, Ye have taken away my gods which I made, and the priest, and ye are gone away: and what have I more? and what *is* this *that* ye say unto me, What aileth thee? 25 And the children of Dan said unto him, Let not thy voice be heard among us, lest angry fellows run upon thee, and thou lose thy life, with the lives of thy household. 26 And the children of Dan went their way: and when Micah saw that they *were* too strong for him, he turned and went back unto his house.

The Danites had sent out their spies to find out a country for them, and they sped well in their search; but here, now that they came to the place (for till this brought it to their mind it does not appear that they had mentioned it to their brethren), they oblige them with a further discovery—they can tell them where there are gods: "Here, *in these houses*, there are an ephod, and teraphim, and a great many fine things for devotion, such as we have not the like in our country; *now therefore consider what you have to do, v.* 14. We consulted them, and had a good answer from them; they are worth having, nay, they are worth stealing (that is, having upon the worst terms), and, if we can but make ourselves masters of these gods, we may the better hope to prosper, and make ourselves masters of Laish." So far they were in the right, that it was desirable to have God's presence with them, but wretchedly mistaken when they took these images (which were fitter to be used in a puppet-play than in acts of devotion) for tokens of God's presence. They thought an oracle would be pretty company for them in their enterprise, and instead of a council of war to consult upon every emergency; and, the place they were going to settle in being so far from Shiloh, they thought they had more need of a *house of gods* among themselves than Micah had that lived so near to it. They might have made as good an ephod and teraphim themselves as these were, and such as would have served their purpose every whit as well; but the reputation which they found them in possession of (though they had had that reputation but a while) amused them into a strange veneration for this *house of gods,* which they would soon have dropped if they had had so much sense as to enquire into its origin, and examine whether there were any thing divine in its institution. Being determined to take these gods along with them, we are here told how they stole the images, cajoled the priest, and frightened Micah from attempting to rescue them.

I. The five men that knew the house and the avenues to it, and particularly the chapel, went in and fetched out the images, with the ephod, and teraphim, and all the appurtenances, while the 600 kept the priest in talk at the gate, *v.* 16—18. See what little care this sorry priest took of his gods; while he was sauntering at the gate, and gazing at the strangers, his treasure (such as it was) was gone. See how impotent these sorry gods were, that could not keep themselves from being stolen. It is mentioned as the reproach of idols that they *themselves had gone into captivity,* Isa. xlvi. 2. O the sottishness of these Danites! How could they imagine those gods should protect them that could not keep themselves from being stolen? Yet because they went by the name of gods, as if it were not enough that they had with them the presence of the invisible God, nor that they stood in relation to the tabernacle, where there were even visible tokens of his presence, nothing will serve them but they must have *gods to go before them,* not of their own making indeed, but, which was as bad, of their own stealing. Their idolatry began in theft, a proper prologue for such an opera. In order to the breaking of the second commandment, they begin with the eighth, and take their neighbour's goods to make them their gods. The holy God *hates robbery for burnt-offerings,* but the devil loves it. Had these Danites seized the images to deface and abolish them, and the priest to punish him, they would have done like Israelites indeed, and would have appeared jealous for their God as their fathers had done (Josh. xxii. 16); but to take them for their own use was such a complicated crime as showed that they neither feared God nor regarded man, but were perfectly lost both to godliness and honesty.

II. They set upon the priest, and flattered him into a good humour, not only to let the gods go, but to go himself along with them; for without him they knew not well how to make use of the gods. Observe, 1. How they tempted him, *v.* 19. They assured him of better preferment with them than what he now had. It would be more honour and profit to be chaplain to a regiment (for they were no more, though they called themselves a *tribe)* than to be only a domestic chaplain to a private gentleman. Let him go with them, and he shall have more dependants no him, more sacrifices brought to his altar, and more fees for consulting his teraphim, than he had here. 2. How they won him. A little persuasion served: *His heart was glad, v.* 20. The proposal took well enough with his rambling fancy, which would never let him stay long at a place, and gratified his covetousness and ambition. He had no reason to say but that he was well off where he was; Micah had not *deceived him, nor changed his wages.* He was not moved with any remorse of conscience for attending on a graven image: had he gone away to Shiloh to minister to the Lord's priests, according to the duty of a Levite, he might have been welcome there (Deut. xviii. 6), and his removal would have been commendable; but, instead of this, he takes the images with him, and carries the infection of the idolatry into a whole city. It would have been very unjust and ungrateful to Micah if he had only gone away himself, but it was much more so to take the images along with him, which he knew the heart of Micah was set upon. Yet better could not be expected from a treacherous Levite. What house can be sure of him who has forsaken the house of the Lord? Or what friend will he be true to that has been false to his God? He could not pretend that he was under compulsive force, for he was *glad in his heart* to go. If ten shekels won him (as bishop Hall expresses it), eleven would lose him; for what can hold those that have made shipwreck of a good conscience? *The hireling flees because he is a hireling.* The priest and his gods went in *the midst of the people.* There they placed him, that they might secure him either from going back himself, if his mind should change, or from being fetched back by Micah; or perhaps this post was assigned to him in imitation of the order of Israel's march through the wilderness, in which the ark and the priests went in the midst of their camp.

III. They frightened Micah back when he pursued them to recover his gods. As soon as ever he perceived that his chapel was plundered, and his chaplain had run away from him, he mustered all the forces he could and pursued the robbers, *v.* 22. His neighbours, and perhaps tenants, that used to join with him in his devotions, were forward to help him on this occasion; they got together, and pursued the robbers, who, having their children and cattle before them (*v.* 21), could make no great haste, so that they soon overtook them, hoping by strength of reason to recover what was stolen, for the disproportion of their numbers was such that they could not hope to do it by strength of arm. The pursuers called after them, desiring to speak a word with them; those in the rear (where it is probable they posted the fiercest and strongest of their company, expecting there to be attacked) turned about and asked Micah what ailed him that he was so much concerned, and what he would have, *v.* 23. He argues with them, and pleads his right, which he thought should prevail; but they, in answer, plead their might, which, it proved, did prevail; for it is common that might overcomes right.

1. He insists upon the wrong they had certainly done him (*v.* 24): "*You have taken away my gods*, my images of God, which I have an incontestable title to, for I made them myself, and which I have such an affection for that I am undone if I lose them; for what have I more that will do me any good if these be lost?" Now, (1.) This discovers to us the folly of idolaters, and the power that Satan has over them. What a folly was it for him to call those his *gods* which he had made, when he only that made us is to be worshipped by us as a God! Folly indeed to set his heart upon such silly idle things, and to look upon himself as undone when he had lost them! (2.) This may discover to us our spiritual idolatry. That creature which we place our happiness in, which we set our affections inordinately upon, and which we can by no means find in our hearts to part with, of which we say, "What have we more?" *that* we make an idol of. That is put in God's place, and is a usurper, which we are concerned about as if our life and comfort, our hope and happiness, and our all, were bound up in it. But, (3.) If all people will thus walk in the name of their god, shall we not be in like manner affected towards our God, the true God? Let us reckon the having of an interest in God and communion with him incomparably the richest portion, and the loss of God the sorest loss. Woe unto us if he depart, for what have we more? Deserted souls that are lamenting after the Lord may well wonder, as Micah did, that you should ask what ails them; for the tokens of God's favour are suspended, his comforts are withdrawn, and what have they more?

2. They insist upon the mischief they would certainly do him if he prosecuted his demand. They would not hear reason, nor do justice, nor so much as offer to pay him the prime cost he had been at upon those images, nor promise to make restitution of what they had taken when they had served their present purpose with them in this expedition and had time to copy them and make others like them for themselves: much less had they any compassion for a loss he so bitterly lamented. They would not so much as give him good words, but resolved to justify their robbery with murder if he did not immediately let fall his claims, *v.* 25. "Take heed *lest angry fellows run upon thee, and thou lose thy life*, and that is worse than losing thy gods." Wicked and unreasonable men reckon it a great provocation to be asked to do justice, and support themselves by their power against right and reason. Micah's crime is asking his own, yet, for this, he is in danger of losing his life and the lives of his household. Micah has not courage enough to venture his life for the rescue of his gods, so little opinion has he of their being able to protect him and bear him out, and therefore tamely gives them up (*v.* 26): *He turned and went back to his house;* and if the loss of his idols did but convince him (as, one would think, it should) of their vanity and impotency, and his own folly in setting his heart upon them, and send him back to the true God from whom he had revolted, he that lost them had a much better bargain than those that by force of arms carried them off. If the loss of our idols cure us of the love of them, and make us say, *What have we to do any more with idols?* the loss will be unspeakable gain. See Isa. ii. 20; xxx. 22.

27 And they took *the things* which Micah had made, and the priest which he had, and came unto Laish, unto a people *that were* at quiet and secure: and they smote them with the edge of the sword, and burnt the city with fire. 28 And *there was* no deliverer, because it *was* far from Zidon, and they had no business with *any* man; and it was in the valley that *lieth* by Beth-rehob. And they built a city, and dwelt therein. 29 And they called the name of the city Dan, after the name of Dan their father, who was born unto Israel: howbeit the name of the city *was* Laish at the first. 30 And the children of Dan set up the graven image: and Jonathan, the son of Gershom, the son of Manasseh, he and his sons were priests to the tribe of Dan until the day of the captivity of the land. 31 And they set them up Micah's graven image, which he made, all the time that the house of God was in Shiloh.

Here is, I. Laish conquered by the Danites. They proceeded on their march, and, because they met with no disaster, perhaps concluded they had not done amiss in robbing Micah. Many justify themselves in their impiety by their prosperity. Observe, 1. What posture they found the people of Laish in, both those of the city and those of the country about. They were quiet and secure, not jealous of the five spies that had been among them to search out the land, nor had they any intelligence of the approach of this enemy, which made them a very easy prey to this little handful of men that came upon them, *v.* 27. Note, Many are brought to destruction by their security. Satan gets advantage against us when we are careless and off our watch. Happy therefore is the man that feareth always. 2. What a complete victory they obtained over them: They *put all the people to the sword,* and burnt down so much of the city as they thought fit to rebuild (*v.* 27, 28), and, for aught that appears, herein they met with no resistance; for the measure of the iniquity of the Canaanites was full, that of the Danites was but beginning to fill. 3. How the conquerors settled themselves in their room, *v.* 28, 29. They built the city, or much of it, anew (the old buildings having gone to decay), and *called the name of it Dan,* to be a witness for them that, though separated so far off from their brethren, they were nevertheless Danites by birth, which might hereafter, by reason of their distance, be called in question. We should feel concerned not to lose the privilege of our relation to God's Israel, and therefore should take all occasions to own it and preserve the remembrance of it to ours after us.

II. Idolatry immediately set up there. God had graciously performed his promise, in putting them in possession of that which fell to their lot, obliging them thereby to be faithful to him who had been so to them. They *inherited the labour of the people, that they might observe his statutes,* Ps. cv. 44, 45. But the first thing they do after they are settled is to break his statutes. As soon as they began to settle themselves they *set up the graven image* (*v.* 30), perversely attributing their success to that idol which, if God had not been infinitely patient, would have been their ruin. Thus a prosperous idolater goes on to offend, *imputing this his power unto his god,* Hab. i. 11. Their Levite, who officiated as priest, is at length *named* here—*Jonathan, the son of Gershom, the son of Manasseh.* The word *Manasseh,* in the original, has the letter נ, *n,* set over the head, which, some of the Jewish rabbin say, is an intimation that it should be left out, and then *Manasseh* will be *Moses,* and this Levite, they say, was grandson to the famous Moses, who indeed had a son named Gershom; but, say they, the historian, in honour of Moses, by a half interposition of that letter, turned the name into Manasseh. The vulgar Latin reads it *Moses.* And if indeed Moses had a grandson that was rakish, and was picked up as a fit tool to be made use of in the setting up of idolatry, it is not the only instance (would to God it were!) of the unhappy degenerating of the posterity of great and good men. Children's children are not always the crown of old men. But the learned bishop Patrick takes this to be an idle conceit of the rabbin, and supposes this Jonathan to be of some other family of the Levites. How long these corruptions continued we are told in the close. 1. That the posterity of this Jonathan continued to act as priests to this family of Dan that was seated at Laish, and in the country about, till the captivity, *v.* 30. After Micah's image was removed this family retained the character of priests, and had respect paid them as such by that city, and it is very probable that Jeroboam had an eye to them when he set up one of his calves there (which they would welcome at Dan, and put some reputation upon, when the priests of the Lord would have nothing to do with them), and that this family officiated as some of his priests. 2. That these images continued till Samuel's time, for so long *the ark of God was at Shiloh;* and it is probable that in his time effectual care was taken to suppress and abolish this idolatry. See how dangerous it is to admit an infection, for spiritual distempers are not so soon cured as caught.

CHAP. XIX.

The three remaining chapters of this book contain a most tragical story of the wickedness of the men of Gibeah, patronised by the tribe of Benjamin, for which that tribe was severely chastised and almost entirely cut off by the rest of the tribes. This seems to have been done not long after the death of Joshua, for it was when there was no king, no judge, in Israel (ver. 1, and ch. xxi. 25), and Phinehas was then high priest, ch. xx. 28. These particular iniquities, the Danites' idolatry, and the Benjamites' immorality, let in that general apostasy, ch. iii. 7. The abuse of the Levite's concubine is here very particularly related. I. Her adulterous elopement from him, ver. 1, 2. II. His reconciliation to her, and the journey he took to fetch her home, ver. 3. III. Her father's kind entertainment of him, ver. 4—9. IV. The abuse he met with at Gibeah, where, being benighted, he was forced to stop. 1. He was neglected by the men of Gibeah (ver. 10—15) and entertained by an Ephraimite that sojourned among them, ver. 16—21. 2. They set upon him in his quarters, as the Sodomites did on Lot's guests, ver. 22—24. 3. They villanously forced his concubine to death, ver. 25—28. V. The course he took to send notice of this to all the tribes of Israel, ver. 29, 30.

AND it came to pass in those days, when *there was* no king in Israel, that there was a certain Levite sojourning on the side of mount Ephraim, who took to him a concubine out of Beth-lehem-judah. 2 And his concubine played the whore against him, and went away from him unto her father's house to Beth-lehem-judah, and was there four whole months. 3 And her husband arose, and went after her, to speak friendly unto her, *and* to bring her again, having his servant with him, and a couple of asses: and she brought him into her father's house: and when the father of the damsel saw him, he rejoiced to meet him. 4 And his father in law, the damsel's father, retained him; and he abode with him three days: so they did eat and drink, and lodged there. 5 And it came to pass on the fourth day, when they arose early in the morning, that he rose up to depart: and the damsel's father said unto his son in law, Comfort thine heart with a morsel of bread, and afterward go your way. 6 And they sat down, and did eat and drink both of them together: for the damsel's father had said unto the man, Be content, I pray thee, and tarry all night, and let thine heart be merry. 7 And when the man rose up to depart, his father in law urged him: therefore he lodged there again. 8 And he arose early in the morning on the fifth day to depart: and the damsel's father said, Comfort thine heart, I pray thee. And they tarried until afternoon, and they did eat both of them. 9 And when the man rose up to depart, he, and his concubine, and his servant, his father in law, the damsel's father, said unto him, Behold, now the day draweth toward evening, I pray you tarry all night: behold, the day groweth to an end, lodge here, that thine heart may be merry; and to morrow get you early on your way, that thou mayest go home. 10 But the man would not tarry that night, but he rose up and departed, and came over against Jebus, which *is* Jerusalem; and *there were* with him two asses saddled, his concubine also *was* with him. 11 *And* when they *were* by Jebus, the day was far spent; and the servant said unto his master, Come, I pray thee, and let us turn in into this city of the Jebusites, and lodge in it. 12 And his master said unto him, We will not turn aside hither into the city of a stranger, that *is* not of the children of Israel; we will pass over to Gibeah. 13 And he said unto his servant, Come, and let us draw near to one of these places to lodge all night, in Gibeah, or in Ramah. 14 And they passed on and went their way; and the sun went down upon them *when they were* by Gibeah, which *belongeth* to Benjamin. 15 And they turned aside thither, to go in *and* to lodge in Gibeah: and when he went in, he sat him down in a street of the city: for *there was* no man that took them into his house to lodging.

The domestic affairs of this Levite would not have been related thus largely but to make way for the following story of the injuries done him, in which the whole nation interested themselves. Bishop Hall's first remark upon this story is, *That there is no complaint of a public ordered state but there is a Levite at one end of it, either as an agent or as a patient.* In Micah's idolatry a Levite was active; in the wickedness of Gibeah a Levite was passive; *no tribe shall sooner feel the want of government than that of Levi;* and, in all the book of Judges, no mention is made of any of that tribe, but of these two. This Levite was of Mount Ephraim, *v.* 1. He married a wife of Bethlehem-Judah. She is called his *concubine,* because she was not endowed, for perhaps he had nothing to endow her with, being himself a sojourner and not settled; but it does not appear that he had any other wife, and the margin calls her *a wife, a concubine, v.* 1. She came from the same city that Micah's Levite came from, as if Bethlehem-Judah owed a double ill turn to Mount Ephraim, for she was as bad for a Levite's wife as the other for a Levite.

I. This Levite's concubine played the whore and eloped from her husband, *v.* 2. The Chaldee reads it only that she *carried herself insolently to him,* or *despised him,* and, he being displeased at it, *she went away from him,* and (which was not fair) was received and entertained at her father's house. Had her husband turned her out of doors unjustly, her father ought to have pitied her affliction; but, when she treacherously departed from her husband to embrace the bosom of a stranger, her father ought not to have countenanced her sin. Perhaps she would not have violated her duty to her husband if she had not known too well where she should be kindly received. Children's ruin is often owing very much to parents' indulgence.

II. The Levite went himself to court her return. It was a sign there was no king, no judge, in Israel, else she would have been prosecuted and put to death as an adulteress; but, instead of that, she is addressed in the kindest manner by her injured husband, who takes a long journey on purpose to beseech her to be reconciled, *v.* 3. If he had put her away, it would have been a crime in him to return to her again, Jer. iii. 1. But, she having gone away, it was a virtue in him to forgive the offence, and, though the party wronged, to make the first motion to her to be friends again. It is part of the character of the wisdom from above that it is gentle and easy to be entreated. He spoke *friendly* to her, or *comfortably* (for so the Hebrew phrase of *speaking to the heart* commonly signifies), which intimates that she was in sorrow, penitent for what she had done amiss, which probably he heard of when he came to fetch her back. Thus God promises concerning adulterous Israel (Hos. ii. 14), *I will bring her into the wilderness, and speak comfortably to her.*

III. Her father made him very welcome, and, by his extraordinary kindness to him, endeavoured to atone for the countenance he had given his daughter in withdrawing from him, and to confirm him in his disposition to be reconciled to her. 1. He entertains him kindly, *rejoices to see him* (*v.* 3), treats him generously for three days, *v.* 4. And the Levite, to show that he was perfectly reconciled, accepted his kindness, and we do not find that he upbraided him or his daughter with what had been amiss, but was as easy and as pleasant as at his first wedding-feast. It becomes all, but especially Levites, to forgive as God does. Every thing among them gave a hopeful prospect of their living comfortably together for the future; but, could they have foreseen what befel them within one day or two, how would all their mirth have been embittered and turned into mourning! When the affairs of our families are in the best posture we ought to rejoice with trembling, because we know not what troubles one day may bring forth. We cannot foresee what evil is near us, but we ought to consider what may be, that we may not be secure, as if to-morrow must needs be as this day and *much more abundant*, Isa. lvi. 12. 2. He is very earnest for his stay, as a further demonstration of his hearty welcome. The affection he had for him, and the pleasure he took in his company, proceeded, (1.) From a civil regard to him as his son-in-law and an ingrafted branch of his own house. Note, Love and duty are due to those to whom we are related by marriage as well as to those who are bone of our bone: and those that show kindness as this Levite did may expect to receive kindness as he did. And, (2.) From a pious respect to him as a Levite, a servant of God's house; if he was such a Levite as he should be (and nothing appears to the contrary) he is to be commended for courting his stay, finding his conversation profitable, and having opportunity to learn from him the *good knowledge of the Lord*, hoping also that *the Lord will do him good because he has a Levite* to be his son-in-law, and will bless him for his sake. [1.] He forces him to stay the fourth day, and this was kind; not knowing when they might be together again, he engages him to stay as long as he possibly could. The Levite, though nobly treated, was very urgent to be gone. A good man's heart is where his business is; for *as a bird that wanders from her nest so is the man that wanders from his place.* It is a sign a man has either little to do at home, or little heart to do what he has to do, when he can take pleasure in being long abroad where he has nothing to do. It is especially good to see a Levite willing to go home to his few sheep in the wilderness. Yet this Levite was overcome by importunity and kind persuasion to stay longer than he intended, *v.* 5—7. We ought to avoid the extreme of an over-easy yielding, to the neglect of our duty on the one hand, and that of moroseness and wilfulness, to the neglect of our friends and their kindness on the other hand. Our Saviour, after his resurrection, was prevailed upon to stay with his friends longer than he at first intimated to be his purpose, Luke xxiv. 28, 29. [2.] He forces him to stay till the afternoon of the fifth day, and this, as it proved, was unkind, *v.* 8, 9. He would by no means let him go before dinner, promises him he shall have dinner early, designing thereby, as he had done the day before, to detain him another night; but the Levite was intent on the *house of the Lord at Shiloh* (*v.* 18), and, being impatient to get thither, would stay no longer. Had they set out early, they might have reached some better lodging-place than that which they were now constrained to take up with, nay, they might have got to Shiloh. Note, Our friends' designed kindnesses often prove, in the event, real injuries; what is meant for our welfare becomes a trap. *Who knows what is good for a man in this life?* The Levite was unwise in setting out so late; he might have got home better if he had staid a night longer and taken the day before him.

IV. In his return home he was forced to lodge at Gibeah, a city in the tribe of Benjamin, afterwards called *Gibeah of Saul*, which lay on his road towards Shiloh and Mount Ephraim. When it drew towards night, and the shadows of the evening were stretched out, they began to think (as it behoves us to do when we observe the day of our life hastening towards a period) where they must lodge. When night came they could not pursue their journey. *He that walketh in darkness knoweth not whither he goes.* They could not but desire rest, for which the night was intended, as the day for labour. 1. The servant proposed that they should lodge in Jebus, afterwards Jerusalem, but as yet in the possession of Jebusites. "Come," said the servant, "let us lodge in this city of the Jebusites," *v.* 11. And, if they had done so, it is probable they would have had much better usage than they met with in Gibeah of Benjamin. Debauched and profligate Israelites are worse and much more dangerous than Canaanites themselves. But the master, as became one of God's tribe, would by no means quarter, no, not one night, in a city of strangers (*v.* 12), not because he questioned his safety among them, but he was not willing, if he could possibly avoid it, to have so much intimacy and familiarity with them as a night's lodging came to, nor to be so much beholden to them. By shunning this place he would witness against the wickedness of those that contracted friendship and familiarity with these devoted nations. Let Israelites, Levites especially, associate with Israelites, and not with the *sons of the stranger.*

2. Having passed by Jebus, which was about five or six miles from Bethlehem (the place whence they came), and not having daylight to bring them to Ramah, they stopped at Gibeah (*v.* 13—15); there they sat down in the street, nobody offering them a lodging. In these countries, at that time, there were no inns, or public-houses, in which, as with us, travellers might have entertainment for their money, but they carried entertainment along with them, as this Levite did (*v.* 19), and depended upon the courtesy and hospitality of the inhabitants for a lodging. Let us take occasion hence, when we are in journeys, to thank God for this, among other conveniences of travelling, that there are inns to entertain strangers, and in which they may be welcome and well accommodated for their money. Surely there is no country in the world wherein one may stay at home with more satisfaction, or go abroad with more comfort, than in our own nation. This traveller, though a Levite (and to those of that tribe God had particularly commanded his people to be kind upon all occasions), met with very cold entertainment at Gibeah: *No man took them into his house.* If they had any reason to think he was a Levite perhaps that made those ill-disposed people the more shy of him. There are those who will have this laid to their charge at the great day, *I was a stranger and you took me not in.*

16 And, behold, there came an old man from his work out of the field at even, which *was* also of mount Ephraim; and he sojourned in Gibeah: but the men of the place *were* Benjamites. 17 And when he had lifted up his eyes, he saw a wayfaring man in the street of the city: and the old man said, Whither goest thou? and whence comest thou? 18 And he said unto him, We *are* passing from Beth-lehem-judah toward the side of mount Ephraim; from thence *am* I: and I went to Beth-lehem-judah, but I *am now* going to the house of the LORD; and there *is* no man that receiveth me to house. 19 Yet there is both straw and provender for our asses; and there is bread and wine also for me, and for thy handmaid, and for the young man *which is* with thy servants: *there is* no want of any thing. 20 And the old man said, Peace *be* with thee; howsoever *let* all thy wants *lie* upon me; only lodge not in the street. 21 So he brought him into his house, and gave provender unto the asses: and they washed their feet, and did eat and drink.

Though there was not one *of* Gibeah, yet it proved there was one *in* Gibeah, that showed some civility to this distressed Levite, who was glad that any one took notice of him. It was strange that some of those wicked people, who, when it was dark, designed so ill to him and his concubine, did not, under pretence of kindness, invite them in, that they might have a fairer opportunity of perpetrating their villany; but either they had not wit enough to be so designing, or not wickedness enough to be so deceiving. Or, perhaps, none of them separately thought of such a wickedness, till in the black and dark night they got together to contrive what mischief they should do. Bad people in confederacy make one another much worse than any of them would be by themselves. When the Levite, and his wife, and servant, were beginning to fear that they must lie in the street all night (and as good have laid in a den of lions) they were at length invited into a house, and we are here told,

I. Who that kind man was that invited them. 1. He was a man of Mount Ephraim, and only sojourned in Gibeah, *v.* 16. Of all the tribes of Israel, the Benjamites had most reason to be kind to poor travellers, for their ancestor, Benjamin, was born upon the road, his mother being then upon a journey, and very near to this place, Gen. xxxv. 16, 17. Yet they were hard-hearted to a traveller in distress, while an honest Ephraimite had compassion on him, and, no doubt, was the more kind to him, when, upon enquiry, he found that he was his countryman, of Mount Ephraim likewise. He that was himself but a sojourner in Gibeah was the more compassionate to a wayfaring man, for he *knew the heart of a stranger,* Exod. xxiii. 9; Deut. x. 19. Good people, that look upon themselves but as strangers and sojourners in this world, should for this reason be tender to one another, because they all belong to the same better country and are not at home here. 2. He was an old man, one that retained some of the expiring virtue of an Israelite. The rising generation was entirely corrupted; if there was any good remaining among them, it was only with those that were old and going off. 3. He was coming home from his work out of the field at eventide. The evening calls home labourers, Ps. civ. 23. But, it should seem, this was the only labourer that this evening brought home to Gibeah. The rest had given themselves up to sloth and luxury, and no marvel there was among them, as in Sodom, abundance of uncleanness, when there was among them, as in Sodom, abundance of idleness, Ezek. xvi. 49. But he that was honestly diligent in his business all day was disposed to be generously hospitable to these poor strangers at night. Let men *labour, that they may have to give,*

Eph. iv. 28. It appears from *v.* 21 that he was a man of some substance, and yet had been himself at work in the field. No man's estate will privilege him in idleness.

II. How free and generous he was in his invitation. He did not stay till they applied to him to beg for a night's lodging; but when he saw them (*v.* 17) enquired into their circumstances, and anticipated them with his kindness. Thus our good God answers before we call. Note, A charitable disposition expects only opportunity, not importunity, to do good, and will succour upon sight, unsought unto. Hence we read of a *bountiful eye*, Prov. xxii. 9. If Gibeah was like Sodom, this old man was like Lot in Sodom, who *sat in the gate* to invite strangers, Gen. xix. 1. Thus *Job opened his doors to the traveller*, and would not suffer him to *lodge in the street*, Job xxxi. 32. Observe, 1. How ready he was to give credit to the Levite's account of himself when he saw no reason at all to question the truth of it. Charity is not apt to distrust, but *hopeth all things* (1 Cor. xiii. 7) and will not make use of Nabal's excuse for his churlishness to David, *Many servants now-a-days break away from their masters*, 1 Sam. xxv. 10. The Levite, in his account of himself, professed that he was now going *to the house of the Lord* (*v.* 18), for there he designed to attend, either with a trespass-offering for the sins of his family, or with a peace-offering for the mercies of his family, or both, before he went to his own house. And, if the men of Gibeah had any intimation of his being bound that way, probably they would therefore be disinclined to entertain him. The Samaritans would not receive Christ because his face was towards Jerusalem, Luke ix. 53. But for this reason, because he was a Levite and was now going to the house of the Lord, this good old man was the more kind to him. Thus he received a disciple *in the name of a disciple*, a servant of God for his Master's sake. 2. How free he was to give him entertainment. The Levite was himself provided with all necessaries (*v.* 19), wanted nothing but a lodging, but his generous host would be himself at the charge of his entertainment (*v.* 20): *Let all thy wants be upon me;* so he *brought him into his house*, *v.* 21. Thus God will, some way or other, raise up friends for his people and ministers, even when they seem forlorn.

22 *Now* as they were making their hearts merry, behold, the men of the city, certain sons of Belial, beset the house round about, *and* beat at the door, and spake to the master of the house, the old man, saying, Bring forth the man that came into thine house, that we may know him. 23 And the man, the master of the house, went out unto them, and said unto them, Nay, my brethren, *nay*, I pray you, do not *so* wickedly; seeing that this man is come into mine house, do not this folly. 24 Behold, *here is* my daughter a maiden, and his concubine; them I will bring out now, and humble ye them, and do with them what seemeth good unto you: but unto this man do not so vile a thing. 25 But the men would not hearken to him: so the man took his concubine, and brought her forth unto them; and they knew her, and abused her all the night until the morning: and when the day began to spring, they let her go. 26 Then came the woman in the dawning of the day, and fell down at the door of the man's house where her lord *was*, till it was light. 27 And her lord rose up in the morning, and opened the doors of the house, and went out to go his way: and, behold, the woman his concubine was fallen down *at* the door of the house, and her hands *were* upon the threshold. 28 And he said unto her, Up, and let us be going. But none answered. Then the man took her *up* upon an ass, and the man rose up, and gat him unto his place. 29 And when he was come into his house, he took a knife, and laid hold on his concubine, and divided her, *together* with her bones, into twelve pieces, and sent her into all the coast of Israel. 30 And it was so, that all that saw it said, There was no such deed done nor seen from the day that the children of Israel came up out of the land of Egypt unto this day: consider of it, take advice, and speak *your minds*.

Here is, I. The great wickedness of the men of Gibeah. One could not imagine that ever it should enter into the heart of men that had the use of human reason, of Israelites that had the benefit of divine revelation, to be so very wicked. "Lord, what is man!" said David, "what a *mean* creature is he!" "Lord, what is man," may we say upon the reading of this story, "what a vile creature is he, when he is given up to his own heart's lusts!" The sinners are here called *sons of Belial*, that is, ungovernable men, men that would endure no yoke, children of the devil (for he is Belial), resembling him, and joining with him in rebellion against God and his government. Sons of Benjamin, of whom Moses had said, *The beloved of the Lord shall dwell in safety by him* (Deut. xxxiii. 12), have become such sons of Belial that an honest man cannot lodge in safety among them. The sufferers were a Levite and his wife, and that kind man that gave them entertainment. We are strangers upon earth, and must expect strange usage. It is said *they were making their hearts merry* when this trouble came upon them, *v.* 22. If the mirth was innocent, it teaches us of what uncertain continuance all our creature comforts and enjoyments are; when we are ever so well pleased with our friends, we know not how near our enemies are; nor, if it be well with us this hour, can we be sure it will be so the next. If the mirth was sinful and excessive, let it be a warning to us to keep a strict guard upon ourselves, that we grow not intemperate in the use of lawful things, nor be transported into indecencies by our cheerfulness; for *the end of that mirth is heaviness.* God can soon change the note of those that are making their hearts merry, and turn their laughter into mourning and their joy into heaviness. Let us see what the wickedness of these Benjamites was.

1. They made a rude and insolent assault, in the night, upon the habitation of an honest man, that not only lived peaceably among them, but kept a good house and was a blessing and ornament to their city. They beset the house round, and, to the great terror of those within, beat as hard as they could at the door, *v.* 22. A man's house is his castle, in which he ought to be both safe and quiet, and, where there is law, it is taken under the special protection of it; but there was no king in Israel to keep the peace and secure honest men from the sons of violence.

2. They had a particular spite at the strangers that were within their gates, that only desired a night's lodging among them, contrary to the laws of hospitality, which all civilized nations have accounted sacred, and which the master of the house pleaded with them (*v.* 23): *Seeing that this man has come into my house.* Those are base and abject spirits indeed that will trample upon the helpless, and use a man the worse for his being a a stranger, whom they know no ill of.

3. They designed in the most filthy and abominable manner (not to be thought of without horror and detestation) to abuse the Levite, whom perhaps they had observed to be young and comely: *Bring him forth that we may know him.* We should certainly have concluded they meant only to enquire whence he came, and to know his character, but that the good man of the house, who understood their meaning too well, by his answer lets us know that they designed the gratification of that most unnatural and worse than brutish lust which was expressly forbidden by the law of Moses, and called an *abomination,* Lev. xviii. 22. Those that are guilty of it are ranked in the New Testament among the worst and vilest of sinners (1 Tim. i. 10), and such as *shall not inherit the kingdom of God,* 1 Cor. vi. 9. Now, (1.) This was the sin of Sodom, and is thence called *Sodomy.* The Dead Sea, which was the standing monument of God's vengeance upon Sodom, for its filthiness, was one of the boundaries of Canaan, and lay not many miles off from Gibeah. We may suppose the men of Gibeah had seen it many a time, and yet would not take warning by it, but did worse than Sodom (Ezek. xvi. 48), and sinned just *after the similitude of their transgression.* Who would have expected (says bishop Hall) such extreme abomination to come out of the loins of Jacob? Even the worst pagans were saints to them. What did it avail them that they had the ark of God in Shiloh when they had Sodom in their streets—God's law in their fringes, but the devil in their hearts? Nothing but hell itself can yield a worse creature than a depraved Israelite. (2.) This was the punishment of their idolatry, that sin to which they were, above all others, most addicted. Because they liked not to retain God in their knowledge, therefore he gave them up to these vile affections, by which they dishonoured themselves as they had by their idolatry dishonoured him and turned his glory into shame, Rom. i. 24, 28. See and admire, in this instance, the patience of God. Why were not these sons of Belial struck blind, as the Sodomites were? Why were not fire and brimstone rained from heaven upon their city? It was because God would leave it to Israel to punish them by the sword, and would reserve his own punishment of them for the future state, in which those that *go after strange flesh* shall *suffer the vengeance of eternal fire,* Jude 7.

4. They were deaf to the reproofs and reasonings of the good man of the house, who, being well acquainted (we may suppose) with the story of Lot and the Sodomites, set himself to imitate Lot, *v.* 23, 24. Compare Gen. xix. 6—8. He went out to them as Lot did, spoke civilly to them, called them brethren, begged of them to desist, pleaded the protection of his house which his guests were under, and represented to them the great wickedness of their attempt: "Do not so wickedly, so very wickedly." He calls it *folly* and *a vile thing.* But in one thing he conformed too far to Lot's example (as we are apt in imitating good men to follow them even in their false steps), in offering them his daughter to do what they would with. He had not power thus to prostitute his daughter, nor ought he to have done this evil that good might come. But this wicked proposal of his may be in

part excused from the great surprise and terror he was in, his concern for his guests, and his having too close a regard to what Lot did in the like case, especially not finding that the angels who were by reproved him for it. And perhaps he hoped that his mentioning this as a more natural gratification of their lust would have sent them back to their common harlots. But *they would not hearken to him, v.* 25. Headstrong lusts are like the deaf adder that stoppeth her ear; they sear the conscience and make it insensible.

5. They got the Levite's wife among them, and abused her to death, *v.* 25. They slighted the old man's offer of his daughter to their lust, either because she was not handsome or because they knew her to be one of great gravity and modesty: but, when the Levite brought them his concubine, they took her with them by force to the place appointed for their filthiness. Josephus, in his narrative of this story, makes her to be the person they had a design upon when they beset the house, and says nothing of their villanous design upon the Levite himself. They saw her (he says) in the street, when they came into the town, and were smitten with her beauty; and perhaps, though she was reconciled to her husband, her looks did not bespeak her to be one of the most modest. Many bring mischief of this kind upon themselves by their loose carriage and behaviour; a little spark may kindle a great fire. One would think the Levite should have followed them, to see what became of his wife, but it is probable he durst not, lest they should do him a mischief. In the miserable end of this woman, we may see the righteous hand of God punishing her for her former uncleanness, when she played the whore against her husband, *v.* 2. Though her father had countenanced her, her husband had forgiven her, and the fault was forgotten now that the quarrel was made up, yet God remembered it against her when he suffered these wicked men thus wretchedly to abuse her; how unrighteous soever they were in their treatment of her, in permitting it the Lord was righteous. Her punishment answered her sin, *Culpa libido fuit, pœna libido fuit—Lust was her sin, and lust was her punishment.* By the law of Moses she was to have been put to death for her adultery. She escaped that punishment from men, yet vengeance pursued her; for, if there was no king in Israel, yet there was a God in Israel, a God that judgeth in the earth. We must not think it enough to make our peace with men, whom by our sins we have wronged, but are concerned, by repentance and faith, to make our peace with God, who sees not as men see, nor makes so light of sin as men often do. The justice of God in this matter does not at all extenuate the horrid wickedness of these men of Gibeah, than which nothing could be more barbarous and inhuman.

II. The notice that was sent of this wickedness to all the tribes of Israel. The poor abused woman made towards her husband's lodgings as soon as ever the approach of the day-light obliged these sons of Belial to let her go (for these works of darkness hate and dread the light), *v.* 25. Down she fell at the door, with her hands on the threshold, begging pardon (as it were) for her former transgression, and in that posture of a penitent, with her mouth in the dust, she expired. There he found her (*v.* 26, 27), supposed her asleep, or overcome with shame and confusion for what had happened, but soon perceived she was dead (*v.* 28), took up her dead body, which, we may suppose, had all over it marks of the hands, the blows, and other abuses, she had received. On this sad occasion he waived his purpose of going to Shiloh, and went directly home. He that went out in hopes to return rejoicing came in again melancholy and disconsolate, sat down and considered, "Is this an injury fit to be passed by?" He cannot call for fire from heaven to consume the men of Gibeah, as those angels did who were, after the same manner, insulted by the Sodomites. There was no king in Israel, nor (for aught that appears) any sanhedrim, or great council, to appeal to, and demand justice from. Phinehas is high priest, but he attends closely to the business of the sanctuary, and will be no judge or divider. He has therefore no other way left him than to appeal to the people: let the community be judge. Though they had no general stated assembly of all the tribes, yet it is probable that each tribe had a meeting of their chiefs within itself. To each of the tribes, in their respective meetings, he sent by special messengers a remonstrance of the wrong that was done him, in all its aggravating circumstances, and with it a piece of his wife's dead body (*v.* 29), both to confirm the truth of the story and to affect them the more with it. He divided it into twelve pieces, *according to the bones,* so some read it, that is, by the joints, sending one to each tribe, even to Benjamin among the rest, with the hope that some among them would be moved to join in punishing so great a villany, and the more warmly because committed by some of their own tribe. It did indeed look very barbarous thus to mangle a dead body, which, having been so wretchedly dishonoured, ought to have been decently interred; but the Levite designed hereby, not only to represent their barbarous usage of his wife, whom they had better have cut in pieces thus than have used as they did, but also to express his own passionate concern and thereby to excite the like in them. And it had the desired effect. All that saw the pieces of the dead body, and were told how the matter was, expressed the same sentiments upon it. 1. That the men of

Gibeah had been guilty of a very heinous piece of wickedness, the like to which had never been known before in Israel, *v.* 30. It was a complicated crime, loaded and blackened with all possible aggravations. They were not such fools as to make a mock at this sin, or turn the story off with a jest. 2. That a general assembly of all Israel should be called, to debate what was fit to be done for the punishment of this wickedness, that a stop might be put to this threatening inundation of debauchery, and the wrath of God might not be poured upon the whole nation for it. It is not a common case, and therefore they stir up one another to come together upon the occasion with this: *Consider of it, take advice, and speak your minds.* We have here the three great rules by which those that sit in council ought to go in every arduous affair. (1.) Let every man retire into himself, and weigh the matter impartially and fully in his own thoughts, and seriously and calmly consider it, without prejudice on either side, before he speaks upon it. (2.) Let them freely talk it over, and every man take advice of his friend, know his opinion and his reasons, and weigh them. (3.) Then let every man speak his mind, and give his vote according to his conscience. In the multitude of such counsellors there is safety.

CHAP. XX.

Into the book of the wars of the Lord the story of this chapter must be brought, but it looks as sad and uncomfortable as any article in all that history; for there is nothing in it that looks in the least bright or pleasant but the pious zeal of Israel against the wickedness of the men of Gibeah, which made it on their side a just and holy war; but otherwise the obstinacy of the Benjamites in protecting their criminals, which was the foundation of the war, the vast loss which the Israelites sustained in carrying on the war, and (though the righteous cause was victorious at last) the issuing of the war in the almost utter extirpation of the tribe of Benjamin, make it, from first to last, melancholy. And yet this happened soon after the glorious settlement of Israel in the land of promise, upon which one would have expected every thing to be prosperous and serene. In this chapter we have, I. The Levite's cause heard in a general convention of the tribes, ver. 1—7. II. A unanimous resolve to avenge his quarrel upon the men of Gibeah, ver. 8—11. III. The Benjamites appearing in defence of the criminals, ver. 12—17. IV. The defeat of Israel in the first and second day's battle, ver. 18—25. V. Their humbling themselves before God upon that occasion, ver. 26—28. VI. The total rout they gave the Benjamites in the third engagement, by a stratagem, by which they were all cut off, except 600 men, ver. 29—48. And all this the effect of the indignities done to one poor Levite and his wife; so little do those that do iniquity consider what will be the end thereof.

THEN all the children of Israel went out, and the congregation was gathered together as one man, from Dan even to Beer-sheba, with the land of Gilead, unto the LORD in Mizpeh. 2 And the chief of all the people, *even* of all the tribes of Israel, presented themselves in the assembly of the people of God, four hundred thousand footmen that drew sword. 3 (Now the children of Benjamin heard that the children of Israel were gone up to Mizpeh.) Then said the children of Israel, Tell *us,* how was this wickedness? 4 And the Levite, the husband of the woman that was slain, answered and said, I came into Gibeah, that *belongeth* to Benjamin, I and my concubine, to lodge. 5 And the men of Gibeah rose against me, and beset the house round about upon me by night, *and* thought to have slain me: and my concubine have they forced, that she is dead. 6 And I took my concubine, and cut her in pieces, and sent her throughout all the country of the inheritance of Israel: for they have committed lewdness and folly in Israel. 7 Behold, ye *are* all children of Israel; give here your advice and counsel. 8 And all the people arose as one man, saying, We will not any *of us* go to his tent, neither will we any *of us* turn into his house. 9 But now this *shall be* the thing which we will do to Gibeah; *we will go up* by lot against it; 10 And we will take ten men of a hundred throughout all the tribes of Israel, and a hundred of a thousand, and a thousand out of ten thousand, to fetch victual for the people, that they may do, when they come to Gibeah of Benjamin, according to all the folly that they have wrought in Israel. 11 So all the men of Israel were gathered against the city, knit together as one man.

Here is, I. A general meeting of all the congregation of Israel to examine the matter concerning the Levite's concubine, and to consider what was to be done upon it, *v.* 1, 2. It does not appear that they were summoned by the authority of any one common head, but they came together by the consent and agreement, as it were, of one common heart, fired with a holy zeal for the honour of God and Israel. 1. The place of their meeting was *Mizpeh;* they gathered together unto the Lord there, for Mizpeh was so very near to Shiloh that their encampment might very well be supposed to reach from Mizpeh to Shiloh. Shiloh was a small town, and therefore, when there was a general meeting of the people to present themselves before God, they chose Mizpeh for their head-quarters, which was the next adjoining city of note, perhaps because they were not willing to give that trouble to Shiloh which so great an assembly would occasion, it being the residence of the priests that attended the tabernacle. 2. The persons that met were all Israel, from Dan (the city very lately so called, *ch.* xviii. 29) in the north to Beersheba in the south, with the land of Gilead (that is, the tribes on the other side Jordan), all *as one man,* so unanimous were they in their concern for the public good. Here was an assembly of the people of God, not a convocation of the Levites and priests, though a Levite was the person principally concerned in the cause, but an assembly of the people, to whom the Levite referred himself with an *Appello populum—I appeal to the people.* The *people of God were* 400,000 *footmen that drew sword,* that is, were armed and disciplined, and fit for service, and some of them perhaps such as had *known the wars of Canaan, ch.* iii. 1. In this assembly of all Israel, the chief (or corners) of the people (for rulers are the corner-stones of the people, that keep all together) presented themselves as the representatives of the rest. They rendered themselves at their respective posts, at the head of the thousands and hundreds, the fifties and tens, over which they presided; for so much order and government, we may suppose, at least, they had among them, though they had no general or commander-in-chief. So that here was, (1.) A general congress of the states for counsel. The chief of the people presented themselves, to lead and direct in this affair. (2.) A general rendezvous of the militia for action, all that drew sword and were men of war (*v.* 17), not hirelings nor pressed men, but the best freeholders, that went at their own charge. Israel were above 600,000 when they came into Canaan, and we have reason to think they were at this time much increased, rather than diminished; but then all between twenty and sixty were military men, now we may suppose more than the one half exempted from bearing arms to cultivate the land; so that these were as the trained bands. The militia of the two tribes and a half were 40,000 (Josh. iv. 13), but the tribes were many more.

II. Notice given to the tribe of Benjamin of this meeting (*v.* 3): *They heard that the children of Israel had gone up to Mizpeh.* Probably they had a legal summons sent them to appear with their brethren, that the cause might be fairly debated, before any resolutions were taken up upon it, and so the mischiefs that followed would have been happily prevented; but the notice they had of this meeting rather hardened and exasperated them than awakened them to think of the things that belonged to their peace and honour.

III. A solemn examination of the crime charged upon the men of Gibeah. A very horrid representation of it had been made by the report of the messengers that were sent to call them together, but it was fit it should be more closely enquired into, because such things are often made worse than really they were; a committee therefore was appointed to examine the witnesses (upon oath, no doubt) and to report the matter. It is only the testimony of the Levite himself that is here recorded, but it is probable his servant, and the old man, were examined, and gave in their testimony, for that more than one were examined appears by the original (*v.* 3), which is, *Tell you us;* and the law was that none should be put to death, much less so many, upon the testimony of one witness only. The Levite gives a particular account of the matter: that he came into Gibeah only as a traveller to lodge there, not giving the least shadow of suspicion that he designed them any ill turn (*v.* 4), and that the men of Gibeah, even those that were of substance among them, that should have been a protection to the stranger within their gates, riotously set upon the house where he lodged, and *thought to slay him;* he could not, for shame relate the demand which they, without shame, made, *ch.* xix. 22. They declared their sin as Sodom, even the sin of Sodom, but his modesty would not suffer him to repeat it; it was sufficient to say they would have slain him, for he would rather have been slain than have submitted to their villany; and, if they had got him into their hands, they would have abused him to death, witness what they had done to his concubine: They have *forced her that she is dead, v.* 5. And, to excite in his countrymen an indignation at this wickedness, he had sent pieces of the mangled body to all the tribes, which had fetched them together to bear their testimony against the *lewdness and folly committed in Israel, v.* 6. All lewdness is folly, but especially lewdness in Israel. For those to defile their own bodies who have the honourable seal of the covenant in their flesh, for those to defy the divine vengeance to whom it is so clearly revealed from heaven—Nabal is their name, and folly is with them. He concludes his declaration with an appeal to the judgment of the court (*v.* 7): *You are all children of Israel,* and therefore you *know law and judgment,* Esth. i. 13. "You are a holy people to God, and have a dread of every thing which will dishonour God and defile the land; you are of the same community, members of the same body, and therefore likely to feel from the distempers of it; you are children of Israel, that ought to take particular care of the Levites, God's tribe, among you, and therefore give your advice and counsel what is to be done."

IV. The resolution they came to hereupon, which was that, being now together, they would not disperse till they had seen vengeance taken upon this wicked city, which was the reproach and scandal of their nation. Observe, 1. Their zeal against the lewdness that was committed. They would not return to their houses, how much soever their families and their affairs at home wanted them, till they had vindicated the honour of God and Israel, and recovered with their swords, if it could not be had otherwise, that satisfaction for the crime which the justice of the nation called for, *v.* 8. By this they showed themselves children of Israel indeed, that they preferred the public interest before their private concerns. 2. Their prudence in sending out a considerable body of their forces to fetch provisions for the rest, *v.* 9, 10. One of ten, and he chosen by lot, 40,000 in all, must go to their respective countries, whence they came, to fetch bread and other necessaries for the subsistence of this great army; for when they came from home they took with them provisions only for a journey to Mizpeh, not for an encampment (which might prove long) before Gibeah. This was to prevent their scattering to forage for themselves, for, if they had done this, it would have been hard to get them all together again, especially all in so good a mind. Note, When there appears in people a pious zeal for any good work it is best to strike while the iron is hot, for such zeal is apt to cool quickly if the prosecution of the work be delayed. Let it never be said that we left that good work to be done to-morrow which we could as well have done to-day. 3. Their unanimity in these counsels, and the execution of them. The resolution was voted, *Nemine contradicente—Without a dissenting voice* (*v.* 8); it was one and all; and, when it was put in execution, they were *knit together as one man, v.* 11. This was their glory and strength, that the several tribes had no separate interests when the common good was concerned.

12 And the tribes of Israel sent men through all the tribe of Benjamin, saying, What wickedness *is* this that is done among you? 13 Now therefore deliver *us* the men, the children of Belial, which *are* in Gibeah, that we may put them to death, and put away evil from Israel. But the children of Benjamin would not hearken to the voice of their brethren the children of Israel: 14 But the children of Benjamin gathered themselves together out of the cities unto Gibeah, to go out to battle against the children of Israel. 15 And the children of Benjamin were numbered at that time out of the cities twenty and six thousand men that drew sword, beside the inhabitants of Gibeah, which were numbered seven hundred chosen men. 16 Among all this people *there were* seven hundred chosen men lefthanded; every one could sling stones at a hair *breadth*, and not miss. 17 And the men of Israel, beside Benjamin, were numbered four hundred thousand men that drew sword: all these *were* men of war.

Here is, I. The fair and just demand which the tribes of Israel, now encamped, sent to the tribe of Benjamin, to deliver up the malefactors of Gibeah to justice, *v.* 12, 13. If the tribe of Benjamin had come up, as they ought to have done, to the assembly, and agreed with them in their resolution, there would have been none to deal with but the men of Gibeah only, but they, by their absence, taking part with the criminals, application must be made to them all. The Israelites were zealous against the wickedness that was committed, yet they were discreet in their zeal, and did not think it would justify them in falling upon the whole tribe of Benjamin unless they, by refusing to give up the criminals, and protecting them against justice, should make themselves guilty, *ex post facto —as accessaries after the fact.* They desire them to consider how great the wickedness was that was committed (*v.* 12), and that it was done among them: and how necessary it was therefore that they should either punish the malefactors with death themselves, according to the law of Moses, or deliver them up to this general assembly, to be so much the more publicly and solemnly punished, that evil might be put away from Israel, the national guilt removed, the infection stopped by cutting off the gangrened part, and national judgments prevented; for the sin was so very like that of the Sodomites that they might justly fear, if they did not punish it, God would rain hail from heaven upon them, as he did, not only upon Sodom, but the neighbouring cities. If the Israelites had not made this reasonable demand, they would have had much more reason to lament the following desolations of Benjamin. All methods of accommodation must be used before we go to war or go to law. The demand was like that of Joab's to Abel, 2 Sam. xx. 20, 21 "Only deliver up the traitor, and we will lay down our arms." On these terms, and no other, God will be at peace with us, that we part with our sins, that we mortify and crucify our lusts, and then all shall be well; his anger will be turned away.

II. The wretched obstinacy and perverseness of the men of Benjamin, who seem to have been as unanimous and zealous in their resolutions to stand by the criminals as the rest of the tribes were to punish them, so little sense had they of their honour, duty, and interest. 1. They were so prodigiously vile as to patronise the wickedness that was committed: They *would not hearken to the voice of their brethren* (*v.* 13), either because those of that tribe were generally more vicious and debauched at this time than the rest of the tribes, and therefore would not bear to have that punished in others of which they knew themselves guilty (some of the most fruitful and pleasant parts of Canaan fell to the lot of this tribe; their land, like that of Sodom, was *as the garden of the Lord,* which perhaps helped to make the inhabitants, like the men of Sodom, wicked, and *sinners before the*

Lord exceedingly, Gen. xiii. 10, 13), or because (as bishop Patrick suggests) they took it ill that the other tribes should meddle with their concerns; they would not do that which they knew was their duty because they were reminded of it by their brethren, by whom they scorned to be taught and controlled. If there were any wise men among them that would have complied with the demand made, yet they were overpowered by the majority, who thus made the crime of the men of Gibeah their own. Thus we have *fellowship with the unfruitful works of darkness* if we say *A confederacy* with those that have, and make ourselves guilty of other men's sins by countenancing and defending them. It seems there is no cause so bad but it will find some patrons, some advocates, to appear for it; but *woe be to those by whom such offences come.* Those will have a great deal to answer for that obstruct the course of necessary justice, and strengthen the hands of the wicked, by saying, *O wicked man! thou shalt not die.*

2. They were so prodigiously vain and presumptuous as to make head against the united force of all Israel. Never, surely, were men so wretchedly infatuated as they were when they took up arms in opposition, (1.) To so good a cause as Israel had. How could they expect to prosper when they fought against justice, and consequently against the just God himself, against those that had the high priest and the divine oracle on their side, and so acted in downright rebellion against the sacred and supreme authority of the nation. (2.) To so great a force as Israel had. The disproportion of their numbers was much greater than that, Luke xiv. 31, 32, where he that had but 10,000 durst not meet him that came against him with 20,000, and therefore desired conditions of peace. There the enemy was but two to one, here above fifteen to one; yet they despised conditions of peace. All the forces they could bring into the field were but 26,000 men, besides 700 men of Gibeah (*v.* 15); yet with these they will dare to face 400,000 men of Israel, *v.* 17. Thus sinners are infatuated to their own ruin, and provoke him to jealousy who is infinitely stronger than they, 1 Cor. x. 22. But it should seem they depended upon the skill of their men to make up what was wanting in numbers, especially a regiment of slingers, 700 men, who, though left-handed, were so dexterous at slinging stones that they would not be a hair's breadth beside their mark, *v.* 16. But these good marksmen were very much out in their aim when they espoused this bad cause. *Benjamin* signifies *the son of the right hand*, yet we find his posterity left-handed.

18 And the children of Israel arose, and went up to the house of God, and asked counsel of God, and said, Which of us shall go up first to the battle against the children of Benjamin? And the LORD said, Judah *shall go up* first. 19 And the children of Israel rose up in the morning, and encamped against Gibeah. 20 And the men of Israel went out to battle against Benjamin; and the men of Israel put themselves in array to fight against them at Gibeah. 21 And the children of Benjamin came forth out of Gibeah, and destroyed down to the ground of the Israelites that day twenty and two thousand men. 22 And the people the men of Israel encouraged themselves, and set their battle again in array in the place where they put themselves in array the first day. 23 (And the children of Israel went up and wept before the LORD until even, and asked counsel of the LORD, saying, Shall I go up again to battle against the children of Benjamin my brother? And the LORD said, Go up against him.) 24 And the children of Israel came near against the children of Benjamin the second day. 25 And Benjamin went forth against them out of Gibeah the second day, and destroyed down to the ground of the children of Israel again eighteen thousand men; all these drew the sword.

We have here the defeat of the men of Israel in their first and second battle with the Benjamites.

I. Before their first engagement they asked counsel of God concerning the order of their battle and were directed, and yet they were sorely beaten. They did not think it was proper to ask of God whether they should go up at all against Benjamin (the case was plain enough, the men of Gibeah must be punished for their wickedness, and Israel must inflict the punishment or it will not be done), but "Who shall go first?" (*v.* 18), that is, "Who shall be general of our army?" for, which soever tribe was appointed to go first, the prince of that tribe must be looked upon as commander-in-chief of the whole body. For, if they had meant it of the order of their march only, it would have been proper to ask, "Who shall go next?" and then, "Who next?" But, if they know that Judah must go first, they know they must all observe the orders of the prince of that tribe. This honour was done to Judah because our Lord Jesus was to spring from that tribe, who was in all things to have the pre-eminence. The tribe that went up first had the most honourable post, but withal the most dangerous, and probably lost most in the engagement. Who would strive for precedency that sees the peril of it? Yet though Judah, that strong and valiant tribe, goes up first, and all the tribes of Israel attend them, *little Benjamin* (so he is called, Ps. lxviii. 27), is too hard for them all. The whole army lays siege to Gibeah, *v.* 19. The Benjamites advance to raise the siege, and the army prepares to give them a warm reception (*v.* 20), turns upon them to fight them, *v.* 20. But between the Benjamites that attacked them in the front with incredible fury, and the men of Gibeah that sallied out upon their rear, they were put into confusion and lost 22,000 men, *v.* 21. Here were no prisoners taken, for there was no quarter given, but all put to the sword.

II. Before their second engagement they again *asked counsel of God*, and more solemnly than before; for they *wept before the Lord until evening* (*v.* 23), lamenting the loss of so many brave men, especially as it was a token of God's displeasure and would give occasion to the Benjamites to triumph in the success of their wickedness. Also at this time they did not ask who should go up first, but whether they should go up at all. They intimate a reason why they should scruple to do it, especially now that Providence had frowned upon them, because Benjamin was their brother, and a readiness to lay down their arms if God should so order them. God bade them go up; he allowed the attempt, for, though Benjamin was their brother, he was a gangrened member of their body and must be cut off. Upon this they encouraged themselves, perhaps more in their own strength than in the divine commission, and made a second attempt upon the forces of the rebels, in the same place where the former battle was fought (*v.* 22), with the hope of retrieving their credit upon the same spot of ground where they had lost it, which they would not superstitiously change, as if there were any thing unlucky in the place. But they were this second time repulsed, with the loss of 18,000 men, *v.* 25. The former day's loss and this amounted to 40,000, which was just a tenth part of the whole army, and the same number that they had drawn out by lot to fetch victuals, *v.* 10. They decimated themselves for that service, and now God again decimated them for the slaughter. But what shall we say to these things, that so just and honourable a cause should thus be put to the worst once and again? Were they not fighting God's battles against sin? Had they not his commission? What, and yet miscarry thus! 1. God's judgments are a great deep, and his way is in the sea. *Clouds and darkness are* often *round about* him, *but judgment and justice are* always *the habitation of his throne.* We may be sure of the righteousness, when we cannot see the reasons, of God's proceedings. 2. God would hereby show them, and us in them, that *the race is not to the swift nor the battle to the strong*, that we are not to confide in numbers, which perhaps the Israelites did with too much assurance. We must never lay the weight on an arm of flesh, which only the Rock of ages will bear. 3. God designed hereby to correct Israel for their sins. They did well to show such a zeal against the wickedness of Gibeah: but *were there not with them, even with them, sins against the Lord their God?* Those must be made to know their own iniquity that are forward in condemning the iniquity of others. Some think it was a rebuke to them for not witnessing against the idolatry of Micah and the Danites, by which their religion was corrupted, as they now did against the lewdness of Gibeah and the Benjamites, by which the public peace was disturbed, though God had particularly ordered them to levy war upon idolaters, Deut. xiii. 12, &c. 4. God would hereby teach us not to think it strange if a good cause should suffer defeat for a while, nor to judge of the merits of it by the success of it. The interest of grace in the heart, and of religion in the world, may be foiled, and suffer great loss, and seem to be quite run down, but judgment will be brought forth to victory at last. *Vincimur in prœlio, sed non in bello—We are foiled in a battle, but not in the whole campaign.* Right may fall, but it shall arise.

26 Then all the children of Israel, and all the people, went up, and came unto the house of God, and wept, and sat there before the LORD, and fasted that day until even, and offered burnt offerings and peace offerings before the LORD. 27 And the children of Israel enquired of the LORD, (for the ark of the covenant of God *was* there in those days, 28 And Phinehas, the son of Eleazar, the son of Aaron, stood before it in those days,) saying, Shall I yet again go out to battle against the children of Benjamin my brother, or shall I cease? And the LORD said, Go up; for to morrow I will deliver them into thine hand. 29 And Israel set liers in wait round about Gibeah. 30 And the children of Israel went up against the children of Benjamin on the third day, and put themselves in array against Gibeah, as at other times. 31 And the children of Benjamin went out against the people, *and* were drawn away from the city; and they began to

smite of the people, *and* kill, as at other times, in the highways, of which one goeth up to the house of God, and the other to Gibeah in the field, about thirty men of Israel. 32 And the children of Benjamin said, They *are* smitten down before us, as at the first. But the children of Israel said, Let us flee, and draw them from the city unto the highways. 33 And all the men of Israel rose up out of their place, and put themselves in array at Baal-tamar: and the liers in wait of Israel came forth out of their places, *even* out of the meadows of Gibeah. 34 And there came against Gibeah ten thousand chosen men out of all Israel, and the battle was sore: but they knew not that evil *was* near them. 35 And the LORD smote Benjamin before Israel: and the children of Israel destroyed of the Benjamites that day twenty and five thousand and a hundred men: all these drew the sword. 36 So the children of Benjamin saw that they were smitten: for the men of Israel gave place to the Benjamites, because they trusted unto the liers in wait which they had set beside Gibeah. 37 And the liers in wait hasted, and rushed upon Gibeah; and the liers in wait drew *themselves* along, and smote all the city with the edge of the sword. 38 Now there was an appointed sign between the men of Israel and the liers in wait, that they should make a great flame with smoke rise up out of the city. 39 And when the men of Israel retired in the battle, Benjamin began to smite *and* kill of the men of Israel about thirty persons: for they said, Surely they are smitten down before us, as *in* the first battle. 40 But when the flame began to arise up out of the city with a pillar of smoke, the Benjamites looked behind them, and, behold, the flame of the city ascended up to heaven. 41 And when the men of Israel turned again, the men of Benjamin were amazed: for they saw that evil was come upon them. 42 Therefore they turned *their backs* before the men of Israel unto the way of the wilderness; but the battle overtook them; and them which *came* out of the cities they destroyed in the midst of them. 43 *Thus* they inclosed the Benjamites round about, *and* chased them, *and* trode them down with ease over against Gibeah toward the sunrising. 44 And there fell of Benjamin eighteen thousand men; all these *were* men of valour. 45 And they turned and fled toward the wilderness unto the rock of Rimmon: and they gleaned of them in the highways five thousand men; and pursued hard after them unto Gidom, and slew two thousand men of them. 46 So that all which fell that day of Benjamin were twenty and five thousand men that drew the sword; all these *were* men of valour. 47 But six hundred men turned and fled to the wilderness unto the rock Rimmon, and abode in the rock Rimmon four months. 48 And the men of Israel turned again upon the children of Benjamin, and smote them with the edge of the sword, as well the men of *every* city, as the beast, and all that came to hand: also they set on fire all the cities that they came to.

We have here a full account of the complete victory which the Israelites obtained over the Benjamites in the third engagement: the righteous cause was victorious at last, when the managers of it amended what had been amiss; for, when a good cause suffers, it is for want of good management. Observe then how the victory was obtained, and how it was pursued.

I. How the victory was obtained. Two things they had trusted too much to in the former engagements—the goodness of their cause and the superiority of their numbers. It was true that they had both right and strength on their side, which were great advantages; but they depended too much upon them, to the neglect of those duties to which now, this third time, when they see their error, they apply themselves.

1. They were previously so confident of the goodness of their cause that they thought it needless to address themselves to God for his presence and blessing. They took it for granted that God would bless them, nay, perhaps they concluded that he owed them his favour, and could not in justice withhold it, since it was in defence of virtue that they appeared and took up arms. But God having shown them that he was under no

obligation to prosper their enterprise, that he neither needed them nor was tied to them, that they were more indebted to him for the honour of being ministers of his justice than he to them for the service, now they became humble petitioners for success. Before they only consulted God's oracle, *Who shall go up first?* And, *Shall we go up?* But now they implored his favour, fasted and prayed, and *offered burnt-offerings and peace-offerings* (*v.* 26), to make an atonement for sin and an acknowledgment of their dependence upon God, and as an expression of their desire towards him. We cannot expect the presence of God with us, unless we thus seek it in the way he has appointed. And when they were in this frame, and thus sought the Lord, then he not only ordered them to go up against the Benjamites the third time, but gave them a promise of victory: *To-morrow I will deliver them into thy hand, v.* 28.

2. They were previously so confident of the greatness of their strength that they thought it needless to use any art, to lay any ambush, or form a stratagem, not doubting but to conquer purely by a strong hand; but now they saw it was requisite to use some policy, as if they had an enemy to deal with them that had been superior in number; accordingly, they set *liers in wait* (*v.* 29), and gained their point, as their fathers did before Ai (Josh. viii.), stratagems of that kind being most likely to take effect after a previous defeat, which has flushed the enemy, and made the pretended flight the less suspected. The management of this artifice is here very largely described. The assurance God had given them of success in this day's action, instead of making them remiss and presumptuous, set all heads and hands on work for the effecting of what God had promised.

(1.) Observe the method they took. The body of the army faced the city of Gibeah, as they had done before, advancing towards the gates, *v.* 30. The Benjamites, the body of whose army was now quartered at Gibeah, sallied out upon them, and charged them with great bravery. The besiegers gave back, retired with precipitation, as if their hearts failed them upon the sight of the Benjamites, which they were willing to believe, proudly imagining that by their former success they had made themselves very formidable. Some loss the Israelites sustained in this counterfeit flight, about thirty men being cut off in their rear, *v.* 31, 39. But, when the Benjamites were all drawn out of the city, the ambush seized the city (*v.* 37), gave a signal to the body of the army (*v.* 38, 40), which immediately turned upon them (*v.* 41), and, it should seem, another considerable party that was posted at Baal-tamar came upon them at the same time (*v.* 33); so that the Benjamites were quite surrounded, which put them into the greatest consternation that could be. A sense of guilt now disheartened them, and the higher their hopes had been raised the more grievous was this confusion. At first *the battle was sore* (*v.* 34), the Benjamites fought with fury; but, when they saw what a snare they were drawn into, they thought one pair of heels (as we say) was worth two pair of hands, and they made the best of their way *towards the wilderness* (*v.* 42); but in vain: *the battle overtook them,* and, to complete their distress, *those who came out of the cities of Israel,* that waited to see the event of the battle, joined with their pursuers, and helped to cut them off. Every man's hand was against them.

(2.) Observe in this story, [1.] That the Benjamites, in the beginning of the battle, were confident that the day was their own: *They are smitten down before us, v.* 32, 39. Sometimes God suffers wicked men to be lifted up in successes and hopes, that their fall may be the sorer. See how short their joy is, and their triumphing but for a moment. *Let not him that girdeth on the harness boast,* except he has reason to boast in God. [2.] Evil was near them and they did not know it, *v.* 34. But (*v.* 41) they saw, when it was too late to prevent it, *that evil had come upon them.* What evils may at any time be near us we cannot tell, but the less they are feared the heavier they fall. Sinners will not be persuaded to see evil near them, but how dreadful will it be when it comes and there is no escaping! 1 Thess. v. 3. [3.] Though the men of Israel played their parts so well in this engagement, yet the victory is ascribed to God (*v.* 35): *The Lord smote Benjamin before Israel.* The battle was his, and so was the success. [4.] They *trode down the men of Benjamin with ease* when God fought against them, *v.* 43. It is an easy thing to trample upon those who have made God their enemy. See Mal. iv. 3.

II. How the victory was prosecuted and improved in a military execution done upon these sinners against their own souls. 1. Gibeah itself, that nest of lewdness, was destroyed in the first place. The ambush that entered the city by surprise *drew themselves along,* that is, dispersed themselves into the several parts of it, which they might easily do, now that all the men of war had sallied out and very presumptuously left it defenceless; and they smote all they found, even women and children, *with the sword* (*v.* 37), and set fire to the city, *v.* 40. Sin brings ruin upon cities. 2. The army in the field was quite routed and cut off: 18,000 men of valour lay dead upon the spot, *v.* 44. 3. Those that escaped from the field were pursued, and cut off in their flight, to the number of 7000, *v.* 45. It is to no purpose to think of out-running divine vengeance. *Evil pursues sinners,* and it will overtake them. 4. Even those that tarried at home were involved in the ruin. They *let their sword devour for ever,* not considering that *it would be bitterness in the latter end,* as Abner pleads long after, when he was at the head of an army of Benjamites, probably with an eye to this very story, 2 Sam. ii. 25, 26. They put to the sword all that breathed, and set fire to *all the cities, v.* 48. So that of all the tribe of Benjamin, for aught that appears, there remained none alive but 600 men that took shelter in the rock Rimmon, and lay close there four months, *v.* 47. Now, (1.) It is difficult to justify this severity as it was Israel's act. The whole tribe of Benjamin was culpable; but must they therefore be treated as devoted Canaanites? That it was done in the heat of war, that this was the way of prosecuting victories which the sword of Israel had been accustomed to, that the Israelites were extremely exasperated against the Benjamites for the slaughter they had made among them in the two former engagements, will go but a little way to excuse the cruelty of this execution. It is true they had sworn that whosoever did not come up to Mizpeh should be *put to death, ch.* xxi. 5. But that, if it was a justifiable oath, yet extended only to the men of war; the rest were not expected to come. Yet, (2.) It is easy to justify the hand of God in it. Benjamin had sinned against him, and God had threatened that, if they forgot him, they should *perish as the nations* that were before them perished (Deut. viii. 20), who were all in this manner cut off. (3.) It is easy likewise to improve it for warning against the beginnings of sin: they are *like the letting forth of water, therefore leave it off before it be meddled with,* for we know not *what will be in the end thereof.* The eternal ruin of souls will be worse, and more fearful, than all these desolations of a tribe. This affair of Gibeah is twice spoken of by the prophet Hosea as the beginning of the corruption of Israel and a pattern to all that followed (Hos. ix. 9): *They have deeply corrupted themselves as in the days of Gibeah;* and (Hos. x. 9), *Thou hast sinned from the days of Gibeah;* and it is added that *the battle in Gibeah against the children of iniquity did not* (that is, did not *at first)* overtake them.

CHAP. XXI.

The ruins of the tribe of Benjamin we read of in the foregoing chapter; now here we have, I. The lamentation which Israel made over these ruins, ver. 1—4, 6, 15. II. The provision they made for the repair of them out of the 600 men that escaped, for whom they procured wives, 1. Of the virgins of Jabesh-Gilead, when they destroyed that city for not sending its forces to the general rendezvous, ver. 5, 7—14. 2. Of the daughters of Shiloh, ver. 16—25. And so this melancholy story concludes.

NOW the men of Israel had sworn in Mizpeh, saying, There shall not any of us give his daughter unto Benjamin to wife. 2 And the people came to the house of God, and abode there till even before God, and lifted up their voices, and wept sore; 3 And said, O LORD God of Isra l, why is this come to pass in Israel, that there should be to day one tribe lacking in Israel? 4 And it came to pass on the morrow, that the people rose early, and built there an altar, and offered burnt offerings and peace offerings. 5 And the children of Israel said, Who *is there* among all the tribes of Israel that came not up with the congregation unto the LORD? For they had made a great oath concerning him that came not up to the LORD to Mizpeh, saying, He shall surely be put to death. 6 And the children of Israel repented them for Benjamin their brother, and said, There is one tribe cut off from Israel this day. 7 How shall we do for wives for them that remain, seeing we have sworn by the LORD that we will not give them of our daughters to wives? 8 And they said, What one *is there* of the tribes of Israel that came not up to Mizpeh to the LORD? And, behold, there came none to the camp from Jabesh-gilead to the assembly. 9 For the people were numbered, and, behold, *there were* none of the inhabitants of Jabesh-gilead there. 10 And the congregation sent thither twelve thousand men of the valiantest, and commanded them, saying, Go and smite the inhabitants of Jabesh-gilead with the edge of the sword, with the women and the children. 11 And this *is* the thing that ye shall do, Ye shall utterly destroy every male, and every woman that hath lain by man. 12 And they found among the inhabitants of Jabesh-gilead four hundred young virgins, that had known no man by lying with any male: and they brought them unto the camp to Shiloh, which *is* in the land of Canaan. 13 And the whole congregation sent *some* to speak to the children of Benjamin that *were* in the rock Rimmon, and to call peaceably unto them. 14 And Benjamin came again at that time; and they gave them wives which they had saved alive of the women of Jabesh-gilead: and yet so they sufficed them not. 15 And the people repented them for Benjamin, because that the LORD had made a breach in the tribes of Israel.

We may observe in these verses,

I. The ardent zeal which the Israelites had expressed against the wickedness of the men of Gibeah, as it was countenanced by the tribe of Benjamin. Occasion is here given to mention two instances of their zeal on this occasion, which we did not meet with before:—1. While the general convention of the states was gathering together, and was waiting for a full house before they would proceed, they bound themselves with the great execration, which they called the *Cherum,* utterly to destroy all those cities that should not send in their representatives and their quota of men upon this occasion, or had sentenced those to that curse who should thus refuse (*v.* 5); for they would look upon such refusers as having no indignation at the crime committed, no concern for the securing of the nation from God's judgments by the administration of justice, nor any regard to the authority of a common consent, by which they were summoned to meet. 2. When they had met and heard the cause they made another solemn oath that none of all the thousands of Israel then present, nor any of those whom they represented (not intending to bind their posterity), should, if they could help it, *marry a daughter* to a Benjamite, *v.* 1. This was made an article of the war, not with any design to extirpate the tribe, but because in general they would treat those who were then actors and abettors of this villany in all respects as they treated the devoted nations of Canaan, whom they were not only obliged to destroy, but with whom they were forbidden to marry; and because, in particular, they judged those unworthy to match with a daughter of Israel that had been so very barbarous and abusive to one of the tender sex, than which nothing could be done more base and villanous, nor a more certain indication given of a mind perfectly lost to all honour and virtue. We may suppose that the Levite's sending the mangled pieces of his wife's body to the several tribes helped very much to inspire them with all this fury, and much more than a bare narrative of the fact, though ever so well attested, would have done, so much does the eye affect the heart.

II. The deep concern which the Israelites did express for the destruction of the tribe of Benjamin when it was accomplished. Observe,

1. The tide of their anger at Benjamin's crime did not run so high and so strong before but the tide of their grief for Benjamin's destruction ran as high and as strong after: *They repented for Benjamin their brother, v.* 6, 15. They did not repent of their zeal against the sin; there is a holy indignation against sin, the fruit of godly sorrow, which is *to salvation, not to be repented of,* 2 Cor. vii. 10, 11. But they repented of the sad consequences of what they had done, that they had carried the matter further than was either just or necessary. It would have been enough to destroy all they found in arms; they needed not to have cut off the husbandmen and shepherds, the women and children. Note, (1.) There may be over-doing in well-doing. Great care must be taken in the government of our zeal, lest that which seemed supernatural in its causes prove unnatural in its effects. That is no good divinity which swallows up humanity. Many a war is ill ended which was well begun. (2.) Even necessary justice is to be done with compassion. God does not punish with delight, nor should men. (3.) Strong passions make work for repentance. What we say and do in a heat our calmer thoughts commonly wish undone again. (4.) In a civil war (according to the usage of the Romans) no victories ought to be celebrated with triumphs, because, which soever side gets, the community loses, as here *there is a tribe cut off from Israel.* What the better is the body for one member's crushing another? Now,

2. How did they express their concern? (1.) By their grief for the breach that was made. They came to the house of God, for thither they brought all their doubts, all their counsels, all their cares, and all their sorrows. There was to be heard on this occasion, not the voice of joy and praise, but only that of lamentation, and mourning, and woe: They *lifted up their voices and wept sore* (*v.* 2), not so much for the 40,000 whom they had lost (these would not be so much missed out of eleven tribes), but for the entire destruction of one whole tribe; for this was the complaint they poured out before God (*v.* 3): *There is one tribe lacking.* God had taken care of every tribe; their number twelve was that which they were known by; every tribe had his station appointed in the camp, and his stone in the high priest's breast-plate; every tribe had his blessing both from Jacob and Moses; and it would be an intolerable reproach to them if they should drop any out of this illustrious jury, and lose one out of twelve, especially Benjamin, the youngest, who was particularly dear to Jacob their common ancestor, and whom all the rest ought to have been in a particular manner tender of. Benjamin is not; what then will become of Jacob? Benjamin become a Benoni, the son of the right hand a son of sorrow! In this trouble they built an altar, not in competition, but in communion with the appointed altar at the door of the tabernacle, which was not large enough to contain all the sacrifices they designed; for they offered burnt offerings and peace offerings, to give thanks for their victory, yet to atone for their own folly in the pursuit of it, and to implore the divine favour in their present strait. Every thing that grieves us should bring us to God. (2.) By their amicable treaty with the poor distressed refugees that were hidden in the rock

Rimmon, to whom they sent an act of indemnity, assuring them, upon the public faith, that they would now no longer treat them as enemies, but receive them as brethren, *v.* 13. The falling out of friends should thus be the renewing of friendship. Even those that have sinned, if at length they repent, must be forgiven and comforted, 2 Cor. ii. 7. (3.) By the care they took to provide wives for them, that their tribe might be built up again, and the ruins of it repaired. Had the men of Israel sought themselves, they would have been secretly pleased with the extinguishing of the families of Benjamin, because then the land allotted to them would escheat to the rest of the tribes, *ob defectum sanguinis—for want of heirs*, and be easily seized for want of occupants; but those have not the spirit of Israelites who aim to raise themselves upon the ruins of their neighbours. They were so far from any design of this kind that all heads were at work to find out ways and means for the rebuilding of this tribe. All the women and children of Benjamin were slain: they had sworn not to marry their daughters to any of them; it was against the divine law that they should match with the Canaanites; to oblige them to that would be, in effect, to bid them *go and serve other gods.* What must they do then for wives for them? While the poor distressed Benjamites that were hidden in the rock feared their brethren were contriving to ruin them, they were at the same time upon a project to prefer them; and it was this:—[1.] There was a piece of necessary justice to be done upon the city of Jabesh-Gilead, which belonged to the tribe of Gad, on the other side Jordan. It was found upon looking over the muster-roll (which was taken, *ch.* xx. 2) that none appeared from that city upon the general summons (*v.* 8, 9), and it was then resolved, before it appeared who were absent, that whatever city of Israel should be guilty of such a contempt of the public authority and interest that city should be an anathema; Jabesh-Gilead lies under that severe sentence, which might by no means be dispensed with. Those that had spared the Canaanites in many places, who were devoted to destruction by the divine command, could not find in their hearts to spare their brethren that were devoted by their own curse. Why did they not now send men to root the Jebusites out of Jerusalem, to avoid whom the poor Levite had been forced to go to Gibeah? *ch.* xix. 11, 12. Men are commonly more zealous to support their own authority than God's. A detachment is therefore sent of 12,000 men, to execute the sentence upon Jabesh-Gilead. Having found that when the whole body of the army went against Gibeah the people were thought too many for God to deliver them into their hands, on this expedition they sent but a few, *v.* 10. Their commission is to put all to the sword, men, women, and children (*v.* 11), according to that law (Lev. xxvii. 29), *Whatsoever is devoted of men*, by those that have power to do it, *shall surely be put to death.* [2.] An expedient is hence formed for providing the Benjamites with wives. When Moses sent the same number of men to avenge the Lord on Midian, the same orders were given as here, that all married women should be slain with their husbands, as one with them, but that the virgins should be saved alive, Num. xxxi. 17, 18. That precedent was sufficient to support the distinction here made between a wife and a virgin, *v.* 11, 12. 400 virgins that were marriageable were found in Jabesh-Gilead, and these were married to so many of the surviving Benjamites, *v.* 14. Their fathers were not present when the vow was made not to marry with Benjamites, so that they were not under any colour of obligation by it: and besides, being a prey taken in war, they were at the disposal of the conquerors. Perhaps the alliance now contracted between Benjamin and Jabesh-Gilead made Saul, who was a Benjamite, the more concerned for that place (1 Sam. xi. 4), though then inhabited by new families.

16 Then the elders of the congregation said, How shall we do for wives for them that remain, seeing the women are destroyed out of Benjamin? 17 And they said, *There must be* an inheritance for them that be escaped of Benjamin, that a tribe be not destroyed out of Israel. 18 Howbeit we may not give them wives of our daughters: for the children of Israel have sworn, saying, Cursed *be* he that giveth a wife to Benjamin. 19 Then they said, Behold, *there is* a feast of the LORD in Shiloh yearly *in a place* which *is* on the north side of Beth-el, on the east side of the highway that goeth up from Beth-el to Shechem, and on the south of Lebonah. 20 Therefore they commanded the children of Benjamin, saying, Go and lie in wait in the vineyards; 21 And see, and, behold, if the daughters of Shiloh come out to dance in dances, then come ye out of the vineyards, and catch you every man his wife of the daughters of Shiloh, and go to the land of Benjamin. 22 And it shall be, when their fathers or their brethren come unto us to complain, that we will say unto them, Be favourable unto them for our sakes: because we reserved

not to each man his wife in the war: for ye did not give unto them at this time, *that* ye should be guilty. 23 And the children of Benjamin did so, and took *them* wives, according to their number, of them that danced, whom they caught: and they went and returned unto their inheritance, and repaired the cities, and dwelt in them. 24 And the children of Israel departed thence at that time, every man to his tribe and to his family, and they went out from thence every man to his inheritance. 25 In those days *there was* no king in Israel: every man did *that which was* right in his own eyes.

We have here the method that was taken to provide the 200 Benjamites that remained with wives. And, though the tribe was reduced to a small number, they were only in care to provide each man with one wife, not with more under pretence of multiplying them the faster. They may not bestow their daughters upon them, but to save their oath, and yet marry some of their daughters to them, they put them into a way of taking them by surprise, and marrying them, which should be ratified by their parents' consent, *ex post facto—afterwards*. The less consideration is used before the making of a vow, the more, commonly, there is need of afterwards for the keeping of it.

I. That which gave an opportunity for the doing of this was a public ball at Shiloh, in the fields, at which all the young ladies of that city and the parts adjacent that were so disposed met to dance, in honour of a *feast of the Lord* then observed, probably the feast of tabernacles (*v.* 19), for that feast (bishop Patrick says) was the only season wherein the Jewish virgins were allowed to dance, and that not so much for their own recreation as to express their holy joy, as David when he danced before the ark, otherwise the present melancholy posture of public affairs would have made dancing unseasonable, as Isa. xxii. 12, 13. The dancing was very modest and chaste. It was not mixed dancing; no men danced with these daughters of Shiloh, nor did any married women so far forget their gravity as to join with them. However their dancing thus in public made them an easy prey to those that had a design upon them, whence bishop Hall observes that the *ambushes of evil spirits carry away many souls from dancing to a fearful desolation*.

II. The elders of Israel gave authority to the Benjamites to do this, to *lie in wait in the vineyards* which surrounded the green they used to dance on, and, when they were in the midst of their sport, to come upon them, and catch every man a wife for himself, and carry them straight away to their own country, *v.* 20, 21. They knew that none of their own daughters would be there, so that the parents of these virgins could not be said to give them, for they knew nothing of the matter. A sorry *salvo* is better than none, to save the breaking of an oath: it were much better to be cautious in making vows, that there be not occasion afterwards, as there was here, *to say before the angel that it was an error*. Here was a very preposterous way of match-making, when both the mutual affection of the young people and the consent of the parents must be presumed to come after; the case was extraordinary, and may by no means be drawn into a precedent. Over hasty marriages often occasion a leisurely repentance; and what comfort can be expected from a match made either by force or fraud? The virgins of Jabesh-Gilead were taken out of the midst of blood and slaughter, but these of Shiloh out of the midst of mirth and joy; the former had reason to be thankful that they had their lives for a prey, and the latter, it is to be hoped, had no cause to complain, after a while, when they found themselves matched, not to men of broken and desperate fortunes, as they seemed to be, who were lately fetched out of a cave, but to men of the best and largest estates in the nation, as they must needs be when the lot of the whole tribe of Benjamin, which consisted of 45,600 men (Num. xxvi. 41), came to be divided again among 600, who had all by survivorship.

III. They undertook to pacify the fathers of these young women. As to the infringement of their paternal authority, they would easily forgive it when they considered to what fair estates their daughters were matched and what mothers in Israel they were likely to be; but the oath they were bound by, not to give their daughters to Benjamites, might perhaps stick with some of them, whose consciences were tender, yet, as to that, this might satisfy them:—1. That the necessity was urgent (*v.* 22): *We reserved not to each man his wife*, owning now that they did ill to destroy all the women, and desiring to atone for their too rigorous construction of their vow to destroy them by the most favourable construction of their vow not to match with them. "And therefore for our sakes, who were too severe, let them keep what they have got." For, 2. In strictness it was not a breach of their vow; they had sworn not to give them their daughters, but they had not sworn to fetch them back if they were forcibly taken, so that if there was any fault the elders must be responsible, not the parents. And *Quod fieri non debuit, factum valet—That which ought not to have been done is yet valid when it is done*. The thing was done, and is ratified only by connivance, according to the law, Num. xxx. 4.

Lastly, In the close of all we have, 1. The settling of the tribe of Benjamin again. The few that remained returned to the inheritance of that tribe, *v.* 23. And soon after from among them sprang Ehud, who was famous in his generation, the second judge of Israel, *ch.* iii. 15. 2. The disbanding and dispersing of the army of Israel, *v.* 24. They did not set up for a standing army, nor pretend to make any alterations or establishments in the government; but, when the affair was over for which they were called together, they quietly departed in God's peace, every man to his family. Public services must not make us think ourselves above our own private affairs and the duty of providing for our own house. 3. A repetition of the cause of these confusions, *v.* 25. Though God was their King, every man would be his own master, as if there was no king. Blessed be God for magistracy.

AN

EXPOSITION,

WITH PRACTICAL OBSERVATIONS,

ON THE BOOK OF

RUTH.

This short history of the domestic affairs of one particular family fitly follows the book of Judges (the events related here happening in the days of the judges), and fitly goes before the books of Samuel, because in the close it introduces David; yet the Jews, in their Bibles, separate it from both, and make it one of the five *Megilloth*, or *Volumes*, which they put together towards the latter end, in this order: *Solomon's Song*, *Ruth*, *Lamentations*, *Ecclesiastes*, and *Esther*. It is probable that Samuel was the penman of it. It relates not miracles nor laws, wars nor victories, nor the revolutions of states, but the affliction first and afterwards the comfort of Naomi, the conversion first and afterwards the preferment of Ruth. Many such events have happened, which perhaps we may think as well worthy to be recorded; but these God saw fit to transmit the knowledge of to us; and even common historians think they have liberty to choose their subject. The design of this book is, I. To lead to providence, to show us how conversant it is about our private concerns, and to teach us in them all to have an eye to it, acknowledging God in all our ways and in all events that concern us. See 1 Sam. ii. 7, 8; Ps. cxiii. 7—9. II. To lead to Christ, who descended from Ruth, and part of whose genealogy concludes the book, whence it is fetched into Matt. i. In the conversion of Ruth the Moabitess, and the bringing of her into the pedigree of the Messiah, we have a type of the calling of the Gentiles in due time into the fellowship of Christ Jesus our Lord. The afflictions of Naomi and Ruth we have an account of, *ch.* i. Instances of their industry and humility, *ch.* ii. The bringing of them into an alliance with Boaz, *ch.* iii. And their happy settlement thereby, *ch.* iv. And let us remember the scene is laid in Bethlehem, the city where our Redeemer was born.

CHAP. I.

In this chapter we have Naomi's afflictions. I. As a distressed housekeeper, forced by famine to remove into the land of Moab, ver. 1, 2. II. As a mournful widow and mother, bewailing the death of her husband and her two sons, ver. 3—5. III. As a careful mother-in-law, desirous to be kind to her two daughters, but at a loss how to be so when she returns to her own country, ver. 6—13. Orpah she parts with in sorrow, ver. 14. Ruth she takes with her in fear, ver. 15—18. IV. As a poor woman sent back to the place of her first settlement, to be supported by the kindness of her friends, ver. 19—22. All these things were melancholy and seemed against her, and yet all were working for good.

NOW it came to pass in the days when the judges ruled, that there was a famine in the land. And a certain man of Beth-lehem-judah went to sojourn in the country of Moab, he, and his wife, and his two sons. 2 And the name of the man *was* Elimelech, and the name of his wife Naomi, and the name of his two sons Mahlon and Chilion, Ephrathites of Beth-lehem-judah. And they came into the country of Moab, and continued there. 3 And Elimelech Naomi's husband died; and she was left, and her two sons. 4 And they took them wives of the women of Moab: the name of the one *was* Orpah, and the name of the other Ruth: and they dwelled there about ten years. 5 And Mahlon and Chilion died also both of them; and the woman was left of her two sons and her husband.

The first words give all the date we have of this story. It was *in the days when the judges ruled* (*v.* 1), not in those disorderly times when *there was no king in Israel;* but under which of the judges these things happened we are not told, and the conjectures of the learned are very uncertain. It must have been towards the beginning of the judges' time, for Boaz, who married Ruth, was born of Rahab, who received the spies in Joshua's time. Some think it was in the days of Ehud, others of Deborah; the learned bishop Patrick inclines to think it was in the days of Gideon, because in his days only we read of a famine by the Midianites' invasion, Judges vi. 3, 4. While the judges were ruling, some one city and some another, Providence takes particular cognizance of Bethlehem, and has an eye to a King, to Messiah himself, who should descend from two Gentile mothers, Rahab and Ruth. Here is,

I. A famine in the land, in the land of Canaan, that land *flowing with milk and honey.* This was one of the judgments which God had threatened to bring upon them for their sins, Lev. xxvi. 19, 20. He has many arrows in his quiver. In the days of the judges they were oppressed by their enemies; and, when by that judgment they were not reformed, God tried this, for when he *judges he will overcome.* When the land had rest, yet it had not plenty; even in Bethlehem, which signifies *the house of bread,* there was scarcity. A *fruitful land is turned into barrenness,* to correct and restrain the luxury and wantonness of those that dwell therein.

II. An account of one particular family distressed in the famine; it is that of *Elimelech.* His name signifies *my God a king,* agreeable to the state of Israel when the judges ruled, for the Lord was their King, and comfortable to him and his family in their affliction, that God was theirs and that he reigns for ever. His wife was *Naomi,* which signifies my *amiable* or *pleasant* one. But his sons' names were *Mahlon* and *Chilion, sickness* and *consumption,* perhaps because weakly children, and not likely to be long-lived. Such are the productions of our pleasant things, weak and infirm, fading and dying.

III. The removal of this family from Bethlehem into the country of Moab on the other side Jordan, for subsistence, because of the famine, *v.* 1, 2. It seems there was plenty in the country of Moab when there was scarcity of bread in the land of Israel. Common gifts of providence are often bestowed in greater plenty upon those that are strangers to God than upon those that know and worship him. *Moab is at ease from his youth,* while Israel *is emptied from vessel to vessel* (Jer. xlviii. 11), not because God loves Moabites better, but because they have *their portion in this life.* Thither Elimelech goes, not to settle for ever, but to sojourn for a time, during the dearth, as Abraham, on a similar occasion, went into Egypt, and Isaac into the land of the Philistines. Now here, 1. Elimelech's care to provide for his family, and his taking his wife and children with him, were without doubt commendable. *If any provide not for his own, he hath denied the faith,* 1 Tim. v. 8. When he was in his straits he did not forsake his house, go seek his fortune himself, and leave his wife and children to shift for their own maintenance; but, as became a tender husband and a loving father, where he went he took them with him, not as the ostrich, Job xxxix. 16. But, 2. I see not how his removal into the country of Moab, upon this occasion, could be justified. Abraham and Isaac were only sojourners in Canaan, and it was agreeable to their condition to remove; but the seed of Israel were now fixed, and ought not to remove into the territories of the heathen. What reason had Elimelech to go more than any of his neighbours? If by any ill husbandry he had wasted his patrimony, and sold his land or mortgaged it (as it should seem, *ch.* iv. 3, 4), which brought him into a more necessitous condition than others, the law of God would have obliged his neighbours to relieve him (Lev. xxv. 35); but that was not his case, for he went out full, *v.* 21. By those who tarried at home it appears that the famine was not so extreme but that there was sufficient to keep life and soul together; and his charge was but small, only two sons. But if he could not be content with the short allowance that his neighbours took up with, and *in the day of famine could not be satisfied* unless he kept as plentiful a table as he had done formerly, if he could not live in hope that there would come years of plenty again in due time, or could not with patience wait for those years, it was his fault, and he did by it dishonour God and the good land he had given them, *weaken the hands of his brethren,* with whom he should have been willing to take his lot, and set an ill example to others. If all should do as he did Canaan would be dispeopled. Note, It is an evidence of a discontented, distrustful, unstable spirit, to be weary of the place in which God hath set us, and to be for leaving it immediately whenever we meet with any uneasiness or inconvenience in it. It is folly to think of escaping that cross which, being laid in our way, we ought to take up. It is our wisdom to make the best of that which is, for it is seldom that changing our place is mending it. Or, if he would remove, why to the country of Moab? If he had made enquiry, it is probable he would have found plenty in some of the tribes of Israel, those, for instance, on the other side Jordan, that bordered on the land of Moab; if he had had that zeal for God and his worship, and that affection for his brethren which became an Israelite, he would not have persuaded himself so easily to go and sojourn among Moabites.

IV. The marriage of his two sons to two of the daughters of Moab after his death, *v.* 4. All agree that this was ill done. The Chaldee says, *They transgressed the decree of the word of the Lord in taking strange wives.* If they would not stay unmarried till their return to the land of Israel, they were not so far off but that they might have fetched themselves wives thence. Little did Elimelech think, when he went to sojourn in Moab, that ever his sons would thus join in affinity with Moabites. But those that bring young people into bad acquaintance, and take them out of the way of public ordinances, though they may think them well-principled and armed against temptation, know not what they do, nor *what will be the end thereof.* It does not appear that the women they married were proselyted to the Jewish religion, for Orpah is said to return to her gods (*v.* 15); the gods of Moab were hers still. It is a groundless tradition of the Jews that Ruth was the daughter of Eglon king of Moab, yet the Chaldee paraphrast inserts it; but this and their other tradition, which he inserts likewise, cannot agree, that Boaz who married Ruth was the same with Ibzan, who judged Israel 200 years after Eglon's death, Judg. xii.

V. The death of Elimelech and his two sons, and the disconsolate condition Naomi was thereby reduced to. Her husband died (*v.* 3) and her two sons (*v.* 5) soon after their marriage, and the Chaldee says, *Their days were shortened,* because they transgressed the law in marrying strange wives. See here, 1. That wherever we go we cannot out-run death, whose fatal arrows fly in all places. 2. That we cannot expect to prosper when we go out of the way of our duty. *He that will save his life* by any indirect course *shall lose it.* 3. That death, when it comes into a family, often makes breach upon breach. One is taken away to prepare another to follow soon after; one is taken away, and that affliction is not duly improved, and therefore God sends another of the same kind. When Naomi had lost her husband she took so much the more complacency and put so much the more confidence in her sons. Under the shadow of these surviving comforts she thinks she shall live among the heathen, and exceedingly glad she was of these gourds; but behold they wither presently, *green and growing up in the morning, cut down and dried up* before night, buried soon after they were married, for neither of them left any children. So uncertain and transient are all our enjoyments here. It is therefore our wisdom to make sure of those comforts that will be made sure and of which death cannot rob us. But how desolate was the condition, and how disconsolate the spirit, of poor Naomi, when the woman *was left of her two sons and her husband!* When *these two things, loss of children and widowhood, come upon her in a moment,* come upon her *in their perfection, by whom shall she be comforted?* Isa. xlvii. 9; li. 19. It is God alone who has wherewithal to comfort those who are thus cast down.

6 Then she arose with her daughters in law, that she might return from the country of Moab: for she had heard in the country of Moab how that the LORD had visited his people in giving them bread. 7 Wherefore she went forth out of the place where she was, and her two daughters in law with her; and they went on the way to return unto the land of Judah. 8 And Naomi said unto her two daughters in law, Go, return each to her mother's house: the LORD deal kindly with you, as ye have dealt with the dead, and with me. 9 The LORD grant you that ye may find rest, each *of you* in the house of her husband. Then she kissed them; and they lifted up their voice, and wept. 10 And they said unto her, Surely we will return with thee unto thy people. 11 And Naomi said, Turn again, my daughters: why will ye go with me? *are* there yet *any more* sons in my womb, that they may be your husbands? 12 Turn again, my daughters, go *your way;* for I am too old to have a husband. If I should say, I have hope, *if* I should have a husband also to night, and should also bear sons; 13 Would ye tarry for them till they were grown? would ye stay for them from having husbands? nay, my daughters; for it grieveth me much for your sakes that the hand of the LORD is gone out against me. 14 And they lifted up their voice, and wept again: and Orpah kissed her mother in law; but Ruth clave unto her. 15 And she said, Behold, thy sister in law is gone back unto her people, and unto her gods: return thou after thy sister in law. 16 And Ruth said, Intreat me not to leave

thee, *or* to return from following after thee: for whither thou goest, I will go; and where thou lodgest, I will lodge: thy people *shall be* my people, and thy God my God: 17 Where thou diest, will I die, and there will I be buried: the LORD do so to me, and more also, *if aught* but death part thee and me. 18 When she saw that she was stedfastly minded to go with her, then she left speaking unto her.

See here, I. The good affection Naomi bore to the land of Israel, *v.* 6. Though she could not stay in it while the famine lasted, she would not stay out of it when the famine ceased. Though the country of Moab had afforded her shelter and supply in a time of need, yet she did not intend it should be her rest for ever; no land should be that but the holy land, in which the sanctuary of God was, of which he had said, *This is my rest for ever*. Observe,

1. God, at last, returned in mercy to his people; for, though he contend long, he will not contend always. As the judgment of oppression, under which they often groaned in the time of the judges, still came to an end, after a while, when God had raised them up a deliverer, so here the judgment of famine: At length God graciously *visited his people in giving them bread*. Plenty is God's gift, and it is his visitation which by bread, the staff of life, *holds our souls in life*. Though this mercy be the more striking when it comes after famine, yet if we have constantly enjoyed it, and never knew what famine meant, we are not to think it the less valuable.

2. Naomi then returned, in duty to her people. She had often enquired of their state, what harvests they had and how the markets went, and still the tidings were discouraging; but like the prophet's servant, who, having looked seven times and seen no sign of rain, at length discerned a cloud no bigger than a man's hand, which soon overspread the heavens, so Naomi at last has good news brought her of plenty in Bethlehem, and then she can think of no other than returning thither again. Her new alliances in the country of Moab could not make her forget her relation to the land of Israel. Note, Though there be a reason for our being in bad places, yet, when the reason ceases, we must by no means continue in them. Forced absence from God's ordinances, and forced presence with wicked people, are great afflictions; but when the force ceases, and such a situation is continued of choice, then it becomes a great sin. It should seem she began to think of returning immediately upon the death of her two sons, (1.) Because she looked upon that affliction to be a judgment upon her family for lingering in the country of Moab; and hearing this to be the *voice of the rod, and of him that appointed it*, she obeys and returns. Had she returned upon the death of her husband, perhaps she might have saved the life of her sons; but, *when God judgeth he will overcome*, and, if one affliction prevail not to awaken us to a sight and sense of sin and duty, another shall. When death comes into a family it ought to be improved for the reforming of what is amiss in the family: when relations are taken away from us we are put upon enquiry whether, in some instance or other, we are not out of the way of our duty, that we may return to it. God *calls our sins to remembrance* when he *slays a son*, 1 Kings xvii. 18. And, if he thus hedge up our way with thorns, it is that he may oblige us to say, We will *go and return to our first husband*, as Naomi here to her country, Hos. ii. 7. (2.) Because the land of Moab had now become a melancholy place to her. It is with little pleasure that she can breathe in that air in which her husband and sons had expired, or go on that ground in which they lay buried out of her sight, but not out of her thoughts; now she will go to Canaan again. Thus God takes away from us the comforts we stay ourselves too much upon and solace ourselves too much in, here in the land of our sojourning, that we may think more of our home in the other world, and by faith and hope may hasten towards it. Earth is embittered to us, that heaven may be endeared.

II. The good affection which her daughters-in-law, and one of them especially, bore to her, and her generous return of their good affection.

1. They were both so kind as to accompany her, some part of the way at least, when she returned towards the land of Judah. Her two daughters-in-law did not go about to persuade her to continue in the land of Moab, but, if she was resolved to go home, would pay her all possible civility and respect at parting; and this was one instance of it: they would *bring her on her way*, at least, to the utmost limits of their country, and help her to carry her luggage as far as they went, for it does not appear that she had any servant to attend her, *v.* 7. By this we see both that Naomi, as became an Israelite, had been very kind and obliging to them and had won their love, in which she is an example to all mothers-in-law, and that Orpah and Ruth had a just sense of her kindness, for they were willing to return it thus far. It was a sign they had dwelt together in unity, though *those* were dead by whom the relation between them came. Though they retained an affection for the gods of Moab (*v.* 15), and Naomi was still faithful to the God of Israel, yet that was no hindrance to either side from love and kindness, and all the good offices that the relation required. Mothers-

in-law and daughters-in-law are too often at variance (Matt. x. 35), and therefore it is the more commendable if they live in love; let all who sustain this relation aim at the praise of doing so.

2. When they had gone a little way with her Naomi, with a great deal of affection, urged them to go back (*v.* 8, 9): *Return each to her mother's house.* When they were dislodged by a sad providence from the house of their husbands it was a mercy to them that they had their parents yet living, that they had their houses to go to, where they might be welcome and easy, and were not turned out to the wide world. Naomi suggests that their own mothers would be more agreeable to them than a mother-in-law, especially when their own mothers had houses and their mother-in-law was not sure she had a place to lay her head in which she could call her own. She dismisses them,

(1.) With commendation. This is a debt owing to those who have conducted themselves well in any relation, they ought to have the praise of it: *You have dealt kindly with the dead and with me,* that is, "You were good wives to your husbands that are gone, and have been good daughters to me, and not wanting to your duty in either relation." Note, When we and our relations are parting, by death or otherwise, it is very comfortable if we have both their testimony and the testimony of our own consciences for us that while we were together we carefully endeavoured to do our duty in the relation. This will help to allay the bitterness of parting; and, while we are together, we should labour so to conduct ourselves as that when we part we may not have cause to reflect with regret upon our miscarriages in the relation.

(2.) With prayer. It is very proper for friends, when they part, to part with prayer. She sends them home with her blessing; and the blessing of a mother-in-law is not to be slighted. In this blessing she twice mentions the name *Jehovah*, Israel's God, and the only true God, that she might direct her daughters to look up to him as the only fountain of all good. To him she prays in general that he would recompense to them the kindness they had shown to her and hers. It may be expected and prayed for in faith that God will deal kindly with those that have dealt kindly with their relations. *He that watereth shall be watered also himself.* And, in particular, that they might be happy in marrying again: *The Lord grant that you may find rest, each of you in the house of her husband.* Note, [1.] It is very fit that, according to the apostle's direction (1 Tim. v. 14), the younger women, and he speaks there of young widows, should *marry, bear children,* and *guide the house.* And it is a pity that those who have approved themselves good wives should not again be blessed with good husbands, especially those that, like these widows have no children. [2.] The married state is a state of rest, such rest as this world affords, rest in the house of a husband, more than can be expected in the house of a mother or a mother-in-law. [3.] This rest is God's gift. If any content and satisfaction be found in our outward condition, God must be acknowledged in it. There are those that are unequally yoked, that find little rest even in the house of a husband. Their affliction ought to make those the more thankful to whom the relation is comfortable. Yet let God be the rest of the soul, and no perfect rest thought of on this side heaven.

(3.) She dismissed them with great affection: *She kissed them,* wished she had somewhat better to give them, but silver and gold she had none. However, this parting kiss shall be the seal of such a true friendship as (though she never see them more) she will, while she lives, retain the pleasing remembrance of. If relations must part, let them thus part in love, that they may (if they never meet again in this world) meet in the world of everlasting love.

3. The two young widows could not think of parting with their good mother-in-law, so much had the good conversation of that pious Israelite won upon them. They not only lifted up their voice and wept, as loth to part, but they professed a resolution to adhere to her (*v.* 10): "*Surely we will return with thee unto thy people,* and take our lot with thee." It is a rare instance of affection to a mother-in-law and an evidence that they had, for her sake, conceived a good opinion of the people of Israel. Even Orpah, who afterwards went back to her gods, now seemed resolved to go forward with Naomi. The sad ceremony of parting, and the tears shed on that occasion, drew from her this protestation, but it did not hold. Strong passions, without a settled judgment, commonly produce weak resolutions.

4. Naomi sets herself to dissuade them from going along with her, *v.* 11—13.

(1.) Naomi urges her afflicted condition. If she had had any sons in Canaan, or any near kinsmen, whom she could have expected to marry the widows, to *raise up seed* to those that were gone, and to redeem the mortgaged estate of the family, it might have been some encouragement to them to hope for a comfortable settlement at Bethlehem. But she had no sons, nor could she think of any near kinsman likely to do the kinsman's part, and therefore argues that she was never likely to have any sons to be husbands for them, for she was too old to have a husband; it became her age to think of dying and going out of the world, not of marrying and beginning the world again. Or, if she had a husband, she could not expect to have children, nor, if she had sons, could she think that these young widows would stay unmarried till her sons that should yet be born would grow up to be marriageable. Yet this was not all: she could not only not propose to herself to marry them like themselves, but she knew not how to maintain them like themselves. The greatest grievance of that poor condition to which she was reduced was that she was not in a capacity to do for them as she would: *It grieveth me* more *for your sakes* than for my own *that the hand of the Lord has gone out against me.* Observe, [1.] She judges herself chiefly aimed at in the affliction, that God's quarrel was principally with her: "*The hand of the Lord has gone out against me.* I am the sinner; it is with me that God has a controversy; it is with me that he is contending; I take it to myself." This well becomes us when we are under affliction; though many others share in the trouble, yet we must hear the voice of the rod as if it spoke only against us and to us, not billeting the rebukes of it at other people's houses, but taking them to ourselves. [2.] She laments most the trouble that redounded to them from it. She was the sinner, but they were the sufferers: *It grieveth me much for your sakes.* A gracious generous spirit can better bear its own burden than it can bear to see it a grievance to others, or others in any way drawn into trouble by it. Naomi could more easily want herself than see her daughters want. "Therefore *turn again, my daughters,* for, alas! I am in no capacity to do you any kindness." But,

(2.) Did Naomi do well thus to discourage her daughters from going with her, when, by taking them with her, she might save them from the idolatry of Moab and bring them to the faith and worship of the God of Israel? Naomi, no doubt, desired to do so. But, [1.] If they did come with her, she would not have them to come upon her account. Those that take upon them a profession of religion only in complaisance to their relations, to oblige their friends, or for the sake of company, will be converts of small value and of short continuance. [2.] If they did come with her, she would have them to make it their deliberate choice, and to sit down first and count the cost, as it concerns those to do that may take up a profession of religion. It is good for us to be told the worst. Our Saviour took this course with him who, in the heat of zeal, spoke that bold word, *Master, I will follow thee whithersoever thou goest.* "Come, come," says Christ, "canst thou fare as I fare? *The Son of man has not where to lay his head;* know this, and then consider whether thou canst find in thy heart to take thy lot with him," Matt. viii. 19, 20. Thus Naomi deals with her daughters-in-law. Thoughts ripened into resolves by serious consideration are likely to be kept always in the imagination of the heart, whereas what is soon ripe is soon rotten.

5. Orpah was easily persuaded to yield to her own corrupt inclination, and to go back to her country, her kindred, and her father's house, now when she stood fair for an effectual call from it. They both *lifted up their voice and wept again* (*v.* 14), being much affected with the tender things that Naomi had said. But it had a different effect upon them: to Orpah it was a savour of death unto death; the representation Naomi had made of the inconveniences they must count upon if they went forward to Canaan sent her back to the country of Moab, and served her as an excuse for her apostasy; but, on the contrary, it strengthened Ruth's resolution, and her good affection to Naomi, with whose wisdom and goodness she was never so charmed as she was upon this occasion; thus to her it was a savour of life unto life. (1.) *Orpah kissed her mother-in-law,* that is, took an affectionate leave of her, bade her farewell for ever, without any purpose to follow her hereafter, as he that said he would follow Christ when he had buried his father or bidden those farewell that were at home. Orpah's kiss showed she had an affection for Naomi and was loth to part from her; yet she did not love her well enough to leave her country for her sake. Thus many have a value and affection for Christ, and yet come short of salvation by him, because they cannot find in their hearts to forsake other things for him. They love him and yet leave him, because they do not love him enough, but love other things better. Thus the young man that went away from Christ went away sorrowful, Matt. xix. 22. But, (2.) *Ruth clave unto her.* Whether, when she came from home, she was resolved to go forward with her or no does not appear; perhaps she was before determined what to do, out of a sincere affection for the God of Israel and to his law, of which, by the good instructions of Naomi, she had some knowledge.

6. Naomi persuades Ruth to go back, urging, as a further inducement, her sister's example (*v.* 15): *Thy sister-in-law has gone back to her people,* and therefore of course gone back *to her gods;* for, whatever she might do while she lived with her mother-in-law, it would be next to impossible for her to show any respect to the God of Israel when she went to live among the worshippers of Chemosh. Those that forsake the communion of saints, and return to the people of Moab, will certainly break off their communion with God, and embrace the idols of Moab. Now, *return thou after thy sister,* that is, "If ever thou wilt return, return now. This is the greatest trial of thy constancy; stand this trial, and thou art mine for ever." Such offences as that of Orpah's revolt must needs come, that those who are perfect and sincere may be made manifest, as Ruth was upon this occasion.

7. Ruth puts an end to the debate by a most solemn profession of her immovable re-

solution never to forsake her, nor to return to her own country and her old relations again, *v.* 16, 17.

(1.) Nothing could be said more fine, more brave, than this. She seems to have had another spirit, and another speech, now that her sister had gone, and it is an instance of the grace of God inclining the soul to the resolute choice of the better part. *Draw me* thus, and *we will run after thee.* Her mother's dissuasions made her the more resolute; as when Joshua said to the people, *You cannot serve the Lord,* they said it with the more vehemence, *Nay, but we will.* [1.] She begs of her mother-in-law to say no more against her going: *Entreat me not to leave thee, or to return from following after thee;* for all thy entreaties now cannot shake that resolution which thy instructions formerly have wrought in me, and therefore let me hear no more of them." Note, It is a great vexation and uneasiness to those that are resolved for God and religion to be tempted and solicited to alter their resolution. Those that would not think of it would not hear of it. *Entreat me not.* The margin reads it, *Be not against me.* Note, We are to reckon those against us, and really our enemies, that would hinder us in our way to the heavenly Canaan. Our relations they may be, but they cannot be our friends, that would dissuade us from and discourage us in the service of God and the work of religion. [2.] She is very particular in her resolution to cleave to her and never to forsake her; and she speaks the language of one resolved for God and heaven. She is so in love, not with her mother's beauty, or riches, or gaiety (all these were withered and gone), but with her wisdom, and virtue, and grace, which remained with her, even in her present poor and melancholy condition, that she resolves to cleave to her. *First,* She will travel with her: *Whither thou goest I will go,* though to a country I never saw and in a low and ill opinion of which I have been trained up; though far from my own country, yet with thee every road shall be pleasant. *Secondly,* She will dwell with her: "*Where thou lodgest I will lodge,* though it be in a cottage, nay, though it be no better a lodging than Jacob had when he had the stones for his pillow. Where thou settest up thy staff I will set up mine, be it where it may." *Thirdly,* She will twist interests with her: *Thy people shall be my people.* From Naomi's character she concludes certainly that that great nation was a wise and an understanding people. She judges of them all by her good mother, who, wherever she went, was a credit to her country (as all those should study to be who profess relation to the better country, that is, the heavenly), and therefore she will think herself happy if she may be reckoned one of them. "Thy people shall be mine to associate with, to be conformable to, and to be concerned for." *Fourthly,* She will join in religion with her. Thus she determined to be hers *usque ad aras—to the very altars:* "*Thy God shall be my God,* and farewell to all the gods of Moab, which are vanity and a lie. I will adore the God of Israel, the only living and true God, trust in him alone, serve him, and in every thing be ruled by him;" this is to take the Lord for our God. *Fifthly,* She will gladly die in the same bed: *Where thou diest will I die.* She takes it for granted they must both die, and that in all probability Naomi, as the elder, would die first, and resolves to continue in the same house, if it might be, till her days also were fulfilled, intimating likewise a desire to partake of her happiness in death; she wishes to die in the same place, in token of her dying after the same manner. "Let me die the death of righteous Naomi, and let my last end be like hers." *Sixthly,* She will desire to be buried in the same grave, and to lay her bones by hers: *There will I be buried,* not desiring to have so much as her dead body carried back to the country of Moab, in token of any remaining kindness for it; but, Naomi and she having joined souls, she desires they may mingle dust, in hopes of rising together, and being together for ever in the other world. [3.] She backs her resolution to adhere to Naomi with a solemn oath: *The Lord do so to me, and more also* (which was an ancient form of imprecation), *if aught but death part thee and me.* An oath for confirmation was an end of this strife, and would leave a lasting obligation upon her never to forsake that good way she was now making choice of. *First,* It is implied that death would separate between them for a time. She could promise to die and be buried in the same place, but not at the same time; it might so happen that she might die first, and this would part them. Note, Death parts those whom nothing else will part. A dying hour is a parting hour, and should be so thought of by us and prepared for. *Secondly,* It is resolved that nothing else should part them; not any kindness from her own family and people, nor any hope of preferment among them, not any unkindness from Israel, nor the fear of poverty and disgrace among them. "No, I will *never leave thee.*" Now,

(2.) This is a pattern of a resolute convert to God and religion. Thus must we be at a point. [1.] We must take the Lord for our God. "This God is *my God for ever and ever;* I have avouched him for mine." [2.] When we take God for our God we must take his people for our people in all conditions; though they be a poor despised people, yet, if they be his, they must be ours. [3.] Having cast in our lot among them, we must be willing to take our lot with them and to fare as they fare. We must submit to the same yoke and draw in it faithfully, take up the same cross and carry it cheerfully, go where God will have us to go, though it should be into banishment, and lodge where he will have us to lodge, though it be in a prison, die where he will have us die, and lay our bones in the graves of the upright, who enter into peace and rest in their beds, though they be but the *graves of the common people.* [4.] We must resolve to continue and persevere, and herein our adherence to Christ must be closer than that of Ruth to Naomi. She resolved that nothing but death should separate them; but we must resolve that death itself shall not separate us from our duty to Christ, and then we may be sure that death itself shall not separate us from our happiness in Christ. [5.] We must bind our souls with a bond never to break these pious resolutions, and swear unto the Lord that we will cleave to him. Fast bind, fast find. He that means honestly does not startle at assurances.

8. Naomi is hereby silenced (*v.* 18): *When she saw that Ruth was stedfastly minded to go with her* (which was the very thing she aimed at in all that she had said, to make her of a stedfast mind in going with her), when she saw that she had gained her point, she was well satisfied, and *left off speaking to her.* She could desire no more than that solemn protestation which Ruth had just now made. See the power of resolution, how it puts temptation to silence. Those that are unresolved, and go in religious ways without a stedfast mind, tempt the tempter, and stand like a door half open, which invites a thief; but resolution shuts and bolts the door, resists the devil, and forces him to flee.

The Chaldee paraphrase thus relates the debate between Naomi and Ruth:—Ruth said, *Entreat me not to leave thee,* for *I will be a proselyte.* Naomi said, *We are commanded to keep sabbaths and good days, on which we may not travel above* 2000 *cubits*—a sabbath-day's journey. *Well,* said Ruth, *whither thou goest I will go.* Naomi said, *We are commanded not to tarry all night with Gentiles. Well,* said Ruth, *where thou lodgest I will lodge.* Naomi said, *We are commanded to keep* 613 *precepts. Well,* said Ruth, *whatever thy people keep I will keep, for they shall be my people.* Naomi said, *We are forbidden to worship any strange god. Well,* said Ruth, *thy God shall be my God.* Naomi said, *We have four sorts of deaths for malefactors, stoning, burning, strangling, and slaying with the sword. Well,* said Ruth, *where thou diest I will die. We have,* said Naomi, *houses of sepulchre. And there,* said Ruth, *will I be buried.*

19 So they two went until they came to Beth-lehem. And it came to pass, when they were come to Beth-lehem, that all the city was moved about them, and they said, *Is* this Naomi? 20 And she said unto them, Call me not Naomi, call me Mara: for the Almighty hath dealt very bitterly with me. 21 I went out full, and the LORD hath brought me home again empty: why *then* call ye me Naomi, seeing the LORD hath testified against me, and the Almighty hath afflicted me? 22 So Naomi returned, and Ruth the Moabitess, her daughter in law, with her, which returned out of the country of Moab: and they came to Beth-lehem in the beginning of barley harvest.

Naomi and Ruth, after many a weary step (the fatigue of the journey, we may suppose, being somewhat relieved by the good instructions Naomi gave to her proselyte and the good discourse they had together), came at last to Bethlehem. And they came very seasonably, *in the beginning of the barley-harvest,* which was the first of their harvests, that of wheat following after. Now Naomi's own eyes might convince her of the truth of what she had heard in the country of Moab, that *the Lord had visited his people in giving them bread,* and Ruth might see this good land in its best state; and now they had opportunity to provide for winter. Our *times are in God's hand,* both the events and the time of them. Notice is here taken,

I. Of the discomposure of the neighbours upon this occasion (*v.* 19): *All the city was moved about them.* Her old acquaintance gathered about her, to enquire concerning her state, and to bid her welcome to Bethlehem again. Or perhaps they were *moved about her,* lest she should be a charge to the town, she looked so bare. By this it appears that she had formerly lived respectably, else there would not have been so much notice taken of her. If those that have been in a high and prosperous condition break, or fall into poverty or disgrace, their fall is the more remarkable. And they said, *Is this Naomi?* The *women* of the city said it, for the word is feminine. Those with whom she had formerly been intimate were surprised to see her in this condition; she was so much broken and altered with her afflictions that they could scarcely believe their own eyes, nor think that this was the same person whom they had formerly seen, so fresh, and fair, and gay: *Is this Naomi?* So unlike is the rose when it is withered to what it was when it was blooming. What a poor figure does Naomi make now, compared with what she made in her prosperity! If any asked this question in contempt, upbraiding her with her miseries ("is this she that could not be content to fare as her neighbours did, but must ramble to a strange country? see what she has got by it!"), their temper was very base and sordid. Nothing more barbarous than to triumph over those that are fallen. But we may suppose that the generality asked it in compassion and commiseration: "Is this she that lived so plentifully, and kept so good a house, and was so charitable to the poor? *How has the gold become dim!*" Those that had seen the magnificence of the first temple wept when they saw the meanness of the second; so these here. Note, Afflictions will make great and surprising changes in a little time. When we see how sickness and old age alter people, change their countenance and temper, we may think of what the Bethlehemites said: "*Is this Naomi?* One would not take it to be the same person." God, by his grace, fit us for all such changes, especially the great change!

II. Of the composure of Naomi's spirit. If some upbraided her with her poverty, she was not moved against them, as she would have been if she had been poor and proud; but, with a great deal of pious patience, bore that and all the other melancholy effects of her affliction (*v.* 20, 21): *Call me not Naomi, call me Mara,* &c. "*Naomi* signifies *pleasant* or *amiable;* but all my pleasant things are laid waste; call me *Mara, bitter* or *bitterness,* for I am now a woman of a sorrowful spirit." Thus does she bring her mind to her condition, which we all ought to do when our condition is not in every thing to our mind. Observe,

1. The change of her state, and how it is described, with a pious regard to the divine providence, and without any passionate murmurings or complaints. (1.) It was a very sad and melancholy change. She *went out full;* so she thought herself when she had her husband with her and two sons. Much of the fulness of our comfort in this world arises from agreeable relations. But she now *came home again empty,* a widow and childless, and probably had sold her goods, and of all the effects she took with her brought home no more than the clothes on her back. So uncertain is all that which we call fulness in the creature, 1 Sam. ii. 5. Even in the fulness of that sufficiency we may be in straits. But there is a fulness, a spiritual and divine fulness, which we can never be emptied of, a good part which shall not be *taken from those that have it.* (2.) She acknowledges the hand of God, his mighty hand, in the affliction. "It is the Lord that has *brought me home again empty;* it is the Almighty that has afflicted me." Note, Nothing conduces more to satisfy a gracious soul under an affliction than the consideration of the hand of God in it. *It is the Lord,* 1 Sam. iii. 18; Job i. 21. Especially to consider that he who afflicts us is *Shaddai,* the *Almighty,* with whom it is folly to contend and to whom it is our duty and interest to submit. It is that name of God by which he enters into covenant with his people: *I am God Almighty, God All-sufficient,* Gen. xvii. 1. He afflicts as a God in covenant, and his all-sufficiency may be our support and supply under all our afflictions. He that empties us of the creature knows how to fill us with himself. (3.) She speaks very feelingly of the impression which the affliction had made upon her: He has *dealt very bitterly with me.* The cup of affliction is a bitter cup, and even that which afterwards *yields the peaceable fruit of righteousness,* yet, for the present, is *not joyous, but grievous,* Heb. xii. 11. Job complains, *Thou writest bitter things against me,* Job xiii. 26. (4.) She owns the affliction to come from God as a controversy: *The Lord hath testified against me.* Note, When God corrects us he *testifies against us* and contends with us (Job x. 17), intimating that he is displeased with us. Every rod has a voice, the voice of a witness.

2. The compliance of her spirit with this change: "*Call me not Naomi,* for I am no more pleasant, either to myself or to my friends; *but call me Mara,* a name more agreeable to my present state." Many that are debased and impoverished yet affect to be called by the empty names and titles of honour they have formerly enjoyed. Naomi did not so. Her humility regards not a glorious name in a dejected state. If God deal bitterly with her, she will accommodate herself to the dispensation, and is willing to be called *Mara, bitter.* Note, It well becomes us to have our hearts humbled under humbling providences. When our condition is brought down our spirits should be brought down with it. And then our troubles are sanctified to us when we thus comport with them; for it is not an affliction itself, but an affliction rightly borne, that does us good. *Perdidisti tot mala, si nondum misera esse didicisti—So many calamities have been lost upon you if you have not yet learned how to suffer.* Sen. ad Helv. *Tribulation works patience.*

CHAP. II.

There is scarcely any chapter in all the sacred history that stoops so low as this to take cognizance of so mean a person as Ruth, a poor Moabitish widow, so mean an action as her gleaning corn in a neighbour's field, and the minute circumstances thereof. But all this was in order to her being grafted into the line of Christ and taken in among his ancestors, that she might be a figure of the espousals of the Gentile church to Christ, Isa. liv. 1. This makes the story remarkable; and many of the passages of it are instructive and very improvable. Here we have, I. Ruth's humility and industry in gleaning corn, Providence directing her to Boaz's field, ver. 1—3. II. The great favour which Boaz showed to her in many instances, ver. 4—16. III. The return of Ruth to her mother-in-law, ver. 18—23.

AND Naomi had a kinsman of her husband's, a mighty man of wealth, of the family of Elimelech; and his name *was* Boaz. 2 And Ruth the Moabitess said unto Naomi, Let me now go to the field, and glean ears of corn after *him* in whose sight I shall find grace. And she said unto her, Go, my daughter. 3 And she went, and came, and gleaned in the field after the reapers: and her hap was to light on a part of the field *be-*

longing unto Boaz, who *was* of the kindred of Elimelech.

Naomi had now gained a settlement in Bethlehem among her old friends; and here we have an account,

I. Of her rich kinsman, Boaz, *a mighty man of wealth, v.* 1. The Chaldee reads it, *mighty in the law.* If he was both, it was a most rare and excellent conjunction, to be mighty in wealth and mighty in the scriptures too; those that are so are mighty indeed. He was grandson of Nahshon, who was prince of the tribe of Judah in the wilderness, and son of Salmon, probably a younger son, by Rahab, the harlot of Jericho. He carries might in his name, *Boaz—in him is strength;* and he was of the family of Elimelech, that family which was now reduced and brought so low. Observe, 1. Boaz, though a rich and great man, had poor relations. Every branch of the tree is not a top-branch. Let not those that are great in the world be ashamed to own their kindred that are mean and despised, lest they be found therein proud, scornful, and unnatural. 2. Naomi, though a poor contemptible widow, had rich relations, whom yet she boasted not of, nor was burdensome to, nor expected any thing from when she returned to Bethlehem in distress. Those that have rich relations, while they themselves are poor, ought to know that it is the wise providence of God that makes the difference (in which we ought to acquiesce), and that to be proud of our relation to such is a great sin, and to trust to it is great folly.

II. Of her poor daughter-in-law, Ruth. 1. Her condition was very low and poor, which was a great trial to the faith and constancy of a young proselyte. The Bethlehemites would have done well if they had invited Naomi and her daughter-in-law first to one good house and then to another (it would have been a great support to an aged widow and a great encouragement to a new convert); but, instead of tasting the dainties of Canaan, they have no way of getting necessary food but by gleaning corn, and otherwise, for aught that appears, they might have starved. Note, *God has chosen the poor of this world;* and poor they are likely to be, for, though God has chosen them, commonly men overlook them. 2. Her character, in this condition, was very good (*v.* 2): *She said to Naomi,* not, "Let me now go to the land of Moab again, for there is no living here, here there is want, but *in my father's house there is bread enough.*" No, she is *not mindful of the country from which she came out,* otherwise she had now a fair occasion to return. The God of Israel shall be her God, and, though he slay her, yet will she trust in him and never forsake him. But her request is, *Let me go to the field, and glean ears of corn.* Those that are well born, and have been well brought up, know not what straits they may be reduced to, nor what mean employments they may be obliged to get their bread by, Lam. iv. 5. When the case is thus melancholy, let Ruth be remembered, who is a great example, (1.) Of humility. When Providence had made her poor she did not say, "To glean, which is in effect to beg, I am ashamed," but cheerfully stoops to the meanness of her circumstances and accommodates herself to her lot. High spirits can more easily starve than stoop; Ruth was none of those. She does not tell her mother she was never brought up to live upon crumbs. Though she was not brought up to it, she is brought down to it, and is not uneasy at it. Nay, it is her own motion, not her mother's injunction. Humility is one of the brightest ornaments of youth, and one of the best omens. Before Ruth's honour was this humility. Observe how humbly she speaks of herself, in her expectation of leave to glean: Let me glean after him *in whose sight I shall find grace.* She does not say, "I will go and glean, and surely nobody will deny me the liberty," but, "I will go and glean, in the hope that somebody will allow me the liberty." Note, Poor people must not demand kindness as a debt, but humbly ask it, and take it as a favour, though in ever so small a matter. It becomes the poor to use entreaties. (2.) Of industry. She does not say to her mother-in-law, "Let me now go a visiting to the ladies of the town, or go a walking in the fields to take the air and be merry; I cannot sit all day moping with you." No, it is not sport, but business, that her heart is upon: "*Let me go and glean ears of corn,* which will turn to some good account." She was one of those virtuous women that love not to eat the bread of idleness, but love to take pains. This is an example to young people. Let them learn betimes to labour, and, *what their hand finds to do, do it with their might.* A disposition to diligence bodes well both for this world and the other. Love not sleep, love not sport, love not sauntering; but love business. It is also an example to poor people to work for their living, and not beg that which they are able to earn. We must not be shy of any honest employment, though it be mean, ἐργον ουδεν ὀνεῖδος—*No labour is a reproach.* Sin is a thing below us, but we must not think any thing else so that Providence calls us to. (3.) Of regard to her mother. Though she was but her mother-in-law, and though, being loosed by death from the law of her husband, she might easily suppose herself thereby loosed from the law of her husband's mother, yet she is dutifully observant of her. She will not go out without letting her know and asking her leave. This respect young people ought to show to their parents and governors; it is part of the honour due to them. She did not say, "Mother, if you will go with me, I will go glean:" but, "Do you sit at home and take your ease, and I will go abroad, and take pains." *Juniores ad labores—Youth should work.* Let young people take advice from the aged, but not put them upon toil. (4.) Of dependence upon Providence, intimated in that, I will *glean after him in whose sight I shall find grace.* She knows not which way to go, nor whom to enquire for, but will trust Providence to raise her up some friend or other that will be kind to her. Let us always keep up good thoughts of the divine providence, and believe that while we do well it will do well for us. And it did well for Ruth; for when she went out alone, without guide or companion, to glean, *her hap was to light on the field of Boaz, v.* 3. To her it seemed casual. She knew not whose field it was, nor had she any reason for going to that more than any other, and therefore it is said to be *her hap;* but Providence directed her steps to this field. Note, God wisely orders small events; and those that seem altogether contingent serve his own glory and the good of his people. Many a great affair is brought about by a little turn, which seemed fortuitous to us, but was directed by Providence with design.

4 And, behold, Boaz came from Bethlehem, and said unto the reapers, The LORD *be* with you. And they answered him, The LORD bless thee. 5 Then said Boaz unto his servant that was set over the reapers, Whose damsel *is* this? 6 And the servant that was set over the reapers answered and said, It *is* the Moabitish damsel that came back with Naomi out of the country of Moab: 7 And she said, I pray you, let me glean and gather after the reapers among the sheaves: so she came, and hath continued even from the morning until now, that she tarried a little in the house. 8 Then said Boaz unto Ruth, Hearest thou not, my daughter? Go not to glean in another field, neither go from hence, but abide here fast by my maidens: 9 *Let* thine eyes *be* on the field that they do reap, and go thou after them: have I not charged the young men that they shall not touch thee? and when thou art athirst, go unto the vessels, and drink of *that* which the young men have drawn. 10 Then she fell on her face, and bowed herself to the ground, and said unto him, Why have I found grace in thine eyes, that thou shouldest take knowledge of me, seeing I *am* a stranger? 11 And Boaz answered and said unto her, It hath fully been showed me, all that thou hast done unto thy mother in law since the death of thine husband: and *how* thou hast left thy father and thy mother, and the land of thy nativity, and art come unto a people which thou knewest not heretofore. 12 The LORD recompense thy work, and a full reward be given thee of the LORD God of Israel, under whose wings thou art come to trust. 13 Then she said, Let me find favour in thy sight, my lord; for that thou hast comforted me, and for that thou hast spoken friendly unto thine handmaid, though I be not like unto one of thine handmaidens. 14 And Boaz said unto her, At mealtime come thou hither, and eat of the bread, and dip thy morsel in the vinegar. And she sat beside the reapers: and he reached her parched *corn,* and she did eat, and was sufficed, and left. 15 And when she was risen up to glean, Boaz commanded his young men, saying, Let her glean even among the sheaves, and reproach her not: 16 And let fall also *some* of the handfuls of purpose for her, and leave *them,* that she may glean *them,* and rebuke her not.

Now Boaz himself appears, and a great deal of decency there appears in his carriage both towards his own servants and towards this poor stranger.

I. Towards his own servants, and those that were employed for him in reaping and gathering in his corn. Harvest-time is busy time, many hands must then be at work. Boaz that had much, being a mighty man of wealth, had much to do, and consequently many to work under him and to live upon him. *As goods are increased those are increased that eat them, and what good has the owner thereof save the beholding of them with his eyes?* Boaz is here an example of a good master.

1. He had a servant that was set over the reapers, *v.* 6. In great families it is requisite there should be one to oversee the rest of the servants, and appoint to each their portion both of work and meat. Ministers are such servants in God's house, and it is requisite that they be both wise and faithful, and *show their Lord all things,* as he here, *v.* 6.

2. Yet he came himself to his reapers, to see how the work went forward, if he found any thing amiss to rectify it, and to give further orders what should be done. This

was both for his own interest (he that wholly leaves his business to others will have it done by the halves; the master's eye makes a fat horse) and it was also for the encouragement of his servants, who would go on the more cheerfully in their work when their master countenanced them so far as to make them a visit. Masters that live at ease should think with tenderness of those that toil for them and bear the burden and heat of the day.

3. Kind and pious salutations were interchanged between Boaz and his reapers.

(1.) He said to them, *The Lord be with you;* and they replied, *The Lord bless thee, v.* 4. Hereby they expressed, [1.] Their mutual respect to each other; he to them as good servants, and they to him as a good master. When he came to them he did not fall a chiding them, as if he came only to find fault and exercise his authority, but he prayed for them: "*The Lord be with you,* prosper you, and give you health and strength, and preserve you from any disaster." Nor did they, as soon as ever he was out of hearing, fall a cursing him, as some ill-natured servants that hate their master's eye, but they returned his courtesy: "*The Lord bless thee,* and make our labours serviceable to thy prosperity." Things are likely to go on well in a house where there is such good-will as this between master and servants. [2.] Their joint-dependence upon the divine providence. They express their kindness to each other by praying one for another. They show not only their courtesy, but their piety, and acknowledgment that all good comes from the presence and blessing of God, which therefore we should value and desire above any thing else both for ourselves and others.

(2.) Let us hence learn to use, [1.] Courteous salutations, as expressions of a sincere good-will to our friends. [2.] Pious ejaculations, lifting up our hearts to God for his favour, in such short prayers as these. Only we must take heed that they do not degenerate into formality, lest in them we *take the name of the Lord our God in vain;* but, if we be serious in them, we may in them keep up our communion with God, and fetch in mercy and grace from him. It appears to have been the usual custom thus to wish reapers good speed, Ps. cxxix. 7, 8.

4. He took an account from his reapers concerning a stranger he met with in the field, and gave necessary orders concerning her, that they should not touch her (*v.* 9) nor reproach her, *v.* 15. Masters must take care, not only that they do no hurt themselves, but that they suffer not their servants and those under them to do hurt. He also ordered them to be kind to her, and *let fall some of the handfuls on purpose for her.* Though it is fit that masters should restrain and rebuke their servants' wastefulness, yet they should not tie them up from being charitable, but give them allowance for that, with prudent directions.

II. Boaz was very kind to Ruth, and showed her a great deal of favour, induced to it by the account he had of her, and what he observed concerning her, God also inclining his heart to countenance her. Coming among his reapers, he observed this stranger among them, and got intelligence from his steward who she was, and here is a very particular account of what passed concerning her.

1. The steward gave to Boaz a very fair account of her, proper to recommend her to his favour, *v* 6, 7. (1.) That she was a stranger, and therefore one of those that by the law of God were to *gather the gleanings of the harvest,* Lev. xix. 9, 10. She is the Moabitish damsel. (2.) That she was allied to his family; she came back with Naomi, the wife of Elimelech, a kinsman of Boaz. (3.) That she was a proselyte, for she came out of the country of Moab to settle in the land of Israel. (4.) That she was very modest, and had not gleaned till she had asked leave. (5.) That she was very industrious, and had continued close to her work from morning even until now. And the poor that are industrious and willing to take pains are fit to be encouraged. Now, in the heat of the day, she tarried a little in the house or booth that was set up in the field for shelter from the weather to repose herself, and some suggest that it is probable she retired for her devotion. But she soon came back to her work, and, except that little intermission, kept close to it all day, though it was not what she had been used to. Servants should be just in the character and reports they give to their masters, and take heed they do not misrepresent any person, nor without cause discourage their master's charity.

2. Boaz was hereupon extremely civil to her in divers instances. (1.) He ordered her to attend his reapers in every field they gathered in and not to glean in the field of another, for she should not need to go any where else to better herself (*v.* 8): *Abide here fast by my maidens;* for those of her own sex were the fittest company for her. (2.) He charged all his servants to be very tender of her and respectful to her, and no doubt they would be so to one to whom they saw their master kind. She was a stranger, and it is probable her language, dress, and mien differed much from theirs; but he charged them that they should not in any thing affront her, or be abusive to her, as rude servants are too apt to be to strangers. (3.) He bade her welcome to the entertainment he had provided for his own servants. He ordered her, not only to drink of the water which was drawn for them (for that seems to be the liquor he means (*v.* 9), drawn from the famous well of Beth-lehem which was by the gate, the water of which David longed for, 2 Sam. xxiii. 15), but *at meal-time to come and eat of their bread* (*v.* 14), yea, and she should be welcome to their sauce too: *Come, dip thy morsel in the*

vinegar, to make it savoury; for God allows us not only nourishing but relishing food, not for necessity only, but for delight. And for encouragement to her, and direction to the servants, he himself, happening to be present when the reapers sat down to meat, *reached her parched corn* to eat. It is no disparagement to the finest hand to be *reached forth to the needy* (Prov. xxxi. 20), and to be employed in serving the poor. Observe, Boaz was not scanty in his provision for his reapers, but sent them so much more than enough for themselves as would be entertainment for a stranger. Thus *there is that scattereth and yet increaseth.* (4.) He commended her for her dutiful respect to her mother-in-law, which, though he did not know her by sight, yet he had heard of (*v.* 11): *It has been fully shown me all that thou hast done unto thy mother-in-law.* Note, Those that do well ought to have the praise of it. But that which especially he commended her for was that she had left her own country, and had become a proselyte to the Jewish religion; for so the Chaldee expounds it: "Thou hast come to be proselyted, and to dwell among *a people whom thou knowest not.*" Those that leave all, to embrace the true religion, are worthy of double honour. (5.) He prayed for her (*v.* 12): *The Lord recompense thy work.* Her strong affection to the commonwealth of Israel, to which she was by birth an alien, was such a work of the divine grace in her as would certainly be crowned with a full reward by him *under whose wings she had come to trust.* Note, Those that by faith come under the wings of the divine grace, and have a full complacency and confidence in that grace, may be sure of a full recompence of reward for their so doing. From this expression, the Jews describe a proselyte to be one that is *gathered under the wings of the divine majesty.* (6.) He encouraged her to go on in her gleaning, and did not offer to take her off from that; for the greatest kindness we can do our poor relations is to assist and encourage their industry. Boaz ordered his servants to let her glean among the sheaves, where other gleaners were not allowed to come, and not to reproach her, that is, not to call her *thief*, or to suspect her of taking more than was allowed her, *v.* 15. All this shows Boaz to have been a man of a generous spirit, and one that, according to the law, considered the heart of a stranger.

3. Ruth received his favours with a great deal of humility and gratitude, and conducted herself with as much propriety in her place as he did himself in his, but little thinking that she should shortly be the mistress of that field she was now gleaning in. (1.) She paid all possible respect to him, and gave him honour, according to the usage of the country (*v.* 10): *She fell on her face, and bowed herself to the ground.* Note, Good breeding is a great ornament to religion; and we must render *honour to whom honour is due.* (2.) She humbly owned herself unworthy of his favours: "*I am a stranger* (*v.* 10) and *not like one of thy handmaids* (*v.* 13), not so well dressed nor so well taught, not so neat nor so handy." Note, It well becomes us all to think meanly of ourselves, and to take notice of that in ourselves which is diminishing, esteeming others better than ourselves. (3.) She gratefully acknowledged his kindness to her; though it was no great expense to him, nor much more than what he was obliged to by the divine law, yet she magnifies and admires it: *Why have I found grace in thy eyes? v.* 10. (4.) She begs the continuance of his good-will: *Let me find favour in thy sight* (*v.* 13), and owns that what he had said had been a cordial to her: *Thou hast comforted me, for that thou hast spoken friendly to me.* Those that are great, and in high places, know not how much good they may do to their inferiors with a kind look or by speaking friendly to them; and so small an expense, one would think, they should not grudge, when it shall be put upon the score of their charity. (5.) When Boaz gave her her dinner with his reapers she only ate so much as would suffice her, and left the rest, and immediately rose up to glean, *v.* 14, 15. She did not, under pretence either of her want or of her labour, eat more than was convenient for her, nor so much as to unfit her for work in the afternoon. Temperance is a friend to industry; and we must eat and drink to strengthen us for business, not to indispose us to it.

17 So she gleaned in the field until even, and beat out that she had gleaned: and it was about an ephah of barley. 18 And she took *it* up, and went into the city: and her mother in law saw what she had gleaned: and she brought forth, and gave to her that she had reserved after she was sufficed. 19 And her mother in law said unto her, Where hast thou gleaned to day? and where wroughtest thou? blessed be he that did take knowledge of thee. And she showed her mother in law with whom she had wrought, and said, The man's name with whom I wrought to day *is* Boaz. 20 And Naomi said unto her daughter in law, Blessed *be* he of the LORD, who hath not left off his kindness to the living and to the dead. And Naomi said unto her, The man *is* near of kin unto us, one of our next kinsmen. 21 And Ruth the Moabitess said, He said unto me also, Thou shalt keep fast by my

young men, until they have ended all my harvest. 22 And Naomi said unto Ruth her daughter in law, *It is* good, my daughter, that thou go out with his maidens, that they meet thee not in any other field. 23 So she kept fast by the maidens of Boaz to glean unto the end of barley harvest and of wheat harvest; and dwelt with her mother in law.

Here, I. Ruth finishes her day's work, *v.* 17. 1. She took care not to lose time, for she gleaned until evening. We must not be weary of well-doing, because in due season we shall reap. She did not make an excuse to sit still, or go home, till the evening. Let us *work the works of him that sent us, while it is day.* She scarcely used, much less did she abuse, the kindness of Boaz; for, though he ordered his servants to leave handfuls for her, she continued to glean the scattered ears. 2. She took care not to lose what she had gathered, but threshed it herself, that she might the more easily carry it home, and might have it ready for use. *The slothful man roasteth not that which he took in hunting,* and so loseth the benefit of it, *but the substance of a diligent man is precious,* Prov. xii. 27. Ruth had gathered it ear by ear, but, when she had put it all together, it was an ephah of barley, about four pecks. Many a little makes a great deal. It is an encouragement to industry that in all labour, even that of gleaning, there is profit, but the *talk of the lips tendeth only to penury.* When she had got her corn into as little compass as she could, she took it up herself, and carried it into the city, though, had she asked them, it is likely some of Boaz's servants would have done that for her. We should study to be as little as possible troublesome to those that are kind to us. She did not think it either too hard or too mean a service to carry her corn herself into the city, but was rather pleased with what she had gotten by her own industry, and careful to secure it; and let us thus take care that we *lose not those things which we have wrought,* which we have gained, 2 John 8.

II. She paid her respects to her mother-in-law, went straight home to her and did not go to converse with Boaz's servants, *showed her what she had gleaned,* that she might see she had not been idle.

1. She entertained her with what she had left of the good dinner Boaz had given her. She gave to her what she had reserved, after she was sufficed (*v.* 18), which refers to *v.* 14. If she had any thing better than another, her mother should have part with her. Thus, having shown industry abroad, she showed piety at home; so children's maintaining their parents is called (1 Tim. v. 4), and it is part of the honour due to them by the fifth commandment, Matt. xv. 6.

2. She gave her an account of her day's work, and how a kind providence had favoured her in it, which made it very comfortable to her; for the gleanings that a righteous man hath are better than the harvests of many wicked, Ps. xxxvii. 16. (1.) Naomi asked her where she had been: *Where hast thou gleaned to-day?* Note, Parents should take care to enquire into the ways of their children, how, and where, and in what company they spend their time. This may prevent many extravagancies which children, left to themselves, run into, by which they bring both themselves and their parents to shame. If we are not our brethren's, yet surely we are our children's keepers: and we know what a son Adonijah proved, that had never been chidden. Parents should examine their children, not to frighten nor discourage them, not so as to make them hate home or tempt them to tell a lie, but to commend them if they have done well, and with mildness to reprove and caution them if they have done otherwise. It is a good question for us to ask ourselves in the close of every day, "*Where have I gleaned to-day?* What improvements have I made in knowledge and grace? What have I done or obtained that will turn to a good account?" (2.) Ruth gave her a particular account of the kindness she had received from Boaz (*v.* 19) and the hopes she had of further kindness from him, he having ordered her to attend his servants throughout all the harvest, *v.* 21. Note, Children should look upon themselves as accountable to their parents and to those that are over them, and not think it a disparagement to them to be examined; let them *do that which is good,* and they shall have praise of the same. Ruth told her mother what kindness Boaz had shown her, that she might take some occasion or another to acknowledge it and return him thanks; but she did not tell her how Boaz had commended her, *v.* 11. Humility teaches us, not only not to praise ourselves, but not to be forward to publish others' praises of us. (3.) We are here told what Naomi said to it. [1.] She prayed heartily for him that had been her daughter's benefactor, even before she knew who it was (*v.* 19): *Blessed be he,* whoever he was, *that did take knowledge of thee,* shooting the arrow of prayer at a venture. But more particularly when she was told who it was (*v.* 20): *Blessed be he of the Lord.* Note, The poor must pray for those that are kind and liberal to them, and thus requite them, when they are not capable of making them any other requital. Let the loins of the poor bless those that refresh them, Job xxix. 13; xxxi. 20. And he that hears the cries of the poor against their oppressors (Exod. xxii. 27), it may be hoped, will hear the prayers of the poor for their benefactors. She now remembered the former kindnesses Boaz had shown to her husband and sons, and joins those to

this: he has not *left off his kindness to the living and to the dead.* If we generously show kindness even to those that seem to have forgotten our former favours, perhaps it may help to revive the remembrance even of those which seem buried. [2.] She acquainted Ruth with the relation their family was in to Boaz: *The man is near of kin to us.* It should seem she had been so long in Moab that she had forgotten her kindred in the land of Israel, till by this providence God brought it to her mind. At least she had not told Ruth of it, though it might have been some encouragement to a young proselyte. Unlike to humble Naomi are many, who, though fallen into decay themselves, are continually boasting of their great relations. Nay, Observe the chain of thought here, and in it a chain of providences, bringing about what was designed concerning Ruth. Ruth names Boaz as one that had been kind to her. Naomi bethinks herself who that should be, and presently recollects herself: "*The man is near of kin to us;* now that I hear his name, I remember him very well." This thought brings in another: "He is *our next kinsman,* our *goel,* that has the right to redeem our estate that was mortgaged, and therefore from him we may expect further kindness. He is the likeliest man in all Bethlehem to set us up." Thus God brings things to our mind, sometimes on a sudden, that prove to have a wonderful tendency to our good. [3.] She appointed Ruth to continue her attendance in the fields of Boaz (*v.* 22): "*Let them not meet thee in any other field,* for that will be construed a contempt of his courtesy." Our blessed Saviour is our *Goel;* it is he that has a right to redeem. If we expect to receive benefit by him, let us closely adhere to him, and his fields, and his family; let us not go to the world and its fields for that which is to be had with him only, and which he has encouraged us to expect from him. Has the Lord dealt bountifully with us? Let us not be found in any other field, nor seek for happiness and satisfaction in the creature. Tradesmen take it ill if those that are in their books go to another shop. We lose divine favours if we slight them. Some think Naomi gave her daughter-in-law a tacit rebuke; she had spoken (*v.* 21) of keeping fast by the young *men.* "Nay," said Naomi (*v.* 22), "*It is good that thou go out with his maidens; they* are fitter company for thee than the *young men.*" But they are too critical. Ruth spoke of the young men because they were the principal labourers, and to them Boaz had given directions concerning her; and Naomi takes it for granted that, while she attended the young men, her society would be with the maidens, as was fit. Ruth dutifully observed her mother's directions; she continued to glean, to the end, not only of barley-harvest, but of the wheat-harvest, which followed it, that she might gather food in harvest to serve for winter, Prov. vi. 6—8. She also kept fast by the maidens of Boaz, with whom she afterwards cultivated an acquaintance, which might do her service, *v.* 23. But she constantly came to her mother at night in due time, as became a virtuous woman, that was for working days, and not for merry nights. And when the harvest was ended (as bishop Patrick expounds it) she did not gad abroad, but kept her aged mother company at home. Dinah went out to see the daughters of the land, and we know what a disgrace her vanity ended in. Ruth kept at home, and helped to maintain her mother, and went out on no other errand than to get provision for her, and we shall find afterwards what preferment her humility and industry ended in. *Seest thou a man diligent in his business?* Honour is before him.

CHAP. III.

We found it very easy, in the former chapter, to applaud the decency of Ruth's behaviour, and to show what good use we may make of the account given us of it; but in this chapter we shall have much ado to vindicate it from the imputation of indecency, and to save it from having an ill use made of it; but the goodness of those times was such as saved what is recorded here from being ill done, and yet the badness of these times is such as that it will not justify any now in doing the like. Here is, I. The directions Naomi gave to her daughter-in-law how to claim Boaz for her husband, ver. 1—5. II. Ruth's punctual observance of those directions, ver. 6, 7. III. The kind and honourable treatment Boaz gave her, ver. 8—15. IV. Her return to her mother-in-law, ver. 16—18.

THEN Naomi her mother in law said unto her, My daughter, shall I not seek rest for thee, that it may be well with thee? 2 And now *is* not Boaz of our kindred, with whose maidens thou wast? Behold, he winnoweth barley to night in the threshing floor. 3 Wash thyself therefore, and anoint thee, and put thy raiment upon thee, and get thee down to the floor: *but* make not thyself known unto the man, until he shall have done eating and drinking. 4 And it shall be, when he lieth down, that thou shalt mark the place where he shall lie, and thou shalt go in, and uncover his feet, and lay thee down; and he will tell thee what thou shalt do. 5 And she said unto her, All that thou sayest unto me I will do.

Here, I. Naomi's care for her daughter's comfort is without doubt very commendable, and is recorded for imitation. She had no thoughts of marrying herself, *ch.* i. 12. But, though she that was old had resolved upon a perpetual widowhood, yet she was far from the thoughts of confining her daughter-in-law to it, that was young. Age must not make itself a standard to youth. On the contrary, she is full of contrivance how to get her well married. Her wisdom projected that for her daughter which her daughter's modesty forbade her to project for herself, *v.* 1. This she did, 1. In justice to the dead, to raise up seed to those that were gone, and so to preserve the family from being extinct. 2. In kindness and gratitude to her daughter-in-law, who had conducted herself very dutifully and respectfully to her. "*My daughter*" (said she, looking upon her in all respects as her own), "*shall I not seek rest for thee,*" that is, a settlement in the married state; "shall I not get thee a good husband, *that it may be well with thee,*" that is, "that thou mayest live plentifully and pleasantly, and not spend all thy days in the mean and melancholy condition we now live in?" Note, (1.) A married state is, or should be, a state of rest to young people. Wandering affections are then fixed, and the heart must be at rest. It is at rest in the house of a husband, and in his heart, *ch.* i. 9. Those are giddy indeed that marriage does not compose. (2.) That which should be desired and designed by those that enter into the married state is *that it may be well with them,* in order to which it is necessary that they choose well; otherwise, instead of being a rest to them, it may prove the greatest uneasiness. Parents, in disposing of their children, must have this in their eye, *that it may be well with them.* And be it always remembered *that is best for us which is best for our souls.* (3.) It is the duty of parents to seek this rest for their children, and to do all that is fit for them to do, in due time, in order to it. And the more dutiful and respectful they are to them, though they can the worse spare them, yet they should the rather prefer them, and the better.

II. The course she took in order to her daughter's preferment was very extraordinary and looks suspicious. If there was any thing improper in it, the fault must lie upon Naomi, who put her daughter upon it, and who knew, or should know, the laws and usages of Israel better than Ruth. 1. It was true that Boaz, being near of kin to the deceased, and (for aught that Naomi knew to the contrary) the nearest of all now alive, was obliged by the divine law to marry the widow of Mahlon, who was the eldest son of Elimelech, and was dead without issue (*v.* 2): "*Is not Boaz of our kindred,* and therefore bound in conscience to take care of our affairs? Why should we not remind him of his duty?" This may encourage us to lay ourselves by faith at the feet of Christ, that he is our near kinsman; having taken our nature upon him, he is *bone of our bone and flesh of our flesh.* 2. It was a convenient time to remind him of it, now that he had got so much acquaintance with Ruth by her constant attendance on his reapers during the whole harvest, which was now ended; and he also, by the kindness he had shown to Ruth in smaller matters, had encouraged Naomi to hope that he would not be unkind, much less unjust, in this greater. And she thought it was a good opportunity to apply to him when he made a winnowing-feast at his threshing-floor (*v.* 2), then and there completing the joy of the harvest, and treating his workmen like a kind master: *He winnoweth barley to-night,* that is, he makes his entertainment to-night. As Nabal and Absalom had feasts at their sheep-shearing, so Boaz at his winnowing. 3. Naomi thought Ruth the most proper person to do it herself; and perhaps it was the usage in that country that in this case the woman should make the demand; so much is intimated by the law, Deut. xxv. 7—9. Naomi therefore orders her daughter-in-law to make herself clean and neat, not to make herself fine (*v.* 3): "*Wash thyself and anoint thee,* not paint thee (as Jezebel), put on thy raiment, but not the attire of a harlot, and go down to the floor," whither, it is probable, she was invited to the supper there made; but she must not make herself known, that is, not make her errand known (she herself could not but be very well known among Boaz's reapers) till the company had dispersed and Boaz had retired. And upon this occasion she would have an easier access to him in private than she could have at his own house. And thus far was well enough. But, 4. Her coming to lie down at his feet, when he was asleep in his bed, had such an appearance of evil, was such an approach towards it, and might have been such an occasion of it, that we know not well how to justify it. Many expositors think it unjustifiable, particularly the excellent Mr. Poole. We must not do evil that good may come. It is dangerous to bring the spark and the tinder together; for how great a matter may a little fire kindle! All agree that it is not to be drawn into a precedent; neither our laws nor our times are the same that were then; yet I am willing to make the best of it. If Boaz was, as they presumed, the next kinsman, she was his wife before God (as we say), and there needed but little ceremony to complete the nuptials; and Naomi did not intend that Ruth should approach to him any otherwise than as his wife. She knew Boaz to be not only an old man (she would not have trusted to that alone in venturing her daughter-in-law so near him), but a grave sober man, a virtuous and religious man, and one that feared God. She knew Ruth to be a modest woman, *chaste, and a keeper at home,* Tit. ii. 5. The Israelites had indeed been once debauched by the daughters of Moab (Num. xxv. 1), but this Moabitess was none of those daughters. Naomi herself designed nothing but what was honest and honourable, and her charity (which *believeth all things* and *hopeth all things)* banished and forbade all suspicion that either Boaz or Ruth would attempt any thing but what was likewise honest and honourable. If what she advised had been then as indecent and immodest (according to the usage of the country) as it seems now to us, we cannot think that if Naomi had had so little virtue (which yet we have no reason to suspect) she would also have had so little wisdom as to put her daughter upon it, since that alone might have marred the match, and have alienated the affections of so grave and good a man as Boaz from her. We must therefore think that the thing did not look so ill then as it does now. Naomi referred her daughter-in-law to Boaz for further directions. When she had thus made her claim, Boaz, who was more learned in the laws, would *tell her what she must do*. Thus must we lay ourselves at the feet of our Redeemer, to receive from him our doom. *Lord, what wilt thou have me to do?* Acts ix. 6. We may be sure, if Ruth had apprehended any evil in that which her mother advised her to, she was a woman of too much virtue and too much sense to promise as she did (*v.* 5): *All that thou sayest unto me I will do.* Thus must *the younger submit to the elder,* and to their grave and prudent counsels, when they have nothing worth speaking of to object against it.

6 And she went down unto the floor, and did according to all that her mother in law bade her. 7 And when Boaz had eaten and drunk, and his heart was merry, he went to lie down at the end of the heap of corn: and she came softly, and uncovered his feet, and laid her down. 8 And it came to pass at midnight, that the man was afraid, and turned himself: and, behold, a woman lay at his feet. 9 And he said, Who *art* thou? and she answered, I *am* Ruth thine handmaid: spread therefore thy skirt over thine handmaid; for thou *art* a near kinsman. 10 And he said, Blessed *be* thou of the LORD, my daughter: *for* thou hast showed more kindness in the latter end than at the beginning, inasmuch as thou followedst not young men, whether poor or rich. 11 And now, my daughter, fear not; I will do to thee all that thou requirest: for all the city of my people doth know that thou *art* a virtuous woman. 12 And now it is true that I *am thy* near kinsman; howbeit there is a kinsman nearer than I. 13 Tarry this night, and it shall be in the morning, *that* if he will perform unto thee the part of a kinsman, well; let him do the kinsman's part: but if he will not do the part of a kinsman to thee, then will I do the part of a kinsman to thee, *as* the LORD liveth: lie down until the morning.

Here is, I. Boaz's good management of his common affairs. It is probable, according to the common usage, 1. When his servants winnowed, he was with them, and had his eye upon them, to prevent, not their stealing any of his corn (he had no reason to fear that), but their waste of it through carelessness in the winnowing of it. Masters may sustain great losses by servants that are heedless, though they be honest, which is a reason why men should be diligent to *know the state of their own flocks,* and look well to them. 2. When he had more than ordinary work to be done, he treated his servants with extraordinary entertainments, and, for their encouragement, did *eat and drink with them.* It well becomes those that are rich and great to be generous to, and also to be familiar with, those that are under them, and employed for them. 3. When Boaz had supped with his workmen, and been awhile pleasant with them, he *went to bed in due time,* so early that by midnight he had his first sleep (*v.* 8), and thus he would be fit for his business betimes next morning. All that are good husbands will keep good hours, and not indulge themselves nor their families in unseasonable mirth. The Chaldee paraphrase tells us (*v.* 7) that *Boaz ate and drank and his heart was good* (and so the Hebrew word is), *and he blessed the name of the Lord, who had heard his prayers, and taken away the famine from the land of Israel.* So that he went sober to bed, his heart was in a good frame, and not overcharged with surfeiting and drunkenness. And he did not go to bed without prayer. Now that he had eaten and was full he blessed the Lord, and now that he was going to rest he committed himself to the divine protection; it was well he did, for he had an unusual temptation before him, though he knew not of it. 4. He had his bed or couch laid *at the end of the heap of corn;* not because he had set his heart upon it, nor only that he might watch and keep it safe from thieves, but it was too late to go home to the city, and here he would be near his work, and ready for it next morning, and he would show that he was not nice or curious in his lodging, neither took state nor consulted his ease, but was, like his father Jacob, a plain man, that, when there was occasion, could make his bed in a barn, and, if need were, sleep contentedly in the straw.

II. Ruth's good assurance in the management of her affair. She observed her mother's orders, went and laid herself down, not by his side, but overcross his bed's feet, in her clothes, and kept awake, waiting for an opportunity to tell her errand. When he awaked in the night, and perceived there was somebody at his feet, and enquired who it was, she told him her name and then her errand (*v.* 9), that she came to put herself under his protection, as the person appointed by the divine law to be her protector: "*Thou art he that has a right to redeem* a family and an estate from perishing, and therefore *let this ruin be under thy hand:* and *spread thy skirt over me*—be pleased to espouse me and my cause." Thus must we by faith apply ourselves to Jesus Christ as our next kinsman, that is able to redeem us, come under his wings, as we are invited (Matt. xxiii. 37), and beg of him to *spread his skirt over us.* "Lord Jesus, take me into thy covenant and under thy care. *I am oppressed, undertake for me.*"

III. The good acceptance Ruth gained with Boaz. What she did had no ill-effect, either one way or other, so that Naomi was not mistaken in her good opinion of her kinsman. He knew her demand was just and honourable, and treated her accordingly, and did not *deal with* his *sister as with a harlot,* Gen. xxxiv. 31. For,

1. He did not offer to violate her chastity, though he had all the opportunity that could be. The Chaldee paraphrase thus descants upon it:—He *subdued his concupiscence, and did not approach to her, but did as Joseph the Just, who would not come near to his Egyptian mistress, and as Phaltiel the Pious, who, when Saul had given him Michal, David's wife* (1 Sam. xxv. 44), *put a sword between himself and her, that he might not touch her.* Boaz knew it was not any sinful lust that brought her thither, and therefore bravely maintained both his own honour and hers.

2. He did not put any ill construction upon what she did, did not reproach her as an impudent woman and unfit to make an honest man a wife. She having approved herself well in the fields, and all her conduct having been modest and decent, he would not, from this instance, entertain the least suspicion of her character nor seem to do so, perhaps blaming himself that he had not offered the service of a kinsman to these distressed widows, and saved her this trouble, and ready to say as Judah concerning his daughter-in-law, *She is more righteous than I.* But on the contrary,

(1.) He commended her, spoke kindly to her, called her his *daughter,* and spoke honourably of her, as a woman of eminent virtue. She had shown in this instance more kindness to her mother-in-law, and to the family into which she had matched, than in any instance yet. It was very kind to leave her own country and come along with her mother to the land of Israel, to dwell with her, and help to maintain her. For this he had blessed her (*ch.* ii. 12); but now he says, Thou hast *shown more kindness in the latter end than at the beginning* (*v.* 10), in that she consulted not her own fancy, but her husband's family, in marrying again. She received not the addresses of *young men* (much less did she seek them), *whether poor or rich,* but was willing to marry as the divine law directed, though it was to an old man, because it was for the honour and interest of the family into which she had matched, and for which she had an entire kindness. Young people must aim, in disposing of themselves, not so much to please their own eye as to please God and their parents.

(2.) He promised her marriage (*v.* 11): "*Fear not* that I will slight thee, or expose thee; no, *I will do all that thou requirest,* for it is the same that the law requires, from the next of kin, and I have no reason to decline it, *for all the city of my people doth know that thou art a virtuous woman,*" *v.* 11. Note, [1.] Exemplary virtue ought to have its due praise (Phil. iv. 8), and it will recommend both men and women to the esteem of the wisest and best. Ruth was a poor woman, and poverty often obscures the lustre of virtue: yet Ruth's virtues, even in a mean condition, were generally taken notice of and could not be hid; nay, her virtues took away the reproach of her poverty. If poor people be but good people, they shall have honour from God and man. Ruth had been remarkable for her humility, which paved the way to this honour. The less she proclaimed her own goodness the more did her neighbours take notice of it. [2.] In the choice of yoke-fellows, virtue should especially be regarded, known approved virtue. Let religion determine the choice, and it will certainly crown the choice and make it comfortable. *Wisdom is better than gold,* and, when it is said to be *good with an inheritance,* the meaning is that an inheritance is worth little without it.

(3.) He made his promise conditional, and could not do otherwise, for it seems there was a kinsman that was nearer than he, to whom the right of redemption did belong, *v.* 12. This he knew, but we may reasonably suppose Naomi (who had been long abroad, and could not be exact in the pedigree of her husband's family) was ignorant of it, otherwise she would never have sent her daughter to make her claim of Boaz. Yet he does not bid her go herself to this other kinsman; this would have been to put too great a hardship upon her: but he promises, [1.] That he would himself propose it to the other kinsman, and know his mind. The Hebrew word for a widow signifies *one that is dumb.* Boaz will therefore *open his mouth for the dumb* (Prov. xxxi. 8), and will say that for this widow which she knew not how to say for herself. [2.] That, if the other kinsman refused to do the kinsman's part, he would do it, would marry the widow, redeem the land, and so repair the family. This promise he backs with a solemn oath, for it was a conditional contract of marriage (*v.* 13): *As the Lord liveth.* Thus keeping the matter in suspense, he bade her wait till morning. Bishop Hall thus sums up this matter in his contemplations:—"Boaz, instead of touching her as a wanton, blesseth her as a father, encourageth her as a friend, promiseth her as a kinsman, rewards her as a patron, and sends her away laden with hopes and gifts, no less chaste, more happy, than she came. O admirable temperance, worthy the progenitor of him in whose lips and heart there was no guile!"

14 And she lay at his feet until the morning: and she rose up before one could know another. And he said, Let it not be known that a woman came into the floor. 15 Also he said, Bring the veil that *thou hast* upon thee, and hold it. And when she held it, he measured six *measures* of barley, and laid *it* on her: and she went into the city. 16 And when she came to her mother in law, she said, Who *art* thou, my daughter? And she told her all that the man had done to her. 17 And she said, These six *measures* of barley gave he me; for he said to me, Go not empty unto thy mother in law. 18 Then said she, Sit still, my daughter, until thou know how the matter will fall: for the man will not be in rest, until he have finished the thing this day.

We are here told, I. How Ruth was dismissed by Boaz. It would not have been safe for her to go home in the dead of the night; therefore *she lay at his feet* (not by his side) *until morning.* But as soon as ever the day broke, that she had light to go home by, she got away, *before one could know another,* that, if she were seen, yet she might not be known to be abroad so unseasonably. She was not shy of being known to be a gleaner in the field, nor ashamed of that mark of her poverty. But she would not willingly be known to be a night-walker, for her virtue was her greatest honour, and that which she most valued. Boaz dismissed her, 1. With a charge to keep counsel (*v.* 14): *Let it not be known that a woman came into the floor,* and lay all night so near to Boaz; for, though they needed not to care much what people said of them while they were both conscious to themselves of an unspotted purity, yet, because few could have come so near the fire as they did and not have been scorched, had it been known it would have occasioned suspicions in some and reflections from others. Good people would have been troubled, and bad people would have triumphed, and therefore *let it not be known.* Note, We must always take care, not only to keep a good conscience, but to keep a good name: either we must not do that which, though innocent, is liable to be misinterpreted, or, if we do, we must not *let it be known.* We must avoid not only sin, but scandal. There was likewise a particular reason for concealment here. If this matter should take wind, it might prejudice the freedom of the other kinsman's choice, and he would make this his reason for refusing Ruth, that Boaz and she had been together. 2. He dismissed her with a good present of corn, which would be very acceptable to her poor mother at home, and an evidence for her that he had not sent her away in dislike, which Naomi might have suspected if he had sent her away empty. He gave it to her in her *veil,* or *apron,* or *mantle,* gave it to her by measure. Like a prudent corn-master, he kept an account of all he delivered out. It was *six measures,* that is, six omers as is supposed, ten of which made an ephah; whatever the measure was, it is probable he gave her as much as she could well carry, *v.* 15. And the Chaldee says, *Strength was given her from the Lord to carry it;* and adds that now *it was told her by the spirit of prophecy that from her should descend six of the most righteous men of their age,* namely, *David, Daniel, his three companions, and the king Messiah.*

II. How she was welcomed by her mother-in-law. She asked her, "*Who art thou, my daughter?* Art thou a bride or no? Must I give thee joy?" So Ruth told her how the matter stood (*v.* 17), whereupon her mother, 1. Advised her to be satisfied in what was done: *Sit still, my daughter, till thou know how the matter will fall* (*v.* 18)—*how it is decreed in heaven,* so the Chaldee reads it, for marriages are made there. She had done all that was fit for her to do, and now she must patiently wait the issue and not be perplexed about it. Let us learn hence to cast our care upon providence, to follow that and attend the motions of it, composing ourselves into an expectation of the event, with a resolution to acquiesce in it, whatever it be. Sometimes that proves best done for us that is least our own doing. "*Sit still,* therefore, *and see how the matter will fall,* and say, Let it fall how it will, I am ready for it." 2. She assured her that Boaz, having undertaken this matter, would approve himself a faithful careful friend: *He will not be at rest till he have finished the matter.* Though it was a busy time with him in his fields and his floor, yet, having undertaken to serve his friend, he would not neglect the business. Naomi believes that Ruth has won his heart, and that therefore he will not be easy till he knows whether she be his or no. This she gives as a reason why Ruth should sit still and not perplex herself about it, that Boaz had undertaken it, and he would be sure to manage it well. Much more reason have good Christians to be *careful for nothing,* but *cast their care on God,* because he has promised to *care for them:* and what need have we to care if he do? *Sit still, and see how the matter will fall,* for *the Lord will perfect that which concerns thee,* and will make it to work for good to thee, Ps. xxxvii. 4, 5; cxxxviii. 8. *Your strength is to sit still,* Isa. xxx. 7.

CHAP. IV.

In this chapter we have the wedding between Boaz and Ruth, in the circumstances of which there was something uncommon, which is kept upon record for the illustration, not only of the law concerning the marrying of a brother's widow (Deut. xxv. 5, &c.), for cases help to expound laws, but of the gospel too, for from this marriage descended David, and the Son of David, whose espousals to the Gentile church were hereby typified. We are here told, I. How Boaz got clear of his rival, and fairly shook him off, ver. 1—8. II. How his marriage with Ruth was publicly solemnized, and attended with the good wishes of his neighbours, ver. 9—12. III. The happy issue that descended from this marriage, Obed, the grandfather of David, ver. 13—17. And so the book concludes with the pedigree of David, ver. 18—22. Perhaps it was to oblige him that the blessed Spirit directed the inserting of this story in the sacred canon, he being desirous that the virtues of his great-grandmother Ruth, together with her Gentile extraction and the singular providences that attended her, should be transmitted to posterity.

THEN went Boaz up to the gate, and sat him down there: and, behold, the kinsman of whom Boaz spake came by; unto whom he said, Ho, such a one! turn aside, sit down here. And he turned aside, and sat down. 2 And he took ten men of the elders of the city, and said, Sit ye down here. And they sat down. 3 And he said unto the kinsman, Naomi, that is come again out of the country of Moab, selleth a parcel of land, which *was* our brother Elimelech's: 4 And I thought to advertise thee, saying, Buy *it* before the inhabitants, and before the elders of my people. If thou wilt redeem *it,* redeem *it:* but if thou wilt not redeem *it, then* tell me, that I may know; for *there is* none to redeem *it* beside thee; and I *am* after thee. And he said, I will redeem *it.* 5 Then said Boaz, What day thou buyest the field of the hand of Naomi, thou must buy *it* also of Ruth the Moabitess, the wife of the dead, to raise up the name of the dead upon his inheritance. 6 And the kinsman said, I cannot redeem *it* for myself, lest I mar mine own inheritance: redeem thou my right to thyself; for I cannot redeem *it.* 7 Now this *was the manner* in former time in Israel concerning redeeming and concerning changing, for to confirm all things; a man plucked off his shoe, and gave *it* to his neighbour: and this *was* a testimony in Israel. 8 Therefore the kinsman said unto Boaz, Buy *it* for thee. So he drew off his shoe.

Here, 1. Boaz calls a court immediately. It is probable he was himself one of the elders (or aldermen) of the city; for he was a mighty man of wealth. Perhaps he was father of the city, and sat chief; for he seems here to have gone up to the gate as one having authority, and not as a common person; like Job, *ch.* xxix. 7, &c. We cannot suppose him less than a magistrate in his city who was grandson to Nahshon, prince of Judah; and his lying at the end of a heap of corn in the threshing-floor the night before was not at all inconsistent, in those days of plainness, with the honour of his sitting judge in the gate. But why was Boaz so hasty, why so fond of the match? Ruth was not rich, but lived upon alms; not honourable, but a poor stranger. She was never said to be beautiful; if ever she had been so, we may suppose that weeping, and travelling, and gleaning, had withered her lilies and roses. But that which made Boaz in love with her, and solicitous to expedite the affair, was that all her neighbours agreed she was a virtuous woman. This set her price with him *far above rubies* (Prov. xxxi. 10); and therefore he thinks, if by marrying her he might do her a real kindness, he should also do himself a very great kindness. He will therefore bring it to a conclusion immediately. It was not court-day, but he got ten men of the elders of the city to meet him in the town-hall over the gate, where public business used to be transacted, *v.* 2. So many, it is probable, by the custom of the city, made a full court. Boaz, though a judge, would not be judge in his own cause, but desired the concurrence of other elders. Honest intentions dread not a public cognizance. 2. He summons his rival to come and hear the matter that was to be proposed to him (*v.* 1): "*Ho, such a one,* sit down here." He called him by his name, no doubt, but the divine historian thought not fit to record it, for, because he refused to raise up the name of the dead, he deserved not to have his name preserved to future ages in this history. Providence favoured Boaz in ordering it so that this kinsman should come by thus opportunely, just when the matter was ready to be proposed to him. Great affairs are sometimes much furthered by small circumstances, which facilitate and expedite them. 3. He proposes to the other kinsman the redemption of Naomi's land, which, it is probable, had been mortgaged for money to buy bread with when the famine was in the land (*v.* 3): "*Naomi has a parcel of land to sell,* namely, the equity of the redemption of it out of the hands of the mortgagee, which she is willing to part with;" or, as some think, it was her jointure for her life, and, wanting money, for a small matter she would sell her interest to the heir at law, who was fittest to be the purchaser. This he gives the kinsman legal notice of (*v.* 4), that he might have the refusal of it.

Whoever had it must pay for it, and Boaz might have said, "My money is as good as my kinsman's; if I have a mind to it, why may not I buy it privately, since I had the first proffer of it, and say nothing to my kinsman?" No, Boaz, though fond enough of the purchase, would not do so mean a thing as to take a bargain over another man's head that was nearer a-kin to it; and we are taught by his example to be not only just and honest, but fair and honourable, in all our dealings, and to do nothing which we are unwilling should see the light, but be above-board. 4. The kinsman seemed forward to redeem the land till he was told that, if he did that, he must marry the widow, and then he flew off. He liked the land well enough, and probably caught at that the more greedily because he hoped that the poor widow being under a necessity of selling he might have so much the better bargain: "*I will redeem it*" (said he) "with all my heart," thinking it would be a fine addition to his estate, *v.* 4. But Boaz told him there was a young widow in the case, and, if he have the land, he must take her with it, *Terra transit cum onere—The estate passes with this incumbrance;* either the divine law or the usage of the country would oblige him to it, or Naomi insisted upon it that she would not sell the land but upon this condition, *v.* 5. Some think this does not relate to the law of marrying the brother's widow (for that seems to oblige only the children of the same father, Deut. xxv. 5, unless by custom it was afterwards made to extend to the next of kin), but to the law of redemption of inheritances (Lev. xxv. 24, 25), for it is a *goel*, a *redeemer*, that is here enquired for; and if so it was not by the law, but by Naomi's own resolution, that the purchaser was to marry the widow. However it was, this kinsman, when he heard the conditions of the bargain, refused it (*v.* 6): "*I cannot redeem it for myself.* I will not meddle with it upon these terms, lest I mar my own inheritance." The land, he thought, would be an improvement of his inheritance, but not the land with the woman; that would mar it. Perhaps he thought it would be a disparagement to him to marry such a poor widow that had come from a strange country, and almost lived upon alms. He fancied it would be a blemish to his family, it would mar his blood, and disgrace his posterity. Her eminent virtues were not sufficient in his eye to counterbalance this. The Chaldee paraphrase makes his reason for this refusal to be that he had another wife, and, if he should take Ruth, it might occasion strife and contention in his family, which would mar the comfort of his inheritance. Or he thought she might bring him a great many children, and they would all expect shares out of his estate, which would scatter it into too many hands, so that the family would make the less figure. This makes many shy of the great redemption: they are not willing to espouse religion. They have heard well of it, and have nothing to say against it; they will give it their good word, but at the same time they will give their good word with it; they are willing to part with it, and cannot be bound to it, for fear of marring their own inheritance in this world. Heaven they could be glad of, but holiness they can dispense with; it will not agree with the lusts they have already espoused, and therefore, let who will purchase heaven at that rate, they cannot. 5. The right of redemption is fairly resigned to Boaz. If this nameless kinsman lost a good bargain, a good estate, and a good wife too, he may thank himself for not considering it better, and Boaz will thank him for making his way clear to that which he valued and desired above any thing. In those ancient times it was not the usage to pass estates by writings, as afterwards (Jer. xxxii. 10, &c.), but by some sign or ceremony, as with us by livery and seisin, as we commonly call it, that is, the delivery of seisin, seisin of a house by giving the key, of land by giving turf and a twig. The ceremony here used was, he that surrendered *plucked off his shoe* (the Chaldee says it was *the glove of his right hand*) and gave it to him to whom he made the surrender, intimating thereby that, whatever right he had to tread or go upon the land, he conveyed and transferred it, upon a valuable consideration, to the purchaser: this was a *testimony in Israel*, *v.* 7. And it was done in this case, *v.* 8. If this kinsman had been bound by the law to marry Ruth, and his refusal had been a contempt of that law, Ruth must have *plucked off his shoe* and *spit in his face*, Deut. xxv. 9. But, though his relation should in some measure oblige him to the duty, yet the distance of his relation might serve to excuse him from the penalty, or Ruth might very well dispense with it, since his refusal was all she desired from him. But bishop Patrick, and the best interpreters, think this had no relation to that law, and that the drawing off of the shoe was not any disgrace as there, but a confirmation of the surrender, and an evidence that it was not fraudulently nor surreptitiously obtained. Note, Fair and open dealing in all matters of contract and commerce is what all those must make conscience of that would approve themselves Israelites indeed, without guile. How much more honourably and honestly does Boaz come by this purchase than if he had secretly undermined his kinsman, and privately struck up a bargain with Naomi, unknown to him. Honesty will be found the best policy.

9 And Boaz said unto the elders, and *unto* all the people, Ye *are* witnesses this day, that I have bought all that *was* Elimelech's, and all that *was* Chilion's and Mahlon's, of the hand

of Naomi. 10 Moreover Ruth the Moabitess, the wife of Mahlon, have I purchased to be my wife, to raise up the name of the dead upon his inheritance, that the name of the dead be not cut off from among his brethren, and from the gate of his place: ye *are* witnesses this day. 11 And all the people that *were* in the gate, and the elders, said, *We are* witnesses. The LORD make the woman that is come into thine house like Rachel and like Leah, which two did build the house of Israel: and do thou worthily in Ephratah, and be famous in Beth-lehem: 12 And let thy house be like the house of Pharez, whom Tamar bare unto Judah, of the seed which the LORD shall give thee of this young woman.

Boaz now sees his way clear, and therefore delays not to perform his promise made to Ruth that he would do the kinsman's part, but in the gate of his city, before the elders and all the people, publishes a marriage-contract between himself and Ruth the Moabitess, and therewith the purchase of all the estate that belonged to the family of Elimelech. If he had not been (*ch.* ii. 1) *a mighty man of wealth,* he could not have compassed this redemption, nor done this service to his kinsman's family. What is a great estate good for, but that it enables a man to do so much the more good in his generation, and especially to those of his own household, if he have but a heart to use it so! Now concerning this marriage it appears,

I. That it was solemnized, or at least published, before many witnesses, *v.* 9, 10. "You are witnesses," 1. "That I have bought the estate. Whoever has it, or any part of it, mortgaged to him, let him come to me and he shall have his money, according to the value of the land," which was computed by the number of years to the year of jubilee (Lev. xxv. 15), when it would have returned of course to Elimelech's family. The more public the sales of estates are the better they are guarded against frauds. 2. "That I have purchased the widow to be my wife." He had no portion with her; what jointure she had was encumbered, and he could not have it without giving as much for it as it was worth, and therefore he might well say he purchased her; and yet, being a virtuous woman, he reckoned he had a good bargain. *House and riches are the inheritance of fathers,* but a prudent wife is more valuable, is from the Lord as a special gift. He designed, in marrying her, to preserve the memory of the dead, that the name of Mahlon, though he left no son to bear it up, might not be cut off from the gate of his place, but by this means might be preserved, that it should be inserted in the public register that Boaz married Ruth the widow of Mahlon, the son of Elimelech, which posterity, whenever they had occasion to consult the register, would take particular notice of. And this history, being preserved for the sake of that marriage and the issue of it, proved an effectual means to perpetuate the name of Mahlon, even beyond the thought or intention of Boaz, to the world's end. And observe that because Boaz did this honour to the dead, as well as this kindness to the living, God did him the honour to bring him into the genealogy of the Messiah, by which his family was dignified above all the families of Israel; while the other kinsman, that was so much afraid of diminishing himself, and marring his inheritance, by marrying the widow, has his name, family, and inheritance, buried in oblivion and disgrace. A tender and generous concern for the honour of the dead and the comfort of poor widows and strangers, neither of which can return the kindness (Luke xiv. 14), is what God will be well pleased with and will surely recompense. Our Lord Jesus is our *Goel,* our *Redeemer,* our everlasting Redeemer. He looked, like Boaz, with compassion on the deplorable state of fallen mankind. At a vast expense he redeemed the heavenly inheritance for us, which by sin was mortgaged, and forfeited into the hands of divine justice, and which we should never have been able to redeem. He likewise purchased a peculiar people, whom he would espouse to himself, though strangers and foreigners, like Ruth, poor and despised, that the name of that dead and buried race might not be cut off for ever. He ventured the marring of his own inheritance, to do this, for, *though he was rich, yet for our sakes he became poor;* but he was abundantly recompensed for it by his Father, who, because he thus humbled himself, hath *highly exalted him, and given him a name above every name.* Let us own our obligations to him, make sure our contract with him, and study all our days how to do him honour. Boaz, by making a public declaration of this marriage and purchase, not only secured his title against all pretenders, as it were by a fine with proclamations, but put honour upon Ruth, showed that he was not ashamed of her, and her parentage and poverty, and left a testimony against clandestine marriages. It is only that which is evil that hates the light and comes not to it. Boaz called witnesses to what he did, for it was what he could justify, and would never disown; and such regard was then had, even to the contemned crowd, that not only the elders, but all the people that were in the gate, passing and re-passing, were appealed to (*v.* 9), and hearkened to (*v.* 11) when they said, *We are witnesses.*

II. That it was attended with many prayers The elders and all the people, when they witnessed to it, wished well to it, and blessed it, *v.* 11, 12. Ruth, it should seem, was now sent for; for they speak of her (*v.* 12) as present: *This young woman;* and, he having taken her to wife, they look upon her as already come into his house. And very heartily they pray for the new-married couple.

1. The senior elder, it is likely, made this prayer, and the rest of the elders, with the people, joined in it, and therefore it is spoken of as made by them all; for in public prayers, though but one speaks, we must all pray. Observe, (1.) Marriages ought to be blessed, and accompanied with prayer, because every creature and every condition are that to us, and no more, that God makes them to be. It is civil and friendly to wish all happiness to those who enter into that condition; and what good we desire we should pray for from the fountain of all good. The minister who gives himself to the word and prayer, as he is the fittest person to exhort, so he is the fittest to bless and pray for those that enter into this relation. (2.) We ought to desire and pray for the welfare and prosperity one of another, so far from envying or grieving at it.

2. Now here, (1.) They prayed for Ruth: *The Lord make the woman that has come into thy house like Rachel and Leah,* that is, "God make her a good wife and a fruitful mother." Ruth was a virtuous woman, and yet needed the prayers of her friends, that by the grace of God she might be made a blessing to the family she had come into. They prayed that she might be like Rachel and Leah, rather than like Sarah and Rebekah, for Sarah had but one son, and Rebekah but one that was in covenant, the other was Esau, who was rejected; but Rachel and Leah did *build up the house of Israel:* all their children were in the church, and their offspring was numerous. "May she be a flourishing, fruitful, faithful *vine by thy house side.*" (2.) They prayed for Boaz, that he might continue to do worthily in the city to which he was an ornament, and might there be more and more famous. They desired that the wife might be a blessing in the private affairs of the house, and the husband a blessing in the public business of the town, that she in her place, and he in his, might be wise, virtuous, and successful. Observe, The way to be famous is to do worthily. Great reputation must be obtained by great merits. It is not enough not to do unworthily, to be harmless and inoffensive, but we must do worthily, be useful and serviceable to our generation. Those that would be truly illustrious must in their places shine as lights. (3.) They prayed for the family: "*Let thy house be like the house of Pharez,*" that is, "let it be very numerous, let it greatly increase and multiply, as the house of Pharez did." The Bethlehemites were of the house of Pharez, and knew very well how numerous it was; in the distribution of the tribes, that grandson of Jacob had the honour which none of the rest had but Manasseh and Ephraim, that his posterity was subdivided into two distinct families, Hezron and Hamul, Num. xxvi. 21. Now they prayed that the family of Boaz, which was one branch of that stock, might in process of time become as numerous and great as the whole stock now was.

13 So Boaz took Ruth, and she was his wife: and when he went in unto her, the LORD gave her conception, and she bare a son. 14 And the women said unto Naomi, Blessed *be* the LORD, which hath not left thee this day without a kinsman, that his name may be famous in Israel. 15 And he shall be unto thee a restorer of *thy* life, and a nourisher of thine old age: for thy daughter in law, which loveth thee, which is better to thee than seven sons, hath borne him. 16 And Naomi took the child, and laid it in her bosom, and became nurse unto it. 17 And the women her neighbours gave it a name, saying, There is a son born to Naomi; and they called his name Obed: he *is* the father of Jesse, the father of David. 18 Now these *are* the generations of Pharez: Pharez begat Hezron, 19 And Hezron begat Ram, and Ram begat Amminadab, 20 And Amminadab begat Nahshon, and Nahshon begat Salmon, 21 And Salmon begat Boaz, and Boaz begat Obed, 22 And Obed begat Jesse, and Jesse begat David.

Here is, I. Ruth a wife Boaz took her, with the usual solemnities, to his house, and *she became his wife* (*v.* 13), all the city, no doubt, congratulating the preferment of a virtuous woman, purely for her virtues. We have reason to think that Orpah, who returned from Naomi to her people and her gods, was never half so well preferred as Ruth was. He that forsakes all for Christ shall find more than all with him; it shall be recompensed a hundred-fold in this present time. Now Orpah wished she had gone with Naomi too; but she, like the other kinsman, stood in her own light. Boaz had prayed that this pious proselyte might receive a full reward of her courage and constancy from the God of Israel, *under whose wings she had come to trust;* and now he became an instrument of that kindness, which was an answer to his prayer, and helped to make his own words good. Now she had the command of those servants with whom she had associated and of those fields in which she had gleaned. Thus sometimes *God raiseth up the poor out of the dust, to set them with princes,* Ps. cxiii. 7, 8.

II. Ruth a mother: *The Lord gave her conception;* for *the fruit of the womb is his reward,* Ps. cxxvii. 3. It is one of the keys he hath in his hand; and he sometimes makes the barren woman that had been long so to be *a joyful mother of children,* Ps. cxiii. 9; Isa. liv. 1.

III. Ruth still a daughter-in-law, and the same that she always was, to Naomi, who was so far from being forgotten that she was a principal sharer in these new joys. The good women that were at the labour when this child was born congratulated Naomi upon it more than either Boaz or Ruth, because she was the match-maker, and it was the family of her husband that was hereby built up. See here, as before, what an air of devotion there was then even in the common expressions of civility among the Israelites. Prayer to God attended the marriage (*v.* 11), and praise to him attended the birth of the child. What a pity it is that such pious language should either be disused among Christians or degenerate into a formality. "*Blessed be the Lord* that has sent thee this grandson," *v.* 14, 15. 1. Who was the preserver of the name of her family, and who, they hoped, would be famous, because his father was so. 2. Who would be hereafter dutiful and kind to her, so they hoped, because his mother was so. If he would but take after her, he would be a comfort to his aged grandmother, a restorer of her life, and, if there should be occasion, would have wherewithal to be the nourisher of her old age. It is a great comfort to those that are going into years to see any of those that descend from them growing up, that are likely, by the blessing of God, to be a stay and support to them, when the years come wherein they will need such, and of which they will say they have no pleasure in them. Observe, They say of Ruth that she loved Naomi, and therefore was better to her than seven sons. See how God in his providence sometimes makes up the want and loss of those relations from whom we expected most comfort in those from whom we expected least. The bonds of love prove stronger than those of nature, and there is a *friend that sticks closer than a brother;* so here there was a daughter-in-law better than an own child. See what wisdom and grace will do. Now here, (1.) The child is named by the neighbours, *v.* 17. The good women would have it called *Obed, a servant,* either in remembrance of the meanness and poverty of the mother or in prospect of his being hereafter a servant, and very serviceable, to his grandmother. It is no dishonour to those that are ever so well born to be servants to God, their friends, and their generation. The motto of the princes of Wales is *Ich dien—I serve.* (2.) The child is nursed by the grandmother, that is, dry-nursed, when the mother had weaned him from the breast, *v.* 16. She laid it in her bosom, in token of her tender affection to it and care of it. Grandmothers are often the most fond.

IV. Ruth is hereby brought in among the ancestors of David and Christ, which was the greatest honour. The genealogy is here drawn from Pharez, through Boaz and Obed, to David, and so leads towards the Messiah, and therefore it is not an endless genealogy.

AN

EXPOSITION,

WITH PRACTICAL OBSERVATIONS,

OF THE FIRST BOOK OF

SAMUEL.

THIS book, and that which follows it, bear the name of *Samuel* in the title, not because he was the penman of them (except of so much of them as fell within his own time, to the twenty-fifth chapter of the first book, in which we have an account of his death), but because the first book begins with a large account of him, his birth and childhood, his life and government; and the rest of these two volumes that are denominated from him contains the history of the reigns of *Saul* and *David,* who were both anointed by him. And, because the history of these two kings takes up the greatest part of these books, the Vulgar Latin calls them the *First* and *Second Books of the Kings,* and the two that follow the *Third* and *Fourth,* which the titles in our English Bibles take notice of with an *alias : otherwise called the First Book of the Kings,* &c. The LXX. call them the first and second Book *of the Kingdoms.* It is needless to contend about it, but there is no occasion to vary from the Hebrew verity. These two books contain the history of the last two of the judges, *Eli* and *Samuel*, who were not, as the rest, men of war, but priests (and so much of them is an appendix to the book of Judges), and of the first two of the kings, *Saul* and *David*, and so much of them is an entrance upon the history of the kings. They contain a considerable part of the sacred history, are sometimes referred to in the New Testament, and often in the titles of David's Psalms, which, if placed in their order, would fall in in these books. It is uncertain who was the penman of them ; it is probable that Samuel wrote the history of his own time, and that, after him, some of the prophets that were with David (Nathan as likely as any) continued it. This first book gives us a full account of Eli's fall and Samuel's rise and good government, *ch.* i.—viii. Of Samuel's resignation of the government and Saul's advancement and mal-administration, *ch.* ix.—xv. The choice of David, his struggles with Saul, Saul's ruin at last, and the opening of the way for David to the throne, *ch.* xvi.—xxxi. And these things are written for our learning.

CHAP. I.

The history of Samuel here begins as early as that of Samson did, even before he was born, as afterwards the history of John the Baptist and our blessed Saviour. Some of the scripture-worthies drop out of the clouds, as it were, and their first appearance is in their full growth and lustre. But others are accounted for from the birth, and from the womb, and from the conception. What God says of the prophet Jeremiah is true of all : "Before I formed thee in the belly I knew thee," Jer. i. 5. But some great men were brought into the world with more observation than others, and were more early distinguished from common persons, as Samuel for one. God, in this matter, acts as a free agent. The story of Samson introduces him as a child of promise, Judg. xiii. But the story of Samuel introduces him as a child of prayer. Samson's birth was foretold by an angel to his mother ; Samuel was asked of God by his mother. Both together intimate what wonders are produced by the word and prayer. Samuel's mother was Hannah, the principal person concerned in the story of this chapter. I. Here is her affliction—she was childless, and this affliction aggravated by her rival's insolence, but in some measure balanced by her husband's kindness, ver. 1—8. II. The prayer and vow she made to God under this affliction, in which Eli the high priest at first censured her, but afterwards encouraged her, ver. 9—18. III. The birth and nursing of Samuel, ver. 19—23. IV. The presenting of him to the Lord, ver. 24—28.

NOW there was a certain man of Ramathaim-zophim, of mount Ephraim, and his name *was* Elkanah, the son of Jeroham, the son of Elihu, the son of Tohu, the son of Zuph, an Ephrathite : 2 And he had two wives ; the name of the one *was* Hannah, and the name of the other Peninnah : and Peninnah had children, but Hannah had no children. 3 And this man went up out of his city yearly to worship and to sacrifice unto the LORD of hosts in Shiloh. And the two sons of Eli, Hophni and Phinehas, the priests of the LORD, *were* there. 4 And when the time was that Elkanah offered, he gave to Peninnah his wife, and to all her sons and her daughters, portions : 5 But unto Hannah he gave a worthy portion ; for he loved Hannah : but the LORD had shut up her womb. 6 And her adversary also provoked her sore, for to make her fret, because the LORD had shut up her womb. 7 And *as* he did so year by year, when she went up to the house of the LORD, so she provoked her ; therefore she wept, and did not eat. 8 Then said Elkanah her husband to her, Hannah, why weepest thou ? and why eatest thou not ? and why is thy heart grieved ? *am* not I better to thee than ten sons ?

We have here an account of the state of the family into which Samuel the prophet was born. His father's name was Elkanah, a Levite, and of the family of the Kohathites (the most honourable house of that tribe) as appears, 1 Chron. vi. 33, 34. His ancestor Zuph was an Ephrathite, that is, of Bethlehem-Judah, which was called *Ephrathah*, Ruth i. 2. There this family of the Levites was first seated, but one branch of it, in process of time, removed to Mount Ephraim, from which Elkanah descended. Micah's Levite came from Bethlehem to Mount Ephraim, Judg. xvii. 8. Ministers' families are as movable as any. Perhaps notice is taken of their being originally Ephrathites to show their alliance to David. This Elkanah lived at Ramah, or Ramathaim, which signifies *the double Ramah*, the higher and lower town, the same with Arimathea of which Joseph was, here called *Ramathaim-zophim.* Zophim signifies *watchmen ;* probably they had one of the schools of the prophets there, for prophets are called *watchmen :* the Chaldee paraphrase calls Elkanah *a disciple of the prophets.* But it seems to me that it was in Samuel that prophecy revived, before his time there being, for a great while, no open vision, *ch.* iii. 1. Nor is there any mention of a prophet of the Lord from Moses to Samuel, except Judg. vi. 8. So that we have no reason to think that there was any nursery or college of prophets here till Samuel himself founded one, *ch.* xix. 19, 20. This is the account of Samuel's parentage, and the place of his nativity. Let us now take notice of the state of the family.

I. It was a devout family. All the families of Israel should be so, but Levites' families in a particular manner. Ministers should be patterns of family religion. Elkanah went up at the solemn feasts to the tabernacle at Shiloh, to *worship and to sacrifice to the Lord of hosts.* I think this is the first time in scripture that God is called *the Lord of hosts—Jehovah Sabaoth,* a name by which he was afterwards very much called and known. Probably Samuel the prophet was the first that used this title of God, for the comfort of Israel, when in his time their hosts were few and feeble and those of their enemies many and mighty; then it would be a support to them to think that the God they served was Lord of hosts, of all the hosts both of heaven and earth; of them he has a sovereign command, and makes what use he pleases of them. Elkanah was a country Levite, and, for aught that appears, had not any place or office which required his attendance at the tabernacle, but he went up as a common Israelite, with his own sacrifices, to encourage his neighbours and set them a good example. When he sacrificed he worshipped, joining prayers and thanksgivings with his sacrifices. In this course of religion he was constant, for he went up yearly. And that which made it the more commendable in him was, 1. That there was a general decay and neglect of religion in the nation. Some among them worshipped other gods, and the generality were remiss in the service of the God of Israel, and yet Elkanah kept his integrity; whatever others did, his resolution was that he and his house should serve the Lord. 2. That Hophni and Phinehas, the sons of Eli, were the men that were now chiefly employed in the service of the house of God; and they were men that conducted themselves very ill in their place, as we shall find afterwards; yet Elkanah went up to sacrifice. God had then tied his people to one place and one altar, and forbidden them, under any pretence whatsoever, to worship elsewhere, and therefore, in pure obedience to that command, he attended at Shiloh. If the priests did not do their duty, he would do his. Thanks be to God, we, under the gospel, are not tied to any one place or family; but the pastors and teachers whom the exalted Redeemer has given to his church are those only whose ministration tends to the *perfecting of the saints* and the *edifying of the body of Christ,* Eph. iv. 11, 12. None have dominion over our faith; but our obligation is to those that are the helpers of our holiness and joy, not to any that by their scandalous immoralities, like Hophni and Phinehas, make the sacrifices of the Lord to be abhorred, though still the validity and efficacy of the sacraments depend not on the purity of him that administers them.

II. Yet it was a divided family, and the divisions of it carried with them both guilt and grief. Where there is piety, it is a pity but there should be unity. The joint-devotions of a family should put an end to divisions in it.

1. The original cause of this division was Elkanah's marrying two wives, which was a transgression of the original institution of marriage, to which our Saviour reduces it. Matt. xix. 5, 8, *From the beginning it was not so.* It made mischief in Abraham's family, and Jacob's, and here in Elkanah's. How much better does the law of God provide for our comfort and ease in this world than we should, if we were left to ourselves! It is probable that Elkanah married Hannah first, and, because he had not children by her so soon as he hoped, he married Peninnah, who bore him children indeed, but was in other things a vexation to him. Thus are men often beaten with rods of their own making.

2. That which followed upon this error was that the two wives could not agree. They had different blessings: Peninnah, like Leah, was fruitful and had many children, which should have made her easy and thankful, though she was but a second wife, and was less beloved; Hannah, like Rachel, was childless indeed, but she was very dear to her husband, and he took all occasions to let both her and others know that she was so, and many a *worthy portion he gave her* (*v.* 5), and this should have made her easy and thankful. But they were of different tempers: Peninnah could not bear the blessing of fruitfulness, but she grew haughty and insolent; Hannah could not bear the affliction of barrenness, but she grew melancholy and discontented: and Elkanah had a difficult part to act between them.

(1.) Elkanah kept up his attendance at God's altar notwithstanding this unhappy difference in his family, and took his wives and children with him, that, if they could not agree in other things, they might agree to worship God together. If the devotions of a family prevail not to put an end to its divisions, yet let not the divisions put a stop to the devotions.

(2.) He did all he could to encourage Hannah, and to keep up her spirits under her affliction, *v.* 4, 5. At the feast he offered peace-offerings, to supplicate for peace in his family; and when he and his family were to eat their share of the sacrifice, in token of their communion with God and his altar, though he carved to Peninnah and her children competent portions, yet to Hannah he gave a worthy portion, the choicest piece that came to the table, the piece (whatever it was) that used to be given on such occasions to those that were most valued; this he did in token of his love to her, and to give all possible assurances of it. Observe, [1.] Elkanah loved his wife never the less for her being barren. *Christ loves his church,* notwithstanding her infirmities, her barrenness; and *so ought men to love their wives,* Eph. v. 25. To abate our just love to any relation for the sake of any infirmity which they cannot help, and which is not their sin but their affliction, is to make God's providence quarrel with his precept, and very unkindly to add affliction to the afflicted. [2.] He studied to show his love so much the more because she was afflicted, insulted, and low-spirited. It is wisdom and duty to support the weakest, and to hold up those that are run down. [3.] He showed his great love to her by the share he gave her of his peace-offerings. Thus we should testify our affection to our friends and relations, by abounding in prayer for them. The better we love them the more room let us give them in our prayers.

(3.) Peninnah was extremely peevish and provoking. [1.] She upbraided Hannah with her affliction, despised her because she was barren, and gave her taunting language, as one whom Heaven did not favour. [2.] She envied the interest she had in the love of Elkanah, and the more kind he was to her the more was she exasperated against her, which was all over base and barbarous. [3.] She did this most when they *went up to the house of the Lord*, perhaps because then they were more together than at other times, or because then Elkanah showed his affection most to Hannah. But it was very sinful at such a time to show her malice, when pure hands were to be lifted up at God's altar without wrath and quarrelling. It was likewise very unkind at that time to vex Hannah, not only because then they were in company, and others would take notice of it, but then Hannah was to mind her devotions, and desired to be most calm and composed, and free from disturbance. The great adversary to our purity and peace is then most industrious to ruffle us when we should be most composed. When the *sons of God* come to *present themselves before the Lord Satan* will be sure to *come among them,* Job i. 6. [4.] She continued to do this from year to year, not once or twice, but it was her constant practice; neither deference to her husband nor compassion to Hannah could break her of it. [5.] That which she designed was to make her fret, perhaps in hopes to break her heart, that she might possess her husband's heart solely, or because she took a pleasure in her uneasiness, nor could Hannah gratify her more than by fretting. Note, It is an evidence of a base disposition to delight in grieving those that are melancholy and of a sorrowful spirit, and in putting those out of humour that are apt to fret and be uneasy. We ought to bear one another's burdens, not add to them.

(4.) Hannah (poor woman) could not bear the provocation: *She wept, and did not eat, v.* 7. It made her uneasy to herself and to all her relations. She did not eat of the feast; her trouble took away her appetite, made her unfit for any company, and a jar in the harmony of family-joy. It was of the *feast upon the sacrifice* that she *did not eat,* for they were not to *eat of the holy things in their mourning,* Deut. xxvi. 14; Lev. x. 19. Yet it was her infirmity so far to give way to the sorrow of the world as to unfit herself for holy joy in God. Those that are of a fretful spirit, and are apt to lay provocations too much to heart, are enemies to themselves, and strip themselves very much of the comforts both of life and godliness. We find that God took notice of this ill effect of discontents and disagreements in the conjugal relation, that the parties aggrieved *covered the altar of the Lord with tears, insomuch that he regarded not the offering,* Mal. ii. 13.

(5.) Elkanah said what he could to her to comfort her. She did not upbraid him with his unkindness in marrying another wife as Sarah did, nor did she render to Peninnah railing for railing, but took the trouble wholly to herself, which made her an object of much compassion. Elkanah showed himself extremely grieved at her grief (*v.* 8): *Hannah, why weepest thou?* [1.] He is much disquieted to see her thus overwhelmed with sorrow. Those that by marriage are made one flesh ought thus far to be of one spirit too, to share in each other's troubles, so that one cannot be easy while the other is uneasy. [2.] He gives her a loving reproof for it: *Why weepest thou? And why is thy heart grieved?* As many as God loves he rebukes, and so should we. He puts her upon enquiring into the cause of her grief. Though she had just reason to be troubled, yet let her consider whether she had reason to be troubled to such a degree, especially so much as to be taken off by it from eating of the holy things. Note, Our sorrow upon any account is sinful and inordinate when it diverts us from our duty to God and embitters our comfort in him, when it makes us unthankful for the mercies we enjoy and distrustful of the goodness of God to us in further mercies, when it casts a damp upon our joy in Christ, and hinders us from doing the duty and taking the comfort of our particular relations. [3.] He intimates that nothing should be wanting on his part to balance her grief: "*Am not I better to thee than ten sons?* Thou knowest thou hast my entire affection, and let that comfort thee." Note, We ought to take notice of our comforts, to keep us from grieving excessively for our crosses; for our crosses we deserve, but our comforts we have forfeited. If we would keep the balance even, we must look at that which is for us, as well as at that which is against us, else we are unjust to Providence and unkind to ourselves. *God hath set the one over-against the other* (Eccl. vii. 14) and so should we.

9 So Hannah rose up after they had eaten in Shiloh, and after they had drunk. Now Eli the priest sat upon a seat by a post of the temple of the LORD. 10 And she *was* in bitterness of soul, and prayed unto the LORD, and wept sore. 11 And she vowed a vow, and said, O LORD

of hosts, if thou wilt indeed look on the affliction of thine handmaid, and remember me, and not forget thine handmaid, but wilt give unto thine handmaid a man child, then I will give him unto the LORD all the days of his life, and there shall no razor come upon his head. 12 And it came to pass, as she continued praying before the LORD, that Eli marked her mouth. 13 Now Hannah, she spake in her heart; only her lips moved, but her voice was not heard: therefore Eli thought she had been drunken. 14 And Eli said unto her, How long wilt thou be drunken? put away thy wine from thee. 15 And Hannah answered and said, No, my lord, I *am* a woman of a sorrowful spirit: I have drunk neither wine nor strong drink, but have poured out my soul before the LORD. 16 Count not thine handmaid for a daughter of Belial: for out of the abundance of my complaint and grief have I spoken hitherto. 17 Then Eli answered and said, Go in peace: and the God of Israel grant *thee* thy petition that thou hast asked of him. 18 And she said, Let thine handmaid find grace in thy sight. So the woman went her way, and did eat, and her countenance was no more *sad*.

Elkanah had gently reproved Hannah for her inordinate grief, and here we find the good effect of the reproof.

I. It brought her to her meat. She ate and drank, *v.* 9. She did not harden herself in sorrow, nor grow sullen when she was reproved for it; but, when she perceived her husband uneasy that she did not come and eat with them, she cheered up her own spirits as well as she could, and came to table. It is as great a piece of self-denial to control our passions as it is to control our appetites.

II. It brought her to her prayers. It put her upon considering, "Do I well to be angry? Do I well to fret? What good does it do me? Instead of binding the burden thus upon my own shoulders, had I not better ease myself of it, and cast it upon the Lord by prayer?" Elkanah had said, *Am not I better to thee than ten sons?* which perhaps occasioned her to think within herself, "Whether *he* be so or no, *God* is, and therefore to him will I apply, and before him will I pour out my complaint, and try what relief that will give me." If ever she will make a more solemn address than ordinary to the throne of grace upon this errand, now is the time. They are at Shiloh, at the door of the tabernacle, where God had promised to meet his people, and which was the *house of prayer*. They had recently offered their peace-offerings, to obtain the favour of God and all good and in token of their communion with him; and, taking the comfort of their being accepted of him, they had feasted upon the sacrifice; and now it was proper to put up her prayer in virtue of that sacrifice, for the peace-offerings typified Christ's mediation as well as the sin-offerings, for by it not only atonement is made for sin, but the audience and acceptance of our prayers and an answer of peace to them are obtained for us: to that sacrifice, in all our supplications, we must have an eye. Now concerning Hannah's prayer we may observe,

1. The warm and lively devotion there was in it, which appeared in several instances, for our direction in prayer. (1.) She improved the present grief and trouble of her spirit for the exciting and quickening of her pious affections in prayer: *Being in bitterness of soul, she prayed, v.* 10. This good use we should make of our afflictions, they should make us the more lively in our addresses to God. Our blessed Saviour himself, *being in an agony, prayed more earnestly*, Luke xxii. 44. (2.) She mingled tears with her prayers. It was not a dry prayer: she wept sore. Like a true Israelite, she *wept and made supplication* (Hos. xii. 4), with an eye to the tender mercy of our God, who knows the troubled soul. The prayer came from her heart, as the tears from her eyes. (3.) She was very particular, and yet very modest, in her petition. She begged a child, a man-child, that it might be fit to serve in the tabernacle. God gives us leave, in prayer, not only to ask good things in general, but to mention that special good thing which we most need and desire. Yet she says not, as Rachel, *Give me children*, Gen. xxx. 1. She will be very thankful for *one*. (4.) She made a solemn vow, or promise, that if God would give her a son she would *give him up to God, v.* 11. He would be by birth a Levite, and so devoted to the service of God, but he should be by her vow a Nazarite, and his very childhood should be sacred. It is probable she had acquainted Elkanah with her purpose before, and had had his consent and approbation. Note, Parents have a right to dedicate their children to God, as living sacrifices and spiritual priests; and an obligation is thereby laid upon them to serve God faithfully *all the days of their life.* Note further, It is very proper, when we are in pursuit of any mercy, to bind our own souls with a bond, that, if God give it us, we will devote it to his honour and cheerfully use it in his service. Not that hereby we can pretend to merit the gift, but thus we are qualified for it and for the comfort of it. In hope of mercy, let us promise duty. (5.)

She spoke all this so softly that none could hear her. Her lips moved, but *her voice was not heard, v.* 13. Hereby she testified her belief of God's knowledge of the heart and its desires. Thoughts are words to him, nor is he one of those gods that must be *cried aloud to,* 1 Kings xviii. 27. It was likewise an instance of her humility and holy shamefacedness in her approach to God. She was none of those that *made her voice to be heard on high,* Isa. lviii. 4. It was a secret prayer, and therefore, though made in a public place, yet was thus made secretly, and not, as the Pharisees prayed, *to be seen of men.* It is true prayer is not a thing we have reason to be ashamed of, but we must avoid all appearances of ostentation. Let what passes between God and our souls be kept to ourselves.

2. The hard censure she fell under for it. Eli was now high priest, and judge in Israel; he sat upon a seat in the temple, to oversee what was done there, *v.* 9. The tabernacle is here called the *temple,* because it was now fixed, and served all the purposes of a temple. There Eli sat to receive addresses and give direction, and somewhere (it is probable in a private corner) he espied Hannah at her prayers, and by her unusual manner fancied she was drunken, and spoke to her accordingly (*v.* 14): *How long wilt thou be drunken?*—the very imputation that Peter and the apostles fell under when the Holy Ghost *gave them utterance,* Acts ii. 13. Perhaps in this degenerate age it was no strange thing to see drunken women at the door of the tabernacle; for otherwise, one would think, the vile lust of Hophni and Phinehas could not have found so easy a prey there, *ch.* ii. 22. Eli took Hannah for one of these. It is one bad effect of the abounding of iniquity, and its becoming fashionable, that it often gives occasion to suspect the innocent. When a disease is epidemical every one is suspected to be tainted with it. Now, (1.) This was Eli's fault; and a great fault it was to pass so severe a censure without better observation or information. If his own eyes had already become dim, he should have employed those about him to enquire. Drunkards are commonly noisy and turbulent, but this poor woman was silent and composed. His fault was the worse that he was the priest of the Lord, who should have had *compassion on the ignorant,* Heb. v. 2. Note, It ill becomes us to be rash and hasty in our censures of others, and to be forward to believe people guilty of bad things, while either the matter of fact on which the censure is grounded is doubtful and unproved or is capable of a good construction. Charity commands us to hope the best concerning all, and forbids censoriousness. Paul had very good information when he did but *partly believe* (1 Cor. xi. 18), hoping it was not so. Especially we ought to be cautious how we censure the devotions of others, lest we call that *hypocrisy, enthusiasm,* or *superstition,* which is really the fruit of an honest zeal, and it is accepted of God. (2.) It was Hannah's affliction; and a great affliction it was, added to all the rest, vinegar to the wounds of her spirit. She had been reproved by Elkanah because she would not eat and drink, and now to be reproached by Eli as if she had eaten and drunk too much was very hard. Note, It is no new thing for those that do well to be ill thought of, and we must not think it strange if at any time it be our lot.

3. Hannah's humble vindication of herself from this crime with which she was charged. She bore it admirably well. She did not retort the charge and upbraid him with the debauchery of his own sons, did not bid him look at home and restrain them, did not tell him how ill it became one in his place thus to abuse a poor sorrowful worshipper at the throne of grace. When we are at any time unjustly censured we have need to set a double watch before the door of our lips, that we do not recriminate, and return censure for censure. Hannah thought it enough to vindicate herself, and so must we, *v.* 15, 16. (1.) In justice to herself, she expressly denies the charge, speaks to him with all possible respect, calls him, *My lord,* intimates how very desirous she was to stand right in his opinion and how loth to lie under his censure. "No, my lord, it is not as you suspect; I have drunk neither wine nor strong drink, not any at all" (though it was proper enough to be given to one of such a *heavy heart,* Prov. xxxi. 6), "much less to any excess; therefore *count not thy handmaid for a daughter of Belial.*" Note, Drunkards are children of Belial (women-drunkards particularly), children of the wicked one, children of disobedience, children that will not endure the yoke (else they would not be drunk), more especially when they are actually drunk. Those that cannot govern themselves will not bear that any one else should. Hannah owns that the crime would have been very great if she had indeed been guilty of it, and he might justly have shut her out of the courts of God's house; but the very manner of her speaking in her own defence was sufficient to demonstrate that she was not drunk. (2.) In justice to him, she gives an account of her present behaviour, which had given occasion to his suspicion: "*I am a woman of a sorrowful spirit,* dejected and discomposed, and that is the reason I do not look as other people; the eyes are red, not with wine, but with weeping. And at this time I have not been talking to myself, as drunkards and fools do, but I have been pouring out my soul before the Lord, who hears and understands the language of the heart, and this out of the abundance of my complaint and grief." She had been more than ordinarily fervent in prayer to God, and this, she tells him, was the true reason of the transport and

disorder she seemed to be in. Note, When we are unjustly censured we should endeavour, not only to clear ourselves, but to satisfy our brethren, by giving them a just and true account of that which they misapprehended.

4. The atonement Eli made for his rash unfriendly censure, by a kind and fatherly benediction, *v.* 17. He did not (as many are apt to do in such a case) take it for an affront to have his mistake rectified and to be convinced of his error, nor did it put him out of humour. But, on the contrary, he now encouraged Hannah's devotions as much as before he had discountenanced them; not only intimated that he was satisfied of her innocency by those words, *Go in peace*, but, being high priest, as one having authority he blessed her in the name of the Lord, and, though he knew not what the particular blessing was that she had been praying for, yet he puts his *Amen* to it, so good an opinion had he now conceived of her prudence and piety: *The God of Israel grant thee thy petition,* whatever it is, *that thou hast asked of him.* Note, By our meek and humble carriage towards those that reproach us because they do not know us, we may perhaps make them our friends, and turn their censures of us into prayers for us.

5. The great satisfaction of mind with which Hannah now went away, *v.* 18. She begged the continuance of Eli's good opinion of her and his good prayers for her, and then she went her way and did eat of what remained of the peace-offerings (none of which was to be left until the morning), *and her countenance was no more sad,* no more as it had been, giving marks of inward trouble and discomposure; but she looked pleasant and cheerful, and all was well. Why, what had happened? Whence came this sudden happy change? She had by prayer committed her case to God and left it with him, and now she was no more perplexed about it. She had prayed for herself, and Eli had prayed for her; and she believed that God would either give her the mercy she had prayed for or make up the want of it to her some other way. Note, Prayer is heart's-ease to a gracious soul; the seed of Jacob have often found it so, being confident that God will never say unto them, *Seek you me in vain,* see Phil. iv. 6, 7. Prayer will smooth the countenance; it should do so.

19 And they rose up in the morning early, and worshipped before the LORD, and returned, and came to their house to Ramah: and Elkanah knew Hannah his wife; and the LORD remembered her. 20 Wherefore it came to pass, when the time was come about after Hannah had conceived, that she bare a son, and called his name Samuel, *saying,* Because I have asked him of the LORD. 21 And the man Elkanah, and all his house, went up to offer unto the LORD the yearly sacrifice, and his vow. 22 But Hannah went not up; for she said unto her husband, *I will not go up* until the child be weaned, and *then* I will bring him, that he may appear before the LORD, and there abide for ever. 23 And Elkanah her husband said unto her, Do what seemeth thee good; tarry until thou have weaned him; only the LORD establish his word. So the woman abode, and gave her son suck until she weaned him. 24 And when she had weaned him, she took him up with her, with three bullocks, and one ephah of flour, and a bottle of wine, and brought him unto the house of the LORD in Shiloh: and the child *was* young. 25 And they slew a bullock, and brought the child to Eli. 26 And she said, Oh my lord, *as* thy soul liveth, my lord, I *am* the woman that stood by thee here, praying unto the LORD. 27 For this child I prayed; and the LORD hath given me my petition which I asked of him: 28 Therefore also I have lent him to the LORD; as long as he liveth he shall be lent to the LORD. And he worshipped the LORD there.

Here is, I. The return of Elkanah and his family to their own habitation, when the days appointed for the feast were over, *v.* 19. Observe how they improved their time at the tabernacle. Every day they were there, even that which was fixed for their journey home, they worshipped God; and they rose up early to do it. It is good to begin the day with God. Let him that is the first have the first. They had a journey before them, and a family of children to take with them, and yet they would not stir till they had worshipped God together. Prayer and provender do not hinder a journey. They had spent several days now in religious worship, and yet they attended once more. We should not be weary of well-doing.

II. The birth and name of this desired son. At length the Lord remembered Hannah, the very thing she desired (*v.* 11), and more she needed not desire, that was enough, for then she conceived and bore a son. Though God seem long to forget his people's burdens, troubles, cares, and prayers, yet he will at length make it to appear that they are not out of his mind. This son the mother called *Samuel, v.* 20. Some make the etymology of this name to be much the same with that of *Ishmael—heard of God,* because the mother's prayers were remarkably heard, and he was an answer to them. Others, because of the reason she gives for the name, make it to signify *asked of God.* It comes nearly to the same; she designed by it to perpetuate the remembrance of God's favour to her in answering her prayers. Thus she designed, upon every mention of his name, to take the comfort to herself and to give God the glory of that gracious condescension. Note, Mercies in answer to prayer are to be remembered with peculiar expressions of thankfulness, as Ps. cxvi. 1, 2. How many seasonable deliverances and supplies may we call *Samuels, asked of God;* and whatever is so we are in a special manner engaged to devote to him. Hannah intended by this name to put her son in mind of the obligation he was under to be the Lord's, in consideration of this, that he was asked of God and was at the same time dedicated to him. A child of prayer is in a special manner bound to be a good child. Lemuel's mother reminds him that he was the *son of her vows,* Prov. xxxi. 2.

III. The close attendance Hannah gave to the nursing of him, not only because he was dear to her, but because he was devoted to God, and for him she nursed him. She therefore nursed him herself, and did not hang him on another's breast. We ought to take care of our children, not only with an eye to the law of nature as they are ours, but with an eye to the covenant of grace as they are given up to God. See Ezek. xvi. 20, 21. This sanctifies the nursing of them, when it is done as unto the Lord. Elkanah went up every year to worship at the tabernacle, and particularly to perform his vow, perhaps some vow he had made distinct from Hannah's if God would give him a son by her, *v.* 21. But Hannah, though she felt a warm regard for the courts of God's house, begged leave of her husband to stay at home; for the women were not under any obligation to go up to the three yearly feasts, as the men were. However Hannah had been accustomed to go, but now desired to be excused, 1. Because she would not be so long absent from her nursery. *Can a woman forget her sucking child?* We may suppose she kept constantly at home, for, if she had gone any where, she would have gone to Shiloh. Note, God will have mercy and not sacrifice. Those that are detained from public ordinances by the nursing and tending of little children may take comfort from this instance, and believe that, if they do that with an eye to God, he will graciously accept them therein, and though they tarry at home they shall divide the spoil. 2. Because she would not go up to Shiloh till her son was big enough, not only to be taken thither, but to be left there; for, if once she took him thither, she thought she could never find in her heart to bring him back again. Note, Those who are stedfastly resolved to pay their vows may yet see good cause to defer the payment of them. *Every thing is beautiful in its season.* No animal was accepted in sacrifice till it had been for some time under the dam, Lev. xxii. 27. Fruit is best when it is ripe. Elkanah agrees to what she proposes (*v.* 23): *Do what seemeth thee good.* So far was he from delighting to cross her that he referred it entirely to her. *Behold how good and pleasant a thing it is,* when yoke-fellows thus draw even in the yoke, and accommodate themselves to one another, each thinking well of what the other does, especially in works of piety and charity. He adds a prayer: *Only the Lord establish his word,* that is, "God preserve the child through the perils of his infancy, that the solemn vow which God signified his acceptance of, by giving us the child, may be performed in its season, and so the whole matter may be accomplished." Note, Those that have in sincerity devoted their children to God may with comfort pray for them, that God will establish the word sealed to them at the same time that they were sealed for him.

IV. The solemn entering of this child into the service of the sanctuary. We may take it for granted that he was presented to the Lord at forty days old, as all the first-born were (Luke ii. 22, 23): but this is not mentioned, because there was nothing in it singular; but now that he was weaned he was presented, not to be redeemed. Some think it was as soon as he was weaned from the breast, which, the Jews say, was not till he was three years old; it is said she gave him suck till she had weaned him, *v.* 23. Others think it was not till he was weaned from childish things, at eight or ten years old. But I see no inconvenience in admitting such an extraordinary child as this into the tabernacle at three years old, to be educated among the children of the priests. It is said (*v.* 24), *The child was young,* but, being intelligent above his years, he was no trouble. None can begin too soon to be religious. *The child was a child,* so the Hebrew reads it, in his learning-age. For *whom shall he teach knowledge* but *those that are* newly *weaned from the milk and drawn from the breasts?* Isa. xxviii. 9. Observe how she presented her child, 1. With a sacrifice; no less than three bullocks, with a meat-offering for each, *v.* 24. A bullock, perhaps, for each year of the child's life. Or one for a burnt-offering, another for a sin-offering, and the third for a peace-offering. So far was she from thinking that, by presenting her son to God, she made God her debtor, that she thought it requisite by these slain offerings to seek God's acceptance of her living sacrifice. All our covenants with God for ourselves and ours must be made by sacrifice, the great sacrifice. 2. With a grateful acknowledgment of God's goodness in answer to prayer. This she makes to Eli, because he had encouraged her to hope for an answer of peace (*v.* 26, 27): "*For this child I prayed.* Here it was obtained by prayer, and here it is resigned to the prayer-hearing God. You have forgotten me, my lord, but I who now appear so cheerful am the woman, the very same, that three years ago stood by thee here weeping and praying, and this was the child I prayed for." Answers of prayer may thus be humbly triumphed in, to the glory of God. Here is a living testimony for God. "I am his witness that he is gracious (see Ps. lxvi. 16—19); for this mercy, this comfort, I prayed, *and the Lord has given me my petition.*" See Ps. xxxiv. 2, 4, 6. Hannah does not remind Eli of it by adverting to the suspicion he had formerly expressed; she does not say, "I am the woman whom you passed that severe censure upon; what do you think of me now?" Good men ought not to be upbraided with their infirmities and oversights. They have themselves repented of them; let them hear no more of them. 3 With a full surrender of all her interest in this child unto the Lord (*v.* 28): *I have lent him to the Lord as long as he liveth.* And she repeats it, because she will never revoke it: *He shall be* (a deodand) *lent* or given *to the Lord.* Not that she designed to call for him back, as we do what we lend, but she uses this word *Shaol, lent,* because it is the same word that she had used before (*v.* 20, *I asked* him of the Lord), only in another conjugation. And (*v.* 27) the Lord gave me the petition which *I asked (Shaalti,* in Kal), therefore *I have lent him (Hishilti,* the same word in Hiphil), and so it gives another etymology of his name *Samuel,* not only *asked of God,* but *lent to God.* And observe, (1.) Whatever we give to God, it is what we have first asked and received from him. All our gifts to him were first his gifts to us. *Of thy own, Lord, have we given thee,* 1 Chron. xxix. 14, 16. (2.) Whatever we give to God may upon this account be said to be *lent* to him, that though we may not recal it, as a thing lent, yet he will certainly repay it, with interest, to our unspeakable advantage, particularly what is given *to his poor,* Prov. xix. 17. When by baptism we dedicate our children to God, let us remember that they were his before by a sovereign right, and that they are ours still so much the more to our comfort. Hannah resigns him to the Lord, not for a certain term of years, as children are sent apprentices, but *durante vitâ—as long as he liveth, he shall be lent unto the Lord,* a Nazarite for life. Such must our covenant with God be, a marriage-covenant; as long as we live we must be his, and never forsake him.

Lastly, The child Samuel did his part beyond what could have been expected from one of his years; for of him that seems to be spoken, *He worshipped the Lord there,* that is, *he said his prayers.* He was no doubt extraordinarily forward (we have known children that have discovered some sense of religion very young), and his mother, designing him for the sanctuary, took particular care to train him up to that which was to be his work in the sanctuary. Note, Little children should learn betimes to worship God. Their parents should instruct them in his worship and bring them to it, put them upon engaging in it as well as they can, and God will graciously accept them and teach them to do better.

CHAP. II.

In this chapter we have, I. Hannah's song of thanksgiving to God for his favour to her in giving her Samuel, ver. 1—10. II. Their return to their family, with Eli's blessing, ver. 11, 20. The increase of their family, ver. 21. Samuel's growth and improvement (ver. 11, 18, 21, 26), and the care Hannah took to clothe him, ver. 19. III. The great wickedness of Eli's sons, ver. 12—17, 22. IV. The over-mild reproof that Eli gave them for it, ver. 23—25. V. The justly dreadful message God sent him by a prophet, threatening the ruin of his family for the wickedness of his sons, ver. 27—36.

AND Hannah prayed, and said, My heart rejoiceth in the LORD, mine horn is exalted in the LORD; my mouth is enlarged over mine enemies; because I rejoice in thy salvation. 2 *There is* none holy as the LORD: for *there is* none beside thee: neither *is there* any rock like our God. 3 Talk no more so exceeding proudly; let *not* arrogancy come out of your mouth: for the LORD *is* a God of knowledge, and by him actions are weighed. 4 The bows of the mighty men *are* broken, and they that stumbled are girded with strength. 5 *They that were* full have hired out themselves for bread; and *they that were* hungry ceased: so that the barren hath borne seven; and she that hath many children is waxed feeble. 6 The LORD killeth, and maketh alive: he bringeth down to the grave, and bringeth up. 7 The LORD maketh poor, and maketh rich: he bringeth low, and lifteth up. 8 He raiseth up the poor out of the dust, *and* lifteth up the beggar from the dunghill, to set *them* among princes, and to make them inherit the throne of glory: for the pillars of the earth *are* the LORD's, and he hath set the world upon them. 9 He will keep the feet of his saints, and the wicked shall be silent in darkness; for by strength shall no man prevail. 10 The adversaries of the LORD shall be broken to pieces; out of heaven shall he thunder upon them: the LORD shall judge the ends of the earth; and he shall give strength unto his king, and exalt the horn of his anointed.

We have here Hannah's thanksgiving, dictated, not only by the spirit of prayer, but by the spirit of prophecy. Her petition for the mercy she desired we had before (*ch.* i 11), and here we have her return of praise; in both *out of the abundance of a heart* deeply affected (in the former with her own wants, and in the latter with God's goodness) *her mouth spoke.* Observe in general, 1. When she had received mercy from God she owned it, with thankfulness to his praise. Not like the nine lepers, Luke xvii. 17. Praise is our rent, our tribute. We are unjust if we do not pay it. 2. The mercy she had received was an answer to prayer, and therefore she thought herself especially obliged to give thanks for it. What we win by prayer we may wear with comfort, and must wear with praise. 3. Her thanksgiving is here called a prayer: *Hannah prayed;* for thanksgiving is an essential part of prayer. In every address to God we must express a grateful regard to him as our benefactor. Nay, and thanksgiving for mercies received shall be accepted as a petition for further mercy. 4. From this particular mercy which she had received from God she takes occasion, with an elevated and enlarged heart, to speak glorious things of God and of his government of the world for the good of his church. Whatever at any time gives rise to our praises in this manner they should be raised. 5. Her prayer was mental. *Her voice was not heard;* but in her thanksgiving she spoke, that all might hear her. She made her supplication *with groanings that could not be uttered,* but now her lips were opened to *show forth God's praise.* 6. This thanksgiving is here left upon record for the encouragement of those of the weaker sex to attend the throne of grace. God will regard their prayers and praises. The virgin Mary's song has great affinity with this of Hannah, Luke i. 46. Three things we have in this thanksgiving:—

I. Hannah's triumph in God, in his glorious perfections, and the great things he had done for her, *v.* 1—3. Observe,

1. What great things she says of God. She takes little notice of the particular mercy she was now rejoicing in, does not commend Samuel for the prettiest child, the most toward and sensible for his age that she ever saw, as fond parents are too apt to do. No, she overlooks the gift, and praises the giver; whereas most forget the giver and fasten only on the gift. Every stream should lead us to the fountain; and the favours we receive from God should raise our admiration of the infinite perfections there are in God. There may be other Samuels, but no other Jehovah. *There is none besides thee.* Note, God is to be praised as a peerless being, and of unparalleled perfection. This glory is due unto his name, to own not only that there is *none like him, but that there is none besides him.* All others were pretenders, Ps. xviii. 31. Four of God's glorious attributes Hannah here celebrates the glory of:—(1.) His unspotted purity. This is that attribute which is most praised in the upper world, by those that always behold his face, Isa. vi. 3; Rev. iv. 8. When Israel triumphed over the Egyptians God was praised *as glorious in holiness,* Exod. xv. 11. So here, in Hannah's triumph, *There is none holy as the Lord.* It is the rectitude of his nature, his infinite agreement with himself, and the equity of his government and judgment in all the administrations of both. At the remembrance of this we ought to give thanks. (2.) His almighty power: *Neither is there any rock* (or *any strength,* for so the word is sometimes rendered) *like our God.* Hannah had experienced a mighty support by staying herself upon him, and therefore speaks as she had found, and seems to refer to that of Moses, Deut. xxxii. 31. (3.) His unsearchable wisdom: *The Lord,* the Judge of all, *is a God of knowledge;* he clearly and perfectly sees into the character of every person and the merits of every cause, and he gives knowledge and understanding to those that seek them of him. (4.) His unerring justice: *By him actions are weighed.* His own are so, in his eternal counsels; the actions of the children of men are so, in the balances of his judgment, so that he will *render to every man according to his work,* and is not mistaken in what any man is or does.

2. How she solaces herself in these things. What we give God the glory of we may take the comfort of. Hannah does so, (1.) In holy joy: *My heart rejoiceth in the Lord;* not so much in her son as in her God; he is to be the gladness of our joy (Ps. xliii. 4), and our joy must not terminate in any thing short of him: "*I rejoice in thy salvation;* not only in this particular favour to me, but in the salvation of thy people Israel, those salvations especially which this child will be an instrument of, and that, above all, by Christ, which those are but the types of." (2.) In holy triumph: "*My horn is exalted;* not only is my reputation saved by my having a son, but greatly raised by having such a son." We read of some of the singers whom David appointed to lift up the horn, an instrument of music, in praising God (1 Chron. xxv. 5), so that, *My horn is exalted* means this, "My praises are very much elevated to an unusual strain." *Exalted in the Lord;* God is to

have the honour of all our exaltations, and in him must we triumph. *My mouth is enlarged*, that is, "Now I have wherewith to answer those that reproached me." He that has his quiver full of arrows, his house full of children, shall not be ashamed to *speak with the enemy in the gate*, Ps. cxxvii. 5.

3. How she herewith silences those that set up themselves as rivals with God and rebels against him (*v.* 3): *Talk no more so exceedingly proudly.* Let not Peninnah and her children upbraid her any more with her confidence in God and praying to him: at length she found it not in vain. See Mic. vii. 10, *Then she that is my enemy shall see it, and shame shall cover her that said, Where is thy God?* Or perhaps it was below her to take so much notice of Peninnah, and her malice, in this song; but this is intended as a check to the insolence of the Philistines, and other enemies of God and Israel, that *set their mouth against the heavens*, Ps. lxxiii. 9. "Let this put them to silence and shame; he that has thus judged for me against my adversary will judge for his people against all theirs."

II. The notice she takes of the wisdom and sovereignty of the divine providence, in its disposals of the affairs of the children of men; such are the vicissitudes of them, and such the strange and sudden turns and revolutions of them, that it is often found a very short step between the height of prosperity and the depth of adversity. *God has* not only *set the one over against the other* (Eccl. vii. 14), but the one very near the other, and no gulf fixed between them, that we may *rejoice as though we rejoiced not* and *weep as though we wept not.*

1. The strong are soon weakened and the weak are soon strengthened, when God pleases, *v.* 4. On the one hand, if he speak the word, *the bows of the mighty men are broken;* they are disarmed, disabled to do as they have before done and as they have designed to do. Those have been worsted in battle who seemed upon all accounts to have the advantage on their side, and thought themselves sure of victory. See Ps. xlvi. 9; xxxvii. 15, 17. Particular persons are soon weakened by sickness and age, and they find that the bow does not long abide in strength; many a mighty man who has gloried in his might has found it a deceitful bow, that failed him when he trusted to it. On the other hand, if the Lord speak the word, those who stumble through weakness, who were so feeble that they could not go straight or steady, are *girded with strength*, in body and mind, and are able to bring great things to pass. Those who were weakened by sickness return to their vigour (Job xxxiii. 25), and those who were brought down by sorrow shall recover their comfort, which will *comfirm the weak hands and the feeble knees*, Isa. xxxv. 3. Victory turns in favour of that side that was given up for gone, and even *the lame take the prey*, Isa. xxxiii. 23.

2. The rich are soon impoverished and the poor strangely enriched on a sudden, *v.* 5. Providence sometimes does so blast men's estates and cross their endeavours, and with a fire not blown consume their increase, that those who were full (their barns full, and their bags full, their *houses full of good things*, Job xxii. 18, and their *bellies full of these hidden treasures*, Ps. xvii. 14) have been reduced to such straits and extremities as to want the necessary supports of life, and to *hire out themselves for bread*, and they must dig, since to *beg they are ashamed. Riches flee away* (Prov. xxiii. 5), and leave those miserable who, when they had them, placed their happiness in them. To those that have been full and free poverty and slavery must needs be doubly grievous. But, on the other hand, sometimes Providence so orders it that *those who are hungry cease*, that is, cease to hire out themselves for bread as they have done. Having, by God's blessing on their industry, got beforehand in the world, and enough to live upon at ease, *they shall hunger no more, nor thirst any more.* This is not to be ascribed to fortune, nor merely to men's wisdom or folly. *Riches are not to men of understanding, nor favour to men of skill* (Eccl. ix. 11), nor is it always men's own fault that they become poor, but (*v.* 7) *the Lord maketh some poor and maketh others rich;* the impoverishing of one is the enriching of another, and it is God's doing. To some he gives power to get wealth, from others he takes away power to keep the wealth they have. Are we poor? God made us poor, which is a good reason why we should be content, and reconcile ourselves to our condition. Are we rich? God made us rich, which is a good reason why we should be thankful, and serve him cheerfully in the abundance of good things he gives us. It may be understood of the same person; those that were rich God makes poor, and after awhile makes rich again, as Job; he gave, he takes away, and then gives again, Let not the rich be proud and secure, for God can soon make them poor; let not the poor despond and despair, for God can in due time enrich them again.

3. Empty families are replenished and numerous families diminished and made few. This is the instance that comes close to the occasion of the thanksgiving: *The barren hath borne seven*, meaning herself, for, though at present she had but one son, yet that one being a Nazarite, devoted to God and employed in his immediate service, he was to her as good as seven. Or it is the language of her faith. Now that she had one she hoped for more, and was not disappointed; she had five more (*v.* 21), so that if we reckon Samuel but for two, as we well may, she has the number she promised herself: the *barren hath borne seven*, while, on the other hand, *she that hath many children has waxed feeble*, and hath left bearing. She

says no more. Peninnah is now mortified and crest-fallen. The tradition of the Jews is that when Hannah bore one child Peninnah buried two. There are many instances both of the increase of families that were inconsiderable and the extinguishing of families that made a figure, Job xxii. 23; Ps.cvii.38,&c.

4. God is the sovereign Lord of life and death (*v.* 6): *The Lord killeth and maketh alive.* Understand it, (1.) Of God's sovereign dominion and universal agency, in the lives and deaths of the children of men. He presides in births and burials. Whenever any die it is God that directs the arrows of death. *The Lord killeth.* Death is his messenger, strikes whom and when he bids; none are brought to the dust but it is he that brings them down, for in his hand are the *keys of death and the grave,* Rev. i. 18. Whenever any are born it is he that *makes them alive. None knows what is the way of the spirit,* but this we know, that it comes from the *Father of spirits.* Whenever any are recovered from sickness, and delivered from imminent perils, it is God that bringeth up; for *to him belong the issues from death.* (2.) Of the distinction he makes between some and others: *He killeth* some, and *maketh,* that is, keepeth, others *alive* that were in the same danger (in war, suppose, or pestilence), two in a bed together, it may be, one taken by death and the other left alive. *Even so, Father, because it seemed good in thy eyes.* Some that were most likely to live are brought down to the grave, and others that were as likely to die are brought up; for living and dying do not go by likelihoods. God's providences towards some are killing, ruining to their comforts, and towards others at the same time reviving. (3.) Of the change he makes with one and the same person: *He killeth and bringeth down to the grave,* that is, he brings even to death's door, and then revives and raises up, when even life was despaired of and a sentence of death received, 2 Cor. i. 8, 9. *He turns to destruction,* and then says, *Return,* Ps. xc. 3. Nothing is too hard for God to do, no, not the quickening of the dead, and putting life into dry bones.

5. Advancement and abasement are both from him. He brings some low and lifts up others (*v.* 7), humbles the proud and gives grace and honour to the lowly, lays those in the dust that would vie with the God above them and trample upon all about them (Job xl. 12, 13), but lifts up those with his salvation that humble themselves before him, Jam. iv. 10. Or it may be understood of the same persons: those whom he had brought low, when they are sufficiently humbled, he lifteth up. This is enlarged upon, *v.* 8. *He raiseth up the poor out of the dust,* a low and mean condition, nay, from the dunghill, a base and servile condition, loathed, and despised, *to set them among princes.* See Ps. cxiii. 7, 8. Promotion comes not by chance, but from the counsel of God, which often prfers those that were very unlikely and that men thought very unworthy. Joseph and Daniel, Moses and David, were thus strangely advanced, from a prison to a palace, from a sheep-hook to a sceptre. The princes they are set among may be tempted to disdain them, but God can establish the honour which he gives thus surprisingly, and make them even to *inherit the throne of glory.* Let not those whom Providence has thus preferred be upbraided with the dust and dunghill they are raised out of, for the meaner their beginnings were the more they are favoured, and God is glorified, in their advancement, if it be by lawful and honourable means.

6. A reason is given for all these dispensations which obliges us to acquiesce in them, how surprising soever they are: *For the pillars of the earth are the Lord's.* (1.) If we understand this literally, it intimates God's almighty power, which cannot be controlled. He upholds the whole creation, founded the earth, and still sustains it by the word of his power. What cannot he do in the affairs of families and kingdoms, far beyond our conception and expectation, *who hangs the earth upon nothing?* Job xxvi. 7. But, (2.) If we understand it figuratively, it intimates his incontestable sovereignty, which cannot be disputed. The princes and great ones of the earth, the directors of states and governments, are the *pillars of the earth,* Ps. lxxv. 3. On these hinges the affairs of the world seem to turn, but they are the Lord's, Ps. xlvii. 9. From him they have their power, and therefore he may advance whom he pleases; and who may say, *What doest thou?*

III. A prediction of the preservation and advancement of all God's faithful friends, and the destruction of all his and their enemies. Having testified her joyful triumph in what God had done, and is doing, she concludes with joyful hopes of what he would do, *v.* 9, 10. Pious affections (says bishop Patrick) in those days rose many times to the height of prophecy, whereby God continued in that nation his true religion, in the midst of their idolatrous inclinations. This prophecy may refer, 1. More immediately to the government of Israel by Samuel, and by David whom he was employed to anoint. The Israelites, God's saints, should be protected and delivered; the Philistines, their enemies, should be conquered and subdued, and particularly by *thunder, ch.* vii. 10. Their dominions should be enlarged, king David strengthened and greatly exalted, and Israel (that in the time of the judges had made so small a figure and had much ado to subsist) should now shortly become great and considerable, and give law to all its neighbours. An extraordinary change that was; and the birth of Samuel was, as it were, the dawning of that day. But, 2. We have reason to think that this prophecy looks further, to the kingdom of Christ, and the administration of that kingdom of grace, of which she now comes to speak, having spoken so largely of the kingdom of providence. And here is the first time that we meet with the name *Messiah*, or *his Anointed.* The ancient expositors, both Jewish and Christian, make it to look beyond David, to the Son of David. Glorious things are here spoken of the kingdom of the Mediator, both before and since his incarnation; for the method of the administration of it, both by the eternal Word and by that Word made flesh, is much the same. Concerning that kingdom we are here assured, (1.) That all the loyal subjects of it shall be carefully and powerfully protected (*v.* 9): *He will keep the feet of his saints.* There are a people in the world that are God's saints, his select and sanctified ones; and he will keep their feet, that is, all that belongs to them shall be under his protection, down to their very feet, the lowest part of the body. If he will keep their feet, much more their head and hearts. Or he will keep their feet, that is, he will secure the ground they stand on, and establish their goings; he will set a guard of grace upon their affections and actions, that their feet may neither wander out of the way nor stumble in the way. When their feet are ready to slip (Ps. lxxiii. 2) *his mercy holdeth them up* (Ps. xciv. 18) and *keepeth them from falling*, Jude 24. While we keep God's ways he will keep our feet. See Ps. xxxvii. 23, 24. (2.) That all the powers engaged against it shall not be able to effect the ruin of it. By strength shall no man prevail. God's strength is engaged for the church; and, while it is so, man's strength shall not prevail against it. The church seems destitute of strength, her friends few and feeble, but prevalency does not go by human strength, Ps. xxxiii. 16. God neither needs it for him (Ps. cxlvii. 10) nor dreads it against him. (3.) That all the enemies of it will certainly be broken and brought down: *The wicked shall be silent in darkness, v.* 9. They shall be struck both blind and dumb, not be able to see their way nor have any thing to say for themselves. Damned sinners are sentenced to utter darkness, and in it they will be for ever speechless, Matt. xxii. 12, 13. The wicked are called *the adversaries of the Lord,* and it is foretold (*v.* 10) that they *shall be broken to pieces.* Their designs against his kingdom among men will all be dashed, and they themselves destroyed; how can those speed better that are in arms against Omnipotence? See Luke xix. 27. God has many ways of doing it, and, rather than fail, from *heaven shall he thunder upon them,* and so, not only put them in terror and consternation, but bring them to destruction. Who can stand before God's thunderbolts? (4.) That the conquests of this kingdom shall extend themselves to distant regions: *The Lord shall judge the ends of the earth.* David's victories and dominions reached far, but the *uttermost parts of the earth* are promised to the Messiah for his *possession* (Ps. ii. 8), to be either reduced to his golden sceptre or ruined by his iron rod. God is Judge of all, and he will judge for his people against his and their enemies, Ps. cx. 5, 6. (5.) That the power and honour of Messiah the prince shall grow and increase more and more: *He shall give strength unto his king,* for the accomplishing of his great undertaking (Ps. lxxxix. 21, and see Luke xxii. 43), strengthen him to go through the difficulties of his humiliation, and in his exaltation he will *lift up the head* (Ps. cx. 7), lift up the horn, the power and honour, of his *anointed,* and *make him higher than the kings of the earth,* Ps. lxxxix. 27. This crowns the triumph, and is, more than any thing, the matter of her exultation. Her *horn is exalted* (*v.* 1) because she foresees the horn of the Messiah will be so. This secures the hope. The subjects of Christ's kingdom will be safe, and the enemies of it will be ruined, for the anointed, the Lord Christ, is girded with strength, and is able to save and destroy unto the uttermost.

11 And Elkanah went to Ramah to his house. And the child did minister unto the LORD before Eli the priest. 12 Now the sons of Eli *were* sons of Belial; they knew not the LORD. 13 And the priest's custom with the people *was, that,* when any man offered sacrifice, the priest's servant came, while the flesh was in seething, with a fleshhook of three teeth in his hand; 14 And he struck *it* into the pan, or kettle, or caldron, or pot; all that the fleshhook brought up the priest took for himself. So they did in Shiloh unto all the Israelites that came thither. 15 Also before they burnt the fat, the priest's servant came, and said to the man that sacrificed, Give flesh to roast for the priest; for he will not have sodden flesh of thee, but raw. 16 And *if* any man said unto him, Let them not fail to burn the fat presently, and *then* take *as much* as thy soul desireth; then he would answer him, *Nay;* but thou shalt give *it me* now: and if not, I will take *it* by force. 17 Wherefore the sin of the young men was very great before the LORD: for men abhorred the offering of the LORD. 18 But Samuel ministered before the LORD, *being* a child, girded with a linen ephod. 19 Moreover

his mother made him a little coat, and brought *it* to him from year to year, when she came up with her husband to offer the yearly sacrifice. 20 And Eli blessed Elkanah and his wife, and said, The LORD give thee seed of this woman for the loan which is lent to the LORD. And they went unto their own home. 21 And the LORD visited Hannah, so that she conceived, and bare three sons and two daughters. And the child Samuel grew before the LORD. 22 Now Eli was very old, and heard all that his sons did unto all Israel; and how they lay with the women that assembled *at* the door of the tabernacle of the congregation. 23 And he said unto them, Why do ye such things? for I hear of your evil dealings by all this people. 24 Nay, my sons; for *it is* no good report that I hear: ye make the LORD's people to transgress. 25 If one man sin against another, the judge shall judge him: but if a man sin against the LORD, who shall intreat for him? Notwithstanding they hearkened not unto the voice of their father, because the LORD would slay them. 26 And the child Samuel grew on, and was in favour both with the LORD, and also with men.

In these verses we have the good character and posture of Elkanah's family, and the bad character and posture of Eli's family. The account of these two is observably interwoven throughout this whole paragraph, as if the historian intended to set the one over against the other, that they might set off one another. The devotion and good order of Elkanah's family aggravated the iniquity of Eli's house; while the wickedness of Eli's sons made Samuel's early piety appear the more bright and illustrious.

I. Let us see how well things went in Elkanah's family and how much better than formerly. 1. Eli dismissed them from the house of the Lord, when they had entered their little son there, with a blessing, *v.* 20. He blessed as one having authority: *The Lord give thee* more children *of this woman, for the loan that is lent to the Lord.* If Hannah had then had many children, it would not have been such a generous piece of piety to part with one out of many for the service of the tabernacle; but when she had but one, an only one whom she loved, her Isaac, to present him to the Lord was such an act of heroic piety as should by no means lose its reward. As when Abraham had offered Isaac he received the promise of a numerous issue (Gen. xxii. 16, 17), so did Hannah, when she had presented Samuel unto the Lord a living sacrifice. Note, What is lent to the Lord will certainly be repaid with interest, to our unspeakable advantage, and oftentimes in kind. Hannah resigns one child to God, and is recompensed with five; for Eli's blessing took effect (*v.* 21): *She bore three sons and two daughters.* There is nothing lost by lending to God or losing for him; it shall be repaid *a hundred-fold,* Matt. xix. 29. 2. They returned to their own habitation. This is twice mentioned, *v.* 11, and again *v.* 20. It was very pleasant to attend at God's house, to bless him, and to be blessed of him. But they have a family at home that must be looked after, and thither they return, cheerfully leaving the dear little one behind them, knowing they left him in a good place; and it does not appear that he cried after them, but was as willing to stay as they were to leave him, so soon did he *put away childish things* and behave like a man. 3. They kept up their constant attendance at the house of God with their *yearly sacrifice, v.* 19. They did not think that their son's ministering there would excuse them, or that that offering must serve instead of other offerings; but, having found the benefit of drawing near to God, they would omit no appointed season for it, and now they had one loadstone more in Shiloh to draw them thither. We may suppose they went thither to see their child oftener than once a year, for it was not ten miles from Ramah; but their annual visit is taken notice of because then they brought their yearly sacrifice, and then Hannah fitted up her son (and some think oftener than once a year) with a new suit of clothes, *a little coat* (*v.* 19) and every thing belonging to it. She undertook to find him with clothes during his apprenticeship at the tabernacle, and took care he should be well provided, that he might appear the more decent and sightly in his ministration, and to encourage him in his towardly beginnings. Parents must take care that their children want nothing that is fit for them, whether they are with them or from them; but those that are dutiful and hopeful, and minister to the Lord, must be thought worthy of double care and kindness. 4. The child Samuel did very well. Four separate times he is mentioned in these verses, and two things we are told of:—(1.) The service he did to the Lord. He did well indeed, for he *ministered to the Lord* (*v.* 11, 18) according as his capacity was. He learned his catechism and was constant to his devotions, soon learned to read, and took a pleasure in the book of the law, and thus he *ministered to the Lord.* He ministered before Eli, that is, under his inspection, and as he ordered him, not before Eli's sons; all parties were agreed that they were unfit to be his tutors. Perhaps he attended immediately on Eli's person, was ready to him to fetch and bring as he had occasion, and that is called *ministering to the Lord.* Some little services perhaps he was employed in about the altar, though much under the age appointed by the law for the Levites' ministration. He could light a candle, or hold a dish, or run on an errand, or shut a door; and, because he did this with a pious disposition of mind it is called *ministering to the Lord,* and great notice is taken of it. After awhile he did his work so well that Eli appointed that he should minister with a *linen ephod* as the priests did (though he was no priest), because he saw that God was with him. Note, Little children must learn betimes to *minister to the Lord.* Parents must train them up to it, and God will accept them. Particularly let them learn to pay respect to their teachers, as Samuel to Eli. None can begin too soon to be religious. See Ps. viii. 2, and Matt. xxi. 15, 16. (2.) The blessing he received from the Lord: He *grew before the Lord,* as a tender plant (*v.* 21), *grew on* (*v.* 26) in strength and stature, and especially in wisdom and understanding and fitness for business. Note, Those young people that serve God as well as they can will obtain grace to improve, that they may serve him better. Those that are planted in God's house shall *flourish,* Ps. xcii. 13. *He was in favour with the Lord and with man.* Note, It is a great encouragement to children to be tractable, and virtuous, and good betimes, that if they be both God and man will love them. Such children are the darlings both of heaven and earth. What is here said of Samuel is said of our blessed Saviour, that great example, Luke ii. 52.

II. Let us now see how ill things went in Eli's family, though seated at the very door of the tabernacle. The nearer the church the further from God.

1. The abominable wickedness of Eli's sons (*v.* 12): *The sons of Eli were sons of Belial.* It is emphatically expressed. Nothing appears to the contrary but that Eli himself was a very good man, and no doubt had educated his sons well, giving them good instructions, setting them good examples, and putting up many a good prayer for them; and yet, when they grew up, they proved *sons of Belial,* profane wicked men, and arrant rakes: *They knew not the Lord.* They could not but have a notional knowledge of God and his law, a form of knowledge (Rom. ii. 20), yet, because their practice was not conformable to it, they are spoken of as wholly ignorant of God; they lived as if they knew nothing at all of God. Note, Parents cannot give grace to their children, nor does it run in the blood. Many that are sincerely pious themselves live to see those that come from them notoriously impious and profane; *for the race is not to the swift.* Eli was high priest and judge in Israel. His sons were priests by their birth. Their character was sacred and honourable, and obliged them, for their reputation-sake, to observe decorum. They were resident at the fountain-head both of magistracy and ministry, and yet they were *sons of Belial,* and their honour, power, and learning, made them so much the worse. They did not go to *serve other gods,* as those did that lived at a distance from the altar, for from the house of God they had their wealth and dignity; but, which was worse, they managed the service of God as if he had been one of the dunghill deities of the heathen. It is hard to say which dishonours God more, idolatry or profaneness, especially the profaneness of the priests. Let us see the wickedness of Eli's sons; and it is a sad sight.

(1.) They profaned the offerings of the Lord, and made a gain to themselves, or rather a gratification of their own luxury, out of them. God had provided competently for them out of the sacrifices. *The offerings of the Lord made by fire* were a considerable branch of their revenue, but not enough to please them; they served not the God of Israel, but their own bellies (Rom. xvi. 18), being such as the prophet calls *greedy dogs that can never have enough,* Isa. lvi. 11. [1.] They robbed the offerers, and seized for themselves some of their part of the sacrifice of the peace-offerings. The priests had for their share the *wave-breast* and the *heave shoulder* (Lev. vii. 34), but these did not content them; when the flesh was boiling for the offerer to feast upon religiously with his friends, they sent a servant with a flesh-hook of three teeth, a trident, and that must be struck into the pot, and whatever that brought up the priest must have (*v.* 13, 14), and the people, out of their great veneration, suffered this to grow into a custom, so that after awhile prescription was pleaded for this manifest wrong. [2.] They stepped in before God himself, and encroached upon his right too. *As if it were a small thing to weary men, they wearied my God also,* Isa. vii. 13. Be it observed, to the honour of Israel, that though the people tamely yielded to their unwarrantable demands from them, yet they were very solicitous that God should not be robbed: *Let them not fail to burn the fat presently, v.* 16 Let the altar have its due, for that is the main matter. Unless God have the fat, they can feast with little comfort upon the flesh. It was a shame that the priests should need to be thus admonished by the people of their duty; but they regarded not the admonition. The priest will be served first, and will take what he thinks fit of the fat too, for he is weary of boiled meat, he must have roast, and, in order to that, they must give it to him raw; and if the offerer dispute it, though not in his own favour (let the priest take what he pleases of his part) but in favour of the altar (let them be sure to *burn the fat* first), even the priest's servant had grown so very imperious that he would either have it now or take it by force, than which there could not be a greater affront to God nor a greater abuse to the people. The effect was, *First,* That God was displeased: *The sin of the young men was very great before the Lord, v.* 17. Nothing is more provoking to God than the profanation of sacred things, and men serving their lusts with the offerings of the Lord. *Secondly,* That religion suffered by it: *Men abhorred the offerings of the Lord.* All good men abhorred their management of the offerings, and too many insensibly fell into a contempt of the offerings themselves for their sakes. It was the people's sin to think the worse of God's institutions, but it was the much greater sin of the priests that gave them occasion to do so. Nothing brings a greater reproach upon religion than ministers' covetousness, sensuality, and imperiousness. In the midst of this sad story comes in the repeated mention of Samuel's devotion. *But Samuel ministered before the Lord,* as an instance of the power of God's grace, in preserving him pure and pious in the midst of this wicked crew; and this helped to keep up the sinking credit of the sanctuary in the minds of the people, who, when they had said all they could against Eli's sons, could not but admire Samuel's seriousness, and speak well of religion for his sake.

(2.) They debauched the women that came to worship at the door of the tabernacle, *v.* 22. They had wives of their own, but were like *fed horses,* Jer. v. 8. To have gone to the harlots' houses, the common prostitutes, would have been abominable wickedness, but to use the interest which as priests they had in those women that had devout dispositions and were religiously inclined, and to bring them to commit this wickedness, was such horrid impiety as one can scarcely think it possible that men who called themselves priests should ever be guilty of. *Be astonished, O heavens! at this, and tremble, O earth!* No words can sufficiently express the villany of such practices as these.

2. The reproof which Eli gave his sons for this their wickedness: *Eli was very old* (*v.* 22) and could not himself inspect the service of the tabernacle as he had done, but left all to his sons, who, because of the infirmities of his age, slighted him, and did what they would. However, he was told of the wickedness of his sons, and we may well imagine what a heart-breaking it was to him, and how much it added to the burdens of his age; but it should seem he did not so much as reprove them till he heard of their debauching the women, and then he thought fit to give them a check. Had he rebuked them for their greediness and luxury, this might have been prevented. Young people should be told of their faults as soon as it is perceived that they begin to be extravagant, lest their hearts be hardened. Now concerning the reproof he gave them observe,

(1.) That it was very just and rational. That which he said was very proper. [1.] He tells them that the matter of fact was too plain to be denied and too public to be concealed: "*I hear of your evil dealings by all this people, v.* 23. It is not the surmise of one or two, but the avowed testimony of many; all your neighbours cry out shame on you, and bring their complaints to me, expecting that I should redress the grievance." [2.] He shows them the bad consequences of it, that they not only sinned, but made Israel to sin, and would have the people's sin to answer for as well as their own: "You that should turn men from iniquity (Mal. ii. 6), *you make the Lord's people to transgress,* and corrupt the nation instead of reforming it; you tempt people to go and serve other gods when they see the God of Israel so ill served." [3.] He warns them of the danger they brought themselves into by it, *v.* 25. He intimates to them what God afterwards told him, that the *iniquity* would not be *purged with sacrifice nor offering, ch.* iii. 14. *If one man sin against another,* the judge (that is, the priest, who was appointed to be the judge in many cases, Deut. xvii. 9) *shall judge him,* shall undertake his cause, arbitrate the matter, and make atonement for the offender; *but if a man sin against the Lord* (that is, if a priest profane the holy things of the Lord, if a man that deals with God for others do himself affront him) *who shall entreat for him?* Eli was himself a judge, and had often made intercession for transgressors, but, says he, "You that *sin against the Lord,*" that is, "against the law and honour of God, in those very things which immediately pertain to him, and by which reconciliation is to be made, how can I entreat for you?" Their condition was deplorable indeed when their own father could not speak a good word for them, nor could have the face to appear as their advocate. Sins against the remedy, the atonement itself, are most dangerous, *treading under foot the blood of the covenant,* for then there *remains no more sacrifice,* Heb. x. 26.

(2.) It was too mild and gentle. He should have rebuked them sharply. Their crimes deserved sharpness; their temper needed it; the softness of his dealing with them would but harden them the more. The animadversion was too easy when he said, *It is no good report.* He should have said, "It is a shameful scandalous thing, and not to be suffered!" Whether it was because he loved them or because he feared them that he dealt thus tenderly with them, it was certainly an evidence of his want of zeal for the honour of God and his sanctuary. He bound them over to God's judgment, but he should have taken cognizance of their crimes himself, as high priest and judge, and have restrained and punished them. What he said was right, but it was not enough. Note, It is sometimes necessary that we put an edge upon the reproofs we give. There are those that must be saved *with fear,* Jude 23.

3. Their obstinacy against this reproof. His lenity did not at all work upon them: They *hearkened not to their father,* though he was also a judge. They had no regard either to his authority or to his affection, which was to them *an evident token of perdition;* it was *because the Lord would slay them.* They had long hardened their hearts, and now God, in a way of righteous judgment, hardened their hearts, and seared their consciences, and withheld from them the grace they had resisted and forfeited. Note, Those that are deaf to the reproofs of wisdom are manifestly marked for ruin. The Lord has *determined to destroy them,* 2 Chron. xxv. 16. See Prov. xxix. 1. Immediately upon this, Samuel's tractableness is again mentioned (*v.* 26), to shame their obstinacy: *The child Samuel grew.* God's grace is his own; he denied it to the sons of the high priest and gave it to the child of an obscure country Levite.

27 And there came a man of God unto Eli, and said unto him, Thus saith the LORD, Did I plainly appear unto the house of thy father, when they were in Egypt in Pharaoh's house? 28 And did I choose him out of all the tribes of Israel *to be* my priest, to offer upon mine altar, to burn incense, to wear an ephod before me? and did I give unto the house of thy father all the offerings made by fire of the children of Israel? 29 Wherefore kick ye at my sacrifice and at mine offering, which I have commanded *in my* habitation; and honourest thy sons above me, to make yourselves fat with the chiefest of all the offerings of Israel my people? 30 Wherefore the LORD God of Israel saith, I said indeed *that* thy house, and the house of thy father, should walk before me for ever: but now the LORD saith, Be it far from me; for them that honour me I will honour, and they that despise me shall be lightly esteemed. 31 Behold, the days come, that I will cut off thine arm, and the arm of thy father's house, that there shall not be an old man in thine house. 32 And thou shalt see an enemy *in my* habitation, in all *the wealth* which *God* shall give Israel: and there shall not be an old man in thine house for ever. 33 And the man of thine, *whom* I shall not cut off from mine altar, *shall be* to consume thine eyes, and to grieve thine heart: and all the increase of thine house shall die in the flower of their age. 34 And this *shall be* a sign unto thee, that shall come upon thy two sons, on Hophni and Phinehas; in one day they shall die both of them. 35 And I will raise me up a faithful priest, *that* shall do according to *that* which *is* in mine heart and in my mind: and I will build him a sure house; and he shall walk before mine anointed for ever. 36 And it shall come to pass, *that* every one that is left in thine house shall come *and* crouch to him for a piece of silver and a morsel of bread, and shall say, Put me, I pray thee, into one of the priests' offices, that I may eat a piece of bread.

Eli reproved his sons too gently, and did not threaten them as he should, and therefore God sent a prophet to him to reprove him sharply, and to threaten him, because, by his indulgence of them, he had strengthened their hands in their wickedness. If good men be wanting in their duty, and by their carelessness and remissness contribute any thing to the sin of sinners, they must expect both to hear of it and to smart for it. Eli's family was now nearer to God than all *the families of the earth, and therefore he will punish them,* Amos iii. 2. The message is sent to Eli himself, because God would bring him to repentance and save him; not to his sons, whom he had determined to destroy. And it might have been a means of awakening him to do his duty at last, and so to have prevented the judgment, but we do not find it had any great effect upon him. The message this prophet delivers from God is very close.

I. He reminds him of the great things God had done for the house of his fathers and for his family. He appeared to Aaron in Egypt (Exod. iv. 27), in the house of bondage, as a token of further favour which he designed for him, *v.* 27. He advanced him to the priesthood, entailed it upon his family, and thereby dignified it above any of the families of Israel. He entrusted him with honourable work, to offer on God's altar, *to burn incense,* and to wear that ephod in which was the breast-plate of judgment. He settled upon him an honourable maintenance, a share out of *all the offerings made by fire, v.* 28. What could he have done more for them, to engage them to be faithful to him? Note, The distinguishing favours we have received from God, especially those of the spiritual priesthood, are great aggravations of sin, and will be remembered against us in the day of account, if we profane our crown and betray our trusts, Deut. xxxii. 6; 2 Sam. xii. 7, 8.

II. He exhibits a high charge against him and his family. His children did wickedly, and he connived at it, and thereby involved himself in the guilt; the indictment therefore runs against them all, *v.* 29. 1. His sons had impiously profaned the holy things of God: "*You kick at my sacrifice which I have commanded;* not only trample upon the institution as a mean thing, but spurn at it as a thing you hate to be tied up to." They did the utmost despite imaginable to the offerings of the Lord when they committed all that outrage and rapine about them that we read of, and violently plundered the pots on which, in effect, *Holiness to the Lord* was written (Zech. xiv. 20), and took that fat to themselves which God had appointed to be burnt on his altar. 2. Eli had bolstered them up in it, by not punishing their insolence and impiety: "Thou for thy part *honourest thy sons above me,*" that is, "thou hadst rather see my offerings disgraced by their profanation of them than see thy sons disgraced by a legal censure upon them for so doing, which ought to have been inflicted, even to suspension and deprivation *ab officio et beneficio—of their office and its emoluments.* Those that allow and countenance their children in any evil way, and do not use their authority to restrain and punish them, do in effect *honour them more than God,* being more tender of their reputation than of his glory and more desirous to humour them than to honour him. 3. They had all shared in the gains of the sacrilege. It is to be feared that Eli himself, though he disliked and reproved the abuses they committed, yet did not forbear to eat of the roast meat they sacrilegiously got, *v.* 15. He was a *fat heavy man* (*ch.* iv. 18), and therefore it is charged upon the whole family (though Hophni and Phinehas were principally guilty), *You make yourselves fat with the chief of all the offerings.* God gave them sufficient to feed them, but that would not suffice; they made themselves fat, and served their lusts with that which God was to be served with. See Hos. iv. 8.

III. He declares the cutting off of the entail of the high priesthood from his family (*v.* 30): "*The Lord God of Israel,* who is jealous for his own honour and Israel's, says, and lets thee know it, that thy commission is revoked and superseded." *I said, indeed, that thy house, and the house of thy father* Ithamar (for from that younger son of Aaron Eli descended), *should walk before me for ever.* Upon what occasion the dignity of the high priesthood was transferred from the family of Eleazar to that of Ithamar does not appear; but it seems this had been done, and Eli stood fair to have that honour perpetuated to his posterity. But observe, the promise carried its own condition along with it: *They shall walk before me for ever,* that is, "they shall have the honour, provided they faithfully do the service." *Walking before God* is the great condition of the covenant, Gen. xvii. 1. Let them set me before their face, and I will set them before my face continually (Ps. xli. 12), otherwise not. But now the Lord says, *Be it far from me.* "Now that you cast me off you can expect no other than that I should cast you off; you will not walk before me as you should, and therefore you shall not." Such wicked and abusive servants God will discard, and turn out of his service. Some think there is a further reach in this recal of the grant, and that it was not only to be fulfilled shortly in the deposing of the posterity of Eli, when Zadok, who descended from Eleazar, was put in Abiathar's room, but it was to have its complete accomplishment at length in the total abolition of the Levitical priesthood by the priesthood of Christ.

IV. He gives a good reason for this revocation, taken from a settled and standing rule of God's government, according to which all must expect to be dealt with (like that by which Cain was tried, Gen. iv. 7): *Those that honour me I will honour, and those that despise me shall be lightly esteemed.*

1. Observe in general, (1.) That God is the fountain of honour and dishonour; he can exalt the meanest and put contempt upon the greatest. (2.) As we deal with God we must expect to be dealt with by him, and yet more favourably than we deserve. See Ps. xviii. 25, 26.

2. Particularly, (1.) Be it spoken, to the everlasting reputation of religion or of serious godliness, that it gives honour to God and puts honour upon men. By it we seek and serve the glory of God, and he will be behind-hand with none that do so, but here and hereafter will secure their glory. The way to be truly great is to be truly good. If we humble and deny ourselves in any thing to honour God, and have a single eye to him in it, we may depend upon this promise, he will put the best honour upon us. See John xii. 26. (2.) Be it spoken, to the everlasting reproach of impiety or profaneness, that this does dishonour to God (despises the greatest and best of beings, whom angels adore) and will bring dishonour upon men, for those that do so shall be lightly esteemed; not only God will lightly esteem them (that perhaps they will not regard, as those that honour him value his honour, of whom therefore it is said, *I will honour them),* but they shall be lightly esteemed by all the world; the very honour they are proud of shall be laid in the dust; they shall see themselves despised by all mankind, their names a reproach; when they are gone, their memory shall rot, and, when they rise again, it shall be to everlasting shame and contempt. The dishonour which their impotent malice puts upon God and his omnipotent justice will return upon their own heads, Ps. lxxix. 12.

V. He foretels the particular judgments

which should come upon his family, to its perpetual ignominy. A curse should be entailed upon his posterity, and a terrible curse it is, and shows how jealous God is in the matters of his worship and how ill he takes it when those who are bound by their character and profession to preserve and advance the interests of his glory are false to their trust, and betray them. If God's ministers be vicious and profane, *of how much sorer punishment will they be thought worthy,* here and for ever, than other sinners! Let such read the doom here passed on Eli's house, and tremble. It is threatened,

1. That their power should be broken (*v.* 31): *I will cut off thy arm, and the arm of thy father's house.* They should be stripped of all their authority, should be deposed, and have no influence upon the people as they had had. God *would make them contemptible and base.* See Mal. ii. 8, 9. The sons had abused their power to oppress the people and encroach upon their rights, and the father had not used his power, as he ought to have done, to restrain and punish them, and therefore it was justly threatened that the arm should be cut off which was not stretched out as it should have been.

2. That their lives should be shortened. He was himself an old man; but instead of using the wisdom, gravity, experience, and authority of his age, for the service of God and the support of religion, he had suffered the infirmities of age to make him more cool and remiss in his duty, and therefore it is here threatened that none of his posterity should live to be old, *v.* 31, 32. It is twice spoken: "*There shall not be an old man in thy house for ever;*" and again (*v.* 33), "*All the increase of thy house,* from generation to generation, *shall die in the flower of their age,* when they are in the midst of the years of their service," so that though the family should not be extinct, yet it should never be considerable, nor should any member of it come to be eminent in his day. Bishop Patrick relates, out of some of the Jewish writers, that long after this, there being a family in Jerusalem none of which commonly lived above eighteen years, upon search it was found that they descended from the house of Eli, on which this sentence was passed.

3. That all their comforts should be embittered. (1.) The comfort they had in the sanctuary, in its wealth and prosperity: *Thou shalt see an enemy in my habitation.* This was fulfilled in the Philistines' invasions and the mischiefs they did to Israel, by which the country was impoverished (*ch.* xiii. 19), and no doubt the priests' incomes were thereby very much impaired. The captivity of the ark was such an act of hostility committed upon God's habitation as broke Eli's heart. As it is a blessing to a family to see *peace upon Israel* (Ps. cxxviii. 5, 6), so the contrary is a sore judgment upon a family, especially a family of priests. (2.) The comfort of their children: "*The man of thine whom I shall not cut off by an untimely death* shall live to be a blot and burden to the family, a scandal and vexation to his relations; he shall be to *consume thy eyes* and *grieve thy heart,* for his foolishness or his sickliness, his wickedness or his poverty." Grief for a dead child is great, but for a bad child often greater.

4. That their substance should be wasted and they should be reduced to extreme poverty (*v.* 36): "*He that is left* alive *in thy house* shall have little joy of his life, for want of a livelihood; he shall come and crouch to the succeeding family for a subsistence." (1.) He shall beg for the smallest alms—*a piece of silver* (and the word signifies the *least* piece) and *a morsel of bread.* See how this answered the sin. Eli's sons must have the best pieces of flesh, but their sons will be glad of *a morsel of bread.* Note, Want is the just punishment of wantonness. Those who could not be content without dainties and varieties are brought, they or theirs, to want necessaries, and the Lord is righteous in thus visiting them. (2.) He shall beg for the meanest office: *Put me into somewhat belonging to the priesthood* (as it is in the original); *make me as one of the hired servants,* the fittest place for a prodigal. Plenty and power are forfeited when they are abused. They should not be able to pretend to any good preferment, not to any place at the altar, but should petition for some poor employment, be the work ever so hard and the wages ever so small, so they might but get bread. This, it is probable, was fully accomplished when Abiathar, who was of Eli's race, was deposed by Solomon for treason, and he and his turned out of office in the temple (1 Kings ii. 26, 27), by which it is easy to think his posterity were reduced to the extremities here described.

5. That God would shortly begin to execute these judgments in the death of Hophni and Phinehas, the sad tidings of which Eli himself should live to hear: *This shall be a sign to thee, v.* 34. When thou hearest it, say, "Now the word of God begins to operate; here is one threatening fulfilled, from which I infer that all the rest will be fulfilled in their order." Hophni and Phinehas had many a time sinned together, and it is here foretold that they should die together both in one day. Bind these tares in a bundle for the fire. This was fulfilled, *ch.* iv. 11.

VI. In the midst of all these threatenings against the house of Eli, here is mercy promised to Israel (*v.* 35): *I will raise me up a faithful priest.* 1. This was fulfilled in Zadoc, of the family of Eleazar, who came into Abiathar's place in the beginning of Solomon's reign, and was faithful to his trust; and the high priests were of his posterity as long as the Levitical priesthood continued. Note, The wickedness of ministers, though it destroy themselves, yet it shall not destroy the ministry. How bad soever the officers are, the office shall continue always to the end of the world. If some betray their trust, yet others shall be raised up that will be true to it. God's work shall never fall to the ground for want of hands to carry it on. The high priest is here said to *walk before God's anointed* (that is, David and his seed) because he wore the breast-plate of judgment, which he was to consult, not in common cases, but for the king, in the affairs of state. Note, Notwithstanding the degeneracy we see and lament in many families, God will secure to himself a succession. If some grow worse than their ancestors, others, to balance that, shall grow better. 2. It has its full accomplishment in the priesthood of Christ, that merciful and faithful high priest whom God raised up when the Levitical priesthood was thrown off, who in all things did his father's mind, and for whom God will build a sure house, build it on a rock, so that the gates of hell cannot prevail against it.

CHAP. III.

In the foregoing chapter we had Samuel a young priest, though by birth a Levite only, for he ministered before the Lord in a linen ephod; in this chapter we have him a young prophet, which was more, God in an extraordinary manner revealing himself to him, and in him reviving, if not commencing, prophecy in Israel. Here is, I. God's first manifestation of himself in an extraordinary manner to Samuel, ver. 1—10. II. The message he sent by him to Eli, ver. 11—14. III. The faithful delivery of that message to Eli, and his submission to the righteousness of God in it, ver. 15—18. IV. The establishment of Samuel to be a prophet in Israel, ver. 19—21.

AND the child Samuel ministered unto the LORD before Eli. And the word of the LORD was precious in those days; *there was* no open vision. 2 And it came to pass at that time, when Eli *was* laid down in his place, and his eyes began to wax dim, *that* he could not see; 3 And ere the lamp of God went out in the temple of the LORD, where the ark of God *was*, and Samuel was laid down *to sleep;* 4 That the LORD called Samuel: and he answered, Here *am* I. 5 And he ran unto Eli, and said, Here *am* I; for thou calledst me. And he said, I called not; lie down again. And he went and lay down. 6 And the LORD called yet again, Samuel. And Samuel arose and went to Eli, and said, Here *am* I; for thou didst call me. And he answered, I called not, my son; lie down again. 7 Now Samuel did not yet know the LORD, neither was the word of the LORD yet revealed unto him. 8 And the LORD called Samuel again the third time. And he arose and went to Eli, and said, Here *am* I; for thou didst call me. And Eli perceived that the LORD had called the child. 9 Therefore Eli said unto Samuel, Go, lie down: and it shall be, if he call thee, that thou shalt say, Speak, LORD; for thy servant heareth. So Samuel went and lay down in his place. 10 And the LORD came, and stood, and called as at other times, Samuel, Samuel. Then Samuel answered, Speak; for thy servant heareth.

To make way for the account of God's revealing himself first to Samuel, we are here told, 1. How industrious Samuel was in serving God, according as his place and capacity were (*v.* 1): *The child Samuel,* though but a child, *ministered unto the Lord before Eli.* It was an aggravation of the wickedness of Eli's sons that the child Samuel shamed them. They rebelled against the Lord, but Samuel ministered to him; they slighted their father's admonitions, but Samuel was observant of them; he ministered before Eli, under his eye and direction It was the praise of Samuel that he was so far from being influenced by their bad example that he did not in the least fall off, but improved and went on. And it was a preparative for the honours God intended him; he that was thus faithful in a little was soon after entrusted with much more. Let those that are young be humble and diligent, which they will find the surest way to preferment. Those are fittest to rule who have learnt to obey. 2. How scarce a thing prophecy then was, which made the call of Samuel to be the greater surprise to himself and the greater favour to Israel: *The word of the Lord was precious in those days.* Now and then a man of God was employed as a messenger upon an extraordinary occasion (as *ch.* ii. 27), but there were no settled prophets, to whom the people might have recourse for counsel, nor from whom they might expect the discoveries of the divine will. And the rarity of prophecy made it the more precious in the account of all those that knew how to put a right value upon it. It was precious, for what there was (it seems) was private: *There was no open vision,* that is, there were none that were publicly known to have visions. Perhaps the impiety and impurity that prevailed in the tabernacle, and no doubt corrupted the whole nation, had provoked God, as a token of his displeasure, to withdraw the Spirit of prophecy, till the decree had gone forth for the raising up of a more faithful priest, and then, as an earnest of that, this faithful prophet was raised up.

The manner of God's revealing himself to Samuel is here related very particularly, for it was uncommon.

I. Eli had retired. Samuel had waited on

him to his bed, and the rest that attended the service of the sanctuary had gone, we may suppose, to their several apartments (*v.* 2): *Eli had laid down in his place;* he went to bed betimes, being unfit for business and soon weary of it, and perhaps loving his ease too well. Probably he kept his chamber much, which gave his sons the greater liberty. And he sought retirement the more because his eyes began to wax dim, an affliction which came justly upon him for winking at his sons' faults.

II. Samuel had laid down to sleep, in some closet near to Eli's room, as his page of the back-stairs, ready within call if the old man should want any thing in the night, perhaps to read to him if he could not sleep. He chose to take Samuel into this office rather than any of his own family, because of the towardly disposition he observed in him. When his own sons were a grief to him, his little servitor was his joy. Let those that are afflicted in their children thank God if they have any about them in whom they are comforted. *Samuel had laid down ere the lamp of God went out, v.* 3. It should seem he lay somewhere so near the holy place that he went to bed by that light, before any of the lamps in the branches of the candlestick went out (for the main lamp never went out), which probably was towards midnight. Till that time Samuel had been employing himself in some good exercise or other, reading and prayer, or perhaps cleaning or making ready the holy place; and then went softly to his bed. Then we may expect God's gracious visits, when we are constant and diligent in our duty.

III. God called him by name, and he took it for Eli's call, and ran to him *v.* 4, 5. Samuel lay awake in his bed, his thoughts, no doubt, well employed (as David's, Ps. lxiii. 6), when the Lord called to him, bishop Patrick thinks out of the most holy place, and so the Chaldee paraphrase reads it, *A voice was heard out of the temple of the Lord;* but Eli, though it is likely he lay nearer, heard it not; yet possibly it might come some other way. Hereupon we have an instance, 1. Of Samuel's industry, and readiness to wait on Eli; supposing it was he that called him, he hastened out of his warm bed and ran to him, to see if he wanted any thing, and perhaps fearing he was not well. "Here am I," said he—a good example to servants, to come when they are called; and to the younger, not only to submit to the elder, but to be careful and tender of them. 2. Of his infirmity, and unacquaintedness with the visions of the Almighty, that he took that to be only Eli's call which was really the call of God. Such mistakes as these we make oftener than we think of. God calls to us by his word, and we take it to be only the call of the minister, and answer it accordingly; he calls to us by his providences, and we look only at the instruments. His voice cries, and it is but here and there a man of wisdom that understands it to be his voice. Eli assured him he did not call him, yet did not chide him for disturbing him with being over-officious, did not call him a *fool,* and tell him he dreamed, but mildly bade him lie down again, he had nothing for him to do. If servants must be ready at their masters' call, masters also must be tender of their servants' comfort: that thy *man-servant and thy maid-servant* may *rest as well as thou.* So *Samuel went and lay down.* God calls many by the ministry of the word, and they say, as Samuel did, "Here am I;" but not looking at God, nor discerning his voice in the call, the impressions of it are soon lost; they lie down again, and their convictions come to nothing.

IV. The same call was repeated, and the same mistake made, a second and third time, *v.* 6—9. 1. God continued to call the child *yet again* (*v.* 6), and *again the third time, v.* 8. Note, The call which divine grace designs to make effectual shall be repeated till it is so, that is, till we come at the call; for the purpose of God, according to which we are called, shall certainly stand. 2. Samuel was still ignorant that it was the Lord that called him (*v.* 7): *Samuel did not yet know the Lord.* He knew the written word, and was acquainted with the mind of God in that, but he did not yet apprehend the way in which God reveals himself to his servants the prophets, especially by a *still small voice;* this was altogether new and strange to him. Perhaps he would have been sooner aware of a divine revelation had it come in a dream or a vision; but this was a way he had not only not known himself, but not heard of. Those that have the greatest knowledge of divine things must remember the time when they were as babes, unskilful in the word of righteousness *When I was a child I understood as a child.* Yet let us not despise the day of small things. *Thus did Samuel* (so the margin reads it) *before he knew the Lord, and before the word of the Lord was revealed unto him;* thus he blundered one time after another, but afterwards he understood his duty better. The witness of the Spirit in the hearts of the faithful is often thus mistaken, by which means they lose the comfort of it; and the strivings of the Spirit with the consciences of sinners are likewise often mistaken, and so the benefit of their convictions is lost. *God speaketh once, yea, twice, but man perceiveth it not,* Job xxxiii. 14. 3. Samuel went to Eli this second and third time, the voice perhaps resembling his, and the child being very near to him; and he tells Eli, with great assurance, "*Thou didst call me* (*v.* 6—8), it could be no one else." Samuels' disposition to come when he was called, though but by Eli, proving him dutiful and active, qualified him for the favour now to be shown him; God chooses to employ such

But there was a special providence in it, that he should go thus often to Eli; for hereby, at length, *Eli perceived that the Lord had called the child, v.* 8. And, (1.) This would be a mortification to him, and he would apprehend it to be a step towards his family's being degraded, that when God had something to say he should choose to say it to the child Samuel, his servant that waited on him, and not to him. And it would humble him the more when afterwards he found it was a message to himself, and yet sent to him by a child. He had reason to look upon this as a further token of God's displeasure. (2.) This would put him upon enquiring what it was that God said to Samuel, and would abundantly satisfy him of the truth and certainty of what should be delivered, and no room would be left for him to suggest that it was but a fancy of Samuel's; for before the message was delivered he himself perceived that God was about to speak to him, and yet must not know what it was till he had it from Samuel himself. Thus even the infirmities and mistakes of those whom God employs are overruled by infinite Wisdom, and made serviceable to his purposes.

V. At length Samuel was put into a posture to receive a message from God, not to be lodged with himself and go no further, but, that he might be a complete prophet, to be published and made an open vision. 1. Eli, perceiving that it was the voice of God that Samuel heard, gave him instructions what to say, *v.* 9. This was honestly done, that though it was a disgrace to him for God's call to pass him by, and be directed to Samuel, yet he put him in the way how to entertain it. Had he been envious of this honour done to Samuel, he would have done what he could to deprive him of it, and, since he did not perceive it himself, would have bidden him lie down and sleep, and never heed it, it was but a dream; but he was of a better spirit than to act so; he gave him the best advice he could, for the forwarding of his advancement. Thus the elder should, without grudging, do their utmost to assist and improve the younger that are rising up, though they see themselves likely to be darkened and eclipsed by them. Let us never be wanting to inform and instruct those that are coming after us, even such as will soon be preferred before us, John i. 30. The instruction Eli gave him was, when God called the next time, to say, *Speak, Lord, for thy servant heareth.* He must call himself God's servant, must desire to know the mind of God. "*Speak, Lord,* speak to me, speak now:" and he must prepare to hear, and promise to attend: *Thy servant heareth.* Note, Then we may expect that God will speak to us, when we set ourselves to hearken to what he says, Ps. lxxxv. 8; Hab. ii. 1. When we come to read the word of God, and to attend on the preaching of it, we should come thus disposed, submitting ourselves to the commanding light and power of it: *Speak, Lord, for thy servant heareth.* 2. It should seem that God spoke the fourth time in a way somewhat different from the other; though the call was, as at other times, a call to him by name, yet now *he stood and called,* which intimates that there was now some visible appearance of the divine glory to Samuel, a vision that stood before him, like that before Eliphaz, though he *could not discern the form thereof,* Job iv. 16. This satisfied him that it was not Eli that called; for he now *saw the voice that spoke with him,* as it is expressed, Rev. i. 12. Now also the call was doubled—*Samuel, Samuel,* as if God delighted in the mention of his name, or to intimate that now he should be made to understand who spoke to him. *God hath spoken once, twice have I heard this,* Ps. lxii. 11. It was an honour to him that God was pleased to *know him by name* (Exod. xxxiii. 12), and then his call was powerful and effectual when he called him by name, and so brought it particularly to him, as *Saul, Saul.* Thus God called to Abraham by name, Gen. xxii. 1. 3. Samuel said, as he was taught, *Speak, for thy servant heareth.* Note, Good words should be put into children's mouths betimes, and apt expressions of pious and devout affections, by which they may be prepared for a better acquaintance with divine things, and trained up to a holy converse with them. Teach young people what they shall say, for *they cannot order their speech by reason of darkness.* Samuel did not now rise and run as before when he thought Eli called, but lay still and listened. The more sedate and composed our spirits are the better prepared they are for divine discoveries. Let all tumultuous thoughts and passions be kept under, and every thing be quiet and serene in the soul, and then we are fit to hear from God. All must be silent when he speaks. But observe, Samuel left out one word; he did not say, *Speak, Lord,* but only, *Speak, for thy servant heareth,* perhaps, as bishop Patrick suggests, out of uncertainty whether it was God that spoke to him or no. However, by this answer, *Speak, for thy servant heareth,* way was made for the message he was now to receive, and Samuel was brought acquainted with the words of God and visions of the Almighty, and this *ere the lamp of God went out* (*v.* 3) *in the temple of the Lord,* which some of the Jewish writers put a mystical sense upon; before the fall of Eli, and the eclipsing of the Urim and Thummim for some time thereby, God called Samuel, and made him an oracle, whence they have an observation among their doctors, *That the sun riseth, and the sun goeth down* (Eccl. i. 5), that is, say they, Ere God maketh the sun of one righteous man to set, he makes the sun of another righteous man to rise. *Smith ex Kimchi.*

11 And the LORD said to Samuel,

Behold, I will do a thing in Israel, at which both the ears of every one that heareth it shall tingle. 12 In that day I will perform against Eli all *things* which I have spoken concerning his house: when I begin, I will also make an end. 13 For I have told him that I will judge his house for ever for the iniquity which he knoweth; because his sons made themselves vile, and he restrained them not. 14 And therefore I have sworn unto the house of Eli, that the iniquity of Eli's house shall not be purged with sacrifice nor offering for ever. 15 And Samuel lay until the morning, and opened the doors of the house of the LORD. And Samuel feared to show Eli the vision. 16 Then Eli called Samuel, and said, Samuel, my son. And he answered, Here *am* I. 17 And he said, What *is* the thing that *the LORD* hath said unto thee? I pray thee hide *it* not from me: God do so to thee, and more also, if thou hide *any* thing from me of all the things that he said unto thee. 18 And Samuel told him every whit, and hid nothing from him. And he said, It *is* the LORD: let him do what seemeth him good.

Here is, I. The message which, after all this introduction, God delivered to Samuel concerning Eli's house. God did not come to him now to tell him how great a man he should be in his day, what a figure he should make, and what a blessing he should be in Israel. Young people have commonly a great curiosity to be told their fortune, but God came to Samuel, not to gratify his curiosity, but to employ him in his service and send him on an errand to another person, which was much better; and yet the matter of this first message, which no doubt made a very great impression upon him, might be of good use to him afterwards, when his own sons proved, though not so bad as Eli's, yet not so good as they should have been, *ch.* viii. 3. The message is short, not nearly so long as that which the man of God brought, *ch.* ii. 27. For, Samuel being a child, it could not be expected that he should remember a long message, and God considered his frame. The memories of children must not be overcharged, no, not with divine things. But it is a sad message, a message of wrath, to ratify the message in the former chapter, and to bind on the sentence there pronounced, because perhaps Eli did not give so much regard to that as he ought to have done. Divine threatenings, the less they are heeded, the surer they will come and the heavier they will fall. Reference is here had to what was there said concerning both the sin and the punishment.

1. Concerning the sin: it is the *iniquity that he knoweth, v.* 13. The man of God told him of it, and many a time his own conscience had told him of it. O what a great deal of guilt and corruption is there in us concerning which we may say, "It is the iniquity *which our own heart knoweth,* we are conscious to ourselves of it!" In short, the iniquity was this: *His sons made themselves vile, and he restrained them not.* Or, as it is in the Hebrew, he *frowned not upon them.* If he did show his dislike of their wicked courses, yet not to that degree that he ought to have done: he did reprove them, but he did not punish them, for the mischief they did, nor deprive them of their power to do mischief, which as a father, high priest, and judge, he might have done. Note, (1.) Sinners do by their own wickedness make themselves vile. They debauch themselves (for *every man is tempted when he is drawn aside of his own lusts,* Jam. i. 14) and thereby they debase themselves, and make themselves not only mean, but odious to the holy God and holy men and angels. Sin is a vile thing, and degrades men more than any thing, Ps. xv. 4. Eli's sons made light of God, and made his offerings vile in the people's eyes; but the shame returned into their own bosom: they *made themselves vile.* (2.) Those that do not restrain the sins of others, when it is in the power of their hand to do it, make themselves partakers of the guilt, and will be charged as accessaries: Those in authority will have a great deal to answer for if they make not the sword they bear a *terror to evil workers.*

2. Concerning the punishment: it is *that which I have spoken concerning his house, v.* 12 and 13. *I have told him that I will judge his house for ever,* that is, that a curse should be entailed upon his family from generation to generation. The particulars of this curse we had before; they are not here repeated, but it is added, (1.) That when that sentence began to be executed it would be very dreadful and amazing to all Israel (*v.* 11): *Both the ears of every one that hears it shall tingle.* Every Israelite would be struck with terror and astonishment to hear of the slaying of Eli's sons, the breaking of Eli's neck, and the dispersion of Eli's family. Lord, how terrible art thou in thy judgments! If this be done in a green tree, what shall be done in the dry? Note, God's judgments upon others should affect us with a holy fear, Ps. cxix. 120. (2.) That these direful first-fruits of the execution would be certain earnests of the progress and full accomplishment of it: *When I begin I will* proceed and *make an end* of all that I have threatened, *v.* 12. It is intimated that it might possibly

be some time before he would begin, but let them not call that forbearance an acquittance, nor that reprieve a pardon; for when at length he does begin he will make thorough work of it, and, though he stay long, he will strike home. (3.) That no room should be left for hope that this sentence might be reversed and the execution stayed or mitigated, *v.* 14. [1.] God would not revoke the sentence, for he backed it with an oath: *I have sworn to the house of Eli;* and God will not go back from what he has sworn either in mercy or judgment. [2.] He would never come to a composition for the forfeiture: "The *iniquity of Eli's house shall not be purged with sacrifice nor offering for ever.* No atonement shall be made for the sin, nor any abatement of the punishment." This was the imperfection of the legal sacrifices, that there were iniquities which they did not reach, which they would not purge; *but the blood of Christ cleanseth from all sin,* and secures all those that by faith are interested in it from that eternal death which is the wages of sin.

II. The delivery of this message to Eli. Observe,

1. Samuel's modest concealment of it, *v.* 15. (1.) He *lay till the morning,* and we may well suppose he lay awake pondering on what he had heard, repeating it to himself, and considering what use he must make of it. After we have received the spiritual food of God's word, it is good to compose ourselves, and give it time to digest. (2.) *He opened the doors of the house of the Lord,* in the morning, as he used to do, being up first in the tabernacle. That he should do so at other times was an instance of extraordinary towardliness in a child, but that he should do so this morning was an instance of great humility. God had highly honoured him above all the children of his people, yet he was not proud of the honour, nor puffed up with it, did not think himself too great and too good to be employed in these mean and servile offices, but, as cheerfully as ever, went and opened the doors of the tabernacle. Note, Those to whom God manifests himself he makes and keeps low in their own eyes, and willing to stoop to any thing by which they may be serviceable to his glory, though but as door-keepers in his house. One would have expected that Samuel would be so full of his vision as to forget his ordinary service, that he would go among his companions, as one in an ecstasy, to tell them what converse he had had with God this night; but he modestly keeps it to himself, tells the vision to no man, but silently goes on in his business. Our secret communion with God is not to be proclaimed upon the house-tops. (3.) *He feared to show Eli the vision.* If he was afraid Eli would be angry with him and chide him, then we have cause to suspect that Eli used to be as severe with this towardly child as he was indulgent to his own wicked sons, and this will bear hard upon him. But we will suppose it was rather because he was afraid to grieve and trouble the good old man that he was so shy. If he had run immediately with the tidings to Eli, this would have looked as if he desired the woeful day and hoped to build his own family upon the ruin of Eli's; therefore it became him not to be forward to declare the vision. No good man can take pleasure in bringing evil tidings, especially not Samuel to Eli, the pupil to the tutor whom he loves and honours.

2. Eli's careful enquiry into it, *v.* 16, 17. As soon as ever he heard Samuel stirring he called for him, probably to his bed-side; and, having before perceived that God had spoken to him, he obliged him, not only by importunity *(I pray thee, hide it not from me),* but, finding him timorous and backward, by an adjuration likewise—*God do so to thee, and more also, if thou hide any thing from me!* He had reason enough to fear that the message prophesied no good concerning him, but evil; and yet, because it was a message from God, he could not contentedly be ignorant of it. A good man desires to be acquainted with all the will of God, whether it make for him or against him. His adjuration—*God do so to thee, if thou hide any thing from me*—may intimate the fearful doom of unfaithful watchmen; if they warn not sinners, they bring upon themselves that wrath and curse which they should have denounced, in God's name, against those that *go on still in their trespasses.*

3. Samuel's faithful delivery of his message at last (*v.* 18): *He told him every whit.* When he saw that he must tell him he never minced the matter, nor offered to make it better than it was, to blunt that which was sharp, or to gild the bitter pill, but delivered the message as plainly and fully as he received it, *not shunning to declare the whole counsel of God.* Christ's ministers must deal thus faithfully.

4. Eli's pious acquiescence in it. He did not question Samuel's integrity, was not cross with him, nor had he any thing to object against the equity of the sentence. He did not complain of the punishment, as Cain did, that it was greater than he either deserved or could bear, but patiently submitted, and accepted the punishment of his iniquity *It is the Lord, let him do what seemeth him good.* He understood the sentence to intend only a temporal punishment, and the entail of disgrace and poverty upon his posterity, and not a final separation of them from the favour of God, and therefore he cheerfully submitted, did not repine, because he knew the demerits of his family; nor did he now intercede for the reversing of the sentence, because God had ratified it with a solemn oath, of which he would not repent. He therefore composes himself into a humble

resignation to God's will, as Aaron, in a case not much unlike. Lev. x. 3, *He held his peace.* In a few words, (1.) He lays down this satisfying truth, "*It is the Lord;* it is he that pronounces the judgment, from whose bar there lies no appeal and against whose sentence there lies no exception. It is he that will execute the judgment, whose power cannot be resisted, his justice arraigned, nor his sovereignty contested. *It is the Lord,* who will thus sanctify and glorify himself, and it is highly fit he should. *It is the Lord,* with whom there is no unrighteousness, who never did nor ever will do any wrong to any of his creatures, nor exact more than their iniquity deserves." (2.) He infers from it this satisfying conclusion: "*Let him do what seemeth him good.* I have nothing to say against his proceedings. He is righteous in all his ways and holy in all his works, and therefore *his will be done. I will bear the indignation of the Lord, because I have sinned against him.*" Thus we ought to quiet ourselves under God's rebukes, and never to strive with our Maker.

19 And Samuel grew, and the LORD was with him, and did let none of his words fall to the ground. 20 And all Israel from Dan even to Beer-sheba knew that Samuel *was* established *to be* a prophet of the LORD. 21 And the LORD appeared again in Shiloh: for the LORD revealed himself to Samuel in Shiloh by the word of the LORD.

Samuel being thus brought acquainted with the visions of God, we have here an account of the further honour done him as a prophet.

I. God did him honour. Having begun to favour him, he carried on and crowned his own work in him: *Samuel grew, for the Lord was with him, v.* 19. All our increase in wisdom and grace is owing to the presence of God with us; this is all in all to our growth. God honoured Samuel, 1. By further manifestations of himself to him. Samuel had faithfully delivered the message he was entrusted with, and therefore God employed him again in his service: *The Lord revealed himself again to Samuel in Shiloh, v.* 21. Note, God will graciously repeat his visits to those that receive them aright. 2. By fulfilling what he spoke by him: *God did let none of his words fall to the ground, v.* 19. Whatever Samuel said, as a prophet, it proved true, and was accomplished in its season. Probably there were some remarkable instances of the truth of Samuel's predictions that happened soon after, which confirmed those that were afterwards to be fulfilled, and gave general satisfaction as to his mission. God will *confirm the word of his servants,* and *perform the counsel of his messengers* (Isa. xliv. 26), and will do what he hath said.

II. Israel did him honour. They all knew and owned *that Samuel was established to be a prophet, v.* 20. 1. He grew famous; all that came up to Shiloh to worship took notice of him, and admired him, and talked of him when they returned home. Early piety will be the greatest honour of young people, and bring them, as much as any thing, and as soon, into reputation. Those that honour God he will honour. 2. He grew useful and very serviceable to his generation. He that began betimes to *be* good soon came to *do* good. His established commission from God, and established reputation with the people, gave him a great opportunity of shining as a light in Israel. When old Eli was rejected, young Samuel was established; for God will never leave himself without a witness nor his church without a guide.

CHAP. IV.

The predictions in the foregoing chapters concerning the ruin of Eli's house here begin to be fulfilled; how long after does not appear, but certainly not long. Such sinners God often makes quick work with. Here is, I. The disgrace and loss Israel sustained in an encounter with the Philistines, ver. 1, 2. II. Their foolish project to fortify themselves by bringing the ark of God into their camp upon the shoulders of Hophni and Phinehas (ver. 3, 4), which made them secure (ver. 5) and struck a fear into the Philistines, but such a fear as roused them, ver. 6—9. III. The fatal consequences of it: Israel was beaten, and the ark taken prisoner, ver. 10, 11. IV. The tidings of this brought to Shiloh, and the sad reception of those tidings. 1. The city was put into confusion, ver. 12, 13. 2. Eli fainted away, fell, and broke his neck, ver. 14—18. 3. Upon hearing what had occurred his daughter-in-law fell in labour, bore a son, but died immediately, ver. 19—22. These were the things which would make the ears of those that heard them to tingle.

AND the word of Samuel came to all Israel. Now Israel went out against the Philistines to battle, and pitched beside Eben-ezer: and the Philistines pitched in Aphek. 2 And the Philistines put themselves in array against Israel: and when they joined battle, Israel was smitten before the Philistines: and they slew of the army in the field about four thousand men. 3 And when the people were come into the camp, the elders of Israel said, Wherefore hath the LORD smitten us to day before the Philistines? Let us fetch the ark of the covenant of the LORD out of Shiloh unto us, that, when it cometh among us, it may save us out of the hand of our enemies. 4 So the people sent to Shiloh, that they might bring from thence the ark of the covenant of the LORD of hosts, which dwelleth *between* the cherubims: and the two sons of Eli, Hophni and Phinehas, *were* there with the ark of the covenant of God. 5 And when the ark of the covenant of the

LORD came into the camp, all Israel shouted with a great shout, so that the earth rang again. 6 And when the Philistines heard the noise of the shout, they said, What *meaneth* the noise of this great shout in the camp of the Hebrews? And they understood that the ark of the LORD was come into the camp. 7 And the Philistines were afraid, for they said, God is come into the camp. And they said, Woe unto us! for there hath not been such a thing heretofore. 8 Woe unto us! who shall deliver us out of the hand of these mighty Gods? these *are* the Gods that smote the Egyptians with all the plagues in the wilderness. 9 Be strong, and quit yourselves like men, O ye Philistines, that ye be not servants unto the Hebrews, as they have been to you: quit yourselves like men, and fight.

The first words of this paragraph, which relate to Samuel, that *his word came to all Israel,* seem not to have any reference to the following story, as if it was by any direction of his that the Israelites went out against the Philistines. Had they consulted him, though but newly initiated as a prophet, his counsel might have stood them in more stead than the presence of the ark did; but perhaps the princes of Israel despised his youth, and would not have recourse to him as an oracle, and he did not as yet interpose in public affairs; nor do we find any mention of his name henceforward till some years after (*ch.* vii. 3), only *his word came to all Israel,* that is, people from all parts that were piously disposed had recourse to him as a prophet and consulted him. Perhaps it is meant of his prophecy against the house of Eli. This was generally known and talked of, and all that were serious and observing compared the events here related, when they came to pass, with the prophecy, and saw it accomplished in them. Here is,

I. A war entered into with the Philistines, *v.* 1. It was an attempt to throw off the yoke of their oppression, and would have succeeded better if they had first repented and reformed, and so begun their work at the right end. It is computed that this was about the middle of the forty years' dominion that the Philistines had over Israel (Judg. xiii. 1) and soon after the death of Samson; so bishop Patrick, who thinks the slaughter he made at his death might encourage this attempt; but Dr. Lightfoot reckons it forty years after Samson's death, for so long Eli judged, *v.* 18.

II. The defeat of Israel in that war, *v.* 2. Israel, who were the aggressors, were smitten, and had 4000 men killed upon the spot. God had promised that one of them should chase a thousand; but now, on the contrary, *Israel is smitten before the Philistines.* Sin, the accursed thing, was in the camp, and gave their enemies all the advantage against them they could wish for.

III. The measures they concerted for another engagement. A council of war was called, and, instead of resolving to fast and pray and amend their lives, so ill taught were they (and no wonder when they had such teachers) that, 1. They quarrelled with God for appearing against them (*v.* 3): *Wherefore has the Lord smitten us?* If they meant this as an enquiry into the cause of God's displeasure, they needed not go far to find that out. It was plain enough; Israel had sinned, though they were not willing to see it and own it. But it rather seems that they expostulate boldly with God about it, are displeased at what God has done, and dispute the matter with him. They own the hand of God in their trouble (so far was right): "It is the Lord that has smitten us;" but, instead of submitting to it, they quarrel with it, and speak as those that are angry at him and his providence, and not aware of any just provocation they have given him: "Wherefore shall we, that are Israelites, be smitten before the Philistines? How absurd and unjust is it!" Note, The foolishness of man perverts his way, and then his heart *frets against the Lord* (Prov. xix. 3) and finds fault with him. 2. They imagined that they could oblige him to appear for them the next time by bringing the ark into their camp. The elders of Israel were so ignorant and foolish as to make the proposal (*v.* 3), and the people soon put it in execution, *v.* 4. They sent to Shiloh for the ark, and Eli had not courage enough to detain it, but sent his ungodly sons, Hophni and Phinehas, along with it, at least permitted them to go, though he knew that wherever they went the curse of God went along with them. Now see here, (1.) The profound veneration the people had for the ark. "O send for that, and it will do wonders for us." The ark was, by institution, a visible token of God's presence. God had said that he would dwell *between the cherubim,* which were over the ark and were carried along with it; now they thought that, by paying a great respect to this sacred chest, they should prove themselves to be Israelites indeed, and effectually engage God Almighty to appear in their favour. Note, It is common for those that have estranged themselves from the vitals of religion to discover a great fondness for the rituals and external observances of it, for those that even deny the power of godliness not only to have, but to have in admiration, the form of it. The temple of the Lord is cried up, and the ark of the Lord stickled for with a great deal of seeming zeal by multitudes that have no regard at all for the Lord of the temple and the God of the ark, as if a fiery concern for the name of Christianity would atone for a profane contempt of the thing. And yet indeed they did but make an idol of the ark, and looked upon it to be as much an image of the God of Israel as those idols which the heathen worshipped were of their gods. To worship the true God, and not to worship him as God, is in effect not to worship him at all. (2.) Their egregious folly in thinking that the ark, if they had it in their camp, would certainly *save them out of the hand of their enemies*, and bring victory back to their side. For, [1.] When the ark set forward Moses prayed, *Rise up, Lord, and let thy enemies be scattered*, well knowing that it was not the ark moving with them, but God appearing for them, that must give them success; and here were no proper means used to engage God to favour them with his presence; what good then would the ark do them, the shell without the kernel? [2.] They were so far from having God's leave to remove his ark that he had plainly enough intimated to them in his law that when they were settled in Canaan his ark should be settled in the place that he should choose (Deut. xii. 5, 11), and that they must come to it, not it to them. How then could they expect any advantage by it when they had not a just and legal possession of it, nor any warrant to remove it from its place? Instead of honouring God by what they did, they really affronted him. Nay, [3.] If there had been nothing else to invalidate their expectations from the ark, how could they expect it should bring a blessing when Hophni and Phinehas were the men that carried it? It would have given too much countenance to their villany if the ark had done any kindness to Israel while it was in the hands of those graceless priests.

IV. The great joy there was in the camp of Israel when the ark was brought into it (*v.* 5): *They shouted, so that the earth rang again.* Now they thought themselves sure of victory, and therefore gave a triumphant shout before the battle, as if the day was without fail their own, intending, by this mighty shout, to animate themselves and their own forces, and to intimidate their adversaries. Note, Carnal people triumph much in the external privileges and performances of religion, and build much upon them, as if these would infallibly save them, and as if the ark, God's throne, in the camp, would bring them to heaven, though the world and the flesh should be upon the throne in the heart.

V. The consternation into which the bringing of the ark into the camp of Israel put the Philistines. The two armies lay so near encamped that the Philistines heard the shout the Israelites gave on this great occasion. They soon understood what it was they triumphed in (*v.* 6), and were afraid of the consequences. For, 1. It had never been done before in their days: *God has come into their camp*, and therefore *woe unto us* (*v.* 7), and again, *woe unto us, v.* 8. The name of the God of Israel was formidable even to those that worshipped other gods, and some apprehensions even the infidels had of the danger of contending with them. Natural conscience suggests this, that those are in a woeful condition who have God against them. Yet see what gross notions they had of the divine presence, as if the God of Israel were not as much in the camp before the ark came thither, which may very well be excused in them, since the notions the Israelites themselves had of that presence were no better. "O," say they, "this is a new design upon us, more frightful than all their stratagems, for *there has not been such a thing heretofore;* this was the most effectual course they could take to dispirit our men and weaken their hands." 2. When it had been done in the days of old, it had wrought wonders: *These are the gods that smote the Egyptians with all the plagues in the wilderness, v.* 8. Here they were as much out in their history as in their divinity: the plagues of Egypt were inflicted before the ark was made and before Israel came into the wilderness; but some confused traditions they had of wonders wrought by or for Israel when this ark was carried before them, which they attributed, not to Jehovah, but to the ark. Now, say they, *Who shall deliver us out of the hand of these mighty gods?* taking the ark for God, as well they might when the Israelites themselves idolized it. Yet, it should seem, they scarcely believed themselves when they spoke thus formidably of *these mighty gods*, but only bantered; for instead of retreating, or proposing conditions of peace, which they would have done had they been really convinced of the power of Israel's God, they stirred up one another to fight so much the more stoutly; this surprising difficulty did but sharpen their resolution (*v.* 9): *Be strong, and quit yourselves like men.* The commanders inspired bold and generous thoughts into the minds of their soldiers when they bade them remember how they had lorded it over Israel, and what an intolerable grief and shame it would be if they flinched now, and suffered Israel to lord it over them.

10 And the Philistines fought, and Israel was smitten, and they fled every man into his tent: and there was a very great slaughter; for there fell of Israel thirty thousand footmen. 11 And the ark of God was taken; and the two sons of Eli, Hophni and Phinehas, were slain.

Here is a short account of the issue of this battle.

I. Israel was smitten, the army dispersed and totally routed, not retiring into the camp, as before (*v.* 2) when they hoped to rally again, but returning to their tents, every man shifting for his own safety and making the best of his way home, despairing to make head any more; and 30,000 were slain in the field of battle, *v.* 10. Israel was put to the worse, 1. Though they had the better cause, were the people of God and the Philistines were uncircumcised; they stood up in necessary defence of their just rights and liberties against invaders, and yet they failed of success, for *their rock had sold them.* A good cause often suffers for the sake of the bad men that undertake it. 2. Though they had the greater confidence, and were the more courageous. They shouted, while the Philistines trembled, and yet, when God pleased so to order it, the Philistines' terrors were turned into triumphs, and Israel's shouts into lamentations. 3. Though they had the ark of God with them. External privileges will secure none that abuse them and do not live up to them. The ark in the camp will add nothing to its strength when there is an Achan in it.

II. The ark itself was taken by the Philistines; and Hophni and Phinehas, who it is likely kept close to it, and when it was in danger ventured far in the defence of it, because by it they got their living, were *both slain, v.* 11. To this sad event the Psalmist refers, Ps. lxxviii. 61, 64, *He delivered his strength into captivity, and his glory into the enemy's hands. Their priests fell by the sword.* 1. The slaughter of the priests, considering their bad character, was no great loss to Israel, but it was a dreadful judgment upon the house of Eli. The word which God had spoken was fulfilled in it (*ch.* ii. 34): *This shall be a sign unto thee,* an earnest of the judgments threatened, *thy two sons shall die both in one day,* and so shall all *the increase of thy house die in the flower of their age, v.* 33. If Eli had done his duty, and *put them, as polluted, from the priesthood* (Neh. vii. 64), they might have lived, though in disgrace; but now God takes the work into his own hands, and chases them out of the world by the sword of the uncircumcised. *The Lord is known by those judgments which he executeth.* It is true the sword devours one as well as another, but these were waited for of the sword, marked for vengeance. They were out of their place; what had they to do in the camp? When men leave the way of their duty they shut themselves out of God's protection. But this was not all; they had betrayed the ark, by bringing it into danger, without a warrant from God, and this filled the measure of their iniquities. But, 2. The taking of the ark was a very great judgment upon Israel, and a certain token of God's hot displeasure against them. Now they are made to see their folly in trusting to their external privileges when they had by their wickedness forfeited them, and fancying that the ark would save them when God had departed from them. Now they are made to reflect, with the utmost regret, upon their own rashness and presumption in bringing the ark into the camp and so exposing it, and wish a thousand times they had left it where God had fixed it. Now they are convinced that God will not be prescribed to by vain and foolish men, and that though he has bound us to his ark he has not bound himself to it, but will rather deliver it into the hands of his sworn enemies than suffer it to be profaned by his false friends, and countenance their superstition. Let none think to shelter themselves from the wrath of God under the cloak of a visible profession, for there will be those cast into outer darkness that have *eaten and drunk in Christ's presence.*

12 And there ran a man of Benjamin out of the army, and came to Shiloh the same day with his clothes rent, and with earth upon his head. 13 And when he came, lo, Eli sat upon a seat by the wayside watching: for his heart trembled for the ark of God. And when the man came into the city, and told *it,* all the city cried out. 14 And when Eli heard the noise of the crying, he said, What *meaneth* the noise of this tumult? And the man came in hastily, and told Eli. 15 Now Eli was ninety and eight years old; and his eyes were dim, that he could not see. 16 And the man said unto Eli, I *am* he that came out of the army, and I fled to day out of the army. And he said, What is there done, my son? 17 And the messenger answered and said, Israel is fled before the Philistines, and there hath been also a great slaughter among the people, and thy two sons also, Hophni and Phinehas, are dead, and the ark of God is taken. 18 And it came to pass, when he made mention of the ark of God, that he fell from off the seat backward by the side of the gate, and his neck brake, and he died: for he was an old man, and heavy. And he had judged Israel forty years.

Tidings are here brought to Shiloh of the fatal issue of their battle with the Philistines. Bad news flies fast. This soon spread through all Israel; every man that fled to his tent brought it, with too plain a proof of it, to his neighbours. But no place was so nearly concerned as Shiloh. Thither therefore an express posted away immediately; it was a man of Benjamin; the Jews fancy it was Saul. *He rent his clothes, and put earth upon his head,* by these signs to proclaim the sorrowful news to all that saw him as he ran, and to show how much he himself was affected with it, *v.* 12. He went straight to Shiloh with it; and here we are told,

I. How the city received it. *Eli sat in the gate* (*v.* 13, 18), but the messenger was loth to tell him first, and therefore passed him by, and told it in the city, with all the aggravating circumstances; and now *both the ears of every one that heard it tingled,* as was foretold, *ch.* iii. 11. Their hearts trembled, and every face gathered blackness. *All the city cried out* (*v.* 13), and well they might, for, besides that this was a calamity to all Israel, it was a particular loss to Shiloh, and the ruin of that place; for, though the ark was soon rescued out of the hands of the Philistines, yet it never returned to Shiloh again; their candlestick was removed out of its place, because they had *left their first love,* and their city dwindled, and sunk, and came to nothing. Now God *forsook the tabernacle of Shiloh,* they having driven him from them; and the tribe of Ephraim, which had for 340 years been blessed with the presence of the ark in it, lost the honour (Ps. lxxviii. 60, 67), and, some time after, it was transferred to the tribe of Judah, the *Mount Sion which he loved,* as it follows there (*v.* 68), because the men of Shiloh knew not *the day of their visitation.* This abandoning of Shiloh Jerusalem is long afterwards reminded of, and told to take warning by. Jer. vii. 12, "*Go see what I did to Shiloh.* From this day, this fatal day, let the desolations of Shiloh be dated." They had therefore reason enough to cry out when they heard that the ark was taken.

II. What a fatal blow it was to old Eli. Let us see, 1. With what fear he expected the tidings. Though old, and blind, and heavy, yet he could not keep his chamber when he was sensible the glory of Israel lay at stake, but placed himself by the way-side, to receive the first intelligence; for *his heart trembled for the ark of God, v.* 13. His careful thoughts represented to him what a dishonour it would be to God, and what an irreparable loss to Israel, if the ark should fall into the Philistines' hands, with what profane triumphs the tidings would be told in Gath and published in the streets of Ashkelon. He also apprehended what imminent danger there was of it. Israel had forfeited the ark (his own sons especially) and the Philistines would aim at it; and now the threatening comes to his mind, that he should *see an enemy in God's habitation* (*ch.* ii. 32); and perhaps his own heart reproached him for not using his authority to prevent the carrying of the ark into the camp. All these things made him tremble. Note, All good men lay the interests of God's church nearer their hearts than any secular interest or concern of their own, and cannot but be in pain and fear for them if at any time they are in peril. How can we be easy if the ark be not safe? 2. With what grief he received the tidings. Though he could not see, he could hear the *tumult* and *crying of the city,* and perceived it to be the voice of lamentation, and mourning, and woe; like a careful magistrate, he asks, *What means the noise of this tumult? v.* 14. He is told there is an express come from the army, who relates the story to him very distinctly, and with great confidence, having himself been an eye-witness of it, *v.* 16, 17. The account of the defeat of the army, and the slaughter of a great number of the soldiers, was very grievous to him as a judge; the tidings of the death of his two sons, of whom he had been so indulgent, and who, he had reason to fear, died impenitent, touched him in a tender part as a father; yet it was not for these that his heart trembled: there is a greater concern upon his spirit, which swallows up the less; he does not interrupt the narrative with any passionate lamentations for his sons, like David for Absalom, but waits for the end of the story, not doubting but that the messenger, being an Israelite, would, without being asked, say something of the ark; and if he could but have said, "Yet the ark of God is safe, and we are bringing that home," his joy for that would have overcome his grief for all the other disasters, and have made him easy; but, when the messenger concludes his story with, *The ark of God is taken,* he is struck to the heart, his spirits fail, and, it should seem, he swooned away, fell off his seat, and partly with the fainting, and partly with the fall, he died immediately, and never spoke a word more. His heart was broken first, and then his neck. So fell the high priest and judge of Israel, so fell his heavy head when he had lived within two of 100 years, so fell the crown from his head when he had judged Israel about forty years: thus did his sun set under a cloud, thus were the folly and wickedness of those sons of his, whom he had indulged, his ruin at last. Thus does God sometimes set marks of his displeasure in this life upon good men who have misconducted themselves, that others may hear, and fear, and take warning. A man may die miserably and yet not die eternally, may come to an untimely end and yet the end be peace. Dr. Lightfoot observes that Eli died the death of an unredeemed ass, whose neck was to be broken, Exod. xiii. 13. Yet we must observe, to Eli's praise, that it was the loss of the ark that was his death, not the slaughter of his sons. He does, in effect, say, "Let me fall with the ark, for what pious Israelite can live with any comfort when God's ordinances are removed?" Farewell all in this world, even life itself, if the ark be gone.

19 And his daughter in law, Phinehas' wife, was with child, *near* to be delivered: and when she heard the tidings that the ark of God was taken, and that her father in law and her husband were dead, she bowed herself and travailed; for her pains came upon her. 20 And about the time of her death the women that stood by her said unto her, Fear not; for thou hast borne a son. But she answered not, neither did she regard *it*. 21 And she named the child I-chabod, saying, The glory is departed from Israel: because the ark of God was taken, and because of her father in law and her husband. 22 And she said, The glory is departed from Israel: for the ark of God is taken.

We have here another melancholy story, that carries on the desolations of Eli's house, and the sorrowful feeling which the tidings of the ark's captivity excited. It is concerning the wife of Phinehas, one of those ungracious sons of Eli that had brought all this mischief on Israel. It cost her her life, though young, as well as that of her father-in-law, that was old; for many a green head, as well as many a hoary head, has been brought by sorrow to the grave: it worketh death. By what is here related of her it appears,

I. That she was a woman of a very tender spirit. Providence so ordered it that, just at this time, she was near her time; and our Saviour hath said, *Woe to those that are with child,* or *give suck,* in such days as these, Matt. xxiv. 19. So little joy will there then be in the birth, even of a man-child, that it will be said, *Blessed are the wombs that bear not,* Luke xxiii. 29. The amazing news coming at this unhappy juncture, it put her into labour, as great frights or other strong passions sometimes do. When she heard of the death of her father-in law whom she reverenced, and her husband whom, bad as he was, she loved, but especially of the loss of the ark, *she travailed, for her pains came* thickly *upon her* (*v.* 19), and the tidings so seized her spirits, at a time when they needed all possible supports, that, though she had strength to bear the child, she, soon after, fainted and died away, being very willing to let life go when she had lost the greatest comforts of her life. Those who are drawing near to that trying hour have need to treasure up for themselves comforts from the covenant of grace, to balance, not only the usual sorrows, but any thing extraordinary that may add to the grief which they do not foresee. Faith, at such a time, will keep from fainting, Ps. xxvii. 13.

II. That she was a woman of a very gracious spirit, though matched to a wicked husband. Her concern for the death of her husband and father-in-law was an evidence of her natural affection; but her much greater concern for the loss of the ark was an evidence of her pious and devout affection to God and sacred things. The former helped to hasten her travail, but it appears by her dying words that the latter lay nearer her heart (*v.* 22): *She said, The glory has departed from Israel,* not lamenting so much the sinking of that particular family to which she was related as the general calamity of Israel in the captivity of the ark. This, this was it that was her grief, that was her death.

1. This made her regardless of her child. The women that attended her, who it is likely were some of the first rank in the city, encouraged her, and, thinking that her concern was mostly about the issue of her pains, when the child was born, *said unto her, Fear not,* now the worst is past, *for thou hast borne a son* (and perhaps it was her first-born), *but she answered not, neither did she regard it.* The sorrows of her travail, if she had no other, would have been *forgotten, for joy that a man-child was born into the world.* John xvi. 21. But what is that joy, (1.) To one that feels herself dying? No joy but that which is spiritual and divine will stand us in any stead then. Death is too serious a thing to admit the relish of any earthly joy; it is all flat and sapless then. (2.) What is it to one that is lamenting the loss of the ark? Small comfort could she have of a child born in Israel, in Shiloh, when the ark is lost, and is a prisoner in the land of the Philistines. What pleasure can we take in our creature-comforts and enjoyments if we want God's word and ordinances, especially if we want the comfort of his gracious presence and the light of his countenance? *As vinegar upon nitre, so is he that sings songs* to such *heavy hearts.*

2. This made her give her child a name which should perpetuate the remembrance of the calamity and her sense of it. She has nothing to say to the child, only it being her province, now that her husband was dead, to name the child, she orders them to call it *I-chabod,* that is, *Where is the glory?* Or, *Alas for the glory!* or, *There is no glory* (*v.* 21), which she thus explains with her dying lips (*v.* 22): "*The glory has departed from Israel; for the ark of God is taken.* Call the child inglorious, for so he is; the beauty of Israel is lost, and there appears no hope of ever retrieving it; never let the name of an Israelite, much less a priest, carry glory in it any more, now that the ark is taken." Note, (1.) The purity and plenty of God's ordinances, and the tokens of his presence in them, are the glory of any people, much more so than their wealth, and trade, and interest, among the nations. 2. Nothing is more cutting, more killing, to

a faithful Israelite, than the want and loss of these. If God go, the glory goes, and all good goes. Woe unto us if he depart!

CHAP. V.

It is now time to enquire what has become of the ark of God; we cannot but think that we shall hear more of that sacred treasure. I should have thought the next news would have been that all Israel, from Dan to Beersheba, had gathered together as one man, with a resolution to bring it back, or die in the attempt; but we find not any motion made of that kind, so little was there of zeal or courage left among them. Nay, we do not find that they desired a treaty with the Philistines about the ransom of it, or offered any thing in lieu of it. "It is gone, and let it go." Many have softness enough to lament the loss of the ark that have not hardiness enough to take one step towards the recovery of it, any more than Israel here. If the ark will help itself it may, for they will not help it. Unworthy they were of the name of Israelites that could thus tamely part with the glory of Israel. God would therefore take the work into his own hands and plead his own cause, since men would not appear for him. We are told in this chapter, I. How the Philistines triumphed over the ark (ver. 1, 2), and, II. How the ark triumphed over the Philistines, 1. Over Dagon their god, ver. 3–5. 2. Over the Philistines themselves, who were sorely plagued with emerods, and made weary of the ark; the men of Ashdod first (ver. 6, 7), then the men of Gath (ver. 8, 9), and lastly those of Ekron, which forced them at length upon a resolution to send the ark back to the land of Israel; for when God judgeth he will overcome.

AND the Philistines took the ark of God, and brought it from Eben-ezer unto Ashdod. 2 When the Philistines took the ark of God, they brought it into the house of Dagon, and set it by Dagon. 3 And when they of Ashdod arose early on the morrow, behold, Dagon *was* fallen upon his face to the earth before the ark of the LORD. And they took Dagon, and set him in his place again. 4 And when they arose early on the morrow morning, behold, Dagon *was* fallen upon his face to the ground before the ark of the LORD; and the head of Dagon and both the palms of his hands *were* cut off upon the threshold; only *the stump of* Dagon was left to him. 5 Therefore neither the priests of Dagon, nor any that come into Dagon's house, tread on the threshold of Dagon in Ashdod unto this day.

Here is, I. The Philistines' triumph over the ark, which they were the more pleased, the more proud, to be now masters of, because before the battle they were possessed with a great fear of it, *ch.* iv. 7. When they had it in their hands God restrained them, that they did not offer any violence to it, did not break it to pieces, as the Israelites were ordered to do by the idols of the heathen, but showed some respect to it, and carefully carried it to a place of safety. Whether their curiosity led them to open it, and to read what was written with the finger of God on the two tables of stone that were in it, we are not told; perhaps they looked no further than the golden outside and the cherubim that covered it, like children that are more affected with the fine binding of their bibles than with the precious matter contained in them. They carried it to Ashdod, one of their five cities, and that in which Dagon's temple was; there they placed the ark of God, *by Dagon* (*v.* 2), either, 1. As a sacred thing, which they designed to pay some religious respect to, in conjunction with Dagon; for the gods of the heathen were never looked upon as averse to partners. Though the nations would not change their gods, yet they would multiply them and add to them. But they were mistaken in the God of Israel when, in putting his ark by Dagon's image, they intended to do him honour; for he is not worshipped at all if he is not worshipped alone. *The Lord our God is one Lord.* Or rather, 2. They placed it there as a trophy of victory, in honour of Dagon their god, to whom no doubt they intended to offer a great sacrifice, as they had done when they had taken Samson (Judg. xvi. 23, 24), boasting that as then they had triumphed over Israel's champion so now over Israel's God. What a reproach was this to God's great name! what a *disgrace to the throne of his glory!* Shall the ark, the symbol of God's presence, be a prisoner to Dagon, a dunghill deity? (1.) So it is, because God will show of how little account the ark of the covenant is if the covenant itself be broken and neglected; even sacred signs are not things that either he is tied to or we can trust to. (2.) So it is for a time, that God may have so much the more glory, in reckoning with those that thus affront him, and get him honour upon them. Having punished Israel, that betrayed the ark, by giving it into the hands of the Philistines, he will next deal with those that abused it, and will fetch it out of their hands again. Thus even the *wrath of man shall praise him;* and he is bringing about his own glory even when he seems to neglect it, Ps. lxxvi. 10. Out of the eater shall come forth meat.

II. The ark's triumph over Dagon. Once and again Dagon was made to fall before it. If they designed to do honour to the ark, God thereby showed that he valued not their honour, nor would he accept it; for he will be worshipped, not *with* any god, but *above* all gods. *He owes a shame* (as bishop Hall expresses it) *to those who will be making matches betwixt himself and Belial.* But they really designed to affront it, and though for some hours Dagon stood by the ark, and it is likely stood above it (the ark as its footstool), yet the next morning, when the worshippers of Dagon came to pay their devotions to his shrine, they found their triumphing short, Job xx. 5.

1. Dagon, that is, the image (for that was all the god), had *fallen upon his face to the earth before the ark*, *v.* 3. God had seemed to forget the ark, but see how the Psalmist speaks of his appearing, at last, to vindicate his own honour. When he had delivered his strength into captivity, and all seemed go-

ing to ruin, *then the Lord awaked as one out of sleep, and like a mighty man that shouteth by reason of wine*, Ps. lxxviii. 59—65. And therefore he prevented the utter desolations of the Jewish church, because he *feared the wrath of the enemy*, Deut. xxxii. 26, 27. Great care was taken, in setting up the images of their gods, to fix them. The prophet takes notice of it, Isa. xli. 7, *He fastened it with nails that it should not be moved;* and again, Isa. xlvi. 7. And yet Dagon's fastenings stood him in no stead. The ark of God triumphs over him upon his own dunghill, in his own temple. Down he comes before the ark, directly towards it (though the ark was set on one side of him), as it were, pointing to the conqueror, to whom he is constrained to yield and do homage. Note, The kingdom of Satan will certainly fall before the kingdom of Christ, error before truth, profaneness before godliness, and corruption before grace in the hearts of the faithful. When the interests of religion seem to be run down and ready to sink, yet even then we may be confident that the day of their triumph will come. Great is the truth, and will prevail. Dagon by falling prostrate before the ark of God, which was a posture of adoration, did as it were direct his worshippers to pay their homage to the God of Israel, as *greater than all gods.* See Exod. xviii. 11.

2. The priests, finding their idol on the floor, make all the haste they can, before it be known, to set him in his place again. A sorry silly thing it was to make a god of, which, when it was down, wanted help to get up again; and sottish wretches those were that could pray for help from that idol that needed, and in effect implored, their help. How could they attribute their victory to the power of Dagon when Dagon himself could not keep his own ground before the ark? But they are resolved Dagon shall be their god still, and therefore set him in his place. Bishop Hall observes hence, It is just with God that those who want grace shall want wit too; and it is the work of superstition to turn men into the stocks and stones they worship. *Those that make them are like unto them.* What is it that the great upholders of the antichristian kingdom are doing at this day but heaving Dagon up, and labouring to set him in his place again, and healing the deadly wound that has been given to the beast? but if the reformation be the cause of God, before which it has begun to fall, it shall not prevail, but shall surely fall before it.

3. The next night Dagon fell the second time, *v.* 4. They rose early, either, as usual, to make their addresses to their god, or earlier than usual, being impatient to know whether Dagon had kept his standing this night; and, to their great confusion, they find his case worse now than before. Whether the matter of which the image was made was apt to break or no, so it was that the head and hands were *cut off upon the threshold,* so that nothing remained but the stump, or, as the margin reads it, *the fishy part of* Dagon; for (as many learned men conjecture) the upper part of this image was in a human shape, the lower in the shape of a fish, as mermaids are painted. Such strong delusions were idolaters given up to, so vain were they in their imaginations, and so wretchedly darkened were their foolish hearts, as to worship the images, not only of creatures, but of nonentities, the mere figments of fancy. Well, the misshapen monster is by this fall made to appear, (1.) Very ridiculous, and worthy to be despised. A pretty figure Dagon made now, when the fall had anatomized him, and shown how the human part and the fishy part were artificially put together, which perhaps the ignorant devotees had been made to believe was done by miracle! (2.) Very impotent, and unworthy to be prayed to or trusted in; for his losing his head and hands proved him utterly destitute both of wisdom and power, and for ever disabled either to advise or act for his worshippers. This they got by setting Dagon in his place again; they had better have let him alone when he was down. But those can speed no better that contend with God, and will set up that which he is throwing down, Mal. i. 4. God, by this, magnified his ark and made it honourable, when they vilified and made it contemptible. He also showed what will be the end of all that which is set up in opposition to him. *Gird yourselves,* but *you shall be broken to pieces,* Isa. viii. 9.

4. The threshold of Dagon's temple was ever looked upon as sacred, and not to be trodden on, *v.* 5. Some think that reference is had to this superstitious usage of Dagon's worshippers in Zeph. i. 9, where God threatens to punish those who, in imitation of them, leaped over the threshold. One would have thought that this incontestable proof of the ark's victory over Dagon would convince the Philistines of their folly in worshipping such a senseless thing, and that henceforward they would pay their homage to the conqueror; but, instead of being reformed, they were hardened in their idolatry, and, as evil men and seducers are wont to do, became worse and worse, 2 Tim. iii. 13. Instead of despising Dagon, for the threshold's sake that beheaded him, they were almost ready to worship the threshold because it was the block on which he was beheaded, and will never set their feet on that on which Dagon lost his head, shaming those who *tread under foot the blood of the covenant* and trample on things truly sacred. Yet this piece of superstition would help to perpetuate the remembrance of Dagon's disgrace; for, with the custom, the reason would be transmitted to posterity, and the children that should be born, enquiring why the threshold of Dagon's temple must not

be trodden on, would be told that Dagon fell before the ark of the Lord. Thus God would have honour even out of their superstition. We are not told that they repaired the broken image; it is probable that they sent the ark of God away first, and then they patched it up again, and set it in its place; for, it seems, they *cannot deliver their souls, nor say, Is there not a lie in our right hand?* Isa. xliv. 20.

6 But the hand of the LORD was heavy upon them of Ashdod, and he destroyed them, and smote them with emerods, *even* Ashdod and the coasts thereof. 7 And when the men of Ashdod saw that *it was* so, they said, The ark of the God of Israel shall not abide with us: for his hand is sore upon us, and upon Dagon our god. 8 They sent therefore and gathered all the lords of the Philistines unto them, and said, What shall we do with the ark of the God of Israel? And they answered, Let the ark of the God of Israel be carried about unto Gath. And they carried the ark of the God of Israel about *thither*. 9 And it was *so*, that, after they had carried it about, the hand of the LORD was against the city with a very great destruction: and he smote the men of the city, both small and great, and they had emerods in their secret parts. 10 Therefore they sent the ark of God to Ekron. And it came to pass, as the ark of God came to Ekron, that the Ekronites cried out, saying, They have brought about the ark of the God of Israel to us, to slay us and our people. 11 So they sent and gathered together all the lords of the Philistines, and said, Send away the ark of the God of Israel, and let it go again to his own place, that it slay us not, and our people: for there was a deadly destruction throughout all the city; the hand of God was very heavy there. 12 And the men that died not were smitten with the emerods: and the cry of the city went up to heaven.

The downfal of Dagon (if the people had made a good use of it, and had been brought by it to repent of their idolatries and to humble themselves before the God of Israel and seek his face) might have prevented the vengeance which God here proceeds to take upon them for the indignities done to his ark, and their obstinate adherence to their idol, in defiance of the plainest conviction. *Lord, when thy hand is lifted up they will not see, but they shall see,* Isa. xxvi. 11. And, if they will not see the glory, they shall feel the weight, of God's hand, for so the Philistines did. *The hand of the Lord was heavy upon them* (*v.* 6), and he not only convinced them of their folly, but severely chastised their insolence. 1. *He destroyed them,* that is, cut many of them off by sudden death, those, we may suppose, that had most triumphed in the captivity of the ark. This is distinguished from the disease with which others were smitten. At Gath it is called *a great destruction* (*v.* 9), *a deadly destruction*, *v.* 11. And it is expressly said (*v.* 12) that those who were *smitten with the emerods were the men that died not* by the other *destruction,* which probably was the pestilence. They boasted of the great slaughter which their sword had made among the Israelites, *ch.* iv. 10. But God lets them know that though he does not see fit to draw Israel's sword against them (they were unworthy to be employed), yet God had a sword of his own, with which he could make a no less dreadful execution among them, which if he whet, and *his hand take hold on judgment, he will render vengeance to his enemies,* Deut. xxxii. 41, 42. Note, Those that contend with God, his ark, and his Israel, will infallibly be ruined at last. If conviction conquer not, destruction shall. 2. Those that were not destroyed *he smote with emerods* (*v.* 6), *in their secret parts* (*v.* 9), so grievous that (*v.* 12) the *cry went up to heaven,* that is, it might be heard a great way off, and perhaps, in the extremity of their pain and misery, they cried, not to Dagon, but to the God of heaven. The Psalmist, speaking of this sore judgment upon the Philistines, describes it thus: God *smote his enemies in the hinder parts,* and *put them to a perpetual reproach,* Ps. lxxviii. 66. The emerods (which we call the piles, and perhaps it was then a more grievous disease than it is now) is threatened among the judgments that would be the fruit of the curse, Deut. xxviii. 27. It was both a painful and shameful disease; a vile disease for vile deserts. By it God would humble their pride, and put contempt upon them, as they had done upon his ark. The disease was epidemical, and perhaps, among them, a new disease. *Ashdod was smitten, and the coasts thereof,* the country round. For contempt of God's ordinances, *many are weak and sick, and many sleep,* 1 Cor. xi. 30. 3. The men of Ashdod were soon aware that it was *the hand of God, the God of Israel, v.* 7. Thus they were constrained to acknowledge his power and dominion, and confess themselves within his jurisdiction, and yet they would not renounce Dagon and submit to Jehovah; but rather, now that he touched their bone and their flesh, and in a tender part, they were ready to curse him to his face, and instead of making their peace with him, and courting the stay of his ark upon better terms, they desired to get clear of it, as the Gadarenes, who, when they had lost their swine, desired Christ to *depart out of their coasts.* Carnal hearts, when they smart under the judgments of God, would rather, if it were possible, put him far from them than enter into covenant and communion with him, and make him their friend. Thus the men of Ashdod resolve, *The ark of the God of Israel shall not abide with us.* 4. It is resolved to change the place of its imprisonment. A great council was called, and the question proposed to all the lords was, "What shall we do with the ark?" And at last it was agreed that it should be carried to Gath, *v.* 8. Some superstitious conceit they had that the fault was in the place, and that the ark would be better pleased with another lodging, further off from Dagon's temple; and therefore, instead of returning it, as they should have done, to its own place, they contrive to send it to another place. *Gath* is pitched upon, a place famed for a race of giants, but their strength and stature are no fence against the pestilence and the emerods: the men of that city were smitten, *both great and small* (*v.* 9), both dwarfs and giants, all alike to God's judgments; none so great as to over-top them, none so small as to be over-looked by them. 5. They were all at last weary of the ark, and very willing to get rid of it. It was sent from Gath to Ekron, and, coming by order of council, the Ekronites could not refuse it, but were much exasperated against their great men for sending them such a fatal present (*v.* 10): *They have sent it to us to slay us and our people.* The ark had the tables of the law in it; and nothing more welcome to faithful Israelites than the word of God (to them it is *a savour of life unto life*), but to uncircumcised Philistines, that persist in enmity to God, nothing more dreadful nor unwelcome: to them it is *a savour of death unto death.* A general assembly is instantly called, to advise about *sending the ark again to its place, v.* 11. While they are consulting about it, the hand of God is doing execution; and their contrivances to evade the judgment do but spread it. Many drop down dead among them. Many more are raging ill of the emerods, *v.* 12. What shall they do? Their triumphs in the captivity of the ark are soon turned into lamentations, and they are as eager to quit it as ever they had been to seize it. Note, God can easily make Jerusalem a burdensome stone to all that heave at it, Zech. xii. 3. Those that fight against God will soon have enough of it, and, first or last, will be made to know that none ever hardened their hearts against him and prospered. The wealth that is got by fraud and injustice, especially that which is got by sacrilege and robbing God, though swallowed greedily, and rolled under the tongue as a sweet morsel, must be vomited up again; for, till it be, the sinner shall not *feel quietness in his belly,* Job xx. 15—20.

CHAP. VI.

In this chapter we have the return of the ark to the land of Israel, whither we are now gladly to attend it, and observe, I. How the Philistines dismissed it, by the advice of their priests (ver. 1—11), with rich presents to the God of Israel, to make an atonement for their sin (ver. 3—5), and yet with a project to bring it back, unless Providence directed the kine, contrary to their inclination, to go to the land of Israel, ver. 8, 9. II. How the Israelites entertained it. 1. With great joy and sacrifices of praise, ver. 12—18. 2. With an over-bold curiosity to look into it, for which many of them were struck dead, the terror of which moved them to send it forward to another city, ver. 19—21.

AND the ark of the LORD was in the country of the Philistines seven months. 2 And the Philistines called for the priests and the diviners, saying, What shall we do to the ark of the LORD? tell us wherewith we shall send it to his place. 3 And they said, If ye send away the ark of the God of Israel, send it not empty; but in any wise return him a trespass offering: then ye shall be healed, and it shall be known to you why his hand is not removed from you. 4 Then said they, What *shall be* the trespass offering which we shall return to him? They answered, Five golden emerods, and five golden mice, *according to* the number of the lords of the Philistines: for one plague *was* on you all, and on your lords. 5 Wherefore ye shall make images of your emerods, and images of your mice that mar the land: and ye shall give glory unto the God of Israel: peradventure he will lighten his hand from off you, and from off your gods, and from off your land. 6 Wherefore then do ye harden your hearts, as the Egyptians and Pharaoh hardened their hearts? when he had wrought wonderfully among them, did they not let the people go, and they departed? 7 Now therefore make a new cart, and take two milch kine, on which there hath come no yoke, and tie the kine to the cart, and bring their calves home from them: 8 And take the ark of the LORD, and lay it upon the cart; and put the jewels of gold, which ye return him *for* a trespass offering, in a coffer by the side thereof; and send it away, that it may go. 9 And see, if it goeth up by the way of his own coast to Beth-shemesh, *then* he hath done us this great evil; but if not, then we shall know that *it is* not his hand *that* smote us; it *was* a chance *that* happened to us.

The first words of the chapter tell us how long the captivity of the ark continued—it was *in the country of the Philistines seven months. In the field of the Philistines* (so it is in the original), from which some gather that, having tried it in all their cities, and found it a plague to the inhabitants of each, at length they sent it into the open fields, upon which mice sprang up out of the ground in great multitudes, and destroyed the corn which was now nearly ripe and marred the land. With that judgment they were plagued (*v.* 5), and yet it is not mentioned in the foregoing chapter; so God let them know that wherever they carried the ark, so long as they carried it captive, they should find it a curse to them. *Cursed shalt thou be in the city, and cursed in the field,* Deut. xxviii. 16. But most take it to signify, as we render it, *The country of the Philistines.* Now, 1. Seven months Israel was punished with the absence of the ark, that special token of God's presence. How bare did the tabernacle look without it! How was the holy city now a desolation, and the holy land a wilderness! A melancholy time no doubt it was to the good people among them, particularly to Samuel; but they had this to comfort themselves with, as we have in the like distress when we are deprived of the comfort of public ordinances, that, wherever the ark is, *the Lord is in his holy temple, the Lord's throne is in heaven,* and by faith and prayer we may have access with boldness to him there. We may have God nigh unto us when the ark is at a distance. 2. Seven months the Philistines were punished with the presence of the ark; so long it was a plague to them, because they would not send it home sooner. Note, Sinners lengthen out their own miseries by obstinately refusing to part with their sins. Egypt's plagues would have been fewer than ten if Pharaoh's heart had not been hardened not to let the people go. But at length it is determined that the ark must be sent back; there is no remedy, they are undone if they detain it.

I. The priests and the diviners are consulted about it, *v.* 2. They were supposed to be best acquainted both with the rules of wisdom and with the rites of worship and atonement. And the Israelites being their neighbours, and famed above all people for the institutions of their religion, they had no doubt the curiosity to acquaint themselves with their laws and usages; and therefore it was proper to ask them, *What shall we do to the ark of Jehovah?* All nations have had a regard to their priests, as the men whose lips keep knowledge. Had the Philistines diviners? We have divines, of whom we should enquire wherewith we shall *come before the Lord* and *bow ourselves before the most high God.*

II. They give their advice very fully, and seem to be very unanimous in it. It was a wonder they did not, as friends to their country, give it, *ex officio—officially,* before they were asked. 1. They urge it upon them that it was absolutely necessary to send the ark back, from the example of Pharaoh and the Egyptians, *v.* 6. Some, it may be, were loth to yield, and were willing to try it out with the ark awhile longer, and to them they apply themselves: *Wherefore do you harden your hearts, as the Egyptians and Pharaoh did?* It seems they were well acquainted with the Mosaic history, and could cite precedents out of it. This good use we should make of the remaining records of God's judgments upon obstinate sinners, we should by them be warned not to harden our hearts as they did. It is much cheaper to learn by other people's experience than by our own. The Egyptians were forced at last to let Israel go; therefore let the Philistines yield in time to let the ark go. 2. They advise that, when they sent it back, they should send a trespass-offering with it, *v.* 3. Whatever the gods of other nations were, they knew the God of Israel was a jealous God, and how strict he was in his demands of sin-offerings and trespass-offerings from his own people; and therefore, since they found how highly he resented the affront of holding his ark captive, those with whom he had such a quarrel must *in any wise return him a trespass-offering,* and they could not expect to be healed upon any other terms. Injured justice demands satisfaction. So far natural light instructed men. But when they began to contrive what that satisfaction should be, they became wretchedly vain in their imaginations. But those who by wilful sin have imprisoned the truth in unrighteousness, as the Philistines did the ark (Rom. i. 18), may conclude that there is no making their peace with him whom they have thus injured but by a sin-offering; and we know but one that can take away sin. 3. They direct that this trespass-offering should be an acknowledgment of the punishment of their iniquity, by which they might take shame to themselves as conquered and yielding, and guilty before God, and might *give glory to the God of Israel* as their mighty conqueror and most just avenger, *v.* 5. They must make images of the *emerods,* that is, of the swellings and sores with which they had been afflicted, so making the reproach of that shameful disease perpetual by their own act and deed (Ps. lxxviii. 66), also images of the *mice that had marred the land,* owning thereby the almighty power of the God of Israel, who could chastise and humble them, even in the day of their triumph, by such small and despicable animals. These images must be made of gold, the most precious metal, to intimate that they would gladly purchase their peace with the God of Israel at any rate, and would not think it bought too dearly with gold, *with much fine gold.* The *golden emerods* must be, in number, five, according to the *number of the lords,* who, it is likely, were all afflicted with them, and were content thus to own it; it was advised that the *golden mice* should be five too, but, because the whole country was infested with them, it should seem, upon second thoughts, they sent more of them, *according to the number both of the fenced cities and of the country villages, v.* 18. Their priests reminded them that *one plague was on them all;* they could not blame one another, for they were all guilty, which they were plainly told by being all plagued. Their proposal to offer a trespass-offering for their offence was conformable enough to divine revelation at that time; but to send such things as these for trespass-offerings was very foreign, and showed them grossly ignorant of the methods of reconciliation appointed by the law of Moses; for there it appears all along that it is blood, and not gold, that makes atonement for the soul. 4. They encourage them to hope that hereby they would take an effectual course to get rid of the plague: *You shall be healed, v.* 3. For, it seems, the disease obstinately resisted all the methods of cure their physicians had prescribed. "Let them therefore send back the ark, and then," say they, "*It shall be known to you why his hand is not removed from you,* that is, by this it will appear whether it is for your detaining the ark that you are thus plagued; for, if it be, upon your delivering it up the plague will cease." God has sometimes put his people upon making such a trial, whether their reformation would not be their relief. *Prove me now herewith, saith the Lord of hosts,* Mal. iii. 10; Hag. ii. 18, 19. Yet they speak doubtfully (*v.* 5): *Peradventure he will lighten his hand from off you;* as if now they began to think that the judgment might come from God's hand, and yet not be removed immediately upon the restitution of the ark; however that was the likeliest way to obtain mercy. Take away the cause and the effect will cease. 5. Yet they put them in a way to make a further trial whether it was the hand of the God of Israel that had smitten them with these plagues or no. They must, in honour of the ark, put it on a new cart or carriage, to be drawn by two milch-cows, that had calves daily sucking them (*v.* 7), unused to draw, and inclined to home, both for the sake of the crib where they were fed and of the calves they nourished, and, besides, altogether unacquainted with the road that led towards the land of Israel. They must have no one to lead or drive them, but must take their own way, which, in all reason, one might expect, would be home again; and yet, unless the God of Israel, after all the other miracles he has wrought, will work one more, and by an invisible power lead these cows, contrary to their natural instinct and inclination, to the land of Israel, and particularly to Beth-shemesh, they will retract their former opinion, and will believe it was not the hand of God that smote them, but it was a chance that *happened to them, v.* 8, 9. Thus did God suffer himself to be tempted and prescribed to, after he had been otherwise affronted, by these uncircumcised Philistines. Would they have been content that the honour of Dagon, their god, should be put upon such an issue as this? See how willing bad men are to shift off their convictions of the hand of God upon them, and to believe, when they are in trouble, that it is *a chance that happens to them;* and, if so, the rod has no voice which they are concerned to hear or heed.

10 And the men did so; and took two milch kine, and tied them to the cart, and shut up their calves at home: 11 And they laid the ark of the LORD upon the cart, and the coffer with the mice of gold and the images of their emerods. 12 And the kine took the straight way to the way of Beth-shemesh, *and* went along the highway, lowing as they went, and turned not aside *to* the right hand or *to* the left; and the lords of the Philistines went after them unto the border of Beth-shemesh. 13 And *they of* Beth-shemesh *were* reaping their wheat harvest in the valley: and they lifted up their eyes, and saw the ark, and rejoiced to see *it.* 14 And the cart came into the field of Joshua, a Beth-shemite, and stood there, where *there was* a great stone: and they clave the wood of the cart, and offered the kine a burnt offering unto the LORD. 15 And the Levites took down the ark of the LORD, and the coffer that *was* with it, wherein the jewels of gold *were,* and put *them* on the great stone: and the men of Beth-shemesh offered burnt offerings and sacrificed sacrifices the same day unto the LORD. 16 And when the five lords of the Philistines had seen *it,* they returned to Ekron the same day. 17 And these are the golden emerods which the Philistines returned *for* a trespass offering unto the LORD; for Ashdod one, for Gaza one, for Ash-

kelon one, for Gath one, for Ekron one; 18 And the golden mice, *according to* the number of all the cities of the Philistines *belonging* to the five lords, *both* of fenced cities, and of country villages, even unto the great *stone of* Abel, whereon they set down the ark of the LORD: *which stone remaineth* unto this day in the field of Joshua, the Beth-shemite.

We are here told,

I. How the Philistines dismissed the ark, *v.* 10, 11. They were made as glad to part with it as ever they had been to take it. As God had fetched Israel out of the house of bondage, so now he fetched the ark out of its captivity, in such a manner as that *Egypt was glad when they departed,* Ps. cv. 38. 1. They received no money or price for the ransom of it, as they hoped to do, even beyond a king's ransom. Thus it is prophesied of Cyrus (Isa. xlv. 13), *He shall let go my captives, not for price nor reward.* Nay, 2. They gave jewels of gold, as the Egyptians did to the Israelites, to be rid of it. Thus the ark that was carried into the land of the Philistines, a trophy of their victory, carried back with it trophies of its own, and lasting monuments of the disgrace of the Philistines. Note, God will be no loser in his glory, at last, by the successes of the church's enemies against his ark, but will get himself honour from those that seek to do dishonour to him.

II. How the kine brought it to the land of Israel, *v.* 12. They *took the straight way to Beth-shemesh,* the next city of the land of Israel, and a priests' city, *and turned not aside.* This was a wonderful instance of the power of God over the brute-creatures, and, all things considered, no less than a miracle, that cattle unaccustomed to the yoke should draw so even, so orderly, and still go forward,—that, without any driver, they should go from home, to which all tame creatures have a natural inclination, and from their own calves, to which they had a natural affection,—that, without any director, they should go the straight road to Beth-shemesh, a city eight or ten miles off, never miss the way, never turn aside into the fields to feed themselves, nor turn back home to feed their calves. They went on lowing for their young ones, by which it appeared that they had not forgotten them, but that nature was sensible of the grievance of going from them; the power of the God of nature therefore appeared so much the greater, in overruling one of the strongest instincts of nature. These two kine, says Dr. Lightfoot, knew their owner, their great owner (Isa. i. 3), whom Hophni and Phinehas knew not, to which I may add they brought home the ark to shame the stupidity of Israel, that made no attempt to fetch it home. God's providence is conversant about the motions even of brute-creatures, and serves its own purposes by them. The lords of the Philistines, with a suitable retinue no doubt, went after them, wondering at the power of the God of Israel; and thus those who thought to triumph over the ark were made to go like menial servants after it.

III. How it was welcomed to the land of Israel: *The men of Beth-shemesh were reaping their wheat-harvest, v.* 13. They were going on with their worldly business, and were in no care about the ark, made no enquiries what had become of it; if they had, it is likely they might have had private intelligence beforehand of its coming, and might have gone to meet it, and conduct it into their own border. But they were as careless as the people that *ceiled their own houses* and *let God's house lie waste.* Note, God will in his own time effect the deliverance of his church, not only though it be fought against by its enemies, but though it be neglected by its friends. Some observe that the returning ark found the men of Beth-shemesh, not idling or sporting in the streets of the city, but busy, reaping their corn in their fields, and well employed. Thus the tidings of the birth of Christ were brought to the shepherds when they were *keeping their flock by night.* The devil visits idle men with his temptations. God visits industrious men with his favours. The same invisible hand that directed the kine to the land of Israel brought them into the field of Joshua, and in that field they stood, some think for the owner's sake, on whom, being a very good man, they suppose God designed to put this honour. I rather think it was for the sake of the great stone in that field, which was convenient to put the ark upon, and which is spoken of, *v.* 14, 15, 18. Now, 1. When the reapers *saw the ark, they rejoiced* (*v.* 13); their joy for that was greater than the joy of harvest, and therefore they left their work to bid it welcome. When the Lord turned again the captivity of his ark they were *like men that dream; then was their mouth filled with laughter,* Ps. cxxvi. 1, 2. Though they had not zeal and courage enough to attempt the rescue or ransom of it, yet, when it did come, they bade it heartily welcome. Note, The return of the ark, and the revival of holy ordinances, after days of restraint and trouble, cannot but be matter of great joy to every faithful Israelite. 3. They offered up the kine for a burnt-offering, to the honour of God, and made use of the wood of the cart for fuel, *v.* 14. Probably the Philistines intended these, when they sent them, to be a part of their trespass-offering, to make atonement, *v.* 3, 7. However, the men of Beth-shemesh looked upon it as proper to make this use of them, because it was by no means fit that ever they should be put to any other use;

never shall that cart carry any common thing that has once carried that sacred symbol of the divine presence: and the kine had been under such an immediate guidance of heaven that God had, as it were, already laid claim to them; they were servants to him, and therefore must be sacrifices to him, and no doubt were accepted, though females, whereas, in strictness, every burnt-offering was to be a male. 3. They deposited the ark, with a chest of jewels that the Philistines presented, upon the great stone in the open field, a cold lodging for the ark of the Lord and a very mean one; vet better so than in Dagon's temple, or in the hands of the Philistines. It is desirable to see the ark in its habitation in all the circumstances of solemnity and splendour; but better have it upon a great stone, and in the fields of the wood, than be without it. The intrinsic grandeur of instituted ordinances ought not to be diminished in our eyes by the meanness and poverty of the place where they are administered. As the burning of the cart and cows that brought home the ark might be construed to signify their hopes that it should never be carried away again out of the land of Israel, so the setting of it upon a great stone might signify their hopes that it should be established again upon a firm foundation. The church is built upon a rock. 4. They offered the sacrifices of thanksgiving to God, some think upon the great stone, more probably upon an altar of earth made for the purpose, *v.* 15. And, the case being extraordinary, the law for offering at the altar in the court of the tabernacle was dispensed with, and the more easily because Shiloh was now dismantled; God himself had forsaken it, and the ark, which was its chief glory, they had with them here. Beth-shemesh, though it lay within the lot of the tribe of Dan, yet belonged to Judah, so that this accidental bringing of the ark hither was an indication of its designed settlement there, in process of time; for, when God *refused the tabernacle of Joseph, he chose the tribe of Judah*, Ps. lxxviii. 67, 68. It was one of those cities which were assigned out of the lot of Judah to the *sons of Aaron*, Josh. xxi. 16. Whither should the ark go but to a priests' city? And it was well they had those of that sacred order ready (for though they are here called *Levites*, *v.* 15, yet it should seem they were priests) both to take down the ark and to offer the sacrifices. 5. The lords of the Philistines returned to Ekron, much affected, we may suppose, with what they had seen of the glory of God and the zeal of the Israelites, and yet not reclaimed from the worship of Dagon; for how seldom *has a nation changed its gods, though they were no gods!* Jer. ii. 11. Though they cannot but think the God of Israel *glorious in holiness and fearful in praises*, yet they are resolved they will think Baal-zebub, the god of Ekron, at least as good as he, and to him they will cleave because he is theirs. 6. Notice is taken of the continuance of the great stone in the same place; there it is *unto this day* (*v.* 18), because it remained a lasting memorial of this great event, and served to support the traditional history by which it was transmitted to posterity. The fathers would say to the children, "This is the stone upon which the ark of God was set when it came out of the Philistines' hands, a thing never to be forgotten."

19 And he smote the men of Beth-shemesh, because they had looked into the ark of the LORD, even he smote of the people fifty thousand and threescore and ten men: and the people lamented, because the LORD had smitten *many* of the people with a great slaughter. 20 And the men of Beth-shemesh said, Who is able to stand before this holy LORD God? and to whom shall he go up from us? 21 And they sent messengers to the inhabitants of Kirjath-jearim, saying, The Philistines have brought again the ark of the LORD; come ye down, *and* fetch it up to you.

Here is, 1. The sin of the men of Beth-shemesh: *They looked into the ark of the Lord*, *v.* 19. Every Israelite had heard great talk of the ark, and had been possessed with a profound veneration for it; but they had been told that it was lodged within a veil, and even the high priest himself might not look upon it but once a year, and then through a cloud of incense. Perhaps this made many say (as we are apt to covet that which is forbidden) what a great deal they would give for a sight of it. Some of these Beth-shemites, we may suppose, for that reason, *rejoiced to see the ark* (*v.* 13) more than for the sake of the public. Yet this did not content them; they might see it, but they would go further, they would take off the covering, which it is likely was nailed or screwed on, and look into it, under pretence of seeing whether the Philistines had not taken the two tables out of it or some way damaged them, but really to gratify a sinful curiosity of their own, which intruded into those things that God had thought fit to conceal from them. Note, It is a great affront to God for vain men to pry into and meddle with the secret things which belong not to them, Deut. xxix. 29; Col. ii. 18. We were all ruined by an ambition of forbidden knowledge. That which made this looking into the ark a great sin was that it proceeded from a very low and mean opinion of the ark. The familiarity they had with it upon this occasion bred contempt and irreverence. Perhaps they presumed upon their being priests; but the dignity of the ministerial office will be so far from excusing that it will aggravate a careless and irreverent treatment of holy things. They should, by their example, have taught others to keep their distance and look upon the ark with a holy awe. Perhaps they presumed upon the kind entertainment they had given the ark, and the sacrifices they had now offered to welcome it home with, for which they thought the ark was indebted to them, and they might be allowed to repay themselves with the satisfaction of looking into it. But let no man think that his service done for God will justify him in any instance of disrespect or irreverence towards the things of God. Or it may be they presumed upon the present mean circumstances the ark was in, newly come out of captivity, and unsettled; now that it stood upon a cold stone, they thought they might make free with it; they should never have such another opportunity of being familiar with it. It is an offence to God if we think meanly of his ordinances because of the meanness of the manner of their administration. Had they looked with an understanding eye upon the ark, and not judged purely by outward appearance, they would have thought that the ark never shone with greater majesty than it did now. It had triumphed over the Philistines, and come out of its house of bondage (like Christ out of the grave) by its own power; had they considered this, they would not have looked into it thus, as a common chest. 2. Their punishment for this sin: *He smote the men of Beth-shemesh, many of them, with a great slaughter.* How jealous is God for the honour of his ark! He will not suffer it to be profaned. *Be not deceived, God is not mocked.* Those that will not fear his goodness, and reverently use the tokens of his grace, shall be made to feel his justice, and sink under the tokens of his displeasure. Those that pry into what is forbidden, and come too near to holy fire, will find it is at their peril. *He smote* 50,070 *men.* This account of the numbers smitten is expressed in a very unusual manner in the original, which, besides the improbability that there should be so many guilty and so many slain, occasions many learned men to question whether we take the matter aright. In the original it is, *He smote in* (or among) *the people three score and ten men, fifty thousand men.* The Syriac and Arabic read it, *five thousand and seventy men.* The Chaldee reads it, *seventy men of the elders, and fifty thousand of the common people. Seventy men as valuable as* 50,000, so some, because they were priests. Some think the seventy men were the Beth-shemites that were slain for looking into the ark, and the 50,000 were those that were slain by the ark, in the land of the Philistines. *He smote seventy men,* that is, *fifty out of a thousand,* which was one in twenty, a half decimation; so some understand it. The Septuagint read it much as we do, *he smote seventy men, and fifty thousand men.* Josephus says only seventy were smitten. 3. The terror that was struck upon the men of Beth-shemesh by this severe stroke. They said, as well they might, *Who is able to stand before this holy Lord God? v.* 20. Some think this expresses their murmuring against God, as if he had dealt hardly and unjustly with them. Instead of quarrelling with themselves and their own sins, they quarrelled with God and his judgments; as *David was displeased,* in a case not much dissimilar, 2 Sam. vi. 8, 9. I rather think it intimates their awful and reverent adoration of God, as the Lord God, as a holy Lord God, and as a God before whom none is able to stand. This they infer from that tremendous judgment, "Who is able to stand before the God of the ark? To stand before God to worship him (blessed be his name) is not impossible; we are through Christ invited, encouraged, and enabled to do it, but to stand before God to contend with him we are not able. Who is able to stand before the throne of his immediate glory, and look full upon it? 1 Tim. vi. 16. Who is able to stand before the tribunal of his inflexible justice, and make his part good there? Ps. cxxx. 3; cxliii. 2. Who is able to stand before the arm of his provoked power, and either resist or bear the strokes of it? Ps. lxxvi. 7. 4. Their desire, hereupon, to be rid of the ark. They asked, *To whom shall he go up from us? v.* 20. They should rather have asked, "How may we make our peace with him, and recover his favour?" Mic. vi. 6, 7. But they begin to be as weary of the ark as the Philistines had been, whereas, if they had treated it with due reverence, who knows but it might have taken up its residence among them, and they had all been blessed for the ark's sake? But thus, when the word of God works with terror on sinners' consciences, they, instead of taking the blame and shame to themselves, quarrel with the word, and put it from them, Jer. vi. 10. They sent messengers to the elders of Kirjath-jearim, a strong city further up in the country, and begged of them to come and fetch the ark up thither, *v.* 21. They durst not touch it to bring it thither themselves, but stood aloof from it as a dangerous thing. Thus do foolish men run from one extreme to the other, from presumptuous boldness to slavish shyness. Kirjath-jearim, that is, *the city of woods,* belonged to Judah, Josh. xv. 9, 60. It lay in the way from Beth-shemesh to Shiloh, so that when they sent to them to fetch it, we may suppose, they intended that the elders of Shiloh should fetch it thence, but God intended otherwise. Thus was it sent from town to town, and no care taken of it by the public, a sign that there was no king in Israel.

CHAP. VII.

In this chapter we have, I. The eclipsing of the glory of the ark, by its privacy in Kirjath-jearim for many years, ver. 1, 2. II. The appearing of the glory of Samuel in his public services for the good of Israel, to whom he was raised up to be a judge, and he was the last that bore that character. This chapter gives us all the account we have of him when he was in the prime of his time; for what we had before was in his childhood (ch. ii. and iii.); what we have of him after was in his old age, ch. viii. 1. We have him here active, 1. In the reformation of Israel from their idolatry, ver. 3, 4. 2. In the reviving of religion among them, ver. 5, 6. 3. In praying for them against the invading Philistines (ver. 7—9), over whom God, in answer to his prayer, gave them a glorious victory, ver. 10, 11. 4. In erecting a thankful memorial of that victory, ver. 12. 5. In the improvement of that victory, ver. 13, 14. 6. In the administration of justice, ver. 15—17. And these were the things for which God was preparing and designing him, in the early vouchsafements of his grace to him.

AND the men of Kirjath-jearim came, and fetched up the ark of the LORD, and brought it into the house of Abinadab in the hill, and sanctified Eleazar his son to keep the ark of the LORD. 2 And it came to pass, while the ark abode in Kirjath-jearim, that the time was long; for it was twenty years: and all the house of Israel lamented after the LORD.

Here we must attend the ark to Kirjath-jearim, and then leave it there, to hear not a word more of it except once (*ch.* xiv. 18), till David fetched it thence, about forty years after, 1 Chron. xiii. 6.

I. We are very willing to attend it thither, for the men of Beth-shemesh have by their own folly made that a burden which might have been a blessing; and gladly would we see it among those to whom it will be a *savour of life unto life,* for in every place where it has been of late it has been a *savour of death unto death.* Now,

1. The men of Kirjath-jearim cheerfully bring it among them, *v.* 1. *They came,* at the first word, *and fetched up the ark of the Lord.* Their neighbours the Beth-shemites, were not more glad to get rid of it than they were to receive it, knowing very well that what slaughter the ark had made at Beth-shemesh was not an act of arbitrary power, but of necessary justice, and those that suffered by it must blame themselves, not the ark; we may depend upon the word which God hath said (Jer. xxv. 6), *Provoke me not, and I will do you no hurt.* Note, The judgments of God on those who profane his ordinances should not make us afraid of the ordinances, but of profaning them and making an ill use of them.

2. They carefully provided for its decent entertainment among them, as a welcome guest, with true affection, and, as an honourable guest, with respect and reverence.

(1.) They provided a proper place to receive it. They had no public building to adorn with it, but they lodged it in the house of Abinadab, which stood upon the highest ground, and, probably, was the best house in their city; or perhaps the master of it was the most eminent man they had for piety, and best affected to the ark. The men of Beth-shemesh left it exposed upon a stone in the open field, and, though it was a city of priests, none of them received it into his house; but the men of Kirjath-jearim, though common Israelites, gave it house-room, and no doubt the best-furnished room in the house to which it was brought. Note, [1.] God will find out a resting-place for his ark; if some thrust it from them, yet the hearts of others shall be inclined to receive it. [2.] It is no new thing for God's ark to be thrust into a private house. Christ and his apostles preached from house to house when they could not have public places at command. [3.] Sometimes priests are shamed and outdone in religion by common Israelites.

(2.) They provided a proper person to attend it: *They sanctified Eleazar his son to keep it;* not the father, either because he was aged and infirm, or because he had the affairs of his house and family to attend, from which they would not take him off. But the son, who, it is probable, was a very pious devout young man, and zealously affected towards the best things. His business was to keep the ark, not only from being seized by malicious Philistines, but from being touched or looked into by too curious Israelites. He was to keep the room clean and decent in which the ark was, that, though it was in an obscure place, it might not look like a neglected thing, which no man looked after. It does not appear that this Eleazar was of the tribe of Levi, much less of the house of Aaron, nor was it needful that he should, for here was no altar either for sacrifice or incense, only we may suppose that some devout Israelites would come and pray before the ark, and those that did so he was there ready to attend and assist. For this purpose they sanctified him, that is, by his own consent, they obliged him to make this his business, and to give a constant attendance to it; they set him apart for it in the name of all their citizens. This was irregular, but was excusable because of the present distress. When the ark has but recently come out of captivity we cannot expect it to be on a sudden in its usual solemnity, but must take things as they are, and make the best of them.

II. Yet we are very loth to leave it here, wishing it well at Shiloh again, but that is made desolate (Jer. vii. 14), or at least wishing it at Nob, or Gibeon, or wherever the tabernacle and the altars are; but, it seems, it must lie by the way for want of some public-spirited men to bring it to its proper place. 1. The time of its continuance here was long, very long, above forty years it lay in these fields of the wood, a remote, obscure, private place, unfrequented and almost unregarded (*v.* 2): *The time that the ark abode in Kirjath-jearim was long,* even till David fetched it thence. It was very strange that all the time that Samuel governed the ark was never brought to its place in the holy of holies, an evidence of the decay of holy zeal among them. God suffered it to be so, to punish them for their neglect of the ark when it was in its place and to show that the great stress which the institution laid upon the ark was but typical of Christ, and those *good things to come which cannot be moved*, Heb. ix. 23; xii. 27. It was a just reproach to the priests that one not of their order was sanctified to keep the ark. 2. Twenty years of this time had passed before the house of Israel was sensible of the want of the ark. The Septuagint read it somewhat more clearly than we do; *and it was twenty years, and* (that is, when) *the whole house of Israel looked up again after the Lord.* So long the ark remained in obscurity, and the Israelites were not sensible of the inconvenience, nor ever made any enquiry after it, what has become of it; though, while it was absent from the tabernacle, the token of God's special presence was wanting, nor could they keep the day of atonement as it should be kept. They were content with the altars without the ark; so easily can formal professors rest satisfied in a round of external performances, without any tokens of God's presence or acceptance. But at length they bethought themselves, and began to lament after the Lord, stirred up to it, it is probable, by the preaching of Samuel, with which an extraordinary working of the Spirit of God set in. A general disposition to repentance and reformation now appears throughout all Israel, and they begin to *look unto him whom they had slighted, and to mourn,* Zech. xii. 10. Dr. Lightfoot thinks this was a matter and time as remarkable as almost any we read of in scripture; and that that great conversion, Acts ii. and iii., is the only parallel to it. Note, (1.) Those that know how to value God's ordinances cannot but reckon it a very lamentable thing to want them. (2.) True repentance and conversion begin in lamenting after the Lord; we must be sensible that by sin we have provoked him to withdraw and are undone if we continue in a state of distance from him, and be restless till we have recovered his favour and obtained his gracious returns. It was better with the Israelites when they wanted the ark, and were lamenting after it, than when they had the ark, and were prying into it, or priding themselves in it. Better see people longing in the scarcity of the means of grace than loathing in the abundance of them.

3 And Samuel spake unto all the house of Israel, saying, If ye do return unto the LORD with all your hearts, *then* put away the strange gods and Ashtaroth from among you, and prepare your hearts unto the LORD, and serve him only: and he will deliver you out of the hand of the Philistines. 4 Then the children of Israel did put away Baalim and Ashtaroth, and served the LORD only. 5 And Samuel said, Gather all Israel to Mizpeh, and I will pray for you unto the LORD. 6 And they gathered together to Mizpeh, and drew water, and poured *it* out before the LORD, and fasted on that day, and said there, We have sinned against the LORD. And Samuel judged the children of Israel in Mizpeh.

We may well wonder where Samuel was and what he was doing all this while, for we have not had him so much as named till now, since *ch.* iv. 1, not as if he were unconcerned, but his labours among his people are not mentioned till there appears the fruit of them. When he perceived that they began to *lament after the Lord* he struck while the iron was hot, and two things he endeavoured to do for them, as a faithful servant of God and a faithful friend to the Israel of God:—

I. He endeavoured to separate between them and their idols, for *there* reformation must begin. He *spoke to all the house of Israel* (*v.* 3), going, as it should seem, from place to place, an itinerant preacher (for we find not that they were gathered together till *v.* 5), and wherever he came this was his exhortation, "*If you do indeed return to the Lord,* as you seem inclined to do, by your lamentations for your departure from him and his from you, then know, 1. That you must renounce and abandon your idols, *put away the strange gods,* for your God will admit no rival; put them away from you, each one from himself, nay, and put them *from among you,* do what you can, in your places, to rid them out of the country. Put away Baalim, the strange gods, and Ashtaroth, the strange goddesses," for such also they had. Or Ashtaroth is particularly named because it was the best-beloved idol, and that which they were most wedded to. Note, True repentance strikes at the darling sin, and will with a peculiar zeal and resolution put away that, the sin which most *easily besets us.* 2. "That you must make a solemn business of returning to God, and do it with a serious consideration and a stedfast resolution, for both are included in *preparing the heart,* directing, disposing, establishing, the heart unto the Lord. 3. That you must be wholly for God, for him and no other, *serve him only,* else you do not serve him at all so as to please him. 4. That this is the only way and a sure way to prosperity and deliverance. Take this course, and *he will deliver you out of the hand of the Philistines;* for it was because you forsook him and served other gods that he delivered you into their hands." This was the purport of Samuel's preaching, and it had a wonderfully good effect (*v.* 4): *They put away Baalim and Ashtaroth,* not only quitted the worship of them, but destroyed their images, demolished their altars, and quite abandoned them. *What have we to do any more with idols?* Hos. xiv. 8; Isa. xxx. 22.

II. He endeavoured to engage them for ever to God and his service. Now that he had them in a good mind he did all he could to keep them in it.

1. He summons all Israel, at least by their elders, as their representatives, to meet him at Mizpeh (*v.* 5), and there he promises to pray for them. And it was worth while for them to come from the remotest part of the country to join with Samuel in seeking God's favour. Note, Ministers should pray for those to whom they preach, that God by his grace would make the preaching effectual. And, when we come together in religious assemblies, we must remember that it is as much our business there to join in public prayers as it is to hear a sermon. He would pray for them that, by the grace of God, they might be parted from their idols, and that then, by the providence of God, they might be delivered from the Philistines. Ministers would profit their people more if they did but pray more for them.

2. They obey his summons, and not only come to the meeting, but conform to the intentions of it, and appear there very well disposed, *v.* 6.

(1.) *They drew water and poured it out before the Lord,* signifying, [1.] Their humiliation and contrition for sin, owning themselves as water spilt upon the ground, which cannot be gathered up again (2 Sam. xiv. 14), so mean, so miserable, before God, Ps. xxii. 14. The Chaldee reads it, *They poured out their hearts in repentance before the Lord.* They wept rivers of tears, and sorrowed after a godly sort, for it was before the Lord and with an eye to him. [2.] Their earnest prayers and supplications to God for mercy. The soul is, in prayer, poured out before God, Ps. lxii. 8. [3.] Their universal reformation; they thus expressed their willingness to part with all their sins, and to retain no more of the relish or savour of them than the vessel does of the water that is poured out of it. They were free and full in their confession, and fixed in their resolution to cast away from them *all their transgressions.* Israel is now *baptized from their idols,* so Dr. Lightfoot. [4.] Some think it signifies their joy in the hope of God's mercy, which Samuel had assured them of. This ceremony was used with that signification at the feast of tabernacles, John vii. 37, 38, and see Isa. xii. 3. Taking it in this sense, it must be read, *They drew water after they had fasted.* In the close of their humiliation they thus expressed their hope of pardon and reconciliation.

(2.) *They fasted,* abstained from food, afflicted their souls, so expressing repentance and exciting devotion.

(3.) They made a public confession: *We have sinned against the Lord,* so giving glory to God and taking shame to themselves. And, if we thus confess our sins, we shall find our God *faithful and just to forgive us our sins.*

3. Samuel judged them at that time in Mizpeh, that is, he assured them, in God's name, of the pardon of their sins, upon their repentance, and that God was reconciled to them. It was a judgment of absolution. Or he received informations against those that did not leave their idols, and proceeded against them according to law. Those that would not judge themselves he judged. Or now he settled courts of justice among them, and appointed the terms and circuits which he observed afterwards, *v.* 16. Now he set those wheels a-going; and, whereas before he acted only as a prophet, now he began to act as a magistrate, to prevent their relapsing into those sins which now they seemed to have renounced.

7 And when the Philistines heard that the children of Israel were gathered together to Mizpeh, the lords of the Philistines went up against Israel. And when the children of Israel heard *it,* they were afraid of the Philistines. 8 And the children of Israel said to Samuel, Cease not to cry unto the LORD our God for us, that he will save us out of the hand of the Philistines. 9 And Samuel took a sucking lamb, and offered *it for* a burnt offering wholly unto the LORD: and Samuel cried unto the LORD for Israel; and the LORD heard him. 10 And as Samuel was offering up the burnt offering, the Philistines drew near to battle against Israel: but the LORD thundered with a great thunder on that day upon the Philistines, and discomfited them; and they were smitten before Israel. 11 And the men of Israel went out of Mizpeh, and pursued the Philistines, and smote them, until *they came* under Bethcar. 12 Then Samuel took a stone, and set *it* between Mizpeh and Shen, and called the name of it Eben-ezer, saying, Hitherto hath the LORD helped us.

Here, I. The Philistines invade Israel (*v.* 7), taking umbrage from that general meeting for repentance and prayer as if it had been a rendezvous for war, and, if so, they thought it prudent to keep the war out of their own country. They had no just cause for this suspicion; but those that seek to do mischief to others will be forward to imagine that others design mischief to them. Now see here, 1. How evil sometimes seems to come out of good. The religious meeting of the Israelites at Mizpeh brought trouble upon them from the Philistines, which perhaps tempted them to wish they had staid at home and to blame Samuel for calling them together. But we may be in God's way and yet meet with distress; nay, when sinners begin to repent and reform, they must expect that Satan will muster all his force against them, and set his instruments on work to the utmost to oppose and discourage them. But, 2. How good is, at length, brought out of that evil. Israel could never be threatened more seasonably than at this time, when they were repenting and praying, nor could they have been better prepared to receive the enemy; nor could the Philistines have acted more impoliticly for themselves than to make war upon Israel at this time, when they were making their peace with God. But God permitted them to do it, that he might have an opportunity immediately of crowning his people's reformation with tokens of his favour, and of confirming the words of his messenger, who had assured them that if they repented God would *deliver them out of the hand of the Philistines.* Thus he makes man's wrath to praise him, and serves the purposes of his grace to his people even by the malicious designs of their enemies against them, Mic. iv. 11, 12.

II. Israel cleaves closely to Samuel, as their best friend, under God, in this distress; though he was no military man, nor ever celebrated as a mighty man of valour, yet, being afraid of the Philistines, for whom they thought themselves an unequal match, they engaged Samuel's prayers for them: *Cease not to cry unto the Lord our God for us, v.* 8. They were here unarmed, unprepared for war, come together to fast and pray, not to fight; prayers and tears therefore being all the weapons many of them are now furnished with, to these they have recourse. And, knowing Samuel to have a great interest in heaven, they earnestly beg of him to improve it for them. They had reason to expect it, because he had promised to *pray for them* (*v.* 5), had promised them deliverance from the Philistines (*v.* 3), and they had been observant of him in all that which he had spoken to them from the Lord. Thus those who sincerely submit to Christ, as their lawgiver and judge, need not doubt of their interest in his intercession. They were very solicitous that Samuel should not cease to pray for them: what military preparations were to be made they would undertake them, but let him continue instant in prayer, perhaps remembering that when Moses did but let down his hand ever so little Amalek prevailed. O what a comfort is it to all believers that our great intercessor above never ceases, is never silent, for he *always appears in the presence of God for us!*

III. Samuel intercedes with God for them, and does it *by sacrifice, v.* 9. He took a sucking lamb, and offered it for a *burnt-offering, a whole burnt-offering, to the Lord,* and, while the sacrifice was in burning, with the smoke of it his prayers ascended up to heaven for Israel. Observe, 1. He made intercession with a sacrifice. Christ intercedes in the virtue of his satisfaction, and in all our prayers we must have an eye to his great oblation, depending upon that for audience and acceptance. Samuel's sacrifice without his prayer would have been an empty shadow, his prayer without the sacrifice would not have been so prevalent, but both together teach us what great things we may expect from God in answer to those prayers which are made with faith in Christ's sacrifice. 2. It was a burnt-offering, which was offered purely for the glory of God, so intimating that the great plea he relied on in his prayer was taken from the honour of God. "Lord, help thy people now for thy name's sake." When we endeavour to give glory to God we may hope he will, in answer to our prayers, work for his own glory. 3. It was but one sucking lamb that he offered; for it is the integrity and intention of the heart that God looks at, more than the bulk or number of the offerings. This one lamb (typifying the Lamb of God) was more acceptable than thousands of rams or bullocks would have been without faith and prayer. Samuel was no priest, but he was a Levite and a prophet; the case was extraordinary, and what he did was by special direction, and therefore was accepted of God. And justly was this reproach put upon the priests because they had corrupted themselves.

IV. God gave a gracious answer to Samuel's prayer (*v.* 9): *The Lord heard him.* He was himself a *Samuel, asked of God,* and many a Samuel, many a mercy in answer to prayer, God gave him. Sons of prayer should be famous for praying, as *Samuel was among those that call upon his name,* Ps. xcix. 6. The answer was a real answer: the Philistines were discomfited (*v.* 10, 11), totally routed, and that in such a manner as highly magnified the prayer of Samuel, the power of God, and the valour of Israel. 1. The prayer of Samuel was honoured; for at the very time when he was offering up his sacrifice, and his prayer with it, the battle began, and turned immediately against the Philistines. Thus *while he was yet speaking God heard,* and answered in thunder, Isa. lxv. 24. God showed that it was Samuel's prayer and sacrifice that he had respect to, and hereby let Israel know that as in a former engagement with the Philistines he had justly chastised their presumptuous confidence in the presence of the ark, on the shoulders of two profane priests, so now he graciously accepted their humble dependence upon the prayer of faith from the mouth and heart of a pious prophet. 2. The power of God was greatly honoured; for he took the work into his own hand, and discomfited them, not with great hail-stones, which would kill them (as Josh. x. 11), but with a great thunder, which frightened them and put them into such terror and consternation that they fainted away, and became a very easy prey to the sword of Israel, before whom, being thus confounded, they were smitten. Josephus adds that the earth quaked under them when first they made the onset and in many places opened and swallowed them up, and that, besides the terror of the thunder, their faces and hands were burnt with lightning, which obliged them to shift for themselves by flight. And, being thus driven to their heels by the immediate hand of God (whom they feared not so much as they had feared his ark, *ch.* iv. 7), then, 3. Honour was put upon the hosts of Israel; they were made use of for the completing of the victory, and had the pleasure of triumphing over their oppressors: *They pursued the Philistines, and smote them.* How soon did they find the benefit of their repentance, and reformation, and return to God! Now that they have thus engaged him for them none of their enemies can stand before them.

V. Samuel erected a thankful memorial of this victory, to the glory of God and for the encouragement of Israel, *v.* 12. He set up an *Eben-ezer, the stone of help.* If ever the people's hard hearts should lose the impressions of this providence, this stone would either revive the remembrance of it, and make them thankful, or remain a standing witness against them for their unthankfulness. 1. The place where this memorial was set up was the same where, twenty years before, the Israelites were smitten before the Philistines, for that was beside Eben-ezer, *ch.* iv. 1. The sin which procured that defeat formerly being pardoned upon their repentance, the pardon was sealed by this glorious victory in the very same place where they then suffered loss; see Hos. i. 10. 2. Samuel himself took care to set up this monument. He had been instrumental by prayer to obtain the mercy, and therefore he thought himself in a special manner obliged to make this grateful acknowledgment of it. 3. The reason he gives for the name is, *Hitherto the Lord hath helped us,* in which he speaks thankfully of what was past, giving the glory of the victory to God only, who had added this to all his former favours; and yet he speaks somewhat doubtfully for the future: "Hitherto things have done well, but what God may yet do with us we know not, *that* we refer to him; but let us praise him for what he has done." Note, The beginnings of mercy and deliverance are to be acknowledged by us with thankfulness so far as they go, though they be not completely finished, nay, though the issue seem uncertain. *Having obtained help from God, I continue hitherto,* says blessed Paul, Acts xxvi. 22.

13 So the Philistines were subdued, and they came no more into the coast of Israel: and the hand of the LORD was against the Philistines all the days of Samuel. 14 And the cities which the Philistines had taken from Israel were restored to Israel, from Ekron even unto Gath; and the coasts thereof did Israel deliver out of the hands of the Philistines. And there was peace between Israel and the Amorites. 15 And Samuel judged Israel all the days of his life. 16 And he went from year to year in circuit to Beth-el, and Gilgal, and Mizpeh, and judged Israel in all those places. 17 And his return *was* to Ramah; for there *was* his house; and there he judged Israel; and there he built an altar unto the LORD.

We have here a short account of the further good services that Samuel did to Israel. Having parted them from their idols, and brought them home to their God, he had put them into a capacity of receiving further benefits by his ministry. Having prevailed in that, he becomes, in other instances, a great blessing to them; yet, writing it himself, he is brief in the relation. We are not told here, but it appears (2 Chron. xxxv. 18) that in the days of Samuel the prophet the people of Israel kept the ordinance of the passover with more than ordinary devotion, notwithstanding the distance of the ark and the desolations of Shiloh. Many good offices, no doubt, he did for Israel, but here we are only told how instrumental he was, 1. In securing the public peace (*v.* 13): "*In his days the Philistines came no more into the coast of Israel,* made no inroads or incursions upon them; they perceived that God now fought for Israel and that his hand was against the Philistines, and this kept them in awe, and restrained the remainder of their wrath." Samuel was a protector and deliverer to Israel, not by dint of sword, as Gideon, nor by strength of arm, as Samson, but by the power of prayer to God and carrying on a work of reformation among the people. Religion and piety are the best securities of a nation. 2. In recovering the public rights, *v.* 14. By his influence Israel had the courage to demand the cities which the Philistines had unjustly taken from them and had long detained; and the Philistines, not daring to contend with one that had so great an interest in heaven, tamely yielded to the demand, and restored (some think) even Ekron and Gath, two of their capital cities, though afterwards they retook them; others think some small towns that lay between Ekron and Gath, which were forced out of the Philistines' hands. This they got by their reformation and religion, they got ground of their enemies and got forward in their affairs. It is added, *There was peace between Israel and the Amorites,* that is, the Canaanites, the remains of the natives. Not that Israel made any league with them, but they were quiet, and not so mischievous to Israel as they had sometimes been. Thus *when a man's ways please the Lord he maketh even his enemies to be at peace with him* and give him no disturbance, Prov. xvi. 7. 3. In administering public justice (*v.* 15, 16): *He judged Israel;* as a prophet he taught them their duty and reproved them for their sins, which is called *judging,* Ezek. xx. 4; xxii. 2. Moses judged Israel when he *made them know the statutes of God and his laws* (Exod. xviii. 16); and thus Samuel judged them to the last, even after Saul was made king; so he promised them then, when Saul was inaugurated (*ch.* xii. 23), *I will* not cease to *teach you the good and the right way.* As a magistrate, he received appeals from the inferior courts and gave judgment upon them, tried causes and determined them, tried prisoners and acquitted or condemned them, according to the law. This he did all his days, till he grew old and past service, and resigned to Saul; and afterwards he exercised authority when application was made to him; nay, he judged even Agag, and Saul himself. But when he was in his prime he rode the circuit, for the convenience of the country, at least of that part of it which lay most under his influence. He. kept courts at Beth-el, Gilgal, and Mizpeh, all in the tribe of Benjamin; but his constant residence was at Ramah, his father's city, and there he judged Israel, thither they resorted to him from all parts with their complaints, *v.* 17. 4. In keeping up the public exercises of religion; for there, where he lived, he built an altar to the Lord, not in contempt of the altar that was at Nob, or Gibeon, or wherever the. tabernacle was; but divine justice having laid Shiloh waste, and no other place being yet chosen for them to bring their offerings to (Deut. xii 11), he looked upon the law which confined them to one place to be for the present suspended, and therefore, being a prophet, and under divine direction, he did as the patriarchs did, he built an altar where he lived, both for the use of his own family and for the good of the country that resorted to it. Great men should use their wealth, power, and interest, for the keeping up of religion in the places where they live.

CHAP. VIII.

Things went so very well with Israel, in the chapter before, under Samuel's administration, that, methinks, it is a pity to find him so quickly, as we do in this chapter, old, and going off, and things working towards a revolution. But so it is; Israel's good days seldom continue long. We have here, I. Samuel decaying, ver. 1. II. His sons degenerating, ver. 2, 3. III. Israel discontented with the present government and anxious to see a change. For, 1. They petition Samuel to set a king over them, ver. 4, 5. 2. Samuel brings the matter to God, ver. 6. 3. God directs him what answer to give them, by way of reproof (ver. 7, 8), and by way of remonstrance, setting forth the consequences of a change of the government, and how uneasy they would soon be under it, ver. 9—18. 4. They insist upon their petition, ver. 19, 20. 5. Samuel promises them, from God, that they shall shortly be gratified, ver. 21, 22. Thus hard is it for people to know when they are well off.

AND it came to pass, when Samuel was old, that he made his sons judges over Israel. 2 Now the name of his firstborn was Joel; and the name of his second, Abiah: *they were* judges in Beer-sheba. 3 And his sons walked not in his ways, but turned aside after lucre, and took bribes, and perverted judgment.

Two sad things we find here, but not strange things:—1. A good and useful man growing old and unfit for service (*v.* 1): *Samuel was old,* and could not judge Israel, as he had done. He is not reckoned to be past sixty years of age now, perhaps not so much; but he was a man betimes, was full of thoughts and cares when he was a child, which perhaps hastened the infirmities of age upon him. The fruits that are the first ripe keep the worst. He had spent his strength and spirits in the fatigue of public business, and now, if he think to shake himself as at other times, he finds he is mistaken: old age has cut his hair. Those that are in the prime of their time ought to be busy in doing the work of life: for, as they go into years, they will find themselves less disposed to it and less able for it. 2. The children of a good man turning aside, and not treading in his steps. Samuel had given his sons so good an education, and they had given him such good hopes of their doing well, and gained such a reputation in Israel, that he made them judges, assistants to him awhile, and afterwards deputies under him at Beer-sheba, which lay remote from Ramah, *v.* 2. Probably the southern countries petitioned for their residence there, that they might not be necessitated to travel far with their causes. We have reason to think that Samuel gave them their commissions, not because they were his sons (he had no ambition to entail the government upon his family, any more than Gideon had), but because, for aught that yet appeared, they were men very fit for the trust; and none so proper to ease the aged judge, and take some of the burden off him, as (*cæteris paribus—other things being equal*) his own sons, who no doubt were respected for their good father's sake, and, having such an advantage at setting out, might soon have been great if they had but been good. But, alas! *his sons walked not in his ways* (*v.* 3), and, when their character was the reverse of his, their relation to so good a man, which otherwise would have been their honour, was really their disgrace. *Degeneranti genus opprobrium—A good extraction is a reproach to him that degenerates from it.* Note, Those that have the most grace themselves cannot give grace to their children. It has often been the grief of good men to see their posterity, instead of treading in their steps, trampling upon them, and, as Job speaks, *marring their path.* Nay, many that have begun well, promised fair, and set out in the right path, so that their parents and friends have had great hopes of them, yet afterwards have turned aside to by-paths, and been the grief of those of whom they should have been the joy. When Samuel's sons were made judges, and settled at a distance from him, then they discovered themselves. Thus, (1.) Many that have been well educated, and have conducted themselves well while they were under their parents' eye, when they have gone abroad into the world and set up for themselves have proved bad. Let none therefore be secure either of themselves or theirs, but depend on divine grace. (2.) Many that have done well in a state of meanness and subjection have been spoiled by preferment and power. Honours change men's minds, and too often for the worse. It does not appear that Samuel's sons were so profane and vicious as Eli's sons; but, whatever they were in other respects, they were corrupt judges, they *turned aside after lucre,* after *the mammon of unrighteousness,* so the Chaldee reads it. Note, *The love of money is the root of all evil.* It is pernicious in any, but especially in judges. Samuel had taken no bribes (*ch.* xii. 3), but his sons had, though, no doubt, he warned them against it when he made them judges; and then they perverted judgment. In determining controversies, they had an eye to the bribe, not to the law, and enquired who bid highest, not who had right on his side. It is sad with a people when the public justice that should do them right, being perverted, does them the greatest wrong.

4 Then all the elders of Israel gathered themselves together, and came to Samuel unto Ramah, 5 And said unto him, Behold, thou art old, and thy sons walk not in thy ways: now make us a king to judge us like all the nations. 6 But the thing displeased Samuel, when they said, Give us a king to judge us. And Samuel prayed unto the LORD. 7 And the LORD said unto Samuel, Hearken unto the voice of the people in all that they say unto thee: for they have not rejected thee, but they have rejected me, that I should not reign over them. 8 According to all the works which they have done since the day that I brought them up out of Egypt even unto this day, wherewith they have forsaken me, and served other gods, so do they also unto thee. 9 Now therefore hearken unto their voice: howbeit yet protest solemnly unto them, and show them the manner of the king that shall reign over them. 10 And Samuel told all the words of the LORD unto the people that asked of him a king. 11 And he said, This will be the manner of the king that shall reign over you: he will take your sons, and appoint *them* for himself, for his chariots, and *to be* his horsemen; and *some* shall run before his chariots. 12 And he will appoint him captains over thousands, and captains over fifties; and *will set them* to ear his ground, and to reap his harvest, and to make his instruments of war, and instruments of his chariots. 13 And he will take your daughters *to be* confectionaries, and *to be* cooks, and *to be* bakers. 14 And he will take your fields, and your vineyards, and your oliveyards, *even* the best *of them,* and give *them* to his servants. 15 And he will take the tenth of your seed, and of your vineyards, and give to his officers, and to his servants. 16 And he will take your menservants, and your maidservants, and your goodliest young men, and your asses, and put *them* to his work. 17 He will take the tenth of your sheep: and ye shall be his servants. 18 And ye shall cry out in that day because of your king which ye shall have chosen you; and the LORD will not hear you in that day. 19 Nevertheless the people refused to obey the voice of Samuel; and they said, Nay; but we will have a king over us; 20 That we also may be like all the nations; and that our king may judge us, and go out before us, and fight our battles. 21 And Samuel heard all the words of the people, and he rehearsed them in the ears of the LORD. 22 And the LORD said to Samuel, Hearken unto their voice and make them a king. And Samuel

said unto the men of Israel, Go ye every man unto his city.

We have here the starting of a matter perfectly new and surprising, which was the setting up of kingly government in Israel. Perhaps the thing had been often talked of among them by those that were given to change and affected that which looked great. But we do not find that it was ever till now publicly proposed and debated. Abimelech was little better than a titular king, though he is said to reign over Israel (Judges ix. 22), and perhaps his fall had for a great while rendered the title of king odious in Israel, as that of Tarquinius did among the Romans; but, if it had, by this time the odium was worn off, and some bold steps are here taken towards so great a revolution as that amounted to. Here is,

I. The address of the elders to Samuel in this matter (*v.* 4, 5): They *gathered themselves together*, by common consent; and not in a riotous tumultuous manner, but with the respect due to his character, they came to him to his house at Ramah with their address, which contained,

1. A remonstrance of their grievances: in short, *Thou art old, and thy sons walk not in thy ways.* Many a fairer occasion that people had had to ask a king, when they were oppressed by their neighbours or embroiled at home for want of *a king in Israel,* but a small thing will serve factious spirits for a colour to desire a change. (1.) It was true that Samuel was old; but if that made him less able to ride the circuit, and sit long on the bench, yet it made him the more wise and experienced, and, upon that account, the fitter to rule. If he was old, had he not grown old in their service? And it was very unkind, ungrateful, nay, and unjust, to cast him off when he was old, who had spent his days in doing them good. God had saved his youth from being despicable (*ch.* iii. 20), yet they make his old age so, which should have been counted worthy of double honour. If old people be upbraided with their infirmities, and laid aside for them, let them not think it strange; Samuel himself was so. (2.) It was true that his sons did not walk in his ways; the more was his grief, but they could not say it was his fault: he had not, like Eli, indulged them in their badness, but was ready to receive complaints against them. And, if that had been the thing desired, we may well suppose, upon the making out of the charge of bribery against them he would have superseded their commissions and punished them. But this would not content the elders of Israel; they had another project in their head.

2. A petition for the redress of these grievances, by setting a king over them: *Make us a king to judge us like all the nations.* Thus far it was well, that they did not rise up in rebellion against Samuel and set up a king for themselves, *vi et armis—by force;* but they applied to Samuel, God's prophet, and humbly begged of him to do it. But it appears by what follows that it was an evil proposal and ill made, and was displeasing to God. God designed them a king, a man after his own heart, when Samuel was dead; but they would anticipate God's counsel, and would have one now that Samuel was old. They had a prophet to judge them, that had immediate correspondence with heaven, and therein they were great and happy above any nation, none having God *so nigh unto them* as they had, Deut. iv. 7. But this would not serve; they must have a king to judge them with external pomp and power, like *all the nations.* A poor prophet in a mantle, though conversant in the visions of the Almighty, looked mean in the eyes of those who judged by outward appearance; but a king in a purple robe, with his guards and officers of state, would look great: and such a one they must have. They knew it was in vain to court Samuel to take upon him the title and dignity of a king, but he must appoint them one. They do not say, "Give us a king that is wise and good, and will judge better than thy sons do," but, "Give us a king," any body that will but make a figure. Thus foolishly did they forsake their own mercies, and, under pretence of advancing the dignity of their nation to that of their neighbours, did really thrust themselves down from their own excellency, and profane their crown by *casting it to the ground.*

II. Samuel's resentment of this address, *v.* 6. Let us see how he took it. 1. It cut him to the heart. Probably it was a surprise to him, and he had not any intimation before of their design, which made it the more grievous. The thing displeased Samuel; not when they upbraided him with his own infirmities and his children's irregularities (he could patiently bear what reflected on himself and his own family), but it *displeased him when they said, Give us a king to judge us,* because that reflected upon God and his honour. 2. It drove him to his knees; he gave them no answer for the present, but took time to consider of what they proposed, and prayed unto the Lord for direction what to do, spreading the case before him and leaving it with him, and so making himselt easy. Samuel was a man much in prayer, and we are encouraged *in every thing to make our requests known to God,* Phil. iv. 6. When any thing disturbs us, it is our interest, as well as our duty, to show before God our trouble, and he gives us leave to be humbly free with him.

III. The instruction God gave him concerning this matter. Those that in straits seek to God shall find him nigh unto them, and ready to direct them. He tells him,

1. That which would be an allay to his displeasure. Samuel was much disturbed

at the proposal: it troubled him greatly to see his prophetic office thus slighted, and all the good turns he had done to Israel thus ungratefully returned; but God tells him he must not think it either hard or strange. (1.) He must not think it hard that they had put this slight upon him, for they had herein put a slight upon God himself: "*They have not rejected thee* only, but *they have rejected me.* I share with thee in the affront," *v.* 7. Note, If God interest himself in the indignities that are done us, and the contempts that are put upon us, we may well afford to bear them patiently; nor need we think the worse of ourselves if *for his sake we bear reproach* (Ps. lxix. 7), but rather rejoice and count it an honour, Col. i. 24. Samuel must not complain that they were weary of his government, though just and gentle, for really they were weary of God's government; this was what they disliked: *They have rejected me, that I should not reign over them.* God *reigns over the heathen* (Ps. xlvii. 8), over all the world, but the government of Israel had hitherto been, in a more peculiar manner than ever any government was, a Theocracy, a divine government; their judges had their call and commission immediately from God; the affairs of their nation were under his peculiar direction. As the constitution, so the administration of their government, was by *Thus saith the Lord;* this method they were weary of, though it was their honour and safety, above any thing, so long as they kept in with God. They were indeed so much the more exposed to calamities if they provoked God to anger by sin, and found they could not transgress at so cheap a rate as other nations could, which perhaps was the true reason why they desired to stand upon the same terms with God that other nations did. (2.) He must not think it strange, nor marvel at the matter, for they do as they always have done: *According to all the works which they have done, since the day that I brought them out of Egypt, so do they unto thee, v.* 8; They had at first been so very respectful and obsequious to Samuel that he began to hope they were cured of their old stubborn disposition; but now he found himself deceived in them, and must not be surprised at it. They had always been rude to their governors, witness Moses and Aaron; nay, *They have forsaken me and served other gods;* the greatness of their crime, in affecting new gods, may make this crime of affecting new governors seem little. Samuel might expect they would deal treacherously, for they were called *transgressors from the womb,* Isa. xlviii. 8. This had been *their manner from their youth up,* Jer. xxii. 21.

2. He tells him that which would be an answer to their demand. Samuel would not have known what to say if God had not instructed him. Should he oppose the motion, it would bespeak a greater fondness of power and dominion than did become a prophet, and an indulgence of his sons. Should he yield to the motion, it would look like the betraying of his trust, and he would become accessory to all the bad consequences of a change. Aaron sinned in gratifying the people when they said, *Make us gods;* Samuel dares not therefore comply with them when they say, *Make us a king,* but he gives them, with assurance, the answer God sent them.

(1.) He must tell them that *they shall have a king. Hearken to the voice of the people, v.* 7, and again, *v.* 9. Not that God was pleased with their request, but, as sometimes he crosses us in love, so at other times he gratifies us in wrath; he did so here. When they said, *Give us a king and princes he gave them a king in his anger* (see Hos. xiii. 10, 11), as he gave them quails, Ps. cvi. 15; lxxviii. 29. God bade Samuel humour them in this matter, [1.] That they might be beaten with their own rod, and might feel, to their cost, the difference between his government and the government of a king; see 2 Chron. xii. 8. It soon appeared how much worse their condition was, in all respects, under Saul, than it had been under Samuel. [2.] To prevent something worse. If they were not gratified, they would either rise in rebellion against Samuel or universally revolt from their religion and admit the gods of the nations, that they might have kings like them. Rather than so, let them have a king. [3.] God knows how to bring glory to himself out of it, and to serve his own wise purposes even by their foolish counsels.

(2.) But he must tell them, withal, that when they have a king they will soon have enough of him, and will, when it is too late, repent of their choice. This he must *protest solemnly to them* (*v.* 9), that, if they would have a king to rule them, as the eastern kings ruled their subjects, they would find the yoke exceedingly heavy. They looked only at the pomp or magnificence of a king, and thought that would make their nation great and considerable among its neighbours, and would strike a terror upon their enemies; but he must bid them consider how they would like to bear the charges of that pomp, and how they would endure that arbitrary power which the neighbouring kings assumed. Note, Those that set their hearts inordinately upon any thing in this world ought, for the moderating of their desires, to consider the inconveniences as well as the conveniences that will attend it, and to set the one over against the other in their thoughts. Those that submit to the government of the world and the flesh are told plainly what hard masters they are, and what a tyranny the dominion of sin is; and yet they will exchange God's government for it.

IV. Samuel's faithful delivery of God's mind to them, *v.* 10. He *told them all the words of the Lord,* how ill he resented it, that he construed it a rejecting of him, and compared it with their serving other gods,—that he would grant their request if they insisted on it, but withal had ordered him to represent to them the certain consequences of their choice, that they would be such that if they had any reason left them, and would allow themselves to consult their own interest, they would withdraw their petition, and beg to continue as they were. Accordingly he lays before them, very particularly, what would be, not the right of a king in general, but *the manner of the king that should reign over them,* according to the pattern of the nations, *v.* 11. Samuel does not speak (as bishop Patrick expounds it) of a just and honest right of a king to do these things, for his right is quite otherwise described in that part of Moses's law which concerns the king's duty, but such a right as the kings of the nations had then acquired. *This shall be the manner of the king,* that is, "thus he must support his dignity at the expense of that which is dearest to you, and thus he will abuse his power, as those that have power are apt to do; and, having the militia in his hand, you will be under a necessity of submitting to him."

1. If they will have such a king as the nations have, let them consider, (1.) That king must have a great retinue, abundance of servants to wait on him, grooms to look after his chariots and horses, gentlemen to ride about with him, and footmen to run before his chariots. This is the chief grandeur of princes, and the imaginary glory of great men, to have a multitude of attendants. And whence must he have these? "Why, he will take your sons, who are free-born, have a liberal education, and whom you now have at your own disposal, and will *appoint them for himself,*" *v.* 11. They must wait upon him, and be at his beck; those that used to work for their parents and themselves must work for him, *ear his ground, and reap his harvest* (*v.* 12), and count it their preferment too, *v.* 16. This would be a great change. (2.) He must keep a great table; he will not be content to dine with his neighbours upon a sacrifice, as Samuel used to do (*ch.* ix. 13); but he must have a variety of dainty dishes, forced meats, and sweet-meats, and delicate sauces; and who must prepare him these? "Why, he will take your daughters, the most ingenious and handy of them, whom you hoped to prefer to houses and tables of their own; and, whether you be willing or no, they must be his confectioners, and cooks, and bakers, and the like." (3.) "He must needs have a standing army, for guards and garrisons; and your sons, instead of being elders of your cities, and living in quiet and honour at home, must be captains over thousands and captains over fifties, and must be disposed of at the pleasure of the sovereign." (4.) "You may expect that he will have great favourites, whom, having dignified and ennobled, he must enrich, and give them estates suitable to their honour; and which way can he do that, but out of your inheritances? *v.* 14. *He will take your fields and vineyards,* which descended to you from your ancestors, and which you hoped to leave to your posterity after you, *even the best of them;* and will not only take them to himself (you could bear that better), but he will *give them to his servants,* who will be your masters, and bear rule over that for which you have laboured, How will you like that?" 5. "He must have great revenues to maintain his grandeur and power with; and whence must he have them but from you? He will take the tenth of the fruits of your ground (*v.* 15), and your cattle, *v.* 17. You think the tenths, the double tenths, which the law of God has appointed for the support of the church, grievous enough, and grudge the payment of them; but, if you have a king, there must issue another tenth out of your estates, which will be levied with more rigour, for the support of the royal dignity. Consider the expense with the magnificence, and whether it will quit cost."

2. These would be their grievances, and, (1.) They would have none but God to complain to. Once they complained to the prince himself, and were answered, according to the manner of the king, Your *yoke is heavy, and I will add to it,* 1 Kings xii. 11. (2.) When they complained to God he *would not hear them, v.* 18. Nor could they expect that he should, both because they had been deaf to his calls and admonitions, and this trouble, in particular, they had brought upon themselves by rejecting him, and would not believe when he told them what would come of it. Note, When we bring ourselves into distress by our own irregular desires and projects we justly forfeit the comfort of prayer and the benefit of divine aids, and, if God be not better to us than we deserve, must have our relief in our own hands, and then it is bad with us.

V. The people's obstinacy in their demand, *v.* 19, 20. One would think such a representation of the consequences as this was, coming from God himself, who can neither deceive by his word nor be deceived in his knowledge, should have prevailed with them to waive their request: but their hearts were upon it, right or wrong, good or evil: "*We will have a king over us,* whatever God or Samuel say to the contrary; we will have a king, whatever it cost us, and whatever inconvenience we bring upon ourselves or our posterity by it." See their folly. 1. They were quite deaf to reason and blind to their own interest. They could not answer Samuel's arguments against it, nor deny the force of them, and yet they grow more violent in their request, and more insolent. Before it was, "Pray, *make us a king;*" now it is, "*Nay, but we will have a king;* yea, that we will, because we will; nor will we bear to have any thing said against it." See the absurdity of inordinate desires, and how they rob men of their reason. 2. They could not stay God's time. God had intimated to them in the law that, in due time, Israel should have a king (Deut. xvii. 14, 15), and perhaps they had some intimation that the time was at hand; but they are all in haste: "We, in our day, will have this king over us." Could they but have waited ten or twelve years longer they would have had David, a king of God's giving in mercy, and all the calamities that attended the setting up of Saul would have been prevented. Sudden resolves and hasty desires make work for a long and leisurely repentance. 3. That which they aimed at in desiring a king was not only, as before, that they might be like the nations, and levelled with the one above whom God had so far advanced them, but that they might have one to judge them, and to go out before them when they took the field, and to fight their battles. Foolish people and unwise! Could they ever desire a battle better fought for them than the last was, by Samuel's prayer and God's thunder? *ch.* vii. 10. Was victory hereby too sure to them? And were they fond of trying the chance of war at the same uncertainty that others did? So sick, it seems, were they of their privileges: and what was the issue? Their first king was slain in a battle, which none of their judges ever were; so was Josiah, one of the last and best.

VI. The dismissing of them with an intimation that very shortly they should have what they asked. 1. *Samuel rehearsed all their words in the ears of the Lord, v.* 21. Not but that God perfectly knew it, without Samuel's report; but thus he dealt faithfully between God and Israel, as a prophet, returning the answer to him that sent him; and thus he waited on God for further direction. God is fully acquainted with the state of the case we are in care and doubt about, but he will know it from us. His rehearsing it *in the ears of the Lord* intimates that it was done in private; for the people were not disposed to join with him in prayer to God for direction in this matter; also it bespeaks a holy familiarity, to which God graciously admits his people: they speak in the ears of the Lord, as one friend whispers with another; their communion with God is *meat they have to eat which the world knows not of,* John iv. 32. 2. God gave direction that they should have a king, since they were so inordinately set upon it (*v.* 22): "*Make them a king,* and let them make their best of him, and thank themselves if that very pomp and power which they are so eager to see their sovereign in be their plague and burden." *So he gave them up to their own hearts' lusts.* Samuel told them this, but sent them home for the present, *every man to his city;* for the designation of the person must be left to God; they had now no more to do. When God saw fit to notify the choice to Samuel they should hear further from him; in the mean time let them keep the peace and expect the issue.

CHAP. IX.

Samuel had promised Israel, from God, that they should have a king; it is strange that the next news is not of candidates setting up for the government, making an interest in the people, or recommending themselves to Samuel, and, by him, to God, to be put in nomination. Why does not the prince of the tribe of Judah, whoever he is, look about him now, remembering Jacob's entail of the sceptre on that tribe? Is there never a bold aspiring man in Israel, to say, "I will be king, if God will choose me?" No, none appears, whether it is owing to a culpable mean-spiritedness or a laudable humility I know not; but surely it is what can scarcely be paralleled in the history of any kingdom; a crown, such a crown, set up, and nobody bids for it. Most governments began in the ambition of the prince to rule, but Israel's in the ambition of the people to be ruled. Had any of those elders who petitioned for a king afterwards petitioned to be king, I should have suspected that person's ambition to have been at the bottom of the motion; but now (let them have the praise of what was good in them) it was not so. God having, in the law, undertaken to choose their king (Deut. xvii. 15), they all sit still, till they hear from heaven, and that they do in this chapter, which begins the story of Saul, their first king, and, by strange steps of Providence, brings him to Samuel to be anointed privately, and so to be prepared for an election by lot, and a public commendation to the people, which follows in the next chapter. Here is, I. A short account of Saul's parentage and person, ver. 1, 2. II. A large and particular account of the bringing of him to Samuel, to whom he had been before altogether a stranger. 1. God, by revelation, had told Samuel to expect him, ver. 15, 16. 2. God, by providence, led him to Samuel. (1.) Being sent to seek his father's asses, he was at a loss, ver. 3–5. (2.) By the advice of his servant, he determined to consult Samuel, ver. 6–10. (3.) By the direction of the young maidens, he found him out, ver. 11–14. (4.) Samuel, being informed of God concerning him (ver. 17), treated him with respect in the gate (ver. 18–21), in the dining-room (ver. 22–24), and at length in private, where he prepared him to hear the surprising news that he must be king, ver. 25–27. And these beginnings would have been very hopeful and promising if it had not been that the sin of the people was the spring of this great affair.

NOW there was a man of Benjamin, whose name *was* Kish, the son of Abiel, the son of Zeror, the son of Bechorath, the son of Aphiah, a Benjamite, a mighty man of power. 2 And he had a son, whose name *was* Saul, a choice young man, and a goodly: and *there was* not among the children of Israel a goodlier person than he: from his shoulders and upward *he was* higher than any of the people.

We are here told, 1. What a good family Saul was of, *v.* 1. He was of the tribe of Benjamin; so was the New-Testament Saul, who also was called *Paul,* and he mentions it as his honour, for Benjamin was a favourite, Rom. xi. 1; Phil. iii. 5. That tribe had been reduced to a very small number by the fatal war with Gibeah, and much ado there was to provide wives for those 600 men that were the poor remains of it out of that diminished tribe, which is here called, with good reason, *the smallest of the tribes of Israel, v.* 21. Saul sprang as a root out of a dry ground. That tribe, though fewest in number, was first in dignity, *God giving more abundant honour to that part which lacked,* 1 Cor. xii. 24. His father was *Kish, a mighty man of power,* or, as the margin reads it, *in substance;* in spirit bold, in body strong, in estate wealthy. The whole lot of the tribe of Benjamin coming to be distributed among 600 men, we may suppose their inheritances were much larger than theirs who were of other tribes, an advantage which somewhat helped to balance the disadvantage of the smallness of their number. 2. What a good figure Saul made, *v.* 2. No mention is here made of his wisdom or virtue, his learning or piety, or any of the accomplishments of his mind, but that he was a tall, proper, handsome man, that had a good face, a good shape, and a good presence, graceful and well proportioned: *Among all the children of Israel there was not a goodlier person than he;* and, as if nature had marked him for pre-eminence and superiority, he was taller by the head and shoulders than any of the people, the fitter to be a match for the giants of Gath, the champions of the Philistines. When God chose a king after his own heart he pitched upon one that was not at all remarkable for the height of his stature, nor any thing in his countenance but the innocence and sweetness that appeared there, *ch.* xvi. 7, 12. But when he chose a king after the people's heart, who aimed at nothing so much as stateliness and grandeur, he pitched upon this huge tall man, who, if he had no other good qualities, yet would look great. It does not appear that he excelled in strength so much as he did in stature; Samson did, and him they slighted, bound, and betrayed into the hands of the Philistines; justly therefore are they now put off with one who, though of uncommon height, is weak as other men. They would have a king like the nations, and the nations commonly chose portly men for their kings.

3 And the asses of Kish Saul's father were lost. And Kish said to Saul his son, Take now one of the servants with thee, and arise, go seek the asses. 4 And he passed through mount Ephraim, and passed through the land of Shalisha, but they found *them* not: then they passed through the land of Shalim, and *there they were* not: and he passed through the land of the Benjamites, but they found *them* not. 5 *And* when they were come to the land of Zuph, Saul said to his servant that *was* with him, Come, let us return; lest my father leave *caring* for the asses, and take thought for us. 6 And he said unto him, Behold now, *there is* in this city a man of God, and *he is* an honourable man; all that he saith cometh surely to pass: now let us go thither; peradventure he can show us our way that we should go. 7 Then said Saul to his servant, But, behold, *if* we go, what shall we bring the man? for the bread is spent in our vessels, and *there is* not a present to bring to the man of God: what have we? 8 And the servant answered Saul again, and said, Behold, I have here at hand the fourth part of a shekel of silver: *that* will I give to the man of God, to tell us our way. 9 (Beforetime in Israel, when a man went to enquire of God, thus he spake, Come, and let us go to the seer: for *he that is* now *called* a Prophet was beforetime called a Seer.) 10 Then said Saul to his servant, Well said; come, let us go. So they went unto the city where the man of God *was.*

Here is, I. A great man rising from small beginnings. It does not appear that Saul had any preferment at all, or was in any post of honour or trust, till he was chosen king of Israel. Most that are advanced rise gradually, but Saul, from the level with his neighbours, stepped at once into the throne, according to that of Hannah, He *raiseth up the poor out of the dust, to set them among princes,* 1 Sam. ii. 8. Saul, it should seem, though he was himself married and had children grown up, yet lived in his father's house, and was subject to him. Promotion comes not by chance nor human probabilities, but God is the Judge.

II. A great event arising from small occurrences. How low does the history begin! Having to trace Saul to the crown, we find him first employed as meanly as any we meet with called out to preferment.

1. Saul's father sends him with one of his servants to seek some asses that he had lost. It may be they had no way then to give public notice of such a number of asses strayed or stolen out of the grounds of Kish the Benjamite. A very good law they had to oblige men to bring back an ox or an ass that went astray, but it is to be feared that was, as other good laws, neglected and forgotten. It is easy to observe here that those who have must expect to lose, that it is wisdom to look after what is lost, that no man should think it below him to know the state of his flocks, that children should be forward to serve their parents' interests. Saul readily went to *seek his father's asses, v.* 3, 4. His taking care of the asses is to be ascribed, not so much to the humility of his spirit as to the plainness and simplicity of those times. But his obedience to his father in it was very commendable. *Seest thou a man diligent in his business,* and dutiful to his superiors, willing to stoop and willing to take pains? he does as Saul stand fair for preferment. The servant of Kish would be faithful only as a servant, but Saul as a son, in his own business, and therefore he was sent with him. Saul and his servants travelled far (probably on foot) in quest of the asses, but in vain:

they found them not. He missed of what he sought, but had no reason to complain of the disappointment, for he met with the kingdom, which he never dreamed of.

2. When he could not find them, he determined to return to his father (*v.* 5), in consideration of his father's tender concern for him, being apprehensive that if they staid out any longer his aged father would begin to fear, as Jacob concerning Joseph, that an evil beast had devoured them or some mischief had befallen them; he will *leave caring for the asses,* as much as he was in care about them, and *will take thought for us.* Children should take care that they do nothing to grieve or frighten their parents, but be tender of their tenderness.

3. His servant proposed (for, it should seem, he had more religion in him than his master) that, since they were now at Ramah, they should call on Samuel, and take his advice in this important affair. Observe here, (1.) They were close by the city where Samuel lived, and that put it into their heads to consult him (*v.* 6): *There is in this city a man of God.* Note, Wherever we are we should improve our opportunities of acquainting ourselves with those that are wise and good. But there are many that will consult a man of God, if he comes in their way, that would not go a step out of their way to get wisdom. (2.) The servant spoke very respectfully concerning Samuel, though he had no personal knowledge of him, but by common fame only: *He is a man of God, and an honourable man.* Note, Men of God are honourable men, and should be so in our eyes. Acquaintance with the things of God, and serviceableness to the kingdom of God, put true honour upon men, and make them great. This was the honour of Samuel, as a man of God, that *all he saith comes surely to pass.* This was observed concerning him when he was a young prophet (*ch.* iii. 19), *God did let none of his words fall to the ground;* and still it held true. (3.) They agreed to consult him concerning *the way that they should go; peradventure he can show us.* All the use they would make of the man of God was to be advised by him whether they should return home, or, if there were yet any hopes of finding the asses, which way they must go next—a poor business to employ a prophet about! Had they said, "Let us give up the asses for lost, and, now that we are so near the man of God, let us go and learn from him the good knowledge of God, let us consult him how we may order our conversations aright, and enquire the law at his mouth, since we may not have such another opportunity, and then we shall not lose our journey"—the proposal would have been such as became Israelites; but to make prophecy, that glory of Israel, serve so mean a turn as this, discovered too much what manner of spirit they were of. Note, Most people would rather be told their fortune than told their duty, how to be rich than how to be saved. If it were the business of the men of God to direct for the recovery of lost asses, they would be consulted much more than they are now that it is their business to direct for the recovery of lost souls; so preposterous is the care of most men! (4.) Saul was thoughtful what present they should bring to the man of God, what fee they should give him for his advice (*v.* 7): *What shall we bring the man?* They could not present him, as Jeroboam's wife did Ahijah, with loaves and cakes (1 Kings xiv. 3), for their bread was spent; but the servant bethought himself that he had in his pocket the fourth part of a shekel, about seven-pence halfpenny in value, and *that* he would give to the man of God to direct them, *v.* 8. "That will do," says Saul; "*let us go,*" *v.* 10. Some think that when Saul talked of giving Samuel a fee he measured him by himself, or by his sons, as if he must be hired to do an honest Israelite a kindness, and was like the false prophets, that *divined for money,* Mic. iii. 11. He came to him as a fortune-teller, rather than as a prophet, and therefore thought the fourth part of a shekel was enough to give him. But it rather seems to be agreeable to the general usage of those times, as it is to natural equity, that those who sowed spiritual things should reap not only eternal things from him that employs them, but temporal things from those for whom they are employed. Samuel needed not their money, nor would he have denied them his advice if they had not brought it (it is probable, when he had it, he gave it to the poor); but they brought it to him as a token of their respect and the value they put upon his office; nor did he refuse it, for they were able to give it, and, though it was but little, it was the widow's mite. But Saul, as he never thought of going to the man of God till the servant proposed it, so, it should seem, he mentioned the want of a present as an objection against their going; he would not own that he had money in his pocket, but, when the servant generously offered to be at the charge, then, "Well said," says Saul; "come, let us go." Most people love a cheap religion, and like it best when they can devolve the expense of it on others. (5.) The historian here takes notice of the name then given to the prophets: they called them *Seers,* or *seeing men* (*v.* 9), not but that the name *prophet* was then used, and applied to such persons, but that of seers was more in use. Note, Those that are prophets must first be seers; those who undertake to speak to others of the things of God must have an insight into those things themselves.

11 *And* as they went up the hill to the city, they found young maidens going out to draw water, and said unto them, Is the seer here? 12 And they

answered them, and said, He is; behold, *he is* before you: make haste now, for he came to day to the city; for *there is* a sacrifice of the people to day in the high place: 13 As soon as ye be come into the city, ye shall straightway find him, before he go up to the high place to eat: for the people will not eat until he come, because he doth bless the sacrifice; *and* afterwards they eat that be bidden. Now therefore get you up; for about this time ye shall find him. 14 And they went up into the city: *and* when they were come into the city, behold, Samuel came out against them, for to go up to the high place. 15 Now the LORD had told Samuel in his ear a day before Saul came, saying, 16 To morrow about this time I will send thee a man out of the land of Benjamin, and thou shalt anoint him *to be* captain over my people Israel, that he may save my people out of the hand of the Philistines: for I have looked upon my people, because their cry is come unto me. 17 And when Samuel saw Saul, the LORD said unto him, Behold the man whom I spake to thee of! this same shall reign over my people.

Here, I. Saul, by an ordinary enquiry, is directed to Samuel, *v.* 11—14. Gibeah of Saul was not twenty miles from Ramah where Samuel dwelt, and was near to Mizpeh where he often judged Israel, and yet, it seems, Saul had lived so very privately, and had taken so little notice of public affairs, that he had never seen Samuel, for when he met him (*v.* 18) he did not know him, so that there was no cause to suspect any secret compact or collusion between them in this matter. *I knew him not,* says John Baptist concerning Christ, John i. 31. Yet I do not think it any commendation to Saul that he was a stranger to Samuel. However,

1. The maid-servants of Ramah, whom they met with at the places of drawing water, could give him and his servant intelligence concerning Samuel; and very particular they were in their directions, *v.* 12, 13. We should always be ready to give what assistance we can to those that are enquiring after God's prophets, and to further them in their enquiries. Even the maid-servants could tell them, (1.) That there was a sacrifice that day in the high place, it being either an ordinary festival or an extraordinary day of prayer and thanksgiving, with which sacrifices were joined. The tabernacle being deprived of the ark, the altar there had not now the reputation it formerly had, nor were they confined to it, as they would be when God had again chosen a place to put his name in; and therefore now other places were allowed. Samuel had built an altar at Ramah (*ch.* vii. 17), and here we have him making use of that altar. (2.) That Samuel came that day to the city, either from his circuit or from his country seat. He was such a public person that his movements were generally known. (3.) That this was just the time of their meeting to feast before the Lord upon the sacrifice: "About this time you will find him in the street going up to the high place." They knew the hour of the solemn feast. (4.) That the people would not eat till Samuel came, not only because he was the worthiest person, and they ought in good manners to stay for him, and he was, as some think, the maker of this feast, the sacrifice being offered at his charge and upon his account; but because, as a man of God, whoever made the feast, *he* must bless the sacrifice, that is, those parts of the sacrifice which they feasted upon, which may be considered, [1.] As a common meal, and so this is an instance of the great duty of craving a blessing upon our meat before we partake of it. We cannot expect benefit from our food without that blessing, and we have no reason to expect that blessing if we do not pray for it. Thus we must give glory to God as our benefactor, and own our dependence upon him and our obligations to him. Or, [2.] As a religious assembly. When the sacrifice was offered, which was the ceremony, Samuel blessed it, that is, he prayed over it, and offered up spiritual sacrifices with it, which were the substance; and afterwards, when the holy duties were performed, they did eat. Let the soul first be served. The feast upon the sacrifice being a sacred rite, it was requisite that it should in a particular manner be blessed, as is the Christian eucharist. They feasted in token of their reconciliation to God by virtue of the sacrifice, and their participation of the benefits of it; and Samuel blessed the feast, that is, he prayed to God to grace the solemnity with his special presence, that it might answer those great ends. Bishop Hall observes what a particular account those maid-servants could give of the usages of those sacred feasts, and infers from it that, "where there is the practice and example of piety in the better sort, there will be a reflection of it upon the meanest. It is no small advantage to live in religious places; for we shall be much to blame if all goodness fall beside us."

2. Saul and his servant followed the directions given them, and very opportunely met Samuel going to the high place, the synagogue of the city, *v.* 14. This seemed purely accidental, but the divine providence ordered

it for the forwarding of this great event. The wise God serves very great and certain purposes by very small and casual occurrences. A sparrow falls not to the ground without our Father.

II. Samuel, by an extraordinary revelation, is informed concerning Saul. He was a seer, and therefore must see this in a way peculiar to himself.

1. God had told him, the day before, that he would, at this time, send him the man that should serve the people of Israel for such a king as they wished to have, *like all the nations*, v. 15, 16. He *told him in his ear*, that is, privately, by a secret whisper to his mind, or perhaps by a still small voice, some soft and gentle sounds conveyed to his ear, probably when he was praying in secret for direction in that and other affairs of the nation. He had spoken *in the ears of the Lord* (*ch.* viii. 21), and now God *spoke in his ear*, in token of friendship and familiarity, for *he revealeth his secret to his servants the prophets*, as secrets in their ear, Amos iii. 7. God told him before, that it might not be a surprise to him; and perhaps it was in expectation of it that he appointed the feast and the sacrifice, for the imploring of God's blessing upon this great and important affair, though he might keep the particular occasion in his own breast, God having only told it to him in his ear. The Hebrew phrase is, *He uncovered the ear of Samuel*, to which some allude for the explication of the way of God's revealing himself to us; he not only speaks, but *uncovers our ear*. We have naturally a covering on our ears, so that we perceive not what God says (Job xxxiii. 14), but, when God will manifest himself to a soul, he uncovers the ear, says, *Ephphatha, Be opened;* he takes *the veil from off the heart*, 2 Cor. iii. 16. Though God had, in displeasure, granted their request for a king, yet here he speaks tenderly of Israel; for even in *wrath he remembers mercy*. (1.) He calls them again and again his people; though a peevish and provoking people, yet mine still. (2.) He sends them a man to be captain over them, that they might not be a body without a head, and to *save them out of the hand of the Philistines*, which perhaps was more than many of them aimed at in desiring a king. (3.) He does it with a gracious respect to them and to their cry: *I have looked upon my people*, and *their cry has come unto me*. He gratified them with what they cried for, as the tender mother humours the froward child, lest it should break its heart. And (as bishop Patrick observes), though he would not hear their cry to relieve them against the oppression of their kings (*ch.* viii. 18), yet he was so gracious as to make those kings instruments of their deliverance from the oppression of their neighbours, which was more than they had reason to expect.

2. When Saul came up towards him in the street God again whispered Samuel in the ear (*v.* 17): *Behold the man whom I spoke to thee of!* Saul being a man of unusual stature, it is natural to think that Samuel fixed his eye upon him at a distance, and perhaps looked the more wistfully towards him because the hour had now come when God would send him the man that should be king of Israel, and he fancied this might be he; but, that he might be fully satisfied, God told him expressly, *That is the man* that shall *restrain* (for magistrates are heirs of restraint) *my people Israel*.

18 Then Saul drew near to Samuel in the gate, and said, Tell me, I pray thee, where the seer's house *is*. 19 And Samuel answered Saul, and said, I *am* the seer: go up before me unto the high place; for ye shall eat with me to day, and to morrow I will let thee go, and will tell thee all that *is* in thine heart. 20 And as for thine asses that were lost three days ago, set not thy mind on them; for they are found. And on whom *is* all the desire of Israel? *Is it* not on thee, and on all thy father's house? 21 And Saul answered and said, *Am* not I a Benjamite, of the smallest of the tribes of Israel? and my family the least of all the families of the tribe of Benjamin? wherefore then speakest thou so to me? 22 And Samuel took Saul and his servant, and brought them into the parlour, and made them sit in the chiefest place among them that were bidden, which *were* about thirty persons. 23 And Samuel said unto the cook, Bring the portion which I gave thee, of which I said unto thee, Set it by thee. 24 And the cook took up the shoulder, and *that* which *was* upon it, and set *it* before Saul. And *Samuel* said, Behold that which is left! set *it* before thee, *and* eat: for unto this time hath it been kept for thee since I said, I have invited the people. So Saul did eat with Samuel that day. 25 And when they were come down from the high place into the city, *Samuel* communed with Saul upon the top of the house. 26 And they arose early: and it came to pass about the spring of the day, that Samuel called Saul to the top of the house, saying, Up, that I may send thee away. And Saul

arose, and they went out both of them, he and Samuel, abroad. 27 *And* as they were going down to the end of the city, Samuel said to Saul, Bid the servant pass on before us, (and he passed on,) but stand thou still a while, that I may show thee the word of God.

Providence having at length brought Samuel and Saul together, we have here an account of what passed between them in the gate, at the feast, and in private.

I. In the gate of the city; passing through that, Saul found him (*v.* 18), and, little thinking that he was Samuel himself, asked him the way to Samuel's house: *Tell me where the seer's house is;* for there he expected to find him. See how mean a figure Samuel made, though so great a man: he took not any state, had no attendants, no ensigns of honour carried before him, nor any distinguishing habit, no, not when he went to church, but appeared, in all respects, so much a common person that Saul, though he was told he should meet him, never suspected that it was he, but, as if he looked more like a porter than a prophet, asked him the way to the seer's house. Thus is great worth oftentimes hidden under a very despicable appearance. Samuel knew that it was not the house, but the man, that he wanted, and therefore answered him, "*I am the seer,* the person you enquire for," *v.* 19. Samuel knew him before he knew Samuel; thus, though all that are called to the kingdom of glory are brought to know God, yet first they were known of him, Gal. iv. 9. Now, 1. Samuel obliges him to stay with him till the next day. The greatest part of this day had been spent in sacrificing, and the rest of it was to be spent in holy feasting, and therefore, "*To-morrow I will let thee go,* and not sooner; now *go up before me to the high place;* let us pray together, and then we will talk together." Saul had nothing in his mind but to find his asses, but Samuel would take him off from that care, and dispose him to the exercises of piety; and therefore bids him *go to the high place,* and go before him, because, it may be, some business obliged Samuel to call by the way. 2. He satisfies him about his asses (*v.* 20): *Set not thy mind on them,* be not in further care about them; *they are found.* By this Saul might perceive that he was a prophet, that he could give him an answer to the enquiry which he had not yet made, and tell him what he thought; and thence he might infer, if a man of God can do this, much more doth God himself *understand our thoughts afar off.* 3. He surprises him with an intimation of preferment before him: "*On whom is all the desire of Israel?* Is it not a king that they are set upon, and there is never a man in Israel that will suit them as thou wilt." It does not appear that the country had as yet any eye upon him for the government, because they had left it wholly to God to choose for them; but such a one as he they wished for, and his advancement would be the advancement of his family and relations, as Abner, and others. 4. To this strange intimation Saul returns a very modest answer, *v.* 21. Samuel, he thought, did but banter him, because he was a tall man, but a very unlikely man to be a king; for, though the historian says (*v.* 1) his father was a *mighty man of power,* yet he himself speaks diminishingly of his tribe and family. "Benjamin, the youngest of Jacob's sons, when grown up to be a man, was called a *little one* (Gen. xliv. 20); that tribe was diminished by the war of Gibeah; and *I am a Benjamite, my family the least,*" probably a younger house, not in any place of honour or trust, no, not in their own tribe. Gideon had expressed himself thus, Judg. vi. 15. A humble disposition is a good presage of preferment.

II. At the public feast; thither Samuel took him and his servant. Though the advancement of Saul would be the deposing of Samuel, yet that good prophet was so far from envying him, or bearing him any ill-will for it, that he was the first and forwardest man to do him honour, in compliance with the will of God. If this be the man whom God has chosen, though he be none of Samuel's particular friends or confidants, yet he is heartily welcome to his table, nay, to his bosom. We may suppose it was no unseasonable kindness to Saul to give him a meal's meat, for it seems, by what he said (*v.* 7), that all their meat and money were spent. But this was not all. Samuel treats him not as a common person, but a person of quality and distinction, to prepare both him and the people for what was to follow. Two marks of honour he put upon him:—1. He set him *in the best place,* as more honourable than any other of the guests, to whom he said, *Give this man place,* Luke xiv. 9. Though we may suppose the magistrates were there, who in their own city would claim precedency, yet the master of the feast made Saul and his servant too (who, if Saul was a king, must be respected as his prime minister of state) *sit in the chief place, v.* 22. Note, Civil respects must be paid to those who in civil things have the precedency given them by the divine providence. 2. He presented him with the *best dish,* which, having had notice from heaven the day before of his coming (*v.* 16), he had designed for him, and ordered the cook to secure for him, when he gave orders for inviting the guests and making preparation for them. And what should this precious dish be, which was so very carefully reserved for the king-elect? One would expect it should be something very nice and delicate. No, it was a plain shoulder of mutton (*v.* 23, 24). The right shoulder of the peace-offerings was to be given to the priests, who were God's receivers (Lev. vii. 32); the next in honour to that was the left shoulder, which probably was always allotted to those that sat at the upper end of the table, and was wont to be Samuel's mess at other times; so that his giving it to Saul now was an implicit resignation of his place to him. Some observe a significancy in this dish. The shoulder denotes strength, and the breast, which some think went with it, denotes affection: he that was king had *the government upon his shoulder*, for he must bear the weight of it; and the people in his bosom, for they must be dear to him.

III. What passed between them in private. Both that evening and early the next morning Samuel communed with Saul upon the flat roof of the house, *v.* 25, 26. We may suppose Samuel now told him the whole story of the people's desire of a king, the grounds of their desire, and God's grant of it, to all which Saul, living very privately, was perhaps a stranger; he satisfied him that he was the person God had pitched upon for the government; and whereas Saul would object that Samuel was in possession, and he would not for all the world take it out of his hands, Samuel, we may suppose, gave him all the assurance he could desire of his willingness to resign. Early in the morning he sent him towards home, brought him part of the way, bade him send his servant before, that they might be private (*v.* 27), and there, as we find in the beginning of the next chapter, he anointed him, and therein showed him the *word of the Lord*, that is, gave him full satisfaction that he was the person chosen to be king, for he would not jest with that sacred rite. It is by the *unction of the Holy Ghost* that Christ, the great prophet, *shows us the word of the Lord.* 1 John ii. 27, *the same anointing teacheth you of all things.*

CHAP. X.

We left Samuel and Saul walking together, probably some private way over the fields down from Ramah, perhaps in the paths of the vineyards, and Saul expecting to hear from Samuel the word of God. Now here we have, I. The anointing of Saul then and there, ver. 1. The signs Samuel gave him, ver. 2–6. And instructions, ver. 7—8. II. The accomplishment of those signs to the satisfaction of Saul, ver 9—13. III. His return to his father's house, ver. 14—16. IV. His public election by lot, and solemn inauguration, ver. 17—25. V. His return to his own city, ver. 26, 27. It is a great work that is here a doing, the setting up not only of a monarch, but of monarchy itself, in Israel; and therefore in all the advances towards it much of God is seen.

THEN Samuel took a vial of oil, and poured *it* upon his head, and kissed him, and said, *Is it* not because the LORD hath anointed thee *to be* captain over his inheritance? 2 When thou art departed from me to day, then thou shalt find two men by Rachel's sepulchre in the border of Benjamin at Zelzah; and they will say unto thee, The asses which thou wentest to seek are found: and, lo, thy father hath left the care of the asses, and sorroweth for you, saying, What shall I do for my son? 3 Then shalt thou go on forward from thence, and thou shalt come to the plain of Tabor, and there shall meet thee three men going up to God to Beth-el, one carrying three kids, and another carrying three loaves of bread, and another carrying a bottle of wine: 4 And they will salute thee, and give thee two *loaves* of bread; which thou shalt receive of their hands. 5 After that thou shalt come to the hill of God, where *is* the garrison of the Philistines: and it shall come to pass, when thou art come thither to the city, that thou shalt meet a company of prophets coming down from the high place with a psaltery, and a tabret, and a pipe, and a harp, before them; and they shall prophesy: 6 And the Spirit of the LORD will come upon thee, and thou shalt prophesy with them, and shalt be turned into another man. 7 And let it be, when these signs are come unto thee, *that* thou do as occasion serve thee; for God *is* with thee. 8 And thou shalt go down before me to Gilgal; and, behold, I will come down unto thee, to offer burnt offerings, *and* to sacrifice sacrifices of peace offerings: seven days shalt thou tarry, till I come to thee, and show thee what thou shalt do.

Samuel is here executing the office of a prophet, giving Saul full assurance from God that he should be king, as he was afterwards, according to these prophecies which went before of him.

I. He *anointed him* and *kissed him, v.* 1. This was not done in a solemn assembly, but it was done by divine appointment, which made up the want of all external solemnities, nor was it ever the less valid for its being done in private, under a hedge, or, as the Jews says, by *a fountain.* God's institutions are great and honourable, though the circumstances of their administration be ever so mean and despicable. 1. Samuel, by anointing Saul, assured him that it was God's act to make him king: *Is it not because the Lord hath anointed thee?* And, in token of that, the high priest was anointed to his office, to signify the conferring of those gifts upon him that were requisite for the discharge of its duties, and the same was intimated in the anointing of kings; for whom God calls he qualifies, and suitable qualifications furnish good proof of a commission. These sacred unctions, then used, pointed at the great Messiah, or anointed one, the king of the church, and high priest of our profession, who was anointed with the oil of the Spirit, not by measure, but without measure, and above all the priests and princes of the Jewish church. It was common oil, no doubt, which Samuel used, and we read not of his blessing it or praying over it. But it was only a vial of oil that he anointed him with, the vessel brittle, because his kingdom would soon be cracked and broken, and the quantity small, because he had but little of the Spirit conferred upon him to what David had, who was therefore anointed with a horn of oil, as were Solomon and Jehu with a box of oil. 2. By kissing him, he assured him of his own approbation of the choice, not only his consent to it, but his complacency in it, though it abridged his power and eclipsed his glory and the glory of his family. "*God has anointed thee,*" says Samuel, "*to be king,* and I am satisfied and very well pleased, in pledge of which take this kiss." It was likewise a kiss of homage and allegiance; hereby he not only owns him to be king, but his' king, and in this sense we are commanded to *kiss the Son,* Ps. ii. 12. God has anointed him, and therefore we must thus acknowledge him and do homage to him. In Samuel's explication of the ceremony, he reminds him, (1.) Of the nature of the government to which he is called. He was anointed to be a captain, a commander indeed, which bespeaks honour and power, but a commander in war, which bespeaks care, and toil, and danger. (2.) Of the origin of it: *The Lord hath anointed thee.* By him he ruled, and therefore must rule for him, in dependence on him, and with an eye to his glory. (3.) Of the end of it. It is over his inheritance, to take care of that, protect it, and order all the affairs of it for the best, as a steward whom a great man sets over his estate, to manage it for his service and give an account of it to him.

II. For his further satisfaction he gives him some signs, which should come to pass immediately, this very day; and they were such as would not only confirm the word of Samuel in general, and prove him a true prophet, but would confirm this word to Saul in particular, that he should be king. 1. He should presently meet with some that would bring him intelligence from home of the care his father's house was in concerning him, *v.* 2. These he would meet hard by Rachel's sepulchre. The first place Samuel directed him to was a sepulchre, the sepulchre of one of his ancestors, for Rachel died in travail with Benjamin; there he must read a lecture of his own mortality, and now that he had a crown in his eye must think of his grave, in which all his honour would be laid in the dust. Here two men would meet him, perhaps sent on purpose to look after him, and would tell him the asses were found, and his father was in pain concerning him, saying, *What shall I do for my son?* He would reckon it happened well that he met with these messengers; and it is good to eye Providence in favourable conjunctures (though the matter be minute) and to be encouraged to trust it in greater matters. 2. He should next meet with others going to Bethel, where, it should seem, there was a high place for religious worship, and these men were bringing their sacrifices thither, *v.* 3, 4. It was a token for good to one that was designed for the government of Israel, wherever he came, to meet with people going to worship God. It is supposed that those kids and loaves, and the bottle of wine which the three men had with them, were designed for sacrifice, with the meat-offerings and drink-offerings that were to attend the sacrifice; yet Samuel tells Saul that they will give him two of their loaves, and he must take them. Such a present would look to us now like the relieving of a beggar. Saul must hereafter remember the time when he received alms, and must therefore be humble and charitable to the poor. But perhaps it would then be construed a fit present for a prince; and, as such, Saul must receive it, the first present that was brought to him, by such as knew not what they did, nor why they did it, but God put it into their hearts, which made it the more fit to be a sign to him. These two loaves, which were the first tribute paid to this newly-anointed king, might serve for an admonition to him not to spend the wealth of his crown in luxury, but still to be content with plain food. Bread is the staff of life. 3. The most remarkable sign of all would be his joining with a company of prophets that he should meet with, under the influence of a spirit of prophecy, which should at that time come upon him. What God works in us by his Spirit serves much more for the confirming of faith than any thing wrought for us by his providence. He here (*v.* 5, 6) tells him, (1.) Where this would happen: *At the hill of God,* where there was a *garrison of the Philistines,* which is supposed to be near Gibeah, his own city, for there was the Philistines' garrison, *ch.* xiii. 3. Perhaps it was one of the articles of Samuel's agreement with them that they should have a garrison there, or, rather, after they were subdued in the beginning of his time they got ground again, so far as to force this garrison into that place, and thence God raised up the man that should chastise them. There was a place that was called the *hill of God,* because of one of the schools of the prophets built upon it; and such respect did even Philistines themselves pay to religion that a garrison of their soldiers suffered a school of God's prophets to live peaceably by them, and did not only not dislodge them, but not restrain nor disturb the public exercises of their devotion. (2.) Upon what occasion; he should meet *a company of prophets with music before them, prophesying*, and with them he should join himself. These prophets were not (as it should seem) divinely inspired to foretel things to come, nor did God reveal himself to them by dreams and visions, but they employed themselves in the study of the law, in instructing their neighbours, and in the acts of piety, especially in praising God, wherein they were wonderfully assisted and enlarged by the Spirit of God. It was happy for Israel that they had not only prophets, but companies of prophets, who gave them good instructions and set them good examples, and helped very much to keep up religion among them. Now the word of the Lord was not precious, as it had been when Samuel was first raised up, who had been instrumental in founding these colleges, or religious houses, whence, it is probable, the synagogues took their rise. What a pity was it that Israel should be weary of the government of such a man, who though he had not, as a man of war, expelled the Philistines, yet (which was a greater kindness to Israel) had, as a man of God, settled the schools of the prophets! Music was then used as a proper means to dispose the mind to receive the impressions of the good Spirit, as it did Elisha's, 2 Kings iii. 15. But we have no reason to look for the same benefit by it now, unless we saw it as effectual as it was then in Saul's case, to drive away the evil spirit. These prophets had been at the high place, probably offering sacrifice, and now they came back singing psalms. We should come from holy ordinances with our hearts greatly enlarged in holy joy and praise. See Ps. cxxxviii. 5. Saul should find himself strongly moved to join with them, and should be turned thereby *into another man* from what he had been while he lived in a private capacity. The Spirit of God, by his ordinances, changes men, wonderfully transforms them; Saul, by praising God in the communion of saints, became another man, but whether a new man or no may be questioned.

III. He directs him to proceed in the administration of his government as Providence should lead him, and as Samuel should advise him. 1. He must follow Providence in ordinary cases (*v.* 7): "*Do as occasion shall serve thee.* Take such measures as thy own prudence shall direct thee." But, 2. In an extraordinary strait that would hereafter befal him at Gilgal, and would be the most critical juncture of all, when he would have special need of divine aids, he must wait for Samuel to come to him, and must tarry *seven days* in expectation of him, *v.* 8. How his failing in this matter proved his fall we find afterwards, *ch.* xiii. 11. It was now a plain intimation to him that he was upon his good behaviour, and, though a king, must act under the direction of Samuel, and do as he should order him. The greatest of men must own themselves in subjection to God and his word.

9 And it was *so*, that when he had turned his back to go from Samuel, God gave him another heart: and all those signs came to pass that day. 10 And when they came thither to the hill, behold, a company of prophets met him; and the Spirit of God came upon him, and he prophesied among them. 11 And it came to pass, when all that knew him beforetime saw that, behold, he prophesied among the prophets, then the people said one to another, What *is* this *that* is come unto the son of Kish? *Is* Saul also among the prophets? 12 And one of the same place answered and said, But who *is* their father? Therefore it became a proverb, *Is* Saul also among the prophets? 13 And when he had made an end of prophesying, he came to the high place. 14 And Saul's uncle said unto him and unto his servant, Whither went ye? And he said, To seek the asses: and when we saw that *they were* no where, we came to Samuel. 15 And Saul's uncle said, Tell me, I pray thee, what Samuel said unto you. 16 And Saul said unto his uncle, He told us plainly that the asses were found. But of the matter of the kingdom, whereof Samuel spake, he told him not.

Saul has now taken his leave of Samuel, much amazed, we may well suppose, at what has been done to him, almost ready to question whether he be awake or no, and whether it be not all a dream. Now here we are told,

I. What occurred by the way, *v.* 9. Those signs which Samuel had given him came to pass very punctually; but that which gave him the greatest satisfaction of all was this, he found immediately that God had given him *another heart*. A new fire was kindled in his breast, such as he had never before been acquainted with: seeking the asses is quite out of his mind, and he thinks of nothing but fighting the Philistines, redressing the grievances of Israel, making laws, administering justice, and providing for the public safety; these are the things that now fill his head. He finds himself raised to such a pitch of boldness and bravery as he never thought he should be conscious of. He has no longer the heart of a husbandman, which is low, and mean, and narrow, and concerned only about his corn and cattle; but the heart of a statesman, a general, a prince. Whom God calls to any service he will make fit for it. If he advance to another station, he will give another heart, to those who sincerely desire to serve him with their power.

II. What occurred when he came near home. They came to *the hill* (*v.* 10), that is, to *Gibeah*, or *Geba*, which signifies *a hill*, and so the Chaldee here takes it as a proper name; he met with the prophets as Samuel had told him, and the Spirit of God came upon him, strongly and suddenly (so the word signifies), but not so as to rest and abide upon him. It came on so as to go off quickly. However, for the present, it had a strange effect upon him; for he immediately joined with the prophets in their devotion, and that with as much decorum and as great a transport of affection as any of them: *He prophesied among them.* Now,

1. His prophesying was publicly taken notice of, *v.* 11, 12. He was now among his acquaintance, who, when they saw him among the prophets, called one another to come and see a strange sight. This would prepare them to accept him as a king, though one of themselves, when they had seen how God had advanced him to the honour of a prophet. The seventy elders prophesied before they were made judges, Num. xi. 25. Now, (1.) They all wondered to see Saul among the prophets: *What is this that has come to the son of Kish?* Though this school of the prophets was near his father's house, yet he had never associated with them, nor shown them any respect, perhaps had sometimes spoken slightly of them; and now to see him prophesying among them was a surprise to them, as it was long after when his namesake, in the New Testament, preached that gospel which he had before persecuted, Acts ix. 21. Where God gives another heart it will soon show itself. (2.) One of them, that was wiser than the rest, asked, "*Who is their father*, or instructor? Is it not God? Are they not all taught of him? Do they not all owe their gifts to him? And is he limited? Cannot he make Saul a prophet, as well as any of them, if he please?" Or, "Is not Samuel their father?" Under God, he was so; and Saul had now lately been with him, which, by his servant, he might know. No marvel for him to prophesy who lay last night under Samuel's roof. (3.) It became a proverb, commonly used in Israel, when they would express their wonder at a bad man's either becoming good, or at least being found in good company, *Is Saul among the prophets?* Note, Saul among the prophets is a wonder to a proverb. Let not the worst be despaired of, yet let not an external show of devotion, and a sudden change for the present, be too much relied on; for Saul among the prophets was Saul still.

2. His being anointed was kept private. When he had done prophesying, (1.) It should seem he uttered all his words before the Lord, and recommended the affair to his favour, for he went straight *to the high place* (*v.* 13), to give God thanks for his mercies to him and to pray for the continuance of those mercies. But, (2.) He industriously concealed from his relations what had passed. His uncle, who met with him either at the high place or as soon as he came home, examined him, *v.* 14. Saul owned, for his servant knew it, that they had been with Samuel, and that he told them the asses were found, but said not a word of *the kingdom*, *v.* 14, 15. This was an instance, [1.] Of his humility. Many a one would have been so elated with this surprising elevation as to proclaim it upon the house-top. But Saul, though he might please himself with it in his own breast, did not pride himself in it among his neighbours. The heirs of the kingdom of glory are well enough pleased that *the world knows them not*, 1 John iii. 1. [2.] Of his prudence. Had he been forward to proclaim it, he would have been envied, and he knew not what difficulty that might have created him. Samuel had communicated it to him as a secret, and he knows how to keep counsel. Thus it appears that he had another heart, a heart fit for government. [3.] Of his dependence upon God. He does not go about to make an interest for himself, but leaves it to God to carry on his own work by Samuel, and, for his own part, sits still, to see how the matter will fall.

17 And Samuel called the people together unto the LORD to Mizpeh; 18 And said unto the children of Israel, Thus saith the LORD God of Israel, I brought up Israel out of Egypt, and delivered you out of the hand of the Egyptians, and out of the hand of all kingdoms, *and* of them that oppressed you: 19 And ye have this day rejected your God, who himself saved you out of all your adversities and your tribulations; and ye have said unto him, *Nay*, but set a king over us. Now therefore present yourselves before the LORD by your tribes, and by your thousands. 20 And when Samuel had caused all the tribes of Israel to come near, the tribe of Benjamin was taken. 21 When he had caused the tribe of Benjamin to come near by their families, the family of Matri was taken, and Saul the son of Kish was taken: and when

they sought him, he could not be found. 22 Therefore they enquired of the LORD further, if the man should yet come thither. And the LORD answered, Behold, he hath hid himself among the stuff. 23 And they ran and fetched him thence: and when he stood among the people, he was higher than any of the people from his shoulders and upward. 24 And Samuel said to all the people, See ye him whom the LORD hath chosen, that *there is* none like him among all the people? And all the people shouted, and said, God save the king. 25 Then Samuel told the people the manner of the kingdom, and wrote *it* in a book, and laid *it* up before the LORD. And Samuel sent all the people away, every man to his house. 26 And Saul also went home to Gibeah; and there went with him a band of men, whose hearts God had touched. 27 But the children of Belial said, How shall this man save us? And they despised him, and brought him no presents. But he held his peace.

Saul's nomination to the throne is here made public, in a general assembly of the elders of Israel, the representatives of their respective tribes at Mizpeh. It is probable that this convention of the states was called as soon as conveniently it might, after Saul was anointed, for, if there must be a change in their government, the sooner the better: it might be of bad consequence to be long in the doing. The people having met in a solemn assembly, in which God was in a peculiar manner present (and therefore it is said they were *called together unto the Lord*, *v.* 17), Samuel acts for God among them.

I. He reproves them for casting off the government of a prophet, and desiring that of a captain. 1. He shows them (*v.* 18) how happy they had been under the divine government; when God ruled them, he *delivered them out of the hand of those that oppressed them,* and what would they desire more? Could the mightiest man of valour do that for them which the Almighty God had done? 2. He likewise shows them (*v.* 19) what an affront they had put upon God (who had himself saved them *out of all their tribulations,* by his own power, and by such as he had immediately called and qualified) in desiring a king to save them. He tells them in plain terms, "*You have this day rejected your God;* you have in effect done it: so he construes it, and he might justly, for your so doing, reject you." Those that can live better by sense than by faith, that stay themselves upon an arm of flesh rather than upon the almighty arm, forsake a fountain of living waters for broken cisterns. And some make their obstinacy in this matter to be a presage of their rejecting Christ, in casting off whom they cast off God, that he should not reign over them.

II. He puts them upon choosing their king by lot. He knew whom God had chosen, and had already anointed him, but he knew also the peevishness of that people, and that there were those among them who would not acquiesce in the choice if it depended upon his single testimony; and therefore, that every tribe and every family of the chosen tribe might please themselves with having a chance for it, he calls them to the lot, *v.* 19. Benjamin is taken out of all the tribes (*v.* 20), and out of that tribe Saul the son of Kish, *v.* 21. By this method it would appear to the people, as it already appeared to Samuel, that Saul was appointed of God to be king; for *the disposal of the lot is of the Lord.* It would also prevent all disputes and exceptions; for *the lot causeth contentions to cease, and parteth between the mighty.* When the tribe of Benjamin was taken, they might easily foresee that they were setting up a family that would soon be put down again; for dying Jacob had, by the spirit of prophecy, entailed the dominion upon Judah. Judah is the tribe that must *rule as a lion; Benjamin* shall only *ravin as a wolf,* Gen. xlix. 10, 27. Those therefore that knew the scriptures could not be very fond of the doing of that which they foresaw must, ere long, be undone again.

III. It is with much ado, and not without further enquiries of the Lord, that Saul is at length produced. When the lot fell upon him, every one expected he should answer to his name at the first call, but, instead of that, none of his friends could find him (*v.* 21), he had *hidden himself among the stuff* (*v.* 22), so little fond was he now of that power which yet, when he was in possession of, he could not without the utmost indignation think of parting with.

1. He withdrew, in hopes that, upon his not appearing, they would proceed to another choice, or thus to express his modesty; for, by what had already passed, he knew he must be the man. We may suppose he was at this time really averse to take upon him the government, (1.) Because he was conscious to himself of unfitness for so great a trust. He had not been bred up to books, or arms, or courts, and feared he should be guilty of some fatal blunder. (2.) Because it would expose him to the envy of his neighbours that were ill-affected towards him. (3.) Because he understood, by what Samuel had said, that the people sinned in asking a king, and it was in anger that God granted their request. (4.) Because the affairs of Israel

were at this time in a bad posture; the Philistines were strong, the Ammonites threatening: and he must be bold indeed that will set sail in a storm.

2. But the congregation, believing that choice well made which God himself made, would leave no way untried to find him out on whom the lot fell. *They enquired of the Lord,* either by the high priest, and his breast-plate of judgment, or by Samuel, and his spirit of prophecy; and the Lord directed them where they should find him, hidden among the carriages, and thence *they fetched him, v.* 23. Note, None will be losers at last by their humility and modesty. Honour, like the shadow, follows those that flee from it, but flees from those that pursue it.

IV. Samuel presents him to the people, and they accept him. He needed not to mount the bench, or scaffold, to be seen; when he stood upon even ground with the rest he was seen above them all, for he was taller than any of them by *head and shoulders, v.* 23. "Look you," said Samuel, "what a king God has chosen for you, just such a one as you wished for; *there is none like him among all the people,* that has so much majesty in his countenance and such a graceful stateliness in his mien; he is in the crowd like a cedar among the shrubs. Let your own eyes be judges, is he not a brave and gallant man?" The people hereupon signified their approbation of the choice, and their acceptance of him; they *shouted and said, Let the king live,* that is, "Let him long reign over us in health and prosperity." Subjects were wont to testify their affection and allegiance to their prince by their good wishes, and those turned (as our translation does this) into addresses to God. Ps. lxxii. 15, *Prayer shall be made for him continually.* See Ps. xx. 1. Samuel had told them they would soon be weary of their king, but, in the mind they are now in, they will never be so: *Let the king live.*

V. Samuel settles the original contract between them, and leaves it upon record, *v.* 25. He had before told them *the manner of the king* (*ch.* viii. 11), how he would abuse his power; now he tells them *the manner of the kingdom,* or rather the law, or judgment, or constitution, of it, what power the prince might challenge and the utmost of the property the subject might claim. He fixed the land-marks between them, that neither might encroach upon the other. Let them rightly understand one another at first, and let the agreement remain in black and white, which will tend to preserve a good understanding between them ever after. The learned bishop Patrick thinks he now repeated and registered what he had told them (*ch.* viii. 11) of the arbitrary power their kings would assume, that it might hereafter be a witness against them that they had drawn the calamity upon themselves, for they were warned what it would come to and yet they would have a king.

VI. The convention was dissolved when the solemnity was over: *Samuel sent every man to his house.* Here were no votes passed, nor, for aught that appears, so much as a motion made, for the raising of money to support the dignity of their new-elected king; if therefore he afterwards thinks fit to take what they do not think fit to give (which yet it was necessary that he should have), they must thank themselves. They went every man to his house, pleased with the name of a king over them, and *Saul also went home to Gibeah,* to his father's house, not puffed up with the name of a kingdom under him. At Gibeah he had no palace, no throne, no court, yet thither he goes. If he must be a king, as one mindful of the rock out of which he was hewn, he will make his own city the royal city, nor will he be ashamed (as too many are when they are preferred) of his mean relations. Such a humble spirit as this puts a beauty and lustre upon great advancements. The condition rising, and the mind not rising with it, behold how good and pleasant it is! But,

1. How did the people stand affected to their new king? The generality of them, it should seem, did not show themselves much concerned: They *went every man to his own house.* Their own domestic affairs lay nearer their hearts than any interests of the public; this was the general temper. But, (1.) There were some so faithful as to attend him: *A band of men whose hearts God had touched, v.* 26. Not the body of the people, but a small company, who because they were fond of their own choice of a king, or because they had so much more sense than their neighbours as to conclude that if he was a king he ought to be respected accordingly, went with him to Gibeah, as his life-guard. They were those *whose hearts God had touched,* in this instance, to do their duty. Note, Whatever good there is in us, or is done by us, at any time, it must be ascribed to the grace of God. If the heart bend at any time the right way, it is because he has touched it. One touch is enough, when it is divine. (2.) There were others so spiteful as to affront him; children of Belial, men that would endure no yoke, that would be pleased with nothing that either God or Samuel did; they *despised him* (*v.* 27) for the meanness of his tribe and family, the smallness of his estate, and the privacy of his education; and they said, *How shall this man save us?* Yet they did not propose any man more likely; nor, whomsoever they had, must their salvation come from the man, but from God. They would not join with their neighbours in testifying an affection to him and his government, by bringing him presents, or addressing him upon his accession to the crown. Perhaps those discontented spirits were most earnest for a king, and yet, now that they had one, they quarrelled with him, because he was not altogether such a one as themselves It

was reason enough for them not to like him because others did. Thus differently are men affected to our exalted Redeemer. God hath set him king upon the holy hill of Sion. There is a remnant that submit to him, rejoice in him, bring him presents, and follow him wherever he goes; and they are those *whose hearts God has touched*, whom he has *made willing in the day of his power.* But there are others who despise him, who ask, *How shall this man save us?* They are offended in him, stumble at his external meanness, and they will be broken by it.

2. How did Saul resent the bad conduct of those that were disaffected to his government? *He held his peace.* Margin, *He was as though he had been deaf.* He was so far from resenting it that he seemed not to take notice of it, which was an evidence of his humility and modesty, and the mercifulness of his disposition, and also that he was well satisfied with his title to the crown; for those are commonly most jealous of their honour, and most revengeful of affronts, that gain their power by improper means. Christ held his peace when he was affronted, for it was the day of his patience; but there is a day of recompence coming.

CHAP. XI.

In this chapter we have the first-fruits of Saul's government, in the glorious rescue of Jabesh-Gilead out of the hands of the Ammonites. Let not Israel thence infer that therefore they did well to ask a king (God could and would have saved them without one); but let them admire God's goodness, that he did not reject them, when they rejected him, and acknowledge his wisdom in the choice of the person whom, if he did not find fit, yet he made fit, for the great trust he called him to, and enabled, in some measure, to merit the crown by his public services, before it was fixed on his head by the public approbation. Here is, I The great extremity to which the city of Jabesh-Gilead, on the other side of Jordan, was reduced by the Ammonites, ver. 1—3. II. Saul's great readiness to come to their relief, whereby he signalized himself, ver. 4—10. III. The good success of his attempt, by which God signalized him, ver. 11. IV. Saul's tenderness, notwithstanding this, towards those that had opposed him, ver. 12, 13. V. The public confirmation and recognition of his election to the government, ver. 14, 15.

THEN Nahash the Ammonite came up, and encamped against Jabesh-gilead: and all the men of Jabesh said unto Nahash, Make a covenant with us, and we will serve thee. 2 And Nahash the Ammonite answered them, On this *condition* will I make *a covenant* with you, that I may thrust out all your right eyes, and lay it *for* a reproach upon all Israel. 3 And the elders of Jabesh said unto him, Give us seven days' respite, that we may send messengers unto all the coasts of Israel: and then, if *there be* no man to save us, we will come out to thee. 4 Then came the messengers to Gibeah of Saul, and told the tidings in the ears of the people: and all the people lifted up their voices, and wept.

The Ammonites were bad neighbours to those tribes of Israel that lay next them, though descendants from just Lot, and, for that reason, dealt civilly with by Israel. See Deut. ii. 19. Jephthah, in his time, had humbled them, but now the sin of Israel had put them into a capacity to make head again, and avenge that quarrel. The city of Jabesh-Gilead had been, some ages ago, destroyed by Israel's sword of justice, for not appearing against the wickedness of Gibeah (Judges xxi. 10); and now being replenished again, probably by the posterity of those that then escaped the sword, it is in danger of being destroyed by the Ammonites, as if some bad fate attended the place. Nahash, king of Ammon (1 Chron. xix. 1), laid siege to it. Now here,

I. The besieged beat a parley (*v.* 1): "*Make a covenant with us, and we will* surrender upon terms, and *serve thee.*" They had lost the virtue of Israelites, else they would not have thus lost the valour of Israelites, nor tamely yielded to serve an Ammonite, without one bold struggle for themselves. Had they not broken their covenant with God, and forsaken his service, they needed not thus to have courted a covenant with a Gentile nation, and offered themselves to serve them.

II. The besiegers offer them base and barbarous conditions; they will spare their lives, and take them to be their servants, upon condition that they shall *put out their right eyes, v.* 2. The Gileadites were content to part with their liberty and estates for the ransom of their blood; and, had the Ammonites taken them at their word, the matter would have been so settled immediately, and the Gileadites would not have sent out for relief. But their abject concessions make the Ammonites more insolent in their demands, and they cannot be content to have them for their servants, but, 1. They must torment them, and put them to pain, exquisite pain, for so the thrusting out of an eye would do. 2. They must disable them for war, and render them incapable, though not of labour (that would have been a loss to their lords), yet of bearing arms; for in those times they fought with shields in their left hands, which covered their left eye, so that a soldier without his right eye was in effect blind. 3. They must put a *reproach upon all Israel*, as weak and cowardly, that would suffer the inhabitants of one of their chief cities to be thus miserably used, and not offer to rescue them.

III. The besieged desire, and obtain, seven days' time to consider of this proposal, *v.* 3. If Nahash had not granted them this respite, we may suppose the horror of the proposal would have made them desperate, and they would rather have died with their swords in their hands than have surrendered to such merciless enemies: therefore Nahash, not imagining it possible that, in so short a time, they should have relief, and being very secure of the advantages he thought he had against them, in a bravado gave them seven days, that the reproach upon Israel, for not rescuing them, might be the greater, and his triumphs the more illustrious. But there was a providence in it, that his security might be his infatuation and ruin.

IV. Notice is sent of this to Gibeah. They said they would send messengers *to all the coasts of Israel* (*v.* 3), which made Nahash the more secure, for that, he thought, would be a work of time, and none would be forward to appear if they had not one common head; and perhaps Nahash had not yet heard of the new-elected king. But the messengers, either of their own accord or by order from their masters, went straight to Gibeah, and, not finding Saul within, told their news to the people, who fell a weeping upon hearing it, *v.* 4. They would sooner lament their brethren's misery and danger than think of helping them, shed their tears for them than shed their blood. They wept, as despairing to help the men of Jabesh-Gilead, and fearing lest, if that frontier-city should be lost, the enemy would penetrate into the very bowels of their country, which now appeared in great hazard.

5 And, behold, Saul came after the herd out of the field; and Saul said, What *aileth* the people that they weep? And they told him the tidings of the men of Jabesh. 6 And the Spirit of God came upon Saul when he heard those tidings, and his anger was kindled greatly. 7 And he took a yoke of oxen, and hewed them in pieces, and sent *them* throughout all the coasts of Israel by the hands of messengers, saying, Whosoever cometh not forth after Saul and after Samuel, so shall it be done unto his oxen. And the fear of the LORD fell on the people, and they came out with one consent. 8 And when he numbered them in Bezek, the children of Israel were three hundred thousand, and the men of Judah thirty thousand. 9 And they said unto the messengers that came, Thus shall ye say unto the men of Jabesh-gilead, To morrow, by *that time* the sun be hot, ye shall have help. And the messengers came and showed *it* to the men of Jabesh; and they were glad. 10 Therefore the men of Jabesh said, To morrow we will come out unto you, and ye shall do with us all that seemeth good unto you. 11 And it was *so* on the morrow, that Saul put the people in three companies; and they came into the midst of the host in the morning watch, and slew the Ammonites until the heat of the day: and it came to pass, that they which remained were scattered, so that two of them were not left together.

What is here related turns very much to the honour of Saul, and shows the happy fruits of that other spirit with which he was endued. Observe here,

I. His humility. Though he was anointed king, and accepted by his people, yet he did not think it below him to know the state of his own flocks, but went himself to see them, and came in the evening, with his servants, *after the herd out of the field, v.* 5. This was an evidence that he was not puffed up with his advancement, as those are most apt to be that are raised from a mean estate. Providence had not yet found him business as a king; he left all to Samuel; and therefore, rather than be idle, he would, for the present, apply himself to his country business again. Though the sons of Belial would, perhaps, despise him the more for it, such as were virtuous and wise, and loved business themselves, would think never the worse of him. He had no revenues settled upon him for the support of his dignity, and he was desirous not to be burdensome to the people, for which reason, like Paul, he worked with his hands; for, if he neglect his domestic affairs, how must he maintain himself and his family? Solomon gives it as a reason why men should look well to their herds because *the crown doth not endure to every generation*, Prov. xxvii. 23, 24. Saul's did not; he must therefore provide something surer.

II. His concern for his neighbours. When he perceived them in tears, he asked, "*What ails the people that they weep?* Let me know, that, if it be a grievance which can be redressed, I may help them, and that, if not, I may weep with them." Good magistrates are in pain if their subjects are in tears.

III. His zeal for the safety and honour of Israel. When he heard of the insolence of the Ammonites, and the distress of a city, a mother in Israel, *the Spirit of God came upon him*, and put great thoughts into his mind, *and his anger was kindled greatly, v.* 6. He was angry at the insolence of the Ammonites, angry at the mean and sneaking spirit of the men of Jabesh-Gilead, angry that they had not sent him notice sooner of the Ammonites' descent and the extremity they were likely to be reduced to. He was angry to see his neighbours weeping, when it was fitter for them to be preparing for war. It was a brave and generous fire that was now kindled in the breast of Saul, and such as became his high station.

IV. The authority and power he exerted

upon this important occasion. He soon let Israel know that, though he had retired to his privacy, he had a care for the public, and knew how to command men into the field, as well as how to drive cattle out of the field, *v.* 5, 7. He sent a summons to all the coasts of Israel, to show the extent of his power beyond his own tribe, even to all the tribes, and ordered all the military men forthwith to appear in arms at a general rendezvous in Bezek. Observe, 1. His modesty, in joining Samuel in commission with himself. He would not execute the office of a king without a due regard to that of a prophet. 2. His mildness in the penalty threatened against those that should disobey his orders. He hews a yoke of oxen in pieces, and sends the pieces to the several cities of Israel, threatening, with respect to him who should decline the public service, not, "Thus shall it be done to *him*," but, "Thus shall it be done to his *oxen*." God had threatened it as a great judgment (Deut. xxviii. 31), *Thy ox shall be slain before thy eyes, and thou shalt not eat thereof.* It was necessary that the command should be enforced with some penalty, but this was not nearly so severe as that which was affixed to a similar order by the whole congregation, Judg. xxi. 5. Saul wished to show that his government was more gentle than that which they had been under. The effect of this summons was that the militia, or trained bands, of the nation, *came out as one man,* and the reason given is, because *the fear of the Lord fell upon them.* Saul did not affect to make them fear him, but they were influenced to observe his orders by the fear of God and a regard to him who had made Saul their king and them members one of another. Note, Religion and the fear of God will make men good subjects, good soldiers, and good friends to the public interests of their country. Those that fear God will make conscience of their duty to all men, particularly to their rulers.

V. His prudent proceedings in this great affair, *v.* 8. He numbered those that came in to him, that he might know his own strength, and how to distribute his forces in the best manner their numbers would allow. It is the honour of princes to know the number of their men, but it is the honour of the King of kings that *there is not any number of his armies,* Job xxv. 3. In this muster, it seems, Judah, though numbered by itself, made no great figure; for, as it was one tribe of twelve, so it was but an eleventh part of the whole number, 30,330, though the rendezvous was at Bezek, in that tribe. They wanted the numbers, or the courage, or the zeal for which that tribe used to be famous; so low was it, just before the sceptre was brought into it in David.

VI. His faith and confidence, and (grounded thereon) his courage and resolution, in this enterprise. It should seem that those very messengers who brought the tidings from Jabesh-Gilead Saul sent into the country to raise the militia, who would be sure to be faithful and careful in their own business, and them he now sends back to their distressed countrymen, with this assurance (in which, it is probable, Samuel encouraged him): "*To-morrow,* by such an hour, before the enemy can pretend that the seven days have expired, *you shall have deliverance, v.* 9. Be you ready to do your part, and we will not fail to do ours. Do you sally out upon the besiegers, while we surround them." Saul knew he had a just cause, a clear call, and God on his side, and therefore doubted not of success. This was good news to the besieged Gileadites, whose right eyes had wept themselves dry for their calamities, and now began to fail with looking for relief and to ache in expectation of the doom of the ensuing day, when they must look their last; the greater the exigence the more welcome the deliverance. When they heard it they were glad, relying on the assurances that were sent to them. And they sent into the enemies' camp (*v.* 10) to tell them that next day they would be ready to meet them, which the enemies understood as an intimation that they despaired of relief, and so were made the more secure by it. If they took not care, by sending out scouts, to rectify their own mistake, they must thank themselves if they were surprised: the besieged were under no obligation to give them notice of the help they were assured of.

VII. His industry and close application to this business. If he had been bred up to war from his youth, and had led regiments as often as he had followed droves, he could not have gone about an affair of this nature more dexterously nor more diligently. When the Spirit of the Lord comes upon men it will make them expert even without experience. A vast army (especially in comparison with the present usage) Saul had now at his foot, and a long march before him, nearly sixty miles, and over Jordan too. No cavalry in his army, but all infantry, which he divides into three battalions, *v.* 11. And observe, 1. With what incredible swiftness he flew to the enemy. In a day and a night he came to the place of action, where his own fate, and that of Israel, must be determined. He had passed his word, and would not break it; nay, he was better than his word, for he promised help next day, *by that time the sun was hot* (*v.* 9), but brought it before day, *in the morning-watch, v.* 11. Whom God helps he *helps right early,* Ps. xlvi. 5. 2. With what incredible bravery he flew upon the enemy. Betimes in the morning, when they lay dreaming of the triumphs they expected that day over the miserable inhabitants of Jabesh-Gilead, before they were aware he was in the midst of their host; and his men, being marched against them in three columns, surrounded them on every side, so that they could have neither heart nor time to make head against them.

Lastly, To complete his honour, God crowned all these virtues with success. Jabesh-Gilead was rescued, and the Ammonites were totally routed; he had now the day before him to complete his victory in, and so complete a victory it was that those who remained, after a great slaughter, were scattered so that *two of them were not left together* to encourage or help one another, *v.* 11. We may suppose that Saul was the more vigorous in this matter, 1. Because there was some alliance between the tribe of Benjamin and the city of Jabesh-Gilead. That city had declined joining with the rest of the Israelites to destroy Gibeah, which was then punished as their crime, but perhaps was now remembered as their kindness, when Saul of Gibeah came with so much readiness and resolution to relieve Jabesh-Gilead. Yet that was not all; two-thirds of the Benjamites that then remained were provided with wives from that city (Judg. xxi. 14), so that most of the mothers of Benjamin were daughters of Jabesh-Gilead, for which city Saul, being a Benjamite, had therefore a particular kindness; and we find they returned his kindness, *ch.* xxxi. 11, 12. 2. Because it was the Ammonites' invasion that induced the people to desire a king (so Samuel says, *ch.* xii. 12), so that if he had not done his part, in this expedition, he would have disappointed their expectations, and for ever forfeited their respect.

12 And the people said unto Samuel, Who *is* he that said, Shall Saul reign over us? bring the men, that we may put them to death. 13 And Saul said, There shall not a man be put to death this day: for to day the LORD hath wrought salvation in Israel. 14 Then said Samuel to the people, Come, and let us go to Gilgal, and renew the kingdom there. 15 And all the people went to Gilgal; and there they made Saul king before the LORD in Gilgal; and there they sacrificed sacrifices of peace offerings before the LORD; and there Saul and all the men of Israel rejoiced greatly.

We have here the improvement of the glorious victory which Saul had obtained, not the improvement of it abroad, though we take it for granted that the men of Jabesh-Gilead, having so narrowly saved their right eyes, would with them now discern the opportunity they had of avenging themselves upon these cruel enemies and disabling them from ever straitening them in like manner again; now shall they be avenged on the Ammonites for their right eyes condemned, as Samson on the Philistines for his two eyes put out, Judg. xvi. 28. But the account here given is of the improvement of this victory at home.

I. The people took this occasion to show their jealousy for the honour of Saul, and their resentment of the indignities done him. Samuel, it seems, was present, if not in the action (it was too far for him to march) yet to meet them when they returned victorious; and to him, as judge, the motion was made (for they knew Saul would not be judge in his own cause) that the sons of Belial that would not have him to reign over them should be brought forth and slain, *v.* 12. Saul's good fortune (as foolish men commonly call it) went further with them to confirm his title than either his choice by lot or Samuel's anointing him. They had not courage thus to move for the prosecution of those that opposed him when he himself looked mean, but, now that his victory made him look great, nothing would serve but they must be put to death.

II. Saul took this occasion to give further proofs of his clemency, for, without waiting for Samuel's answer, he himself quashed the motion (*v.* 13): *There shall not a man be put to death this day,* no, not those men, those bad men, that had abused him, and therein reflected on God himself, 1. Because it was a day of joy and triumph: "*To day the Lord has wrought salvation in Israel;* and, since God has been so good to us all, let us not be harsh one to another. Now that God has made the heart of Israel in general so glad, let not us make sad the hearts of any particular Israelites." 2. Because he hoped they were by this day's work brought to a better temper, were now convinced that this man, under God, could save them, now honoured him whom before they had despised; and, if they are but reclaimed, he is secured from receiving any disturbance by them, and therefore his point is gained. If an enemy be made a friend, that will be more to our advantage than to have him slain. And all good princes consider that their power is for edification, not for destruction.

III. Samuel took this occasion to call the people together *before the Lord in Gilgal,* *v.* 14, 15. 1. That they might publicly give God thanks for their late victory. There they *rejoiced greatly,* and, that God might have the praise of that which they had the comfort of, they *sacrificed to him,* as the giver of all their successes, *sacrifices of peace-offerings.* 2. That they might confirm Saul in the government, more solemnly than had been yet done, that he might not retire again to his obscurity. Samuel would have the kingdom renewed; he would renew his resignation, and the people should renew their approbation, and so in concurrence with, or rather in attendance upon, the divine nomination, they made Saul king, making it their own act and deed to submit to him.

CHAP. XII.

We left the general assembly of the states together, in the close of the foregoing chapter; in this chapter we have Samuel's speech to them, when he resigned the government into the hands of Saul, in which, I. He clears himself from all suspicion or imputation of mismanagement, while the administration was in his hands, ver. 1—5. II. He reminds them of the great things God had done for them and for their fathers, ver. 6—13. III. He sets before them good and evil, the blessing and the curse, ver. 14, 15. IV. He awakens them to regard what he said to them, by calling to God for thunder, ver. 16—19. V. He encourages them with hopes that all should be well, ver. 20—25. This is his farewell sermon to that august assembly and Saul's coronation sermon.

AND Samuel said unto Israel, Behold, I have hearkened unto your voice in all that ye said unto me, and have made a king over you. 2 And now, behold, the king walketh before you: and I am old and gray-headed; and, behold, my sons *are* with you: and I have walked before you from my childhood unto this day. 3 Behold, here I *am:* witness against me before the LORD, and before his anointed: whose ox have I taken? or whose ass have I taken? or whom have I defrauded? whom have I oppressed? or of whose hand have I received *any* bribe to blind mine eyes therewith? and I will restore it you. 4 And they said, Thou hast not defrauded us, nor oppressed us, neither hast thou taken aught of any man's hand. 5 And he said unto them, The LORD *is* witness against you, and his anointed *is* witness this day, that ye have not found aught in my hand. And they answered, *He is* witness.

Here, I. Samuel gives them a short account of the late revolution, and of the present posture of their government, by way of preface to what he had further to say to them, *v.* 1, 2. 1. For his own part, he had spent his days in their service; he began betimes to be useful among them, and had continued long so: "*I have walked before you,* as a guide to direct you, as a shepherd that leads his flock (Ps. lxxx. 1), *from my childhood unto this day.*" As soon as he was illuminated with the light of prophecy, in his early days, he began to be a burning and shining light to Israel; "and now my best days are done: *I am old and gray-headed;*" therefore they were the more unkind to cast him off, yet therefore he was the more willing to resign, finding the weight of government heavy upon his stooping shoulders. He was old, and therefore the more able to advise them, and the more observant they should have been of what he said, for *days shall speak* and *the multitude of years shall teach wisdom;* and there is a particular reverence due to the aged, especially aged magistrates and aged ministers. "I am old, and therefore not likely to live long, perhaps may never have an opportunity of speaking to you again, and therefore take notice of what I say." 2. As for his sons, "*Behold*" (says he), "*they are with you,* you may, if you please, call them to an account for any thing they have done amiss. They are present with you, and have not, upon this revolution, fled from their country. They are upon the level with you, subjects to the new king as well as you; if you can prove them guilty of any wrong, you may prosecute them now by a due course of law, punish them, and oblige them to make restitution." 3. As for their new king, Samuel had gratified them in setting him over them (*v.* 1): "*I have hearkened to your voice in all that you said to me,* being desirous to please you, if possible, and make you easy, though to the discarding of myself and family; and now will you hearken to me, and take my advice?" The change was now perfected: "*Behold, the king walketh before you*" (*v.* 2); he appears in public, ready to serve you in public business. Now that you have made yourselves like the nations in your civil government, and have cast off the divine administration in that, take heed lest you make yourselves like the nations in religion and cast off the worship of God.

II. He solemnly appeals to them concerning his own integrity in the administration of the government (*v.* 3): *Witness against me, whose ox have I taken?* Observe,

1. His design in this appeal. By this he intended, (1.) To convince them of the injury they had done him in setting him aside, when they had nothing amiss to charge him with (his government had no fault but that it was too cheap, too easy, too gentle), and also of the injury they had done themselves in turning off one that did not so much as take an ox or an ass from them, to put themselves under the power of one that would take from them their fields and vineyards, nay, and their very sons and daughters (*ch.* viii. 11), so unlike would the manner of the king be from Samuel's manner. (2.) To preserve his own reputation. Those that heard of Samuel's being rejected as he was would be ready to suspect that certainly he had done some evil thing, or he would never have been so ill treated; so that it was necessary for him to make this challenge, that it might appear upon record that it was not for any iniquity in his hands that he was laid aside, but to gratify the humour of a giddy people, who owned they could not have a better man to rule them, only they desired a bigger man. There is a just debt which every man owes to his own good name, especially men in public stations, which is to guard it against unjust aspersions and suspicions, that we may finish our course with honour as well as joy. (3.) As he designed hereby to leave a good name behind him, so he designed to leave his suc-

cessor a good example before him; let him write after his copy, and he will write fair. (4.) He designed, in the close of his discourse, to reprove the people, and therefore he begins with a vindication of himself; for he that will, with confidence, tell another of his sin, must see to it that he himself be clear.

2. In the appeal itself observe,

(1.) What it is that Samuel here acquits himself from. [1.] He had never, under any pretence whatsoever, taken that which was not his own, ox or ass, had never distrained their cattle for tribute, fines, or forfeitures, nor used their service without paying for it. [2.] He had never defrauded those with whom he dealt, nor oppressed those that were under his power. [3.] He had never taken bribes to pervert justice, nor was ever biassed by favour or affection to give judgment in a cause against his conscience.

(2.) How he calls upon those that had slighted him to bear witness concerning his conduct: "*Here I am; witness against me.* If you have any thing to lay to my charge, do it *before the Lord and the king*, the proper judges." He puts honour upon Saul, by owning himself accountable to him if guilty of any wrong.

III. Upon this appeal he is honourably acquitted. He did not expect that they would do him honour at parting, though he well deserved it, and therefore mentioned not any of the good services he had done them, for which they ought to have applauded him, and returned him the thanks of the house; all he desired was that they should do him justice, and that they did (*v.* 4), readily owning, 1. That he had not made his government oppressive to them, nor used his power to their wrong. 2. That he had not made it expensive to them: *Neither hast thou taken aught of any man's hand* for the support of thy dignity. Like Nehemiah, he did *not require the bread of the governor* (Neh. v. 18), had not only been righteous, but generous, had *coveted no man's silver, or gold, or apparel*, Acts xx. 33.

IV. This honourable testimony borne to Samuel's integrity is left upon record to his honour (*v.* 5): "*The Lord is witness*, who searcheth the heart, *and his anointed is witness*, who trieth overt acts;" and the people agree to it: "*He is witness.*" Note, The testimony of our neighbours, and especially the testimony of our own consciences for us, that we have in our places lived honestly, will be our comfort under the slights and contempts that are put upon us. Demetrius is a happy man, that has a *good report of all men and of the truth itself*, 3 John 12.

6 And Samuel said unto the people, *It is* the LORD that advanced Moses and Aaron, and that brought your fathers up out of the land of Egypt. 7 Now therefore stand still, that I may reason with you before the LORD of all the righteous acts of the LORD, which he did to you and to your fathers. 8 When Jacob was come into Egypt, and your fathers cried unto the LORD, then the LORD sent Moses and Aaron, which brought forth your fathers out of Egypt, and made them dwell in this place. 9 And when they forgat the LORD their God, he sold them into the hand of Sisera, captain of the host of Hazor, and into the hand of the Philistines, and into the hand of the king of Moab, and they fought against them. 10 And they cried unto the LORD, and said, We have sinned, because we have forsaken the LORD, and have served Baalim and Ashtaroth: but now deliver us out of the hand of our enemies, and we will serve thee. 11 And the LORD sent Jerubbaal, and Bedan, and Jephthah, and Samuel, and delivered you out of the hand of your enemies on every side, and ye dwelled safe. 12 And when ye saw that Nahash the king of the children of Ammon came against you, ye said unto me, Nay; but a king shall reign over us: when the LORD your God *was* your king. 13 Now therefore behold the king whom ye have chosen, *and* whom ye have desired! and, behold, the LORD hath set a king over you. 14 If ye will fear the LORD, and serve him, and obey his voice, and not rebel against the commandment of the LORD, then shall both ye and also the king that reigneth over you continue following the LORD your God: 15 But if ye will not obey the voice of the LORD, but rebel against the commandment of the LORD, then shall the hand of the LORD be against you, as *it was* against your fathers.

Samuel, having sufficiently secured his own reputation, instead of upbraiding the people upon it with their unkindness to him, sets himself to instruct them, and keep them in the way of their duty, and then the change of the government would be the less damage to them.

I. He reminds them of the great goodness of God to them and to their fathers, gives them an abstract of the history of their nation, that, by the consideration of the great things God had done for them, they might be for ever engaged to love him and serve him. "Come," says he (*v.* 7), "stand still, stand in token of reverence when God is speaking to you, stand still in token of attention and composedness of mind, and give me leave to reason with you." Religion has reason on its side, Isa. i. 18. The work of ministers is to reason with people, not only to exhort and direct, but to persuade, to convince men's judgments, and so to gain their wills and affections. Let reason rule men, and they will be good. He reasons of the righteous acts of the Lord, that is, "both the benefits he hath bestowed upon you, in performance of his promises, and the punishments he has inflicted on you for your sins." His favours are called *his righteous acts* (Judg. v. 11), because in them he is just to his own honour. He not only puts them in mind of what God had done for them in their days, but of what he had done of old, in the days of their fathers, because the present age had the benefit of God's former favours. We may suppose that his discourse was much larger than as here related. 1. He reminds them of their deliverance out of Egypt. Into that house of bondage Jacob and his family came down poor and little; when they were oppressed they cried unto God, who advanced Moses and Aaron, from mean beginnings, to be their deliverers, and the founders of their state and settlement in Canaan, *v.* 6, 8. 2. He reminds them of the miseries and calamities which their fathers brought themselves into by forgetting God and serving other gods, *v.* 9. They enslaved themselves, for they were sold as criminals and captives into the hand of oppressors. They exposed themselves to the desolation of war, and their neighbours fought against them. 3. He reminds them of their fathers' repentance and humiliation before God for their idolatries: *They said, We have sinned*, *v.* 10. Let not them imitate the sins of their fathers, for what they had done amiss they had many a time wished undone again. In the day of their distress they had sought unto God, and had promised to serve him; let their children then reckon that good at all times which they found good in bad times. 4. He reminds them of the glorious deliverances God had wrought for them, the victories he had blessed them with, and their happy settlements, many a time, after days of trouble and distress, *v.* 11. He specifies some of their judges, Gideon and Jephthah, great conquerors in their time; among the rest he mentions Bedan, whom we read not of any where else: he might be some eminent person, that was instrumental of salvation to them, though not recorded in the book of Judges, such a one as Shamgar, of whom it is said that he *delivered* Israel, but not that he *judged* them, Judg. iii. 31. Perhaps this Bedan guarded and delivered them on one side, at the same time when some other of the judges appeared and acted for them on another side. Some think it was the same with Jair (so the learned Mr. Poole), others the same with Samson, who was Ben Dan, a son of Dan, of that tribe, and the Spirit of the Lord came upon him Be-Dan, in Dan, in the camp of Dan. Samuel mentions himself, not to his own praise, but to the honour of God, who had made him an instrument of subduing the Philistines. 5. At last he puts them in mind of God's late favour to the present generation, in gratifying them with a king, when they would prescribe to God by such a one to save them out of the hand of Nahash king of Ammon, *v.* 12, 13. Now it appears that this was the immediate occasion of their desiring a king: Nahash threatened them; they desired Samuel to nominate a general; he told them that God was commander-in-chief in all their wars and they needed no other, that what was wanting in them should be made up by his power: *The Lord is your king.* But they insisted on it, *Nay, but a king shall reign over us.* "And now," said he, "you have a king, a king of your own asking—let that be spoken to your shame; but a king of God's making—let that be spoken to his honour and the glory of his grace." God did not cast them off, even when they in effect cast him off.

II. He shows them that they are now upon their good behaviour, they and their king. Let them not think that they had now cut themselves off from all dependence upon God, and that now, having a king of their own, the making of their own fortunes (as men foolishly call it) was in their own hands; no, still their judgment must proceed from the Lord. He tells them plainly,

1. That their obedience to God would certainly be their happiness, *v.* 14. If they would not revolt from God to idols, nor rebel against him by breaking his commandments, but would persevere in their allegiance to him, would fear his wrath, serve his interests, and obey his will, then they and their king should certainly be happy; but observe how the promise is expressed: *Then you shall continue following the Lord your God;* that is, (1.) "You shall continue in the way of your duty to God, which will be your honour and comfort." Note, To those that are sincere in their religion God will give grace to persevere in it: those that follow God faithfully will be divinely strengthened to continue following him. And observe, Following God is a work that is its own wages. It is the matter of a promise as well as of a precept. (2.) "You shall continue under the divine guidance and protection:" *You shall be after the Lord,* so it is in the original, that is, "he will go before you to lead and prosper you, and make your way plain. *The Lord is with you while you are with him.*"

2. That their disobedience would as cer-

tainly be their ruin (*v.* 15): "*If you rebel,* think not that your having a king will secure you against God's judgments, and that having in this instance made yourselves *like the nations* you may sin at as cheap a rate as they can. No, *the hand of the Lord will be against you, as it was against your fathers* when they offended him, in the days of the the judges." We mistake if we think that we can evade God's justice by shaking off his dominion. If God shall not rule us, yet he will judge us.

16 Now therefore stand and see this great thing, which the LORD will do before your eyes. 17 *Is it* not wheat harvest to day? I will call unto the LORD, and he shall send thunder and rain; that ye may perceive and see that your wickedness *is* great, which ye have done in the sight of the LORD, in asking you a king. 18 So Samuel called unto the LORD; and the LORD sent thunder and rain that day: and all the people greatly feared the LORD and Samuel. 19 And all the people said unto Samuel, Pray for thy servants unto the LORD thy God, that we die not: for we have added unto all our sins *this* evil, to ask us a king. 20 And Samuel said unto the people, Fear not: ye have done all this wickedness: yet turn not aside from following the LORD, but serve the LORD with all your heart; 21 And turn ye not aside; for *then should ye go* after vain *things,* which cannot profit nor deliver; for they *are* vain. 22 For the LORD will not forsake his people for his great name's sake: because it hath pleased the LORD to make you his people. 23 Moreover as for me, God forbid that I should sin against the LORD in ceasing to pray for you: but I will teach you the good and the right way: 24 Only fear the LORD, and serve him in truth with all your heart: for consider how great *things* he hath done for you. 25 But if ye shall still do wickedly, ye shall be consumed, both ye and your king.

Two things Samuel here aims at:—

I. To convince the people of their sin in desiring a king. They were now rejoicing before God in and with their king (*ch.* xi. 15), and offering to God the sacrifices of praise, which they hoped God would accept; and this perhaps made them think that there was no harm in their asking a king, but really they had done well in it. Therefore Samuel here charges it upon them as their sin, as wickedness, *great wickedness in the sight of the Lord.* Note, Though we meet with prosperity and success in a way of sin, yet we must not therefore think the more favourably of it. They have a king, and if they conduct themselves well their king may be a very great blessing to them, and yet Samuel will have them perceive and see that their *wickedness was great in asking a king.* We must never think well of that which God in his law frowns upon, though in his providence he may seem to smile upon it. Observe,

1. The expressions of God's displeasure against them for asking a king. At Samuel's word, God sent prodigious thunder and rain upon them, at a season of the year when, in that country, the like was never seen or known before, *v.* 16—18. Thunder and rain have natural causes and sometimes terrible effects. But Samuel made it to appear that this was designed by the almighty power of God on purpose to convince them that they had done very *wickedly in asking a king;* not only by its coming in an unusual time, in wheat-harvest, and this on a fair clear day, when there appeared not to the eye any signs of a storm, but by his giving notice of it before. Had there happened to be thunder and rain at the time when he was speaking to them, he might have improved it for their awakening and conviction, as we may in a like case: but, to make it no less than a miracle, before it came, (1.) He spoke to them of it (*v.* 16, 17): *Stand and see this great thing.* He had before told them to *stand and hear* (*v.* 7); but, because he did not see that his reasoning with them affected them (so stupid were they and unthinking), now he bids them *stand and see.* If what he said in a *still small voice* did not reach their hearts, nor his doctrine which dropped as the dew, they shall hear God speaking to them in dreadful claps of thunder and the great rain of his strength. He appealed to this as a sign: "*I will call upon the Lord, and he will send thunder, will* send it just now, to confirm the word of his servant, and to make you see that I spoke truly when I told you that God was angry with you for *asking a king.*" And the event proved him a true prophet; the sign and wonder came to pass. (2.) He spoke to God for it. Samuel called unto the Lord, and, in answer to his prayer, even while he was yet speaking, *the Lord sent thunder and rain.* By this Samuel made it to appear, not only what a powerful influence God has upon this earth, that he could, of a sudden, when natural causes did not work towards it, produce this dreadful rain and thunder, and bring them out of his treasures (Ps. cxxxv. 7), but also what a powerful interest *he* had in heaven, that God would thus *hearken to the voice of a man* (Josh. x. 14) and answer him *in the secret place of thunder,*

Ps. lxxxi. 7. Samuel, that son of prayer, was still famous for success in prayer. Now by this extraordinary thunder and rain sent on this occasion, [1.] God testified his displeasure against them in the same way in which he had formerly testified it, and at the prayer of Samuel too, against the Philistines. *The Lord discomfited them with a great thunder, ch.* vii. 10. Now that Israel rebelled, and vexed his Holy Spirit, he turned to be their enemy, and fought against them with the same weapons which, not long before, had been employed against their adversaries, Isa. lxiii. 10. [2.] He showed them their folly in desiring a king to save them, rather than God or Samuel, promising themselves more from an arm of flesh than from the arm of God or from the power of prayer. Could their king *thunder with a voice like God?* Job. xl. 9. Could their prince command such forces as the prophet could by his prayers? [3.] He intimated to them that how serene and prosperous soever their condition seemed to be now that they had a king, like the weather in wheat-harvest, yet, if God pleased, he could soon change the face of their heavens, and persecute them with his tempest, as the Psalmist speaks.

2. The impressions which this made upon the people. It startled them very much, as well it might. (1.) *They greatly feared the Lord and Samuel.* Though when they had a king they were ready to think they must fear him only, God made them know that *he is greatly to be feared* and his prophets for his sake. Now they were rejoicing in their king, God taught them to rejoice with trembling. (2.) They owned their sin and folly in desiring a king: *We have added to all our sins this evil, v.* 19. Some people will not be brought to a sight of their sins by any gentler methods than storms and thunders. Samuel did not extort this confession from them till the matter was settled and the king confirmed, lest it should look as if he designed by it rather to establish himself in the government than to bring them to repentance. Now that they were *flattering themselves in their own eyes, their iniquity was found to be hateful,* Ps. xxxvi. 2. (3.) They earnestly begged Samuel's prayers (*v.* 19); *Pray for thy servants, that we die not.* They were apprehensive of their danger from the wrath of God, and could not expect that he should hear their prayers for themselves, and therefore they entreat Samuel to pray for them. Now they see their need of him whom awhile ago they slighted. Thus many that will not have *Christ to reign over them* would yet be glad to have him intercede for them, to turn away the wrath of God. And the time may come when those that have despised and ridiculed praying people will value their prayers, and desire a share in them. "*Pray*" (say they) "*to the Lord thy God*; we know not how to call him ours, but, if thou hast any interest in him, improve it for us."

II. He aims to confirm the people in their religion, and engage them for ever to cleave unto the Lord. The design of his discourse is much the same with Joshua's, *ch.* xxiii. and xxiv.

1. He would not that the terrors of the Lord should frighten them from him, for they were intended to frighten them to him (*v.* 20): "*Fear not; though you have done all this wickedness,* and though God is angry with you for it, yet do not therefore abandon his service, nor *turn from following him.*" *Fear not,* that is, "despair not, fear not with amazement, the weather will clear up after the storm. Fear not; for, though God will frown upon his people, yet he will not forsake them (*v.* 22) *for his great name's sake;* do not you forsake him then." Every transgression in the covenant, though it displease the Lord, yet does not throw us out of covenant, and therefore God's just rebukes must not drive us from our hope in his mercy. The fixedness of God's choice is owing to the freeness of it; we may therefore hope he will not forsake his people, because it has *pleased him to make them his people.* Had he chosen them for their good merits, we might fear he would cast them off for their bad merits; but, choosing them *for his name's sake,* for his name's sake he will not leave them.

2. He cautions them against idolatry: "*Turn not aside* from God and the worship of him" (*v.* 20, and again *v.* 21); "for if you turn aside from God, whatever you turn aside to, you will find it is a vain thing, that can never answer your expectations, but will certainly deceive you if you trust to it; it is a broken reed, a broken cistern." Idols are so; they are vanity and a lie: whatever we make a god of, we shall find it so. Creatures in their own place are good things, but when put in God's place they are vain things. Idols could not profit those that sought to them in their wants, nor deliver those that sought to them in their straits, for they were vain, and not what they pretended to be. *An idol is nothing in the world,* 1 Cor. viii. 4.

3. He comforts them with an assurance that he would continue his care and concern for them, *v.* 23. They desired him to pray for them, *v.* 19. He might have said, "Go to Saul, the king that you have put in my room," and get him to pray for you; but so far is he from upbraiding them with their disrespect to him that he promised them much more than they asked. (1.) They asked it of him as a favour; he promised it as a duty, and startles at the thought of neglecting it. *Pray for you!* says he, *God forbid that I should sin against the Lord in not doing it.* Note, It is a sin against God not to pray for the Israel of God, especially for those of them that are under our charge: and good men are afraid of the guilt of omissions. (2.) They asked him to pray for them at this time, and upon this occasion, but he promised to continue his prayers for them and not to cease as

long as he lived. Our rule is to *pray without ceasing;* we sin if we restrain prayer in general, and in particular if we cease praying for the church. (3.) They asked him only to pray for them, but he promised to do more for them, not only to pray for them, but to teach them; though they were not willing to be under his government as a judge, he would not therefore deny them his instructions as a prophet. And they might be sure he would teach them no other than the *good and the right way:* and the right way is certainly the good way: the way of duty is the way of pleasure and profit.

4. He concludes with an earnest exhortation to practical religion and serious godliness, *v.* 24, 25. The great duty here pressed upon us is to *fear the Lord.* He had said (*v.* 20), "*Fear not* with a slavish fear," but here, "Fear the Lord, with a filial fear. As the fruit and evidence of this, serve him in the duties of religious worship and of a godly conversation, in truth and sincerity, and not in show and profession only, with your heart, and *with all your heart*, not dissembling, not dividing. And two things he urges by way of motive:—(1.) That they were bound in gratitude to serve God, considering *what great things he had done for them,* to engage them for ever to his service. (2.) That they were bound in interest to serve him, considering what great things he would do against them if they should still do wickedly: "*You shall be destroyed* by the judgments of God, *both you and your king* whom you are so proud of and expect so much from, and who will be a blessing to you if you keep in with God." Thus, as a faithful watchman, he gave them warning, and so delivered his own soul.

CHAP. XIII.

Those that desired a king like all the nations fancied that, when they had one, they should look very great and considerable; but in this chapter we find it proved much otherwise. While Samuel was joined in commission with Saul things went well, ch. xi. 7. But, now that Saul began to reign alone, all went to decay, and Samuel's words began to be fulfilled: "You shall be consumed, both you and your king;" for never was the state of Israel further gone in a consumption than in this chapter. I. Saul appears here a very silly prince. 1. Infatuated in his counsels, ver. 1—3. 2. Invaded by his neighbours, ver. 4, 5. 3. Deserted by his soldiers, ver. 6, 7. 4. Disordered in his own spirit, and sacrificing in confusion, ver. 8—10. 5. Chidden by Samuel, ver. 11—13. 6. Rejected of God from being king, ver. 14. II. The people appear here a very miserable people. 1. Disheartened and dispersed, ver. 6, 7. 2. Diminished, ver. 15, 16. 3. Plundered, ver. 17, 18. 4. Disarmed, ver. 19—23. This they got by casting off God's government, and making themselves like the nations: all their glory departed from them.

SAUL reigned one year; and when he had reigned two years over Israel, 2 Saul chose him three thousand *men* of Israel; *whereof* two thousand were with Saul in Michmash and in mount Beth-el, and a thousand were with Jonathan in Gibeah of Benjamin: and the rest of the people he sent every man to his tent. 3 And Jonathan smote the garrison of the Philistines that *was* in Geba, and the Philistines heard *of it.* And Saul blew the trumpet throughout all the land, saying, Let the Hebrews hear. 4 And all Israel heard say *that* Saul had smitten a garrison of the Philistines, and *that* Israel also was had in abomination with the Philistines. And the people were called together after Saul to Gilgal. 5 And the Philistines gathered themselves together to fight with Israel, thirty thousand chariots, and six thousand horsemen, and people as the sand which *is* on the sea shore in multitude: and they came up, and pitched in Michmash, eastward from Beth-aven. 6 When the men of Israel saw that they were in a strait, (for the people were distressed,) then the people did hide themselves in caves, and in thickets, and in rocks, and in high places, and in pits. 7 And *some of* the Hebrews went over Jordan to the land of Gad and Gilead. As for Saul, he *was* yet in Gilgal, and all the people followed him trembling.

We are not told wherein it was that the people of Israel offended God, so as to forfeit his presence and turn his hand against them, as Samuel had threatened (*ch.* xii. 15); but doubtless they left God, else he would not have left them, as here it appears he did; for,

I. Saul was very weak and impolitic, and did not order his affairs with discretion. *Saul was the son of one year* (so the first words are in the original), a phrase which we make to signify the date of his reign, but ordinarily it signifies the date of one's birth, and therefore some understand it figuratively—he was as innocent and good as a child of a year old; so the Chaldee paraphrase: he was *without fault, like the son of a year.* But, if we admit a figurative sense, it may as well intimate that he was ignorant and imprudent, and as unfit for business as a child of a year old: and the subsequent particulars make this more accordant with his character than the former. But we take it rather, as our own translation has it, *Saul reigned one year,* and nothing happened that was considerable, it was a year of no action; but in his second year he did as follows:—1. He chose a band of 3000 men, of whom he himself commanded 2000, and his son Jonathan 1000, *v.* 2. The rest of the people he dismissed to their tents. If he intended these only for the guard of his person and his honorary attendants, it was impolitic to have so many, if for a standing army, in apprehension of danger from the Philistines, it was no less impolitic to have so few; and perhaps the confidence he put in this select number, and his disbanding the rest of that brave army with which he had lately beaten the Ammonites (*ch.* xi. 8—11), was looked upon as an affront to the kingdom, excited general disgust, and was the reason he had so few at his call when he had occasion for them. The prince that relies on a particular party weakens his own interest in the whole community. 2. He ordered his son Jonathan to surprise and destroy the garrison of the Philistines that lay near him in Geba, *v.* 3. I wish there were no ground for supposing that this was a violation or infraction of some articles with the Philistines, and that it was done treacherously and perfidiously. The reason why I suspect it is because it is said that, for doing it, *Israel was had in abomination*, or, as the word is, *did stink with the Philistines* (*v.* 4), as men void of common honesty and whose word could not be relied on. If it was so, we will lay the blame, not on Jonathan who did it, but on Saul, his prince and father, who ordered him to do it, and perhaps kept him in ignorance of the truth of the matter. Nothing makes the name of Israel odious to those that are without so much as the fraud and dishonesty of those that are called by that worthy name. If professors of religion cheat and overreach, break their word and betray their trust, religion suffers by it, and is *had in abomination with the Philistines.* Whom may one trust if not an Israelite, one that, it is expected, should be *without guile?* 3. When he had thus exasperated the Philistines, then he began to raise forces, which, if he had acted wisely, he would have done before. When the Philistines had a vast army ready to pour in upon him, to avenge the wrong he had done them, then was he *blowing the trumpet through the land,* among a careless, if not a disaffected people, saying, *Let the Hebrews hear* (*v.* 3), and so as many as thought fit came to Saul to Gilgal, *v.* 4. But now the generality, we may suppose, drew back (either in dislike of Saul's politics or in dread of the Philistines' power), who, if he had summoned them sooner, would have been as ready at his beck as they were when he marched against the Ammonites. We often find that after-wit would have done much better before and have prevented much inconvenience.

II. Never did the Philistines appear in such a formidable body as they did now, upon this provocation which Saul gave them. We may suppose they had great assistance from their allies, for (*v.* 5), besides 6000 horse, which in those times, when horses were not so much used in war as they are now, was a great body, they had an incredible number of chariots, 30,000 in all: most of them, we may suppose, were carriages for the bag and baggage of so vast an army, not chariots of war. But their foot was *innumerable as the sand of the sea-shore,* so jealous were they for the honour of their nation and so much enraged at the baseness of the Israelites in destroying their garrison. If Saul had asked counsel of God before he had given the Philistines this provocation, he and his people might the better have borne this threatening trouble which they had now brought on themselves by their own folly.

III. Never were the people of Israel so faint-hearted, so sneaking, so very cowardly, as they were now. Some considerable numbers, it may be, came to Saul to Gilgal; but, hearing of the Philistines' numbers and preparations, their spirits sunk within them, some think because they did not find Samuel there with Saul. Those that, awhile ago, were weary of him, and wished for a king, now had small joy of their king unless they could see him under Samuel's direction. Sooner or later, men will be made to see that God and his prophets are their best friends. Now that they saw the Philistines making war upon them, and Samuel not coming in to help them, they knew not what to do; *men's hearts failed them for fear.* And, 1. Some absconded. Rather than run upon death among the Philistines, they buried themselves alive in caves and thickets, *v.* 6. See what work sin makes; it exposes men to perils, and then robs them of their courage and dispirits them. A single person, by faith, can say, *I will not be afraid of* 10,000 (Ps iii. 6); but here thousands of degenerate Israelites tremble at the approach of a great crowd of Philistines. Guilt makes men cowards. 2. Others fled (*v.* 7): They *went over Jordan to the land of Gilead,* as far as they could from the danger, and to a place where they had lately been victorious over the Ammonites. Where they had triumphed they hoped to be sheltered. 3. Those that staid with Saul *followed him trembling,* expecting no other than to be cut off, and having their hands and hearts very much weakened by the desertion of so many of their troops. And perhaps Saul himself, though he had so much honour as to stand his ground, yet had no courage to spare wherewith to inspire his trembling soldiers.

8 And he tarried seven days, according to the set time that Samuel *had appointed:* but Samuel came not to Gilgal; and the people were scattered from him. 9 And Saul said, Bring hither a burnt offering to me, and peace offerings. And he offered the burnt offering. 10 And it came to pass, that as soon as he had made an end of offering the burnt offering, behold, Samuel came; and Saul went out to meet him, that he might salute him. 11 And Samuel said, What

hast thou done? And Saul said, Because I saw that the people were scattered from me, and *that* thou camest not within the days appointed, and *that* the Philistines gathered themselves together at Michmash; 12 Therefore said I, The Philistines will come down now upon me to Gilgal, and I have not made supplication unto the LORD: I forced myself therefore, and offered a burnt offering. 13 And Samuel said to Saul, Thou hast done foolishly: thou hast not kept the commandment of the LORD thy God, which he commanded thee: for now would the LORD have established thy kingdom upon Israel for ever. 14 But now thy kingdom shall not continue: the LORD hath sought him a man after his own heart, and the LORD hath commanded him *to be* captain over his people, because thou hast not kept *that* which the LORD commanded thee.

Here is, I. Saul's offence in offering sacrifice before Samuel came. Samuel, when he anointed him, had ordered him to tarry for him seven days in Gilgal, promising that, at the end of those days, he would be sure to come to him, and both offer sacrifices for him and direct him what he should do. This we had *ch.* x. 8. Perhaps that order, though inserted there, was given him afterwards, or was given him as a general rule to be observed in every public congress at Gilgal, or, as is most probable, though not mentioned again, was lately repeated with reference to this particular occasion; for it is plain that Saul himself understood it as obliging him from God now to stay till Samuel came, else he would not have made so many excuses as he did for not staying, *v.* 11. This order Saul broke. He staid till the seventh day, yet had not patience to wait till the end of the seventh day. Perhaps he began to reproach Samuel as false to his word, careless of his country, and disrespectful of his prince, and thought it more fit that Samuel should wait for him than he for Samuel. However, 1. He presumed to offer sacrifice without Samuel, and nothing appears to the contrary but that he did it himself, though he was neither priest nor prophet, as if, because he was a king, he might do any thing, a piece of presumption which king Uzziah paid dearly for, 2 Chron. xxvi. 16, &c. 2. He determined to engage the Philistines without Samuel's directions, though he had promised to *show him what he should do.* So self-sufficient Saul was that he thought it not worth while to stay for a prophet of the Lord either to pray for him or to advise him. This was Saul's offence, and that which aggravated it was, (1.) That, for aught that appears, he did not send any messenger to Samuel, to know his mind, to represent the case to him, and to receive fresh directions from him, though he had enough about him that were swift enough of foot at this time. (2.) That when Samuel came he rather seemed to boast of what he had done than to repent of it; for he *went forth to salute him,* as his brother-sacrificer, and seemed pleased with the opportunity he had of letting Samuel know that he needed him not, but could do well enough without him. He went out to *bless him,* so the word is, as if he now thought himself a complete priest, empowered to bless as well as sacrifice, whereas he should have gone out to be blessed by him. (3.) That he charged Samuel with breach of promise: *Thou camest not within the days appointed* (*v.* 11), and therefore if any thing was amiss Samuel must bear the blame, who was God's minister; whereas he did come according to his word, before the seven days had expired. Thus the *scoffers of the latter days* think the promise of Christ's coming is broken, because he does not come in their time, though it is certain he will come at the set time. (4.) That when he was charged with disobedience he justified himself in what he had done, and gave no sign at all of repentance for it. It is not sinning that ruins men, but sinning and not repenting, falling and not getting up again. See what excuses he made, *v,* 11, 12. He would have this act of disobedience pass, [1.] For an instance of his prudence. The people were most of them scattered from him, and he had no other way than this to keep those with him that remained and to prevent their deserting too. If Samuel neglected the public concerns, he would not. [2.] For an instance of his piety. He would be thought very devout, and in great care not to engage the Philistines till he had by prayer and sacrifice engaged God on his side: "*The Philistines,*" said he, "*will come down upon me, before I have made my supplication to the Lord,* and then I am undone. What! go to war before I have said my prayers! Thus he covered his disobedience to God's command with a pretence of concern for God's favour. Hypocrites lay a great stress upon the external performances of religion, thinking thereby to excuse their neglect of the *weightier matters of the law.* And yet, lastly, He owns it went against his conscience to do it: *I forced myself and offered a burnt-offering,* perhaps boasting that he had broken through his convictions and got the better of them, or at least thinking this extenuated his fault, that he knew he should not have done as he did, but did it with reluctancy. Foolish man! to think that God would be well pleased with sacrifices offered in direct opposition both to his general and particular command.

II. The sentence passed upon Saul for this offence. Samuel found him standing by his burnt-offering, but, instead of an answer of peace, was sent to him with heavy tidings, and let him know that *the sacrifice of the wicked is abomination to the Lord,* much more when he brings it, as Saul did, *with a wicked mind.* 1. He shows him the aggravations of his crime, and says to this king, *Thou art wicked,* which it is not for any but a prophet of the Lord to say, Job xxxiv. 18. He charges him with being an enemy to himself and his interest—*Thou hast done foolishly,* and a rebel to God and his government—"*Thou hast not kept the commandment of the Lord thy God,* that commandment wherewith he intended to try thy obedience." Note, Those that disobey the commandments of God do foolishly for themselves. Sin is folly, and sinners are the greatest fools. 2. He reads his doom (*v.* 14): "*Thy kingdom shall not continue* long to thee or thy family; God has his eye upon another, *a man after his own heart,* and not like thee, that will have thy own will and way." The sentence is in effect the same with *Mene tekel,* only now there seems room left for Saul's repentance, upon which this sentence would have been reversed; but, upon the next act of disobedience, it was made irreversible, *ch.* xv. 29. And now, better a thousand times he had continued in obscurity tending his asses than to be enthroned and so soon dethroned. But was not this hard, to pass so severe a sentence upon him and his house for a single error, an error that seemed so small, and in excuse for which he had so much to say? No, *The Lord is righteous in all his ways* and does no man any wrong, *will be justified when he speaks and clear when he judges.* By this, (1.) He shows that there is no sin little, because no little god to sin against; but that every sin is a forfeiture of the heavenly kingdom, for which we stood fair. (2.) He shows that disobedience to an express command, though in a small matter, is a great provocation, as in the case of our first parents. (3.) He warns us to *take heed of our spirits,* for that which to men may seem but a small offence, yet to him that knows from what principle and with what disposition of mind it is done, may appear a heinous crime. (4.) God, in rejecting Saul for an error seemingly little, sets off, as by a foil, the lustre of his mercy in forgiving such great sins as those of David, Manasseh, and others. (5.) We are taught hereby how necessary it is that we *wait on our God continually.* Saul lost his kingdom for want of two or three hours' patience.

15 And Samuel arose, and gat him up from Gilgal unto Gibeah of Benjamin. And Saul numbered the people *that were* present with him, about six hundred men. 16 And Saul, and Jonathan his son, and the people *that were* present with them, abode in Gibeah of Benjamin: but the Philistines encamped in Michmash. 17 And the spoilers came out of the camp of the Philistines in three companies: one company turned unto the way *that leadeth to* Ophrah, unto the land of Shual: 18 And another company turned the way *to* Beth-horon: and another company turned *to* the way of the border that looketh to the valley of Zeboim toward the wilderness. 19 Now there was no smith found throughout all the land of Israel: for the Philistines said, Lest the Hebrews make *them* swords or spears: 20 But all the Israelites went down to the Philistines, to sharpen every man his share, and his coulter, and his ax, and his mattock. 21 Yet they had a file for the mattocks, and for the coulters, and for the forks, and for the axes, and to sharpen the goads. 22 So it came to pass in the day of battle, that there was neither sword nor spear found in the hand of any of the people that *were* with Saul and Jonathan: but with Saul and with Jonathan his son was there found. 23 And the garrison of the Philistines went out to the passage of Michmash.

Here, 1. Samuel departs in displeasure. Saul has set up for himself, and now he is left to himself: *Samuel gat him from Gilgal* (*v.* 15), and it does not appear that he either prayed with Saul or directed him. Yet in going up to Gibeah of Benjamin, which was Saul's city, he intimated that he had not quite abandoned him, but waited to do him a kindness another time. Or he went to the college of the prophets there, to pray for Saul when he did not think fit to pray with him. 2. Saul goes after him to Gibeah, and there musters his army, and finds his whole nnmber to be but 600 men, *v.* 15, 16. Thus were they for their sin *diminished and brought low.* 3. The Philistines ravage the country, and put all the adjacent parts under contribution. The body of their army, or standing camp (as it is called in the margin, *v.* 23), lay in an advantageous pass at Michmash, but thence they sent out three separate parties or detachments that took several ways, to plunder the country, and bring in provisions for the army, *v.* 17, 18. By these the land of Israel was both terrified and impoverished, and the Philistines were animated and enriched. This the sin of Israel brought upon them, Isa. xlii. 24. 4. The Israelites that take the field with Saul are unarmed, having only slings and clubs, not a sword or spear among them all, except what Saul and Jonathan themselves have, *v.* 19, 22. See here, (1.) How politic the Philistines were, when they had power in their hands, and did what they pleased in Israel. They put down all the smiths' shops, transplanted the smiths into their own country, and forbade any Israelite, under severe penalties, to exercise the trade or mystery of working in brass or iron, though they had rich mines of both (Deut. viii. 9) in such plenty that it was said of Asher, *his shoes shall be iron and brass,* Deut. xxxiii. 25. This was subtilely done of the Philistines, for hereby they not only prevented the people of Israel from making themselves weapons of war (by which they would be both disused to military exercises and unfurnished when there was occasion), but obliged them to a dependence upon them even for the instruments of husbandry; they must go to them, that is, to some or other of their garrisons, which were dispersed in the country, to have all their iron-work done, and no more might an Israelite do than use a file (*v.* 20, 21), and no doubt the Philistines' smiths brought the Israelites long bills for work done. (2.) How impolitic Saul was, that did not, in the beginning of his reign, set himself to redress this grievance. Samuel's not doing it was very excusable; he fought with other artillery; thunder and lightning, in answer to his prayer, were to him instead of sword and spear; but for Saul, that pretended to be a king like the kings of the nations, to leave his soldiers without swords and spears, and take no care to provide them, especially when he might have done it out of the spoils of the Ammonites whom he conquered in the beginning of his reign, was such a piece of negligence as could by no means be excused. (3.) How slothful and mean-spirited the Israelites were, that suffered the Philistines thus to impose upon them and had no thought nor spirit to help themselves. It was reckoned very bad with them when there was *not a shield or spear found among* 40,000 *in Israel* (Judg. v. 8), and it was no better now, when there was never an Israelite with a sword by his side but the king and his son, never a soldier, never a gentleman; surely they were reduced to this, or began to be so, in Samson's time, for we never find him with sword or spear in his hand. If they had not been dispirited, they could not have been disarmed, but it was sin that made them naked to their shame.

CHAP. XIV.

We left the host of Israel in a very ill posture, in the close of the foregoing chapter; we saw in them no wisdom, nor strength, nor goodness, to give us ground to expect any other than that they should all be cut off by the army of the Philistines; yet here we find that infinite power which works without means, and that infinite goodness which gives without merit, glorified in a happy turn to their affairs, that still Samuel's words may be made good: "The Lord will not forsake his people, for his great name's sake," ch. xii. 22. In this chapter we have, I. The host of the Philistines trampled upon, and triumphed over, by the faith and courage of Jonathan, who unknown to his father (ver. 1—3), with his armour-bearer only, made a brave attack upon them, encouraging himself in the Lord his God, ver. 4—7. He challenged them (ver. 8—12), and, upon their acceptance of the challenge, charged them with such fury, or rather such faith, that he put them to flight, and set them one against another (ver. 13—15), which gave opportunity to Saul and his forces, with other Israelites, to follow the blow, and gain a victory, ver. 16—23. II. The host of Israel troubled and perplexed by the rashness and folly of Saul, who adjured the people to eat no food till night, which 1. Brought Jonathan to a præmunire, ver. 24—30. 2. Was a temptation to the people, when the time of their fast had expired, to eat with the blood, ver. 31—35. Jonathan's error, through ignorance, had like to have been his death, but the people rescued him, ver. 36—46. III. In the close we have a general account of Saul's exploits (ver. 47, 48) and of his family, ver. 49—52.

NOW it came to pass upon a day, that Jonathan the son of Saul said unto the young man that bare his armour, Come, and let us go over to the Philistines' garrison, that *is* on the other side. But he told not his father. 2 And Saul tarried in the uttermost part of Gibeah under a pomegranate tree which *is* in Migron: and the people that *were* with him *were* about six hundred men; 3 And Ahiah, the son of Ahitub, I-chabod's brother, the son of Phinehas, the son of Eli, the LORD's priest in Shiloh, wearing an ephod. And the people knew not that Jonathan was gone. 4 And between the passages, by which Jonathan sought to go over unto the Philistines' garrison, *there was* a sharp rock on the one side, and a sharp rock on the other side: and the name of the one *was* Bozez, and the name of the other Seneh. 5 The forefront of the one *was* situate northward over against Michmash, and the other southward over against Gibeah. 6 And Jonathan said to the young man that bare his armour, Come, and let us go over unto the garrison of these uncircumcised: it may be that the LORD will work for us: for *there is* no restraint to the LORD to save by many or by few. 7 And his armour-bearer said unto him, Do all that *is* in thine heart: turn thee; behold, I *am* with thee according to thy heart. 8 Then said Jonathan, Behold, we will pass over unto *these* men, and we will discover ourselves unto them. 9 If they say thus unto us, Tarry until we come to you; then we will stand still in our place, and will not go up unto them. 10 But if they say thus, Come up unto us; then we will go up: for the LORD hath delivered them into our hand: and this *shall be* a sign unto us. 11 And both of them discovered themselves unto the garrison of the Philistines: and the Philistines said, Behold, the Hebrews come forth out of the holes where they had hid themselves. 12 And the men of the garrison answered Jonathan and his armourbearer, and said, Come up to us, and we will show you a thing. And Jonathan said unto his armourbearer, Come up after me: for the LORD hath delivered them into the hand of Israel. 13 And Jonathan climbed up upon his hands and upon his feet, and his armourbearer after him: and they fell before Jonathan; and his armourbearer slew after him. 14 And that first slaughter, which Jonathan and his armourbearer made, was about twenty men, within as it were an half acre of land, *which* a yoke *of oxen might plough.* 15 And there was trembling in the host, in the field, and among all the people: the garrison, and the spoilers, they also trembled, and the earth quaked: so it was a very great trembling.

We must here take notice,

I. Of the goodness of God in restraining the Philistines, who had a vast army of valiant men in the field, from falling upon that little handful of timorous trembling people that Saul had with him, whom they would easily have swallowed up at once. It is an invisible power that sets bounds to the malice of the church's enemies, and suffers them not to do that which we should think there is nothing to hinder them from.

II. Of the weakness of Saul, who seems here to have been quite at a loss, and unable to help himself. 1. He pitched his tent under a tree, and had but 600 men with him, *v.* 2. Where were now the 3000 men he had chosen, and put such a confidence in? *ch.* xiii. 2. Those whom he trusted too much to failed him when he most needed them. He durst not stay in Gibeah, but got into some obscure place, in the uttermost part of the city, under a pomegranate-tree, under *Rimmon* (so the word is), *Ha-Rimmon,* that Rimmon near Gibeah, in the caves of which those 600 Benjamites that escaped hid themselves, Judg. xx. 47. Some think that there Saul took shelter, so mean and abject was his spirit, now that he had fallen under God's displeasure, every hour expecting the Philistines upon him, and thereby the accomplishment of Samuel's threatening, *ch.* xiii. 14. Those can never think themselves safe that see themselves cast out of God's protection. 2. Now he sent for a priest, and the ark, a priest from Shiloh, and the ark from Kirjath-jearim, *v.* 3, 18. Saul had once offended by offering sacrifice himself, *ch.* xiii. 9. Now he resolves never to fall into that error again, and therefore sends for a priest, and hopes to compromise the matter with God Almighty by a particular reformation, as many do whose hearts are unhumbled and unchanged. Samuel, the Lord's prophet, had forsaken him, but he thinks he can make up that loss by commanding Ahiah, the Lord's priest, to attend him, and *he* will not make him stay for him nor reprove him, as Samuel had done, but will do just as he bids him, *v.* 18, 19. Many love to have such ministers as will be what they would have them to be, and prophesy smooth things to them; and their caressing them because they are priests, they hope, will atone for their enmity to those ministers that deal faithfully and plainly with them. He will also have the ark brought, perhaps to upbraid Samuel, who in the days of his government, for aught that appears, had not made any public use of it; or in hopes that this would make up the deficiency of his forces; one would have supposed that they would never bring the ark into the camp again, since, the last time, it not only did not save them, but did itself fall into the Philistines' hands. But it is common for those that have lost the substance of religion to be most fond of the shadows of it, as here is a deserted prince courting a deserted priest.

III. Of the bravery and piety of Jonathan, the son of Saul, who was much fitter than the father to wear the crown. "A sweet imp (says bishop Hall) out of a crab-stock."

1. He resolved to go *incognito—unknown to any one,* into the camp of the Philistines; he did not acquaint his father with his design, for he knew he would forbid him; nor the people, for he knew they would all discourage him, and, because he resolved not to heed their objections, he resolved not to hear them, nor ask their advice, *v.* 1, 3. Nor had he so great an opinion of the priest as to consult him, but, being conscious of a divine impulse putting him upon it, he threw himself into the mouth of danger, in hope of doing service to his country. The way of access to the enemies' camp is described (*v.* 4, 5) as being peculiarly difficult, and their natural entrenchments impregnable, yet this does not discourage him; the strength and sharpness of the rocks do but harden and whet his resolutions. Great and generous souls are animated by opposition and take a pleasure in breaking through it.

2. He encouraged his armour-bearer, a

young man that attended him, to go along with him in this daring enterprise, (*v.* 6): "*Come, and let us* put our lives in our hands, *and go over to the* enemies' *garrison*, and try what we can do to put them into confusion." See whence he draws his encouragements. (1.) "They are uncircumcised, and have not the seal of the covenant in their flesh, as we have. Fear not, we shall do well enough with them, for they are not under the protection of God's covenant as we are, cannot call him theirs as we can, by the sign of circumcision." If such as are enemies to us are also strangers to God, we need not fear them. (2.) "God is able to make us two victorious over their unnumbered regiments. *There is no restraint in the Lord*, no limitation to the holy One of Israel, but it is all one to him *to save by many or by few*." This is a truth easily granted in general, that it is all alike to Omnipotence what the instruments are by which it works; and yet it is not so easy to apply it to a particular case; when we are but few and feeble then to believe that God can not only save us, but save by us, this is an instance of faith, which, wherever it is, shall obtain a good report. Let this strengthen the weak and encourage the timid: let it be pleaded with God for the enforcing of our petitions and with ourselves for the silencing of our fears: *It is nothing with God to help, whether with many or with those that have no power*, 2 Chron. xiv. 11. (3.) "Who knows but he that can use us for his glory will do it? *It may be the Lord will work for us*, work with us, work a sign or miracle for us." So the Chaldee. We may encourage ourselves with hope that God will appear for us, though we have not ground on which to build an assurance. An active faith will venture far in God's cause upon an *it may be*. Jonathan's armour-bearer, or esquire, as if he had learned to carry, not his arms only, but his heart, promised to stand by him and to follow him whithersoever he went, *v.* 7. We have reason to think that Jonathan felt a divine impulse and impression putting him upon this bold adventure, in which he was encouraged by his servant's concurrence, otherwise the danger was so great which he ran upon that he would have tempted God rather than trusted him. And perhaps he had an actual regard to that word of Joshua (Josh. xxiii. 10), *One man of you shall chase a thousand*, borrowed from Moses, Deut. xxxii. 30.

3. How bold soever his resolution was, he resolved to follow Providence in the execution of it, which, he believed, would guide him *with its eye* (Ps. xxxii. 8), and which therefore he would carefully attend and take hints of direction from. See how he put himself upon Providence, and resolved to be determined by it. "Come" (says he to his confidant), we will discover ourselves to the enemy, as those that are not afraid to look them in the face (*v.* 8), and then, if they be so cautious as to bid us stand, we will advance no further, taking it for an intimation of Providence that God would have us act defensively, and we will prepare as well as we can to give them a warm reception (*v.* 9); but if they be so presumptuous as to challenge us, and the first sentinel we meet with bid us march on, we will push forward, and make as brisk an onset, assuredly gathering thence that it is the will of God we should act offensively, and then not doubting but he will *stand by us*," *v.* 10. And upon this issue he puts it, firmly believing, as we all should, (1.) That God has the governing of the hearts and tongues of all men, even of those that know him not, nor have any regard to him, and serves his own purposes by them, though they mean not so, neither do their hearts think so. Jonathan knew God could discover his mind to him if he pleased, and would do it, since he depended upon him, as surely by the mouth of a Philistine as by the mouth of a priest. (2.) That God will, some way or other, direct the steps of those that *acknowledge him in all their ways*, and seek unto him for direction, with full purpose of heart to follow it. Sometimes we find most comfort in that which is least our own doing, and into which we have been led by the unexpected, but well observed, turns of Providence.

4. Providence gave him the sign he expected, and he answered the signal. He and his armour-bearer did not surprise the Philistines when they were asleep, but discovered themselves to them by day-light, *v.* 11. The guards of the Philistines, (1.) Disdained them, upbraided them with the cowardice of many of their people, and looked upon them to be of the regiment of sneakers: *Behold, the Hebrews come forth out of their holes*. If some of Christ's soldiers play the coward, others that play the man may perhaps be upbraided with it. (2.) They defied them (*v.* 12): *Come, and we will show you a thing*, as if they came like children to gaze about them; but, meaning, as Goliath (*ch.* xvii. 44), that they would *give them as meat to the fowls of the air*. They bantered them, not doubting but to make a prey of them. This greatly emboldened Jonathan. With it he encouraged his servant; he had spoken with uncertainty (*v.* 6): *It may be the Lord will work for us;* but now he speaks with assurance (*v.* 12): *The Lord has delivered them*, not into our hands (he sought not his own glory), but *into the hand of Israel*, for he aimed at nothing but the advantage of the public. His faith being thus strengthened, no difficulty can stand before him; he climbs up the rock upon all four (*v.* 13), though he has nothing to cover him, nor any but his own servant to second him, nor any human probability of any thing but death before him.

5. The wonderful success of this daring enterprise. The Philistines, instead of falling

upon Jonathan, to slay him, or take him prisoner, fell before him (*v.* 13) unaccountably, upon the first blow he gave. They fell, that is, (1.) They were many of them slain by him and his armour-bearer, *v.* 14. Twenty Philistines fell presently. It was not so much the name of Jonathan that made them yield so tamely (though some think that this had become terrible to them, since he smote one of their garrisons, *ch.* xiii. 3), but it was God's right hand and his arm that got him this victory. (2.) The rest were put to flight, and fell foul upon one another (*v.* 15): *There was trembling in the host.* There was no visible cause for fear; they were so numerous, bold, and advantageously posted; the Israelites had fled before them; not an enemy made head against them, but one gentleman and his man; and yet they shook like an aspen-leaf. The consternation was general: they all trembled; even *the spoilers,* those that had been most bold and forward, shared in the common fright, the joints of their loins were loosed, and their knees smote one against another, and yet none of them could tell why or wherefore. It is called *a trembling of God* (so the original phrase is), signifying not only, as we render it, a very great trembling, which they could not resist nor reason themselves clear of, but that it was supernatural, and came immediately from the hand of God. He that made the heart knows how to make it tremble. To complete the confusion, even the earth quaked, and made them ready to fear that it would sink under them. Those that will not fear the eternal God, he can make afraid of a shadow. See Prov. xxi. 1; Isa. xxxiii. 14.

16 And the watchmen of Saul in Gibeah of Benjamin looked; and, behold, the multitude melted away, and they went on beating down *one another.* 17 Then said Saul to the people that *were* with him, Number now, and see who is gone from us. And when they had numbered, behold, Jonathan and his armourbearer *were* not *there.* 18 And Saul said unto Ahiah, Bring hither the ark of God. For the ark of God was at that time with the children of Israel. 19 And it came to pass, while Saul talked unto the priest, that the noise that *was* in the host of the Philistines went on and increased: and Saul said unto the priest, Withdraw thine hand. 20 And Saul and all the people that *were* with him assembled themselves, and they came to the battle: and, behold, every man's sword was against his fellow, *and there was* a very great discomfiture. 21 Moreover the Hebrews *that* were with the Philistines before that time, which went up with them into the camp *from the country* round about, even they also *turned* to be with the Israelites that *were* with Saul and Jonathan. 22 Likewise all the men of Israel which had hid themselves in mount Ephraim, *when* they heard that the Philistines fled, even they also followed hard after them in the battle. 23 So the LORD saved Israel that day: and the battle passed over unto Beth-aven.

We have here the prosecution and improvement of the wonderful advantages which Jonathan and his armour-bearer gained against the Philistines.

I. The Philistines were, by the power of God, set against one another. They melted away like snow before the sun, and *went on beating down one another* (*v.* 16), for (*v.* 20) *every man's sword was against his fellow.* When they fled for fear, instead of turning back upon those that chased them, they reckoned those only their enemies that stood in their way, and treated them accordingly. The Philistines were very secure, because all the swords and spears were in their hands. Israel had none except what Saul and Jonathan had. But now God showed them the folly of that confidence, by making their own swords and spears the instruments of their destruction, and more fatal in their own hands than if they had been in the hands of Israel. See the like done, Judg. vii. 22; 2 Chron. xx. 23.

II. The Israelites were hereby animated against them.

1. Notice was soon taken of it by the watchmen of Saul, those that stood sentinel at Gibeah, *v.* 16. They were aware that the host of the enemy was in great confusion, and that a great slaughter was made among them, and yet, upon search, they found none of their own forces absent, but only Jonathan and his servant (*v.* 17), which no doubt greatly animated them, and assured them that it could be no other than the Lord's doing, when there was no more of man's doing than what those two could do against a great host.

2. Saul began to enquire of God, but soon desisted. His spirit had not come down so far as to allow him to consult Samuel, though, it is probable, he was near him; for we read (*ch.* xiii. 15) that he had come to Gibeah of Benjamin; but he called for the ark (*v.* 18), desiring to know whether it would be safe for him to attack the Philistines, upon the disorder they perceived them to be in. Many will consult God about their safety that would never consult him about

their duty. But, perceiving by his scouts that the noise in the enemy's camp increased, he commanded the priest that officiated to break off abruptly: "*Withdraw thy hand* (*v.* 19), consult no more, wait no longer for an answer. He was very unwise indeed if (as some think) he forbade him to lift up his hands in prayer; for when Joshua was actually engaged with Amalek Moses continued still to lift up his hands. It is rather a prohibition to his enquiring of the Lord, either, (1.) Because now he thought he did not need an answer, the case was plain enough. And yet the more evident it was that God did all the more reason he had to enquire whether he would give him leave to do any thing. Or, (2.) Because now he would not stay for it; he was in such haste to fight a falling enemy that he would not stay to make an end of his devotions, nor hear what answer God would give him. A little thing will divert a vain and carnal mind from religious exercises. He that believeth will not make haste, such haste as this, nor reckon any business so urgent as not to allow time to take God along with him.

3. He, and all the little force he had, made a vigorous attack upon the enemy; and all the people *were cried together* (so the word is, *v* 20), for want of the silver trumpets wherewith God appointed them to sound an alarm in the day of battle, Num. x. 9. They summoned them together by shouting, and their number was not so great but that they might soon be got together. And now they seem bold and brave when the work is done to their hands. Our Lord Jesus has conquered our spiritual enemies, routed and dispersed them, so that we are cowards indeed if we will not stand to our arms when it is only to pursue the victory and to divide the spoil.

4. Every Hebrew, even those from whom one would least have expected it, now turned his hand against the Philistines. (1.) Those that had deserted and gone over to the enemy, and were among them, now fought against them, *v.* 21. Some think, they were such as had been taken prisoners by them, and now they were as goads in their sides. It rather seems that they went in to them voluntarily, but, now that they saw them falling, recovered the hearts of Israelites, and did valiantly for their country. (2.) Those that had fled their colours, and hid themselves in the mountains, returned to their posts, and joined in with the pursuers (*v.* 22), hoping by their great zeal and officiousness, now that the danger was over and the victory sure, to atone for their former cowardice. It was not much to their praise to appear now, but it would have been more their reproach if they had not appeared. Those are remiss and faint-hearted indeed that will not act in the cause of God when they see it victorious, as well as righteous. Thus all hands were at work against the Philistines, and every Israelite slew as many as he could, without sword or spear; yet it is said (*v.* 23), it was *the Lord that saved Israel that day.* He did it by them, for without him they could do nothing. *Salvation is of the Lord.*

24 And the men of Israel were distressed that day: for Saul had adjured the people, saying, Cursed *be* the man that eateth *any* food until evening, that I may be avenged on mine enemies. So none of the people tasted *any* food. 25 And all *they of* the land came to a wood; and there was honey upon the ground. 26 And when the people were come into the wood, behold, the honey dropped; but no man put his hand to his mouth: for the people feared the oath. 27 But Jonathan heard not when his father charged the people with the oath: wherefore he put forth the end of the rod that *was* in his hand, and dipped it in a honeycomb, and put his hand to his mouth; and his eyes were enlightened. 28 Then answered one of the people, and said, Thy father straitly charged the people with an oath, saying, Cursed *be* the man that eateth *any* food this day. And the people were faint. 29 Then said Jonathan, My father hath troubled the land: see, I pray you, how mine eyes have been enlightened, because I tasted a little of this honey. 30 How much more, if haply the people had eaten freely to day of the spoil of their enemies which they found? for had there not been now a much greater slaughter among the Philistines? 31 And they smote the Philistines that day from Michmash to Aijalon: and the people were very faint. 32 And the people flew upon the spoil, and took sheep, and oxen, and calves, and slew *them* on the ground: and the people did eat *them* with the blood. 33 Then they told Saul, saying, Behold, the people sin against the LORD, in that they eat with the blood. And he said, Ye have transgressed: roll a great stone unto me this day. 34 And Saul said, Disperse yourselves among the people, and say unto them, Bring me hither every man his ox

and every man his sheep, and slay *them* here, and eat; and sin not against the LORD in eating with the blood. And all the people brought every man his ox with him that night, and slew *them* there. 35 And Saul built an altar unto the LORD: the same was the first altar that he built unto the LORD.

We have here an account of the distress of the children of Israel, even in the day of their triumphs. Such alloys are all present joys subject to. And such obstructions does many a good cause meet with, even when it seems most prosperous, through the mismanagement of instruments.

I. Saul forbade the people, under the penalty of a curse, to taste any food that day, *v.* 24. Here we will suppose, 1. That as king he had power to put his soldiers under this interdict, and to bind it on with a curse; and therefore they submitted to it, and God so far owned it as to discover, by the lot, that Jonathan was the delinquent that had meddled with the accursed thing (though ignorantly), on which account God would not be at that time enquired of by them. 2. That he did it with a good intention, lest the people, who perhaps had been kept for some time at short allowance, when they found plenty of victuals in the deserted camp of the Philistines, should fall greedily upon that, and so lose time in pursuing the enemy, and some of them, it may be, glut themselves to such a degree as not to be fit for any more service that day. To prevent this, he forbade them to taste any food, and laid himself, it is likely, under the same restraint. And yet his making this severe order was, (1.) Impolitic and very unwise; for, if it gained time, it lost strength, for the pursuit. (2.) It was imperious, and disobliging to the people, and worse than *muzzling the mouth of the ox when he treads out the corn.* To forbid them to feast would have been commendable, but to forbid them so much as to taste, though ever so hungry, was barbarous. (3.) It was impious to enforce the prohibition with a curse and an oath. Had he no penalty less than an anathema wherewith to support his military discipline? Death for such a crime would have been too much, but especially death with a curse. Though superiors may chide and correct, they may not curse their inferiors; our rule is, *Bless, and curse not.* When David speaks of an enemy he had that loved cursing perhaps he meant Saul, Ps. cix. 17, 18.

II. The people observed his order, but it had many inconveniences attending it. 1. The soldiers were tantalized; for, in their pursuit of the enemy, it happened that they went through a wood so full of wild honey that it dropped from the trees upon the ground, the Philistines having perhaps, in their flight, broken in upon the honey-combs, for their own refreshment, and left them running. Canaan flowed with honey, and here is an instance of it. They sucked honey out of *the rock, the flinty rock* (Deut. xxxii. 13); yet, for fear of the curse, they did not so much as taste the honey, *v.* 25, 26. Those are worthy the name of Israelites that can deny themselves and their own appetites even when they are most craving, and the delights of sense most tempting, for fear of guilt and a curse, and the table becoming a snare. Let us never feed ourselves, much less feast ourselves, without fear. 2. Jonathan fell under the curse through ignorance. He heard not of the charge his father had given; for, having bravely forced the lines, he was then following the chase, and therefore might justly be looked upon as exempted from the charge and not intended in it. But it seems it was taken for granted, and he himself did not object against it afterwards, that it extended to him, though absent upon so good an occasion. He, not knowing any peril in it, took up a piece of a honey-comb, upon the end of his staff, and sucked it (*v.* 27), and was sensibly refreshed by it: *His eyes were enlightened,* which began to grow dim through hunger and faintness; it made his countenance look pleasant and cheerful, for it was such as a stander-by might discern (*v.* 29): *See how my eyes have been enlightened.* He thought no harm, nor feared any, till one of the people acquainted him with the order, and then he found himself in a snare. Many a good son has been thus entangled and distressed, in more ways than one, by the rashness of an inconsiderate father. Jonathan, for his part, lost the crown he was heir to by his father's folly, which, it may be, this was an ill omen of. 3. The soldiers were faint, and grew feeble, in the pursuit of the Philistines. Jonathan foresaw this would be the effect of it; their spirits would flag, and their strength would fail, for want of sustenance. Such is the nature of our bodies that they soon grow unfit for service if they be not supplied with fresh recruits. Daily work cannot be done without daily bread, which our Father in heaven graciously gives us. It is *bread* that *strengthens man's heart;* therefore Jonathan reasoned very well, *If the people had eaten freely,* there would have been *a much greater slaughter* (*v.* 30); but, as it was, they were *very faint, too much fatigued* (so the Chaldee), and began to think more of their meat than of their work. 4. The worst effect of all was that at evening, when the restraint was taken off and they returned to their food again, they were so greedy and eager upon it that they ate the flesh with the blood, expressly contrary to the law of God, *v.* 32. Two hungry meals, we say, make the third a glutton; it was so here. They would not stay to have their meat either duly killed (for they slew the cattle upon the ground, and did not hang them up, as they used to do, that the blood might all run out of them) or duly dressed, but fell greedily upon it before it was half boiled or half roasted, *v.* 32. Saul, being informed of it, reproved them for the sin (*v.* 33.): *You have transgressed;* but did not, as he should have done, reflect upon himself as having been accessory to it, and having *made the Lord's people to transgress.* To put a stop to this irregularity, Saul ordered them to set up a great stone before him, and let all that had cattle to kill, for their present use, bring them thither, and kill them under his eye upon that stone (*v.* 33), and the people did so (*v.* 34), so easily were they restrained and reformed when their prince took care to do his part. If magistrates would but use their power as they might, people would be made better than they are with more ease than is imagined.

III. On this occasion Saul built an altar (*v.* 35), that he might offer sacrifice, either by way of acknowledgment of the victory they had obtained or by way of atonement for the sin they had been guilty of. *The same was the first altar that he built,* and perhaps the rolling of the great stone to kill the beasts on reminded him of converting it into an altar, else he would not have thought of it. Saul was turning aside from God, and yet now he began to build altars, being most zealous (as many are) for the form of godliness when he was denying the power of it. See Hos. viii. 14, *Israel has forgotten his Maker, and buildeth temples.* Some read it, *He began to build that altar;* he laid the first stone, but was so hasty to pursue his victory that he could not stay to finish it.

36 And Saul said, Let us go down after the Philistines by night, and spoil them until the morning light, and let us not leave a man of them. And they said, Do whatsoever seemeth good unto thee. Then said the priest, Let us draw near hither unto God. 37 And Saul asked counsel of God, Shall I go down after the Philistines? wilt thou deliver them into the hand of Israel? But he answered him not that day. 38 And Saul said, Draw ye near hither, all the chief of the people: and know and see wherein this sin hath been this day. 39 For, *as* the LORD liveth, which saveth Israel, though it be in Jonathan my son, he shall surely die. But *there was* not a man among all the people *that* answered him. 40 Then said he unto all Israel, Be ye on one side, and I and Jonathan my son will be on the other side. And the people said unto Saul, Do what seemeth good unto thee. 41 Therefore Saul said unto the LORD God of Israel, Give a perfect *lot.* And Saul and Jonathan were taken: but the people escaped. 42 And Saul said, Cast *lots* between me and Jonathan my son. And Jonathan was taken. 43 Then Saul said to Jonathan, Tell me what thou hast done. And Jonathan told him, and said, I did but taste a little honey with the end of the rod that *was* in mine hand, *and,* lo, I must die. 44 And Saul answered, God do so and more also: for thou shalt surely die, Jonathan. 45 And the people said unto Saul, Shall Jonathan die, who hath wrought this great salvation in Israel? God forbid: *as* the LORD liveth, there shall not one hair of his head fall to the ground; for he hath wrought with God this day. So the people rescued Jonathan, that he died not. 46 Then Saul went up from following the Philistines: and the Philistines went to their own place.

Here is, I. Saul's boasting against the Philistines. He proposed, as soon as his soldiers had got their suppers, to pursue them all night, and *not leave a man of them,* *v.* 36. Here he showed much zeal, but little discretion; for his army, thus fatigued, could as ill spare a night's sleep as a meal's meat. But it is common for rash and foolish men to consider nobody but themselves, and, so that they may but have their humour, not to care what hardships they put upon those that are under them. However, the people were so obsequious to their king that they would by no means oppose the motion, but resolved to make the best of it, and, if he will go on, they will follow him: *Do whatsoever seemeth good to thee.* Only the priest thought it convenient to go on with the devotions that were broken off abruptly (*v.* 19), and to consult the oracle: *Let us draw near hither unto God.* Princes and great men have need of such about them as will thus be their remembrancers, wherever they go, to take God along with them. And, when the priest proposed it, Saul could not for shame reject the proposal, but *asked counsel of God* (*v.* 37): "*Shall I go down after the Philistines?* And shall I speed?"

II. His falling foul on his son Jonathan: and the rest of this paragraph is wholly concerning him; for, while he is prosecuted, the Philistines make their escape. We know not what mischief may ensue upon one rash resolve.

1. God, by giving an intimation of his displeasure, put Saul upon searching for an accursed thing. When, by the priest, he consulted the oracle, God *answered him not, v.* 37. Note, When God denies our prayers it concerns us to enquire what the sin is that has provoked him to do so. *Let us see where the sin is, v.* 38. For God's ear is not heavy that it cannot hear, but it is sin that separates between us and him. If God turns away our prayer, we have reason to suspect it is for some iniquity regarded in our hearts, which we are concerned to find out, that we may put it away, may mortify it, and put it to death. Saul swears by his Maker that whoever was the Achan that troubled the camp, by eating the forbidden fruit, should certainly die, though it were Jonathan himself, that is, though ever so dear to himself and the people, little thinking that Jonathan was the man (*v.* 39): *He shall surely die,* the curse shall be executed upon him. But none of the people answered him, that is, none of those who knew Jonathan had broken the order would inform against him.

2. Jonathan was discovered by lot to be the offender. Saul would have lots cast between himself and Jonathan on the one side, and the people on the other, perhaps because he was as confident of Jonathan's innocency in this matter as of his own, *v.* 40. The people, seeing him in a heat, durst not gainsay any thing he proposed, but acquiesced: *Do as seemeth good unto thee.* Before he cast lots, he prayed that *God would give a perfect lot* (*v.* 41), that is, make a full discovery of this matter, or, as it is in the margin, that he would show the innocent. This was with an air of impartial justice. Judges should desire that truth may come out, whoever may suffer by it. Lots should be cast with prayer, because they are a solemn appeal to Providence, and by them we beg of God to direct and determine us (Acts i. 24), for which reason some have condemned games that depend purely upon lot or chance as making too bold with a sacred thing. Jonathan at length was taken (*v.* 42), Providence designing hereby to countenance and support a lawful authority, and to put an honour upon the administration of public justice in general, reserving another way to bring off one that had done nothing worthy of death.

3. Jonathan ingenuously confesses the fact, and Saul, with an angry curse, passes sentence upon him. Jonathan denies not the truth, nor goes about to conceal it, only he thinks it hard that he must *die for it, v.* 43. He might very fairly have pleaded his invincible ignorance of the law, or have insisted upon his merit, but he submitted to the necessity with a great and generous mind: "God's and my father's will be done:" thus he showed as much valour in receiving the messengers of death himself as in sending them among the Philistines. It is as brave to yield in some cases as it is in other cases to fight. Saul is not mollified by his filial submission nor the hardness of his case; but as one that affected to be thought firm to his word, and much more to his oath; even when it bound him hardest, with another imprecation he gives judgment upon Jonathan (*v.* 44): "*God do so and more also* to me if I do not execute the law upon thee, *for thou shalt surely die, Jonathan.*" (1.) He passed this sentence too hastily, without consulting the oracle. Jonathan had a very good plea in arrest of the judgment. What he had done was not *malum in se—bad in itself;* and, as for the prohibition of it, he was ignorant of that, so that he could not be charged with rebellion or disobedience. (2.) He did it in fury. Had Jonathan been worthy to die, yet it would have become a judge, much more a father, to pass sentence with tenderness and compassion, and not with such an air of triumph, like a man perfectly divested of all humanity and natural affection. Justice is debased when it is administered with wrath and bitterness. (3.) He backed it with a curse upon himself if he did not see the sentence executed; and this curse did return upon his own head. Jonathan escaped, but God did so to Saul, and more also; for he was rejected of God and made anathema. Let none upon any occasion dare to use such imprecations as these, lest God say Amen to them, and *make their own tongues to fall upon them,* Ps. lxiv. 8. This stone will return upon him that rolleth it. Yet we have reason to think that Saul's bowels yearned towards Jonathan, so that he really punished himself, and very justly, when he seemed so severe upon Jonathan. God made him feel the smart of his own rash edict, which might make him fear being again guilty of the like. By all these vexatious accidents God did likewise correct him for his presumption in offering sacrifice without Samuel. An expedition so ill begun could not end without some rebukes.

4. The people rescued Jonathan out of his father's hands, *v.* 45. Hitherto they had expressed themselves very observant of Saul. What seemed good to him they acquiesced in, *v.* 36, 40. But, when Jonathan is in danger, Saul's word is no longer a law to them, but with the utmost zeal they oppose the execution of his sentence: "*Shall Jonathan die*—that blessing, that darling, of his country? Shall that life be sacrificed to a punctilio of law and honour which was so bravely exposed for the public service, and to which we owe our lives and triumphs? No, we will never stand by and see him thus treated whom God delights to honour." It is good to see Israelites zealous for the protection of those whom God has made instruments of public good. Saul had sworn that Jonathan should die, but they oppose their oath to his, and swear he shall not die: "*As the Lord liveth there shall not* only not his head, but not *a hair of his head fall to the*

ground;" they did not rescue him by violence, but by reason and resolution; and Josephus says they made their prayer to God that he might be loosed from the curse. They plead for him that *he has wrought with God this day;* that is, "he has owned God's cause, and God has owned his endeavours, and therefore his life is too precious to be thrown away upon a nicety." We may suppose Saul had not so perfectly forgotten the relation of a father but that he was willing enough to have Jonathan rescued, and well pleased to have that done which yet he would not do himself: and he that knows the heart of a father knows not how to blame him.

5. The design against the Philistines is quashed by this incident (*v.* 46): *Saul went up from following them,* and so an opportunity was lost of completing the victory. When Israel's shields are clashing with one another the public safety and service suffer by it.

47 So Saul took the kingdom over Israel, and fought against all his enemies on every side, against Moab, and against the children of Ammon, and against Edom, and against the kings of Zobah, and against the Philistines: and whithersoever he turned himself, he vexed *them.* 48 And he gathered a host, and smote the Amalekites, and delivered Israel out of the hands of them that spoiled them. 49 Now the sons of Saul were Jonathan, and Ishui, and Melchi-shua: and the names of his two daughters *were these;* the name of the firstborn Merab, and the name of the younger Michal: 50 And the name of Saul's wife *was* Ahinoam, the daughter of Ahimaaz: and the name of the captain of his host *was* Abner, the son of Ner, Saul's uncle. 51 And Kish *was* the father of Saul; and Ner the father of Abner *was* the son of Abiel. 52 And there was sore war against the Philistines all the days of Saul: and when Saul saw any strong man, or any valiant man, he took him unto him.

Here is a general account of Saul's court and camp. 1. Of his court and family, the names of his sons and daughters (*v.* 49), and of his wife and his cousin-german that was general of his army, *v.* 50. There is mention of another wife of Saul's (2 Sam. xxi. 8), Rizpah, a secondary wife, and of the children he had by her. 2. Of his camp and military actions. (1.) How he levied his army: *When he saw any strong valiant man,* that was remarkably fit for service, *he took him unto him* (*v.* 52), as Samuel had told them the manner of the king would be (*ch.* viii. 11); and, if he must have a standing army, it was his prudence to fill it up with the ablest men he could make choice of. (2.) How he employed his army. He guarded his country against the insults of its enemies on every side, and prevented their incursions, *v.* 47, 48. It is supposed that he acted only defensively against those that used to invade the borders of Israel; *and whithersoever he turned himself,* as there was occasion, *he vexed them,* by checking and disappointing them. But the enemies he struggled most with were the Philistines, with whom he had *sore war all his days, v.* 52. He had little reason to be proud of his royal dignity, nor had any of his neighbours cause to envy him, for he had little enjoyment of himself after he took the kingdom. He could not vex his enemies without some vexation to himself, such thorns are crowns quilted with.

CHAP. XV.

In this chapter we have the final rejection of Saul from being king, for his disobedience to God's command in not utterly destroying the Amalekites. By his wars and victories he hoped to magnify and perpetuate his own name and honour, but, by his mismanagement of them, he ruined himself, and laid his honour in the dust. Here is, I. The commission God gave him to destroy the Amalekites, with a command to do it utterly, ver. 1—3. II. Saul's preparation for this expedition, ver. 4—6. III. His success, and partial execution of this commission, ver. 7—9. IV. His examination before Samuel, and sentence passed upon him, notwithstanding the many frivolous pleas he made to excuse himself, ver. 10—31. V. The slaying of Agag, ver. 32, 33. VI. Samuel's final farewell to Saul, v. 34, 35.

SAMUEL also said unto Saul, The LORD sent me to anoint thee *to be* king over his people, over Israel: now therefore hearken thou unto the voice of the words of the LORD. 2 Thus saith the LORD of hosts, I remember *that* which Amalek did to Israel, how he laid *wait* for him in the way, when he came up from Egypt. 3 Now go and smite Amalek, and utterly destroy all that they have, and spare them not; but slay both man and woman, infant and suckling, ox and sheep, camel and ass. 4 And Saul gathered the people together, and numbered them in Telaim, two hundred thousand footmen, and ten thousand men of Judah. 5 And Saul came to a city of Amalek, and laid wait in the valley. 6 And Saul said unto the Kenites, Go, depart, get you down from among the Amalekites, lest I destroy you with them: for ye showed kindness to all the children of Israel, when they came up out of Egypt. So the Kenites departed from among the Amalekites. 7 And Saul smote the Amalekites from Havilah *until* thou comest to

Shur, that *is* over against Egypt. 8 And he took Agag the king of the Amalekites alive, and utterly destroyed all the people with the edge of the sword. 9 But Saul and the people spared Agag, and the best of the sheep, and of the oxen, and of the fatlings, and the lambs, and all *that was* good, and would not utterly destroy them: but every thing *that was* vile and refuse, that they destroyed utterly.

Here, I. Samuel, in God's name, solemnly requires Saul to be obedient to the command of God, and plainly intimates that he was now about to put him upon a trial, in one particular instance, whether he would be obedient or no, *v.* 1. And the making of this so expressly the trial of his obedience did very much aggravate his disobedience. 1. He reminds him of what God had done for him: "*The Lord sent me to anoint thee to be a king.* God gave thee thy power, and therefore he expects thou shouldst use thy power for him. He put honour upon thee, and now thou must study how to do him honour. He made thee king over Israel, and now thou must plead Israel's cause and avenge their quarrels. Thou art advanced to command Israel, but know that thou art a subject to the God of Israel and must be commanded by him." Men's preferment, instead of releasing them from their obedience to God, obliges them so much the more to it. Samuel had himself been employed to anoint Saul, and therefore was the fitter to be sent with these orders to him. 2. He tells him, in general, that, in consideration of this, whatever God commanded him to do he was bound to do it: *Now therefore hearken to the voice of the Lord.* Note, God's favours to us lay strong obligations upon us to be obedient to him. This we must render, Ps. cxvi. 12.

II. He appoints him a particular piece of service, in which he must now show his obedience to God more than in any thing he had done yet. Samuel premises God's authority to the command: *Thus says the Lord of hosts,* the Lord of all hosts, of Israel's hosts. He also gives him a reason for the command, that the severity he must use might not seem hard: *I remember that which Amalek did to Israel, v.* 2. God had an ancient quarrel with the Amalekites, for the injuries they did to his people Israel when he brought them out of Egypt. We have the story, Exod. xvii. *v.* 8, &c., and the crime is aggravated, Deut. xxv. 18. He basely smote the hindmost of them, and feared not God. God then swore that he would have *war with Amalek from generation to generation,* and that in process of time he *would utterly put out the remembrance of Amalek;* this is the work that Saul is now appointed to do (*v.* 3): "*Go and smite Amalek.* Israel is now strong, and the measure of the iniquity of Amalek is now full; now go and make a full riddance of that devoted nation." He is expressly commanded to kill and slay all before him, *man and woman, infant and suckling,* and not spare them out of pity; also *ox and sheep, camel and ass,* and not spare them out of covetousness. Note, 1. Injuries done to God's Israel will certainly be reckoned for sooner or later, especially the opposition given them when they are coming out of Egypt. 2. God often bears long with those that are marked for ruin. The sentence passed is not executed speedily. 3. Though he bear long, he will not bear always. The year of recompence for the controversy of Israel will come at last. Though divine justice strikes slowly it strikes surely. 4. The longer judgment is delayed many times the more severe it is when it comes. 5. God chooses out instruments to do his work that are fittest for it. This was bloody work, and therefore Saul who was a rough and severe man must do it.

III. Saul hereupon musters his forces, and makes a descent upon the country of Amalek. It was an immense army that he brought into the field (*v.* 4): 200,000 *footmen.* When he was to engage the Philistines, and the success was hazardous, he had but 600 attending him, *ch.* xiii. 15. But now that he was to attack the Amalekites by express order from heaven, in which he was sure of victory, he had thousands at his call. But, whatever it was at other times, it was not now for the honour of Judah that their forces were numbered by themselves, for their quota was scandalously short (whatever was the reason), but a twentieth part of the whole, for they were but 10,000, when the other ten tribes (for I except Levi) brought into the field 200,000. The day of Judah's honour drew near, but had not yet come. Saul numbered them in *Telaim,* which signifies *lambs.* He numbered them *like lambs* (so the vulgar Latin), numbered them *by the paschal lambs* (so the Chaldee), allowing ten to a lamb, a way of numbering used by the Jews in the later times of their nation. Saul drew all his forces to the *city of Amalek,* that city that was their metropolis (*v.* 5), that he might provoke them to give him battle.

IV. He gave friendly advice to the Kenites to separate themselves from the Amalekites among whom they dwelt, while this execution was in doing, *v.* 6. Herein he did prudently and piously, and, it is probable, according to the direction Samuel gave him. The Kenites were of the family and kindred of Jethro, Moses's father-in-law, a people that dwelt in tents, which made it easy for them, upon every occasion, to remove to other lands not appropriated. Many of them, at this time, dwelt among the Amalekites, where, though they dwelt in tents, they were fortified by nature, for *they put their nest in a rock*, being hardy people that could live any where, and affected fastnesses, Num. xxiv. 21. Balaam had foretold that they should be wasted, Num. xxiv. 22. However Saul must not waste them. But, 1. He acknowledges the kindness of their ancestors to Israel, when they came out of Egypt. Jethro and his family had been very helpful and serviceable to them in their passage through the wilderness, had been to them instead of eyes, and this is remembered to their posterity many ages after. Thus a good man leaves the divine blessing for an inheritance to his children's children; those that come after us may be reaping the benefit of our good works when we are in our graves. God is not unrighteous to forget the kindnesses shown to his people; but they shall be remembered another day, at furthest in the great day, *and recompensed in the resurrection of the just. I was hungry, and you gave me meat.* God's remembering the kindness of the Kenites' ancestors in favour to them, at the same time when he was punishing the injuries done by the ancestors of the Amalekites, helped to clear the righteousness of God in that dispensation. If he entail favours, why may he not entail frowns? He espouses his people's cause, so as to *bless those that bless them;* and therefore so as to *curse those that curse them,* Num. xxiv. 9; Gen. xii. 3. They cannot themselves requite the kindnesses nor avenge the injuries done them, but God will do both. 2. He desires them to remove their tents from among the Amalekites: *Go, depart, get you down from among them.* When destroying judgments are abroad God will take care to separate between the precious and the vile, and to hide the meek of the earth in the day of his anger. It is dangerous being found in the company of God's enemies, and it is our duty and interest to *come out from among them,* lest we share in their sins and plagues, Rev. xviii. 4. The Jews have a saying, *Woe to the wicked man and woe to his neighbour.*

V. Saul prevailed against the Amalekites, for it was rather an execution of condemned malefactors than a war with contending enemies. The issue could not be dubious when the cause was just and the call so clear: *He smote them* (*v.* 7), *utterly destroyed them, v.* 8. Now they paid dearly for the sin of their ancestors. God sometimes *lays up iniquity for the children.* They were idolaters, and were guilty of many other sins, for which they deserved to fall under the wrath of God; yet, when God would reckon with them, he fastened upon the sin of their ancestors in abusing his Israel as the ground of his quarrel. Lord, How unsearchable are thy judgments, yet how incontestable is thy righteousness!

VI. Yet he did his work by halves, *v.* 9. 1. He *spared Agag,* because he was a king like himself, and perhaps in hope to get a great ransom for him. 2. He spared the best of the cattle, and destroyed only the refuse, that was good for little. Many of the people, we may suppose, made their escape, and took their effects with them into other countries, and therefore we read of Amalekites after this; but that could not be helped. It was Saul's fault that he did not destroy such as came to his hands and were in his power. That which was now destroyed was in effect sacrificed to the justice of God, as the God to whom vengeance belongeth; and for Saul to think the torn and the sick, the lame and the lean, good enough for that, while he reserved for his own fields and his own table the firstlings and the fat, was really to honour himself more than God.

10 Then came the word of the LORD unto Samuel, saying, 11 It repenteth me that I have set up Saul *to be* king: for he is turned back from following me, and hath not performed my commandments. And it grieved Samuel; and he cried unto the LORD all night. 12 And when Samuel rose early to meet Saul in the morning, it was told Samuel, saying, Saul came to Carmel, and, behold, he set him up a place, and is gone about, and passed on, and gone down to Gilgal. 13 And Samuel came to Saul: and Saul said unto him, Blessed *be* thou of the LORD: I have performed the commandment of the LORD. 14 And Samuel said, What *meaneth* then this bleating of the sheep in mine ears, and the lowing of the oxen which I hear? 15 And Saul said, They have brought them from the Amalekites: for the people spared the best of the sheep and of the oxen, to sacrifice unto the LORD thy God; and the rest we have utterly destroyed. 16 Then Samuel said unto Saul, Stay, and I will tell thee what the LORD hath said to me this night. And he said unto him, Say on. 17 And Samuel said, When thou *wast* little in thine own sight, *wast* thou not *made* the head of the tribes of Israel, and the LORD anointed thee king over Israel? 18 And the LORD sent thee on a journey, and said, Go and utterly destroy the sinners the Amalekites, and fight against them until they be consumed. 19 Wherefore then didst thou not obey the voice of the LORD, but didst fly upon the

spoil, and didst evil in the sight of the LORD? 20 And Saul said unto Samuel, Yea, I have obeyed the voice of the LORD, and have gone the way which the LORD sent me, and have brought Agag the king of Amalek, and have utterly destroyed the Amalekites. 21 But the people took of the spoil, sheep and oxen, the chief of the things which should have been utterly destroyed, to sacrifice unto the LORD thy God in Gilgal. 22 And Samuel said, Hath the LORD *as great* delight in burnt offerings and sacrifices, as in obeying the voice of the LORD? Behold, to obey *is* better than sacrifice, *and* to hearken than the fat of rams. 23 For rebellion *is as* the sin of witchcraft, and stubbornness *is as* iniquity and idolatry. Because thou hast rejected the word of the LORD, he hath also rejected thee from *being* king.

Saul is here called to account by Samuel concerning the execution of his commission against the Amalekites; and remarkable instances we are here furnished with of the strictness of the justice of God and the treachery and deceitfulness of the heart of man. We are here told,

I. What passed between God and Samuel, in secret, upon this occasion, *v.* 10, 11. 1. God determines Saul's rejection, and acquaints Samuel with it: *It repenteth me that I have set up Saul to be king.* Repentance in God is not, as it is in us, a change of his mind, but a change of his method or dispensation. He does not alter his will, but wills an alteration. The change was in Saul: *He has turned back from following me;* this construction God put upon the partiality of his obedience, and the prevalency of his covetousness. And hereby he did himself make God his enemy. God repented that he had given Saul the kingdom and the honour and power that belonged to it: but he never repented that he had given any man wisdom and grace, and his fear and love; these gifts and callings of God are without repentance. 2. Samuel laments and deprecates it. *It grieved Samuel* that Saul had forfeited God's favour, and that God had resolved to cast him off; and he *cried unto the Lord all night,* spent a whole night in interceding for him, that this decree might not go forth against him. When others were in their beds sleeping, he was upon his knees praying and wrestling with God. He did not thus deprecate his own exclusion from the government; nor was he secretly pleased, as many a one would have been, that Saul, who succeeded him, was so soon laid aside, but on the contrary prayed earnestly for his establishment, so far was he from desiring that woeful day. The rejection of sinners is the grief of good people; God delights not in their death, nor should we.

II. What passed between Samuel and Saul in public. Samuel, being sent of God to him with these heavy tidings, went, as Ezekiel, in *bitterness of soul,* to meet him, perhaps according to an appointment when Saul went forth on this expedition, for Saul had come to Gilgal (*v.* 12), the place where he was made king (*ch.* xi. 15), and where now he would have been confirmed if he had approved himself well in this trial of his obedience. But Samuel was informed that Saul had set up a triumphal arch, or some monument of his victory, at Carmel, a city in the mountains of Judah, seeking his own honour more than the honour of God, for he set up this place (or *hand,* as the word is) for himself (he had more need to have been repenting of his sin and making his peace with God than boasting of his victory), and also that he had marched in great state to Gilgal, for this seems to be intimated in the manner of expression: *He has gone about, and passed on, and gone down,* with a great deal of pomp and parade. There Samuel gave him the meeting, and,

1. Saul makes his boast to Samuel of his obedience, because that was the thing by which he was now to signalize himself (*v.* 13): "*Blessed be thou of the Lord,* for thou sentest me upon a good errand, in which I have had great success, and *I have performed the commandment of the Lord.*" It is very likely, if his conscience had not flown in his face at this time and charged him with disobedience, he would not have been so forward to proclaim his obedience; for by this he hoped to prevent Samuel's reproving him. Thus sinners think, by justifying themselves, to escape being *judged of the Lord;* whereas the only way to do that is by *judging ourselves.* Those that boast most of their religion may justly be suspected of partiality and hypocrisy in it.

2. Samuel convicts him by a plain demonstration of his disobedience. "Hast thou performed the commandment of the Lord? *What means then the bleating of the sheep?* *v.* 14. Saul would needs have it thought that God Almighty was wonderfully beholden to him for the good service he had done; but Samuel shows him that God was so far from being a debtor to him that he had just cause of action against him, and produces for evidence the *bleating of the sheep, and the lowing of the oxen,* which perhaps Saul appointed to bring up the rear of his triumph, but Samuel appeals to them as witnesses against him. He needed not go far to disprove his professions. The noise the cattle made (like the *rust of the silver,* Jam. v. 3) would be a *witness against him.* Note, It is no new thing for the plausible profes-

sions and protestations of hypocrites to be contradicted and disproved by the most plain and undeniable evidence. Many boast of their obedience to the command of God; but what mean then their indulgence of the flesh, their love of the world, their passion and uncharitableness, and their neglect of holy duties, which witness against them?

3. Saul insists upon his own justification against this charge, *v.* 15. The fact he cannot deny; the sheep and oxen were brought from the Amalekites. But, (1.) It was not his fault, for *the people spared them;* as if they durst have done it without the express orders of Saul, when they knew it was against the express orders of Samuel. Note, Those that are willing to justify themselves are commonly very forward to condemn others, and to lay the blame upon any rather than take it to themselves. Sin is a brat that nobody cares to have laid at his doors. It is the sorry subterfuge of an impenitent heart, that will not confess its guilt, to lay the blame on those that were tempters, or partners, or only followers in it. (2.) It was with a good intention: "It was *to sacrifice to the Lord thy God.* He is thy God, and thou wilt not be against any thing that is done, as this is, for his honour." This was a false plea, for both Saul and the people designed their own profit in sparing the cattle. But, if it had been true, it would still have been frivolous, for God hates robbery for burnt-offering. God appointed these cattle to be sacrificed to him in the field, and therefore will give those no thanks that bring them to be sacrificed at his altar; for he will be served in his own way, and according to the rule he himself has prescribed. Nor will a good intention justify a bad action.

4. Samuel overrules, or rather overlooks, his plea, and proceeds, in God's name, to give judgment against him. He premises his authority. What he was about to say was what the Lord had said to him (*v.* 16), otherwise he would have been far from passing so severe a censure upon him. Those who complain that their ministers are too harsh with them should remember that, while they keep to the word of God, they are but messengers, and must say as they are bidden, and therefore be willing, as Saul himself here was, that they should *say on.* Samuel delivers his message faithfully. (1.) He reminds Saul of the honour God had done him in making him king (*v.* 17), *when he was little in his own sight.* God regarded the lowness of his state and rewarded the lowliness of his spirit. Note, Those that are advanced to honour and wealth ought often to remember their mean beginnings, that they may never think highly of themselves, but always study to do great things for the God that has advanced them. (2.) He lays before him the plainness of the orders he was to execute (*v.* 18): *The Lord sent thee on a journey;* so easy was the service, and so certain the success, that it was rather to be called a *journey* than a *war.* The work was honourable, to destroy the sworn enemies of God and Israel; and had he denied himself, and set aside the consideration of his own profit so far as to have destroyed all that belonged to Amalek, he would have been no loser by it at last, nor have gone this *warfare on his own charges.* God would no doubt have made it up to him, so that he should have no need of spoil. And therefore, (3.) He shows him how inexcusable he was in aiming to make a profit of this expedition, and to enrich himself by it (*v.* 19): "*Wherefore then didst thou fly upon the spoil,* and convert that to thy own use which was to have been destroyed for God's honour?" See what evil the love of money is the root of; but see what is the sinfulness of sin, and that in it which above any thing else makes it evil in the sight of the Lord. It is disobedience: *Thou didst not obey the voice of the Lord.*

5. Saul repeats his vindication of himself, as that which, in defiance of conviction, he resolved to abide by, *v.* 20, 21. He denies the charge (*v.* 20): "*Yea, I have obeyed,* I have done all I should do;" for he had done all which he thought he needed to do, so much wiser was he in his own eyes than God himself. God bade him kill all, and yet he puts in among the instances of his obedience that he had brought Agag alive, which he thought was as good as if he had killed him. Thus carnal deceitful hearts think to excuse themselves from God's commandments with their own equivalents. He insists upon it that he has *utterly destroyed the Amalekites* themselves, which was the main thing intended; but, as to the spoil, he owns it should have been *utterly destroyed;* so that he knew his *Lord's will,* and was under no mistake about the command. But he thought that would be wilful waste; the cattle of the Midianites was taken for a prey in Moses's time (Num. xxxi. 32, &c.), and why not the cattle of the Amalekites now? Better it should be a prey to the Israelites than to the fowls of the air and the wild beasts; and therefore he connived at the people's carrying it away. But it was their doing and not his; and, besides, it was for *sacrifice to the Lord* here at Gilgal, whither they were now bringing them. See what a hard thing it is to convince the children of disobedience of their sin and to strip them of their fig-leaves.

6. Samuel gives a full answer to his apology, since he did insist upon it, *v.* 22, 23. He appeals to his own conscience: *Has the Lord as great delight in sacrifices as in obedience?* Though Saul was not a man of any great acquaintance with religion, yet he could not but know this, (1.) That nothing is so pleasing to God as obedience, no, not sacrifice and offering, and the fat of rams. See here what we should seek and aim at in all the exercises of religion, even acceptance

with God, that he may delight in what we do. If God be well pleased with us and our services, we are happy, we have gained our point; but otherwise *to what purpose is it?* Isa. i. 11. Now here we are plainly told that humble, sincere, and conscientious obedience to the will of God, is more pleasing and acceptable to him than *all burnt-offerings and sacrifices*. A careful conformity to moral precepts recommends us to God more than all ceremonial observances, Mic. vi. 6—8; Hos. vi. 6. Obedience is enjoined by the eternal law of nature, but sacrifice only by a positive law. Obedience was the law of innocency, but sacrifice supposes sin come into the world, and is but a feeble attempt to take that away which obedience would have prevented. God is more glorified and self more denied by obedience than by sacrifice. It is much easier to bring a bullock or lamb to be burnt upon the altar than to bring *every high thought into obedience* to God and the will subject to his will. Obedience is the glory of angels (Ps. ciii. 20), and it will be ours. (2.) That nothing is so provoking to God as disobedience, setting up our wills in competition with his. This is here called *rebellion* and *stubbornness*, and is said to be as bad as *witchcraft* and *idolatry*, *v.* 23. It is as bad to set up other gods as to live in disobedience to the true God. Those that are governed by their own corrupt inclinations, in opposition to the command of God, do, in effect, consult the *teraphim* (as the word here is for idolatry) or the diviners. It was disobedience that made us all sinners (Rom. v. 19), and this is the malignity of sin, that it is the *transgression of the law*, and consequently it is *enmity to God*, Rom. viii. 7. Saul was a king, but, if he disobey the command of God, his royal dignity and power will not excuse him from the guilt of rebellion and stubbornness. It is not the rebellion of the people against their prince, but of a prince against God, that this text speaks of.

7. He reads his doom: in short, "*Because thou hast rejected the word of the Lord*, hast *despised it* (so the Chaldee), hast *made nothing of it* (so the LXX.), hast cast off the government of it, therefore he has *rejected thee*, despised and made nothing of thee, but cast thee off *from being king*. He that made thee king has determined to unmake thee again." Those are unfit and unworthy to rule over men who are not willing that God should rule over them.

24 And Saul said unto Samuel, I have sinned: for I have transgressed the commandment of the LORD, and thy words: because I feared the people, and obeyed their voice. 25 Now therefore, I pray thee, pardon my sin, and turn again with me, that I may worship the LORD. 26 And Samuel said unto Saul, I will not return with thee: for thou hast rejected the word of the LORD, and the LORD hath rejected thee from being king over Israel. 27 And as Samuel turned about to go away, he laid hold upon the skirt of his mantle, and it rent. 28 And Samuel said unto him, The LORD hath rent the kingdom of Israel from thee this day, and hath given it to a neighbour of thine, *that is* better than thou. 29 And also the Strength of Israel will not lie nor repent: for he *is* not a man, that he should repent. 30 Then he said, I have sinned: *yet* honour me now, I pray thee, before the elders of my people, and before Israel, and turn again with me, that I may worship the LORD thy God. 31 So Samuel turned again after Saul; and Saul worshipped the LORD.

Saul is at length brought to put himself into the dress of a penitent; but it is too evident that he only acts the part of a penitent, and is not one indeed. Observe,

I. How poorly he expressed his repentance. It was with much ado that he was made sensible of his fault, and not till he was threatened with being deposed. This touched him in a tender part. Then he began to relent, and not till then. When Samuel told him he was *rejected from being king*, then he said, *I have sinned*, *v.* 24. His confession was not free nor ingenuous, but extorted by the rack, and forced from him. We observe here several bad signs of the hypocrisy of his repentance, and that it came short even of Ahab's. 1. He made his application to Samuel only, and seemed most solicitous to stand right in his opinion and to gain his favour. He makes a little god of him, only to preserve his reputation with the people, because they all knew Samuel to be a prophet, and the man that had been the instrument of his preferment. Thinking it would please Samuel, and be a sort of bribe to him, he puts it into his confession: *I have transgressed the commandment of the Lord and thy word;* as if he had been in God's stead, *v.* 24. David, though convinced by the ministry of Nathan, yet, in his confession, has his eye to God alone, not to Nathan. Ps. li. 4 *Against thee, thee only have I sinned.* But Saul, ignorantly enough, confesses his sin as a transgression of Samuel's word; whereas his word was no other than a declaration of the *commandment of the Lord.* He also applies to Samuel for forgiveness (*v.* 25): *I pray thee, pardon my sin;* as if any could forgive sin but God only. Those wretchedly deceive themselves who, when they have fallen into scandalous sin, think it enough to make their peace with the church and their ministers, by the show and plausible profession of repentance, without taking care to make their peace with God by the sincerity of it. The most charitable construction we can put upon this of Saul is to suppose that he looked upon Samuel as a sort of mediator between him and God, and intended an address to God in his application to him. However it was very weak. 2. He excused his fault even in the confession of it, and that is never the fashion of a true penitent (*v.* 24): I did it *because I feared the people, and obeyed their voice.* We have reason enough to think that it was purely his own doing and not the people's; however, if they were forward to do it, it is plain, by what we have read before, that he knew how to keep up his authority among them and did not stand in any awe of them. So that the excuse was false and frivolous; whatever he pretended, he did not really fear the people. But it is common for sinners, in excusing their faults, to plead the thoughts and workings of their own minds, because those are things which, how groundless soever, no man can disprove; but they forget that God searcheth the heart. 3. All his care was to save his credit, and preserve his interest in the people, lest they should revolt from him, or at least despise him. Therefore he courts Samuel with so much earnestness (*v.* 25) to turn again with him, and assist in a public thanksgiving for the victory. Very importunate he was in this matter when he laid hold on the skirt of his mantle to detain him (*v.* 27), not that he cared for Samuel, but he feared that if Samuel forsook him the people would do so too. Many seem zealously affected to good ministers and good people only for the sake of their own interest and reputation, while in heart they hate them. But his expression was very gross when he said (*v.* 30), *I have sinned, yet honour me, I pray thee, before my people.* Is this the language of a penitent? No, but the contrary: "*I have sinned,* shame me now, for to me belongs shame, and no man can loathe me so much as I loathe myself." Yet how often do we meet with the copies of this hypocrisy of Saul! It is very common for those who are convicted of sin to show themselves very solicitous to be honoured before the people. Whereas he that has lost the honour of an innocent can pretend to no other than that of a penitent, and it is the honour of a penitent to take shame to himself.

II. How little he got by these thin shows of repentance. What point did he gain by them? 1. Samuel repeated the sentence passed upon him, so far was he from giving any hopes of the repeal of it, *v.* 26, the same with *v.* 23. *He that covers his sins shall never prosper,* Prov. xxviii. 13. Samuel refused to turn back with him, but *turned about to go away, v.* 27. As the thing appeared to him upon the first view, he thought it altogether unfit for him so far to countenance one whom God had rejected as to join with him in giving thanks to God for a victory which was made to serve rather Saul's covetousness than God's glory. Yet afterwards he did turn again with him (*v.* 31), upon further thoughts, and probably by divine direction, either to prevent a mutiny among the people or perhaps not to do honour to Saul (for, though Saul worshipped the Lord, *v.* 31, it is not said Samuel presided in that worship), but to do justice on Agag, *v.* 32. 2. He illustrated the sentence by a sign, which Saul himself, by his rudeness, gave occasion for. When Samuel was turning from him he tore his clothes to detain him (*v.* 27), so loth was he to part with the prophet; but Samuel put a construction upon this accident which none but a prophet could do. He made it to signify the *rending of the kingdom* from him (*v.* 28), and that, like this, was his own doing. "He hath rent it from thee, and *given it to a neighbour better than thou,*" namely, to David, who afterwards, upon occasion, cut off the skirt of Saul's robe (1 Sam. xxiv. 4), upon which Saul said (1 Sam. xxiv. 20), *I know that thou shalt surely be king,* perhaps remembering this sign, the tearing of the skirt of Samuel's mantle. 3. He ratified it by a solemn declaration of its being irreversible (*v.* 29): *The Strength of Israel will not lie.* The *Eternity* or *Victory of Israel,* so some read it; *the holy One,* so the Arabic; *the most noble One,* so the Syriac; the *triumphant King of Israel,* so bishop Patrick. "He is determined to depose thee, and he will not change his purpose. *He is not a man that he should repent.*" Men are fickle and alter their minds, feeble and cannot effect their purposes; something happens which they could not foresee, by which their measures are broken. But with God it is not so. God has sometimes repented of the evil which he thought to have done, upon the sinner's repenting; but here repentance was hidden from Saul, and therefore hidden from God's eyes.

32 Then said Samuel, Bring ye hither to me Agag the king of the Amalekites. And Agag came unto him delicately. And Agag said, Surely the bitterness of death is past. 33 And Samuel said, As thy sword hath made women childless, so shall thy mother be childless among women. And Samuel hewed Agag in pieces before the LORD in Gilgal. 34 Then Samuel went to Ramah; and Saul went up to his house to Gibeah of Saul. 35 And Samuel came no more to see Saul until the day of his

death: nevertheless Samuel mourned for Saul: and the LORD repented that he had made Saul king over Israel.

Samuel, as a prophet, is here set over kings, Jer. i. 10.

I. He destroys king Agag, doubtless by such special direction from heaven as none now can pretend to. He *hewed Agag in pieces.* Some think he only ordered it to be done; or perhaps he did it with his own hands, as a sacrifice to God's injured justice (*v.* 33), and sacrifices used to be cut in pieces. Now observe in this,

1. How Agag's present vain hopes were frustrated: He *came delicately,* in a stately manner, to show that he was a king, and therefore to be treated with respect, or in a soft effeminate manner, as one never used to hardship, that *could not set the sole of his foot to the ground for tenderness and delicacy* (Deut. xxviii. 56), to move compassion: and he said, "Surely, now that the heat of the battle is over, *the bitterness of death is past, v.* 32. Having escaped the sword of Saul," that man of war, he thought he was in no danger from Samuel, an old prophet, a man of peace. Note, (1.) There is bitterness in death, it is terrible to nature. *Surely death is bitter,* so divers versions read those words of Agag; as the LXX. read the former clause, *He came trembling.* Death will dismay the stoutest heart. (2.) Many think the bitterness of death is past when it is not so; they put that evil day far from them which is very near. True believers may, through grace, say this, upon good grounds, though death be not past, the bitterness of it is. *O death! where is thy sting?*

2. How his former wicked practices were now punished. Samuel calls him to account, not only for the sins of his ancestors, but his own sins: *Thy sword has made women childless, v.* 33. He trod in the steps of his ancestors' cruelty, and those under him, it is likely, did the same; justly therefore is all the righteous blood shed by Amalek required of this generation, Matt. xxiii. 36. Agag, that was delicate and luxurious himself, was cruel and barbarous to others. It is commonly so: those who are indulgent of their appetites are not less indulgent of their passions. But blood will be reckoned for; even kings must account to the King of kings for the guiltless blood they shed or cause to be shed. It was that crime of king Manasseh which the Lord would not pardon, 2 Kings xxiv. 4. See Rev. xiii. 10.

II. He deserts king Saul, takes leave of him (*v.* 34), and *never came any more to see him* (*v.* 35), to advise or assist him in any of his affairs, because Saul did not desire his company nor would he be advised by him. He looked upon him as rejected of God, and therefore he forsook him. Though he might sometimes see him accidentally (as *ch* xix. 24), yet he never came to see him out of kindness or respect. Yet he *mourned for Saul,* thinking it a very lamentable thing that a man who stood so fair for great things should ruin himself so foolishly. He mourned for the bad state of the country, to which Saul was likely to have been so great a blessing, but now would prove a curse and a plague. He mourned for his everlasting state, having no hopes of bringing him to repentance. When he wept for him, it is likely, he made supplication, but the Lord had *repented that he had made Saul king,* and resolved to undo that work of his, so that Samuel's prayers prevailed not for him. Observe, We must mourn for the rejection of sinners, 1. Though we withdraw from them, and dare not converse familiarly with them. Thus the prophet determines to leave his people and go from them, and yet to *weep day and night for them,* Jer. ix. 1, 2. 2. Though they do not mourn for themselves. Saul seems unconcerned at the tokens of God's displeasure which he lay under, and yet Samuel mourns day and night for him. Jerusalem was secure when Christ wept over it.

CHAP. XVI.

At this chapter begins the story of David, one that makes as great a figure in the sacred story as almost any of the worthies of the Old Testament, one that both with his sword and with his pen served the honour of God and the interests of Israel as much as most ever did, and was as illustrious a type of Christ. Here, I. Samuel is appointed and commissioned to anoint a king among the sons of Jesse at Bethlehem, ver. 1—5. II. All his elder sons are passed by and David the youngest is pitched upon and anointed, ver. 6—13. III. Saul growing melancholy, David is pitched upon to relieve him by music, ver. 14—23. Thus small are the beginnings of that great man.

AND the LORD said unto Samuel, How long wilt thou mourn for Saul, seeing I have rejected him from reigning over Israel? fill thine horn with oil, and go, I will send thee to Jesse the Beth-lehemite: for I have provided me a king among his sons. 2 And Samuel said, How can I go? if Saul hear *it,* he will kill me. And the LORD said, Take a heifer with thee, and say, I am come to sacrifice to the LORD. 3 And call Jesse to the sacrifice, and I will show thee what thou shalt do: and thou shalt anoint unto me *him* whom I name unto thee. 4 And Samuel did that which the LORD spake, and came to Beth-lehem. And the elders of the town trembled at his coming, and said, Comest thou peaceably? 5 And he said, Peaceably: I am come to sacrifice unto the LORD: sanctify yourselves, and come with me to the sacrifice. And he sanctified Jesse and his sons, and called them to the sacrifice.

Samuel had retired to his own house in Ramah, with a resolution not to appear any more in public business, but to addict himself wholly to the instructing and training up of the sons of the prophets, over whom he presided, as we find, *ch.* xix. 20. He promised himself more satisfaction in young prophets than in young princes; and we do not find that, to his dying day, God called him out to any public action relating to the state, but only here to anoint David.

I. God reproves him for continuing so long to mourn for the rejection of Saul. He does not blame him for mourning on that occasion, but for exceeding in his sorrow: *How long wilt thou mourn for Saul? v.* 1. We do not find that he mourned at all for the setting aside of his own family and the deposing of his own sons; but for the rejecting of Saul and his seed he mourns without measure, for the former was done by the people's foolish discontent, this by the righteous wrath of God. Yet he must find time to recover himself, and not go mourning to his grave, 1. Because God has rejected him, and he ought to acquiesce in the divine justice, and forget his affection to Saul; if God will be glorified in his ruin, Samuel ought to be satisfied. Besides, to what purpose should he weep? The decree has gone forth, and all his prayers and tears cannot prevail for the reversing of it, 2 Sam. xii. 22, 23. 2. Because Israel shall be no loser by it, and Samuel must prefer the public welfare before his own private affection to his friend. "Mourn not for Saul, for I *have provided me a king.* The people provided themselves a king and he proved bad, now I will provide myself one, *a man after my own heart.*" See Ps. lxxxix. 20; Acts xiii. 22. "If Saul be rejected, yet Israel shall not be *as sheep having no shepherd.* I have another in store for them; let thy joy of him swallow up thy grief for the rejected prince."

II. He sends him to Bethlehem, to anoint one of the sons of Jesse, a person probably not unknown to Samuel. *Fill thy horn with oil.* Saul was anointed with a glass vial of oil, scanty and brittle, David with a horn of oil, which was more plentiful and durable; hence we read of a *horn of salvation in the house of his servant David,* Luke i. 69.

III. Samuel objects the peril of going on this errand (*v.* 2): *If Saul hear it, he will kill me.* By this it appears, 1. That Saul had grown very wicked and outrageous since his rejection, else Samuel would not have mentioned this. What impiety would he not be guilty of who durst kill Samuel? 2. That Samuel's faith was not so strong as one would have expected, else he would not have thus feared the rage of Saul. Would not he that sent him protect him and bear him out? But the best men are not perfect in their faith, nor will fear be wholly cast out any where on this side heaven. But this may be understood as Samuel's desire of direction from heaven how to manage this matter prudently, so as not to expose himself, or any other, more than needed.

IV. God orders him to cover his design with a sacrifice: *Say, I have come to sacrifice;* and it was true he did, and it was proper that he should, when he came to anoint a king, *ch.* xi. 15. As a prophet, he might sacrifice when and where God appointed him; and it was not at all inconsistent with the laws of truth to say he came to sacrifice when really he did so, though he had also a further end, which he thought fit to conceal. Let him give notice of a sacrifice, and invite Jesse (who, it is probable, was the principal man of the city) and his family to come to the feast upon the sacrifice; and, says God, *I will show thee what thou shalt do.* Those that go about God's work in God's way shall be directed step by step, wherever they are at a loss, to do it in the best manner.

V. Samuel went accordingly to Bethlehem, not in pomp, or with any retinue, only a servant to lead the heifer which he was to sacrifice; yet *the elders of Bethlehem trembled at his coming,* fearing it was an indication of God's displeasure against them and that he came to denounce some judgment for the iniquities of the place. Guilt causes fear. Yet indeed it becomes us to stand in awe of God's messengers, and to tremble at his word. Or they feared it might be an occasion of Saul's displeasure against them, for probably they knew how much he was exasperated at Samuel, and feared he would pick a quarrel with them for entertaining him. They asked him, "*Comest thou peaceably?* Art thou in peace thyself, and not flying from Saul? Art thou at peace with us, and not come with any message of wrath?" We should all covet earnestly to stand upon good terms with God's prophets, and dread having the word of God, or their prayers, against us. When the Son of David was born king of the Jews all Jerusalem was troubled, Matt. ii. 3. Samuel kept at home, and it was a strange thing to see him so far from his own house: they therefore concluded it must needs be some extraordinary occasion that brought him, and feared the worst till he satisfied them (*v.* 5): "*I come peaceably,* for *I come to sacrifice,* not with a message of wrath against you, but with the methods of peace and reconciliation; and therefore you may bid me welcome and need not fear my coming; therefore *sanctify yourselves,* and prepare to join with me in the sacrifice, that you may have the benefit of it." Note, Before solemn ordinances there must be a solemn preparation. When we are to offer spiritual sacrifices it concerns us, by sequestering ourselves from the world and renewing the dedication of ourselves to God, to sanctify ourselves. When our Lord Jesus came into the world, though men had reason enough to tremble, fearing that his errand was to condemn the world, yet he gave full assurance that he came peaceably, for he came to sacrifice, and he brought his offering along with him: *A body hast thou prepared me.* Let us sanctify ourselves, that we may have an interest in his sacrifice. Note, Those that come to sacrifice should come peaceably; religious exercises must not be performed tumultuously.

VI. He had a particular regard to Jesse and his sons, for with them his private business lay, with which, it is likely, he acquainted Jesse at his first coming, and took up his lodging at his house. He spoke to all the elders to *sanctify themselves*, but he *sanctified Jesse and his sons* by praying with them and instructing them. Perhaps he had acquaintance with them before, and it appears (*ch.* xx. 29, where we read of the sacrifices that family had) that it was a devout religious family. Samuel assisted them in their family preparations for the public sacrifice, and, it is probable, chose out David, and anointed him, at the family-solemnities, before the sacrifice was offered or the holy feast solemnized. Perhaps he offered private sacrifices, like Job, *according to the number of them all* (Job i. 5), and, under colour of that, called for them all to appear before him. When signal blessings are coming into a family they ought to sanctify themselves.

6 And it came to pass, when they were come, that he looked on Eliab, and said, Surely the LORD's anointed *is* before him. 7 But the LORD said unto Samuel, Look not on his countenance, or on the height of his stature; because I have refused him: for *the LORD seeth* not as man seeth; for man looketh on the outward appearance, but the LORD looketh on the heart. 8 Then Jesse called Abinadab, and made him pass before Samuel. And he said, Neither hath the LORD chosen this. 9 Then Jesse made Shammah to pass by. And he said, Neither hath the LORD chosen this. 10 Again, Jesse made seven of his sons to pass before Samuel. And Samuel said unto Jesse, The LORD hath not chosen these. 11 And Samuel said unto Jesse, Are here all *thy* children? And he said, There remaineth yet the youngest, and, behold, he keepeth the sheep. And Samuel said unto Jesse, Send and fetch him: for we will not sit down till he come hither. 12 And he sent, and brought him in. Now he *was* ruddy, *and* withal of a beautiful countenance, and goodly to look to. And the LORD said, Arise, anoint him: for this *is* he. 13 Then Samuel took the horn of oil, and anointed him in the midst of his brethren: and the Spirit of the LORD came upon David from that day forward. So Samuel rose up, and went to Ramah.

If the sons of Jesse were told that God would provide himself a king among them (as he had said, *v.* 1), we may well suppose they all made the best appearance they could, and each hoped he should be the man; but here we are told,

I. How all the elder sons, who stood fairest for the preferment, were passed by.

1. Eliab, the eldest, was privately presented first to Samuel, probably none being present but Jesse only, and Samuel thought he must needs be the man: *Surely this is the Lord's anointed*, *v.* 6. The prophets themselves, when they spoke from under the divine direction, were as liable to mistake as other men; as Nathan, 2 Sam. vii. 3. But God rectified the prophet's mistake by a secret whisper to his mind: *Look not on his countenance*, *v.* 7. It was strange that Samuel, who had been so wretchedly disappointed in Saul, whose countenance and stature recommended him as much as any man's could, should be so forward to judge of a man by that rule. When God would please the people with a king he chose a comely man; but, when he would have one after his own heart, he should not be chosen by the outside. Men judge by the sight of the eyes, but God does not, Isa. xi. 3. *The Lord looks on the heart*, that is, (1.) He knows it. We can tell how men look, but he can tell what they are. Man looks on the eyes (so the original word is), and is pleased with the liveliness and sprightliness that appear in them; but God looks on the heart, and sees the thoughts and intents of that. (2.) He judges of men by it. The good disposition of the heart, the holiness or goodness of that, recommends us to God, and is *in his sight of great price* (1 Pet. iii. 4), not the majesty of the look, or the strength and stature of the body. Let us reckon that to be true beauty which is within, and judge of men, as far as we are capable, by their minds, not their mien.

2. When Eliab was set aside, Abinadad and Shammah, and, after them, four more of the sons of Jesse, seven in all, were presented to Samuel, as likely for his purpose; but Samuel, who now attended more carefully than he did at first to the divine direction, rejected them all: *The Lord has not chosen these*, *v.* 8, 10. Men dispose of their honours and estates to their sons according to their seniority of age and priority of birth, but God does not. *The elder shall serve the younger.* Had it been left to Samuel, or Jesse, to make the choice, one of these would certainly have been chosen; but God will magnify his sovereignty in passing by some that were most

promising as well as in fastening on others that were less so.

II. How David at length was pitched upon. He was the youngest of all the sons of Jesse; his name signifies *beloved*, for he was a type of the beloved Son. Observe, 1. How he was in the fields, *keeping the sheep* (*v.* 11), and was left there, though there was a sacrifice and a feast at his father's house. The youngest are commonly the fondlings of the family, but, it should seem, David was least set by of all the sons of Jesse; either they did not discern or did not duly value the excellent spirit he was of. Many a great genius lies buried in obscurity and contempt; and God often exalts those whom men despise and gives *abundant honour to that part which lacked.* The Son of David was he whom men despised, *the stone which the builders refused*, and yet he has *a name above every name.* David was taken *from following the ewes to feed Jacob* (Ps. lxxviii. 71), as Moses from keeping the flock of Jethro, an instance of his humility and industry, both which God delights to put honour upon. We should think a military life, but God saw a pastoral life (which gives advantage for contemplation and communion with heaven), the best preparative for kingly power, at least for those graces of the Spirit which are necessary to the due discharge of that trust which attends it. David was keeping sheep, though it was a time of sacrifice; for there is mercy that takes precedence of sacrifice. 2. How earnest Samuel was to have him sent for: "*We will not sit down* to meat" (perhaps it was not the feast upon the sacrifice, but a common meal) "*till he come hither;* for, if all the rest be rejected, this must be he." He that was designed not to sit at table at all is now waited for as the principal guest. If God will exalt those of low degree, who can hinder? 3. What appearance he made when he did come. No notice is taken of his clothing. No doubt that was according to his employment, mean and coarse, as shepherds' coats commonly are, and he did not change his clothes as Joseph did (Gen. xli. 14); but he had a very honest look, not stately, as Saul's, but sweet and lovely: *He was ruddy, of a beautiful countenance, and goodly to look to* (*v.* 12), that is, he had a clear complexion, a good eye, and a lovely face; the features were extraordinary, and there was something in his looks that was very charming. Though he was so far from using any art to help his beauty that his employment exposed it to the sun and wind, yet nature kept its own, and, by the sweetness of his aspect, gave manifest indications of an amiable temper and disposition of mind. Perhaps his modest blush, when he was brought before Samuel, and received by him with surprising respect, made him look much the handsomer. 4. The anointing of him. The Lord told Samuel in his ear (as he had done, *ch.* ix. 15) that this was he whom he must anoint, *v* 12. Samuel objects not to the meanness of his education, his youth, or the little respect he had in his own family, but, in obedience to the divine command, took his horn of oil and *anointed him* (*v.* 13), signifying thereby, (1.) A divine designation to the government, after the death of Saul, of which hereby he gave him a full assurance. Not that he was at present invested with the royal power, but it was entailed upon him, to come to him in due time. (2.) A divine communication of gifts and graces, to fit him for the government, and make him a type of him who was to be the Messiah, the anointed One, who received the Spirit, not by measure, but without measure. He is said to be anointed *in the midst of his brethren,* who yet, possibly, did not understand it as a designation to the government, and therefore did not envy David (as Joseph's brethren did him), because they saw no further marks of dignity put upon him, no, not so much as a coat of divers colours. But bishop Patrick reads it, *He anointed him from the midst of his brethren,* that is, he singled him out from the rest, and privately anointed him, but with a charge to keep his own counsel, and not to let his own brethren know it, as by what we find (*ch.* xvii. 28), it should seem, Eliab did not. It is computed that David was now about twenty years old; if so, his troubles by Saul lasted ten years, for he was thirty years old when Saul died. Dr. Lightfoot reckons that he was about twenty-five, and that his troubles lasted but five years. 5. The happy effects of this anointing: The *Spirit of the Lord came upon David from that day forward, v.* 13. The anointing of him was not an empty ceremony, but a divine power went along with that instituted sign, and he found himself inwardly advanced in wisdom, and courage, and concern for the public, with all the qualifications of a prince, though not at all advanced in his outward circumstances. This would abundantly satisfy him that his election was of God. The best evidence of our being predestinated to the kingdom of glory is our being sealed with the Spirit of promise, and our experience of a work of grace in our own hearts. Some think that his courage, by which he slew the lion and the bear, and his extraordinary skill in music, were the effects and evidences of the Spirit's coming upon him. However, this made him the sweet psalmist of Israel, 2 Sam. xxiii. 1. Samuel, having done this, went to Ramah in safety, and we never read of him again but once (*ch.* xix. 18), till we read of his death; now he retired to die in peace, since his eyes had seen the salvation, even the sceptre brought into the tribe of Judah.

14 But the Spirit of the LORD departed from Saul, and an evil spirit from the LORD troubled him. 15 And Saul's servants said unto him,

Behold now, an evil spirit from God troubleth thee. 16 Let our lord now command thy servants, *which are* before thee, to seek out a man, *who is* a cunning player on a harp: and it shall come to pass, when the evil spirit from God is upon thee, that he shall play with his hand, and thou shalt be well. 17 And Saul said unto his servants, Provide me now a man that can play well, and bring *him* to me. 18 Then answered one of the servants, and said, Behold, I have seen a son of Jesse the Beth-lehemite, *that is* cunning in playing, and a mighty valiant man, and a man of war, and prudent in matters, and a comely person, and the LORD *is* with him. 19 Wherefore Saul sent messengers unto Jesse, and said, Send me David thy son, which *is* with the sheep. 20 And Jesse took an ass *laden* with bread, and a bottle of wine, and a kid, and sent *them* by David his son unto Saul. 21 And David came to Saul, and stood before him: and he loved him greatly; and he became his armourbearer. 22 And Saul sent to Jesse, saying, Let David, I pray thee, stand before me; for he hath found favour in my sight. 23 And it came to pass, when the *evil* spirit from God was upon Saul, that David took a harp, and played with his hand: so Saul was refreshed, and was well, and the evil spirit departed from him.

We have here Saul falling and David rising.

I. Here is Saul made a terror to himself (*v.* 14): *The Spirit of the Lord departed from him.* He having forsaken God and his duty, God, in a way of righteous judgment, withdrew from him those assistances of the good Spirit with which he was directed, animated, and encouraged in his government and wars. He lost all his good qualities. This was the effect of his rejecting God, and an evidence of his being rejected by him. Now God took his mercy from Saul (as it is expressed, 2 Sam. vii. 15); for, when the Spirit of the Lord departs from us, all good goes. When men grieve and quench the Spirit, by wilful sin, he departs, and will not always strive. The consequence of this was that *an evil spirit from God troubled him.* Those that drive the good Spirit away from them do of course become a prey to the evil spirit. If God and his grace do not rule us, sin and Satan will have possession of us. The devil, by the divine permission, troubled and terrified Saul, by means of the corrupt humours of his body and passions of his mind. He grew fretful, and peevish, and discontented, timorous and suspicious, ever and anon starting and trembling; he was sometimes, says Josephus, as if he had been choked or strangled, and a perfect demoniac by fits. This made him unfit for business, precipitate in his counsels, the contempt of his enemies, and a burden to all about him.

II. Here is David made a physician to Saul, and by this means brought to court, a physician that helped him against the worst of diseases, when none else could. David was newly anointed privately to the kingdom. It would be of use to him to go to court and see the world; and here his doing so is brought about for him without any contrivance of his own or his friends. Note, Those whom God designs for any service his providence shall concur with his grace to prepare and qualify for it. Saul is distempered; his servants have the honesty and courage to tell him what his distemper is (*v.* 15), *an evil spirit,* not by chance but *from God* and his providence, *troubleth thee.* Now, 1. The means they all advised him to for his relief was music (*v.* 16): "Let us have a *cunning player on the harp* to attend thee." How much better friends had they been to him if they had advised him, since the evil spirit was from the Lord, to give all diligence to make his peace with God by true repentance, to send for Samuel to pray with him and to intercede with God for him! then might he not only have had some present relief, but the good Spirit would have returned to him. But their project is to make him merry, and so cure him. Many whose consciences are convinced and startled are for ever ruined by such methods as these, which drown all care of the soul in the delights of sense. Yet Saul's servants did not amiss to send for music as a help to cheer up the spirits, if they had but withal sent for a prophet to give him good counsel. And (as bishop Hall observes) it was well they did not send for a witch or diviner, by his enchantments to cast out the evil spirit, which has been the abominably wicked practice of some that have worn the Christian name, who consult the devil in their distresses and make hell their refuge. It will be no less than a miracle of divine grace if those who thus agree with Satan ever break off from him again. 2. One of his servants recommended David to him, as a fit person to be employed in the use of these means, little imagining that he was the man whom Samuel meant when he told Saul of a neighbour of his, better than he, who should have the kingdom, *ch.* xv. 28. It is a very high character which this servant of Saul's here gives of David (*v.* 18), that he was not only fit for his purpose as a comely person and skilful in playing, but a man of courage and conduct, a mighty valiant man, and prudent in all matters, fit to be further preferred, and (which crowned his character) *the Lord is with him.* By this it appears that though David, after he was anointed, returned to his country business, and there remained on his head no marks of the oil, so careful was he to keep that secret, yet the workings of the Spirit signified by the oil could not be hid, but made him shine in obscurity, so that all his neighbours observed with wonder the great improvements of his mind on a sudden. David, even in his shepherd's garb, has become an oracle, a champion, and every thing that is great. His fame reached the court soon, for Saul was inquisitive after such young men, *ch.* xiv. 52. When the Spirit of God comes upon a man he will make his face to shine. 3. David is hereupon sent for to court. And it seems, (1.) His father was very willing to part with him, sent him very readily, and a present with him to Saul, *v.* 20. The present was, according to the usage of those times, bread and wine (compare, *ch.* x. 3, 4), therefore acceptable because expressive of the homage and allegiance of him that sent it. Probably Jesse, who knew what his son David was designed for, was aware that Providence was herein fitting him for it. and therefore he would not force Providence by sending him to court uncalled, yet he followed Providence very cheerfully when he saw it plainly putting him into the way of preferment. Some suggest that when Jesse received that message, *Send me David thy son,* he began to be afraid that Saul had got some intimation of his being anointed, and sent for him to do him a mischief, and therefore Jesse sent a present to pacify him; but it is probable that the person, whoever he was, that brought the message, gave him an account on what design he was sent for. (2.) Saul became very kind to him (*v.* 21), *loved him greatly,* and designed to *make him his armour-bearer,* and (contrary to the manner of the king, *ch.* viii. 11) asked his father's leave to keep him in his service (*v.* 22): *Let David, I pray thee, stand before me.* And good reason he had to respect him, for he did him a great deal of service with his music, *v.* 23. Only his instrumental music with his harp is mentioned, but it should seem, by the account Josephus gives, that he added vocal music to it, and sung hymns, probably divine hymns, songs of praise, to his harp. David's music was Saul's physic. [1.] Music has a natural tendency to compose and exhilarate the mind, when it is disturbed and saddened. Elisha used it for the calming of his spirits, 2 Kings iii. 15. On some it has a greater influence and effect than on others, and, probably, Saul was one of those. Not that it charmed the evil spirit, but it made his spirit sedate, and allayed those tumults of the animal spirits by which the devil had advantage against him. The beams of the sun (it is the learned Bochart's comparison) cannot be cut with a sword, quenched with water, or blown out with wind, but, by closing the window-shutters, they may be kept out of the chamber. Music cannot work upon the devil, but it may shut up the passages by which he has access to the mind. [2.] David's music was extraordinary, and in mercy to him, that he might gain a reputation at court, as one that had the Lord with him. God made his performances in music more successful, in this case, than those of others would have been. Saul found, even after he had conceived an enmity to David, that no one else could do him the same service (*ch.* xix. 9, 10), which was a great aggravation of his outrage against him. It is a pity that music, which may be so serviceable to the good temper of the mind, should ever be abused by any to the support of vanity and luxury, and made an occasion of drawing the heart away from God and serious things: if this be to any the effect of it, it drives away the good Spirit, not the evil spirit.

CHAP. XVII.

David is the man whom God now delights to honour, for he is a man after his own heart. We read in the foregoing chapter how, after he was anointed, Providence made him famous in the court; we read in this chapter how Providence made him much more famous in the camp, and, by both, not only marked him for a great man, but fitted him for the throne for which he was designed. In the court he was only Saul's physician; but in the camp Israel's champion; there he fairly fought, and beat Goliath of Gath. In the story observe, I. What a noble figure Goliath made, and how daringly he challenged the armies of Israel, ver. 1—11 II. What a mean figure David made, when Providence brought him to the army, ver. 12—30. III. The unparalleled bravery wherewith David undertook to encounter this Philistine, ver. 31—39. IV. The pious resolution with which he attacked him, ver. 40—47. V. The glorious victory he obtained over him with a sling and a stone, and the advantage which the Israelites thereby gained against the Philistines, ver. 48—54. VI. The great notice which was hereupon taken of David at court, ver. 55—58.

NOW the Philistines gathered together their armies to battle, and were gathered together at Shochoh, which *belongeth* to Judah, and pitched between Shochoh and Azekah, in Ephes-dammim. 2 And Saul and the men of Israel were gathered together, and pitched by the valley of Elah, and set the battle in array against the Philistines. 3 And the Philistines stood on a mountain on the one side, and Israel stood on a mountain on the other side: and *there was* a valley between them. 4 And there went out a champion out of the camp of the Philistines, named Goliath, of Gath, whose height *was* six cubits and a span. 5 And *he had* a helmet of brass upon his head, and he *was* armed with a coat of mail: and the weight of the coat *was* five thousand shekels of brass. 6 And *he had* greaves of brass upon his legs, and a target of brass between his shoulders. 7

And the staff of his spear *was* like a weaver's beam; and his spear's head *weighed* six hundred shekels of iron: and one bearing a shield went before him. 8 And he stood and cried unto the armies of Israel, and said unto them, Why are ye come out to set *your* battle in array? *am* not I a Philistine, and ye servants to Saul? choose you a man for you, and let him come down to me. 9 If he be able to fight with me, and to kill me, then will we be your servants: but if I prevail against him, and kill him, then shall ye be our servants, and serve us. 10 And the Philistine said, I defy the armies of Israel this day; give me a man, that we may fight together. 11 When Saul and all Israel heard those words of the Philistine, they were dismayed, and greatly afraid.

It was not long ago that the Philistines were soundly beaten, and put to the worse, before Israel, and they would have been totally routed if Saul's rashness had not prevented; but here we have them making head again. Observe,

I. How they *defied Israel with their armies, v.* 1. They made a descent upon the Israelites' country, and possessed themselves, as it should seem, of some part of it, for they encamped in a place *which belonged to Judah.* Israel's ground would never have been footing for Philistine-armies if Israel had been faithful to their God. The Philistines (it is probable) had heard that Samuel had fallen out with Saul and forsaken him, and no longer assisted and advised him, and that Saul had grown melancholy and unfit for business, and this news encouraged them to make this attempt for the retrieving of the credit they had lately lost. The enemies of the church are watchful to take all advantages, and they never have greater advantages than when her protectors have provoked God's Spirit and prophets to leave them. Saul mustered his forces, and faced them, *v.* 2, 3. And here we must take notice, 1. That the evil spirit, for the present, had left Saul, *ch.* xvi. 23. David's harp having given him some relief, perhaps the alarms and affairs of the war prevented the return of the distemper. Business is a good antidote against melancholy. Let the mind have something without to fasten on and employ itself about, and it will be the less in danger of preying upon itself. God, in mercy to Israel, suspended the judgment for a while; for how distracted must the affairs of the public have been if at this juncture the prince had been distracted! 2. That David for the present had returned to Bethlehem, and had left the court, *v.* 15. When Saul had no further occasion to use him for the relief of his distemper, though, being anointed, he had a very good private reason, and, having a grant of the place of Saul's armour-bearer, he had a very plausible pretence to have continued his attendance, as a retainer to the court, yet he went home to Bethlehem, and returned to keep his father's sheep; this was a rare instance, in a young man that stood so fair for preferment, of humility and affection to his parents. He knew better than most do how to come down again after he had begun to rise, and strangely preferred the retirements of a pastoral life before all the pleasures and gaieties of the court. None more fit for honour than he, nor that deserved it better, and yet none more dead to it.

II. How they defied Israel with their champion Goliath, whom they were almost as proud of as he was of himself, hoping by him to recover their reputation and dominion. Perhaps the army of the Israelites was superior in number and strength to that of the Philistines, which made the Philistines decline a battle, and stand at bay with them, desiring rather to put the issue upon a single combat, in which, having such a champion, they hoped to gain the victory. Now concerning this champion observe,

1. His prodigious size. He was of the sons of Anak, who at Gath kept their ground in Joshua's time (Josh. xi. 22), and kept up a race of giants there, of which Goliath was one, and, it is probable, one of the largest. He was in height *six cubits and a span, v.* 4 The learned bishop Cumberland has made it out that the scripture-cubit was above twenty-one inches (above three inches more than our half-yard) and a span was half a cubit, by which computation Goliath wanted but eight inches of four yards in height, eleven feet and four inches, a monstrous stature, and which made him very formidable, especially if he had strength and spirit proportionable.

2. His armour. Art, as well as nature, made him terrible. He was well furnished with defensive armour (*v.* 5, 6): *A helmet of brass on his head, a coat of mail,* made of brass plates laid over one another, like the scales of a fish; and, because his legs would lie most within the reach of an ordinary man, he wore brass boots, and had a large corselet of brass about his neck. The coat is said to weigh 5000 shekels, and a shekel was half an ounce avoirdupoise, a vast weight for a man to carry, all the other parts of his armour being proportionable. But some think it should be translated, not the *weight* of the coat, but the *value* of it, was 5000 shekels; so much it cost. His offensive weapons were extraordinary, of which his spear only is here described, *v.* 7. It was like a weaver's beam. His arm could manage that which an ordinary man could scarcely heave. His

shield only, which was the lightest of all his accoutrements, was carried before him by his esquire, probably for state; for he that was clad in brass little needed a shield.

3. His challenge. The Philistines having chosen him for their champion, to save themselves from the hazard of a battle, he here throws down the gauntlet, and bids defiance to the armies of Israel, *v.* 8—10. He came into the valley that lay between the camps, and, his voice probably being as much stronger than other people's as his arm was, he cried so as to make them all hear him, *Give me a man, that we may fight together.* He looked upon himself with admiration, because he was so much taller and stronger than all about him; his heart (says bishop Hall) nothing but a lump of proud flesh. He looked upon Israel with disdain, because they had none among them of such a monstrous bulk, and defies them to find a man among them bold enough to enter the list with him. (1.) He upbraids them with their folly in drawing an army together: "*Why have you come to set the battle in array?* How dare you oppose the mighty Philistines?" Or, "Why should the two armies engage, when the controversy may be sooner decided, with only the expense of one life and the hazard of another?" (2.) He offers to put the war entirely upon the issue of the duel he proposes: "If your champion kill me, we will be your servants; if I kill him, you shall be ours." This, says bishop Patrick, was only a bravado, for no nation would be willing thus to venture its all upon the success of one man, nor is it justifiable; notwithstanding Goliath's stipulation here, when he was killed the Philistines did not stand to his word, nor submit themselves as servants to Israel. When he boasts, *I am a Philistine, and you are servants to Saul,* he would have it thought a great piece of condescension in him, who was a chief ruler, to enter the lists with an Israelite; for he looked on them as no better than slaves. The Chaldee paraphrase brings him in boasting that he was the man that had killed Hophni and Phinehas and taken the ark prisoner, but that the Philistines had never given him so much as the command of a regiment in recompence of his services, whereas Saul had been made king for his services: "Let him therefore take up the challenge."

4. The terror this struck upon Israel: *Saul and all his army were greatly afraid, v.* 11. The people would not have been dismayed but that they observed Saul's courage failed him; and it is not to be expected that, if the leader be a coward, the followers should be bold. We found before, when the Spirit of the Lord came upon Saul (*ch.* xi. 6), none could be more daring nor forward to answer the challenge of Nahash the Ammonite, but now that the *Spirit of the Lord had departed from him* even the big looks and big words of a single Philistine make him change colour. But where was Jonathan all this while? Why did not he accept the challenge, who, in the last war, had so bravely engaged a whole army of Philistines? Doubtless he did not feel himself stirred up of God to it, as he did in the former case. As the best, so the bravest men, are no more than what God makes them. Jonathan must now sit still, because the honour of engaging Goliath is reserved for David. In great and good actions, the wind of the Spirit blows when and where he listeth. Now the pious Israelites lament their king's breach with Samuel.

12 Now David *was* the son of that Ephrathite of Beth-lehem-judah, whose name *was* Jesse; and he had eight sons: and the man went among men *for* an old man in the days of Saul. 13 And the three eldest sons of Jesse went *and* followed Saul to the battle: and the names of his three sons that went to the battle *were* Eliab the firstborn, and next unto him Abinadab, and the third Shammah. 14 And David *was* the youngest: and the three eldest followed Saul. 15 But David went and returned from Saul to feed his father's sheep at Beth-lehem. 16 And the Philistine drew near morning and evening, and presented himself forty days. 17 And Jesse said unto David his son, Take now for thy brethren an ephah of this parched *corn,* and these ten loaves, and run to the camp to thy brethren; 18 And carry these ten cheeses unto the captain of *their* thousand, and look how thy brethren fare, and take their pledge. 19 Now Saul, and they, and all the men of Israel, *were* in the valley of Elah, fighting with the Philistines. 20 And David rose up early in the morning, and left the sheep with a keeper, and took, and went, as Jesse had commanded him; and he came to the trench, as the host was going forth to the fight, and shouted for the battle. 21 For Israel and the Philistines had put the battle in array, army against army. 22 And David left his carriage in the hand of the keeper of the carriage, and ran into the army, and came and saluted his brethren. 23 And as he talked with them, behold, there came up the champion,

the Philistine of Gath, Goliath by name, out of the armies of the Philistines, and spake according to the same words: and David heard *them*. 24 And all the men of Israel, when they saw the man, fled from him, and were sore afraid. 25 And the men of Israel said, Have ye seen this man that is come up? surely to defy Israel is he come up: and it shall be, *that* the man who killeth him, the king will enrich him with great riches, and will give him his daughter, and make his father's house free in Israel. 26 And David spake to the men that stood by him, saying, What shall be done to the man that killeth this Philistine, and taketh away the reproach from Israel? for who *is* this uncircumcised Philistine, that he should defy the armies of the living God? 27 And the people answered him after this manner, saying, So shall it be done to the man that killeth him. 28 And Eliab his eldest brother heard when he spake unto the men; and Eliab's anger was kindled against David, and he said, Why camest thou down hither? and with whom hast thou left those few sheep in the wilderness? I know thy pride, and the naughtiness of thine heart; for thou art come down that thou mightest see the battle. 29 And David said, What have I now done? *Is there* not a cause? 30 And he turned from him toward another, and spake after the same manner: and the people answered him again after the former manner.

Forty days the two armies lay encamped facing one another, each advantageously posted, but neither forward to engage. Either they were parleying and treating of an accommodation or they were waiting for recruits; and perhaps there were frequent skirmishes between small detached parties. All this while, twice a day, morning and evening, did the insulting champion appear in the field and repeat his challenge, his own heart growing more and more proud for his not being answered and the people of Israel more and more timorous, while God designed hereby to ripen him for destruction and to make Israel's deliverance the more illustrious. All this while David is keeping his father's sheep, but at the end of forty days Providence brings him to the field to win and wear the laurel which no other Israelite dares venture for. We have in these verses,

I. The present state of his family. His father was old (*v.* 12): *He went among men for an old man,* was taken notice of for his great age, above what was usual at that time, and therefore was excused from public services, and went not in person to the wars, but sent his sons; he had the honours paid him that were due to his age, his hoary head was a crown of glory to him. David's three elder brethren, who perhaps envied his place at the court, got their father to send for him home, and let them go to the camp, where they hoped to signalize themselves and eclipse him (*v.* 13, 14), while David himself was so far from being proud of the services he had done his prince, or ambitious of further preferment, that he not only returned from court to the obscurity of his father's house, but to the care, and toil, and (as it proved, *v.* 34) the peril, of *keeping his father's sheep*. It was the praise of this humility that it came after he had the honour of a courtier, and the reward of it that it came before the honour of a conqueror. *Before honour is humility.* Now he had that opportunity of meditation and prayer, and other acts of devotion, which fitted him for what he was destined to more than all the military exercises of that inglorious camp could do.

II. The orders his father gave him to go and visit his brethren in the camp. He did not himself ask leave to go, to satisfy his curiosity, or to gain experience and make observations; but his father sent him on a mean and homely errand, on which any of his servants might have gone. He must carry some bread and cheese to his brethren, ten loaves with some parched corn for themselves (*v.* 17) and ten cheeses (which, it seems, he thought too good for them) for a present to their colonel, *v.* 18. David must still be the drudge of the family, though he was to be the greatest ornament of it. He had not so much as an ass at command to carry his load, but must take it on his back, and yet run to the camp. Jesse, we thought, was privy to his being anointed, and yet industriously kept him thus mean and obscure, probably to hide him from the eye of suspicion and envy, knowing that he was anointed to a crown in reversion. He must observe how his brethren fared, whether they were not reduced to short allowance, now that the encampment continued so long, that, if need were, he might send them more provisions. And he must take their pledge, that is, if they had pawned any thing, he must redeem it; *take notice of their company,* so some observe, whom they associate with, and what sort of life they lead. Perhaps David, like Joseph, had formerly brought to his father their evil report, and now he sends him to enquire concerning their manners. See the care of pious parents about their children when they are abroad from them, especially in places of temptation; they are solicitous how they conduct themselves, and particularly what company they keep. Let children think of this, and conduct themselves accordingly, remembering that, when they are from under their parents' eye, they are still under God's eye.

III. David's dutiful obedience to his father's command. His prudence and care made him be up early (*v.* 20), and yet not to leave his sheep without a keeper, so faithful was he in a few things and therefore the fitter to be made ruler over many things, and so well had he learnt to obey before he pretended to command. God's providence brought him to the camp very seasonably, when both sides had set the battle in array, and, as it should seem, were more likely to come to an engagement than they had yet been during all the forty days, *v.* 21. Both sides were now preparing to fight. Jesse little thought of sending his son to the army just at that critical juncture, but the wise God orders the time and all the circumstances of actions and affairs so as to serve his designs of securing the interests of Israel and advancing the men after his own heart. Now observe here,

1. How brisk and lively David was, *v.* 22. What articles he brought he honestly took care of, and left them with those that had the charge of the bag and baggage; but, though he had come a long journey with a great load, he *ran into the army*, to see what was doing there, and to pay his respects to his brethren. *Seest thou a man* thus *diligent in his business*, he is in the way of preferment, *he shall stand before kings.*

2. How bold and daring the Philistine was, *v.* 23. Now that the armies were drawn out into a line of battle he appeared first to renew his challenge, vainly imagining that he was in the eager chase of his own glory and triumph, whereas really he was but courting his own destruction.

3. How timorous and faint-hearted the men of Israel were. Though they had, for forty days together, been used to his haughty looks and threatening language, and, having seen no execution done by either, might have learned to despise both, yet, upon his approach, they *fled from him and were greatly afraid*, *v.* 24. One Philistine could never thus have chased 1000 Israelites, and put 10,000 to flight, unless their Rock, being treacherously forsaken by them, had justly *sold them, and shut them up*, Deut. xxxii. 30.

4. How high Saul bid for a champion. Though he was the tallest of all the men of Israel, and, if he had not been so, while he kept close to God might himself have safely taken up the gauntlet which this insolent Philistine threw down, yet, the Spirit of the Lord having departed from him, he durst not do it, nor press Jonathan to do it; but whoever will do it shall have as good preferment as he can give him, *v.* 25. If the hope of wealth and honour will prevail with any man to expose himself so far, it is proclaimed that the bold adventurer, if he come off, shall marry the king's daughter and have a good portion with her; but, as it should seem, whether he come off or no, his *father's house shall be free in Israel*, from all toll, tribute, custom, and services to the crown, or shall be ennobled and advanced to the peerage.

5. How much concerned David was to assert the honour of God and Israel against the impudent challenges of this champion. He asked what reward was promised to him that should slay this Philistine (*v.* 26), though he knew already, not because he was ambitious of the honour, but because he would have it taken notice of, and reported to Saul, how much he resented the indignity hereby done to Israel and Israel's God. He might have presumed so far upon his acquaintance and interest at court as to go himself to Saul to offer his service; but his modesty would not let him do this. It was one of his own rules, before it was one of his son's proverbs, *Put not forth thyself in the presence of the king, and stand not in the place of great men* (Prov. xxv. 6); yet his zeal put him upon that method which he hoped would bring him into this great engagement. Two considerations, it seems, fired David with a holy indignation:—(1.) That the challenger was one that was uncircumcised, a stranger to God and out of covenant with him. (2.) That the challenged were the armies of the living God, devoted to him, employed by him and for him, so that the affronts offered to them reflected upon the living God himself, and *that* he could not bear. When therefore some had told him what was the reward proposed for killing the Philistine (*v.* 27) he asked others (*v.* 30), with the same resentment, which he expected would at length come to Saul's ear.

6. How he was brow-beaten and discouraged by his eldest brother Eliab, who, taking notice of his forwardness, fell into a passion upon it, and gave David very abusive language, *v.* 28. Consider this, (1.) As the fruit of Eliab's jealousy. He was the eldest brother, and David the youngest, and perhaps it had been customary with him (as it is with too many elder brothers) to trample upon him and take every occasion to chide him. But those who thus exalt themselves over their juniors may perhaps live to see themselves, by a righteous providence, abased, and those to whom they are abusive exalted. Time may come when the elder may serve the younger. But Eliab was now vexed that his younger brother should speak those bold words against the Philistine which he himself durst not say. He knew what honour David had already had in the court, and, if he should now get honour in the camp (from which he thought he had found

means effectually to seclude him, *v.* 15), the glory of his elder brethren would be eclipsed and stained; and therefore (such is the nature of jealousy) he would rather that Goliath should triumph over Israel than that David should be the man that should triumph over him. *Wrath is cruel and anger is outrageous, but who can stand before envy,* especially the envy of a brother, the keenness of which Jacob, and Joseph, and David experienced? See Prov. xviii. 19. It is very ill-favoured language that Eliab here gives him; not only unjust and unkind, but, at this time, basely ungrateful; for David was now sent by his father, as Joseph by his, on a kind visit to his brethren. Eliab intended, in what he said, not only to grieve and discourage David himself, and quench that noble fire which he perceived glowing in his breast, but to represent him to those about him as an idle proud lad, not fit to be taken notice of. He gives them to understand that his business was only to keep sheep, and falsely insinuates that he was a careless unfaithful shepherd; though he had left his charge in good hands (*v.* 20), yet he must tauntingly be asked, *With whom hast thou left those few sheep?* Though he came down now to the camp in obedience to his father and kindness to his brethren, and Eliab knew this, yet his coming is turned to his reproach: "Thou hast come down, not to do any service, but to gratify thy own curiosity, and only to look about thee;" and thence he will infer *the pride and naughtiness of his heart,* and pretends to know it as certainly as if he were in his bosom. David could appeal to God concerning his humility and sincerity (Ps. xvii. 3; cxxxi. 1) and at this time gave proofs of both, and yet could not escape this hard character from his own brother. See the folly, absurdity, and wickedness, of a proud and envious passion; how groundless its jealousies are, how unjust its censures, how unfair its representations, how bitter its invectives, and how indecent its language. God, by his grace, keep us from such a spirit! (2.) As a trial of David's meekness, patience, and constancy. A short trial it was, and he approved himself well in it; for, [1.] He bore the provocation with admirable temper (*v.* 29): "*What have I now done?* What fault have I committed, for which I should thus be chidden? *Is there not a cause* for my coming to the camp, when my father sent me? *Is there not a cause* for my resenting the injury done to Israel's honour by Goliath's challenges?" He had right and reason on his side, and knew it, and therefore did not render railing for railing, but with a soft answer turned away his brother's wrath. This conquest of his own passion was in some respects more honourable than his conquest of Goliath. *He that hath rule over his own spirit is better than the mighty.* It was no time for David to quarrel with his brother when the Philistines were upon them. The more threatening the church's enemies are the more forbearing her friends should be with one another. [2.] He broke through the discouragement with admirable resolution. He would not be driven off from his thoughts of engaging the Philistine by the ill-will of his brother. Those that undertake great and public services must not think it strange if they be discountenanced and opposed by those from whom they had reason to expect support and assistance; but must humbly go on with their work, in the face not only of their enemies' threats, but of their friends' slights and suspicions.

31 And when the words were heard which David spake, they rehearsed *them* before Saul: and he sent for him. 32 And David said to Saul, Let no man's heart fail because of him; thy servant will go and fight with this Philistine. 33 And Saul said to David, Thou art not able to go against this Philistine to fight with him: for thou *art but* a youth, and he a man of war from his youth. 34 And David said unto Saul, Thy servant kept his father's sheep, and there came a lion, and a bear, and took a lamb out of the flock: 35 And I went out after him, and smote him, and delivered *it* out of his mouth: and when he arose against me, I caught *him* by his beard, and smote him, and slew him. 36 Thy servant slew both the lion and the bear: and this uncircumcised Philistine shall be as one of them, seeing he hath defied the armies of the living God. 37 David said moreover, The LORD that delivered me out of the paw of the lion, and out of the paw of the bear, he will deliver me out of the hand of this Philistine. And Saul said unto David, Go, and the Lord be with thee. 38 And Saul armed David with his armour, and he put a helmet of brass upon his head; also he armed him with a coat of mail. 39 And David girded his sword upon his armour, and he assayed to go; for he had not proved *it.* And David said unto Saul, I cannot go with these; for I have not proved *them.* And David put them off him.

David is at length presented to Saul for his champion (*v.* 31) and he bravely undertakes to fight the Philistine (*v.* 32): *Let no man's heart fail because of him.* It would have reflected too much upon the valour of his prince if he had said, *Let not thy heart fail;* therefore he speaks generally: *Let no man's heart fail.* A little shepherd, come but this morning from keeping sheep, has more courage than all the mighty men of Israel, and encourages them. Thus does God often send good words to his Israel, and do great things for them, by the weak and foolish things of the world. David only desires a commission from Saul to go and fight with the Philistine, but says nothing to him of the reward he had proposed, because that was not the thing he was ambitious of, but only the honour of serving God and his country: nor would he seem to question Saul's generosity. Two things David had to do with Saul:—

I. To get clear of the objection Saul made against his undertaking. "Alas!" says Saul, "thou hast a good heart to it, but art by no means an equal match for this Philistine. To engage with him is to throw away a life which may better be reserved for more agreeable services. *Thou art but a youth,* rash and inconsiderate, weak and unversed in arms: he is a man that has the head and hands of a man, *a man of war,* trained up and inured to it *from his youth* (*v.* 33), and how canst thou expect but that he will be too hard for thee?" David, as he had answered his brother's passion with meekness, so he answered Saul's fear with faith, and *gives a reason of the hope* which was in him that he should conquer the Philistine, to the satisfaction of Saul. We have reason to fear that Saul had no great acquaintance with nor regard to the word of God, and therefore David, in reasoning with him, fetched not his arguments and encouragements thence, how much soever he had an eye to it in his own mind. But he argues from experience; though he was but a youth, and never in the wars, yet perhaps he had done as much as the killing of Goliath came to, for he had had, by divine assistance, spirit enough to encounter and strength enough to subdue a lion once and another time a bear that robbed him of his lambs, *v.* 34—36. To these he compares this uncircumcised Philistine, looks upon him to be as much a ravenous beast as either of them, and therefore doubts not but to deal as easily with him; and hereby he gives Saul to understand that he was not so inexperienced in hazardous combats as he took him to be.

1. He tells his story like a man of spirit. He is not ashamed to own that he kept his father's sheep, which his brother had just now upbraided him with. So far is he from concealing it that from his employment as a shepherd he fetches the experience that now animated him. But he lets those about him know that he was no ordinary shepherd. Whatever our profession or calling is, be it ever so mean, we should labour to excel in it, and do the business of it in the best manner. When David kept sheep, (1.) He approved himself very careful and tender of his flock, though it was not his own, but his father's. He could not see a lamb in distress but he would venture his life to rescue it. This temper made him fit to be a king, to whom the lives of subjects should be dear and their blood precious (Ps. lxxii. 14), and fit to be a type of Christ, the good Shepherd, who *gathers the lambs in his arms and carries them in his bosom* (Isa. xl. 11), and who not only ventured, but *laid down his life for his sheep.* Thus too was David fit to be an example to ministers with the utmost care and diligence to watch for souls, that they be not a prey to the roaring lion. (2.) He approved himself very bold and brave in the defence of his flock. This was that which he was now concerned to give proof of, and better evidence could not be demanded than this: "Thy servant not only rescued the lambs, but, to revenge the injury, *slew both the lion and the bear.*"

2. He applies his story like a man of faith. He owns (*v.* 37) it was *the Lord that delivered him from the lion and the bear;* to him he gives the praise of that great achievement, and thence he infers, *He will deliver me out of the hand of this Philistine.* "The lion and the bear were enemies only to me and my sheep, and it was in defence of my own interest that I attacked them; but this Philistine is an enemy to God and Israel, *defies the armies of the living God,* and it is for their honour that I attack him." Note, (1.) Our experiences ought to be improved by us as our encouragements to trust in God and venture in the way of duty. He that has delivered does and will. (2.) By the care which common Providence takes of the inferior creatures, and the protection they are under, we may be encouraged to depend upon that special Providence which surrounds the Israel of God. He that sets bounds to the waves of the sea and the rage of wild beasts can and will restrain the wrath of wicked men. Paul seems to allude to this of David (2 Tim. iv. 17, 18), *I was delivered out of the mouth of the lion,* and therefore, I trust, *the Lord shall deliver me.* And perhaps David here thought of the story of Samson, and encouraged himself with it; for his slaying a lion was a happy presage of his many illustrious victories over the Philistines in single combat. Thus David took off Saul's objection against his undertaking, and gained a commission to fight the Philistine, with which Saul gave him a hearty good wish; since he would not venture himself, he prayed for him that would: *Go, and the Lord be with thee,* a good word, if it was not spoken customarily, and in a formal manner, as too often it is. But David has somewhat to do likewise,

II. To get clear of the armour wherewith Saul would, by all means, have him dressed up when he went upon this great action (*v.* 38): *He armed David with his armour,* not that which he wore himself, the disproportion of his stature would not admit that, but some that he kept in his armoury, little thinking that he on whom he now put his helmet and coat of mail must shortly inherit his crown and robe. David, being not yet resolved which way to attack his enemy, *girded on his sword,* not knowing, as yet, but he should have occasion to make use of it; but he found the armour would but encumber him, and would be rather his burden than his defence, and therefore he desires leave of Saul to put them off again: *I cannot go with these, for I have not proved them,* that is, "I have never been accustomed to such accoutrements as these." We may suppose Saul's armour was both very fine and very firm, but what good would it do David if it were not fit, or if he knew not how to manage himself in it? Those that aim at things above their education and usage, and covet the attire and armour of princes, forget that that is the best for us which we are fit for and accustomed to; if we had our desire, we should wish to be in our own coat again, and should say, "We cannot go with these;" we had therefore better go without them.

40 And he took his staff in his hand, and chose him five smooth stones out of the brook, and put them in a shepherd's bag which he had, even in a scrip; and his sling *was* in his hand: and he drew near to the Philistine. 41 And the Philistine came on and drew near unto David; and the man that bare the shield *went* before him. 42 And when the Philistine looked about, and saw David, he disdained him: for he was *but* a youth, and ruddy, and of a fair countenance. 43 And the Philistine said unto David, *Am* I a dog, that thou comest to me with staves? And the Philistine cursed David by his gods. 44 And the Philistine said to David, Come to me, and I will give thy flesh unto the fowls of the air, and to the beasts of the field. 45 Then said David to the Philistine, Thou comest to me with a sword, and with a spear, and with a shield: but I come to thee in the name of the LORD of hosts, the God of the armies of Israel, whom thou hast defied. 46 This day will the LORD deliver thee into mine hand; and I will smite thee, and take thine head from thee; and I will give the carcases of the host of the Philistines this day unto the fowls of the air, and to the wild beasts of the earth; that all the earth may know that there is a God in Israel. 47 And all this assembly shall know that the LORD saveth not with sword and spear: for the battle *is* the LORD's, and he will give you into our hands.

We are now coming near this famous combat, and have in these verses the preparations and remonstrances made on both sides.

I. The preparations made on both sides for the encounter. The Philistine was already fixed, as he had been daily for the last forty days. Well might he go with his armour, for he had sufficiently proved it. Only we are told (*v.* 41) that he *came on and drew near,* a signal, it is likely, being given that his challenge was accepted, and, as if he distrusted his helmet and coat of mail, a man went before him, *carrying his shield,* for his own hands were full with his sword and spear, *v.* 45. But what arms and ammunition is David furnished with? Truly none but what he brought with him as a shepherd; no breastplate, nor corselet, but his plain shepherd's coat; no spear, but his staff; no sword nor bow, but his sling; no quiver, but his scrip; nor any arrows, but, instead of them, five smooth stones picked up out of the brook, *v.* 40. By this it appeared that his confidence was purely in the power of God, and not in any sufficiency of his own, and that now at length he who put it into his heart to fight the Philistine put it into his head with what weapons to do it.

II. The conference which precedes the encounter, in which observe,

1. How very proud Goliath was, (1.) With what scorn he looked upon his adversary, *v.* 42. He looked about, expecting to meet some tall strong man, but, when he saw what a mean figure he made with whom he was to engage, he disdained him, thought it below him to enter the lists with him, fearing that the contemptibleness of the champion he contended with would lessen the glory of his victory. He took notice of his person, that he was but a youth, not come to his strength, *ruddy and of a fair countenance,* fitter to accompany the virgins of Israel in their dances (if mixed dancing was then in use) than to lead on the men of Israel in their battles. He took notice of his array with great indignation (*v.* 43): "*Am I a dog, that thou comest to me with staves?* Dost thou think to beat me as easily as thou dost thy shepherd's dog?" (2.) With what confidence he presumed upon his success. He cursed David by his gods, imprecating the impotent vengeance of his idols against him, thinking these fire-balls thrown about him

would secure his success: and therefore, in confidence of that, he darts his grimaces, as if threatening words would kill (*v.* 44): "*Come to me, and I will give thy flesh to the fowls of the air,* it will be a tender and delicate feast for them." Thus the security and presumption of fools destroy them.

2. How very pious David was. His speech savours nothing of ostentation, but God is all in all in it, *v.* 45—47. (1.) He derives his authority from God: "*I come to thee* by warrant and commission from heaven, *in the name of the Lord,* who has called me to and anointed me for this undertaking, who, by his universal providence, is the *Lord of hosts,* of all hosts, and therefore has power to do what he pleases, and, by the special grace of his covenant, is *the God of the armies of Israel,* and therefore has engaged and will employ his power for their protection, and against thee who hast impiously defied them." The name of God David relied on, as Goliath did on his sword and spear. See Ps. xx. 7; cxviii. 10, 11. (2.) He depends for success upon God, *v.* 46. David speaks with as much assurance as Goliath had done, but upon better ground; it is his faith that says, "*This day will the Lord deliver thee into my hand,* and not only thy carcase, but the carcases of the host of the Philistines, shall be given to the birds and beasts of prey." (3.) He devotes the praise and glory of all to God. He did not, like Goliath, seek his own honour, but the honour of God, not doubting but by the success of this action, [1.] All the world should be made to know that there is a God, and that the God of Israel is the one only living and true God, and all other pretended deities are vanity and a lie. [2.] All Israel (whom he calls not this army, but *this assembly,* or church, because they were now religiously attending the *goings of their God and King,* as they used to do *in the sanctuary)* shall *know that the Lord saveth not with sword and spear* (*v.* 47), but can, when he pleases, save without either and against both, Ps. xlvi. 9. David addresses himself to this combat rather as a priest that was going to offer a sacrifice to the justice of God than as a soldier that was going to engage an enemy of his country.

48 And it came to pass, when the Philistine arose, and came and drew nigh to meet David, that David hasted, and ran toward the army to meet the Philistine. 49 And David put his hand in his bag, and took thence a stone, and slang *it,* and smote the Philistine in his forehead, that the stone sunk into his forehead; and he fell upon his face to the earth. 50 So David prevailed over the Philistine with a sling and with a stone, and smote the Philistine, and slew him; but *there was* no sword in the hand of David. 51 Therefore David ran, and stood upon the Philistine, and took his sword, and drew it out of the sheath thereof, and slew him, and cut off his head therewith. And when the Philistines saw their champion was dead, they fled. 52 And the men of Israel and of Judah arose, and shouted, and pursued the Philistines, until thou come to the valley, and to the gates of Ekron. And the wounded of the Philistines fell down by the way to Shaaraim, even unto Gath, and unto Ekron. 53 And the children of Israel returned from chasing after the Philistines, and they spoiled their tents. 54 And David took the head of the Philistine, and brought it to Jerusalem; but he put his armour in his tent. 55 And when Saul saw David go forth against the Philistine, he said unto Abner, the captain of the host, Abner, whose son *is* this youth? And Abner said, *As* thy soul liveth, O king, I cannot tell. 56 And the king said, Enquire thou whose son the stripling *is.* 57 And as David returned from the slaughter of the Philistine, Abner took him, and brought him before Saul with the head of the Philistine in his hand. 58 And Saul said to him, Whose son *art* thou, *thou* young man? And David answered, *I am* the son of thy servant Jesse the Beth-lehemite.

Here is, 1. The engagement between the two champions, *v.* 48. To this engagement the Philistine advanced with a great deal of state and gravity; if he must encounter a pigmy, yet it shall be with the magnificence of a giant and a grandee. This is intimated in the manner of expression: He *arose, and came, and drew nigh,* like a stalking mountain, overlaid with brass and iron, *to meet David.* David advanced with no less activity and cheerfulness, as one that aimed more to do execution than to make a figure: He *hasted, and ran,* being lightly clad, to *meet the Philistine.* We may imagine with what tenderness and compassion the Israelites saw such a pleasing youth as this throwing himself into the mouth of destruction, but he knew whom he had believed and for whom he acted. 2. The fall of Goliath in this engagement. He was in no haste, because in no fear, but confident that he should soon at one stroke cleave his adversary's head; but, while he was preparing to do it solemnly, David did his business effectually, without any parade: he slang a stone which hit him in the forehead, and, in the twinkling of an eye, fetched him to the ground, *v.* 49. Goliath knew there were famous slingers in Israel (Judg. xx. 16), yet was either so forgetful or presumptuous as to go with the beaver of his helmet open, and thither, to the only part left exposed, not so much David's art as God's providence directed the stone, and brought it with such force that it sunk into his head, notwithstanding the impudence with which his forehead was brazened. See how frail and uncertain life is, even when it thinks itself best fortified, and how quickly, how easily, and with how small a matter, the passage may be opened for life to go out and death to enter. Goliath himself *has not power over the spirit to retain the spirit,* Eccl. viii. 8. Let not the strong man glory in his strength, nor the armed man in his armour. See how God resists the proud and pours contempt upon those that bid defiance to him and his people. None ever hardened his heart against God and prospered. One of the Rabbin thinks that when Goliath said to David, *Come, and I will give thy flesh to the fowls of the air,* he threw up his head so hastily that his helmet fell off, and so left his broad forehead a fair mark for David. To complete the execution, David drew Goliath's own sword, a two-handed weapon for David, and with it *cut off his head, v.* 51. What need had David to take a sword of his own? his enemy's sword shall serve his purpose, when he has occasion for one. God is greatly glorified when his proud enemies are cut off with their own sword and he makes *their own tongues to fall upon them,* Ps. lxiv. 8. David's victory over Goliath was typical of the triumphs of the son of David over Satan and all the powers of darkness, whom he *spoiled, and made a show of them openly* (Col. ii. 15), and we through him are *more than conquerors.* 3. The defeat of the Philistines' army hereupon. They relied wholly upon the strength of their champion, and therefore, when they saw him slain, they did not, as Goliath had offered, throw down their arms and surrender themselves servants to Israel (*v.* 9), but took to their heels, being wholly dispirited, and thinking it to no purpose to oppose one before whom such a mighty man had fallen: *They fled* (*v.* 51), and this put life into the Israelites, who *shouted and pursued them* (David, it is probable, leading them on in the pursuit) even to the gates of their own cities, *v.* 52. In their return from the chase they seized all the baggage, plundered the tents (*v.* 53), and enriched themselves with the spoil. 4. David's disposal of his trophies, *v.* 54. He brought the head of the Philistine to Jerusalem, to be a terror to the Jebusites, who held the strong-hold of Sion: it is probable that he carried it in triumph to other cities. *His armour he laid up in his tent;* only the sword was preserved behind the ephod in the tabernacle, as consecrated to God, and a memorial of the victory to his honour, *ch.* xxi. 9. 5. The notice that was taken of David. Though he had been at court formerly, yet, having been for some time absent (*v.* 15), Saul had forgotten him, being melancholy and mindless, and little thinking that his musician would have spirit enough to be his champion; and therefore, as if he had never seen him before, he asked whose son he was. Abner was a stranger to him, but brought him to Saul (*v.* 57), and he gave a modest account of himself, *v.* 58. And now he was introduced to the court with much greater advantages than before, in which he owned God's hand performing all things for him.

CHAP. XVIII.

In the course of the foregoing chapter we left David in triumph; now in this chapter we have, I. The improvement of his triumphs; he soon became, 1. Saul's constant attendant, ver. 2. 2. Jonathan's covenant friend, ver. 1, 3, 4. 3. The darling of his country, ver. 5, 7, 16. II. The allays of his triumphs. This is the vanity that accompanies even a right work, that "for it a man is envied," Eccl. iv. 4. So David was by Saul. 1. He hated him, and sought to kill him himself, ver. 8—11. 2. He feared him, and contrived how he might have some mischief done him, ver. 12—17. He proposed to marry his daughter to him; but, [1.] Cheated him of the eldest to provoke him (ver. 19), and, [2.] Gave him the younger, upon conditions which would endanger his life, ver. 20—25. But David performed his conditions bravely (ver. 26, 27), and grew to be more and more esteemed, ver. 28—30. Still David is rising, but (as all that aim at the crown of life must expect) he had a great deal of difficulty and opposition to grapple with.

AND it came to pass, when he had made an end of speaking unto Saul, that the soul of Jonathan was knit with the soul of David, and Jonathan loved him as his own soul. 2 And Saul took him that day, and would let him go no more home to his father's house. 3 Then Jonathan and David made a covenant, because he loved him as his own soul. 4 And Jonathan stripped himself of the robe that *was* upon him, and gave it to David, and his garments, even to his sword, and to his bow, and to his girdle. 5 And David went out whithersoever Saul sent him, *and* behaved himself wisely: and Saul set him over the men of war, and he was accepted in the sight of all the people, and also in the sight of Saul's servants.

David was anointed to the crown to take it out of Saul's hand, and over Jonathan's head, and yet here we find,

I. That Saul, who was now in possession of the crown, reposed a confidence in him, God so ordering it, that he might by his preferment at court be prepared for future service. Saul now took David home with him, and would not suffer him to return again to his retirement, *v.* 2. And David having signalized himself above the men of war, in taking up the challenge which they declined, *Saul set him over the men of war* (*v.* 5), not that he made him general (Abner was in that post), but perhaps captain of the life-guard; or, though he was youngest, he ordered him to have the precedency, in recompence of his great services. He employed him in the affairs of government; *and David went out whithersoever Saul sent him,* showing himself as dutiful as he was bold and courageous. Those that hope to rule must first learn to obey. He had approved himself a dutiful son to Jesse his father, and now a dutiful servant to Saul his master; those that are good in one relation it is to be hoped will be so in another.

II. That Jonathan, who was heir to the crown, entered into covenant with him, God so ordering it, that David's way might be the clearer when his rival was his friend. 1. Jonathan conceived an extraordinary kindness and affection for him (*v.* 1): *When he had made an end of speaking to Saul* he fell perfectly in love with him. Whether it refers to his conference with Saul before the battle (*ch.* xvii. 34, 37), or to that after (*v.* 51), in which it is probable much more was said than is there set down, is uncertain. But, in both, David expressed himself with so much prudence, modesty, and piety, such a felicity of expression, with so much boldness and yet so much sweetness, and all this so natural and unaffected, and the more surprising because of the disadvantages of his education and appearance, *that the soul of Jonathan was* immediately *knit* unto *the soul of David.* Jonathan had formerly set upon a Philistine army with the same faith and bravery with which David had now attacked a Philistine giant; so that there was between them a very near resemblance of affections, dispositions, and counsels, which made their spirits unite so easily, so quickly, so closely, that they seemed but as one soul in two bodies. None had so much reason to dislike David as Jonathan had, because he was to put him by the crown, yet none regards him more. Those that are governed in their love by principles of wisdom and grace will not suffer their affections to be alienated by any secular regards or considerations: the greater thoughts will swallow up and overrule the less. 2. He testified his love to David by a generous present he made him, *v.* 4. He was uneasy at seeing so great a soul, though lodged in so fair body, yet disguised in the mean and despicable dress of a poor shepherd, and therefore takes care to put him speedily into the habit of a courtier (for he gave him a robe) and of a soldier, for he gave him, instead of his staff and sling, a sword and bow, and, instead of his shepherd's scrip, a girdle, either a belt or a sash; and, which made the present much more obliging, they were the same that he himself had worn, and (as a presage of what would follow) he stripped himself of them to dress David in them. Saul's would not fit him, but Jonathan's did. Their bodies were of a size, a circumstance which well agreed with the suitableness of their minds. When Saul put these marks of honour on David he put them off again, because he would first earn them and then wear them; but, now that he had given proofs of the spirit of a prince and a soldier, he was not ashamed to wear the habits of a prince and a soldier. David is seen in Jonathan's clothes, that all may take notice he is a Jonathan's second self. Our Lord Jesus has thus shown his love to us, that he stripped himself to clothe us, emptied himself to enrich us; nay, he did more than Jonathan, he clothed himself with our rags, whereas Jonathan did not put on David's. 3. He endeavoured to perpetuate this friendship. So entirely satisfied were they in each other, even at the first interview, that they made a covenant with each other, *v.* 3. Their mutual affection was sincere; and he that bears an honest mind startles not at assurances. True love desires to be constant. Those who love Christ as their own souls will be willing to join themselves to him in an everlasting covenant.

III. That both court and country agree to bless him. It is but seldom that they agree in their favourites; yet David was *accepted in the sight of all the people, and also* (which was strange) *in the sight of Saul's servants, v.* 5. The former cordially loved him, the latter could not for shame but caress and compliment him. And it was certainly a great instance of the power of God's grace in David that he was able to bear all this respect and honour flowing in upon him on a sudden without being lifted up above measure. Those that climb so fast have need of good heads and good hearts. It is more difficult to know how to abound than how to be abased.

6 And it came to pass as they came, when David was returned from the slaughter of the Philistine, that the women came out of all cities of Israel, singing and dancing, to meet king Saul, with tabrets, with joy, and with instruments of music. 7 And the women answered *one another* as they played, and said, Saul hath slain his thousands, and David his ten thousands. 8 And Saul was very wroth, and the saying displeased him; and he said, They have ascribed unto David ten thousands, and to me they have ascribed *but* thousands: and *what* can he have more but the kingdom? 9 And Saul eyed David from that day and forward. 10 And it

came to pass on the morrow, that the evil spirit from God came upon Saul, and he prophesied in the midst of the house: and David played with his hand, as at other times: and *there was* a javelin in Saul's hand. 11 And Saul cast the javelin; for he said, I will smite David even to the wall *with it.* And David avoided out of his presence twice.

Now begin David's troubles, and they not only tread on the heels of his triumphs, but take rise from them, such is the vanity of that in this world which seems greatest.

I. He was too much magnified by the common people. Some time after the victory Saul went a triumphant progress through the cities of Israel that lay next him, to receive the congratulations of the country. And, when he made his public entry into any place, the women were most forward to show him respect, as was usual then in public triumphs (*v.* 6), and they had got a song, it seems, which they sang in their dances (made by some poet or other, that was a great admirer of David's bravery, and was more just than wise, in giving his achievements in the late action the preference before Saul's), the burden of which was, *Saul has slain his thousands, and David his ten thousands.* Such a difference as this Moses made between the numbers of Ephraim and Manasseh, Deut. xxxiii. 17.

II. This mightily displeased Saul, and made him envy David, *v.* 8, 9. He ought to have considered that they referred only to this late action, and intended not to diminish any of Saul's former exploits; and that in the action now celebrated it was undeniably true that David, in killing Goliath, did in effect slay all the Philistines that were slain that day and defeated the whole army; so that they did but give David his due. It may be, he that composed the song only used a poetical liberty, and intended not any invidious comparison between Saul and David; or, if he did, it was below the great mind of a prince to take notice of such a reflection upon his personal honour, when it appeared that the glory of the public was sincerely intended. But Saul was very wroth, and presently suspected some treasonable design at the bottom of it: *What can he have more but the kingdom?* This made him eye David as one he was jealous of and sought advantages against (*v.* 9): his countenance was not towards him as it had been. Proud men cannot endure to hear any praised but themselves, and think all the honour lost that goes by themselves. It is a sign that the Spirit of God has departed from men if they be peevish in their resentment of affronts, envious and suspicious of all about them, and ill-natured in their conduct; for the wisdom from above makes us quite otherwise.

III. In his fury he aimed to kill David, *v,* 10, 11. *Jealousy is the rage of a man;* it made Saul outrageous against David and impatient to get him out of the way. 1. His fits of frenzy returned upon him. The very next day after he conceived malice against David the evil spirit from God, that had formerly haunted him, seized him again Those that indulge themselves in envy and uncharitableness *give place to the devil,* and prepare for the re-entry of the unclean spirit, with seven others more wicked. Where envy is there is confusion. Saul pretended a religious ecstasy: *He prophesied in the midst of the house,* that is, he had the gestures and motions of a prophet, and humoured the thing well enough to decoy David into a snare, and that he might be fearless of any danger and off his guard; and perhaps designing, if he could but kill him, to impute it to a divine impulse and to charge it upon the spirit of prophecy with which he seemed to be animated: but really it was a hellish fury that actuated him. 2. David, though advanced to a much higher post of honour, disdained not, for his master's service, to return to his harp: *He played with his hand as at other times.* Let not the highest think any thing below them whereby they may do good and be serviceable to those they are obliged to. 3. He took this opportunity to aim at the death of David. A sword in a madman's hand is a dangerous thing, especially such a madman as Saul was, that was mad with malice. Yet he had a javelin or dart in his hand, which he projected, endeavouring thereby to slay David, not in a sudden passion, but deliberately: *I will smite David to the wall with it,* with such a desperate force did he throw it. Justly does David complain of his enemies that they hated him with *a cruel hatred,* Ps. xxv. 19. No life is thought too precious to be sacrificed to malice. If a grateful sense of the great service David had done to the public could not assuage Saul's fury, yet one would think he should have allowed himself to consider the kindness David was now doing him, in relieving him, as no one else could, against the worst of troubles. Those are possessed with a devilish spirit indeed that render evil for good. Compare David, with his harp in his hand, aiming to serve Saul, and Saul, with his javelin in his hand, aiming to slay David; and observe the meekness and usefulness of God's persecuted people and the brutishness and barbarity of their persecutors. *The bloodthirsty hate the upright, but the just seek his soul,* Prov. xxix. 10. 4. David happily avoided the blow twice (namely, now, and afterwards, *ch.* xix. 10); he did not throw the javelin at Saul again, but withdrew, not fighting but flying for his own preservation; though he had both strength and courage enough, and colour of right, to make resistance and revenge the injury, yet he did no more than secure himself, by getting out of the way of it. David, no doubt, had a watchful eye upon Saul's hand, and the javelin in it, and did as bravely in running from it as he did lately in running upon Goliath. Yet his safety must be ascribed to the watchful eye of God's providence upon him, saving his servant from the hurtful sword; and by this narrow escape it seemed he was designed for something extraordinary.

12 And Saul was afraid of David, because the LORD was with him, and was departed from Saul. 13 Therefore Saul removed him from him, and made him his captain over a thousand; and he went out and came in before the people. 14 And David behaved himself wisely in all his ways; and the LORD *was* with him. 15 Wherefore when Saul saw that he behaved himself very wisely, he was afraid of him. 16 But all Israel and Judah loved David, because he went out and came in before them. 17 And Saul said to David, Behold my elder daughter Merab, her will I give thee to wife: only be thou valiant for me, and fight the LORD's battles. For Saul said, Let not my hand be upon him, but let the hand of the Philistines be upon him. 18 And David said unto Saul, Who *am* I? and what *is* my life, *or* my father's family in Israel, that I should be son in law to the king? 19 But it came to pass at the time when Merab Saul's daughter should have been given to David, that she was given unto Adriel the Meholathite to wife. 20 And Michal Saul's daughter loved David: and they told Saul, and the thing pleased him. 21 And Saul said, I will give him her, that she may be a snare to him, and that the hand of the Philistines may be against him. Wherefore Saul said to David, Thou shalt this day be my son in law in *the one of* the twain. 22 And Saul commanded his servants, *saying*, Commune with David secretly, and say, Behold, the king hath delight in thee, and all his servants love thee: now therefore be the king's son in law. 23 And Saul's servants spake those words in the ears of David. And David said, Seemeth it to you *a* light *thing* to be a king's son in law, seeing that I *am* a poor man, and lightly esteemed? 24 And the servants of Saul told him, saying, On this manner spake David. 25 And Saul said, Thus shall ye say to David, The king desireth not any dowry, but a hundred foreskins of the Philistines, to be avenged of the king's enemies. But Saul thought to make David fall by the hand of the Philistines. 26 And when his servants told David these words, it pleased David well to be the king's son in law: and the days were not expired. 27 Wherefore David arose and went, he and his men, and slew of the Philistines two hundred men; and David brought their foreskins, and they gave them in full tale to the king, that he might be the king's son in law. And Saul gave him Michal his daughter to wife. 28 And Saul saw and knew that the LORD *was* with David, and *that* Michal Saul's daughter loved him. 29 And Saul was yet the more afraid of David; and Saul became David's enemy continually. 30 Then the princes of the Philistines went forth: and it came to pass, after they went forth, *that* David behaved himself more wisely than all the servants of Saul; so that his name was much set by.

Saul had now, in effect, proclaimed war with David. He began in open hostility when he threw the javelin at him. Now we are here told how his enmity proceeded, and how David received the attacks of it.

I. See how Saul expressed his malice against David. 1. He was *afraid of him, v.* 12. Perhaps he pretended to be afraid that David would do him mischief, to force his way to the crown. Those that design ill against others are commonly willing to have it thought that others design ill against them. But David's withdrawing (*v.* 11) was a plain evidence that he was far from such a thought. However, he really stood in awe of him, as Herod feared John, Mark vi. 20. Saul was sensible that he had lost the favourable presence of God himself, and that David had it, and for this reason he feared him. Note, Those are truly great and to be reverenced that have God with them. The more *wisely David behaved himself* the more *Saul feared him, v.* 15, and again *v.* 29. Men think the way to be feared is to hector and threaten, which makes them feared by fools only, but despised by the wise and good; whereas the way to be both feared and loved, feared by those to whom we would wish to be a terror and loved by those to whom we would wish to be a delight, is to *behave ourselves wisely.* Wisdom makes the face to shine and commands respect. 2. He removed him from court, and gave him a regiment in the country, *v.* 13. He made him captain over 1000, that he might be from under his eye, because he hated the sight of him; and that he might not secure the interest of the courtiers. Yet herein he did impoliticly; for it gave David an opportunity of ingratiating himself with the people, who therefore *loved him* (*v.* 16) because he *went out and came in before them,* that is, he presided in the business of his country, civil as well as military, and gave universal satisfaction. 3. He stirred him up to take all occasions of quarrelling with the Philistines and engaging them (*v.* 17), insinuating to him that hereby he would do good service to his prince *(be thou valiant for me),* and good service to his God *(fight the Lord's battles),* and a kindness to himself too, for hereby he would qualify himself for the honour he designed him, which was to marry his eldest daughter to him. This he had merited by killing Goliath, for it was promised by proclamation to him that should do that exploit (*ch.* xvii. 25); but David was so modest as not to demand it, and now, when Saul proposed it, it was with design of mischief to him, to make him venture upon hazardous attempts, saying in his heart, *Let the hand of the Philistines be upon him,* hoping they would some time or other be the death of him; yet how could he expect this when he saw that God was with him? 4. He did what he could to provoke him to discontent and mutiny, by breaking his promise with him, and giving his daughter to another when the time came that she should have been given to him, *v.* 19. This was as great an affront as he could possibly put upon him, and touched him both in his honour and in his love. He therefore thought David's resentment of it would break out in some indecency or other, in word or deed, which might give him an advantage against him to take him off by the course of law. Thus evil men seek mischief. 5. When he was disappointed in this, he proffered him his other daughter (who it seems had a secret kindness for David, *v.* 20), but with this design, that she might be *a snare to him, v.* 21. (1.) Perhaps he hoped that she would, even after her marriage to David, take part with her father against her husband, and give him an opportunity of doing David an unkindness. However, (2.) The conditions of the marriage, he hoped, would be his destruction; for (so zealous will Saul seem against the Philistines) the conditions of the marriage must be that he killed 100 Philistines, and, as proofs that those he had slain were uncircumcised, he must bring in their foreskins cut off; this would be a just reproach upon the Philistines, who hated circumcision as it was an ordinance of God; and perhaps David, in doing this, would the more exasperate them against him, and make them seek to be revenged on him, which was the thing that Saul desired and designed, much more than to be avenged on the Philistines: *For Saul thought to make David fall by the Philistines, v.* 25. See here, [1.] What cheats bad men put upon themselves. Saul's conscience would not suffer him, except when the evil spirit was actually upon him, to aim at David's life himself, for even he could not but conceive a horror at the thought of murdering such an innocent and excellent person; but he thought that to expose him designedly to the Philistines had nothing bad in it *(Let not my hand be upon him, but the hand of the Philistines),* whereas that malicious design against him was as truly murder before God as if he had slain him with his own hands. [2.] What cheats they put upon the world. Saul pretended extraordinary kindness for David even when he aimed at his ruin, and was actually plotting it: *Thou shalt be my son-in-law,* says he (*v.* 21), notwithstanding he hated him implacably. Perhaps David refers to this when (Ps. lv. 21) he speaks of his enemy as one whose words were *smoother than butter, but war was in his heart.* It is probable that Saul's employing his servants to persuade David to enter into a treaty of a match with his daughter Michal (*v.* 22) arose from an apprehension that either his having cheated him about his elder daughter (*v.* 19) or the hardness of the terms he intended now to propose would make him decline it.

II. See how David conducted himself when the tide of Saul's displeasure ran thus high against him.

1. *He behaved himself wisely in all his ways.* He perceived Saul's jealousy of him, which made him very cautious and circumspect in every thing he said and did, and careful to give no offence. He did not complain of hard measure nor make himself the head of a party, but managed all the affairs he was entrusted with as one that made it his business to do real service to his king and country, looking upon that to be the end of his preferment. And then *the Lord was with him* to give him success in all his undertakings. Though he procured Saul's ill-will by it, yet he obtained God's favour. Compare this with Ps. ci. 2, where it is David's promise, *I will behave myself wisely;* and that promise he here performed; and it is his prayer, *O, when wilt thou come unto me?* And that prayer God here answered: *The Lord was with him.* However blind fortune may seem to favour fools, God will own and bless those that behave themselves wisely.

2. When it was proposed to him to be son-in-law to the king he once and again received the proposal with all possible modesty

and humility. When Saul proposed his elder daughter to him (*v.* 18) he said, *Who am I, and what is my life?* When the courtiers proposed the younger, he took no notice of the affront Saul had put upon him in disposing of the elder from him, but continued in the same mind (*v.* 23): *Seemeth it a light thing to you to be a king's son-in-law, seeing that I am a poor man and lightly esteemed?* He knew Michal loved him, and yet did not offer to improve his interest in her affections for the gaining of her without her father's consent, but waited till it was proposed to him. And then see, (1.) How highly he speaks of the honour offered him: *To be son-in-law to the king.* Though this king was but an upstart, in his original as mean as himself, in his management no better than he should be, yet, being a crowned head, he speaks of him and the royal family with all due respect. Note, Religion is so far from teaching us to be rude and unmannerly that it does not allow us to be so. We must *render honour to whom honour is due.* (2.) How humbly he speaks of himself: *Who am I?* This did not proceed from a mean, abject, sneaking spirit, for when there was occasion he made it appear that he had as high a sense of honour as most men; nor was it from his jealousy of Saul (though he had reason enough to fear a snake under the green grass), but from his true and deep humility: *Who am I, a poor man, and lightly esteemed?* David had as much reason as any man to value himself. He was of an ancient and honourable family of Judah, a comely person, a great statesman and soldier; his achievements were great, for he had won Goliath's head and Michal's heart. He knew himself destined by the divine counsels to the throne of Israel, and yet, *Who am I, and what is my life?* Note, It well becomes us, however God has advanced us, always to have low thoughts of ourselves. *He that humbleth himself shall be exalted.* And, if David thus magnified the honour of being son-in-law to the king, how should we magnify the honour of being sons (not in law, but in gospel) to the King of kings! *Behold what manner of love the Father has bestowed upon us!* Who are we that we should be thus dignified?

3. When the slaying of 100 Philistines was made the condition of David's marrying Saul's daughter he readily closed with it (*v.* 26): *It pleased David well to be the king's son-in-law* upon those terms; and, before the time given him for the action had expired, he doubled the demand, and slew 200, *v.* 27. He would not seem to suspect that Saul designed his hurt by it (though he had reason enough), but would rather act as if Saul had meant to consult his honour, and therefore cheerfully undertook it, as became a brave soldier and a true lover, though we may suppose it uneasy to Michal. David hereby discovered likewise, (1.) A great confidence in the divine protection. He knew God was with him, and therefore, whatever Saul hoped, David did not fear falling by the Philistines, though he must needs expose himself much by such an undertaking as this. (2.) A great zeal for the good of his country, which he would not decline any occasion of doing service to, though with the hazard of his life. (3.) A right notion of honour, which consists not so much in being preferred as in deserving to be so. David was then pleased with the thoughts of being the king's son-in-law when he found the honour set at this high price, being more solicitous how to merit it than how to obtain it; nor could he wear it with satisfaction till he had won it.

4. Even after he was married he continued his good services to Israel. When the princes of the Philistines began to move towards another war David was ready to oppose them, and *behaved himself more wisely than all the servants of Saul, v.* 30. The law dispensed with men from going to war the first year after they were married (Deut. xxiv. 5), but David loved his country too well to make use of that dispensation. Many that have shown themselves forward to serve the public when they have been in pursuit of preferment have declined it when they have gained their point; but David acted from more generous principles.

III. Observe how God brought good to David out of Saul's project against him. 1. Saul gave him his daughter to be a snare to him, but in this respect that marriage was a kindness to him, that his being Saul's son-in-law made his succeeding him much the less invidious, especially when so many of his sons were slain with him, *ch.* xxxi. 2. 2. Saul thought, by putting him upon dangerous services, to have him taken off, but that very thing confirmed his interest in the people; for the more he did against the Philistines the better they loved him, so that *his name was much set by* (*v.* 30), which would make his coming to the crown the more easy. Thus God makes even the wrath of man to praise him and serves his designs of kindness to his own people by it.

CHAP. XIX.

Immediately after David's marriage, which one would have hoped would secure him Saul's affection, we find his troubles coming upon him faster than ever and Saul's enmity to him the cause of all. His death was vowed, and four fair escapes of his from the hurtful sword of Saul we have an account of in this chapter: the first by the prudent mediation of Jonathan (ver. 1—7), the second by his own quickness (ver. 8—10), the third by Michal's fidelity (ver. 11—17), the fourth by Samuel's protection, and a change, for the present, wrought upon Saul, ver. 18—24. Thus God has many ways of preserving his people. Providence is never at a loss.

AND Saul spake to Jonathan his son, and to all his servants, that they should kill David. 2 But Jonathan Saul's son delighted much in David: and Jonathan told David, saying, Saul my father seeketh to kill thee: now therefore, I pray thee, take heed to thyself until the morning, and abide in a secret *place*, and hide thyself: 3 And I will go out and stand beside my father in the field where thou *art*, and I will commune with my father of thee; and what I see, that I will tell thee. 4 And Jonathan spake good of David unto Saul his father, and said unto him, Let not the king sin against his servant, against David; because he hath not sinned against thee, and because his works *have been* to thee-ward very good: 5 For he did put his life in his hand, and slew the Philistine, and the LORD wrought a great salvation for all Israel: thou sawest *it*, and didst rejoice: wherefore then wilt thou sin against innocent blood, to slay David without a cause? 6 And Saul hearkened unto the voice of Jonathan: and Saul sware, *As* the LORD liveth, he shall not be slain. 7 And Jonathan called David, and Jonathan showed him all those things. And Jonathan brought David to Saul, and he was in his presence, as in times past.

Saul and Jonathan appear here in their different characters, with reference to David.

I. Never was enemy so unreasonably cruel as Saul. He spoke to his son and all his servants *that they should kill David*, *v.* 1. His projects to take him off had failed, and therefore he proclaims him an out-law, and charges all about him, upon their allegiance, to take the first opportunity to kill David. It is strange that he was not ashamed thus to avow his malice when he could give no reason for it, and that knowing all his servants loved David (for so he had said himself, *ch.* xviii. 22), he was not afraid of provoking them to rebel by this bloody order. Either malice was not then so politic, or justice was not so corrupted as it has been since, or else Saul would have had him indicted, and have suborned witnesses to swear treason against him, and so have had him taken off, as Naboth was, by colour of law. But there is least danger from this undisguised malice. It was strange that he who knew how well Jonathan loved him should expect him to kill him; but he thought that because he was heir to the crown he must needs be as envious at David as himself was. And Providence ordered it thus that he might befriend David's safety.

II. Never was friend so surprisingly kind as Jonathan. *A friend in need is a friend indeed.* Such a one Jonathan was to David, He not only continued to delight much in him, though David's glory eclipsed his, but bravely appeared for him now that the stream ran so strongly against him.

1. He took care for his present security by letting him know his danger (*v.* 2): "*Take heed to thyself*, and keep out of harm's way." Jonathan knew not but that some of the servants might be either so obsequious to Saul or so envious at David as to put the orders in execution which Saul had given, if they could light on David.

2. He took pains to pacify his father and reconcile him to David. The next morning he ventured to commune with him concerning David (*v.* 3), not that night, perhaps because he observed Saul to be drunk and not fit to be spoken to, or because he hoped that, when he had slept upon it, he would himself revoke the order, or because he could not have an opportunity of speaking to him till morning.

(1.) His intercession for David was very prudent. It was managed with a great deal of the meekness of wisdom; and he showed himself faithful to his friends by speaking good of him, though he was in danger of incurring his father's displeasure by it—a rare instance of valuable friendship! He pleads, [1.] The good services David had done to the public, and particularly to Saul: *His work has been to thee-ward very good, v.* 4. Witness the relief he had given him against his distemper with his harp, and his bold encounter with Goliath, that memorable action, which did, in effect, save Saul's life and kingdom. He appeals to himself concerning this: *Thou thyself sawest it, and didst rejoice.* In that and other instances it appeared that David was a favourite of heaven and a friend to Israel, as well as a good servant to Saul, for by him *the Lord wrought a great salvation for all Israel;* so that to order him to be slain was not only base ingratitude to so good a servant, but a great affront to God and a great injury to the public. [2.] He pleads his innocency. Though he had formerly done many good offices, yet, if he had now been chargeable with any crimes, it would have been another matter; but *he has not sinned against thee* (*v.* 1), his *blood is innocent* (*v.* 5), and, if he be slain, it is without cause. And Jonathan had therefore reason to protest against it because he could not entail any thing upon his family more pernicious than the guilt of innocent blood.

(2.) His intercession, being thus prudent, was prevalent. God inclined the heart of Saul to hearken to the voice of Jonathan. Note, We must be willing to hear reason, and to take all reproofs and good advice even from our inferiors, parents from their own children. How forcible are right words! Saul was, for the present, so far convinced of the unreasonableness of his enmity to

David that, [1.] He recalled the bloody warrant for his execution (*v.* 6): *As the Lord liveth, he shall not be slain.* Whether Saul swore here with due solemnity or no does not appear; perhaps he did, and the matter was of such moment as to deserve it and of such uncertainty as to need it. But at other times Saul swore rashly and profanely, which made the sincerity of this oath justly questionable; for it may be feared that those who can so far jest with an oath as to make a by-word of it, and prostitute it to a trifle, have not such a due sense of the obligation of it but that, to serve a turn, they will prostitute it to a lie Some suspect that Saul said and swore this with a malicious design to bring David within his reach again, intending to take the first opportunity to slay him. But, as bad as Saul was, we can scarcely think so ill of him; and therefore we suppose that he spoke as he thought for the present, but the convictions soon wore off and his corruptions prevailed and triumphed over them. [2.] He renewed the grant of his place at court. Jonathan brought him to Saul, and *he was in his presence as in times past* (*v.* 7), hoping that now the storm was over, and that his friend Jonathan would be instrumental to keep his father always in this good mind.

8 And there was war again: and David went out, and fought with the Philistines, and slew them with a great slaughter; and they fled from him. 9 And the evil spirit from the LORD was upon Saul, as he sat in his house with his javelin in his hand: and David played with *his* hand. 10 And Saul sought to smite David even to the wall with the javelin; but he slipped away out of Saul's presence, and he smote the javelin into the wall: and David fled, and escaped that night.

Here, I. David continues his good services to his king and country. Though Saul had requited him evil for good, and even his usefulness was the very thing for which Saul envied him, yet he did not therefore retire in sullenness and decline public service. Those that are ill paid for doing good, yet must not be *weary of well doing*, remembering what a bountiful benefactor our heavenly Father is, even to the froward and unthankful. Notwithstanding the many affronts Saul had given to David, yet we find him, 1. As bold as ever in using his sword for the service of his country, *v.* 8. The war broke out again with the Philistines, which gave David occasion again to signalize himself. It was with a great deal of bravery that he charged them; and he came off victorious, slaying many and putting the rest to flight. 2. As cheerful as ever in using his harp for the service of the prince. When Saul was disturbed with his former fits of melancholy *David played with his hand, v.* 9. He might have pleaded that this was a piece of service now below him; but a humble man will think nothing below him by which he may do good. He might have objected the danger he was in the last time he performed this service for Saul, *ch.* xviii. 10. But he had learned to render good for evil, and to trust God with his safety in the way of his duty. See how David was affected when his enemy was sick (Ps. xxxv. 13, 14), which perhaps refers to Saul's sickness.

II. Saul continues his malice against David. He that but the other day had sworn by his Maker that David *should not be slain* now endeavours to slay him himself. So implacable, so incurable, is the enmity of the seed of the serpent against that of the woman, so deceitful and desperately wicked is the heart of man without the grace of God, Jer. xvii. 9. The fresh honours David had won in this last war with the Philistines, instead of extinguishing Saul's ill-will to him, and confirming his reconciliation, revived his envy and exasperated him yet more. And, when he indulged this wicked passion, no marvel that *the evil spirit came upon him* (*v.* 9), for when we *let the sun go down upon our wrath we give place to the devil* (Eph. iv. 26, 27), we make room for him and invite him. Discomposures of mind, though helped forward by the agency of Satan, commonly owe their origin to men's own sins and follies. Saul's fear and jealousy made him a torment to himself, so that he could not sit in his house without a javelin in his hand, pretending it was for his preservation, but designing it for David's destruction; for he endeavoured to nail him to the wall, running at him so violently that he struck the *javelin into the wall* (*v.* 10), so strong was the devil in him, so strong his own rage and passion. Perhaps he thought that, if he killed David now, he would be excusable before God and man, as being *non compos mentis—not in his right mind,* and that it would be imputed to his distraction. But God cannot be deceived by pretences, whatever men may be.

III. God continues his care of David and still watches over him for good. Saul missed his blow. David was too quick for him and fled, and by a kind providence escaped that night. To these preservations, among others, David often refers in his Psalms, when he speaks of God's being his shield and buckler, his rock and fortress, and delivering his *soul from death.*

11 Saul also sent messengers unto David's house, to watch him, and to slay him in the morning: and Michal David's wife told him, saying, If thou save not thy life to night, to

morrow thou shalt be slain. 12 So Michal let David down through a window: and he went, and fled, and escaped. 13 And Michal took an image, and laid *it* in the bed, and put a pillow of goats' *hair* for his bolster, and covered *it* with a cloth. 14 And when Saul sent messengers to take David, she said, He *is* sick. 15 And Saul sent the messengers *again* to see David, saying, Bring him up to me in the bed, that I may slay him. 16 And when the messengers were come in, behold, *there was* an image in the bed, with a pillow of goats' *hair* for his bolster. 17 And Saul said unto Michal, Why hast thou deceived me so, and sent away mine enemy, that he is escaped? And Michal answered Saul, He said unto me, Let me go; why should I kill thee?

Here is, I. Saul's further design of mischief to David. When David had escaped the javelin, supposing he went straight to his own house, as indeed he did, Saul sent some of his guards after him to lay wait at the door of his house, and to assassinate him in the morning as soon as he stirred out, *v.* 11. Josephus says the design was to seize him and to hurry him before a court of justice that was ordered to condemn him and put him to death as a traitor; but we are here told it was a shorter way they were to take with him: they were ordered to *slay him.* Well might David complain that his enemies were *bloody men,* as he did in the psalm which he penned at this time, and upon this occasion (Ps. lix.), when Saul sent, and they watched the house to kill him. See *v.* 2, 3, and 7. He complains that *swords were in their lips.*

II. David's wonderful deliverance out of this danger. Michal was the instrument of it, whom Saul gave him to be a snare to him, but she proved his protector and helper. Often is the devil out-shot with his own bow. How Michal came to know the danger her husband was in does not appear; perhaps she had notice sent her from court, or rather was herself aware of the soldiers about the house, when they were going to bed, though they kept so still and silent that they said, *Who does hear?* which David takes notice of, Ps. lix. 7. She, knowing her father's great indignation at David, soon suspected the design, and bestirred herself for her husband's safety. 1. She got David out of the danger. She told him how imminent the peril was (*v.* 11): *To-morrow thou wilt be slain.* As Josephus paraphrases it, she told him that if the sun saw him there next morning it would never see him more; and then put him in a way of escape. David himself was better versed in the art of fighting than of flying, and had it been lawful it would have been easy for him to have cleared his house, by dint of sword, from those that haunted it; but *Michal let him down through a window* (*v.* 12), all the doors being guarded; and so he *fled and escaped.* And now it was that, either in his own closet before he went or in the hiding-place to which he fled, he penned that fifty-ninth Psalm, which shows that, in his fright and hurry, his mind was composed, and, in this great danger, his faith was strong and fixed on God; and, whereas the plot was to slay him *in the morning,* he speaks there with the greatest assurance (*v.* 16), *I will sing aloud of thy mercy in the morning.* 2. She practised a deception upon Saul and those whom he employed to be the instruments of his cruelty. When the doors of the house were opened in the morning, and David did not appear, the messengers would search the house for him, and did so. But Michal told them he was sick in bed (*v.* 14), and, if they would not believe her, they might see, for (*v.* 13) she had put a wooden image in the bed, and wrapped it up close and warm as if it had been David asleep, not in a condition to be spoken to: the goats' hair about the image was to resemble David's hair, the better to impose upon them. Michal can by no means be justified in telling a lie, and covering it thus with a cheat. God's truth needed not her lie. But she intended hereby to keep Saul in suspense for a while, that David might have time to secure himself, not doubting but those messengers would pursue him if they found he had gone. The messengers had so much humanity as not to offer him any disturbance when they heard he was sick; for to those that are in this misery pity should be shown; but Saul, when he heard it, gave positive orders that he should be brought to him sick or well: *Bring him to me in the bed, that I may slay him, v.* 15. It was base and barbarous thus to triumph over a sick man; and to vow the death of one who for aught that he knew was dying by the hand of nature. So earnestly did he thirst after his blood, and so greedy was his revenge, that he could not be pleased to see him dead, unless he himself was the death of him; though awhile ago he had said, *Let not my hand be upon him.* Thus when men lay the reins on the neck of their passions they grow more and more outrageous. When the messengers were sent again, the cheat was discovered, *v.* 16. But by this time it was to be hoped that David was safe, and therefore Michal was not then much concerned at the discovery. Saul chid her for helping David to escape (*v.* 17): *Why hast thou deceived me so?* What a base spirit was Saul of, to expect that, because Michal was his daughter, she must therefore betray her own husband to him unjustly. Ought she not to forsake and forget her father and her father's house, to cleave to her husband? Those that themselves will be held by no bonds of reason or religion are ready to think that others should as easily break those bonds. In answer to Saul's chiding, Michal is not so careful of her husband's reputation as she had been of his person, when she makes this her excuse: *He said, Let me go, why should I kill thee?* As her insinuating that she would have hindered his flight was false (it was she that put him upon it and furthered it), so it was an unjust unworthy reflection upon him to suggest that he threatened to kill her if she would not let him go, and might confirm Saul in his rage against him. David was far from being so barbarous a man and so imperious a husband, so brutish in his resolves and so haughty in his menaces, as she here represented him. But David suffered both from friends and foes, and so did the son of David.

18 So David fled, and escaped, and came to Samuel to Ramah, and told him all that Saul had done to him. And he and Samuel went and dwelt in Naioth. 19 And it was told Saul, saying, Behold, David *is* at Naioth in Ramah. 20 And Saul sent messengers to take David: and when they saw the company of the prophets prophesying, and Samuel standing *as* appointed over them, the Spirit of God was upon the messengers of Saul, and they also prophesied. 21 And when it was told Saul, he sent other messengers, and they prophesied likewise. And Saul sent messengers again the third time, and they prophesied also. 22 Then went he also to Ramah, and came to a great well that *is* in Sechu: and he asked and said, Where *are* Samuel and David? And *one* said, Behold, *they be* at Naioth in Ramah. 23 And he went thither to Naioth in Ramah: and the Spirit of God was upon him also, and he went on, and prophesied, until he came to Naioth in Ramah. 24 And he stripped off his clothes also, and prophesied before Samuel in like manner, and lay down naked all that day and all that night. Wherefore they say, *Is* Saul also among the prophets?

Here is, I. David's place of refuge. Having got away in the night from his own house, he fled not to Bethlehem to his relations, nor to any of the cities of Israel that had caressed and cried him up, to make an interest in them for his own preservation; but he ran straight to Samuel and *told him all that Saul had done to him*, *v.* 18. 1. Because Samuel was the man that had given him assurance of the crown, and his faith in that assurance now beginning to fail, and he being ready to say in his haste (or *in his flight*, as some read it, Ps. cxvi. 11), *All men are liars* ("not only Saul that promised me my life, but Samuel himself that promised me the throne"), whither should he go but to Samuel, for such encouragements, in this day of distress, as would support his faith? In flying to Samuel he made God his refuge, trusting in the *shadow of his wings;* where else can a good man think himself safe? 2. Because Samuel, as a prophet, was best able to advise him what to do in this day of his distress. In the psalm he penned the night before he had lifted up his prayer to God, and now he takes the first opportunity of waiting upon Samuel to receive direction and instruction from God. If we expect answers of peace to our prayers, we must have our ears open to God's word. 3. Because with Samuel there was a college of prophets with whom he might join in praising God, and the pleasure of this exercise would be the greatest relief imaginable to him in his present distress. He met with little rest or satisfaction in Saul's court, and therefore went to seek it in Samuel's church. And, doubtless, what little pleasure is to be had in this world those have it that live a life of communion with God; to this David retired in the time of trouble, Ps. xxvii. 4—6.

II. David's protection in this place: *He and Samuel went and dwelt* (or *lodged*) *in Naioth,* where the school of the prophets was, in Ramah, as in a privileged place, for the Philistines themselves would not disturb that meeting, *ch.* x. 10. But Saul, having notice of it by some of his spies (*v.* 19), sent officers to seize David, *v.* 20. When they did not bring him he sent more; when they returned not he sent the third time (*v.* 21), and, hearing no tidings of these, he went himself, *v.* 22. So impatient was he in his thirst after David's blood, so restless to compass his design against him, that, though baffled by one providence after another, he could not perceive that David was under the special protection of Heaven. It was below the king to go himself on such an errand as this; but persecutors will stoop to any thing, and stick at nothing, to gratify their malice. Saul lays aside all public business to hunt David. How was David delivered, now that he was just ready to fall (like his own lamb formerly) into the mouth of the lions? Not as he delivered his lamb, by slaying the lion, or, as Elijah was delivered, by consuming the messengers with *fire from heaven*, but by turning the lions for the present into lambs.

1. When the messengers came into the congregation where David was among the prophets *the Spirit of God* came upon them, and *they prophesied*, that is, they joined with

the rest in praising God. Instead of seizing David, they themselves were seized. And thus, (1.) God secured David; for either they were put into such an ecstasy by the spirit of prophecy that they could not think of any thing else, and so forgot their errand and never minded David, or they were by it put, for the present, into so good a frame that they could not entertain the thought of doing so bad a thing. 2. He put an honour upon the sons of the prophets and the communion of saints, and showed how he can, when he pleases, strike an awe upon the worst of men, by the tokens of his presence in the assemblies of the faithful, and force them to acknowledge that *God is with them of a truth,* 1 Cor. xiv. 24, 25. See also the benefit of religious societies, and what good impressions may be made by them on minds that seemed unapt to receive such impressions. And where may the influences of the Spirit be expected but in the congregations of the saints? (3.) He magnified his power over the spirits of men. He that made the heart and tongue can manage both to serve his own purposes. Balaam prophesied the happiness of Israel, whom he would have cursed; and some of the Jewish writers think these messengers prophesied the advancement of David to the throne of Israel.

2. Saul himself was likewise seized with the spirit of prophecy before he came to the place. One would have thought that so bad a man as he was in no danger of being turned into a prophet; yet, when God will take this way of protecting David, even Saul has no sooner come (as bishop Hall expresses it) within smell of the smoke of Naioth but he prophesies, as his messengers did, *v.* 23. He stripped off his royal robe and warlike habiliments, because they were either too fine or too heavy for this service, and fell into a trance as it should seem, or into a rapture, which continued all that day and night. The saints at Damascus were delivered from the rage of the New-Testament Saul by a change wrought on his spirit, but of another nature from this. This was only amazing, but that sanctifying—this for a day, that for ever. Note, Many have great gifts and yet no grace, prophesy in Christ's name and yet are disowned by him, Matt. vii. 22, 23. Now the proverb recurs, *Is Saul among the prophets?* See *ch.* x. 12. Then it was different from what it had been, but now *contrary.* He is rejected of God, and actuated by an evil spirit, and yet among the prophets.

CHAP. XX.

David, having several times narrowly escaped Saul's fury, begins to consider at last whether it may not be necessary for him to retire into the country and to take up arms in his own defence. But he will not do so daring a thing without consulting his faithful friend Jonathan; how he did this, and what passed between them, we have an account in this chapter, where we have as surprising instances of supernatural love as we had in the chapter before of unnatural hatred. I. David complains to Jonathan of his present distress, and engages him to be his friend, ver. 1—8. II. Jonathan faithfully promises to get and give him intelligence how his father stood affected to him, and renews the covenant of friendship with him, ver. 9—23. III. Jonathan, upon trial, finds, to his grief, that his father was implacably enraged against David, ver. 24—34. IV. He gives David notice of this, according to the appointment between them, ver. 35—42.

AND David fled from Naioth in Ramah, and came and said before Jonathan, What have I done? what *is* mine iniquity? and what *is* my sin before thy father that he seeketh my life? 2 And he said unto him, God forbid; thou shalt not die: behold, my father will do nothing either great or small, but that he will show it me: and why should my father hide this thing from me? it *is* not *so.* 3 And David sware moreover, and said, Thy father certainly knoweth that I have found grace in thine eyes; and he saith, Let not Jonathan know this, lest he be grieved; but truly *as* the LORD liveth, and *as* thy soul liveth, *there is* but a step between me and death. 4 Then said Jonathan unto David, Whatsoever thy soul desireth, I will even do *it* for thee. 5 And David said unto Jonathan, Behold, to morrow *is* the new moon, and I should not fail to sit with the king at meat: but let me go, that I may hide myself in the field unto the third *day* at even. 6 If thy father at all miss me, then say, David earnestly asked *leave* of me that he might run to Beth-lehem his city: for *there is* a yearly sacrifice there for all the family. 7 If he say thus, *It is* well; thy servant shall have peace: but if he be very wroth, *then* be sure that evil is determined by him. 8 Therefore thou shalt deal kindly with thy servant; for thou hast brought thy servant into a covenant of the LORD with thee: notwithstanding, if there be in me iniquity, slay me thyself; for why shouldest thou bring me to thy father?

Here, I. David makes a representation to Jonathan of his present troubles. While Saul lay bound by his trance at Naioth David escaped to the court, and got to speak with Jonathan. And it was happy for him that he had such a friend at court, when he had such an enemy on the throne. If there be those that hate and despise us, let us not be disturbed at that, for there are those also that love and respect us. God hath set the one over against the other, and so must we. Jonathan was a friend that loved at all times, loved David as well now in his distress, and bade him as welcome into his arms, as he had done when he was in his triumph (*ch.* xviii. 1), and he was *a brother that was born for adversity,* Prov. xvii. 17. Now, 1. David appeals to Jonathan himself concerning his innocency, and he needed not say much to him for the proof of it, only he desired him that if he knew of any just offence he had given his father he would tell him, that he might humble himself and beg his pardon: *What have I done? v.* 1. 2. He endeavours to convince him that, notwithstanding his innocency, Saul sought his life. Jonathan, from a principle of filial respect to his father, was very loth to believe that he designed or would ever do so wicked a thing, *v.* 2. He the rather hoped so because he knew nothing of any such design, and he had usually been made privy to all his counsels. Jonathan, as became a dutiful son, endeavoured to cover his father's shame, as far as was consistent with justice and fidelity to David. Charity is not forward to think evil of any, especially of a parent, 1 Cor. xiii. 5. David therefore gives him the assurance of an oath concerning his own danger, swears the peace upon Saul, that he was in fear of his life by him: "*As the Lord liveth,* than which nothing more sure in itself, and as *thy soul liveth,* than which nothing more certain to thee, whatever thou thinkest, *there is but a step between me and death,*" *v.* 3. And, as for Saul's concealing it from Jonathan, it was easy to account for that; he knew the friendship between him and David, and therefore, though in other things he advised with him, yet not in that. None more fit than Jonathan to serve him in every design that was just and honourable, but he knew him to be a man of more virtue than to be his confidant in so base a design as the murder of David.

II. Jonathan generously offers him his service (*v.* 4): *Whatsoever thou desirest,* he needed not insert the proviso of lawful and honest (for he knew David too well to think he would ask any thing that was otherwise), *I will even do it for thee.* This is true friendship. Thus Christ testifies his love to us: *Ask, and it shall be done for you;* and we must testify ours to him by keeping his commandments.

III. David only desires him to satisfy himself, and then to satisfy him whether Saul did really design his death or no. Perhaps David proposed this more for Jonathan's conviction than his own, for he himself was well satisfied. 1. The method of trial he proposed was very natural, and would certainly discover how Saul stood affected to him. The two next days Saul was to dine publicly, upon occasion of the solemnities of the new moon, when extraordinary sacrifices were offered and feasts made upon the sacrifices. Saul was rejected of God, and the Spirit of the Lord had departed from him, yet he kept up his observance of the holy feasts. There may be the remains of external devotion where there is nothing but the ruins of real virtue. At these solemn feasts Saul had either all his children to sit with him, and David had a seat as one of them, or all his great officers, and David had a seat as one of *them.* However it was, David resolved his seat should be empty (and that it never used to be at a sacred feast) those two days (*v.* 5), and he would abscond till the solemnity was over, and put it upon this issue: if Saul admitted an excuse for his absence, and dispensed with it, he would conclude he had changed his mind and was reconciled to him; but if he resented it, and was put into a passion by it, it was easy to conclude he designed him a mischief, since it was certain he did not love him so well as to desire his presence for any other end than that he might have an opportunity to do him a mischief, *v.* 7. 2. The excuse he desired Jonathan to make for his absence, we have reason to think, was true, that he was invited by his elder brother to Bethlehem, his own city, to celebrate this new moon with his relations there, because, besides the monthly solemnity in which they held communion with all Israel, they had now a yearly sacrifice, and a holy feast upon it, for *all the family, v.* 6. They kept a day of thanksgiving in their family for the comforts they enjoyed, and of prayer for the continuance of them. By this it appears that the family David was of was a very religious family, a house that had a church in it. 3. The arguments he used with Jonathan to persuade him to do this kindness for him were very pressing, *v.* 8. (1.) That he had entered into a league of friendship with him, and it was Jonathan's own proposal: *Thou hast brought thy servant into a covenant of the Lord with thee.* (2.) That he would by no means urge him to espouse his cause if he was not sure that it was a righteous cause: "*If there be iniquity in me,* I am so far from desiring or expecting that the covenant between us should bind thee to be a confederate with me in that iniquity that I freely release thee from it, and wish that thy hand may be first upon me: *Slay me thyself.*" No honest man will urge his friend to do a dishonest thing for his sake.

9 And Jonathan said, Far be it from thee: for if I knew certainly that evil were determined by my father to come upon thee, then would not I tell it thee? 10 Then said David to Jonathan, Who shall tell me? or what *if* thy father answer thee roughly? 11 And Jonathan said unto David, Come, and let us go out into the field. And they went out both of them into the field. 12 And Jonathan said unto David, O LORD God of Israel, when I have sounded

my father about to morrow any time, *or* the third *day*, and, behold, *if there be* good toward David, and I then send not unto thee, and show it thee; 13 The LORD do so and much more to Jonathan: but if it please my father *to do* thee evil, then I will show it thee, and send thee away, that thou mayest go in peace: and the LORD be with thee, as he hath been with my father. 14 And thou shalt not only while yet I live show me the kindness of the LORD, that I die not: 15 But *also* thou shalt not cut off thy kindness from my house for ever: no, not when the LORD hath cut off the enemies of David every one from the face of the earth. 16 So Jonathan made *a covenant* with the house of David, *saying*, Let the LORD even require *it* at the hand of David's enemies. 17 And Jonathan caused David to swear again, because he loved him: for he loved him as he loved his own soul. 18 Then Jonathan said to David, To morrow *is* the new moon: and thou shalt be missed, because thy seat will be empty. 19 And *when* thou hast stayed three days, *then* thou shalt go down quickly, and come to the place where thou didst hide thyself when the business was *in hand*, and shalt remain by the stone Ezel. 20 And I will shoot three arrows on the side *thereof*, as though I shot at a mark. 21 And, behold, I will send a lad, *saying*, Go, find out the arrows. If I expressly say unto the lad, Behold, the arrows *are* on this side of thee, take them; then come thou: for *there is* peace to thee, and no hurt; *as* the LORD liveth. 22 But if I say thus unto the young man, Behold, the arrows *are* beyond thee; go thy way: for the LORD hath sent thee away. 23 And *as touching* the matter which thou and I have spoken of, behold, the LORD *be* between thee and me for ever.

Here, I. Jonathan protests his fidelity to David in his distress. Notwithstanding the strong confidence David had in Jonathan, yet, because he might have some reason to fear that his father's influence, and his own interest, should make him warp, or grow cool towards him, Jonathan thought it requisite solemnly to renew the professions of his friendship to him (*v.* 9): "*Far be it from thee* to think that I suspect thee of any crime for which I should either slay thee myself or deliver thee to my father; no, if thou hast any jealousy of that, *Come let us go into the field* (*v.* 11), and talk it over more fully." He did not challenge him to the field to fight him for an affront, but to fix him in his friendship. He faithfully promised him that he would let him know how, upon trial, he found his father affected towards him, and would make the matter neither better nor worse than it was. "If there be *good towards thee*, I will *show it thee*, that thou mayest be easy (*v.* 12), if evil, I will *send thee away*, that thou mayest be safe" (*v.* 13); and thus he would help to deliver him from the evil if it were real and from the fear of evil if it were but imaginary. For the confirmation of his promise he appeals to God, 1. As a witness (*v.* 12): "*O Lord God of Israel*, thou knowest I mean sincerely, and think as I speak." The strength of his passion made the manner of his speaking concise and abrupt. 2. As a judge: "*The Lord do so and much more to Jonathan* (*v.* 13), if I speak deceitfully, or break my word with my friend." He expressed himself thus solemnly that David might be abundantly assured of his sincerity. And thus God has confirmed his promises to us, that we might have *strong consolation*, Heb. vi. 17, 18. Jonathan adds to his protestations his hearty prayers: "*The Lord be with thee*, to protect and prosper thee, *as he has been* formerly *with my father*, though now he has withdrawn." Thus he intimates his belief that David would be in his father's place, and his good wishes that he might prosper in it better than his father now did.

II. He provides for the entail of the covenant of friendship with David upon his posterity, *v.* 14—16. He engages David to be a friend to his family when he was gone (*v.* 15): *Thou shalt* promise that thou wilt *not cut off thy kindness from my house for ever*. This he spoke from a natural affection he had to his children, whom he desired it might go well with after his decease, and for whose future welfare he desired to improve his present interest. It also intimates his firm belief of David's advancement, and that it would be in the power of his hand to do a kindness or unkindness to his seed; for, in process of time, *the Lord would cut off his enemies*, Saul himself not excepted; then "*Do not thou cut off thy kindness from my house*, nor revenge my father's wrongs upon my children." The house of David must likewise be bound to the house of Jonathan from generation to generation; he *made a covenant* (*v.* 16) *with the house of David*. Note, True friends cannot but covet to transmit to theirs after them their mutual affections. *Thy own friend, and thy father's friend, forsake not.* This kindness, 1. He calls *the kindness of the Lord,* because it is such kindness as God shows to those whom he takes into covenant with himself; for he is a God to them and to their seed; they are *beloved for the fathers' sakes.* 2. He secures it by an imprecation (*v.* 16): *The Lord require it at the hand of David's seed* (for of David himself he had no suspicion) if they prove so far David's enemies as to deal wrongfully with the posterity of Jonathan, David's friend. He feared lest David, or some of his, should hereafter be tempted, for the clearing and confirming of their title to the throne, to do by his seed as Abimelech had done by the sons of Gideon (Judg. ix. 5), and this he would effectually prevent; but the reason given (*v.* 17) why Jonathan was so earnest to have the friendship entailed is purely generous, and has nothing of self in it; it was because *he loved him as he loved his own soul,* and therefore desired that he and his might be beloved by him. David, though now in disgrace at court and in distress, was as amiable in the eyes of Jonathan as ever he had been, and he loved him never the less for his father's hating him, so pure were the principles on which his friendship was built. Having himself sworn to David, he caused David to swear to him, and (as we read it) *to swear again,* which David consented to (for he that bears an honest mind does not startle at assurances), to swear by his love to him, which he looked upon as a sacred thing. Jonathan's heart was so much upon it that, when they parted this time, he concluded with a solemn appeal to God: *The Lord be between me and thee for ever* (*v.* 23), that is, "God himself be judge between us and our families for ever, if on either side this league of friendship be violated." It was in remembrance of this covenant that David was kind to Mephibosheth, 2 Sam. ix. 7; xxi. 7. It will be a kindness to ourselves and ours to secure an interest in those whom God favours and to make his friends ours.

III. He settles the method of intelligence, and by what signs and tokens he would give him notice how his father stood affected towards him. David would be missed the first day, or at least the second day, of the new moon, and would be enquired after, *v.* 18. On the third day, by which time he would have returned from Bethlehem, he must be at such a place (*v.* 19), and Jonathan would come towards that place with his bow and arrows to shoot for diversion (*v.* 20), would send his lad to fetch his arrows, and, if they were shot short of the lad, David must take it for a signal of safety, and not be afraid to show his head (*v.* 21); but, if he shot beyond the lad, it was a signal of danger, and he must shift for his safety, *v.* 22. This expedient he fixed lest he should not have the opportunity, which yet it proved he had, of talking with David, and making the report by word of mouth.

24 So David hid himself in the field: and when the new moon was come, the king sat him down to eat meat. 25 And the king sat upon his seat, as at other times, *even* upon a seat by the wall: and Jonathan arose, and Abner sat by Saul's side, and David's place was empty. 26 Nevertheless Saul spake not any thing that day: for he thought, Something hath befallen him, he *is* not clean: surely he *is* not clean. 27 And it came to pass on the morrow, *which was* the second *day* of the month, that David's place was empty: and Saul said unto Jonathan his son, Wherefore cometh not the son of Jesse to meat, neither yesterday, nor to day? 28 And Jonathan answered Saul, David earnestly asked *leave* of me *to go* to Beth-lehem: 29 And he said, Let me go, I pray thee; for our family hath a sacrifice in the city; and my brother, he hath commanded me *to be there:* and now, if I have found favour in thine eyes, let me get away, I pray thee, and see my brethren. Therefore he cometh not unto the king's table. 30 Then Saul's anger was kindled against Jonathan, and he said unto him, Thou son of the perverse rebellious *woman,* do not I know that thou hast chosen the son of Jesse to thine own confusion, and unto the confusion of my mother's nakedness? 31 For as long as the son of Jesse liveth upon the ground, thou shalt not be established, nor thy kingdom. Wherefore now send and fetch him unto me, for he shall surely die. 32 And Jonathan answered Saul his father, and said unto him, Wherefore shall he be slain? what hath he done? 33 And Saul cast a javelin at him to smite him: whereby Jonathan knew that it was determined of his father to slay David. 34 So Jonathan arose from the table in fierce anger, and did eat no meat the second day of the month: for he was grieved for David, because his father had done him shame.

Jonathan is here effectually convinced of that which he was so loth to believe, that his father had an implacable enmity to David, and would certainly be the death of him if it were in his power; and he had like to have paid very dearly himself for the conviction.

I. David is missed from the feast on the first day, but nothing is said of him. *The king sat upon his seat*, to feast upon the peace-offerings *as at other times* (*v.* 25), and yet had his heart as full of envy and malice against David as it could hold. He should first have been reconciled to him, and then have come and offered his gift; but, instead of that, he hoped, at this feast, to drink the blood of David. What an abomination was that sacrifice which was brought with such a wicked mind as this! Prov. xxi. 27. When the king came to take his seat Jonathan arose, in reverence to him both as a father and as his sovereign; every one knew his place, but David's was empty. It did not use to be so. None more constant than he in attending holy duties; nor had he been absent now but that he must have come at the peril of his life; self-preservation obliged him to withdraw. In imminent peril present opportunities may be waived, nay, we ought not to throw ourselves into the mouth of danger. Christ himself absconded often, till he knew that his hour had come. But that day Saul took no notice that he missed David, but said within himself, "*Surely he is not clean*, *v.* 26. Some ceremonial pollution has befallen him, which forbids him to eat of the holy things till he has *washed his clothes, and bathed his flesh in water, and been unclean until the evening*." Saul knew what conscience David made of the law, and that he would rather keep away from the holy feast than come in his uncleanness. Blessed be God, no uncleanness is now a restraint upon us, but what we may by faith and repentance be washed from in the fountain opened, Ps. xxvi. 6.

II. He is enquired for the second day, *v.* 27. Saul asked Jonathan, who he knew was his confidant, *Wherefore cometh not the son of Jesse to meat?* He was his own son by marriage, but he calls him in disdain, *the son of Jesse*. He asks for him as if he were not pleased that he should be absent from a religious feast; and so it should be an example to masters of families to see to it that those under their charge be not absent from the worship of God, either in public or in the family. It is a bad thing for us, except in case of necessity, to omit any opportunity of statedly attending on God in solemn ordinances. Thomas lost a sight of Christ by being once absent from a meeting of the disciples. But that which displeased Saul was that hereby he missed the opportunity he expected of doing David a mischief.

III. Jonathan makes his excuse, *v.* 28, 29. 1. That he was absent upon a good occasion, keeping the feast in another place, though not here, sent for by his elder brother, who was now more respectful to him than he had been (*ch.* xvii. 28), and that he had gone to pay his respects to his relations, for the keeping up of brotherly love; and no master would deny a servant liberty to do that in due time. He pleads, 2. That he did not go without leave humbly asked and obtained from Jonathan, who, as his superior officer, was proper to be applied to for it. Thus he represents David as not wanting in any instance of respect and duty to the government.

IV. Saul hereupon breaks out into a most extravagant passion, and rages like a lion disappointed of his prey. David was out of his reach, but he falls upon Jonathan for his sake (*v.* 30, 31), gives him base language, not fit for a gentleman, a prince, to give to any man, especially his own son, heir apparent to his crown, a son that served him, the greatest stay and ornament of his family, before a great deal of company, at a feast, when all should be in good humour, at a sacred feast, by which all irregular passions should be mortified and subdued; yet he does in effect call him, 1. A bastard: *Thou son of the perverse rebellious woman;* that is, according to the foolish filthy language of men's brutish passion now a day, "Thou son of a whore." He tells him he was born *to the confusion of his mother*, that is, he had given the world cause to suspect that he was not the legitimate son of Saul, because he loved him whom Saul hated and supported him who would be the destruction of their family. 2. A traitor: *Thou son of perverse rebellion* (so the word is), that is, "thou perverse rebel." At other times he reckoned no counsellor or commander that he had more trusty and well-beloved than Jonathan; yet now in this passion he represents him as dangerous to his crown and life. 3. A fool: *Thou hast chosen the son of Jesse* for thy friend *to thy own confusion*, for while he lives *thou shalt never be established*. Jonathan indeed did wisely and well for himself and family to secure an interest in David, whom Heaven had destined to the throne, yet, for this, he is branded as most impolitic. It is good taking God's people for our people and going with those that have him with them. It will prove to our advantage at last, however for the present it may be thought a disparagement, and a prejudice to our secular interest. It is probable Saul knew that David was anointed to the kingdom by the same hand that anointed him, and then not Jonathan, but himself, was the fool, to think to defeat the counsels of God. Yet nothing will serve him but David must die, and Jonathan must fetch him to execution. See how ill Saul's passion looks, and let it warn us against the indulgence of any thing like it in ourselves. Anger is madness, and *he that hates his brother is a murderer.*

V. Jonathan is sorely grieved and put into disorder by his father's barbarous passion, and the more because he had hoped better things, *v.* 2. He was troubled for his father, that he should be such a brute, troubled for his friend, whom he knew to be a friend of God, that he should be so basely abused; he was *grieved for David* (*v.* 34), and troubled for himself too, because *his father had done him shame,* and, though most unjustly, yet he must submit to it. One would pity Jonathan to see how he was put, 1. Into the peril of sin. Much ado that wise and good man had to keep his temper, upon such a provocation as this. His father's reflections upon himself he made no return to; it becomes inferiors to bear with meekness and silence the contempts put upon them in wrath and passion. *When thou art the anvil lie thou still.* But his dooming David to die he could not bear: to that he replied with some heat (*v.* 32), *Wherefore shall he be slain? What has he done?* Generous spirits can much more easily bear to be abused themselves than to hear their friends abused. 2. Into the peril of death. Saul was now so outrageous that he threw his javelin at Jonathan, *v.* 33. He seemed to be in great care (*v.* 31) that Jonathan should be established in his kingdom, and yet now he himself aims at his life. What fools, what savage beasts and worse does anger make men! How necessary is it to put a hook in its nose and a bridle in its jaws! Jonathan was fully satisfied that evil was determined against David, which put him out of frame exceedingly: he *rose from table,* thinking it high time when his life was struck at, and *would eat no meat,* for they were not to eat of the holy things in their mourning. All the guests, we may suppose, were discomposed, and the mirth of the feast was spoiled. *He that is cruel troubles his own flesh,* Prov. xi. 17.

35 And it came to pass in the morning, that Jonathan went out into the field at the time appointed with David, and a little lad with him. 36 And he said unto his lad, Run, find out now the arrows which I shoot. *And* as the lad ran, he shot an arrow beyond him. 37 And when the lad was come to the place of the arrow which Jonathan had shot, Jonathan cried after the lad, and said, *Is* not the arrow beyond thee? 38 And Jonathan cried after the lad, Make speed, haste. stay not. And Jonathan's lad gathered up the arrows, and came to nis master. 39 But the lad knew not any thing: only Jonathan and David knew the matter. 40 And Jonathan gave his artillery unto his lad, and said unto him, Go, carry *them* to the city. 41 *And* as soon as the lad was gone, David arose out of *a place* toward the south, and fell on his face to the ground, and bowed himself three times: and they kissed one another, and wept one with another, until David exceeded. 42 And Jonathan said to David, Go in peace, forasmuch as we have sworn both of us in the name of the LORD, saying, The LORD be between me and thee, and between my seed and thy seed for ever. And he arose and departed: and Jonathan went into the city.

Here is, 1. Jonathan's faithful performance of his promise to give David notice of the success of his dangerous experiment. He went at the time and to the place appointed (*v.* 35), within sight of which he knew David lay hid, sent his footboy to fetch his arrows, which he would shoot at random (*v.* 36), and gave David the fatal signal by shooting an arrow beyond the lad (*v.* 37): *Is not the arrow beyond thee?* That word [*beyond*] David knew the meaning of better than the lad. Jonathan dismissed the lad, who knew nothing of the matter, and, finding the coast clear and no danger of a discovery, he presumed upon one minute's personal conversation with David after he had bidden him flee for his life. 2. The most sorrowful parting of these two friends, who, for aught that appears, never came together again but once, and that was by stealth *in a wood, ch.* xxiii. 16. (1.) David addressed himself to Jonathan with the reverence of a servant rather than the freedom of a friend: *He fell on his face to the ground, and bowed himself three times,* as one deeply sensible of his obligations to him for the good services he had done him. (2.) They took leave of each other with the greatest affection imaginable, with kisses and tears; they wept on each other's neck *till David exceeded, v.* 41. The separation of two such faithful friends was equally grievous to them both, but David's case was the more deplorable; for, when Jonathan was returning to his family and friends, David was leaving all his comforts, even those of God's sanctuary, and therefore his grief exceeded Jonathan's, or perhaps it was because his temper was more tender and his passions were stronger. (3.) They referred themselves to the covenant of friendship that was between them, both of them comforting themselves with this in this mournful separation: "*We have sworn both of us in the name of the Lord,* for ourselves and our heirs, that we and they will be faithful and kind to each other from generation to generation." Thus, while we are at home in the body and absent from the Lord, this is our comfort, that he has *made with us an everlasting covenant.*

CHAP. XXI.

David has now quite taken leave both of Saul's court and of his camp, has bidden farewell to his alter idem—his other self, the beloved Jonathan; and henceforward to the end of this book he is looked upon and treated as an outlaw and proclaimed a traitor.

We still find him shifting from place to place for his own safety, and Saul pursuing him. His troubles are very particularly related in this and the following chapters, not only to be a key to the Psalms, but that he might be, as other prophets, an example to the saints in all ages, "of suffering affliction, and of patience," and especially that he might be a type of Christ, who, being anointed to the kingdom, humbled himself, and was therefore highly exalted. But the example of the suffering Jesus was a copy without a blot, that of David was not so; witness the records of this chapter, where we find David in his flight, I. Imposing upon Ahimelech the priest, to get from him both victuals and arms, ver. 1—9. II. Imposing upon Achish, king of Gath, by feigning himself mad, ver. 10—15. Justly are troubles called temptations, for many are by them drawn into sin.

THEN came David to Nob, to Ahimelech the priest: and Ahimelech was afraid at the meeting of David, and said unto him, Why *art* thou alone, and no man with thee? 2 And David said unto Ahimelech the priest, The king hath commanded me a business, and hath said unto me, Let no man know any thing of the business whereabout I send thee, and what I have commanded thee: and I have appointed *my* servants to such and such a place. 3 Now therefore what is under thine hand? give *me* five *loaves of* bread in mine hand, or what there is present. 4 And the priest answered David, and said, *There is* no common bread under mine hand, but there is hallowed bread; if the young men have kept themselves at least from women. 5 And David answered the priest, and said unto him, Of a truth women *have been* kept from us about these three days, since I came out, and the vessels of the young men are holy, and *the bread is* in a manner common, yea, though it were sanctified this day in the vessel. 6 So the priest gave him hallowed *bread:* for there was no bread there but the showbread, that was taken from before the LORD, to put hot bread in the day when it was taken away. 7 Now a certain man of the servants of Saul *was* there that day, detained before the LORD; and his name *was* Doeg, an Edomite, the chiefest of the herdmen that *belonged* to Saul. 8 And David said unto Ahimelech, And is there not here under thine hand spear or sword? for I have neither brought my sword nor my weapons with me, because the king's business required haste. 9 And the priest said, The sword of Goliath the Philistine, whom thou slewest in the valley of Elah, behold, it *is here* wrapped in a cloth behind the ephod: if thou wilt take that, take *it:* for *there is* no other save that here. And David said, *There is* none like that; give it me.

Here, I. David, in distress, flies to the tabernacle of God, now pitched at Nob, supposed to be a city in the tribe of Benjamin. Since Shiloh was forsaken, the tabernacle was often removed, though the ark still remained at Kirjath-jearim. Hither David came in his flight from Saul's fury (*v.* 1), and applied to Ahimelech the priest. Samuel the prophet could not protect him, Jonathan the prince could not. He therefore has recourse next to Ahimelech the priest. He foresees he must now be an exile, and therefore comes to the tabernacle, 1. To take an affecting leave of it, for he knows not when he shall see it again, and nothing will be more afflictive to him in his banishment than his distance from the house of God, and his restraint from public ordinances, as appears by many of his psalms. He had given an affectionate farewell to his friend Jonathan, and cannot go till he has given the like to the tabernacle. 2. To enquire of the Lord there, and to beg direction from him in the way both of duty and safety, his case being difficult and dangerous. That this was his business appears *ch.* xxii. 10, where it is said that *Ahimelech enquired of the Lord for him,* as he had done formerly, *v.* 15. It is a great comfort to us in a day of trouble that we have a God to go to, to whom we may open our case, and from whom we may ask and expect direction.

II. Ahimelech the priest is surprised to see him in so poor an equipage; having heard that he had fallen into disgrace at court, he looked shy upon him, as most are apt to do upon their friends when the world frowns upon them. He was afraid of incurring Saul's displeasure by entertaining him, and took notice how mean a figure he now made to what he used to make: *Why art thou alone?* He had some with him (as appears Mark ii. 26), but they were only his own servants; he had none of the courtiers, no persons of quality with him, as he used to have at other times, when he came to enquire of the Lord. He says (Ps. xlii. 4) he was wont to *go with a multitude to the house of God;* and, having now but two or three with him, Ahimelech might well ask, *Why art thou alone?* He that was suddenly advanced from the solitude of a shepherd's life to the crowds and hurries of the camp is now as soon reduced to the desolate condition of an exile and is *alone like a sparrow on the house-top,* such changes are there in this world and so uncertain are its smiles! Those that are courted to-day may be deserted to-morrow.

III. David, under pretence of being sent

by Saul upon public services, solicits Ahimelech to supply his present wants, *v.* 2, 3.

1. Here David did not behave like himself. He told Ahimelech a gross untruth, that Saul had ordered him business to despatch, that his attendants were dismissed to such a place, and that he was charged to observe secresy and therefore durst not communicate it, no, not to the priest himself. This was all false. What shall we say to this? The scripture does not conceal it, and we dare not justify it. It was ill done, and proved of bad consequence; for it *occasioned the death of the priests of the Lord,* as David reflected upon it afterwards with regret, *ch.* xxii. 22. It was needless for him thus to dissemble with the priest, for we may suppose that, if he had told him the truth, he would have sheltered and relieved him as readily as Samuel did, and would have known the better how to advise him and enquire of God for him. People should be free with their faithful ministers. David was a man of great faith and courage, and yet now both failed him, and he fell thus foully through fear and cowardice, and both owing to the weakness of his faith. Had he trusted God aright, he would not have used such a sorry sinful shift as this for his own preservation. It is written, not for our imitation, no, not in the greatest straits, but for our admonition. *Let him that thinks he stands take heed lest he fall;* and let us all pray daily, *Lord, lead us not into temptation.* Let us all take occasion from this to lament, (1.) The weakness and infirmity of good men; the best are not perfect on this side heaven. There may be true grace where yet there are many failings. (2.) The wickedness of bad times, which forces good men into such straits as prove temptations too strong for them. Oppression makes a wise man do foolishly.

2. Two things David begged of Ahimelech, *bread* and a *sword.*

(1.) He wanted bread: *Five loaves, v.* 3. Travelling was then troublesome, when men generally carried their provisions with them in kind, having little money and no public houses, else David would not now have had to seek for bread. It seems David had known the *seed of the righteous begging bread* occasionally, but not constantly, Ps. xxxvii. 25. Now, [1.] The priest objected that he had none but hallowed bread, *show-bread,* which had stood a week on the golden table in the sanctuary, and was taken thence for the use of the priests and their families, *v.* 4. It seems the priest kept no good house, but wanted either a heart to be hospitable or provisions wherewithal to be so. Ahimelech thinks that the young men that attended David might not eat of this bread unless they had for some time abstained from women, even from their own wives; this was required at the *giving of the law* (Exod. xix. 15), but otherwise we never find this made the matter of any ceremonial purity on the one side or pollution on the other, and therefore the priest here seems to be over-nice, not to say superstitious. [2.] David pleads that he and those that were with him, in this case of necessity, might lawfully eat of the hallowed bread, for they were not only able to answer his terms of keeping from women for three days past, but *the vessels* (that is, the bodies) *of the young men were holy,* being *possessed in sanctification and honour at all times* (1 Thess. iv. 4, 5), and therefore God would take particular care of them, that they wanted not necessary supports, and would have his priest to do so. Being thus holy, holy things were not forbidden to them. Poor and pious Israelites were in effect priests to God, and, rather than be starved, might feed on the bread which was appropriated to the priests. Believers are spiritual priests, and the offerings of the Lord shall be their inheritance; they eat the bread of their God. He pleads that the bread is in a manner common, now that what was primarily the religious use of it is over; especially (as our margin reads it) *when there is other bread (hot, v. 6) sanctified this day in the vessel,* and put in the room of it upon the table. This was David's plea, and the Son of David approves it, and shows from it that mercy is to be preferred to sacrifice, that ritual observances must give way to moral duties, and that that may be done in a case of an urgent providential necessity which may not otherwise be done. He brings it to justify his disciples in plucking the ears of corn on the sabbath day, for which the Pharisees censured them, Matt. xii. 3, 4. [3.] Ahimelech hereupon supplies him: *He gave him hallowed bread* (*v.* 6), and some think it was about this that *he enquired of the Lord, ch.* xxii. 10. As a faithful servant he would not dispose of his master's provisions without his master's leave. This bread, we may suppose, was the more agreeable to David for its being hallowed, so precious were all sacred things to him. The show-bread was but twelve loaves in all, yet out of these he gave David five (*v.* 3), though they had no more in the house; but he trusted Providence.

(2.) He wanted a sword. Persons of quality, though officers of the army, did not then wear their swords so constantly as now they do, else surely David would not have been without one. It was a wonder that Jonathan did not furnish him with his, as he had before done, *ch.* xviii. 4. However, it happened that he had now no weapons with him, the reason of which he pretends to be because he came away in haste, *v.* 8. Those that are furnished with the sword of the Spirit and the shield of faith cannot be disarmed of them, nor need they, at any time, to be at a loss. But the priests, it seems, had no swords: the weapons of their warfare were not carnal. There was not a sword to be found about the tabernacle but the sword of Goliath, which was laid up behind the ephod, as a monument of the glorious victory David obtained over him. Probably David had an eye to that when he asked the priest to help him with a sword; for, that being mentioned, O! says he, *there is none like that, give it to me, v.* 9. He could not use Saul's armour, for he had not proved it; but this sword of Goliath he had made trial of and done execution with. By this it appears that he was now well grown in strength and stature, that he could wear and wield such a sword as that. God had *taught his hands to war,* so that he could do wonders, Ps. xviii. 34. Two things we may observe concerning this sword:—[1.] That God had graciously given it to him, as a pledge of his singular favour; so that whenever he drew it, nay, whenever he looked upon it, it would be a great support to his faith, by bringing to mind that great instance of the particular care and countenance of the divine providence respecting him. Experiences are great encouragements. [2.] That he had gratefully given it back to God, dedicating it to him and to his honour as a token of his thankfulness; and now in his distress it stood him greatly in stead. Note, What we devote to God's praise, and serve him with, is most likely to redound, one way or other, to our own comfort and benefit. What we gave we have.

Thus was David well furnished with arms and victuals; but it fell out very unhappily that there was one of Saul's servants then attending before the Lord, *Doeg* by name, that proved a base traitor both to David and to Ahimelech. He was by birth an Edomite (*v.* 7), and though proselyted to the Jewish religion, to get the preferment he now had under Saul, yet he retained the ancient and hereditary enmity of Edom to Israel. He was master of the herds, which perhaps was then a place of as much honour as master of the horse is now. Some occasion or other he had at this time to wait on the priest, either to be purified from some pollution or to pay some vow; but, whatever his business was, it is said, he was *detained before the Lord.* He must attend and could not help it, but he was sick of the service, *snuffed at it, and said, What a weariness is it!* Mal. i. 13. He would rather have been any where else than before the Lord, and therefore, instead of minding the business he came about, was plotting to do David a mischief and to be revenged on Ahimelech for detaining him. God's sanctuary could never secure itself from such wolves in sheep's clothing. See Gal. ii. 4.

10 And David arose, and fled that day for fear of Saul, and went to Achish the king of Gath. 11 And the servants of Achish said unto him, *Is* not this David the king of the land? did they not sing one to another of him in dances, saying, Saul hath slain his thousands, and David his ten thousands? 12 And David laid up these words in his heart, and was sore afraid of Achish the king of Gath. 13 And he changed his behaviour before them, and feigned himself mad in their hands, and scrabbled on the doors of the gate, and let his spittle fall down upon his beard. 14 Then said Achish unto his servants, Lo, ye see the man is mad: wherefore *then* have ye brought him to me? 15 Have I need of mad men, that ye have brought this *fellow* to play the mad man in my presence? shall this *fellow* come into my house?

David, though king elect, is here an exile—designed to be master of vast treasures, yet just now begging his bread—anointed to the crown, and yet here forced to flee from his country. Thus do God's providences sometimes seem to run counter to his promises, for the trial of his people's faith, and the glorifying of his name, in the accomplishment of his counsels, notwithstanding the difficulties that lay in the way. Here is, 1. David's flight into the land of the Philistines, where he hoped to be hid, and to remain undiscovered in the court or camp of Achish king of Gath, *v.* 10. Israel's darling is necessitated to quit the land of Israel, and he that was the Philistine's great enemy (upon I know not what inducements) goes to seek for shelter among them. It should seem that as, though the Israelites loved him, yet the king of Israel had a personal enmity to him, which obliged him to leave his own country, so, though the Philistines hated him, yet the king of Gath had a personal kindness for him, valuing his merit, and perhaps the more for his killing Goliath of Gath, who, it may be, had been no friend to Achish. To him David now went directly, as to one he could confide in, as afterwards (*ch.* xxvii. 2, 3), and Achish would now have protected him but that he was afraid of disobliging his own people. God's persecuted people have often found better usage from Philistines than from Israelites, in the Gentile theatres than in the Jewish synagogues. The king of Judah imprisoned Jeremiah, and the king of Babylon set him at liberty. 2. The disgust which the servants of Achish took at his being there, and their complaint of it to Achish (*v.* 11): "*Is not this David?* Is not this he that has triumphed over the Philistines? witness that burden of the song which was so much talked of, *Saul has slain his thousands,* but *David,* this very man, *his ten thousands.* Nay, Is not this he that (if our intelligence from the land of Israel be true) is, or is to be, *king of the land?*" As such, he must be an enemy to our country; and is it safe or honourable for us to protect or entertain such a man?" Achish perhaps had intimated to them that it would be policy to entertain David, because he was now an enemy to Saul, and he might be hereafter a friend to them. It is common for the outlaws of a nation to be sheltered by the enemies of that nation. But the servants of Achish objected to his politics, and thought it not at all fit that he should stay among them. 3. The fright which this put David into. Though he had some reason to put confidence in Achish, yet, when he perceived the servants of Achish jealous of him, he began to be afraid that Achish would be obliged to deliver him up to them, and he was *sorely afraid* (*v.* 12), and perhaps he was the more apprehensive of his own danger, when he was thus discovered, because he wore Goliath's sword, which, we may suppose, was well known in Gath, and with which he had reason to expect they would cut off his head, as he had cut off Goliath's with it. David now learned by experience what he has taught us (Ps. cxviii. 9), *that it is better to trust in the Lord than to put confidence in princes.* Men of high degree are a lie, and, if we make them our hope, they may prove our fear. It was at this time that David penned Psalm lv. (*Michtam, a golden psalm*), *when the Philistines took him in Gath,* where having shown before God his distresses, he resolves (*v.* 3), "*What time I am afraid I will trust in thee;* and therefore (*v.* 11) *will not be afraid what man can do unto me,* no, not the sons of the giant." 4. The course he took to get out of their hands: *He feigned himself mad, v.* 13. He used the gestures and fashions of a natural fool, or one that had gone out of his wits, supposing they would be ready enough to believe that the disgrace he had fallen into, and the troubles he was now in, had driven him distracted. This dissimulation of his cannot be justified (it was a mean thing thus to disparage himself, and inconsistent with truth thus to misrepresent himself, and therefore not becoming the honour and sincerity of such a man as David); yet it may in some degree be excused, for it was not a downright lie and it was like a stratagem in war, by which he imposed upon his enemies for the preservation of his own life. What David did here in pretence and for his own safety, which made it partly excusable, drunkards do really, and only to gratify a base lust: they make fools of themselves and change their behaviour; their words and actions commonly are either as silly and ridiculous as an idiot's or as furious and outrageous as a madman's, which has often made me wonder that ever men of sense and honour should allow themselves in it. 5. His escape by this means, *v.* 14, 15. I am apt to think Achish was aware that the delirium was but counterfeit, but, being desirous to protect David (as we find afterwards he was very kind to him, even when the lords of the Philistines favoured him not, *ch.* xxviii. 1, 2; xxix. 6), he pretended to his servants that he really thought he was mad, and therefore had reason to question whether it was David or no; or, if it were, they need not fear him, what harm could he do them now that his reason had departed from him? They suspected that Achish was inclined to entertain him: "Not I," says he. "He is a madman. I'll have nothing to do with him. You need not fear that I should employ him, or give him any countenance. He humours the thing well enough when he asks, "*Have I need of madmen? Shall this fool come into my house?* I will show him no kindness, but then you shall do him no hurt, for, if he be a madman, he is to be pitied." He therefore *drove him away,* as it is in the title of Ps. xxxiv, which David penned upon this occasion, and an excellent psalm it is, and shows that he did not change his spirit when he changed his behaviour, but even in the greatest difficulties and hurries his *heart was fixed,* trusting in the Lord; and he concludes that psalm with this assurance, that *none of those that trust in God shall be desolate,* though they may be, as he now was, solitary and distressed, *persecuted, but not forsaken.*

CHAP. XXII.

David, being driven from Achish, returns into the land of Israel to be hunted by Saul. I. David sets up his standard in the cave of Adullam, entertains his relations (ver. 1), enlists soldiers (ver. 2), but removes his aged parents to a more quiet settlement (ver. 3, 4), and has the prophet Gad for his counsellor, ver. 5. Saul resolves to pursue him and find him out, complains of his servants and Jonathan (ver 6—8), and, finding by Doeg's information that Ahimelech had been kind to David, he ordered him and all the priests that were with him, eighty-five in all, to be put to death, and all that belonged to them destroyed (ver. 9—19) from the barbarous execution of which sentence Abiathar escaped to David, ver. 20—23.

DAVID therefore departed thence, and escaped to the cave Adullam: and when his brethren and all his father's house heard *it,* they went down thither to him. 2 And every one *that was* in distress, and every one that *was* in debt, and every one *that was* discontented, gathered themselves unto him; and he became a captain over them: and there were with him about four hundred men. 3 And David went thence to Mizpeh of Moab: and he said unto the king of Moab, Let my father and my mother, I pray thee, come forth, *and be* with you, till I know what God will do for me. 4 And he brought them before the king of Moab: and they dwelt with him all the while that David was in the hold. 5 And the prophet Gad said unto David, Abide not in the hold; depart, and get thee into the land of Judah. Then David departed, and came into the forest of Hareth.

Here, I. David shelters himself in the cave of Adullam, *v.* 1. Whether it was a natural or artificial fastness does not appear; it is probable that the access to it was so difficult that David thought himself able, with Goliath's sword, to keep it against all the forces of Saul, and therefore buried himself alive in it, while he was waiting to see (as he says here, *v.* 3) what God would do with him. The promise of the kingdom implied a promise of preservation to it, and yet David used proper means for his own safety, otherwise he would have tempted God. He did not do any thing that aimed to destroy Saul, but only to secure himself. He that might have done great service to his country as a judge or general is here shut up in a cave, and thrown by as a vessel in which there was no pleasure. We must not think it strange if sometimes shining lights be thus eclipsed and hidden under a bushel. Perhaps the apostle refers to this instance of David, among others, when he speaks of some of the Old-Testament worthies that *wandered in deserts, in dens and caves of the earth,* Heb. xi. 38. It was at this time that David penned Psalm cxlii., which is entitled, *A prayer when David was in the cave;* and there he complains that *no man would know him* and that refuge failed him, but hopes that shortly the *righteous would compass him about.*

II. Thither his relations flocked to him, *his brethren and all his father's house,* to be protected by him, to give assistance to him, and to take their lot with him. *A brother is born for adversity.* Now Joab, and Abishai, and the rest of his relations, came to him, to suffer and venture with him, in hopes shortly to be advanced with him; and they were so. The first three of his worthies were those that first owned him when he was in the cave, 1 Chron. xi. 15, &c.

III. Here he began to raise forces in his own defence, *v.* 2. He found by the late experiments he had made that he could not save himself by flight, and therefore was necessitated to do it by force, wherein he never acted offensively, never offered any violence to his prince nor gave any disturbance to the peace of the kingdom, but only used his forces as a guard to his own person. But, whatever defence his soldiers were to him, they did him no great credit, for the regiment he had was made up not of great men, nor rich men, nor stout men, no, nor good men, but men *in distress, in debt, and discontented,* men of broken fortunes and restless spirits, that were put to their shifts, and knew not well what to do with themselves. When David had fixed his head-quarters in the cave of Adullam, they came and enlisted themselves under him to the number of about 400. See what weak instruments God sometimes makes use of, by which to bring about his own purposes. The Son of David is ready to receive distressed souls, that will appoint him their captain and be commanded by him.

IV. He took care to settle his parents in a place of safety. No such place could he find in all the land of Israel while Saul was so bitterly enraged against him and all that belonged to him for his sake; he therefore goes with them to the king of Moab, and puts them under his protection, *v.* 3, 4. Observe here, 1. With what a tender concern he provided for his aged parents. It was not fit they should be exposed either to the frights or to the fatigues which he must expect during his struggle with Saul (their age would by no means bear such exposure); therefore the first thing he does is to find them a quiet habitation, whatever became of himself. Let children learn from this to *show piety at home and requite their parents* (1 Tim. v. 4), in every thing consulting their ease and satisfaction. Though ever so highly preferred, and ever so much employed, let them not forget their aged parents. 2. With what a humble faith he expects the issue of his present distresses: *Till I know what God will do for me.* He expresses his hopes very modestly, as one that had entirely cast himself upon God and committed his way to him, expecting a good issue, not from his own arts, or arms, or merits, but from what the wisdom, power, and goodness of God would do for him. Now David's father and mother forsook him, but God did not, Ps. xxvii. 10.

V. He had the advice and assistance of the prophet Gad, who probably was one of the sons of the prophets that were brought up under Samuel, and was by him recommended to David for his chaplain or spiritual guide. Being a prophet, he would pray for him and instruct him in the mind of God; and David, though he was himself a prophet, was glad of his assistance. He advised him to go into the land of Judah (*v.* 5), as one that was confident of his own innocency, and was well assured of the divine protection, and was desirous, even in his present hard circumstances, to do some service to his tribe and country. Let him not be ashamed to own his own cause nor decline the succours that would be offered him. Animated by this word, there he determined to appear publicly. Thus are *the steps of a good man ordered by the Lord.*

6 When Saul heard that David was discovered, and the men that *were* with him, (now Saul abode in Gibeah under a tree in Ramah, having his spear in his hand, and all his servants *were* standing about him;) 7 Then Saul said unto his servants that stood about him, Hear now, ye Benjamites; will the son of Jesse give

every one of you fields and vineyards, *and* make you all captains of thousands, and captains of hundreds; 8 That all of you have conspired against me, and *there is* none that showeth me that my son hath made a league with the son of Jesse, and *there is* none of you that is sorry for me, or showeth unto me that my son hath stirred up my servant against me, to lie in wait, as at this day? 9 Then answered Doeg the Edomite, which was set over the servants of Saul, and said, I saw the son of Jesse coming to Nob, to Ahimelech the son of Ahitub. 10 And he enquired of the LORD for him, and gave him victuals, and gave him the sword of Goliath the Philistine. 11 Then the king sent to call Ahimelech the priest, the son of Ahitub, and all his father's house, the priests that *were* in Nob: and they came all of them to the king. 12 And Saul said, Hear now, thou son of Ahitub. And he answered, Here I *am*, my lord. 13 And Saul said unto him, Why have ye conspired against me, thou and the son of Jesse, in that thou hast given him bread, and a sword, and hast enquired of God for him, that he should rise against me, to lie in wait, as at this day? 14 Then Ahimelech answered the king, and said, And who *is so* faithful among all thy servants as David, which is the king's son in law, and goeth at thy bidding, and is honourable in thine house? 15 Did I then begin to enquire of God for him? be it far from me: let not the king impute *any* thing unto his servant, *nor* to all the house of my father: for thy servant knew nothing of all this, less or more. 16 And the king said, Thou shalt surely die, Ahimelech, thou, and all thy father's house. 17 And the king said unto the footmen that stood about him, Turn, and slay the priests of the LORD; because their hand also *is* with David, and because they knew when he fled, and did not show it to me. But the servants of the king would not put forth their hand to fall upon the priests of the LORD. 18 And the king said to Doeg, Turn thou, and fall upon the priests. And Doeg the Edomite turned, and he fell upon the priests, and slew on that day fourscore and five persons that did wear a linen ephod. 19 And Nob, the city of the priests, smote he with the edge of the sword, both men and women, children and sucklings, and oxen, and asses, and sheep, with the edge of the sword.

We have seen the progress of David's troubles; now here we have the progress of Saul's wickedness. He seems to have laid aside the thoughts of all other business and to have devoted himself wholly to the pursuit of David. He heard at length, by the common fame of the country, that David *was discovered* (that is, that he appeared publicly and enlisted men into his service); and hereupon he called all his servants about him, and sat down under a tree, or grove, in the high place at Gibeah, with his spear in his hand for a sceptre, intimating the force by which he designed to rule, and the present temper of his spirit, or its distemper rather, which was to kill all that stood in his way. In this bloody court of inquisition,

I. Saul seeks for information against David and Jonathan, *v.* 7, 8. Two things he was willing to suspect and desirous to see proved, that he might wreak his malice upon two of the best and most excellent men he had about him:—1. That his servant David did *lie in wait* for him and seek his life, which was utterly false. He really sought David's life, and therefore pretended that David sought his life, though he could not charge him with any overt act that gave the least shadow of suspicion. 2. That his son Jonathan stirred him up to do so, and was confederate with him in compassing and imagining the death of the king. This also was notoriously false. A league of friendship there was between David and Jonathan, but no conspiracy in any evil thing; none of the articles of their covenant carried any mischief to Saul. If Jonathan had agreed, after the death of Saul, to resign to David, in compliance with the revealed will of God, what harm would that do to Saul? Yet thus the best friends to their prince and country have often been odiously represented as enemies to both; even Christ himself was so. Saul took it for granted that Jonathan and David were in a plot against him, his crown and dignity, and was displeased with his servants that they did not give him information of it, supposing that they could not but know it; whereas really there was no such thing. See the nature of a jealous malice, and its pitiful arts to extort discoveries of things that are not. He looked upon all about him as his enemies because they did not say just as he said; and told them, (1.) That they were very unwise, and acted against the interest both of their tribe (for they were Benjamites, and David, if he were advanced, would bring the honour into Judah which was now in Benjamin) and of their families; for David would never be able to give them such rewards as he had for them, of *fields and vineyards*, and such preferments, to be colonels and captains. (2.) That they were unfaithful: *You have conspired against me.* What a continual agitation and torment are those in that give way to a spirit of jealousy! *If a ruler hearken to lies, all his servants are wicked* (Prov. xxix. 12), that is, they seem to be so in his eyes. (3.) That they were very unkind. He thought to work upon their good nature with that word: *There is none of you that is* so much as *sorry for me*, or *solicitous for me*, as some read it. By these reasonings he stirred them up to act vigorously, as the instruments of his malice, that they might take away his suspicions of them.

II. Though he could not learn any thing from his servants against David or Jonathan, yet he got information from Doeg against Ahimelech the priest.

1. An indictment is brought against Ahimelech by Doeg, and he himself is evidence against him, *v.* 9, 10. Perhaps Doeg, as bad as he was, would not have given this information if Saul had not extorted it, for had he been very forward to it he would have done it sooner: but now he thinks they must be all deemed traitors if none of them be accusers, and therefore tells Saul what kindness Ahimelech had shown to David, which he himself happened to be an eye-witness of. He had *enquired of God for him* (which the priest used not to do but for public persons and about public affairs) and he had furnished him with *bread and a sword.* All this was true; but it was not the whole truth. He ought to have told Saul further that David had made Ahimelech believe he was then going upon the king's business; so that what service he did to David, however it proved, was designed in honour to Saul, and this would have cleared Ahimelech, whom Saul had in his power, and would have thrown all the blame upon David, who was out of his reach.

2. Ahimelech is seized, or summoned rather to appear before the king, and upon this indictment he is arraigned. The king sent for him and all the priests who then attended the sanctuary, whom he supposed to be aiding and abetting; and they, not being conscious of any guilt, and therefore not apprehensive of any danger, *came all of them to the king* (*v.* 11), and none of them attempted to make an escape, or to flee to David for shelter, as they would have done now that he had set up his standard if they had been as much in his interests as Saul suspected they were. Saul arraigns Ahimelech himself with the utmost disdain and indignation (*v.* 12): *Hear now, thou son of Ahitub;* not so much as calling him by his name, much less giving him his title of distinction. By this it appears that he had cast off the fear of God, that he showed no respect at all to his priests, but took a pleasure in affronting them and insulting them. Ahimelech holds up his hand at the bar in those words: "*Here I am, my lord*, ready to hear my charge, knowing I have done no wrong." He does not object to the jurisdiction of Saul's court, nor insist upon an exemption as a priest, no, not though he is a high priest, to which office that of the judge, or chief magistrate, had not long since been annexed; but Saul having now the sovereignty vested in him, in things pertaining to the king, even the high priest sets himself on a level with common Israelites. *Let every soul be subject* (even clergymen) *to the higher powers.*

3. His indictment is read to him (*v.* 13), that he, as a false traitor, had joined himself with the son of Jesse in a plot to depose and murder the king. "His design" (says Saul) "was to *rise up against me*, and thou didst assist him with victuals and arms." See what bad constructions the most innocent actions are liable to, how unsafe those are that live under a tyrannical government, and what reason we have to be thankful for the happy constitution and administration of the government we are under.

4. To this indictment he pleads, Not guilty, *v.* 14, 15. He owns the fact, but denies that he did it traitorously or maliciously, or with any design against the king. He pleads that he was so far from knowing of any quarrel between Saul and David that he really took David to have been then as much in favour at court as ever he had been. Observe, He does not plead that David had told him an untruth, and with that had imposed upon him, though really it was so, because he would not proclaim the weakness of so good a man, no, not for his own vindication, especially to Saul, who sought all occasions against him; but he insists upon the settled reputation David had, as the most faithful of all the servants of Saul, the honour the king had put upon him in marrying his daughter to him, the use the king had often made of him, and the trust he had reposed in him: "He *goes at thy bidding, and is honourable in thy house*, and therefore any one would think it a meritorious piece of service to the crown to show him respect, so far from apprehending it to be a crime." He pleads that he had been wont to *enquire of God for him* when he was sent by Saul upon any expedition, and did it now as innocently as ever he had done it. He protests his abhorrence of the thought of being in a plot against the king: "*Be it far from me.* I mind my own business, and meddle not with state matters." He begs the king's favour: "*Let him not impute* any crime to us;" and concludes with a declaration of his in-

nocency: *Thy servant knew nothing of all this.* Could any man plead with more evidences of sincerity? Had he been tried by a jury of honest Israelites, he would certainly have been acquitted, for who can find any fault in him? But,

5. Saul himself gives judgment against him (*v.* 16): *Thou shalt surely die, Ahimelech,* as a rebel, *thou and all thy father's house.* What could be more unjust? *I saw under the sun the place of judgment, that wickedness was there,* Eccl. iii. 16. (1.) It was unjust that Saul should himself, himself alone, give judgment in his own cause, without any appeal to judge or prophet, to his privy council, or to a council of war. (2.) That so fair a plea should be overruled and rejected without any reason given, or any attempt to disprove the allegations of it, but purely with a high hand. (3.) That sentence should be passed so hastily and with so much precipitation, the judge taking no time himself to consider of it, nor allowing the prisoner any time to move in arrest of judgment. (4.) That the sentence should be passed not only on Ahimelech himself, who was the only person accused by Doeg, but on *all his father's house,* against whom nothing was alleged: must the children be put to death for the fathers? (5.) That the sentence should be pronounced in passion, not for the support of justice, but for the gratification of his brutish rage.

6. He issues out a warrant (a verbal warrant only) for the immediate execution of this bloody sentence.

(1.) He ordered his footmen to be the executioners of this sentence, but they refused, *v.* 17. Hereby he intended to put a further disgrace upon the priests; they may not die by the hands of the men of war (as 1 Kings ii. 29) or his usual ministers of justice, but his footmen must triumph over them, and wash their hands in their blood. [1.] Never was the command of a prince more barbarously given: *Turn and slay the priests of the Lord.* This is spoken with such an air of impiety as can scarcely be paralleled. Had he seemed to forget their sacred office or relation to God, and taken no notice of that, he would thereby have intimated some regret that men of that character should fall under his displeasure; but to call them *the priests of the Lord,* when he ordered his footmen to cut their throats, looked as if, upon that very account, he hated them. God having rejected him, and ordered another to be anointed in his room, he seems well pleased with this opportunity of being revenged on the priests of the Lord, since God himself was out of his reach. What wickedness will not the evil spirit hurry men to, when he gets the dominion! He alleged, in his order, that which was utterly false and unproved to him, that they knew when David fled; whereas they knew nothing of the matter. But malice and murder are commonly supported with lies. [2.] Never was the command of a prince more honourably disobeyed. The footmen had more sense and grace than their master. Though they might expect to be turned out of their places, if not punished and put to death for their refusal, yet, come on them what would, they would not offer to fall upon the priests of the Lord, such a reverence had they for their office, and such a conviction of their innocence.

(2.) He ordered Doeg (the accuser) to be the executioner, and he obeyed. One would have thought that the footmen's refusal would awaken Saul's conscience, and that he would not insist upon the doing of a thing so barbarous as that his footmen startled at the thought of it. But his mind was blinded and his heart hardened, and, if they will not do it, the hands of the witness shall be upon the victims, Deut. xvii. 7. The most bloody tyrants have found out instruments of their cruelty as barbarous as themselves. Doeg is no sooner commanded to fall upon the priests than he does it willingly enough, and, meeting with no resistance, slays with his own hand (for aught that appears) on that same day eighty-five priests that were ot the age of ministration, between twenty and fifty, for they *wore a linen ephod* (*v.* 18), and perhaps appeared at this time before Saul in their habits, and were slain in them. This (one would think) was enough to satiate the most blood-thirsty; but the horseleech of persecution still cries, "Give, give." Doeg, by Saul's order no doubt, having murdered the priests, went to their city Nob, and put all to the sword there (*v.* 19), *men, women, and children,* and the cattle too. Barbarous cruelty, and such as one cannot think of without horror! Strange that ever it should enter into the heart of man to be so impious, so inhuman! We may see in this, [1.] The desperate wickedness of Saul when the Spirit of the Lord had departed from him. Nothing so vile but those may be hurried to it who have provoked God to give them up to their hearts' lusts. He that was so compassionate as to spare Agag and the cattle of the Amalekites, in disobedience to the command of God, could now, with unrelenting bowels, see the priests of the Lord murdered, and nothing spared of all that belonged to them. For that sin God left him to this. [2.] The accomplishment of the threatenings long since pronounced against the house of Eli; for Ahimelech and his family were descendants from him. Though Saul was unrighteous in doing this, yet God was righteous in permitting it. Now God performed against Eli that at which the ears of those that heard it must needs tingle, as he had told him that he would *judge his house for ever ch.* iii. 11—13. No word of God shall fall to the ground. [3.] This may be considered as a great judgment upon Israel, and the just punishment of their desiring a king before the time God intended them one,

How deplorable was the state of religion at this time in Israel! Though the ark had long been in obscurity, yet it was some comfort to them that they had the altar, and priests to serve at it; but now to see their priests weltering in their own blood, and the heirs of the priesthood too, and the city of the priests made a desolation, so that the altar of God must needs be neglected for want of attendants, and this by the unjust and cruel order of their own king to satisfy his brutish rage—this could not but go to the heart of all pious Israelites, and make them wish a thousand times they had been satisfied with the government of Samuel and his sons. The worst enemies of their nation could not have done them a greater mischief.

20 And one of the sons of Ahimelech the son of Ahitub, named Abiathar, escaped, and fled after David. 21 And Abiathar showed David that Saul had slain the LORD's priests. 22 And David said unto Abiathar, I knew *it* that day, when Doeg the Edomite *was* there, that he would surely tell Saul: I have occasioned *the death* of all the persons of thy father's house. 23 Abide thou with me, fear not: for he that seeketh my life seeketh thy life: but with me thou *shalt be* in safeguard.

Here is, 1. The escape of Abiathar, the son of Ahimelech, out of the desolations of the priests' city. Probably when his father went to appear, upon Saul's summons, he was left at home to attend the altar, by which means he escaped the first execution, and, before Doeg and his bloodhounds came to Nob, he had intelligence of the danger, and had time to shift for his own safety. And whither should he go but to David? *v.* 20. Let those that suffer for the Son of David *commit the keeping of their souls to him,* 1 Pet. iv. 19. 2. David's resentment of the melancholy tidings he brought. He gave David an account of the bloody work Saul had made among the priests of the Lord (*v.* 21), as the disciples of John, when their master was beheaded, *went and told Jesus,* Matt. xiv. 12. And David greatly lamented the calamity itself, but especially his being accessory to it: *I have occasioned the death of all the persons of thy father's house, v.* 22. Note, It is a great trouble to a good man to find himself in any way an occasion of the calamities of the church and ministry. David knew Doeg's character so well that he feared he would do some such mischief as this when he saw him at the sanctuary: *I knew he would tell Saul.* He calls him *Doeg the Edomite,* because he retained the heart of an Edomite, though, by embracing the profession of the Jewish religion, he had put on the mask of an Israelite. 3. The protection he granted to Abiathar. He perceived him to be terrified, as he had reason to be, and therefore bade him not to fear, he would be as careful for him as for himself: *With me thou shalt be in safeguard, v.* 23. David, having now time to recollect himself, speaks with assurance of his own safety, and promises that Abiathar shall have the full benefit of his protection. It is promised to the Son of David that God will *hide him in the shadow of his hand* (Isa. xlix. 2), and, with him, all that are his may be sure that they shall be in safeguard, Ps. xci. 1. David had now not only a prophet, but a priest, a high-priest, with him, to whom he was a blessing and they to him, and both a happy omen of his success. Yet it appears (by *ch.* xxviii. 6) that Saul had a high priest too, for he had a urim to consult: it is supposed that he preferred Ahitub the father of Zadok, of the family of Eleazar (1 Chron. vi. 8). for even those that hate the power of godliness yet will not be without the form. It must not be forgotten here that David at this time penned Psalm lii., as appears by the title of that psalm, wherein he represents Doeg not only as malicious and spiteful, but as false and deceitful, because though what he said was, for the substance of it, true, yet he put false colours upon it, with a design to do mischief. Yet even then, when the priesthood had become as a withered branch, he looks upon himself as a *green olive-tree in the house of God,* Ps. lii. 8. In this great hurry and distraction that David was continually in, yet he found both time and a heart for communion with God, and found comfort in it.

CHAP. XXIII.

Saul, having made himself drunk with the blood of the priests of the Lord, is here, in this chapter, seeking David's life, who appears here doing good, and suffering ill, at the same time. Here is, I. The good service he did to his king and country, in rescuing the city of Keilah out of the hands of the Philistines, ver. 1—6. II. The danger he was thereby brought into from the malice of the prince he served and the treachery of the city he saved, and his deliverance, by divine direction, from that danger, ver. 7—13. III. David in a wood, and his friend Jonathan visiting him there and encouraging him, ver. 14—18. IV. The information which the Ziphites brought to Saul of David's haunts, and the expedition Saul made, in pursuit of him, ver. 19—25. The narrow escape David had of falling into his hands, ver. 26—29. "Many are the troubles of the righteous, but the Lord delivereth them out of them all."

THEN they told David, saying, Behold, the Philistines fight against Keilah, and they rob the threshingfloors. 2 Therefore David enquired of the LORD, saying, Shall I go and smite these Philistines? And the LORD said unto David, Go and smite the Philistines, and save Keilah. 3 And David's men said unto him, Behold, we be afraid here in Judah: how much more then if we come to Keilah against the armies of the Philistines? 4 Then David enquired of the LORD yet again. And the LORD answered him and said, Arise, go down to Keilah; for I will deliver the Philistines into thine hand. 5 So David and his men went to Keilah, and fought with the Philistines, and brought away their cattle, and smote them with a great slaughter. So David saved the inhabitants of Keilah. 6 And it came to pass, when Abiathar the son of Ahimelech fled to David to Keilah, *that* he came down *with* an ephod in his hand.

Now we find why the prophet Gad (by divine direction, no doubt) ordered David to go into the land of Judah, *ch.* xxii. 5. It was that, since Saul neglected the public safety, he might take care of it, notwithstanding the ill treatment that was given him; for he must render good for evil, and therein be a type of him who not only ventured his life, but laid down his life, for those that were his enemies.

I. Tidings are brought to David, as to the patron and protector of his country's liberties, that the Philistines had made a descent upon the city of Keilah and plundered the country thereabouts, *v.* 1. Probably it was the departure both of God and David from Saul that encouraged the Philistines to make this incursion. When princes begin to persecute God's people and ministers, let them expect no other than vexation on all sides. The way for any country to be quiet is to let God's church be quiet in it. If Saul fight against David, the Philistines shall fight against his country.

II. David is forward enough to come in for their relief, but is willing to enquire of the Lord concerning it. Here is an instance, 1. Of David's generosity and public-spiritedness. Though his head and hands were full of his own business, and he had enough to do, with the little force he had, to secure himself, yet he was concerned for the safety of his country and could not sit still to see that ravaged: nay, though Saul, whose business it was to guard the borders of his land, hated him and sought his life, yet he was willing, to the utmost of his power, to serve him and his interests against the common enemy, and bravely abhorred the thought of sacrificing the common welfare to his private revenge. Those are unlike to David who sullenly decline to do good because they have not been so well considered as they deserved for the services they have done. 2. Of David's piety and regard to God. He enquired of the Lord by the prophet Gad; for it should seem (by *v.* 6) that Abiathar came not to him with the ephod till he was in Keilah. His enquiry is, *Shall I go and smite these Philistines?* He enquires both concerning the duty (whether he might lawfully take Saul's work out of his hand, and act without a commission from him) and concerning the event, whether he might safely venture against such a force as the Philistines had with such a handful of men at his feet, and such a dangerous enemy as Saul was at his back. It is our duty, and will be our case and comfort, whatever happens, to acknowledge God in all our ways and to seek direction from him.

III. God appointed him once and again to go against the Philistines, and promised him success: *Go, and smite the Philistines, v.* 2. His men opposed it, *v.* 3. No sooner did he begin to have soldiers of his own than he found it hard enough to manage them. They objected that they had enemies enough among their own countrymen, they needed not to make the Philistines their enemies. Their hearts failed them when they only apprehended themselves in danger from Saul's band of pursuers, much more when they came to engage the Philistine-armies. To satisfy them, therefore, he *enquired of the Lord again,* and now received, not only a full commission, which would warrant him to fight though he had no orders from Saul *(Arise, go down to Keilah)*, but also a full assurance of victory: *I will deliver the Philistines into thy hand, v.* 4. This was enough to animate the greatest coward he had in his regiment.

IV. He went accordingly against the Philistines, routed them, and rescued Keilah, (*v.* 5), and it should seem he made a sally into the country of the Philistines, for he carried off their cattle by way of reprisal for the wrong they did to the men of Keilah in robbing their threshing-floors. Here notice is taken (*v.* 6) that it was while David remained in Keilah, after he had cleared it of the Philistines, that Abiathar came to him with the ephod in his hand, that is, the high priest's ephod, in which the urim and thummim were. It was a great comfort to David, in his banishment, that when he could not go to the house of God he had some of the choicest treasures of that house brought to him, the high priest and his breast-plate of judgment.

7 And it was told Saul that David was come to Keilah. And Saul said, God hath delivered him into mine hand; for he is shut in, by entering into a town that hath gates and bars. 8 And Saul called all the people together to war, to go down to Keilah, to besiege David and his men. 9 And David knew that Saul secretly practised mischief against him; and he said to Abiathar the priest, Bring hither the ephod. 10 Then said David, O LORD God of Israel, thy servant hath certainly heard that Saul seeketh to come to Keilah, to destroy

the city for my sake. 11 Will the men of Keilah deliver me up into his hand? will Saul come down, as thy servant hath heard? O LORD God of Israel, I beseech thee, tell thy servant. And the LORD said, He will come down. 12 Then said David, Will the men of Keilah deliver me and my men into the hand of Saul? And the LORD said, They will deliver *thee* up. 13 Then David and his men, *which were* about six hundred, arose and departed out of Keilah, and went whithersoever they could go. And it was told Saul that David was escaped from Keilah; and he forbare to go forth.

Here is, I. Saul contriving within himself the destruction of David (*v.* 7, 8): *He heard that he had come to Keilah;* and did he not hear what brought him thither? Was it not told him that he had bravely relieved Keilah and delivered it out of the hands of the Philistines? This, one would think, should have put Saul upon considering what honour and dignity should be done to David for this. But, instead of that, he catches at it as an opportunity of doing David a mischief. An ungrateful wretch he was, and for ever unworthy to have any service or kindness done him. Well might David complain of his enemies that they rewarded him *evil for good,* and that for his love they were his adversaries, Ps. xxxv. 12; cix. 4. Christ was used thus basely, John x. 32. Now observe, 1. How Saul abused the *God of Israel,* in making his providence to patronise and give countenance to his malicious designs, and thence promising himself success in them: *God hath delivered him into my hand;* as if he who was rejected of God were in this instance owned and favoured by him, and David infatuated. He vainly triumphs before the victory, forgetting how often he had had fairer advantages against David than he had now and had yet missed his aim. He impiously connects God with his cause, because he thought he had gained one point. Therefore David prays (Ps. cxl. 8), *Grant not, O Lord! the desires of the wicked; further not his wicked device, lest they exalt themselves.* We must not think that one smiling providence either justifies an unrighteous cause or secures its success. 2. How Saul abused the Israel of God, in making them the servants of his malice against David. He called all the people together to war, and they must with all speed march to Keilah, pretending to oppose the Philistines, but intending to besiege David and his men, though concealing that design; for it is said (*v.* 9) that he *secretly practised mischief against him.* Miserable is that people whose prince is a tyrant, for, while some are sufferers by his tyranny, others (which is worse) are made servants to it and instruments of it.

II. David consulting with God concerning his own preservation. He knew by the information brought him that Saul was plotting his ruin (*v.* 9) and therefore applied to his great protector for direction. No sooner is the ephod brought to him than he makes use of it: *Bring hither the ephod.* We have the scriptures, those lively oracles, in our hands; let us take advice from them in doubtful cases. "Bring hither the Bible."

1. David's address to God upon this occasion is, (1.) Very solemn and reverent. Twice he calls God the *Lord God of Israel,* and thrice calls himself his *servant, v.* 10, 11. Those that address God must know their distance, and who they are speaking to. (2.) Very particular and express. His representation of the case is so (*v.* 10): "Thy servant has certainly heard on good authority" (for he would not call for the ephod upon every idle rumour) "that Saul has a design upon Keilah;" he does not say, "to destroy me," but, "to destroy the city" (as he had lately done the city of Nob) "for my sake." He seems more solicitous for their safety than for his own, and will expose himself any where rather than they shall be brought into trouble by his being among them. Generous souls are thus minded. His queries upon the case are likewise very particular. God allows us to be so in our addresses to him: "Lord, direct me in this matter, about which I am now at a loss." He does indeed invert the due order of his queries, but God in his answer puts him into method. That question should have been put first, and was first answered, "Will Saul come down, as thy servant has heard?" "Yea," says the oracle, "he will come down; he has resolved it, is preparing for it, and will do it, unless he hear that thou hast quitted the town." "Well, but if he do come down will the men of Keilah stand by me in holding the city against him, or will they open to him the gates, and deliver me into his hand?" If he had asked the men (the magistrates or elders) of Keilah themselves what they would do in that case, they could not have told him, not knowing their own minds, nor what they should do when it came to the trial, much less which way the superior vote of their council would carry it; or they might have told him they would protect him, and yet afterwards have betrayed him; but God could tell him infallibly: "When Saul besieges their city, and demands of them that they surrender thee into his hands, how fond soever they now seem of thee, as their saviour, they will deliver thee up rather than stand the shock of Saul's fury." Note, [1.] God knows all men better than they know themselves, knows their length, their strength, what is in them, and what they will do if

they come into such and such circumstances. [2.] He therefore knows not only what *will* be, but what *would* be if it were not prevented; and therefore knows how to deliver the godly out of temptation, and how to render to every man according to his works.

2. David, having thus far notice given him of his danger, quitted Keilah, *v.* 13. His followers had now increased in number to 600; with these he went out, not knowing whither he went, but resolving to follow Providence and put himself under its protection. This broke Saul's measures. He thought God had delivered David into his hand, but it proved that God delivered him out of his hand, as a bird out of the snare of the fowler. When *Saul heard that David had escaped from Keilah, he forbore to go forth* with the body of the army, as he intended (*v.* 8), and resolved to take only his own guards, and go in quest of him. Thus does God baffle the designs of his people's enemies and turn their counsels head-long.

14 And David abode in the wilderness in strong holds, and remained in a mountain in the wilderness of Ziph. And Saul sought him every day, but God delivered him not into his hand. 15 And David saw that Saul was come out to seek his life: and David *was* in the wilderness of Ziph in a wood. 16 And Jonathan Saul's son arose, and went to David into the wood, and strengthened his hand in God. 17 And he said unto him, Fear not: for the hand of Saul my father shall not find thee; and thou shalt be king over Israel, and I shall be next unto thee; and that also Saul my father knoweth. 18 And they two made a covenant before the LORD: and David abode in the wood, and Jonathan went to his house.

Here is, I. David absconding. He abode in a *wilderness, in a mountain* (*v.* 14), *in a wood, v.* 15. We must here, 1. Commend his eminent virtues, his humility, modesty, fidelity to his prince, and patient attendance on the providence of his God, that he did not draw up his forces against Saul, fight him in the field, or surprise him by some stratagem or other, and so avenge his own quarrel and that of the Lord's priests upon him, and put an end to his own troubles and the calamities of the country under Saul's tyrannical government. No, he makes no such attempt; he keeps God's way, waits God's time, and is content to secure himself in woods and wildernesses, though with some it might seem a reproach to that courage for which he had been famous. But, 2. We must also lament his hard fate, that an innocent man should be thus terrified and put in fear of his life, that a man of honour should be thus disgraced, a man of merit thus recompensed for his services, and a man that delighted in the service both of God and his country should be debarred from both and wrapped up in obscurity. What shall we say to this? Let it make us think the worse of this world, which often gives such bad treatment to its best men; let it reconcile even great and active men to privacy and restraint, if Providence make these their lot, for they were David's; and let it make us long for that kingdom where goodness shall for ever be in glory and holiness in honour, and the righteous shall shine as the sun, which cannot be put under a bushel.

II. Saul hunting him, as his implacable enemy. He sought him every day, so restless was his malice, *v.* 14. He sought no less than his life, so cruel was his malice, *v.* 15. As it had been from the beginning, so it was now, and will be, *he that is born after the flesh persecuteth him that is born after the spirit,* Gal. iv. 29.

III. God defending him, as his powerful protector. God delivered him not into Saul's hand, as Saul hoped (*v.* 7); and, unless God delivered him into his hand, he could not prevail against him, John xix. 11.

IV. Jonathan comforting him as his faithful and constant friend. True friends will find out means to get together. David, it is likely, appointed time and place for this interview, and Jonathan observed the appointment, though he exposed himself thereby to his father's displeasure, and, had it been discovered, it might have cost him his life. True friendship will not shrink from danger, but can easily venture, will not shrink from condescension, but can easily stoop, and exchange a palace for a wood, to serve a friend. The very sight of Jonathan was reviving to David; but, besides this, he said that to him which was very encouraging. 1. As a pious friend, he directed him to God, the foundation of his confidence and the fountain of his comfort: He *strengthened his hand in God.* David, though a strong believer, needed the help of his friends for the perfecting of what was lacking in his faith; and herein Jonathan was helpful to him, by reminding him of the promise of God, the holy oil wherewith he was anointed, the presence of God with him hitherto, and the many experiences he had had of God's goodness to him. Thus he strengthened his hands for action, by encouraging his heart, not in the creature, but in God. Jonathan was not in a capacity of doing any thing to strengthen him, but he assured him God would. 2. As a self-denying friend, he took a pleasure in the prospect of David's advancement to that honour which was his own birthright, *v.* 17. "Thou shalt live to be king, and I shall think it preferment enough to be next thee, near thee, though under thee, and will never pretend to be a rival with thee." This resignation which Jonathan made to David of his title would be a great satisfaction to him, and make his way much the more clear. This, he tells him, Saul knew very well, Jonathan having sometimes heard him say as much, whence it appears what a wicked man Saul was, to persecute one whom God favoured, and what a foolish man he was, in thinking to prevent that which God had determined and which would certainly come to pass. How could he disannul what God had purposed? 3. As a constant friend, he renewed his league of friendship with him. They made a covenant now, this third time, before the Lord, calling him to witness to it, *v.* 18. True love takes delight in repeating its engagements, giving and receiving fresh assurances of the firmness of the friendship. Our covenant with God should be often renewed, and therein our communion with him kept up. David and Jonathan now parted, and never came together again, that we find, in this world; for Jonathan said what he wished, not what he had ground to expect, when he promised himself that he should be next to David in his kingdom.

19 Then came up the Ziphites to Saul to Gibeah, saying, Doth not David hide himself with us in strong holds in the wood, in the hill of Hachilah, which *is* on the south of Jeshimon? 20 Now therefore, O king, come down according to all the desire of thy soul to come down; and our part *shall be* to deliver him into the king's hand. 21 And Saul said, Blessed *be* ye of the LORD; for ye have compassion on me. 22 Go, I pray you, prepare yet, and know and see his place where his haunt is, *and* who hath seen him there: for it is told me *that* he dealeth very subtilly. 23 See therefore, and take knowledge of all the lurking places where he hideth himself, and come ye again to me with the certainty, and I will go with you: and it shall come to pass, if he be in the land, that I will search him out throughout all the thousands of Judah. 24 And they arose, and went to Ziph before Saul: but David and his men *were* in the wilderness of Maon, in the plain on the south of Jeshimon. 25 Saul also and his men went to seek *him*. And they told David: wherefore he came down into a rock, and abode in the wilderness of Maon. And when Saul heard *that*, he pursued after David in the wilderness of Maon. 26 And Saul went on this side of the mountain, and David and his men on that side of the mountain: and David made haste to get away for fear of Saul; for Saul and his men compassed David and his men round about to take them. 27 But there came a messenger unto Saul, saying, Haste thee, and come; for the Philistines have invaded the land. 28 Wherefore Saul returned from pursuing after David, and went against the Philistines; therefore they called that place Sela-hammahlekoth. 29 And David went up from thence, and dwelt in strong holds at En-gedi.

Here, 1. The Ziphites offer their service to Saul, to betray David to him, *v.* 19, 20. He was sheltering himself in the wilderness of Ziph (*v.* 14, 15), putting the more confidence in the people of that country because they were of his own tribe. They had reason to think themselves happy that they had an opportunity of serving one who was the ornament of their tribe and was likely to be much more so, who was so far from plundering the country, or giving it any disturbance with his troops, that he was ready to protect it and do them all the good offices that there was occasion for. But, to ingratiate themselves with Saul, they went to him, and not only informed him very particularly where David quartered (*v.* 19), but invited him to come with his forces into their country in pursuit of him, and promised to deliver him into his hand, *v.* 20. Saul had not sent to examine or threaten them, but of their own accord, and even without asking a reward (as Judas did—*What will you give me?*), they offered to betray David to him who, they knew, thirsted after his blood. 2. Saul thankfully receives their information, and gladly lays hold of the opportunity of hunting David in their wilderness, in hopes to make a prey of him at length. He intimates to them how kindly he took it (*v.* 21): *Blessed be you of the Lord* (so near is God to his mouth, though far from his heart), *for you have compassion on me.* It seems he looked upon himself as a miserable man and an object of pity; his own envy and ill-nature made him so, otherwise he might have been easy and have needed no man's compassion. He likewise insinuates the little concern that the generality of his people showed for him. "You have compassion on me, which others have not." Saul gives them instructions to search more particularly for his haunts (*v.* 22), "for" (says he) "I hear he deals very subtilely," representing him as a man crafty to do mischief, whereas all his subtlety was to secure himself. It was strange that Saul did not go down with them immediately, but he hoped by their means to set his game with the more certainty, and thus divine Providence gave David time to shift for himself. But the Ziphites had laid their spies upon all the places where he was likely to be discovered, and therefore Saul might come and seize him if he was in the land, *v.* 23. Now he thought himself sure of his prey and pleased himself with the thoughts of devouring it. 3. The imminent peril that David was now brought into. Upon intelligence that the Ziphites had betrayed him, he retired from the hill of Hachilah to the wilderness of Maon (*v.* 24), and at this time he penned the 54th Psalm, as appears by the title, wherein he calls the Ziphites *strangers,* though they were Israelites, because they used him barbarously; but he puts himself under the divine protection: "*Behold, God is my helper,* and then all shall be well" Saul, having got intelligence of him, pursued him closely (*v.* 25), till he came so near him that there was but a mountain between them (*v.* 26), David and his men on one side of the mountain flying and Saul and his men on the other side pursuing, David in fear and Saul in hope. But this mountain was an emblem of the divine Providence coming between David and the destroyer, like the pillar of cloud between the Israelites and the Egyptians. David was concealed by this mountain and Saul confounded by it. David now flees *as a bird to his mountain* (Ps. xi. 1) and finds God to him as the shadow of a great rock. Saul hoped with his numerous forces to enclose David, and compass him in and his men; but the ground did not prove convenient for his design, and so it failed. A new name was given to the place in remembrance of this (*v.* 28): *Selah-hammah-lekoth—the rock of division,* because it divided between Saul and David. 4. The deliverance of David out of this danger. Providence gave Saul a diversion, when he was just ready to lay hold of David; notice was brought him that the Philistines were *invading the land* (*v.* 27), probably that part of the land where his own estate lay, which would be seized, or at least spoiled, by the invaders; for the little notice he took of Keilah's distress and David's relief of it, in the beginning of this chapter, gives us cause to suspect that he would not now have left pursuing David, and gone to oppose the Philistines, if some private interests of his own had not been at stake. However it was, he found himself under a necessity of *going against the Philistines* (*v.* 28), and by this means David was delivered when he was on the brink of destruction. Saul was disappointed of his prey, and God was glorified as David's wonderful protector. When the Philistines invaded the land they were far from intending any kindness to David by it, yet the overruling providence of God, which orders all events and the times of them, made it very serviceable to him. The wisdom of God is never at a loss for ways and means to preserve his people. As this Saul was diverted, so another Saul was converted, just then when he was *breathing out threatenings and slaughter against the saints of the Lord,* Acts ix. 1. 5. David, having thus escaped, took shelter in some natural fortresses, which he found in the wilderness of En-gedi, *v.* 29. And this Dr. Lightfoot thinks was the wilderness of Judah, in which David was when he penned Psalm lxiii., which breathes as much pious and devout affection as almost any of his psalms; for in all places and in all conditions he still kept up his communion with God.

CHAP. XXIV.

We have hitherto had Saul seeking an opportunity to destroy David, and, to his shame, he could never find it. In this chapter David had a fair opportunity to destroy Saul, and, to his honour, he did not make use of it; and his sparing Saul's life was as great an instance of God's grace in him as the preserving of his own life was of God's providence over him. Observe, I. How maliciously Saul sought David's life, ver. 1, 2. II. How generously David saved Saul's life (when he had him at an advantage) and only cut off the skirt of his robe, ver. 3—8. III. How pathetically he reasoned with Saul, upon this, to bring him to a better temper towards him, ver. 9—15. IV. The good impression this made upon Saul for the present, ver. 16—22.

AND it came to pass, when Saul was returned from following the Philistines, that it was told him, saying, Behold, David *is* in the wilderness of En-gedi. 2 Then Saul took three thousand chosen men out of all Israel, and went to seek David and his men upon the rocks of the wild goats. 3 And he came to the sheepcotes by the way, where *was* a cave; and Saul went in to cover his feet: and David and his men remained in the sides of the cave. 4 And the men of David said unto him, Behold the day of which the LORD said unto thee, Behold, I will deliver thine enemy into thine hand, that thou mayest do to him as it shall seem good unto thee. Then David arose, and cut off the skirt of Saul's robe privily. 5 And it came to pass afterward, that David's heart smote him, because he had cut off Saul's skirt. 6 And he said unto his men, The LORD forbid that I should do this thing unto my master, the LORD's anointed, to stretch forth mine hand against him, seeing he *is* the anointed of the LORD. 7 So David stayed his servants with these words, and suffered them not to rise against Saul. But Saul rose up out of the cave, and went on *his* way. 8 David also arose afterward, and went out of the cave, and cried after Saul, saying, My lord the king. And when Saul looked behind him, David stooped with his face to the earth, and bowed himself.

Here, I. Saul renews his pursuit of David, *v.* 1, 2. No sooner had he come home safely from chasing the Philistines, in which it should seem he had good success, than he enquired after David to do him a mischief, and resolved to have another thrust at him, *as if he had been delivered to do all these abominations,* Jer. vii. 10. By the frequent incursions of the Philistines, he might have seen how necessary it was to recal David from his banishment and restore him to his place in the army again; but so far is he from doing this that now more than ever he is exasperated against him, and, hearing that he is *in the wilderness of En-gedi,* he draws out 3000 choice men, and goes with them at his feet in pursuit of him *upon the rocks of the wild goats,* where, one would think, David should not have been envied a habitation nor Saul desirous of disturbing him; for what harm could he fear from one who was no better accommodated? But it is not enough for Saul that David is thus cooped up; he cannot be easy while he is alive.

II. Providence brings Saul alone into the same cave wherein David and his men had hidden themselves, *v.* 3. In those countries there were very large caves in the sides of the rocks or mountains, partly natural, but probably much enlarged by art for the sheltering of sheep from the heat of the sun; hence we read of places where the flocks did rest at noon (Cant. i. 7), and this cave seems to be spoken of as one of the sheep-cotes. In the sides of this cave David and his men remained, perhaps not all his men, the whole 600, but only some few of his particular friends, the rest being disposed of in similar retirements. Saul, passing by, turned in himself alone, not in search of David (for, supposing him to be an aspiring ambitious man, he thought to find him rather climbing with the wild goats upon the rocks than retiring with the sheep into a cave), but thither he turned aside to *cover his feet,* that is, to sleep awhile, it being a cool and quiet place, and very refreshing in the heat of the day: probably he ordered his attendants to march before, reserving only a very few to wait for him at the mouth of the cave. Some by the covering of the feet understand the easing of nature, and think that this was Saul's errand into the cave: but the former interpretation is more probable.

III. David's servants stir him up to kill Saul now that he has so fair an opportunity to do it, *v.* 4. They reminded him that this was the day which he had long looked for, and of which God had spoken to him in general when he was anointed to the kingdom, which should put a period to his troubles and open the passage to his advancement. Saul now lay at his mercy, and it was easy to imagine how little mercy he would find with Saul and therefore what little reason he had to show mercy to him. "By all means" (say his servants) "give him the fatal blow now." See how apt we are to misunderstand, 1. The promises of God. God had assured David that he would deliver him from Saul, and his men interpret this as a warrant to destroy Saul. 2. The providences of God. Because it was now in his power to kill him, they concluded he might lawfully do it.

IV. David *cut off the skirt of his robe,* but soon repented that he had done this: *His heart smote him* for it (*v.* 5); though it did Saul no real hurt, and served David for a proof that it was in his power to have killed him (*v.* 11), yet, because it was an affront to Saul's royal dignity, he wished he had not done it. Note, It is a good thing to have a heart within us smiting us for sins that seem little; it is a sign that conscience is awake and tender, and will be the means of preventing greater sins.

V. He reasons strongly both with himself and with his servants against doing Saul any hurt. 1. He reasons with himself (*v.* 6): *The Lord forbid that I should do this thing.* Note, Sin is a thing which it becomes us to startle at, and to resist the temptations to, not only with resolution, but with a holy indignation. He considered Saul now, not as his enemy, and the only person that stood in the way of his preferment (for then he would be induced to hearken to the temptation), but as God's anointed (that is, the person whom God had appointed to reign as long as he lived, and who, as such, was under the particular protection of the divine law), and as his master, to whom he was obliged to be faithful. Let servants and subjects learn hence to be dutiful and loyal, whatever hardships are put upon them, 1 Pet. ii. 18. 2. He reasons with his servants: *He suffered them not to rise against Saul, v.* 7. He would not only not do this evil thing himself, but he would not suffer those about him to do it. Thus did he render good for evil to him from whom he had received evil for good, and was herein both a type of Christ, who saved his persecutors, and an example to all Christians not to be *overcome of evil, but to overcome evil with good.*

VI. He followed Saul out of the cave, and, though he would not take the opportunity to slay him, yet he wisely took the opportunity, if possible, to slay his enmity, by convincing him that he was not such a man as he took him for. 1. Even in showing his head now he testified that he had an honourable opinion of Saul. He had too much reason to believe that, let him say what he would, Saul would immediately be the death of him as soon as he saw him, and yet he bravely lays aside that jealousy, and thinks Saul so much a man of sense as to hear his reasoning when he had so much to say in his own vindication and such fresh and sensible proofs to give of his own integrity. 2. His behaviour was very respectful: He *stooped with his face to the earth, and bowed himself*, giving honour to whom honour was due, and teaching us to order ourselves lowly and reverently to all our superiors, even to those that have been most injurious to us.

9 And David said to Saul, Wherefore hearest thou men's words, saying, Behold, David seeketh thy hurt? 10 Behold, this day thine eyes have seen how that the LORD had delivered thee to day into mine hand in the cave: and *some* bade *me* kill thee: but *mine eye* spared thee; and I said, I will not put forth mine hand against my lord; for he *is* the LORD's anointed. 11 Moreover, my father, see, yea, see the skirt of thy robe in my hand: for in that I cut off the skirt of thy robe, and killed thee not, know thou and see that *there is* neither evil nor transgression in mine hand, and I have not sinned against thee; yet thou huntest my soul to take it. 12 The LORD judge between me and thee, and the LORD avenge me of thee: but mine hand shall not be upon thee. 13 As saith the proverb of the ancients, Wickedness proceedeth from the wicked: but mine hand shall not be upon thee. 14 After whom is the king of Israel come out? after whom dost thou pursue? after a dead dog, after a flea. 15 The LORD therefore be judge, and judge between me and thee, and see, and plead my cause, and deliver me out of thine hand.

We have here David's warm and pathetic speech to Saul, wherein he endeavours to convince him that he did him a great deal of wrong in persecuting him thus and to persuade him therefore to be reconciled.

I. He calls him *father* (*v.* 11), for he was not only, as king, the father of his country, but he was, in particular, his father-in-law. From a father one may expect compassion and a favourable opinion. For a prince to seek the ruin of any of his good subjects is as unnatural as for a father to seek the ruin of his own children.

II. He lays the blame of his rage against him upon his evil counsellors: *Wherefore hearest thou men's words? v.* 9. It is a piece of respect due to crowned heads, if they do amiss, to charge it upon those about them, who either advised them to it or should have advised them against it. David had reason enough to think that Saul persecuted him purely from his own envy and malice, yet he courteously supposes that others put him on to do it, and made him believe that David was his enemy and sought his hurt. Satan, the great accuser of the brethren, has his agents in all places, and particularly in the courts of those princes that encourage them and give ear to them, who make it their business to represent the people of God as enemies to Cæsar and hurtful to kings and provinces, that, being thus dressed up in bear-skins, they may "be baited."

III. He solemnly protests his own innocence, and that he is far from designing any hurt or mischief to Saul: "*There is neither evil nor transgression in my hand, v.* 11. I am not chargeable with any crime, nor conscious of any guilt, and, had I a window in my breast, thou mightest through it see the sincerity of my heart in this protestation: *I have not sinned against thee* (however I have sinned against God), *yet thou huntest my soul,*" that is, "my life." Perhaps it was about this time that David penned the seventh psalm, concerning the affair of Cush the Benjamite (that is, Saul, as some think), wherein he thus appeals to God (*v.* 3—5): *If there be iniquity in my hands, then let the enemy persecute my soul and take it,* putting in a parenthesis, with reference to the story of this chapter, *Yea, I have delivered him that without cause is my enemy.*

IV. He produces undeniable evidence to prove the falsehood of the suggestion upon which Saul's malice against him was grounded. David was charged with seeking Saul's hurt: "*See,*" says he, "*yea, see the skirt of thy robe, v.* 11. Let this be a witness for me, and an unexceptionable witness it is; had that been true of which I am accused, I should now have had thy head in my hand and not the skirt of thy robe, for I could as easily have cut off that as this." To corroborate this evidence he shows him, 1. That God's providence had given him opportunity to do it: *The Lord delivered thee,* very surprisingly, *to day into my hand,* whence many a one would have gathered an intimation that it was the will of God he should now give the determining blow to him whose neck lay so fair for it. When Saul had but a very small advantage against David he cried out, *God has delivered him into my hand* (*ch.* xxiii. 7), and resolved to make the best of that advantage; but David did not so. 2. That his counsellors and those about him had earnestly besought him to do it: *Some bade me kill thee.* He had blamed Saul for hearkening to men's words and justly; "for," says he, "if I had done so, thou wouldest not have been alive now." 3. That it was upon a good principle that he refused to do it; not because Saul's attendants were at hand, who, it may be, would have avenged his death; no, it was not by the fear of them, but by the fear of God, that he was restrained from it. "He is my lord, and the Lord's anointed, whom I ought to protect, and to whom I owe faith and allegiance, and therefore I said, I will not touch a hair of his head." Such a happy command he had of himself that his nature, in the midst of the greatest provocation, was not suffered to rebel against his principles.

V. He declares it to be his fixed resolution never to be his own avenger: "*The Lord avenge me of thee*, that is, deliver me out of thy hand; but, whatever comes of it, *my hand shall not be upon thee*" (*v.* 12), and again (*v.* 13), for *saith the proverb of the ancients, Wickedness proceedeth from the wicked.* The wisdom of the ancients is transmitted to posterity by their proverbial sayings. Many such we receive by tradition from our fathers; and the counsels of common persons are very much directed by this, "As the old saying is." Here is one that was in use in David's time: *Wickedness proceedeth from the wicked*, that is, 1. Men's own iniquity will ruin them at last, so some understand it. Froward furious men will cut their own throats with their own knives. Give them rope enough, and they will hang themselves. In this sense it comes in very fitly as a reason why *his hand should not be upon him.* 2. Bad men will do bad things; according as men's principles and dispositions are, so will their actions be. This also agrees very well with the connexion. If David had been a wicked man, as he was represented, he would have done this wicked thing; but he durst not, because of the fear of God. Or thus: Whatever injuries bad men do us (which we are not to wonder at; he that lies among thorns must expect to be scratched), yet we must not return them; never render railing for railing. Though *wickedness proceed from the wicked*, yet let it not therefore proceed from us by way of retaliation. Though the dog bark at the sheep, the sheep does not bark at the dog. See Isa. xxxii. 6—8.

VI. He endeavours to convince Saul that as it was a bad thing, so it was a mean thing, for him to give chase to such an inconsiderable person as he was (*v.* 14): *Whom does the king of Israel pursue* with all this care and force? *A dead dog; a flea; one flea*, so it is in the Hebrew. It is below so great a king to enter the lists with one that is so unequal a match for him, one of his own servants, bred a poor shepherd, now an exile, neither able nor willing to make any resistance. To conquer him would not be to his honour, to attempt it was his disparagement. If Saul would consult his own reputation, he would slight such an enemy (supposing he were really his enemy) and would think himself in no danger from him. David was so far from aspiring that he was, in his own account, as a dead dog. Mephibosheth thus calls himself, 2 Sam. ix. 8. This humble language would have wrought upon Saul if he had had any spark of generosity in him. *Satis est prostrâsse leoni—Enough for the lion that he has laid his victim low.* What credit would it be to Saul to trample upon a dead dog? What pleasure could it be to him to hunt a flea, a single flea, which (as some have observed), if it be sought, is not easily found, if it be found, is not easily caught, and, if it be caught, is a poor prize, especially for a prince. *Aquila non captat muscas—The eagle does not dart upon flies.* David thinks Saul had no more reason to fear him than to fear a flea-bite.

VII. He once and again appeals to God as the righteous Judge (*v.* 12 and *v.* 15): *The Lord judge between me and thee.* Note, The justice of God is the refuge and comfort of oppressed innocence. If men wrong us, God will right us, at furthest, in the judgment of the great day. With him David leaves his cause, and so rests satisfied, waiting his time to appear for him.

16 And it came to pass, when David had made an end of speaking these words unto Saul, that Saul said, *Is* this thy voice, my son David? And Saul lifted up his voice, and wept. 17 And he said to David, Thou *art* more righteous than I: for thou hast rewarded me good, whereas I have rewarded thee evil. 18 And thou hast showed this day how that thou hast dealt well with me: forasmuch as when the LORD had delivered me into thine hand, thou killedst me not. 19 For if a man find his enemy, will he let him go well away? wherefore the LORD reward thee good for that thou hast done unto me this day. 20 And now, behold, I know well that thou shalt surely be king, and that the kingdom of Israel shall be established in thine hand. 21 Swear now therefore unto me by the LORD, that thou wilt not cut off my seed after me, and that thou wilt not destroy my name out of my father's house. 22 And David sware unto Saul. And Saul went home; but David and his men gat them up unto the hold.

Here we have,

I. Saul's penitent reply to David's speech. It was strange that he had patience to hear him out, considering how outrageous he was against him, and how cutting David's discourse was. But God restrained him and his men; and we may suppose Saul struck with amazement at the singularity of the event, and much more when he found how much he had lain at David's mercy. His heart must have been harder than a stone if this had not affected him. 1. He melted into tears, and we will not suppose them to have been counterfeit but real expressions of his present concern at the sight of his own iniquity, so plainly proved upon him. He speaks as one quite overcome with David's kindness: *Is this thy voice, my son David?* And, as one that relented at the thought of his own folly and ingratitude, he *lifted up his voice and wept, v.* 16. Many mourn for their sins that do not truly repent of them, weep bitterly for them, and yet continue in love and league with them. 2. He ingenuously acknowledges David's integrity and his own iniquity (*v.* 17): *Thou art more righteous than I.* Now God made good to David that word on which he had caused him to hope, that he would *bring forth his righteousness as the light,* Ps. xxxvii. 6. Those who take care to keep a good conscience may leave it to God to secure them the credit of it. This fair confession was enough to prove David innocent (even his enemy himself being judge), but not enough to prove Saul himself a true penitent. He should have said, *Thou art righteous, but I am wicked;* but the utmost he will own is this: *Thou art more righteous than I.* Bad men will commonly go no further than this in their confessions; they will own they are not so good as some others are; there are those that are better than they, and more righteous. He now owns himself under a mistake concerning David (*v.* 18): "*Thou hast shown this day* that thou art so far from seeking my hurt *that thou hast dealt well with me.*" We are too apt to suspect others to be worse affected towards us than really they are, and than perhaps they are proved to be; and when, afterwards, our mistake is discovered, we should be forward to recal our suspicions, as Saul does here. 3. He prays God to recompense David for this his generous kindness to him. He owns that David's sparing him, when he had him in his power, was an uncommon and unparalleled instance of tenderness to an enemy; no man would have done the like; and therefore, either because he thought himself not able to give him a full recompence for so great a favour, or because he found himself not inclined to give him any recompence at all, he turns him over to God for his pay: *The Lord reward thee good, v.* 19. Poor beggars can do no less than pray for their benefactors, and Saul did no more. 4. He prophesies his advancement to the throne (*v.* 20): I *know well that thou shalt surely be king.* He knew it before, by the promise Samuel had made him of it compared with the excellent spirit that appeared in David, which highly aggravated his sin and folly in persecuting him as he did; he had as much reason to say concerning David as David concerning him, *How can I put forth my hand against the Lord's anointed?* But now he knew it by the interest he found David had in the people, the special providence of God in protecting him, and the generous kingly spirit he had now given a proof of in sparing his enemy. Now he knew it, that is, now that he was in a good temper he was willing to own that he knew it and to submit to the conviction of it. Note, Sooner or later, God will force even those that are of the synagogue of Satan to know and own those that he has loved, and to worship before their feet; for so is the promise, Rev. iii. 9. This acknowledgment which Saul made of David's incontestable title to the crown was a great encouragement to David himself and a support to his faith and hope. 5. He binds David with an oath hereafter to show the same tenderness of his seed and of his name as he had now shown of his person, *v.* 21. David had more reason to oblige Saul by an oath that he would not destroy him, yet he insists not on that (if the laws of justice and honour would not bind him, an oath would not), but Saul knew David to be a conscientious man, and would think his interests safe if he could get them secured by his oath. Saul by his disobedience had ruined his own soul, and never took care by repentance to prevent that ruin, and yet is very solicitous that his name might not be destroyed nor his seed cut off. However, *David swore unto him, v.* 22. Though he might be tempted, not only in revenge, but in prudence, to extirpate Saul's family, yet he binds himself not to do it, knowing that God could and would establish the kingdom to him and his, without the use of such bloody methods. This oath he afterwards religiously observed; he supported Mephibosheth, and executed those as traitors that slew Ishbosheth. The hanging up of seven of Saul's posterity, to atone for the destruction of the Gibeonites, was God's appointment, not David's act, and therefore not the violation of this oath.

II. Their parting in peace. 1. Saul, for the present, desisted from the persecution. He went home convinced, but not converted; ashamed of his envy of David, yet retaining in his breast that root of bitterness; vexed that, when at last he had found David, he could not at that time find in his heart to destroy him, as he had designed. God has many ways to tie the hands of persecutors, when he does not turn their hearts. 2. David continued to shift for his own safety. He knew Saul too well to trust him, and therefore *got him up into the hold.* It is dangerous venturing upon the mercy of a reconciled enemy. We read of those who believed in Christ, and yet he *did not commit himself to them because he knew all men.* Those that like David are innocent as doves must thus like him be *wise as serpents.*

CHAP. XXV.

We have here some intermission of David's troubles by Saul. Providence favoured him with a breathing time, and yet this chapter gives us instances of the troubles of David. If one vexation seem to be over, we must not be secure; a storm may arise from some other point, as here to David. I. Tidings of the death of Samuel could not but trouble him, ver. 1. But, II. The abuse he received from Nabal is more largely recorded in this chapter. 1. The character of Nabal, ver. 2, 3. 2. The humble request sent to him, ver. 4—9. 3. His churlish answer, ver. 10—12. 4. David's angry resentment of it, ver. 13, 21, 22. 5. Abigail's prudent care to prevent the mischief it was likely to bring upon her family, ver. 14—20. 6. Her address to David to pacify him, ver. 23—31. 7. David's favourable reception of her, ver. 32—35. 8. The death of Nabal, ver. 36—38. 9. Abigail's marriage to David, ver. 39—44.

AND Samuel died; and all the Israelites were gathered together, and lamented him, and buried him in his house at Ramah. And David arose, and went down to the wilderness of Paran.

We have here a short account of Samuel's death and burial. 1. Though he was a great man, and one that was admirably well qualified for public service, yet he spent the latter end of his days in retirement and obscurity, not because he was superannuated (for he knew how to preside in a college of the prophets, *ch.* xix. 20), but because Israel had rejected him, for which God thus justly chastised them, and because his desire was to be quiet and to enjoy himself and his God in the exercises of devotion now in his advanced years, and in this desire God graciously indulged him. Let old people be willing to rest themselves, though it look like burying themselves alive. 2. Though he was a firm friend to David, for which Saul hated him, as also for dealing plainly with him, yet he died in peace even in the worst of the days of the tyranny of Saul, who, he sometimes feared, would kill him, *ch.* xvi. 2. Though Saul loved him not, yet he feared him, as Herod did John, and feared the people, for all knew him to be a prophet. Thus is Saul restrained from hurting him. 3. All Israel lamented him; and they had reason, for they had all a loss in him. His personal merits commanded this honour to be done him at his death. His former services to the public, when he judged Israel, made this respect to his name and memory a just debt; it would have been very ungrateful to have withheld it. The sons of the prophets had lost the founder and president of their college, and whatever weakened them was a public loss. But that was not all: Samuel was a constant intercessor for Israel, prayed daily for them, *ch.* xii. 23. If he go, they part with the best friend they have. The loss is the more grievous at this juncture when Saul has grown so outrageous and David is driven from his country; never more need of Samuel than now, yet now he is removed. We will hope that the Israelites lamented Samuel's death the more bitterly because they remembered against themselves their own sin and folly in rejecting him and desiring a king. Note, (1.) Those have hard hearts who can bury their faithful ministers with dry eyes, who are not sensible of the loss of those who have prayed for them and taught them the way of the Lord. (2.) When God's providence removes our relations and friends from us we ought to be humbled for our misconduct towards them while they were with us. 4. They buried him, not in the school of the prophets at Naioth, but in his own house (or perhaps in the garden pertaining to it) at Ramah, where he was born. 5. David, hereupon, went down to the wilderness of Paran, retiring perhaps to mourn the more solemnly for the death of Samuel. Or, rather, because now that he had lost so good a friend, who was (and he hoped would be) a great support to him, he apprehended his danger to be greater than ever, and therefore withdrew to a wilderness, out of the limits of the land of Israel; and now it was that he *dwelt in the tents of Kedar*, Ps. cxx. 5. In some parts of this wilderness of Paran Israel wandered when they came out of Egypt. The place would bring to mind God's care concerning them, and David might improve that for his own encouragement, now in his wilderness-state.

2 And *there was* a man in Maon, whose possessions *were* in Carmel; and the man *was* very great, and he had three thousand sheep, and a thousand goats: and he was shearing his sheep in Carmel. 3 Now the name of the man *was* Nabal; and the name of his wife Abigail: and *she was* a woman of good understanding, and of a beautiful countenance: but the man *was* churlish and evil in his doings; and he *was* of the house of Caleb. 4 And David heard in the wilderness that Nabal did shear his sheep. 5 And David sent out ten young men, and David said unto the young men, Get you up to Carmel, and go to Nabal, and greet him in my name: 6 And thus shall ye say to him that liveth *in prosperity*, Peace *be* both to thee, and peace *be* to thine house, and peace *be* unto all that thou hast. 7 And now I have heard that thou hast shearers: now thy shepherds which were with us, we hurt them not, neither was there aught missing unto them, all the while they were in Carmel. 8 Ask thy young men, and they will show thee. Wherefore let the young men find favour in thine eyes: for we come in a good day: give, I pray thee, whatsoever cometh to thine hand unto thy ser-

vants, and to thy son David. 9 And when David's young men came, they spake to Nabal according to all those words in the name of David, and ceased. 10 And Nabal answered David's servants, and said, Who *is* David? and who *is* the son of Jesse? there be many servants now a days that break away every man from his master. 11 Shall I then take my bread, and my water, and my flesh that I have killed for my shearers, and give *it* unto men, whom I know not whence they *be?*

Here begins the story of Nabal.

I. A short account of him, who and what he was (*v.* 2, 3), a man we should never have heard of if there had not happened some communication between him and David. Observe, 1. His name: *Nabal—a fool;* so it signifies. It was a wonder that his parents would give him that name and an ill omen of what proved to be his character. Yet indeed we all of us deserve to be so called when we come into the world, for *man is born like the wild ass's colt* and *foolishness is bound up in our hearts.* 2. His family: He was of the house of Caleb, but was indeed of another spirit. He inherited Caleb's estate; for Maon and Carmel lay near Hebron, which was given to Caleb (Josh. xv. 54, 55; xiv. 14), but he was far from inheriting his virtues. He was a disgrace to his family, and then it was no honour to him. *Degeneranti genus opprobrium—A good extraction is a reproach to him who degenerates from it.* The LXX., and some other ancient versions, read it appellatively, not, He was a Calebite, but, He was a dogged man, of a currish disposition, surly and snappish, and always snarling. He was ἄνθρωπος κυνικός*—a man that was a cynic.* 3. His wealth: He was very great, that is, very rich (for riches make men look great in the eye of the world), otherwise, to one that takes his measures aright, he really looked very mean. Riches are common blessings, which God often gives to Nabals, to whom he gives neither wisdom nor grace. 4. His wife—Abigail, a woman of great understanding. Her name signifies, *the joy of her father;* yet he could not promise himself much joy of her when he married her to such a husband, enquiring more after his wealth than after his wisdom. Many a child is thrown away upon a great heap of the dirt of worldly wealth, married to that, and to nothing else that is desirable. Wisdom is good with an inheritance, but an inheritance is good for little without wisdom. Many an Abigail is tied to a Nabal; and if it be so, be her understanding, like Abigail's, ever so great, it will be little enough for her exercises. 5. His character. He had no sense either of honour or honesty; not of honour, for he was churlish, cross, and ill-humoured; not of honesty, for he was evil in his doings, hard and oppressive, and a man that cared not what fraud and violence he used in getting and saving, so he could but get and save. This is the character given of Nabal by him who knows what every man is.

II. David's humble request to him, that he would send him some victuals for himself and his men.

1. David, it seems, was in such distress that he would be glad to be beholden to him, and did in effect come a begging to his door. What little reason have we to value the wealth of this world when so great a churl as Nabal abounds and so great a saint as David suffers want! Once before we had David begging his bread, but then it was of Ahimelech the high priest, to whom one would not grudge to stoop. But to send a begging to Nabal was what such a spirit as David had could not admit without some reluctancy; yet, if Providence bring him to these straits, he will not say that to beg he is ashamed. Yet see Ps. xxxvii. 25.

2. He chose a good time to send to Nabal, when he had many hands employed about him in shearing his sheep, for whom he was to make a plentiful entertainment, so that good cheer was stirring. Had he sent at another time, Nabal would have pretended he had nothing to spare, but now he could not have that excuse. It was usual to make feasts at their sheep-shearings, as appears by Absalom's feast on that occasion (2 Sam. xiii. 24), for wool was one of the staple commodities of Canaan.

3. David ordered his men to deliver their message to him with a great deal of courtesy and respect: "*Go to Nabal, and greet him in my name.* Tell him I sent you to present my service to him, and to enquire how he does and his family," *v.* 5. He puts words in their mouths (*v.* 6): *Thus shall you say to him that liveth;* our translators add, *in prosperity,* as if those live indeed that live as Nabal did, with abundance of the wealth of this world about them; whereas, in truth, those that *live in pleasure* are *dead while they live,* 1 Tim. v. 6. This was, methinks too high a compliment to pass upon Nabal, to call him *the man that liveth.* David knew better things, that in God's favour is life, not in the world's smiles; and by the rough answer he was well enough served, for this too smooth address to such a muck-worm. Yet his good wishes were very commendable. "*Peace be to thee,* all good both to soul and body. *Peace be to thy house and to all that thou hast.*" Tell him I am a hearty well-wisher to his health and prosperity. He bids them call him his *son David* (*v.* 8), intimating that, for his age and estate, David honoured him as a father, and therefore hoped to receive some fatherly kindness from him.

4. He pleaded the kindness which Nabal's shepherds had received from David and his men; and one good turn requires another. He appeals to Nabal's own servants, and shows that when David's soldiers were quartered among Nabal's shepherds, (1.) They did not hurt them themselves, did them no injury, gave them no disturbance, were not a terror to them, nor took any of the lambs out of the flock. Yet, considering the character of David's men, men in distress, and debt, and discontented, and the scarcity of provisions in his camp, it was not without a great deal of care and good management that they were kept from plundering. (2.) They protected them from being hurt by others. David himself does but *intimate* this, for he would not boast of his good offices: *Neither was there aught missing to them, v.* 7. But Nabal's servants, to whom he appealed, went further (*v.* 16): *They were a wall unto us, both by night and day.* David's soldiers were a guard to Nabal's shepherds when the bands of the *Philistines robbed the threshing-floors* (*ch.* xxiii. 1) and would have robbed the sheepfolds. From those plunderers Nabal's flocks were protected by David's care, and therefore he says, *Let us find favour in thy eyes.* Those that have shown kindness may justly expect to receive kindness.

5. He was very modest in his request. Though David was anointed king, he insisted not upon royal dainties, but, "Give whatsoever comes to thy hand, and we will be thankful for it." Beggars must not be choosers. Those that deserved to have been served first will now be glad of what is left. They plead, *We come in a good day,* a festival, when not only the provision is more plentiful, but the heart and hand are usually more open and free than at other times, when much may be spared and yet not be missed. David demands not what he wanted as a debt, either by way of tribute as he was a king, or by way of contribution as he was a general, but asks it as a boon to a friend, that was his humble servant. David's servants delivered their message faithfully and very handsomely, not doubting but to go back well laden with provisions.

III. Nabal's churlish answer to this modest petition, *v.* 10, 11. One could not have imagined it possible that any man should be so very rude and ill-conditioned as Nabal was. David called himself his *son,* and asked bread and a fish, but, instead thereof, Nabal gave him a stone and a scorpion; not only denied him, but abused him. If he had not thought fit to send him any supplies for fear of Ahimelech's fate, who paid dearly for his kindness to David; yet he might have given a civil answer, and made the denial as modest as the request was. But, instead of that, he falls into a passion, as covetous men are apt to do when they are asked for any thing, thinking thus to cover one sin with another, and by abusing the poor to excuse themselves from relieving them. But God will not thus be mocked. 1. He speaks scornfully of David as an insignificant man, not worth taking notice of. The Philistines could say of him, *This is* David *the king of the land,* that *slew his ten thousands* (*ch.* xxi. 11), yet Nabal his near neighbour, and one of the same tribe, affects not to know him, or not to know him to be a man of any merit or distinction: *Who is David? And who is the son of Jesse?* He could not be ignorant how much the country was obliged to David for his public services, but his narrow soul thinks not of paying any part of that debt, nor so much as of acknowledging it; he speaks of David as an inconsiderable man, obscure, and not to be regarded. Think it not strange if great men and great merits be thus disgraced. 2. He upbraids him with his present distress, and takes occasion from it to represent him as a bad man, that was fitter to be set in the stocks for a vagrant than to have any kindness shown him. How naturally does he speak the churlish clownish language of those that hate to give alms! *There are many servants now-a-days* (as if there had been none such in former days) *that break every man from his master,* suggesting that David was one of them himself ("He might have kept his place with his master Saul, and then he needed not have sent to me for provisions"), and also that he entertained and harboured those that were fugitives like himself. It would make one's blood rise to hear so great and good a man as David thus vilified and reproached by such a base churl as Nabal. *But the vile person will speak villany,* Isa. xxxii. 5—7. If men bring themselves into straits by their own folly, yet they are to be pitied and helped, and not trampled upon and starved. But David was reduced to this distress, not by any fault, no, nor any indiscretion, of his own, but purely by the good services he had done to his country and the honours which his God had put upon him; and yet he was represented as a fugitive and runagate. Let this help us to bear such reproaches and misrepresentations of us with patience and cheerfulness, and make us easy under them, that it has often been the lot of the excellent ones of the earth. Some of the best men that ever the world was blest with were counted as the *off-scouring of all things,* 1 Cor. iv. 13. 3. He insists much upon the property he had in the provisions of his table, and will by no means admit any body to share in them. "It is my bread and my flesh, yes, and my water too (though *usus communis aquarum—water is every one's property*), and it is prepared for my shearers," priding himself in it that it was all his own; and who denied it? Who offered to dispute his title? But this, he thinks, will justify him in keeping it all to himself, and giving David none;

for may he not do what he will with his own? Whereas we mistake if we think we are absolute lords of what we have and may do what we please with it. No, we are but stewards, and must use it as we are directed, remembering it is not our own, but his that entrusted us with it. Riches are *τα ἀλλότρια* (Luke xvi. 12); they are *another's*, and we ought not to talk too much of their being our own.

12 So David's young men turned their way, and went again, and came and told him all those sayings. 13 And David said unto his men, Gird ye on every man his sword. And they girded on every man his sword; and David also girded on his sword: and there went up after David about four hundred men; and two hundred abode by the stuff. 14 But one of the young men told Abigail, Nabal's wife, saying, Behold, David sent messengers out of the wilderness to salute our master; and he railed on them. 15 But the men *were* very good unto us, and we were not hurt, neither missed we any thing, as long as we were conversant with them, when we were in the fields: 16 They were a wall unto us both by night and day, all the while we were with them keeping the sheep. 17 Now therefore know and consider what thou wilt do; for evil is determined against our master, and against all his household: for he *is such* a son of Belial, that *a man* cannot speak to him.

Here is, I. The report made to David of the abuse Nabal had given to his messengers (*v.* 12): *They turned their way.* They showed their displeasure, as became them to do, by breaking off abruptly from such a churl, but prudently governed themselves so well as not to render railing for railing, not to call him as he deserved, much less to take by force what ought of right to have been given them, but came and told David that he might do as he thought fit. Christ's servants, when they are thus abused, must leave it to him to plead his own cause and wait till he appear in it. The servant showed his lord what affronts he had received, but did not return them, Luke xiv. 21.

II. David's hasty resolution hereupon. He girded on his sword, and ordered his men to do so too, to the number of 400, *v.* 13. And what he said we are told, *v.* 21, 22. 1. He repented of the kindness he had done to Nabal, and looked upon it as thrown away upon him. He said, "*Surely in vain have I kept all that this fellow hath in the wilderness.* I thought to oblige him and make him my friend, but I see it is to no purpose. He has no sense of gratitude, nor is he capable of receiving the impressions of a good turn, else he could not have used me thus. He hath *requited me evil for good.*" But, when we are thus requited, we should not repent of the good we have done, nor be backward to do good another time. God is kind to the evil and unthankful, and why may not we? 2. He determined to destroy Nabal and all that belonged to him, *v.* 22. Here David did not act like himself. His resolution was bloody, to cut off all the males of Nabal's house, and spare none, man nor man-child. The ratification of his resolution was passionate: *So, and more also do God* (he was going to say *to me*, but that would better become Saul's mouth (*ch.* xiv. 44) than David's, and therefore he decently turns it off) *to the enemies of David. Is this thy voice, O David?* Can the man after God's own heart speak thus unadvisedly with his lips? Has he been so long in the school of affliction, where he should have learned patience, and yet so passionate? Is this he who used to be dumb and deaf when he was reproached (Ps. xxxviii. 13), who but the other day spared him who sought his life, and yet now will not spare any thing that belongs to him who has only put an affront upon his messengers? He who at other times used to be calm and considerate is now put into such a heat by a few hard words that nothing will atone for them but the blood of a whole family. Lord, what is man! What are the best of men, when God leaves them to themselves, to try them, that they may know what is in their hearts? From Saul David expected injuries, and against those he was prepared and stood upon his guard, and so kept his temper; but from Nabal he expected kindness, and therefore the affront he gave him was a surprise to him, found him off his guard, and, by a sudden and unexpected attack, put him for the present into disorder. What need have we to pray, *Lord, lead us not into temptation!*

III. The account given of this matter to Abigail by one of the servants, who was more considerate than the rest, *v.* 14. Had this servant spoken to Nabal, and shown him the danger he had exposed himself to by his own rudeness, he would have said, "Servants are now-a-days so saucy, and so apt to prescribe, that there is no enduring them," and, it may be, would have turned him out of doors. But Abigail, being a woman of good understanding, took cognizance of the matter, even from her servant, who, 1. Did David justice in commending him and his men for their civility to Nabal's shepherds, *v.* 15, 16. "The men were very good to us, and, though they were themselves exposed, yet they protected us and were a wall unto us." Those who do that which is good shall, one way or other, have the praise of the same. Nabal's own servant will be a witness for David that he is a man of honour and conscience, whatever Nabal himself says of him. And, 2. He did Nabal no wrong in condemning him for his rudeness to David's messengers: *He railed on them* (*v.* 14), *he flew upon them* (so the word is) with an intolerable rage; "for," say they, "it is his usual practice, *v.* 17. He is such a son of Belial, so very morose and intractable, that a man cannot speak to him but he flies into a passion immediately." Abigail knew it too well herself. 3. He did Abigail and the whole family a kindness in making her sensible what was likely to be the consequence. He knew David so well that he had reason to think he would highly resent the affront, and perhaps had had information of David's orders to his men to march that way; for he is very positive *evil is determined against our master, and all his household,* himself among the rest, would be involved in it. Therefore he desires his mistress to consider what was to be done for their common safety. They could not resist the force David would bring down upon them, nor had they time to send to Saul to protect them; something therefore must be done to pacify David.

18 Then Abigail made haste, and took two hundred loaves, and two bottles of wine, and five sheep ready dressed, and five measures of parched *corn*, and a hundred clusters of raisins, and two hundred cakes of figs, and laid *them* on asses. 19 And she said unto her servants, Go on before me; behold, I come after you. But she told not her husband Nabal. 20 And it was *so, as* she rode on the ass, that she came down by the covert of the hill, and, behold, David and his men came down against her; and she met them. 21 Now David had said, Surely in vain have I kept all that this *fellow* hath in the wilderness, so that nothing was missed of all that *pertained* unto him: and he hath requited me evil for good. 22 So and more also do God unto the enemies of David, if I leave of all that *pertain* to him by the morning light any that pisseth against the wall. 23 And when Abigail saw David, she hasted, and lighted off the ass, and fell before David on her face, and bowed herself to the ground, 24 And fell at his feet, and said, Upon me, my lord, *upon* me *let this* iniquity *be:* and let thine handmaid, I pray thee, speak in thine audience, and hear the words of thine handmaid. 25 Let not my lord, I pray thee, regard this man of Belial, *even* Nabal: for as his name *is*, so *is* he; Nabal *is* his name, and folly *is* with him: but I thine handmaid saw not the young men of my lord, whom thou didst send. 26 Now therefore, my lord, *as* the LORD liveth, and *as* thy soul liveth, seeing the LORD hath withholden thee from coming to *shed* blood, and from avenging thyself with thine own hand, now let thine enemies, and they that seek evil to my lord, be as Nabal. 27 And now this blessing which thine handmaid hath brought unto my lord, let it even be given unto the young men that follow my lord. 28 I pray thee, forgive the trespass of thine handmaid: for the LORD will certainly make my lord a sure house; because my lord fighteth the battles of the LORD, and evil hath not been found in thee *all* thy days. 29 Yet a man is risen to pursue thee, and to seek thy soul: but the soul of my lord shall be bound in the bundle of life with the LORD thy God; and the souls of thine enemies, them shall he sling out, *as out* of the middle of a sling. 30 And it shall come to pass, when the LORD shall have done to my lord according to all the good that he hath spoken concerning thee, and shall have appointed thee ruler over Israel; 31 That this shall be no grief unto thee, nor offence of heart unto my lord, either that thou hast shed blood causeless, or that my lord hath avenged himself: but when the LORD shall have dealt well with my lord, then remember thine handmaid.

We have here an account of Abigail's prudent management for the preserving of her husband and family from the destruction that was just coming upon them; and we find that she did her part admirably well and fully answered her character. The passion of fools often makes those breaches in a little time which the wise, with all their wisdom, have much ado to make up again. It is hard to say whether Abigail was more miserable in such a husband or Nabal happy in such a wife. A *virtuous woman is a crown to her husband,* to protect as well as adorn, and will *do him good and not evil.* Wisdom in such a case as this was better than weapons of war. 1. It was her wisdom that what she did she did quickly, and without delay; she made haste, *v.* 18. It was no time to trifle or linger when all was in danger. Those that desire conditions of peace must send when the enemy is yet a great way off, Luke xiv. 32. 2. It was her wisdom that what she did she did herself, because, being a woman of great prudence and very happy address, she knew better how to manage it than any servant she had. The virtuous woman will herself *look well to the ways of her household,* and not devolve this duty wholly upon others.

Abigail must endeavour to atone for Nabal's faults. Now he had been in two ways rude to David's messengers, and in them to David: He had denied them the provisions they asked for, and he had given them very provoking language. Now,

I. By a most generous present, Abigail atones for his denial of their request. If Nabal had given them what came next to hand, they would have gone away thankful; but Abigail prepares the very best the house afforded and abundance of it (*v.* 18), according to the usual entertainments of those times, not only *bread* and *flesh,* but *raisins* and *figs,* which were their dried sweet-meats. Nabal grudged them *water,* but she took *two bottles (casks* or *rundlets) of wine,* loaded her asses with these provisions, and sent them before; for *a gift pacifieth anger,* Prov. xxi. 14. Jacob thus pacified Esau. When the *instruments of the churl are evil, the liberal devises liberal things,* and loses nothing by it; for by *liberal things shall he stand,* Isa. xxxii. 7, 8. Abigail not only lawfully, but laudably, disposed of all these goods of her husband's without his knowledge (even when she had reason to think that if he had known what she did he would not have consented to it), because it was not to gratify her own pride or vanity, but for the necessary defence of him and his family, which otherwise would have been inevitably ruined. Husbands and wives, for their common good and benefit, have a joint-interest in their worldly possessions; but if either waste, or unduly spend in any way, it is a robbing of the other.

II. By a most obliging demeanour, and charming speech, she atones for the abusive language which Nabal had given them. She met David upon the march, big with resentment, and meditating the destruction of Nabal (*v.* 20); but with all possible expressions of complaisance and respect she humbly begs his favour, and solicits him to pass by the offence. Her demeanour was very submissive: *She bowed herself to the ground before David* (*v.* 23) *and fell at his feet, v.* 24. Yielding pacifies great offences. She put herself into the place and posture of a penitent and of a petitioner, and was not ashamed to do it, when it was for the good of her house, in the sight both of her own servants and of David's soldiers. She humbly begs of David that he will give her the hearing: *Let thy handmaid speak in thy audience.* But she needed not thus to bespeak his attention and patience; what she said was sufficient to command it, for certainly nothing could be more fine nor more moving. No topic of argument is left untouched; every thing is well placed and well expressed, most pertinently and pathetically urged, and improved to the best advantage, with such a force of natural rhetoric as cannot easily be paralleled.

1. She speaks to him all along with the deference and respect due to so great and good a man, calls him *My lord,* over and over, to expiate her husband's crime in saying, "Who is David?" She does not upbraid him with the heat of his passion, though he deserved to be reproved for it; nor does she tell him how ill it became his character; but endeavours to soften him and bring him to a better temper, not doubting but that then his own conscience would upbraid him with it.

2. She takes the blame of the ill-treatment of his messengers upon herself: "*Upon me, my lord, upon me, let this iniquity be, v.* 24. If thou wilt be angry, be angry with me, rather than with my poor husband, and look upon it *as the trespass of thy handmaid,*" *v.* 28. Sordid spirits care not how much others suffer for their faults, while generous spirits can be content to suffer for the faults of others. Abigail here discovered the sincerity and strength of her conjugal affection and concern for her family: whatever Nabal was, he was her husband.

3. She excuses her husband's fault by imputing it to his natural weakness and want of understanding (*v.* 25): "*Let not my lord* take notice of his rudeness and ill manners, for it is like him; it is not the first time that he has behaved so churlishly; he must be borne with, for it is for want of wit: *Nabal is his name*" (which signifies *a fool),* "*and folly is with him.* It was owing to his folly, not his malice. He is simple, but not spiteful. Forgive him, for he knows not what he does." What she said was too true, and she said it to excuse his fault and prevent his ruin, else she would not have done well to give such a bad character as this of her own husband, whom she ought to make the best of, and not to speak ill of.

4. She pleads her own ignorance of the matter: "*I saw not the young men,* else they should have had a better answer, and should not have gone without their errand," intimating hereby that though her husband was foolish, and unfit to manage his affairs himself, yet he had so much wisdom as to be ruled by her and take her advice.

5. She takes it for granted that she has gained her point already, perhaps perceiving,

by David's countenance, that he began to change his mind (*v.* 26): *Seeing the Lord hath withholden thee.* She depends not upon her own reasonings, but God's grace, to mollify him, and doubts not but that grace would work powerfully upon him; and then, "*Let all thy enemies be as Nabal,* that is, if thou forbear to avenge thyself, no doubt God will avenge thee on him, as he will on all thy other enemies." Or it intimates that it was below him to take vengeance on so weak and impotent an enemy as Nabal was, who, as he would do him no kindness, so he could do him no hurt, for he needed to wish no more concerning his enemies than that they might be as unable to resist him as Nabal was. Perhaps she refers to his sparing Saul, when, but the other day, he had him at his mercy. "Didst thou forbear to avenge thyself on that lion that would devour thee, and wilt thou shed the blood of this dog that can but bark at thee?" The very mentioning of what he was about to do, to shed blood and to avenge himself, was enough to work upon such a tender gracious spirit as David had; and it should seem, by his reply (*v.* 33), that it affected him.

6. She makes a tender of the present she had brought, but speaks of it as unworthy of David's acceptance, and therefore desires it may be given to the *young men that followed him* (*v.* 27), and particularly to those ten that were his messengers to Nabal, and whom he had treated so rudely.

7. She applauds David for the good services he had done against the common enemies of his country, the glory of which great achievements, she hoped, he would not stain by any personal revenge: "*My lord fighteth the battles of the Lord* against the Philistines, and therefore he will leave it to God to fight his battles against those that affront him, *v.* 28. *Evil has not been found in thee all thy days.* Thou never yet didst wrong to any of thy countrymen (though persecuted as a traitor), and therefore thou wilt not begin now, nor do a thing which Saul will improve for the justifying of his malice against thee."

8. She foretels the glorious issue of his present troubles. "It is true *a man pursues thee* and *seeks thy life*" (she names not Saul, out of respect to his present character as king), "but thou needest not look with so sharp and jealous an eye upon every one that affronts thee;" for all these storms that now ruffle thee will be blown over shortly. She speaks it with assurance, (1.) That God would keep him safe: *The soul of my lord shall be bound in the bundle of life with the Lord thy God,* that is, God shall *hold thy soul in life* (as the expression is, Ps. lxvi. 9) as we hold those things which are bundled up or which are precious to us, Ps. cxvi. 15. *Thy soul shall be treasured up in the treasure of lives* (so the Chaldee), under lock and key as our treasure is. "Thou shalt abide under the special protection of the divine providence." The *bundle of life is with the Lord our God,* for in his hand our breath is, and our times Those are safe, and may be easy, that have him for their protector. The Jews understand this not only of the *life that now is,* but of that *which is to come,* even the happiness of separate souls, and therefore use it commonly as an inscription on their gravestones. "Here we have laid the body, but trust that *the soul is bound up in the bundle of life, with the Lord our God.*" There it is safe, while the dust of the body is scattered. (2.) That God would make him victorious over his enemies. Their souls he shall *sling out, v.* 29. The stone is bound up in the sling, but it is in order to be thrown out again; so the souls of the godly shall be bundled as corn for the barn, but the souls of the wicked as tares for the fire. (3.) That God would settle him in wealth and power: "*The Lord will certainly make my lord a sure house,* and no enemy thou hast can hinder it; therefore *forgive this trespass,*" that is, "show mercy, as thou hopest to find mercy. God will make thee great, and it is the glory of great men to pass by offences."

9. She desires him to consider how much more comfortable it would be to him in the reflection to have forgiven this affront than to have revenged it, *v.* 30, 31. She reserves this argument for the last, as a very powerful one with so good a man, that the less he indulged his passion the more he consulted his peace and the repose of his own conscience, which every wise man will be tender of. (1.) She cannot but think that if he should avenge himself it would afterwards be a grief and an offence of heart to him. Many have done that in a heat which they have a thousand times wished undone again. The sweetness of revenge is soon turned into bitterness. (2.) She is confident that if he pass by the offence it will afterwards be no grief to him; but, on the contrary, it would yield him unspeakable satisfaction that his wisdom and grace had got the better of his passion. Note, When we are tempted to sin we should consider how it will appear in the reflection. Let us never do any thing for which our own consciences will afterwards have occasion to upbraid us, and which we shall look back upon with regret: *My heart shall not reproach me.*

10. She recommends herself to his favour: *When the Lord shall have dealt well with my lord, then remember thy handmaid,* as one that kept thee from doing that which would have disgraced thy honour, disquieted thy conscience, and made a blot in thy history. We have reason to remember those with respect and gratitude who have been instrumental to keep us from sin.

32 And David said to Abigail, Blessed *be* the LORD God of Israel, which sent thee this day to meet me:

33 And blessed *be* thy advice, and blessed *be* thou, which hast kept me this day from coming to *shed* blood, and from avenging myself with mine own hand. 34 For in very deed, *as* the LORD God of Israel liveth, which hath kept me back from hurting thee, except thou hadst hasted and come to meet me, surely there had not been left unto Nabal by the morning light any that pisseth against the wall. 35 So David received of her hand *that* which she had brought him, and said unto her, Go up in peace to thine house; see, I have hearkened to thy voice, and have accepted thy person.

As an ear-ring of gold, and an ornament of fine gold, so is a wise reprover upon an obedient ear, Prov. xxv. 12. Abigail was a wise reprover of David's passion, and he gave an obedient ear to the reproof, according to his own principle (Ps. cxli. 5): *Let the righteous smite me, it shall be a kindness.* Never was such an admonition either better given or better taken.

I. David gives God thanks for sending him this happy check to a sinful way (*v.* 32): *Blessed be the Lord God of Israel, who sent thee this day to meet me.* Note, 1. God is to be acknowledged in all the kindnesses that our friends do us either for soul or body. Whoever meet us with counsel, direction, comfort, caution, or seasonable reproof, we must see God sending them. 2. We ought to be very thankful for those happy providences which are means of preventing sin.

II. He gives Abigail thanks for interposing so opportunely between him and the mischief he was about to do: *Blessed be thy advice, and blessed be thou, v.* 33. Most people think it enough if they take a reproof patiently, but we meet with few that will take it thankfully and will commend those that give it to them and accept it as a favour. Abigail did not rejoice more that she had been instrumental to save her husband and family from death than David did that Abigail had been instrumental to save him and his men from sin.

III. He seems very apprehensive of the great danger he was in, which magnified the mercy of his deliverance. 1. He speaks of the sin as very great. He was coming to shed blood, a sin of which when in his right mind he had a great horror, witness his prayer, *Deliver me from blood-guiltiness.* He was coming to *avenge himself with his own hand*, and that would be stepping into the throne of God, who has said, *Vengeance is mine; I will repay.* The more heinous any sin is the greater mercy it is to be kept from it. He seems to aggravate the evil of his design with this, that it would have been an injury to so wise and good a woman as Abigail: God has *kept me back from hurting thee, v.* 34. Or perhaps, at the first sight of Abigail, he was conscious of a thought to do her a mischief for offering to oppose him, and therefore reckons it a great mercy that God gave him patience to hear her speak. 2. He speaks of the danger of his falling into it as very imminent: "*Except thou hadst hasted*, the bloody execution had been done." The nearer we were to the commission of sin the greater was the mercy of a seasonable restraint—*Almost gone* (Ps. lxxiii. 2) and yet upheld.

IV. He dismissed her with an answer of peace, *v.* 35. He does, in effect, own himself overcome by her eloquence: "*I have hearkened to thy voice*, and will not prosecute the intended revenge, for I *have accepted thy person*, am well pleased with thee and what thou hast said." Note, 1. Wise and good men will hear reason, and let that rule them, though it come from those that are every way their inferiors, and though their passions are up and their spirits provoked. 2. Oaths cannot bind us to that which is sinful. David had solemnly vowed the death of Nabal. He did evil to make such a vow, but he would have done worse if he had performed it. 3. A wise and faithful reproof is often better taken, and speeds better, than we expected, such is the hold God has of men's consciences. See Prov. xxviii. 23.

36 And Abigail came to Nabal; and, behold, he held a feast in his house, like the feast of a king; and Nabal's heart *was* merry within him, for he *was* very drunken: wherefore she told him nothing, less or more, until the morning light. 37 But it came to pass in the morning, when the wine was gone out of Nabal, and his wife had told him these things, that his heart died within him, and he became *as* a stone. 38 And it came to pass about ten days *after*, that the LORD smote Nabal, that he died. 39 And when David heard that Nabal was dead, he said, Blessed *be* the LORD, that hath pleaded the cause of my reproach from the hand of Nabal, and hath kept his servant from evil: for the LORD hath returned the wickedness of Nabal upon his own head. And David sent and communed with Abigail, to take her to him to wife. 40 And when the servants of David were come to Abigail to Carmel, they spake unto her, saying, David sent us unto thee, to take thee to him to

wife. 41 And she arose, and bowed herself on *her* face to the earth, and said, Behold, *let* thine handmaid *be* a servant to wash the feet of the servants of my lord. 42 And Abigail hasted, and arose, and rode upon an ass, with five damsels of her's that went after her; and she went after the messengers of David, and became his wife. 43 David also took Ahinoam of Jezreel; and they were also both of them his wives. 44 But Saul had given Michal his daughter, David's wife, to Phalti the son of Laish, which *was* of Gallim.

We are now to attend Nabal's funeral and Abigail's wedding.

I. Nabal's funeral. The apostle speaks of some that were *twice dead,* Jude 12. We have here Nabal *thrice* dead, though but just now wonderfully rescued from the sword of David and delivered from so great a death; for the preservations of wicked men are but reservations for some further sorer strokes of divine wrath. Here is,

1. *Nabal dead drunk, v.* 36. Abigail came home, and, it should seem, he had so many people and so much plenty about him that he neither missed her nor the provisions she took to David; but she found him in the midst of his jollity, little thinking how near he was to ruin by one whom he had foolishly made his enemy. Sinners are often most secure when they are most in danger and destruction is at the door. Observe, (1.) How extravagant he was in the entertainment of his company: *He held a feast like the feast of a king,* so magnificent and abundant, though his guests were but his sheep-shearers. This abundance might have been allowed if he had considered what God gave him his estate for, not to look great with, but to do good with. It is very common for those that are most niggardly in any act of piety or charity to be most profuse in gratifying a vain humour or a base lust. A mite is grudged to God and his poor; but, to make a *fair show in the flesh, gold is lavished out of the bag.* If Nabal had not answered to his name, he would never have been thus secure and jovial, till he had enquired whether he was safe from David's resentments; but (as bishop Hall observes) thus foolish are carnal men, that give themselves over to their pleasures before they have taken any care to make their peace with God. (2.) How sottish he was in the indulgence of his own brutish appetite: *He was very drunk,* a sign he was *Nabal, a fool,* that could not use his plenty without abusing it, could not be pleasant with his friends without making a beast of himself. There is not a surer sign that a man has but little wisdom, nor a surer way to ruin the little he has, than drinking to excess. Nabal, that never thought he could bestow too little in charity, never thought he could bestow too much in luxury. Abigail, finding him in this condition (and probably those about him little better, when the master of the feast set them so bad an an example), had enough to do to set the disordered house to-rights a little, but told Nabal nothing of what she had done with reference to David, nothing of his folly in provoking David, of his danger or of his deliverance, for, being drunk, he was as incapable to hear reason as he was to speak it. To give good advice to those that are in drink is to *cast pearls before swine;* it is better to stay till they are sober.

2. Nabal again dead with melancholy, *v.* 37. Next morning, when he had come to himself a little, his wife told him how near to destruction he had brought himself and his family by his own rudeness, and with what difficulty she had interposed to prevent it; and, upon this, *his heart died within him and he became as a stone.* Some suggest that the expense of the satisfaction made to David, by the present Abigail brought him, broke his heart: it seems rather that the apprehension he now had of the danger he had narrowly escaped put him into a consternation, and seized his spirits so that he could not recover it. He grew sullen, and said little, ashamed of his own folly, put out of countenance by his wife's wisdom. How is he changed! His heart over-night merry with wine, next morning heavy as a stone; so deceitful are carnal pleasures, so transient the laughter of the fool. *The end of that mirth is heaviness.* Drunkards are sometimes sad when they reflect upon their own folly. Joy in God makes the heart always light. Abigail could never, by her wise reasonings, bring Nabal to repentance; but now, by her faithful reproof, she brings him to despair.

3. Nabal, at last, dead indeed: *About ten days after,* when he had been kept so long under this pressure and pain, *the Lord smote him that he died* (*v.* 38), and, it should seem, he never held up his head; it is just with God (says bishop Hall) that those who live without grace should die without comfort, nor can we expect better while we go on in our sins. Here is no lamentation made for Nabal. He departed without being lamented. Every one wished that the country might never sustain a greater loss. *David,* when he heard the news of his death, *gave God thanks* for it, *v.* 39. He blessed God, (1.) That he had kept him from killing him: *Blessed be the Lord, who hath kept his servant from evil.* He rejoices that Nabal died a natural death and not by his hand. We should take all occasions to mention and magnify God's goodness to us in keeping us from sin. (2.) That he had taken the work into his own hands, and had vindicated David's honour, and not suffered him to go unpunished who

had been abusive to him; hereby his interest would be confirmed, and all would stand in awe of him, as one for whom God fought. (3.) That he had thereby encouraged him and all others to commit their cause to God, when they are in any way injured, with an assurance that, in his own time, he will redress their wrongs if they sit still and leave the matter to him.

II. Abigail's wedding. David was so charmed with the beauty of her person, and the uncommon prudence of her conduct and address, that, as soon as was convenient, after he heard she was a widow, he informed her of his attachment to her (*v.* 39), not doubting but that she who approved herself so good a wife to so bad a husband as Nabal would much more make a good wife to him, and having taken notice of her respect to him and her confidence of his coming to the throne. 1. He courted by proxy, his affairs, perhaps, not permitting him to come himself. 2. She received the address with great modesty and humility (*v.* 41), reckoning herself unworthy of the honour, yet having such a respect for him that she would gladly be one of the poorest servants in his family, to wash the feet of the other servants. None so fit to be preferred as those that can thus humble themselves. 3. She agreed to the proposal, went with his messengers, took a retinue with her agreeable to her quality, and *she became his wife*, *v.* 42. She did not upbraid him with his present distresses, and ask him how he could maintain her, but valued him, (1.) Because she knew he was a very good man. (2.) Because she believed he would, in due time, be a very great man. She married him in faith, not questioning but that, though now he had not a house of his own that he durst bring her to, yet God's promise to him would at length be fulfilled. Thus those who join themselves to Christ must be willing now to suffer with him, believing that hereafter they shall reign with him.

Lastly, On this occasion we have some account of David's wives. 1. One that he had lost before he married Abigail, Michal, Saul's daughter, his first, and the wife of his youth, to whom he would have been constant if she would have been so to him, but Saul had given her to another (*v.* 44), in token of his displeasure against him and disclaiming the relation of a father-in-law to him. 2. Another that he married besides Abigail (*v.* 43), and, as should seem, before her, for she is named first, *ch.* xxvii. 3. David was carried away by the corrupt custom of those times; but from the beginning it was not so, nor is it so now that Messias has come, and the times of reformation, Matt. xix. 4, 5. Perhaps Saul's defrauding David of his only rightful wife was the occasion of his running into this irregularity; for, when the knot of conjugal affection is once loosed, it is scarcely ever tied fast again. When David could not keep his first wife he thought that would excuse him if he did not keep to his second. But we deceive ourselves if we think to make others' faults a cloak for our own.

CHAP. XXVI.

David's troubles from Saul here begin again; and the clouds return after the rain, when one would have hoped the storm had blown over, and the sky had cleared upon that side; but after Saul had owned his fault in persecuting David, and acknowledged David's title to the crown, yet here he revives the persecution, so perfectly lost was he to all sense of honour and virtue. I. The Ziphites informed him where David was (ver. 1), and thereupon he marched out with a considerable force in quest of him, ver. 2, 3. II. David gained intelligence of his motions (ver. 4), and took a view of his camp, ver. 5. III. He and one of his men ventured into his camp in the night and found him and all his guards fast asleep, ver. 6, 7. IV. David, though much urged to it by his companions, would not take away Saul's life, but only carried off his spear and his cruse of water, ver. 8—12. V. He produced these as a further witness for him that he did not design any ill to Saul, and reasoned with him upon his conduct, ver. 13—20. VI. Saul was hereby convinced of his error, and once more desisted from persecuting David, ver. 21—25. The story is much like that which we had ch. xxiv. In both David is delivered out of Saul's hand, and Saul out of David's.

AND the Ziphites came unto Saul to Gibeah, saying, Doth not David hide himself in the hill of Hachilah, *which is* before Jeshimon? 2 Then Saul arose, and went down to the wilderness of Ziph, having three thousand chosen men of Israel with him, to seek David in the wilderness of Ziph. 3 And Saul pitched in the hill of Hachilah, which *is* before Jeshimon, by the way. But David abode in the wilderness, and he saw that Saul came after him into the wilderness. 4 David therefore sent out spies, and understood that Saul was come in very deed. 5 And David arose, and came to the place where Saul had pitched: and David beheld the place where Saul lay, and Abner the son of Ner, the captain of his host: and Saul lay in the trench and the people pitched round about him.

Here, 1. Saul gets information of David's movements and acts offensively. The Ziphites came to him and told him where David now was, in the same place where he was when they formerly betrayed him, *ch.* xxiii. 19. Perhaps (though it is not mentioned) Saul had given them intimation, under-hand, that he continued his design against David, and would be glad of their assistance. If not, they were very officious to Saul, aware of what would please him, and very malicious against David, to whom they despaired of ever reconciling themselves, and therefore they stirred up Saul (who needed no such spur) against him, *v.* 1. For aught we know, Saul would have continued in the same good mind that he was in (*ch.* xxiv. 17), and would not have given David this fresh trouble, if the Ziphites had not put him on. See what need we have to pray to God that, since we have so much of the tinder of corruption in our own hearts, the sparks of temptation may be kept far from us, lest, if they come together, we be set on fire of hell. Saul readily caught at the information, and went down with an army of 3000 men to the place where David hid himself, *v.* 2. How soon do unsanctified hearts lose the good impressions which their convictions have made upon them and return with the dog to their vomit!

2. David gets information of Saul's movements and acts defensively. He did not march out to meet and fight him; he sought only his own safety, not Saul's ruin; therefore he *abode in the wilderness* (*v.* 3), putting thereby a great force upon himself, and curbing the bravery of his own spirit by a silent retirement, showing more true valour than he could have done by an irregular resistance. (1.) He had spies who informed him of Saul's descent, *that he had come in very deed* (*v.* 4); for he would not believe that Saul would deal so basely with him till he had the utmost evidence of it. (2.) He observed with his own eyes how Saul was encamped, *v.* 5. He came towards the place where Saul and his men had pitched their tents, so near as to be able, undiscovered, to take a view of their entrenchments, probably in the dusk of the evening.

6 Then answered David and said to Ahimelech the Hittite, and to Abishai the son of Zeruiah, brother to Joab, saying, Who will go down with me to Saul to the camp? And Abishai said, I will go down with thee. 7 So David and Abishai came to the people by night: and, behold, Saul lay sleeping within the trench, and his spear stuck in the ground at his bolster: but Abner and the people lay round about him. 8 Then said Abishai to David, God hath delivered thine enemy into thine hand this day: now therefore let me smite him, I pray thee, with the spear even to the earth at once, and I will not *smite* him the second time. 9 And David said to Abishai, Destroy him not: for who can stretch forth his hand against the LORD's anointed, and be guiltless? 10 David said furthermore, *As* the LORD liveth, the LORD shall smite him; or his day shall come to die; or he shall descend into battle, and perish. 11 The LORD forbid that I should stretch forth mine hand against the LORD's anointed: but, I pray thee, take thou now the spear that *is* at his bolster, and the cruse of water, and let us go. 12 So David took the spear and the cruse of water from Saul's bolster; and they gat them away, and no man saw *it*, nor knew *it*, neither awaked: for they *were* all asleep; because a deep sleep from the LORD was fallen upon them.

Here is, I. David's bold adventure into Saul's camp in the night, accompanied only by his kinsman Abishai, the son of Zeruiah. He proposed it to him and to another of his confidants (*v.* 6), but the other either declined it as too dangerous an enterprise, or at least was content that Abishai, who was forward to it, should run the risk of it rather than himself. Whether David was prompted to do this by his own courage, or by an extraordinary impression upon his spirits, or by the oracle, does not appear; but, like Gideon, he ventured through the guards, with a special assurance of the divine protection.

II. The posture he found the camp in *Saul lay sleeping in the trench*, or, as some read it, *in his chariot, and in the midst of his carriages*, with *his spear stuck in the ground* by him, to be ready if his quarters should be beaten up (*v* 7); and all the soldiers, even those that were appointed to stand sentinel, were *fast asleep*, *v.* 12. Thus were their eyes closed and their hands bound, *for a deep sleep from the Lord had fallen upon them;* something extraordinary there was in it that they should all be asleep together, and so fast asleep that David and Abishai walked and talked among them, and yet none of them stirred. Sleep, when God gives it to his beloved, is their rest and refreshment; but he can, when he pleases, make it to his enemies their imprisonment. Thus are the *stout-hearted spoiled; they have slept their sleep, and none of the men of might have found their hands, at thy rebuke, O God of Jacob!* Ps. lxxvi. 5, 6. *It was a deep sleep from the Lord*, who has the command of the powers of nature, and makes them to serve his purposes as he pleases. Whom God will disable, or destroy, he binds up with *a spirit of slumber*, Rom. xi. 8. How helpless do Saul and all his forces lie, all, in effect, disarmed and chained! and yet nothing is done to them; they are only rocked asleep. How easily can God weaken the strongest, befool the wisest, and baffle the most watchful! Let all his friends therefore trust him and all his enemies fear him.

III. Abishai's request to David for a commission to dispatch Saul with the spear that stuck at his bolster, which (now that he lay so fair) he undertook to do at one blow, *v.* 8. He would not urge David to kill him himself, because he had declined doing this before when he had a similar opportunity; but he begged earnestly that David would give him leave to do it, pleading that he was his enemy, not only cruel and implacable, but false and perfidious, whom no reason would rule nor kindness work upon, and that *God had now delivered him into his hand,* and did in effect bid him strike. The last advantage he had of this kind was indeed but accidental, when Saul happened to be in the cave with him at the same time. But in this there was something extraordinary; the deep sleep that had fallen on Saul and all his guards was manifestly from the Lord, so that it was a special providence which gave him this opportunity; he ought not therefore to let it slip.

IV. David's generous refusal to suffer any harm to be done to Saul, and in it a resolute adherence to his principles of loyalty, *v.* 9. David charged Abishai not to destroy him, would not only not do it himself, but not permit another to do it. And he gave two reasons for it:—1. It would be a sinful affront to God's ordinance. Saul was the Lord's anointed, king of Israel by the special appointment and nomination of the God of Israel, the power that was, and to resist him was to *resist the ordinance of God,* Rom. xiii. 2. No man could do it and be guiltless. The thing he feared was guilt and his concern respected his innocence more than his safety. 2. It would be a sinful anticipation of God's providence. God had sufficiently shown him, in Nabal's case, that, if he left it to him to avenge him, he would do it in due time. Encouraged therefore by his experience in that instance, he resolves to wait till God shall think fit to avenge him on Saul, and he will by no means *avenge himself* (*v.* 10): "*The Lord shall smite him,* as he did Nabal, with some sudden stroke, or he shall *die in battle* (as it proved he did soon after), or, if not, *his day shall come to die* a natural death, and I will contentedly wait till then, rather than force my way to the promised crown by any indirect methods." The temptation indeed was very strong; but, if he should yield, he would sin against God, and therefore he will resist the temptation with the utmost resolution (*v.* 11): "*The Lord forbid that I should stretch forth my hand against the Lord's anointed;* no, I will never do it, nor suffer it to be done." Thus bravely does he prefer his conscience to his interest and trusts God with the issue.

V. The improvement he made of this opportunity for the further evidence of his own integrity. He and Abishai carried away the spear and cruse of water which Saul had by his bed-side (*v.* 12), and, which was very strange, none of all the guards were aware of it. If a physician had given them the strongest opiate or stupifying dose, they could not have been faster locked up with sleep. Saul's spear which he had by him for defence, and his cup of water which he had for his refreshment, were both stolen from him while he slept. Thus do we lose our strength and our comfort when we are careless, and secure, and off our watch.

13 Then David went over to the other side, and stood on the top of a hill afar off; a great space *being* between them: 14 And David cried to the people, and to Abner the son of Ner, saying, Answerest thou not, Abner? Then Abner answered and said, Who *art* thou *that* criest to the king? 15 And David said to Abner, *Art* not thou a *valiant* man? and who *is* like to thee in Israel? wherefore then hast thou not kept thy lord the king? for there came one of the people in to destroy the king thy lord. 16 This thing *is* not good that thou hast done. *As* the LORD liveth, ye *are* worthy to die, because ye have not kept your master, the LORD's anointed. And now see where the king's spear *is,* and the cruse of water that *was* at his bolster. 17 And Saul knew David's voice, and said, *Is* this thy voice, my son David? And David said, *It is* my voice, my lord, O king. 18 And he said, Wherefore doth my lord thus pursue after his servant? for what have I done? or what evil *is* in mine hand? 19 Now therefore, I pray thee, let my lord the king hear the words of his servant. If the LORD have stirred thee up against me, let him accept an offering: but if *they be* the children of men, cursed *be* they before the LORD; for they have driven me out this day from abiding in the inheritance of the LORD, saying, Go, serve other gods. 20 Now therefore, let not my blood fall to the earth before the face of the LORD: for the king of Israel is come out to seek a flea, as when one doth hunt a partridge in the mountains.

David having got safely from Saul's camp himself, and having brought with him proofs sufficient that he had been there, posts himself conveniently, so that they might hear him and yet not reach him (*v.* 13), and then begins to reason with them upon what had passed.

I. He reasons ironically with Abner, and keenly banters him. David knew well that it was from the mighty power of God that Abner and the rest of the guards were cast into so deep a sleep, and that God's immediate hand was in it; but he reproaches

Abner as unworthy to be captain of the life-guards, since he could sleep when the king his master lay so much exposed. By this it appears that the hand of God locked them up in this deep sleep that, as soon as ever David had got out of danger, a very little thing awakened them, even David's voice at a great distance roused them, *v.* 14. Abner got up (we may suppose it early in a summer's morning) and enquired who called, and disturbed the king's repose. "It is I," says David, and then he upbraids him with his sleeping when he should have been upon his guard. Perhaps Abner, looking upon David as a despicable enemy and one that there was no danger from, had neglected to set a watch; however, he himself ought to have been more wakeful. David, to put him into confusion, told him, 1. That he had lost his honour (*v.* 15): "*Art not thou a man?* (so the word is), a man in office, that art bound, by the duty of thy place, to inspect the soldiery? Art not thou in reputation for a valiant man? So thou wouldst be esteemed, a man of such courage and conduct that there is none like thee; but now thou art shamed for ever. Thou a general! Thou, a sluggard!" 2. That he deserved to lose his head (*v.* 16): "*You are all worthy to die*, by martial law, for being off your guard, when you had the king himself asleep in the midst of you. *Ecce signum—Behold this token.* See where the king's spear is, in the hand of him whom the king himself is pleased to count his enemy. Those that took away this might as easily and safely have taken away his life. Now see who are the king's best friends, you that neglected him and left him exposed or I that protected him when he was exposed. You pursue me as worthy to die, and irritate Saul against me; but who is worthy to die now?" Note, Sometimes those that unjustly condemn others are justly left to fall into condemnation themselves.

II. He reasons seriously and affectionately with Saul. By this time he was so well awake as to hear what was said, and to discern who said it (*v.* 17): *Is this thy voice, my son David?* In the same manner he had expressed his relentings, *ch.* xxiv. 16. He had given his wife to another and yet calls him *son*, thirsted after his blood and yet is glad to hear his voice. Those are bad indeed that have never any convictions of good, nor ever sincerely utter good expressions. And now David has as fair an opportunity of reaching Saul's conscience as he had just now of taking away his life. This he lays hold on, though not of that, and enters into a close argument with him, concerning the trouble he still continued to give him, endeavouring to persuade him to let fall the prosecution and be reconciled.

1. He complains of the very melancholy condition he was brought into by the enmity of Saul against him. Two things he laments:—(1.) That he was driven from his master and from his business: "*My lord pursues after his servant, v.* 18. How gladly would I serve thee as formerly if my service might be accepted! but, instead of being owned as a servant, I am pursued as a rebel, and my lord is my enemy, and he whom I would follow with respect compels me to flee from him." (2.) That he was driven from his God and from his religion; and this was a much greater grievance than the former (*v.* 19): "They have *driven me out from the inheritance of the Lord,* have made Canaan too hot for me, at least the inhabited parts of it, have forced me into the deserts and mountains, and will, ere long, oblige me entirely to quit the country." And that which troubled him was not so much that he was driven out from his own inheritance as that he was driven out from the *inheritance of the Lord,* the holy land. It should be more comfortable to us to think of God's title to our estates and his interest in them than of our own, and that with them we may honour him than that with them we may maintain ourselves. Nor was it so much his trouble that he was constrained to live among strangers as that he was constrained to live among the worshippers of strange gods and was thereby thrust into temptation to join with them in their idolatrous worship. His enemies did, in effect, send him to *go and serve other gods,* and perhaps he had heard that some of them had spoken to that purport of him. Those that forbid our attendance on God's ordinances do what in them lies to estrange us from God and to make us heathens. If David had not been a man of extraordinary grace, and firmness to his religion, the ill usage he met with from his own prince and people, who were Israelites and worshippers of the true God, would have prejudiced him against the religion they professed and have driven him to communicate with idolaters. "If these be Israelites," he might have said, "let me live and die with Philistines;" and no thanks to them that their conduct had not that effect. We are to reckon that the greatest injury that can be done us which exposes us to sin. Of those who thus led David into temptation he here says, *Cursed be they before the Lord.* Those fall under a curse that thrust out those whom God receives, and send those to the devil who are dear to God.

2. He insists upon his own innocency: *What have I done or what evil is in my hand? v.* 18. He had the testimony of his conscience for him that he had never done nor ever designed any mischief to the person, honour, or government, of his prince, nor to any of the interests of his country. He had lately had Saul's own testimony concerning him (*ch.* xxiv. 17): *Thou art more righteous than I.* It was very unreasonable and wicked for Saul to pursue him as a criminal, when he could not charge him with any crime.

3. He endeavours to convince Saul that his pursuit of him is not only wrong, but mean, and much below him: "*The king of Israel,* whose dignity is great, and who has so much other work to do, *has come out to seek a flea, as when one doth hunt a partridge in the mountains,*" *v.* 20—a poor game for the king of Israel to pursue. He compares himself to a partridge, a very innocent harmless bird, which, when attempts are made upon its life, flies if it can, but makes no resistance. And would Saul bring the flower of his army into the field only to hunt one poor partridge? What a disparagement was this to his honour! What a stain would it be on his memory to trample upon so weak and patient as well as so innocent an enemy! James v. 6, *You have killed the just, and he doth not resist you.*

4. He desires that the core of the controversy may be searched into and some proper method taken to bring it to an end, *v.* 19. Saul himself could not say that justice put him on thus to persecute David, or that he was obliged to do it for the public safety. David was not willing to say (though it was very true) that Saul's own envy and malice put him on to do it; and therefore he concludes it must be attributed either to the righteous judgment of God or to the unrighteous designs of evil men. Now, (1.) "*If the Lord have stirred thee up against me,* either in displeasure to me (taking this way to punish me for my sins against him, though, as to thee, I am guiltless) or in displeasure to thee, if it be the effect of that evil spirit from the Lord which troubles thee, *let him accept an offering* from us both—let us join in making our peace with God, reconciling ourselves to him, which may be done, by sacrifice; and then I hope the sin will be pardoned, whatever it is, and the trouble, which is so great a vexation both to thee and me, will come to an end." See the right method of peace-making; let us first make God our friend by Christ the great Sacrifice, and then all other enmities shall be slain, Eph. ii. 16; Prov. xvi. 7. But, (2.) "If thou art incited to it by wicked men, that incense thee against me, *cursed be they before they Lord,*" that is, they are very wicked people, and it is fit that they should be abandoned as such, and excluded from the king's court and councils. He decently lays the blame upon the evil counsellors who advised the king to that which was dishonourable and dishonest, and insists upon it that they be removed from about him and forbidden his presence, as men cursed before the Lord, and then he hoped he should gain his petition, which is (*v.* 20), "*Let not my blood fall to the earth,* as thou threatenest, for it is *before the face of the Lord,* who will take cognizance of the wrong and avenge it." Thus pathetically does David plead with Saul for his life, and, in order to that, for his favourable opinion of him.

21 Then said Saul, I have sinned: return, my son David: for I will no more do thee harm, because my soul was precious in thine eyes this day: behold, I have played the fool, and have erred exceedingly. 22 And David answered and said, Behold the king's spear! and let one of the young men come over and fetch it. 23 The LORD render to every man his righteousness and his faithfulness: for the LORD delivered thee into *my* hand to day, but I would not stretch forth mine hand against the LORD's anointed. 24 And, behold, as thy life was much set by this day in mine eyes, so let my life be much set by in the eyes of the LORD, and let him deliver me out of all tribulation. 25 Then Saul said to David, Blessed *be* thou, my son David: thou shalt both do great *things,* and also shalt still prevail. So David went on his way, and Saul returned to his place.

Here is, I. Saul's penitent confession of his fault and folly in persecuting David and his promise to do so no more. This second instance of David's respect to him wrought more upon him than the former, and extorted from him better acknowledgements, *v.* 21. 1. He owns himself melted and quite overcome by David's kindness to him: "*My soul was precious in thy eyes this day,* which, I thought, had been odious!" 2. He acknowledges he has done very wrong to persecute him, that he has therein acted against God's law *(I have sinned),* and against his own interest *(I have played the fool),* in pursuing him as an enemy who would have been one of his best friends, if he could but have thought so. "Herein (says he) I have *erred exceedingly,* and wronged both thee and myself." Note, Those that sin play the fool and err exceedingly, those especially that hate and persecute God's people, Job xix. 28. 3. He invites him to court again: *Return, my son David.* Those that have understanding will see it to be their interest to have those about them that *behave themselves wisely,* as David did, and have God with them. 4. He promises him that he will not persecute him as he has done, but protect him: *I will no more do thee harm.* We have reason to think, according to the mind he was now in, that he meant as he said, and yet neither his confession nor his promise of amendment came from a principle of true repentance.

II. David's improvement of Saul's convictions and confessions and the evidence he had to produce of his own sincerity. He desired that one of the footmen might fetch the spear (*v.* 22), and then (*v.* 23), 1. He appeals to God as judge of the controversy: *The Lord render to every man his righteousness.* David, by faith, is sure that he will do it because he infallibly knows the true characters of all persons and actions and is inflexibly just to render to every man according to his work, and, by prayer, he desires he would do it. Herein he does, in effect, pray against Saul, who had dealt unrighteously and unfaithfully with him (*Give them according to their deeds,* Ps. xxviii. 4); but he principally intends it as a prayer for himself, that God would protect him in his righteousness and faithfulness, and also reward him, since Saul so ill requited him. 2. He reminds Saul again of the proof he had now given of his respect to him from a principle of loyalty: *I would not stretch forth my hand against the Lord's anointed,* intimating to Saul that the anointing oil was his protection, for which he was indebted to the Lord and ought to express his gratitude to him (had he been a common person David would not have been so tender of him), perhaps with this further implication, that Saul knew, or had reason to think, David was the Lord's anointed too, and therefore, by the same rule, Saul ought to be as tender of David's life as David had been of his. 3. Not relying much upon Saul's promises, he puts himself under God's protection and begs his favour (*v.* 24): "*Let my life be much set by in the eyes of the Lord,* how light soever thou makest of it." Thus, for his kindness to Saul, he takes God to be his paymaster, which those may with a holy confidence do that *do well and suffer for it.*

III. Saul's prediction of David's advancement. He commends him (*v.* 25): *Blessed be thou, my son David.* So strong was the conviction Saul was now under of David's honesty that he was not ashamed to condemn himself and applaud David, even in the hearing of his own soldiers, who could not but blush to think that they had come out so furiously against a man whom their master, when he meets him, caresses thus. He foretels his victories, and his elevation at last: *Thou shalt do great things.* Note, Those who make conscience of doing that which is truly good may come, by the divine assistance, to do that which is truly great. He adds, "*Thou shalt also still prevail,* more and more," he means against himself, but is loth to speak that out. The princely qualities which appeared in David—his generosity in sparing Saul, his military authority in reprimanding Abner for sleeping, his care of the public good, and the signal tokens of God's presence with him—convinced Saul that he would certainly be advanced to the throne at last, according to the prophecies concerning him.

Lastly, A palliative cure being thus made of the wound, they parted friends. Saul returned to Gibeah *re infectâ—without accomplishing his design,* and ashamed of the expedition he had made; but David could not take his word so far as to return with him. Those that have once been false are not easily trusted another time. Therefore *David went on his way.* And, after this parting, it does not appear that ever Saul and David saw one another again.

CHAP. XXVII.

David was a man after God's own heart, and yet he had his faults, which are recorded, not for our imitation, but for our admonition; witness the story of this chapter, in which, though, I. We find, to his praise, that he prudently took care of his own safety and his family's (ver. 2—4) and valiantly fought Israel's battles against the Canaanites (ver. 8—9), yet, II. We find, to his dishonour, 1. That he began to despair of his deliverance, ver. 1. 2. That he deserted his own country, and went to dwell in the land of the Philistines, ver. 1, 5—7. 3. That he imposed upon Achish with an equivocation, if not a lie, concerning his expedition, ver. 10—12.

AND David said in his heart, I shall now perish one day by the hand of Saul: *there is* nothing better for me than that I should speedily escape into the land of the Philistines; and Saul shall despair of me, to seek me any more in any coast of Israel: so shall I escape out of his hand. 2 And David arose, and he passed over with the six hundred men that *were* with him unto Achish, the son of Maoch, king of Gath. 3 And David dwelt with Achish at Gath, he and his men, every man with his household, *even* David with his two wives, Ahinoam the Jezreelitess, and Abigail the Carmelitess, Nabal's wife. 4 And it was told Saul that David was fled to Gath: and he sought no more again for him. 5 And David said unto Achish, If I have now found grace in thine eyes, let them give me a place in some town in the country, that I may dwell there: for why should thy servant dwell in the royal city with thee? 6 Then Achish gave him Ziklag that day: wherefore Ziklag pertaineth unto the kings of Judah unto this day. 7 And the time that David dwelt in the country of the Philistines was a full year and four months.

Here is, I. The prevalency of David's fear, which was the effect of the weakness of his faith (*v.* 1): *He said to his heart* (so it may be read), in his communings with it concerning his present condition, *I shall now perish one day by the hand of Saul.* He represented to himself the restless rage and malice of Saul (who could not be wrought into a reconciliation) and the treachery of his own countrymen, witness that of the Ziphites, once and again; he looked upon his own forces, and observed how few they were, and that no recruits had come in to him for a great while, nor could he perceive that he got any ground; and hence, in a melancholy mood, he draws this dark conclusion: *I shall one day perish by the hand of Saul.* But, *O thou of little faith! wherefore dost thou doubt?* Was he not anointed to be king? Did not that imply an assurance that he should be preserved to the kingdom? Though he had no reason to trust Saul's promises, had he not all the reason in the world to trust the promises of God? His experience of the particular care Providence took of him ought to have encouraged him. He that has delivered does and will. But unbelief is a sin that easily besets even good men. When *without are fightings, within are fears,* and it is a hard matter to get over them. *Lord, increase our faith!*

II. The resolution he came to hereupon. Now that Saul had, for this time, returned to his place, he determined to take this opportunity of retiring into the Philistines' country. Consulting his own heart only, and not the ephod or the prophet, he concludes, *There is nothing better for me than that I should speedily escape into the land of the Philistines.* Long trials are in danger of tiring the faith and patience even of very good men. Now, 1. Saul was an enemy to himself and his kingdom in driving David to this extremity. He weakened his own interest when he expelled from his service, and forced into the service of his enemies, so great a general as David was, and so brave a regiment as he had the command of. 2. David was no friend to himself in taking this course. God had appointed him to set up his standard *in the land of Judah, ch.* xxii. 5. There God had wonderfully preserved him, and employed him sometimes for the good of his country; why then should he think of deserting his post? How could he expect the protection of the God of Israel if he went out of the borders of the land of Israel? Could he expect to be safe among the Philistines, out of whose hands he had lately escaped so narrowly by feigning himself mad? Would he receive obligations from those now whom he knew he must not return kindness to when he should come to be king, but be under an obligation to make war upon? Hereby he would gratify his enemies, who bade him go and serve other gods that they might have wherewith to reproach him, and very much weaken the hands of his friends, who would not have wherewith to answer that reproach. See what need we have to pray, *Lord, lead us not into temptation.*

III. The kind reception he had at Gath. Achish bade him welcome, partly out of generosity, being proud of entertaining so brave a man, partly out of policy, hoping to engage him for ever to his service, and that his example would invite many more to desert and come over to him. No doubt he gave David a solemn promise of protection, which he could rely upon when he could not trust Saul's promises. We may blush to think that the word of a Philistine should go further than the word of an Israelite, who, if an Israelite indeed, would be without guile, and that the city of Gath should be a place of refuge for a good man when the cities of Israel refuse him a safe abode. David, 1. Brought his men with him (*v.* 2) that they might guard him, and might themselves be safe where he was, and to recommend himself the more to Achish, who hoped to have service out of him. 3. He brought his family with him, his *wives* and *his household,* so did all *his men, v.* 2, 3. Masters of families ought to take care of those that are committed to them, to protect and provide for those of their own house, and to *dwell with them as men of knowledge.*

IV. Saul's desisting from the further prosecution of him (*v.* 4): *He sought no more again for him;* this intimates that notwithstanding the professions of repentance he had lately made, if he had had David in his reach, he would have aimed another blow. But, because he dares not come where he is, he resolves to let him alone. Thus many seem to leave their sins, but really their sins leave them; they would persist in them if they could. Saul sought no more for him, contenting himself with his banishment, since he could not have his blood, and hoping, it may be (as he had done, *ch.* xviii. 25), that he would, some time or other, *fall by the hand of the Philistines;* and, though he would rather have the pleasure of destroying him himself, yet, if they do it, he will be satisfied, so that it be done effectually.

V. David's removal from Gath to Ziklag.

1. David's request for leave to remove was prudent and very modest, *v.* 5. (1.) It was really prudent. David knew what it was to be envied in the court of Saul, and had much more reason to fear in the court of Achish, and therefore declines preferment there, and wishes for a settlement in the country, where he might be private, more within himself, and less in other people's way. In a town of his own he might have the more free exercise of his religion, and keep his men better to it, and not have his righteous soul vexed, as it was at Gath, with the idolatries of the Philistines. (2.) As it was presented to Achish it was very modest. He does not prescribe to him what place he should assign him, only begs it may be in some town in the country, where he pleased (beggars must not be choosers); but he gives this for a reason, "*Why should thy servant dwell in the royal city,* to crowd thee, and disoblige those about thee?" Note, Those that would stand fast must not covet to stand high; and humble souls aim not to dwell in royal cities.

2. The grant which Achish made to him, upon that request, was very generous and kind (*v.* 6, 7): *Achish gave him Ziklag.* Hereby, (1.) Israel recovered their ancient right; for Ziklag was in the lot of the tribe of Judah (Josh. xv. 31), and afterwards, out of that lot, was assigned, with some other cities, to Simeon, Josh. xix. 5. But either it was never subdued, or the Philistines had, in some struggle with Israel, made themselves masters of it. Perhaps they had got it unjustly, and Achish, being a man of sense and honour, took this occasion to restore it. *The righteous God judgeth righteously.* (2.) David gained a commodious settlement, not only at a distance from Gath, but bordering upon Israel, where he might keep up a correspondence with his own countrymen, and whither they might resort to him at the revolution that was now approaching. Though we do not find that he augmented his forces at all while Saul lived (for, *ch.* xxx. 10, he had but his *six hundred men*), yet, immediately after Saul's death, that was the rendezvous of his friends. Nay, it should seem, while he kept himself close because of Saul, multitudes resorted to him, at least to assure him of their sincere intentions, 1 Chron. xii. 1—22. And this further advantage David gained, that Ziklag was annexed to the crown, at least the royalty of it pertained to the kings of Judah, ever after, *v.* 6. Note, There is nothing lost by humility and modesty, and a willingness to retire. Real advantages follow those that flee from imaginary honours. Here David continued for some days, even *four months,* as it may very well be read (*v.* 7), or some days above four months: the LXX. read it, *some months;* so long he waited for the set time of his accession to the throne; for *he that believeth shall not make haste.*

8 And David and his men went up, and invaded the Geshurites, and the Gezrites, and the Amalekites: for those *nations were* of old the inhabitants of the land, as thou goest to Shur, even unto the land of Egypt. 9 And David smote the land, and left neither man nor woman alive, and took away the sheep, and the oxen, and the asses, and the camels, and the apparel, and returned, and came to Achish. 10 And Achish said, Whither have ye made a road to day? And David said, Against the south of Judah, and against the south of the Jerahmeelites, and against the south of the Kenites. 11 And David saved neither man nor woman alive, to bring *tidings* to Gath, saying, Lest they should tell on us, saying, So did David, and so *will be* his manner all the while he dwelleth in the country of the Philistines. 12 And Achish believed David, saying, He hath made his people Israel utterly to abhor him; therefore he shall be my servant for ever.

Here is an account of David's actions while he was in the land of the Philistines, a fierce attack he made upon some remains of the devoted nations, his success in it, and the representation he gave of it to Achish. 1. We may acquit him of injustice and cruelty in this action because those people whom he cut off were such as heaven had long since doomed to destruction, and he that did it was one whom heaven had ordained to dominion; so that the thing was very fit to be done, and he was very fit to do it. It was not for him that was anointed to fight the Lord's battles to sit still in sloth, however he might think fit, in modesty, to retire He desired to be safe from Saul only that he might expose himself for Israel. He avenged an old quarrel that God had with these nations, and at the same time fetched in provisions for himself and his army, for by their swords they must live. The Amalekites were to be all cut off. Probably the Geshurites and Gezrites were branches of Amalek. Saul was rejected for sparing them, David makes up the deficiency of his obedience before he succeeds him. He smote them, and *left none alive, v.* 8, 9. The service paid itself, for they carried off abundance of spoil, which served for the subsistence of David's forces. 2. Yet we cannot acquit him of dissimulation with Achish in the account he gave him of this expedition. (1.) David, it seems, was not willing that he should know the truth, and therefore spared none to carry tidings to Gath (*v.* 11), not because he was ashamed of what he had done as a bad thing, but because he was afraid, if the Philistines knew it, they would be apprehensive of danger to themselves or their allies by harbouring him among them and would expel him from their coasts. It would be easy to conclude, *If so he did, so will be his manner,* and therefore he industriously conceals it from them, which, it seems, he could do by putting them all to the sword, for none of their neighbours would inform against him, nor perhaps would soon come to the knowledge of what was done, intelligence not being so readily communicated then as now. (2.) He hid it from Achish with an equivocation not at all becoming his character Being asked which way he had made his sally, he answered, *Against the south of Judah, v.* 13. It was true he had invaded those countries that lay south of Judah, but he made Achish believe he had invaded those that lay south in Judah, the Ziphites for example, that had once and again betrayed him; so Achish understood him, and thence inferred that he *had made his people Israel to abhor him,* and so rivetted himself in the interest of Achish. The fidelity of Achish to him, his good opinion of him, and the confidence he put in him, aggravate his sin in deceiving him thus, which, with some other such instances, David seems penitently to reflect upon when he prays, *Remove from me the way of lying.*

CHAP. XXVIII.

Preparations are herein making for that war which will put an end to the life and reign of Saul, and so make way for David to the throne. In this war, I. The Philistines are the aggressors and Achish their king makes David his confidant, ver. 1, 2. II. The Israelites prepare to receive them, and Saul their king makes the devil his privy-counsellor, and thereby fills the measure of his iniquity. Observe, 1. The despairing condition which Saul was in, ver. 3—6. 2. The application he made to a witch, to bring him up Samuel, ver. 7—14. 3. His discourse with the apparition, ver. 15—19. The damp it struck upon him, ver. 20—25.

AND it came to pass in those days, that the Philistines gathered their armies together for warfare, to fight with Israel. And Achish said unto David, Know thou assuredly, that thou shalt go out with me to battle, thou and thy men. 2 And David said to Achish, Surely thou shalt know what thy servant can do. And Achish said to David, Therefore will I make thee keeper of mine head for ever. 3 Now Samuel was dead, and all Israel had lamented him, and buried him in Ramah, even in his own city. And Saul had put away those that had familiar spirits, and the wizards, out of the land. 4 And the Philistines gathered themselves together, and came and pitched in Shunem: and Saul gathered all Israel together, and they pitched in Gilboa. 5 And when Saul saw the host of the Philistines, he was afraid, and his heart greatly trembled. 6 And when Saul enquired of the LORD, the LORD answered him not, neither by dreams, nor by Urim, nor by prophets.

Here is, I. The design of the Philistines against Israel. They resolved to *fight them, v.* 1. If the Israelites had not forsaken God, there would have been no Philistines remaining to molest them; if Saul had not forsaken him, they would by this time have been put out of all danger by them. The Philistines took an opportunity to make this attempt when they had David among them, whom they feared more than Saul and all his forces.

II. The expectation Achish had of assistance from David in this war, and the encouragement David gave him to expect it: "*Thou shalt go with me to battle,*" says Achish. "If I protect thee, I may demand service from thee;" and he will think himself happy if he may have such a man as David on his side, who prospered whithersoever he went. David gave him an ambiguous answer: "We will see what will be done; it will be time enough to talk of that hereafter; but *surely thou shalt know what thy servant can do*" (*v.* 2), that is, "I will consider in what post I may be best able to serve thee, if thou wilt but give me leave to choose it." Thus he keeps himself free from a promise to serve him and yet keeps up his expectation of it; for Achish took it in no other sense than as an engagement to assist him, and promised him, thereupon, that he would make him captain of the guards, protector, or prime-minister of state.

III. The drawing of the armies, on both sides, into the field (*v.* 4): *The Philistines pitched in Shunem,* which was in the tribe of Issachar, a great way north from their country. The land of Israel, it seems, was ill-guarded, when the Philistines could march their army into the very heart of the country. Saul, while he pursued David, left his people naked and exposed. On some of the adjacent mountains of Gilboa Saul mustered his forces, and prepared to engage the Philistines, which he had little heart to do now that the *Spirit of the Lord had departed from him.*

IV. The terror Saul was in, and the loss he was at, upon this occasion: He *saw the host of the Philistines,* and by his own view of them, and the intelligence his spies brought him, he perceived they were more numerous, better armed, and in better heart, than his own were, which made him afraid, so that *his heart greatly trembled, v.* 5. Had he kept close to God, he needed not have been afraid at the sight of an army of Philistines; but now that he had provoked God to forsake him his interest failed, his armies dwindled and looked mean, and, which was worse, his spirits failed him, his heart sunk within him, a guilty conscience made him tremble at the shaking of a leaf. Now he remembered the guilty blood of the Amalekites which he had spared, and the innocent blood of the priests which he had spilt. His sins were set in order before his eyes, which put him into confusion, embarrassed all his counsels, robbed him of all his courage, and produced in him a certain fearful looking for of judgment and fiery indignation. Note, Troubles are terrors to the children of disobedience. In this distress *Saul enquired of the Lord, v.* 6. Need drives those to God who in the day of their prosperity slighted his oracles and altars. *Lord, in trouble have they visited thee,* Isa. xxvi. 16. Did ever any seek the Lord and not find him? Yes, Saul did; *the Lord answered him not,* took no notice either of his petitions or of his enquiries; gave him no directions what to do, nor any encouragement to hope that he would be with him. *Should he be enquired of at all* by such a one as Saul? Ezek. xiv. 3. No, he could not expect an answer of peace, for, 1. He enquired in such a manner that it was as if he had *not enquired at all.* Therefore it is said (1 Chron. x. 14), *He enquired not of the Lord;* for he did it faintly and coldly, and with a secret design, if God did not answer him, to consult the devil. He did not enquire in faith, but with a double unstable mind. 2. He enquired of the Lord when it was too late, when the days of his probation were over and he was finally rejected. *Seek the Lord while he may be found,* for there is a time when he will not be found. 3. He had forfeited the benefit of all the methods of enquiry. Could he that hated and persecuted Samuel and David, who were both prophets, expect to be answered by prophets? Could he that had slain the high priest, expect to be answered by Urim? Or could he that had sinned away the Spirit of grace, expect to be answered by dreams? No. *Be not deceived, God is not mocked.*

V. The mention of some things that had happened a good while ago, to introduce the following story, *v.* 3. 1. The death of Samuel. Samuel was dead, which made the Philistines the more bold and Saul the more afraid; for, had Samuel been alive, Saul probably thought that his presence and countenance, his good advice and good prayers, would have availed him in his distress. 2. Saul's edict against witchcraft. He had put the laws in execution against *those that had familiar spirits,* who must not be *suffered to live,* Exod. xxii. 18. Some think that he did this in the beginning of his reign, while he was under Samuel's influence; others think that it was lately done, for it is spoken of here (.*v* 9) as a late edict. Perhaps when Saul was himself troubled with an evil spirit he suspected that he was bewitched, and, for that reason, cut off all that had familiar spirits. Many seem zealous against sin, when they themselves are any way hurt by it (they will inform against swearers if they swear at them, or against drunkards if in their drink they abuse them), who otherwise have no concern for the glory of God, nor any dislike of sin as sin. However it was commendable in Saul thus to use his power for the terror and restraint of these evil-doers. Note, Many seem enemies to sin in others, while they indulge it in themselves. Saul will drive the devil out of his kingdom, and yet harbour him in his heart, by envy and malice.

7 Then said Saul unto his servants, Seek me a woman that hath a familiar spirit, that I may go to her, and enquire of her. And his servants said to him, Behold, *there is* a woman that hath a familiar spirit at En-dor. 8 And Saul disguised himself, and put on other raiment, and he went, and two men with him, and they came to the woman by night: and he said, I pray thee, divine unto me by the familiar spirit, and bring me *him* up, whom I shall name unto thee. 9 And the woman said unto him, Behold, thou knowest what Saul hath done, how he hath cut off those that have familiar spirits, and the wizards, out of the land: wherefore then layest thou a snare for my life, to cause me to die? 10 And Saul sware to her by the LORD, saying, *As* the LORD liveth, there shall no punishment happen to thee for this thing. 11 Then said the woman, Whom shall I bring up unto thee? And he said, Bring me up Samuel. 12 And when the woman saw Samuel, she cried with a loud voice: and the woman spake to Saul, saying, Why hast thou deceived me? for thou *art* Saul. 13 And the king said unto her, Be not afraid: for what sawest thou? And the woman said unto Saul, I saw gods ascending out of the earth. 14 And he said unto her, What form *is* he of? And she said, An old man cometh up: and he *is* covered with a mantle. And Saul perceived that it *was* Samuel, and he stooped with *his* face to the ground, and bowed himself.

Here, I. Saul seeks for a witch, *v.* 7. When God *answered him not,* if he had humbled himself by repentance and persevered in seeking God, who knows but that at length he might have been entreated for him? but, since he can discern no comfort either from heaven or earth (Isa. viii. 21, 22), he resolves to knock at the gates of hell, and to see if any there will befriend him and give him advice: *Seek me a woman that has a familiar spirit, v.* 7. And his servants were too officious to serve him in this evil affair; they presently recommended one to him at Endor (a city not far off) who had escaped the execution of Saul's edict. To her he resolves to apply. Herein he is chargeable, 1. With contempt of the God of Israel; as if any creature could do him a kindness when God had left him and frowned upon him. 2. With contradiction to himself. He knew the heinousness of the sin of witchcraft, else he would not have cut off those that had familiar spirits; yet now he had recourse to that as an oracle which he had before condemned as an abomination. It is common for men to inveigh severely against those sins which they are in no temptation to, but afterwards to be themselves overcome by them. Had one told Saul, when he was destroying the witches, that he himself would, ere long, consult with one, he would have said, as Hazael did, *What? Is thy servant a dog?* But who knows what mischiefs those will run into that forsake God and are forsaken of him?

II. Hearing of one he hastens to her, but goes by night, and in disguise, only with two servants, and probably on foot, *v.* 8. See how those that are led captive by Satan are forced, 1. To disparage themselves. Never did Saul look so mean as when he went sneaking to a sorry witch to know his fortune. 2. To dissemble. Evil works are works of darkness, and they hate the light, neither care for coming to it. Saul went to the witch, not in his robes, but in the habit of a common soldier, not only lest the witch herself, if she had known him, should decline to serve him, either fearing he came to trepan her or resolving to be avenged on him for his edict against those of her profession, but lest his own people should know it and abhor him for it. Such is the power of natural conscience that even those who do evil blush and are ashamed to do it.

III. He tells her his errand and promises her impunity. 1. All he desires of her is to bring up one from the dead, whom he had a mind to discourse with. It was necromancy, or divination by the dead, that he hoped to serve his purpose by. This was expressly forbidden by the law (Deut. xviii. 11), seeking *for the living to the dead,* Isa. viii. 19. *Bring me up him whom I shall name, v.* 8. This supposes that it was generally taken for granted that souls exist after death, and that when men die there is not an end of them: it supposes too that great knowledge was attributed to separate souls. But to think that any good souls would come up at the beck of an evil spirit, or that God, who had denied a man the benefit of his own institutions, would suffer him to reap any real advantage by a cursed diabolical invention, was very absurd. 2. She signifies her fear of the law, and her suspicion that this stranger came to draw her into a snare (*v.* 9): *Thou knowest what Saul has done.* Providence ordered it so that Saul should be told to his face of his edict against witches, at this very time when he was consulting one, for the greater aggravation of his sin. She insists upon the peril of the law, perhaps to raise her price; for, though no mention is made of her fee, no doubt she demanded and had a large one. Observe how sensible she is of danger from the edict of Saul, and what care she is in to guard against it; but not at all apprehensive of the obligations of God's law and the terrors of his wrath. She considered what *Saul* had done, not what *God* had done, against such practices, and feared a snare laid for her life more than a snare laid for her soul. It is common for sinners to be more afraid of punishment from men than of God's righteous judgment. But, 3. Saul promises with an oath not to betray her, *v.* 10. It was his duty as a king to punish her and he knew it, yet he swears not to do it; as if he could by his own oath bind himself from doing that which, by the divine command, he was bound to do. But he promised more than he could perform when he said, *There shall no punishment happen to thee;* for he that could not secure himself could much less secure her from divine vengeance.

IV. Samuel, who was lately dead, is the person whom Saul desired to have some talk with; and the witch, with her enchantments, gratifies his desire, and brings them together. 1. As soon as Saul had given the witch the assurance she desired (that he would not discover her) she applied to her witchcrafts, and asked very confidently, *Whom shall I bring up to thee? v.* 11. Note, Hopes of impunity embolden sinners in their evil ways and harden their hearts. 2. Saul desires to speak with Samuel: *Bring me up Samuel.* Samuel had anointed him to the kingdom and had formerly been his faithful friend and counsellor, and therefore with him he wished to advise. While Samuel was living at Ramah, not far from Gibeah of Saul, and presided there in the school of the prophets, we never read of Saul's going to him to consult him in any of the difficulties he was in (it would have been well for him if he had); then he slighted him, and perhaps hated him, looking upon him to be in David's interest. But now that he is dead, "O for Samuel again! By all means, *bring me up Samuel.*" Note, Many that despise and persecute God's saints and ministers when they are living would be glad to have them again when they are gone. *Send Lazarus to me,* and *send Lazarus to my father's house,* Luke xvi. 24—27. The sepulchres of the righteous are garnished. 3. Here is a seeming defector chasm in the story. Saul said, *Bring me up Samuel,* and the very next words are, *When the woman saw Samuel,* (*v.* 12), whereas one would have expected to be told how she performed the operation, what spells and charms she used, or that some little intimation would be given of what she said or did; but the profound silence of the scripture concerning it forbids our coveting to *know the depths of Satan* (Rev. ii. 24) or to have our curiosity gratified with an account of the mysteries of iniquity. It has been said of the books of some of the popish confessors that, by their descriptions of sin, they have taught men to commit it; but the scripture conceals sinful art, that we may be *simple concerning evil,* Rom. xvi. 19. 4. The witch, upon sight of the apparition, was aware that her client was Saul, her familiar spirit, it is likely, informing her of it (*v.* 12): "*Why hast thou deceived me* with a disguise; for thou art Saul, the very man that I am afraid of above any man?" Thus she gave Saul to understand the power of her art, in that she could discover him through his disguise; and yet she feared lest, hereafter, at least, he should take advantage against her for what she was now doing. Had she believed that it was really Samuel whom she saw, she would have had more reason to be afraid of him, who was a good prophet, than of Saul, who was a wicked king. But the wrath of earthly princes is feared by most more than the wrath of the King of kings. 5. Saul (who, we may suppose, was kept at a distance in the next room) bade her not to be afraid of him, but go on with the operation, and enquired *what she saw? v.* 13. *O,* says the woman, *I saw gods* (that is, a spirit) *ascending out of the earth;* they called angels *gods,* because spiritual beings. Poor gods that ascend *out of the earth!* But she speaks the language of the heathen, who had their infernal deities and had them in veneration. If Saul had thought it necessary to his conversation with Samuel that the body of Samuel should be called out of the grave, he would have taken the witch with him to Ramah, where his sepulchre was; but the design was wholly upon his soul, which yet, if it became visible, was expected to appear in the usual resemblance of the body; and God permitted the devil, to answer the design, to put on Samuel's shape, that those who would not *receive the love of the truth* might be *given up to strong delusions and believe a lie.* That it could not be the soul of Samuel himself they might easily apprehend when it *ascended out of the earth,* for the *spirit of a man,* much more of a good man, *goes upward,* Eccl. iii. 21. But, if people will be deceived, it is just with God to say, "Let them be deceived." That the devil, by the divine permission, should be able to personate Samuel is not strange, since he can *transform himself into an angel of light!* nor is it strange that he should be permitted to do it upon this occasion, that Saul might be driven to despair, by enquiring of the devil, since he would not, in a right manner, enquire of the Lord, by which he might have had comfort. Saul, being told of gods ascending, was eager to know what was the form of this deity, and in what shape he appeared, so far was he from conceiving any horror at it, his heart being wretchedly *hardened by the deceitfulness of sin.* Saul, it seems, was not permitted to see any manner of similitude himself, but he must take the woman's word for it, that she saw *an old man covered with a mantle, or robe,* the habit of a judge, which Samuel had sometimes worn, and some think it was for the sake of that, and the majesty of its aspect, that she called this apparition *Elohim, a god* or *gods;* for so magistrates are styled, Ps. lxxxii. 1. 6. Saul, perceiving, by the woman's description, that it was Samuel, *stooped with his face to the ground,* either, as it is generally taken, in reverence to Samuel, though he saw him not, or perhaps to listen to that soft and muttering voice which he now expected to hear (for those that had familiar spirits *peeped and muttered,* Isa. viii. 19); and it should seem Saul bowed himself (probably by the witch's direction) that he might hear what was whispered and listen carefully to it; for the *voice of one that has a familiar spirit* is said to come *out of the ground, and to whisper out of the dust,* Isa. xxix. 4. He would stoop to that who would not stoop to the word of God.

15 And Samuel said to Saul, Why hast thou disquieted me, to bring me up? And Saul answered, I am sore distressed; for the Philistines make war against me, and God is departed from me, and answereth me no more, neither by prophets, nor by dreams: therefore I have called thee, that thou mayest make known unto me what I shall do. 16 Then said Samuel, Wherefore then dost thou ask of me, seeing the LORD is departed from thee, and is become thine enemy? 17 And the LORD hath done to him, as he spake by me: for the LORD hath rent the kingdom out of thine hand, and given it to thy neighbour, *even* to David: 18 Because thou obeyedst not the voice of the LORD, nor executedst his fierce wrath upon Amalek, therefore hath the LORD done this thing unto thee this day. 19 Moreover the LORD will also deliver Israel with thee into the hand of the Philistines: and to morrow *shalt* thou and thy sons *be* with me: the LORD also shall deliver the host of Israel into the hand of the Philistines.

We have here the conference between Saul and Satan. Saul came in disguise (*v.* 8), but Satan soon discovered him, *v.* 12. Satan comes in disguise, in the disguise of Samuel's mantle, and Saul cannot discover him. Such is the disadvantage we labour under, in wrestling with *the rulers of the darkness of this world,* that they know us, while we are ignorant of their wiles and devices.

I. The spectre, or apparition, personating Samuel, asks why he is sent for (*v.* 15): *Why hast thou disquieted me to bring me up?* To us this discovers that it was an evil spirit that personated Samuel; for (as bishop Patrick observes) it is not in the power of witches to disturb the rest of good men and to bring them back into the world when they please; nor would the true Samuel have acknowledged such a power in magical arts: but to Saul this was a proper device of Satan's, to draw veneration from him, to possess him with an opinion of the power of divination, and so to rivet him in the devil's interests.

II. Saul makes his complaint to this counterfeit Samuel, mistaking him for the true; and a most doleful complaint it is: "*I am sorely distressed,* and know not what to do, *for the Philistines make war against me;* yet I should do well enough with them if I had but the tokens of God's presence with me; but, alas! *God has departed from me.*" He complained not of God's withdrawings till he fell into trouble, till the *Philistines made war against him,* and then he began to lament God's departure. He that in his prosperity enquired not after God in his adversity thought it hard that God answered him not, nor took any notice of his enquiries, either by dreams or prophets, neither gave answers immediately himself nor sent them by any of his messengers. He does not, like a penitent, own the righteousness of God in this; but, like a man enraged, flies out against God as unkind and flies off from him: *Therefore I have called thee;* as if Samuel, a servant of God, would favour those whom God frowned upon, or as if a dead prophet could do him more service than the living ones. One would think, from this, that he really desired to meet with the devil, and expected no other (though under the covert of Samuel's name), for he desires advice otherwise than from God, therefore from the devil, who is a rival with God. "God denies me, *therefore I come to thee. Flectere si nequeo superos, Acheronta movebo.*" —*If I fail with heaven, I will move hell.*

III. It is cold comfort which this evil spirit in Samuel's mantle gives to Saul, and is manifestly intended to drive him to despair and self-murder. Had it been the true Samuel, when Saul desired to be told what he should do he would have told him to repent and make his peace with God, and recal David from his banishment, and would then have told him that he might hope in this way to find mercy with God; but, instead of that, he represents his case as helpless and hopeless, serving him as he did Judas, to whom he was first a tempter and then a tormentor, persuading him first to sell his master and then to hang himself. 1. He upbraids him with his present distress (*v.* 16), tells him, not only that God had departed from him, but that he had become his enemy, and therefore he must expect no comfortable answer from him: "*Wherefore dost thou ask me?* How can I be thy friend when God is thy enemy, or thy counsellor when he has left thee?" 2. He upbraids him with the anointing of David to the kingdom, *v.* 17. He could not have touched upon a string that sounded more unpleasant in the ear of Saul than this. Nothing is said to reconcile him to David, but all tends rather to exasperate him against David and widen the breach. Yet, to make him believe that he was Samuel, the apparition affirmed that it was God who spoke by him. The devil knows how to speak with an air of religion, and can teach *false apostles to transform themselves into the apostles of Christ* and imitate their language. Those who use spells and charms, and plead, in defence of them, that they find nothing in them but what is good, may remember what good words the devil here spoke, and yet with what a malicious design. 3. He upbraids him with his disobedience to the command of God in not destroying the Amalekites, *v.* 18. Satan had helped him to palliate and excuse that sin when Samuel was dealing with him to bring him to repentance, but now he aggravates it, to make him despair of God's mercy. See what those get that hearken to Satan's temptations. He himself will be their accuser, and insult over them. And see whom those resemble that allure others to that which is evil and reproach them for it when they have done. 4. He foretels his approaching ruin, *v.* 19. (1.) That his army should be routed by the Philistines. This is twice mentioned: *The Lord shall deliver Israel into the hand of the Philistines.* This he might foresee, by considering the superior strength and number of the Philistines, the weakness of the armies of Israel, Saul's terror, and especially God's departure from them. Yet, to personate a prophet, he very gravely ascribes it once and again to God: *The Lord shall do it.* (2.) That he and his sons should be slain in the battle: *To-morrow,* that is, in a little time (and, supposing that it was now after midnight, I see not but it may be taken strictly for the very next day after that which had now begun), *thou and thy sons shall be with me,* that is, in the state of the dead, separate from the body. Had this been the true Samuel, he could not have foretold the event unless God had revealed it to him; and, though it were an evil spirit, God might by him foretel it; as we read of an evil spirit that foresaw Ahab's fall at Ramoth-Gilead and was instrumental in it (1 Kings xxii. 20, &c.), as perhaps this evil spirit was, by the divine permission, in Saul's destruction. That evil spirit flattered Ahab, this frightened Saul, and both that they might fall; so miserable are those that are under the power of Satan; for, *whether he rage or laugh, there is no rest,* Prov. xxix. 9.

20 Then Saul fell straightway all along on the earth, and was sore afraid, because of the words of Samuel: and there was no strength in him; for he had eaten no bread all the day, nor all the night. 21 And the woman came unto Saul, and saw that he was sore troubled, and said unto him, Behold, thine handmaid

hath obeyed thy voice, and I have put my life in my hand, and have hearkened unto thy words which thou spakest unto me. 22 Now therefore, I pray thee, hearken thou also unto the voice of thine handmaid, and let me set a morsel of bread before thee; and eat, that thou mayest have strength, when thou goest on thy way. 23 But he refused, and said, I will not eat. But his servants, together with the woman, compelled him; and he hearkened unto their voice. So he arose from the earth, and sat upon the bed. 24 And the woman had a fat calf in the house; and she hasted, and killed it, and took flour, and kneaded *it*, and did bake unleavened bread thereof: 25 And she brought *it* before Saul, and before his servants; and they did eat. Then they rose up, and went away that night.

We are here told how Saul received this terrible message from the ghost he consulted. He desired to be told *what he should do* (*v.* 15), but was only told what he had not done and what should be done to him. Those that expect any good counsel or comfort otherwise than from God, and in the way of his institutions, will be as wretchedly disappointed as Saul here was. Observe,

I. How he sunk under the load, *v.* 20. He was indeed unfit to bear it, having *eaten nothing all the day* before, nor *that night.* He came fasting from the camp, and continued fasting; not for want of food, but for want of an appetite. The fear he was in of the power of the Philistines (*v.* 5) took away his appetite, or perhaps the struggle he had with his own conscience, after he had entertained the thought of consulting the witch, made him to nauseate even his necessary food, though ever so dainty. This made him an easy prey to this fresh terror that now came upon him like an armed man. *He fell all along on the earth,* as if the archers of the Philistines had already hit him, *and there was no strength in him* to bear up against these heavy tidings. Now he had enough of consulting witches, and found them miserable comforters. When God in his word speaks terror to sinners he opens to them, at the same time, a door of hope if they repent: but those that apply to the gates of hell for succour must there expect darkness without any glimpse of light.

II. With what difficulty he was persuaded to take so much relief as was necessary to carry him back to his post in the camp. The witch, it should seem, had left Saul alone with the spectre, to have his talk with him by himself; but perhaps hearing him fall and groan, and perceiving him to be in great agony, she came to him (*v.* 21), and was very importunate with him to take some refreshment, that he might be able to get clear from her house, fearing that if he should be ill, especially if he should die there, she should be punished for it as a traitor, though she had escaped punishment as a witch. This, it is probable, rather than any sentiment of kindness, made her solicitous to help him. But what a deplorable condition had he brought himself to when he needed so wretched a comforter! 1. She showed herself very importunate with him to take some refreshment. She pleaded (*v* .21) that she had obeyed his voice to the endangering of her life, and why therefore should not he hearken to her voice for the relieving of his life? *v.* 22. She had a fat calf at hand (and the word signifies one that was made use of in treading out the corn, and therefore could the worse be spared); this she prepared for his entertainment, *v.* 24. Josephus is large in applauding the extraordinary courtesy and liberality of this woman, and recommending what she did as an example of compassion to the distressed, and readiness to communicate for their relief, though we have no prospect of being recompensed. 2. He showed himself very averse to it: *He refused, and said, I will not eat* (*v.* 23), choosing rather to die obscurely by famine than honourably by the sword. Had he laboured only under a defect of animal spirits, food might have helped him; but, alas! his case was out of the reach of such succours. What are dainty meats to a wounded conscience? *As vinegar upon nitre, so is he that sings songs to a heavy heart,* so disagreeable and unwelcome. 3. The woman at length, with the help of his servants, overpersuaded him, against his inclination and resolution, to take some refreshment. Not by force, but by friendly advice, they *compelled him* (*v.* 23), and of no other than such a rational and courteous compulsion are we to understand that in the parable, *Compel them to come in,* Luke xiv. 23. *How forcible are right words,* when men are pressed by them to that which is for their own interest! Job vi. 25. Saul was somewhat revived with this entertainment; so that he and his servants, when they had eaten, *rose up and went away* before it was light (*v.* 25), that they might hasten to their business and that they might not be seen to come out of such a scandalous house. Josephus here much admires the bravery and magnanimity of Saul, that, though he was assured he should lose both his life and honour, yet he would not desert his army, but resolutely returned to the camp, and stood ready for an engagement. I wonder more at the hardness of his heart, that he did not again apply to God by repentance and prayer, in hopes yet to obtain at least a reprieve; but he desperately ran headlong upon his own ruin. Perhaps, indeed, now that rage and envy possessed him to the uttermost, he was the better reconciled to his hard fate, being told that his sons, and Jonathan among the rest, whom he hated for his affection to David, should die with him. If he must fall, he cared not what desolations of his family and kingdom accompanied his fall, hoping it would be the worse for his successor. Ἐμοῦ θανόντος γαῖα μιχθέτω πυρί.—*I care not if, when I am dead, the world should be set on fire.* He begged not, as David, "Let thy hand be against me, but not against thy people."

CHAP. XXIX.

How Saul, who was forsaken of God, when he was in a strait was more and more perplexed and embarrassed with his own counsels, we read in the foregoing chapter. In this chapter we find how David, who kept close to God, when he was in a strait was extricated and brought off by the providence of God, without any contrivance of his own. We have him, I. Marching with the Philistines, ver. 1, 2. II. Excepted against by the lords of the Philistines, ver. 3—5. III. Happily dismissed by Achish from that service which did so ill become him, and which yet he knew not how to decline, ver. 6—11.

NOW the Philistines gathered together all their armies to Aphek: and the Israelites pitched by a fountain which *is* in Jezreel. 2 And the lords of the Philistines passed on by hundreds, and by thousands: but David and his men passed on in the rereward with Achish. 3 Then said the princes of the Philistines, What *do* these Hebrews *here?* And Achish said unto the princes of the Philistines, *Is* not this David, the servant of Saul the king of Israel, which hath been with me these days, or these years, and I have found no fault in him since he fell *unto me* unto this day? 4 And the princes of the Philistines were wroth with him; and the princes of the Philistines said unto him, Make this fellow return, that he may go again to his place which thou hast appointed him, and let him not go down with us to battle, lest in the battle he be an adversary to us; for wherewith should he reconcile himself unto his master? *should it* not *be* with the heads of these men? 5 *Is* not this David, of whom they sang one to another in dances, saying, Saul slew his thousands, and David his ten thousands?

Here is, I. The great strait that David was in, which we may suppose he himself was aware of, though we read not of his asking advice from God, nor of any project of his own to get clear of it. The two armies of the Philistines and the Israelites were encamped and ready to engage, *v.* 1. Achish, who had been kind to David, had obliged him to come himself and bring the forces he had into his service. David came accordingly, and, upon a review of the army, was found with Achish, in the post assigned him in the rear, *v.* 2. Now, 1. If, when the armies engaged, he should retire, and quit his post, he would fall under the indelible reproach, not only of cowardice and treachery, but of base ingratitude to Achish, who had been his protector and benefactor and had reposed a confidence in him, and from whom he had received a very honourable commission. Such an unprincipled thing as this he could by no means persuade himself to do. 2. If he should, as was expected from him, fight for the Philistines against Israel, he would incur the imputation of being an enemy to the Israel of God and a traitor to his country, would make his own people hate him, and unanimously oppose his coming to the crown, as unworthy the name of an Israelite, much more the honour and trust of a king of Israel, when he had fought against them under the banner of the uncircumcised. If Saul should be killed (as it proved he was) in this engagement, the fault would be laid at David's door, as if he had killed him. So that on each side there seemed to be both sin and scandal. This was the strait he was in; and a great strait it was to a good man, greater to see sin before him than to see trouble. Into this strait he brought himself by his own unadvisedness, in quitting the land of Judah, and going among the uncircumcised. It is strange if those that associate themselves with wicked people, and grow intimate with them, come off without guilt, or grief, or both. What he himself proposed to do does not appear. Perhaps he designed to act only as keeper to the king's head, the post assigned him (*ch.* xxviii. 2) and not to do any thing offensively against Israel. But it would have been very hard to come so near the brink of sin and not to fall in. Therefore, though God might justly have left him in this difficulty, to chastise him for his folly, yet, because his heart was upright with him, he would *not suffer him to be tempted above what he was able, but with the temptation made a way for him to escape,* 1 Cor. x. 13.

II. A door opened for his deliverance out of this strait. God inclined the hearts of the princes of the Philistines to oppose his being employed in the battle, and to insist upon his being dismissed. Thus their enmity befriended him, when no friend he had was capable of doing him such a kindness. 1. It was a proper question which they asked, upon the mustering of the forces, "*What do these Hebrews here?* *v.* 3. What confidence can we put in them, or what service can we expect from them?" A *Hebrew is out of his place,* and, if he has the spirit of a *Hebrew, is out of his element,* when he is in the camp of the Philistines, and deserves to be made uneasy there. David used to *hate the congregation of evil doers,* however he came now to be among them, Ps. xxvi. 5. It was an honourable testimony which Achish, on this occasion, gave to David. He looked upon him as a refugee, that fled from a wrongful prosecution in his own country, and had put himself under his protection, whom therefore he was obliged, in justice, to take care of, and thought he might in prudence employ; "for (says he) he has been with me *these days*, or *these years*," that is, a considerable time, many days at his court and a year or two in his country, and he never found any fault in him, nor saw any cause to distrust his fidelity, or to think any other than that he had heartily come over to him. By this it appears that David had conducted himself with a great deal of caution, and had prudently concealed the affection he still retained for his own people. We have need to *walk in wisdom towards those that are without, to keep our mouth when the wicked is before us*, and to be upon the reserve. 3. Yet the princes are peremptory in it, that he must be sent home; and they give good reasons for their insisting on it. (1.) Because he had been an old enemy to the Philistines; witness what was sung in honour of his triumphs over them: *Saul slew his thousands, and David his ten thousands, v.* 5. "It will be a reproach to us to harbour and trust so noted a destroyer of our people; nor can it be thought that he will now act heartily against Saul who then acted so vigorously with him and for him." Who would be fond of popular praise or applause when, even that may, another time, be turned against a man to his reproach? (2.) Because he might be a most dangerous enemy to them, and do them more mischief than all Saul's army could (*v.* 4): "He may *in the battle be an adversary to us*, and surprise us with an attack in the rear, while their army charges us in the front; and we have reason to think he will do so, that, by betraying us, he may reconcile himself to his master. Who can trust a man who, besides his affection to his country, will think it his interest to be false to us?" It is dangerous to put confidence in a reconciled enemy.

6 Then Achish called David, and said unto him, Surely, *as* the LORD liveth, thou hast been upright, and thy going out and thy coming in with me in the host *is* good in my sight: for I have not found evil in thee since the day of thy coming unto me unto this day: nevertheless the lords favour thee not. 7 Wherefore now return, and go in peace, that thou displease not the lords of the Philistines. 8 And David said unto Achish, But what have I done? and what hast thou found in thy servant so long as I have been with thee unto this day, that I may not go fight against the enemies of my lord the king? 9 And Achish answered and said to David, I know that thou *art* good in my sight, as an angel of God: notwithstanding the princes of the Philistines have said, He shall not go up with us to the battle. 10 Wherefore now rise up early in the morning with thy master's servants that are come with thee: and as soon as ye be up early in the morning, and have light, depart. 11 So David and his men rose up early to depart in the morning, to return into the land of the Philistines. And the Philistines went up to Jezreel.

If the reasons Achish had to trust David were stronger than the reasons which the princes offered why they should distrust him (as I do not see that, in policy, they were, for the princes were certainly in the right), yet Achish was but one of five, though the chief, and the only one that had the title of king; accordingly, in a council of war held on this occasion, he was over-voted, and obliged to dismiss David, though he was extremely fond of him. Kings cannot always do as they would, nor have such as they would about them.

I. The discharge Achish gives him is very honourable, and not a final discharge, but only from the present service. 1. He signifies the great pleasure and satisfaction he had taken in him and in his conversation: *Thou art good in my sight as an angel of God, v.* 9. Wise and good men will gain respect, wherever they go, from all that know how to make a right estimate of persons and things, though of different professions in religion. What Achish says of David, God, by the prophet, says *of the house of David* (Zech. xii. 8), that it shall be *as the angel of the Lord.* But the former is a court-compliment; the latter is a divine promise. 2. He gives him a testimonial of his good behaviour, *v.* 6. It is very full and in obliging terms: "*Thou hast been upright*, and thy whole conduct has been *good in my sight*, and *I have not found evil in thee.*" Saul would not have given him such a testimonial, though he had done far more service to him than Achish. God's people should behave themselves always so inoffensively as if possible to get the good word of all they have dealings with; and it is a debt we owe to those who have acquitted themselves well to give them the praise of it. 3. He lays all the blame of his dismission upon the princes, who would by no means suffer him to continue in the camp. "The king loves thee entirely, and would venture his life in thy hand; *but the lords favour thee not*, and we must not disoblige them, nor can we oppose them; therefore *return and go in peace.*" He had better part with his favourite than occasion a disgust among his generals and a mutiny in his army. Achish intimates a reason why they were uneasy. It was not so much for David's own sake as for the sake of his soldiers that attended him, whom he calls *his master's servants* (namely, Saul's), *v.* 10. They could trust him, but not them. (4.) He orders him to be gone early, as soon as it was light (*v.* 10), to prevent their further resentments, and the jealousies they would have been apt to conceive if he had lingered.

II. His reception of this discourse is very complimental; but, I fear, not without some degree of dissimulation. "What?" says David, "must I leave *my lord the king,* whom I am bound by office to protect, just now when he is going to expose himself in the field? Why may not I go and *fight against the enemies of my lord the king?*" *v.* 8. He seemed anxious to serve him when he was at this juncture really anxious to leave him, but he was not willing that Achish should know that he was. No one knows how strong the temptation is to compliment and dissemble which those are in that attend great men, and how hard it is to avoid it.

III. God's providence ordered it wisely and graciously for him. For, besides that the snare was broken and he was delivered out of the dilemma to which he was first reduced, it proved a happy hastening of him to the relief of his own city, which sorely wanted him, though he did not know it. Thus the disgrace which the lords of the Philistines put upon him proved, in more ways than one, an advantage to him. *The steps of a good man are ordered by the Lord, and he delighteth in his way.* What he does with us we know not now, but we shall know hereafter, and shall see it was all for good.

CHAP. XXX.

When David was dismissed from the army of the Philistines he did not go over to the camp of Israel, but, being expelled by Saul, observed an exact neutrality, and silently retired to his own city Ziklag, leaving the armies ready to engage. Now here we are told, I. What a melancholy posture he found the city in, all laid waste by the Amalekites, and what distress it occasioned him and his men, ver. 1—6. II. What course he took to recover what he had lost. He enquired of God, and took out a commission from him (ver. 7, 8), pursued the enemy (ver. 9, 10), gained intelligence from a straggler (ver. 11—15), attacked and routed the plunderers (ver. 16, 17), and recovered all that they had carried off, ver. 18—20. III. What method he observed in the distribution of the spoil, ver. 21—31.

AND it came to pass, when David and his men were come to Ziklag on the third day, that the Amalekites had invaded the south, and Ziklag, and smitten Ziklag, and burned it with fire; 2 And had taken the women captives, that *were* therein: they slew not any, either great or small, but carried *them* away, and went on their way. 3 So David and his men came to the city, and, behold, *it was* burned with fire; and their wives, and their sons, and their daughters, were taken captives. 4 Then David and the people that *were* with him lifted up their voice and wept, until they had no more power to weep. 5 And David's two wives were taken captives, Ahinoam the Jezreelitess, and Abigail the wife of Nabal the Carmelite. 6 And David was greatly distressed; for the people spake of stoning him, because the soul of all the people was grieved, every man for his sons and for his daughters: but David encouraged himself in the LORD his God.

Here we have, I. The descent which the Amalekites made upon Ziklag in David's absence, and the desolations they made there. They surprised the city when it was left unguarded, plundered it, burnt it, and carried all the women and children captives, *v.* 1, 2. They intended, by this, to revenge the like havoc that David had lately made of them and their country, *ch.* xxvii. 8. He that had made so many enemies ought not to have left his own concerns so naked and defenceless. Those that make bold with others must expect that others will make as bold with them and provide accordingly. Now observe in this, 1. The cruelty of Saul's pity (as it proved) in sparing the Amalekites; if he had utterly destroyed them, as he ought to have done, these would not have been in being to do this mischief. 2. How David was corrected for being so forward to go with the Philistines against Israel. God showed him that he had better have staid at home and looked after his own business. When we go abroad in the way of our duty we may comfortably hope that God will take care of our families in our absence, but not otherwise. 3. How wonderfully God inclined the hearts of these Amalekites to carry the women and children away captives, and not to kill them. When David invaded them he put all to the sword (*ch.* xxvii. 9), and no reason can be given why they did not retaliate upon this city, but that God restrained them; for he has all hearts in his hands, and says to the fury of the most cruel men, *Hitherto thou shalt come, and no further.* Whether they spared them to lead them in triumph, or to sell them, or to use them for slaves, God's hand must be acknowledged, who designed to make use of the Amalekites for the correction, not for the destruction, of the house of David.

II. The confusion and consternation that David and his men were in when they found their houses in ashes and their wives and children gone into captivity. Three days' march they had from the camp of the Philistines to Ziklag, and now that they came thither weary, but hoping to find rest in their houses and joy in their families, behold a black and dismal scene was presented to them (*v.* 3), which made them all weep (David himself not excepted), though they were men of war, *till they had no more power to weep, v.* 4. The mention of David's wives, *Ahinoam and Abigail,* and their being carried captive, intimates that this circumstance went nearer his heart than any thing else. Note, It is no disparagement to the boldest and bravest spirits to lament the calamities of relations and friends. Observe, 1. This trouble came upon them when they were absent. It was the ancient policy of Amalek to take Israel at an advantage. 2. It met them at their return, and, for aught that appears, their own eyes gave them the first intelligence of it. Note, When we go abroad we cannot foresee what evil tidings may meet us when we come home again. The going out may be very cheerful, and yet the coming in be very doleful. *Boast not thyself* therefore *of to-morrow,* nor of to-night either, *for thou knowest not what a day,* or a piece of a day, *may bring forth,* Prov. xxvii. 1. If, when we come off a journey, we find our *tabernacles in peace,* and not laid waste as David here found his, let the Lord be praised for it.

III. The mutiny and murmuring of David's men against him (*v.* 6): *David was greatly distressed,* for, in the midst of all his losses, his own people spoke of stoning him, 1. Because they looked upon him as the occasion of their calamities, by the provocation he had given the Amalekites, and his indiscretion in leaving Ziklag without a garrison in it. Thus apt are we, when we are in trouble, to fly into a rage against those who are in any way the occasion of our trouble, while we overlook the divine providence, and have not that regard to the operations of God's hand in it which would silence our passions, and make us patient. 2. Because now they began to despair of that preferment which they had promised themselves in following David. They hoped ere this to have been all princes; and now to find themselves all beggars was such a disappointment to them as made them grow outrageous, and threaten the life of him on whom, under God, they had the greatest dependence. What absurdities will not ungoverned passions plunge men into? This was a sore trial to the man after God's own heart, and could not but go very near him. Saul had driven him from his country, the Philistines had driven him from their camp, the Amalekites had plundered his city, his wives were taken prisoners, and now, to complete his woe, his own familiar friends, in whom he trusted, whom he had sheltered, and who did eat of his bread, instead of sympathizing with him and offering him any relief, *lifted up the heel against him,* and threatened to stone him. Great faith must expect such severe exercises. But it is observable that David was reduced to this extremity just before his accession to the throne. At this very time, perhaps, the stroke was struck which opened the door to his advancement. Things are sometimes at the worst with the church and people of God just before they begin to mend.

IV. David's pious dependence upon the divine providence and grace in this distress: *But David encouraged himself in the Lord his God.* His men fretted at their loss. *The soul of the people was bitter,* so the word is. Their own discontent and impatience added *wormwood and gall* to the affliction and misery, and made their case doubly grievous. But 1. David bore it better, though he had more reason than any of them to lament it; they gave liberty to their passions, but he set his graces on work, and by encouraging himself in God, while they dispirited each other, he kept his spirit calm and sedate. Or, 2. There may be a reference to the threatening words his men gave out against him. They *spoke of stoning him;* but he, not offering to avenge the affront, nor terrified by their menaces, *encouraged himself in the Lord his God,* believed, and considered with application to his present case, the power and providence of God, his justice and goodness, the method he commonly takes of bringing low and then raising up, his care of his people that serve him and trust in him, and the particular promises he had made to him of bringing him safely to the throne; with these considerations he supported himself, not doubting but the present trouble would end well. Note, Those that have taken the Lord for their God may take encouragement from their relation to him in the worst of times. It is the duty and interest of all good people, whatever happens, to encourage themselves in God as their Lord and their God, assuring themselves that he can and will bring light out of darkness, peace out of trouble, and good out of evil, to all that love him and are *the called according to his purpose,* Rom. viii. 28. It was David's practice, and he had the comfort of it, *What time I am afraid I will trust in thee.* When he was at his wits' end he was not at his faith's end.

7 And David said to Abiathar the priest, Ahimelech's son, I pray thee, bring me hither the ephod. And Abiathar brought thither the ephod to David. 8 And David enquired at the LORD, saying, Shall I pursue after this troop? shall I overtake them? And he answered him, Pursue: for thou shalt surely overtake *them,* and without fail recover *all.* 9 So David went, he and the six hundred men that *were* with him, and came to the brook Besor, where those that were left behind stayed. 10 But David pursued, he and four hundred men: for two hundred abode behind,

which were so faint that they could not go over the brook Besor. 11 And they found an Egyptian in the field, and brought him to David, and gave him bread, and he did eat; and they made him drink water; 12 And they gave him a piece of a cake of figs, and two clusters of raisins: and when he had eaten, his spirit came again to him: for he had eaten no bread, nor drunk *any* water, three days and three nights. 13 And David said unto him, To whom *belongest* thou? and whence *art* thou? And he said, I *am* a young man of Egypt, servant to an Amalekite; and my master left me, because three days agone I fell sick. 14 We made an invasion *upon* the south of the Cherethites, and upon *the coast* which *belongeth* to Judah, and upon the south of Caleb; and we burned Ziklag with fire. 15 And David said to him, Canst thou bring me down to this company? And he said, Swear unto me by God, that thou wilt neither kill me, nor deliver me into the hands of my master, and I will bring thee down to this company. 16 And when he had brought him down, behold, *they were* spread abroad upon all the earth, eating and drinking, and dancing, because of all the great spoil that they had taken out of the land of the Philistines, and out of the land of Judah. 17 And David smote them from the twilight even unto the evening of the next day: and there escaped not a man of them, save four hundred young men, which rode upon camels, and fled. 18 And David recovered all that the Amalekites had carried away: and David rescued his two wives. 19 And there was nothing lacking to them, neither small nor great, neither sons nor daughters, neither spoil, nor any *thing* that they had taken to them: David recovered all. 20 And David took all the flocks and the herds, *which* they drave before those *other* cattle, and said, This *is* David's spoil.

Solomon observes that *the righteous is delivered out of trouble* and *the wicked cometh in his stead,* that *the just falleth seven times a-day and riseth again;* so it was with David. Many were his troubles, but *the Lord delivered him out of them all,* and particularly out of this of which we have here an account.

I. He enquired of the Lord both concerning his duty—*Shall I pursue after this troop?* and concerning the event—*Shall I overtake them? v.* 8. It was a great advantage to David that he had the high priest with him and the breast-plate of judgment, which, as a public person, he might consult in all his affairs, Num. xxvii. 21. We cannot think that he left Abiathar and the ephod at Ziklag, for then he and it would have been carried away by the Amalekites, unless we may suppose them hidden by a special providence, that they might be ready for David to consult at his return. If we conclude that David had his priest and ephod with him in the camp of the Philistines, it was certainly a great neglect in him that he did not enquire of the Lord by them concerning his engagement to Achish. Perhaps he was ashamed to own his religion so far among the uncircumcised; but now he begins to apprehend that this trouble is brought upon him to correct him for that oversight, and therefore the first thing he does is to call for the ephod. It is well if we get this good by our afflictions, to be reminded by them of neglected duties, and particularly to be quickened by them to enquire of the Lord. See 1 Chron. xv. 13. David had no room to doubt but that his war against these Amalekites was just, and he had an inclination strong enough to set upon them when it was for the recovery of that which was dearest to him in this world; and yet he would not go about it without asking counsel of God, thereby owning his dependence upon God and submission to him. If we thus, in all our ways, acknowledge God, we may expect that he will direct our steps, as he did David's here, answering him above what he asked, with an assurance that he should recover all.

II. He went himself in person, and took with him all the force he had, in pursuit of the Amalekites, *v.* 9, 10. See how quickly, how easily, how effectually the mutiny among the soldiers was quelled by his patience and faith. When they *spoke of stoning him* (*v.* 6), if he had spoken of hanging them, or had ordered that the ringleaders of the faction should immediately have their heads struck off, though it would have been just, yet it might have been of pernicious consequence to his interest in this critical juncture; and, while he and his men were contending, the Amalekites would have clearly carried off their spoil. But when he, as a deaf man, heard not, smothered his resentments, and *encouraged himself in the Lord his God,* the tumult of the people was stilled by his gentleness and the power of God on their hearts; and, being thus mildly treated, they are now as ready to follow his foot as they were but a little before to fly in his face. Meekness is the security of any government. All his men were willing to go along with him in pursuit of the Amalekites, and he needed them all; but he was forced to drop a third part of them by the way; 200 out of 600 were so fatigued with their long march, and so sunk under the load of their grief, that they could not pass the brook Besor, but staid behind there. This was, 1. A great trial of David's faith, whether he could go on, in a dependence upon the word of God, when so many of his men failed him. When we are disappointed and discouraged in our expectations from second causes, then to go on with cheerfulness, confiding in the divine power, this is giving glory to God, by believing against hope, in hope. 2. A great instance of David's tenderness to his men, that he would by no means urge them beyond their strength, though the case itself was so very urgent. The Son of David thus considers the frame of his followers, who are not all alike strong and vigorous in their spiritual pursuits and conflicts; but, where we are weak, there he is kind; nay, more there he is strong, 2 Cor. xii. 9, 10.

III. Providence threw one in their way that gave them intelligence of the enemy's motions, and guided theirs; a poor Egyptian lad, scarcely alive, is made instrumental of a great deal of good to David. *God chooses the foolish things of the world,* with them *to confound the wise.* Observe, 1. His master's cruelty to him. He had got out of him all the service he could, and when the lad fell sick, probably being over-toiled with his work, he barbarously left him to perish in the field, when he was in no such haste but he might have put him into some of the carriages, and brought him home, or, at least, have left him wherewithal to support himself. That master has the spirit of an Amalekite, not of an Israelite, that can thus use a servant worse than one would use a beast. *The tender mercies of the wicked are cruel.* This Amalekite thought he should now have servants enough of the Israelite-captives, and therefore cared not what became of his Egyptian slave, but could willingly let him die in a ditch for want of necessaries, while he himself was *eating and drinking, v.* 16. Justly did Providence make this poor servant, that was thus basely abused, instrumental towards the destruction of a whole army of Amalekites and his master among the rest; for God hears the cry of oppressed servants. 2. David's compassion to him. Though he had reason to think he was one of those that had helped to destroy Ziklag, yet, finding him in distress, he generously relieved him, not only with *bread and water* (*v.* 11), but with *figs and raisins, v.* 12. Though the Israelites were in haste, and had no great plenty for themselves, yet they would not *forbear to deliver one that was drawn unto death,* nor say, *Behold, we knew it not,* Prov. xxiv. 11, 12. Those are unworthy the name of Israelites who shut up the bowels of their compassion from persons in distress. It was also prudently done to relieve this Egyptian; for, though despicable, he was capable of doing them service: so it proved, though they were not certain of this when they relieved him. It is a good reason why we should neither do an injury nor deny a kindness to any man that we know not but, some time or other, it may be in his power to return either a kindness or an injury. 3. The intelligence David received from this poor Egyptian when he had come to himself. He gave him an account concerning his party. (1.) What they had done (*v.* 14): *We made an invasion,* &c. The countries which David had pretended to Achish to have made an incursion upon (*ch.* xxvii. 10) they really had invaded and laid waste. What was then false now proved too true. (2.) Whither they had gone, *v.* 15. This he promised David to inform him of upon condition he would spare his life and protect him from his master, who, if he could hear of him again (he thought), would add cruelty to cruelty. Such an opinion this poor Egyptian had of the obligation of an oath that he desired no greater security for his life than this: *Swear unto me by God,* not by the gods of Egypt or Amalek, but by the one supreme God.

IV. David, being directed to the place where they lay, securely celebrating their triumphs, fell upon them, and, as he used to pray, *saw his desire upon his enemies.* 1. The spoilers were cut off. The Amalekites, finding the booty was rich, and having got with it (as they thought) out of the reach of danger, were making themselves very merry with it, *v.* 16. All thoughts of war were laid aside, nor were they in any haste to house their prey, but *spread themselves abroad on the earth* in the most careless manner that could be, and there they were found *eating, and drinking, and dancing,* probably in honour of their idol-gods, to whom they gave the praise of their success. In this posture David surprised them, which made the conquest of them, and the blow he gave them, the more easy to him and the more dismal to them. Then are sinners nearest to ruin when they cry, *Peace and safety,* and *put the evil day far from them.* Nor does any thing give our spiritual enemies more advantage against us than sensuality and the indulgence of the flesh. *Eating, and drinking, and dancing,* have been the soft and pleasant way in which many have gone down to the congregation of the dead. Finding them thus off their guard, and from their arms (many of them, it may be, drunk, and unable to make any resistance), he put them all to the sword, and only 400 escaped, *v.* 17. Thus is the triumphing of the wicked short, and wrath comes on them, as on Belshazzar, when they are in the midst of their jollity. 2. The spoil was recovered and brought off, and nothing was lost, but a great deal gotten. (1.) They retrieved all their own (*v.* 18, 19): *David rescued his two wives;* this is mentioned particularly, because this pleased David more than all the rest of his achievements. Providence had so ordered it that the Amalekites carefully preserved all that they had taken, concluding that they kept it for themselves, though really they preserved it for the right owners, so that there was nothing lacking to them; so it proved, when they concluded all was gone: so much better is God oftentimes to us than our own fears. Our Lord Jesus was indeed the Son of David and the Son of Abraham, in this resembling them both (Abraham, Gen. xiv. 16, and David here), that he *took the prey from the mighty, and led captivity captive.* But this was not all. (2.) They took all that belonged to the Amalekites besides (*v.* 20): *Flocks and herds,* either such as were taken from the Philistines and others, which David had the disposal of by the law of war; or perhaps he made a sally into the enemy's country, and fetched off these flocks and herds thence, as interest for his own. This drove was put in the van of the triumph, with this proclamation, "*This is David's spoil.* This we may thank him for." Those who lately spoke of stoning him now caressed him and cried him up, because they got by him more than they had then lost. Thus are the world and its sentiments governed by interest.

21 And David came to the two hundred men, which were so faint that they could not follow David, whom they had made also to abide at the brook Besor: and they went forth to meet David, and to meet the people that *were* with him: and when David came near to the people, he saluted them. 22 Then answered all the wicked men and *men* of Belial, of those that went with David, and said, Because they went not with us, we will not give them *aught* of the spoil that we have recovered, save to every man his wife and his children, that they may lead *them* away, and depart. 23 Then said David, Ye shall not do so, my brethren, with that which the LORD hath given us, who hath preserved us, and delivered the company that came against us into our hand. 24 For who will hearken unto you in this matter? but as his part *is* that goeth down to the battle, so *shall* his part *be* that tarrieth by the stuff: they shall part alike. 25 And it was *so* from that day forward, that he made it a statute and an ordinance for Israel unto this day. 26 And when David came to Ziklag, he sent of the spoil unto the elders of Judah, *even* to his friends, saying, Behold a present for you of the spoil of the enemies of the LORD; 27 To *them* which *were* in Beth-el, and to *them* which *were* in south Ramoth, and to *them* which *were* in Jattir, 28 And to *them* which *were* in Aroer, and to *them* which *were* in Siphmoth, and to *them* which *were* in Eshtemoa, 29 And to *them* which *were* in Rachal, and to *them* which *were* in the cities of the Jerahmeelites, and to *them* which *were* in the cities of the Kenites, 30 And to *them* which *were* in Hormah, and to *them* which *were* in Chorashan, and to *them* which *were* in Athach, 31 And to *them* which *were* in Hebron, and to all the places where David himself and his men were wont to haunt.

We have here an account of the distribution of the spoil which was taken from the Amalekites. When the Amalekites had carried away a rich booty from the land of Judah and the Philistines they spent it in sensuality, in eating, and drinking, and making merry with it; but David disposed of the spoil taken after another manner, as one that knew that justice and charity must govern us in the use we make of whatever we have in this world. What God gives us he designs we should do good with, not serve our lusts with. In the distribution of the spoil,

I. David was just and kind to those who abode by the stuff. They came forth to meet the conquerors, and to congratulate them on this success, though they could not contribute to it (*v.* 21); for we should rejoice in a good work done, though Providence had laid us aside and rendered us incapable of lending a hand to it. David received their address very kindly, and was so far from upbraiding them with their weakness that he showed himself solicitous concerning them. He saluted them; *he asked them of peace* (so the word is), enquired how they did, because he had left them faint and not well; or wished them peace, bade them be of good cheer, they should lose nothing by staying behind; for of this they seemed afraid, as perhaps David saw by their countenances.

1. There were those that opposed their coming in to share in the spoil; some of David's soldiers, probably the same that spoke of stoning him, spoke now of defrauding

their brethren; they are called wicked men and *men of Belial, v.* 22. Let not the best of men think it strange if they have those attending them that are very bad and they cannot prevail to make them better. We may suppose that David had instructed his soldiers, and prayed with them, and yet there were many among them that were wicked men and men of Belial, often terrified with the apprehensions of death and yet wicked men still and men of Belial. These made a motion that the 200 men who abode by the stuff should only have their wives and children given them, but none of their goods. Well might they be called *wicked men;* for this bespeaks them, (1.) Very covetous themselves and greedy of gain; for hereby the more would fall to their share. Awhile ago they would gladly have given half their own to recover the other half, yet now that they have all their own they are not content unless they can have their brethren's too; so soon do men forget their low estate. All seek their own, and too often more than their own. (2.) Very barbarous to their brethren; for, to give them their wives and children, and not their estates, was to give them the mouths without the meat. What joy could they have of their families if they had nothing to maintain them with? Was this to do as they would be done by? Those are men of Belial indeed who delight in putting hardships upon their brethren, and care not who is starved, so they may be fed to the full.

2. David would by no means admit this, but ordered that those who tarried behind should come in for an equal share in the spoils with those that went to the battle, *v.* 23, 24. This he did, (1.) In gratitude to God. The spoil we have is that which God has given us; we have it from him, and therefore must use it under his direction as good stewards. Let this check us when we are tempted to misapply that which God has entrusted us with of this world's goods. "Nay, I must not do so with that which God has given me, not serve Satan and a base lust with those things which are not only the creatures of his power, but the gifts of his bounty. God has recompensed us by *delivering the company that came against us into our hand,* let not us then wrong our brethren. God has been kind to us in preserving us and giving us victory, let not us be unkind to them." God's mercy to us should make us merciful to one another. (2.) In justice to them. It was true they tarried behind; but, [1.] It was not for want of good-will to the cause or to their brethren, but because they had not strength to keep up with them. It was not their fault, but their infelicity; and therefore they ought not to suffer for it. [2.] Though they tarried behind now, they had formerly engaged many times in battle and done their part as well as the best of their brethren, and their former services must be considered now that there was something to enjoy. [3.] Even now they did good service, for they abode by the stuff, to guard that which somebody must take care of, else that might have fallen into the hands of some other enemy. Every post of service is not alike a post of honour, yet those that are in any way serviceable to the common interest, though in a meaner station, ought to share in the common advantages, as in the natural body every member has its use and therefore has its share of the nourishment. *First,* Thus David overruled the wicked men, and men of Belial, with reason, but with a great deal of mildness; for the force of reason is sufficient, without the force of passion. He calls them *his brethren, v.* 23. Superiors often lose their authority by haughtiness, but seldom by courtesy and condescension. *Secondly,* Thus he settled the matter for the time to come, made it a statute of his kingdom (a statute of distributions, *primo Davidis—in the first year of David's reign),* an ordinance of war (*v.* 25), that *as his part is that goes down to the battle,* and hazards his life in the high places of the field, so shall his be that guards the carriages. Abraham returned the spoils of Sodom to the right owners, and quitted his title to them *jure belli—derived from the laws of war.* If we help others to recover their right, we must not think that this alienates the property and makes it ours. God appointed that the spoil of Midian should be divided between the soldiers and the whole congregation, Num. xxxi. 27. The case here was somewhat different, but governed by the same general rule—that we are members one of another. The disciples, at first, *had all things common,* and we should still be *ready to distribute, willing to communicate,* 1 Tim. vi. 18. When *kings of armies did flee apace, she that tarried at home did divide the spoil,* Ps. lxviii. 12.

II. David was generous and kind to all his friends. When he had given every one his own with interest there was a considerable overplus, which David, as general, had the disposal of; probably the spoil of the tents of the Amalekites consisted much in plate and jewels (Judg. viii. 24, 26), and these, because he thought they would but make his own soldiers proud and effeminate, he thought fit to make presents of to his friends, even the *elders of Judah, v.* 26. Several places are here named to which he sent of these presents, all of them in or near the tribe of Judah. The first place named is *Bethel,* which signifies *the house of God;* that place shall be first served for its name's sake; or perhaps it means not the city so called, but the place where the ark was, which was therefore *the house of God.* Thither David sent the first and best, to those that attended there, for his sake who is the first and best. *Hebron* is named last (*v.* 31), probably because thither he sent the residuum, which was the largest share, having an eye upon that place as fittest for his head-quarters, 2 Sam. ii. 1. In David's sending these presents observe, 1. His generosity. He aimed not to enrich himself, but to serve his country; and therefore God afterwards enriched him, and set him to rule the country he had served. It becomes gracious souls to be generous. *There is that scatters, and yet increases.* 2. His gratitude. He sent presents to *all the places where he and his men were wont to haunt* (*v.* 31), that is, to all that he had received kindness from, that had sheltered him and sent him intelligence or provisions. Note, Honesty, as well as honour, obliges us to requite the favours that have been done us, or at least to make a real acknowledgment of them as far as is in the power of our hand. 3. His piety. He calls his present *a blessing;* for no present we give to our friends will be a comfort to them but as it is made so by the blessing of God: it intimates that his prayers for them accompanied his present. He also sent it out of *the spoil of the enemies of the Lord* (so he calls them, not *his* enemies), that they might rejoice in the victory for the Lord's sake, and might join with him in thanksgivings for it. 4. His policy. He sent these presents among his countrymen to engage them to be ready to appear for him upon his accession to the throne, which he now saw at hand. *A man's gift maketh room for him.* He was fit to be a king who thus showed the bounty and liberality of a king. Munificence recommends a man more than magnificence. The Ziphites had none of his presents, nor the men of Keilah; and thus he showed that, though he was such a saint as not to revenge affronts, yet he was not such a fool as not to take notice of them.

CHAP. XXXI.

In the foregoing chapter we had David conquering, yea, more than a conqueror. In this chapter we have Saul conquered and worse than a captive. Providence ordered it that both these things should be doing just at the same time. The very same day, perhaps, that David was triumphing over the Amalekites, were the Philistines triumphing over Saul. One is set over against the other, that men may see what comes of trusting in God and what comes of forsaking him. We left Saul ready to engage the Philistines, with a shaking hand and an aching heart, having had his doom read him from hell, which he would not regard when it was read him from heaven. Let us now see what becomes of him. Here is, I. His army routed, ver. 1. II. His three sons slain, ver. 2. III. Himself wounded (ver. 3), and slain by his own hand, ver. 4. The death of his armour-bearer (ver. 5) and all his men, ver 6. IV. His country possessed by the Philistines, ver. 7. His camp plundered, and his dead body deserted, ver. 8. His fall triumphed in, ver. 9. His body publicly exposed (ver. 10) and with difficulty rescued by the men of Jabesh-Gilead, ver. 11—13. Thus fell the man that was rejected of God.

NOW the Philistines fought against Israel: and the men of Israel fled from before the Philistines, and fell down slain in mount Gilboa. 2 And the Philistines followed hard upon Saul and upon his sons; and the Philistines slew Jonathan, and Abinadab, and Melchi-shua, Saul's sons. 3 And the battle went sore against Saul, and the archers hit him; and he was sore wounded of the archers. 4 Then said Saul unto his armourbearer, Draw thy sword, and thrust me through therewith; lest these uncircumcised come and thrust me through, and abuse me. But his armourbearer would not; for he was sore afraid. Therefore Saul took a sword, and fell upon it. 5 And when his armourbearer saw that Saul was dead, he fell likewise upon his sword, and died with him. 6 So Saul died, and his three sons, and his armourbearer, and all his men, that same day together. 7 And when the men of Israel that *were* on the other side of the valley, and *they* that *were* on the other side Jordan, saw that the men of Israel fled, and that Saul and his sons were dead, they forsook the cities, and fled; and the Philistines came and dwelt in them.

The day of recompence has now come, in which Saul must account for the blood of the Amalekites which he had sinfully spared, and that of the priests which he had more sinfully spilt; that of David too, which he would have spilt, must come into the account. Now his day has come to fall, as David foresaw, when he should descend into battle and perish, *ch.* xxvi. 10. Come and see the *righteous judgments of God.*

I. He sees his soldiers fall about him, *v.* 1. Whether the Philistines were more numerous, better posted, and better led on, or what other advantages they had, we are not told; but it seems they were more vigorous, for they made the onset; they fought against Israel, and the Israelites fled and fell. The best of the troops were put into disorder, and multitudes slain, probably those whom Saul had employed in pursuing David. Thus those who had followed him and served him in his sin went before him in his fall and shared with him in his plagues.

II. He sees his sons fall before him. The victorious Philistines pressed most forcibly upon the king of Israel and those about him. His three sons were next him, it is probable, and they were all three slain before his face, to his great grief (for they were the hopes of his family) and to his great terror, for they were now the guard of his person, and he could conclude no other than that his own turn would come next. His sons are named (*v.* 2), and it grieves us to find Jonathan among them: that wise, valiant, good man, who was as much David's friend as Saul was his enemy, yet falls with the rest. Duty to his father would not permit him to stay at home, or to retire when the armies engaged; and Providence so orders it that he falls in the common fate of his family, though he never involved himself in the guilt of it; so that the observation of Eliphaz does not hold (Job iv. 7), *Who ever perished being innocent?* For here was one. What shall we say to it? 1. God would hereby complete the vexation of Saul in his dying moments, and the judgment that was to be executed upon his house. If the family must fall, Jonathan, that is one of it, must fall with it. 2. He would hereby make David's way to the crown the more clear and open. For, though Jonathan himself would have cheerfully resigned all his title and interest to him (we have no reason to suspect any other), yet it is very probable that many of the people would have made use of his name for the support of the house of Saul, or at least would have come in but slowly to David. If Ish-bosheth (who was now left at home as one unfit for action, and so escaped) had so many friends, what would Jonathan have had, who had been the darling of the people and had never forfeited their favour? Those that were so anxious to have a king like the nations would be zealous for the right line, especially if that threw the crown upon such a head as Jonathan's. This would have embarrassed David; and, if Jonathan could have prevailed to bring in all his interest to David, then it would have been said that Jonathan had made him king, whereas God was to have all the glory. *This is the Lord's doing.* So that though the death of Jonathan would be a great affliction to David, yet, by making him mindful of his own frailty, as well as by facilitating his accession to the throne, it would be an advantage to him. 3. God would hereby show us that the difference between good and bad is to be made in the other world, not in this. *All things come alike to all.* We cannot judge of the spiritual or eternal state of any by the manner of their death; for in that *there is one event to the righteous and to the wicked.*

III. He himself is sorely wounded by the Philistines and then slain by his own hand. The archers hit him (*v.* 3), so that he could neither fight nor fly, and therefore must inevitably fall into their hands. Thus, to make him the more miserable, destruction comes gradually upon him, and he dies so as to feel himself die. To such an extremity was he now reduced that, 1. He was desirous to die by the hand of his own servant rather than by the hand of the Philistines, lest they should abuse him as they had abused Samson. Miserable man! He finds himself dying, and all his care is to keep his body out of the hands of the Philistines, instead of being solicitous to resign his soul into the hands of God who gave it, Eccl. xii. 7. As he lived, so he died, proud and jealous, and a terror to himself and all about him. Those who rightly understand the matter think it of small account, in comparison, how it is with them in death, so it may but be well with them after death. Those are in a deplorable condition indeed who, being *bitter in soul, long for death, but it cometh not* (Job iii. 20, 21), especially those who, despairing of the mercy of God, like Judas, leap into a hell before them, to escape a hell within them. 2. When he could not obtain that favour he became his own executioner, thinking hereby to avoid shame, but running upon a heinous sin, and with it entailing upon his own name a mark of perpetual infamy, as *felo de se—a self-murderer.* Jonathan, who received his death-wound from the hand of the Philistines and bravely yielded to the fate of war, died on the bed of honour; but Saul died as a fool dieth, as a coward dieth—a proud fool, a sneaking coward; he died as a man that had neither the fear of God nor hope in God, neither the reason of a man nor the religion of an Israelite, much less the dignity of a prince or the resolution of a soldier. Let us all pray, *Lord, lead us not into temptation,* this temptation. His armour-bearer would not run him through, and he did well to refuse it; for no man's servant ought to be a slave to his master's lusts or passions of any kind. The reason given is that *he was sorely afraid,* not of death, for he himself ran wilfully upon that immediately; but, having a profound reverence for the king his master, he could not conquer that so far as to do him any hurt; or perhaps he feared lest his trembling hand should give him but half a blow, and so put him to the greater misery.

IV. His armour-bearer who refused to kill him refused not to die with him, but *fell likewise upon his sword, v.* 5. This was an aggravating circumstance of the death of Saul, that, by the example of his wickedness in murdering himself, he drew in his servant to be guilty of the same wickedness, and *perished not alone in his iniquity.* The Jews say that Saul's armour-bearer was Doeg, whom he preferred to that dignity for killing the priests, and, if so, justly does his *violent dealing return on his own head.* David had foretold concerning him that God would *destroy him for ever,* Ps. lii. 5.

V. The country was put into such confusion by the rout of Saul's army that the inhabitants of the neighbouring cities (*on that side Jordan,* as it might be read) quitted them, and the Philistines, for a time, had possession of them, till things were settled in Israel (*v.* 7), to such a sad pass had Saul by his wickedness brought his country, which might have remained in the hands of the uncircumcised if David had not been raised up to repair the breaches of it. See what a king he proved for whom they rejected God and Samuel. They had still done wickedly (it is to be feared) as well as he, and therefore *were consumed both they and their king,* as the prophet had foretold concerning them, *ch.* xii. 25. And to this reference is had long after. Hos. xiii. 10, 11, "*Where are thy saviours in all thy cities, of whom thou saidst, Give me a king and princes? I gave thee a king in my anger, and took him away in my wrath;* that is, he was a plague to thee living and dying; thou couldst expect no other."

8 And it came to pass on the morrow, when the Philistines came to strip the slain, that they found Saul and his three sons fallen in mount Gilboa. 9 And they cut off his head, and stripped off his armour, and sent into the land of the Philistines round about, to publish *it in* the house of their idols, and among the people. 10 And they put his armour in the house of Ashtaroth: and they fastened his body to the wall of Beth-shan. 11 And when the inhabitants of Jabesh-gilead heard of that which the Philistines had done to Saul; 12 All the valiant men arose, and went all night, and took the body of Saul and the bodies of his sons from the wall of Beth-shan, and came to Jabesh, and burnt them there. 13 And they took their bones, and buried *them* under a tree at Jabesh, and fasted seven days.

The scripture makes no mention of the souls of Saul and his sons, what became of them after they were dead (secret things belong not to us), but of their bodies only.

I. How they were basely abused by the Philistines. The day after the battle, when they had recovered their fatigue, they came to strip the slain, and, among the rest, found the bodies of Saul and his three sons, *v.* 8. Saul's armour-bearer perhaps intended to honour his master by following the example of his self-murder, and to show thereby how well he loved him; but, if he had consulted his reason more than his passions, he would have spared that foolish compliment, not only in justice to his own life, but in kindness to his master, to whom, by the opportunity of survivorship, he might have done all the service that could be done him by any man after he was dead; for he might, in the night, have conveyed away his body, and those of his sons, and buried them decently. But such false and foolish notions these vain men have (though they would be wise) of giving and receiving honour. Nay, it should seem, Saul might have saved himself the fatal thrust and have made his escape: for the pursuers (in fear of whom he slew himself) came not to the place where he was till the next day. But whom God will destroy he infatuates and utterly *consumes with his terrors.* See Job xviii. 5, &c. Finding Saul's body (which now that it lay extended on the bloody turf was distinguishable from the rest by its length, as it was, while erect, by its height, when he proudly overlooked the surrounding crowd), they will, in that, triumph over Israel's crown, and meanly gratify a barbarous and brutish revenge by insulting the deserted corpse, which, when alive, they had stood in awe of. 1. They cut off his head. Had they designed in this to revenge the cutting off of Goliath's head they would rather have cut off the head of David, who did that execution, when he was in their country. They intended it, in general, for a reproach to Israel, who promised themselves that a crowned and an anointed head would save them from the Philistines, and a particular reproach to Saul, who was taller by the head than other men (which perhaps he was wont to boast of), but was now shorter by the head. 2. They stripped him of his armour (*v.* 9), and sent that to be set up as a trophy of their victory, in the house of Ashtaroth their goddess (*v.* 10); and we are told, 1 Chron. x. 10 (though it is omitted here), that they fastened his head in the temple of Dagon. Thus did they ascribe the honour of their victory, not as they ought to have done to the real justice of the true God, but to the imaginary power of their false gods, and by this respect paid to pretended deities shame those who give not the praise of their achievements to the living God. Ashtaroth, the idol that Israel had many a time gone a whoring after, now triumphs over them. 3. They sent expresses throughout their country, and ordered public notice to be given in the houses of their gods of the victory they had obtained (*v.* 9), that public rejoicings might be made and thanks given to their gods. This David regretted sorely, 2 Sam. i. 20. *Tell it not in Gath.* 4. They fastened his body and the bodies of his sons (as appears, *v.* 12) to the wall of *Beth-shan,* a city that lay not far from Gilboa and very near to the river Jordan. Hither the dead bodies were dragged and here hung up in chains, to be devoured by the birds of prey. Saul slew himself to avoid being abused by the Philistines, and never was royal corpse so abused as his was, perhaps the more if they understood that he slew himself for that reason. He that thinks to save his honour by sin will certainly lose it. See to what a height of insolence the Philistines had arrived just before David was raised up, who perfectly subdued them. Now that they had slain Saul and his sons they thought the land of Israel was their own for ever, but they soon found themselves deceived. When God has accomplished his whole work by them he will accomplish it upon them. See Isa. x. 6, 7.

II. How they were bravely rescued by the

men of Jabesh-Gilead. Little more than the river Jordan lay between Beth-shan and Jabesh-Gilead, and Jordan was in that place passable by its fords; a bold adventure was therefore made by the valiant men of that city, who in the night passed the river, took down the dead bodies, and gave them decent burial, *v.* 11, 13. This they did, 1. Out of a common concern for the honour of Israel, or the land of Israel, which ought not to be defiled by the exposing of any dead bodies, and especially of the crown of Israel, which was thus profaned by the uncircumcised. 2. Out of a particular sense of gratitude to Saul, for his zeal and forwardness to rescue them from the Ammonites when he first came to the throne, *ch.* xi. It is an evidence of a generous spirit and an encouragement to beneficence when the remembrance of kindnesses is thus retained, and they are thus returned in an extremity. The men of Jabesh-Gilead would have done Saul better service if they had sent their valiant men to him sooner, to strengthen him against the Philistines. But his day had come to fall, and now this is all the service they can do him, in honour to his memory. We find not that any general mourning was made for the death of Saul, as was for the death of Samuel (*ch.* xxv. 1), only those Gileadites of Jabesh did him honour at his death; for, (1.) They made a burning for the bodies, to perfume them. So some understand the burning of them. They burnt spices over them, *v.* 12. And that it was usual thus to do honour to their deceased friends, at least their princes, appears by the account of Asa's funeral (2 Chron. xvi. 14), that *they made a very great burning for him.* Or (as some think) they burnt the flesh, because it began to putrefy. (2.) They buried the bodies, when, by burning over them, they had sweetened them (or, if they burnt them, they buried the bones and ashes), under a tree, which served for a grave-stone and monument. And, (3.) They *fasted seven days,* that is, each day of the seven they fasted till the evening; thus they lamented the death of Saul and the present distracted state of Israel, and perhaps joined prayers with their fasting for the re-establishment of their shattered state. Though, *when the wicked perish there is shouting* (that is, it is to be hoped a better state of things will ensue, which will be matter of joy), yet humanity obliges us to show a decent respect to dead bodies, especially those of princes.

This book began with the birth of Samuel, but now it ends with the burial of Saul, the comparing of which two together will teach us to prefer the honour that comes from God before any of the honours which this world pretends to have the disposal of.

AN

EXPOSITION,

WITH PRACTICAL OBSERVATIONS,

OF THE SECOND BOOK OF

SAMUEL.

THIS book is the history of the reign of king David. We had in the foregoing book an account of his designation to the government, and his struggles with Saul, which ended at length in the death of his persecutor. This book begins with his accession to the throne, and is entirely taken up with the affairs of the government during the forty years he reigned, and therefore is entitled by the LXX. *The Third Book of the Kings.* It gives us an account of David's triumphs and his troubles. I. His triumphs over the house of Saul (*ch.* i.—iv.), over the Jebusites and Philistines (*ch.* v.), at the bringing up of the ark (*ch.* vi. and vii.), over the neighbouring nations that opposed him (*ch.* viii. — x.); and so far the history is agreeable to what we might expect from David's character and the choice made of him. But his cloud has a dark side. II. We have his troubles, the causes of them, his sin in the matter of Uriah (*ch.* xi. and xii.), the troubles themselves from the sin of Amnon (*ch.* xiii.), the rebellion of Absalom (*ch.* xiv.—xix.) and of Sheba (*ch.* xx.), and the plague in Israel for his numbering the people (*ch.* xxiv.), besides the famine of the Gibeonites *ch.* xxi. His song we have (*ch.* xxii.), and his words and worthies, *ch.* xxiii. Many things in his history are very instructive; but for the hero who is the subject of it, though in many instances he appears here very great, and very good, and very much the favourite of heaven, yet it must be confessed that his honour shines brighter in his Psalms than in his Annals.

CHAP. I.

In the close of the foregoing book (with which this is connected as a continuation of the same history) we had Saul's exit; he went down slain to the pit, though he was the terror of the mighty in the land of the living. We are now to look towards the rising sun, and to enquire where David is, and what he is doing. In this chapter we have, I. Tidings brought him to Ziklag of the death of Saul and Jonathan, by an Amalekite, who undertook to give him a particular narrative of it, ver. 1—10. II. David's sorrowful reception of these tidings, ver. 11, 12. III. Justice done upon the messenger, who boasted that he had helped Saul to dispatch himself, ver. 13—16. IV. An elegy which David penned upon this occasion, ver. 17—27. And in all this David's breast appears very happily free from the sparks both of revenge and ambition, and he observes a very suitable demeanour.

NOW it came to pass after the death of Saul, when David was returned from the slaughter of the Amalekites, and David had abode two days in Ziglag; 2 It came even to pass on the third day, that, behold, a man came out of the camp from Saul with his clothes rent, and earth upon his head: and *so* it was, when he came to David, that he fell to the earth, and did obeisance. 3 And David said unto him, From whence comest thou? And he said unto him, Out of the camp of Israel am I escaped. 4 And David said unto him, How went the matter? I pray thee, tell me. And he answered, That the people are fled from the battle, and many of the people also are fallen and dead; and Saul and Jonathan his son are dead also. 5 And David said unto the young man that told him, How knowest thou that Saul and Jonathan his son be dead? 6 And the young man that told him said, As I happened by chance upon mount Gilboa, behold, Saul leaned upon his spear; and, lo, the chariots and horsemen followed hard after him. 7 And when he looked behind him, he saw me, and called unto me. And I answered, Here *am* I. 8 And he said unto me, Who *art* thou? And I answered him, I *am* an Amalekite. 9 He said unto me again, Stand, I pray thee, upon me, and slay me: for anguish is come upon me, because my life *is* yet whole in me. 10 So I stood upon him, and slew him, because I was sure that he could not live after that he was fallen: and I took the crown that *was* upon his head, and the bracelet that *was* on his arm, and have brought them hither unto my lord.

Here is, I. David settling again in Ziklag, his own city, after he had rescued his family and friends out of the hands of the Amalekites (*v.* 1): He *abode in Ziklag.* Thence he was now sending presents to his friends (1 Sam. xxx. 26), and there he was ready to receive those that came into his interests; not men in distress and debt, as his first followers were, but persons of quality in their country, *mighty men, men of war,* and *captains of thousands* (as we find, 1 Chron. xii. 1, 8, 20); such came day by day to him, God stirring up their hearts to do so, till he had a *great host, like the host of God,* as it is said, 1 Chron. xii. 22. The secret springs of revolutions are unaccountable, and must be resolved into that Providence which turns all hearts as the rivers of water.

II. Intelligence brought him thither of the death of Saul. It was strange that he did not leave some spies about the camp, to bring him early notice of the issue of the engagement, a sign that he desired not Saul's woeful day, nor was impatient to come to the throne, but willing to wait till those tidings were brought to him which many a one would have sent more than half-way to meet. He that believes does not make haste, takes good news when it comes and is not uneasy while it is in the coming. 1. The messenger presents himself to David as an express, in the posture of a mourner for the deceased prince and a subject to the succeeding one. He came with his clothes rent, and made obeisance to David (*v.* 2), pleasing himself with the fancy that he had the honour to be the first that did him homage as his sovereign, but it proved he was the first that received from him sentence of death as his judge. He told David he came from the camp of Israel, and intimated the bad posture it was in when he said he had escaped out of it, having much ado to get away with his life, *v.* 3. 2. He gives him a general account of the issue of the battle. David was very desirous to know how the matter went, as one that had more reason than any to be concerned for the public; and he told him very distinctly that the army of Israel was routed, many slain, and, among the rest, Saul and Jonathan, *v.* 4. He named only Saul and Jonathan, because he knew David would be most solicitous to know their fate; for Saul was the man whom he most feared and Jonathan the man whom he most loved. 3. He gives him a more particular account of the death of Saul. It is probable that David had heard, by the report of others, what the issue of the war was, for multitudes resorted to him, it should seem, in consequence; but he was desirous to know the certainty of the report concerning Saul and Jonathan, either because he was not forward to believe it or because he would not proceed upon it to make his own claims till he was fully assured of it. He therefore asks, *How knowest thou that Saul and Jonathan are dead?* in answer to which the young man tells him a very ready story, putting it past doubt that Saul was dead, for he himself had been not only an eye-witness of his death, but an instrument of it, and therefore David might rely upon his testimony. He says nothing, in his narrative, of the death of Jonathan, knowing how ungrateful that would be to David, but accounts only for Saul, thinking (as David understood it well enough, *ch.* iv. 10) that he should be welcome for that, and rewarded as one that brought good tidings. The account he gives of this matter is, (1.) Very particular. That he happened to go to the place where Saul was (*v.* 6) as a passenger, not as a soldier, and therefore an indifferent person, that he found Saul endeavouring to run himself through with his own spear, none of his attendants being willing to do it for him; and, it seems, he could not do it dexterously for himself: his hand and heart failed him. The miserable man had not courage enough either to live or die; he therefore called this stranger to him (*v.* 7), enquired what countryman he was, for, provided he was not a Philistine, he would gladly receive from his hand the *coup de grace* (as the French call it concerning those that are broken on the wheel)—*the merciful stroke,* that might dispatch him out of his pain. Understanding that he was an Amalekite (neither one of his subjects nor one of his enemies), he begs this favour from him (*v.* 9): *Stand upon me, and slay me.* He is now sick of his dignity and willing to be trampled upon, sick of his life and willing to be slain. Who then would be inordinately fond of life or honour? The case may he such, even with those that have no hope in their death, that yet they may *desire to die, and death flee from them,* Rev. ix. 6. *Anguish has come upon me;* so we read it, as a complaint of the pain and terror his spirit was seized with. If his conscience now brought to mind the javelin he had cast at David, his pride, malice, and perfidiousness, and especially the murder of the priests, no marvel that anguish came upon him: moles (they say) open their eyes when they are dying. Sense of unpardoned guilt will make death indeed the king of terrors. Those that have baffled their convictions will perhaps, in their dying moments, be overpowered by them. The margin reads it as a complaint of the inconvenience of his clothes; that his coat of mail which he had for defence, or his embroidered coat which he had for ornament, hindered him, that he could not get the spear far enough into his body, or so straitened him, now that his body swelled with anguish, that he could not expire. Let no man's clothes be his pride, for it may so happen that they may be his burden and snare. "Hereupon," saith our young man, "*I stood uponhim, and slew him*" (*v.* 10) at which word, perhaps, he observed David look upon him with some show of displeasure, and therefore he excuses himself in the next words: "*For I was sure he could not live;* his life was whole in him indeed, but he would certainly have fallen into the hands of the Philistines or given himself another thrust." (2.) It is doubtful whether this story be true. If it be, the righteousness of God is to be observed, that Saul, who spared the Amalekites in contempt of the divine command, received his death's wound from an Amalekite. But most interpreters think that it was false, and that, though he might happen to be present, yet he was not assisting in the death of Saul, but told David so in expectation that he would reward him for it, as having done him a piece of good service. Those who would rejoice at the fall of an enemy are apt to measure others by themselves, and to think that they will do so too. But a man after God's own heart is not to be judged of by common men. I am not clear whether this young man's story was true or no: it may consist with the narrative in the chapter before, and be an addition to it, as Peter's account of the death of Judas (Acts i. 18) is to the narrative, Matt. xxvii. 5. What is there called *a sword* may here be called *a spear,* or when he fell upon his sword he leaned on his spear. (3.) However he produced that which was proof sufficient of the death of Saul, the crown that was upon his head and the bracelet that was on his arm. It should seem Saul was so foolishly fond of these as to wear them in the field of battle, which made him a fair mark for the archers, by distinguishing him from those about him; but as *pride* (we say) *feels no cold,* so it fears no danger, from that which gratifies it. These fell into the hands of this Amalekite. Saul spared the best of their spoil, and now the best of his came to one of that devoted nation. He brought them to David, as the rightful owner of them now that Saul was dead, not doubting but by his officiousness herein to recommend himself to the best preferments in his court or camp. The tradition of the Jews is that this Amalekite was the son of Doeg (for the Amalekites were descendants from Edom), and that Doeg, who they suppose was Saul's armour-bearer, before he slew himself gave Saul's crown and bracelet (the ensigns of his royalty) to his son, and bade him carry them to David, to curry favour with him. But this is a groundless conceit. Doeg's son, it is likely, was so well known to Saul that he needed not ask him as he did this Amalekite (*v.* 8), *Who art thou?* David had been long waiting for the crown, and now it was brought to him by an Amalekite. See how God can serve his own purposes of kindness to his people, even by designing (ill-designing) men, who aim at nothing but to set up themselves.

11 Then David took hold on his clothes, and rent them; and likewise all the men that *were* with him: 12 And they mourned, and wept, and

fasted until even, for Saul, and for Jonathan his son, and for the people of the LORD, and for the house of Israel; because they were fallen by the sword. 13 And David said unto the young man that told him, Whence *art* thou? And he answered, I *am* the son of a stranger, an Amalekite. 14 And David said unto him, How wast thou not afraid to stretch forth thine hand to destroy the LORD's anointed? 15 And David called one of the young men, and said, Go near, *and* fall upon him. And he smote him that he died. 16 And David said unto him, Thy blood *be* upon thy head; for thy mouth hath testified against thee, saying, I have slain the LORD's anointed.

Here is, I. David's reception of these tidings. So far was he from falling into a transport of joy, as the Amalekite expected, that he fell into a passion of weeping, *rent his clothes* (*v.* 11), *mourned and fasted* (*v.* 12), not only for his people Israel and Jonathan his friend but for Saul his enemy. This he did, not only as a man of honour, in observance of that decorum which forbids us to insult over those that are fallen, and requires us to attend our relations to the grave with respect, whatever we lost by their life or got by their death, but as a good man and a man of conscience, that had forgiven the injuries Saul had done him and bore him no malice. He knew it, before his son wrote it (Prov. xxiv. 17, 18), that if we *rejoice when our enemy falls the Lord sees it, and it displeases him;* and that *he who is glad at calamities shall not go unpunished,* Prov. xvii. 5. By this it appears that those passages in David's psalms which express his desire of, and triumph in, the ruin of his enemies, proceeded not from a spirit of revenge, nor any irregular passion, but from a holy zeal for the glory of God and the public good; for by what he did here, when he heard of Saul's death, we may perceive that his natural temper was very tender, and that he was kindly affected even to those that hated him. He was very sincere, no question, in his mourning for Saul, and it was not pretended, or a copy of his countenance only. His passion was so strong, on this occasion, that it moved those about him; *all that were with him,* at least in complaisance to him, *rent their clothes,* and they *fasted till even,* in token of their sorrow; and probably it was a religious fast: they humbled themselves under the hand of God, and prayed for the repairing of the breaches made upon Israel by this defeat.

II. The reward he gave to him that brought him the tidings. Instead of preferring him, he put him to death, judged him out of his own mouth, as a murderer of his prince, and ordered him to be forthwith executed for the same. What a surprise was this to the messenger, who thought he should have favour shown him for his pains. In vain did he plead that he had Saul's order for it, that it was a real kindness to him, that he must inevitably have died; all those pleas are overruled: "*Thy mouth has testified against thee, saying, I have slain the Lord's anointed* (*v.* 16), therefore thou must die." Now,

1. David herein did not do unjustly. For, (1.) The man was an Amalekite. This, lest he should have mistaken it in his narrative, he made him own a second time, *v.* 13. That nation, and all that belonged to it, were doomed to destruction, so that, in slaying him, David did what his predecessor should have done and was rejected for not doing. (2.) He did himself confess the crime, so that the evidence was, by the consent of all laws, sufficient to convict him; for every man is presumed to make the best of himself. If he did as he said, he deserved to die for treason (*v.* 14), doing that which, it is probable, he heard Saul's own armour-bearer refuse to do; if not, yet by boasting that he had done it he plainly showed that if there had been occasion he would have done it, and would have made nothing of it; and, by boasting of it to David, he showed what opinion he had of him, that he would rejoice in it, as one altogether like himself, which was an intolerable affront to him who had himself once and again refused to *stretch forth his hand against the Lord's anointed.* And his lying to David, if indeed it was a lie, was highly criminal, and proved, as sooner or later that sin will prove, lying against his own head.

2. He did honourably and well. Hereby he demonstrated the sincerity of his grief, discouraged all others from thinking by doing the like to ingratiate themselves with him, and did that which might probably oblige the house of Saul and win upon them, and recommend him to the people as one that was zealous for public justice, without regard to his own private interest. We may learn from it that to give assistance to any in murdering themselves, directly or indirectly, if done wittingly, incurs the guilt of blood, and that the lives of princes ought to be, in a special manner, precious to us.

17 And David lamented with this lamentation over Saul and over Jonathan his son: 18 (Also he bade them teach the children of Judah *the use of* the bow: behold, *it is* written in the book of Jasher.) 19 The beauty of Israel is slain upon thy high places: how are the mighty fallen! 20 Tell *it* not in Gath, publish *it* not in the streets of Ashkelon; lest the

daughters of the Philistines rejoice, lest the daughters of the uncircumcised triumph. 21 Ye mountains of Gilboa, *let there be* no dew, neither *let there be* rain, upon you, nor fields of offerings: for there the shield of the mighty is vilely cast away, the shield of Saul, *as though he had* not *been* anointed with oil. 22 From the blood of the slain, from the fat of the mighty, the bow of Jonathan turned not back, and the sword of Saul returned not empty. 23 Saul and Jonathan *were* lovely and pleasant in their lives, and in their death they were not divided: they were swifter than eagles, they were stronger than lions. 24 Ye daughters of Israel, weep over Saul, who clothed you in scarlet, with *other* delights, who put on ornaments of gold upon your apparel. 25 How are the mighty fallen in the midst of the battle! O Jonathan, *thou wast* slain in thine high places. 26 I am distressed for thee, my brother Jonathan: very pleasant hast thou been unto me: thy love to me was wonderful, passing the love of women. 27 How are the mighty fallen, and the weapons of war perished!

When David had rent his clothes, mourned, and wept, and fasted, for the death of Saul, and done justice upon him who made himself guilty of it, one would think he had made full payment of the debt of honour he owed to his memory; yet this is not all: we have here a poem he wrote on that occasion; for he was a great master of his pen as well as of his sword. By this elegy he designed both to express his own sorrow for this great calamity and to impress the like on the minds of others, who ought to lay it to heart. The putting of lamentations into poems made them, 1. The more moving and affecting. The passion of the poet, or singer, is, by this way, wonderfully communicated to the readers and hearers. 2. The more lasting. Thus they were made, not only to spread far, but to continue long, from generation to generation. Those might gain information by poems that would not read history. Here we have,

I. The orders David gave with this elegy (*v.* 18): *He bade them teach the children of Judah* (his own tribe, whatever others did) *the use of the bow,* either, 1. The bow used in war. Not but that the children of Judah knew how to use the bow (it was so commonly used in war, long before this, that the sword and bow were put for all weapons of war, Gen. xlviii. 22), but perhaps they had of late made more use of slings, as David in killing Goliath, because cheaper, and David would have them now to see the inconvenience of these (for it was the archers of the Philistines that bore so hard upon Saul, 1 Sam. xxxi. 3), and to return more generally to the use of the bow, to exercise themselves in this weapon, that they might be in a capacity to avenge the death of their prince upon the Philistines, and to outdo them at their own weapon. It was a pity but those that had such good heads and hearts as the children of Judah should be well armed. David hereby showed his authority over and concern for the armies of Israel, and set himself to rectify the errors of the former reign. But we find that the companies which had now come to David to Ziklag were armed with bows (1 Chron. xii. 2); therefore, 2. Some understand it either of some musical instrument called *a bow* (to which he would have the mournful ditties sung) or of the elegy itself: *He bade them teach the children of Judah Kesheth, the bow,* that is, this song, which was so entitled for the sake of Jonathan's bow, the achievements of which are here celebrated. Moses commanded Israel to learn his song (Deut. xxxi. 19), so David his. Probably he bade the Levites teach them. It is *written in the book of Jasher,* there it was kept upon record, and thence transcribed into this history. That book was probably a collection of state-poems; what is said to be written in that book (Josh. x. 13) is also poetical, a fragment of an historical poem. Even songs would be forgotten and lost if they were not committed to writing, that best conservatory of knowledge.

II. The elegy itself. It is not a divine hymn, nor given by inspiration of God to be used in divine service, nor is there any mention of God in it; but it is a human composition, and therefore was inserted, not in the book of Psalms (which, being of divine original, is preserved), but in the book of Jasher, which, being only a collection of common poems, is long since lost. This elegy proves David to have been,

1. A man of an excellent spirit, in four things:—

(1.) He was very generous to Saul, his sworn enemy. Saul was his father-in-law, his sovereign, and the anointed of the Lord; and therefore, though he had done him a great deal of wrong, David does not wreak his revenge upon his memory when he is in his grave; but like a good man, and a man of honour, [1.] He conceals his faults; and, though there was no preventing their appearance in his history, yet they should not appear in this elegy. Charity teaches us to make the best we can of every body and to say nothing of those of whom we can say no good, especially when they are gone. *De mortuis nil nisi bonum—Say nothing but good concerning the dead.* We ought to deny ourselves the satisfaction of making personal reflections upon those who have been injurious to us, much more drawing their character thence, as if every man must of necessity be a bad man that has done ill by us. Let the corrupt part of the memory be buried with the corrupt part of the man—earth to earth, ashes to ashes; let the blemish be hidden and a veil drawn over the deformity. [2.] He celebrates that which was praiseworthy in him. He does not commend him for that which he was not, says nothing of his piety or fidelity. Those funeral commendations which are gathered out of the spoils of truth are not at all to the praise of those on whom they are bestowed, but very much the dispraise of those who unjustly misplace them. But he has this to say in honour of Saul himself, *First*, That he was *anointed with oil* (*v.* 21), the sacred oil, which signified his elevation to, and qualification for, the government. Whatever he was otherwise, the *crown of the anointing oil of his God was upon him,* as is said of the high priest (Lev. xxi. 12), and on that account he was to be honoured, because God, the fountain of honour, had honoured him. *Secondly*, That he was a man of war, a *mighty man* (*v.* 19—21), that he had often been victorious over the enemies of Israel and *vexed them whithersoever he turned,* 1 Sam. xiv. 47. His *sword returned not empty*, but satiated with blood and spoil, *v.* 22. His disgrace and fall at last must not make his former successes and services to be forgotten. Though his sun set under a cloud, time was when it shone brightly. *Thirdly*, That take him with Jonathan he was a man of a very agreeable temper, that recommended himself to the affections of his subjects (*v.* 23): *Saul and Jonathan were lovely and pleasant*. Jonathan was always so, and Saul was so as long as he concurred with him. Take them together, and in the pursuit of the enemy, never were men more bold, more brave; they were *swifter than eagles and stronger than lions.* Observe, Those that were most fierce and fiery in the camp were no less sweet and lovely in the court, as amiable to the subject as they were formidable to the foe; a rare combination of softness and sharpness they had, which makes any man's temper very happy. It may be understood of the harmony and affection that for the most part subsisted between Saul and Jonathan: they were lovely and pleasant one to another, Jonathan a dutiful son, Saul an affectionate father; and therefore dear to each other in their lives, and *in their death they were not divided,* but kept close together in the stand they made against the Philistines, and fell together in the same cause. *Fourthly,* That he had enriched his country with the spoils of conquered nations, and introduced a more splendid attire. When they had a king like the nations, they must have clothes like the nations; and herein he was, in a particular manner, obliging to his female subjects, *v.* 24. The *daughters of Israel* he *clothed in scarlet,* which was their delight.

(2.) He was very grateful to Jonathan, his sworn friend. Besides the tears he shed over him, and the encomiums he gives of him in common with Saul, he mentions him with some marks of distinction (*v.* 25): *O Jonathan! thou wast slain in thy high places!* which (compared with *v.* 19) intimates that he meant him by *the beauty of Israel,* which, he there says, was slain upon the high places. He laments Jonathan as his particular friend (*v.* 26): *My brother, Jonathan;* not so much because of what he would have been to him if he had lived, very serviceable no doubt in his advancement to the throne and instrumental to prevent those long struggles which, for want of his assistance, he had with the house of Saul (had this been the only ground of his grief it would have been selfish), but he lamented him for what he had been: "*Very pleasant hast thou been unto me;* but that pleasantness is now over, and *I am distressed for thee.*" He had reason to say that Jonathan's love to him was wonderful; surely never was the like, for a man to love one who he knew was to take the crown over his head, and to be so faithful to his rival: this far surpassed the highest degree of conjugal affection and constancy. See here, [1.] That nothing is more delightful in this world than a true friend, that is wise and good, that kindly receives and returns our affection, and is faithful to us in all our true interests. [2.] That nothing is more distressful than the loss of such a friend; it is parting with a piece of one's self. It is the vanity of this world that what is most pleasant to us we are most liable to be distressed in. The more we love the more we grieve.

(3.) He was deeply concerned for the honour of God; for this is what he has an eye to when he fears lest *the daughters of the uncircumcised,* that are out of covenant with God, should triumph over Israel, and the God of Israel, *v.* 20. Good men are touched in a very sensible part by the reproaches of those that reproach God.

(4.) He was deeply concerned for the public welfare. It was the beauty of Israel that was slain (*v.* 19) and the honour of the public that was disgraced: The *mighty have fallen* (this is three times lamented, *v.* 19, 25, 27), and so the strength of the people is weakened. Public losses are most laid to heart by men of public spirit. David hoped God would make him instrumental to repair those losses and yet laments them.

2. A man of a fine imagination, as well as a wise and holy man. The expressions are all excellent, and calculated to work upon the passions. (1.) The embargo he would fain lay upon Fame is elegant (*v.* 20): *Tell it not in Gath.* It grieved him to the heart to think that it would be proclaimed in the

cities of the Philistines, and that they would insult over Israel upon it, and the more in remembrance of the triumphs of Israel over them formerly, when they sang, *Saul has slain his thousands;* for this would now be retorted. (2.) The curse he entails on the mountains of Gilboa, the theatre on which this tragedy was acted: *Let there be no dew upon you, nor fields of offerings, v.* 21. This is a poetical strain, like that of Job, *Let the day perish wherein I was born.* Not as if David wished that any part of the land of Israel might be barren, but, to express his sorrow for the thing, he speaks with a seeming indignation at the place. Observe, [1.] How the fruitfulness of the earth depends upon heaven. The worst thing he could wish to the mountains of Gilboa was barrenness and unprofitableness to man: those are miserable that are useless. It was the curse Christ pronounced on the fig-tree, *Never fruit grow on thee more,* and that took effect—the fig-tree withered away: this, on the mountains of Gilboa, did not. But, when he wished them barren, he wished there might be no rain upon them; and, if the heavens be brass, the earth will soon be iron. [2.] How the fruitfulness of the earth must therefore be devoted to heaven, which is intimated in his calling the fruitful fields *fields of offerings.* Those fruits of their land that were offered to God were the crown and glory of it: and therefore the failure of the offerings is the saddest consequent of the failure of the corn. See Joel i. 9. To want that wherewith we should honour God is worse than to want that wherewith we should sustain ourselves. This is the reproach David fastens upon the mountains of Gilboa, which, having been stained with royal blood, thereby forfeited celestial dews. In this elegy Saul had a more honourable interment than that which the men of Jabesh-Gilead gave him.

CHAP. II.

David had paid due respect to the memory of Saul his prince and Jonathan his friend, and what he did was as much his praise as theirs; he is now considering what is to be done next. Saul is dead, now therefore David arise. I. By direction from God he went up to Hebron, and was there anointed king, ver. 1—4. II. He returned thanks to the men of Jabesh-Gilead for burying Saul, ver. 5—7. III. Ishbosheth, the son of Saul, is set up in opposition to him, ver. 8—11. IV. A warm encounter happens between David's party and Ishbosheth's, in which, 1. Twelve of each side engaged hand to hand and were all slain, ver. 12—16. 2. Saul's party was beaten, ver. 17. 3. Asahel, on David's side, was slain by Abner, ver. 18—23. 4. Joab, at Abner's request, sounds a retreat, ver. 24—28. 5. Abner makes the best of his way (ver. 29), and the loss on both sides is computed, ver. 30—32. So that here we have an account of a civil war in Israel, which, in process of time, ended in the complete settlement of David on the throne.

AND it came to pass after this, that David enquired of the LORD, saying, Shall I go up into any of the cities of Judah? And the LORD said unto him, Go up. And David said, Whither shall I go up? And he said, Unto Hebron. 2 So David went up thither, and his two wives also, Ahinoam the Jezreelitess, and Abigail Nabal's wife the Carmelite. 3 And his men that *were* with him did David bring up, every man with his household: and they dwelt in the cities of Hebron. 4 And the men of Judah came, and there they anointed David king over the house of Judah. And they told David, saying, *That* the men of Jabesh-gilead *were they* that buried Saul. 5 And David sent messengers unto the men of Jabesh-gilead, and said unto them, Blessed *be* ye of the LORD, that ye have showed this kindness unto your lord, *even* unto Saul, and have buried him. 6 And now the LORD show kindness and truth unto you: and I also will requite you this kindness, because ye have done this thing. 7 Therefore now let your hands be strengthened, and be ye valiant: for your master Saul is dead, and also the house of Judah have anointed me king over them.

When Saul and Jonathan were dead, though David knew himself anointed to be king, and now saw his way very clear, yet he did not immediately send messengers through all the coasts of Israel to summon all people to come in and swear allegiance to him, upon pain of death, but proceeded leisurely; for he that believeth doth not make haste, but waits God's time for the accomplishment of God's promises. Many had come in to his assistance from several tribes while he continued at Ziklag, as we find (1 Chron. xii. 1—22), and with such a force he might have come in by conquest. But he that will rule with meekness will not rise with violence. Observe here,

I. The direction he sought and had from God in this critical juncture, *v.* 1. He doubted not of success, yet he used proper means, both divine and human. Assurance of hope in God's promise will be so far from slackening that it will quicken pious endeavours. If I be elected to the crown of life, it does not follow, Then I will do nothing; but, Then I will do all that he directs me, and follow the guidance of him who chose me. This good use David made of his election, and so will all whom God has chosen. 1. David, according to the precept, *acknowledged God in his way.* He enquired of the Lord by the breast-plate of judgment, which Abiathar brought to him. We must apply to God not only when we are in distress, but even when the world smiles upon us and second causes work in favour of us. His enquiry was, *Shall I go up to any of the cities of Judah?* Shall I stir hence? Though

Ziklag be in ruins, he will not quit it without direction from God. "If I stir hence, *Shall I go to one of the cities of Judah?*" not limiting God to them (if God should so direct him, he would go to any of the cities of Israel), but thus expressing his prudence (in the cities of Judah he would find most friends), and his modesty—he would look no further at present than his own tribe. In all our motions and removals it is comfortable to see God going before us; and we may, if by faith and prayer we set him before us. 2. God, according to the promise, directed his path, bade him go up, told him whither, unto Hebron, a priests' city, one of the cities of refuge, so it was to David, and an intimation that God himself would be to him a little sanctuary. The sepulchres of the patriarchs, adjoining to Hebron, would remind him of the ancient promise, on which God had caused him to hope. God sent him not to Bethlehem, his own city, because that was *little among the thousands of Judah* (Mic. v. 2), but to Hebron, a more considerable place, and which perhaps was then as the county-town of that tribe.

II. The care he took of his family and friends in his removal to Hebron. 1. He took his wives with him (*v.* 2), that, as they had been companions with him in tribulation, they might be so in the kingdom. It does not appear that as yet he had any children; his first was born in Hebron, *ch.* iii. 2. 2. He took his friends and followers with him, *v.* 3. They had accompanied him in his wanderings, and therefore, when he gained a settlement, they settled with him. Thus, if we *suffer with Christ, we shall reign with him,* 2 Tim. ii. 12. Nay, Christ does more for his good soldiers than David could do for his; David found lodging for them—*They dwelt in the cities of Hebron,* the adjacent towns; but to those who *continue with Christ in his temptations he appoints a kingdom,* and will *feast them at his own table,* Luke xxii. 29, 30.

III. The honour done him by the men of Judah: They *anointed him king over the house of Judah, v.* 4. The tribe of Judah had often stood by itself more than any other of the tribes. In Saul's time it was numbered by itself as a distinct body (1 Sam. xv. 4) and those of this tribe had been accustomed to act separately. They did so now; yet they did it for themselves only; they did not pretend to anoint him king *over all Israel* (as Judg. ix. 22), but only *over the house of Judah.* The rest of the tribes might do as they pleased, but, as for them and their house, they would be ruled by him whom God had chosen. See how David rose gradually; he was first anointed king *in reversion,* then *in possession* of one tribe only, and at last of all the tribes. Thus the kingdom of the Messiah, the Son of David, is set up by degrees; he is Lord of all by divine designation, but *we see not yet all things put under him,* Heb. ii. 8. David's reigning at first over the house of Judah only was a tacit intimation of Providence that his kingdom would in a short time be reduced to that again, as it was when the ten tribes revolted from his grandson; and it would be an encouragement to the godly kings of Judah that David himself at first reigned over Judah only.

IV. The respectful message he sent to the men of Jabesh-Gilead, to return them thanks for their kindness to Saul. Still he studies to honour the memory of his predecessor, and thereby to show that he was far from aiming at the crown from any principle of ambition or enmity to Saul, but purely because he was called of God to it. It was told him that the men of Jabesh-Gilead buried Saul, perhaps by some that thought he would be displeased at them as over-officious. But he was far from that. 1. He commends them for it, *v.* 5. According as our obligations were to love and honour any while they lived, we ought to show respect to their remains (that is, their bodies, names, and families) when they are dead. "Saul was your lord," says David, "and therefore you did well to show him this kindness and do him this honour." 2. He prays to God to bless them for it, and to recompense it to them: *Blessed are you,* and blessed *may you be* of the Lord, who will deal kindly with those in a particular manner that *dealt kindly with the dead,* as it is in Ruth i. 8. Due respect and affection shown to the bodies, names, and families of those that are dead, in conscience towards God, is a piece of charity which shall in no wise lose its reward: *The Lord show kindness and truth to you* (*v.* 6), that is, kindness according to the promise. What kindness God shows is in truth, what one may trust to. 3. He promises to make them amends for it: *I also will requite you.* He does not turn them over to God for a recompence that he may excuse himself from rewarding them. Good wishes are good things, and instances of gratitude, but they are too cheap to be rested in where there is an ability to do more. 4. He prudently takes this opportunity to gain them to his interest, *v.* 7. They had paid their last respects to Saul, and he would have them to be the last: "*The house of Judah have anointed me king,* and it will be your wisdom to concur with them and in that to be valiant." We must not so dote on the dead, how much soever we have valued them, as to neglect or despise the blessings we have in those that survive, whom God has raised up to us in their stead.

8 But Abner the son of Ner, captain of Saul's host, took Ish-bosheth the son of Saul, and brought him over to Mahanaim; 9 And made him king over Gilead, and over the Ashurites, and over Jezreel, and over

Ephraim, and over Benjamin, and over all Israel. 10 Ish-bosheth Saul's son *was* forty years old when he began to reign over Israel, and reigned two years. But the house of Judah followed David. 11 And the time that David was king in Hebron over the house of Judah was seven years and six months. 12 And Abner the son of Ner, and the servants of Ish-bosheth the son of Saul, went out from Mahanaim to Gibeon. 13 And Joab the son of Zeruiah, and the servants of David, went out, and met together by the pool of Gibeon: and they sat down, the one on the one side of the pool, and the other on the other side of the pool. 14 And Abner said to Joab, Let the young men now arise, and play before us. And Joab said, Let them arise. 15 Then there arose and went over by number twelve of Benjamin, which *pertained* to Ish-bosheth the son of Saul, and twelve of the servants of David. 16 And they caught every one his fellow by the head, and *thrust* his sword in his fellow's side; so they fell down together: wherefore that place was called Helkath-hazzurim, which *is* in Gibeon. 17 And there was a very sore battle that day; and Abner was beaten, and the men of Israel, before the servants of David.

Here is, I. A rivalship between two kings—David, whom God made king, and Ishbosheth, whom Abner made king. One would have thought, when Saul was slain, and all his sons that had sense and spirit enough to take the field with him, David would come to the throne without any opposition, since all Israel knew, not only how he had signalized himself, but how manifestly God had designated him to it; but such a spirit of contradiction is there, in the devices of men, to the counsels of God, that such a weak and silly thing as Ishbosheth, who was not thought fit to go with his father to the battle, shall yet be thought fit to succeed him in the government, rather than David shall come peaceably to it. Herein David's kingdom was typical of the Messiah's, against which *the heathens rage* and the *rulers take counsel*, Ps. ii. 1, 2. 1. Abner was the person who set up Ishbosheth in competition with David, perhaps in his zeal for the lineal succession (since they must have a king like the nations, in *this* they must be like them, that the crown must descend from father to son), or rather in his affection to his own family and relations (for he was Saul's uncle), and because he had no other way to secure to himself the post of honour he was in, as captain of the host. See how much mischief the pride and ambition of one man may be the occasion of. Ishbosheth would never have set up himself if Abner had not set him up, and made a tool of him to serve his own purposes. 2. Mahanaim, the place where he first made his claim, was on the other side Jordan, where it was thought David had the least interest, and being at a distance from his forces they might have time to strengthen themselves. But, having set up his standard there, the unthinking people of all the tribes of Israel (that is, the generality of them) submitted to him (*v.* 9), and Judah only was entirely for David. This was a further trial of the faith of David in the promise of God, and of his patience, whether he could wait God's time for the performance of that promise. 3. Some difficulty there is about the time of the continuance of this competition. David reigned about seven years over Judah only (*v.* 11), and yet (*v.*10) Ishbosheth reigned over Israel but two years: before those two years, or after, or both, it was in general for the house of Saul (*ch.* iii. 6), and not any particular person of that house, that Abner declared. Or these two years he reigned before the war broke out (*v.* 12), which continued long, even the remaining five years, *ch.* iii. 1.

II. An encounter between their two armies. 1. It does not appear that either side brought their whole force into the field, for the slaughter was but small, *v.* 30, 31. We may wonder, (1.) That the men of Judah did not appear and act more vigorously for David, to reduce all the nation into obedience to him; but, it is likely, David would not suffer them to act offensively, choosing rather to wait till the thing would do itself or rather till God would do it for him, without the effusion of Israelitish blood; for to him, as a type of Christ, that was very precious, Ps. lxxii. 14. Even those that were his adversaries he looked upon as his subjects, and would treat them accordingly. (2.) That the men of Israel could in a manner stand neuter, and sit down tamely under Ishbosheth, for so many years, especially considering what characters many of the tribes displayed at this time (as we find, 1 Chron. xii. 23, &c.): *Wise men, mighty men, men of valour, expert in war,* and not of double heart, and yet for seven years together, for aught that appears, most of them seemed indifferent in whose hand the public administration was. Divine Providence serves its own purposes by the stupidity of men at some times and the activity of the same persons at other times; they are unlike themselves, and yet the motions of Providence are uniform.

2. In this battle Abner was the aggressor.

David sat still to see how the matter would fall, but the house of Saul, and Abner at the head of it, gave the challenge, and they went by the worst. Therefore *go not forth hastily to strive,* nor be forward to begin quarrels, *lest thou know not what to do in the end thereof,* Prov. xxv. 8. A fool's lips and hands enter into contention.

3. The seat of the war was Gibeon. Abner chose it because it was in the lot of Benjamin, where Saul had the most friends; yet, since he offered battle, Joab, David's general, would not decline it, but there joined issue with him, and met him *by the pool of Gibeon, v.* 13. David's cause, being built upon God's promise, feared not the disadvantages of the ground. The pool between them gave both sides time to deliberate.

4. The engagement was at first proposed by Abner, and accepted by Joab, to be between twelve and twelve of a side. (1.) It should seem this trial of skill began in sport. Abner made the motion (*v.* 14): *Let the young men arise and play before us,* as gladiators. Perhaps Saul had used his men to these barbarous pastimes, like a tyrant indeed, and Abner had learnt of him to make a jest of wounds and death and divert himself with the scenes of blood and horror. He meant, "Let them *fight* before us," when he said, "Let them *play* before us." *Fools* thus *make a mock at sin.* But he is unworthy the name of a man that can be thus prodigal of human blood, that can thus *throw about firebrands, arrows, and death,* and say, *Am not I in sport?* Prov. xxvi. 18, 19. Joab, having been bred up under David, had so much wisdom as not to make such a proposal, yet had not resolution enough to resist and gainsay it when another made it; for he stood upon a point of honour, and thought it a blemish to his reputation to refuse a challenge, and therefore said, *Let them arise;* not that he was fond of the sport, or expected that the duels would be decisive, but he would not be hectored by his antagonist. How many precious lives have thus been sacrificed to the caprices of proud men! Twelve of each side were accordingly called out as champions to enter the lists, a double jury of life and death, not of others', but their own; and the champions on Abner's side seem to have been most forward, for they took the field first (*v.* 15), having perhaps been bred up in a foolish ambition thus to serve the humour of their commander-in-chief. But, (2.) However it began, it ended in blood (*v.* 16): They thrust *every man his sword into his fellow's side* (spurred on by honour, not by enmity); so they *fell down together,* that is, all the twenty-four were slain, such an equal match were they for one another, and so resolute, that neither side would either beg or give quarter; they did as it were by agreement (says *Josephus*) dispatch one another with mutual wounds. Those that strike at other men's lives often throw away their own, and death only conquers and rides in triumph. The wonderful obstinacy of both sides was remembered in the name given to the place: *Helkath-hazzurim—the field of rocky men,* men that were not only strong in body, but of firm and unshaken constancy, that stirred not at the sight of death. Yet *the stout-hearted were spoiled, and slept their sleep,* Ps. lxxvi. 5. Poor honour for men to purchase at so vast an expense! Those that lose their lives for Christ shall find them.

5. The whole army at length engaged, and Abner's forces were routed, *v.* 17. The former was a drawn battle, in which all were killed on both sides, and therefore they must put it upon another trial, in which (as it often happens) those that gave the challenge went away with loss. David had God on his side; his side therefore was victorious.

18 And there were three sons of Zeruiah there, Joab, and Abishai, and Asahel: and Asahel *was as* light of foot as a wild roe. 19 And Asahel pursued after Abner; and in going he turned not to the right hand nor to the left from following Abner. 20 Then Abner looked behind him, and said, *Art* thou Asahel? And he answered, I *am.* 21 And Abner said to him, Turn thee aside to thy right hand or to thy left, and lay thee hold on one of the young men, and take thee his armour. But Asahel would not turn aside from following of him. 22 And Abner said again to Asahel, Turn thee aside from following me: wherefore should I smite thee to the ground? how then should I hold up my face to Joab thy brother? 23 Howbeit he refused to turn aside: wherefore Abner with the hinder end of the spear smote him under the fifth *rib,* that the spear came out behind him; and he fell down there, and died in the same place: and it came to pass, *that* as many as came to the place where Asahel fell down and died stood still. 24 Joab also and Abishai pursued after Abner: and the sun went down when they were come to the hill of Ammah, that *lieth* before Giah by the way of the wilderness of Gibeon.

We have here the contest between Abner and Asahel. Asahel, the brother of Joab and cousin-german to David, was one of the principal commanders of David's forces, and was famous for swiftness in running: he was *as light of foot as a wild roe* (*v.* 18); this he got the name of by swift pursuing, not swift flying. Yet, we may suppose, he was not comparable to Abner as a skilful experienced soldier; we must therefore observe,

I. How rash he was in aiming to make Abner his prisoner. He pursued after him, and no other, *v.* 19. Proud of his relation to David and Joab, his own swiftness, and the success of his party, no less a trophy of victory would now serve the young warrior than Abner himself, either slain or bound, which he thought would put an end to the war and effectually open David's way to the throne. This made him very eager in the pursuit, and careless of the opportunities he had of seizing others in his way, on his right hand and on his left; his eye was on Abner only. The design was brave, had he been *par negotio—equal to its accomplishment:* but let not the swift man glory in his swiftness, any more than the strong man in his strength; *magnis excidit ausis—he perished in an attempt too vast for him.*

II. How generous Abner was in giving him notice of the danger he exposed himself to, and advising him not to *meddle to his own hurt,* 2 Chron. xxv. 19. 1. He bade him content himself with a less prey (*v.* 21): "*Lay hold of one of the young men,* plunder him and make him thy prisoner, meddle with thy match, but pretend not to one who is so much superior to thee." It is wisdom in all contests to compare our own strength with that of our adversaries, and to take heed of being partial to ourselves in making the comparison, lest we prove in the issue *enemies to ourselves,* Luke xiv. 31. 2. He begged of him not to put him upon the necessity of slaying him in his own defence, which he was very loth to do, but must do rather than be slain by him, *v.* 22. Abner, it seems, either loved Joab or feared him; for he was very loth to incur his displeasure, which he would certainly do if he slew Asahel. It is commendable for enemies to be thus respectful one to another. Abner's care how he should lift up his face to Joab gives cause to suspect that he really believed David would have the kingdom at last, according to the divine designation, and then, in opposing him, he acted against his conscience.

III. How fatal Asahel's rashness was to him. He refused to turn aside, thinking that Abner spoke so courteously because he feared him; but what came of it? Abner, as soon as he came up to him, gave him his death's wound with a back stroke (*v.* 23): *He smote him with the hinder end of his spear,* from which he feared no danger. This was a pass which Asahel was not acquainted with, nor had learned to stand upon his guard against; but Abner, perhaps, had formerly used it, and done execution with it; and here it did effectual execution. Asahel died immediately of the wound. See here, 1. How death often comes upon us by ways that we least suspect. Who would fear the hand of a flying enemy or the butt-end of a spear? yet from these Asahel receives his death's wound. 2. How we are often betrayed by the accomplishments we are proud of. Asahel's swiftness, which he presumed so much upon, did him no kindness, but forwarded his fate, and with it he ran upon his death, instead of running from it. Asahel's fall was not only Abner's security from him, but put a full stop to the conqueror's pursuit and gave Abner time to rally again; for all that came to the place stood still, only Joab and Abishai, instead of being disheartened, were exasperated by it, pursued Abner with so much the more fury (*v.* 24), and overtook him at last about sunset, when the approaching night would oblige them to retire.

25 And the children of Benjamin gathered themselves together after Abner, and became one troop, and stood on the top of a hill. 26 Then Abner called to Joab, and said, Shall the sword devour for ever? knowest thou not that it will be bitterness in the latter end? how long shall it be then, ere thou bid the people return from following their brethren? 27 And Joab said, *As* God liveth, unless thou hadst spoken, surely then in the morning the people had gone up every one from following his brother. 28 So Joab blew a trumpet, and all the people stood still, and pursued after Israel no more, neither fought they any more. 29 And Abner and his men walked all that night through the plain, and passed over Jordan, and went through all Bithron, and they came to Mahanaim. 30 And Joab returned from following Abner: and when he had gathered all the people together, there lacked of David's servants nineteen men and Asahel. 31 But the servants of David had smitten of Benjamin, and of Abner's men, *so that* three hundred and threescore men died. 32 And they took up Asahel, and buried him in the sepulchre of his father, which *was in* Beth-lehem. And Joab and his men went all night, and they came to Hebron at break of day.

Here, I. Abner, being conquered, meanly begs for a cessation of arms. He rallied the remains of his forces on the top of a hill (*v.* 25), as if he would have made head again, but becomes a humble supplicant to Joab for a little breathing-time, *v.* 26. He that was most forward to fight was the first that had enough of it. He that made a jest of bloodshed (*Let the young men arise and play before us, v.* 14) is now shocked at it, when he finds himself on the losing side, and the sword he made so light of drawing threatening to touch himself. Observe how his note is changed. Then it was but playing with the sword; now, *Shall the sword devour for ever?* It had devoured but one day, yet to him it seemed for ever, because it went against him; and very willing he is now that the sun should not go down upon the wrath. Now he can appeal to Joab himself concerning the miserable consequences of a civil war: *Knowest thou not that it will be bitterness in the latter end?* It will be reflected upon with regret when the account comes to be made up; for, whoever gets in a civil war, the community is sure to lose. Perhaps he refers to the bitterness that there was in the tribes of Israel, in the end of their war with Benjamin, when they wept sorely for the desolations which they themselves had made, Judg. xxi. 2. Now he begs of Joab to sound a retreat, and pleads that they were brethren, who ought not thus to bite and devour one another. He that in the morning would have Joab bid the people fall upon their brethren now would have him bid them lay down their arms. See here, 1. How easy it is for men to use reason when it makes for them who would not use it if it made against them. If Abner had been the conqueror, we should not have had him complaining of the voraciousness of the sword and the miseries of a civil war, nor pleading that both sides were brethren; but, finding himself beaten, all these reasonings are mustered up and improved for the securing of his retreat and the saving of his scattered troops from being cut off. 2. How the issue of things alters men's minds. The same thing which looked pleasant in the morning at night looked dismal. Those that are forward to enter into contention will perhaps repent it before they have done with it, and therefore had better leave it off before it be meddled with, as Solomon advises. It is true of every sin (O that men would consider it in time!) that it will be *bitterness in the latter end. At the last it bites like a serpent* those on whom it fawned.

II. Joab, though a conqueror, generously grants it, and sounds a retreat, knowing very well his master's mind and how averse he was to the shedding of blood. He does indeed justly upbraid Abner with his forwardness to engage, and lays the blame upon him that there had been so much bloodshed as there was (*v.* 27): "*Unless thou hadst spoken,*" that is, "hadst given orders to fight, hadst bidden the young men arise and play before us, none of us would have struck a stroke, nor drawn a sword against our brethren. Thou complainest that the sword devours, but who first unsheathed it? Who began? Now thou wouldst have the people parted, but remember who set them on to fight. We should have retired in the morning if thou hadst not given the challenge." Those that are forward to make mischief are commonly the first to complain of it. This might have served to excuse Joab if he had pushed on his victory, and made a full end of Abner's forces; but like one that pitied the mistake of his adversaries, and scorned to make an army of Israelites pay dearly for the folly of their commander, he very honourably, by sound of trumpet, put a stop to the pursuit (*v.* 28) and suffered Abner to make an orderly retreat. It is good husbandry to be sparing of blood. As the soldiers were here very obsequious to the general's orders, so he, no doubt, observed the instructions of his prince, who sought the welfare of all Israel and therefore not the hurt of any.

III. The armies being separated, both retired to the places whence they came, and both marched in the night, Abner to Mahanaim, on the other side Jordan (*v.* 29), and Joab to Hebron, where David was, *v.* 32. The slain on both sides are computed. On David's side only nineteen men were missing, besides Asahel (*v.* 30), who was worth more than all; on Abner's side 360, *v.* 31. In civil wars formerly great slaughters had been made (as Judg. xii. 6, 20, 44), in comparison with which this was nothing. It is to be hoped that they had grown wiser and more moderate. Asahel's funeral is here mentioned; the rest they buried in the field of battle, but he was carried to Bethlehem, and buried in the sepulchre of his father, *v.* 32. Thus are distinctions made between the dust of some and that of others; but in the resurrection no other difference will be made but that between godly and ungodly, which will remain for ever.

CHAP. III.

The battle between Joab and Abner did not end the controversy between the two houses of Saul and David, but it is in this chapter working towards a period. Here is, I. The gradual advance of David's interest, ver. 1. II. The building up of his family, ver. 2—5. III. Abner's quarrel with Ish-bosheth, and his treaty with David, ver. 6—12. IV. The preliminaries settled, ver. 13—16. V. Abner's undertaking and attempt to bring Israel over to David, ver. 17—21. VI. The treacherous murder of Abner by Joab, when he was carrying on this matter, ver. 22—27. VII. David's great concern and trouble for the death of Abner, ver. 28—39.

NOW there was long war between the house of Saul and the house of David: but David waxed stronger and stronger, and the house of Saul waxed weaker and weaker. 2 And unto David were sons born in Hebron: and his firstborn was Amnon, of Ahinoam the Jezreelitess; 3 And his second, Chileab, of Abigail the wife of Nabal the Carmelite; and the third, Absalom the son of Maacah the daughter of Talmai king of Geshur; 4 And the fourth, Adonijah the son of Haggith; and the fifth, Shephatiah the son of Abital; 5 And the sixth, Ithream, by Eglah David's wife. These were born to David in Hebron. 6 And it came to pass, while there was war between the house of Saul and the house of David, that Abner made himself strong for the house of Saul.

Here is, I. The struggle that David had with the house of Saul before his settlement in the throne was completed, *v.* 1. 1. Both sides contested. Saul's house, though beheaded and diminished, would not fall tamely. It is not strange that there was war between them, but one would wonder it should be a long war, when David's house had right on its side, and therefore God on its side; but, though truth and equity will triumph at last, God may for wise and holy ends prolong the conflict. The length of this war tried the faith and patience of David, and made his establishment at last the more welcome to him. 2. David's side got ground. The house of Saul waxed weaker and weaker, lost places, lost men, sunk in its reputation, grew less considerable, and was foiled in every engagement. But the house of David grew stronger and stronger. Many deserted the declining cause of Saul's house, and prudently came into David's interest, being convinced that he would certainly win the day. The contest between grace and corruption in the hearts of believers, who are sanctified but in part, may fitly be compared to this recorded here. There is a long war between them, the flesh lusting against the spirit and the spirit against the flesh; but, as the work of sanctification is carried on, corruption, like the house of Saul, grows weaker and weaker; while grace, like the house of David, grows stronger and stronger, till it come to a perfect man, and judgment be brought forth unto victory.

II. The increase of his own house. Here is an account of six sons he had by six several wives, in the seven years he reigned in Hebron. Perhaps this is here mentioned as that which strengthened David's interest. Every child, whose welfare was embarked in the common safety, was a fresh security given to the commonwealth for his care of it. He that has his quiver filled with these arrows shall *speak with his enemy in the gate*, Ps. cxxvii. 5. As the death of Saul's sons weakened his interest, so the birth of David's strengthened his. 1. It was David's fault thus to multiply wives, contrary to the law (Deut. xvii. 17), and it was a bad example to his successors. 2. It does not appear that in these seven years he had above one son by each of these wives; some have had as numerous a progeny, and with much more honour and comfort, by one wife. 3. We read not that any of these sons came to be famous (three of them were infamous, Amnon, Absalom, and Adonijah); we have therefore reason to rejoice with trembling in the building up of our families. 4. His son by Abigail is called *Chileab* (*v.* 3), whereas (1 Chron. iii. 1) he is called *Daniel*. Bishop Patrick mentions the reason which the Hebrew doctors give for these names, that his first name was *Daniel—God has judged me* (namely, against Nabal), but David's enemies reproached him, and said, "It is Nabal's son, and not David's," to confute which calumny Providence so ordered it that, as he grew up, he became, in his countenance and features, extremely like David, and resembled him more than any of his children, upon which he gave him the name of *Chileab*, which signifies, *like his father*, or the father's picture. 5. Absalom's mother is said to be the daughter of Talmai king of Geshur, a heathen prince. Perhaps David thereby hoped to strengthen his interest, but the issue of the marriage was one that proved his grief and shame. 6. The last is called *David's wife*, which therefore, some think, was Michal, his first and most rightful wife, called here by another name: and, though she had no child after she mocked David, she might have had before.

Thus was David's house strengthened; but it was Abner that *made himself strong for the house of Saul*, which is mentioned (*v.* 6) to show that, if he failed them, they would fall of course.

7 And Saul had a concubine, whose name *was* Rizpah, the daughter of Aiah: and *Ishbosheth* said to Abner, Wherefore hast thou gone in unto my father's concubine? 8 Then was Abner very wroth for the words of Ishbosheth, and said, *Am* I a dog's head, which against Judah do show kindness this day unto the house of Saul thy father, to his brethren, and to his friends, and have not delivered thee into the hand of David, that thou chargest me to day with a fault concerning this woman? 9 So do God to Abner, and more also, except as the LORD hath sworn to David, even so I do to him; 10 To translate the kingdom from the house of Saul, and to set up the throne of David over Israel and over Judah, from Dan even to Beer-sheba. 11 And he could not answer Abner a word again, because he feared him. 12 And Abner sent messengers to David on his behalf, saying, Whose *is* the land? saying *also*, Make thy league with me, and, behold, my hand *shall be* with thee,

to bring about all Israel unto thee. 13 And he said, Well; I will make a league with thee: but one thing I require of thee, that is, Thou shalt not see my face, except thou first bring Michal Saul's daughter, when thou comest to see my face. 14 And David sent messengers to Ish-bosheth Saul's son, saying, Deliver *me* my wife Michal, which I espoused to me for a hundred foreskins of the Philistines. 15 And Ish-bosheth sent, and took her from *her* husband, *even* from Phaltiel the son of Laish. 16 And her husband went with her along weeping behind her to Bahurim. Then said Abner unto him, Go, return. And he returned. 17 And Abner had communication with the elders of Israel, saying, Ye sought for David in times past *to be* king over you: 18 Now then do *it*: for the LORD hath spoken of David, saying, By the hand of my servant David I will save my people Israel out of the hand of the Philistines, and out of the hand of all their enemies. 19 And Abner also spake in the ears of Benjamin: and Abner went also to speak in the ears of David in Hebron all that seemed good to Israel, and that seemed good to the whole house of Benjamin. 20 So Abner came to David to Hebron, and twenty men with him. And David made Abner and the men that *were* with him a feast. 21 And Abner said unto David, I will arise and go, and will gather all Israel unto my lord the king, that they may make a league with thee, and that thou mayest reign over all that thine heart desireth. And David sent Abner away; and he went in peace.

Here, I. Abner breaks with Ish-bosheth, and deserts his interest, upon a little provocation which Ish-bosheth unadvisedly gave him. God can serve his own purposes by the sins and follies of men. 1. Ish-bosheth accused Abner of no less a crime than debauching one of his father's concubines, *v.* 7. Whether it was so or no does not appear, nor what ground he had for the suspicion: but, however it was, it would have been Ish-bosheth's prudence to be silent, considering how much it was his interest not to disoblige Abner. If the thing was false, and his jealousy groundless, it was very disingenuous and ungrateful to entertain unjust surmises of one who had ventured his all for him, and was certainly the best friend he had in the world. 2. Abner resented the charge very strongly. Whether he was guilty of the *fault concerning this woman* or no he does not say (*v.* 8), but we suspect he was guilty, for he does not expressly deny it; and, though he was, he lets Ish-bosheth know, (1.) That he scorned to be reproached with it by him, and would not take reproof at his hands. "What!" says Abner, "*Am I a dog's head,* a vile and contemptible animal, that thou exposest me thus? *v.* 8. Is this my recompence for the kindness I have shown to thee and thy father's house, and the good services I have done you?" He magnifies the service with this, that it was against Judah, the tribe on which the crown was settled, and which would certainly have it at last, so that, in supporting the house of Saul, he acted both against his conscience and against his interest, for which he deserved a better requital than this: and yet, perhaps, he would not have been so zealous for the house of Saul if he had not thereby gratified his own ambition and hoped to find his own account in it. Note, Proud men will not bear to be reproved, especially by those whom they think they have obliged. (2.) That he would certainly be revenged on him, *v.* 9, 10. With the utmost degree of arrogance and insolence he lets him know that, as he had raised him up, so he could pull him down again and would do it. He knew that God had sworn to David to give him the kingdom, and yet opposed it with all his might from a principle of ambition; but now he complies with it from a principle of revenge, under colour of some regard to the will of God, which was but a pretence. Those that are slaves to their lusts have many masters, which drive, some one way and some another, and, according as they make head, men are violently hurried into self-contradictions. Abner's ambition made him zealous for Ish-bosheth, and now his revenge made him as zealous for David. If he had sincerely regarded God's promise to David, and acted with an eye to that, he would have been steady and uniform in his counsels, and acted in consistency with himself. But, while Abner serves his own lusts, God by him serves his own purposes, makes even his wrath and revenge to praise him, and ordains strength to David by it. *Lastly,* See how Ish-bosheth was thunder-struck by Abner's insolence: He *could not answer him again, v.* 11. If Ish-bosheth had had the spirit of a man, especially of a prince, he might have answered him that his merits were the aggravation of his crimes, that he would not be served by so base a man, and doubted not but to do well enough without him. But he was conscious to himself of his own weakness, and therefore said not a word, lest he should make bad worse. His heart failed him, and he now became, as David had foretold concerning his enemies, like a bowing wall and a *tottering fence*, Ps. lxii. 3.

II. Abner treats with David. We must suppose that he began to grow weary of Ish-bosheth's cause, and sought an opportunity to desert it, or else, however he might threaten Ish-bosheth with it, for the quashing of the charge against himself, he would not have made good his angry words so soon as he did, *v.* 12. He *sent messengers to David*, to tell him that he was at his service. "*Whose is the land?* Is it not thine? For thou hast the best title to the government and the best interest in the people's affections." Note, God can find out ways to make those serviceable to the kingdom of Christ who yet have no sincere affection for it and who have vigorously set themselves against it. Enemies are sometimes made a footstool, not only to be trodden upon, but to ascend by. The earth helped the woman.

III. David enters into a treaty with Abner, but upon condition that he shall procure him the restitution of Michal his wife, *v.* 13. Hereby, 1. David showed the sincerity of his conjugal affection to his first and most rightful wife; neither her marrying another, nor his, had alienated him from her. Many waters could not quench that love. 2. He testified his respect to the house of Saul. So far was he from trampling upon it, now that it was fallen, that even in his elevation he valued himself not a little on his relation to it. He cannot be pleased with the honours of the throne unless he have Michal, Saul's daughter, to share with him in them, so far is he from bearing any malice to the family of his enemy. Abner sent him word that he must apply to Ish-bosheth, which he did (*v.* 14), pleading that he had purchased her at a dear rate, and she was wrongfully taken from him. Ish-bosheth durst not deny his demand, now that he had not Abner to stand by him, but took her from Phaltiel, to whom Saul had married her (*v.* 15), and Abner conducted her to David, not doubting but that then he should be doubly welcome when he brought him a wife in one hand and a crown in the other. Her latter husband was loth to part with her, and followed her *weeping* (*v.* 16), but there was no remedy: he must thank himself; for when he took her he knew that another had a right to her. Usurpers must expect to resign. Let no man therefore set his heart on that to which he is not entitled. If any disagreement has separated husband and wife, as they expect the blessing of God let them be reconciled, and come together again; let all former quarrels be forgotten, and let them live together in love, according to God's holy ordinance.

IV. Abner uses his interest with the elders of Israel to bring them over to David, knowing that whichever way they went the common people would follow of course. Now that it serves his own turn he can plead in David's behalf that he was, 1. Israel's choice (*v.* 17): "*You sought for him in times past to be king over you*, when he had signalized himself in so many engagements with the Philistines and done you so much good service; no man can pretend to greater personal merit than David nor to less than Ish-bosheth. You have tried them both, *Detur digniori—Give the crown to him that best deserves it.* Let David be your king." 2. God's choice (*v.* 18): "*The Lord hath spoken of David.* Compare *v.* 9. When God appointed Samuel to anoint him he did, in effect, promise that by his hand he would save Israel; for for that end he was made king. God having promised, by David's hand, to save Israel, it is both your duty, in compliance with God's will, and your interest, in order to your victories over your enemies, to submit to him; and it is the greatest folly in the world to oppose him." Who would have expected such reasonings as these out of Abner's mouth? But thus God will make the enemies of his people to know and own *that he has loved them*, Rev. iii. 9. He particularly applied to the men of Benjamin, those of his own tribe, on whom he had the greatest influence, and whom he had drawn in to appear for the house of Saul. He was the man that had deceived them, and therefore he was concerned to undeceive them. Thus the multitude are as they are managed.

V. David concludes the treaty with Abner; and he did wisely and well therein; for, whatever induced Abner to it, it was a good work to put an end to the war, and to settle the Lord's anointed on the throne; and it was as lawful for David to make use of his agency as it is for a poor man to receive alms from a Pharisee, who gives it in pride and hypocrisy. Abner reported to David the sense of the people and the success of his communications with them, *v.* 19. He came now, not as at first privately, but with a retinue of twenty men, and David entertained them with *a feast* (*v.* 20) in token of reconciliation and joy and as a pledge of the agreement between them: it was a feast upon a covenant, like that, Gen. xxvi. 30. *If thy enemy hunger, feed him;* but, if he submit, feast him. Abner, pleased with his entertainment, the prevention of his fall with Saul's house (which would have been inevitable if he had not taken this course), and much more with the prospect he had of preferment under David, undertakes in a little time to perfect the revolution, and to bring all Israel into obedience to David, *v.* 21. He tells David he shall *reign over all that his heart desired.* He knew David's elevation took rise from God's appointment, yet he insinuates that it sprang from his own ambition and desire of rule; thus (as bad men often do) he measured that good man by himself. However, David and he parted very good friends, and the affair between them was well settled. Thus it behoves all who fear God and keep his commandments to avoid strife, even with the wicked, to live at peace with all men, and to show the world that they are children of the light.

22 And, behold, the servants of David and Joab came from *pursuing* a troop, and brought in a great spoil with them: but Abner *was* not with David in Hebron; for he had sent him away, and he was gone in peace. 23 When Joab and all the host that *was* with him were come, they told Joab, saying, Abner the son of Ner came to the king, and he hath sent him away, and he is gone in peace. 24 Then Joab came to the king, and said, What hast thou done? behold, Abner came unto thee; why *is* it *that* thou hast sent him away, and he is quite gone? 25 Thou knowest Abner the son of Ner, that he came to deceive thee, and to know thy going out and thy coming in, and to know all that thou doest. 26 And when Joab was come out from David, he sent messengers after Abner, which brought him again from the well of Sirah: but David knew *it* not. 27 And when Abner was returned to Hebron, Joab took him aside in the gate to speak with him quietly, and smote him there under the fifth *rib*, that he died, for the blood of Asahel his brother. 28 And afterward when David heard *it*, he said, I and my kingdom *are* guiltless before the LORD for ever from the blood of Abner the son of Ner: 29 Let it rest on the head of Joab, and on all his father's house; and let there not fail from the house of Joab one that hath an issue, or that is a leper, or that leaneth on a staff, or that falleth on the sword, or that lacketh bread. 30 So Joab and Abishai his brother slew Abner, because he had slain their brother Asahel at Gibeon in the battle. 31 And David said to Joab, and to all the people that *were* with him, Rend your clothes, and gird you with sackcloth, and mourn before Abner. And king David *himself* followed the bier. 32 And they buried Abner in Hebron: and the king lifted up his voice, and wept at the grave of Abner; and all the people wept. 33 And the king lamented over Abner, and said, Died Abner as a fool dieth? 34 Thy hands *were* not bound, nor thy feet put into fetters: as a man falleth before wicked men, *so* fellest thou. And all the people wept again over him. 35 And when all the people came to cause David to eat meat while it was yet day, David sware, saying, So do God to me, and more also, if I taste bread, or aught else, till the sun be down. 36 And all the people took notice *of it*, and it pleased them: as whatsoever the king did pleased all the people. 37 For all the people and all Israel understood that day that it was not of the king to slay Abner the son of Ner. 38 And the king said unto his servants, Know ye not that there is a prince and a great man fallen this day in Israel? 39 And I *am* this day weak, though anointed king; and these men the sons of Zeruiah *be* too hard for me: the LORD shall reward the doer of evil according to his wickedness.

We have here an account of the murder of Abner by Joab, and David's deep resentment of it.

I. Joab very insolently fell foul upon David for treating with Abner. He happened to be abroad upon service when Abner was with David, pursuing a troop, either of Philistines or of Saul's party; but, upon his return, he was informed that Abner was just gone (*v.* 22, 23), and that a great many kind things had passed between David and him. He had all the reason in the world to be satisfied of David's prudence and to acquiesce in the measures he took, knowing him to be a wise and good man himself and under a divine conduct in all his affairs; and yet, as if he had the same sway in David's cause that Abner had in Ish-bosheth's, he chides David, and reproaches him to his face as impolitic (*v.* 24, 25): *What hast thou done?* As if David were accountable to him for what he did: "*Why hast thou sent him away*, when thou mightest have made him a prisoner? He came as a spy, and will certainly betray thee." I know not whether to wonder more that Joab had impudence enough to give such an affront to his prince or that David had patience enough to take it. He does, in effect, call David *a fool* when he tells him he knew Abner came to deceive him and yet he trusted him. We find no answer that David gave him, not because he feared him, as Ish-bosheth did Abner (*v.* 11), but because he despised him, or because Joab had not so much good manners as to stay for an answer.

II. He very treacherously sent for Abner back, and, under colour of a private conference with him, barbarously killed him with his own hand. That he made use of David's name, under pretence of giving him some further instructions, is intimated in that, *but David knew it not, v.* 26. Abner, designing no harm, feared none, but very innocently returned to Hebron, and, when he found Joab waiting for him at the gate, turned aside with him to speak with him privately, forgetting what he himself had said when he slew Asahel, *How shall I hold up my face to Joab thy brother?* (*ch.* ii. 22), and there Joab murdered him (*v.* 27), and it is intimated (*v.* 30) that Abishai was privy to the design, and was aiding and abetting, and would have come in to his brother's assistance if there had been occasion; he is therefore charged as an accessary: *Joab and Abishai slew Abner,* though perhaps he only knew it who is privy to the thoughts and intents of men's hearts. Now in this, 1. It is certain that the Lord was righteous. Abner had maliciously, and against the convictions of his conscience, opposed David. He had now basely deserted Ish-bosheth, and betrayed him, under pretence of regard to God and Israel, but really from a principle of pride, and revenge, and impatience of control. God will not therefore use so bad a man, though David might, in so good a work as the uniting of Israel. Judgments are prepared for such scorners as Abner was. But, 2. It is as certain that Joab was unrighteous, and, in what he did, did wickedly. David was a man after God's own heart, but could not have those about him, no, not in places of the greatest trust, after his own heart. Many a good prince, and a good master, has been forced to employ bad men. (1.) Even the pretence for doing this was very unjust. Abner had indeed slain his brother Asahel, and Joab and Abishai pretended herein to be the avengers of his blood (*v.* 27, 30); but Abner slew Asahel in an open war, wherein Abner indeed had given the challenge, but Joab himself had accepted it and had slain many of Abner's friends. He did it likewise in his own defence, and not till he had given him fair warning (which he would not take), and he did it with reluctancy; but Joab here shed *the blood of war in peace,* 1 Kings ii. 5. (2.) That which we have reason to think was at the bottom of Joab's enmity to Abner made it much worse. Joab was now general of David's forces; but, if Abner should come into his interest, he would possibly be preferred before him, being a senior officer, and more experienced in the art of war. This Joab was jealous of, and could better bear the guilt of blood than the thoughts of a rival. (3.) He did it treacherously, and under pretence of speaking peaceably to him, Deut. xxvii. 24. Had he challenged him, he would have done like a soldier; but to assassinate him was done villanously and like a coward. *His words were softer than oil, yet were they drawn swords,* Ps. lv. 21. Thus he basely slew Amasa, *ch.* xx. 9, 10. (4.) The doing of it was a great affront and injury to David, who was now in treaty with Abner, as Joab knew. Abner was now actually in his master's service, so that, through his side, he struck at David himself. (5.) It was a great aggravation of the murder that he did it in the gate, openly and avowedly, as one that was not ashamed, nor could blush. The gate was the place of judgment and the place of concourse, so that he did it in defiance of justice, both the just sentence of the magistrates and the just resentment of the crowd, as one that neither feared God nor regarded man, but thought himself above all control: and Hebron was a Levites' city and a city of refuge.

III. David laid deeply to heart and in many ways expressed his detestation of this execrable villany.

1. He washed his hands from the guilt of Abner's blood. Lest any should suspect that Joab had some secret intimation from David to do as he did (and the rather because he went so long unpunished), he here solemnly appeals to God concerning his innocency: *I and my kingdom are guiltless* (and my kingdom is so because I am so) *before the Lord for ever, v.* 28. It is a comfort to be able to say, when any bad thing is done, that we had no hand in it. *We have not shed this blood,* Deut. xxi. 7. However we may be censured or suspected, *our hearts shall not reproach us.*

2. He entailed the curse for it upon Joab and his family (*v.* 29): "*Let it rest on the head of Joab.* Let the blood cry against him, and let divine vengeance follow him. Let the iniquity be visited upon his children and children's children, in some hereditary disease or other. The longer the punishment is delayed, the longer let it last when it shall come. Let his posterity be stigmatized, blemished with an issue or a leprosy, which will shut them out from society; let them be beggars, or cripples, or come to some untimely end, that it may be said, He is one of Joab's race." This intimates that the guilt of blood brings a curse upon families; if men do not avenge it, God will, and will lay up the iniquity for the children. But methinks a resolute punishment of the murderer himself would better have become David than this passionate imprecation of God's judgments upon his posterity.

3. He called upon all about him, even Joab himself, to lament the death of Abner (*v.* 31): *Rend your clothes and mourn before Abner,* that is, before the hearse of Abner, as Abraham is said to mourn *before his dead* (Gen.

xxiii. 2, 3), and he gives a reason why they should attend his funeral with sincere and solemn mourning (*v.* 38), because there is *a prince and a great man fallen this day in Israel.* His alliance to Saul, his place as general, his interest, and the great services he had formerly done, were enough to denominate him *a prince and a great man.* When he could not call him a saint or a good man, he said nothing of that, but what was true he gave him the praise of, though he had been his enemy, that he was *a prince and a great man.* "Such a man has fallen in Israel, and fallen *this day,* just when he was doing the best deed he ever did in his life, *this day,* when he was likely to be so serviceable to the public peace and welfare and could so ill be spared." (1.) Let them all lament it. The humbling change death puts all men under is to be lamented, especially as affecting princes and great men. Alas! alas! (see Rev. xviii. 10) how mean, how little, are those made by death who made themselves the terror of the mighty in the land of the living! But we are especially obliged to lament the fall of useful men in the midst of their usefulness and when there is most need of them. A public loss must be every man's grief, for every man shares in it. Thus David took care that honour should be done to the memory of a man of merit, to animate others. (2.) Let Joab, in a particular manner, lament it, which he has less heart but more reason to do than any of them. If he could be brought to do it sincerely, it would be an expression of repentance for his sin in slaying him. If he did it in show only, as it is likely he did, yet it was a sort of penance imposed upon him, and a present commutation of the punishment. If he do not as yet expiate the murder with his blood, let him do something towards it with tears. This, perhaps, Joab submitted to with no great reluctancy, now he had gained his point. Now that he is on the bier, no matter in what pomp he lies. *Sit divus, modo non sit vivus—Let him be canonized, so that he be but killed.*

4. David himself followed the corpse as chief mourner, and made a funeral oration at the grave. He attended the bier (*v.* 31) *and wept at the grave, v.* 32. Though Abner had been his enemy, and might possibly have proved no very firm friend, yet because he had been a man of bravery in the field, and might have done great service in the public counsels at this critical juncture, all former quarrels are forgotten and David is a true mourner for his fall. What he said over the grave fetched fresh floods of tears from the eyes of all that were present, when they thought they had already paid the debt in full (*v.* 33, 34): *Died Abner as a fool dieth?* (1.) He speaks as one vexed that Abner was fooled out of his life, that so great a man as he, so famed for conduct and courage, should be imposed upon by a colour of friendship, slain by surprise, and so die as a fool dies. The wisest and stoutest of men have no fence against treachery. To see Abner, who thought himself the main hinge on which the great affairs of Israel turned, so considerable as himself to be able to turn the scale of a trembling government, his head full of great projects and great prospects, to see him made a fool of by a base rival, and falling on a sudden a sacrifice to his ambition and jealousy—this stains the pride of all glory, and should put one out of conceit with worldly grandeur. *Put not your trust in princes,* Ps. cxlvi. 3, 4. And let us therefore make that sure which we cannot be fooled out of. A man may have his life, and all that is dear to him, taken from him, and not be able to prevent it with all his wisdom, care, and integrity; but there is that which no thief can break through to steal. See here how much more we are beholden to God's providence than to our own prudence for the continuance of our lives and comforts. Were it not for the hold God has of the consciences of bad men, how soon would the weak and innocent become an easy prey to the strong and merciless and the wisest die as fools! Or, (2.) He speaks as one boasting that Abner did not fool himself out of his life: "*Died Abner as a fool dies?* No, he did not, not as a criminal, a traitor or felon, that forfeits his life into the hands of public justice; his hands were not pinioned, nor his feet fettered, as those of malefactors are. Abner falls not before just men, by a judicial sentence; but as *a man, an innocent man, falleth before wicked men,* thieves and robbers, so fellest thou." *Died Abner as Nabal died?* so the LXX. read it. Nabal died as he lived, like himself, like a sot; but Abner's fate was such as might have been the fate of the wisest and best man in the world. Abner did not throw away his life as Asahel did, who wilfully ran upon the spear, after fair warning, but he was struck by surprise. Note, It is a sad thing to die like a fool, as those do that in any way shorten their own days, and much more those that make no provision for another world.

5. He fasted all that day, and would by no means be persuaded to eat any thing till night, *v.* 35. It was then the custom of great mourners to refrain for the time from bodily refreshments, as *ch.* i. 12; 1 Sam. xxxi. 13. How incongruous is it then to turn the house of mourning into a house of feasting! This respect which David paid to Abner was very pleasing to the people and satisfied them that he was not, in the least, accessory to the murder (*v.* 36, 37), of which he was solicitous to avoid the suspicion, lest Joab's villany should make him odious, as that of Simeon and Levi did Jacob, Gen. xxxiv. 30. On this occasion it is said, *Whatever the king did pleased all the people.* This intimates, (1.) His good affection to them. He studied to

please them in every thing and carefully avoided what might be disobliging. (2.) Their good opinion of him. They thought every thing he did well done. Such a mutual willingness to please, and easiness to be pleased, will make every relation comfortable.

6. He bewailed it that he could not with safety do justice on the murderers, *v.* 30. He was weak, his kingdom was newly planted, and a little shake would overthrow it. Joab's family had a great interest, were bold and daring, and to make them his enemies now might be of bad consequence. These sons of Zeruiah were too hard for him, too big for the law to take hold of; and therefore, though by man, by the magistrate, the blood of a murderer *should be shed* (Gen. ix. 6), David bears the sword in vain, and contents himself, as a private person, to leave them to the judgment of God: *The Lord shall reward the doer of evil according to his wickedness.* Now this is a diminution, (1.) To David's greatness. He is anointed king, and yet is kept in awe by his own subjects, and some of them are too hard for him. Who would be fond of power when a man may have the name of it, and must be accountable for it, and yet be hampered in the use of it? (2.) To David's goodness. He ought to have done his duty, and trusted God with the issue. *Fiat justitia, ruat cœlum—Let justice be done, though the heavens should fall asunder.* If the law had had its course against Joab, perhaps the murder of Ishbosheth, Amnon, and others, would have been prevented. It was carnal policy and cruel pity that spared Joab. Righteousness supports the throne and will never shake it. Yet it was only a reprieve that David gave to Joab; on his death-bed he left it to Solomon (who could the better wield the sword of justice because he had no occasion to draw the sword of war) to avenge the blood of Abner. Evil pursues sinners, and will overtake them at last. David preferred Abner's son Jaasiel, 1 Chron. xxvii. 21.

CHAP. IV.

When Abner was slain David was at a loss for a friend to perfect the reduction of those tribes that were yet in Ish-bosheth's interest. Which way to adopt for the accomplishment of it he could not tell; but here Providence brings it about by the removal of Ish-bosheth. I. Two of his own servants slew him, and brought his head to David, ver. 1—8. II. David, instead of rewarding them, put them to death for what they had done, ver. 9—12.

AND when Saul's son heard that Abner was dead in Hebron, his hands were feeble, and all the Israelites were troubled. 2 And Saul's son had two men *that were* captains of bands: the name of the one *was* Baanah, and the name of the other Rechab, the sons of Rimmon a Beerothite, of the children of Benjamin: (for Beeroth also was reckoned to Benjamin: 3 And the Beerothites fled to Gittaim, and were sojourners there until this day.) 4 And Jonathan, Saul's son, had a son *that was* lame of *his* feet. He was five years old when the tidings came of Saul and Jonathan out of Jezreel, and his nurse took him up, and fled: and it came to pass, as she made haste to flee, that he fell, and became lame. And his name *was* Mephibosheth. 5 And the sons of Rimmon the Beerothite, Rechab and Baanah, went, and came about the heat of the day to the house of Ish-bosheth, who lay on a bed at noon. 6 And they came thither into the midst of the house, *as though* they would have fetched wheat; and they smote him under the fifth *rib*: and Rechab and Baanah his brother escaped. 7 For when they came into the house, he lay on his bed in his bedchamber, and they smote him, and slew him, and beheaded him, and took his head, and gat them away through the plain all night. 8 And they brought the head of Ish-bosheth unto David to Hebron, and said to the king, Behold the head of Ish-bosheth the son of Saul thine enemy, which sought thy life; and the LORD hath avenged my lord the king this day of Saul, and of his seed.

Here is, I. The weakness of Saul's house. Still it grew weaker and weaker. 1. As for Ishbosheth, who was in possession of the throne, his hands were feeble, *v.* 1. All the strength they ever had was from Abner's support, and now that he was dead he had no spirit left in him. Though Abner had, in a passion, deserted his interest, yet he hoped, by his means, to make good terms with David; but now even this hope fails him, and he sees himself forsaken by his friends and at the mercy of his enemies. All the Israelites that adhered to him were troubled and at a loss what to do, whether to proceed in their treaty with David or no. 2. As for Mephibosheth, who in the right of his father Jonathan had a prior title, his feet were lame, and he was unfit for any service, *v.* 4. He was but five years old when his father and grandfather were killed. His nurse, hearing of the Philistines' victory, was apprehensive that, in pursuit of it, they would immediately send a party to Saul's house, to cut off all that pertained to it, and would especially aim at her young master, who was now next heir to the crown. Under the apprehension of this, she fled with the child in her arms, to secure it either in some secret place where he could not be found, or in some strong place where he could not be got at; and, making more haste than good speed, she fell with the child, and by the fall some bone was broken or put out, and not well set, so that he was lame of it as long as he lived, and unfit either for court or camp. See what sad accidents children are liable to in their infancy, the effect of which may be felt by them, to their great uneasiness, all their days. Even the children of princes and great men, the children of good men, for such a one Jonathan was, children that are well tended, and have nurses of their own to take care of them, yet are not always safe. What reason have we to be thankful to God for the preservation of our limbs and senses to us, through the many perils of the weak and helpless state of infancy, and to own his goodness in giving his angels a charge concerning us, to bear us up in their arms, out of which there is no danger of falling, Ps. xci. 12.

II. The murder of Saul's son. We are here told,

1. Who were the murderers: *Baanah and Rechab*, *v.* 2, 3. They were own brothers, as Simeon and Levi, and partners in iniquity. They were or had been Ish-bosheth's own servants, employed under him, so much the more base and treacherous was it in them to do him a mischief. They were Benjamites, of his own tribe. They were of the city of Beeroth; for some reason which we cannot now account for care is here taken to let us know (in a parenthesis) that that city belonged to the lot of Benjamin, so we find (Josh. xviii. 25), but that the inhabitants, upon some occasion or other, perhaps upon the death of Saul, retired to Gittaim, another city which lay not far off in the same tribe, and was better fortified by nature, being situate (if we may depend upon Mr. Fuller's map) between the two rocks Bozez and Seneh. There the Beerothites were when this was written, and probably took root there, and never returned to Beeroth again, which made Beeroth, that had been one of the cities of the Gibeonites (Josh. ix. 17), to be forgotten, and Gittaim to be famous long after, as we find, Neh. xi. 33.

2. How the murder was committed, *v.* 5—7. See here, (1.) The slothfulness of Ish-bosheth. He lay upon his bed at noon. It does not appear that the country was at any time of the year so hot as to oblige the inhabitants to retire at noon, as we are told they do in Spain in the heat of summer; but Ishbosheth was a sluggish man, loved his ease and hated business: and when he should have been, at this critical juncture, at the head of his forces in the field, or at the head of his counsels in a treaty with David, he was lying upon his bed and sleeping, for his hands were feeble (*v.* 1), and so were his head and heart. When those difficulties dispirit us which should rather invigorate us and sharpen our endeavours we betray both our crowns and lives. *Love not sleep, lest thou come to poverty and ruin.* The idle soul is an easy prey to the destroyer. (2.) The treachery of Baanah and Rechab. They came into the house, under pretence of fetching wheat for the victualling of their regiments; and such was the plainness of those times that the king's corn-chamber and his bed-chamber lay near together, which gave them an opportunity, when they were fetching wheat, to murder him as he lay on the bed. We know not when and where death will meet us. When we lie down to sleep we are not sure but that we may sleep the sleep of death before we awake; nor do we know from what unsuspected hand a fatal stroke may come. Ish-bosheth's own men, who should have protected his life, took it away.

3. The murderers triumphed in what they had done. As if they had performed some very glorious action, and the doing of it for David's advantage was enough not only to justify it, but to sanctify it, they made a present of Ish-bosheth's head to David (*v.* 8): *Behold the head of thy enemy,* than which they thought nothing could be more acceptable to him; yea, and they made themselves instruments of God's justice, ministers to bear his sword, though they had no commission: *The Lord hath avenged thee this day of Saul and of his seed.* Not that they had any regard either to God or to David's honour; they aimed at nothing but to make their own fortunes (as we say) and to get preferment in David's court; but, to ingratiate themselves with him, they pretended a concern for his life, a conviction of his title, and a zealous desire to see him in full possession of the throne. Jehu pretended *zeal for the Lord of hosts* when an ambition to set up himself and his own family was the spring of his actions.

9 And David answered Rechab and Baanah his brother, the sons of Rimmon the Beerothite, and said unto them, *As* the LORD liveth, who hath redeemed my soul out of all adversity, 10 When one told me, saying, Behold, Saul is dead, thinking to have brought good tidings, I took hold of him, and slew him in Ziklag, who *thought* that I would have given him a reward for his tidings: 11 How much more, when wicked men have slain a righteous person in his own house upon his bed? shall I not therefore now require his blood of your hand, and take you away from the earth? 12 And David commanded his young men, and they slew them, and cut off their hands and their feet, and hanged *them* up over the pool in Hebron. But they took the

head of Ish-bosheth, and buried *it* in the sepulchre of Abner in Hebron.

We have here justice done upon the murderers of Ish-bosheth.

I. Sentence passed upon them. There needed no evidence, their own tongues witnessed against them; they were so far from denying the fact that they gloried in it. David therefore shows them the heinousness of the crime, and that blood called for blood from his hand, who was now the chief magistrate, and was by office the avenger of blood. And, perhaps, he was the more vigorous in the prosecution because for reasons of state he had spared Joab: "*Shall I not require the blood of the slain at the hand of the slayers*, and, since they cannot make restitution, take theirs instead of it?" Observe, 1. How he aggravates the crime, *v.* 11. Ish-bosheth was a righteous person, he had done them no wrong, nor designed them any. As to himself, David was satisfied that what opposition he gave him was not from malice, but mistake, from an idea he had of his own title to the crown, and the influence of others upon him, who urged him to put in for it. Note, Charity teaches us to make the best, not only of our friends, but of our enemies, and to think those may be righteous persons who yet, in some instances, do us wrong. I must not presently judge a man a bad man because I think him so to me. David owns Ish-bosheth an honest man, though he had created him a great deal of trouble unjustly. The manner of it much aggravated the crime. To slay him in his own house, which should have been his castle, and upon his bed, when he was in no capacity of making any opposition, this is treacherous and barbarous, and all that is base, and that which the heart of every man who is not perfectly lost to all honour and humanity will rise with indignation at the thought of. Assassinating is confessedly the most odious and villanous way of murdering. *Cursed is he that smiteth his neighbour secretly.* 2. He quotes a precedent (*v.* 10): he had put him to death who had brought him the tidings of the death of Saul, because he thought it would be good tidings to David. Nothing is here said of that Amalekite's helping Saul to kill himself, only of his bringing the tidings of his death, by which it should seem that the story he told was upon enquiry found to be false, and that he lied against his own head. "Now" (says David) "did I treat him as a criminal, and not a favourite" (as he expected), "who brought me Saul's crown, and shall those be held guiltless that bring me Ish-bosheth's head?" 3. He ratifies the sentence with an oath (*v.* 9): *As the Lord liveth, who hath redeemed my soul out of all adversity.* He expresses himself thus resolutely, to prevent the making of any intercession for the criminals by those about him, and thus piously to intimate that his dependence was upon God for the putting of him in possession of the promised throne, and that he would not be beholden to any man to help him to it by any indirect or unlawful practices. God had redeemed him from all adversity hitherto, helped him over many a difficulty and through many a danger, and therefore he would depend upon him to crown and complete his own work. He speaks of his redemption from all adversity as a thing done, though he had many a storm yet before him, because he knew that he who had delivered would deliver. 4. Hereupon he signs a warrant for the execution of these men, *v.* 12. This may seem severe, when they intended him a kindness in what they did; but, (1.) He would thus show his detestation of the villany When he heard that *the Lord smote Nabal, he gave thanks* (1 Sam. xxv. 38, 39), *for he is the God to whom vengeance belongeth*; but, if wicked men smite Ish-bosheth, they deserve to die for taking God's work out of his hand. (2.) He would thus show his resentment of the great affront they put upon him in expecting that he should patronize and reward it; they could scarcely have done him a greater injury than thus to think him altogether such a one as themselves, one that cared not what blood he waded through to the crown.

II. Execution done. The murderers were put to death according to law, and their hands and feet were hung up; not their whole bodies, the law forbade that; but only their hands and feet, *in terrorem—to frighten others*, to be monuments of David's justice, and to make that to be taken notice of which would recommend him to the esteem of the people, as a man fit to rule, and that aimed not at his own preferment, nor had any enmity to the house of Saul, but only and sincerely designed the public welfare. But what a confusion was this to the two murderers! What a horrid disappointment! And such those will meet with who think to serve the interests of the Son of David by any immoral practices, by war and persecution, fraud and rapine, who, under colour of religion, murder princes, break solemn contracts, lay countries waste, *hate their brethren, and cast them out, and say, Let the Lord be glorified, kill them, and think they do God good service.* However men may canonize such methods of serving the church and the catholic cause, Christ will let them know, another day, that Christianity was not intended to destroy humanity; and those who thus think to merit heaven shall not escape the damnation of hell.

CHAP. V.

How far Abner's deserting the house of Saul, his murder, and the murder of Ish-bosheth, might contribute to the perfecting of the revolution, and the establishing of David as king over all Israel, does not appear; but, it should seem, that happy change followed presently thereupon, which in this chapter we have an account of. Here is, I. David anointed king by all the tribes, ver. 1—5. II. Making himself master of the strong-hold of Zion, ver. 6—10. III. Building himself a house and strengthening himself in his kingdom, ver. 11, 12. IV. His children that

were born after this, ver. 13—16. V. His victories over the Philistines, ver. 17—25.

THEN came all the tribes of Israel to David unto Hebron, and spake, saying, Behold, we *are* thy bone and thy flesh. 2 Also in time past, when Saul was king over us, thou wast he that leddest out and broughtest in Israel: and the LORD said to thee, Thou shalt feed my people Israel, and thou shalt be a captain over Israel. 3 So all the elders of Israel came to the king to Hebron; and king David made a league with them in Hebron before the LORD: and they anointed David king over Israel. 4 David *was* thirty years old when he began to reign, *and* he reigned forty years. 5 In Hebron he reigned over Judah seven years and six months: and in Jerusalem he reigned thirty and three years over all Israel and Judah.

Here is, I. The humble address of all the tribes to David, beseeching him to take upon him the government (for they were now as sheep having no shepherd), and owning him for their king. Though David might by no means approve the murder of Ish-bosheth, yet he might improve the advantages he gained thereby, and accept the applications made to him thereupon. Judah had submitted to David as their king above seven years ago, and their ease and happiness, under his administration, encouraged the rest of the tribes to make their court to him. What numbers came from each tribe, with what zeal and sincerity they came, and how they were entertained for three days at Hebron, when they were all of one heart to make David king, we have a full account, 1 Chron. xii. 23—40. Here we have only the heads of their address, containing the grounds they went upon in making David king. 1. Their relation to him was some inducement: "*We are thy bone and thy flesh* (*v.* 1), not only thou art our bone and our flesh, not a stranger, unqualified by the law to be king (Deut. xvii. 15), but we are thine," that is, "we know that thou considerest us as thy bone and thy flesh, and hast as tender a concern for us as a man has for his own body, which Saul and his house had not. *We are thy bone and thy flesh,* and therefore thou wilt be as glad as we shall be to put an end to this long civil war; and thou wilt take pity on us, protect us, and do thy utmost for our welfare." Those who take Christ for their king may thus plead with him: "*We are thy bone and thy flesh,* thou hast made thyself in all things *like unto thy brethren* (Heb. ii. 17); therefore be thou our ruler, and let this ruin be under thy hand," Isa. iii. 6. 2. His former good services to the public were a further inducement (*v.* 2): "*When Saul was king* he was but the cypher, thou wast the figure, *thou wast he that leddest out* Israel to battle, and broughtest them in in triumph; and therefore who so fit now to fill the vacant throne?" He that is faithful in a little deserves to be entrusted with more. Former good offices done for us should be gratefully remembered by us when there is occasion. 3. The divine appointment was the greatest inducement of all: *The Lord said, Thou shalt feed my people Israel,* that is, thou shalt rule them; for princes are to feed their people as shepherds, in every thing consulting the subjects' benefit, feeding them and not fleecing them. "And thou shalt be not only a king to govern in peace, but a captain to preside in war, and be exposed to all the toils and perils of the camp." Since God has said so, now at length, when need drives them to it, they are persuaded to say so too.

II. The public and solemn inauguration of David, *v.* 3. A convention of the states was called; all the elders of Israel came to him; the contract was settled, the *pacta conventa —covenants,* sworn to, and subscribed on both sides. He obliged himself to protect them as their judge in peace and captain in war; and they obliged themselves to obey him. He *made a league* with them to which God was a witness: it was *before the Lord.* Hereupon he was, for the third time, anointed king. His advances were gradual, that his faith might be tried and that he might gain experience. And thus his kingdom typified that of the Messiah, which was to come to its height by degrees; for *we see not yet all things put under him* (Heb. ii. 8), but we shall see it, 1 Cor. xv. 25.

III. A general account of his reign and age. He was thirty years old when he began to reign, upon the death of Saul, *v.* 4. At that age the Levites were at first appointed to begin their administration, Num. iv. 3. About that age the Son of David entered upon his public ministry, Luke iii. 23. Then men come to their full maturity of strength and judgment. He reigned, in all, forty years and six months, of which seven years and a half in Hebron and thirty-three years in Jerusalem, *v.* 5. Hebron had been famous, Josh. xiv. 15. It was a priest's city. But Jerusalem was to be more so, and to be the holy city. Great kings affected to raise cities of their own, Gen. x. 11, 36, 32—35. David did so, and Jerusalem was the city of David. It is a name famous to the end of the Bible (Rev. xxi.), where we read of a new Jerusalem.

6 And the king and his men went to Jerusalem unto the Jebusites, the inhabitants of the land: which spake unto David, saying, Except thou take away the blind and the lame, thou shalt not come in hither: thinking,

David cannot come in hither. 7 Nevertheless David took the strong hold of Zion: the same *is* the city of David. 8 And David said on that day, Whosoever getteth up to the gutter, and smiteth the Jebusites, and the lame and the blind, *that are* hated of David's soul, *he shall be chief and captain.* Wherefore they said, The blind and the lame shall not come into the house. 9 So David dwelt in the fort, and called it the city of David. And David built round about from Millo and inward. 10 And David went on, and grew great, and the LORD God of hosts *was* with him.

If Salem, the place of which Melchizedec was king, was Jerusalem (as seems probable from Ps. lxxvi. 2), it was famous in Abraham's time. Joshua, in his time, found it the chief city of the south part of Canaan, Josh. x. 1—3. It fell to Benjamin's lot (Josh. xviii. 28), but joined close to Judah's, Josh. xv. 8. The children of Judah had taken it (Judg. i. 8), but the children of Benjamin suffered the Jebusites to dwell among them (Judg. i. 21), and they grew so upon them that it became a *city of Jebusites*, Judg. xix 11. Now the very first exploit David did, after he was anointed king over all Israel, was to gain Jerusalem out of the hand of the Jebusites, which, because it belonged to Benjamin, he could not well attempt till that tribe, which long adhered to Saul's house (1 Chron. xii. 29), submitted to him. Here we have,

I. The Jebusites' defiance of David and his forces. They said, *Except thou take away the blind and the lame, thou shalt not come in hither*, *v.* 6. They sent David this provoking message, because, as it is said afterwards, on another occasion, they could not believe that *ever an enemy would enter into the gates of Jerusalem*, Lam. iv. 12. They confided either, 1. In the protection of their gods, which David, in contempt, had called *the blind and the lame*, for *they have eyes and see not, feet and walk not.* "But," say they, "these are the guardians of our city, and except thou take these away (which thou canst never do) thou canst not come in hither." Some think they were constellated images of brass set up in the recess of the fort, and entrusted with the custody of the place. They called their idols their *Mauzzim*, or *strong-holds* (Dan. xi. 38) and as such relied on them. *The name of the Lord is our strong tower*, and his arm is strong, his eyes are piercing. Or, 2. In the strength of their fortifications, which they thought were made so impregnable by nature or art, or both, that the blind and the lame were sufficient to defend them against the most powerful assailant. The strong-hold of Zion they especially depended on, as that which could not be forced. Probably they set blind and lame people, invalids or maimed soldiers, to make their appearance upon the walls, in scorn of David and his men, judging them an equal match for him. Though there remain but wounded men among them, yet they should serve to beat back the besiegers. Compare Jer. xxxvii. 10. Note, The enemies of God's people are often very confident of their own strength and most secure when their day to fall draws nigh.

II. David's success against the Jebusites. Their pride and insolence, instead of daunting him, animated him, and when he made a general assault he gave this order to his men: "*He that smiteth the Jebusites, let him also throw down into the ditch*, or gutter, *the lame and the blind*, which are set upon the wall to affront us and our God." It is probable they had themselves spoken blasphemous things, and were therefore hated of David's soul. Thus *v.* 8 may be read; we fetch our reading of it from 1 Chron. xi. 6, which speaks only of smiting the Jebusites, but nothing of the blind and the lame. The Jebusites had said that if these images of theirs did not protect them *the blind and the lame should not come into the house*, that is, they would never again trust their palladium (so Mr. Gregory understands it) nor pay the respect they had paid to their images; and David, having gained the fort, said so too, that these images, which could not protect their worshippers, should never have any place there more.

III. His fixing his royal seat in Sion. He himself dwelt in the fort (the strength whereof, which had given him opposition, and was a terror to him, now contributed to his safety), and he built houses round about for his attendants and guards (*v.* 9) from Millo (the town-hall, or state-house) and inward. He proceeded and prospered in all he set his hand to, grew great in honour, strength, and wealth, more and more honourable in the eyes of his subjects and formidable in the eyes of his enemies; for *the Lord God of hosts was with him.* God has all creatures at his command, makes what use he pleases of them, and serves his own purposes by them; and he was with him, to direct, preserve, and prosper him. Those that have the Lord of hosts for them need not fear what hosts of men or devils can do against them. Those who grow great must ascribe their advancement to the presence of God with them, and give him the glory of it. The church is called *Sion*, and the *city of the living God.* The Jebusites, Christ's enemies, must first be conquered and dispossessed, the blind and the lame taken away, and then Christ divides the spoil, sets up his throne there, and makes it his residence by the Spirit.

11 And Hiram king of Tyre sent messengers to David, and cedar trees,

and carpenters, and masons: and they built David a house. 12 And David perceived that the LORD had established him king over Israel, and that he had exalted his kingdom for his people Israel's sake. 13 And David took *him* more concubines and wives out of Jerusalem, after he was come from Hebron: and there were yet sons and daughters born to David. 14 And these *be* the names of those that were born unto him in Jerusalem; Shammuah, and Shobab, and Nathan, and Solomon, 15 Ibhar also, and Elishua, and Nepheg, and Japhia, 16 And Elishama, and Eliada, and Eliphalet.

Here is, I. David's house built, a royal palace, fit for the reception of the court he kept and the homage that was paid to him, *v.* 11. The Jews were husbandmen and shepherds, and did not much addict themselves either to merchandise or manufactures; and therefore Hiram, king of Tyre, a wealthy prince, when he sent to congratulate David on his accession to the throne, offered him workmen to build him a house. David thankfully accepted the offer, and Hiram's workmen built David a house to his mind. Many have excelled in arts and sciences who were strangers to the covenants of promise. Yet David's house was never the worse, nor the less fit to be dedicated to God, for being built by the sons of the stranger. It is prophesied of the gospel church, *The sons of the strangers shall build up thy walls, and their kings shall minister unto thee,* Isa. lx. 10.

II. David's government settled and built up, *v.* 12. 1. His kingdom was established, there was nothing to shake it, none to disturb his possession or question his title. He that made him king established him, because he was to be a type of Christ, with whom God's hand should be established, and his *covenant stand fast,* Ps. lxxxix. 21—28. Saul was made king, but not established; so Adam in innocency. David was established king, so is the Son of David, with all who through him are made to our God *kings and priests.* 2. It was exalted in the eyes both of its friends and enemies. Never had the nation of Israel looked so great or made such a figure as it began now to do. Thus it is promised of Christ that he shall be *higher than the kings of the earth,* Ps. lxxxix. 27. God has *highly exalted him,* Phil. ii. 9. 3. David perceived, by the wonderful concurrence of providences to his establishment and advancement, that God was with him. *By this I know that thou favourest me,* Ps. xli. 11. Many have the favour of God and do not perceive it, and so want the comfort of it: but to be exalted to that and established in it, and to perceive it, is happiness enough. 4. He owned that it was for his people Israel's sake that God had done great things for him, that he might be a blessing to them and they might be happy under his administration. God did not make Israel his subjects for his sake, that he might be great, and rich, and absolute: but he made him their king for their sake, that he might lead, and guide, and protect them. Kings are *ministers of God to their people for good,* Rom. xiii. 4.

III. David's family multiplied and increased. All the sons that were born to him after he came to Jerusalem are here mentioned together, eleven in all, besides the six that were born to him before in Hebron, *ch.* iii. 2, 5. *There* the mothers are mentioned, not *here;* only, in general, it is said that he *took more concubines and wives, v.* 13. Shall we praise him for this? We praise him not; we justify him not; nor can we scarcely excuse him. The bad example of the patriarchs might make him think there was no harm in it, and he might hope it would strengthen his interest, by multiplying his alliances, and increasing the royal family. *Happy is the man that has his quiver full of these arrows.* But one vine by the side of the house, with the blessing of God, may send boughs to the sea and branches to the rivers. Adam, by one wife, peopled the world, and Noah repeopled it. David had many wives, and yet that did not keep him from coveting his neighbour's wife and defiling her; for men that have once broken the fence will wander endlessly. Of David's concubines, see 2 Sam. xv. 16; xvi. 22; xix. 5. Of his sons, see 1 Chron. iii. 1—9.

17 But when the Philistines heard that they had anointed David king over Israel, all the Philistines came up to seek David; and David heard *of it,* and went down to the hold. 18 The Philistines also came and spread themselves in the valley of Rephaim. 19 And David enquired of the LORD, saying, Shall I go up to the Philistines? wilt thou deliver them into mine hand? And the LORD said unto David, Go up: for I will doubtless deliver the Philistines into thine hand. 20 And David came to Baal-perazim, and David smote them there, and said, The LORD hath broken forth upon mine enemies before me, as the breach of waters. Therefore he called the name of that place Baal-perazim. 21 And there they left their images, and David and his men burned them. 22 And the

Philistines came up yet again, and spread themselves in the valley of Rephaim. 23 And when David enquired of the LORD, he said, Thou shalt not go up; *but* fetch a compass behind them, and come upon them over against the mulberry trees. 24 And let it be, when thou hearest the sound of a going in the tops of the mulberry trees, that then thou shalt bestir thyself: for then shall the LORD go out before thee, to smite the host of the Philistines. 25 And David did so, as the LORD had commanded him; and smote the Philistines from Geba until thou come to Gazer.

The particular service for which David was raised up was to *save Israel out of the hand of the Philistines, ch.* iii. 18. This therefore divine Providence, in the first place, gives him an opportunity of accomplishing. Two great victories obtained over the Philistines we have here an account of, by which David not only balanced the disgrace and retrieved the loss Israel had sustained in the battle wherein Saul was slain, but went far towards the total subduing of those vexatious neighbours, the last remains of the devoted nations.

I. In both these actions the Philistines were the aggressors, stirred first towards their own destruction, and pulled it on their own heads. 1. In the former they *came up to seek David* (*v.* 17), because they *heard that he was anointed king over Israel.* He that under Saul had slain his ten thousands, what would he do when he himself came to be king! They therefore thought it was time to look about them, and try to crush his government in its infancy, before it was well settled. Their success against Saul, some years ago, perhaps encouraged them to make this attack upon David; but they considered not that David had that presence of God with him which Saul had forfeited and lost. The kingdom of the Messiah, as soon as ever it was set up in the world, was thus vigorously attacked by the powers of darkness, who, with the combined force both of Jews and Gentiles, made head against it. The heathen raged, and the kings of the earth set themselves to oppose it; but all in vain, Ps. ii. 1, &c. The destruction will turn, as this did, upon Satan's own kingdom. They took counsel together, but were *broken in pieces,* Isa. viii. 9, 10. 2. In the latter they *came up yet again,* hoping to recover what they had lost in the former engagement, and their hearts being hardened to their destruction, *v.* 22. 3. In both they *spread themselves in the valley of Rephaim,* which lay very near Jerusalem. That city they hoped to make themselves masters of before David had completed the fortifications of it. Jerusalem, from its infancy, has been aimed at, and struck at, with a particular enmity. Their spreading themselves intimates that they were very numerous and that they made a very formidable appearance. We read of the church's enemies *going up on the breadth of the earth* (Rev. xx. 9), but the further they spread themselves the fairer mark they are to God's arrows.

II. In both, David, though forward enough to go forth against them (for as soon as he heard it he *went down to the hold,* to secure some important and advantageous post, *v.* 17), yet entered not upon action till he had *enquired of the Lord* by the breast-plate of judgment, *v.* 19, and again, *v.* 23. His enquiry was twofold:—1. Concerning his duty: "*Shall I go up?* Shall I have a commission from heaven to engage them?" One would think he needed not doubt this; what was he made king for, but to fight the battles of the Lord and Israel? But a good man loves to see God going before him in every step he takes. "Shall I go up *now?*" It is to be done, but is it to be done at this time? *In all thy ways acknowledge him.* And besides, though the Philistines were public enemies, yet some of them had been his particular friends. Achish had been kind to him in his distress, and had protected him. "Now," says David, "ought not I, in remembrance of that, rather to make peace with them than to make war with them?" "No," says God, "they are Israel's enemies, and are doomed to destruction, and therefore scruple not, but *go up.*" 2. Concerning his success. His conscience asked the former question, *Shall I go up?* His prudence asked this, *Wilt thou deliver them into my hand?* Hereby he owns his dependence on God for victory, that he could not conquer them unless God delivered them into his hand, and refers his cause to the good pleasure of God: *Wilt thou do it?* Yea, says God, *I will doubtless do it.* If God send us, he will bear us out and stand by us. The assurance God has given us of victory over our spiritual enemies, that he will tread Satan under our feet shortly, should animate us in our spiritual conflicts. We do not fight at uncertainty. David had now a great army at command and in good heart, yet he relied more on God's promise than his own force.

II. In the former of these engagements David routed the army of the Philistines by dint of sword (*v.* 20): He *smote them;* and when he had done, 1. He gave his God the glory; he said, "*The Lord has broken forth upon my enemies before me.* I could not have done it if he had not done it before me; he opened the breach like the breach of waters in a dam, which when once opened grows wider and wider." The principal part of the work was God's doing; nay, he did all; what David did was not worth speaking of; and therefore, *Not unto us, but unto the Lord, give glory.* He hoped likewise that this breach, like that of waters, was as the opening of the sluice, to let in a final desolation upon them; and, to perpetuate the remembrance of it, he called the place *Baal-perazim, the master of the breaches,* because, God having broken in upon their forces, he soon had the mastery of them. Let posterity take notice of it to God's honour. 2. He put their gods to shame. They brought the images of their gods into the field as their protectors, in imitation of the Israelites bringing the ark into their camp; but, being put to flight, they could not stay to carry off their images, for they were a *burden to the weary beasts* (Isa. xlvi. 1), and therefore they left them to fall with the rest of their baggage into the hands of the conqueror. Their images failed them, and gave them no assistance, and therefore they left their images to shift for themselves. God can make men weary of those things that they have been most fond of, and compel them to desert what they dote upon, and cast even *the idols of silver and gold to the moles and the bats,* Isa. ii. 20, 21. David and his men converted to their own use the rest of the plunder, but the images they burnt, as God had appointed (Deut. vii. 5): "*You shall burn their graven images with fire,* in token of your detestation of idolatry, and lest they should be a snare." Bishop Patrick well observes here that when the ark fell into the Philistines' hands it consumed them, but, when these images fell into the hands of Israel, they could not save themselves from being consumed.

IV. In the latter of these engagements God gave David some sensible tokens of his presence with him, bade him not fall upon them directly, as he had done before, but *fetch a compass behind them, v.* 23. 1. God appoints him to draw back, as *Israel stood still to see the salvation of the Lord.* 2. He promised him to charge the enemy himself, by an invisible host of angels, *v.* 24. "Thou shalt hear the *sound of a going,* like the march of an army in the air, *upon the tops of the mulberry trees.*" Angels tread light, and he that can walk upon the clouds can, when he pleases, walk on the tops of trees, or (as bishop Patrick understands it) at the head of the mulberry-trees, that is, of the wood, or hedge-row of those trees. "And, by that sign, thou shalt know that *the Lord goes out before thee;* though thou see him not, yet thou shalt hear him, and faith shall come and be confirmed by hearing. He goes forth *to smite the host of the Philistines.*" When David had himself smitten them (*v.* 20), he ascribed it to God: *The Lord has broken forth upon my enemies,* to reward him for which thankful acknowledgment the next time God did it himself alone, without putting him to any toil or peril. Those that own God in what he has done for them will find him doing more. But observe, Though God promised to *go before him and smite the Philistines,* yet David, when he heard the sound of the going must bestir himself and be ready to pursue the victory. Note, God's grace must quicken our endeavours. If God work in us both to will and to do, it does not follow that we must sit still, as those that have nothing to do, but we must therefore *work out our own salvation* with all possible care and diligence, Phil. ii. 12, 13. The sound of the going was, (1.) A signal to David when to move; it is comfortable going out when God goes before us. And, (2.) Perhaps it was an alarm to the enemy, and put them into confusion. Hearing the march of an army against their front, they retreated with precipitation, and fell into David's army which lay behind them in their rear. Of those whom God fights against it is said (Lev. xxvi. 36), *The sound of a shaken leaf shall chase them.* (3.) The success of this is briefly set down, *v.* 25. David observed his orders, waited till God moved, and stirred then, but not till then. Thus he was trained up in a dependence on God and his providence. God performed his promise, went before him, and routed all the enemies' force, and David failed not to improve his advantages; he smote the Philistines, even to the borders of their own country. When the kingdom of the Messiah was to be set up, the apostles that were to beat down the devil's kingdom must not attempt any thing till they received the promise of the Spirit, who *came with a sound from heaven as of a rushing mighty wind* (Acts ii. 2), which was typified by this sound of the going on the tops of the mulberry trees; and, when they heard that, they must bestir themselves, and did so; they went forth conquering and to conquer.

CHAP. VI.

The obscurity of the ark, during the reign of Saul, had been as great a grievance to Israel as the insults of the Philistines. David, having humbled the Philistines and mortified them, in gratitude for that favour, and in pursuance of his designs for the public welfare, is here bringing up the ark to his own city, that it might be near him, and be an ornament and strength to his new foundation. Here is, I. An attempt to do it, which failed and miscarried. The design was well laid, ver. 1, 2. But, 1. They were guilty of an error in carrying it in a cart, ver. 3—5. 2. They were punished for that error by the sudden death of Uzzah (ver. 6, 7), which was a great terror to David (ver. 8, 9) and put a stop to his proceedings, ver. 10, 11. II. The great joy and satisfaction with which it was at last done, ver. 12—15. And, 1. The good understanding between David and his people, ver. 17—19. 2. The uneasiness between David and his wife upon that occasion, ver. 16, 20—23. And, when we consider that the ark was both the token of God's presence and a type of Christ, we shall see that this story is very instructive.

AGAIN, David gathered together all *the* chosen *men* of Israel, thirty thousand. 2 And David arose, and went with all the people that *were* with him from Baale of Judah, to bring up from thence the ark of God, whose name is called by the name of the LORD of hosts, that dwelleth *between* the cherubims. 3 And they set the ark of God upon a new cart, and brought it out of the house of Abinadab that *was* in Gibeah, and Uzzah and Ahio, the sons of Abinadab, drave the new cart. 4 And they brought it out of the house of Abinadab which *was* at Gibeah, accompanying the ark of God: and Ahio went before the ark. 5 And David and all the house of Israel played before the LORD on all manner of *instruments made of* fir wood, even on harps, and on psalteries, and on timbrels, and on cornets, and on cymbals.

We have not heard a word of the ark since it was lodged in Kirjath-jearim, immediately after its return out of its captivity among the Philistines (1 Sam. vii. 1, 2), except that, once, Saul called for it, 1 Sam. xiv. 18. That which in former days had made so great a figure is now thrown aside, as a neglected thing, for many years. And, if now the ark was for so many years in a house, let it not seem strange that we find the church so long in the wilderness, Rev. xii. 14. Perpetual visibility is no mark of the true church. God is graciously present with the souls of his people even when they want the external tokens of his presence. But now that David is settled in the throne the honour of the ark begins to revive, and *Israel's care of it to flourish again, wherein also,* no doubt, the good people among them *had been careful, but they lacked opportunity.* See Phil. iv. 10.

I. Here is honourable mention made of the ark. Because it had not been spoken of a great while, now that it is spoken of observe how it is described (*v.* 2): it is *the ark of God whose name is called by the name of the Lord of hosts that dwelleth between the cherubim,* or *at which the name, even the name of the Lord of hosts, was called upon,* or *upon which the name of the Lord of hosts was called,* or *because of which the name is proclaimed, the name of the Lord of hosts* (that is, God was greatly magnified in the miracles done before the ark)), or *the ark of God, who is called the name* (Lev. xxiv. 11, 16), *the name of the Lord of hosts, sitting on the cherubim upon it.* Let us learn hence, 1. To think and speak highly of God. He is the name above every name, *the Lord of hosts,* that has all the creatures in heaven and earth at his command, and receives homage from them all, and yet is pleased to dwell between the cherubim, over the propitiatory or mercy-seat, graciously manifesting himself to his people, reconciled in a Mediator, and ready to do them good. 2. To think and speak honourably of holy ordinances, which are to us, as the ark was to Israel, the tokens of God's presence (Matt. xxviii. 2)), and the means of our communion with him, Ps. xxvii. 4. It is the honour of the ark that it is the ark of God; he is jealous for it, is magnified in it, his name is called upon it. The divine institution puts a beauty and grandeur upon holy ordinances, which otherwise have no form nor comeliness. Christ is our ark. In and by him God manifests his favour and communicates his grace to us, and accepts our adoration and addresses.

II. Here is an honourable attendance given to the ark upon the removal of it. Now, at length, it is enquired after, David made the motion (1 Chron. xiii. 1—3), and the heads of the congregation agreed to it, *v.* 4. All the chosen men of Israel are called together to grace the solemnity, to pay their respect to the ark, and to testify their joy in its restoration. The nobility and gentry, elders and officers, came to the number of 30,000 (*v.* 1), and the generality of the common people besides (1 Chron. xiii. 5); for, some think, it was done at one of the three great festivals. This would make a noble cavalcade, and would help to inspire the young people of the nation, who perhaps had scarcely heard of the ark, with a great veneration for it, for this was certainly a treasure of inestimable value which the king himself and all the great men waited upon, and were a guard to.

III. Here are great expressions of joy upon the removal of the ark, *v.* 5. David himself, and all that were with him that were musically inclined, made use of such instruments as they had to excite and express their rejoicing upon this occasion. It might well put them into a transport of joy to see the ark rise out of obscurity and move towards a public station. It is better to have the ark in a house than not at all, better in a house than a captive in Dagon's temple; but it is very desirable to have it in a tent pitched on purpose for it, where the resort to it may be more free and open. As secret worship is better the more secret it is, so public worship is better the more public it is; and we have reason to rejoice when restraints are taken off, and the ark of God finds welcome in the city of David, and has not only the protection and support, but the countenance and encouragement, of the civil powers; for joy of this they *played before the Lord.* Note, Public joy must always be as *before the Lord,* with an eye to him and terminating in him, and must not degenerate into that which is carnal and sensual. Dr. Lightfoot supposes that, upon this occasion, David penned the 68th Psalm, because it begins with that ancient prayer of Moses at the removing of the ark, *Let God arise, and let his enemies be scattered;* and notice is taken there (*v.* 25) of the *singers and players on instruments* that attended, and (*v.* 27) of the princes of several of the tribes; and perhaps those words in the last verse, *O God, thou art terrible out of thy holy places,* were added upon occasion of the death of Uzzah.

IV. Here is an error that they were guilty of in this matter, that they carried the ark in a cart or carriage, whereas the priests should have carried it upon their shoulders, *v.* 3.

The Kohathites that had the charge of the ark had no waggons assigned them, because *their service was to bear it upon their shoulders*, Num. vii. 9. The ark was no such heavy burden but that they might, among them, have carried it as far as Mount Sion upon their shoulders, they needed not to put it in a cart like a common thing. It was no excuse for them that the Philistines had done so and were not punished for it; they knew no better, nor had they any priests or Levites with them to undertake the carrying of it; better carry it in a cart than that any of Dagon's priests should carry it. Philistines may cart the ark with impunity; but, if Israelites do so, they do it at their peril. And it mended the matter very little that it was a new cart; old or new, it was not what God had appointed. I wonder how so wise and good a man as David was, that conversed so much with the law of God, came to be guilty of such an oversight. We will charitably hope that it was because he was so extremely intent upon the substance of the service that he forgot to take care of this circumstance.

6 And when they came to Nachon's threshing-floor, Uzzah put forth *his hand* to the ark of God, and took hold of it; for the oxen shook *it*. 7 And the anger of the LORD was kindled against Uzzah; and God smote him there for *his* error; and there he died by the ark of God. 8 And David was displeased, because the LORD had made a breach upon Uzzah: and he called the name of the place Perez-uzzah to this day. 9 And David was afraid of the LORD that day, and said, How shall the ark of the LORD come to me? 10 So David would not remove the ark of the LORD unto him into the city of David: but David carried it aside into the house of Obed-edom the Gittite. 11 And the ark of the LORD continued in the house of Obed-edom the Gittite three months: and the LORD blessed Obed-edom, and all his household.

We have here Uzzah struck dead for touching the ark, when it was upon its journey towards the city of David, a sad providence, which damped their mirth, stopped the progress of the ark, and, for the present, dispersed this great assembly, which had come together to attend it, and sent them home in a fright.

I. Uzzah's offence seems very small. He and his brother Ahio, the sons of Abinadab, in whose house the ark had long been lodged, having been used to attend it, to show their willingness to prefer the public benefit to their own private honour and advantage, undertook to drive the cart in which the ark was carried, this being perhaps the last service they were likely to do it; for others would be employed about it when it came to the city of David. Ahio went before, to clear the way, and, if need were, to lead the oxen. Uzzah followed close to the side of the cart. It happened that the oxen shook it, *v.* 6. The critics are not agreed about the signification of the original word: *They stumbled* (so our margin); *they kicked* (so some), perhaps against the goad with which Uzzah drove them; *they stuck in the mire*, so some. By some accident or other the ark was in danger of being overthrown. Uzzah thereupon laid hold of it, to save it from falling, we have reason to think with a very good intention, to preserve the reputation of the ark and to prevent a bad omen. Yet this was his crime. Uzzah was a Levite, but priests only might touch the ark. The law was express concerning the Kohathites, that, though they were to carry the ark by the staves, yet *they must not touch any holy thing, lest they die*, Num. iv. 15. Uzzah's long familiarity with the ark, and the constant attendance he had given to it, might occasion his presumption, but would not excuse it.

II. His punishment for this offence seems very great (*v.* 7): *The anger of the Lord was kindled against him* (for in sacred things he is a jealous God) and he *smote him there for his rashness*, as the word is, and struck him dead upon the spot. There he sinned, and there he died, *by the ark of God;* even the mercy-seat would not save him. Why was God thus severe with him? 1. The touching of the ark was forbidden to the Levites expressly under pain of death—*lest they die;* and God, by this instance of severity, would show how he might justly have dealt with our first parents, when they had eaten that which was forbidden under the same penalty—*lest you die.* 2. God saw the presumption and irreverence of Uzzah's heart. Perhaps he affected to show, before this great assembly, how bold he could make with the ark, having been so long acquainted with it. Familiarity, even with that which is most awful, is apt to breed contempt. 3. David afterwards owned that Uzzah died for an error they were all guilty of, which was carrying the ark in a cart. Because it was not carried on the Levites' shoulders, *the Lord made that breach upon us*, 1 Chron. xv. 13. But Uzzah was singled out to be made an example, perhaps because he had been most forward in advising that way of conveyance; however he had fallen into another error, which was occasioned by that. Perhaps the ark was not covered, as it should have been, with the covering of badgers' skins (Num. iv. 6), and that was a further provocation. 4. God would hereby strike an awe upon the thousands of Israel, would convince them that the ark was never the less venerable for its having been so long in mean circumstances, and thus he would teach them to rejoice with trembling, and always to treat holy things with reverence and holy fear. 5. God would hereby teach us that a good intention will not justify a bad action; it will not suffice to say of that which is ill done that it was well meant. He will let us know that he can and will secure his ark, and needs not any man's sin to help him to do it. 6. If it was so great a crime for one to lay hold on the ark of the covenant that had no right to do so, what is it for those to lay claim to the privileges of the covenant that come not up to the terms of it? To the wicked God says, *What hast thou to do to take my covenant in thy mouth?* Ps. l. 16. *Friend, how camest thou in hither?* If the ark was so sacred, and not to be touched irreverently, what is the *blood of the covenant?* Heb. x. 29.

III. David's feelings on the infliction of this stroke were keen, and perhaps not altogether as they should have been. He should have humbled himself under God's hand, confessed his error, acknowledged God's righteousness, and deprecated the further tokens of his displeasure, and then have gone on with the good work he had in hand. But we find, 1. He was displeased. It is not said because Uzzah had affronted God, but because God had made a breach upon Uzzah (*v.* 8): *David's anger was kindled.* It is the same word that is used for God's displeasure, *v.* 7. Because God was angry, David was angry and out of humour. As if God might not assert the honour of his ark, and frown upon one that touched it rudely, without asking David leave. Shall mortal man pretend to be more just than God, arraign his proceedings, or charge him with iniquity? David did not now act like himself, like *a man after God's own heart.* It is not for us to be displeased at any thing that God does, how unpleasing soever it is to us. The death of Uzzah was indeed an eclipse to the glory of a solemnity which David valued himself upon more than any thing else, and might give birth to some speculations among those that were disaffected to him, as if God were departing from him too; but he ought nevertheless to have subscribed to the righteousness and wisdom of God in it, and not to have been displeased at it. When we lie under God's anger we must keep under our own. 2. He was afraid, *v.* 9. It should seem he was afraid with amazement; for he said, *How shall the ark of the Lord come to me?* As if God sought advantages against all that were about him, and was so extremely tender of his ark that there was no dealing with it; and therefore better for him to keep it at a distance. *Qui procul a Jove, procul a fulmine—To retire from Jove is to retire from the thunder-bolt.* He should rather have said, "Let the ark come to me, and I will take warning by this to treat it with more reverence." *Provoke me not* (says God, Jer. xxv. 6) *and I will do you no hurt.* Or this may be looked upon as a good use which David made of this tremendous judgment. He did not say, "Surely Uzzah was a sinner above all men, because he suffered such things," but is concerned for himself, as one conscious, not only of his own unworthiness of God's favour, but his obnoxiousness to God's displeasure. "God might justly strike me dead as he did Uzzah. *My flesh trembles for fear of thee,*" Ps. cxix. 120. This God intends in his judgments, that others may hear and fear. David therefore will not bring the ark into his own city (*v.* 10) till he is better prepared for its reception. 3. He took care to perpetuate the remembrance of this stroke by a new name he gave to the place: *Perez-uzzah, the breach of Uzzah, v.* 8. He had been lately triumphing in the breach made upon his enemies, and called the place *Baal-perazim, a place of breaches.* But here is a breach upon his friends. When we see one breach, we should consider that we know not where the next will be. The memorial of this stroke would be a warning to posterity to take heed of all rashness and irreverence in dealing about holy things; for *God will be sanctified in those that come nigh unto him.* 4. He lodged the ark in a good house, the house of Obed-edom a Levite, which happened to be near the place where this disaster happened, and there, (1.) It was kindly entertained and welcomed, and continued there *three months, v.* 10, 11. Obed-edom knew what slaughter the ark had made among the Philistines that imprisoned it and the Bethshemites that looked into it. He saw Uzzah struck dead for touching it, and perceived that David himself was afraid of meddling with it; yet he cheerfully invites it to his own house, and opens his doors to it without fear, knowing it was a *savour of death unto death* only to those that treated it ill. "O the courage," says bishop Hall, "of an honest and faithful heart! nothing can make God otherwise than amiable to his own people: even his very justice is lovely." (2.) It paid well for its entertainment: *The Lord blessed Obed-edom and all his household.* The same hand that punished Uzzah's proud presumption rewarded Obed-edom's humble boldness, and made the ark to him a *savour of life unto life.* Let none think the worse of the gospel for the judgments inflicted on those that reject it, but set in opposition to them the blessings it brings to those that duly receive it. None ever had, nor ever shall have, reason to say that *it is in vain to serve God.* Let masters of families be encouraged to keep up religion in their families, and to serve God and the interests of his kingdom with their houses and estates, for that is the way to bring a blessing upon all they have. The ark is a guest which none shall lose by that bid it welcome. Josephus says that, whereas before Obed-edom was poor, on a sudden, in these three months, his estate increased, to the envy of his neighbours. Piety is the best friend to prosperity. In wisdom's left hand are riches and honour. His household shared in the blessing. It is good living in a family that entertains the ark, for all about it will fare the better for it.

12 And it was told king David, saying, The LORD hath blessed the house of Obed-edom, and all that *pertaineth* unto him, because of the ark of God. So David went and brought up the ark of God from the house of Obed-edom into the city of David with gladness. 13 And it was *so*, that when they that bare the ark of the LORD had gone six paces, he sacrificed oxen and fatlings. 14 And David danced before the LORD, with all *his* might; and David *was* girded with a linen ephod. 15 So David and all the house of Israel brought up the ark of the LORD with shouting, and with the sound of the trumpet. 16 And as the ark of the LORD came into the city of David, Michal Saul's daughter looked through a window, and saw king David leaping and dancing before the LORD; and she despised him in her heart. 17 And they brought in the ark of the LORD, and set it in his place, in the midst of the tabernacle that David had pitched for it: and David offered burnt offerings and peace offerings before the LORD. 18 And as soon as David had made an end of offering burnt offerings and peace offerings, he blessed the people in the name of the LORD of hosts. 19 And he dealt among all the people, *even* among the whole multitude of Israel, as well to the women as men, to every one a cake of bread, and a good piece *of flesh,* and a flagon *of wine.* So all the people departed every one to his house.

We have here the second attempt to bring the ark home to the city of David; and this succeeded, though the former miscarried.

I. It should seem the blessing with which the house of Obed-edom was blessed for the ark's sake was a great inducement to David to bring it forward; for when that was told him (*v.* 12) he hastened to fetch it to him. For, 1. It was an evidence that God was reconciled to them, and his anger was turned away. As David could read God's frowns upon them all in Uzzah's stroke, so he could read God's favour to them all in Obed-edom's prosperity; and, if God be at peace with them, they can cheerfully go on with their design. 2. It was an evidence that the ark was not such a burdensome stone as it was taken to be, but, on the contrary, happy was the man that had it near him. Christ is indeed a *stone of stumbling, and a rock of offence,* to those that are disobedient; but to those who believe he is a *corner-stone, elect, precious,* 1 Pet. ii. 6—8. When David heard that Obed-edom had such joy of the ark, then he would have it in his own city. Note, The experience others have had of the gains of godliness should encourage us to be religious Is the ark a blessing to others' houses? let us bid it welcome to ours; we may have it, and the blessing of it, without fetching it from our neighbours.

II. Let us see how David managed the matter now. 1. He rectified the former error. He did not put the ark in a cart now, but ordered those whose business it was to carry it on their shoulders. This is implied here (*v.* 13) and expressed 1 Chron. xv. 15. Then we make a good use of the judgments of God on ourselves and others when we are awakened by them to reform and amend whatever has been amiss. 2. At their first setting out he offered sacrifices to God (*v.* 13) by way of atonement for their former errors and in a thankful acknowledgment of the blessings bestowed on the house of Obed-edom. Then we are likely to speed in our enterprises when we begin with God and give diligence to make our peace with him. When we attend upon God in holy ordinances our eye must be to the great sacrifice, to which we owe it that we are taken into covenant and communion with God, Ps. l. 5. 3. He himself attended the solemnity with the highest expressions of joy that could be (*v.* 14): *He danced before the Lord with all his might;* he leaped for joy, as one transported with the occasion, and the more because of the disappointment he met with the last time. It is a pleasure to a good man to see his errors rectified and himself in the way of his duty. His dancing, I suppose, was not artificial, by any certain rule or measure, nor do we find that any danced with him; but it was a natural expression of his great joy and exultation of mind. He did it with all his might; so we should perform all our religious services, as those that are intent upon them and desire to do them in the best manner. All our might is little enough to be employed in holy duties: the work deserves it all. On this occasion David laid aside his imperial purple, and put on a plain linen ephod, which was light and convenient for dancing, and was used in religious exercises by those who were no priests, for Samuel wore one, 1 Sam. ii. 18. That great prince thought it no disparagement to him to appear in the habit of a minister to the ark. 4. All the people triumphed in this advancement of the ark (*v.* 15): *They brought it up* into the royal city *with shouting*, and *with sound of trumpet*, so expressing their own joy in loud acclamations, and giving notice to all about them to rejoice with them. The public and free administration of ordinances, not only under the protection, but under the smiles, of the civil powers, is just matter of rejoicing to any people. 5. The ark was safely brought to, and honourably deposited in, the place prepared for it, *v.* 17. They set it in *the midst of the tabernacle*, or tent, *which David had pitched for it;* not the tabernacle which Moses reared, for that was at Gibeon (2 Chron. i. 13), and, we may suppose, being made of cloth, in so many hundred years it had gone to decay and was not fit to be removed; but this was a tent set up on purpose to receive the ark. He would not bring it into a private house, no, not his own, lest it should seem to be too much engrossed, and people's resort to it, to pray before it, should be less free; yet he would not build a house for it, lest that should supersede the building of a more stately temple in due time, and therefore, for the present, he placed it within curtains, under a canopy, in imitation of Moses's tabernacle. As soon as ever it was lodged, he offered burnt-offerings and peace-offerings, in thankfulness to God that the business was now done without any more errors or breaches, and in supplication to God for the continuance of his favour. Note, All our joys must be sanctified both with praises and prayers; *for with such sacrifices God is well pleased.* Now, it should seem, he penned the 132d Psalm. 6. The people were then dismissed with great satisfaction. He sent them away, (1.) With a gracious prayer: *He blessed them in the name of the Lord of hosts* (*v.* 18), having not only a particular interest in heaven as a prophet, but an authority over them as a prince; for *the less is blessed of the better*, Heb. vii. 7. He prayed to God to bless them, and particularly to reward them for the honour and respect they had now shown to his ark, assuring them they should be no losers by their journey, but the blessing of God upon their affairs at home would more than bear their charges. He testified his desire for their welfare by this prayer for them, and let them know they had a king that loved them. (2.) With a generous treat; for so it was, rather than a distribution of alms. The great men, it is probable, he entertained at his own house, but to the *multitude of Israel, men* and *women* (and *children*, says Josephus), he dealt to every one a *cake of bread (a spice-cake*, so some), *a good piece of flesh—a handsome decent piece* (so some)—*a part of the peace-offerings* (so Josephus), that they might feast with him *upon the sacrifice*, and a *flagon*, or bottle, *of wine*, *v.* 19. Probably he ordered this provision to be made for them at their respective quarters, and this he did, [1.] In token of his joy and gratitude to God. When the heart is enlarged in cheerfulness the hand should be opened in liberality. The feast of Purim was observed with *sending portions one to another*, Esth. ix. 22. As those to whom God is merciful ought to show mercy in forgiving, so those to whom God is bountiful ought to exercise bounty in giving. [2.] To recommend himself to the people, and confirm his interest in them; for *every one is a friend to him that giveth gifts.* Those that cared not for his prayers would love him for his generosity; and this would encourage them to attend him another time if he saw cause to call them together.

20 Then David returned to bless his household. And Michal the daughter of Saul came out to meet David, and said, How glorious was the king of Israel to day, who uncovered himself to day in the eyes of the handmaids of his servants, as one of the vain fellows shamelessly uncovereth himself! 21 And David said unto Michal, *It was* before the LORD, which chose me before thy father, and before all his house, to appoint me ruler over the people of the LORD, over Israel: therefore will I play before the LORD. 22 And I will yet be more vile than thus, and will be base in mine own sight: and of the maidservants which thou hast spoken of, of them shall I be had in honour. 23 Therefore Michal the daughter of Saul had no child unto the day of her death.

David, having dismissed the congregation with a blessing, *returned to bless his household* (*v.* 20), that is, to pray with them and for them, and to offer up his family thanksgiving for this national mercy. Ministers must not think that their public performances will excuse them from their family-worship; but when they have, with their instructions and prayers, blessed the solemn assemblies, they must return in the same manner to bless their households, for with them they are in a particular manner charged. David, though he had prophets, and priests, and Levites, about him, to be his chaplains, yet did not devolve the work upon them, but himself *blessed his household.* It is angels' work to worship God, and therefore surely that can be no disparagement to the greatest of men.

Never did David return to his house with so much pleasure and satisfaction as he did now that he had got the ark into his neighbourhood; and yet even this joyful day concluded with some uneasiness, occasioned by the pride and peevishness of his wife. Even the palaces of princes are not exempt from domestic troubles. David had pleased all the multitude of Israel, but Michal was not pleased with his dancing before the ark. For this, when he was at a distance, she scorned him, and when he came home she scolded him. She was not displeased at his generosity to the people, nor did she grudge the entertainment he gave them; but she thought he degraded himself too much in dancing before the ark. It was not her covetousness, but her pride, that made her fret.

I. When she saw David in the street dancing before the Lord she *despised him in her heart, v.* 16. She thought this mighty zeal of his for the ark of God, and the transport of joy he was in upon its coming home to him, was but a foolish thing, and unbecoming so great a soldier, and statesman, and monarch, as he was. It would have been enough for him to encourage the devotion of others, but she looked upon it as a thing below him to appear so very devout himself. "What a fool" (thinks she) "does my husband make of himself now! How fond is he of this ark, that might as well have lain still where it had lain for so many years! Much devotion has almost made him mad." Note, The exercises of religion appear very mean in the eyes of those that have little or no religion themselves.

II. When he came home in the very best disposition she began to upbraid him, and was so full of disdain and indignation that she could not contain till she had him in private, but went out to meet him with her reproaches. Observe,

1. How she taunted him (*v.* 20): "*How glorious was the king of Israel to-day!* What a figure didst thou make to-day in the midst of the mob! How unbecoming thy post and character!" Her contempt of him and his devotion began in the heart, but out of the abundance of that the mouth spoke. That which displeased her was his affection to the ark, which she wished he had no greater kindness for than she had: but she basely represents his conduct, in dancing before the ark, as lewd and immodest; and, while really she was displeased at it as a diminution to his honour, she pretended to dislike it as a reproach to his virtue, that he *uncovered himself in the eyes of the maid-servants,* as no man would have done but *one of the vain fellows* that cared not how much he shamed himself. We have no reason to think that this was true in fact. David, no doubt, observed decorum, and governed his zeal with discretion. But it is common for those that reproach religion thus to put false colours upon it and lay it under the most odious characters. To have abused any man thus for his pious zeal would have been very profane, but to abuse her own husband thus, whom she ought to have reverenced, and one whose prudence and virtue were above the reach of malice itself to disparage, one who had shown such affection for her that he would not accept a crown unless he might have her restored to him (*ch.* iii. 13), was a most base and wicked thing, and showed her to have more of Saul's daughter in her than of David's wife or Jonathan's sister.

2. How he replied to her reproach. He did not upbraid her with her treacherous departure from him to embrace the bosom of a stranger. He had forgiven that, and therefore had forgotten it, though, it may be, his own conscience, on this occasion, upbraided him with his folly in receiving her again (for that is said to pollute the land, Jer. iii. 1), but he justifies himself in what he did.

(1.) He designed thereby to honour God (*v.* 21): *It was before the Lord,* and with an eye to him. Whatever invidious construction she was pleased to put upon it, he had the testimony of his conscience for him that he sincerely aimed at the glory of God, for whom he thought he could never do enough. Here he reminds her indeed of the setting aside of her father's house, to make way for him to the throne, that she might not think herself the most proper judge of propriety: "*God chose me before thy father, and appointed me to be ruler over Israel,* and now I am the fountain of honour; and, if the expressions of a warm devotion to God were looked upon as mean and unfashionable in thy father's court, yet *I will play before the Lord,* and thereby bring them into reputation again. And, if this be to be vile (*v.* 22), *I will be yet more vile.*" Note, [1.] We should be afraid of censuring the devotion of others though it may not agree with our sentiments, because, for aught that we know, the heart may be upright in it, and who are we that we should despise those whom God has accepted? [2.] If we can approve ourselves to God in what we do in religion, and do it as before the Lord, we need not value the censures and reproaches of men. If we appear right in God's eyes, no matter how mean we appear in the eyes of the world. [3.] The more we are vilified for well-doing the more resolute we should be in it, and hold our religion the faster, and bind it the closer to us, for the endeavours of Satan's agents to shake us and to shame us out of it. *I will be yet more vile.*

(2.) He designed thereby to humble himself: "*I will be base in my own sight,* and will think nothing too mean to stoop to for the honour of God." In the throne of judgment, and in the field of battle, none shall do more to support the grandeur and authority of a prince than David shall; but in acts of devotion he lays aside the thoughts of majesty, humbles himself to the dust before the Lord, joins in with the meanest services done in honour of the ark, and thinks all this no diminution to him. The greatest of men is less than the least of the ordinances of Jesus Christ.

(3.) He doubted not but even this would turn to his reputation among those whose reproach Michal pretended to fear: *Of the maid-servants shall I be had in honour.* The common people would be so far from thinking the worse of him for these pious condescensions that they would esteem and honour him so much the more. Those that are truly pious are sometimes *manifested in the consciences* even of those that speak ill of them, 2 Cor. v. 11. Let us never be driven from our duty by the fear of reproach; for to be steady and resolute in it will perhaps turn to our reputation more than we think it will. Piety will have its praise. Let us not then be indifferent in it, nor afraid or ashamed to own it.

David was contented thus to justify himself, and did not any further animadvert upon Michal's insolence; but God punished her for it, writing her for ever childless from this time forward, *v.* 23. She unjustly reproached David for his devotion, and therefore God justly put her under the perpetual reproach of barrenness. *Those that honour God he will honour;* but those that despise him, and his servants and service, *shall be lightly esteemed.*

CHAP. VII.

Still the ark is David's care as well as his joy. In this chapter we have, I. His consultation with Nathan about building a house for it; he signifies his purpose to do it (ver. 1, 2) and Nathan approves his purpose, ver. 3. II. His communion with God about it. 1. A gracious message God sent him about it, accepting his purpose, countermanding the performance, and promising him an entail of blessings upon his family, ver. 4—17. 2. A very humble prayer which David offered up to God in return to that gracious message, thankfully accepting God's promises to him, and earnestly praying for the performance of them, ver. 18—29. And, in both these, there is an eye to the Messiah and his kingdom.

AND it came to pass, when the king sat in his house, and the LORD had given him rest round about from all his enemies; 2 That the king said unto Nathan the prophet, See now, I dwell in a house of cedar, but the ark of God dwelleth within curtains. 3 And Nathan said to the king, Go, do all that *is* in thine heart; for the LORD *is* with thee.

Here is, I. David at rest. *He sat in his house* (*v.* 1), quiet and undisturbed, having no occasion to take the field: *The Lord had given him rest round about,* from all those that were enemies to his settlement in the throne, and he sets himself to enjoy that rest. Though he was a man of war, he was *for peace* (Ps. cxx. 7) and did not delight in war. He had not been long at rest, nor was it long before he was again engaged in war; but at present he enjoyed a calm, and he was in his element when he was sitting in his house, meditating in the law of God.

II. David's thought of building a temple for the honour of God. He had built a palace for himself and a city for his servants; and now he thinks of building a habitation for the ark. 1. Thus he would make a grateful return for the honours God put upon him. Note, When God, in his providence, has remarkably done much for us, it should put us upon contriving what we may do for him and his glory. *What shall I render unto the Lord?* 2. Thus he would improve the present calm, and make a good use of the rest God had given him. Now that he was not called out to serve God and Israel in the high places of the field, he would employ his thoughts, and time, and estate, in serving him another way, and not indulge himself in ease, much less in luxury. When God, in his providence, gives us rest, and finds us little to do of worldly business, we must do so much the more for God and our souls. How different were the thoughts of David when he sat in his palace from Nebuchadnezzar's when he *walked in his!* Dan. iv. 29, 30. That proud man thought of nothing but the might of his own power, and the honour of his own majesty; this humble soul is full of contrivance how to glorify God, and give honour to him. And how God resisteth the proud, and giveth grace and glory to the humble, the event showed. David considered (*v.* 2) the stateliness of his own habitation *(I dwell in a house of cedar)*, and compared with that the meanness of the habitation of the ark *(the ark dwells within curtains)*, and thought this incongruous, that he should dwell in a palace and the ark in a tent. David had been uneasy till he found out *a place for the ark* (Ps. cxxxii. 4, 5), and now he is uneasy till he finds out a better place. Gracious grateful souls, (1.) Never think they can do enough for God, but, when they have done much, are still projecting to do more and devising liberal things. (2.) They cannot enjoy their own accommodations while they see the church of God in distress and under a cloud. David can take little pleasure in a house of cedar for himself, unless the ark have one. Those who *stretched themselves upon beds of ivory,* and were *not grieved for the affliction of Joseph,* though they had David's music, had not David's spirit (Amos vi. 4, 6) nor those who dwelt in their ceiled houses while God's house lay waste.

III. His communicating this thought to Nathan the prophet. He told him, as a friend and confidant, whom he used to advise with. Could not David have gone about it himself? Was it not a good work? Was not he himself a prophet? Yes, but *in the multitude of counsellors there is safety.* David told him, that by him he might know the mind of God. It was certainly a good work, but it was uncertain whether it was the will of God that David should have the doing of it.

IV. Nathan's approbation of it: *Go, do all that is in thy heart; for the Lord is with thee, v.* 3. We do not find that David told him that he purposed to build a temple, only that it was a trouble to him that there was not one built, from which Nathan easily gathered what was in his heart, and bade him go on and prosper. Note, We ought to do all we can to encourage and promote the good purposes and designs of others, and put in a good word, as we have opportunity, to forward a good work. Nathan spoke this, not in God's name, but as from himself; not as a prophet, but as a wise and good man; it was agreeable to the revealed will of God, which requires that all in their places should lay out themselves for the advancement of religion and the service of God, though it seems his secret will was otherwise, that David should not do this. It was Christ's prerogative always to speak the mind of God, which he perfectly knew. Other prophets spoke it only when the spirit of prophecy was upon them; but, if in any thing they mistook (as Samuel, 1 Sam. xvi. 6, and Nathan here) God soon rectified the mistake.

4 And it came to pass that night, that the word of the LORD came unto Nathan, saying, 5 Go and tell my servant David, Thus saith the LORD, Shalt thou build me a house for me to dwell in? 6 Whereas I have not dwelt in *any* house since the time that I brought up the children of Israel out of Egypt, even to this day, but have walked in a tent and in a tabernacle. 7 In all *the places* wherein I have walked with all the children of Israel spake I a word with any of the tribes of Israel, whom I commanded to feed my people Israel, saying, Why build ye not me a house of cedar? 8 Now therefore so shalt thou say unto my servant David, Thus saith the LORD of hosts, I took thee from the sheepcote, from following the sheep, to be ruler over my people, over Israel: 9 And I was with thee whithersoever thou wentest, and have cut off all thine enemies out of thy sight, and have made thee a great name, like unto the name of the great *men* that *are* in the earth. 10 Moreover I will appoint a place for my people Israel, and will plant them, that they may dwell in a place of their own, and move no more; neither shall the children of wickedness afflict them any more, as beforetime, 11 And as since the time that I commanded judges *to be* over my people Israel, and have caused thee to rest from all thine enemies. Also the LORD telleth thee that he will make thee a house. 12 And when thy days be fulfilled, and thou shalt sleep with thy fathers, I will set up thy seed after thee, which shall proceed out of thy bowels, and I will establish his kingdom. 13 He shall build a house for my name, and I will establish the throne of his kingdom for ever. 14 I will be his father, and he shall be my son. If he commit iniquity, I will chasten him with the rod of men, and with the stripes of the children of men: 15 But my mercy shall not depart away from him, as I took *it* from Saul, whom I put away before thee. 16 And thine house and thy kingdom shall be established for ever before thee: thy throne shall be established for ever. 17 According to all these words, and according to all this vision, so did Nathan speak unto David.

We have here a full revelation of God's favour to David and the kind intentions of that favour, the notices and assurances of which God sent him by Nathan the prophet, whom he entrusted to deliver this long message to him. The design of it is to take him off from his purpose of building the temple and it was therefore sent, 1. By the same hand that had given him encouragement to do it, lest, if it had been sent by any other, Nathan should be despised and insulted and David should be perplexed, being encouraged by one prophet and discouraged by another. 2. The same night, that Nathan might not continue long in an error nor David have his head any further filled with thoughts of that which he must never bring to pass. God might have said this to David himself immediately, but he chose to send it by Nathan, to support the honour of his prophets, and to preserve in David a regard to them. Though he be the head, they must be the eyes by which he must see the visions of the Almighty, and the tongue by which he must hear the word of God. He that delivered this long message to Nathan assisted his memory to retain it, that he might deliver it fully (he being resolved to deliver it faithfully) as he received it of the Lord. Now in this message,

I. David's purpose to build God a house is superseded. God took notice of that purpose, for he knows what is in man; and he was well pleased with it, as appears 1 Kings viii. 18, *Thou didst well that it was in thy heart;* yet he forbade him to go on with his purpose (*v.* 5): "*Shalt thou build me a house?* No, *thou shalt not* (as it is explained in the parallel place, 1 Chron. xvii. 4); there is other work appointed for thee to do, which must be done first." David is a man of war, and he must enlarge the borders of Israel, by carrying on their conquests. David is a sweet psalmist, and he must prepare psalms for the use of the temple when it is built, and settle the courses of the Levites; but his son's genius will better suit for building the house, and he will have a better treasure to bear the charge of it, and therefore let it be reserved for him to do. *As every man hath received the gift, so let him minister.* The building of a temple was to be a work of time, and preparation made for it; but it was a thing that had never been spoken of till now. God tells him, 1. That hitherto he had never had a house built for him (*v.* 6), a tabernacle had served hitherto, and it might serve awhile longer. God regards not outward pomp in his service; his presence was as surely with his people when the ark was in a tent as when it was in a temple. David was uneasy that the ark was in curtains (a mean and movable habitation), but God never complained of it as any uneasiness to him. He did not dwell, but walk, and yet fainted not, nor was weary. Christ, like the ark, when here on earth walked in a tent or tabernacle, for he *went about doing good,* and dwelt not in any house of his own, till he ascended on high, to the mansions above, in his Father's house, and there he sat down. The church, like the ark, in this world is ambulatory, dwells in a tent, because its present state is both pastoral and military; its continuing city is to come. David, in his psalms, often calls the tabernacle a temple (as Ps. v. 7; xxvii. 4; xxix. 9; lxv. 4; cxxxviii. 2), because it answered the intention of a temple, though it was made but of curtains. Wise and good men value not the show, while they have the substance. David perhaps had more true devotion, and sweeter communion with God, in a house of curtains, than any of his successors in the house of cedar. 2. That he had never given any orders or directions, or the least intimation, to any of the sceptres of Israel, that is, to any of the judges, 1 Chron. xvii. 6 (for rulers are called *sceptres,* Ezek. xix. 14, the great Ruler is called so, Num. xxiv. 17), concerning the building of the temple, *v.* 7. That worship only is acceptable which is instituted; why should David therefore design what God never ordained? Let him wait for a warrant, and then let him do it. Better a tent of God's appointing than a temple of his own inventing.

II. David is reminded of the great things God had done for him, to let him know that he was a favourite of heaven, though he had not the favour to be employed in this service, as also that God was not indebted to him for his good intentions, but, whatever he did for God's honour, God was beforehand with him, *v.* 8, 9. 1. He had raised him from a very mean and low condition: *He took him from the sheep-cote.* It is good for those who have come to great preferment to be often reminded of their small beginnings, that they may always be humble and thankful. 2. He had given him success and victory over his enemies (*v.* 9): "*I was with thee whithersoever thou wentest,* to protect thee when pursued, to prosper thee when pursuing. *I have cut off all thy enemies,* that stood in the way of thy advancement and settlement." 3. He had crowned him not only with power and dominion in Israel, but with honour and reputation among the nations about: *I have made thee a great name.* He had become famous for his courage, conduct, and great achievements, and was more talked of than any of the great men of his day. A great name is what those who have it have great reason to be thankful for and may improve to good purposes, but what those who have it not have no reason to be ambitious of: a good name is more desirable. A man may pass through the world very obscurely and yet very comfortably.

III. A happy establishment is promised to God's Israel, *v.* 10, 11. This comes in in a parenthesis, before the promises made to David himself, to let him understand that what God designed to do for him was for Israel's sake, that they might be happy under his administration, and to give him the satisfaction of foreseeing peace upon Israel, when it was promised him that he should *see his children's children,* Ps. cxxviii. 6. A good king cannot think himself happy unless his kingdom be so. The promises that follow relate to his family and posterity; these therefore, which speak of the settlement of Israel, intend the happiness of his own reign. Two things are promised:—1. A quiet place: *I will appoint a place for my people Israel.* It was appointed long ago, yet they were disappointed, but now that appointment should be made good. Canaan should be clearly their own without any ejection or molestation. 2. A quiet enjoyment of that place: *The children of wickedness* (meaning especially the Philistines, who had been so long a plague to them) *shall not afflict them any more; but, as in the time that I caused judges to be over my people Israel, I will cause thee to rest from all thy enemies* (so *v.* 11 may be read), that is, "I will continue and complete that rest; the land shall rest from war, as it did under the judges."

IV. Blessings are entailed upon the family and posterity of David. David had purposed to build God a house, and, in requital, God promises to *build him a house, v.* 11. Whatever we do for God, or sincerely design to do though Providence prevents our doing it, we *shall in no wise lose our reward.* He had promised to make him a name (*v.* 9); here he promises to make him a house, which should bear up that name. It would be a great satisfaction to David, while he lived, to have the inviolable assurance of a divine promise that his family should flourish when he was dead. Next to the happiness of our souls, and the church of God, we should desire the happiness of our seed, that those who come of us may be praising God on earth when we are praising him in heaven.

1. Some of these promises relate to Solomon, his immediate successor, and to the royal line of Judah. (1.) That God would advance him to the throne. Those words, *when thy days be fulfilled, and thou shalt sleep with thy fathers,* intimate that David himself should come to his grave in peace; and then *I will set up thy seed.* This favour was so much the greater because it was more than God had done for Moses, or Joshua, or any of the judges whom he called to feed his people. David's government was the first that was entailed; for the promise made to Christ of the kingdom was to reach to his spiritual seed. *If children, then heirs.* (2.) That he would settle him in the throne: *I will establish his kingdom* (*v.* 12), *the throne of his kingdom, v.* 13. His title shall be clear and uncontested, his interest confirmed, and his administration steady. (3.) That he would employ him in that good work of building the temple, which David had only the satisfaction of designing: *He shall build a house for my name, v.* 13. The work shall be done, though David shall not have the doing of it. (4.) That he would take him into the covenant of adoption (*v.* 14, 15): *I will be his father, and he shall be my son.* We need no more to make us and ours happy than to have God to be a Father to us and them; and all those to whom God is a Father he by his grace makes his sons, by giving them the disposition of children. If he be a careful, tender, bountiful Father to us, we must be obedient, tractable, dutiful children to him. The promise here speaks *as unto sons.* [1.] That his Father would correct him when there was occasion; for *what son is he whom the Father chasteneth not?* Afflictions are an article of the covenant, and are not only consistent with, but flow from, God's fatherly love. "*If he commit iniquity,* as it proved he did (1 Kings xi. 1), *I will chasten him* to bring him to repentance, but it shall be *with the rod of men,* such a rod as men may wield—I will not *plead against him with the great power* of God," Job xxiii. 6. Or rather such a rod as *men may bear*—"I will consider his frame, and correct him with all possible tenderness and compassion when there is need, and no more than there is need of; it shall be with *the stripes,* the *touches* (so the word is) *of the children of men;* not a stroke, or wound, but a gentle touch." [2.] That yet he would not disinherit him (*v.* 15): *My mercy* (and that is the inheritance of sons) *shall not depart from him.* The revolt of the ten tribes from the house of David was their correction for iniquity, but the constant adherence of the other two to that family, which was a competent support of the royal dignity, perpetuated the mercy of God to the seed of David, according to this promise; though that family was cut short, yet it was not cut off, as the house of Saul was. Never any other family swayed the sceptre of Judah than that of David. This is that covenant of royalty celebrated (Ps. lxxxix. 3, &c.) as typical of the covenant of redemption and grace.

2. Others of them relate to Christ, who is often called *David* and the *Son of David,* that Son of David to whom these promises pointed and in whom they had their full accomplishment. He was of the *seed of David,* Acts xiii. 23. To him God *gave the throne of his father David* (Luke i. 32), all power both in heaven and earth, and authority to execute judgment. He was to build the gospel temple, a house for God's name, Zech. vi. 12, 13. That promise, *I will be his Father, and he shall be my Son,* is expressly applied to Christ by the apostle, Heb. i. 5. But the establishing of his house, and his throne, and his *kingdom, for ever* (*v.* 13, and again, and a third time *v.* 16, *for ever*), can be applied to no other than Christ and his kingdom. David's house and kingdom have long since come to an end; it is only the Messiah's kingdom that is everlasting, and *of the increase of his government and peace there shall be no end.* The supposition of committing iniquity cannot indeed be applied to the Messiah himself, but it is applicable (and very comfortable) to his spiritual seed. True believers have their infirmities, for which they may expect to be corrected, but they shall not be cast off. Every transgression in the covenant will not throw us out of covenant. Now, (1.) This message Nathan faithfully delivered to David (*v.* 17); though, in forbidding him to build the temple, he contradicted his own words, yet he was not backward to do it when he was better informed concerning the mind of God. (2.) These promises God faithfully performed to David and his seed in due time. Though David came short of making good his purpose to build God a house, yet God did not come short of making good his promise to build him a house. Such is the tenour of the covenant we are under; though there are many failures in our performances, there are none in God's.

18 Then went king David in, and sat before the LORD, and he said, Who *am* I, O Lord GOD? and what *is* my house, that thou hast brought me hitherto? 19 And this was yet a small thing in thy sight, O Lord GOD; but thou hast spoken also of thy servant's house for a great while to come. And *is* this the manner of man, O Lord GOD? 20 And what can David say more unto thee?

for thou, Lord GOD, knowest thy servant. 21 For thy word's sake, and according to thine own heart, hast thou done all these great things, to make thy servant know *them.* 22 Wherefore thou art great, O LORD God: for *there is* none like thee, neither *is there any* God beside thee, according to all that we have heard with our ears. 23 And what one nation in the earth *is* like thy people, *even* like Israel, whom God went to redeem for a people to himself, and to make him a name, and to do for you great things and terrible, for thy land, before thy people, which thou redeemedst to thee from Egypt, *from* the nations and their gods? 24 For thou hast confirmed to thyself thy people Israel *to be* a people unto thee for ever: and thou, LORD, art become their God. 25 And now, O LORD God, the word that thou hast spoken concerning thy servant, and concerning his house, establish *it* for ever, and do as thou hast said. 26 And let thy name be magnified for ever, saying, The LORD of hosts *is* the God over Israel: and let the house of thy servant David be established before thee. 27 For thou, O LORD of hosts, God of Israel, hast revealed to thy servant, saying, I will build thee a house: therefore hath thy servant found in his heart to pray this prayer unto thee. 28 And now, O Lord GOD, thou *art* that God, and thy words be true, and thou hast promised this goodness unto thy servant: 29 Therefore now let it please thee to bless the house of thy servant, that it may continue for ever before thee: for thou, O Lord GOD, hast spoken *it:* and with thy blessing let the house of thy servant be blessed for ever.

We have here the solemn address David made to God, in answer to the gracious message God had sent him. We are not told what he said to Nathan; no doubt he received him very kindly and respectfully as God's messenger. But his answer to God he took himself, and did not send by Nathan. When ministers deliver God's message to us, it is not to them, but to God, that our hearts must reply; he understands the language of the heart, and to him we may come boldly. David had no sooner received the message than, while the impressions of it were fresh, he retired to return an answer. Observe,

I. The place he retired to: He *went in before the Lord,* that is, into the tabernacle where the ark was, which was the token of God's presence; before *that* he presented himself. God's will now is that men pray every where; but, wherever we pray, we must set ourselves as before the Lord and set him before us.

II. The posture he put himself into: He *sat before the Lord.* 1. It denotes the posture of his body. Kneeling or standing is certainly the most proper gesture to be used in prayer; but the Jews, from this instance, say, "It was allowed to the kings of the house of David to sit in the temple, and to no other." But this will by no means justify the ordinary use of that gesture in prayer, whatever may be allowed in a case of necessity. *David went in, and took his place before the Lord,* so it may be read; but, when he prayed, he stood up as the manner was. Or he *went in and continued before the Lord,* staid some time silently meditating, before he began his prayer, and then remained longer than usual in the tabernacle. Or, 2. It may denote the frame of his spirit at this time. He went in, and composed himself before the Lord; thus we should do in all our approaches to God. *O God, my heart is fixed, my heart is fixed.*

III. The prayer itself, which is full of the breathings of pious and devout affection towards God.

1. He speaks very humbly of himself and his own merits. So he begins as one astonished: *Who am I, O Lord God! and what is my house? v.* 18. God had reminded him of the meanness of his original (*v.* 8) and he subscribed to it; he had low thoughts, (1.) Of his personal merits: *Who am I?* He was upon all accounts a very considerable and valuable man. His endowments both of body and mind were extraordinary. His gifts and graces were eminent. He was a man of honour, success, and usefulness, the darling of his country and the dread of its enemies. Yet, when he comes to speak of himself before God, he says, "*Who am I?* A man not worth taking notice of." (2.) Of the merits of his family: *What is my house?* His house was of the royal tribe, and descended from the prince of that tribe; he was allied to the best families of the country, and yet, like Gideon, thinks his family poor in Judah and himself *the least in his father's house,* Judg. vi. 15. David thus humbled himself when Saul's daughter was proposed to him for a wife (1 Sam. xviii. 18), but now with much more reason. Note, It very well becomes the greatest and best of men, even in the midst of the highest advancements, to have low and mean thoughts of themselves; for the greatest of men are worms, the best are sinners, and those that are highest ad-

vanced have nothing but what they have received: "*What am I, that thou hast brought me hitherto,* brought me to the kingdom, and to a settlement in it, and rest from all my enemies?" It intimates that he could not have reached this himself by his own management, if God had not brought him to it. All our attainments must be looked upon as God's vouchsafements.

2. He speaks very highly and honourably of God's favours to him. (1.) In what he had done for him: "*Thou hast brought me hitherto,* to this great dignity and dominion. Hitherto thou hast helped me." Though we should be left at uncertainty concerning further mercy, we have great reason to be thankful for that which has been done for us hitherto, Acts xxvi. 22. (2.) In what he had yet further promised him. God had done great things for him already, and yet, as if those had been nothing, he had promised to do much more, *v.* 19. Note, What God has laid out upon his people is much, but what he has laid up for them is infinitely more, Ps. xxxi. 19. The present graces and comforts of the saints are invaluable gifts; and yet, as if these were too little for God to bestow upon his children, he has spoken concerning them for a great while to come, even as far as eternity itself reaches. Of this we must own, as David here, [1.] That it is far beyond what we could expect: *Is this the manner of men?* that is, *First,* Can man expect to be so dealt with by his Maker? *Is this the law of Adam?* Note, Considering what the character and condition of man are, it is very surprising and amazing that God should deal with him as he does. Man is a mean creature, and therefore under a law of distance—unprofitable to God, and therefore under a law of disesteem and disregard—guilty and obnoxious, and therefore under a law of death and damnation. But how unlike are God's dealings with man to this law of Adam! He is brought near to God, purchased at a high rate, taken into covenant and communion with God; could this ever have been thought of? *Secondly,* Do men usually deal thus with one another? No, the way of our God is far above the manner of men. Though he be high, he has respect to the lowly; and is this the manner of men? Though he is offended by us, he beseeches us to be reconciled, waits to be gracious, multiplies his pardons: and is this the manner of men? Some give another sense of this, reading it thus: *And this is the law of man, the Lord Jehovah,* that is, "This promise of one whose kingdom shall be established for ever must be understood of one that is a man and yet the Lord Jehovah, this must be the law of such a one. A Messiah from my loins must be man, but, reigning for ever, must be God." [2.] That beyond this there is nothing we can desire: "*And what can David say more unto thee?* *v.* 20. What can I ask or wish for more? *Thou, Lord, knowest thy servant,* knowest what will make me happy, and what thou hast promised is enough to do so." The promise of Christ includes all. If that man, the Lord God, be ours, what can we ask or think of more? Eph. iii. 20. The promises of the covenant of grace are framed by him that knows us, and therefore knows how to adapt them to every branch of our necessity. He knows us better than we know ourselves; and therefore let us be satisfied with the provision he has made for us. What can we say more for ourselves in our prayers than he has said for us in his promises?

3. He ascribes all to the free grace of God (*v.* 21), both the great things he had done for him and the great things he had made known to him. All was, (1.) For his word's sake, that is, for the sake of Christ the eternal Word; it is all owing to his merit. Or, "That thou mayest magnify thy word of promise above all thy name, in making it the stay and store-house of thy people." (2.) According to thy own heart, thy gracious counsels and designs, *ex mero motu—of thy own good pleasure. Even so, Father, because it seemed good in thy eyes.* All that God does for his people in his providences, and secures to them in his promises, is for his pleasure and for his praise, the pleasure of his will and the praise of his word.

4. He adores the greatness and glory of God (*v.* 22): *Thou art great, O Lord God! for there is none like thee.* God's gracious condescension to him, and the honour he had put upon him, did not at all abate his awful veneration for the divine Majesty; for the nearer any are brought to God the more they see of his glory, and the dearer we are in his eyes the greater he should be in ours. And this we acknowledge concerning God, that there is no being like him, nor any God besides him, and that what we have seen with our eyes of his power and goodness is according to all that we have heard with our ears, and the one half not told us.

5. He expresses a great esteem for the Israel of God, *v.* 23, 24. As there was none among the gods to be compared with Jehovah, so none among the nations to be compared with Israel, considering,

(1.) The works he had done for them. He went to redeem them, applied himself to it as a great work, went about it with solemnity. *Elohim halecu, dii iverunt—Gods went,* as if there was the same consultation and concurrence of all the persons in the blessed Trinity about the work of redemption that there was about the work of creation, when God said, *Let us make man. Whom those that were sent of God went to redeem;* so the Chaldee, meaning, I suppose, Moses and Aaron. The redemption of Israel, as described here, was typical of our redemption by Christ in that, [1.] They were redeemed from the nations and their gods; so are we from all iniquity and all conformity to this present world. Christ came to save his people from their sins. [2.] They were redeemed to be a peculiar people unto God, purified and appropriated to himself, that he might make himself a great name and do for them great things. The honour of God, and the eternal happiness of the saints, are the two things aimed at in their redemption.

(2) The covenant he had made with them, *v.* 24. It was, [1.] Mutual: "They to be a people to thee, and thou to be a God to them; all their interests consecrated to thee, and all thy attributes engaged for them." [2.] Immutable: "Thou hast confirmed them." He that makes the covenant makes it sure and will make it good.

6. He concludes with humble petitions to God. (1.) He grounds his petitions upon the message which God had sent him (*v.* 27): *Thou hast revealed this to thy servant,* that is, "Thou hast of thy own good will given me the promise that thou wilt build me a house, else I could never have found in my heart to pray such a prayer as this. I durst not have asked such great things if I had not been directed and encouraged by thy promise to ask them. They are indeed too great for me to beg, but not too great for thee to give. Thy servant has found in his heart to pray this prayer;" so it is in the original, and the LXX. Many, when they go to pray, have their hearts to seek, but David's heart was found, that is, it was fixed, gathered in from its wanderings, and entirely engaged to the duty and employed in it. That prayer which is found in the tongue only will not please God; it must be found in the heart; the heart must be lifted up and poured out before God. *My son, give God thy heart.* (2.) He builds his faith and hopes to speed upon the fidelity of God's promise (*v.* 25): "*Thou art that God* (thou art *he,* even *that God,* the *Lord of hosts,* and *God of Israel,* or *that God whose words are true,* that God whom one may depend upon); and *thou hast promised this goodness unto thy servant,* which I am therefore bold to pray for." (3.) Thence he fetches the matter of his prayer, and refers to that as the guide of his prayers. [1.] He prays for the performance of God's promise (*v.* 25): "Let the word be made good to me, *on which thou hast caused me to hope* (Ps. cxix. 49) *and do as thou hast said;* I desire no more, and I expect no less; so full is the promise, and so firm." Thus we must turn God's promises into prayers, and then they shall be turned into performances; for, with God, saying and doing are not two things, as they often are with men. God will do as he hath said. [2.] He prays for the glorifying of God's name (*v.* 26): *Let thy name be magnified for ever.* This ought to be the summary and centre of all our prayers, the Alpha and the Omega of them. Begin with *Hallowed be thy name,* and end with *Thine is the glory for ever.* "Whether I be magnified or no, *let thy name be magnified.*" And he reckons that nothing magnifies God's name more than this, to say, with suitable affections, *The Lord of hosts is the God over Israel.* This bespeaks the *God of Israel gloriously great,* that he is the *Lord of hosts;* and this bespeaks the *Lord of hosts* gloriously good, that he is *God over Israel.* In both, *let his name be magnified for ever.* Let all the creatures and all the churches give him the glory of these two. David desired the performance of God's promise for the honour, not of his own name, but of God's. Thus the Son of David prayed, *Father, glorify thy name* (John xii. 28), and (John xvii. 1), *Glorify thy Son, that thy Son may also glorify thee.* [3.] He prays for his house, for to that the promise has special reference, *First,* That it might be happy (*v.* 29): *Let it please thee to bless the house of thy servant;* and again, *with thy blessing.* "Let the house of thy servant be truly and eternally blessed. *Those whom thou blessest are blessed indeed.*" The care of good men is very much concerning their families; and the best entail on their families is that of the blessing of God. The repetition of this request is not a vain repetition, but expressive of the value he had of the divine blessing, and his earnest desire of it, as all in all to the happiness of his family. *Secondly,* That the happiness of it might remain: "Let it be *established before thee* (*v.* 26); let it *continue for ever before thee,*" *v.* 29. He prayed, 1. That the entail of the crown might not be cut off, but remain in his family, that none of his might ever forfeit it, but that they might walk before God, which would be their establishment. 2. That his kingdom might have its perfection and perpetuity in the kingdom of the Messiah. When Christ for ever sat down on the right hand of God (Heb. x. 12), and received all possible assurance that his seed and throne shall be as the days of heaven, this prayer of David the son of Jesse for his seed was abundantly answered, that it might *continue before God for ever.* See Ps. lxxii. 17. The perpetuity of the Messiah's kingdom is the desire and faith of all good people.

CHAP. VIII.

David having sought first the kingdom of God and the righteousness thereof, settling the ark as soon as he was himself well settled, we are here told how all other things were added to him. Here is an account, I. Of his conquests. He triumphed, 1. Over the Philistines, ver. 1. 2. Over the Moabites, ver. 2. 3. Over the king of Zobah, ver. 3, 4. 4. Over the Syrians, ver. 5—8, 13. 5. Over the Edomites, ver. 14. II. Of the presents that were brought him and the wealth he got from the nations he subdued, which he dedicated to God, ver. 9—12. III. Of his court, the administration of his government (ver. 15), and his chief officers, ver. 16—18. This gives us a general idea of the prosperity of David's reign.

AND after this it came to pass, that David smote the Philistines, and subdued them: and David took Metheg-ammah out of the hand of the Philistines. 2 And he smote Moab, and measured them with a line, casting them down to the ground; even with two lines measured he to put to death, and with one full line to keep alive. And *so* the Moabites became David's servants, *and* brought gifts. 3 David smote also Hadadezer, the son of Rehob, king of Zobah, as he went to recover his border at the river Euphrates. 4 And David took from him a thousand *chariots*, and seven hundred horsemen, and twenty thousand footmen: and David houghed all the chariot *horses*, but reserved of them *for* a hundred chariots. 5 And when the Syrians of Damascus came to succour Hadadezer, king of Zobah, David slew of the Syrians two and twenty thousand men. 6 Then David put garrisons in Syria of Damascus: and the Syrians became servants to David, *and* brought gifts. And the LORD preserved David whithersoever he went. 7 And David took the shields of gold that were on the servants of Hadadezer, and brought them to Jerusalem. 8 And from Betah, and from Berothai, cities of Hadadezer, king David took exceeding much brass.

God had given David rest from all his enemies that opposed him and made head against him; and he, having made a good use of that rest, has now commission given him to make war upon them, and to act offensively for the avenging of Israel's quarrels and the recovery of their rights; for as yet they were not in full possession of that country to which by the promise of God they were entitled.

I. He quite subdued the Philistines, *v.* 1. They had attacked him when they thought him weak (*ch.* v. 17), and went by the worst then; but, when he found himself strong, he attacked them, and made himself master of their country. They had long been vexatious and oppressive to Israel. Saul got no ground against them; but David completed Israel's deliverance out of their hands, which Samson had begun long before, Judg. xiii. 5. *Metheg-ammah* was *Gath* (the chief and royal city of the Philistines) and the towns belonging to it, among which there was a constant garrison kept by the Philistines on the hill Ammah (2 Sam. ii. 24), which was *Metheg*, a *bridle* (so it signifies) or *curb* upon the people of Israel; this David took out of their hand and used it as a curb upon them. Thus, when the strong man is disarmed, the armour wherein he trusted is taken from him, and used against him, Luke xi. 22. And after the long and frequent struggles which the saints have had with the powers of darkness, like Israel with the Philistines, the Son of David shall tread them all under their feet and make the saints more than conquerors.

II. He smote the Moabites, and made them tributaries to Israel, *v.* 2. He divided the country into three parts, two of which he destroyed, casting down the strong-holds, and putting all to the sword; the third part he spared, to till the ground and be servants to Israel. Dr. Lightfoot says, "He laid them on the ground and measured them with a cord, who should be slain and who should live;" and this is called *meting out the valley of Succoth*, Ps. lx. 6. The Jews say he used this severity with the Moabites because they had slain his parents and brethren, whom he put under the protection of the king of Moab during his exile, 1 Sam. xxii. 3, 4. He did it in justice, because they had been dangerous enemies to the Israel of God; and in policy, because, if left in their strength, they still would have been so. But observe, Though it was necessary that two-thirds should be cut off, yet the line that was to keep alive, though it was but one, is ordered to be a full line. Be sure to give that length enough; let the line of mercy be stretched to the utmost *in favorem vitæ—so as to favour life.* Acts of indemnity must be construed so as to enlarge the favour. Now Balaam's prophecy was fulfilled, *A sceptre shall arise out of Israel, and shall smite the corners of Moab*, to the utmost of which the fatal line extended, Num. xxiv. 17. The Moabites continued tributaries to Israel till after the death of Ahab, 2 Kings iii. 4, 5. Then they rebelled and were never reduced.

III. He smote the Syrians or Aramites. Of them there were two distinct kingdoms, as we find them spoken of in the title of the 60th Psalm: *Aram Naharaim,—Syria of the rivers,* whose head city was Damascus (famed for its rivers, 2 Kings v. 12), and *Aram Zobah,* which joined to it, but extended to Euphrates. These were the two northern crowns. 1. David began with the Syrians of Zobah, *v.* 3, 4. As he went to settle his border at the river Euphrates (for so far the land conveyed by the divine grant to Abraham and his seed did extend, Gen. xv. 18), the king of Zobah opposed him, being himself possessed of those countries which belonged to Israel; but David routed his forces, and took his chariots and horsemen. The horsemen are here said to be 700, but 1 Chron. xviii. 4 they are said to be 7000. If they divided their horse by ten in a company, as it is probable they did, the captains and companies were 700, but the horsemen were 7000. David houghed the horses, cut the sinews of their hams, and so lamed them, and made them unserviceable, at least in war, God having forbidden them to *multiply horses*, Deut. xvii. 16. David reserved only 100 chariots out of 1000 for his own use: for he placed his strength not in chariots nor horses, but in the living

God (Ps. xx. 7), and wrote it from his own observation that a *horse is a vain thing for safety,* Ps. xxxiii. 16, 17. 2. The Syrians of Damascus coming in to the relief of the king of Zobah fell with him. 22,000 were slain in the field, *v.* 5. So that it was easy for David to make himself master of the country, and garrison it for himself, *v.* 6. The enemies of God's church, that think to secure themselves, will prove, in the end, to ruin themselves, by their confederacies with each other. *Associate yourselves, and you shall be broken in pieces,* Isa. viii. 9.

IV. In all these wars, 1. David was protected: *The Lord preserved him whithersoever he went.* It seems, he went in person, and, in the cause of God and Israel, jeoparded his own life in the high places of the field; but God covered his head in the day of battle, which he often speaks of, in his psalms, to the glory of God. 2. He was enriched. He took the shields of gold which the servants of Hadadezer had in their custody (*v.* 7) and much brass from several cities of Syria (*v.* 8), which he was entitled to, not only *jure belli—by the uncontrollable right of the longest sword* ("Get it, and take it"); but by commission from heaven, and the ancient entail of these countries on the seed of Abraham.

9 When Toi king of Hamath heard that David had smitten all the host of Hadadezer, 10 Then Toi sent Joram his son unto king David, to salute him, and to bless him, because he had fought against Hadadezer, and smitten him: for Hadadezer had wars with Toi. And *Joram* brought with him vessels of silver, and vessels of gold, and vessels of brass: 11 Which also king David did dedicate unto the LORD, with the silver and gold that he had dedicated of all nations which he subdued; 12 Of Syria, and of Moab, and of the children of Ammon, and of the Philistines, and of Amalek, and of the spoil of Hadadezer, son of Rehob, king of Zobah. 13 And David gat *him* a name when he returned from smiting of the Syrians in the valley of salt, *being* eighteen thousand *men.* 14 And he put garrisons in Edom; throughout all Edom put he garrisons, and all they of Edom became David's servants. And the LORD preserved David whithersoever he went.

Here is, 1. The court made to David by the king of Hamath, who, it seems was at this time at war with the king of Zobah. He, hearing of David's success against his enemy, sent his own son ambassador to him (*v.* 9, 10), to congratulate him on his victory, to return him thanks for the favour he had done him in breaking the power of one he was in fear of, and to beg his friendship. Thus he not only secured but strengthened himself. And David lost nothing by taking this little prince under his protection, any more than the old Romans did by the like policy; for the wealth he had from the countries he conquered by way of spoil he had from this by way of present or gratuity: *Vessels of silver and gold.* Better get by composition than by compulsion. 2. The offering David made to God of the spoils of the nations and all the rich things that were brought him. He dedicated all to the Lord, *v.* 11, 12. This crowned all his victories, and made them far to out-shine Alexander's or Cæsar's, that they sought their own glory, but he aimed at the glory of God. All the precious things he was master of were dedicated things, that is, they were designed for the building of the temple; and a good omen it was of kindness to the Gentiles in the fulness of time, and of the making of God's house a house of prayer for all people, that the temple was built of the spoils and presents of Gentile nations, in allusion to which we find *the kings of the earth* bringing *their glory and honour into the new Jerusalem,* Rev. xxi. 24. Their gods of gold David burnt (2 Sam. v. 21), but their vessels of gold he dedicated. Thus in the conquest of a soul, by the grace of the Son of David, what stands in opposition to God must be destroyed, every lust mortified and crucified, but what may glorify him must be dedicated and the property of it altered. Even the merchandise and the hire must be *holiness to the Lord* (Isa. xxiii. 18), the gain *consecrated to the Lord of the whole earth* (Mic. iv. 13), and then it is truly our own and that most comfortably. 3. The reputation he got, in a particular manner, by his victory over the Syrians and their allies the Edomites, who acted in conjunction with them, as appears by comparing the title of the 60th Psalm, which was penned on this occasion, with *v.* 13. *He got himself a name* for all that conduct and courage which are the praise of a great and distinguished general. Something extraordinary, it is likely, there was in that action, which turned very much to his honour, yet he is careful to transfer the honour to God, as appears by the psalm he penned on this occasion, *v.* 12. It is through God that we do valiantly. 4. His success against the Edomites. They all became David's servants, *v.* 14. Now, and not till now, Isaac's blessing was accomplished, by which Jacob was made Esau's Lord (Gen. xxvii. 37—40) and the Edomites continued long tributary to the kings of Judah, as the Moabites were to the kings of Israel, till, in Joram's time, they revolted (2 Chron. xxi. 8) as Isaac had there foretold that Esau should, in process of time, break the yoke from off his neck. Thus David by his conquests, (1.) Secured peace to his son, that he might have time to build the temple. And, (2.) Procured wealth for his son, that he might have wherewith to build it. God employs his servants variously, some in one employment, others in another, some in the spiritual battles, others in the spiritual buildings; and one prepares work for the other, that God may have the glory of all All David's victories were typical of the success of the gospel against the kingdom of Satan, in which the Son of David rode forth, conquering and to conquer, and he shall reign till he has brought down all opposing rule, principality, and power: and he has, as David had (*v.* 2), a line to kill and a line to save; for the same gospel is to some a savour of life unto life, to others a savour of death unto death.

15 And David reigned over all Israel; and David executed judgment and justice unto all his people. 16 And Joab the son of Zeruiah *was* over the host; and Jehoshaphat the son of Ahilud *was* recorder; 17 And Zadok the son of Ahitub, and Ahimelech the son of Abiathar, *were* the priests; and Seraiah *was* the scribe; 18 And Benaiah the son of Jehoiada *was over* both the Cherethites and the Pelethites; and David's sons were chief rulers.

David was not so engaged in his wars abroad as to neglect the administration of the government at home.

I. His care extended itself to all the parts of his dominion: *He reigned over all Israel* (*v.* 15); not only he had a right to reign over all the tribes, but he did so; they were all safe under his protection, and shared in the fruits of his good government.

II. He did justice with an unbiassed unshaken hand: *He executed judgment unto all his people,* neither did wrong nor denied or delayed right to any. This intimates, 1. His industry and close application to business, his easiness of access and readiness to admit all addresses and appeals made to him. All his people, even the meanest, and those too of the meanest tribes, were welcome to his council-board. 2. His impartiality and the equity of his proceedings, in administering justice. He never perverted justice though favour or affection, nor had respect of persons in judgment. Herein he was a type of Christ, who was faithful and true, and who doth *in righteousness both judge and make war,* Rev. xix. 11. See Ps. lxxii. 1, 2.

III. He kept good order and good officers in his court. David being the first king that had an established government (for Saul's reign was short and unsettled) he had the modelling of the administration. In Saul's time we read of no other great officer than Abner, that was captain of the host. But David appointed more officers. Here are, 1. Two military officers: Joab that was general of the forces in the field, and Banaiah that was over the Cherethites and Pelethites, who were either the city train-bands *(archers and slingers,* so the Chaldee), or rather the life-guards, or standing force, that attended the king's person, the pretorian band, the militia. They were ready to do service at home, to assist in the administering of justice, and to preserve the public peace. We find them employed in proclaiming Solomon, 1 Kings i. 38. 2. Two ecclesiastical officers: *Zadok and Ahimelech were priests,* that is, they were most employed in the priests' work under Abiathar, the high priest. 3. Two civil officers: one that was recorder, or remembrancer, to put the king in mind of business in its season (he was prime minister of state, yet not entrusted with the custody of the king's conscience, as they say of our lord chancellor, but only of the king's memory; let the king be put in mind of business and he would do it himself); another that was scribe, or secretary of state, that drew up public orders and despatches, and recorded judgments given. 4. David's sons, as they grew up to be fit for business, were made chief rulers; they had places of honour and trust assigned them, in the household, or in the camp, or in the courts of justice, according as their genius led them. They were chief about the king (so it is explained, 1 Chron. xviii. 17), employed near him, that they might be under his eye. Our Lord Jesus has appointed officers in his kingdom, for his honour and the good of the community; when he ascended on high *he gave these gifts* (Eph. iv. 8—11), *to every man his work,* Mark xiii. 34. David made his sons chief rulers; but all believers, Christ's spiritual seed, are better preferred, for they are *made to our God kings and priests,* Rev. i. 6.

CHAP. IX.

The only thing recorded in this chapter is the kindness David showed to Jonathan's seed for his sake. I. The kind enquiry he made after the remains of the house of Saul, and his discovery of Mephibosheth, ver. 1—4. II. The kind reception he gave to Mephibosheth, when he was brought to him, ver. 5—8. III. The kind provision he made for him and his, ver. 9—13.

AND David said, Is there yet any that is left of the house of Saul, that I may show him kindness for Jonathan's sake? 2 And *there was* of the house of Saul a servant whose name *was* Ziba. And when they had called him unto David, the king said unto him, *Art* thou Ziba? And he said, Thy servant *is he.* 3 And the king said, Is there not yet any of the house of Saul, that I may show the kindness of God unto him? And Ziba said unto the king, Jonathan hath yet a son, *which is* lame on *his* feet. 4 And the king said unto him, Where *is* he? And Ziba said unto the king, Behold, he *is* in the house of Machir, the son of Ammiel, in Lodebar. 5 Then king David sent, and fetched him out of the house of Machir the son of Ammiel, from Lodebar. 6 Now when Mephibosheth, the son of Jonathan, the son of Saul, was come unto David, he fell on his face, and did reverence. And David said, Mephibosheth. And he answered, Behold thy servant! 7 And David said unto him, Fear not: for I will surely show thee kindness for Jonathan thy father's sake, and will restore thee all the land of Saul thy father; and thou shalt eat bread at my table continually. 8 And he bowed himself, and said, What *is* thy servant, that thou shouldest look upon such a dead dog as I *am?*

Here is, I. David's enquiry after the remains of the ruined house of Saul, *v.* 1. This was a great while after his accession to the throne, for it should seem that Mephibosheth, who was but five years old when Saul died, had now a son born, *v.* 12. David had too long forgotten his obligations to Jonathan, but now, at length, they are brought to his mind. It is good sometimes to bethink ourselves whether there be any promises or engagements that we have neglected to make good; better do it late than never. The compendium which Paul gives us of the life of David is this (Acts xiii. 36), that he *served his generation according to the will of God,* that is, he was a man that made it his business to do good; witness this instance, where we may observe,

1. That he sought an opportunity to do good. He might perhaps have satisfied his conscience with the performance of his promise to Jonathan if he had been only ready, upon request or application made to him by any of his seed, to help and succour them. But he does more, he enquires of those about him first (*v.* 1), and, when he met with a person that was likely to inform him, asked him particularly, *Is there any yet left of the house of Saul, that I may show him kindness? v.* 3. "Is there any, not only to whom I may do justice (Num. v. 8), but to whom I may show kindness?" Note, Good men should seek opportunities of doing good. *The liberal deviseth liberal things,* Isa. xxxii. 8. For, the most proper objects of our kindness and charity are such as will not be frequently met with without enquiry. The most necessitous are the least clamorous.

2. Those he enquired after were the remains of the house of Saul, to whom he would show kindness for Jonathan's sake: *Is there any left of the house of Saul?* Saul had a very numerous family (1 Chron. viii. 33), enough to replenish a country, and was yet so emptied that none of it appeared; but it was a matter of enquiry, *Is there any left?* See how the providence of God can empty full families; see how the sin of man will do it. Saul's was a bloody house, no marvel it was thus reduced, *ch.* xxi. 1. But, though God visited the iniquity of the father upon the children, David would not. "Is there any left that I can show kindness to, not for Saul's own sake, but for Jonathan's?" (1.) Saul was David's sworn enemy, and yet he would show kindness to his house with all his heart and was forward to do it. He does not say, "Is there any left of the house of Saul, that I may find some way to take them off, and prevent their giving disturbance to me or my successor?" It was against Abimelech's mind that any one was left of the house of Gideon (Judg. ix. 5), and against Athaliah's mind that any one was left of *the seed royal,* 2 Chron. xxii. 10, 11. Those were usurped governments. David's needed no such vile supports. He was desirous to show kindness to the house of Saul, not only because he trusted in God and feared not what they could do unto him, but because he was of a charitable disposition and forgave what they had done to him. Note, We must evince the sincerity of our forgiving those that have been any way unjust or injurious to us by being ready, as we have opportunity, to show kindness both to them and theirs. We must not only not avenge ourselves upon them, but we must love them, and *do them good* (Matt. v. 44), and not be backward to do any office of love and good-will to those that have done us many an injury. 1 Pet. iii. 9,—*but, contrariwise, blessing.* This is the way to overcome evil, and to find mercy for ourselves and ours, when we or they need it. (2.) Jonathan was David's sworn friend, and therefore he would show kindness to his house. This teaches us, [1.] To be mindful of our covenant. The kindness we have promised we must conscientiously perform, though it should not be claimed. God is faithful to us; let us not be unfaithful to one another. [2.] To be mindful of our friendships, our old friendships. Note, Kindness to our friends, even to them and theirs, is one of the laws of our holy religion. *He that has friends must show himself friendly,* Prov. xviii. 24. If Providence has raised us, and our friends and their families are brought low, yet we must not forget former acquaintance, but rather look upon that as giving us so much the fairer opportunity of being kind to them: then our friends have most need of us and we are in the best capacity to help them. Though there be not a solemn league of friendship tying us to this constancy of love, yet there is a sacred law of friendship no less obliging, that to him that is in misery pity should be shown by his friend, Job vi.

14. *A brother is born for adversity.* Friendship obliges us to take cognizance of the families and surviving relations of those we have loved, who, when they left us, left behind them their bodies, their names, and their posterity, to be kind to.

3. The kindness he promised to show them he calls the *kindness of God;* not only great kindness, but, (1.) Kindness in pursuance of the covenant that was between him and Jonathan, to which God was a witness. See 1 Sam. xx. 42. (2.) Kindness after God's example; for we must be merciful as he is. He spares those whom he has advantage against, and so must we. Jonathan's request to David was (1 Sam. xx. 14, 15), "*Show me the kindness of the Lord, that I die not,* and the same to my seed." The kindness of God is some greater instance of kindness than one can ordinarily expect from men. (3.) It is kindness done after a godly sort, and with an eye to God, and his honour and favour.

II. Information given him concerning Mephibosheth, the son of Jonathan. Ziba was an old retainer to Saul's family, and knew the state of it. He was sent for and examined, and informed the king that Jonathan's son was living, but *lame* (how he came to be so we read before, *ch.* iv. 4), and that he lived in obscurity, probably among his mother's relations in Lo-debar, in Gilead, on the other side Jordan, where he was *forgotten, as a dead man out of mind,* but bore this obscurity the more easily because he could remember little of the honour he fell from.

III. The bringing of him to court. The king sent (Ziba, it is likely) to bring him up to Jerusalem with all convenient speed, *v.* 5. Thus he eased Machir of his trouble, and perhaps recompensed him for what he had laid out on Mephibosheth's account. This Machir appears to have been a very generous free-hearted man, and to have entertained Mephibosheth, not out of any disaffection to David or his government, but in compassion to the reduced son of a prince, for afterwards we find him kind to David himself when he fled from Absalom. He is named (*ch.* xvii. 27) among those that furnished the king with what he wanted at Mahanaim, though David, when he sent for Mephibosheth from him, little thought that the time would come when he himself would gladly be beholden to him: and perhaps Machir was then the more ready to help David in recompence for his kindness to Mephibosheth. Therefore we should be forward to give, because we know not but we ourselves may some time be in want, Eccl. xi. 2. *And he that watereth shall be watered also himself,* Prov. xi. 25. Now,

1. Mephibosheth presented himself to David with all the respect that was due to his character. Lame as he was, *he fell on his face, and did homage, v.* 6. David had thus made his honours to Mephibosheth's father, Jonathan, when he was next to the throne (1 Sam. xx. 41, *he bowed himself to him three times),* and now Mephibosheth, in like manner, addresses him, when affairs are so completely reversed. Those who, when they are in inferior relations, show respect, shall, when they come to be advanced, have respect shown to them.

2. David received him with all the kindness that could be. (1.) He spoke to him as one surprised, but pleased to see him. "Mephibosheth! Why, is there such a man living?" He remembered his name, for it is probable that he was born about the time of the intimacy between him and Jonathan. (2.) He bade him not be afraid: *Fear not, v.* 7. It is probable that the sight of David put him into some confusion, to free him from which he assures him that he sent for him, not out of any jealousy he had of him, nor with any bad design upon him, but to show him kindness. Great men should not take a pleasure in the timorous approaches of their inferiors (for the great God does not), but should encourage them. (3.) He gives him, by grant from the crown, *all the land of Saul his father,* that is, his paternal estate, which was forfeited by Ishbosheth's rebellion and added to his own revenue. This was a real favour, and more than giving him a kind word. True friendship will be generous. (4.) Though he had thus given him a good estate, sufficient to maintain him, yet for Jonathan's sake (whom perhaps he saw some resemblance of in Mephibosheth's face), he will take him to be a constant guest at his own table, where he will not only be comfortably fed, but have company and attendance suitable to his birth and quality. Though Mephibosheth was lame and unsightly, and does not appear to have had any great fitness for business, yet, for his good father's sake, David took him to be one of his family.

3. Mephibosheth accepts this kindness with great humility and self-abasement. He was not one of those that take every favour as a debt, and think every thing too little that their friends do for them; but, on the contrary, speaks as one amazed at the grants David made him (*v.* 8): *What is thy servant, that thou shouldst look upon such a dead dog as I am?* How does he vilify himself! Though the son of a prince, and the grandson of a king, yet his family being under guilt and wrath, and himself poor and lame, he calls himself *a dead dog* before David. Note, It is good to have the heart humble under humbling providences. If, when divine Providence brings our condition down, divine grace brings our spirits down with it, we shall be easy. And those who thus humble themselves shall be exalted. How does he magnify David's kindness! It would have been easy to lessen it if he had been so disposed. Had David restored him his father's estate? It was but giving him his own. Did he take him to his table? This was policy, that he might have an eye upon him. But Mephibosheth considered all that

David said and did as very kind, and himself as less than the least of all his favours. See 1 Sam. xviii. 18.

9 Then the king called to Ziba, Saul's servant, and said unto him, I have given unto thy master's son all that pertained to Saul and to all his house. 10 Thou therefore, and thy sons, and thy servants, shall till the land for him, and thou shalt bring in *the fruits*, that thy master's son may have food to eat: but Mephibosheth thy master's son shall eat bread alway at my table. Now Ziba had fifteen sons and twenty servants. 11 Then said Ziba unto the king, According to all that my lord the king hath commanded his servant, so shall thy servant do. As for Mephibosheth, *said the king*, he shall eat at my table, as one of the king's sons. 12 And Mephibosheth had a young son, whose name *was* Micha. And all that dwelt in the house of Ziba *were* servants unto Mephibosheth. 13 So Mephibosheth dwelt in Jerusalem: for he did eat continually at the king's table: and was lame on both his feet.

The matter is here settled concerning Mephibosheth. 1. This grant of his father's estate is confirmed to him, and Ziba called to be a witness to it (*v.* 9); and, it should seem, Saul had a very good estate, for his father was a mighty man of substance (1 Sam. ix. 1), and he had fields and vineyards to bestow, 1 Sam. xxii. 7. Be it ever so much, Mephibosheth is now master of it all. 2. The management of the estate is committed to Ziba, who knew what it was and how to make the most of it, in whom, having been his father's servant, he might confide, and who, having a numerous family of sons and servants, had hands sufficient to be employed about it, *v.* 10. Thus Mephibosheth is made very easy, having a good estate without care, and is in a fair way of being very rich, having much coming in and little occasion to spend, himself being kept at David's table. Yet he must have food to eat besides his own bread, provisions for his son and servants; and Ziba's sons and servants would come in for their share of his revenue, for which reason perhaps their number is here mentioned, *fifteen sons and twenty servants*, who would require nearly all there was; *for as goods are increased those are increased that eat them, and what good has the owner thereof save the beholding of them with his eyes?* Eccl. v. 11. *All that dwelt in the house of Ziba were servants to Mephibosheth* (*v.* 12), that is, they all lived upon him, and made a prey of his estate, under pretence of waiting on him and doing him service. The Jews have a saying, "He that multiplies servants multiplies thieves." Ziba is now pleased, for he loves wealth, and will have abundance. "As *the king has commanded, so will thy servant do, v.* 11. Let me alone with the estate: and *as for Mephibosheth*" (they seem to be Ziba's words), "if the king please, he need not trouble the court, *he shall eat at my table*, and be as well treated *as one of the king's sons.*" But David will have him at his own table, and Mephibosheth is as well pleased with his post as Ziba with his. How unfaithful Ziba was to him we shall find afterwards, *ch.* xvi. 3. Now because David was a type of Christ, his Lord and son, his root and offspring, let his kindness to Mephibosheth serve to illustrate the kindness and love of God our Saviour towards fallen man, which yet he was under no obligation to, as David was to Jonathan. Man was convicted of rebellion against God, and, like Saul's house, under a sentence of rejection from him, was not only brought low and impoverished, but lame and impotent, made so by the fall. The Son of God enquires after this degenerate race, that enquired not after him, comes to seek and save them. To those of them that humble themselves before him, and commit themselves to him, he restores the forfeited inheritance, he entitles them to a better paradise than that which Adam lost, and takes them into communion with himself, sets them with his children at his table, and feasts them with the dainties of heaven. *Lord, what is man, that thou shouldst thus magnify him!*

CHAP. X.

This chapter gives us an account of a war David had with the Ammonites and the Syrians their allies, with the occasion and success of it. I. David sent a friendly embassy to Hanun king of the Ammonites, ver. 1, 2. He, upon a base surmise that it was ill intended, abused David's ambassadors, ver. 3, 4. III. David resenting it (ver. 5), the Ammonites prepared for war against him, ver. 6. IV. David carried the war into their country, sent against them Joab and Abishai, who addressed themselves to the battle with a great deal of conduct and bravery, ver. 7--12. V. The Ammonites, and the Syrians their allies, were totally routed, ver. 13, 14. VI. The forces of the Syrians, which rallied again, were a second time defeated, ver. 15—19. Thus did David advance his own reputation for gratitude, in returning kindness, and for justice, in repaying injuries.

AND it came to pass after this, that the king of the children of Ammon died, and Hanun his son reigned in his stead. 2 Then said David, I will show kindness unto Hanun the son of Nahash, as his father showed kindness unto me. And David sent to comfort him by the hand of his servants for his father. And David's servants came into the land of the children of Ammon. 3 And the princes of the children of Ammon said unto Hanun their lord, Thinkest thou that David doth honour thy father, that he hath sent comforters unto thee? hath not David *rather* sent his servants unto thee, to search the city, and to spy it out, and to overthrow it? 4 Wherefore Hanun took David's servants, and shaved off the one half of their beards, and cut off their garments in the middle, *even* to their buttocks, and sent them away. 5 When they told *it* unto David, he sent to meet them, because the men were greatly ashamed: and the king said, Tarry at Jericho until your beards be grown, and *then* return.

Here is, I. The great respect David paid to his neighbour, the king of the Ammonites, *v.* 1, 2. 1. The inducement to it was some kindness he had formerly received from Nahash the deceased king. He *showed kindness to me*, says David (*v.* 2), and therefore (having lately had satisfaction in showing kindness to Mephibosheth for his father's sake) he resolves to show kindness to his son, and to keep up a friendly correspondence with him. Thus the pleasure of doing one kind and generous action should excite us to another. Nahash had been an enemy to Israel, a cruel enemy (1 Sam. xi. 2), and yet had shown kindness to David, perhaps only in contradiction to Saul, who was unkind to him: however, if David receives kindness, he is not nice in examining the grounds and principles of it, but resolvess gratefully to return it. If a Pharisee give alms in pride, though God will not reward him, yet he that receives the alms ought to return thanks for it. God knows the heart, but we do not. 2. The particular instance of respect was sending an embassy to condole with him on his father's death, as is common among princes in alliance with each other: *David sent to comfort him.* Note, It is a comfort to children, when their parents are dead, to find that their parents' friends are theirs, and that they intend to keep up an acquaintance with them. It is a comfort to mourners to find that there are those who mourn with them, are sensible of their loss and share with them in it. It is a comfort to those who are honouring the memory of their deceased relations to find there are others who likewise honour it and who had a value for those whom they valued.

II. The great affront which Hanun the king of the Ammonites put upon David in his ambassadors. 1. He hearkened to the spiteful suggestions of his princes, who insinuated that David's ambassadors, under pretence of being comforters, were sent as spies, *v.* 3. False men are ready to think others as false as themselves; and those that bear ill-will to their neighbours are resolved not to believe that their neighbours bear any good-will to them. They would not thus have imagined that David dissembled but that they were conscious to themselves that they could have dissembled, to serve a turn. Unfounded suspicion argues a wicked mind. Bishop Patrick's note on this is that "there is nothing so well meant but it may be ill interpreted, and is wont to be so by men who love nobody but themselves." Men of the greatest honour and virtue must not think it strange if they be thus misrepresented. *Charity thinketh no evil.* 2. Entertaining this vile suggestion, he basely abused David's ambassadors, like a man of a sordid villanous spirit, that was fitter to rake a kennel than to wear a crown. If he had any reason to suspect that David's messengers came on a bad design, he would have done prudently enough to be upon the reserve with them, and to dismiss them as soon as he could; but it is plain he only sought an occasion to put the utmost disgrace he could upon them, out of an antipathy to their king and their country. They were themselves men of honour, and much more so as they represented the prince that sent them; they and their reputation were under the special protection of the law of nations; they put a confidence in the Ammonites, and came among them unarmed; yet Hanun used them like rogues and vagabonds, and worse, *shaved off the one half of their beards, and cut off their garments in the midst*, to expose them to the contempt and ridicule of his servants, that they might make sport with them, and that these men might seem vile.

III. David's tender concern for his servants that were thus abused. He sent to meet them, and to let them know how much he interested himself in their quarrel and how soon he would avenge it, and directed them to stay at Jericho, a private place, where they would not have occasion to come into company, till that half of their beards which was shaved off had grown to such a length that the other half might be decently cut to it, *v.* 5. The Jews wore their beards long, reckoning it an honour to appear aged and grave; and therefore it was not fit that persons of their rank and figure should appear at court unlike their neighbours. Change of raiment, it is likely, they had with them, to put on, instead of that which was cut off; but the loss of their beards would not be so soon repaired; yet in time these would grow again, and all would be well. Let us learn not to lay too much to heart unjust reproaches; after awhile they will wear off of themselves, and turn only to the shame of their authors, while the injured reputation in a little time grows again, as these beards did. God will *bring forth thy righteousness as the light*, therefore *wait patiently for him*, Ps. xxxvii. 6, 7.

Some have thought that David, in the indignity he received from the king of Ammon, was but well enough served for courting and complimenting that pagan prince, whom he knew to be an inveterate enemy to Israel, and might now remember how, when he would have put out the right eyes of the men of Jabesh-Gilead, he designed that, as he did this, for a *reproach upon all Israel,* 1 Sam. xi. 2. What better usage could he expect from such a spiteful family and people? Why should he covet the friendship of a people whom Israel must have so little to do with as that an Ammonite might not *enter into the congregation of the Lord, even to the tenth generation?* Deut. xxiii. 3.

6 And when the children of Ammon saw that they stank before David, the children of Ammon sent and hired the Syrians of Beth-rehob, and the Syrians of Zoba, twenty thousand footmen, and of king Maacah a thousand men, and of Ish-tob twelve thousand men. 7 And when David heard of *it*, he sent Joab, and all the host of the mighty men. 8 And the children of Ammon came out, and put the battle in array at the entering in of the gate: and the Syrians of Zoba, and of Rehob, and Ish-tob, and Maacah, *were* by themselves in the field. 9 When Joab saw that the front of the battle was against him before and behind, he chose of all the choice *men* of Israel, and put *them* in array against the Syrians: 10 And the rest of the people he delivered into the hand of Abishai his brother, that he might put *them* in array against the children of Ammon. 11 And he said, If the Syrians be too strong for me, then thou shalt help me: but if the children of Ammon be too strong for thee, then I will come and help thee. 12 Be of good courage, and let us play the men for our people, and for the cities of our God: and the LORD do that which seemeth him good. 13 And Joab drew nigh, and the people that *were* with him, unto the battle against the Syrians: and they fled before him. 14 And when the children of Ammon saw that the Syrians were fled, then fled they also before Abishai, and entered into the city. So Joab returned from the children of Ammon, and came to Jerusalem.

Here we have, I. The preparation which the Ammonites made for war, *v.* 6. They saw they had made themselves very odious to David and obnoxious to his just displeasure. This they might easily have foreseen when they abused his ambassadors, which was no other than a challenge to war, and a bold defiance of him. Yet, it seems, they had not considered how unable they were, with their thousands, to meet his; for now they found themselves an unequal match, and were forced to hire forces of other nations into their service. Thus sinners daringly provoke God, and expose themselves to his wrath, and never consider that he is *stronger than they,* 1 Cor. x. 22. The Ammonites gave the affront first, and they were the first that raised forces to justify it. Had they humbled themselves, and begged David's pardon, probably an honorary satisfaction might have atoned for the offence. But, when they were thus desperately resolved to stand by what they had done, they courted their own ruin.

II. The speedy descent which David's forces made upon them, *v.* 7. When David heard of their military preparations, he sent Joab with a great army to attack them, *v.* 7. Those that are at war with the Son of David not only give the provocation, but begin the war; for he *waits to be gracious,* but they *strengthen themselves against him,* and therefore, *if they turn not, he will whet his sword,* Ps. vii. 12. God has forces to send against those that set his wrath at defiance (Isa. v. 19), which will convince them, when it is too late, that *none ever hardened his heart against God and prospered.* It was David's prudence to carry the war into their country, and fight them at the entering in of the gate of their capital city, *Rabbah,* as some think, or *Medeba,* a city in their borders, before which they pitched to guard their coast, 1 Chron. xix. 7. Such are the terrors and desolations of war that every good prince will, in love to his people, keep it as much as may be at a distance from them.

III. Preparations made on both sides for an engagement. 1. The enemy disposed themselves into two bodies, one of Ammonites, which, being their own, were posted at the gate of the city; the other of Syrians, whom they had taken into their pay, and who were therefore posted at a distance in the field, to charge the forces of Israel in the flank or rear, while the Ammonites charged them in the front, *v.* 8. 2. Joab, like a wise general, was soon aware of the design, and accordingly divided his forces: the choicest men he took under his own command, to fight the Syrians, whom probably he knew to be the better soldiers, and, being hired men, better versed in the arts of war, *v.* 9. The rest of the forces he put under the command of Abishai his brother, to engage the Ammonites, *v.* 10. It should seem, Joab found the enemy so well prepared to receive them that his conduct and courage were never so tried as now.

IV. Joab's speech before the battle, *v.* 11. 12. It is not long, but pertinent, and brave. 1. He prudently concerts the matter with Abishai his brother, that the dividing of the forces might not be the weakening of them, but that, which part soever was borne hard upon, the other should come in to its assistance. He supposes the worst, that one of them should be obliged to give back; and in that case, upon a signal given, the other should send a detachment to relieve it. Note, Mutual helpfulness is brotherly duty. If occasion be, *thou shalt help me, and I will help thee.* Christ's soldiers should thus strengthen one another's hands in their spiritual warfare. The strong must succour and help the weak. Those that through grace are conquerors over temptation must counsel, and comfort, and pray for, those that are tempted. *When thou art converted, strengthen thy brethren,* Luke xxii. 32. The members of the natural body help one another, 1 Cor. xii. 21. 2. He bravely encourages himself, and his brother, and the rest of the officers and soldiers, to do their utmost. Great dangers put an edge upon true courage. When Joab saw the front of the battle was against him, both before and behind, instead of giving orders to make an honourable retreat, he animated his men to charge so much more furiously: *Be of good courage and let us play the men,* not for pay and preferment, for honour and fame, but *for our people, and for the cities of our God,* for the public safety and welfare, in which the glory of God is so much interested. *God and our country* was the word. "Let us be valiant, from a principle of love to Israel, that are our people, descended from the same stock, for whom we are employed, and in whose peace we shall have peace; and from a principle of love to God, for they are his cities that we are fighting in the defence of." The relation which any person or thing stands in to God should endear it to us, and engage us to do our utmost in its service. 3. He piously leaves the issue with God: "When we have done our part, according to the duty of our place, *let the Lord do that which seemeth to him good.*" Let nothing be wanting in us, whatever the success be; let God's work be done by us, and then God's will be done concerning us. When we make conscience of doing our duty we may, with the greatest satisfaction, leave the event with God, not thinking that our valour binds him to prosper us, but that still he may do as he pleases, yet hoping for his salvation in his own way and time.

V. The victory Joab obtained over the confederate forces of Syria and Ammon, *v.* 13, 14. He provided for the worst, and put the case that the Syrians and Ammonites might prove too strong for him (*v.* 11), but he proved too strong for them both. We do not hinder our success by preparing for disappointment. The Syrians were first routed by Joab, and then the Ammonites by Abishai; the Ammonites seem not to have fought at all, but, upon the retreat of the Syrians, to have fled into the city. It is a temptation to soldiers to fly when they have a city at their backs to fly to. It is one thing when men may either fight or fly and another thing when they must either fight or die.

15 And when the Syrians saw that they were smitten before Israel, they gathered themselves together. 16 And Hadarezer sent, and brought out the Syrians that *were* beyond the river: and they came to Helam; and Shobach the captain of the host of Hadarezer *went* before them. 17 And when it was told David, he gathered all Israel together, and passed over Jordan, and came to Helam. And the Syrians set themselves in array against David, and fought with him. 18 And the Syrians fled before Israel; and David slew *the men of* seven hundred chariots of the Syrians, and forty thousand horsemen, and smote Shobach the captain of their host, who died there. 19 And when all the kings *that were* servants to Hadarezer saw that they were smitten before Israel, they made peace with Israel, and served them. So the Syrians feared to help the children of Ammon any more.

Here is, 1. A new attempt of the Syrians to recover their lost honour and to check the progress of David's victorious arms. The forces that were lately dispersed rallied again, and *gathered themselves together, v.* 15. Even the baffled cause will make head as long as there is any life in it; the enemies of the Son of David do so, Matt. xxii. 34; Rev. xix. 19. These, being conscious of their insufficiency, called in the aid of their allies and dependencies on the other side of *the river* (*v.* 16), and, being thus recruited, they hoped to make their part good against Israel, but *they knew not the thoughts of the Lord, for he gathered them as sheaves into the floor;* see Mic. iv. 11—13. 2. The defeat of this attempt by the vigilance and valour of David, who, upon notice of their design, resolved not to stay till they attacked him, but went in person at the head of his army over Jordan (*v.* 17), and, in a pitched battle, routed the Syrians (*v.* 18), slew 7000 men, who belonged to 700 chariots, and 40,000 other soldiers, horse and foot, as appears by comparing 1 Chron. xix. 18. Their general was killed in the battle, and David came home in triumph, no doubt. 3. The consequence of this victory over the Syrians.

(1.) David gained several tributaries, *v.* 19. *The kings*, or petty princes, that had been subject to Hadarezer, when they saw how powerful David was, very wisely *made peace with Israel*, whom they found they could not make war with, *and served them*, since they were able to give them protection. Thus the promise made to Abraham (Gen. xv. 18), and repeated to Joshua (*ch.* i. 4), that the borders of Israel should extend to the river Euphrates, was performed, at length. (2.) The Ammonites lost their old allies: *The Syrians feared to help the children of Ammon*, not because they had an unrighteous cause (justifying a crime which was a breach of the law of nations), but because they found it was an unsuccessful cause. It is dangerous helping those that have God against them; for, when they fall, their helpers will fall with them.

Jesus Christ, the Son of David, sent his ambassadors, his apostles and ministers, after all his servants the prophets, to the Jewish church and nation; but they treated them shamefully, as Hanun did David's ambassadors, mocked them, abused them, slew them; and it was this that filled the measure of their iniquity, and brought upon them ruin without remedy (Matt. xxi. 35, 41; xxii. 7; compare 2 Chron. xxvi. 16); for Christ takes the affronts and injuries done to his ministers as done to himself and will avenge them accordingly.

CHAP. XI.

What David said of the mournful report of Saul's death may more fitly be applied to the sad story of this chapter, the adultery and murder David was guilty of.—"Tell it not in Gath, publish it not in the streets of Ashkelon." We wish we could draw a veil over it, and that it might never be known, might never be said, that David did such things as are here recorded of him. But it cannot, it must not, be concealed. The scripture is faithful in relating the faults even of those whom it most applauds, which is an instance of the sincerity of the penmen, and an evidence that it was not written to serve any party: and even such stories as these "were written for our learning," that "he that thinks he stands may take heed lest he fall," and that others' harms may be our warnings. Many, no doubt, have been emboldened to sin, and hardened in it, by this story, and to them it is a "savour of death unto death;" but many have by it been awakened to a holy jealousy over themselves, and constant watchfulness against sin, and to them it is a "savour of life unto life." Those are very great sins, and greatly aggravated, which here we find David guilty of. I. He committed adultery with Bath-sheba, the wife of Uriah, ver. 1—5. II. He endeavoured to father the spurious brood upon Uriah, ver. 6—13. III. When that project failed, he plotted the death of Uriah by the sword of the children of Ammon, and effected it, ver. 14—25. IV. He married Bath-sheba, ver. 26, 27. Is this David? Is this the man after God's own heart? How is his behaviour changed, worse than it was before Ahimelech! How has this gold become dim! Let him that readeth understand what the best of men are when God leaves them to themselves.

AND it came to pass, after the year was expired, at the time when kings go forth *to battle*, that David sent Joab, and his servants with him, and all Israel; and they destroyed the children of Ammon, and besieged Rabbah. But David tarried still at Jerusalem. 2 And it came to pass in an eveningtide, that David arose from off his bed, and walked upon the roof of the king's house: and from the roof he saw a woman washing herself; and the woman *was* very beautiful to look upon. 3 And David sent and enquired after the woman. And *one* said, *Is* not this Bath-sheba, the daughter of Eliam, the wife of Uriah the Hittite? 4 And David sent messengers, and took her; and she came in unto him, and he lay with her; for she was purified from her uncleanness; and she returned unto her house. 5 And the woman conceived, and sent and told David, and said, I *am* with child.

Here is, I. David's glory, in pursuing the war against the Ammonites, *v.* 1. We cannot take that pleasure in viewing this great action which hitherto we have taken in observing David's achievements, because the beauty of it was stained and sullied by sin; otherwise we might take notice of David's wisdom and bravery in following his blow. Having routed the army of the Ammonites in the field, as soon as ever the season of the year permitted he sent more forces to waste the country and further to avenge the quarrel of his ambassadors. Rabbah, their metropolis, made a stand, and held out a great while. To this city Joab laid close siege, and it was at the time of this siege that David fell into this sin.

II. David's shame, in being himself conquered, and led captive by his own lust. The sin he was guilty of was adultery, against the letter of the seventh commandment, and (in the judgment of the patriarchal age) a heinous crime, and *an iniquity to be punished by the judges* (Job xxxi. 11), a sin which *takes away the heart*, and *gets a man a wound and dishonour*, more than any other, and the *reproach of which is not wiped away*.

1. Observe the occasions which led to this sin. (1.) Neglect of his business. When he should have been abroad with his army in the field, fighting the battles of the Lord, he devolved the care upon others, and he himself *tarried still at Jerusalem*, *v.* 1. To the war with the Syrians David went in person, *ch.* x. 17. Had he been now at his post at the head of his forces, he would have been out of the way of this temptation. When we are out of the way of our duty we are in the way of temptation. (2.) Love of ease, and the indulgence of a slothful temper: *He came off his bed at evening-tide*, *v.* 2. There he had dozed away the afternoon in idleness, which he should have spent in some exercise for his own improvement or the good of others He used to pray, not only morning and evening, but at noon, in the day of his trouble: it is to be feared he had, this noon, omitted to do so. Idleness gives great advantage to the tempter. Standing waters gather filth. The bed of sloth often proves the bed of lust. (3.) A wandering eye: *He*

saw a woman washing herself, probably from some ceremonial pollution, according to the law. The sin came in at the eye, as Eve's did. Perhaps he sought to see her, at least he did not practise according to his own prayer, *Turn away my eyes from beholding vanity,* and his son's caution in a like case, *Look not thou on the wine when it is red.* Either he had not, like Job, *made a covenant with his eyes,* or, at this time, he had forgotten it.

2. The steps of the sin. When he saw her, lust immediately conceived, and, (1.) He enquired who she was (*v.* 3), perhaps intending only, if she were unmarried, to take her to wife, as he had taken several; but, if she were a wife, having no design upon her. (2.) The corrupt desire growing more violent, though he was told she was a wife, and whose wife she was, yet he sent messengers for her, and then, it may be, intended only to please himself with her company and conversation. But, (3.) When she came *he lay with her,* she too easily consenting, because he was a great man, and famed for his goodness too. Surely (thinks she) that can be no sin which such a man as David is the mover of. See how the way of sin is down-hill; when men begin to do evil they cannot soon stop themselves. *The beginning* of lust, as *of strife, is like the letting forth of water;* it is therefore wisdom to leave it off before it be meddled with. The foolish fly fires her wings, and fools away her life at last, by playing about the candle.

3. The aggravations of the sin. (1.) He was now in years, fifty at least, some think more, when those lusts which are more properly youthful, one would think, should not have been violent in him. (2.) He had many wives and concubines of his own; this is insisted on, *ch.* xii. 8. (3.) Uriah, whom he wronged, was one of his own worthies, a person of honour and virtue, one that was now abroad in his service, hazarding his life in the high places of the field for the honour and safety of him and his kingdom, where he himself should have been. (4.) Bath-sheba, whom he debauched, was a lady of good reputation, and, till she was drawn by him and his influence into this wickedness, had no doubt preserved her purity. Little did she think that ever she could have done so bad a thing as to *forsake the guide of her youth, and forget the covenant of her God;* nor perhaps could any one in the world but David have prevailed against her. The adulterer not only wrongs and ruins his own soul, but, as much as he can, another's soul too. (5.) David was a king, whom God had entrusted with the sword of justice and the execution of the law upon other criminals, particularly upon adulterers, who were, by the law, to be put to death; for him therefore to be guilty of those crimes himself was to make himself a pattern, when he should have been a terror, to evil doers. With what face could he rebuke or punish that in others which he was conscious to himself of being guilty of? See Rom. ii. 22. Much more might be said to aggravate the sin; and I can think but of one excuse for it, which is that it was done but once; it was far from being his practice; it was by the surprise of a temptation that he was drawn into it. He was not one of those of whom the prophet complains that *they were as fed horses, neighing every one after his neighbour's wife* (Jer. v. 8); but this once God left him to himself, as he did Hezekiah, *that he might know what was in his heart,* 2 Chron. xxxii. 31. Had he been told of it before, he would have said, as Hazael, *What! is thy servant a dog?* But by this instance we are taught what need we have to pray every day, *Father, in heaven, lead us not into temptation,* and to watch, that we enter not into it.

6 And David sent to Joab, *saying,* Send me Uriah the Hittite. And Joab sent Uriah to David. 7 And when Uriah was come unto him, David demanded *of him* how Joab did, and how the people did, and how the war prospered. 8 And David said to Uriah, Go down to thy house, and wash thy feet. And Uriah departed out of the king's house, and there followed him a mess *of meat* from the king. 9 But Uriah slept at the door of the king's house with all the servants of his lord, and went not down to his house. 10 And when they had told David, saying, Uriah went not down unto his house, David said unto Uriah, Camest thou not from *thy* journey? why *then* didst thou not go down unto thine house? 11 And Uriah said unto David, The ark, and Israel, and Judah, abide in tents; and my lord Joab, and the servants of my lord, are encamped in the open fields; shall I then go into mine house, to eat and to drink, and to lie with my wife? *as* thou livest, and *as* thy soul liveth, I will not do this thing. 12 And David said to Uriah, Tarry here to day also, and to morrow I will let thee depart. So Uriah abode in Jerusalem that day, and the morrow. 13 And when David had called him, he did eat and drink before him; and he made him drunk: and at even he went out to lie on his bed with the servants of his lord, but went not down to his house.

Uriah, we may suppose, had now been absent from his wife some weeks, making the campaign in the country of the Ammonites, and not intending to return till the end of it. The situation of his wife would *bring to light the hidden works of darkness;* and when Uriah, at his return, should find how he had been abused, and by whom, it might well be expected, 1. That he would prosecute his wife, according to law, and have her stoned to death; for *jealousy is the rage of a man*, especially a man of honour, and he that is thus injured *will not spare in the day of vengeance*, Prov. vi. 34. This Bath-sheba was apprehensive of when she sent to let David know she was with child, intimating that he was concerned to protect her, and, it is likely, if he had not promised her so to do (so wretchedly abusing his royal power), she would not have consented to him. Hope of impunity is a great encouragement to iniquity. 2. It might also be expected that since he could not prosecute David by law for an offence of this nature he would take his revenge another way, and raise a rebellion against him. There have been instances of kings who by provocations of this nature, given to some of their powerful subjects, have lost their crowns. To prevent this double mischief, David endeavours to father the child which should be born upon Uriah himself, and therefore sends for him home to stay a night or two with his wife. Observe,

I. How the plot was laid. Uriah must come home from the army under pretence of bringing David an account *how the war prospered*, and how they went on with the siege of Rabbah, *v.* 7. Thus does he pretend a more than ordinary concern for his army when that was the least thing in his thoughts; if he had not had another turn to serve, an express of much less figure than Uriah might have sufficed to bring him a report of the state of the war. David, having had as much conference with Uriah as he thought requisite to cover the design, sent him to his house, and, that he might be the more pleasant there with the wife of his youth, sent a dish of meat after him for their supper, *v.* 8. When that project failed the first night, and Uriah, being weary of his journey and more desirous of sleep than meat, lay all night in the guard-chamber, the next night *he made him drunk* (*v.* 13), or made him merry, tempted him to drink more than was fit, that he might forget his vow (*v* 11), and might be disposed to go home to his own bed, to which perhaps, if David could have made him dead drunk, he would have ordered him to be carried. It is a very wicked thing, upon any design whatsoever, to make a person drunk. *Woe to him* that does so, Hab. ii. 15, 16. God will put a cup of trembling into the hands of those who put into the hands of others the cup of drunkenness. Robbing a man of his reason is worse than robbing him of his money, and drawing him into sin worse than drawing him into any trouble whatsoever. Every good man, especially every magistrate, should endeavour to prevent this sin, by admonishing, restraining, and denying the glass to those whom they see falling into excess; but to further it is to do the devil's work, to officiate as factor for him.

II. How this plot was defeated by Uriah's firm resolution not to lie in his own bed. Both nights he slept with the life-guard, and *went not down to his house*, though, it is probable, his wife pressed him to do it as much as David, *v.* 9, 12. Now, 1. Some think he suspected what was done, being informed of his wife's attendance at court, and therefore he would not go near her. But, if he had had any suspicion of that kind, surely he would have opened the letter that David sent by him to Joab. 2. Whether he suspected any thing or no, Providence put this resolution into his heart, and kept him to it, for the discovering of David's sin, and that the baffling of his design to conceal it might awaken David's conscience to confess it and repent of it. 3. The reason he gave to David for this strange instance of self-denial and mortification was very noble, *v.* 11. While the army was encamped in the field, he would not lie at ease in his own house. "The ark is in a tent," whether at home, in the tent David had pitched for it, or abroad, with Joab in the camp, is not certain. "Joab, and all the mighty men of Israel, lie hard and uneasy, and much exposed to the weather and to the enemy; and shall I go and take my ease and pleasure at my own house?" No, he protests he will not do it. Now, (1.) This was in itself a generous resolution, and showed Uriah to be a man of a public spirit, bold and hardy, and mortified to the delights of sense. In times of public difficulty and danger it does not become us to repose ourselves in security, or roll ourselves in pleasure, or, with the king and Haman, to sit down to drink when the *city Shushan was perplexed*, Esth. iii. 15. We should voluntarily endure hardness when the church of God is constrained to endure it. (2.) It might have been of use to awaken David's conscience, and make his heart to smite him for what he had done. [1.] That he had basely abused so brave a man as Uriah was, a man so heartily concerned for him and his kingdom, and that acted for him and it with so much vigour. [2.] That he was himself so unlike him. The consideration of the public hardships and hazards kept Uriah from lawful pleasures, yet could not keep David, though more nearly interested, from unlawful ones. Uriah's severity to himself should have shamed David for his indulgence of himself. The law was, *When the host goeth forth against the enemy then*, in a special manner, *keep thyself from every wicked thing*, Deut. xxiii. 9. Uriah outdid that law, but David violated it.

14 And it came to pass in the morning, that David wrote a letter to Joab, and sent *it* by the hand of Uriah. 15 And he wrote in the letter, saying, Set ye Uriah in the forefront of the hottest battle, and retire ye from him, that he may be smitten, and die. 16 And it came to pass, when Joab observed the city, that he assigned Uriah unto a place where he knew that valiant men *were*. 17 And the men of the city went out, and fought with Joab: and there fell *some* of the people of the servants of David; and Uriah the Hittite died also. 18 Then Joab sent and told David all the things concerning the war; 19 And charged the messenger, saying, When thou hast made an end of telling the matters of the war unto the king, 20 And if so be that the king's wrath arise, and he say unto thee, Wherefore approached ye so nigh unto the city when ye did fight? knew ye not that they would shoot from the wall? 21 Who smote Abimelech the son of Jerubbesheth? did not a woman cast a piece of a millstone upon him from the wall, that he died in Thebez? why went ye nigh the wall? then say thou, Thy servant Uriah the Hittite is dead also. 22 So the messenger went, and came and showed David all that Joab had sent him for. 23 And the messenger said unto David, Surely the men prevailed against us, and came out unto us into the field, and we were upon them even unto the entering of the gate. 24 And the shooters shot from off the wall upon thy servants; and *some* of the king's servants be dead, and thy servant Uriah the Hittite is dead also. 25 Then David said unto the messenger, Thus shalt thou say unto Joab, Let not this thing displease thee, for the sword devoureth one as well as another: make thy battle more strong against the city, and overthrow it: and encourage thou him. 26 And when the wife of Uriah heard that Uriah her husband was dead, she mourned for her husband. 27 And when the mourning was past, David sent and fetched her to his house, and she became his wife, and bare him a son. But the thing that David had done displeased the LORD.

When David's project of fathering the child upon Uriah himself failed, so that, in process of time, Uriah would certainly know the wrong that had been done him, to prevent the fruits of his revenge, the devil put it into David's heart to take him off, and then neither he nor Bath-sheba would be in any danger (what prosecution could there be when there was no prosecutor?), suggesting further that, when Uriah was out of the way, Bath-sheba might, if he pleased, be his own for ever. Adulteries have often occasioned murders, and one wickedness must be covered and secured with another. The beginnings of sin are therefore to be dreaded; for who knows where they will end? It is resolved in David's breast (which one would think could never possibly have harboured so vile a thought) that Uriah must die. That innocent, valiant, gallant man, who was ready to die for his prince's honour, must die by his prince's hand. David has sinned, and Bath-sheba has sinned, and both against him, and therefore he must die; David determines he must. Is this the man whose heart smote him because he had cut off Saul's skirt? *Quantum mutatus ab illo!—But ah, how changed!* Is this he that executed judgment and justice to all his people? How can he now do so unjust a thing? See how fleshly lusts war against the soul, and what devastations they make in that war; how they blind the eyes, harden the heart, sear the conscience, and deprive men of all sense of honour and justice. *Whoso committeth adultery with a woman lacketh understanding* and quite loses it; *he that doth it destroys his own soul*, Prov. vi. 32. But, as the eye of the adulterer, so the hand of the murderer seeks concealment, Job xxiv. 14, 15. Works of darkness hate the light. When David bravely slew Goliath it was done publicly, and he gloried in it; but, when he basely slew Uriah, it must be done clandestinely, for he is ashamed of it, and well he may. Who would do a thing that he dare not own? The devil, having, as a poisonous serpent, put it into David's heart to murder Uriah, as a subtle serpent he puts it into his head how to do it. Not as Absalom slew Amnon, by commanding his servants to assassinate him, nor as Ahab slew Naboth by suborning witnesses to accuse him, but by exposing him to the enemy, a way of doing it which, perhaps, would not seem so odious to conscience and the world, because soldiers expose themselves of course. If Uriah had not been in that dangerous post, another must; he has (as we say) a chance for his life; if he fight stoutly, he may perhaps come off; and, if he die, it is in the field of honour, where a soldier would choose to die; and yet all this will not save it from being a wilful murder, of malice prepense.

I. Orders are sent to Joab to set Uriah in the front of the hottest battle, and then to desert him, and abandon him to the enemy, *v.* 14, 15. This was David's project to take off Uriah, and it succeeded, as he designed. Many were the aggravations of this murder. 1. It was deliberate. He took time to consider of it; and though he had time to consider of it, for he wrote a letter about it, and though he had time to have countermanded the order afterwards before it could be put in execution, yet he persisted in it. 2. He sent the letter by Uriah himself, than which nothing could be more base and barbarous, to make him accessory to his own death. And what a paradox was it that he could bear such a malice against him in whom yet he could repose such a confidence as that he would carry letters which he must not know the purport of. 3. Advantage must be taken of Uriah's own courage and zeal for his king and country, which deserve the greatest praise and recompence, to betray him the more easily to his fate. If he had not been forward to expose himself, perhaps he was a man of such importance that Joab could not have exposed him; and that this noble fire should be designedly turned upon himself was a most detestable instance of ingratitude. 4. Many must be involved in the guilt. Joab, the general, to whom the blood of his soldiers, especially the worthies, ought to be precious, must do it; he, and all that retire from Uriah when they ought in conscience to support and second him, become guilty of his death. 5. Uriah cannot thus die alone: the party he commands is in danger of being cut off with him; and it proved so: some of the people, even the servants of David (so they are called, to aggravate David's sin in being so prodigal of their lives), fell with him, *v.* 17. Nay, this wilful misconduct by which Uriah must be betrayed might be of fatal consequence to the whole army, and might oblige them to raise the siege. 6. It will be the triumph and joy of the Ammonites, the sworn enemies of God and Israel; it will gratify them exceedingly. David prayed for himself, that he might not fall into the hands of man, nor flee from his enemies (*ch.* xxiv. 13, 14); yet he sells his servant Uriah to the Ammonites, and not for any iniquity in his hand.

II. Joab executes these orders. In the next assault that is made upon the city Uriah has the most dangerous post assigned him, is encouraged to hope that if he be repulsed by the besieged he shall be relieved by Joab, in dependence on which he marches on with resolution, but, succours not coming on, the service proves too hot, and he is slain in it, *v.* 16, 17. It was strange that Joab would do such a thing merely upon a letter, without knowing the reason. But, 1. Perhaps he supposed Uriah had been guilty of some great crime, to enquire into which David had sent for him, and that, because he would not punish him openly, he took this course with him to put him to death. 2. Joab had been guilty of blood, and we may suppose it pleased him very well to see David himself falling into the same guilt, and he was willing enough to serve him in it, that he might continue to be favourable to him. It is common for those who have done ill themselves to desire to be countenanced therein by others doing ill likewise, especially by the sins of those that are eminent in the profession of religion. Or, perhaps, David knew that Joab had a pique against Uriah, and would gladly be avenged on him; otherwise Joab, when he saw cause, knew how to dispute the king's orders, as *ch.* xix. 5; xxiv. 3.

III. He sends an account of it to David. An express is despatched away immediately with a report of this last disgrace and loss which they had sustained, *v.* 18. And, to disguise the affair, 1. He supposes that David would appear to be angry at his bad conduct, would ask why they came so near the wall (*v.* 20), did they not know that Abimelech lost his life by doing so? *v.* 21. We had the story (Judg. ix. 53), which book, it is likely, was published as a part of the sacred history in Samuel's time; and (be it noted to their praise, and for imitation) even the soldiers were conversant with their bibles, and could readily quote the scripture-story, and make use of it for admonition to themselves not to run upon the same attempts which they found had been fatal. 2. He slyly orders the messenger to soothe it with telling him that Uriah the Hittite was dead also, which gave too broad an intimation to the messenger, and by him to others, that David would be secretly pleased to hear that; for murder will out. And, when men do such base things, they must expect to be bantered and upbraided with them, even by their inferiors. The messenger delivered his message agreeably to orders, *v.* 22—24. He makes the besieged to sally out first upon the besiegers *(they came out unto us into the field)*, represents the besiegers as doing their part with great bravery *(we were upon them even to the entering of the gate*—we forced them to retire into the city with precipitation), and so concludes with a slight mention of the slaughter made among them by some shot from the wall: *Some of the king's servants are dead,* and particularly *Uriah the Hittite,* an officer of note, stood first in the list of the slain.

IV. David receives the account with a secret satisfaction, *v.* 25. Let not Joab be displeased, for David is not. He blames not his conduct, nor thinks they did wrong in approaching so near the wall; all is well now that Uriah is put out of the way. This point being gained, he can make light of the loss, and turn it off easily with an excuse: *The sword devours one as well as another;* it was a chance of war, nothing more common. He orders Joab to make the battle more strong next time, while he, by his sin, was weakening it, and provoking God to blast the undertaking.

V. He marries the widow in a little time. She submitted to the ceremony of mourning for her husband as short a time as custom would admit (*v.* 26), and then David took her to his house as his wife, and she bore him a son. Uriah's revenge was prevented by his death, but the birth of the child so soon after the marriage published the crime. Sin will have shame. Yet that was not the worst of it: *The thing that David had done displeased the Lord.* The whole *matter of Uriah* (as it is called, 1 Kings xv. 5), the adultery, falsehood, murder, and this marriage at last, it was all displeasing to the Lord. He had pleased himself, but displeased God. Note, God sees and hates sin in his own people. Nay, the nearer any are to God in profession the more displeasing to him their sins are; for in them there is more ingratitude, treachery, and reproach, than in the sins of others. Let none therefore encourage themselves in sin by the example of David; for those that sin as he did will fall under the displeasure of God as he did. Let us therefore stand in awe and sin not, not sin after the similitude of his transgression.

CHAP. XII.

The foregoing chapter gave us the account of David's sin; this gives us the account of his repentance. Though he fell, he was not utterly cast down, but, by the grace of God, recovered himself, and found mercy with God. Here is, I. His conviction, by a message Nathan brought him from God, which was a parable that obliged him to condemn himself (ver. 1—6), and the application of the parable, in which Nathan charged him with the sin (ver. 7—9) and pronounced sentence upon him, ver. 10—12. II. His repentance and remission, with a proviso, ver. 13, 14. III. The sickness and death of the child, and his behaviour while it was sick and when it was dead (ver. 15—23), in both which David gave evidence of his repentance. IV. The birth of Solomon, and God's gracious message concerning him, in which God gave an evidence of his reconciliation to David, ver. 24, 25. V. The taking of Rabbah (ver. 26—31), which is mentioned as a further instance that God did not deal with David according to his sins.

AND the LORD sent Nathan unto David. And he came unto him, and said unto him, There were two men in one city; the one rich, and the other poor. 2 The rich *man* had exceeding many flocks and herds: 3 But the poor *man* had nothing, save one little ewe lamb, which he had bought and nourished up: and it grew up together with him, and with his children; it did eat of his own meat, and drank of his own cup, and lay in his bosom, and was unto him as a daughter. 4 And there came a traveller unto the rich man, and he spared to take of his own flock and of his own herd, to dress for the wayfaring man that was come unto him; but took the poor man's lamb, and dressed it for the man that was come to him. 5 And David's anger was greatly kindled against the man; and he said to Nathan, *As* the LORD liveth, the man that hath done this *thing* shall surely die: 6 And he shall restore the lamb fourfold, because he did this thing, and because he had no pity. 7 And Nathan said to David, Thou *art* the man. Thus saith the LORD God of Israel, I anointed thee king over Israel, and I delivered thee out of the hand of Saul: 8 And I gave thee thy master's house, and thy master's wives into thy bosom, and gave thee the house of Israel and of Judah; and if *that had been* too little, I would moreover have given unto thee such and such things. 9 Wherefore hast thou despised the commandment of the LORD, to do evil in his sight? thou hast killed Uriah the Hittite with the sword, and hast taken his wife *to be* thy wife, and hast slain him with the sword of the children of Ammon. 10 Now therefore the sword shall never depart from thine house; because thou hast despised me, and hast taken the wife of Uriah the Hittite to be thy wife. 11 Thus saith the LORD, Behold, I will raise up evil against thee out of thine own house, and I will take thy wives before thine eyes, and give *them* unto thy neighbour, and he shall lie with thy wives in the sight of this sun. 12 For thou didst *it* secretly: but I will do this thing before all Israel, and before the sun. 13 And David said unto Nathan, I have sinned against the LORD. And Nathan said unto David, The LORD also hath put away thy sin; thou shalt not die. 14 Howbeit, because by this deed thou hast given great occasion to the enemies of the LORD to blaspheme, the child also *that is* born unto thee shall surely die.

It seems to have been a great while after David had been guilty of adultery with Bathsheba before he was brought to repentance for it. For, when Nathan was sent to him, the child was born (*v.* 14), so that it was about nine months that David lay under the guilt of that sin, and, for aught that appears, unrepented of. What shall we think of David's state all this while? Can we imagine that his heart never smote him for it, or that he never lamented it in secret before God? I would willingly hope that he did, and that Nathan was sent to him, immediately upon the birth of the child, when the thing by that means came to be publicly known and talked of, to draw from him an open confession of the sin, to the glory of God, the admonition of others, and that he might receive, by Nathan, absolution with certain limitations. But, during these nine months, we may well suppose his comforts and the exercises of his graces suspended, and his communion with God interrupted; during all that time, it is certain, he penned no psalms, his harp was out of tune, and his soul like a tree in winter, that has life in the root only. Therefore, after Nathan had been with him, he prays, *Restore unto me the joy of thy salvation, and open thou my lips,* Ps. li. 12, 15. Let us observe,

I. The messenger God sent to him. We were told by the last words of the foregoing chapter that the thing David had done displeased the Lord, upon which, one would think, it should have followed that the Lord sent enemies to invade him, terrors to take hold on him, and the messengers of death to arrest him. No, he sent a prophet to him —Nathan, his faithful friend and confidant, to instruct and counsel him, *v.* 1. David did not send for Nathan (though he had never had so much occasion as he had now for his confessor), but God sent Nathan to David. Note, Though God may suffer his people to fall into sin, he will not suffer them to lie still in it. *He went on frowardly in the way of his heart,* and, if left to himself, would have wandered endlessly, but (saith God) *I have seen his ways, and will heal him,* Isa. lvii. 17, 18. He sends after us before we seek after him, else we should certainly be lost. Nathan was the prophet by whom God had sent him notice of his kind intentions towards him (*ch.* vii. 4), and now, by the same hand, he sends him this message of wrath. God's word in the mouth of his ministers must be received, whether it speak terror or comfort. Nathan was obedient to the heavenly vision, and went on God's errand to David. He did not say, "David has sinned, I will not come near him." No; *count him not an enemy, but admonish him as a brother,* 2 Thess. iii. 15. He did not say, "David is a king, I dare not reprove him." No; if God sends him, he *sets his face like a flint,* Isa. l. 7.

II. The message Nathan delivered to him, in order to his conviction.

1. He fetched a compass with a parable, which seemed to David as a complaint made to him by Nathan against one of his subjects that had wronged his poor neighbour, in order to his redressing the injury and punishing the injurious. Nathan, it is likely, used to come to him upon such errands, which made this the less suspected. It becomes those who have interest in princes, and have free access to them, to intercede for those that are wronged, that they may have justice done them. (1.) Nathan represented to David a grievous injury which a rich man had done to an honest neighbour that was not able to contend with him: *The rich man had many flocks and herds* (*v.* 2); the poor man had one lamb only; so unequally is the world divided; and yet infinite wisdom, righteousness, and goodness, make the distribution, that the rich may learn charity and the poor contentment. This poor man had but one lamb, a ewe-lamb, a little ewe-lamb, having not wherewithal to buy or keep more. But it was a *cade*-lamb (as we call it); *it grew up with his children, v.* 3. He was fond of it, and it was familiar with him at all times. The rich man, having occasion for a lamb to entertain a friend with, took the poor man's lamb from him by violence and made use of that (*v.* 4), either out of covetousness, because he grudged to make use of his own, or rather out of luxury, because he fancied the lamb that was thus tenderly kept, and ate and drank like a child, must needs be more delicate food than any of his own and have a better relish. (2.) In this he showed him the evil of the sin he had been guilty of in defiling Bath-sheba. He had many wives and concubines, whom he kept at a distance, as rich men keep their flocks in their fields. Had he had but one, and had she been dear to him, as the ewe-lamb was to its owner, had she been dear to him *as the loving hind and the pleasant roe, her breasts would have satisfied him at all times,* and he would have looked no further, Prov. v. 19. Marriage is a remedy against fornication, but marrying many is not; for, when once the law of unity is transgressed, the indulged lust will hardly stint itself. Uriah, like the poor man, had only one wife, who was to him as his own soul, and always lay in his bosom, for he had no other, he desired no other, to lie there. The traveller or wayfaring man was, as bishop Patrick explains it from the Jewish writers, the evil imagination, disposition, or desire, which came into David's heart, which he might have satisfied with some of his own, yet nothing would serve but Uriah's darling. They observe that this evil disposition is called a traveller, for in the beginning it is only so, but, in time, it becomes a guest, and, in conclusion, is master of the house. For he that is called a traveller in the beginning of the verse is called a *man (ish—a husband)* in the close of it. Yet some observe that in David's breast lust was but as a wayfaring man that tarries only for a night; it did not constantly dwell and rule there.

(3.) By this parable he drew from David a sentence against himself. For David supposing it to be a case in fact, and not doubting the truth of it when he had it from Nathan himself, gave judgment immediately against the offender, and confirmed it with an oath, *v.* 5, 6. [1.] That, for his injustice in taking away the lamb, he should restore four-fold, according to the law (Exod. xxii. 1), *four sheep for a sheep.* [2.] That for his tyranny and cruelty, and the pleasure he took in abusing a poor man, he should be put to death. If a poor man steal from a rich man, to satisfy his soul when he is hungry, he shall make restitution, though it cost him *all the substance of his house,* Prov. vi. 30, 31 (and Solomon there compares the sin of adultery with that, *v* 32); but if a rich man steal for stealing sake, not for want but wantonness, merely that he may be imperious and vexatious, he deserves to die for it; for to him the making of restitution is no punishment, or next to none. If the sentence be thought too severe, it must be imputed to the present roughness of David's temper, being under guilt, and not having himself as yet received mercy.

2. He closed in with him, at length, in the application of the parable. In beginning with a parable he showed his prudence, and great need there is of prudence in giving reproofs. It is well managed if, as here, the offender can be brought, ere he is aware, to convict and condemn himself. But here, in his application, he shows his faithfulness, and deals as plainly and roundly with king David himself as if he had been a common person. In plain terms, "*Thou art the man* who hast done this wrong, and a much greater, to thy neighbour; and therefore, by thy own sentence, thou deservest to die, and shalt be judged out of thy own mouth. Did he deserve to die who took his neighbour's lamb? and dost not thou who hast taken thy neighbour's wife? Though he took the lamb, he did not cause the owner thereof to lose his life, as thou hast done, and therefore much more art thou worthy to die." Now he speaks immediately from God, and in his name. He begins with, *Thus saith the Lord God of Israel,* a name sacred and venerable to David, and which commanded his attention. Nathan now speaks, not as a petitioner for a poor man, but as an ambassador from the great God, with whom is no respect of persons.

(1.) God, by Nathan, reminds David of the great things he had done and designed for him, anointing him to be king, and preserving him to the kingdom (*v.* 7), giving him power over the house and household of his predecessor, and of others that had been his masters, Nabal for one. He had given him the house of Israel and Judah. The wealth of the kingdom was at his service and every body was willing to oblige him. Nay, he was ready to bestow any thing upon him to make him easy: *I would have given thee such and such things, v.* 8. See how liberal God is in his gifts; we are not straitened in him. Where he has given much, yet he gives more. And God's bounty to us is a great aggravation of our discontent and desire of forbidden fruit. It is ungrateful to covet what God has prohibited, while we have liberty to pray for what God has promised, and that is enough.

(2.) He charges him with a high contempt of the divine authority, in the sins he had been guilty of: *Wherefore hast thou* (presuming upon thy royal dignity and power) *despised the commandment of the Lord? v.* 9. This is the spring and this is the malignity of sin, that it is making light of the divine law and the law-maker; as if the obligation of it were weak, the precepts of it trifling, and the threats not at all formidable. Though no man ever wrote more honourably of the law of God than David did, yet, in this instance, he is justly charged with a contempt of it. His adultery with Bath-sheba, which began the mischief, is not mentioned, perhaps because he was already convinced of that, but, [1.] The murder of Uriah is twice mentioned: "*Thou hast killed Uriah with the sword,* though not with thy sword, yet, which is equally heinous, with thy pen, by ordering him to be set in the forefront of the battle." Those that contrive wickedness and command it are as truly guilty of it as those that execute it. It is repeated with an aggravation: *Thou hast slain him with the sword of the children of Ammon,* those uncircumcised enemies of God and Israel. [2.] The marrying of Bath-sheba is likewise twice mentioned, because he thought there was no harm in that (*v.* 9): *Thou hast taken his wife to be thy wife,* and again, *v.* 10. To marry her whom he had before defiled, and whose husband he had slain, was an affront upon the ordinance of marriage, making that not only to palliate, but in a manner to consecrate, such villanies. In all this he *despised the word of the Lord* (so it is in the Hebrew), not only his commandment in general which forbade such things, but the particular word of promise which God had, by Nathan, sent to him some time before, that he would build him a house. If he had had a due value and veneration for this sacred promise, he would not thus have polluted his house with lust and blood.

(3.) He threatens an entail of judgments upon his family for this sin (*v.* 10): "*The sword shall never depart from thy house,* not in thy time nor afterwards, but, for the most part, thou and thy posterity shall be engaged in war." Or it points at the slaughters that should be among his children, Amnon, Absalom, and Adonijah, all falling by the sword. God had promised that his mercy should not depart from him and his house (*ch.* vii. 15), yet here threatens that the sword should not depart. Can the mercy and the sword consist with each other? Yes, those may lie under great and long afflictions who yet shall not be excluded from the grace of the covenant. The reason given is, *Because thou hast despised me.* Note, Those who despise the word and law of God despise God himself and shall be lightly esteemed. It is particularly threatened, [1.] That his children should be his grief: *I will raise up evil against thee out of thy own house.* Sin brings trouble into a family, and one sin is often made the punishment of another. [2.] That his wives should be his shame, that by an unparalleled piece of villany they should be publicly debauched before all Israel, *v.* 11, 12. It is not said that this should be done by his own son, lest the accomplishment should have been hindered by the prediction being too plain; but it was done by Absalom, at the counsel of Ahithophel, *ch.* xvi. 21, 22. *He that defiled his neighbour's wife should have his own defiled,* for thus that sin used to be punished, as appears by Job's imprecation, Job xxxi. 10, *Then let my wife grind unto another,* and that threatening, Hos. iv. 14. The sin was secret, and industriously concealed, but the punishment should be open, and industriously proclaimed, to the shame of David, whose sin in the matter of Uriah, though committed many years before, would then be called to mind and commonly talked of upon that occasion. As face answers to face in a glass, so does the punishment often answer to the sin; here is *blood for blood and uncleanness for uncleanness.* And thus God would show how much he hates sin, even in his own people, and that, wherever he find it, he will not let it go unpunished.

3. David's penitent confession of his sin hereupon. He says not a word to excuse himself or extenuate his sin, but freely owns it: *I have sinned against the Lord, v.* 13. It is probable that he said more to this purport; but this is enough to show that he was truly humbled by what Nathan said, and submitted to the conviction. He owns his guilt—*I have sinned,* and aggravates it—It was *against the Lord:* on this string he harps in the psalm he penned on this occasion. Ps. li. 1, *Against thee, thee only, have I sinned.*

4. His pardon declared, upon this penitent confession, but with a proviso. When David said *I have sinned,* and Nathan perceived that he was a true penitent,

(1.) He did, in God's name, assure him that his sin was forgiven: "*The Lord also has put away thy sin* out of the sight of his avenging eye; *thou shalt not die,*" that is, "not die eternally, nor be for ever put away from God, as thou wouldest have been if he had not put away the sin." The obligation to punishment is hereby cancelled and vacated. *He shall not come into condemnation:* that is the nature of forgiveness. "Thy iniquity shall not be thy everlasting ruin. *The sword shall not depart from thy house,* but, [1.] It shall not cut thee off, thou shalt come to thy grave in peace." David deserved to die as an adulterer and murderer, but God would not cut him off as he might justly have done. [2.] "Though thou shalt all thy days be *chastened of the Lord,* yet thou *shalt not be condemned with the world.*" See how ready God is to forgive sin. To this instance, perhaps, David refers, Ps. xxxii. 5, *I said, I will confess, and thou forgavest.* Let not great sinners despair of finding mercy with God if they truly repent; for who is a God like unto him, pardoning iniquity?

(2.) Yet he pronounces a sentence of death upon the child, *v.* 14. Behold the sovereignty of God! The guilty parent lives, and the guiltless infant dies; but all souls are his, and he may, in what way he pleases, glorify himself in his creatures. [1.] David had, by his sin, wronged God in his honour; he had *given occasion to the enemies of the Lord to blaspheme.* The wicked people of that generation, the infidels, idolaters, and profane, would triumph in David's fall, and speak ill of God and of his law, when they saw one guilty of such foul enormities that professed such an honour both for him and it. "These are your professors! This is he that prays and sings psalms, and is so very devout! What good can there be in such exercises, if they will not restrain men from adultery and murder?" They would say, "Was not Saul rejected for a less matter? why then must David live and reign still?" not considering that God *sees not as man sees, but searches the heart.* To this day there are those who reproach God, and are hardened in sin, through the example of David. Now, though it is true that none have any just reason to speak ill of God, or of his word and ways, for David's sake, and it is their sin that do so, yet he shall be reckoned with that laid the stumbling-block in their way, and gave, though not cause, yet colour, for the reproach. Note, There is this great evil in the scandalous sins of those that profess religion, and relation to God, that they furnish the enemies of God and religion with matter for reproach and blasphemy, Rom. ii. 24. [2.] God will therefore vindicate his honour by showing his displeasure against David for this sin, and letting the world see that though he loves David he hates his sin; and he chooses to do it by the *death of the child.* The landlord may distrain on any part of the premises where he pleases. Perhaps the diseases and deaths of infants were not so common in those days as they are now, which might make this, as an unusual thing, the more evident token of God's displeasure; according to the word he had often said, that he would *visit the sins of the fathers upon the children.*

15 And Nathan departed unto his

house. And the LORD struck the child that Uriah's wife bare unto David, and it was very sick. 16 David therefore besought God for the child; and David fasted, and went in, and lay all night upon the earth. 17 And the elders of his house arose, *and went* to him, to raise him up from the earth: but he would not, neither did he eat bread with them. 18 And it came to pass on the seventh day, that the child died. And the servants of David feared to tell him that the child was dead: for they said, Behold, while the child was yet alive, we spake unto him, and he would not hearken unto our voice: how will he then vex himself, if we tell him that the child is dead? 19 But when David saw that his servants whispered, David perceived that the child was dead: therefore David said unto his servants, Is the child dead? And they said, He is dead. 20 Then David arose from the earth, and washed, and anointed *himself*, and changed his apparel, and came into the house of the LORD, and worshipped: then he came to his own house; and when he required, they set bread before him, and he did eat. 21 Then said his servants unto him, What thing *is* this that thou hast done? thou didst fast and weep for the child, *while it was* alive; but when the child was dead, thou didst rise and eat bread. 22 And he said, While the child was yet alive, I fasted and wept: for I said, Who can tell *whether* God will be gracious to me, that the child may live? 23 But now he is dead, wherefore should I fast? can I bring him back again? I shall go to him, but he shall not return to me. 24 And David comforted Bath-sheba his wife, and went in unto her, and lay with her: and she bare a son, and he called his name Solomon: and the LORD loved him. 25 And he sent by the hand of Nathan the prophet; and he called his name Jedidiah, because of the LORD.

Nathan, having delivered his message, staid not at court, but went home, probably to pray for David, to whom he had been preaching. God, in making use of him as an instrument to bring David to repentance, and as the herald both of mercy and judgment, put an honour upon the ministry, *and magnified his word above all his name.* David named one of his sons by Bath-sheba *Nathan,* in honour of this prophet (1 Chron. iii. 5), and it was that son of whom Christ, the great prophet, lineally descended, Luke iii. 31. When Nathan retired, David, it is probable, retired likewise, and penned the 51st Psalm, in which (though he had been assured that his sin was pardoned) he prays earnestly for pardon, and greatly laments his sin; for then will true penitents be ashamed of what they have done when God is *pacified towards them,* Ezek. xvi. 63.

Here is, I. The child's illness: *The Lord struck* it, *and it was very sick,* perhaps with convulsions, or some other dreadful distemper, *v.* 15. The diseases and death of infants that have *not sinned after the similitude of Adam's transgression,* especially as they are sometimes sadly circumstanced, are sensible proofs of the original sin in which they are conceived.

II. David's humiliation under this token of God's displeasure, and the intercession he made with God for the life of the child (*v.* 16, 17): *He fasted, and lay all night upon the earth,* and would not suffer any of his attendants either to feed him or help him up. This was an evidence of the truth of his repentance. For, 1. Hereby it appeared that he was willing to bear the shame of his sin, to have it ever before him, and to be continually upbraided with it; for this child would be a continual memorandum of it, both to himself and others, if he lived: and therefore he was so far from desiring its death, as most in such circumstances do, that he prayed earnestly for its life. True penitents patiently *bear the reproach of their youth,* and of their youthful lusts, Jer. xxxi. 19. 2. A very tender compassionate spirit appeared in this, and great humanity, above what is commonly found in men, especially men of war, towards little children, even their own; and this was another sign of a broken contrite spirit. Those that are penitent will be pitiful. 3. He discovered, in this, a great concern for another world, which is an evidence of repentance. Nathan had told him that certainly the child should die; yet, while it is in the reach of prayer, he earnestly intercedes with God for it, chiefly (as we may suppose) that its soul might be safe and happy in another world, and that his sin might not come against the child, and that it might not fare the worse for that in the future state. 4. He discovered, in this, a holy dread of God and of his displeasure. He deprecated the death of the child chiefly as it was a token of God's anger against him and his house, and was inflicted in performance of a threatening; therefore he prayed thus earnestly that, if it were the will of God, the child might live, because that would be to him a token of God's being reconciled to him. *Lord, chasten me not in thy hot displeasure.* Ps. vi. 1.

III. The death of the child: It *died on the seventh day* (*v.* 18), when it was seven days old, and therefore not circumcised, which David might perhaps interpret as a further token of God's displeasure, that it died before it was brought under the seal of the covenant; yet he does not therefore doubt of its being happy, for the benefits of the covenant do not depend upon the seals. David's servants, judging of him by themselves, were afraid to tell him that *the child was dead,* concluding that then he would disquiet himself most of all; so that he knew not till he asked, *v.* 19.

IV. David's wonderful calmness and composure of mind when he understood the child was dead. Observe,

1. What he did. (1.) He laid aside the expressions of his sorrow, washed and anointed himself, and called for clean linen, that he might decently appear before God in his house. (2.) *He went up to the tabernacle and worshipped,* like Job when he heard of the death of his children. He went to acknowledge the hand of God in the affliction, and to humble himself under it, and to submit to his holy will in it, to thank God that he himself was spared and his sin pardoned, and to pray that God would not proceed in his controversy with him, nor stir up all his wrath. *Is any afflicted? Let him pray.* Weeping must never hinder worshipping. (3.) *Then he went to his own house* and refreshed himself, as one who found benefit by his religion in the day of his affliction; for, having worshipped, *he did eat,* and his countenance was no more sad.

2. The reason he gave for what he did. His servants thought it strange that he should afflict himself so for the sickness of the child and yet take the death of it so easily, and asked him the reason of it (*v.* 21), in answer to which he gives this plain account of his conduct, (1.) That while the child was alive he thought it his duty to importune the divine favour towards it, *v.* 22. Nathan had indeed said the child should die, but, for aught that he knew, the threatening might be conditional, as that concerning Hezekiah: upon his great humiliation and earnest prayer, he that had so often *heard the voice of his weeping* might be pleased to reverse the sentence, and spare the child: *Who can tell whether God will yet be gracious to me?* God gives us leave to be earnest with him in prayer for particular blessings, from a confidence in his power and general mercy, though we have no particular promise to build upon: we cannot be sure, yet let us pray, *for who can tell but God will be gracious to us,* in this or that particular? When our relations and friends have fallen sick, the prayer of faith has prevailed much; while there is life there is hope, and, while there is hope, there is room for prayer. (2.) That now the child was dead he thought it as much his duty to be satisfied in the divine disposal concerning it (*v.* 23): *Now, wherefore should I fast?* Two things checked his grief:—[1.] *I cannot bring him back again;* and again, *He shall not return to me.* Those that are dead are out of the reach of prayer; nor can our tears profit them. We can neither weep nor pray them back to this life. Wherefore then should we fast? *To what purpose is this waste?* Yet David fasted and wept for Jonathan when he was dead, in honour to him. [2.] *I shall go to him. First,* To him to the grave. Note, The consideration of our own death should moderate our sorrow at the death of our relations. It is the common lot; instead of mourning for their death, we should think of our own: and, whatever loss we have of them now, we shall die shortly, and go to them. *Secondly,* To him to heaven, to a state of blessedness, which even the Old-Testament saints had some expectation of. Godly parents have great reason to hope concerning their children that die in infancy that it is well with their souls in the other world; for *the promise is to us and to our seed,* which shall be performed to those that do not put a bar in their own door, as infants do not. *Favores sunt ampliandi—Favours received should produce the hope of more.* God calls those his children that are born unto him; and, if they be his, he will save them. This may comfort us when our children are removed from us by death, they are better provided for, both in work and wealth, than they could have been in this world. We shall be with them shortly, to part no more.

V. The birth of Solomon. Though David's marrying Bath-sheba had displeased the Lord, yet he was not therefore commanded to divorce her; so far from this that God gave him that son by her on whom the covenant of royalty should be entailed. Bath-sheba, no doubt, was greatly afflicted with the sense of her sin and the tokens of God's displeasure. But, God having restored to David the joys of his salvation, he comforted her with the same comforts with which he himself was comforted of God (*v.* 24): He *comforted Bath-sheba.* And both he and she had reason to be comforted in the tokens of God's reconciliation to them, 1. Inasmuch as, by his providence, he gave them a son, not as the former, who was given in anger and taken away in wrath, but a child graciously given, and written among the living in Jerusalem. They called him *Solomon—peaceful,* because his birth was a token of God's being at peace with them, because of the prosperity which was entailed upon him, and because he was to be a type of Christ, the prince of peace. God had removed one son from them, but now gave them another instead of him, like *Seth instead of Abel,* Gen. iv. 25. Thus God often balances the griefs of his people with comforts in the same thing wherein he hath afflicted them, setting the one over-against the other. David had very patiently submitted to the will of God in the death of the other child, and now God made up the loss of that, abundantly to his advantage, in the birth of this. The way to have our creature-comforts either continued or restored, or the loss of them made up some other way, is cheerfully to resign them to God. 2. Inasmuch as, by his grace, he particularly owned and favoured that son: *The Lord loved him* (*v.* 24 and 25), ordered him, by the prophet Nathan, to be called *Jedidiah—Beloved of the Lord:* though a seed of evil-doers (for such David and Bath-sheba were), yet so well ordered was the covenant, and the crown entailed by it, that it took away all attainders and corruption of blood, signifying that those who were by nature children of wrath and disobedience should, by the covenant of grace, not only be reconciled, but made favourites. And, in this name, he typified Jesus Christ, that blessed Jedidiah, the son of God's love, concerning whom God declared again and again, *This is my beloved Son, in whom I am well pleased.*

26 And Joab fought against Rabbah of the children of Ammon, and took the royal city. 27 And Joab sent messengers to David, and said, I have fought against Rabbah, and have taken the city of waters. 28 Now therefore gather the rest of the people together, and encamp against the city, and take it: lest I take the city, and it be called after my name. 29 And David gathered all the people together, and went to Rabbah, and fought against it, and took it. 30 And he took their king's crown from off his head, the weight whereof *was* a talent of gold with the precious stones: and it was *set* on David's head. And he brought forth the spoil of the city in great abundance. 31 And he brought forth the people that *were* therein, and put *them* under saws, and under harrows of iron, and under axes of iron, and made them pass through the brickkiln: and thus did he unto all the cities of the children of Ammon. So David and all the people returned unto Jerusalem.

We have here an account of the conquest of Rabbah, and other cities of the Ammonites. Though this comes in here after the birth of David's child, yet it is most probable that it was effected a good while before, and soon after the death of Uriah, perhaps during the days of Bath-sheba's mourning for him. Observe, 1. That God was very gracious in giving David this great success against his enemies, notwithstanding the sin he had been guilty of just at that time when he was engaged in this war, and the wicked use he had made of the sword of the children of Ammon in the murder of Uriah. Justly might he have made that sword, thenceforward, a plague to David and his kingdom; yet he breaks it, and makes David's sword victorious, even before he repents, that this *goodness of God might lead him to repentance.* Good reason had David to own that God *dealt not with him according to his sins,* Ps. ciii. 10. 2. That Joab acted very honestly and honourably; for when he had taken *the city of waters,* the royal city, where the palace was, and from which the rest of the city was supplied with water (and therefore, upon the cutting off of that, would be obliged speedily to surrender), he sent to David to come in person to complete this great action, that he might have the praise of it, *v.* 26—28. Herein he showed himself a faithful servant, that sought his master's honour, and his own only in subordination to his, and left an example to the servants of the Lord Jesus, in every thing they do, to consult his honour. *Not unto us, but to thy name, give glory.* 3. That David was both too haughty and too severe upon this occasion, and neither so humble nor so tender as he should have been. (1.) He seems to have been too fond of the crown of the king of Ammon, *v.* 30. Because it was of extraordinary value, by reason of the precious stones with which it was set, David would have it set upon his head, though it would have been better to have cast it at God's feet, and at this time to have put his own mouth in the dust, under guilt. The heart that is truly humbled for sin is dead to worldly glory and looks upon it with a holy contempt. (2.) He seems to have been too harsh with his prisoners of war, *v.* 31. Taking the city by storm, after it had obstinately held out against a long and expensive siege, if he had put all whom he found in arms to the sword in the heat of battle, it would have been severe enough; but to kill them afterwards in cold blood, and by cruel tortures, with saws and harrows, tearing them to pieces, did not become him who, when he entered upon the government, promised to sing of mercy as well as judgment, Ps. ci. 1. Had he made examples of those only who had abused his ambassadors, or advised or assisted in it, that being a violation of the law of nations, it might have been looked upon as a piece of necessary justice for terror to other nations; but to be thus severe with all the cities of the children of Ammon (that is, the garrisons or soldiers of the cities) was extremely rigorous, and a sign that David's heart was not yet made soft by repentance, else the bowels of his compassion would not have been thus shut up—a sign that he had not yet found mercy, else he would have been more ready to show mercy.

CHAP. XIII.

The righteous God had lately told David, by Nathan the prophet, that, to chastise him for his sin in the matter of Uriah, he would "raise up evil against him out of his own house," ch. xii. 11. And here, in the very next chapter, we find the evil beginning to rise; henceforward he was followed with one trouble after another, which made the latter part of his reign less glorious and pleasant than the former part. Thus God chastened him with the rod of men, yet assured him that his "loving-kindness he would not utterly take away." Adultery and murder were David's sins, and those sins among his children (Amnon defiling his sister Tamar, and Absalom murdering his brother Amnon) were the beginnings of his punishment, and the more grievous because he had reason to fear that his bad example might help to bring them to these wickednesses. In this chapter we have, I. Amnon ravishing Tamar, assisted in his plot to do it by Jonadab his kinsman, and villanously executing it, ver. 1—20. II. Absalom murdering Amnon for it, ver. 21—39. Both were great griefs to David, and the more because he was unwittingly made accessory to both, by sending Tamar to Amnon and Amnon to Absalom.

AND it came to pass after this that Absalom the son of David had a fair sister, whose name *was* Tamar; and Amnon the son of David loved her. 2 And Amnon was so vexed, that he fell sick for his sister Tamar; for she *was* a virgin; and Amnon thought it hard for him to do any thing to her. 3 But Amnon had a friend, whose name *was* Jonadab, the son of Shimeah David's brother: and Jonadab *was* a very subtle man. 4 And he said unto him, Why *art* thou, *being* the king's son, lean from day to day? wilt thou not tell me? And Amnon said unto him, I love Tamar, my brother Absalom's sister. 5 And Jonadab said unto him, Lay thee down on thy bed, and make thyself sick: and when thy father cometh to see thee, say unto him, I pray thee, let my sister Tamar come, and give me meat, and dress the meat in my sight, that I may see *it*, and eat *it* at her hand. 6 So Amnon lay down, and made himself sick: and when the king was come to see him, Amnon said unto the king, I pray thee, let Tamar my sister come, and make me a couple of cakes in my sight, that I may eat at her hand. 7 Then David sent home to Tamar, saying, Go now to thy brother Amnon's house, and dress him meat. 8 So Tamar went to her brother Amnon's house; and he was laid down. And she took flour, and kneaded *it*, and made cakes in his sight, and did bake the cakes. 9 And she took a pan, and poured *them* out before him; but he refused to eat. And Amnon said, Have out all men from me. And they went out every man from him. 10 And Amnon said unto Tamar, Bring the meat into the chamber, that I may eat of thine hand. And Tamar took the cakes which she had made, and brought *them* into the chamber to Amnon her brother. 11 And when she had brought *them* unto him to eat, he took hold of her, and said unto her, Come lie with me, my sister. 12 And she answered him, Nay, my brother, do not force me; for no such thing ought to be done in Israel: do not thou this folly. 13 And I, whither shall I cause my shame to go? and as for thee, thou shalt be as one of the fools in Israel. Now therefore, I pray thee, speak unto the king; for he will not withhold me from thee. 14 Howbeit he would not hearken unto her voice: but, being stronger than she, forced her, and lay with her. 15 Then Amnon hated her exceedingly; so that the hatred wherewith he hated her *was* greater than the love wherewith he had loved her. And Amnon said unto her, Arise, be gone. 16 And she said unto him, *There is* no cause: this evil in sending me away *is* greater than the other that thou didst unto me. But he would not hearken unto her. 17 Then he called his servant that ministered unto him, and said, Put now this *woman* out from me, and bolt the door after her. 18 And *she had* a garment of divers colours upon her: for with such robes were the king's daughters *that were* virgins apparelled. Then his servant brought her out, and bolted the door after her. 19 And Tamar put ashes on her head, and rent her garment of divers colours that *was* on her, and laid her hand on her head, and went on crying. 20 And Absalom her brother said unto her, Hath Amnon thy brother been with thee? but hold now thy peace my sister: he *is* thy brother; regard not this thing. So Tamar remained desolate in her brother Absalom's house.

We have here a particular account of the abominable wickedness of Amnon in ravishing his sister, a subject not fit to be enlarged upon nor indeed to be mentioned without blushing, that ever any man should be so vile, especially that a son of David should be so. Amnon's character, we have reason to think, was bad in other things; if he had not forsaken God, he would never have been given up to these vile affections. Godly parents have often been afflicted with wicked children; grace does not run in the blood, but corruption does. We do not find that David's children imitated him in his devotion; but his false steps they trod in, and in those did much worse, and repented not. Parents know not how fatal the consequences may be if in any instance they give their children bad examples. Observe the steps of Amnon's sin.

I. The devil, as an unclean spirit, put it into his heart to lust after his sister Tamar. Beauty is a snare to many; it was so to her. She was fair, and therefore Amnon coveted her, *v.* 1. Those that are peculiarly handsome have no reason, on that account, to be proud, but great reason to stand upon their watch. Amnon's lust was, 1. Unnatural in itself, to lust after his sister, which even natural conscience startles at and cannot think of without horror. Such a spirit of contradiction there is in man's corrupt nature that still it desires forbidden fruit, and the more strongly it is forbidden the more greedily it is desired. Can he entertain the thought of betraying that virtue and honour of which, as a brother, he ought to have been the protector? But what wickedness so vile as not to find admittance into an unsanctified unguarded heart, left to itself? 2. It was very uneasy to him. He was so vexed that he could not gain an opportunity to solicit her chastity (for innocent converse with her was not denied him) that he *fell sick*, *v.* 2. Fleshly lusts are their own punishment, and not only *war against the soul*, but against the body too, and are the *rottenness of the bones*. See what a hard master sinners serve, and how heavy his yoke is.

II. The devil, as a subtle serpent, put it into his head how to compass this wicked design. Amnon had a friend (so he called him, but he was really an enemy to him), a kinsman, that had in him more of David's blood (for he was his nephew) than of David's spirit, for he was a subtle man, cunning to carry on any bad design, especially an intrigue of this nature, *v.* 3.

1. He took notice that Amnon looked ill, and, being a subtle man, concluded that he was love-sick (*v.* 4), and asks him, "*Why art thou, being the king's son, lean from day to day?* Why dost thou pine, being the king's eldest son, and heir to the crown. *Being the king's son,*" (1.) "Thou hast the pleasures of the court to divert thee; take those pleasures then, and with them drive away the sorrow, whatever it is." Content and comfort are not always to be found in royal palaces. With much more reason may we ask dejected and disconsolate saints why they, who are the children of the King of kings and heirs of the crown of life, are thus *lean from day to day.* (2.) "Thou hast the power of a prince to command what thou wantest and wishest for; use that power therefore, and gratify thyself. Pine not away for that which, lawful or unlawful, thou, being the king's son, mayest have. *Quicquid libet licet—Your will is law.*" Thus Jezebel to Ahab in a like case (1 Kings xxi. 7), *Dost not thou govern Israel?* The abuse of power is the most dangerous temptation of the great.

2. Amnon having the impudence to own his wicked lust, miscalling it *love (I love Tamar)*, Jonadab put him in a way to compass his design, *v.* 5. Had he been what he pretended (Amnon's friend), he would have startled at the mention of such horrid wickedness, would have laid before him the evil of it, what an offence it was to God and what a wrong to his own soul to entertain such a vile thought, of what fatal consequence it would be to him to cherish and prosecute it; he would have used his subtlety to divert Amnon from it, by recommending some other person to him, whom he might lawfully marry. But he seems not at all surprised at it, objects not either the unlawfulness or the difficulty, the reproach or so much as his father's displeasure, but puts him in the way to get Tamar to his bed-side, and then he might do as he pleased. Note, The case of those is very miserable whose friends, instead of admonishing and reproving them, flatter them and forward them in their sinful ways, and are their counsellors and contrivers to do wickedly. Amnon is already sick, but goes about; he must take upon him to be so ill (and his thin looks will give colour enough to the pretence) as not to be able to get up, and to have no appetite to any thing but just that which pleases his fancy. Dainty meat is abhorred, Job xxxiii. 20. The best dish from the king's table cannot please him; but, if he can eat any thing, it must be from his sister Tamar's fair hand. This is what he is advised to.

3. Amnon followed these directions, and thus got Tamar within his reach: ***He made himself sick***, *v.* 6. Thus he ***lieth in wait secretly, as a lion in his den, to catch the poor***, and to ***draw them into his net***, Ps. x. 8—10. David was always fond of his children, and concerned if any thing ailed them; he no sooner hears that Amnon is sick than he comes himself to visit him. Let parents learn hence to be tender of their children and compassionate towards them. The sick child commonly *the mother* comforteth (Isa. lxvi. 13), but let not the *father* be unconcerned. We may suppose that when David came to see his sick son he gave him good

counsel to make a right use of his affliction, and prayed with him, which yet did not alter his wicked purpose. At parting, the indulgent father asks, "Is there any thing thou hast a mind to, that I can procure for thee?" "Yes, Sir," says the dissembling son, "my stomach is weak, and I know not of any thing I can eat, unless it be a cake of my sister Tamar's making, and I cannot be satisfied that it is so unless I see her make it, and it will do me the more good if I eat it at her hand.' David saw no reason to suspect any mischief intended. God hid his heart from understanding in this matter. He therefore immediately orders Tamar to go and attend her sick brother, *v.* 7. He does it very innocently, but afterwards, no doubt, reflected upon it with great regret. Tamar as innocently goes to her brother's chamber, neither dreading any abuse (why should she from a brother, a sick brother?) nor disdaining, in obedience to her father and love to her brother (though but her half-brother), to be his nurse, *v.* 8, 9. Though she was a king's daughter, a great beauty (*v.* 1), and well dressed (*v.* 18), yet she did not think it below her to knead cakes and bake them, nor would she have done this now if she had not been used to it. Good house-wifery is not a thing below the greatest ladies, nor ought they to think it a disparagement to them. The virtuous woman, whose husband sits among the elders, yet *works willingly with her hands,* Prov. xxxi. 13. Modern ages have not been destitute of such instances, nor is it so unfashionable as some would make it. Preparing for the sick should be more the care and delight of the ladies than preparing for the nice, charity more than curiosity.

4. Having got her to him, he contrives to have her alone; for *the adulterer* (much more so vile an adulterer as this) is in care that *no eye see him,* Job xxiv. 15. The meat is ready, but he cannot eat while he is looked at by those about him; they must all be turned out, *v.* 9. The sick must be humoured, and think they have a privilege to command. Tamar is willing to humour him; her chaste and virtuous soul has not the least thought of that which his polluted breast is full of; and therefore she makes no scruple of being alone with him *in the inner chamber, v.* 10. And now the mask is thrown off, the meat is thrown by, and the wicked wretch calls her *sister,* and yet impudently courts her to *come and lie with him, v.* 11. It was a base affront to her virtue to think it possible to persuade her to consent to such wickedness when he knew her behaviour to be always exemplarily modest and virtuous. But it is common for those that live in uncleanness to think others such as themselves, at least tinder to their sparks.

III. The devil, as a strong tempter, deafens his ear to all the reasonings with which she resisted his assaults and would have persuaded him to desist. We may well imagine what a surprise and terror it was to the young lady to be thus attacked, how she blushed and how she trembled; yet, in this great confusion, nothing could be said more pertinently, nor with greater strength of argument, than what she said to him. 1. She calls him *brother,* reminding him of the nearness of the relation, which made it unlawful for him to marry her, much more to debauch her. It was expressly forbidden (Lev. xviii. 9) under a severe penalty, Lev. xx. 17. Great care must be taken lest the love that should be among relations degenerate into lust. 2. She entreats him not to force her, which intimates that she would never consent to it in any degree; and what satisfaction could he take in offering violence? 3. She lays before him the great wickedness of it. It is *folly;* all sin is so, especially uncleanness. It is wickedness of the worst kind. Such abominations ought not to be committed in Israel, among the professing people of God, that have better statutes than the heathen have. We are Israelites; if we do such things, we are more inexcusable than others, and our condemnation will be more intolerable, for we *reproach the Lord,* and *that worthy name by which we are called.* 4. She represents to him the shame of it, which perhaps might influence him more than the sin of it: "For my part, *whither shall I cause my shame to go?* If it should be concealed, yet I shall blush to think of it as long as I live; and, if ever it be known, how shall I be able to look any of my friends in the face? For thy part, *thou shalt be as one of the fools in Israel,"* that is, "Thou wilt be looked upon as an atrocious debauchee, the worst of men; thou wilt lose thy interest in the esteem of all that are wise and good, and so wilt be set aside as unfit to rule, though the first-born; for Israel will never submit to the government of such a fool." Prospect of shame, especially everlasting shame, should deter us from sin. 5. To divert him from his wicked purpose at this time, and (if possible) to get clear of him, she intimates to him that probably the king, rather than he should die for love of her, would dispense with the divine law and let him marry her: not as if she thought he had such a dispensing power, or would pretend to it; but she was confident that, upon notice given to the king by himself of this wicked desire, which he would scarcely have believed from any one else, he would take an effectual course to protect her from him. But all her arts and all her arguments availed not. His proud spirit cannot bear a denial; but her comfort, and honour, and all that was dear to her, must be sacrificed to his brutish and outrageous lust, *v.* 14. It is to be feared that Amnon, though young, had long lived a lewd life, which his father either knew not or punished not; for a man could not, of a sudden, arrive at such a pitch of wickedness as this. But is this his love to Tamar? Is this the recompence he gives her for her readiness to attend him in his sickness? Will he deal with his sister as with a harlot? Base villain! God deliver all that are modest and virtuous from such wicked and unreasonable men.

IV. The devil, as a tormentor and betrayer, immediately turns his love of her into hatred (*v.* 15): *He hated her with great hatred, greatly,* so it is in the margin, and grew as outrageous in his malice as he had been in his lust.

1. He basely turned her out of doors by force; nay, as if he now disdained to touch her with his own hands, he ordered his servant to *pull her out* and *bolt the door after her, v.* 17. Now, (1.) The innocent injured lady had reason to resent this as a great affront, and in some respects (as she says, *v.* 16) worse than the former; for nothing could have been done more barbarous and ill-natured, or more disgraceful to her. Had he taken care to conceal what was done, her honour would have been lost to herself only. Had he gone down on his knees and begged her pardon, it might have been some little reparation. Had he given her time to compose herself after the horrid confusion she was put into, she might have kept her countenance when she went out, and so have kept her counsel. But to dismiss her thus hurried, thus rudely, as if she had done some wicked thing, obliged her, in her own defence, to proclaim the wrong that had been done her. (2.) We may learn from it both the malignity of sin (unbridled passions are as bad as unbridled appetites) and the mischievous consequences of sin (at last, it bites like a serpent); for here we find, [1.] That sins, sweet in the commission, afterwards become odious and painful, and the sinner's own conscience makes them so to himself. Amnon hated Tamar because she would not consent to his wickedness, and so take part of the blame upon herself, but to the last resisted it, and reasoned against it, and so threw all the blame upon him. Had he hated the sin, and loathed himself for it, we might have hoped he was penitent. *Godly sorrow worketh indignation,* 2 Cor. vii. 11. But to hate the person he had abused showed that his conscience was terrified, but his heart not at all humbled. See what deceitful pleasures those of the flesh are, how soon they pass away, and turn into loathing; see Ezek. xxiii. 17. [2.] That sins, secret in the commission, afterwards become open and public, and the sinners themselves often make them so. Their own tongues fall upon them. The Jewish doctors say that, upon the occasion of this wickedness of Amnon, a law was made that a young man and a young woman should never be alone together; for, said they, if the king's daughter be so used, what will become of the children of private men?

2. We must now leave the criminal to the terrors of his own guilty conscience, and enquire what becomes of the poor victim. (1.) She bitterly lamented the injury she had received, as it was a stain to her honour, though no real blemish to her virtue. She tore her fine clothes in token of her grief, and put ashes upon her head, to deform herself, loathing her own beauty and ornaments, because they had occasioned Amnon's unlawful love; and she went on crying for another's sin, *v.* 19. (2.) She retired to her brother Absalom's house, because he was her own brother, and there she lived in solitude and sorrow, in token of her modesty and detestation of uncleanness. Absalom spoke kindly to her, bade her pass by the injury for the present, designing himself to revenge it, *v.* 20. It should seem by Absalom's question *(Has Amnon been with thee?)* that Amnon was notorious for such lewd practices, so that it was dangerous for a modest woman to be with him; this Absalom might know, and yet Tamar be wholly ignorant of it.

21 But when king David heard of all these things, he was very wroth. 22 And Absalom spake unto his brother Amnon neither good nor bad: for Absalom hated Amnon, because he had forced his sister Tamar. 23 And it came to pass after two full years, that Absalom had sheepshearers in Baal-hazor, which *is* beside Ephraim: and Absalom invited all the king's sons. 24 And Absalom came to the king, and said, Behold now, thy servant hath sheepshearers; let the king, I beseech thee, and his servants go with thy servant. 25 And the king said to Absalom, Nay, my son, let us not all now go, lest we be chargeable unto thee. And he pressed him: howbeit he would not go, but blessed him. 26 Then said Absalom, If not, I pray thee, let my brother Amnon go with us. And the king said unto him, Why should he go with thee? 27 But Absalom pressed him, that he let Amnon and all the king's sons go with him. 28 Now Absalom had commanded his servants, saying, Mark ye now when Amnon's heart is merry with wine, and when I say unto you, Smite Amnon; then kill him, fear not: have not I commanded you? be courageous, and be valiant. 29 And the servants of Absalom did unto Amnon as Absalom had commanded. Then all the

king's sons arose, and every man gat him up upon his mule, and fled.

What Solomon says of the beginning of strife is as true of the beginning of all sin, it is as the letting forth of water; when once the flood-gates are plucked up, an inundation follows; one mischief begets another, and it is hard to say what shall be in the end thereof.

I. We are here told how David resented the tidings of Amnon's sin: *He was very wroth, v.* 21. So he had reason to be, that his own son should do such a wicked thing and draw him to be accessory to it. It would be a reproach to him for not giving him a better education; it would be a blot upon his family, the ruin of his daughter, a bad example to his kingdom, and a wrong to his son's soul. But was it enough for him to be angry? He ought to have punished his son for it, and have put him to open shame; both as a father and as a king he had power to do it. But the LXX. here adds these words: *But he saddened not the spirit of his son Amnon, because he loved him, because he was his first-born.* He fell into Eli's error, whose sons *made themselves vile, and he frowned not on them.* If Amnon was dear to him, his punishing him would have been so much the greater punishment to himself for his own uncleanness. But he cannot bear the shame those must submit to who correct that in others which they are conscious of in themselves, and therefore his anger must serve instead of his justice; and this hardens sinners, Eccl. viii. 11.

II. How Absalom resented it. He resolves already to do the part of a judge in Israel; and, since his father will not punish Amnon, he will, from a principle, not of justice or zeal for virtue, but of revenge, because he reckons himself affronted in the abuse done to his sister. Their mother was daughter to a heathen prince (*ch.* iii. 3), which perhaps they were upbraided with sometimes by their brethren, as children of a stranger. As such a one Absalom thought his sister was now treated; and, if Amnon thought her fit to be made his harlot, he would think him fit to be made his slave. This enraged him, and nothing less than the blood of Amnon will quench his rage. Here we have,

1. The design conceived: *Absalom hated Amnon* (*v.* 22), and *he that hateth his brother is a murderer* already, and, like *Cain, is of that wicked one,* 1 John iii. 12, 15. Absalom's hatred of his brother's crime would have been commendable, and he might justly have prosecuted him for it by a due course of law, for example to others, and the making of some compensation to his injured sister; but to hate his person, and design his death by assassination, was to put a great affront upon God, by offering to repair the breach of his seventh commandment by the violation of his sixth, as if they were not all alike sacred. *But he that said, Do not commit adultery, said also, Do not kill,* James ii. 11.

2. The design concealed. He said nothing to Amnon of this matter, either good or bad, appeared as if he did not know it, and maintained towards him his usual civility, only waiting for a fair opportunity to do him a mischief. That malice is the worst, (1.) Which is hidden closely, and has no vent given to it. If Absalom had reasoned the matter with Amnon, he might have convinced him of his sin and brought him to repentance; but, saying nothing, Amnon's heart was hardened, and his own more and more embittered against him; therefore rebuking our neighbour is opposed to hating him in our hearts, Lev. xix. 17. Let passion have vent and it will spend itself. (2.) Which is gilded over with a show of friendship; so Absalom's was, *his words smoother than butter but war in his heart.* See Prov. xxvi. 26. (3.) Which is harboured long. Two full years Absalom nursed this root of bitterness, *v.* 24. It may be, at first, he did not intend to kill his brother (for, if he had, he might have had as fair an opportunity to do it as he had at last), and only waited for an occasion to disgrace him or do him some other mischief; but in time his hatred ripened to this, that he would be no less than the death of him. If the *sun going down* once *upon the wrath gives such place to the devil* (as is intimated, Eph. iv. 26, 27), what would the sunsets of two full years do?

3. The design laid. (1.) Absalom has a feast at his house in the country, as Nabal had, on occasion of his sheep-shearing, *v.* 23. Attentive as Absalom was to his person (*ch.* xiv. 26), and as high as he looked, he *knew the state of his flocks and looked well to his herds.* Those who have no other care about their estates in the country than how to spend them in the town take a ready way to see the end of them. Whem Absalom had sheepshearers he would himself be with them. (2.) To this feast he invites the king his father, and all the princes of the blood (*v.* 24), not only that he might have this opportunity to pay his respects to them, but that he might make himself the more respected among his neighbours. Those that are akin to great folks are apt to value themselves too much on their kindred. (3.) The king would not go himself, because he would not put him to the expense of his entertainment, *v.* 25. It seems Absalom had an estate in his own hands, on which he lived like himself; the king had given it to him, but would have him to be a good husband of it: in both these he is an example to parents, when their children have grown up, to give them a competency to live upon, according to their rank, and then to take care that they do not live above it, especially that they be no way accessory to their doing so. It is prudent for young house-keepers to begin as they can

hold out, and not to spend the wool upon the shearing of it. (4.) Absalom got leave for Amnon, and all the rest of the king's sons, to come and grace his table in the country, *v.* 26, 27. Absalom had so effectually concealed his enmity to Amnon that David saw no reason to suspect any design upon him in that particular invitation: "Let my brother Amnon go;" but this would make the stroke more cutting to David that he was himself drawn in to consent to that which gave the opportunity for it, as before, *v.* 7. It seems, David's sons, though grown up, continued to pay such a deference to their father as not to go such a small journey as this without his leave. Thus ought children, even when they have become men and women, to honour their parents, consult them, and do nothing material without their consent, much less against their mind.

4. The design executed, *v.* 28, 29. (1.) Absalom's entertainment was very plentiful; for he resolves that they shall all be merry with wine, at least concludes that Amnon will be so, for he knew that he was apt to drink to excess. But, (2.) The orders he gave to his servants concerning Amnon, that they should mingle his blood with his wine, were very barbarous. Had he challenged him, and, in reliance upon the goodness of his cause and the justice of God, fought him himself, though that would have been bad enough, yet it would have been more honourable and excusable (our ancient law, in some cases, allowed trial by battle); but to murder him, as he did, was to copy Cain's example, only that the reason made a difference: Abel was slain for his righteousness, Amnon for his wickedness. Observe the aggravations of this sin:—[1.] He would have Amnon slain *when his heart was merry with wine,* and he was consequently least apprehensive of danger, least able to resist it, and also least fit to go out of the world; as if his malice aimed to destroy both soul and body, not giving him time to say, *Lord, have mercy upon me.* What a dreadful surprise hath death been to many, whose hearts have been *overcharged with surfeiting and drunkenness!* [2.] His servants must be employed to do it, and so involved in the guilt. He was to give the word of command—*Smite Amnon;* and then they, in obedience to him, and, upon presumption that his authority would bear them out, must *kill him.* What an impious defiance does he bid to the divine law, when, though the command of God is express, *Thou shalt not kill,* he bids them kill Amnon, with this warrant, "*Have not I commanded you?* That is enough. *Be courageous,* and fear neither God nor man." Those servants are ill taught who obey their masters in contradiction to God, and those are wicked masters who have taught them to do so. Those are too obsequious that will damn their souls to please their masters, whose big words cannot secure them from God's wrath. Masters must always command their servants as those that know they also have a Master in heaven. [3.] He did it in the presence of *all the king's sons,* of whom it is said (*ch.* viii. 18) that they were *chief rulers;* so that it was an affront to public justice which they had the administration of, and to the king his father whom they represented, and a contempt of that sword which should have been a terror to his evil deeds, while his evil deeds, on the contrary, were a terror to those that bore it. [4.] There is reason to suspect that Absalom did this, not only to revenge his sister's quarrel, but to make way for himself to the throne, which he was ambitious of, and which he would stand fair for if Amnon the eldest son was taken off. When the word of command was given Absalom's servants failed not to execute it, being buoyed up with an opinion that their master, being now next heir to the crown (for Chileab was dead, as bishop Patrick thinks), would save them from harm. Now the threatened sword is drawn in David's house which should not depart from it. *First,* His eldest son falls by it, himself being, by his wickedness, the cause of it, and his father, by his connivance, accessory to it. *Secondly,* All his sons flee from it, and come home in terror, not knowing how far their brother Absalom's bloody design might extend. See what mischief sin makes in families.

30 And it came to pass, while they were in the way, that tidings came to David, saying, Absalom hath slain all the king's sons, and there is not one of them left. 31 Then the king arose, and tare his garments, and lay on the earth; and all his servants stood by with their clothes rent. 32 And Jonadab, the son of Shimeah David's brother, answered and said, Let not my lord suppose *that* they have slain all the young men the king's sons; for Amnon only is dead: for by the appointment of Absalom this hath been determined from the day that he forced his sister Tamar. 33 Now therefore let not my lord the king take the thing to his heart, to think that all the king's sons are dead: for Amnon only is dead. 34 But Absalom fled. And the young man that kept the watch lifted up his eyes, and looked, and, behold, there came much people by the way of the hill side behind him. 35 And Jonadab said unto the king, Behold, the king's sons come: as thy servant said, so it is. 36 And it came to pass, as soon as

he had made an end of speaking, that, behold, the king's sons came, and lifted up their voice and wept: and the king also and all his servants wept very sore. 37 But Absalom fled, and went to Talmai, the son of Ammihud, king of Geshur. And *David* mourned for his son every day. 38 So Absalom fled, and went to Geshur, and was there three years. 39 And *the soul of* king David longed to go forth unto Absalom: for he was comforted concerning Amnon, seeing he was dead.

Here is, I. The fright that David was put into by a false report brought to Jerusalem that Absalom had *slain all the king's sons, v.* 30. It is common for fame to make bad worse; and the first news of such a thing as this represents it as more dreadful than afterwards it proves. Let us not therefore be afraid of evil tidings, while they want confirmation, but, when we hear the worst, hope the best, at least hope better. However, this false news gave as much affliction to David, for the present, as if it had been true; he *tore his garments, and lay on the earth,* while as yet it was only a flying story, *v.* 31. It was well that David had grace; he had need enough of it, for he had strong passions.

II. The rectifying of the mistake in two ways:—1. By the sly suggestions of Jonadab, David's nephew, who could tell him, *Amnon only is dead,* and not all the king's sons (*v.* 32, 33), and could tell him too that it was done by the appointment of Absalom, and designed from the day Amnon forced his sister Tamar. What a wicked man was he, if he knew all this or had any cause to suspect it, that he did not make David acquainted with it sooner, that means might be used to make up the quarrel, or at least that David might not throw Amnon into the mouth of danger by letting him go to Absalom's house. If we do not our utmost to prevent mischief, we make ourselves accessory to it. *If we say, Behold, we knew it not; doth not he that pondereth the heart consider* whether we did or no? See Prov. xxiv. 11, 12. It is well if Jonadab was not as guilty of Amnon's death as he was of his sin; such friends do those prove who are hearkened to as counsellors to do wickedly: he that would not be so kind as to prevent Amnon's sin would not be so kind as to prevent his ruin, when, it should seem, he might have done both. 2. By the safe return of all the king's sons except Amnon. They and their attendants were speedily discovered by the watch (*v.* 34, 35), and soon arrived, to show themselves alive, but to bring the certain sad news that Absalom had murdered their brother Amnon. The grief David had been in for that which was not made him the better able to bear that which was, by giving him a sensible occasion, when he was undeceived, to thank God that all his sons were not dead: yet that Amnon was dead, and slain by his own brother in such a treacherous barbarous manner, was enough to put the king and court, the king and kingdom, into real mourning. Sorrow is never more reasonable than when there is sin in the case.

III. Absalom's flight from justice: *Absalom* immediately *fled, v.* 34. He was now as much afraid of the king's sons as they were of him; they fled from his malice, he from their justice. No part of the land of Israel could shelter him. The cities of refuge gave no protection to a wilful murderer Though David had let Amnon's incest go unpunished, Absalom could not promise himself his pardon for this murder; so express was the law in this case, and so well known David's justice, and his dread of blood-guiltiness. He therefore made the best of his way to his mother's relations, and was entertained by his grandfather *Talmai, king of Geshur* (*v.* 37), and there he was protected *three years* (*v.* 38), David not demanding him, and Talmai not thinking himself obliged to send him back unless he were demanded.

IV. David's uneasiness for his absence. He mourned for Amnon a good while (*v.* 37); but, he being past recal, time wore off that grief: he was *comforted concerning Amnon.* It also wore off too much his detestation of Absalom's sin; instead of loathing him as a murderer, he *longs to go forth to him, v.* 39. At first he could not find in his heart to do justice on him; now he can almost find in his heart to take him into his favour again. This was David's infirmity. Something God saw in his heart that made a difference, else we should have thought that he, as much as Eli, *honoured his sons more than God.*

CHAP. XIV.

How Absalom threw himself out of his royal father's protection and favour we read in the foregoing chapter, which left him an exile, outlawed, and proscribed; in this chapter we have the arts that were used to bring him and his father together again, and how, at last, it was done, which is here recorded to show the folly of David in sparing him and indulging him in his wickedness, for which he was soon after severely corrected by his unnatural rebellion. I. Joab, by bringing a feigned issue (as the lawyers speak) to be tried before him, in the case of a poor widow of Tekoah, gains from him a judgment in general, That the case might be so as that the putting of a murderer to death ought to be dispensed with, ver. 1—20. II. Upon the application of this, he gains from him an order to bring Absalom back to Jerusalem, while yet he was forbidden the court, ver. 21—24. III. After an account of Absalom, his person, and family, we are told how at length he was introduced by Joab into the king's presence, and the king was thoroughly reconciled to him, ver. 25—33.

NOW Joab the son of Zeruiah perceived that the king's heart *was* toward Absalom. 2 And Joab sent to Tekoah, and fetched thence a wise woman, and said unto her, I pray thee, feign thyself to be a mourner, and put on now mourning apparel, and anoint not thyself with oil, but be as a woman that had a long time mourned for the dead: 3 And come to the king, and speak on this manner unto him. So Joab put the words in her mouth. 4 And when the woman of Tekoah spake to the king, she fell on her face to the ground, and did obeisance, and said, Help, O king. 5 And the king said unto her, What aileth thee? And she answered, I *am* indeed a widow woman, and mine husband is dead. 6 And thy handmaid had two sons, and they two strove together in the field, and *there was* none to part them, but the one smote the other, and slew him. 7 And, behold, the whole family is risen against thine handmaid, and they said, Deliver him that smote his brother, that we may kill him, for the life of his brother whom he slew; and we will destroy the heir also: and so they shall quench my coal which is left, and shall not leave to my husband *neither* name nor remainder upon the earth. 8 And the king said unto the woman, Go to thine house, and I will give charge concerning thee. 9 And the woman of Tekoah said unto the king, My lord, O king, the iniquity *be* on me, and on my father's house: and the king and his throne *be* guiltless. 10 And the king said, Whosoever saith *aught* unto thee, bring him to me, and he shall not touch thee any more. 11 Then said she, I pray thee, let the king remember the LORD thy God, that thou wouldest not suffer the revengers of blood to destroy any more, lest they destroy my son. And he said, *As* the LORD liveth, there shall not one hair of thy son fall to the earth. 12 Then the woman said, Let thine handmaid, I pray thee, speak *one* word unto my lord the king. And he said, Say on. 13 And the woman said, Wherefore then hast thou thought such a thing against the people of God? for the king doth speak this thing as one which is faulty, in that the king doth not fetch home again his banished. 14 For we must needs die, and *are* as water spilt on the ground, which cannot be gathered up again; neither doth God respect *any* person: yet doth he devise means, that his banished be not expelled from him. 15 Now therefore that I am come to speak of this thing unto my lord the king, *it is* because the people have made me afraid: and thy handmaid said, I will now speak unto the king; it may be that the king will perform the request of his handmaid. 16 For the king will hear, to deliver his handmaid out of the hand of the man *that would* destroy me and my son together out of the inheritance of God. 17 Then thine handmaid said, The word of my lord the king shall now be comfortable: for as an angel of God, so *is* my lord the king to discern good and bad: therefore the LORD thy God will be with thee. 18 Then the king answered and said unto the woman, Hide not from me, I pray thee, the thing that I shall ask thee. And the woman said, Let my lord the king now speak. 19 And the king said, *Is not* the hand of Joab with thee in all this? And the woman answered and said, *As* thy soul liveth, my lord the king, none can turn to the right hand or to the left from aught that my lord the king hath spoken: for thy servant Joab, he bade me, and he put all these words in the mouth of thine handmaid: 20 To fetch about this form of speech hath thy servant Joab done this thing: and my lord *is* wise, according to the wisdom of an angel of God, to know all *things* that *are* in the earth.

Here is, I. Joab's design to get Absalom recalled out of banishment, his crime pardoned, and his attainder reversed, *v.* 1. Joab made himself very busy in this affair. 1 As a courtier that was studious, by all ways possible, to ingratiate himself with his prince and improve his interest in his favour: He *perceived that the king's heart was towards Absalom,* and that, the heat of his displeasure being over, he still retained his old affection for him, and only wanted a friend to court him to be reconciled, and to contrive for him how he might do it without impeaching the honour of his justice. Joab, finding how David stood affected, undertook this good office. 2. As a friend to Absalom, for whom perhaps he had a particular kindness, whom at least he looked upon as the rising sun, to whom it was his interest to recommend himself. He plainly foresaw that his father would at length be reconciled to him, and therefore thought he should make both his friends if he were instrumental to bring it about. 3. As a statesman, and one concerned for the public welfare. He knew how much Absalom was the darling of the people, and, if David should die while he was in banishment, it might occasion a civil war between those that were for him and those that were against him; for it is probable that though all Israel loved his person, yet they were much divided upon his case. 4. As one who was himself a delinquent, by the murder of Abner. He was conscious to himself of the guilt of blood, and that he was himself obnoxious to public justice, and therefore whatever favour he could procure to be shown to Absalom would corroborate his reprieve.

II. His contrivance to do it by laying somewhat of a parallel case before the king, which was done so dexterously by the person he employed that the king took it for a real case, and gave judgment upon it, as he had done upon Nathan's parable; and, the judgment being in favour of the criminal, the manager might, by that, discover his sentiments so far as to venture upon the application of it, and to show that it was the case of his own family, which, it is probable, she was instructed not to proceed to if the king's judgment upon her case should be severe.

1. The person he employed is not named, but she is said to be *a woman of Tekoah*, one whom he knew to be fit for such an undertaking: and it was requisite that the scene should be laid at a distance, that David might not think it strange that he had not heard of the case before. It is said, She was *a wise woman*, one that had a quicker wit and a readier tongue than most of her neighbours, *v.* 2. The truth of the story would be the less suspected when it came, as was supposed, from the person's own mouth.

2. The character she put on was that of a disconsolate widow, *v.* 2. Joab knew such a one would have an easy access to the king, who was always ready to comfort the mourners, especially the mourning widows, having himself mentioned it among the titles of God's honour that he is *a Judge of the widows*, Ps. lxviii. 5. God's ear, no doubt, is more open to the cries of the afflicted, and his heart too, than that of the most merciful princes on earth can be.

3. It was a case of compassion which she had to represent to the king, and a case in which she could have no relief but from the chancery in the royal breast, the law (and consequently the judgment of all the inferior courts) being against her. She tells the king that she had buried her husband (*v.* 5),—that she had two sons that were the support and comfort of her widowed state,—that these two (as young men are apt to do) fell out and fought, and one of them unhappily killed the other (*v.* 6),—that, for her part, she was desirous to protect the manslayer (for, as Rebekah argued concerning her two sons, *Why should she be deprived of them both in one day?* Gen. xxvii. 45), but though she, who was nearest of kin to the slain, was willing to let fall the demands of an avenger of blood, yet the other relations insisted upon it that the surviving brother should be put to death according to law, not out of any affection either to justice or to the memory of the slain brother, but that, by destroying the heir (which they had the impudence to own was the thing they aimed at), the inheritance might be theirs: and thus they would cut off, (1.) Her comfort: "*They shall quench my coal,* deprive me of the only support of my old age, and put a period to all my joy in this world, which is reduced to this one coal." (2.) Her husband's memory: "His family will be quite extinct, and they will *leave* him *neither name nor remainder,*" *v.* 7.

4. The king promised her his favour and a protection for her son. Observe how she improved the king's compassionate concessions. (1.) Upon the representation of her case he promised to consider of it and to give orders about it, *v.* 8. This was encouraging, that he did not dismiss her petition with "*Currat lex—Let the law take its course;* blood calls for blood, and let it have what it calls for:" but he will take time to enquire whether the allegations of her petition be true. (2.) The woman was not content with this, but begged that he would immediately give judgment in her favour; and if the matter of fact were not as she represented it, and consequently a wrong judgment given upon it, let her bear the blame, and free *the king and his throne from guilt, v.* 9. Yet her saying this would not acquit the king if he should pass sentence without taking due cognizance of the case. (3.) Being thus pressed, he made a further promise that she should not be injured nor insulted by her adversaries, but he would protect her from all molestation, *v.* 10. Magistrates ought to be the patrons of oppressed widows. (4.) Yet this does not content her, unless she can get her son's pardon, and protection for him too. Parents are not easy, unless their children be safe, safe for both worlds: "*Let not the avenger of blood destroy my son* (*v.* 11), for I am undone if I lose him; as good take my life as his. *Therefore let the king remember the Lord thy God,*" that is, [1.] "Let him confirm this merciful sentence with an oath, making mention of the Lord our God, by way of appeal to him, that the sentence may be indisputable and irreversible; and then I shall be easy." See Heb. vi. 17, 18. [2.] "Let him consider what good reason there is for this merciful sentence, and then he himself will be confirmed in it. *Remember* how gracious and merciful *the Lord thy God* is, how he bears long with sinners and does not deal with them according

to their deserts, but is ready to forgive. *Remember* how *the Lord thy God* spared Cain, who slew his brother, and protected him from the avengers of blood, Gen. iv. 15. *Remember* how *the Lord thy God* forgave thee the blood of Uriah, and let the king, that has found mercy, show mercy." Note, Nothing is more proper, nor more powerful, to engage us to every duty, especially to all acts of mercy and kindness, than to remember the Lord our God. (5.) This importunate widow, by pressing the matter thus closely, obtains at last a full pardon for her son, ratified with an oath as she desired: *As the Lord liveth, there shall not one hair of thy son fall to the earth,* that is, "I will undertake he shall come to no damage upon this account." The Son of David has assured all that put themselves under his protection that, though they should be put to death for his sake, *not a hair of their head shall perish* (Luke xxi. 16—18), though they should lose for him, they shall not lose by him. Whether David did well thus to undertake the protection of a murderer, whom the cities of refuge would not protect, I cannot say. But, as the matter of fact appeared to him, there was not only great reason for compassion to the mother, but room enough for a favourable judgment concerning the son: he had slain his brother, but he *hated him not in time past;* it was upon a sudden provocation, and, for aught that appeared, it might be done in his own defence. He pleaded not this himself, but the judge must be of counsel for the prisoner; and therefore, *Let mercy* at this time *rejoice against judgment.*

5. The case being thus adjudged in favour of her son, it is now time to apply it to the king's son, Absalom. The mask here begins to be thrown off, and another scene opened. The king is surprised, but not at all displeased, to find his humble petitioner, of a sudden, become his reprover, his privy-counsellor, an advocate for the prince his son, and the mouth of the people, undertaking to represent to him their sentiments. She begs his pardon, and his patience, for what she had further to say (*v.* 12), and has leave to say it, the king being very well pleased with her wit and humour. (1.) She supposes Absalom's case to be, in effect, the same with that which she had put as her son's; and therefore, if the king would protect her son, though he had slain his brother, much more ought he to protect his own, and to *fetch home his banished, v.* 13. *Mutato nomine, de te fabula narratur—Change but the name, to you the tale belongs.* She names not Absalom, nor needed she to name him. David longed so much after him, and had him so much in his thoughts, that he was soon aware whom she meant by his banished. And in those two words were two arguments which the king's tender spirit felt the force of: "He is banished, and has for three years undergone the disgrace and terror, and all the inconveniences, of banishment. *Sufficient to such a one is this punishment.* But he is *thy* banished, thy own son, a piece of thyself, thy dear son, whom thou lovest." It is true, Absalom's case differed very much from that which she had put. Absalom did not slay his brother upon a hasty passion, but maliciously, and upon an old grudge; not in the field, where there were no witnesses, but at table, before all his guests. Absalom was not an only son, as hers was; David had many more, and one lately born, more likely to be his successor than Absalom, for he was called *Jedidiah,* because God loved him. But David was himself too well affected to the cause to be critical in his remarks upon the disparity of the cases, and was more desirous than she could be to bring that favourable judgment to his own son which he had given concerning hers. (2.) She reasons upon it with the king, to persuade him to recal Absalom out of banishment, give him his pardon, and take him into his favour again. [1.] She pleads the interest which the people of Israel had in him. "What is done against him is done *against the people of God,* who have their eye upon him as heir of the crown, at least have their eye upon the house of David in general, with which the covenant is made, and which therefore they cannot tamely see the diminution and decay of by the fall of so many of its branches in the flower of their age. Therefore *the king speaks as one that is faulty,* for he will provide that my husband's name and memory be not cut off, and yet takes no care though his own be in danger, which is of more value and importance than ten thousand of ours." [2.] She pleads man's mortality (*v.* 14): "*We must needs die.* Death is appointed for us; we cannot avoid the thing itself, nor defer it till another time. We are all under a fatal necessity of dying; and, when we are dead, we are past recal, as water spilt upon the ground; nay, even while we are alive, we are so, we have lost our immortality, past retrieve. Amnon must have died, some time, if Absalom had not killed him; and, if Absalom be now put to death for killing him, that will not bring him to life again." This was poor reasoning, and would serve against the punishment of any murderer: but, it should seem, Amnon was a man little regarded by the people and his death little lamented, and it was generally thought hard that so dear a life as Absalom's should go for one so little valued as Amnon's. [3.] She pleads God's mercy and his clemency towards poor guilty sinners: "*God does not take away the soul, or life, but devises means that his banished,* his children that have offended him, and are obnoxious to his justice, as Absalom is to thine, *be not* for ever *expelled from him,*" *v.* 14. Here are two great instances of the mercy of God to sinners, properly urged as reasons for showing mercy:—*First,* The patience he exercises

towards them. His law is broken, yet he does not immediately take away the life of those that break it, does not strike sinners dead, as justly he might, in the act of sin, but bears with them, and waits to be gracious. God's vengeance had suffered Absalom to live; why then should not David's justice suffer him? *Secondly,* The provision he has made for their restoration to his favour, that though by sin they have banished themselves from him, yet they might not be expelled, or cast off, for ever. Atonement might be made for sinners by sacrifice. Lepers, and others ceremonially unclean, were banished, but provision was made for their cleansing, that, though for a time excluded, they might not be finally expelled. The state of sinners is a state of banishment from God. Poor banished sinners are likely to be for ever expelled from God if some course be not taken to prevent it. It is against the mind of God that they should be so, for he is not willing that any should perish. Infinite wisdom has devised proper means to prevent it; so that it is the sinners' own fault if they be cast off. This instance of God's good-will towards us all should incline us to be merciful and compassionate one towards another, Matt. xviii. 32, 33.

6. She concludes her address with high compliments to the king, and strong expressions of her assurance that he would do what was just and kind both in the one case and in the other (*v.* 15—17); for, as if the case had been real, still she pleads for herself and her son, yet meaning Absalom. (1.) She would not have troubled the king thus, but that the people made her afraid. Understanding it of her own case, all her neighbours made her apprehensive of the ruin she and her son were upon the brink of, from the avengers of blood, the terror of which made her thus bold in her application to the king himself. Understanding it of Absalom's case, she gives the king to understand, what he did not know before, that the nation was disgusted at his severity towards Absalom to such a degree that she was really afraid it would occasion a general mutiny or insurrection, for the preventing of which great mischief she ventured to speak to the king himself. The fright she was in must excuse her rudeness. (2.) She applied to him with a great confidence in his wisdom and clemency: "I said, *I will speak to the king* myself, and ask nobody to speak for me; for the king will hear reason, even from so mean a creature as I am, will hear the cries of the oppressed, and will not suffer the poorest of his subjects to be *destroyed out of the inheritance of God,*" that is, "driven out of the land of Israel, to seek for shelter among the uncircumcised, as Absalom is, whose case is so much the worse, that, being shut *out of the inheritance of God,* he wants God's law and ordinances, which might help to bring him to repentance, and is in danger of being infected with the idolatry of the heathen among whom he sojourns, and of bringing home the infection. To engage the king to grant her request, she expressed a confident hope that his answer would be comfortable, and such as angels bring (as bishop Patrick explains it), who are messengers of divine mercy. What this woman says by way of compliment the prophet says by way of promise (Zech. xii. 8), that, when *the weak shall be as David, the house of David shall be as the angel of the Lord.* "And, in order to this, *the Lord thy God will be with thee,* to assist thee in this and every judgment thou givest." Great expectations are great engagements, especially to persons of honour, to do their utmost not to disappoint those that depend upon them.

7. The hand of Joab is suspected by the king, and acknowledged by the woman, to be in all this, *v.* 18—20. (1.) The king soon suspected it. For he could not think that such a woman as this would appeal to him, in a matter of such moment, of her own accord; and he knew none so likely to set her on as Joab, who was a politic man and a friend of Absalom. (2.) The woman very honestly owned it: "*Thy servant Joab bade me.* If it be well done, let him have the thanks; if ill, let him bear the blame." Though she found it very agreeable to the king, yet she would not take the praise of it to herself, but speaks the truth as it was, and gives us an example to do likewise, and never to tell a lie for the concealing of a well-managed scheme. *Dare to be true; nothing can need a lie.*

21 And the king said unto Joab, Behold now, I have done this thing: go therefore, bring the young man Absalom again. 22 And Joab fell to the ground on his face, and bowed himself, and thanked the king: and Joab said, To day thy servant knoweth that I have found grace in thy sight, my lord, O king, in that the king hath fulfilled the request of his servant. 23 So Joab arose and went to Geshur, and brought Absalom to Jerusalem. 24 And the king said, Let him turn to his own house, and let him not see my face. So Absalom returned to his own house, and saw not the king's face. 25 But in all Israel there was none to be so much praised as Absalom for his beauty: from the sole of his foot even to the crown of his head there was no blemish in him. 26 And when he polled his head, (for it was at every

year's end that he polled *it:* because *the hair* was heavy on him, therefore he polled it:) he weighed the hair of his head at two hundred shekels after the king's weight. 27 And unto Absalom there were born three sons, and one daughter, whose name *was* Tamar: she was a woman of a fair countenance.

Observe here, I. Orders given for the bringing back of Absalom. The errand on which the woman came to David was so agreeable, and her management of it so very ingenious and surprising, that he was brought into a peculiarly kind humour: *Go* (says he to Joab), *bring the young man Absalom again, v.* 21. He was himself inclined to favour him, yet, for the honour of his justice, he would not do it but upon intercession made for him, which may illustrate the methods of divine grace. It is true God has thoughts of compassion towards poor sinners, not willing that any should perish, yet he is reconciled to them through a Mediator, who intercedes with him on their behalf, and to whom he has given these orders, *Go, bring them again. God was in Christ reconciling the world to himself,* and he came to this land of our banishment to bring us to God. Joab, having received these orders, 1. Returns thanks to the king for doing him the honour to employ him in an affair so universally grateful, *v.* 22. Joab took it as a kindness to himself, and (some think) as an indication that he would never call him to an account for the murder he had been guilty of. But, if he meant so, he was mistaken, as we shall find, 1 Kings ii. 5, 6. 2. Delays not to execute David's orders; he brought Absalom to Jerusalem, *v.* 23. I see not how David can be justified in suspending the execution of the ancient law (Gen. ix. 6), *Whoso sheds man's blood, by man shall his blood be shed,* in which a righteous magistrate ought not to *acknowledge even his brethren, or know his own children.* God's laws were never designed to be like cobwebs, which catch the little flies, but suffer the great ones to break through. God justly made Absalom, whom his foolish pity spared, a scourge to him. But, though he allowed him to return to his own house, he forbade him the court, and would not see him himself, *v.* 24. He put him under this interdict, (1.) For his own honour, that he might not seem to countenance so great a criminal, nor to forgive him too easily. (2.) For Absalom's greater humiliation. Perhaps he had heard something of his conduct when Joab went to fetch him, which gave him too much reason to think that he was not truly penitent; he therefore put him under this mark of his displeasure, that he might be awakened to a sight of his sin and to sorrow for it, and might make his peace with God, upon the first notice of which, no doubt, David would be forward to receive him again into his favour.

II. Occasion taken hence to give an account of Absalom. Nothing is said of his wisdom and piety. Though he was the son of such a devout father, we read nothing of his devotion. Parents cannot give grace to their children, though they give them ever so good an education. All that is here said of him is, 1. That he was a very handsome man; there was not his equal in all Israel for beauty, (*v.* 25), a poor commendation for a man that had nothing else in him valuable. Handsome are those that handsome do. Many a polluted deformed soul dwells in a fair and comely body; witness Absalom's, that was polluted with blood, and deformed with unnatural disaffection to his father and prince. In his body there was no blemish, but in his mind nothing but wounds and bruises. Perhaps his comeliness was one reason why his father was so fond of him and protected him from justice. Those have reason to fear affliction in their children who are better pleased with their beauty than with their virtue. 2. That he had a very fine head of hair. Whether it was the length, or colour, or extraordinary softness of it, something there was which made it very valuable and very much an ornament to him, *v.* 26. This notice is taken of his hair, not as the hair of a Nazarite (he was far from that strictness), but as the hair of a beau. He let it grow till it was a burden to him, and was heavy on him, nor would he cut it as long as ever he could bear it; as pride feels no cold, so it feels no heat, and that which feeds and gratifies it is not complained of, though very uneasy. When he did poll it at certain times, for ostentation he had it weighed, that it might be seen how much it excelled other men's, and it weighed 200 shekels, which some reckon to be three pounds and two ounces of our weight; and with the oil and powder, especially if powdered (as Josephus says the fashion then was) with gold-dust, bishop Patrick thinks it is not at all incredible that it should weigh so much. This fine hair proved his halter, *ch.* xviii. 9. 3. That his family began to be built up. It is probable that it was a good while before he had a child; and then it was that, despairing of having one, he set up that pillar which is mentioned *ch.* xviii. 18, to bear up his name; but afterwards he had three sons and one daughter, *v.* 27. Or perhaps these sons, while he was hatching his rebellion, were all cut off by the righteous hand of God, and thereupon he set up that monument.

28 So Absalom dwelt two full years in Jerusalem, and saw not the king's face. 29 Therefore Absalom sent for Joab, to have sent him to the king; but he would not come to him: and

when he sent again the second time, he would not come. 30 Therefore he said unto his servants, See, Joab's field is near mine, and he hath barley there; go and set it on fire. And Absalom's servants set the field on fire. 31 Then Joab arose, and came to Absalom unto *his* house, and said unto him, Wherefore have thy servants set my field on fire? 32 And Absalom answered Joab, Behold, I sent unto thee, saying, Come hither, that I may send thee to the king, to say, Wherefore am I come from Geshur? *it had been* good for me *to have been* there still: now therefore let me see the king's face; and if there be *any* iniquity in me, let him kill me. 33 So Joab came to the king, and told him: and when he had called for Absalom, he came to the king, and bowed himself on his face to the ground before the king: and the king kissed Absalom.

Three years Absalom had been an exile from his father-in-law, and now two years a prisoner at large in his own house, and, in both, better dealt with than he deserved; yet his spirit was still unhumbled, his pride unmortified, and, instead of being thankful that his life is spared, he thinks himself sorely wronged that he is not restored to all his places at court. Had he truly repented of his sin, his distance from the gaieties of the court, and his solitude and retirement in his own house, especially being in Jerusalem the holy city, would have been very agreeable to him. If a murderer must live, yet let him be for ever a recluse. But Absalom could not bear this just and gentle mortification. He longed to see the king's face, pretending it was because he loved him, but really because he wanted an opportunity to supplant him. He cannot do his father a mischief till he is reconciled to him; this therefore is the first branch of his plot; this snake cannot sting again till he be warmed in his father's bosom. He gained this point, not by pretended submissions and promises of reformation, but (would you think it?) by insults and injuries. 1. By his insolent carriage towards Joab, he brought him to mediate for him. Once and again he sent to Joab to come and speak with him, for he durst not go to him; but Joab would not come (*v.* 29), probably because Absalom had not owned the kindness he had done him in bringing him to Jerusalem so gratefully as he thought he should have done; proud men take every service done them for a debt. One would think that a person in Absalom's circumstances should have sent to Joab a kindly message, and offered him a large gratuity: courtiers expect noble presents. But, instead of this, he bids his servants set Joab's corn-fields on fire (*v.* 30), as spiteful a thing as he could do. Samson could not think of a greater injury to do the Philistines than this. Strange that Absalom should think, by doing Joab a mischief, to prevail with him to do him a kindness, or to recommend himself to the favour of his prince or people by showing himself so very malicious and ill-natured, and such an enemy to the public good, for the fire might spread to the corn of others. Yet by this means he brings Joab to him, *v.* 31. Thus God, by afflictions, brings those to him that kept at a distance from him. Absalom was obliged by the law to make restitution (Exod. xxii. 6), yet we do not find either that he offered it or that Joab demanded it. Joab (it might be) thought he could not justify his refusal to go and speak with him; and therefore Absalom thought he could justify his taking this way to fetch him. And now Joab (perhaps frightened at the surprising boldness and fury of Absalom, and apprehensive that he had made an interest in the people strong enough to bear him out in doing the most daring things, else he would never have done this) not only puts up with this injury, but goes on his errand to the king. See what some men can do by threats, and carrying things with a high hand. 2. By his insolent message (for I can call it no better) to the king, he recovered his place at court, to see the king's face, that is, to become a privy counsellor, Esth. i. 14. (1.) His message was haughty and imperious, and very unbecoming either a son or a subject, *v.* 32. He undervalued the favour that had been shown him in recalling him from banishment, and restoring him to his own house, and that in Jerusalem: *Wherefore have I come from Geshur?* He denies his own crimes, though most notorious, and will not own that there was any iniquity in him, insinuating that therefore he had been wronged in the rebuke he had been under. He defies the king's justice: "Let him kill me, if he can find in his heart," knowing he loved him too well to do it. (2.) Yet with this message he carried his point, *v.* 33. David's strong affection for him construed all this to be the language of a great respect to his father, and an earnest desire of his favour, when, alas! it was far otherwise. See how easily wise and good men may be imposed upon by their own children that design ill, especially when they are blindly fond of them. Absalom, by the posture of his body, testified his submission to his father: *He bowed himself on his face to the ground;* and David, with a kiss, sealed his pardon. Did the bowels of a father prevail to reconcile him to an impenitent son, and shall penitent sinners question the compassion of him who is the Father of mercy? If

Ephraim bemoan himself, God soon bemoans him, with all the kind expressions of a fatherly tenderness: *He is a dear son, a pleasant child,* Jer. xxxi. 20.

CHAP. XV.

Absalom's name signifies "the peace of his father," yet he proves his greatest trouble; so often are we disappointed in our expectations from the creature. The sword entailed upon David's house had hitherto been among his children, but now it begins to be drawn against himself, with this aggravation, that he may thank himself for it, for, had he done justice upon the murderer, he would have prevented the traitor. The story of Absalom's rebellion begins with this chapter, but we must go over three or four more before we see the end of it. In this chapter we have, I. The arts Absalom used to insinuate himself into the people's affections, ver. 1—6. II. His open avowal of his pretensions to the crown at Hebron, whither he went under colour of a vow, and the strong party that appeared for him there, ver. 7—12. III. The notice brought of this to David, and his flight from Jerusalem thereupon, ver. 13—18. In his flight we are told, 1. What passed between him and Ittai, ver. 19—22. 2. The concern of the country for him, ver. 23. 3. His conference with Zadok, ver. 24—29. 4. His tears and prayers upon this occasion, ver. 30, 31. 5. Matters concerted by him with Hushai, ver. 32—37. Now the word of God was fulfilled, that he would "raise up evil against him out of his own house," ch. xii. 11.

AND it came to pass after this, that Absalom prepared him chariots and horses, and fifty men to run before him. 2 And Absalom rose up early, and stood beside the way of the gate: and it was *so,* that when any man that had a controversy came to the king for judgment, then Absalom called unto him, and said, Of what city *art* thou? And he said, Thy servant *is* of one of the tribes of Israel. 3 And Absalom said unto him, See, thy matters *are* good and right; but *there is* no man *deputed* of the king to hear thee. 4 Absalom said moreover, Oh that I were made judge in the land, that every man which hath any suit or cause might come unto me, and I would do him justice! 5 And it was *so,* that when any man came nigh *to him* to do him obeisance, he put forth his hand, and took him, and kissed him. 6 And on this manner did Absalom to all Israel that came to the king for judgment: so Absalom stole the hearts of the men of Israel.

Absalom is no sooner restored to his place at court than he aims to be in the throne. He that was unhumbled under his troubles became insufferably proud when they were over; and he cannot be content with the honour of being the king's son, and the prospect of being his successor, but he must be king now. His mother was a king's daughter; on that perhaps he valued himself, and despised his father, who was but the son of Jesse. She was the daughter of a heathen king, which made him the less concerned for the peace of Israel. David, in this unhappy issue of that marriage, smarted for his being unequally yoked with an unbeliever. When Absalom was restored to the king's favour, if he had had any sense of gratitude, he would have studied how to oblige his father, and make him easy; but, on the contrary, he meditates how to undermine him, by stealing the hearts of the people from him. Two things recommend a man to popular esteem—greatness and goodness.

I. Absalom looks great, *v.* 1. He had learned of the king of Geshur (what was not allowed to the kings of Israel) to multiply horses, which made him look desirable, while his father, on his mule, looked despicable. The people desired a king like the nations; and such a one Absalom will be, appearing in pomp and magnificence, above what had been seen in Jerusalem. Samuel had foretold that this would be *the manner of the king:* He shall *have chariots and horsemen, and some shall run before his chariots* (1 Sam. viii. 11); and this is Absalom's manner. Fifty footmen (in rich liveries we may suppose) running before him, to give notice of his approach, would highly gratify his pride and the people's foolish fancy. David thinks that this parade is designed only to grace his court, and connives at it. Those parents know not what they do who indulge a proud humour in their children; for I have seen more young people ruined by pride than by any one lust whatsoever.

II. Absalom will seem very good too, but with a very bad design. Had he proved himself a good son and a good subject, and set himself to serve his father's interest, he would have done his present duty, and shown himself worthy of future honours, after his father's death. Those that know how to obey well know how to rule. But to show how good a judge and how good a king he will be is but to deceive himself and others. Those are good indeed that are good in their own place, not that pretend how good they would be in other people's places. But this is all the goodness we find in Absalom.

1. He wishes that he were a judge in Israel, *v.* 4. He had all the pomp and all the pleasure he could wish, lived as great and in as much ease as any man could; yet this will not content him, unless he have power too: *O that I were a judge in Israel!* He that should himself have been judged to death for murder has the impudence to aim at being a judge of others. We read not of Absalom's wisdom, virtue, or learning in the laws, nor had he given any proofs of his love to justice, but the contrary; yet he wishes he were judge. Note, Those are commonly most ambitious of preferment that are least fit for it; the best qualified are the most modest and self-diffident, while it is no better than the spirit of an Absalom that says, *O that I were a judge in Israel!*

2. He takes a very bad course for the accomplishing of his wish. Had he humbly petitioned his father to employ him in the administration of justice, and studied to qualify himself for it (according to the rule,

Exod. xviii. 21), no doubt he would have been sure of the next judge's place that fell; but this is too mean a post for his proud spirit. It is below him to be subordinate, though to the king his father; he must be supreme or nothing. He wants to be such a judge that every man who has any cause shall come to him: in all causes, and over all persons, he must preside, little thinking what a fatigue this would be to have every man come to him. Moses himself could not bear it. Those know not what power is that grasp at so much, so very much. To gain the power he aims at, he endeavours to instil into the people's minds,

(1.) A bad opinion of the present administration, as if the affairs of the kingdom were altogether neglected, and no care taken about them. He got round him all he could that had business at the council-board, enquired what their business was; and, [1.] Upon a slight and general enquiry into their cause, he pronounced it good: *Thy matters are right.* A fit man indeed to be a judge, who would give judgment upon hearing one side only! For he has a bad cause indeed that cannot put a good colour upon it, when he himself has the telling of the story. But, [2.] He told them that it was to no purpose to appeal to the throne: "*There is no man deputed of the king to hear thee.* The king is himself old, and past business, or so taken up with his devotions that he never minds business; his sons are so addicted to their pleasures that, though they have the name of chief rulers, they take no care of the affairs committed to them." He further seems to insinuate what a great want there was of him while he was banished and confined, and how much the public suffered by his exile; what his father said truly in Saul's reign (Ps. lxxv. 3) he says falsely: *The land and all the inhabitants of it are dissolved,* all will go to wreck and ruin, unless *I bear up the pillars of it.* Every appellant shall be made to believe that he will never have justice done him, unless Absalom be viceroy or lord-justice. It is the way of turbulent, factious, aspiring men, to reproach the government they are under. *Presumptuous are they, self-willed, and not afraid to speak evil of dignities,* 2 Pet. ii. 10. Even David himself, the best of kings, and his administration, could not escape the worst of censures. Those that aim to usurp cry out of grievances, and pretend to design nothing but the redress of them: as Absalom here.

(2.) A good opinion of his own fitness to rule. That the people might say, "O that Absalom were a judge!" (and they are apt enough to desire changes), he recommends himself to them, [1.] As very diligent. He rose up early, and appeared in public before the rest of the king's sons were stirring, and he stood beside the way of the gate, where the courts of judgment sat, as one mightily concerned to see justice done and public business despatched. [2.] As very inquisitive and prying, and desirous to be acquainted with every one's case. He would know of what city every one was that came for judgment, that he might inform himself concerning every part of the kingdom and the state of it, *v.* 2. [3.] As very familiar and humble. If any Israelite offered to do obeisance to him he took him and embraced him as a friend. No man's conduct could be more condescending, while his heart was as proud as Lucifer's. Ambitious projects are often carried on by *a show of humility,* Col. ii. 23. He knew what a grace it puts upon greatness to be affable and courteous, and how much it wins upon common people: had he been sincere in it, it would have been his praise; but to fawn upon the people that he might betray them was abominable hypocrisy. *He croucheth, and humbleth himself, to draw them into his net,* Ps. x. 9, 10.

7 And it came to pass after forty years, that Absalom said unto the king, I pray thee, let me go and pay my vow, which I have vowed unto the LORD, in Hebron. 8 For thy servant vowed a vow while I abode at Geshur in Syria, saying, If the LORD shall bring me again indeed to Jerusalem, then I will serve the LORD. 9 And the king said unto him, Go in peace. So he arose, and went to Hebron. 10 But Absalom sent spies throughout all the tribes of Israel, saying, As soon as ye hear the sound of the trumpet, then ye shall say, Absalom reigneth in Hebron. 11 And with Absalom went two hundred men out of Jerusalem, *that were* called; and they went in their simplicity, and they knew not any thing. 12 And Absalom sent for Ahithophel the Gilonite, David's counsellor, from his city, *even* from Giloh, while he offered sacrifices. And the conspiracy was strong: for the people increased continually with Absalom.

We have here the breaking out of Absalom's rebellion, which he had long been contriving. It is said to be *after forty years, v.* 7. But whence it is to be dated we are not told; not from David's beginning his reign, for then it would fall in the last year of his life, which is not probable; but either from his first anointing by Samuel seven years before, or rather (I think) from the people's desiring a king, and the first change of the government into a monarchy, which might be about ten years before David began to reign; it is fitly dated thence, to show that the same restless spirit was still working, and still they were given to change: as fond now of a new man as then of a new model. So it fell about the thirtieth year of David's reign. Absalom's plot being now ripe for execution,

I. The place he chose for the rendezvous of his party was Hebron, the place where he was born, and where his father began his reign and continued it several years, which would give some advantage to his pretensions. Every one knew Hebron to be a royal city; and it lay in the heart of Judah's lot, in which tribe, probably, he thought his interest strong.

II. The pretence he had both to go thither and to invite his friends to him there was to offer a sacrifice to God, in performance of a vow he had made during his banishment, *v.* 7, 8. We have cause enough to suspect that he had not made any such vow; it does not appear that he was so religiously inclined. But he that stuck not at murder and treason would not make conscience of a lie to serve his purpose. If he said he had made such a vow, nobody could disprove him. Under this pretence, 1. He got leave of his father to go to Hebron. David would be well pleased to hear that his son, in his exile, was so desirous to return to Jerusalem, not only his father's city, but the city of the living God,—that he looked up to God, to bring him back,—that he had vowed, if he were brought back, to serve the Lord, whose service he had hitherto neglected,—and that now, being brought back, he remembered his vow, and resolved to perform it. If he think fit to do it in Hebron, rather than in Sion or Gibeon, the good king is so well pleased with the thing itself that he will not object against his choice of the place. See how willing tender parents are to believe the best concerning their children, and, upon the least indication of good, to hope, even concerning those that have been untoward, that they will repent and reform. But how easy is it for children to take advantage of their good parents' credulity, and to impose upon them with the show of religion, while still they are what they were! David was overjoyed to hear that Absalom inclined to *serve the Lord,* and therefore readily gave him leave to go to Hebron, and to go thither with solemnity. 2. He got a good number of sober substantial citizens to go along with him, *v.* 11. There went 200 men, probably of the principal men of Jerusalem, whom he invited to join with him in his feast upon his sacrifice; and they went in their simplicity, not in the least suspecting that Absalom had any bad design in this journey. He knew that it was to no purpose to tempt them into his plot: they were inviolably firm to David. But he drew them in to accompany him, that the common people might think that they were in his interest, and that David was deserted by some of his best friends. Note, It is no new thing for very good men, and very good things, to be made use of by designing men to put a colour upon bad practices. When religion is made a stalking-horse, and sacrifice a shoeing-horn, to sedition and usurpation it is not to be wondered at if some that were well affected to religion, as these followers of Absalom here, are imposed upon by the fallacy, and drawn in to give countenance to that, with their names, which in their heart they abhor, not having known the depths of Satan.

III. The project he laid was to get himself proclaimed king throughout all the tribes of Israel upon a signal given, *v.* 10. Spies were sent abroad, to be ready in every country to receive the notice with satisfaction and acclamations of joy, and to make the people believe that the news was both very true and very good, and that they were all concerned to take up arms for their new king. Upon the sudden spreading of this proclamation, "*Absalom reigns in Hebron,*" some would conclude that David was dead, others that he had resigned: and thus those that were in the secret would draw in many to appear for Absalom, and to come in to his assistance, who, if they had rightly understood the matter, would have abhorred the thought of it, but, being drawn in, would adhere to him. See what artifices ambitious men use for the compassing of their ends; and in matters of state, as well as in matters of religion, let us not be forward to believe every spirit, but try the spirits.

IV. The person he especially courted and relied upon in this affair was Ahithophel, a politic thinking man, and one that had a clear head and a great compass of thought, that had been David's counsellor, his guide and his acquaintance (Ps. lv. 13), his *familiar friend, in whom he trusted, who did eat of his bread,* Ps. xli. 9. But, upon some disgust of David's against him, or his against David, he was banished, or retired from public business, and lived privately in the country. How should a man of such good principles as David, and a man of such corrupt principles as Ahithophel, long agree? A fitter tool Absalom could not find in all the kingdom than one that was so great a statesman, and yet was disaffected to the present ministry. While Absalom was offering his sacrifices, in performance of his pretended vow, he sent for this man. So much was his heart on the projects of his ambition that he could not stay to make an end of his devotion, which showed what his eye was upon in all, and that it was but for a pretence that he made long offerings.

V. The party that joined with him proved at last very considerable. The people increased continually with Absalom, which made the conspiracy strong and formidable. Every one whom he had complimented and caressed (pronouncing his matters right and good, especially if afterwards the cause went against him) not only came himself, but made all the interest he could for him, so that he wanted not for numbers. The majority is no certain rule to judge of equity by. *All the world wondered after the beast.* Whether Absalom formed this design merely in the height of his ambition and fondness to rule, or whether there was not in it also malice against his father and revenge for his banishment and confinement, though this punishment was so much less than he deserved, does not appear. But, generally, that which aims at the crown aims at the head that wears it.

13 And there came a messenger to David, saying, The hearts of the men of Israel are after Absalom. 14 And David said unto all his servants that *were* with him at Jerusalem, Arise, and let us flee; for we shall not *else* escape from Absalom: make speed to depart, lest he overtake us suddenly, and bring evil upon us, and smite the city with the edge of the sword. 15 And the king's servants said unto the king, Behold, thy servants *are ready to do* whatsoever my lord the king shall appoint. 16 And the king went forth, and all his household after him. And the king left ten women, *which were* concubines, to keep the house. 17 And the king went forth, and all the people after him, and tarried in a place that was far off. 18 And all his servants passed on beside him; and all the Cherethites, and all the Pelethites, and all the Gittites, six hundred men which came after him from Gath, passed on before the king. 19 Then said the king to Ittai the Gittite, Wherefore goest thou also with us? return to thy place, and abide with the king: for thou *art* a stranger, and also an exile. 20 Whereas thou camest *but* yesterday, should I this day make thee go up and down with us? seeing I go whither I may, return thou, and take back thy brethren: mercy and truth *be* with thee. 21 And Ittai answered the king, and said, *As* the LORD liveth, and *as* my lord the king liveth, surely in what place my lord the king shall be, whether in death or life, even there also will thy servant be. 22 And David said to Ittai, Go and pass over. And Ittai the Gittite passed over, and all his men, and all the little ones that *were* with him. 23 And all the country wept with a loud voice, and all the people passed over: the king also himself passed over the brook Kidron, and all the people passed over, toward the way of the wilderness.

Here is, I. The notice brought to David of Absalom's rebellion, *v.* 13. The matter was bad enough, and yet it seems to have been made worse to him (as such things commonly are) than really it was; for he was told that *the hearts of the men of Israel* (that is, the generality of them, at least the leading men) were *after Absalom.* But David was the more apt to believe it because now he could call to mind the arts that Absalom had used to inveigle them, and perhaps reflected upon it with regret that he had not done more to counterwork him, and secure his own interest, which he had been too confident of. Note, It is the wisdom of princes to make sure of the hearts of their subjects; for, if they have them, they have their purses, and arms, and all, at their service.

II. The alarm this gave to David, and the resolutions he came to thereupon. We may well imagine him in a manner thunderstruck, when he heard that the son he loved so dearly, and had been so indulgent to, was so unnaturally and ungratefully in arms against him. Well might he say with Cæsar, Καὶ σὺ τεκνον—*What, thou my son?* Let not parents raise their hopes too high from their children, lest they be disappointed. David did not call a council, but, consulting only with God and his own heart, determined immediately to quit Jerusalem, *v.* 14. He took up this strange resolve, so disagreeable to his character as a man of courage, either, 1. As a penitent, submitting to the rod, and lying down under God's correcting hand. Conscience now reminded him of his sin in the matter of Uriah, and the sentence he was under for it, which was that *evil should arise against him out of his own house.* "Now," thinks he, "the word of God begins to be fulfilled, and it is not for me to contend with it or fight against it; God is righteous and I submit." Before unrighteous Absalom he could justify himself and stand it out; but before the righteous God he must condemn himself and yield to his judgments. Thus he *accepts the punishment of his iniquity.* Or, 2. As a politician. Jerusalem was a great city, but not tenable; it should seem, by David's prayer (Ps. li. 18), that the walls of it were not built up, much less was it regularly fortified. It was too large to be garrisoned by so small a force as David had now with him. He had reason to fear that the generality of the inhabitants were too well affected to Absalom to be true to him. Should he fortify himself here, he might lose the country, in which, especially among those that lay furthest from Absalom's tampering, he hoped to have the most friends. And he had such a kindness for Jerusalem that he was loth to make it the seat of war, and expose it to the calamities of a siege; he will rather quit it tamely to the rebels. Note, Good men, when they suffer themselves, care not how few are involved with them in suffering.

III. His hasty flight from Jerusalem. His servants agreed to the measures he took, faithfully adhered to him (*v.* 15), and assured him of their inviolable allegiance, whereupon, 1. He went out of Jerusalem himself on foot, while his son Absalom had chariots and horses. It is not always the best man, nor the best cause, that makes the best figure. See here, not only the servant, but the traitor, on horseback, while the prince, the rightful prince, *walks as a servant upon the earth,* Eccl. x. 7. Thus he chose to do, to abase himself so much the more under God's hand, and in condescension to his friends and followers, with whom he would walk, in token that he would live and die with them. 2. He took his household with him, his wives and children, that he might protect them in this day of danger, and that they might be a comfort to him in this day of grief. Masters of families, in their greatest frights, must not neglect their households. *Ten women,* that *were concubines,* he *left* behind, *to keep the house,* thinking that the weakness of their sex would secure them from murder, and their age and relation to him would secure them from rape; but God overruled this for the fulfilling of his word. 3. He took his life-guard with him, or band of pensioners, the Cherethites and Pelethites, who were under the command of Benaiah, and the Gittites, who were under the command of Ittai, *v.* 18. These Gittites seem to have been, by birth, Philistines of Gath, who came, a regiment of them, 600 in all, to enter themselves in David's service, having known him at Gath, and being greatly in love with him for his virtue and piety, and having embraced the Jews' religion. David made them of his *garde du corps—his body-guard,* and they adhered to him in his distress. The Son of David *found not such great faith in Israel* as in a Roman centurion and a woman of Canaan. 4. As many as would, of the people of Jerusalem, he took with him, and made a halt at some distance from the city, to draw them up, *v.* 17. He compelled none. Those whose hearts were with Absalom, to Absalom let them go, and so shall their doom be: they will soon have enough of him. Christ enlists none but volunteers.

IV. His discourse with Ittai the Gittite, who commanded the Philistine-proselytes.

1. David dissuaded him from going along with him, *v.* 19, 20. Though he and his men might be greatly serviceable to him, yet, (1.) He would try whether he was hearty for him, and not inclined to Absalom. He therefore bids him return to his post in Jerusalem, and serve the new king. If he was no more than a soldier of fortune (as we say), he would be for that side which would pay and prefer him best; and to that side let him go. (2.) If he was faithful to David, yet David would not have him exposed to the fatigues and perils he now counted upon. David's tender spirit cannot bear to think that a stranger and an exile, a proselyte and a new convert, who ought, by all means possible, to be encouraged and made easy, should, at his first coming, meet with such hard usage: "*Should I make thee go up and down with us?* No, return with thy brethren." Generous souls are more concerned at the share others have in their troubles than at their own. Ittai shall therefore be dismissed with a blessing: *Mercy and truth be with thee,* that is, God's mercy and truth, mercy according to promise, the promise made to those who renounce other gods and put themselves under the wings of the divine Majesty. This is a very proper pious farewell, when we part with a friend, "*Mercy and truth be with thee,* and then thou art safe, and mayest be easy, wherever thou art." David's dependence was upon the mercy and truth of God for comfort and happiness, both for himself and his friends; see Ps. lxi. 7.

2. Ittai bravely resolved not to leave him, *v.* 21. Where David is, *whether in life or death,* safe or in peril, there will this faithful friend of his be; and he confirms this resolution with an oath, that he might not be tempted to break it. Such a value has he for David, not for the sake of his wealth and greatness (for then he would have deserted him now that he saw him thus reduced), but for the sake of his wisdom and goodness, which were still the same, that, whatever comes of it, he will never leave him. Note, That is a friend indeed who loves at all times, and will adhere to us in adversity. Thus should we cleave to the Son of David with full purpose of heart that *neither life nor death shall separate us from his love.*

V. The common people's sympathy with David in his affliction. When he and his attendants *passed over the brook Kidron* (the very same brook that Christ passed over when he entered upon his sufferings, John xviii. 1), *towards the way of the wilderness,* which lay between Jerusalem and Jericho, *all the country wept with a loud voice, v.* 23. Cause enough there was for weeping, 1. To see a prince thus reduced, one that had lived so great forced from his palace and in fear of his life, with a small retinue seeking shelter in a desert, to see the city of David, which he himself won, built, and fortified, made an unsafe abode for David himself. It would move the compassion even of strangers to see a man fallen thus low from such a height, and this by the wickedness of his own son; a piteous case it was. Parents that are abused and ruined by their own children merit the tender sympathy of their friends as much as any of the sons or daughters of affliction. Especially, 2. To see their own prince thus wronged, who had been so great a blessing to their land, and had not done any thing to forfeit the affections of his people; to see him in this distress, and themselves unable to help him, might well draw floods of tears from their eyes.

24 And lo Zadok also, and all the Levites *were* with him, bearing the ark of the covenant of God: and they set down the ark of God; and Abiathar went up, until all the people had done passing out of the city. 25 And the king said unto Zadok, Carry back the ark of God into the city: if I shall find favour in the eyes of the LORD, he will bring me again, and show me *both* it, and his habitation: 26 But if he thus say, I have no delight in thee; behold, *here am* I, let him do to me as seemeth good unto him. 27 The king said also unto Zadok the priest, *Art not* thou a seer? return into the city in peace, and your two sons with you, Ahimaaz thy son, and Jonathan the son of Abiathar. 28 See, I will tarry in the plain of the wilderness, until there come word from you to certify me. 29 Zadok therefore and Abiathar carried the ark of God again to Jerusalem: and they tarried there. 30 And David went up by the ascent of *mount* Olivet, and wept as he went up, and had his head covered, and he went barefoot: and all the people that *was* with him covered every man his head, and they went up, weeping as they went up.

Here we have, I. The fidelity of the priests and Levites and their firm adherence to David and his interest. They knew David's great affection to them and their office, notwithstanding his failings. The method Absalom took to gain people's affections made no impression upon them; he had little religion in him, and therefore they steadily adhered to David. Zadok and Abiathar, and all the Levites, if he go, will accompany him, and take the ark with them, that, by it, they may ask counsel of God for him, *v.* 24. Note, Those that are friends to the ark in their prosperity will find it a friend to them in their adversity. Formerly David would not rest till he had found a resting-place for the ark; and now, if the priests may have their mind, the ark shall not rest till David return to his rest.

II. David's dismission of them back into the city, *v.* 25, 26. Abiathar was high priest (1 Kings ii. 35), but Zadok was his assistant, and attended the ark most closely, while Abiathar was active in public business, *v.* 24. Therefore David directs his speech to Zadok, and an excellent speech it is, and shows him to be in a very good frame under his affliction, and that still he holds fast his integrity. 1. He is very solicitous for the safety of the ark: "By all means *carry the ark back into the city,* let not that be unsettled and exposed with me, lodge that again in the tent pitched for it; surely Absalom, bad as he is, will do that no harm." David's heart, like Eli's, trembles for the ark of God. Note, It argues a good principle to be more concerned for the church's prosperity than for our own, to *prefer Jerusalem* before our *chief joy* (Ps. cxxxvii. 6), the success of the gospel, and the flourishing of the church, above our own wealth, credit, ease, and safety, even when they are most in hazard. 2. He is very desirous to return to the enjoyment of the privileges of God's house. He will reckon it the greatest instance of God's favour to him if he may but once more be brought back to see it and his habitation. This will be more his joy than to be brought back to his own palace and throne again. Note, Gracious souls measure their comforts and conveniences in this world by the opportunity they give them of communion with God. Hezekiah wished for the recovery of his health for this reason, that he might *go up to the house of the Lord,* Isa. xxxviii. 22. 3. He is very submissive to the holy will of God concerning the issue of this dark dispensation. He hopes the best (*v.* 25), and hopes for it from the favour of God, which he looks upon to be the fountain of all good: "If God favour me so far, I shall be settled again as formerly." But he provides for the worst: "If he deny me this favour—if he thus say, *I have no delight in thee*—I know I deserve the continuance of his displeasure; his holy will be done." See him here patiently awaiting the event: "*Behold, here am I,* as a servant expecting orders;" and see him willing to commit himself to God concerning it: "*Let him do to me as seemeth good to him.* I have nothing to object. All is well that God does." Observe with what satisfaction and holy complacency he speaks of the divine disposal: not only, "He can do what he will," subscribing to his power (Job ix. 12), or, "He has a right to do what he will," subscribing to his sovereignty (Job xxxiii. 13), or, "He will do what he will," subscribing to his unchangeableness (Job xxiii. 13, 15), but, "*Let him do what he will,*" subscribing to his wisdom and goodness. Note, It is our interest, as well as duty, cheerfully to acquiesce in the will of God, whatever befals us. That we may not complain of what is, let us see God's hand in all events; and, that we may not be afraid of what shall be, let us see all events in God's hand.

III. The confidence David put in the priests that they would serve his interest to the utmost of their power in his absence. He calls Zadok a *seer* (*v.* 27), that is, a wise man, a man that can see into business and discern time and judgment: "Thou hast thy *eyes in thy head* (Eccl. ii. 14), and therefore art capable of doing me service, especially by sending me intelligence of the enemy's motions and resolutions." One friend that is a seer, in such an exigency as this, was worth twenty that were not so quick-sighted. For the settling of a private correspondence with the priests in his absence, he appoints, 1. Whom they should send to him—their two sons, Ahimaaz and Jonathan, whose coat, it might be hoped, would be their protection, and of whose prudence and faithfulness he had probably had experience. 2. Whither they should send. He would encamp *in the plain of the wilderness* till he heard from them (*v.* 28), and then would move according to the information and advice they should send him. Hereupon they returned to the city, to await the event. It was a pity that any disturbance should be given to a state so happy as this was, when the prince and the priests had such an entire affection for and confidence in each other.

IV. The melancholy posture that David and his men put themselves into, when, at the beginning of their march, they went up the *mount of Olives*, *v.* 30.

1. David himself, as a deep mourner, covered his head and face for shame and blushing, went bare-foot, as a prisoner or a slave, for mortification, and went weeping. Did it become a man of his reputation for courage and greatness of spirit thus to cry like a child, only for fear of an enemy at a distance, against whom he might easily have made head, and perhaps with one bold stroke have routed him? Yes, it did not ill become him, considering how much there was in this trouble, (1.) Of the unkindness of his son. He could not but weep to think that one who came out of his bowels, and had so often lain in his arms, should thus lift up the heel against him. God himself is said to be grieved with the rebellions of his own children (Ps. xcv. 10) and even *broken with their whorish heart*, Ezek. vi. 9. (2.) There was much of the displeasure of his God in it. This infused the wormwood and gall into the *affliction and misery*, Lam. iii. 19. His sin was *ever before him* (Ps. li. 3), but never so plain nor ever appearing so black as now. He never wept thus when Saul hunted him: but a wounded conscience makes troubles lie heavily, Ps. xxxviii. 4.

2. When David wept all his company wept likewise, being much affected with his grief and willing to share in it. It is our duty to *weep with those that weep*, especially our superiors, and those that are better than we; for, *if this be done in the green tree, what will be done in the dry?* We must weep with those that weep for sin. When Hezekiah humbled himself for his sin all Jerusalem joined with him, 2 Chron. xxxii. 26. To prevent suffering with sinners, let us sorrow with them.

31 And *one* told David, saying, Ahithophel *is* among the conspirators with Absalom. And David said, O LORD, I pray thee, turn the counsel of Ahithophel into foolishness. 32 And it came to pass, that *when* David was come to the top *of the mount*, where he worshipped God, behold, Hushai the Archite came to meet him with his coat rent, and earth upon his head: 33 Unto whom David said, If thou passest on with me, then thou shalt be a burden unto me: 34 But if thou return to the city, and say unto Absalom, I will be thy servant, O king; *as* I *have been* thy father's servant hitherto, so *will* I now also *be* thy servant: then mayest thou for me defeat the counsel of Ahithophel. 35 And *hast thou* not there with thee Zadok and Abiathar the priests? therefore it shall be, *that* what thing soever thou shalt hear out of the king's house, thou shalt tell *it* to Zadok and Abiathar the priests 36 Behold, *they have* there with them their two sons, Ahimaaz Zadok's *son*, and Jonathan Abiathar's *son*; and by them ye shall send unto me every thing that ye can hear. 37 So Hushai David's friend came into the city, and Absalom came into Jerusalem.

Nothing, it seems, appeared to David more threatening in Absalom's plot than that Ahithophel was in it; for one good head, in such a design, is worth a thousand good hands. Absalom was himself no politician, but he had got one entirely in his interest that was, and would be the more dangerous because he had been all along acquainted with David's counsels and affairs; if therefore he can be baffled, Absalom is as good as routed and the head of the conspiracy cut off. This David endeavours to do.

I. By prayer. When he heard that Ahithophel was in the plot he lifted up his heart to God in this short prayer: *Lord, turn the counsel of Ahithophel into foolishness, v.* 31. He had not opportunity for a long prayer, but he was not one of those that thought he should be heard for his much speaking. It was a fervent prayer: "*Lord, I pray thee,* do this." God is well pleased with the importunity of those that come to him with their petitions. David is particular in this prayer; he names the person whose counsels he prays against. God gives us leave, in prayer, to be humbly and reverently free with him, and to mention the particular care, and fear, and grief, that lies heavily upon us. David prayed not against Ahithophel's person, but against his counsel, that God would *turn it into foolishness*, that, though he was a wise man, he might at this time give foolish counsel, or, if he gave wise counsel, that it might be rejected as foolish, or, if it were followed, that by some providence or other it might be defeated, and not attain the end. David prayed this in a firm belief that God has all hearts in his hand, and tongues too, that, when he pleases, he can *take away the understanding of the aged and make the judges fools*, (Job xii. 17; Isa. iii. 2, 3), and in hope that God would own and plead his just and injured cause. Note, We may pray in faith, and should pray with fervency, that God will turn that counsel into foolishness which is taken against his people.

II. By policy. We must second our prayer with our endeavours, else we tempt God. It is good service to countermine the policy of the church's enemies. When David came to the top of the mount, he *worshipped God*, *v.* 32. Note, Weeping must not hinder worshipping, but quicken it rather. Now he penned the third Psalm, as appears by the title; and some think that his singing this was the worship he now paid to God. Just now Providence brought Hushai to him. While he was yet speaking, God heard, and sent him the person that should be instrumental to befool Ahithophel. He came to condole with David on his present trouble, with his coat rent and earth upon his head; but David, having a great deal of confidence in his conduct and faithfulness, resolved to employ him as a spy upon Absalom. He would not take him with him (*v.* 33), for he had now more need of soldiers than counsellors, but sent him back to Jerusalem, to wait for Absalom's arrival, as a deserter from David, and to offer him his service, *v.* 34. Thus he might insinuate himself into his counsels, and defeat Ahithophel, either by dissuading Absalom from following his advice or by discovering it to David, that he might know where to stand upon his guard. How this gross dissimulation, which David put Hushai upon, can be justified, as a stratagem in war, I do not see. The best that can be made of it is that Absalom, if he rebel against his father, must stand upon his guard against all mankind, and, if he will be deceived, let him be deceived. David recommended Hushai to Zadok and Abiathar, as persons proper to be consulted with (*v.* 35), and to their two sons, as trusty men to be sent on errands to David, *v.* 36. Hushai, thus instructed, came to Jerusalem (*v.* 37), whither also Absalom soon after came with his forces. How soon do royal palaces and royal cities change their masters! But we look for a kingdom which cannot be thus shaken and in the possession of which we cannot be disturbed.

CHAP. XVI.

In the close of the foregoing chapter we left David flying from Jerusalem, and Absalom entering into it; in this chapter, I. We are to follow David in his melancholy flight; and there we find him, 1. Cheated by Ziba, ver. 1—4. 2. Cursed by Shimei, which he bears with wonderful patience, ver. 5—14. II. We are to meet Absalom in his triumphant entry; and there we find him, 1. Cheated by Hushai, ver. 15—19. 2. Counselled by Ahithophel to go in unto his father's concubines, ver. 20—23.

AND when David was a little past the top *of the hill*, behold, Ziba the servant of Mephibosheth met him, with a couple of asses saddled, and upon them two hundred *loaves* of bread, and a hundred bunches of raisins, and a hundred of summer fruits, and a bottle of wine. 2 And the king said unto Ziba, What meanest thou by these? And Ziba said, The asses *be* for the king's household to ride on; and the bread and summer fruit for the young men to eat; and the wine, that such as be faint in the wilderness may drink. 3 And the king said, And where *is* thy master's son? And Ziba said unto the king, Behold, he abideth at Jerusalem: for he said, To day shall the house of Israel restore me the kingdom of my father. 4 Then said the king to Ziba, Behold, thine *are* all that *pertained* unto Mephibosheth. And Ziba said, I humbly beseech thee *that* I may find grace in thy sight, my lord, O king.

We read before how kind David was to Mephibosheth the son of Jonathan, how he prudently entrusted his servant Ziba with the management of his estate, while he generously entertained him at his own table, *ch.* ix. 10. This matter was well settled; but, it seems, Ziba is not content to be manager, he longs to be master, of Mephibosheth's estate. Now, he thinks, is his time to make himself so; if he can procure a grant of it from the crown, whether David or Absalom get the better it is all one to him, he hopes he shall secure his prey, which he promises himself by fishing in troubled waters. In order hereunto, 1. He made David a handsome present of provisions, which was the more welcome because it came seasonably (*v.* 1), and with this he designed to incline him to himself; for *a man's gift maketh room for him, and bringeth him before great men*, Prov. xviii. 16. Nay, *Whithersoever it turneth, it prospereth*, Prov. xvii 8. David inferred from this that Ziba was a very discreet and generous man, and well affected to him, when, in all, he designed nothing but to make his own market and to get Mephibosheth's estate settled upon himself. Shall the prospect of advantage in this world make men generous to the rich? and shall not the belief of an abundant recompence in the resurrection of the just make us charitable to the poor? Luke xiv. 14. Ziba was very considerate in the present he brought to David; it was what would do him some good in his present distress, *v.* 2. Observe, The wine was intended for those that were faint, not for the king's own drinking, or the courtiers; it seems, they did not commonly use it, but it was for cordials for those *that were ready to perish,* Prov. xxxi. 6. Blessed art thou, O land! when thy princes use wine for strength, as David did, and not for drunkenness, as Absalom did, *ch.* xiii. 28. See Eccl. x. 17. Whatever Ziba intended in this present, God's providence sent it to David for his support very graciously. God makes use of bad men for good purposes to his people, and sends them meat by ravens. 2. Having by his present insinuated himself into David's affection, and gained credit with him, the next thing he has to do for the compassing of his end is to incense him against Mephibosheth, which he does by a false accusation, representing him as ungratefully designing to raise himself by the present broils, and to recover the crown to his own head, now that David and his son were contending for it. David enquires for him as one of his family, which gives Ziba occasion to tell this false story of him, *v.* 3. What immense damages do masters often sustain by the lying tongues of their servants! David knew Mephibosheth not to be an ambitious man, but easy in his place, and well-affected to him and his government; nor could he be so weak as to expect with his lame legs to climb the ladder of preferment; yet David gives credit to the calumny, and, without further enquiry or consideration, convicts Mephibosheth of treason, seizes his lands as forfeited, and grants them to Ziba: *Behold, thine are all that pertained to Mephibosheth* (*v.* 4), a rash judgment, and which afterwards he was ashamed of, when the truth came to light, *ch.* xix. 29. Princes cannot help it, but they will be sometimes (as our law speaks) deceived in their grants; but they ought to use all means possible to discover the truth and to guard against malicious designing men, who would impose upon them, as Ziba did upon David. Having by his wiles gained his point, Ziba secretly laughed at the king's credulity, congratulated himself on his success, and departed, with a great compliment upon the king, that he valued his favour more than Mephibosheth's estate: "Let me *find grace in thy sight, O king!* and I have enough." Great men ought always to be jealous of flatterers, and remember that nature has given them two ears, that they may hear both sides.

5 And when king David came to Bahurim, behold, thence came out a man of the family of the house of Saul, whose name *was* Shimei, the son of Gera: he came forth, and cursed still as he came. 6 And he cast stones at David, and at all the servants of king David: and all the people and all the mighty men *were* on his right hand and on his left. 7 And thus said Shimei when he cursed, Come out, come out, thou bloody man, and thou man of Belial: 8 The LORD hath returned upon thee all the blood of the house of Saul, in whose stead thou hast reigned; and the LORD hath delivered the kingdom into the hand of Absalom thy son: and, behold, thou *art taken* in thy mischief, because thou *art* a bloody man. 9 Then said Abishai the son of Zeruiah unto the king, Why should this dead dog curse my lord the king? let me go over, I pray thee, and take off his head. 10 And the king said, What have I to do with you, ye sons of Zeruiah? so let him curse, because the LORD hath said unto him, Curse David. Who shall then say, Wherefore hast thou done so? 11 And David said to Abishai, and to all his servants, Behold, my son, which came forth of my bowels, seeketh my life: how much more now *may this* Benjamite *do it?* let him alone, and let him curse; for the LORD hath bidden him. 12 It may be that the LORD will look on mine affliction, and that the LORD will requite me good for his cursing this day. 13 And as David and his men went by the way, Shimei went along on the hill's side over against him, and cursed as he went, and threw stones at him, and cast dust. 14 And the king, and all the people that *were* with him, came weary, and refreshed themselves there.

We here find how David bore Shimei's curses much better than he had borne Ziba's flatteries. By the latter he was brought to pass a wrong judgment on another, by the former to pass a right judgment on himself. The world's smiles are more dangerous than its frowns. Observe here,

I. How insolent and furious Shimei was, and how his malice took occasion from David's present distress to be so much the more outrageous. David, in his flight, had come to Bahurim, a city of Benjamin in or near which this Shimei lived, who, being of the house of Saul (with the fall of which all his hopes of preferment fell), had an implacable enmity to David, unjustly looking upon him as the ruin of Saul and his family only because, by the divine appointment, he succeeded Saul. While David was in prosperity and power, Shimei hated him as much as he did now, but he durst not then say any thing against him. God knows what is in the hearts of those that are disaffected to him and his government, but earthly princes do not. Now he came forth, and cursed David with all the bad words and wishes he could invent, *v.* 5. Observe,

1. Why he took this opportunity to give vent to his malice. (1.) Because now he thought he might do it safely; yet, if David had thought proper to resent the provocation, it would have cost Shimei his life. (2.) Because now it would be most grievous to David, would add affliction to his grief, and pour vinegar into his wounds. He complains of those as most barbarous who *talk to the grief of those whom God has wounded,* Ps. lxix. 26. So Shimei did, loading him with curses whom no generous eye could look upon without compassion. (3.) Because now he thought that Providence justified his reproaches, and that David's present afflictions proved him to be as bad a man as he was willing to represent him. Job's friends condemned him upon this false principle. Those that are under the rebukes of a gracious God must not think it strange if these bring upon them the reproaches of evil men. If once it be said, *God hath forsaken him,* presently it follows, *Persecute and take him,* Ps. lxxi. 11. But it is the character of a base spirit thus to trample upon those that are down, and insult over them.

2. How his malice was expressed. See, (1.) What this wretched man did: *He cast stones at David* (*v.* 6), as if his king had been a dog, or the worst of criminals, whom all Israel must stone with stones till he die. Perhaps he kept at such a distance that the stones he threw could not reach David, nor any of his attendants, yet he showed what he would have done if it had been in his power. *He cast dust* (*v.* 13), which, probably, would blow into his own eyes, like the curses he threw, which, being causeless, would return upon his own head. Thus, while his malice made him odious, the impotency of it made him ridiculous and contemptible. Those that fight against God cannot hurt him, though they hate him. *If thou sinnest, what doest thou against him?* Job xxxv. 6. It was an aggravation of his wickedness that David was attended with his mighty men on his right hand and on his left, so that he was not in so forlorn a condition as he thought (*persecuted but not forsaken*), and that he continued to do it, and did it the more passionately, for David's bearing it patiently. (2.) What he said. With the stones he shot his arrows, even bitter words (*v.* 7, 8), in contempt of that law, *Thou shalt not curse the gods,* Exod. xxii. 28. David was a man of honour and conscience, and in great reputation for every thing that was just and good; what could this foul mouth say against him? Why, truly, what was done long since to the house of Saul was the only thing which he could recollect, and with this he upbraided David because it was the thing that he himself was a loser by. See how apt we are to judge of men and their character by what they are to us, and to conclude that those are certainly evil men that have ever so justly been, or that we ever so unjustly think have been, instruments of evil to us. So partial are we to ourselves that no rule can be more fallacious than this. No man could be more innocent of the blood of the house of Saul than David was. Once and again he spared Saul's life, while Saul sought his. When Saul and his sons were slain by the Philistines and David his men were many miles off; and, when they heard it, they lamented it. From the murder of Abner and Ish-bosheth he had sufficiently cleared himself; and yet all *the blood of the house of Saul* must be laid at his door. Innocency is no fence against malice and falsehood; nor are we to think it strange if we be charged with that from which we have been most careful to keep ourselves. It is well for us that men are not to be our judges, but he whose judgment is according to truth. The blood of the house of Saul is here most unjustly charged upon David, [1.] As that which gave him his character, and denominated him a bloody man and a man of Belial, *v.* 7. And, if a man of blood, no doubt a man of Belial, that is, a child of the devil, who is called *Belial* (2 Cor. vi. 15), and who was a murderer from the beginning. Bloody men are the worst of men. [2.] As that which brought the present trouble upon him: "Now that thou art dethroned, and driven out to the wilderness, *the Lord has returned upon thee the blood of the house of Saul.*" See how forward malicious men are to press God's judgments into the service of their own passion and revenge. If any who have, as they think, wronged them, should come into trouble, the injury done to them must be made the cause of the trouble. But we must take heed lest we wrong God by making his providence thus to patronise our foolish and unjust resentments. As the *wrath of man works not the righteousness of God,* so the righteousness of God serves not the wrath of man. [3.] As that which would now be his utter ruin; for he endeavours to make him despair of ever recovering his throne again. Now they said, *There is no help for him in God* (Ps. iii. 2), *the Lord hath delivered the kingdom into the hand of Absalom* (n t Mephibosheth—the house of Saul never dreamed

of making *him* king, as Ziba suggested), *and thou art taken in thy mischief*, that is, "the mischief that will be thy destruction, and all because thou art a bloody man." Thus Shimei cursed.

II. See how patient and submissive David was under this abuse. The sons of Zeruiah, Abishai particularly, were forward to maintain David's honour with their swords; they resented the affront keenly, as well they might: *Why should this dead dog* be suffered to *curse the king? v.* 9. If David will but give them leave, they will put these lying cursing lips to silence, and take off his head; for his throwing stones at the king was an overt act, which abundantly proved that he compassed and imagined his death. But the king would by no means suffer it: *What have I to do with you? So let him curse.* Thus Christ rebuked the disciples, who, in zeal for his honour, would have commanded fire from heaven on the town that affronted him, Luke ix. 55. Let us see with what considerations David quieted himself. 1. The chief thing that silenced him was that he had deserved this affliction. This is not mentioned indeed; for a man may truly repent, and yet needs not, upon all occasions, proclaim his penitent reflections. Shimei unjustly upbraided him with the blood of Saul: from *that* his conscience acquitted him, but, at the same time, it charged him with the blood of Uriah. "The reproach is too true" (thinks David), "though false as he means it." Note, A humble tender spirit will turn reproaches into reproofs, and so get good by them, instead of being provoked by them. 2. He observes the hand of God in it: *The Lord hath said unto him, Curse David* (*v.* 10), and again, *So let him curse, for the Lord hath bidden him, v.* 11. As it was Shimei's sin, it was not from God, but from the devil and his own wicked heart, nor did God's hand in it excuse or extenuate it, much less justify it, any more than it did the sin of those who put Christ to death, Acts ii. 23; iv. 28. But, as it was David's affliction, it was from the Lord, one of the evils which he raised up against him. David looked above the instrument of his trouble to the supreme director, as Job, when the plunderers had stripped him, acknowledged, *The Lord hath taken away.* Nothing more proper to quiet a gracious soul under affliction than an eye to the hand of God in it. *I opened not my mouth, because thou didst it.* The scourge of the tongue is God's rod. 3. He quiets himself under the less affliction with the consideration of the greater (*v.* 11): *My son seeks my life, much more may this Benjamite.* Note, Tribulation works patience in those that are sanctified. The more we bear the better able we should be to bear still more; what tries our patience should improve it. The more we are inured to trouble the less we should be surprised at it, and not think it strange. Marvel not that enemies are injurious, when even friends are unkind; nor that friends are unkind, when even children are undutiful. 4. He comforts himself with hopes that God would, in some way or other, bring good to him out of his affliction, would balance the trouble itself, and recompense his patience under it: "*The Lord will requite me good for his cursing.* If God bid Shimei grieve me, it is that he himself may the more sensibly comfort me; surely he has mercy in store for me, which he is preparing me for by this trial." We may depend upon God as our pay-master, not only for our services, but for our sufferings. *Let them curse, but bless thou.* David, at length, is housed at Bahurim (*v.* 14), where he meets with refreshment, and is hidden from this strife of tongues.

15 And Absalom, and all the people the men of Israel, came to Jerusalem, and Ahithophel with him. 16 And it came to pass, when Hushai the Archite, David's friend, was come unto Absalom, that Hushai said unto Absalom, God save the king, God save the king. 17 And Absalom said to Hushai, *Is* this thy kindness to thy friend? why wentest thou not with thy friend? 18 And Hushai said unto Absalom, Nay; but whom the LORD, and this people, and all the men of Israel, choose, his will I be, and with him will I abide. 19 And again, whom should I serve? *should I* not *serve* in the presence of his son? as I have served in thy father's presence, so will I be in thy presence. 20 Then said Absalom to Ahithophel, Give counsel among you what we shall do. 21 And Ahithophel said unto Absalom, Go in unto thy father's concubines, which he hath left to keep the house; and all Israel shall hear that thou art abhorred of thy father: then shall the hands of all that *are* with thee be strong. 22 So they spread Absalom a tent upon the top of the house; and Absalom went in unto his father's concubines in the sight of all Israel. 23 And the counsel of Ahithophel, which he counselled in those days, *was* as if a man had enquired at the oracle of God: so *was* all the counsel of Ahithophel both with David and with Absalom.

Absalom had notice sent him speedily by some of his friends at Jerusalem that David had withdrawn, and with what a small retinue he had gone; so that the coasts were clear, Absalom might take possession of Jerusalem when he pleased. The gates were open, and there was none to oppose him. Accordingly he came without delay (*v.* 15), extremely elevated, no doubt, with this success at first, and that that in which, when he formed his design, he probably apprehended the greatest difficulty, was so easily and effectually done. Now that he is master of Jerusalem he concludes all his own, the country will follow of course. God suffers wicked men to prosper awhile in their wicked plots, even beyond their expectation, that their disappointment may be the more grievous and disgraceful. The most celebrated politicians of that age were Ahithophel and Hushai. The former Absalom brings with him to Jerusalem (*v.* 15), the other meets him there (*v.* 16), so that he cannot but think himself sure of success, when he has both these to be his counsellors; on them he relies, and consults not the ark, though he has that with him. But miserable counsellors were they both; for,

I. Hushai would never counsel him to do wisely. He was really his enemy, and designed to betray him, while he pretended to be in his interest; so that Absalom could not have a more dangerous man about him. 1. Hushai complimented him upon his accession to the throne, as if he had been abundantly satisfied in his title, and well pleased that he had come to the possession, *v.* 16. What arts of dissimulation are those tempted to use who govern themselves by fleshly wisdom! and how happy are those who have not known these depths of Satan, but have their conversation in the world with simplicity and godly sincerity! 2. Absalom was surprised to find *him* for him who was known to be David's intimate friend and confidant. He asks him, *Is this thy kindness to thy friend?* (*v.* 17), pleasing himself with this thought, that all would be his, since Hushai was. He doubts not of his sincerity, but easily believes what he wishes to be true, that David's best friends are so in love with himself as to take the first opportunity to declare for him, *though the pride of his heart deceived him,* Obad. 3. 3. Hushai confirmed him in the belief that he was hearty for him. For, though David is his friend, yet he is for the king in *possession, v.* 18. Whom the people choose, and Providence smiles upon, he will be faithful to; and he is for the king in *succession* (*v.* 19), the rising sun. It was true, he loved his father; but he had had his day, and it was over; and why should he not love his successor as well? Thus he pretended to give reasons for a resolution he abhorred the thought of.

II. Ahithophel counselled him to do wickedly, and so did as effectually betray him as he did who was designedly false to him; for those that advise men to sin certainly advise them to their hurt; and that government which is founded in sin is founded in the sand.

1. It seems, Ahithophel was noted as a deep politician; his counsel was as if a man had enquired at the oracle of God, *v.* 23. Such reputation was he in for subtlety and sagacity in public affairs, such reaches had he beyond other privy-counsellors, such reasons would he give for his advice, and such success generally his projects had, that all people, good and bad, both David and Absalom, had a profound regard for his sentiments, too much by far, when they regarded him *as an oracle of God;* shall the prudence of any mortal compare with him who only is wise? Let us observe from this account of Ahithophel's fame for policy, (1.) That many excel in worldly wisdom who are utterly destitute of heavenly grace, because those who set up for oracles themselves are apt to despise the oracles of God. *God has chosen the foolish things of the world;* and the greatest statesmen are seldom the greatest saints. (2.) That frequently the greatest politicians act most foolishly for themselves. Ahithophel was cried up for an oracle, and yet very unwisely took part with Absalom, who was not only a usurper, but a rash youth, never likely to come to good, whose fall, and the fall of all that adhered to him, any one, with the tenth part of the policy that Ahithophel pretended to, might foresee. Well, after all, honesty is the best policy, and will be found so in the long run. But,

2. His policy in this case defeated its own aim. Observe,

(1.) The wicked counsel Ahithophel gave to Absalom. Finding that David had left his concubines to keep the house, he advised him to *lie with them* (*v.* 21), a very wicked thing. The divine law had made it a capital crime, Lev. xx. 11. The apostle speaks of it as a piece of villany *not so much as named among the Gentiles,* 1 Cor. v. 1. Reuben lost his birthright for it. But Ahithophel advised Absalom to it as a politic thing, because it would give assurance to all Israel, [1.] That he was in good earnest in his pretensions. No doubt he resolved to make himself master of all that belonged to his predecessor when he began with his concubines. [2.] That he was resolved never to make peace with his father upon any terms; for by this he would render himself so odious to his father that he would never be reconciled to him, which perhaps the people were jealous of and that they must be sacrificed to the reconciliation. Having drawn the sword, he did, by this provocation, throw away the scabbard, which would strengthen the hands of his party and keep them firmly to him. This was Ahithophel's cursed policy, which bespoke him rather *an oracle of the devil than of God.*

(2.) Absalom's compliance with this counsel. It entirely suited his lewd and wicked mind, and he delayed not to put it in execution, *v.* 22. When an unnatural rebellion was the opera, what fitter prologue could there be to it than such unnatural lust? Thus was his wickedness all of a piece, and such as a conscience not quite seared could not entertain the thoughts of without the utmost horror. Nay, the client outdoes what his counsel advises. Ahithophel advised him to do it, that all Israel might hear of it; but, as if that were not enough, so perfectly lost is he to all honour and virtue that he will do it, and all Israel shall *see* it. A tent is accordingly spread on the top of the house for the purpose; so impudently does he declare his sin as Sodom. Yet, in this, the word of God was fulfilled in the letter of it: God had threatened, by Nathan, that, for defiling Bath-sheba, David should have his own wives publicly debauched (*ch.* xii. 11, 12), and some think that Ahithophel, in advising it, designed to be revenged on David for the injury done to Bath-sheba, who was his grand-daughter: for she was the daughter of Eliam (*ch.* xi. 3), who was the son of Ahithophel, *ch.* xxiii. 34. Job speaks of this as the just punishment of adultery (*Let my wife grind to another,* Job xxxi. 9, 10), and the prophet, Hos. iv. 13, 14. What to think of these concubines, who submitted to this wickedness, I know not; but, how unrighteous soever Absalom and they were, we must say, *The Lord is righteous:* nor shall any word of his fall to the ground.

CHAP. XVII.

The contest between David and Absalom is now hasting towards a crisis. It must be determined by the sword, and preparation is made accordingly in this chapter. I. Absalom calls a council of war, in which Ahithophel urges despatch (ver. 1—4), but Hushai recommends deliberation (ver. 5—13); and Hushai's counsel is agreed to (ver. 14), for vexation at which Ahithophel hangs himself, ver. 23. II. Secret intelligence is sent to David (but with much difficulty) of their proceedings, ver. 15—21. III. David marches to the other side Jordan (ver. 22—24), and there his camp is victualled by some of his friends in that country, ver. 27—29. IV. Absalom and his forces march after him into the land of Gilead on the other side Jordan, ver. 25, 26. There we shall, in the next chapter, find the cause decided by a battle: hitherto, every thing has looked black upon poor David, but now the day of his deliverance begins to dawn.

MOREOVER Ahithophel said unto Absalom, Let me now choose out twelve thousand men, and I will arise and pursue after David this night: 2 And I will come upon him while he *is* weary and weak handed, and will make him afraid: and all the people that *are* with him shall flee; and I will smite the king only: 3 And I will bring back all the people unto thee: the man whom thou seekest *is* as if all returned: *so* all the people shall be in peace. 4 And the saying pleased Absalom well, and all the elders of Israel. 5 Then said Absalom, Call now Hushai the Archite also, and let us hear likewise what he saith. 6 And when Hushai was come to Absalom, Absalom spake unto him, saying, Ahithophel hath spoken after this manner: shall we do *after* his saying? if not; speak thou. 7 And Hushai said unto Absalom, The counsel that Ahithophel hath given *is* not good at this time. 8 For, said Hushai, thou knowest thy father and his men, that they *be* mighty men, and they *be* chafed in their minds, as a bear robbed of her whelps in the field: and thy father *is* a man of war, and will not lodge with the people. 9 Behold, he is hid now in some pit, or in some *other* place: and it will come to pass, when some of them be overthrown at the first, that whosoever heareth it will say, There is a slaughter among the people that follow Absalom. 10 And he also *that is* valiant, whose heart *is* as the heart of a lion, shall utterly melt: for all Israel knoweth that thy father *is* a mighty man, and *they* which *be* with him *are* valiant men. 11 Therefore I counsel that all Israel be generally gathered unto thee, from Dan even to Beer-sheba, as the sand that *is* by the sea for multitude; and that thou go to battle in thine own person. 12 So shall we come upon him in some place where he shall be found, and we will light upon him as the dew falleth on the ground: and of him and of all the men that *are* with him there shall not be left so much as one. 13 Moreover, if he be gotten into a city, then shall all Israel bring ropes to that city, and we will draw it into the river, until there be not one small stone found there. 14 And Absalom and all the men of Israel said, The counsel of Hushai the Archite *is* better than the counsel of Ahithophel. For the LORD had appointed to defeat the good counsel of Ahithophel, to the intent that the LORD might bring evil upon Absalom.

Absalom is now in peaceable possession of Jerusalem; the palace-royal is his own, as are *the thrones of judgment, even the thrones of the house of David.* His good father reigned in Hebron, and only over the tribe of Judah, above seven years, and was not hasty to destroy his rival; his government was built upon a divine promise, the performance of which he was sure of in due time, and therefore he waited patiently in the mean time. But the young man, Absalom, not only hastens from Hebron to Jerusalem, but is impatient there till he has destroyed his father, cannot be content with his throne till he has his life; for his government is founded in iniquity, and therefore feels itself tottering and thinks itself obliged to do every thing with violence. That so profligate a wretch as Absalom should aim at the life of so good a father is not so strange (there are here and there monsters in nature); but that the body of the people of Israel, to whom David had been so great a blessing in all respects, should join with him in his attempt, is very amazing. But their fathers often mutinied against Moses. The best of parents, and the best of princes, will not think it strange if they be made uneasy by those who should be their support and joy, when they consider what sons and what subjects David himself had.

David and all that adhered to him must be cut off. This was resolved, for aught that appears, *nemine contradicente—unanimously*. None durst mention his personal merits, and the great services done to his country, in opposition to this resolve, nor so much as ask, "*Why, what evil has he done* to forfeit his crown, much less his head?" None durst propose that his banishment should suffice, for the present, nor that agents should be sent to treat with him to resign the crown, which, having so tamely quitted the city, they might think he would easily be persuaded to do. It was not long since that Absalom himself fled for a crime, and David contented himself with his being an exile, though he deserved death, nay, he mourned and longed for him; but so perfectly void of all natural affection is this ungrateful Absalom that he eagerly thirsts after his own father's blood. It is past dispute that David must be destroyed; all the question is how he may be destroyed.

I. Ahithophel advises that he be pursued immediately, this very night, with a flying army (which he himself undertakes the command of), that the king only be smitten and his forces dispersed, and then the people that were now for him would fall in with Absalom of course, and there would not be such a long war as had been between the house of Saul and David: *The man whom thou seekest is as if all returned, v.* 1—3. By this it appears that Absalom had declared his design to be upon David's life, and Ahithophel concurs with him in it. *Smite the shepherd, and the sheep will be scattered,* and be an easy prey to the wolf. Thus he contrives to include the war in a little compass, by fighting neither with small nor great but the king of Israel only, and to conclude it in a little time, by falling upon him immediately. Nothing could be more fatal to David than the taking of these measures. It was too true that he was weary and weak-handed, that a little thing would make him afraid, else he would not have fled from his house upon the first alarm of Absalom's rebellion; it was probable enough that upon a fierce attack, especially in the night, the small force he had would be put into confusion and disorder, and it would be an easy thing to *smite the king only,* and then the business would be done, the whole nation would be reduced, of course, and *all the people,* says he, *shall be in peace.* See how a general ruin is called by usurpers a *general peace;* but thus the devil's palace is in peace, while he, as a strong man armed, keeps it. Compare with this the plot of Caiaphas (that second Ahithophel) against the Son of David, to crush his interest by destroying him. Let that *one man die for the people,* John xi. 50. *Kill the heir, and the inheritance shall be ours,* Matt. xxi. 38. But the counsel of them both was turned into foolishness. Yet the children of light may, in their generation, learn wisdom from the children of this world. What our hand finds to do let us do quickly, and with all our might. It is prudence to be vigorous and expeditious, and not to lose time, particularly in our spiritual warfare. If Satan flee from us, let us follow our blow. Those that have quarrelled with crowned heads have generally observed the decorum of declaring only against their evil counsellors, and calling them to an account (*The king himself can do no wrong,* it is they that do it); but Absalom's bare-faced villany strikes at the king directly, nay, at the king only; for (would you think it?) this saying, *I will smite the king only,* pleased Absalom well (*v.* 4), nor had he so much sense of honour and virtue left him as to pretend to startle at it or even to be reluctant in this barbarous and monstrous resolution. What good can stand before the heat of a furious ambition?

II. Hushai advises that they be not too hasty in pursuing David, but take time to draw up all their force against him, and to overpower him with numbers, as Ahithophel had advised to take him by surprise. Now Hushai, in giving this counsel, really intended to serve David and his interest, that he might have time to send him notice of his proceedings, and that David might gain time to gather an army and to remove into those countries beyond Jordan, in which, lying more remote, Absalom had probably least interest. Nothing would be of greater advantage to David in this juncture than time to turn himself in; that he may have this, Hushai counsels Absalom to do nothing rashly, but to proceed with caution and secure his success by securing his strength. Now,

1. Absalom gave Hushai a fair invitation to advise him. All the elders of Israel approved of Ahithophel's counsel, yet God overruled the heart of Absalom not to proceed upon it, till he had consulted Hushai (*v.* 5): *Let us hear what he saith.* Herein he thought he did wisely (two heads are better than one), but God taketh the wise in their own craftiness See Mr. Poole's note on this.

2. Hushai gave very plausible reasons for what he said.

(1.) He argued against Ahithophel's counsel, and undertook to show the danger of following his advice. It is with modesty, and all possible deference to Ahithophel's settled reputation, that he begs leave to differ from him, *v.* 7. He acknowledges that the counsel of Ahithophel is usually the best, and such as may be relied on; but, with submission to that noble peer, he is of opinion that his counsel is not good at this time, and that it is by no means safe to venture so great a cause as that in which they are now engaged upon so small a number, and such a hasty sally, as Ahithophel advises, remembering the defeat of Israel before Ai, Josh. vii. 4. It has often proved of bad consequence to despise an enemy. See how plausibly Hushai reasoned. [1.] He insisted much upon it that David was a great soldier, a man of great conduct, courage, and experience; all knew and owned this, even Absalom himself: "*Thy father is a man of war* (*v.* 8), *a mighty man* (*v.* 10), and not so weary and weak-handed as Ahithophel imagines. His retiring from Jerusalem must be imputed, not to his cowardice, but his prudence." [2.] His attendants, though few, were mighty men (*v.* 8), valiant men (*v.* 10), men of celebrated bravery and versed in all the arts of war. Ahithophel, who perhaps had worn the gown more than the sword, would find himself an unequal match for them. *One of them would chase a thousand.* [3.] They were all exasperated against Absalom, who was the author of all this mischief, were chafed in their minds, and would fight with the utmost fury; so that, what with their courage, and what with their rage, there would be no standing before them, especially for such raw soldiers as Absalom's generally were. Thus did he represent them as formidable as Ahithophel had made them despicable. [4.] He suggested that probably David and some of his men would lie in ambush, in some pit, or other close place, and fall upon Absalom's soldiers before they were aware, the terror of which would put them to flight; and the defeat, though but of a small party, would dispirit all the rest, especially their own consciences at the same time accusing them of treason against one that, they were sure, was not only God's anointed, *but a man after his own heart, v.* 9. "It will soon be given out that there is a slaughter among Absalom's men, and then they will all make the best of their way, and the heart of Ahithophel himself, though now it seems like the heart of a lion, will utterly melt. In short, he will not find it so easy a matter to deal with David and his men as he thinks it is; and, if he be foiled, we shall all be routed."

(2.) He offered his own advice, and gave his reasons; and, [1.] He counselled that which he knew would gratify Absalom's proud vain-glorious humour, though it would not be really serviceable to his interest. *First,* He advised that all Israel should be gathered together, that is, the militia of all the tribes. His taking it for granted that they are all for him, and giving him an opportunity to see them all together under his command, would gratify him as much as any thing. *Secondly,* He advises that Absalom go to battle in his own person, as if he looked upon him to be a better soldier than Ahithophel, more fit to give command and have the honour of the victory, insinuating that Ahithophel had put a slight upon him in offering to go without him. See how easy it is to betray proud men, by applauding them, and feeding their pride. [2.] He counselled that which seemed to secure the success, at last, infallibly, without running any hazard. For, if they could raise such vast numbers as they promised themselves, wherever they found David they could not fail to crush him. *First,* If in the field, they should fall upon him, as the dew that covers the face of the ground, and cut off all his men with him, *v.* 12. Perhaps Absalom was better pleased with the design of cutting off all the men that were with him, having a particular antipathy to some of David's friends, than with Ahithophel's project of smiting the king only. Thus Hushai gained his point by humouring his revenge, as well as his pride. *Secondly,* If in a city, they need not fear conquering him, for they should have hands enough, if occasion were, to draw the city itself into its river with ropes, *v.* 13. This strange suggestion, how impracticable soever, being new, served for an amusement, and recommended itself by pleasing the fancy, for they would all smile at the humour of it.

(3.) By all these arts, Hushai gained not only Absalom's approbation of his advice, but the unanimous concurrence of this great council of war; they all agreed that the counsel of Hushai was better than the counsel of Ahithophel, *v.* 14. See here, [1.] How much the policy of man can do: if Hushai had not been there, Ahithophel's counsel would certainly have prevailed; and, though all had given their opinion, nothing could be really more for Absalom's interest than that which he advised; yet Hushai, with his management, brings them all over to his side, and none of them are aware that he says all this in favour of David and his interest, but all say as he says. See how the unthinking are imposed upon by the designing part of mankind; what tools, what fools, great men make of one another by their intrigues; and what tricks there are often in courts and councils, which those are happiest that are least conversant with. [2.] See how much more the providence of God can do. Hushai managed the plot with dexterity, yet the success is ascribed to God, and his agency on the minds of those concerned: *The Lord had appointed to defeat the good counsel of*

Ahithophel. Be it observed, to the comfort of all that fear God, he turns all men's hearts as the rivers of water, though *they know not the thoughts of the Lord. He stands in the congregation of the mighty*, has an overruling hand in all counsels and a negative voice in all resolves, and laughs at men's projects against his anointed.

15 Then said Hushai unto Zadok and to Abiathar the priests, Thus and thus did Ahithophel counsel Absalom and the elders of Israel: and thus and thus have I counselled. 16 Now therefore send quickly, and tell David, saying, Lodge not this night in the plains of the wilderness, but speedily pass over; lest the king be swallowed up, and all the people that *are* with him. 17 Now Jonathan and Ahimaaz stayed by En-rogel; for they might not be seen to come into the city: and a wench went and told them; and they went and told king David. 18 Nevertheless a lad saw them, and told Absalom: but they went both of them away quickly, and came to a man's house in Bahurim, which had a well in his court; whither they went down. 19 And the woman took and spread a covering over the well's mouth, and spread ground corn thereon; and the thing was not known. 20 And when Absalom's servants came to the woman to the house, they said, Where *is* Ahimaaz and Jonathan? And the woman said unto them, They be gone over the brook of water. And when they had sought and could not find *them*, they returned to Jerusalem. 21 And it came to pass, after they were departed, that they came up out of the well, and went and told king David, and said unto David, Arise, and pass quickly over the water: for thus hath Ahithophel counselled against you.

We must now leave David's enemies pleasing themselves with the thoughts of a sure victory by following Hushai's counsel, and sending a summons, no doubt, to all the tribes of Israel, to come to the general rendezvous at a place appointed, pursuant to that counsel; and we next find David's friends consulting how to get him notice of all this, that he might steer his course accordingly. Hushai tells the priests what had passed in council, *v.* 15. But, it should seem, he was not sure but that yet Ahithophel's counsel might be followed, and was therefore jealous lest, if he made not the best of his way, the king would be *swallowed up, and all the people that were with him, v.* 16. Perhaps, as he was called in to give his advice (*v.* 5), so he was dismissed before they came to that resolve (*v.* 14) in favour of his advice, or he feared they might afterwards change their mind. However, it was good to provide against the worst, and therefore to hasten those valuable lives out of the reach of these destroyers. Such strict guards did Absalom set upon all the avenues to Jerusalem that they had much ado to get this necessary intelligence to David. 1. The young priests that were to be the messengers were forced to retire secretly out of the city, by *En-rogel*, which signifies, as some say, *the fountain of a spy*. Surely it went ill with Jerusalem when two such faithful priests as they were might not be seen to come into the city. 2. Instructions were sent to them by a poor simple young woman, who probably went to that well under pretence of fetching water, *v.* 17. If she carried the message by word of mouth, there was danger of her making some mistake or blunder in it; but Providence can make an ignorant girl a trusty messenger, and serve its wise counsels by the foolish things of the world. 3. Yet, by the vigilance of Absalom's spies, they were discovered, and information was brought to Absalom of their motions: *A lad saw them and told him, v.* 18. 4. They, being aware that they were discovered, sheltered themselves in a friend's house in Bahurim, where David had refreshed himself but just before, *ch.* xvi. 14. There they were happily hidden in a well, which now, in summer time, perhaps was dry, *v.* 18. The woman of the house very ingeniously covered the mouth of the well with a cloth, on which she spread corn to dry, so that the pursuers were not aware that there was a well; else they would have searched it, *v.* 19. Thus far the woman did well; but we know not how to justify her further concealing them with a lie, *v.* 20. We must not do evil that good may come of it. However, hereby the messengers were protected, and the pursuers were defeated and returned to Absalom without their prey. It was well that Absalom did not hereupon fall upon their two fathers, Zadok and Abiathar, as Saul on Ahimelech for his kindness to David: but God restrained him. Being thus preserved, they brought their intelligence very faithfully to David (*v.* 21), with this advice of his friends, that he should not delay to pass over Jordan, near to which, it seems, he now was. There, as some think, he penned the 42d and 43d Psalms, looking back upon *Jerusalem from the land of Jordan*, Ps. xlii. 6.

22 Then David arose, and all the people that *were* with him, and they passed over Jordan: by the morning light there lacked not one of them that

was not gone over Jordan. 23 And when Ahithophel saw that his counsel was not followed, he saddled *his* ass, and arose, and gat him home to his house, to his city, and put his household in order, and hanged himself, and died, and was buried in the sepulchre of his father. 24 Then David came to Mahanaim. And Absalom passed over Jordan, he and all the men of Israel with him. 25 And Absalom made Amasa captain of the host instead of Joab: which Amasa *was* a man's son, whose name *was* Ithra an Israelite, that went in to Abigail the daughter of Nahash, sister to Zeruiah Joab's mother. 26 So Israel and Absalom pitched in the land of Gilead. 27 And it came to pass, when David was come to Mahanaim, that Shobi the son of Nahash of Rabbah of the children of Ammon, and Machir the son of Ammiel of Lodebar, and Barzillai the Gileadite of Rogelim, 28 Brought beds, and basons, and earthen vessels, and wheat, and barley, and flour, and parched *corn*, and beans, and lentiles, and parched *pulse*, 29 And honey, and butter, and sheep, and cheese of kine, for David, and for the people that *were* with him, to eat: for they said, The people *is* hungry, and weary, and thirsty, in the wilderness.

Here is, I. The transporting of David and his forces over Jordan, pursuant to the advice he had received from his friends at Jerusalem, *v.* 22. He, and all that were with him, went over in the night, whether in ferry-boats, which probably always plied there, or through the fords, does not appear. But special notice is taken of this, that there lacked not one of them: none deserted him, though his distress was great, none staid behind sick or weary, nor were any lost or cast away in passing the river. Herein some make him a type of the Messiah, who said, in a difficult day, *Of all that thou hast given me have I lost none.* Having got over Jordan, he marched many miles forward to Mahanaim, a Levites' city in the tribe of Gad, in the utmost border of that tribe, and not far from Rabbah, the chief city of the Ammonites. This city, which Ishbosheth had made his royal city (*ch.* ii. 8), David now made his head-quarters, *v.* 24. And now he had time to raise an army wherewith to oppose the rebels and give them a warm reception.

II. The death of Ahithophel, *v.* 23. He died by his own hands, *felo de se—a suicide.* He hanged himself for vexation that his counsel was not followed; for thereby, 1. He thought himself slighted, and an intolerable slur cast upon his reputation for wisdom. His judgment always used to sway at the council-board, but now another's opinion is thought wiser and better than his. His proud heart cannot bear the affront; it rises and swells, and the more he thinks of it the more violent his resentments grow, till they bring him at last to this desperate resolve, not to live to see another preferred before him. All men think him a wise man, but he thinks himself the only wise man; and therefore, to be avenged upon mankind for not thinking so too, he will die, that wisdom may die with him. The world is not worthy of such an oracle as he is, and therefore he will make them know the want of him. See what real enemies those are to themselves that think too well of themselves, and what mischiefs those run upon that are impatient of contempt. That will break a proud man's heart that will not break a humble man's sleep. 2. He thought himself endangered and his life exposed. He concluded that, because his counsel was not followed, Absalom's cause would certainly miscarry, and then, whoever would find David's mercy, he concluded that he, who was the greatest criminal, and had particularly advised him to lie with his father's concubines, must be sacrificed to his justice. To prevent therefore the shame and terror of a public and solemn execution, he does justice upon himself, and, after all his reputation for wisdom, by this his last act puts a far greater disgrace upon himself than Absalom's privy-council had put upon him, and answers his name *Ahithophel,* which signifies, *the brother of a fool.* Nothing indicates so much folly as self-murder. Observe, How deliberately he did it, and of malice prepense against himself; not in a heat, but he went home to his city, to his house, to do it; and, which is strange, took time to consider of it, and yet did it. And, to prove himself *compos mentis—in his senses,* when he did it, he first put his household in order, made his will as a man of sane memory and understanding, settled his estate, balanced his accounts; yet he that had sense and prudence enough to do this had not consideration enough to revoke the sentence his pride and passion had passed upon his own neck, nor so much as to suspend the execution of it till he saw the event of Absalom's rebellion. Now herein we may see, (1.) Contempt poured upon the wisdom of man. He that was more renowned for policy than any man played the fool with himself more abundantly. *Let not the wise man glory in his wisdom,* when he sees him that was so great an oracle dying *as a fool dies.* (2.) Honour done to the justice of God. When the wicked are thus *snared in the work of their own hands, and sunk in a pit of their own digging, the Lord is known by the judgment which he executeth,* and we must say, *Higgaion, Selah;* it is a thing to be marked and meditated upon, Ps. vii. 15, 16. (3.) Prayer answered, and an honest cause served even by its enemies. Now, as David had prayed, Ahithophel's counsel was *turned into foolishness to himself.* Dr. Lightfoot supposes that David penned the 55th Psalm upon occasion of Ahithophel's being in the plot against him, and that he is the man complained of (*v.* 13) that had been *his equal, his guide, and his acquaintance;* and, if so, this was an immediate answer to his prayer there (*v.* 15): *Let death seize upon them, and let them go down quickly into hell.* Ahithophel's death was an advantage to David's interest; for had he digested that affront (as those must resolve often to do that will live in this world), and continued his post at Absalom's elbow, he might have given him counsel afterwards that might have been of pernicious consequence to David. It is well that that breath is stopped and that head laid from which nothing could be expected but mischief. It seems, it was not then usual to disgrace the dead bodies of self-murderers, for Ahithophel was *buried,* we may suppose honourably buried, *in the sepulchre of his father,* though he deserved no better than the *burial of an ass.* See Eccl. viii. 10.

III. Absalom's pursuit of his father. He had now got all the men of Israel with him, as Hushai advised, and he himself, at the head of them, *passed over Jordan, v.* 24. Not content that he had driven his good father to the utmost corner of his kingdom, he resolved to chase him out of the world. He *pitched in the land of Gilead* with all his forces, ready to give David battle, *v.* 26. Absalom made one Amasa his general (*v.* 25), whose father was by birth Jether, an Ishmaelite (1 Chron. ii. 17), but by religion Ithra (as he is here called), an Israelite; probably he was not only proselyted, but, having married a near relation of David's, was, by some act of the state, naturalized, and is therefore called an Israelite. His wife, Amasa's mother, was Abigail, David's sister, whose other sister, Zeruiah, was Joab's mother (1 Chron. ii. 16), so that Amasa was in the same relation to David that Joab was. In honour to his family, even while he was in arms against his father, Absalom made him commander-in-chief of all his forces. Jesse is here called *Nahash,* for many had two names; or perhaps this was his wife's name.

IV. The friends David met with in this distant country. Even Shobi, a younger brother of the royal family of the Ammonites, was kind to him, *v.* 27. It is probable that he had detested the indignity which his brother Hanun had done to David's ambassadors, and for that had received favours from David, which he now returned. Those that think their prosperity most confirmed know not but, some time or other, they may stand in need of the kindness of those that now lie at their mercy, and may be glad to be beholden to them, which is a reason why we should, as we have opportunity, *do good to all men,* for *he that watereth shall be watered also himself,* when there is occasion. Machir, the son of Ammiel, was he that maintained Mephibosheth (*ch.* ix. 4), till David eased him of that charge, and is now repaid for it by that generous man, who, it seems, was the common patron of distressed princes. Barzillai we shall hear of again. These, compassionating David and his men, now that they were weary with a long march, brought him furniture for his house, *beds and basins,* and provision for his table, *wheat and barley,* &c., *v.* 28, 29. He did not put them under contribution, did not compel them to supply him, much less plunder them; but in token of their dutiful affection to him, their firm adherence to his government, and their sincere concern for him in his present straits, of their own good will they brought in plenty of all that which he had occasion for. Let us learn hence to be generous and open-handed, according as our ability is, to all in distress, especially great men, to whom it is most grievous, and good men, who deserve better treatment; and see how God sometimes makes up to his people that comfort from strangers which they are disappointed of in their own families.

CHAP. XVIII.

This chapter puts a period to Absalom's rebellion and life, and so makes way for David to his throne again, whither the next chapter brings him back in peace and triumph. We have here, I. David's preparations to engage the rebels, ver. 1—5. II. The total defeat of Absalom's party, and their dispersion, ver. 6—8. III. The death of Absalom, and his burial, ver. 9—18. IV. The bringing of the tidings to David, who tarried at Mahanaim, ver. 19—32. V. His bitter lamentation for Absalom, ver. 33.

AND David numbered the people that *were* with him, and set captains of thousands and captains of hundreds over them. 2 And David sent forth a third part of the people under the hand of Joab, and a third part under the hand of Abishai the son of Zeruiah, Joab's brother, and a third part under the hand of Ittai the Gittite. And the king said unto the people, I will surely go forth with you myself also. 3 But the people answered, Thou shalt not go forth: for if we flee away, they will not care for us; neither if half of us die, will they care for us: but now *thou art* worth ten thousand of us: therefore now *it is* better that thou succour us out of the city. 4 And the king said unto them, What seemeth you best I will do. And the king stood by the gate side, and all the people came out by hundreds and by thousands.

5 And the king commanded Joab and Abishai and Ittai, saying, *Deal* gently for my sake with the young man, *even* with Absalom. And all the people heard when the king gave all the captains charge concerning Absalom. 6 So the people went out into the field against Israel: and the battle was in the wood of Ephraim; 7 Where the people of Israel were slain before the servants of David, and there was there a great slaughter that day of twenty thousand *men.* 8 For the battle was there scattered over the face of all the country; and the wood devoured more people that day than the sword devoured.

Which way David raised an army here, and what reinforcements were sent him, we are not told; many, it is likely, from all the coasts of Israel, at least from the neighbouring tribes, came in to his assistance, so that, by degrees, he was able to make head against Absalom, as Ahithophel foresaw. Now here we have,

I. His army numbered and marshalled, *v.* 1, 2. He had, no doubt, committed his cause to God by prayer, for that was his relief in all his afflictions; and then he took an account of his forces. Josephus says they were, in all, but about 4000. These he divided into regiments and companies, to each of which he appointed proper officers, and then disposed them, as is usual, into the right wing, the left wing, and the centre, two of which he committed to his two old experienced generals, Joab and Abishai, and the third to his new friend Ittai. Good order and good conduct may sometimes be as serviceable in an army as great numbers. Wisdom teaches us to make the best of the strength we have, and let it reach to the utmost.

II. Himself over-persuaded not to go in person to the battle. He was Absalom's false friend that persuaded him to go, and served his pride more than his prudence; David's true friends would not let him go, remembering what they had been told of Ahithophel's design to *smite the king only.* David showed his affection to them by being willing to venture with them (*v.* 2), and they showed theirs to him by opposing it. We must never reckon it an affront to be gainsaid for our good, and by those that therein consult our interest. 1. They would by no means have him to expose himself, for (say they) *thou art worth* 10,000 *of us.* Thus ought good princes to be valued by their subjects, who, for their safety, must be willing to expose themselves. 2. They would not so far gratify the enemy, who would rejoice more in his fall than in the defeat of the whole army. 3. He might be more serviceable to them by tarrying in the city, with a reserve of his forces there, whence he might send them recruits. That may be a post of real service which yet is not a post of danger. The king acquiesced in their reasons, and changed his purpose (*v.* 4): *What seemeth to you best I will do.* It is no piece of wisdom to be stiff in our resolutions, but to be willing to hear reason, even from our inferiors, and to be overruled by their advice when it appears to be for our own good. Whether the people's prudence had an eye to it or no, God's providence wisely ordered it, that David should not be in the field of battle; for then his tenderness would certainly have interposed to save the life of Absalom, whom God had determined to destroy.

III. The charge he gave concerning Absalom, *v.* 5. When the army was drawn out, rank and file, Josephus says, he encouraged them, and prayed for them, but withal bade them all take heed of doing Absalom any hurt. How does he render good for evil! Absalom would have David only smitten. David would have Absalom only spared. What foils are these to each other! Never was unnatural hatred to a father more strong than in Absalom; nor was ever natural affection to a child more strong than in David. Each did his utmost, and showed what man is capable of doing, how bad it is possible for a child to be to the best of fathers and how good it is possible for a father to be to the worst of children; as if it were designed to be a resemblance of man's wickedness towards God and God's mercy towards man, of which it is hard to say which is more amazing. "*Deal gently,*" says David, "by all means, *with the young man, even with Absalom, for my sake;* he is a young man, rash and heady, and his age must excuse him; he is mine, whom I love; if you love me, be not severe with him." This charge supposes David's strong expectation of success. Having a good cause and a good God, he doubts not but Absalom would lie at their mercy, and therefore bids them deal gently with him, spare his life and reserve him for his judgment.

Bishop Hall thus descants on this: "What means this ill-placed love? This unjust mercy? Deal gently with a traitor? Of all traitors, with a son? Of all sons, with an Absalom? That graceless darling of so good a father? And all this, for thy sake, whose crown, whose blood, he hunts after? For whose sake must he be pursued, if forborne for thine? Must the cause of the quarrel be the motive of mercy? Even in the holiest parents, nature may be guilty of an injurious tenderness, of a bloody indulgence. But was not this done in type of that immeasurable mercy of the true King and Redeemer of Israel, who prayed for his persecutors, for his murderers, *Father, forgive them? Deal gently with them for my sake.*" When God sends an affliction to correct his children, it is with this charge, "Deal gently with them for my sake;" for he knows our frame.

IV. A complete victory gained over Absalom's forces. The battle was fought *in the wood of Ephraim* (*v.* 6), so called from some memorable action of the Ephraimites there, though it lay in the tribe of Gad. David thought fit to meet the enemy with his forces at some distance, before they came up to Mahanaim, lest he should bring that city into trouble which had so kindly sheltered him. The cause shall be decided by a pitched battle. Josephus represents the fight as very obstinate, but the rebels were at length totally routed and 20,000 of them slain, *v.* 7. Now they smarted justly for their treason against their lawful prince, their uneasiness under so good a government, and their base ingratitude to so good a governor; and they found what it was to take up arms for a usurper, who with his kisses and caresses had wheedled them into their own ruin. Now where are the rewards, the preferments, the golden days, they promised themselves from him? Now they see what it is to take counsel *against the Lord and his anointed,* and to think of *breaking his bands asunder.* And that they might see that God fought against them, 1. They are conquered by a few, an army, in all probability, much inferior to theirs in number. 2. By that flight with which they hoped to save themselves they destroyed themselves. *The wood,* which they sought to for shelter, *devoured more than the sword,* that they might see how, when they thought themselves safe from David's men, and said, *Surely the bitterness of death is past,* yet the justice of God pursued them and suffered them not to live. What refuge can rebels find from divine vengeance? The pits and bogs, the stumps and thickets, and, as the Chaldee paraphrast understands it, the wild beasts of the wood, were probably the death of multitudes of the dispersed distracted Israelites, besides the 20,000 that were slain with the sword. God herein fought for David, and yet fought against him; for all these that were slain were his own subjects, and the common interest of his kingdom was weakened by the slaughter. The Romans allowed no triumph for a victory in a civil war.

9 And Absalom met the servants of David. And Absalom rode upon a mule, and the mule went under the thick boughs of a great oak, and his head caught hold of the oak, and he was taken up between the heaven and the earth; and the mule that *was* under him went away. 10 And a certain man saw *it,* and told Joab, and said, Behold, I saw Absalom hanged in an oak. 11 And Joab said unto the man that told him, And, behold, thou sawest *him,* and why didst thou not smite him there to the ground? and I would have given thee ten *shekels* of silver, and a girdle. 12 And the man said unto Joab, Though I should receive a thousand *shekels* of silver in mine hand, *yet* would I not put forth mine hand against the king's son: for in our hearing the king charged thee and Abishai and Ittai, saying, Beware that none *touch* the young man Absalom. 13 Otherwise I should have wrought falsehood against mine own life: for there is no matter hid from the king, and thou thyself wouldest have set thyself against *me.* 14 Then said Joab, I may not tarry thus with thee. And he took three darts in his hand, and thrust them through the heart of Absalom, while he *was* yet alive in the midst of the oak. 15 And ten young men that bare Joab's armour compassed about and smote Absalom, and slew him. 16 And Joab blew the trumpet, and the people returned from pursuing after Israel: for Joab held back the people. 17 And they took Absalom, and cast him into a great pit in the wood, and laid a very great heap of stones upon him: and all Israel fled every one to his tent. 18 Now Absalom in his lifetime had taken and reared up for himself a pillar, which *is* in the king's dale: for he said, I have no son to keep my name in remembrance: and he called the pillar after his own name: and it is called unto this day, Absalom's place.

Here is Absalom quite at a loss, at his wit's end first, and then at his life's end. He that began the fight, big with the expectation of triumphing over David himself, with whom, if he had had him in his power, he would not have dealt gently, is now in the greatest consternation, when he *meets the servants of David, v.* 9. Though they were forbidden to meddle with him, he durst not look them in the face; but, finding they were near him, he clapped spurs to his mule and made the best of his way, through thick and thin, and so rode headlong upon his own destruction. Thus *he that fleeth from the fear shall fall into the pit, and he that getteth up out of the pit shall be taken in the snare,* Jer. xlviii. 44. David is inclined to spare him, but divine justice passes sentence upon him as a traitor, and sees it executed—that he hang by the neck, be caught alive, be embowelled, and his body disposed of disgracefully.

I. He is hanged by the neck. Riding furiously, neck or nothing, *under the thick boughs of a great oak* which hung low and had never been cropped, either the twisted branches, or some one forked bough of the oak, caught hold of his head, either by his neck, or, as some think, by his long hair, which had been so much his pride, and was now justly made a halter for him, and there he hung, so astonished that he could not use his hands to help himself or so entangled that his hands could not help him, but the more he struggled the more he was embarrassed. This set him up for a fair mark to the servants of David, and he had the terror and shame of seeing himself thus exposed, while he could do nothing for his own relief, neither fight nor fly. Observe concerning this, 1. That his *mule went away* from *under him*, as if glad to get clear of such a burden, and resign it to the ignominious tree. Thus the whole creation groans under the burden of man's corruption, but shall shortly be delivered from its load, Rom. viii. 21, 22. 2. That he hung *between heaven and earth*, as unworthy of either, as abandoned of both; earth would not keep him, heaven would not take him, hell therefore opens her mouth to receive him. 3. That this was a very surprising unusual thing. It was fit that it should be so, his crime being so monstrous: if, in his flight, his mule had thrown him, and left him half-dead upon the ground, till the servants of David had come up and dispatched him, the same thing would have been done as effectually; but that would have been too common a fate for so uncommon a criminal. God will here, as in the case of those other rebels, Dathan and Abiram, *create a new thing*, that it may be understood how much *this man has provoked the Lord*, Num. xvi. 29, 30. Absalom is here hung up, *in terrorem—to frighten* children from disobedience *to their parents*. See Prov. xxx. 17.

II. He is caught alive by one of the servants of David, who goes directly and tells Joab in what posture he found that archrebel, *v.* 10. Thus was he set up for a spectacle, as well as a mark, that the righteous might see him and *laugh at him* (Ps. lii. 6), while he had this further vexation in his breast, that of all the friends he had courted and confided in, and thought he had sure in his interest, though he hung long enough to have been relieved, yet he had none at hand to disentangle him. Joab chides the man for not dispatching him (*v.* 11), telling him, if he had given that bold stroke, he would have rewarded him with ten half-crowns and a girdle, that is, a captain's commission, which perhaps was signified by the delivery of a belt or girdle; see Isa. xxii. 21. But the man, though zealous enough against Absalom, justified himself in not doing it: "Dispatch him!" says he, "not for all the world; it would have cost me my head: and thou thyself wast witness to the king's charge concerning him (*v.* 12), and, for all thy talk, wouldst have been my prosecutor if I had done it," *v.* 13. Those that love the treason hate the traitor. Joab could not deny this, nor blame the man for his caution, and therefore makes him no answer, but breaks off the discourse, under colour of haste (*v.* 14): *I may not tarry thus with thee.* Superiors should consider a reproof before they give it, lest they be ashamed of it afterwards, and find themselves unable to make it good.

III. He is (as I may say) embowelled and quartered, as traitors are, so pitifully mangled is he as he hangs there, and receives his death in such a manner as to see all its terrors and feel all its pain. 1. Joab throws three darts into his body, which put him, no doubt, to exquisite torment, while he is yet *alive in the midst of the oak*, *v.* 14. I know not whether Joab can be justified in this direct disobedience to the command of his sovereign; was this to *deal gently with the young man?* Would David have suffered him to do it if he had been upon the spot? Yet this may be said for him, that, while he broke the order of a too indulgent father, he did real service both to his king and country, and would have endangered the welfare of both if he had not done it. *Salus populi suprema lex—The safety of the people is the supreme law.* 2. Joab's young men, ten of them, smite him, before he is dispatched, *v.* 15. They surrounded him, made a ring about him in triumph, and then *smote him and slew him.* So *let all thy enemies perish, O Lord!* Joab hereupon sounds a retreat, *v.* 16. The danger is over, now that Absalom is slain; the people will soon return to their allegiance to David, and therefore no more blood shall be spilt; no prisoners are taken, to be tried as traitors and made examples; let every man return to his tent; they are all the king's subjects, all his good subjects again.

IV. His body is disposed of disgracefully (*v.* 17, 18): They *cast it into a great pit in the wood;* they would not bring it to his father (for that circumstance would but have added to his grief), nor would they preserve it to be buried, according to his order, but threw it into the next pit with indignation. Now where is the beauty he had been so proud of and for which he had been so much admired? Where are his aspiring projects, and the castles he had built in the air? His thoughts perish, and he with them. And, to signify how heavy *his iniquity lay upon his bones*, as the prophet speaks (Ezek. xxxii. 27), they raised a *great heap of stones upon him*, to be a monument of his villany, and to signify that he ought to have been stoned as a rebellious son, Deut. xxi. 21. Travellers say that the place is taken notice of to this day, and that it is common for passengers to throw a stone to this heap, with words to this purport: *Cursed be the memory of rebellious Absalom, and cursed for ever be all wicked children that rise up in rebellion against their parents.* To aggravate the ignominy of Absalom's burial, the historian takes notice of a pillar he had erected in the valley of Kidron, near Jerusalem, to be a monument for himself, and keep his name in remembrance (*v.* 18), at the foot of which, it is probable, he designed to be buried. What foolish insignificant projects do proud men fill their heads with! And what care do many people take about the disposal of their bodies, when they are dead, that have no care at all what shall become of their precious souls! Absalom had three sons (*ch.* xiv. 27), but, it seems, now he had none; God had taken them away by death; and justly is a rebellious son written childless. To make up the want, he erects this pillar for a memorial; yet in this also Providence crosses him, and a rude heap of stones shall be his monument, instead of this marble pillar. Thus *those that exalt themselves shall be abased.* His care was to have his name kept in remembrance, and it is so, to his everlasting dishonour. He could not be content in the obscurity of the rest of David's sons, of whom nothing is recorded but their names, but would be famous, and is therefore justly made for ever infamous. The pillar shall bear his name, but not to his credit; it was designed for Absalom's glory, but proved Absalom's folly.

19 Then said Ahimaaz the son of Zadok, Let me now run, and bear the king tidings, how that the LORD hath avenged him of his enemies. 20 And Joab said unto him, Thou shalt not bear tidings this day, but thou shalt bear tidings another day: but this day thou shalt bear no tidings, because the king's son is dead. 21 Then said Joab to Cushi, Go tell the king what thou hast seen. And Cushi bowed himself unto Joab, and ran. 22 Then said Ahimaaz the son of Zadok yet again to Joab, But howsoever, let me, I pray thee, also run after Cushi. And Joab said, Wherefore wilt thou run, my son, seeing that thou hast no tidings ready? 23 But howsoever, *said he,* let me run. And he said unto him, Run. Then Ahimaaz ran by the way of the plain, and overran Cushi. 24 And David sat between the two gates: and the watchman went up to the roof over the gate unto the wall, and lifted up his eyes, and looked, and behold a man running alone. 25 And the watchman cried, and told the king. And the king said, If he *be* alone, *there is* tidings in his mouth. And he came apace, and drew near. 26 And the watchman saw another man running: and the watchman called unto the porter, and said, Behold *another* man running alone. And the king said, He also bringeth tidings. 27 And the watchman said, Methinketh the running of the foremost is like the running of Ahimaaz the son of Zadok. And the king said, He *is* a good man, and cometh with good tidings. 28 And Ahimaaz called, and said unto the king, All is well. And he fell down to the earth upon his face before the king, and said, Blessed *be* the LORD thy God, which hath delivered up the men that lifted up their hand against my lord the king. 29 And the king said, Is the young man Absalom safe? And Ahimaaz answered, When Joab sent the king's servant, and *me* thy servant, I saw a great tumult, but I knew not what *it was.* 30 And the king said *unto him,* Turn aside, *and* stand here. And he turned aside, and stood still. 31 And, behold, Cushi came; and Cushi said, Tidings, my lord the king: for the LORD hath avenged thee this day of all them that rose up against thee. 32 And the king said unto Cushi, *Is* the young man Absalom safe? And Cushi answered, The enemies of my lord the king, and all that rise against thee to do *thee* hurt, be as *that* young man *is.* 33 And the king was much moved, and went up to the chamber over the gate, and wept: and as he went, thus he said, O my son Absalom, my son, my son Absalom! would God I had died for thee, O Absalom, my son, my son!

Absalom's business is done; and we are now told,

I. How David was informed of it. He staid behind at the city of Mahanaim, some miles from the wood where the battle was, and in the utmost border of the land. Absalom's scattered forces all made homeward towards Jordan, which was the contrary way from Mahanaim, so that his watchmen could not perceive how the battle went, till an express came on purpose to bring advice of the issue, which the king sat in the gate expecting to hear, *v.* 24.

1. Cushi was the man Joab ordered to carry the tidings (*v.* 21), an *Ethiopian,* so his name signifies, and some think that he was so by birth, a black that waited on Joab, probably one of the ten that had helped to dispatch Absalom (*v.* 15) as some think, though it was dangerous for one of those to bring the news to David, lest his fate should be the same with theirs that reported to him Saul's death, and Ish-bosheth's.

2. Ahimaaz, the young priest (one of those who brought David intelligence of Absalom's motions, *ch.* xvii. 17), was very forward to be the messenger of these tidings, so transported was he with joy that this cloud was blown over; let him go and tell the king that *the Lord hath avenged him of his enemies, v.* 19. This he desired, not so much in hope of a reward (he was above that) as that he might have the pleasure and satisfaction of bringing the king, whom he loved, this good news. Joab knew David better than Ahimaaz did, and that the tidings of Absalom's death, which must conclude the story, would spoil the acceptableness of all the rest; and he loves Ahimaaz too well to let him be the messenger of those tidings (*v.* 20); they are fitter to be brought by a footman than by a priest. However, when Cushi was gone, Ahimaaz begged hard for leave to run after him, and with great importunity obtained it, *v.* 22, 23. One would wonder why he should be so very fond of this office, when another was employed in it. (1.) Perhaps it was to show his swiftness; observing how heavily Cushi ran, and that he took the worse way, though the nearest, he had a mind to show how fast he could run, and that he could go the furthest way about and yet beat Cushi. No great praise for a priest to be swift of foot, yet perhaps Ahimaaz was proud of it. (2.) Perhaps it was in prudence and tenderness to the king that he desired it. He knew he could get before Cushi, and therefore was willing to prepare the king, by a vague and general report, for the plain truth which Cushi was ordered to tell him. If bad news must come, it is best that it come gradually, and will be the better borne.

3. They are both discovered by the watchman on the gate of Mahanaim, Ahimaaz first (*v.* 24), for, though Cushi had the lead, Ahimaaz soon outran him; but presently after Cushi appeared, *v.* 26. (1.) When the king hears of one running alone he concludes he is an express (*v.* 25): *If he be alone, there are tidings in his mouth;* for if they had been beaten, and were flying back from the enemy, there would have been many. (2.) When he hears it is Ahimaaz he concludes he brings good news, *v.* 27. Ahimaaz, it seems, was so famous for running that he was known by it at a distance, and so eminently good that it is taken for granted, if he be the messenger, the news must needs be good: *He is a good man,* zealously affected to the king's interest, and would not bring bad news. It is pity but the good tidings of the gospel should always be brought by good men; and how welcome should the messengers be to us for the irmessage sake!

4. Ahimaaz is very forward to proclaim the victory (*v.* 28), cries at a distance, "Peace, there is peace;" peace after war, which is doubly welcome. "*All is well,* my lord O king! the danger is over, and we may return, when the king pleases, to Jerusalem." And, when he comes near, he tells him the news more particularly, "They are all cut off *that lifted up their hand against the king;*" and, as became a priest, while he gives the king the joy of it, he gives God the glory of it, the God of peace and war, the God of salvation and victory: "*Blessed be the Lord thy God,* that has done this for thee, as thy God, pursuant to the promises made to uphold thy throne," *ch.* vii. 16. When he said this, *he fell down upon his face,* not only in reverence to the king, but in humble adoration of God, whose name he praised for this success. By directing David thus to give God thanks for his victory, he prepared him for the approaching news of its allay. The more our hearts are fixed and enlarged in thanksgiving to God for our mercies the better disposed we shall be to bear with patience the afflictions mixed with them. Poor David is so much a father that he forgets he is a king, and therefore cannot rejoice in the news of a victory, till he know whether the *young man Absalom be safe,* for whom his heart seems to tremble, almost as Eli's, in a similar case, for the ark of God. Ahimaaz soon discerned, what Joab intimated to him, that the death of the king's son would make the tidings of the day very unwelcome, and therefore in his report left that matter doubtful; and, though he gave occasion to suspect how it was, yet, that the thunderclap might not come too suddenly upon the poor perplexed king, he refers him to the next messenger, whom they saw coming, for a more particular account of it. "When Joab sent the king's servant (namely, *Cushi) and me thy servant,* to bring the news, *I saw a great tumult,* occasioned by something extraordinary, as you will hear by and by; but I have nothing to say about it. I have delivered that which was my message. Cushi is better able to inform you than I am. I will not be the messenger of evil tidings; nor will I pretend to know that which I cannot give a perfect account of." He is therefore told to stand by till Cushi come (*v.* 30), and now, we may suppose, he gives the king a more particular account of the victory, which was the thing he came to bring the news of.

5. Cushi, the slow post, proves the sure one, and besides the confirmation of the

news of the victory which Ahimaaz had brought—*The Lord has avenged thee of all those that rose up against thee* (*v.* 31)—he satisfied the king's enquiry concerning Absalom, *v.* 32. *Is he safe?* says David. "Yes," says Cushi, "he is safe in his grave;" but he tells the news so discreetly that, how unwelcome soever the message is, the messenger can have no blame. He did not tell him plainly that Absalom was hanged, and run through, and buried under a heap of stones; but only that his fate was what he desired might be the fate of all that were traitors against the king, his crown and dignity: "*The enemies of my lord the king,* whoever they are, *and all that rise against thee to do thee hurt, be as that young man is;* I need wish them no worse."

II. How David received the intelligence. He forgets all the joy of his deliverance, and is quite overwhelmed with the sorrowful tidings of Absalom's death, *v.* 33. As soon as he perceived by Cushi's reply that Absalom was dead, he asked no more questions, but fell into a passion of weeping, retired from company, and abandoned himself to sorrow; as he was going up to his chamber he was overheard to say, "*O my son Absalom! my son, my son Absalom!* alas for thee! I lament thee. How hast thou fallen! *Would God I had died for thee,* and that thou hadst remained alive this day" (so the Chaldee adds) "*O Absalom! my son, my son!*" I wish I could see reason to think that this arose from a concern about Absalom's everlasting state, and that the reason why he wished he had *died for him* was because he had good hopes of his own salvation, and of Absalom's repentance if he had lived. It rather seems to have been spoken inconsiderately, and in a passion, and it was his infirmity. He is to be blamed, 1. For showing so great a fondness for a graceless son only because he was handsome and witty, while he was justly abandoned both of God and man. 2. For quarrelling, not only with divine providence, in the disposals of which he ought silently to have acquiesced, but with divine justice, the judgments of which he ought to have adored and subscribed to. See how Bildad argues (Job viii. 3, 4), *If thy children have sinned against him, and he have cast them away in their transgression,* thou shouldst submit, *for doth God pervert judgment?* See Lev. x. 3. 3. For opposing the justice of the nation, which, as king, he was entrusted with the administration of, and which, with other public interests, he ought to have preferred before any natural affection. 4. For despising the mercy of his deliverance, and the deliverance of his family and kingdom, from Absalom's wicked designs, as if this were no mercy, nor worth giving thanks for, because it cost the life of Absalom. 5. For indulging a strong passion, and speaking unadvisedly with his lips. He now forgot his own reasonings upon the death of another child (*Can I bring him back again?*) and his own resolution to *keep his mouth as with a bridle* when *his heart was hot within him,* as well as his own practice at other times, when he *quieted himself as a child that was weaned from his mother.* The best men are not always in an equally good frame. What we over-loved we are apt to over-grieve for: in each affection, therefore, it is wisdom to have rule over our own spirits and to keep a strict guard upon ourselves when that is removed from us which was very dear to us. Losers think they may have leave to speak; but little said is soon amended. The penitent patient sufferer *sitteth alone and keepeth silence* (Lam. iii. 28), or rather, with *Job,* says, *Blessed be the name of the Lord.*

CHAP. XIX.

We left David's army in triumph and yet David himself in tears: now here we have, I. His return to himself, by the persuasion of Joab, ver. 1—8. II. His return to his kingdom from his present banishment. 1. The men of Israel were forward of themselves to bring him back, ver. 9, 10. 2. The men of Judah were dealt with by David's agents to do it (ver. 11—14) and did it, ver. 15. III. At the king's coming over Jordan, Shimei's treason is pardoned (ver. 16—23), Mephibosheth's failure is excused (ver. 24—30), and Barzillai's kindness is thankfully owned, and recompensed to his son, ver. 31—39. IV. The men of Israel quarrelled with the men of Judah, for not calling them to the ceremony of the king's restoration, which occasioned a new rebellion, an account of which we have in the next chapter, ver. 40—43.

AND it was told Joab, Behold, the king weepeth and mourneth for Absalom. 2 And the victory that day was *turned* into mourning unto all the people: for the people heard say that day how the king was grieved for his son. 3 And the people gat them by stealth that day into the city, as people being ashamed steal away when they flee in battle. 4 But the king covered his face, and the king cried with a loud voice, O my son Absalom, O Absalom, my son, my son! 5 And Joab came into the house to the king, and said, Thou hast shamed this day the faces of all thy servants, which this day have saved thy life, and the lives of thy sons and of thy daughters, and the lives of thy wives, and the lives of thy concubines; 6 In that thou lovest thine enemies, and hatest thy friends. For thou hast declared this day, that thou regardest neither princes nor servants: for this day I perceive, that if Absalom had lived, and all we had died this day, then it had pleased thee well. 7 Now therefore arise, go forth, and speak comfortably unto thy servants: for I swear by the LORD, if thou go not forth, there will not tarry one with thee this night: and that will be worse unto thee than all the evil that befel thee from thy youth until now. 8 Then the king arose, and sat in the gate. And they told unto all the people, saying, Behold, the king doth sit in the gate. And all the people came before the king: for Israel had fled every man to his tent.

Soon after the messengers had brought the news of the defeat and death of Absalom to the court of Mahanaim, Joab and his victorious army followed, to grace the king's triumphs and receive his further orders. Now here we are told,

I. What a damp and disappointment it was to them to find the king in tears for Absalom's death, which they construed as a token of his displeasure against them for what they had done, whereas they expected him to have met them with joy and thanks for their good services: *It was told Joab, v.* 1. The report of it ran through the army (*v.* 2), *how the king was grieved for his son.* The people will take particular notice what their princes say and do. The more eyes we have upon us, and the greater our influence is, the more need we have to speak and act wisely and to govern our passions strictly. When they came to the city they found the king in close mourning, *v.* 4. He covered his face, and would not so much as look up, nor take any notice of the generals when they attended him. It could not but surprise them to find, 1. How the king proclaimed his passion, of which he ought to have been ashamed, and which he would have striven to smother and conceal if he had consulted either his reputation for courage, which was lessened by his mean submission to the tyranny of so absurd a passion, or his interest in the people, which would be prejudiced by his discountenancing what was done in zeal for his honour and the public safety. Yet see how he avows his grief: *He cries with a loud voice, O my son Absalom!* "My servants have all come home safe, but where is my son? He is dead; and, dying in sin, I fear he is lost for ever. I cannot now say, *I shall go to him,* for my soul shall not be gathered with such sinners; what shall be done for thee, *O Absalom! my son, my son!*" 2. How he prolonged his passion, even till the army had come up to him, which must be some time after he received the first intelligence. If he had contented himself with giving vent to his passion for an hour or two when he first heard the news, it would have been excusable, but to continue it thus for so bad a son as Absalom, like Jacob for so good a son as Joseph, with a resolution to go to the grave mourning and to stain his triumphs with his tears, was very unwise and very unworthy. Now see how ill this was taken by the people. They were loth to blame the king, for *whatever he did used to please them* (*ch.* iii. 36), but they took it as a great mortification to them. *Their victory was turned into mourning, v.* 2. *They stole into the city as men ashamed, v.* 3 In compliment to their sovereign, they would not rejoice in that which they perceived so afflictive to him, and yet they could not but be uneasy that they were thus obliged to conceal their joy. Superiors ought not to put such hardships as these on their inferiors.

II. How plainly and vehemently Joab reproved David for this indiscreet management of himself in this critical juncture. David never more needed the hearts of his subjects than now, nor was ever more concerned to secure his interest in their affections; and therefore whatever tended to disoblige them now was the most impolitic thing he could do, and the greatest wrong imaginable to his friends that adhered to him. Joab therefore censures him, *v.* 5—7. He speaks a great deal of reason, but not with the respect and deference which he owed to his prince. *Is it fit to say to a king, Thou art wicked?* A plain case may be fairly pleaded with those that are above us, and they may be reproved for what they do amiss, but it must not be done with rudeness and insolence. David did indeed need to be roused and alarmed; and Joab thought it no time to dally with him. If superiors do that which is foolish, they must neither think it strange nor take it ill if their inferiors tell them of it, perhaps too bluntly. 1. Joab magnifies the services of David's soldiers: "*This day they have saved thy life,* and therefore deserve to be taken notice of, and have reason to resent it if they be not." It is implied that Absalom, whom he honoured with his tears, sought his ruin and the ruin of his family, while those whom by his tears he puts a slight upon were such as preserved from ruin him and all that was dear to him. Great mischiefs have arisen to princes from the contempt of great merits. 2. He aggravates the discouragement David had given them: "*Thou hast shamed their faces;* for, while they have shown such a value for thy life, thou hast shown no value for theirs, but preferrest a spoiled wicked youth, a false traitor to his king and country, whom we are happily rid of, before all thy wise counsellors, brave commanders, and loyal subjects. What can be more absurd than to love thy enemies and to hate thy friends?" 3. He advises him to present himself immediately at the head of his troops, to smile upon them, welcome them home, congratulate their success, and return them thanks for their services. Even those that may be commanded yet expect to be thanked when they do well, and ought to be. 4. He threatens him with another rebellion if he would not do this, intimating that rather than serve so ungrateful a prince he himself would head a revolt from him, and then (so confident is Joab of his own interest in the people) "*there will not tarry with thee one man.* If I go, they will all go.

Thou hast now nothing to mourn for; but, if thou persist, I will give thee something to mourn for (as Josephus expresses it) with a true and more bitter mourning."

II. How prudently and mildly David took the reproof and counsel given him, *v.* 8. He shook off his grief, anointed his head, and washed his face, that he might not appear unto men to mourn, and then made his appearance in public in the gate, which was as the guild-hall of the city. Hither the people flocked to him to congratulate his and their safety, and all was well. Note, When we are convinced of a fault, we must amend, though we are told of it by our inferiors, and indecently, or in heat and passion.

9 And all the people were at strife throughout all the tribes of Israel, saying, The king saved us out of the hand of our enemies, and he delivered us out of the hand of the Philistines; and now he is fled out of the land for Absalom. 10 And Absalom, whom we anointed over us, is dead in battle. Now therefore why speak ye not a word of bringing the king back? 11 And king David sent to Zadok and to Abiathar the priests, saying, Speak unto the elders of Judah, saying, Why are ye the last to bring the king back to his house? seeing the speech of all Israel is come to the king, *even* to his house. 12 Ye *are* my brethren, ye *are* my bones and my flesh: wherefore then are ye the last to bring back the king? 13 And say ye to Amasa, *Art* thou not of my bone, and of my flesh? God do so to me, and more also, if thou be not captain of the host before me continually in the room of Joab. 14 And he bowed the heart of all the men of Judah, even as *the heart of* one man; so that they sent *this word* unto the the king, Return thou, and all thy servants. 15 So the king returned, and came to Jordan. And Judah came to Gilgal, to go to meet the king, to conduct the king over Jordan.

It is strange that David did not immediately upon the defeat and dispersion of Absalom's forces march with all expedition back to Jerusalem, to regain the possession of his capital city, while the rebels were in confusion and before they could rally again. What occasion was there to bring him back? Could not he himself go back with the victorious army he had with him in Gilead? He could, no doubt; but, 1. He would go back as a prince, with the consent and unanimous approbation of the people, and not as a conqueror forcing his way: he would restore their liberties, and not take occasion to seize them, or encroach upon them. 2. He would go back in peace and safety, and be sure that he should meet with no difficulty or opposition in his return, and therefore would be satisfied that the people were well-affected to him before he would stir. 3. He would go back in honour, and like himself, and therefore would go back, not at the head of his forces, but in the arms of his subjects; for the prince that has wisdom and goodness enough to make himself his people's darling, without doubt, looks greater and makes a much better figure than the prince that has strength enough to make himself his people's terror. It is resolved therefore that David must be brought back to Jerusalem his own city, and his own house there, with some ceremony, and here we have that matter concerted.

I. The men of Israel (that is, the ten tribes) were the first that talked of it, *v.* 9, 10. The people were at strife about it; it was the great subject of discourse and dispute throughout all the country. Some perhaps opposed it: "Let him either come back himself or stay where he is;" others appeared zealous for it, and reasoned as follows here, to further the design, 1. That David had formerly helped them, had fought their battles, subdued their enemies, and done them much service, and therefore it was a shame that he should continue banished from their country who had been so great a benefactor to it. Note, Good services done to the public, though they may be forgotten for a while, yet will be remembered again when men come to their right minds. 2. That Absalom had now disappointed them. "We were foolishly sick of the cedar, and chose the branch to reign over us; but we have had enough of him: he is consumed, and we narrowly escaped being consumed with him. Let us therefore return to our allegiance, and think of bringing the king back." Perhaps this was all the strife among them, not a dispute whether the king should be brought back or no (all agreed it was to be done), but whose fault it was that it was not done. As is usual in such cases, every one justified himself and blamed his neighbour. The people laid the fault on the elders, and the elders on the people, and one tribe upon another. Mutual excitements to the doing of a good work are laudable, but not mutual accusations for the not doing of it; for usually when public services are neglected all sides must share in the blame; every one might do more than he does, in the reformation of manners, the healing of divisions, and the like.

II. The men of Judah, by David's contrivance, were the first that did it. It is strange that they, being David's own tribe, were not so forward as the rest. David had intelligence of the good disposition of all the rest towards him, but nothing from Judah, though he had always been particularly careful of them. But we do not always find the most kindness from those from whom we have most reason to expect it. Yet David would not return till he knew the sense of his own tribe. *Judah was his lawgiver*, Ps. lx. 7. That his way home might be the more clear, 1. He employed Zadok and Abiathar, the two chief priests, to treat with the elders of Judah, and to excite them to give the king an invitation back to his house, even to his house, which was the glory of their tribe, *v.* 11, 12. No men more proper to negociate this affair than the two priests, who were firm to David's interest, were prudent men, and had great influence with the people. Perhaps the men of Judah were remiss and careless, and did it not, because nobody put them on to do it, and then it was proper to stir them up to it. Many will follow in a good work who will not lead: it is a pity that they should continue idle for want of being spoken to. Or perhaps they were so sensible of the greatness of the provocation they had given to David, by joining with Absalom, that they were afraid to bring him back, despairing of his favour; he therefore warrants his agents to assure them of it, with this reason: "*You are my brethren, my bone and my flesh*, and therefore I cannot be severe with you." The Son of David has been pleased to call us *brethren, his bone and his flesh*, which encourages us to hope that we shall find favour with him. Or perhaps they were willing to see what the rest of the tribes would do before they stirred, with which they are here upbraided: "The speech of all Israel has come to the king to invite him back, and shall Judah be the last, that should have been the first? Where is now the celebrated bravery of that royal tribe? Where is its loyalty?" Note, We should be stirred up to that which is great and good by the examples both of our ancestors and of our neighbours, and by the consideration of our rank. Let not the first in dignity be last in duty. 2. He particularly courted into his interest Amasa, who had been Absalom's general, but was his own nephew as well as Joab, *v.* 13. He owns him for his kinsman, and promises him that, if he will appear for him now, he will make him captain-general of all his forces in the room of Joab, will not only pardon him (which, it may be, Amasa questioned), but prefer him. Sometimes there is nothing lost in purchasing the friendship of one that has been an enemy. Amasa's interest might do David good service at this juncture. But, if David did wisely for himself in designating Amasa for this post (Joab having now grown intolerably haughty), he did not do kindly by Amasa in letting his design be known, for it occasioned his death by Joab's hand, *ch.* xx. 10. 3. The point was hereby gained. He bowed the heart of the men of Judah to pass a vote, *nemine contradicente—unanimously*, for the recal of the king, *v.* 14. God's providence, by the priests' persuasions and Amasa's interest, brought them to this resolve. David stirred not till he received this invitation, and then he came as far back as Jordan, at which river they were to meet him, *v.* 15. Our Lord Jesus will rule in those that invite him to the throne in their hearts and not till he be invited. He first bows the heart and makes it willing in the day of his power, and then *rules in the midst of his enemies*, Ps. cx. 2, 3.

16 And Shimei the son of Gera, a Benjamite, which *was* of Bahurim, hasted and came down with the men of Judah to meet king David. 17 And *there were* a thousand men of Benjamin with him, and Ziba the servant of the house of Saul, and his fifteen sons and his twenty servants with him; and they went over Jordan before the king. 18 And there went over a ferry boat to carry over the king's household, and to do what he thought good. And Shimei the son of Gera fell down before the king, as he was come over Jordan; 19 And said unto the king, Let not my lord impute iniquity unto me, neither do thou remember that which thy servant did perversely the day that my lord the king went out of Jerusalem, that the king should take it to his heart. 20 For thy servant doth know that I have sinned: therefore, behold, I am come the first this day of all the house of Joseph to go down to meet my lord the king. 21 But Abishai the son of Zeruiah answered and said, Shall not Shimei be put to death for this, because he cursed the LORD's anointed? 22 And David said, What have I to do with you, ye sons of Zeruiah, that ye should this day be adversaries unto me? shall there any man be put to death this day in Israel? for do not I know that I *am* this day king over Israel? 23 Therefore the king said unto Shimei, Thou shalt not die. And the king sware unto him.

Perhaps Jordan was never passed with so much solemnity, nor with so many remarkable occurrences, as it was now, since Israel passed it under Joshua. David, in his afflictive flight, remembered God particularly *from the land of Jordan* (Ps. xlii. 6), and now that land, more than any other, was graced with the glories of his return. David's soldiers furnished themselves with accommodations for their passage over this river, but, for his own family, *a ferry-boat* was sent on purpose, *v.* 18. *A fleet of boats,* say some; *a bridge of boats was made,* say others; the best convenience they had to serve him with. Two remarkable persons met him on the banks of Jordan, both of whom had abused him wretchedly when he was in his flight.

I. Ziba, who had abused him with his fair tongue, and, by accusing his master, had obtained from the king a grant of his estate, *ch.* xvi. 4. A greater abuse he could not have done him, than, by imposing upon his credulity, to draw him in to do a thing so unkind to the son of his friend Jonathan. He comes now, with a retinue of sons and servants, to meet the king (*v.* 17), that he may obtain the king's favour, and so come off the better when Mephibosheth shall shortly undeceive him, and clear himself, *v.* 26.

II. Shimei, who had abused him with his foul tongue, railed at him, and cursed him, *ch.* xvi. 5. If David had been defeated, no doubt he would have continued to trample upon him, and have gloried in what he had done; but now that he sees him coming home in triumph, and returning to his throne, he thinks it his interest to make his peace with him. Those who now slight and abuse the Son of David would be glad to make their peace too when he shall come in his glory; but it will be too late. Shimei, to recommend himself to the king, 1. Came with good company, with the men of Judah, as one in their interest. 2. He brought a regiment of the men of Benjamin with him, 1000, of which perhaps he was chiliarch, or commander-in-chief, offering his own and their service to the king; or perhaps they were volunteers, whom by his interest he had got together to meet the king, which was the more obliging because of all the tribes of Israel there were none, except these and Judah, that appeared to pay him this respect. 3. What he did he hastened to do; he lost no time. *Agree with thy adversary quickly, while thou art in the way.* Here is, (1.) The criminal's submission (*v.* 18—20): *He fell down before the king,* as a penitent, as a supplicant; and, that he might be thought sincere, he did it publicly before all David's servants, and his friends the men of Judah, yea, and before his own thousand. The offence was public, therefore the submission ought to be so. He owns his crime: *Thy servant doth know that I have sinned.* He aggravates it: *I did perversely.* He begs the king's pardon: *Let not the king impute iniquity to thy servant,* that is, deal with me as I deserve. He intimates that it was below the king's great and generous mind to *take it to his heart;* and pleads his early return to his allegiance, that he was *the first of all the house of Joseph* (that is, of Israel, who in the beginning of David's reign had distinguished themselves from Judah by their adherence to Ishbosheth, *ch.* ii. 10) that came *to meet the king.* He came first, that by his example of duty the rest might be induced, and by his experience of the king's clemency the rest might be encouraged, to follow. (2.) A motion made for judgment against him (*v.* 21): "*Shall not Shimei be put to death* as a traitor? Let him, of all men, be made an example." This motion was made by Abishai, who would have ventured his life to have been the death of Shimei when he was cursing, *ch.* xvi. 9. David did not think fit to have it done then, because his judicial power was cut short; but, now that it was restored, why should not the law have its course? Abishai herein consulted what he supposed to be David's feelings more than his true interest. Princes have need to arm themselves against temptations to severity. (3.) His discharge by the king's order, *v.* 22, 23. He rejected Abishai's motion with displeasure: *What have I to do with you, you sons of Zeruiah?* The less we have to do with those who are of an angry revengeful spirit, and who put us upon doing what is harsh and rigorous, the better. He looks upon these prosecutors as adversaries to him, though they pretended friendship and zeal for his honour. Those who advise us to what is wrong are really *Satans,* adversaries to us. [1.] They were adversaries to his inclination, which was to clemency. He knew that he was *this day king in Israel,* restored to, and re-established in, his kingdom, and therefore his honour inclined him to forgive. It is the glory of kings to forgive those that humble and surrender themselves: *Satis est prostrâsse leoni—It suffices the lion that he has laid his victim prostrate.* His joy inclined him to forgive. The pleasantness of his spirit on this great occasion forbade the entrance of any thing that was sour and peevish: joyful days should be forgiving days. Yet this was not all; his experience of God's mercy in restoring him to his kingdom, his exclusion from which he attributed to his sin, inclined him to show mercy to Shimei. Those that are forgiven must forgive. David had severely revenged the abuses done to his ambassadors by the Ammonites (*ch.* xii. 31), but easily passes by the abuse done to himself by an Israelite. That was an affront to Israel in general, and touched the honour of his crown and kingdom; this was purely personal, and therefore (according to the usual disposition of good men) he could the more easily forgive it. [2.] They were adversaries to his interest. If he should put to death Shimei, who cursed him, those would expect the same fate who had taken up arms and actually levied war against him, which would drive them from him, while he was endeavouring to draw them to him. Acts of severity are seldom acts of policy. *The throne is established by mercy.* Shimei, hereupon, had his pardon signed and sealed with an oath, yet being bound, no doubt, to his good behaviour, and liable to be prosecuted if he afterwards misbehaved; and thus he was reserved to be, in due time, as much a monument of the justice of the government as he was now of its clemency, and in both of its prudence.

24 And Mephibosheth the son of Saul came down to meet the king, and had neither dressed his feet, nor trimmed his beard, nor washed his clothes, from the day the king departed until the day he came *again* in peace. 25 And it came to pass, when he was come to Jerusalem to meet the king, that the king said unto him, Wherefore wentest not thou with me, Mephibosheth? 26 And he answered, My lord, O king, my servant deceived me: for thy servant said, I will saddle me an ass, that I may ride thereon, and go to the king; because thy servant *is* lame. 27 And he hath slandered thy servant unto my lord the king; but my lord the king *is* as an angel of God: do therefore *what is* good in thine eyes. 28 For all *of* my father's house were but dead men before my lord the king; yet didst thou set thy servant among them that did eat at thine own table. What right therefore have I yet to cry any more unto the king? 29 And the king said unto him, Why speakest thou any more of thy matters? I have said, Thou and Ziba divide the land. 30 And Mephibosheth said unto the king, Yea, let him take all, forasmuch as my lord the king is come again in peace unto his own house.

The day of David's return was a day of bringing to remembrance, a day of account, in which what had passed in his flight was called over again; among other things, after the case of Shimei, that of Mephibosheth comes to be enquired into, and he himself brings it on.

I. He went down in the crowd *to meet the king* (*v.* 24), and, as a proof of the sincerity of his joy in the king's return, we are here told what a true mourner he was for the king's banishment. During that melancholy time, when one of the greatest glories of Israel had departed, Mephibosheth continued in a very melancholy state. He was never trimmed, nor put on clean linen, but wholly neglected himself, as one abandoned to grief for the king's affliction and the kingdom's misery. In times of public calamity we ought to abridge our enjoyments in the delights of sense, in conformity to the season. There are times when God calls to weeping and mourning, and we must comply with the call.

II. When the king came to Jerusalem (since he could not sooner have an opportunity) he made his appearance before him (*v.* 25); and when the king asked him why he, being one of his family, had staid behind, and not accompanied him in his exile, he opened his case fully to the king. 1. He complained of Ziba, his servant, who should have been his friend, but had been in two ways his enemy; for, first, he had hindered him from going along with the king, by taking the ass himself which he was ordered to make ready for his master (*v.* 26), basely taking advantage of his lameness and his inability to help himself; and, secondly, he had accused him to David of a design to usurp the government, *v.* 27. How much mischief is it in the power of a wicked servant to do to the best master! 2. He gratefully acknowledged the king's great kindness to him when he and all his father's house lay at the king's mercy, *v.* 28. When he might justly have been dealt with as a rebel, he was treated as a friend, as a child: *Thou didst set thy servant among those that did eat at thy own table.* This shows that Ziba's suggestion was improbable; for could Mephibosheth be so foolish as to aim higher when he lived so easily, so happily as he did? And could he be so very disingenuous as to design any harm to David, of whose great kindness to him he was thus sensible? (3.) He referred his cause to the king's pleasure (*Do what is good in thy eyes* with me and my estate), depending on the king's wisdom, and his ability to discern between truth and falsehood (*My lord the king is as an angel from God),* and disclaiming all pretensions of his own merit: "So much kindness I have received above what I deserved, and *what right have I to cry any more unto the king?* Why should I trouble the king with my complaints when I have already been so troublesome to him? Why should I think any thing hard that is put upon me when I have hitherto been so kindly treated?" We were all *as dead men before God;* yet he has not only spared us, *but taken us to sit at his table.* How little reason then have we to complain of any trouble we are in, and how much reason to take all well that God does!

III. David hereupon recals the sequestration of Mephibosheth's estate; being deceived in his grant, he revokes it, and confirms his former settlement of it: "*I have said, Thou and Ziba divide the land* (*v.* 29), that is, Let it be as I first ordered it (*ch* ix. 10); the property shall still be vested in thee, but Ziba shall have the occupancy: he shall till the land, paying thee a rent." Thus Mephibosheth is where he was; no harm is done, only Ziba goes away unpunished for his false and malicious information against his master. David either feared him too much, or loved him too well, to do justice upon him according to that law, Deut. xix. 18, 19; and he was now in the humour of forgiving and resolved to make every body easy.

IV. Mephibosheth drowns all his cares about his estate in his joy for the king's return (*v.* 30): "*Yea, let him take all,* the presence and favour of the king shall be to me instead of all. A good man can contentedly bear his own private losses and disappointments, while he sees Israel in peace, and the throne of the Son of David exalted and established. Let Ziba take all, so that David may be in peace.

31 And Barzillai the Gileadite came down from Rogelim, and went over Jordan with the king, to conduct him over Jordan. 32 Now Barzillai was a very aged man, *even* fourscore years old: and he had provided the king of sustenance while he lay at Mahanaim; for he *was* a very great man. 33 And the king said unto Barzillai, Come thou over with me, and I will feed thee with me in Jerusalem. 34 And Barzillai said unto the king, How long have I to live, that I should go up with the king unto Jerusalem? 35 I *am* this day fourscore years old: *and* can I discern between good and evil? can thy servant taste what I eat or what I drink? can I hear any more the voice of singing men and singing women? wherefore then should thy servant be yet a burden unto my lord the king? 36 Thy servant will go a little way over Jordan with the king: and why should the king recompense it me with such a reward? 37 Let thy servant, I pray thee, turn back again, that I may die in mine own city, *and be buried* by the grave of my father and of my mother. But behold thy servant Chimham; let him go over with my lord the king; and do to him what shall seem good unto thee. 38 And the king answered, Chimham shall go over with me, and I will do to him that which shall seem good unto thee: and whatsoever thou shalt require of me, *that* will I do for thee. 39 And all the people went over Jordan. And when the king was come over, the king kissed Barzillai, and blessed him; and he returned unto his own place.

David had already graced the triumphs of his restoration with the generous remission of the injuries that had been done to him; we have him here gracing them with a no less generous reward of the kindnesses that had been shown to him. Barzillai, the Gileadite, who had a noble seat at Rogelim, not far from Mahanaim, was the man who, of all the nobility and gentry of that country, had been most kind to David in his distress. If Absalom had prevailed, it is likely he would have suffered for his loyalty; but now he and his shall be no losers by it. Here is,

I. Barzillai's great respect to David, not only as a good man, but as his rightful sovereign: He *provided him with much sustenance,* for himself and his family, *while he lay at Mahanaim, v.* 32. God had given him a large estate, *for he was a very great man,* and, it seems, he had a large heart to do good with it: what else but that is a large estate good for? To reduced greatness generosity obliges us, and to oppressed goodness piety obliges us, to be in a particular manner kind, to the utmost of our power. Barzillai, to show that he was not weary of David, though he was so great a charge to him, attended him to Jordan, and went over with him, *v.* 31. Let subjects learn hence to render *tribute to whom tribute is due* and *honour to whom honour,* Rom. xiii. 7.

II. The kind invitation David gave him to court (*v.* 33): *Come thou over with me.* He invited him, 1. That he might have the pleasure of his company and the benefit of his counsel; for we may suppose that he was very wise and good, as well as very rich, otherwise he would not have been called here *a very great man;* for it is what a man is, more than what he has, that renders him truly great. 2. That he might have an opportunity of returning his kindness: "*I will feed thee with me;* thou shalt fare as sumptuously as I fare, and this at Jerusalem, the royal and holy city." David did not take Barzillai's kindness to him as a debt (he was not one of those arbitrary princes who think that whatever their subjects have is theirs when they please), but accepted it and rewarded it as a favour. We must always study to be grateful to our friends, especially to those who have helped us in distress.

III. Barzillai's reply to this invitation, wherein,

1. He admires the king's generosity in making him this offer, lessening his service, and magnifying the king's return for it: *Why should the king recompense it with such a reward? v.* 36. Will the master thank that servant who only does what was his duty to do? He thought he had done himself honour enough in doing the king any service. Thus, when the saints shall be called to inherit the kingdom in consideration of what

they have done for Christ in this world, they will be amazed at the disproportion between the service and the recompence. Matt. xxv. 37, *Lord, when saw we thee hungry, and fed thee?*

2. He declines accepting the invitation. He begs his majesty's pardon for refusing so generous an offer: he should think himself very happy in being near the king, but, (1.) He is old, and unfit to remove at all, especially to court. He is old, and unfit for the *business* of the court: "Why *should I go up with the king to Jerusalem?* I can do him no service there, in the council, the camp, the treasury, or the courts of justice; for *how long have I to live? v.* 34. Shall I think of going into business, now that I am going out of the world?" He is old, and unfit for the *diversions* of the court, which will be ill-bestowed, and even thrown away, upon one that can relish them so little, *v.* 35. As it was in Moses's time, so it was in Barzillai's, and it is not worse now, that, *if men be so strong that they come to fourscore years, their strength then is labour and sorrow,* Ps. xc. 10. These were then, and are still, years of which men say they *have no pleasure in them,* Eccl. xii. 1. Dainties are insipid when desire fails; and songs to the aged ear are little better than those sung to a heavy heart, very disagreeable: how should they be otherwise when the daughters of music are brought low? Let those that are old learn of Barzillai to be dead to the delights of sense; let grace second nature, and make a virtue of the necessity. Nay, Barzillai, being old, thinks he shall be *a burden to the king,* rather than any credit to him; and a good man would not go any where to be burdensome, or, if he must be so, will rather be so to his own house than to another's. (2.) He is dying, and must begin to think of his long journey, his removal out of the world, *v.* 37. It is good for us all, but it especially becomes old people, to think and speak much of dying. "Talk of going to court!" says Barzillai; "Let me go home and *die in my own city,* the place of my father's sepulchre; let me die *by the grave of my father,* that my bones may be quietly carried to the place of their rest. The grave is ready for me, let me go and get ready for it, go and die in my nest."

3. He desires the king to be kind to his son Chimham: *Let him go over with my lord the king,* and have preferment at court. What favour is done to him Barzillai will take as done to himself. Those that are old must not grudge young people those delights which they themselves are past the enjoyment of, nor confine them to their retirements. Barzillai will go back himself, but he will not make Chimham go back with him; though he could ill spare Chimham, yet, thinking it would gratify and advance him, he is willing to do it.

IV. David's farewell to Barzillai. 1. He sends him back into his country with a kiss and a blessing (*v.* 39), signifying that in gratitude for his kindnesses he would love him and pray for him, and with a promise that whatever request he should at any time make to him he would be ready to oblige him (*v.* 38): *Whatsoever thou shalt think of,* when thou comest home, to *ask of me,* that *will I do for thee.* What is the chief excellency of power but this, that it gives men a capacity of doing the more good? 2. He takes Chimham forward with him, and leaves it to Barzillai to choose him his preferment. I will *do to him what shall seem good to thee, v.* 38. And, it should seem, Barzillai, who had experienced the innocency and safety of retirement, begged a country seat for him near Jerusalem, but not in it; for, long after, we read of a place near Beth-lehem, David's city, which is called *the habitation of Chimham,* allotted to him, probably, not out of the crown-lands or the forfeited estates, but out of David's paternal estate.

40 Then the king went on to Gilgal, and Chimham went on with him: and all the people of Judah conducted the king, and also half the people of Israel. 41 And, behold, all the men of Israel came to the king, and said unto the king, Why have our brethren the men of Judah stolen thee away, and have brought the king, and his household, and all David's men with him, over Jordan? 42 And all the men of Judah answered the men of Israel, Because the king *is* near of kin to us: wherefore then be ye angry for this matter? have we eaten at all of the king's *cost?* or hath he given us any gift? 43 And the men of Israel answered the men of Judah, and said, We have ten parts in the king, and we have also more *right* in David than ye: why then did ye despise us, that our advice should not be first had in bringing back our king? And the words of the men of Judah were fiercer than the words of the men of Israel.

David came over Jordan attended and assisted only by the men of Judah; but when he had advanced as far as Gilgal, the first stage on this side Jordan, *half the people of Israel* (that is, of their elders and great men) had come to wait upon him, to kiss his hand, and congratulate him on his return, but found they came too late to witness the solemnity of his first entrance. This put them out of humour, and occasioned a quarrel between them and the men of Judah, which was a damp to the joy of the day, and the beginning of further mischief. Here is,

1. The complaint which the men of Israel brought to the king against the men of Judah (*v.* 41), that they had performed the ceremony of bringing the king over Jordan, and not given them notice, that they might have come to join in it. This reflected upon them, as if they were not so well affected to the king and his restoration as the men of Judah were, whereas the king himself knew that they had spoken of it before the men of Judah thought of it, *v.* 11. It seemed likewise as if they intended to monopolize the king's favours when he had come back, and to be looked upon as his only friends. See what mischief comes from pride and jealousy. 2. The excuse which the men of Judah made for themselves, *v.* 42. (1.) They plead relation to the king: "*He is near of kin to us,* and therefore in a matter of mere ceremony, as this was, we may claim precedency. It was into our country that he was to be brought, and therefore who so fit as we to bring him?" (2.) They deny the insinuated charge of self-seeking in what they had done: "*Have we eaten at all of the king's cost?* No, we have all borne our own charges. *Hath he given us any gift?* No, we have no design to engross the advantages of his return; you have come time enough to share in them." Too many that attend princes do so only for what they can get. 3. The men of Israel's vindication of their charge, *v.* 43. They pleaded, "*We have ten parts in the king*" (Judah having Simeon only, whose lot lay within his, to join with him), "and therefore it is a slight upon us that our advice was not asked about *bringing back the king.*" See how uncertain the multitude is. They were lately striving against the king, to drive him out; now they are striving about him, which shall honour him most. A good man and a good cause will thus recover their credit and interest, though, for a time, they may seem to have lost them. See what is commonly the origin of strife, nothing so much as impatience of contempt or the least seeming slight. The men of Judah would have done better if they had taken their brethren's advice and assistance; but, since they did not, why should the men of Israel be so grievously offended? If a good work be done, and well done, let us not be displeased, nor the work disparaged, though we had no hand in it. 4. The scripture takes notice, by way of blame, which of the contending parties managed the cause with most passion: *The words of the men of Judah were fiercer than* those *of the men of Israel.* Though we have right and reason on our side, yet, if we express ourselves with fierceness, God takes notice of it and is much displeased with it.

CHAP. XX.

How do the clouds return after the rain! No sooner is one of David's troubles over than another arises, as it were out of the ashes of the former, wherein the threatening is fulfilled, that the sword should never depart from his house. I. Before he reaches Jerusalem a new rebellion is raised by Sheba, ver. 1, 2. II. His first work, when he comes to Jerusalem, is to condemn his concubines to perpetual imprisonment, ver. 3. III. Amasa, whom he entrusts to raise an army against Sheba, is too slow in his motions, which puts him into a fright, ver. 4—6. IV. One of his generals barbarously murders the other, when they are taking the field, ver. 7—13. V. Sheba is at length shut up in the city of Abel (ver. 14, 15), but the citizens deliver him up to Joab, and so his rebellion is crushed, ver. 16—22. The chapter concludes with a short account of David's great officers, ver. 23—26.

AND there happened to be there a man of Belial, whose name *was* Sheba, the son of Bichri, a Benjamite: and he blew a trumpet, and said, We have no part in David, neither have we inheritance in the son of Jesse: every man to his tents, O Israel. 2 So every man of Israel went up from after David, *and* followed Sheba the son of Bichri: but the men of Judah clave unto their king, from Jordan even to Jerusalem. 3 And David came to his house at Jerusalem; and the king took the ten women *his* concubines, whom he had left to keep the house, and put them in ward, and fed them, but went not in unto them. So they were shut up unto the day of their death, living in widowhood.

David, in the midst of his triumphs, has here the affliction to see his kingdom disturbed and his family disgraced.

I. His subjects revolting from him at the instigation of *a man of Belial,* whom they followed when they forsook the *man after God's own heart.* Observe, 1. That this happened immediately upon the crushing of Absalom's rebellion. We must not think it strange, while we are in this world, if the end of one trouble be the beginning of another: deep sometimes calls unto deep. 2. That the people were now just returning to their allegiance, when, of a sudden, they flew off from it. When a reconciliation is newly made, it ought to be handled with great tenderness and caution, lest the peace break again before it be settled. A broken bone, when it is set, must have time to knit. 3. That the ring-leader of this rebellion was Sheba, a Benjamite by birth (*v.* 1), who had his habitation in Mount Ephraim, *v.* 21. Shimei and he were both of Saul's tribe, and both retained the ancient grudge of that house. Against the kingdom of the Messiah there is an hereditary enmity in the serpent's seed, and a succession of attempts to overthrow it (Ps. ii. 1, 2); but he that sits in heaven laughs at them all. 4. That the occasion of it was that foolish quarrel, which we read of in the close of the foregoing chapter, between the elders of Israel and the elders of Judah, about bringing the king back. It was a point of honour that was disputed between them, which had most interest in David. "We are more numerous," say the elders of Israel. "We are nearer akin to him," say the elders of Judah. Now one would think David very safe and happy when his subjects are striving which shall love him best, and be most forward to show him respect; yet even that strife proves the occasion of a rebellion. The men of Israel complained to David of the slight which the men of Judah had put upon them. If he had now countenanced their complaint, commended their zeal, and returned them thanks for it, he might have confirmed them in his interest; but he seemed partial to his own tribe: *Their words prevailed above the words of the men of Israel;* as some read the last words of the foregoing chapter. David inclined to justify them, and, when the men of Israel perceived this, they flew off with indignation. "If the king will suffer himself to be engrossed by the men of Judah, let him and them make their best of one another, and we will set up one for ourselves. We thought we had ten parts in David, but such an interest will not be allowed us; the men of Judah tell us, in effect, *we have no part in him,* and therefore we will have none, nor will we attend him any further in his return to Jerusalem, nor own him for our king." This was proclaimed by Sheba (*v.* 1), who probably was a man of note, and had been active in Absalom's rebellion; the disgusted Israelites took the hint, and *went up from after David to follow Sheba* (*v.* 2), that is, the generality of them did so, only the men of Judah adhered to him. Learn hence, (1.) That it is as impolitic for princes to be partial in their attentions to their subjects as it is for parents to be so to their children; both should carry it with an even hand. (2.) Those know not what they do that make light of the affections of their inferiors, by not countenancing and accepting it. Their hatred may be feared whose love is despised. (3.) *The beginning of strife is as the letting forth of water;* it is *therefore* wisdom to *leave it off before it be meddled with,* Prov. xvii. 14. How great a matter doth a little of this fire kindle! (4.) The perverting of words is the subverting of peace; and much mischief is made by forcing invidious constructions upon what is said and written and drawing consequences that were never intended. The men of Judah said, *The king is near of kin to us.* "By this," say the men of Israel, "you mean that *we have no part in him;*" whereas they meant no such thing. (5.) People are very apt to run into extremes. *We have ten parts in David,* said they; and, almost in the next breath, *We have no part in him.* To-day *Hosanna,* to-morrow *Crucify.*

II. His concubines imprisoned for life, and he himself under a necessity of putting them in confinement, because they had been defiled by Absalom, *v.* 3. David had multiplied wives, contrary to the law, and they proved a grief and shame to him. Those whom he had sinfully taken pleasure in he was now, 1. Obliged, in duty, to put away, they being rendered unclean to him by the vile uncleanness his son had committed with them. Those whom he had loved must now be loathed. 2. Obliged, in prudence, to shut up in privacy, not to be seen abroad for shame, lest the sight of them should give occasion to people to speak of what Absalom had done to them, which ought not to be so much as named, 1 Cor. v. 1. That that villany might be buried in oblivion, they must be buried in obscurity. 3. Obliged, in justice, to shut up in prison, to punish them for their easy submission to Absalom's lust, despairing perhaps of David's return, and giving him up for gone. Let none expect to do ill and fare well.

4 Then said the king to Amasa, Assemble me the men of Judah within three days, and be thou here present. 5 So Amasa went to assemble *the men of* Judah: but he tarried longer than the set time which he had appointed him. 6 And David said to Abishai, Now shall Sheba the son of Bichri do us more harm than *did* Absalom: take thou thy lord's servants, and pursue after him, lest he get him fenced cities, and escape us. 7 And there went out after him Joab's men, and the Cherethites, and the Pelethites, and all the mighty men: and they went out of Jerusalem, to pursue after Sheba the son of Bichri. 8 When they *were* at the great stone which *is* in Gibeon, Amasa went before them. And Joab's garment that he had put on was girded unto him, and upon it a girdle *with* a sword fastened upon his loins in the sheath thereof; and as he went forth it fell out. 9 And Joab said to Amasa, *Art* thou in health, my brother? And Joab took Amasa by the beard with the right hand to kiss him. 10 But Amasa took no heed to the sword that *was* in Joab's hand: so he smote him therewith in the fifth *rib,* and shed out his bowels to the ground, and struck him not again; and he died. So Joab and Abishai his brother pursued after Sheba the son of Bichri. 11 And one of Joab's men stood by him, and said, He that favoureth Joab, and he that *is* for David, *let him go* after Joab. 12 And Amasa wallowed in blood in the midst of the highway. And when the man saw that all the people stood

still, he removed Amasa out of the highway into the field, and cast a cloth upon him, when he saw that every one that came by him stood still. 13 When he was removed out of the highway, all the people went on after Joab, to pursue after Sheba the son of Bichri.

We have here Amasa's fall just as he began to rise. He was nephew to David (*ch.* xvii. 25), had been Absalom's general, and commander-in-chief of his rebellious army; but, that being routed, he came over into David's interest, upon a promise that he should be general of his forces instead of Joab. Sheba's rebellion gives David an occasion to fulfil his promise sooner than he could wish, but Joab's envy and emulation rendered its fulfilment of ill consequence both to him and David.

I. Amasa has a commission to raise forces for the suppressing of Sheba's rebellion, and is ordered to raise them with all possible expedition, *v.* 4. It seems, the men of Judah, though forward to attend the king's triumphs, were backward enough to fight his battles; else, when they were all in a body attending him to Jerusalem, they might immediately have pursued Sheba, and have crushed that cockatrice in the egg. But most love a loyalty, as well as a religion, that is cheap and easy. Many boast of their being akin to Christ that yet are very loth to venture for him. Amasa is sent to assemble the men of Judah within three days; but he finds them so backward and unready that he cannot do it within the time appointed (*v.* 5), though the promotion of Amasa, who had been their general under Absalom, was very obliging to them, and a proof of the clemency of David's government.

II. Upon Amasa's delay, Abishai, the brother of Joab, is ordered to take the guards and standing forces, and with them to pursue Sheba (*v.* 6, 7), for nothing could be of more dangerous consequence than to give him time. David gives these orders to Abishai, because he resolves to mortify Joab, and degrade him, not so much, I doubt, for the blood of Abner, which he had shed basely, as for the blood of Absalom, which he had shed justly and honourably. "Now (says bishop Hall) Joab smarteth for a loyal disobedience. How slippery are the stations of earthly honours and subject to continual mutability! Happy are those who are in favour with him in whom there is no shadow of change." Joab, without orders, though in disgrace, goes along with his brother, knowing he might be serviceable to the public, or perhaps now meditating the removal of his rival.

III. Joab, near Gibeon, meets with Amasa, and barbarously murders him, *v.* 8—10. It should seem, the great stone in Gibeon was the place appointed for the general rendezvous. There the rivals met; and Amasa, relying upon his commission, went before, as general both of the new-raised forces which he had got together, and of the veteran troops which Abishai had brought in; but Joab there took an opportunity to kill him with his own hand; and, 1. He did it subtilely, and with contrivance, and not upon a sudden provocation. He girded his coat about him, that it might not hang in his way, and girded his belt upon his coat, that his sword might be the readier to his hand; he also put his sword in a sheath too big for it, that, whenever he pleased, it might, upon a little shake, fall out, as if it fell by accident, and so he might take it into his hand, unsuspected, as if he were going to return it into the scabbard, when he designed to sheath it in the bowels of Amasa. The more there is of plot in a sin the worse it is. 2. He did it treacherously, and under pretence of friendship, that Amasa might not be upon his guard. He called him *brother,* for they were own cousins, enquired of his welfare *(Art thou in health?)* and *took him by the beard,* as one he was free with, to kiss him, while with the drawn sword in his other hand he was aiming at his heart. Was this done like a gentleman, like a soldier, like a general? No, but like a villain, like a base coward. Just thus he slew Abner, and went unpunished for it, which encouraged him to do the like again. 3. He did it impudently, not in a corner, but at the head of his troops, and in their sight, as one that was neither ashamed nor afraid to do it, that was so hardened in blood and murders that he could neither blush nor tremble. 4. He did it at one blow, gave the fatal push with a good-will, as we say, so that he needed not strike him again; with such a strong and steady hand he gave this one stroke that it was fatal. 5. He did it in contempt and defiance of David and the commission he had given to Amasa; for that commission was the only ground of his quarrel with him, so that David was struck at through the side of Amasa, and was, in effect, told to his face that Joab would be general, in spite of him. 6. He did it very unseasonably, when they were going against a common enemy and were concerned to be unanimous. This ill-timed quarrel might have scattered their forces, or engaged them one against another, and so have made them all an easy prey to Sheba. So contentedly could Joab sacrifice the interest both of king and kingdom to his personal revenge.

IV. Joab immediately resumes his general's place, and takes care to lead the army on in pursuit of Sheba, that, if possible, he might prevent any prejudice to the common cause by what he had done. 1. He leaves one of his men to make proclamation to the forces that were coming up that they were still engaged in David's cause, but under Joab's command, *v.* 11. He knew what an interest he had in the soldiery, and how many favoured him rather than Amasa, who had been a traitor, was now a turn-coat, and had never been successful; on this he boldly relied, and called them all to follow him. What man of Judah would not be for his old king and his old general? But one would wonder with what face a murderer could pursue a traitor; and how, under such a heavy load of guilt, he had courage to enter upon danger. Surely his conscience was seared with a hot iron. 2. care is taken to remove the dead body out of the way, because at that they made a stand (as *ch.* ii. 23), and to cover it with a cloth, *v.* 12, 13. Wicked men think themselves safe in their wickedness if they can but conceal it from the eye of the world: if it be hidden, it is with them as if it were never done. But the covering of blood with a cloth cannot stop its cry in God's ear for vengeance, or make it the less loud. However, since this was no time to arraign Joab for what he had done, and the common safety called for expedition, it was prudent to remove that which retarded the march of the army; and then they all went on after Joab, while David, who no doubt had notice soon brought him of this tragedy, could not but reflect upon it with regret that he had not formerly done justice upon Joab for the death of Abner, and that he now had exposed Amasa by preferring him. And perhaps his conscience reminded him of his employing Joab in the murder of Uriah, which had helped to harden him in cruelty.

14 And he went through all the tribes of Israel unto Abel, and to Beth-maachah, and all the Berites: and they were gathered together, and went also after him. 15 And they came and besieged him in Abel of Beth-maachah, and they cast up a bank against the city, and it stood in the trench: and all the people that *were* with Joab battered the wall, to throw it down. 16 Then cried a wise woman out of the city, Hear, hear; say, I pray you, unto Joab, Come near hither, that I may speak with thee. 17 And when he was come near unto her, the woman said, *Art* thou Joab? And he answered, I *am he*. Then she said unto him, Hear the words of thine handmaid. And he answered, I do hear. 18 Then she spake, saying, They were wont to speak in old time, saying, They shall surely ask *counsel* at Abel: and so they ended *the matter*. 19 I *am one of them that are* peaceable *and* faithful in Israel: thou seekest to destroy a city and a mother in Israel: why wilt thou swallow up the inheritance of the LORD? 20 And Joab answered and said, Far be it, far be it from me, that I should swallow up or destroy. 21 The matter *is* not so: but a man of mount Ephraim, Sheba the son of Bichri by name, hath lifted up his hand against the king, *even* against David: deliver him only, and I will depart from the city. And the woman said unto Joab, Behold, his head shall be thrown to thee over the wall. 22 Then the woman went unto all the people in her wisdom. And they cut off the head of Sheba the son of Bichri, and cast *it* out to Joab. And he blew a trumpet, and they retired from the city, every man to his tent. And Joab returned to Jerusalem unto the king.

We have here the conclusion of Sheba's attempt.

I. The rebel, when he had rambled over all the tribes of Israel, and found them not so willing, upon second thoughts, to follow him, as they had been upon a sudden provocation to desert David (having only picked up a few like himself, that sided with him), at length entered Abel-Beth-maacah, a strong city in the north, in the lot of Naphtali, where we find it placed, 2 Kings xv. 29. Here he took shelter, whether by force or with consent does not appear; but his adherents were mostly Berites, of Beeroth in Benjamin, *v.* 14. One bad man will find or make more.

II. Joab drew up all his force against the city, besieged it, battered the wall, and made it almost ready for a general storm, *v.* 15. Justly is that place attacked with all this fury which dares harbour a traitor; nor will that heart fare better which indulges those rebellious lusts that will not have Christ to reign over them.

III. A discreet good woman of the city of Abel brings this matter, by her prudent management, to a good issue, so as to satisfy Joab and yet save the city. Here is,

1. Her treaty with Joab, and her capitulation with him, by which he is engaged to raise the siege, upon condition that Sheba be delivered up. It seems, none of all the men of Abel, none of the elders or magistrates, offered to treat with Joab, no, not when they were reduced to the last extremity. They were stupid and unconcerned for the public safety, or they stood in awe of Sheba, or they despaired of gaining any good terms with Joab, or they had not sense enough to manage the treaty. But this one woman with her wisdom saved the city. Souls know

no difference of sexes. Though the man be the head, it does not therefore follow that he has the monopoly of the brains, and therefore he ought not, by any salique law, to have the monopoly of the crown. Many a masculine heart, and more than masculine, has been found in a female breast; nor is the treasure of wisdom the less valuable for being lodged in the weaker vessel. In the treaty between this nameless heroine and Joab,

(1.) She gains his audience and attention, *v.* 16, 17. We may suppose it was the first time he had ever treated with a woman in martial affairs.

(2.) She reasons with him on behalf of her city, and very ingeniously. [1.] That it was a city famous for wisdom (*v.* 18), as we translate it. She pleads that this city had been long in such reputation for prudent knowing men that it was the common referee of the country, and all agreed to abide by the award of its elders. Their sentence was an oracle; let them be consulted and the matter is ended, all sides will acquiesce. Now shall such a city as this be laid in ashes and never treated with? [2.] That the inhabitants were generally peaceable and faithful in Israel, *v.* 19. She could speak, not for herself only, but for all those whose cause she pleaded, that they were not of turbulent and seditious spirits, but of known fidelity to their prince and peaceableness with their fellow-subjects; they were neither seditious nor litigious. [3.] That it was a mother in Israel, a guide and nurse to the towns and country about; and that it was a part of *the inheritance of the Lord*, a city of Israelites, not of heathen; and the destruction of it would lessen and weaken that nation which God had chosen for his heritage. [4.] That they expected him to offer them peace before he made an attack upon them, according to that known law of war, Deut. xx. 10. So the margin reads (*v.* 18): *They plainly spoke in the beginning* (of the siege), *saying, Surely they will ask of Abel,* that is, "The besiegers will demand the traitor, and will ask us to surrender him; and, if they do, we will soon come to an agreement, and so end the matter." Thus she tacitly upbraids Joab for not offering them peace, but hopes it is not too late to beg it.

(3.) Joab and Abel's advocate soon agree that Sheba's head shall be the ransom of the city. Joab, though in a personal quarrel he had lately swallowed up and destroyed Amasa, yet, when he acts as a general, will by no means bear the imputation of delighting in bloodshed: "*Far be it from me that I should* delight to *swallow up or destroy*, or design it, but when it is necessary for the public safety, *v.* 20. The matter is not so. Our quarrel is not with your city; we would hazard our lives for its protection. Our quarrel is only with the traitor that is harboured among you; deliver him up, and we have done." A great deal of mischief would be prevented if contending parties would but understand one another. The city obstinately holds out, believing Joab aims at its ruin. Joab furiously attacks it, believing the citizens all confederates with Sheba. Whereas both were mistaken; let both sides be undeceived, and the matter is soon accommodated. The single condition of peace is the surrender of the traitor. It is so in God's dealing with the soul, when it is besieged by conviction and distress: sin is the traitor; the beloved lust is the rebel; part with that, cast away the transgression, and all shall be well. No peace on any other terms. Our wise woman immediately agrees to the proposal: *Behold, his head shall be thrown to thee presently.*

2. Her treaty with the citizens. She went to them in her wisdom (and perhaps she had as much need of it in dealing with them as in dealing with Joab) and persuaded them to cut off Sheba's head, probably by some public order of their government, and it was thrown over the wall to Joab. He knew the traitor's face, and therefore looked no further, intending not that any of his adherents should suffer. The public safety was secured, and he felt no wish to gratify the public revenge. Joab hereupon raised the siege, and marched back to Jerusalem, with the trophies rather of peace than victory.

23 Now Joab *was* over all the host of Israel: and Benaiah the son of Jehoiada *was* over the Cherethites and over the Pelethites: 24 And Adoram *was* over the tribute: and Jehoshaphat the son of Ahilud *was* recorder: 25 And Sheva *was* scribe: and Zadok and Abiathar *were* the priests: 26 And Ira also the Jairite was a chief ruler about David.

Here is an account of the state of David's court after his restoration. Joab retained the office of general, being too great to be displaced. Benaiah, as before, was captain of the guards. Here is one new office erected, which we had not (*ch.* viii. 16—18), that of *treasurer*, or one *over the tribute*, for it was not till towards the latter end of his time that David began to raise taxes. Adoram was long in this office, but it cost him his life at last, 1 Kings xii. 18.

CHAP. XXI.

The date of the events of this chapter is uncertain. I incline to think that they happened as they are here placed, after Absalom's and Sheba's rebellion, and towards the latter end of David's reign. That the battles with the Philistines, mentioned here, were long after the Philistines were subdued, appears by comparing 1 Chron. xviii. 1 with ch. xx. 4. The numbering of the people was just before the fixing of the place of the temple (as appears 1 Chron. xxii. 1), and that was towards the close of David's life; and, it should seem, the people were numbered just after the three years' famine for the Gibeonites, for that which is threatened as "three" years' famine (1 Chron. xxi. 12) is called "seven" years (2 Sam. xxiv. 12, 13), three more, with the year current, added to those three. We have here, I. The Gibeonites avenged, 1. By a famine in the land, ver. 1. 2. By the putting of seven of Saul's posterity to death (ver. 2—9), care, however, being taken of their dead bodies, and of the bones of Saul, ver. 10—14. II. The giants of the Philistines slain in several battles, ver. 15—22.

THEN there was a famine in the days of David three years, year after year; and David enquired of the LORD. And the LORD answered, *It is* for Saul, and for *his* bloody house, because he slew the Gibeonites. 2 And the king called the Gibeonites, and said unto them; (now the Gibeonites *were* not of the children of Israel, but of the remnant of the Amorites; and the children of Israel had sworn unto them: and Saul sought to slay them in his zeal to the children of Israel and Judah.) 3 Wherefore David said unto the Gibeonites, What shall I do for you? and wherewith shall I make the atonement, that ye may bless the inheritance of the LORD? 4 And the Gibeonites said unto him, We will have no silver nor gold of Saul, nor of his house; neither for us shalt thou kill any man in Israel. And he said, What ye shall say, *that* will I do for you. 5 And they answered the king, The man that consumed us, and that devised against us *that* we should be destroyed from remaining in any of the coasts of Israel, 6 Let seven men of his sons be delivered unto us, and we will hang them up unto the LORD in Gibeah of Saul, *whom* the LORD did choose. And the king said, I will give *them*. 7 But the king spared Mephibosheth, the son of Jonathan the son of Saul, because of the LORD's oath that *was* between them, between David and Jonathan the son of Saul. 8 But the king took the two sons of Rizpah the daughter of Aiah, whom she bare unto Saul, Armoni and Mephibosheth; and the five sons of Michal the daughter of Saul, whom she brought up for Adriel the son of Barzillai the Meholathite: 9 And he delivered them into the hands of the Gibeonites, and they hanged them in the hill before the LORD: and they fell *all* seven together, and were put to death in the days of harvest, in the first *days*, in the beginning of barley harvest.

Here, I. We are told of the injury which Saul had, long before this, done to the Gibeonites, which we had no account of in the history of his reign, nor should we have heard of it here but that it came now to be reckoned for. The Gibeonites were of the remnant of the Amorites (*v.* 2), who by a stratagem had made peace with Israel, and had the public faith pledged to them by Joshua for their safety. We had the story Josh. ix., where it was agreed (*v.* 23) that they should have their lives secured, but be deprived of their lands and liberties, that they and theirs should be tenants in villanage to Israel. It does not appear that they had broken their part of the covenant, either by denying their service or attempting to recover their lands or liberties; nor was this pretended; but Saul, under colour of zeal for the honour of Israel, that it might not be said that they had any of the natives among them, aimed to root them out, and, in order to that, slew many of them. Thus he would seem wiser than his predecessors the judges, and more zealous for the public interest; and perhaps he designed it for an instance of his royal prerogative and the power which as king he assumed to rescind the former acts of government and to disannul the most solemn leagues. It may be, he designed, by this severity towards the Gibeonites, to atone for his clemency towards the Amalekites. Some conjecture that he sought to cut off the Gibeonites at the same time when he put away the witches (1 Sam. xxviii. 3), or perhaps many of them were remarkably pious, and he sought to destroy them when he slew the priests their masters. That which made this an exceedingly sinful sin was that he not only shed innocent blood, but therein violated the solemn oath by which the nation was bound to protect them. See what brought ruin on Saul's house: it was a bloody house.

II. We find the nation of Israel chastised with a sore famine, long after, for this sin of Saul. Observe, 1. Even in the land of Israel, that fruitful land, and in the reign of David, that glorious reign, there was a famine, not extreme (for then notice would sooner have been taken of it and enquiry made into the cause of it), but great drought, and scarcity of provisions, the consequence of it, for three years together. If corn miss one year, commonly the next makes up the deficiency; but, if it miss three years successively, it will be a sore judgment; and the man of wisdom will by it hear God's voice crying to the country to repent of the abuse of plenty. 2. David enquired of God concerning it. Though he was himself a prophet, he must consult the oracle, and know God's mind in his own appointed way. Note, When we are under God's judgments we ought to enquire into the grounds of the controversy. *Lord, show me wherefore thou contendest with me.* It is strange that David did not sooner consult the oracle, not till the third year; but perhaps, till then, he apprehended it not to be an extraordinary judgment for some particular sin. Even good men are often slack and remiss in doing their duty. We continue in ignorance, and under mistake, because we delay to enquire. 3. God was ready in his answer, though David was slow in his enquiries: *It is for Saul.* Note, God's judgments often look a great way back, which obliges us to do so when we are under his rebukes. It is not for us to object against the people's smarting for the sin of their king (perhaps they were aiding and abetting), nor against this generation's suffering for the sin of the last. God often *visiteth the sins of the fathers upon the children, and his judgments are a great deep.* He gives not account of any of his matters. Time does not wear out the guilt of sin; nor can we build hopes of impunity upon the delay of judgments. There is no statute of limitation to be pleaded against God's demands. *Nullum tempus occurrit Deo—God may punish when he pleases.*

III. We have vengeance taken upon the house of Saul for the turning away of God's wrath from the land, which, at present, smarted for his sin.

1. David, probably by divine direction, referred it to the Gibeonites themselves to prescribe what satisfaction should be given them for the wrong that had been done them, *v.* 3. They had many years remained silent, had not appealed to David, nor given the kingdom any disturbance with their complaints or demands; and now, at length, God speaks for them (*I heard not, for thou wilt hear,* Ps. xxxviii. 14, 15); and they are recompensed for their patience with this honour, that they are made judges in their own case, and have a blank given them to write their demands on: *What you shall say, that will I do* (*v.* 4), that atonement may be made, and that *you may bless the inheritance of the Lord, v.* 3. It is sad for any family or nation to have the prayers of oppressed innocency against them, and therefore the expense of a just restitution is well bestowed for the retrieving of *the blessing of those that were ready to perish,* Job xxix. 13. "My servant Job, whom you have wronged, shall pray for you," says God, "and then I will be reconciled to you, and not till then." Those understand not themselves that value not the prayers of the poor and despised.

2. They desired that seven of Saul's posterity might be put to death, and David granted their demand. (1.) They required no *silver, nor gold, v.* 4. Note, Money is no satisfaction for blood, see Num. xxxv. 31—33. It is the ancient law that blood calls for blood (Gen. ix. 6); and those over-value money, and under-value life, that sell the blood of their relations for corruptible things, *such as silver and gold.* The Gibeonites had now a fair opportunity to get a discharge from their servitude, in compensation for the wrong done them, according to the equity of that law (Exod. xxi. 26), *If a man strike out his servant's eye, he shall let him go free for his eye's sake.* But they did not insist on this; though the covenant was broken on the other side, it should not be broken on theirs. They were *Nethinim,* given to God and his people Israel, and they would not seem weary of the service. (2.) They required no lives but of Saul's family. He had done them the wrong, and therefore his children must pay for it. We sue the heirs for the parents' debts. Men may not extend this principle so far as life, Deut. xxiv. 16. *The children,* in an ordinary course of law, *shall never be put to death for the parents.* But this case of the Gibeonites was altogether extraordinary. God had made himself an immediate party to the cause, and no doubt put it into the heart of the Gibeonites to make this demand, for he owned what was done (*v.* 14), and his judgments are not subject to the rules which men's judgments must be subject to. Let parents take heed of sin, especially the sin of cruelty and oppression, for their poor children's sake, who may be smarting for it by the just hand of God when they themselves are in their graves. Guilt and a curse are a bad entail upon a family. It should seem, Saul's posterity trod in his steps, for it is called *a bloody house;* it was the spirit of the family, and therefore they are justly reckoned with for his sin, as well as for their own. (3.) They would not impose it upon David to do this execution: *Thou shalt not for us kill any man* (*v.* 4), but we will do it ourselves, *we will hang them up unto the Lord* (*v.* 6), that, if there were any hardship in it, they might bear the blame, and not David or his house. By our old law, if a murderer had judgment given against him upon an appeal, the relations that appealed had the executing of him. (4.) They did not require this out of malice against Saul or his family (had they been revengeful, they would have moved it themselves long before), but out of love to the people of Israel, whom they saw plagued for the injury done to them: "*We will hang them up unto the Lord* (*v.* 6), to satisfy his justice, not to gratify any revenge of our own—for the good of the public, not for our own reputation." (5.) The nomination of the persons they left to David, who took care to secure Mephibosheth for Jonathan's sake, that, while he was avenging the breach of one oath, he might not himself break another (*v.* 7); but he delivered up two of Saul's sons whom he had by a concubine, and five of his grandsons, whom his daughter Merab bore to Adriel (1 Sam. xviii. 19), but his daughter Michal brought up, *v.* 8. Now Saul's treachery was punished, in giving Merab to Adriel, when he had promised her to David, with a design to provoke him. "It is a dangerous matter," says bishop Hall upon this, "to offer injury to any of God's faithful ones; if their meekness have easily remitted it, their God will not pass it over without a severe retribution, though it may be long first. (6.) The place, time, and manner, of their

execution, all added to the solemnity of their being sacrificed to divine justice. [1.] They were hanged up, as anathemas, under a peculiar mark of God's displeasure; for the law had said, *He that is hanged is accursed of God*, Deut. xxi. 23; Gal. iii. 13. Christ being made a curse for us, and dying to satisfy for our sins and to turn away the wrath of God, became obedient to this ignominious death. [2.] They were hanged up in Gibeah of Saul (*v.* 6), to show that it was for his sin that they died. They were hanged, as it were, before their own door, to expiate the guilt of the house of Saul; and thus God accomplished the ruin of that family, for the blood of the priests, and their families, which, doubtless, now came in remembrance before God, and inquisition was made for it, Ps. ix. 12. Yet the blood of the *Gibeonites* only is mentioned, because that was shed in violation of a sacred oath, which, though sworn long before, though obtained by a wile, and the promise made to Canaanites, yet is thus severely reckoned for. The despising of the oath, and breaking of the covenant, will be recompensed on the head of those who thus profane God's sacred name, Ezek. xvii. 18, 19. And thus God would show that with him rich and poor meet together. Even royal blood must go to atone for the blood of Gibeonites, who were but the vassals of the congregation. [3.] They were put to death *in the days of harvest* (*v.* 9), *at the beginning of harvest* (*v.* 10), to show that they were thus sacrificed for the turning away of that wrath of God which had withheld from them their harvest-mercies for some years past, and to obtain his favour in the present harvest. Thus there is no way of appeasing God's anger but by mortifying and crucifying our lusts and corruptions. In vain do we expect mercy from God, unless we do justice upon our sins. Those executions must not be complained of as cruel which have become necessary to the public welfare. Better that seven of Saul's bloody house be hanged than that all Israel be famished.

10 And Rizpah the daughter of Aiah took sackcloth, and spread it for her upon the rock, from the beginning of harvest until water dropped upon them out of heaven, and suffered neither the birds of the air to rest on them by day, nor the beasts of the field by night. 11 And it was told David what Rizpah the daughter of Aiah, the concubine of Saul, had done. 12 And David went and took the bones of Saul and the bones of Jonathan his son from the men of Jabesh-gilead, which had stolen them from the street of Beth-shan, where the Philistines had hanged them, when the Philistines had slain Saul in Gilboa: 13 And he brought up from thence the bones of Saul and the bones of Jonathan his son; and they gathered the bones of them that were hanged. 14 And the bones of Saul and Jonathan his son buried they in the country of Benjamin in Zelah, in the sepulchre of Kish his father: and they performed all that the king commanded. And after that God was intreated for the land.

Here we have, I. Saul's sons not only hanged, but hanged in chains, their dead bodies left hanging, and exposed, till the judgment ceased, which their death was to turn away, by the sending of rain upon the land. They died as sacrifices, and thus they were, in a manner, offered up, not consumed all at once by fire, but gradually by the air. They died as anathemas, and by this ignominious usage they were represented as execrable, because iniquity was laid upon them. When our blessed Saviour was made sin for us he was made a curse for us. But how shall we reconcile this with the law which expressly required that those who were hanged should be buried on the same day? Deut. xxi. 23. One of the Jewish rabbin wishes this passage of story expunged, *that the name of God might be sanctified*, which, he thinks, is dishonoured by his acceptance of that which was a violation of his law: but this was an extraordinary case, and did not fall within that law; nay, the very reason for that law is a reason for this exception. He that is thus left hanged is accursed; therefore ordinary malefactors must not be so abused; but therefore these must, because they were sacrificed, not to the justice of the nation, but for the crime of the nation (no less a crime than the violation of the public faith) and for the deliverance of the nation from no less a judgment than a general famine. Being thus made as the *off-scouring of all things*, they were made a *spectacle to the world* (1 Cor. iv. 9, 13), God appointing, or at least allowing it.

II. Their dead bodies watched by Rizpah, the mother of two of them, *v.* 10. It was a great affliction to her, now in her old age, to see her two sons, who, we may suppose, had been a comfort to her, and were likely to be the support of her declining years, cut off in this dreadful manner. None know what sorrows they are reserved for. She may not see them decently interred, but they shall be decently attended. She attempts not to violate the sentence passed upon them, that they should hang there till God sent rain; she neither steals nor forces away their dead bodies, though the divine law might have been cited to bear her out; but she patiently submits, pitches a tent of sackcloth near the gibbets, where, with her servants and friends, she protects the dead bodies from birds and beasts of prey. Thus, 1. She indulged her grief, as mourners are too apt to do, to no good purpose. When sorrow, in such cases, is in danger of growing excessive, we should rather study how to divert and pacify it than how to humour and gratify it. Why should we thus harden ourselves in sorrow? 2. She testified her love. Thus she let the world know that her sons died, not for any sin of their own, not as stubborn and rebellious sons, *whose eye had despised to obey their mother;* if that had been the case, she would have suffered the *ravens of the valley to pick it out* and *the young eagles to eat it*, Prov. xxx. 17. But they died for their father's sin, and therefore her mind could not be alienated from them by their hard fate. Though there is no remedy, but they must die, yet they shall die pitied and lamented.

III. The solemn interment of their dead bodies, with the bones of Saul and Jonathan, in the burying-place of their family. David was so far from being displeased at what Rizpah had done that he was himself stirred up by it to do honour to the house of Saul, and to these branches of it among the rest; thus it appeared that it was not out of any personal disgust to the family that he delivered them up, and that he had not desired the woeful day, but that he was obliged to do it for the public good. 1. He now bethought himself of removing the bodies of Saul and Jonathan from the place where the men of Jabesh-Gilead had decently, but privately and obscurely, interred them, *under a tree*, 1 Sam. xxxi. 12, 13. Though the shield of Saul was vilely cast away, as if he had not been anointed with oil, yet let not royal dust be lost in the graves of the common people. Humanity obliges us to respect human bodies, especially of the great and good, in consideration both of what they have been and what they are to be. 2. With them he buried the bodies *of those that were hanged;* for, when God's anger was turned away, they were no longer to be looked upon as a curse, *v.* 13, 14. When *water dropped upon them out of heaven* (*v.* 10), that is, when God sent rain to water the earth (which perhaps was not many days after they were hung up), then they were taken down, for then it appeared *that God was entreated for the land.* When justice is done on earth vengeance from heaven ceases. Through Christ, who was hanged on a tree and so made a curse for us, to expiate our guilt (though he was himself guiltless), God is pacified, and is entreated for us: and it is said (Acts xiii. 29) that *when they had fulfilled all that was written of him*, in token of the completeness of the sacrifice and of God's acceptance of it, *they took him down from the tree and laid him in a sepulchre.*

15 Moreover the Philistines had yet war again with Israel: and David went down, and his servants with him, and fought against the Philistines: and David waxed faint. 16 And Ishbi-benob, which *was* of the sons of the giant, the weight of whose spear *weighed* three hundred *shekels* of brass in weight, he being girded with a new *sword*, thought to have slain David. 17 But Abishai the son of Zeruiah, succoured him, and smote the Philistine, and killed him. Then the men of David sware unto him, saying, Thou shalt go no more out with us to battle, that thou quench not the light of Israel. 18 And it came to pass after this, that there was again a battle with the Philistines at Gob: then Sibbechai the Hushathite slew Saph, which *was* of the sons of the giant. 19 And there was again a battle in Gob with the Philistines, where Elhanan the son of Jaare-oregim, a Beth-lehemite, slew *the brother of* Goliath the Gittite, the staff of whose spear *was* like a weaver's beam. 20 And there was yet a battle in Gath, where there was a man of *great* stature, that had on every hand six fingers, and on every foot six toes, four and twenty in number; and he also was born to the giant. 21 And when he defied Israel, Jonathan the son of Shimeah the brother of David slew him. 22 These four were born to the giant in Gath, and fell by the hand of David, and by the hand of his servants.

We have here the story of some conflicts with the Philistines, which happened, as it should seem, in the latter end of David's reign. Though he had so subdued them that they could not bring any great numbers into the field, yet, as long as they had any giants among them to be their champions, they would never be quiet, but took all occasions to disturb the peace of Israel, to challenge them, or make incursions upon them.

I. David himself was engaged with one of the giants. The Philistines began the war yet again, *v.* 15. The enemies of God's Israel are restless in their attempts against them. David, though old, desired not a writ of ease from the public service, but he *went down* in person to fight *against the Philistines (Senescit, non segnescit—He grows old, but not indolent)*, a sign that he fought not for his own glory (at this age he was loaded with glory, and needed no more), but for the good of his kingdom. But in this engagement we find him, 1. In distress and danger. He thought he could bear the fatigues of war as well as he had done formerly; his will was good, and he hoped he could do as at other times. But he found himself deceived; age had cut his hair, and, after a little toil, he *waxed faint.* His body could not keep pace with his mind. The champion of the Philistines was soon aware of his advantage, perceived that David's strength failed him, and, being himself strong and well-armed, *he thought to slay David;* but God was not in his thoughts, and therefore in that very day they all perished. The enemies of God's people are often very strong, very subtle, and very sure of success, like Isbi-benob, but there is no strength, nor counsel, nor confidence against the Lord. 2. Wonderfully rescued by Abishai, who came seasonably in to his relief, *v.* 17. Herein we must own Abishai's courage and fidelity to his prince (to save whose life he bravely ventured his own), but much more the good providence of God, which brought him in to David's succour in the moment of his extremity. Such a cause and such a champion, though distressed, shall not be deserted. When *Abishai succoured him,* gave him a cordial, it may be, to relieve his fainting spirits, or appeared as his second, *he* (namely, David, so I understand it) *smote the Philistine and killed him;* for it is said (*v.* 22) that David had himself a hand in slaying the giants. David fainted, but he did not flee; though his strength failed him, he bravely kept his ground, and then God sent him this help in the time of need, which, though brought him by his junior and inferior, he thankfully accepted, and, with a little recruiting, gained his point, and came off a conqueror. Christ, in his agonies, was strengthened by an angel. In spiritual conflicts, even strong saints sometimes wax faint; then Satan attacks them furiously; but those that stand their ground and resist him shall be relieved, and made more than conquerors. 3. David's servants hereupon resolved that he should never expose himself thus any more. They had easily persuaded him not to fight against Absalom (*ch.* xviii. 3), but against the Philistines he would go, till, having had this narrow escape, it was resolved in council, and confirmed with an oath, that *the light of Israel* (its guide and glory, so David was) should never be put again into such hazard of being blown out. The lives of those who are as valuable to their country as David was ought to be preserved with a double care, both by themselves and others.

II. The rest of the giants fell by the hand of David's servants. 1. Saph was slain by Sibbechai, one of David's worthies, *v.* 18. 1 Chron. xi. 29. 2. Another, who was brother to Goliath, was slain by Elhanan, who is mentioned *ch.* xxiii. 24. 3. Another, who was of very unusual bulk, who had more fingers and toes than other people (*v.* 20), and such an unparalleled insolence that, though he had seen the fall of other giants, yet he defied Israel, was slain by *Jonathan the son of Shimea.* Shimea had one son named *Jonadab* (2 Sam. xiii. 3), whom I should have taken for the same with this Jonathan, but that the former was noted for subtlety, the latter for bravery. These giants were probably the remains of the sons of Anak, who, though long feared, fell at last. Now observe, (1.) It is folly for the strong man to *glory in his strength.* David's servants were no bigger nor stronger than other men; yet thus, by divine assistance, they mastered one giant after another. God chooses by the weak things to confound the mighty. (2.) It is common for those to go down slain to the pit who have been *the terror of the mighty in the land of the living,* Ezek. xxxii. 27. (3.) The most powerful enemies are often reserved for the last conflict. David began his glory with the conquest of one giant, and here concludes it with the conquest of four. Death is a Christian's last enemy, and a son of Anak; but, through him that triumphed for us, we hope to be more than conquerors at last, even over that enemy.

CHAP. XXII.

This chapter is a psalm, a psalm of praise; we find it afterwards inserted among David's psalms (Ps. xviii.) with some little variation. We have it here as it was first composed for his own closet and his own harp; but there we have it as it was afterwards delivered to the chief musician for the service of the church, a second edition with some amendments; for, though it was calculated primarily for David's case, yet it might indifferently serve the devotion of others, in giving thanks for their deliverances; or it was intended that his people should thus join with him in his thanksgivings, because, being a public person, his deliverances were to be accounted public blessings and called for public acknowledgments. The inspired historian, having largely related David's deliverances in this and the foregoing book, and one particularly in the close of the foregoing chapter, thought fit to record this sacred poem as a memorial of all that had been before related. Some think that David penned this psalm when he was old, upon a general review of the mercies of his life and the many wonderful preservations God had blessed him with, from first to last. We should in our praises, look as far back as we can, and not suffer time to wear out the sense of God's favours. Others think that he penned it when he was young, upon occasion of some of his first deliverances, and kept it by him for his use afterwards, and that, upon every new deliverance, his practice was to sing this song. But the book of Psalms shows that he varied as there was occasion, and confined not himself to one form. Here is, 1. The title of the psalm, ver. 1. II. The psalm itself, in which, with a very warm devotion and very great fluency and copiousness of expression, 1. He gives glory to God. 2. He takes comfort in him; and he finds matter for both, (1.) In the experiences he had of God's former favours. (2.) In the expectations he had of his further favours. These are intermixed throughout the whole psalm.

AND David spake unto the LORD the words of this song in the day *that* the LORD had delivered him out of the hand of all his enemies, and out of the hand of Saul.

Observe here, I. That it has often been the lot of God's people to have many enemies, and to be in imminent danger of falling into their hands. David was a man after God's heart, but not after men's heart: many were those that hated him, and sought his ruin; Saul is particularly named, either,

1. As distinguished from his enemies of the heathen nations. Saul hated David, but David did not hate Saul, and therefore would not reckon him among his enemies; or, rather, 2. As the chief of his enemies, who was more malicious and powerful than any of them. Let not those whom God loves marvel if the world hate them.

II. Those that trust God in the way of duty shall find him a present help to them in their greatest dangers. David did so. God delivered him out of the hand of Saul. He takes special notice of this. Remarkable preservations should be mentioned in our praises with a particular emphasis. He delivered him also *out of the hand of all his enemies,* one after another, sometimes in one way, sometimes in another; and David, from his own experience, has assured us *that, though many are the troubles of the righteous, yet the Lord delivers them out of them all,* Ps. xxxiv. 19. We shall never be delivered from all our enemies till we get to heaven; and to that heavenly kingdom God will preserve all that are his, 2 Tim. iv. 18.

III. Those that have received many signal mercies from God ought to give him the glory of them. Every new mercy in our hand should put a new song into our mouth, even praises to our God. Where there is a grateful heart, out of the abundance of that the mouth will speak. David spoke, not only to himself, for his own pleasure, nor merely to those about him, for their instruction, but *to the Lord,* for his honour, *the words of this song.* Then we sing with grace when we sing to the Lord. In distress he *cried with his voice* (Ps. cxlii. 1), therefore with his voice he gave thanks. Thanksgiving to God is the sweetest vocal music.

IV. We ought to be speedy in our thankful returns to God: *In the day that God delivered him he sang this song.* While the mercy is fresh, and our devout affections are most excited by it, let the thank-offering be brought, that it may be kindled with the fire of those affections.

2 And he said, The LORD *is* my rock, and my fortress, and my deliverer; 3 The God of my rock; in him will I trust: *he is* my shield, and the horn of my salvation, my high tower, and my refuge, my saviour; thou savest me from violence. 4 I will call on the LORD, *who is* worthy to be praised: so shall I be saved from mine enemies. 5 When the waves of death compassed me, the floods of ungodly men made me afraid; 6 The sorrows of hell compassed me about; the snares of death prevented me; 7 In my distress I called upon the LORD, and cried to my God: and he did hear my voice out of his temple, and my cry *did enter* into his ears. 8 Then the earth shook and trembled; the foundations of heaven moved and shook, because he was wroth. 9 There went up a smoke out of his nostrils, and fire out of his mouth devoured: coals were kindled by it. 10 He bowed the heavens also, and came down; and darkness *was* under his feet. 11 And he rode upon a cherub, and did fly: and he was seen upon the wings of the wind. 12 And he made darkness pavilions round about him, dark waters, *and* thick clouds of the skies. 13 Through the brightness before him were coals of fire kindled. 14 The LORD thundered from heaven, and the most High uttered his voice. 15 And he sent out arrows, and scattered them; lightning, and discomfited them. 16 And the channels of the sea appeared, the foundations of the world were discovered, at the rebuking of the LORD, at the blast of the breath of his nostrils. 17 He sent from above, he took me; he drew me out of many waters; 18 He delivered me from my strong enemy, *and* from them that hated me: for they were too strong for me. 19 They prevented me in the day of my calamity: but the LORD was my stay. 20 He brought me forth also into a large place: he delivered me, because he delighted in me. 21 The LORD rewarded me according to my righteousness: according to the cleanness of my hands hath he recompensed me. 22 For I have kept the ways of the LORD, and have not wickedly departed from my God. 23 For all his judgments *were* before me: and *as for* his statutes, I did not depart from them. 24 I was also upright before him, and have kept myself from mine iniquity. 25 Therefore the LORD hath recompensed me according to my righteousness; according to my cleanness in his eye sight. 26 With the merciful thou wilt show thyself merciful, *and* with the upright man thou wilt show thyself upright. 27 With the pure thou wilt show thyself

pure; and with the froward thou wilt show thyself unsavoury. 28 And the afflicted people thou wilt save: but thine eyes *are* upon the haughty, *that* thou mayest bring *them* down. 29 For thou *art* my lamp, O LORD: and the LORD will lighten my darkness. 30 For by thee I have run through a troop: by my God have I leaped over a wall. 31 *As for* God, his way *is* perfect; the word of the LORD *is* tried: he *is* a buckler to all them that trust in him. 32 For who *is* God, save the LORD? and who *is* a rock, save our God? 33 God *is* my strength *and* power: and he maketh my way perfect. 34 He maketh my feet like hinds' *feet:* and setteth me upon my high places. 35 He teacheth my hands to war; so that a bow of steel is broken by mine arms. 36 Thou hast also given me the shield of thy salvation: and thy gentleness hath made me great. 37 Thou hast enlarged my steps under me; so that my feet did not slip. 38 I have pursued mine enemies, and destroyed them; and turned not again until I had consumed them. 39 And I have consumed them, and wounded them, that they could not arise: yea, they are fallen under my feet. 40 For thou hast girded me with strength to battle: them that rose up against me hast thou subdued under me. 41 Thou hast also given me the necks of mine enemies, that I might destroy them that hate me. 42 They looked, but *there was* none to save; *even* unto the LORD, but he answered them not. 43 Then did I beat them as small as the dust of the earth, I did stamp them as the mire of the street, *and* did spread them abroad. 44 Thou also hast delivered me from the strivings of my people, thou hast kept me *to be* head of the heathen: a people *which* I knew not shall serve me. 45 Strangers shall submit themselves unto me: as soon as they hear, they shall be obedient unto me. 46 Strangers shall fade away, and they shall be afraid out of their close places. 47 The LORD liveth; and blessed *be* my rock; and exalted be the God of the rock of my salvation. 48 It *is* God that avengeth me, and that bringeth down the people under me, 49 And that bringeth me forth from mine enemies: thou also hast lifted me up on high above them that rose up against me: thou hast delivered me from the violent man. 50 Therefore I will give thanks unto thee, O LORD, among the heathen, and I will sing praises unto thy name. 51 *He is* the tower of salvation for his king: and showeth mercy to his anointed, unto David, and to his seed for evermore.

Let us observe, in this song of praise,

I. How David adores God, and gives him the glory of his infinite perfections. There is none like him, nor any to be compared with him (*v.* 32): *Who is God, save the Lord?* All others that are adored as deities are counterfeits and pretenders. None is to be relied on but he. *Who is a rock, save our God?* They are dead, but *the Lord liveth, v.* 47. They disappoint their worshippers when they most need them. But *as for God his way is perfect, v.* 31. Men begin in kindness, but end not—promise, but perform not; but God will finish his work, and his word is tried, and what we may trust.

II. How he triumphs in the interest he has in this God, and his relation to him, which he lays down as the foundation of all the benefits he has received from him: *He is my God;* as such he cries to him (*v.* 7), and cleaves to him (*v.* 22); "and, if *my God,* then *my rock*" (*v.* 2), that is, "my strength and my power (*v.* 33), the rock under which I take shelter (he who is to me as the shadow of a great rock in a weary land), the rock on which I build my hope," *v.* 3. Whatever is my strength and support, it is *the God of my rock that makes it so;* nay, he is *the God of the rock of my salvation* (*v.* 47): my saving strength is in him and from him. David often hid himself in a rock (1 Sam. xxiv. 2), but God was his chief hiding-place. "He is my fortress, in which I am safe and think myself so—*my high tower,* or stronghold, in which I am out of the reach of real evils—the *tower of salvation* (*v.* 51), which can never be scaled, nor battered, nor undermined. Salvation itself saves me. Am I in distress? he is my deliverer—struck at, shot at? he is my shield—pursued? he is my refuge—oppressed? he is my saviour, that rescues me out of the hand of those that seek my ruin. Nay, he is the *horn of my salvation,* by which I am strongly protected, and my enemies are strongly pushed." Christ is spoken of as the *horn of salvation* in the house of David, Luke i. 69 "Am I burdened, and ready to sink? *The Lord is my stay* (*v.* 19), by whom I am supported. Am I in the dark, benighted, at a loss? *Thou art my lamp, O Lord!* to show me my way, and thou wilt dispel *my darkness," v.* 29. If we sincerely take the Lord for our God, all this, and much more, he will be to us, all we need and can desire.

III. What improvement he makes of his interest in God. If he be mine, 1. *In him will I trust* (*v.* 3), that is, "I will resign myself to his direction, and then depend upon his power, and wisdom, and goodness, to conduct me well. 2. *On him I will call* (*v.* 4), for *he is worthy to be praised.* What we have found in God that is worthy to be praised should engage us to pray to him, and thereby we do in effect praise him and give glory to him. 3. *To him will I give thanks* (*v.* 50), and that publicly. When he was among the heathen he would neither be afraid nor ashamed to own his obligations to the God of Israel.

IV. The full and large account he keeps for himself, and gives to others, of the great and kind things God had done for him. This takes up most of the song. He gives God the glory both of his deliverances and of his successes, showing both the perils he was delivered from and the power he was advanced to.

1. He magnifies the great salvations God had wrought for him. God sometimes brings his people into very great difficulties and dangers, that he may have the honour of saving them and they the comfort of being saved by him. He owns, *Thou hast saved me from violence* (*v.* 3), *from my enemies* (*v.* 4), *from my strong enemy,* meaning Saul, who, if God had not succoured him, would have been too hard for him, *v.* 18. Thou hast given me *the shield of thy salvation, v.* 36. To magnify the salvation, he observes,

(1.) That the danger was very great and threatening out of which he was delivered. Men *rose up against him* (*v.* 40, 49) that *hated him* (*v.* 41), a *violent man* (*v.* 49), namely, Saul, who was malicious in his designs against him and vigorous in his pursuit. This is expressed figuratively, *v.* 5, 6. He was surrounded with death on every side, threatened to be overwhelmed, and saw no way of escape. So violently did the waves of death beat upon him, so strongly did the cords and snares of death hold him, that he could not help himself, any more than a man in the grave can. The floods of Belial, the wicked one, and his wicked instruments, made him afraid; he trembled to see not only earth, but death and hell, in arms against him.

(2.) That his deliverance was an answer to prayer, *v.* 7. He has here left us a good example, when we are in distress, to cry unto God with importunity, as children in a fright cry to their parents; and great encouragement to do so, in that he found God ready to answer prayer out of his temple in heaven, where he is continually served and adored.

(3.) That God appeared in a singular and extraordinary manner for him and against his enemies. The expressions are borrowed from the descent of the divine Majesty upon Mount Sinai, *v.* 8, 9, &c. We do not find that in any of David's battles God fought for him with thunder (as in Samuel's time), or with hail (as in Joshua's time), or with the stars in their courses (as in Deborah's time); but these lofty metaphors are used, [1.] To set forth the glory of God, which was manifested in his deliverance. God's wisdom and power, his goodness and faithfulness, his justice and holiness, and his sovereign dominion over all the creatures and all the counsels of men, which appeared in favour of David, were as clear and bright a discovery of God's glory to an eye of faith as such miraculous interpositions would have been to an eye of sense. [2.] To set forth God's displeasure against his enemies. God so espoused his cause that he showed himself an enemy to all his enemies; his anger is set forth by a *smoke out of his nostrils,* and *fire out of his mouth* (*v.* 9), *coals kindled* (*v.* 13), *arrows, v.* 15. Who knows the power and terror of his wrath? [3.] To set forth the extraordinary confusion which his enemies were put into, and the consternation that seized them; as if the earth had trembled and the *foundations of the world* had been discovered, *v.* 8, 16. Who can stand before God when he is angry? [4.] To show how ready God was to help him: *He rode upon a cherub and did fly, v.* 11. God hastened to his succour, and came to him with seasonable relief, though he had seemed at a distance; yet he was *a God hiding himself* (Isa. xlv. 15), for he made *darkness his pavilion* (*v.* 12), for the amazement of his enemies and the protection of his own people.

(4.) That God manifested his particular favour and kindness to him in these deliverances (*v.* 20): *He delivered me, because he delighted in me.* The deliverance came not from common providence, but covenant-love; he was herein treated as a favourite: so he perceived by the communications of divine grace and comfort to his soul with these deliverances, and the communion he had with God in them. Herein he was a type of Christ, whom God upheld because he *delighted in him,* Isa. xlii. 1, 2.

2. He magnifies the great successes God had crowned him with. He had not only preserved but prospered him. He was blessed, (1.) With liberty and enlargement. He was *brought into a large place* (*v.* 20), where he had room to thrive; and his *steps were enlarged under him,* so that he had room to stir (*v.* 37), being no longer straitened and confined. (2.) With military skill, and strength, and swiftness. Though he was bred up to the crook, he was well instructed in the arts of war and qualified for the toils and perils of it. God, having called him to

fight his battles, qualified him for the service. He made him very ingenious (*He teacheth my hands to war, v.* 35. And this ingenuity was as good as strength, for it follows, "so *that a bow of steel is broken by my arms,*" not so much by main force as by dexterity), and very vigorous and valiant (*Thou hast girded me with strength to battle, v.* 40. He gives God the glory of all his courage and ability for service), and very expeditious: *He maketh my feet* swift *like hinds' feet* (*v.* 34), which is of great advantage both in charging and retreating. (3.) With victory over his enemies, not only Saul and Absalom, but the Philistines, Moabites, Ammonites, Syrians, and other neighbouring nations, whom he subdued and made tributaries to Israel. His wonderful victories are here described, *v.* 38—43. They were *speedy* victories (*I turned not again till I had consumed them, v.* 38), and *complete* victories. The enemies of Israel were *wounded, destroyed, consumed,* fell *under his feet*, trampled upon, and disabled to rise, and their necks lay at his mercy. They cried both to earth and heaven for help, but in vain. *There was none to save,* none that durst appear for them. God *answered them not*, for they were not on his side, nor did they cry unto him till they were brought to the last extremity. Being thus abandoned, they became an easy prey to David's righteous and victorious sword, so that he *beat them as small as the dust of the earth,* which is scattered by the wind and trodden on by every foot. (4.) With advancement to honour and power. To this he was anointed before his troubles began, and at length, *post tot discrimina rerum—after all his dangers and disasters,* he gained his point. God *made his way perfect* (*v.* 33), gave him success in all his undertakings, *set him upon his high places* (*v.* 34), denoting both safety and dignity. God's gentleness, his grace and tender mercy, *made him great* (*v.* 36), gave him great wealth, and great authority, and a name like that of the great men of the earth. He was *kept to be the head of the heathen* (*v.* 44); his signal preservations evinced that he was designed and reserved for something great—to rule over all Israel, notwithstanding the *strivings of the people*, and so that those whom *he had not known should serve him,* many of the nations that lay remote. Thus he was *lifted up on high,* as high as the throne, above those that *rose up against him, v.* 49.

V. The comfortable reflections he makes upon his own integrity, which God, by those wonderful deliverances, had graciously owned and witnessed to, *v.* 21—25. He means especially his integrity with reference to Saul and Ishbosheth, Absalom and Sheba, and those who either opposed his coming to the crown or endeavoured to dethrone him. They falsely accused him and misrepresented him, but he had the testimony of his conscience for him that he was not an ambitious aspiring man, a false and bloody man, as they called him,—that he had never taken any indirect unlawful courses to secure or raise himself, but in his whole conduct had kept in the way of his duty,—and that in the whole course of his conversation he had, for the main, made religion his business, so that he could take God's favours to him as the rewards of his righteousness, not of debt, but of grace. God had recompensed him, though not for his righteousness, as if that had merited any thing at the hand of God, yet according to his righteousness, which he was well pleased with, and had an eye to. His conscience witnessed for him, 1. That he had made the word of God his rule, and had kept to it, *v.* 23. Wherever he was, God's judgments were before him as his guide; whithersoever he went, he took his religion along with him; and though he was forced to depart from his country, and sent, as it were, to serve other gods, yet, as for God's statutes, he did not depart from them, but kept the way of the Lord and walked in it. 2. That he had carefully avoided the bye-paths of sin. He had not wickedly departed from his God. He could not say but that he had taken some false steps, but he had not deserted God, nor forsaken his way. Sins of infirmity he could not acquit himself from, but the grace of God had kept him from presumptuous sins. Though he had sometimes *weakly* departed from his duty, he had never *wickedly* departed from his God. By this it appeared that he was *upright before God,* or *to God* (in his sight, and with an eye to him), that he *kept himself from his own iniquity,* not only from that particular sin of killing Saul when it was in the power of his hand to do it, but, in general, he was afraid of sin and watchful against it, and made conscience of what he said and did. The matter of Uriah is an exception (1 Kings xv. 5), like that in Hezekiah's character, 2 Chron. xxxii. 31. Note, A careful abstaining from our own iniquity is one of the best evidences of our own integrity; and the testimony of our conscience for us that we have done so will be such a rejoicing as will not only lessen the griefs of an afflicted state, but increase the comforts of a prosperous state. David reflected with more comfort upon his victories over his own iniquity than upon his conquest of Goliath and all the hosts of the uncircumcised Philistines; and the witness of his own heart to his uprightness was sweeter though more silent music than theirs that sang, *David has slain his ten thousands.* If a great man be a good man, his goodness will be much more his satisfaction than his greatness. Let favour be shown to the upright, and his uprightness will sweeten it, will double it.

VI. The comfortable prospects he has of God's further favour. As he looks back, so he looks forward, with pleasure, and assures himself of the kindness God has in store for all the saints, for himself, and also for his seed.

1. For all good people, *v.* 26—28. As God had dealt with him according to his uprightness, so he will with all others. He takes occasion here to lay down the established rules of God's procedure with the children of men:—

(1.) That he will do good to those that are upright in their hearts. As we are found towards God, he will be found towards us. [1.] God's mercy and grace will be the joy of those that are merciful and gracious. Even the merciful need mercy, and they shall obtain it. [2.] God's uprightness, his justice and faithfulness, will be the joy of those that are upright, just, and faithful, both towards God and man. [3.] God's purity and holiness will be the joy of those that are pure and holy, who therefore give thanks at the remembrance thereof. And, if any of these good people be *afflicted people, he will save* them, either out of their afflictions or by and after them. On the other hand,

(2.) That those who turn aside to crooked ways he will *lead forth with the workers of iniquity*, as he says in another psalm. *With the froward he will wrestle;* and those with whom God wrestles are sure to be foiled. *Woe unto him that strives with his Maker!* God will walk contrary to those that walk contrary to him and be displeased with those that are displeased with him. As for the haughty, his eyes are upon them, marking them out, as it were, to be brought down; for *he resists the proud.*

2. For himself. He foresaw that his conquests and kingdom would be yet further enlarged, *v.* 45, 46. Even the *sons of the stranger,* that would hear the report of his victories and the tokens of God's presence with him, would be possessed with a fear of him, would be forced to submit to him, though feignedly, and would be obedient to him. The successes which he had had he looked upon as earnests of more and means of more. Who durst oppose him by whom so many had been overcome? Thus the Son of David goes on *conquering and to conquer,* Rev. vi. 2. His gospel, which has been victorious, shall be so more and more.

3. For his seed: He *showeth mercy to his Messiah* (*v.* 51), not only to David himself, but to that seed of his for evermore. David was himself anointed of God, not a usurper, but duly called to the government and qualified for it; therefore he doubted not but God would show mercy to him, that mercy which he had promised not to take from him nor from his posterity (*ch.* vii. 15, 16); on that promise he depends, with an eye to Christ, who alone is his *seed for evermore,* whose throne and kingdom still continue, and will to the end, whereas the seed and lineage of David are long since extinct. See Ps. lxxxix. 28, 29. Thus all his joys and all his hopes terminate, as ours should, in the great Redeemer.

CHAP. XXIII.

The historian is now drawing towards a conclusion of David's reign, and therefore gives us an account here, I. Of some of his last words, which he spoke by inspiration, and which seem to have reference to his seed that was to be for evermore, spoken of in the close of the foregoing chapter, ver. 1—7. II. Of the great men, especially the military men, that were employed under him, the first three (ver. 8—17), two of the next three (ver. 18—23), and then the thirty, ver. 24—39.

NOW these *be* the last words of David. David the son of Jesse said, and the man *who was* raised up on high, the anointed of the God of Jacob, and the sweet psalmist of Israel, said, 2 The Spirit of the LORD spake by me, and his word *was* in my tongue. 3 The God of Israel said, the Rock of Israel spake to me, He that ruleth over men *must be* just, ruling in the fear of God. 4 And *he shall be* as the light of the morning, *when* the sun riseth, *even* a morning without clouds; *as* the tender grass *springing* out of the earth by clear shining after rain. 5 Although my house *be* not so with God; yet he hath made with me an everlasting covenant, ordered in all *things,* and sure: for *this is* all my salvation, and all *my* desire, although he make *it* not to grow. 6 But *the sons* of Belial *shall be* all of them as thorns thrust away, because they cannot be taken with hands: 7 But the man *that* shall touch them must be fenced with iron and the staff of a spear; and they shall be utterly burned with fire in the *same* place.

We have here the last will and testament of king David, or a codicil annexed to it, after he had settled the crown upon Solomon and his treasures upon the temple which was to be built. The last words of great and good men are thought worthy to be in a special manner remarked and remembered. David would have those taken notice of, and added either to his Psalms (as they are here to that in the foregoing chapter) or to the chronicles of his reign. Those words especially in *v.* 5, though recorded before, we may suppose he often repeated for his own consolation, even to his last breath, and therefore they are called his *last words.* When we find death approaching we should endeavour both to honour God and to edify those about us with our last words. Let those that have had long experience of God's goodness and the pleasantness of wisdom, when they come to finish their course, leave a record of that experience and bear their testimony to the truth of the promise. We have upon record the last words of Jacob and Moses, and here of David, designed, as those, for a legacy to those that were left behind. We are here told,

I. Whose last will and testament this is. This is related either, as is usual, by the testator himself, or, rather, by the historian, *v.* 1. He is described, 1. By the meanness of his original: He was *the son of Jesse.* It is good for those who are advanced to be corner-stones and top-stones to be reminded, and often to remind themselves, of *the rock out of which they were hewn.* 2. The height of his elevation: He *was raised up on high,* as one favoured of God, and designed for something great, raised up as a prince, to sit higher than his neighbours, and as a prophet, to see further; for, (1.) He was *the anointed of the God of Jacob,* and so was serviceable to the people of God in their civil interests, the protection of their country and the administration of justice among them. (2.) He was *the sweet psalmist of Israel,* and so was serviceable to them in their religious exercises. He penned the psalms, set the tunes, appointed both the singers and the instruments of music, by which the devotions of good people were much excited and enlarged. Note, The singing of psalms is a sweet ordinance, very agreeable to those that delight in praising God. It is reckoned among the honours to which David was raised up that he was a psalmist: in that he was as truly great as in his being *the anointed of the God of Jacob.* Note, It is true preferment to be serviceable to the church in acts of devotion and instrumental to promote the blessed work of prayer and praise. Observe, Was David a prince? He was so for Jacob. Was he a psalmist? He was so for Israel. Note, The dispensation of the Spirit is given to every man to profit withal, and therefore, *as every man has received the gift, so let him minister the same.*

II. What the purport of it is. It is an account of his communion with God. Observe,

1. What God said to him both for his direction and for his encouragement as a king, and to be, in like manner, of use to his successors. Pious persons take a pleasure in calling to mind what they have heard from God, in recollecting his word, and revolving it in their minds. Thus what God spoke once David heard twice, yea often. See here,

(1.) Who spoke: *The Spirit of the Lord, the God of Israel,* and *the Rock of Israel,* which some think is an intimation of the Trinity of persons in the Godhead—the Father *the God of Israel,* the Son *the Rock of Israel,* and *the Spirit* proceeding from the Father and the Son, *who spoke by the prophets,* and particularly by David, and whose word was not only in his heart, but in his tongue, for the benefit of others. David here avows his divine inspiration, that in his psalms, and in this composition, *The Spirit of God spoke by him.* He, and other holy men, spoke and wrote *as they were moved by the Holy Ghost.* This puts an honour upon the book of Psalms, and recommends them to our use in our devotions, that they are words which the Holy Ghost teaches.

(2.) What was spoken. Here seems to be a distinction made between what the Spirit of God spoke *by* David, which includes all his psalms, and what the Rock of Israel spoke *to* David, which concerned himself and his family. Let ministers observe that those by whom God speaks to others are concerned to hear and heed what he speaks to themselves. Those whose office it is to teach others their duty must be sure to learn and do their own. Now that which is here said (*v.* 3, 4) may be considered, [1.] With application to David, and his royal family. And so here is, *First,* The duty of magistrates enjoined them. When a king was spoken to from God he was not to be complimented with the height of his dignity and the extent of his power, but to be told his duty. "Must is for the king," we say. Here is a *must* for the king: *He must be just, ruling in the fear of God;* and so must all inferior magistrates in their places Let rulers remember that they rule over men—not over beasts which they may enslave and abuse at pleasure, but over reasonable creatures and of the same rank with themselves. They rule over men that have their follies and infirmities, and therefore must be borne with. They rule over men, but under God, and for him; and therefore, 1. They must be just, both to those over whom they rule, in allowing them their rights and properties, and between those over whom they rule, using their power to right the injured against the injurious; see Deut. i. 16, 17. It is not enough that they do no wrong, but they must not suffer wrong to be done. 2. They must rule in the fear of God, that is, they must themselves be possessed with a fear of God, by which they will be effectually restrained from all acts of injustice and oppression. Nehemiah was so (Neh. v. 15) *So did not I, because of the fear of God),* and Joseph, Gen. xlii. 18. They must also endeavour to promote the fear of God (that is, the practice of religion) among those over whom they rule. The magistrate is to be the keeper of both tables, and to protect both godliness and honesty. *Secondly,* Prosperity promised them if they do this duty. *He that* rules *in the fear of God shall be as the light of the morning, v.* 4. Light is sweet and pleasant, and he that does his duty shall have the comfort of it; his rejoicing will be the testimony of his conscience. Light is bright, and a good prince is illustrious; his justice and piety will be his honour. Light is a blessing, nor are there any greater and more extensive blessings to the public than princes that *rule in the fear of God.* As *the light of the morning,* which is most welcome after the darkness of the night (so was David's government after Saul's, Ps. lxxv. 3), which is increasing, shines more and more to the perfect day, such is the growing lustre of a good government. It is likewise compared to the tender grass, which the earth produces for the service of man; it brings with it a harvest of blessings. See Ps. lxxii. 6, 16, which were also some of the last words of David, and seem to refer to those recorded here. [2.] With application to Christ, the Son of David, and then it must all be taken as a prophecy, and the original will bear it: *There shall be a ruler among men,* or over men, that *shall be just,* and *shall rule in the fear of God,* that is, shall order the affairs of religion and divine worship according to his Father's will; and he shall be as *the light of the morning,* &c., for he is the light of the world, and *as the tender grass,* for he is the *branch of the Lord,* and the *fruit of the earth,* Isa. iv. 2. Compare this with those promises of Christ which speak of his *reigning in righteousness* and being *of quick understanding in the fear of the Lord,* Isa. xi. 1—5; xxxii. 1, 2; Ps. lxxii. 2. God, by the Spirit, gave David the foresight of this, to comfort him under the many calamities of his family and the melancholy prospects he had of the degeneracy of his seed.

2. What comfortable use he made of this which God spoke to him, and what were his devout meditations on it, by way of reply, *v.* 5. It is not unlike his meditation on occasion of such a message, 2 Sam. vii. 18, &c. That which goes before the Rock of Israel spoke *to* him; this the Spirit of God spoke *by* him, and it is a most excellent confession of his faith and hope in the everlasting covenant. Here is,

(1.) Trouble supposed: *Although my house be not so with God,* and *although he make it not to grow.* David's family was not so with God as is described (*v.* 3, 4), and as he could wish, not so good, not so happy; it had not been so while he lived; he foresaw it would not be so when he was gone, that his house would be neither so pious nor so prosperous as one might have expected the offspring of such a father to be. [1.] *Not so with God.* Note, We and ours are that really which we are with God. This was what David's heart was upon concerning his children, that they might be right with God, faithful to him and zealous for him. But the children of godly parents are often neither so holy nor so happy as might be expected. We must be made to know that it is corruption, not grace, that runs in the blood, that the race is not to the swift, but that God gives his Spirit as a free-agent. [2.] *Not made to grow,* in number, in power; it is God that makes families to grow or not to grow, Ps. cvii. 41. Good men have often the melancholy prospect of a declining family. David's house was typical of the church of Christ, which is his house, Heb. iii. 3. Suppose this be not so with God as we could wish, suppose it be diminished, distressed, disgraced, and weakened, by errors and corruptions, yea, almost extinct, yet God has made a covenant with the church's head, the Son of David, that he will preserve to him a seed, that the gates of hell shall never prevail against his house. This our Saviour comforted himself with in his sufferings, that the covenant with him stood firm, Isa. liii. 10—12.

(2.) Comfort ensured: *Yet he hath made with me an everlasting covenant.* Whatever trouble a child of God may have the prospect of, still he has some comfort or other to balance it with (2 Cor. iv. 8, 9), and there is none like this of the Psalmist, which may be understood, [1.] Of the covenant of royalty (in the type) which God made with David and his seed, touching the kingdom, Ps. cxxxii. 11, 12. But, [2.] It must look further, to the covenant of grace made with all believers, that God will be, in Christ, to them a God, which was signified by the covenant of royalty, and therefore the promises of the covenant are called *the sure mercies of David,* Isa. lv. 3. It is this only that is the everlasting covenant, and it cannot be imagined that David, who, in so many of his psalms, speaks so clearly concerning Christ and the grace of the gospel, should forget it in his last words. God has made a covenant of grace with us in Jesus Christ, and we are here told, *First,* That it is an *everlasting* covenant, from everlasting in the contrivance and counsel of it, and to everlasting in the continuance and consequences of it. *Secondly,* That it is *ordered,* well ordered in all things, admirably well, to advance the glory of God and the honour of the Mediator, together with the holiness and comfort of believers. It is herein well ordered, that whatever is required in the covenant is promised, and that every transgression in the covenant does not throw us out of covenant, and that it puts our salvation, not in our own keeping, but in the keeping of a Mediator. *Thirdly,* That it is *sure,* and *therefore* sure because well ordered; the general offer of it is sure; the promised mercies are sure on the performance of the conditions. The particular application of it to true believers is sure; it is sure to all the seed. *Fourthly,* That it is *all our salvation.* Nothing but this will save us, and this is sufficient: it is this only upon which our salvation depends. *Fifthly,* That therefore it must be *all our desire.* Let me have an interest in this covenant and the promises of it, and I have enough, I desire no more.

3. Here is the doom of the sons of Belial read, *v.* 6, 7. (1.) They shall be thrust away as thorns—rejected, abandoned. They are like thorns, not to be touched with hands, so passionate and furious that they cannot be managed or dealt with by a wise and faithful reproof, but must be restrained by law and the sword of justice (Ps. xxxii. 9); and therefore, like thorns, (2.) They shall, at length, be utterly burnt with fire in the same place, Heb. vi. 8. Now this is intended, [1.] As a direction to magistrates to use their

power for the punishing and suppressing of wickedness. Let them *thrust away the sons of Belial*; see Ps. ci. 8. Or, [2.] As a caution to magistrates, and particularly to David's sons and successors, to see that they be not themselves sons of Belial (as too many of them were), for then neither the dignity of their place nor their relation to David would secure them from being thrust away by the righteous judgments of God. Though men could not deal with them, God would. Or, [3.] As a prediction of the ruin of all the implacable enemies of Christ's kingdom. There are enemies without, that openly oppose it and fight against it, and enemies within, that secretly betray it and are false to it; both are sons of Belial, children of the wicked one, of the serpent's seed; both are as thorns, grievous and vexatious: but both shall be so thrust away as that Christ will set up his kingdom in despite of their enmity, will go *through them* (Isa. xxvii. 4), and will, in due time, bless his church with such peace that there shall be *no pricking brier nor grieving thorn*. And those that will not repent, to give glory to God, shall, in the judgment-day (to which the Chaldee paraphrast refers this), be burnt with unquenchable fire. See Luke xix. 27.

8 These *be* the names of the mighty men whom David had: The Tachmonite that sat in the seat, chief among the captains; the same *was* Adino the Eznite: *he lift up his spear* against eight hundred, whom he slew at one time. 9 And after him *was* Eleazar the son of Dodo the Ahohite, *one* of the three mighty men with David, when they defied the Philistines *that* were there gathered together to battle, and the men of Israel were gone away: 10 He arose, and smote the Philistines until his hand was weary, and his hand clave unto the sword: and the LORD wrought a great victory that day; and the people returned after him only to spoil. 11 And after him *was* Shammah the son of Agee the Hararite. And the Philistines were gathered together into a troop, where was a piece of ground full of lentiles: and the people fled from the Philistines. 12 But he stood in the midst of the ground, and defended it, and slew the Philistines: and the LORD wrought a great victory. 13 And three of the thirty chief went down, and came to David in the harvest time unto the cave of Adullam: and the troop of the Philistines pitched in the valley of Rephaim. 14 And David *was* then in a hold, and the garrison of the Philistines *was* then *in* Beth-lehem. 15 And David longed, and said, Oh that one would give me drink of the water of the well of Beth-lehem, which *is* by the gate! 16 And the three mighty men brake through the host of the Philistines, and drew water out of the well of Beth-lehem, that *was* by the gate, and took *it*, and brought *it* to David: nevertheless he would not drink thereof, but poured it out unto the LORD. 17 And he said, Be it far from me, O LORD, that I should do this: *is not this* the blood of the men that went in jeopardy of their lives? therefore he would not drink it. These things did these three mighty men. 18 And Abishai, the brother of Joab, the son of Zeruiah, was chief among three. And he lifted up his spear against three hundred, *and* slew *them*, and had the name among three. 19 Was he not most honourable of three? therefore he was their captain: howbeit he attained not unto the *first* three. 20 And Benaiah the son of Jehoiada, the son of a valiant man, of Kabzeel, who had done many acts, he slew two lionlike men of Moab: he went down also and slew a lion in the midst of a pit in time of snow: 21 And he slew an Egyptian, a goodly man: and the Egyptian had a spear in his hand; but he went down to him with a staff, and plucked the spear out of the Egyptian's hand, and slew him with his own spear. 22 These *things* did Benaiah the son of Jehoiada, and had the name among three mighty men. 23 He was more honourable than the thirty, but he attained not to the *first* three. And David set him over his guard. 24 Asahel the brother of Joab *was* one of the thirty; Elhanan the son of Dodo of Beth-lehem, 25 Shammah the Harodite, Elika the Harodite, 26 Helez the Paltite, Ira the son of Ikkesh the Tekoite, 27 Abiezer the Anethothite, Mebunnai the Hushathite, 28 Zalmon the Ahohite, Maharai the Netophathite, 29 Heleb

the son of Baanah, a Netophathite, Ittai the son of Ribai out of Gibeah of the children of Benjamin, 30 Benaiah the Pirathonite, Hiddai of the brooks of Gaash, 31 Abi-albon the Arbathite, Azmaveth the Barhumite, 32 Eliahba the Shaalbonite, of the sons of Jashen, Jonathan, 33 Shammah the Hararite, Ahiam the son of Sharar the Hararite, 34 Eliphelet the son of Ahasbai, the son of the Maachathite, Eliam the son of Ahithophel the Gilonite, 35 Hezrai the Carmelite, Paarai the Arbite, 36 Igal the son of Nathan of Zobah, Bani the Gadite, 37 Zelek the Ammonite, Nahari the Beerothite, armourbearer to Joab the son of Zeruiah, 38 Ira an Ithrite, Gareb an Ithrite, 39 Uriah the Hittite: thirty and seven in all.

I. The catalogue which the historian has here left upon record of the great soldiers that were in David's time is intended, 1. For the honour of David, who trained them up in the arts and exercises of war, and set them an example of conduct and courage. It is the reputation as well as the advantage of a prince to be attended and served by such brave men as are here described. 2. For the honour of those worthies themselves, who were instrumental to bring David to the crown, settle and protect him in the throne, and enlarge his conquests. Note, Those that in public stations venture themselves, and lay out themselves, to serve the interests of their country, are worthy of double honour, both to be respected by those of their own age and to be remembered by posterity. 3. To excite those that come after to a generous emulation. 4. To show how much religion contributes to the inspiring of men with true courage. David, both by his psalms and by his offerings for the service of the temple, greatly promoted piety among the grandees of the kingdom (1 Chron. xxix. 6), and, when they became famous for piety, they became famous for bravery.

II. Now these mighty men are here divided into three ranks:—

1. The first three, who had done the greatest exploits and thereby gained the greatest reputation—Adino (*v.* 8), Eleazar (*v.* 9, 10), and Shammah, *v.* 11, 12. I do not remember that we read of any of these, or of their actions, any where in all the story of David but here and in the parallel place, 1 Chron. xi. Many great and remarkable events are passed by in the annals, which relate rather the blemishes than the glories of David's reign, especially after his sin in the matter of Uriah; so that we may conclude his reign to have been really more illustrious than it has appeared to us while reading the records of it. The exploits of this brave triumvirate are here recorded. They signalized themselves in the wars of Israel against their enemies, especially the Philistines. (1.) Adino slew 800 at once with his spear. (2.) Eleazar defied the Philistines, as they by Goliath, had defied Israel, but with better success and greater bravery; for when the men of Israel had gone away, he not only kept his ground, but *arose, and smote the Philistines,* on whom God struck a terror equal to the courage with which this great hero was inspired. His hand was weary, and yet it clave to his sword; as long as he had any strength remaining he held his weapon and followed his blow. Thus, in the service of God, we should keep up the willingness and resolution of the spirit, notwithstanding the weakness and weariness of the flesh—faint, yet pursuing (Judg. viii. 4), the hand weary, yet not quitting the sword. Now that Eleazar had beaten the enemy, the men of Israel, who had gone away from the battle (*v.* 9), returned to spoil, *v.* 10. It is common for those who quit the field when any thing is to be done to hasten to it when any thing is to be gotten. (3.) Shammah met with a party of the enemy, that were foraging, and routed them, *v.* 11, 12. But observe, both concerning this exploit and the former, it is here said, *The Lord wrought a great victory.* Note, How great soever the bravery of the instruments is, the praise of the achievement must be given to God. These fought the battles, but God wrought the victory. Let not the strong man then glory in his strength, nor in any of his military operations, but *let him that glories glory in the Lord.*

2. The next three were distinguished from, and dignified above, the thirty, but attained not to the first three, *v.* 23. All great men are not of the same size. Many a bright and benign star there is which is not of the first magnitude, and many a good ship not of the first rate. Of this second triumvirate two only are named, Abishai and Benaiah, whom we have often met with in the story of David, and who seem to have been not inferior in serviceableness, though they were in dignity, to the first three. Here is,

(1.) A brave action of these three in conjunction. They attended David in his troubles, when he absconded, in the cave of Adullam (*v.* 13), suffered with him, and therefore were afterwards preferred by him. When David and his brave men who attended him, who had acted so vigorously against the Philistines, were, by the iniquity of the times, in Saul's reign, driven to shelter themselves from his rage in caves and strong holds, no marvel that the Philistines pitched in the valley of Rephaim, and put a garrison even in Bethlehem itself, *v.* 13, 14. If the church's guides are so misled as to persecute some of her best friends and champions, the common enemy will, no doubt, get advantage by it. If David had had his liberty, Bethlehem would not have been now in the Philistines' hands. But, being so, we are here told, [1.] How earnestly David longed for the water of the well of Bethlehem. Some make it a public-spirited wish, and that he meant, "O that we could drive the garrison of the Philistines out of Bethlehem, and make that beloved city of mine our own again!" the well being put for the city, as the river often signifies the country it passes through. But, if he meant so, those about him did not understand him; therefore it seems rather to be an instance of his weakness. It was harvest-time; the weather was hot; he was thirsty; perhaps good water was scarce, and therefore he earnestly wished, "O that I could but have one draught of the water of the well of Bethlehem!" With the water of that well he had often refreshed himself when he was a youth, and nothing now will serve him but that, though it is almost impossible to come at it. He strangely indulged a humour which he could give no reason for. Other water might quench his thirst as well, but he had a fancy for that above any. It is folly to entertain such fancies and greater folly to insist upon the gratification of them. We ought to check our appetites when they go out inordinately towards those things that really are more pleasant and grateful than other things *(Be not desirous of dainties)*, much more when they are thus set upon such things as only please a humour. [2.] How bravely his three mighty men, Abishai, Benaiah, and another not named, ventured through the camp of the Philistines, upon the very mouth of danger, and fetched water from the well of Bethlehem, without David's knowledge, *v.* 16. When he wished for it he was far from desiring that any of his men should venture their lives for it; but those three did, to show, *First*, How much they valued their prince, and with what pleasure they could run the greatest hazards and undergo the greatest hardships in his service. David, though anointed king, was as yet an exile, a poor prince that had no external advantages to recommend him to the affection and esteem of his attendants, nor was he in any capacity to prefer or reward them; yet those three were thus zealous for his satisfaction, firmly believing the time of recompence would come. Let us be willing to venture in the cause of Christ, even when it is a suffering cause, as those who are assured that it will prevail and that we shall not lose by it at last. Were they so forward to expose themselves upon the least hint of their prince's mind and so ambitious to please him? And shall not we covet to approve ourselves to our Lord Jesus by a ready compliance with every intimation of his will given us by his word, Spirit, and providence? *Secondly*, How little they feared the Philistines. They were glad of an occasion to defy them. Whether they broke through the host clandestinely, and with such art that the Philistines did not discover them, or openly, and with such terror in their looks that the Philistines durst not oppose them, is not certain; it should seem, they forced their way, sword in hand. But see, [3.] How self-denyingly David, when he had this far-fetched dear-bought water, *poured it out before the Lord*, *v.* 17. *First*, Thus he would show the tender regard he had to the lives of his soldiers, and how far he was from being prodigal of their blood, Ps. lxxii. 14. In God's sight the death of his saints is precious. *Secondly*, Thus he would testify his sorrow for speaking that foolish word which occasioned those men to put their lives in their hands. Great men should take heed what they say, lest any bad use be made of it by those about them. *Thirdly*, Thus he would prevent the like rashness in any of his men for the future. *Fourthly*, Thus he would cross his own foolish fancy, and punish himself for entertaining and indulging it, and show that he had sober thoughts to correct his rash ones, and knew how to deny himself even in that which he was most fond of. Such generous mortifications become the wise, the great, and the good. *Fifthly*, Thus he would honour God and give glory to him. The water purchased at this rate he thought too precious for his own drinking and fit only to be poured out to God as a drink-offering If it was the blood of these men, it was God's due, for the blood was always his. *Sixthly*, Bishop Patrick speaks of some who think that David hereby showed that it was not material water he longed for, but the Messiah, who had the water of life, who, he knew, should be born at Bethlehem, which the Philistines therefore should not be able to destroy. *Seventhly*, Did David look upon that water as very precious which was got at the hazard of these men's blood, and shall not we much more value those benefits for the purchasing of which our blessed Saviour shed his blood? Let us not undervalue the blood of the covenant, as those do that undervalue the blessings of the covenant.

(2.) The brave actions of two of them on other occasions. Abishai slew 300 men at once, *v.* 18, 19. Benaiah did many great things. [1.] He slew two Moabites that were lion-like men, so bold and strong, so fierce and furious. [2.] He slew a lion in a pit, either in his own defence, as Samson, or perhaps in kindness to the country, a lion that had done mischief. It being in a time of snow, he was more stiff and the lion more fierce and ravenous, and yet he mastered him. [3.] He slew an Egyptian, on what occasion it is not said; he was well armed, but Benaiah attacked him with no other weapon than a walking staff, dexterously wrested his spear out of his hand, and slew him with it, *v.* 21. For these and similar exploits David preferred him to be captain of the life-guard or standing forces, *v.* 23.

3. Inferior to the second three, but of great note, were the thirty-one here mentioned by name, *v.* 24, &c. Asahel is the first, who was slain by Abner in the beginning of David's reign, but lost not his place in this catalogue. Elhanan is the next, brother to Eleazar, one of the first three, *v.* 9. The surnames here given them are taken, as it should seem, from the places of their birth or habitation, as many surnames with us originally were. From all parts of the nation, the most wise and valiant were picked up to serve the king. Several of those who are here named we find captains of the twelve courses which David appointed, one for each month in the year, 1 Chron. xxvii. Those that did worthily were preferred according to their merits. One of them was the son of Ahithophel (*v.* 34), the son famous in the camp as the father at the council-board. But to find Uriah the Hittite bringing up the rear of these worthies, as it revives the remembrance of David's sin, so it aggravates it, that a man who deserved so well of his king and country should be so ill treated. Joab is not mentioned among all these, either, (1.) Because he was so great that he did not need to be mentioned; the first of the first three sat chief among the captains, but Joab was over them as general. Or, (2.) Because he was so bad that he did not deserve to be mentioned; for though he was confessedly a great soldier, and one that had so much religion in him as to dedicate of his spoils to the house of God (1 Chron. xxvi. 28), yet he lost as much honour by slaying two of David's friends as ever he got by slaying his enemies.

Christ, the Son of David, has his worthies too, who, like David's, are influenced by his example, fight his battles against the spiritual enemies of his kingdom, and in his strength are more than conquerors. Christ's apostles were his immediate attendants, did and suffered great things for him, and at length came to reign with him. They are mentioned with honour in the New Testament, as these in the Old, especially, Rev. xxi. 14. Nay, all the good soldiers of Jesus Christ have their names better preserved than even these worthies have; for they are written in heaven. This honour have all his saints.

CHAP. XXIV.

The last words of David, which we read in the chapter before, were admirably good, but in this chapter we read of some of his last works, which were none of the best; yet he repented, and did his first works again, and so he finished well. We have here, I. His sin, which was numbering the people in the pride of his heart, ver. 1—9. II. His conviction of the sin, and repentance for it, ver. 10. III. The judgment inflicted upon him for it, ver. 11—15. IV. The staying of the judgment, ver. 16, 17. V. The erecting of an altar in token of God's reconciliation to him and his people, ver. 18—25.

AND again the anger of the LORD was kindled against Israel, and he moved David against them to say, Go, number Israel and Judah. 2 For the king said to Joab the captain of the host, which *was* with him, Go now through all the tribes of Israel, from Dan even to Beer-sheba, and number ye the people, that I may know the number of the people. 3 And Joab said unto the king, Now the LORD thy God add unto the people, how many soever they be, a hundredfold, and that the eyes of my lord the king may see *it:* but why doth my lord the king delight in this thing? 4 Notwithstanding the king's words prevailed against Joab, and against the captains of the host. And Joab and the captains of the host went out from the presence of the king, to number the people of Israel. 5 And they passed over Jordan, and pitched in Aroer, on the right side of the city that *lieth* in the midst of the river of Gad, and toward Jazer: 6 Then they came to Gilead, and to the land of Tahtim-hodshi; and they came to Dan-jaan, and about to Zidon, 7 And came to the strong hold of Tyre, and to all the cities of the Hivites, and of the Canaanites: and they went out to the south of Judah, *even* to Beer-sheba. 8 So when they had gone through all the land, they came to Jerusalem at the end of nine months and twenty days. 9 And Joab gave up the sum of the number of the people unto the king: and there were in Israel eight hundred thousand valiant men that drew the sword; and the men of Judah *were* five hundred thousand men.

Here we have,

I. The orders which David gave to Joab to number the people of Israel and Judah, *v.* 1, 2. Two things here seem strange:—1. The sinfulness of this. What harm was there in it? Did not Moses twice number the people without any crime? Does not political arithmetic come in among the other policies of a prince? Should not the shepherd know the number of his sheep? Does not the Son of David know all his own by name? Might not he make good use of this calculation? What evil has he done, if he do this? *Answer,* It is certain that it was a sin, and a great sin; but where the evil of it lay is not so certain. (1.) Some think the fault was that he numbered those that were under twenty years old if they were but of stature and strength able to bear arms, and that this was the reason why this account was not enrolled, because it was illegal, 1 Chron. xxvii. 23, 24

(2.) Others think the fault was that he did not require the half-shekel, which was to be paid for the service of the sanctuary whenever the people were numbered, as a *ransom for their souls*, Exod. xxx. 12. (3.) Others think that he did it with a design to impose a tribute upon them for himself, to be put into his treasury, and this by way of poll, so that when he knew their numbers he could tell what it would amount to. But nothing of this appears, nor was David ever a raiser of taxes. (4.) This was the fault, that he had no orders from God to do it, nor was there any occasion for the doing of it. It was a needless trouble both to himself and to his people. (5.) Some think that it was an affront to the ancient promise which God made to Abraham, that his seed should be innumerable as the dust of the earth; it savoured of distrust of that promise, or a design to show that it was not fulfilled in the letter of it. He would number those of whom God had said that they could not be numbered. Those know not what they do that go about to disprove the word of God. (6.) That which was the worst thing in numbering the people was that David did it in the pride of his heart, which was Hezekiah's sin in showing his treasures to the ambassadors. [1.] It was a proud conceit of his own greatness in having the command of so numerous a people, as if their increase, which was to be ascribed purely to the blessing of God, had been owing to any conduct of his own. [2.] It was a proud confidence in his own strength. By publishing among the nations the number of his people, he thought to appear the more formidable, and doubted not that, if he should have any war, he should overpower his enemies with the multitude of his forces, trusting in an arm of flesh more than he should have done who had written so much of trusting in God only. God judges not of sin as we do. What appears to us harmless, or at least but a small offence, may be a great sin in the eye of God, who sees men's principles, and is a discerner of the thoughts and intents of the heart. But his judgment, we are sure, is according to truth.

2. The spring from which it is here said to arise is yet more strange, *v.* 1. It is not strange that *the anger of the Lord should be kindled against Israel.* There was cause enough for it. They were unthankful for the blessings of David's government, and strangely drawn in to take part with Absalom first and afterwards with Sheba. We have reason to think that their peace and plenty made them secure and sensual, and that God was therefore displeased with them. But that, in this displeasure, he should move David to number the people is very strange. We are sure that God is not the author of sin; he tempts no man: we are told (1 Chron. xxi. 1) that *Satan provoked David to number Israel.* Satan, as an enemy, suggested it for a sin, as he put it into the heart of Judas to betray Christ. God, as righteous Judge, permitted it, with a design, from this sin of David, to take an occasion to punish Israel for other sins, for which he might justly have punished them without this. But, as before he brought a famine upon them for the sin of Saul, so now a pestilence for the sin of David, that princes may from these instances learn, when the judgments of God are abroad, to suspect that their sins are the ground of the controversy, and may therefore repent and reform themselves, which should have a great influence upon national repentance and reformation, and that people may learn to pray for those in authority, that God would keep them from sin, because, if they sin, the kingdom smarts.

II. The opposition which Joab made to these orders. Even he was aware of David's folly and vain-glory in this design. He observed that David gave no reason for it, only, *Number the people, that I may know the number of the people;* and therefore he endeavoured to divert his pride, and in a much more respectful manner than he had before endeavoured to divert his passion upon the death of Absalom; then he spoke rudely and insolently (*ch.* xix. 5—7), but now as became him: *Now the Lord thy God add unto the people a hundred fold, v.* 3. There was no occasion to tax them, nor to enlist them, nor to make any distribution of them. They were all easy and happy; and Joab wished both that their number might increase and that the king, though old, might live to see their increase, and have the satisfaction of it. "*But why doth my lord the king delight in this thing?* What need is there of doing it?" *Pauperis est numerare pecus—Leave it to the poor to count their flocks.* Especially why should David, who speaks so much of delighting in God and the exercises of devotion, and who, being old, one would think, should have put away childish things, take a pleasure (so he calls it modestly, but he means taking pride) in a thing of this nature? Note, Many things, not in themselves sinful, turn into sin to us by our inordinately delighting in them. Joab was aware of David's vanity herein, but he himself was not. It would be good for us to have a friend that would faithfully admonish us when we say or do any thing proud or vain-glorious, for we often do so and are not ourselves aware of it.

III. The orders executed notwithstanding. *The king's word prevailed, v.* 4. He would have it done; Joab must not gainsay it, lest he be thought to grudge his time and pains in the king's service. It is an unhappiness to great men to have those about them that will aid them and serve them in that which is evil. Joab, according to order, applied himself with some reluctancy to this unpleasing task, and took the captains of the host to help him. They began in the most distant places, in the east first, on the other side Jordan (*v.* 5), then they went towards Dan in the north (*v.* 6), so to Tyre on the east, and thence to Beersheba in the south, *v.* 7. Above nine months were spent in taking this account, a great deal of trouble and amazement were occasioned by it in the country (*v.* 8), and the sum total was, at length, brought to the king at Jerusalem, *v.* 9. Whether the numbers answered David's expectation or no we are not told, nor whether the account fed his pride or mortified it. The people were very many, but, it may be, not so many as he thought they were. They had not increased in Canaan as they had in Egypt, nor were much more than double to what they were when they came into Canaan under Joshua, about 400 years before; yet it is an evidence that Canaan was a very fruitful land that so many thousands were maintained within so narrow a compass.

10 And David's heart smote him after that he had numbered the people. And David said unto the LORD, I have sinned greatly in that I have done: and now, I beseech thee, O LORD, take away the iniquity of thy servant; for I have done very foolishly. 11 For when David was up in the morning, the word of the LORD came unto the prophet Gad, David's seer, saying, 12 Go and say unto David, Thus saith the LORD, I offer thee three *things;* choose thee one of them, that I may *do it* unto thee. 13 So Gad came to David, and told him, and said unto him, Shall seven years of famine come unto thee in thy land? or wilt thou flee three months before thine enemies, while they pursue thee? or that there be three days' pestilence in thy land? now advise, and see what answer I shall return to him that sent me. 14 And David said unto Gad, I am in a great strait: let us now fall into the hand of the LORD; for his mercies *are* great: and let me not fall into the hand of man. 15 So the LORD sent a pestilence upon Israel from the morning even to the time appointed: and there died of the people from Dan even to Beer-sheba seventy thousand men. 16 And when the angel stretched out his hand upon Jerusalem to destroy it, the LORD repented him of the evil, and said to the angel that destroyed the people, It is enough: stay now thine hand. And the angel of the LORD was by the threshingplace of Araunah the Jebusite. 17 And David spake unto the LORD when he saw the angel that smote the people, and said, Lo, I have sinned, and I have done wickedly: but these sheep, what have they done? let thine hand, I pray thee, be against me, and against my father's house.

We have here David repenting of the si. and yet punished for it, God repenting of the judgment and David thereby made more penitent.

I. Here is David's penitent reflection upon and confession of his sin in numbering the people. While the thing was in doing, during all those nine months, we do not find that David was sensible of his sin, for had he been so he would have countermanded the orders he had given; but, when the account was finished and laid before him, that very night his conscience was awakened, and he felt the pain of it just then when he promised himself the pleasure of it. When he was about to feast on the satisfaction of the number of his people, it was turned into the gall of asps within him; sense of the sin cast a damp upon the joy, *v.* 10. 1. He was convinced of his sin: *His heart smote him* before the prophet came to him (I think it should not be read *for* (*v.* 11), but *and when David was up,* so it is in the original), his conscience showed him the evil of what he had done; now that appeared sin, and exceedingly sinful, which before he saw no harm in. He reflected upon it with great regret and his heart reproached him for it. Note, It is a good thing, when a man has sinned, to have a heart within him to smite him for it; it is a good sign of a principle of grace in the heart, and a good step towards repentance and reformation. 2. He confessed it to God and begged earnestly for the forgiveness of it. (1.) He owned that he had sinned, sinned greatly, though to others it might seem no sin at all, or a very little one. True penitents, whose consciences are tender and well informed, see that evil in sin which others do not see. (2.) He owned that he had *done foolishly, very foolishly,* because he had done it in the pride of his heart; and it was folly for him to be proud of the numbers of his people, when they were God's people, not his, and, as many as they were, God could soon make them fewer. (3.) He cried to God for pardon: *I beseech thee, O Lord! take away the iniquity of thy servant. If we confess our sins,* we may pray in faith that God *will forgive them,* and take away, by pardoning mercy, that iniquity which we cast away by sincere repentance.

II. The just and necessary correction which he suffered for this sin. David had been full of tossings to and fro all night under the sense of his sin, having no rest in his bones because of it, *and he arose in the morning* expecting to hear of God's displeasure against him for what he had done, or designing to speak with Gad his seer concerning it. Gad is called his *seer* because he had him always at hand to advise with in the things of God, and made use of him as his confessor and counsellor; but God prevented him, and directed the prophet Gad what to say to him (*v.* 11), and,

1. Three things are taken for granted, (1.) That David must be corrected for his fault. It is too great a crime, and reflects too much dishonour upon God, to go unpunished, even in David himself. Of the seven things that God hates, pride is the first, Prov. vi. 17. Note, Those who truly repent of their sins, and have them pardoned, are yet often made to smart for them in this world. (2.) The punishment must answer to the sin. He was proud of the numbers of his people, and therefore the judgment he must be chastised with for this sin must be such as will make them fewer. Note, What we make the matter of our pride it is just with God to take from us, or embitter to us, and, some way or other, to make the matter of our punishment. (3.) It must be such a punishment as the people must have a large share in, *for God's anger was kindled against Israel, v.* 1. Though it was David's sin that immediately opened the sluice, the sins of the people all contributed to the deluge.

2. As to the punishment that must be inflicted,

(1.) David is told to choose what rod he will be beaten with, *v.* 12, 13. His heavenly Father must correct him, but, to show that he does not do it willingly, he gives David leave to make choice whether it shall be by war, famine, or pestilence, three sore judgments, which greatly weaken and diminish a people. God, by putting him thus to his choice, designed, [1.] To humble him the more for his sin, which he would see to be exceedingly sinful when he came to consider each of these judgments as exceedingly dreadful. Or, [2.] To upbraid him with the proud conceit he had of his own sovereignty over Israel. He that is so great a prince begins to think he may have what he will. "Come then," says God, "which wilt thou have of these three things?" Compare Jer. xxxiv. 17, *I proclaim a liberty for you,* but it is such a liberty as this of David's, *to the sword, to the pestilence, and to the famine;* and Jer. xv. 2, *Such as are for death to death.* Or, [3.] To give him some encouragement under the correction, letting him know that God did not cast him out of communion with himself, but that still his secret was with him, and in afflicting him he considered his frame and what he could best bear. Or, [4.] That he might the more patiently bear the rod when it was a rod of his own choosing. The prophet bids him advise with himself, and then tell him what answer he should *return to him that sent him.* Note, Ministers are sent of God to us, and they must give an account of the success of their embassy. It concerns us therefore to consider what answer they shall return from us, that they may give up their account of us with joy.

(2.) He objects only against the judgments of the sword, and, for the other two, he refers the matter to God, but intimates his choice of the pestilence rather (*v.* 14): *I am in a great strait;* and well he might be *when fear, and the pit, and the snare, were before him,* and, if he escape one, he must inevitably fall into the other, Jer. xlviii. 43, 44. Note, Sin brings men into straits; wise and good men often distress themselves by their own folly. [1.] He begs that he may *not fall into the hand of man.* "Whatever comes, *let us not flee three months before our enemies;*" this would sully all the glory of David's triumphs and give occasion to the enemies of God and Israel to *behave themselves proudly.* See Deut. xxxii. 26, 27. "Their tender mercies are cruel; and in three months they will do that damage to the nation which many years will not repair." But, [2.] He casts himself upon God: *Let us fall now into the hand of the Lord, for his mercies are great.* Men are *God's hand* (so they are called, Ps. xvii. 14, the sword of his sending), yet there are some judgments which come more immediately from his hand than others, as famine and pestilence, and David refers it to God which of these shall be the scourge, and God chooses the shortest, that he may the sooner testify his being reconciled. But some think that David, by these words, intimates his choice of the pestilence. The land had not yet recovered the famine under which it smarted three years upon the Gibeonites' account, and therefore, "Let us not be corrected with that rod, for that also will be the triumph of our neighbours," hence we read of *the reproach of famine* (Ezek. xxxvi. 30); "but, if Israel must be diminished, let it be by the pestilence, for that is *falling into the hands of the Lord,*" who usually inflicted that judgment by the hand of his own immediate servants, the angels, as in the death of the first-born of Egypt. That is a judgment to which David himself, and his own family, lie as open as the meanest subject, but not so either to famine or sword, and therefore David, tenderly conscious of his guilt, chooses that. Sword and famine will devour one as well as another, but, it may be thought, the destroying angel will draw his sword against those who are known to God to be most guilty. This will be of the shortest continuance, and he dreads the thought of lying long under the tokens of God's displeasure. *It is a dreadful thing,* the apostle says, *to fall into the hands of the living God* (Heb. x. 31), a fearful thing indeed for sinners that have, by their impenitency, shut themselves out from all hope of his mercy. But David, a penitent, dares cast himself into

God's hand, knowing he shall find that *his mercies are great.* Good men, even when they are under God's frowns, yet will entertain no other than good thoughts of him. *Though he slay me, yet will I trust in him.*

(3.) A pestilence is accordingly sent (*v.* 15), which, for the extent of it, spread from Dan to Beersheba, from one end of the kingdom to the other, which showed it to come immediately from God's hand and not from any natural causes. David has his choice; he suffers by miracle, and not by ordinary means. For the continuance of it, it lasted from morning (this very morning on which it was put to David's choice) to the time appointed, that is, to the third day (so Mr. Poole), or only to the evening of the first day, the time appointed for the evening sacrifice, so bishop Patrick and others, who reckon that the pestilence lasted but nine hours, and that, in compassion to David, God shortened the time he had first mentioned. The execution the pestilence did was very severe. *There died* 70,000 *men,* that were all well, and sick, and dead, in a few hours. What a great cry, may we suppose, was there now throughout all the land of Israel, as there was in Egypt when the first-born were slain! but that was at midnight, this in the daytime, Ps. xci. 6. See the power of the angels, when God gives them commission, either to save or to destroy. Joab is nine months in passing with his pen, the angel but nine hours in passing with his sword, through all the coasts and corners of the land of Israel. See how easily God can bring down the proudest sinners, and how much we owe daily to the divine patience. David's adultery is punished, for the present, only with the death of one infant, his pride with the death of all those thousands, so much does God hate pride. The number slain amounted to almost half a decimation, 70,000 being about one in twenty. Now, we may suppose, David's flesh *trembled for fear of God and he was afraid of his judgments,* Ps. cxix. 120.

III. God's gracious relaxation of the judgment, when it began to be inflicted upon Jerusalem (*v.* 16): *The angel stretched out his hand upon Jerusalem,* as if he intended to do greater execution there than any where else, even *to destroy it.* The country had drunk of the bitter cup, but Jerusalem must drink the dregs. It should seem that was last numbered, and therefore was reserved to be last plagued; perhaps there was more wickedness, especially more pride (and that was the sin now chastised), in Jerusalem than elsewhere, therefore the hand of the destroyer is stretched out upon that; but then *the Lord repented him of the evil,* changed not his mind, but his way, and said to the destroying angel, *It is enough; stay now thy hand,* and *let mercy rejoice against judgment.* Jerusalem shall be spared for the ark's sake, for it is the place God hath chosen to put his name there. See here how ready God is to forgive and how little pleasure he takes in punishing; and let it encourage us to meet him by repentance in the way of his judgments. This was on Mount Moriah. Dr. Lightfoot observes that in the very place where Abraham, by a countermand from heaven, was stayed from slaying his son, this angel, by a like countermand, was stayed from destroying Jerusalem. It is for the sake of the great sacrifice that our forfeited lives are preserved from the destroying angel.

IV. David's renewed repentance for his sin upon this occasion, *v.* 17. He saw the angel (God opening his eyes for that purpose), saw his sword stretched out to destroy, a flaming sword, saw him ready to sheath it upon the orders given him to stay proceedings; seeing all this, he spoke, not to the angel (he knew better than to address himself to the servant in the presence of the Master, or to give that honour to the creature which is the Creator's due), but *to the Lord, and said, Lo, I have sinned.* Note, True penitents, the more they perceive of God's sparing pardoning mercy the more humbled they are for sin and the more resolved against it. They shall be ashamed *when I am pacified towards them,* Ezek. xvi. 63. Observe, 1. How he criminates himself, as if he could never speak ill enough of his own fault: "*I have sinned, and I have done wickedly;* mine is the crime, and therefore on me be the cross. *Let thy hand be against me, and my father's house.* I am the sinner, let me be the sufferer;" so willing was he to accept the punishment of his iniquity, though he was worth 10,000 of them. 2. How he intercedes for the people, whose bitter lamentations made his heart to ache, and his ears to tingle: *These sheep, what have they done?* Done! Why they had done much amiss; it was their sin that provoked God to leave David to himself to do as he did; yet, as becomes a penitent, he is severe upon his own faults, while he extenuates theirs. Most people, when God's judgments are abroad, charge others with being the cause of them, and care not who falls by them, so they can escape. But David's penitent and public spirit was otherwise affected. Let this remind us of the grace of our Lord Jesus, who gave himself for our sins and was willing that God's hand should be against him, that we might escape. The shepherd was smitten that the sheep might be spared.

18 And Gad came that day to David, and said unto him, Go up, rear an altar unto the LORD in the threshingfloor of Araunah the Jebusite. 19 And David, according to the saying of Gad, went up as the LORD commanded. 20 And Araunah looked and saw the king and his servants

coming on toward him: and Araunah went out, and bowed himself before the king on his face upon the ground. 21 And Araunah said, Wherefore is my lord the king come to his servant? And David said, To buy the threshingfloor of thee, to build an altar unto the LORD, that the plague may be stayed from the people. 22 And Araunah said unto David, Let my lord the king take and offer up what *seemeth* good unto him: behold, *here be* oxen for burnt sacrifice, and threshing instruments and *other* instruments of the oxen for wood. 23 All these *things* did Araunah, *as* a king, give unto the king. And Araunah said unto the king, The LORD thy God accept thee. 24 And the king said unto Araunah, Nay; but I will surely buy *it* of thee at a price: neither will I offer burnt offerings unto the LORD my God of that which doth cost me nothing. So David bought the threshingfloor and the oxen for fifty shekels of silver. 25 And David built there an altar unto the LORD, and offered burnt offerings and peace offerings. So the LORD was intreated for the land, and the plague was stayed from Israel.

Here is, I. A command sent to David to erect an altar in the place where he saw the angel, *v.* 18. This was to intimate to David, 1. That, upon his repeated submission and humiliation, God was now thoroughly reconciled to him; *for, if the Lord had been pleased to kill him, he would not have accepted an offering,* and therefore would not have ordered him to *build an altar.* God's encouraging us to offer to him spiritual sacrifices is a comfortable evidence of his reconciling us to himself. 2. That peace is made between God and sinners by sacrifice, and not otherwise, even by Christ the great propitiation, of whom all the legal sacrifices were types. It is for his sake that the destroying angel is told to stay his hand. 3. That when God's judgments are graciously stayed we ought to acknowledge it with thankfulness to his praise. This altar was to be for thank-offerings. See Isa. xii. 1.

II. The purchase which David made of the ground in order hereunto. It seems the owner was a Jebusite, Araunah by name, proselyted no doubt to the Jewish religion, though by birth a Gentile, and therefore allowed, not only to dwell among the Israelites, but to have a possession of his own in a city, Lev. xxv. 29, 30. The piece of ground was a threshing-floor, a mean place, *yet* thus dignified—a place of labour, *therefore* thus dignified. Now,

1. David went in person to the owner, to treat with him. See his justice, that he would not so much as use this place in the present exigence, though the proprietor was an alien, though he himself was a king, and though he had express orders from God to rear an altar there, till he had bought it and paid for it. God *hates robbery for burnt-offering.* See his humility, how far he was from taking state; though a king, he was now a penitent, and therefore, in token of his self-abasement, he neither sent for Araunah to come to him nor sent another to deal with him, but went himself (*v.* 19), and, though it looked like a diminution of himself, he lost no honour by it. Araunah, when he saw him, went and *bowed himself to the ground before him, v.* 20. Great men will never be the less respected for their humility, but the more.

2. Araunah, when he understood his business (*v.* 21), generously offered him, not only the ground to build his altar on, but *oxen for sacrifices,* and other things that might be of use to him in the service (*v.* 22), and all this *gratis,* and a good prayer into the bargain: *The Lord thy God accept thee!* This he did, (1.) Because he had a generous spirit with a great estate. *He gave as a king* (*v.* 23); though an ordinary subject, he had the spirit of a prince. In the Hebrew it is, *He gave, even the king to the king,* whence it is supposed that Araunah had been king of the Jebusites in that place, or was descended from their royal family, though now a tributary to David. (2.) Because he highly esteemed David, though his conqueror, upon the score of his personal merits, and never thought he could do too much to oblige him. (3.) Because he had an affection for Israel, and earnestly desired that *the plague might be stayed;* and the honour of its being stayed at *his threshing-floor,* he would account a valuable consideration for all he now tendered to David.

3. David resolved to pay the full value of it, and did so, *v.* 24. Here were two generous souls well met. Araunah is very willing to give; but David is determined to buy, and for a good reason: he will not offer that to God which costs him nothing. He would not take advantage of the pious Jebusite's generosity. He thanked him, no doubt, for his kind offer, but paid him *fifty shekels of silver* for the floor and the oxen for the present service, and afterwards 600 shekels of gold for the ground adjoining, to build the temple on. Note, Those know not what religion is whose chief care it is to make it cheap and easy to themselves, and who are best pleased with that which costs them least pains or money. What have we our substance for but to honour God with it? and how can it be better bestowed?

III. The building of the altar, and the

offering of the proper sacrifices upon it (*v.* 25), burnt-offerings to the glory of God's justice in the execution that had been done, and peace-offerings to the glory of his mercy in the seasonable staying of the process. Hereupon God showed (it is supposed by fire from heaven consuming the sacrifices) that *he was entreated for the land,* and that it was in mercy that the plague was removed and in token of God's being reconciled both to prince and people. Christ is our altar, our sacrifice; in him alone we may expect to find favour with God, to escape his wrath, and the sword, the flaming sword, of the cherubim who *keep the way of the tree of life.*

AN EXPOSITION, WITH PRACTICAL OBSERVATIONS, OF THE FIRST BOOK OF KINGS.

MANY histories are books of kings and their reigns, to which the affairs of their kingdoms are reduced; this is a piece of honour that has commonly been paid to crowned heads. The holy Scripture is the history of the kingdom of God among men, under the several administrations of it; but there the King is one and his name one. The particular history now before us accounts for the affairs of the kingdoms of Judah and Israel, yet with special regard to the kingdom of God among them; for still it is a sacred history, much more instructive and not less entertaining than any of the histories of the kings of the earth, to which (those of them that are of any certainty) it is prior in time; for though there were kings in Edom before there was any king in Israel, Gen. xxxvi. 31 (foreigners, in that point of state, got the precedency), yet the history of the kings of Israel lives, and will live, in holy Writ, to the end of the world, whereas that of the kings of Edom is long since buried in oblivion; for the honour that comes from God is durable, while the honour of the world is like a mushroom, which comes up in a night and perishes in a night.—The Bible began with the story of patriarchs, and prophets, and judges, men whose converse with heaven was more immediate, the record of which strengthens our faith, but is not so easily accommodated to our case, now that we expect not visions, as the subsequent history of affairs like ours under the direction of common providence; and here also we find, though not many types and figures of the Messiah, yet great expectations of him; for not only prophets, but kings, desired to see the great mysteries of the gospel, Luke x. 24.—The two books of Samuel are introductions to the books of the Kings, as they relate the origin of the royal government in Saul and of the royal family in David. These two books give us an account of David's successor, Solomon, the division of his kingdom, and the succession of the several kings both of Judah and Israel, with an abstract of their history down to the captivity. And as from the book of Genesis we may collect excellent rules of economics, for the good governing of families, so from these books we may collect rules of politics, for the directing of public affairs. There is in these books special regard had to the house and lineage of David, from which Christ came. · Some of his sons trod in his steps, and others did not. The characters of the kings of Judah may be thus briefly given:—David the devout, Solomon the wise, Rehoboam the simple, Abijah the valiant, Asa the upright, Jehoshaphat the religious, Jehoram the wicked, Ahaziah the profane, Joash the backslider, Amaziah the rash, Uzziah the mighty, Jotham the peaceable, Ahaz the idolater, Hezekiah the reformer, Manasseh the penitent, Amon the obscure, Josiah the tender-hearted, Jehoahaz, Jehoiakim, Jehoiachin, and Zedekiah, all wicked, and such as brought ruin quickly on themselves and their kingdom. The number of the good and bad is nearly equal, but the reigns of the good were generally long and those of the bad short, the consideration of which will make the state of Israel not altogether so bad in this period as at first it seems. In this first book we have, I. The death of David, *ch.* i. and ii. II. The glorious reign of Solomon, and his building the temple (*ch.* iii.—x.), but the cloud his sun set under, *ch.* xi. III. The division of the kingdoms in Rehoboam, and his reign and Jeroboam's, *ch.* xii.—xiv. IV. The reigns of Abijah and Asa over Judah, Baasha and Omri over Israel, *ch.* xv. and xvi. V. Elijah's miracles, *ch.* xvii.—xix. VI. Ahab's success against Benhadad, his wickedness and fall, *ch.* xx.— xxii. And in all this history it appears that kings, though gods to us, are men to God, mortal and accountable.

CHAP. I.

In this chapter we have, I. David declining in his health, ver. 1—4. II. Adonijah aspiring to the kingdom, and treating his party, in order to it, ver. 5—10. III. Nathan and Bathsheba contriving to secure the succession to Solomon, and prevailing for an order from David for that purpose, ver. 11—31. IV. The anointing of Solomon accordingly, and the people's joy therein, ver. 32—40. V. The effectual stop this put to Adonijah's usurpation, and the dispersion of his party thereupon, ver. 41—49. VI. Solomon's dismission of Adonijah upon his good behaviour, ver. 50—53.

NOW king David was old *and* stricken in years; and they covered him with clothes, but he gat no heat. 2 Wherefore his servants said unto him, Let there be sought for my lord the king a young virgin: and let her stand before the king, and let her cherish him, and let her lie in thy bosom, that my lord the king may get heat. 3 So they sought for a fair damsel throughout all the coasts of Israel, and found Abishag a Shunammite, and brought her to the king. 4 And the damsel *was* very fair, and cherished the king, and ministered to him; but the king knew her not.

David, as recorded in the foregoing chapter, had, by the great mercy of God, escaped the sword of the destroying angel. But our deliverances from or through diseases and dangers are but reprieves; if the candle be not blown out, it will burn out of itself. We have David here sinking under the infirmities of old age, and brought by them to the gates of the grave. He that *cometh up out of the pit shall fall into the snare;* and, one way or other, *we must needs die.* 1. It would have troubled one to see David so infirm. He was old, and his natural heat so wasted that no clothes could keep him warm, *v.* 1. David had been a valiant active man and a man of business, and very vehement had the flame always been in his breast; and yet now his blood is chilled and stagnated, he is confined to his bed, and there can get no heat. He was now seventy years old. Many, at that age, are as lively and fit for business as ever: but David was now chastised for his former sins, especially that in the matter of Uriah, and felt from his former toils and the hardships he had gone through in his youth, which then he made nothing of, but was now the worse for. *Let not the strong man glory in his strength,* which may soon be weakened by sickness, or at last will be weakened by old age. Let young people *remember their Creator in the days of their youth,* before these evil days come. What our hand finds to do for God, and our souls, and our generation, let us do with all our might, because the night comes, the night of old age, in which no man can work; and, when our strength has gone, it will be a comfort to remember that we used it well. 2. It would have troubled one to see his physicians so weak and unskilful that they knew no other way of relieving him than by outward applications. No cordials, no spirits, but, (1.) *They covered him with clothes,* which, where there is any inward heat, will keep it in, and so increase it; but, where it is not, they have none to communicate, no, not royal clothing. Elihu makes it a difficulty to understand *how our garments are warm upon us* (Job xxxvii. 17); but, if God deny his blessing, men *clothe themselves, and there is none warm* (Hag. i. 6), David here was not. (2.) They foolishly prescribed nuptials to one that should rather have been preparing for his funeral (*v.* 2—4); but they knew what would gratify their own corruptions, and perhaps were too willing to gratify his, under colour of consulting his health. His prophets should have been consulted as well as his physicians in an affair of this nature. However, this might be excused then, when even good men ignorantly allowed themselves to have many wives. We now have not so learned of Christ, but are taught that one man must have but one wife (Matt. xix. 5), and further that *it is good for a man not to touch a woman,* 1 Cor. vii. 1. That Abishag was married to David before she lay with him, and was his secondary wife, appears from its being imputed as a great crime to Adonijah that he desired to marry her (*ch.* ii. 22) after his father's death.

5 Then Adonijah the son of Haggith exalted himself, saying, I will be king: and he prepared him chariots and horsemen, and fifty men to run before him. 6 And his father had not displeased him at any time in saying, Why hast thou done so? and he also *was a* very goodly *man;* and *his mother* bare him after Absalom. 7 And he conferred with Joab the son of Zeruiah, and with Abiathar the priest: and they following Adonijah helped *him.* 8 But Zadok the priest, and Benaiah the son of Jehoiada, and Nathan the prophet, and Shimei, and Rei, and the mighty men which *belonged* to David, were not with Adonijah. 9 And Adonijah slew sheep and oxen and fat cattle by the stone of Zoheleth, which *is* by En-rogel, and called all his brethren the king's sons, and all the men of Judah the king's servants: 10 But Nathan the prophet, and Benaiah, and the mighty men, and Solomon his brother, he called not.

David had much affliction in his children. Amnon and Absalom had both been his grief; the one his first-born, the other his third, 2. Sam. iii. 2, 3. His second, whom he had by Abigail, we will suppose he had comfort in; his fourth was Adonijah (2 Sam. iii. 4); he was one of those that were born in Hebron; we have heard nothing of him till now, and here we are told that he was a comely person, and that he was next in age, and (as it proved) next in temper, to Absalom, *v.* 6. And, further, that in his father's eyes he had been a jewel, but was now a thorn.

I. His father had made a fondling of him, *v.* 6. He had not displeased him at any time. It is not said that he never displeased his father; it is probable that he had done so frequently, and his father was secretly troubled at his misconduct and lamented it before God. But his father had not displeased him, by crossing him in his humours, denying him any thing he had a mind to, or by calling him to an account as to what he had done and where he had been, or by keeping him to his book or his business, or reproving him for what he saw or heard of that he did amiss; he never said to him, *Why hast thou done so?* because he saw it was uneasy to him, and he could not bear it without fretting. It was the son's fault that he was displeased at reproof and took it for an affront, whereby he lost the benefit of it; and it was the father's fault that, because he saw it displeased him, he did not reprove him; and now he justly smarted for indulging him. Those who honour their sons more than God, as those do who keep them not under good discipline, thereby forfeit the honour they might expect from their sons.

II. He, in return, made a fool of his father. Because he was old, and confined to his bed, he thought no notice was to be taken of him, and therefore *exalted himself*, and said, *I will be king*, *v.* 5. Children that are indulged learn to be proud and ambitious, which is the ruin of a great many young people. The way to keep them humble is to keep them under. Observe Adonijah's insolence, 1. He looked upon the days of mourning for his father to be at hand, and therefore he prepared to succeed him, though he knew that by the designation both of God and David Solomon was to be the man; for public notice had been given of it by David himself, and the succession settled, as it were by act of parliament, in pursuance of God's appointment, 1 Chron. xxii. 9; xxiii. 1. This entail Adonijah attempted by force to cut off, in contempt both of God and his father. Thus is the kingdom of Christ opposed, and there are those that say, "We will not have him to reign over us." 2. He looked upon his father as superannuated and good for nothing, and therefore he entered immediately upon the possession of the throne. He cannot wait till his father's head be laid low, but it must now be said, *Adonijah reigns* (*v.* 18), and, *God save king Adonijah*, *v.* 25. His father is not fit to govern, for he is old and past ruling; nor Solomon, for he is young, and not yet able to rule; and therefore Adonijah will take the government upon him. It argues a very base and wicked mind for children to insult over their parents because of the infirmities of their age. 3. In pursuance of this ambitious project, (1.) He got a great retinue (*v.* 5), *chariots and horsemen*, both for state and strength, to wait on him, and to fight for him. (2.) He made great interest with no less than Joab, the general of the army, and Abiathar the high priest, *v.* 7. That he should make his court to those who by their influence in church and camp were capable of doing him great service is not strange; but we may well wonder by what arts they could be drawn to follow him and help him. They were old men, who had been faithful to David in the most difficult and troublesome of his times, men of sense and experience, who, one would think, would not easily be wheedled. They could not propose any advantage to themselves by supporting Adonijah, for they were both at the top of their preferment and stood fast in it. They could not be ignorant of the entail of the crown upon Solomon, which it was not in their power to cut off, and therefore it was their interest to oblige him. But God, in this matter, left them to themselves, perhaps to correct them for some former misconduct with a scourge of their own making. We are told (*v.* 8) who those were that were of such approved fidelity to David that Adonijah had not the confidence so much as to propose his project to them—Zadok, Benaiah, and Nathan. A man that has given proofs of his resolute adherence to that which is good shall not be asked to do a bad thing. (3.) He prepared a great entertainment (*v.* 9) at En-rogel, not far from Jerusalem; his guests were the king's sons, and the king's servants, whom he feasted and caressed to bring them over to his party; but Solomon was not invited, either because he despised him or because he despaired of him, *v.* 10. Such as serve their own belly, and will be in the interest of those that will feast them what side soever they are of, are an easy prey to seducers, Rom. xvi. 18. Some think that Adonijah slew these sheep and oxen, even fat ones, for sacrifice, and that it was a religious feast he made, beginning his usurpation with a show of devotion, as Absalom under the colour of a vow (2 Sam. xv. 7), which he might do the more plausibly when he had the high priest himself on his side. It is a pity that any occasion should ever be given to say, *In nomine Domini incipit omne malum—In the name of the Lord begins all evil*, and that all religious exercises should be made to patronise all religious practices.

11 Wherefore Nathan spake unto Bath-sheba the mother of Solomon, saying, Hast thou not heard that Adonijah the son of Haggith doth reign, and David our lord knoweth

it not? 12 Now therefore come, let me, I pray thee give thee counsel, that thou mayest save thine own life, and the life of thy son Solomon. 13 Go and get thee in unto king David, and say unto him, Didst not thou my lord, O king, swear unto thine handmaid, saying, Assuredly Solomon thy son shall reign after me, and he shall sit upon my throne? why then doth Adonijah reign? 14 Behold, while thou yet talkest there with the king, I also will come in after thee, and confirm thy words. 15 And Bath-sheba went in unto the king into the chamber: and the king was very old; and Abishag the Shunammite ministered unto the king. 16 And Bath-sheba bowed, and did obeisance unto the king. And the king said, What wouldest thou? 17 And she said unto him, My lord, thou swarest by the LORD thy God unto thine handmaid, *saying*, Assuredly Solomon thy son shall reign after me, and he shall sit upon my throne. 18 And now, behold, Adonijah reigneth: and now, my lord the king, thou knowest *it* not: 19 And he hath slain oxen and fat cattle and sheep in abundance, and hath called all the sons of the king, and Abiathar the priest, and Joab the captain of the host: but Solomon thy servant hath he not called. 20 And thou, my lord, O king, the eyes of all Israel *are* upon thee, that thou shouldest tell them who shall sit on the throne of my lord the king after him. 21 Otherwise it shall come to pass, when my lord the king shall sleep with his fathers, that I and my son Solomon shall be counted offenders. 22 And, lo, while she yet talked with the king, Nathan the prophet also came in. 23 And they told the king, saying, Behold Nathan the prophet. And when he was come in before the king, he bowed himself before the king with his face to the ground. 24 And Nathan said, My lord, O king, hast thou said, Adonijah shall reign after me, and he shall sit upon my throne? 25 For he is gone down this day, and hath slain oxen and fat cattle and sheep in abundance, and hath called all the king's sons, and the captains of the host, and Abiathar the priest; and, behold, they eat and drink before him, and say, God save king Adonijah. 26 But me, *even* me thy servant, and Zadok the priest, and Benaiah the son of Jehoiada, and thy servant Solomon, hath he not called. 27 Is this thing done by my lord the king, and thou hast not showed *it* unto thy servant, who should sit on the throne of my lord the king after him? 28 Then king David answered and said, Call me Bath-sheba. And she came into the king's presence, and stood before the king. 29 And the king sware, and said, *As* the LORD liveth, that hath redeemed my soul out of all distress, 30 Even as I sware unto thee by the LORD God of Israel, saying, Assuredly Solomon thy son shall reign after me, and he shall sit upon my throne in my stead; even so will I certainly do this day. 31 Then Bath-sheba bowed with *her* face to the earth, and did reverence to the king, and said, Let my lord king David live for ever.

We have here the effectual endeavours that were used by Nathan and Bathsheba to obtain from David a ratification of Solomon's succession, for the crushing of Adonijah's usurpation. 1. David himself knew not what was doing. Disobedient children think that they are well enough off if they can but keep their good old parents ignorant of their bad courses; but a *bird of the air will carry the voice*. 2. Bathsheba lived retired, and knew nothing of it either, till Nathan informed her. Many get very comfortably through this world that know little how the world goes. 3. Solomon, it is likely, knew of it, but was as a deaf man that heard not. Though he had years, and wisdom above his years, yet we do not find that he stirred to oppose Adonijah, but quietly composed himself and left it to God and his friends to order the matter. Hence David, in his Psalm for Solomon, observes that while men, in pursuit of the world, in vain *rise early and sit up late, God giveth his beloved* (his *Jedidiahs*) *sleep*, in giving them to be easy, and to gain their point without agitation, Ps. cxxvii. 1, 2. How then is the design brought about?

I. Nathan the prophet alarms Bathsheba by acquainting her with the case, and puts her in a way to get an order from the king for the confirming of Solomon's title. He was concerned, because he knew God's mind, and David's and Israel's interest; it was by him that God had named Solomon *Jedidiah* (2 Sam. xii. 25), and therefore he could not sit still and see the throne usurped, which he knew was Solomon's right by the will of him from whom promotion cometh. When crowns were disposed of by immediate direction from heaven, no marvel that prophets were so much interested and employed in that matter; but now that common providence rules the affairs of the kingdom of men (Dan. iv. 32) the subordinate agency must be left to common persons, and let not prophets intermeddle in them, but keep to the affairs of the kingdom of God among men. Nathan applied to Bathsheba, as one that had the greatest concern for Solomon, and could have the freest access to David. He informed her of Adonijah's attempt (*v.* 11), and that it was not with David's consent or knowledge. He suggested to her that not only Solomon was in danger of losing the crown, but that he and she too were in danger of losing their lives if Adonijah prevailed. A humble spirit may be indifferent to a crown, and may be content, notwithstanding the prospect of it, to sit down short of the possession of it. But the law of self-preservation, and the sixth commandment, obliges us to use all possible endeavours to secure our own life and the life of others. Now, says Nathan, let me *give thee counsel how to save thy own life and the life of thy son, v.* 12. Such as this is the counsel that Christ's ministers give us in his name, to give all diligence, not only *that no man take our crown* (Rev. iii. 11), but that we *save our lives,* even the lives of our souls. He directs her (*v.* 13) to go to the king, to remind him of his word and oath, that Solomon should be his successor; and to ask him in the most humble manner, *Why doth Adonijah reign?* He thought David was not so cold but this would warm him. Conscience, as well as a sense of honour, would put life into him upon such an occasion as this; and he promised (*v.* 14) that, while she was reasoning with the king upon this matter, he would come in and second her, as if he came accidentally, which perhaps the king might look upon as a special providence (and he was one that took notice of such evidences, 1 Sam. xxv. 32, 33), or, at least, it would help to awaken him so much the more.

II. Bathsheba, according to Nathan's advice and direction, loses no time, but immediately makes her application to the king, on the same errand on which Esther came to king Ahasuerus, to intercede for her life. She needed not wait for a call as Esther did, she knew she should be welcome at any time; but it is remarked that when she visited the king Abishag was ministering to him (*v.* 15), and Bathsheba took no displeasure either at him or her for it, also that she *bowed and did obeisance to the king* (*v.* 16), in token of her respect to him both as her prince and as her husband; such a genuine daughter was she of Sarah, who obeyed Abraham, calling him *lord.* Those that would find favour with superiors must show them reverence, and be dutiful to those whom they expect to be kind to them. Her address to the king, on this occasion, is very discreet. 1. She reminded him of his promise made to her, and confirmed with a solemn oath, that Solomon should succeed him, *v.* 17. She knew how fast this would hold such a conscientious man as David was. 2. She informed him of Adonijah's attempt, which he was ignorant of (*v.* 18): "Adonijah reigns, in competition with thee for the present and in contradiction to thy promise for the future. The fault is not thine, for thou knewest it not; but now that thou knowest it thou wilt, in pursuance of thy promise, take care to suppress this usurpation." She told him who were Adonijah's guests, and who were in his interest, and added, but "*Solomon thy servant has he not called,* which plainly shows he looks upon him as his rival, and aims to undermine him, *v.* 19. It is not an oversight, but a contempt of the act of settlement, that Solomon is neglected." 3. She pleads that it is very much in his power to obviate this mischief (*v.* 20): *The eyes of all Israel are upon thee,* not only as a *king,* for we cannot suppose it the prerogative of any prince to bequeath his subjects by will (as if they were his goods and chattels) to whom he pleases, but as a *prophet.* All Israel knew that David was not only himself *the anointed of the God of Jacob,* but that the *Spirit of the Lord spoke by him* (2 Sam. xxiii. 1, 2), and therefore waiting for and depending upon a divine designation, in a matter of such importance, David's word would be an oracle and a law to them; this therefore (says Bathsheba) they expect, and it will end the controversy and effectually quash all Adonijah's pretensions. *A divine sentence is in the lips of the king.* Note, Whatever power, interest, or influence, men have, they ought to improve it to the utmost for the preserving and advancing of the kingdom of the Messiah, of which Solomon's kingdom was a type. 4. She suggested the imminent peril which she and her son would be in if this matter was not settled in David's life-time, *v.* 21. "If Adonijah prevail, as he is likely to do (having Joab the general and Abiathar the priest on his side) unless speedily suppressed, Solomon and all his friends will be looked upon as traitors and dealt with accordingly." Usurpers are most cruel. If Adonijah had got into the throne, he would not have dealt so fairly with Solomon as Solomon did with him. Those hazard every thing who stand in the way of such as against right force their entrance.

III. Nathan the prophet, according to his promise, seasonably stepped in, and seconded her, while she was speaking, before the king had given his answer, lest, if he had heard Bathsheba's representation only, his answer should be dilatory and only that he would consider of it: but out of the mouth of two witnesses, two such witnesses, the word would be established, and he would immediately give positive orders. The king is told that Nathan the prophet has come, and he is sure to be always welcome to the king, especially when either he is not well or has any great affair upon his thoughts; for, in either case, a prophet will be, in a particular manner, serviceable to him. Nathan knows he must render honour to whom honour is due, and therefore pays the king the same respect now that he finds him sick in bed as he would have done if he had found him in his throne: He *bowed himself with his face to the ground, v.* 23. He deals a little more plainly with the king than Bathsheba had done. In this his character would support him, and the present languor of the king's spirits made it necessary that they should be roused. 1. He makes the same representation of Adonijah's attempt as Bathsheba had made (*v.* 25, 26), adding that his party had already got to such a height of assurance as to shout, *God save king Adonijah,* as if king David were already dead, taking notice also that they had not invited him to their feast (*Me thy servant has he not called),* thereby intimating that they resolved not to consult either God or David in the matter, for Nathan was *secretioribus consiliis—intimately acquainted with the mind of both.* 2. He makes David sensible how much he was concerned to clear himself from having a hand in it: *Hast thou said, Adonijah shall reign after me?* (*v.* 24), and again (*v.* 27), "*Is this thing done by my lord the king?* If it be, he is not so faithful either to God's word or to his own as we all took him to be; if it be not, it is high time that we witness against the usurpation, and declare Solomon his successor. If it be, why is not Nathan made acquainted with it, who is not only, in general, the king's confidant, but is particularly concerned in this matter, having been employed to notify to David the mind of God concerning the succession; but, if my lord the king knows nothing of the matter (as certainly he does not), what daring insolence are Adonijah and his party guilty of!" Thus he endeavoured to incense David against them, that he might act the more vigorously for the support of Solomon's interest. Note, Good men would do their duty if they were reminded of it, and put upon it, and told what occasion there is for them to appear; and those who thus are their remembrancers do them a real kindness, as Nathan here did to David.

IV. David, hereupon, made a solemn declaration of his firm adherence to his former resolution, that Solomon should be his successor. Bathsheba is called in (*v.* 28), and to her, as acting for and on behalf of her son, the king gives these fresh assurances. 1. He repeats his former promise and oath, owns that he had *sworn unto her by the Lord God of Israel that Solomon should reign after him, v.* 30. Though he is old, and his memory begins to fail him, yet he remembers this. Note, An oath is so sacred a thing that the obligations of it cannot be broken, and so solemn a thing that the impressions of it, one would think, cannot be forgotten. 2. He ratifies it with another, because the occasion called for it: *As the Lord liveth, that hath redeemed my soul out of all distress, even so will I certainly do this day,* without dispute, without delay. His form of swearing seems to be what he commonly used on solemn occasions, for we find it, 2 Sam. iv. 9. And it carries in it a grateful acknowledgment of the goodness of God to him, in bringing him safely through the many difficulties and hardships which had lain in his way, and which he now makes mention of to the glory of God (as Jacob, when he lay a dying, Gen. xlviii. 16), thus setting to his seal, from his own experience, that that was true which the Spirit of the Lord spoke by him. Ps. xxxiv. 22, *The Lord redeemeth the soul of his servants.* Dying saints ought to be witnesses for God, and speak of him as they have found. Perhaps he speaks thus, on this occasion, for the encouragement of his son and successor to trust in God in the distresses he also might meet with.

V. Bathsheba receives these assurances (*v.* 31), 1. With great complaisance to the king's person; she did reverence to him while Adonijah and his party affronted him. 2. With hearty good wishes for the king's health: *Let him live.* So far was she from thinking that he lived too long that she prayed he might live for ever, if it were possible, to adorn the crown he wore and to be a blessing to his people. We should earnestly desire the prolonging of useful lives, however it may be the postponing of any advantages of our own.

32 And king David said, Call me Zadok the priest, and Nathan the prophet, and Benaiah the son of Jehoiada. And they came before the king. 33 The king also said unto them, Take with you the servants of your lord, and cause Solomon my son to ride upon mine own mule, and bring him down to Gihon: 34 And let Zadok the priest and Nathan the prophet anoint him there king over Israel: and blow ye with the trumpet, and say, God save king Solomon. 35 Then ye shall come up after him, that he may come and sit upon my throne; for he shall be king in my stead: and I have appointed him to be ruler

over Israel and over Judah. 36 And Benaiah the son of Jehoiada answered the king, and said, Amen: the LORD God of my lord the king say so *too.* 37 As the LORD hath been with my lord the king, even so be he with Solomon, and make his throne greater than the throne of my lord king David. 38 So Zadok the priest, and Nathan the prophet, and Benaiah the son of Jehoiada, and the Cherethites, and the Pelethites, went down, and caused Solomon to ride upon king David's mule, and brought him to Gihon. 39 And Zadok the priest took a horn of oil out of the tabernacle, and anointed Solomon. And they blew the trumpet; and all the people said, God save king Solomon. 40 And all the people came up after him, and the people piped with pipes, and rejoiced with great joy, so that the earth rent with the sound of them.

We have here the effectual care David took both to secure Solomon's right and to preserve the public peace, by crushing Adonijah's project in the bud. Observe,

I. The express orders he gave for the proclaiming of Solomon. The persons he entrusted with this great affair were Zadok, Nathan, and Benaiah, men of power and interest whom David had always reposed a confidence in and found faithful to him, and whom Adonijah had passed by in his invitation, *v.* 10. David orders them forthwith, with all possible solemnity, to proclaim Solomon. They must take with them *the servants of their lord,* the life-guards, and all the servants of the household. They must set Solomon on the mule the king used to ride, for he kept not such stables of horses as his son afterwards did. He appoints them whither to go (*v.* 33 and *v.* 34, 35), and what to do. 1. Zadok and Nathan, the two ecclesiastical persons, must, in God's name, anoint him king; for though he was not the first of his family, as Saul and David were, yet he was a younger son, was made king by divine appointment, and his title was contested, which made it necessary that hereby it should be settled. This unction was typical of the designation and qualification of the Messiah, or Christ, the anointed one, on whom the Spirit, that oil of gladness, was poured without measure, Heb. i. 9; Ps. lxxxix. 20. And all real Christians, being *heirs of the kingdom* (Jam. ii. 5), do from him *receive the anointing,* 1 John ii. 27. 2. The great officers, civil and military, are ordered to give public notice of this, and to express the public joy upon this occasion by sound of trumpet, by which the law of Moses directed the gracing of great solemnities; to this must be added the acclamations of the people: "*Let king Solomon live,* let him prosper, let his kingdom be established and perpetuated, and let him long continue in the enjoyment of it;" so it had been promised concerning him. Ps. lxxii. 15, *He shall live.* 3. They must then bring him in state to the city of David, and he must sit upon the throne of his father, as his substitute now, or viceroy, to despatch public business during his weakness and be his successor after his death: *He shall be king in my stead.* It would be a great satisfaction to David himself, and to all parties concerned, to have this done immediately, that upon the demise of the king there might be no dispute, or agitation, in the public affairs. David was far from grudging his successor the honour of appearing such in his life-time, and yet perhaps was so taken up with his devotions on his sick-bed that, if he had not been put in mind of it by others, this great good work, which was so necessary to the public repose, would have been left undone.

II. The great satisfaction which Benaiah, in the name of the rest, professed in these orders. The king said, "Solomon shall reign for me, and reign after me." "Amen" (says Benaiah heartily); "as the king says, so say we; we are entirely satisfied in the nomination, and concur in the choice; we give our vote for Solomon, *nemine contradicente—unanimously,* and since we can bring nothing to pass, much less establish it, without the concurrence of a propitious providence, *The Lord God of my lord the king say so too!*" *v.* 36. This is the language of his faith in that promise of God on which Solomon's government was founded. If we say as God says in his word, we may hope that he will say as we say by his providence. To this he adds a prayer for Solomon (*v.* 37), that God would be with him as he had been with David, and make his throne greater. He knew David was not one of those that envy their children's greatness, and that therefore he would not be disquieted at this prayer, nor take it as an affront, but would heartily say *Amen* to it. The wisest and best man in the world desires his children may be wiser and better than he, for he himself desires to be wiser and better than he is; and wisdom and goodness are true greatness.

III. The immediate execution of these orders, *v.* 38—40. No time was lost, but Solomon was brought in state to the place appointed, and there Zadok (who, though he was not as yet high priest, was, we may suppose, the suffragan, the Jews called him the *sagan,* or second priest) anointed him by the direction of Nathan the prophet and David the king, *v.* 39. In the tabernacle, where the ark was now lodged, was kept, among other sacred things, the holy oil for many religious services thence Zadok took a *horn of oil,* which denotes both power and plenty, and therewith anointed Solomon. We do not find that Abiathar pretended to anoint Adonijah: he was made king by a feast, not by an unction. Whom God calls, he will qualify, which was signified by the anointing; usurpers had it not. *Christ* signifies *anointed,* and he is the king whom God hath *set upon his holy hill of Sion,* according to decree, Ps. ii. 6, 7. Christians also are *made to our God* (and *by* him) *kings,* and they have an *unction from the Holy One,* 1 John ii. 20. The people, hereupon, express their great joy and satisfaction in the elevation of Solomon, surround him with their Hosannas—*God save king Solomon,* and attend him with their music and shouts of joy, *v.* 40. Hereby they declared their concurrence in the choice, and that he was not forced upon them, but cheerfully accepted by them. The power of a prince can be little satisfaction to himself, unless he knows it to be a satisfaction to his people. Every Israelite indeed rejoices in the exaltation of the Son of David.

41 And Adonijah and all the guests that *were* with him heard *it* as they had made an end of eating. And when Joab heard the sound of the trumpet, he said, Wherefore *is this* noise of the city being in an uproar? 42 And while he yet spake, behold, Jonathan the son of Abiathar the priest came: and Adonijah said unto him, Come in; for thou *art* a valiant man, and bringest good tidings. 43 And Jonathan answered and said to Adonijah, Verily our lord king David hath made Solomon king. 44 And the king hath sent with him Zadok the priest, and Nathan the prophet, and Benaiah the son of Jehoiada, and the Cherethites, and the Pelethites, and they have caused him to ride upon the king's mule: 45 And Zadok the priest and Nathan the prophet have anointed him king in Gihon: and they are come up from thence rejoicing, so that the city rang again. This *is* the noise that ye have heard. 46 And also Solomon sitteth on the throne of the kingdom. 47 And moreover the king's servants came to bless our lord king David, saying, God make the name of Solomon better than thy name, and make his throne greater than thy throne. And the king bowed himself upon the bed. 48 And also thus said the king, Blessed *be* the LORD God of Israel, which hath given *one* to sit on my throne this day, mine eyes even seeing *it.* 49 And all the guests that *were* with Adonijah were afraid, and rose up, and went every man his way. 50 And Adonijah feared because of Solomon, and arose, and went, and caught hold on the horns of the altar. 51 And it was told Solomon, saying, Behold, Adonijah feareth king Solomon; for, lo, he hath caught hold on the hornsof the altar, saying, Let king Solomon swear unto me to day that he will not slay his servant with the sword. 52 And Solomon said, If he will show himself a worthy man, there shall not a hair of him fall to the earth: but if wickedness shall be found in him, he shall die. 53 So king Solomon sent, and they brought him down from the altar. And he came and bowed himself to king Solomon: and Solomon said unto him, Go to thine house.

We have here,

I. The tidings of Solomon's inauguration brought to Adonijah and his party, in the midst of their jollity: *They had made an end of eating,* and, it should seem, it was a great while before they made an end, for all the affair of Solomon's anointing was ordered and finished while they were at dinner, glutting themselves. Thus those who *serve not our Lord Christ,* but oppose him, are commonly such as *serve their own belly* (Rom. xvi. 18) and make *a god of it,* Phil. iii. 19. Their long feast intimates likewise that they were very secure and confident of their interest, else they would not have lost so much time. The old world and Sodom were *eating and drinking,* secure and sensual, when their destruction came, Luke xvii. 26, &c. When *they made an end of eating,* and were preparing themselves to proclaim their king, and bring him in triumph into the city, they *heard the sound of the trumpet* (*v.* 41), and a *dreadful sound it was in their ears,* Job xv. 21. Joab was an old man, and was alarmed at it, apprehending the city to be in an uproar; but Adonijah was very confident that the messenger, being a *worthy man, brought good tidings, v.* 42. Usurpers flatter themselves with the hopes of success, and those are commonly least timorous whose condition is most dangerous. But how can those who do evil deeds expect to have good tidings? No, the worthiest man will bring them the worst news, as the priest's son did here to Adonijah, *v.* 43. "*Verily,* the best tidings I have to bring you is that *Solomon is made king,* so that your pretensions are all quashed." He relates to them very particularly, 1. With what great solemnity *Solomon* was *made king* (*v.* 44, 45), and that he was now *sitting on the throne of the kingdom, v.* 46. Adonijah thought to have stepped into the throne before him, but Solomon was too quick for him. 2. With what general satisfaction Solomon was made king, so that that which was done was not likely to be undone again. (1.) The people were pleased, witness their joyful acclamations, *v.* 45. (2.) The courtiers were pleased: *The king's servants* attended him with an address of congratulation upon this occasion, *v.* 47. We have here the heads of their address: They *blessed king David,* applauded his prudent care for the public welfare, acknowledged their happiness under his government, and prayed heartily for his recovery. They also prayed for Solomon, that God would make his name better than his father's, which it might well be when he had his father's foundation to build upon. A child, on a giant's shoulders, is higher than the giant himself. (3.) The king himself was pleased: He *bowed himself upon the bed,* not only to signify his acceptance of his servants' address, but to offer up his own address to God (*v.* 48): "*Blessed be the Lord God of Israel,* who, as Israel's God, for Israel's good, has brought this matter to such a happy issue, *my eyes even seeing it.*" Note, It is a great satisfaction to good men, when they are going out of the world, to see the affairs of their families in a good posture, their children rising up in their stead to serve God and their generation, and especially to see peace upon Israel and the establishment of it.

II. The effectual crush which this gave to Adonijah's attempt. It spoiled the sport of his party, dispersed the company, and obliged every man to shift for his own safety. *The triumphing of the wicked is short.* They were building a castle in the air, which, having no foundation, would soon fall and crush them. They were afraid of being taken in the fact, while they were together hatching their treason, and therefore each one made the best of his way.

III. The terror Adonijah himself was in, and the course he took to secure himself. He was now as much depressed as he had been elevated, *v.* 42, 50. He had despised Solomon as not worthy to be his guest (*v.* 10), but now he dreads him as his judge: He *feared because of Solomon.* Thus those who oppose Christ and his kingdom will shortly be made to tremble before him, and call in vain to rocks and mountains to shelter them from his wrath. He *took hold on the horns of the altar,* which was always looked upon as a sanctuary, or place of refuge (Exod. xxi. 14), intimating hereby that he durst not stand a trial, but threw himself upon the mercy of his prince, in suing for which he relied upon no other plea than the mercy of God, which was manifested in the institution and acceptance of the sacrifices that were offered on that altar and the remission of sin thereupon. Perhaps Adonijah had formerly slighted the service of the altar, yet now he courts the protection of it. Many who in the day of their security neglect the great salvation, under the arrests of the terrors of the Lord would gladly be beholden to Christ and his merit, and, when it is too late, will *catch hold of the horns of the altar.*

IV. His humble address to Solomon for mercy. By those who brought Solomon tidings where he was, he sent a request for his life (*v.* 51): *Let king Solomon swear to me that he will not slay his servant.* He owns Solomon for his prince, and himself his servant, dares not justify himself, but *makes supplication to his judge.* It was a great change with him. He that in the morning was grasping at a crown is before night begging for his life. Then Adonijah reigned, now Adonijah trembles, and cannot think himself safe unless Solomon promise, with an oath, not to put him to death.

V. The orders Solomon gave concerning him. He discharged him upon his good behaviour, *v.* 52, 53. He considered that Adonijah was his brother, and that it was the first offence. Perhaps, being so soon made sensible of his error and then not persisting in his rebellion, he might prove not only a peaceable, but a serviceable subject, and therefore, if he will conduct himself well for the future, what is past shall be pardoned: but if he be found disaffected, turbulent, and aspiring, this offence shall be remembered against him, he shall be called up upon his former conviction (as our law speaks), and execution shall be awarded against him. Thus the Son of David receives those to mercy that have been rebellious: if they will return to their allegiance, and be faithful to their Sovereign, their former crimes shall not be mentioned against them; but, if still they continue in the interests of the world and the flesh, this will be their ruin. Adonijah is sent for, and told upon what terms he stands, which he signifies his grateful submission to, and then is told to go to his house and live retired there. Solomon not only gave him his life, but his estate, thus *establishing his throne by mercy.*

CHAP. II.

In this chapter we have David setting and Solomon at the same time rising. I. The conclusion of David's reign with his life. 1. The charge he gives to Solomon upon his death-bed, in general, to serve God (ver. 1—4), in particular, concerning Joab, Barzillai, and Shimei, ver. 5—9. 2. His death and burial, and the years of his reign, ver. 10, 11. II. The beginning of Solomon's reign, ver. 12. Though he was to be a prince of peace, he began his reign with some remarkable acts of justice, 1. Upon Adonijah, whom he put to death for his aspiring pretensions, ver. 13—25. 2. Upon Abiathar, whom he deposed from the high priesthood for siding with Adonijah, ver. 26, 27. 3. Upon Joab, whom he put to death for his late treasons and former murders, ver. 28—35. 4. Upon Shimei, whom, for cursing David, he confined to Jerusalem (ver. 36—38), and three years after, for transgressing the rules, put to death, ver. 39—46.

NOW the days of David drew nigh that he should die; and he charged Solomon his son, saying,

2 I go the way of all the earth: be thou strong therefore, and show thyself a man; 3 And keep the charge of the LORD thy God, to walk in his ways, to keep his statutes, and his commandments, and his judgments, and his testimonies, as it is written in the law of Moses, that thou mayest prosper in all that thou doest, and whithersoever thou turnest thyself: 4 That the LORD may continue his word which he spake concerning me, saying, If thy children take heed to their way, to walk before me in truth with all their heart and with all their soul, there shall not fail thee (said he) a man on the throne of Israel. 5 Moreover thou knowest also what Joab the son of Zeruiah did to me, *and* what he did to the two captains of the hosts of Israel, unto Abner the son of Ner, and unto Amasa the son of Jether, whom he slew, and shed the blood of war in peace, and put the blood of war upon his girdle that *was* about his loins, and in his shoes that *were* on his feet. 6 Do therefore according to thy wisdom, and let not his hoar head go down to the grave in peace. 7 But show kindness unto the sons of Barzillai the Gileadite, and let them be of those that eat at thy table: for so they came to me when I fled because of Absalom thy brother. 8 And, behold, *thou hast* with thee Shimei the son of Gera, a Benjamite of Bahurim, which cursed me with a grievous curse in the day when I went to Mahanaim: but he came down to meet me at Jordan, and I sware to him by the LORD, saying, I will not put thee to death with the sword. 9 Now therefore hold him not guiltless: for thou *art* a wise man, and knowest what thou oughtest to do unto him; but his hoar head bring thou down to the grave with blood. 10 So David slept with his fathers, and was buried in the city of David. 11 And the days that David reigned over Israel *were* forty years: seven years reigned he in Hebron, and thirty and three years reigned he in Jerusalem.

David, that great and good man, is here a dying man (*v.* 1), and a dead man, *v.* 10. It is well there is another life after this, for death stains all the glory of this, and lays it in the dust. We have here,

I. The charge and instructions which David, when he was dying, gave to Solomon, his son and declared successor. He feels himself declining, and is not backward to own it, nor afraid to hear or speak of dying: *I go the way of all the earth, v.* 2. Heb. *I am walking in it.* Note, Death is a way; not only a period of this life, but a passage to a better. It is *the way of all the earth,* of all mankind who dwell on earth, and are themselves earth, and therefore must return to their earth. Even the sons and heirs of heaven must *go the way of all the earth,* they must needs die; but they walk with pleasure in this way, *through the valley of the shadow of death,* Ps. xxiii. 4. Prophets, and even kings, must go this way to brighter light and honour than prophecy or sovereignty. David is going this way, and therefore gives Solomon directions what to do.

1. He charges him, in general, to keep God's commandments and to make conscience of his duty, *v.* 2—4. He prescribes to him, (1.) A good rule to act by—the divine will: "Govern thyself by that." David's charge to him is to *keep the charge of the Lord* his *God.* The authority of a dying father is much, but nothing to that of a living God. There are great trusts which we are charged with by the Lord our God—let us keep them carefully, as those that must give account; and excellent statutes, which we must be ruled by—let us also keep them. The written word is our rule. Solomon must himself do *as was written in the law of Moses.* (2.) A good spirit to act with: *Be strong and show thyself a man,* though in years but a child. Those that would keep the charge of the Lord their God must put on resolution. (3.) Good reasons for all this. This would effectually conduce, [1.] To the prosperity of his kingdom. It is the way to *prosper in all thou doest,* and to succeed with honour and satisfaction in every undertaking. [2.] To the perpetuity of it: *That the Lord may continue* and so confirm *his word which he spoke concerning me.* Those that rightly value the treasure of the promise, that sacred *depositum,* cannot but be solicitous to preserve the entail of it, and very desirous that those who come after them may do nothing to cut it off. Let each, in his own age, successively, keep God's charge, and then God will be sure to continue his word. We never let fall the promise till we let fall the precept. God had promised David that the Messiah should come from his loins, and that promise was absolute: but the promise that there should not fail him *a man on the throne of Israel* was conditional—if his seed behave themselves as they should. If Solomon, in his day, fulfil the condition, he does his part towards the perpetuating of the pro-

mise. The condition is that he walk before God in all his institutions, in sincerity, with zeal and resolution; and, in order hereunto, that he *take heed to his way*. In order to our constancy in religion, nothing is more necessary than caution and circumspection.

2. He gives him directions concerning some particular persons, what to do with them, that he might make up his deficiencies in justice to some and kindness to others. (1.) Concerning Joab, *v.* 5. David was now conscious to himself that he had not done well to spare him, when he had made himself once and again obnoxious to the law, by the murder of Abner first and afterwards of Amasa, both of them great men, *captains of the hosts of Israel*. He slew them treacherously *(shed the blood of war in peace)*, and injuriously to David: *Thou knowest what* he *did to me* therein. The murder of a subject is a wrong to the prince, it is a loss to him, and is against the peace of our sovereign lord the king. These murders were particularly against David, reflecting upon his reputation, he being, at that time, in treaty with the victims, and hazarded his interest, which they were very capable of serving. Magistrates are the avengers of the blood of those they have the charge of. It aggravated Joab's crime that he was neither ashamed of the sin nor afraid of the punishment, but daringly wore the girdle and shoes that were stained with innocent blood, in defiance of the justice both of God and the king. David refers him to Solomon's wisdom (*v.* 6), with an intimation that he left him to his justice. Say not, "He has a hoary head; it is a pity it should be cut off, for it will shortly fall of itself." No, let it not *go down to the grave in peace*. Though he has been long reprieved, he shall be reckoned with at last; time does not wear out the guilt of any sin, particularly that of murder. (2.) Concerning Barzillai's family, to whom he orders him to be kind for Barzillai's sake, who, we may suppose, by this time, was dead, *v.* 7. When David, upon his death-bed, was remembering the injuries that had been done, he could not forget the kindnesses that had been shown, but leaves it as a charge upon his son to return them. Note, The kindnesses we have received from our friends must not be buried either in their graves or ours, but our children must return them to theirs. Hence, perhaps, Solomon fetched that rule (Prov. xxvii. 10), *Thy own friend, and thy father's friend, forsake not*. Paul prays for the house of Onesiphorus, who had often refreshed him. (3.) Concerning Shimei, *v.* 8, 9. [1.] His crime is remembered: *He cursed me with a grievous curse;* the more grievous because he insulted him when he was in misery and poured vinegar into his wounds. The Jews say that one thing which made this a grievous curse was that, besides all that is mentioned (2 Sam. xvi.), Shimei upbraided him with his descent from Ruth the Moabitess. [2.] His pardon is not forgotten. David owned he had sworn to him that he would not himself put him to death, because he seasonably submitted, and cried *Peccavi—I have sinned*, and he was not willing, especially at that juncture, to use the sword of public justice for the avenging of wrongs done to himself. But, [3.] His case, as it now stands, is left with Solomon, as one that knew what was fit to be done and would do as he found occasion. David intimates to him that his pardon was not designed to be perpetual, but only a reprieve for David's life: "*Hold him not guiltless;* do not think him any true friend to thee or thy government, nor fit to be trusted. He has no less malice than he had then, though he has more sense to conceal it. He is still a debtor to the public justice for what he did then; and, though I promised him that I would not put him to death, I never promised that my successor should not. His turbulent spirit will soon give thee an occasion, which thou shouldst not fail to take, for the bringing of his *hoary head to the grave with blood*." This proceeded not from personal revenge, but a prudent zeal for the honour of the government and the covenant God had made with his family, the contempt of which ought not to go unpunished. Even a hoary head, if a guilty and forfeited head, ought not to be any man's protection from justice. *The sinner, being a hundred years old, shall be accursed*, Isa. lxv. 20.

II. David's death and burial (*v.* 10): He *was buried in the city of David*, not in the burying place of his father, as Saul was, but in his own city, which he was the founder of. There were set the thrones, and there the tombs, of the house of David. Now *David, after he had served his own generation, by the will of God, fell asleep, and was laid to his fathers, and saw corruption*, Acts xiii. 36, and see Acts ii. 29. His epitaph may be taken from 2 Sam. xxiii. 1. Here lies *David the son of Jesse, the man who was raised up on high, the anointed of the God of Jacob, and the sweet psalmist of Israel*, adding his own words (Ps. xvi. 9), *My flesh also shall rest in hope*. Josephus says that, besides the usual magnificence with which his son Solomon buried him, he put into his sepulchre a vast deal of money; and that 1300 years after (so he reckons) it was opened by Hircanus the high priest, in the time of Antiochus, and 3000 talents were taken out for the public service. The years of his reign are here computed (*v.* 11) to be forty years; the odd six months which he reigned above seven years in Hebron are not reckoned, but the even sum only.

12 Then sat Solomon upon the throne of David his father; and his kingdom was established greatly. 13 And Adonijah the son of Haggith came to Bath-sheba the mother of

Solomon. And she said, Comest thou peaceably? And he said, Peaceably. 14 He said moreover, I have somewhat to say unto thee. And she said, Say on. 15 And he said, Thou knowest that the kingdom was mine, and *that* all Israel set their faces on me, that I should reign: howbeit the kingdom is turned about, and is become my brother's: for it was his from the LORD. 16 And now I ask one petition of thee, deny me not. And she said unto him, Say on. 17 And he said, Speak, I pray thee, unto Solomon the king, (for he will not say thee nay,) that he give me Abishag the Shunammite to wife. 18 And Bath-sheba said, Well; I will speak for thee unto the king. 19 Bath-sheba therefore went unto king Solomon, to speak unto him for Adonijah. And the king rose up to meet her, and bowed himself unto her, and sat down on his throne, and caused a seat to be set for the king's mother; and she sat on his right hand. 20 Then she said, I desire one small petition of thee: *I pray thee,* say me not nay. And the king said unto her, Ask on, my mother: for I will not say thee nay. 21 And she said, Let Abishag the Shunammite be given to Adonijah thy brother to wife. 22 And king Solomon answered and said unto his mother, And why dost thou ask Abishag the Shunammite for Adonijah? ask for him the kingdom also; for he *is* mine elder brother; even for him, and for Abiathar the priest, and for Joab the son of Zeruiah. 23 Then king Solomon sware by the LORD, saying, God do so to me, and more also, if Adonijah have not spoken this word against his own life. 24 Now therefore, *as* the LORD liveth, which hath established me, and set me on the throne of David my father, and who hath made me a house, as he promised, Adonijah shall be put to death this day. 25 And king Solomon sent by the hand of Benaiah the son of Jehoiada; and he fell upon him that he died.

Here is, I. Solomon's accession to the throne, *v.* 12. He came to it much more easily and peaceably than David did, and much sooner saw his government established. It is happy for a kingdom when the end of one good reign is the beginning of another, as it was here.

II. His just and necessary removal of Adonijah his rival, in order to the establishment of his throne. Adonijah had made some bold pretensions to the crown, but was soon obliged to let them fall and throw himself upon Solomon's mercy, who dismissed him upon his good behaviour, and, had he been easy, he might have been safe. But here we have him betraying himself into the hands of Solomon's justice, and falling by it, the righteous God leaving him to himself, that he might be punished for his former treason and that Solomon's throne might be established. Many thus ruin themselves, because they know not when they are well off, or well done to; and sinners, by presuming on God's patience, treasure up wrath to themselves. Now observe,

1. Adonijah's treasonable project, which was to marry Abishag, David's concubine, not because he was in love with her, but because, by her, he hoped to renew his claim to the crown, which might stand him in stead, or because it was then looked upon as a branch of the government to have *the wives of the predecessor,* 2 Sam. xii. 8. Absalom thought his pretensions much supported by lying with his father's concubines. Adonijah flatters himself that if he may succeed him in his bed, especially with the best of his wives, he may by that means step up to succeed him in his throne. Restless and turbulent spirits reach high. It was but a small game to play at, as it should seem, yet he hoped to make it an after-game for the kingdom, and now to gain that by a wife which he could not gain by force.

2. The means he used to compass this. He durst not make suit to Abishag immediately (he knew she was at Solomon's disposal, and he would justly resent it if his consent were not first obtained, as even Ish-bosheth did, in a like case, 2 Sam. iii. 7), nor durst he himself apply immediately to Solomon, knowing that he lay under his displeasure; but he engaged Bathsheba to be his friend in this matter, who would be forward to believe it a matter of love, and not apt to suspect it a matter of policy. Bathsheba was surprised to see Adonijah in her apartment, and asked him if he did not come with a design to do her a mischief, because she had been instrumental to crush his late attempt. "No," says he, "I come *peaceably* (*v.* 13), and to beg a favour" (*v.* 14), that she would use the great interest she had in her son to gain his consent, that he might marry Abishag (*v.* 16, 17), and, if he may but obtain this, he will thankfully accept it, (1.) As a compensation for his loss of the kingdom. He insinuates (*v.* 15), "*Thou knowest the kingdom was mine,* as my father's

eldest son, living at the time of his death, *and all Israel set their faces on me.*" This was false; they were but a few that he had on his side; yet thus he would represent himself as an object of compassion, that had been deprived of a crown, and therefore might well be gratified in a wife. If he may not inherit his father's throne, yet let him have something valuable that was his father's, to keep for his sake, and let it be Abishag. (2.) As his reward for his acquiescence in that loss. He owns Solomon's right to the kingdom: "*It was his from the Lord.* I was foolish in offering to contest it; and now that it is turned about to him I am satisfied." Thus he pretends to be well pleased with Solomon's accession to the throne, when he is doing all he can to give him disturbance. *His words were smoother than butter, but war was in his heart.*

3. Bathsheba's address to Solomon on his behalf. She promised to speak to the king for him (*v.* 18) and did so, *v.* 19. Solomon received her with all the respect that was due to a mother, though he himself was a king: He *rose up to meet her, bowed himself to her,* and caused her *to sit on his right hand,* according to the law of the fifth commandment. Children, not only when grown up, but when grown great, must give honour to their parents, and behave dutifully and respectfully towards them. *Despise not thy mother when she is old.* As a further instance of the deference he paid to his mother's wisdom and authority, when he understood she had a petition to present to him, he promised not to say her nay, a promise which both he and she understood with this necessary limitation, provided it be just and reasonable and fit to be granted; but, if it were otherwise, he was sure he should convince her that it was so, and that then she would withdraw it. She tells him her errand at last (*v.* 21): *Let Abishag be given to Adonijah thy brother.* It was strange that she did not suspect the treason, but more strange that she did not abhor the incest, that was in the proposal. But either she did not take Abishag to be David's wife, because the marriage was not consummated, or she thought it might be dispensed with to gratify Adonijah, in consideration of his tame submission to Solomon. This was her weakness and folly: it was well that she was not regent. Note, Those that have the ear of princes and great men, as it is their wisdom not to be too prodigal of their interest, so it is their duty never to use it for the assistance of sin or the furtherance of any wicked design. Let not princes be asked that which they ought not to grant. It ill becomes a good man to prefer a bad request or appear in a bad cause.

4. Solomon's just and judicious rejection of the request. Though his mother herself was the advocate, and called it *a small petition,* and perhaps it was the first she had troubled him with since he was king, yet he denied it, without violation of the general promise he had made, *v.* 20. If Herod had not had a mind to cut off John Baptist's head, he would not have thought himself obliged to do it by a general promise, like this, made to Herodias. The best friend we have in the world must not have such an interest in us as to bring us to do a wrong thing, either unjust or unwise. (1.) Solomon convinces his mother of the unreasonableness of the request, and shows her the tendency of it, which, before, she was not aware of. His reply is somewhat sharp: "*Ask for him the kingdom also, v.* 22. To ask that he may succeed the king in his bed is, in effect, to ask that he may succeed him in his throne; for that is it he aims at." Probably he had information, or cause for a strong suspicion, that Adonijah was plotting with Joab and Abiathar to give him disturbance, which warranted him to put this construction upon Adonijah's request. (2.) He convicts and condemns Adonijah for his pretensions, and both with an oath. He convicts him out of his own mouth, *v.* 23. His own tongue shall fall upon him; and a heavier load a man needs not fall under. Bathsheba may be imposed upon, but Solomon cannot; he plainly sees what Adonijah aims at, and concludes, "He has *spoken this word against his own life;* he is snared in the words of his own lips; now he shows what he would be at." He condemns him to die immediately: *He shall be put to death this day, v.* 24. God had himself declared with an oath that he would establish David's throne (Ps. lxxxix. 35), and therefore Solomon pledges the same assurance to secure that establishment, by cutting off the enemies of it. "As God liveth, that establisheth the government, Adonijah shall die, that would unsettle it." Thus the ruin of the enemies of Christ's kingdom is as sure as the stability of his kingdom, and both are as sure as the being and life of God, the founder of it. The warrant is immediately signed for his execution, and no less a man than Benaiah, the son of Jehoiada, general of the army, is ordered to be the executioner, *v.* 25. It is strange that Adonijah may not be heard to speak for himself: but Solomon's wisdom did not see it needful to examine the matter any further; it was plain enough that Adonijah aimed at the crown, and Solomon could not be safe while he lived. Ambitious turbulent spirits commonly prepare for themselves the instruments of death. Many a head has been lost by catching at a crown.

26 And unto Abiathar the priest said the king, Get thee to Anathoth, unto thine own fields; for thou *art* worthy of death: but I will not at this time put thee to death, because thou barest the ark of the Lord GOD before David my father, and because

thou hast been afflicted in all wherein my father was afflicted. 27 So Solomon thrust out Abiathar from being priest unto the LORD; that he might fulfil the word of the LORD, which he spake concerning the house of Eli in Shiloh. 28 Then tidings came to Joab: for Joab had turned after Adonijah, though he turned not after Absalom. And Joab fled unto the tabernacle of the LORD, and caught hold on the horns of the altar. 29 And it was told king Solomon that Joab was fled unto the tabernacle of the LORD; and, behold, *he is* by the altar. Then Solomon sent Benaiah the son of Jehoiada, saying, Go, fall upon him. 30 And Benaiah came to the tabernacle of the LORD, and said unto him, Thus saith the king, Come forth. And he said, Nay; but I will die here. And Benaiah brought the king word again, saying, Thus said Joab, and thus he answered me. 31 And the king said unto him, Do as he hath said, and fall upon him, and bury him; that thou mayest take away the innocent blood, which Joab shed, from me, and from the house of my father. 32 And the LORD shall return his blood upon his own head, who fell upon two men more righteous and better than he, and slew them with the sword, my father David not knowing *thereof, to wit,* Abner the son of Ner, captain of the host of Israel, and Amasa the son of Jether, captain of the host of Judah. 33 Their blood shall therefore return upon the head of Joab, and upon the head of his seed for ever: but upon David, and upon his seed, and upon his house, and upon his throne, shall there be peace for ever from the LORD. 34 So Benaiah the son of Jehoiada went up, and fell upon him, and slew him: and he was buried in his own house in the wilderness.

Abiathar and Joab were both aiding and abetting in Adonijah's rebellious attempt, and it is probable were at the bottom of this new motion made by Adonijah for Abishag, and it should seem Solomon knew it, *v.* 22. This was, in both, an intolerable affront both to God and to the government, and the worse because of their high station and the great influence their examples might have upon many. They therefore come next to be reckoned with. They are both equally guilty of the treason, but, in the judgment passed upon them, a difference is made and with good reason.

I. Abiathar, in consideration of his old services, is only degraded, *v.* 26, 27. 1. Solomon convicts him, and by his great wisdom finds him guilty: "*Thou art worthy of death,* for joining with Adonijah, when thou knewest on whose head God intended to set the crown." 2. He calls to mind the respect he had formerly shown to David his father, and that he had both ministered to him in holy things *(had borne before him the ark of the Lord),* and also had tenderly sympathized with him in his afflictions and been afflicted in them all, particularly when he was in exile and distress both by Saul's persecution and Absalom's rebellion. Note, Those that show kindness to God's people shall have it remembered to their advantage one time or other. 3. For this reason he spares Abiathar's life, but deposes him from his offices, and confines him to his country seat at Anathoth, forbids him the court, the city, the tabernacle, the altar, and all intermeddling in public business, with an intimation likewise that he was upon his good behaviour, and that though Solomon did not put him to death at this time he might another time, if he did not conduct himself well. But, for the present, he was only thrust out from being priest, as rendered unworthy that high station by the opposition he had given to that which he knew to be the will of God. Saul, for a supposed crime, had barbarously slain Abiathar's father, and eighty-five priests, their families, and city. Solomon spares Abiathar himself, though guilty of a real crime. Thus was Saul's government ruined and Solomon's established. As men are to God's ministers, they will find him to them. 4. The depriving of Abiathar was the fulfilling of the threatening against the house of Eli (1 Sam. ii. 30), for he was the last high priest of that family. It was now above eighty years since the ruin was threatened; but God's judgments, though not executed speedily, will be executed surely.

II. Joab, in consideration of his old sins, is put to death.

1. His guilty conscience sent him to the horns of the altar. He heard that Adonijah was executed and Abiathar deposed, and therefore, fearing his turn would be next, he fled for refuge to the altar. Many that, in the day of their security, care not for the service of the altar, will be glad of the protection of it in the day of their distress. Some think Joab designed thereby to devote himself for the future to a constant attendance upon the altar, hoping thereby to obtain his pardon, as some that have lived a dissolute life all their days have thought to atone for their crimes by retiring into a monastery when

they are old, leaving the world when it has left them, and no thanks to them.

2. Solomon ordered him to be put to death there for the murder of Abner and Amasa; for these were the crimes upon which he thought fit to ground the sentence, rather than upon his treasonable adherence to Adonijah. Joab was indeed worthy of death for turning after Adonijah, in contempt of Solomon and his designation to the throne, *though he had not turned after Absalom, v.* 28. Former fidelity will not serve to excuse any after treachery; yet, besides that, Joab had merited well of the house of David, to which and to his country he had done a great deal of good service in his day, in consideration of which, it is probable, Solomon would have pardoned him his offence against him (for clemency gives great reputation and establishment to an infant government), and would have only displaced him as he did Abiathar; but he must die for the murders he had formerly been guilty of, which his father had charged Solomon to call him to an account for. The debt he owed to the innocent blood that was shed, by answering its cries with the blood of him that shed it, he could not pay himself, but left it to his son to pay it, who, having power wherewithal, failed not to do it. On this he grounds the sentence, aggravating the crime (*v.* 32), that he *fell upon two men more righteous and better than he*, that had done him no wrong nor meant him any, and, had they lived, might probably have done David better service (if the blood shed be not only innocent, but excellent, the life more valuable than common lives, the crime is the more heinous), that David knew not of it, and yet the case was such that he would be suspected as privy to it; so that Joab endangered his prince's reputation in taking away the life of his rivals, which was a further aggravation. For these crimes, (1.) He must die, and die by the sword of public justice. *By man must his blood be shed*, and it lies upon his own head (*v.* 32), as theirs does whom he had murdered, *v.* 33. Woe to the head that lies under the guilt of blood! Vengeance for murder was long in coming upon Joab; but, when it did come, it remained the longer, being here entailed *upon the head of his seed for ever* (*v.* 33), who, instead of deriving honour, as otherwise they might have done, from his heroic actions, derived guilt, and shame, and a curse, from his villanous actions, on account of which they fared the worse in this world. The seed of such evil doers shall never be renowned. (2.) He must die at the altar, rather than escape. Joab resolved not to stir from the altar (*v.* 30), hoping thereby either to secure himself or else to render Solomon odious to the people, as a profaner of the holy place, if he should put him to death there. Benaiah made a scruple of either killing him there or dragging him thence; but Solomon knew the law, that the altar of God should give no protection to wilful murderers. Exod. xxi. 14, *Thou shalt take him from my altar that he may die*, may die a sacrifice. In case of such sins as the blood of beasts would atone for the altar was a refuge, but not in Joab's case. He therefore orders him to be executed there, if he could not be got thence, to show that he feared not the censure of the people in doing his duty, but would rectify their mistake, and let them know that the administration of justice is better than sacrifice, and that the holiness of any place should never countenance the wickedness of any person. Those who, by a lively faith, take hold on Christ and his righteousness, with a resolution, if they perish, to perish there, shall find in him a more powerful protection than Joab found at the horns of the altar. Benaiah slew him (*v.* 34), with the solemnity, no doubt, of a public execution. The law being thus satisfied, he was *buried in his own house in the wilderness*, privately, like a criminal, not pompously, like a soldier; yet no indignity was done to his dead body. It is not for man to lay the iniquity upon the bones, whatever God does.

3. Solomon pleased himself with this act of justice, not as it gratified any personal revenge, but as it was the fulfilling of his father's orders and a real kindness to himself and his own government. (1.) Guilt was hereby removed, *v.* 31. By returning the innocent blood that had been shed upon the head of him that shed it, it was taken away from him and from the house of his father, which implies that the blood which is not required from the murderer will be required from the magistrate, at least there is danger lest it should. Those that would have their houses safe and built up must put away iniquity far from them. (2.) Peace was hereby secured (*v.* 33) upon David. He does not mean his person, but, as he explains himself in the next words, Upon *his seed, his house, and his throne*, shall there be *peace for ever from the Lord;* thus he expresses his desire that it may be so and his hope that it shall be so. "Now that justice is done, and the cry of blood is satisfied, the government will prosper." Thus *righteousness and peace kiss each other*. Now that such a turbulent man as Joab is removed there shall be peace. *Take away the wicked from before the king, and his throne shall be established in righteousness*, Prov. xxv. 5. Solomon, in this blessing of peace upon his house and throne, piously looks upward to God as the author of it and forward to eternity as the perfection of it. "It shall be peace from the Lord, and peace for ever from the Lord." The Lord of peace himself give us that peace which is everlasting.

35 And the king put Benaiah the son of Jehoiada in his room over the host: and Zadok the priest did the

king put in the room of Abiathar. 36 And the king sent and called for Shimei, and said unto him, Build thee a house in Jerusalem, and dwell there, and go not forth thence any whither. 37 For it shall be, *that* on the day thou goest out, and passest over the brook Kidron, thou shalt know for certain that thou shalt surely die: thy blood shall be upon thine own head. 38 And Shimei said unto the king, The saying *is* good: as my lord the king hath said, so will thy servant do. And Shimei dwelt in Jerusalem many days. 39 And it came to pass after the end of three years, that two of the servants of Shimei ran away unto Achish son of Maachah king of Gath. And they told Shimei, saying, Behold, thy servants *be* in Gath. 40 And Shimei arose, and saddled his ass, and went to Gath to Achish to seek his servants: and Shimei went, and brought his servants from Gath. 41 And it was told Solomon that Shimei had gone from Jerusalem to Gath, and was come again. 42 And the king sent and called for Shimei, and said unto him, Did I not make thee to swear by the LORD, and protested unto thee, saying, Know for a certain, on the day thou goest out, and walkest abroad any whither, that thou shalt surely die? and thou saidst unto me, The word *that* I have heard *is* good. 43 Why then hast thou not kept the oath of the LORD, and the commandment that I have charged thee with? 44 The king said moreover to Shimei, Thou knowest all the wickedness which thine heart is privy to, that thou didst to David my father: therefore the LORD shall return thy wickedness upon thine own head; 45 And king Solomon *shall be* blessed, and the throne of David shall be established before the LORD for ever. 46 So the king commanded Benaiah the son of Jehoiada; which went out, and fell upon him, that he died. And the kingdom was established in the hand of Solomon.

Here is, I. The preferment of Benaiah and Zadok, two faithful friends to Solomon and his government, *v.* 35. Joab being put to death, Benaiah was advanced to be general of the forces in his room, and, Abiathar being deposed, Zadok was made high priest in his room, and therein was fulfilled that word of God, when he threatened to cut off the house of Eli (1 Sam. ii. 35), *I will raise me up a faithful priest, and will build him a sure house.* Though sacred offices may be disgraced, they shall not be destroyed, by the mal-administration of those that are entrusted with them, nor shall God's work ever stand still for want of hands to carry it on. No wonder that he who was a king so immediately of God's making was empowered to make whom he thought fit high priest; and he exercised this power with equity, for the ancient right was in Zadok, he being of the family of Eleazar, whereas Eli and his house were of Ithamar.

II. The course that was taken with Shimei. He is sent for, by a messenger, from his house at Bahurim, expecting perhaps no better than Adonijah's doom, being conscious of his enmity to the house of David; but Solomon knows how to make a difference of crimes and criminals. David had promised Shimei his life for his time. Solomon is not bound by that promise, yet he will not go directly contrary to it. 1. He confines him to Jerusalem, and forbids him, upon any pretence whatsoever, to go out of the city any further than the brook Kidron, *v.* 36, 37. He would not suffer him to continue at his country seat lest he should make mischief among his neighbours, but took him to Jerusalem, where he kept him prisoner at large. This might make Shimei's confinement easy to himself, for Jerusalem was beautiful for situation, *the joy of the whole earth,* the royal city, the holy city (he had no reason to complain of being shut up in such a paradise); it would also make it the more safe for Solomon, for there he would have him under his eye and be able to watch his motions; and he plainly tells him that if he ever go out of the rules he shall certainly die for it. This was a fair trial of his obedience, and such a test of his loyalty as he had no reason to complain of. He has his life upon easy terms: he shall live if he will but be content to live at Jerusalem. 2. Shimei submits to the confinement, and thankfully takes his life upon those terms. He enters into recognizance (*v.* 38), under the penalty of death, not to stir out of Jerusalem, and owns that the saying is good. Even those that perish cannot but own the conditions of pardon and life unexceptionable, so that their blood, like Shimei's, must rest upon their own heads. Shimei promised, with an oath, to keep within his bounds, *v.* 42. 3. Shimei forfeits his recognizance, which was the thing Solomon expected; and God was righteous in suffering him to do it, that he might now suffer for his old sins. Two of his servants (it seems, though he was a prisoner, he lived like himself, well attended) ran from him to the land of the Philistines, *v.* 39. Thither he pursued them, and thence brought them back to Jerusalem, *v.* 40. For the keeping of it private he *saddled his ass* himself, probably went in the night, and came home he thought undiscovered. "Seeking his servants," says bishop Hall, "he lost himself; these earthly things either are, or should be, our servants. How commonly do we see men run out of the bounds set by God's law, to hunt after them, till their souls incur a fearful judgment!" 4. Solomon takes the forfeiture. Information is given him that Shimei has transgressed, *v.* 41. The king sends for him, and, (1.) Charges him with the present crime (*v.* 42, 43), that he had put a great contempt upon the authority and wrath both of God and the king, that he had broken *the oath of the Lord* and disobeyed the commandment of his prince, and by this it appeared what manner of spirit he was of, that he would not be held by the bonds of gratitude or conscience. Had he represented to Solomon the urgency of the occasion, and begged leave to go, perhaps Solomon might have given him leave; but to presume either upon his ignorance or his connivance was to affront him in the highest degree. (2.) He condemns him for his former crime, cursing David, and throwing stones at him in the day of his affliction: *The wickedness which thy heart is privy to, v.* 44. There was no need to examine witnesses for the proof of the fact, his own conscience was instead of a thousand witnesses. That wickedness which men's *own hearts* alone *are privy to* is enough, if duly considered, to fill them with confusion, in expectation of its return upon *their own heads;* for, if the heart be privy to it, God is greater than the heart and knoweth all things. Others knew of Shimei's cursing David, but Shimei himself knew of the wicked principles of hatred and malice against David which he displayed in cursing him and that his submission was but feigned and forced. (3.) He blessed himself and his government (*v.* 45): *King Solomon shall be blessed,* notwithstanding Shimei's impotent curses, which perhaps, in fury and despair, he now vented freely: *Let them curse, but bless thou.* And *the throne of David shall be established,* by taking away those that would undermine it. It is a comfort, in reference to the enmity of the church's enemies, that, how much soever they rage, it is a vain thing they imagine. Christ's throne is established, and they cannot shake it. (4.) He gives orders for the execution of Shimei immediately, *v.* 46. All judgment is committed to the Lord Jesus, and, though he be King of peace, he will be found a King of righteousness; and this will shortly be his word of command concerning all his enemies, that would not have him to reign over them: *Bring them forth, and slay them before me;* the reproaches of those that blasphemed him will fall on themselves, to their eternal condemnation.

CHAP. III.

Solomon's reign looked bloody in the foregoing chapter, but the necessary acts of justice must not be called cruelty; in this chapter it appears with another face. We must not think the worse of God's mercy to his subjects for his judgments on rebels. We have here, I. Solomon's marriage to Pharaoh's daughter, ver. 1. II. A general view of his religion, ver. 2—4. III. A particular account of his prayer to God for wisdom, and the answer to that prayer, ver. 5—15. IV. A particular instance of his wisdom in deciding the controversy between the two harlots, ver. 16—28. And very great he looks here, both at the altar and on the bench, and therefore on the bench because at the altar.

AND Solomon made affinity with Pharaoh king of Egypt, and took Pharaoh's daughter, and brought her into the city of David, until he had made an end of building his own house, and the house of the LORD, and the wall of Jerusalem round about. 2 Only the people sacrificed in high places, because there was no house built unto the name of the LORD, until those days. 3 And Solomon loved the LORD, walking in the statutes of David his father: only he sacrificed and burnt incense in high places. 4 And the king went to Gibeon to sacrifice there; for that *was* the great high place: a thousand burnt offerings did Solomon offer upon that altar.

We are here told concerning Solomon,

I. Something that was unquestionably good, for which he is to be praised and in which he is to be imitated. 1. He *loved the Lord, v.* 3. Particular notice was taken of God's love to him, 2 Sam. xii. 24. He had his name from it: *Jedidiah—beloved of the Lord.* And here we find he returned that love, as John, the beloved disciple, was most full of love. Solomon was a wise man, a rich man, a great man; yet the brightest encomium of him is that which is the character of all the saints, even the poorest, He *loved the Lord. He loved the worship of the Lord,* so the Chaldee; all that love God love his worship, love to hear from him and speak to him, and so to have communion with him. 2. He *walked in the statutes of David his father,* that is, in the statutes that David gave him, *ch.* ii. 2, 3; 1 Chron. xxviii. 9, 10 (his dying father's charge was sacred, and as a law to him), or in God's statutes, which David his father walked in before him; he kept close to God's ordinances, carefully observed them and diligently attended them. Those that truly *love God* will make conscience of *walking in his statutes.* 3. He was very free and generous in what he did for the honour of God. When he offered sacrifice he offered like a king, in some proportion to his great wealth, a *thousand burnt-offerings, v.* 4. Where God sows plentifully he expects to reap accordingly; and those that truly love God and his worship will not grudge the expenses of their religion. We may be tempted to say, *To what purpose is this waste?* Might not these cattle have been given to the poor? But we must never think that wasted which is laid out in the service of God. It seems strange how so many beasts should be burnt upon one altar in one feast, though it continued seven days; but the fire on the altar is supposed to be more quick and devouring than common fire, for it represented that fierce and mighty wrath of God which fell upon the sacrifices, that the offerers might escape. *Our God is a consuming fire.* Bishop Patrick quotes it as a tradition of the Jews that the smoke of the sacrifices ascended directly in a straight pillar, and was not scattered, otherwise it would have choked those that attended, when so many sacrifices were offered as were here.

II. Here is something concerning which it may be doubted whether it was good or no. 1. His marrying Pharaoh's daughter, *v.* 1. We will suppose she was proselyted, otherwise the marriage would not have been lawful; yet, if so, surely it was not advisable. He that *loved the Lord* should, for his sake, have fixed his love upon one of the Lord's people. Unequal matches of the sons of God with the daughters of men have often been of pernicious consequence; yet some think that he did this with the advice of his friends, that she was a sincere convert (for the gods of the Egyptians are not reckoned among the strange gods which his strange wives drew him in to the worship of, *ch.* xi. 5, 6), and that the book of Canticles and the 45th Psalm were penned on this occasion, by which these nuptials were made typical of the mystical espousals of the church to Christ, especially the Gentile church. 2. His worshipping in the high places, and thereby tempting the people to do so too, *v.* 2, 3. Abraham built his altars on mountains (Gen. xii. 8; xxii. 2), and worshipped in a grove, Gen. xxi. 33. Thence the custom was derived, and was proper, till the divine law confined them to one place, Deut. xii. 5, 6. David kept to the ark, and did not care for the high places, but Solomon, though in other things he *walked in the statutes of his father,* in this came short of him. He showed thereby a great zeal for sacrificing, but to obey would have been better. This was an irregularity. Though there was as yet no house built, there was a tent pitched, to the name of the Lord, and the ark ought to have been the centre of their unity. It was so by divine institution; from it the high places separated; yet while they worshipped God only, and in other things according to the rule, he graciously overlooked their weakness, and accepted their services; and it is owned that *Solomon loved the Lord,* though he *burnt incense in the high places,* and let not men be more severe than God is.

5 In Gibeon the LORD appeared to Solomon in a dream by night: and God said, Ask what I shall give thee. 6 And Solomon said, Thou hast showed unto thy servant David my father great mercy, according as he walked before thee in truth, and in righteousness, and in uprightness of heart with thee; and thou hast kept for him this great kindness, that thou hast given him a son to sit on his throne, as *it is* this day. 7 And now, O LORD my God, thou hast made thy servant king instead of David my father: and I *am but* a little child: I know not *how* to go out or come in. 8 And thy servant *is* in the midst of thy people which thou hast chosen, a great people, that cannot be numbered nor counted for multitude. 9 Give therefore thy servant an understanding heart to judge thy people, that I may discern between good and bad: for who is able to judge this thy so great a people? 10 And the speech pleased the LORD, that Solomon had asked this thing. 11 And God said unto him, Because thou hast asked this thing, and hast not asked for thyself long life; neither hast asked riches for thyself, nor hast asked the life of thine enemies; but hast asked for thyself understanding to discern judgment; 12 Behold, I have done according to thy words: lo, I have given thee a wise and an understanding heart; so that there was none like thee before thee, neither after thee shall any arise like unto thee. 13 And I have also given thee that which thou hast not asked, both riches, and honour: so that there shall not be any among the kings like unto thee all thy days. 14 And if thou wilt walk in my ways, to keep my statutes and my commandments, as thy father David did walk, then I will lengthen thy days. 15 And Solomon awoke: and, behold, *it was* a dream. And he came to Jerusalem, and stood before the ark of the covenant of the LORD, and offered up burnt offerings, and offered peace offerings, and made a feast to all his servants.

We have here an account of a gracious visit which God paid to Solomon, and the communion he had with God in it, which put a greater honour upon Solomon than all the wealth and power of his kingdom did.

I. The circumstances of this visit, *v.* 5. 1. The place. It was in Gibeon; that was the great high place, and should have been the only one, because there the tabernacle and the brazen altar were, 2 Chron. i. 3. There Solomon offered his great sacrifices, and there God owned him more than in any other of the high places. The nearer we come to the rule in our worship the more reason we have to expect the tokens of God's presence. Where God records his name, there he will meet us and bless us. 2. The time. It was by night, the night after he had offered that generous sacrifice, *v.* 4. The more we abound in God's work the more comfort we may expect in him; if the day has been busy for him, the night will be easy in him. Silence and retirement befriend our communion with God. His kindest visits are often in the night, Ps. xvii. 3. 3. The manner. It was in a dream, when he was asleep, his senses locked up, that God's access to his mind might be the more free and immediate. In this way God used to speak to the prophets (Num. xii. 6) and to private persons, for their own benefit, Job xxxiii. 15, 16. These divine dreams, no doubt, were plainly distinguishable from those in which there are divers vanities, Eccl. v. 7.

II. The gracious offer God made him of the favour he should choose, whatever it might be, *v.* 5. He saw the glory of God shine about him, and heard a voice saying, *Ask what I shall give thee.* Not that God was indebted to him for his sacrifices, but thus he would testify his acceptance of them, and signify to him what great mercy he had in store for him, if he were not wanting to himself. Thus he would try his inclinations and put an honour upon the prayer of faith. God, in like manner, condescends to us, and puts us in the ready way to be happy by assuring us that we shall have what we will for the asking, John xvi. 23; 1 John v. 14. What would we more? *Ask, and it shall be given you.*

III. The pious request Solomon hereupon made to God. He readily laid hold of this offer. Why do we neglect the like offer made to us, like Ahaz, who said, *I will not ask?* Isa. vii. 12. Solomon prayed in his sleep, God's grace assisting him; yet it was a lively prayer. What we are most in care about, and which makes the greatest impression upon us when we are awake, commonly affects us when we are asleep; and by our dreams, sometimes, we may know what our hearts are upon and how our pulse beats. Plutarch makes virtuous dreams one evidence of increase in virtue. Yet this must be attributed to a higher source. Solomon's making such an intelligent choice as this when he was asleep, and the powers of reason were least active, showed that it came purely from the grace of God, which wrought in him these gracious desires. If his *reins* thus *instruct him in the night season,* he must *bless the Lord* who *gave him counsel,* Ps. xvi. 7. Now, in this prayer,

1. He acknowledges God's great goodness to his father David, *v.* 6. He speaks honourably of his father's piety, that he had *walked before God in uprightness of heart,* drawing a veil over his faults. It is to be hoped that those who praise their godly parents will imitate them. But he speaks more honourably of God's goodness to his father, the mercy he had shown to him while he lived, in giving him to be sincerely religious and then recompensing his sincerity, and the great kindness he had kept for him, to be bestowed on his family when he was gone, in *giving him a son to sit on his throne.* Children should give God thanks for his mercies to their parents, for the sure mercies of David. God's favours are doubly sweet when we observe them transmitted to us through the hands of those that have gone before us. The way to get the entail perpetuated is to bless God that it has hitherto been preserved.

2. He owns his own insufficiency for the discharge of that great trust to which he is called, *v.* 7, 8. And here is a double plea to enforce his petition for wisdom:—(1.) That his place required it, as he was successor to David ("*Thou hast made me king instead of David,* who was a very wise and good man: Lord, give me wisdom, that I may keep up what he wrought, and carry on what he began") and as he was ruler over Israel: "Lord, give me wisdom to rule well; for they are a numerous people, that will not be managed without much care, and they are thy people, whom thou hast chosen, and therefore to be ruled for thee, and the more wisely they are ruled the more glory thou wilt have from them." (2.) That he wanted it. As one that had a humble sense of his own deficiency, he pleads, "*Lord, I am but a little child* (so he calls himself, a child in understanding, though his father called him *a wise man, ch.* ii. 9); *I know not how to go out or come in* as I should, nor to do so much as the common daily business of the government, much less what to do in a critical juncture." Note, Those who are employed in public stations ought to be very sensible of the weight and importance of their work and their own insufficiency for it, and then they are qualified for receiving divine instruction. Paul's question *(Who is sufficient for these things?)* is much like Solomon's here, *Who is able to judge this thy so great a people? v.* 9. Absalom, who was a fool, wished himself a judge; Solomon, who was a wise man, trembles at the undertaking and suspects his own fitness for it. The more knowing and considerate men are the better acquainted they are with their own

weakness and the more jealous of themselves.

3. He begs of God to give him wisdom (*v.* 9): *Give therefore thy servant an understanding heart.* He calls himself *God's servant,* pleased with that relation to God (Ps. cxvi. 16) and pleading it with him: "I am devoted to thee, and employed for thee; give me that which is requisite to the services in which I am employed." Thus his good father prayed, and thus he pleaded. Ps. cxix. 125, *I am thy servant, give me understanding.* An understanding heart is God's gift, Prov. ii. 6. We must pray for it (James i. 5), and pray for it with application to our particular calling and the various occasions we have for it; as Solomon, *Give me an understanding,* not to please my own curiosity with, or puzzle my neighbours, but *to judge thy people.* That is the best knowledge which will be serviceable to us in doing our duty; and such that knowledge is which enables us to *discern between good and bad,* right and wrong, sin and duty, truth and falsehood, so as not to be imposed upon by false colours in judging either of others' actions or of our own.

4. The favourable answer God gave to his request. It was a pleasing prayer (*v.* 10): *The speech pleased the Lord.* God is well pleased with his own work in his people, the desires of his own kindling, the prayers of his Spirit's inditing. By this choice Solomon made it appear that he desired to be good more than great, and to serve God's honour more than to advance his own. Those are accepted of God who prefer spiritual blessings to temporal, and are more solicitous to be found in the way of their duty than in the way to preferment. But that was not all; it was a prevailing prayer, and prevailed for more than he asked. (1.) God gave him wisdom, *v.* 12. He fitted him for all that great work to which he had called him, gave him such a right understanding of the law which he was to judge by, and the cases he was to judge of, that he was unequalled for a clear head, a solid judgment, and a piercing eye. Such an insight, and such a foresight, never was prince so blessed with. (2.) He gave him riches and honour over and above into the bargain (*v.* 13), and it was promised that in these he should as much exceed his predecessors, his successors, and all his neighbours, as in wisdom. These also are God's gift, and, as far as is good for them, are promised to all that *seek first the kingdom of God and the righteousness thereof,* Matt. vi. 33. Let young people learn to prefer grace to gold in all that they choose, because *godliness has the promise of the life that now is,* but *the life that now is* has not *the promise of godliness.* How completely blessed was Solomon, that had both wisdom and wealth! He that has wealth and power without wisdom and grace is in danger of doing hurt with them; he that has wisdom and grace without wealth and power is not capable of doing so much good with them as he that has both. Wisdom is good, is so much the better, with an inheritance, Eccles. vii. 11. But, if we make sure of wisdom and grace, these will either bring outward prosperity with them or sweeten the want of it. God promised Solomon riches and honour absolutely, but long life upon condition (*v.* 14). *If thou wilt walk in my ways, as David did, then I will lengthen thy days.* He failed in the condition; and therefore, though he had riches and honour, he did not live so long to enjoy them as in the course of nature he might have done. Length of days is wisdom's right-hand blessing, typical of eternal life; but it is in her left hand that riches and honour are, Prov. iii. 16. Let us see here, [1.] That the way to obtain spiritual blessings is to be importunate for them, to wrestle with God in prayer for them, as Solomon did for wisdom, asking that only, as the *one thing needful.* [2.] That the way to obtain temporal blessings is to be indifferent to them and to refer ourselves to God concerning them. Solomon had wisdom given him because he did ask it and wealth because he did not ask it.

5. The grateful return Solomon made for the visit God was pleased to pay him, *v.* 15. He awoke, we may suppose in a transport of joy, awoke, and *his sleep was sweet to him,* as the prophet speaks (Jer. xxxi. 26); being satisfied of God's favour, he was satisfied with it, and he began to think *what he should render to the Lord.* He had made his prayer at the high place at Gibeon, and there God had graciously met him; but he comes to Jerusalem to give thanks *before the ark of the covenant,* blaming himself, as it were, that he had not prayed there, the ark being the token of God's presence, and wondering that God had met him any where else. God's passing by our mistakes should persuade us to amend them. There he, (1.) Offered a great sacrifice to God. We must give God praise for his gifts in the promise, though not yet fully performed. David used to *praise God's word,* as well as his *works* (Ps. lvi. 10, and particularly, 2 Sam. vii. 18), and Solomon trod in his steps. (2.) He made a great feast upon the sacrifice, that those about him might rejoice with him in the grace of God.

16 Then came there two women, *that were* harlots, unto the king, and stood before him. 17 And the one woman said, O my lord, I and this woman dwell in one house; and I was delivered of a child with her in the house. 18 And it came to pass the third day after that I was delivered, that this woman was delivered also: and we *were* together; *there was* no stranger with us in the house,

save we two in the house. 19 And this woman's child died in the night; because she overlaid it. 20 And she arose at midnight, and took my son from beside me, while thine handmaid slept, and laid it in her bosom, and laid her dead child in my bosom. 21 And when I rose in the morning to give my child suck, behold, it was dead: but when I had considered it in the morning, behold, it was not my son, which I did bear. 22 And the other woman said, Nay; but the living *is* my son, and the dead *is* thy son. And this said, No; but the dead *is* thy son, and the living *is* my son. Thus they spake before the king. 23 Then said the king, The one saith, This *is* my son that liveth, and thy son *is* the dead: and the other saith, Nay; but thy son *is* the dead, and my son *is* the living. 24 And the king said, Bring me a sword. And they brought a sword before the king. 25 And the king said, Divide the living child in two, and give half to the one, and half to the other. 26 Then spake the woman whose the living child *was* unto the king, for her bowels yearned upon her son, and she said, O my lord, give her the living child, and in no wise slay it. But the other said, Let it be neither mine nor thine, *but* divide *it*. 27 Then the king answered and said, Give her the living child, and in no wise slay it: she *is* the mother thereof. 28 And all Israel heard of the judgment which the king had judged; and they feared the king: for they saw that the wisdom of God *was* in him, to do judgment.

An instance is here given of Solomon's wisdom, to show that the grant lately made him had a real effect upon him. The proof is fetched, not from the mysteries of state and the policies of the council-board, though there no doubt he excelled, but from the trial and determination of a cause between party and party, which princes, though they devolve them upon their judges, must not think it below them to take cognizance of. Observe,

I. The case opened, not by lawyers, but by the parties themselves, though they were women, which made it the easier to such a piercing eye as Solomon had to discern between right and wrong by their own showing. These two women were harlots, kept a public house, and their children, some think, were born of fornication, because here is no mention of their husbands. It is probable the cause had been heard in the inferior courts, before it was brought before Solomon, and had been found special, the judges being unable to determine it, that Solomon's wisdom in deciding it at last might be the more taken notice of. These two women, who lived in a house together, were each of them delivered of a son within three days of one another, *v.* 17, 18. They were so poor that they had no servant or nurse to be with them, so slighted, because harlots, that they had no friend or relation to accompany them. One of them overlaid her child, and, in the night, exchanged it with the other (*v.* 19, 20), who was soon aware of the cheat put upon her, and appealed to public justice to be righted, *v.* 21. See, 1. What anxiety is caused by little children, how uncertain their lives are, and to how many dangers they are continually exposed. The age of infancy is the valley of the shadow of death; and the lamp of life, when first lighted, is easily blown out. It is a wonder of mercy that so few perish in the perils of nursing. 2. How much better it was in those times with children born in fornication than commonly it is now. Harlots then loved their children, nursed them, and were loth to part with them; whereas now they are often sent to a distance, abandoned, or killed. But thus it was foretold that *in the last days perilous times should come*, when people should be without natural affection, 2 Tim. iii. 1, 3.

II. The difficulty of the case. The question was, Who was the mother of this living child, which was brought into court, to be finally adjudged either to the one or to the other? Both mothers were vehement in their claim, and showed a deep concern about it. Both were peremptory in their asseverations: "It is mine," says one. "Nay, it is mine," says the other. Neither will own the dead child, though it would be cheaper to bury that than to maintain the other: but it is the living one they strive for. The living child is therefore the parents' joy because it is their hope; and may not the dead children be so? See Jer. xxxi. 17. Now the difficulty of the case was that there was no evidence on either side. The neighbours, though it is probable that some of them were present at the birth and circumcision of the children, yet had not taken so much notice of them as to be able to distinguish them. To put the parties to the rack would have been barbarous; not she who had justice on her side, but she who was most hardy, would have had the judgment in her favour. Little stress is to be laid on extorted evidence. Judges and juries have need of wisdom to find out truth when it thus lies hid.

III. The determination of it. Solomon, having patiently heard what both sides had to say, sums up the evidence, *v.* 23. And now the whole court is in expectation what course Solomon's wisdom will take to find out the truth. One knows not what to say to it; another, perhaps, would determine it by lot. Solomon calls for a sword, and gives orders to divide the living child between the two contenders. Now, 1. This seemed a ridiculous decision of the case, and a brutal cutting of the knot which he could not untie. "Is this," think the sages of the law, "the wisdom of Solomon?" little dreaming what he aimed at in it. *The hearts of kings,* such kings, *are unsearchable,* Prov. xxv. 3. There was a law concerning the dividing of a living ox and a dead one (Exod. xxi. 35), but that did not reach this case. But, 2. It proved an effectual discovery of the truth. Some think that Solomon did himself discern it, before he made this experiment, by the countenances of the women and their way of speaking: but by this he gave satisfaction to all the company, and silenced the pretender. To find out the true mother, he could not try which the child loved best, and must therefore try which loved the child best; both pretended to a motherly affection, but their sincerity will be tried when the child is in danger. (1.) She that knew the child was not her own, but in contending for it stood upon a point of honour, was well content to have it divided. She that had overlaid her own child cared not what became of this, so that the true mother might not have it: *Let it be neither mine nor thine, but divide it.* By this it appeared that she knew her own title to be bad, and feared Solomon would find it so, though she little suspected she was betraying herself, but thought Solomon in good earnest. If she had been the true mother she would not have forfeited her interest in the child by agreeing so readily to this bloody decision. But, (2.) She that knew the child was her own, rather than the child should be butchered, gives it up to her adversary. How feelingly does she cry out, *O, my lord! give her the living child,* v. 26. "Let me see it hers, rather than not see it at all." By this tenderness towards the child it appeared that she was not the careless mother that had overlaid the dead child, but was the true mother of the living one, that could not endure to see its death, having compassion on the son of her womb. "The case is plain," says Solomon; "what need of witnesses? *Give her the living child;* for you all see, by this undissembled compassion, *she is the mother of it.*" Let parents show their love to their children by taking care of them, especially by taking care of their souls, and, with a holy violence, snatching them as brands out of the burning. Those are most likely to have the comfort of children that do their duty to them. Satan pretends to the heart of man, but by this it appears that he is only a pretender, that he would be content to divide with God, whereas the rightful sovereign of the heart will have all or none.

IV. We are told what a great reputation Solomon got among his people by this and other instances of his wisdom, which would have a great influence upon the ease of his government: *They feared the king* (*v.* 28), highly reverenced him, durst not in any thing oppose him, and were afraid of doing an unjust thing; for they knew, if ever it came before him, he would certainly discover it, *for they saw that the wisdom of God was in him,* that is, that wisdom with which God had promised to endue him. This *made his face to shine,* Eccl. viii. 1. This *strengthened him,* Eccl. vii. 19. This was better to him *than weapons of war,* Eccl. ix. 18. For this he was both feared and loved.

CHAP. IV.

An instance of the wisdom God granted to Solomon we had in the close of the foregoing chapter. In this we have an account of his wealth and prosperity, the other branch of the promise there made him. We have here, I. The magnificence of his court, his ministers of state (ver. 1—6), and the purveyors of his household (ver. 7—19), and their office, ver. 27, 28. II. The provisions for his table, ver. 22, 23. III. The extent of his dominion, ver. 21—24. IV. The numbers, ease, and peace, of his subjects, ver. 20—25. V. His stables, ver. 26. VI. His great reputation for wisdom and learning, ver. 29—34. Thus great was Solomon, but our Lord Jesus was greater than he (Matt. xii. 42), though he took upon him the form of a servant; for divinity, in its lowest humiliation, infinitely transcends royalty in its highest elevation.

SO king Solomon was king over all Israel. 2 And these *were* the princes which he had; Azariah the son of Zadok the priest, Elihoreph and Ahiah, the sons of Shisha, scribes; Jehoshaphat the son of Ahilud, the recorder. 4 And Benaiah the son of Jehoiada *was* over the host: and Zadok and Abiathar *were* the priests: 5 And Azariah the son of Nathan *was* over the officers: and Zabud the son of Nathan *was* principal officer, *and* the king's friend: 6 And Ahishar *was* over the household: and Adoniram the son of Abda *was* over the tribute. 7 And Solomon had twelve officers over all Israel, which provided victuals for the king and his household: each man his month in a year made provision. 8 And these *are* their names: The son of Hur, in mount Ephraim: 9 The son of Dekar, in Makaz, and in Shaalbim, and Beth-shemesh, and Elon-beth-hanan: 12 The son of Hesed, in Aruboth; to him *pertained* Sochoh, and all the land of Hepher: 11 The son of Abinadab, in all the region of Dor; which had Taphath the daughter of Solomon to wife: 12 Baana the son of Ahilud; *to him pertained* Taanach and Megiddo, and all Beth-shean, which *is* by Zartanah beneath Jezreel, from Beth-shean to Abel-meholah, *even* unto *the place that is* beyond Jokneam: 13 The son of Geber, in Ramoth-gilead; to him *pertained* the towns of Jair the son of Manasseh, which *are* in Gilead; to him *also pertained* the region of Argob, which *is* in Bashan, threescore great cities with walls and brasen bars: 14 Ahinadab the son of Iddo *had* Mahanaim: 15 Ahimaaz *was* in Naphtali; he also took Basmath the daughter of Solomon to wife: 16 Baanah the son of Hushai *was* in Asher and in Aloth: 17 Jehoshaphat the son of Paruah, in Issachar: 18 Shimei the son of Elah, in Benjamin: 19 Geber the son of Uri *was* in the country of Gilead, *in* the country of Sihon king of the Amorites, and of Og king of Bashan; and *he was* the only officer which *was* in the land.

Here we have,

I. Solomon upon his throne (*v.* 1): *So king Solomon was king,* that is, he was confirmed and established king *over all Israel,* and not, as his successors, only over two tribes. He was a king, that is, he did the work and duty of a king, with the wisdom God had given him. Those preserve the name and honour of their place that mind the business of it and make conscience of it.

II. The great officers of his court, in the choice of whom, no doubt, his wisdom much appeared. It is observable, 1. That several of them are the same that were in his father's time. Zadok and Abiathar were then priests (2 Sam. xx. 25), so they were now; only then Abiathar had the precedency, now Zadok. Jehoshaphat was then recorder, or keeper of the great seal, so he was now. Benaiah, in his father's time, was a principal man in military affairs, and so he was now. Shisha was his father's scribe, and his sons were his, *v.* 3. Solomon, though a wise man, would not affect to be wiser than his father in this matter. When sons come to inherit their father's wealth, honour, and power, it is a piece of respect to their memory, *cæteris paribus—where it can properly be done,* to employ those whom they employed, and trust those whom they trusted. Many pride themselves in being the reverse of their good parents. 2. The rest were priests' sons. His prime-minister of state was *Azariah the son of Zadok the priest.* Two others of the first rank were the sons of Nathan the prophet, *v.* 5. In preferring them he testified the grateful respect he had for their good father, whom he loved *in the name of a prophet.*

III. The purveyors for his household, whose business it was to send in provisions from several parts of the country, for the king's tables and cellars (*v.* 7) and for his stables (*v.* 27, 28), that thus, 1. His house might always be well furnished at the best hand. Let great men learn hence good house-keeping and yet good husbandry in their house-keeping, to be generous in spending according to their ability, but prudent in providing. It is the character of the virtuous woman that she *bringeth her food from afar* (Prov. xxxi. 14), not far-fetched and dear-bought, but the contrary, every thing bought where it is cheapest. 2. That thus he himself, and those who immediately attended him, might be eased of a great deal of care, and the more closely apply themselves to the business of the state, not troubled about much serving, provision for that being got ready to their hand. 3. That thus all the parts of the kingdom might be equally benefited by the taking off of the commodities that were the productions of their country and the circulating of the coin. Industry would hereby be encouraged, and consequently wealth increased, even in those tribes that lay most remote from the court. The providence of God extends itself to all *places of his dominions* (Ps. ciii. 22); so should the prudence and care of princes. 4. The dividing of this trust into so many hands was prudent, that no man might be continually burdened with the care of it nor grow exorbitantly rich with the profit of it, but that Solomon might have those, in every district, who, having a dependence upon the court, would be serviceable to him and his interest as there was occasion. These commissioners of the victualling-office, not for the army or navy (Solomon was engaged in no war), but for the household, are here named, several of them only by their surnames, as great men commonly call their servants: *Ben-hur, Ben-dekar, &c.,* though several of them have also their proper names prefixed. Two of them married Solomon's daughters, Ben-Abinadab (*v.* 11) and Ahimaaz (*v.* 15), and no disparagement to them to marry men of business. Better match with the officers of their father's court that were Israelites than with the sons of princes that were *strangers to the covenant of promise.* The son of Geber was in Ramoth-Gilead (*v.* 19), and Geber himself was in the country of Sihon and Og, which included that and Mahanaim, *v.* 14. He is therefore said to be *the only officer in that land,* because the other two, mentioned *v.* 13, 14, depended on him, and were subordinate to him.

20 Judah and Israel *were* many, as the sand which *is* by the sea in multitude, eating and drinking, and making merry. 21 And Solomon

reigned over all kingdoms from the river unto the land of the Philistines, and unto the border of Egypt: they brought presents, and served Solomon all the days of his life. 22 And Solomon's provision for one day was thirty measures of fine flour, and threescore measures of meal, 23 Ten fat oxen, and twenty oxen out of the pastures, and a hundred sheep, beside harts, and roebucks, and fallowdeer, and fatted fowl. 24 For he had dominion over all *the region* on this side the river, from Tiphsah even to Azzah, over all the kings on this side the river: and he had peace on all sides round about him. 25 And Judah and Israel dwelt safely, every man under his vine and under his fig tree, from Dan even to Beer-sheba, all the days of Solomon. 26 And Solomon had forty thousand stalls of horses for his chariots, and twelve thousand horsemen. 27 And those officers provided victual for king Solomon, and for all that came unto king Solomon's table, every man in his month: they lacked nothing. 28 Barley also and straw for the horses and dromedaries brought they unto the place where *the officers* were, every man according to his charge.

Such a kingdom, and such a court, surely never any prince had, as Solomon's are here described to be.

I. Such a kingdom. Never did the crown of Israel shine so brightly as it did when Solomon wore it, never in his father's days, never in the days of any of his successors; nor was that kingdom ever so glorious a type of the kingdom of the Messiah as it was then. The account here given of it is such as fully answers the prophecies which we have concerning it in Ps. lxxii., which is a psalm for Solomon, but with reference to Christ. 1. The territories of his kingdom were large and its tributaries many; so it was foretold that he should *have dominion from sea to sea,* Ps. lxxii. 8—11. Solomon reigned not only over all Israel, who were his subjects by choice, but over all the neighbouring kingdoms, who were his subjects by constraint. All the princes from the river Euphrates north-east to the border of Egypt south-west, not only added to his honour by doing him homage and holding their crowns from him, but added to his wealth by serving him, and bringing him presents, *v.* 21. David, by his successful wars, compelled them to this subjection, and Solomon, by his admirable wisdom, made it easy and reasonable; for it is fit that the fool should be *servant to the wise in heart.* If they gave him presents, he gave them instructions, and still *taught the people knowledge,* not only his own people, but those of other nations: and *wisdom is better than gold.* He had *peace on all sides, v.* 24. None of all the nations that were subject to him offered to shake off his yoke, or to give him any disturbance, but rather thought themselves happy in their dependence upon him. Herein his kingdom typified the Messiah's; for to him it is promised that he shall have the *heathen for his inheritance* and that *princes shall worship him,* Isa. xlix. 6, 7; liii. 12. 2. The subjects of his kingdom, and its inhabitants, were many and cheerful. (1.) They were numerous and the country was exceedingly populous (*v.* 20): *Judah and Israel were many,* and that good land was sufficient to maintain them all. *They were as the sand of the sea in multitude.* Now was fulfilled the promise made to Abraham concerning the increase of his seed (Gen. xxii. 17), as well as that concerning the extent of their dominion, Gen. xv. 18. This was their strength and beauty, the honour of their prince, the terror of their enemies, and an advancement of the wealth of the nation. If they grew so numerous that the place was any where too strait for them, they might remove with advantage into the countries that were subject to them. God's spiritual Israel are many, at least they will be so when they come all together, Rev. vii. 9. (2.) They were easy, they dwelt safely, or with confidence and assurance (*v.* 25), not jealous of their king or of his officers, not disaffected either to him or one to another, nor under any apprehension of danger from enemies foreign or domestic. They were happy and knew it, safe and willing to think themselves so. They dwelt every man under *his vine and fig-tree.* Solomon invaded no man's property, took not to himself their vineyards and olive-yards, as sometimes was the manner of the king (1 Sam. viii. 14), but what they had they could call their own: he protected every man in the possession and enjoyment of his property. Those that had vines and fig-trees ate the fruit of them themselves; and so great was the peace of the country that they might, if they pleased, dwell as safely under the shadow of them as within the walls of a city. Or, because it was usual to have *vines by the sides of their houses* (Ps. cxxviii. 3), they are said to *dwell under their vines.* (3.) They were cheerful in the use of their plenty, *eating and drinking, and making merry, v.* 20. Solomon did not only keep a good table himself, but enabled all his subjects, according to their rank, to do so too, and taught them that God gave them their abundance that they might use it soberly and pleasantly, not that they might hoard it up. *There is nothing better* than for a man to eat *the labour of his hands* (Eccl ii. 24), and that *with a merry heart*, Eccl. ix. 7. His father, in the Psalms, had led his people into the comforts of communion with God, and now he led them into the comfortable use of the good things of this life. This pleasant posture of Israel's affairs extended, in place, from Dan to Beer-sheba—no part of the country was exposed nor upon any account uneasy; and it continued a long time, *all the days of Solomon*, without any material interruption. Go where you would, you might see all the marks of plenty, peace, and satisfaction. The spiritual peace, and joy, and holy security, of all the faithful subjects of the Lord Jesus were typified by this. *The kingdom of God is not*, as Solomon's was, *meat and drink*, but, what is infinitely better, *righteousness, and peace, and joy in the Holy Ghost.*

II. Such a court Solomon kept as can scarcely be paralleled. We may guess at the vast number of his attendants, and the great resort there was to him, by the provision that was made daily for his table. Of bread there were so many measures of flour and meal as, it is computed, would richly serve 3000 men (Carellus computes above 4800 men), and the provision of flesh (*v.* 23) was rather more in proportion. What vast quantities were here of beef, mutton, and venison, and the choicest of all *fatted things*, as some read that which we translate *fatted fowl!* Ahasuerus, once in his reign, made a *great feast*, to *show the riches of his kingdom*, Esth. i. 3, 4. But it was much more the honour of Solomon that he kept a constant table and a very noble one, not of dainties or deceitful meats (he himself witnessed against them, Prov. xxiii. 3), but substantial food, for the entertainment of those who came to hear his wisdom. Thus Christ fed those whom he taught, 5000 at a time, more than ever Solomon's table would entertain at once: and all believers have in him a continual feast. Herein he far outdoes Solomon, that he feeds all his subjects, not with the bread that perishes, but *with that which endures to eternal life.* It added much both to the strength and glory of Solomon's kingdom that he had such abundance of horses, 40,000 for chariots and 12,000 for his troops, 1000 horse, perhaps, in every tribe, for the preserving of the public peace, *v.* 26. God had commanded that their king should not multiply horses (Deut. xvii. 16), nor, according to the account here given, considering the extent and wealth of Solomon's kingdom, did he multiply horses in proportion to his neighbours; for we find even the Philistines bringing into the field 30,000 chariots (1 Sam. xiii. 5) and the Syrians at least 40,000 horse, 2 Sam. x. 18. The same officers that provided for his house provided also for his stable, *v.* 27, 28. Every one knew his place, and work, and time; and so this great court was kept without confusion. Solomon, that had vast incomes, lived at a vast expense, and perhaps wrote that with application to himself, Eccl. v. 11. *When goods increase those are increased that eat them; and what good is there to the owners thereof, saving the beholding of them with their eyes,* unless withal they have the satisfaction of doing good with them?

29 And God gave Solomon wisdom and understanding exceeding much, and largeness of heart, even as the sand that *is* on the sea shore. 30 And Solomon's wisdom excelled the wisdom of all the children of the east country, and all the wisdom of Egypt. 31 For he was wiser than all men; than Ethan the Ezrahite, and Heman, and Chalcol, and Darda, the sons of Mahol: and his fame was in all nations round about. 32 And he spake three thousand proverbs: and his songs were a thousand and five. 33 And he spake of trees, from the cedar tree that *is* in Lebanon even unto the hyssop that springeth out of the wall: he spake also of beasts, and of fowl, and of creeping things, and of fishes. 34 And there came of all people to hear the wisdom of Solomon, from all kings of the earth, which had heard of his wisdom.

Solomon's wisdom was more his glory than his wealth, and here we have a general account of it.

I. The fountain of his wisdom: *God gave it him, v.* 29. He owns it himself. Prov. ii. 6, *The Lord giveth wisdom.* He gives the powers of reason (Job xxxviii. 36), preserves and improves them. The ordinary advances of them are owing to his providence, the sanctification of them to his grace, and this extraordinary pitch at which they arrived in Solomon to a special grant of his favour to him in answer to prayer.

II. The fulness of it: *He had wisdom and understanding, exceeding much,* great knowledge of distant countries and the histories of former times, a quickness of thought, strength of memory, and clearness of judgment, such as never any man had. It is called *largeness of heart;* for the heart is often put for the intellectual powers. He had a vast compass of knowledge, could take things entire, and had an admirable faculty of laying things together. Some, by his *largeness of heart*, understand his courage and boldness, and that great assurance with which he delivered his dictates and determinations. Or it may be meant of his disposition to do good with his knowledge. He was very free and communicative, had the gift of utterance as well as wisdom, was as free of his learning as he was of his meat, and grudged neither to any that were about him. Note, It is very desirable that those who have large gifts of any kind should have large hearts to use them for the good of others; and this is *from the hand of God*, Eccl. ii. 24. He shall *enlarge the heart*, Ps. cxix. 32. The greatness of Solomon's wisdom is illustrated by comparison. Chaldea and Egypt were nations famous for learning; thence the Greeks borrowed theirs; but the greatest scholars of these nations came short of Solomon, *v.* 30. If nature excels art, much more does grace. The knowledge which God gives by special favour goes beyond that which man gets by his own labour. Some wise men there were in Solomon's time, who were in great repute, particularly Heman, and others who were Levites, and employed by David in the temple-music, 1 Chron. xv. 19. Heman was *his seer in the word of God*, 1 Chron. xxv. 5. Chalcol and Darda were own brothers, and they also were noted for learning and wisdom. But *Solomon excelled them all* (*v.* 30), he out-did them and confounded them; his counsel was much more valuable.

III. The fame of it. It was talked of *in all nations round about*. His great wealth and glory made his wisdom much more illustrious, and gave him those opportunities of showing it which those cannot have that live in poverty and obscurity. The jewel of wisdom may receive great advantage by the setting of it.

IV. The fruits of it; by these the tree is known: he did not bury his talent, but showed his wisdom,

1. In his compositions. Those in divinity, written by divine inspiration, are not mentioned here, for they are extant, and will remain to the world's end monuments of his wisdom, and are, as other parts of scripture, of use to make us *wise unto salvation*. But, besides these, it appears by what he spoke, or dictated to be written from him, (1.) That he was a moralist, and a man of great prudence, for he spoke 3000 *proverbs*, wise sayings, apophthegms, of admirable use for the conduct of human life. The world is much governed by proverbs, and was never better furnished with useful ones than by Solomon. Whether those proverbs of Solomon that we have were any part of the 3000 is uncertain. (2.) That he was a poet and a man of great wit: *His songs were* 1005, of which one only is extant, because that only was divinely inspired, which is therefore called his *Song of songs*. His wise instructions were communicated by proverbs, that they might be familiar to those whom he designed to teach and ready on all occasions, and by *songs*, that they might be pleasant and move the affections. (3.) That he was a natural philosopher, and a man of great learning and insight into the mysteries of nature. From his own and others' observations and experience, he wrote both of plants and animals (*v.* 33), descriptions of their natures and qualities, and (some think) of the medicinal use of them.

2. In his conversation. There came persons from all parts, who were more inquisitive after knowledge than their neighbours, to *hear the wisdom of Solomon, v.* 34. Kings that had heard of it sent their ambassadors to hear it and to bring them instructions from it. Solomon's court was the staple of learning, and the rendezvous of philosophers, that is, the lovers of wisdom, who all came to light their candle at his lamp and to borrow from him. Let those who magnify the modern learning above that of the ancients produce such a treasure of knowledge any where in these latter ages as that was which Solomon was master of; yet this puts an honour upon human learning, that Solomon was praised for it, and recommends it to the great men of the earth, as well worthy their diligent search. But,

Lastly, Solomon was, herein, a type of Christ, *in whom are hidden all the treasures of wisdom and knowledge*, and hidden for use; for he is *made of God to us wisdom*.

CHAP. V.

The great work which Solomon was raised up to do was the building of the temple; his wealth and wisdom were given him to qualify him for that. In this, especially, he was to be a type of Christ, for "he shall build the temple of the Lord," Zech. vi. 12. In this chapter we have an account of the preparations he made for that and his other buildings. Gold and silver his good father had prepared in abundance, but timber and stones he must get ready; and about these we have him treating with Hiram king of Tyre. I. Hiram congratulated him on his accession to the throne, ver. 1. II. Solomon signified to him his design to build the temple and desired him to furnish him with workmen, ver. 2–6. III. Hiram agreed to do it, ver. 7–9. IV. Solomon's work was accordingly well done and Hiram's workmen were well paid, ver. 10–18.

AND Hiram king of Tyre sent his servants unto Solomon; for he had heard that they had anointed him king in the room of his father: for Hiram was ever a lover of David. 2 And Solomon sent to Hiram, saying, 3 Thou knowest how that David my father could not build a house unto the name of the LORD his God for the wars which were about him on every side, until the LORD put them under the soles of his feet. 4 But now the LORD my God hath given me rest on every side, *so that there is* neither adversary nor evil occurrent. 5 And, behold, I purpose to build a house unto the name of the LORD my God, as the LORD spake unto David my father, saying, Thy son, whom I will set upon thy throne in thy room, he shall build a house unto my name. 6 Now therefore command thou that they hew me cedar trees out of Lebanon; and my servants shall be with thy servants: and unto thee will I give hire for thy servants according to all that thou shalt appoint: for thou knowest that *there is* not among us any that can skill to hew timber like unto the Sidonians. 7 And it came to pass, when Hiram heard the words of Solomon, that he rejoiced greatly, and said, Blessed *be* the LORD this day, which hath given unto David a wise son over this great people. 8 And Hiram sent to Solomon, saying, I have considered the things which thou sentest to me for: *and* I will do all thy desire concerning timber of cedar, and concerning timber of fir. 9 My servants shall bring *them* down from Lebanon unto the sea: and I will convey them by sea in floats unto the place that thou shalt appoint me, and will cause them to be discharged there, and thou shalt receive *them:* and thou shalt accomplish my desire, in giving food for my household.

We have here an account of the amicable correspondence between Solomon and Hiram. Tyre was a famous trading city, that lay close upon the sea, in the border of Israel; its inhabitants (as should seem) were none of the devoted nations, nor ever at enmity with Israel, and therefore David never offered to destroy them, but lived in friendship with them. It is here said of Hiram their king that he was *ever a lover of David;* and we have reason to think he was a worshipper of the true God, and had himself renounced, though he could not reform, the idolatry of his city. David's character will win the affections even of those that are without. Here is,

I. Hiram's embassy of compliment to Solomon, *v.* 1. He sent, as is usual among princes, to condole with him on the death of David, and to renew his alliances with him upon his succession to the government. It is good keeping up friendship and communion with the families in which religion is uppermost.

II. Solomon's embassy of business to Hiram, sent, it is likely, by messengers of his own. In wealth, honour, and power, Hiram was very much inferior to Solomon, yet Solomon had occasion to be beholden to him and begged his favour. Let us never look with disdain on those below us, because we know not how soon we may need them. Solomon, in his letter to Hiram, acquaints him,

1. With his design to build a temple to the honour of God. Some think that temples among the heathen took their first rise and copy from the tabernacle which Moses erected in the wilderness, and that there were none before that; however there were many houses built in honour of the false gods before this was built in honour of the God of Israel, so little is external splendour a mark of the true church. Solomon tells Hiram, who was himself no stranger to the affair, (1.) That David's wars were an obstruction to him, that he could not build this temple, though he designed it, *v.* 3. They took up much of his time, and thoughts, and cares, were a constant expense to him and a constant employment of his subjects; so that he could not do it so well as it must be done, and therefore, it not being essential to religion, he must leave it to be done by his successor. See what need we have to pray that God will *give peace in our time,* because, in time or war, the building of the gospel temple commonly goes on slowly. (2.) That peace gave him an opportunity to build it, and therefore he resolved to set about it immediately: *God has given me rest* both at home and abroad, and there is no adversary (*v.* 4), no *Satan* (so the word is), no instrument of Satan to oppose it, or to divert us from it. Satan does all he can to hinder temple work (1 Thess. ii. 18; Zech. iii. 1), but when he is bound (Rev. xx. 2) we should be busy. When there is *no evil occurrent,* then let us be vigorous and zealous in that which is good and get it forward. When the churches have rest let them be edified, Acts ix. 31. Days of peace and prosperity present us with a fair gale, which we must account for if we improve not. As God's providence excited Solomon to think of building the temple, by giving him wealth and leisure, so his promise encouraged him. God had told David that his *son should build him a house, v.* 5. He will take it as a pleasure to be thus employed, and will not lose the honour designed him by that promise. It may stir us up much to good undertakings to be assured of good success in them. Let God's promise quicken our endeavours.

2. With his desire that Hiram would assist him herein. Lebanon was the place whence timber must be had, a noble forest in the north of Canaan, particularly expressed in the grant of that land to Israel—*all Lebanon,* Josh. xiii. 5. So that Solomon was proprietor of all its productions. The *cedars of Lebanon* are spoken of as, in a special manner, the *planting of the Lord* (Ps. civ. 16), being designed for Israel's use and particularly for temple service. But Solomon owned that though the trees were his the Israelites had not *skill to hew timber* like the Sidonians, who were Hiram's subjects. Canaan was *a land of wheat and barley* (Deut. viii. 8), which employed Israel in the affairs of husbandry, so that they were not at all versed in manufactures: in them the Sidonians excelled. Israel, in the things of God, are a *wise and understanding people;* and yet, in curious

arts, inferior to their neighbours. True piety is a much more valuable gift of heaven than the highest degree of ingenuity. Better be an Israelite skilful in the law than a Sidonian skilful to hew timber. But, the case being thus, Solomon courts Hiram to send him workmen, and promises (*v.* 6) both to *assist* them *(my servants shall be with thy servants,* to work under them), and to *pay* them *(unto thee will I give hire for thy servants);* for the labourer, even in church-work, though it be indeed its own wages, *is worthy of his hire.* The evangelical prophet, foretelling the glory of the church in the days of the Messiah, seems to allude to this story, Isa. lx., where he prophesies, (1.) That the *sons of strangers* (such were the Tyrians and Sidonians) shall *build up the wall* of the gospel temple, *v.* 10. Ministers were raised up among the Gentiles for the edifying of the body of Christ. (2.) That *the glory of Lebanon* shall be brought to it to *beautify it, v.* 13. All external endowments and advantages shall be made serviceable to the interests of Christ's kingdom.

3. Hiram's reception of, and return to, this message.

(1.) He received it with great satisfaction to himself: He *rejoiced greatly* (*v.* 7) that Solomon trod in his father's steps, and carried on his designs, and was likely to be so great a blessing to his kingdom. In this Hiram's generous spirit rejoiced, and not merely in the prospect he had of making an advantage to himself by Solomon's employing him. What he had the pleasure of he gave God the praise of: *Blessed be the Lord, who has given to David* (who was himself a wise man) *a wise son* to rule *over this great people.* See here, [1.] With what pleasure Hiram speaks of Solomon's wisdom and the extent of his dominion. Let us learn not to envy others either those secular advantages or those endowments of the mind wherein they excel us. What a great comfort it is to those that wish well to the Israel of God to see religion and wisdom kept up in families from one generation to another, especially in great families and those that have great influence on others! where it is so, God must have the glory of it. If to godly parents be given a godly seed (Mal. ii. 15), it is a token for good, and a happy indication that the entail of the blessing shall not be cut off.

(2.) He answered it with great satisfaction to Solomon, granting him what he desired, and showing himself very forward to assist him in this great and good work to which he was laying his hand. We have here his articles of agreement with Solomon concerning this affair, in which we may observe Hiram's prudence. [1.] He deliberated upon the proposal, before he returned an answer (*v.* 8): *I have considered the things.* It is common for those that make bargains rashly afterwards to wish them unmade again. The virtuous woman *considers a field* and then *buys it,* Prov. xxxi. 16. Those do not lose time who take time to consider. [2.] He descended to particulars in the articles, that there might be no misunderstanding afterwards, to occasion a quarrel. Solomon had spoken of hewing the trees (*v.* 6), and Hiram agrees to what he desired concerning that (*v.* 8); but nothing had been said concerning carriage, and this matter therefore must be settled. Land-carriage would be very troublesome and chargeable; he therefore undertakes to bring all the timber down from Lebanon by sea, a coasting voyage. Conveyance by water is a great convenience to trade, for which God is to have praise, who taught man that discretion. Observe what a definite bargain Hiram made. Solomon must appoint the place where the timber shall be delivered, and thither Hiram will undertake to bring it and be responsible for its safety. As the Sidonians excelled the Israelites in timber-work, so they did in sailing; for Tyre and Sidon were *situate at the entry of the sea* (Ezek. xxvii. 3): they therefore were fittest to take care of the water-carriage. *Tractant fabrilia fabri—Every artist has his trade assigned.* And, [3.] If Hiram undertake for the work, and *do all Solomon's desire concerning the timber* (*v.* 8), he justly expects that Solomon shall undertake for the wages: "*Thou shalt accomplish my desire in giving food for my household* (*v.* 9), not only for the workmen, but for my own family." If Tyre supply Israel with craftsmen, Israel will supply Tyre with corn, Ezek. xxvii. 17. Thus, by the wise disposal of Providence, one country has need of another and is benefited by another, that there may be mutual correspondence and dependence, to the glory of God our common parent.

10 So Hiram gave Solomon cedar trees and fir trees *according to* all his desire. 11 And Solomon gave Hiram twenty thousand measures of wheat *for* food to his household, and twenty measures of pure oil: thus gave Solomon to Hiram year by year. 12 And the LORD gave Solomon wisdom, as he promised him: and there was peace between Hiram and Solomon; and they two made a league together. 13 And king Solomon raised a levy out of all Israel; and the levy was thirty thousand men. 14 And he sent them to Lebanon, ten thousand a month by courses: a month they were in Lebanon, *and* two months at home: and Adoniram *was* over the levy. 15 And Solomon had threescore and ten thousand that bare burdens, and fourscore thousand hewers in the mountains; 16 Beside the chief of Solomon's officers

which *were* over the work, three thousand and three hundred, which ruled over the people that wrought in the work. 17 And the king commanded, and they brought great stones, costly stones, *and* hewed stones, to lay the foundation of the house. 18 And Solomon's builders and Hiram's builders did hew *them*, and the stonesquarers: so they prepared timber and stones to build the house.

Here is, I. The performance of the agreement between Solomon and Hiram. Each of the parties made good his engagement. 1. Hiram delivered Solomon the timber, according to his bargain, *v.* 10. The trees were Solomon's, but perhaps—*Materiam superabat opus—The workmanship was of more value than the article.* Hiram is therefore said to deliver the trees. 2. Solomon conveyed to Hiram the corn which he had promised him, *v.* 11. Thus let justice be followed (as the expression is, Deut. xvi. 20), justice on both sides, in every bargain.

II. The confirmation of the friendship that was between them hereby. *God gave Solomon wisdom* (*v.* 12), which was more and better than any thing Hiram did or could give him; but this made Hiram love him, and enabled Solomon to improve his kindness, so that they were both willing to ripen their mutual love into a mutual league, that it might be lasting. It is wisdom to strengthen our friendship with those whom we find to be honest and fair, lest new friends prove not so firm and so kind as old ones.

III. The labourers whom Solomon employed in preparing materials for the temple. 1. Some were Israelites, who were employed in the more easy and honourable part of the work, felling trees and helping to square them, in conjunction with Hiram's servants; for this he appointed 30,000, but employed only 10,000 at a time, so that for one month's work they had two months' vacation, both for rest and for the despatch of their own affairs at home, *v.* 13, 14. It was temple service, yet Solomon takes care that they shall not be over-worked. Great men ought to consider that their servants must rest as well as they. 2. Others were captives of other nations, who were to bear burdens and to hew stone (*v.* 15), and we read not that these had their resting times as the other had, for they were doomed to servitude. 3. There were some employed as directors and overseers (*v.* 16), 3300 that ruled over the people, and they were as necessary and useful in their place as the labourers in theirs; here were many hands and many eyes employed, for preparation was now to be made, not only for the temple, but for all the rest of Solomon's buildings, at Jerusalem, and here in the forest of Lebanon, and in other places of his dominion, of which see *ch.* ix. 17—19. He speaks of the vastness of his undertakings (Eccl. ii. 4, *I made me great works),* which required this vast number of workmen.

IV. The laying of the foundation of the temple; for that is the building his heart is chiefly upon, and therefore he begins with that, *v.* 17, 18. It should seem, Solomon was himself present, and president, at the founding of the temple, and that the first stone (as has been usual in famous buildings) was laid with some solemnity. *Solomon commanded and they brought costly stones* for the foundation; he would do every thing like himself, generously, and therefore would have some of the costliest stones laid, or buried rather, in the foundation, though, being out of sight, worse might have served. Christ, who is laid for a foundation, is an elect and precious stone (Isa. xxviii. 16), and the foundations of the church are said to be *laid with sapphires,* Isa. liv. 11, compare Rev. xxi. 19. That sincerity which is our gospel perfection obliges us to lay our foundation firm and to bestow most pains on that part of our religion which lies out of the sight of men.

CHAP. VI.

Great and long preparation had been making for the building of the temple, and here, at length, comes an account of the building of it; a noble piece of work it was, one of the wonders of the world, and, taking in its spiritual significancy, one of the glories of the church. Here is, I. The time when it was built (ver. 1), and how long it was in the building, ver. 37, 38. II. The silence with which it was built, ver. 7. III. The dimensions of it, ver. 2, 3. IV. The message God sent to Solomon, when it was in the building, ver. 11—13. V. The particulars: windows (ver. 4), chambers (ver. 5, 6, 8—10), the walls and flooring (ver. 15—18), the oracle (ver. 19—22), the cherubim (ver. 23—30), the doors (ver. 31—35), and the inner court, ver. 36. Many learned men have well bestowed their pains in expounding the description here given of the temple according to the rules of architecture, and solving the difficulties which, upon search, they find in it; but in that matter, having nothing new to offer, we will not be particular or curious; it was then well understood, and every man's eyes that saw this glorious structure furnished him with the best critical exposition of this chapter.

AND it came to pass in the four hundred and eightieth year after the children of Israel were come out of the land of Egypt, in the fourth year of Solomon's reign over Israel, in the month Zif, which *is* the second month, that he began to build the house of the LORD. 2 And the house which king Solomon built for the LORD, the length thereof *was* threescore cubits, and the breadth thereof twenty *cubits,* and the height thereof thirty cubits. 3 And the porch before the temple of the house, twenty cubits *was* the length thereof, according to the breadth of the house; *and* ten cubits *was* the breadth thereof before the house. 4 And for the house he made windows of narrow lights. 5 And against the wall of the house he built chambers round about, *against* the walls of the house round about, *both* of the temple and of the oracle: and he made chambers round about: 6 The nethermost chamber *was* five cubits broad, and the middle *was* six cubits broad, and the third *was* seven cubits broad: for without *in the wall* of the house he made narrowed rests round about, that *the beams* should not be fastened in the walls of the house. 7 And the house, when it was in building, was built of stone made ready before it was brought thither: so that there was neither hammer nor ax *nor* any tool of iron heard in the house, while it was in building. 8 The door for the middle chamber *was* in the right side of the house: and they went up with winding stairs into the middle *chamber*, and out of the middle into the third. 9 So he built the house, and finished it; and covered the house with beams and boards of cedar. 10 And *then* he built chambers against all the house, five cubits high: and they rested on the house with timber of cedar.

Here, I. The temple is called *the house of the Lord* (*v.* 1), because it was, 1. Directed and modelled by him. Infinite Wisdom was the architect, and gave David the plan or pattern by the Spirit, not by word of mouth only, but, for the greater certainty and exactactness, in writing (1 Chron. xxviii. 11, 12), as he had given to Moses in the mount a draught of the tabernacle. 2. Dedicated and devoted to him and to his honour, to be employed in his service, so his as never any other house was, for he manifested his glory in it (so as never in any other) in a way agreeable to that dispensation; for, when there were carnal ordinances, there was a *worldly sanctuary*, Heb ix. 1, 10. This gave it its *beauty of holiness*, that it was *the house of the Lord*, which far transcended all its other beauties.

II. The time when it began to be built is exactly set down. 1. It was just 480 years after the bringing of the children of Israel out of Egypt. Allowing forty years to Moses, seventeen to Joshua, 299 to the Judges, forty to Eli, forty to Samuel and Saul, forty to David, and four to Solomon before he began the work, we have just the sum of 480. So long it was after that holy state was founded before that holy house was built, which, in less than 430 years, was burnt by Nebuchadnezzar. It was thus deferred because Israel had, by their sins, rendered themselves unworthy of this honour, and because God would show how little he values external pomp and splendour in his service: he was in no haste for a temple. David's tent, which was clean and convenient, though it was neither stately nor rich, nor, for aught that appears, ever consecrated, is called the *house of the Lord* (2 Sam. xii. 20), and served as well as Solomon's temple; yet, when God gave Solomon great wealth, he put it into his heart thus to employ it, and graciously accepted him, chiefly because it was to be a shadow of good things to come, Heb. ix. 9. 2. It was in the fourth year of Solomon's reign, the first three years being taken up in settling the affairs of his kingdom, that he might not find any embarrassment from them in this work. It is not time lost which is spent in composing ourselves for the work of God, and disentangling ourselves from every thing which might distract or divert us. During this time he was adding to the preparations which his father had made (1 Chron. xxii. 14), hewing the stone, squaring the timber, and getting every thing ready, so that he is not to be blamed for slackness in deferring it so long. We are truly serving God when we are preparing for his service and furnishing ourselves for it.

III. The materials are brought in, ready for their place (*v.* 7), so ready that there was *neither hammer nor ax heard in the house while it was in building.* In all building Solomon prescribes it as a rule of prudence to *prepare the work in the field*, and *afterwards build*, Prov. xxiv. 27. But here, it seems, the preparation was more than ordinarily full and exact, to such a degree that, when the several parts came to be put together, there was nothing defective to be added, nothing amiss to be amended. It was to be the temple of the God of peace, and therefore no iron tool must be heard in it. Quietness and silence both become and befriend religious exercises: God's work should be done with as much care and as little noise as may be. The temple was thrown down with axes and hammers, and those that threw it down roared *in the midst of the congregation* (Ps. lxxiv. 4, 6); but it was built up in silence. Clamour and violence often hinder the work of God, but never further it.

IV. The dimensions are laid down (*v.* 2, 3) according to the rules of proportion. Some observe that the length and breadth were just double to that of the tabernacle. Now that Israel had grown more numerous the place of their meeting needed to be enlarged (Isa. liv. 1, 2), and now that they had grown richer they were the better able to enlarge it. Where God sows plentifully he expects to reap so.

V. An account of the windows (*v.* 4): They were *broad within, and narrow without*, *Marg.* Such should the eyes of our mind be, reflecting nearer on ourselves than on other people, looking much within, to judge ourselves, but little without, to censure our brethren. The narrowness of the lights intimated the darkness of that dispensation, in comparison with the gospel day.

VI. The chambers are described (*v.* 5, 6), which served as vestries, in which the utensils of the tabernacle were carefully laid up, and where the priests dressed and undressed themselves and left the clothes in which they ministered: probably in some of these chambers they feasted upon the holy things. Solomon was not so intent upon the magnificence of the house as to neglect the conveniences that were requisite for the offices thereof, that every thing might be done decently and in order. Care was taken that the beams should not be fastened in the walls to weaken them, *v.* 6. Let not the church's strength be impaired under pretence of adding to its beauty or convenience.

11 And the word of the LORD came to Solomon, saying, 12 *Concerning* this house which thou art in building, if thou wilt walk in my statutes, and execute my judgments, and keep all my commandments to walk in them; then will I perform my word with thee, which I spake unto David thy father: 13 And I will dwell among the children of Israel, and will not forsake my people Israel. 14 So Solomon built the house, and finished it.

Here is, I. The word God sent to Solomon, when he was engaged in building the temple. God let him know that he took notice of what he was doing, *the house he was now building*, *v.* 12. None employ themselves for God without having his eye upon them. "*I know thy works,* thy good works." He assured him that if he would proceed and persevere in obedience to the divine law, and keep in the way of duty and the true worship of God, the divine loving-kindness should be drawn out both to himself *(I will perform my word with thee)* and to his kingdom: "Israel shall be ever owned as my people; I will *dwell among them,* and *not forsake* them." This word God sent him probably by a prophet, 1. That by the promise he might be encouraged and comforted in his work. Perhaps sometimes the great care, expense, and fatigue of it, made him ready to wish he had never begun it; but this would help him through the difficulties of it, that the promised establishment of his family and kingdom would abundantly recompense all his pains. An eye to the promise will carry us cheerfully through our work; and those who wish well to the public will think nothing too much that they can do to secure and perpetuate to it the tokens of God's presence. 2. That, by the condition annexed, he might be awakened to consider that though he built the temple ever so strong the glory of it would soon depart, unless he and his people continued *to walk in God's statutes.* God plainly let him know that all this charge which he and his people were at, in erecting this temple, would neither excuse them from obedience to the law of God nor shelter them from his judgments in case of disobedience. Keeping God's commandments is better, and more pleasing to him, than building churches.

II. The work Solomon did for God: *So he built the house* (*v.* 14), *so* animated by the message God had sent him, *so* admonished not to expect that God should own his building unless he were obedient to his laws: "Lord, I proceed upon these terms, being firmly resolved to walk in thy statutes." The strictness of God's government will never drive a good man from his service, but quicken him in it. Solomon built and finished, he went on with the work, and God went along with him till it was completed. It is spoken both to God's praise and his: he grew not weary of the work, met not with any obstructions (as Ezra iv. 24), did not out-build his property, nor do it by halves, but, having begun to build, was both able and willing to finish; for he was a wise builder.

15 And he built the walls of the house within with boards of cedar, both the floor of the house, and the walls of the ceiling: *and* he covered *them* on the inside with wood, and covered the floor of the house with planks of fir. 16 And he built twenty cubits on the sides of the house, both the floor and the walls with boards of cedar: he even built *them* for it within, *even* for the oracle, *even* for the most holy *place.* 17 And the house, that *is* the temple before it, was forty cubits *long.* 18 And the cedar of the house within *was* carved with knops and open flowers: all *was* cedar; there was no stone seen. 19 And the oracle he prepared in the house within, to set there the ark of the covenant of the LORD. 20 And the oracle in the forepart *was* twenty cubits in length, and twenty cubits in breadth, and twenty cubits in the height thereof: and he overlaid it with pure gold; and *so* covered the altar *which was of* cedar. 21 So Solomon overlaid the house within with pure gold: and he made a partition by the chains of gold before the oracle; and he overlaid it with gold. 22 And

the whole house he overlaid with gold, until he had finished all the house: also the whole altar that *was* by the oracle he overlaid with gold. 23 And within the oracle he made two cherubims *of* olive tree, *each* ten cubits high. 24 And five cubits *was* the one wing of the cherub, and five cubits the other wing of the cherub: from the uttermost part of the one wing unto the uttermost part of the other *were* ten cubits. 25 And the other cherub *was* ten cubits: both the cherubims *were* of one measure and one size. 26 The height of the one cherub *was* ten cubits, and so *was it* of the other cherub. 27 And he set the cherubims within the inner house: and they stretched forth the wings of the cherubims, so that the wing of the one touched the *one* wall, and the wing of the other cherub touched the other wall; and their wings touched one another in the midst of the house. 28 And he overlaid the cherubims with gold. 29 And he carved all the walls of the house round about with carved figures of cherubims and palm trees and open flowers, within and without. 30 And the floor of the house he overlaid with gold, within and without. 31 And for the entering of the oracle he made doors *of* olive tree: the lintel *and* side posts *were* a fifth part *of the wall*. 32 The two doors also *were of* olive tree; and he carved upon them carvings of cherubims and palm trees and open flowers, and overlaid *them* with gold, and spread gold upon the cherubims, and upon the palm trees. 33 So also made he for the door of the temple posts *of* olive tree, a fourth part *of the wall*. 34 And the two doors *were of* fir tree: the two leaves of the one door *were* folding, and the two leaves of the other door *were* folding. 35 And he carved *thereon* cherubims and palm trees and open flowers: and covered *them* with gold fitted upon the carved work. 36 And he built the inner court with three rows of hewed stone, and a row of cedar beams. 37 In the fourth year was the foundation of the house of the LORD laid, in the month Zif: 38 And in the eleventh year, in the month Bul, which *is* the eighth month, was the house finished throughout all the parts thereof, and according to all the fashion of it. So was he seven years in building it.

Here, I. We have a particular account of the details of the building.

1. The wainscot of the temple. It was of cedar (*v.* 15), which was strong and durable, and of a very sweet smell. The wainscot was curiously carved with knops (like eggs or apples) and flowers, no doubt as the fashion then was, *v.* 18.

2. The gilding. It was not like ours, washed over, but *the whole house*, all the inside of the temple (*v.* 22), even the floor (*v.* 30), he *overlaid with gold*, and the most holy place with *pure gold*, *v.* 21. Solomon would spare no expense necessary to make it every way sumptuous. Gold was under foot there, as it should be in all the living temples: the abundance of it lessened its worth.

3. The oracle, or *speaking-place* (for so the word signifies), *the holy of holies*, so called because thence God spoke to Moses, and perhaps to the high priest, when he consulted with the breast-plate of judgment. In this place *the ark of the covenant was to be set*, *v.* 19. Solomon made every thing new, and more magnificent than it had been, except the ark, which was still the same that Moses made, with its mercy-seat and cherubim; that was the token of God's presence, which is always the same with his people whether they meet in tent or temple, and changes not with their condition.

4. The cherubim. Besides those at the ends of the mercy-seat, which covered the ark, (1.) Solomon set up two more, very large ones, images of young men (as some think), with wings made of olive-wood, and all overlaid with gold, *v.* 23, &c. This most holy place was much larger than that in the tabernacle, and therefore the ark would have seemed lost in it, and the dead wall would have been unsightly, if it had not been thus adorned. (2.) He carved cherubim upon all the walls of the house, *v.* 29. The heathen set up images of their gods and worshipped them; but these were designed to represent the servants and attendants of the God of Israel, the holy angels, not to be themselves worshipped *(see thou do it not)*, but to show how great he is whom we are to worship.

5. The doors. The folding doors that led into the oracle were but a fifth part of the wall (*v.* 31), those into the temple were a fourth part (*v.* 33); but both were beautified with cherubim engraven on them, *v.* 32, 35.

6. The inner court, in which the brazen altar was at which the priests ministered. This was separated from the court where the people were by a low wall, three rows of

hewn stone tipped with a cornice of cedar (*v.* 36), that over it the people might see what was done and hear what the priests said to them; for, even under that dispensation, they were not kept wholly either in the dark or at a distance.

7. The time spent in this building. It was but seven years and a half from the founding to the finishing of it, *v.* 38. Considering the vastness and elegance of the building, and the many appurtenances to it which were necessary to fit it for use, it was soon done. Solomon was in earnest in it, had money enough, had nothing to divert him from it, and many hands made quick work. He finished it (as the margin reads it) with all the appurtenances thereof, and with all the ordinances thereof, not only built the place, but set forward the work for which it was built.

II. Let us now see what was typified by this temple. 1. Christ is the true temple; he himself spoke of the temple of his body, John ii. 21. God himself prepared him his body, Heb. x. 5. *In him dwelt the fulness of the Godhead*, as the *Shechinah* in the temple. In him meet all God's spiritual Israel. Through him we have access with confidence to God. All the angels of God, those blessed cherubim, have a charge to worship him. 2. Every believer is a living temple, in whom the Spirit of God dwells, 1 Cor. iii. 16. Even the body is such by virtue of its union with the soul, 1 Cor. vi. 19. We are not only wonderfully made by the divine providence, but more wonderfully made anew by the divine grace. This living temple is built upon Christ as its foundation and will be perfected in due time. 3. The gospel church is the mystical temple; it grows to a *holy temple in the Lord* (Eph. ii. 21), enriched and beautified with the gifts and graces of the Spirit, as Solomon's temple with gold and precious stones. Only Jews built the tabernacle, but Gentiles joined with them in building the temple. Even strangers and foreigners are built up *a habitation of God,* Eph. ii. 19, 22. The temple was divided into the holy place and the most holy, the courts of it into the outer and inner; so there are the visible and the invisible church. The door into the temple was wider than that into the oracle. Many enter into profession that come short of salvation. This temple is built firm, upon a rock, not to be taken down as the tabernacle of the Old Testament was. The temple was long in preparing, but was built at last. The top-stone of the gospel church will, at length, be brought forth with shoutings, and it is a pity that there should be the clashing of axes and hammers in the building of it. Angels are ministering spirits, attending the church on all sides and all the members of it. 4. Heaven is the everlasting temple. There the church will be fixed, and no longer movable. The streets of the new Jerusalem, in allusion to the flooring of the temple, are said to be *of pure gold,* Rev. xxi. 21. The cherubim there always attend the throne of glory. The temple was uniform, and in heaven there is the perfection of beauty and harmony. In Solomon's temple there was no noise of axes and hammers. Every thing is quiet and serene in heaven; all that shall be stones in that building must in the present state of probation and preparation be fitted and made ready for it, must be hewn and squared by divine grace, and so made meet for a place there.

CHAP. VII.

As, in the story of David, one chapter of wars and victories follows another, so, in the story of Solomon, one chapter concerning his buildings follows another. In this chapter we have, I. His fitting up several buildings for himself and his own use, ver. 1—12. II. His furnishing the temple which he had built for God, 1. With two pillars, ver. 13—22. 2. With a molten sea, ver. 23—26. 3. With ten basins of brass (ver. 27—37), and ten lavers upon them, ver. 38, 39. 4. With all the other utensils of the temple, ver. 40—50. 5. With the things that his father had dedicated, ver. 51. The particular description of these things was not needless when it was written, nor is it now useless.

BUT Solomon was building his own house thirteen years, and he finished all his house. 2 He built also the house of the forest of Lebanon; the length thereof *was* a hundred cubits, and the breadth thereof fifty cubits, and the height thereof thirty cubits, upon four rows of cedar pillars, with cedar beams upon the pillars. 3 And *it was* covered with cedar above upon the beams, that *lay* on forty five pillars, fifteen *in* a row. 4 And *there were* windows *in* three rows, and light *was* against light *in* three ranks. 5 And all the doors and posts *were* square, with the windows: and light *was* against light *in* three ranks. 6 And he made a porch of pillars; the length thereof *was* fifty cubits, and the breadth thereof thirty cubits: and the porch *was* before them: and the *other* pillars and the thick beam *were* before them. 7 Then he made a porch for the throne where he might judge, *even* the porch of judgment: and *it was* covered with cedar from one side of the floor to the other. 8 And his house where he dwelt *had* another court within the porch, *which* was of the like work. Solomon made also a house for Pharaoh's daughter, whom he had taken *to wife*, like unto this porch. 9 All these *were of* costly stones, according to the measures of hewed stones, sawed with saws, within and without, even from the foundation unto the coping, and *so* on the

outside toward the great court. 10 And the foundation *was of* costly stones, even great stones stones of ten cubits, and stones of eight cubits. 11 And above *were* costly stones, after the measures of hewed stones, and cedars. 12 And the great court round about *was* with three rows of hewed stones, and a row of cedar beams, both for the inner court of the house of the LORD, and for the porch of the house.

Never had any man so much of the spirit of building as Solomon had, nor to better purpose; he began with the temple, built for God first, and then all his other buildings were comfortable. The surest foundations of lasting prosperity are those which are laid in an early piety, Matt. vi. 33. 1. He built a house for himself (*v.* 1), *where he dwelt*, *v.* 8. His father had built a good house; but it was no reflection upon his father for him to build a better, in proportion to the estate wherewith God had blessed him. Much of the comfort of this life is connected with an agreeable house. He was thirteen years building this house, whereas he built the temple in little more than seven years; not that he was more exact, but less eager and intent, in building his own house than in building God's. He was in no haste for his own palace, but impatient till the temple was finished and fit for use. Thus we ought to prefer God's honour before our own ease and satisfaction. 2. He built *the house of the forest at Lebanon* (*v.* 2), supposed to be a country seat near Jerusalem, so called from the pleasantness of its situation and the trees that encompassed it. I rather incline to think that it was a house built in the forest of Lebanon itself, whither (though far distant from Jerusalem) Solomon (having so many chariots and horses, and those dispersed into chariot-cities, which probably were his stages) might frequently retire with ease. It does not appear that his throne (mentioned *v.* 7) was at the house of the forest of Lebanon, and it was not at all improper to put his shields there as in a magazine. Express notice is taken of his buildings, not only in Jerusalem, but in Lebanon (*ch.* ix. 19), and we read of the tower of Lebanon, which looks towards Damascus (Cant. vii. 4), which probably was part of this house. A particular account is given of this house, that being built in Lebanon, a place famed for cedars, the pillars, and beams, and roof, were all cedar (*v.* 2, 3), and, being designed for pleasant prospects, there were three tiers of windows on each side, *light against light* (*v.* 4, 5), or, as it may be read, *prospect against prospect*. Those whose lost i cast in the country may be well reconciled to a country life by this, that some of the greatest princes have thought those the most pleasant of their days which they have spent in their country retirements. 3. He built piazzas before one of his houses, either that at Jerusalem or that in Lebanon, which were very famous—a porch of pillars (*v.* 6), perhaps for an exchange or a guard-house, or for those to walk in that attended him about business till they could have audience, or for state and magnificence. He himself speaks of Wisdom's building her house, and *hewing out her seven pillars* (Prov. ix. 1), for the shelter of those that, three verses before (*ch.* viii. 34), are said to *watch daily at her gates and to wait at the posts of her doors.* 4. At his house where he dwelt in Jerusalem he built a great hall, or porch of judgment, where was set the throne, or king's bench, for the trial of causes, in which he himself was appealed to *(placita coram ipso rege tenenda—causes were to be adjusted in the king's presence)*, and this was richly wainscoted with cedar, from the floor to the roof, *v.* 7. He had there also *another court within the porch*, nearer his house, of similar work, for his attendants to walk in, *v* 8. 5. He built a house for his wife, where she kept her court, *v.* 8. It is said to be *like the porch*, because built of cedar like it, though not in the same form; this, no doubt, was nearer adjoining to his own palace, yet perhaps if it had been as near as it ought to have been Solomon would not have multiplied wives as he did.

The wonderful magnificence of all these buildings is taken notice of, *v.* 9, &c. All the materials were the best of their kind. The foundation-stones were costly for their size, four or five yards square, or at least so many yards long (*v.* 10), and the stones of the building were costly for the workmanship, hewn and sawn, and in all respects finely wrought, *v.* 9, 11. The court of his own house was like that of the temple (*v.* 12, compare *ch.* vi. 36); so well did he like the model of God's courts that he made his own by it.

13 And king Solomon sent and fetched Hiram out of Tyre. 14 He *was* a widow's son of the tribe of Naphtali, and his father *was* a man of Tyre, a worker in brass: and he was filled with wisdom, and understanding, and cunning to work all works in brass. And he came to king Solomon, and wrought all his work. 15 For he cast two pillars of brass, of eighteen cubits high apiece: and a line of twelve cubits did compass either of them about. 16 And he made two chapiters *of* molten brass, to set upon the tops of the pillars: the height of the one chapiter *was* five cubits, and the height of the

other chapiter *was* five cubits: 17 *And* nets of checker work, and wreaths of chain work, for the chapiters which *were* upon the top of the pillars; seven for the one chapiter, and seven for the other chapiter. 18 And he made the pillars, and two rows round about upon the one network, to cover the chapiters that *were* upon the top, with pomegranates: and so did he for the other chapiter. 19 And the chapiters that *were* upon the top of the pillars *were* of lily work in the porch, four cubits. 20 And the chapiters upon the two pillars *had pomegranates* also above, over against the belly which *was* by the network: and the pomegranates *were* two hundred in rows round about upon the other chapiter. 21 And he set up the pillars in the porch of the temple: and he set up the right pillar, and called the name thereof Jachin: and he set up the left pillar, and called the name thereof Boaz. 22 And upon the top of the pillars *was* lily work: so was the work of the pillars finished. 23 And he made a molten sea, ten cubits from the one brim to the other; *it was* round all about, and his height *was* five cubits: and a line of thirty cubits did compass it round about. 24 And under the brim of it round about *there were* knops compassing it, ten in a cubit, compassing the sea round about: the knops *were* cast in two rows, when it was cast. 25 It stood upon twelve oxen, three looking toward the north, and three looking toward the west, and three looking toward the south, and three looking toward the east: and the sea *was set* above upon them, and all their hinder parts *were* inward. 26 And it *was* a handbreadth thick, and the brim thereof was wrought like the brim of a cup, with flowers of lilies: it contained two thousand baths. 27 And he made ten bases of brass; four cubits *was* the length of one base, and four cubits the breadth thereof, and three cubits the height of it. 28 And the work of the bases *was* on this *manner*: they had borders, and the borders *were* between the ledges: 29 And on the borders that *were* between the ledges *were* lions, oxen, and cherubims: and upon the ledges *there was* a base above: and beneath the lions and oxen *were* certain additions made of thin work. 30 And every base had four brasen wheels, and plates of brass: and the four corners thereof had undersetters: under the laver *were* undersetters molten, at the side of every addition. 31 And the mouth of it within the chapiter and above *was* a cubit: but the mouth thereof *was* round *after* the work of the base, a cubit and a half: and also upon the mouth of it *were* gravings with their borders, foursquare, not round. 32 And under the borders *were* four wheels; and the axletrees of the wheels *were joined* to the base: and the height of a wheel *was* a cubit and half a cubit. 33 And the work of the wheels *was* like the work of a chariot wheel: their axletrees, and their naves, and their felloes, and their spokes, *were* all molten. 34 And *there were* four undersetters to the four corners of one base: *and* the undersetters *were* of the very base itself. 35 And in the top of the base *was there* a round compass of half a cubit high: and on the top of the base the ledges thereof and the borders thereof *were* of the same. 36 For on the plates of the ledges thereof, and on the borders thereof, he graved cherubims, lions, and palm trees, according to the proportion of every one, and additions round about. 37 After this *manner* he made the ten bases: all of them had one casting, one measure, *and* one size. 38 Then made he ten lavers of brass: one laver contained forty baths: *and* every laver was four cubits: *and* upon every one of the ten bases one laver. 39 And he put five bases on the right side of the house, and five on the left side of the house: and he set the sea on the right side of the house eastward over against the south. 40 And Hiram made the lavers, and the shovels, and the basons. So Hiram made an end of doing all the work that he made king Solomon for the house of the LORD: 41 The two pillars, and the *two* bowls of the chapiters that *were* on the top of the two pillars; and the two networks, to cover the two bowls of the chapiters which *were* upon the top of the pillars; 42 And four hundred pomegranates for the two networks, *even* two rows of pomegranates for one network, to cover the two bowls of the chapiters that *were* upon the pillars; 43 And the ten bases, and ten lavers on the bases; 44 And one sea, and twelve oxen under the sea; 45 And the pots, and the shovels, and the basons: and all these vessels, which Hiram made to king Solomon for the house of the LORD, *were of* bright brass. 46 In the plain of Jordan did the king cast them, in the clay ground between Succoth and Zarthan. 47 And Solomon left all the vessels *unweighed,* because they were exceeding many: neither was the weight of the brass found out.

We have here an account of the brass-work about the temple. There was no iron about the temple, though we find David preparing for the temple *iron for things of iron,* 1 Chron. xxix. 2. What those things were we are not told, but some of the things of brass are here described and the rest mentioned.

I. The brasier whom Solomon employed to preside in this part of the work was Hiram, or Huram (2 Chron. iv. 11), who was by his mother's side an Israelite, of the tribe of Naphtali, by his father's side a man of Tyre, *v.* 14. If he had the ingenuity of a Tyrian, and the affection of an Israelite to the house of God (the head of a Tyrian and the heart of an Israelite), it was happy that the blood of the two nations mixed in him, for thereby he was qualified for the work to which he was designed. As the tabernacle was built with the wealth of Egypt, so the temple with the wit of Tyre. God will serve himself by the common gifts of the children of men.

II. The brass he made use of was the best he could get. All the brazen vessels were of *bright brass* (*v.* 45), *good* brass, so the Chaldee, that which was strongest and looked finest. God, who is the best, must be served and honoured with the best.

III. The place where all the brazen vessels were cast was the plain of Jordan, because the ground there was stiff and clayey, fit to make moulds of for the casting of the brass (*v.* 46), and Solomon would not have this dirty smoky work done in or near Jerusalem.

IV. The quantity was not accounted for The vessels were *unnumbered* (so it may be read (*v.* 47) as well as *unweighed*), *because they were exceedingly numerous,* and it would have been an endless thing to keep the account of them; *neither was the weight of the brass,* when it was delivered to the workmen, searched or enquired into; so honest were the workmen, and such great plenty of brass they had, that there was no danger of wanting. We must ascribe it to Solomon's care that he provided so much, not to his carelessness that he kept no account of it.

V. Some particulars of the brass-work are described.

1. Two brazen pillars, which were set up *in the porch of the temple* (*v.* 21), whether under the cover of the porch or in the open air is not certain; it was between the temple and the court of the priests. These pillars were neither to hang gates upon nor to rest any building upon, but purely for ornament and significancy. (1.) What an ornament they were we may gather from the account here given of the curious work that was about them, chequer-work, chain-work, network, lily-work, and pomegranates in rows, and all of bright brass, and framed no doubt according to the best rules of proportion, to please the eye. (2.) Their significancy is intimated in the names given them (*v.* 21): *Jachin—he will establish;* and *Boaz—in him is strength.* Some think they were intended for memorials of the pillar of cloud and fire which led Israel through the wilderness: I rather think them designed for memorandums to the priests and others that came to worship at God's door, [1.] To depend upon God only, and not upon any sufficiency of their own, for strength and establishment in all their religious exercises. When we come to wait upon God, and find our hearts wandering and unfixed, then by faith let us fetch in help from heaven: *Jachin—God will fix this roving mind. It is a good thing that the heart be established with grace.* We find ourselves weak and unable for holy duties, but this is our encouragement: *Boaz—in him is our strength,* who works in us both to will and to do. *I will go in the strength of the Lord God.* Spiritual strength and stability are to be had at the door of God's temple, where we must wait for the gifts of grace in the use of the means of grace. [2.] It was a memorandum to them of the strength and establishment of the temple of God among them. Let them keep close to God and duty, and they should never lose their dignities and privileges, but the grant should be confirmed and perpetuated to them. The gospel church is what God will establish, what he will strengthen, and what the gates of hell can never prevail against. But, with respect to this temple, when it was destroyed particular notice was taken of the destroying

of these pillars (2 Kings xxv. 13, 17), which had been the tokens of its establishment, and would have been so if they had not forsaken God.

2. A brazen sea, a very large vessel, above five yards in diameter, and which contained above 500 barrels of water for the priests' use, in washing themselves and the sacrifices, and keeping the courts of the temple clean, *v.* 23, &c. It stood raised upon the figures of twelve oxen in brass, so high that either they must have stairs to climb up to it or cocks at the bottom to draw water from it. The Gibeonites, or Nethinim, who were to draw water for the house of God, had the care of filling it. Some think Solomon made the images of oxen to support this great cistern in contempt of the golden calf which Israel had worshipped, that (as bishop Patrick expresses it) the people might see there was nothing worthy of adoration in those figures; they were fitter to make posts of than to make gods of. Yet this prevailed not to prevent Jerusalem's setting up the calves for deities. In the court of the tabernacle there was only a laver of brass provided to wash in, but in the court of the temple a sea of brass, intimating that by the gospel of Christ much fuller preparation is made for our cleansing than was by the law of Moses. That had a laver, this has a sea, *a fountain opened*, Zech. xiii. 1.

3. Ten bases, or stands, or settles, of brass, on which were put ten lavers, to be filled with water for the service of the temple, because there would not be room at the molten sea for all that had occasion to wash there. The bases on which the lavers were fixed are very largely described here, *v.* 27, &c. They were curiously adorned and set upon wheels, that the lavers might be removed as there was occasion; but ordinarily they stood in two rows, five on one side of the court and five on the other, *v.* 39. Each laver contained forty baths, that is, about ten barrels, *v.* 38. Those must be very *clean that bear the vessels of the Lord.* Spiritual priests and spiritual sacrifices must be washed in the laver of Christ's blood and of regeneration. We must wash often, for we daily contract pollution, must cleanse our hands and purify our hearts. Plentiful provision is made for our cleansing; so that if we have our lot for ever among the unclean it will be our own fault.

4. Besides these, there was a vast number of brass pots made to boil the flesh of the peace-offerings in, which the priests and offerers were to feast upon before the Lord (see 1 Sam. ii. 14); also shovels, wherewith they took out the ashes of the altar. Some think the word signifies *flesh-hooks,* with which they took meat out of the pot. The basins also were made of brass, to receive the blood of the sacrifices. These are put for all the utensils of the brazen altar, Exod. xxxviii. 3. While they were about it they made abundance of them, that they might have a good stock by them when those that were first in use wore out and went to decay. Thus Solomon, having wherewithal to do so, provided for posterity.

48 And Solomon made all the vessels that *pertained* unto the house of the LORD: the altar of gold, and the table of gold, whereupon the showbread *was,* 49 And the candlesticks of pure gold, five on the right *side,* and five on the left, before the oracle, with the flowers, and the lamps, and the tongs *of* gold, 50 And the bowls, and the snuffers, and the basons, and the spoons, and the censers *of* pure gold: and the hinges *of* gold, *both* for the doors of the inner house, the most holy *place, and* for the doors of the house, *to wit,* of the temple. 51 So was ended all the work that king Solomon made for the house of the LORD. And Solomon brought in the things which David his father had dedicated; *even* the silver, and the gold, and the vessels, did he put among the treasures of the house of the LORD.

Here is, 1. The making of the gold work of the temple, which it seems was done last, for with it the work of the house of God ended. All within doors was gold, and all made new (except the ark, with its mercy-seat and cherubim), the old being either melted down or laid by—the golden altar, table, and candlestick, with all their appurtenances. The altar of incense was still *one,* for Christ and his intercession are so: but he made ten golden tables, 2 Chron. iv. 8 (though here mention is made of that one only *on which the show-bread was* (*v.* 48), which we may suppose was larger than the rest and to which the rest were as sideboards), and *ten golden candlesticks* (*v.* 49), intimating the much greater plenty both of spiritual food and heavenly light which the gospel blesses us with than the law of Moses did or could afford. Even the hinges of the door were of gold (*v.* 50), that every thing might be alike magnificent, and bespeak Solomon's generosity. Some suggest that every thing was made thus splendid in God's temple to keep the people from idolatry, for none of the idol-temples were so rich and fine as this: but how little the expedient availed the event showed. 2. The bringing in of the dedicated things, which David had devoted to the honour of God, *v.* 51. What was not expended in the building and furniture was laid up in the treasury, for repairs, exigencies, and the constant charge of the temple-service What the parents have dedicated to God the children ought by no means to alienate or recal, but should cheerfully devote what was intended for pious and charitable uses, that they may, with their estates, inherit the blessing.

CHAP. VIII.

The building and furniture of the temple were very glorious, but the dedication of it exceeds in glory as much as prayer and praise, the work of saints, exceed the casting of metal and the graving of stones, the work of the craftsman. The temple was designed for the keeping up of the correspondence between God and his people; and here we have an account of the solemnity of their first meeting there. I. The representatives of all Israel were called together (ver. 1, 2), to keep a feast to the honour of God, for fourteen days, ver. 65. II. The priests brought the ark into the most holy place, and fixed it there, ver. 3–9. III. God took possession of it by a cloud, ver. 10, 11. IV. Solomon, with thankful acknowledgments to God, informed the people touching the occasion of their meeting, ver. 12–21. V. In a long prayer he recommended to God's gracious acceptance all the prayers that should be made in or towards this place, ver. 22–53. VI. He dismissed the assembly with a blessing and an exhortation, ver. 54–61. VII. He offered abundance of sacrifices, on which he and his people feasted, and so parted, with great satisfaction, ver. 62–66. These were Israel's golden days, days of the Son of man in type.

THEN Solomon assembled the elders of Israel, and all the heads of the tribes, the chief of the fathers of the children of Israel, unto king Solomon in Jerusalem, that they might bring up the ark of the covenant of the LORD out of the city of David, which *is* Zion. 2 And all the men of Israel assembled themselves unto king Solomon at the feast in the month Ethanim, which *is* the seventh month. 3 And all the elders of Israel came, and the priests took up the ark. 4 And they brought up the ark of the LORD, and the tabernacle of the congregation, and all the holy vessels that *were* in the tabernacle, even those did the priests and the Levites bring up. 5 And king Solomon, and all the congregation of Israel, that were assembled unto him, *were* with him before the ark, sacrificing sheep and oxen, that could not be told nor numbered for multitude. 6 And the priests brought in the ark of the covenant of the LORD unto his place, into the oracle of the house, to the most holy *place*, *even* under the wings of the cherubims. 7 For the cherubims spread forth *their* two wings over the place of the ark, and the cherubims covered the ark and the staves thereof above. 8 And they drew out the staves, that the ends of the staves were seen out in the holy *place* before the oracle, and they were not seen without: and there they are unto this day. 9 *There was* nothing in the ark save the two tables of stone, which Moses put there at Horeb, when the LORD made *a covenant* with the children of Israel, when they came out of the land of Egypt. 10 And it came to pass, when the priests were come out of the holy *place*, that the cloud filled the house of the LORD, 11 So that the priests could not stand to minister because of the cloud: for the glory of the LORD had filled the house of the LORD.

The temple, though richly beautified, yet while it was without the ark was like a body without a soul, or a candlestick without a candle, or (to speak more properly) a house without an inhabitant. All the cost and pains bestowed on this stately structure are lost if God do not accept them; and, unless he please to own it as the place where he will record his name, it is after all but a ruinous heap. When therefore *all the work* is ended (*ch.* vii. 51), the *one thing needful* is yet behind, and that is the bringing in of the ark. This therefore is the end which must crown the work, and which here we have an account of the doing of with great solemnity.

I. Solomon presides in this service, as David did in the bringing up of the ark to Jerusalem; and neither of them thought it below him to follow the ark nor to lead the people in their attendance on it. Solomon glories in the title of the *preacher* (Eccl. i. 1), and the *master of assemblies*, Eccl. xii. 11. This great assembly he summons (*v.* 1), and he is the centre of it, for to him they all assembled (*v.* 2) *at the feast in the seventh month*, namely, the feast of tabernacles, which was appointed on the fifteenth day of that month, Lev. xxiii. 34. David, like a very *good* man, brings the ark to a *convenient* place, near him; Solomon, like a very *great* man, brings it to a *magnificent* place. As every man has received the gift, so let him minister; and let children proceed in God's service where their parents left off.

II. All Israel attend the service, their judges and the chief of their tribes and families, all their officers, civil and military, and (as they speak in the north) the heads of their clans. A convention of these might well be called *an assembly of all Israel.* These came together, on this occasion, 1. To do honour to Solomon, and to return him the thanks of the nation for all the good offices he had done in kindness to them. 2. To do honour to the ark, to pay respect to it, and testify their universal joy and satisfaction in its settlement. The advancement of the ark in external splendour, though it has often proved too strong a temptation to its hypocritical followers, yet, because it may prove an advantage to its true interests, is to be rejoiced in (with trembling) by all that wish well to it. Public mercies call for public acknowledgments. Those that appeared before the Lord did not appear empty, for they all sacrificed sheep and oxen innumerable, *v.* 5. The people in Solomon's time were very rich, very easy, and very cheerful, and therefore it was fit that, on this occasion, they should consecrate not only their cheerfulness, but a part of their wealth, to God and his honour.

III. The priests do their part of the service. In the wilderness, the Levites were to carry the ark, because then there were not priests enough to do it; but here (it being the last time that the ark was to be carried) the priests themselves did it, as they were ordered to do when it surrounded Jericho. We are here told, 1. What was in the ark, nothing but the two tables of stone (*v.* 9), a treasure far exceeding all the dedicated things both of David and Solomon. The pot of manna and Aaron's rod were *by* the ark, but not *in* it. 2. What was brought up with the ark (*v.* 4): *The tabernacle of the congregation.* It is probable that both that which Moses set up in the wilderness, which was in Gibeon, and that which David pitched in Zion, were brought to the temple, to which they did, as it were, surrender all their holiness, merging it in that of the temple, which must henceforward be the place where God must be sought unto. Thus will all the church's holy things on earth, that are so much its joy and glory, be swallowed up in the perfection of holiness above. 3. Where it was fixed in its place, the place appointed for its rest after all its wanderings (*v.* 6): *In the oracle of the house,* whence they expected God to speak to them, even in the most holy place, which was made so by the presence of the ark, *under the wings of the* great *cherubim* which Solomon set up (*ch.* vi. 27), signifying the special protection of angels, under which God's ordinances and the assemblies of his people are taken. The staves of the ark were drawn out, so as to be seen from under the wings of the cherubim, to direct the high priest to the mercy-seat, over the ark, when he went in, once a year, to sprinkle the blood there; so that still they continued of some use, though there was no longer occasion for them to carry it by.

IV. God graciously owns what is done and testifies his acceptance of it, *v.* 10, 11. The priests might come into the most holy place till God manifested his glory there; but, thenceforward, none might, at their peril, approach the ark, except the high priest, on the day of atonement. Therefore it was not till the priests had come out of the oracle that the *Shechinah* took possession of it, in a cloud, which filled not only the most holy place, but the temple, so that the priests who burnt incense at the golden altar could not bear it. By this visible emanation of the divine glory, 1. God put an honour upon the ark, and owned it as a token of his presence. The glory of it had been long diminished and eclipsed by its frequent removes, the meanness of its lodging, and its being exposed too much to common view; but God will now show that it is as dear to him as ever, and he will have it looked upon with as much veneration as it was when Moses first brought it into his tabernacle. 2. He testified his acceptance of the building and furnishing of the temple as good service done to his name and his kingdom among men. 3. He struck an awe upon this great assembly; and, by what they saw, confirmed their belief of what they read in the books of Moses concerning the glory of God's appearances to their fathers, that hereby they might be kept close to the service of the God of Israel and fortified against temptations to idolatry. 4. He showed himself ready to hear the prayer Solomon was now about to make; and not only so, but took up his residence in this house, that all his praying people might there be encouraged to make their applications to him. But the glory of God appeared in a cloud, a dark cloud, to signify, (1.) The darkness of that dispensation in comparison with the light of the gospel, by which, *with open face, we behold, as in a glass, the glory of the Lord.* (2.) The darkness of our present state in comparison with the vision of God, which will be the happiness of heaven, where the divine glory is unveiled. Now we can only say what he is not, but then we shall see him as he is.

12 Then spake Solomon, The LORD said that he would dwell in the thick darkness. 13 I have surely built thee a house to dwell in, a settled place for thee to abide in for ever. 14 And the king turned his face about, and blessed all the congregation of Israel: (and all the congregation of Israel stood;) 15 And he said, Blessed *be* the LORD God of Israel, which spake with his mouth unto David my father, and hath with his hand fulfilled *it*, saying, 16 Since the day that I brought forth my people Israel out of Egypt, I chose no city out of all the tribes of Israel to build a house, that my name might be therein; but I chose David to be over my people Israel. 17 And it was in the heart of David my father to build a house for the name of the LORD God of Israel. 18 And the LORD said unto David my father, Whereas it was in thine heart to build a house unto my name, thou didst well that it was in thine heart. 19 Nevertheless

thou shalt not build the house; but thy son that shall come forth out of thy loins, he shall build the house unto my name. 20 And the LORD hath performed his word that he spake, and I am risen up in the room of David my father, and sit on the throne of Israel, as the LORD promised, and have built a house for the name of the LORD God of Israel. 21 And I have set there a place for the ark, wherein *is* the covenant of the LORD, which he made with our fathers, when he brought them out of the land of Egypt.

Here, I. Solomon encourages the priests, who came out of the temple from their ministration, much astonished at the dark cloud that overshadowed them. The disciples of Christ *feared when they entered into the cloud,* though it was a *bright cloud* (Luke ix. 34), so did the priests when they found themselves wrapped in a thick cloud. To silence their fears, 1. He reminds them of that which they could not but know, that this was a token of God's presence (*v.* 12): *The Lord said he would dwell in the thick darkness.* It is so far from being a token of his displeasure that it is an indication of his favour; for he had said, *I will appear in a cloud,* Lev. xvi. 2. Note, Nothing is more effectual to reconcile us to dark dispensations than to consider what God hath said, and to compare his word and works together; as Lev. x. 3, *This is that which the Lord hath said.* God is light (1 John i. 5), and he dwells in light (1 Tim. vi. 16), but he dwells with men *in the thick darkness*, makes that his pavilion, because they could not bear the dazzling brightness of his glory. *Verily thou art a God that hidest thyself.* Thus our holy faith is exercised and our holy fear is increased. Where God dwells in light faith is swallowed up in vision and fear in love. 2. He himself bids it welcome, as worthy of all acceptation; and since God, by this cloud, came down to take possession, he does, in a few words, solemnly give him possession (*v.* 13): "*Surely I come,*" says God. "*Amen,*" says Solomon, "*Even so, come, Lord.* The house is thy own, entirely thy own, *I have surely built it for thee,* and furnished it for thee; it is for ever thy own, *a settled place for thee to abide in for ever;* it shall never be alienated nor converted to any other use; the ark shall never be removed from it, never unsettled again." It is Solomon's joy that God has taken possession; and it is his desire that he would keep possession. Let not the priests therefore dread that in which Solomon so much triumphs.

II. He instructs the people, and gives them a plain account concerning this house, which they now saw God take possession of. He spoke briefly to the priests, to satisfy them (a word to the wise), but *turned his face about* (*v.* 14) from them *to the congregation* that stood in the outer court, and addressed himself to them largely.

1. He blessed them. When they saw the dark cloud enter the temple they blessed themselves, being astonished at it and afraid lest the thick darkness should be utter darkness to them. The amazing sight, such as they had never seen in their days, we may suppose, drove every man to his prayers, and the vainest minds were made serious by it. Solomon therefore set in with their prayers, and blessed them all, as one having authority (for *the less is blessed of the better*); in God's name, he spoke peace to them, and a blessing, like that with which the angel blessed Gideon when he was in a fright, upon a similar occasion. Judg. vi. 22, 23, *Peace be unto thee. Fear not; thou shalt not die.* Solomon *blessed them,* that is, he pacified them, and freed them from the consternation they were in. To receive this blessing, they all stood up, in token of reverence and readiness to hear and accept it. It is a proper posture to be in when the blessing is pronounced.

2. He informed them concerning this house which he had built and was now dedicating.

(1.) He began his account with a thankful acknowledgment of the good hand of his God upon him hitherto: *Blessed be the Lord God of Israel, v.* 15. What we have the pleasure of God must have the praise of. He thus engaged the congregation to lift up their hearts in thanksgivings to God, which would help to still the tumult of spirit which, probably, they were in. "Come," says he, "let God's awful appearances not drive us from him, but draw us to him; *let us bless the Lord God of Israel.*" Thus Job, under a dark scene, *blessed the name of the Lord.* Solomon here blessed God, [1.] For his promise which he *spoke with his mouth to David.* [2.] For the performance, that he had now *fulfilled it with his hand.* We have then the best sense of God's mercies, and most grateful both to ourselves and to our God, when we run up those streams to the fountain of the covenant, and compare what God does with what he has said.

(2.) Solomon is now making a solemn surrender or dedication of this house unto God, delivering it to God by his own act and deed. Grants and conveyances commonly begin with recitals of what has been before done, leading to what is now done: accordingly, here is a recital of the special causes and considerations moving Solomon to build this house. [1.] He recites the want of such a place. It was necessary that this should be premised; for, according to the dispensation they were under, there must be but one place in which they must expect God to record his name. If, therefore, there were any other chosen, this would be a usurpation. But he shows, from what God himself had said, that there was no other (*v.* 16): *I chose no city to build a house in for my name;* therefore there is occasion for the building of this. [2.] He recites David's purpose to build such a place. God chose the person first that should rule his people (*I chose David, v.* 16) and then put it into *his heart to build a house* for God's name, *v.* 17. It was not a project of his own, for the magnifying of himself; but his good father, of blessed memory, laid the first design of it, though he lived not to lay the first stone. [3.] He recites God's promise concerning himself. God approved his father's purpose (*v.* 18): *Thou didst well, that it was in thy heart.* Note, Sincere intentions to do good shall be graciously approved and accepted of God, though Providence prevent our putting them in execution. *The desire of a man is his kindness.* See 2 Cor. viii. 12. God accepted David's good will, yet would not permit him to do the good work, but reserved the honour of it for his son (*v.* 19): *He shall build the house to my name;* so that what he had done was not of his own head, nor for his own glory, but the work itself was according to his father's design and his doing it was according to God's designation. [4.] He recites what he himself had done, and with what intention: *I have built a house,* not for my own name, but *for the name of the Lord God of Israel* (*v.* 20), and *set there a place for the ark, v.* 21. Thus all the right, title, interest, claim, and demand, whatsoever, which he or his had or might have in or to this house, or any of its appurtenances, he resigns, surrenders, and gives up, to God for ever. It is for his name, and his ark. In this, says he, *the Lord hath performed his word that he spoke.* Note, Whatever good we do, we must look upon it as the performance of God's promise to us, rather than the performance of our promises to him. The more we do for God the more we are indebted to him; for our sufficiency is of him, and not of ourselves.

22 And Solomon stood before the altar of the LORD in the presence of all the congregation of Israel, and spread forth his hands toward heaven: 23 And he said, LORD God of Israel, *there is* no God like thee, in heaven above, or on earth beneath, who keepest covenant and mercy with thy servants that walk before thee with all their heart: 24 Who hast kept with thy servant David my father that thou promisedst him: thou spakest also with thy mouth, and hast fulfilled *it* with thine hand, as *it is* this day. 25 Therefore now, LORD God of Israel, keep with thy servant David my father that thou promisedst him, saying, There shall not fail thee a man in my sight to sit on the throne of Israel; so that thy children take heed to their way, that they walk before me as thou hast walked before me. 26 And now, O God of Israel, let thy word, I pray thee, be verified, which thou spakest unto thy servant David my father. 27 But will God indeed dwell on the earth? behold, the heaven and heaven of heavens cannot contain thee; how much less this house that I have builded? 28 Yet have thou respect unto the prayer of thy servant, and to his supplication, O LORD my God, to hearken unto the cry and to the prayer, which thy servant prayeth before thee to day: 29 That thine eyes may be open toward this house night and day, *even* toward the place of which thou hast said, My name shall be there: that thou mayest hearken unto the prayer which thy servant shall make toward this place. 30 And hearken thou to the supplication of thy servant, and of thy people Israel, when they shall pray toward this place: and hear thou in heaven thy dwelling place: and when thou hearest, forgive. 31 If any man trespass against his neighbour, and an oath be laid upon him to cause him to swear, and the oath come before thine altar in this house: 32 Then hear thou in heaven, and do, and judge thy servants, condemning the wicked, to bring his way upon his head; and justifying the righteous, to give him according to his righteousness. 33 When thy people Israel be smitten down before the enemy, because they have sinned against thee, and shall turn again to thee, and confess thy name, and pray, and make supplication unto thee in this house: 34 Then hear thou in heaven, and forgive the sin of thy people Israel, and bring them again unto the land which thou gavest unto their fathers. 35 When heaven is shut up, and there is no rain, because they have sinned against

thee: if they pray toward this place, and confess thy name, and turn from their sin, when thou afflictest them: 36 Then hear thou in heaven, and forgive the sin of thy servants, and of thy people Israel, that thou teach them the good way wherein they should walk, and give rain upon thy land, which thou hast given to thy people for an inheritance. 37 If there be in the land famine, if there be pestilence, blasting, mildew, locust, *or* if there be caterpillar; if their enemy besiege them in the land of their cities; whatsoever plague, whatsoever sickness *there be;* 38 What prayer and supplication soever be *made* by any man, *or* by all thy people Israel, which shall know every man the plague of his own heart, and spread forth his hands toward this house: 39 Then hear thou in heaven thy dwelling place, and forgive, and do, and give to every man according to his ways, whose heart thou knowest; (for thou, *even* thou only, knowest the hearts of all the children of men;) 40 That they may fear thee all the days that they live in the land which thou gavest unto our fathers. 41 Moreover concerning a stranger, that *is* not of thy people Israel, but cometh out of a far country for thy name's sake; 42 (For they shall hear of thy great name, and of thy strong hand, and of thy stretched out arm;) when he shall come and pray toward this house; 43 Hear thou in heaven thy dwelling place, and do according to all that the stranger calleth to thee for: that all people of the earth may know thy name, to fear thee, as *do* thy people Israel; and that they may know that this house, which I have builded, is called by thy name. 44 If thy people go out to battle against their enemy, whithersoever thou shalt send them, and shall pray unto the LORD toward the city which thou hast chosen, and *toward* the house that I have built for thy name: 45 Then hear thou in heaven their prayer and their supplication, and maintain their cause. 46 If they sin against thee, (for *there is* no man that sinneth not,) and thou be angry with them, and deliver them to the enemy, so that they carry them away captives unto the land of the enemy, far or near; 47 *Yet* if they shall bethink themselves in the land whither they were carried captives, and repent, and make supplication unto thee in the land of them that carried them captives, saying, We have sinned, and have done perversely, we have committed wickedness; 48 And *so* return unto thee with all their heart, and with all their soul, in the land of their enemies, which led them away captive, and pray unto thee toward their land, which thou gavest unto their fathers, the city which thou hast chosen, and the house which I have built for thy name: 49 Then hear thou their prayer and their supplication in heaven thy dwelling place, and maintain their cause, 50 And forgive thy people that have sinned against thee, and all their transgressions wherein they have transgressed against thee, and give them compassion before them who carried them captive, that they may have compassion on them: 51 For they *be* thy people, and thine inheritance, which thou broughtest forth out of Egypt, from the midst of the furnace of iron: 52 That thine eyes may be open unto the supplication of thy servant, and unto the supplication of thy people Israel, to hearken unto them in all that they call for unto thee. 53 For thou didst separate them from among all the people of the earth, *to be* thine inheritance, as thou spakest by the hand of Moses thy servant, when thou broughtest our fathers out of Egypt, O Lord GOD.

Solomon having made a general surrender of this house to God, which God had signified his acceptance of by taking possession, next follows Solomon's prayer, in which he makes a more particular declaration of the uses of that surrender, with all humility and reverence, desiring that God would agree thereto. In short, it is his request that this temple may be deemed and taken, not only for a house of sacrifice (no mention is made of that in all this prayer, that was taken for granted), but a *house of prayer for all people;* and herein it was a type of the gospel church; see Isa. lvi. 7, compared with Matt. xxi. 13. Therefore Solomon opened this house, not only with an extraordinary sacrifice, but with an extraordinary prayer.

I. The person that prayed this prayer was great. Solomon did not appoint one of the priests to do it, nor one of the prophets, but did it himself, *in the presence of all the congregation of Israel, v.* 22. 1. It was well that he was able to do it, a sign that he had made a good improvement of the pious education which his parents gave him. With all his learning, it seems, he learnt to pray well, and knew how to express himself to God in a suitable manner, *pro re nata—on the spur of the occasion,* without a prescribed form. In the crowd of his philosophical transactions, his proverbs, and songs, he did not forget his devotions. He was a gainer by prayer (*ch.* iii. 11, &c.), and, we may suppose, gave himself much to it, so that he excelled, as we find here, in praying gifts. 2. It was well that he was willing to do it, and not shy of performing divine service before so great a congregation. He was far from thinking it any disparagement to him to be his own chaplain and the mouth of the assembly to God; and shall any think themselves too great to do this office for their own families? Solomon, in all his other glory, even on his ivory throne, looked not so great as he did now. Great men should thus support the reputation of religious exercises and so honour God with their greatness. Solomon was herein a type of Christ, the great intercessor for all over whom he rules.

II. The posture in which he prayed was very reverent, and expressive of humility, seriousness, and fervency in prayer. He *stood before the altar of the Lord,* intimating that he expected the success of his prayer in virtue of that sacrifice which should be offered up in the fulness of time, typified by the sacrifices offered at that altar. But when he addressed himself to prayer, 1. He *kneeled down,* as appears, *v.* 54, where he is said to *rise from his knees;* compare 2 Chron. vi. 13. Kneeling is the most proper posture for prayer, Eph. iii. 14. The greatest of men must not think it below them to *kneel before the Lord their Maker.* Mr. Herbert says, "Kneeling never spoiled silk stockings." 2. *He spread forth his hands towards heaven,* and (as it should seem by *v.* 54) continued so to the end of the prayer, hereby expressing his desire towards, and expectations from, God, as a *Father in heaven.* He spread forth his hands, as it were to offer up the prayer from an open enlarged heart and to present it to heaven, and also to receive thence, with both arms, the mercy which he prayed for. Such outward expressions of the fixedness and fervour of devotion ought not to be despised or ridiculed.

III. The prayer itself was very long, and perhaps much longer than is here recorded. At the throne of grace we have liberty of speech, and should use our liberty. It is not making long prayers, but making them for a pretence, that Christ condemns. In this excellent prayer Solomon does, as we should in every prayer,

1. Give glory to God. This he begins with, as the most proper act of adoration. He addresses himself to God as the *Lord God of Israel,* a God in covenant with them And, (1.) He gives him the praise of what he is, in general, the best of beings in himself (*"There is no God like thee,* none of the powers in heaven or earth to be compared with thee"), and the best of masters to his people: *"Who keepest covenant and mercy with thy servants;* not only as good as thy word in keeping covenant, but better than thy word in keeping mercy, doing that for them of which thou hast not given them an express promise, provided they *walk before thee with all their heart,* are zealous for thee, with an eye to thee." (2.) He gives him thanks for what he had done, in particular, for his family (*v.* 24): *"Thou hast kept with thy servant David,* as with thy other servants, *that which thou promisedst him."* The promise was a great favour to him, his support and joy, and now performance is the crown of it: *Thou hast fulfilled it, as it is this day.* Fresh experiences of the truth of God's promises call for enlarged praises.

2. He sues for grace and favour from God. (1.) That God would perform to him and his the mercy which he had promised, *v.* 25, 26. Observe how this comes in. He thankfully acknowledges the performance of the promise in part; hitherto God had been faithful to his word: *"Thou hast kept with thy servant David that which thou promisedst him,* so far that his son fills his throne and has built the intended temple; *therefore now keep with thy servant David that which thou hast* further *promised him,* and which yet remains to be fulfilled in its season." Note, The experiences we have had of God's performing his promises should encourage us to depend upon them and plead them with God: and those who expect further mercies must be thankful for former mercies. Hitherto God has helped, 2 Cor. i. 10. Solomon repeats the promise (*v.* 25): *There shall not fail thee a man to sit on the throne,* not omitting the condition, *so that thy children take heed to their way;* for we cannot expect God's performance of the promise but upon our performance of the condition. And then he humbly begs this entail (*v.* 26): *Now, O God of Israel! let thy word be verified.* God's promises (as we have often observed) must be both the guide of our desires and the ground of our hopes and expectations in prayer. David had prayed (2 Sam. vii. 25): *Lord, do as thou hast said.* Note, Children should learn of their godly parents how to pray, and plead in prayer.

(2.) That God would have respect to this temple which he had now taken possession of, and that his eyes might be *continually open towards it* (*v.* 29), that he would graciously own it, and so put an honour upon it. To this purpose,

[1.] He premises, *First,* A humble admiration of God's gracious condescension (*v.* 27): "*But will God indeed dwell on the earth?* Can we imagine that a Being infinitely high, and holy, and happy, will stoop so low as to let it be said of him that he *dwells upon the earth* and blesses the worms of the earth with his presence—the earth, that is corrupt, and overspread with sin—cursed, and reserved to fire? *Lord, how is it?*" *Secondly,* A humble acknowledgment of the incapacity of the house he had built, though very capacious, to contain God: "*The heaven of heavens cannot contain thee,* for no place can include him who is present in all places; even this house is too little, too mean to be the residence of him that is infinite in being and glory." Note, When we have done the most we can for God we must acknowledge the infinite distance and disproportion between us and him, between our services and his perfections.

[2.] This premised, he prays in general, *First,* That God would graciously hear and answer the prayer he was now praying, *v.* 28. It was a humble prayer *(the prayer of thy servant),* an earnest prayer (such a prayer as is a *cry),* a prayer made in faith *(before thee,* as the Lord, and my God): "Lord, *hearken to it, have respect to it,* not as the prayer of Israel's king (no man's dignity in the world, or titles of honour, will recommend him to God), but as the prayer of thy servant." *Secondly,* That God would in like manner hear and answer all the prayers that should, at any time hereafter, be made in or towards this house which he had now built, and of which God had said, *My name shall be there* (*v.* 29), his own prayers *(Hearken to the prayers which thy servant shall make),* and the prayers of all Israel, and of every particular Israelite (*v.* 30): "*Hear it in heaven, that* is indeed *thy dwelling-place,* of which this is but a figure; and, *when thou hearest, forgive* the sin that separates between them and God, even the *iniquity of their holy things.*" *a.* He supposes that God's people will ever be a praying people; he resolves to adhere to that duty himself. *b.* He directs them to have an eye, in their prayers, to that place where God was pleased to manifest his glory as he did not any where else on earth. None but priests might come into that place; but, when they worshipped in the courts of the temple, it must be with an eye towards it, not as the object of their worship (that were idolatry), but as an instituted medium of their worship, helping the weakness of their faith, and typifying the mediation of Jesus Christ, who is the true temple, to whom we must have an eye in every thing wherein we have to do with God. Those that were at a distance looked towards Jerusalem, for the sake of the temple, even when it was in ruins, Dan. vi. 10. *c.* He begs that God will *hear the prayers,* and *forgive the sins,* of all that look this way in their prayers. Not as if he thought all the devout prayers offered up to God by those who had no knowledge of this house, or regard to it, were therefore rejected; but he desired that the sensible tokens of the divine presence with which this house was blessed might always give sensible encouragement and comfort to believing petitioners.

[3.] More particularly, he here puts divers cases in which he supposed application would be made to God by prayer in or towards this house of prayer.

First, If God were appealed to by an oath for the determining of any controverted right between man and man, and the oath were taken before this altar, he prayed that God would, in some way or other, discover the truth, and judge between the contending parties, *v.* 31, 32. He prayed that, in difficult matters, this throne of grace might be a throne of judgment, from which God would right the injured that believingly appealed to it, and punish the injurious that presumptuously appealed to it. It was usual to swear by the temple and altar (Matt. xxiii. 16, 18), which corruption perhaps took its rise from this supposition of an oath taken, not *by* the temple or altar, but *at* or *near* them, for the greater solemnity.

Secondly, If the people of Israel were groaning under any national calamity, or any particular Israelite under any personal calamity, he desired that the prayers they should make in or towards this house might be heard and answered.

a. In case of public judgments, war (*v.* 33), want of rain (*v.* 35), famine, or pestilence (*v.* 37), and he ends with an *et cetera*—any plague or sickness; for no calamity befals other people which may not befal God's Israel. Now he supposes, (*a.*) That the cause of the judgment would be sin, and nothing else. "If they be *smitten before the enemy,* if there be no rain, it is *because they have sinned against thee.*" It is sin that makes all the mischief. (*b.*) That the consequence of the judgment would be that they would cry to God, and make supplication to him in or towards that house. Those that slighted him before would solicit him then. *Lord, in trouble have they visited thee. In their afflictions they will seek me early* and earnestly. (*c.*) That the condition of the removal of the judgment was something more than barely praying for it. He could not, he would not, ask that their prayer might be answered unless they did also *turn from their sin* (*v.* 35) and *turn again to God* (*v.* 33), that is, unless they did truly repent and reform. On no other terms may we look for salvation in this world or the other. But, if they did thus qualify themselves for mercy, he prays, [*a.*] That God would hear from heaven, his holy temple above, to which they must look, through *this* temple. [*b.*] That he would forgive their sin; for then only are judgments removed in mercy when sin is pardoned. [*c.*] That he would *teach them the good way wherein they should walk*, by his Spirit, with his word and prophets; and thus they might be both profited by their trouble (for *blessed is the man whom God chastens and teaches)*, and prepared for deliverance, which then comes in love when it finds us brought back to the good way of God and duty. [*d.*] That he would then remove the judgment, and redress the grievance, whatever it might be—not only accept the prayer, but give in the mercy prayed for.

b. In case of personal afflictions, *v.* 38—40. "If any man of Israel has an errand to thee, here let him find thee, here let him find favour with thee." He does not mention particulars, so numerous, so various, are the grievances of the children of men. (*a.*) He supposes that the complainants themselves would very sensibly feel their own burden, and would open that case to God which otherwise they kept to themselves and did not make any man acquainted with: They *shall know every man the plague of his own heart*, what it is that pains him, and (as we say) where the shoe pinches, and shall spread their hands, that is, spread their case, as Hezekiah spread the letter, in prayer, towards this house; whether the trouble be of body or mind, they shall represent it before God. Inward burdens seem especially meant. Sin is the plague of our own heart; our indwelling corruptions are our spiritual diseases. Every Israelite indeed endeavours to know these, that he may mortify them and watch against the risings of them. These he complains of. This is the burden he groans under: *O wretched man that I am!* These drive him to his knees, drive him to the sanctuary. Lamenting these, *he spreads forth his hands* in prayer. (*b.*) He refers all cases of this kind, that should be brought hither, to God. [*a.*] To his omniscience: *Thou, even thou only, knowest the hearts of all the children of men*, not only the plagues of their hearts, their several wants and burdens" (these he knows, but he will know them from us), "but the desire and intent of the heart, the sincerity or hypocrisy of it. Thou knowest which prayer comes from the heart, and which from the lips only." The hearts of kings are not unsearchable to God. [*b.*] To his justice: *Give to every man according to his ways;* and he will not fail to do so, by the rules of grace, not the law, for then we should all be undone. [*c.*] To his mercy: *Hear, and forgive, and do* (*v.* 39), *that they may fear thee all their days, v.* 40. This use we should make of the mercy of God to us in hearing our prayers and forgiving our sins, we should thereby be engaged to fear him while we live. *Fear the Lord and his goodness. There is forgiveness with him, that he may be feared.*

c. The case of the stranger that is not an Israelite is next mentioned, a proselyte that comes to the temple to pray to the God of Israel, being convinced of the folly and wickedness of worshipping the gods of his country. (*a.*) He supposed that there would be many such (*v.* 41, 42), that the fame of God's great works which he had wrought for Israel, by which he proved himself to be above all gods, nay, to be God alone, would reach to distant countries: "Those that live remote *shall hear of thy strong hand, and thy stretched-out arm;* and this will bring all thinking considerate people to pray towards this house, that they may obtain the favour of a God that is able to do them a real kindness." (*b.*) He begged that God would accept and answer the proselyte's prayer (*v.* 43): *Do according to all that the stranger calleth to thee for.* Thus early, thus ancient, were the indications of favour towards the *sinners of the Gentiles:* as there was then *one law for the native and for the stranger* (Exod. xii. 49), so there was one gospel for both. (*c.*) Herein he aimed at the glory of God and the propagating of the knowledge of him: "O let the stranger, in a special manner, speed well in his addresses, that he may carry away with him to his own country a good report of the God of Israel, *that all people may know thee and fear thee* (and, if they know thee aright, they will fear thee) *as do thy people Israel.*" So far was Solomon from monopolizing the knowledge and service of God, and wishing to have them confined to Israel only (which was the envious desire of the Jews in the days of Christ and his apostles), that he prayed that *all people might fear God as Israel did.* Would to God that all the children of men might receive the adoption, and be made God's children! *Father*, thus *glorify thy name.*

d. The case of an army going forth to battle is next recommended by Solomon to the divine favour. It is supposed that the army is encamped at a distance, somewhere a great way off, sent by divine order *against the enemy, v.* 44. "When they are ready to engage, and consider the perils and doubtful issues of battle, and put up a prayer to God for protection and success, with their eye *towards this city and temple*, then *hear their prayer*, encourage their hearts, strengthen their hands, cover their heads, and so maintain their cause and give them victory." Soldiers in the field must not think it enough that those who tarry at home pray for them, but must pray for themselves, and they are here encouraged to hope for a gracious answer. Praying should always go along with fighting.

e. The case of poor captives is the last that is here mentioned as a proper object of divine compassion. (*a.*) He supposes that

Israel will sin. He knew them, and himself, and the nature of man, too well to think this a foreign supposition; *for there is no man that sinneth not,* that does not enough to justify God in the severest rebukes of his providence, no man but what is in danger of falling into gross sin, and will if God leave him to himself. (*b.*) He supposes, what may well be expected, that, if Israel revolt from God, God will be *angry with them,* and *deliver them into the hand of their enemies,* to be carried captive into a strange country, *v.* 46. (*c.*) He then supposes that they will bethink themselves, will consider their ways (for afflictions put men upon consideration), and, when once they are brought to consider, they will repent and pray, will confess their sins, and humble themselves, saying, *We have sinned and have done perversely* (*v.* 47), and *in the land of their enemies will return to God,* whom they had forsaken in their own land. (*d.*) He supposes that in their prayers they will look towards their own land, the holy land, Jerusalem, the holy city, and the temple, the holy house, and directs them so to do (*v.* 48), for his sake who gave them that land, chose that city, and to whose honour that house was built. (*e.*) He prays that then God would *hear their prayers, forgive their sins, plead their cause,* and incline their enemies to *have compassion on them, v.* 49, 50. God has all hearts in his hand, and can, when he pleases, turn the strongest stream the contrary way, and make those to pity his people who have been their most cruel persecutors. See this prayer answered, Ps. cvi. 46. He *made them to be pitied of those that carried them captive,* which, if it did not release them, yet eased their captivity. (*f.*) He pleads their relation to God, and his interest in them: "They are thy people, whom thou hast taken into thy covenant and under thy care and conduct, thy inheritance, from which, more than from any other nation, thy rent and tribute of glory issue and arise (*v.* 51), *separated from among all people* to be so and by distinguishing favours appropriated to thee," *v.* 53.

Lastly, After all these particulars, he concludes with this general request, that God would hearken to all his praying people *in all that they call unto him for, v.* 52. No place now, under the gospel, can be imagined to add any acceptableness to the prayers made in or towards it, as the temple then did. That was a shadow: the substance is Christ; whatever we ask in his name, it shall be given us

54 And it was *so,* that when Solomon had made an end of praying all this prayer and supplication unto the LORD, he arose from before the altar of the LORD, from kneeling on his knees with his hands spread up to heaven. 55 And he stood, and blessed all the congregation of Israel with a loud voice, saying, 56 Blessed *be* the LORD, that hath given rest unto his people Israel, according to all that he promised: there hath not failed one word of all his good promise, which he promised by the hand of Moses his servant. 57 The LORD our God be with us, as he was with our fathers: let him not leave us, nor forsake us: 58 That he may incline our hearts unto him, to walk in all his ways, and to keep his commandments, and his statutes, and his judgments, which he commanded our fathers. 59 And let these my words, wherewith I have made supplication before the LORD, be nigh unto the LORD our God day and night, that he maintain the cause of his servant, and the cause of his people Israel at all times, as the matter shall require: 60 That all the people of the earth may know that the LORD *is* God, *and that there is* none *else.* 61 Let your heart therefore be perfect with the LORD our God, to walk in his statutes, and to keep his commandments, as at this day.

Solomon, after his sermon in Ecclesiastes, gives us the conclusion of the whole matter; so he does here, after this long prayer; it is called his *blessing the people, v.* 55. He pronounced it standing, that he might be the better heard, and because he blessed as one having authority. Never were words more fitly spoken, nor more pertinently. Never was congregation dismissed with that which was more likely to affect them and abide with them.

I. He gives God the glory of the great and kind things he had done for Israel, *v.* 56. He stood up to *bless the congregation* (*v.* 55), but began with blessing God; for we must in *every thing give thanks.* Do we expect God should do well for us and ours? let us take all occasions to speak well of him and his. He blesses God who has given, he does not say wealth, and honour, and power, and victory, to Israel, but *rest,* as if that were a blessing more valuable than any of those. Let not those who have rest undervalue that blessing, though they want some others. He compares the blessings God had bestowed upon them with the promises he had given them, that God might have the honour of his faithfulness and the truth of that word of his which he has *magnified above all his name.* 1. He refers to the *promises given by the hand of Moses,* as he did (*v.* 15, 24) to those which were made to David. There were promises given by Moses, as well as precepts. It was long ere God gave Israel the promised rest, but they had it at last, after many trials. The day will come when God's spiritual Israel will *rest from all their labours.* 2. He does, as it were, write a receipt in full on the back of these bonds: *There has not failed one word of all his good promises.* This discharge he gives in the name of all Israel, to the everlasting honour of the divine faithfulness, and the everlasting encouragement of all those that build upon the divine promises.

II. He blesses himself and the congregation, expressing his earnest desire and hope of these four things:—1. The presence of God with them, which is all in all to the happiness of a church and nation and of every particular person. This great congregation was now shortly to be scattered, and it was not likely that they would ever be all together again in this world. Solomon therefore dismisses them with this blessing: "*The Lord be present with us,* and that will be comfort enough when we are absent from each other. *The Lord our God be with us, as he was with our fathers* (*v.* 57); *let him not leave us,* let him be to us to day, and to ours for ever, what he was to those that went before us." 2. The power of his grace upon them: "*Let him be with us,* and continue with us, not that he may enlarge our coasts and increase our wealth, but *that he may incline our hearts to himself, to walk in all his ways and to keep his commandments,*" *v.* 58. Spiritual blessings are the best blessings, with which we should covet earnestly to be blessed. Our hearts are naturally averse to our duty, and apt to decline from God; it is his grace that inclines them, grace that must be obtained by prayer. 3. An answer to the prayer he had now made: "*Let these my words be nigh unto the Lord our God day and night, v.* 59. Let a gracious return be made to every prayer that shall be made here, and that will be a continual answer to this prayer." What Solomon asks here for his prayer is still granted in the intercession of Christ, of which his supplication was a type; that powerful prevailing intercession *is before the Lord our God day and night,* for our great Advocate attends continually to this very thing, and we may depend upon him to maintain our cause (against the adversary that accuses us *day* and *night,* Rev. xii. 10) *and the* common *cause of his people Israel, at all times,* upon all occasions, as the matter shall require, so as to speak for us *the word of the day in its day,* as the original here reads it, from which we shall receive grace sufficient, suitable, and seasonable, *in every time of need.* 4. The glorifying of God in the enlargement of his kingdom among men. Let Israel be thus blessed, thus favoured; not that all people may become tributaries to us (Solomon sees his kingdom as great as he desires), but *that all people may know that the Lord is God,* and he only, and may come and worship him, *v.* 60. With this Solomon's prayers, like *the prayers of his father David, the son of Jesse, are ended* (Ps. lxxii. 19, 20): *Let the whole earth be filled with his glory.* We cannot close our prayers with a better summary than this, *Father, glorify thy name.*

III. He solemnly charges his people to continue and persevere in their duty to God. Having spoken to God for them, he here speaks from God to them, and those only would fare the better for his prayers that were made better by his preaching. His admonition, at parting, is, "*Let your heart be perfect with the Lord our God, v.* 61. Let your obedience be universal, without dividing—upright, without dissembling—constant, without declining;" this is evangelical perfection.

62 And the king, and all Israel with him, offered sacrifice before the LORD. 63 And Solomon offered a sacrifice of peace offerings, which he offered unto the LORD, two and twenty thousand oxen, and a hundred and twenty thousand sheep. So the king and all the children of Israel dedicated the house of the LORD. 64 The same day did the king hallow the middle of the court that *was* before the house of the LORD: for there he offered burnt offerings, and meat offerings, and the fat of the peace offerings: because the brasen altar that *was* before the LORD *was* too little to receive the burnt offerings, and meat offerings, and the fat of the peace offerings. 65 And at that time Solomon held a feast, and all Israel with him, a great congregation, from the entering in of Hamath unto the river of Egypt, before the LORD our God, seven days and seven days, *even* fourteen days. 66 On the eighth day he sent the people away: and they blessed the king, and went unto their tents joyful and glad of heart for all the goodness that the LORD had done for David his servant, and for Israel his people.

We read before that Judah and Israel were eating and drinking, and very cheerful under their own vines and fig-trees; here we have them so in God's courts. Now they found Solomon's words true concerning Wisdom's ways, that they are ways of pleasantness.

I. They had abundant joy and satisfaction while they attended at God's house, for there, 1. Solomon offered a great sacrifice, 22,000 oxen and 120,000 sheep, enough to have drained the country of cattle if it had not been a very fruitful land. The heathen thought themselves very generous when they offered sacrifices by *hundreds (hecatombs* they called them), but Solomon out-did them: he offered them by *thousands.* When Moses dedicated his altar, the peace-offerings were twenty-four *bullocks, and of rams, goats, and lambs,* 180 (Num. vii. 88); then the people were poor, but now that they had increased in wealth more was expected from them. Where God sows plentifully he must reap accordingly. All these sacrifices could not be offered in one day, but in the several days of the feast. Thirty oxen a day served Solomon's table, but thousands shall go to God's altar. Few are thus minded, to spend more on their souls than on their bodies. The flesh of the peace-offerings, which belonged to the offerer, it is likely, Solomon treated the people with. Christ fed those who attended him. The brazen altar was not large enough to receive all these sacrifices, so that, to serve the present occasion, they were forced to offer many of them *in the middle of the court,* (*v.* 64), some think on altars, altars of earth or stone, erected for the purpose and taken down when the solemnity was over, others think on the bare ground. Those that will be generous in serving God need not stint themselves for want of room and occasion to be so. 2. He kept a feast, the feast of tabernacles, as it should seem, after the feast of dedication, and both together lasted fourteen days (*v.* 65), yet they said not, *Behold, what a weariness is this!*

II. They carried this joy and satisfaction with them to their own houses. When they were dismissed they blessed the king (*v.* 66), applauded him, admired him, and returned him the thanks of the congregation, and then *went to their tents joyful and glad of heart,* all easy and pleased. God's goodness was the matter of their joy, so it should be of ours at all times. They rejoiced in God's blessing both on the royal family and on the kingdom; thus should we go home rejoicing from holy ordinances, and go on our way rejoicing for God's goodness to our Lord Jesus (of whom David his servant was a type, in the advancement and establishment of his throne, pursuant to the covenant of redemption), and to all believers, his spiritual Israel, in their sanctification and consolation, pursuant to the covenant of grace. If we rejoice not herein always it is our own fault.

CHAP. IX.

In this chapter we have, I. The answer which God, in a vision, gave to Solomon's prayer, and the terms he settled with him, ver. 1—9. II. The interchanging of grateful kindnesses between Solomon and Hiram, ver. 10—14. III. His workmen and buildings, ver. 15—24. IV. His devotion, ver. 25. V. His trading navy, ver. 26—28.

AND it came to pass, when Solomon had finished the building of the house of the LORD, and the king's house, and all Solomon's desire which he was pleased to do, 2 That the LORD appeared to Solomon the second time, as he had appeared unto him at Gibeon. 3 And the LORD said unto him, I have heard thy prayer and thy supplication, that thou hast made before me: I have hallowed this house, which thou hast built, to put my name there for ever; and mine eyes and mine heart shall be there perpetually. 4 And if thou wilt walk before me, as David thy father walked, in integrity of heart, and in uprightness, to do according to all that I have commanded thee, *and* wilt keep my statutes and my judgments: 5 Then I will establish the throne of thy kingdom upon Israel for ever, as I promised to David thy father, saying, There shall not fail thee a man upon the throne of Israel. 6 *But* if ye shall at all turn from following me, ye or your children, and will not keep my commandments *and* my statutes which I have set before you, but go and serve other gods, and worship them: 7 Then will I cut off Israel out of the land which I have given them; and this house, which I have hallowed for my name, will I cast out of my sight; and Israel shall be a proverb and a byword among all people. 8 And at this house, *which* is high, every one that passeth by it shall be astonished, and shall hiss; and they shall say, Why hath the LORD done thus unto this land, and to this house? 9 And they shall answer, Because they forsook the LORD their God, who brought forth their fathers out of the land of Egypt, and have taken hold upon other gods, and have worshipped them, and served them: therefore hath the LORD brought upon them all this evil.

God had given a real answer to Solomon's prayer, and tokens of his acceptance of it, immediately, by the *fire from heaven* which consumed the sacrifices (as we find 2 Chron. vii. 1); but here we have a more express and distinct answer to it. Observe,

I. In what way God gave him this answer. He appeared to him, as he had done at Gibeon, in the beginning of his reign, in a dream or vision, *v.* 2. The comparing of it with that intimates that it was the very night after he had finished the solemnities of his festival, for so that was, 2 Chron. i. 6, 7. And then *v.* 1, speaking of Solomon's finishing all his buildings, which was not till many years after the dedication of the temple, must be read thus, *Solomon finished* (as it is 2 Chron. vii. 11), and *v.* 2 must be read, *and the Lord had appeared.*

II. The purport of this answer. 1. He assures him of his special presence in the temple he had built, in answer to the prayer he had made (*v.* 3): *I have hallowed this house.* Solomon had dedicated it, but it was God's prerogative to hallow it—to sanctify or consecrate it. Men cannot make a place holy, yet what we, in sincerity, devote to God, we may hope he will graciously accept as his; and *his eyes and his heart shall be upon it.* Apply it to persons, the living temples. Those whom God hallows or sanctifies, whom he sets apart for himself, have his eye, his heart, his love and care, and this perpetually. 2. He shows him that he and his people were for the future *upon their good behaviour.* Let them not be secure now, as if they might live as they please now that they have the *temple of the Lord* among them, Jer. vii. 4. No, this house was designed to protect them in their allegiance to God, but not in their rebellion or disobedience. God deals plainly with us, sets before us good and evil, the blessing and the curse, and lets us know what we must trust to. God here tells Solomon, (1.) That the establishment of his kingdom depended upon the constancy of his obedience (*v.* 4, 5): "*If thou wilt walk before me as David did,* who left thee a good example and encouragement enough to follow it (an advantage thou wilt be accountable for if thou do not improve it), *if thou wilt walk as he did, in integrity of heart and uprightness*" (for that is the main matter—no religion without sincerity), "*then I will establish the throne of thy kingdom,* and not otherwise," for on that condition the promise was made, Ps. cxxxii. 12. If we perform our part of the covenant, God will not fail to perform his; if we improve the grace God has given us, he will confirm us to the end. Let not the children of godly parents expect the entail of the blessing, unless they tread in the steps of those that have gone before them to heaven, and keep up the virtue and piety of their ancestors. (2.) That the ruin of his kingdom would be the certain consequence of his or his children's apostasy from God (*v.* 6): "But know thou, and let thy family and kingdom know it, and be admonished by it, that *if you shall altogether turn from following me*" (so it is thought it should be read), "if you forsake my service, desert my altar, and go and serve other gods" (for that was the covenant-breaking sin), "if you or your children break off from me, this house will not save you. But, [1.] Israel, though a holy nation, will be cut off (*v.* 7), by one judgment after another, till they become a proverb and a by-word, and the most despicable people under the sun, though now the most honourable." This supposes the destruction of the royal family, though it is not particularly threatened; the king is, of course, undone, if the kingdom be. [2.] "The temple, though a holy house, which God himself has *hallowed for his name,* shall be abandoned and laid desolate (*v.* 8, 9): *This house which is high.*" They prided themselves in the stateliness and magnificence of the structure, but let them know that it is not so high as to be out of the reach of God's judgments, if they vilify it so as to exchange it for groves and idol-temples, and yet, at the same time, magnify it so as to think it will secure the favour of God to them though they ever so much corrupt themselves. *This house which is high.* Those that *now pass by it are astonished* at the bulk and beauty of it; the richness, contrivance, and workmanship, are admired by all spectators, and it is called a stupendous fabric; but, if you forsake God, its height will make its fall the more amazing, and those that pass by will be as much astonished at its ruins, while the guilty, self-convicted, self-condemned, Israelites, will be forced to acknowledge, with shame, that they themselves were the ruin of it; for when it shall be asked, *Why hath the Lord done thus to his house?* they cannot but answer, It was *because they forsook the Lord their God.* See Deut. xxix. 24, 25. Their sin will be read in their punishment. They deserted the temple, and therefore God deserted it; they profaned it with their sins and laid it common, and therefore God profaned it with his judgments and laid it waste. God gave Solomon fair warning of this, now that he had newly built and dedicated it, that he and his people might not be high-minded, but fear.

10 And it came to pass at the end of twenty years, when Solomon had built the two houses, the house of the LORD, and the king's house, 11 (*Now* Hiram the king of Tyre had furnished Solomon with cedar trees and fir trees, and with gold, according to all his desire,) that then king Solomon gave Hiram twenty cities in the land of Galilee. 12 And Hiram came out from Tyre to see the cities which Solomon had given him; and they pleased him not. 13 And he said, What cities *are* these which thou hast given me, my brother? And he called them the land of Cabul unto this day. 14 And Hiram sent to the king sixscore talents of gold.

What agreement was made between Solomon and Hiram, when the building-work was to be begun, we read before, *ch.* v. Here we have an account of their fair and friendly parting when the work was done. 1. Hiram made good his bargain to the utmost. He had furnished Solomon with materials for his buildings, according to all his desire (*v.* 11), and with gold, *v.* 15. So far was he from envying Solomon's growing greatness and reputation, and being jealous of him, that he helped to magnify him. Solomon's power, with Solomon's wisdom, needs not be dreaded by any of his neighbours. God honours him; therefore Hiram will. 2. Solomon, no doubt, made good his bargain, and gave Hiram *food for his household*, as was agreed, *ch.* v. 9. But here we are told that, over and above that, he gave him twenty cities (small ones we may suppose, like those mentioned here, *v.* 19) *in the land of Galilee*, *v.* 11. It should seem, these were not allotted to any of the tribes of Israel (for the border of Asher came up to them, Josh. xix. 27, which intimates that it did not include them), but continued in the hands of the natives till Solomon made himself master of them, and then made a present of them to Hiram. It becomes those that are great and good to be generous. Hiram came to see these cities, and did not like them (*v.* 12): *They pleased him not.* He called the country the land of *Cabul*, a Phenician word (says Josephus) which signifies *displeasing*, *v.* 13. He therefore returned them to Solomon (as we find, 2 Chron. viii. 2), who repaired them, and then *caused the children of Israel to inhabit them*, which intimates that before they did not; but, when Solomon received back what he had given, no doubt he honourably gave Hiram an equivalent in something else. But what shall we think of this? Did Solomon act meanly in giving Hiram what was not worth his acceptance? Or was Hiram humoursome and hard to please? I am willing to believe it was neither the one nor the other. The country was truly valuable, and so were the cities in it, but not agreeable to Hiram's genius. The Tyrians were merchants, trading men, that lived in fine houses, and became rich by navigation, but knew not how to value a country that was fit for corn and pasture (that was business that lay out of their way); and therefore Hiram desired Solomon to take them again, he knew not what to do with them, and, if he would please to gratify him, let it be in his own element, by becoming his partner in trade, as we find he did, *v.* 27. Hiram, who was used to the clean streets of Tyre, could by no means agree with the miry lanes in the land of Cabul, whereas the best lands have commonly the worst roads through them. See how the providence of God suits both the accommodation of this earth to the various dispositions of men and the dispositions of men to the various accommodations of the earth, and all for the good of mankind in general. Some take delight in husbandry, and wonder what pleasure sailors can take on a rough sea; others take as much delight in navigation, and wonder what pleasure husbandmen can take in a dirty country, like the land of Cabul. It is so in many other instances, in which we may observe the wisdom of him whose all souls are and all lands.

15 And this *is* the reason of the levy which king Solomon raised; for to build the house of the LORD, and his own house, and Millo, and the wall of Jerusalem, and Hazor, and Megiddo, and Gezer. 16 *For* Pharaoh king of Egypt had gone up and taken Gezer, and burnt it with fire, and slain the Canaanites that dwelt in the city, and given it *for* a present unto his daughter, Solomon's wife. 17 And Solomon built Gezer, and Beth-horon the nether. 18 And Baalath, and Tadmor in the wilderness, in the land, 19 And all the cities of store that Solomon had, and cities for his chariots, and cities for his horsemen, and that which Solomon desired to build in Jerusalem, and in Lebanon, and in all the land of his dominion. 20 *And* all the people *that were* left of the Amorites, Hittites, Perizzites, Hivites, and Jebusites, which *were* not of the children of Israel, 21 Their children that were left after them in the land, whom the children of Israel also were not able utterly to destroy, upon those did Solomon levy a tribute of bondservice unto this day. 22 But of the children of Israel did Solomon make no bondmen: but they *were* men of war, and his servants, and his princes, and his captains, and rulers of his chariots, and his horsemen. 23 These *were* the chief of the officers that *were* over Solomon's work, five hundred and fifty, which bare rule over the people that wrought in the work. 24 But Pharaoh's daughter came up out of the city of David unto her house which *Solomon* had built for her: then did he build Millo. 25 And three times in a year did Solomon offer burnt offerings and peace offerings upon the altar which he built unto the LORD, and he burnt incense upon the altar that *was* before the

LORD. So he finished the house. 26 And king Solomon made a navy of ships in Ezion-geber, which *is* beside Eloth, on the shore of the Red sea, in the land of Edom. 26 And Hiram sent in the navy his servants, shipmen that had knowledge of the sea, with the servants of Solomon. 28 And they came to Ophir, and fetched from thence gold, four hundred and twenty talents, and brought *it* to king Solomon.

We have here a further account of Solomon's greatness.

I. His buildings. He raised a great levy both of men and money, because he projected a great deal of building, which would both employ many hands and put him to a vast expense, *v.* 15. And he was a wise builder, who sat down first, and counted the cost, and would not begin to build till he found himself able to finish. Perhaps there was some complaint of the heaviness of the taxes, which the historian excuses from the greatness of his undertakings. He raised it, not for war (as other princes), which would spend the blood of his subjects, but for building, which would require only their labour and purses. Perhaps David observed Solomon's genius to lie towards building, and foresaw he would have his head and hands full of it, when he penned that song of degrees for Solomon, which begins, *Except the Lord build the house, those labour in vain that build it* (Ps. cxxvii. 1), directing him to acknowledge God in all his ways, and, by prayer and faith in his providence, to take him along with him in all his designs of this kind. And Solomon verily began his work at the right end, for he built God's house first, and finished that before he began his own; and then God blessed him, and he prospered in all his other buildings. If we begin with God, he will go on with us. Let the first-fruits be his, and the after-fruits will the more comfortably be ours, Matt. vi. 33. Solomon built a church first and then he was enabled to build houses, and cities, and walls. Those consult not their own interest that defer to the last what they design for pious uses. The further order in Solomon's buildings is observable. God's house first for religion, then his own for his own convenience, then a house for his wife, to which she removed as soon as it was ready for her (*v.* 24), then Millo, the town-house or guild-hall, then the wall of Jerusalem, the royal city, then some cities of note and strength in the country, which were decayed and unfortified, Hazor, Megiddo, &c. As he rebuilt these at his own charge, the inhabitants would be not only his subjects, but his tenants, which would increase the revenues of the crown for the benefit of his successors. Among the rest, he built Gezer, which Pharaoh took out of the hands of the Canaanites, and made a present of to his daughter, Solomon's wife, *v.* 16. See how God *maketh the earth to help the woman.* Solomon was not himself a warlike prince, but the king of Egypt, who was, took cities for him to build. Then he built cities for convenience, for store, for his chariots, and for his horsemen, *v.* 19. And, *lastly*, he built for pleasure in Lebanon, for his hunting perhaps, or other diversions there. Let piety begin, and profit proceed, and leave pleasure to the last.

II. His workmen and servants. In doing such great works, he must needs employ abundance of workmen. The honour of great men is borrowed from their inferiors, who do that which they have the credit of. 1. Solomon employed those who remained of the conquered and devoted nations in all the slavish work, *v.* 20, 21. We may suppose that they renounced their idolatry and submitted to Solomon's government, so that he could not, in honour, utterly destroy them, and they were so poor that he could not levy money on them; therefore he served himself of their labour. Herein he observed God's law (Lev. xxv. 44, *Thy bondmen shall be of the heathen),* and fulfilled Noah's curse upon Canaan, *A servant of servants shall he be unto his brethren,* Gen. ix. 25. 2. He employed Israelites in the more creditable services (*v.* 22, 23): *Of them he made no bondmen,* for they were God's freemen, but he made them soldiers and courtiers, and gave them offices, as he saw them qualified, among his chariots and horsemen, appointing some to support the service of the inferior labourers. Thus he preserved the dignity and liberty of Israel and honoured their relation to God as a kingdom of priests.

III. His piety and devotion (*v.* 25): *Three times in a year* he offered burnt-offerings extraordinary (namely, at the three yearly feasts, the passover, pentecost, and feast of tabernacles) in honour of the divine institution, besides what he offered at other times, both statedly and upon special occasions. With his sacrifices he burnt incense, not himself (that was king Uzziah's crime), but the priest for him, at his charge, and for his particular use. It is said, He offered *on the altar which he* himself *built.* He took care to build it, and then, 1. He himself made use of it. Many will assist the devotions of others that neglect their own. Solomon did not think his building an altar would excuse him from sacrificing, but rather engage him the more to it. 2. He himself had the benefit and comfort of it. Whatever pains we take, for the support of religion, to the glory of God and the edification of others, we ourselves are likely to have the advantage of it.

IV. His merchandise. He built a fleet of trading ships at Ezion-geber (*v.* 26), a port on the coast of the Red Sea, the furthest stage of the Israelites when they wandered in the wilderness, Num. xxxiii. 35. Probably that wilderness now began to be peopled by the Edomites, which it was not then. To them this port had belonged, but, David having subdued the Edomites, it now pertained to the crown of Judah. The fleet traded to Ophir in the East Indies, supposed to be that which is now called *Ceylon*. Gold was the commodity traded for, substantial wealth. It should seem, Solomon had before been Hiram's partner, or put a venture into his ships, which made him a rich return of 120 talents (*v.* 14), which encouraged him to build a fleet of his own. The success of others in any employment should quicken our industry; for *in all labour there is profit*. Solomon sent his own servants as factors, and merchants, and super-cargoes, but hired Tyrians for sailors, for they had *knowledge of the sea, v.* 27. Thus one nation needs another, Providence so ordering it that there may be mutual commerce and assistance; for not only as Christians, but as men, we are members one of another. The fleet brought home to Solomon 420 *talents of gold, v.* 28. Canaan, the holy land, the glory of all lands, had no gold in it, which teaches us that that part of the wealth of this world which is for hoarding and trading is not the best part of it, but that which is more immediately for the present support and comfort of life, our own and others'; such were the productions of Canaan. Solomon got much by his merchandise, but, it should seem, David got much more by his conquests. What were Solomon's 420 *talents* to David's 100,000 *talents of gold?* 1 Chron. xxii. 14; xxix. 4. Solomon got much by his merchandise, and yet has directed us to a better trade, within reach of the poorest, having assured us from his own experience of both that the *merchandise of wisdom is better than the merchandise of silver and the gain thereof than fine gold,* Prov. iii. 14.

CHAP. X.

Still Solomon looks great, and every thing in this chapter adds to his magnificence. We read nothing indeed of his charity, of no hospitals he built, or alms-houses; he made his kingdom so rich that it did not need them; yet, no question, many poor were relieved from the abundance of his table. A church he had built, never to be equalled; schools or colleges he need not build any, his own palace is an academy, and his court a rendezvous of wise and learned men, as well as the centre of all the circulating riches of that part of the world. I. What abundance of wisdom there was there appears from the application the queen of Sheba made to him, and the great satisfaction she had in her entertainment there (ver. 1—13), and others likewise, ver. 24. II. What abundance of wealth there was there appears here by the gold imported, with other things, yearly (ver. 14, 15), and in a triennial return, ver. 22. Gold presented (ver. 25), and gold used in targets and shields (ver. 16, 17), and vessels, ver. 21. A stately throne made, ver. 18—20. His chariots and horsemen, ver. 26. His trade with Egypt, ver. 28, 29. And the great plenty of silver and cedars among his people, ver. 27. So that, putting all together, it must be owned, as it is here said (ver. 23), that "king Solomon exceeded all the kings of the earth for riches, and for wisdom." Yet what was he to the King of kings? Where Christ is, by his word and Spirit, "Behold, a greater than Solomon is there."

AND when the queen of Sheba heard of the fame of Solomon concerning the name of the LORD, she came to prove him with hard questions. 2 And she came to Jerusalem with a very great train, with camels that bare spices, and very much gold, and precious stones: and when she was come to Solomon, she communed with him of all that was in her heart. 3 And Solomon told her all her questions: there was not *any* thing hid from the king, which he told her not. 4 And when the queen of Sheba had seen all Solomon's wisdom, and the house that he had built, 5 And the meat of his table, and the sitting of his servants, and the attendance of his ministers, and their apparel, and his cupbearers, and his ascent by which he went up unto the house of the LORD; there was no more spirit in her. 6 And she said to the king, It was a true report that I heard in mine own land of thy acts and of thy wisdom. 7 Howbeit I believed not the words, until I came, and mine eyes had seen *it*: and, behold, the half was not told me: thy wisdom and prosperity exceedeth the fame which I heard. 8 Happy *are* thy men, happy *are* these thy servants, which stand continually before thee, *and* that hear thy wisdom. 9 Blessed be the LORD thy God, which delighted in thee, to set thee on the throne of Israel: because the LORD loved Israel for ever, therefore made he thee king, to do judgment and justice. 10 And she gave the king a hundred and twenty talents of gold, and of spices very great store, and precious stones: there came no more such abundance of spices as these which the queen of Sheba gave to king Solomon. 11 And the navy also of Hiram, that brought gold from Ophir, brought in from Ophir great plenty of almug trees, and precious stones. 12 And the king made of the almug trees pillars for the house of the LORD, and for the king's house, harps also and psalteries for singers: there came no such almug trees, nor were seen unto this day. 13 And king Solomon gave unto the queen of Sheba all her desire, whatsoever she asked, beside *that* which Solomon gave her of his royal bounty. So she turned and went to her own country, she and her servants.

We have here an account of the visit which the queen of Sheba made to Solomon, no doubt when he was in the height of his piety and prosperity. Our Saviour calls her *the queen of the south,* for Sheba lay south of Canaan. The common opinion is that it was in Africa; and the Christians in Ethiopia, to this day, are confident that she came from their country, and that Candace was her successor, who is mentioned Acts viii. 27. But it is more probable that she came from the south part of Arabia the happy. It should seem she was a queen regent, sovereign of her country. Many a kingdom would have been deprived of its greatest blessings if a Salique law had been admitted into its constitution. Observe,

I. On what errand the queen of Sheba came—not to treat of trade or commerce, to adjust the limits of their dominions, to court his alliance for their mutual strength or his assistance against some common enemy, which are the common occasions of the congress of crowned heads and their interviews, but she came, 1. To satisfy her curiosity; for she had heard of his fame, especially for wisdom, and she came to prove him, whether he was so great a man as he was reported to be, *v.* 1. Solomon's fleet sailed near the coast of her country, and probably might put in there for fresh water; perhaps it was thus that *she heard of the fame of Solomon,* that he excelled in wisdom all the children of the east, and nothing would serve her but she would go herself and know the truth of the report. 2. To receive instruction from him. She came to *hear his wisdom,* and thereby to improve her own (Matt. xii. 42), that she might be the better able to govern her own kingdom by his maxims of policy. Those whom God has called to any public employment, particularly in the magistracy and ministry, should, by all means possible, be still improving themselves in that knowledge which will more and more qualify them for it, and enable them to discharge their trust well. But, it should seem, that which she chiefly aimed at was to be instructed in the things of God. She was religiously inclined, and had heard not only of the fame of Solomon, but *concerning the name of the Lord* (*v.* 1), the great name of that God whom Solomon worshipped and from whom he received his wisdom, and with this God she desired to be better acquainted. Therefore does our Saviour mention her enquiries after God, by Solomon, as an aggravation of the stupidity of those who enquire not after God by our Lord Jesus Christ, though he, having lain in his bosom, was much better able to instruct them.

II. With what equipage she came, with a very great retinue, agreeable to her rank, intending to try Solomon's wealth and generosity, as well as his wisdom, what entertainment he could and would give to a royal visitant, *v.* 2. Yet she came not as one begging, but brought enough to bear her charges, and abundantly to recompense Solomon for his attention to her, nothing mean or common, but gold, and precious stones, and spices, because she came to trade for wisdom, which she would purchase at any rate.

III. What entertainment Solomon gave her. He despised not the weakness of her sex, blamed her not for leaving her own business at home to come so long a journey, and put herself and him to so much trouble and expense merely to satisfy her curiosity; but he made her welcome and all her train, gave her liberty to put all her questions, though some perhaps were frivolous, some captious, and some over-curious; he allowed her to *commune with him of all that was in her heart* (*v.* 2) and gave her a satisfactory answer to *all her questions* (*v.* 3), whether natural, moral, political, or divine. Were they designed to try him? he gave them such turns as abundantly satisfied her of his uncommon knowledge. Were they designed for her own instruction? (as we suppose most of them were), she received abundant instruction from him, and he made things surprisingly easy which she apprehended insuperably difficult, and satisfied her that there was *a divine sentence in the lips of* this *king.* But he informed her no doubt, with particular care, concerning God, and his law and instituted worship. He had taken it for granted (*ch.* viii. 42) that *strangers would hear of his great name,* and would come thither to enquire after him; and now that so great a stranger came we may be sure he was not wanting to assist and encourage her enquiries, and give her a description of the temple, and the officers and services of it, that she might be persuaded to serve the Lord whom she now sought.

IV. How she was affected with what she saw and heard in Solomon's court. Divers things are here mentioned which she admired, the buildings and furniture of his palace, the provision that was made every day for his table (when she saw that perhaps she wondered where there were mouths for all that meat, but when she saw the multitude of his attendants and guests she was as ready to wonder where was the meat for all those mouths), the orderly sitting of his servants, every one in his place, and the ready attendance of his ministers, without any confusion, their rich liveries, and the propriety with which his cup-bearers waited at his table. These things she admired, as adding much to his magnificence. But, above all these, the first thing mentioned (which contained all) is his wisdom (*v.* 4), of the transcendency of which she now had incontestable proofs: and the last thing mentioned, which crowned all, is his piety, the *ascent by which he went up to the house of the Lord,* with what gravity and seriousness, and an air of devotion in his countenance, he appeared, when he went to the temple to worship God, with as much humility then as majesty at other times. Many of the ancient versions read it, The *burnt-offerings which he offered in the house of the Lord;* she observed with what a generous bounty he brought his sacrifices, and with what a pious fervour he attended the offering of them; never did she see so much goodness with so much greatness. Every thing was so surprising that there was no more spirit in her, but she stood amazed; she had never seen the like.

V. How she expressed herself upon this occasion. 1. She owned her expectation far out-done, though it was highly raised by the report she heard, *v.* 6, 7. She is far from repenting her journey or calling herself a *fool* for undertaking it, but acknowledges it was well worth her while to come so far for the sight of that which she could not believe the report of. Usually things are represented to us, both by common fame and by our own imagination, much greater than we find them when we come to examine them; but here the truth exceeded both fame and fancy. Those who, through grace, are brought to experience the delights of communion with God will say that the one-half was not told them of the pleasures of Wisdom's ways and the advantages of her gates. Glorified saints, much more, will say that it was a true report which they heard of the happiness of heaven, but that the thousandth part was not told them, 1 Cor. ii. 9. 2. She pronounced those happy that constantly attended him, and waited on him at table: "*Happy are thy men, happy are these thy servants* (*v.* 8); they may improve their own wisdom by hearing thine." She was tempted to envy them and to wish herself one of them. Note, It is a great advantage to be in good families, and to have opportunity of frequent converse with those that are wise, and good, and communicative. Many have this happiness who know not how to value it. With much more reason may we say this of Christ's servants, *Blessed are those that dwell in his house, they will be still praising him.* 3. She blessed God, the giver of Solomon's wisdom and wealth, and the author of his advancement, who had made him king, (1.) In kindness to him, that he might have the larger opportunity of doing good with his wisdom: He *delighted in thee, to set thee on the throne of Israel, v.* 9. Solomon's preferment began in the prophet's calling him *Jedidiah, because the Lord loved him,* 2 Sam. xii. 25. It more than doubles our comforts if we have reason to hope they come from God's delight in us. *It was his pleasure concerning thee* (so it may be read) to *set thee on the throne,* not for thy merit's sake, but because it so seemed good unto him. (2.) In kindness to the people, *because the Lord loved Israel for ever,* designed them a lasting bliss, long to survive him that laid the foundations of it. "He has made thee king, not that thou mayest live in pomp and pleasure, and do what thou wilt, but *to do judgment and justice.*" This she kindly reminded Solomon of, and no doubt he took it kindly. Both magistrates and ministers must be more solicitous to do the duty of their places than to secure the honours and profits of them. To this she attributes his prosperity, not to his wisdom, for bread is not always *to the wise* (Eccl. ix. 11), but whoso *doeth judgment and justice,* it shall be *well with him,* Jer. xxii. 15. Thus *giving of thanks* must be *made for kings,* for good kings, for such kings; they are what God makes them to be.

VI. How they parted. 1. She made a noble present to Solomon of *gold and spices, v.* 10. David had foretold concerning Solomon that *to him should be given of the gold of Sheba,* Ps. lxxii. 15. The present of gold and spices which the wise men of the east brought to Christ was signified by this, Matt. ii. 11. Thus she paid for the wisdom she had learned and did not think she bought it dearly. Let those that are taught of God give him their hearts, and the present will be more acceptable than this of gold and spices. Mention is made of the great abundance Solomon had of his own, notwithstanding she presented and he accepted this gold. What we present to Christ he needs not, but will have us so to express our gratitude. The almug-trees are here spoken of (*v.* 11, 12) as extraordinary, because perhaps much admired by the queen of Sheba. 2. Solomon was not behind-hand with her: *He gave her whatsoever she asked,* patterns, we may suppose, of those things that were curious, by which she might make the like; or perhaps he gave her his precepts of wisdom and piety in writing, *besides that which he gave her of his royal bounty, v.* 13. Thus those who apply to our Lord Jesus will find him not only greater than Solomon, and wiser, but more kind; whatsoever we ask, it shall be done for us; nay, he will, out of his divine bounty, which infinitely exceeds royal bounty, even Solomon's, do for us *more than we are able to ask or think.*

14 Now the weight of gold that came to Solomon in one year was six hundred threescore and six talents of gold, 15 Beside *that he had* of the merchantmen, and of the traffick of the spice merchants, and of all the kings of Arabia, and of the governors of the country. 16 And king Solomon made two hundred targets *of* beaten gold: six hundred *shekels* of gold went to one target. 17 And *he made* three hundred shields *of* beaten gold; three pound of gold went to

one shield; and the king put them in the house of the forest of Lebanon. 18 Moreover the king made a great throne of ivory, and overlaid it with the best gold. 19 The throne had six steps, and the top of the throne *was* round behind: and *there were* stays on either side on the place of the seat, and two lions stood beside the stays. 20 And twelve lions stood there on the one side and on the other upon the six steps: there was not the like made in any kingdom. 21 And all king Solomon's drinking vessels *were of* gold, and all the vessels of the house of the forest of Lebanon *were of* pure gold; none *were of* silver: it was nothing accounted of in the days of Solomon. 22 For the king had at sea a navy of Tharshish with the navy of Hiram: once in three years came the navy of Tharshish, bringing gold, and silver, ivory, and apes, and peacocks. 23 So king Solomon exceeded all the kings of the earth for riches and for wisdom. 24 And all the earth sought to Solomon, to hear his wisdom, which God had put in his heart. 25 And they brought every man his present, vessels of silver, and vessels of gold, and garments, and armour, and spices, horses, and mules, a rate year by year. 26 And Solomon gathered together chariots and horsemen: and he had a thousand and four hundred chariots, and twelve thousand horsemen, whom he bestowed in the cities for chariots, and with the king at Jerusalem. 27 And the king made silver *to be* in Jerusalem as stones, and cedars made he *to be* as the sycamore trees that *are* in the vale, for abundance. 28 And Solomon had horses brought out of Egypt, and linen yarn: the king's merchants received the linen yarn at a price. 29 And a chariot came up and went out of Egypt for six hundred *shekels* of silver, and a horse for a hundred and fifty; and so for all the kings of the Hittites, and for the kings of Syria, did they bring *them* out by their means.

We have here a further account of Solomon's prosperity.

I. How he increased his wealth. Though he had much, he still coveted to have more, being willing to try the utmost the things of this world could do to make men happy. 1. Besides the gold that came from Ophir (*ch.* ix. 28), he brought so much into his country from other places that the whole amounted, every year, to 666 *talents* (*v.* 14), an ominous number, compare Rev. xiii. 18, and Ezra ii. 13. 2. He received a great deal in customs from the merchants, and in land-taxes from the countries his father had conquered and made tributaries to Israel, *v.* 15. 3. He was Hiram's partner in a Tharshish fleet, of and for Tyre, which imported once in three years, not only gold, and silver, and ivory, substantial goods and serviceable, but apes to play with and peacocks to please the eye with their feathers, *v.* 22. I wish this may not be an evidence that Solomon and his people, being overcharged with prosperity, by this time grew childish and wanton. 4. He had presents made him, every year, from the neighbouring princes and great men, to engage the continuance of his friendship, not so much because they feared him or were jealous of him as because they loved him and admired his wisdom, had often occasion to consult him as an oracle, and sent him these presents by way of recompence for his advice in politics, and (whether it became his grandeur and generosity or no we will not enquire) he took all that came, even garments and spices, horses and mules, *v.* 24, 25. 5. He traded to Egypt for horses and linen-yarn (or, as some read it, *linen-cloth)*, the staple commodities of that country, and had his own merchants or factors whom he employed in this traffic and who were accountable to him, *v.* 28, 29. The custom to be paid to the king of Egypt for exported chariots and horses out of Egypt was very high, but (as bishop Patrick understands it) Solomon, having married his daughter, got him to compound for the customs, so that he could bring them up cheaper than his neighbours, which obliged them to buy them of him, which he was wise enough no doubt to make his advantange of. This puts an honour upon the trading part of a nation, and sets a tradesman not so much below a gentleman as some place him, that Solomon, one of the greatest men that ever was, thought it no disparagement to him to deal in trade. In all labour there is profit.

II. What use he made of his wealth. He did not hoard it up in his coffers, that he might have it to look upon and leave behind him. He has, in his Ecclesiastes, so much exposed the folly of hoarding that we cannot suppose he would himself be guilty of it. No, God that had given him riches, and wealth, and honour, gave him also power to eat thereof, and to take his portion, Eccles. v. 19.

1. He laid out his gold in fine things for himself, which he might the better be allowed

to do when he had before laid out so much in fine things for the house of God. (1.) He made 200 targets, and 300 shields, of beaten gold (*v.* 16, 17), not for service, but for state, to be carried before him when he appeared in pomp. With us, magistrates have *swords* and *maces* carried before them, as the Romans had their *rods* and *axes*, in token of their power to correct and punish the bad, to whom they are to be a terror. But Solomon had *shields* and *targets* carried before him, to signify that he took more pleasure in using his power for the defence and protection of the good, to whom he would be a praise. Magistrates are *shields of the earth*. (2.) He made a stately throne, on which he sat, to give laws to his subjects, audience to ambassadors, and judgment upon appeals, *v.* 18—20. It was made of ivory, or elephants' teeth, which was very rich; and yet, as if he had so much gold that he knew not what to do with it, he *overlaid that with gold*, the best gold. Yet some think he did not cover the ivory all over, but here and there. He rolled it, flowered it, or inlaid it, with gold. The stays or arms of this stately chair were supported by the images of lions in gold; so were the steps and paces by which he went up to it, to be a memorandum to him of that courage and resolution wherewith he ought to execute judgment, not fearing the face of man. *The righteous*, in that post, *is bold as a lion*. (3.) He made all his drinking vessels, and all the furniture of his table, even at his country seat, of pure gold, *v.* 21. He did not grudge himself what he had, but took the credit and comfort of it, such as it was. That is good that does us good.

2. He made it circulate among his subjects, so that the kingdom was as rich as the king; for he had no separate interests of his own to consult, but sought the welfare of his people. Those princes are not governed by Solomon's maxims who think it policy to keep their subjects poor. Solomon was herein a type of Christ, who is not only rich himself, but enriches all that are his. Solomon was instrumental to bring so much gold into the country, and disperse it, that *silver was nothing accounted of*, *v.* 21. There was such plenty of it in Jerusalem that it was as the stones; and cedars, that used to be great rarities, were as common *as sycamore trees*, *v.* 27. Such is the nature of worldly wealth, plenty of it makes it the less valuable; much more should the enjoyment of spiritual riches lessen our esteem of all earthly possessions. If *gold in abundance* would make silver to seem so despicable, shall not wisdom, and grace, and the foretastes of heaven, which are far better than gold, make earthly wealth seem much more despicable?

Lastly, Well, thus rich, thus great, was Solomon, and thus did he *exceed all the kings of the earth*, *v.* 23. Now let us remember, 1. That this was he who, when he was *setting out in the world*, did not ask for the wealth and honour of it, but asked for *a wise and understanding heart*. The more moderate our desires are towards earthly things the better qualified we are for the enjoyment of them and the more likely to have them. See, in Solomon's greatness, the performance of God's promise (*ch.* iii. 13), and let it encourage us to *seek first the righteousness of God's kingdom*. 2. That this was he who, having tasted all these enjoyments, wrote a whole book to show the vanity of all worldly things and the vexation of spirit that attends them, their insufficiency to make us happy and the folly of setting our hearts upon them, and to recommend to us the practice of serious godliness, as that which is the whole of man, and will do infinitely more towards the making of us easy and happy than all the wealth and power that he was master of, and which, through the grace of God, is within our reach, when the thousandth part of Solomon's greatness is a thousand times more than we can ever be so vain as to promise ourselves in this world.

CHAP. XI.

This chapter begins with as melancholy a "but" as almost any we find in all the Bible. Hitherto we have read nothing of Solomon but what was great and good; but the lustre both of his goodness and of his greatness is here sullied and eclipsed, and his sun sets under a cloud. I. The glory of his piety is stained by his departure from God and his duty, in his latter days, marrying strange wives and worshipping strange gods, ver. 4—8. II. The glory of his prosperity is stained by God's displeasure against him and the fruits of that displeasure. 1. He sent him an angry message, ver. 9—13. 2. He stirred up enemies, who gave him disturbance, Hadad (ver. 14—22), Rezon, ver. 23—25. 3. He gave away ten tribes of his twelve, from his posterity after him, to Jeroboam, whom therefore he sought in vain to slay (ver. 26—40), and this is all that remains here to be told concerning Solomon, except his death and burial (ver. 41—43), for there is nothing perfect under the sun, but all is so above the sun.

BUT king Solomon loved many strange women, together with the daughter of Pharaoh, women of the Moabites, Ammonites, Edomites, Zidonians, *and* Hittites; 2 Of the nations *concerning* which the LORD said unto the children of Israel, Ye shall not go in to them, neither shall they come in unto you: *for* surely they will turn away your heart after their gods: Solomon clave unto these in love. 3 And he had seven hundred wives, princesses, and three hundred concubines: and his wives turned away his heart. 4 For it came to pass, when Solomon was old, *that* his wives turned away his heart after other gods: and his heart was not perfect with the LORD his God, as *was* the heart of David his father. 5 For Solomon went after Ashtoreth the goddess of the Zidonians, and after Milcom the abomination of the Ammonites. 6 And Solomon did evil in the sight of the LORD, and went not fully after the LORD, as *did* David his father. 7 Then did Solomon build a high place for Chemosh, the abomination of Moab, in the hill that *is* before Jerusalem, and for Molech, the abomination of the children of Ammon. 8 And likewise did he for all his strange wives, which burnt incense and sacrificed unto their gods.

This is a sad story, and very surprising, of Solomon's defection and degeneracy.

I. Let us enquire into the occasions and particulars of it. Shall Solomon fall, that was the beauty of Israel, and so great a blessing of his generation? Yes, it is too true, and the scripture is faithful in relating it, and repeating it, and referring to it long after, Neh. xiii. 26. *There was no king like Solomon who was beloved of his God, yet even him did outlandish women cause to sin.* There is the summary of his apostasy; it was the woman that *deceived him,* and was *first in the transgression.*

1. He doted on strange women, *many strange women.* Here his revolt began. (1.) He gave himself to women, which his mother had particularly cautioned him against. Prov. xxxi. 3, *Give not thy strength unto women* (perhaps alluding to Samson, who lost his strength by giving information of it to a woman), for it is that which, as much as any thing, destroys kings. His father David's fall began with the lusts of the flesh, which he should have taken warning by. The love of women has *cast down many wounded* (Prov. vii. 26) and *many* (says bishop Hall) *have had their head broken by their own rib.* (2.) He took many women, so many that, at last, they amounted to 700 wives and 300 concubines, 1000 in all, and not one good one among them, as he himself owns in his penitential sermon (Eccl. vii. 28), for no woman of established virtue would be one of such a set. God had, by his law, particularly forbidden the kings to multiply either horses or wives, Deut. xvii. 16, 17. How he broke the former law, in multiplying horses, and having them *out of Egypt* too (which was expressly prohibited in that law) we read *ch.* x. 29, and here we are told how he broke the latter (which proved of more fatal consequence) in multiplying wives. Note, Less sins, made bold with, open the door to greater. David had multiplied wives too much, and perhaps that made Solomon presume it lawful. Note, If those that are in reputation for religion in any thing set a bad example, they know not what a deal of mischief they may do by it, particularly to their own children. One bad act of a good man may be of more pernicious consequence to others than twenty of a wicked man. Probably Solomon, when he began to multiply wives, intended not to exceed his father's number. But the way of sin is down-hill; those that have got into it cannot easily stop themselves. Divine wisdom has appointed one woman for one man, did so at first; and those who do not think one enough will not think two or three enough. Unbridled lust will be unbounded, and the loosened hind will wander endlessly. But this was not all: (3.) They were strange women, Moabites, Ammonites, &c., of the nations which God had particularly forbidden them to intermarry with, *v.* 2. Some think it was in policy that he married these foreigners, by them to get intelligence of the state of those countries. I rather fear it was because the daughters of Israel were too grave and modest for him, and those foreigners pleased him with the looseness and wantonness of their dress, and air, and conversation. Or, perhaps, it was looked upon as a piece of state to have his seraglio, as his other treasures, replenished with that which was far-fetched; as if that were too great an honour for the best of his subjects which would really have been a disgrace to the meanest of them—to be his mistresses. And, (4.) To complete the mischief, *Solomon clave unto these in love, v.* 2. He not only kept them, but was extravagantly fond of them, set his heart upon them, spent his time among them, thought every thing well they said and did, and despised Pharaoh's daughter, his rightful wife, who had been dear to him, and all the ladies of Israel, in comparison of them. Solomon was master of a great deal of knowledge, but to what purpose, when he had no better a government of his appetites?

2. He was drawn by them to the worship of strange gods, as Israel to Baal-peor by the daughters of Moab. This was the bad consequence of his multiplying wives. We have reason to think it impaired his health, and hastened upon him the decays of age; it exhausted his treasure, which, though vast indeed, would be found little enough to maintain the pride and vanity of all these women; perhaps it occasioned him, in his latter end, to neglect his business, by which he lost his supplies from abroad, and was forced, for the keeping up of his grandeur, to burden his subjects with those taxes which they complained of, *ch.* xii. 4. But none of these consequences were so bad as this: *His wives turned away his heart after other gods, v.* 3, 4. (1.) He grew cool and indifferent in his own religion and remiss in the service of the God of Israel: *His heart was not perfect with the Lord his God* (*v.* 4), nor did he *follow him fully* (*v.* 6), like David. We cannot suppose that he quite cast off the worship of God, much less that he restrained or hindered it (the temple-service went on as usual); but he grew less frequent, and less serious, in *his ascent to the house of the Lord* and his attendance on his altar. He left his first love, lost his zeal for God, and did not persevere

to the end as he had begun; therefore it is said *he was not perfect*, because he was not *constant;* and he followed not God fully, because he turned from following him, and did not continue to the end. His father David had many faults, but he never neglected the worship of God, nor grew remiss in that, as Solomon did (his wives using all their arts to divert him from it), and *there* began his apostasy. (2.) He tolerated and maintained his wives in their idolatry and made no scruple of joining with them in it. Pharaoh's daughter was proselyted (as is supposed) to the Jews' religion, but, when he began to grow careless in the worship of God himself, he used no means to convert his other wives to it; in complaisance to them, he built chapels for their gods (*v.* 7, 8), maintained their priests, and occasionally did himself attend their altars, making a jest of it, asking, "What harm is there in it? Are not all religions alike?" which (says bishop Patrick) has been the *disease of some great wits.* When he humoured one thus, the rest would take it ill if he did not, in like manner, gratify them, so that he did it for all his wives (*v.* 8), and at last came to such a degree of impiety that he set up a high place for *Chemosh in the hill that is before Jerusalem,* the *mount of Olives,* as if to confront the temple which he himself had built. These high places continued here, not utterly demolished, till Josiah's time, 2 Kings xxiii. 13. This is the account here given of Solomon's apostasy.

II. Let us now pause awhile, and lament Solomon's fall; and we may justly stand and wonder at it. *How has the gold become dim! How has the most fine gold changed! Be astonished, O heavens! at this, and be horribly afraid,* as the prophet exclaims in a like case, Jer. ii. 12.

1. How strange, (1.) That Solomon, in his old age, should be ensnared with fleshly lusts, youthful lusts. As we must never presume upon the strength of our resolutions, so neither upon the weakness of our corruptions, so as to be secure and off our guard. (2.) That so wise a man as Solomon was, so famed for a quick understanding and sound judgment, should suffer himself to be made such a fool of by these foolish women. (3.) That one who had so often and so plainly warned others of the danger of the love of women should himself be so wretchedly bewitched with it; it is easier to see a mischief, and to show it to others, than to shun it ourselves. (4.) That so good a man, so zealous for the worship of God, who had been so conversant with divine things, and who prayed that excellent prayer at the dedication of the temple, should do these sinful things. Is this Solomon? Have all his wisdom and devotion come to this at last? Never was gallant ship so wrecked; never was crown so profaned.

2. What shall we say to all this? Why God permitted it it is not for us to enquire; his way is in the sea and his path in the great waters; he knew how to bring glory to himself out of it. God foresaw it when he said concerning him that should build the temple, *If he commit iniquity,* &c., 2 Sam. vii. 14. But it concerns us to enquire what good use we may make of it. (1.) Let him that thinks he stands take heed lest he fall. We see how weak we are of ourselves, without the grace of God; let us therefore live in a constant dependence on that grace. (2.) See the danger of a prosperous condition, and how hard it is to overcome the temptations of it. Solomon, like Jeshurun, waxed fat and then kicked. The food convenient, which Agur prayed for, is safer and better than the food abundant, which Solomon was even surfeited with. (3.) See what need those have to stand upon their guard who have made a great profession of religion, and shown themselves forward and zealous in devotion, because the devil will set upon them most violently, and, if they misbehave, the reproach is the greater. It is the evening that commends the day; let us therefore fear, lest, having run well, we seem to come short.

9 And the LORD was angry with Solomon, because his heart was turned from the LORD God of Israel, which had appeared unto him twice, 10 And had commanded him concerning this thing, that he should not go after other gods: but he kept not that which the LORD commanded. 11 Wherefore the LORD said unto Solomon, Forasmuch as this is done of thee, and thou hast not kept my covenant and my statutes, which I have commanded thee, I will surely rend the kingdom from thee, and will give it to thy servant. 12 Notwithstanding in thy days I will not do it for David thy father's sake: *but* I will rend it out of the hand of thy son. 13 Howbeit I will not rend away all the kingdom; *but* will give one tribe to thy son for David my servant's sake, and for Jerusalem's sake which I have chosen.

Here is, I. God's anger against Solomon for his sin. The thing he did *displeased the Lord.* Time was when the Lord *loved Solomon* (2 Sam xii. 24) and delighted in him (*ch.* x. 9), but now *the Lord was angry with Solomon* (*v.* 9), for there was in his sin, 1. The most base ingratitude that could be. He turned from the Lord *who had appeared unto him twice,* once before he began to build the temple (*ch.* iii. 5) and once after he had dedicated it, *ch.* ix. 2. God keeps account of the gracious visits he makes us, whether we do or no, knows how often he has appeared *to* us and *for* us, and will remember it against us if we *turn from him*. God's appearing to Solomon was such a sensible confirmation of his faith as should have for ever prevented his worshipping *any other god;* it was also such a distinguishing favour, and put such an honour upon him, as he ought never to have forgotten, especially considering what God said to him in both these appearances. 2. The most wilful disobedience. This was the very thing concerning which *God had commanded him—that he should not go after other gods,* yet he was not restrained by such an express admonition, *v.* 10. Those who have dominion over men are apt to forget God's dominion over them; and, while they demand obedience from their inferiors, to deny it to him who is the Supreme.

II. The message he sent him hereupon (*v.* 11): *The Lord said unto Solomon* (it is likely by a prophet) that he must expect to smart for his apostasy. And here, 1. The sentence is just, that, since he had revolted from God, part of his kingdom should revolt from his family; he had given God's glory to the creature, and therefore God would give his crown to his servant: "*I will rend the kingdom from thee,* in thy posterity, and will *give it to thy servant,* who shall bear rule over much of that for which thou hast laboured." This was a great mortification to Solomon, who pleased himself no doubt with the prospect of the entail of his rich kingdom upon his heirs for ever. Sin brings ruin upon families, cuts off entails, alienates estates, and lays men's honour in the dust. 2. Yet the mitigations of it are very kind, for David's sake (*v.* 12, 13), that is, for the sake of the promise made to David. Thus all the favour God shows to man is for *Christ's sake,* and for the sake of the covenant made with him. The kingdom shall be rent from Solomon's house, but, (1.) Not immediately. Solomon shall not live to see it done, but it shall be rent *out of the hand of his son,* a son that was born to him by one of his strange wives, for his mother was an Ammonitess (1 Kings xiv. 31) and probably had been a promoter of idolatry. What comfort can a man take in leaving children and an estate behind him if he do not leave a blessing behind him? Yet, if judgments be coming, it is a favour to us if they come not in our days, as 2 Kings xx. 19. (2.) Not wholly. One tribe, that of Judah, the strongest and most numerous, shall remain to the house of David (*v.* 13), for Jerusalem's sake, which David built, and for the sake of the temple there, which Solomon built; these shall not go into other hands. Solomon did not quickly nor wholly turn away from God; therefore God did not quickly nor wholly take the kingdom from him.

Upon this message which God graciously sent to Solomon, to awaken his conscience and bring him to repentance, we have reason to hope that he humbled himself before God, confessed his sin, begged pardon, and returned to his duty, that he then published his repentance in the book of Ecclesiastes, where he bitterly laments his own folly and madness (*ch.* vii. 25, 26), and warns others to take heed of the like evil courses, and to *fear God* and *keep his commandments,* in consideration of *the judgment to come,* which, it is likely, had made him tremble, as it did Felix. That penitential sermon was as true an indication of a heart broken for sin and turned from it as David's penitential psalms were, though of another nature. God's grace in his people works variously. Thus, though Solomon fell, *he was not utterly cast down;* what God had said to David concerning him was fulfilled: *I will chasten him with the rod of men, but my mercy shall not depart from him,* 2 Sam. vii. 14, 15. Though God may suffer those whom he loves to fall into sin, he will not suffer them to lie still in it. Solomon's defection, though it was much his reproach and a great blemish to his personal character, yet did not so far break in upon the character of his reign but that it was afterwards made the pattern of a good reign, 2 Chron. xi. 17, where the kings are said to have done well, while *they walked in the way of David and Solomon.* But, though we have all this reason to hope he repented and found mercy, yet the Holy Ghost did not think fit expressly to record his recovery, but left it doubtful, for warning to others not to sin upon presumption of repenting, for it is but a peradventure whether *God will give them repentance,* or, if he do, whether he will give the evidence of it to themselves or others. Great sinners may recover themselves and have the benefit of their repentance, and yet be denied both the comfort and credit of it; the guilt may be taken away, and yet not the reproach.

14 And the LORD stirred up an adversary unto Solomon, Hadad the Edomite: he *was* of the king's seed in Edom. 15 For it came to pass, when David was in Edom, and Joab the captain of the host was gone up to bury the slain, after he had smitten every male in Edom; 16 (For six months did Joab remain there with all Israel, until he had cut off every male in Edom:) 17 That Hadad fled, he and certain Edomites of his father's servants with him, to go into Egypt; Hadad *being* yet a little child. 18 And they arose out of Midian, and came to Paran: and they took men with them out of Paran, and they came to Egypt, unto Pharaoh king of Egypt; which gave him a house, and appointed him victuals, and gave him

land. 19 And Hadad found great favour in the sight of Pharaoh, so that he gave him to wife the sister of his own wife, the sister of Tahpenes the queen. 20 And the sister of Tahpenes bare him Genubath his son, whom Tahpenes weaned in Pharaoh's house: and Genubath was in Pharaoh's household among the sons of Pharaoh. 21 And when Hadad heard in Egypt that David slept with his fathers, and that Joab the captain of the host was dead, Hadad said to Pharaoh, Let me depart, that I may go to mine own country. 22 Then Pharaoh said unto him, But what hast thou lacked with me, that, behold, thou seekest to go to thine own country? And he answered, Nothing: howbeit let me go in any wise. 23 And God stirred him up *another* adversary, Rezon the son of Eliadah, which fled from his lord Hadadezer king of Zobah: 24 And he gathered men unto him, and became captain over a band, when David slew them *of Zobah:* and they went to Damascus, and dwelt therein, and reigned in Damascus. 25 And he was an adversary to Israel all the days of Solomon, beside the mischief that Hadad *did:* and he abhorred Israel, and reigned over Syria.

While Solomon kept closely to God and to his duty there was *no adversary nor evil occurrent* (*ch.* v. 4), nothing to create him any disturbance or uneasiness in the least; but here we have an account of two adversaries that appeared against him, inconsiderable, and that could not have done any thing worth taking notice of if Solomon had not first made God his enemy. What hurt could Hadad or Rezon have done to so great and powerful a king as Solomon was if he had not, by sin, made himself mean and weak? And then those little people menace and insult him. If God be on our side, we need not fear the greatest adversary; but, if he be against us, he can make us fear the least, and the very grasshopper shall be a burden. Observe,

I. Both these adversaries God stirred up, *v.* 14, 23. Though they themselves were moved by principles of ambition or revenge, God made use of them to serve his design of correcting Solomon. The principal judgment threatened was deferred, namely, the rending of the kingdom from him, but he himself was made to feel the smart of the rod, for his greater humiliation. Note, Whoever are, in any way, adversaries to us, we must take notice of the hand of God stirring them up to be so, as he bade Shimei curse David; we must look through the instruments of our trouble to the author of it and hear the Lord's controversy in it.

II. Both these adversaries had the origin of their enmity to Solomon and Israel laid in David's time, and in his conquests of their respective countries, *v.* 15, 24. Solomon had the benefit and advantage of his father's successes both in the enlargement of his dominion and the increase of his treasure, and would never have known any thing but the benefit of them if he had kept closely to God; but now he finds evils to balance the advantages, and that David had made himself enemies, who were thorns in his sides. Those that are too free in giving provocation ought to consider that perhaps it may be remembered in time to come and returned with interest to theirs after them; having so few friends in this world, it is our wisdom not to make ourselves more enemies than we needs must.

1. Hadad, an Edomite, was an adversary to Solomon. We are not told what he did against him, nor which way he gave him disturbance, only, in general, that he was an adversary to him: but we are told, (1.) What induced him to bear Solomon a grudge. David had conquered Edom, 2 Sam. viii. 14. Joab put all the males to the sword, *v.* 15, 16. A terrible execution he made, avenging on Edom their old enmity to Israel, yet perhaps with too great a severity. From this general slaughter, while Joab was burying the slain (for he left not any alive of their own people to bury them, and buried they must be, or they would be an annoyance to the country, Ezek. xxxix. 12), Hadad, a branch of the royal family, then a little child, was taken and preserved by some of the king's servants, and conveyed to Egypt, *v.* 17. They halted by the way, in Midian first, and then in Paran, where they furnished themselves with men, not to fight for them or force their passage, but to attend them, that their young master might go into Egypt with an equipage agreeable to his quality. There he was kindly sheltered and entertained by Pharaoh, as a distressed prince, was well provided for, and so recommended himself that, in process of time, he married the queen's sister (*v.* 19), and by her had a child, which the queen herself conceived such a kindness for that she brought him up in Pharaoh's house, among the king's children. (2.) What enabled him to do Solomon a mischief. Upon the death of David and Joab, he returned to his own country, in which, it should seem, he settled and remained quiet while Solomon continued wise and watchful for the public good, but from which he had opportunity of making inroads upon Israel when Solomon, having sinned away his wisdom

as Samson did his strength (and in the same way), grew careless of public affairs, was off his guard himself, and had forfeited the divine protection. What vexation Hadad gave to Solomon we are not here told, but only how loth Pharaoh was to part with him and how earnestly he solicited his stay (*v.* 22): *What hast thou lacked with me?* "Nothing," says Hadad; "but let me go to my own country, my native air, my native soil." Peter Martyr has a pious reflection upon this: "Heaven is our home, and we ought to keep up a holy affection to that, and desire towards it, even when the world, the place of our banishment, smiles most upon us. Does it ask, What have you lacked, that you are so willing to be gone? We may answer, "Nothing that the world can do for us; but still let us go thither, where our hope, and honour, and treasure are."

2. Rezon, a Syrian, was another adversary to Solomon. When David conquered the Syrians, he headed the remains, lived at large by spoil and rapine, till Solomon grew careless, and then he got possession of Damascus, reigned there (*v.* 24) and over the country about (*v.* 25), and he created troubles to Israel, probably in conjunction with Hadad, all the days of Solomon (namely, after his apostasy), or he was an enemy to Israel during all Solomon's reign, and upon all occasions vented his then impotent malice against them, but till Solomon's revolt, when his defence had departed from him, he could not do them any mischief. It is said of him that *he abhorred Israel.* Other princes loved and admired Israel and Solomon, and courted their friendship, but here was one that abhorred them. The greatest and best of princes and people, however much they may in general be respected, will yet perhaps be hated and abhorred by some.

26 And Jeroboam the son of Nebat, an Ephrathite of Zereda, Solomon's servant, whose mother's name *was* Zeruah, a widow woman, even he lifted up *his* hand against the king. 27 And this *was* the cause that he lifted up *his* hand against the king: Solomon built Millo, *and* repaired the breaches of the city of David his father. 28 And the man Jeroboam *was* a mighty man of valour: and Solomon seeing the young man that he was industrious, he made him ruler over all the charge of the house of Joseph. 29 And it came to pass at that time when Jeroboam went out of Jerusalem, that the prophet Ahijah the Shilonite found him in the way; and he had clad himself with a new garment; and they two *were* alone in the field: 30 And Ahijah caught the new garment that *was* on him, and rent it *in* twelve pieces: 31 And he said to Jeroboam, Take thee ten pieces: for thus saith the LORD, the God of Israel, Behold, I will rend the kingdom out of the hand of Solomon, and will give ten tribes to thee: 32 (But he shall have one tribe for my servant David's sake, and for Jerusalem's sake, the city which I have chosen out of all the tribes of Israel:) 33 Because that they have forsaken me, and have worshipped Ashtoreth the goddess of the Zidonians, Chemosh the god of the Moabites, and Milcom the god of the children of Ammon, and have not walked in my ways, to do *that which is* right in mine eyes, and *to keep* my statutes and my judgments, as *did* David his father. 34 Howbeit I will not take the whole kingdom out of his hand: but I will make him prince all the days of his life for David my servant's sake, whom I chose, because he kept my commandments and my statutes: 35 But I will take the kingdom out of his son's hand, and will give it unto thee, *even* ten tribes. 36 And unto his son will I give one tribe, that David my servant may have a light alway before me in Jerusalem, the city which I have chosen me to put my name there. 37 And I will take thee, and thou shalt reign according to all that thy soul desireth, and shalt be king over Israel. 38 And it shall be, if thou wilt hearken unto all that I command thee, and wilt walk in my ways, and do *that is* right in my sight, to keep my statutes and my commandments, as David my servant did; that I will be with thee, and build thee a sure house, as I built for David, and will give Israel unto thee. 39 And I will for this afflict the seed of David, but not for ever. 40 Solomon sought therefore to kill Jeroboam. And Jeroboam arose, and fled into Egypt, unto Shishak king of Egypt, and was in Egypt until the death of Solomon.

We have here the first mention of that infamous name *Jeroboam the son of Nebat, that made Israel to sin;* he is here brought upon the stage as an adversary to Solomon, whom God had expressly told (*v.* 11) that he would give the greatest part of his kingdom to his servant, and Jeroboam was the man. We have here an account,

I. Of his extraction, *v.* 26. He was of the tribe of Ephraim, the next in honour to Judah. His mother was a widow, to whom Providence had made up the loss of a husband in a son that was active and ingenious, and (we may suppose) a great support and comfort to her.

II. Of his elevation. It was Solomon's wisdom, when he had work to do, to employ proper persons in it. He observed Jeroboam to be a very industrious young man, one that minded his business, took a pleasure in it, and did it with all his might, and therefore he gradually advanced him, till at length he made him receiver-general for the two tribes of Ephraim and Manasseh, or perhaps put him into an office equivalent to that of lord-lieutenant of those two counties, for he was ruler of the burden, or tribute, that is, either of the taxes or of the militia of the house of Joseph. Note, Industry is the way to preferment. *Seest thou a man diligent in his business,* that will take care and pains, and go through with it? he shall *stand before kings,* and not always be on the level with mean men. Observe a difference between David, and both his predecessor and his successor: when Saul saw a *valiant man he took him to himself* (1 Sam. xiv. 52); when Solomon saw an *industrious* man he preferred him; but David's *eyes were upon the faithful in the land,* that they might *dwell with him:* if he saw a godly man, he preferred him, for he was a man after God's own heart, whose *countenance beholds the upright.*

III. Of his designation to the government of the ten tribes after the death of Solomon. Some think he was himself plotting against Solomon, and contriving to rise to the throne, that he was turbulent and aspiring. The Jews say that when he was employed by Solomon in building Millo he took opportunities of reflecting upon Solomon as oppressive to his people, and suggesting that which would alienate them from his government. It is not indeed probable that he should say much to that purport, for Solomon would have got notice of it, and it would have hindered his preferment; but it is plainly intimated that he had it in his thoughts, for the prophet tells him (*v.* 37), *Thou shalt reign according to all that thy soul desireth.* But this was the *cause,* or rather this was the *story,* of the lifting up of his hand against the king: Solomon made him ruler over the tribes of Joseph, and, as he was going to take possession of his government, he was told by a prophet in God's name that he should be king, which emboldened him to aim high, and in some instances to oppose the king and give him vexation. 1. The prophet by whom this message was sent was *Ahijah of Shiloh;* we shall read of him again, *ch.* xiv. 2. It seems, Shiloh was not so perfectly forsaken and forgotten of God but that, in remembrance of the former days, it was blessed with a prophet. He delivered his message to Jeroboam in the way, his servants being probably ordered to retire, as in a like case (1 Sam. ix. 27), when Samuel delivered his message to Saul. God's word was not the less sacred and sure for being delivered to him thus obscurely, under a hedge it may be. 2. The sign by which it was represented to him was the rending of a garment into twelve pieces, and giving him ten, *v.* 30, 31. It is not certain whether the garment was Jeroboam's, as is commonly taken for granted, or Ahijah's, which is more probable: *He* (that is, the prophet) *had clad himself with a new garment,* on purpose that he might with it give him a sign. The rending of the kingdom from Saul was signified by the rending of Samuel's mantle, not Saul's, 1 Sam. xv. 27, 28. And it was more significant to give Jeroboam ten pieces of that which was not his own before than of that which was. The prophets, both true and false, used such signs, even in the New Testament, as Agabus, Acts xxi. 10, 11. 3. The message itself, which is very particular. (1.) He assures him that he shall be king over ten of the twelve tribes of Israel, *v.* 31. The meanness of his extraction and employment shall be no hindrance to his advancement, when the God of Israel says (by whom kings reign), *I will give ten tribes unto thee.* (2.) He tells him the reason; not for his good character or deserts, but for the chastising of Solomon's apostasy: "Because he, and his family, and many of his people with him, *have forsaken me, and worshipped other gods,*" *v.* 33. It was because they had done ill, not because he was likely to do much better. Thus Israel must know that it is not *for their righteousness* that they are made masters of Canaan, but for the wickedness of the Canaanites, Deut. ix. 4. Jeroboam did not deserve so good a post, but Israel deserved so bad a prince. In telling him that the reason why he rent the kingdom from the house of Solomon was because they had forsaken God, he warns him to take heed of sinning away his preferment in like manner. (3.) He limits his expectations to the ten tribes only, and to them in reversion after the death of Solomon, lest he should aim at the whole and give immediate disturbance to Solomon's government. He is here told, [1.] That two tribes (called here *one tribe,* because little Benjamin was in a manner lost in the thousands of Judah) should remain sure to the house of David, and he must never make any attempt upon them: *He shall have one tribe* (*v.* 32), and again (*v.* 36), *That David may have a lamp,* that is, a shining name and memory (Ps.

cxxxii. 17), and his family, as a royal family, may not be extinct. He must not think that David was rejected, as Saul was. No, God would not take his loving-kindness from him, as he did from Saul. The house of David must be supported and kept in reputation, for all this, because out of it the Messiah must arise. *Destroy it not,* for that *blessing is in it.* [2.] That Solomon must keep possession during his life, *v.* 34, 35. Jeroboam therefore must not offer to dethrone him, but wait with patience till his day shall come to fall. Solomon shall be *prince, all the days of his life,* not for his own sake (he had forfeited his crown to the justice of God), but for *David my servant's sake, because he kept my commandments.* Children that do not tread in their parents' steps yet often fare the better in this world for their good parents' piety. (4.) He gives him to understand that he will be upon his good behaviour. The grant of the crown must run *quamdiu se bene gesserit—during good behaviour.* "If thou wilt *do what is right in my sight, I will build thee a sure house,* and not otherwise" (*v.* 38), intimating that, if he forsook God, even his advancement to the throne would in time lay his family in the dust; whereas the seed of David, though afflicted, should not be afflicted for ever (*v.* 39), but should flourish again, as it did in many of the illustrious kings of Judah, who reigned in glory when Jeroboam's family was extirpated.

IV. Jeroboam's flight into Egypt, *v.* 40. In some way or other Solomon came to know of all this, probably from Jeroboam's own talk of it; he could not conceal it as Saul did, nor keep his own counsel; if he had, he might have staid in his country, and been preparing there for his future advancement; but letting it be known, 1. Solomon foolishly sought to kill his successor. Had not he taught others that, whatever devices are in men's hearts, *the counsel of the Lord shall stand?* And yet does he himself think to defeat that counsel? 2. Jeroboam prudently withdrew into Egypt. Though God's promise would have secured him any where, yet he would use means for his own preservation, and was content to live in exile and obscurity for a while, being sure of a kingdom at last. And shall not we be so, who have a better kingdom in reserve?

41 And the rest of the acts of Solomon, and all that he did, and his wisdom, *are* they not written in the book of the acts of Solomon? 42 And the time that Solomon reigned in Jerusalem over all Israel *was* forty years. 43 And Solomon slept with his fathers, and was buried in the city of David his father: and Rehoboam his son reigned in his stead.

We have here the conclusion of Solomon's story, and in it, 1. Reference is had to another history then extant, but (not being divinely inspired) since lost, *the Book of the Acts of Solomon, v.* 41. Probably this book was written by a chronologer or historiographer, whom Solomon employed to write his annals, out of which the sacred writer extracted what God saw fit to transmit to the church. 2. A summary of the years of his reign (*v.* 42): *He reigned in Jerusalem* (not, as his father, part of his time in Hebron and part in Jerusalem), *over all Israel* (not as his son, and his father in the beginning of his time, over Judah only), *forty years.* His reign was as long as his father's, but not his life. Sin shortened his days. 3. His death and burial, and his successor, *v.* 43. (1.) He followed his fathers to the grave, slept with them, and was buried in David's burying-place, with honour no doubt. (2.) His son followed him in the throne. Thus the graves are filling with the generations that go off, and houses are filling with those that are growing up. As the grave cries, "Give, give," so land is never lost for want of an heir.

CHAP. XII.

The glory of the kingdom of Israel was in its height and perfection in Solomon; it was long in coming to it, but it soon declined, and began to sink and wither in the very next reign, as we find in this chapter, where we have the kingdom divided, and thereby weakened and made little in comparison with what it had been. Here is, I. Rehoboam's accession to the throne and Jeroboam's return out of Egypt, ver. 1, 2. II. The people's petition to Rehoboam for the redress of grievances, and the rough answer he gave, by the advice of his young counsellors, to that petition, ver. 3—15. III. The revolt of the ten tribes thereupon, and their setting up Jeroboam, ver. 16—20. IV. Rehoboam's attempt to reduce them and the prohibition God gave to that attempt, ver. 21—24. V. Jeroboam's establishment of his government upon idolatry, ver. 25—33. Thus did Judah become weak, being deserted by their brethren, and Israel, by deserting the house of the Lord.

AND Rehoboam went to Shechem: for all Israel were come to Shechem to make him king. 2 And it came to pass, when Jeroboam the son of Nebat, who was yet in Egypt, heard *of it,* (for he was fled from the presence of king Solomon, and Jeroboam dwelt in Egypt;) 3 That they sent and called him. And Jeroboam and all the congregation of Israel came, and spake unto Rehoboam, saying, 4 Thy father made our yoke grievous: now therefore make thou the grievous service of thy father, and his heavy yoke which he put upon us, lighter, and we will serve thee. 5 And he said unto them, Depart yet *for* three days, then come again to me. And the people departed. 6 And king Rehoboam consulted with the old men, that stood before Solomon his father while he yet lived, and said, How do ye advise that I may answer this people? 7 And they spake unto him, saying, If thou wilt be a servant unto this people this day, and wilt serve them, and answer them, and speak good words to them, then they will be thy servants for ever. 8 But he forsook the counsel of the old men, which they had given him, and consulted with the young men that were grown up with him, *and* which stood before him: 9 And he said unto them, What counsel give ye that we may answer this people, who have spoken to me, saying, Make the yoke which thy father did put upon us lighter? 10 And the young men that were grown up with him spake unto him, saying, Thus shalt thou speak unto this people that spake unto thee, saying, Thy father made our yoke heavy, but make thou *it* lighter unto us; thus shalt thou say unto them, My little *finger* shall be thicker than my father's loins. 11 And now whereas my father did lade you with a heavy yoke, I will add to your yoke: my father hath chastised you with whips, but I will chastise you with scorpions. 12 So Jeroboam and all the people came to Rehoboam the third day, as the king had appointed, saying, Come to me again the third day. 13 And the king answered the people roughly, and forsook the old men's counsel that they gave him; 14 And spake to them after the counsel of the young men, saying, My father made your yoke heavy, and I will add to your yoke: my father *also* chastised you with whips, but I will chastise you with scorpions. 15 Wherefore the king hearkened not unto the people; for the cause was from the LORD, that he might perform his saying, which the LORD spake by Ahijah the Shilonite unto Jeroboam the son of Nebat.

Solomon had 1000 wives and concubines, yet we read but of one son he had to bear up his name, and he a fool. It is said (Hos. iv. 10), *They shall commit whoredom, and shall not increase.* Sin is a bad way of building up a family. Rehoboam was the son of the wisest of men, yet did not inherit his father's wisdom, and then it stood him in little stead to inherit his father's throne. Neither wisdom nor grace runs in the blood. Solomon came to the crown very young, yet he was then a wise man. Rehoboam came to the crown at forty years old, when men will be wise if ever they will, yet he was then foolish. Wisdom does not go by age, nor is it the multitude of years nor the advantage of education that reaches it. Solomon's court was a mart of wisdom and the rendezvous of learned men, and Rehoboam was the darling of the court; and yet all was not sufficient to make him a wise man. *The race is not to the swift, nor the battle to the strong.* No dispute is made of Rehoboam's succession; upon the death of his father, he was immediately proclaimed. But,

I. The people desired a treaty with him at Shechem, and he condescended to meet them there. 1. Their pretence was to make him king, but the design was to unmake him. They would give him a public inauguration in another place than the city of David, that he might not seem to be king of Judah only. They had ten parts in him, and would have him among themselves for once, that they might recognize his title. 2. The place was ominous: at *Shechem,* where Abimelech set up himself (Judg. ix.); yet it had been famous for the convention of the states there, Josh. xxiv. 1. Rehoboam, we may suppose, knew of the threatening, that the kingdom should be rent from him, and hoped by going to Shechem, and treating there with the ten tribes, to prevent it: yet it proved the most impolitic thing he could do, and hastened the rupture.

II. The representatives of the tribes addressed him, praying to be eased of the taxes they were burdened with. The meeting being appointed, they sent for Jeroboam out of Egypt to come and be their speaker. This they needed not to have done: he knew what God had designed him for, and would have come though he had not been sent for, for now was his time to expect the possession of the promised crown. In their address, 1. They complain of the last reign: *Thy father made our yoke grievous, v.* 4. They complain not of his father's idolatry and revolt from God; that which was the greatest grievance of all was none to them, so careless and indifferent were they in the matters of religion, as if God or Moloch were all one, so they might but live at ease and pay no taxes. Yet the complaint was groundless and unjust. Never did people live more at ease than they did, nor in greater plenty. Did they pay taxes? It was to advance the strength and magnificence of their kingdom. If Solomon's buildings cost them money, they cost them no blood, as war would do. Were many servile hands employed about them? They were not the hands of the Israelites. Were the taxes a burden? How could that be, when Solomon imported bullion in such plenty that silver was, in a manner, as common as the stones? So that they did but render to Solomon the things that were Solomon's. Nay, suppose there was some hardship put upon them, were they not told before that this would be the manner of the king and yet they would have one? The best government cannot secure itself from reproach and censure, no, not Solomon's. Factious spirits will never want something to complain of. I know nothing in Solomon's administration that could make the people's yoke grievous, unless perhaps the women whom in his latter days he doted on were connived at in oppressing them. 2. They demand relief from him, and on this condition will continue in their allegiance to the house of David. They asked not to be wholly free from paying taxes, but to have the burden made lighter; this was all their care, to save their money, whether their religion was supported and the government protected or no. All seek their own.

III. Rehoboam consulted with those about him concerning the answer he should give to this address. It was prudent to take advice, especially having so weak a head of his own; yet, upon this occasion, it was impolitic to take time himself to consider, for thereby he gave time to the disaffected people to ripen things for a revolt, and his deliberating in so plain a case would be improved as an indication of the little concern he had for the people's ease. They saw what they must expect, and prepared accordingly. Now, 1. The grave experienced men of his council advised him by all means to give the petitioners a kind answer, to give them good words, to promise them fair, and this day, this critical day, to serve them, that is, to tell them that he was their servant, and that he would redress all their grievances and make it his business to please them and make them easy. "Deny thyself (say they) so far as to do this for this once, and they will be *thy servants for ever.* When the present heat is allayed with a soft answer, and the assembly dismissed, their cooler thoughts will reconcile and fix them to Solomon's family still." Note, The way to rule is to serve, to do good, and stoop to do it, to become all things to all men and so win their hearts. Those who are in power really sit highest, and easiest, and safest, when they take this method. 2. The young men of his council were hot and haughty, and they advised him to return a severe and threatening answer to the people's demands. It was an instance of Rehoboam's weakness, (1.) That he did not prefer aged counsellors, but had a better opinion of the young men that had grown up with him and with whom he was familiar, *v.* 8. Days should speak. It was a folly for him to think that, because they had been his agreeable companions in the sports and pleasures of his youth, they were therefore fit to have the management of the affairs of his kingdom. Great wits have not always the most wisdom; nor are those to be relied on as our best friends that know how to make us merry, for that will not make us happy. It is of great consequence to young people, that are setting out in the world, whom they associate with, accommodate themselves to, and depend upon for advice. If they reckon those that feed their pride, gratify their vanity, and further them in their pleasures, their best friends, they are already marked for ruin. (2.) That he did not prefer moderate counsels, but was pleased with those that put him upon harsh and rigorous methods, and advised him to double the taxes, whether there was occasion for so doing or no, and to tell them in plain terms that he would do so, *v.* 10, 11. These young counsellors thought the old men expressed themselves but dully, *v.* 7. They affect to be witty in their advice, and value themselves on that. The old men did not undertake to put words into Rehoboam's mouth, only counselled him to speak good words; but the young men will furnish him with very quaint and pretty phrases, with pointed and pert similitudes: *My little finger shall be thicker than my father's loins,* &c. That is not always the best sense that is best worded.

IV. He answered the people according to the counsel of the young men, *v.* 14, 15. He affected to be haughty and imperious, and fancied he could carry all before him with a high hand, and therefore would rather run the risk of losing them than deny himself so far as to give them good words. Note, Many ruin themselves by consulting their humour more than their interest. See,

1. How Rehoboam was infatuated in his counsels. He could not have acted more foolishly and impoliticly. (1.) He owned their reflections upon his father's government to be true: *My father made your yoke heavy;* and therein he was unjust to his father's memory, which he might easily have vindicated from the imputation. (2.) He fancied himself better able to manage them, and impose upon them, than his father was, not considering that he was vastly inferior to him in capacity. Could he think to support the blemishes of his father's reign who could never pretend to come near the glories of it? (3.) He threatened not only to squeeze them by taxes, but to chastise them by cruel laws and severe executions of them, which should be not as whips only, but as scorpions, whips with rowels in them, that will fetch blood at every lash. In short, he would use them as brute beasts, load them and beat them at his pleasure: not caring whether they loved him or no, he would make them fear him. (4.) He gave this provocation to a people that by long ease and prosperity were made wealthy, and strong, and proud, and would not be trampled upon (as a poor cowed dispirited people may), to a people that were now disposed to revolt, and had one ready to head them. Never, surely, was man so

blinded by pride and affectation of arbitrary power, than which nothing is more fatal.

2. How God's counsels were hereby fulfilled. It was *from the Lord, v.* 15. He left Rehoboam to his own folly, and *hid from his eyes* the *things which belonged to his peace*, that the kingdom might be rent from him. Note, God serves his own wise and righteous purposes by the imprudences and iniquities of men, and snares sinners in the work of their own hands. Those that lose the kingdom of heaven throw it away, as Rehoboam did his, by their own wilfulness and folly.

16 So when all Israel saw that the king hearkened not unto them, the people answered the king, saying, What portion have we in David? neither *have we* inheritance in the son of Jesse: to your tents, O Israel: now see to thine own house, David. So Israel departed unto their tents. 17 But *as for* the children of Israel which dwelt in the cities of Judah, Rehoboam reigned over them. 18 Then king Rehoboam sent Adoram, who *was* over the tribute; and all Israel stoned him with stones, that he died. Therefore king Rehoboam made speed to get him up to his chariot, to flee to Jerusalem. 19 So Israel rebelled against the house of David unto this day. 20 And it came to pass, when all Israel heard that Jeroboam was come again, that they sent and called him unto the congregation, and made him king over all Israel: there was none that followed the house of David, but the tribe of Judah only. 21 And when Rehoboam was come to Jerusalem, he assembled all the house of Judah, with the tribe of Benjamin, a hundred and fourscore thousand chosen men, which were warriors, to fight against the house of Israel, to bring the kingdom again to Rehoboam the son of Solomon. 22 But the word of God came unto Shemaiah the man of God, saying, 23 Speak unto Rehoboam, the son of Solomon, king of Judah, and unto all the house of Judah and Benjamin, and to the remnant of the people, saying, 24 Thus saith the LORD, Ye shall not go up, nor fight against your brethren the children of Israel: return every man to his house; for this thing is from me. They hearkened therefore to the word of the LORD, and returned to depart, according to the word of the LORD.

We have here the rending of the kingdom of the ten tribes from the house of David, to effect which,

I. The people were bold and resolute in their revolt. They highly resented the provocation that Rehoboam had given them, were incensed at his menaces, concluded that that government would in the progress of it be intolerably grievous which in the beginning of it was so very haughty, and therefore immediately came to this resolve, one and all: *What portion have we in David? v.* 16. They speak here very unbecomingly of David, that great benefactor of their nation, calling him *the son of Jesse*, no greater a man than his neighbours. How soon are good men, and their good services to the public, forgotten! The rashness of their resolution was also much to be blamed. In time, and with prudent management, they might have settled the original contract with Rehoboam to mutual satisfaction. Had they enquired who gave Rehoboam this advice, and taken a course to remove those evil counsellors from about him, the rupture might have been prevented: otherwise their jealousy for their liberty and property well became that free people. *Israel is not a servant, is not a home-born slave; why should he be spoiled?* Jer. ii. 14. They are willing to be ruled, but not to be ridden. Protection draws allegiance, but destruction cannot. No marvel that *Israel falls away from the house of David* (*v.* 19) if the house of David fall away from the great ends of their advancement, which was to be *ministers of God to them for good*. But thus to rebel against the seed of David, whom God had advanced to the kingdom (entailing it on his seed), and to set up another king in opposition to that family, was a great sin; see 2 Chron. xiii. 5—8. To this God refers, Hos. viii. 4. *They have set up kings, but not by me.* And it is here mentioned to the praise of the tribe of Judah that they *followed the house of David* (*v.* 17, 20), and, for aught that appears, they found Rehoboam better than his word, nor did he rule with the rigour which at first he threatened.

II. Rehoboam was imprudent in the further management of this affair, and more and more infatuated. Having foolishly thrown himself into a quick-sand, he sunk the further in with plunging to get out. 1. He was very unadvised in sending Adoram, who was *over the tribute*, to treat with them, *v.* 18. The tribute was the thing, and, for the sake of that, Adoram was the person, they most complained of. The very sight of him, whose name was odious among them, exasperated them, and made them outrageous. He was one to whom they could not so much as give a patient hearing, but *stoned him to death* in a popular tumult. Rehoboam was now as unhappy in the choice of his ambassador as before of his counsellors. 2. Some think he was also unadvised in quitting his ground, and making so much haste to Jerusalem, for thereby he deserted his friends and gave advantage to his enemies, who had gone to their tents indeed (*v.* 16) in disgust, but did not offer to make Jeroboam king till Rehoboam had gone, *v.* 20. See how soon this foolish prince went from one extreme to the other. He hectored and talked big when he thought all was his own, but sneaked and looked very mean when he saw himself in danger. It is common for those that are most haughty in their prosperity to be most abject in adversity.

III. God forbade his attempt to recover by the sword what he had lost. What was done was of God, who would not suffer that it should be undone again (as it would be if Rehoboam got the better and reduced the ten tribes), nor that more should be done to the prejudice of the house of David, as would be if Jeroboam got the better and conquered the two tribes. The thing must rest as it is, and therefore God forbids the battle. 1. It was brave in Rehoboam to design the reducing of the revolters by force. His courage came to him when he had come to Jerusalem, *v.* 21. There he thought himself among his firm friends, who generously adhered to him and appeared for him. Judah and Benjamin (who feared the Lord and the king, and meddled not with those that were given to change) presently raised an army of 180,000 men, for the recovery of their king's right to the ten tribes, and were resolved to stand by him (as we say) with their lives and fortunes, having either not such cause, or rather not such a disposition, to complain, as the rest had. 2. It was more brave in Rehoboam to desist when God, by a prophet, ordered him to lay down his arms. He would not lose a kingdom tamely, for then he would have been unworthy the title of a prince; and yet he would not contend for it in opposition to God, for then he would have been unworthy the title of an Israelite. To proceed in this war would be not only to *fight against their brethren* (*v.* 24), whom they ought to love, but to fight against their God, to whom they ought to submit: *This thing is from me.* These two considerations should reconcile us to our losses and troubles, that God is the author of them and our brethren are the instruments of them; let us not therefore meditate revenge. Rehoboam and his people *hearkened to the word of the Lord*, disbanded the army, and acquiesced. Though, in human probability, they had a fair prospect of success (for their army was numerous and resolute, Jeroboam's party weak and unsettled), though it would turn to their reproach among their neighbours to lose so much of their strength and never have one push for it, to make a flourish and do nothing, yet, (1.) They regarded the command of God though sent by a poor prophet. When we know God's mind we must submit to it, how much soever it crosses our own mind. (2.) They consulted their own interest, concluding that though they had all the advantages, even that of right, on their side, yet they could not prosper if they fought in disobedience to God; and it was better to sit still than to rise up and fall. In the next reign God allowed them to fight, and gave them victory (2 Chron. xiii.), but not now.

25 Then Jeroboam built Shechem in mount Ephraim, and dwelt therein; and went out from thence, and built Penuel. 26 And Jeroboam said in his heart, Now shall the kingdom return to the house of David: 27 If this people go up to do sacrifice in the house of the LORD at Jerusalem, then shall the heart of this people turn again unto their lord, *even* unto Rehoboam king of Judah, and they shall kill me, and go again to Rehoboam, king of Judah. 28 Whereupon the king took counsel, and made two calves *of* gold, and said unto them, It is too much for you to go up to Jerusalem: behold thy gods, O Israel, which brought thee up out of the land of Egypt. 29 And he set the one in Beth-el, and the other put he in Dan. 30 And this thing became a sin: for the people went *to worship* before the one, *even* unto Dan. 31 And he made a house of high places, and made priests of the lowest of the people, which were not of the sons of Levi. 32 And Jeroboam ordained a feast in the eighth month, on the fifteenth day of the month, like unto the feast that *is* in Judah, and he offered upon the altar. So did he in Beth-el, sacrificing unto the calves that he had made: and he placed in Beth-el the priests of the high places which he had made. 33 So he offered upon the altar which he had made in Beth-el the fifteenth day of the eighth month, *even* in the month which he had devised of his own heart; and ordained a feast unto the children of Israel: and he offered upon the altar, and burnt incense.

We have here the beginning of the reign of Jeroboam. He built Shechem first and then Penuel—beautified and fortified them, and probably had a palace in each of them for himself (*v.* 25), the former in Ephraim, the latter in Gad, on the other side Jordan. This might be proper; but he formed another project for the establishing of his kingdom which was fatal to the interests of religion in it.

I. That which he designed was by some effectual means to secure those to himself who had now chosen him for their king, and to prevent their return to the house of David, *v.* 26, 27. It seems, 1. He was jealous of the people, afraid that, some time or other, they would kill him and go again to Rehoboam. Many that have been advanced in one tumult have been hurled down in another. Jeroboam could not put any confidence in the affections of his people, though now they seemed extremely fond of him; for what is got by wrong and usurpation cannot be enjoyed nor kept with any security or satisfaction. 2. He was distrustful of the promise of God, could not take his word that, if he would keep close to his duty, *God would build him a sure house* (*ch.* xi. 38); but he would contrive ways and means, and sinful ones too, for his own safety. A practical disbelief of God's all-sufficiency is at the bottom of all our treacherous departures from him.

II. The way he took to do this was by keeping the people from going up to Jerusalem to worship. That was the place God had chosen, to put his name there. Solomon's temple was there, which God had, in the sight of all Israel, and in the memory of many now living, taken solemn possession of in a cloud of glory. At the altar there the priest of the Lord attended, there all Israel were to keep the feasts, and thither they were to bring their sacrifices. Now,

1. Jeroboam apprehended that, if the people continued to do this, they would in time return to the house of David, allured by the magnificence both of the court and of the temple. If they cleave to their old religion, they will go back to their old king. We may suppose, if he had treated with Rehoboam for the safe conduct of himself and his people to and from Jerusalem at the times appointed for their solemn feasts, it would not have been denied him; therefore he fears not their being driven back by force, but their going back voluntarily to Rehoboam.

2. He therefore dissuaded them from going up to Jerusalem, pretending to consult their ease: "*It is too much for you* to go so far to worship God, *v.* 28. It is a heavy yoke, and it is time to shake it off; *you have gone long enough to Jerusalem*" (so some read it); "the temple, now that you are used to it, does not appear so glorious and sacred as it did at first" (sensible glories wither by degrees in men's estimation); "you have freed yourselves from other burdens, free yourselves from this: why should we now be tied to one place any more than in Samuel's time?"

3. He provided for the assistance of their devotion at home. Upon consultation with some of his politicians, he came to this resolve, to set up two golden calves, as tokens or signs of the divine presence, and persuade the people that they might as well stay at home and offer sacrifice to those as go to Jerusalem to worship before the ark: and some are so charitable as to think they were made to represent the mercy-seat and the cherubim over the ark; but more probably he adopted the idolatry of the Egyptians, in whose land he had sojourned for some time and who worshipped their god Apis under the similitude of a bull or calf. (1.) He would not be at the charge of building a golden temple, as Solomon had done; two golden calves are the most that he can afford. (2.) He intended, no doubt, by these to represent, or rather make present, not any false god, as Moloch or Chemosh, but the true God only, the God of Israel, the God that brought them up out of the land of Egypt, as he declares, *v.* 28. So that it was no violation of the first commandment, but the second. And he chose thus to engage the people's devotion because he knew there were many among them so in love with images that for the sake of the calves they would willingly quit God's temple, where all images were forbidden. (3.) He set up two, by degrees to break people off from the belief of the unity of the godhead, which would pave the way to the polytheism of the Pagans. He set up these two at Dan and Beth-el (one the utmost border of his country northward), the other southward, as if they were the guardians and protectors of the kingdom. Beth-el lay close to Judah. He set up one there, to tempt those of Rehoboam's subjects over to him who were inclined to image-worship, in lieu of those of his subjects that would continue to go to Jerusalem. He set up the other at Dan, for the convenience of those that lay most remote, and because Micah's images had been set up there, and great veneration paid to them for many ages, Judg. xviii. 30, 31. *Beth-el* signifies *the house of God,* which gave some colour to the superstition; but the prophet called it *Beth-aven, the house of vanity,* or iniquity.

4. The people complied with him herein, and were fond enough of the novelty: They *went to worship before the one, even unto Dan* (*v.* 30), to that at Dan first because it was first set up, or *even* to that at Dan, though it lay such a great way off. Those that thought it much to go to Jerusalem, to worship God according to his institution, made no difficulty of going twice as far, to Dan, to worship him according to their own inventions. Or they are said to go to one of the calves at Dan because Abijah, king of Judah, within twenty years, recovered Beth-el (2 Chron. xiii. 19), and it is likely removed the golden calf, or forbade the use of it, and then they had only that at Dan to go to. *This became a sin;*

and a great sin it was, against the express letter of the second commandment. God had sometimes dispensed with the law concerning worshipping in one place, but never allowed the worship of him by images. Hereby they justified their fathers in making the calf at Horeb, though God had so fully shown his displeasure against them for it and threatened to visit for it in the day of visitation (Exod. xxxii. 34), so that it was as great a contempt of God's wrath as it was of his law; and thus they added sin to sin. Bishop Patrick quotes a saying of the Jews, That till Jeroboam's time the Israelites sucked but one calf, but from that time they sucked two.

5. Having set up the gods, he fitted up accommodations for them; and wherein he varied from the divine appointment we are here told, which intimates that in other things he imitated what was done in Judah (*v.* 32) as well as he could. See how one error multiplied into many. (1.) He made a house of high-places, or of altars, one temple at Dan, we may suppose, and another at Beth-el (*v.* 31), and in each many altars, probably complaining of it as an inconvenience that in the temple at Jerusalem there was but one. The multiplying of altars passed with some for a piece of devotion, but God, by the prophet, puts another construction upon it, Hos. viii. 11. *Ephraim has made many altars to sin.* (2.) He made priests of the lowest of the people; and the lowest of the people were good enough to be priests to his calves, and too good. He made priests *from the extremest parts of the people,* that is, some out of every corner of the country, whom he ordered to reside among their neighbours, to instruct them in his appointments and reconcile them to them. Thus were they dispersed as the Levites, but *were not of the sons of Levi.* But the priests of the high-places, or altars, he ordered to reside in Beth-el, as the priests at Jerusalem (*v.* 32), to attend the public service. (3.) The feast of tabernacles, which God had appointed on the fifteenth day of the seventh month, he adjourned to the fifteenth day of the eighth month (*v.* 32), *the month which he devised of his own heart,* to show his power in ecclesiastical matters, *v.* 33. The passover and pentecost he observed in their proper season, or did not observe them at all, or with little solemnity in comparison with this. (4.) He himself assuming a power to make priests, no marvel if he undertook to do the priests' work with his own hands: *He offered upon the altar.* This is twice mentioned (*v.* 32, 33), as also that he burnt incense. This was connived at in him because it was of a piece with the rest of his irregularities; but in king Uzziah it was immediately punished with the plague of leprosy. He did it himself, to make himself look great among the people and to get the reputation of a devout man, also to grace the solemnity of his new festival, with which, it is likely, at this time he joined the feast of the dedication of his altar. And thus, [1.] Jeroboam sinned himself, yet perhaps excused himself to the world and his own conscience with this, that he did not do so ill as Solomon did, who worshipped other gods. [2.] He *made Israel to sin,* drew them off from the worship of God and entailed idolatry upon their seed. And hereby they were punished for deserting the thrones *of the house of David.* The learned Mr. Whiston, in his chronology, for the adjusting of the annals of the two kingdoms of Judah and Israel, supposes that Jeroboam changed the calculation of the year and made it to contain but eleven months, and that by those years the reigns of the kings of Israel are measured till Jehu's revolution and no longer, so that during this interval eleven years of the annals of Judah answer to twelve in those of Israel.

CHAP. XIII.

In the close of the foregoing chapter we left Jeroboam attending his altar at Beth-el, and there we find him in the beginning of this, when he received a testimony from God against his idolatry and apostasy. This was sent to him by a prophet, a man of God that lived in Judah, who is the principal subject of the story of this chapter, where we are told, I. What passed between him and the new king. 1. The prophet threatened Jeroboam's altar (ver. 1, 2), and gave him a sign (ver. 3), which immediately came to pass, ver. 5. 2. The king threatened the prophet, and was himself made another sign, by the withering of his hand (ver. 4), and the restoring of it upon his submission and the prophet's intercession, ver. 6. 3. The prophet refused the kindness offered him thereupon, ver. 7—10. II. What passed between him and the old prophet. 1. The old prophet fetched him back by a lie, and gave him entertainment, ver. 11—19. 2. He, for accepting it, in disobedience to the divine command, is threatened with death, ver. 20—22. And, 3. The threatening is executed, for he is slain by a lion (ver. 23, 24), and buried at Beth-el, ver. 25—32. 4. Jeroboam is hardened in his idolatry, ver. 33, 34. "Thy judgments, Lord, are a great deep."

AND, behold, there came a man of God out of Judah by the word of the LORD unto Beth-el: and Jeroboam stood by the altar to burn incense. 2 And he cried against the altar in the word of the LORD, and said, O altar, altar, thus saith the LORD; Behold, a child shall be born unto the house of David, Josiah by name; and upon thee shall he offer the priests of the high places that burn incense upon thee, and men's bones shall be burnt upon thee. 3 And he gave a sign the same day, saying, This *is* the sign which the LORD hath spoken; Behold, the altar shall be rent, and the ashes that *are* upon it shall be poured out. 4 And it came to pass, when king Jeroboam heard the saying of the man of God, which had cried against the altar in Beth-el, that he put forth his hand from the altar, saying, Lay hold on him. And his hand, which he put forth against him, dried up, so that he could not pull it in again to him. 5 The altar also was rent, and the ashes poured out from the altar, according to the sign which the man of God had given by the word of the LORD. 6 And the king answered and said unto the man of God, Intreat now the face of the LORD thy God, and pray for me, that my hand may be restored me again. And the man of God besought the LORD, and the king's hand was restored him again, and became as *it was* before. 7 And the king said unto the man of God, Come home with me, and refresh thyself, and I will give thee a reward. 8 And the man of God said unto the king, If thou wilt give me half thine house, I will not go in with thee, neither will I eat bread nor drink water in this place: 9 For so was it charged me by the word of the LORD, saying, Eat no bread, nor drink water, nor turn again by the same way that thou camest. 10 So he went another way, and returned not by the way that he came to Beth-el.

Here is, I. A messenger sent to Jeroboam, to signify to him God's displeasure against his idolatry, *v.* 1. The army of Judah that aimed to ruin him was countermanded, and might not draw a sword against him (*ch.* xii. 24); but a prophet of Judah is, instead thereof, sent to reclaim him from his evil way, and is sent in time, while he is but dedicating his altar, before his heart is hardened by the deceitfulness of his sin; for God delights not in the death of sinners, but would rather they would turn and live. How bold was the messenger that durst attack the king in his pride and interrupt the solemnity he was proud of! Those that go on God's errand must not fear the face of man; they know who will bear them out. How kind was he that sent him to warn Jeroboam of the wrath of God *revealed from heaven* against his *ungodliness* and *unrighteousness!*

II. The message delivered in God's name, not whispered, but cried with a loud voice, denoting both the prophet's courage, that he was neither afraid nor ashamed to own it, and his earnestness, that he desired to be heard and heeded by all that were present, who were not a few, on this great occasion. It was directed, not to Jeroboam nor to the people, but to the altar, the stones of which would sooner hear and yield than those who were mad upon their idols and deaf to divine calls. Yet, in threatening the altar, God threatened the founder and worshippers, to whom it was as dear as their own souls, and who might conclude, "If God's wrath fasten upon the lifeless guiltless altar, how shall we escape?" That which was foretold concerning the altar (*v.* 2) was that, in process of time, a prince of the house of David, Josiah by name, should pollute this altar by sacrificing the idolatrous priests themselves upon it, and burning the bones of dead men. Let Jeroboam know and be sure, 1. That the altar he now consecrated should be desecrated. Idolatrous worship will not continue, but the word of the Lord will endure for ever. 2. That the *priests of the high places* he now made should themselves be made sacrifices to the justice of God, and the first and only sacrifices upon this altar that would be pleasing to him. If the offering be such as is an abomination to God, it will follow, of course, that the offerers must themselves fall under his wrath, which will abide upon them, since it is not otherwise transmitted. 3. That this should be done by a branch *of the house of David.* That family which he and his kingdom had despised and treacherously deserted should recover so much power as to demolish that altar which he thought to establish; so that right and truth should at length prevail, both in civil and sacred matters, notwithstanding the present triumphs of those that were given to change the fear both *of God and the king.* It was about 356 years ere this prediction was fulfilled, yet it was spoken of as sure and nigh at hand, for a thousand years with God are but as one day. Nothing more contingent and arbitrary than the giving of names to persons, yet Josiah was here named above 300 years before he was born. Nothing future is hidden from God. There are *names in the book* of the divine prescience (Phil. iv. 3), names *written in heaven.*

III. A sign is given for the confirming of the truth of this prediction, that the altar should be shaken to pieces by an invisible power and the ashes of the sacrifice scattered (*v.* 3), which came to pass immediately, *v.* 5. This was, 1. A proof that the prophet was sent of God, *who confirmed the word with this sign following,* Mark xvi. 20. 2. A present indication of God's displeasure against these idolatrous sacrifices. How could the gift be acceptable when the altar that should sanctify it was an abomination? 3. It was a reproach to the people, whose hearts were harder than these stones and rent not under the word of the Lord. 4. It was a specimen of what should be done to it in the accomplishment of this prophecy by Josiah; it was now rent, in token of its being then ruined.

IV. Jeroboam's hand withered, which he stretched out to seize or smite the man of God, *v.* 4. Instead of trembling at the message, as he might well have done, he assaulted him that brought it, in defiance of the wrath of which he was warned and contempt of that grace which sent him the warning. *Rebuke a sinner* and *he will hate thee,* and do thee a mischief if he can; yet God's prophets must rather expose themselves than betray their trust: he that employs them will protect them, and restrain the wrath of man, as he did Jeroboam's here by withering his hand, so that he could neither hurt the prophet nor draw it in to help himself. When his hand was stretched out to burn incense to his calves it was not withered; but, when it is stretched out against a prophet, he shall have no use of it till he humble himself. Of all the wickedness of the wicked there is none more provoking to God than their malicious attempts against his prophets, of whom he has said, *Touch them not, do them no harm.* As this was a punishment of Jeroboam, and answering to the sin, so it was the deliverance of the prophet. God has many ways of disabling the enemies of his church from executing their mischievous purposes. Jeroboam's inability to pull in his hand made him a spectacle to all about him, that they might see and fear. If God, in justice, harden the hearts of sinners, so that the hand they have stretched out in sin they cannot pull in again by repentance, that is a spiritual judgment, represented by this, and much more dreadful.

V. The sudden healing of the hand that was suddenly dried up, upon his submission, *v.* 6. That word of God which should have touched his conscience humbled him not, but this which *touched his bone and his flesh* brings down his proud spirit. He looks for help now, 1. Not from his calves, but from God only, from his power and his favour. He wounded, and no hand but his can make whole. 2. Not by his own sacrifice or incense, but by the prayer and intercession of the prophet, whom he had just now threatened and aimed to destroy. The time may come when those that hate the preaching would be glad of the prayers of faithful ministers. "Pray to the Lord thy God," says Jeroboam; "thou hast an interest in him; improve it for me." But observe, He did not desire the prophet to pray that his sin might be pardoned, and his heart changed, only that *his hand might be restored;* thus Pharaoh would have Moses to pray that God would *take away this death* only (Exod. x. 17), not this *sin.* The prophet, as became a man of God, renders good for evil, upbraids not Jeroboam with his impotent malice, nor triumphs in his submission, but immediately addresses himself to God for him. Those only are entitled to the blessing Christ pronounced on the persecuted that learn of him to pray for their persecutors, Matt. v. 10, 44. When the prophet thus honoured God, by showing himself of a forgiving spirit, God put this further honour upon him, that at his word he recalled the judgment and by another miracle healed the withered hand, that by the goodness of God Jeroboam might be led to repentance, and, if he were not broken by the judgment, yet might be melted by the mercy. With both he seemed affected for the present, but the impressions wore off.

VI. The prophet's refusal of Jeroboam's kind invitation, in which observe, 1. That God forbade his messenger to eat or drink in Beth-el (*v.* 9), to show his detestation of their execrable idolatry and apostasy from God, and to teach us not to have fellowship with the works of darkness, lest we have infection from them or give encouragement to them. He must not *turn back the same way,* but deliver his message, as it were, *in transitu—as he passes along.* He shall not seem to be sent on purpose (they were unworthy such a favour), but as if he only called by the way, his spirit being stirred, like Paul's at Athens, as he *passed and saw their devotions.* God would, by this command, try his prophet, as he did Ezekiel, whether he would not be *rebellious, like that rebellious house,* Ezek. ii. 8. 2. That Jeroboam was so affected with the cure of his hand that though we read not of his thanksgivings to God for the mercy, or of his sending an offering to the altar at Jerusalem in acknowledgment of it, yet he was willing to express his gratitude to the prophet and pay him for his prayers, *v.* 7. Favours to the body will make even graceless men seem grateful to good ministers. 3. That the prophet, though hungry and weary, and perhaps poor, in obedience to the divine command refused both the entertainment and the reward proffered him. He might have supposed his acceptance of it would give him an opportunity of discoursing further with the king, in order to his effectual reformation, now that he was convinced; yet he will not think himself wiser than God, but, like a faithful careful messenger, hastens home when he has done his errand. Those have little learned the lessons of self-denial that cannot forbear one forbidden meal.

11 Now there dwelt an old prophet in Beth-el; and his sons came and told him all the works that the man of God had done that day in Beth-el: the words which he had spoken unto the king, them they told also to their father. 12 And their father said unto them, What way went he? For his sons had seen what way the man of God went, which came from Judah. 13 And he said unto his sons, Saddle me the ass. So they saddled him the ass: and he rode thereon, 14 And went after the man of God, and found him sitting under an oak: and he said unto him, *Art* thou the man of God that camest from Judah? And he said, I *am.* 15 Then he said unto him, Come home with me, and eat bread.

16 And he said, I may not return with thee, nor go in with thee: neither will I eat bread nor drink water with thee in this place: 17 For it was said to me by the word of the LORD, Thou shalt eat no bread nor drink water there, nor turn again to go by the way that thou camest. 18 He said unto him, I *am* a prophet also as thou *art;* and an angel spake unto me by the word of the LORD, saying, Bring him back with thee into thine house, that he may eat bread and drink water. *But* he lied unto him. 19 So he went back with him, and did eat bread in his house, and drank water. 20 And it came to pass, as they sat at the table, that the word of the LORD came unto the prophet that brought him back: 21 And he cried unto the man of God that came from Judah, saying, Thus saith the LORD, Forasmuch as thou hast disobeyed the mouth of the LORD, and hast not kept the commandment which the LORD thy God commanded thee, 22 But camest back, and hast eaten bread and drank water in the place of the which *the LORD* did say to thee, Eat no bread, and drink no water; thy carcase shall not come unto the sepulchre of thy fathers.

The man of God had honestly and resolutely refused the king's invitation, though he promised him a reward; yet he was over-persuaded by an old prophet to come back with him, and dine in Beth-el, contrary to the command given him. Here we find how dearly his dinner cost him. Observe with wonder,

I. The old prophet's wickedness. I cannot but call him a false prophet and a bad man, it being much easier to believe that from one of such a bad character should be extorted a confirmation of what the man of God said (as we find, *v.* 32) than that a true prophet, and a good man, should tell such a deliberate lie as he did, and father it upon God. *A good tree could never bring forth such corrupt fruit.* Perhaps he was trained up among the sons of the prophets, in one of Samuel's colleges not far off, whence he retained the name of a prophet, but, growing worldly and profane, the spirit of prophecy had departed from him. If he had been a good prophet he would have reproved Jeroboam's idolatry, and not have suffered his sons to attend his altars, as, it should seem, they did. Now, 1. Whether he had any good design in fetching back the man of God is not certain. One may hope that he did it in compassion to him, concluding he wanted refreshment, and out of a desire to be better acquainted with him and more fully to understand his errand than he could from the report of his sons; yet his sons having told him all that passed, and particularly that the prophet was forbidden to eat or drink there, which he had openly told Jeroboam, I suppose it was done with a bad design, to draw him into a snare, and so to expose him; for false prophets have ever been the worst enemies to the true prophets, usually aiming to destroy them, but sometimes, as here, to debauch them and draw them from their duty. Thus they *gave the Nazarites wine to drink* (Amos ii. 12), that they might glory in their fall. But, 2. It is certain that he took a very bad method to bring him back. When the man of God had told him, "I may not, and therefore I will not, return to eat bread with thee" (his resolutions concurring with the divine command, *v.* 16, 17), he wickedly pretended that he had an order from heaven to fetch him back. He imposed upon him by asserting his quondam character as a prophet: *I am a prophet also as thou art;* he pretended he had a vision of an angel that sent him on this errand. But it was all a lie; it was a banter upon prophecy, and profane in the highest degree. When this old prophet is spoken of (2 Kings xxiii. 18) he is called *the prophet that came out of Samaria,* whereas there was no such place as Samaria till long after, *ch.* xvi. 24. Therefore I take it he is so called there, though he was of Beth-el, because he was like those who were afterwards *the prophets of Samaria,* who *caused God's people Israel to err,* Jer. xxiii. 13.

II. The good prophet's weakness, in suffering himself to be thus imposed upon: *He went back with him, v.* 19. He that had resolution enough to refuse the invitation of the king, who promised him a reward, could not resist the insinuations of one that pretended to be a prophet. Good people are more in danger of being drawn from their duty by the plausible pretences of divinity and sanctity than by external inducements; we have therefore need to *beware of false prophets,* and not *believe every spirit.*

III. The proceedings of divine justice hereupon; and here we may well wonder that the wicked prophet, who told the lie and did the mischief, went unpunished, while the holy man of God, that was drawn by him into sin, was suddenly and severely punished for it. What shall we make of this! The judgments of God are unfathomable. *The deceived and the deceiver are his,* and he *giveth not account of any of his matters.* Certainly there must be a judgment to come, when these things will be called over again, and when those that sinned most and suffered least, in this world, will receive according to their works. 1. The message delivered to the man of God was strange. His crime is recited, *v.* 21, 22. It was, in one word, disobedience to an express command. Judgment is given upon it: *Thy carcase shall not come to the sepulchre of thy fathers,* that is, "Thou shalt never reach thy own house, but shalt be a carcase quickly, nor shall thy dead body be brought to *the place of thy fathers' sepulchres,* to be interred." 2. Yet it was more strange that the old prophet himself should be the messenger. Of this we can give no account but that God would have it so, as he spoke to Balaam by his ass and read Saul his doom by the devil in Samuel's likeness. We may think God designed hereby, (1.) To startle the lying prophet, and make him sensible of his sin. The message could not but affect him the more when he himself had the delivering of it, and had so strong an impression made upon his spirit by it that he cried out, as one in an agony, *v.* 21. He had reason to think, if he must die for his disobedience in a small matter who sinned by surprise, of how much sorer punishment he should be thought worthy who had belied an angel of God and cheated a man of God by a deliberate forgery. *If this were done to the green tree, what shall be done to the dry?* Perhaps it had a good effect upon him. Those who preach God's wrath to others have hard hearts indeed if they fear it not themselves. (2.) To put the greater mortification upon the prophet that was deceived, and to show what those must expect who hearken to the great deceiver. Those that yield to him as a tempter will be terrified by him as a tormentor; whom he now fawns upon he will afterwards fly upon, and whom he now draws into sin he will do what he can to drive to despair.

23 And it came to pass, after he had eaten bread, and after he had drunk, that he saddled for him the ass, *to wit,* for the prophet whom he had brought back. 24 And when he was gone, a lion met him by the way, and slew him: and his carcase was cast in the way, and the ass stood by it, the lion also stood by the carcase. 25 And, behold, men passed by, and saw the carcase cast in the way, and the lion standing by the carcase: and they came and told *it* in the city where the old prophet dwelt. 26 And when the prophet that brought him back from the way heard *thereof,* he said, It *is* the man of God, who was disobedient unto the word of the LORD: therefore the LORD hath delivered him unto the lion, which hath torn him, and slain him, according to the word of the LORD, which he spake unto him. 27 And he spake to his sons, saying, Saddle me the ass. And they saddled *him.* 28 And he went and found his carcase cast in the way, and the ass and the lion standing by the carcase: the lion had not eaten the carcase, nor torn the ass. 29 And the prophet took up the carcase of the man of God, and laid it upon the ass, and brought it back: and the old prophet came to the city, to mourn and to bury him. 30 And he laid his carcase in his own grave; and they mourned over him, *saying,* Alas, my brother! 31 And it came to pass, after he had buried him, that he spake to his sons, saying, When I am dead, then bury me in the sepulchre wherein the man of God *is* buried; lay my bones beside his bones: 32 For the saying which he cried by the word of the LORD against the altar in Beth-el, and against all the houses of the high places which *are* in the cities of Samaria, shall surely come to pass. 33 After this thing Jeroboam returned not from his evil way, but made again of the lowest of the people priests of the high places: whosoever would, he consecrated him, and he became *one* of the priests of the high places. 34 And this thing became sin unto the house of Jeroboam, even to cut *it* off, and to destroy *it* from off the face of the earth.

Here is, I. The death of the deceived disobedient prophet. The old prophet that had deluded him, as if he would make him some amends for the wrong he had done him or help to prevent the mischief threatened him, furnished him with an ass to ride home on; but by the way a lion set upon him, and killed him, *v.* 23, 24. He did but return back to refresh himself when he was hungry, and behold he must die for it; see 1 Sam. xiv. 43. But we must consider, 1. That his offence was great, and it would by no means justify him that he was drawn into it by a lie; he could not be so certain of the countermand sent by another as he was of the command given to himself, nor had he any ground to think that the command would be recalled, when the reason of it remained in force, which was that he might testify his detestation of the wickedness of that place. He had great reason to suspect the honesty of this old prophet, who did not himself bear his testimony, nor did God think fit to make use of him as a witness against the idolatry of the city he lived in. However, he should have taken time to beg direction from God, and not have complied so soon. Did he think this old prophet's house safer to eat in than other houses at Beth-el, when God had forbidden him to eat in any? That was to refine upon the command, and make himself wiser than God. Did he think to excuse himself that he was hungry? Had he never read that *man lives not by bread alone?* 2. That his death was for the glory of God; for by this it appeared, (1.) That nothing is more provoking to him than disobedience to an express command, though in a small matter, which makes his proceedings against our first parents, for eating the forbidden fruit, the easier to be accounted for. (2.) That God is displeased at the sins of his own people, and no man shall be protected in disobedience by the sanctity of his profession, the dignity of his office, his nearness to God, or any good services he has done for him. Perhaps God by this intended, in a way of righteous judgment, to harden Jeroboam's heart, since he was not reformed by the withering of his hand; for he would be apt to make a bad use of it, and to say that the prophet was well enough served for meddling with his altar, he had better have staid at home; nay, he would say that Providence had punished him for his insolence, and the lion had done that which his withered hand might not do. However, by this God intended to warn all those whom he employs strictly to observe their orders, at their peril.

II. The wonderful preservation of his dead body, which was a token of God's mercy remembered in the midst of wrath. The lion that gently strangled him, or tore him, did not devour his dead body, nor so much as tear the ass, *v.* 24, 25, 28. Nay, what was more, he did not set upon the travellers that passed by and saw it, nor upon the old prophet (who had reason enough to fear it) when he came to take up the corpse. His commission was to kill the prophet; hitherto he should go, but no further. Thus God showed that, though he was angry with him, his anger was turned away, and the punishment went *no further than death.*

III. The care which the old prophet took of his burial. When he heard of this unusual accident, he concluded it was *the man of God, who was disobedient* to his Master (and whose fault was that?), *therefore the Lord has delivered him to the lion, v.* 26. It would well have become him to ask why the lion was not sent against him and his house, rather than against the good man whom he had cheated. He *took up the corpse, v.* 29. If there be any truth in the vulgar opinion, surely the corpse bled afresh when he touched it, for he was in effect the murderer, and it was but a poor reparation for the injury to inter the dead body. Perhaps when he cheated him into his ruin he intended to laugh at him; yet now his conscience so far relents that he weeps over him, and, like Joab at Abner's funeral, is compelled to be a mourner for him whom he had been the death of. They said, *Alas! my brother, v.* 30. The case was indeed very lamentable that so good a man, a prophet so faithful, and so bold in God's cause, should, for one offence, die as a criminal, while an old lying prophet lives at ease and an idolatrous prince in pomp and power. *Thy way, O God! is in the sea, and thy path in the great waters.* We cannot judge of men by their sufferings, nor of sins by their present punishments; with some the flesh is destroyed that the spirit may be saved, while with others the flesh is pampered that the soul may ripen for hell.

IV. The charge which the old prophet gave his sons concerning his own burial, that they should be sure to bury him in the same grave where the man of God was buried (*v.* 3): "*Lay my bones beside his bones,* close by them, as near as may be, so that my dust may mingle with his." Though he was a lying prophet, yet he desired to *die the death of a* true prophet. "Gather not my soul with the sinners of Beth-el, but with the man of God." The reason he gives is because *what he cried against the altar of Beth-el,* that men's bones should be burnt upon it, *shall surely come to pass, v.* 32. Thus, 1. He ratifies the prediction, that *out of the mouth of two witnesses* (and one of them such a one as St. Paul quotes, Titus i. 12, *one of themselves, even a prophet of their own)* the *word might be established,* if possible to convince and reclaim Jeroboam. 2. He does honour to the deceased prophet, as one whose *word* would not fall to the ground, though *he* did. Ministers die, die prematurely it may be; but the word of the Lord endures for ever, and does not die with them. 3. He consults his own interest. It was foretold that men's bones should be burnt upon Jeroboam's altar: "Lay mine (says he) close to his, and then they will not be disturbed;" and it was, accordingly, their security, as we find, 2 Kings xxiii. 18. Sleeping and waking, living and dying, it is safe being in good company. No mention is made here of the inscription on the prophet's tomb; but it is spoken of 2 Kings xxiii. 17, where Josiah asks, *What title is that?* and is told, *It is the sepulchre of the man of God that came from Judah, who proclaimed these things which thou hast done;* so that the epitaph upon the prophet's grave preserved the remembrance of his prophecy, and was a standing testimony against the idolatries of Beth-el, which it would not have been so remarkably if he had died and been buried elsewhere. The cities of Israel are here called *cities of Samaria,* though that name was not yet known; for, however the old prophet spoke, the inspired historian wrote in the language of his own time.

V. The obstinacy of Jeroboam in his idolatry (*v.* 33): *He returned not from his evil way;* some hand was found that durst repair the altar God had rent, and then Jeroboam offered sacrifice on it again, and the more boldly because the prophet who disturbed him before was in his grave (Rev. xi. 10) and because the prophecy was for a great while to come. Various methods had been used to reclaim him, but neither threats nor signs, neither judgments nor mercies, wrought upon him, so strangely was he wedded to his calves. He did not reform, no, not his priesthood, but whoever would, he filled his hand, and made him priest, though ever so illiterate or immoral, and of what tribe soever; *and this became sin,* that is, a snare first, and then a ruin, to Jeroboam's house, to *cut it off, v.* 34. Note, The diminution, disquiet, and desolation of families, are the fruit of sin; he promised himself that the calves would secure the crown to his family, but it proved they lost it, and sunk his family. Those betray themselves that think by any sin to support themselves.

CHAP. XIV.

The kingdom being divided into that of Judah and that of Israel, we must henceforward, in these books of Kings, expect and attend their separate history, the succession of their kings, and the affairs of their kingdoms, accounted for distinctly. In this chapter we have, I. The prophecy of the destruction of Jeroboam's house, ver. 7—16. The sickness of his child was the occasion of it (ver. 1—6), and the death of his child the earnest of it (ver. 17, 18), together with the conclusion of his reign, ver. 19, 20. II. The history of the declension and diminution of Rehoboam's house and kingdom (ver. 21—28) and the conclusion of his reign, ver. 29—31. In both we may read the mischievous consequences of sin and the calamities it brings on kingdoms and families.

AT that time Abijah the son of Jeroboam fell sick. 2 And Jeroboam said to his wife, Arise, I pray thee, and disguise thyself, that thou be not known to be the wife of Jeroboam; and get thee to Shiloh: behold, there *is* Ahijah the prophet, which told me that *I should be* king over this people. 3 And take with thee ten loaves, and cracknels, and a cruse of honey, and go to him: he shall tell thee what shall become of the child. 4 And Jeroboam's wife did so, and arose, and went to Shiloh, and came to the house of Ahijah. But Ahijah could not see; for his eyes were set by reason of his age. 5 And the LORD said unto Ahijah, Behold, the wife of Jeroboam cometh to ask a thing of thee for her son; for he *is* sick: thus and thus shalt thou say unto her: for it shall be, when she cometh in, that she shall feign herself *to be* another *woman.* 6 And it was *so,* when Ahijah heard the sound of her feet, as she came in at the door, that he said, Come in, thou wife of Jeroboam: why feignest thou thyself *to be* another? for I *am* sent to thee *with* heavy *tidings.*

How Jeroboam persisted in his contempt of God and religion we read in the close of the foregoing chapter. Here we are told how God proceeded in his controversy with him; for when God judges he will overcome, and sinners shall either bend or break before him.

I. His child fell sick, *v.* 1. It is probable that he was his eldest son, and heir-apparent to the crown; for at his death all the kingdom went into mourning for him, *v.* 13. His dignity as a prince, his age as a young prince, and his interest in heaven as a pious prince, could not exempt him from sickness, dangerous sickness. Let none be secure of the continuance of their health, but improve it, while it continues, for the best purposes. Lord, *behold, he whom thou lovest,* thy favourite, he whom Israel loves, their darling, *is sick. At that time,* when Jeroboam prostituted and profaned the priesthood (*ch.* xiii. 33), his child sickened. When sickness comes into our families we should enquire whether there be not some particular sin harboured in our houses, which the affliction is sent to convince us of and reclaim us from.

II. He sent his wife in disguise to enquire of Ahijah the prophet *what should become of the child, v.* 2, 3. The sickness of his child touched him in a tender part. The withering of this branch of the family would, perhaps, be as sore an affliction to him as the withering of that branch of his body, *ch.* xiii. 4. Such is the force of natural affection; our children are ourselves but once removed. Now,

1. Jeroboam's great desire, under this affliction, is to know *what shall become of the child,* whether he will live or die. (1.) It would have been more prudent if he had desired to know what means they should use for the recovery of the child, what they should give him, and what they should do to him; but by this instance, and those of Ahaziah (2 Kings i. 2) and Benhadad (2 Kings viii. 8), it should seem they had then such a foolish notion of fatality as took them off from all use of means; for, if they were sure the patient would live, they thought means needless; if he would die, they thought them useless; not considering that duty is ours, events are God's, and that he that ordained the end ordained the means. Why should a prophet be desired to show that which a little time will show? (2.) It would have been more pious if he had desired to know wherefore God contended with him, had begged the prophet's prayers, and cast

away his idols from him; then the child might have been restored to him, as his hand was. But most people would rather be told their fortune than their faults or their duty.

2. That he might know the child's doom, he sent to Ahijah the prophet, who lived obscurely and neglected in Shiloh, blind through age, yet still blest with the visions of the Almighty, which need not bodily eyes, but are rather favoured by the want of them, the eyes of the mind being then most intent and least diverted. Jeroboam sent not to him for advice about the setting up of his calves, or the consecrating of his priests, but had recourse to him in his distress, when the gods he served could give him no relief. *Lord, in trouble have those visited thee* who before slighted thee. Some have by sickness been reminded of their forgotten ministers and praying friends. He sent to Ahijah, because he had *told him he should be king*, *v.* 2. "He was once the messenger of good tidings, surely he will be so again." Those that by sin disqualify themselves for comfort, and yet expect their ministers, because they are good men, should speak peace and comfort to them, greatly wrong both themselves and their ministers.

3. He sent his wife to enquire of the prophet, because she could best put the question without naming names, or making any other description than this, "Sir, I have a son ill; will he recover or not?" The heart of her husband safely trusted in her that she would be faithful both in delivering the message and bringing him the answer; and it seems there were none of all his counsellors in whom he could repose such a confidence; otherwise the sick child could very ill spare her, for mothers are the best nurses, and it would have been much fitter for her to have staid at home to tend him than go to Shiloh to enquire what would become of him. If she go, she must go *incognito—in disguise*, must change her dress, cover her face, and go by another name, not only to conceal herself from her own court and the country through which she passed (as if it were below her quality to go upon such an errand, and what she had reason to be ashamed of, as Nicodemus that came to Jesus by night, whereas it is no disparagement to the greatest to attend God's prophets), but also to conceal herself from the prophet himself, that he might only answer her question concerning her son, and not enter upon the unpleasing subject of her husband's defection. Thus some people love to prescribe to their ministers, limit them to smooth things, and care not for having the *whole counsel of God declared* to them, lest it prove to prophesy *no good concerning them, but evil.* But what a strange notion had Jeroboam of God's prophet when he believed that he could and would certainly tell what would *become of the child*, and yet either could not or would not discover who was the mother! Could he see into the thick darkness of futurity, and yet not see through the thin veil of this disguise? Did Jeroboam think the God of Israel like his calves, just what he pleased? *Be not deceived, God is not mocked.*

III. God gave Ahijah notice of the approach of Jeroboam's wife, and that she came in disguise, and full instructions what to say to her (*v.* 5), which enabled him, as she came in at the door, to call her by her name, to her great surprise, and so to discover to all about him who she was (*v.* 6): *Come in, thou wife of Jeroboam, why feignest thou thyself to be another?* He had no regard, 1. To her rank. She was a queen, but what was that to him, who had a message to deliver to her immediately from God, before whom all the children of men stand upon the same level? Nor, 2. To her present. It was usual for those who consulted prophets to bring them tokens of respect, which they accepted, and yet were no hirelings. She brought him a handsome country present (*v.* 3), but he did not think himself obliged by that to give her any finer language than the nature of her message required. Nor, 3. To her industrious concealment of herself. It is a piece of civility not to take notice of those who desire not to be taken notice of; but the prophet was no courtier, nor gave flattering titles; plain dealing is best, and she shall know, at the first word, what she has to trust to: *I am sent to thee with heavy tidings.* Note, Those who think by their disguises to hide themselves from God will be wretchedly confounded when they find themselves disappointed in the day of discovery. Sinners now appear in the garb of saints, and are taken to be such; but how will they blush and tremble when they find themselves stripped of their false colours, and are called by their own name: "Go out, thou treacherous false-hearted hypocrite. *I never knew thee. Why feignest thou thyself to be another?*" Tidings of a portion with hypocrites will be heavy tidings. God will judge men according to what they are, not according to what they seem.

7 Go, tell Jeroboam, Thus saith the LORD God of Israel, Forasmuch as I exalted thee from among the people, and made thee prince over my people Israel, 8 And rent the kingdom away from the house of David, and gave it thee: and *yet* thou hast not been as my servant David, who kept my commandments, and who followed me with all his heart, to do *that* only *which was* right in mine eyes; 9 But hast done evil above all that were before thee: for thou hast gone and made thee other gods, and molten images, to provoke

me to anger, and hast cast me behind thy back: 10 Therefore, behold, I will bring evil upon the house of Jeroboam, and will cut off from Jeroboam him that pisseth against the wall, *and* him that is shut up and left in Israel, and will take away the remnant of the house of Jeroboam, as a man taketh away dung, till it be all gone. 11 Him that dieth of Jeroboam in the city shall the dogs eat; and him that dieth in the field shall the fowls of the air eat: for the LORD hath spoken *it.* 12 Arise thou therefore, get thee to thine own house: *and* when thy feet enter into the city, the child shall die. 13 And all Israel shall mourn for him, and bury him: for he only of Jeroboam shall come to the grave, because in him there is found *some* good thing toward the LORD God of Israel in the house of Jeroboam. 14 Moreover the LORD shall raise him up a king over Israel, who shall cut off the house of Jeroboam that day: but what? even now. 15 For the LORD shall smite Israel, as a reed is shaken in the water, and he shall root up Israel out of this good land, which he gave to their fathers, and shall scatter them beyond the river, because they have made their groves, provoking the LORD to anger. 16 And he shall give Israel up because of the sins of Jeroboam, who did sin, and who made Israel to sin. 17 And Jeroboam's wife arose, and departed, and came to Tirzah: *and* when she came to the threshold of the door, the child died; 18 And they buried him; and all Israel mourned for him, according to the word of the LORD, which he spake by the hand of his servant Ahijah the prophet. 19 And the rest of the acts of Jeroboam, how he warred, and how he reigned, behold, they *are* written in the book of the chronicles of the kings of Israel. 20 And the days which Jeroboam reigned *were* two and twenty years: and he slept with his fathers, and Nadab his son reigned in his stead.

When those that set up idols, and keep them up, go to enquire of the Lord, he determines to answer them, not according to the pretensions of their enquiry, but *according to the multitude of their idols,* Ezek. xiv. 4. So Jeroboam is answered here.

I. The prophet anticipates the enquiry concerning the child, and foretels the ruin of Jeroboam's house for the wickedness of it. No one else durst have carried such a message: a servant would have smothered it, but his own wife cannot be suspected of ill-will to him.

1. God calls himself the *Lord God of Israel.* Though Israel had forsaken God, God had not cast them off, nor given them a bill of divorce for their whoredoms. He is Israel's God, and therefore will take vengeance on him who did them the greatest mischief he could do them, debauched them and drew them away from God.

2. He upbraids Jeroboam with the great favour he had bestowed upon him, in making him king, exalting him from among the people, the common people, to be prince over God's chosen Israel, and taking the kingdom *from the house of David,* to bestow it upon him. Whether we keep an account of God's mercies to us or no, he does, and will set even them in order before us, if we be ungrateful, to our greater confusion; otherwise he gives and upbraids not.

3. He charges him with his impiety and apostasy, and his idolatry particularly: *Thou hast done evil above all that were before thee, v.* 9. Saul, that was rejected, never worshipped idols; Solomon did it but occasionally, in his dotage, and never made Israel to sin. Jeroboam's calves, though pretended to be set up in honour of the God of Israel, that brought *them up out of Egypt,* yet are here called *other gods,* or *strange gods,* because in them he worshipped God as the heathen worshipped their strange gods, because by them he *changed the truth of God into a lie* and represented him as altogether different from what he is, and because many of the ignorant worshippers terminated their devotion in the image, and did not at all regard the God of Israel. Though they were calves of gold, the richness of the metal was so far from making them acceptable to God that they *provoked him to anger,* designedly affronted him, under colour of pleasing him. In doing this, (1.) He had not set David before him (*v.* 8): *Thou hast not been as my servant David,* who, though he had his faults and some bad ones, yet never forsook the worship of God nor grew loose nor cold to that; his faithful adherence to that gained him this honourable character, that he *followed God with all his heart,* and herein he was proposed for an example to all his successors. Those did not do well that did not do like David. (2.) He had not *set God before him,* but (*v.* 9), "*Thou hast cast me behind thy back,* my law, my fear; thou hast neglected me, forgotten me, and preferred thy policies before my precepts."

4. He foretels the utter ruin of Jeroboam's house, *v.* 10, 11. He thought, by his idolatry, to establish his government, and by that he not only lost it, but brought destruction upon his family, the universal destruction of all the males, whether shut up or left, married or unmarried. (1.) Shameful destruction. They shall be taken away as dung, which is loathsome and which men are glad to be rid of. He worshipped dunghill-deities, and God removed his family as a great dunghill. Noble and royal families, if wicked, are no better in God's account. (2.) Unusual destruction. Their very dead bodies should be meat for the dogs in the street, or the birds of prey in the field, *v.* 11. Thus evil pursues sinners. See this fulfilled, *ch.* xv. 29.

5. He foretels the immediate death of the sick child, *v.* 12, 13.

(1.) In mercy to him, lest, if he live, he be infected with the sin, and so involved in the ruin, of his father's house. Observe the character given of him: *In him was found some good thing towards the Lord God of Israel, in the house of Jeroboam.* He had an affection for the true worship of God and disliked the worship of the calves. Note, [1.] Those are good *in whom are good things towards the Lord God of Israel,* good inclinations, good intentions, good desires, towards him. [2.] Where there is but *some* good thing of that kind it will be found: God, who seeks it, sees it be it ever so little and is pleased with it. [3.] A little grace goes a great way with great people. It is so rare to find princes well affected to religion that, when they are so, they are worthy of double honour. [4.] Pious dispositions are in a peculiar manner amiable and acceptable when they are found in those that are young. The divine image in miniature has a peculiar beauty and lustre in it. [5.] Those that are good in bad times and places shine very brightly in the eyes of God. A good child *in the house of Jeroboam* is a miracle of divine grace: to be there untainted is like being in the fiery furnace unhurt, unsinged. Observe the care taken of him: he only, of all Jeroboam's family, shall die in honour, shall be buried, and shall be lamented as one that lived desired. Note, Those that are distinguished by divine grace shall be distinguished by divine providence. This hopeful child dies first of all the family, for God often *takes those soonest whom he loves best.* Heaven is the fittest place for them; this earth is not worthy of them.

(2.) In wrath to the family. [1.] It was a sign the family would be ruined when *he* was taken by whom it might have been reformed. The righteous are removed from the evil to come in this world, to the good to come in a better world. It is a bad omen to a family when the best in it are buried out of it; when what was valuable is picked out the rest is for the fire. [2.] It was likewise a present affliction to the family and kingdom, by which both ought to have been bettered; and this aggravated the affliction to the poor mother that she should not reach home time enough to see her son alive: *When thy feet enter into the city,* just then *the child shall die.* This was to be a sign to her of the accomplishment of the rest of the threatenings, as 1 Sam. ii. 34.

6. He foretels the setting up of another family to rule over Israel, *v.* 14. This was fulfilled in Baasha of Issachar, who conspired against Nadab the son of Jeroboam, in the second year of his reign, murdered him and all his family. *"But what? Even now.* Why do I speak of it as a thing at a distance? It is at the door. It shall be done *even now."* Sometimes God makes quick work with sinners; he did so with the house of Jeroboam. It was not twenty-four years from his first elevation to the final extirpation of his family.

7. He foretels the judgments which should come upon the people of Israel for conforming to the worship which Jeroboam had established. *If the blind lead the blind,* both the blind leaders and the blind followers shall *fall into the ditch.* It is here foretold, *v.* 15, (1.) That they should never be easy, nor rightly settled in their land, but continually *shaken like a reed in the water.* After they left the house of David, the government never continued long in one family, but one undermined and destroyed another, which must needs occasion great disorders and disturbances among the people. (2.) That they should, ere long, be totally expelled out of their land, that good land, and given up to ruin, *v.* 16. This was fulfilled in the captivity of the ten tribes by the king of Assyria. Families and kingdoms are ruined by sin, ruined by the wickedness of the heads of them. *Jeroboam did sin, and made Israel to sin.* If great men do wickedly, they involve many others both in the guilt and in the snare; multitudes *follow their pernicious ways.* They go to hell with a long train, and their condemnation will be the more intolerable, for they must answer, not only for their own sins, but for the sins which others have been drawn into and kept in by their influence.

II. Jeroboam's wife has nothing to say against the word of the Lord, but she goes home with a heavy heart to their house in *Tirzah,* a *sweet delightful place,* so the name signifies, famed for its beauty, Cant. vi. 4. But death, which will stain its beauty and embitter all its delights, cannot be shut out from it. Hither she came, and here we leave her attending the funeral of her son, and expecting the fate of her family. 1. *The child died* (*v.* 17), and justly did all Israel mourn, not only for the loss of so hopeful a prince, whom they were not worthy of, but because his death plucked up the flood-gates, and made a breach, at which an inundation of judgments broke in. 2. Jeroboam himself died soon after, *v.* 20. It is said (2 Chron.

xiii. 20), *The Lord struck him* with some sore disease, so that he died miserably, when he had reigned twenty-two years, and left his crown to a son who lost it, and his life too, and all the lives of his family, within two years after. For a further account of him the reader is referred to the annals of his reign, drawn up by his own secretaries, or to the public records, like those in the Tower, called here, *The Book*, or register, *of the Chronicles of the Kings of Israel*, to which recourse might then be had; but, not being divinely inspired, these records are long since lost.

21 And Rehoboam the son of Solomon reigned in Judah. Rehoboam *was* forty and one years old when he began to reign, and he reigned seventeen years in Jerusalem, the city which the LORD did choose out of all the tribes of Israel, to put his name there. And his mother's name *was* Naamah an Ammonitess. 22 And Judah did evil in the sight of the LORD, and they provoked him to jealousy with their sins which they had committed, above all that their fathers had done. 23 For they also built them high places, and images, and groves, on every high hill, and under every green tree. 24 And there were also sodomites in the land: *and* they did according to all the abominations of the nations which the LORD cast out before the children of Israel. 25 And it came to pass in the fifth year of king Rehoboam, *that* Shishak king of Egypt came up against Jerusalem: 26 And he took away the treasures of the house of the LORD, and the treasures of the king's house; he even took away all: and he took away all the shields of gold which Solomon had made. 27 And king Rehoboam made in their stead brasen shields, and committed *them* unto the hands of the chief of the guard, which kept the door of the king's house. 28 And it was *so*, when the king went into the house of the LORD, that the guard bare them, and brought them back into the guard chamber. 29 Now the rest of the acts of Rehoboam, and all that he did, *are* they not written in the book of the chronicles of the kings of Judah? 30 And there was war between Rehoboam and Jeroboam all *their* days. 31 And Rehoboam slept with his fathers, and was buried with his fathers in the city of David. And his mother's name *was* Naamah an Ammonitess. And Abijam his son reigned in his stead.

Judah's story and Israel's are intermixed in this book. Jeroboam out-lived Rehoboam, four or five years, yet his history is despatched first, that the account of Rehoboam's reign may be laid together; and a sad account it is.

I. Here is no good said of the king. All the account we have of him here is, 1. That he was forty-one years old when he began to reign, by which reckoning he was born in the last year of David, and had his education, and the forming of his mind, in the best days of Solomon; yet he lived not up to these advantages. Solomon's defection at last did more to corrupt him than his wisdom and devotion had done to give him good principles. 2. That he reigned seventeen years in Jerusalem, *the city where God put his name*, where he had opportunity enough to know his duty, if he had but had a heart to do it. 3. That his mother was Naamah, an Ammonitess; this is twice mentioned, *v.* 21, 31. It was strange that David would marry his son Solomon to an Ammonitess (for it was done while he lived), but it is probable that Solomon was in love with her, because she was *Naamah*, a *beauty* (so it signifies), and his father was loth to cross him, but it proved to have a very bad influence upon posterity. Probably she was daughter to Shobi the Ammonite, who was kind to David (2 Sam. xvii. 27), and David was too willing to requite him by matching his son into his family. None can imagine how lasting and how fatal the consequences may be of being unequally yoked with unbelievers. 4. That he had continual war with Jeroboam (*v.* 30), which could not but be a perpetual uneasiness to him. 5. That when he had reigned but seventeen years he died, and left his throne to his son. His father, and grandfather, and grandson, that reigned well, reigned long, forty years apiece. But sin often shortens men's lives and comforts.

II. Here is much evil said of the subjects, both as to their character and their condition.

1. See here how wicked and profane they were. It is a most sad account that is here given of their apostasy from God, *v.* 22—24. Judah, the only professing people God had in the world, *did evil in his sight*, in contempt and defiance of him and the tokens of his special presence with them; *they provoked him to jealousy*, as the adulterous wife provokes her husband by breaking the marriage-covenant. Their fathers had been bad enough, especially in the times of the judges, but they

did abominable things, *above all that their fathers had done.* The magnificence of their temple, the pomp of their priesthood, and all the secular advantages with which their religion was attended, could not prevail to keep them to it. Nothing less than the *pouring out of the Spirit from on high* will keep God's Israel in their allegiance to him. The account here given of the wickedness of the Jews agrees with that which the apostle gives of the wickedness of the Gentile world (Rom. i. 21, 24), so that both *Jew and Gentile are* alike *under sin,* Rom. iii. 9. (1.) They became *vain in their imaginations* concerning God, and *changed his glory into an image,* for they built themselves *high places, images, and groves* (*v.* 23), profaning God's name by affixing to it their images, and God's ordinances by serving their idols with them. They foolishly fancied that they exalted God when they worshipped him on high hills and pleased him when they worshipped him under the pleasant shadow of green trees. (2.) They were given up to vile affections (as those idolaters Rom. i. 26, 27), for there were *sodomites in the land* (*v.* 24), *men with men working that which is unseemly,* and not to be thought of, much less mentioned, without abhorrence and indignation. They dishonoured God by one sin and then God left them to dishonour themselves by another. They profaned the privileges of a holy nation, therefore God gave them up to their own hearts' lusts, to imitate the abominations of the accursed Canaanites; and herein the Lord was righteous. And, when they did *like those that were cast out,* how could they expect any other than to be cast out like them?

2. See here how weak and poor they were; and this was the consequence of the former. Sin exposes, impoverishes, and weakens any people. Shishak, king of Egypt, came against them, and so far, either by force or surrender, made himself master of Jerusalem itself that he took away the treasures both of the temple and of the exchequer, of the house of the Lord and of the king's house, which David and Solomon had amassed, *v.* 25, 26. These, it is likely, tempted him to make his descent; and, to save the rest, Rehoboam perhaps tamely surrendered them, as Ahab, *ch.* xx. 4. He also took away the golden shields that were made but in his father's time, *v.* 26. These the king of Egypt carried off as trophies of his victory; and, instead of them, Rehoboam made brazen shields, which the life-guard carried before him when he went to church in state, *v.* 27, 28. This was an emblem of the diminution of his glory. Sin makes the gold become dim, changes the most fine gold, and turns it into brass. We commend Rehoboam for going to *the house of the Lord,* perhaps the oftener for the rebuke he had been under, and do not condemn him for going in pomp. Great men should honour God with their honour, and then they are themselves most honoured by it.

CHAP. XV.

In this chapter we have an abstract of the history, I. Of two of the kings of Judah, Abijam, the days of whose reign were few and evil (ver. 1—8), and Asa, who reigned well and long, ver. 9—24. II. Of two of the kings of Israel, Nadab the son of Jeroboam, and Baasha the destroyer of Jeroboam's house, ver. 25—34.

NOW in the eighteenth year of king Jeroboam the son of Nebat reigned Abijam over Judah. 2 Three years reigned he in Jerusalem. And his mother's name *was* Maachah, the daughter of Abishalom. 3 And he walked in all the sins of his father, which he had done before him: and his heart was not perfect with the LORD his God, as the heart of David his father. 4 Nevertheless for David's sake did the LORD his God give him a lamp in Jerusalem, to set up his son after him, and to establish Jerusalem: 5 Because David did *that which was* right in the eyes of the LORD, and turned not aside from any *thing* that he commanded him all the days of his life, save only in the matter of Uriah the Hittite. 6 And there was war between Rehoboam and Jeroboam all the days of his life. 7 Now the rest of the acts of Abijam, and all that he did, *are* they not written in the book of the chronicles of the kings of Judah? And there was war between Abijam and Jeroboam. 8 And Abijam slept with his fathers; and they buried him in the city of David: and Asa his son reigned in his stead.

We have here a short account of the short reign of Abijam the son of Rehoboam king of Judah. He makes a better figure, 2 Chron. xiii., where we have an account of his war with Jeroboam, the speech which he made before the armies engaged, and the wonderful victory he obtained by the help of God. There he is called *Abijah—My father is the Lord,* because no wickedness is there laid to his charge. But here, where we are told of his faults, *Jah,* the name of God, is, in disgrace to him, taken away from his name, and he is called *Abijam.* See Jer. xxii. 24.

I. Few particulars are related concerning him. 1. Here began his reign in the beginning of Jeroboam's eighteenth year; for Rehoboam reigned but seventeen, *ch.* xiv. 21. Jeroboam indeed survived Rehoboam, but Rehoboam's Abijah lived to succeed him and to be a terror to Jeroboam, while Jeroboam's Abijah (whom we read of *ch.* xiv. 1) died before him. 2. He reigned scarcely three years, for he died before the end of Jeroboam's twentieth year, *v.* 9. Being made proud and secure by his great victory over Jeroboam (2 Chron. xiii. 21), God cut him off, to make way for his son Asa, who would be a better man. 3. *His mother's name was Maachah, the daughter of Abishalom,* that is, Absalom, David's son, as I am the rather inclined to think because two other of Rehoboam's wives were his near relations (2 Chron. xi. 18), one the daughter of Jerimoth, David's son, and another the daughter of Eliab, David's brother. He took warning by his father not to marry strangers; yet thought it below him to marry his subjects, except they were of the royal family. 4. He carried on his father's wars with Jeroboam. As there was continual war between Rehoboam and Jeroboam, not set battles (these were forbidden, *ch.* xii. 24), but frequent encounters, especially upon the borders, one making incursions and reprisals on the other, so there was between Abijam and Jeroboam (*v.* 7), till Jeroboam, with a great army, invaded him, and then Abijam, not being forbidden to act in his own defence, routed him, and weakened him, so that he compelled him to be quiet during the rest of his reign, 2 Chron. xiii. 20.

II. But, in general, we are told, 1. That he was not like David, had no hearty affection for the ordinances of God, though, to serve his purpose against Jeroboam, he pleaded his possession of the temple and priesthood, as that upon which he valued himself, 2 Chron. xiii. 10—12. Many boast of their profession of godliness who are strangers to the power of it, and plead the truth of their religion who yet are not true to it. *His heart was not perfect with the Lord his God.* He seemed to have zeal, but he wanted sincerity; he began pretty well, but he fell off, and *walked in all the sins of his father,* followed his bad example, though he had seen the bad consequences of it. He that was all his days in war ought to have been so wise as to make and keep his peace with God, and not to make him his enemy, especially having found him so good a friend in his war with Jeroboam, 2 Chron. xiii. 18. *Let favour be shown to the wicked, yet will he not learn righteousness,* Isa. xxvi. 10. 2. That yet it was for David's sake that he was advanced, and continued upon the throne; it was *for his sake* (*v.* 4, 5) that God thus *set up his son after him;* not for his own sake, nor for the sake of his father, in whose steps he trod, *but for the sake of David,* whose example he would not follow. Note, It aggravates the sin of a degenerate seed that they fare the better for the piety of their ancestors and owe their blessings to it, and yet will not imitate it. They stand upon that ground, and yet despise it, and trample upon it, and unreasonably ridicule and oppose that which they enjoy the benefit of. The kingdom of Judah was supported, (1.) That David might have a lamp, pursuant to the divine ordination of *a lamp for his anointed,* Ps. cxxxii. 17. (2.) That Jerusalem might be established, not only that the honours put upon it in David's and Solomon's time might be preserved to it, but that it might be reserved to the honours designed for it in after-times. The character here given of David is very great—*that he did that which was right in the eyes of the Lord;* but the exception is very remarkable—*save only in the matter of Uriah,* including both his murder and the debauching of his wife. That was a bad matter; it was a remaining blot upon his name, a bar in his escutcheon, and the reproach of it was not wiped away, though the guilt was. David was guilty of other faults, but they were nothing in comparison of that; yet even that being repented of, though it be mentioned for warning to others, did not prevail to throw him out of the covenant, nor to cut off the entail of the promise upon his seed.

9 And in the twentieth year of Jeroboam king of Israel reigned Asa over Judah. 10 And forty and one years reigned he in Jerusalem. And his mother's name *was* Maachah, the daughter of Abishalom. 11 And Asa did *that which was* right in the eyes of the LORD, as *did* David his father. 12 And he took away the sodomites out of the land, and removed all the idols that his fathers had made. 13 And also Maachah his mother, even her he removed from *being* queen, because she had made an idol in a grove; and Asa destroyed her idol, and burnt *it* by the brook Kidron. 14 But the high places were not removed: nevertheless Asa's heart was perfect with the LORD all his days. 15 And he brought in the things which his father had dedicated, and the things which himself had dedicated, into the house of the LORD, silver, and gold, and vessels. 16 And there was war between Asa and Baasha king of Israel all their days. 17 And Baasha king of Israel went up against Judah, and built Ramah, that he might not suffer any to go out or come in to Asa king of Judah. 18 Then Asa took all the silver and the gold *that were* left in the treasures of the house of the LORD, and the treasures of the king's house, and delivered them into the hand of his servants: and king Asa sent them to Ben-hadad, the son of Tabrimon, the

son of Hezion, king of Syria, that dwelt at Damascus, saying, 19 *There is* a league between me and thee, *and* between my father and thy father: behold, I have sent unto thee a present of silver and gold; come and break thy league with Baasha king of Israel, that he may depart from me. 20 So Ben-hadad hearkened unto king Asa, and sent the captains of the hosts which he had against the cities of Israel, and smote Ijon, and Dan, and Abel-beth-maachah, and all Cinneroth, with all the land of Naphtali. 21 And it came to pass, when Baasha heard *thereof*, that he left off building of Ramah, and dwelt in Tirzah. 22 Then king Asa made a proclamation throughout all Judah; none *was* exempted: and they took away the stones of Ramah, and the timber thereof, wherewith Baasha had builded; and king Asa built with them Geba of Benjamin, and Mizpah. 23 The rest of all the acts of Asa, and all his might, and all that he did, and the cities which he built, *are* they not written in the book of the chronicles of the kings of Judah? Nevertheless in the time of his old age he was diseased in his feet. 24 And Asa slept with his fathers, and was buried with his fathers in the city of David his father: and Jehoshaphat his son reigned in his stead.

We have here a short account of the reign of Asa; we shall find a more copious history of it 2 Chron. xiv., xv., and xvi. Here is,

I. The length of it: *He reigned forty-one years in Jerusalem, v.* 10. In the account we have of the kings of Judah we find the number of the good kings and the bad ones nearly equal; but then we may observe, to our comfort, that the reign of the good kings was generally long, but that of the bad kings short, the consideration of which will make the state of God's church not altogether so bad within that period as it appears at first sight. Length of days is in Wisdom's right hand. *Honour thy father*, much more thy heavenly Father, *that thy days may be long*.

II. The general good character of it (*v.* 11): *Asa did that which was right in the eyes of the Lord*, and that is right indeed which is so in God's eyes; those are approved whom he commends. He did *as did David his father*, kept close to God, and to his instituted worship, was hearty and zealous for that, which gave him this honourable character, that he was like David, though he was not a a prophet, or psalmist, as David was. If we come up to the graces of those that have gone before us it will be our praise with God, though we come short of their gifts. Asa was like David, though he was neither such a conqueror nor such an author; for *his heart was perfect with the Lord all his days* (*v.* 14), that is, he was both cordial and constant in his religion. What he did for God he was sincere in, steady and uniform, and did it from a good principle, with a single eye to the glory of God.

III. The particular instances of Asa's piety. His times were times of reformation. For,

1. He removed that which was evil. There reformation begins; and a great deal of work of that kind his hand found to do. For, though it was but twenty years after the death of Solomon that he began to reign, yet very gross corruption had spread far and taken deep root. Immorality he first struck at: *He took away the sodomites out of the land*, suppressed the brothels; for how can either prince or people prosper while those cages of unclean and filthy birds, more dangerous than pest-houses, are suffered to remain? Then he proceeded against idolatry: *He removed all the idols*, even those *that his father had made, v.* 12. His father having made them, he was the more concerned to remove them, that he might cut off the entail of the curse, and prevent the visiting of that iniquity upon him and his. Nay (which redounds much to his honour, and shows his heart was perfect with God), when he found idolatry in the court, he rooted it out thence, *v.* 13. When it appeared that Maachah his mother, or rather his grandmother (but called his *mother* because she had the educating of him in his childhood), had an idol in a grove, though she was his mother, his grandmother,—though, it is likely, she had a particular fondness for it,—though, being old, she could not live long to patronise it,—though she kept it for her own use only, yet he would by no means connive at her idolatry. Reformation must begin at home. Bad practices will never be suppressed in the country while they are supported in the court. Asa, in every thing else, will honour and respect his mother; he loves her well, but he loves God better, and (like the Levite, Deut. xxxiii. 9) readily forgets the relation when it comes in competition with his duty. If she be an idolater, (1.) Her idol shall be destroyed, publicly exposed to contempt, defaced, and burnt to ashes *by the brook Kidron*, on which, it is probable, he strewed the ashes, in imitation of Moses (Exod. xxxii. 20) and in token of his detestation of idolatry and his indignation at it wherever he found it. Let no remains of a court-idol appear. (2.) She shall be deposed, He removed her from being queen, or from the queen, that is, from conversing with his wife; he banished her from the court, and

confined her to an obscure and private life. Those that have power are happy when thus they have hearts to use it well.

2. He re-established that which was good (*v.* 15): He *brought into the house of God the dedicated things* which he himself had vowed out of the spoils of the Ethiopians he had conquered, and which his father had vowed, but lived not to bring in pursuant to his vow. We must not only cease to do evil, but learn to do well, not only cast away the idols of our iniquity, but dedicate ourselves and our all to God's honour and glory. When those who, in their infancy, were by baptism devoted to God, make it their own act and deed to join themselves to him and vigorously employ themselves in his service, this is bringing in the dedicated things which they and their fathers have dedicated: it is necessary justice—rendering to God the things that are his.

IV. The policy of his reign. He built cities himself, to encourage the increase of his people (*v.* 23) and to invite others to him by the conveniences of habitation; and he was very zealous to hinder Baasha from building Ramah, because he designed it for the cutting off of communication between his people and Jerusalem and to hinder those who in obedience to God would come to worship there. An enemy must by no means be suffered to fortify a frontier town.

V. The faults of his reign. In both the things for which he was praised he was found defective. The fairest characters are not without some *but* or other in them. 1. Did he take away the idols? That was well; *but the high places were not removed* (*v.* 14); therein his reformation fell short. He removed all images which were rivals with the true God or false representations of him; but the altars which were set up in high places, and to which those sacrifices were brought which should have been offered on the altar in the temple, those he suffered to stand, thinking there was no great harm in them, they having been used by good men before the temple was built, and being loth to disoblige the people, who had a kindness to them and were wedded to them both by custom and convenience; whereas in Judah and Benjamin, the only tribes under Asa's government which lay so near Jerusalem and the altars there, there was less pretence for them than in those tribes which lay more remote. They were against the law, which obliged them to worship *at one place,* Deut. xii. 11. They lessened men's esteem of the temple and the altars there, and were an open gap for idolatry to enter in at, while the people were so much addicted to it. It was not well that Asa, when his hand was in, did not remove these. *Nevertheless his heart was perfect with the Lord.* This affords us a comfortable note, That those may be found honest and upright with God, and be accepted of him, who yet, in some instances, come short of doing the good they might and should do. The perfection which is made the indispensable condition of the new covenant is not to be understood of sinlessness (then we were all undone), but sincerity. 2. Did he bring in the dedicated things? That was well; but he afterwards alienated the dedicated things, when he took the gold and silver out of the house of God and sent them as a bribe to Benhadad, to hire him to break his league with Baasha, and, by making an inroad upon his country, to give him a diversion from the building of Ramah, *v.* 18, 19. Here he sinned, (1.) In tempting Benhadad to break his league, and so to violate the public faith. If he did wrong in doing it, as certainly he did, Asa did wrong in persuading him to do it. (2:) In that he could not trust God, who had done so much for him, to free him out of this strait, without using such indirect means to help himself. (3.) In taking the gold out of the treasury of the temple, which was not to be made use of but on extraordinary occasions. The project succeeded. Benhadad made a descent upon the land of Israel, which obliged Baasha to retire with his whole force from Ramah (*v.* 20, 21), which gave Asa a fair opportunity to demolish his works there, and the timber and stones served him for the building of some cities of his own, *v.* 22. But, though the design prospered, we find it was displeasing to God; and though Asa valued himself upon the policy of it, and promised himself that it would effectually secure his peace, he was told by the prophet that he had done foolishly, and that *thenceforth he should have wars;* see 2 Chron. xvi. 7—9.

VI. The troubles of his reign. For the most part he prospered; but, 1. Baasha king of Israel was a very troublesome neighbour to him. He reigned twenty-four years, and all his days had war, more or less, with Asa, *v.* 16. This was the effect of the division of the kingdoms, that they were continually vexing one another, and so weakened one another, which made them both an easier prey to the common enemy. 2. In his old age he was himself afflicted with the gout: He was *diseased in his feet,* which made him less fit for business and peevish towards those about him.

VII. The conclusion of his reign. The acts of it were more largely recorded in the common history (to which reference is here had, *v.* 23) than in this sacred one. He reigned long, but finished at last with honour, and left his throne to a successor no way inferior to him.

25 And Nadab the son of Jeroboam began to reign over Israel in the second year of Asa king of Judah, and reigned over Israel two years. 26 And he did evil in the sight of the LORD, and walked in the way of his father, and in his sin

wherewith he made Israel to sin. 27 And Baasha the son of Ahijah, of the house of Issachar, conspired against him; and Baasha smote him at Gibbethon, which *belonged* to the Philistines; for Nadab and all Israel laid siege to Gibbethon. 28 Even in the third year of Asa king of Judah did Baasha slay him, and reigned in his stead. 29 And it came to pass, when he reigned, *that* he smote all the house of Jeroboam; he left not to Jeroboam any that breathed, until he had destroyed him, according unto the saying of the LORD, which he spake by his servant Ahijah the Shilonite: 30 Because of the sins of Jeroboam which he sinned, and which he made Israel sin, by his provocation wherewith he provoked the LORD God of Israel to anger. 31 Now the rest of the acts of Nadab, and all that he did, *are* they not written in the book of the chronicles of the kings of Israel? 32 And there was war between Asa and Baasha king of Israel all their days. 33 In the third year of Asa king of Judah began Baasha the son of Ahijah to reign over all Israel in Tirzah, twenty and four years. 34 And he did evil in the sight of the LORD, and walked in the way of Jeroboam, and in his sin wherewith he made Israel to sin.

We are now to take a view of the miserable state of Israel, while the kingdom of Judah was happy under Asa's good government. It was threatened that they should be as *a reed shaken in the water* (*ch.* xiv. 15), and so they were, when, during the single reign of Asa, the government of their kingdom was in six or seven different hands, as we find in this and the following chapter. Jeroboam was upon the throne in the beginning of his reign and Ahab at the end of it, and between them were Nadab, Baasha, Elah, Zimri, Tibni, and Omri, undermining and destroying one another. This they got by deserting the house both of God and of David. Here we have, 1. The ruin and extirpation of the family of Jeroboam, according to the word of the Lord by Ahijah. His son Nadab succeeded him. If the death of his brother Abijah had had a due influence upon him to make him religious, and the honour done him at his death had engaged him to follow his good example, his reign might have been long and glorious; but he *walked in the way of his father* (*v.* 26), kept up the worship of his calves, and forbade his subjects to go up to Jerusalem to worship, *sinned and made Israel to sin,* and therefore God brought ruin upon him quickly, in the second year of his reign. He was besieging Gibbethon, a city which the Philistines had taken from the Danites, and was endeavouring to re-take it; and there, in the midst of his army, did Baasha, with others, conspire against him and kill him (*v.* 27), and so little interest had he in the affections of his people that his army did not only not avenge his death, but chose his murderer for his successor. Whether Baasha did it upon a personal pique against Nadab, or to be avenged on the house of Jeroboam for some affront received from them, or whether under pretence of freeing his country from the tyranny of a bad prince, or whether merely from a principle of ambition, to make way for himself to the throne, does not appear; but he *slew him,* and *reigned in his stead, v.* 28. And the first thing he did when he came to the crown was to *cut off all the house of Jeroboam,* that he might the better secure himself and his own usurped government. He thought it not enough to imprison or banish them, but he destroyed them, left not only no males (as was foretold, *ch.* xiv. 10), but none that breathed. Herein he was barbarous, but God was righteous. Jeroboam's sin was punished (*v.* 30); for those that provoke God do it *to their own confusion;* see Jer. vii. 19. Ahijah's prophecy was accomplished (*v.* 29); for no word of God shall fall to the ground. Divine threatenings are not bugbears. 2. The elevation of Baasha. He shall be tried awhile, as Jeroboam was. Twenty-four years he reigned (*v.* 33), but showed that it was not from any dislike to Jeroboam's sin that he destroyed his family, but from malice and ambition; for, when he had rooted out the sinner, he himself clave to the sin, and *walked in the way of Jeroboam* (*v.* 34), though he had seen the end of that way; so strangely was his heart hardened with the deceitfulness of sin.

CHAP. XVI.

This chapter relates wholly to the kingdom of Israel, and the revolutions of that kingdom—many in a little time. The utter ruin of Jeroboam's family, after it had been twenty-four years a royal family, we read of in the foregoing chapter. In this chapter we have, I. The ruin of Baasha's family, after it had been but twenty-six years a royal family, foretold by a prophet (ver. 1—7), and executed by Zimri, one of his captains, ver. 8—14. II. The seven days' reign of Zimri, and his sudden fall, ver. 15—20. III. The struggle between Omri and Tibni, and Omri's prevalency, and his reign, ver. 21—28. IV. The beginning of the reign of Ahab, of whom we shall afterwards read much, ver. 29—33. V. The rebuilding of Jericho, v. 34. All this while, in Judah, things went well.

THEN the word of the LORD came to Jehu the son of Hanani against Baasha, saying, 2 Forasmuch as I exalted thee out of the dust, and made thee prince over my people Israel; and thou hast walked in the way of Jeroboam, and hast made my people Israel to sin, to provoke me to anger with their sins; 3

Behold, I will take away the posterity of Baasha, and the posterity of his house; and will make thy house like the house of Jeroboam the son of Nebat. 4 Him that dieth of Baasha in the city shall the dogs eat; and him that dieth of his in the fields shall the fowls of the air eat. 5 Now the rest of the acts of Baasha, and what he did, and his might, *are* they not written in the book of the chronicles of the kings of Israel? 6 So Baasha slept with his fathers, and was buried in Tirzah: and Elah his son reigned in his stead. 7 And also by the hand of the prophet Jehu the son of Hanani came the word of the LORD against Baasha, and against his house, even for all the evil that he did in the sight of the LORD, in provoking him to anger with the work of his hands, in being like the house of Jeroboam; and because he killed him. 8 In the twenty and sixth year of Asa king of Judah began Elah the son of Baasha to reign over Israel in Tirzah, two years. 9 And his servant Zimri, captain of half *his* chariots, conspired against him, as he was in Tirzah, drinking himself drunk in the house of Arza steward of *his* house in Tirzah. 10 And Zimri went in and smote him, and killed him, in the twenty and seventh year of Asa king of Judah, and reigned in his stead. 11 And it came to pass, when he began to reign, as soon as he sat on his throne, *that* he slew all the house of Baasha: he left him not one that pisseth against a wall, neither of his kinsfolks, nor of his friends. 12 Thus did Zimri destroy all the house of Baasha, according to the word of the LORD, which he spake against Baasha by Jehu the prophet, 13 For all the sins of Baasha, and the sins of Elah his son, by which they sinned, and by which they made Israel to sin, in provoking the LORD God of Israel to anger with their vanities. 14 Now the rest of the acts of Elah, and all that he did, *are* they not written in the book of the chronicles of the kings of Israel?

Here is, I. The ruin of the family of Baasha foretold. He was a man likely enough to have raised and established his family—active, politic, and daring; but he was an idolater, and this brought destruction upon his family.

1. God sent him warning of it before. (1.) That, if he were thereby wrought upon to repent and reform, the ruin might be prevented; for God threatens, that he may not strike, as one that desires not the death of sinners. (2.) That, if not, it might appear that the destruction when it did come, whoever might be instruments of it, was the act of God's justice and the punishment of sin.

2. The warning was sent by *Jehu the son of Hanani.* The father was a seer, or prophet, at the same time (2 Chron. xvi. 7), and was sent to Asa king of Judah; but the son, who was young and more active, was sent on this longer and more dangerous expedition to Baasha king of Israel. *Juniores ad labores—Toil and adventure are for the young.* This Jehu was a prophet and the son of a prophet. Prophecy, thus happily entailed, was worthy of so much the more honour. This Jehu continued long in his usefulness, for we find him reproving Jehoshaphat (2 Chron. xix. 2) above forty years after, and writing the annals of that prince, 2 Chron. xx. 34. The message which this prophet brought to Baasha is much the same with that which Ahijah sent to Jeroboam by his wife.

(1.) He reminds Baasha of the great things God had done for him (*v.* 2): *I exalted thee out of the dust* to the *throne of glory,* a great instance of the divine sovereignty and power, 1 Sam. ii. 8. Baasha seemed to have raised himself by his own treachery and cruelty, yet there was a hand of Providence in it, to bring about God's counsel, concerning Jeroboam's house; and God's owning his advancement as his act and deed does by no means amount to the patronising of his ambition and treachery. It is God that puts power into bad men's hands, which he makes to serve his good purposes, notwithstanding the bad use they make of it. *I made thee prince over my people.* God calls Israel his people still, though wretchedly corrupted, because they retained the covenant of circumcision, and there were many good people among them; it was not till long after that they were called *Loammi, not a people,* Hos. i. 9.

(2.) He charges him with high crimes and misdemeanours. [1.] That he had caused *Israel to sin,* had seduced God's subjects from their allegiance and brought them to pay to dunghill-deities the homage due to him only, and herein he had *walked in the way of Jeroboam* (*v.* 2), and been *like his house, v.* 7. [2.] That he had himself *provoked God to anger with the work of his hands,* that is, by worshipping images, the *work of men's hands;* though perhaps others made them, yet he served them and thereby avowed the making of them, and they are therefore called the *work of his hands.* [3.] That he had *destroyed the house of Jeroboam* (*v.* 7), *because he killed him,* namely, Jeroboam's son and all his: if he had done that with an eye to God, to his will and glory, and from a holy indignation against the sins of Jeroboam and his house, he would have been accepted and applauded as a minister of God's justice; but, as he did it, he was only the tool of God's justice, but a servant to his own lusts, and is justly punished for the malice and ambition which actuated and governed him in all he did. Note, Those who are in any way employed in denouncing or executing the justice of God (magistrates or ministers) are concerned to do it from a good principle and in a holy manner, lest it turn into sin to them and they make themselves obnoxious by it.

(3.) He foretels the same destruction to come upon his family which he himself had been employed to bring upon the family of Jeroboam, *v.* 3, 4. Note, Those who resemble others in their sins may expect to resemble them in their plagues, especially those who seem zealous against such sins in others as they allow themselves in; the house of Jehu was reckoned with for the blood of the house of Ahab, Hos. i. 4.

II. A reprieve granted for some time, so long that Baasha himself dies in peace, and is buried with honour in his own royal city (*v.* 6), so far is he from being a prey either to the dogs or to the fowls, which yet was threatened to his house, *v.* 4. He lives not either to see or feel the punishment threatened, yet he was himself the greatest delinquent. Certainly there must be a future state, in which impenitent sinners will suffer in their own persons, and not escape, as often they do in this world. Baasha died under no visible stroke of divine vengeance for aught that appears, but *God laid up his iniquity for his children,* as Job speaks, *ch.* xxi. 19. Thus he often visits sin. Observe, Baasha is punished by the destruction of his children after his death, and his children are punished by the abuse of their bodies after their death; that is the only thing which the threatening specifies (*v.* 4), that the dogs and the fowls of the air should eat them, as if herein were designed a tacit intimation that there are punishments after death, when death has done its worst, which will be the sorest punishments and are most to be dreaded; these judgments on the body and posterity signified judgments on the soul when separated from the body, by him who, *after he has killed, has power to cast into hell.*

III. Execution done at last. Baasha's son Elah, like Jeroboam's son Nadab, reigned two years, and then was slain by Zimri, one of his own soldiers, as Nadab was by Baasha; so like was his house made to that of Jeroboam, as was threatened, *v.* 3. Because his idolatry was like his, and one of the sins for which God contended with him being the destruction of Jeroboam's family, the more the destruction of his own resembled that, the nearer did the punishment resemble the sin, as face answers to face in a glass.

1. As then, so now, the king himself was first slain, but Elah fell more ingloriously than Nadab. Nadab was slain in the field of action and honour, he and his army then besieging Gibbethon (*ch.* xv. 27); but the siege being then raised upon that disaster, and the city remaining still in the Philistines' hands, the army of Israel was now renewing the attempt (*v.* 15) and Elah should have been with them to command in chief, but he loved his own ease and safety better than his honour or duty, or the public good, and therefore staid behind to take his pleasure; and, when he was *drinking himself drunk in his servant's house,* Zimri killed him, *v.* 9, 10. Let it be a warning to drunkards, especially to those who designedly drink themselves drunk, that they know not but death may surprise them in that condition. (1.) Death comes easily upon men when they are drunk. Besides the chronic diseases which men frequently bring themselves into by hard drinking, and which cut them off in the midst of their days, men in that condition are more easily overcome by an enemy, as Amnon by Absalom, and are liable to more bad accidents, being unable to help themselves. (2.) Death comes terribly upon men in that condition. Finding them in the act of sin, and incapacitated for any act of devotion, that day *comes upon them unawares* (Luke xxi. 34), like a thief.

2. As then, so now, the whole family was cut off, and rooted out. The traitor was the successor, to whom the unthinking people tamely submitted, as if it were all one to them what king they had, so that they had one. The first thing Zimri did was to *slay all the house of Baasha;* thus he held by cruelty what he got by treason. His cruelty seems to have extended further than Baasha's did against the house of Jeroboam, for he left to Elah *none of his kinsfolks or friends* (*v.* 11), *none of his avengers* (so the word is), none that were likely to avenge his death; yet divine justice soon avenged it so remarkably that it was used as a proverb long after, *Had Zimri peace who slew his master?* 2 Kings ix. 31. In this, (1.) The word of God was fulfilled, *v.* 12. (2.) The sins of Baasha and Elah were reckoned for, with which they *provoked God by their vanities, v.* 13. Their idols are called their *vanities,* for they cannot profit nor help. Miserable are those whose deities are vanities.

15 In the twenty and seventh year of Asa king of Judah did Zimri reign seven days in Tirzah. And the people *were* encamped against Gibbethon, which *belonged* to the Philistines. 16 And the people *that were* encamped

heard say, Zimri hath conspired, and hath also slain the king: wherefore all Israel made Omri, the captain of the host, king over Israel that day in the camp. 17 And Omri went up from Gibbethon, and all Israel with him, and they besieged Tirzah. 18 And it came to pass, when Zimri saw that the city was taken, that he went into the palace of the king's house, and burnt the king's house over him with fire, and died, 19 For his sins which he sinned in doing evil in the sight of the LORD, in walking in the way of Jeroboam, and in his sin which he did, to make Israel to sin. 20 Now the rest of the acts of Zimri, and his treason that he wrought, *are* they not written in the book of the chronicles of the kings of Israel? 21 Then were the people of Israel divided into two parts: half of the people followed Tibni the son of Ginath, to make him king; and half followed Omri. 22 But the people that followed Omri prevailed against the people that followed Tibni the son of Ginath: so Tibni died, and Omri reigned. 23 In the thirty and first year of Asa king of Judah began Omri to reign over Israel, twelve years: six years reigned he in Tirzah. 24 And he bought the hill Samaria of Shemer for two talents of silver, and built on the hill, and called the name of the city which he built, after the name of Shemer, owner of the hill, Samaria. 25 But Omri wrought evil in the eyes of the LORD, and did worse than all that *were* before him. 26 For he walked in all the way of Jeroboam the son of Nebat, and in his sin wherewith he made Israel to sin, to provoke the LORD God of Israel to anger with their vanities. 27 Now the rest of the acts of Omri which he did, and his might that he showed, *are* they not written in the book of the chronicles of the kings of Israel? 28 So Omri slept with his fathers, and was buried in Samaria: and Ahab his son reigned in his stead.

Solomon observes (Prov. xxviii. 2) that *for the transgression of a land many were the princes thereof* (so it was here in Israel), *but by a man of understanding the state thereof shall be prolonged*—so it was with Judah at the same time under Asa. When men forsake God they are out of the way of rest and establishment. Zimri, and Tibni, and Omri, are here striving for the crown. Proud aspiring men ruin one another, and involve others in the ruin. These confusions end in the settlement of Omri; we must therefore take him along with us through this part of the story.

I. How he was chosen, as the Roman emperors often were, by the army in the field, now encamped before Gibbethon. Notice was soon brought thither that Zimri had slain their king (*v.* 16) and set up himself in Tirzah, the royal city, whereupon they chose Omri king in the camp, that they might without delay avenge the death of Elah upon Zimri. Though he was idle and intemperate, yet he was their king, and they would not tamely submit to his murderer, nor let the treason go unpunished. They did not attempt to avenge the death of Nadab upon Baasha, perhaps because the house of Baasha had ruled with more gentleness than the house of Jeroboam; but Zimri shall feel the resentments of the provoked army. The siege of Gibbethon is quitted (Philistines are sure to gain when Israelites quarrel) and Zimri is prosecuted.

II. How he conquered Zimri, who is said to have reigned seven days (*v.* 15), so long before Omri was proclaimed king and himself proclaimed traitor; but we may suppose it was a longer time before he died, for he continued long enough to show his inclination to the way of Jeroboam, and to make himself obnoxious to the justice of God by supporting his idolatry, *v.* 19. Tirzah was a beautiful city, but not fortified, so that Omri soon made himself master of it (*v.* 17), forced Zimri into the palace, which being unable to defend, and yet unwilling to surrender, he burnt, and himself in it, *v.* 18. Unwilling that his rival should ever enjoy that sumptuous palace, he burnt it; and fearing that if he fell into the hands of the army, either alive or dead, he should be ignominiously treated, he burnt himself in it. See what desperate practices men's wickedness sometimes brings them to, and how it hurries them into their own ruin; see the disposition of incendiaries, who set palaces and kingdoms on fire, though they are themselves in danger of perishing in the flame.

III. How he struggled with Tibni, and at length got clear of him: *Half of the people followed this Tibni* (*v.* 21), probably those who were in Zimri's interest, with whom others joined, who would not have a king chosen in the camp (lest he should rule by the sword and a standing army), but in a convention of the states. The contest between these two lasted some years, and, it is likely, cost a great deal of blood on both sides, for it was in the twenty-seventh year of Asa that Omri was first elected (*v.* 15) and thence the twelve years of his reign are to be dated; but it was not till the thirty-first year of Asa that he began to reign without a rival; then Tibni died, it is likely in battle, *and Omri reigned*, *v.* 22. Sir Walter Raleigh, in his History of the World (*l.* ii. *c.* 19 § 6), enquires here why it was that in all these confusions and revolutions of the kingdom of Israel they never thought of returning to the house of David, and uniting themselves again to Judah, *for then it was better with them than now;* and he thinks the reason was because the kings of Judah assumed a more absolute, arbitrary, and despotic power than the kings of Israel. It was the heaviness of the yoke that they complained of when they first revolted from the house of David, and the dread of that made them ever after averse to it, and attached to kings of their own, who ruled more by law and the rules of a limited monarchy.

IV. How he reigned when he was at length settled on the throne. 1. He made himself famous by building Samaria, which, ever after, was the royal city of the kings of Israel (the palace at Tirzah being burnt), and in process of time grew so considerable that it gave name to the middle part of Canaan (which lay between Galilee on the north and Judea on the south) and to the inhabitants of that country, who were called *Samaritans*. He bought the ground for *two talents of silver*, somewhat more than £700 of our money, for a talent was £353. 11*s.* 10½*d.* Perhaps Shemer, who sold him the ground, let him have it considerably the cheaper upon condition that the city should be called after his name, for otherwise it would have borne the name of the purchaser; it was called *Samaria*, or *Shemeren* (as it is in the Hebrew), from Shemer, the former owner, *v.* 24. The kings of Israel changed their royal seats, Shechem first, then Tirzah, now Samaria; but the kings of Judah were constant to Jerusalem, the city of God. Those that cleave to the Lord fix, but those that leave him ever wander. 2. He made himself infamous by his wickedness; for *he did worse than all that were before him*, *v.* 25. Though he was brought to the throne with much difficulty, and Providence had remarkably favoured him in his advancement, yet he was more profane, or more superstitious, and a greater persecutor, than either of the houses of Jeroboam or Baasha. He went further than they had done in *establishing iniquity by a law*, and forcing his subjects to comply with him in it; for we read of the statutes of Omri, the keeping of which made *Israel a desolation*, Mic. vi. 16. Jeroboam caused Israel to sin by temptation, example, and allurement; but Omri did it by compulsion.

V. How he ended his reign, *v.* 27, 28. He was in some repute for the might which he showed. Many a bad man has been a stout man. He died in his bed, as did Jeroboam and Baasha themselves; but, like them, left it to his posterity to fill up the measure, and then pay off the scores, of his iniquity.

29 And in the thirty and eighth year of Asa king of Judah began Ahab the son of Omri to reign over Israel: and Ahab the son of Omri reigned over Israel in Samaria twenty and two years. 30 And Ahab the son of Omri did evil in the sight of the LORD above all that *were* before him. 31 And it came to pass, as if it had been a light thing for him to walk in the sins of Jeroboam the son of Nebat, that he took to wife Jezebel the daughter of Ethbaal king of the Zidonians, and went and served Baal, and worshipped him. 32 And he reared up an altar for Baal in the house of Baal, which he had built in Samaria. 33 And Ahab made a grove; and Ahab did more to provoke the LORD God of Israel to anger than all the kings of Israel that were before him. 34 In his days did Hiel the Beth-elite build Jericho: he laid the foundation thereof in Abiram his first-born, and set up the gates thereof in his youngest *son* Segub, according to the word of the LORD, which he spake by Joshua the son of Nun.

We have here the beginning of the reign of Ahab, of whom we have more particulars recorded than of any of the kings of Israel We have here only a general idea given us of him, as the worst of all the kings, that we may expect what the particulars will be. He reigned twenty-two years, long enough to do a great deal of mischief.

I. He exceeded all his predecessors in wickedness, *did evil above all that were before him* (*v.* 30), and, as if it were done with a particular enmity both to God and Israel, to affront him and ruin them, it is said, *He did more* purposely *to provoke the Lord God of Israel to anger*, and, consequently, to send judgments on his land, *than all the kings of Israel that were before him*, *v.* 33. It was bad with the people when every successive king was worse than his predecessor. What would they come to at last? He had seen the ruin of other wicked kings and their families; yet, instead of taking warning, his heart was hardened and enraged against God by it. He thought it *a light thing to walk in the sins of Jeroboam*, *v.* 31. It was nothing to break the second commandment by image-worship, he would set aside the first also by introducing other gods; his little finger should fall heavier upon God's ordinances than Jeroboam's loins. Making light of less sins makes way for greater, and those that endeavour to extenuate other people's sins will but aggravate their own.

II. He married a wicked woman, who he knew would bring in the worship of Baal, and seemed to marry her with that design. *As if it had been a light thing to walk in the sins of Jeroboam, he took to wife Jezebel* (*v.* 31), a zealous idolater, extremely imperious and malicious in her natural temper, addicted to witchcrafts and whoredoms (2 Kings ix. 22), and every way vicious. The false prophetess spoken of Rev. ii. 20 is there called *Jezebel*, for a wicked woman could not be called by a worse name than hers; what mischiefs she did, and what mischief at last befel her (2 Kings ix. 33), we shall find in the following story; this one strange wife debauched Israel more than all the strange wives of Solomon.

III. He set up the worship of Baal, forsook the God of Israel and served the god of the Sidonians, Jupiter instead of Jehovah, the sun (so some think), a deified hero of the Phenicians (so others): he was weary of the golden calves, and thought they had been worshipped long enough; such vanities were they that those who had been fondest of them at length grew sick of them, and, like adulterers, must have variety. In honour of this mock deity, whom they called *Baal—lord*, and for the convenience of his worship, 1. Ahab built a temple in Samaria, the royal city, because the temple of God was in Jerusalem, the royal city of the other kingdom. He would have Baal's temple near him, that he might the better frequent it, protect it, and put honour upon it. 2. He reared an altar in that temple, on which to offer sacrifice to Baal, by which they acknowledged their dependence upon him and sought his favour. O the stupidity of idolaters, who are at a great expense to make one their friend whom they might have chosen whether they would make a god of or no! 3. He made a grove about his temple, either a natural one, by planting shady trees there, or, if those would be too long in growing, an artificial one in imitation of it; for it is not said he *planted*, but he *made* a grove, something that answered the intention, which was to conceal and so countenance the abominable impurities that were committed in the filthy worship of Baal. *Lucus, à lucendo, quia non lucet—He that doeth evil hateth the light*

IV. One of his subjects, in imitation of his presumption, ventured to build Jericho, in defiance of the curse Joshua had long since pronounced on him that should attempt it, *v.* 34. It comes in as an instance of the height of impiety to which men had arrived, especially at Bethel, where one of the calves was, for of that city this daring sinner was. Observe, 1. How ill he did. Like Achan he meddled with the accursed thing, turned that to his own use which was devoted to God's honour. He began to build, in defiance of the curse well known in Israel, jesting with it perhaps as a bugbear, or fancying its force worn out by length of time, for it was above 500 years since it was pronounced, Josh. vi. 26. He went on to build, in defiance of the execution of the curse in part; for, though his eldest son died when he began, yet he would proceed in contempt of God and his wrath revealed from heaven against his ungodliness. 2. How ill he sped He built for his children, but God wrote him childless; his eldest son died when he began, the youngest when he finished, and all the rest (it is supposed) between. Note, Those whom God curses are cursed indeed; none ever hardened his heart against God and prospered. God keep us back from presumptuous sins, those great transgressions!

CHAP. XVII.

So sad was the character both of the princes and people of Israel, as described in the foregoing chapter, that one might have expected God would cast off a people that had so cast him off; but, as an evidence to the contrary, never was Israel so blessed with a good prophet as when it was so plagued with a bad king. Never was king so bold to sin as Ahab; never was prophet so bold to reprove and threaten as Elijah, whose story begins in this chapter and is full of wonders. Scarcely any part of the Old-Testament history shines brighter than this history of the spirit and power of Elias; he only, of all the prophets, had the honour of Enoch, the first prophet, to be translated, that he should not see death, and the honour of Moses, the great prophet, to attend our Saviour in his transfiguration. Other prophets prophesied and wrote, he prophesied and acted, but wrote nothing; but his actions cast more lustre on his name than their writings did on theirs. In this chapter we have, I. His prediction of a famine in Israel, through the want of rain, ver. 1. II. The provision made for him in that famine, 1. By the ravens at the brook Cherith, ver. 2—7. 2. When that failed, by the widow at Zarephath, who received him in the name of a prophet and had a prophet's reward; for (1.) He multiplied her meal and her oil, ver. 8—16. (2.) He raised her dead son to life, ver. 17—24. Thus his story begins with judgments and miracles, designed to awaken that stupid generation that had so deeply corrupted themselves.

AND Elijah the Tishbite, *who was* of the inhabitants of Gilead, said unto Ahab, *As* the LORD God of Israel liveth, before whom I stand, there shall not be dew nor rain these years, but according to my word. 2 And the word of the LORD came unto him, saying, 3 Get thee hence, and turn thee eastward, and hide thyself by the brook Cherith, that *is* before Jordan. 4 And it shall be, *that* thou shalt drink of the brook; and I have commanded the ravens to feed thee there. 5 So he went and did according unto the word of the LORD: for he went and dwelt by the brook Cherith, that *is* before Jordan. 6 And the ravens brought him bread and flesh in the morning, and bread and flesh in the evening; and he drank of the brook. 7 And it came to pass after a while, that the brook dried up, because there had been no rain in the land.

The history of Elijah begins somewhat abruptly. Usually, when a prophet enters, we have some account of his parentage, are told whose son he was and of what tribe; but Elijah drops (so to speak) out of the clouds, as if, like Melchisedek, he were without father, without mother, and without descent, which made some of the Jews fancy that he was an angel sent from heaven; but the apostle has assured us that *he was a man subject to like passions as we are* (James v. 17), which perhaps intimates, not only that he was liable to the common infirmities of human nature, but that, by his natural temper, he was a man of strong passions, more hot and eager than most men, and therefore the more fit to deal with the daring sinners of the age he lived in: so wonderfully does God suit men to the work he designs them for. Rough spirits are called to rough services. The reformation needed such a man as Luther to break the ice. Observe, 1. The prophet's name: *Elijahu*—"*My God Jehovah is he*" (so it signifies), "is he who sends me and will own me and bear me out, is he to whom I would bring Israel back and who alone can effect that great work." 2. His country: He was *of the inhabitants of Gilead,* on the other side Jordan, either of the tribe of Gad or the half of Manasseh, for Gilead was divided between them; but whether a native of either of those tribes is uncertain. The obscurity of his parentage was no prejudice to his eminency afterwards. We need not enquire whence men are, but what they are: if it be a good thing, no matter though it come out of Nazareth. Israel was sorely wounded when God sent them this balm from Gilead and this physician thence. He is called a *Tishbite* from Thisbe, a town in that country. Two things we have an account of here in the beginning of his story:—

I. How he foretold a famine, a long and grievous famine, with which Israel should be punished for their sins. That fruitful land, for want of rain, should be turned into barrenness, for the iniquity of those that dwelt therein. He went and told Ahab this; did not whisper it to the people, to make them disaffected to the government, but proclaimed it to the king, in whose power it was to reform the land, and so to prevent the judgment. It is probable that he reproved Ahab for his idolatry and other wickedness, and told him that unless he repented and reformed this judgment would be brought upon his land. There should be *neither dew nor rain for some years,* none but *according to my word,* that is, "Expect none till you hear from me again." The apostle teaches us to understand this, not only of the word of prophecy, but the word of prayer, which turned the key of the clouds, James v. 17, 18. He prayed earnestly (in a holy indignation at Israel's apostasy, and a holy zeal for the glory of God, whose judgments were defied) *that it might not rain;* and, according to his prayers, the heavens became as brass, till he *prayed again that it might rain.* In allusion to this story it is said of God's witnesses (Rev. xi. 6), *These have power to shut heaven, that it rain not in the days of their prophecy.* Elijah lets Ahab know, 1. That *the Lord Jehovah* is the *God of Israel,* whom he had forsaken. 2. That he is a *living God,* and not like the gods he worshipped, which were dead dumb idols. 3. That he himself was God's servant in office, and a messenger sent from him: "It is he *before whom I stand,* to minister to him," or "whom I now represent, in whose stead I stand, and in whose name I speak, in defiance of the prophets of Baal and the groves." 4. That, notwithstanding the present peace and prosperity of the kingdom of Israel, God was displeased with them for their idolatry and would chastise them for it by the want of rain (which, when he withheld it, it was not in the power of the gods they served to bestow; for *are there any of the vanities of the heathen that can give rain?* Jer. xiv. 22), which would effectually prove their impotency, and the folly of those who left the living God, to make their court to such as could do neither good nor evil; and this he confirms with a solemn oath—*As the Lord God of Israel liveth,* that Ahab might stand the more in awe of the threatening, the divine life being engaged for the accomplishment of it. 5. He lets Ahab know what interest he had in heaven: It shall be *according to my word.* With what dignity does he speak when he speaks in God's name, as one who well understood that commission of a prophet (Jer. i. 10), *I have set thee over the nations and over the kingdoms.* See the power of prayer and the truth of God's word; for he performeth the counsel of his messengers.

II. How he was himself taken care of in that famine. 1. How he was hidden. God bade him *go and hide himself by the brook Cherith, v.* 3. This was intended, not so much for his preservation, for it does not appear that Ahab immediately sought his life, but as a judgment to the people, to whom, if he had publicly appeared, he might have been a blessing both by his instructions and his intercession, and so have shortened the days of their calamity; but God had determined it should last three years and a half, and therefore, so long, appointed Elijah to abscond, that he might not be solicited to revoke the sentence, the execution of which he had said should be *according to his word.* When God *speaks concerning a nation, to pluck up and destroy,* he finds some way or other to remove those that would stand in the gap to turn away his wrath. It bodes ill to a people when good men and good ministers are ordered to hide themselves. When God intended to *send rain upon the earth* then he bade Elijah go and *show himself to Ahab, ch.* xviii. 1. For the present, in obedience to the divine command, he went and dwelt all alone in some obscure unfrequented place, where he was not discovered, probably among the reeds of the brook. If Providence calls us to solitude and retirement, it becomes us to acquiesce; when we cannot be useful we must be patient, and when we cannot work for God we must sit still quietly for him. 2. How he was fed. Though he could not work there, having nothing to do but to meditate and pray (which would help to prepare him for his usefulness afterwards), yet he shall eat, for he is in the way of his duty, and *verily he shall be fed, in the day of famine he shall be satisfied.* When the woman, the church, is *driven into the wilderness,* care is taken that she be fed and nourished there, time, times, and half a time, that is, three years and a half, which was just the time of Elijah's concealment. See Rev. xii. 6, 14. Elijah must drink of the brook, and the ravens were appointed to *bring him meat* (*v.* 4) and did so, *v.* 6. Here, (1.) The provision was plentiful, and good, and constant, bread and flesh twice a day, daily bread and food convenient. We may suppose that he fared not so sumptuously as the prophets of the groves, who *did eat at Jezebel's table* (*ch.* xviii. 19), and yet better than the rest of the Lord's prophets, whom Obadiah fed with bread and water, *ch.* xviii. 4. It ill becomes God's servants, especially his servants the prophets, to be nice and curious about their food and to affect dainties and varieties; if nature be sustained, no matter though the palate be not pleased; instead of envying those who have daintier fare, we should think how many there are, better than we, who live comfortably upon coarser fare and would be glad of our leavings. Elijah had but one meal brought him at a time, every morning and every evening, to teach him not to take thought for the morrow. Let those who have but from hand to mouth learn to live upon Providence, and trust it for *the bread of the day in the day;* thank God for bread this day, and let to-morrow bring bread with it. (2.) The caterers were very unlikely; the *ravens* brought it to him. Obadiah, and others in Israel that had not bowed the knee to Baal, would gladly have entertained Elijah; but he was a man by himself, and must be fed in an extraordinary way. He was a figure of John the baptist, whose meat was locusts and wild honey. God could have sent angels to minister to him, as he did afterwards (*ch.* xix. 5) and as he did to our Saviour (Matt. iv. 11), but he chose to send by winged messengers of another nature, to show that when he pleases he can serve his own purposes by the meanest creatures as effectually as by the mightiest. If it be asked whence the ravens had this provision, how and where it was cooked, and whether they came honestly by it, we must answer, as Jacob did (Gen. xxvii. 20), *The Lord our God brought it to them,* whose the earth is and the fulness thereof, the world and those that dwell therein. But why ravens? [1.] They are birds of prey, ravenous devouring creatures, more likely to have taken his meat from him, or to have picked out his eyes (Prov. xxx. 17); but thus Samson's riddle is again unriddled, *Out of the eater comes forth meat.* [2.] They are unclean creatures *Every raven after his kind* was, by the law, forbidden to be eaten (Lev. xi. 15), yet Elijah did not think the meat they brought ever the worse for that, but ate and gave thanks, asking no question for conscience' sake. Noah's dove was to him a more faithful messenger than his raven; yet here the ravens are faithful and constant to Elijah. [3.] Ravens feed on insects and carrion themselves, yet they brought the prophet man's meat and wholesome food. It is a pity that those who bring the bread of life to others should themselves take up with *that which is not bread.* [4.] Ravens could bring but a little, and broken meat, yet Elijah was content with such things as he had, and thankful that he was fed, though not feasted. [5.] Ravens neglect their own young ones, and do not feed them; yet when God pleases they shall feed his prophet. Young lions and young ravens may lack, and suffer hunger, but not those that fear the Lord, Ps. xxxiv. 10 [6.] Ravens are themselves fed by special providence (Job xxxviii. 41; Ps. cxlvii. 9), and now they fed the prophet. Have we experienced God's special goodness to us and ours? Let us reckon ourselves obliged thereby to be kind to those that are his, for his sake. Let us learn hence, *First,* To acknowledge the sovereignty and power of God over all the creatures; he can make what use he pleases of them, either for judgment or mercy. *Secondly,* To encourage ourselves in God in the greatest straits, and never to distrust him. He that could furnish a table in the wilderness, and make ravens purveyors, cooks, and servitors to his prophet, is able to supply all our need according to his riches in glory.

Thus does Elijah, for a great while, *eat his morsels alone,* and his provision of water, which he has in an ordinary way from the brook, fails him before that which he has by miracle. The powers of nature are limited, but not the powers of the God of nature. Elijah's brook dried up (*v.* 7) *because there was no rain.* If the heavens fail, earth fails of course; such are all our creature-comforts; we lose them when we most need them, like the brooks in summer, Job vi. 15. But there is *a river which makes glad the city of God* and which never runs dry (Ps. xlvi. 4), *a well of water that springs up to eternal life.* Lord, give us that living water!

8 And the word of the LORD came unto him, saying, 9 Arise, get thee

to Zarephath, which *belongeth* to Zidon, and dwell there: behold, I have commanded a widow woman there to sustain thee. 10 So he arose and went to Zarephath. And when he came to the gate of the city, behold, the widow woman *was* there gathering of sticks: and he called to her, and said, Fetch me, I pray thee, a little water in a vessel, that I may drink. 11 And as she was going to fetch *it*, he called to her, and said, Bring me, I pray thee, a morsel of bread in thine hand. 12 And she said, *As* the LORD thy God liveth, I have not a cake, but a handful of meal in a barrel, and a little oil in a cruse: and, behold, I *am* gathering two sticks, that I may go in and dress it for me and my son, that we may eat it, and die. 13 And Elijah said unto her, Fear not; go *and* do as thou hast said: but make me thereof a little cake first, and bring *it* unto me, and after make for thee and for thy son. 14 For thus saith the LORD God of Israel, The barrel of meal shall not waste, neither shall the cruse of oil fail, until the day *that* the LORD sendeth rain upon the earth. 15 And she went and did according to the saying of Elijah: and she, and he, and her house, did eat *many* days. 16 *And* the barrel of meal wasted not, neither did the cruse of oil fail, according to the word of the LORD, which he spake by Elijah.

We have here an account of the further protection Elijah was taken under, and the further provision made for him in his retirement. *At destruction and famine he shall laugh* that has God for his friend to guard and maintain him. The brook Cherith is dried up, but God's care of his people, and kindness to them, never slacken, never fail, but are still the same, are still continued and drawn out to those that know him, Ps. xxxvi. 10. When the brook was dried up Jordan was not; why did not God send him thither? Surely because he would show that he has a variety of ways to provide for his people and is not tied to any one. God will now provide for him where he shall have some company and opportunity of usefulness, and not be, as he had been, buried alive. Observe,

I. The place he is sent to, to *Zarephath*, or *Surepta*, a city of Sidon, out of the borders of the land of Israel, *v.* 9. Our Saviour takes notice of this as an early and ancient indication of the favour of God designed for the poor Gentiles, in the fulness of time, Luke iv. 25, 26. *Many widows were in Israel in the days of Elias*, and some, it is likely, that would have bidden him welcome to their houses; yet he is sent to honour and bless with his presence a city of Sidon, a Gentile city, and so becomes (says Dr. Lightfoot) *the first prophet of the Gentiles.* Israel had corrupted themselves with the idolatries of the nations and become worse than they; justly therefore is *the casting off of them the riches of the world.* Elijah was hated and driven out by his countrymen; therefore, lo, he turns to the Gentiles, as the apostles were afterwards ordered to do, Acts xviii. 6. But why to a city of Sidon? Perhaps because the worship of Baal, which was now the crying sin of Israel, came lately thence with Jezebel, who was a Sidonian (*ch.* xvi. 31); therefore thither he shall go, that thence may be fetched the destroyer of that idolatry, "Even out of Sidon have I called my prophet, my reformer." Jezebel was Elijah's greatest enemy; yet, to show her the impotency of her malice, God will find a hiding-place for him even in her country. Christ never went among the Gentiles except once *into the coast of Sidon*, Matt. xv. 21.

II. The person that is appointed to entertain him, not one of the rich merchants or great men, of Sidon, not such a one as Obadiah, that was governor of Ahab's house and fed the prophets; but a poor widow woman, destitute and desolate, is commanded (that is, is made both able and willing) to sustain him. It is God's way, and it is his glory, to make use of the *weak and foolish things of the world* and put honour upon them. He is, in a special manner, the widows' God, and feeds them, and therefore they must study what they shall render to him.

III. The provision made for him there. Providence brought the widow woman to meet him very opportunely at the gate of the city (*v.* 10), and, by what is here related of what passed between Elijah and her, we find,

1. Her case and character; and it appears, (1.) That she was very poor and necessitous. She had nothing to live upon but a handful of meal and a little oil, needy at the best, and now, by the general scarcity, reduced to the last extremity. When she has eaten the little she has, for aught she yet sees, she must die for want, she and her son, *v.* 12. She had no fuel but the sticks she gathered in the streets, and, having no servant, she must gather them herself (*v.* 10), being thus more in a condition to receive alms than give entertainment. To her Elijah was sent, that he might still live upon Providence as much as he did when the ravens fed him. It was in compassion to the low estate of his handmaiden that God sent the prophet to her, not to beg of her, but to board with her, and

he would pay well for his table. (2.) That she was very humble and industrious. He found her gathering sticks, and preparing to bake her own bread, *v.* 10, 12. Her mind was brought to her condition, and she complained not of the hardship she was brought to, nor quarrelled with the divine Providence for withholding rain, but accommodated herself to it as well as she could. Such as are of this temper in a day of trouble are best prepared for honour and relief from God. (3.) That she was very charitable and generous. When this stranger desired her to go and fetch him some water to drink, she readily went, at the first word, *v.* 10, 11. She objected not to the present scarcity of it, nor asked him what he would give her for a draught of water (for now it was worth money), nor hinted that he was a stranger, an Israelite, with whom perhaps the Sidonians cared not for having any dealings, any more than the Samaritans, John iv. 9. She did not excuse herself on account of her weakness through famine, or the urgency of her own affairs, did not tell him she had something else to do than to go on his errands, but left off gathering the sticks for herself to fetch water for him, which perhaps she did the more willingly, being moved with the gravity of his aspect. We should be ready to do any office of kindness even to strangers; if we have not wherewith to give to the distressed, we must be the more ready to work for them. A cup of cold water, though it cost us no more than the labour of fetching, shall in no wise lose its reward. (4.) That she had a great confidence in the word of God. It was a great trial for her faith and obedience when, having told the prophet how low her stock of meal and oil was and that she had but just enough for herself and her son, he bade her *make a cake for him,* and make *his* first, and then *prepare for herself and her son.* If we consider, it will appear as great a trial as could be in so small a matter. "Let the children first be served" (might she have said); "charity begins at home. I cannot be expected to give, having but little, and not knowing, when that is gone, where to obtain more." She had much more reason than Nabal to ask, "Shall I take my meat and my oil and *give it to one that I know not whence he is?*" Elijah, it is true, made mention of *the God of Israel* (*v.* 14), but what was that to a Sidonian? Or if she had a veneration for the name *Jehovah,* and valued the God of Israel as the true God, yet what assurance had she that this stranger was his prophet or had any warrant to speak in his name? It was easy for a hungry vagrant to impose upon her. But she gets over all these objections, and obeys the precept in dependence upon the promise: She *went and did according to the saying of Elijah, v.* 15. *O woman! great was thy faith;* one has not found the like, *no, not in Israel:* all things considered, it exceeded that of the widow who, when she had but two mites, cast them into the treasury. She took the prophet's word, that she should not lose by it, but it should be repaid with interest. Those that can venture upon the promise of God will make no difficulty of exposing and emptying themselves in his service, by giving him his dues out of a little and giving him his part first. Those that deal with God must deal upon trust; seek first his kingdom, and then other things shall be added. By the law, the first-fruits were God's, the tithe was taken out first, and the heave-offering of their dough was first offered, Num. xv. 20, 21. But surely the increase of this widow's faith, to such a degree as to enable her thus to deny herself and to depend upon the divine promise, was as great a miracle in the kingdom of grace as the increase of her oil was in the kingdom of providence. Happy are those who can thus, against hope, believe and obey in hope.

2. The care God took of her guest: *The barrel of meal wasted not, nor did the cruse of oil fail,* but still as they took from them more was added to them by the divine power, *v.* 16. Never did corn or olive so increase in the growing (says bishop Hall) as these did in the using; but the *multiplying of the seed sown* (2 Cor. ix. 10) in the common course of providence is an instance of the power and goodness of God not to be overlooked because common. The meal and the oil multiplied, not in the hoarding, but in the spending; for *there is that scattereth and yet increaseth.* When God blesses a little, it will go a great way, even beyond expectation; as, on the contrary, though there be abundance, if he blow upon it, it comes to little, Hag. i. 9; ii. 16. (1.) This was a maintenance for the prophet. Still miracles shall be his daily bread. Hitherto he had been fed with bread and flesh, now he was fed with bread and oil, which they used as we do butter. Manna was both, for the *taste of it was as the taste of fresh oil,* Num. xi. 8. This Elijah was thankful for, though he had been used to flesh twice a day and now had none at all. Those that cannot live without flesh, once a day at least, because they have been used to it, could not have boarded contentedly with Elijah, no, not to live upon a miracle. (2.) It was a maintenance for *the poor widow and her son,* and a recompence to her for entertaining the prophet. There is nothing lost by being kind to God's people and ministers; she that received a prophet had a prophet's reward; she gave him house-room, and he repaid her with food for her household. Christ has promised to those who open their doors to him that he will come in to them, and *sup with them,* and *they with him,* Rev. iii. 20. Like Elijah here, he brings to those who bid him welcome, not only his own entertainment, but theirs too. See how the reward answered the service. She generously made one cake for the pro-

phet, and was repaid with many for herself and her son. When Abraham offers his only son to God he is told he shall be the father of multitudes. What is laid out in piety or charity is let out to the best interest, upon the best securities. One poor meal's meat this poor widow gave the prophet, and, in recompence of it, *she and her son did eat many days* (*v.* 15), above two years, in a time of general scarcity; and to have their food from God's special favour, and to eat it in such good company as Elijah's, made it more than doubly sweet. It is promised to those that trust in God that they *shall not be ashamed in the evil time, but in the days of famine they shall be satisfied*, Ps. xxxvii. 19.

17 And it came to pass after these things, *that* the son of the woman, the mistress of the house, fell sick; and his sickness was so sore, that there was no breath left in him. 18 And she said unto Elijah, What have I to do with thee, O thou man of God? art thou come unto me to call my sin to remembrance, and to slay my son? 19 And he said unto her, Give me thy son. And he took him out of her bosom, and carried him up into a loft, where he abode, and laid him upon his own bed. 20 And he cried unto the LORD, and said, O LORD my God, hast thou also brought evil upon the widow with whom I sojourn, by slaying her son? 21 And he stretched himself upon the child three times, and cried unto the LORD, and said, O LORD my God, I pray thee, let this child's soul come into him again. 22 And the LORD heard the voice of Elijah; and the soul of the child came into him again, and he revived. 23 And Elijah took the child, and brought him down out of the chamber into the house, and delivered him unto his mother: and Elijah said, See, thy son liveth. 24 And the woman said to Elijah, Now by this I know that thou *art* a man of God, *and* that the word of the LORD in thy mouth *is* truth.

We have here a further recompence made to the widow for her kindness to the prophet; as if it were a small thing to be kept alive, her son, when dead, is restored to life, and so restored to her. Observe,

I. The sickness and death of the child. For aught that appears he was her only son, the comfort of her widowed estate. He was fed miraculously, and yet that did not secure him from sickness and death. *Your fathers did eat manna, and are dead,* but *there is bread of which a man may eat and not die,* which was given for the life of the world, John vi. 49, 50. The affliction was to this widow as a thorn in the flesh, lest she should be lifted up above measure with the favours that were done her and the honours that were put upon her. 1. She was nurse to a great prophet, was employed to sustain him, and had strong reason to think the Lord would do her good; yet now she loses her child. Note, We must not think it strange if we meet with very sharp afflictions, even when we are in the way of duty, and of eminent service to God. 2. She was herself nursed by miracle, and kept a good house without charge or care, by a distinguishing blessing from heaven; and in the midst of all this satisfaction she was thus afflicted. Note, When we have the clearest manifestations of God's favour and good-will towards us, even then we must prepare for the rebukes of Providence. Our mountain never stands so strong but it may be moved, and therefore, in this world, we must always rejoice with trembling.

II. Her pathetic complaint to the prophet of this affliction. It should seem, the child died suddenly, else she would have applied to Elijah, while he was sick, for the cure of him; but being dead, dead in her bosom, she expostulates with the prophet upon it, rather to give vent to her sorrow than in any hope of relief, *v.* 18. 1. She expresses herself passionately: *What have I to do with thee, O thou man of God?* How calmly had she spoken of her own and her child's death when she expected to die for want (*v.* 12)—*that we may eat, and die!* Yet now that her child dies, and not so miserably as by famine, she is extremely disturbed at it. We may speak lightly of an affliction at a distance, but when it *toucheth us we are troubled*, Job iv. 5. Then she spoke deliberately, now in haste; the death of her child was now a surprise to her, and it is hard to keep our spirits composed when troubles come upon us suddenly and unexpectedly, and in the midst of our peace and prosperity. She calls him *a man of God*, and yet quarrels with him as if he had occasioned the death of her child, and is ready to wish she had never seen him, forgetting past mercies and miracles: "What have I done against thee?" (so some understand it), "Wherein have I offended thee, or been wanting in my duty? *Show me wherefore thou contendest with me.*" 2. Yet she expresses herself penitently: "*Hast thou come to call my sin to* thy *remembrance*, as the cause of the affliction, and so to call it to *my* remembrance, as the effect of the affliction?" Perhaps she knew of Elijah's intercession against Israel, and, being conscious to herself of sin, perhaps her former worshipping of Baal the god of the Sidonians, she apprehends he had made intercession against her. Note, (1.) When God removes our comforts from us he remembers our sins against us, perhaps the iniquities of our youth, though long since past, Job xiii. 26. Our sins are the death of our children. (2.) When God thus remembers our sins against us he designs thereby to make us remember them against ourselves and repent of them.

III. The prophet's address to God upon this occasion. He gave no answer to her expostulation, but brought it to God, and laid the case before him, not knowing what to say to it himself. He took the dead child from the mother's bosom to his own bed, *v.* 19. Probably he had taken a particular kindness to the child, and found the affliction his own more than by sympathy. He retired to his chamber, and, 1. He humbly reasons with God concerning the death of the child, *v.* 20. He sees death striking by commission from God: *Thou hast brought this evil;* for is there any evil of this kind in the city, in the family, and the Lord has not done it? He pleads the greatness of the affliction to the poor mother: "It is *evil upon the widow;* thou art the widow's God, and dost not usually bring evil upon widows; it is affliction added to the afflicted." He pleads his own concern: "It is the widow *with whom I sojourn;* wilt thou, that art my God, bring evil upon one of the best of my benefactors? I shall be reflected upon, and others will be afraid of entertaining me, if I bring death into the house where I come." 2. He earnestly begs of God to restore the child to life again, *v.* 21. We do not read before this of any that were raised to life; yet Elijah, by a divine impulse, prays for the resurrection of this child, which yet will not warrant us to do the like. David expected not, by fasting and prayer, to bring his child back to life (2 Sam. xii. 23), but Elijah had a power to work miracles, which David had not. He *stretched himself upon the child,* to affect himself with the case and to show how much he was affected with it and how desirous he was of the restoration of the child—he would if he could put life into him by his own breath and warmth; also to give a sign of what God would do by his power, and what he does by his grace, in raising dead souls to a spiritual life; the Holy Ghost comes upon them, overshadows them, and puts life into them. He is very particular in his prayer: *I pray thee let this child's soul come into him again,* which plainly supposes the existence of the soul in a state of separation from the body, and consequently its immortality, which Grotius thinks God designed by this miracle to give intimation and evidence of, for the encouragement of his suffering people.

IV. The resurrection of the child, and the great satisfaction it gave to the mother: the child revived, *v.* 22. See the power of prayer and the power of him that hears prayer, who *kills and makes alive.* Elijah brought him to his mother, who, we may suppose, could scarcely believe her own eyes, and therefore Elijah assures her it is her own: "It is *thy son that liveth;* see it is thy own, and not another," *v.* 23. The good woman hereupon cries out, *Now I know that thou art a man of God;* though she knew it before, by the increase of her meal, yet the death of her child she took so unkindly that she began to question it (a good man surely would not serve her so); but now she was abundantly satisfied that he had both the power and goodness of a man of God, and will never doubt of it again, but give up herself to the direction of his word and the worship of the God of Israel. Thus the death of the child (like that of Lazarus, John xi. 4) was for the glory of God and the honour of his prophet.

CHAP. XVIII.

We left the prophet Elijah wrapt up in obscurity. It does not appear that either the increase of the provision or the raising of the child had caused him to be taken notice of at Zarephath, for then Ahab would have discovered him; he would rather do good than be known to do it. But in this chapter his appearance was as public as before his retirement was close; the days appointed for his concealment (which was part of the judgment upon Israel) being finished, he is now commanded to show himself to Ahab, and to expect rain upon the earth, ver. 1. Pursuant to this order we have here, I. His interview with Obadiah, one of Ahab's servants, by whom he sends notice to Ahab of his coming, ver. 2—16. II. His interview with Ahab himself, ver. 17—20. III. His interview with all Israel upon Mount Carmel, in order to a public trial of titles between the Lord and Baal; a most distinguished solemnity it was, in which, 1. Baal and his prophets were confounded. 2. God and Elijah were honoured, ver. 21—39. IV. The execution he did upon the prophets of Baal, ver. 40 V. The return of the mercy of rain, at the word of Elijah, ver. 41—46. It is a chapter in which are many things very observable.

AND it came to pass *after* many days, that the word of the LORD came to Elijah in the third year, saying, Go, show thyself unto Ahab; and I will send rain upon the earth. 2 And Elijah went to show himself unto Ahab. And *there was* a sore famine in Samaria. 3 And Ahab called Obadiah, which *was* the governor of *his* house. (Now Obadiah feared the LORD greatly: 4 For it was *so,* when Jezebel cut off the prophets of the LORD, that Obadiah took a hundred prophets, and hid them by fifty in a cave, and fed them with bread and water.) 5 And Ahab said unto Obadiah, Go into the land, unto all fountains of water, and unto all brooks: peradventure we may find grass to save the horses and mules alive, that we lose not all the beasts. 6 So they divided the land between them to pass throughout it: Ahab went one way by himself, and Obadiah went another way by himself. 7 And as Obadiah was in the way, behold, Elijah met him: and he knew him, and fell on his face, and said, *Art* thou that my lord Elijah? 8

And he answered him, I *am:* go, tell thy lord, Behold, Elijah *is here.* 9 And he said, What have I sinned, that thou wouldest deliver thy servant into the hand of Ahab, to slay me? 10 *As* the LORD thy God liveth, there is no nation or kingdom, whither my lord hath not sent to seek thee: and when they said, *He is* not *there;* he took an oath of the kingdom and nation, that they found thee not. 11 And now thou sayest, Go, tell thy lord, Behold, Elijah *is here.* 12 And it shall come to pass, *as soon as* I am gone from thee, that the Spirit of the LORD shall carry thee whither I know not; and *so* when I come and tell Ahab, and he cannot find thee, he shall slay me: but I thy servant fear the LORD from my youth. 13 Was it not told my lord what I did when Jezebel slew the prophets of the LORD, how I hid a hundred men of the LORD's prophets by fifty in a cave, and fed them with bread and water? 14 And now thou sayest, Go, tell thy lord, Behold, Elijah *is here:* and he shall slay me. 15 And Elijah said, *As* the LORD of hosts liveth, before whom I stand, I will surely show myself unto him to day. 16 So Obadiah went to meet Ahab, and told him: and Ahab went to meet Elijah.

In these verses we find,

I. The sad state of Israel at this time, upon two accounts:—

1. *Jezebel cut off the prophets of the Lord* (*v.* 4), *slew them, v.* 13. Being an idolater, she was a persecutor, and made Ahab one. Even in those bad times, when the calves were worshipped and the temple at Jerusalem deserted, yet there were some good people that feared God and served him, and some good prophets that instructed them in the knowledge of him and assisted them in their devotions. The priests and the Levites had all gone to Judah and Jerusalem (2 Chron. xi. 13, 14), but, instead of them, God raised up these prophets, who read and expounded the law in private meetings, or in the families that retained their integrity, for we read not of any synagogues at this time; they had not the spirit of prophecy as Elijah, nor did they offer sacrifice, or burn incense, but taught people to live well, and keep close to the God of Israel. These Jezebel aimed to extirpate, and put many of them to death, which was as much a public calamity as a public iniquity, and threatened the utter ruin of religion's poor remains in Israel. Those few that escaped the sword were forced to abscond, and hide themselves in caves, where they were buried alive and cut off, though not from life, yet from usefulness, which is the end and comfort of life; and, when the prophets were persecuted and driven into corners, no doubt their friends, those few good people that were in the land, were treated in like manner. Yet, bad as things were,

(1.) There was one very good man, who was a great man at court, *Obadiah,* who answered his name—*a servant of the Lord,* one who feared God and was faithful to him, and yet was steward of the household to Ahab. Observe his character: He *feared the Lord greatly* (*v.* 3), was not only a good man, but zealously and eminently good; his great place put a lustre upon his goodness, and gave him great opportunities of doing good; and he *feared the Lord from his youth* (*v.* 12), he began betimes to be religious and had continued long. Note, Early piety, it is to be hoped, will be eminent piety; those that are good betimes are likely to be very good; he that feared God from his youth came to fear him greatly. He that will thrive must rise betimes. But it is strange to find such an eminently good man governor of Ahab's house, an office of great honour, power, and trust. [1.] It was strange that so wicked a man as Ahab would prefer him to it and continue him in it; certainly it was because he was a man of celebrated honesty, industry, and ingenuity, and one in whom he could repose a confidence, whose eyes he could trust as much as his own, as appears here, *v.* 5. Joseph and Daniel were preferred because there were none so fit as they for the places they were preferred to. Note, Those who profess religion should study to recommend themselves to the esteem even of those that are without by their integrity, fidelity, and application to business. [2.] It was strange that so good a man as Obadiah would accept of preferment in a court so addicted to idolatry and all manner of wickedness. We may be sure it was not made necessary to qualify him for preferment that he should be of the king's religion, that he should conform to the *statutes of Omri, or the law of the house of Ahab.* Obadiah would not have accepted the place if he could not have had it without bowing the knee to Baal, nor was Ahab so impolitic as to exclude those from offices that were fit to serve him, merely because they would not join with him in his devotions. That man that is true to his God will be faithful to his prince. Obadiah therefore could with a good conscience enjoy the place, and therefore would not decline it, nor give it up, though he foresaw he could not do the good he desired to do in it. Those that fear God need not go out of the world, bad as it is. [3.] It was strange that either he did not reform

Ahab or Ahab corrupt him; but it seems they were both fixed; he that was filthy would be filthy still, and he that was holy would be holy still. Those fear God greatly that keep up the fear of him in bad times and places; thus Obadiah did. God has his remnant among all sorts, high and low; there were saints in Nero's household, and in Ahab's.

(2.) This great good man used his power for the protection of God's prophets. He hid 100 of them in two caves, when the persecution was hot, and *fed them with bread and water, v.* 4. He did not think it enough to fear God himself, but, having wealth and power wherewith to do it, he thought himself obliged to assist and countenance others that feared God; nor did he think his being kind to them would excuse him from being good himself, but he did both, he both feared God greatly himself and patronised those that feared him likewise. See how wonderfully God raises up friends for his ministers and people, for their shelter in difficult times, even where one would least expect them. Bread and water were now scarce commodities, yet Obadiah will find a competence of both for God's prophets, to keep them alive for service hereafter, though now they were laid aside.

2. When Jezebel cut off God's prophets God cut off the necessary provisions by the extremity of the drought. Perhaps Jezebel persecuted God's prophets under pretence that they were the cause of the judgment, because Elijah had foretold it. *Christianos ad leones—Away with Christians to the lions.* But God made them know the contrary, for the famine continued till Baal's prophets were sacrificed, and so great a scarcity of water there was that the king himself and Obadiah went in person throughout the land to seek for grass for the cattle, *v.* 5, 6. Providence ordered it so, that Ahab might, with his own eyes, see how bad the consequences of this judgment were, that so he might be the better inclined to hearken to Elijah, who would direct him into the only way to put an end to it. Ahab's care was not to *lose all the beasts*, many being already lost; but he took no care about his soul, not to lose that; he took a deal of pains to seek grass, but none to seek the favour of God, fencing against the effect, but not enquiring how to remove the cause. The land of Judah lay close to the land of Israel, yet we find no complaint there of the want of rain; for *Judah yet ruled with God, and was faithful with the saints* and prophets (Hos. xi. 12), by which distinction Israel might plainly have seen the ground of God's controversy, when God *caused it to rain upon one city and not upon another* (Amos iv. 7, 8); but they blinded their eyes, and hardened their hearts, and would not see.

II. The steps taken towards redressing the grievance, by Elijah's appearing again upon the stage, to act as a *Tishbite,* a *converter* or *reformer* of Israel, for so (some think) that title of his signifies. Turn them again to the Lord God of hosts, from whom they have revolted, and all will be well quickly; this must be Elijah's doing. See Luke i. 16, 17.

1. Ahab had made diligent search for him (*v.* 10), had offered rewards to any one that would discover him, sent spies *into every tribe and lordship* of his own dominions, as some understand it, or, as others, into all the neighbouring nations and kingdoms that were in alliance with him; and, when they denied that they knew any thing of him, he would not believe them unless they swore it, and, as should seem, promised likewise upon oath that, if ever they found him among them, they would discover him and deliver him up. It should seem, he made this diligent search for him, not so much that he might punish him for what he had done in denouncing the judgment as that he might oblige him to undo it again, by recalling the sentence, because he had said it should be *according to his word*, having such an opinion of him as men foolishly conceive of witches (that, if they can but compel them to bless that which they have bewitched, it will be well again), or such as the king of Moab had of Balaam. I incline to this because we find, when they came together, Elijah, knowing what Ahab wanted him for, appointed him to meet him on Mount Carmel, and Ahab complied with the appointment, though Elijah took such a way to revoke the sentence and bless the land as perhaps he little thought of.

2. God, at length, ordered Elijah to present himself to Ahab, because the time had now come when he would *send rain upon the earth* (*v.* 1), or rather *upon the land.* Above two years he had lain hid with the widow at Zarephath, after he had been concealed one year by the brook Cherith; so that the third year of his sojourning there, here spoken of (*v.* 1), was the fourth of the famine, which lasted in all three years and six months, as we find, Luke iv. 25; James v. 17. Such was Elijah's zeal, no doubt, against the idolatry of Baal, and such his compassion to his people, that he thought it long to be thus confined to a corner; yet he appeared not till God bade him: "*Go and show thyself to Ahab,* for now thy hour has come, even *the time to favour Israel.*" Note, It bodes well to any people when God calls his ministers out of their corners, and bids them show themselves—asign that he will *give rain on the earth;* at least we may the better be content with the bread of affliction while *our eyes see our teachers,* Isa. xxx. 20, 21.

3. Elijah first surrendered, or rather discovered, himself to Obadiah. He knew, by the Spirit, where to meet him, and we are here told what passed between them.

(1.) Obadiah saluted him with great respect, fell on his face, and humbly asked, *Art thou that my lord Elijah? v.* 7. As he had shown the tenderness of a father to the sons of the prophets, so he showed the reverence of a son to this father of the prophets; and by this made it appear that he did indeed *fear God greatly*, that he did honour to one that was his extraordinary ambassador and had a great interest in heaven.

(2.) Elijah, in answer to him, [1.] Transfers the title of honour he gave him to Ahab: "Call him thy lord, not me;" that is a fitter title for a prince than for a prophet, *who seeks not honour from men.* Prophets should be called *seers*, and *shepherds*, and *watchmen*, and *ministers*, rather than *lords*, as those that mind duty more than dominion. [2.] He bids Obadiah go and tell the king that he is there to speak with him: *Tell thy lord, Behold, Elijah* is forth-coming, *v.* 8. He would have the king know before, that it might not be a surprise to him and that he might be sure it was the prophet's own act to present himself to him.

(3.) Obadiah begs to be excused from carrying this message to Ahab, for it might prove as much as his life was worth. [1.] He tells Elijah what great search Ahab had made for him and how much his heart was upon it to find him out, *v.* 10. [2.] He takes it for granted that Elijah would again withdraw (*v.* 12): *The Spirit of the Lord shall carry thee* (as it is likely he had done sometimes, when Ahab thought he had been sure of him) *whither I know not.* See 2 Kings ii. 16. He thought Elijah was not in good earnest when he bade him tell Ahab where he was, but intended only to expose the impotency of his malice; for he knew Ahab was not worthy to receive any kindness from the prophet and it was not fit that the prophet should receive any mischief from him. [3.] He is sure Ahab would be so enraged at the disappointment that he would put him to death for making a fool of him, or for not laying hands on Elijah himself, when he had him in his reach, *v.* 12. Tyrants and persecutors, in their passion, are often unreasonably outrageous, even towards their friends and confidants. [4.] He pleads that he did not deserve to be thus exposed, and put in peril of his life: *What have I said amiss? v.* 9. Nay (*v.* 13), *Was it not told my lord how I hid the prophets?* He mentions this, not in pride or ostentation, but to convince Elijah that though he was Ahab's servant he was not in his interest, and therefore deserved not to be bantered as one of the tools of his persecution. He that had protected so many prophets, he hoped, should not have his own life hazarded by so great a prophet.

(4.) Elijah satisfied him that he might with safety deliver this message to Ahab, by assuring him, with an oath, that he would, this very day, present himself to Ahab, *v.* 15. Let but Obadiah know that he spoke seriously and really intended it, and he will make no scruple to carry the message to Ahab. Elijah swears by *the Lord of hosts,* who has all power in his hands, and is therefore able to protect his servants against all the powers of hell and earth.

(5.) Notice is hereby soon brought to Ahab that Elijah had sent him a challenge to meet him immediately at such a place, and Ahab accepts the challenge: *He went to meet Elijah, v.* 16. We may suppose it was a great surprise to Ahab to hear that Elijah, whom he had so long sought and not found, was now found without seeking. He went in quest of grass, and found him from whose word, at God's mouth, he must expect rain. Yet his guilty conscience gave him little reason to hope for it, but, rather, to fear some other more dreadful judgment. Had he, by his spies, surprised Elijah, he would have triumphed over him; but, now that he was thus surprised by him, we may suppose he even trembled to look him in the face, hated him, and yet feared him, as Herod did John.

17 And it came to pass, when Ahab saw Elijah, that Ahab said unto him, *Art* thou he that troubleth Israel? 18 And he answered, I have not troubled Israel; but thou, and thy father's house, in that ye have forsaken the commandments of the LORD, and thou hast followed Baalim. 19 Now therefore send, *and* gather to me all Israel unto mount Carmel, and the prophets of Baal four hundred and fifty, and the prophets of the groves four hundred, which eat at Jezebel's table. 20 So Ahab sent unto all the children of Israel, and gathered the prophets together unto mount Carmel.

We have here the meeting between Ahab and Elijah, as bad a king as ever the world was plagued with and as good a prophet as ever the church was blessed with. 1. Ahab, like himself, basely accused Elijah. He durst not strike him, remembering that Jeroboam's hand withered when it was stretched out against a prophet, but gave him bad language, which was no less an affront to him that sent him. It was a very coarse compliment with which he accosted him at the first word: *Art thou he that troubleth Israel? v.* 17. How unlike was this to that with which his servant Obadiah saluted him (*v.* 7): *Art thou that my lord Elijah?* Obadiah feared God greatly; Ahab had sold himself to work wickedness; and both discovered their character by the manner of their address to the prophet. One may guess how people stand affected to God by observing how they stand affected to his people and ministers. Elijah now came to bring blessings to Israel, tidings of the return of the rain; yet he was thus affronted. Had it been true that he was the *troubler of Israel,* Ahab, as king, would have been bound to animadvert upon him. There are those who trouble Israel by their wickedness, whom the conservators of the public peace are concerned to enquire after. But it was utterly false concerning Elijah; so far was he from being an enemy to Israel's welfare that he was the stay of it, *the chariots and horsemen of Israel.* Note, It has been the lot of the best and most useful men to be called and counted *the troublers of the land,* and to be run down as public grievances. Even Christ and his apostles were thus misrepresented, Acts xvii. 6. 2. Elijah, like himself, boldly returned the charge upon the king, and proved it upon him, that he was *the troubler of Israel, v.* 18. Elijah is not the Achan: "*I have not troubled Israel,* have neither done them any wrong nor designed them any hurt." Those that procure God's judgments do the mischief, not he that merely foretels them and gives warning of them, that the nation may repent and prevent them. *I would have healed Israel, but they would not be healed.* Ahab is the Achan, the troubler, who follows Baalim, those accursed things. Nothing creates more trouble to a land than the impiety and profaneness of princes and their families. 3. As one having authority immediately from the King of kings, he ordered a convention of the states to be forthwith summoned to meet at Mount Carmel, where there had been an altar built to God, *v.* 30. Probably on that mountain they had an eminent high place, where formerly the pure worship of God had been kept up as well as it could be any where but at Jerusalem. Thither all Israel must come, to give Elijah the meeting; and the prophets of Baal who were dispersed all the country over, with those of the groves who were Jezebel's domestic chaplains, must there make their personal appearance. 4. Ahab issued out writs accordingly, for the convening of this great assembly (*v.* 20), either because he feared Elijah and durst not oppose him (Saul stood in awe of Samuel more than of God), or because he hoped Elijah would bless the land, and speak the word that they might have rain, and upon those terms they would be all at his beck. Those that slighted and hated his counsels would gladly be beholden to him for his prayers. Now God *made those who said they were Jews and were not, but were of the synagogue of Satan, to come, and,* in effect, *to worship at his feet, and to know that God had loved him,* Rev. iii. 9.

21 And Elijah came unto all the people, and said, How long halt ye between two opinions? if the LORD *be* God, follow him: but if Baal, *then* follow him. And the people answered him not a word. 22 Then said Elijah unto the people, I, *even* I only, remain a prophet of the LORD; but Baal's prophets *are* four hundred and fifty men. 23 Let them therefore give us two bullocks; and let them choose one bullock for themselves, and cut it in pieces, and lay *it* on wood, and put no fire *under:* and I will dress the other bullock, and lay *it* on wood, and put no fire *under:* 24 And call ye on the name of your gods, and I will call on the name of the LORD: and the God that answereth by fire, let him be God. And all the people answered and said, It is well spoken. 25 And Elijah said unto the prophets of Baal, Choose you one bullock for yourselves, and dress *it* first; for ye *are* many; and call on the name of your gods, but put no fire *under.* 26 And they took the bullock which was given them, and they dressed *it,* and called on the name of Baal from morning even until noon, saying, O Baal, hear us But *there was* no voice, nor any that answered. And they leaped upon the altar which was made. 27 And it came to pass at noon, that Elijah mocked them, and said, Cry aloud: for he *is* a god; either he is talking, or he is pursuing, or he is in a journey, *or* peradventure he sleepeth, and must be awaked. 28 And they cried aloud, and cut themselves after their manner with knives and lancets, till the blood gushed out upon them. 29 And it came to pass, when midday was past, and they prophesied until the *time* of the offering of the *evening* sacrifice, that *there was* neither voice, nor any to answer, nor any that regarded. 30 And Elijah said unto all the people, Come near unto me. And all the people came near unto him. And he repaired the altar of the LORD *that was* broken down. 31 And Elijah took twelve stones, according to the number of the tribes of the sons of Jacob, unto whom the word of the LORD came, saying, Israel shall be thy name: 32 And with the stones he built an altar in the name of the LORD: and he made a trench about the altar, as great as would contain two measures of seed. 33 And he put the wood in order,

and cut the bullock in pieces, and laid *him* on the wood, and said, Fill four barrels with water, and pour *it* on the burnt sacrifice, and on the wood. 34 And he said, Do *it* the second time. And they did *it* the second time. And he said, Do *it* the third time. And they did *it* the third time. 35 And the water ran round about the altar; and he filled the trench also with water. 36 And it came to pass at *the time of* the offering of the *evening* sacrifice, that Elijah the prophet came near, and said, LORD God of Abraham, Isaac, and of Israel, let it be known this day that thou *art* God in Israel, and *that* I *am* thy servant, and *that* I have done all these things at thy word. 37 Hear me, O LORD, hear me, that this people may know that thou *art* the LORD God, and *that* thou hast turned their heart back again. 38 Then the fire of the LORD fell, and consumed the burnt sacrifice, and the wood, and the stones, and the dust, and licked up the water that *was* in the trench. 39 And when all the people saw *it*, they fell on their faces: and they said, The LORD, he *is* the God; the LORD, he *is* the God. 40 And Elijah said unto them, Take the prophets of Baal; let not one of them escape. And they took them: and Elijah brought them down to the brook Kishon, and slew them there.

Ahab and the people expected that Elijah would, in this solemn assembly, *bless the land*, and pray for rain; but he had other work to do first. The people must be brought to repent and reform, and then they may look for the removal of the judgment, but not till then. This is the right method. God will first *prepare our heart*, and then *cause his ear to hear*, will first *turn us to him*, and then *turn to us*, Ps. x. 17; lxxx. 3. Deserters must not look for God's favour till they return to their allegiance. Elijah might have looked for rain seventy times seven times, and not have seen it, if he had not thus begun his work at the right end. Three years and a half's famine would not bring them back to God. Elijah would endeavour to convince their judgments, and no doubt it was by special warrant and direction from heaven that he put the controversy between God and Baal upon a public trial. It was great condescension in God that he would suffer so plain a case tobe disputed, and would permit Baal to be a competitor with him; but thus God would have every mouth to be stopped and all flesh to become silent before him. God's cause is so incontestably just that it needs not fear to have the evidences of its equity searched into and weighed.

I. Elijah reproved the people for mixing the worship of God and the worship of Baal together. Not only some Israelites worshipped God and others Baal, but the same Israelites sometimes worshipped one and sometimes the other. This he calls (*v.* 21) *halting between two opinions*, or *thoughts*. They worshipped God to please the prophets, but worshipped Baal to please Jezebel and curry favour at court. They thought to trim the matter, and play on both sides, as the Samaritans, 2 Kings xvii. 33. Now Elijah shows them the absurdity of this. He does not insist upon their relation to Jehovah—"Is he not yours, and the God of your fathers, while Baal is the god of the Sidonians? And *will a nation change their god?*" Jer. ii. 11. No, he waives the prescription, and enters upon the merits of the cause:—"There can be but one God, but one infinite and but one supreme: there needs but one God, one omnipotent, one all-sufficient. What occasion for addition to that which is perfect? Now if, upon trial, it appears that Baal is that one infinite omnipotent Being, that one supreme Lord and all-sufficient benefactor, you ought to renounce Jehovah and cleave to Baal only: but, if Jehovah be that one God, Baal is a cheat, and you must have no more to do with him." Note, 1. It is a very bad thing to *halt between God and Baal*. "In reconcilable differences (says bishop Hall) nothing more safe than indifferency both of practice and opinion; but, in cases of such necessary hostility as betwixt God and Baal, *he that is not with God is against him*." Compare Mark ix. 38, 39, with Matt. xii. 30. The service of God and the service of sin, the dominion of Christ and the dominion of our lusts, these are the two thoughts which it is dangerous halting between. Those halt between them that are unresolved under their convictions, unstable and unsteady in their purposes, promise fair, but do not perform, begin well, but do not hold on, that are inconsistent with themselves, or indifferent and lukewarm in that which is good. *Their heart is divided* (Hos. x. 2), whereas God will have all or none. 2. We are fairly put to our choice *whom we will serve*, Josh. xxiv. 15. If we can find one that has more right to us, or will be a better master to us, than God, we may take him at our peril. God demands no more from us than he can make out a title to. To this fair proposal of the case, which Elijah here makes, the people knew not what to say: *They answered him not a word.* They could say nothing to justify themselves, and they would say nothing to condemn themselves, but, as people confounded, let him say what he would.

II. He proposed to bring the matter to a fair trial; and it was so much the fairer because Baal had all the external advantages on his side. The king and court were all for Baal; so was the body of the people. The managers of Baal's cause were 450 men, fat and well fed (*v.* 22), besides 400 more, their supporters or seconds, *v.* 19. The manager of God's cause was but one man, lately a poor exile, hardly kept from starving; so that God's cause has nothing to support it but its own right. However, it is put to this experiment, "Let each side prepare a sacrifice, and pray to its God, and *the God that answereth by fire, let him be God;* if neither shall thus answer, let the people turn Atheists; if both, let them continue to *halt between two.*" Elijah, doubtless, had a special commission from God to put it to this test, otherwise he would have tempted God and affronted religion; but the case was extraordinary, and the judgment upon it would be of use, not only then, but in all ages. It is an instance of the courage of Elijah that he durst stand alone in the cause of God against such powers and numbers; and the issue encourages all God's witnesses and advocates never to fear the face of man. Elijah does not say, "The God that answers by *water*" (though that was the thing the country needed), but "that *answers by fire, let him be God;*" because the atonement was to be made by sacrifice, before the judgment could be removed in mercy. The God therefore that has power to pardon sin, and to signify it by consuming the sin-offering, must needs be the God that can relieve us against the calamity. He that can give fire can give rain; see Matt. ix. 2, 6.

III. The people join issue with him: *It is well spoken, v.* 24. They allow the proposal to be fair and unexceptionable. "God has often answered by fire; if Baal cannot do so, let him be cast out for a usurper." They were very desirous to see the experiment tried, and seemed resolved to abide by the issue, whatever it should be. Those that were firm for God doubted not but it would end to his honour; those that were indifferent were willing to be determined; and Ahab and the prophets of Baal durst not oppose for fear of the people, and hoped that either *they* could obtain fire from heaven (though they never had yet), and the rather because, as some think, they worshipped the sun in Baal, or that *Elijah* could not, because not at the temple, where God was wont thus to manifest his glory. If, in this trial, they could but bring it to a drawn battle, their other advantages would give them the victory. Let it go on therefore to a trial.

IV. The prophets of Baal try first, but in vain, with their god. They covet the precedency, not only for the honour of it, but that, if they can but in the least seem to gain their point, Elijah may not be admitted to make the trial. Elijah allows it to them (*v.* 25), gives them the lead for their greater confusion; only, knowing that the working of Satan is with lying wonders, he takes care to prevent a fraud: Be sure to *put no fire under.* Now in their experiment observe,

1. How importunate and noisy the prophets of Baal were in their applications to him. They got their sacrifices ready; and we may well imagine what a noise 450 men made, when they cried as one man, and with all their might, *O Baal! hear us, O Baal! answer us;* as it is in the margin: and this for some hours together, longer than Diana's worshippers made their cry, *Great is Diana of the Ephesians,* Acts xix. 34. How senseless, how brutish, were they in their addresses to Baal! (1.) Like fools, *they leaped upon the altar,* as if they would themselves become sacrifices with their bullock; or thus they expressed their great earnestness of mind. *They leaped up and down,* or danced about the altar (so some): they hoped, by their dancing, to please their deity, as Herodias did Herod, and so to obtain their request. (2.) Like madmen they *cut themselves in pieces with knives and lancets* (*v.* 28) for vexation that they were not answered, or in a sort of prophetic fury, hoping to obtain the favour of their god by offering to him their own blood, when they could not obtain it with the blood of their bullock. God never required his worshippers thus to honour him; but the service of the devil, though in some instances it pleases and pampers the body, yet in other things it is really cruel to it, as in envy and drunkenness. It seems, this was the manner of the worshippers of Baal. God expressly forbade his worshippers to cut themselves, Deut. xiv. 1. He insists upon it that we mortify our lusts and corruptions; but corporeal penances and severities, such as the Papists use, which have no tendency to that, are no pleasure to him. *Who has required these things at your hands?*

2. How sharp Elijah was upon them, *v.* 27. He stood by them, and patiently heard them for so many hours praying to an idol, yet with secret indignation and disdain; and at noon, when the sun was at the hottest, and they too expecting fire (then if ever), he upbraided them with their folly; and notwithstanding the gravity of his office, and the seriousness of the work he had before him, bantered them: "*Cry aloud, for he is a god,* a goodly god that cannot be made to hear without all this clamour. Surely you think he is talking or meditating (as the word is) or he is pursuing some deep thoughts, (in a brown study, as we say), thinking of somewhat else and not minding his own matter, when not your credit only, but all his honour lies at stake, and his interest in Israel. His new conquest will be lost if he do not look about him quickly." Note, The worship of idols is a most ridiculous thing, and it is but justice to represent it so and expose it to scorn. This will, by no means, justify those

who ridicule the worshippers of God in Christ because the worship is not performed just in their way. Baal's prophets were so far from being convinced and put to shame by the just reproach Elijah cast upon them that it made them the more violent and led them to act more ridiculously. *A deceived heart had turned them aside,* they *could not deliver their souls* by saying, *Is there not a lie in our right hand?*

3. How deaf Baal was to them. Elijah did not interrupt them, but let them go on till they were tired, and quite despaired of success, which was not *till the time of the evening sacrifice, v.* 29. During all that time some of them prayed, while others of them prophesied, sang hymns, perhaps to the praise of Baal, or rather encouraged those that were praying to proceed, telling them that Baal would answer them at last; but there was *no answer, nor any that regarded.* Idols could do neither good nor evil. The prince of the power of the air, if God had permitted him, could have caused *fire to come down from heaven* on this occasion, and gladly would have done it for the support of his Baal. We find that the beast which deceives the world does it. *He maketh fire come down from heaven in the sight of men and* so *deceiveth them,* Rev. xiii. 13, 14. But God would not suffer the devil to do it now, because the trial of his title was put on that issue by consent of parties.

V. Elijah soon obtains from his God an answer by fire. The Baalites are forced to give up their cause, and now it is Elijah's turn to produce his. Let us see if he speed better.

1. He fitted up an altar. He would not make use of theirs, which had been polluted with their prayers to Baal, but, finding the ruins of an altar there, which had formerly been used in the service of the Lord, he chose to repair that (*v.* 30), to intimate to them that he was not about to introduce any new religion, but to revive the faith and worship of their fathers' God, and reduce them to their first love, their first works. He could not bring them to the altar at Jerusalem unless he could unite the two kingdoms again (which, for correction to both, God designed should not now be done), therefore, by his prophetic anthority, he builds an altar on Mount Carmel, and so owns that which had formerly been built there. When we cannot carry a reformation so far as we would we must do what we can, and rather comply with some corruptions than not do our utmost towards the extirpation of Baal. He repaired this altar with *twelve stones, according to the number of the twelve tribes, v.* 31. Though ten of the tribes had revolted to Baal, he would look upon them as belonging to God still, by virtue of the ancient covenant with their fathers: and, though those ten were unhappily divided from the other two in civil interest, yet in the worship of the God of Israel they had communion with each other, and they twelve were one. Mention is made of God's calling their father Jacob by the name of *Israel, a prince with God* (*v.* 31), to shame his degenerate seed, who worshipped a god which they saw could not hear nor answer them, and to encourage the prophet who was now to wrestle with God as Jacob did; he also shall be a prince with God. Ps. xxiv. 6, *Thy face, O Jacob!* Hos. xii. 4. *There he spoke with us.*

2. Having built his altar *in the name of the Lord* (*v.* 32), by direction from him and with an eye to him, and not for his own honour, he prepared his sacrifice, *v.* 33. *Behold the bullock and the wood; but where is the fire?* Gen. xxii. 7, 8. *God will provide himself fire.* If we, in sincerity, offer our hearts to God, he will, by his grace, kindle a holy fire in them. Elijah was no priest, nor were his attendants Levites. Carmel had neither tabernacle nor temple; it was a great way distant from the ark of the testimony and the place God had chosen; this was not the altar that sanctified the gift; yet never was any sacrifice more acceptable to God than this. The particular Levitical institutions were so often dispensed with (as in the time of the Judges, Samuel's time, and now) that one would be tempted to think they were more designed for types to be fulfilled in the evangelical anti-types than for laws to be fulfilled in the strict observance of them. Their perishing thus in the using, as the apostle speaks of them (Col. ii. 22), was to intimate the utter abolition of them after a little while, Heb. viii. 13.

3. He ordered abundance of water to be poured upon his altar, which he had prepared a trench for the reception of (*v.* 32), and, some think, made the altar hollow. Twelve barrels of water (probably sea-water, for the sea was near, and so much fresh water in this time of drought was too precious for him to be so prodigal of it), thrice four, he poured upon his sacrifice, to prevent the suspicion of any fire under (for, if there had been any, this would have put it out), and to make the expected miracle the more illustrious.

4. He then solemnly addressed himself to God by prayer before his altar, humbly beseeching him to *turn to ashes his burnt-offering* (as the phrase is, Ps. xx. 3), and to testify his acceptance of it. His prayer was not long, for he used no vain repetitions, nor thought he should be *heard for his much speaking;* but it was very grave and composed, and showed his mind to be calm and sedate, and far from the heats and disorders that Baal's prophets were in, *v.* 36, 37. Though he was not at the *place* appointed, he chose the appointed *time of the offering of the evening sacrifice,* thereby to testify his communion with the altar at Jerusalem. Though he expected an answer by fire, yet he came near to the altar with boldness, and

feared not that fire. He addressed himself to God as *the God of Abraham, Isaac, and Israel,* acting faith on God's ancient covenant, and reminding people too (for prayer may prevail) of their relation both to God and to the patriarchs. Two things he pleads here:—(1.) The glory of God: "Lord, hear me, and answer me, *that it may be known* (for it is now by the most denied or forgotten) *that thou art God in Israel,* to whom alone the homage and devotion of Israel are due, and *that I am thy servant,* and do all that I have done, am doing, and shall do, as thy agent, *at thy word,* and not to gratify any humour or passion of my own. Thou employest me; Lord, make it appear that thou dost so;" see Num. xvi. 28, 29. Elijah sought not his own glory but in subserviency to God's, and for his own necessary vindication. (2.) The edification of the people: "*That they may know that thou art the Lord,* and may experience thy grace, *turning their heart,* by this miracle, as a means, *back again to thee,* in order to thy return in a way of mercy to them."

5. God immediately answered him by fire, *v.* 38. Elijah's God was neither talking nor pursuing, needed not to be either awakened or quickened; while he was yet speaking, *the fire of the Lord fell,* and not only, as at other times (Lev. ix. 24; 1 Chron. xxi. 26; 2 Chron. vii. 1) *consumed the sacrifice and the wood,* in token of God's acceptance of the offering, but *licked up all the water in the trench,* exhaling that, and drawing it up as a vapour, in order to the intended rain, which was to be the fruit of this sacrifice and prayer, more than the product of natural causes. Compare Ps. cxxxv. 7. *He causeth vapours to ascend, and maketh lightnings for the rain;* for this rain he did both. As for those who fall as victims to the fire of God's wrath, no water can shelter them from it, any more than briers or thorns, Isa. xxvii. 4, 5. But this was not all; to complete the miracle, the fire consumed the *stones of the altar, and* the very *dust,* to show that it was no ordinary fire, and perhaps to intimate that, though God accepted this occasional sacrifice from this altar, yet for the future they ought to demolish all the altars on their high places, and, for their constant sacrifices, make use of that at Jerusalem only. Moses's altar and Solomon's were consecrated by the fire from heaven; but this was destroyed, because no more to be used. We may well imagine what a terror the fire struck on guilty Ahab and all the worshippers of Baal, and how they fled from it as far and as fast as they could, saying, *Lest it consume us also,* alluding to Num. xvi. 34.

VI. What was the result of this fair trial. The prophets of Baal had failed in their proof, and could give no evidence at all to make out their pretensions on behalf of their god, but were perfectly non-suited. Elijah had, by the most convincing and undeniable evidence, proved his claims on behalf of the God of Israel. And now, 1. The people, as the jury, gave in their verdict upon the trial, and they are all agreed in it; the case is so plain that they need not go from the bar to consider of their verdict or consult about it: *They fell on their faces,* and all, as one man, said, "*Jehovah, he is the God,* and not Baal; we are convinced and satisfied of it: *Jehovah, he is the God*" (*v.* 39), whence, one would think, they should have inferred, "If he be the God, he shall be our God, and we will serve him only," as Josh. xxiv. 24. Some, we hope, had their hearts thus turned back, but the generality of them were convinced only, not converted, yielded to the truth of God, that he is the God, but consented not to his covenant, that he should be theirs. Blessed are those that have not seen what *they* saw and yet have believed and been wrought upon by it more than those that saw it. Let it for ever be looked upon as a point adjudged against all pretenders (for it was carried, upon a full hearing, against one of the most daring and threatening competitors that ever the God of Israel was affronted by) that *Jehovah, he is God,* God alone. 2. The prophets of Baal, as criminals, are seized, condemned, and executed, according to law, *v.* 40. If Jehovah be the true God, Baal is a false God, to whom these Israelites had revolted, and seduced others to the worship of him; and therefore, by the express law of God, they were to be put to death, Deut. xiii. 1—11. There needed no proof of the fact; all Israel were witnesses of it: and therefore Elijah (acting still by an extraordinary commission, which is not to be drawn into a precedent) orders them all to be slain immediately as the troublers of the land, and Ahab himself is so terrified, for the present, with the fire from heaven, that he dares not oppose it. These were the 450 prophets of Baal; the 400 prophets of the groves (who, some think, were Sidonians), though summoned (*v.* 19), yet, as it should seem, did not attend, and so escaped this execution, which fair escape perhaps Ahab and Jezebel thought themselves happy in; but it proved they were reserved to be the instruments of Ahab's destruction, some time after, by encouraging him to go up to Ramoth-Gilead *ch.* xxii. 6.

41 And Elijah said unto Ahab, Get thee up, eat and drink; for *there is* a sound of abundance of rain. 42 So Ahab went up to eat and to drink. And Elijah went up to the top of Carmel; and he cast himself down upon the earth, and put his face between his knees, 43 And said to his servant, Go up now, look toward the sea. And he went up, and looked,

and said, *There is* nothing. And he said, Go again seven times. 44 And it came to pass at the seventh time, that he said, Behold, there ariseth a little cloud out of the sea, like a man's hand. And he said, Go up, say unto Ahab, Prepare *thy chariot*, and get thee down, that the rain stop thee not. 45 And it came to pass in the mean while, that the heaven was black with clouds and wind, and there was a great rain. And Ahab rode, and went to Jezreel. 46 And the hand of the LORD was on Elijah; and he girded up his loins, and ran before Ahab to the entrance of Jezreel.

Israel being thus far reformed that they had acknowledged the Lord to be God, and had consented to the execution of Baal's prophets, that they might not seduce them any more, though this was far short of a thorough reformation, yet it was so far accepted that God thereupon opened the bottles of heaven, and poured out blessings upon his land, that very evening (as it should seem) on which they did this good work, which should have confirmed them in their reformation; see Hag. ii. 18, 19.

I. Elijah sent Ahab to *eat and drink,* for joy that God *had now accepted his works,* and that rain was coming; see Eccl. ix. 7. Ahab had continued fasting all day, either religiously, it being a day of prayer, or for want of leisure, it being a day of great expectation; but now let him *eat and drink,* for, though others perceive no sign of it, Elijah, by faith, hears *the sound of abundance of rain, v.* 41. God reveals his secrets to his servants the prophets; and yet, without a revelation, we may foresee that when man's judgments run down like a river God's mercy will. Rain is *the river of God,* Ps lxv. 9.

II. He himself retired to pray (for though God had promised rain, he must ask it, Zech. x. 1), and to give thanks for God's answer by fire, now hoping for an answer by water. What he said we are not told; but, 1. He withdrew to a strange place, to the *top of Carmel,* which was very high and very private. Hence we read of those that *hide themselves in the top of Carmel,* Amos ix. 3. There he would be alone. Those who are called to appear and act in public for God must yet find time to be private with him and keep up their converse with him in solitude. There he set himself, as it were, *upon his watch-tower,* like the prophet, Hab. ii. 1. 2. He put himself into a strange posture. He cast himself down on his knees upon the earth, in token of humility, reverence, and importunity, and *put his face between his knees* (that is, bowed his head so low that it touched his knees), thus abasing himself in the sense of his own meanness now that God had thus honoured him.

III. He ordered his servant to bring him notice as soon as he discerned a cloud arising out of the sea, the Mediterranean Sea, which he had a large prospect of from the top of Carmel. The sailors at this day call it *Cape Carmel.* Six times his servant goes to the point of the hill and sees nothing, brings no good news to his master; yet Elijah continues praying, will not be diverted so far as to go and see with his own eyes, but still sends his servant to see if he can discover any hopeful cloud, while he keeps his mind close and intent in prayer, and abides by it, as one that has taken up his father Jacob's resolution, *I will not let thee go except thou bless me.* Note, Though the answer of our fervent and believing supplications may not come quickly, yet we must continue instant in prayer, and not faint nor desist; for *at the end it shall speak and not lie.*

IV. A little cloud at length appeared, no bigger than a man's hand, which presently overspread the heavens and watered the earth, *v.* 44, 45. Great blessings often arise from small beginnings, and showers of plenty from a cloud of a span long. Let us therefore never *despise the day of small things,* but hope and wait for great things from it. This was not as a morning cloud, which passes away (though Israel's goodness was so), but one that produced a plentiful rain (Ps. lxviii. 9), and an earnest of more.

V. Elijah hereupon hastened Ahab home, and attended him himself. Ahab rode in his chariot, at ease and in state, *v.* 45. Elijah ran on foot before him. If Ahab had paid the respect to Elijah that he deserved he would have taken him into his chariot, as the eunuch did Philip, that he might honour him before the elders of Israel, and confer with him further about the reformation of the kingdom. But his corruptions got the better of his convictions, and he was glad to get clear of him, as Felix of Paul, when he dismissed him, and adjourned his conference with him to a more convenient season. But, since Ahab invites him not to ride with him, he will *run before him* (*v.* 46) as one of his footmen, that he may not seem to be lifted up with the great honour God had put upon him or to abate in his civil respect to his prince, though he reproved him faithfully. God's ministers should make it appear that, how great soever they look when they deliver God's messages, yet they are far from affecting worldly grandeur: let them leave that to the kings of the earth.

CHAP. XIX.

We left Elijah at the entrance of Jezreel, still appearing publicly, and all the people's eyes upon him. In this chapter we have him again absconding, and driven into obscurity, at a time when he could ill be spared; but we are to look upon it as a punishment to Israel for the insincerity and inconstancy of their reformation. When people will not learn it is just with God to remove their teachers into corners. Now observe, I. How he was driven into banishment by the malice of Jezebel his sworn enemy, ver. 1—3. II. How he was met, in his banishment, by

the favour of God, his covenant-friend. I. How God fed him, ver. 4—8. 2. How he conversed with him, and manifested himself to him (ver. 9, 11—13), heard his complaint (ver. 10—14), directed him what to do (ver. 15—17), and encouraged him, ver. 18. III. How his hands were strengthened, at his return out of banishment, by the joining of Elisha with him, ver. 19—21.

AND Ahab told Jezebel all that Elijah had done, and withal how he had slain all the prophets with the sword. 2 Then Jezebel sent a messenger unto Elijah, saying, So let the gods do *to me*, and more also, if I make not thy life as the life of one of them by to-morrow about this time. 3 And when he saw *that*, he arose, and went for his life, and came to Beer-sheba, which *belongeth* to Judah, and left his servant there. 4 But he himself went a day's journey into the wilderness, and came and sat down under a juniper tree: and he requested for himself that he might die; and said, It is enough; now, O LORD, take away my life; for I *am* not better than my fathers. 5 And as he lay and slept under a juniper tree, behold, then an angel touched him, and said unto him, Arise *and* eat. 6 And he looked, and, behold, *there was* a cake baken on the coals, and a cruse of water at his head. And he did eat and drink, and laid him down again. 7 And the angel of the LORD came again the second time, and touched him, and said, Arise *and* eat; because the journey *is* too great for thee. 8 And he arose, and did eat and drink, and went in the strength of that meat forty days and forty nights unto Horeb the mount of God.

One would have expected, after such a public and sensible manifestation of the glory of God and such a clear decision of the controversy depending between him and Baal, to the honour of Elijah, the confusion of Baal's prophets, and the universal satisfaction of the people—after they had seen both fire and water come from heaven at the prayer of Elijah, and both in mercy to them, the one as it signified the acceptance of their offering, the other as it *refreshed their inheritance, which was weary*—that now they would all, as one man, return to the worship of the God of Israel and take Elijah for their guide and oracle, that he would thenceforward be prime-minister of state, and his directions would be as laws both to king and kingdom. But it is quite otherwise; he is neglected whom God honoured; no respect is paid to him, no care taken of him, nor any use made of him, but, on the contrary, the land of Israel, to which he had been, and might have been, so great a blessing, is now made too hot for him. 1. Ahab incensed Jezebel against him. That queen-consort, it seems, was in effect queen-regent, as she was afterwards when she was queen-dowager, an imperious woman that managed king and kingdom and did what she would. Ahab's conscience would not let him persecute Elijah (some remains he had in him of the blood and spirit of an Israelite, which tied his hands), but he told Jezebel all that Elijah had done (*v.* 1), not to convince, but to exasperate her. It is not said he told her what *God* had done, but what *Elijah* had done, as if he, by some spell or charm, had brought fire from heaven, and the hand of the Lord had not been in it. Especially he represented to her, as that which would make her outrageous against him, that he had slain the prophets; the prophets of Baal he calls *the prophets*, as if none but they were worthy of the name. His heart was set upon them, and he aggravated the slaying of them as Elijah's crime, without taking notice that it was a just reprisal upon Jezebel for killing God's prophets, *ch.* xviii. 4. Those who, when they cannot for shame or fear do mischief themselves, yet stir up others to do it, will have it laid to their charge as if they had themselves done it. 2. Jezebel sent him a threatening message (*v.* 2), that she had vowed and sworn to be the death of him within twenty-four hours. Something prevents her from doing it just now, but she resolves it shall not be long undone. Note, Carnal hearts are hardened and enraged against God by that which should convince and conquer them and bring them into subjection to him. She swears by her gods, and, raging like one distracted, curseth herself if she slay not him, without any proviso of a divine permission. Cruelty and confidence often meet in persecutors. *I will pursue, I will overtake,* Exod. xv. 9. But how came she to send him word of her design, and so to give him an opportunity of making his escape? Did she think him so daring that he would not flee, or herself so formidable that she could prevent him? Or was there a special providence in it, that she should be thus infatuated by her own fury? I am apt to think that though she desired nothing more than his blood, yet, at this time, she durst not meddle with him *for fear of the people, all counting him a prophet*, a great prophet, and therefore sent this message to him merely to frighten him and get him out of the way, for the present, that he might not carry on what he had begun. The backing of her threats with an oath and imprecation does not at all prove that she really intended to slay him, but only that she intended to make him believe so. The gods she swore by could do her no harm. 3. Elijah, hereupon, in a great fright, fled for his life, it is likely by night, and came to Beer-sheba, *v.* 3. Shall we praise him for this? We praise him not. Where was the courage with which he had lately confronted Ahab and all the prophets of Baal? Nay, which kept him by his sacrifice when the fire of God fell upon it? He that stood undaunted in the midst of the terrors both of heaven and earth trembles at the impotent menaces of a proud passionate woman. *Lord, what is man!* Great faith is not always alike strong. He could not but know that he might be very serviceable to Israel at this juncture, and had all the reason in the world to depend upon God's protection while he was doing God's work; yet he fled. In his former danger God had bidden him hide himself (*ch.* xvii. 3), therefore he supposed he might do so now. 4. From Beer-sheba he went forward into the wilderness, that vast howling wilderness in which the Israelites wandered. Beer-sheba was so far distant from Jezreel, and within the dominion of so good a king as Jehoshaphat, that he could not but be safe there; yet, as if his fears haunted him even when he was out of the reach of danger, he could not rest there, but went a day's journey into the desert. Yet perhaps he retired thither not so much for his safety as that he might be wholly retired from the world, in order to a more free and intimate communion with God. *He left his servant at Beer-sheba* that he might be private in the wilderness, as Abraham left his servants at the bottom of the hill when he went up into the mount to worship God, and as Christ in the garden was *withdrawn from his disciples,* or perhaps it was because he would not expose his servant, who was young and tender, to the hardships of the wilderness, which would have been putting new wine into old bottles. We ought thus to consider the frame of those who are under our charge, for God considers ours. 5. Being wearied with his journey, he grew cross (like children when they are sleepy) and *wished he might die, v.* 4. He *requested for his life* (so it is in the margin), *that he might die;* for death is life to a good man; the death of the body is the life of the soul. Yet that was not the reason why he wished to die; it was not the deliberate desire of grace, as Paul's, to *depart and be with Christ,* but the passionate wish of his corruption, as Job's. Those that are, in this manner, forward to die are not in the fittest frame for dying. Jezebel has sworn his death, and therefore he, in a fret, prays for it, runs from death to death, yet with this difference, he wishes to die by the hand of the Lord, whose tender mercies are great, and not to fall into the hands of man, whose tender mercies are cruel. He would rather die in the wilderness than as Baal's prophet died, according to Jezebel's threatening (*v.* 2), lest the worshippers of Baal should triumph and blaspheme the God of Israel, whom they will think themselves too hard for, if they can run down his advocate. He pleads, "It is enough. I have done enough, and suffered enough. I am weary of living." Those that have secured a happiness in the other world will soon have enough of this world. He pleads, "*I am not better than my fathers,* not better able to bear those fatigues, and therefore why should I be longer burdened with them than they were?" But is this *that my lord Elijah?* Can that great and gallant spirit shrink thus? God thus left him to himself, to show that when he was bold and strong it was *in the Lord and the power of his might,* but of himself he was *no better than his fathers* or brethren. 6. God, by an angel, fed him in that wilderness, into the wants and perils of which he had wilfully thrown himself, and in which, if God had not graciously succoured him, he would have perished. How much better does God deal with his froward children than they deserve! Elijah, in a pet, wished to die; God needed him not, yet he designed further to employ and honour him, and therefore sent an angel to *keep him alive.* Our case would be bad sometimes if God should take us at our word and grant us our foolish passionate requests. Having prayed that he might die, he *laid down and slept* (*v.* 5), wishing it may be to die in his sleep, and not to awake again; but he is awakened out of his sleep, and finds himself not only well provided for with bread and water (*v.* 6), but, which was more, attended by an angel, who guarded him when he slept, and twice called him to his food when it was ready for him, *v.* 5, 7. He needed not to complain of the unkindness of men when it was thus made up by the ministration of angels. Thus provided for, he had reason to think he had fared better than the *prophets of the groves,* that *did eat at Jezebel's table.* Wherever God's children are, as they are still upon their Father's ground, so they are still under their Father's eye and care. They may lose themselves in a wilderness, but God has not lost them; there they may *look at him that lives and sees them, as Hagar,* Gen. xvi. 13. 7. He was carried, in the strength of this meat, to Horeb, *the mount of God, v.* 8. Thither the Spirit of the Lord led him, probably beyond his own intention, that he might have communion with God in the same place where Moses had, the law that was given by Moses being revived by him. The angel bade him eat the second time, because of the greatness *of the journey* that was *before him, v.* 7. Note God knows what he designs us for, though we do not, what service, what trials, and will take care for us when we, for want of foresight, cannot for ourselves, that we be furnished for them with *grace sufficient.* He that appoints what the voyage shall be will victual the ship accordingly. See how many different ways God took to keep Elijah alive; he fed him by ravens, with multiplied meals —then by an angel—and now, to show that *man lives not by bread alone,* he kept him alive forty days without meat, not resting and sleeping, which might make him the less to crave sustenance, but continually traversing the mazes of the desert, a day for a year of Israel's wanderings; yet he neither needs food nor desires it. The place, no doubt, reminds him of the manna, and encourages him to hope that God will sustain him here, and in due time bring him hence, as he did Israel, though, like him, fretful and distrustful.

9 And he came thither unto a cave, and lodged there; and, behold, the word of the LORD *came* to him, and he said unto him, What doest thou here, Elijah? 10 And he said, I have been very jealous for the LORD God of hosts: for the children of Israel have forsaken thy covenant, thrown down thine altars, and slain thy prophets with the sword; and I, *even* I only, am left; and they seek my life, to take it away. 11 And he said, Go forth, and stand upon the mount before the LORD. And, behold, the LORD passed by, and a great and strong wind rent the mountains, and brake in pieces the rocks before the LORD; *but* the LORD *was* not in the wind: and after the wind an earthquake; *but* the LORD *was* not in the earthquake: 12 And after the earthquake a fire; *but* the LORD *was* not in the fire: and after the fire a still small voice. 13 And it was *so*, when Elijah heard *it*, that he wrapped his face in his mantle, and went out, and stood in the entering in of the cave. And, behold, *there came* a voice unto him, and said, What doest thou here, Elijah? 14 And he said, I have been very jealous for the LORD God of hosts: because the children of Israel have forsaken thy covenant, thrown down thine altars, and slain thy prophets with the sword; and I, *even* I only, am left; and they seek my life, to take it away. 15 And the LORD said unto him, Go, return on thy way to the wilderness of Damascus: and when thou comest, anoint Hazael *to be* king over Syria: 16 And Jehu the son of Nimshi shalt thou anoint *to be* king over Israel: and Elisha the son of Shaphat of Abel-meholah shalt thou anoint *to be* prophet in thy room. 17 And it shall come to pass, *that* him that escapeth the sword of Hazael shall Jehu slay: and him that escapeth from the sword of Jehu shall Elisha slay. 18 Yet I have left *me* seven thousand in Israel, all the knees which have not bowed unto Baal, and every mouth which hath not kissed him.

Here is, I. Elijah housed in a cave at Mount Horeb, which is called *the mount of God,* because on it God had formerly manifested his glory. And perhaps this was the same cave, or cleft of a rock, in which Moses was hidden when the Lord *passed by before him and proclaimed his name,* Exod xxxiii. 22. What Elijah proposed to himself in coming to lodge here, I cannot conceive, unless it was to indulge his melancholy, or to satisfy his curiosity and assist his faith and devotion with the sight of that famous place where the law was given and where so many great things were done, and hoping to meet with God himself there, where Moses met with him, or in token of his abandoning his people Israel, who hated to be reformed (in the latter case, it agrees with Jeremiah's wish (Jer. ix. 2), *O that I had in the wilderness a lodging place of wayfaring men, that I might leave my people, and go from them, for they are all adulterers)* and so it was a bad omen of God's forsaking them; or it was because he thought he could not be safe any where else, and to this instance of the hardships this good man was reduced to the apostle refers, Heb. xi. 38. *They wandered in deserts and in mountains, and in dens and caves of the earth.*

II. The visit God paid to him there and the enquiry he made concerning him: *The word of the Lord came to him.* We cannot go any where to be out of the reach of God's eye, his arm, and his word. *Whither can I flee from thy Spirit?* Ps. cxxxix. 7, &c. God will take care of his out-casts; and those who, for his sake, are driven out from among men, he will find, and own, and gather with everlasting loving-kindnesses. John saw the visions of the Almighty when he was in banishment in the isle of Patmos, Rev. i. 9. The question God puts to the prophet is, *What doest* thou *here, Elijah? v.* 9, and again *v.* 13. This is a reproof, 1. For his fleeing hither. "What brings thee so far from home? Dost thou flee from Jezebel? Couldst thou not depend upon almighty power for thy protection?" Lay the emphasis upon the pronoun *thou.* "What *thou!* So great a man, so great a prophet, so famed for resolution—dost thou flee thy country, forsake thy colours thus?" This cowardice would have been more excusable in another, and not so bad an example. *Should such a man as I flee?* Neh. vi. 11. *Howl, fir-trees, if the cedars be* thus *shaken.* 2. For his fixing here. "What doest thou here, in this cave? Is this a place for a prophet of the Lord to lodge in? Is this a time for such men to retreat, when the public has such need of them?" In the retirement to which God sent Elijah (*ch.* xvii.) he was a blessing to a poor widow at Sarepta, but here he had no opportunity of doing good. Note, It concerns us often to enquire whether we be in our place and in the way of our duty. "Am I where I should be, whither God calls me, where my business lies, and where I may be useful?"

III. The account he gives of himself, in answer to the question put to him (*v.* 10), and repeated, in answer to the same question, *v.* 14.

1. He excuses his retreat, and desires it may not be imputed to his want of zeal for reformation, but to his despair of success. For God knew, and his own conscience witnessed for him, that as long as there was any hope of doing good he had been *very jealous for the Lord God of Hosts;* but now that he had *laboured in vain,* and all his endeavours were to no purpose, he thought it was time to give up the cause, and mourn for what he could not mend. *Abi in cellam, et dic, Miserere mei—"Away to thy cell, and cry, Have compassion on me."*

2. He complains of the people, their obstinacy in sin, and the height of impiety to which they had arrived: "*The children of Israel have forsaken thy covenant,* and that is the reason I have forsaken them; who can stay among them, to see every thing that is sacred ruined and run down?" This the apostle calls his *making intercession against Israel,* Rom. xi. 2, 3. He had often been, of choice, their advocate, but now he is necessitated to be their accuser, before God. Thus John v. 45, *There is one that accuseth you, even Moses, whom you trust.* Those are truly miserable that have the testimony and prayers of God's prophets against them. (1.) He charges them with having forsaken God's covenant; though they retained circumcision, the sign and seal of it, yet they had quitted his worship and service, which was the intention of it. Those who neglect God's ordinances, and let fall their communion with him, do really forsake his covenant, and break their league with him. (2.) With having *thrown down his altars,* not only deserted them and suffered them to go to decay, but, in their zeal for the worship of Baal, wilfully demolished them. This alludes to the private altars which the prophets of the Lord had, and which good people attended, who could not go up to Jerusalem and would not worship the calves nor Baal. These separate altars, though breaking in upon the unity of the church, yet, being erected and attended by those that sincerely aimed at the glory of God and served him faithfully, the seeming schism was excused. God owned them for his altars, as well as that at Jerusalem, and the putting of them down is charged upon Israel as a crying sin. But this was not all. (3.) *They have slain thy prophets with the sword,* who, it is probable, ministered at those altars. Jezebel, a foreigner, slew them (*ch.* xviii. 4), but the crime is charged upon the body of the people because the generality of them were *consenting to their death,* and pleased with it.

3. He gives the reasons why he retired into this desert and took up his residence in this cave. (1.) It was because he could not appear to any purpose: "*I only am left,* and have none to second or support me in any good design. They all said, *The Lord he is God,* but none of them would stand by me nor offer to shelter me. That point then gained was presently lost again, and Jezebel can do more to debauch them than I can to reform them. What can one do against thousands?" Despair of success hinders many a good enterprise. No one is willing to venture alone, forgetting that those are not alone who have God with them. (2.) It was because he could not appear with any safety: "*They seek my life to take it away;* and I had better spend my life in a useless solitude than lose my life in a fruitless endeavour to reform those that hate to be reformed."

IV. God's manifestation of himself to him. Did he come hither to meet with God? He shall find that God will not fail to give him the meeting. Moses was put into the cave when God's glory passed before him; but Elijah was called out of it: *Stand upon the mount before the Lord, v.* 11. He *saw no manner of similitude,* any more than Israel did when God *talked to them in Horeb.* But, 1. He heard a strong wind, and saw the terrible effects of it, for it rent the mountains and tore the rocks. Thus was the trumpet sounded before the Judge of heaven and earth, by his angels, whom he makes *spirits,* or *winds* (Ps. civ. 4), sounded so loud that the earth not only rang, but rent again. 2. He felt the shock of an earthquake. 3. He saw an eruption of fire, *v.* 12. These were to usher in the designed manifestation of the divine glory, angels being employed in them, whom he *maketh a flame of fire,* and who, as his ministers, march before him, to *prepare in this desert a highway for our God.* But, 4. At last he perceived a *still small voice,* in which *the Lord was,* that is, by which he spoke to him, and not out of the wind, or the earthquake, or the fire. Those struck an awe upon him, awakened his attention, and inspired humility and reverence; but God chose to make known his mind to him in whispers soft, not in those dreadful sounds. When he perceived this, (1.) *He wrapped his face in his mantle,* as one afraid to look upon the glory of God, and apprehensive that it would dazzle his eyes and overcome him. The angels *cover their faces* before God in token of reverence, Isa. vi. 2. Elijah hid his face in token of shame for having been such a coward as to flee from his duty when he had such a God of power to stand by him in it. The wind, and earthquake, and fire, did not make him cover his face, but the still voice did. Gracious souls are more affected by the tender mercies of the Lord than by his terrors. (2.) He stood at the entrance of the cave, ready to hear what God had to say to him. This method of God's manifesting himself here at Mount Horeb seems to refer to the discoveries God formerly made of himself at this place to Moses. [1.] Then there was a tempest, an earthquake, and fire (Heb. xii. 18); but, when God would show Moses his glory, he *proclaimed his goodness*; and so here: *He was, the Word* was, in the *still small voice*. [2.] Then the law was thus given to Israel, with the appearances of terror first and then with a voice of words; and Elijah being now called to revive that law, especially the first two commandments of it, is here taught how to manage it; he must not only awaken and terrify the people with amazing signs, like the earthquake and fire, but he must endeavour, with a still small voice, to convince and persuade them, and not forsake them when he should be addressing them. Faith comes by hearing the word of God; miracles do but make way for it. [3.] Then God spoke to his people with terror; but in the gospel of Christ, which was to be introduced by the spirit and power of Elias, he would speak by a still small voice, the dread of which should not make us afraid; see Heb. xii. 18, &c.

V. The orders God gives him to execute. He repeats the question he had put to him before, "*What doest thou here?* This is not a place for thee now." Elijah gives the same answer (*v.* 14), complaining of Israel's apostasy from God and the ruin of religion among them. To this God gives him a reply. When he wished *he might die* (*v.* 4) God answered him not according to his folly, but was so far from letting him die that he not only kept him alive then, but provided that he should never die, but be translated. But when he complained of his discouragement (and whither should God's prophets go with their complaints of that kind but to their Master?) God gave him an answer. He sends him back with directions to appoint Hazael king of Syria (*v.* 15), Jehu king of Israel, and Elisha his successor in the eminency of the prophetical office (*v.* 16), which is intended as a prediction that by these God would chastise the degenerate Israelites, plead his own cause among them, and *avenge the quarrel of his covenant, v.* 17. Elijah complained that the wickedness of Israel was unpunished. The judgment of famine was too gentle, and had not reclaimed them; it was removed before they were reformed: "*I have been jealous,*" says he, "for God's name, but he himself has not appeared jealous for it." "Well," says God, "be content; it is all in good time; *judgments are prepared for those scorners,* though they are not yet inflicted; the persons are pitched upon, and shall now be nominated, for they are now in being, who shall do the business." 1. "When Hazael comes to be king of Syria, he shall make bloody work among the people (2 Kings viii. 12) and so correct them for their idolatry." 2. "When Jehu comes to be king of Israel he shall make bloody work with the royal family, and shall utterly destroy the house of Ahab, that set up and maintained idolatry." 3. "Elisha, while thou art on earth, shall strengthen thy hands; and, when thou art gone, shall carry on thy work, and be a remaining witness against the apostasy of Israel, and even he shall slay the children of Bethel, that idolatrous city." Note, The wicked are reserved to judgment. *Evil pursues sinners,* and there is no escaping it; to attempt an escape is but to run from one sword's point upon another. See Jer. xlviii. 44, *He that flees from the fear shall fall into the pit; and he that gets up out of the pit shall be taken in the snare.* Elisha, with the *sword of the Spirit,* shall terrify and wound the consciences of those who escape Hazael's sword of war and Jehu's sword of justice. *With the breath of his lips shall he slay the wicked,* Isa. xi. 4; 2 Thess. ii. 8; Hos. vi. 5. It is a great comfort to good men and good ministers to think that God will never want instruments to do his work in his time, but, when they are gone, others shall be raised up to carry it on.

VI. The comfortable information God gives him of the number of Israelites who retained their integrity, though he thought he was left alone (*v.* 18): *I have left* 7000 *in Israel* (besides Judea) *who have not bowed the knee to Baal.* Note, 1. In times of the greatest degeneracy and apostasy God has always had, and will have, a remnant faithful to him, some that keep their integrity and do not go down the stream. The apostle mentions this answer of God to Elijah (Rom. xi. 4) and applies it to his own day, when the Jews generally rejected the gospel. *Yet,* says he, *at this time also there is a remnant, v.* 5. 2. It is God's work to preserve that remnant, and distinguish them from the rest, for without his grace they could not have distinguished themselves: *I have left me;* it is therefore said to be a remnant *according to the election of grace.* 3. It is but a little remnant, in comparison with the degenerate race; what are 7000 to the thousands of Israel? Yet, when those of every age come together, they will be found many more, 12,000 *sealed out of each tribe,* Rev. vii. 4. 4. God's faithful ones are often his hidden ones (Ps. lxxxiii. 3), and the visible church is scarcely visible, the wheat lost in the chaff and the gold in the dross, till the sifting, refining, separating day comes. 5. *The Lord knows those that are his,* though we do not; he sees in secret. 6. There are more good people in the world than some wise and holy men think there are. Their jealousy of themselves, and for God, makes them think the corruption is universal; but God sees not as they do. When we come to heaven, as we shall miss a great many whom we thought to meet there, so we shall meet a great many whom we little thought to find there. God's love often proves larger than man's charity and more extensive.

19 So he departed thence, and found Elisha the son of Shaphat, who *was* plowing *with* twelve yoke *of oxen* before him, and he with the twelfth: and Elijah passed by him, and cast his mantle upon him. 20 And he left the oxen, and ran after Elijah, and said, Let me, I pray thee, kiss my father and my mother, and *then* I will follow thee. And he said unto him, Go back again; for what have I done to thee? 21 And he returned back from him, and took a yoke of oxen, and slew them, and boiled their flesh with the instruments of the oxen, and gave unto the people, and they did eat. Then he arose, and went after Elijah, and ministered unto him.

Elisha was named last in the orders God gave to Elijah, but he was first called, for by him the other two were to be called. He must come in Elijah's room; yet Elijah is forward to raise him, and is far from being jealous of his successor, but rejoices to think that he shall leave the work of God in such good hands. Concerning the call of Elisha observe, 1. That it was an unexpected surprising call. Elijah found him by divine direction, or perhaps he was before acquainted with him and knew where to find him. He found him, not in the schools of the prophets, but *in the field*, not reading, nor praying, nor sacrificing, but *ploughing*, *v.* 19. Though a great man (as appears by his feast, *v.* 21), master of the ground, and oxen, and servants, yet he did not think it any disparagement to him to follow his business himself, and not only to inspect his servants, but himself to lay his hand to the plough. Idleness is no man's honour, nor is husbandry any man's disgrace. An honest calling in the world does not at all put us out of the way of our heavenly calling, any more than it did Elisha, who was taken from following the plough to feed Israel and to sow the *seed of the word*, as the apostles were taken from fishing to catch men. Elisha enquired not after Elijah, but was anticipated with this call. We love God, and choose him, because he chose us, and loved us, first. 2. That it was a powerful call. Elijah did but *cast his mantle upon him* (*v.* 19), in token of friendship, that he would take him under his care and tuition as he did under his mantle, and to be one with him in the same clothes, or in token of his being clothed with the spirit of Elijah (now he put some of his honour upon him, as Moses on Joshua, Num. xxvii. 20); but, when Elijah went to heaven, he had the mantle entire, 2 Kings ii. 13. And immediately he *left the oxen* to go as they would, and *ran after Elijah*, and assured him that he would follow him presently, *v.* 20. An invisible hand touched his heart, and unaccountably inclined him by a secret power, without any external persuasions, to quit his husbandry and give himself to the ministry. It is in a day of power that Christ's subjects are made willing (Ps. cx. 3), nor would any come to Christ unless they were thus drawn. Elisha came to a resolution presently, but begged a little time, not to *ask* leave, but only to *take* leave, of his parents. This was not an excuse for delay, like his (Luke ix. 61) that desired he might *bid those farewell that were at home*, but only a reservation of the respect and duty he owed to his father and mother. Elijah bade him go back and do it, he would not hinder him; nay, if he would, he might go back, and not return, for any thing he had done to him. He will not force him, nor take him against his will; let him sit down and count the cost, and make it his own act. The efficacy of God's grace preserves the native liberty of man's will, so that those who are good are good of choice and not by constraint, not pressed men, but volunteers. 3. That it was a pleasant and acceptable call to him, which appears by the farewell-feast he made for his family (*v.* 21), though he not only quitted all the comforts of his father's house, but exposed himself to the malignity of Jezebel and her party. It was a discouraging time for prophets to set out in. A man that had consulted with flesh and blood would not be fond of Elijah's mantle, nor willing to wear his coat; yet Elisha cheerfully, and with a great deal of satisfaction, leaves all to accompany him. Thus Matthew made a great feast when he left the receipt of custom to follow Christ. 4. That it was an effectual call. Elijah did not stay for him, lest he should seem to compel him, but left him to his own choice, and he soon arose, went after him, and not only associated with him, but *ministered to him* as his servitor, *poured water on his hands*, 2 Kings iii. 11. It is of great advantage to young ministers to spend some time under the direction of those that are aged and experienced, whose years teach wisdom, and not to think much, if occasion be, to minister to them. Those that would be fit to teach must have time to learn; and those that hope hereafter to rise and rule must be willing at first to stoop and serve.

CHAP. XX.

This chapter is the history of a war between Ben-hadad king of Syria and Ahab king of Israel, in which Ahab was, once and again, victorious We read nothing of Elijah or Elisha in all this story; Jezebel's rage, it is probable, had abated, and the persecution of the prophets began to cool, which gleam of peace Elijah improved. He appeared not at court, but, being told how many thousands of good people there were in Israel more than he thought of, employed himself, as we may suppose, in founding religious houses, schools, or colleges of prophets, in several parts of the country, to be nurseries of religion, that they might help to reform the nation when the throne and court would not be reformed. While he was thus busied, God favoured the nation with the successes we here read of, which were the more remarkable because obtained against Ben-hadad king of Syria, whose successor, Hazael, was ordained to be a scourge to Israel. They must shortly suffer by the Syrians, and yet now triumphed over them, that, if possible, they might be led to repentance by the goodness of God. Here is, I. Ben-hadad's descent upon Israel, and his insolent demand, ver. 1—11. II. The defeat Ahab gave him, encouraged and directed by a prophet, ver. 12—21. III. The Syrians rallying again, and the second defeat Ahab gave them, ver. 22—30. IV. The covenant of peace Ahab made with Ben-hadad, when he had him at his mercy (ver. 31—34), for which he is reproved and threatened by a prophet, ver. 35—43.

AND Ben-hadad the king of Syria gathered all his host together: and *there were* thirty and two kings with him, and horses, and chariots: and he went up and besieged Samaria, and warred against it. 2 And he sent messengers to Ahab king of Israel into the city, and said unto him, Thus saith Ben-hadad, 3 Thy silver and thy gold *is* mine; thy wives also and thy children, *even* the goodliest, *are* mine. 4 And the king of Israel answered and said, My lord, O king, according to thy saying, I *am* thine, and all that I have. 5 And the messengers came again, and said, Thus speaketh Ben-hadad, saying, Although I have sent unto thee, saying, Thou shalt deliver me thy silver, and thy gold, and thy wives, and thy children; 6 Yet I will send my servants unto thee to-morrow about this time, and they shall search thine house, and the houses of thy servants; and it shall be, *that* whatsoever is pleasant in thine eyes, they shall put *it* in their hand, and take *it* away. 7 Then the king of Israel called all the elders of the land, and said, Mark, I pray you, and see how this *man* seeketh mischief: for he sent unto me for my wives, and for my children, and for my silver, and for my gold; and I denied him not. 8 And all the elders and all the people said unto him, Hearken not *unto him*, nor consent. 9 Wherefore he said unto the messengers of Ben-hadad, Tell my lord the king, All that thou didst send for to thy servant at the first I will do: but this thing I may not do. And the messengers departed, and brought him word again. 10 And Ben-hadad sent unto him, and said, The gods do so unto me, and more also, if the dust of Samaria shall suffice for handfuls for all the people that follow me. 11 And the king of Israel answered and said, Tell *him*, Let not him that girdeth on *his harness* boast himself as he that putteth it off.

Here is, I. The threatening descent which Benhadad made upon Ahab's kingdom, and the siege he laid to Samaria, his royal city, *v.* 1. What the ground of the quarrel was we are not told; covetousness and ambition were the principle, which would never want some pretence or other. David in his time had quite subdued the Syrians and made them tributaries to Israel, but Israel's apostasy from God makes them formidable again. Asa had tempted the Syrians to invade Israel once (*ch.* xv. 18—20), and now they did it of their own accord. It is dangerous bringing a foreign force into the country: posterity may pay dearly for it. Ben-hadad had with him thirty-two kings, who were either tributaries to him, and bound in duty to attend him, or confederates with him, and bound in interest to assist him. How little did the title of king look when all these poor petty governors pretended to it!

II. The treaty between these two kings. Surely Israel's defence had departed from them, or else the Syrians could not have marched so readily, and with so little opposition, to Samaria, the head and heart of the country, a city lately built, and therefore, we may suppose, not well fortified, but likely to fall quickly into the hands of the invaders; both sides are aware of this, and therefore,

1. Ben-hadad's proud spirit sends Ahab a very insolent demand, *v.* 2, 3. A parley is sounded, and a trumpeter (we may suppose) is sent into the city, to let Ahab know that he will raise the siege upon condition that Ahab become his vassal (nay, his *villain*), and not only pay him a tribute out of what he has, but make over his title to Ben-hadad, and hold all at his will, even his wives and children, the goodliest of them. The manner of expression is designed to gall them; "All shall be mine, without exception."

2. Ahab's poor spirit sends Ben-hadad a very disgraceful submission. It is general indeed (he cannot mention particulars in his surrender with so much pleasure as Benhadad did in his demand), but it is effectual: *I am thine, and all that I have, v.* 4. See the effect of sin. (1.) If he had not by sin provoked God to depart from him, Ben-hadad could not have made such a demand. Sin brings men into such straits, by putting them out of divine protection. If God may not rule us, our enemies shall. A rebel to God is a slave to all besides. Ahab had prepared his silver and gold for Baal, Hos. ii. 8. Justly therefore is it taken from him; such

an alienating amounts to a forfeiture. (2.) If he had not by sin wronged his own conscience, and set that against him, he could not have made such a mean surrender. Guilt dispirits men, and makes them cowards. He knew Baal could not help, and had no reason to think that God would, and therefore was content to buy his life upon any terms. Skin for skin, and all that is dear to him, he will give for it; he will rather live a beggar than not die a prince.

3. Ben-hadad's proud spirit rises upon his submission, and becomes yet more insolent and imperious, *v.* 5, 6. Ahab had laid his all at his feet, at his mercy, expecting that one king would use another generously, that this acknowledgment of Ben-hadad's sovereignty would content him, the honour was sufficient for the present, and he might hereafter make use of it if he saw cause *(Satis est prostrasse leoni—It suffices the lion to have laid his victim prostrate);* but this will not serve. (1.) Ben-hadad is as covetous as he is proud, and cannot go away unless he have the possession as well as the dominion. He thinks it not enough to call it his, unless he have it in his hands. He will not so much as lend Ahab the use of his own goods above a day longer. (2.) He is as spiteful as he is haughty. Had he come himself to select what he had a mind for, it would have shown some respect to a crowned head; but he will send his servants to insult the prince, and hector over him, to rifle the palace, and strip it of all its ornaments; nay, to give Ahab the more vexation, they shall be ordered, not only to take what they please, but, if they can learn which are the persons or things that Ahab is in a particular manner fond of, to take those: *Whatsoever is pleasant in thy eyes they shall take away.* We are often crossed in that which we most dote upon; and that proves least safe which is most dear. (3.) He is as unreasonable as he is unjust, and will construe the surrender Ahab made for himself as made for all his subjects too, and will have them also to lie at his mercy: "They shall search, not only thy house, but *the houses of thy servants* too, and plunder them at discretion." Blessed be God for peace and property, and that what we have we can call our own.

4. Ahab's poor spirit begins to rise too, upon this growing insolence; and, if it becomes not bold, yet it becomes desperate, and he will rather hazard his life than give up all thus. (1.) Now he takes advice of his privy-council, who encourage him to stand it out. He speaks but poorly (*v.* 7), appeals to them whether Ben-hadad be not an unreasonable enemy, and do not seek mischief. What else could he expect from one who, without any provocation given him, had invaded his country and besieged his capital city? He owns to them how he had truckled to him before, and will have them advise him what he should do in this strait; and they speak bravely *(Hearken not to him, nor consent, v. 8)*, promising no doubt to stand by him in the refusal. (2.) Yet he expresses himself very modestly in his denial, *v.* 9 He owns Ben-hadad's dominion over him: "*Tell my lord the king* I have no design to affront him, nor to recede from the surrender I have already made; what I offered at first I will stand to, *but this thing I may not do;* I must not give what is none of my own." It was a mortification to Ben-hadad that even such an abject spirit as Ahab's durst deny him; yet it should seem, by his manner of expressing himself, that he durst not have done it if his people had not animated him.

5. Ben-hadad proudly swears the ruin of Samaria. The threatening waves of his wrath, meeting with this check, rage and foam, and make a noise. In his fury, he imprecates the impotent revenge of his gods, *if the dust of Samaria serve for handfuls for his army* (*v.* 10), so numerous, so resolute, an army will he bring into the field against Samaria, and so confident is he of their success; it will be done as easily as the taking up of a handful of dust; all shall be carried away, even the ground on which the city stands. Thus confident is his pride, thus cruel is his malice; this prepares him to be ruined, though such a prince and such a people are unworthy of the satisfaction of seeing him ruined.

6. Ahab sends him a decent rebuke to his assurance, dares not defy his menaces, only reminds him of the uncertain turns of war (*v.* 11): "Let not him that begins a war, and is girding on his sword, his armour, his harness, boast of victory, or think himself sure of it, *as if he had put it off,* and had come home a conqueror." This was one of the wisest words that ever Ahab spoke, and is a good item or memento to us all; it is folly to boast beforehand of any day, since we know not what it may bring forth (Prov. xxvii. 1), but especially to boast of a day of battle, which may prove as much against us as we promise ourselves it will be for us. It is impolitic to despise an enemy, and to be too sure of victory is the way to be beaten. Apply it to our spiritual conflicts. Peter fell by his confidence. While we are here we are but girding on the harness, and therefore must never boast as though we had put it off. *Happy is the man that feareth always,* and is never off his watch.

12 And it came to pass, when *Ben-hadad* heard this message, as he *was* drinking, he and the kings in the pavilions, that he said unto his servants, Set *yourselves in array.* And they set *themselves in array* against the city. 13 And, behold, there came a prophet unto Ahab king of Israel, saying, Thus saith the LORD, Hast

thou seen all this great multitude? behold, I will deliver it into thine hand this day; and thou shalt know that I *am* the LORD. 14 And Ahab said, By whom? And he said, Thus saith the LORD, *Even* by the young men of the princes of the provinces. Then he said, Who shall order the battle? And he answered, Thou. 15 Then he numbered the young men of the princes of the provinces, and they were two hundred and thirty two: and after them he numbered all the people, *even* all the children of Israel, *being* seven thousand. 16 And they went out at noon. But Ben-hadad *was* drinking himself drunk in the pavilions, he and the kings, the thirty and two kings that helped him. 17 And the young men of the princes of the provinces went out first; and Ben-hadad sent out, and they told him, saying, There are men come out of Samaria. 18 And he said, Whether they be come out for peace, take them alive; or whether they be come out for war, take them alive. 19 So these young men of the princes of the provinces came out of the city, and the army which followed them. 20 And they slew every one his man: and the Syrians fled; and Israel pursued them: and Ben-hadad the king of Syria escaped on a horse with the horsemen. 21 And the king of Israel went out, and smote the horses and chariots, and slew the Syrians with a great slaughter.

The treaty between the besiegers and the besieged being broken off abruptly, we have here an account of the battle that ensued immediately.

I. The Syrians, the besiegers, had their directions from a drunken king, who gave orders over his cups, as he was *drinking* (*v.* 12), *drinking himself drunk* (*v.* 16) *with the kings in the pavilions*, and this at noon. Drunkenness is a sin which armies and their officers have of old been addicted to. Say not thou then that the former days were, in this respect, better than these, though these are bad enough. Had he not been very secure he would not have sat to drink; and, had he not been intoxicated, he would not have been so very secure. Security and sensuality went together in the old world, and Sodom, Luke xvii. 26, &c. Ben-hadad's drunkenness was the forerunner of his fall, as Belshazzar's was, Dan. v. How could he prosper that preferred his pleasure before his business, and kept his kings to drink with him when they should have been at their respective posts to fight for him? In his drink, 1. He orders the town to be invested, the engines fixed, and every thing got ready for the making of a general attack (*v.* 12), but stirs not from his drunken club to see it done. *Woe unto thee, O land! when thy king is* such *a child.* 2. When the besieged made a sally (and, by that time, he was far gone) he gave orders to take them alive (*v.* 18), not to kill them, which might have been done more easily and safely, but to seize them, which gave them an opportunity of killing the aggressors; so imprudent was he in the orders he gave, as well as unjust, in ordering them to be taken prisoners though they came for peace and to renew the treaty. Thus, as is usual, he drinks, and forgets the law, both the policies and the justice of war.

II. The Israelites, the besieged, had their directions from an inspired prophet, one of the prophets of the Lord, whom Ahab had hated and persecuted: *And behold a prophet, even one, drew near to the king of Israel;* so it may be read, *v.* 13.

1. Behold, and wonder, that God should send a prophet with a kind and gracious message to so wicked a prince as Ahab was; but he did it, (1.) For his people Israel's sake, who, though wickedly degenerated, were the seed of Abraham his friend and Jacob his chosen, the children of the covenant, and not yet cast off. (2.) That he might magnify his mercy, in doing good to one so evil and unthankful, might either bring him to repentance or leave him the more inexcusable. (3.) That he might mortify the pride of Ben-hadad and check his insolence. Ahab's idolatry shall be punished hereafter, but Ben-hadad's haughtiness shall be chastised now; for God resists the proud, and is pleased to say that *he fears the wrath of the enemy*, Deut. xxxii. 26, 27. There was but one prophet perhaps to be had in Samaria, and he drew near with this message, intimating that he had been forced to keep at a distance. Ahab, in his prosperity, would not have borne the sight of him, but now he bids him welcome, when none of the prophets of the groves can give him any assistance. He enquired not for a prophet of the Lord, but God sent one to him unasked, for he waits to be gracious.

2. Two things the prophet does:—(1.) He animates Ahab with an assurance of victory, which was more than all the elders of Israel could give him (*v.* 8), though they promised to stand by him. This prophet, who is not named (for he *spoke in God's name)*, tells him from God that this very day the siege shall be raised, and the army of the Syrians routed, *v.* 13. When the prophet said, *Thus saith*

the Lord, we may suppose Ahab began to tremble, expecting a message of wrath; but he is revived when it proves a gracious one. He is informed what use he ought to make of this blessed turn of affairs: "*Thou shalt know that I am Jehovah*, the sovereign Lord of all." God's foretelling a thing that was so very unlikely proved that it was his own doing. (2.) He instructs him what to do for the gaining of this victory. [1.] He must not stay till the enemy attacked him, but must sally out upon them and surprise them in their trenches. [2.] The persons employed must be the *young men of the princes of the provinces*, the pages, the footmen, who were few in number, only 232, utterly unacquainted with war, and the unlikeliest men that could be thought of for such a bold attempt; yet these must do it, these weak and foolish things must be instruments of confounding the wise and strong, that, while Ben-hadad's boasting is punished, Ahab's may be prevented and precluded, and the *excellency of the power may appear to be of God*. [3.] Ahab must himself so far testify his confidence in the word of God as to command in person, though, in the eye of reason, he exposed himself to the utmost danger by it. But it is fit that those who have the benefit of God's promises should enter upon them. Yet, [4.] He is allowed to make use of what other forces he has at hand, to follow the blow, when these young men have broken the ice. All he had in Samaria, or within call, were but 7000 men, *v.* 15. It is observable that it is the same number with theirs that had not *bowed the knee to Baal* (*ch.* xix. 18), though, it is likely, not the same men.

III. The issue was accordingly. The proud Syrians were beaten, and the poor despised Israelites were more than conquerors. The young men gave an alarm to the Syrians just at noon, at high dinner-time, supported by what little force they had, *v.* 16. Ben-hadad despised them at first (*v.* 18), but when they had, with unparalleled bravery and dexterity, *slain every one his man*, and so put the army into disorder, that proud man durst not face them, but mounted immediately, drunk as he was, and made the best of his way, *v.* 20. See how God *takes away the spirit of princes*, and makes himself *terrible to the kings of the earth*. Now where are the silver and gold he demanded of Ahab? Where are the handfuls of Samaria's dust? Those that are most secure are commonly least courageous. Ahab failed not to improve this advantage, but *slew the Syrians with a great slaughter*, *v.* 21. Note, God oftentimes makes one wicked man a scourge to another.

22 And the prophet came to the king of Israel, and said unto him, Go, strengthen thyself, and mark, and see what thou doest: for at the return of the year the king of Syria will come up against thee. 23 And the servants of the king of Syria said unto him, Their gods *are* gods of the hills; therefore they were stronger than we; but let us fight against them in the plain, and surely we shall be stronger than they. 24 And do this thing, Take the kings away, every man out of his place, and put captains in their rooms: 25 And number thee an army, like the army that thou hast lost, horse for horse, and chariot for chariot: and we will fight against them in the plain, *and* surely we shall be stronger than they. And he hearkened unto their voice, and did so. 26 And it came to pass at the return of the year, that Ben-hadad numbered the Syrians, and went up to Aphek, to fight against Israel. 27 And the children of Israel were numbered, and were all present, and went against them: and the children of Israel pitched before them like two little flocks of kids; but the Syrians filled the country. 28 And there came a man of God, and spake unto the king of Israel, and said, Thus saith the LORD, Because the Syrians have said, The LORD *is* God of the hills, but he *is* not God of the valleys, therefore will I deliver all this great multitude into thine hand, and ye shall know that I *am* the LORD. 29 And they pitched one over against the other seven days. And *so* it was, that in the seventh day the battle was joined: and the children of Israel slew of the Syrians a hundred thousand footmen in one day. 30 But the rest fled to Aphek, into the city; and *there* a wall fell upon twenty and seven thousand of the men *that were* left. And Ben-haded fled, and came into the city, into an inner chamber.

We have here an account of another successful campaign which Ahab, by divine aid, made against the Syrians, in which he gave them a greater defeat than in the former. Strange! Ahab idolatrous and yet victorious, a persecutor and yet a conqueror! God has wise and holy ends in suffering wicked men to prosper, and glorifies his own name thereby.

I. Ahab is admonished by a prophet to

prepare for another war, *v.* 22. It should seem, he was now secure, and looked but a little way before him. Those that are careless of their souls are often as careless of their outward affairs; but the prophet (to whom God made known the following counsels of the Syrians) told him they would renew their attempt at the return of the year, hoping to retrieve the honour they had lost and be avenged for the blow they had received. He therefore bade him strengthen himself, put himself into a posture of defence, and be ready to give them a warm reception. God had decreed the end, but Ahab must use the means, else he tempts God: "Help thyself, strengthen thyself, and God will help and strengthen thee." The enemies of God's Israel are restless in their malice, and, though they may take some breathing-time for themselves, yet they are still *breathing out threatenings and slaughter* against the church. It concerns us always to expect assaults from our spiritual enemies, and therefore to mark and see what we do.

II. Ben-hadad is advised by those about him concerning the operations of the next campaign. 1. They advised him to *change his ground, v.* 23. They took it for granted that it was not Israel, but Israel's gods, that beat them (so great a regard was then universally had to invisible powers); but they speak very ignorantly of Jehovah—that he was *many,* whereas he is one and his name one,—that he was *their* God only, a local deity, peculiar to that nation, whereas he is the Creator and ruler of all the world,—and that he was a God *of the hills* only, because David their great prophet had said, *I will lift up my eyes to the hills whence cometh my help* (Ps. cxxi. 1), and that *his foundation was in the holy mountain* (Ps. lxxxvii. 1; lxxviii. 54), and much was said of his *holy hill* (Ps. xv. 1; xxiv. 3); supposing him altogether such a one as their imaginary deities, they fancied he was confined to his hills, and could not or would not come down from them, and therefore an army in the valley would be below his cognizance and from under his protection. Thus vain were the *Gentiles in their imaginations* concerning God, so wretchedly were *their foolish hearts darkened,* and, *professing themselves to be wise, they became fools.* 2. They advised him to change his officers (*v.* 24, 25), not to employ the kings, who were commanders by birth, but captains rather, who were commanders by merit, who were inured to war, would not affect to make a show like the kings, but would go through with business. Let every man be employed in that which he is brought up to and used to, and preferred to that which he is fit for. Syria, it seems, was rich and populous, when it could furnish recruits sufficient, after so great a defeat, *horse for horse, chariot for chariot.*

III. Both armies take the field. Ben-hadad, with his Syrians, encamps near Aphek, in the tribe of Asher. It is probable that Asher was a city in his own possession, one of those which his father had won (*v.* 34), and the country about it was flat and level, and fit for his purpose, *v.* 26. Ahab, with his forces, posted himself at some distance over against them, *v.* 27. The disproportion of numbers was very remarkable. *The children of Israel,* who were cantoned in two battalions, looked like *two little flocks of kids,* their numbers small, their equipage mean, and the figure they made contemptible; *but the Syrians filled the country* with their numbers, their noise, their chariots, their carriages, and their baggage.

IV. Ahab is encouraged to fight the Syrians, notwithstanding their advantages and confidence. A man of God is sent to him, to tell him that this numerous army shall *all be delivered into his hand* (*v.* 28), but not for his sake; be it known to him, he is utterly unworthy for whom God will do this. God would not do it because Ahab had praised God or prayed to him (we do not read that he did either), but because the Syrians had blasphemed God, and had said, He is *the God of the hills and not of the valleys;* therefore God will do it in his own vindication, and to preserve the honour of his own name. If the Syrians had said, "Ahab and his people have forgotten their God, and so put themselves out of his protection, and therefore we may venture to attack them," God would probably have delivered Israel into their hands; but when they go upon a presumption so very injurious to the divine omnipotence, and the honour of him who is Lord of all hosts, not only in hills and valleys, but in heaven and earth, which they are willingly ignorant of, they shall be undeceived, at the expense of that vast army which is so much their pride and confidence.

V. After the armies had faced one another seven days (the Syrians, it is likely, boasting, and the Israelites trembling), they engaged, and the Syrians were totally routed, 100,000 men slain by the sword of Israel in the field of battle (*v.* 29), and 27,000 men, that thought themselves safe *under the walls of Aphek,* a fortified city (from the walls of which the shooters might annoy the enemy if they pursued them, 2 Sam. xi. 24), found their bane where they hoped for protection: the wall fell upon them, probably overthrown by an earthquake, and, the cities of Canaan being walled up to heaven, it reached a great way, and they were all killed, or hurt, or overwhelmed with dismay. Ben-hadad, who thought his city Aphek would hold out against the conquerors, finding it thus unwalled, and the remnant of his forces dispirited and dispersed, had nothing but secresy to rely upon for safety, and therefore hid himself in *a chamber within a chamber,* lest the pursuers should seize him. See how the greatest confidence often ends in the greatest cowardice. "Now is the God of Israel the *God of the valleys* or no?" He shall know now that he is forced *into an inner chamber to hide himself,* see *ch.* xxii. 25.

31 And his servants said unto him, Behold now, we have heard that the kings of the house of Israel *are* merciful kings: let us, I pray thee, put sackcloth on our loins, and ropes upon our heads, and go out to the king of Israel: peradventure he will save thy life. 32 So they girded sackcloth on their loins, and *put* ropes on their heads, and came to the king of Israel, and said, Thy servant Ben-hadad saith, I pray thee, let me live. And he said, *Is* he yet alive? he *is* my brother. 33 Now the men did diligently observe whether *any thing would come* from him, and did hastily catch *it:* and they said, Thy brother Ben-hadad. Then he said, Go ye, bring him. Then Ben-hadad came forth to him; and he caused him to come up into the chariot. 34 And *Ben-hadad* said unto him, The cities, which my father took from thy father, I will restore; and thou shalt make streets for thee in Damascus, as my father made in Samaria. Then *said Ahab,* I will send thee away with this covenant. So he made a covenant with him, and sent him away. 35 And a certain man of the sons of the prophets said unto his neighbour in the word of the LORD, Smite me, I pray thee. And the man refused to smite him. 36 Then said he unto him, Because thou hast not obeyed the voice of the LORD, behold, as soon as thou art departed from me, a lion shall slay thee. And as soon as he was departed from him, a lion found him, and slew him. 37 Then he found another man, and said, Smite me, I pray thee. And the man smote him, so that in smiting he wounded *him.* 38 So the prophet departed, and waited for the king by the way, and disguised himself with ashes upon his face. 39 And as the king passed by, he cried unto the king: and he said, Thy servant went out into the midst of the battle; and, behold, a man turned aside, and brought a man unto me, and said, Keep this man: if by any means he be missing, then shall thy life be for his life, or else thou shalt pay a talent of silver. 40 And as thy servant was busy here and there, he was gone. And the king of Israel said unto him, So *shall* thy judgment *be;* thyself hast decided *it.* 41 And he hasted, and took the ashes away from his face; and the king of Israel discerned him that he *was* of the prophets. 42 And he said unto him, Thus saith the LORD, Because thou hast let go out of *thy* hand a man whom I appointed to utter destruction, therefore thy life shall go for his life, and thy people for his people. 43 And the king of Israel went to his house heavy and displeased, and came to Samaria.

Here is an account of what followed upon the victory which Israel obtained over the Syrians.

I. Ben-hadad's tame and mean submission. Even in his inner chamber he feared, and would, if he could, flee further, though none pursued. His servants, seeing him and themselves reduced to the last extremity, advised that they should surrender at discretion, and make themselves prisoners and petitioners to Ahab for their lives, *v.* 31. The servants will put their lives in their hands, and venture first, and their master will act according as they speed. Their inducement to take this course is the great reputation the kings of Israel had for clemency above any of their neighbours: "We have heard that they are merciful kings, not oppressive to their subjects that are under their power" (as governments then went, that of Israel was one of the most easy and gentle), "and therefore not cruel to their enemies when they lie at their mercy." Perhaps they had this notion of the kings of Israel because they had heard that the God of Israel proclaimed his name *gracious and merciful,* and they concluded their kings would make their God their pattern. It was an honour to the kings of Israel to be thus represented, as indeed every Israelite is then dressed as becomes him when he *puts on bowels of mercies.* "They are merciful kings, therefore we may hope to find mercy upon our submission." This encouragement poor sinners have to repent and humble themselves before God. "Have we not heard that the God of Israel is a merciful God? Have we not found him so? Let us therefore rend our hearts and return to him." Joel ii. 13. That is evangelical repentance which flows from an apprehension of the mercy of God in Christ; *there is forgiveness with him.* Two things Ben-hadad's servants undertake to represent to Ahab:—1. Their master a penitent; for they *girded sackcloth on their loins*, as mourners, and *put ropes on their heads*, as condemned criminals going to execution, pretending to be sorry that they had invaded his country and disturbed his repose, and owning that they deserved to be hanged for it. Here they are ready to do penance for it, and throw themselves at the feet of him whom they had injured. Many pretend to repent of their wrong-doing, when it does not succeed, who, if they had prospered in it, would have justified it and gloried in it. 2. Their master a beggar, a beggar for his life: *Thy servant Ben-hadad saith, "I pray thee, let me live, v.* 32. Though I live a perpetual exile from my own country, and captive in this, yet, upon any terms, *let me live."* What a great change is here, (1.) In his condition! How has he fallen from the height of power and prosperity to the depths of disgrace and distress, and all the miseries of poverty and slavery! See the uncertainty of human affairs; such turns are they subject to that the spoke which was uppermost may soon come to be undermost. (2.) In his temper—in the beginning of the chapter hectoring, swearing, and threatening, and none more high in his demands, but here crouching and whining and none more low in his requests! How meanly does he beg his life at the hand of him upon whom he had there been trampling! The most haughty in prosperity are commonly most abject in adversity: an even spirit will be the same in both conditions. See how God glorifies himself when he *looks upon proud men and abases them, and hides them in the dust together,* Job xl. 11—13.

II. Ahab's foolish acceptance of his submission, and the league he suddenly made with him upon it. He was proud to be thus courted by him whom he had feared, and enquired for him with great tenderness: *Is he yet alive? He is my brother,* brother-king, though not brother-Israelite; and Ahab valued himself more upon his royalty than on his religion, and others accordingly. "*Is he thy brother, Ahab?* Did he use thee like a brother when he sent thee that barbarous message? *v.* 5, 6. Would he have called thee brother if he had been the conqueror? Would he now have called himself *thy servant* if he had not been reduced to the utmost strait? Canst thou suffer thyself to be thus imposed upon by a forced and counterfeit submission?" This word *brother* they caught at (*v.* 33), and were thereby encouraged to go and fetch him to the king. He that calls him *brother* will let him live. Let poor penitents hear God, in his word, calling them *children* (Jer. xxxi. 20), catch at it, echo to it, and call him *Father*. Ben-hadad, upon his submission, shall not only be honourably conveyed (he *took him up into the chariot*), but treated with as an ally (*v.* 34): he *made a covenant with him,* not consulting God's prophets, or the elders of the land, or himself, concerning what was fit to be insisted on, but, as if Ben-hadad had been conqueror, he shall make his own terms. He might now have demanded some of Ben-hadad's cities, when all of them lay at the mercy of his victorious army; but was content with the restitution of his own. He might now have demanded the stores, and treasures, and magazines of Damascus, to augment the wealth and strength of his own kingdom, but was content with a poor liberty, at his own expense, to build streets there, a point of honour and no advantage, or no more than what the kings of Syria had had in Samaria, though they had never had so much power as he had now to support the demand of it. With this covenant he sent him away, without so much as reproving him for his blasphemous reflections upon the God of Israel, for whose honour Ahab had no concern. Note, There are those on whom success is ill bestowed; they know not how to serve God, or their generation, or even their own true interests, with their prosperity. *Let favour be shown to the wicked, yet will he not learn righteousness.*

III. The reproof given to Ahab for his clemency to Ben-hadad and his covenant with him. It was given him by a prophet, in the name of the Lord, the Jews say by Micaiah, and not unlikely, for Ahab complains of him (*ch.* xxii. 8) that he used to *prophesy evil concerning him.* This prophet designed to reprove Ahab by a parable, that he might oblige him to condemn himself, as Nathan and the woman of Tekoa did David. To make his parable the more plausible, he finds it necessary to put himself into the posture of a wounded soldier. 1. With some difficulty he gets himself wounded, for he would not wound himself with his own hands. He commanded one of his brother prophets, his *neighbour*, or *companion* (for so the word signifies), to smite him, and this in God's name (*v.* 35), but finds him not so willing to give the blow as he is to receive it; he refused to smite him: others, he thought, were forward enough to smite prophets, they need not smite one another. We cannot but think it was from a good principle he declined it. "If it must be done, let another do it, not I; I cannot find it in my heart to strike my friend." Good men can much more easily receive a wrongful blow than give one; yet because he disobeyed an express command of God (which was so much the worse if he was himself a prophet), like that other disobedient prophet (*ch.* xiii. 24), he was presently *slain by a lion, v.* 36. This was intended, not only to show, in general, how provoking disobedience is (Col. iii. 6), but to intimate to Ahab (who no doubt was told the story) that if a good prophet were thus punished for sparing his friend and God's, when God said, *Smite*, of much sorer punishment should a wicked king be thought worthy, who spared his enemy and God's, when God said, *Smite.* *Shall mortal man* pretend to *be more just than God, more pure* or more compassionate *than his Maker?* We must be merciful as he is merciful, and not otherwise. The next he met with made no difficulty of smiting him *(Volenti non fit injuria—He that asks for an injury is not wronged by it)* and did it so that he *wounded him, v.* 37. He fetched blood with the blow, probably in his face. 2. Wounded as he was, and disguised with ashes that he might not be known to be a prophet, he made his application to the king in a story wherein he charged himself with such a crime as the king was now guilty of in sparing Ben-hadad, and waited for the king's judgment upon it. The case in short is this—A prisoner taken in the battle was committed to his custody by a man (we may suppose one that had authority over him as his superior officer) with this charge, *If he be missing, thy life shall be for his life, v.* 39. The prisoner has made his escape through his carelessness. Can the chancery in the king's breast relieve him against his captain, who demands his life in lieu of the prisoner's? "By no means," says the king, "thou shouldst either not have undertaken the trust or been more careful and faithful to it; there is no remedy (*Currat lex—Let the law take its course*), thou hast forfeited thy bond, and execution must go out upon it: *So shall thy doom be, thou thyself hast decided it.*" Now the prophet has what he would have, puts off his disguise, and is known by Ahab himself to be a prophet (*v.* 41) and plainly tells him, "*Thou art the man.* Is it *my* doom? No, it is *thine; thou thyself hast decided it.* Out of thy own mouth art thou judged. God, thy superior and commander-in-chief, delivered into thy hands one plainly marked for destruction both by his own pride and God's providence, and thou hast not carelessly lost him, but wittingly and willingly dismissed him, and so hast been false to thy trust, and lost the end of thy victory; expect therefore no other than that *thy life shall go for his life,* which thou hast spared" (and so it did, *ch.* xxii. 35), "and thy *people for his people,* whom likewise thou hast spared," and so they did afterwards, 2 Kings x. 32, 33. When their other sins brought them low, this came into the account. There is a time when *keeping back the sword from blood* is *doing the work of the Lord deceitfully,* Jer. xlviii. 10. Foolish pity spoils the city. 3. We are told how Ahab resented this reproof. He *went to his house heavy and displeased (v.* 43), not truly penitent, or seeking to undo what he had done amiss, but enraged at the prophet, exasperated against God (as if he had been too severe in the sentence passed upon him), and yet vexed at himself, every way out of humour, notwithstanding his victory. He who by his providence had mortified the pride of one king, by his word cast a damp upon the triumphs of another. *Be wise therefore, O you kings! and be instructed to serve the Lord with fear and rejoice with trembling,* Ps. ii. 10, 11.

CHAP. XXI.

Ahab is still the unhappy subject of the sacred history; from the great affairs of his camp and kingdom this chapter leads us into his garden, and gives us an account of some ill things (and ill indeed they proved to him) relating to his domestic affairs. I. Ahab is sick for Naboth's vineyard, ver. 1—4. II. Naboth dies by Jezebel's plot, that the vineyard may escheat to Ahab, ver. 5—14. III. Ahab goes to take possession, ver. 15—16. IV. Elijah meets him, and denounces the judgments of God against him for his injustice, ver. 17—24. V. Upon his humiliation a reprieve is granted, ver. 25—29.

AND it came to pass after these things, *that* Naboth the Jezreelite had a vineyard, which *was* in Jezreel, hard by the palace of Ahab king of Samaria. 2 And Ahab spake unto Naboth, saying, Give me thy vineyard, that I may have it for a garden of herbs, because it *is* near unto my house: and I will give thee for it a better vineyard than it; *or,* if it seem good to thee, I will give thee the worth of it in money. 3 And Naboth said to Ahab, The LORD forbid it me, that I should give the inheritance of my fathers unto thee. 4 And Ahab came into his house heavy and displeased because of the word which Naboth the Jezreelite had spoken to him: for he had said, I will not give thee the inheritance of my fathers. And he laid him down upon his bed, and turned away his face, and would eat no bread.

Here is, 1. Ahab coveting his neighbour's vineyard, which unhappily lay near his palace and conveniently for a kitchen-garden. Perhaps Naboth had been pleased that he had a vineyard which lay so advantageously for a prospect of the royal gardens, or the vending of its productions to the royal family; but the situation of it proved fatal to him. If he had had no vineyard, or it had lain obscure in some remote place, he would have preserved his life. But many a man's possessions have been his snare, and his neighbourhood to greatness has been of pernicious consequence. Ahab sets his eye and heart on this vineyard, *v.* 2. It will be a pretty addition to his demesne, a convenient out-let to his palace; and nothing will serve him but it must be his own. He is welcome to the fruits of it, welcome to walk in it; Naboth perhaps would have made him a lease of it for his life, to please him; but nothing will please him unless he have an absolute property in it, he and his heirs for ever. Yet he is not such a tyrant as to take it by force, but fairly proposes either to give Naboth the full value of it in money or a better vineyard in exchange. He had tamely quitted the great advantages God had given him of enlarging his dominion for the honour of his kingdom, by his victory over the Syrians, and now is eager to enlarge his garden, only for the convenience of his house, as if to be penny wise would atone for being pound foolish. To desire a convenience to his estate was not evil (there would be no buying if there were no desire of what is bought; the virtuous woman *considers a field and buys it*); but to desire any thing inordinately, though we would compass it by lawful means, is a fruit of selfishness, as if we must engross all the conveniences, and none must live, or live comfortably, by us, contrary to the law of contentment, and the letter of the tenth commandment, *Thou shalt not covet thy neighbour's house*. 2. The repulse he met with in this desire. Naboth would by no means part with it (*v.* 3): *The Lord forbid it me;* and the Lord did forbid it, else he would not have been so rude and uncivil to his prince as not to gratify him in so small a matter. Canaan was in a peculiar manner God's land; the Israelites were his tenants; and this was one of the conditions of their leases, that they should not alienate (no, not to one another) any part of that which fell to their lot, unless in case of extreme necessity, and then only till the year of jubilee, Lev. xxv. 28. Now Naboth foresaw that, if his vineyard were sold to the crown, it would never return to his heirs, no, not in the jubilee. He would gladly oblige the king, but he must obey God rather than men, and therefore in this matter desires to be excused. Ahab knew the law, or should have known it, and therefore did ill to ask that which his subject could not grant without sin. Some conceive that Naboth looked upon his earthly inheritance as an earnest of his lot in the heavenly Canaan, and therefore would not part with the former, lest it should amount to a forfeiture of the latter. He seems to have been a conscientious man, who would rather hazard the king's displeasure than offend God, and probably was one of the 7000 that had not bowed the knee to Baal, for which, it may be, Ahab owed him a grudge. 3. Ahab's great discontent and uneasiness hereupon. He was as before (*ch.* xx. 43) *heavy and displeased* (*v.* 4), grew melancholy upon it, threw himself upon his bed, would not eat nor admit company to come to him. He could by no means digest the affront. His proud spirit aggravated the indignity Naboth did him in denying him, as a thing not to be suffered. He cursed the squeamishness of Naboth's conscience, which he pretended to consult the peace of, and secretly meditated revenge. Nor could he bear the disappointment; it cut him to the heart to be crossed in his desires, and he was perfectly sick for vexation. Note, (1.) Discontent is a sin that is its own punishment and makes men torment themselves; it makes the spirit sad, the body sick, and all the enjoyments sour; it is the heaviness of the heart and the rottenness of the bones. (2.) It is a sin that is its own parent. It arises not from the condition, but from the mind. As we find Paul contented in a prison, so Ahab discontent in a palace. He had all the delights of Canaan, that pleasant land, at command, the wealth of a kingdom, the pleasures of a court, and the honours and powers of a throne; and yet *all this avails him nothing* without Naboth's vineyard. Inordinate desires expose men to continual vexations, and those that are disposed to fret, be they ever so happy, will always find something or other to fret at.

5 But Jezebel his wife came to him, and said unto him, Why is thy spirit so sad, that thou eatest no bread? 6 And he said unto her, Because I spake unto Naboth the Jezreelite, and said unto him, Give me thy vineyard for money; or else, if it please thee, I will give thee *another* vineyard for it: and he answered, I will not give thee my vineyard. 7 And Jezebel his wife said unto him, Dost thou now govern the kingdom of Israel? arise, *and* eat bread, and let thine heart be merry: I will give thee the vineyard of Naboth the Jezreelite. 8 So she wrote letters in Ahab's name, and sealed *them* with his seal, and sent the letters unto the elders and to the nobles that *were* in his city, dwelling with Naboth. 9 And she wrote in the letters, saying, Proclaim a fast, and set Naboth on high among the people: 10 And set two men, sons of Belial, before him, to bear witness against him, saying, Thou didst blaspheme God and the king. And *then* carry him out, and stone him, that he may die. 11 And the men of his city, *even* the elders and the nobles who were the inhabitants in his city, did as Jezebel had sent unto them, *and* as it *was* written in the letters which she had sent unto them. 12 They proclaimed a fast, and set Naboth on high among the people. 13 And there came in two men, children of Belial, and sat before him: and the men of Belial witnessed against him, *even* against Naboth, in the presence of the people, saying, Naboth did blaspheme God and the king. Then they car-

ried him forth out of the city, and stoned him with stones, that he died. 14 Then they sent to Jezebel, saying, Naboth is stoned, and is dead. 15 And it came to pass, when Jezebel heard that Naboth was stoned, and was dead, that Jezebel said to Ahab, Arise, take possession of the vineyard of Naboth the Jezreelite, which he refused to give thee for money: for Naboth is not alive, but dead. 16 And it came to pass, when Ahab heard that Naboth was dead, that Ahab rose up to go down to the vineyard of Naboth the Jezreelite, to take possession of it.

Nothing but mischief is to be expected when Jezebel enters into the story—*that cursed woman*, 2 Kings ix. 34.

I. Under pretence of comforting her afflicted husband, she feeds his pride and passion, and blows the coals of his corruptions. It became her to take notice of his grief and to enquire into the cause of it, *v.* 5. Those have forgotten both the duty and affection of the conjugal relation that interest not themselves in each other's troubles. He told her what troubled him (*v.* 6), yet invidiously concealed Naboth's reason for his refusal, representing it as peevish, when it was conscientious—*I will not give it thee*, whereas he said, *I may not*. What! says Jezebel (*v.* 7), *Dost thou govern Israel? Arise, and eat bread.* She does well to persuade him to shake off his melancholy, and not to sink under his burden, to be easy and cheerful; whatever was his grief, grieving would not redress it, but pleasantness would alleviate it. Her plea is, *Dost thou now govern Israel?* This is capable of a good sense: "Does it become so great a prince as thou art to cast thyself down for so small a matter? Thou shamest thyself, and profanest thy crown; it is below thee to take notice of so inconsiderable a thing. Art thou fit to govern Israel, who hast no better a government of thy own passions? Or hast thou so rich a kingdom at command and canst not thou be without this one vineyard?" We should learn to quiet ourselves, under our crosses, with the thoughts of the mercies we enjoy, especially our hopes of the kingdom. But she meant it in a bad sense: "*Dost thou govern Israel*, and shall any subject thou hast deny thee any thing thou hast a mind to? Art thou a king? It is below thee to buy and pay, much more to beg and pray; use thy prerogative, and take by force what thou canst not compass by fair means; instead of resenting the affront thus, revenge it. If thou knowest not how to support the dignity of a king, let me alone to do it; give me but leave to make use of thy name, and I will soon *give thee the vineyard of Naboth;* right or wrong, it shall be thy own shortly, and cost thee nothing." Unhappy princes those are, and hurried apace towards their ruin, who have those about them that stir them up to acts of tyranny and teach them how to abuse their power.

II. In order to gratify him, she projects and compasses the death of Naboth. No less than his blood will serve to atone for the affront he has given to Ahab, which she thirsts after the more greedily because of his adherence to the law of the God of Israel.

1. Had she aimed only at his land, her false witnesses might have sworn him out of that by a forged deed (she could not have set up so weak a title but the elders of Jezreel would have adjudged it good); but *the adultress will hunt for the precious life*, Prov. vi. 26. Revenge is sweet. Naboth must die, and die as a malefactor, to gratify it.

(1.) Never were more wicked orders given by any prince than those which Jezebel sent to the magistrates of Jezreel, *v.* 8—10. She borrows the privy-seal, but the king shall not know what she will do with it. It is probable this was not the first time he had lent it to her, but that with it she had signed warrants for the slaying of the prophets. She makes use of the king's name, knowing the thing would please him when it was done, yet fearing he might scruple at the manner of doing it; in short, she commands them, upon their allegiance, to put Naboth to death, without giving them any reason for so doing. Had she sent witnesses to inform against him, the judges (who must go *secundum allegata et probata—according to allegations and proofs)* might have been imposed upon, and their sentence might have been rather their unhappiness than their crime; but to oblige them to find the witnesses, sons of Belial, to suborn them themselves, and then to give judgment upon a testimony which they knew to be false, was such an impudent defiance to every thing that is just and sacred as we hope cannot be paralleled in any story. She must have looked upon the elders of Jezreel as men perfectly lost to every thing that is honest and honourable when she expected these orders should be obeyed. But she will put them in a way how to do it, having as much of the serpent's subtlety as she had of his poison. [1.] It must be done under colour of religion: "*Proclaim a fast;* signify to your city that you are apprehensive of some dreadful judgment coming upon you, which you must endeavour to avert, not only by prayer, but by finding out and by putting away the accursed thing; pretend to be afraid that there is some great offender among you undiscovered, for whose sake God is angry with your city; charge the people, if they know of any such, on that solemn occasion to inform against him, as they regard the welfare of the city; and at last let Naboth be fastened upon as the suspected person, probably because he does not join with his neighbours in their worship. This may serve for a pretence to *set him on high among the people,* to call him to the bar. Let proclamation be made that, if any one can inform the court against the prisoner, and prove him to be the Achan, they shall be heard; and then let the witnesses appear to give evidence against him." Note, There is no wickedness so vile, so horrid, but religion has sometimes been made a cloak and cover for it. We must not think at all the worse of fasting and praying for their having been sometimes thus abused, but much the worse of those wicked designs that have at any time been carried on under the shelter of them. [2.] It must be done *under colour of justice* too, and with the formalities of a legal process. Had she sent to them to hire some of their banditti, some desperate ruffians, to assassinate him, to stab him as he went along the streets in the night, the deed would have been bad enough; but to destroy him by a course of law, to use that power for the murdering of the innocent which ought to be their protection, was such a *violent perversion of justice and judgment* as was truly monstrous, yet such as we are directed *not to marvel at,* Eccl. v. 8. The crime they must lay to his charge was *blaspheming God and the king*—a complicated blasphemy. Surely she could not think to put a blasphemous sense upon the answer he had given to Ahab, as if denying him his vineyard were blaspheming the king, and giving the divine law for the reason were blaspheming God. No, she pretends not any ground at all for the charge: though there was no colour of truth in it, the witnesses must swear it, and Naboth must not be permitted to speak for himself, or cross-examine the witnesses, but immediately, under pretence of a universal detestation of the crime, they must *carry him out and stone him.* His blaspheming God would be the forfeiture of his life, but not of his estate, and therefore he is also charged with treason, in *blaspheming the king,* for which his estate was to be confiscated, that so Ahab might have his vineyard.

(2.) Never were wicked orders more wickedly obeyed than these were by the magistrates of Jezreel. They did not so much as dispute the command nor make any objections against it, though so palpably unjust, but punctually observed all the particulars of it, either because they feared Jezebel's cruelty or because they hated Naboth's piety, or both: They did *as it was written in the letters* (*v.* 11, 12), neither made any difficulty of it, nor met with any difficulty in it, but cleverly carried on the villany. They stoned Naboth to death (*v.* 13), and, as it should seem, his sons with him, or after him; for, when God came to make inquisition for blood, we find this article in the account (2 Kings ix. 26), *I have seen the blood of Naboth and the blood of his sons.* Perhaps they were secretly murdered, that they might not claim their father's estate nor complain of the wrong done him.

2. Let us take occasion from this sad story, (1.) To stand amazed at the wickedness of the wicked, and the power of Satan in the children of disobedience. What a holy indignation may we be filled with to see *wickedness in the place of judgment!* Eccl. iii. 16. (2.) To lament the hard case of oppressed innocency, and to mingle our tears with *the tears of the oppressed that have no comforter,* while *on the side of the oppressors there is power,* Eccl. iv. 1. (3.) To commit the keeping of our lives and comforts to God, for innocency itself will not always be our security. (4.) To rejoice in the belief of a judgment to come, in which such wrong judgments as these will be called over. Now we see that *there are just men to whom it happens according to the work of the wicked* (Eccl. viii. 14), but all will be set to rights in the great day.

III. Naboth being taken off, Ahab takes possession of his vineyard. 1. The elders of Jezreel sent notice to Jezebel very unconcernedly, sent it to her as a piece of agreeable news, *Naboth is stoned and is dead, v.* 14. Here let us observe that, as obsequious as the elders of Jezreel were to Jezebel's orders which she sent from Samaria for the murder of Naboth, so obsequious were the elders of Samaria afterwards to Jehu's orders which he sent from Jezreel for the murder of Ahab's seventy sons, only that was not done by course of law, 2 Kings x. 6, 7. Those tyrants that by their wicked orders debauch the consciences of their inferior magistrates may perhaps find at last the wheel return upon them, and that those who will not stick to do one cruel thing for them will be as ready to do another cruel thing against them. 2. Jezebel, jocund enough that her plot succeeded so well, brings notice to Ahab that *Naboth is not alive, but dead;* therefore, says she, *Arise, take possession of his vineyard, v.* 15. He might have taken possession by one of his officers, but so pleased is he with this accession to his estate that he will make a journey to Jezreel himself to enter upon it; and it should seem he went in state too, as if he had obtained some mighty victory, for Jehu remembers long after that he and Bidkar attended him at this time, 2 Kings ix. 25. If Naboth's sons were all put to death, Ahab thought himself entitled to the estate, *ob defectum sanguinis —in default of heirs* (as our law expresses it); if not, yet, Naboth dying as a criminal, he claimed it *ob delictum criminis—as forfeited by his crime.* Or, if neither would make him a good title, the absolute power of Jezebel would give it to him, and who would dare to oppose her will? Might often prevails against right, and wonderful is the divine patience that suffers it to do so. God is certainly *of purer eyes than to behold ini-*

quity, and yet for a time *keeps silence when the wicked devours the man that is more righteous than he,* Hab. i. 13.

17 And the word of the LORD came to Elijah the Tishbite, saying, 18 Arise, go down to meet Ahab king of Israel, which *is* in Samaria: behold, *he is* in the vineyard of Naboth, whither he is gone down to possess it. 19 And thou shalt speak unto him, saying, Thus saith the LORD, Hast thou killed, and also taken possession? And thou shalt speak unto him, saying, Thus saith the LORD, In the place where dogs licked the blood of Naboth shall dogs lick thy blood, even thine. 20 And Ahab said to Elijah, Hast thou found me, O mine enemy? And he answered, I have found *thee:* because thou hast sold thyself to work evil in the sight of the LORD. 21 Behold, I will bring evil upon thee, and will take away thy posterity, and will cut off from Ahab him that pisseth against the wall, and him that is shut up and left in Israel, 22 And will make thine house like the house of Jeroboam the son of Nebat, and like the house of Baasha the son of Ahijah, for the provocation wherewith thou hast provoked *me* to anger, and made Israel to sin. 23 And of Jezebel also spake the LORD, saying, The dogs shall eat Jezebel by the wall of Jezreel. 24 Him that dieth of Ahab in the city the dogs shall eat; and him that dieth in the field shall the fowls of the air eat. 25 But there was none like unto Ahab, which did sell himself to work wickedness in the sight of the LORD, whom Jezebel his wife stirred up. 26 And he did very abominably in following idols, according to all *things* as did the Amorites, whom the LORD cast out before the children of Israel. 27 And it came to pass, when Ahab heard those words, that he rent his clothes, and put sackcloth upon his flesh, and fasted, and lay in sackcloth, and went softly. 28 And the word of the LORD came to Elijah the Tishbite, saying, 29 Seest thou how Ahab humbleth himself before me? because he humbleth himself before me, I will not bring the evil in his days: *but* in his son's days will I bring the evil upon his house.

In these verses we may observe,

I. The very bad character that is given of Ahab (*v.* 25, 26), which comes in here to justify God in the heavy sentence passed upon him, and to show that though it was passed upon occasion of his sin in the matter of Naboth (which David's sin in the matter of Uriah did too much resemble), yet God would not have punished him so severely if he had not been guilty of many other sins, especially idolatry; whereas David, except in that one matter, *did that which was right.* But, as to Ahab, there was *none like him,* so ingenious and industrious in sin, and that made a trade of it. He *sold himself to work wickedness,* that is, he made himself a perfect slave to his lusts, and was as much at their beck and command as ever any servant was at his master's. He was wholly given up to sin, and, upon condition he might have the pleasures of it, he would take the wages of it, which is death, Rom. vi. 23. Blessed Paul complained that he was *sold under sin* (Rom. vii. 14), as a poor captive against his will; but Ahab was voluntary: he *sold himself to sin;* of choice, and as his own act and deed, he submitted to the dominion of sin. It was no excuse of his crimes that *Jezebel his wife stirred him up* to do wickedly, and made him, in many respects, worse than otherwise he would have been. To what a pitch of impiety did he arrive who had such tinder of corruption in his heart and such a temper in his bosom to strike fire into it! In many things he did ill, but he did *most abominably in following idols,* like the Canaanites; his immoralities were very provoking to God, but his idolatries were especially so. Israel's case was sad when a prince of such a character as this reigned over them.

II. The message with which Elijah was sent to him, when he went to take possession of Naboth's vineyard, *v.* 17—19.

1. Hitherto God kept silence, did not intercept Jezebel's letters, nor stay the process of the elders of Jezreel; but now Ahab is reproved and his *sin set in order before his eyes.* (1.) The person sent is Elijah. A prophet of lower rank was sent with messages of kindness to him, *ch.* xx. 13. But the father of the prophets is sent to try him, and condemn him, for his murder. (2.) The place is Naboth's vineyard and the time just when he is taking possession of it; then, and there, must his doom be read him. By taking possession, he avowed all that was done, and made himself guilty *ex post facto —as an accessary after the fact.* There he was taken in the commission of the errors, and therefore the conviction would come upon him with so much the more force. "What

hast thou to do in this vineyard? What good canst thou expect from it when it is *purchased with blood* (Hab. ii. 12) and thou hast *caused the owner thereof to lose his life?"* Job xxxi. 39. Now that he is pleasing himself with his ill-gotten wealth, and giving direction for the turning of this vineyard into a flower-garden, his *meat in his bowels is turned. He shall not feel quietness. When he is about to fill his belly, God shall cast the fury of his wrath upon him,* Job xx. 14, 20, 23.

2. Let us see what passed between him and the prophet.

(1.) Ahab vented his wrath against Elijah, fell into a passion at the sight of him, and, instead of humbling himself before the prophet, as he ought to have done (2 Chron. xxxvi. 12), was ready to fly in his face. *Hast thou found me, O my enemy? v.* 20. This shows, [1.] That he hated him. The last time we found them together they parted very good friends, *ch.* xviii. 46. Then Ahab had countenanced the reformation, and therefore then all was well between him and the prophet; but now he had relapsed, and was worse than ever. His conscience told him he had made God his enemy, and therefore he could not expect Elijah should be his friend. Note, That man's condition is very miserable that has made the word of God his enemy, and his condition is very desperate that reckons the ministers of that word his enemies because they *tell him the truth,* Gal. iv. 16. Ahab, having sold himself to sin, was resolved to stand to his bargain, and could not endure him that would have helped him to recover himself, [2.] That he feared him: *Hast thou found me?* intimating that he shunned him all he could, and it was now a terror to him to see him. The sight of him was like that of the handwriting upon the wall to Belshazzar; it made his *countenance change, the joints of his loins were loosed, and his knees smote one against another.* Never was poor debtor or criminal so confounded at the sight of the officer that came to arrest him. Men may thank themselves if they make God and his word a terror to them.

(2.) Elijah denounced God's wrath against Ahab: *I have found thee* (says he, *v.* 20), *because thou hast sold thyself to work evil.* Note, Those that give up themselves to sin will certainly be found out, sooner or later, to their unspeakable horror and amazement. Ahab is now set to the bar, as Naboth was, and trembles more than he did. [1.] Elijah finds the indictment against him, and convicts him upon the notorious evidence of the fact (*v.* 19): *Hast thou killed, and also taken possession?* He was thus charged with the murder of Naboth, and it would not serve him to say the law killed him (perverted justice is the highest injustice), nor that, if he was unjustly prosecuted, it was not his doing —he knew nothing of it; for it was to please him that it was done, and he had shown himself pleased with it, and so had made himself guilty of all that was done in the unjust prosecution of Naboth. He killed, for he took possession. If he takes the garden, he takes the guilt with it. *Terra transit cum onere—The land with the incumbrance.* [2.] He passes judgment upon him. He told him from God that his family should be ruined and rooted out (*v.* 21) and all his posterity cut off,—that his house should be made like the houses of his wicked predecessors, Jeroboam and Baasha (*v.* 22), particularly that those who died in the city should be meat for dogs and those who died in the field meat for birds (*v.* 24), which had been foretold of Jeroboam's house (*ch.* xiv. 11), and of Baasha's (*ch.* xvi. 4),—that Jezebel, particularly, should be devoured by dogs (*v.* 23), which was fulfilled (2 Kings ix. 36),—and, as for Ahab himself, that the dogs should *lick his blood* in the very same place where they licked Naboth's (*v.* 19—"*Thy blood, even thine,* though it be royal blood, though it swell thy veins with pride and boil in thy heart with anger, shall ere long be an entertainment for the dogs"), which was fulfilled, *ch.* xxii. 38. This intimates that he should die a violent death, should come to his grave with blood, and that disgrace should attend him, the foresight of which must needs be a great mortification to such a proud man. Punishments after death are here most insisted on, which, though such as affected the body only, were perhaps designed as figures of the soul's misery after death.

III. Ahab's humiliation under the sentence passed upon him, and the favourable message sent him thereupon. 1. Ahab was a kind of penitent. The message Elijah delivered to him in God's name put him into a fright for the present, so that he *rent his clothes* and *put on sackcloth, v.* 27. He was still a proud hardened sinner, and yet thus reduced. Note, God can make the stoutest heart to tremble and the proudest to humble itself. His word is quick and powerful, and is, when he pleases to make it so, like a *fire and a hammer,* Jer. xxiii. 29. It made Felix tremble. Ahab put on the garb and guise of a penitent, and yet his heart was unhumbled and unchanged. After this, we find, he hated a faithful prophet, *ch.* xxii. 8. Note, It is no new thing to find the show and profession of repentance where yet the truth and substance of it are wanting. Ahab's repentance was only what might be seen of men: *Seest thou* (says God to Elijah) *how Ahab humbles himself;* it was external only, the garments rent, but not the heart. A hypocrite may go very far in the outward performance of holy duties and yet come short. 2. He obtained hereby a reprieve, which I may call a kind of pardon. Though it was but an outside repentance (lamenting the judgment only, and not the sin), though he did not leave his idols, nor restore the vineyard to Naboth's heirs, yet, because he did hereby give some glory to God, God took notice of it, and bade Elijah take notice of it: *Seest thou how Ahab humbles himself? v.* 29. In consideration of this the threatened ruin of his house, which had not been fixed to any time, should be *adjourned to his son's days.* The sentence should not be revoked, but the execution suspended. Now, (1.) This discovers the great goodness of God, and his readiness to show mercy, which here *rejoices against judgment.* Favour was shown to this wicked man that God might magnify his goodness (says bishop Sanderson) even to the hazard of his other divine perfections; as if (says he) God would be thought unholy, or untrue, or unjust (though he be none of these), or any thing, rather than unmerciful. (2.) This teaches us to take notice of that which is good even in those who are not so good as they should be: let it be commended as far as it goes. (3.) This gives a reason why wicked people sometimes prosper long; God is rewarding their external services with external mercies. (4.) This encourages all those that truly repent and unfeignedly believe the holy gospel. If a pretending partial penitent shall go to his house reprieved, doubtless a sincere penitent shall *go to his house justified.*

CHAP. XXII.

This chapter finishes the history of Ahab's reign. It was promised in the close of the foregoing chapter that the ruin of his house should not come in his days, but his days were soon at an end. His war with the Syrians at Ramoth-Gilead is that which we have an account of in this chapter. I. His preparations for that war. He consulted, 1. His privy-council, ver. 1—3. 2. Jehoshaphat, ver. 4. 3. His prophets. (1.) His own, who encouraged him to go on this expedition (ver. 5, 6), Zedekiah particularly, ver. 11, 12. (2.) A prophet of the Lord, Micaiah, who was desired to come by Jehoshaphat (ver. 7, 8), sent for (ver. 9, 10—13, 14), upbraided Ahab with his confidence in the false prophets (ver. 15), but foretold his fall in this expedition (ver. 16—18), and gave him an account how he came to be thus imposed upon by his prophets, ver. 19—23. He is abused by Zedekiah (ver. 24, 25), and imprisoned by Ahab, ver. 26—28 II. The battle itself, in which, 1. Jehoshaphat is exposed But, 2. Ahab is slain, ver. 29—40. In the close of the chapter we have a short account, (1.) Of the good reign of Jehoshaphat king of Judah, ver. 41—50. (2.) Of the wicked reign of Ahaziah king of Israel, ver. 51—53.

AND they continued three years without war between Syria and Israel. 2 And it came to pass in the third year, that Jehoshaphat the king of Judah came down to the king of Israel. 3 And the king of Israel said unto his servants, Know ye that Ramoth in Gilead *is* our's, and we *be* still, *and* take it not out of the hand of the king of Syria? 4 And he said unto Jehoshaphat, Wilt thou go with me to battle to Ramoth-gilead? And Jehoshaphat said to the king of Israel, I *am* as thou *art,* my people as thy people, my horses as thy horses. 5 And Jehoshaphat said unto the king of Israel, Enquire, I pray thee, at the word of the LORD to day. 6 Then the king of Israel gathered the prophets together, about four hundred men, and said unto them, Shall I go against Ramoth-gilead to battle, or shall I forbear? And they said, Go up; for the LORD shall deliver *it* into the hand of the king. 7 And Jehoshaphat said, *Is there* not here a prophet of the LORD besides, that we might enquire of him? 8 And the king of Israel said unto Jehoshaphat, *There is* yet one man, Micaiah the son of Imlah, by whom we may enquire of the LORD: but I hate him; for he doth not prophesy good concerning me, but evil. And Jehoshaphat said, Let not the king say so. 9 Then the king of Israel called an officer, and said, Hasten *hither* Micaiah the son of Imlah. 10 And the king of Israel and Jehoshaphat the king of Judah sat each on his throne, having put on their robes, in a void place in the entrance of the gate of Samaria; and all the prophets prophesied before them. 11 And Zedekiah the son of Chenaanah made him horns of iron: and he said, Thus saith the LORD, With these shalt thou push the Syrians, until thou have consumed them. 12 And all the prophets prophesied so, saying, Go up to Ramoth-gilead, and prosper: for the LORD shall deliver *it* into the king's hand. 13 And the messenger that was gone to call Micaiah spake unto him, saying, Behold now, the words of the prophets *declare* good unto the king with one mouth: let thy word, I pray thee, be like the word of one of them, and speak *that which is* good. 14 And Micaiah said, *As* the LORD liveth, what the LORD saith unto me, that will I speak.

Though Ahab continued under guilt and wrath, and the dominion of the lusts to which he had sold himself, yet, as a reward for his professions of repentance and humiliation, though the time drew near when he should descend into battle and perish, yet we have him blessed with a three years' peace (*v.* 1) and an honourable visit made him by Jehoshaphat king of Judah, *v.* 2. The Jews have a fabulous conceit, that when Ahab humbled himself for his sin, and lay in sackcloth, he sent for Jehoshaphat to come to him, to chastise him; and that he staid with him for some time, and gave him so many stripes every day. This is a groundless tradition He came now, it is probable, to consult him about the affairs of their kingdoms. It is strange that so great a man as Jehoshaphat would pay so much respect to a kingdom revolted from the house of David, and that so good a man should show so much kindness to a king revolted from the worship of God. But, though he was a godly man, his temper was too easy, which betrayed him into snares and inconveniences. The Syrians durst not give Ahab any disturbance. But,

I. Ahab here meditates a war against the Syrians, and advises concerning it with those about him, *v.* 3. The king of Syria gave him the provocation; when he lay at his mercy, he promised to restore him his cities (*ch.* xx. 34), and Ahab foolishly took his word, when he ought not to have dismissed him till the cities were put into his possession. But now he knows by experience, what he ought before to have considered, that as the kisses, so the promises, *of an enemy are deceitful*, and there is no confidence to be put in leagues extorted by distress. Ben-hadad is one of those princes that think themselves bound by their word no further and no longer than it is for their interest. Whether any other cities were restored we do not find, but Ramoth-Gilead was not, a considerable city in the tribe of Gad, on the other side Jordan, a Levites' city, and one of the cities of refuge. Ahab blames himself, and his people, that they did not bestir themselves to recover it out of the hands of the Syrians, and to chastise Ben-hadad's violation of his league; and resolves to let that ungrateful perfidious prince know that as he had given him peace he could give him trouble. Ahab has a good cause, yet succeeds not. Equity is not to be judged of by prosperity.

II. He engages Jehoshaphat, and draws him in, to join with him in this expedition, for the recovery of Ramoth-Gilead, *v.* 4. And here I do not wonder that Ahab should desire the assistance of so pious and prosperous a neighbour. Even bad men have often coveted the friendship of the good. It is desirable to have an interest in those that have an interest in heaven, and to have those with us that have God with them. But it is strange that Jehoshaphat will go so entirely into Ahab's interests as to say, *I am as thou art, and my people as thy people.* I hope not; Jehoshaphat and his people are not so wicked and corrupt as Ahab and his people. Too great a complaisance to evil-doers has brought many good people, through unwariness, into a dangerous fellowship with *the unfruitful works of darkness.* Jehoshaphat had like to have paid dearly for his compliment when, in battle, he was taken for Ahab. Yet some observe that in joining with Israel against Syria he atoned for his father's fault in joining with Syria against Israel, *ch.* xv. 19, 20.

III. At the special instance and request of Jehoshaphat, he asks counsel of the prophets concerning this expedition. Ahab thought it enough to consult with his statesmen, but Jehoshaphat moves that they should *enquire of the word of the Lord, v.* 5. Note, 1. Whithersoever a good man goes he desires to take God along with him, and will acknowledge him in all his ways, ask leave of him, and look up to him for success. 2. Whithersoever a good man goes he ought to take his religion along with him, and not be ashamed to own it, no, not when he is with those who have no kindness for it. Jehoshaphat has not left behind him, at Jerusalem, his affection, his veneration, for *the word of the Lord*, but both avows it and endeavours to introduce it into Ahab's court. If Ahab drew him into his wars, he will draw Ahab into his devotions.

IV. Ahab's 400 prophets, the standing regiment he had of them (*prophets of the groves* they called them), agreed to encourage him in this expedition and to assure him of success, *v.* 6. He put the question to them with a seeming fairness: *Shall I go or shall I forbear?* But they knew which way his inclination was and designed only to humour the two kings. To please Jehoshaphat, they made use of the name *Jehovah:* He shall *deliver it into the hand of the king;* they stole the word from the true prophets (Jer. xxiii. 30) and spoke their language. To please Ahab they said, *Go up.* They had indeed probabilities on their side: Ahab had, not long since, beaten the Syrians twice; he had now a good cause, and was much strengthened by his alliance with Jehoshaphat. But they pretended to speak by prophecy, not by rational conjecture, by divine, not human, foresight: "Thou shalt certainly recover Ramoth-Gilead." Zedekiah, a leading man among these prophets, in imitation of the true prophets, illustrated his false prophecy with a sign, *v.* 11. He made himself a pair of iron horns, representing the two kings, and their honour and power (both of which were signified by horns, exaltation and force), and with these the Syrians must be pushed. All the prophets agreed, as one man, that Ahab should return from this expedition a conqueror, *v.* 12. Unity is not always the mark of a true church and a true ministry. Here were 400 men that prophesied with one mind and one mouth, and yet all in an error.

V. Jehoshaphat cannot relish this sort of preaching; it is not like what he was used to. The false prophets cannot so mimic the true but that he who had spiritual senses exercised could discern the fallacy, and therefore he enquired for a *prophet of the Lord besides, v.* 7. He is too much of a courtier to say any thing by way of reflection on the king's chaplains, but he waits to see a *prophet of the Lord*, intimating that he could not look upon these to be so. They *seemed to be somewhat* (whatever they were, it made no matter to him), but, in conference, they *added nothing to him,* they gave him no satisfaction, Gal. ii. 6. One faithful prophet of the Lord was worth them all.

VI. Ahab has another, but one he hates, Micaiah by name, and, to please Jehoshaphat, he is willing to have him sent for, *v.* 8—10. Ahab owned they might *enquire of the Lord by him,* that he was a true prophet, and one that knew God's mind. And yet, 1. He hated him, and was not ashamed to own to the king of Judah that he did so, and to give this for a reason, He *doth not prophesy good concerning me, but evil.* And whose fault was that? If Ahab had done well, he would have heard nothing but good from heaven; if he do ill, he may thank himself for all the uneasiness which the reproofs and threats of God's word gave him. Note, Those are wretchedly hardened in sin, and are ripening apace for ruin, who hate God's ministers because they deal plainly with them and faithfully warn them of their misery and danger by reason of sin, and reckon those their enemies that *tell them the truth.* 2. He had (it should seem) imprisoned him; for, when he committed him (*v.* 26), he bade the officer carry him back, namely, to the place whence he came. We may suppose that this was he that reproved him for his clemency to Ben-hadad (*ch.* xx. 38, &c.) and for so doing was cast into prison, where he had lain these three years. This was the reason why Ahab knew where to find him so readily, *v.* 9. But his imprisonment had not excluded him from divine visits: the spirit of prophecy continued with him there. He was bound, but *the word of the Lord was not.* Nor did it in the least abate his courage, nor make him less confident or faithful in delivering his message. Jehoshaphat gave too gentle a reproof to Ahab for expressing his indignation against a faithful prophet: *Let not the king say so, v.* 8. He should have said, "Thou art unjust to the prophet, unkind to thyself, and puttest an affront upon his Lord and thine, in saying so." Such sinners as Ahab must be rebuked sharply. However he so far yielded to the reproof that, for fear of provoking Jehoshaphat to break off from his alliance with him, he orders Micaiah to be sent for with all speed, *v.* 9. The two kings sat each in their robes and chairs of state, in the gate of Samaria, ready to receive this poor prophet, and to hear what he had to say; for many will give God's word the hearing that will not lend it an obedient ear. They were attended with a crowd of flattering prophets, that could not think of prophesying any thing but what was very sweet and very smooth to two such glorious princes now in confederacy. Those that love to be flattered shall not want flatterers.

VII. Micaiah is pressed by the officer that fetches him to follow the cry, *v.* 13. That officer was unworthy the name of an Israelite who pretended to prescribe to a prophet; but he thought him altogether such a one as the rest, who studied to please men and not God. He told Micaiah how unanimous the other prophets were in foretelling the king's good success, how agreeable it was to the king, intimating that it was his interest to say as they said—he might thereby gain, not only enlargement, but preferment. Those that dote upon worldly things themselves think every body else should do so too, and true or false, right or wrong, speak and act for their secular interest only. He intimated likewise that it would be to no purpose to contradict such a numerous and unanimous vote; he would be ridiculed, as affecting a foolish singularity, if he should. But Micaiah, who knows better things, protests, and backs his protestation with an oath, that he will deliver his message from God with all faithfulness, whether it be pleasing or displeasing to his prince (*v.* 14): "*What the Lord saith to me, that will I speak,* without addition, diminution, or alteration." This was nobly resolved, and as became one who had his eye to a greater King than either of these, arrayed with brighter robes, and sitting on a higher throne.

15 So he came to the king. And the king said unto him, Micaiah, shall we go against Ramoth-gilead to battle, or shall we forbear? And he answered him, Go, and prosper: for the LORD shall deliver *it* into the hand of the king. 16 And the king said unto him, How many times shall I adjure thee that thou tell me nothing but *that which is* true in the name of the LORD? 17 And he said, I saw all Israel scattered upon the hills, as sheep that have not a shepherd: and the LORD said, These have no master: let them return every man to his house in peace. 18 And the king of Israel said unto Jehoshaphat, Did I not tell thee that he would prophesy no good concerning me, but evil? 19 And he said, Hear thou therefore the word of the LORD: I saw the LORD sitting on his throne, and all the host of heaven standing by him on his right hand and on his left. 20 And the LORD said, Who shall persuade Ahab, that he may go up and fall at Ramoth-gilead? And one said on this manner, and another said on that manner. 21 And there came forth a spirit, and stood before the LORD, and said, I will persuade

him. 22 And the LORD said unto him, Wherewith? And he said, I will go forth, and I will be a lying spirit in the mouth of all his prophets. And he said, Thou shalt persuade *him*, and prevail also: go forth, and do so. 23 Now therefore, behold, the LORD hath put a lying spirit in the mouth of all these thy prophets, and the LORD hath spoken evil concerning thee. 24 But Zedekiah the son of Chenaanah went near, and smote Micaiah on the cheek, and said, Which way went the Spirit of the LORD from me to speak unto thee? 25 And Micaiah said, Behold, thou shalt see in that day, when thou shalt go into an inner chamber to hide thyself. 26 And the king of Israel said, Take Micaiah, and carry him back unto Amon the governor of the city, and to Joash the king's son; 27 And say, Thus saith the king, Put this *fellow* in the prison, and feed him with bread of affliction and with water of affliction, until I come in peace. 28 And Micaiah said, If thou return at all in peace, the LORD hath not spoken by me. And he said, Hearken, O people, every one of you.

Here Micaiah does well, but, as is common, suffers ill for so doing.

I. We are told how faithfully he delivered his message, as one that was more solicitous to please God than to humour either the great or the many. In three ways he delivers his message, and all displeasing to Ahab:—

1. He spoke as the rest of the prophets had spoken, but ironically: *Go, and prosper*, *v.* 15. Ahab put the same question to him that he had put to his own prophets *(Shall we go, or shall we forbear?)* seeming desirous to know God's mind, when, like Balaam, he was strongly bent to do his own, which Micaiah plainly took notice of when he bade him go, but with such an air and pronunciation as plainly showed he spoke it by way of derision; as if he had said, "I know you are determined to go, and I hear your own prophets are unanimous in assuring you of success; go then, and take what follows. They say, *The Lord shall deliver it into the hand of the king;* but I do not tell thee that *thus saith the Lord;* no, he saith otherwise." Note, Those deserve to be bantered that love to be flattered; and it is just with God to give up those to their own counsels that give up themselves to their own lusts, Eccl. xi. 9. In answer to this Ahab adjured him to tell him the truth, and not to jest with him (*v.* 16), as if he sincerely desired to know both what God would have him to do and what he would do with him, yet intending to represent the prophet as a perverse ill-humoured man, that would not tell him the truth till he was thus put to his oath, or adjured to do it.

2. Being thus pressed, he plainly foretold that the king would be cut off in this expedition, and his army scattered, *v.* 17. He saw them in a vision, or in a dream, dispersed upon the mountains, as sheep that had no one to guide them. *Smite the shepherd, and the sheep will be scattered,* Zech. xiii. 7. This intimates, (1.) That Israel should be deprived of their king, who was their shepherd. God took notice of it, *These have no master.* (2.) That they would be obliged to retire *re infectâ—without accomplishing their object.* He does not foresee any great slaughter in the army, but that they should make a dishonourable retreat. *Let them return every man to his house in peace,* put into disorder indeed for the present, but no great losers by the death of their king; he shall fall in war, but they shall go home in peace. Thus Micaiah, in his prophecy, testified what he had seen and heard (let them take it how they pleased), while the others prophesied merely *out of their own hearts;* see Jer. xxiii. 28. "The prophet that has a dream let him tell that, and so quote his authority; *and he that has my word, let him speak my word faithfully,* and not his own; for *what is the chaff to the wheat?*" Now Ahab finds himself aggrieved, turns to Jehoshaphat, and appeals to him whether Micaiah had not manifestly a spite against him, *v.* 18. Those that bear malice to others are generally willing to believe that others bear malice to them, though they have no cause for it, and therefore to put the worst constructions upon all they say. What evil did Micaiah prophesy to Ahab in telling him that, if he proceeded in this expedition, it would be fatal to him, while he might choose whether he would proceed in it or no? The greatest kindness we can do to one that is going in a dangerous way is to tell him of his danger.

3. He informed the king how it was that all his prophets encouraged him to proceed, that God permitted Satan by them to deceive him into his ruin, and he by vision knew of it; it was represented to him, and he represented it to Ahab, that the God of heaven had determined he should fall at Ramoth-Gilead (*v.* 19, 20), that the favour he had wickedly shown to Ben-hadad might be punished by him and his Syrians, and that he being in some doubt whether he should go to Ramoth-Gilead or no, and resolving to be advised by his prophets, they should persuade him to it and prevail (*v.* 21, 22); and hence it was that they encouraged him with so much assurance (*v.* 23); it was a lie from the father of lies, but by divine permission.

This matter is here represented after the manner of men. We are not to imagine that God is ever put upon new counsels, or is ever at a loss for means whereby to effect his purposes, nor that he needs to consult with angels, or any creature, about the methods he should take, nor that he is the author of sin or the cause of any man's either telling or believing a lie; but, besides what was intended by this with reference to Ahab himself, it is to teach us, (1.) That God is a great king above all kings, and has a throne above all the thrones of earthly princes. "You have your thrones," said Micaiah to these two kings, "and you think you may do what you will, and we must all say as you would have us; but *I saw the Lord sitting upon his throne*, and every man's judgment proceeding from him, and therefore I must say as he says; he is not a man, as you are." (2.) That he is continually attended and served by an innumerable company of angels, those heavenly hosts, who stand by him, ready to go where he sends them and to do what he bids them, messengers of mercy *on his right hand*, of wrath *on his left hand*. (3.) That he not only takes cognizance of, but presides over, all the affairs of this lower world, and overrules them *according to the counsel of his own will*. The rise and fall of princes, the issues of war, and all the great affairs of state, which are the subject of the consultations of wise and great men, are no more above God's direction than the meanest concerns of the poorest cottages are below his notice. (4.) That God has many ways of bringing about his own counsels, particularly concerning the fall of sinners when they are ripe for ruin; he can do it either in this manner or in that manner. (5.) That there are malicious and lying spirits which go about continually seeking to devour, and, in order to that, seeking to deceive, and especially to put lies into the mouths of prophets, by them to entice many to their destruction. (6.) It is not without the divine permission that the devil deceives men, and even thereby God serves his own purposes. *With him are strength and wisdom, the deceived and the deceiver are his*, Job xii. 16. When he pleases, for the punishment of those who receive not the truth in the love of it, he not only *lets Satan loose to deceive them* (Rev. xx. 7, 8), but *gives men up to strong delusions to believe* him, 2 Thess. ii. 11, 12. (7.) Those are manifestly marked for ruin that are thus given up. God has certainly *spoken evil concerning those* whom he has given up to be imposed upon by lying prophets. Thus Micaiah gave Ahab fair warning, not only of the danger of proceeding in this war, but of the danger of believing those that encouraged him to proceed. Thus we are warned to *beware of false prophets*, and to try the spirits; the lying spirit never deceives so fatally as *in the mouth of prophets*.

II. We are told how he was abused for delivering his message thus faithfully, thus plainly, in a way so very proper both to convince and to affect. 1. Zedekiah, a wicked prophet, impudently insulted him in the face of the court, *smote him on the cheek*, to reproach him, to silence him and stop his mouth, and to express his indignation at him (thus was our blessed Saviour abused, Matt. xxvi. 67, that Judge of Israel, Mic. v. 1); and as if he not only had the spirit of the Lord, but the monopoly of this Spirit, that he might not go without his leave, he asks, *Which way went the Spirit of the Lord from me to speak to thee? v.* 24. The false prophets were always the worst enemies the true prophets had, and not only stirred up the government against them, but were themselves abusive to them, as Zedekiah here. To strike within the verge of the court, especially in the king's presence, is looked upon by our law as a high misdemeanour; yet this wicked prophet gives this abuse to a prophet of the Lord, and is not reprimanded nor bound to his good behaviour for it. Ahab was pleased with it, and Jehoshaphat had not courage to appear for the injured prophet, pretending it was out of his jurisdiction; but Micaiah, though he returns not his blow (God's prophets are no strikers nor persecutors, dare not avenge themselves, render blow for blow, or be in any way accessory to the breach of the peace), yet, since he boasted so much of the Spirit, as those commonly do that know least of his operations, he leaves him to be convinced of his error by the event: *Thou shalt know when thou hidest thyself in an inner chamber, v.* 25. It is likely Zedekiah went with Ahab to the battle, and took his horns of iron with him to encourage the soldiers, to see with pleasure the accomplishment of his prophecy, and return in triumph with the king; but, the army being routed, he fled among the rest from the sword of the enemy, sheltered himself as Ben-hadad had done in *a chamber within a chamber* (*ch.* xx. 30), lest he should perish, as he knew he deserved to do, with those whom he had deluded, as Balaam did (Num. xxxi. 8), and lest the blind prophet should *fall into the ditch* with the blinded prince whom he had misled. Note, Those that will not have their mistakes rectified in time by the word of God will be undeceived, when it is too late, by the judgments of God. 2. Ahab, that wicked king, committed him to prison (*v.* 27), not only ordered him to be taken into custody, or remitted to the prison whence he came, but to be fed with bread and water, coarse bread and puddle-water, till he should return, not doubting but that he should return a conqueror, and then he would put him to death for a false prophet (*v.* 27)—hard usage for one that would have prevented his ruin! But by this it appeared that God had *determined to destroy him*, as 2 Chron. xxv. 16. How confident is Ahab of success.

He doubts not but he shall return in peace, forgetting what he himself had reminded Ben-hadad of, *Let not him that girdeth on the harness boast*; but there was little likelihood of his coming home in peace when he left one of God's prophets behind him in prison. Micaiah put it upon the issue, and called all the people to be witnesses that he did so: "*If thou return in peace, the Lord has not spoken by me, v.* 28. Let me incur the reproach and punishment of a false prophet, if the king come home alive." He ran no hazard by this appeal, for he knew whom he had believed; he that is terrible to the kings of the earth, and treads upon princes as mortar, will rather let thousands of them fall to the ground than one jot or tittle of his own word; he will not fail to *confirm the word of his servants,* Isa. xliv. 26.

29 So the king of Israel and Jehoshaphat the king of Judah went up to Ramoth-gilead. 30 And the king of Israel said unto Jehoshaphat, I will disguise myself, and enter into the battle; but put thou on thy robes. And the king of Israel disguised himself, and went into the battle. 31 But the king of Syria commanded his thirty and two captains that had rule over his chariots, saying, Fight neither with small nor great, save only with the king of Israel. 32 And it came to pass, when the captains of the chariots saw Jehoshaphat, that they said, Surely it *is* the king of Israel. And they turned aside to fight against him: and Jehoshaphat cried out. 33 And it came to pass, when the captains of the chariots perceived that it *was* not the king of Israel, that they turned back from pursuing him. 34 And a *certain* man drew a bow at a venture, and smote the king of Israel between the joints of the harness: wherefore he said unto the driver of his chariot, Turn thine hand, and carry me out of the host; for I am wounded. 35 And the battle increased that day: and the king was stayed up in his chariot against the Syrians, and died at even: and the blood ran out of the wound into the midst of the chariot. 36 And there went a proclamation throughout the host about the going down of the sun, saying, Every man to his city, and every man to his own country. 37 So the king died, and was brought to Samaria; and they buried the king in Samaria. 38 And *one* washed the chariot in the pool of Samaria; and the dogs licked up his blood; and they washed his armour; according unto the word of the LORD which he spake. 39 Now the rest of the acts of Ahab, and all that he did, and the ivory house which he made, and all the cities that he built, *are* they not written in the book of the chronicles of the kings of Israel? 40 So Ahab slept with his fathers; and Ahaziah his son reigned in his stead.

The matter in contest between God's prophet and Ahab's prophets is here soon determined, and it is made to appear which was in the right. Here,

I. The two kings march with their forces to Ramoth-Gilead, *v.* 29. That the king of Israel, who hated God's prophet, should so far disbelieve his admonition as to persist in his resolution, notwithstanding, is not strange; but that Jehoshaphat, that pious prince, who had desired to enquire by a *prophet of the Lord,* as disrelishing and discrediting Ahab's prophets, should yet proceed, after so fair a warning, is matter of astonishment. But by the easiness of his temper he was carried away with the delusion (as Barnabas was with the dissimulation, Gal. ii. 13) of his friends. He gave too much heed to Ahab's prophets, because they pretended to speak from God too, and in his country he had never been imposed upon by such cheats. He was ready to give his opinion with the majority, and to conclude that it was 400 to one but they should succeed. Micaiah had not forbidden them to go; nay, at first, he said, *Go, and prosper.* If it came to the worst, it was only Ahab's fall that was foretold, and therefore Jehoshaphat hoped he might safely venture.

II. Ahab adopts a contrivance by which he hopes to secure himself and expose his friend (*v.* 30): "*I will disguise myself,* and go in the habit of a common soldier, but let *Jehoshaphat put on his robes,* to appear in the dress of a general." He pretended thereby to do honour to Jehoshaphat, and to compliment him with the sole command of the army in this action. He shall direct and give orders, and Ahab will serve as a soldier under him. But he intended, 1. To make a liar of a good prophet. Thus he hoped to elude the danger, and so to defeat the threatening, as if, by disguising himself, he could escape the divine cognizance and the judgments that pursued him. 2. To make a fool of a good king, whom he did not cordially love, because he was one that adhered to God and so condemned his apostasy. He knew that if any perished it must be the shepherd (so Micaiah had foretold); and perhaps he had intimation of the charge the enemy had to fight chiefly *against the king of Israel*, and therefore basely intended to betray Jehoshaphat to the danger, that he might secure himself. Ahab was marked for ruin; one would not have been in his coat for a great sum; yet he will over-persuade this godly king to muster for him. See what those get that join in affinity with vicious men, whose consciences are debauched, and who are lost to every thing that is honourable. How can it be expected that he should be true to his friend that has been false to his God?

III. Jehoshaphat, having more piety than policy, put himself into the post of honour, though it was the post of danger, and was thereby brought into peril of his life, but God graciously delivered him. The king of Syria charged his captains to level their force, not against the king of Judah, for with him he had no quarrel, but against the king of Israel only (*v.* 31), to aim at his person, as if against him he had a particular enmity. Now Ahab was justly repaid for sparing Ben-hadad, who, as the seed of the serpent commonly do, stung the bosom in which he was fostered and saved from perishing. Some think that he designed only to have him taken prisoner, that he might now give him as honourable a treatment as he had formerly received from him. Whatever was the reason, this charge the officers received, and endeavoured to oblige their prince in this matter; for, seeing Jehoshaphat in his royal habit, they took him for the king of Israel, and surrounded him. Now, 1. By his danger God let him know that he was displeased with him for joining in confederacy with Ahab. Jehoshaphat had said, in compliment to Ahab (*v.* 4), *I am as thou art;* and now he was indeed taken for him. Those that associate with evil doers are in danger of sharing in their plagues. 2. By his deliverance God let him know that, though he was displeased with him, yet he had not deserted him. Some of the captains that knew him perceived their mistake, and so retired from the pursuit of him; but it is said (2 Chron. xviii. 31) that *God moved them* (for he has all hearts in his hand) *to depart from him.* To him he cried out, not in cowardice, but devotion, and from him his relief came: Ahab was in no care to succour him. God is a friend that will not fail us when other friends do.

IV. Ahab receives his mortal wound in the battle, notwithstanding his endeavours to secure himself in the habit of a private sentinel. Let no man think to hide himself from God's judgment, no, not in masquerade. *Thy hand shall find out all thy enemies,* whatever disguise they are in, *v.* 34. The Syrian that shot him little thought of doing such a piece of service to God and his king; for he *drew a bow at a venture,* not aiming particularly at any man, yet God so directed the arrow that, 1. He hit the right person, the man that was marked for destruction, whom, if they had taken alive, as was designed, perhaps Ben-hadad would have spared. Those cannot escape with life whom God hath doomed to death. 2. He hit him in the right place, *between the joints of the harness,* the only place about him where this arrow of death could find entrance. No armour is of proof against the darts of divine vengeance. Case the criminal in steel, and it is all one, *he that made him can make his sword to approach him.* That which to us seems altogether casual is done by the determinate counsel and fore-knowledge of God.

V. The army is dispersed by the enemy and sent home by the king. Either Jehoshaphat or Ahab ordered the retreat of the sheep, when the shepherd was smitten: *Every man to his city,* for it is to no purpose to attempt any thing more, *v.* 36. Ahab himself lived long enough to see that part of Micaiah's prophecy accomplished that all Israel should be scattered *upon the mountains of Gilead* (*v.* 17), and perhaps with his dying lips did himself give orders for it; for though he would be carried out of the army, to have his wounds dressed (*v.* 34), yet he would be *held up in his chariot,* to see if his army were victorious. But, when he saw the battle increase against them, his spirits sunk, and he died, but his death was so lingering that he had time to feel himself die; and we may well imagine with what horror he now reflected upon the wickedness he had committed, the warnings he had slighted, Baal's altars, Naboth's vineyard, Micaiah's imprisonment. Now he sees himself flattered into his own ruin, and Zedekiah's horns of iron pushing, not the Syrians, but himself, into destruction. Thus is he *brought to the king of terrors* without *hope in his death.*

VI. The royal corpse is brought to Samaria and buried there (*v.* 37), and hither are brought the bloody chariot and bloody armour in which he died, *v.* 38. One particular circumstance is taken notice of, because there was in it the accomplishment of a prophecy, that when they brought the chariot to the pool of Samaria, to be washed, the dogs (and swine, says the LXX.) gathered about it, and, as is usual, *licked the blood,* or, as some think, the water in which it was washed, with which the blood was mingled: the dogs made no difference between royal blood and other blood. Now Naboth's blood was avenged (*ch.* xxi. 19), and that word of David, as well as Elijah's word, was fulfilled (Ps. lxviii. 23), *That thy foot may be dipped in the blood of thy enemies, and the tongue of thy dogs in the same.* The dogs licking the guilty blood was perhaps designed to represent the terrors that prey upon the guilty soul after death.

Lastly, The story of Ahab is here concluded in the usual form, *v.* 39, 40. Among his works mention is made of an ivory house which he built, so called because many parts of it were inlaid with ivory; perhaps it was intended to vie with the stately palace of the kings of Judah, which Solomon built.

41 And Jehoshaphat the son of Asa began to reign over Judah in the fourth year of Ahab king of Israel. 42 Jehoshaphat *was* thirty and five years old when he began to reign; and he reigned twenty and five years in Jerusalem. And his mother's name *was* Azubah the daughter of Shilhi. 43 And he walked in all the ways of Asa his father; he turned not aside from it, doing *that which was* right in the eyes of the LORD: nevertheless the high places were not taken away; *for* the people offered and burnt incense yet in the high places. 44 And Jehoshaphat made peace with the king of Israel. 45 Now the rest of the acts of Jehoshaphat, and his might that he showed, and how he warred, *are* they not written in the book of the chronicles of the kings of Judah? 46 And the remnant of the Sodomites, which remained in the days of his father Asa, he took out of the land. 47 *There was* then no king in Edom: a deputy *was* king. 48 Jehoshaphat made ships of Tharshish to go to Ophir for gold: but they went not; for the ships were broken at Ezion-geber. 49 Then said Ahaziah the son of Ahab unto Jehoshaphat, Let my servants go with thy servants in the ships. But Jehoshaphat would not. 50 And Jehoshaphat slept with his fathers, and was buried with his fathers in the city of David his father: and Jehoram his son reigned in his stead. 51 Ahaziah the son of Ahab began to reign over Israel in Samaria the seventeenth year of Jehoshaphat king of Judah, and reigned two years over Israel. 52 And he did evil in the sight of the LORD, and walked in the way of his father, and in the way of his mother, and in the way of Jeroboam the son of Nebat, who made Israel to sin: 53 For he served Baal, and worshipped him, and provoked to anger the LORD God of Israel, according to all that his father had done.

Here is, I. A short account of the reign of Jehoshaphat king of Judah, of which we shall have a much fuller narrative in the book of Chronicles, and of the greatness and goodness of that prince, neither of which was lessened or sullied by any thing but his intimacy with the house of Ahab, which, upon several accounts, was a diminution to him. His confederacy with Ahab in war we have already found dangerous to him, and his confederacy with Ahaziah his son in trade sped no better. He offered to go partner with him in a fleet of merchant-ships, that should fetch gold from Ophir, as Solomon's navy did, *v.* 49. See 2 Chron. xx. 35, 36. But, while they were preparing to set sail, they were exceedingly damaged and disabled by a storm *(broken at Ezion-geber)*, which a prophet gave Jehoshaphat to understand was a rebuke to him for his league with wicked Ahaziah (2 Chron. xx. 37); and therefore, as we are told here (*v.* 49), when Ahaziah desired a second time to be a partner with him, or, if that could not be obtained, that he might but send his servants with some effects on board Jehoshaphat's ships, he refused: *Jehoshaphat would not.* The rod of God, expounded by the word of God, had effectually broken him off from his confederacy with that ungodly unhappy prince. Better buy wisdom dear than be without it; but experience is therefore said to be the mistress of fools because those are fools that will not learn till they are taught by experience, and particularly till they are taught the danger of associating with wicked people. Now Jehoshaphat's reign appears here to have been none of the longest, but one of the best. 1. It was none of the longest, for he reigned but twenty-five years (*v.* 42), but then it was in the prime of his time, between thirty-five and sixty, and these twenty-five, added to his father's happy forty-one, give us a grateful idea of the flourishing condition of the kingdom of Judah, and of religion in it, for a great while, even when things were very bad, upon all accounts, in the kingdom of Israel. If Jehoshaphat reigned not so long as his father, to balance this he had not those blemishes on the latter end of his reign that his father had (2 Chron. xvi. 9, 10, 12), and it is better for a man that has been in reputation for wisdom and honour to die in the midst of it than to outlive it. 2. Yet it was one of the best, both in respect of piety and prosperity. (1.) He did well: He *did that which was right in the eyes of the Lord* (*v.* 43), observed the commands of his God, and trod in the steps of his good father; and he persevered therein: He *turned not aside from it.* Yet every man's character has some *but* or other, so had his; the *high places were not taken away,* no, not out of Judah and Benjamin, though those tribes lay so near Jerusalem that they might easily bring their offerings and incense to the altar there, and could not pretend, as some other of the tribes, the inconveniency of lying remote. But old corruptions are with difficulty rooted out, especially when they have formerly had the patronage of those that were good, as the high places had of Samuel, Solomon, and some others. (2.) His affairs did well. He prevented the mischiefs which had attended their wars with the kingdom of Israel, establishing a lasting peace (*v.* 44), which would have been a greater blessing if he had contented himself with a peace, and not carried it on to an affinity with Israel; he put a deputy, or viceroy, in Edom, so that that kingdom was tributary to him (*v.* 47), and therein the prophecy concerning Esau and Jacob was fulfilled, that *the elder should serve the younger*. And, in general, mention is made of his might and his wars, *v.* 45. He pleased God, and God blessed him with strength and success. His death is spoken of (*v.* 50), to shut up his story, yet, in the history of the kings of Israel, we find mention of him afterwards, 2 Kings iii. 7.

II. The beginning of the story of Ahaziah the son of Ahab, *v.* 51—53. His reign was very short, not two years. Some sinners God makes quick work with. It is a very bad character that is here given him. He not only kept up Jeroboam's idolatry, but the worship of Baal likewise; though he had heard of the ruin of Jeroboam's family, and had seen his own father drawn into destruction by the prophets of Baal, who had often been proved false prophets, yet he received no instruction, took no warning, but followed the example of his wicked father and the counsel of his more wicked mother Jezebel, who was still living. Miserable are the children that not only derive a stock of corruption from their parents, but are thus taught by them to trade with it; and unhappy, most unhappy parents, are those that help to damn their children's souls.

AN

EXPOSITION,

WITH PRACTICAL OBSERVATIONS,

OF THE SECOND BOOK OF

KINGS.

THIS second book of the Kings (which the LXX., numbering from Samuel, called the *fourth)* is a continuation of the former book; and, some think, might better have been made to begin with the fifty-first verse of the foregoing chapter, where the reign of Ahaziah begins. The former book had an illustrious beginning, in the glories of the kingdom of Israel, when it was entire; this has a melancholy conclusion, in the desolations of the kingdoms of Israel first, and then of Judah, after they had been long broken into two: for a kingdom divided against itself cometh to destruction. But, as Elijah's mighty works were very much the glory of the former book, towards the latter end of it, so were Elisha's the glory of this, towards the beginning of it. These prophets out-shone their princes; and therefore, as far as they go, the history shall be accounted for in them. Here is, I. Elijah fetching fire from heaven and ascending in fire to heaven, *ch.* i. and ii. II. Elisha working many miracles, both for prince and people, Israelites and foreigners, *ch.* iii.—vii. III. Hazael and Jehu anointed, the former for the correction of Israel, the latter for the destruction of the house of Ahab and the worship of Baal, *ch.* viii.—x. IV. The reign of several of the kings, both of Judah and Israel, *ch.* xi.—xvi. V. The captivity of the ten tribes, *ch.* xvii. VI. The good and glorious reign of Hezekiah, *ch.* xviii.—xx. VII. Manasseh's wicked reign, and Josiah's good one, *ch.* xxi.—xxiii. VIII. The destruction of Jerusalem by the king of Babylon, *ch.* xxiv., xxv. This history, in the several passages of it, confirms that observation of Solomon, *That righteousness exalts a nation, but sin is the reproach of any people.*

CHAP. I.

We here find Ahaziah, the genuine son and successor of Ahab, on the throne of Israel. His reign continued not two years; he died by a fall in his own house, of which, after the mention of the revolt of Moab (ver. 1), we have here an account. I. The message which, on that occasion, he sent to the god of Ekron, ver. 2. II. The message he received from the God of Israel, ver. 3—8. III. The destruction of the messengers he sent to seize the prophet, once and again, ver. 9—12. IV. His compassion to, and compliance with, the third messenger, upon his submission, and the delivery of the message to the king himself, ver. 13—16. V. The death of Ahaziah, ver. 17, 18. In the story we may observe how great the prophet looks and how little the prince.

THEN Moab rebelled against Israel after the death of Ahab. 2 And Ahaziah fell down through a lattice in his upper chamber that *was* in Samaria, and was sick: and he sent messengers, and said unto them, Go, enquire of Baal-zebub the god of Ekron whether I shall recover of this disease. 3 But the angel of the LORD said to Elijah the Tishbite, Arise, go up to meet the messengers of the king of Samaria, and say unto them, *Is it* not because *there is* not a God in Israel, *that* ye go to enquire of Baal-zebub the god of Ekron? 4 Now therefore thus saith the LORD, Thou shalt not come down from that bed on which thou art gone up, but shalt surely die. And Elijah departed. 5 And when the messengers turned back unto him, he said unto them, Why are ye now turned back? 6 And they said unto him, There came a man up to meet us, and said unto us, Go, turn again unto the king that sent you, and say unto him, Thus saith the LORD, *Is it* not because *there is* not a God in Israel, *that* thou sendest to enquire of Baal-zebub the god of Ekron? therefore thou shalt not come down from that bed on which thou art gone up, but shalt surely die. 7 And he said unto them, What manner of man *was he* which came up to meet you, and told you these words? 8 And they answered him, *He was* a hairy man, and girt with a girdle of leather about his loins. And he said, It *is* Elijah the Tishbite.

We have here Ahaziah, the wicked king of Israel, under God's rebukes both by his providence and by his prophet, by his rod and by his word.

I. He is crossed in his affairs. How can those expect to prosper that *do evil in the sight of the Lord*, and *provoke him to anger?* When he rebelled against God, and revolted from his allegiance to him, Moab rebelled against Israel, and revolted from the subjection they had long paid to the kings of Israel, *v.* 1. The Edomites that bordered on Judah, and were tributaries to the kings of Judah, still continued so, as we find in the chapter before (*v.* 47), till, in the wicked reign of Joram, they broke that yoke (*ch.* viii. 22) as the Moabites did now. If men break their covenants with us, and neglect their duty, we must reflect upon our breach of covenant with God, and the neglect of our duty to him. Sin weakens and impoverishes us. We shall hear of the Moabites, *ch.* iii. 5.

II. He is seized with sickness in body, not from any inward cause, but by a severe accident. *He fell down through a lattice*, and was much bruised with the fall; perhaps it threw him into a fever, *v.* 2. Wherever we go, there is but a step between us and death. A man's house is his castle, but not to secure him against the judgments of God. The cracked lattice is as fatal to the son, when God pleases to make it so, as the bow drawn at a venture was to the father. Ahaziah would not attempt to reduce the Moabites, lest he should perish in the field of battle: but he is not safe, though he tarry at home. Royal palaces do not always yield firm footing. The snare is laid for the sinner in the ground where he thinks least of it, Job xviii. 9, 10. The whole creation, which groans under the burden of man's sin, will at length sink and break under the weight, like this lattice. He is never safe that has God for his enemy.

III. In his distress he sends messengers to enquire of the god of Ekron whether he should recover or no, *v.* 2. And here, 1. His enquiry was very foolish: *Shall I recover?* Even nature itself would rather have asked, "What means may I use that I may recover?" But as one solicitous only to know his fortune, not to know his duty, his question is only this, *Shall I recover?* to which a little time would give an answer. We should be more thoughtful what will become of us after death than how, or when, or where, we shall die, and more desirous to be told how we may conduct ourselves well in our sickness, and get good to our souls by it, than whether we shall recover from it. 2. His sending to Baal-zebub was very wicked; to make a dead and dumb idol, perhaps newly erected (for idolaters were fond of new gods), his oracle, was no less a reproach to his reason than to his religion. Baal-zebub, which signifies *the lord of a fly*, was one of their Baals that perhaps gave his answers, either by the power of the demons or the craft of the priests, with a humming noise, like that of a great fly, or that had (as they fancied) rid their country of the swarms of flies wherewith it was infested, or of some pestilential disease brought among them by flies. Perhaps this dunghill-deity was as famous then as the oracle of Delphos was, long afterwards, in Greece. In the New Testament *the prince of the devils* is called *Beel-zebub* (Matt. xii. 24), for the gods of the Gentiles were devils, and this perhaps grew to be one of the most famous.

IV. Elijah, by direction from God, meets the messengers, and turns them back with an answer that shall save them the labour of going to Ekron. Had Ahaziah sent for Elijah, humbled himself, and begged his prayers, he might have had an answer of peace; but if he send to the god of Ekron, instead of the God of Israel, this, like Saul's consulting the witch, shall fill the measure of his iniquity, and bring upon him a sentence of death. Those that will not enquire of the word of God for their comfort shall be made to hear it, whether they will or no, to their amazement.

1. He faithfully reproves his sin (*v.* 3): *Is it not because there is not* (that is, because you think there is not) a God in Israel *(because there is no God, none in Israel,* so it may be read), *that you go to enquire of Baalzebub, the god of Ekron,* a despicable town of the Philistines (Zech. ix. 7), long since vanquished by Israel? Here, (1.) The sin was bad enough, giving that honour to the devil which is due to God alone, which was done as much by their enquiries as by their sacrifices. Note, It is a very wicked thing, upon any occasion or pretence whatsoever, to consult with the devil. This wickedness reigned in the heathen world (Isa. xlvii. 12, 13) and remains too much even in the Christian world, and the devil's kingdom is supported by it. (2.) The construction which Elijah, in God's name, puts upon it, makes it much worse: "It is because you think not only that the God of Israel is not able to tell you, but that there is no God at all in Israel, else you would not send so far for a divine answer." Note, A practical and constructive atheism is the cause and malignity of our departures from God. Surely we think there is *no God in Israel* when we live at large, make flesh our arm, and seek a portion in the things of this world.

2. He plainly reads his doom: Go, tell him *he shall surely die, v.* 4. "Since he is so anxious to know his fate, this is it; let him make the best of it." The certain fearful looking for of judgment and indignation which this message must needs cause cannot but cut him to the heart.

V. The message being delivered to him by his servants, he enquires of them by whom it was sent to him, and concludes, by their description of him, that it must be Elijah, *v.* 7, 8. For, 1. His dress was the same that he had seen him in, in his father's court. He was clad in a hairy garment, and had a leathern girdle about him, was plain and homely in his garb. John Baptist, the Elias of the New Testament, herein resembled him, for his clothes were made of hair-cloth, and he was girt with a leathern girdle, Matt. iii. 4. He that was clothed with the Spirit despised all rich and gay clothing. 2. His message was such as he used to deliver to his father, to whom he never prophesied good, but evil. Elijah is one of those witnesses that still torment the inhabitants of the earth, Rev. xi. 10. He that was a thorn in Ahab's eyes will be so in the eyes of his son while he treads in the steps of his father's wickedness; and he is ready to cry out, as his father did, *Hast thou found me, O my enemy?* Let sinners consider that the word which *took hold of their fathers* is still as quick and powerful as ever. See Zech. i. 6; Heb. iv. 12.

9 Then the king sent unto him a captain of fifty with his fifty. And he went up to him: and, behold, he sat on the top of a hill. And he spake unto him, Thou man of God, the king hath said, Come down. 10 And Elijah answered and said to the captain of fifty, If I *be* a man of God, then let fire come down from heaven, and consume thee and thy fifty. And there came down fire from heaven, and consumed him and his fifty. 11 Again also he sent unto him another captain of fifty with his fifty. And he answered and said unto him, O man of God, thus hath the king said, Come down quickly. 12 And Elijah answered and said unto them, If I *be* a man of God, let fire come down from heaven, and consume thee and thy fifty. And the fire of God came down from heaven, and consumed him and his fifty. 13 And he sent again a captain of the third fifty with his fifty. And the third captain of fifty went up, and came and fell on his knees before Elijah, and besought him, and said unto him, O man of God, I pray thee, let my life, and the life of these fifty thy servants, be precious in thy sight. 14 Behold, there came down fire from heaven, and burnt up the two captains of the former fifties with their fifties: therefore let my life now be precious in thy sight. 15 And the angel of the LORD said unto Elijah, Go down with him: be not afraid of him. And he arose, and went down with him unto the king. 16 And he said unto him, Thus saith the LORD, Forasmuch as thou hast sent messengers to enquire of Baalzebub the god of Ekron, *is it* not be-

cause *there is* no God in Israel to enquire of his word? therefore thou shalt not come down off that bed on which thou art gone up, but shalt surely die. 17 So he died according to the word of the LORD which Elijah had spoken. And Jehoram reigned in his stead in the second year of Jehoram the son of Jehoshaphat king of Judah; because he had no son. 18 Now the rest of the acts of Ahaziah which he did, *are* they not written in the book of the chronicles of the kings of Israel?

Here, I. The king issues out a warrant for the apprehending of Elijah. If the God of Ekron had told him he should die, it is probable he would have taken it quietly; but now that a prophet of the Lord tells him so, reproving him for his sin and reminding him of the God of Israel, he cannot bear it. So far is he from making any good improvement of the warning given him that he is enraged against the prophet; neither his sickness, nor the thoughts of death, made any good impressions upon him, nor possessed him with any fear of God. No external alarms will startle and soften secure sinners, but rather exasperate them. Did the king think Elijah a prophet, a true prophet? Why then durst he persecute him? Did he think him a common person? What occasion was there to send such a force, in order to seize him? Thus a band of men must take our Lord Jesus.

II. The captain that was sent with his fifty soldiers found Elijah on the top of a hill (some think Carmel), and commanded him, in the king's name, to surrender himself, *v.* 9. Elijah was now so far from absconding, as formerly, into the close recesses of a cave, that he makes a bold appearance on the top of a hill; experience of God's protection makes him more bold. The captain calls him *a man of God,* not that he believed him to be so, or reverenced him as such a one, but because he was commonly called so. Had he really looked upon him as a prophet, he would not have attempted to make him his prisoner; and, had he thought him entrusted with the word of God, he would not have pretended to command him with the word of a king.

III. Elijah calls for fire from heaven, to consume this haughty daring sinner, not to secure himself (he could have done that some other way), nor to avenge himself (for it was not his own cause that he appeared and acted in), but to prove his mission, and to *reveal the wrath of God* from *heaven against the ungodliness and unrighteousness of men.* This captain had, in scorn, called him *a man of God:* "If I be so," says Elijah, "thou shalt pay dearly for making a jest of it." He valued himself upon his commission (the king has said, *Come down),* but Elijah will let him know that the God of Israel is superior to the king of Israel and has a greater power to enforce his commands. It was not long since Elijah had fetched fire from heaven, to consume the sacrifice (1 Kings xviii. 38), in token of God's acceptance of that sacrifice as an atonement for the sins of the people; but, they having slighted that, now the fire falls, not on the sacrifice, but on the sinners themselves, *v.* 10. See here, 1. What an interest the prophets had in heaven; what the Spirit of God in them demanded the power of God effected. Elijah did but speak, and it was done. He that formerly had fetched water from heaven now fetches fire. O the power of prayer! *Concerning the work of my hands, command you me,* Isa. xlv. 11. 2. What an interest heaven had in the prophets! God was always ready to plead their cause, and avenge the injuries done to them; kings shall still be *rebuked for their sakes,* and charged to do *his prophets no harm;* one Elijah is more to God than 10,000 captains and their fifties. Doubtless Elijah did this by a divine impulse, and yet our Saviour would not allow the disciples to draw it into a precedent, Luke ix. 54. They were now not far from the place where Elias did this act of justice upon provoking Israelites, and would needs, in like manner, call for fire upon those provoking Samaritans. "No," says Christ, "by no means, *you know not what manner of spirit you are of,*" that is, (1.) "You do not consider *what manner of spirit,* as disciples, you are called to, and how different from that of the Old-Testament dispensation; it was agreeable enough to that dispensation of terror, and of the letter, for Elias to call for fire, but the dispensation of the Spirit and of grace will by no means allow of it." (2.) "You are not aware what manner of spirit you are, upon this occasion, actuated by, and how different from that of Elias: he did it in holy zeal, you in passion; he was concerned for God's glory, you for your own reputation only. God judges men's practices by their principles, and his judgment is according to truth.

IV. This is repeated a second time; would one think it? 1. Ahaziah sends, a second time, to apprehend Elijah (*v.* 11), as if he were resolved not to be baffled by omnipotence itself. Obstinate sinners must be convinced and conquered, at last, by the fire of hell, for fire from heaven, it seems, will not subdue them. 2. Another captain is ready with his fifty, who, in his blind rage against the prophet, and his blind obedience to the king, dares engage in that service which had been fatal to the last undertakers. This is as impudent and imperious as the last, and more in haste; not only, "*Come down quietly,* and do not struggle," but without taking any notice of what had been done, he says, "*Come down quickly,* and do not trifle, the king's business requires haste;

come down, or I will fetch thee down." 3. Elijah relents not, but calls for another flash of lightning, which instantly lays this captain and his fifty dead upon the spot. Those that will sin like others must expect to suffer like them; God is inflexibly just.

V. The third captain humbled himself and cast himself upon the mercy of God and Elijah. It does not appear that Ahaziah ordered him to do so (his stubborn heart is as hard as ever; so regardless is he of the terrors of the Lord, so little affected with the manifestations of his wrath, and withal so prodigal of the lives of his subjects, that he sends a third with the same provoking message to Elijah), but he took warning by the fate of his predecessors, who, perhaps, lay dead before his eyes; and, instead of summoning the prophet down, fell down before him, and begged for his life and the lives of his soldiers, acknowledging their own evil deserts and the prophet's power (*v.* 13, 14): *Let my life be precious in thy sight.* Note, There is nothing to be got by contending with God: if we would prevail with him, it must be by supplication; if we would not fall before God, we must bow before him; and those are wise for themselves who learn submission from the fatal consequences of the obstinacy of others.

VI. Elijah does more than grant the request of this third captain. God is not so severe with those that stand it out against him but he is as ready to show mercy to those that repent and submit to him; never any found it in vain to cast themselves upon the mercy of God. This captain, not only has his life spared, but is permitted to carry his point: Elijah, being so commanded by the angel, *goes down with him to the king, v.* 15. Thus he shows that he before refused to come, not because he feared the king or court, but because he would not be imperiously compelled, which would lessen the honour of his master; he *magnifies his office.* He comes boldly to the king, and tells him to his face (let him take it as he may) what he had before sent to him (*v.* 16), that he shall surely and shortly die; he mitigates not the sentence, either for fear of the king's displeasure or in pity to his misery. The God of Israel has condemned him, let him send to see whether the god of Ekron can deliver him. So thunder-struck is Ahaziah with this message, when it comes from the prophet's own mouth, that neither he nor any of those about him durst offer him any violence, nor so much as give him an affront; but out of that den of lions he comes unhurt, like Daniel. Who can harm those whom God will shelter?

Lastly, The prediction is accomplished in a few days. Ahaziah died (*v.* 17), and, dying childless, left his kingdom to his brother Jehoram. His father reigned wickedly twenty-two years, he not two. Sometimes the *wicked live, become old, yea, are mighty in power;* but those who therefore promise themselves prosperity in impiety may perhaps find themselves deceived; for (as bishop Hall observes here), "Some sinners live long, to aggravate their judgment, others die soon, to hasten it;" but it is certain that *evil pursues sinners,* and, sooner or later, it will overtake them; nor will any thing fill the measure sooner than that complicated iniquity of Ahaziah—honouring the devil's oracles and hating God's oracles.

CHAP. II.

In this chapter we have, I. That extraordinary event, the translation of Elijah. In the close of the foregoing chapter we had a wicked king leaving the world in disgrace, here we have a holy prophet leaving it in honour; the departure of the former was his greatest misery, of the latter his greatest bliss: men are as their end is. Here is, 1. Elijah taking leave of his friends, the sons of the prophets, and especially Elisha, who kept close to him, and walked with him through Jordan, ver. 1—10. 2. Elijah taken into heaven by the ministry of angels (ver. 11), and Elisha's lamentation of the loss this earth had of him, ver. 12. II. The manifestation of Elisha, as a prophet in his room. 1. By the dividing of Jordan, ver. 13, 14. 2. By the respect which the sons of the prophets paid him, ver. 15—18. 3. By the healing of the unwholesome waters of Jericho, ver. 19—22. 4. By the destruction of the children of Bethel that mocked him, ver. 23—25. This revolution in prophecy makes a greater figure than the revolution of a kingdom.

AND it came to pass, when the LORD would take up Elijah into heaven by a whirlwind, that Elijah went with Elisha from Gilgal. 2 And Elijah said unto Elisha, Tarry here, I pray thee; for the LORD hath sent me to Beth-el. And Elisha said *unto him, As* the LORD liveth, and *as* thy soul liveth, I will not leave thee. So they went down to Beth-el. 3 And the sons of the prophets that *were* at Beth-el came forth to Elisha, and said unto him, Knowest thou that the LORD will take away thy master from thy head to day? And he said, Yea, I know *it;* hold ye your peace. 4 And Elijah said unto him, Elisha, tarry here, I pray thee; for the LORD hath sent me to Jericho. And he said, *As* the LORD liveth, and *as* thy soul liveth, I will not leave thee. So they came to Jericho. 5 And the sons of the prophets that *were* at Jericho came to Elisha, and said unto him, Knowest thou that the LORD will take away thy master from thy head to day? And he answered, Yea, I know *it;* hold ye your peace. 6 And Elijah said unto him, Tarry, I pray thee, here; for the LORD hath sent me to Jordan. And he said, *As* the LORD liveth, and *as* thy soul liveth, I will not leave thee. And they two went on. 7 And fifty men of the sons of the prophets went, and stood to view afar off: and they two stood by Jordan. 8 And Elijah took his mantle, and wrapped *it* together, and smote the waters, and they were divided hither and thither, so that they two went over on dry ground.

Elijah's times, and the events concerning him, are as little dated as those of any great man in scripture; we are not told of his age, nor in what year of Ahab's reign he first appeared, nor in what year of Joram's he disappeared, and therefore cannot conjecture how long he flourished; it is supposed about twenty years in all. Here we are told,

I. That God had determined to take him up into heaven by a whirlwind, *v.* 1. He would do it, and it is probable let him know of his purpose some time before, that he would shortly take him from the world, not by death, but translate him body and soul to heaven, as Enoch was, only causing him to undergo such a change as would be necessary to the qualifying of him to be an inhabitant in that world of spirits, and such as those shall undergo who will be found alive at Christ's coming. It is not for us to say why God would put such a peculiar honour upon Elijah above any other of the prophets; he was a man *subject to like passions as we are*, knew sin, and yet never tasted death. Wherefore is he thus dignified, thus distinguished, as a man whom the King of kings did delight to honour? We may suppose that herein, 1. God looked back upon his past services, which were eminent and extraordinary, and intended a recompence for those and an encouragement to the sons of the prophets to tread in the steps of his zeal and faithfulness, and, whatever it cost them, to witness against the corruptions of the age they lived in. 2. He looked down upon the present dark and degenerate state of the church, and would thus give a very sensible proof of another life after this, and draw the hearts of the faithful few upward towards himself, and that other life. 3. He looked forward to the evangelical dispensation, and, in the translation of Elijah, gave a type and figure of the ascension of Christ and the *opening of the kingdom of heaven to all believers.* Elijah had, by faith and prayer, conversed much with heaven, and now he is taken thither, to assure us that if we have our conversation in heaven, while we are here on earth, we shall be there shortly, the soul shall (and that is the man) be happy there, there for ever.

II. That Elisha had determined, as long as he continued on earth to cleave to him, and not to leave him. Elijah seemed desirous to shake him off, would have had him stay behind at Gilgal, at Bethel, at Jericho, *v.* 2, 4, 6. Some think out of humility; he knew what glory God designed for him, but would not seem to glory in it, nor desired it should be seen of men (God's favourites covet not to have it proclaimed before them that they are so, as the favourites of earthly princes do), or rather it was to try him, and make his constant adherence to him the more commendable, like Naomi's persuading Ruth to go back. In vain does Elijah entreat him to tarry here and tarry there; he resolves to tarry nowhere behind his master, till he goes to heaven, and leaves him behind on this earth. "Whatever comes of it, *I will not leave thee;*" and why so? Not only because he loved him, but, 1. Because he desired to be edified by his holy heavenly converse as long as he staid on earth; it had always been profitable, but, we may suppose, was now more so than ever. We should do all the spiritual good we can one to another, and get all we can one by another, while we are together, because we are to be *together but a little while.* 2. Because he desired to be satisfied concerning his departure, and to see him when he was taken up, that his faith might be confirmed and his acquaintance with the invisible world increased. He had long followed Elijah, and he would not leave him now when he hoped for the parting blessing. Let not those that follow Christ come short by tiring at last.

III. That Elijah, before his departure, visited the schools of the prophets and took leave of them. It seems that there were such schools in many of the cities of Israel, probably even in Samaria itself. Here we find *sons of the prophets*, and considerable numbers of them, even at Bethel, where one of the calves was set up, and at Jericho, which was lately built in defiance of a divine curse. At Jerusalem, and in the kingdom of Judah, they had priests and Levites, and the temple-service, the want of which, in the kingdom of Israel, God graciously made up by those colleges, where men were trained up and employed in the exercises of religion and devotion, and whither good people resorted to solemnize the appointed feasts with praying and hearing, when they had not conveniences for sacrifice or incense, and thus religion was kept up in a time of general apostasy. Much of God was among these prophets, and *more were the children of the desolate* than the *children of the married wife.* None of all the high priests were comparable to those two great men Elijah and Elisha, who, for aught we know, never attended in the temple at Jerusalem. These seminaries of religion and virtue, which Elijah, it is probable, had been instrumental to found, he now visits, before his departure, to instruct, encourage, and bless them. Note, Those that are going to heaven themselves ought to be concerned for those they leave behind them on earth, and to leave with them their experiences, testimonies, counsels, and prayers, 2 Pet. i. 15. When Christ said, with triumph, *Now I am no more in the world,* he added, with tenderness, *But these are. Father, keep them.*

IV. That the sons of the prophets had intelligence (either from Elijah himself, or by the spirit of prophecy in some of their own society), or suspected by the solemnity of Elijah's farewell, that he was now shortly to be removed; and, 1. They told Elisha of it, both at Bethel (*v.* 3) and at Jericho (*v.* 5): *Knowest thou that the Lord will take away thy master from thy head to day?* This they said, not as upbraiding him with his loss, or expecting that when his master was gone he would be upon the level with them, but to show how full they were of the thoughts of this matter and big with expectation of the event, and to admonish Elisha to prepare for the loss. Know we not that our nearest relations, and dearest friends, must shortly be taken from us? *The Lord will* take them; we lose them not till he calls for them whose they are, and who *taketh away and none can hinder him.* He takes away superiors from our head, inferiors from our feet, equals from our arms; let us therefore carefully do the duty of every relation, that we may reflect upon it with comfort when it comes to be dissolved. Elisha knew it too well, and *sorrow had filled his heart* upon this account (as the disciples in a like case, John xvi. 6), and therefore he did not need to be told of it, did not care for hearing of it, and would not be interrupted in his contemplations on this great concern, or in the least diverted from his attendance upon his master: *I know it; hold you your peace.* He speaks not this peevishly, or in contempt of the sons of the prophets, but as one that was himself and would have them composed and sedate, and with an awful silence expecting the event: *I know it; be silent,* Zech. ii. 13. 2. They went themselves to be witnesses of it at a distance, though they might not closely attend (*v.* 7): *Fifty of them stood to view afar off,* intending to satisfy their curiosity, but God so ordered it that they might be eye-witnesses of the honour heaven did to that prophet, who was *despised and rejected of men.* God's works are well worthy our notice; when a *door is opened in heaven* the call is, *Come up hither, come and see.*

V. That the miraculous dividing of the river Jordan was the preface to Elijah's translation into the heavenly Canaan, as it had been to the entrance of Israel into the earthly Canaan, *v.* 8. He must go on to the other side Jordan to be translated, because it was his native country, and that he might be near the place where Moses died, and that thus honour might be put on that part of the country which was most despised. He and Elisha might have gone over Jordan by a ferry, as other passengers did, but God would magnify Elijah in his exit, as he did Joshua in his entrance, by the dividing of this river, Josh. iii. 7. As Moses with his rod divided the sea, so Elijah with his mantle divided Jordan, both being the *insignia—the badges* of their office. These waters of old yielded to the ark, now to the prophet's mantle, which, to those that wanted the ark was an equivalent token of God's presence. When God will take up his faithful ones to heaven death is the Jordan which, immediately before their translation, they must pass through, and they find a way through it, a safe and comfortable way; the death of Christ has divided those waters, that the ransomed of the Lord may pass over. *O death! where is thy sting,* thy hurt, thy terror?

9 And it came to pass, when they were gone over, that Elijah said unto Elisha, Ask what I shall do for thee, before I be taken away from thee. And Elisha said, I pray thee, let a double portion of thy spirit be upon me. 10 And he said, Thou hast asked a hard thing: *nevertheless,* if thou see me *when I am* taken from thee, it shall be so unto thee; but if not, it shall not be *so.* 11 And it came to pass, as they still went on, and talked, that, behold, *there appeared* a chariot of fire, and horses of fire, and parted them both asunder; and Elijah went up by a whirlwind into heaven. 12 And Elisha saw *it,* and he cried, My father, my father, the chariot of Israel, and the horsemen thereof. And he saw him no more: and he took hold of his own clothes, and rent them in two pieces.

Here, I. Elijah makes his will, and leaves Elisha his heir, now anointing him to be prophet in his room, more than when he *cast his mantle upon him,* 1 Kings xix. 19.

1. Elijah, being greatly pleased with the constancy of Elisha's affection and attendance, bade him ask what he should do for him, what blessing he should leave him at parting; he does not say (as bishop Hall observes), "*Ask of me when I am gone,* in heaven I shall be better able to befriend thee," but, "Ask before I go." Our friends on earth may be spoken to, and can give us an answer, but we know not that we can have access to any friend in heaven but Christ, and God in him. *Abraham is ignorant of us.*

2. Elisha, having this fair opportunity to enrich himself with the best riches, prays for a *double portion of his spirit.* He asks not for wealth, nor honour, nor exemption from trouble, but to be qualified for the service of God and his generation; he asks, (1.) For the Spirit, not that the gifts and graces of the Spirit were in Elijah's power to give, therefore he says not, "Give me the Spirit" (he knew very well it was God's gift), but, "*Let it be upon me,* intercede with God for this for me." Christ bade his disciples ask what they would, not one, but all, and

promised to send the Spirit, with much more authority and assurance than Elijah could. (2.) For *his* spirit, because he was to be a prophet in his room, to carry on his work, to father the sons of the prophets and face their enemies, because he had the same difficulties to encounter and the same perverse generation to deal with that he had, so that, if he have not his spirit, he has not *strength according to the day.* (3.) For a *double portion of his spirit;* he does not mean double to whât Elijah had, but double to what the rest of the prophets had, from whom so much would not be expected as from Elisha, who had been brought up under Elijah. It is a holy ambition to *covet earnestly the best gifts,* and those which will render us most serviceable to God and our brethren. Note, We all ought, both ministers and people, to set before us the example of our predecessors, to labour after their spirit, and to be earnest with God for that grace which carried them through their work and enabled them to finish well.

3. Elijah promised him that which he asked, but under two provisos, *v.* 10. (1.) Provided he put a due value upon it and esteem it highly: this he teaches him to do by calling it *a hard thing,* not too hard for God to do, but too great for him to expect. Those are best prepared for spiritual blessings that are most sensible of their worth and their own unworthiness to receive them. (2.) Provided he kept close to his master, even to the last, and was observant of him: *If thou see me when I am taken from thee, it shall be* so, otherwise not. A diligent attendance upon his master's instructions, and a careful observance of his example, particularly now in his last scene, were the condition and would be a proper means of obtaining much of his spirit. Taking strict notice of the manner of his ascenison would likewise be of great use to him. The comforts of departing saints, and their experiences, will mightily help both to gild our comforts and to steel our resolutions. Or, perhaps, this was intended only as a sign: "If God favour thee so far as to give thee a sight of me when I ascend, take that for a token that he will do this for thee, and depend upon it." Christ's disciples saw him ascend, and were thereupon assured that they should, in a little time, be filled with his Spirit, Acts i. 8. Elisha, we may suppose, hereupon prayed earnestly, *Lord, show me this token for good.*

II. Elijah is carried up to heaven in a fiery chariot, *v.* 11. Like Enoch, he was translated, *that he should not see death;* and was (as Mr. Cowley expresses it) *the second man that leaped the ditch where all the rest of mankind fell, and went not downward to the sky.* Many curious questions might be asked about this matter, which could not be answered. Let it suffice that we are here told,

1. What his Lord, when he came, found him doing. He was talking with Elisha, instructing and encouraging him, directing him in his work, and quickening him to it, for the good of those whom he left behind. He was not meditating nor praying, as one wholly taken up with the world he was going to, but engaged in edifying discourse, as one concerned about the kingdom of God among men. We mistake if we think our preparation for heaven is carried on only by contemplation and the acts of devotion. Usefulness to others will pass as well in our account as any thing. Thinking of divine things is good, but talking of them (if it come from the heart) is better, because for edification, 1 Cor. xiv. 4. Christ ascended as he was blessing his disciples.

2. What convoy his Lord sent for him—*a chariot of fire and horses of fire,* which appeared either descending upon them from the clouds or (as bishop Patrick thinks) running towards them upon the ground: in this form the angels appeared. The souls of all the faithful are carried by an invisible guard of angels into the bosom of Abraham; but, Elijah being to carry his body with him, this heavenly guard was visible, not in a human shape, as usual, though they might so have borne him up in their arms, or carried him as on eagles' wings, but that would have been to carry him like a child, like a lamb (Isa. xl. 11, 31); they appear in the form of a chariot and horses, that he may ride in state, may ride in triumph, like a prince, like a conqueror, yea, *more than a conqueror.* The angels are called in scripture *cherubim* and *seraphim,* and their appearance here, though it may seem below their dignity, answers to both those names; for (1.) *Seraphim* signifies *fiery,* and God is said to make them *a flame of fire,* Ps. civ. 4. (2.) *Cherubim* (as many think) signifies *chariots,* and they are called *the chariots of God* (Ps. lxviii. 17), and he is said to *ride upon a cherub* (Ps. xviii. 10), to which perhaps there is an allusion in Ezekiel's vision of four living creatures, and wheels, like horses and chariots; in Zechariah's vision they are so represented, Zech. i. 8; vi. 1. Compare Rev. vi. 2, &c. See the readiness of the angels to do the will of God, even in the meanest services, for the good of those that shall be heirs of salvation. Elijah must remove to the world of angels, and therefore, to show how desirous they were of his company, some of them would come to fetch him. The chariot and horses appeared like fire, not for burning, but brightness, not to torture or consume him, but to render his ascension conspicuous and illustrious in the eyes of those that stood afar off to view it. Elijah had burned with holy zeal for God and his honour, and now with a heavenly fire he was refined and translated.

3. How he was separated from Elisha. This chariot parted them both asunder. Note. The dearest friends must part. Elisha had protested he would not leave him, yet now is left behind by him.

4. Whither he was carried. He *went up by a whirlwind into heaven.* The fire tends upward; the whirlwind helped to carry him through the atmosphere, out of the reach of the magnetic virtue of this earth, and then how swiftly he ascended through the pure ether to the world of holy and blessed spirits we cannot conceive.

"But where he stopped will ne'er be known,
'Till Phenix-nature, aged grown,
To a better being shall aspire,
Mounting herself, like him, to eternity in fire."
COWLEY.

Elijah had once, in a passion, wished he might die; yet God was so gracious to him as not only not to take him at his word then, but to honour him with this singular privilege, that he should never see death; and by this instance, and that of Enoch, (1.) God showed how men should have left the world if they had not sinned, not by death, but by a translation. (2.) He gave a glimpse of that life and immortality which are brought to light by the gospel, of the glory reserved for the bodies of the saints, and the *opening of the kingdom of heaven to all believers,* as then to Elijah. It was also a figure of Christ's ascension.

III. Elisha pathetically laments the loss of that great prophet, but attends him with an encomium, *v.* 12. 1. He saw it; thus he received the sign by which he was assured of the grant of his request for a double portion of Elijah's spirit. He looked stedfastly towards heaven, whence he was to expect that gift, as the disciples did, Acts i. 10. He saw it awhile, but the vision was presently out of his sight; and *he saw him no more.* 2. He rent his own clothes, in token of the sense he had of his own and the public loss. Though Elijah had gone triumphantly to heaven, yet this world could ill spare him, and therefore his removal ought to be much regretted by the survivors. Surely their hearts are hard whose eyes are dry when God, by taking away faithful useful men, calls for weeping and mourning. Though Elijah's departure made way for Elisha's eminency, especially since he was now sure of a double portion of his spirit, yet he lamented the loss of him, for he loved him, and could have served him for ever. 3. He gave him a very honourable character, as the reason why he thus lamented the loss of him. (1.) He himself had lost the guide of his youth: *My father, my father.* He saw his own condition like that of a fatherless child thrown upon the world, and lamented it accordingly. Christ, when he left his disciples, did not leave them orphans (John xiv. 15), but Elijah must. (2.) The public had lost its best guard; he was *the chariot of Israel, and the horsemen thereof.* He would have brought them all to heaven, as in this chariot, if it had not been their own fault; they used not chariots and horses in their wars, but Elijah was to them, by his counsels, reproofs, and prayers, better than the strongest force of chariot and horse, and kept off the judgments of God. His departure was like the routing of an army, an irreparable loss. "Better have lost all our men of war than this man of God."

13 He took up also the mantle of Elijah that fell from him, and went back, and stood by the bank of Jordan; 14 And he took the mantle of Elijah that fell from him, and smote the waters, and said, Where *is* the LORD God of Elijah? and when he also had smitten the waters, they parted hither and thither: and Elisha went over. 15 And when the sons of the prophets which *were* to view at Jericho saw him, they said, The spirit of Elijah doth rest on Elisha. And they came to meet him, and bowed themselves to the ground before him. 16 And they said unto him, Behold now, there be with thy servants fifty strong men; let them go, we pray thee, and seek thy master: lest peradventure the Spirit of the LORD hath taken him up, and cast him upon some mountain, or into some valley. And he said, Ye shall not send. 17 And when they urged him till he was ashamed, he said, Send. They sent therefore fifty men; and they sought three days, but found him not. 18 And when they came again to him, (for he tarried at Jericho,) he said unto them, Did I not say unto you, Go not?

We have here an account of what followed immediately after the translation of Elijah.

I. The tokens of God's presence with Elisha, and the marks of his elevation into Elijah's room, to be, as he had been, a father to the sons of the prophets, and the chariots and horsemen of Israel.

1. He was possessed of Elijah's mantle, the badge of his office, which, we may suppose, he put on and wore for his master's sake, *v.* 13. When Elijah went to heaven, though he did not let fall his body as others do, he let fall his mantle instead of it; for he was unclothed, that he might be clothed upon with immortality: he was going to a world where he needed not the mantle to adorn him, nor to shelter him from the weather, nor to wrap his face in, as 1 Kings xix. 13. He left his mantle as a legacy to Elisha, and, though in itself it was of small value, yet as it was a token of the descent of the Spirit upon him, it was more than if he had bequeathed to him thousands of gold and silver.

Elisha took it up, not as a sacred relic to be worshipped, but as a significant garment to be worn, and a recompence to him for his own garments which he had rent. He loved this cloak ever since it was first cast over him, 1 Kings xix. 19. He that then so cheerfully obeyed the summons of it, and became Elijah's servant, is now dignified with it, and becomes his successor. There are remains of great and good men, which, like this mantle, ought to be gathered up and preserved by the survivors, their sayings, their writings, their examples, that, as their works follow them in the reward of them, they may stay behind in the benefit of them.

2. He was possessed of Elijah's power to divide Jordan, *v.* 14. Having parted with his father, he returns to his sons in the schools of the prophets. Jordan was between him and them; it had been divided to make way for Elijah to his glory; he will try whether it will divide to make way for him to his business, and by that he will know that God is with him, and that he has the double portion of Elijah's spirit. Elijah's last miracle shall be Elisha's first; thus he begins where Elijah left off and there is no vacancy. In dividing the waters, (1.) He made use of Elijah's mantle, as Elijah himself had done (*v.* 8), to signify that he designed to keep to his master's methods, and would not introduce any thing new, as those affect to do that think themselves wiser than their predecessors. (2.) He applied to Elijah's God: *Where is the Lord God of Elijah?* He does not ask, "Where is Elijah?" as poring upon the loss of him, as if he could not be easy now that he was gone,—or as doubting of his happy state, as if, like the sons of the prophets here, he knew not what had become of him,—or as curiously enquiring concerning him, and the particulars of that state he was removed to (no, that is a hidden life, it does not yet appear what we shall be),—nor as expecting help from him; no, Elijah is happy, but is neither omniscient nor omnipotent; but he asks, *Where is the Lord God of Elijah?* Now that Elijah was taken to heaven God had abundantly proved himself the God of Elijah; if he had not prepared for him that city, and done better for him there than ever he did for him in this world, he *would have been ashamed to be called his God*, Heb. xi. 16; Matt. xxvii. 31, 32. Now that Elijah was taken to heaven Elisha enquired, [1.] After God. When our creature-comforts are removed, we have a God to go to, that lives for ever. [2.] After *the God of Elijah*, the God that Elijah served, and honoured, and pleaded for, and adhered to when all Israel had deserted him. This honour is done to those who cleave to God in times of general apostasy, that God will be, in a peculiar manner, their God. "The God that owned, and protected, and provided for Elijah, and many ways honoured him, especially now at last, where is he? Lord, am not I promised Elijah's spirit? Make good that promise." The words which next follow in the original, *Aph-his—even he*, which we join to the following clause, *when he also had smitten the waters*, some make an answer to this question, *Where is Elijah's God? Etiam ille adhuc superest*—"*He is in being still*, and nigh at hand. We have lost Elijah, but we have not lost Elijah's God. He *has not forsaken the earth;* it is even he that is still with me." Note, *First*, It is the duty and interest of the saints on earth to enquire after God, and apply to him as the Lord God of the saints that have gone before to heaven, *the God of our fathers. Secondly*, It is very comfortable to those who enquire after God that they know where to find him; it is *even he* that *is in his holy temple* (Ps. xi. 4) and *nigh to all who call upon him*, Ps. cxlv. 18. *Thirdly*, Those that walk in the spirit and steps of their godly faithful predecessors shall certainly experience the same grace that they experienced; Elijah's God will be Elisha's too. The Lord God of the holy prophets is the same yesterday, to-day, and for ever; and what will it avail us to have the mantles of those that are gone, their places, their books, if we have not their spirit, their God?

3. He was possessed of Elijah's interest in the sons of the prophets, *v.* 15. Some of the fellows of the college at Jericho, who had placed themselves conveniently near Jordan, to see what passed, were surprised to see Jordan divided before Elisha in his return, and took that as a convincing evidence that *the spirit of Elijah did rest upon him*, and that therefore they ought to pay the same respect and deference to him that they had paid to Elijah. Accordingly they went to meet him, to congratulate him on his safe passage through fire and water, and the honour God had put upon him; and they *bowed themselves to the ground before him.* They were trained up in the schools; Elisha was taken from the plough; yet when they perceived that God was with him, and that this was *the man whom he delighted to honour*, they readily submitted to him as their head and father, as the people to Joshua when Moses was dead, Josh. i. 17. Those that appear to have God's Spirit and presence with them ought to have our esteem and best affections, notwithstanding the meanness of their extraction and education. Whomsoever God honours, we must. This ready submission of the sons of the prophets, no doubt, was a great encouragement to Elisha, and helped to clear his call.

II. The needless search which the sons of the prophets made for Elijah. 1. They suggested that possibly he was dropped, either alive or dead, upon some mountain, or in some valley; and it would be a satisfaction to them if they sent some strong men, whom they had at command, in quest of him, *v.* 16. Some of them perhaps started this as a demurrer to the choice of Elisha: "Let us first be sure that Elijah has quite gone. Can we think Elijah thus neglected by heaven, that chosen vessel thus cast away as a vessel in which was no pleasure?" 2. Elisha consented not to their motion till they overcame him with importunity, *v.* 17. They urged him till he was ashamed to oppose it any further, lest he should be thought wanting in his respect to his old master or loth to resign the mantle again. Wise men may yield to that, for the sake of peace and the good opinion of others, which yet their judgment is against as needless and fruitless. 3. The issue made them as much ashamed of their proposal as they, by their importunity, had made Elisha ashamed of his opposing it. Their messengers, after they had tired themselves with fruitless search, returned with a *non est inventus—he is not to be found,* and gave Elisha an opportunity of upbraiding his friends with their folly: *Did I not say unto you, Go not? v.* 18. This would make them the more willing to acquiesce in his judgment another time. Traversing hills and valleys will never bring us to Elijah, but the imitation of his holy faith and zeal will, in due time.

19 And the men of the city said unto Elisha, Behold, I pray thee, the situation of this city *is* pleasant, as my lord seeth: but the water *is* naught, and the ground barren. 20 And he said, Bring me a new cruse, and put salt therein. And they brought *it* to him. 21 And he went forth unto the spring of the waters, and cast the salt in there, and said, Thus saith the LORD, I have healed these waters; there shall not be from thence any more death or barren *land.* 22 So the waters were healed unto this day, according to the saying of Elisha which he spake. 23 And he went up from thence unto Beth-el: and as he was going up by the way, there came forth little children out of the city, and mocked him, and said unto him, Go up, thou bald head; go up, thou bald head. 24 And he turned back, and looked on them, and cursed them in the name of the LORD. And there came forth two she bears out of the wood, and tare forty and two children of them. 25 And he went from thence to mount Carmel, and from thence he returned to Samaria.

Elisha had, in this respect, a double portion of Elijah's spirit, that he wrought more miracles than Elijah. Some reckon them in number just double. Two are recorded in these verses—a miracle of mercy to Jericho and a miracle of judgment to Bethel, Ps. ci. 1.

I. Here is a blessing upon the waters of Jericho, which was effectual to heal them. Jericho was built in disobedience to a command, in defiance to a threatening, and at the expense of the lives of all the builder's children; yet, when it was built, it was not ordered to be demolished again, nor were God's prophets or people forbidden to dwell in it, but even within those walls that were built by iniquity we find a nursery of piety. Fools, they say, build houses for wise men to dwell in. Here the wealth of the sinner provided a habitation for the just. We find Christ at Jericho, Luke xix. 1. Hither Elisha came, to confirm the souls of the disciples with a more particular account of Elijah's translation than their spies, who saw at a distance, could give them. Here he staid while the fifty men were searching for him. And, 1. The men of Jericho represented to him their grievance, *v.* 19. God's faithful prophets love to be employed; it is wisdom to make use of them during the little while that their light is with us. They had not applied to Elijah concerning the matter, perhaps because he was not so easy of access as Elisha was; but now, we may hope, by the influence of the divinity-school in their city, they were reformed. The situation was pleasant and afforded a good prospect; but they had neither wholesome water to drink nor fruitful soil to yield them food, and what pleasure could they take in their prospect? Water is a common mercy, which we should estimate by the greatness of the calamity which the want or unwholesomeness of it would be. Some think that it was not all the ground about Jericho that was barren and had bad water, but some one part only, and *that* where the sons of the prophets had their lodgings, who are here called *the men of the city.* 2. He soon redressed their grievance. Prophets should endeavour to make every place they come to, some way or other, the better for them, endeavouring to sweeten bitter spirits, and to make barren souls fruitful, by the due application of the word of God. Elisha will heal their waters; but, (1.) They must furnish him with salt in a new cruse, *v.* 20. If salt had been proper to season the water, yet what could so small a quantity do towards it and what the better for being in a new cruse? But thus those that would be helped must be employed and have their faith and obedience tried. God's works of grace are wrought, not by any operations of ours, but in observance of his institutions. (2.) He cast the salt *into the spring of the waters,* and so healed the streams and the ground they watered. Thus the way to reform men's lives is to renew their hearts; let those be seasoned with the salt of grace, for *out of them are the issues of life. Make the tree good and the fruit will be good.* Purify the heart and that will cleanse the hands. (3.) He did not pretend to do this by his own power, but in God's name: *Thus saith the Lord, I have healed these waters.* He is but the instrument, the channel through which God is pleased to convey this healing virtue. By doing them this kindness with a *Thus saith the Lord,* they would be made the more willing, hereafter, to receive from him a reproof, admonition, or command, with the same preface. If, in God's name, he can help them, in God's name let him teach and rule them. *Thus saith the Lord,* out of Elisha's mouth, must, ever after, be of mighty force with them. (4.) The cure was lasting, and not for the present only: *The waters were healed unto this day, v.* 22. What God does *shall be for ever,* Eccl. iii. 14. When he, by his Spirit, *heals a soul,* there shall be *no more death nor barrenness;* the property is altered: what was useless and offensive becomes grateful and serviceable.

II. Here is a curse upon the children of Bethel, which was effectual to destroy them; for it was not a curse causeless. At Bethel there was another school of prophets. Thither Elisha went next, in this his primary visitation, and the scholars there no doubt welcomed him with all possible respect, but the townsmen were abusive to him. One of Jeroboam's calves was at Bethel; this they were proud of, and fond of, and hated those that reproved them. The law did not empower them to suppress this pious academy, but we may suppose it was their usual practice to jeer the prophets as they went along the streets, to call them by some nickname or other, that they might expose them to contempt, prejudice their youth against them, and, if possible, drive them out of their town. Had the abuse done to Elisha been the first offence of that kind, it is probable that it would not have been so severely punished. But *mocking the messengers of the Lord,* and *misusing the prophets,* was one of the *crying sins of Israel,* as we find, 2 Chron. xxxvi. 16. Now here we have, 1. An instance of that sin. The little *children of Bethel,* the boys and girls that were playing in the streets (notice, it is likely, having come to the town of his approach), went out to meet him, not with their hosannas, as they ought to have done, but with their scoffs; they gathered about him and mocked him, as if he had been a fool, or one fit to make sport with. Among other things that they used to jeer the prophets with, they had this particular taunt for him, *Go up, thou bald head, go up, thou bald head.* It is a wicked thing to reproach persons for their natural infirmities or deformities; it is adding affliction to the afflicted; and, if they are as God made them, the reproach reflects upon him. But this was such a thing as scarcely deserved to be called a blemish, and would never have been turned to his reproach if they had had any thing else to reproach him with. It was his character as a prophet that they designed to abuse. The honour God had crowned him with should have been sufficient to cover his bald head and protect him from their scoffs. They bade him *go up,* perhaps reflecting on the assumption of Elijah: "Thy master," they say, "has gone up; why dost not thou go up after him? Where is the fiery chariot? When shall we be rid of thee too?" These children said as they were taught; they had learned of their idolatrous parents to call foul names and give bad language, especially to prophets. These young cocks, as we say, crowed after the old ones. Perhaps their parents did at this time send them out and set them on, that, if possible, they might keep the prophet out of their town. 2. A specimen of that ruin which came upon Israel at last, for misusing God's prophets, and of which this was intended to give them fair warning. Elisha heard their taunts, a good while, with patience; but at length the fire of holy zeal for God was kindled in his breast by the continued provocation, and he *turned and looked upon them,* to try if a grave and severe look would put them out of countenance and oblige them to retire, to see if he could discern in their faces any marks of ingenuousness; but they *were not ashamed, neither could they blush;* and therefore he *cursed them in the name of the Lord,* both imprecated and denounced the following judgment, not in personal revenge for the indignity done to himself, but as the mouth of divine justice to punish the dishonour done to God. His summons was immediately obeyed. two she-bears (bears perhaps robbed of their whelps) came out of an adjacent wood, and presently killed forty-two children, *v.* 24. Now in this, (1.) The prophet must be justified, for he did it by divine impulse. Had the curse come from any bad principle God would not have said *Amen* to it. We may think it would have been better to have called for two rods for the correction of these children than two bears for the destruction of them. But Elisha knew, by the Spirit, the bad character of these children. He knew what a generation of vipers those were, and what mischievous enemies they would be to God's prophets if they should live to be men, who began so early to be abusive to them. He intended hereby to punish the parents and to make them afraid of God's judgments. (2.) God must be glorified as a righteous God, that hates sin, and will reckon for it. even in little children. Let the hideous shrieks and groans of this wicked wretched brood make our flesh tremble for fear of God. Let little children be afraid of speaking wicked words, for God notices what they say. Let them not mock any for their defects in mind or body, but pity them rather; especially let them know that it is at their peril if they jeer God's people or ministers, and scoff at any for well-doing. Let parents, that would have comfort in their children, train them up well, and do their utmost betimes to drive out the foolishness that is bound up in their hearts; for, as bishop Hall says, "In vain do we look for good from those children whose education we have neglected; and in vain do we grieve for those miscarriages which our care might have prevented." Elisha comes to Bethel, and fears not the revenges of the bereaved parents; God, who bade him do what he did, he knew would bear him out. Thence he goes to Mount Carmel (*v.* 25), where it is probable there was a religious house fit for retirement and contemplation. Thence he returned to Samaria, where, being a public place, this father of the prophets might be most serviceable. Bishop Hall observes here, "That he can never be a profitable seer who is either always or never alone."

CHAP. III.

We are now called to attend the public affairs of Israel, in which we shall find Elisha concerned. Here is, I. The general character of Jehoram, king of Israel, ver. 1—3. II. A war with Moab, in which Jehoram and his allies were engaged, ver. 4—8. III. The straits which the confederate army were reduced to in their expedition against Moab, and their consulting Elisha in that distress, with the answer of peace he gave them, ver. 9—19. IV. The glorious issue of this campaign (ver. 20—25) and the barbarous method the king of Moab took to oblige the confederate army to retire, ver. 26, 27. The house of Ahab is doomed to destruction; and, though in this chapter we have both its character and its condition better than before, yet the threatened ruin is not far off.

NOW Jehoram the son of Ahab began to reign over Israel in Samaria the eighteenth year of Jehoshaphat king of Judah, and reigned twelve years. 2 And he wrought evil in the sight of the LORD; but not like his father, and like his mother: for he put away the image of Baal that his father had made. 3 Nevertheless he cleaved unto the sins of Jeroboam the son of Nebat, which made Israel to sin; he departed not therefrom. 4 And Mesha king of Moab was a sheepmaster, and rendered unto the king of Israel a hundred thousand lambs, and a hundred thousand rams, with the wool. 5 But it came to pass, when Ahab was dead, that the king of Moab rebelled against the king of Israel.

Jehoram, the son of Ahab, and brother of Ahaziah, is here upon the throne of Israel; and, though he was but a bad man, yet two commendable things are here recorded of him:—

I. That he removed his father's idols. He did evil in many things, but not like his father Ahab or his mother Jezebel, *v.* 2. Bad he was, but not so bad, so *overmuch wicked,* as Solomon speaks, Eccl. vii. 17. Perhaps Jehoshaphat, though by his alliance with the house of Ahab he made his own family worse, did something towards making Ahab's better. Jehoram saw his father and brother cut off for worshipping Baal, and wisely took warning by God's judgments on them, and *put away the image of Baal,* resolving to worship the God of Israel only, and consult none but his prophets. So far was well, yet it did not prevent the destruction of Ahab's family, nay, that destruction came *in his days,* and fell immediately *upon him* (*ch.* ix. 24), though he was one of the best of the family, for then the measure of its iniquity was full. Jehoram's reformation was next to none; for, 1. He only put away the image of Baal *which his father had made,* and this probably in compliment to Jehoshaphat, who otherwise would not have come into confederacy with him, any more than with his brother, 1 Kings xxii. 49. Bu he did not destroy the worship of Baal among the people, for Jehu found it prevalent, *ch.* x. 19. It was well to reform his family, but it was not enough; he ought to have used his power for the reforming of his kingdom. 2. When he put away the image of Baal, he adhered to the worship of the calves, that politic sin of Jeroboam, *v.* 3. *He departed not therefrom,* because that was the state engine by which the division between the two tribes was supported. Those do not truly, nor acceptably, repent or reform, who only part with the sins that they lose by, but continue their affection to the sins that they get by. 3. He only *put away* the image of Baal, he did not break it in pieces, as he ought to have done. He laid it aside for the present, yet not knowing but he might have occasion for it another time; and Jezebel, for reasons of state, was content to worship her Baal in private.

II. That he did what he could to recover his brother's losses. As he had something more of the religion of an Israelite than his father, so he had something more of the spirit of a king than his brother. Moab rebelled against Israel immediately upon the death of Ahab, *ch.* i. 1. And we do not find that Ahaziah made any attempt to chastise or reduce them, but tamely let go his interest in them, rather than entertain the cares, undergo the fatigues, and run the hazards, of a war with them. His folly and pusillanimity herein, and his indifference to the public good, were the more aggravated because the tribute which the king of Moab paid was a very considerable branch of the revenue of the crown of Israel: 100,000 *lambs, and* 100,000 *wethers, v.* 4. The riches of kings then lay more in cattle than coin, and they thought it not below them to *know the state of their flocks and herds* themselves, because, as Solomon observes, *the crown doth not endure to every generation,* Prov. xxvii. 23, 24. Taxes were then paid not so much in money as in the commodities of the country, which was an ease to the subject, whether it was an advantage to the prince or no. The revolt of Moab was a great loss to Israel, yet Ahaziah sat still in sloth and ease. But an upper chamber in his house proved as fatal to him as the high places of the field could have been (*ch.* i 2), and the breaking of his lattice let into his throne a man of a more active genius, that would not lose the dominion of Moab without making at least one push for its preservation.

6 And king Jehoram went out of Samaria the same time, and numbered all Israel. 7 And he went and sent to Jehoshaphat the king of Judah, saying, The king of Moab hath rebelled against me: wilt thou go with me against Moab to battle? And he said, I will go up: I *am* as thou *art*, my people as thy people, *and* my horses as thy horses. 8 And he said, Which way shall we go up? And he answered, The way through the wilderness of Edom. 9 So the king of Israel went, and the king of Judah, and the king of Edom: and they fetched a compass of seven days' journey: and there was no water for the host, and for the cattle that followed them. 10 And the king of Israel said, Alas! that the LORD hath called these three kings together, to deliver them into the hand of Moab! 11 But Jehoshaphat said, *Is there* not here a prophet of the LORD, that we may enquire of the LORD by him? And one of the king of Israel's servants answered and said, Here *is* Elisha the son of Shaphat, which poured water on the hands of Elijah. 12 And Jehoshaphat said, The word of the LORD is with him. So the king of Israel and Jehoshaphat and the king of Edom went down to him. 13 And Elisha said unto the king of Israel, What have I to do with thee? get thee to the prophets of thy father, and to the prophets of thy mother. And the king of Israel said unto him, Nay: for the LORD hath called these three kings together, to deliver them into the hand of Moab. 14 And Elisha said, *As* the LORD of hosts liveth, before whom I stand, surely, were it not that I regard the presence of Jehoshaphat the king of Judah, I would not look toward thee, nor see thee. 15 But now bring me a minstrel. And it came to pass, when the minstrel played, that the hand of the LORD came upon him. 16 And he said, Thus saith the LORD, Make this valley full of ditches. 17 For thus saith the LORD, Ye shall not see wind, neither shall ye see rain; yet that valley shall be filled with water, that ye may drink, both ye, and your cattle, and your beasts. 18 And this is *but* a light thing in the sight of the LORD: he will deliver the Moabites also into your hand. 19 And ye shall smite every fenced city, and every choice city, and shall fell every good tree, and stop all wells of water, and mar every good piece of land with stones.

Jehoram has no sooner got the sceptre into his hand than he takes the sword into his hand, to reduce Moab. Crowns bring great cares and perils to the heads that wear them; no sooner in honour than in war Now here we have,

I. The concerting of this expedition between Jehoram king of Israel and Jehoshaphat king of Judah. Jehoram levied an army (*v.* 6), and such an opinion he had of the godly king of Judah that, 1. He courted him to be his confederate: *Wilt thou go with me against Moab?* And he gained him. Jehoshaphat said, *I will go up. I am as thou art*, *v.* 7. Judah and Israel, though unhappily divided from each other, yet can unite against Moab a common enemy. Jehoshaphat upbraids them not with their revolt from the house of David, nor makes it an article of their alliance that they shall return to their allegiance, though he had good reason to insist upon it, but treats with Israel as a sister-kingdom. Those are no friends to their own peace and strength who can never find in their hearts to forgive and forget an old injury, and unite with those that have formerly broken in upon their rights. *Quod initio non valuit, tractu temporis invalescit—That which was originally destitute of authority in the progress of time acquires it.* 2. He consulted him as his confidant, *v.* 8. He took advice of Jehoshaphat, who had more wisdom and experience than himself, which way they should make their descent upon the country of Moab; and he advised that they should not march against them the nearest way, over Jordan, but go round *through the wilderness of Edom*, that they might take the king of Edom (who was tributary to him) and his forces along with them. If two be better than one, much more will not a *threefold cord be easily broken.* Jehoshaphat had like to have paid dearly for joining with

Ahab, yet he joined with his son, and this expedition also had like to have been fatal to him. There is nothing got by being yoked with unbelievers.

II. The great straits that the army of the confederates was reduced to in this expedition. Before they saw the face of an enemy they were all in danger of perishing for want of water, *v.* 9. This ought to have been considered before they ventured a march through the wilderness, the same wilderness (or very near it) where their ancestors wanted water, Num. xx. 2. God suffers his people, by their own improvidence, to bring themselves into distress, that the wisdom, power, and goodness of his providence may be glorified in their relief. What is more cheap and common than water? It is *drink to every beast of the field*, Ps. civ. 11. Yet the want of it will soon humble and ruin kings and armies. The king of Israel sadly lamented the present distress, and the imminent danger it put them in of falling into the hands of their enemies the Moabites, to whom, when weakened by thirst, they would be an easy prey, *v.* 10. It was he that had *called these kings together;* yet he charges it upon Providence, and reflects upon that as unkind: The Lord has *called them together.* Thus *the foolishness of man perverteth his way*, and then *his heart fretteth against the Lord*, Prov. xix. 3.

III. Jehoshaphat's good motion to ask counsel of God in this exigency, *v.* 11. The place they were now in could not but remind them of the *wonders of which their fathers told them,* the waters fetched out of the rock for Israel's seasonable supply. The thought of this, we may suppose, encouraged Jehoshaphat to ask, *Is there not here a prophet of the Lord,* like unto Moses? He was the more concerned because it was by his advice that they fetched this compass through the wilderness, *v.* 8. It was well that Jehoshaphat enquired of the Lord now, but it would have been much better if he had done it sooner, before he engaged in this war, or steered this course; so the distress might have been prevented. Good men are sometimes remiss and forgetful, and neglect their duty till necessity and affliction drive them to it.

IV. Elisha recommended as a proper person for them to consult with, *v.* 11. And here we may wonder, 1. That Elisha should follow the camp, especially in such a tedious march as this, as a volunteer, unasked, unobserved, and in no post of honour at all; not in the office of *priest of the war* (Deut. xx. 2) or president of the council of war, but in such obscurity that none of the kings knew they had such a jewel in the treasures of their camp, nor so good a friend in their retinue. We may suppose it was by special direction from heaven that Elisha attended the war, as *the chariot of Israel and the horsemen thereof.* Thus does God anticipate his people with the blessings of his goodness and provide his oracles for those that provide them not for themselves. It would often be bad with us if God did not take more care of us, both for soul and body, than we take for ourselves. 2. That a servant of the king of Israel knew of his being there when the king himself did not. Probably it was such a servant as Obadiah was to his father Ahab, one that *feared the Lord;* to such a one Elisha made himself known, not to the kings. The account he gives of him is that it was he that *poured water on the hands of Elijah*, that is, he was his servant, and particularly attended him when he washed his hands. He that will be great, let him learn to minister: he that will rise high, let him begin low.

V. The application which the kings made to Elisha. They went down to him to his quarters, *v.* 12. Jehoshaphat had such an esteem for a prophet with whom the word of the Lord was that he would condescend to visit him in his own person and not send for him up to him. The other two were moved by the straits they were in to make their court to the prophet. He that humbled himself was thus exalted, and looked great, when three kings came to knock at his door, and beg his assistance; see Rev. iii. 9.

VI. The entertainment which Elisha gave them. 1. He was very plain with the wicked king of Israel (*v.* 13): "*What have I to do with thee?* How canst thou expect an answer of peace from me? *Get thee to the prophets of thy father and mother*, whom thou hast countenanced and maintained in thy prosperity, and let them help thee now in thy distress." Elisha was not imposed upon, as Jehoshaphat was, by his partial and hypocritical reformation; he knew that, though he had put away the image of Baal, Baal's prophets were still dear to him, and perhaps some of them were now in his camp. "*Go,*" said he, "*go to them. Get you to the gods whom you have served*, Judg. x. 14. The world and the flesh have ruled you, let them help you; why should God be *enquired of by* you?" Ezek. xiv. 3. Elisha tells him to his face, in a holy indignation at his wickedness, that he can scarcely find in his heart to *look towards him* or to *see him, v.* 14. Jehoram is to be respected as a prince, but as a wicked man he is a vile person, and is to be contemned, Ps. xv. 4. Elisha, as a subject, will honour him, but as a prophet he will cause him to know his iniquity. For those that had such an extraordinary commission it was fit (though not for a common person) to say to a king, *Thou art wicked*, Job xxxiv. 18. Jehoram has so much self-command as to take this plain dealing patiently; he cares not now for hearing of the prophets of Baal, but is a humble suitor to the God of Israel and his prophet, representing the present case as very deplorable and humbly recommending it to the prophet's compassionate consideration. In effect, he owns himself unworthy, but let not the other kings be ruined for his sake. 2. Elisha showed a great respect to the godly king of Judah, *regarded his presence,* and, for his sake, would *enquire of the Lord* for them all. It is good being with those that have God's favour and his prophet's love. Wicked people often fare the better for the friendship and society of those that are godly. 3. He composed himself to receive instructions from God. His mind was somewhat ruffled and disturbed at the sight of Jehoram; though he was not put into a sinful heat or passion, nor had spoken unadvisedly, yet his zeal for the present indisposed him for prayer and the operations of the Spirit, which required a mind very calm and sedate. He therefore called for a musician (*v.* 15), a devout musician, one accustomed to play upon his harp and sing psalms to it. To hear God's praises sweetly sung, as David had appointed, would cheer his spirits, and settle his mind, and help to put him into a right frame both to speak to him and to hear from him. We find a company of prophets prophesying with *a psaltery and a tabret before them,* 1 Sam. x. 5. Those that desire communion with God must keep their spirits quiet and serene. Elisha being refreshed, and having the tumult of his spirits laid by this divine music, *the hand of the Lord came upon him,* and his visit did him more honour than that of three kings. 4. God, by him, gave them assurance that the issue of the present distress would be comfortable and glorious. (1.) They should speedily be supplied with water, *v.* 16, 17. To try their faith and obedience, he bids them *make the valley full of ditches* to receive the water. Those that expect God's blessings must prepare room for them, *dig the pools* for the rain to fill, as they did in the valley of Baca, and so made even that a well, Ps. lxxxiv. 6. To raise their wonder, he tells them they shall have water enough, and yet there shall be *neither wind nor rain.* Elijah, by prayer, obtained water out of the clouds, but Elisha fetches it nobody knows whence. The spring of these waters shall be as secret as the head of the Nile. God is not tied to second causes. Ordinarily it is by a plentiful rain that God *confirms his inheritance* (Ps. lxviii. 9), but here it is done without rain, at least without rain in that place. Some of the *fountains of the great deep,* it is likely, *were broken up* on this occasion; and, to increase the miracle, *that valley* only (as it should seem) *was filled with water,* and no other place had any share of it. (2.) That supply should be an earnest of victory (*v.* 18): "*This is but a light thing in the sight of the Lord;* you shall not only be saved from perishing, but shall return in triumph." As God gives freely to the unworthy, so he gives richly, like himself, more than we are *able to ask or think.* His grants out-do our requests and expectations. Those that sincerely seek for the dew of God's grace shall have it, and by it be made *more than conquerors.* It is promised that they shall be masters of the rebellious country, and they are permitted to lay it waste and ruin it, *v.* 19. The law forbade them to fell fruit-trees to be employed in their sieges (Deut. xx. 19), but not when it was intended, in justice, for the starving of a country that had forfeited its fruits, by denying *tribute to those to whom tribute was due.*

20 And it came to pass in the morning, when the meat offering was offered, that, behold, there came water by the way of Edom, and the country was filled with water. 21 And when all the Moabites heard that the kings were come up to fight against them, they gathered all that were able to put on armour, and upward, and stood in the border. 22 And they rose up early in the morning, and the sun shone upon the water, and the Moabites saw the water on the other side *as* red as blood: 23 And they said, This *is* blood: the kings are surely slain, and they have smitten one another: now therefore, Moab, to the spoil. 24 And when they came to the camp of Israel, the Israelites rose up and smote the Moabites, so that they fled before them: but they went forward smiting the Moabites, even in *their* country. 25 And they beat down the cities, and on every good piece of land cast every man his stone, and filled it; and they stopped all the wells of water, and felled all the good trees: only in Kir-haraseth left they the stones thereof; howbeit the slingers went about *it,* and smote it. 26 And when the king of Moab saw that the battle was too sore for him, he took with him seven hundred men that drew swords, to break through *even* unto the king of Edom: but they could not. 27 Then he took his eldest son that should have reigned in his stead, and offered him *for* a burnt offering upon the wall. And there was great indignation against Israel: and they departed from him, and returned to *their own* land.

I. We have here the divine gift of both those things which God had promised by Elisha—water and victory, and the former not only a pledge of the latter, but a means of it. God, who created, and commands, all the waters, both above and beneath the firmament, sent them an abundance of water on a sudden, which did them double service.

1. It relieved their armies, which were ready to perish, *v.* 20. And, which was very observable, this relief came just at the time of the *offering of the morning sacrifice* upon the altar at Jerusalem, a certain time, and universally known. That time Elisha chose for his *hour of prayer* (it is likely *looking towards the temple,* for so they were to do in their prayers when they were *going out to battle* and encamped at a distance, 1 Kings viii. 44), in token of his communion with the temple-service, and his expectation of success by virtue of the great sacrifice. We now cannot pitch upon any hour more acceptable than another, because our high priest is always appearing for us, to present and plead his sacrifice. That time God chose for the hour of mercy to put an honour upon the daily sacrifice, which had been despised. God answered Daniel's prayer just at the *time of the evening sacrifice* (Dan. ix. 21); for he will acknowledge his own institutions.

2. It deceived their enemies, who were ready to triumph, into their destruction. Notice was given to the Moabites of the advances of the confederate army, to oppose which *all that were able to put on armour* were posted upon the frontiers, where they were ready to give the Israelites a warm reception (*v.* 21), promising themselves that it would be easy dealing with an army fatigued by so long a march through the wilderness of Edom. But see here,

(1.) How easily they were drawn into their own delusions. Observe the steps of their self-deceit. [1.] They saw the water in the valley where the army of Israel encamped, and conceited it was blood (*v.* 22), because they knew the valley to be dry, and (there having been no rain) could not imagine it should be water. The sun shone upon it, and probably *the sky was red and lowering,* a presage of *foul weather that day* (Matt. xvi. 3), and so it proved to them. But, this making the water look red, their own fancies, which made them willing to believe what made for them, suggested, *This is blood,* God permitting them thus to impose upon themselves. [2.] If their camp was thus full of blood, they conclude, "Certainly the kings have fallen out (as confederates of different interests are apt to do) and they have *slain one another* (*v.* 23), for who else should slay them?" And, [3.] "If the armies have slain one another, we have nothing to do but to divide the prey. *Now therefore, Moab, to the spoil.*" These were the gradual suggestions of some sanguine spirits among them, that thought themselves wiser and happier in their conjectures than their neighbours; and the rest, being desirous it should be so, were forward to believe it was so. *Quod volumus facile credimus—What we wish we readily believe.* Thus those that are to be destroyed are first deceived (Rev. xx. 8), and none are so effectually deceived as those that deceive themselves.

(2.) How fatally they thereby ran upon their own destruction. They rushed carelessly into the camp of Israel, to plunder it, but were undeceived when it was too late. The Israelites, animated by the assurances Elisha had given them of victory, fell upon them with the utmost fury, routed them, and pursued them into their own country (*v.* 24), which they laid waste (*v.* 25), destroyed the cities, marred the ground, stopped up the wells, felled the timber, and left only the royal city standing, in the walls of which they made great breaches with their battering engines. This they got by rebelling against Israel. Who ever *hardened his heart against God and prospered?*

II. In the close of the chapter we are told what the king of Moab did when he found himself reduced to the last extremity by the besiegers, and that his capital city was likely to fall into their hands. 1. He attempted that which was bold and brave. He got together 700 choice men, and with them sallied out upon the intrenchments of the king of Edom, who, being but a mercenary in this expedition, would not, he hoped, make any great resistance if vigorously attacked, and so he might make his escape that way. But it would not do; even the king of Edom proved too hard for him, and obliged him to retire, *v.* 26. 2. This failing, he did that which was brutish and barbarous; he took his own son, his eldest son, that was to succeed him, than whom nothing could be more dear to himself and his people, and *offered him for a burnt-offering upon the wall, v.* 27. He designed by this, (1.) To obtain the favour of Chemosh his god, which, being a devil, delighted in blood and murder, and the destruction of mankind. The dearer any thing was to them the more acceptable those idolaters thought it must needs be if offered in sacrifice to their gods, and therefore burnt their children in the fire to their honour. (2.) To terrify the besiegers, and oblige them to retire. Therefore he did it *upon the wall,* in their sight, that they might see what desperate courses he resolved to take rather than surrender, and how dearly he would sell his city and life. He intended hereby to render them odious, and to exasperate and enrage his own subjects against them. This effect it had: *There was great indignation against Israel* for driving him to this extremity, whereupon they raised the siege and returned. Tender and generous spirits will not do that, though just, which will drive any man distracted, or make him desperate.

CHAP. IV.

Great service Elisha had done, in the foregoing chapter, for the three kings: to his prayers and prophecies they owed their lives and triumphs. One would have expected that the next chapter would tell us what honours and what dignities were

conferred on Elisha for this, that he should immediately be preferred at court, and made prime-minister of state, that Jehoshaphat should take him home with him, and advance him in his kingdom. No, the wise man delivered the army, but no man remembered the wise man, Eccl. ix. 15. Or, if he had preferment offered him, he declined it: he preferred the honour of doing good in the schools of the prophets before that of being great in the courts of princes. God magnified him, and that sufficed him—magnified him indeed, for we have him here employed in working no fewer than five miracles. I. He multiplied the poor widow's oil, ver. 1—7. II. He obtained for the good Shunammite the blessing of a son in her old age, ver. 8—17. III. He raised that child to life when it was dead, ver. 18—37. IV. He healed the deadly pottage, ver. 38—41. V. He fed 100 men with twenty small loaves, ver. 42—44.

NOW there cried a certain woman of the wives of the sons of the prophets unto Elisha, saying, Thy servant my husband is dead; and thou knowest that thy servant did fear the LORD: and the creditor is come to take unto him my two sons to be bondmen. 2 And Elisha said unto her, What shall I do for thee? tell me, what hast thou in the house? And she said, Thine handmaid hath not any thing in the house, save a pot of oil. 3 Then he said, Go, borrow thee vessels abroad of all thy neighbours, *even* empty vessels; borrow not a few. 4 And when thou art come in, thou shalt shut the door upon thee and upon thy sons, and shalt pour out into all those vessels, and thou shalt set aside that which is full. 5 So she went from him, and shut the door upon her and upon her sons, who brought *the vessels* to her; and she poured out. 6 And it came to pass, when the vessels were full, that she said unto her son, Bring me yet a vessel. And he said unto her, *There is* not a vessel more. And the oil stayed. 7 Then she came and told the man of God. And he said, Go, sell the oil, and pay thy debt, and live thou and thy children of the rest.

Elisha's miracles were for use, not for show; this recorded here was an act of real charity. Such also were the miracles of Christ, not only great wonders, but great favours to those for whom they were wrought. God magnifies his goodness with his power.

I. Elisha readily receives a poor widow's complaint. She was a prophet's widow; to whom therefore should she apply, but to him that was a father to the sons of the prophets, and concerned himself in the welfare of their families? It seems, the prophets had wives as well as the priests, though prophecy went not by entail, as the priesthood did. Marriage is honourable in all, and not inconsistent with the most sacred professions. Now, by the complaint of this poor woman (*v.* 1), we are given to understand, 1. That her husband, being *one of the sons of the prophets*, was well known to Elisha. Ministers of eminent gifts and stations should make themselves familiar with those that are every way their inferiors, and know their character and state. 2. That he had the reputation of a godly man. Elisha knew him to be one that feared the Lord, else he would have been unworthy of the honour and unfit for the work of a prophet. He was one that kept his integrity in a time of general apostasy, one of the 7000 that had not bowed the knee to Baal. 3. That he was dead, though a good man, a good minister. The prophets—do they live for ever? Those that were clothed with the Spirit of prophecy were not thereby armed against the stroke of death. 4. That he died poor, and in debt more than he was worth. He did not contract his debts by prodigality, and luxury, and riotous living, for he was one that feared the Lord, and therefore durst not allow himself in such courses: nay, religion obliges men not to live above what they have, nor to spend more than what God gives them, no, not in expenses otherwise lawful; for thereby, of necessity, they must disable themselves, at last, to give every one his own, and so prove guilty of a continued act of injustice all along. Yet it may be the lot of those that fear God to be in debt, and insolvent, through afflictive providences, losses by sea, or bad debts, or their own imprudence, for the *children of light* are not always *wise for this world.* Perhaps this prophet was impoverished by persecution: when Jezebel ruled, prophets had much ado to live, and especially if they had families. 5. That the creditors were very severe with her. Two sons she had to be the support of her widowed state, and their labour is reckoned *assets* in her hand; that must go therefore, and they must be bondmen for seven years (Exod. xxi. 2) to work out this debt. Those that leave their families under a load of debt disproportionable to their estates know not what trouble they entail. In this distress the poor widow goes to Elisha, in dependence upon the promise that the seed of the righteous shall not be forsaken. The generation of the upright may expect help from God's providence and countenance from his prophets.

II. He effectually relieves this poor widow's distress, and puts her in a way both to pay her debt and to maintain herself and her family. He did not say, *Be warmed, be filled*, but gave her real help. He did not give her some small matter for her present provision, but set her up in the world to sell oil, and put a stock into her hand to begin with. This was done by miracle, but it is an indication to us what is the best method of charity, and the greatest kindness one can do to poor people, which is, if possible, to help them into a way of improving what little they have by their own industry and ingenuity.

1. He directed her what to do, considered her case · *What shall I do for thee?* The sons of the prophets were poor, and it would signify little to make a collection for her among them: but the God of the holy prophets is able to supply all her need; and, if she has a little committed to her management, her need must be supplied by his blessing and increasing that little. Elisha therefore enquired what she had to make money of, and found she had nothing to sell but one pot of oil, *v.* 2. If she had had any plate or furniture, he would have bidden her part with it, to enable her to be just to her creditors. We cannot reckon any thing really, nor comfortably, our own, but what is so when all our debts are paid. If she had not had this pot of oil, the divine power could have supplied her; but, having this, it will work upon this, and so teach us to make the best of what we have. The prophet, knowing her to have credit among her neighbours, bids her borrow of them *empty vessels* (*v.* 3), for, it seems, she had old her own, towards the satisfying of hei creditors. He directs her to shut the door upon herself and her sons, while she filled all those vessels out of that one. She must shut the door, to prevent interruptions from the creditors and others while it was in the doing, that they might not seem proudly to boast of this miraculous supply, and that they might have opportunity for prayer and praise to God upon this extraordinary occasion. Observe, (1.) The oil was to be multiplied in the pouring, as the other widow's meal in the spending. The way to increase what we have is to use it; to him that so hath shall be given. It is not hoarding the talents, but trading with them, that doubles them. (2.) It must be poured out by herself, not by Elisha nor by any of the sons of the prophets, to intimate that it is in connexion with our own careful and diligent endeavours that we may expect the blessing of God to enrich us both for this world and the other. What we have will increase best in our own hand.

2. She did it accordingly. She did not tell the prophet he designed to make a fool of her; but firmly believing the divine power and goodness, and in pure obedience to the prophet, she borrowed vessels large and many of her neighbours, and poured out her oil into them. One of her sons was employed to bring her empty vessels, and the other carefully to set aside those that were full, while they were all amazed to find their pot, like a fountain of living water, always flowing, and yet always full. They saw not the spring that supplied it, but believed it to be in him *in whom all our springs are.* Job's metaphor was now verified in the letter (Job xxix. 6), *The rock poured me out rivers of oil.* Perhaps this was in the tribe of Asher, part of whose blessing it was that he should *dip his foot in oil,* Deut. xxxiii. 24.

3. The oil continued flowing as long as she had any empty vessels to receive it; when every vessel was full the oil stayed (*v.* 6), for it was not fit that this precious liquor should run over, and be as water spilt on the ground, which cannot be gathered up again. Note, We are never straitened in God, in his power and bounty, and the riches of his grace; all our straitness is in ourselves. It is our faith that fails, not his promise. He gives above what we ask: were there more vessels, there is enough in God to fill them—enough for all, enough for each. Was not this pot of oil exhausted as long as there were any vessels to be filled from it? And shall we fear lest the golden oil which flows from the very root and fatness of the good olive should fail, as long as there are any lamps to be supplied from it? Zech. iv. 12.

4. The prophet directed her what to do with the oil she had, *v.* 7. She must not keep it for her own use, to *make her face to shine.* Those whom Providence has made poor must be content with poor accommodations for themselves (this is *knowing how to want*), and must not think, when they get a little of that which is better than ordinary, to feed their own luxury: no, (1.) She must sell the oil to those that were rich, and could afford to bestow it on themselves. We may suppose, being produced by miracle, it was the best of its kind, like the wine (John ii. 10), so that she might have both a good price and a good market for it. Probably the merchants bought it to export, for oil was one of the commodities that Israel traded in, Ezek. xxvii. 17. (2.) She must pay her debt with the money she received for her oil. Though her creditors were too rigorous with her, yet they must not therefore lose their debt. Her first care, now that she has wherewithal to do so, must be to discharge that, even before she makes any provision for her children. It is one of the fundamental laws of our religion that we render to all their due, pay every just debt, give every one his own, though we leave ever so little for ourselves; and this, not of constraint, but willingly and without grudging; not only for wrath, to avoid being sued, but also for conscience' sake. Those that possess an honest mind cannot with pleasure eat their daily bread, unless it be their own bread. (3.) The rest must not be laid up, but she and her children must live upon it, not upon the oil, but upon the money received from it, with which they must put themselves into a capacity of getting an honest livelihood. No doubt she did as the man of God directed; and hence, [1.] Let those that are poor and in distress be encouraged to trust God for supply in the way of duty. *Verily thou shalt be fed,* though not feasted. It is true we cannot now expect miracles, yet we may expect mercies, if we wait on God and seek to him. Let widows particularly, and prophets' widows in a special manner, depend upon him to preserve them and their father-

less children alive, for to them he will be a husband, a father. [2.] Let those whom God has blessed with plenty use it for the glory of God and under the direction of his word: let them do justly with it, as this widow did, and serve God cheerfully in the use of it, and, as Elisha, be ready to do good to those that need them, be eyes to the blind, and feet to the lame.

8 And it fell on a day, that Elisha passed to Shunem, where *was* a great woman; and she constrained him to eat bread. And *so* it was, *that* as oft as he passed by, he turned in thither to eat bread. 9 And she said unto her husband, Behold now, I perceive that this *is* a holy man of God, which passeth by us continually. 10 Let us make a little chamber, I pray thee, on the wall; and let us set for him there a bed, and a table, and a stool, and a candlestick: and it shall be, when he cometh to us, that he shall turn in thither. 11 And it fell on a day, that he came thither, and he turned into the chamber, and lay there. 12 And he said to Gehazi his servant, Call this Shunammite. And when he had called her, she stood before him. 13 And he said unto him, Say now unto her, Behold, thou hast been careful for us with all this care; what *is* to be done for thee? wouldest thou be spoken for to the king, or to the captain of the host? And she answered, I dwell among mine own people. 14 And he said, What then *is* to be done for her? And Gehazi answered, Verily she hath no child, and her husband is old. 15 And he said, Call her. And when he had called her, she stood in the door. 16 And he said, About this season, according to the time of life, thou shalt embrace a son. And she said, Nay, my lord, *thou* man of God, do not lie unto thine handmaid. 17 And the woman conceived, and bare a son at that season that Elisha had said unto her, according to the time of life.

The giving of a son to such as were old, and had been long childless, was an ancient instance of the divine power and favour, in the case of Abraham, and Isaac, and Manoah, and Elkanah; we find it here among the wonders wrought by Elisha. This was wrought in recompence for the kind entertainment which a good woman gave him, as the promise of a son was given to Abraham when he entertained angels. Observe here,

I. The kindness of the Shunammite woman to Elisha. Things are bad enough in Israel, yet not so bad but that God's prophet finds friends, wherever he goes. Shunem was a city in the tribe of Issachar, that lay in the road between Samaria and Carmel, a road that Elisha often travelled, as we find *ch.* ii. 25. *There* lived *a great woman,* who kept a good house, and was very hospitable, her husband having a good estate, and his heart safely trusting in her, and in her discreet management, Prov. xxxi. 11. So famous a man as Elisha could not pass and repass unobserved. Probably he had been accustomed to take some private obscure lodgings in the town; but this pious matron, having notice once of his being there, pressed him with great importunity, and, with much difficulty, constrained him to dine with her, *v.* 8. He was modest and loth to be troublesome, humble and affected not to associate with those of the first rank; so that it was not without some difficulty that he was first drawn into an acquaintance there; but afterwards, whenever he went that way in his circuit, he constantly called there. So well pleased was she with her guest, and so desirous of his company, that she would not only bid him welcome to her table, but provide a lodging-room for him in her house, that he might make the longer stay, not doubting but her house would be blessed for his sake, and all under her roof edified by his pious instructions and example—a good design, yet she would not do it without acquainting her husband, would neither lay out his money nor invite strangers to his house without his consent asked and obtained, *v.* 9, 10. She suggests to him, 1. That the stranger she would invite was *a holy man of God,* who therefore would do good to their family, and God would recompense the kindness done to him; perhaps she had heard how well paid the widow of Sarepta was for entertaining Elijah. 2. That the kindness she intended him would be no great charge to them; she would build him only a little chamber. Perhaps she had no spare room in the house, or none private and retired enough for him, who spent much of his time in contemplation, and cared not for being disturbed with the noise of the family. The furniture shall be very plain; no costly hangings, no stands, no couches, no looking-glasses, but a bed, and a table, a stool, and a candlestick, all that was needful for his convenience, not only for his repose, but for his study, his reading and writing. Elisha seemed highly pleased with these accommodations, for he turned in and lay there (*v.* 11), and, as it should seem, his man in the same chamber, for he was far from taking state.

II. Elisha's gratitude for this kindness. Being exceedingly pleased with the quietness of his apartment, and the friendliness of his entertainment, he began to consider with himself what recompence he should make her. Those that receive courtesies should study to return them; it ill becomes men of God to be ungrateful, or to sponge upon those that are generous. 1. He offered to use his interest for her in the king's court (*v.* 13): *Thou hast been careful for us with all this care* (thus did he magnify the kindness he received, as those that are humble are accustomed to do, though in the purse of one so rich, and in the breast of one so free, it was as nothing); now *what shall be done for thee?* As the liberal devise liberal things, so the grateful devise grateful things. "*Wouldst thou be spoken for to the king, or the captain of the host,* for an office for thy husband, civil or military? Hast thou any complaint to make, any petition to present, any suit at law depending, that needs the countenance of the higher powers? Wherein can I serve thee?" It seems Elisha had got such an interest by his late services that, though he chose not to prefer himself by it, yet he was capable of preferring his friends. A good man can take as much pleasure in serving others as in raising himself. But she needs not any good offices of this kind to be done for her: *I dwell* (says she) *among my own people,* that is, "We are well off as we are, and do not aim at preferment." It is a happiness to *dwell among our own people,* that love and respect us, and to whom we are in a capacity of doing good; and a greater happiness to be content to do so, to be easy, and to know when we are well off. Why should those that live comfortably among their own people covet to live delicately in kings' palaces? It would be well with many if they did but know when they were well off. Some years after this we find this Shunammite had occasion to be spoken for to the king, though now she needed it not, *ch.* viii. 3, 4. Those that dwell among their own people must not think their mountain stands so strong as that it cannot be moved; they may be driven, as this good woman was, to sojourn among strangers. Our continuing city is above. 2. He did use his interest for her in the court of heaven, which was far better. Elisha consulted with his servant what kindness he should do for her, to such a freedom did this great prophet admit even his servant. Gehazi reminded him that she was childless, had a great estate, but no son to leave it to, and was past hopes of having any, her husband being old. If Elisha could obtain this favour from God for her, it would be the removal of that which at present was her only grievance. Those are the most welcome kindnesses which are most suited to our necessities. He sent for her immediately. She very humbly and respectfully *stood in the door* (*v.* 15), according to her accustomed modesty, and then he assured her that within a year she should bring forth a son, *v.* 16. She had received this prophet *in the name of a prophet,* and now she had not a courtier's reward, in being spoken for to the king, but a prophet's reward, a signal mercy given by prophets and in answer to prayer: the promise was a surprise to her, and she begged that she might not be flattered by it: "*Nay, my lord, thou* art a *man of God,* and therefore I hope speakest seriously, and dost not jest with me, nor lie unto thy handmaid." The event, within the time limited, confirmed the truth of the promise: *She bore a son* at the season that Elisha spoke of, *v.* 17. God built up her house, in reward of her kindness in building the prophet a chamber. We may well imagine what joy this brought to the family. *Sing, O barren! thou that didst not bear.*

18 And when the child was grown, it fell on a day, that he went out to his father to the reapers. 19 And he said unto his father, My head, my head. And he said to a lad, Carry him to his mother. 20 And when he had taken him, and brought him to his mother, he sat on her knees till noon, and *then* died. 21 And she went up, and laid him on the bed of the man of God, and shut *the door* upon him, and went out. 22 And she called unto her husband, and said, Send me, I pray thee, one of the young men, and one of the asses, that I may run to the man of God, and come again. 23 And he said, Wherefore wilt thou go to him to day? *it is* neither new moon, nor sabbath. And she said, *It shall be* well. 24 Then she saddled an ass, and said to her servant, Drive, and go forward; slack not *thy* riding for me, except I bid thee. 25 So she went and came unto the man of God to mount Carmel. And it came to pass, when the man of God saw her afar off, that he said to Gehazi his servant, Behold, *yonder is* that Shunammite: 26 Run now, I pray thee, to meet her, and say unto her, *Is it* well with thee? *is it* well with thy husband? *is it* well with the child? And she answered, *It is* well. 27 And when she came to the man of God to the hill, she caught him by the feet: but Gehazi came near to thrust her away. And the man of

God said, Let her alone; for her soul *is* vexed within her: and the LORD hath hid *it* from me, and hath not told me. 28 Then she said, Did I desire a son of my lord? did I not say, Do not deceive me? 29 Then he said to Gehazi, Gird up thy loins, and take my staff in thine hand, and go thy way: if thou meet any man, salute him not; and if any salute thee, answer him not again: and lay my staff upon the face of the child. 30 And the mother of the child said, *As* the LORD liveth, and *as* thy soul liveth, I will not leave thee. And he arose, and followed her. 31 And Gehazi passed on before them, and laid the staff upon the face of the child; but *there was* neither voice, nor hearing. Wherefore he went again to meet him, and told him, saying, The child is not awaked. 32 And when Elisha was come into the house, behold, the child was dead, *and* laid upon his bed. 33 He went in therefore, and shut the door upon them twain, and prayed unto the LORD. 34 And he went up, and lay upon the child, and put his mouth upon his mouth, and his eyes upon his eyes, and his hands upon his hands: and he stretched himself upon the child; and the flesh of the child waxed warm. 35 Then he returned, and walked in the house to and fro; and went up, and stretched himself upon him: and the child sneezed seven times, and the child opened his eyes. 36 And he called Gehazi, and said, Call this Shunammite. So he called her. And when she was come in unto him, he said, Take up thy son. 37 Then she went in, and fell at his feet, and bowed herself to the ground, and took up her son, and went out.

We may well suppose that, after the birth of this son, the prophet was doubly welcome to the good Shunammite. He had thought himself indebted to her, but henceforth, as long as she lives, she will think herself in his debt, and that she can never do too much for him. We may also suppose that the child was very dear to the prophet, as the son of his prayers, and very dear to the parents, as the son of their old age. But here is,

I. The sudden death of the child, though so much a darling. He was so far past the perils of infancy that he was able to go to the field to his father, who no doubt was pleased with his engaging talk, and his joy of his son was greater than the joy of his harvest; but either the cold or the heat of the open field overcame the child, who was bred tenderly, and he complained to his father that his head ached, *v.* 19. Whither should we go with our complaints, but to our heavenly Father? Thither the Spirit of adoption brings believers with all their grievances, all their desires, teaching them to cry, with groanings that cannot be uttered, "*My head, my head;* my heart, my heart." The father sent him to his mother's arms, his mother's lap, little suspecting any danger in his indisposition, but hoping he would drop asleep in his mother's bosom and awake well; but the sickness proved fatal; he slept the sleep of death (*v.* 20), was well in the morning and dead by noon: all the mother's care and tenderness could not keep him alive. A child of promise, a child of prayer, and given in love, yet taken away. Little children lie open to the arrests of sickness and death. But how admirably does the prudent pious mother guard her lips under this surprising affliction! Not one peevish murmuring word comes from her. She has a strong belief that the child will be raised to life again: like a genuine daughter of Abraham's faith, as well as loins, she accounts that God is able to raise him from the dead, for thence at first she *received him in a figure*, Heb. xi. 19. She had heard of the raising of the widow's son of Sarepta, and that the spirit of Elijah rested on Elisha; and such confidence had she of God's goodness that she was very ready to believe that he who so soon took away what he had given would restore what he had now taken away. By this faith *women received their dead raised to life*, Heb. xi. 35. In this faith she makes no preparation for the burial of her dead child, but for its resurrection; for she *lays him on the prophet's bed* (*v.* 21), expecting that he will stand her friend. *O woman! great is thy faith.* He that wrought it would not frustrate it.

II. The sorrowful mother's application to the prophet on this sad occasion; for it happened very opportunely that he was now at the college upon Mount Carmel, not far off.

1. She begged leave of her husband to go to the prophet, yet not acquainting him with her errand, lest he should not have faith enough to let her go, *v.* 22. He objected, *It is neither new moon nor sabbath* (*v.* 23), which intimates that on those feasts of the Lord she used to go to the assembly in which he presided, with other good people, to hear the word, and to join with him in prayers and praises. She did not think it enough to have his help sometimes in her own family, but, though a great woman, at-

tended on public worship, for which this was none of the times appointed; *therefore,* said the husband, "why wilt thou go to day? What is the matter?" "No harm," said she, "*It shall be well,* so you will say yourself hereafter." See how this husband and wife vied with each other in showing mutual regard; she was so dutiful to him that she would not go till she had acquainted him with her journey, and he so kind to her that he would not oppose it, though she did not think fit to acquaint him with her business. 2. She made all the haste she could to the prophet (*v.* 24), and he, seeing her at a distance, sent his servant to enquire whether any thing was amiss, *v.* 25, 26. The questions were particular: *Is it well with thee? Is it well with thy husband? Is it well with the child?* Note, It well becomes the men of God, with tenderness and concern, to enquire about the welfare of their friends and their families. The answer was general: *It is well.* Gehazi was not the man that she came to complain to, and therefore she put him off with this; she said little, and little said is soon amended (Ps. xxxix. 1, 2), but what she did say was very patient: "It is well with me, with my husband, with the child"—all well, and yet the child dead in the house. Note, When God calls away our dearest relations by death it becomes us quietly to say, "It is well both with us and them;" it is well, for all is well that God does; all is well with those that are gone if they have gone to heaven, and all well with us that stay behind if by the affliction we are furthered in our way thither. 3. When she came to the prophet she humbly reasoned with him concerning her present affliction. She threw herself at his feet, as one troubled and in grief, which she never showed till she came to him who, she believed, could help her, *v.* 27. When her passion would do her service she knew how to discover it, as well as how to conceal it when it would do her disservice. Gehazi knew his master would not be pleased to see her lie at his feet, and therefore would have raised her up; but Elisha waited to hear from her, since he might not know immediately from God, what was the cause of her trouble. God discovered things to his prophets as he saw fit, not always as they desired; God did not show this to the prophet, because he might know it from the good woman herself. What she said was very pathetic. She appealed to the prophet, (1.) Concerning her indifference to this mercy which was now taken from her: "*Did I desire a son of my lord?* No, thou knowest I did not; it was thy own proposal, not mine; I did not fret for the want of a son, as Hannah, nor beg, as Rachel, *Give me children or else I die.*" Note, When any creature-comfort is taken from us, it is well if we can say, through grace, that we did not set our hearts inordinately upon it; for, if we did, we have reason to fear it was given in anger and taken away in wrath. (2.) Concerning her entire dependence upon the prophet's word: *Did I not say, Do not deceive me?* Yes, she did say so (*v.* 16), and this reflection upon it may be considered either, [1.] As quarrelling with the prophet for deceiving her. She was ready to think herself mocked with the mercy when it was so soon removed, and that it would have been better she had never had this child than to be deprived of him when she began to have comfort in him. Note, The loss of a mercy should not make us undervalue the gift of it. Or, [2.] As pleading with the prophet for the raising of the child to life again: "*I said, Do not deceive me,* and I know thou wilt not." Note, However the providence of God may disappoint us, we may be sure the promise of God never did, nor ever will, deceive us: hope in that will not make us ashamed.

III. The raising of the child to life again. We may suppose that the woman gave Elisha a more express account of the child's death, and he gave her a more express promise of his resurrection, than is here related, where we are briefly told,

1. That Elisha sent Gehazi to go in all haste to the dead child, gave him his staff, and bade him lay that on the face of the child, *v.* 29. I know not what to make of this. Elisha knew that Elijah raised the dead child with a very close application, stretching himself upon the child, and praying again and again; and could he think to raise this child by so slight a ceremony as this, especially when nothing hindered him from coming himself? Shall such a power as this be delegated, and to no better a man than Gehazi? Bishop Hall suggests that it was done out of human conceit, and not by divine instinct, and therefore it failed of the effect; God will not have such great favours made too cheap, nor shall they be too easily come by, lest they be undervalued.

2. The woman resolved not to go back without the prophet himself (*v.* 30): *I will not leave thee.* She had no great expectation from the staff, she would have the hand, and she was in the right of it. Perhaps God intended hereby to teach us not to put that confidence in creatures, that are servants, which the power of the Creator, their Master and ours, will alone bear the weight of. Gehazi returns *re infectâ—without success,* without the tidings of any sign of life in the child (*v.* 31): *The child is not awaked,* intimating, to the comfort of the mother, that its death was but a sleep, and that he expected it would shortly be awaked. In the raising of dead souls to spiritual life ministers can do no more by their own power than Gehazi here could; they lay the word, like the prophet's staff, before their faces, but there is neither voice nor hearing, till Christ, by his Spirit, comes himself. The letter alone kills; it is the Spirit that gives

life. It is not prophesying upon dry bones that will put life into them, breath must come from heaven and breathe upon those slain.

3. The prophet, by earnest prayer, obtained from God the restoring of this dead child to life again. He found the child dead upon his own bed (*v.* 32), *and shut the door upon them twain, v.* 33. Even the dead child is spoken of as a person, one of the *twain*, for it was still in being and not lost. He shut out all company, that he might not seem to glory in the power God had given him, or to use it for ostentation and to be seen of men. Observe,

(1.) How closely the prophet applied himself to this great operation, perhaps being sensible that he had tempted God too much in thinking to effect it by the staff in Gehazi's hand, for which he thought himself rebuked by the disappointment. He now found it a harder task than he then thought, and therefore addressed himself to it with great solemnity. [1.] He *prayed unto the Lord* (*v.* 33), probably as Elijah had done, *Let this child's soul come into him again.* Christ raised the dead to life as one having authority—*Damsel, arise—Young man, I say unto thee, Arise—Lazarus, come forth* (for he was powerful and faithful as a Son, the Lord of life), but Elijah and Elisha did it by petition, as servants. [2.] He *lay upon the child* (*v.* 34), as if he would communicate to him some of his vital heat or spirits. Thus he expressed the earnestness of his desire, and gave a sign of that divine power which he depended upon for the accomplishment of this great work. He first *put his mouth to the child's mouth,* as if, in God's name, he would breathe into him the breath of life; then *his eyes to the child's eyes,* to open them again to the light of life; then *his hands to the child's hands,* to put strength into them. He then *returned, and walked in the house,* as one full of care and concern, and wholly intent upon what he was about. Then he went up stairs again, and, the second time, *stretched himself upon the child, v.* 35. Those that would be instrumental in conveying spiritual life to dead souls must thus affect themselves with their case, and accommodate themselves to it, and labour fervently in prayer for them.

(2.) How gradually the operation was performed. At the first application, *the flesh of the child waxed warm* (*v.* 34), which gave the prophet encouragement to continue instant in prayer. After a while, *the child sneezed seven times,* which was an indication, not only of life, but liveliness. Some have reported it as an ancient tradition that when God breathed into Adam the breath of life the first evidence of his being alive was sneezing, which gave rise to the usage of paying respect to those that sneeze. Some observe here that sneezing clears the head, and there lay the child's distemper.

(3.) How joyfully the child was restored alive to his mother (*v.* 36, 37), and all parties concerned *were not a little comforted,* Acts xx. 12. See the power of God, who kills and makes alive again. See the power of prayer; as it has the key of the clouds, so it has the key of death. See the power of faith; that fixed law of nature (that death is a way whence there is no returning) shall rather be dispensed with than this believing Shunammite shall be disappointed.

38 And Elisha came again to Gilgal: and *there was* a dearth in the land; and the sons of the prophets *were* sitting before him: and he said unto his servant, Set on the great pot, and seethe pottage for the sons of the prophets. 39 And one went out into the field to gather herbs, and found a wild vine, and gathered thereof wild gourds his lap full, and came and shred *them* into the pot of pottage: for they knew *them* not. 40 So they poured out for the men to eat. And it came to pass, as they were eating of the pottage, that they cried out, and said, O *thou* man of God, *there is* death in the pot. And they could not eat *thereof.* 41 But he said, Then bring meal. And he cast *it* into the pot; and he said, Pour out for the people, that they may eat. And there was no harm in the pot. 42 And there came a man from Baal-shalisha, and brought the man of God bread of the firstfruits, twenty loaves of barley, and full ears of corn in the husk thereof. And he said, Give unto the people, that they may eat. 43 And his servitor said, What, should I set this before a hundred men? He said again, Give the people, that they may eat: for thus saith the LORD, They shall eat, and shall leave *thereof.* 44 So he set *it* before them, and they did eat, and left *thereof,* according to the word of the LORD.

We have here Elisha in his place, in his element, among the sons of the prophets, teaching them, and, as a father, providing for them; and happy it was for them that they had one over them who naturally cared for their state, under whom they were well fed and well taught. There was a dearth in the land, for the wickedness of those that dwelt therein, the same that we read of, *ch.* viii. 1. It continued seven years, just as long again as that in Elijah's time. A famine of bread there was, but not of hearing the word of God, for Elisha had the sons of the prophets sitting before him, to hear his wisdom, who were taught, that they might teach others. Two instances we have here of the care he took about their meat. Christ twice fed those to whom he preached. Elisha was in the more care about it now because of the dearth, that the sons of the prophets might not be ashamed in this evil time, but, even in *the days of famine, might be satisfied,* Ps. xxxvii. 19.

I. He made hurtful food to become safe and wholesome. 1. On the lecture-day, the sons of the prophets being all to attend, he ordered his servant to provide food for their bodies, while he was breaking to them the bread of life for their souls. Whether there was any flesh-meat for them does not appear; he orders only that pottage should be seethed for them of herbs, *v.* 38. The sons of the prophets should be examples of temperance and mortification, not desirous of dainties, but content with plain food. If they have neither savoury meats nor sweet meats, nay, if a mess of pottage be all the dinner, let them remember that this great prophet entertained himself and his guests no better. 2. One of the servitors, who was sent to gather herbs (which, it should seem, must serve instead of flesh for the pottage), by mistake brought in that which was noxious, or at least very nauseous, and shred it into the pottage: *wild gourds* they are called, *v.* 39. Some think it was *coloquintida,* a herb strongly cathartic, and, if not qualified, dangerous. The sons of the prophets, it seems, were better skilled in divinity than in natural philosophy, and read their Bibles more than their herbals. If any of the fruits of the earth be hurtful, we must look upon it as an effect of the curse *(thorns and thistles shall it bring forth unto thee),* for the original blessing made all good. 3. The guests complained to Elisha of the unwholesomeness of their food. Nature has given man the sense of tasting, not only that wholesome food may be pleasant, but that that which is unwholesome may be discovered before it comes to the stomach; the mouth tries meat by tasting it, Job. xii. 11. This pottage was soon found by the taste of it to be dangerous, so that they cried out, *There is death in the pot,* *v.* 40. The table often becomes a snare, and that which should be for our welfare proves a trap, which is a good reason why we should not feed ourselves without fear; when we are receiving the supports and comforts of life we must keep up an expectation of death and a fear of sin. 4. Elisha immediately cured the bad taste and prevented the bad consequences of this unwholesome pottage; as before he had healed the bitter waters with salt, so now the bitter broth with meal, *v.* 41. It is probable that there was meal in it before, but that was put in by a common hand, only to thicken the pottage; this was the same thing, but cast in by Elisha's hand, and with intent to heal the pottage, by which it appears that the change was not owing to the meal (that was the sign only, not the means), but to the divine power. Now all was well, not only no death, but no harm in the pot. We must acknowledge God's goodness in making our food wholesome and nourishing. *I am the Lord that healeth thee.*

II. He made a little food to go a great way. 1. Elisha had a present brought him of twenty barley-loaves and some ears of corn (*v.* 42), a present which, in those ages, would not be despicable at any time, but now in a special manner valuable, when there was a dearth in the land. It is said to be of *the first-fruits,* which was God's due out of their increase; and when the priests and Levites were all at Jerusalem, out of their reach, the religious people among them, with good reason, looked upon the prophets as God's receivers, and brought their first-fruits to them, which helped to maintain their schools. 2. Having freely received, he freely gave, ordering it all to be set before the sons of the prophets, reserving none for himself, none for hereafter. "*Let the morrow take thought for the things of itself,* give it all to the people that they may eat." It well becomes the men of God to be generous and open-handed, and the fathers of the prophets to be liberal to the sons of the prophets. 3. Though the loaves were little, it is likely no more than what one man would ordinarily eat at a meal, yet with twenty of them he satisfied 100 men, *v.* 43, 44. His servant thought that to set so little meat before so many men was but to tantalize them, and shame his master for making so great an invitation to such short commons; but he, in God's name, pronounced it a full meal for them, and so it proved; they did eat, and left thereof, not because their stomachs failed them, but because the bread increased in the eating. God has promised his church (Ps. cxxxii. 15) *that he will abundantly bless her provision, and satisfy her poor with bread;* for whom he feeds he fills, and what he blesses comes to much, as what he blows upon comes to little, Hag. i. 9. Christ's feeding his hearers was a miracle far beyond this; but both teach us that those who wait upon God in the way of duty may hope to be both protected and supplied by a particular care of divine Providence.

CHAP. V.

Two more of Elisha's miracles are recorded in this chapter. I. The cleansing of Naaman, a Syrian, a stranger, from his leprosy, and there, 1. The badness of his case, ver. 1. 2. The providence that brought him to Elisha, the intelligence given him by a captive maid, ver. 2—4. A letter from the king of Syria to the king of Israel, to introduce him, ver. 5—7. And the invitation Elisha sent him, ver. 8. 3. The method prescribed for his cure, his submission, with much ado, to that method, and his cure thereby, ver. 9—14. 4. The grateful acknowledgments he made to Elisha hereupon, ver. 15—19. II. The smiting of Gehazi, his own servant, with that leprosy. 1. Gehazi's sins, which were belying his master to Naaman (ver. 20—24), and lying to his master when he examined him, ver. 25. 2. His punishment for these sins. Naaman's leprosy was entailed on his family, ver. 26, 27. And, if Naaman's cure was typical of the calling of the Gentiles, as our Saviour seems to make it (Luke iv. 27), Gehazi's stroke may be looked upon as typical of the blinding and rejecting of the Jews, who envied God's grace to the Gentiles, as Gehazi envied Elisha's favour to Naaman.

NOW Naaman, captain of the host of the king of Syria, was a great man with his master, and honourable, because by him the LORD had given deliverance unto Syria: he was also a mighty man in valour, *but he was* a leper. 2 And the Syrians had gone out by companies, and had brought away captive out of the land of Israel a little maid; and she waited on Naaman's wife. 3 And she said unto her mistress, Would God my lord *were* with the prophet that *is* in Samaria! for he would recover him of his leprosy. 4 And *one* went in, and told his lord, saying, Thus and thus said the maid that *is* of the land of Israel. 5 And the king of Syria said, Go to, go, and I will send a letter unto the king of Israel. And he departed, and took with him ten talents of silver, and six thousand *pieces* of gold, and ten changes of raiment. 6 And he brought the letter to the king of Israel, saying, Now when this letter is come unto thee, behold, I have *therewith* sent Naaman my servant to thee, that thou mayest recover him of his leprosy. 7 And it came to pass, when the king of Israel had read the letter, that he rent his clothes, and said, *Am* I God, to kill and to make alive, that this man doth send unto me to recover a man of his leprosy? wherefore consider, I pray you, and see how he seeketh a quarrel against me. 8 And it was *so*, when Elisha the man of God had heard that the king of Israel had rent his clothes, that he sent to the king, saying, Wherefore hast thou rent thy clothes? let him come now to me, and he shall know that there is a prophet in Israel.

Our Saviour's miracles were intended for the lost sheep of the house of Israel, yet one, like a crumb, fell from the table to a woman of Canaan; so this one miracle Elisha wrought for Naaman, a Syrian; for God does good to all, and will have all men to be saved. Here is,

I. The great affliction Naaman was under, in the midst of all his honours, *v.* 1. He was a great man, in a great place; not only rich and raised, but particularly happy for two things:—1. That he had been very serviceable to his country. God made him so: *By him the Lord had* often *given deliverance to Syria,* success in their wars even with Israel. The preservation and prosperity even of those that do not know God and serve him must be ascribed to him, for *he is the Saviour of all men,* but *especially of those that believe.* Let Israel know that when the Syrians prevailed it was from the Lord. 2. That he was very acceptable to his prince, was his favourite, and prime-minister of state; so great was he, so high, so honourable, and a mighty man of valour; but he was a leper, was under that loathsome disease, which made him a burden to himself. Note, (1.) No man's greatness, or honour, or interest, or valour, or victory, can set him out of the reach of the sorest calamities of human life; there is many a sickly crazy body under rich and gay clothing. (2.) Every man has some *but* or other in his character, something that blemishes and diminishes him, some allay to his grandeur, some damp to his joy; he may be very happy, very good, yet, in something or other, not so good as he should be nor so happy as he would be. Naaman was as great as the world could make him, and yet (as bishop Hall expresses it) the basest slave in Syria would not change skins with him.

II. The notice that was given him of Elisha's power, by a little maid that waited on his lady, *v.* 2, 3. This maid was, by birth, an Israelite, providentially carried captive into Syria, and there preferred into Naaman's family, where she published Elisha's fame to the honour of Israel and Israel's God. The unhappy dispersing of the people of God has sometimes proved the happy occasion of the diffusion of the knowledge of God, Acts viii. 4. This little maid, 1. As became a true-born Israelite, consulted the honour of her country, and could give an account, though but a girl, of the famous prophet they had among them. Children should betimes acquaint themselves with the wondrous works of God, that, wherever they go, they may have them to talk of. See Ps. viii. 2. 2. As became a good servant, she desired the health and welfare of her master, though she was a captive, a servant by force; much more should servants of choice seek their masters' good. The Jews in Babylon were to seek the peace of the land of their captivity, Jer. xxix. 7. *Elisha* had *not cleansed any leper in Israel* (Luke iv. 27), yet this little maid, from the other miracles he had wrought, inferred that he *could* cure her master, and from his common beneficence inferred that he *would* do it, though he was a Syrian. Servants may be blessings to the families where they are, by telling what they know of the glory of God and the honour of his prophets.

III. The application which the king of Syria hereupon made to the king of Israel on Naaman's behalf. Naaman took notice of the intelligence, though given by a simple maid, and did not despise it for the sake of her meanness, when it tended to his bodily health. He did not say, "The girl talks like a fool; how can any prophet of Israel do that for me which all the physicians of Syria have attempted in vain?" Though he neither loved nor honoured the Jewish nation, yet, if one of that nation can but cure him of his leprosy, he will thankfully acknowledge the obligation. O that those who are spiritually diseased would hearken thus readily to the tidings brought them of the great Physician! See what Naaman did upon this little hint. 1. He would not send for the prophet to come to him, but such honour would he pay to one that had so much of a divine power with him as to be able to cure diseases that he would go to him himself, though he himself was sickly, unfit for society, the journey long, and the country an enemy's; princes, he thinks, must stoop to prophets when they need them. 2. He would not go *incognito—in disguise*, though his errand proclaimed his loathsome disease, but went in state, and with a great retinue, to do the more honour to the prophet. 3. He would not go empty-handed, but took with him gold, silver, and raiment, to present to his physician. Those that have wealth, and want health, show which they reckon the more valuable blessing; what will they not give for ease, and strength, and soundness of body? 4. He would not go without a letter to the king of Israel from the king his master, who did himself earnestly desire his recovery. He knows not where in Samaria to find this wonder-working prophet, but takes it for granted the king knows where to find him; and, to engage the prophet to do his utmost for Naaman, he will go to him supported with the interest of two kings. If the king of Syria must entreat his help, he hopes the king of Israel, being his liege-lord, may command it. The gifts of the subject must all be (he thinks) for the service and honour of the prince, and therefore he desires the king that he would *recover the leper* (*v.* 6), taking it for granted that there was a greater intimacy between the king and the prophet than really there was.

IV. The alarm this gave to the king of Israel, *v.* 7. He apprehended there was in this letter, 1. A great affront upon God, and therefore he rent his clothes, according to the custom of the Jews when they heard or read that which they thought blasphemous; and what less could it be than to attribute to him a divine power? *"Am I a God, to kill* whom I will, and *make alive* whom I will? No, I pretend not to such an authority." Nebuchadnezzar did, as we find, Dan. v. 19. "*Am I a God, to kill* with a word, *and make alive* with a word? No, I pretend not to such a power;" thus this great man, this bad man, is made to own that he is but a man. Why did he not, with this consideration, correct himself for his idolatry, and reason thus:—Shall I worship those as gods that can neither kill nor make alive, can *do neither good nor evil?* 2. A bad design upon himself. He appeals to those about him for this: *"See how he seeketh a quarrel against me;* he requires me to recover the leper, and if I do not, though I cannot, he will make that a pretence to wage war with me," which he suspects the rather because Naaman is his general. Had he rightly understood the meaning of the letter, that when the king wrote to him to recover the leper he meant that he would take care he might be recovered, he would not have been in this fright. Note, We often create a great deal of uneasiness to ourselves by misinterpreting the words and actions of others that are well intended: it is charity to ourselves to think no evil. If he had bethought himself of Elisha, and his power, he would easily have understood the letter, and have known what he had to do; but he is put into this confusion by making himself a stranger to the prophet: the captive maid had him more in her thoughts than the king had.

V. The proffer which Elisha made of his services. He was willing to do any thing to make his prince easy, though he was neglected and his former good services were forgotten by him. Hearing on what occasion the king had rent his clothes, he sent to him to let him know that if his patient would come to him he should not lose his labour (*v.* 8): *He shall know that there is a prophet in Israel* (and it were sad with Israel if there were not), that there is a prophet in Israel who can do that which the king of Israel dares not attempt, which the prophets of Syria cannot pretend to. It was not for his own honour, but for the honour of God, that he coveted to make them all know *that there was a prophet in Israel,* though obscure and overlooked.

9 So Naaman came with his horses and with his chariot, and stood at the door of the house of Elisha. 10 And Elisha sent a messenger unto him, saying, Go and wash in Jordan seven times, and thy flesh shall come again to thee, and thou shalt be clean. 11 But Naaman was wroth, and went away, and said, Behold, I thought, He will surely come out to me, and stand, and call on the name of the LORD his God, and strike his hand over the place, and recover the leper. 12 *Are* not Abana and Pharpar, rivers of Damascus, better than all the waters of Israel? may I not wash in them, and be clean? So he turned and went away in a rage. 13 And

his servants came near, and spake unto him, and said, My father, *if* the prophet had bid thee *do some* great thing, wouldest thou not have done *it?* how much rather then, when he saith to thee, Wash, and be clean? 14 Then went he down, and dipped himself seven times in Jordan, according to the saying of the man of God: and his flesh came again like unto the flesh of a little child, and he was clean.

We have here the cure of Naaman's leprosy.

I. The short and plain direction which the prophet gave him, with assurance of success. Naaman designed to do honour to Elisha when he came in his chariot, and with all his retinue, to Elisha's door, *v.* 9. Those that showed little respect to prophets at other times were very complaisant to them when they needed them. He attended at Elisha's door as a beggar for an alms. Those that would be cleansed from their spiritual leprosy must wait at *Wisdom's gate, and watch at the posts of her doors.* Naaman expected to have his compliment returned, but Elisha gave him his answer without any formality, would not go to the door to him, lest he should seem too much pleased with the honour done him, but sent a messenger to him, saying, *Go wash in Jordan seven times,* and promising him that if he did so his disease should be cured. The promise was express: *Thou shalt be clean.* The method prescribed was plain: *Go wash in Jordan.* This was not intended as any means of the cure; for, though cold bathing is recommended by many as a very wholesome thing, yet some think that in the case of a leprosy it was rather hurtful. But it was intended as a sign of the cure, and a trial of his obedience. Those that will be helped of God must do as they are bidden. But why did Elisha send a messenger to him with these directions? 1. Because he had retired, at this time, for devotion, was intent upon his prayers for the cure, and would not be diverted; or, 2. Because he knew Naaman to be a proud man, and he would let him know that before the great God all men stand upon the same level.

II. Naaman's disgust at the method prescribed, because it was not what he expected. Two things disgusted him:—

1. That Elisha, as he thought, put a slight upon his person, in sending him orders by a servant, and not coming to him himself, *v.* 11. Being big with the expectation of a cure, he had been fancying how this cure would be wrought, and the scheme he had laid was this: "*He will surely come out to me,* that is the least he can do to me, a peer of Syria, to me that have come to him in all this state, to me that have so often been victorious over Israel. *He will stand,* and *call on the name of his God,* and name me in his prayer, and then he will *wave his hand over the place,* and so effect the cure." And, because the thing was not done just thus, he fell into a passion, forgetting, (1.) That he was a leper, and the law of Moses, which Elisha would religiously observe, shut lepers out from society—a leper, and therefore he ought not to insist upon the punctilios of honour. Note, Many have hearts unhumbled under humbling providences; see Num. xii. 14. (2.) That he was a petitioner, suing for a favour which he could not demand; and beggars must not be choosers, patients must not prescribe to their physician. See in Naaman the folly of pride. A cure will not content him unless he be cured with ceremony, with a great deal of pomp and parade; he scorns to be healed, unless he be humoured.

2. That Elisha, as he thought, put a slight upon his country. He took it hard that he must be sent to wash in Jordan, a river of Israel, when he thought *Abana and Pharpar, rivers of Damascus, better than all the waters of Israel.* How magnificently does he speak of these two rivers that watered Damascus, which soon after fell into one, called by geographers *Chrysoroas—the golden stream!* How scornfully does he speak of all the waters of Israel, though God had called the land of Israel *the glory of all lands,* and particularly for its *brooks of water!* Deut. viii. 7. So common it is for God and man to differ in their judgments. How slightly does he speak of the prophet's directions! *May I not wash in them and be clean?* He might wash in them and be clean from dirt, but not wash in them and be clean from leprosy. He was angry that the prophet bade him wash and be clean; he thought that the prophet must do all and was not pleased that he was bidden to do any thing,—or he thought this too cheap, too plain, too common a thing for so great a man to be cured by,—or he did not believe it would at all effect the cure, or, if it would, what medicinal virtue was there in Jordan more than in the rivers of Damascus? But he did not consider, (1.) That Jordan belonged to Israel's God, from whom he was to expect the cure, and not from the gods of Damascus; it watered the Lord's land, the holy land, and, in a miraculous cure, relation to God was much more considerable than the depth of the channel or the beauty of the stream. (2.) That Jordan nad more than once before this obeyed the commands of omnipotence. It had of old yielded a passage to Israel, and of late to Elijah and Elisha, and therefore was fitter for such a purpose than those rivers which had only observed the common law of their creation, and had never been thus distinguished; but, above all, (3.) Jordan was the river appointed, and, if he expected a cure from the divine power, he ought to acquiesce in the divine will, without asking why or wherefore. Note,

It is common for those that are wise in their own conceit to look with contempt on the dictates and prescriptions of divine wisdom, and to prefer their own fancies before them; those that are for *establishing their own righteousness* will not *submit to the righteousness of God,* Rom. x. 3. Naaman talked himself into such a heat (as passionate men usually do) that he turned away from the prophet's door in a rage, ready to swear he would never have any thing more to say to Elisha; and who then would be the loser? Note, *Those that observe lying vanities forsake their own mercies,* Jonah ii. 8. Proud men are the worst enemies to themselves and forego their own redemption.

III. The modest advice which his servants gave him, to observe the prophet's prescriptions, with a tacit reproof of his resentments, *v.* 13. Though at other times they kept their distance, and now saw him in a passion, yet, knowing him to be a man that would hear reason at any time, and from any body (a good character of great men, and a very rare one), they drew near, and made bold to argue the matter a little with him. They had conceived a great opinion of the prophet (having, perhaps, heard more of him from the common people, whom they had conversed with, than Naaman had heard from the king and courtiers, whom he had conversed with), and therefore begged of him to consider: "*If the prophet had bidden thee to do some great thing,* had ordered thee into a tedious course of physic, or to submit to some painful operation, blistering, or cupping, or salivating, *Wouldst thou not have done it?* No doubt thou wouldst. And wilt thou not submit to so easy a method as this, *Wash and be clean?*" Observe, 1. His own servants gave him this reproof and counsel, which was no more disparagement to him than that he had intelligence of one that could cure him from his wife's maid, *v.* 3. Note, It is a great mercy to have those about us that will be free with us, and faithfully tell us of our faults and follies, though they be our inferiors. Masters must be willing to hear reason from their servants, Job xxxi. 13, 14. As we should be deaf to the counsel of the ungodly, though given by the greatest and most venerable names, so we should have our ear open to good advice, though brought us by those who are much below us: no matter who speaks, if the thing be well said. 2. The reproof was very modest and respectful. They call him *Father;* for servants must honour and obey their masters with a kind of filial affection. In giving reproof or counsel we must make it appear that it comes from love and true honour, and that we intend, not reproach, but reformation. 3. It was very rational and considerate. If the rude and unthinking servants had stirred up their master's angry resentment, and offered to avenge his quarrel upon the prophet, who (he thought) affronted him, how mischievous would the consequences have been! Fire from heaven, probably, upon them all! But they, to our great surprise, took the prophet's part. Elisha, though it is likely he perceived that what he had said had put Naaman out of humour, did not care to pacify him: it was at his peril if he persisted in his wrath. But his servants were made use of by Providence to reduce him to temper. They reasoned with him, (1.) From his earnest desire of a cure: *Wouldst thou not do* any thing? Note, When diseased sinners come to this, that they are content to do any thing, to submit to any thing, to part with any thing, for a cure, then, and not till then, there begin to be some hopes of them. Then they will take Christ on his own terms when they are made willing to have Christ upon any terms. (2.) From the easiness of the method prescribed: "It is but, *Wash and be clean.* It is but trying; the experiment is cheap and easy, it can do no hurt, but may do good." Note, The methods prescribed for the healing of the leprosy of sin are so plain that we are utterly inexcusable if we do not observe them. It is but, "Believe, and be saved"—"Repent, and be pardoned"—"Wash, and be clean."

IV. The cure effected, in the use of the means prescribed, *v.* 14. Naaman, upon second thoughts, yielded to make the experiment, yet, it should seem, with no great faith or resolution; for, whereas the prophet bade him wash in Jordan seven times, he did but dip himself so many times, as lightly as he could. However God was pleased so far to honour himself and his word as to make that effectual. *His flesh came again, like the flesh of a child,* to his great surprise and joy. This men get by yielding to the will of God, by attending to his institutions. His being cleansed by washing put an honour on the law for cleansing lepers. God will magnify his word above all his name.

15 And he returned to the man of God, he and all his company, and came, and stood before him: and he said, Behold, now I know that *there is* no God in all the earth, but in Israel: now therefore, I pray thee, take a blessing of thy servant. 16 But he said, *As* the LORD liveth, before whom I stand, I will receive none. And he urged him to take *it;* but he refused. 17 And Naaman said, Shall there not then, I pray thee, be given to thy servant two mules' burden of earth? for thy servant will henceforth offer neither burnt offering nor sacrifice unto other gods, but unto the LORD. 18 In this thing the LORD pardon thy servant, *that* when my master goeth into the house of

Rimmon to worship there, and he leaneth on my hand, and I bow myself in the house of Rimmon: when I bow down myself in the house of Rimmon, the LORD pardon thy servant in this thing. 19 And he said unto him, Go in peace. So he departed from him a little way.

Of the ten lepers that our Saviour cleansed, the only one that *returned to give thanks* was a *Samaritan*, Luke xvii. 16. This Syrian did so, and here expresses himself,

I. Convinced of the power of the God of Israel, not only that he is God, but that he is God alone, and that indeed *there is no God in all the earth but in Israel* (*v.* 15)—a noble confession, but such as intimates the misery of the Gentile world; for the nations that had many gods really had no God, but were without God in the world. He had formerly thought the gods of Syria gods indeed, but now experience had rectified his mistake, and he knew Israel's God was God alone, the sovereign Lord of all. Had he seen other lepers cleansed, perhaps the sight would not have convinced him, but the mercy of the cure affected him more than the miracle of it. Those are best able to speak of the power of divine grace who have themselves experienced it.

II. Grateful to Elisha the prophet: "Therefore, for his sake whose servant thou art, I have a present for thee, silver, and gold, and raiment, whatever thou wilt please to accept." He valued the cure, not by the easiness of it to the prophet, but the acceptableness of it to himself, and would gladly pay for it accordingly. But Elisha generously refused the fee, though urged to accept it; and, to prevent further importunity, backed his refusal with an oath: *As the Lord liveth, I will receive none* (*v.* 16), not because he did not need it, for he was poor enough, and knew what to do with it, and how to bestow it among the sons of the prophets, nor because he thought it unlawful, for he received presents from others; but he would not be beholden to this Syrian, nor should *he* say, *I have made Elisha rich*, Gen. xiv. 23. It would be much for the honour of God to show this new convert that the servants of the God of Israel were taught to look upon the wealth of this world with a holy contempt, which would confirm him in his belief that *there was no God but in Israel*. See 1 Cor. ix. 18; 2 Cor. xi. 9.

III. Proselyted to the worship of the God of Israel. He will not only offer a sacrifice to the Lord, in thanks for his present cure, but he resolves he will never offer sacrifice to any other gods, *v.* 17. It was a happy cure of his leprosy which cured him of his idolatry, a more dangerous disease. But here are two instances of his weakness and infirmity in his conversion:—1. In one instance he over-did it, that he would not only worship the God of Israel, but he would have clods of earth out of the prophet's garden, or at least of the prophet's ordering, to *make an altar of*, *v.* 17. He that awhile ago had spoken very slightly of the waters of Israel (*v.* 12) now is in another extreme, and over-values the earth of Israel, supposing (since God had appointed *altars of earth*, Exod. xx. 24) that an altar of that earth would be most acceptable to him, not considering that all *the earth is the Lord's and the fulness thereof*. Or perhaps the transport of his affection and veneration for the prophet, not only upon the account of his power, but of his virtue and generosity, made him, as we say, love the very ground he went upon and desire to have some of it home with him. The modern compliment equivalent to this would be, "Pray, sir, let me have your picture." 2. In another instance he under-did it, that he reserved to himself a liberty to bow in the house of Rimmon, in complaisance to the king his master, and according to the duty of his place at court (*v.* 18), *in this thing* he must be excused. He owns he ought not to do it, but that he cannot otherwise keep his place,—protests that his bowing is not, nor ever shall be, as it had been, in honour to the idol, but only in honour to the king,—and therefore he hopes God will forgive him. Perhaps, all things considered, this might admit of some apology, though it was not justifiable. But, as to us, I am sure, (1.) If, in covenanting with God, we make a reservation for any known sin, which we will continue to indulge ourselves in, that reservation is a defeasance of his covenant. We must cast away all our transgressions and not except any house of Rimmon. (2.) Though we are encouraged to pray for the remission of the sins we have committed, yet, if we ask for a dispensation to go on in any sin for the future, we mock God, and deceive ourselves. (3.) Those that know not how to quit a place at court when they cannot keep it without sinning against God, and wronging their consciences, do not rightly value the divine favour. (4.) Those that truly hate evil will make conscience of abstaining from all appearances of evil. Though Naaman's dissembling his religion cannot be approved, yet because his promise to offer no sacrifice to any god but the God of Israel only was a great point gained with a Syrian, and because, by asking pardon in this matter, he showed such a degree of conviction and ingenuousness as gave hopes of improvement, the prophet took fair leave of him, and bade him *Go in peace*, *v.* 19. Young converts must be tenderly dealt with.

20 But Gehazi, the servant of Elisha the man of God, said, Behold, my master hath spared Naaman this

Syrian, in not receiving at his hands that which he brought: but, *as* the LORD liveth, I will run after him, and take somewhat of him. 21 So Gehazi followed after Naaman. And when Naaman saw *him* running after him, he lighted down from the chariot to meet him, and said, *Is* all well? 22 And he said, All *is* well. My master hath sent me, saying, Behold, even now there be come to me from mount Ephraim two young men of the sons of the prophets: give them, I pray thee, a talent of silver, and two changes of garments. 23 And Naaman said, Be content, take two talents. And he urged him, and bound two talents of silver in two bags, with two changes of garments, and laid *them* upon two of his servants; and they bare *them* before him. 24 And when he came to the tower, he took *them* from their hand, and bestowed *them* in the house: and he let the men go, and they departed. 25 But he went in, and stood before his master. And Elisha said unto him, Whence *comest thou*, Gehazi? And he said, Thy servant went no whither. 26 And he said unto him, Went not mine heart *with thee*, when the man turned again from his chariot to meet thee? *Is it* a time to receive money, and to receive garments, and oliveyards, and vineyards, and sheep, and oxen, and menservants, and maidservants? 27 The leprosy therefore of Naaman shall cleave unto thee, and unto thy seed for ever. And he went out from his presence a leper *as white* as snow.

Naaman, a Syrian, a courtier, a soldier, had many servants, and we read how wise and good they were, *v.* 13. Elisha, a holy prophet, a man of God, has but one servant, and he proves a base, lying, naughty fellow. Those that heard of Elisha at a distance honoured him, and got good by what they heard; but he that stood continually before him, to hear his wisdom, had no good impressions made upon him either by his doctrine or miracles. One would have expected that Elisha's servant should be a saint (even Ahab's servant, Obadiah, was), but even Christ himself had a Judas among his followers. The means of grace cannot give grace. The best men, the best ministers, have often had those about them that have been their grief and shame. The nearer the church the further from God. *Many come from the east and west to sit down with Abraham when the children of the kingdom shall be cast out.* Here is,

I. Gehazi's sin. It was a complicated sin. 1. The love of money, that root of all evil, was at the bottom of it. His master contemned Naaman's treasures, but he coveted them, *v.* 20. His heart (says bishop Hall) was packed up in Naaman's chests, and he must run after him to fetch it. Multitudes, by coveting worldly wealth, have *erred from the faith* and *pierced themselves with many sorrows.* 2. He blamed his master for refusing Naaman's present, condemned him as foolish in not taking gold when he might have it, envied and grudged his kindness and generosity to this stranger, though it was for the good of his soul. In short, he thought himself wiser than his master. 3. When Naaman, like a person of accomplished manners, alighted from his chariot to meet him (*v.* 21), he told him a deliberate lie, that his master sent him to him, and so he received that courtesy to himself which Naaman intended to his master. 4. He abused his master, and basely misrepresented him to Naaman as one that had soon repented of his generosity, that was fickle, and did not know his own mind, that would say and unsay, swear and unswear, that would not do an honourable thing but he must presently undo it again. His story of the two sons of the prophets was as silly as it was false; if he would have begged a token for two young scholars, surely less than a talent of silver might serve them. 5. There was danger of his alienating Naaman from that holy religion which he had espoused, and lessening his good opinion of it. He would be ready to say, as Paul's enemies suggested concerning him (2 Cor. xii. 16, 17), that, though Elisha himself did not burden him, yet being crafty he caught him with guile, sending those that made a gain of him. We hope that he understood afterwards that Elisha's hand was not in it, and that Gehazi was forced to restore what he had unjustly got, else it might have driven him to his idols again. 6. His seeking to conceal what he had unjustly got added much to his sin. (1.) He hid it, as Achan did his gain, by sacrilege, in the tower, a secret place, a strong place, till he should have an opportunity of laying it out, *v.* 24. Now he thought himself sure of it, and applauded his own management of a fraud by which he had imposed, not only upon the prudence of Naaman, but upon Elisha's spirit of discerning, as Ananias and Sapphira upon the apostles. 2. He denied it: He *went in, and stood before his master,* ready to receive his orders. None looked more observant of his master, though really none more injurious to him; he thought, as Ephraim, *I have become rich, but they shall find no iniquity in me,* Hos. xii. 8.

His master asked him where he had been. "Nowhere, sir" (said he), "out of the house." Note, One lie commonly begets another: the way of that sin is down-hill; therefore dare to be true.

II. The punishment of this sin. Elisha immediately called him to an account for it; and observe,

1. How he was convicted. He thought to impose upon the prophet, but was soon given to understand that the Spirit of prophecy could not be deceived, and that it was in vain to lie to the Holy Ghost. Elisha could tell him, (1.) What he had done, though he had denied it. "Thou sayest thou wentest nowhere, but *went not my heart with thee?*" *v.* 26. Had Gehazi yet to learn that prophets had spiritual eyes? or could he think to hide any thing from a seer, from him with whom the secret of the Lord was? Note, It is folly to presume upon sin in hopes of secresy. When thou goest aside into any by-path does not thy own conscience go with thee? Does not the eye of God go with thee? *He that covers his sin shall not prosper,* particularly *a lying tongue is but for a moment,* Prov. xii. 19. Truth will transpire, and often comes to light strangely, to the confusion of those that make lies their refuge. (2.) What he designed, though he kept that in his own breast. He could tell him the very thoughts and intents of his heart, that he was projecting, now that he had got these two talents, to purchase ground and cattle, to leave Elisha's service, and to set up for himself. Note, All the foolish hopes and contrivances of carnal worldlings are open before God. And he tells him also the evil of it: "*Is it a time to receive money?* Is this an opportunity of enriching thyself? Couldst thou find no better way of getting money than by belying thy master and laying a stumbling-block before a young convert?" Note, Those that are for getting wealth at any time, and by any ways and means whatsoever, right or wrong, lay themselves open to a great deal of temptation. Those that will be rich *(per fas, per nefas; rem, rem, quocunque modo rem—by fair means, by foul means; careless of principle, intent only on money) drown themselves in destruction and perdition,* 1 Tim. vi. 9. War, and fire, and plague, and shipwreck, are not, as many make them, things to get money by. It is not a time to increase our wealth when we cannot do it but in such ways as are dishonourable to God and religion or injurious to our brethren or the public.

2. How he was punished for it: *The leprosy of Naaman shall cleave to thee, v.* 27. If he will have his money, he shall take his disease with it, *Transit cum onere—It passes with this incumbrance.* He was contriving to entail lands upon his posterity; but, instead of them, he entails a loathsome disease on the heirs of his body, from generation to generation. The sentence was immediately executed on himself; no sooner said than done: He *went out from his presence a leper as white as snow.* Thus he is stigmatized and made infamous, and carries the mark of his shame wherever he goes: thus he loads himself and family with a curse, which shall not only for the present proclaim his villany, but for ever perpetuate the remembrance of it. Note, *The getting of treasures by a lying tongue is a vanity tossed to and fro of those that seek death,* Prov. xxi. 6. Those who get wealth by fraud and injustice cannot expect either the comfort or the continuance of it. What was Gehazi profited, though he gained his two talents, when thereby he lost his health, his honour, his peace, his service, and, if repentance prevented not, his soul for ever? See Job xx. 12, &c.

CHAP. VI.

In this chapter we have, I. A further account of the wondrous works of Elisha. 1. His making iron to swim, ver. 1—7. 2. His disclosing to the king of Israel the secret counsels of the king of Syria, ver. 8—12. 3. His saving himself out of the hands of those who were sent to apprehend him, ver. 13—23. II. The besieging of Samaria by the Syrians and the great distress the city was reduced to, ver. 24—33. The relief of it is another of the wonders wrought by Elisha's word, which we shall have the story of in the next chapter. Elisha is still a great blessing both to church and state, both to the sons of the prophets and to his prince.

AND the sons of the prophets said unto Elisha, Behold now, the place where we dwell with thee is too strait for us. 2 Let us go, we pray thee, unto Jordan, and take thence every man a beam, and let us make us a place there, where we may dwell. And he answered, Go ye. 3 And one said, Be content, I pray thee, and go with thy servants. And he answered, I will go. 4 So he went with them. And when they came to Jordan, they cut down wood. 5 But as one was felling a beam, the ax head fell into the water: and he cried, and said, Alas, master! for it was borrowed. 6 And the man of God said, Where fell it? And he showed him the place. And he cut down a stick, and cast *it* in thither; and the iron did swim. 7 Therefore said he, Take *it* up to thee. And he put out his hand, and took it.

Several things may be observed here,

I. Concerning the sons of the prophets, and their condition and character. The college here spoken of seems to be that at Gilgal, for there Elisha was (*ch.* iv. 38), and it was near Jordan; and, probably, wherever Elisha resided as many as could of the sons of the prophets flocked to him for the advantage of his instructions, counsels, and prayers. Every one would covet to dwell with him and be near him. Those that would be teachers should lay out themselves to get the best advantages for learning. Now observe,

1. Their number increased so that they

wanted room: *The place is too strait for us* (*v.* 1)—a good hearing, for it is a sign many are added to them. Elisha's miracles doubtless drew in many. Perhaps they increased the more now that Gehazi was cashiered, and, it is likely, an honester man put in his room, to take care of their provisions; for it should seem (by that instance, *ch.* iv. 43) that Naaman's case was not the only one in which he grudged his master's generosity.

2. They were humble men and did not affect that which was gay or great. When they wanted room they did not speak of sending for cedars, and marble stones, and curious artificers, but only of getting every man a beam, to run up a plain hut or cottage with. It becomes the sons of the prophets, who profess to look for great things in the other world, to be content with mean things in this.

3. They were poor men, and men that had no interest in great ones. It was a sign that Joram was king, and Jezebel ruled too, or the sons of the prophets, when they wanted room, would have needed only to apply to the government, not to consult among themselves about the enlargement of their buildings. God's prophets have seldom been the world's favourites. Nay, so poor were they that they had not wherewithal to hire workmen (but must leave their studies, and work for themselves), no, nor to buy tools, but must borrow of their neighbours. Poverty then is no bar to prophecy.

4. They were industrious men, and willing to take pains. They desired not to live, like idle drones (idle *monks*, I might have said), upon the labours of others, but only desired leave of their president to work for themselves. As the sons of the prophets must not be so taken up with contemplation as to render themselves unfit for action, so much less must they so indulge themselves in their ease as to be averse to labour. He that must eat or die must work or starve, 2 Thess. iii. 8, 10. Let no man think an honest employment either a burden or disparagement.

5. They were men that had a great value and veneration for Elisha; though they were themselves prophets, they paid much deference to him. (1.) They would not go about to build at all without his leave, *v.* 2. It is good for us all to be suspicious of our own judgment, even when we think we have most reason for it, and to be desirous of the advice of those who are wiser and more experienced; and it is especially commendable in the sons of the prophets to take their fathers along with them, and to act in all things of moment under their direction, *permissu superiorum—by permission of their superiors.* (2.) They would not willingly go to fell timber without his company: "*Go with thy servants* (*v.* 3), not only to advise us in any exigence, but to keep good order among us, that, being under thy eye, we may behave as becomes us." Good disciples desire to be always under good discipline.

6. They were honest men, and men that were in care to give all men their own. When one of them, accidentally fetching too fierce a stroke (as those that work seldom are apt to be violent), threw off his axe-head into the water, he did not say, "It was a mischance, and who can help it? It was the fault of the helve, and the owner deserves to stand to the loss." No, he cries out with deep concern, *Alas, master! For it was borrowed, v.* 5. Had the axe been his own, it would only have troubled him that he could not be further serviceable to his brethren; but now, besides that, it troubles him that he cannot be just to the owner, to whom he ought to be not only just but grateful. Note, We ought to be as careful of that which is borrowed as of that which is our own, that it receive no damage, because we must love our neighbour as ourselves and do as we would be done by. It is likely this prophet was poor, and had not wherewithal to pay for the axe, which made the loss of it so much the greater trouble. To those that have an honest mind the sorest grievance of poverty is not so much their own want or disgrace as their being by it rendered unable to pay their just debts.

II. Concerning the father of the prophets, Elisha. 1. That he was a man of great condescension and compassion; he went with the sons of the prophets to the woods, when they desired his company, *v.* 3. Let no man, especially no minister, think himself too great to stoop to do good, but be tender to all. 2. That he was a man of great power; he could make iron to swim, contrary to its nature (*v.* 6), for the God of nature is not tied up to its laws. He did not throw the helve after the hatchet, but cut down a new stick, and cast it into the river. We need not double the miracle by supposing that the stick sunk to fetch up the iron, it was enough that it was a signal of the divine summons to the iron to rise. God's grace can thus raise the stony iron heart which has sunk into the mud of this world, and raise up affections naturally earthly, to things above.

8 Then the king of Syria warred against Israel, and took counsel with his servants, saying, In such and such a place *shall be* my camp. 9 And the man of God sent unto the king of Israel, saying, Beware that thou pass not such a place; for thither the Syrians are come down. 10 And the king of Israel sent to the place which the man of God told him and warned him of, and saved himself there, not once nor twice. 11 Therefore the heart of the king of Syria was sore troubled for this thing; and he

called his servants, and said unto them, Will ye not show me which of us *is* for the king of Israel? 12 And one of his servants said, None, my lord, O king: but Elisha, the prophet that *is* in Israel, telleth the king of Israel the words that thou speakest in thy bedchamber.

Here we have Elisha, with his spirit of prophecy, serving the king, as before helping the sons of the prophets; for that, as other gifts, is given to every man to profit withal; and, whatever abilities any man has of doing good, he is by them made a debtor both to the wise and unwise. Observe here,

I. How the king of Israel was informed by Elisha of all the designs and motions of his enemy, the king of Syria, more effectually than he could have been by the most vigilant and faithful spies. If the king of Syria, in a secret council of war, determined in what place to make an inroad upon the coasts of Israel, where he thought it would be the greatest surprise and they would be least able to make resistance, before his forces could receive his orders the king of Israel had notice of them from Elisha, and so had opportunity of preventing the mischief; and this many a time, *v.* 8—10. See here, 1. That the enemies of God' s Israel are politic in their devices, and restless in their attempts, against him. *They shall not know, nor see, till we come in the midst among them, and slay them,* Neh. iv. 11. 2. All those devices are known to God, even those that are deepest laid. He knows not only what men do, but what they design, and has many ways of countermining them. 3. It is a great advantage to us to be warned of our danger, that we may stand upon our guard against it. The work of God's prophets is to give us warning; if, being warned, we do not save ourselves, it is our own fault, and our blood will be upon our own head. The king of Israel would regard the warnings Elisha gave him of his danger by the Syrians, but not the warnings he gave him of his danger by his sins. Such warnings are little heeded by the most; they will save themselves from death, but not from hell.

II. How the king of Syria resented this. He suspected treachery among his senators, and that his counsels were betrayed, *v.* 11. But one of his servants, that had heard, by Naaman and others, of Elisha's woundrous works, concludes it must needs be he that gave this intelligence to the king of Israel, *v.* 12. What could not he discover who could tell Gehazi his thoughts? Here a confession of the boundless knowledge, as before of the boundless power, of Israel's God, is extorted from Syrians. Nothing done, said, thought, by any person, in any place, at any time, is out of the reach of God's cognizance.

13 And he said, Go and spy where he *is,* that I may send and fetch him. And it was told him, saying, Behold, *he is* in Dothan. 14 Therefore sent he thither horses, and chariots, and a great host: and they came by night, and compassed the city about. 15 And when the servant of the man of God was risen early, and gone forth, behold, a host compassed the city both with horses and chariots. And his servant said unto him, Alas, my master! how shall we do? 16 And he answered, Fear not: for they that *be* with us *are* more than they that *be* with them. 17 And Elisha prayed, and said, LORD, I pray thee, open his eyes, that he may see. And the LORD opened the eyes of the young man; and he saw: and, behold, the mountain *was* full of horses and chariots of fire round about Elisha. 18 And when they came down to him, Elisha prayed unto the LORD, and said, Smite this people, I pray thee, with blindness. And he smote them with blindness according to the word of Elisha. 9 And Elisha said unto them, This *is* not the way, neither *is* this the city: follow me, and I will bring you to the man whom ye seek. But he led them to Samaria. 20 And it came to pass, when they were come into Samaria, that Elisha said, LORD, open the eyes of these *men,* that they may see. And the LORD opened their eyes, and they saw; and, behold, *they were* in the midst of Samaria. 21 And the king of Israel said unto Elisha, when he saw them, My father, shall I smite *them?* shall I smite *them?* 22 And he answered, Thou shalt not smite *them:* wouldest thou smite those whom thou hast taken captive with thy sword and with thy bow? set bread and water before them, that they may eat and drink, and go to their master. 23 And he prepared great provision for them: and when they had eaten and drunk, he sent them away, and they went to their master. So the bands of Syria came no more into the land of Israel.

Here is, 1. The great force which the king

of Syria sent to seize Elisha. He found out where he was, at Dothan (*v.* 13), which was not far from Samaria; thither he sent a great host, who were to come upon him by night, and to bring him dead or alive, *v.* 14. Perhaps he had heard that when only one captain and his fifty men were sent to take Elijah they were baffled in the attempt, and therefore he sent an *army* against Elisha, as if the fire from heaven that consumed fifty men could not as easily consume 50,000. Naaman could tell him that Elisha dwelt not in any strong-hold, nor was attended with any guards, nor had any such great interest in the people that he needed to fear a tumult among them; what occasion then was there for this great force? But thus he hoped to make sure of him, especially coming upon him by surprise. Foolish man! Did he believe that Elisha had informed the king of Israel of his secret counsels or not? If not, what quarrel had he with him? If he did, could he be so weak as to imagine that Elisha would not discover the designs laid against himself, and that, having interest enough in heaven to discover them, he would not have interest enough to defeat them? Those that fight against God, his people, and prophets, know not what they do.

II. The grievous fright which the prophet's servant was in, when he perceived the city surrounded by the Syrians, and the effectual course which the prophet took to pacify him and free him from his fears. It seems, Elisha accustomed his servant to rise early, that is the way to bring something to pass, and to do the work of a day in its day. Being up, we may suppose he heard the noise of soldiers, and thereupon looked out, and was aware of an army compassing the city (*v.* 15), with great assurance no doubt of success, and that they should have this troublesome prophet in their hands presently. Now observe, 1. What a consternation he was in. He ran straight to Elisha, to bring him an account of it: "*Alas, master!*" (said he) "*what shall we do?* We are undone; it is to no purpose to think either of fighting or flying, but we must unavoidably fall into their hands." Had he but studied David's Psalms, which were than extant, he might have learnt *not to be afraid of* 10,000 of people (Ps. iii. 6), no, not of *a host encamped against him*, Ps. xxvii. 3. Had he considered that he was embarked with his master, by whom God had done great things, and whom he would not now leave to *fall into the hands of the uncircumcised*, and who, having saved others, would no doubt save himself, he would not have been thus at a loss. If he had only said, *What shall I do?* it would have been the more excusable, and like that of the disciples: *Lord, save us, we perish;* but he needed not to include his master as being in distress, nor to say, *What shall we do?* 2. How his master quieted him, (1.) By word. What he said to him (*v.* 16) is spoken to all the faithful servants of God, when *without are fightings and within are fears:* "*Fear not* with that fear which has torment and amazement, *for those that are with us*, to protect us, *are more than those that are against us*, to destroy us—angels unspeakably more numerous—God infinitely more powerful." When we are magnifying the causes of our fear we ought to possess ourselves with clear, and great, and high thoughts of God and the invisible world. *If God be for us*, we know what follows, Rom. viii. 31. (2.) By vision, *v.* 17. [1.] It seems Elisha was much concerned for the satisfaction of his servant. Good men desire, not only to be easy themselves, but to have those about them easy. Elisha had lately parted with his old man, and this, having newly come into his service, had not the advantage of experience; his master was therefore desirous to give him other convincing evidence of that omnipotence which employed him and was therefore employed for him. Note, Those whose faith is strong ought tenderly to consider and compassionate those who are weak and of a timorous spirit, and to do what they can to strengthen their hands. [2.] He saw himself safe, and wished no more than that his servant might see what he saw, a guard of angels round about him; such as were his master's convoy to the gates of heaven were his protectors against the gates of hell—*chariots of fire, and horses of fire.* Fire is both dreadful and devouring; that power which was engaged for Elisha's protection could both terrify and consume the assailants. As angels are God's messengers, so they are his soldiers, his hosts (Gen. xxxii. 2), his legions, or regiments (Matt. xxvi. 53), for the good of his people. [3.] For the satisfaction of his servant there needed no more than the opening of his eyes; *that* therefore he prayed for, and obtained for him: *Lord, open his eyes that he may see.* The eyes of his body were open, and with them he saw the danger. "Lord, open the eyes of his faith, that with them he may see the protection we are under." Note, *First*, The greatest kindness we can do for those that are fearful and faint-hearted is to pray for them, and so to recommend them to the mighty grace of God. *Secondly*, The opening of our eyes will be the silencing of our fears. In the dark we are most apt to be frightened. The clearer sight we have of the sovereignty and power of heaven the less we shall fear the calamities of this earth.

III. The shameful defeat which Elisha gave to the host of Syrians who came to seize him. They thought to make a prey of him, but he made fools of them, perfectly played with them, so far was he from fearing them or any damage by them. 1. He prayed to God to smite them with blindness, and they were all struck blind immediately, not stone-blind, nor so as to be themselves aware that they were blind, for they could see the light, but their sight was so altered that they could not know the persons and places they were before acquainted with, *v.* 18. They were so confounded that those among them whom they depended upon for information did not know this place to be Dothan nor this person to be Elisha, but *groped at noon day as in the night* (Isa. lix. 10; Job xii. 24, 25); their memory failed them, and their distinguishing faculty. See the power of God over the minds and understanding of men, both ways; he enlightened the eyes of Elisha's friend, and darkened the eyes of his foes, that they might see indeed, but not perceive, Isa. vi. 9. *For this* twofold judgment Christ came into this world, *that those who see not might see, and that those who see might be made blind* (John ix. 39), a savour of life to some, of death to others.

2. When they were thus bewildered and confounded he led them to Samaria (*v.* 19), promising that he would show them the man whom they sought, and he did so. He did not lie to them when he told them, *This is not the way, nor is this the city* where Elisha is; for he had now come out of the city; and, if they would see him, they must go to another city to which he would direct them. Those that fight against God and his prophets deceive themselves, and are justly given up to delusions. 3. When he had brought them to Samaria he prayed to God so to open their eyes and restore them their memories that they might see where they were (*v.* 20), *and behold,* to their great terror, *they were in the midst of Samaria,* where, it is probable, there was a standing force sufficient to cut them all off, or make them prisoners of war. Satan, the god of this world, blinds men's eyes, and so deludes them into their own ruin; but, when God enlightens their eyes, they then see themselves in the midst of their enemies, captives to Satan and in danger of hell, though before they thought their condition good. The enemies of God and his church, when they fancy themselves ready to triumph, will find themselves conquered and triumphed over. 4. When he had them at his mercy he made it appear that he was influenced by a divine goodness as well as a divine power. (1.) He took care to protect them from the danger into which he had brought them, and was content to show them what he could have done; he needed not the sword of an angel to avenge his cause, the sword of the king of Israel is at his service if he please (*v.* 21): *My father* (so respectfully does the king now speak to him, though, soon after, he swore his death), *shall I smite them?* And, again, as if he longed for the assault, *Shall I smite them?* Perhaps, he remembered how God was displeased at his father for *letting go out of his hands* those whom he had put it in his power to destroy, and he would not offend in like manner; yet such a reverence has he for the prophet that he will not strike a stroke without his commission. But the prophet would by no means suffer him to meddle with them; they were brought hither to be convinced and shamed, not to be killed, *v.* 22. Had they been *his* prisoners, taken captive by his sword and bow, when they asked quarter it would have been barbarous to deny, and, when he had given it to them, it would have been perfidious to do them any hurt, and against the law of arms to kill men in cool blood. But they were not his prisoners; they were God's prisoners and the prophet's, and therefore he must do them no harm. Those that humble themselves under God's hand take the best course to secure themselves. (2.) He took care to provide for them; he ordered the king to treat them handsomely and then dismiss them fairly, which he did, *v.* 23. [1.] It was the king's praise that he was so obsequious to the prophet, contrary to his inclination, and, as it seemed, to his interest, 1 Sam. xxiv. 19. Nay, so willing was he to oblige Elisha that, whereas he was ordered only to set *bread and water* before them (which are good fare for captives), he *prepared great provision* for them, for the credit of his court and country and of Elisha. [2.] It was the prophet's praise that he was so generous to his enemies, who, though they came to take him, could not but go away admiring him, as both the mightiest and kindest man they ever met with. The great duty of loving enemies, and doing good to those that hate us, was both commanded in the Old Testament (Prov. xxv. 21, 22, *If thy enemy hunger, feed him,* Exod. xxiii. 4, 5) and practised, as here by Elisha. His predecessor had given a specimen of divine justice when he called for flames of fire on the heads of his persecutors to consume them, but he gave a specimen of divine mercy in heaping coals of fire on the heads of his persecutors to melt them. Let not us then be *overcome of evil, but overcome evil with good*

IV. The good effect this had, for the present, upon the Syrians. They *came no more into the land of Israel* (*v.* 23), namely, upon this errand, to take Elisha; they saw it was to no purpose to attempt that, nor would any of their bands be persuaded to make an assault on so great and good a man. The most glorious victory over an enemy is to turn him into a friend.

24 And it came to pass after this, that Ben-hadad king of Syria gathered all his host, and went up, and besieged Samaria. 25 And there was a great famine in Samaria: and, behold, they besieged it, until an ass's head was *sold* for fourscore *pieces* of silver, and the fourth part of a cab of dove's dung for five *pieces* of silver. 26 And as the king of Israel was passing by upon the wall, there cried a woman unto him, saying, Help, my

lord, O king. 27 And he said, If the LORD do not help thee, whence shall I help thee? out of the barnfloor, or out of the winepress? 28 And the king said unto her, What aileth thee? And she answered, This woman said unto me, Give thy son, that we may eat him to day, and we will eat my son to morrow. 29 So we boiled my son, and did eat him: and I said unto her on the next day, Give thy son, that we may eat him: and she hath hid her son. 30 And it came to pass, when the king heard the words of the woman, that he rent his clothes; and he passed by upon the wall, and the people looked, and, behold, *he had* sackcloth within upon his flesh. 31 Then he said, God do so and more also to me, if the head of Elisha the son of Shaphat shall stand on him this day. 32 But Elisha sat in his house, and the elders sat with him; and *the king* sent a man from before him: but ere the messenger came to him, he said to the elders, See ye how this son of a murderer hath sent to take away mine head? look, when the messenger cometh, shut the door, and hold him fast at the door: *is* not the sound of his master's feet behind him? 33 And while he yet talked with them, behold, the messenger came down unto him: and he said, Behold, this evil *is* of the LORD; what should I wait for the LORD any longer?

This last paragraph of this chapter should, of right, have been the first of the next chapter, for it begins a new story, which is there continued and concluded. Here is,

I. The siege which the king of Syria laid to Samaria and the great distress which the city was reduced to thereby. The Syrians had soon forgotten the kindnesses they had lately received in Samaria, and very ungratefully, for aught that appears without any provocation, sought the destruction of it, *v.* 24. There are base spirits that can never feel obliged. The country, we may suppose, was plundered and laid waste when this capital city was brought to the last extremity, *v.* 25. The dearth which had of late been in the land was probably the occasion of the emptiness of their stores, or the siege was so sudden that they had not time to lay in provisions; so that, while the sword devoured without, the famine within was more grievous (Lam. iv. 9): for, it should seem, the Syrians designed not to storm the city, but to starve it. So great was the scarcity that an ass's head, that has but little flesh on it and that unsavoury, unwholesome, and ceremonially unclean, was sold for five pounds, and a small quantity of fitches, or lentiles, or some such coarse corn, then called *dove's dung*, no more of it than the quantity of six eggs, for five pieces of silver, about twelve or fifteen shillings. Learn to value plenty, and to be thankful for it; see how contemptible money is, when, in time of famine, it is so freely parted with for any thing that is eatable.

II. The sad complaint which a poor woman had to make to the king, in the extremity of the famine. He was *passing by upon the wall* to give orders for the mounting of the guard, the posting of the archers, the repair of the breaches, and the like, when a woman of the city cried to him, *Help, my lord, O king! v.* 26. Whither should the subject, in distress, go for help but to the prince, who is, by office, the protector of right and the avenger of wrong? He returns but a melancholy answer (*v.* 27): *If the Lord do not help thee, whence shall I?* Some think it was a *quarrelling* word, and the language of his fretfulness: "Why dost thou expect any thing from me, when God himself deals thus hardly with us?" Because he could not help her as he would, out of the floor or the wine-press, he would not help her at all. We must take heed of being made cross by afflictive providences. It rather seems to be a *quieting* word: "Let us be content, and make the best of our affliction, looking up to God, for, till he help us, I cannot help thee." 1. He laments the emptiness of the floor and the wine-press. These were not as they had been; even the king's failed. We read (*v.* 23) of great provisions which he had at command, sufficient for the entertainment of an army, yet now he has not wherewithal to relieve one poor woman. Scarcity sometimes follows upon great plenty; we cannot be sure that *to-morrow shall be as this day*, Isa. lvi. 12.; Ps. xxx. 6. 2. He acknowledges himself thereby disabled to help, unless God would help them. Note, Creatures are helpless things without God, for every creature is that, all that, and only that, which he makes it to be. However, though he cannot help her, he is willing to hear her (*v.* 28): "*What ails thee?* Is there any thing singular in thy case, or dost thou fare worse than thy neighbours?" Truly yes; she and one of her neighbours had made a barbarous agreement, that, all provisions failing, they should boil and eat her son first and then her neighbour's; hers was eaten (who can think of it without horror?) and now her neighbour hid hers, *v.* 28, 29. See an instance of the dominion which the flesh has got above the spirit, when the most natural affections of the mind may be thus overpowered by the natural appetites of the body.

See the word of God fulfilled; among the threatenings of God's judgments upon Israel for their sins this was one (Deut. xxviii. 53—57), that they should eat the flesh of their own children, which one would think incredible, yet it came to pass.

III. The king's indignation against Elisha upon this occasion. He lamented the calamity, *rent his clothes, and had sackcloth upon his flesh* (*v.* 30), as one heartily concerned for the misery of his people, and that it was not in his power to help them; but he did not lament his own iniquity, nor the iniquity of his people, which was the procuring cause of the calamity; he was not sensible that his *ways and his doings had procured this to himself; this is his wickedness, for it is bitter. The foolishness of man perverteth his way,* and then *his heart fretteth against the Lord.* Instead of vowing to pull down the calves at Dan and Beth-el, or letting the law have its course against the prophets of Baal and of the groves, he swears *the death of Elisha, v.* 31. Why, what is the matter? What has Elisha done? His head is the most innocent and valuable in all Israel, and yet that must be devoted, and made an anathema. Thus in the days of the persecuting emperors, when the empire groaned under any extraordinary calamity, the fault was laid on the Christians, and they were doomed to destruction. *Christianos ad leones—Away with the Christians to the lions.* Perhaps Jehoram was in this heat against Elisha because he had foretold this judgment, or had persuaded him to hold out, and not surrender, or rather because he did not, by his prayers, raise the siege, and relieve the city, which he thought he could do, but would not; whereas till they repented and reformed, and were ready for deliverance, they had no reason to expect that the prophet should pray for it.

IV. The foresight Elisha had of the king's design against him, *v.* 32. He sat in his house well composed, and the elders with him, well employed no doubt, while the king was like a wild bull in a net, or like the troubled sea when it cannot rest; he told the elders there was an officer coming from the king to cut off his head, and bade them stop him at the door, and not let him in, for the king his master was just following him, to revoke the order, as we may suppose. The same spirit of prophecy that enabled Elisha to tell what was done at a distance authorized him to call the king *the son of a murderer,* which, unless we could produce such an extraordinary commission, it is not for us to imitate; far be it from us to despise dominion and to speak evil of dignities. He appealed to the elders whether he had deserved so ill at the king's hands: "See whether in this he be not the son of a murderer?" For *what evil had Elisha done?* He *had not desired the woeful day,* Jer. xvii. 16.

V. The king's passionate speech, when he came to prevent the execution of his edict for the beheading of Elisha. He seems to have been in a struggle between his convictions and his corruptions, knew not what to say, but, seeing things brought to the last extremity, he even abandoned himself to despair (*v.* 33): *This evil is of the Lord.* Therein his notions were right and well applied; it is a general truth that all penal evil is of the Lord, as the first cause, and sovereign judge (Amos iii. 6), and this we ought to apply to particular cases: if all evil, then this evil, whatever it is we are now groaning under, whoever are the instruments, God is the principal agent of it. But his inference from this truth was foolish and wicked: *What should I wait for the Lord any longer?* When Eli, and David, and Job, said, *It is of the Lord,* they grew patient upon it, but this bad man grew outrageous upon it: "I will neither fear worse nor expect better, for worse cannot come and better never will come: we are all undone, and there is no remedy." It is an unreasonable thing to be weary of waiting for God, for he is a God of judgment, and blessed are all those that wait for him.

CHAP. VII.

Relief is here brought to Samaria and her king, when the case is, in a manner, desperate, and the king despairing. I. It is foretold by Elisha, and an unbelieving lord shut out from the benefit of it, ver. 1, 2. II. It is brought about, 1. By an unaccountable fright into which God put the Syrians (ver. 6), which caused them to retire precipitately, ver. 7. 2. By the seasonable discovery which four lepers made of this (ver. 3—5), and the account which they gave of it to the court, ver. 8—11. 3. By the cautious trial which the king made of the truth of it, ver. 12—15. III. The event answered the prediction both in the sudden plenty (ver. 16), and the death of the unbelieving lord (ver. 17—20); for no word of God shall fall to the ground.

THEN Elisha said, Hear ye the word of the LORD; Thus saith the LORD, To morrow about this time *shall* a measure of fine flour *be sold* for a shekel, and two measures of barley for a shekel, in the gate of Samaria. 2 Then a lord on whose hand the king leaned answered the man of God, and said, Behold, *if* the LORD would make windows in heaven, might this thing be? And he said, Behold, thou shalt see *it* with thine eyes, but shalt not eat thereof.

Here, I. Elisha foretels that, notwithstanding the great straits to which the city of Samaria is reduced, yet within twenty-four hours they shall have plenty, *v.* 1. The king of Israel despaired of it and grew weary of waiting: then Elisha foretold it, when things were at the worst. Man's extremity is God's opportunity of magnifying his own power; his time to appear for his people is when *their strength is gone,* Deut. xxxii. 36. When they had given over expecting help it came. *When the son of man comes shall he find faith on the earth?* Luke xviii. 8. The king said, *What shall I wait for the Lord any longer?* And perhaps some of the elders were ready to say the same: "Well," said Elisha, "you hear what these say; *now hear you the word of the Lord,* hear what he says, hear it and heed it, hear it and believe it: to-morrow corn shall be sold at the usual rate in the gate of Samaria;" that is, the siege shall be raised, for the gate of the city shall be opened, and the market shall be held there as formerly. The return of peace is thus expressed (Judg. v. 11), *Then shall the people of the Lord go down to the gates,* to buy and sell there. 2. The consequence of that shall be great plenty. This would, in time, follow of course, but that corn should be thus cheap in so short a time was quite beyond what could be thought of. Though the king of Israel had just now threatened Elisha's life, God promises to save his life and the life of his people; for *where sin abounded grace doth much more abound.*

II. A peer of Israel that happened to be present openly declared his disbelief of this prediction, *v.* 2. He was a courtier whom the king had an affection for, as the man of his right hand, on whom he leaned, that is, on whose prudence he much relied, and in whom he reposed much confidence. He thought it impossible, unless God should rain corn out of the clouds, as once he did manna; no less than the repetition of Moses's miracle will serve him, though that of Elijah might have served to answer this intention, the increasing of the meal in the barrel.

III. The just doom passed upon him for his infidelity, that he should see this great plenty for his conviction, and yet not eat of it to his comfort. Note, Unbelief is a sin by which men greatly dishonour and displease God, and deprive themselves of the favours he designed for them. The murmuring Israelites saw Canaan, but could not enter in because of unbelief. Such (says bishop Patrick) will be the portion of those that believe not the promise of eternal life; they shall see it at a distance—Abraham afar off, but shall never taste of it; for they forfeit the benefit of the promise if they cannot find in their heart to take God's word.

3 And there were four leprous men at the entering in of the gate: and they said one to another, Why sit we here until we die? 4 If we say, We will enter into the city, then the famine *is* in the city, and we shall die there: and if we sit still here, we die also. Now therefore come, and let us fall unto the host of the Syrians: if they save us alive, we shall live; and if they kill us, we shall but die. 5 And they rose up in the twilight, to go unto the camp of the Syrians: and when they were come to the uttermost part of the camp of Syria, behold, *there was* no man there. 6 For the Lord had made the host of the Syrians to hear a noise of chariots, and a noise of horses, *even* the noise of a great host: and they said one to another, Lo, the king of Israel hath hired against us the kings of the Hittites, and the kings of the Egyptians, to come upon us. 7 Wherefore they arose and fled in the twilight, and left their tents, and their horses, and their asses, even the camp as it *was,* and fled for their life. 8 And when these lepers came to the uttermost part of the camp, they went into one tent, and did eat and drink, and carried thence silver, and gold, and raiment, and went and hid *it;* and came again, and entered into another tent, and carried thence *also,* and went and hid *it.* 9 Then they said one to another, We do not well: this day *is* a day of good tidings, and we hold our peace: if we tarry till the morning light, some mischief will come upon us: now therefore come, that we may go and tell the king's household. 10 So they came and called unto the porter of the city: and they told them, saying, We came to the camp of the Syrians, and, behold, *there was* no man there, neither voice of man, but horses tied, and asses tied, and the tents as they *were.* 11 And he called the porters; and they told *it* to the king's house within.

We are here told,

I. How the siege of Samaria was raised in the evening, at the edge of night (*v.* 6, 7), not by might or power, but by the Spirit of the Lord of hosts, striking terror upon the spirits of the besiegers. Here was not a sword drawn against them, not a drop of blood shed, it was not by thunder or hailstones that they were discomfited, nor were they slain, as Sennacherib's army before Jerusalem, by a destroying angel; but, 1. *The Lord made them to hear a noise of chariots and horses.* The Syrians that besieged Dothan had their *sight* imposed upon, *ch.* vi. 18. These had their *hearing* imposed upon. For God knows how to work upon every sense, pursuant to his own counsels: as *he makes the hearing ear and the seeing eye,* so he makes *the deaf and the blind,* Exod. iv. 11. Whether the noise was really made in the air by the ministry of angels, or whether it was only a sound in their ears, is not certain; which soever it was, it was from God, who both *brings the wind out of his treasures*, and *forms the spirit of man within him*. The sight of horses and chariots had encouraged the prophet's servant, *ch.* vi. 17. The noise of horses and chariots terrified the hosts of Syria. For notices from the invisible world are either very comfortable or very dreadful, according as men are at peace with God or at war with him. 2. Hearing this noise, they concluded the king of Israel had certainly procured assistance from some foreign power: *He has hired against us the kings of the Hittites and the kings of the Egyptians.* There was, for aught we know, but one king of Egypt, and what kings there were of the Hittites nobody can imagine; but, as they were imposed upon by that dreadful sound in their ears, so they imposed upon themselves by the interpretation they made of it. Had they supposed the king of Judah to have come with his forces, there would have been more of probability in their apprehensions than to dream of the *kings of the Hittites and the Egyptians.* If the fancies of any of them raised this spectre, yet their reasons might soon have laid it: how could the king of Israel, who was closely besieged, hold intelligence with those distant princes? What had he to hire them with? It was impossible but some notice would come, before, of the motions of so great a host; but *there were they in great fear where no fear was.* 3. Hereupon they all fled with incredible precipitation, as for their lives, left their camp as it was: even their horses, that might have hastened their flight, they could not stay to take with them, *v.* 7. None of them had so much sense as to send out scouts to discover the supposed enemy, much less courage enough to face the enemy, though fatigued with a long march. *The wicked flee when none pursues.* God can, when he pleases, dispirit the boldest and most brave, and make the stoutest heart to tremble. Those that will not fear God he can make to fear at the shaking of a leaf.

II. How the Syrians' flight was discovered by four leprous men. Samaria was delivered, and did not know it. The watchmen on the walls were not aware of the retreat of the enemy, so silently did they steal away. But Providence employed four lepers to be the intelligencers, who had their lodging without the gate, being excluded from the city, as ceremonially unclean: the Jews say they were Gehazi and his three sons; perhaps Gehazi might be one of them, which might cause him to be taken notice of afterwards by the king, *ch.* viii. 4. See here, 1. How these lepers reasoned themselves into a resolution to make a visit in the night to the camp of the Syrians, *v.* 3, 4. They were ready to perish for hunger; none passed through the gate to relieve them. Should they go into the city, there was nothing to be had there, they must die in the streets; should they sit still, they must pine to death in their cottage. They therefore determine to go over to the enemy, and throw themselves upon their mercy: if they killed them, better die by the sword than by famine, one death than a thousand; but perhaps they would save them alive, as objects of compassion. Common prudence will put us upon that method which may better our condition, but cannot make it worse. The prodigal son resolves to return to his father, whose displeasure he had reason to fear, rather than perish with hunger in the far country. These lepers conclude, "If they kill us, we shall but die;" and happy they who, in another sense, can thus speak of dying. "We shall but die, that is the worst of it, not die and be damned, not be hurt of the second death." According to this resolution, they went, in the beginning of the night, to the camp of the Syrians, and, to their great surprise, found it wholly deserted, not a man to be seen or heard in it, *v.* 5. Providence ordered it, that these lepers came as soon as ever the Syrians had fled, for they fled in the twilight, the evening twilight (*v.* 7), and in the twilight the lepers came (*v.* 5), and so no time was lost. 2. How they reasoned themselves into a resolution to bring tidings of this to the city. They feasted in the first tent they came to (*v.* 8) and then began to think of enriching themselves with the plunder; but they corrected themselves (*v.* 9): "*We do not well* to conceal these good tidings from the community we are members of, under colour of being avenged upon them for excluding us from their society; it was the law that did it, not they, and therefore let us bring them the news. Though it awake them from sleep, it will be *life from the dead* to them." Their own consciences told them that some mischief would befal them if they acted separately, and sought themselves only. Selfish narrow-spirited people cannot expect to prosper; the most comfortable advantage is that which our brethren share with us in. According to this resolution, they returned to the gate, and acquainted the sentinel with what they had discovered (*v.* 10), who straightway brought the intelligence to court (*v.* 11), and it was not the less acceptable for being first brought by lepers.

12 And the king arose in the night, and said unto his servants, I will now show you what the Syrians have done to us. They know that we *be* hungry; therefore are they gone out of the camp to hide themselves in the field, saying, When they come out of the city, we shall catch them alive, and get into the city. 13 And one of his servants answered and said,

Let *some* take, I pray thee, five of the horses that remain, which are left in the city, (behold, they *are* as all the multitude of Israel that are left in it: behold, *I say*, they *are* even as all the multitude of the Israelites that are consumed :) and let us send and see. 14 They took therefore two chariot horses; and the king sent after the host of the Syrians, saying, Go and see. 15 And they went after them unto Jordan: and, lo, all the way *was* full of garments and vessels, which the Syrians had cast away in their haste. And the messengers returned, and told the king. 16 And the people went out, and spoiled the tents of the Syrians. So a measure of fine flour was *sold* for a shekel, and two measures of barley for a shekel, according to the word of the LORD. 17 And the king appointed the lord on whose hand he leaned to have the charge of the gate: and the people trode upon him in the gate, and he died, as the man of God had said, who spake when the king came down to him. 18 And it came to pass as the man of God had spoken to the king, saying, Two measures of barley for a shekel, and a measure of fine flour for a shekel, shall be to morrow about this time in the gate of Samaria: 19 And that lord answered the man of God, and said, Now, behold, *if* the LORD should make windows in heaven, might such a thing be? And he said, Behold, thou shalt see it with thine eyes, but shalt not eat thereof. 20 And so it fell out unto him: for the people trode upon him in the gate, and he died.

Here we have,

I. The king's jealousy of a stratagem in the Syrian's retreat, *v.* 12. He feared that they had withdrawn into an ambush, to draw out the besieged, that they might fall on them with more advantage. He knew he had no reason to expect that God should appear thus wonderfully for him, having forfeited his favour by his unbelief and impatience. He knew no reason the Syrians had to fly, for it does not appear that he or any of his attendants heard the noise of the chariots which the Syrians were frightened at. Let not those who, like him, are *unstable in all their ways, think to receive any thing from God;* nay, a guilty conscience fears the worst and makes men suspicious.

II. The course they took for their satisfaction, and to prevent their falling into a snare. They sent out spies to see what had become of the Syrians, and found they had all fled indeed, commanders as well as common soldiers. They could track them by the garments which they threw off, and left by the way, for their greater expedition, *v.* 15. He that gave this advice seems to have been very sensible of the deplorable condition the people were in (*v.* 13); for speaking of the horses, many of which were dead and the rest ready to perish for hunger, he says, and repeats it, "*They are as all the multitude of Israel.* Israel used to glory in their multitude, but now they are diminished and brought low." He advised to send five horsemen, but, it should seem, there were only two horses fit to be sent, and those chariot-horses, *v.* 14. Now the Lord repented himself concerning his servants, when he saw that their strength was gone, Deut. xxxii. 36.

III. The plenty that was in Samaria, from the plunder of the camp of the Syrians, *v.* 16. Had the Syrians been governed by the modern policies of war, when they could not take their baggage and their tents with them they would rather have burnt them (as it is common to do with the forage of a country) than let them fall into their enemies' hands; but God determined that the besieging of Samaria, which was intended for its ruin, should turn to its advantage, and that Israel should now be enriched with the spoil of the Syrians as of old with that of the Egyptians. Here see, 1. The *wealth of the sinner laid up for the just* (Job. xxvii. 16, 17) and the spoilers spoiled, Isa. xxxiii. 1. 2. The wants of Israel supplied in a way that they little thought of, which should encourage us to depend upon the power and goodness of God in our greatest straits. 3. The word of Elisha fulfilled to a tittle: *A measure of fine flour was sold for a shekel;* those that spoiled the camp had not only enough to supply themselves with, but an overplus to sell at an easy rate for the benefit of others, and so even *those that tarried at home did divide the spoil*, Ps. lxviii. 12; Isa. xxxiii. 23. God's promise may be safely relied on, for no word of his shall fall to the ground.

IV. The death of the unbelieving courtier, that questioned the truth of Elisha's word. Divine threatenings will as surely be accomplished as divine promises. *He that believeth not shall be damned* stands as firm as *He that believeth shall be saved.* This lord, 1. Was preferred by the king to the *charge of the gate* (*v.* 17), to keep the peace, and to see that there was no tumult or disorder in dividing and disposing of the spoil. So much trust did the king repose in him, in his prudence and gravity, and so much did he delight to honour him. He that will be great, let him serve the public. 2. Was trodden to death by the people in the gate, either by accident, the crowd being exceedingly great, and he in the thickest of it, or perhaps designedly, because he abused his power, and was imperious in restraining the people from satisfying their hunger. However it was, God's justice was glorified, and the word of Elisha was fulfilled. He saw the plenty, for the silencing and shaming of his unbelief, corn cheap without *opening windows in heaven,* and therein saw his own folly in prescribing to God; but he did not eat of the plenty he saw. *When he was about to fill his belly* God *cast the fury of his wrath upon him* (Job xx. 23) and it came between the cup and the lip. Justly are those thus tantalized with the world's promises that think themselves tantalized with the promises of God. If believing shall not be seeing, seeing shall not be enjoying. This matter is repeated, and the event very particularly compared with the prediction (*v.* 18—20), that we might take special notice of it, and might learn, (1.) How deeply God resents our distrust of him, of his power, providence, and promise. When Israel said, *Can God furnish a table? the Lord heard it and was wroth.* Infinite wisdom will not be limited by our folly. God never promises the end without knowing where to provide the means. (2.) How uncertain life and the enjoyments of it are. Honour and power cannot secure men from sudden and inglorious deaths. He whom the king leaned upon the people trod upon; he who fancied himself the stay and support of the government was trampled under foot as the mire in the streets. Thus hath the pride of men's glory been often stained. (3.) How certain God's threatenings are, and how sure to alight on the guilty and obnoxious heads. Let all men fear before the great God, who *treads upon princes as mortar* and is *terrible to the kings of the earth.*

CHAP. VIII.

The passages of story recorded in this chapter oblige us to look back. I. We read before of a Shunammite woman that was a kind benefactor to Elisha; now here we are told how she fared the better for it, afterwards, in the advice Elisha gave her, and the favour the king showed her for his sake, ver. 1—6. II. We read before of the designation of Hazael to be king of Syria (1 Kings xix. 15), and here we have an account of his elevation to that throne and the way he forced for himself to it, by killing his master, ver. 7—15. III. We read before of Jehoram's reigning over Judah in the room of his father Jehoshaphat (1 Kings xxii. 50), now here we have a short and sad history of his short and wicked reign (ver. 16—24), and the beginning of the history of the reign of his son Ahaziah, ver. 25—29.

THEN spake Elisha unto the woman, whose son he had restored to life, saying, Arise, and go thou and thine household, and sojourn wheresoever thou canst sojourn: for the LORD hath called for a famine: and it shall also come upon the land seven years. 2 And the woman arose, and did after the saying of the man of God: and she went with her household, and sojourned in the land of the Philistines seven years. 3 And it came to pass at the seven years' end, that the woman returned out of the land of the Philistines: and she went forth to cry unto the king for her house and for her land. 4 And the king talked with Gehazi the servant of the man of God, saying, Tell me, I pray thee, all the great things that Elisha hath done. 5 And it came to pass, as he was telling the king how he had restored a dead body to life, that, behold, the woman, whose son he had restored to life, cried to the king for her house and for her land. And Gehazi said, My lord, O king, this *is* the woman, and this *is* her son, whom Elisha restored to life. 6 And when the king asked the woman, she told him. So the king appointed unto her a certain officer, saying, Restore all that *was* her's, and all the fruits of the field since the day that she left the land, even until now.

Here we have,

I. The wickedness of Israel punished with a long famine, one of God's sore judgments often threatened in the law. *Canaan,* that fruitful land, *was turned into barrenness,* for the *iniquity of those that dwelt therein.* The famine in Samaria was soon relieved by the raising of the siege, but neither that judgment nor that mercy had a due influence upon them, and therefore *the Lord called for another famine;* for when he judgeth he will overcome. If less judgments do not prevail to bring men to repentance, he will send greater and longer; they are at his beck, and will come when he calls for them. He does, by his ministers, call for reformation and obedience, and, if those calls be not regarded, we may expect he will call for some plague or other, for he will be heard. This famine continued seven years, as long again as that in Elijah's time; for, if men will walk contrary to him, he will heat the furnace yet hotter.

II. The kindness of the good Shunammite to the prophet rewarded by the care that was taken of her in that famine; she was not indeed fed by miracle, as the widow of Sarepta was, but, 1. She had notice given her of this famine before it came, that she might provide accordingly, and was directed to remove to some other country; any where but in Israel she would find plenty. It was a great advantage to Egypt in Joseph's time that they had notice of the famine before it came, so it was to this Shunammite; others would be forced to remove at last, after they had long borne the grievances of the famine, and had wasted their substance, and could not settle elsewhere upon such good terms as she might that went early, before the crowd, and took her stock with her unbroken. It is our happiness to foresee an evil, and our wisdom, when we foresee it, to hide ourselves. 2. Providence gave her a comfortable settlement in *the land of the Philistines*, who, though subdued by David, yet were not wholly rooted out. It seems the famine was peculiar to the land of Israel, and other countries that joined close to them had plenty at the same time, which plainly showed the immediate hand of God in it (as in the plagues of Egypt, when they distinguished between the Israelites and the Egyptians) and that the sins of Israel, against whom this judgment was directly levelled, were more provoking to God than the sins of their neighbours, because of their profession of relation to God. *You only have I known, therefore will I punish you*, Amos iii. 2. Other countries had rain when they had none, were free from locusts and caterpillars when they were eaten up with them; for some think this was the famine spoken of, Joel i. 3, 4. It is strange that when there was plenty in the neighbouring countries there were not those that made it their business to import corn into the land of Israel, which might have prevented the inhabitants from removing; but, as they were befooled with their idolatries, so they were infatuated even in the matters of their civil interest.

III. Her petition to the king at her return, favoured by the seasonableness of her application to him. 1. When the famine was over she *returned out of the land of the Philistines;* that was no proper place for an Israelite to dwell any longer than there was a necessity for so doing, for there she could not keep her new moons and her sabbaths as she used to do in her own country, among the schools of the prophets, *ch.* iv. 23. 2. At her return she found herself kept out of the possession of her own estate, it being either confiscated to the exchequer, seized by the lord, or usurped in her absence by some of the neighbours; or perhaps the person she had entrusted with the management of it proved false, and would neither resign it to her nor come to an account with her for the profits: so hard is it to find a person that one can put a confidence in *in a time of trouble*, Prov. xxv 19; Mic. vii. 5. 3. She made her application to the king himself for redress; for, it seems (be it observed to his praise), he was easy of access, and did himself take cognizance of the complaints of his injured subjects. Time was when she dwelt so securely among her own people that she had no occasion to be *spoken for to the king, or to the captain of the host* (*ch.* iv. 13); but now her own familiar friends, in whom she trusted, proved so unjust and unkind that she was glad to appeal to the king against them. Such uncertainty there is in the creature that that may fail us which we most depend upon and that befriend us which we think we shall never need. 4. She found the king talking with Gehazi about Elisha's miracles, *v.* 4. It was his shame that he needed now to be informed concerning them, when he might have acquainted himself with them as they were done from Elisha himself, if he had not been willing to shut his eyes against the convincing evidence of his mission; yet it was his praise that he was now better disposed, and would rather talk with a leper that was capable of giving a good account of them than continue ignorant of them. The law did not forbid all conversation with lepers, but only dwelling with them. There being then no priests in Israel, perhaps the king, or some one appointed by him, had the inspection of lepers, and passed the judgment upon them, which might bring him acquainted with Gehazi. 5. This happy coincidence befriended both Gehazi's narrative and her petition. Providence is to be acknowledged in ordering the circumstances of events, for sometimes those that are minute in themselves prove of great consequence, as this did, for, (1.) It made the king ready to believe Gehazi's narrative when it was thus confirmed by the persons most nearly concerned: "*This is the woman, and this her son;* let them speak for themselves," *v.* 5. Thus did God even force him to believe what he might have had some colour to question if he had only had Gehazi's word for it, because he was branded for a liar, witness his leprosy. (2.) It made him ready to grant her request; for who would not be ready to favour one whom heaven had thus favoured, and to support a life which was given once and again by miracle? In consideration of this the king gave orders that her land should be restored to her and all the profits that were made of it in her absence. If it was to himself that the land and profits had escheated, it was generous and kind to make so full a restitution; he would not (as Pharaoh did in Joseph's time) enrich the crown by the calamities of his subjects. If it was by some other person that her property was invaded, it was an act of justice in the king, and part of the duty of his place, to give her redress, Ps. lxxxii. 3,4; Prov. xxxi. 9. It is not enough for those in authority that they do no wrong themselves, but they must support the right of those that are wronged.

7 And Elisha came to Damascus; and Ben-hadad the king of Syria was sick; and it was told them, saying, The man of God is come hither. 8 And the king said unto Hazael, Take a present in thine hand, and go, meet the man of God, and enquire of the LORD by him, saying, Shall I recover of this disease? 9 So Hazael went

to meet him, and took a present with him, even of every good thing of Damascus, forty camels' burden, and came and stood before him, and said, Thy son Ben-hadad king of Syria hath sent me to thee, saying, Shall I recover of this disease? 10 And Elisha said unto him, Go, say unto him, Thou mayest certainly recover: howbeit the LORD hath showed me that he shall surely die. 11 And he settled his countenance stedfastly, until he was ashamed: and the man of God wept. 12 And Hazael said, Why weepeth my lord? And he answered, Because I know the evil that thou wilt do unto the children of Israel: their strong holds wilt thou set on fire, and their young men wilt thou slay with the sword, and wilt dash their children, and rip up their women with child. 13 And Hazael said, But what, *is* thy servant a dog, that he should do this great thing? And Elisha answered, The LORD hath showed me that thou *shalt be* king over Syria. 14 So he departed from Elisha, and came to his master; who said to him, What said Elisha to thee? And he answered, He told me, *that* thou shouldest surely recover. 15 And it came to pass on the morrow, that he took a thick cloth, and dipped *it* in water, and spread *it* on his face, so that he died: and Hazael reigned in his stead.

Here, I. We may enquire what brought Elisha to Damascus, the chief city of Syria. Was he sent to any but the *lost sheep of the house of Israel?* It seems he was. Perhaps he went to pay a visit to Naaman his convert, and to confirm him in his choice of the true religion, which was the more needful now because, it should seem, he was now out of his place (for Hazael is supposed to be captain of the host); either he resigned it or was turned out of it, because he would not bow, or not bow heartily, in the house of Rimmon. Some think he went to Damascus upon account of the famine, or rather he went thither in obedience to the orders God gave Elijah, 1 Kings xix. 15, "*Go to Damascus to anoint Hazael,* thou, or thy successor."

II. We may observe that Ben-hadad, a great king, rich and mighty, lay sick. No honour, wealth, or power, will secure men from the common diseases and disasters of human life; palaces and thrones lie as open to the arrests of sickness and death as the meanest cottage.

III. We may wonder that the king of Syria, in his sickness, should make Elisha his oracle.

1. Notice was soon brought him that *the man of God* (for by that title he was well known in Syria since he cured Naaman) had come to Damascus, *v.* 7. "Never in better time," says Ben-hadad. "*Go, and enquire of the Lord by him.*" In his health he *bowed in the house of Rimmon,* but now that he is sick he distrusts his idol, and sends to enquire of the God of Israel. Affliction brings those to God who in their prosperity had made light of him; sometimes sickness opens men's eyes and rectifies their mistakes. This is the more observable, (1.) Because it was not long since a king of Israel had, in his sickness, sent to enquire of the god of Ekron (*ch.* i. 2), as if there had been no God in Israel. Note, God sometimes fetches to himself that honour from strangers which is denied him and alienated from him by his own professing people. (2.) Because it was not long since this Ben-hadad had sent a great force to treat Elisha as an enemy (*ch.* vi. 14), yet now he courts him as a prophet. Note, Among other instances of the change of men's minds by sickness and affliction, this is one, that it often gives them other thoughts of God's ministers, and teaches them to value the counsels and prayers of those whom they had hated and despised.

2. To put an honour upon the prophet, (1.) He sends *to* him, and does not send *for* him, as if, with the centurion, he thought himself not worthy that the man of God should come under his roof. (2.) He sends to him by Hazael, his prime-minister of state, and not by a common messenger. It is no disparagement to the greatest of men to attend the prophets of the Lord. Hazael must go and meet him at the place where he had appointed a meeting with his friends. (3.) He sends him a noble present, *of every good thing of Damascus,* as much as loaded forty camels (*v.* 9), testifying hereby his affection to the prophet, bidding him welcome to Damascus, and providing for his sustenance while he sojourned there. It is probable that Elisha accepted it (why should he not?), though he refused Naaman's. (4.) He orders Hazael to call him *his son Ben-hadad,* conforming to the language of Israel, who called the prophets *fathers.* (5.) He puts an honour upon him as one acquainted with the secrets of heaven, when he enquires of him, *Shall I recover?* It is natural to us to desire to know things to come in time, while things to come in eternity are little thought of or enquired after.

IV. What passed between Hazael and Elisha is especially remarkable.

1. Elisha answered his enquiry concerning the king, that he might recover, the disease was not mortal, but that he should die an-

other way (*v.* 10), not a natural but a violent death. There are many ways out of the world, and sometimes, while men think to avoid one, they fall by another.

2. He looked Hazael in the face with an unusual concern, till he made Hazael blush and himself weep, *v.* 11. The man of God could outface the man of war. It was not in Hazael's countenance that Elisha read what he would do, but God did, at this time, reveal it to him, and it fetched tears from his eyes. The more foresight men have the more grief they are liable to.

3. When Hazael asked him why he wept he told him what a great deal of mischief he foresaw he would do to the Israel of God (*v.* 12), what desolations he would make of their strong-holds, and barbarous destruction of their men, women, and children. The sins of Israel provoked God to give them up into the hands of their cruel enemies, yet Elisha wept to think that ever Israelites should be thus abused; for, though he foretold, he did not desire the woeful day. See what havock war makes, what havock sin makes, and how the nature of man is changed by the fall, and stripped even of humanity itself.

4. Hazael was greatly surprised at this prediction (*v.* 13): *What,* says he, *Is thy servant a dog, that he should do this great thing?* This great thing he looks upon to be, (1.) An act of great power, not to be done but by a crowned head. "It must be some mighty potentate that can think to prevail thus against Israel, and therefore not I." Many are raised to that dominion which they never thought of and it often proves *to their own hurt,* Eccl. viii. 9. (2.) An act of great barbarity, which could not be done but by one lost to all honour and virtue: "Therefore," says he, "it is what I shall never find in my heart to be guilty of: *Is thy servant a dog,* to rend, and tear, and devour? Unless I were a dog, I could not do it." See here, [1.] What a bad opinion he had of the sin; he looked upon it to be great wickedness, fitter for a brute, for a beast of prey, to do than a man. Note, It is possible for a wicked man, under the convictions and restraints of natural conscience, to express great abhorrence of a sin, and yet afterwards to be well reconciled to it. [2.] What a good opinion he had of himself, how much better than he deserved; he thought it impossible he should do such barbarous things as the prophet foresaw. Note, We are apt to think ourselves sufficiently armed against those sins which yet we are afterwards overcome by, as Peter, Matt. xxvi. 35.

5. In answer to this Elisha only told him *he should be king over Syria;* then he would have power to do it, and then he would find in his heart to do it. *Honours change men's tempers and manners,* and seldom for the better: "Thou knowest not what thou wilt do when thou comest to be king, but I tell thee this thou wilt do." Those that are little and low in the world cannot imagine how strong the temptations of power and prosperity are, and, if ever they arrive at them, they will find how deceitful their hearts were and how much worse than they suspected.

V. What mischief Hazael did to his master hereupon. If he took any occasion to do it from what Elisha had said the fault was in him, not in the word. 1. He basely cheated his master, and belied the prophet (*v.* 14): *He told me thou shouldst certainly recover.* This was abominably false; he told him he should die (*v.* 10), but he unfairly and unfaithfully concealed that, either because he was loth to put the king out of humour with bad news or because hereby he might the more effectually carry on that bloody design which he conceived when he was told he should be his successor. The devil ruins men by telling them they shall certainly recover and do well, so rocking them asleep in security, than which nothing is more fatal. This was an injury to the king, who lost the benefit of this warning to prepare for death, and an injury to Elisha, who would be counted a false prophet. 2. He barbarously murdered his master, and so made good the prophet's word, *v.* 15. He dipped a thick cloth in cold water, and spread it upon his face, under pretence of cooling and refreshing him, but so that it stopped his breath, and stifled him presently, he being weak (and not able to help himself) or perhaps asleep: such a bubble is the life of the greatest of men, and so much exposed are princes to violence. Hazael, who was Ben-hadad's confidant, was his murderer, and, some think, was not suspected, nor did the truth ever come out but by the pen of this inspired historian. We found this haughty monarch (1 Kings xx.) *the terror of the mighty in the land of the living,* but he *goes down slain to the pit* with *his iniquity upon his bones,* Ezek. xxxii. 27.

16 And in the fifth year of Joram the son of Ahab king of Israel, Jehoshaphat *being* then king of Judah, Jehoram the son of Jehoshaphat king of Judah began to reign. 17 Thirty and two years old was he when he began to reign; and he reigned eight years in Jerusalem. 18 And he walked in the way of the kings of Israel, as did the house of Ahab: for the daughter of Ahab was his wife: and he did evil in the sight of the LORD. 19 Yet the LORD would not destroy Judah for David his servant's sake, as he promised him to give him alway a light, *and* to his children. 20 In his days Edom revolted from

under the hand of Judah, and made a king over themselves. 21 So Joram went over to Zair, and all the chariots with him: and he rose by night, and smote the Edomites which compassed him about, and the captains of the chariots: and the people fled into their tents. 22 Yet Edom revolted from under the hand of Judah unto this day. Then Libnah revolted at the same time. 23 And the rest of the acts of Joram, and all that he did, *are* they not written in the book of the chronicles of the kings of Judah? 24 And Joram slept with his fathers, and was buried with his fathers in the city of David: and Ahaziah his son reigned in his stead.

We have here a brief account of the life and reign of Jehoram (or Joram), one of the worst of the kings of Judah, but the son and successor of Jehoshaphat, one of the best. Note, 1. Parents cannot give grace to their children. Many that have themselves been godly have had the grief and shame of seeing those that came forth out of their bowels wicked and vile. Let not the families that are thus afflicted think it strange. 2. If the children of good parents prove wicked, commonly they are worse than others. The unclean spirit brings in seven others more wicked than himself, Luke xi. 26. 3. A nation is sometimes justly punished with the miseries of a bad reign for not improving the blessings and advantages of a good one.

Concerning this Jehoram observe,

I. The general idea here given of his wickedness (*v.* 18): *He did as the house of Ahab,* and worse he could not do. His character is taken from the bad example he followed, for men are according to the company they converse with and the copies they write after. No mistake is more fatal to young people than a mistake in the choice of those whom they would recommend themselves to and take their measures from, and whose good opinion they value themselves by. Jehoram chose the house of Ahab for his pattern rather than his father's house, and this choice was his ruin. We have a particular account of his wickedness (2 Chron. xxi.), murder, idolatry, persecution, every thing that was bad.

II. The occasions of his wickedness. His father was a very good man, and no doubt took care to have him taught the good knowledge of the Lord, but, 1. It is certain he did ill to marry him to the daughter of Ahab; no good could come of an alliance with an idolatrous family, but all mischief with such a daughter of such a mother as Athaliah the daughter of Jezebel. The degeneracy of the old world took rise from the unequal yoking of professors with profane. Those that are ill-matched are already half-ruined. 2. I doubt he did not do well to make him king in his own life-time. It is said here (*v.* 16) that he *began to reign, Jehoshaphat being then king;* hereby he gratified his pride (than which nothing is more pernicious to young people), indulged him in his ambition, in hopes to reform him by humouring him, and so brought a curse upon his family, as Eli did, *whose sons made themselves vile and he restrained them not.* Jehoshaphat had made this wicked son of his viceroy once when he went with Ahab to Ramoth-Gilead, from which Jehoshaphat's seventeenth year (1 Kings xxii. 51) is made Jehoram's second (2 Kings i. 17), but afterwards, in his twenty-second year, he made him partner in his government, and thence Joram's eight years are to be dated, three years before his father's death. It has been hurtful to many young men to come too soon to their estates. Samuel got nothing by *making his sons judges.*

III. The rebukes of Providence which he was under for his wickedness. 1. The Edomites revolted, who had been under the government of the kings of Judah ever since David's time, about 150 years, *v.* 20. He attempted to reduce them, and gave them a defeat (*v.* 21), but he could not improve the advantage he had got, so as to recover his dominion over them: *Yet Edom revolted* (*v.* 22), and the Edomites were, after this, bitter enemies to the Jews, as appears by the prophecy of Obadiah and Ps. cxxxvii. 7. Now Isaac's prophecy was fulfilled, that this Esau the elder should serve Jacob the younger; yet, in process of time, he should *break that yoke from off his neck,* Gen. xxvii. 40. 2. Libnah revolted. This was a city in Judah, in the heart of his country, a priests' city; the inhabitants of this city shook off his government *because he had forsaken God,* and would have compelled them to do so too, 2 Chron. xxi. 10, 11. In order that they might preserve their religion they set up for a free state. Perhaps other cities did the same. 3. His reign was short. God cut him off in the midst of his days, when he was but forty years old, and had reigned but eight years. *Bloody and deceitful men shall not live out half their days.*

IV. The gracious care of Providence for the keeping up of the kingdom of Judah, and the house of David, notwithstanding the apostasies and calamities of Jehoram's reign (*v.* 19): *Yet the Lord would not destroy Judah.* He could easily have done it; he might justly have done it; it would have been no loss to him to have done it; yet he would not do it, for David's sake, not for the sake of any merit of his which could challenge this favour to his family as a debt, but for the sake of a promise made to him that he should always have a lamp (that is, a succession of kings from one generation to another, by which his name should be kept bright and illustrious, as a lamp is kept burning by a constant fresh supply of oil), that his family should never be extinct till it terminated in the Messiah, that Son of David on whom was to be *hung all the glory of his Father's house* and in whose everlasting kingdom that promise to David is fulfilled (Ps. cxxxii. 17), *I have ordained a lamp for my anointed.*

V. The conclusion of this impious and inglorious reign, *v.* 23, 24. Nothing peculiar is here said of him; but we are told (2 Chron. xxi. 19, 20) that he *died of sore diseases* and *died without being desired.*

25 In the twelfth year of Joram the son of Ahab king of Israel did Ahaziah the son of Jehoram king of Judah begin to reign. 26 Two and twenty years old *was* Ahaziah when he began to reign; and he reigned one year in Jerusalem. And his mother's name *was* Athaliah, the daughter of Omri king of Israel. 27 And he walked in the way of the house of Ahab, and did evil in the sight of the LORD, as *did* the house of Ahab: for he *was* the son in law of the house of Ahab. 28 And he went with Joram the son of Ahab to the war against Hazael king of Syria in Ramoth-gilead; and the Syrians wounded Joram. 29 And king Joram went back to be healed in Jezreel of the wounds which the Syrians had given him at Ramah, when he fought against Hazael king of Syria. And Ahaziah the son of Jehoram king of Judah went down to see Joram the son of Ahab in Jezreel, because he was sick.

As among common persons there are some that we call *little men*, who make no figure, are little regarded, and less valued, so among kings there are some whom, in comparison with others, we may call *little kings.* This Ahaziah was one of these; he looks mean in the history, and in God's account vile, because wicked. It is too plain an evidence of the affinity between Jehoshaphat and Ahab that they had the same names in their families at the same time, in which, we may suppose, they designed to compliment one another. Ahab had two sons, Ahaziah and Jehoram, who reigned successively; Jehoshaphat had a son and grandson named Jehoram and Ahaziah, who, in like manner, reigned successively. Names indeed do not make natures, but it was a bad omen to Jehoshaphat's family to borrow names from Ahab's; or, if he lent the names to that wretched family, he could not communicate with them the devotion of their significations, *Ahaziah—Taking hold of the Lord,* and *Jehoram—The Lord exalted.* Ahaziah king of Israel had reigned but two years, Ahaziah king of Judah reigned but one. We are here told that his relation to Ahab's family was the occasion, 1. Of his wickedness (*v.* 27): *He walked in the way of the house of Ahab,* that idolatrous bloody house; for his mother was Ahab's daughter (*v.* 26), so that he sucked in wickedness with his milk. *Partus sequitur ventrem—The child may be expected to resemble the mother.* When men choose wives for themselves they must remember they are choosing mothers for their children, and are concerned to choose accordingly. 2. Of his fall. Joram, his mother's brother, courted him to join with him for the recovery of Ramoth-Gilead, an attempt fatal to Ahab; so it was to Joram his son, for in that expedition he was wounded (*v.* 28), and returned to Jezreel to be cured, leaving his army there in possession of the place. Ahaziah likewise returned, but went to Jezreel to see how Jehoram did, *v.* 29. Providence so ordered it, that he who had been debauched by the house of Ahab might be cut off with them, when the measure of their iniquity was full, as we shall find in the next chapter. Those who partake with sinners in their sins must expect to partake with them in their plagues.

CHAP. IX.

Hazael and Jehu were the men that were designed to be the instruments of God's justice in punishing and destroying the house of Ahab. Elijah was told to appoint them to this service; but, upon Ahab's humiliation, a reprieve was granted, and so it was left to Elisha to appoint them. Hazael's elevation to the throne of Syria we read of in the foregoing chapter; and we must now attend Jehu to the throne of Israel; for him that escapeth the sword of Hazael, as Joram and Ahaziah did, Jehu must slay, of which this chapter gives us an account. I. A commission is sent to Jehu by the hand of one of the prophets, to take upon him the government, and destroy the house of Ahab, ver. 1—10. II. Here is his speedy execution of this commission. 1. He communicates it to his captains, ver. 11–15. 2. He marches directly to Jezreel (ver. 16—20), and there dispatches, (1.) Joram king of Israel, ver. 21—26. (2.) Ahaziah king of Judah, ver. 27—29. (3.) Jezebel, ver. 30–37.

AND Elisha the prophet called one of the children of the prophets, and said unto him, Gird up thy loins, and take this box of oil in thine hand, and go to Ramoth-gilead: 2 And when thou comest thither, look out there Jehu the son of Jehoshaphat the son of Nimshi, and go in, and make him arise up from among his brethren, and carry him to an inner chamber; 3 Then take the box of oil, and pour *it* upon his head, and say, Thus saith the LORD, I have anointed thee king over Israel. Then open the door, and flee, and tarry not. 4. So the young man, *even* the young man the prophet, went to Ramoth-gilead. 5 And when he came, behold, the captains of the hosts *were* sitting; and he said, I have an errand to thee, O captain. And Jehu said, Unto which of all us? And he said, To thee, O captain. 6 And he arose, and went into the house; and he poured the oil on his head, and said unto him, Thus saith the LORD God of Israel, I have anointed thee king over the people of the LORD, *even* over Israel. 7 And thou shalt smite the house of Ahab thy master, that I may avenge the blood of my servants the prophets, and the blood of all the servants of the LORD, at the hand of Jezebel. 8 For the whole house of Ahab shall perish: and I will cut off from Ahab him that pisseth against the wall, and him that is shut up and left in Israel: 9 And I will make the house of Ahab like the house of Jeroboam the son of Nebat, and like the house of Baasha the son of Ahijah: 10 And the dogs shall eat Jezebel in the portion of Jezreel, and *there shall be* none to bury *her*. And he opened the door, and fled.

We have here the anointing of Jehu to be king, who was, at this time, a commander (probably commander-in-chief) of the forces employed at Ramoth-Gilead, *v.* 14. There he was fighting for the king his master, but received orders from a higher king to fight against him. It does not appear that Jehu aimed at the government, or that he ever thought of it, but the commission given him was a perfect surprise to him. Some think that he had been anointed before by Elijah, whom God ordered to do it, but privately, and with an intimation that he must not act till further orders, as Samuel anointed David long before he was to come to the throne: but that is not at all probable, for then we must suppose Elijah had anointed Hazael too. No, when God bade him do these things he bade him anoint Elisha to *be prophet in his room*, to do them when he was gone, as God should direct him.. Here is,

I. The commission sent.

1. Elisha did not go himself to anoint Jehu, because he was old and unfit for such a journey and so well known that he could not do it privately, could not go and come without observation; therefore he sends *one of the sons of the prophets* to do it, *v.* 1. They not only reverenced him as their father (*ch.* ii. 15), but observed and obeyed him as their father. This service of anointing Jehu, (1.) Had danger in it (1 Sam. xvi. 2), and therefore it was not fit that Elisha should expose himself, but one of the sons of the prophets, whose life was of less value, and who could do it with less danger. (2.) It required labour and was therefore fitter for a young man in his full strength. Let youth work and age direct. (3.) Yet it was an honourable piece of service, to anoint a king, and he that did it might hope to be preferred for it afterwards, and therefore, for the encouragement of the young prophets, Elisha employed one of them: he would not engross all the honours to himself, nor grudge the young prophets a share in them

2. When he sent him, (1.) He put the oil into his hand with which he must anoint Jehu: *Take this box of oil.* Solomon was anointed with *oil out of the tabernacle,* 1 Kings i. 39. That could not now be had, but oil from a prophet's hand was equivalent to oil out of God's house. Probably it was not the constant practice to anoint kings, but upon the disturbance of the succession, as in the case of Solomon, or the interruption of it, as in the case of Joash (*ch.* xi. 12), or the translation of the government to a new family, as here and in the case of David; yet it might be used generally, though the scripture does not mention it. (2.) He put *the words into his mouth* which he must say (*v.* 3)—*I have anointed thee king,* and, no doubt, told him all the rest that he said, *v.* 7—10. Those whom God sends on his errands shall not go without full instructions. (3.) He also ordered him, [1.] To do it privately, to single out Jehu from the rest of the captains and anoint him *in an inner chamber* (*v.* 2), that Jehu's confidence in his commission might be tried, when he had no witness to attest it. His being suddenly animated for the service would be proof sufficient of his being anointed to it. There needed no other proof. The thing signified was the best evidence of the sign. [2.] To do it expeditiously. When he went about it he must *gird up his loins;* when he had done it he must *flee and not tarry* for a fee, or a treat, or to see what Jehu would do. It becomes the sons of the prophets to be quick and lively at their work, to go about it and go through it as men that hate sauntering and trifling. They should be as angels that fly swiftly.

II. The commission delivered. The young prophet did his business with despatch, was at Ramoth-Gilead presently, *v.* 4. There he found the general officers sitting together, either at dinner or in a council of war, *v.* 5. With the assurance that became a messenger from God, notwithstanding the meanness of his appearance, he called Jehu out from the rest, not waiting his leisure, or begging his pardon for disturbing him, but as one having authority: *I have an errand to thee, O captain.* Perhaps Jehu had some intimation of his business; and therefore, that he might not seem too forward to catch at the honour, he asked, *To which of all us?* that it might not be said afterwards he got it by speaking first, but they might all be satisfied he was indeed the person designed. When the prophet had him alone he anointed him, *v.* 6. The anointing of the Spirit is a hidden thing, that new name which none knows but those that have it. Herewith,

1. He invests him with the royal dignity: *Thus saith the Lord God of Israel,* whose messenger I am, in his name *I have anointed thee king over the people of the Lord.* He gives him an incontestable title, but reminds him that he was made king, (1.) *By the God of Israel;* from him he must see his power derived (for by him king sreign), for him he must use it, and to him he must be accountable. Magistrates are the ministers of God, and must therefore act in dependence upon him and with an entire devotedness to him and to his glory. (2.) *Over the Israel of God.* Though the people of Israel were wretchedly corrupted, and had forfeited all the honour of relationship to God, yet they are here called the *people of the Lord,* for he had a right to them and had not yet given them a bill of divorce. Jehu must look upon the people he was made king of as the *people of the Lord,* not as his vassals, but God's freemen, his sons, his first-born, not to be abused or tyrannized over, *God's people,* and therefore to be ruled for him, and according to his laws.

2. He instructs him in his present service, which was to destroy all the house of Ahab (*v.* 7), not that he might clear his own way to the throne, and secure to himself the possession of it, but that he might execute the judgments of God upon that guilty and obnoxious family. He calls Ahab his *master,* that the relation might be no objection. "He was thy master, and to lift up thy hand against his son and successor would be not only base ingratitude, but treason, rebellion, and all that is bad, if thou hadst not an immediate command from God to do it. But thou art under higher obligations to thy Master in heaven than to thy master Ahab. He has determined that *the whole house of Ahab shall perish,* and *by thy hand;* fear not: has not he commanded thee? Fear not sin; his command will justify thee and bear thee out: fear not danger; his command will secure and prosper thee." That he might intelligently, and in a right manner, do this great execution on the house of Ahab, he tells him, (1.) What was their crime, what the ground of the controversy, and wherefore God had this quarrel with them, that he might have an eye to that which God had an eye to, and that was *the blood of God's servants, the prophets* and others, faithful worshippers, which they had shed, and which must now be required at the hand of Jezebel. That they were idolaters was bad enough, and merited all that was brought upon them; yet that is not mentioned here, but the controversy God has with them is for their being persecutors, not so much their *throwing down God's altars* as their *slaying his prophets with the sword.* Nothing fills the measure of the iniquity of any prince or people as this does nor brings a surer or a sorer ruin. This was the sin that brought on Jerusalem its first destruction (2 Chron. xxxvi. 16) and its final one, Matt. xxiii. 37, 38. Jezebel's whoredoms and witchcrafts were not so provoking as her persecuting the prophets, killing some and driving the rest into corners and caves, 1 Kings xviii. 4. (2.) What was their doom. They were sentenced to utter destruction; not to be corrected, but to be cut off and rooted out. This Jehu must know, that his eye might not spare for pity, favour, or affection. All that belonged to Ahab must be slain, *v.* 8. A pattern is given him of the destruction intended, in the destruction of the families of Jeroboam and Baasha (*v.* 9), and he is particularly directed to throw Jezebel to the dogs, *v.* 10. The whole stock of royal blood was little enough, and too little, to atone for the blood of the prophets, the saints and martyrs, which, in God's account, is of great price.

The prophet, having done this errand, made the best of his way home again, and left Jehu alone to consider what he had to do and beg direction from God.

11 Then Jehu came forth to the servants of his lord: and *one* said unto him, *Is* all well? wherefore came this mad *fellow* to thee? And he said unto them, Ye know the man, and his communication. 12 And they said, *It is* false; tell us now. And he said, Thus and thus spake he to me, saying, Thus saith the LORD, I have anointed thee king over Israel. 13 Then they hasted, and took every man his garment, and put *it* under him on the top of the stairs, and blew with trumpets, saying, Jehu is king. 14 So Jehu the son of Jehoshaphat the son of Nimshi conspired against Joram. (Now Joram had kept Ramoth-gilead, he and all Israel, because of Hazael king of Syria. 15 But king Joram was returned to be healed in Jezreel of the wounds which the Syrians had given him, when he fought with Hazael king of Syria.) And Jehu said, If it be your minds, *then* let none go forth *nor* escape out of the city to go to tell *it* in Jezreel.

Jehu, after some pause, returned to his place at the board, taking no notice of what had passed, but, as it should seem, designing, for the present, to keep it to himself, if they had not urged him to disclose it. Let us therefore see what passed between him and the captains.

I. With what contempt the captains speak

of the young prophet (*v.* 11): "*Wherefore came this mad fellow to thee?* What business had he with thee? And why wouldst thou humour him so far as to retire for conversation with him? Are prophets company for captains?" They called him *a mad fellow*, because he was one of those that would not *run with them to an excess of riot* (1 Pet. iv. 4), but lived a life of self-denial, mortification, and contempt of the world, and spent their time in devotion; for these things they thought the prophets were fools and the *spiritual men were mad*, Hos. ix. 7. Note, Those that have no religion commonly speak with disdain of those that are religious, and look upon them as mad. They said of our Saviour, *He is beside himself*, of John Baptist, *He has a devil* (is a poor melancholy man), of St. Paul, *Much learning has made him mad.* The highest wisdom is thus represented as folly, and those that best understand themselves are looked upon as beside themselves. Perhaps Jehu intended it for a rebuke to his friends when he said, "*You know the man* to be a prophet, why then do you call him a mad fellow? You know the way of his communication to be not from madness, but inspiration." Or, "Being a prophet, you may guess what his business is, to tell me of my faults, and to teach me my duty; I need not inform you concerning it." Thus he thought to put them off, but they urged him to tell them. "It is false," say they, "we cannot conjecture what was his errand, and therefore tell us." Being thus pressed to it, he told them that the prophet had *anointed him king*, and it is probable showed them the oil upon his head, *v.* 12. He knew not but some of them, either out of loyalty to Joram or envy of him, might oppose him, and go near to crush his interest in its infancy; but he relied on the divine appointment, and was not afraid to own it, knowing whom he had trusted: he that raised him would stand by him.

II. With what respect they compliment the new king upon the first notice of his advancement, *v.* 13. How meanly soever they thought of the prophet that anointed him, and of his office, they expressed a great veneration for the royal dignity of him that was anointed, and were very forward to proclaim him with sound of trumpet. In token of their subjection and allegiance to him, their affection to his person and government, and their desire to see him high and easy in it, they put their garments under him, that he might stand or sit upon them *on the top of the stairs*, in sight of the soldiers, who, upon the first intimation, came together to grace the solemnity. God put it into their hearts thus readily to own him, for he turns the hearts of people as well as kings, like the rivers of water, into what channel he pleases. Perhaps they were disquieted at Joram's government, or had a particular affection for Jehu; or, however this might be, things it seems were ripe for the revolution, and they all came into Jehu's interest and *conspired against Joram*, *v.* 14.

III. With what caution Jehu proceeded. He had advantages against Joram, and he knew how to improve them. He had the army with him. Joram had left it, and had gone home badly wounded. Jehu's good conduct appears in two things:—1. That he complimented the captains, and would do nothing without their advice and consent ("If it be your minds, we will do so and so, else not"), thereby intimating the deference he paid to their judgment and the confidence he had in their fidelity, both which tended to please and fix them. It is the wisdom of those that would rise fast, and stand firm, to take their friends along with them. 2. That he contrived to surprise Joram; and, in order thereto, to come upon him with speed, and to prevent his having notice of what was now done: "*Let none go forth to tell it in Jezreel*, that, as a snare, the ruin may come on him and his house." The suddenness of an attack sometimes turns to as good an account as the force of it.

16 So Jehu rode in a chariot, and went to Jezreel; for Joram lay there. And Ahaziah king of Judah was come down to see Joram. 17 And there stood a watchman on the tower in Jezreel, and he spied the company of Jehu as he came, and said, I see a company. And Joram said, Take a horseman, and send to meet them, and let him say, *Is it* peace? 18 So there went one on horseback to meet him, and said, Thus saith the king, *Is it* peace? And Jehu said, What hast thou to do with peace? turn thee behind me. And the watchman told, saying, The messenger came to them, but he cometh not again. 19 Then he sent out a second on horseback, which came to them, and said, Thus saith the king, *Is it* peace? And Jehu answered, What hast thou to do with peace? turn thee behind me. 20 And the watchman told, saying, He came even unto them, and cometh not again: and the driving *is* like the driving of Jehu the son of Nimshi; for he driveth furiously. 21 And Joram said, Make ready. And his chariot was made ready. And Joram king of Israel and Ahaziah king of Judah went out, each in his chariot, and they went out against Jehu, and met him in the portion of Naboth the Jezreelite. 22 And it came to pass,

when Joram saw Jehu, that he said, *Is it* peace, Jehu? And he answered, What peace, so long as the whoredoms of thy mother Jezebel and her witchcrafts *are so* many? 23 And Joram turned his hands, and fled, and said to Ahaziah, *There is* treachery, O Ahaziah. 24 And Jehu drew a bow with his full strength, and smote Jehoram between his arms, and the arrow went out at his heart, and he sunk down in his chariot. 25 Then said *Jehu* to Bidkar his captain, Take up, *and* cast him in the portion of the field of Naboth the Jezreelite: for remember how that, when I and thou rode together after Ahab his father, the LORD laid this burden upon him; 26 Surely I have seen yesterday the blood of Naboth, and the blood of his sons, saith the LORD; and I will requite thee in this plat, saith the LORD. Now therefore take *and* cast him into the plat *of ground*, according to the word of the LORD. 27 But when Ahaziah the king of Judah saw *this*, he fled by the way of the garden house. And Jehu followed after him, and said, Smite him also in the chariot. *And they did so* at the going up to Gur, which *is* by Ibleam. And he fled to Megiddo, and died there. 28 And his servants carried him in a chariot to Jerusalem, and buried him in his sepulchre with his fathers in the city of David. 29 And in the eleventh year of Joram the son of Ahab began Ahaziah to reign over Judah.

From Ramoth-Gilead to Jezreel was more than one day's march; about the mid-way between them the river Jordan must be crossed. We may suppose Jehu to have marched with all possible expedition, and to have taken the utmost precaution to prevent the tidings from getting to Jezreel before him; and, at length, we have him within sight first, and then within reach, of the devoted king.

I. Joram's watchman discovers him first at a distance, him and his retinue, and gives notice to the king of the approach of a company, whether of friends or foes he cannot tell. But the king (impatient to know what is the matter, and perhaps jealous that the Syrians, who had wounded him, had traced him by the blood to his own palace, and were coming to seize him) sent first one messenger, and then another, to bring him intelligence, *v.* 17—19. He had scarcely recovered from the fright he was put into in the battle, and his guilty conscience put him into a continual terror. Each messenger asked the same question: "*Is it peace?* are you for us or for our adversaries? Do you bring good tidings or bad?" Each had the same answer: *What hast thou to do with peace? Turn thee behind me, v.* 18, 19. As if he had said, "It is not to thee, but to him that sent thee, that I will give answer; for thy part, if thou consult thy own safety, *turn thee behind me*, and enlist thyself among my followers." The watchman gave notice that the messengers were taken prisoners, and at length observed that the leader of this troop drove like Jehu, who it seems was noted for driving furiously, thereby discovering himself to be a man of a hot eager spirit, intent upon his business, and pushing forward with all his might. A man of such a violent temper was fittest for the service to which Jehu was designated. The wisdom of God is seen in the choice of proper instruments to be employed in his work. But it is not much for any man's reputation to be known by his fury. He that has rule over his own spirit is better than the mighty. The Chaldee paraphrase gives this a contrary sense: *The leading is like that of Jehu, for he leads quietly.* And, it should seem, he did not come up very fast, for then there would not have been time for all this that passed. And some think he chose to march slowly, that he might give Joram time to come out to him, and so dispatch him before he entered the city.

II. Joram himself goes out to meet him, and takes Ahaziah king of Judah along with him, neither of them equipped for war, as not expecting an enemy, but in haste to have their curiosity satisfied. How strangely has Providence sometimes ordered it, that men have been in haste to meet their ruin when their day has come to fall.

1. The place where Joram met Jehu was ominous: *In the portion of Naboth the Jezreelite, v.* 21. The very sight of that ground was enough to make Joram tremble and Jehu triumph; for Joram had the guilt of Naboth's blood fighting against him and Jehu had the force of Elijah's curse fighting for him. The circumstances of events are sometimes so ordered by divine Providence as to make the punishment answer to the sin as face answers to face in a glass.

2. Joram's demand was still the same: "*Is it peace, Jehu?* Is all well? Dost thou come home thus flying from the Syrians or more than a conqueror over them?" It seems, he looked for peace, and could not entertain any other thought. Note, It is very common for great sinners, even when they are upon the brink of ruin, to flatter themselves with an opinion that all is well with them, and to cry peace to themselves.

3. Jehu's reply was very startling. He

answered him with a question: *What peace* canst thou expect, *so long as the whoredoms of thy mother Jezebel* (who, though queen dowager, was in effect queen regent) *and her witchcrafts are so many?* See how plainly Jehu deals with him. Formerly he durst not do so, but now he had another spirit. Note, Sinners will not always be flattered; one time or other, they will have their own given them, Ps. xxxvi. 2. Observe, (1.) He charges upon him his mother's wickedness, because he had at first learned it and then with his kingly power protected it. She stands impeached for whoredom, corporal and spiritual (serving idols and serving them with the very acts of lewdness), for witchcraft likewise, enchantments and divinations, used in honour of her idols; and these multiplied, the whoredoms and the witchcrafts many; for those that abandon themselves to wicked courses know not where they will stop. One sin begets another. (2.) Upon that account he throws him off from all pretensions to peace: "What peace can come to that house in which there is so much wickedness unrepented of?" Note, The way of sin can never be the way of peace, Isa. lvii. 21. What peace can sinners have with God, what peace with their own consciences, what good, what comfort, can they expect in life, in death, or after death, who go on still in their trespasses? No peace so long as sin is persisted in; but, as soon as it is repented of and forsaken, there is peace.

4. The execution was done immediately. When Joram heard of his mother's crimes his heart failed him; he presently concluded the long-threatened day of reckoning had now come, and cried out, "*There is treachery, O Ahaziah!* Jehu is our enemy, and it is time for us to shift for our safety." Both fled, and, (1.) Joram king of Israel was slain presently, *v.* 24. Jehu dispatched him with his own hands. The bow was not drawn at a venture, as that which sent the fatal arrow through the joints of his father's harness, but Jehu directed the arrow between his shoulders as he fled (it was one of God's arrows which he *has ordained against the persecutor*, Ps. vii. 13), and it reached to his heart, so that he died upon the spot. He was now the top branch of Ahab's house, and therefore was first cut off. He died a criminal, under the sentence of the law, which Jehu, the executioner, pursues in the disposal of the dead body. Naboth's vineyard was hard by, which put him in mind of that circumstance of the doom Elijah passed upon Ahab, "*I will requite thee in this plat, said the Lord* (*v.* 25, 26), *for the blood of Naboth* himself, and *for the blood of his sons,*" who were either put to death with him as partners in his crime, or secretly murdered afterwards, lest they should bring an appeal, or find some way to avenge their father's death, or break their hearts for the loss of him, or (his whole estate being confiscated, as well as his vineyard) lose their livelihoods, which was in effect to lose their lives. For this the house of Ahab must be reckoned with; and that very piece of ground which he, with so much pride and pleasure, had made himself master of at the expense of the guilt of innocent blood, now became the theatre on which his son's dead body lay exposed a spectacle to the world. Thus *the Lord is known by the judgment which he executeth. Higgaion. Selah.* (2.) Ahaziah king of Judah was pursued, and slain in a little time, and not far off, *v.* 27, 28. [1.] Though he was now in Joram's company, he would not have been slain but that he was joined with the house of Ahab both in affinity and in iniquity. He was one of them (so he had made himself by his sins) and therefore he must fare as they fared. Jehu justly construed his commission as extending to them. Yet, [2.] Perhaps he would not at this time have fallen with them if he had not been found in company with them. It is a dangerous thing to associate with evil-doers; we may be entangled both in guilt and misery by it.

30 And when Jehu was come to Jezreel, Jezebel heard *of it;* and she painted her face, and tired her head, and looked out at a window. 31 And as Jehu entered in at the gate, she said, *Had* Zimri peace, who slew his master? 32 And he lifted up his face to the window, and said, Who *is* on my side? who? And there looked out to him two *or* three eunuchs. 33 And he said, Throw her down. So they threw her down: and *some* of her blood was sprinkled on the wall, and on the horses: and he trode her under foot. 34 And when he was come in, he did eat and drink, and said, Go, see now this cursed *woman*, and bury her: for she *is* a king's daughter. 35 And they went to bury her: but they found no more of her than the skull, and the feet, and the palms of *her* hands. 36 Wherefore they came again, and told him. And he said, This is the word of the LORD, which he spake by his servant Elijah the Tishbite, saying, In the portion of Jezreel shall dogs eat the flesh of Jezebel: 37 And the carcase of Jezebel shall be as dung upon the face of the field in the portion of Jezreel; *so* that they shall not say, This *is* Jezebel.

The greatest delinquent in the house of Ahab was Jezebel: it was she that introduced Baal, slew the Lord's prophets, contrived the murder of Naboth, stirred up her husband first, and then her sons, to do wickedly; a *cursed woman* she is here called (*v.* 34), a curse to the country, and whom all that wished well to their country had a curse for. Three reigns her reign had lasted, but now, at length, her day had come to fall. We read of a false prophetess in the church of Thyatira that is compared to Jezebel, and called by her name (Rev. ii. 20), her wickedness the same, seducing God's servants to idolatry, a long *space given her to repent* (*v.* 21) as to Jezebel, and a fearful ruin brought upon her at last (*v.* 22, 23), as here upon Jezebel. So that Jezebel's destruction may be looked upon as typical of the destruction of idolaters and persecutors, especially that great whore, that mother of harlots, that hath made herself *drunk with the blood of saints* and the nations *drunk with the wine of her fornications*, when God shall put it into the heart of the kings of the earth to hate her, Rev. xvii. 5, 6, 16. Now here we have,

I. Jezebel daring the judgment. She heard that Jehu had slain her son, and slain him for her whoredoms and witchcrafts, and thrown his dead body into the portion of Naboth, according to the word of the Lord, and that he was now coming to Jezreel, where she could not but expect herself to fall next a sacrifice to his revenging sword. Now see how she meets her fate; she posted herself in a window at the entering of the gate, to affront Jehu and set him at defiance. 1. Instead of hiding herself, as one afraid of divine vengeance, she exposed herself to it and scorned to flee, mocked at fear and was not affrighted. See how a heart hardened against God will brave it out to the last, *run upon him, even upon his neck*, Job xv. 26. But never did any thus harden their hearts against him and prosper. 2. Instead of humbling herself, and putting herself into close mourning for her son, she *painted her face, and tired her head*, that she might appear like herself, that is (as she thought), great and majestic, hoping thereby to daunt Jehu, to put him out of countenance, and to stop his career. *The Lord God called to baldness and girding with sackcloth*, but behold painting and dressing, walking contrary to God, Isa. xxii. 12, 13. There is not a surer presage of ruin than an unhumbled heart under humbling providences. Let painted faces look in Jezebel's glass, and see how they like themselves. 3. Instead of trembling before Jehu, the instrument of God's vengeance, she thought to make him tremble with that threatening question, *Had Zimri peace, who slew his master?* Observe, (1.) She took no notice of the hand of God gone out against her family, but flew in the face of him that was only the sword in his hand. We are very apt, when we are in trouble, to break out into a passion against the instruments of our trouble, when we ought to be submissive to God and angry at ourselves only. (2.) She pleased herself with the thought that what Jehu was now doing would certainly end in his own ruin, and that he would not have peace in it. He had cut her off from all pretensions to peace (*v.* 22), and now she thought to cut him off likewise. Note, It is no new thing for those that are doing God's work to be looked upon as out of the way of peace. Active reformers, faithful reprovers, are threatened with trouble; but let them be in nothing terrified, Phil. i. 28. (3.) She quoted a precedent, to deter him from the prosecution of this enterprise: "*Had Zimri peace?* No, he had not; he came to the throne by blood and treachery, and within seven days was constrained to burn the palace over his head and himself in it: and canst thou expect to fare any better?" Had the case been parallel, it would have been proper enough to give him this memorandum; for the judgments of God upon those that have gone before us in any sinful way should be warnings to us to take heed of treading in their steps. But the instance of Zimri was misapplied to Jehu. Zimri had no warrant for what he did, but was incited to it merely by his own ambition and cruelty; whereas Jehu was anointed by one of the sons of the prophets, and did this by order from heaven, which would bear him out. In comparing persons and things we must carefully distinguish between the precious and the vile, and take heed lest from the fate of sinful men we read the doom of useful men.

II. Jehu demanding aid against her. He looked up to the window, not daunted at the menaces of her impudent but impotent rage, and cried, *Who is on my side? Who? v.* 32. He was called out to do God's work, in reforming the land and punishing those that had debauched it; and here he calls out for assistance in the doing of it, looked if there were any to help, any to uphold, Isa. lxiii. 5. He lifts up a standard, and makes proclamation, as Moses (Exod. xxxii. 26), *Who is on the Lord's side?* And the Psalmist (Ps. xciv. 16), *Who will rise up for me against the evil-doers?* Note, When reformation-work is set on foot, it is time to ask, "Who sides with it?"

III. Her own attendants delivering her up to his just revenge. Two or three chamberlains looked out to Jehu with such a countenance as encouraged him to believe they were on his side, and to them he called, not to seize or secure her till further orders, but immediately to throw her down, which was one way of stoning malefactors, casting them headlong from some steep place. Thus was vengeance taken on her for the stoning of Naboth. They threw her down, *v.* 33. If God's command would justify Jehu, his command would justify them. Perhaps they had a secret dislike of Jezebel's wickedness, and hated her, though they served her; or, it may be, she was barbarous and injurious to those about her, and they were pleased with this opportunity of being avenged on her; or, observing Jehu's success, they hoped thus to ingratiate themselves with him, and keep their places in his court. However it was, thus she was most shamefully put to death, dashed against the wall and the pavement, and then trodden on by the horses, which were all besmeared with her blood and brains. See the end of pride and cruelty, and say, *The Lord is righteous.*.

IV. The very dogs completing her shame and ruin, according to the prophecy. When Jehu had taken some refreshment in the palace, he bethought himself of showing so much respect to Jezebel's sex and quality as to bury her. As bad as she was, she was a daughter, a king's daughter, a king's wife, a king's mother: *Go and bury her, v.* 34. But, though he had forgotten what the prophet said (*v.* 10, *Dogs shall eat Jezebel*), God had not forgotten it. While he was eating and drinking, the dogs had devoured her dead body, the dogs that *went about the city* (Ps. lix. 6) and fed upon the carrion, so that there was nothing left but her bare skull (the painted face gone) and her feet and hands. The hungry dogs had no respect to the dignity of her extraction; a king's daughter was no more to them than a common person. When we pamper our bodies, and use them deliciously, let us think how vile they are, and that shortly they will be either a feast for worms under ground or beasts above ground. When notice was brought of this to Jehu, he remembered the threatening (1 Kings xxi. 23), *The dogs shall eat Jezebel by the wall of Jezreel.* Nothing should remain of her but the monuments of her infamy. She had been used to appear on public days in great state, and the cry was, "This is Jezebel. What a majestic port and figure! How great she looks!" But now it shall be said no more. We have often seen the wicked buried (Eccl. viii. 10), yet sometimes, as here, they have no burial, Eccl. vi. 3. Jezebel's name nowhere remained, but as stigmatized in sacred writ: they could not so much as say, "This is Jezebel's dust, This is Jezebel's grave," or "This is Jezebel's seed." Thus the name of the wicked shall rot—rot above ground.

CHAP. X.

We have in this chapter, I. A further account of Jehu's execution of his commission. He cut off, 1. All Ahab's sons, ver. 1—10. 2. All Ahab's kindred, ver. 11—14, 17. 3. Ahab's idolatry: his zeal against this he took Jonadab to be witness to (ver. 15, 16), summoned all the worshippers of Baal to attend (ver 18—23), and slew them all (ver. 24, 25), and then abolished that idolatry, ver. 26—28. II. A short account of the administration of his government. 1. The old idolatry of Israel, the worship of the calves, was retained, ver. 29—31. 2. This brought God's judgments upon them by Hazael, with which his reign concludes, ver. 32—36.

AND Ahab had seventy sons in Samaria. And Jehu wrote letters, and sent to Samaria, unto the rulers of Jezreel, to the elders, and to them that brought up Ahab's *children*, saying, 2 Now as soon as this letter cometh to you, seeing your master's sons *are* with you, and *there are* with you chariots and horses, a fenced city also, and armour; 3 Look even out the best and meetest of your master's sons, and set *him* on his father's throne, and fight for your master's house. 4 But they were exceedingly afraid, and said, Behold, two kings stood not before him: how then shall we stand? 5 And he that *was* over the house, and he that *was* over the city, the elders also, and the bringers up *of the children*, sent to Jehu, saying, We *are* thy servants, and will do all that thou shalt bid us; we will not make any king: do thou *that which is* good in thine eyes. 6 Then he wrote a letter the second time to them, saying, If ye *be* mine, and *if* ye will hearken unto my voice, take ye the heads of the men your master's sons, and come to me to Jezreel by to morrow this time. Now the king's sons, *being* seventy persons, *were* with the great men of the city, which brought them up. 7 And it came to pass, when the letter came to them, that they took the king's sons, and slew seventy persons, and put their heads in baskets, and sent him *them* to Jezreel. 8 And there came a messenger, and told him, saying, They have brought the heads of the king's sons. And he said, Lay ye them in two heaps at the entering in of the gate until the morning. 9 And it came to pass in the morning, that he went out, and stood, and said to all the people, Ye *be* righteous: behold, I conspired against my master, and slew him: but who slew all these? 10 Know now that there shall fall unto the earth nothing of the word of the LORD, which the LORD spake concerning the house of Ahab: for the LORD hath done *that* which he spake by his servant Elijah. 11 So Jehu slew all that remained of the house of Ahab in Jezreel, and all his great men, and his kinsfolks, and his priests, until he left him none remaining. 12 And he arose and departed, and came to Samaria. *And* as he *was* at the shearing house in the way, 13 Jehu met with the brethren of Ahaziah king of Judah, and said, Who *are* ye? And they answered, We *are* the brethren of Ahaziah; and we go down to salute the children of the king and the children of the queen. 14 And he said, Take them alive. And they took them alive, and slew them at the pit of the shearing house, *even* two and forty men; neither left he any of them.

We left Jehu in quiet possession of Jezreel, triumphing over Joram and Jezebel; and we must now attend his further motions. He knew the whole house of Ahab must be cut off, and therefore proceeded in this bloody work, and did not do it deceitfully, or by halves, Jer. xlviii. 10.

I. He got the heads of all the sons of Ahab cut off by their own guardians at Samaria. Seventy sons (or grandsons) Ahab had, Gideon's number, Judg. viii. 30. In such a number that bore his name his family was likely to be perpetuated, and yet it is extirpated all at once. Such a quiver full of arrows could not protect his house from divine vengeance. Numerous families, if vicious, must not expect to be long prosperous. These sons of Ahab were now at Samaria, a strong city, perhaps brought thither upon occasion of the war with Syria, as a place of safety, or upon notice of Jehu's insurrection; with them were the rulers of Jezreel, that is, the great officers of the court, who went to Samaria to secure themselves or to consult what was to be done. Those of them that were yet under tuition had their tutors with them, who were entrusted with their education in learning, agreeable to their birth and quality, but, it is to be feared, brought them up in the idolatries of their father's house and made them all worshippers of Baal. Jehu did not think fit to bring his forces to Samaria to destroy them, but, that the hand of God might appear the more remarkably in it, made their guardians their murderers. 1. He sent a challenge to their friends to stand by them, *v.* 2, 3. "You that are hearty well-wishers to the house of Ahab, and entirely in its interests, now is your time to appear for it. Samaria is a strong city; you are in possession of it; you have forces at command; you may choose out the likeliest person of all the royal family to head you; you know you are not tied to the eldest, unless he be *the best and meetest of your master's sons.* If you have any spirit in you, show it, and set one of them on his father's throne, and stand by him with your lives and fortunes." Not that he desired they should do this, or expected they would, but thus he upbraided them with their cowardice and utter inability to contest with the divine counsels. "Do if you dare, and see what will come of it." Those that have forsaken their religion have often, with it, lost both their sense and their courage, and deserve to be upbraided with it. 2. Hereby he gained from them a submission. They prudently reasoned with themselves: "*Behold, two kings stood not before him,* but fell as sacrifices to his rage; *how then shall we stand?*" *v.* 4. Therefore they sent him a surrender of themselves: "*We are thy servants,* thy subjects, and *will do all that thou shalt bid us,* right or wrong, and will set up nobody in competition with thee." They saw it was to no purpose to contend with him, and therefore it was their interest to submit to him. With much more reason may we thus argue ourselves into a subjection to the great God. Many kings and great men have fallen before his wrath, for their wickedness; and how then shall we stand? *Do we provoke the Lord to jealousy? Are we stronger than he?* No, we must either bend or break. 3. This was improved so far as to make them the executioners of those whom they had the tuition of (*v.* 6): *If you be mine, bring me the heads of your master's sons by to-morrow at this time.* Though he knew it must be done, and was loth to do it himself, one would think he could not expect they should do it. Could they betray such a trust? Could they be cruel to their master's sons? It seems, so low did they stoop in their adoration to the rising sun that they did it; they cut off the heads of those seventy princes, and sent them in baskets a present to Jehu, *v.* 7. Learn hence not to trust in a friend nor to put confidence in a guide not governed by conscience. One can scarcely expect that he who has been false to his God should ever be faithful to his prince. But observe God's righteousness in their unrighteousness. These elders of Jezreel had been wickedly obsequious to Jezebel's order for the murder of Naboth, 1 Kings xxi. 11. She gloried, it is likely, in the power she had over them; and now the same base spirit makes them as pliable to Jehu and as ready to obey his orders for the murder of Ahab's sons. Let none aim at arbitrary power, lest they be found rolling a stone which, some time or other, will return upon them. Princes that make their people slaves take the readiest way to make them rebels; and by forcing men's consciences, as Jezebel did, they lose their hold of them. When the separated heads were presented to Jehu, he slily upbraided those that were the executioners, yet owned the hand of God in it. (1.) He seems to blame those that had been the executioners of this vengeance. The heads were laid in two heaps at the gate, the proper place of judgment. There he acquitted the people before God and the world (*v.* 9, *You are righteous*), and, by what the rulers of Samaria had now done, comparatively acquitted himself: "I slew but one; they have slain all these: I did it by conspiracy and with design; they have done this merely in compliance and with an implicit obedience. Let not the people of Samaria, nor any of the friends of the house of Ahab, ever reproach me for what I have done, when their own elders, and the very guardians of the orphans, have done this." It is common for those who have done something base to attempt the mitigation of their own reproach by drawing others in to do something worse. But, (2.) He resolves all into the righteous judgment of God (*v.* 10): *The Lord hath done that which he spoke by Elijah.* God is not the author of any man's sin, but even by that which men do from bad principles God serves his own purposes and glorifies his own name; and he is righteous in that wherein men are unrighteous. When the Assyrian is made the *rod of God's anger,* and the instrument of his justice, *he meaneth not so, neither does his heart think so,* Isa. x. 7.

II. He proceeded to destroy all that remained of the house of Ahab, not only those that descended from him, but those that were in any relation to him, all the officers of his household, ministers of state, and those in command under him, called here his *great men* (*v.* 11), all his kinsfolks and acquaintance, who had been partners with him in his wickedness, and his priests, or domestic chaplains, whom he employed in his idolatrous services and who strengthened his hand that he should not turn from his evil way. Having done this in Jezreel, he did the same in Samaria (*v.* 17), *slew all that remained to Ahab in Samaria.* This was bloody work, and is not now, in any case, to be drawn into a precedent. Let the guilty suffer, but not the guiltless for their sakes. Perhaps such terrible destructions as these were intended as types of the final destruction of all the ungodly. God has a sword, bathed in heaven, which will come down upon the people of his curse, and *be filled with blood.* Isa. xxxiv. 5, 6. Then *his eye will not spare, neither will he pity.*

III. Providence bringing the brethren of Ahaziah in his way, as he was going on with this execution, he slew them likewise, *v.* 12—14. The brethren of Ahaziah were slain by the Arabians (2 Chron. xxii. 1), but these were the sons of his brethren, as it is there explained (*v.* 8), and they are said to be princes of Judah, and to minister to Ahaziah. Several things concurred to make them obnoxious to the vengeance Jehu was now executing. 1. They were branches of Ahab's house, being descended from Athaliah, and therefore fell within his commission. 2. They were tainted with the wickedness of the house of Ahab. 3. They were now going to make their court to the princes of the house of Ahab, to *salute the children of the king and the queen,* Joram and Jezebel, which showed that they were linked to them in affection as well as in affinity. These princes, forty-two in number, being appointed as sheep for the sacrifice, were slain with solemnity, *at the pit of the shearing-house. The Lord is known by these judgments which he executeth.*

15 And when he was departed thence, he lighted on Jehonadab the son of Rechab *coming* to meet him: and he saluted him, and said to him, Is thine heart right, as my heart *is* with thy heart? And Jehonadab answered, It is. If it be, give *me* thine hand. And he gave *him* his hand; and he took him up to him into the chariot. 16 And he said, Come with me, and see my zeal for the LORD. So they made him ride in his chariot. 17 And when he came to Samaria, he slew all that remained unto Ahab in Samaria, till he had destroyed him, according to the saying of the LORD, which he spake to Elijah. 18 And Jehu gathered all the people together, and said unto them, Ahab served Baal a little; *but* Jehu shall serve him much. 19 Now therefore call unto me all the prophets of Baal, all his servants, and all his priests; let none be wanting: for I have a great sacrifice *to do* to Baal; whosoever shall be wanting, he shall not live. But Jehu did *it* in subtlety, to the intent that he might destroy the worshippers of Baal. 20 And Jehu said, Proclaim a solemn assembly for Baal. And they proclaimed *it.* 21 And Jehu sent through all Israel: and all the worshippers of Baal came, so that there was not a man left that came not. And they came into the house of Baal; and the house of Baal was full from one end to another. 22 And he said unto him that *was* over the vestry, Bring forth vestments for all the worshippers of Baal. And he brought them forth vestments. 23 And Jehu went, and Jehonadab the son of Rechab, into the house of Baal, and said unto the worshippers of Baal, Search, and look that there be here with you none of the servants of the LORD, but the worshippers of Baal only. 24 And when they went in to offer sacrifices and burnt offerings, Jehu appointed fourscore men without, and said, *If* any of the men whom I

have brought into your hands escape, *he that letteth him go*, his life *shall be* for the life of him. 25 And it came to pass, as soon as he had made an end of offering the burnt offering, that Jehu said to the guard and to the captains, Go in, *and* slay them; let none come forth. And they smote them with the edge of the sword; and the guard and the captains cast *them* out, and went to the city of the house of Baal. 26 And they brought forth the images out of the house of Baal, and burned them. 27 And they brake down the image of Baal, and brake down the house of Baal, and made it a draught house unto this day. 28 Thus Jehu destroyed Baal out of Israel.

Jehu, pushing on his work, is here,

I. Courting the friendship of a good man, *Jehonadab the son of Rechab, v.* 15, 16. This Jehonadab, though mortified to the world and meddling little with the business of it (as appears by his charge to his posterity, which they religiously observed 300 years after, not to drink wine nor dwell in cities, Jer. xxxv. 6, &c.), yet, upon this occasion, went to meet Jehu, that he might encourage him in the work to which God had called him. The countenance of good men is a thing which great men, if they be wise, will value, and value themselves by. David prayed, *Let those that fear thee turn to me*, Ps. cxix. 79. This Jehonadab, though no prophet, priest, or Levite, no prince or ruler, was, we may suppose, very eminent for prudence and piety, and generally respected for that life of self-denial and devotion which he lived: Jehu, though a soldier, knew him and honoured him. He did not indeed think of sending for him, but when he met him (though it is likely he drove now as furiously as ever) he stopped to speak to him; and we are here told what passed between them. 1. Jehu saluted him; he *blessed him* (so the word is), paid him the respect and showed him the good-will that were due to so great an example of serious godliness. 2. Jehonadab assured him that he was sincerely in his interest and a hearty well-wisher to his cause. Jehu professed that *his heart was right with him*, that he had a true affection for his person and a veneration for the crown of his Nazariteship, and desired to know whether he had the same affection for him and satisfaction in that crown of royal dignity which God had put upon his head: *Is thy heart right?* a question we should often put to ourselves. "I make a plausible profession, have gained a reputation among men, but *is my heart right?* Am I sincere and inward with God?" Jehonadab gave him his word *(It is)*, and gave him his hand as a pledge of his heart, *yielded to him* (so giving the hand is rendered, 2 Chron. xxx. 8), concurred and covenanted with him, and owned him in the work both of revenge and of reformation he was now about. 3. Jehu took him up into his chariot and took him along with him to Samaria. He put some honour upon him, by taking him into the chariot with him (Jehonadab was not accustomed to ride in a chariot, much less with a king); but he received more honour from him, and from the countenance he gave to his present work. All sober people would think the better of Jehu when they saw Jehonadab in the chariot with him. This was not the only time in which the piety of some has been made to serve the policy of others, and designing men have strengthened themselves by drawing good men into their interests. Jehonadab is a stranger to the arts of fleshly wisdom, and has his *conversation in simplicity and godly sincerity;* and therefore, if Jehu be a servant of God and an enemy to Baal, he will be his faithful friend. "Come then" (says Jehu), "come with me, *and see my zeal for the Lord;* and then thou wilt see reason to espouse my cause." This is commonly taken as not well said by Jehu, and as giving cause to suspect that his heart was not right with God in what he did, and that the zeal he pretended for the Lord was really zeal for himself and his own advancement. For, (1). He boasted of it, and spoke as if God and man were mightily indebted to him for it. (2.) He desired it might be seen and taken notice of, like the Pharisees, who did all to be seen of men. An upright heart approves itself to God and covets no more than his acceptance. If we aim at the applause of men, and make their praise our highest end, we are upon a false bottom. Whether Jehu looked any further we cannot judge; however Jehonadab went with him, and, it is likely, animated and assisted him in the further execution of his commission (*v.* 17), destroying all Ahab's friends in Samaria. A man may hate cruelty and yet love justice, may be far from thirsting after blood and yet may *wash his feet in the blood of the wicked*, Ps. lviii. 10.

II. Contriving the destruction of all the worshippers of Baal. The service of Baal was the crying sin of the house of Ahab: that root of this idolatry was plucked up, but multitudes yet remained that were infected with it, and would be in danger of infecting others. The law of God was express, that they were to be put to death; but they were so numerous, and so dispersed throughout all parts of the kingdom, and perhaps so alarmed with Jehu's beginnings, that it would be a hard matter to find them all out and an endless task to prosecute and execute them one by one. Jehu's project therefore is to cut them all off together. 1. By a wile, by a fraud, he brought them together to the temple of Baal. He pretended he would worship Baal more than ever Ahab had done, *v.* 18. Perhaps he spoke this ironically, or to try the body of the people whether they would oppose such a resolution as this, and would resent his threatening to increase his predecessor's idolatries, as they did Rehoboam's threatening to increase his predecessor's exactions, and say, "If it be so, we have no part in Jehu, nor inheritance in the son of Nimshi." But it rather seems to have been spoken purposely to deceive the worshippers of Baal, and then it cannot be justified. The truth of God needs not any man's lie. He issued a proclamation, requiring the attendance of all the worshippers of Baal to join with him in a sacrifice to Baal (*v.* 19, 20), not only the prophets and priests, but all, throughout the kingdom, who worshipped Baal, who were not nearly so many as they had been in Elijah's time. Jehu's friends, we may suppose, were aware of what he designed, and were not offended at it; but the bigoted besotted Baalites began to think themselves very happy, and that now they should see golden days again. *Joram* had *put away the image of Baal, ch.* iii. 2. If Jehu will restore it, they have what they would have, and come up to Samaria with joy from all parts to celebrate the solemnity; and they are pleased to see the house of Baal crowded (*v.* 21), to see his priests in their vestments (*v.* 22), and themselves perhaps with some badges or other to notify their relation to Baal, for there were vestments for all his worshippers 2. He took care that none of the servants of the Lord should be among them, *v.* 23. This they took as a provision to preserve the worship of Baal from being profaned by strangers; but it was a wonder that they did not, by this, see themselves brought into a snare and discern a design upon them. No marvel if those that suffer themselves to be deceived by Baal (as all idolaters were by their idols), are deceived by Jehu to their destruction. 3. He gave order for the cutting of them all off, and Jehonadab joined with him therein, *v.* 23. When a strict search was made lest any of the servants of God should, either for company or curiosity, have got among them—lest any wheat should be mixed with those tares, and when eighty men were set to stand guard at all the avenues to Baal's temple, that none might escape (*v.* 24), then the guards were sent in to put them all to the sword and to *mingle their blood with their sacrifices*, in a way of just revenge, as they themselves had sometimes done, when, in their blind devotion, they *cut themselves with knives and lancets till the blood gushed out*, 1 Kings xviii. 28. This was accordingly done, and the doing of it, though seemingly barbarous, was, considering the nature of their crime, really righteous. *The Lord, whose name is jealous, is a jealous God.* 4. The idolaters being thus destroyed, the idolatry itself was utterly abolished. The buildings about the house of Baal (which were so many and so stately that they are here called a *city*), where Baal's priests and their families lived, were destroyed; all the little images, statues, pictures, or shrines, which beautified Baal's temple, with the great image of Baal himself, were brought out and burnt (*v.* 26, 27), and the temple of Baal was broken down, and made a dunghill, the common sink, or sewer, of the city, that the remembrance of it might be blotted out or made infamous. Thus was the worship of Baal quite destroyed, at least for the present, out of Israel, though it had once prevailed so far that there were but 7000 of all the thousands of Israel that had not bowed the knee to Baal, and those concealed. Thus will God destroy all the gods of the heathen, and, sooner or later, triumph over them all.

29 Howbeit *from* the sins of Jeroboam the son of Nebat, who made Israel to sin, Jehu departed not from after them, *to wit*, the golden calves that *were* in Beth-el, and that *were* in Dan. 30 And the LORD said unto Jehu, Because thou hast done well in executing *that which is* right in mine eyes, *and* hast done unto the house of Ahab according to all that *was* in mine heart, thy children of the fourth *generation* shall sit on the throne of Israel. 31 But Jehu took no heed to walk in the law of the LORD God of Israel with all his heart: for he departed not from the sins of Jeroboam, which made Israel to sin. 32 In those days the LORD began to cut Israel short: and Hazael smote them in all the coasts of Israel; 33 From Jordan eastward, all the land of Gilead, the Gadites, and the Reubenites, and the Manassites, from Aroer, which *is* by the river Arnon, even Gilead and Bashan. 34 Now the rest of the acts of Jehu, and all that he did, and all his might, *are* they not written in the book of the chronicles of the kings of Israel? 35 And Jehu slept with his fathers: and they buried him in Samaria. And Jehoahaz his son reigned in his stead. 36 And the time that Jehu reigned over Israel in Samaria *was* twenty and eight years.

Here is all the account of the reign of Jehu, though it continued twenty-eight years. The progress of it answered not to the glory of its beginning. We have here,

I. God's approbation of what Jehu had done. Many, it is probable, censured him as treacherous and barbarous—called him a rebel, a usurper, a murderer, and prognosticated ill concerning him, that a family thus raised would soon be ruined; but God said, *Well done* (*v.* 30), and then it signified little who said otherwise. 1. God pronounced that to be right which he had done. It is justly questionable whether he did it from a good principle and whether he did not take some false steps in the doing of it; and yet (says God), *Thou hast done well in executing that which is right in my eyes.* The extirpating of idolaters and idolatry was a thing right in God's eyes, for it is an iniquity he visits as surely and severely as any: it was *according to all that was in his heart,* all he desired, all he designed. Jehu went through with his work. 2. God promised him a reward, that his children of the fourth generation from him should *sit upon the throne of Israel.* This was more than what took place in any of the dignities or royal families of that kingdom; of the house of Ahab there were indeed four kings, Omri, Ahab, Ahaziah, and Joram, but the last two were brothers, so that it reached but to the third generation, and that whole family continued but about forty-five years in all, whereas Jehu's continued in four, besides himself, and in all about 120 years. Note, No services done for God shall go unrewarded.

II. Jehu's carelessness in what he was further to do. By this it appeared that his heart was not right with God, that he was partial in his reformation. 1. He did not put away all the evil. He departed from the sins of Ahab, but not from the sins of Jeroboam—discarded Baal, but adhered to the calves. The worship of Baal was indeed the greater evil, and more heinous in the sight of God, but the worship of the calves was a great evil, and true conversion is not only from gross sin, but from all sin—not only from false gods, but from false worships. The worship of Baal weakened and diminished Israel, and made them beholden to the Sidonians, and therefore he could easily part with that; but the worship of the calves was a politic idolatry, was begun and kept up for reasons of state, to prevent the return of the ten tribes to the house of David, and therefore Jehu clave to that. True conversion is not only from wasteful sins, but from gainful sins—not only from those sins that are destructive to the secular interest, but from those that support and befriend it, in forsaking which is the great trial whether we can deny ourselves and trust God. 2. He put away evil, but he did not mind that which was good (*v.* 31): *He took no heed to walk in the law of the Lord God of Israel.* He abolished the worship of Baal, but did not keep up the worship of God, nor walk in his law. He had shown great care and zeal for the rooting out of a false religion; but in the true religion, (1.) He showed no care, took no heed, lived at large, was not at all solicitous to please God and to do his duty, took no heed to the scriptures, to the prophets, to his own conscience, but walked at all adventures. Those that are heedless, it is to be feared, are graceless; for, where there is a good principle in the heart, it will make men cautious and circumspect, desirous to please God and jealous of doing any thing to offend him. (2.) He showed no zeal; what he did in religion he did not do with his heart, with all his heart, but did it as if he did it not, without any liveliness or concern. It seems, he was a man that had little religion himself, and yet God made use of him as an instrument of reformation in Israel. It is a pity but that those that do good to others should always be good themselves.

III. The judgment that came upon Israel in his reign. We have reason to fear that when Jehu took no heed himself to walk in God's law the people were generally as careless as he, both in their devotions and in their conversations. There was a general decay of piety and increase of profaneness; and therefore it is not strange that the next news we hear is, *In those days the Lord began to cut Israel short, v.* 32. Their neighbours encroached upon them on every side; they were short in their duty to God, and therefore God cut them short in their extent, wealth, and power. Hazael king of Syria was, above any other, vexatious and mischievous to them, *smote them in all the coasts of Israel,* particularly the countries on the other side Jordan, which lay next him, and most exposed; on these he made continual inroads, and laid them waste. Now the Reubenites and Gadites smarted for the choice which their ancestors made of an inheritance on that side Jordan, which Moses reproved them for, Num. xxxii. Now Hazael did what Elisha foresaw and foretold he would do. Yet, for doing it, God had a quarrel with him and with his kingdom, as we may find, Amos i. 3, 4. Because those of Damascus have *threshed Gilead with threshing instruments of iron,* therefore (says God) *I will send a fire into the house of Hazael, which shall devour the palaces of Benhadad.*

Lastly, The conclusion of Jehu's reign, *v.* 34—36. Notice is taken, in general, of his might; but, because he took no heed to serve God, the memorials of his mighty enterprises and achievements are justly buried in oblivion.

CHAP. XI.

The revolution in the kingdom of Israel was soon perfected in Jehu's settlement; we must now enquire into the affairs of the kingdom of Judah, which lost its head (such as it was) at the same time, and by the same hand, as Israel lost its head; but things continued longer there in distraction than in Israel, yet, after some years, they were brought into a good posture, as we find in this chapter. I. Athaliah usurps the government and destroys all the seed-royal, ver. 1. II. Joash, a child of a year old, is wonderfully preserved, ver. 2, 3. III. At six years' end he is produced, and, by the agency of Jehoiada, made king, ver. 4—12. IV. Athaliah is slain, ver. 13—16. V. Both the civil and religious interests of the kingdom are well settled in the hands of Joash, ver. 17—21. And thus, after some interruption, things returned with advantage into the old channel.

AND when Athaliah the mother of Ahaziah saw that her son was dead, she arose and destroyed all the seed royal. 2 But Jehosheba, the daughter of king Joram, sister of Ahaziah, took Joash the son of Ahaziah, and stole him from among the king's sons *which were* slain; and they hid him, *even* him and his nurse, in the bedchamber from Athaliah, so that he was not slain. 3 And he was with her hid in the house of the LORD six years. And Athaliah did reign over the land.

God had assured David of the continuance of his family, which is called his *ordaining a lamp for his anointed;* and this cannot but appear a great thing, now that we have read of the utter extirpation of so many royal families, one after another. Now here we have David's promised lamp almost extinguished and yet wonderfully preserved.

I. It was almost extinguished by the barbarous malice of Athaliah, the queen-mother, who, when she heard that her son Ahaziah was slain by Jehu, *arose and destroyed all the seed-royal* (*v.* 1), all that she knew to be akin to the crown. Her husband Jehoram had slain all his brethren the sons of Jehoshaphat, 2 Chron. xxi. 4. The Arabians had slain all Jehoram's sons except Ahaziah, 2 Chron. xxii. 1. Jehu had slain all their sons (2 Chron. xxii. 8) and Ahaziah himself. Surely never was royal blood so profusely shed. Happy the men of inferior birth, who live below envy and emulation! But, as if all this were but a small matter, Athaliah destroyed all that were left of the seed-royal. It was strange that one of the tender sex could be so barbarous, that one who had been herself a king's daughter, a king's wife, and a king's mother, could be so barbarous to a royal family, and a family into which she was herself ingrafted; but she did it, 1. From a spirit of ambition. She thirsted after rule, and thought she could not get to it any other way. That none might reign with her, she slew even the infants and sucklings that might have reigned after her. For fear of a competitor, not any must be reserved for a successor. 2. From a spirit of revenge and rage against God. The house of Ahab being utterly destroyed, and her son Ahaziah among the rest, because he was akin to it, she resolved, as it were, by way of reprisal, to destroy the house of David, and cut off his line, in defiance of God's promise to perpetuate it—a foolish attempt and fruitless, for who can disannul what God hath purposed? Grandmothers have been thought more fond of their grandchildren than they were of their own; yet Ahaziah's own mother is the wilful murderer of Ahaziah's own sons, and in their infancy too, when she was obliged, above any other, to nurse them and take care of them. Well might she be called *Athaliah, that wicked woman* (2 Chron. xxiv. 7), Jezebel's own daughter; yet herein God was righteous, and visited the iniquity of Joram and Ahaziah, those degenerate branches of David's house, upon their children.

II. It was wonderfully preserved by the pious care of one of Joram's daughters (who was wife to Jehoiada the priest), who stole away one of the king's sons, Joash by name, and hid him, *v.* 2, 3. This was a brand plucked out of the fire; what number were slain we are not told, but, it seems, this being a child in the nurse's arms was not missed, or not enquired after, or at least not found. The person that delivered him was his own aunt, the daughter of wicked Joram; for God will raise up protectors for those whom he will have protected. The place of his safety was the house of the Lord, one of the chambers belonging to the temple, a place Athaliah seldom troubled. His aunt, by bringing him hither, put him under God's special protection, and so hid him by faith, as Moses was hidden. Now were David's words made good to one of his seed (Ps. xxvii. 5), *In the secret of his tabernacle shall he hide me.* With good reason did this Joash, when he grew up, set himself to repair the house of the Lord, for it had been a sanctuary to him. Now was the promise made to David bound up in one life, and yet it did not fail. Thus to the son of David will God, according to his promise, secure a spiritual seed, which, though sometimes reduced to a small number, brought very low, and seemingly lost, will be perpetuated to the end of time, hidden sometimes and unseen, but hidden in God's pavilion and unhurt. It was a special providence that Joram, though a king, a wicked king, married his daughter to Jehoiada a priest, a godly priest. Some perhaps thought it a disparagement to the royal family to marry a daughter to a clergyman, but it proved a happy marriage, and the saving of the royal family from ruin; for Jehoiada's interest in the temple gave *her* an opportunity to preserve the child, and her interest in the royal family gave *him* an opportunity to set him on the throne. See the wisdom and care of Providence, and how it prepares for what it designs; and see what blessings those lay up in store for their families that marry their children to those that are wise and good.

4 And the seventh year Jehoiada sent and fetched the rulers over hundreds, with the captains and the guard, and brought them to him into the house of the LORD, and made a covenant with them, and took an oath of them in the house of the LORD, and showed them the king's son. 5

And he commanded them, saying, This *is* the thing that ye shall do; A third part of you that enter in on the sabbath shall even be keepers of the watch of the king's house; 6 And a third part *shall be* at the gate of Sur; and a third part at the gate behind the guard: so shall ye keep the watch of the house, that it be not broken down. 7 And two parts of all you that go forth on the sabbath, even they shall keep the watch of the house of the LORD about the king. 8 And ye shall compass the king round about, every man with his weapons in his hand: and he that cometh within the ranges, let him be slain: and be ye with the king as he goeth out and as he cometh in. 9 And the captains over the hundreds did according to all *things* that Jehoiada the priest commanded: and they took every man his men that were to come in on the sabbath, with them that should go out on the sabbath, and came to Jehoiada the priest. 10 And to the captains over hundreds did the priest give king David's spears and shields, that *were* in the temple of the LORD. 11 And the guard stood, every man with his weapons in his hand, round about the king, from the right corner of the temple to the left corner of the temple, *along* by the altar and the temple. 12 And he brought forth the king's son, and put the crown upon him, and *gave him* the testimony; and they made him king, and anointed him; and they clapped their hands, and said, God save the king.

Six years Athaliah tyrannised. We have not a particular account of her reign; no doubt it was of a piece with the beginning. While Jehu was extirpating the worship of Baal in Israel, she was establishing it in Judah, as appears, 2 Chron. xxiv. 7. The court and kingdom of Judah had been debauched by their alliance with the house of Ahab, and now one of that house is a curse and a plague to both: sinful friendships speed no better. All this while, Joash lay hid, entitled to a crown and intended for it, and yet buried alive in obscurity. Though the sons and heirs of heaven are now hidden, *the world knows them not* (1 John iii. 1), yet the time is fixed when they shall appear in glory, as Joash in his seventh year; by that time he was ready to be shown, not a babe, but, having served his first apprenticeship to life and arrived at his first climacterical year, he had taken a good step towards manhood; by that time the people had grown weary of Athaliah's tyranny and ripe for a revolution. How that revolution was effected we are here told.

I. The manager of this great affair was Jehoiada the priest, probably the high priest, or at least the *sagan* (as the Jews called him) or suffragan to the high priest. By his birth and office he was a man in authority, whom the people were bound by the law to observe and obey, especially when there was no rightful king upon the throne, Deut. xvii. 12. By marriage he was allied to the royal family, and, if all the seed-royal were destroyed, his wife, as daughter to Joram, had a better title to the crown than Athaliah had. By his eminent gifts and graces he was fitted to serve his country, and better service he could not do it than to free it from Athaliah's usurpation; and we have reason to think he did not make this attempt till he had first asked counsel of God and known his mind, either by prophets or Urim, perhaps by both.

II. The management was very discreet and as became so wise and good a man as Jehoiada was.

1. He concerted the matter with the *rulers of hundreds and the captains,* the men in office, ecclesiastical, civil, and military; he got them to him to the temple, consulted with them, laid before them the grievances they at present laboured under, gave them an oath of secresy, and, finding them free and forward to join with him, *showed them the king's son* (*v.* 4), and so well satisfied were they with his fidelity that they saw no reason to suspect an imposition. We may well think what a pleasing surprise it was to the good people among them, who feared that the house and lineage of David were quite cut off, to find such a spark as this in the embers.

2. He posted the priests and Levites, who were more immediately under his direction, in the several avenues to the temple, to keep the guard, putting them under the command of the *rulers of hundreds, v.* 9. David had divided the priests into courses, which waited by turns. Every sabbath-day morning a new company came into waiting, but the company of the foregoing week did not go out of waiting till the sabbath evening, so that on the sabbath day, when double service was to be done, there was a double number to do it, both those that were to come in and those that were to go out. These Jehoiada employed to attend on this great occasion; he armed them out of the magazines of the temple with David's spears and shields, either his own or those he had taken from his enemies, which he devoted to God's honour, *v.*10. If they were old and unfashionable, yet those that used them might, by their being David's, be reminded of God's covenant with him,

which they were now acting in the defence of. Two things they were ordered to do:—(1.) To protect the young king from being insulted; they must *keep the watch of the king's house* (*v.* 5), *compass the king, and be with him* (*v.* 8), to guard him from Athaliah's partizans, for still there were those that thirsted after royal blood. (2.) To preserve the holy temple from being profaned by the concourse of people that would come together on this occasion (*v.* 6): *Keep the watch of the house, that it be* neither broken through nor broken down, and so strangers should crowd in, or such as were unclean. He was not so zealous for the projected revolution as to forget his religion. In times of the greatest hurry care must be taken, *Ne detrimentum capiat ecclesia—That the holy things of God be not trenched upon.* It is observable that Jehoiada appointed to each his place as well as his work (*v.* 6, 7), for good order contributes very much to the expediting and accomplishing of any great enterprise. Let every man know, and keep, and make good, his post, and then the work will be done quickly.

3. When the guards were fixed, then the king was brought forth, *v.* 12. *Rejoice greatly, O daughter of Sion!* for even in thy holy mountain thy king appears, a child indeed, but not such a one as brings a woe upon the land, for he is the son of nobles, the son of David (Eccl. x. 17)—a child indeed, but he had a good guardian, and, which was better, a good God, to go to. Jehoiada, without delay, proceeded to the coronation of this young king; for, though he was not yet capable of despatching business, he would be growing up towards it by degrees. This was done with great solemnity, *v.* 12. (1.) In token of his being invested with kingly power, he *put the crown upon him,* though it was yet too large and heavy for his head. The regalia, it is probable, were kept in the temple, and so the crown was ready at hand. (2.) In token of his obligation to govern by law, and to make the word of God his rule, he gave him the testimony, put into his hand a Bible, in which he must *read all the days of his life,* Deut. xvii. 18, 19. (.3) In token of his receiving the Spirit, to qualify him for this great work to which he before was called, he anointed him. Though notice is taken of the anointing of the kings only in case of interruption, as here, and in Solomon's case, yet I know not but the ceremony might be used for all their kings, at least those of the house of David, because their royalty was typical of Christ's, who was to be anointed above his fellows, above all the sons of David. (4.) In token of the people's acceptance of him and subjection to his government, they clapped their hands for joy, and expressed their hearty good wishes to him: *Let the king live;* and thus they made him king, made him their king, consented to, and concurred with, the divine appointment. They had reason to rejoice in the period now put to Athaliah's tyranny, and the prospect they had of the restoration and establishment of religion by a king under the tuition of so good a man as Jehoiada. They had reason to bid him welcome to the crown whose right it was, and to pray, *Let him live,* concerning him who came to them as life from the dead and in whom the house of David was to live. With such acclamations of joy and satisfaction must the kingdom of Christ be welcomed into our hearts when his throne is set up there and Satan the usurper is deposed *Hosanna, blessed is he that comes:* clap hands, and say, "Let King Jesus live, for ever live and reign, in my soul, and in all the world;" it is promised (Ps. lxxii. 15), *He shall live, and prayer shall be made for him,* and his kingdom, *continually.*

13 And when Athaliah heard the noise of the guard *and* of the people, she came to the people into the temple of the LORD. 14 And when she looked, behold, the king stood by a pillar, as the manner *was,* and the princes and the trumpeters by the king, and all the people of the land rejoiced, and blew with trumpets: and Athaliah rent her clothes, and cried, Treason, Treason. 15 But Jehoiada the priest commanded the captains of the hundreds, the officers of the host, and said unto them, Have her forth without the ranges: and him that followeth her kill with the sword. For the priest had said, Let her not be slain in the house of the LORD. 16 And they laid hands on her; and she went by the way by the which the horses came into the king's house: and there was she slain.

We may suppose it was designed when they had finished the solemnity of the king's inauguration, to pay a visit to Athaliah, and call her to an account for her murders, usurpation, and tyranny; but, like her mother Jezebel, she saved them the labour, went out to meet them, and hastened her own destruction. 1. Hearing the noise, she came in a fright to see what was the matter, *v.* 13. Jehoiada and his friends began in silence, but now that they found their strength, they proclaimed what they were doing. It seems, Athaliah was little regarded, else she would have had intelligence brought her of this daring attempt before with her own ears she heard the noise; had the design been discovered before it was perfected, it might have been quashed, but now it was too late. When she heard the noise it was strange that she was so ill advised as to come herself, and, for aught that appears, to come alone. Surely she was not so neglected as to have none to go for her, or none to go with her, but she was wretchedly infatuated by the transport both of fear and indignation she was in. Whom God will destroy he befools. 2. Seeing what was done she cried out for help. She saw the king's place by the pillar possessed by one to whom the princes and people did homage (*v.* 14) and had reason to conclude her power at an end, which she knew was usurped; this made her rend her clothes, like one distracted, and cry, "Treason! treason! Come and help against the traitors." Josephus adds that she cried to have him killed that possessed the king's place. What was now doing was the highest justice, yet it was branded as the highest crime; she herself was the greatest traitor, and yet was first and loudest in crying Treason! treason! Those that are themselves most guilty are commonly most forward to reproach others. 3. Jehoiada gave orders to put her to death as an idolater, a usurper, and an enemy to the public peace. Care was taken, (1.) That she should not be killed in the temple, or any of the courts of it, in reverence to that holy place, which must not be stained with the blood of any human sacrifice, though ever so justly offered. (2.) That whoever appeared for her should die with her: "Him that follows her, to protect or rescue her, any of her attendants that resolve to adhere to her and will not come into the interests of their rightful sovereign, *kill with the sword,* but not unless they follow her now," *v.* 15. According to these orders, she endeavouring to make her escape the back way to the palace, through the stalls, they pursued her, and there killed her, *v.* 16. *So let all thy enemies perish, O Lord!* thus give the bloody harlot blood to drink, for she is worthy.

17 And Jehoiada made a covenant between the LORD and the king and the people, that they should be the LORD'S people; between the king also and the people. 18 And all the people of the land went into the house of Baal, and brake it down; his altars and his images brake they in pieces thoroughly, and slew Mattan the priest of Baal before the altars. And the priest appointed officers over the house of the LORD. 19 And he took the rulers over hundreds, and the captains, and the guard, and all the people of the land; and they brought down the king from the house of the LORD, and came by the way of the gate of the guard to the king's house. And he sat on the throne of the kings. 20 And all the people of the land rejoiced, and the city was in quiet: and they slew Athaliah with the sword *beside* the king's house. 21 Seven years old *was* Jehoash when he began to reign.

Jehoiada had now got over the hardest part of his work, when, by the death of Athaliah, the young prince had his way to the throne cleared of all opposition. He had now to improve his advantages for the perfecting of the revolution and the settling of the government. Two things we have an account of here:—

I. The good foundations he laid, by an original contract, *v.* 17. Now that prince and people were together in God's house, as it should seem before they stirred, Jehoiada took care that they should jointly covenant with God, and mutually covenant with each other, that they might rightly understand their duty both to God and to one another, and be firmly bound to it. 1. He endeavoured to settle and secure the interests of religion among them, by a covenant between them and God. King and people would then cleave most firmly to each other when both had joined themselves to the Lord. God had already, on his part, promised to be their God (Jehoiada could show them that in the book of the testimony); now the king and people on their part must covenant and agree that *they will be the Lord's people:* in this covenant, the king stands upon the same level with his subjects and is as much bound as any of them to serve the Lord. By this engagement they renounced Baal, whom many of them had worshipped, and resigned themselves to God's government. It is well with a people when all the changes that pass over them help to revive, strengthen, and advance the interests of religion among them. And those are likely to prosper who set out in the world under fresh and sensible obligations to God and their duty. By our bonds to God the bonds of every relation are strengthened. They *first gave themselves to the Lord,* and then *to us,* 2 Cor. viii. 5. 2. He then settled both the coronation-oath and the oath of allegiance, the *pacta conventa—covenant,* between the king and the people, by which the king was obliged to govern according to law and to protect his subjects, and they were obliged, while he did so, to obey him and to bear faith and true allegiance to him. Covenants are of use both to remind us of and to bind us to those duties which are already binding on us. It is good, in all relations, for the parties to understand one another fully, particularly in that between prince and subject, that the one may understand the limits of his power and prerogative, the other those of his liberty and property; and never may the ancient landmarks which our fathers have set before them be removed.

II. The good beginnings he raised on

those foundations. 1. Pursuant to their covenant with God they immediately abolished idolatry, which the preceding kings, in compliance with the house of Ahab, had introduced (*v.* 18): *All the people of the land,* the mob, got together, to show their zeal against idolatry; and every one, now that they were so well headed, would lend a hand to pull down Baal's temple, his altars, and his images. All his worshippers, it should seem, deserted him; only his priest Mattan stuck to his altar. Though all men forsook Baal, he would not, and there he was slain, the best sacrifice that ever was offered upon that altar. Having destroyed Baal's temple, they appointed *officers over the house of God,* to see that the service of God was regularly performed by the proper persons, in due time, and according to the instituted manner. 2. Pursuant to their covenant with one another they expressed a mutual readiness to and satisfaction in each other. (1.) The king was brought in state to the royal palace, and sat there on the throne of judgment, *the thrones of the house of David* (*v.* 19), ready to receive petitions and appeals, which he would refer it to Jehoiada to give answers to and to give judgment upon. (2.) The people rejoiced, and Jerusalem was in quiet (*v.* 20), and Josephus says they kept a feast of joy many days, making good Solomon's observation (Prov. xi. 10), *When it goes well with the righteous the city rejoices, and when the wicked perish there is shouting.*

CHAP. XII.

This chapter gives us the history of the reign of Joash, which does not answer to that glorious beginning of it which we had an account of in the foregoing chapter; he was not so illustrious at forty years old as he was at seven, yet his reign is to be reckoned one of the better sort, and appears much worse in Chronicles (2 Chron. xxiv.) than it does here, for there we find the blood of one of God's prophets laid a this door; here we are only told, I. That he did well while Jehoiada lived, ver. 1—3. II. That he was careful and active to repair the temple, ver. 4—16. III. That after a mean compact with Hazael (ver. 17, 18) he died ingloriously, ver. 19—21.

IN the seventh year of Jehu Jehoash began to reign; and forty years reigned he in Jerusalem. And his mother's name *was* Zibiah of Beer-sheba. 2 And Jehoash did *that which was* right in the sight of the LORD all his days wherein Jehoiada the priest instructed him. 3 But the high places were not taken away: the people still sacrificed and burnt incense in the high places.

The general account here given of Joash is, 1. That he reigned forty years. As he began his reign when he was very young, he might, in the course of nature, have continued much longer, for he was cut off when he was but forty-seven years old, *v.* 1. 2. That he did that which was right as long as Jehoiada lived to instruct him, *v.* 2. Many young men have come too soon to an estate—have had wealth, and power, and liberty, before they knew how to use them—and it has been of bad consequence to them; but against this danger Joash was well guarded by having such a good director as Jehoiada was, so wise, and experienced, and faithful to him, and by having so much wisdom as to hearken to him and be directed by him, even when he was grown up. Note, It is a great mercy to young people, and especially to young princes, and all young men of consequence, to be under good direction, and to have those about them that will instruct them to do *that which is right in the sight of the Lord;* and they then do wisely and well for themselves when they are willing to be counselled and ruled by such. *A child left to himself brings his mother to shame,* but a child left to such a tuition may bring himself to honour and comfort. 3. That the *high places were not taken away, v.* 3. Up and down the country they had altars both for sacrifice and incense, to the honour of the God of Israel only, but in competition with, and at least in tacit contempt of, his altar at Jerusalem. These private altars, perhaps, had been more used in the late bad reigns than formerly, because it was not safe to go up to Jerusalem, nor was the temple-service performed as it should have been; and, it may be, Jehoiada connived at them, because some well-meaning people were glad of them when they could not have better, and he hoped that the reforming of the temple, and putting things into a good posture there, would by degrees draw people from their high places and they would dwindle of themselves; or perhaps neither the king nor the priest had zeal enough to carry on their reformation so far, nor courage and strength enough to encounter such an inveterate usage.

4 And Jehoash said to the priests, All the money of the dedicated things that is brought into the house of the LORD, *even* the money of every one that passeth *the account,* the money that every man is set at, *and* all the money that cometh into any man's heart to bring into the house of the LORD, 5 Let the priests take *it* to them, every man of his acquaintance: and let them repair the breaches of the house, wheresoever any breach shall be found. 6 But it was *so, that* in the three and twentieth year of king Jehoash the priests had not repaired the breaches of the house. 7 Then king Jehoash called for Jehoiada the priest, and the *other* priests, and said unto them, Why repair ye not the breaches of the house? now therefore receive no *more* money of your acquaintance, but deliver it for the breaches of the house. 8 And the

priests consented to receive no *more* money of the people, neither to repair the breaches of the house. 9 But Jehoiada the priest took a chest, and bored a hole in the lid of it, and set it beside the altar, on the right side as one cometh into the house of the LORD: and the priests that kept the door put therein all the money *that was* brought into the house of the LORD. 10 And it was *so*, when they saw that *there was* much money in the chest, that the king's scribe and the high priest came up, and they put up in bags, and told the money that was found in the house of the LORD. 11 And they gave the money, being told, into the hands of them that did the work, that had the oversight of the house of the LORD: and they laid it out to the carpenters and builders, that wrought upon the house of the LORD, 12 And to masons, and hewers of stone, and to buy timber and hewed stone to repair the breaches of the house of the LORD, and for all that was laid out for the house to repair *it*. 13 Howbeit there were not made for the house of the LORD bowls of silver, snuffers, basons, trumpets, any vessels of gold, or vessels of silver, of the money *that was* brought into the house of the LORD: 14 But they gave that to the workmen, and repaired therewith the house of the LORD. 15 Moreover they reckoned not with the men, into whose hand they delivered the money to be bestowed on workmen: for they dealt faithfully. 16 The trespass money and sin money was not brought into the house of the LORD: it was the priests'.

We have here an account of the repairing of the temple in the reign of Joash.

I. It seems, the temple had gone out of repair. Though Solomon built it very strong, of the best materials and in the best manner, yet in time it went to decay, and there were *breaches found in it* (*v.* 5), in the roofs, or walls, or floors, the ceiling, or wainscoting, or windows, or the partitions of the courts. Even temples themselves are the worse for the wearing; but the heavenly temple will never wax old. Yet it was not only the teeth of time that made these breaches, the sons of Athaliah had *broken up the house of God* (2 Chron. xxiv. 7), and, out of enmity to the service of the temple, had damaged the buildings of it, and the priests had not taken care to repair the breaches in time, so that they went worse and worse. Unworthy were those husbandmen to have this valuable vineyard let out to them upon such easy terms who could not afford to keep the winepress in due and tenantable repair, Matt. xxi. 33. Justly did their great Lord sue them for this permissive waste, and by his judgments recover *locum vastatum—for dilapidations* (as the law speaks), when this neglected temple was laid even with the ground.

II. The king himself was (as it should seem) the first and forwardest man that took care for the repair of it. We do not find that the priests complained of it or that Jehoiada himself was active in it, but the king was zealous in the matter, 1. Because he was king, and God expects and requires from those who have power that they use it for the maintenance and support of religion, the redress of grievances, and reparation of decays, for the exciting and engaging of ministers to do their part and people theirs. 2. Because the temple had been both his nursery and his sanctuary when he was a child, in a grateful remembrance of which he now appeared zealous for the honour of it. Those who have experienced the comfort and benefit of religious assemblies will make the reproach of them their burden (Zeph. iii. 18), the support of them their care, and the prosperity of them their chief joy.

III. The priests were ordered to collect money for these repairs, and to take care that the work was done. The king had the affairs of his kingdom to mind, and could not himself inspect this affair, but he employed the priests to manage it, the fittest persons, and most likely, one would think, to be hearty in it. 1. He gave them orders for the levying of the money of the dedicated things. They must not stay till it was paid in, but they must call for it where they knew it was due, in their respective districts, as redemption-money (by virtue of the law, Exod. xxx. 12), or as estimation-money (by virtue of the law, Lev. xxvii. 2, 3), or as a free-will offering, *v.* 4. This they were to gather every man of his acquaintance, and it was supposed that there was no man but had acquaintance with some or other of the priests. Note, We should take the opportunity that God gives us of exciting those we have a particular acquaintance with to that which is good. 2. He gave them orders for laying out the money they had levied in *repairing the breaches of the house*, *v.* 5.

IV. This method did not answer the intention, *v.* 6. Little money was raised. Either the priests were careless, and did not call on the people to pay in their dues, or the people had so little confidence in the priests' management that they were backward to pay money into their hands; if they were distrusted without cause, it was the people's shame; if with, it was more theirs. But what money was raised was not applied to the proper use: *The breaches of the house were not repaired;* the priests thought it might serve as well as it had done, and therefore put off repairing from time to time. Church work is usually slow work, but it is a pity that churchmen, of all men, should be slow at it. Perhaps what little money they raised they thought it necessary to use for the maintenance of the priests, which must needs fall much short when ten tribes had wholly revolted and the other two were wretchedly corrupted.

V. Another method was therefore taken. The king had his heart much set upon having *the breaches of the house repaired, v.* 7. His apostasy, at last, gives us cause to question whether he had as good an affection for the service of the temple as he had for the structure. Many have been zealous for building and beautifying churches, and for other forms of godliness, who yet have been strangers to the power of it. However, we commend his zeal, and blame him not for reproving even his tutor Jehoiada himself when he saw him remiss; and so convincing was his reproof that the priests owned themselves unworthy to be any longer employed, and consented to the taking of some other measures, and the giving up of the money they had received into other hands, *v.* 8. It was honestly done, when they found they had not spirit to do it themselves, not to hinder other people from doing it. Another course was taken,

1. For raising money, *v.* 9, 10. The money was not paid into private hands, but put into a public chest, and then people brought it in readily and in great abundance, not only their dues, but their free-will offerings for so good a work. The high priest and the secretary of state counted the money out of the chest, and laid it by *in specie* for the use to which it was appropriated. When public distributions are made faithfully public contributions will be made cheerfully. The money that was given, (1.) Was dropped into the chest through a hole in the lid, past recal, to intimate that what has been once resigned to God must never be resumed. *Every man, as he purposeth in his heart, so let him give.* (2.) The chest was put on the right hand as they went in, which, some think, is alluded to in that rule of charity which our Saviour gives, *Let not thy left hand know what thy right hand doeth.* But, while they were getting all they could for the repair of the temple, they did not break in upon that which was the stated maintenance of the priests, *v.* 16. The trespass-money and the sin-money (which were given to them by that law, Lev. v. 15, 16) were reserved to them. Let not the servants of the temple be starved under colour of repairing the breaches of it.

2. For laying out the money that was raised.

(1.) They did not put it into the hands of the priests, who were not versed in affairs of this nature, having other work to mind, but *into the hands of those that did the work,* or at least *had the oversight of it, v.* 11. Those were fittest to be entrusted with this business whose employment lay that way. *Tractant fabrilia fabri—Every artist has his trade assigned;* but let not those who are called to war the holy warfare entangle themselves in the affairs of this life. Those that were thus entrusted did the business, [1.] Carefully, purchasing materials and paying workmen, *v.* 12. Business is done with expedition when those are employed in it that understand it and know which way to go about it. [2.] Faithfully; such a reputation they got for honesty that there was no occasion to examine their bills or audit their accounts. Let all that are entrusted with public money, or public work, learn hence to deal faithfully, as those that know God will reckon with them, whether men do or no. Those that think it is no sin to cheat the government, cheat the country, or cheat the church, will be of another mind when God shall set their sins in order before them.

(2.) They did not lay it out in ornaments for the temple, in vessels of gold or silver, but in necessary repairs first (*v.* 13), whence we may learn, in all our expenses to give that the preference which is most needful, and, in dealing for the public, to deal as we would for ourselves. After the repairs were finished we find the overplus turned into plate for the service of the temple, 2 Chron. xxiv. 14.

17 Then Hazael king of Syria went up, and fought against Gath, and took it: and Hazael set his face to go up to Jerusalem. 18 And Jehoash king of Judah took all the hallowed things that Jehoshaphat, and Jehoram, and Ahaziah, his fathers, kings of Judah, had dedicated, and his own hallowed things, and all the gold *that was* found in the treasures of the house of the LORD, and in the king's house, and sent *it* to Hazael king of Syria: and he went away from Jerusalem. 19 And the rest of the acts of Joash, and all that he did, *are* they not written in the book of the chronicles of the kings of Judah? 20 And his servants arose, and made a conspiracy, and slew Joash in the house of Millo, which goeth down to Silla. 21 For Jozachar the son of Shimeath, and Jehozabad the son of Shomer, his servants, smote him, and he died; and

they buried him with his fathers in the city of David: and Amaziah his son reigned in his stead.

When Joash had revolted from God and become both an idolater and a persecutor the hand of the Lord went out against him, and his *last state was worse than his first*.

I. His wealth and honour became an easy prey to his neighbours. Hazael, when he had chastised Israel (*ch.* x. 32), threatened Judah and Jerusalem likewise, took Gath, a strong city (*v.* 17), and thence intended to march with his forces against Jerusalem, the royal city, the holy city, but whose defence, on account of its sinfulness, had departed. Joash had neither spirit nor strength to make head against him, but gave him all the hallowed things, and all the gold that was found both in his exchequer and in the treasures of the temple (*v.* 18), to bribe him to march another way. If it were lawful to do this for the public safety, better part with the gold of the temple than expose the temple itself; yet, 1. If he had not forsaken God, and forfeited his protection, his affairs would not have been brought to this extremity, but he might have forced Hazael to retire. 2. He diminished himself, and made himself very mean, lost the honour of a prince and a soldier, and of an Israelite too, in alienating the dedicated things. 3. He impoverished himself and his kingdom. And, 4. He tempted Hazael to come again, when he could carry home so rich a booty without striking a stroke. And it had this effect, for the next year the host of Syria came up against Jerusalem, destroyed the prince, and plundered the city, 2 Chron. xxiv. 23, 24.

II. His life became an easy prey to his own servants. They conspired against him and slew him (*v.* 20, 21), not aiming at his kingdom, for they opposed not his son's succeeding him, but to be avenged on him for some crime he had committed; and we are told in Chronicles that his murdering the prophet, Jehoiada's son, was the provocation. In this, how unrighteous soever they were (vengeance was not theirs, nor did it belong to them to repay), God was righteous; and this was not the only time that he let even kings know that it was at their peril if they touched his anointed and did his prophets any harm, and that, when he comes to make inquisition for blood, the blood of prophets will run the account very high. Thus fell Joash, who began in the spirit and ended in the flesh. God usually sets marks of his displeasure upon apostates, even in this life; for they, of all sinners, do most *reproach the Lord*.

CHAP. XIII.

This chapter brings us again to the history of the kings of Israel, and particularly of the family of Jehu. We have here an account of the reign, I. Of his son Jehoahaz, which continued seventeen years. 1. His bad character in general (ver. 1, 2), the trouble he was brought into (ver. 3), and the low ebb of his affairs, ver. 7. 2. His humiliation before God, and God's compassion towards him, ver. 4, 5, and again, ver. 23. 3. His continuance in his idolatry notwithstanding, ver. 6. 4. His death, ver. 8, 9. II. Of his grandson Joash, which continued sixteen years. Here is a general account of his reign in the usual form (ver. 10—13), but a particular account of the death of Elisha in his time. 1. The kind visit the king made him (ver. 14), the encouragement he gave the king in his wars with Syria, ver. 15—19. 2. His death and burial (ver. 20), and a miracle wrought by his bones, ver. 21. And, lastly, the advantages Joash gained against the Syrians, according to his predictions, ver. 24, 25.

IN the three and twentieth year of Joash the son of Ahaziah king of Judah Jehoahaz the son of Jehu began to reign over Israel in Samaria, *and reigned* seventeen years. 2 And he did *that which* was evil in the sight of the LORD, and followed the sins of Jeroboam the son of Nebat, which made Israel to sin; he departed not therefrom. 3 And the anger of the LORD was kindled against Israel, and he delivered them into the hand of Hazael king of Syria, and into the hand of Ben-hadad the son of Hazael, all *their* days. 4 And Jehoahaz besought the LORD, and the LORD hearkened unto him: for he saw the oppression of Israel, because the king of Syria oppressed them. 5 (And the LORD gave Israel a saviour, so that they went out from under the hand of the Syrians: and the children of Israel dwelt in their tents, as beforetime. 6 Nevertheless they departed not from the sins of the house of Jeroboam, who made Israel sin, *but* walked therein: and there remained the grove also in Samaria.) 7 Neither did he leave of the people to Jehoahaz but fifty horsemen, and ten chariots, and ten thousand footmen; for the king of Syria had destroyed them, and had made them like the dust by threshing. 8 Now the rest of the acts of Jehoahaz, and all that he did, and his might, *are* they not written in the book of the chronicles of the kings of Israel? 9 And Jehoahaz slept with his fathers; and they buried him in Samaria: and Joash his son reigned in his stead.

This general account of the reign of Jehoahaz, and of the state of Israel during his seventeen years, though short, is long enough to let us see two things which are very affecting and instructive:—

I. The glory of Israel raked up in the ashes, buried and lost, and turned into shame. How unlike does Israel appear here to what it had been and might have been! How is its crown profaned and its honour laid in the dust! 1. It was the honour of

Israel that they worshipped the only living and true God, who is a Spirit, an eternal mind, and had rules by which to worship him of his own appointment; but by *changing the glory of their incorruptible God into the similitude of an ox, the truth of God into a lie,* they lost this honour, and levelled themselves with the nations that worshipped the work of their own hands. We find here that the king *followed the sins of Jeroboam* (*v.* 2), and the people departed *not from them, but walked therein, v.* 6. There could not be a greater reproach than these two idolized calves were to a people that were instructed in the service of God and entrusted with the lively oracles. In all the history of the ten tribes we never find the least shock given to that idolatry, but, in every reign, still the calf was their god, and they separated themselves to that shame. 2. It was the honour of Israel that they were taken under the special protection of heaven; God himself was their defence, the shield of their help and the sword of their excellency. Happy wast thou, O Israel! upon this account. But here, as often before, we find them stripped of this glory, and exposed to the insults of all their neighbours. They by their sins provoked God to anger, and then he *delivered them into the hands of Hazael and Benhadad, v.* 3. *Hazael oppressed Israel, v.* 22. Surely never was any nation so often plucked and pillaged by their neighbours as Israel was. This the people brought upon themselves by sin; when they had provoked God to pluck up their hedge, the goodness of their land did but tempt their neighbours to prey upon them. So low was Israel brought in this reign, by the many depredations which the Syrians made upon them, that the militia of the kingdom and all the force they could bring into the field were but *fifty horsemen, ten chariots, and* 10,000 *footmen,* a despicable muster, *v.* 7. Have the thousands of Israel come to this? *How has the gold become dim!* The debauching of a nation will certainly be the debasing of it.

II. Some sparks of Israel's ancient honour appearing in these ashes. It is not quite forgotten, notwithstanding all these quarrels, that this people is the Israel of God and he is the God of Israel. For, 1. It was the ancient honour of Israel that they were a praying people: and here we find somewhat of that honour revived; for Jehoahaz their king, in his distress, *besought the Lord* (*v.* 4), applied for help, not to the calves (what help could they give him?) but to the Lord. It becomes kings to be beggars at God's door, and the greatest of men to be humble petitioners at the footstool of his throne. Need will drive them to it. 2. It was the ancient honour of Israel that they had *God nigh unto them in all that which they called upon him for* (Deut. iv. 7), and so he was here. Though he might justly have rejected the prayer as an abomination to him, yet *the Lord hearkened unto Jehoahaz,* and to his prayer for himself and for his people (*v.* 4), and *he gave Israel a saviour* (*v.* 5), not Jehoahaz himself, for all his days Hazael oppressed Israel (*v.* 22), but his son, to whom, in answer to his father's prayers, God gave success against the Syrians, so that he recovered the cities which they had taken from his father, *v.* 25. This gracious answer God gave to the prayer of Jehoahaz, not for his sake, or the sake of that unworthy people, but in remembrance of his covenant with Abraham (*v.* 23), which, in such exigencies as these, he had long since promised to have respect to, Lev. xxvi. 42. See how swift God is to show mercy, how ready to hear prayers, how willing to find out a reason to be gracious, else he would not look so far back as that ancient covenant which Israel had so often broken and forfeited all the benefit of. Let this invite and engage us for ever to him, and encourage even those that have forsaken him to return and repent; for *there is forgiveness with him, that he may be feared.*

10 In the thirty and seventh year of Joash king of Judah began Jehoash the son of Jehoahaz to reign over Israel in Samaria, *and reigned* sixteen years. 11 And he did *that which was* evil in the sight of the LORD; he departed not from all the sins of Jeroboam the son of Nebat, who made Israel sin: *but* he walked therein. 12 And the rest of the acts of Joash, and all that he did, and his might wherewith he fought against Amaziah king of Judah, *are* they not written in the book of the chronicles of the kings of Israel? 13 And Joash slept with his fathers; and Jeroboam sat upon his throne: and Joash was buried in Samaria with the kings of Israel. 14 Now Elisha was fallen sick of his sickness whereof he died. And Joash the king of Israel came down unto him, and wept over his face, and said, O my father, my father, the chariot of Israel, and the horsemen thereof. 15 And Elisha said unto him, Take bow and arrows. And he took unto him bow and arrows. 16 And he said to the king of Israel, Put thine hand upon the bow. And he put his hand *upon it:* and Elisha put his hands upon the king's hands. 17 And he said, Open the window eastward. And he opened *it.* Then Elisha said, Shoot. And he shot. And he said, The arrow of the LORD's deliverance, and the

arrow of deliverance from Syria: for thou shalt smite the Syrians in Aphek, till thou have consumed *them.* 18 And he said, Take the arrows. And he took *them.* And he said unto the king of Israel, Smite upon the ground. And he smote thrice, and stayed. 19 And the man of God was wroth with him, and said, Thou shouldest have smitten five or six times; then hadst thou smitten Syria till thou hadst consumed *it:* whereas now thou shalt smite Syria *but* thrice.

We have here Jehoash, or Joash, the son of Jehoahaz and grandson of Jehu, upon the throne of Israel. Probably the house of Jehu intended some respect to the house of David when they gave this heir-apparent to the crown the same name with him that was then king of Judah.

I. The general account here given of him and his reign is much the same with what we have already met with, and has little in it remarkable, *v.* 10—13. He was none of the worst, and yet, because he kept up that ancient and politic idolatry of the house of Jeroboam, it is said, *He did that which was evil in the sight of the Lord.* That one evil was enough to leave an indelible mark of infamy upon his name; for, how little evil soever men saw in it, it was, *in the sight of the Lord,* a very wicked thing; and we are sure that his judgment is according to truth. It is observable how lightly the inspired penman passes over his acts, and his might wherewith he warred, leaving it to the common historians to record them, while he takes notice only of the respect he showed to Elisha. One good action shall make a better figure in God's book than twenty great ones; and, in his account, it gains a man a much better reputation to honour a prophet than to conquer a king and his army.

II. The particular account of what passed between him and Elisha has several things in it remarkable.

1. Elisha fell sick, *v.* 14. Observe, (1.) He lived long; for it was now about sixty years since he was first called to be a prophet. It was a great mercy to Israel, and especially to the sons of the prophets, that he was continued so long a burning and shining light. Elijah finished his testimony in a fourth part of that time. God's prophets have their day set them, some longer, others shorter, as Infinite Wisdom sees fit. (2.) All the latter part of his time, from the anointing of Jehu, which was forty-five years before Joash began his reign, we find no mention made of him, or of any thing he did, till we find him here upon his death-bed. He might be useful to the last, and yet not so famous as he had sometimes been. The time of his flourishing was less than the time of his living. Let not old people complain of obscurity, but rather be well pleased with retirement. (3.) The spirit of Elijah rested on Elisha, and yet he was not sent for to heaven in a fiery chariot, as Elijah was, but went the common road out of the world, and was *visited with the visitation of all men.* If God honour some above others, who yet are not inferior to them in gifts or graces, who shall find fault? *May he not do what he will with his own?*

2. King Joash visited him in his sickness, and *wept over him, v.* 14. This was an evidence of some good in him, that he had a value and affection for a faithful prophet; so far was he from hating and persecuting him as a troubler of Israel that he loved and honoured him as one of the greatest blessings of his kingdom, and lamented the loss of him. There have been those who would not be obedient to the word of God, and yet have had the faithful ministers of it so manifested in their consciences that they could not but have an honour for them. Observe here, (1.) When the king heard of Elisha's sickness he came to visit him, and to receive his dying counsel and blessing; and it was no disparagement to him, though a king, thus to honour one whom God honoured. Note, It may turn much to our spiritual advantage to attend the sick-beds and death-beds of good ministers and other good men, that we may learn to die, and may be encouraged in religion by the living comforts they have from it in a dying hour. (2.) Though Elisha was very old, had been a great while useful, and, in the course of nature, could not continue long, yet the king, when he saw him sick and likely to die, wept over him. The aged are most experienced and therefore can worst be spared. In many causes, one old witness is worth ten young ones. (3.) He lamented him in the same words with which Elisha had himself lamented the removal of Elijah: *My father, my father.* It is probable he had heard or read them in that famous story. Note, Those that give just honours to the generation that goes before them are often recompensed with the like from the generation that comes after them. He that watereth, that watereth with tears, shall be watered, shall be so watered, also himself, when it comes to his own turn, Prov. xi. 25. (4.) This king was herein selfish; he lamented the loss of Elisha because he was as the chariot and horsemen of Israel, and therefore could be ill spared when Israel was so poor in chariots and horsemen, as we find they were (*v.* 7), when they had in all but fifty horsemen and ten chariots. Those who consider how much good men contribute to the defence of a nation, and the keeping off of God's judgments, will see cause to lament the removal of them.

3. Elisha gave the king great assurances of his success against the Syrians, Israel's present oppressors, and encouraged him to

prosecute the war against them with vigour. Elisha was aware that therefore he was loth to part with him because he looked upon him as the great bulwark of the kingdom against that common enemy, and depended much upon his blessings and prayers in his designs against them. "Well," says Elisha, "if that be the cause of your grief, let not that trouble thee, for thou shalt be victorious over the Syrians when I am in my grave. *I die, but God will surely visit you.* He has the residue of the Spirit, and can raise up other prophets to pray for you." God's grace is not tied to one hand. He can bury his workmen and yet carry on his work. To animate the king against the Syrians he gives him a sign, orders him to *take bow and arrows* (*v.* 15), to intimate to him that, in order to the deliverance of his kingdom from the Syrians, he must put himself into a military posture and resolve to undergo the perils and fatigues of war. God would be the agent, but he must be the instrument. And that he should be successful he gives him a token, by directing him,

(1.) To shoot an arrow towards Syria, *v.* 16, 17. The king, no doubt, knew how to manage a bow better than the prophet did, and yet, because the arrow now to be shot was to have its significancy from the divine institution, as if he were now to be disciplined, he received the words of command from the prophet: *Put thy hand upon the bow—Open the window—Shoot.* Nay, as if he had been a child that never drew a bow before, *Elisha put his hands upon the king's hands,* to signify that in all his expeditions against the Syrians he must look up to God for direction and strength, must reckon his own hands not sufficient for him, but go on in a dependence upon divine aid. *He teacheth my hands to war,* Ps. xviii. 34; cxliv. 1. The trembling hands of a dying prophet, as they signified the concurrence and communication of the power of God, gave this arrow more force than the hands of the king in his full strength. The Syrians had made themselves masters of the country that lay eastward, *ch.* x. 33. Thitherward therefore the arrow was directed, and such an interpretation given by the prophet of the shooting of this arrow, though shot in one respect at random, as made it, [1.] A commission to the king to attack the Syrians, notwithstanding their power and possession. [2.] A promise of success therein. It is the *arrow of the Lord's deliverance, even the arrow of deliverance from Syria.* It is God that commands deliverance; and, when he will effect it, who can hinder? The arrow of deliverance is his. He shoots out his arrows, and the work is done, Ps. xviii. 14. "*Thou shalt smite the Syrians in Aphek,* where they are now encamped, or where they are to have a general rendezvous of their forces, *till thou have consumed* those of them that are vexatious and oppressive to thee and thy kingdom."

(2.) To ***strike with the arrows***, *v.* 18, 19. The prophet having in God's name assured him of victory over the Syrians, he will now try him and see what improvement he will make of his victories, whether he will push them on with more zeal than Ahab did when Benhadad lay at his mercy. For the trial of this he bids him *smite with the arrows on the ground:* "Believe them brought to the ground by the *arrow of the Lord's deliverance,* and laid at thy feet; and now show me what thou wilt do to them when thou hast them down, whether thou wilt do as David did when God *gave him the necks of his enemies, beat them small as the dust before the wind,*" Ps. xviii. 40, 42. The king showed not that eagerness and flame which one might have expected upon this occasion, but smote thrice, and no more. Either out of foolish tenderness to the Syrians, he smote as if he were afraid of hurting them, at least of ruining them, willing to show mercy to those that never did, nor ever would, show mercy to him or his people. Or, perhaps, he smote thrice, and very coldly, because he thought it but a silly thing, that it looked idle and childish for a king to beat the floor with his arrows; and thrice was often enough for him to play the fool merely to please the prophet. But, by contemning the sign, he lost the thing signified, sorely to the grief of the dying prophet, who was angry with him, and told him he should have smitten five or six times. Not being straitened in the power and promise of God, why should he be straitened in his own expectations and endeavours? Note, It cannot but be a trouble to good men to see those they wish well to stand in their own light and forsake their own mercies, to see them lose their advantages against their spiritual enemies, and to give them advantage.

20 And Elisha died, and they buried him. And the bands of the Moabites invaded the land at the coming in of the year. 21 And it came to pass, as they were burying a man, that, behold, they spied a band *of men;* and they cast the man into the sepulchre of Elisha: and when the man was let down, and touched the bones of Elisha, he revived, and stood up on his feet. 22 But Hazael king of Syria oppressed Israel all the days of Jehoahaz. 23 And the LORD was gracious unto them, and had compassion on them, and had respect unto them, because of his covenant with Abraham, Isaac, and Jacob, and would not destroy them, neither cast he them from his presence as yet. 24 So Hazael king of Syria died; and

Ben-hadad his son reigned in his stead. 25 And Jehoash the son of Jehoahaz took again out of the hand of Ben-hadad the son of Hazael the cities, which he had taken out of the hand of Jehoahaz his father by war. Three times did Joash beat him, and recovered the cities of Israel.

We must here attend,

I. The sepulchre of Elisha: he died in a good old age, and they buried him; and what follows shows, 1. What power there was in his life to keep off judgments; for, as soon as he was dead, the bands of the Moabites invaded the land—not great armies to face them in the field, but roving sculking bands, that murdered and plundered by surprise. God has many ways to chastise a provoking people. The king was apprehensive of danger only from the Syrians, but, behold, the Moabites invade him. Trouble comes sometimes from that point whence we least feared it. The mentioning of this immediately upon the death of Elisha intimates that the removal of God's faithful prophets is a presage of judgments coming. When ambassadors are recalled heralds may be expected. 2. What power there was in his dead body: it communicated life to another dead body, *v.* 21. This great miracle, though very briefly related, was a decided proof of his mission and a confirmation of all his prophecies. It was also a plain indication of another life after this. When Elisha died, there was not an end of him, for then he could not have done this. From operation we may infer existence. By this it appeared that the Lord was still the God of Elisha; therefore Elisha still lived, for *God is not the God of the dead, but of the living.* And it may, perhaps, have a reference to Christ, by whose death and burial the grave is made to all believers a safe and happy passage to life. It likewise intimated that though Elisha was dead, yet, in virtue of the promises made by him, Israel's interests, though they seemed quite sunk and lost, should revive and flourish again. The neighbours were carrying the dead body of a man to the grave, and, fearing to fall into the hands of the Moabites, a party of whom they saw at a distance near the place where the body was to be interred, they laid the corpse in the next convenient place, which proved to be Elisha's sepulchre. The dead man, upon touching Elisha's bones, revived, and, it is likely, went home again with his friends. Josephus relates the story otherwise, That some thieves, having robbed and murdered an honest traveller, threw his dead body into Elisha's grave, and it immediately revived. Elijah was honoured *in* his departure. Elisha was honoured *after* his departure. God thus dispenses honours as he pleases, but, one way or other, the rest of all the saints will be glorious, Isa. xi. 10. It is good being near the saints and having our lot with them both in life and death.

II. The sword of Joash king of Israel; and we find it successful against the Syrians. 1. The cause of his success was God's favour (*v.* 23): *The Lord was gracious to them, had compassion on them* in their miseries and *respect unto them.* The several expressions here of the same import call upon us to observe and admire the triumphs of divine goodness in the deliverance of such a provoking people. It was of the Lord's mercies that they were not consumed, because he would not destroy them as yet. He foresaw they would destroy themselves at last, but as yet he would reprieve them, and give them space to repent. The slowness of God's processes against sinners must be construed to the honour of his mercy, not the impeachment of his justice. 2. The effect of his success was Israel's benefit. He recovered out of the hands of Benhadad the cities of Israel which the Syrians were possessed of, *v.* 25. This was a great kindness to the cities themselves, which were hereby brought from under the yoke of oppression, and to the whole kingdom, which was much strengthened by the reduction of those cities. Thrice Joash beat the Syrians, just as often as he had struck the ground with the arrows, and then a full stop was put to the course of his victories. Many have repented, when it was too late, of their distrusts and the straitness of their desires.

CHAP. XIV.

This chapter continues the history of the succession in the kingdoms both of Judah and Israel. I. In the kingdom of Judah here is, 1. The entire history (as much as is recorded in this book) of Amaziah's reign. (1.) His good character, ver. 1–4. (2.) The justice he executed on the murderers of his father, ver. 5, 6. (3.) His victory over the Edomites, ver. 7. (4.) His war with Joash, and his defeat in that war, ver. 8–14. (5.) His fall, at last, by a conspiracy against him, ver 17–20. 2. The beginning of the history of Azariah, ver. 21, 22. II. In the kingdom of Israel, the conclusion of the reign of Joash (ver, 15, 16), and the entire history of Jeroboam his son, the second of that name, ver. 23–29. How many great men are made to stand in a little compass in God's book!

IN the second year of Joash son of Jehoahaz king of Israel reigned Amaziah the son of Joash king of Judah. 2 He was twenty and five years old when he began to reign, and reigned twenty and nine years in Jerusalem. And his mother's name *was* Jehoaddan of Jerusalem. 3 And he did *that which was* right in the sight of the LORD, yet not like David his father: he did according to all things as Joash his father did. 4 Howbeit the high places were not taken away: as yet the people did sacrifice and burn incense on the high places. 5 And it came to pass, as soon as the kingdom was confirmed in his hand, that he slew his servants which had slain the king his father.

6 But the children of the murderers he slew not: according unto that which is written in the book of the law of Moses, wherein the LORD commanded, saying, The fathers shall not be put to death for the children, nor the children be put to death for the fathers; but every man shall be put to death for his own sin. 7 He slew of Edom in the valley of salt ten thousand, and took Selah by war, and called the name of it Joktheel unto this day.

Amaziah, the son and successor of Joash, is the king whom here we have an account of. Let us take a view of him,

I. In the temple; and there he acted, in some measure, well, like Joash, but not like David, *v.* 3. He began well, but did not persevere: He *did that which was right in the sight of the Lord,* kept up his attendance on God's altars and his attention to God's word, yet not like David. It is not enough to do that which our pious predecessors did, merely to keep up the usage, but we must do it *as* they did it, from the same principle of faith and devotion and with the same sincerity and resolution. It is here taken notice of, as before, that *the high places were not taken away, v.* 4. It is hard to get clear of those corruptions which, by long usage, have gained both prescription and a favourable opinion.

II. On the bench; and there we have him doing justice on the traitors that murdered his father, not as soon as ever he came to the crown, lest it should occasion some disturbance, but he prudently deferred it till *the kingdom was confirmed in his hand, v.* 5. To weaken a factious party gradually, when it is not safe to provoke, often proves the way to ruin it effectually. Justice strikes surely by striking slowly, and is often executed most prudently when it is not executed presently. Wisdom here is profitable to direct. Amaziah did thus, 1. According to the rule of the law, that ancient rule, that *he that sheds man's blood by man shall his blood be shed.* Never let traitors or murderers expect to come to their graves like other men. *Let them flee to the pit, and let no man stay them.* 2. Under the limitation of the law: *The children of the murderers he slew not,* because the law of Moses had expressly provided that *the children should not be put to death for the fathers, v.* 6. It is probable that this is taken notice of because there were those about him that advised him to that rigour, both in revenge (because the crime was extraordinary—the murder of a king) and in policy, that the children might not plot against him, in revenge of their father's death. But against these insinuations he opposed the express law of God (Deut. xxiv. 16), which he was to judge by, and which he resolved to adhere to and trust God with the issue. God visits the iniquity of the fathers upon the children, because every man is guilty before him and owes him a death; so that, if he require the life for the father's sin, he does no wrong, the sinner having forfeited it already by his own. But he does not allow earthly princes to do thus: the children, before them, are innocent, and therefore must not suffer as guilty.

III. In the field; and there we find him triumphing over the Edomites, *v.* 7. Edom had *revolted from under the hand of Judah* in Joram's time, *ch.* viii. 22. Now he makes war upon them to bring them back to their allegiance, kills 10,000, and takes the chief city of Arabia the stony (called *Selah—a rock),* and gave it a new name. We shall find a larger account of this expedition, 2 Chron. xxv. 5, &c.

8 Then Amaziah sent messengers to Jehoash, the son of Jehoahaz son of Jehu, king of Israel, saying, Come, let us look one another in the face. 9 And Jehoash the king of Israel sent to Amaziah king of Judah, saying, The thistle that *was* in Lebanon sent to the cedar that *was* in Lebanon, saying, Give thy daughter to my son to wife: and there passed by a wild beast that *was* in Lebanon, and trode down the thistle. 10 Thou hast indeed smitten Edom, and thine heart hath lifted thee up: glory *of this,* and tarry at home: for why shouldest thou meddle to *thy* hurt, that thou shouldest fall, *even* thou, and Judah with thee? 11 But Amaziah would not hear. Therefore Jehoash king of Israel went up; and he and Amaziah king of Judah looked one another in the face at Beth-shemesh, which *belongeth* to Judah. 12 And Judah was put to the worse before Israel; and they fled every man to their tents. 13 And Jehoash king of Israel took Amaziah king of Judah, the son of Jehoash the son of Ahaziah, at Beth-shemesh, and came to Jerusalem, and brake down the wall of Jerusalem from the gate of Ephraim unto the corner gate, four hundred cubits. 14 And he took all the gold and silver, and all the vessels that were found in the house of the LORD, and in the treasures of the king's house, and hostages, and returned to Samaria.

For several successions after the division

of the kingdoms that of Judah suffered much by the *enmity* of Israel. After Asa's time, for several successions, it suffered more by the *friendship* of Israel, and by the alliance and affinity made with them. But now we meet with hostility between them again, which had not been for some ages before.

I. Amaziah, upon no provocation, and without showing any cause of quarrel, challenged Joash into the field (*v.* 8): *Come, let us look one another in the face;* let us try our strength in battle." Had he challenged him to a personal duel only, the error would have remained with himself, but each must bring all their forces into the field, and thousands of lives on both sides must be sacrificed to his capricious humour. Hereby he showed himself proud, presumptuous, and prodigal of blood. Some think that he intended to avenge the injury which the dismissed disgusted Israelites had lately done to his country, in their return (2 Cron. xxv. 13), and that he had also the vanity to think of subduing the kingdom of Israel, and reuniting it to Judah. A *fool's lips thus enter into contention, and his mouth calleth for strokes.* Those that challenge are chargeable with that beginning of strife, which is as the letting forth of water. He that is eager either to fight or to go to law may perhaps have enough of it quickly, and be the first that repents it.

II. Joash sent him a grave rebuke for his challenge, with advice to withdraw it, *v.* 9. 10. 1. He mortifies his pride, by comparing himself to a cedar, a stately tree, and Amaziah to a thistle, a sorry weed, telling him he was so far from fearing him that he despised him, and scorned as much to have any thing to do with him, or make any alliance with him, as the cedar would to match his daughter to a thistle. The ancient house of David he thinks not worthy to be named the same day with the house of Jehu, though an upstart. How may a humble man smile to hear two proud and scornful men set their wits on work to vilify and undervalue one another! 2. He foretels his fall: *A wild beast trode down the thistle,* and so put an end to his treaty with the cedar; so easily does Joash think his forces can crush Amaziah, and so unable does he think him to make any resistance. 3. He shows him the folly of his challenge: " *Thou hast indeed smitten Edom,* a weak, unarmed, undisciplined body of men, and therefore thinkest thou canst carry all before thee and subdue the regular forces of Israel with as much ease. *Thy heart has lifted thee up.*" See where the root of all sin lies; it is in the heart, thence it flows, and that must bear the blame. It is not Providence, the event, the occasion (whatever it is), that makes men proud, or secure, or discontented, or the like, but it is their own heart that does it. "Thou art proud of the blow thou hast given to Edom, as if that had made thee formidable to all mankind. Those wretchedly deceive themselves that magnify their own performances, and, because they have been blessed with some little success and reputation, conclude themselves fit for any thing and no less sure of it. 4. He counsels him to be content with the honour he has won, and not to hazard that, by grasping at more that was out of his reach: *Why shouldst thou meddle to thy hurt,* as fools often do, that will be meddling? Prov. xx. 3. Many would have had wealth and honour enough if they had but known when they had enough. He warns him of the consequence, that it would be fatal not to himself only, but to his kingdom, which he ought to protect.

III. Amaziah persisted in his resolution, and the issue was bad; he had better have tarried at home, for Joash gave him such a look in the face as put him to confusion. Challengers commonly prove to be on the losing side. 1. His army was routed and dispersed, *v.* 12. Josephus says, When they were to engage they were struck with such terror that they did not strike a stroke, but every one made the best of his way. 2. He himself was taken prisoner by the king of Israel, and then had enough of *looking him in the face.* Amaziah's pedigree comes in here somewhat abruptly *(the son of Joash, the son of Ahaziah),* because perhaps he had gloried in the dignity of his ancestors, or because he now smarted for their iniquity. 3. The conqueror entered Jerusalem, which tamely opened to him, and yet he broke down their wall (and, as Josephus says, drove his chariot in triumph through the breach), in reproach to them, and that he might, when he pleased, take possession of the royal city. 4. He plundered Jerusalem, took away all that was valuable, and returned to Samaria, laden with spoils, *v.* 14. It was said of Joash that he did that which was *evil in the sight of the Lord,* and of Amaziah that he did *that which was right;* and yet Joash triumphs thus over Amaziah, and why so? Because God would show, in Amaziah's fate, that he resists the proud, or because, whatever they were otherwise, Joash had lately been respectful to one of God's prophets (*ch.* xiii. 14), but Amaziah had been abusive to another (2 Chron. xxv. 16), and God will honour those who honour him in his prophets, but those who despise them, and him in them, shall be lightly esteemed.

15 Now the rest of the acts of Jehoash which he did, and his might, and how he fought with Amaziah king of Judah, *are* they not written in the book of the chronicles of the kings of Israel? 16 And Jehoash slept with his fathers, and was buried in Samaria with the kings of Israel; and Jeroboam his son reigned in his

stead. 17 And Amaziah the son of Joash king of Judah lived after the death of Jehoash son of Jehoahaz king of Israel fifteen years. 18 And the rest of the acts of Amaziah, *are* they not written in the book of the chronicles of the kings of Judah? 19 Now they made a conspiracy against him in Jerusalem: and he fled to Lachish; but they sent after him to Lachish, and slew him there. 20 And they brought him on horses: and he was buried at Jerusalem with his fathers in the city of David. 21 And all the people of Judah took Azariah, which *was* sixteen years old, and made him king instead of his father Amaziah. 22 He built Elath, and restored it to Judah, after that the king slept with his fathers.

Here are three kings brought to their graves in these few verses:—1. Joash king of Israel, *v.* 15, 16. We attended his funeral once before, *ch.* xiii. 12, 13. But, because the historian had occasion to give a further account of his life and actions, he again mentions his death and burial. 2. Amaziah king of Judah. Fifteen years he survived his conqueror the king of Israel, *v.* 17. A man may live a great while after he has been shamed, may be thoroughly mortified (as Amaziah no doubt was) and yet not dead. His acts are said to be found written in his annals (*v.* 18), but not his might; for his cruelty when he was a conqueror over the Edomites, and his insolence when he challenged the king of Israel, showed him void of true courage. He was slain by his own subjects, who hated him for his maladministration (*v.* 19) and made Jerusalem too hot for him, the ignominious breach made in their walls being occasioned by his folly and presumption. He fled to Lachish. How long he continued concealed or sheltered there we are not told, but, at last, he was there murdered, *v.* 19. No further did the rage of the rebels extend, for they brought him in a chariot to Jerusalem, and buried him there among his ancestors. 3. Azariah succeeded Amaziah, but not till twelve years after his father's death, for Amaziah died in the fifteenth year of Jeroboam (as appears by comparing *v.* 23 with *v.* 2), but Azariah did not begin his reign till the twenty-seventh of Jeroboam (*ch.* xv. 1), for he was but four years old at the death of his father, so that, for twelve years, till he came to be sixteen, the government was in the hands of protectors. He reigned very long (*ch.* xv. 2) and yet the account of his reign is here industriously huddled up, and broken off abruptly (*v.* 22): *He built Elath* (which had belonged to the Edomites, but, it is probable, was recovered by his father (*v.* 7), *after that the king slept with his fathers,* as if that had been all he did that was worth mentioning, or rather it is meant of king Amaziah: he built it soon after Amaziah died.

23 In the fifteenth year of Amaziah the son of Joash king of Judah Jeroboam the son of Joash king of Israel began to reign in Samaria, *and reigned* forty and one years. 24 And he did *that which was* evil in the sight of the LORD: he departed not from all the sins of Jeroboam the son of Nebat, who made Israel to sin. 25 He restored the coast of Israel from the entering of Hamath unto the sea of the plain, according to the word of the LORD God of Israel, which he spake by the hand of his servant Jonah, the son of Amittai, the prophet, which *was* of Gath-hepher. 26 For the LORD saw the affliction of Israel, *that it was* very bitter: for *there was* not any shut up, nor any left, nor any helper for Israel. 27 And the LORD said not that he would blot out the name of Israel from under heaven: but he saved them by the hand of Jeroboam the son of Joash. 28 Now the rest of the acts of Jeroboam, and all that he did, and his might, how he warred, and how he recovered Damascus, and Hamath, *which belonged* to Judah, for Israel, *are* they not written in the book of the chronicles of the kings of Israel? 29 And Jeroboam slept with his fathers, *even* with the kings of Israel; and Zachariah his son reigned in his stead.

Here is an account of the reign of Jeroboam the second. I doubt it is an indication of the affection and adherence of the house of Jehu to the sins of *Jeroboam the son of Nebat, who made Israel to sin,* that they called an heir-apparent to the crown by his name, thinking that an honourable name which in the book of God is infamous and stigmatized as much as any.

I. His reign was long, the longest of all the reigns of the kings of Israel: *He reigned forty-one years;* yet his contemporary Azariah, the king of Judah, reigned longer, even fifty-two years. This Jeroboam reigned just as long as Asa had done (1 Kings xv. 10), yet one did that which was good and the other that which was evil. We cannot measure men's characters by the length of their lives or by their outward prosperity. *There is one event to the righteous and to the wicked.*

II. His character was the same with that of the rest of those kings: *He did that which was evil* (*v.* 24), for *he departed not from the sins of Jeroboam;* he kept up the worship of the calves, and never left that, thinking there was no harm in it, because it had been the way of all his ancestors and predecessors. But a sin is never the less evil in God's sight, whatever it is in ours, for its being an ancient usage; and a frivolous plea it will be against doing good, that we have been accustomed to do evil.

III. Yet he prospered more than most of them, for though, in that one thing, he did evil in the sight of the Lord, yet it is likely, in other respects, there was some good found in him and therefore God owned him, 1. By prophecy. He raised up Jonah the son of Amittai, a Galilean (so much were those mistaken that said, *Out of Galilee ariseth no prophet,* John vii. 52), and by him intimated the purposes of his favour to Israel, notwithstanding their provocations, encouraged him and his kingdom to take up arms for the recovery of their ancient possessions, and (which would contribute not a little to their success) assured them of victory. It is a sign that God has not cast off his people if he continue faithful ministers among them; when Elisha, who strengthened the hands of Joash, was removed, Jonah was sent to encourage his son. Happy is the land that has a succession of prophets running parallel with a succession of princes, that the word of the Lord may endure for ever. Of this Jonah we read much in that little book of scripture that bears his name. It is probable that it was when he was a young man, and fit for such an expedition, that God sent him to Nineveh, and that it was when he had yet been but a little conversant with the visions of God that he flew off and fretted as he did; and, if so, this is an undoubted evidence of the forgiveness of his faults and follies, that he was afterwards employed as a messenger of mercy to Israel. A commission amounts to a pardon, and he that had himself found mercy, notwithstanding his provocations, could the better encourage them with the hope of mercy notwithstanding theirs. Some that have been foolish and passionate, and have gone about their work very awkwardly at first, yet afterwards have proved useful and eminent. Men must not be thrown away for every fault. 2. By providence. The event was *according to the word of the Lord:* his arms were successful; he *restored the coast of Israel,* recovered those frontier-towns and countries that lay from Hamath in the north to the sea of the plain, (that is, the sea of Sodom) in the south, all which the Syrians had possessed themselves of, *v.* 25. Two reasons are here given why God blessed them with those victories:—(1.) Because their distress was very great, which made them the objects of his compassion, *v.* 26. Though he saw not any signs of their repentance and reformation, yet *he saw their affliction, that it was very bitter.* Those that lived in those countries which the enemies were masters of were miserably oppressed and enslaved, and could call nothing their own; the rest, we may suppose, were much impoverished by the frequent incursions the enemy made upon them to plunder them, and continually terrified by their threatenings, so that *there was none shut up or left,* both towns and countries were laid waste and stripped of their wealth, and no helper appeared. To this extremity were they reduced, in many parts of the country, in the beginning of Jeroboam's reign, when God, in mere pity to them, heard the cry of their affliction (for no mention is made here of the cry of their prayers), and wrought this deliverance for them by the hand of Jeroboam. Let those whose case is pitiable take comfort from the divine pity: we read of God's bowels of mercy (Isa. lxiii. 15; Jer. xxxi. 20) and that he is full of compassion, Ps. lxxxvi. 15. (2.) Because the decree had not yet gone forth for their utter destruction; he had not as yet said *he would blot out the name of Israel* (*v.* 27), and because he had not said it he would not do it. If this be understood of the dispersion of the ten tribes, he did say it and do it not long after (reprieves are not pardons)—if of the utter extirpation of the name of Israel, he never said it, nor will ever do it, for that name still remains under heaven in the *gospel Israel,* and will to the end of time; and because they, at present, bore that name which was to have this lasting honour, he showed them this favour, as well as for the sake of the ancient honour of that name, *ch.* xiii. 23.

IV. Here is the conclusion of Jeroboam's reign. We read (*v.* 28) of his might, and how he warred, but (*v.* 29) he *slept with his fathers;* for the mightiest must yield to death, and there is no discharge in that war. Many prophets there had been in Israel, a constant succession of them in every age, but none of the prophets had left any of their prophecies in writing till those of this age began to do it, and their prophecies are part of the canon of scripture. It was in the reign of this Jeroboam that *Hosea* (who continued very long a prophet) began to prophesy, and he was the first that wrote his prophecies; therefore the word of the Lord by him is called *the beginning of the word of the Lord,* Hos. i. 2. Then *that part of the word of the Lord* began to be written. At the same time *Amos* prophesied, and wrote his prophecy, soon afterwards *Micah,* and then *Isaiah,* in the days of Ahaz and Hezekiah. Thus God never left himself without witness, but, in the darkest and most degenerate ages of the church, raised up some to be burning and shining lights in it to their own age by their preaching and living, and a few by their writings to reflect light upon us on whom the ends of the world have come.

CHAP. XV.

In this chapter, I. The history of two of the kings of Judah is briefly recorded:—1. Of Azariah, or Uzziah, ver. 1—7. 2. Of Jotham his son, ver. 32—38. II. The history of many of the kings of Israel that reigned at the same time is given us in short, five in succession, all of whom, except one, went down slain to the pit, and their murderers were their successors. 1. Zachariah, the last of the house of Jehu, reigned six months, and then was slain and succeeded by Shallum, ver. 8—12. 2. Shallum reigned one month, and then was slain and succeeded by Menahem, ver. 13—15. 3. Menahem reigned ten years (or tyrannised rather, such were his barbarous cruelties (ver. 16) and unreasonable exactions, ver. 20), and then died in his bed, and left his son to succeed him first, and then suffer for him, ver. 16—22. 4. Pekahiah reigned two years, and then was slain and succeeded by Pekah, ver. 23—26. 5. Pekah reigned twenty years, and then was slain and succeeded by Hoshea, the last of all the kings of Israel (ver. 27—31), for things were now working and hastening apace towards the final destruction of that kingdom.

IN the twenty and seventh year of Jeroboam king of Israel began Azariah son of Amaziah king of Judah to reign. 2 Sixteen years old was he when he began to reign, and he reigned two and fifty years in Jerusalem. And his mother's name *was* Jecholiah of Jerusalem. 3 And he did *that which was* right in the sight of the LORD, according to all that his father Amaziah had done; 4 Save that the high places were not removed: the people sacrificed and burnt incense still on the high places. 5 And the LORD smote the king, so that he was a leper unto the day of his death, and dwelt in a several house. And Jotham the king's son *was* over the house, judging the people of the land. 6 And the rest of the acts of Azariah, and all that he did, *are* they not written in the book of the chronicles of the kings of Judah? 7 So Azariah slept with his fathers; and they buried him with his fathers in the city of David: and Jotham his son reigned in his stead.

This is a short account of the reign of Azariah. 1. Most of it is general, and the same that has been given of others; he began young and reigned long (*v.* 2), did, for the most part, that which was right, *v.* 3 (it was happy for the kingdom that a good reign was a long one), only he had not zeal and courage enough to take away the high places, *v.* 4. 2. That which is peculiar, *v.* 5 (that God smote him with a leprosy) is more largely related, with the occasion of it, 2 Chron. xxvi. 16, &c., where we have also a fuller account of the glories of the former part of his reign, as well as of the disgraces of the latter part of it. He did that which was right, as Amaziah had done; like him, he began well, but failed before he finished. Here we are told, (1.) That he was a leper. The greatest of men are not only subject to the common calamities, but also to the common infirmities, of human nature; and, if they be guilty of any heinous sin, they lie as open as the meanest to the most grievous strokes of divine vengeance. (2.) God smote him with this leprosy, to chastise him for his presumptuous invasion of the priests' office. If great men be proud men, some way or other God will humble them, and make them know he is both above them and against them, for he resisteth the proud. (3.) That he was a leper *to the day of his death.* Though we have reason to think he repented and the sin was pardoned, yet, for warning to others, he was continued under this mark of God's displeasure as long as he lived, and perhaps it was for the good of his soul that he was so. (4.) That he *dwelt in a separate house,* as being made ceremonially unclean by the law, to the discipline of which, though a king, he must submit. He that presumptuously intruded into God's temple, and pretended to be a priest, was justly shut out from his own palace, and shut up as a prisoner or recluse, ever after. We suppose that his *separate house* was made as convenient and agreeable as might be. Some translate it a *free house,* where he had liberty to take his pleasure. However, it was a great mortification to one that had been so much a man of honour, and a man of business, as he had been, to be cut off from society and dwell always in a *separate house:* it would almost make life itself a burden, even to kings, though they have never any to converse with but their inferiors; the most contemplative men would soon be weary of it. (5.) That his son was his viceroy in the affairs both of his court (for *he was over the house*) and of his kingdom (for he was *judging the people of the land);* and it was both a comfort to him and a blessing to his kingdom that he had such a son to fill up his room.

8 In the thirty and eighth year of Azariah king of Judah did Zachariah the son of Jeroboam reign over Israel in Samaria six months. 9 And he did *that which was* evil in the sight of the LORD, as his fathers had done: he departed not from the sins of Jeroboam the son of Nebat, who made Israel to sin. 10 And Shallum the son of Jabesh conspired against him, and smote him before the people, and slew him, and reigned in his stead. 11 And the rest of the acts of Zachariah, behold, they *are* written in the book of the chronicles of the kings of Israel. 12 This *was* the word of the LORD which he spake unto Jehu, saying, Thy sons shall sit on the throne

of Israel unto the fourth *generation.* And so it came to pass. 13 Shallum the son of Jabesh began to reign in the nine and thirtieth year of Uzziah king of Judah; and he reigned a full month in Samaria. 14 For Menahem the son of Gadi went up from Tirzah, and came to Samaria, and smote Shallum the son of Jabesh in Samaria, and slew him, and reigned in his stead. 15 And the rest of the acts of Shallum, and his conspiracy which he made, behold, they *are* written in the book of the chronicles of the kings of Israel. 16 Then Menahem smote Tiphsah, and all that *were* therein, and the coasts thereof from Tirzah; because they opened not *to him,* therefore he smote *it; and* all the women therein that were with child he ripped up. 17 In the nine and thirtieth year of Azariah king of Judah began Menahem the son of Gadi to reign over Israel, *and reigned* ten years in Samaria. 18 And he did *that which was* evil in the sight of the LORD: he departed not all his days from the sins of Jeroboam the son of Nebat, who made Israel to sin. 19 *And* Pul the king of Assyria came against the land: and Menahem gave Pul a thousand talents of silver, that his hand might be with him to confirm the kingdom in his hand. 20 And Menahem exacted the money of Israel, *even* of all the mighty men of wealth, of each man fifty shekels of silver, to give to the king of Assyria. So the king of Assyria turned back, and stayed not there in the land. 21 And the rest of the acts of Menahem, and all that he did, *are* they not written in the book of the chronicles of the kings of Israel? 22 And Menahem slept with his fathers; and Pekahiah his son reigned in his stead. 23 In the fiftieth year of Azariah king of Judah Pekahiah the son of Menahem began to reign over Israel in Samaria, *and reigned* two years. 24 And he did *that which was* evil in the sight of the LORD: he departed not from the sins of Jeroboam the son of Nebat, who made Israel to sin. 25 But Pekah the son of Remaliah, a captain of his, conspired against him, and smote him in Samaria, in the palace of the king's house, with Argob and Arieh, and with him fifty men of the Gileadites: and he killed him, and reigned in his room. 26 And the rest of the acts of Pekahiah, and all that he did, behold, they are written in the book of the chronicles of the kings of Israel. 27 In the two and fiftieth year of Azariah king of Judah Pekah the son of Remaliah began to reign over Israel in Samaria, *and reigned* twenty years. 28 And he did *that which was* evil in the sight of the LORD: he departed not from the sins of Jeroboam the son of Nebat, who made Israel to sin. 29 In the days of Pekah king of Israel came Tiglath-pileser king of Assyria, and took Ijon, and Abel-beth-maachah, and Janoah, and Kedesh, and Hazor, and Gilead, and Galilee, all the land of Naphtali, and carried them captive to Assyria. 30 And Hoshea the son of Elah made a conspiracy against Pekah the son of Remaliah, and smote him, and slew him, and reigned in his stead, in the twentieth year of Jotham the son of Uzziah. 31 And the rest of the acts of Pekah, and all that he did, behold, they *are* written in the book of the chronicles of the kings of Israel.

The best days of the kingdom of Israel were while the government was in Jehu's family. In his reign, and the next three reigns, though there were many abominable corruptions and miserable grievances in Israel, yet the crown went in succession, the kings died in their beds, and some care was taken of public affairs; but, now that those days are at an end, the history which we have in these verses of about thirty-three years represents the affairs of that kingdom in the utmost confusion imaginable. Woe to those that were with child (*v.* 16) and to those that gave suck in those days, for then must needs be great tribulations, when, for *the transgression of the land, many were the princes thereof.*

I. Let us observe something, in general, concerning these unhappy revolutions and the calamities which must needs attend them—these bad times, as they may truly be called. 1. God had tried the people of Israel both with judgments and mercies, explained and enforced by his servants the prophets, and yet they continued impenitent and unreformed, and therefore God justly brought these miseries upon them, as Moses had warned them. If you will yet *walk contrary to me, I will punish you yet seven times more,* Lev. xxvi. 21, &c. 2. God made good his promise to Jehu, that his sons to the fourth generation after him should sit upon the throne of Israel, which was a greater favour than was shown to any of the royal families either before or after his. God had said it should be so (*ch.* x. 30) and we are told in this chapter (*v.* 12) that so it came to pass. See how punctual God is to his promises. These calamities God long designed for Israel, and they deserved them, yet they were not inflicted till that word had taken effect to the full. Thus God rewarded Jehu for his zeal in destroying the worship of Baal and the house of Ahab; and yet, when the measure of the sins of the house of Jehu was full, God avenged upon it the blood then shed, called *the blood of Jezreel,* Hos. i. 4. 3. All these kings did that which was *evil in the sight of the Lord,* for *they walked in the sins of Jeroboam the son of Nebat.* Though at variance with one another, yet in this they agreed, to keep up idolatry, and the people loved to have it so; though they were emptied from vessel to vessel, that *taste remained in them,* and *that scent was not changed.* It was sad indeed when their government was so often altered, yet never for the better—that among all those contending interests none of them should think it as much their interest to destroy the calves as others had done to support them. 4. Each of these (except one) conspired against his predecessor, and slew him—*Shallum, Menahem, Pekah,* and *Hoshea,* all traitors and murderers, and yet all kings awhile, one of them ten, another twenty, and another nine years; for God may suffer wickedness to prosper and to carry away the wealth and honours awhile, but, sooner or later, blood shall have blood, and he that dealt treacherously shalt be dealt treacherously with. One wicked man is often made a scourge to another, and every wicked man, at length, a ruin to himself. 5. The ambition of the great men made the nation miserable. Here is Tiphsah, a city of Israel, barbarously destroyed, with all the coasts thereof, by one of these pretenders (*v.* 16), and no doubt it was through blood that each of them waded to the throne, nor could any of these kings perish alone. No land can have greater pests, nor Israel worse troubles, than such men as care not how much the welfare and repose of their country are sacrificed to their revenge and affectation of dominion. 6. While the nation was thus shattered by divisions at home the kings of Assyria, first one (*v.* 19) and then another (*v.* 29), came against it and did what they pleased. Nothing does more towards the making of a nation an easy prey to a common enemy than intestine broils and contests for the sovereignty. Happy the land where that is settled. 7. This was the condition of Israel just before they were quite ruined and carried away captive, for that was in the ninth year of Hoshea, the last of these usurpers. If they had, in these days of confusion and perplexity, humbled themselves before God and sought his face, that final destruction might have been prevented; but when God judgeth he will overcome. These factions, the fruit of an evil spirit sent among them, hastened that captivity, for a kingdom thus divided against itself will soon come to desolation.

II. Let us take a short view of the particular reigns.

1. Zachariah, the son of Jeroboam, began to reign in the thirty-eighth year of Azariah, or Uzziah, king of Judah, *v.* 8. Some of the most critical chronologers' reckon that between Jeroboam and his son Zachariah the throne was vacant twenty-two years, others eleven years, through the disturbances and dissensions that were in the kingdom; and then it was not strange that Zachariah was deposed before he was well seated on the throne: he reigned but six months, and then Shallum *slew him before the people,* perhaps as Cæsar was slain in the senate, or he put him to death publicly as a criminal, with the approbation of the people, to whom he had, some way or other, made himself odious; so ended the line of Jehu.

2. But had Shallum peace, who slew his master? No, he had not (*v.* 13), one month of days measured his reign and then he was cut off; perhaps to this the prophet, who then lived, refers (Hos. v. 7), *Now shall a month devour them with their portions.* That dominion seldom lasts long which is founded in blood and falsehood. Menahem, either provoked by his crime or animated by his example, soon served him as he had served his master—*slew him and reigned in his stead, v.* 14. Probably he was general in the army, which then lay encamped at Tirzah, and, hearing of Shallum's treason and usurpation, hastened to punish it, as Omri did that of Zimri in a like case, 1 Kings xvi. 17.

3. Menahem held the kingdom ten years, *v.* 17. But, whereas we have heard that the *kings of the house of Israel were merciful kings* (1 Kings xx. 31), this Menahem (the scandal of his country) was so prodigiously cruel to those of his own nation who hesitated a little at submitting to him that he not only ruined a city, and the coasts thereof, but, forgetting that he himself was born of a woman, *ripped up all the women with child, v.* 16. We may well wonder that ever it should enter into the heart of any man to be so barbarous, and to be so perfectly lost to humanity itself. By these cruel methods he hoped to strengthen himself and to frighten all others into his interests; but it seems he did not gain his point, for when the king of Assyria came against him, (1.) So little confidence had he in his people that he durst not meet him as an enemy, but was obliged, at a vast expense, to purchase a peace with him. (2.) Such

need had he of help *to confirm the kingdom in his hand* that he made it part of his bargain with him (a bargain which, no doubt, the king of Assyria knew how to make a good hand of another time) that he should assist him against his own subjects that were disaffected to him. The money wherewith he purchased his friendship was a vast sum, no less than 1000 talents of silver (*v.* 19), which Menahem exacted, it is probable, by military execution, *of all the mighty men of wealth,* very considerately sparing the poor, and laying the burden (as was fit) on those that were best able to bear it; being raised, it was given *to the king of Assyria,* as pay for his army, fifty shekels of silver for each man in it. Thus he got clear of the king of Assyria for this time; he staid not to quarter in the land (*v.* 20), but his army now got so rich a booty with so little trouble that it encouraged them to come again, not long after, when they laid all waste. Thus was *he* the betrayer of his country that should have been the protector of it.

4. Pekahiah, the son of Menahem, succeeded his father, but reigned only two years, and then was treacherously slain by Pekah, falling under the load both of his own and of his father's wickedness. It is repeated concerning him as before that he *departed not from the sins of Jeroboam.* Still this is mentioned, to show that God was righteous in bringing that destruction upon them which came not long after, because they hated to be reformed, *v.* 24. Pekah, it seems, had some persons of figure in his interest, two of whom are here named (*v.* 25), and with their help he compassed his design.

5. Pekah, though he got the kingdom by treason, kept it twenty years (*v.* 27), so long it was before his violent dealing returned upon his own head, but it returned at last. This Pekah, son of Remaliah, (1.) Made himself more considerable abroad than any of these usurpers, for he was, even in the latter end of his time (in the reign of Ahaz, which began in his seventeenth year), a great terror to the kingdom of Judah, as we find, Isa. vii. 1, &c. (2.) He lost a great part of his kingdom to the king of Assyria. Several cities are here named (*v.* 29) which were taken from him, all the land of Gilead on theother side Jordan, and Galilee in the north containing the tribes of Naphtali and Zebulon, were seized, and the inhabitants carried captive into Assyria. By this judgment God punished him for his attempt upon Judah and Jerusalem. It was then foretold that within two or three years after he made that attempt, before a child, then born, should be able to cry *My father and my mother,* the riches of Samaria should be *taken away before the king of Assyria* (Isa. viii. 4), and here we have the accomplishment of that prediction. (3.) Soon after this he forfeited his life to the resentments of his countrymen, who, it is probable, were disgusted at him for leaving them exposed to a foreign enemy, while he was invading Judah, of which Hoshea took advantage and, to gain his crown, seized his life, *slew him, and reigned in his stead.* Surely he was fond of a crown indeed who, at this time, would run such a hazard as a traitor did; for the crown of Israel, now that it had lost the choicest of its flowers and jewels, was lined more than ever with thorns, had of late been fatal to all the heads that had worn it, was forfeited to divine justice, and now ready to be laid in the dust—a crown which a wise man would not have taken up in the street, yet Hoshea not only ventured *upon* it but ventured *for* it, and it cost him dear.

32 In the second year of Pekah the son of Remaliah king of Israel began Jotham the son of Uzziah king of Judah to reign. 33 Five and twenty years old was he when he began to reign, and he reigned sixteen years in Jerusalem. And his mother's name *was* Jerusha, the daughter of Zadok. 34 And he did *that which was* right in the sight of the LORD: he did according to all that his father Uzziah had done. 35 Howbeit the high places were not removed: the people sacrificed and burned incense still in the high places. He built the higher gate of the house of the LORD. 36 Now the rest of the acts of Jotham, and all that he did, *are* they not written in the book of the chronicles of the kings of Judah? 37 In those days the LORD began to send against Judah Rezin the king of Syria, and Pekah the son of Remaliah. 38 And Jotham slept with his fathers, and was buried with his fathers in the city of David his father: and Ahaz his son reigned in his stead.

We have here a short account of the reign of Jotham king of Judah, of whom we are told, 1. That he reigned very well, *did that which was right in the sight of the Lord, v.* 34. Josephus gives him a very high character, stating that he was pious towards God, just towards men, and laid out himself for the public good,—that, whatever was amiss, he took care to have it rectified,—and, in short, wanted no virtue that became a good prince. Though the high places were not taken away, yet to draw people from them, and keep them close to God's holy place, he showed great respect to the temple, and built the higher gate which he went through to the temple. If magistrates cannot do all they would for the suppressing of vice and profaneness, let them do so much the more for the support and advancement of piety and virtue, and the bringing of them into reputation. If they cannot pull down the high places of sin, yet let them build and beautify the high gate of God's house. 2. That he died in the midst of his days, *v.* 33. Of most of the kings of Judah we are told how old they were when they began their reign, and by that may compute how old they were when they died; but no account is kept of the *age* of any of the kings of Israel that I remember, only of the years of their *reigns.* This honour God would put upon the kings of the house of David above those of other families. And by these accounts it appears that there was none of all the kings of Judah that reached David's age, seventy, the common age of man. Asa's age I do not find. Uzziah lived to be sixty-eight, Manasseh sixty-seven, and Jehoshaphat sixty; and these were the three oldest; many of those that were of note did not reach fifty. This Jotham died at forty-one. He was too great a blessing to be continued long to such an unworthy people. His death was a judgment, especially considering the character of his son and successor. 3. That in his days the confederacy was formed against Judah by Rezin and Remaliah's son, the king of Syria and the king of Israel, which appeared so very formidable in the beginning of the reign of Ahaz that, upon notice of it, the heart of that prince was moved and *the heart of the people, as the trees of the wood are moved with the wind,* Isa. vii. 2. The confederates were unjust in the attempt, yet it is here said (*v.* 37), *The Lord began to send them against Judah,* as he bade Shimei curse David, and took away from Job what the Sabeans robbed him of. Men are God's hand—the sword, the rod in his hand—which he makes use of as he pleases to serve his own righteous counsels, though men be unrighteous in their intentions. This storm gathered in the reign of pious Jotham, but he came to his grave in peace and it fell upon his degenerate son.

CHAP. XVI.

This chapter is wholly taken up with the reign of Ahaz; and we have quite enough of it, unless it were better. He had a good father, and a better son, and yet was himself one of the worst of the kings of Judah. I. He was a notorious idolater, ver. 1—4. II. With the treasures of the temple, as well as his own, he hired the king of Assyria to invade Syria and Israel, ver. 5—9. III. He took pattern from an idol's altar which he saw at Damascus for a new altar in God's temple, ver. 10—16. IV. He abused and embezzled the furniture of the temple, ver. 17, 18. And so his story ends, ver. 19, 20.

IN the seventeenth year of Pekah the son of Remaliah Ahaz the son of Jotham king of Judah began to reign. 2 Twenty years old *was* Ahaz when he began to reign, and reigned sixteen years in Jerusalem, and did not *that which was* right in the sight of the LORD his God, like David his father. 3 But he walked in the way of the kings of Israel, yea, and made his son to pass through the fire, according to the abominations of the heathen, whom the LORD cast out from before the children of Israel. 4 And he sacrificed and burnt incense in the high places, and on the hills, and under every green tree.

We have here a general character of the reign of Ahaz. Few and evil were his days—few, for he died at thirty-six—evil, for we are here told, 1. That he *did not that which was right like David* (*v.* 2), that is, he had none of that concern and affection for the instituted service and worship of God for which David was celebrated. He had no love for the temple, made no conscience of his duty to God, nor had any regard to his law. Herein he was unlike David; it was his honour that he was of the house and lineage of David, and it was owing to God's ancient covenant with David that he was now upon the throne, which aggravated his wickedness; for he was a reproach to that honourable name and family, which therefore was really a reproach to him (*Degeneranti genus opprobrium—A good extraction is a disgrace to him who degenerates from it*), and though he enjoyed the benefit of David's piety he did not tread in the steps of it. 2. That he walked *in the way of the kings of Israel* (*v.* 3), who all worshipped the calves. He was not joined in any affinity with them, as Jehoram and Ahaziah were with the house of Ahab, but, *ex mero motu—without any instigation,* walked in their way. The kings of Israel pleaded policy and reasons of state for their idolatry, but Ahaz had no such pretence: in him it was the most unreasonable impolitic thing that could be. They were his enemies, and had proved enemies to themselves too by their idolatry; yet he walked in their way. 3. That he *made his sons to pass through the fire,* to the honour of his dunghill-deities. He burnt them, so it is expressly said of him (2 Chron. xxviii. 3), burnt some of them, and perhaps made others of them (Hezekiah himself not excepted, though afterwards he was never the worse for it) to pass between two fires, or to be drawn through a flame, in token of their dedication to the idol. 4. That he did *according to the abominations of the heathen whom the Lord had cast out.* It was an instance of his great folly that he would be guided in his religion by those whom he saw fallen into the ditch before his eyes, and follow them; and it was an instance of his great impiety that he would conform to those usages which God had declared to be abominable to him, and set himself to write after the copy of those whom God had cast out, thus walking directly contrary to God. 5. That he *sacrificed in the high places, v.* 4. If his father had but had zeal enough to take them away, the debauching of his sons might have been prevented; but those that connive at sin know not what dangerous snares they lay for those that come after them. He forsook God's house, was weary of that place where, in his father's time, he had often been detained before the Lord, and performed his devotions on high hills, where he had a better prospect, and under green trees, where he had a more pleasant shade. It was a religion little worth, which was guided by fancy, not by faith.

5 Then Rezin king of Syria and Pekah son of Remaliah king of Israel came up to Jerusalem to war: and they besieged Ahaz, but could not overcome *him*. 6 At that time Rezin king of Syria recovered Elath to Syria, and drave the Jews from Elath: and the Syrians came to Elath, and dwelt there unto this day. 7 So Ahaz sent messengers to Tiglath-pileser king of Assyria, saying, I *am* thy servant and thy son: come up, and save me out of the hand of the king of Syria, and out of the hand of the king of Israel, which rise up against me. 8 And Ahaz took the silver and gold that was found in the house of the LORD, and in the treasures of the king's house, and sent *it for* a present to the king of Assyria. 9 And the king of Assyria hearkened unto him: for the king of Assyria went up against Damascus, and took it, and carried *the people of* it captive to Kir, and slew Rezin.

Here is, 1. The attempt of his confederate neighbours, the kings of Syria and Israel, upon him. They thought to make themselves masters of Jerusalem, and to set a king of their own in it, Isa. vii. 6. In this they fell short, but the king of Syria recovered Elath, a considerable port upon the Red Sea, which Amaziah had taken from the Syrians, *ch.* xiv. 22. What can those keep that have lost their religion? Let them expect, thenceforward, to be always on the losing hand. 2. His project to get clear of them. Having forsaken God, he had neither courage nor strength to make head against his enemies, nor could he, with any boldness, ask help of God; but he made his court to the king of Assyria, and got him to come in for his relief. Those whose hearts condemn them will go any where in a day of distress rather than to God. Was it because there was not a God in Israel that he sent to the Assyrian for help? Was the rock of ages removed out of its place, that he stayed himself on this broken reed? The sin itself was its own punishment; for, though it is true that he gained his point (the king of Assyria hearkened to him, and, to serve his own turn, made a descent upon Damascus, whereby he gave a powerful diversion to the king of Syria (*v.* 9), and obliged him to let fall his design against Ahaz, carrying the Syrians captive to Kir, as Amos had expressly foretold, *ch.* i. 5), yet, considering all, he made but a bad bargain; for, to compass this, (1.) He enslaved himself (*v.* 7): *I am thy servant and thy son,* that is, "I will be as dutiful and obedient to thee as to a master or father, if thou wilt but do me this good turn." Had he thus humbled himself to God, and implored his favour, he might have been delivered upon easier terms; he might have saved his money, and needed only to have parted with his sins. But, if the prodigal forsake his father's house, he soon becomes a slave to the worst of masters, Luke xv. 15. (2.) He impoverished himself; for he took the silver and gold that were laid up in the treasury both of the temple and of the kingdom, and sent it to the king of Assyria, *v.* 8. Both church and state must be squeezed and exhausted, to gratify this his new patron and guardian. I know not what authority he had thus to dispose of the public stock; but it is common for those that have brought themselves into straits by one sin to help themselves out by another; and those that have alienated themselves from God will make no difficulty of alienating any of his rights.

10 And king Ahaz went to Damascus to meet Tiglath-pileser king of Assyria, and saw an altar that *was* at Damascus: and king Ahaz sent to Urijah the priest the fashion of the altar, and the pattern of it, according to all the workmanship thereof. 11 And Urijah the priest built an altar according to all that king Ahaz had sent from Damascus: so Urijah the priest made *it* against king Ahaz came from Damascus. 12 And when the king was come from Damascus, the king saw the altar: and the king approached to the altar, and offered thereon. 13 And he burnt his burnt offering and his meat offering, and poured his drink offering, and sprinkled the blood of his peace offerings, upon the altar. 14 And he brought also the brasen altar, which *was* before the LORD, from the forefront of the house, from between the altar and the house of the LORD, and put it on the north side of the altar. 15 And king Ahaz commanded Urijah the priest, saying, Upon the great altar burn the morning burnt offering, and the evening meat offering, and the king's burnt sacrifice, and his

meat offering, with the burnt offering of all the people of the land, and their meat offering, and their drink offerings; and sprinkle upon it all the blood of the burnt offering, and all the blood of the sacrifice: and the brasen altar shall be for me to enquire *by*. 16 Thus did Urijah the priest, according to all that king Ahaz commanded.

Though Ahaz had himself sacrificed in high places, on hills, and under every green tree (*v.* 4), yet God's altar had hitherto continued in its place and in use, and the *king's burnt-offering and his meat-offering* (*v.* 15) had been offered upon it by the priests that attended it; but here we have it taken away by wicked Ahaz, and another altar, an idolatrous one, put in the room of it—a bolder stroke than the worst of the kings had yet given to religion. We have here,

I. The model of this new altar, taken from one at Damascus, by the king himself, *v.* 10. The king of Assyria having taken Damascus, thither Ahaz went, to congratulate him on his success, to return him thanks for the kindness he had done him by this expedition, and, as his servant and son, to receive his commands. Had he been faithful to his God, he would not have needed to crouch thus meanly to a foreign power. At Damascus, either while viewing the rarities of the place, or rather while joining with them in their devotions (for, when he was there, he thought it no harm to do as they did), he saw an altar that pleased his fancy extremely, not such a plain old-fashioned one as that which he had been trained up in attendance upon at Jerusalem, but curiously carved, it is likely, and adorned with image-work; there were many pretty things about it which he thought significant, surprising, very charming, and calculated to excite his devotion. Solomon had but a dull fancy, he thought, compared with the ingenious artist that made this altar. Nothing will serve him but he must have an altar just like this: a pattern of it must be taken immediately; he cannot stay till he returns himself, but sends it before him in all haste, with orders to Urijah the priest to get one made exactly according to this model and have it ready against he came home. The pattern God showed to Moses in the mount or to David by the Spirit was not comparable to this pattern sent from Damascus. The hearts of idolaters walked after their eyes, which are therefore said to *go a whoring after their idols;* but the true worshippers worship the true God by faith.

II. The making of it by Urijah the priest, *v.* 11. This Urijah, it is likely, was the chief priest who at this time presided in the temple-service. To him Ahaz sent an intimation of his mind (for we read not of any express orders he gave him), to get an altar made by this pattern. And, without any dispute or objection, he put it in hand immediately, being perhaps as fond of it as the king was, at least being very willing to humour the king and desirous to curry favour with him. Perhaps he might have this excuse for gratifying the king herein, that, by this means, he might keep him to the temple at Jerusalem and prevent his totally deserting it for the high places and the groves. "Let us oblige him in this," thinks Urijah, "and then he will bring all his sacrifices to us; for by this craft we get our living." But, whatever pretence he had, it was a most base wicked thing for him that was a priest, a chief priest, to make this altar, in compliance with an idolatrous prince, for hereby, 1. He prostituted his authority and profaned the crown of his priesthood, making himself a servant to the lusts of men. There is not a greater disgrace to the ministry than obsequiousness to such wicked commands as this was. 2. He betrayed his trust. As priest, he was bound to maintain and defend God's institutions, and to oppose and witness against all innovations; and, for him to assist and serve the king in setting up an altar to confront the altar which by divine appointment he was consecrated to minister at, was such a piece of treachery and perfidiousness as may justly render him infamous to all posterity. Had he only connived at the doing of it,—had he been frightened into it by menaces,—had he endeavoured to dissuade the king from it, or but delayed the doing of it till he came home, that he might first talk with him about it,—it would not have been so bad; but so willingly to walk after his commandment, as if he were glad of the opportunity to oblige him, was such an affront to the God he served as was utterly inexcusable.

III. The dedicating of it. Urijah, perceiving that the king's heart was much upon it, took care to have it ready against he came down, and set it near the brazen altar, but somewhat lower and further from the door of the temple. The king was exceedingly pleased with it, approached it with all possible veneration, and offered thereon his burnt-offering, &c., *v.* 12, 13. His sacrifices were not offered to the God of Israel, but to the gods of Damascus (as we find 2 Chron. xxviii. 23), and, when he borrowed the Syrians' altar, no marvel that he borrowed their gods. Naaman, the Syrian, embraced the God of Israel when he got earth from the land of Israel to make an altar of.

IV. The removal of God's altar, to make room for it. Urijah was so modest that he put this altar at the lower end of the court, and left God's altar in its place, *between this and the house of the Lord*, *v.* 14. But that would not satisfy Ahaz; he removed God's altar to an obscure corner in the north side of the court, and put his own before the sanctuary, in the place of it. He thinks his new altar is much more stately, and much more sightly, and disgraces that; and therefore "let that be laid aside as a vessel in which there is no pleasure." His superstitious invention, at first, jostled *with* God's sacred institution, but at length jostled it *out*. Note, Those will soon come to make nothing of God that will not be content to make him their all. Ahaz durst not (perhaps for fear of the people) quite demolish the brazen altar and knock it to pieces; but, while he ordered all the sacrifices to be offered upon this new altar (*v.* 15), *The brazen altar* (says he) *shall be for me to enquire by*. Having thrust it out from the use for which it was instituted, which was to sanctify the gifts offered upon it, he pretends to advance it above its institution, which it is common for superstitious people to do. The altar was never designed for an oracle, yet Ahaz will have it for that use. The Romish church seemingly magnifies Christ's sacraments, yet wretchedly corrupts them. But some give another sense of Ahaz's purpose: "As for the brazen altar, I will consider what to do with it, and give order about it." The Jews say that, afterwards, of the brass of it he made that famous dial which was called *the dial of Ahaz, ch.* xx. 11. The base compliance of the poor-spirited priest with the presumptuous usurpations of an ill-spirited king is again taken notice of (*v.* 16): *Urijah the priest did according to all that king Ahaz commanded.* Miserable is the case of great men when those that should reprove them for their sins strengthen and serve them in their sins.

17 And king Ahaz cut off the borders of the bases, and removed the laver from off them; and took down the sea from off the brasen oxen that *were* under it, and put it upon a pavement of stones. 18 And the covert for the sabbath that they had built in the house, and the king's entry without, turned he from the house of the LORD for the king of Assyria. 19 Now the rest of the acts of Ahaz which he did, *are* they not written in the book of the chronicles of the kings of Judah? 20 And Ahaz slept with his fathers, and was buried with his fathers in the city of David: and Hezekiah his son reigned in his stead.

Here is, I. Ahaz abusing the temple, not the building itself, but some of the furniture of it. 1. He defaced the bases on which the lavers were set (1 Kings vii. 28, 29) and took down the molten sea, *v.* 17. These the priests used for washing; against them therefore he seems to have had a particular spite. It is one of the greatest prejudices that can be done to religion to obstruct the purifying of the priests, the Lord's ministers. 2. He removed *the covert for the sabbath*, erected either in honour of the sabbath or for the conveniency of the priests, when, on the sabbath, they officiated in greater numbers than on other days. Whatever it was, it should seem that in removing it he intended to put a contempt upon the sabbath, and so to open as wide an inlet as any to all manner of impiety. 3. The king's entry, which led to the house of the Lord, for the convenience of the royal family (perhaps that ascent which Solomon had made, and which the queen of Sheba admired, 1 Kings x. 5), he turned another way, to show that he did not intend to frequent the house of the Lord any more. This he did for the king of Assyria, to oblige him, who perhaps returned his visit, and found fault with this entry, as an inconvenience and disparagement to his palace. When those that have had a ready passage to the house of the Lord, to please their neighbours, turn it another way, they are going down the hill apace towards their ruin.

II. Ahaz resigning his life in the midst of his days, at thirty-six years of age (*v.* 19) and leaving his kingdom to a better man, Hezekiah his son (*v.* 20), who proved as much a friend to the temple as he had been an enemy to it. Perhaps this very son he had made to pass through the fire, and thereby dedicated him to Moloch; but God, by his grace, snatched him as a brand out of the burning.

CHAP. XVII.

This chapter gives us an account of the captivity of the ten tribes, and so finishes the history of that kingdom, after it had continued about 265 years, from the setting up of Jeroboam the son of Nebat. In it we have, I. A short narrative of this destruction, ver. 1—6. II. Remarks upon it, and the causes of it, for the justifying of God in it and for warning to others, ver. 7—23. III. An account of the nations which succeeded them in the possession of their land, and the mongrel religion set up among them, ver. 24—41.

IN the twelfth year of Ahaz king of Judah began Hoshea the son of Elah to reign in Samaria over Israel nine years. 2 And he did *that which was* evil in the sight of the LORD, but not as the kings of Israel that were before him. 3 Against him came up Shalmaneser king of Assyria; and Hoshea became his servant, and gave him presents. 4 And the king of Assyria found conspiracy in Hoshea: for he had sent messengers to So king of Egypt, and brought no present to the king of Assyria, as *he had done* year by year: therefore the king of Assyria shut him up, and bound him in prison. 5 Then the king of Assyria came up throughout all the land, and went up to Samaria, and besieged it three years. 6 In the ninth year of Hoshea the king of Assyria took Samaria,

and carried Israel away into Assyria, and placed them in Halah and in Habor *by* the river of Gozan, and in the cities of the Medes.

We have here the reign and ruin of Hoshea, the last of the kings of Israel, concerning whom observe,

I. That, though he forced his way to the crown by treason and murder (as we read *ch.* xv. 30), yet he gained not the possession of it till seven or eight years after; for it was in the fourth year of Ahaz that he slew Pekah, but did not himself begin to reign till the twelfth year of Ahaz, *v.* 1. Whether by the king of Assyria, or by the king of Judah, or by some of his own people, does not appear, but it seems so long he was kept out of the throne he aimed at. Justly were his bad practices thus chastised, and the word of the prophet was thus fulfilled (Hos. x. 3), *Now they shall say We have no king, because we feared not the Lord.*

II. That, though he was bad, yet not so bad as the kings of Israel had been before him (*v.* 2), not so devoted to the calves as they had been. One of them (that at Dan), the Jews say, had been, before this, carried away by the king of Assyria in the expedition recorded *ch.* xv. 29, (to which perhaps the prophet refers, Hos. viii. 5, *Thy calf, O Samaria! has cast thee off*), which made him put the less confidence in the other. And some say that this Hoshea took off the embargo which the former kings had put their subjects under, forbidding them to go up to Jerusalem to worship, which he permitted those to do that had a mind to it. But what shall we think of this dispensation of providence, that the destruction of the kingdom of Israel should come in the reign of one of the best of its kings? *Thy judgments,* O God! *are a great deep.* God would hereby show that in bringing this ruin upon them he designed to punish, 1. Not only the sins of that generation, but of the foregoing ages, and to reckon for the iniquities of their fathers, who had been long in filling the measure and treasuring up wrath against this day of wrath. 2. Not only the sins of their kings, but the sins of the people. If Hoshea was not so bad as the former kings, yet the people were as bad as those that went before them, and it was an aggravation of their badness, and brought ruin the sooner, that their king did not set them so bad an example as the former kings had done, nor hinder them from reforming; he gave them leave to do better, but they did as bad as ever, which laid the blame of their sin and ruin wholly upon themselves.

III. That the destruction came gradually. They were for some time made tributaries before they were made captives to the king of Assyria (*v.* 3), and, if that less judgment had prevailed to humble and reform them, the greater would have been prevented.

IV. That they brought it upon themselves by the indirect course they took to shake off the yoke of the king of Assyria, *v.* 4. Had the king and people of Israel applied to God, made their peace with him and their prayers to him, they might have recovered their liberty, ease, and honour; but they withheld their tribute, and trusted to the king of Egypt to assist them in their revolt, which, if it had taken effect, would have been but to change their oppressors. But Egypt became to them the staff of a broken reed. This provoked the king of Assyria to proceed against them with the more severity. Men get nothing by struggling with the net, but entangle themselves the more.

V. That it was an utter destruction that came upon them. 1. The king of Israel was made a prisoner; he was shut up and bound, being, it is probable, taken by surprise, before Samaria was besieged. 2. The land of Israel was made a prey. The army of the king of Assyria came up throughout all the land, made themselves masters of it (*v.* 5), and treated the people as traitors to be punished with the sword of justice rather than as fair enemies. 3. The royal city of Israel was besieged, and at length taken. Three years it held out after the country was conquered, and no doubt a great deal of misery was endured at that time which is not particularly recorded; but the brevity of the story, and the passing of this matter over lightly, methinks, intimate that they were abandoned of God and he did not now regard the affliction of Israel, as sometimes he had done. 4. The people of Israel were carried captives into Assyria, *v.* 6. The generality of the people, those that were of any note, were forced away into the conqueror's country, to be slaves and beggars there. (1.) Thus he was pleased to exercise a dominion over them, and to show that they were entirely at his disposal. (2.) By depriving them of their possessions and estates, real and personal, and exposing them to all the hardships and reproaches of a removal to a strange country, under the power of an imperious army, he chastised them for their rebellion and their endeavour to shake off his yoke. (3.) Thus he effectually prevented all such attempts for the future and secured their country to himself. (4.) Thus he got the benefit of their service in his own country, as Pharaoh did that of their fathers; and so this unworthy people were lost as they were found, and ended as they began, in servitude and under oppression. (5) Thus he made room for those of his own country that had little, and little to do, at home, to settle in a good land, a land flowing with milk and honey. In all these several ways he served himself by this captivity of the ten tribes. We are here told in what places of his kingdom he disposed of them—in *Halah* and *Habor*, in places, we may suppose, far distant from each other, lest they should keep up a correspondence, incorporate again, and become formidable. There, we have reason to think, after some time they were so mingled with the nations that they were lost, and *the name of Israel was no more in remembrance*. Those that forgot God were themselves forgotten; those that studied to be like the nations were buried among them; and those that would not serve God in their own land were made to serve their enemies in a strange land. It is probable that they were the men of honour and estates who were carried captive, and that many of the meaner sort of people were left behind, many of every tribe, who either went over to Judah or became subject to the Assyrian colonies, and their posterity were *Galileans* or *Samaritans*. But thus ended Israel as a nation; now they became *Lo-ammi—not a people*, and *Lo-ruhamah—unpitied*. Now Canaan spued them out. When we read of their entry under Hoshea the son of Nun who would have thought that such as this should be their exit under Hoshea the son of Elah? Thus Rome's glory in Augustus sunk, many ages after, in Augustulus. Providence so ordered the eclipsing of the honour of the ten tribes that the honour of Judah (the royal tribe) and Levi (the holy tribe), which yet remained, might shine the brighter. Yet we find a number sealed of every one of the twelve tribes (Rev. vii.) except Dan. James writes to the twelve tribes scattered abroad (Jam. i. 1) and Paul speaks of the twelve tribes which *instantly served God day and night* (Acts xxvi. 7); so that though we never read of those that were carried captive, nor have any reason to credit the conjecture of some (that they yet remain a distinct body in some remote corner of the world), yet a remnant of them did escape, to keep up the name of Israel, till it came to be worn by the gospel church, the spiritual Israel, in which it will ever remain, Gal. vi. 16.

7 For *so* it was, that the children of Israel had sinned against the LORD their God, which had brought them up out of the land of Egypt, from under the hand of Pharaoh king of Egypt, and had feared other gods, 8 And walked in the statutes of the heathen, whom the LORD cast out from before the children of Israel, and of the kings of Israel, which they had made. 9 And the children of Israel did secretly *those* things that *were* not right against the LORD their God, and they built them high places in all their cities, from the tower of the watchmen to the fenced city. 10 And they set them up images and groves in every high hill, and under every green tree: 11 And there they burnt incense in all the high places, as *did* the heathen whom the LORD carried away before them; and wrought wicked things to provoke the LORD to anger: 12 For they served idols, whereof the LORD had said unto them, Ye shall not do this thing. 13 Yet the LORD testified against Israel, and against Judah, by all the prophets, *and by* all the seers, saying, Turn ye from your evil ways, and keep my commandments *and* my statutes, according to all the law which I commanded your fathers, and which I sent to you by my servants the prophets. 14 Notwithstanding they would not hear, but hardened their necks, like to the neck of their fathers, that did not believe in the LORD their God. 15 And they rejected his statutes, and his covenant that he made with their fathers, and his testimonies which he testified against them; and they followed vanity, and became vain, and went after the heathen that *were* round about them, *concerning* whom the LORD had charged them, that they should not do like them. 16 And they left all the commandments of the LORD their God, and made them molten images, *even* two calves, and made a grove, and worshipped all the host of heaven, and served Baal. 17 And they caused their sons and their daughters to pass through the fire, and used divination and enchantments, and sold themselves to do evil in the sight of the LORD, to provoke him to anger. 18 Therefore the LORD was very angry with Israel, and removed them out of his sight: there was none left but the tribe of Judah only. 19 Also Judah kept not the commandments of the LORD their God, but walked in the statutes of Israel which they made. 20 And the LORD rejected all the seed of Israel, and afflicted them, and delivered them into the hand of spoilers, until he had cast them out of his sight. 21 For he rent Israel from the house of David; and they made Jeroboam the son of Nebat king: and Jeroboam drave Israel from following the LORD, and

made them sin a great sin. 22 For the children of Israel walked in all the sins of Jeroboam which he did; they departed not from them; 23 Until the LORD removed Israel out of his sight, as he had said by all his servants the prophets. So was Israel carried away out of their own land to Assyria unto this day.

Though the destruction of the kingdom of the ten tribes was but briefly related, it is in these verses largely commented upon by our historian, and the reasons of it assigned, not taken from the second causes—the weakness of Israel, their impolitic management, and the strength and growing greatness of the Assyrian monarch (these things are overlooked)—but only from the First Cause. Observe, 1. It was *the Lord that removed Israel out of his sight;* whoever were the instruments, he was the author of this calamity. It was *destruction from the Almighty;* the Assyrian was but the *rod of his anger,* Isa. x. 5. It was *the Lord that rejected the seed of Israel,* else their enemies could not have seized upon them, *v.* 20. *Who gave Jacob for a spoil, and Israel to the robbers? Did not the Lord?* Isa. xlii. 24. We lose the benefit of national judgments if we do not eye the hand of God in them, and the fulfilling of the scripture, for that also is taken notice of here (*v.* 23): *The Lord removed Israel* out of his favour, and out of their own land, *as he had said by all his servants the prophets.* Rather shall heaven and earth pass than one tittle of God's word fall to the ground. When God's word and his works are compared, it will be found not only that they agree, but that they illustrate each other. But why would God ruin a people that were raised and incorporated, as Israel was, by miracles and oracles? Why would he undo that which he himself had done at so vast an expense? Was it purely an act of sovereignty? No, it was an act of necessary justice. For, 2. They provoked him to do this by their wickedness. Was it God's doing? Nay, it was their own; by their *way and their doings* they *procured all this to themselves,* and it was their own wickedness that did correct them. This the sacred historian shows here at large, that it might appear that God did them no wrong and that others might hear and fear. Come and see what it was that did all this mischief, that broke their power and laid their honour in the dust; it was sin; that, and nothing else, separated between them and God. This is here very movingly laid open as the cause of all the desolations of Israel. He here shows,

I. What God had done for Israel, to engage them to serve him. 1. He gave them their liberty (*v.* 7): He *brought them from under the hand of Pharaoh* who oppressed them, asserted their freedom (*Israel is my son),* and effected their freedom with a high hand. Thus they were bound in duty and gratitude to be his servants, for he had loosed their bonds; nor would he that rescued them out of the hand of the king of Egypt have contradicted himself so far as to deliver them into the hand of the king of Assyria, as he did, if they had not, by their iniquity, betrayed their liberty and sold themselves. 2. He gave them their law, and was himself their king. They were immediately under a divine regimen. They could not plead ignorance of good and evil, sin and duty, for God had particularly charged them against those very things which here he charges them with (*v.* 15), *That they should not do like the heathen.* Nor could they be in any doubt concerning their obligation to observe the laws which they are here charged with rejecting, for they were *the commandments and statutes* of the Lord their God (*v.* 13), so that no room was left to dispute whether they should keep them or no. He had not *dealt so with other nations,* Ps. cxlvii. 19, 20. 3. He gave them *their land,* for he *cast out the heathen from before them* (*v.* 8), to make room for them; and the casting out of them for their idolatries was as fair a warning as could be given to Israel not to do like them.

II. What they had done against God, notwithstanding these engagements which he had laid upon them. 1. In general· They *sinned against the Lord their God* (*v.* 7), they *did those things that were not right* (*v.* 9), but *secretly.* So wedded were they to their evil practices that when they could not do them publicly, could not for shame or could not for fear, they would do them secretly—an evidence of their atheism, that they thought what was done in secret was from under the eye of God himself and would not be required. Again, they wrought wicked things in such a direct contradiction to the divine law that they seemed as if they were done on purpose to *provoke the Lord to anger* (*v.* 11), in contempt of his authority and defiance of his justice. They *rejected God's statutes and his covenant* (*v.* 15), would not be bound up either by his command or the consent they themselves had given to the covenant, but threw off the obligations of both, and therefore God justly rejected them, *v.* 20. See Hos. iv. 6. They *left all the commandments of the Lord their God* (*v.* 16), left the way, left the work, which those commandments prescribed them and directed them in. Nay, lastly, they *sold themselves to do evil in the sight of the Lord,* that is, they wholly addicted themselves to sin, as slaves to the service of those to whom they are sold, and, by their obstinately persisting in sin, so hardened their own hearts that at length it had become morally impossible for them to recover themselves, as one that has sold himself has put his liberty past recal. 2. In particular. Though they were guilty (no doubt) of many immoralities, and violated all the commands of the second table, yet nothing is here specified but their idolatry. *This* was the sin that did most easily beset them; this was, of all sins, most provoking to God: it was the spiritual adultery that broke the marriage-covenant, and was the inlet of all other wickedness. Hence it is again and again mentioned here as the sin that ruined them. (1.) They feared other gods (*v.* 7), that is, worshipped them and paid their homage to them, as if they feared their displeasure. (2.) They *walked in the statutes of the heathen,* which were contrary to God's statutes (*v.* 8), did *as did the heathen* (*v.* 11), *went after the heathen that were round about them* (*v.* 15), so prostituting the honour of their peculiarity, and defeating God's design concerning them, which was that they should be distinguished from the heathen. Must those that were taught of God go to school to the heathen—those that were appropriated to God take their measures from the nations that were abandoned by him? (3.) They *walked in the statutes of the* idolatrous *kings of Israel* (*v.* 8), *in all the sins of Jeroboam, v.* 22. When their kings assumed a power to alter and add to the divine institutions they submitted to them, and thought the command of their kings would bear them out in disobedience to the command of their God. (4.) They *built themselves high places in all their cities, v.* 9. If in any place there was but the tower of the watchmen (a country town that had no walls, but only a tower to shelter the watch in time of danger), or but a lodge for shepherds, it must be honoured with a high place, and that with an altar. If there was a fenced city, it must be further fortified with a high place. Having forsaken God's holy place, they knew no end of high places, in which every man followed his own fancy and directed his devotion to what god he pleased. Sacred things were hereby profaned and laid common, when their altars were *as heaps in the furrows of the field,* Hos. xii. 11. (5.) They *set them up images and groves—Asherim* (even *wooden images,* so some think the term, which we translate *groves,* should be rendered) or *Ashtaroth* (so others)—directly contrary to the second commandment, *v.* 10. They served idols (*v.* 12), the works of their own hands and creatures of their own fancy, though God had warned them particularly not to do this thing. (6.) They *burnt incense in all the high places,* to the honour of strange gods, for it was to the dishonour of the true God, *v.* 11. (7.) They followed vanity. Idols are called so, because they could do neither good nor evil, but were the most insignificant things that could be; those that worshipped them were like unto them, and so they became vain and good for nothing (*v.* 16), vain in their devotions, which were brutish and ridiculous, and so became vain in their whole conversation. (8.) Besides the molten images, even the two calves, they *worshipped all the host of heaven*—the sun, moon, and stars: for it is not meant of the heavenly host of angels; they could not rise so far above sensible things as to think of them. And, withal, they served Baal, the deified heroes of the Gentiles, *v.* 16. (9.) *They caused their children to pass through the fire,* in token of their dedicating them to their idols. (10.) They used divinations and enchantments, that they might receive directions from the gods to whom they paid their devotions.

III. What means God used with them, to bring them off from their idolatries, and to how little purpose. He testified against them, showed them their sins and warned them of the fatal consequences of them by all the prophets and all the *seers* (for so the prophets had been formerly called), and pressed them to *turn from their evil ways, v.* 13. We have read of prophets, more or less, in every reign. Though they had forsaken God's family of priests, he did not leave them without a succession of prophets, who made it their business to teach them the good knowledge of the Lord, but all in vain (*v.* 14); they would not hear, but hardened their necks, persisted in their idolatries, and were like their fathers, that would not bow their necks to God's yoke, because they *did not believe in him,* did not receive his truths, nor would venture upon his promises: it seems to refer to their fathers in the wilderness; the same sin that kept them out of Canaan turned these out, and that was unbelief.

IV. How God punished them for their sins. He *was very angry with them* (*v.* 18); for, in the matter of his worship, he is a jealous God, and resents nothing more deeply than giving that honour to any creature which is due to himself only. He afflicted them (*v.* 20) and *delivered them into the hand of spoilers,* in the days of the judges and of Saul, and afterwards in the days of most of their kings, to see if they would be awakened by the judgments of God to consider and amend their ways; but, when all these corrections did not prevail to drive out the folly, God first *rent Israel from the house of David,* under which they might have been happy. As Judah was hereby weakened, so Israel was hereby corrupted; for they made a man king who *drove them from following the Lord and caused them to sin a great sin, v.* 21. This was a national judgment, and the punishment of their former idolatries; and, at length, he *removed them quite out of his sight* (*v.* 18, 23), without giving them any hopes of a return out of their captivity.

Lastly, Here is a complaint against Judah in the midst of all (*v.* 19): *Also Judah kept not the commandments of God;* though they were not as yet quite so bad as Israel, yet they *walked in the statutes of Israel;* and this aggravated the sin of Israel, that they communicated the infection of it to Judah;

see Ezek. xxiii. 11. Those that bring sin into a country or family bring a plague into it and will have to answer for all the mischief that follows.

24 And the king of Assyria brought *men* from Babylon, and from Cuthah, and from Ava, and from Hamath, and from Sepharvaim, and placed *them* in the cities of Samaria instead of the children of Israel: and they possessed Samaria, and dwelt in the cities thereof. 25 And *so* it was at the beginning of their dwelling there, *that* they feared not the LORD: therefore the LORD sent lions among them, which slew *some* of them. 26 Wherefore they spake to the king of Assyria, saying, The nations which thou hast removed, and placed in the cities of Samaria, know not the manner of the God of the land: therefore he hath sent lions among them, and, behold, they slay them, because they know not the manner of the God of the land. 27 Then the king of Assyria commanded, saying, Carry thither one of the priests whom ye brought from thence; and let him go and dwell there, and let him teach them the manner of the God of the land. 28 Then one of the priests whom they had carried away from Samaria came and dwelt in Beth-el, and taught them how they should fear the LORD. 29 Howbeit every nation made gods of their own, and put *them* in the houses of the high places which the Samaritans had made, every nation in their cities wherein they dwelt. 30 And the men of Babylon made Succoth-benoth, and the men of Cuth made Nergal, and the men of Hamath made Ashima, 31 And the Avites made Nibhaz and Tartak, and the Sepharvites burnt their children in fire to Adrammelech and Anammelech, the gods of Sepharvaim. 32 So they feared the LORD, and made unto themselves of the lowest of them priests of the high places, which sacrificed for them in the houses of the high places. 33 They feared the LORD, and served their own gods, after the manner of the nations whom they carried away from thence. 34 Unto this day they do after the former manners: they fear not the LORD, neither do they after their statutes, or after their ordinances, or after the law and commandment which the LORD commanded the children of Jacob, whom he named Israel; 35 With whom the LORD had made a covenant, and charged them, saying, Ye shall not fear other gods, nor bow yourselves to them, nor serve them, nor sacrifice to them: 36 But the LORD, who brought you up out of the land of Egypt with great power and a stretched out arm, him shall ye fear, and him shall ye worship, and to him shall ye do sacrifice. 37 And the statutes, and the ordinances, and the law, and the commandment, which he wrote for you, ye shall observe to do for evermore; and ye shall not fear other gods. 38 And the covenant that I have made with you ye shall not forget; neither shall ye fear other gods. 39 But the LORD your God ye shall fear; and he shall deliver you out of the hand of all your enemies. 40 Howbeit they did not hearken, but they did after their former manner. 41 So these nations feared the LORD, and served their graven images, both their children, and their children's children: as did their fathers, so do they unto this day.

Never was land lost, we say, for want of an heir. When the children of Israel were dispossessed, and turned out of Canaan, the king of Assyria soon transplanted thither the supernumeraries of his own country, such as it could well spare, who should be servants to him and masters to the Israelites that remained; and here we have an account of these new inhabitants, whose story is related here that we may take our leave of Samaria, as also of the Israelites that were carried captive into Assyria.

I. Concerning the Assyrians that were brought into the land of Israel we are here told, 1. That they possessed Samaria and *dwelt in the cities thereof*, *v.* 24. It is common for lands to change their owners, but sad that the holy land should become a heathen land again. See what work sin makes. 2. That at their first coming God *sent lions among them*. They were probably insufficient to people the country, which occasioned *the beasts of the field to multiply against them* (Exod. xxiii. 29); yet, besides the natural cause, there was a manifest hand of God in it, who is Lord of hosts, of all the creatures, and can serve his own purposes by which he pleases, small or great, lice or lions. God ordered them this rough welcome to check their pride and insolence, and to let them know that though they had conquered Israel the God of Israel had power enough to deal with them—that he could have prevented their settling here, by ordering lions into the service of Israel, and that he permitted it, not for their righteousness, but the wickedness of his own people—and that they were now under his visitation. They had lived without God in their own land, and were not plagued with lions; but, if they do so in this land, it is at their peril. 3. That they sent a remonstrance of this grievance to the king their master, setting forth, it is likely, the loss their infant colony had sustained by the lions and the continual fear they were in of them, and stating that they looked upon it to be a judgment upon them for not worshipping the God of the land, which they could not, because they knew not how, *v.* 26. The God of Israel was the God of the whole world, but they ignorantly call him the *God of the land,* apprehending themselves therefore within his reach, and concerned to be upon good terms with him. Herein they shamed the Israelites, who were not so ready to hear the voice of God's judgments as they were, and who had not served the *God of that land,* though he was the God of their fathers and their great benefactor, and though they were well instructed in the manner of his worship. Assyrians begged to be taught that which Israelites hated to be taught. 4. That the king of Assyria took care to have them taught *the manner of the God of the land* (*v.* 27, 28), not out of any affection to that God, but to save his subjects from the lions. On this errand he sent back one of the priests whom he had carried away captive. A prophet would have done them more good, for this was but one of the priests of the calves, and therefore chose to dwell at Bethel for old acquaintance' sake, and, though he might teach them to do better than they did, he was not likely to teach them to do well, unless he had taught his own people better. However, he came and dwelt among them, to teach them how they should *fear the Lord.* Whether he taught them out of the book of the law, or only by word of mouth, is uncertain. 5. That, being thus taught, they made a mongrel religion of it, worshipped the God of Israel for fear and their own idols for love (*v.* 33): *They feared the Lord,* but they *served their own gods.* They all agreed to worship the God of the land according to the manner, to observe the Jewish festivals and rites of sacrificing, but every nation made gods of their own besides, not only for their private use in their own families, but to be put *in the houses of their high places,* *v.* 92. The idols of each country are here named, *v.* 30, 31. The learned are at a loss for the signification of several of these names, and cannot agree by what representations these gods were worshipped. If we may credit the traditions of the Jewish doctors, they tell us that Succoth-Benoth was worshipped in a hen and chickens, Nergal in a cock, Ashima in a smooth goat, Nibhaz in a dog, Tartak in an ass, Adrammelech in a peacock, Anammelech in a pheasant. Our own tell us, more probably, that Succoth-Benoth (signifying *the tents of the daughters)* was Venus. Nergal, being worshipped by the Cuthites, or Persians, was *the fire.* Adrammelech and Anammelech were only distinctions of Moloch. See how vain idolaters were in their imaginations, and wonder at their sottishness. Our very ignorance concerning these idols teaches us the accomplishment of that word which God has spoken, that these false gods should all perish (Jer. x. 11); they are all buried in oblivion, while the name of the true God shall continue for ever. 6. This medley superstition is here said to *continue unto this day* (*v.* 41), till the time when this book was written and long after, above 300 years in all, till the time of Alexander the Great, when Manasse, brother to Jaddus the high priest of the Jews, having married the daughter of Sanballat, governor of the Samaritans, went over to them, got leave of Alexander to build a temple in Mount Gerizim, drew over many of the Jews to him, and prevailed with the Samaritans to cast away all their idols and to worship the God of Israel only; yet their worship was mixed with so much superstition that our Saviour told them they knew not what they worshipped, John iv. 22.

II. Concerning the Israelites that were carried into the land of Assyria. The historian has occasion to speak of them (*v.* 33), showing that their successors in the land did as they had done *(after the manner of the nations whom they carried away),* they worshipped both the God of Israel and those other gods; but what did the captives do in the land of their affliction? Were they reformed, and brought to repentance, by their troubles? No, they did after the former manner, *v.* 34. When the two tribes were afterwards carried into Babylon, they were cured by it of their idolatry, and therefore, after seventy years, they were brought back with joy; but the ten tribes were hardened in the furnace, and therefore were justly lost in it and left to perish. This obstinacy of theirs is here aggravated by the consideration, 1. Of the honour God had put upon them, as the seed of Jacob, *whom he named Israel,* and from him they were so named, but were a reproach to *that worthy name by which they were called.* 2. Of the covenant he made with them, and the charge he gave them upon that covenant, which is here very fully recited, that they should *fear and serve the Lord Jehovah* only, who had *brought them up out of Egypt* (*v.* 36), that, having received his statutes and ordinances in writing, they should *observe to do them for evermore* (*v.* 37), and never forget that covenant which God had made with them, the promises and conditions of that covenant, especially that great article of it which is here thrice repeated, because it had been so often inculcated and so much insisted on, that they *should not fear other gods.* He had told them that, if they kept close to him, he would *deliver them out of the hand of all their enemies* (*v* 39); yet when they were in the hand of their enemies, and stood in need of deliverance, they were so stupid, and had so little sense of their own interest, that they did after the former manner (*v.* 40), they served both the true God and false gods, as if they knew no difference. *Ephraim is joined to idols, let him alone.* So they did, and so did the nations that succeeded them. Well might the apostle ask, *What then, Are we better than they? No, in no wise, for both Jews and Gentiles are all under sin,* Rom. iii. 9.

CHAP. XVIII.

When the prophet had condemned Ephraim for lies and deceit he comforted himself with this, that Judah yet "ruled with God, and was faithful with the Most Holy," Hos. xi. 12. It was a very melancholy view which the last chapter gave us of the desolations of Israel; but this chapter shows us the affairs of Judah in a good posture at the same time, that it may appear God has not quite cast off the seed of Abraham, Rom. xi. 1. Hezekiah is here upon the throne, I. Reforming his kingdom, ver. 1—6. II. Prospering in all his undertakings (ver. 7, 8), and this at the same time when the ten tribes were led captive, ver. 9—12. III. Yet invaded by Sennacherib, the king of Assyria, ver. 13. 1. His country put under contribution, ver. 14—16. 2. Jerusalem besieged, ver. 17. 3. God blasphemed, himself reviled, and his people solicited to revolt, in a virulent speech made by Rabshakeh, ver. 18—37. But how well it ended, and how much to the honour and comfort of our great reformer, we shall find in the next chapter.

NOW it came to pass in the third year of Hoshea son of Elah king of Israel, *that* Hezekiah the son of Ahaz king of Judah began to reign. 2 Twenty and five years old was he when he began to reign; and he reigned twenty and nine years in Jerusalem. His mother's name also *was* Abi, the daughter of Zachariah. 3 And he did *that which was* right in the sight of the LORD, according to all that David his father did. 4 He removed the high places, and brake the images, and cut down the groves, and brake in pieces the brasen serpent that Moses had made: for unto those days the children of Israel did burn incense to it: and he called it Nehushtan. 5 He trusted in the LORD God of Israel; so that after him was none like him among all the kings of Judah, nor *any* that were before him. 6 For he clave to the LORD, *and* departed not from following him, but kept his commandments, which the LORD commanded Moses. 7 And the LORD was with him; *and* he prospered whithersoever he went forth: and he rebelled against the king of Assyria, and served him not. 8 He smote the Philistines, *even* unto Gaza, and the borders thereof, from the tower of the watchmen to the fenced city.

We have here a general account of the reign of Hezekiah. It appears, by comparing his age with his father's, that he was born when his father was about eleven or twelve years old, divine Providence so ordering that he might be of full age, and fit for business, when the measure of his father's iniquity should be full. Here is,

I. His great piety, which was the more wonderful because his father was very wicked and vile, one of the worst of the kings, yet he was one of the best, which may intimate to us that what good there is in any is not of nature, but of grace, free grace, sovereign grace, which, contrary to nature, grafts into the good olive that which was wild by nature (Rom. xi. 24), and also that grace gets over the greatest difficulties and disadvantages: Ahaz, it is likely, gave his son a bad education as well as a bad example; Urijah his priest perhaps had the tuition of him; his attendants and companions, we may suppose, were such as were addicted to idolatry; and yet Hezekiah became eminently good. When God's grace will work what can hinder it?

1. He was a genuine son of David, who had a great many degenerate ones (*v.* 3): *He did that which was right, according to all that David his father did,* with whom the covenant was made, and therefore he was entitled to the benefit of it. We have read of some of them who did that which was right, *but not like David, ch.* xiv. 3. They did not love God's ordinances, nor cleave to them, as he did; but Hezekiah was a second David, had such a love for God's word, and God's house, as he had. Let us not be frightened with an apprehension of the continual decay of virtue, as if, when times and men are bad, they must needs, of course, grow worse and worse; that does not follow, for, after many bad kings, God raised up one that was like David himself.

2. He was a zealous reformer of his kingdom, and as we find (2 Chron. xxix. 3) he began betimes to be so, fell to work as soon as ever he came to the crown, and lost no time. He found his kingdom very corrupt, the people in all things too superstitious. They had always been so, but in the last reign worse than ever. By the influence of his wicked father, a deluge of idolatry had overspread the land; his spirit was stirred against this idolatry, we may suppose (as Paul's at Athens), while his father lived, and therefore, as soon as ever he had power in his hands, he set himself to abolish it (*v.* 4), though,

considering how the people were wedded to it, he might think it could not be done without opposition. (1.) The images and the groves were downright idolatrous and of heathenish original. These he broke and destroyed. Though his own father had set them up, and shown an affection for them, yet he would not protect them. We must never dishonour God in honour to our earthly parents. (2.) The high places, though they had sometimes been used by the prophets upon special occasions and had been hitherto connived at by the good kings, were nevertheless an affront to the temple and a breach of the law which required them to worship there only, and, being from under the inspection of the priests, gave opportunity for the introducing of idolatrous usages. Hezekiah therefore, who made God's word his rule, not the example of his predecessors, removed them, made a law for the removal of them, the demolishing of the chapels, tabernacles, and altars there erected, and the suppressing of the use of them, which law was put in execution with vigour; and, it is probable, the terrible judgments which the kingdom of Israel was now under for their idolatry made Hezekiah the more zealous and the people the more willing to comply with him. It is well when our neighbours' harms are our warnings. (3.) The brazen serpent was originally of divine institution, and yet, because it had been abused to idolatry, he broke it to pieces. The children of Israel had brought that with them to Canaan; where they set it up we are not told, but, it seems, it had been carefully preserved, as a memorial of God's goodness to their fathers in the wilderness and a traditional evidence of the truth of that story, Num. xxi. 9, for the encouragement of the sick to apply to God for a cure and of penitent sinners to apply to him for mercy. But in process of time, when they began to worship the creature more than the Creator, those that would not worship images borrowed from the heathen, as some of their neighbours did, were drawn in by the tempter to burn incense to the brazen serpent, because that was made by order from God himself and had been an instrument of good to them. But Hezekiah, in his pious zeal for God's honour, not only forbade the people to worship it, but, that it might never be so abused any more, he showed the people that it was *Nehushtan,* nothing else but *a piece of brass,* and that therefore it was an idle wicked thing to burn incense to it; he then broke it to pieces, that is, as bishop Patrick expounds it, ground it to powder, which he scattered in the air, that no fragment of it might remain. If any think that the just honour of the brazen serpent was hereby diminished they will find it abundantly made up again, John iii. 14, where our Saviour makes it a type of himself. Good things, when idolized, are better parted with than kept.

3. Herein he was a nonsuch, *v.* 5. None of all the kings of Judah were like him, *either before or after him.* Two things he was eminent for in his reformation:—(1.) Courage and confidence in God. In abolishing idolatry, there was danger of disobliging his subjects, and provoking them to rebel; but *he trusted in the Lord God of Israel* to bear him out in what he did and save him from harm. A firm belief of God's all-sufficiency to protect and reward us will conduce much to make us sincere, bold, and vigorous, in the way of our duty, like Hezekiah. When he came to the crown he found his kingdom compassed with enemies, but he did not seek for succour to foreign aids, as his father did, but trusted in the God of Israel to be the keeper of Israel. (2.) Constancy and perseverance in his duty. For this there was none like him, that he clave to the Lord with a fixed resolution and never *departed from following him, v.* 6. Some of his predecessors that began well fell off: but he, like Caleb, followed the Lord *fully.* He not only abolished all idolatrous usages, but kept God's commandments, and in every thing made conscience of his duty.

II. His great prosperity, *v.* 7, 8. He was with God, and then God was with him, and, having the special presence of God with him, *he prospered whithersoever he went,* had wonderful success in all his enterprises, in his wars, his buildings, and especially his reformation, for that good work was carried on with less difficulty than he could have expected. Those that do God's work with an eye to his glory, and with confidence in his strength, may expect to prosper in it. Great is the truth and will prevail. Finding himself successful, 1. He threw off the yoke of the king of Assyria, which his father had basely submitted to. This is called *rebelling against him,* because so the king of Assyria called it; but it was really an asserting of the just rights of his crown, which it was not in the power of Ahaz to alienate. If it was imprudent to make this bold struggle so soon, yet I see not that it was, as some think, unjust; when he had thrown out the idolatry of the nations he might well throw off the yoke of their oppression. The surest way to liberty is to serve God. 2. He made a vigorous attack upon the Philistines, and smote them even unto Gaza, both the country villages and the fortified towns, *the tower of the watchmen and the fenced cities,* reducing those places which they had made themselves masters of in his father's time, 2 Chron. xxviii. 18. When he had purged out the corruptions his father had brought in he might expect to recover the possessions his father had lost. Of his victories over the Philistines Isaiah prophesied, Isa. xiv. 28, &c.

9 And it came to pass in the fourth year of king Hezekiah, which *was* the seventh year of Hoshea son of Elah

king of Israel, *that* Shalmaneser king of Assyria came up against Samaria, and besieged it. 10 And at the end of three years they took it: *even* in the sixth year of Hezekiah, that *is* the ninth year of Hoshea king of Israel, Samaria was taken. 11 And the king of Assyria did carry away Israel unto Assyria, and put them in Halah and in Habor *by* the river of Gozan, and in the cities of the Medes: 12 Because they obeyed not the voice of the LORD their God, but transgressed his covenant, *and* all that Moses the servant of the LORD commanded, and would not hear *them*, nor do *them*. 13 Now in the fourteenth year of king Hezekiah did Sennacherib king of Assyria come up against all the fenced cities of Judah, and took them. 14 And Hezekiah king of Judah sent to the king of Assyria to Lachish, saying, I have offended; return from me: that which thou puttest on me will I bear. And the king of Assyria appointed unto Hezekiah king of Judah three hundred talents of silver and thirty talents of gold. 15 And Hezekiah gave *him* all the silver that was found in the house of the LORD, and in the treasures of the king's house. 16 At that time did Hezekiah cut off *the gold from* the doors of the temple of the LORD, and *from* the pillars which Hezekiah king of Judah had overlaid, and gave it to the king of Assyria.

The kingdom of Assyria had now grown considerable, though we never read of it till the last reign. Such changes there are in the affairs of nations and families: those that have been despicable become formidable, and those, on the contrary, are brought low that have made a great noise and figure. We have here an account,

I. Of the success of Shalmaneser, king of Assyria, against Israel, his besieging Samaria (*v.* 9), taking it (*v.* 10), and carrying the people into captivity (*v.* 11), with the reason why God brought this judgment upon them (*v.* 12): *Because they obeyed not the voice of the Lord their God.* This was related more largely in the foregoing chapter, but it is here repeated, 1. As that which stirred up Hezekiah and his people to purge out idolatry with so much zeal, because they saw the ruin which it brought upon Israel. When their neighbour's house was on fire, and their own in danger, it was time to cast away the accursed thing. 2. As that which Hezekiah much lamented, but had not strength to prevent. Though the ten tribes had revolted from, and often been vexatious to, the house of David, no longer ago than in his father's reign, yet being of the seed of Israel he could not be glad at their calamities. 3. As that which laid Hezekiah and his kingdom open to the king of Assyria, and made it much more easy for him to invade the land. It is said of the ten tribes here that they would neither *hear* God's commandments nor *do* them, *v.* 12. Many will be content to give God the hearing that will give him no more (Ezek. xxxiii. 31), but these, being resolved not to do their duty, did not care to hear of it.

II. Of the attempt of Sennacherib, the succeeding king of Assyria, against Judah, in which he was encouraged by his predecessor's success against Israel, whose honours he would vie with and whose victories he would push forward. The descent he made upon Judah was a great calamity to that kingdom, by which God would try the faith of Hezekiah and chastise the people, who are called *a hypocritical nation* (Isa. x. 6), because they did not comply with Hezekiah's reformation, nor willingly part with their idols, but kept them up in their hearts, and perhaps in their houses, though their high places were removed. Even times of reformation may prove troublesome times, made so by those that oppose it, and then the blame is laid upon the reformers. This calamity will appear great upon Hezekiah if we consider, 1. How much he lost of his country, *v.* 13. The king of Assyria took all or most of the fenced cities of Judah, the frontier-towns and the garrisons, and then all the rest fell into his hands of course. The confusion which the country was put into by this invasion is described by the prophet, Isa. x. 28—32. 2. How dearly he paid for his peace. He saw Jerusalem itself in danger of falling into the enemies' hand, as Samaria had done, and was willing to purchase its safety at the expense, (1.) Of a mean submission: "*I have offended* in denying the usual tribute, and am ready to make satisfaction as shall be demanded," *v.* 14. Where was Hezekiah's courage? Where his confidence in God? Why did he not advise with Isaiah before he sent this crouching message? (2.) Of a vast sum of money—300 talents of silver and thirty of gold (above £200,000), not to be paid annually, but as a present ransom. To raise this sum, he was forced not only to empty the public treasures (*v.* 15), but to take the golden plates off from the doors of the temple, and from the pillars, *v.* 16. Though *the temple sanctified the gold* which he had dedicated, yet, the necessity being urgent, he thought he might make as bold with that as his father David (whom he took for his pattern) did with the show-bread, and that it was neither impious nor imprudent to give a part for the preservation of the whole. His father Ahaz had plundered the temple in contempt of it, 2 Chron. xxviii. 24. He had repaid with interest what his father took; and now, with all due reverence, he only begged leave to borrow it again in an exigency and for a greater good, with a resolution to restore it in full as soon as he should be in a capacity to do so.

17 And the king of Assyria sent Tartan and Rabsaris and Rab-shakeh from Lachish to king Hezekiah with a great host against Jerusalem. And they went up and came to Jerusalem. And when they were come up, they came and stood by the conduit of the upper pool, which *is* in the highway of the fuller's field. 18 And when they had called to the king, there came out to them Eliakim the son of Hilkiah, which *was* over the household, and Shebna the scribe, and Joah the son of Asaph the recorder. 19 And Rab-shakeh said unto them, Speak ye now to Hezekiah, Thus saith the great king, the king of Assyria, What confidence *is* this wherein thou trustest? 20 Thou sayest, (but *they are but* vain words,) *I have* counsel and strength for the war. Now on whom dost thou trust, that thou rebellest against me? 21 Now, behold, thou trustest upon the staff of this bruised reed, *even* upon Egypt, on which if a man lean, it will go into his hand, and pierce it: so *is* Pharaoh king of Egypt unto all that trust on him. 22 But if ye say unto me, We trust in the LORD our God: *is* not that he, whose high places and whose altars Hezekiah hath taken away, and hath said to Judah and Jerusalem, Ye shall worship before this altar in Jerusalem? 23 Now therefore, I pray thee, give pledges to my lord the king of Assyria, and I will deliver thee two thousand horses, if thou be able on thy part to set riders upon them. 24 How then wilt thou turn away the face of one captain of the least of my master's servants, and put thy trust on Egypt for chariots and for horsemen? 25 Am I now come up without the LORD against this place to destroy it? The LORD said to me, Go up against this land, and destroy it. 26 Then said Eliakim the son of Hilkiah, and Shebna, and Joah, unto Rab-shakeh, Speak, I pray thee, to thy servants in the Syrian language; for we understand *it:* and talk not with us in the Jews' language in the ears of the people that *are* on the wall. 27 But Rab-shakeh said unto them, Hath my master sent me to thy master, and to thee, to speak these words? *hath he* not *sent me* to the men which sit on the wall, that they may eat their own dung, and drink their own piss with you? 28 Then Rab-shakeh stood and cried with a loud voice in the Jews' language, and spake, saying, Hear the word of the great king, the king of Assyria: 29 Thus saith the king, Let not Hezekiah deceive you: for he shall not be able to deliver you out of his hand: 30 Neither let Hezekiah make you trust in the LORD, saying, The LORD will surely deliver us, and this city shall not be delivered into the hand of the king of Assyria. 31 Hearken not to Hezekiah: for thus saith the king of Assyria, Make *an agreement* with me by a present, and come out to me, and *then* eat ye every man of his own vine, and every one of his fig tree, and drink ye every one the waters of his cistern: 32 Until I come and take you away to a land like your own land, a land of corn and wine, a land of bread and vineyards, a land of oil olive and of honey, that ye may live, and not die: and hearken not unto Hezekiah, when he persuadeth you, saying, The LORD will deliver us. 33 Hath any of the gods of the nations delivered at all his land out of the hand of the king of Assyria? 34 Where *are* the gods of Hamath, and of Arpad where *are* the gods of Sepharvaim, Hena, and Ivah? have they delivered Samaria out of mine hand? 35 Who *are* they among all the gods of the countries, that have delivered their country out of mine hand, that the LORD should deliver Jerusalem out of mine hand? 36 But the people held their peace, and answered him not a word: for

the king's commandment was, saying, Answer him not. 37 Then came Eliakim the son of Hilkiah, which *was* over the household, and Shebna the scribe, and Joah the son of Asaph the recorder, to Hezekiah with *their* clothes rent, and told him the words of Rab-shakeh.

Here is, I. Jerusalem besieged by Sennacherib's army, *v.* 17. He sent three of his great generals with a great host against Jerusalem. Is this the great king, the king of Assyria? No, never call him so; he is a base, false, perfidious man, and worthy to be made infamous to all ages; let him never be named with honour that could do such a dishonourable thing as this, to take Hezekiah's money, which he gave him upon condition he should withdraw his army, and then, instead of quitting his country according to the agreement, to advance against his capital city, and not send him his money again either. Those are wicked men indeed, and, let them be ever so great, we will call them so, whose principle it is not to make their promises binding any further than is for their interest. Now Hezekiah had too much reason to repent his treaty with Sennacherib, which had made him much the poorer and never the safer.

II. Hezekiah, and his princes and people, railed upon by Rabshakeh, the chief speaker of the three generals, and one that had the most satirical genius. He was no doubt instructed what to say by Sennacherib, who intended hereby to pick a new quarrel with Hezekiah. He had promised, upon the receipt of Hezekiah's money, to withdraw his army, and therefore could not for shame make a forcible attack upon Jerusalem immediately; but he sent Rabshakeh to persuade Hezekiah to surrender it, and, if he should refuse, the refusal would serve him for a pretence (and a very poor one) to besiege it, and, if it hold out, to take it by storm. Rabshakeh had the impudence to desire audience of the king himself at the conduit of the upper pool, without the walls; but Hezekiah had the prudence to decline a personal treaty, and sent three commissioners (the prime ministers of state) to hear what he had to say, but with a charge to them not to answer that fool *according to his folly* (*v.* 36), for they could not convince him, but would certainly provoke him, and Hezekiah had learned of his father David to believe that God would hear when he, *as a deaf man, heard not*, Ps. xxxviii. 13—15. One interruption they gave him in his discourse, which was only to desire that he would speak to them now in the Syrian language, and they would consider what he said and report it to the king, and, if they did not give him a satisfactory answer, then he might appeal to the people, by speaking *in the Jews' language*, *v.* 26. This was a reasonable request, and agreeable to the custom of treaties, which is that the plenipotentiaries should settle matters between themselves before any thing be made public; but Hilkiah did not consider what an unreasonable man he had to deal with, else he would not have made this request, for it did but exasperate Rabshakeh, and make him the more rude and boisterous, *v.* 27. Against all the rules of decency and honour, instead of treating with the commissioners, he menaces the soldiery, persuades them to desert or mutiny, threatens if they hold out to reduce them to the last extremities of famine, and then goes on with his discourse, the scope of which is to persuade Hezekiah, and his princes and people, to surrender the city. Observe how, in order to this,

1. He magnifies his master the king of Assyria. Once and again he calls him, *That great king, the king of Assyria*, *v.* 19, 28. What an idol did he make of that prince whose creature he was! God is the great King, but Sennacherib was in his eye a little god, and he would possess them with the same veneration for him that he had, and thereby frighten them into a submission to him. But to those who by faith see the King of kings in his power and glory even the king of Assyria looks mean and little. What are the greatest of men when either they come to compare with God or God comes to contend with them? Ps. lxxxii. 6, 7.

2. He endeavours to make them believe that it will be much for their advantage to surrender. If they held out, they must expect no other than to eat their own dung, by reason of the want of provisions, which would be entirely cut off from them by the besiegers; but if they would capitulate, seek his favour with a present and cast themselves upon his mercy, he would give them very good treatment, *v.* 31. I wonder with what face Rabshakeh could speak of making an agreement with a present when his master had so lately broken the agreement Hezekiah made with him with that great present, *v.* 14. Can those expect to be trusted that have been so grossly perfidious? But, *Ad populum phaleras—Gild the chain and the vulgar will let you bind them.* He thought to soothe up all with a promise that if they would surrender upon discretion, though they must expect to be prisoners and captives, yet it would really be happy for them to be so. One would wonder he should ever think to prevail by such gross suggestions as these, but that the devil does thus impose upon sinners every day by his temptations. He will needs persuade them, (1.) That their imprisonment would be to their advantage, for they should *eat every man of his own vine* (*v.* 31); though the property of their estates would be vested in the conquerors, yet they should have the free use of them. But he does not explain it now to them as he would afterwards, that it must be understood just as

much, and just as long, as the conqueror pleases. (2.) That their captivity would be much more to their advantage: *I will take you away to a land like your own land;* and what the better would they be for that, when they must have nothing in it to call their own?

3. That which he aims at especially is to convince them that it is to no purpose for them to stand it out: *What confidence is this wherein thou trustest?* So he insults over Hezekiah, *v.* 19. To the people he says (*v.* 29), "*Let not Hezekiah deceive you* into your own ruin, for *he shall not be able to deliver you;* you must either bend or break." It were well if sinners would submit to the force of this argument, in making their peace with God—That it is *therefore* our wisdom to yield to him, because it is in vain to contend with him: what confidence is that which those trust in who stand it out against him? *Are we stronger than he?* Or what shall we get by setting briars and thorns before a consuming fire? But Hezekiah was not so helpless and defenceless as Rabshakeh would here represent him. Three things he supposes Hezekiah might trust to, and he endeavours to make out the insufficiency of these:—(1.) His own military preparations: *Thou sayest, I have counsel and strength for the war;* and we find that so he had, 2 Chron. xxxii. 3. But this Rabshakeh turns off with a slight: "*They are but vain words;* thou art an unequal match for us," *v.* 20. With the greatest haughtiness and disdain imaginable, he challenges him to produce 2000 men of all his people that know how to manage a horse, and will venture to give him 2000 horses if he can. He falsely insinuates that Hezekiah has no men, or none fit to be soldiers, *v.* 23. Thus he thinks to run him down with confidence and banter, and will lay him any wager that one captain of the least of his master's servants is able to baffle him and all his forces. (2.) His alliance with Egypt. He supposes that Hezekiah trusts to Egypt for chariots and horsemen (*v.* 24), because the king of Israel had done so, and of this confidence he truly says, It is *a broken reed* (*v.* 21), it will not only fail a man when he leans on it and expects it to bear his weight, but *it will run into his hand and pierce it,* and rend his shoulder, as the prophet further illustrates this similitude, with application to Egypt, Ezek. xxix. 6, 7. So is the king of Egypt, says he; and truly so had the king of Assyria been to Ahaz, who trusted in him, but he *distressed him, and strengthened him not,* 2 Chron. xxviii. 20. Those that trust to any arm of flesh will find it no better than a broken reed; but God is the rock of ages. (3.) His interest in God and relation to him. This was indeed the confidence in which Hezekiah trusted, *v.* 22. He supported himself by depending on the power and promise of God; with this he encouraged himself and his people (*v.* 30): *The Lord will surely deliver us,* and again *v.* 32. This Rabshakeh was sensible was their great stay, and therefore he was most large in his endeavours to shake this, as David's enemies, who used all the arts they had to drive him from his confidence in God (Ps. iii. 2; xi. 1), and thus did Christ's enemies, Matt. xxvii. 43. Three things Rabshakeh suggested to discourage their confidence in God, and they were all false:—[1.] That Hezekiah had forfeited God's protection, and thrown himself out of it, by *destroying the high places and the altars, v.* 22. Here he measures the God of Israel by the gods of the heathen, who delighted in the multitude of altars and temples, and concludes that Hezekiah has given a great offence to the God of Israel, in confining his people to one altar: thus is one of the best deeds he ever did in his life misconstrued as impious and profane, by one that did not, or would not, know the law of the God of Israel. If that be represented by ignorant and malicious men as evil and a provocation to God which is really good and pleasing to him, we must not think it strange. If this was to be sacrilegious, Hezekiah would ever be so. [2.] That God had given orders for the destruction of Jerusalem at this time (*v.* 25): *Have I now come up without the Lord?* This is all banter and rhodomontade. He did not himself think he had any commission from God to do what he did (by whom should he have it?) but he made this pretence to amuse and terrify the *people that were on the wall.* If he had any colour at all for what he said, it might be taken from the notice which perhaps he had had, by the writings of the prophets, of the hand of God in the destruction of the ten tribes, and he thought he had as good a warrant for the seizing of Jerusalem as of Samaria. Many that have fought against God have pretended commissions from him. [3.] That if Jehovah, the God of Israel, should undertake to protect them from the king of Assyria, yet he was not able to do it. With this blasphemy he concluded his speech (*v.* 33—35), comparing the God of Israel with the gods of the nations whom he had conquered and putting him upon the level with them, and concluding that because they could not defend and deliver their worshippers the God of Israel could not defend and deliver his. See here, *First,* His pride. When he conquered a city he reckoned himself to have conquered its gods, and valued himself mightily upon it. His high opinion of the idols made him have a high opinion of himself as too hard for them. *Secondly,* His profaneness. The God of Israel was not a local deity, but the God of the whole earth, the only living and true God, the ancient of days, and had often proved himself to be above all gods; yet he makes no more of him than of the upstart fictitious gods of Hamath and Arpad, unfairly arguing that

the gods (as some now say the priests) of all religions are the same, and himself above them all. The tradition of the Jews is that Rabshakeh was an apostate Jew, which made him so ready in the Jews' language; if so, his ignorance of the God of Israel was the less excusable and his enmity the less strange, for apostates are commonly the most bitter and spiteful enemies, witness Julian. A great deal of art and management, it must be owned, there were in this speech of Rabshakeh, but, withal, a great deal of pride, malice, falsehood, and blasphemy. One grain of sincerity would have been worth all this wit and rhetoric.

Lastly, We are told what the commissioners on Hezekiah's part did. 1. They held their peace, not for want of something to say both on God's behalf and Hezekiah's: they might easily and justly have upbraided him with his master's treachery and breach of faith, and have asked him, What religion encourages you to hope that such conduct will prosper? at least they might have given him that grave hint which Ahab gave to Benhadad's like insolent demands—*Let not him that girdeth on the harness boast as though he had put it off.* But the king had commanded them not to answer him, and they observed their instructions. There is a time to keep silence, as well as a time to speak, and there are those to whom to offer any thing religious or rational is to cast pearls before swine. What can be said to a madman? It is probable that their silence made Rabshakeh yet more proud and secure, and so his heart was lifted up and hardened to his destruction. 2. They rent their clothes in detestation of his blasphemy and in grief for the despised afflicted condition of Jerusalem, the reproach of which was a burden to them. 3. They faithfully reported the matter to the king, their master, and *told him the words of Rabshakeh,* that he might consider what was to be done, what course they should take and what answer they should return to Rabshakeh's summons.

CHAP. XIX.

Jerusalem's great distress we read of in the foregoing chapter, and left it besieged, insulted, threatened, terrified, and just ready to be swallowed up by the Assyrian army. But in this chapter we have an account of its glorious deliverance, not by sword or bow, but by prayer and prophecy, and by the hand of an angel. I. Hezekiah, in great concern, sent to the prophet Isaiah, to desire his prayers (ver. 1—5) and received from him an answer of peace, ver. 6, 7. II. Sennacherib sent a letter to Hezekiah to frighten him into a surrender, ver. 8—13. III. Hezekiah thereupon, by a very solemn prayer, recommended his case to God, the righteous Judge, and begged help from him, ver. 14—19. IV. God, by Isaiah, sent him a very comfortable message, assuring him of deliverance, ver. 20—34. V. The army of the Assyrians was all cut off by an angel and Sennacherib himself slain by his own sons, ver. 35—37. And so God glorified himself and saved his people.

AND it came to pass when king Hezekiah heard *it,* that he rent his clothes, and covered himself with sackcloth, and went into the house of the LORD. 2 And he sent Eliakim, which *was* over the household, and Shebna the scribe, and the elders of the priests, covered with sackcloth, to Isaiah the prophet the son of Amoz. 3 And they said unto him, Thus saith Hezekiah, This day *is* a day of trouble, and of rebuke, and blasphemy: for the children are come to the birth, and *there is* not strength to bring forth. 4 It may be the LORD thy God will hear all the words of Rab-shakeh, whom the king of Assyria his master hath sent to reproach the living God: and will reprove the words which the LORD thy God hath heard: wherefore lift up *thy* prayer for the remnant that are left. 5 So the servants of king Hezekiah came to Isaiah. 6 And Isaiah said unto them, Thus shall ye say to your master, Thus saith the LORD, Be not afraid of the words which thou hast heard, with which the servants of the king of Assyria have blasphemed me. 7 Behold, I will send a blast upon him, and he shall hear a rumour, and shall return to his own land; and I will cause him to fall by the sword in his own land.

The contents of Rabshakeh's speech being brought to Hezekiah, one would have expected (and it is likely Rabshakeh did expect) that he would call a council of war and it would be debated whether it was best to capitulate or no. Before the siege, he had *taken counsel with his princes and his mighty men,* 2 Chron. xxxii. 3. But that would not do now; his greatest relief is that he has a God to go to, and what passed between him and his God on this occasion we have here an account of.

I. Hezekiah discovered a deep concern at the dishonour done to God by Rabshakeh's blasphemy. When he heard it, though at second hand, he *rent his clothes and covered himself with sackcloth, v.* 1. Good men were wont to do so when they heard of any reproach cast on God's name; and great men must not think it any disparagement to them to sympathize with the injured honour of the great God. Royal robes are not too good to be rent, nor royal flesh too good to be clothed with sackcloth, in humiliation for indignities done to God and for the perils and terrors of his Jerusalem. To this God now called, and was displeased with those who were not thus affected. Isa. xxii. 12—14, *Behold joy and gladness, slaying oxen and killing sheep,* though it was a *day of trouble and perplexity in the valley of vision* (*v.* 5), which refers to this very event. The king was in sackcloth, but many of his subjects were in soft clothing.

II. He *went up to the house of the Lord,*

according to the example of the psalmist, who, when he was grieved at the pride and prosperity of the wicked, *went into the sanctuary of God* and there *understood their end,* Ps. lxxiii. 17. He went to the house of God, to meditate and pray, and get his spirit into a sedate composed frame, after this agitation. He was not considering what answer to return to Rabshakeh, but refers the matter to God. "*Thou shalt answer, Lord, for me.*"—Herbert. In the house of the Lord he found a place both of rest and refuge, a treasury, a magazine, a council-chamber, and all he needed, all in God. Note, When the church's enemies are very daring and threatening it is the wisdom and duty of the church's friends to apply to God, appeal to him, and leave their cause with him.

III. He sent to the prophet Isaiah, by honourable messengers, in token of the great respect he had for him, to desire his prayers, *v.* 2—4. Eliakim and Shebna were two of those that had heard the words of Rabshakeh and were the better able both to acquaint and to affect Isaiah with the case. The elders of the priests were themselves to pray for the people in time of trouble (Joel ii. 17); but they must go to engage Isaiah's prayers, because he could pray better and had a better interest in heaven. The messengers were to go in sackcloth, because they were to represent the king, who was so clothed.

1. Their errand to Isaiah was, "*Lift up thy prayer for the remnant that is left,* that is, for Judah, which is but a remnant now that the ten tribes are gone—for Jerusalem, which is but a remnant now that the defenced cities of Judah are taken." Note, (1.) It is very desirable, and what we should be desirous of when we are in trouble, to have the prayers of our friends for us. In begging to have them we honour God, we honour prayer, and we honour our brethren. (2.) When we desire the prayers of others for us we must not think we are excused from praying for ourselves. When Hezekiah sent to Isaiah to pray for him he himself *went into the house of the Lord* to offer up his own prayers. (3.) Those who speak from God to us we should in a particular manner desire to speak to God for us. *He is a prophet, and he shall pray for thee,* Gen. xx. 7. The great prophet is the great intercessor. (4.) Those are likely to prevail with God that *lift up* their prayers, that is, that lift up their hearts in prayer. (5.) When the interests of God's church are brought very low, so that there is but a remnant left, few friends, and those weak and at a loss, then it is time to *lift up our prayer for that remnant.*

2. Two things are urged to Isaiah, to engage his prayers for them:—(1.) Their fears of the enemy (*v.* 3): "He is insolent and haughty; it is *a day of rebuke and blasphemy.* We are despised. God is dishonoured. Upon this account it is a day of trouble. Never were such a king and kingdom so trampled on and abused as we are: *our soul is exceedingly filled with the contempt of the proud,* and it is *a sword in our bones* to hear them reproach our confidence in God, and say, Where is now your God? and, which is worst of all, we see not which way we can help ourselves and get clear of the reproach. Our cause is good, our people are faithful; but we are quite overpowered with numbers. The children are brought to the birth; now is the time, the critical moment, when, if ever, we must be relieved. One successful blow given to the enemy would accomplish our wishes. But, alas! we are not able to give it: *There is not strength to bring forth.* Our case is as deplorable, and calls for as speedy help, as that of a woman in travail, that is quite spent with her throes, so that she has not strength to bear the child. Compare with this Hos. xiii. 13. We are ready to perish; *if thou canst do any thing, have compassion upon us and help us.*" (2.) Their hopes in God. To him they look, on him they depend, to appear for them. One word from him will turn the scale, and save the sinking remnant. If he but reprove the words of Rabshakeh (that is, disprove them, *v.* 4)—if he undertake to convince and confound the blasphemer—all will be well. And this they trust he will do, not for their merit's sake, but for his own honour's sake, because he has *reproached the living God,* by levelling him with deaf and dumb idols. They have reason to think the issue will be good, for they can interest God in the quarrel. Ps. lxxiv. 22, *Arise, O God! plead thy own cause.* "He is the Lord thy God," say they to Isaiah—"*thine,* whose glory thou art concerned for, and whose favour thou art interested in. He has heard and known the blasphemous words of Rabshakeh, and therefore, it may be, he will hear and rebuke them. We hope he will. Help us with thy prayers to bring the cause before him, and then we are content to leave it with him."

IV. God, by Isaiah, sent to Hezekiah, to assure him that he would glorify himself in the ruin of the Assyrians. Hezekiah sent to Isaiah, not to enquire concerning the event, as many did that sent to the prophets (*Shall I recover?* or the like), but to desire his assistance in his duty. It was this that he was solicitous about; and therefore God let him know what the event should be, in recompence of his care to do his duty, *v.* 6, 7. 1. God interested himself in the cause: *They have blasphemed me.* 2. He encouraged Hezekiah, who was much dismayed: *Be not afraid of the words which thou hast heard;* they are but words (though swelling and fiery words), and words are but wind. 3. He promised to frighten the king of Assyria worse than Rabshakeh had frightened him: "*I will send a blast upon him* (that pestilential breath which killed his army), upon which terrors shall seize him and drive him into his own country, where death shall meet him."

This short threatening from the mouth of God would do execution, when all the impotent menaces that came from Rabshakeh's mouth would vanish into air.

8 So Rab-shakeh returned, and found the king of Assyria warring against Libnah: for he had heard that he was departed from Lachish. 9 And when he heard say of Tirhakah king of Ethiopia, Behold, he is come out to fight against thee: he sent messengers again unto Hezekiah, saying, 10 Thus shall ye speak to Hezekiah king of Judah, saying, Let not thy God in whom thou trustest deceive thee, saying, Jerusalem shall not be delivered into the hand of the king of Assyria. 11 Behold, thou hast heard what the kings of Assyria have done to all lands, by destroying them utterly: and shalt thou be delivered? 12 Have the gods of the nations delivered them which my fathers have destroyed; *as* Gozan, and Haran, and Rezeph, and the children of Eden which *were* in Thelasar? 13 Where *is* the king of Hamath, and the king of Arpad, and the king of the city of Sepharvaim, of Hena, and Ivah? 14 And Hezekiah received the letter of the hand of the messengers, and read it: and Hezekiah went up into the house of the LORD, and spread it before the LORD. 15 And Hezekiah prayed before the LORD, and said, O LORD God of Israel, which dwellest *between* the cherubims, thou art the God, *even* thou alone, of all the kingdoms of the earth; thou hast made heaven and earth. 16 LORD, bow down thine ear, and hear: open, LORD, thine eyes, and see: and hear the words of Sennacherib, which hath sent him to reproach the living God. 17 Of a truth, LORD, the kings of Assyria have destroyed the nations and their lands, 18 And have cast their gods into the fire; for they *were* no gods, but the work of men's hands, wood and stone: therefore they have destroyed them. 19 Now therefore, O LORD our God, I beseech thee, save thou us out of his hand, that all the kingdoms of the earth may know that thou *art* the LORD God, *even* thou only.

Rabshakeh, having delivered his message and received no answer (whether he took this silence for a consent or a slight does not appear), left his army before Jerusalem, under the command of the other generals, and went himself to attend the king his master for further orders. He found him besieging Libnah, a city that had revolted from Judah, *ch.* viii. 22. Whether he had taken Lachish or no is not certain; some think he departed from it because he found the taking of it impracticable, *v.* 8. However, he was now alarmed with the rumour that the king of the Cushites, who bordered upon the Arabians, was coming out against him with a great army, *v.* 9. This made him very desirous to gain Jerusalem with all speed. To take it by force would cost him more time and men than he could well spare, and therefore he renewed his attack upon Hezekiah to persuade him tamely to surrender it. Having found him an easy man once (*ch.* xviii. 14), when he said, *That which thou puttest on me I will bear*, he hoped again to frighten him into a submission, but in vain. Here,

I. Sennacherib sent a letter to Hezekiah, a railing letter, a blasphemous letter, to persuade him to surrender Jerusalem, because it would be to no purpose for him to think of standing it out. His letter is to the same purport with Rabshakeh's speech; there is nothing new offered in it. Rabshakeh had said to the people, *Let not Hezekiah deceive you, ch.* xviii. 29. Sennacherib writes to Hezekiah, *Let not thy God deceive thee, v.* 10. Those that have the God of *Jacob for their help, and whose hope is in the Lord their God*, need not fear being deceived by him, as the heathen were by their gods. To terrify Hezekiah, and drive him from his anchor, he magnifies himself and his own achievements. See how proudly he boasts, 1. Of the lands he had conquered (*v.* 11): *All lands*, and destroyed utterly! How are the mole-hills of his victories swelled to mountains! So far was he from destroying all lands that at this time the land of Cush, and Tirhakah its king, were a terror to him. What vast hyperboles may one expect in proud men's praises of themselves! 2. Of the gods he had conquered, *v.* 12. "Each vanquished nation had its gods, which were so far from being able to deliver them that they fell with them: and shall thy God deliver thee?" 3. Of the kings he had conquered (*v.* 13), the *king of Hamath and the king of Arpad.* Whether he means the prince or the idol, he means to make himself appear greater than either, and therefore very formidable, and the *terror of the mighty in the land of the living.*

II. Hezekiah encloses this in another letter, a praying letter, a believing letter, and sends it to the King of kings, who judges among the gods. Hezekiah was not so haughty as not to receive the letter, though we may suppose the superscription did not give him his due titles; when he had received it he was not so careless as not to read it; when he had read it he was not in such a passion as to write an answer to it in the same provoking language; but he immediately went up to the temple, presented himself, and then *spread the letter before the Lord* (*v.* 14); not as if God needed to have the letter shown to him (he knew what was in it before Hezekiah did), but hereby he signified that he acknowledged God in all his ways,—that he desired not to aggravate the injuries his enemies did him nor to make them appear worse than they were, but desired they might be set in a true light,—and that he referred himself to God, and his righteous judgment, upon the whole matter. Hereby likewise he would affect himself in the prayer he came to the temple to make; and we have need of all possible helps to quicken us in that duty. In the prayer which Hezekiah prayed over this letter, 1. He adores the God whom Sennacherib had blasphemed (*v.* 15), calls him *the God of Israel*, because Israel was his peculiar people, and *the God that dwelt between the cherubim*, because there was the peculiar residence of his glory upon earth; but he gives glory to him as *the God of the whole earth*, and not, as Sennacherib fancied him to be, *the God of Israel only*, and confined to the temple. "Let them say what they will, thou art sovereign Lord, for thou art the God, the God of gods, sole Lord, even thou alone, universal Lord *of all the kingdoms of the earth*, and rightful Lord, *for thou hast made heaven and earth*. Being Creator of all, by an incontestable title thou art owner and ruler of all." 2. He appeals to God concerning the insolence and profaneness of Sennacherib (*v.* 16): "*Lord, hear; Lord, see.* Here it is under his own hand; here it is in black and white." Had Hezekiah only been abused, he would have passed it by; but it is God, the living God, that is reproached, the jealous God. *Lord, what wilt thou do for thy great name?* 3. He owns Sennacherib's triumphs over the gods of the heathen, but distinguishes between them and the God of Israel (*v.* 17, 18): He has indeed *cast their gods into the fire*; for *they were no gods*, unable to help either themselves or their worshippers, and therefore no wonder that he has destroyed them; and, in destroying them, though he knew it not, he really served the justice and jealousy of the God of Israel, who has determined to extirpate all the gods of the heathen. But those are deceived who think they can therefore be too hard for him. He is none of the gods whom men's hands have made, but he has himself made all things, Ps. cxv. 3, 4. 4. He prays that God will now glorify himself in the defeat of Sennacherib and the deliverance of Jerusalem out of his hands (*v.* 19): "*Now therefore save us*; for if we be conquered, as other lands are, they will say that thou art conquered, as the gods of those lands were: but, Lord, distinguish thyself, by distinguishing us, and let all the world know, and be made to confess, that *thou art the Lord God*, the self-existent sovereign God, *even thou only*, and that all pretenders are vanity and a lie." Note, The best pleas in prayer are those which are taken from God's honour; and therefore the Lord's prayer begins with *Hallowed be thy name*, and concludes with *Thine is the glory*.

20 Then Isaiah the son of Amoz sent to Hezekiah, saying, Thus saith the LORD God of Israel, *That* which thou hast prayed to me against Sennacherib king of Assyria I have heard. 21 This *is* the word that the LORD hath spoken concerning him; The virgin the daughter of Zion hath despised thee, *and* laughed thee to scorn; the daughter of Jerusalem hath shaken her head at thee. 22 Whom hast thou reproached and blasphemed? and against whom hast thou exalted *thy* voice, and lifted up thine eyes on high? *even* against the Holy *One* of Israel. 23 By thy messengers thou hast reproached the LORD, and hast said, With the multitude of my chariots I am come up to the height of the mountains, to the sides of Lebanon, and will cut down the tall cedar trees thereof, *and* the choice fir trees thereof: and I will enter into the lodgings of his borders, *and into* the forest of his Carmel. 24 I have digged and drunk strange waters, and with the sole of my feet have I dried up all the rivers of besieged places. 25 Hast thou not heard long ago *how* I have done it, *and* of ancient times that I have formed it? now have I brought it to pass, that thou shouldest be to lay waste fenced cities *into* ruinous heaps. 26 Therefore their inhabitants were of small power, they were dismayed and confounded; they were *as* the grass of the field, and *as* the green herb, *as* the grass on the house tops, and *as* corn blasted before it be grown up. 27 But I know thy abode, and thy going out and thy coming in, and thy rage against me. 28 Because thy rage against me and thy tumult is

come up into mine ears, therefore I will put my hook in thy nose, and my bridle in thy lips, and I will turn thee back by the way by which thou camest. 29 And this *shall be* a sign unto thee, Ye shall eat this year such things as grow of themselves, and in the second year that which springeth of the same; and in the third year sow ye, and reap, and plant vineyards, and eat the fruits thereof. 30 And the remnant that is escaped of the house of Judah shall yet again take root downward, and bear fruit upward. 31 For out of Jerusalem shall go forth a remnant, and they that escape out of mount Zion: the zeal of the LORD *of hosts* shall do this. 32 Therefore thus saith the LORD concerning the king of Assyria, He shall not come into this city, nor shoot an arrow there, nor come before it with shield, nor cast a bank against it. 33 By the way that he came, by the same shall he return, and shall not come into this city, saith the LORD. 34 For I will defend this city, to save it, for mine own sake, and for my servant David's sake.

We have here the gracious copious answer which God gave to Hezekiah's prayer. The message which he sent him by the same hand (*v.* 6, 7), one would think, was an answer sufficient to his prayer; but, that he might have strong consolation, he was encouraged by two immutable things, *in which it was impossible for God to lie*, Heb. vi. 18. In general, God assured him that his prayer was heard, his prayer against Sennacherib, *v.* 20. Note, The case of those that have the prayers of God's people against them is miserable. For, if the oppressed cry to God against the oppressor, *he will hear*, Exod. xxii. 23. God hears and answers, hears *with the saving strength of his right hand*, Ps. xx. 6.

This message bespeaks two things :—

I. Confusion and shame to Sennacherib and his forces. It is here foretold that he should be humbled and broken. The prophet elegantly directs his speech to him, as he does, Isa. x. 5. *O Assyrian! the rod of my anger.* Not that this message was sent to him, but what is here said to him he was made to know by the event. Providence spoke it to him with a witness; and perhaps his own heart was made to whisper this to him: for God has more ways than one of speaking to sinners in his wrath, so as to *vex them in his sore displeasure*, Ps. ii. 5. Sennacherib is here represented,

1. As the scorn of Jerusalem, *v.* 21. He thought himself the terror of the daughter of Zion, that chaste and beautiful virgin, and that by his threats he could force her to submit to him: "But, being a virgin in her Father's house and under his protection, she defies thee, despises thee, laughs thee to scorn. Thy impotent malice is ridiculous; he that sits in heaven laughs at thee, and therefore so do those that abide under his shadow." By this word God intended to silence the fears of Hezekiah and his people. Though to an eye of sense the enemy looked formidable, to an eye of faith he looked despicable.

2. As an enemy to God; and that was enough to make him miserable. Hezekiah pleaded this: "Lord, he has reproached thee," *v.* 16. "He has," saith God, "and I take it as against myself (*v.* 22): *Whom hast thou reproached?* Is it not the Holy One of Israel, whose honour is dear to him, and who has power to vindicate it, which the gods of the heathen have not?" *Nemo me impune lacesset—No one shall provoke me with impunity.*

3. As a proud vainglorious fool, that spoke *great swelling words of vanity*, and *boasted of a false gift*, by his boasts, as well as by his threats, reproaching the Lord. For, (1.) He magnified his own achievements out of measure and quite above what really they were (*v.* 23, 24): *Thou hast said* so and so. This was not in the letter he wrote, but God let Hezekiah know that he not only saw what was written there, but heard what he said elsewhere, probably in the speeches he made to his councils or armies. Note, God takes notice of the boasts of proud men, and will call them to an account, that he *may look upon them and abase them*, Job xl. 11. What a mighty figure does Sennacherib think he makes! Driving his chariots to the tops of the highest mountains, forcing his way through woods and rivers, breaking through all difficulties, making himself master of all he had a mind to. Nothing could stand before him or be withheld from him; no hills too high for him to climb, no trees too strong for him to fell, no waters too deep for him to dry up; as if he had the power of a God, to speak and it is done. (2.) He took to himself the glory of doing these great things, whereas they were all *the Lord's doing*, *v.* 25, 26. Sennacherib, in his letter, had appealed to what Hezekiah had heard (*v.* 11): *Thou hast heard what the kings of Assyria have done;* but, in answer to that, he is reminded of what God has done for Israel of old, drying up the Red Sea, leading them through the wilderness, planting them in Canaan. "What are all thy doings to these? And as for the desolations thou hast made in the earth, and particularly in Judah, thou art but the instrument in God's hand, a mere tool: it is *I that have brought it to pass.* I gave thee thy power, gave thee thy success,

and made thee what thou art, raised thee up to lay waste fenced cities and so to punish them for their wickedness, and *therefore their inhabitants were of small power.*" What a foolish insolent thing was it for him to exalt himself above God, and against God, upon that which he had done by him and under him. Sennacherib's boasts here are expounded in Isa. x. 13, 14, *By the strength of my hand I have done it, and by my wisdom,* &c.; and they are answered (*v.* 15), *Shall the axe boast itself against him that heweth therewith?* It is surely absurd for the fly upon the wheel to say, What a dust do I make! or for the sword in the hand to say, What execution I do! If God be the principal agent in all that is done, boasting is for ever excluded.

4. As under the check and rebuke of that God whom he blasphemed. All his motions were, (1.) Under the divine cognizance (*v.* 27): "*I know thy abode,* and what thou dost secretly devise and design, *thy going out and coming in,* marches and counter-marches, and *thy rage against me* and my people, the tumult of thy passions, the tumult of thy preparations, the noise and bluster thou makest: I know it all." That was more than Hezekiah did, who wished for intelligence of the enemy's motions; but what need was there for this when the eye of God was a constant spy upon him? 2 Chron. xvi. 9. (2.) Under the divine control (*v.* 28): "*I will put my hook in thy nose,* thou great Leviathan (Job xli. 1, 2), *my bridle in thy jaws,* thou great Behemoth. I will restrain thee, manage thee, turn thee where I please, send thee home like a fool as thou camest, *re infectâ—disappointed of thy aim.*" Note, It is a great comfort to all the church's friends that God has a hook in the nose and a bridle in the jaws of all her enemies, can make even their wrath to serve and praise him and then restrain the remainder of it. *Here shall its proud waves be stayed.*

II. Salvation and joy to Hezekiah and his people. This shall be a sign to them of God's favour, and that he is reconciled to them, and *his anger is turned away* (Isa. xii. 1), a wonder in their eyes (for so a sign sometimes signifies), a token for good, and an earnest of the further mercy God has in store for them, that a good issue shall be put to their present distress in every respect.

1. Provisions were scarce and dear; and what should they do for food? The fruits of the earth were devoured by the Assyrian army, Isa. xxxii. 9, 10, &c. Why, they shall not only dwell in the land, but *verily they shall be fed.* If God save them, he will not starve them, nor let them die by famine, when they have escaped the sword: "*Eat you this year that which groweth of itself,* and you shall find enough of that. Did the Assyrians reap what you sowed? You shall reap what you did not sow." But the next year was the sabbatical year, when the land was to rest, and they must neither sow nor reap. What must they do that year? Why, *Jehovah-jireh—The Lord will provide.* God's blessing shall save them seed and labour, and, that year too, the voluntary productions of the earth shall serve to maintain them, to remind them that the earth brought forth before there was a man to till it, Gen. i. 11. And then, the third year, their husbandry should return into its former channel, and they should sow and reap as they used to do. 2. The country was laid waste, families were broken up and scattered, and all was in confusion; how should it be otherwise when it was over-run by such an army? As to this, it is promised that *the remnant that has escaped of the house of Judah* (that is, of the country people) shall yet again be planted in their own habitations, upon their own estates, shall take root there, shall increase and grow rich, *v.* 30. See how their prosperity is described: it is *taking root downwards,* and *bearing fruit upwards,* being well fixed and well provided for themselves, and then doing good to others. Such is the prosperity of the soul: it is taking root downwards by faith in Christ, and then being fruitful in fruits of righteousness. 3. The city was shut up, none went out or came in; but now the remnant in Jerusalem and Zion shall go forth freely, and there shall be none to hinder them, or make them afraid, *v.* 31. Great destruction had been made both in city and country, but in both there was a remnant that escaped, which typified the saved remnant of Israelites indeed (as appears by comparing Isa. x. 22, 23, which speaks of this very event, with Rom. ix. 27, 28), and they shall go forth into the glorious liberty of the children of God. 4. The Assyrians were advancing towards Jerusalem, and would in a little time besiege it in form, and it was in great danger of falling into their hands. But it is here promised that the siege they feared should be prevented,—that, though the enemy had now (as it should seem) encamped before the city, yet they should never *come into the city,* no, nor so much as *shoot an arrow* into it (*v.* 32, 33),—that he should be forced to retire with shame, and a thousand times to repent his undertaking. God himself undertakes to defend the city (*v.* 34), and that person, that place, cannot but be safe, the protection of which he undertakes. 5. The honour and truth of God are engaged for the doing of all this. These are great things, but how will they be effected? Why, *the zeal of the Lord of hosts shall do this, v.* 31. He is Lord of hosts, has all creatures at his beck, therefore he is able to do it; he is *jealous for Jerusalem with great jealousy* (Zech. i. 14); having espoused her a chaste virgin to himself, he will not suffer her to be abused, *v.* 21. "You have reason to think yourselves unworthy that such great things should be done for you; but God's own

zeal will do it." His zeal, (1.) For his own honour (*v.* 34): "I will do it for my own sake, to make myself an everlasting name." God's reasons of mercy are fetched from within himself. (2.) For his own truth: "I will do it for my servant David's sake; not for the sake of his merit, but the promise made to him and the covenant made with him, those sure mercies of David." Thus all the deliverances of the church are wrought for the sake of Christ, the Son of David.

35 And it came to pass that night, that the angel of the LORD went out, and smote in the camp of the Assyrians a hundred fourscore and five thousand: and when they arose early in the morning, behold, they *were* all dead corpses. 36 So Sennacherib king of Assyria departed, and went and returned, and dwelt at Nineveh. 37 And it came to pass, as he was worshipping in the house of Nisroch his god, that Adrammelech and Sharezer his sons smote him with the sword: and they escaped into the land of Armenia. And Esarhaddon his son reigned in his stead.

Sometimes it was long ere prophecies were accomplished and promises performed; but here the word was no sooner spoken than the work was done.

I. The army of Assyria was entirely routed. That night which immediately followed the sending of this message to Hezekiah when the enemy had just set down before the city and were preparing (as we now say) to open the trenches, that night was the main body of their army slain upon the spot by an angel, *v.* 35. Hezekiah had not force sufficient to sally out upon them and attack their camp, nor would God do it by sword or bow; but he sent his angel, a destroying angel, in the dead of the night, to make an assault upon them, which their sentinels, though ever so wakeful, could neither discover nor resist. It was *not by the sword of a mighty man or of a mean man,* that is, not of any man at all, but of an angel, that the Assyrian army was to fall (Isa. xxxi. 8), such an angel as slew the first-born of Egypt. Josephus says it was done by a pestilential disease, which was instant death to them. The number slain was very great, 185,000 men, and Rabshakeh, it is likely, among the rest. When the besieged *arose, early in the morning, behold they were all dead corpses,* scarcely a living man among them. Some think the 76th Psalm was penned on this occasion, where we read that the *stout-hearted were spoiled and slept their sleep,* their last, their long sleep, *v.* 5. See how great, in power and might, the holy angels are, when one angel, in one night, could make so great a slaughter. See how weak the mightiest of men are before almighty God: who ever hardened himself against him and prospered? The pride and blasphemy of the king are punished by the destruction of his army. All these lives are sacrificed to God's glory and Zion's safety. The prophet shows that *therefore* God suffered this vast rendezvous to be made, *that they might be gathered as sheaves into the floor,* Mic. iv. 12, 13.

II. The king of Assyria was hereby put into the utmost confusion. Ashamed to see himself, after all his proud boasts, thus defeated and disabled to pursue his conquests and secure what he had (for this, we may suppose, was the flower of his army), and continually afraid of falling under the like stroke himself, *He departed, and went, and returned;* the manner of the expression intimates the great disorder and distraction of mind he was in, *v.* 36. And it was not long before God cut him off too, by the hands of *two of his own sons, v.* 37. 1. Those that did it were very wicked, to kill their own father (whom they were bound to protect) and in the act of his devotion; monstrous villany! But, 2. God was righteous in it. Justly are the sons suffered to rebel against their father that begat them, when he was in rebellion against the God that made him. Those whose children are undutiful to them ought to consider whether they have not been so to their Father in heaven. The God of Israel had done enough to convince him that he was the only true God, whom therefore he ought to worship; yet he persists in his idolatry, and seeks to his false god for protection against a God of irresistible power. Justly is his blood mingled with his sacrifices, since he will not be convinced by such a plain and dear-bought demonstration of his folly in worshipping idols. His sons that murdered him were suffered to escape, and no pursuit was made after them, his subjects perhaps being weary of the government of so proud a man and thinking themselves well rid of him. And his sons would be looked upon as the more excusable in what they had done if it be true (as bishop Patrick suggested) that he was now vowing to sacrifice them to his god, so that it was for their own preservation that they sacrificed him. His successor was another son, *Esarhaddon,* who (as it should seem) did not aim, like his father, to enlarge his conquests, but rather to improve them; for he it was that first sent colonies of Assyrians to inhabit the country of Samaria, though it is mentioned before (*ch.* xvii. 24), as appears, Ezra iv. 2, where the Samaritans say it was *Esarhaddon that brought them thither.*

CHAP. XX.

In this chapter we have, I. Hezekiah's sickness, and his recovery from that, in answer to prayer, in performance of a promise, in the use of means, and confirmed with a sign, ver. 1—11. II. Hezekiah's sin, and his recovery from that, ver. 12—19. In both of these, Isaiah was God's messenger to him. III The conclusion of his reign, ver. 20, 21.

IN those days was Hezekiah sick unto death. And the prophet Isaiah the son of Amoz came to him, and said unto him, Thus saith the LORD, Set thine house in order; for thou shalt die, and not live. 2 Then he turned his face to the wall, and prayed unto the LORD, saying, 3 I beseech thee, O LORD, remember now how I have walked before thee in truth and with a perfect heart, and have done *that which is* good in thy sight. And Hezekiah wept sore. 4 And it came to pass, afore Isaiah was gone out into the middle court, that the word of the LORD came to him, saying, 5 Turn again, and tell Hezekiah the captain of my people, Thus saith the LORD, the God of David thy father, I have heard thy prayer, I have seen thy tears: behold, I will heal thee: on the third day thou shalt go up unto the house of the LORD. 6 And I will add unto thy days fifteen years; and I will deliver thee and this city out of the hand of the king of Assyria; and I will defend this city for mine own sake, and for my servant David's sake. 7 And Isaiah said, Take a lump of figs. And they took and laid *it* on the boil, and he recovered. 8 And Hezekiah said unto Isaiah, What *shall be* the sign that the LORD will heal me, and that I shall go up into the house of the LORD the third day? 9 And Isaiah said, This sign shalt thou have of the LORD, that the LORD will do the thing that he hath spoken: shall the shadow go forward ten degrees, or go back ten degrees? 10 And Hezekiah answered, It is a light thing for the shadow to go down ten degrees: nay, but let the shadow return backward ten degrees. 11 And Isaiah the prophet cried unto the LORD: and he brought the shadow ten degrees backward, by which it had gone down in the dial of Ahaz.

The historian, having shown us blaspheming Sennacherib destroyed in the midst of the prospects of life, here shows us praying Hezekiah delivered in the midst of the prospects of death—the days of the former shortened, of the latter prolonged.

I. Here is Hezekiah's sickness. *In those days*, that is, in the same year in which the king of Assyria besieged Jerusalem; for he reigning in all twenty-nine years, and surviving this fifteen years, this must be in his fourteenth year, and so was that, *ch.* xviii. 13. Some think it was at the time that the Assyrian army was besieging the city or preparing for it, because God promises (*v.* 6): *I will defend the city*, which promise was afterwards repeated, when the danger came to be most imminent, *ch.* xix. 34. Others think it was soon after the defeat of Sennacherib; and then it shows us the uncertainty of all our comforts in this world. Hezekiah, in the midst of his triumphs in the favour of God, and over the forces of his enemies, is seized with sickness, and under the arrest of death. We must therefore always rejoice with trembling. It should seem he was sick of the plague, for we read of the boil or plague-sore, *v.* 7. The same disease which was killing to the Assyrians was trying to him; God took it from him, and put it upon his enemies. Neither greatness nor goodness can exempt us from sickness, from sore and mortal sicknesses. Hezekiah, lately favoured of heaven above most men, yet is sick unto death—in the midst of his days (under forty) and yet sick and dying; and perhaps he was the more apprehensive of its being fatal to him because his father died when he was about his age, two or three years younger. "In the midst of life we are in death."

II. Warning brought him to prepare for death. It is brought by Isaiah, who had been twice, as stated in the former chapter, a messenger of good tidings to him. We cannot expect to receive from God's prophets any other than what they have received from the Lord, and we must welcome that, be it pleasing or unpleasing. The prophet tells him, 1. That his disease is mortal, and, if he be not recovered by a miracle of mercy, will certainly be fatal: *Thou shalt die, and not live.* 2. That therefore he must, with all speed, get ready for death: *Set thy house in order.* This we should feel highly concerned to do when we are in health, but are most loudly called to do when we come to be sick. Set the heart in order by renewed acts of repentance, and faith, and resignation to God, with cheerful farewells to this world and welcomes to another; and, if not done before (which is the best and wisest course), set the house in order, make thy will, settle thy estate, put thy affairs in the best posture thou canst, for the ease of those that shall come after thee. Isaiah speaks not to Hezekiah of his *kingdom*, only of his *house*. David, being a prophet, had authority to appoint who should reign after him, but other kings did not pretend to bequeath their crowns as part of their goods and chattels.

III. His prayer hereupon: *He prayed unto the Lord*, *v.* 2. Is any sick? Let him be prayed for, let him be prayed with, and let him pray. Hezekiah had found, as recorded in the foregoing chapter, that it was not in vain to wait upon God, but that the prayers of faith bring in answers of peace; therefore will he *call upon God as long as he lives.* Happy experiences of the prevalency of prayer are engagements and encouragements to continue instant in prayer. He had now received the sentence of death within himself, and, if it was reversible, it must be reversed by prayer. When God purposes mercy he will, *for this, be enquired of,* Ezek. xxxvi. 37. We have not if we ask not, or ask amiss. If the sentence was irreversible, yet prayer is one of the best preparations for death, because by it we fetch in strength and grace from God to enable us to finish well. Observe,

1. The circumstances of this prayer. (1.) He *turned his face to the wall,* probably as he lay in his bed. This he did perhaps for privacy; he could not retire to his closet as he used to do, but he retired as well as he could, turned from the company that were about him, to converse with God. When we cannot be so private as we would be in our devotions, nor perform them with the usual outward expressions of reverence and solemnity, yet we must not therefore omit them, but compose ourselves to them as well as we can. Or, as some think, he turned his face towards the temple, to show how willingly he would have gone up thither, to pray this prayer (as he did, *ch.* xix. 1, 14), if he had been able, and remembering what encouragements were given to all the prayers that should be made in or towards that house. Christ is our temple; to him we must have an eye in all our prayers, for no man, no service, *comes to the Father but by him.* (2.) He *wept sorely.* Some gather from this that he was unwilling to die. It is in the nature of man to have some dread of the separation of soul and body, and it was not strange if the Old-Testament saints, to whom another world was but darkly revealed, were not so willing to leave this as Paul and other New-Testament saints were. There was also something peculiar in Hezekiah's case: he was now in the midst of his usefulness, had begun a good work of reformation, which he feared would, through the corruption of the people, fall to the ground, if he should die. If this was before the defeat of the Assyrian army, as some think, he might therefore be loth to die, because his kingdom was in imminent danger of being ruined. However, it does not appear that he had now any son: Manasseh, that succeeded him, was not born till three years after; and, if he should die childless, both the peace of his kingdom and the promise to David would be in danger. But perhaps these were only tears of importunity, and expressions of a lively affection in prayer. Jacob wept and made supplication; and our blessed Saviour, though most willing to die, yet offered up strong cries, with tears, to him whom he knew to be *able to save him,* Heb. v. 7. Let Hezekiah's prayer interpret his tears, and in *that* we find nothing that intimates him to have been under any of that fear of death which has either bondage or torment.

2. The prayer itself: "*Remember now, O Lord! how I have walked before thee in truth;* and either spare me to live, that I may continue thus to walk, or, if my work be done, receive me to that glory which thou hast prepared for those that have thus walked." Observe here, (1.) The description of Hezekiah's piety. He had had his conversation in the world with right intentions ("I have walked before thee, as under thy eye and with an eye ever towards thee"), from a right principle ("*in truth, and with an upright heart*"), and by a right rule—"*I have done that which is good in thy sight.*" (2.) The comfort he now had in reflecting upon it; it made his sick-bed easy. Note, The testimony of conscience for us that we have walked with God in our integrity will be much our support and rejoicing when we come to look death in the face, 2 Cor. i. 12. (3.) The humble mention he makes of it to God. *Lord, remember it now;* not as if God needed to be put in mind of any thing by us (he is greater than our hearts, and knows all things), or as if the reward were of debt, and might be demanded as due (it is Christ's righteousness only that is the purchase of mercy and grace); but our own sincerity may be pleaded as the condition of the covenant which God has wrought in us: "It is the work of thy own hands. Lord, own it." Hezekiah does not pray, "Lord, spare me," or, "Lord, take me; God's will be done;" but, *Lord, remember me; whether I live or die, let me be thine.*

IV. The answer which God immediately gave to this prayer of Hezekiah. The prophet had got but to the middle court when he was sent back with another message to Hezekiah (*v.* 4, 5), to tell him that he should recover; not that there is with God yea and nay, or that he ever says and unsays; but upon Hezekiah's prayer, which he foresaw and which his Spirit inclined him to, God did that for him which otherwise he would not have done. God here calls Hezekiah *the captain of his people,* to intimate that he would reprieve him for his people's sake, because, in this time of war, they could ill spare such a captain: he calls himself *the God of David,* to intimate that he would reprieve him out of a regard to the covenant made with David and the promise that he would always ordain a lamp for him. In this answer, 1. God honours his prayers by the notice he takes of them and the refeence he has to them in this message: *I have heard thy prayers, I have seen thy tears.* Prayers that have much life and affection in them are in a special manner pleasing to God. 2. God exceeds his prayers; he only begged that God would remember his integrity, but God here promises, (1.) To restore him from his illness: *I will heal thee.* Diseases are his servants; as they go where he sends them, so they come when he remands them. Matt. viii. 8, 9. *I am the Lord that healeth thee,* Exod. xv. 26. (2.) To restore him to such a degree of health that *on the third day he should go up to the house of the Lord,* to return thanks. God knew Hezekiah's heart, how dearly he loved the habitation of God's house and the place where his honour dwelt, and that as soon as he was well he would go to attend on public ordinances; thitherward he turned his face when he was sick, and thitherward he would turn his feet when he was recovered; and therefore, because nothing would please him better, he promises him this, *Let my soul live, and it shall praise thee.* The man whom Christ healed was soon after *found in the temple,* John v. 14. (3.) To add fifteen years to his life. This would not bring him to be an old man; it would reach but to fifty-four or fifty-five; yet that was longer than he had lately expected to live. His lease was renewed, which he thought was expiring. We have not the instance of any other that was told before-hand just how long he should live; that good man no doubt made a good use of it; but God has wisely kept us at uncertainties, that we may be always ready. (4.) To deliver Jerusalem from the king of Assyria, *v.* 6. This was the thing which Hezekiah's heart was upon as much as his own recovery, and therefore the promise of this is here repeated. If this was after the raising of the siege, yet there was cause to fear Sennacherib's rallying again. "No," says God, "*I will defend this city.*"

V. The means which were to be used for his recovery, *v.* 7. Isaiah was his physician. He ordered an outward application, a very cheap and common thing: "Lay a *lump of figs to the boil,* to ripen it and bring it to a head, that the matter of the disease may be discharged that way." This might contribute something to the cure, and yet, considering to what a height the disease had come, and how suddenly it was checked, the cure was no less than miraculous. Note, 1. It is our duty, when we are sick, to make use of such means as are proper to help nature, else we do not trust God, but tempt him. 2. Plain and ordinary medicines must not be despised, for many such God has graciously made serviceable to man, in consideration of the poor. 3. What God appoints he will bless and make effectual.

VI. The sign which was given for the encouragement of his faith. 1. He begged it, not in any distrust of the power or promise of God, or as if he staggered at that, but because he looked upon the things promised to be very great things and worthy to be so confirmed, and because it had been usual with God thus to glorify himself and favour his people; and he remembered how much God was displeased with his father for refusing to ask a sign, Isa. vii. 10—12. Observe, Hezekiah asked, *What is the sign,* not that I shall go up to the thrones of judgment or up to the gate, but *up to the house of the Lord?* He desired to recover that he might glorify God *in the gates of the daughter of Zion.* It is not worth while to live for any other purpose than to serve God. 2. It was put to his choice whether the sun should go back or go forward; for it was equal to Omnipotence, and it would be the more likely to confirm his faith if he chose that which he thought the more difficult of the two. Perhaps to this that of this prophet may refer (Isa. xlv. 11), *Ask me of things to come concerning my sons, and concerning the work of my hands command you me.* It is supposed that the degrees were half hours, and that it was just noon when the proposal was made, and the question is, "Shall the sun go back to its place at seven in the morning or forward to its place at five in the evening?" 3. He humbly desired the sun might go back ten degrees, because, though either would be a great miracle, yet, it being the natural course of the sun to go forward, its going back would seem more strange, and would be more significant of Hezekiah's *returning to the days of his youth* (Job xxxiii. 25) and the lengthening out of the day of his life. It was accordingly done, upon the prayer of Isaiah (*v.* 11): He *cried unto the Lord* by special warrant and direction, and God brought the sun back ten degrees, which appeared to Hezekiah (for the sign was intended for him) by the going back of the shadow upon the dial of Ahaz, which, it is likely, he could see through his chamber-window; and the same was observed upon all other dials, even in Babylon, 2 Chron. xxxii. 31. Whether this retrograde motion of the sun was gradual or *per saltum—suddenly—*whether it went back at the same pace that it used to go forward, which would make the day ten hours longer than usual—or whether it darted back on a sudden, and, after continuing a little while, was restored again to its usual place, so that no change was made in the state of the heavenly bodies (as the learned bishop Patrick thinks)—we are not told; but this work of wonder shows the power of God in heaven as well as on earth, the great notice he takes of prayer, and the great favour he bears to his chosen. The most plausible idolatry of the heathen was theirs that worshipped the sun; yet that was hereby convicted of the most egregious folly and absurdity, for by this it appeared that their god was under the check of the God of Israel. Dr. Lightfoot suggests that the fifteen songs of degrees (Ps. cxx., &c.) might perhaps be so called because selected by Hezekiah to be sung to his stringed instruments (Isa. xxxviii. 20) in remembrance of the degrees on the dial which the sun went back and the fifteen years added to his life; and he observes how much of these psalms is applicable to Jerusalem's distress and deliverance and Hezekiah's sickness and recovery.

12 At that time Berodach-baladan, the son of Baladan, king of Babylon, sent letters and a present unto Hezekiah: for he had heard that Hezekiah had been sick. 13 And Hezekiah hearkened unto them, and showed them all the house of his precious things, the silver, and the gold, and the spices, and the precious ointment, and *all* the house of his armour, and all that was found in his treasures: there was nothing in his house, nor in all his dominion, that Hezekiah showed them not. 14 Then came Isaiah the prophet unto king Hezekiah, and said unto him, What said these men? and from whence came they unto thee? And Hezekiah said, They are come from a far country, *even* from Babylon. 15 And he said, What have they seen in thine house? And Hezekiah answered, All *the things* that *are* in mine house have they seen: there is nothing among my treasures that I have not showed them. 16 And Isaiah said unto Hezekiah, Hear the word of the LORD. 17 Behold, the days come, that all that *is* in thine house, and that which thy fathers have laid up in store unto this day, shall be carried into Babylon: nothing shall be left, saith the LORD. 18 And of thy sons that shall issue from thee, which thou shalt beget, shall they take away; and they shall be eunuchs in the palace of the king of Babylon. 19 Then said Hezekiah unto Isaiah, Good *is* the word of the LORD which thou hast spoken. And he said, *Is it* not *good*, if peace and truth be in thy days? 20 And the rest of the acts of Hezekiah, and all his might, and how he made a pool, and a conduit, and brought water into the city, *are* they not written in the book of the chronicles of the kings of Judah? 21 And Hezekiah slept with his fathers: and Manasseh his son reigned in his stead.

Here is, I. An embassy sent to Hezekiah by the king of Babylon, to congratulate him on his recovery, *v.* 12. The kings of Babylon had hitherto been only deputies and tributaries to the kings of Assyria, and Nineveh was the royal city. We find Babylon subject to the king of Assyria, *ch.* xvii. 24. But this king of Babylon began to set up for himself, and by degrees things were so changed that Assyria became subject to the kings of Babylon. This king of Babylon sent to compliment Hezekiah, and ingratiate himself with him upon a double account. 1. Upon the account of religion. The Babylonians worshipped the sun, and, perceiving what honour their god had done to Hezekiah, in going back for his sake, they thought themselves obliged to do honour to him likewise. It is good having those our friends whom we perceive to be the favourites of heaven. 2. Upon the account of civil interest. If the king of Babylon was now meditating a revolt from the king of Assyria, it was policy to get Hezekiah into his interest, in answer to whose prayers, and for whose protection, heaven had given that fatal blow to the king of Assyria. He found himself obliged to Hezekiah, and his God, for the weakening of the Assyrian forces, and had reason to think he could not have a more powerful and valuable ally than one that had so good an interest in the upper world. He therefore made his court to him with all possible respect by ambassadors, letters, and a present.

II. The kind entertainment Hezekiah gave to these ambassadors, *v.* 13. It was his duty to be civil to them, and receive them with the respect due to ambassadors; but he exceeded, and was courteous to a fault. 1. He was too fond of them. He *hearkened unto them.* Though they were idolaters, yet he became intimate with them, was forward to come into a confederacy with the king their master, and granted them all they came for. He was more open and free than he should have been, and stood not so much upon his guard. What reason had he that was in covenant with God so eagerly to catch at an alliance with a heathen prince, or to value himself at all upon his respectful notice? What honour could this embassy add to one whom God had so highly favoured, that he should please himself so much with it? 2. He was too fond of showing them his palace, his treasures, and his magazines, that they might see, and might report to their master, what a great king he was, and how well worthy of the honour their master did him. It is not said that he showed them the temple, the book of the law, and the manner of his worship, that he might proselyte them to the true religion, which he had now a fair opportunity of doing; but in compliment to them, lest he should affront them, he waived that, and showed them the rich furniture of his closet, that house of his precious things, the wealth he had heaped up since the king of Assyria had emptied his coffers, his *silver, and gold, and spices.* All the valuable things he had he showed them, either himself or by his officers. And what harm was there in this? What is more commonly, and (as we think) more innocently, done, than to show strangers the riches and rarities of a country—to show our friends our houses and their furniture, our gardens, stables, and libraries? But if we do this in the pride of our hearts, as Hezekiah did, to gain applause from men, and not giving praise to God, it turns into sin to us, as it did to him.

III. The examination of Hezekiah concerning this matter, *v.* 14, 15. Isaiah, who had often been his comforter, is now his reprover. The blessed Spirit is both, John xvi. 7, 8. Ministers must be both, as there is occasion. Isaiah spoke in God's name, and therefore called him to account as one having authority: "Who are these? Whence come they? What is their business? What have they seen?" Hezekiah not only submitted to the examination (did not ask him, "Why should you concern yourself and question me about this affair?"), but made an ingenuous confession: *There is nothing among my treasures that I have not shown them.* Why then did he not bring them to Isaiah, and show him to them who was without doubt the best treasure he had in his dominions, and who by his prayers and prophecies had been instrumental in all those wonders which these ambassadors came to enquire into? I hope Hezekiah had the same value for Isaiah now that he had in his distress; but it would have become him to show it by bringing these ambassadors to him in the first place, which might have prevented the false step he took.

IV. The sentence passed upon him for his pride and vanity, and the too great relish he had of the things of the world, after that intimate acquaintance he had so lately been admitted into with divine things. The sentence is (*v.* 17, 18), 1. That the treasures he was so proud of should hereafter become a prey, and his family should be robbed of them all. It is just with God to take that from us which we make the matter of our pride and in which we put our confidence. 2. That the king of Babylon, with whom he was so fond of an alliance, should be the enemy that should make a prey of them. Not that it was for this sin that that judgment should he brought upon them: the sins of Manasseh, his idolatries and murders, were the cause of that calamity; but it is now foretold to Hezekiah, to convince him of the folly of his pride and of the value he had for the king of Babylon, and to make him ashamed of it. Hezekiah was fond of assisting the king of Babylon to rise, and to reduce the exorbitant power of the kings of Assyria; but he is told that the snake he is cherishing will ere long sting the bosom that cherishes it, and that his royal seed shall become the king of Babylon's slave (which was fulfilled, Dan. i. 1, &c.), than which there could not be any thing more mortifying to Hezekiah to think of. Babylon will be the ruin of those that are fond of Babylon. Wise therefore and happy are those that *come out from her,* Rev. xviii. 4.

V. Hezekiah's humble and patient submission to this sentence, *v.* 19. Observe how he argues himself into this submission. 1. He lays it down for a truth that "*good is the word of the Lord,* even this word, though a threatening; for every word of his is so. It is not only just, but good; for, as he does no wrong to any, so he means no hurt to good men. It is good; for he will bring good out of it, and do me good by the foresight of it." We should believe this concerning every providence, that it is good, is working for good. 2. He takes notice of that in this word which was good, that he should not live to see this evil, much less to share in it. He makes the best of the bad: "Is it not good? Yes, certainly it is, and better than I deserve." Note, (1.) True penitents, when they are under divine rebukes, call them not only just, but good; not only submit to the punishment of their iniquity, but accept of it. So Hekeziah did, and by this it appeared that he was indeed *humbled for the pride of his heart.* (2.) When at any time we are under dark dispensations, or have dark prospects, public or personal, we must take notice of what is *for* us as well as what is *against* us, that we may by thanksgiving honour God, and may in our patience possess our own souls. (3.) As to public affairs, it is good, and we are bound to think it so, *if peace and truth be in our days.* That is, [1.] Whatever else we want, it is good if we have peace and truth, if we have the true religion professed and protected, Bibles and ministers, and enjoy these in peace, not terrified with the alarms of war or persecution. [2.] Whatever trouble may come when we are gone, it is good if all be well in our days. Not that we should be unconcerned for posterity; it is a grief to foresee evils: but we should own that the deferring of judgments is a great favour in general, and to have them deferred so long as that we may die in peace is a particular favour to us, for charity begins at home. We know not how we shall bear the trial, and therefore have reason to think it well if we may but get safely to heaven before it comes.

Lastly, Here is the conclusion of Hezekiah's life and story, *v.* 20, 21. In 2 Chron. *ch.* xxix.—xxxii. much more is recorded of Hezekiah's work of reformation than in this book of Kings; and it seems that in the civil chronicles, not now extant, there were many things recorded of his might and the good offices he did for Jerusalem, particularly his bringing water by pipes into the city. To have water in plenty, without striving for it and without being terrified with the noise of archers in the drawing of it, to have it at hand and convenient for us, is to be reckoned a great mercy; for the want of water would be a great calamity. But here this historian leaves him *asleep with his fathers,* and a son in his throne that proved very untoward; for parents cannot give grace to their children. Wicked Ahaz was the son of a godly father and the father of a godly son; holy Hezekiah was the son of a wicked father and the father of a wicked son. When the land was not reformed, as it should have been, by a good reign, it was plagued and ripened for ruin by a bad one; yet then tried again with a good one, that it might appear how loth God was to cut off his people.

CHAP. XXI.

In this chapter we have a short but sad account of the reigns of two of the kings of Judah, Manasseh and Amon. I. Concerning Manasseh, all the account we have of him here is, 1. That he devoted himself to sin, to all manner of wickedness, idolatry, and murder, ver. 1—9 and ver. 16. 2. That therefore God devoted him, and Jerusalem for his sake, to ruin, ver. 10—18. In the book of Chronicles we have an account of his troubles, and his repentance. II. Concerning Amon we are only told that he lived in sin (ver. 19—22), died quickly by the sword, and left good Josiah his successor, ver. 23—26. By these two reigns Jerusalem was much debauched and much weakened, and so hastened apace towards its destruction, which slumbered not.

MANASSEH *was* twelve years old when he began to reign, and reigned fifty and five years in Jerusalem. And his mother's name *was* Hephzi-bah. 2 And he did *that which was* evil in the sight of the LORD, after the abominations of the heathen, whom the LORD cast out before the children of Israel. 3 For he built up again the high places which Hezekiah his father had destroyed; and he reared up altars for Baal, and made a grove, as did Ahab king of Israel; and worshipped all the host of heaven and served them. 4 And he built altars in the house of the LORD, of which the LORD said, In Jerusalem will I put my name. 5 And he built altars for all the host of heaven in the two courts of the house of the LORD. 6 And he made his son pass through the fire, and observed times, and used enchantments, and dealt with familiar spirits and wizards: he wrought much wickedness in the sight of the LORD, to provoke *him* to anger. 7 And he set a graven image of the grove that he had made in the house, of which the LORD said to David, and to Solomon his son, In this house, and in Jerusalem, which I have chosen out of all tribes of Israel, will I put my name for ever: 8 Neither will I make the feet of Israel move any more out of the land which I gave their fathers; only if they will observe to do according to all that I have commanded them, and according to all the law that my servant Moses commanded them. 9 But they hearkened not: and Manasseh seduced them to do more evil than did the nations whom the LORD destroyed before the children of Israel.

How delightful were our meditations on the last reign! How many pleasing views had we of Sion in its glory (that is, in its purity and in its triumphs), of the king in his beauty! (for Isa. xxxiii. 17 refers to Hezekiah), and (as it follows there, *v.* 20) Jerusalem was *a quiet habitation* because *a city of righteousness,* Isa. i. 26. But now we have melancholy work upon our hands, unpleasant ground to travel, and cannot but drive heavily. *How has the gold become dim and the most fine gold changed!* The beauty of Jerusalem is stained, and all her glory, all her joy, sunk and gone. These verses give such an account of this reign as make it, in all respects, the reverse of the last, and, in a manner, the ruin of it.

I. Manasseh began young. He was but *twelve years old when he began to reign* (*v.* 1), born when his father was about forty-two years old, three years after his sickness. If he had sons before, either they were dead, or set by as unpromising. As yet they knew of nothing bad in *him,* and they hoped he would prove good; but he proved very bad, and perhaps his coming to the crown so young might help to make it so, which yet will by no means excuse him, for his grandson Josiah came to it younger than he and yet acted well. But being young, 1. He was puffed up with his honour and proud of it; and thinking himself very wise, because he was very great, valued himself upon his undoing what his father had done. It is too common for novices to be lifted up with pride, and so to *fall into the condemnation of the devil.* 2. He was easily wrought upon and drawn aside by seducers, that lay in wait to deceive. Those that were enemies to Hezekiah's reformation, and retained an affection for the old idolatries, flattered him, and so gained his ear, and used his power at their pleasure. Many have been undone by coming too soon to their honours and estates.

II. He reigned long, longest of any of the kings of Judah, fifty-five years. This was the only very bad reign that was a long one: Joram's was but eight years, and Ahaz's sixteen; as for Manasseh's, we hope that in the beginning of his reign for some time affairs continued to move in the course that his father left them in, and that in the latter end of his reign, after his repentance, religion got head again; and, no doubt, when things were at the worst God had his remnant that kept their integrity. Though he reigned long, yet some of this time he was a prisoner in Babylon, which may well be looked upon as a drawback from these years, though they are reckoned in the number because then he repented and began to reform.

III. He reigned very ill.

1. In general, (1.) *He did that which was evil in the sight of the Lord,* and which, having been well educated, he could not but know was so (*v.* 2): *He wrought much wickedness in the sight of the Lord,* as if on purpose to provoke him to anger, *v.* 6. (2.) *He did after the abominations of the heathen* (*v.* 2) and as did Ahab (*v.* 3), not taking warning by the destruction both of the nations of Canaan and the house of Ahab for their idolatry; nay (*v.* 9), he *did more evil than did the nations whom the Lord destroyed.* When the holy seed degenerate, they are commonly worse than the worst of the profane.

2. More particularly, (1.) He *rebuilt the high places which his father had destroyed, v.* 3. Thus did he trample upon the dust, and affront the memory, of his worthy father, though he knew how much he was favoured of God and honoured of men. He concurred, it is probable, with Rabshakeh's sentiments (*ch.* xviii. 22), that Hezekiah had done ill in destroying those high places, and pretended the honour of God, and the edification and convenience of the people, in rebuilding them. This he began with, but proceeded to that which was much worse; for, (2.) He set up other gods, *Baal* and *Ashtaroth* (which we translate *a grove),* and all the host of heaven, the sun and moon, the other planets, and the constellations; these he worshipped and served (*v.* 3), gave their names to the images he made, and then did homage to them and prayed for help from them. To these he built altars (*v.* 5), and offered sacrifices, no doubt, on these altars. (3.) He *made his son pass through the fire,* by which he dedicated him a votary to Moloch, in contempt of the seal of circumcision by which he had been dedicated to God. (4.) He made the devil his oracle, and, in contempt both of urim and prophecy, he *used enchantments and dealt with familiar spirits* (*v.* 6) like Saul. Conjurers and fortune-tellers (who pretended, by the stars or the clouds, lucky and unlucky days, good and bad omens, the flight of birds, or the entrails of beasts, to foretel things to come) were great men with him, his intimates, his confidants; their arts pleased his fancy, and gained his belief, and his counsels were under their direction. (5.) We find afterwards (*v.* 16) that he shed innocent blood very much in gratification of his own passion and revenge; some perhaps were secretly murdered, others taken off by colour of law. Probably much of the blood he shed was theirs that opposed idolatry and witnessed against it, that would not bow the knee to Baal. The *blood of the prophets* is, in a particular manner, charged upon Jerusalem, and it is probable that he put to death many of them. The tradition of the Jews is that he caused the prophet Isaiah to be sawn asunder; and many think the apostle refers to this in Heb. xi. 37, where he speaks of those that had so suffered.

3. Three things are here mentioned as aggravations of Manasseh's idolatry:—(1.) That he set up his images and altars *in the house of the Lord* (*v.* 4), in the two courts of the temple (*v.* 5), in the very house of which God had said to Solomon, *Here will I put my name, v.* 7. Thus he defied God to his face, and impudently affronted him with his rivals immediately under his eye, as one that was neither afraid of God's wrath nor ashamed of his own folly and wickedness. Thus he desecrated what had been consecrated to God, and did, in effect, turn God out of his own house and put the rebels in possession of it. Thus, when the faithful worshippers of God came to the place he had appointed for the performance of their duty to him, they found, to their great grief and terror, other gods ready to receive their offerings. God had said that here he would record his name, here he would put it for ever, and here it was accordingly preserved, while the idolatrous altars were kept at a distance; but Manasseh, by bringing them into God's house, did what he could to alter the property, and to make the name of the God of Israel to be no more in remembrance. (2.) That hereby he put a great slight upon the word of God, and his covenant with Israel. Observe the favour he had shown to that people in putting his name among them,—the kindness he intended them, never to *make them move out of that good land,*—and the reasonableness of his expectations from them, *only if they will observe to do according to all that I have commanded them, v.* 7, 8. Upon these good terms did Israel stand with God, and had as fair a prospect of being happy as any people could have; but *they hearkened not, v.* 9. They would not be kept close to God either by his precepts or by his promises; both were cast behind their back. (3.) That hereby he seduced the people of God, debauched them, and drew them into idolatry, *v.* 9. He caused Judah to sin (*v.* 11), as Jeroboam had caused *Israel to sin.* His very example was enough to corrupt the generality of unthinking people, who would do as their king did, right or wrong. All that aimed at preferment would do as the court did; and others thought it safest to comply, for fear of making their king their enemy. Thus, one way or other, the holy city became a harlot, and Manasseh made her so. Those will have a great deal to answer for that not only are wicked themselves, but help to make others so.

10 And the LORD spake by his servants the prophets, saying, 11 Because Manasseh king of Judah hath done these abominations *and* hath

done wickedly above all that the Amorites did, which *were* before him, and hath made Judah also to sin with his idols: 12 Therefore thus saith the LORD God of Israel, Behold, I *am* bringing *such* evil upon Jerusalem and Judah, that whosoever heareth of it, both his ears shall tingle. 13 And I will stretch over Jerusalem the line of Samaria, and the plummet of the house of Ahab: and I will wipe Jerusalem as *a man* wipeth a dish, wiping *it*, and turning *it* upside down. 14 And I will forsake the remnant of mine inheritance, and deliver them into the hand of their enemies; and they shall become a prey and a spoil to all their enemies; 15 Because they have done *that which was* evil in my sight, and have provoked me to anger, since the day their fathers came forth out of Egypt, even unto this day. 16 Moreover Manasseh shed innocent blood very much, till he had filled Jerusalem from one end to another; beside his sin wherewith he made Judah to sin, in doing *that which was* evil in the sight of the LORD. 17 Now the rest of the acts of Manasseh, and all that he did, and his sin that he sinned, *are* they not written in the book of the chronicles of the kings of Judah? 18 And Manasseh slept with his fathers, and was buried in the garden of his own house, in the garden of Uzza: and Amon his son reigned in his stead.

Here is the doom of Judah and Jerusalem read, and it is a heavy doom. The prophets were sent, in the first place, to teach them the knowledge of God, to remind them of their duty and direct them in it. If they succeeded not in that, their next work was to reprove them for their sins, and to set them in view before them, that they might repent and reform, and return to their duty. If in this they prevailed not, but sinners went on frowardly, their next work was to foretel the judgments of God, that the terror of them might awaken those to repentance who would not be made sensible of the obligations of his love, or else that the execution of them, in their season, might be a demonstration of the divine mission of the prophets that foretold them. The prophets were deputed judges to those that would not hear and receive them as teachers. We have here,

I. A recital of the crime. The indictment is read upon which the judgment is grounded, *v.* 11. Manasseh had done wickedly himself, though he knew better things, had even justified the Amorites, whose copy he wrote after, by outdoing them in impieties, and debauched the people of God, whom he had taught to sin and forced to sin; and besides that (though that was bad enough) *he had filled Jerusalem with innocent blood* (*v.* 16), had multiplied his murders in every corner of the city, and filled the measure of Jerusalem's blood-guiltiness (Matt. xxiii. 32) up to the brim, and all this against the crown and dignity of the King of kings, the peace of his kingdom, and the statutes in these cases made and provided.

II. A prediction of the judgment God would bring upon them for this: *They have done that which was evil,* and therefore *I am bringing evil upon them* (*v.* 12); it will come and it is not far off. The judgment should be, 1. Very terrible and amazing; the very report of it should *make men's ears to tingle* (*v.* 12), that is, their hearts to tremble. It should make a great noise in the world and occasion many speculations. 2. It should be copied out (as the sins of Jerusalem had been) from Samaria and the house of Ahab, *v.* 13. When God lays righteousness to the line it shall be the line of Samaria, measuring out to Jerusalem that which had been the lot of Samaria; when he lays judgment to the plummet it shall be *the plummet of the house of Ahab,* marking out for the same ruin to which that wretched family was devoted. See Isa. xxviii. 17. Note, Those who resemble and imitate others in their sins must expect to fare as they fared. 3. That it should be an utter destruction: *I will wipe it as a man wipes a dish.* This intimates, (1.) That every thing should be put into disorder, and their state subverted; they should be turned upside down, and all their foundations put out of course. (2.) That the city should be emptied of its inhabitants, which had been the filth of it, as a dish is emptied when it is wiped: "They shall all be carried captive, the *land shall enjoy her sabbaths,* and be laid by as a dish when it is wiped." See the comparison of the boiled pot, not much unlike this, Ezek. xxiv. 1—14. (3.) That yet this should be in order to the purifying, not the destroying, of Jerusalem. The dish shall not be dropped, not broken to pieces, or melted down, but only wiped. This shall be the fruit, the taking away of the sinners first, and then of the sin. 4. That *therefore* they should be destroyed, because they should be deserted (*v.* 14): *I will forsake the remnant of my inheritance.* Justly are those that forsake God forsaken of him; nor does he ever leave any till they have first left him: but, when God has forsaken a people, their defence has departed, and they become a prey, an easy prey, to all their enemies. Sin is spoken of here as the alpha and omega of their miseries. (1.) Old guilt came in remembrance, as that which began to fill the measure (*v.* 15): "*They have provoked me to anger* from their conception and birth as a people, *since the day their fathers came out of Egypt.*" The men of this generation, treading in their fathers' steps, are justly reckoned with for their fathers' sins. (2.) The guilt of blood was that which filled the measure, *v.* 16. Nothing has a louder cry, nor brings a sorer vengeance, than that.

This is all we have here of Manasseh; he stands convicted and condemned; but we hope in the book of Chronicles to hear of his repentance, and acceptance with God. Meantime, we must be content, in this place, to have only one intimation of his repentance (for so we are willing to take it), that he was buried, it is likely by his own order, *in the garden of his own house* (*v.* 18); for, being truly humbled for his sins, he judged himself *no more worthy to be called a son*, a son of David, and therefore not worthy to have even his dead body buried *in the sepulchres of his fathers.* True penitents take shame to themselves, not honour; yet, having lost the credit of an innocent, the credit of a penitent was the next best he was capable of. And better it is, and more honourable, for a sinner to die repenting, and be buried in a garden, than to die impenitent, and be buried in the abbey.

19 Amon *was* twenty and two years old when he began to reign, and he reigned two years in Jerusalem. And his mother's name *was* Meshullemeth, the daughter of Haruz of Jotbah. 20 And he did *that which was* evil in the sight of the LORD, as his father Manasseh did. 21 And he walked in all the way that his father walked in, and served the idols that his father served, and worshipped them: 22 And he forsook the LORD God of his fathers, and walked not in the way of the LORD. 23 And the servants of Amon conspired against him, and slew the king in his own house. 24 And the people of the land slew all them that had conspired against king Amon; and the people of the land made Josiah his son king in his stead. 25 Now the rest of the acts of Amon which he did, *are* they not written in the book of the chronicles of the kings of Judah? 26 And he was buried in his sepulchre in the garden of Uzza: and Josiah his son reigned in his stead.

Here is a short account of the short and inglorious reign of Amon, the son of Manasseh. Whether Manasseh, in his blind and brutish zeal for his idols, had sacrificed his other sons—or whether, having been dedicated to his idols, they were refused by the people—so it was that his successor was a son not born till he was forty-five years old. And of him we are here told, 1. That his reign was very wicked: *He forsook the God of his fathers* (*v.* 22), disobeyed the commands given to his fathers, and disclaimed the covenant made with his fathers, *and walked not in the way of the Lord,* but *in all the way which his father walked in, v.* 20, 21. He trod in the steps of his father's idolatry, and revived that which he, in the latter end of his days, had put down. Note, Those who set bad examples, though they may repent themselves, yet cannot be sure that those whom they have drawn into sin by their example will repent; it is often otherwise. 2. That his end was very tragical. He having rebelled against God, his own servants *conspired against him and slew him,* probably upon some personal disgust, when he had reigned but two years, *v.* 23. His servants, who should have guarded him, murdered him; his own house, that should have been his castle of defence, was the place of his execution. He had profaned God's house with his idols, and now God suffered his own house to be polluted with his blood. How unrighteous soever those were that did it, God was righteous who suffered it to be done. Two things the people of the land did, by their representatives, hereupon:—(1.) They did justice on the traitors that had slain the king, and put them to death; for, though he was a *bad* king, he was *their* king, and it was a part of their allegiance to him to avenge his death. Thus they cleared themselves from having any hand in the crime, and did what was incumbent on them to deter others from the like villanous practices. (2.) They did a kindness to themselves in *making Josiah his son king in his stead,* whom probably the conspirators had a design to put by, but the people stood by him and settled him in the throne, encouraged, it may be, by the indications he gave, even in his early days, of a good disposition. Now they made a happy change from one of the worst to one of the best of all the kings of Judah. "Once more," says God, "they shall be tried with a reformation; and, if that succeed, well; if not, then after that I will cut them down." Amon was buried in the same garden where his father was, *v.* 26. If his father put himself under that humiliation, the people will put him under it.

CHAP. XXII.

This chapter begins the story of the reign of good king Josiah, whose goodness shines the brighter because it came just after so much wickedness, which he had the honour to reform, and just before so great a destruction, which yet he had not the honour to prevent. Here, after his general character (ver. 1, 2), we have a particular account of the respect he paid, I. To God's house, which he repaired, ver. 3—7. II. To God's book, which he was much affected with the reading of, ver. 8—11. III. To God's messengers, whom he thereupon consulted, ver. 12—14. And by whom he received from God an answer threatening Jerusalem's destruction (ver. 15—17), but promising favour to him

(ver 18—20), upon which he set about that glorious work of reformation which we have an account of in the next chapter.

JOSIAH *was* eight years old when he began to reign, and he reigned thirty and one years in Jerusalem. And his mother's name *was* Jedidah, the daughter of Adaiah of Boscath. 2 And he did *that which was* right in the sight of the LORD, and walked in all the way of David his father, and turned not aside to the right hand or to the left. 3 And it came to pass in the eighteenth year of king Josiah, *that* the king sent Shaphan the son of Azaliah, the son of Meshullam, the scribe, to the house of the LORD, saying, 4 Go up to Hilkiah the high priest, that he may sum the silver which is brought into the house of the LORD, which the keepers of the door have gathered of the people: 5 And let them deliver it into the hand of the doers of the work, that have the oversight of the house of the LORD: and let them give it to the doers of the work which *is* in the house of the LORD, to repair the breaches of the house, 6 Unto carpenters and builders, and masons, and to buy timber and hewn stone to repair the house. 7 Howbeit there was no reckoning made with them of the money that was delivered into their hand, because they dealt faithfully. 8 And Hilkiah the high priest said unto Shaphan the scribe, I have found the book of the law in the house of the LORD. And Hilkiah gave the book to Shaphan, and he read it. 9 And Shaphan the scribe came to the king, and brought the king word again, and said, Thy servants have gathered the money that was found in the house, and have delivered it into the hand of them that do the work, that have the oversight of the house of the LORD. 10 And Shaphan the scribe showed the king, saying, Hilkiah the priest hath delivered me a book. And Shaphan read it before the king.

Concerning Josiah we are here told,

I. That he was very young when he began to reign (*v.* 1), only eight years old. Solomon says, *Woe unto thee, O land! when thy king is a child;* but happy art thou, O land! when thy king is *such* a child. Our English Israel had once a king that was such a child, Edward VI. Josiah, being young, had not received any bad impressions from the example of his father and grandfather, but soon saw their errors, and God gave him grace to take warning by them. See Ezek. xviii. 14, &c.

II. That he *did that which was right in the sight of the Lord, v.* 2. See the sovereignty of divine grace—the father passed by and left to perish in his sin, the son a chosen vessel. See the triumphs of that grace—Josiah born of a wicked father, no good education nor good example given him, but many about him who no doubt advised him to tread in his father's steps and few that gave him any good counsel, and yet the grace of God made him an eminent saint, *cut him off from the wild olive* and *grafted him into the good olive,* Rom. xi. 24. Nothing is too hard for that grace to do. He walked in a good way, and turned not aside (as some of his predecessors had done who began well) *to the right hand nor to the left.* There are errors on both hands, but God kept him in the right way; he fell neither into superstition nor profaneness.

III. That he took care for the repair of the temple. This he did in the eighteenth year of his reign, *v.* 3. Compare 2 Chron. xxxiv. 8. He began much sooner to *seek the Lord* (as appears, 2 Chron. xxxiv. 3), but it is to be feared the work of reformation went slowly on and met with much opposition, so that he could not effect what he desired and designed, till his power was thoroughly confirmed. The consideration of the time we unavoidably lost in our minority should quicken us, when we have come to years, to act with so much the more vigour in the service of God. Having begun late we have need work hard. He sent Shaphan, the secretary of state, to Hilkiah the high priest, to take an account of the money that was collected for this use by the doorkeepers (*v.* 4); for, it seems, they took much the same way of raising the money that Joash took, *ch.* xii. 9. When people gave by a little at a time the burden was insensible, and, the contribution being voluntary, it was not complained of. This money, so collected, he ordered him to lay out for the repair of the temple, *v.* 5, 6. And now, it seems, the workmen (as in the days of Joash) acquitted themselves so well that *there was no reckoning made with them* (*v.* 7), which is certainly mentioned to the praise of the workmen, that they gained such a reputation for honesty, but whether to the praise of those that employed them I know not; a man should count money (we say) after his own father; it would not have been amiss to have *reckoned with the workmen,* that others also might be satisfied of their honesty.

IV. That, in repairing the temple, *the book of the law* was happily found and brought to the king, *v.* 8, 10. Some think this book was the autograph, or original manuscript, of the five books of Moses, under his own hand; others think it was only an ancient and authentic copy. Most likely it was that which, by the command of Moses, was laid up in the most holy place, Deut. xxxi. 24, &c. 1. It seems, this book of the law was lost or missing. Perhaps it was carelessly mislaid and neglected, thrown by into a corner (as some throw their Bibles), by those that knew not the value of it, and forgotten there; or it was maliciously concealed by some of the idolatrous kings, or their agents, who were restrained by the providence of God or their own consciences from burning and destroying it, but buried it, in hopes it would never see the light again; or, as some think, it was carefully laid up by some of its friends, lest it should fall into the hands of its enemies. Whoever were the instruments of its preservation, we ought to acknowledge the hand of God in it. If this was the only authentic copy of the Pentateuch then in being, which had (as I may say) so narrow a turn for its life and was so near perishing, I wonder the hearts of all good people did not tremble for that sacred treasure, as Eli's for the ark, and I am sure we now have reason to thank God, upon our knees, for that happy providence by which Hilkiah found this book at this time, found it when *he sought it not*, Isa. lxv. 1. If the holy scriptures had not been of God, they would not have been in being at this day; God's care of the Bible is a plain indication of his interest in it. 2. Whether this was the only authentic copy in being or no, it seems the things contained in it were new both to the king himself and to the high priest; for the king, upon the reading of it, rent his clothes. We have reason to think that neither the command for the king's writing a copy of the law, nor that for the public reading of the law every seventh year (Deut. xvii. 18; xxxi. 10, 11), had been observed for a long time; and when the instituted means of keeping up religion are neglected religion itself will soon go to decay. Yet, on the other hand, if the book of the law was lost, it seems difficult to determine what rule Josiah went by in doing that which was *right in the sight of the Lord*, and how the priests and people kept up the rites of their religion. I am apt to think that the people generally took up with abstracts of the law, like our abridgments of the statutes, which the priests, to save themselves the trouble of writing and the people of reading the book at large, had furnished them with—a sort of ritual, directing them in the observances of their religion, but leaving out what they thought fit, and particularly the promises and threatenings (Lev. xxvi. and Deut. xxviii. &c.), for I observe that these were the portions of the law which Josiah was so much affected with (*v.* 13), for these were new to him. No summaries, extracts, or collections, out of the Bible (though they may have their use) can be effectual to convey and preserve the knowledge of God and his will like the Bible itself. It was no marvel that the people were so corrupt when the book of the law was such a scarce thing among them; where that vision is not the people perish. Those that endeavoured to debauch them no doubt used all the arts they could to get that book out of their hands. The church of Rome could not keep up the use of images but by forbidding the use of the scripture. 3. It was a great instance of God's favour, and a token for good to Josiah and his people, that the book of the law was thus seasonably brought to light, to direct and quicken that blessed reformation which Josiah had begun. It is a sign that God has mercy in store for a people when he magnifies his law among them and makes that honourable, and furnishes them with means for the increase of scripture-knowledge. The translating of the scriptures into vulgar tongues was the glory, strength, and joy of the Reformation from Popery. It is observable that they were about a good work, repairing the temple, when they found the book of the law. Those that do their duty according to their knowledge shall have their knowledge increased To him that hath shall be given. The book of the law was an abundant recompence for all their care and cost about the repair of the temple. 4. Hilkiah the priest was exceedingly well pleased with the discovery. "O," says he to Shaphan, "rejoice with me, for *I have found the book of the law*, εὕρηκα, εὕρηκα, —*I have found, I have found*, that jewel of inestimable value. Here, carry it to the king; it is the richest jewel of his crown. Read it before him. He walks in *the way of David his father*, and, if he be like him, he will love the book of the law and bid that welcome; that will be his delight and his counsellor.

11 And it came to pass, when the king had heard the words of the book of the law, that he rent his clothes. 12 And the king commanded Hilkiah the priest, and Ahikam the son of Shaphan, and Achbor the son of Michaiah, and Shaphan the scribe, and Asahiah a servant of the king's, saying, 13 Go ye, enquire of the LORD for me, and for the people, and for all Judah, concerning the words of this book that is found: for great *is* the wrath of the LORD that is kindled against us, because our fathers have not hearkened unto the words of this book, to do according unto all that which is written concerning us. 14 So Hilkiah the priest, and Ahikam, and Achbor, and Shaphan, and Asahiah, went unto Huldah the prophetess, the wife of Shallum the son of Tikvah, the son of

Harhas, keeper of the wardrobe; (now she dwelt in Jerusalem in the college;) and they communed with her. 15 And she said unto them, Thus saith the LORD God of Israel, Tell the man that sent you to me, 16 Thus saith the LORD, Behold, I will bring evil upon this place, and upon the inhabitants thereof, *even* all the words of the book which the king of Judah hath read: 17 Because they have forsaken me, and have burned incense unto other gods, that they might provoke me to anger with all the works of their hands; therefore my wrath shall be kindled against this place, and shall not be quenched. 18 But to the king of Judah which sent you to enquire of the LORD, thus shall ye say to him, Thus saith the LORD God of Israel, *As touching* the words which thou hast heard; 19 Because thine heart was tender, and thou hast humbled thyself before the LORD, when thou heardest what I spake against this place, and against the inhabitants thereof, that they should become a desolation and a curse, and hast rent thy clothes, and wept before me; I also have heard *thee*, saith the LORD. 20 Behold therefore, I will gather thee unto thy fathers, and thou shalt be gathered into thy grave in peace; and thine eyes shall not see all the evil which I will bring upon this place. And they brought the king word again.

We hear no more of the repairing of the temple: no doubt that good work went on well; but the book of the law that was found in it occupies us now, and well it may. It is not laid up in the king's cabinet as a piece of antiquity, a rarity to be admired, but it is read before the king. Those put the truest honour upon their Bibles that study them and converse with them daily, feed on that bread and walk by that light. Men of honour and business must look upon an acquaintance with God's word to be their best business and honour. Now here we have,

I. The impressions which the reading of the law made upon Josiah. He rent his clothes, as one ashamed of the sin of his people and afraid of the wrath of God; he had long thought the case of his kingdom bad, by reason of the idolatries and impieties that had been found among them, but he never thought it so bad as he perceived it to be by the book of the law now read to him. The rending of his clothes signified the rending of his heart for the dishonour done to God, and the ruin he saw coming upon his people.

II. The application he made to God hereupon: *Go, enquire of the Lord for me, v.* 13.

1. Two things we may suppose he desired to know:—"Enquire, (1.) What we shall do; what course we shall take to turn away God's wrath and prevent the judgments which our sins have deserved." Convictions of sin and wrath should put us upon this enquiry, *What shall we do to be saved? Wherewithal shall we come before the Lord?* If you will thus enquire, enquire quickly, before it be too late. (2.) "What we may expect and must provide for." He acknowledges, "*Our fathers have not hearkened to the words of this book;* if this be the rule of right, certainly our fathers have been much in the wrong." Now that *the commandment came sin revived*, and appeared sin; in the glass of the law, he saw the sins of his people more nnmerous and more heinous than he had before seen them, and more exceedingly sinful. He infers hence, "Certainly *great is the wrath that is kindled against us;* if this be the word of God, as no doubt it is, and he will be true to his word, as no doubt he will be, we are all undone. I never thought the threatenings of the law so severe, and the curses of the covenant so terrible, as now I find them to be; it is time to look about us if these be in force against us." Note, Those who are truly apprehensive of the weight of God's wrath cannot but be very solicitous to obtain his favour, and inquisitive how they may make their peace with him. Magistrates should enquire for their people, and study how to prevent the judgments of God that they see hanging over them.

2. This enquiry Josiah sent, (1.) By some of his great men, who are named *v.* 12, and again *v.* 14. Thus he put an honour upon the oracle, by employing those of the first rank to attend it. (2.) To Huldah the prophetess, *v.* 14. The spirit of prophecy, that inestimable treasure, was sometimes put not only into *earthen* vessels, but into the *weaker* vessels, *that the excellency of the power might be of God.* Miriam helped to lead Israel out of Egypt (Mic. vi. 4), Deborah judged them, and now Huldah instructed them in the mind of God, and her being a wife was no prejudice at all to her being a prophetess; *marriage is honourable in all.* It was a mercy to Jerusalem that when Bibles were scarce they had prophets, as afterwards, when prophecy ceased, that they had more Bibles; for God never leaves himself without witness, because he will leave sinners without excuse. Jeremiah and Zephaniah prophesied at this time, yet the king's messengers made Huldah their oracle, probably because her husband having a place at court (for he was keeper of the wardrobe) they had had

more and longer acquaintance with her and greater assurances of her commission than of any other; they had, it is likely, consulted her upon other occasions, and had found that the word of God in her mouth was truth. She was near, for she dwelt at Jerusalem, in a place called *Mishneh,* the second rank of buildings from the royal palace. The Jews say that she prophesied among the women, the court ladies, being herself one of them, who it is probable had their apartments in that place. Happy the court that had a prophetess within the verge of it, and knew how to value her.

III. The answer he received from God to his enquiry. Huldah returned it not in the language of a courtier—"Pray give my humble service to his Majesty, and let him know that this is the message I have for him from the God of Israel;" but in the dialect of a prophetess, speaking from him before whom all stand upon the same level—*Tell the man that sent you to me, v.* 15. Even kings, though gods to us, are men to God, and shall so be dealt with; for *with him there is no respect of persons.*

1. She let him know what judgments God had in store for Judah and Jerusalem (*v.* 16, 17): *My wrath shall be kindled against this place;* and what is hell itself but the fire of God's wrath kindled against sinners? Observe, (1.) The degree and duration of it. It is so kindled that *it shall not be quenched;* the decree has gone forth; it is too late now to think of preventing it; the iniquity of Jerusalem shall not be purged with sacrifice or offering. Hell is unquenchable fire. (2.) The reference it has, [1.] To their sins: "They have committed them, as it were, with design, and on purpose to provoke me to anger. It is a fire of their own kindling; they would provoke me, and at length I am provoked." [2.] To God's threatenings: "The evil I bring is according to the words of the book which the king of Judah has read; the scripture is fulfilled in it. Those that would not be bound by the precept shall be bound by the penalty." God will be found no less terrible to impenitent sinners than his word makes him to be.

2. She let him know what mercy God had in store for him. (1.) Notice is taken of his great tenderness and concern for the glory of God and the welfare of his kingdom (*v.* 19): *Thy heart was tender.* Note, God will distinguish those that distinguish themselves. The generality of the people were hardened and their hearts unhumbled, so were the wicked kings his predecessors, but Josiah's heart was tender. He received the impressions of God's word, trembled at it and yielded to it; he was exceedingly grieved for the dishonour done to God by the sins of his fathers and of his people; he was afraid of the judgments of God, which he saw coming upon Jerusalem, and earnestly deprecated them. This is tenderness of heart, and thus he *humbled himself before the Lord,* and expressed these pious affections by rending his clothes and weeping before God, probably in his closet; but he that sees in secret says it was *before him,* and he heard it, and put every tear of tenderness into his bottle. Note, Those that most fear God's wrath are least likely to feel it. It should seem that those words (Lev. xxvi. 32) much affected Josiah, *I will bring the land into desolation;* for when he heard of *the desolation and of the curse,* that is, that God would forsake them and *separate them to evil* (for till it came to that they were neither desolate nor accursed), then he rent his clothes: the threatening went to his heart. (2.) A reprieve is granted till after his death (*v.* 20): *I will gather thee to thy fathers.* The saints then, no doubt, had a comfortable prospect of happiness on the other side death, else being gathered to their fathers would not have been so often made the matter of a promise as we find it was. Josiah could not prevail to prevent the judgment itself, but God promised him he should not live to see it, which (especially considering that he died in the midst of his days, before he was forty years old) would have been but a small reward for his eminent piety if there had not been another world in which he should be abundantly recompensed, Heb xi. 16. When the righteous is *taken away from the evil to come he enters into peace,* Isa. lvii. 1, 2. This is promised to Josiah here: *Thou shalt go to thy grave in peace,* which refers not to the manner of his death (for he was killed in a battle), but to the time of it; it was a little before the captivity in Babylon, that great trouble, in comparison with which the rest were as nothing, so that he might be truly said to die in peace that did not live to share in that. He died in the love and favour of God, which secure such a peace as no circumstances of dying, no, not dying in the field of war, could alter the nature of, or break in upon.

CHAP. XXIII.

We have here, I. The happy continuance of the goodness of Josiah's reign, and the progress of the reformation he began, reading the law (ver. 1, 2), renewing the covenant (ver. 3), cleansing the temple (ver. 4), and rooting out idols and idolatry, with all the relics thereof, in all places, as far as his power reached (ver. 5—20), keeping a solemn passover (ver. 21—23), and clearing the country of witches (ver. 24); and in all this acting with extraordinary vigour, ver. 25. II. The unhappy conclusion of it in his untimely death, as a token of the continuance of God's wrath against Jerusalem, ver. 26—30. III. The more unhappy consequences of his death, in the bad reigns of his two sons Jehoahaz and Jehoiakim, that came after him, ver. 31—37.

AND the king sent, and they gathered unto him all the elders of Judah and of Jerusalem. 2 And the king went up into the house of the LORD, and all the men of Judah and all the inhabitants of Jerusalem with him, and the priests, and the prophets, and all the people, both small and great: and he read in their ears all the words of the book of the covenant which was found in the house of the LORD. 3 And the king stood by a pillar, and made a covenant before the LORD, to walk after the LORD, and to keep his commandments and his testimonies and his statutes with all *their* heart and all *their* soul, to perform the words of this covenant that were written in this book. And all the people stood to the covenant.

Josiah had received a message from God that there was no preventing the ruin of Jerusalem, but that he should deliver only his own soul; yet he did not therefore sit down in despair, and resolve to do nothing for his country because he could not do all he would. No, he would do his duty, and then leave the event to God. A public reformation was the thing resolved on; if any thing could prevent the threatened ruin it must be that; and here we have the preparations for that reformation. 1. He summoned a general assembly of the states, the elders, the magistrates or representatives of Judah and Jerusalem, to meet him *in the house of the Lord,* with the priests and prophets, the ordinary and extraordinary ministers, that, they all joining in it, it might become a national act and so be the more likely to prevent national judgments; they were all called to attend (*v.* 1, 2), that the business might be done with the more solemnity, that they might all advise and assist in it, and that those who were against it might be discouraged from making any opposition. Parliaments are no diminution at all to the honour and power of good princes, but a great support to them. 2. Instead of making a speech to this convention, he ordered the book of the law to be read to them; nay, it should seem, he read it himself (*v.* 2), as one much affected with it and desirous that they should be so too. Josiah thinks it not below him to be a reader, any more than Solomon did to be a preacher, nay, and David himself to be a door-keeper in the house of God. Besides the convention of the great men, he had a congregation of the *men of Judah and the inhabitants of Jerusalem* to hear the law read. It is really the interest of princes to promote the knowledge of the scriptures in their dominions. If the people be but as stedfastly resolved to obey by law as he is to govern by law, the kingdom will be happy. All people are concerned to know the scripture, and all in authority to spread the knowledge of it. 3. Instead of proposing laws for the confirming of them in their duty, he proposed an association by which they should all jointly engage themselves to God, *v.* 3. The book of the law was the book of the covenant, that, if they would be to God a people, he would be to them a God; they here engage themselves to do their part, not doubting but that then God would do his. (1.) The covenant was that they should walk after the Lord, in compliance with his will, in his ordinances and his providences, should answer all his calls and attend all his motions—that they should make conscience of all his commandments, moral, ceremonial, and judicial, and should carefully observe them *with all their heart and all their soul,* with all possible care and caution, sincerity, vigour, courage, and resolution, and so fulfil the conditions of this covenant, in dependence upon the promises of it. (2.) The covenanters were, in the first place, the king himself, who stood by his pillar (*ch.* xi. 14) and publicly declared his consent to this covenant, to set them an example, and to assure them not only of his protection but of his presidency and all the furtherance his power could give them in their obedience. It is no abridgment of the liberty even of princes themselves to be in bonds to God. *All the people* likewise *stood to the covenant,* that is, they signified their consent to it and promised to abide by it. It is of good use to oblige ourselves to our duty with all possible solemnity, and this is especially seasonable after notorious backslidings to sin and decays in that which is good. He that bears an honest mind does not shrink from positive engagements: fast bind, fast find.

4 And the king commanded Hilkiah the high priest, and the priests of the second order, and the keepers of the door, to bring forth out of the temple of the LORD all the vessels that were made for Baal, and for the grove, and for all the host of heaven: and he burned them without Jerusalem in the fields of Kidron, and carried the ashes of them unto Beth-el. 5 And he put down the idolatrous priests, whom the kings of Judah had ordained to burn incense in the high places in the cities of Judah, and in the places round about Jerusalem; them also that burned incense unto Baal, to the sun, and to the moon, and to the planets, and to all the host of heaven. 6 And he brought out the grove from the house of the LORD, without Jerusalem, unto the brook Kidron, and burned it at the brook Kidron, and stamped *it* small to powder, and cast the powder thereof upon the graves of the children of the people. 7 And he brake down the houses of the sodomites, that *were* by the house of the LORD, where the women wove hangings for the grove. 8 And he brought all the priests out of the

cities of Judah, and defiled the high places where the priests had burned incense, from Geba to Beer-sheba, and brake down the high places of the gates that *were* in the entering in of the gate of Joshua the governor of the city, which *were* on a man's left hand at the gate of the city. 9 Nevertheless the priests of the high places came not up to the altar of the LORD in Jerusalem, but they did eat of the unleavened bread among their brethren. 10 And he defiled Topheth, which *is* in the valley of the children of Hinnom, that no man might make his son or his daughter to pass through the fire to Molech. 11 And he took away the horses that the kings of Judah had given to the sun, at the entering in of the house of the LORD, by the chamber of Nathan-melech the chamberlain, which *was* in the suburbs, and burned the chariots of the sun with fire. 12 And the altars that *were* on the top of the upper chamber of Ahaz, which the kings of Judah had made, and the altars which Manasseh had made in the two courts of the house of the LORD, did the king beat down, and brake *them* down from thence, and cast the dust of them into the brook Kidron. 13 And the high places that *were* before Jerusalem, which *were* on the right hand of the mount of corruption, which Solomon the king of Israel had builded for Ashtoreth the abomination of the Zidonians, and for Chemosh the abomination of the Moabites, and for Milcolm the abomination of the children of Ammon, did the king defile. 14 And he brake in pieces the images, and cut down the groves, and filled their places with the bones of men. 15 Moreover the altar that *was* at Beth-el, *and* the high place which Jeroboam the son of Nebat, who made Israel to sin, had made, both that altar and the high place he brake down, and burned the high place, *and* stamped *it* small to powder, and burned the grove. 16 And as Josiah turned himself, he spied the sepulchres that *were* there in the mount, and sent, and took the bones out of the sepulchres, and burned *them* upon the altar, and polluted it, according to the word of the LORD which the man of God proclaimed, who proclaimed these words. 17 Then he said, What title *is* that that I see? And the men of the city told him, *It is* the sepulchre of the man of God, which came from Judah, and proclaimed these things that thou hast done against the altar of Beth-el. 18 And he said, Let him alone; let no man move his bones. So they let his bones alone, with the bones of the prophet that came out of Samaria. 19 And all the houses also of the high places that *were* in the cities of Samaria, which the kings of Israel had made to provoke *the LORD* to anger, Josiah took away, and did to them according to all the acts that he had done in Beth-el. 20 And he slew all the priests of the high places that *were* there upon the altars, and burned men's bones upon them, and returned to Jerusalem. 21 And the king commanded all the people, saying, Keep the passover unto the LORD your God, as *it is* written in the book of this covenant. 22 Surely there was not holden such a passover from the days of the judges that judged Israel, nor in all the days of the kings of Israel, nor of the kings of Judah; 23 But in the eighteenth year of king Josiah, *wherein* this passover was holden to the LORD in Jerusalem. 24 Moreover the *workers with* familiar spirits, and the wizards, and the images, and the idols, and all the abominations that were spied in the land of Judah and in Jerusalem, did Josiah put away, that he might perform the words of the law which were written in the book that Hilkiah the priest found in the house of the LORD.

We have here an account of such a reformation as we have not met with in all the history of the kings of Judah, such thorough riddance made of all the abominable things and such foundations laid of a glorious good work; and here I cannot but wonder at two things:—1. That so many wicked things should have got in, and kept standing so long, as we find here removed. 2. That notwithstanding the removal of these wicked things, and the hopeful prospects here given of a happy settlement, yet within a few years

Jerusalem was utterly destroyed, and even this did not save it; for the generality of the people, after all, hated to be reformed. *The founder melteth in vain,* and therefore *reprobate silver shall men call them,* Jer. vi. 29, 30. Let us here observe,

I. What abundance of wickedness there was, and had been, in Judah and Jerusalem. One would not have believed it possible that in Judah, where God was known—in Israel, where his name was great—in Salem, in Sion, where his dwelling-place was, such abominations should be found as here we have an account of. Josiah had now reigned eighteen years, and had himself set the people a good example, and kept up religion according to law; and yet, when he came to make inquisition for idolatry, the depth and extent of the dunghill he had to carry away appeared almost incredible. 1. Even in the house of the Lord, that sacred temple which Solomon built, and dedicated to the honour and for the worship of the God of Israel, there were found vessels, all manner of utensils, for the worship of Baal, *and of the grove* (or *Ashtaroth),* and *of all the host of heaven, v.* 4. Though Josiah had suppressed the worship of idols, yet the utensils made for that worship were all carefully preserved, even in the temple itself, to be used again whenever the present restraint should be taken off; nay, even the grove itself, the image of it, was yet standing in the temple (*v.* 6); some make it the image of Venus, the same with Ashtaroth. 2. Just *at the entering in of the house of the Lord* was a stable for horses kept (would you think it?) for a religious use; they were holy horses, *given to the sun* (*v.* 11), as if he needed them who *rejoiceth as a strong man to run a race* (Ps. xix. 5), or rather they would thus represent to themselves the swiftness of his motion, which they much admired, making their religion to conform to the poetical fictions of the chariot of the sun, the follies of which even a little philosophy, without any divinity, would have exposed and made them ashamed of. Some say that those horses were to be led forth in pomp every morning to meet the rising sun, others that the worshippers of the sun rode out upon them to adore the rising sun; it should seem that they drew the chariots of the sun, which the people worshipped. Strange that ever men who had the written word of God among them should be thus *vain in their imaginations!* 3. Hard *by the house of the Lord* there were *houses of the Sodomites,* where all manner of lewdness and filthiness, even that which was most unnatural, was practised, and under pretence of religion too, in honour of their impure deities. Corporal and spiritual whoredom went together, and the vile affections to which the people were given up were the punishment of their vain imaginations. Those that dishonoured their God were justly left thus to dishonour themselves, Rom. i. 24, &c. There were women that *wove hangings for the grove* (*v.* 7), tents which encompassed the image of Venus, where the worshippers committed all manner of lewdness, and this *in the house of the Lord.* Those did ill that made our Father's house a house of merchandise; those did worse that made it a den of thieves; but those did worst of all that made it *(Horrendum dictu!—Horrible to relate!)* a brothel, in an impudent defiance of the holiness of God and of his temple. Well might the apostle call them *abominable idolatries.* 4. There were many idolatrous altars found (*v.* 12), some in the palace, *on the top of the upper chamber of Ahaz.* The roofs of their houses being flat, they made them their high places, and set up altars upon them (Jer. xix. 13; Zeph. i. 5), domestic altars. The kings of Judah did so: and, though Josiah never used them, yet to this time they remained there. Manasseh had built altars for his idols in the house of the Lord. When he repented he removed them, and *cast them out of the city* (2 Chron. xxxiii. 15), but, not destroying them, his son Amon, it seems, had brought them again into the courts of the temple; there Josiah found them, and thence he *broke them down, v.* 12. 5. There was *Tophet, in the valley of the son of Hinnom,* very near Jerusalem, where the image of Moloch (that god of unnatural cruelty, as others were of unnatural uncleanness) was kept, to which some sacrificed their children, burning them in the fire, others dedicated them, making them to pass through the fire (*v.* 10), *labouring in the very fire,* Hab. ii. 13. It is supposed to have been called *Tophet* from *toph,* a drum, because they beat drums at the burning of the children, that their shrieks might not be heard. 6. There were *high places before Jerusalem,* which *Solomon had built, v.* 13. The altars and images on those high places, we may suppose, had been taken away by some of the preceding godly kings, or perhaps Solomon himself had removed them when he became a penitent; but the buildings, or some parts of them, remained, with other high places, till Josiah's time. Those that introduce corruptions into religion know not how far they will reach nor how long they will last. Antiquity is no certain proof of verity. There were also high places all the kingdom over, from *Geba to Beer-sheba* (*v.* 8), and *high places of the gates, in the entering in of the gate of the governor.* In these high places (bishop Patrick thinks) they burnt incense to those tutelar gods to whom their idolatrous kings had committed the protection of their city; and probably the governor of the city had a private altar for his *penates—his household-gods.* 7. There were idolatrous priests, that officiated at all those idolatrous altars (*v.* 5), chemarim, black men, or that wore black. See Zeph. i. 4. Those that sacrificed to Osiris, or that wept for Tammuz (Ezek. viii. 14), or that worshipped the infernal deities, put on black garments as mourners. These idolatrous priests the kings of *Judah had ordained to burn incense in the high places;* they were, it should seem, priests of the house of Aaron, who thus profaned their dignity, and there were others also who had no right at all to the priesthood, who burnt incense to Baal. 8. There were conjurers and wizards, and such as *dealt with familiar spirits, v.* 24. When they worshipped the devil as their god no marvel that they consulted him as their oracle.

II. What a full destruction good Josiah made of all those relics of idolatry. Such is his zeal for the Lord of hosts, and his holy indignation against all that is dipleasing to him, that nothing shall stand before him. The law was that the monuments of the Canaanites' idolatry must be all destroyed (Deut. vii. 5), much more those of the idolatry of the Israelites, in whom it was much more impious, profane, and perfidious. 1. He ordered Hilkiah, and the other priests, to clear the temple. This was their province, *v.* 4. Away with all the vessels that were made for Baal. They must never be employed in the service of God, no, nor reserved for any common use; they must all be burnt, and the ashes of them carried to Bethel. That place had been the common source of idolatry, for there was set up one of the calves, and, that lying next to Judah, the infection had thence spread into that kingdom, and therefore Josiah made it the lay-stall of idolatry, the dunghill to which he carried the filth and offscouring of all things, that, if possible, it might be made loathsome to those that had been fond of it. 2. The idolatrous priests were all put down. Those of them that were not of the house of Aaron, or had sacrificed to Baal or other false gods, he put to death, according to the law, *v.* 20. He *slew them upon their own altars,* the most acceptable sacrifice that ever had been offered upon them, a sacrifice to the justice of God. Those that were descendants from Aaron, and yet had burnt incense in the high places, but to the true God only, he forbade ever to approach the altar of the Lord; they had forfeited that honour (*v.* 9): He *brought them out of the cities of Judah* (*v.* 8), that they might not do mischief in the country by secretly keeping up their old idolatrous usages; but he allowed them to *eat of the unleavened bread* (the bread of the meat-offering, Lev. ii. 4, 5) *among their brethren,* with whom they were to reside, that being under their eye they might be kept from doing hurt and taught to do well; that bread, that unleavened bread (heavy and unpleasant as it was), was better than they deserved, and that would serve to keep them alive. But whether they were permitted to eat of all the sacrifices, as blemished priests were (Lev. xxi. 22), which is called, in general, *the bread of their God,* may be justly questioned. 3. All the images were broken to pieces and burnt. The image of the grove (*v.* 6), some goddess or other, was reduced to ashes, and the *ashes cast upon the graves of the common people* (*v.* 6), the common burying-place of the city. By the law a ceremonial uncleanness was contracted by the touch of a grave, so that in casting them here he declared them most impure, and none could touch them without thereby making themselves unclean. *He cast it into the graves* (so the Chaldee), intimating that he would have all idolatry buried out of his sight, as a loathsome thing, and forgotten, as dead men are out of mind, *v.* 14. He *filled the places of the groves with the bones of men;* as he carried the ashes of the images to the graves, to mingle them with dead men's bones, so he carried dead men's bones to the places where the images had been, and put them in the room of them, that, both ways, idolatry might be rendered loathsome, and the people kept both from the dust of the images and from the ruins of the places where they had been worshipped. Dead men and dead gods were much alike and fittest to go together. 4. All the wicked houses were suppressed, those nests of impiety that harboured idolaters, the houses of the Sodomites, *v.* 7. "Down with them, down with them, rase them to the foundations." The high places were in like manner broken down and levelled with the ground (*v.* 8), even that which belonged to the governor of the city; for no man's greatness or power may protect him in idolatry or profaneness. Let governors be obliged, in the first place, to reform, and then the governed will be the sooner influenced. He defiled the high places (*v.* 8 and again *v.* 13), did all he could to render them abominable, and put the people out of conceit with them, as Jehu did when he made the house of Baal a draught-house, 2 Kings x. 27. Tophet, which, contrary to other places of idolatry, was in a valley, whereas they were on hills or high places, was likewise defiled (*v.* 10), was made the burying-place of the city. Concerning this we have a whole sermon, Jer. xix. 1, 2, &c., where it is said, *They shall bury in Tophet,* and the whole city is threatened to be made like Tophet. 5. The horses that had been given to the sun were taken away and put to common use, and so were delivered from the vanity to which they were made subject; and the chariots of the sun (what a pity was it that those horses and chariots should be kept as the chariots and horsemen of Israel!) he burnt with fire; and, if the sun be a flame, they never resembled him so much as they did when they were chariots of fire. 6. The workers with familiar spirits and the wizards were put away, *v.* 24. Those of them that were convicted of witchcraft, it is likely, he put to death, and so deterred others from those diabolical practices. In all this he had a sincere regard to *the words of the law which were written in the book* lately found, *v.* 24.

He made that law his rule and kept that in his eye throughout this reformation.

III. How his zeal extended itself to the cities of Israel that were within his reach. The ten tribes were carried captive and the Assyrian colonies did not fully people the country, so that, it is likely, many cities had put themselves under the protection of the kings of Judah, 2 Chron. xxx. 1; xxxiv. 6. These he here visits, to carry on his reformation. As far as our influence goes our endeavours should go to do good and bring the wickedness of the wicked to an end.

1. He defiled and demolished Jeroboam's altar at Bethel, with the high place and the grove that belonged to it, *v.* 15, 16. The golden calf, it should seem, was gone *(thy calf, O Samaria! has cast thee off),* but the altar was there, which those that were wedded to their old idolatries made use of still. This was, (1.) Defiled, *v.* 16. Josiah, in his pious zeal, was ransacking the old seats of idolatry, and spied the sepulchres in the mount, in which probably the idolatrous priests were buried, not far from the altar at which they had officiated, and which they were so fond of that they were desirous to lay their bones by it; these he opened, took out the bones, and *burnt them upon the altar,* to show that thus he would have done by the priests themselves if they had been alive, as he did by those whom he found alive, *v.* 20. Thus he polluted the altar, desecrated it, and made it odious. It is threatened against idolaters (Jer. viii. 1, 2) that *their bones shall be spread before the sun;* that which is there threatened and this which is here executed (bespeaking their *iniquity to be upon their bones,* Ezek. xxxii. 27) are an intimation of a punishment after death, reserved for those that live and die impenitent in that or any other sin; the burning of the bones, if that were all, is a small matter, but, if it signify the torment of the soul in a worse flame (Luke xvi. 24), it is very dreadful. This, as it was Josiah's act, seems to have been the result of a very sudden resolve; he would not have done it but that he happened to turn himself, and spy the sepulchres; and yet it was foretold above 350 years before, when this altar was first built by Jeroboam, 1 Kings xiii. 2. God always foresees, and has sometimes foretold as certain, that which yet to us seems most contingent. *The king's heart is in the hand of the Lord;* king Josiah's was so, and he turned it (or ever he himself was aware, Cant. vi. 12) to do this. No word of God shall fall to the ground. (2.) It was demolished. He broke down the altar and all its appurtenances (*v.* 15), burnt what was combustible, and, since an idol is nothing in the world, he went as far towards the annihilating of it as he could; for he *stamped it small to powder* and made it *as dust before the wind.*

2. He destroyed all the houses of the high places, all those synagogues of Satan that were *in the cities of Samaria, v.* 19. These the kings of Israel built, and God raised up this king of Judah to pull them down, for the honour of the ancient house of David, from which the ten tribes had revolted; the priests he justly made sacrifices *upon their own altars, v.* 20.

3. He carefully preserved the sepulchre of that man of God who came from Judah to foretel this, which now a king who came from Judah executed. This was that good prophet who *proclaimed these things against the altar of Bethel,* and yet was himself slain by a lion for disobeying the word of the Lord; but to show that God's displeasure against him went no further than his death, but ended there, God so ordered it that when all the graves about his were disturbed his was safe (*v.* 17, 18) and no man moved his bones. He had entered into peace, and therefore should rest in his bed, Isa. lvii. 2. The old lying prophet, who desired to be buried as near him as might be, it should seem, knew what he did; for his dust also, being mingled with that of the good prophet, was preserved for his sake; see Num. xxiii. 10.

IV. We are here told what a solemn passover Josiah and his people kept after all this. When they had cleared the country of the old leaven they then applied themselves to the keeping of the feast. When Jehu had destroyed the worship of Baal, yet he took no heed to walk in the commandments and ordinances of God; but Josiah considered that we must learn to do well, and not *only* cease to do evil, and that the way to keep out all abominable customs is to keep up all instituted ordinances (see Lev. xviii. 30), and therefore he commanded all the people to keep the passover, which was not only a memorial of their deliverance out of Egypt, but a token of their dedication to him that brought them out and their communion with him. This he found written in the *book of the law,* here called *the book of the covenant;* for, though the divine authority may deal with us in a way of absolute command, divine grace condescends to federal transactions, and therefore he observed it. We have not such a particular account of this passover as of that in Hezekiah's time, 2 Chron. xxx. But, in general, we are told that *there was not holden such a passover* in any of the foregoing reigns, no, not *from the days of the judges* (*v.* 22), which, by the way, intimates that, though the account which the book of Judges gives of the state of Israel under that dynasty looks but melancholy, yet there were then some golden days. This passover, it seems, was extraordinary for the number and devotion of the communicants, their sacrifices and offerings, and their exact observance of the laws of the feast; and it was not now as in Hezekiah's passover, when many communicated that were not cleansed according to the purification of the sanctuary, and the Levites were permitted to do the priests' work. We have reason to think that during all the remainder of Josiah's reign religion flourished and the feasts of the Lord were very carefully observed; but in this passover the satisfaction they took in the covenant lately renewed, the reformation in pursuance of it, and the revival of an ordinance of which they had lately found the divine original in the book of the law, and which had long been neglected or carelessly kept, put them into great transports of holy joy; and God was pleased to recompense their zeal in destroying idolatry with uncommon tokens of his presence and favour. All this concurred to make it a distinguished passover.

25 And like unto him was there no king before him, that turned to the LORD with all his heart, and with all his soul, and with all his might, according to all the law of Moses; neither after him arose there *any* like him. 26 Notwithstanding the LORD turned not from the fierceness of his great wrath, wherewith his anger was kindled against Judah, because of all the provocations that Manasseh had provoked him withal. 27 And the LORD said, I will remove Judah also out of my sight, as I have removed Israel, and will cast off this city Jerusalem which I have chosen, and the house of which I said, My name shall be there. 28 Now the rest of the acts of Josiah, and all that he did, *are* they not written in the book of the chronicles of the kings of Judah? 29 In his days Pharaoh-nechoh king of Egypt went up against the king of Assyria to the river Euphrates: and king Josiah went against him; and he slew him at Megiddo, when he had seen him. 30 And his servants carried him in a chariot dead from Megiddo, and brought him to Jerusalem, and buried him in his own sepulchre. And the people of the land took Jehoahaz the son of Josiah, and anointed him, and made him king in his father's stead.

Upon the reading of these verses we must say, Lord, though *thy righteousness* be *as the great mountains*—evident, conspicuous, and past dispute, yet *thy judgments are a great deep,* unfathomable and past finding out, Ps. xxxvi. 6. What shall we say to this?

I. It is here owned that Josiah was one of the best kings that ever sat upon the throne of David, *v.* 25. As Hezekiah was a nonsuch for faith and dependence upon God in straits (*ch.* xviii. 5), so Josiah was a nonsuch for sincerity and zeal in carrying on a work of reformation. For this there was none like him, 1. That he *turned to the Lord* from whom his fathers had revolted. It is true religion to turn to God as one we have chosen and love. He did what he could to turn his kingdom also to the Lord. 2. That he did this *with his heart and soul;* his affections and aims were right in what he did. Those make nothing of their religion that do not make heart-work of it. 3. That he did it with *all his heart,* and *all his soul,* and *all his might*—with vigour, and courage, and resolution: he could not otherwise have broken through the difficulties he had to grapple with. What great things may we bring to pass in the service of God if we be but lively and hearty in it! 4. That he did this *according to all the law of Moses,* in an exact observance of that law and with an actual regard to it. His zeal did not transport him into any irregularities, but, in all he did, he walked by rule.

II. Notwithstanding this he was cut off by a violent death in the midst of his days, and his kingdom was ruined within a few years after. Consequent upon such a reformation as this, one would have expected nothing but the prosperity and glory both of king and kingdom; but, quite contrary, we find both under a cloud. 1. Even the reformed kingdom continues marked for ruin. For all this (*v.* 26) *the Lord turned not from the fierceness of his great wrath.* That is certainly true, which God spoke by the prophet (Jer. xviii. 7, 8), that if a nation, doomed to destruction, *turn from the evil* of sin, God will *repent of the evil* of punishment; and therefore we must conclude that Josiah's people, though they submitted to Josiah's power, did not heartily imbibe Josiah's principles. They were turned by force, and did not voluntarily *turn from their evil way,* but still continued their affection for their idols; and therefore he that knows men's hearts would not recal the sentence, which was, That Judah should be removed, as Israel had been, and Jerusalem itself cast off, *v.* 27. Yet even this destruction was intended to be their effectual reformation; so that we must say, not only that the criminals had filled their measure and were ripe for ruin, but also that the disease had come to a crisis, and was ready for a cure; and this shall be all the fruit, even the taking away of sin. 2. As an evidence of this, even the reforming king is cut off in the midst of his usefulness—in mercy to him, that he might not see the evil which was coming upon his kingdom, but in wrath to his people, for his death was an inlet to their desolations. The king of Egypt waged war, it seems, with the king of Assyria: so the king of Babylon is now called. Josiah's kingdom lay between them. He therefore thought himself concerned to oppose the king of Egypt, and check the growing, threatening, greatness of his power; for though, at this time, he protested that he had no design against Josiah, yet, if he should prevail to unite the river of Egypt and the river Euphrates, the land of Judah would soon be overflowed between them. Therefore *Josiah went against him,* and was killed in the first engagement, *v.* 29, 30. Here, (1.) We cannot justify Josiah's conduct. He had no clear call to engage in this war, nor do we find that he asked counsel of God by urim or prophets concerning it. What had he to do to appear and act as a friend and ally to the king of Assyria? *Should he help the ungodly and love those that hate the Lord?* If the kings of Egypt and Assyria quarrelled, he had reason to think God would bring good out of it to him and his people, by making them instrumental to weaken one another. Some understand the promise made to him that he should *come to his grave in peace* in a sense in which it was not performed because, by his miscarriage in this matter, he forfeited the benefit of it. God has promised to keep us *in all our ways;* but, if we go out of our way, we throw ourselves out of his protection. I understand the promise so as that I believe it was fulfilled, for he *died in peace* with God and his own conscience, and saw not, nor had any immediate prospect of, the destruction of Judah and Jerusalem by the Chaldeans; yet I understand the providence to be a rebuke to him for his rashness. (2.) We must adore God's righteousness in taking away such a jewel from an unthankful people that knew not how to value it. They greatly lamented his death (2 Chron. xxxv. 25), urged to it by Jeremiah, who told them the meaning of it, and what a threatening omen it was; but they had not made a due improvement of the mercies they enjoyed by his life, of which God taught them the worth by the want.

31 Jehoahaz *was* twenty and three years old when he began to reign; and he reigned three months in Jerusalem. And his mother's name *was* Hamutal, the daughter of Jeremiah of Libnah. 32 And he did *that which was* evil in the sight of the LORD, according to all that his fathers had done. 33 And Pharaoh-nechoh put him in bands at Riblah in the land of Hamath, that he might not reign in Jerusalem; and put the land to a tribute of a hundred talents of silver, and a talent of gold. 34 And Pharaoh-nechoh made Eliakim the son of Josiah king in the room of Josiah his father, and turned his name to Jehoiakim, and took Jehoahaz away: and he came to Egypt, and died there. 35 And Jehoiakim gave the silver and the gold to Pharaoh; but he taxed the land to give the money according to the commandment of Pharaoh: he exacted the silver and the gold of the people of the land, of every one according to his taxation, to give *it* unto Pharaoh-nechoh. 36 Jehoiakim *was* twenty and five years old when he began to reign; and he reigned eleven years in Jerusalem. And his mother's name *was* Zebudah, the daughter of Pedaiah of Rumah. 37 And he did *that which was* evil in the sight of the LORD, according to all that his fathers had done.

Jerusalem saw not a good day after Josiah was laid in his grave, but one trouble came after another, till within twenty-two years it was quite destroyed. Of the reign of two of his sons here is a short account; the former we find here a prisoner and the latter a tributary to the king of Egypt, and both so in the very beginning of their reign. This king of Egypt having slain Josiah, though he had not had any design upon Judah, yet, being provoked by the opposition which Josiah gave him, now, it should seem, he bent all his force against his family and kingdom. If Josiah's sons had trodden in his steps, they would have fared the better for his piety; but, deviating from them, they fared the worse for his rashness.

I. Jehoahaz, a younger son, was first made king by *the people of the land,* probably because he was observed to be of a more active warlike genius than his elder brother, and likely to make head against the king of Egypt and to avenge his father's death, which perhaps the people were more solicitous about, in point of honour, than the keeping up and carrying on of his father's reformation; and the issue was accordingly. 1. He did ill, *v.* 32. Though he had a good education and a good example given him, and many a good prayer, we may suppose, put up for him, yet he *did that which was evil in the sight of the Lord,* and, it is to be feared, began to do so in his father's lifetime, for his reign was so short that he could not, in that, show much of his character. He did *according to all that his* wicked *fathers had done.* Though he had not time to do much, yet he had chosen his patterns, and showed whom he intended to follow and whose steps he resolved to tread in; and, having done this, he is here reckoned to have done according to all the evil which those did whom he proposed to imitate. It is of great consequence to young people whom they choose to take for their patterns and whom they emulate. An error in this choice is fatal. Phil. iii. 17, 18. 2. Doing ill, no wonder that he fared ill. He was but three months a prince, and was then made a prisoner, and lived and died so. The king of Egypt seized him, and put him in bands (*v.* 33), fearing lest he should give him disturbance, and carried him to Egypt, where he died soon after, *v.* 34. This Jehoahaz is that young lion whom Ezekiel speaks of in his *lamentation for the princes of Israel,* that learnt to *catch the prey and devour men* (that was the evil which he did in the sight of the Lord); but *the nations heard of him, he was taken in their pit, and they brought him with chains into the land of Egypt,* Ezek. xix. 1—4. See Jer. xxii. 10—12.

II. Eliákim, another son of Josiah, was made king by the king of Egypt, it is not said *in the room of Jehoahaz* (his reign was so short that it was scarcely worth taking notice of), but *in the room of Josiah.* The crown of Judah had hitherto always descended from a father to a son, and never, till now, from one brother to another; once the succession had so happened in the house of Ahab, but never, till now, in the house of David. The king of Egypt, having used his power in making him king, further showed it in changing his name; he called him *Jehoiakim,* a name that has reference to Jehovah, for he had no design to make him renounce or forget the religion of his country. "All people will walk in the name of their God, and let him do so." The king of Babylon did not do so by those whose names he changed, Dan. i. 7. Of this Jehoiakim we are here told, 1. That the king of Egypt made him poor, exacted from him a vast tribute of 100 *talents of silver and a talent of gold* (*v.* 33), which, with much difficulty, he squeezed out of his subjects and gave to Pharaoh, *v.* 35. Formerly the Israelites had spoiled the Egyptians; now the Egyptians spoil Israel. See what woeful changes sin makes. 2. That which made him poor, yet did not make him good. Notwithstanding the rebukes of Providence he was under, by which he should have been convinced, humbled, and reformed, he *did that which was evil in the sight of the Lord* (*v.* 37), and so prepared against himself greater judgments; for such God will send if less do not do the work for which they are sent.

CHAP. XXIV.

Things are here ripening for, and hastening towards, the utter destruction of Jerusalem. We left Jehoiakim on the throne, placed there by the king of Egypt: now here we have, I. The troubles of his reign, how he was brought into subjection by the king of Babylon, and severely chastised for attempting to shake off the yoke (ver. 1—6), and how Egypt also was conquered by Nebuchadnezzar, ver. 7. II. The desolations of his son's reign, which continued but three months; and then he and all his great men, being forced to surrender at discretion, were carried captives to Babylon, ver. 8—16. III. The preparatives of the next reign (which was the last of all) for the utter ruin of Jerusalem, which the next chapter will give us an account of, ver. 17—20.

IN his days Nebuchadnezzar king of Babylon came up, and Jehoiakim became his servant three years: then he turned and rebelled against him. 2 And the LORD sent against him bands of the Chaldees, and bands of the Syrians, and bands of the Moabites, and bands of the children of Ammon, and sent them against Judah to destroy it, according to the word of the LORD, which he spake by his servants the prophets. 3 Surely at the commandment of the LORD came *this* upon Judah, to remove *them* out of his sight, for the sins of Manasseh, according to all that he did; 4 And also for the innocent blood that he shed: for he filled Jerusalem with innocent blood; which the LORD would not pardon. 5 Now the rest of the acts of Jehoiakim, and all that he did, *are* they not written in the book of the chronicles of the kings of Judah? 6 So Jehoiakim slept with his fathers: and Jehoiachin his son reigned in his stead. 7 And the king of Egypt came not again any more out of his land: for the king of Babylon had taken from the river of Egypt unto the river Euphrates all that pertained to the king of Egypt.

We have here the first mention of a name which makes a great figure both in the histories and in the prophecies of the Old Testament; it is that of *Nebuchadnezzar,* king of Babylon (*v.* 1), that head of gold. He was a potent prince, and one that was the terror of the mighty in the land of the living; and yet his name would not have been known in sacred writ if he had not been employed in the destruction of Jerusalem and the captivity of the Jews.

I. He made Jehoiakim his tributary and kept him in subjection three years, *v.* 1. Nebuchadnezzar began his reign in the fourth year of Jehoiakim. In his eighth year he made him his prisoner, but restored him upon his promise of faithfulness to him. That promise he kept about three years, but then rebelled, probably in hopes of assistance from the king of Egypt. If Jehoiakim had served his God as he should have done, he would not have been servant to the king of Babylon; but God would thus make him know the difference between his service and *the service of the kings of the countries,* 2 Chron. xii. 8. If he had been content with his servitude, and true to his word, his condition would have been no worse; but, rebelling against the king of Babylon, he plunged himself into more trouble.

II. When he rebelled Nebuchadnezzar sent his forces against him to destroy his country, bands of Chaldeans, Syrians, Moabites, Ammonites, who were all now in the service and pay of the king of Babylon (*v.* 2), and withal retained, and now showed, their ancient enmity to the Israel of God. Yet no mention is here made of their commission from the king of Babylon, but only of that from the King of kings: *The Lord sent against him* all these bands; and again (*v.* 3), *Surely at the commandment of the Lord came this upon Judah,* else the commandment of Nebuchadnezzar could not have brought it. Many are serving God's purposes who are not aware of it. Two things God intended in suffering Judah to be thus harassed:—1. The punishment of the sins of Manasseh, which God now visited upon *the third and fourth generation.* So long he waited before he visited them, to see if the nation would repent; but they continued impenitent, notwithstanding Josiah's endeavours to reform them, and ready to relapse, upon the first turn, into their former idolatries. Now that the old bond was put in suit they were called up upon the former judgment; that was revived which God had *laid up in store,* and *sealed among his treasures* (Deut. xxxii. 34; Job xiv. 17), and in remembrance of that he removed Judah out of his sight, and let the world know that *time will not wear out the guilt of sin* and that reprieves are not pardons. All that Manasseh did was called to mind, but especially the *innocent blood that he shed,* much of which, we may suppose, was the blood of God's witnesses and worshippers, *which the Lord would not pardon.* Is there then any unpardonable sin but the blasphemy against the Holy Ghost? This is meant of the remitting of the temporal punishment. Though Manasseh repented, and we have reason to think even the persecutions and murders he was guilty of were pardoned, so that he was delivered from the wrath to come; yet, as they were national sins, they lay still charged upon the land, crying for national judgments. Perhaps some were now living who were aiding and abetting; and the present king was guilty of innocent blood, as appears Jer. xxii. 17. See what a provoking sin murder is, how loud it cries, and how long. See what need nations have to lament the sins of their fathers, lest they smart for them. God intended hereby the accomplishment of the prophecies; it was *according to the word of the Lord, which he spoke by his servants the prophets.* Rather shall Judah be *removed out of his sight,* nay, rather shall *heaven and earth pass away,* than any word of God fall to the ground. Threatenings will be fulfilled as certainly as promises, if the sinner's repentance prevent not.

III. The king of Egypt was likewise subdued by the king of Babylon, and a great part of his country taken from him, *v.* 7. It was but lately that he had oppressed Israel, *ch.* xxiii. 33. Now he is himself brought down and disabled to attempt any thing for the recovery of his losses or the assistance of his allies. He dares not *come any more out of his land.* Afterwards he attempted to give Zedekiah some relief, but was obliged to retire, Jer. xxxvii. 7.

IV. Jehoiakim, seeing his country laid waste and himself ready to fall into the enemy's hand, as it should seem, died of a broken heart, in the midst of his days (*v.* 6). So *Jehoiakim slept with his fathers;* but it is not said that he was *buried with them,* for no doubt the prophecy of Jeremiah was fulfilled, that he should not be lamented, as his father was, but *buried with the burial of an ass* (Jer. xxii. 18, 19), and his dead body cast out, Jer. xxxvi. 30.

8 Jehoiachin *was* eighteen years old when he began to reign, and he reigned in Jerusalem three months. And his mother's name *was* Nehushta, the daughter of Elnathan of Jerusalem. 9 And he did *that which was* evil in the sight of the LORD, according to all that his father had done. 10 At that time the servants of Nebuchadnezzar king of Babylon came up against Jerusalem, and the city was besieged. 11 And Nebuchadnezzar king of Babylon came against the city, and his servants did besiege it. 12 And Jehoiachin the king of Judah went out to the king of Babylon, he, and his mother, and his servants, and his princes, and his officers: and the king of Babylon took him in the eighth year of his reign. 13 And he carried out thence all the treasures of the house of the LORD, and the treasures of the king's house, and cut in pieces all the vessels of gold which Solomon king of Israel had made in the temple of the LORD, as the LORD had said. 14 And he carried away all Jerusalem, and all the princes, and all the mighty men of valour, *even* ten thousand captives, and all the craftsmen and smiths: none remained, save the poorest sort of the people of the land. 15 And he carried away Jehoiachin to Babylon, and the king's mother, and the king's wives, and his officers, and the mighty of the land, *those* carried he into captivity from Jerusalem to Babylon. 16 And all the men of might, *even* seven thousand, and craftsmen and smiths a thousand, all *that were* strong *and* apt for war, even them the king of

Babylon brought captive to Babylon. 17 And the king of Babylon made Mattaniah his father's brother king in his stead, and changed his name to Zedekiah. 18 Zedekiah *was* twenty and one years old when he began to reign, and he reigned eleven years in Jerusalem. And his mother's name *was* Hamutal, the daughter of Jeremiah of Libnah. 19 And he did *that which was* evil in the sight of the LORD, according to all that Jehoiakim had done. 20 For through the anger of the LORD it came to pass in Jerusalem and Judah, until he had cast them out from his presence, that Zedekiah rebelled against the king of Babylon.

This should have been the history of king Jehoiachin's *reign*, but, alas! it is only the history of king Jehoiachin's *captivity*, as it is called, Ezek. i. 2. He came to the crown, not to have the honour of wearing it, but the shame of losing it. *Ideo tantum venerat, ut exiret—He came in only to go out.*

I. His reign was short and inconsiderable. He reigned but three months, and then was removed and carried captive to Babylon, as his father, it is likely, would have been if he had lived but so much longer. What an unhappy young prince was this, that was thrust into a falling house, a sinking throne! What an unnatural father had he, who begat him to suffer for him, and by his own sin and folly had left himself nothing to bequeath to his son but his own miseries! Yet this young prince reigned long enough to show that he justly smarted for his fathers' sins, for he trod in their steps (*v.* 9): *He did that which was evil in the sight of the Lord*, as they had done; he did nothing to cut off the entail of the curse, to discharge the incumbrances of his crown, and therefore (*transit cum onere—the incumbrance descends with the crown*) with his own iniquity that of his fathers shall come into the account.

II. The calamities that came upon him, and his family, and people, in the very beginning of his reign, were very grievous. 1. Jerusalem was besieged by the king of Babylon, *v.* 10, 11. He had sent his forces to ravage the country, *v.* 2. Now he came himself, and laid siege to the city. Now the word of God was fulfilled (Deut. xxviii. 49, &c.), *The Lord shall bring a nation against thee from far, of fierce countenance*, that shall first *eat of the fruit of thy land* and then *besiege thee in all thy gates*. 2. Jehoiachin immediately surrendered at discretion. As soon as he heard the king of Babylon had come in person against the city, his name having at this time become very formidable, he beat a parley and went out to him, *v.* 12. Had he made his peace with God, and taken the method that Hezekiah did in the like case, he needed not to have feared the king of Babylon, but might have held out with courage, honour, and success (one should have chased a thousand); but, wanting the faith and piety of an Israelite, he had not the resolution of a man, of a soldier, of a prince. He and his royal family, his mother and wives, his servants and princes, delivered themselves up prisoners of war; this was the consequence of their being servants of sin. 3. Nebuchadnezzar rifled the treasuries both of the church and of the state, and carried away the silver and gold of both, *v.* 13. Now the word of God by Isaiah was fulfilled (*ch.* xx. 17), *All that is in thy house shall be carried to Babylon.* Even the vessels of the temple which Solomon had made, and laid up in store to be used as the old ones were worn out, he cut off from the temple, and began to cut them in pieces, but, upon second thoughts, reserved them for his own use, for we find Belshazzar drinking wine in them, Dan. v. 2, 3. 4. He carried away a great part of Jerusalem into captivity, to weaken it, that he might effectually secure to himself the dominion of it and prevent its revolt, and to enrich himself with the wealth or service of those he took away. There had been some carried away eight years before this, in the first year of Nebuchadnezzar and the third of Jehoiakim, among whom were Daniel and his fellows. See Dan. i. 1, 6. They had approved themselves so well that this politic prince coveted more of them. Now he carried off, (1.) The young king himself and his family (*v.* 15), and we find (*ch.* xxv. 27—29) that for thirty-seven years he continued a close prisoner. (2.) All the great men, the princes and officers, whose riches were *kept for the owners thereof to their hurt* (Eccl. v. 13), tempting the enemies to make a prey of them first. (3.) All the military men, the *mighty men of valour* (*v.* 14), *the mighty of the land* (*v.* 15), *the men of might, even all that were strong and apt for war*, *v.* 16. These could not defend themselves, and the conqueror would not leave them to defend their country, but took them away, to be employed in his service. (4.) All the craftsmen and smiths who made weapons of war; in taking them he did, in effect, disarm the city, according to the Philistines' policy, 1 Sam. xiii. 19. In this captivity Ezekiel the prophet was carried away (Ezek. i. 1, 2) and Mordecai, Esth. ii. 6 This Jehoiachin was also called *Jeconiah* (1 Chron. iii. 16), and in contempt (Jer. xxii 24, where his captivity is foretold) *Coniah*.

III. The successor whom the king of Babylon appointed in the room of Jehoiachin. God had written him childless (Jer. xxii. 30) and therefore his uncle was entrusted with the government. The king of Babylon made Mattaniah king, the son of Josiah; and to remind him, and let all the world know, that he was his creature, he changed his name and called him *Zedekiah, v.* 17. God had sometimes charged it upon his people, *They have set up kings, but not by me* (Hos. viii. 4), and now, to punish them for that, the king of Babylon shall have the setting up of their kings. Those are justly deprived of their liberty that use it, and insist upon it, against God's authority. This Zedekiah was the last of the kings of Judah. The name which the king of Babylon gave him signifies *The justice of the Lord,* and was a presage of the glorifying of God's justice in his ruin. 1. See how impious this Zedekiah was. Though the judgments of God upon his three immediate predecessors might have been a warning to him not to tread in their steps, yet *he did that which was evil,* like all the rest, *v.* 19. 2. See how impolitic he was. As his predecessor lost his courage, so he his wisdom, with his religion, for he *rebelled against the king of Babylon* (*v.* 20), whose tributary he was, and so provoked him whom he was utterly unable to contend with, and who, if he had continued true to him, would have protected him. This was the most foolish thing he could do, and hastened the ruin of his kingdom. This came to pass *through the anger of the Lord, that he might cast them out from his presence.* Note, When those that are entrusted with the counsels of a nation act unwisely, and against their true interest, we ought to take notice of the displeasure of God in it. It is for the sins of a people that God *removes the speech of the trusty and takes away the understanding of the aged,* and *hides from their eyes the things that belong to* the public *peace.* Whom God will destroy he infatuates.

CHAP. XXV.

Ever since David's time Jerusalem had been a celebrated place, beautiful for situation and the joy of the whole earth; while the book of psalms lasts that name will sound great. In the New Testament we read much of it, when it was, as here, ripening again for its ruin. In the close of the Bible we read of a new Jerusalem Every thing therefore that concerns Jerusalem is worthy our regard. In this chapter we have, I. The utter destruction of Jerusalem by the Chaldeans, the city besieged and taken (ver. 1—4), the houses burnt (ver. 8, 9), the wall broken down (ver. 10), and the inhabitants carried away into captivity, ver. 11, 12. The glory of Jerusalem was, 1. That it was the royal city, where were set "the thrones of the house of David;" but that glory has now departed, for the prince is made a most miserable prisoner, the seed royal is destroyed (ver. 5—7), and the principal officers are put to death, ver. 18—21. 2. That it was the holy city, where was the testimony of Israel; but that glory has departed, for Solomon's temple is burnt to the ground (ver. 9) and the sacred vessels that remained are carried away to Babylon, ver. 13—17. Thus has Jerusalem become as a widow, Lam. i. 1. Ichabod—Where is the glory? II. The distraction and dispersion of the remnant that was left in Judah under Gedaliah, ver. 22—26. III. The countenance which, after thirty-seven years' imprisonment, was given to Jehoiachin the captive king of Judah, ver. 27—30.

AND it came to pass in the ninth year of his reign, in the tenth month, in the tenth *day* of the month, *that* Nebuchadnezzar king of Babylon came, he, and all his host, against Jerusalem, and pitched against it; and they built forts against it round about. 2 And the city was besieged unto the eleventh year of king Zedekiah. 3 And on the ninth *day* of the *fourth* month the famine prevailed in the city, and there was no bread for the people of the land. 4 And the city was broken up, and all the men of *war* fled by night by the way of the gate between two walls, which *is* by the king's garden: (now the Chaldees *were* against the city round about:) and *the king* went the way toward the plain. 5 And the army of the Chaldees pursued after the king, and overtook him in the plains of Jericho: and all his army were scattered from him. 6 So they took the king, and brought him up to the king of Babylon to Riblah; and they gave judgment upon him. 7 And they slew the sons of Zedekiah before his eyes, and put out the eyes of Zedekiah, and bound him with fetters of brass, and carried him to Babylon.

We left king Zedekiah in rebellion against the king of Babylon (*ch.* xxiv. 20), contriving and endeavouring to shake off his yoke, when he was no way able to do it, nor took the right method by making God his friend first. Now here we have an account of the fatal consequences of that attempt.

I. The king of Babylon's army laid siege to Jerusalem, *v.* 1. What should hinder them when the country was already in their possession? *ch.* xxiv. 2. They *built forts against the city round about,* whence, by such arts of war as they then had, they battered it, sent into it instruments of death, and kept out of it the necessary supports of life. Formerly Jerusalem had been compassed with the favour of God as with a shield, but now their defence had departed from them and their enemies surrounded them on every side. Those that by sin have provoked God to leave them will find that *innumerable evils will compass them about.* Two years this siege lasted; at first the army retired, for fear of the king of Egypt (Jer. xxxvii. 11), but, finding him not so powerful as they thought, they soon returned, with a resolution not to quit the city till they had made themselves masters of it.

II. During this siege the famine prevailed (*v.* 3), so that for a long time they *ate their bread by weight and with care,* Ezek. iv. 16. Thus they were punished for their gluttony and excess, their *fulness of bread* and *feeding themselves without fear.* At length *there was no bread for the people of the land,* that is, the common people, the soldiers, whereby they were weakened and rendered unfit for service. Now they ate their own children for want of food. See this foretold by one prophet (Ezek. v. 10) and bewailed by another, Lam. iv. 3, &c. Jeremiah earnestly persuaded the king to surrender (Jer. xxxviii. 17), but his heart was hardened to his destruction.

III. At length the city was taken by storm: it was *broken up*, *v.* 4. The besiegers made a breach in the wall, at which they forced their way into it. The besieged, unable any longer to defend it, endeavoured to quit it, and make the best of their way; and many, no doubt, were put to the sword, the victorious army being much exasperated by their obstinacy.

IV. The king, his family, and all his great men, made their escape in the night, by some secret passages which the besiegers either had not discovered or did not keep their eye upon, *v.* 4. But those as much deceive themselves who think to escape God's judgments as those who think to brave them; the feet of him that flees from them will as surely fail as the hands of him that fights against them. When God judges he will overcome. Intelligence was given to the Chaldeans of the king's flight, and which way he had gone, so that they soon overtook him, *v.* 5. His guards were scattered from him, every man shifting for his own safety. Had he put himself under God's protection, that would not have failed him now. He presently fell into the enemies' hands, and here we are told what they did with him. 1. He was brought to the king of Babylon, and tried by a council of war for rebelling against him who set him up, and to whom he had sworn fidelity. God and man had a quarrel with him for this; see Ezek. xvii. 16, &c. The king of Babylon now lay at Riblah (which lay between Judea and Babylon), that he might be ready to give orders both to his court at home and his army abroad. 2. His *sons were slain before his eyes*, though children, that this doleful spectacle, the last his eyes were to behold, might leave an impression of grief and horror upon his spirit as long as he lived. In slaying his sons, they showed their indignation at his falsehood, and in effect declared that neither he nor any of his were fit to be trusted, and therefore that they were not fit to live. 3. His eyes were put out, by which he was deprived of that common comfort of human life which is given even to *those that are in misery, and to the bitter in soul*, the light of the sun, by which he was also disabled for any service. He dreaded being mocked, and therefore would not be persuaded to yield (Jer. xxxviii. 19), but that which he feared came upon him with a witness, and no doubt added much to his misery; for, as those that are deaf suspect that every body talks of them, so those that are blind suspect that every body laughs at them. By this two prophecies that seemed to contradict one another were both fulfilled. Jeremiah prophesied that Zedekiah should be brought to Babylon, Jer. xxxii. 5; xxxiv. 3. Ezekiel prophesied that he should not see Babylon, Ezek. xii. 13. He was brought thither, but, his eyes being put out, he did not see it. Thus he ended his days, before he ended his life. 4. He was *bound in fetters of brass* and so *carried to Babylon*. He that was blind needed not be bound (his blindness fettered him), but, for his greater disgrace, they led him bound; only, whereas common malefactors are laid in irons (Ps. cv. 18; cvii. 10), he, being a prince, was bound with fetters of brass; but that the metal was somewhat nobler and lighter was little comfort, while still he was in fetters. Let it not seem strange if those that have been held in the cords of iniquity come to be thus *held in the cords of affliction*, Job xxxvi. 8.

8 And in the fifth month, on the seventh *day* of the month, which *is* the nineteenth year of king Nebuchadnezzar king of Babylon, came Nebuzar-adan, captain of the guard, a servant of the king of Babylon, unto Jerusalem: 9 And he burnt the house of the LORD, and the king's house, and all the houses of Jerusalem, and every great *man's* house burnt he with fire. 10 And all the army of the Chaldees, that *were with* the captain of the guard, brake down the walls of Jerusalem round about. 11 Now the rest of the people *that were* left in the city, and the fugitives that fell away to the king of Babylon, with the remnant of the multitude, did Nebuzar-adan the captain of the guard carry away. 12 But the captain of the guard left of the poor of the land *to be* vinedressers and husbandmen. 13 And the pillars of brass that *were* in the house of the LORD, and the bases, and the brasen sea that *was* in the house of the LORD, did the Chaldees break in pieces, and carried the brass of them to Babylon. 14 And the pots, and the shovels, and the snuffers, and the spoons, and all the vessels of brass wherewith they ministered, took they away. 15 And the firepans, and the bowls, *and* such things as *were* of gold, *in* gold, and of silver, *in* silver, the captain of the guard took away. 16 The two pillars, one sea, and the bases which Solomon had made for the house of the LORD; the brass of all these vessels was without weight. 17 The height of the one pillar *was* eighteen cubits, and the chapiter upon it *was* brass: and the height of the chapiter three cubits: and the wreath-

en work, and pomegranates upon the chapiter round about, all of brass: and like unto these had the second pillar with wreathen work. 18 And the captain of the guard took Seraiah the chief priest, and Zephaniah the second priest, and the three keepers of the door: 19 And out of the city he took an officer that was set over the men of war, and five men of them that were in the king's presence, which were found in the city, and the principal scribe of the host, which mustered the people of the land, and threescore men of the people of the land *that were* found in the city: 20 And Nebuzar-adan captain of the guard took these, and brought them to the king of Babylon to Riblah: 21 And the king of Babylon smote them, and slew them at Riblah in the land of Hamath. So Judah was carried away out of their land.

Though we have reason to think that the army of the Chaldeans were much enraged against the city for holding out with so much stubbornness, yet they did not therefore put all to fire and sword as soon as they had taken the city (which is too commonly done in such cases), but about a month after (compare *v.* 8 with *v.* 3) Nebuzar-adan was sent with orders to complete the destruction of Jerusalem. This space God gave them to repent, after all the foregoing days of his patience, but in vain; their hearts (for aught that appears) were still hardened, and therefore execution is awarded to the utmost. 1. The city and temple are burnt, *v.* 9. It does not appear that the king of Babylon designed to send any colonies to people Jerusalem and therefore he ordered it to be laid in ashes, as a nest of rebels. At the burning of the king's house and *the houses of the great men* one cannot so much wonder (the inhabitants had, by their sins, made them combustible), but that the *house of the Lord* should perish in these flames, that that holy and beautiful house should be burnt with fire (Isa. lxiv. 11), is very strange. That house which David prepared for, and which Solomon built at such a vast expense—that house which had the eye and heart of God perpetually upon it (1 Kings ix. 3)—might not that have been snatched as a brand out of this burning? No, it must not be fire-proof against God's judgments. This stately structure must be turned into ashes, and it is probable the ark in it, for the enemies, having heard how dearly the Philistines paid for the abusing of it, durst not seize that, nor did any of its friends take care to preserve it, for then we should have heard of it again in the second temple. One of the apocryphal writers does indeed tell us that the prophet Jeremiah got it out of the temple, and conveyed it to a cave in Mount Nebo on the other side Jordan, and hid it there (2 Macc. ii. 4, 5), but that could not be, for Jeremiah was a close prisoner at that time. By the burning of the temple God would show how little he cares for the external pomp of his worship when the life and power of religion are neglected. The people trusted to the temple, as if that would protect them in their sins (Jer. vii. 4), but God, by this, let them know that when they had profaned it they would find it but a refuge of lies. This temple had stood about 420, some say 430 years. The people having forfeited the promises made concerning it, those promises must be understood of the gospel-temple, which is God's rest for ever. It is observable that the second temple was burnt by the Romans the same month, and the same day of the month, that the first temple was burnt by the Chaldeans, which, Josephus says, was the tenth of August. 2. The walls of Jerusalem are demolished (*v.* 10), as if the victorious army would be revenged on them for having kept them out so long, or at least prevent the like opposition another time. Sin unwalls a people and takes away their defence. These walls were never repaired till Nehemiah's time. 3. The residue of the people are carried away captive to Babylon, *v.* 11. Most of the inhabitants had perished by sword or famine, or had made their escape when the king did (for it is said, *v.* 5, *His army was scattered from him*), so that there were very few left, who with the deserters, making in all but 832 persons (as appears, Jer. lii. 29), were carried away into captivity; only *the poor of the land were left behind* (*v.* 12), to till the ground and dress the vineyards for the Chaldeans. Sometimes poverty is a protection; for those that have nothing have nothing to lose. When the rich Jews, who had been oppressive to the poor, were made strangers, nay, prisoners, in an enemy's country, the poor whom they had despised and oppressed had liberty and peace in their own country. Thus Providence sometimes remarkably humbles the proud and favours those of low degree. 4. The brazen vessels, and other appurtenances of the temple, are carried away, those of silver and gold being most of them gone before. Those two famous columns of brass, *Jachin* and *Boaz*, which signified the strength and stability of the house of God, were broken to pieces and the brass of them was carried to Babylon, *v.* 13. When the things signified were sinned away what should the signs stand there for? Ahaz had profanely *cut off the borders of the bases*, and put *the brazen sea upon a pavement of stones* (2 Kings xvi. 17); justly therefore are the bases themselves, and the brazen sea, delivered into the enemy's hand. It is just with God to take away his ordinances from those that profane and abuse them, that curtail and depress them. Some things remained of gold and silver (*v.* 15) which were now carried off; but most of this plunder was brass, such a vast quantity of it that it is said to be *without weight*, *v.* 16. The carrying away of *the vessels wherewith they ministered* (*v.* 14) put an end to the ministration. It was a righteous thing with God to deprive those of the benefit of his worship who had slighted it so long and preferred false worships before it. Those that would have many altars shall now have none. 5. Several of the great men are slain in cold blood—Seraiah the chief priest (who was the father of Ezra as appears, Ezra vii. 1), the second priest (who, when there was occasion, officiated for him), and three door-keepers of the temple (*v.* 18), the general of the army, five privy-counsellors (afterwards they made them up seven, Jer. lii. 25), the secretary of war, or pay-master of the army, and sixty country gentlemen who had concealed themselves in the city. These, being persons of some rank, were brought to the king of Babylon (*v.* 19, 20), who ordered them to be all put to death (*v.* 21), when, in reason, they might have hoped that surely the bitterness of death was past. These the king of Babylon's revenge looked upon as most active in opposing him; but divine justice, we may suppose, looked upon them as ringleaders in that idolatry and impiety which were punished by these desolations. This completed the calamity: *So Judah was carried away out of their land*, about 860 years after they were put in possession of it by Joshua. Now the scripture was fulfilled, *The Lord shall bring thee, and the king which thou shalt set over thee, into a nation which thou hast not known*, Deut. xxviii. 36. Sin kept their fathers forty years out of Canaan, and now turned *them* out. The Lord is known by those judgments which he executes, and makes good that word which he has spoken, Amos iii. 2. *You only have I known of all the families of the earth, therefore I will punish you for all your iniquities.*

22 And *as for* the people that remained in the land of Judah, whom Nebuchadnezzar king of Babylon had left, even over them he made Gedaliah the son of Ahikam, the son of Shaphan, ruler. 23 And when all the captains of the armies, they and their men, heard that the king of Babylon had made Gedaliah governor, there came to Gedaliah to Mizpah, even Ishmael the son of Nethaniah, and Johanan the son of Careah, and Seraiah the son of Tanhumeth the Netophathite, and Jaazaniah the son of a Maachathite, they and their men. 24 And Gedaliah sware to them, and to their men, and said unto them, Fear not to be the servants of the Chaldees: dwell in the land, and serve the king of Babylon; and it shall be well with you. 25 But it came to pass in the seventh month, that Ishmael the son of Nethaniah, the son of Elishama, of the seed royal, came, and ten men with him, and smote Gedaliah, that he died, and the Jews and the Chaldees that were with him at Mizpah. 26 And all the people, both small and great, and the captains of the armies, arose, and came to Egypt: for they were afraid of the Chaldees. 27 And it came to pass in the seven and thirtieth year of the captivity of Jehoiachin king of Judah, in the twelfth month, on the seven and twentieth *day* of the month, *that* Evil-merodach king of Babylon in the year that he began to reign did lift up the head of Jehoiachin king of Judah out of prison; 28 And he spake kindly to him, and set his throne above the throne of the kings that *were* with him in Babylon; 29 And changed his prison garments: and he did eat bread continually before him all the days of his life. 30 And his allowance *was* a continual allowance given him of the king, a daily rate for every day, all the days of his life.

In these verses we have,

I. The dispersion of the remaining people. The city of Jerusalem was quite laid waste. Some people there were in the land of Judah (*v.* 22) that had weathered the storm, and (which was no small favour at this time, Jer. xlv. 5) had *their lives given them for a prey*. Now see, 1. What a good posture they were put into. The king of Babylon appointed Gedaliah, one of themselves, to be their governor and protector under him, a very good man, and one that would make the best of the bad, *v.* 22. His father Ahikam was one that countenanced and protected Jeremiah when the princes had vowed his death, Jer. xxvi. 24. It is probable that this Gedaliah, by the advice of Jeremiah, had gone over to the Chaldeans, and had conducted himself so well that the king of Babylon entrusted him with the government. He resided not at Jerusalem, but at Mizpah, in the land of Benjamin, a place famous in Samuel's time. Thither those came who had fled from Zedekiah (*v.* 4) and put themselves under his protection (*v.* 23), which he assured them of if they would be patient and peaceable under the government of the king of Babylon, *v.* 24. Gedaliah, though he had not the pomp and power of a sovereign prince, yet might have been a greater blessing to them than many of their kings had been, especially having such a privy-council as Jeremiah, who was now with them, and interested himself in their affairs, Jer. xl. 5, 6. 2. What a fatal breach was made upon them, soon afterwards, by the death of Gedaliah, within two months after he entered upon his government. The utter extirpation of the Jews, for the present, was determined, and therefore it was in vain for them to think of taking root again: the whole land must be plucked up, Jer. xlv. 4. Yet this hopeful settlement is dashed to pieces, not by the Chaldeans, but by some of themselves. The things of their peace were so hidden from their eyes that they knew not when they were well off, nor would believe when they were told. (1.) They had a good governor of their own, and him they slew, out of spite to the Chaldeans, because he was appointed by Nebuchadnezzar, *v.* 25. Ishmael, who was of the royal family, envying Gedaliah's advancement and the happy settlement of the people under him, though he could not propose to set up himself, resolved to ruin him, and basely slew him and all his friends, both Jews and Chaldeans. Nebuchadnezzar would not, could not, have been a more mischievous enemy to their peace than this degenerate branch of the house of David was. (2.) They were as yet in their own good land, but they forsook it, and went to Egypt, for fear of the Chaldeans, *v.* 26. The Chaldeans had reason enough to be offended at the murder of Gedaliah; but if those that remained had humbly remonstrated, alleging that it was only the act of Ishmael and his party, we may suppose that those who were innocent of it, nay, who suffered greatly by it, would not have been punished for it: but, under pretence of this apprehension, contrary to the counsel of Jeremiah, they all went to Egypt, where, it is probable, they mixed with the Egyptians by degrees, and were never heard of more as Israelites. Thus was there a full end made of them by their own folly and disobedience, and Egypt had the last of them, that the last verse of that chapter of threatenings might be fulfilled, after all the rest, Deut. xxviii. 68, *The Lord shall bring thee into Egypt again.* These events are more largely related by the prophet Jeremiah, *ch.* xl. to *ch.* xlv. *Quæque ipse miserrima vidit, et quorum pars magna fuit—Which scenes he was doomed to behold, and in which he bore a melancholy part.*

II. The reviving of the captive prince. Of Zedekiah we hear no more after he was carried blind to Babylon; it is probable that he did not live long, but that when he died he was buried with some marks of honour, Jer. xxxiv. 5. Of Jehoiachin, or Jeconiah, who surrendered himself (*ch.* xxiv. 12), we are here told that as soon as Evil-merodach came to the crown, upon the death of his father Nebuchadnezzar, he released him out of prison (where he had lain thirty-seven years, and was now fifty-five years old), *spoke kindly to him,* paid more respect to him than to any other of the kings his father had left in captivity (*v.* 28), gave him princely clothing instead of his prison-garments, maintained him in his own palace (*v.* 29), and allowed him a pension for himself and his family in some measure corresponding to his rank, *a daily rate for every day as long as he lived.* Consider this, 1. As a very happy change of Jehoiachin's condition. To have honour and liberty after he had been so long in confinement and disgrace, the plenty and pleasure of a court after he had been so long accustomed to the straits and miseries of a prison, was like the return of the morning after a very dark and tedious night. Let none say that they shall never see good again because they have long seen little but evil; the most miserable know not what blessed turn Providence may yet give to their affairs, nor what comforts they are reserved for, *according to the days wherein they have been afflicted,* Ps. xc. 15. However the death of afflicted saints is to them such a change as this was to Jehoiachin: it will release them out of their prison, shake off the body, that prison-garment, and open the way to their advancement; it will send them to the throne, to the table, of the King of kings, the glorious liberty of God's children. 2. As a very generous act of Evil-merodach's. He thought his father made the yoke of his captives too heavy, and therefore, with the tenderness of a man and the honour of a prince, made it lighter. It should seem all the kings he had in his power were favoured, but Jehoiachin above them all, some think for the sake of the antiquity of his family and the honour of his renowned ancestors, David and Solomon. None of the kings of the nations, it is likely, had descended from so long a race of kings in a direct lineal succession, and by a male line, as the king of Judah. The Jews say that this Evil-merodach had been himself imprisoned by his own father, when he returned from his madness, for some mismanagement at that time, and that in prison he contracted a friendship with Jehoiachin, in consequence of which, as soon as he had it in his power, he showed him this kindness as a sufferer, as a fellow-sufferer. Some suggest that Evil-merodach had learned from Daniel and his fellows the principles of the true religion, and was well affected to them, and upon that account favoured Jehoiachin. 3. As a kind dispensation of Providence, for the encouragement of the Jews in captivity, and the support of their faith and hope concerning their enlargement in due time. This happened just about the midnight of their captivity. Thirty-six of the seventy years were now past, and almost as many were yet behind, and now to see their king thus advanced would be a comfortable earnest to them of their own release in due time, in the set time. *Unto the upright there* thus *ariseth light in the darkness,* to encourage them to hope, even in the *cloudy and dark day,* that at *evening time it shall be light;* when therefore we are perplexed, let us not be in despair

AN

EXPOSITION,

WITH PRACTICAL OBSERVATIONS,

OF THE FIRST BOOK OF

CHRONICLES.

In common things repetition is thought needless and nauseous; but, in sacred things, *precept must be upon precept and line upon line. To me,* says the apostle, *to write the same things is not grievous, but for you it is safe,* Phil. iii. 1. These books of Chronicles are in a great measure repetition; so are much of the second and third of the four evangelists: and yet there are no tautologies either here or there, no *vain repetitions.* We may be ready to think that of all the books of holy scripture we could best spare these two books of Chronicles. Perhaps we might, and yet we could ill spare them; for there are many most excellent useful things in them, which we find not elsewhere. And as for what we find here which we have already met with, 1. It might be of great use to those who lived when these books were first published, before the canon of the Old Testament was completed and the particles of it put together; for it would remind them of what was more fully related in the other books. Abstracts, abridgments, and references, are of use in divinity as well as law. That, perhaps, may not be said in vain which yet has been said before. 2. It is still of use, that *out of the mouth of two witnesses every word may be established,* and, being inculcated, may be remembered. The penman of these books is supposed to be Ezra, that *ready scribe in the law of the Lord,* Ezra vii. 6. It is a groundless story of that apocryphal writer (2 Esdr. xiv. 21, &c.) that, all the law being burnt, Ezra was divinely inspired to write it all over again, which yet might take rise from the books of Chronicles, where we find, though not all the same story repeated, yet the names of all those who were the subjects of that story. These books are called in the Hebrew *words of days*—journals or annals, because, by divine direction, collected out of some public and authentic records. The collection was made after the captivity, and yet the language of the originals, written before, is sometimes retained, as 2 Chron. v. 9, *there it is unto this day,* which must have been written before the destruction of the temple. The LXX. call it a book Παραλειπομένων—of *things left,* or overlooked, by the preceding historians; and several such things there are in it. It is the rereward, the gathering host, of this sacred camp, which gathers up what remained, that nothing might be lost. In this first book we have, I. A collection of sacred genealogies, from Adam to David: and they are none of those which the apostle calls *endless genealogies,* but have their use and end in Christ, *ch.* i.—ix. Divers little passages of history are here inserted which we had not before. II. A repetition of the history of the translation of the kingdom from Saul to David, and of the triumph of David's reign, with large additions, *ch.* x.—xxi. III. An original account of the settlement David made of the ecclesiastical affairs, and the preparation he made for the building of the temple, *ch.* xxii.—xxix. These are *words of days,* of the oldest days, of the best days, of the Old-Testament church. The reigns of kings and dates of kingdoms, as well as the lives of common persons, are reckoned by *days;* for a little time often gives a great turn, and yet all time is nothing to eternity.

CHAP. I.

This chapter and many that follow it repeat the genealogies we have hitherto met with in the sacred history, and put them all together, with considerable additions. We may be tempted, it may be, to think it would have been well if they had not been written, because, when they come to be compared with other parallel places, there are differences found, which we can scarcely accommodate to our satisfaction; yet we must not therefore stumble at the word, but bless God that the things necessary to salvation are plain enough. And, since the wise God has thought fit to write these things to us, we should not pass them over unread. All scripture is profitable, though not all alike profitable; and we may take occasion for good thoughts and meditations even from those parts of scripture that do not furnish so much matter for profitable remarks as some other parts. These genealogies, 1. Were then of great use, when they were here preserved, and put into the hands of the Jews after their return from Babylon; for the captivity, like the deluge, had put all into confusion, and they, in that dispersion and despair, would be in danger of losing the distinctions of their tribes and families. This therefore revives the ancient landmarks even of some of the tribes that were carried captive into Assyria. Perhaps it might invite the Jews to study the sacred writings which had been neglected, to find the names of their ancestors, and the rise of their families in them. 2. They are still of some use for the illustrating of the scripture-story, and especially for the clearing of the pedigrees of the Messiah, that it might appear that our blessed Saviour was, according to the prophecies which went before of him, the son of David, the son of Judah, the son of Abraham, the son of Adam. And, now that he has come for whose sake these registers were preserved, the Jews since have so lost all their genealogies that even that of the priests, the most sacred of all, is forgotten, and they know not of any one man in the world that can prove himself of the house of Aaron. When the building is reared the scaffolds are removed. When the promised Seed has come the line that was to lead to him is broken off. In this chapter we have an abstract of all the genealogies in the book of Genesis, till we come to Jacob. I. The descents from Adam to Noah and his sons, out of Gen. v., ver. 1—4. II. The posterity of Noah's sons, by which the earth was repeopled, out of Gen. x., ver. 5—23. III. The descents from Shem to Abraham, out of Gen. xi., ver. 24—28. IV. The posterity of Ishmael, and of Abraham's sons by Keturah, out of Gen. xxv., ver. 29—35. V. The posterity of Esau, out of Gen. xxxvi., ver. 36—54. These, it is likely, were passed over lightly in Genesis; and therefore, according to the law of the school, we are made to go over that lesson again which we did not learn well.

ADAM, Sheth, Enosh, 2 Kenan, Mahalaleel, Jered, 3 Henoch, Methuselah, Lamech, 4 Noah, Shem, Ham, and Japheth, 5 The sons of Japheth; Gomer, and Magog, and Madai, and Javan, and Tubal, and Meshech, and Tiras. 6 And the sons of Gomer: Ashchenaz, and Riphath, and Togarmah. 7 And the sons of Javan; Elishah, and Tarshish, Kittim, and Dodanim. 8 The sons of Ham; Cush, and Mizraim, Put, and Canaan. 9 And the sons of Cush; Seba, and Havilah, and Sabta, and Raamah, and Sabtecha. And the sons of Raamah; Sheba and Dedan. 10 And Cush begat Nimrod: he began to be mighty upon the earth. 11 And Mizraim begat Ludim, and Anamim, and Lehabim, and Naphtuhim, 12 And Pathrusim, and Casluhim, (of whom came the Philistines,) and Caphthorim. 13 And Canaan begat Zidon his firstborn, and Heth, 14 The Jebusite also, and the Amorite, and the Girgashite, 15 And the Hivite, and the Arkite, and the Sinite, 16 And the Arvadite, and the Zemarite, and the Hamathite. 17 The sons of Shem; Elam, and Asshur, and Arphaxad, and Lud, and Aram, and Uz, and Hul, and Gether, and Meshech. 18 And Arphaxad begat Shelah, and Shelah begat Eber. 19 And unto Eber were born two sons: the name of the one *was* Peleg; because in his days the earth was divided: and his brother's name *was* Joktan. 20 And Joktan begat Almodad, and Sheleph, and Hazarmaveth, and Jerah, 21 Hadoram also, and Uzal, and Diklah, 22 And Ebal, and Abimael, and Sheba, 23 And Ophir, and Havilah, and Jobab. All these *were* the sons of Joktan. 24 Shem, Arphaxad, Shelah, 25 Eber, Peleg, Reu, 26 Serug, Nahor, Terah, 27 Abram; the same *is* Abraham.

This paragraph has *Adam* for its first word and *Abraham* for its last. Between the creation of the former and the birth of the latter were 2000 years, almost the one-half of which time Adam himself lived. Adam was the common father of our flesh, Abraham the common father of the faithful. By the breach which the former made of the covenant of innocency, we were all made miserable; by the covenant of grace made with the latter, we all are, or may be, made happy. We all are, by nature, the seed of Adam, branches of that wild olive. Let us see to it that, by faith, we become the seed of Abraham (Rom. iv. 11, 12), that we be grafted into the good olive and partake of its root and fatness

I. The first four verses of this paragraph, and the last four, which are linked together by Shem (*v.* 4, 24), contain the sacred line of Christ from Adam to Abraham, and are inserted in his pedigree, Luke iii. 34—38, the order ascending as here it descends. This genealogy proves the falsehood of that reproach, *As for this man, we know not whence he is.* Bishop Patrick well observes here that, a genealogy being to be drawn of the families of the Jews, this appears as the peculiar glory of the Jewish nation, that they alone were able to derive their pedigree from the first man that God created, which no other nation pretended to, but abused themselves and their posterity with fabulous accounts of their originals, the Arcadians fancying that they were before the moon, the people of Thessaly that they sprang from stones, the Athenians that they grew out of the earth, much like the vain imaginations which some of the philosophers had of the origin of the universe. The account which the holy scripture gives both of the creation of the world and of the rise of nations carries with it as clear evidences of its own truth as those idle traditions do of their own vanity and falsehood.

II. All the verses between repeat the account of the replenishing of the earth by the sons of Noah after the flood. 1. The historian begins with those who were strangers to the church, the sons of Japhet, who were planted in the isles of the Gentiles, those western parts of the world, the countries of Europe. Of these he gives a short account (*v.* 5—7), because with these the Jews had hitherto had little or no dealings. 2. He proceeds to those who had many of them been enemies to the church, the sons of Ham, who moved southward towards Africa and those parts of Asia which lay that way. Nimrod the son of Cush began to be an oppressor, probably to the people of God in his time. But Mizraim, from whom came the Egyptians, and Canaan, from whom came the Canaanites, are both of them names of great note in the Jewish story; for with their descendants the Israel of God had severe struggles to get out of the land of Egypt and into the land of Canaan; and therefore the branches of Mizraim are particularly recorded (*v.* 11, 12), and of Canaan, *v.* 13—16. See at what a rate God valued Israel when he gave *Egypt for their ransom* (Isa. xliii. 3), and cast out all these nations before them, Ps. lxxx. 8. 3. He then gives an account of those that were the ancestors and allies of the church, the posterity of Shem, *v.* 17—23. These peopled Asia, and spread themselves eastward. The Assyrians, Syrians, Chaldeans, Persians, and Arabians, descended from these. At first the originals of the respective nations were known; but at this day, we have reason to think, the nations are so mingled with one another, by the enlargement of commerce and dominion, the transplanting of colonies, the carrying away of captives, and many other circumstances, that no one nation, no, nor the greatest part of any, is descended entire from any one of these fountains. Only this we are sure of, that God has *created of one blood all nations of men;* they have all descended from one Adam, one Noah. *Have we not all one father? Has not one God created us?* Mal. ii. 10. Our register hastens to the line of Abraham, breaking off abruptly from all the other families of the sons of Noah but that of Arphaxad, from whom Christ was to come. The great promise of the Messiah (says bishop Patrick) was translated from Adam to Seth, from him to Shem, from him to Eber, and so to the Hebrew nation, who were entrusted, above all nations, with that sacred treasure, till the promise was performed and the Messiah had come, and then that nation was made *not a people.*

28 The sons of Abraham; Isaac, and Ishmael. 29 These *are* their generations: The firstborn of Ishmael, Nebaioth; then Kedar, and Adbeel, and Mibsam, 30 Mishma, and Dumah, Massa, Hadad, and Tema, 31 Jetur, Naphish, and Kedemah. These are the sons of Ishmael. 32 Now the sons of Keturah, Abraham's concubine: she bare Zimran, and Jokshan, and Medan, and Midian, and Ishbak, and Shuah. And the sons of Jokshan; Sheba, and Dedan. 33 And the sons of Midian; Ephah, and Epher, and Henoch, and Abida, and Eldaah. All these *are* the sons of Keturah. 34 And Abraham begat Isaac. The sons of Isaac; Esau and Israel. 35 The sons of Esau; Eliphaz, Reuel, and Jeush, and Jaalam, and Korah. 36 The sons of Eliphaz; Teman, and Omar, Zephi, and Gatam, Kenaz, and Timna, and Amalek. 37 The sons of Reuel; Nahath, Zerah, Shammah, and Mizzah. 38 And the sons of Seir; Lotan, and Shobal, and Zibeon, and Anah, and Dishon, and Ezar, and Dishan. 39 And the sons of Lotan; Hori, and Homam: and Timna *was* Lotan's sister. 40 The sons of Shobal; Alian, and Manahath, and Ebal, Shephi, and Onam. And the sons of Zibeon; Aiah, and Anah. 41 The sons of Anah; Dishon. And the sons of Dishon; Amram, and Eshban, and Ithran, and Cheran. 42 The sons of Ezer; Bilhan, and Zavan, *and* Jakan. The sons of Dishan; Uz, and Aran. 43 Now these *are* the kings that reigned in the land of Edom before *any* king reigned over the children of Israel; Bela the son of Beor: and the name of his city *was* Dinhabah. 44 And when Bela was dead, Jobab the son of Zerah of Bozrah reigned in his stead. 45 And when Jobab was dead, Husham of the land of the Temanites reigned in his stead. 46 And when Husham was dead, Hadad the son of Bedad, which smote Midian in the field of Moab, reigned in his stead: and the name of his city *was* Avith. 47 And when Hadad was dead, Samlah of Masrekah reigned in his stead. 48 And when Samlah was dead, Shaul of Rehoboth by the river reigned in his stead. 49 And when Shaul was dead, Baal-hanan the son of Achbor reigned in his stead. 50 And when Baal-hanan was dead, Hadad reigned in his stead: and the name of his city *was* Pai; and his wife's name *was* Mehetabel, the daughter of Matred, the daughter of Mezahab. 51 Hadad died also. And the dukes of Edom were; duke Timnah, duke Aliah, duke Jetheth, 52 Duke Aholibamah, duke Elah, duke Pinon, 53 Duke Kenaz, duke Teman, duke Mibzar, 54 Duke Magdiel, duke Iram. These *are* the dukes of Edom.

All nations but the seed of Abraham are already shaken off from this genealogy: they have no part nor lot in this matter. *The Lord's portion is his people.* Of them he keeps an account, knows them by name; but those who are strangers to him he beholds afar off. Not that we are to conclude that therefore no particular persons of any other nation but the seed of Abraham found favour with God. It was a truth, before Peter perceived it, *that in every nation he that feared God and wrought righteousness was accepted of him.* Multitudes will be brought to heaven out of *all nations* (Rev. vii. 9), and we are willing to hope there were many, very many, good people in the world, that lay out of the pale of God's covenant of peculiarity with Abraham, whose names were in the book of life, though not descended from any of the following families written in this book. *The Lord knows those that are his.* But Israel was a chosen nation, elect in type; and no other nation, in its national capacity, was so dignified and privileged as the Jewish nation was. That is the holy nation which is the subject of the sacred story; and therefore we are next to shake off all the seed of Abraham but the posterity of Jacob only, which were all incorporated into one nation and joined to the Lord, while the other descendants from Abraham, for aught that appears, were estranged both from God and from one another.

I. We shall have little to say of the *Ishmaelites.* They were the sons of the bondwoman, that were to be cast out and not to be heirs with the child of the promise; and their case was to represent that of the unbelieving Jews, who were rejected (Gal. iv. 22, &c.), and therefore there is little notice taken of that nation. Ishmael's twelve sons are just named here (*v.* 29—31), to show the performance of the promise God made to Abraham, in answer to his prayer for him, that, for Abraham's sake, he should become a great nation, and particularly that he should beget twelve princes, Gen. xvii. 20.

II. We shall have little to say of the *Midianites,* who descended from Abraham's children by Keturah. They were *children of the east* (probably Job was one of them), and were separated from Isaac, the heir of the promise (Gen. xxv. 6), and therefore they are only named here, *v.* 32. The sons of Jokshan, the son of Keturah, are named also, and the sons of Midian (*v.* 32, 33), who became most eminent, and perhaps gave denomination to all these families, as Judah to the Jews.

III. We shall not have much to say of the *Edomites* They had an inveterate enmity to God's Israel; yet because they descended from Esau, the son of Isaac, we have here an account of their families, and the names of some of their famous men, *v.* 35 to the end. Some slight differences there are between some of the names here, and as we had them in Gen. xxxvi., whence this whole account is taken. Three or four names that were written with a *Vau* there are written with a *Jod* here, probably the pronunciation being altered, as is usual in other languages. We now write many words very differently from what they were written but 200 years ago. Let us take occasion, from the reading of these genealogies, to think, 1. Of the multitudes that have gone through this world, have acted their part in it, and then quitted it. Job, even in his early day, saw not only *every man drawing after him,* but *innumerable before him,* Job xxi. 33. All these, and all theirs, had their day; many of them made a mighty noise and figure in the world; but their day came to fall, and their place knew them no more. The paths of death are trodden paths, but *vestigia nulla retrorsum—none can retrace their steps.* 2. Of the providence of God, which keeps up the generations of men, and so preserves that degenerate race, though guilty and obnoxious, in being upon earth. How easily could he cut it off without either a deluge or a conflagration! Write but all the children of men childless, as some are, and in a few years the earth will be eased of the burden under which it groans; but the divine patience lets the trees that cumber the ground not only grow, but propagate. As one generation, even of sinful men, passes away, another comes (Eccl. i. 4; Num. xxxii. 14), and will do so while the earth remains. *Destroy it not, for a blessing is in it.*

CHAP. II.

We have now come to what was principally intended, the register of the children of Israel, that distinguished people, that were to "dwell alone, and not be reckoned among the nations." Here we have, I. The names of the twelve sons of Israel, ver. 1, 2. II. An account of the tribe of Judah, which has the precedency, not so much for the sake of David as for the sake of the Son of David, our Lord, who sprang out of Judah, Heb. vii. 14. 1. The first descendants from Judah, down to Jesse, ver. 3—12. 2 The children of Jesse, ver. 13—17. 3. The posterity of Hezron, not only through Ram, from whom David came, but through Caleb (ver. 18—20), Segub (ver. 21—24), Jerahmeel (ver. 25—33, and so to ver. 41), and more by Caleb (ver. 42—49), with the family of Caleb the son of Hur, ver. 50—55. The best exposition we can have of this and the following chapters, and which will give the clearest view of them, is found in those genealogical tables which were published with some of the first impressions of the last English Bible about 100 years ago, and continued for some time; and it is a pity but they were revived in some of our later editions, for they are of great use to those who diligently search the scriptures. They are said to be drawn up by that great master in scripture-learning, Mr. Hugh Broughton. We meet with them sometimes in old Bibles.

THESE *are* the sons of Israel; Reuben, Simeon, Levi, and Judah, Issachar, and Zebulon, 2 Dan, Joseph, and Benjamin, Naphtali, Gad, and Asher. 3 The sons of Judah; Er, and Onan, and Shelah: *which* three were born unto him of the daughter of Shua the Canaanitess. And Er, the firstborn of Judah, was evil in the sight of the LORD; and he slew him. 4 And Tamar his daughter in law bare him Pharez and Zerah. All the sons of Judah *were* five. 5 The sons of Pharez; Hezron, and

Hamul. 6 And the sons of Zerah; Zimri, and Ethan, and Heman, and Calcol, and Dara: five of them in all. 7 And the sons of Carmi; Achar, the troubler of Israel, who transgressed in the thing accursed. 8 And the sons of Ethan; Azariah. 9 The sons also of Hezron, that were born unto him; Jerahmeel, and Ram, and Chelubai. 10 And Ram begat Amminadab; and Amminadab begat Nahshon, prince of the children of Judah; 11 And Nahshon begat Salma, and Salma begat Boaz, 12 And Boaz begat Obed, and Obed begat Jesse, 13 And Jesse begat his firstborn Eliab, and Abinadab the second, and Shimma the third, 14 Nethaneel the fourth, Raddai the fifth, 15 Ozem the sixth, David the seventh: 16 Whose sisters *were* Zeruiah, and Abigail. And the sons of Zeruiah; Abishai, and Joab, and Asahel, three. 17 And Abigail bare Amasa: and the father of Amasa *was* Jether the Ishmeelite.

Here is, I. The family of Jacob. His twelve sons are here named, that illustrious number so often celebrated almost throughout the whole Bible, from the first to the last book of it. At every turn we meet with the twelve tribes that descended from these twelve patriarchs. The personal character of several of them was none of the best (the first four were much blemished), and yet the covenant was entailed on their seed; for it was of grace, free grace, that it was said, *Jacob have I loved—not of works, lest any man should boast.*

II. The family of Judah. That tribe was most praised, most increased, and most dignified, of any of the tribes, and therefore the genealogy of it is the first and largest of them all. In the account here given of the first branches of that illustrious tree, of which Christ was to be the top branch, we meet, 1. With some that were very bad. Here is Er, Judah's eldest son, that was *evil in the sight of the Lord,* and was cut off, in the beginning of his days, by a stroke of divine vengeance: The *Lord slew him, v.* 3. His next brother, Onan, was no better, and fared no better. Here is Tamar, with whom Judah, her father-in-law, committed incest, *v.* 4. And here is Achan, called *Achar—a troubler,* that troubled Israel by taking of the accursed thing, *v.* 7. Note, The best and most honourable families may have those belonging to them that are blemishes. 2. With some that were very wise and good, as Heman and Ethan, Calcol and Dara, who were not perhaps the immediate sons of Zerah, but descendants from him, and are named because they were the glory of their father's house; for, when the Holy Ghost would magnify the wisdom of Solomon, he declares him wiser than these four men, who, though the sons of Mahol, are called Ezrahites, from Zerah, 1 Kings iv. 31. That four brothers should be eminent for wisdom and grace was a rare thing. 3. With some that were very great, as Nahshon, who was prince of the tribe of Judah when the camp of Israel was formed in the wilderness, and so led the van in that glorious march, and Salman, or Salmon, who was in that post of honour when they entered into Canaan, *v.* 10, 11.

III. The family of Jesse, of which a particular account is kept for the sake of David, and the Son of David, who is *a rod out of the stem of Jesse,* Isa. xi. 1. Hence it appears that David was a seventh son, and that his three great commanders, Joab, Abishai, and Asahel, were the sons of one of his sisters, and Amasa of another. Three of the four went down slain to the pit, though they were the terror of the mighty.

18 And Caleb the son of Hezron begat *children* of Azubah *his* wife, and of Jerioth: her sons *are* these; Jesher, and Shobab, and Ardon. 19 And when Azubah was dead, Caleb took unto him Ephrath, which bare him Hur. 20 And Hur begat Uri, and Uri begat Bezaleel. 21 And afterward Hezron went in to the daughter of Machir the father of Gilead, whom he married when he *was* threescore years old; and she bare him Segub. 22 And Segub begat Jair, who had three and twenty cities in the land of Gilead. 23 And he took Geshur, and Aram, with the towns of Jair, from them, with Kenath, and the towns thereof, *even* threescore cities. All these *belonged to* the sons of Machir the father of Gilead. 24 And after that Hezron was dead in Caleb-ephratah, then Abiah Hezron's wife bare him Ashur the father of Tekoa. 25 And the sons of Jerahmeel the firstborn of Hezron were, Ram the firstborn, and Bunah, and Oren, and Ozem, *and* Ahijah. 26 Jerahmeel had also another wife, whose name *was* Atarah; she *was* the mother of Onam. 27 And the sons of Ram the firstborn of Jerahmeel were, Maaz, and Jamin, and Eker. 28 And the sons of Onam were, Shammai, and

Jada. And the sons of Shammai; Nadab, and Abishur. 29 And the name of the wife of Abishur *was* Abihail, and she bare him Ahban, and Molid. 30 And the sons of Nadab; Seled, and Appaim: but Seled died without children. 31 And the sons of Appaim; Ishi. And the sons of Ishi; Sheshan. And the children of Sheshan; Ahlai. 32 And the sons of Jada the brother of Shammai; Jether, and Jonathan: and Jether died without children. 33 And the sons of Jonathan; Peleth, and Zaza. These were the sons of Jerahmeel. 34 Now Sheshan had no sons, but daughters. And Sheshan had a servant, an Egyptian, whose name *was* Jarha. 35 And Sheshan gave his daughter to Jarha his servant to wife; and she bare him Attai. 36 And Attai begat Nathan, and Nathan begat Zabad, 37 And Zabad begat Ephlal, and Ephlal begat Obed, 38 And Obed begat Jehu, and Jehu begat Azariah, 39 And Azariah begat Helez, and Helez begat Eleasah, 40 And Eleasah begat Sisamai, and Sisamai begat Shallum, 41 And Shallum begat Jekamiah, and Jekamiah begat Elishama. 42 Now the sons of Caleb the brother of Jerahmeel *were*, Mesha his firstborn, which *was* the father of Ziph; and the sons of Mareshah the father of Hebron. 43 And the sons of Hebron; Korah, and Tappuah, and Rekem, and Shema. 44 And Shema begat Raham, the father of Jorkoam: and Rekem begat Shammai. 45 And the son of Shammai *was* Maon: and Maon *was* the father of Beth-zur. 46 And Ephah, Caleb's concubine, bare Haran, and Moza, and Gazez: and Haran begat Gazez. 47 And the sons of Jahdai; Regem, and Jotham, and Gesham, and Pelet, and Ephah, and Shaaph. 48 Maachah, Caleb's concubine, bare Sheber, and Tirhanah. 49 She bare also Shaaph the father of Madmannah, Sheva the father of Machbenah, and the father of Gibea: and the daughter of Caleb *was* Achsa. 50 These were the sons of Caleb the son of Hur, the firstborn of Ephratah; Shobal the father of Kirjath-jearim, 51 Salma the father of Beth-lehem, Hareph the father of Beth-gader. 52 And Shobal the father of Kirjath-jearim had sons; Haroeh, *and* half of the Manahethites. 53 And the families of Kirjath-jearim; the Ithrites, and the Puhites, and the Shumathites, and the Mishraites; of them came the Zareathites, and the Eshtaulites. 54 The sons of Salma; Beth-lehem, and the Netophathites, Ataroth, the house of Joab, and half of the Manahethites, the Zorites. 55 And the families of the scribes which dwelt at Jabez; the Tirathites, the Shimeathites, *and* Suchathites. These *are* the Kenites that came of Hemath, the father of the house of Rechab.

The persons mentioned in the former paragraph are most of them such as we read of, and most of them such as we read much of, in other scriptures; but very few of those to whom this paragraph relates are mentioned any where else. It should seem, the tribe of Judah were more full and exact in their genealogies than any other of the tribes, in which we must acknowledge a special providence, for the clearing of the genealogy of Christ. 1. Here we find Bezaleel, who was head-workman in building the tabernacle, Exod. xxxi. 2. 2 Hezron, who was the son of Pharez (*v.* 5), was the father of all this progeny, his sons, Caleb and Jerahmeel, being very fruitful, and he himself likewise, even in his old age, for he left his wife pregnant when he died, *v.* 24. This Hezron was one of the seventy that went down with Jacob into Egypt, Gen. xlvi. 12. There his family thus increased, as other oppressed families there did. We cannot but suppose that he died during the Israelites' bondage in Egypt; and yet it is here said he died in Caleb-Ephratah (that is, Bethlehem), in the land of Canaan, *v.* 24. Perhaps, though the body of the people continued in Egypt, yet some that were more active than the rest, at least before their bondage came to be extreme, visited Canaan sometimes and got footing there, though afterwards they lost it. The achievements of Jair, here mentioned (*v.* 22, 23), we had an account of in Num. xxxii. 41; and, it is supposed, they were long after the conquest of Canaan. The Jews say, Hezron married his third wife when he was sixty years old (*v.* 21), and another afterwards (*v.* 24), because he had a great desire of posterity in the family of Pharez, from whom the Messiah was to descend. 3. Here is mention of one that *died without children* (*v.* 30), and another (*v.* 32), and of one that *had no sons, but daughters*, *v.* 34. Let those that are in any of these ways afflicted not think their case new or singular. Providence orders these affairs of families by an incontestable sovereignty, as pleaseth him, giving children, or withholding them, or giving all of one sex. He is not bound to please us, but we are bound to acquiesce in his good pleasure. To those that love him he will himself be better than ten sons, and give them in his house a place and a name better than of sons and daughters. Let not those therefore that are written childless envy the families that are built up and replenished. Shall our eye be evil because God's is good? 4. Here is mention of one who had an only daughter, and married her to his servant an Egyptian, *v.* 34, 35. If it be mentioned to his praise, we must suppose that this Egyptian was proselyted to the Jewish religion and that he was very eminent for wisdom and virtue, otherwise it would not have become a true-born Israelite to match a daughter to him, especially an only daughter. If Egyptians become converts, and servants do worthily, neither their parentage nor their servitude should be a bar to their preferment. Such a one this Egyptian servant might be that she who married him might live as happily with him as if she had married one of the rulers of her tribe. 5. The pedigree of several of these terminates, not in a person, but in a place or country, as one is said to be *the father of Kirjath-jearim* (*v.* 50), another of Bethlehem (*v.* 51), which was afterwards David's city, because these places fell to their lot in the division of the land. 6. Here are some that are said to be *families of scribes* (*v.* 55), such as kept up learning in their family, especially scripture-learning, and taught the people the good knowledge of God. Among all these great families we are glad to find some that were *families of scribes. Would to God that all the Lord's people were prophets*—all the families of Israel families of scribes, well instructed to the kingdom of heaven, and able to bring out of their treasury things new and old!

CHAP. III.

Of all the families of Israel none was so illustrious as the family of David. That is the family which was mentioned in the foregoing chapter, ver. 15. Here we have a full account of it. I. David's sons, ver. 1—9. II. His successors in the throne as long as the kingdom continued, ver. 10—16. III. The remains of his family in and after the captivity, ver. 17--24. From this family, "as concerning the flesh, Christ came."

NOW these were the sons of David, which were born unto him in Hebron; the firstborn Amnon, of Ahinoam the Jezreelitess; the second Daniel, of Abigail the Carmelitess: 2 The third, Absalom the son of Maachah the daughter of Talmai king of Geshur: the fourth, Adonijah the son of Haggith: 3 The fifth, Shephatiah of Abital: the sixth, Ithream by Eglah his wife. 4 *These* six were born unto him in Hebron; and there he reigned seven years and six months: and in Jerusalem he reigned thirty and three years. 5 And these were born unto him in Jerusalem; Shimea, and Shobab, and Nathan, and Solomon, four, of Bath-shua the daughter of Ammiel: 6 Ibhar also, and Elishama, and Eliphelet, 7 And Nogah, and Nepheg, and Japhia, 8 And Elishama, and Eliada, and Eliphelet, nine. 9 *These were* all the sons of David, beside the sons of the concubines, and Tamar their sister.

We had an account of David's sons, 2 Sam. iii. 2, &c., and v. 14, &c. 1. He had many sons; and no doubt wrote as he thought, Ps. cxxvii. 5. *Happy is the man that hath his quiver full of* these arrows. 2. Some of them were a grief to him, as Amnon, Absalom, and Adonijah; and we do not read of any of them that imitated his piety or devotion except Solomon, and he came far short of it. 3. One of them, which Bath-sheba bore to him, he called Nathan, probably in honour of Nathan the prophet, who reproved him for his sin in that matter and was instrumental to bring him to repentance. It seems he loved him the better for it as long as he lived. It is wisdom to esteem those our best friends that deal faithfully with us. From this son of David our Lord Jesus descended, as appears Luke iii. 31. 4. Here are two Elishamas, and two Eliphelets, *v.* 6, 8. Probably the two former were dead, and therefore David called two more by their names, which he would not have done if there had been any ill omen in this practice as some fancy. 5. David had many concubines; but their children are not named, as not worthy of the honour (*v.* 9), the rather because the concubines had dealt treacherously with David in the affair of Absalom. 6. Of all David's sons Solomon was chosen to succeed him, perhaps not for any personal merits (his wisdom was God's gift), but so, *Father, because it seemed good unto thee.*

10 And Solomon's son *was* Rehoboam, Abia his son, Asa his son, Jehoshaphat his son, 11 Joram his son, Ahaziah his son, Joash his son, 12 Amaziah his son, Azariah his son, Jotham his son, 13 Ahaz his son, Hezekiah his son, Manasseh his son, 14 Amon his son, Josiah his son. 15 And the sons of Josiah *were*, the firstborn Johanan, the second Jehoiakim, the third Zedekiah, the fourth Shallum. 16 And the sons of Jehoiakim; Jeconiah his son, Zedekiah his son. 17 And the sons of Jeconiah; Assir,

Salathiel, his son, 18 Malchiram also, and Pedaiah, and Shenazar, Jecamiah, Hoshama, and Nedabiah. 19 And the sons of Pedaiah *were*, Zerubbabel, and Shimei: and the sons of Zerubbabel; Meshullam, and Hananiah, and Shelomith their sister: 20 And Hashubah, and Ohel, and Berechiah, and Hasadiah, Jushab-hesed, five. 21 And the sons of Hananiah; Pelatiah, and Jesaiah: the sons of Rephaiah, the sons of Arnan, the sons of Obadiah, the sons of Shechaniah. 22 And the sons of Shechaniah; Shemaiah: and the sons of Shemaiah; Hattush, and Igeal, and Bariah, and Neariah, and Shaphat, six. 23 And the sons of Neariah; Elioenai, and Hezekiah, and Azrikam, three. 24 And the sons of Elioenai *were*, Hodaiah, and Eliashib, and Pelaiah, and Akkub, and Johanan, and Dalaiah, and Anani, seven.

David having nineteen sons, we may suppose them to have raised many noble families in Israel whom we never hear of in the history. But the scripture gives us an account only of the descendants of Solomon here, and of Nathan Luke iii. The rest had the honour to be the sons of David; but these only had the honour to be related to the Messiah. The sons of Nathan were his fathers as man, the sons of Solomon his predecessors as king. We have here, 1. The great and celebrated names by which the line of David is drawn down to the captivity, the kings of Judah in a lineal succession, the history of whom we have had at large in the two books of Kings and shall meet with again in the second book of Chronicles. Seldom has a crown gone in a direct line from father to son for seventeen descents together, as here. This was the recompence of David's piety. About the time of the captivity the lineal descent was interrupted, and the crown went from one brother to another and from a nephew to an uncle, which was a presage of the eclipsing of the glory of that house. 2. The less famous, and most of them very obscure, names, in which the house of David subsisted after the captivity. The only famous man of that house that we meet with at their return from captivity was Zerubbabel, elsewhere called *the son of Salathiel*, but appearing here to be his grandson (*v.* 17—19), which is usual in scripture. Belshazzar is called *Nebuchadnezzar's son*, but was his grandson. Salathiel is said to be *the son* of Jeconiah because adopted by him, and because, as some think, he succeeded him in the dignity to which he was restored by Evil-merodach. Otherwise Jeconiah was written childless: he was *the signet God plucked from his right hand* (Jer. xxii. 24), and in his room Zerubbabel was placed, and therefore God saith to him (Hag. ii. 23), *I will make thee as a signet.* The posterity of Zerubbabel here bear not the same names that they do in the genealogies (Matt. i., or Luke iii.), but those no doubt were taken from the then herald's office, the public registers which the priests kept of all the families of Judah, especially that of David. The last person named in this chapter is Anani, of whom bishop Patrick says that the Targum adds these words, *He is the king Messiah, who is to be revealed,* and some of the Jewish writers give this reason, because it is said (Dan. vii. 13), the son of man came *gnim gnanani—with the clouds of heaven.* The reason indeed is very foreign and far-fetched; but that learned man thinks it may be made use of as an evidence that their minds were always full of the thoughts of the Messiah and that they expected it would not be very long after the days of Zerubbabel before the set time of his approach would come.

CHAP. IV.

In this chapter we have, I. A further account of the genealogies of the tribe of Judah, the most numerous and most famous of all the tribes. The posterity of Shobal the son of Hur (ver. 1—4), of Ashur the posthumous son of Hezron (who was mentioned, ch. ii. 24), with something particular concerning Jabez (ver. 5—10), of Chelub and others (ver. 11—20), of Shelah, ver. 21—23. II. An account of the posterity and cities of Simeon, their conquest of Gedon, and of the Amalekites in Mount Seir, ver. 24—43.

THE sons of Judah; Pharez, Hezron, and Carmi, and Hur, and Shobal. 2 And Reaiah the son of Shobal begat Jahath; and Jahath begat Ahumai, and Lahad. These *are* the families of the Zorathites. 3 And these *were of* the father of Etam; Jezreel, and Ishma, and Idbash: and the name of their sister *was* Hazelelponi: 4 And Penuel the father of Gedor, and Ezer the father of Hushah. These *are* the sons of Hur, the firstborn of Ephratah, the father of Bethlehem. 5 And Ashur the father of Tekoa had two wives, Helah and Naarah. 6 And Naarah bare him Ahuzam, and Hepher, and Temeni, and Haahashtari. These *were* the sons of Naarah. 7 And the sons of Helah *were*, Zereth, and Jezoar, and Ethnan. 8 And Coz begat Anub, and Zobebah, and the families of Aharhel the son of Harum. 9 And Jabez was more honourable than his brethren: and his mother called his name Jabez, saying, Because I bare him with sorrow. 10 And Jabez called on the God of Israel, saying, Oh that thou wouldest bless me indeed, and enlarge my coast, and that thine hand might be with me, and that thou wouldest keep *me* from evil, that it may not grieve me! And God granted him that which he requested.

One reason, no doubt, why Ezra is here most particular in the register of the tribe of Judah is because it was that tribe which, with its appendages, Simeon, Benjamin, and Levi, made up the kingdom of Judah, which not only long survived the other tribes in Canaan, but in process of time, now when this was written, returned out of captivity, when the generality of the other tribes were lost in the kingdom of Assyria. The most remarkable person in this paragraph is Jabez. It is not said whose son he was, nor does it appear in what age he lived; but, it should seem, he was the founder of one of the families of Aharhel, mentioned *v.* 8. Here is,

I. The reason of his name: his mother gave him the name with this reason, *Because I bore him with sorrow, v.* 9. All children are borne with sorrow (for the sentence upon the woman is, *In sorrow shalt thou bring forth children)*, but some with much more sorrow than others. Usually the sorrow in bearing is afterwards forgotten *for joy that the child is born;* but here it seems it was so extraordinary that it was remembered when the child came to be circumcised, and care was taken to perpetuate the remembrance of it while he lived. Perhaps the mother called him Jabez, as Rachel called her son Benoni, when she was dying of the sorrow. Or, if she recovered it, yet thus she recorded it, 1. That it might be a continual memorandum to herself, to be thankful to God as long as she lived for supporting her under and bringing her through that sorrow. It may be of use to be often reminded of our sorrows, that we may always have such thoughts of things as we had in the day of our affliction, and may learn to rejoice with trembling. 2. That it might likewise be a memorandum to him what this world is into which she bore him, a vale of tears, in which he must expect *few days and full of trouble.* The sorrow he carried in his name might help to put a seriousness upon his spirit. It might also remind him to love and honour his mother, and labour, in every thing, to be a comfort to her who brought him into the world with so much sorrow. It is piety in children thus to requite their parents, 1 Tim. v. 4.

II. The eminence of his character: *He was more honourable than his brethren,* qualified above them by the divine grace and dignified above them by the divine providence; they did virtuously, but he excelled them all. Now the sorrow with which his mother bore him was abundantly recompensed. That son which of all her children cost her most dear she was most happy in, and was made glad in proportion to the affliction, Ps. xc. 15. We are not told upon what account he was *more honourable than his brethren,* whether because he raised a greater estate, or was preferred to the magistracy, or signalized himself in war; we have most reason to think it was upon the account of his learning and piety, not only because these, above any thing, put honour upon a man, but because we have reason to think that in these Jabez was eminent. 1. In learning, because we find that *the families of the scribes dwelt at Jabez (ch.* ii. 55), a city which, it is likely, took its name from him. The Jews say that he was a famous doctor of the law and left many disciples behind him. And it should seem, by the mentioning of him so abruptly here, that his name was well known when Ezra wrote this. 2. In piety, because we find here that he was a praying man. His inclination to devotion made him truly honourable, and by prayer he obtained those blessings from God which added much to his honour. The way to be truly great is to be truly good and to pray much.

III. The prayer he made, probably like Solomon's prayer for wisdom, just when he was setting out in the world. He set himself to acknowledge God in all his ways, put himself under the divine blessing and protection, and prospered accordingly. Perhaps these were the heads on which he enlarged in his daily prayers; for this purpose it was his constant practice to pray alone, and with his family, as Daniel. Some think that it was upon some particular occasion, when he was straitened and threatened by his enemies, that he prayed this prayer. Observe,

1. To whom he prayed, not to any of the gods of the Gentiles; no, he *called on the God of Israel,* the living and true God, who alone can hear and answer prayer, and in prayer had an eye to him as the God of Israel, a God in covenant with his people, the God with whom Jacob wrestled and prevailed and was thence called Israel.

2. What was the nature of his prayer. (1.) As the *margin* reads it, it was a solemn vow—*If thou wilt bless me indeed, &c.*, and then the sense is imperfect, but may easily be filled up from Jacob's vow, or some such like—*then thou shalt be my God.* He did not express his promise, but left it to be understood, either because he was afraid to promise in his own strength or because he resolved to devote himself entirely to God. He does, as it were, give God a blank paper, let him write what he pleases: "Lord, if thou wilt bless me and keep me, do what thou wilt with me, I will be at thy command and disposal for ever." (2.) As the *text* reads it, it was the language of a most ardent and affectionate desire: *O that thou wouldst bless me!*

3. What was the matter of his prayer.

Four things he prayed for :—(1.) That God would bless him indeed : "That, *blessing, thou wilt bless me,* bless me greatly with manifold and abundant blessings." Perhaps he had an eye to the promise God made to Abraham (Gen. xxii. 17), *In blessing, I will bless thee.* "Let that blessing of Abraham come upon me." Spiritual blessings are the best blessings ; and those are blessed indeed who are blessed with them. God's blessings are real things and produce real effects. We can but wish a blessing : he commands it. Those whom he blesses are blessed indeed. (2.) That he would enlarge his coast, that he would prosper his endeavours for the increase of what fell to his lot either by work or war. That God would enlarge our hearts, and so enlarge our portion in himself and in the heavenly Canaan, ought to be our desire and prayer. (3.) That God's hand might be with him. The prayer of Moses for this tribe of Judah was, That his own *hands might be sufficient for him,* Deut. xxxiii. 7 ; but Jabez expects not that this can be the case, unless he have *God's* hand with him and the presence of his power. God's hand with us, to lead us, protect us, strengthen us, and to work all our works in us and for us, is indeed a hand sufficient for us, all-sufficient. (4.) That he would keep him from evil, the evil of sin, the evil of trouble, all the evil designs of his enemies, that they might not hurt him, nor grieve him, nor make him a *Jabez* indeed, *a man of sorrow :* in the original there is an allusion to his name. *Father in heaven, deliver me from evil.*

4. What was the success of his prayer : *God granted him that which he requested,* prospered him remarkably, and gave him success in his undertakings, in his studies, in his worldly business, in his conflicts with the Canaanites, and so he became *more honourable than his brethren.* God was of old always ready to hear prayer, and *his ear is not yet heavy.*

11 And Chelub the brother of Shuah begat Mehir, which *was* the father of Eshton. 12 And Eshton begat Beth-rapha, and Paseah, and Tehinnah the father of Ir-nahash. These *are* the men of Rechah. 13 And the sons of Kenaz ; Othniel, and Seraiah : and the sons of Othniel ; Hathath. 14 And Meonothai begat Ophrah : and Seraiah begat Joab, the father of the valley of Charashim ; for they were craftsmen. 15 And the sons of Caleb the son of Jephunneh ; Iru, Elah, and Naam : and the sons of Elah, even Kenaz. 16 And the sons of Jehaleleel; Ziph, and Ziphah, Tiria, and Asareel. 17 And the sons of Ezra *were,* Jether, and Mered, and Epher, and Jalon : and she bare Miriam, and Shammai, and Ishbah the father of Eshtemoa. 18 And his wife Jehudijah bare Jered the father of Gedor, and Heber the father of Socho, and Jekuthiel the father of Zanoah. And these *are* the sons of Bithiah the daughter of Pharaoh, which Mered took. 19 And the sons of *his* wife Hodiah the sister of Naham, the father of Keilah the Garmite, and Eshtemoa the Maachathite. 20 And the sons of Shimon *were,* Amnon, and Rinnah, Ben-hanan, and Tilon. And the sons of Ishi *were,* Zoheth, and Ben-zoheth. 21 The sons of Shelah the son of Judah *were,* Er the father of Lecah, and Laadah the father of Mareshah, and the families of the house of them that wrought fine linen, of the house of Ashbea, 22 And Jokim, and the men of Chozeba, and Joash, and Saraph, who had the dominion in Moab, and Jashubi-lehem. And *these are* ancient things. 23 These *were* the potters, and those that dwelt among plants and hedges : there they dwelt with the king for his work.

We may observe in these verses, 1. That here is a whole family of craftsmen, handicraft tradesmen, that applied themselves to all sorts of manufactures, in which they were ingenious and industrious above their neighbours, *v.* 14. There was a valley where they lived which was, from them, called *the valley of craftsmen.* Those that are craftsmen are not therefore to be looked upon as mean men. These craftsmen, though two of a trade often disagree, yet chose to live together, for the improving of arts by comparing notes, and that they might support one another's reputation. 2. That one of these married the daughter of Pharaoh (*v.* 18), which was the common name of the kings of Egypt. If an Israelite in Egypt before the bondage began, while Joseph's merits were yet fresh in mind, was preferred to be the king's son-in-law, it is not to be thought strange : few Israelites could, like Moses, refuse an alliance with the court. 3. That another is said to be the *father of the house of those that wrought fine linen, v.* 21. It is inserted in their genealogy as their honour that they were the best weavers in the kingdom, and they brought up their children, from one generation to another, to the same business, not aiming to make them gentlemen. This Laadah is said to be the *father of those that wrought fine linen*, as before the flood Jubal is said to be *the father of musicians* and Jabal of *shepherds*, &c. His posterity inhabited the city of Mareshah, the manufacture or staple commodity of which place was linen-cloth, with which their kings and priests were clothed. 4. That another family had had *dominion in Moab*, but were now in *servitude in Babylon*, *v.* 22, 23. (1.) It was found among the *ancient things* that they had the *dominion in Moab*. Probably in David's time, when that country was conquered, they transplanted themselves thither, and were put in places of power there, which they held for several generations; but this was a great while ago, time out of mind. (2.) Their posterity were now potters and gardeners, as is supposed in Babylon, where they *dwelt with the king for his work*, got a good livelihood by their industry, and therefore cared not for returning with their brethren to their own land, after the years of captivity had expired. Those that now have dominion know not what their posterity may be reduced to, nor what mean employments they may be glad to take up with. But those were unworthy the name of *Israelites* that would dwell among *plants and hedges* rather than be at the pains to return to Canaan.

24 The sons of Simeon *were*, Nemuel, and Jamin, Jarib, Zerah, *and* Shaul: 25 Shallum his son, Mibsam his son, Mishma his son. 26 And the sons of Mishma; Hamuel his son, Zacchur his son, Shimei his son. 27 And Shimei had sixteen sons and six daughters; but his brethren had not many children, neither did all their family multiply, like to the children of Judah. 28 And they dwelt at Beer-sheba, and Moladah, and Hazar-shual, 29 And at Bilhah, and at Ezem, and at Tolad, 30 And at Bethuel, and at Hormah, and at Ziklag, 31 And at Beth-marcaboth, and Hazar-susim, and at Beth-birei, and at Shaaraim. These *were* their cities unto the reign of David. 32 And their villages *were*, Etam, and Ain, Rimmon, and Tochen, and Ashan, five cities: 33 And all their villages that *were* round about the same cities, unto Baal. These *were* their habitations, and their genealogy. 34 And Meshobab, and Jamlech, and Joshah the son of Amaziah, 35 And Joel, and Jehu the son of Josibiah, the son of Seraiah, the son of Asiel, 36 And Elioenai, and Jaakobah, and Jeshohaiah, and Asaiah, and Adiel, and Jesimiel, and Benaiah, 37 And Ziza the son of Shiphi, the son of Allon, the son of Jedaiah, the son of Shimri, the son of Shemaiah; 38 These mentioned by *their* names *were* princes in their families: and the house of their fathers increased greatly. 39 And they went to the entrance of Gedor, *even* unto the east side of the valley, to seek pasture for their flocks. 40 And they found fat pasture and good, and the land *was* wide, and quiet, and peaceable; for *they* of Ham had dwelt there of old. 41 And these written by name came in the days of Hezekiah king of Judah, and smote their tents, and the habitations that were found there, and destroyed them utterly unto this day, and dwelt in their rooms: because *there was* pasture there for their flocks. 42 And *some* of them, *even* of the sons of Simeon, five hundred men, went to mount Seir, having for their captains Pelatiah, and Neariah, and Rephaiah, and Uzziel, the sons of Ishi. 43 And they smote the rest of the Amalekites that were escaped, and dwelt there unto this day.

We have here some of the genealogies of the tribe of Simeon (though it was not a tribe of great note), especially the princes of that tribe, *v.* 38. Of this tribe it is said that they *increased greatly*, but *not like the children of Judah*, *v.* 27. Those whom God increases ought to be thankful, though they see others that are more increased. Here observe, 1. The cities allotted them (*v.* 28), of which see Joshua xix. 1, &c. When it is said that they were theirs *unto the reign of David* (*v.* 31) intimation is given that when the ten tribes revolted from the house of David many of the Simeonites quitted these cities, because they lay within Judah, and seated themselves elsewhere. 2. The ground they got elsewhere. When those of this tribe that revolted from the house of David were carried captive with the rest into Assyria those that adhered to Judah were remarkably owned of God and prospered in their endeavours to enlarge their coasts. It was in the days of Hezekiah that a generation of Simeonites, whose tribe had long crouched and truckled, was animated to make these bold efforts. (1.) Some of them attacked a place in Arabia, as it should seem, called *the entrance of Gedor*, inhabited by the posterity of accursed Ham (*v.* 40), made themselves masters of it, and dwelt there.

This adds to the glory of Hezekiah's pious reign, that, as his kingdom in general prospered, so did particular families. It is said that they found fat pastures, and yet *the land was quiet;* even when the kings of Assyria were giving disturbance to all their neighbours this land escaped their alarms. The inhabitants being shepherds, who molested none, were not themselves molested, till the Simeonites came and drove them out and succeeded them, not only in the plenty, but in the peace, of their land. Those who dwell (as we do) in a fruitful country, and whose land is wide, and quiet, and peaceable, have reason to own themselves indebted to that God who *appoints the bounds of our habitation.* (2.) Others of them, to the number of 500, under the command of four brethren, here named, made a descent upon Mount Seir, and smote the remainder of the devoted Amalekites, and took possession of their country, *v.* 42, 43. Now the curses on Ham and Amalek had a further accomplishment, when they seemed dormant, if not dead; as had also the curse on Simeon, that he should be divided and scattered (Gen. xlix. 7): yet to him it was turned into a blessing, for the families of Simeon, which thus transplanted themselves into those distant countries, are said to *dwell there unto this day* (*v.* 43), by which it should seem they escaped the calamities of the captivity. Providence sometimes sends those out of trouble that are designed for preservation.

CHAP. V.

This chapter gives us some account of the two tribes and a half that were seated on the other side Jordan. I. Of Reuben, ver. 1—10. II. Of Gad, ver. 11—17. III. Of the half-tribe of Manasseh, ver. 23, 24. IV. Concerning all three acting in conjunction we are told, 1. How they conquered the Hagarites, ver. 18—22. 2. How they were, at length, themselves conquered, and made captives, by the king of Assyria, because they had forsaken God, ver. 25, 26.

NOW the sons of Reuben the firstborn of Israel, (for he *was* the firstborn; but, forasmuch as he defiled his father's bed, his birthright was given unto the sons of Joseph the son of Israel: and the genealogy is not to be reckoned after the birthright. 2 For Judah prevailed above his brethren, and of him *came* the chief ruler; but the birthright *was* Joseph's:) 3 The sons, *I say*, of Reuben the firstborn of Israel *were*, Hanoch, and Pallu, Hezron, and Carmi. 4 The sons of Joel; Shemaiah his son, Gog his son, Shimei his son, 5 Micah his son, Reaia his son, Baal his son, 6 Beerah his son, whom Tilgath-pilneser king of Assyria carried away *captive:* he *was* prince of the Reubenites. 7 And his brethren by their families, when the genealogy of their generations was reckoned, *were* the chief, Jeiel, and Zechariah, 8 And Bela the son of Azaz, the son of Shema, the son of Joel, who dwelt in Aroer, even unto Nebo and Baal-meon: 9 And eastward he inhabited unto the entering in of the wilderness from the river Euphrates: because their cattle were multiplied in the land of Gilead. 10 And in the days of Saul they made war with the Hagarites, who fell by their hand: and they dwelt in their tents throughout all the east *land* of Gilead. 11 And the children of Gad dwelt over against them, in the land of Bashan unto Salcah: 12 Joel the chief, and Shapham the next, and Jaanai, and Shaphat in Bashan. 13 And their brethren of the house of their fathers *were*, Michael, and Meshullam, and Sheba, and Jorai, and Jachan, and Zia, and Heber, seven. 14 These *are* the children of Abihail the son of Huri, the son of Jaroah, the son of Gilead, the son of Michael, the son of Jeshishai, the son of Jahdo, the son of Buz; 15 Ahi the son of Abdiel, the son of Guni, chief of the house of their fathers. 16 And they dwelt in Gilead in Bashan, and in her towns, and in all the suburbs of Sharon, upon their borders. 17 All these were reckoned by genealogies in the days of Jotham king of Judah, and in the days of Jeroboam king of Israel.

We have here an extract out of the genealogies,

I. Of the tribe of Reuben, where we have,

1. The reason why this tribe is thus postponed. It is confessed that Reuben was the first-born of Israel, and, upon that account, might challenge the precedency; but he forfeited his birthright by defiling his father's concubine, and was, for that, sentenced *not to excel*, Gen. xlix. 4. Sin lessens men, thrusts them down from their excellency. Seventh-commandment sins especially leave an indelible stain upon men's names and families, a reproach which time will not wipe away. Reuben's seed, to the last, bear the disgrace of Reuben's sin. Yet, though that tribe was degraded, it was not discarded or disinherited. The sullying of the honour of an Israelite is not the losing of his happiness. Reuben loses his birthright, yet it does not devolve upon Simeon

the next in order; for it was typical, and therefore must attend, not the course of nature, but the choice of grace. The advantages of the birthright were dominion and a double portion. Reuben having forfeited these, it was thought too much that both should be transferred to any one, and therefore they were divided. (1.) Joseph had the double portion; for two tribes descended from him, Ephraim and Manasseh, each of whom had a child's part (for so Jacob by faith blessed them, Heb. xi. 21; Gen. xlviii. 15, 22), and each of those tribes was as considerable, and made as good a figure, as any one of the twelve, except Judah. But, (2.) Judah had the dominion; on him the dying patriarch entailed the sceptre, Gen. xlix. 10. Of him came the chief ruler, David first, and, in the fulness of time, Messiah the Prince, Mic. v. 2. This honour was secured to Judah, though the birthright was Joseph's; and, having this, he needed not envy Joseph the double portion.

2. The genealogy of the princes of this tribe, the chief family of it (many, no doubt, being omitted), to Beerah, who was head of this clan when the king of Assyria carried them captive, *v.* 4—6. Perhaps he is mentioned as prince of the Reubenites at that time because he did not do his part to prevent the captivity.

3. The enlargement of the coasts of this tribe. They increasing, and their cattle being multiplied, they crowded out their neighbours the Hagarites, and extended their conquests, though not to the river Euphrates, yet to the wilderness which abutted upon that river, *v.* 9, 10. Thus God did for his people as he promised them: he cast out the enemy from before them by little and little, and gave them their land as they had occasion for it, Exod. xxiii. 30.

II. Of the tribe of Gad. Some great families of that tribe are here named (*v.* 12), seven that were the children of Abihail, whose pedigree is carried upwards from the son to the father (*v.* 14, 15), as that *v.* 4, 5, is brought downwards from father to son. These genealogies were perfected in the days of Jotham king of Judah, but were begun some years before, in the reign of Jeroboam II. king of Israel. What particular reason there was for taking these accounts then does not appear; but it was just before they were carried away captive by the Assyrians, as appears 2 Kings xv. 29, 31. When the judgments of God were ready to break out against them for their wretched degeneracy and apostasy then were they priding themselves in their genealogies, that they were the children of the covenant; as the Jews, in our Saviour's time, who, when they were ripe for ruin, boasted, *We have Abraham to our father.* Or there might be a special providence in it, and a favourable intimation that though they were, for the present, cast out, they were not cast off for ever. What we design to call for hereafter we keep an inventory of.

18 The sons of Reuben, and the Gadites, and half the tribe of Manasseh, of valiant men, men able to bear buckler and sword, and to shoot with bow, and skilful in war, *were* four and forty thousand seven hundred and threescore, that went out to the war. 19 And they made war with the Hagarites, with Jetur, and Nephish, and Nodab. 20 And they were helped against them, and the Hagarites were delivered into their hand, and all that *were* with them: for they cried to God in the battle, and he was intreated of them; because they put their trust in him. 21 And they took away their cattle; of their camels fifty thousand, and of sheep two hundred and fifty thousand, and of asses two thousand, and of men a hundred thousand. 22 For there fell down many slain, because the war *was* of God. And they dwelt in their steads until the captivity. 23 And the children of the half tribe of Manasseh dwelt in the land: they increased from Bashan unto Baal-hermon and Senir, and unto mount Hermon. 24 And these *were* the heads of the house of their fathers, even Epher, and Ishi, and Eliel, and Azriel, and Jeremiah, and Hodaviah, and Jahdiel, mighty men of valour, famous men, *and* heads of the house of their fathers. 25 And they transgressed against the God of their fathers, and went a whoring after the gods of the people of the land, whom God destroyed before them. 26 And the God of Israel stirred up the spirit of Pul king of Assyria, and the spirit of Tilgath-pilneser king of Assyria, and he carried them away, even the Reubenites, and the Gadites, and the half tribe of Manasseh, and brought them unto Halah, and Habor, and Hara, and to the river Gozan, unto this day.

The heads of the half-tribe of Manasseh, that were seated on the other side Jordan, are named here, *v.* 23, 24. Their lot, at first, was Bashan only; but afterwards they increased so much in wealth and power that they spread far north, even unto Hermon.

Two things only are here recorded concerning these tribes on the other side Jordan, in which they were all concerned. They all shared,

I. In a glorious victory over the Hagarites, so the Ishmaelites were now called, to remind them that they were *the sons of the bond-woman*, that was *cast out*. We are not told when this victory was obtained: whether it be the same with that of the Reubenites (which is said *v.* 10 to be *in the days of Saul)*, or whether that success of one of these tribes animated and excited the other two to join with them in another expedition, is not certain. It seems, though in Saul's time the common interests of the kingdom were weak and low, some of the tribes that acted separately did well for themselves. We are here told,

1. What a brave army these frontier-tribes brought into the field against the Hagarites, 44,000 men and upwards, all strong, and brave, and skilful in war, so many effective men, that knew how to manage their weapons, *v.* 18. How much more considerable might Israel have been than they were in the time of the judges if all the tribes had acted in conjunction!

2. What course they took to engage God for them: They *cried to God*, and *put their trust in him, v.* 20. Now they acted as Israelites indeed. (1.) As the seed of believing Abraham, they *put their trust in God*. Though they had a powerful army, they relied not on that, but on the divine power. They depended on the commission they had from God to wage war with their neighbours for the enlarging of their coasts, if there was occasion, even with those that were very far off, besides the devoted nations. See Deut. xx. 15. They depended on God's providence to give them success. (2.) As the seed of praying Jacob, *they cried unto God*, especially *in the battle*, when perhaps, at first, they were in danger of being overpowered. See the like done, 2 Chron. xiii. 14. In distress, God expects we should cry to him; he distrains upon us for this tribute, this rent. In our spiritual conflicts, we must look up to heaven for strength; and it is the believing prayer that will be the prevailing prayer.

3. We are told what success they had: *God was entreated of them*, though need drove them to him; so ready is he to hear and answer prayer. They were helped against their enemies; for God never yet failed any that trusted in him. And then they routed the enemy's army, though far superior in number to theirs, slew many (*v.* 22), took 100,000 prisoners, enriched themselves greatly with the spoil, and settled themselves in their country (*v.* 21, 22), and all this *because the war was of God*, undertaken in his fear and carried on in a dependence upon him. If the battle be the Lord's, there is reason to hope it will be successful. Then we may expect to prosper in any enterprise, and then only, when we take God along with us.

II. They shared, at length, in an inglorious captivity. Had they kept close to God and their duty, they would have continued to enjoy both their ancient lot and their new conquests; but they *transgressed against the God of their fathers, v.* 25. They lay upon the borders, and conversed most with the neighbouring nations, by which means they learned their idolatrous usages and transmitted the infection to the other tribes; for this God had a controversy with them. He was *a husband to them*, and no marvel that his jealousy burnt like fire when they *went a whoring after other gods*. Justly is a bill of divorce given to the adulteress. *God stirred up the spirit of the kings of Assyria*, first one and then another, against them, served his own purposes by the designs of those ambitious monarchs, employed them to chastise these revolters first, and, when that humbled them not, then wholly to *root them out, v.* 26. These tribes were first placed, and they were first displaced. They would have the best land, not considering that it lay most exposed. But those who are governed more by sense than by reason or faith in their choices may expect to fare accordingly.

CHAP. VI.

Though Joseph and Judah shared between them the forfeited honours of the birthright, yet Levi was first of all the tribes, dignified and distinguished with an honour more valuable than either the precedency or the double portion, and that was the priesthood. That tribe God set apart for himself; it was Moses's tribe, and perhaps for his sake was thus favoured. Of that tribe we have an account in this chapter. I. Their pedigree, the first fathers of the tribe (ver. 1—3), the line of the priests, from Aaron to the captivity (ver. 4—15), and of some other of their families, ver. 16—30. II. Their work, the work of the Levites (ver. 31—48), of the priests, ver. 49—53. III. The cities appointed them in the land of Canaan, ver. 54—81.

THE sons of Levi; Gershom, Kohath, and Merari 2 And the sons of Kohath; Amram, Izhar, and Hebron, and Uzziel. 3 And the children of Amram; Aaron, and Moses, and Miriam. The sons also of Aaron; Nadab, and Abihu, Eleazar, and Ithamar. 4 Eleazar begat Phinehas, Phinehas begat Abishua, 5 And Abishua begat Bukki, and Bukki begat Uzzi, 6 And Uzzi begat Zerahiah, and Zerahiah begat Meraioth, 7 Meraioth begat Amariah, and Amariah begat Ahitub, 8 And Ahitub begat Zadok, and Zadok begat Ahimaaz, 9 And Ahimaaz begat Azariah, and Azariah begat Johanan, 10 And Johanan begat Azariah, (he *it is* that executed the priest's office in the temple that Solomon built in Jerusalem:) 11 And Azariah begat Amariah, and Amariah begat Ahitub. 12 And Ahitub begat Zadok, and Zadok begat Shallum, 13 And Shallum begat Hilkiah, and Hilkiah begat Azariah, 14 And Azariah begat Seraiah, and Seraiah begat Jehozadak, 15 And Jehozadak went *into captivity* when the LORD carried away Judah and Jerusalem by the hand of Nebuchadnezzar. 16 The sons of Levi; Gershom, Kohath, and Merari. 17 And these *be* the names of the sons of Gershom; Libni, and Shimei. 18 And the sons of Kohath *were*, Amram, and Izhar, and Hebron, and Uzziel. 19 The sons of Merari; Mahli, and Mushi. And these *are* the families of the Levites according to their fathers. 20 Of Gershom; Libni his son, Jahath his son, Zimmah his son, 21 Joah his son, Iddo his son, Zerah his son, Jeaterai his son. 22 The sons of Kohath; Amminadab his son, Korah his son, Assir his son, 23 Elkanah his son, Ebiasaph his son, and Assir his son, 24 Tahath his son, Uriel his son, Uzziah his son, and Shaul his son. 25 And the sons of Elkanah; Amasai, and Ahimoth. 26 *As for* Elkanah: the sons of Elkanah; Zophai his son, and Nahath his son, 27 Eliab his son, Jeroham his son, Elkanah his son. 28 And the sons of Samuel; the firstborn Vashni, and Abiah. 29 The sons of Merari; Mahli, Libni his son, Shimei his son, Uzza his son, 30 Shimei his son, Haggiah his son, Asaiah his son.

The priests and Levites were more concerned than any other Israelites to preserve their pedigree clear and to be able to prove it, because all the honours and privileges of their office depended upon their descent. And we read of those who, though perhaps they really were children of the priests, yet, because they could not find the register of their genealogies, nor make out their descent by any authentic record, were, *as polluted, put from the priesthood,* and forbidden to eat of the holy things, Ezra ii. 62, 63. It is but very little that is here recorded of the genealogies of this sacred tribe. 1. The first fathers of it are here named twice, *v.* 1, 16. Gershom, Kohath, and Merari, are three names which we were very conversant with in the book of Numbers, when the families of the Levites were marshalled and had their work assigned them. Aaron, and Moses, and Miriam, we have known much more of than their names, and cannot pass them over here without remembering that this was that Moses and Aaron whom God honoured in making them the instruments of Israel's deliverance and settlement and *figures of him that was to come,* Moses as a prophet and Aaron as a priest. And the mention of Nadab and Abihu (though, having no children, there was no occasion to bring them into the genealogy) cannot but remind us of the terrors of that divine justice which they were made monuments of for offering strange fire, that we may always fear before him. 2. The line of Eleazar, the successor of Aaron, is here drawn down to the time of the captivity, *v.* 4—15. It begins with Eleazar, who came out of the house of bondage in Egypt, and ends with Jehozadak, who went into the house of bondage in Babylon. Thus, for their sins, they were left as they were found, which might also intimate that the Levitical priesthood did not make any thing perfect, but this was to be done by the *bringing in of a better hope.* All these here named were not high priests; for, in the time of the judges, that dignity was, upon some occasion or other, brought into the family of Ithamar, of which Eli was; but in Zadok it returned again to the right line. Of Azariah it is here said (*v.* 10), *He it is that executed the priest's office in the temple that Solomon built.* It is supposed that this was that Azariah who bravely opposed the presumption of king Uzziah when he invaded the priest's office (2 Chron. xxvi. 17, 18), though he ventured his neck by so doing. This was done like a priest, like one that was truly zealous for his God. He that thus boldly maintained and defended the priest's office, and made good its barriers against such a daring insult, might well be said to *execute it;* and this honour is put upon him for it; while Urijah, one of his successors, for a base compliance with king Ahaz, in building him an idolatrous altar, has the disgrace put upon him of being left out of this genealogy, as perhaps some others are. But some think that this remark upon this Azariah should have been added to his grandfather of the same name (*v.* 9), who was the son of Ahimaaz, and that he was the priest who first officiated in Solomon's temple. 3. Some other of the families of the Levites are here accounted for. One of the families of Gershom (that of Libni) is here drawn down as far as Samuel, who had the honour of a prophet added to that of a Levite. One of the families of Merari (that of Mahli) is likewise drawn down for several descents, *v.* 29, 30.

31 And these *are they* whom David set over the service of song in the house of the LORD, after that the ark had rest. 32 And they ministered before the dwelling place of the

tabernacle of the congregation with singing, until Solomon had built the house of the LORD in Jerusalem: and *then* they waited on their office according to their order. 33 And these *are* they that waited with their children. Of the sons of the Kohathites: Heman a singer, the son of Joel, the son of Shemuel, 34 The son of Elkanah, the son of Jeroham, the son of Eliel, the son of Toah, 35 The son of Zuph, the son of Elkanah, the son of Mahath, the son of Amasai, 36 The son of Elkanah, the son of Joel, the son of Azariah, the son of Zephaniah, 37 The son of Tahath, the son of Assir, the son of Ebiasaph, the son of Korah, 38 The son of Izhar, the son of Kohath, the son of Levi, the son of Israel. 39 And his brother Asaph, who stood on his right hand, *even* Asaph the son of Berachiah, the son of Shimea, 40 The son of Michael, the son of Baaseiah, the son of Malchiah, 41 The son of Ethni, the son of Zerah, the son of Adaiah, 42 The son of Ethan, the son of Zimmah, the son of Shimei, 43 The son of Jahath, the son of Gershom, the son of Levi. 44 And their brethren the sons of Merari *stood* on the left hand: Ethan the son of Kishi, the son of Abdi, the son of Malluch, 45 The son of Hashabiah, the son of Amaziah, the son of Hilkiah, 46 The son of Amzi, the son of Bani, the son of Shamer, 47 The son of Mahli, the son of Mushi, the son of Merari, the son of Levi. 48 Their brethren also the Levites *were* appointed unto all manner of service of the tabernacle of the house of God. 49 But Aaron and his sons offered upon the altar of the burnt offering, and on the altar of incense, *and were appointed* for all the work of the *place* most holy, and to make an atonement for Israel, according to all that Moses the servant of God had commanded. 50 And these *are* the sons of Aaron; Eleazar his son, Phinehas his son, Abishua his son, 51 Bukki his son, Uzzi his son, Zerahiah his son, 52 Meraioth his son, Amariah his son, Ahitub his son, 53 Zadok his son, Ahimaaz his son.

When the Levites were first ordained in the wilderness much of the work then appointed them lay in carrying and taking care of the tabernacle and the utensils of it, while they were in their march through the wilderness. In David's time their number was increased; and, though the greater part of them were dispersed all the nation over, to teach the people the good knowledge of the Lord, yet those that attended the house of God were so numerous that there was not constant work for them all; and therefore David, by special commission and direction from God, new-modelled the Levites, as we shall find in the latter part of this book. Here we are told what the work was which he assigned them.

I. Singing-work, *v.* 31. David was raised up on high to be the sweet psalmist of Israel (2 Sam. xxiii. 1), not only to pen psalms, but to appoint the singing of them in the house of the Lord (not so much because he was musical as because he was devout), and this he did *after that the ark had rest.* While that was in captivity, obscure, and unsettled, the harps were hung upon the willow-trees: singing was then thought unseasonable (when the bridegroom is taken away they shall fast); but the harps being resumed, and the songs revived, at the bringing up of the ark, they were continued afterwards. For we should rejoice as much in the prolonging of our spiritual privileges as in the restoring of them. When the service of the ark was much superseded by its rest they had other work cut out for them (for Levites should never be idle) and were employed in the service of song. Thus when the people of God come to the rest which remains for them above they shall take leave of all their burdens and be employed in everlasting songs. These singers kept up that service in the tabernacle till the temple was built, and then they *waited on their office* there, *v.* 32. When they came to that stately magnificent house they kept as close both to their office and to their order as they had done in the tabernacle. It is a pity that the preferment of the Levites should ever make them remiss in their business. We have here an account of the three great masters who were employed in the service of the sacred song, with their respective families; for they *waited with their children,* that is, such as descended from them or were allied to them, *v.* 33. Heman, Asaph, and Ethan, were the three that were appointed to this service, one of each of the three houses of the Levites, that there might be an equality in the distribution of this work and honour, and that every one might know his post, such an admirable order was there in this choir service. 1. Of the house of Kohath was Heman with his family (*v.* 33), a man of a sorrowful spirit, if it be the same Heman that penned the 88th psalm, and yet a singer. He was the grandson of Samuel the prophet, the son of Joel, of whom it is said that *he walked not in the ways of Samuel* (1 Sam. viii. 2, 3); but it seems, though the son did not, the grandson did. Thus does the blessing entailed on the seed of the upright sometimes pass over one generation and fasten upon the next. And this Heman, though the grandson of that mighty prince, did not think it below him to be a precentor in the house of God. David himself was willing to be a door-keeper. Rather we may look upon this preferment of the grandson in the church as a recompence for the humble modest resignation which the grandfather made of his authority in the state. Many such ways God has of making up his people's losses and balancing their disgraces. Perhaps David, in making Heman the chief, had some respect to his old friend Samuel. 2. Of the house of Gershom was Asaph, called *his brother*, because in the same office and of the same tribe, though of another family. He was posted on Heman's right hand in the choir, *v.* 39. Several of the psalms bear his name, being either penned by him or tuned by him as the chief musician. It is plain that he was the penman of some psalms; for we read of those that praised the Lord in the words of David and of Asaph. He was a seer as well as a singer, 2 Chron. xxix. 30. His pedigree is traced up here, through names utterly unknown, as high as Levi, *v.* 39--43. 3. Of the house of Merari was Ethan (*v.* 44), who was appointed to Heman's left hand. His pedigree is also traced up to Levi, *v.* 47. If these were the Heman and Ethan that penned the 88th and 89th psalms, there appears no reason here why they should be called *Ezrahites* (see the titles of those psalms), as there does why those should be called so who are mentioned *ch.* ii. 6, and who were the sons of Zerah.

II. There was serving-work, abundance of service to be done *in the tabernacle of the house of God* (*v.* 48), to provide water and fuel,—to wash and sweep, and carry out ashes,—to kill, and flay, and boil the sacrifices; and to all such services there were Levites appointed, those of other families, or perhaps those that were not fit to be singers, that had either no good voice or no good ear. *As every one has received the gift, so let him minister.* Those that could not sing must not therefore be laid aside as good for nothing; though they were not fit for that service, there was other service they might be useful in.

III. There was sacrificing-work, and that was to be done by the priests only, *v.* 49. They only were to sprinkle the blood and burn the incense; as for *the work of the most holy place*, that was to be done by the high priest only. Each had his work, and they both needed one another and both helped one another in it. Concerning the work of the priests we are here told, 1. What was the end they were to have in their eye. They were to *make an atonement for Israel*, to mediate between the people and God; not to magnify and enrich themselves, but to serve the public. They were *ordained for men*. 2. What was the rule they were to have in their eye. They presided in God's house, yet must do as they were bidden, according to all that God commanded. That law the highest are subject to.

54 Now these *are* their dwelling places throughout their castles in their coasts, of the sons of Aaron, of the families of the Kohathites: for their's was the lot. 55 And they gave them Hebron in the land of Judah, and the suburbs thereof round about it. 56 But the fields of the city, and the villages thereof, they gave to Caleb the son of Jephunneh. 57 And to the sons of Aaron they gave the cities of Judah, *namely*, Hebron, *the city* of refuge, and Libnah with her suburbs, and Jattir, and Eshtemoa, with their suburbs, 58 And Hilen with her suburbs, Debir with her suburbs, 59 And Ashan with her suburbs, and Beth-shemesh with her suburbs: 60 And out of the tribe of Benjamin; Geba with her suburbs, and Alemeth with her suburbs, and Anathoth with her suburbs. All their cities throughout their families *were* thirteen cities. 61 And unto the sons of Kohath, *which were* left of the family of that tribe, *were cities given* out of the half tribe, *namely*, *out of* the half *tribe* of Manasseh, by lot, ten cities. 62 And to the sons of Gershom throughout their families out of the tribe of Issachar, and out of the tribe of Asher, and out of the tribe of Naphtali, and out of the tribe of Manasseh in Bashan, thirteen cities. 63 Unto the sons of Merari *were given* by lot, throughout their families, out of the tribe of Reuben, and out of the tribe of Gad, and out of the tribe of Zebulun, twelve cities. 64 And the children of Israel gave to the Levites *these* cities with their suburbs. 65 And they gave by lot out of the tribe of the children of Judah, and out of the tribe of the children of Simeon, and out of the tribe of the children of Benjamin, these cities, which are called

by *their* names. 66 And *the residue* of the families of the sons of Kohath had cities of their coasts out of the tribe of Ephraim. 67 And they gave unto them, *of* the cities of refuge, Shechem in mount Ephraim with her suburbs; *they gave* also Gezer with her suburbs, 68 And Jokmeam with her suburbs, and Beth-horon with her suburbs, 69 And Aijalon with her suburbs, and Gath-rimmon with her suburbs: 70 And out of the half tribe of Manasseh; Aner with her suburbs, and Bileam with her suburbs, for the family of the remnant of the sons of Kohath. 71 Unto the sons of Gershom *were given* out of the family of the half tribe of Manasseh, Golan in Bashan with her suburbs, and Ashtaroth with her suburbs: 72 And out of the tribe of Issachar; Kedesh with her suburbs, Daberath with her suburbs, 73 And Ramoth with her suburbs, and Anem with her suburbs; 74 And out of the tribe of Asher; Mashal with her suburbs, and Abdon with her suburbs, 75 And Hukok with her suburbs, and Rehob with her suburbs: 76 And out of the tribe of Naphtali; Kedesh in Galilee with her suburbs, and Hammon with her suburbs, and Kirjathaim with her suburbs. 77 Unto the rest of the children of Merari *were given* out of the tribe of Zebulun, Rimmon with her suburbs, Tabor with her suburbs: 78 And on the other side Jordan by Jericho, on the east side of Jordan, *were given them* out of the tribe of Reuben, Bezer in the wilderness with her suburbs, and Jahzah with her suburbs, 79 Kedemoth also with her suburbs, and Mephaath with her suburbs: 80 And out of the tribe of Gad; Ramoth in Gilead with her suburbs, and Mahanaim with her suburbs, 81 And Heshbon with her suburbs, and Jazer with her suburbs.

We have here an account of the Levites' cities. They are here called their *castles* (*v.* 54), not only because walled and fortified, and well guarded by the country (for it is the interest of every nation to protect its ministers), but because they and their possessions were, in a particular manner, the care of the divine providence: as God was their portion, so God was their protection; and a cottage will be a castle to those that abide under the shadow of the Almighty. This account is much the same with that which we had, Josh. xxi. We need not be critical in comparing them (what good will it do us?) nor will it do any hurt to the credit of the holy scripture if the names of some of the places be not spelt just the same here that they were there. We know it is common for cities to have several names. *Sarum* and *Salisbury*, *Salop* and *Shrewsbury*, are more unlike than *Hilen* (*v.* 58) and *Holon* (Josh. xxi. 15), *Ashan* (*v.* 59) and *Ain* (Josh. xxi. 16), *Alemeth* (*v.* 60) and *Almon* (Josh. xxi. 18); and time changes names. We are only to observe that in this appointment of cities for the Levites God took care, 1. For the accomplishment of dying Jacob's prediction concerning this tribe, that it should be *scattered in Israel*, Gen. xlix. 7. 2. For the diffusing of the knowledge of himself and his law to all parts of the land of Israel. Every tribe had Levites' cities in it; and so every room was furnished with a candle, so that none could be ignorant of his duty but it was either his own fault or the Levites'. 3. For a comfortable maintenance for those that ministered in holy things. Besides their tithes and offerings, they had glebe-lands and cities of their own to dwell in. Some of the most considerable cities of Israel fell to the Levites' lot. Every tribe had benefit by the Levites, and therefore every tribe must contribute to their support. *Let him that is taught in the word communicate to him that teacheth*, and do it cheerfully.

CHAP. VII.

In this chapter we have some account of the genealogies, I. Of Issachar, ver. 1—5. II. Of Benjamin, ver. 6—12. III. Of Naphtali, ver. 13. IV. Of Manasseh, ver. 14—19. V. Of Ephraim, ver. 20—29. VI. Of Asher, ver. 30—40. Here is no account either of Zebulun or Dan. Why they only should be omitted we can assign no reason; only it is the disgrace of the tribe of Dan that idolatry began in that colony of the Danites which fixed in Laish, and called it Dan, and there one of the golden calves was set up by Jeroboam. Dan is omitted, Rev. vii.

NOW the sons of Issachar *were*, Tola, and Puah, Jashub, and Shimrom, four. 2 And the sons of Tola; Uzzi, and Rephaiah, and Jeriel, and Jahmai, and Jibsam, and Shemuel, heads of their father's house, *to wit*, of Tola: *they were* valiant men of might in their generations; whose number *was* in the days of David two and twenty thousand and six hundred. 3 And the sons of Uzzi; Izrahiah: and the sons of Izrahiah; Michael, and Obadiah, and Joel, Ishiah, five: all of them chief men. 4 And with them, by their generations, after the house of their fathers, *were* bands of soldiers for war, six and thirty thousand *men*: for they had many wives and sons.

5 And their brethren among all the families of Issachar *were* valiant men of might, reckoned in all by their genealogies fourscore and seven thousand. 6 *The sons* of Benjamin; Bela, and Becher, and Jediael, three. 7 And the sons of Bela; Ezbon, and Uzzi, and Uzziel, and Jerimoth, and Iri, five; heads of the house of *their* fathers, mighty men of valour; and were reckoned by their genealogies twenty and two thousand and thirty and four. 8 And the sons of Becher; Zemira, and Joash, and Eliezer, and Elioenai, and Omri, and Jerimoth, and Abiah, and Anathoth, and Alameth. All these *are* the sons of Becher. 9 And the number of them, after their genealogy by their generations, heads of the house of their fathers, mighty men of valour, *was* twenty thousand and two hundred. 10 The sons also of Jediael; Bilhan: and the sons of Bilhan; Jeush, and Benjamin, and Ehud, and Chenaanah, and Zethan, and Tharshish, and Ahishahar. 11 All these the sons of Jediael, by the heads of their fathers, mighty men of valour, *were* seventeen thousand and two hundred *soldiers*, fit to go out for war *and* battle. 12 Shuppim also, and Huppim, the children of Ir, *and* Hushim, the sons of Aher. 13 The sons of Naphtali; Jahziel, and Guni, and Jezer, and Shallum, the sons of Bilhah. 14 The sons of Manasseh; Ashriel, whom she bare: (*but* his concubine the Aramitess bare Machir the father of Gilead: 15 And Machir took to wife *the sister* of Huppim and Shuppim, whose sister's name *was* Maachah;) and the name of the second *was* Zelophehad: and Zelophehad had daughters. 16 And Maachah the wife of Machir bare a son, and she called his name Peresh; and the name of his brother *was* Sheresh; and his sons *were* Ulam and Rakem. 17 And the sons of Ulam; Bedan. These *were* the sons of Gilead, the son of Machir, the son of Manasseh. 18 And his sister Hammoleketh bare Ishod, and Abiezer, and Mahalah. 19 And the sons of Shemidah were, Ahian, and Shechem, and Likhi, and Aniam.

We have here a short view given us,

I. Of the tribe of Issachar, whom Jacob had compared to a *strong ass, couching between two burdens* (Gen. xlix. 14), an industrious tribe, that minded their country business very closely and *rejoiced in their tents,* Deut. xxxiii. 18. And here it appears, 1. That they were a numerous tribe; for they had many wives. So fruitful their country was that they saw no danger of over-stocking the pasture, and so ingenious the people were that they could find work for all hands. Let no people complain of their numbers, provided they suffer none to be idle. 2. That they were a valiant tribe, *men of might* (*v.* 2, 5), *chief men, v.* 3. Those that were inured to labour and business were of all men the fittest to serve their country when there was occasion. The number of the respective families, as taken in the days of David, is here set down, amounting in the whole to above 145,000 men fit for war. The account, some think, was taken when Joab numbered the people, 2 Sam. xxiv. But I rather think it refers to some other computation that was made, perhaps among themselves, because it is said (1 Chron. xxvii. 24) that that account was not inserted in the chronicles of king David, it having offended God.

II. Of the tribe of Benjamin. Some account is here given of this tribe, but a much larger in the next chapter. The militia of this tribe scarcely reached to 60,000; but they are said to be *mighty men of valour, v.* 7, 9, 11. *Benjamin shall ravin as a wolf,* Gen. xlix. 27. It was the honour of this tribe that it produced Saul the first king, and more its honour that it adhered to the rightful kings of the house of David when the other tribes revolted. Here is mention (*v.* 12) of Hushim the sons of Aher. The sons of Dan are said to be *Hushim* (Gen. xlvi. 23), and therefore some read Aher appellatively, *Hushim*—the *sons of another* (that is, another of Jacob's sons) or the sons of a stranger, which Israelites should not be, but such the Danites were when they set up Micah's graven and molten image among them.

III. Of the tribe of Naphtali, *v.* 13. The first fathers only of that tribe are named, the very same that we find, Gen. xlvi. 24, only that *Shillem* there is *Shallum* here. None of their descendants are named, perhaps because their genealogies were lost.

IV. Of the tribe of Manasseh, that part of it which was seated within Jordan; for of the other part we had some account before, *ch.* v. 23, &c. Of this tribe observe, 1. That one of them married an Aramitess, that is, a Syrian, *v.* 14. This was during their bondage in Egypt, so early did they begin to mingle with the nations. 2. That, though the father married a Syrian, Machir, the son of that marriage, perhaps seeing the inconvenience of it in his father's house, took to wife a daughter of Benjamin, *v.* 15. It is good for the children to take warning by their father's mistakes and not stumble at the same stone. 3. Here is mention of Bedan (*v.* 17), who perhaps is the same with that Bedan who is mentioned as one of Israel's deliverers, 1 Sam. xii. 11. Jair perhaps, who was of Manasseh (Judg. x. 3), was the man.

20 And the sons of Ephraim; Shuthelah, and Bered his son, and Tahath his son, and Eladah his son, and Tahath his son, 21 And Zabad his son, and Shuthelah his son, and Ezer, and Elead, whom the men of Gath *that were* born in *that* land slew, because they came down to take away their cattle. 22 And Ephraim their father mourned many days, and his brethren came to comfort him. 23 And when he went in to his wife, she conceived, and bare a son, and he called his name Beriah, because it went evil with his house. 24 (And his daughter *was* Sherah, who built Beth-horon the nether, and the upper, and Uzzen-sherah.) 25 And Rephah *was* his son, also Resheph, and Telah his son, and Tahan his son, 26 Laadan his son, Ammihud his son, Elishama his son, 27 Non his son, Jehoshuah his son. 28 And their possessions and habitations *were*, Beth-el and the towns thereof, and eastward Naaran, and westward Gezer, with the towns thereof; Shechem also and the towns thereof, unto Gaza and the towns thereof: 29 And by the borders of the children of Manasseh, Beth-shean and her towns, Taanach and her towns, Megiddo and her towns, Dor and her towns. In these dwelt the children of Joseph the son of Israel. 30 The sons of Asher; Imnah, and Isuah, and Ishuai, and Beriah, and Serah their sister. 31 And the sons of Beriah; Heber, and Malchiel, who *is* the father of Birzavith. 32 And Heber begat Japhlet, and Shomer, and Hotham, and Shua their sister. 33 And the sons of Japhlet; Pasach, and Bimhal, and Ashvath. These *are* the children of Japhlet. 34 And the sons of Shamer; Ahi, and Rohgah, Jehubbah, and Aram. 35 And the sons of his brother Helem; Zophah, and Imna, and Shelesh, and Amal. 36 The sons of Zophah; Suah, and Harnepher, and Shual, and Beri, and Imrah, 37 Bezer, and Hod, and Shamma, and Shilshah, and Ithran, and Beera. 38 And the sons of Jether; Jephunneh, and Pispah, and Ara. 39 And the sons of Ulla; Ara, and Haniel, and Rezia. 40 All these *were* the children of Asher, heads of *their* father's house, choice *and* mighty men of valour, chief of the princes. And the number throughout the genealogy of them that were apt to the war *and* to battle *was* twenty and six thousand men.

We have here an account,

I. Of the tribe of Ephraim. Great things we read of that tribe when it came to maturity. Here we have an account of the disasters of its infancy, while it was in Egypt as it should seem; for Ephraim himself was alive when those things were done, which yet is hard to imagine if it were, as is here computed, seven generations off. Therefore I am apt to think that either it was another Ephraim or that those who were slain were the immediate sons of that Ephraim that was the son of Joseph. In this passage, which is related here only, we have, 1. The great breach that was made upon the family of Ephraim. The men of Gath, Philistines, giants, slew many of the sons of that family, *because they came down to take away their cattle, v.* 21. It is uncertain who were the aggressors here. Some make the men of Gath the aggressors, men *born in the land of Egypt,* but now resident in Gath, supposing that they came down into the land of Goshen, to drive away the Ephraimites' cattle, and slew the owners, because they stood up in the defence of them. Many a man's life has been exposed and betrayed by his wealth; so far is it from being a strong city. Others think that the Ephraimites made a descent upon the men of Gath to plunder them, presuming that the time had come when they should be put in possession of Canaan; but they paid dearly for their rashness and precipitation. Those that will not wait God's time cannot expect God's blessing. I rather think that the men of Gath came down upon the Ephraimites, because the Israelites in Egypt were shepherds, not soldiers, abounded in cattle of their own, and therefore were not likely to venture their lives for their neighbours' cattle: and the words may be read, *The men of Gath slew them, for they came down to take away their cattle.* Zabad the son of Ephraim, and Shuthelah, and Ezer, and Elead (his grandchildren), were, as Dr. Lightfoot thinks, the men that were slain. Jacob had foretold that the seed of Ephraim should become a *multitude of nations* (Gen. xlviii. 19), and yet that plant is thus nipped in the bud. God's providences often seem to contradict his promises; but, when they do so, they really magnify the promise, and make the performance of it, notwithstanding, so much the more illustrious. The Ephraimites were the posterity of Joseph, and yet his power could not protect them, though some think he was yet living. The sword devours one as well as another. 2. The great grief which oppressed the father of the family hereupon: *Ephraim mourned many days.* Nothing brings the aged to the grave with more sorrow than their following the young that descend from them to the grave first, especially if in blood. It is often the burden of those that live to be old that they see those go before them of whom they said, *These same shall comfort us.* It was a brotherly friendly office which his brethren did, when *they came to comfort him* under this great affliction, to express their sympathy with him and concern for him, and to suggest that to him which would support and quiet him under this sad providence. Probably they reminded him of the promise of increase with which Jacob had blessed him when he laid his right hand upon his head. Although his house was not so with God as he hoped, but a house of mourning, a shattered family, yet that promise was sure, 2 Sam. xxiii. 5. 3. The repair of this breach, in some measure, by the addition of another son to his family in his old age (*v.* 23), like Seth, *another seed instead of that of Abel whom Cain slew,* Gen. iv. 25. When God thus restores comfort to his mourners, *makes glad according to the days wherein he afflicted,* setting the mercies over against the crosses, we ought therein to take notice of the kindness and tenderness of divine Providence; it is as if *it repented God concerning his servants,* Ps. xc. 13, 15. Yet joy that a man was born into his family could not make him forget his grief; for he gives a melancholy name to this son, *Beriah—in trouble,* for he was born when the family was in mourning, when *it went evil with his house.* It is good to have in remembrance the affliction and the misery, the wormwood and the gall, that our souls may be *humbled within us,* Lam. iii. 19, 20. What name more proper for *man that is born of a woman* than *Beriah,* because born into a troublesome world? It is added, as a further honour to the house of Ephraim, (1.) That a daughter of that tribe, *Sherah* by name, at the time of Israel's settling in Canaan, built some cities, either at her own charge or by her own care; one of them bore her name, *Uzzen-sherah, v.* 24. A virtuous woman may be as great an honour and blessing to a family as a mighty man. (2.) That a son of that tribe was employed in the conquest of Canaan, *Joshua the son of Nun, v.* 27. In this also the breach made on Ephraim's family was further repaired; and perhaps the resentment of this injury formerly done by the Canaanites to the Ephraimites might make him more vigorous in the war.

II. Of the tribe of Asher. Some men of note of that tribe are here named. Their militia was not numerous in comparison with some other tribes, only 26,000 men in all; but their princes were *choice and mighty men of valour, chief of the princes* (*v.* 40), and perhaps it was their wisdom that they coveted not to make their trained bands numerous, but rather to have a few, and those apt to the war and serviceable men.

CHAP. VIII.

We had some account given us of Benjamin in the foregoing chapter; here we have a larger catalogue of the great men of that tribe. 1. Because of that tribe Saul came, the first king of Israel, to the story of whom the sacred writer is hastening, ch. x. 1. 2. Because that tribe clave to Judah, inhabited much of Jerusalem, was one of the two tribes that went into captivity, and returned back; and that story also he has an eye to, ch. ix. 1. Here is, I. Some of the heads of that tribe named, ver. 1—32. II. A more particular account of the family of Saul, ver. 33—40.

NOW Benjamin begat Bela his first-born, Ashbel the second, and Aharah the third, 2 Nohah the fourth, and Rapha the fifth. 3 And the sons of Bela were, Addar, and Gera, and Abihud, 4 And Abishua, and Naaman, and Ahoah, 5 And Gera, and Shephuphan, and Huram. 6 And these *are* the sons of Ehud: these are the heads of the fathers of the inhabitants of Geba, and they removed them to Manahath: 7 And Naaman, and Ahiah, and Gera, he removed them, and begat Uzza, and Ahihud. 8 And Shaharaim begat *children* in the country of Moab, after he had sent them away; Hushim and Baara *were* his wives. 9 And he begat of Hodesh his wife, Jobab, and Zibia, and Mesha, and Malcham, 10 And Jeuz, and Shachia, and Mirma. These *were* his sons, heads of the fathers. 11 And of Hushim he begat Abitub, and Elpaal. 12 The sons of Elpaal: Eber, and Misham, and Shamed, who built Ono, and Lod, with the towns thereof: 13 Beriah also, and Shema, who *were* heads of the fathers of the inhabitants of Aijalon, who drove away the inhabitants of Gath: 14 And Ahio, Shashak, and Jeremoth, 15 And Zebadiah, and Arad, and Ader, 16 And Michael, and Ispah, and Joha, the sons of Beriah; 17 And Zebadiah, and Meshullum, and Hezeki, and Heber, 18 Ismerai also, and Jezliah, and Jobab, the sons of Elpaal; 19 And Jakim, and Zichri, and Zabdi, 20 And Elienai, and Zilthai, and Eliel, 21 And Adaiah, and Beraiah, and Shimrath, the sons of Shimhi; 22 And Ishpan, and Heber, and Eliel, 23 And Abdon, and Zichri, and Hanan, 24 And Hananiah, and Elam, and Antothijah, 25 And Iphedeiah, and Penuel, the sons of Shashak; 26 Shamsherai, and Shehariah, and Athaliah, 27 And Jaresiah, and Eliah, and Zichri, the sons of Jeroham. 28 These *were* heads of the fathers, by their generations, chief *men*. These dwelt in Jerusalem. 29 And at Gibeon dwelt the father of Gibeon; whose wife's name *was* Maachah: 30 And his firstborn son Abdon, and Zur, and Kish, and Baal, and Nadab, 31 And Gedor, and Ahio, and Zacher. 32 And Mikloth begat Shimeah. And these also dwelt with their brethren in Jerusalem, over against them.

There is little or nothing of history in all these verses; we have not therefore much to observe. 1. As to the difficulties that occur in this and the foregoing genealogies we need not perplex ourselves. I presume Ezra took them as he found them *in the books of the kings of Israel and Judah* (*ch.* ix. 1), according as they were given in by the several tribes, each observing what method they thought fit. Hence some *as*cend, others *de*scend; some have *numbers* affixed, others *places;* some have historical remarks intermixed, others have not; some are shorter, others longer; some agree with other records, others differ; some, it is likely, were torn, erased, and blotted, others more legible. Those of Dan and Reuben were entirely lost. This holy man wrote as he was moved by the Holy Ghost; but there was no necessity for the making up of the defects, no, nor for the rectifying of the mistakes, of these genealogies by inspiration. It was sufficient that he copied them out as they came to his hand, or so much of them as was requisite to the present purpose, which was the directing of the returned captives to settle as nearly as they could with those of their own family, and in the places of their former residence. We may suppose that many things in these genealogies which to us seem intricate, abrupt, and perplexed, were plain and easy to them then (who knew how to fill up the deficiencies) and abundantly answered the intention of the publishing of them. 2 Many great and mighty nations there were now in being upon earth, and many illustrious men in them, whose names are buried in perpetual oblivion, while the names of multitudes of the Israel of God are here carefully preserved in everlasting remembrance. They are *Jasher, Jeshurun—just ones,* and *the memory of the just is blessed.* Many of these, we have reason to fear, came short of everlasting honour (for even the wicked kings of Judah come into the genealogy), yet the perpetuating of their names here was a figure of the writing of the names of all God's spiritual Israel in the Lamb's book of life. 3. This tribe of Benjamin was once brought to a very low ebb, in the time of the judges, upon the occasion of the iniquity of Gibeah, when only 600 men escaped the sword of justice; and yet, in these genealogies, it makes as good a figure as almost any of the tribes: for it is the honour of God to help the weakest and raise up those that are most diminished and abased. 4. Here is mention of one Ehud (*v.* 6), in the preceding verse of one Gera (*v.* 5) and (*v.* 8) of one that descended from him, that *begat children in the country of Moab,* which inclines me to think it was that Ehud who was the second of the judges of Israel; for he is said to be *the son of Gera* and *a Benjamite* (Judg. iii. 15), and he delivered Israel from the oppression of the Moabites by killing the king of Moab, which might give him a greater sway in the country of Moab than we find evidence of in his history and might occasion some of his posterity to settle there. 5. Here is mention of some of the Benjamites that *drove away the inhabitants of Gath* (*v.* 13), perhaps those that had slain the Ephraimites (*ch.* vii. 21) or their posterity, by way of reprisal: and one of those that did this piece of justice was named *Beriah* too, that name in which the memorial of that injury was preserved. 6. Particular notice is taken of those that *dwelt in Jerusalem* (*v.* 28 and again *v.* 32), that those whose ancestors had had their residence there might thereby be induced, at their return from captivity, to settle there too, which, for aught that appears, few were willing to do, because it was the post of danger: and therefore we find (Neh. xi. 2) *the people blessed those that willingly offered themselves to dwell at Jerusalem,* the greater part being inclined to prefer the cities of Judah. Those whose godly parents had their conversation in the new Jerusalem should thereby be engaged to set their faces thitherward and pursue the way thither, whatever it cost them.

33 And Ner begat Kish, and Kish begat Saul, and Saul begat Jonathan, and Malchi-shua, and Abinadab, and Esh-baal. 34 And the son of Jonathan *was* Merib-baal; and Merib-baal begat Micah. 35 And the sons of Micah *were,* Pithon, and Melech, and

Tarea, and Ahaz. 34 And Ahaz begat Jehoadah, and Jehoadah begat Alemeth, and Azmaveth, and Zimri; and Zimri begat Moza, 37 And Moza begat Binea: Rapha *was* his son, Eleasah his son, Azel his son: 38 And Azel had six sons, whose names *are* these, Azrikam, Bocheru, and Ishmael, and Sheariah, and Obadiah, and Hanan. All these *were* the sons of Azel. 39 And the sons of Eshek his brother *were*, Ulam his firstborn, Jehush the second, and Eliphelet the third. 40 And the sons of Ulam were mighty men of valour, archers, and had many sons, and sons' sons, a hundred and fifty. All these *are* of the sons of Benjamin.

It is observable that among all the genealogies of the tribes there is no mention of any of the kings of Israel after their defection from the house of David, much less of their families; not a word of Jeroboam's house or Baasha's, of Umri's or Jehu's; for they were all idolaters. But of the family of Saul, which was the royal family before the elevation of David, we have here a particular account. 1. Before Saul, Kish and Ner only are named, his father and grandfather, *v.* 33. His pedigree is carried higher 1 Sam. ix. 1, only there Kish is said to be *the son of Abiel*, here *of Ner*. He was in truth the son of Ner but the grandson of Abiel, as appears by 1 Sam. xiv. 51, where it is said that *Ner was the son of Abiel*, and that Abner, who was the son of Ner, was Saul's uncle (that is, his father's brother); therefore his father was also the son of Ner. It is common in all languages to put sons for grandsons and other descendants, much more in the scanty language of the Hebrews. 2. After Saul, divers of his sons are named, but the posterity of none of them, save Jonathan only, who was blessed with a numerous issue and those honoured with a place in the sacred genealogies for the sake of his sincere kindness to David. The line of Jonathan is drawn down here for about ten generations. Perhaps David was, in a particular manner, careful to preserve that, and assigned it a page by itself, because of the covenant made between his seed and Jonathan's seed for ever, 1 Sam. xx. 15, 23, 42. This genealogy ends in Ulam, whose family became famous in the tribe of Benjamin for the number of its valiant men. Of that one man's posterity there were, as it should seem, at one time, 150 archers brought into the field of battle, that were *mighty men of valour*, *v.* 40. That is taken notice of concerning them which is more a man's praise than his pomp or wealth is, that they were qualified to serve their country.

CHAP. IX.

This chapter intimates to us that one end of recording all these genealogies was to direct the Jews, now that they had returned out of captivity, with whom to incorporate and where to reside; for here we have an account of those who first took possession of Jerusalem after their return from Babylon, and began the rebuilding of it upon the old foundation. I. The Israelites, ver. 2—9. II. The priests, ver. 10—13. III. The Levites and other Nethinim, ver. 14—26. IV. Here is the particular charge of some of the priests and Levites, ver. 27—34. V. A repetition of the genealogy of king Saul, ver. 35—44.

SO all Israel were reckoned by genealogies; and, behold, they *were* written in the book of the kings of Israel and Judah, *who* were carried away to Babylon for their transgression. 2 Now the first inhabitants that *dwelt* in their possessions in their cities *were*, the Israelites, the priests, Levites, and the Nethinims. 3 And in Jerusalem dwelt of the children of Judah, and of the children of Benjamin, and of the children of Ephraim, and Manasseh; 4 Uthai the son of Ammihud, the son of Omri, the son of Imri, the son of Bani, of the children of Pharez the son of Judah. 5 And of the Shilonites; Asaiah the firstborn, and his sons. 6 And of the sons of Zerah; Jeuel, and their brethren, six hundred and ninety. 7 And of the sons of Benjamin; Sallu the son of Meshullam, the son of Hodaviah, the son of Hasenuah, 8 And Ibneiah the son of Jeroham, and Elah the son of Uzzi, the son of Michri, and Meshullam the son of Shephathiah, the son of Reuel, the son of Ibnijah; 9 And their brethren, according to their generations, nine hundred and fifty and six. All these men *were* chief of the fathers in the house of their fathers. 10 And of the priests; Jedaiah, and Jehoiarib, and Jachin, 11 And Azariah the son of Hilkiah, the son of Meshullam, the son of Zadok, the son of Meraioth, the son of Ahitub, the ruler of the house of God; 12 And Adaiah the son of Jeroham, the son of Pashur, the son of Malchijah, and Maasiai the son of Adiel, the son of Jahzerah, the son of Meshullam, the son of Meshillemith, the son of Immer; 13 And their brethren, heads of the house of their fathers, a thousand and seven hundred and threescore; very able men for the work of the service of the house of God.

The first verse looks back upon the foregoing genealogies, and tells us they were gathered out of *the books of the kings of Israel and Judah,* not that which we have in the canon of scripture, but another civil record, which was authentic, as the king's books with us. Mentioning Israel and Judah, the historian takes notice of their being *carried away to Babylon for their transgression.* Let that judgment never be forgotten, but ever be remembered, for warning to posterity to take heed of those sins that brought it upon them. Whenever we speak of any calamity that has befallen us, it is good to add this, "it was for my transgression," that God may be justified and clear when he judges. Then follows an account of the first inhabitants, after their return from captivity, that dwelt in their cities, especially in Jerusalem. 1. The Israelites. That general name is used (*v.* 2) because with those of Judah and Benjamin there were many of Ephraim and Manasseh, and the other ten tribes (*v.* 3), such as had escaped to Judah when the body of the ten tribes were carried captive or returned to Judah upon the revolutions in Assyria, and so went into captivity with them, or met them when they were in Babylon, associated with them, and so shared in the benefit of their enlargement. It was foretold that the *children of Judah and of Israel* should be *gathered together and come up out of the land* (Hos. i. 11), and that they should be one nation again, Ezek. xxxvii. 22. Trouble drives those together that have been at variance; and the pieces of metal that had been separated will run together again when melted in the same crucible. Many both of Judah and Israel staid behind in captivity; but some of both, whose spirit God stirred up, enquired the way to Zion again. Divers are here named, and many more numbered, who were *chief of the fathers* (*v.* 9), who ought to be remembered with honour, as Israelites indeed. 2. The priests, *v.* 10. It was their praise that they came with the first. Who should lead in a good work if the priests, the Lord's ministers, do not? It was the people's praise that they would not come without them; for who but the priests should keep knowledge? Who but the priests should bless them in the name of the Lord? (1.) It is said of one of them that he was *the ruler of the house of God* (*v.* 11) not the chief ruler, for Joshua was then the high priest, but the sagan, the next under him, his deputy, who perhaps applied more diligently to the business than the high priest himself. In the house of God it is requisite that there be rulers, not to make new laws, but to take care that the laws of God be duly observed by priests as well as people. (2.) It is said of many of them that they were *very able men for the service of the house of God, v.* 13. In the house of God there is service to be done, constant service; and it is well for the church when those are employed in that service who are qualified for it, *able ministers of the New Testament,* 2 Cor. iii. 6. The service of the temple was such as required at all times, especially in this critical juncture, when they had newly come out of Babylon, great courage and vigour of mind, as well as strength of body; and therefore they are praised as *mighty men of valour.*

14 And of the Levites; Shemaiah the son of Hasshub, the son of Azrikam, the son of Hashabiah, of the sons of Merari; 15 And Bakbakkar, Heresh, and Galal, and Mattaniah the son of Micah, the son of Zichri, the son of Asaph; 16 And Obadiah the son of Shemaiah, the son of Galal, the son of Jeduthun, and Berechiah the son of Asa, the son of Elkanah, that dwelt in the villages of the Netophathites. 17 And the porters *were,* Shallum, and Akkub, and Talmon, and Ahiman, and their brethren: Shallum *was* the chief; 18 Who hitherto *waited* in the king's gate eastward: they *were* porters in the companies of the children of Levi. 19 And Shallum the son of Kore, the son of Ebiasaph, the son of Korah, and his brethren, of the house of his father, the Korahites, *were* over the work of the service, keepers of the gates of the tabernacle: and their fathers, *being* over the host of the LORD, *were* keepers of the entry. 20 And Phinehas the son of Eleazar was the ruler over them in time past, *and* the LORD *was* with him. 21 *And* Zechariah the son of Meshelemiah *was* porter of the door of the tabernacle of the congregation. 22 All these *which were* chosen to be porters in the gates *were* two hundred and twelve. These were reckoned by their genealogy in their villages, whom David and Samuel the seer did ordain in their set office. 23 So they and their children *had* the oversight of the gates of the house of the LORD, *namely,* the house of the tabernacle, by wards. 24 In four quarters were the porters, toward the east, west, north, and south. 25 And their brethren, *which were* in their villages, *were* to come after seven days from time to time with them. 26 For these Levites, the four chief porters, were in *their* set office, and were over the chambers and trea-

suries of the house of God. 27 And they lodged round about the house of God, because the charge *was* upon them, and the opening thereof every morning *pertained* to them. 28 And *certain* of them had the charge of the ministering vessels, that they should bring them in and out by tale. 29 *Some* of them also *were* appointed to oversee the vessels, and all the instruments of the sanctuary, and the fine flour, and the wine, and the oil, and the frankincense, and the spices. 30 And *some* of the sons of the priests made the ointment of the spices. 31 And Mattithiah, *one* of the Levites, who *was* the firstborn of Shallum the Korahite, had the set office over the things that were made in the pans. 32 And *other* of their brethren, of the sons of the Kohathites, *were* over the showbread, to prepare *it* every sabbath. 33 And these *are* the singers, chief of the fathers of the Levites, *who remaining* in the chambers *were* free: for they were employed in *that* work day and night. 34 These chief fathers of the Levites *were* chief throughout their generations; these dwelt at Jerusalem.

We have here a further account of the good posture which the affairs of religion were put into immediately upon the return of the people out of Babylon. They had smarted for their former neglect of ordinances and under the late want of ordinances. Both these considerations made them very zealous and forward in setting up the worship of God among them; and so they began their worship of God at the right end. Instances hereof we have here.

I. Before the house of the Lord was built they had the house of the tabernacle, a plain and movable tent, which they made use of in the mean time. Those that cannot yet reach to have a temple must not be without a tabernacle, but be thankful for that and make the best of it. Never let God's work be left undone for want of a place to do it in.

II. In allotting to the priests and Levites their respective employments, they had an eye to the model that was drawn up by David, and Samuel the seer, *v.* 22. Samuel, in his time, had drawn the scheme of it, and laid the foundation, though the ark was then in obscurity, and David afterwards finished it, and both acted by immediate direction from God. Or David, as soon as he was anointed had this matter in his mind and consulted, Samuel about it, though he was then in his troubles, and the plan was formed in concert between them. This perhaps had been little regarded for many ages; but now, after a long interruption, it was revived. In dividing the work, they observed these ancient land-marks.

III. The most of them dwelt at Jerusalem (*v.* 34), yet there were some that dwelt in the villages (*v.* 16, 22), because, it may be, there was not yet room for them in Jerusalem. However they were employed in the service of the tabernacle (*v.* 25): *They were to come after seven days from time to time.* They had their week's attendance in their turns.

IV. Many of the Levites were employed as porters at the gates of the house of God, four chief porters (*v.* 26), and, under them, others, to the number of 212, *v.* 22. They had the oversight of the gates (*v.* 23), were keepers of the *thresholds,* as in the margin (*v.* 19), and keepers of the entry. This seemed a mean office; and yet David would rather have it than *dwell in the tents of wickedness,* Ps. lxxxiv. 10. Their office was, 1. To open the doors of God's house every morning (*v.* 27) and shut them at night. 2. To keep off the unclean, and hinder those from thrusting in that were forbidden by the law. 3. To direct and introduce into the courts of the Lord those that came thither to worship, and to show them where to go and what to do, that they might not incur punishment. This required care, and diligence, and constant attendance. Ministers have work to do of this kind.

V. Here is one Phinehas, a son of Eleazar, that is said to be a *ruler over them in time past* (*v.* 20), not the famous high priest of that name, but (as is supposed) an eminent Levite, of whom it is here said that *the Lord was with him,* or (as the Chaldee reads it) *the Word of the Lord was his helper*—the eternal Word, who is *Jehovah, the mighty one on whom help is laid.*

VI. It is said of some of them that, because the charge was upon them, *they lodged round about the house of God, v.* 27. It is good for ministers to be near their work, that they may give themselves wholly to it. The Levites pitched about the tabernacle when they marched through the wilderness. Then they were porters in one sense, bearing the burdens of the sanctuary, now porters in another sense, attending the gates and the doors—in both instances keeping the charge of the sanctuary.

VII. Every one knew his charge. Some were entrusted with the plate, the ministering vessels, to bring them in and out by tale, *v.* 28. Others were appointed to prepare the fine flour, wine, oil, &c., *v.* 29. Others, that were priests, made up the holy anointing oil, *v.* 30. Others took care of the meat-offerings, *v.* 31. Others of the showbread, *v.* 32. As in other great houses, so in God's house, the work is likely to be done well when every one knows the duty of his place and makes a business of it. God is the God of order: but that which is every body's work will be nobody's work.

VIII. The singers *were employed in that work day and night, v.* 33. They were the *chief fathers of the Levites* that made a business of it, not mean singing-men, that made a trade of it. They remained in the chambers of the temple, that they might closely and constantly attend it, and were therefore excused from all other services. It should seem, some companies were continually singing, at least at stated hours, both day and night. Thus was God continually praised, as it is fit he should be who is continually doing good. Thus devout people might, at any hour, have assistance in their devotion. Thus was that temple a figure of the heavenly one, where they *rest not day nor night* from praising God, Rev. iv. 8. *Blessed are those that dwell in thy house; they will be still praising thee.*

35 And in Gibeon dwelt the father of Gibeon, Jehiel, whose wife's name *was* Maachah; 36 And his firstborn son Abdon, then Zur, and Kish, and Baal, and Ner, and Nadab, 37 And Gedor, and Ahio, and Zechariah, and Mikloth, 38 And Mikloth begat Shimeam. And they also dwelt with their brethren at Jerusalem, over against their brethren. 39 And Ner begat Kish; and Kish begat Saul; and Saul begat Jonathan, and Malchi-shua, and Abinadab, and Esh-baal. 40 And the son of Jonathan *was* Merib-baal: and Merib-baal begat Micah. 41 And the sons of Micah *were*, Pithon, and Melech, and Tahrea, *and Ahaz.* 42 And Ahaz begat Jarah; and Jarah begat Alemeth, and Azmaveth, and Zimri; and Zimri begat Moza; 43 And Moza begat Binea; and Rephaiah his son, Eleasah his son, Azel his son. 44 And Azel had six sons, whose names *are* these, Azrikam, Bocheru, and Ishmael, and Sheariah, and Obadiah, and Hanan: these *were* the sons of Azel.

These verses are the very same with *ch.* viii. 29—38, giving an account of the ancestors of Saul and the posterity of Jonathan. *There* it is the conclusion of the genealogy of Benjamin; *here* it is an introduction to the story of Saul. We take the repetition as we find it; but if we admit that there are in the originals, especially in these books, some errors of the transcribers, I should be tempted to think this repetition arose from a blunder. Some one, in copying out these genealogies, having written those words, *v.* 34 *(These dwelt at Jerusalem)*, cast his eye on the same words, *ch.* viii. 28 *(These dwelt in Jerusalem)*, and so went on with what followed there, instead of going on with what followed here; and, when he perceived his mistake, was loth to make a blot in his book, and so let it stand. We have a rule in our law, *Redundans non nocet—Redundancies do no harm.*

CHAP. X.

The design of Ezra, in these books of the Chronicles, was to preserve the records of the house of David, which, though much sunk and lessened in a common eye by the captivity, yet grew more and more illustrious in the eyes of those that lived by faith by the nearer approach of the Son of David. And therefore he repeats, not the history of Saul's reign, but only of his death, by which way was made for David to the throne. In this chapter we have, I. The fatal rout which the Philistines gave to Saul's army, and the fatal stroke which he gave himself, ver. 1—7. II. The Philistines' triumph therein, ver 8—10. III. The respect which the men of Jabesh-Gilead showed the royal corpse, ver. 11, 12. IV. The reason of Saul's rejection, ver. 13, 14.

NOW the Philistines fought against Israel; and the men of Israel fled from before the Philistines, and fell down slain in mount Gilboa. 2 And the Philistines followed hard after Saul, and after his sons; and the Philistines slew Jonathan, and Abinadab, and Malchi-shua, the sons of Saul. 3 And the battle went sore against Saul, and the archers hit him, and he was wounded of the archers. 4 Then said Saul to his armourbearer, Draw thy sword, and thrust me through therewith; lest these uncircumcised come and abuse me. But his armourbearer would not; for he was sore afraid. So Saul took a sword, and fell upon it. 5 And when his armour bearer saw that Saul was dead, he fell likewise on the sword, and died. 6 So Saul died, and his three sons, and all his house died together. 7 And when all the men of Israel that *were* in the valley saw that they fled, and that Saul and his sons were dead, then they forsook their cities, and fled: and the Philistines came and dwelt in them.

This account of Saul's death is the same with that which we had, 1 Sam. xxxi. 1, &c. We need not repeat the exposition of it. Only let us observe, 1. Princes sin and the people suffer for it. It was a bad time with Israel when they *fled before the Philistines* and *fell down slain* (*v.* 1), when they quitted their cities, and *the Philistines came and dwelt in them, v.* 7. We do not find that they were at this time guilty of idolatry, as they had been before, in the days of the judges, and were afterwards, in the days of the kings. Samuel had reformed them, and they were reformed: and yet they are thus *given to the spoil and to the robbers.* No doubt there was enough in them to deserve this judgment; but that which divine Justice had chiefly an eye to was the sin of Saul. Note, Princes and great men should in a special manner take heed of provoking God's wrath; for, if they kindle that fire, they know not how many may be consumed by it for their sakes. 2. Parents sin and the children suffer for it. When the measure of Saul's iniquity was full, and his day came to fall (which David foresaw, 1 Sam. xxvi. 10), he not only descended into battle and perished himself, but his sons (all but Ish-bosheth) perished with him, and Jonathan among the rest, that gracious generous, man; for *all things come alike to all.* Thus was the iniquity of the fathers visited upon the children, and they fell as parts of the condemned father. Note, Those that love their seed must leave their sins, lest they perish not alone in their iniquity, but bring ruin on their families with themselves, or entail a curse upon them when they are gone. 3. Sinners sin and at length suffer for it themselves, though they be long reprieved; for, though sentence be not executed speedily, it will be executed. It was so upon Saul; and the manner of his fall was such as, in various particulars, answered to his sin. (1.) He had thrown a javelin more than once at David and missed him; but the archers hit him, and he was wounded of the archers. (2.) He had commanded Doeg to slay the priests of the Lord; and now, in despair, he commands his armour-bearer to *draw his sword and thrust him through.* (3.) He had disobeyed the command of God in not destroying the Amalekites, and his armour-bearer disobeys him in not destroying him. (4.) He that was the murderer of the priests is justly left to himself to be his own murderer; and his family is cut off who cut off the city of the priests. See, and say, *The Lord is righteous.*

8 And it came to pass on the morrow, when the Philistines came to strip the slain, that they found Saul and his sons fallen in mount Gilboa. 9 And when they had stripped him, they took his head, and his armour, and sent into the land of the Philistines round about, to carry tidings unto their idols, and to the people. 10 And they put his armour in the house of their gods, and fastened his head in the temple of Dagon. 11 And when all Jabesh-gilead heard all that the Philistines had done to Saul, 12 They arose, all the valiant men, and took away the body of Saul, and the bodies of his sons, and brought them to Jabesh, and buried their bones under the oak in Jabesh, and fasted seven days. 13 So Saul died for his transgression which he committed against the LORD, *even* against the word of the LORD, which he kept not, and also for asking *counsel* of *one that had* a familiar spirit, to enquire *of it;* 14 And enquired not of the LORD: therefore he slew him, and turned the kingdom unto David the son of Jesse.

Here, I. From the triumph of the Philistines over the body of Saul we may learn, 1. That the greater dignity men are advanced to the greater disgrace they are in danger of falling into. Saul's dead body, because he was a king, was abused more than any other of the slain. Advancement makes men a mark for malice. 2. That, if we give not to God the glory of our successes, even the Philistines will rise up in judgment against us and condemn us; for, when they had obtained a victory over Saul, they *sent tidings to their idols*—poor idols, that knew not what was done a few miles off till the tidings were brought them, nor then either! They also put Saul's armour *in the house of their gods, v.* 10. Shall Dagon have so honourable a share in their triumphs and the true and living God be forgotten in ours?

II. From the triumph of the men of Jabesh-Gilead in the rescue of the bodies of Saul and his sons we learn that there is a respect due to the remains of the deceased, especially of deceased princes. We are not to enquire concerning the eternal state; that must be left to God: but we must treat the dead body as those who remember it has been united to an immortal soul and must be so again.

III. From the triumphs of divine Justice in the ruin of Saul we may learn, 1. That the sin of sinners will certainly find them out, sooner or later: *Saul died for his transgression.* 2. That no man's greatness can exempt him from the judgments of God. 3. Disobedience is a killing thing. Saul died for *not keeping the word of the Lord,* by which he was ordered to destroy the Amalekites. 4. Consulting with witches is a sin that fills the measure of iniquity as soon as any thing. Saul enquired of one that *had a familiar spirit,* and *enquired not of the Lord, therefore he slew him, v.* 13, 14. Saul slew himself, and yet it is said, *God slew him.* What is done by wicked hands is yet done *by the determinate counsel and foreknowledge of God.* Those that abandon themselves to the devil shall be abandoned to him; so shall their doom be. It is said (1 Sam. xxviii. 6) that Saul did *enquire of the Lord* and he *answered him not:* but here it is said, *Saul did not enquire of God;* for he did not till he was brought to the last extremity, and then it was too late.

CHAP. XI.

In this chapter is repeated, I. The elevation of David to the throne, immediately upon the death of Saul, by common consent, ver. 1—3. II. His gaining the castle of Zion out of the hands of the Jebusites, ver. 4—9. III. The catalogue of the worthies and great men of his kingdom, ver. 10—47.

THEN all Israel gathered themselves to David unto Hebron, saying, Behold, we *are* thy bone and thy flesh. 2 And moreover in time past, even when Saul was king, thou *wast* he that leddest out and broughtest in Israel: and the LORD thy God said unto thee, Thou shalt feed my people Israel, and thou shalt be ruler over my people Israel. 3 Therefore came all the elders of Israel to the king to Hebron; and David made a covenant with them in Hebron before the LORD; and they anointed David king over Israel, according to the word of the LORD by Samuel. 4 And David and all Israel went to Jerusalem, which *is* Jebus; where the Jebusites *were*, the inhabitants of the land. 5 And the inhabitants of Jebus said to David, Thou shalt not come hither. Nevertheless David took the castle of Zion, which *is* the city of David. 6 And David said, Whosoever smiteth the Jebusites first shall be chief and captain. So Joab the son of Zeruiah went first up, and was chief. And David dwelt in the castle; therefore they called it the city of David. 8 And he built the city round about, even from Millo round about: and Joab repaired the rest of the city. 9 So David waxed greater and greater: for the LORD of hosts *was* with him.

David is here brought to the possession.

I. Of the throne of Israel, after he had reigned seven years in Hebron, over Judah only. In consideration of his relation to them (*v.* 1), his former good services, and especially the divine designation (*v.* 2), they anointed him their king: he covenanted to protect them, and they to bear faith and true allegiance to him, *v.* 3. Observe, 1. God's counsels will be fulfilled at last, whatever difficulties lie in the way. If God had said, *David shall rule,* it is in vain to oppose it. 2. Men that have long stood in their own light, when they have long wearied themselves with their lying vanities, it is to be hoped, will understand the things that belong to their peace and return to *their own mercies.* 3. Between prince and people there is an original contract, which both ought religiously to observe. If ever any prince might have claimed an absolute despotic power, David might, and might as safely as any have been entrusted with it; and yet he made a covenant with the people, took the coronation-oath, to rule by law.

II. Of the strong-hold of Zion, which was held by the Jebusites till David's time. Whether David had a particular eye upon it as a place fit to make a royal city, or whether he had a promise of it from God, it seems that one of his first exploits was to make himself master of that fort; and, when he had it, he called it the *city of David, v.* 7. To this reference is had, Ps. ii. 6. *I have set my king upon my holy hill of Zion.* See here what quickens and engages resolution in great undertakings. 1. Opposition. When the Jebusites set David at defiance, and said, *Thou shalt not come hither,* he resolved to force it, whatever it cost him. 2. Prospect of preferment. When David proposed to give the general's place to him that would lead the attack upon the castle of Zion, Joab was fired with the proposal, and he *went up first, and was chief.* It has been said, "Take away honour out of the soldier's eye and you cut off the spurs from his heels."

10 These also *are* the chief of the mighty men whom David had, who strengthened themselves with him in his kingdom, *and* with all Israel, to make him king, according to the word of the LORD concerning Israel. 11 And this *is* the number of the mighty men whom David had; Jashobeam, an Hachmonite, the chief of the captains: he lifted up his spear against three hundred slain *by him* at one time. 12 And after him *was* Eleazar, the son of Dodo, the Ahohite, who *was one* of the three mighties. 13 He was with David at Pas-dammim, and there the Philistines were gathered together to battle, where was a parcel of ground full of barley; and the people fled from before the Philistines. 14 And they set themselves in the midst of *that* parcel, and delivered it, and slew the Philistines; and the LORD saved *them* by a great deliverance. 15 Now three of the thirty captains went down to the rock to David, into the cave of Adullam; and the host of the Philistines encamped in the valley of Rephaim. 16 And David *was* then in the hold, and the Philistines' garrison *was* then at Beth-lehem. 17 And David longed, and said, Oh that one would give me drink of the water

of the well of Beth-lehem, that *is* at the gate! 18 And the three brake through the host of the Philistines, and drew water out of the well of Beth-lehem, that *was* by the gate, and took *it*, and brought *it* to David: but David would not drink *of* it, but poured it out to the LORD, 19 And said, My God forbid it me, that I should do this thing: shall I drink the blood of these men that have put their lives in jeopardy? for with the *jeopardy of* their lives they brought it. Therefore he would not drink it. These things did these three mightiest. 20 And Abishai the brother of Joab, he was chief of the three: for lifting up his spear against three hundred, he slew *them*, and had a name among the three. 21 Of the three, he was more honourable than the two; for he was their captain: howbeit he attained not to the *first* three. 22 Benaiah the son of Jehoiada, the son of a valiant man of Kabzeel, who had done many acts; he slew two lionlike men of Moab: also he went down and slew a lion in a pit in a snowy day. 23 And he slew an Egyptian, a man of *great* stature, five cubits high; and in the Egyptian's hand *was* a spear like a weaver's beam; and he went down to him with a staff, and plucked the spear out of the Egyptian's hand, and slew him with his own spear. 24 These *things* did Benaiah the son of Jehoiada, and had a name among the three mighties. 25 Behold, he was honourable among the thirty, but attained not to the *first* three: and David set him over his guard. 26 Also the valiant men of the armies *were*, Asahel the brother of Joab, Elhanan the son of Dodo of Beth-lehem, 27 Shammoth the Harorite, Helez the Pelonite, 28 Ira the son of Ikkesh the Tekoite, Abiezer the Antothite, 29 Sibbecai the Hushathite, Ilai the Ahohite, 30 Maharai the Netophathite, Heled the son of Baanah the Netophathite, 31 Ithai the son of Ribai of Gibeah, *that pertained* to the children of Benjamin, Benaiah the Pirathonite, 32 Hurai of the brooks of Gaash, Abiel the Arbathite, 33 Azmaveth the Baharumite, Eliahba the Shaalbonite, 34 The sons of Hashem the Gizonite, Jonathan the son of Shage the Hararite, 35 Ahiam the son of Sacar the Hararite, Eliphal the son of Ur, 36 Hepher the Mecherathite, Ahijah the Pelonite, 37 Hezro the Carmelite, Naarai the son of Ezbai, 38 Joel the brother of Nathan, Mibhar the son of Haggeri, 39 Zelek the Ammonite, Naharai the Berothite, the armourbearer of Joab the son of Zeruiah, 40 Ira the Ithrite, Gareb the Ithrite, 41 Uriah the Hittite, Zabad the son of Ahlai, 42 Adina the son of Shiza the Reubenite, a captain of the Reubenites, and thirty with him, 43 Hanan the son of Maachah, and Joshaphat the Mithnite, 44 Uzziah the Ashterathite, Shama and Jehiel the sons of Hothan the Aroerite, 45 Jediael the son of Shimri, and Joha his brother, the Tizite, 46 Eliel the Mahavite, and Jeribai, and Joshaviah, the sons of Elnaam, and Ithmah the Moabite. 47 Eliel, and Obed, and Jasiel the Mesobaite.

We have here an account of David's worthies, the great men of his time that served him and were preferred by him. The first edition of this catalogue we had, 2 Sam. xxiii. 8, &c. This is much the same, only that those named here from *v.* 41 to the end are added. Observe,

I. The connexion of this catalogue with that which is said concerning David, *v.* 9. 1. *David waxed greater and greater*, and these were his mighty men. Much of the strength and honour of great men is borrowed from their servants and depends upon them, which cannot but somewhat diminish pomp and power in the opinion of those that are wise. David is great because he has great men about him; take these away, and he is where he was. 2. *The Lord of hosts was with him, and these were the mighty men which he had.* God was with him and wrought for him, but by men and means and the use of second causes. By *this* it appeared that God was with him, that he inclined the hearts of those to come over to him that were able to serve his interest. As, if God be for us, none can be against us, so, if God be for us, all shall be for us that we have occasion for. Yet David ascribed his success and increase, not to the hosts he had, but to the *Lord of hosts*, not to the mighty men that were with him, but to the mighty God, whose presence with us is all in all.

II. The title of this catalogue (*v.* 10): *These are the men who strengthened themselves with him.* In strengthening him they strengthened themselves and their own interest; for his advancement was theirs. What we do in our places for the support of the kingdom of the Son of David we shall be gainers by. In strengthening it we strengthen ourselves. It may be read, *They held strongly with him and with all Israel.* Note, When God has work to do he will not want fit instruments to do it with. If it be work that requires mighty men, mighty men shall be either found or made to effect it, *according to the word of the Lord.*

III. That which made all these men honourable was the good service that they did to their king and country; they helped to make David king (*v.* 10)—a good work. They slew the Philistines, and other public enemies, and were instrumental to save Israel. Note, The way to be great is to do good. Nor did they gain this honour without labour and the hazard of their lives. The honours of Christ's kingdom are prepared for those that *fight the good fight of faith,* that labour and suffer, and are willing to venture all, even life itself, for Christ and a good conscience. It is by a patient continuance in well-doing that we must seek for glory, and honour, and immortality; and those that are faithful to the Son of David shall find their names registered and enrolled much more to their honour than these are in the records of fame.

IV. Among all the great exploits of David's mighty men, here is nothing great mentioned concerning David himself but his *pouring out water before the Lord* which he had *longed for, v.* 18, 19. Four very honourable dispositions of David appeared in that action, which, for aught I know, made it as great as any of the achievements of those worthies. 1. Repentance for his own weakness. It is really an honour to a man, when he is made sensible that he has said or done any thing unadvisedly, to unsay it and undo it again by repentance, as it is a shame to a man when he has said or done amiss to stand to it. 2. Denial of his own appetite. He longed for the water of the well of Bethlehem; but, when he had it, he would not drink it, because he would not so far humour himself and gratify a foolish fancy. He that has such a rule as this *over his own spirit is better than the mighty.* It is an honour to a man to have the command of himself; but he that will command himself must sometimes cross himself. 3. Devotion towards God. That water which he thought too good, too precious, for his own drinking, he *poured out to the Lord* for a *drink-offering.* If we have any thing better than another, let God be honoured with it, who is the best, and should have the best. 4. Tenderness of his servants. It put him into the greatest confusion imaginable to think that three brave men should hazard their lives to fetch water for him. In his account it turns the water into blood. It is the honour of great men not to be prodigal of the blood of those they employ, but, in all the commands they give them, to put their own souls into their souls' stead.

V. In the wonderful achievements of these heroes the power of God must be acknowledged. How could one slay 300 and another the same number (*v.* 11, 20), another two lion-like men (*v.* 22), and another an Egyptian giant (*v.* 23), if they had not had the extraordinary presence of God with them, according to that promise, Josh. xxiii. 10, *One man of you shall chase a thousand, for the Lord your God fighteth for you?*

VI. One of these worthies is said to be *an Ammonite* (*v.* 39), another *a Moabite* (*v.* 46), and yet the law was that an *Ammonite* and *a Moabite should not enter into the congregation of the Lord,* Deut. xxiii. 3. These, it is likely, had approved themselves so hearty for the interest of Israel that in their case it was thought fit to dispense with that law, and the rather because it was an indication that the Son of David would have worthies among the Gentiles: with him there is neither Greek nor Jew.

CHAP. XII.

What the mighty men did towards making David king we read in the foregoing chapter. Here we are told what the many did towards it. It was not all at once, but gradually, that David ascended the throne. His kingdom was to last; and therefore, like fruits that keep longest, it ripened slowly. After he had long waited for the vacancy of the throne, it was at two steps, and those above seven years distant, that he ascended it. Now we are here told, I. What help came in to him to Ziklag, to make him king of Judah, ver. 1—22. II. What help came in to him in Hebron, to make him king over all Israel, above seven years after, ver. 23—40.

NOW these *are* they that came to David to Ziklag, while he yet kept himself close because of Saul the son of Kish: and they *were* among the mighty men, helpers of the war. 2 *They were* armed with bows, and could use both the right hand and the left in *hurling* stones and *shooting* arrows out of a bow, *even* of Saul's brethren of Benjamin. 3 The chief *was* Ahiezer, then Joash, the sons of Shemaah the Gibeathite; and Jeziel, and Pelet, the sons of Azmaveth; and Berachah, and Jehu the Antothite, 4 And Ismaiah the Gibeonite, a mighty man among the thirty, and over the thirty; and Jeremiah, and Jahaziel, and Johanan, and Josabad the Gederathite, 5 Eluzai, and Jerimoth, and Bealiah, and Shemariah, and Shephatiah the Haruphite, 6 Elkanah, and Jesiah, and Azareel, and Joezer, and Jashobeam, the Korhites, 7 And Joelah, and Zebadiah, the sons of Jeroham of Gedor. 8 And of the Gadites there separated themselves unto David into the hold to the wilderness men of might, *and* men of war *fit* for the battle, that could handle shield and buckler, whose faces *were like* the faces of lions, and *were* as swift as the roes upon the mountains; 9 Ezer the first, Obadiah the second, Eliab the third, 10 Mishmannah the fourth, Jeremiah the fifth, 11 Attai the sixth, Eliel the seventh, 12 Johanan the eighth, Elzabad the ninth, 13 Jeremiah the tenth, Machbanai the eleventh. 14 These *were* of the sons of Gad, captains of the host: one of the least *was* over a hundred, and the greatest over a thousand. 15 These *are* they that went over Jordan in the first month, when it had overflown all his banks; and they put to flight all *them* of the valleys, *both* toward the east, and toward the west. 16 And there came of the children of Benjamin and Judah to the hold unto David. 17 And David went out to meet them, and answered and said unto them, If ye be come peaceably unto me to help me, mine heart shall be knit unto you: but if *ye be come* to betray me to mine enemies, seeing *there is* no wrong in mine hands, the God of our fathers look *thereon*, and rebuke *it*. 18 Then the spirit came upon Amasai, *who was* chief of the captains, *and he said*, Thine *are we*, David, and on thy side, thou son of Jesse: peace, peace, *be* unto thee, and peace *be* to thine helpers; for thy God helpeth thee. Then David received them, and made them captains of the band. 19 And there fell *some* of Manasseh to David, when he came with the Philistines against Saul to battle: but they helped them not: for the lords of the Philistines upon advisement sent him away, saying, He will fall to his master Saul to *the jeopardy of* our heads. 20 As he went to Ziklag, there fell to him of Manasseh, Adnah, and Jozabad, and Jediael, and Michael, and Jozabad, and Elihu, and Zilthai, captains of the thousands that *were* of Manasseh. 21 And they helped David against the band *of the rovers:* for they *were* all mighty men of valour, and were captains in the host. 22 For at *that* time day by day there came to David to help him, until *it was* a great host, like the host of God.

We have here an account of those that appeared and acted as David's friends, upon the death of Saul, to bring about the revolution. All the forces he had, while he was persecuted, was but 600 men, who served for his guards; but, when the time had come that he must begin to act offensively, Providence brought in more to his assistance. Even while he *kept himself close, because of Saul* (*v.* 1), while he did not appear, to invite or encourage his friends and well-wishers to come in to him (not foreseeing that the death of Saul was so near), God was inclining and preparing them to come over to him with seasonable succours. Those that trust God to do his work for them in his own way and time shall find his providence outdoing all their forecast and contrivance. The war was God's, and he found out helpers of the war, whose forwardness to act for the man God designed for the government is here recorded to their honour.

I. Some, even of Saul's brethren, of the tribe of Benjamin, and a-kin to him, came over to David, *v.* 2. What moved them to it we are not told. Probably a generous indignation at the base treatment which Saul, one of their tribe, gave him, animated them to appear the more vigorously for him, that the guilt and reproach of it might not lie upon them. These Benjamites are described to be men of great dexterity, that were trained up in shooting and slinging, and used both hands alike—ingenious active men; a few of these might do David a great deal of service. Several of the leading men of them are here named. See Judg. xx. 16.

II. Some of the tribe of Gad, though seated on the other side Jordan, had such a conviction of David's title to the government, and fitness for it, that they *separated themselves from their brethren* (a laudable separation it was) to go to David, though he was *in the hold in the wilderness* (*v.* 8), probably some of his strong holds in the wilderness of Engedi. They were but few, eleven in all, here named, but they added much to David's strength. Those that had hitherto come in to his assistance were most of them men of broken fortunes, distressed, discontented, and soldiers of fortune, that came to him rather for protection than to do him any service, 1 Sam. xxii. 2. But these Gadites were brave men, *men of war, and fit for the battle, v.* 8. For, 1. They were *able-bodied men*, men of incredible swiftness, not to fly from, but to fly upon, the enemy, and to pursue the scattered forces. In this they were *as swift as the roes upon the mountains*, so that no man could escape from them; and yet they had *faces like the faces of lions*, so that no man could out-fight them. 2. They were disciplined men, trained up to military exercises; they could handle shield and buckler, use both offensive and defensive weapons. 3. They were officers of the militia in their own tribe (*v.* 14), so that though they did not bring soldiers with them they had them at command, hundreds, thousands. 4. They were daring men, that could break through the greatest difficulties. Upon some expedition or other, perhaps this to David, they swam over Jordan, when it *overflowed all its banks*, *v.* 15. Those are fit to be employed in the cause of God that can venture thus in a dependence upon the divine protection. 5. They were men that would go through with the business they engaged in. What enemies those were that they met with in the valleys, when they had passed Jordan, does not appear; but they put them to flight with their lion-like faces, and pursued them with matchless fury, both *towards the east and towards the west;* which way soever they turned, they followed their blow, and did not do their work by halves.

III. Some of Judah and Benjamin came to him, *v.* 16. Their leader was Amasai, whether the same with that Amasa that afterwards sided with Absalom (2 Sam. xvii. 25) or no does not appear. Now here we have,

1. David's prudent treaty with them, *v.* 17. He was surprised to see them, and could not but conceive some jealousy of the intentions of their coming, having been so often in danger by the treachery of the men of Ziph and the men of Keilah, who yet were all men of Judah. He might well be timorous whose life was so much struck at; he might well be suspicious who had been deceived in so many that he said, in his haste, *All men are liars.* No marvel that he meets these men of Judah with caution. Observe,

(1.) How he puts the matter to themselves, how fairly he deals with them. As they are, they shall find him; so shall all that deal with the Son of David. [1.] If they be faithful and honourable, he will be their rewarder: "*If you have come peaceably unto me, to help me*, though you have come late and have left me exposed a great while, though you bring no great strength with you to turn the scale for me, yet I will thankfully accept your good-will, and *my heart shall be knit unto you;* I will love you and honour you, and do you all the kindness I can." Affection, respect, and service, that are cordial and sincere, will find favour with a good man, as they do with a good God, though clogged with infirmities, and turning to no great account. But, [2.] If they be false, and come to betray him into the hands of Saul, under colour of friendship, he leaves them to God to be their avenger, as he is, and will be, of every thing that is treacherous and perfidious. Never was man more violently run upon, and run down, than David was (except the Son of David himself), and yet he had the testimony of his conscience that there was no wrong in his hands. He meant no harm to any man, which was his rejoicing in the day of evil, and enabled him, when he feared treachery, to commit his cause to him that judges righteously. He will not be judge in his own cause, though a wise man, nor avenge himself, though a man of valour; but let the righteous God, who hath said, *Vengeance is mine*, do both. *The God of our fathers look thereon and rebuke it.*

(2.) In this appeal observe, [1.] He calls God the *God of our fathers*, both his fathers and theirs. Thus he reminded them not to deal ill with him; for they were both descendants from the same patriarchs, and both dependents on the same God. Thus he encouraged himself to believe that God would right him if he should be abused; for he was the *God of his fathers* and therefore a blessing was entailed on him, and a God to all Israel and therefore not only a Judge to all the earth, but particularly concerned in determining controversies between contesting Israelites. [2.] He does not imprecate any fearful judgment upon them, though they should deal treacherously, but very modestly refers his cause to the divine wisdom and justice: The Lord *look thereon*, and judge as he sees (for he sees men's hearts), and *rebuke it.* It becomes those that appeal to God to express themselves with great temper and moderation; for the wrath of man *works not the righteousness of God.*

2. Their hearty closure with him, *v.* 18. Amasai was their spokesman, on whom the *Spirit of the Lord came*, not a spirit of prophecy, but a spirit of wisdom and resolution, according to the occasion, putting words into his mouth, unpremeditated, which were proper both to give David satisfaction and to animate those that accompanied him. Nothing could be said finer, more lively, or more pertinent to the occasion. For himself and all his associates, (1.) He professed a very cordial adherence to David, and his interest, against all that opposed him, and a resolution to stand by him with the hazard of all that was dear to him: *Thine are we, David, and on thy side, thou son of Jesse.* In calling him *son of Jesse* they reminded themselves that he was lineally descended from Nahshon and Salmon, who in their days were princes of the tribe of Judah. Saul called him so in disdain (1 Sam. xx. 27; xxii. 7), but they looked upon it as his honour. They were convinced that he was on God's side, and that God was on his side; and therefore, *Thine are we, David, and on thy side.* It is good, if we must side, to side with those that side with God and have God with them. (2.) He wished prosperity to David and his cause, not drinking a health, but praying for peace to him and all his friends and well-wishers: "*Peace, peace, be unto thee*, all the good thy heart desires, and *peace be to thy helpers*, among whom we de-

sire to be reckoned, that peace may be on us." (3.) He assured him of help from heaven: "*For thy God helpeth thee;* therefore we wish peace may be, and therefore we doubt not but peace shall be, to thee and thy helpers. God is thy God, and those that have him for their God no doubt have him for their helper in every time of need and danger." From these expressions of Amasai we may take instruction how to testify our affection and allegiance to the Lord Jesus. His we must be without reservation or power of revocation. On his side we must be forward to appear and act. To his interest we must be hearty well-wishers: "Hosanna! prosperity to his gospel and kingdom;" for his God helpeth him, and will till he shall have put down all opposing rule, principality, and power.

3. David's cheerful acceptance of them into his interest and friendship. Charity and honour teach us to let fall our jealousies as soon as satisfaction is given us: *David received them,* and preferred them to be *captains of the band.*

IV. Some of Manasseh likewise joined in with him, *v.* 19. Providence gave them a fair opportunity to do so when he and his men marched through their country upon this occasion. Achish took David with him when he went out to fight with Saul; but the lords of the Philistines obliged him to withdraw. We have the story, 1 Sam. xxix. 4, &c. In his return some great men of Manasseh, who had no heart to join with Saul against the Philistines, struck in with David, and very seasonably, to help him *against the band of Amalekites* who had plundered Ziklag; they were not many, but they were all mighty men and did David good service upon that occasion, 1 Sam. xxx. See how Providence provides. David's interest grew strangely just when he had occasion to make use of it, *v.* 22. Auxiliary forces flocked in daily, *till he had a great host.* When the promise comes to the birth, leave it to God to find strength to bring forth.

23 And these *are* the numbers of the bands *that were* ready armed to the war, *and* came to David to Hebron, to turn the kingdom of Saul to him, according to the word of the LORD. 24 The children of Judah that bare shield and spear *were* six thousand and eight hundred, ready armed to the war. 25 Of the children of Simeon, mighty men of valour for the war, seven thousand and one hundred. 26 Of the children of Levi four thousand and six hundred. 27 And Jehoiada *was* the leader of the Aaronites, and with him *were* three thousand and seven hundred; 28 And Zadok, a young man mighty of valour, and of his father's house twenty and two captains. 29 And of the children of Benjamin, the kindred of Saul, three thousand: for hitherto the greatest part of them had kept the ward of the house of Saul. 30 And of the children of Ephraim twenty thousand and eight hundred, mighty men of valour, famous throughout the house of their fathers. 31 And of the half tribe of Manasseh eighteen thousand, which were expressed by name, to come and make David king. 32 And of the children of Issachar, *which were men* that had understanding of the times, to know what Israel ought to do; the heads of them *were* two hundred; and all their brethren *were* at their commandment. 33 Of Zebulun, such as went forth to battle, expert in war, with all instruments of war, fifty thousand, which could keep rank: *they were* not of double heart. 34 And of Naphtali a thousand captains, and with them with shield and spear thirty and seven thousand. 35 And of the Danites expert in war twenty and eight thousand and six hundred. 36 And of Asher, such as went forth to battle, expert in war, forty thousand. 37 And on the other side of Jordan, of the Reubenites, and the Gadites, and of the half tribe of Manasseh, with all manner of instruments of war for the battle, a hundred and twenty thousand. 38 All these men of war, that could keep rank, came with a perfect heart to Hebron, to make David king over all Israel: and all the rest also of Israel *were* of one heart to make David king. 39 And there they were with David three days, eating and drinking: for their brethren had prepared for them. 40 Moreover they that were nigh them, *even* unto Issachar and Zebulun and Naphtali, brought bread on asses, and on camels, and on mules, and on oxen, *and* meat, meal, cakes of figs, and bunches of raisins, and wine, and oil, and oxen, and sheep abundantly: for *there was* joy in Israel.

We have here an account of those who

were active in perfecting the settlement of David upon the throne, after the death of Ishbosheth. We read (*ch.* xi. 1, and before, 2 Sam. v. 1) that *all the tribes of Israel came,* either themselves or by their representatives, to Hebron, to make David king: now here we have an account of the quota which every tribe brought in *ready armed to the war,* in case there should be any opposition, *v.* 23. We may observe here,

I. That those tribes that lived nearest brought in the fewest—Judah but 6800 (*v.* 24), Simeon but 7100 (*v.* 25); whereas Zebulun, that lay remote, brought 50,000, Asher 40,000, and the two tribes and a half on the other side Jordan 120,000. Not as if the next adjacent tribes were cold in the cause; but they showed as much of their prudence in bringing few, since all the rest lay so near within call, as the others did of their zeal in bringing so many. The men of Judah had enough to do to entertain those that came from afar.

II. The Levites themselves, and the priests (called here the *Aaronites),* appeared very hearty in this cause, and were ready, if there were occasion, to fight for David, as well as pray for him, because they knew he was called of God to the government, *v.* 26—28.

III Even some of the kindred of Saul came over to David (*v.* 29), not so many as of the other tribes, because a foolish affection for their own tribe, and a jealousy for the honour of it, kept many of them long in the sinking interest of Saul's family. Kindred should never over-rule conscience. Call no man *Father* to this extent, but God only.

IV. It is said of most of these that they were *mighty men of valour* (*v.* 25, 28, 30), of others that they were *expert in war* (*v.* 35, 36), and of them all that they *could keep rank, v.* 38. They had a great deal of martial fire, and yet were governable and subject to the rules of order—warm hearts but cool heads.

V. Some were so considerate as to bring with them arms, and all instruments for war (*v.* 24, 33, 37), for how could they think that David should be able to furnish them?

VI. The men of Issachar were the fewest of all, only 200, and yet as serviceable to David's interest as those that brought in the greatest numbers, these few being in effect the whole tribe. For, 1. They were men of great skill above any of their neighbours, men that *had understanding of the times, to know what Israel ought to do.* They understood the natural times, could *discern the face of the sky,* were weather-wise, could advise their neighbours in the proper times for ploughing, sowing, reaping, &c. Or the ceremonial times, the times appointed for the solemn feasts; therefore they are said to *call the people to the mountain* (Deut. xxxiii. 19), for almanacks were not then so common as now. Or, rather, the political times; they understood public affairs, the temper of the nation, and the tendencies of the present events. It is the periphrasis of statesmen that they *know the times,* Esth. i. 13. Those of that tribe were greatly intent on public affairs, had good intelligence from abroad and made a good use of it. They knew *what Israel ought to do:* from their observation and experience they learned both their own and others' duty and interest. In this critical juncture they knew Israel ought to make David king. It was not only expedient, but necessary; the present posture of affairs called for it. The men of Issachar dealt mostly in country business, and did not much intermeddle in public affairs, which gave them an opportunity of observing others and conversing with themselves. A stander-by sees sometimes more than a gamester. 2. They were men of great interests; for *all their brethren were at their commandment.* The commonalty of that tribe having *bowed their shoulders to bear* (Gen. xlix. 15), the great men had them at their beck. Hence we read of *the princes of Issachar,* Judg. v. 15. They knew how to rule, and the rest knew how to obey. It is happy indeed when those that should lead are intelligent and judicious, and those who are to follow are modest and obsequious.

VII. It is said of them all that they engaged in this enterprise *with a perfect heart* (*v.* 38), and particularly of the men of Zebulun that they were *not of double heart, v.* 33. They were, in this matter, *Israelites indeed, in whom was no guile.* And this was their perfection, that they were of one heart, *v.* 38. None had any separate interests, but all for the public good.

VIII. The men of Judah, and others of the adjacent tribes, prepared for the victualling of their respective camps when they came to Hebron, *v.* 39, 40. Those that were at the least pains in travelling to this convention, or congress of the states, thought themselves obliged to be at so much the more charge in entertaining the rest, that there might be something of an equality. A noble feast was made (was *made for laughter,* Eccl. x. 19) upon this occasion, for there was *joy in Israel, v.* 40. And good reason; for *when the righteous* bear *rule the city rejoices.* Thus, when the throne of Christ is set up in a soul, there is, or ought to be, great joy in that soul: and provision is made for the feasting of it, not as here for two or three days, but for the whole life, nay, for eternity.

CHAP. XIII.

In the foregoing chapter we have David made king, by which the civil government was happily settled. In this chapter care is taken about religion. I. David consults with the representatives of the people about bringing up the ark out of its obscurity into a public place; and it is resolved on, ver. 1—4. II. With a great deal of solemnity and joy, it is carried from Kirjath-jearim, ver. 5—8. III. Uzza is struck dead for touching it, which, for the present, spoils the solemnity and stops the proceedings, ver. 9—14.

AND David consulted with the captains of thousands and hundreds, *and* with every leader. 2 And David said unto all the congregation of Israel, If *it seem* good unto you, and *that it be* of the LORD our God, let us send abroad unto our brethren every where, *that are* left in all the land of Israel, and with them *also* to the priests and Levites *which are* in their cities *and* suburbs, that they may gather themselves unto us: 3 And let us bring again the ark of our God to us: for we enquired not at it in the days of Saul. 4 And all the congregation said that they would do so: for the thing was right in the eyes of all the people. 5 So David gathered all Israel together, from Shihor of Egypt even unto the entering of Hemath, to bring the ark of God from Kirjath-jearim. 6 And David went up, and all Israel, to Baalah, *that is*, to Kirjath-jearim, which *belonged* to Judah, to bring up thence the ark of God the LORD, that dwelleth *between* the cherubims, whose name is called *on it.* 7 And they carried the ark of God in a new cart out of the house of Abinadab: and Uzza and Ahio drave the cart. 8 And David and all Israel played before God with all *their* might, and with singing, and with harps, and with psalteries, and with timbrels, and with cymbals, and with trumpets.

Here is, I. David's pious proposal to bring up the ark of God to Jerusalem, that the royal city might be the holy city, *v.* 1—3. This part of the story we had not in Samuel. We may observe in this proposal,

1. That as soon as David was well seated on his throne he had thoughts concerning the ark of God: *Let us bring the ark to us*, *v.* 3. Two things he aimed at herein:—(1.) To do honour to God, by showing respect to his ark, the token of his presence. As soon as he had power in his hand he would use it for the advancement and encouragement of religion. Note, It ought to be the first and great care of those that are enriched and preferred to honour God with their honours, and to serve him, and the interests of his kingdom among men, with their wealth and power. David said not, "What pompous thing shall I do now?" or, "What pleasant thing?" but, "What pious thing?" (2.) To have the comfort and benefit of that sacred oracle. "Let us bring it to us, not only that we may be a credit to it, but that it may be a blessing to us." Those that honour God profit themselves. Note, It is the wisdom of those who are setting out in the world to take God's ark with them, to make his oracles their counsellors and his laws their rule. Those are likely to proceed in the favour of God who thus begin in the fear of God.

2. That he consulted with the leaders of the people about it, *v.* 1. Though it was without doubt a very good work, and, being king, he had the authority to command the doing of it, yet he chose rather to do it by consultation, (1.) That he might show respect to the great men of the kingdom and put honour upon them. Though they made him king, yet he would not rule with a high hand. He did not say, "We will and command, and it is our royal pleasure, that you do so and so; and we will be obeyed;" but, "*If it seem good to you*, and you think that the motion comes from the Lord our God, let us send out orders for this purpose." No prince that is wise will covet to be absolute. The people's allegiance is best secured by taking their concurrence in their representatives. Happy then art thou, O Britain! (2.) That he might be advised by them in the manner of doing it, whether just now, whether publicly. David was a very intelligent man himself, and yet consulted with his captains; *for in the multitude of counsellors there is safety.* It is wisdom to make use of the wisdom of others. (3.) That, they joining in it, it might pass the better for a national act and so might procure a national blessing.

3. That he would have all the people summoned to attend on this occasion, both for the honour of the ark and for the people's satisfaction and edification, *v.* 2. Observe, (1.) He calls the common people *brethren*, which bespeaks his humility and condescension (notwithstanding his advancement), and the tender concern he had for them. Thus our Lord Jesus is not ashamed to call his people brethren, Heb. ii. 11. (2.) He speaks of the people as a remnant that had escaped: *Our brethren that are left in all the land of Israel.* They had been under scattering providences. Their wars with the Philistines, and with the house of Saul, had wasted the country and cut off many. We now hope to see an end of these troubles. Let those that are left be quickened by late judgments, and present mercies, to seek unto God. (3.) He takes care that the priests and Levites especially should be summoned to attend the ark; for it was their province in a particular manner. Thus Christian magistrates should stir up ministers to do their duty when they see them remiss.

4. That all this is upon supposition that it is *of the Lord their God.* "Though it should *seem good to you* and me, yet, if it be not *of the Lord our God*, we will not do it." Whatever we undertake, this must be our enquiry, "Is it of the Lord? Is it agreeable to his mind? Can we approve ourselves to him in it? May we expect that he will own us?"

5. That thus it was requisite they should amend what had been amiss in the last reign, and, as it were, atone for their neglect: "*For we enquired not at it in the days of Saul*, and

this was the reason why things went so ill with us: let that original error be amended, and then we may hope to see our affairs in a better posture." Observe, David makes no peevish reflections upon Saul. He does not say, "Saul never cared for the ark, at least in the latter end of his reign;" but, in general, *We enquired not at it*, making himself with others guilty of the neglect. It better becomes us to judge ourselves than others. Humble good men lament their own share in national guilt, and take shame to themselves, Dan. ix. 5, &c.

II. The people's ready agreement to this proposal (*v.* 4): *The thing* was *right in the eyes of all the people.* Nobody could say to the contrary, but that it was a very good work and very seasonable; so that it was resolved, *nemine contradicente—unanimously*, that they would do so. Those that prudently propose a good work, and lead in it, will perhaps find a more ready concurrence in it than they expected. Great men know not what a great deal of good they are capable of doing by their influence on others.

III. The solemnity of bringing up the ark, *v.* 5, &c., which we read before, 2 Sam. vi. 1, &c. Here therefore we shall only observe, 1. That it is worth while to travel far to attend the ark of God. They came out of all parts of the country, from the *river of Egypt*, the utmost part south, to the entering of Hemath, which lay furthest north (*v.* 5), to grace this solemnity. 2. That we have reason greatly to rejoice in the revival of neglected ordinances and the return of the tokens of God's presence. When the light of religion shines out of obscurity, when it is openly and freely professed, is brought into reputation, and countenanced by princes and great ones, it is such a happy omen to a people as is worthy to be welcomed with all possible expressions of joy. 3. When, after long disuse, ordinances come to be revived, it is too common for even wise and good men to make some mistakes. Who would have thought that David would commit such an error as this, to carry the ark upon a cart? *v.* 7. Because the Philistines so carried it, and a special providence drove the cart (1 Sam. vi. 12), he thought they might do so too. But we must walk by rule, not by example when it varies from the rule, no, not even by those examples which Providence has owned.

9 And when they came unto the threshingfloor of Chidon, Uzza put forth his hand to hold the ark; for the oxen stumbled. 10 And the anger of the LORD was kindled against Uzza, and he smote him, because he put his hand to the ark: and there he died before God. 11 And David was displeased, because the LORD had made a breach upon Uzza: wherefore that place is called Perez-uzza to this day. 12 And David was afraid of God that day, saying, How shall I bring the ark of God *home* to me? 13 So David brought not the ark *home* to himself to the city of David, but carried it aside into the house of Obed-edom the Gittite. 14 And the ark of God remained with the family of Obed-edom in his house three months. And the LORD blessed the house of Obed-edom, and all that he had.

This breach upon Uzza, which caused all the joy to cease, we had an account of, 2 Sam. vi. 6, &c. 1. Let the sin of Uzza warn us all to take heed of presumption, rashness, and irreverence, in dealing about holy things (*v.* 9), and not to think that a good intention will justify a bad action. In our communion with God we must carefully watch over our own hearts, lest familiarity breed contempt, and we think God is in any way beholden to us. 2. Let the punishment of Uzza convince us that the God with whom we have to do is a jealous God. His death, like that of Nadab and Abihu, proclaims aloud that God will be *sanctified in those that come nigh unto him* (Lev. x. 3), and that the nearer any are to him the more displeased he is with their presumptions. Let us not dare to trifle with God in our approaches to him; and yet let us, through Christ, *come boldly to the throne of grace;* for we are under the dispensation of liberty and grace, not of bondage and terror. 3. Let the damp this gave to the joy of Israel be a memorandum to us always to rejoice with trembling, and to *serve the Lord with fear*, even when we *serve him with gladness.* 4. Let David's displeasure upon this occasion caution us to take heed to our spirits when we are under divine rebukes, lest, instead of submitting to God, we quarrel with him. If God be angry with us, shall we dare to be angry with him? 5. Let the stop thus put to the solemnity caution us not to be driven off from our duty by those providences which are only intended to drive us from our sins. David should have gone on with this work notwithstanding the breach made upon Uzza; so might the breach have been made up. 6. Let the blessing which the ark brought with it to the house of Obed-edom encourage us to welcome God's ordinances into our houses, as those that believe the ark is a guest that nobody shall lose by; nor let it be the less precious to us for its being to some a stone of stumbling and a rock of offence. If the gospel be to some a savour of death unto death, as the ark was to Uzza, yet let us receive it in the love of it and it will be to us a savour of life unto life.

CHAP. XIV.

In this chapter we have, I. David's kingdom established, ver. 1, 2. II. His family built up, ver. 3—7. III. His enemies, the Philistines, routed in two campaigns, ver. 8—17. This is repeated here from 2 Sam. v. 11, &c.

NOW Hiram king of Tyre sent messengers to David, and timber of cedars, with masons and carpenters, to build him a house. 2 And David perceived that the LORD had confirmed him king over Israel, for his kingdom was lifted up on high, because of his people Israel. 3 And David took more wives at Jerusalem: and David begat more sons and daughters. 4 Now these *are* the names of *his* children which he had in Jerusalem; Shammua, and Shobab, Nathan, and Solomon, 5 And Ibhar, and Elishua, and Elpalet, 6 And Nogah, and Nepheg, and Japhia, 7 And Elishama, and Beeliada, and Eliphalet.

We may observe here, 1. There is no man that has such a sufficiency in himself but he has need of his neighbours and has reason to be thankful for their help: David had a very large kingdom, Hiram a very little one; yet David could not build himself a house to his mind unless Hiram furnished him with both workmen and materials, *v.* 1. This is a reason why we should despise none, but, as we have opportunity, be obliging to all. 2. It is a great satisfaction to a wise man to be settled, and to a good man to see the special providence of God in his settlement. The people had made David king; but he could not be easy, nor think himself happy, till he perceived that *the Lord had confirmed him king over Israel, v.* 2. "Who shall unfix me if God hath fixed me?" 3. We must look upon all our advancements as designed for our usefulness. *David's kingdom was lifted up on high,* not for his own sake, that he might look great, but *because of his people Israel,* that he might be a guide and protector to them. We are blessed in order that we may be blessings. See Gen. xii. 2. We are not born, nor do we live, for ourselves. 4. It is difficult to thrive without growing secure and indulgent to the flesh. It was David's infirmity that when he was settled in his kingdom *he took more wives* (*v.* 3), yet the numerous issue he had added to his honour and strength. Lo, *children are a heritage of the Lord.* We had an account of David's children, not only in Samuel, but in this book (*ch.* iii. 1, &c.) and now here again; for it was their honour to have such a father.

8 And when the Philistines heard that David was anointed king over all Israel, all the Philistines went up to seek David. And David heard *of it,* and went out against them. 9 And the Philistines came and spread themselves in the valley of Rephaim. 10 And David enquired of God, saying, Shall I go up against the Philistines? and wilt thou deliver them into mine hand? And the LORD said unto him, Go up; for I will deliver them into thine hand. 11 So they came up to Baal-perazim; and David smote them there. Then David said, God hath broken in upon mine enemies by mine hand like the breaking forth of waters: therefore they called the name of that place Baal-perazim. 12 And when they had left their gods there, David gave a commandment, and they were burned with fire. 13 And the Philistines yet again spread themselves abroad in the valley. 14 Therefore David enquired again of God; and God said unto him, Go not up after them; turn away from them, and come upon them over against the mulberry trees. 15 And it shall be, when thou shalt hear a sound of going in the tops of the mulberry trees, *that* then thou shalt go out to battle: for God is gone forth before thee to smite the host of the Philistines. 16 David therefore did as God commanded him: and they smote the host of the Philistines from Gibeon even to Gazer. 17 And the fame of David went out into all lands; and the LORD brought the fear of him upon all nations.

This narrative of David's triumph over the Philistines is much the same with that, 2 Sam. v. 17, &c. 1. Let the attack which the Philistines made upon David forbid us to be secure in any settlement or advancement, and engage us to expect molestation in this world. When we are most easy something or other may come to be a terror or vexation to us. Christ's kingdom will thus be insulted by the serpent's seed, especially when it makes any advances. 2. Let David's enquiry of God, once and again, upon occasion of the Philistines' invading him, direct us in all our ways to acknowledge God—in distress to fly to him, when we are wronged to appeal to him, and, when we know not what to do, to ask counsel at his oracles, to put ourselves under his direction, and to beg of him to show us the right way. 3. Let David's success encourage us to resist our spiritual enemies, in observance of divine directions and in dependence on divine strength. Resist the devil, and he shall flee as the Philistines did before David. 4. Let the sound of the going in the tops of the mulberry trees direct us to attend God's motions both in his providence and in the influences of his Spirit. When we perceive God to go before us let us gird up our loins, gird on our armour, and follow him. 5. Let David's burning the gods of the Philistines, when they fell into his hands, teach us a holy indignation against idolatry and all the remains of it. 6. Let David's thankful acknowledgment of the hand of God in his successes direct us to bring all our sacrifices of praise to God's altar. *Not unto us, O Lord! not unto us, but to thy name give glory.* 7. Let the reputation which David obtained, not only in his own kingdom, but among his neighbours, be looked upon as a type and figure of the exalted honour of the Son of David (*v.* 17): *The fame of David went out into all lands;* he was generally talked of, and admired by all people, and *the Lord brought the fear of him upon all nations.* All looked upon him as a formidable enemy and a desirable ally. Thus has God highly exalted our Redeemer, and given him a name above every name.

CHAP. XV.

The bringing in of the ark to the city of David was a very good work; it was resolved upon (ch. xiii. 4), and attempted, but not perfected; it lay by the way in the house of Obed-edom. Now this chapter gives us an account of the completing of that good work. I. How it was done more regularly than before. 1. A place was prepared for it, ver. 1. 2. The priests were ordered to carry it, ver. 2—15. 3. The Levites had their offices assigned them in attending on it, ver. 16—24. II. How it was done more successfully than before, ver. 25. 1. The Levites made no mistake in their work, ver. 26. 2. David and the people met with no damp upon their joy, ver. 27, 28. As for Michal's despising David, it was nothing, ver. 29.

AND *David* made him houses in the city of David, and prepared a place for the ark of God, and pitched for it a tent. 2 Then David said, None ought to carry the ark of God but the Levites: for them hath the LORD chosen to carry the ark of God, and to minister unto him for ever. 3 And David gathered all Israel together to Jerusalem, to bring up the ark of the LORD unto his place, which he had prepared for it. 4 And David assembled the children of Aaron, and the Levites: 5 Of the sons of Kohath; Uriel the chief, and his brethren a hundred and twenty: 6 Of the sons of Merari; Asaiah the chief, and his brethren two hundred and twenty: 7 Of the sons of Gershom; Joel the chief, and his brethren a hundred and thirty: 8 Of the sons of Elizaphan; Shemaiah the chief, and his brethren two hundred: 9 Of the sons of Hebron; Eliel the chief, and his brethren fourscore: 10 Of the sons of Uzziel; Amminadab the chief, and his brethren a hundred and twelve. 11 And David called for Zadok and Abiathar the priests, and for the Levites, for Uriel, Asaiah, and Joel, Shemaiah, and Eliel, and Amminadab, 12 And said unto them, Ye *are* the chief of the fathers of the Levites: sanctify yourselves, *both* ye and your brethren, that ye may bring up the ark of the LORD God of Israel unto *the place that* I have prepared for it. 13 For because ye *did it* not at the first, the LORD our God made a breach upon us, for that we sought him not after the due order. 14 So the priests and the Levites sanctified themselves to bring up the ark of the LORD God of Israel. 15 And the children of the Levites bare the ark of God upon their shoulders with the staves thereon, as Moses commanded according to the word of the LORD. 16 And David spake to the chief of the Levites to appoint their brethren *to be* the singers with instruments of music, psalteries and harps and cymbals, sounding, by lifting up the voice with joy. 17 So the Levites appointed Heman the son of Joel; and of his brethren, Asaph the son of Berechiah; and of the sons of Merari their brethren, Ethan the son of Kushaiah; 18 And with them their brethren of the second *degree,* Zechariah, Ben, and Jaaziel, and Shemiramoth, and Jehiel, and Unni, Eliab, and Benaiah, and Maaseiah, and Mattithiah, and Elipheleh, and Mikneiah, and Obed-edom, and Jeiel, the porters. 19 So the singers, Heman, Asaph, and Ethan, *were appointed* to sound with cymbals of brass; 20 And Zechariah, and Aziel, and Shemiramoth, and Jehiel, and Unni, and Eliab, and Maaseiah, and Benaiah, with psalteries on Alamoth; 21 And Mattithiah, and Elipheleh, and Mikneiah, and Obed-edom, and Jeiel, and Azaziah, with harps on the Sheminith to excel. 22 And Chenaniah, chief of the Levites, *was* for song: he instructed about the song, because he *was* skilful. 23 And Berechiah and Elkanah *were* doorkeepers for the ark. 24 And Shebaniah, and Jehoshaphat, and Nethaneel, and Amasai, and Zechariah, and Benaiah, and Eliezer, the priests, did blow with the trumpets before the ark of God: and Obed-edom and Jehiah *were* doorkeepers for the ark.

Preparation is here made for the bringing of the ark home to the city of David from the house of Obed-edom. It is here owned that in the former attempt, though it was a very good work and in it they *sought God*, yet they *sought him not after the due order, v.* 13. "We did not go about our work considerately; and therefore we sped so ill." Note, It is not enough that we do that which is good, but we must do it well—not enough that we seek God in a due ordinance, but we must seek him in a due order. Note, also, When we have suffered for our irregularities we must learn thereby to be more regular; then we answer the end of chastisement. Let us see how the matter was mended. 1. David now prepared a place for the reception of the ark, before he brought it to him; and thus he sought in the due order. He had not time to *build a house*, but he *pitched a tent* for it (*v.* 1), probably according to the pattern shown to Moses in the mount, or as near it as might be, of curtains and boards. Observe, When he made houses for himself in the city of David he prepared a place for the ark. Note, Wherever we build for ourselves, we must be sure to make room for God's ark, for a church in the house. 2. David now ordered that the Levites or priests should carry the ark upon their shoulders. Now he bethought himself of that which he could not but know before, that *none ought to carry the ark but the Levites, v.* 2. The Kohathites carried it in their ordinary marches, and therefore had no waggons allotted them, because their work was to *bear upon their shoulders*, Num. vii. 9. But upon extraordinary occasions, as when they passed Jordan and compassed Jericho, the priests carried it. This rule was express, and yet David himself forgot it, and put the ark upon a cart. Note, Even those that are very knowing in the word of God, yet have it not always so ready to them as were to be wished when they have occasion to use it. Wise and good men may be guilty of an oversight, which, as soon as they are aware of, they will correct. David did not go about to justify what had been done amiss, nor to lay the blame on others, but owned himself guilty, with others, of not seeking God in a due order, and now took care not only to summon the Levites to the solemnity, as he did all Israel (*v.* 3), and had done before (*ch.* xiii. 2), but to see that they assembled (*v.* 4), especially the sons of Aaron, *v.* 11. To them he gives that solemn charge (*v.* 12): *You are the chief of the fathers of the Levites*, therefore do you *bring up the ark of the Lord*. It is expected that those who are advanced above others in dignity should go before others in duty. "You are the chief, and therefore more is expected from you than from others, both by way of service yourselves and influence on the rest. You did it not at first, neither did your duty yourselves nor took care to instruct us, and we smarted for it: *The Lord made a breach upon us;* we have all smarted for your neglect; *this has been by your means* (see Mal. i. 9): therefore *sanctify yourselves*, and mind your business. When those that have suffered for doing ill thus learn to do better the correction is well bestowed. 3. The Levites and priests sanctified themselves (*v.* 14) and were ready to carry the ark on their shoulders, according to the law, *v.* 15. Note, Many that are very remiss in their duty, if they were but faithfully told of it, would reform and do better. The breach upon Uzza made the priests more careful to sanctify themselves, that is, to cleanse themselves from all ceremonial pollution and to compose themselves for the solemn service of God, so as to strike a reverence upon the people. Some are made examples, that others may be made exemplary and very cautious. 4. Officers were appointed to be ready to bid the ark welcome, with every possible expression of joy, *v.* 16. David ordered the chief of the Levites to nominate those that they knew to be proficients for this service. Heman, Asaph, and Ethan, were now first appointed, *v.* 17. They undertook to sound with symbols (*v.* 19), others with psalteries (*v.* 20), others with harps, on the *Skeminith*, or *eighth*, eight notes higher or lower than the rest, according to the rules of concert, *v.* 21. Some that were priests blew with the trumpet (*v.* 24), as was usual at the removal of the ark (Num. x. 8) and at solemn feasts, Ps. lxxxi. 3. And one was appointed for song (*v.* 22), for he was skilful in it, could sing well himself and instruct others. Note, As every man has *received the gift*, so he ought to *minister the same*, 1 Pet. iv. 10. And those that excel in any endowment should not only use it for the common good themselves, but teach others also, and not grudge to make others as wise as themselves. This way of praising God by musical instruments had not hitherto been in use. But David, being a prophet, instituted it by divine direction, and added it to the other *carnal ordinances* of that dispensation, as the apostle calls them, Heb. ix. 10. The New Testament keeps up singing of psalms, but has not appointed church-music. Some were appointed to be porters (*v.* 18), others door-keepers for the ark (*v.* 23, 24), and one of these was Obed-edom, who reckoned it no doubt a place of honour, and accepted it as a recompence for the entertainment he had given to the ark. He had been for three months housekeeper to the ark, and indeed its landlord. But, when he might not be so any longer, such an affection had he for it that he was glad to be its doorkeeper.

25 So David, and the elders of Israel, and the captains over thousands, went to bring up the ark of the covenant of the LORD out of the house of Obed-edom with joy. 26 And it came to pass, when God helped the Levites that bare the ark of the covenant of the LORD, that they offered seven bullocks and seven rams. 27 And David *was* clothed with a robe of fine linen, and all the Levites that bare the ark, and the singers, and Chenaniah the master of the song with the singers: David also *had* upon him an ephod of linen. 28 Thus all Israel brought up the ark of the covenant of the LORD with shouting, and with sound of the cornet, and with trumpets, and with cymbals, making a noise with psalteries and harps. 29 And it came to pass, *as* the ark of the covenant of the LORD came to the city of David, that Michal the daughter of Saul looking out at a window saw king David dancing and playing: and she despised him in her heart.

All things being got ready for the carrying of the ark to the city of David, and its reception there, we have here an account of the solemnity of this conveyance thither from the house of Obed-edom.

I. God helped the Levites that carried it. The ark was no very great burden, that those who carried it needed any extraordinary help. But, 1. It is good to take notice of the assistance of the divine providence even in those things that fall within the compass of our natural powers: if God did not help us, we could not stir a step. 2. In all our religious exercises we must particularly derive help from heaven. See Acts xxvi. 22. All our sufficiency for holy duties is from God. 3. The Levites, remembering the breach upon Uzza, were probably ready to tremble when they took up the ark; but God helped them, that is, he encouraged them to it, silenced their fears, and strengthened their faith. 4. God helped them to do it decently and well, and without making any mistake. If we perform any religious duties so as to escape a breach, and come off with our lives, we must own it is God that helps us; for, if left to ourselves, we should be guilty of some fatal miscarriages. God's ministers that bear the vessels of the Lord have special need of divine help in their ministrations, that God in them may be glorified and his church edified. And, if God help the Levites, the people have the benefit of it.

II. When they experienced the tokens of God's presence with them they offered sacrifices of praise to him, *v.* 26. This also he helped them to do. They offered these bullocks and rams perhaps by way of atonement for the former error, that it might not now be remembered against them, as well as by way of acknowledgment for the help now received.

III. There were great expressions of rejoicing used: the sacred music was played, David danced, the singers sang, and the common people shouted, *v.* 27, 28. This we had before, 2 Sam. vi. 14, 15. Learn hence, 1. That we serve a good master, who delights to have his servants sing at their work. 2. That times of public reformation are, and should be, times of public rejoicing. Those are unworthy of the ark that are not glad of it. 3. It is not any disparagement to the greatest of men to show themselves zealous in the acts of devotion. Michal indeed despised David (*v.* 29); but *her* despising him did not make him at all despicable; he did not regard it himself, nor did any that were wise and good (and why should we covet the esteem of any but such?) think the worse of him.

CHAP. XVI.

This chapter concludes that great affair of the settlement of the ark in the royal city, and with it the settlement of the public worship of God during the reign of David. Here is, I. The solemnity with which the ark was fixed, ver. 1–6. II. The psalm David gave to be sung on this occasion, ver. 7–36. III. The settling of the stated public worship of God in order thenceforward, ver. 37–43.

SO they brought the ark of God, and set it in the midst of the tent that David had pitched for it: and they offered burnt sacrifices and peace offerings before God. 2 And when David had made an end of offering the burnt offerings and the peace offerings, he blessed the people in the name of the LORD. 3 And he dealt to every one of Israel, both man and woman, to every one a loaf of bread, and a good piece of flesh, and a flagon *of wine*. 4 And he appointed *certain* of the Levites to minister before the ark of the LORD, and to record, and to thank and praise the LORD God of Israel: 5 Asaph the chief, and next to him Zechariah, Jeiel, and Shemiramoth, and Jehiel, and Mattithiah, and Eliab, and Benaiah, and Obed-edom: and Jeiel with psalteries and with harps; but Asaph made a sound with cymbals; 6 Benaiah also and Jahaziel the priests with trumpets continually before the ark of the covenant of God.

It was a glorious day when the ark of God was safely lodged in the tent David had pitched for it. That good man had his heart much upon it, could not sleep contentedly till it was done, Ps. cxxxii. 4, 5

I. The circumstances of the ark were now, 1. Better than what they had been. It had been obscure in a country town, in the fields of the wood; now it was removed to a public place, to the royal city, where all might resort to it. It had been neglected, as a despised broken vessel; now it was attended with veneration, and God was enquired of by it. It had borrowed a room in a private house, which it enjoyed by courtesy; now it had a habitation of its own entirely to itself, was set in the midst of it, and not crowded into a corner. Note, Though God's word and ordinances may be clouded and eclipsed for a time, they shall at length shine out of obscurity. Yet, 2. They were much short of what was intended in the next reign, when the temple was to be built. This was but a tent, a poor mean dwelling; yet this was the tabernacle, the temple, which David in his psalms often speaks of with so much affection. David, who pitched a tent for the ark and continued stedfast to it, did far better than Solomon, who built a temple for it and yet in his latter end turned his back upon it. The church's poorest times were its purest.

II. Now David was easy in his mind, the ark was fixed, and fixed near him. Now see how he takes care, 1. That God shall have the glory of it. Two ways he gives him honour upon this occasion:—(1.) By sacrifices (*v.* 1), burnt-offerings in adoration of his perfections, peace-offerings in acknowledgment of his favours. (2.) By songs; he appointed Levites to record this story in a song for the benefit of others, or to celebrate it themselves by *thanking and praising the God of Israel, v.* 4. All our rejoicings must express themselves in thanksgivings to him from whom all our comforts are received. 2. That the people shall have the joy of it. They shall fare the better for this day's solemnity; for he gives them all what is worth coming for, not only a royal treat in honour of the day (*v.* 3), in which David showed himself generous to his subjects, as he had found God gracious to him (those whose hearts are enlarged with holy joy should show it by being open-handed); but (which is far better) he gives them also a *blessing in the name of the Lord,* as a father, as a prophet, *v.* 2. He prayed to God for them, and commended them to his grace. *In the name of the Word of the Lord* (so the Targum), the essential eternal Word, who is Jehovah, and through whom all blessings come to us.

7 Then on that day David delivered first *this psalm* to thank the LORD into the hand of Asaph and his brethren. 8 Give thanks unto the LORD, call upon his name, make known his deeds among the people. 9 Sing unto him, sing psalms unto him, talk ye of all his wondrous works. 10 Glory ye in his holy name: let the heart of them rejoice that seek the LORD. 11 Seek the LORD and his strength, seek his face continually. 12 Remember his marvellous works that he hath done, his wonders, and the judgments of his mouth; 13 O ye seed of Israel his servant, ye children of Jacob, his chosen ones. 14 He *is* the LORD our God; his judgments *are* in all the earth. 15 Be ye mindful always of his covenant; the word *which* he commanded to a thousand generations; 16 *Even of the covenant* which he made with Abraham, and of his oath unto Isaac; 17 And hath confirmed the same to Jacob for a law, *and* to Israel *for* an everlasting covenant, 18 Saying, Unto thee will I give the land of Canaan, the lot of your inheritance; 19 When ye were but few, even a few, and strangers in it. 20 And *when* they went from nation to nation, and from *one* kingdom to another people; 21 He suffered no man to do them wrong: yea, he reproved kings for their sakes, 22 *Saying,* Touch not mine anointed, and do my prophets no harm. 23 Sing unto the LORD, all the earth; show forth from day to day his salvation. 24 Declare his glory among the heathen; his marvellous works among all nations. 25 For great *is* the LORD, and greatly to be praised: he also *is* to be feared above all gods. 26 For all the gods of the people *are* idols: but the LORD made the heavens. 27 Glory and honour *are* in his presence; strength and gladness *are* in his place. 28 Give unto the LORD, ye kindreds of the people, give unto the LORD glory and strength. 29 Give unto the LORD the glory *due* unto his name: bring an offering, and come before him: worship the LORD in the beauty of

holiness. 30 Fear before him, all the earth: the world also shall be stable, that it be not moved. 31 Let the heavens be glad, and let the earth rejoice: and let *men* say among the nations, The LORD reigneth. 32 Let the sea roar, and the fulness thereof: let the fields rejoice, and all that *is* therein. 33 Then shall the trees of the wood sing out at the presence of the LORD, because he cometh to judge the earth. 34 O give thanks unto the LORD; for *he is* good; for his mercy *endureth* for ever. 35 And say ye, Save us, O God of our salvation, and gather us together, and deliver us from the heathen, that we may give thanks to thy holy name, *and* glory in thy praise. 36 Blessed *be* the LORD God of Israel for ever and ever. And all the people said, Amen, and praised the LORD.

We have here the thanksgiving psalm which David, by the Spirit, composed, and delivered to the chief musician, to be sung upon occasion of the public entry the ark made into the tent prepared for it. Some think he appointed this hymn to be daily used in the temple service, as duly as the day came; whatever other psalms they sung, they must not omit this. David had penned many psalms before this, some in the time of his troubles by Saul. This was composed before, but was now first delivered into the hand of Asaph, for the use of the church. It is gathered out of several psalms (from the beginning to *v.* 23 is taken from Ps. cv. 1, &c.; and then *v.* 23 to *v.* 34 is the whole 96th psalm, with little variation; *v.* 34 is taken from Ps. cxxxvi. 1 and divers others; and then the last two verses are taken from the close of Ps. cvi.), which some think warrants us to do likewise, and make up hymns out of David's psalms, a part of one and a part of another put together so as may be most proper to express and excite the devotion of Christians. These psalms will be best expounded in their proper places (if the Lord will); here we take them as they are put together, with a design to *thank the Lord* (*v.* 7), a great duty, to which we need to be excited and in which we need to be assisted. 1. Let God be glorified in our praises; let his honour be the centre in which all the lines meet. Let us glorify him by our thanksgivings *(Give thanks to the Lord)*, by our prayers *(Call on his name, v. 8)*, by our songs *(Sing psalms unto him)*, by our discourse—*Talk of all his wondrous works, v.* 9. Let us glorify him as *a great God, and greatly to be praised* (*v.* 25), as supreme God (above all gods), as sole God, for all others are idols, *v.* 26. Let us glorify him as most bright and blessed in himself *(Glory and honour are in his presence, v.* 27), as Creator *(The Lord made the heavens)*, as the ruler of the whole creation *(His judgments are in all the earth, v.* 14), and as ours—*He is the Lord our God.* Thus must we *give unto the Lord the glory due to his name* (*v.* 28, 29), and own it, and much more, his due. 2. Let others be edified and instructed: *Make known his deeds among the people* (*v.* 8), *declare his glory among the heathen* (*v.* 24), that those who are strangers to him may be led into acquaintance with him, allegiance to him, and the adoration of him. Thus must we serve the interests of his kingdom among men, that all the earth may *fear before him, v.* 30. 3. Let us be ourselves encouraged to triumph and trust in God. Those that give glory to God's name are allowed to *glory in it* (*v.* 10), to value themselves upon their relation to God and venture themselves upon his promise to them. *Let the heart of those rejoice that seek the Lord,* much more of those that have found him. *Seek him, and his strength, and his face;* that is, seek him by the ark of his strength, in which he manifests himself. 4. Let the everlasting covenant be the great matter of our joy and praise (*v.* 15): *Be mindful of his covenant.* In the parallel place it is, *He will be ever mindful of it,* Ps. cv. 8. Seeing God never will forget it, we never must. The covenant is said to be *commanded,* because God has obliged us to obey the conditions of it, and because he has both authority to make the promise and ability to make it good. This covenant was ancient, yet never to be forgotten. It was made with Abraham, Isaac, and Jacob, who were long since dead (*v.* 16—18), yet still sure to the spiritual seed, and the promises of it pleadable. 5. Let God's former mercies to his people of old, to our ancestors and our predecessors in profession, be commemorated by us now with thankfulness to his praise. Let it be remembered how God protected the patriarchs in their unsettled condition. When they came strangers to Canaan and were sojourners in it, when they were few and might easily have been swallowed up, when they were continually upon the remove and so exposed, when there were many that bore them ill-will and sought to do them mischief, yet no man was suffered to do them wrong—not the Canaanites, Philistines, Egyptians. Kings were reproved and plagued for their sakes. Pharaoh was so, and Abimelech. They were the *anointed of the Lord,* sanctified by his grace, sanctified to his glory, and had received the unction of the Spirit. They were his prophets, instructed in the things of God themselves and commissioned to instruct others (and prophets are said to be *anointed,* 1 Kings xix. 16; Isa. lxi. 1); therefore, if any touch them, they touch the apple of God's eye; if any harm them, it is at their peril, *v.* 19—22. 6. Let the great salvation of the Lord be especially the subject of our praises (*v.* 23): *Show forth from day to day his salvation,* that is (says bishop Patrick), his promised salvation by Christ. We have reason to celebrate that from day to day; for we daily receive the benefit of it, and it is a subject that can never be exhausted. 7. Let God be praised by a due and constant attendance upon him in the ordinances he has appointed: *Bring an offering,* then the fruit of the *ground,* now the fruit of the *lips,* of the *heart* (Heb. xiii. 15), and *worship him in the beauty of holiness,* in the holy place and in a holy manner, *v.* 29. Holiness is the beauty of the Lord, the beauty of all sanctified souls and all religious performances. 8. Let God's universal monarchy be the fear and joy of all people. Let us reverence it: *Fear before him, all the earth.* And let us rejoice in it: *Let the heavens be glad and rejoice,* because *the Lord reigns,* and by his providence establishes the world, so that, though it be moved, it cannot be removed, nor the measures broken which Infinite Wisdom has taken in the government of it, *v.* 30, 31. 9. Let the prospect of the judgment to come inspire us with an awful pleasure. Let earth and sea, fields and woods, though in the great day of the Lord they will all be consumed, yet rejoice that he will come, doth come, to *judge the earth, v.* 32, 33. 10. In the midst of our praises we must not forget to pray for the succour and relief of those saints and servants of God that are in distress (*v.* 35): *Save us, gather us, deliver us from the heathen,* those of us that are scattered and oppressed. When we are rejoicing in God's favours to us we must remember our afflicted brethren, and pray for their salvation and deliverance as our own. We are members one of another; and therefore when we mean, "Lord, save *them,*" it is not improper to say, "Lord, save *us.*" *Lastly,* Let us make God the Alpha and Omega of our praises. David begins with (*v.* 8), *Give thanks to the Lord;* he concludes (*v.* 36), *Blessed be the Lord.* And whereas in the place whence this doxology is taken (Ps. cvi. 48) it is added, *Let all the people say, Amen, Hallelujah,* here we find they did according to that directory: *All the people said, Amen, and praised the Lord.* When the Levites had finished this psalm of prayer and praise, then, and not till then, the people that attended signified their consent and concurrence by saying, *Amen.* And so they praised the Lord, much affected no doubt with this newly instituted way of devotion, which had been hitherto used in the schools of the prophets only, 1 Sam. x. 5 And, if this way of praising God *please the Lord better than an ox or a bullock that has horns and hoofs, the humble shall see it and be glad,* Ps. lxix. 31, 32.

37 So he left there before the ark of the covenant of the LORD Asaph and his brethren, to minister before the ark continually, as every day's work required: 38 And Obed-edom with their brethren, threescore and eight; Obed-edom also the son of Jeduthun and Hosah *to be* porters: 39 And Zadok the priest, and his brethren the priests, before the tabernacle of the LORD in the high place that *was* at Gibeon, 40 To offer burnt offerings unto the LORD upon the altar of the burnt offering continually morning and evening, and *to do* according to all that is written in the law of the LORD, which he commanded Israel; 41 And with them Heman and Jeduthun, and the rest that were chosen, who were expressed by name, to give thanks to the LORD, because his mercy *endureth* for ever; 42 And with them Heman and Jeduthun with trumpets and cymbals for those that should make a sound, and with musical instruments of God. And the sons of Jeduthun *were* porters. 43 And all the people departed every man to his house: and David returned to bless his house.

The worship of God is not only to be the work of a solemn day now and then, brought in to grace a triumph; but it ought to be the work of every day. David therefore settles it here for a constancy, puts it into a method, which he obliged those that officiated to observe in their respective posts. In the tabernacle of Moses, and afterwards in the temple of Solomon, the ark and the altar were together; but, ever since Eli's time, they had been separated, and still continued so till the temple was built. I cannot conceive what reason there was why David, who knew the law and was zealous for it, did not either bring the ark to Gibeon, where the tabernacle and the altar were, or bring them to Mount Zion, where the ark was. Perhaps the curtains and hangings of Moses's tabernacle were so worn with time and weather that they were not fit to be removed, nor fit to be a shelter for the ark; and yet he would not make all new, but only a tent for the ark, because the time was at hand when the temple should be built. Whatever was the reason, all David's time they were asunder, but he took care that neither of them should be neglected. 1. At Jerusalem, where the ark was, Asaph and his brethren were appointed to attend, to *minister before the ark continually,* with songs of praise, *as every day's work required, v.* 37. No sacrifices were offered there, nor incense burnt, because the altars were not there; but David's prayers were *directed as incense, and the lifting up of his hands as the evening sacrifice* (Ps. cxli. 2), so early did spiritual worship take place of ceremonial. 2. Yet the ceremonial worship, being of divine institution, must by no means be omitted; and therefore at Gibeon were the altars where the priests attended, for their work was to sacrifice and burn incense, which they did *continually, morning and evening, according to the law of Moses, v.* 39, 40. These must be kept up because, however in their own nature they were inferior to the moral services of prayer and praise, yet, as they were types of the mediation of Christ, they had a great deal of honour put upon them, and the observance of them was of great consequence. Here Zadok attended, to preside in the service of the altar; as (it is probable) Abiathar settled at Jerusalem, to attend the ark, because he had the breast-plate of judgment, which must be consulted before the ark: this is the reason why we read that in David's time both Zadok and Abiathar were the priests (2 Sam. viii. 17; xx. 25), one where the altar was and the other where the ark was. At Gibeon, where the altars were, David also appointed *singers to give thanks to the Lord,* and the burden of all their songs must be, *For his mercy endureth for ever, v.* 41. They did it *with musical instruments of God,* such instruments as were appointed and appropriated to this service, not such as they used on other occasions. Between common mirth and holy joy there is a vast difference, and the limits and distances between them must be carefully observed and kept up. Matters being thus settled, and the affairs of religion put into a happy channel, (1.) The people were satisfied, and went home pleased. (2.) David returned to bless his house, resolving to keep up his family worship still, which public worship must not supersede.

CHAP. XVII.

This excellent chapter is the same with 2 Sam. vii. It will be worth while to look back upon what was there said upon it. Two things in general we have in it:—I. God's gracious acceptance of David's purpose to build him a house, and the promise he made thereupon, ver. 1—15. II. David's gracious acceptance of God's good promise to build him a house, and the prayer he made thereupon, ver. 16—27.

NOW it came to pass, as David sat in his house, that David said to Nathan the prophet, Lo, I dwell in a house of cedars, but the ark of the covenant of the LORD *remaineth* under curtains. 2 Then Nathan said unto David, Do all that *is* in thine heart; for God *is* with thee. 3 And it came to pass the same night, that the word of God came to Nathan, saying, 4 Go and tell David my servant, Thus saith the LORD, Thou shalt not build me a house to dwell in: 5 For I have not dwelt in a house since the day that I brought up Israel unto this day; but have gone from tent to tent, and from *one* tabernacle *to another.* 6 Wheresoever I have walked with all Israel, spake I a word to any of the judges of Israel, whom I commanded to feed my people, saying, Why have ye not built me a house of cedars? 7 Now therefore thus shalt thou say unto my servant David, Thus saith the LORD of hosts, I took thee from the sheepcote, *even* from following the sheep, that thou shouldest be ruler over my people Israel: 8 And I have been with thee whithersoever thou hast walked, and have cut off all thine enemies from before thee, and have made thee a name like the name of the great men that *are* in the earth. 9 Also I will ordain a place for my people Israel, and will plant them, and they shall dwell in their place, and shall be moved no more; neither shall the children of wickedness waste them any more, as at the beginning, 10 And since the time that I commanded judges *to be* over my people Israel. Moreover I will subdue all thine enemies. Furthermore I tell thee that the LORD will build thee a house. 11 And it shall come to pass, when thy days be expired that thou must go *to be* with thy fathers, that I will raise up thy seed after thee, which shall be of thy sons; and I will establish his kingdom. 12 He shall build me a house, and I will establish his throne for ever. 13 I will be his father, and he shall be my son: and I will not take my mercy away from him, as I took *it* from *him* that was before thee: 14 But I will settle him in mine house and in my kingdom for ever: and his throne shall be established for evermore. 15 According to all these words, and according to all this vision, so did Nathan speak unto David.

Let us observe here,

I. How desirous and solicitous good people should be to serve the interests of God's kingdom in the world, to the utmost of their capacity. David could not be easy in a house of cedar while the ark was lodged within curtains, *v.* 1. The concerns of the public should always be near our hearts. What pleasure can we take in our own prosperity if we see not the good of Jerusalem? When David is advanced to wealth and power see what his cares and projects are. Not, "What shall I do for my children to get portions for them? What shall I do to fill my coffers and enlarge my dominions?" But, "What shall I do for God, to serve and honour him?" Those that are contriving where to bestow their fruits and their goods would do well to enquire what condition the ark is in, and whether some may not be well bestowed upon it.

II. How ready God's prophets should be to encourage every good purpose. Nathan was no sooner aware of David's good design than he bade him *go and do all that was within his heart* (*v.* 2), for he had no reason to doubt but that God was with him in it. Ministers should stir up the gifts and graces that are in others as well as in themselves.

III. How little God affects external pomp and splendour in his service. His ark was content with a tabernacle (*v.* 5) and he never so much as mentioned the building of a house for it; no, not when he had fixed his people in great and goodly cities which they builded not, Deut. vi. 10. He commanded the judges to *feed his people*, but never bade them *build him a house*, *v.* 6. We may well be content awhile with mean accommodations; God's ark was so.

IV. How graciously God accepts his people's good purposes, yea, though he himself prevents the performance of them. David must not *build this house*, *v.* 4. He must prepare for it, but not do it; as Moses must bring Israel within sight of Canaan, but must then leave it to Joshua to put them in possession of it. It is the prerogative of Christ to be both the author and finisher of his work. Yet David must not think that, because he was not permitted to build the temple, 1. His preferment was in vain; no, "*I took thee from the sheep-cote*, though not to be a builder of the temple, yet to be *ruler over my people Israel;* that is honour enough for thee; leave the other to one that shall come after thee," *v.* 7. Why should one man think to engross all the business and to bring every good work to perfection? let something be left for those that succeed. God had given him victories, and made him a name (*v.* 8), and, further, intended by him to establish his people Israel and secure them against their enemies, *v.* 9. That must be *his* work, who is a man of war and fit for it, and he must let the building of churches be left to one that was never cut out for a soldier. Nor, 2. Must he think that his good purpose was in vain, and that he should lose the reward of it; no, it being God's act to prevent the execution of it, he shall be as fully recompensed as if he had done it: "*The Lord will build thee a house,* and annex the crown of Israel to it," *v.* 10. If there be a willing mind, it shall not only be accepted, but thus rewarded. Nor, 3. Must he think that because *he* might not do this good work therefore it would never be done, and that it was in vain to think of it; no, *I will raise up thy seed, and he shall build me a house*, *v.* 11, 12. God's temple shall be built in the time appointed, though we may not have the honour of helping to build it or the satisfaction of seeing it built. Nor, 4. Must he confine his thoughts to the temporal prosperity of his family, but must entertain himself with the prospect of the kingdom of the Messiah, who should descend from his loins, and whose throne should be *established for evermore*, *v.* 14. Solomon was not himself so settled in God's house as he should have been, nor was his family settled in the kingdom: "But there shall one descend from thee whom I will settle in my house and in my kingdom," which intimates that he should be both a high priest over the house of God and should have the sole administration of the affairs of God's kingdom among men, all power both in heaven and in earth, in the house and in the kingdom, in the church and in the world. He shall be *a priest upon his throne*, and *the counsel of peace shall be between them both*, and *he shall build the temple of the Lord*, Zech. vi. 12, 13.

16 And David the king came and sat before the LORD, and said, Who *am* I, O LORD God, and what *is* mine house, that thou hast brought me hitherto? 17 And *yet* this was a small thing in thine eyes, O God; for thou hast *also* spoken of thy servant's house for a great while to come, and hast regarded me according to the estate of a man of high degree, O LORD God. 18 What can David *speak* more to thee for the honour of thy servant? for thou knowest thy servant. 19 O LORD, for thy servant's sake, and according to thine own heart, hast thou done all this greatness, in making known all *these* great things. 20 O LORD, *there is* none like thee, neither *is there any* God beside thee, according to all that we have heard with our ears. 21 And what one nation in the earth *is* like thy people Israel, whom God went to redeem *to be* his own people, to make thee a name of greatness and terribleness, by driving out nations from before thy people, whom thou hast redeemed out of Egypt? 22 For thy people Israel didst thou make thine own people for ever; and thou, LORD, be-

camest their God. 23 Therefore now, LORD, let the thing that thou hast spoken concerning thy servant and concerning his house be established for ever, and do as thou hast said. 24 Let it even be established, that thy name may be magnified for ever, saying, The LORD of hosts *is* the God of Israel, *even* a God to Israel: and *let* the house of David thy servant *be* established before thee. 25 For thou, O my God, hast told thy servant that thou wilt build him a house: therefore thy servant hath found *in his heart* to pray before thee. 26 And now, LORD, thou art God, and hast promised this goodness unto thy servant: 27 Now therefore let it please thee to bless the house of thy servant, that it may be before thee for ever: for thou blessest, O LORD, and *it shall be* blessed for ever.

We have here David's solemn address to God, in answer to the gracious message he had now received from him. By faith he receives the promises, embraces them, and is persuaded of them, as the patriarchs, Heb. xi. 13. How humbly does he here abase himself, and acknowledge his own unworthiness! How highly does he advance the name of God and admire his condescending grace and favour! With what devout affections does he magnify the God of Israel and what a value has he for the Israel of God! With what assurance does he build upon the promise, and with what a lively faith does he put it in suit! What an example is this to us of humble, believing, fervent prayer! The Lord enable us all thus to seek him! These things were largely observed, 2 Sam. vii. We shall therefore here observe only those few expressions in which the prayer, as we find it here, differs from the record of it there, and has something added to it.

I. That which is there expressed by way of question *(Is this the manner of men, O Lord God?)* is here an acknowledgment: "*Thou hast regarded me according to the estate of a man of high degree.* Thou hast made me a great man, and then treated me accordingly." God, by the covenant-relations into which he admits believers, the titles he gives them, the favours he bestows on them, and the preparations he has made for them, regards them according to the estate of men of high degree, though they are mean and vile. Having himself distinguished them, he treats them as persons of distinction, according to the quality he has been pleased to put upon them. Some give these words here another reading: *Thou hast looked upon me in the form of a man who art in the highest, the Lord God;* or, *Thou hast made me to see according to the form of a man the majesty of the Lord God.*" And so it points at the Messiah; for, as Abraham, so David, saw his day and was glad, saw it by faith, saw him in *fashion as a man, the Word made flesh,* and yet saw his *glory as* that *of the only-begotten of the Father.* And this was that which God spoke concerning his house for a great while to come, the foresight of which affected him more than any thing. And let it not be thought strange that David should speak so plainly of the two natures of Christ who in spirit called him *Lord,* though he knew he was to be his *Son* (Ps. cx. 1), and foresaw him *lower than the angels* for a little while, but afterwards *crowned with glory and honour,* Heb. ii. 6, 7.

II. After the words *What can David say more unto thee,* it is here added, *for the honour of thy servant? v.* 18. Note, The honour God puts upon his servants, by taking them into covenant and communion with himself, is so great that they need not, they cannot, desire to be more highly honoured. Were they to sit down and wish, they could not speak more for their own honour than the word of God has spoken.

III. It is very observable that what in Samuel is said to be *for thy word's sake* is here said to be *for thy servant's sake, v.* 19. Jesus Christ is both *the Word of God* (Rev. xix. 13) and *the servant of God* (Isa. xlii. 1), and it is for his sake, upon the score of his mediation, that the promises are both made and made good to all believers; it is in him that they are *yea and amen.* For his sake is all this kindness done, for his sake it is made known; to him we owe all this greatness and from him we are to expect all these great things; they are *the unsearchable riches of Christ,* which, if by faith we see in themselves and see in the hand of the Lord Jesus, we cannot but magnify as great things, the only true greatness, and speak honourably of accordingly.

IV. In Samuel, the Lord of hosts is said to be the *God over Israel;* here he is said to be *the God of Israel, even a God to Israel, v.* 24. His being the God *of* Israel bespeaks his having the name of *their God* and so calling himself; his being a God *to* Israel bespeaks his answering to the name, his filling up the relation, and doing all that to them which might be expected from him. There were those that were called *gods* of such and such nations, gods of Assyria and Egypt, gods of Hamad and Arpad; but they were no gods to them, for they stood them in no stead at all, were mere ciphers, nothing but a name. But *the God of Israel* is a *God to Israel;* all his attributes and perfections redound to their real benefit and advantage. *Happy therefore, thrice happy, is the people whose God is Jehovah;* for he will be a God to them, a God all-sufficient.

V. The closing words in Samuel are, *With thy blessing let the house of thy servant be blessed for ever.* That is the language of a holy desire. But the closing words here are the language of a most holy faith: *For thou blessest, O Lord! and it shall be blessed for ever, v.* 27. 1. He was encouraged to beg a blessing because God had intimated to him that he had blessings in store for him and his family: "*Thou blessest, O Lord!* and therefore unto thee shall all flesh come for a blessing; unto thee do I come for the blessing promised to me." Promises are intended to direct and excite prayer. Has God said, *I will bless?* Let our hearts answer, *Lord, bless me.* 2. He was earnest for the blessing because he believed that those whom God blesses are truly and eternally blessed: *Thou blessest, and it shall be blessed.* Men can but *beg* the blessing; it is God that *commands* it. What he designs he effects; what he promises he performs; saying and doing are not two things with him. Nay, *it shall be blessed for ever.* His blessings shall not be revoked, cannot be opposed, and the benefits conferred by them are such as will survive time and days. David's prayer concludes as God's promise did (*v.* 14) with that which is *for ever.* God's word looks at things eternal, and so should our desires and hopes.

CHAP. XVIII.

David's piety and his prayer we had an account of in the foregoing chapter; here follows immediately that which one might reasonably expect, an account of his prosperity; for those that seek first the kingdom of God and the righteousness thereof, as David did, shall have other things added to them as far as God sees good for them. Here is, I. His prosperity abroad. He conquered the Philistines (ver. 1), the Moabites (ver. 2), the king of Zobah (ver. 3, 4), the Syrians (ver. 5—8), made the king of Hamath his tributary (ver. 9—11), and the Edomites, ver. 12, 13. II. His prosperity at home. His court and kingdom flourished, ver. 14—17. All this we had an account of before, 2 Sam. viii.

NOW after this it came to pass, that David smote the Philistines, and subdued them, and took Gath and her towns out of the hand of the Philistines. 2 And he smote Moab; and the Moabites became David's servants, *and* brought gifts. 3 And David smote Hadarezer king of Zobah unto Hamath, as he went to stablish his dominion by the river Euphrates. 4 And David took from him a thousand chariots, and seven thousand horsemen, and twenty thousand footmen: David also houghed all the chariot *horses,* but reserved of them a hundred chariots. 5 And when the Syrians of Damascus came to help Hadarezer king of Zobah, David slew of the Syrians two and twenty thousand men. 6 Then David put *garrisons* in Syria-damascus; and the Syrians became David's servants, *and* brought gifts. Thus the LORD preserved David whithersoever he went. 7 And David took the shields of gold that were on the servants of Hadarezer, and brought them to Jerusalem. 8 Likewise from Tibhath, and from Chun, cities of Hadarezer, brought David very much brass, wherewith Solomon made the brasen sea, and the pillars, and the vessels of brass.

After this, it is said (*v.* 1), David did those great exploits. After the sweet communion he had had with God by the word and prayer, as mentioned in the foregoing chapter, he went on in his work with extraordinary vigour and courage, *conquering and to conquer.* Thus Jacob, after his vision, lifted up his feet, Gen. xxix. 1.

We have taken a view of these victories before, and shall now only observe, 1. Those that have been long enemies to the Israel of God will be brought down at last. The Philistines had, for several generations, been vexatious to Israel, but now *David subdued them, v.* 1. Thus shall all opposing *rule, principality, and power,* be, at the end of time, put down by the Son of David, and the most inveterate enemies shall fall before him. 2. Such is the uncertainty of this world that frequently men lose their wealth and power when they think to confirm it. Hadarezer was smitten *as he went to establish his dominion, v.* 3. 3. *A horse is a vain thing for safety,* so David said (Ps. xxxiii. 17), and it seems he believed what he said, for he *houghed the chariot-horses, v.* 4. Being resolved not to trust to them (Ps. xx. 7), he would not use them. 4. The enemies of God's church are often made to ruin themselves by helping one another, *v.* 5. The Syrians of Damascus were smitten when they came to help Hadarezer. When hand thus joins in hand they shall not only not go unpunished, but thereby they shall be gathered *as the sheaves into the floor,* Mic. iv. 11, 12. 5. The *wealth of the sinner* sometimes proves to have been *laid up for the just.* The *Syrians brought gifts, v.* 6. Their shields of gold and their brass were brought to Jerusalem, *v.* 7, 8. As the tabernacle was built of the spoils of the Egyptians, so the temple of the spoils of other Gentile nations, a happy presage of the interest the Gentiles should have in the gospel church.

9 Now when Tou king of Hamath heard how David had smitten all the host of Hadarezer king of Zobah; 10 He sent Hadoram his son to king David, to enquire of his welfare, and to congratulate him, because he had fought against Hadarezer, and smitten him; (for Hadarezer had war

with Tou;) and *with him* all manner of vessels of gold and silver and brass. 11 Them also king David dedicated unto the LORD, with the silver and the gold that he brought from all *these* nations; from Edom, and from Moab, and from the children of Ammon, and from the Philistines, and from Amalek. 12 Moreover Abishai the son of Zeruiah slew of the Edomites in the valley of salt eighteen thousand. 13 And he put garrisons in Edom; and all the Edomites became David's servants. Thus the LORD preserved David whithersoever he went. 14 So David reigned over all Israel, and executed judgment and justice among all his people. 15 And Joab the son of Zeruiah *was* over the host; and Jehoshaphat the son of Ahilud, recorder. 16 And Zadok the son of Ahitub, and Abimelech the son of Abiathar, *were* the priests; and Shavsha was scribe; 17 And Benaiah the son of Jehoiada *was* over the Cherethites and the Pelethites; and the sons of David *were* chief about the king.

Here let us learn, 1. That it is our interest to make those our friends who have the presence of God with them. The king of Hamath, hearing of David's great success, sent to congratulate him and to court his favour with a noble present, *v.* 9, 10. It is in vain to contend with the Son of David. *Kiss the Son,* therefore, *lest he be angry;* let the kings and judges of the earth, and all inferior people too, be thus wise, thus instructed. The presents we are to bring him are not *vessels of gold and silver,* as here (those shall be welcome to him who have no such presents to bring), but our hearts and sincere affections, our whole selves, we must present to him as living sacrifices. 2. That what God blesses us with we must honour him with. The presents of his friends, as well as the spoils of his enemies, *David dedicated unto the Lord* (*v.* 11), that is, he laid them up towards the building and enriching of the temple. That is most truly and most comfortably our own which we have consecrated unto the Lord, and which we use for his glory. Let our *merchandise and our hire be holiness to the Lord,* Isa. xxiii. 18. 3. That those who take God along with them whithersoever they go may expect to prosper, and be preserved, whithersoever they go. It was said before (*v.* 6) and here it is repeated (*v.* 13) that *the Lord preserved David whithersoever he went.* Those are always under the eye of God that have God always in their eye. 4. God gives men power, not that they may look great with it, but that they may do good with it. When David reigned over all Israel he *executed judgment and justice among all his people,* and so answered the end of his elevation. He was not so intent on his conquests abroad as to neglect the administration of justice at home. Herein he served the purposes of the kingdom of providence, and of that God who *sits in the throne judging right;* and he was an eminent type of the Messiah, the *sceptre of whose kingdom is a right sceptre.*

CHAP. XIX.

The story is here repeated of David's war with the Ammonites and the Syrians their allies, and the victories he obtained over them, which we read just as it is here related, 2 Sam. x. Here is, I. David's civility to the king of Ammon, in sending an embassy of condolence to him on occasion of his father's death, ver. 1, 2. II. His great incivility to David, in the base usage he gave to his ambassadors, ver. 3, 4. III. David's just resentment of it, and the war which broke out thereupon, in which the Ammonites acted with policy in bringing the Syrians to their assistance (ver. 6, 7), Joab did bravely (ver. 8—13), and Israel was once and again victorious, ver. 14—19.

NOW it came to pass after this, that Nahash the king of the children of Ammon died, and his son reigned in his stead. 2 And David said, I will show kindness unto Hanun the son of Nahash, because his father showed kindness to me. And David sent messengers to comfort him concerning his father. So the servants of David came into the land of the children of Ammon to Hanun, to comfort him. 3 But the princes of the children of Ammon said to Hanun, Thinkest thou that David doth honour thy father, that he hath sent comforters unto thee? are not his servants come unto thee for to search, and to overthrow, and to spy out the land? 4 Wherefore Hanun took David's servants, and shaved them, and cut off their garments in the midst hard by their buttocks, and sent them away. 5 Then there went *certain,* and told David how the men were served. And he sent to meet them: for the men were greatly ashamed. And the king said, Tarry at Jericho until your beards be grown, and *then* return.

Let us here observe, 1. That it becomes good people to be neighbourly, and especially to be grateful. David will pay respect to Hanun because he is his neighbour; and religion teaches us to be civil and obliging to all, to honour all men, and to be ready to do all offices of kindness to those we live among; nor must difference in religion be any obstruction to this. But, besides this, David remembered the kindness which his father showed to him. Those that have received kindness must return it as they have ability and opportunity: those that have received it from the parents must return it to the children when they are gone. 2. That, as saith the proverb of the ancients, *Wickedness proceedeth from the wicked,* 1 Sam. xxiv. 13. The vile person will speak villany, and the instruments of the churl will be evil, to *destroy those with lying words that speak right,* Isa. xxxii. 6, 7. Those that are base, and design ill themselves, are apt to be jealous and to suspect ill of others without cause. Hanun's servants suggested that David's ambassadors came as spies, as if so great and mighty a man as David needed to do so mean a thing (if he had any design upon the Ammonites, he could effect it by open force, and had no occasion for any fraudulent practices), or as if a man of such virtue and honour would do so base a thing. Yet Hanun hearkened to the suggestion, and, against the law of nations, treated David's ambassadors villanously. 3. Masters ought to protect their servants, and with the greatest tenderness to concern themselves for them if they come by any loss or damage in their service. David did so for his ambassadors, *v.* 5. Christ will do so for his ministers; and let all masters thus *give unto their servants that which is just and equal.*

6 And when the children of Ammon saw that they had made themselves odious to David, Hanun and the children of Ammon sent a thousand talents of silver to hire them chariots and horsemen out of Mesopotamia, and out of Syria-maachah, and out of Zobah. 7 So they hired thirty and two thousand chariots, and the king of Maachah and his people; who came and pitched before Medeba. And the children of Ammon gathered themselves together from their cities, and came to battle. 8 And when David heard *of it,* he sent Joab, and all the host of the mighty men. 9 And the children of Ammon came out, and put the battle in array before the gate of the city: and the kings that were come *were* by themselves in the field. 10 Now when Joab saw that the battle was set against him before and behind, he chose out of all the choice of Israel, and put *them* in array against the Syrians. 11 And the rest of the people he delivered unto the hand of Abishai his brother, and they set *themselves* in array against the children of Ammon. 12 And he said, If the Syrians be too strong for me, then thou shalt help me: but if the children of Ammon be too strong for thee, then I will help thee. 13 Be of good courage, and let us behave ourselves valiantly for our people, and for the cities of our God: and let the LORD do *that which is* good in his sight. 14 So Joab and the people that *were* with him drew nigh before the Syrians unto the battle; and they fled before him. 15 And when the children of Ammon saw that the Syrians were fled, they likewise fled before Abishai his brother, and entered into the city. Then Joab came to Jerusalem. 16 And when the Syrians saw that they were put to the worse before Israel, they sent messengers, and drew forth the Syrians that *were* beyond the river: and Shophach the captain of the host of Hadarezer *went* before them. 17 And it was told David; and he gathered all Israel, and passed over Jordan, and came upon them, and set *the battle* in array against them. So when David had put the battle in array against the Syrians, they fought with him. 18 But the Syrians fled before Israel; and David slew of the Syrians seven thousand *men which fought in* chariots, and forty thousand footmen, and killed Shophach the captain of the host. 19 And when the servants of Hadarezer saw that they were put to the worse before Israel, they made peace with David, and became his servants: neither would the Syrians help the children of Ammon any more.

We may see here, 1. How the hearts of sinners that are marked for ruin are hardened to their destruction. The children of Ammon saw that *they had made themselves odious to David* (*v.* 6), and then it would have been their wisdom to desire conditions of peace, to humble themselves and offer any satisfaction for the injury they had done him, the rather because they had made themselves not only odious to David, but obnoxious to the justice of God, who is *King of nations,* and will assert the injured rights and maintain the violated laws of nations. But, instead of this, they prepared for war, and so brought upon themselves, by David's hand, those desolations which he never intended them. 2. How the courage of brave men is heightened and invigorated by difficulties

When Joab saw that the battle was set against him before and behind (*v.* 10), instead of meditating a retreat, he doubled his resolution; and, though he could not double, he divided his army, and not only spoke, but acted, like a gallant man, that had great presence of mind when he saw himself surrounded. He engaged with his brother for mutual assistance (*v.* 12), excited himself and the rest of the officers to act vigorously in their respective posts, with an eye to God's glory and their country's good, not to any honour and advantage of their own, and then left the issue to God: *Let the Lord do that which is right in his sight.* 3. How vain the greatest art and strength are against justice and equity. The Ammonites did their utmost to make the best of their position: they brought as good a force into the field, and disposed it with as much policy as possible; yet, having a bad cause, and acting in defence of wrong, it would not do; they were put to the worst. Right will prevail and triumph at last. 4. To how little purpose it is for those to rally again, and reinforce themselves, that have not God on their side. The Syrians, though in no way concerned in the merits of the cause, but serving only as mercenaries to the Ammonites, when they were beaten, thought themselves concerned to retrieve their honour, and therefore called in the assistance of the Syrians on the other side Euphrates; but to no purpose, for still they *fled before Israel* (*v.* 18); they lost 7000 men, who are said to be the men of 700 chariots, 2 Sam. x. 18. For, as now in a man of war for sea-service they allot ten men to a gun, so then, in land-service, ten men to a chariot. 5. Those who have *meddled with strife that belongs not to them,* and have found that they *meddled to their own hurt,* do well to learn wit at length and meddle no further. The Syrians, finding that Israel was the conquering side, not only broke off their alliance with the Ammonites and would help them no more (*v.* 19), *but made peace with David and became his servants.* Let those who have in vain stood it out against God be thus wise for themselves, and *agree with him quickly, while they are in the way.* Let them become his servants; for they cannot but see themselves undone if they be his enemies.

CHAP. XX.

Here is a repetition of the story of David's wars, I. With the Ammonites, and the taking of Rabbah, ver. 1—3. II. With the giants of the Philistines, ver. 4—8.

AND it came to pass, that after the year was expired, at the time that kings go out *to battle,* Joab led forth the power of the army, and wasted the country of the children of Ammon, and came and besieged Rabbah. But David tarried at Jerusalem. And Joab smote Rabbah, and destroyed it. 2 And David took the crown of their king from off his head, and found it to weigh a talent of gold, and *there were* precious stones in it; and it was set upon David's head: and he brought also exceeding much spoil out of the city. 3 And he brought out the people that *were* in it, and cut *them* with saws, and with harrows of iron, and with axes. Even so dealt David with all the cities of the children of Ammon. And David and all the people returned to Jerusalem.

How the army of the Ammonites and their allies was routed in the field we read in the foregoing chapters. Here we have the destruction of Rabbah, the metropolis of their kingdom (*v.* 1), the putting of their king's crown upon David's head (*v.* 2), and the great severity that was used towards the people, *v.* 3. Of this we had a more full account in 2 Sam. xi., xii., and cannot but remember it by this sad token, that while Joab was besieging Rabbah David fell into that great sin in the matter of Uriah. But it is observable that, though the rest of the story is repeated, that is not: a hint only is given of it in those words which lie here in a parenthesis—*But David tarried at Jerusalem.* If he had been abroad with his army, he would have been out of the way of that temptation; but, indulging his ease, he fell into uncleanness. Now, as the relating of the sin David fell into is an instance of the impartiality and fidelity of the sacred writers, so the avoiding of the repetition of it here, when there was a fair occasion given to speak of it again, is designed to teach us that, though there may be a just occasion to speak of the faults and miscarriages of others, yet we should not take delight in the repetition of them. That should always be looked upon as an unpleasing subject which, though sometimes one cannot help falling upon, yet one would not choose to dwell upon, any more than we should love to rake in a dunghill. The persons, or actions, we can say no good of, we had best say nothing of.

4 And it came to pass after this, that there arose war at Gezer with the Philistines; at which time Sibbechai the Hushathite slew Sippai, *that was* of the children of the giant: and they were subdued. 5 And there was war again with the Philistines; and Elhanan the son of Jair slew Lahmi the brother of Goliath the Gittite, whose spear staff *was* like a weaver's beam. 6 And yet again there was war at Gath, where was a man of *great* stature, whose fingers and toes *were* four and

twenty, six *on each hand,* and six *on each foot:* and he also was the son of the giant. 7 But when he defied Israel, Jonathan the son of Shimea David's brother slew him. 8 These were born unto the giant in Gath; and they fell by the hand of David, and by the hand of his servants.

The Philistines were nearly subdued (*ch.* xviii. 1); but, as in the destruction of the Canaanites by Joshua the sons of Anak were last subdued (Josh. xi. 21), so here in the conquest of the Philistines the giants of Gath were last brought down. In the conflicts between grace and corruption there are some sins which, like these giants, keep their ground a great while and are not mastered without much difficulty and a long struggle: but judgment will be brought forth unto victory at last. Observe, 1. We never read of giants among the Israelites, as we do of giants among the Philistines—giants of Gath, but not giants of Jerusalem. The growth of God's plants is in usefulness, not in bulk. Those who covet to have *cubits added to their stature* do not consider that it will but make them more unwieldy. In the balance of the sanctuary David far outweighs Goliath. 2. The servants of David, though men of ordinary stature, were too hard for the giants of Gath in every encounter, because they had God on their side, who takes pleasure in abasing lofty looks, and mortifying the giants that are in the earth, as he did of old by the deluge, though they were men of renown. Never let the church's friends be disheartened by the power and pride of the church's enemies. We need not fear great men against us while we have the great God for us. What will a finger more on each hand do, or a toe more on each foot, in contest with Omnipotence? 3. These giants *defied Israel* (*v.* 7) and were thus made to pay for their insolence. None are more visibly marked for ruin than those who reproach God and his Israel. God will do great things rather than suffer the enemy to *behave themselves proudly,* Deut. xxxii. 27. The victories of the Son of David, like those of David himself, are gradual. *We see not yet all things put under him;* but it will be seen shortly: and death itself, the last enemy, like these giants, will be triumphed over.

CHAP. XXI.

As this rehearsal makes no mention of David's sin in the matter of Uriah, so neither of the troubles of his family that followed upon it; not a word of Absalom's rebellion, or Sheba's. But David's sin, in numbering the people, is here related, because, in the atonement made for that sin, an intimation was given of the spot of ground on which the temple should be built. Here is, I. David's sin, in forcing Joab to number the people, ver. 1—6. II. David's sorrow for what he had done, as soon as he perceived the sinfulness of it, ver. 7, 8. III. The sad dilemma (or trilemma rather) he was brought to, when it was put to him to choose how he would be punished for this sin, and what rod he would be beaten with, ver. 9—13. IV. The woeful havoc which was made by the pestilence in the country, and the narrow escape which Jerusalem had from being laid waste by it, ver. 14—17. V. David's repentance, and sacrifice, upon this occasion, and the staying of the plague thereupon, ver. 18—30. This awful story we met with, and meditated upon, 2 Sam. xxiv.

AND Satan stood up against Israel, and provoked David to number Israel. 2 And David said to Joab and to the rulers of the people, Go, number Israel from Beer-sheba even to Dan; and bring the number of them to me, that I may know *it.* 3 And Joab answered, The LORD make his people a hundred times so many more as they *be:* but, my lord the king, *are* they not all my lord's servants? why then doth my lord require this thing? why will he be a cause of trespass to Israel? 4 Nevertheless the king's word prevailed against Joab. Wherefore Joab departed, and went throughout all Israel, and came to Jerusalem. 5 And Joab gave the sum of the number of the people unto David. And all *they of* Israel were a thousand thousand and a hundred thousand men that drew sword: and Judah *was* four hundred threescore and ten thousand men that drew sword. 6 But Levi and Benjamin counted he not among them: for the king's word was abominable to Joab.

Numbering the people, one would think, was no bad thing. Why should not the shepherd know the number of his flock? But God sees not as man sees. It is plain it was wrong in David to do it, and a great provocation to God, because he did it in the pride of his heart; and there is no sin that has in it more of contradiction and therefore more of offence to God than pride. The sin was David's; he alone must bear the blame of it. But here we are told,

I. How active the tempter was in it (*v.* 1): *Satan stood up against Israel, and provoked David* to do it. It is said (2 Sam. xxiv. 1) that *the anger of the Lord was kindled against Israel, and he moved David* to do it. The righteous judgments of God are to be observed and acknowledged even in the sins and unrighteousness of men. We are sure that God is not the author of sin—he *tempts no man;* and therefore, when it is said that he moved David to do it, it must be explained by what is intimated here, that, for wise and holy ends, he permitted the devil to do it. Here we trace this foul stream to its fountain. That Satan, the enemy of God and all good, should *stand up against Israel,* is not strange; it is what he aims at, to weaken the strength, diminish the numbers, and eclipse the glory of God's Israel, to whom he is *Satan,* a sworn *adversary.* But that he should influence David, the man after God's own heart, to do a wrong thing, may well be wondered at. One would think him one of those whom the wicked one touches not. No, even the best saints, till they come to heaven, must never think themselves out of the reach of Satan's temptations. Now, when Satan meant to do Israel a mischief, what course did he take? He did not *move God against them to destroy them* (as Job, *ch.* ii. 3), but he provoked David, the best friend they had, to number them, and so to offend God, and set him against them. Note, 1. The devil does us more mischief by tempting us to sin against our God than he does by accusing us before our God. He destroys none but by their own hands. 2. The greatest spite he can do to the church of God is to tempt the rulers of the church to pride; for none can conceive the fatal consequences of that sin in all, especially in church-rulers. *You shall not be so,* Luke xxii. 26.

II. How passive the instrument was. Joab, the person whom David employed, was an active man in public business; but to this he was perfectly forced, and did it with the greatest reluctance imaginable.

1. He put in a remonstrance against it before he began it. No man more forward than he in any thing that really tended to the honour of the king or the welfare of the kingdom; but in this matter he would gladly be excused. For, (1.) It was a needless thing. There was no occasion at all for it. God had promised to multiply them, and he needed not question the accomplishment of that promise. They were all his servants, and he needed not doubt of their loyalty and affection to him. Their number was as much his strength as he could desire. (2.) It was a dangerous thing. In doing it he might be a cause of trespass to Israel, and might provoke God against them. This Joab apprehended, and yet David himself did not. The most learned in the laws of God are not always the most quick-sighted in the application of those laws.

2. He was quite weary of it before he had done it; for *the king's word was abominable to Joab, v.* 6. Time was when whatever king David did *pleased all the people,* 2 Sam. iii. 36. But now there was a general disgust at these orders, which confirmed Joab in his dislike of them, so that, though the produce of this muster was really very great, yet he had no heart to perfect it, but left two tribes unnumbered (*v.* 5, 6), two considerable ones, Levi and Benjamin, and perhaps was not very exact in numbering the rest, because he did not do it with any pleasure, which might be one occasion of the difference between the sums here and 2 Sam. xxiv. 9.

7 And God was displeased with this thing; therefore he smote Israel. 8 And David said unto God, I have sinned greatly, because I have done this thing: but now, I beseech thee, do away the iniquity of thy servant; for I have done very foolishly. 9 And the LORD spake unto Gad, David's seer, saying, 10 Go and tell David, saying, Thus saith the LORD, I offer thee three *things:* choose thee one of them, that I may do *it* unto thee. 11 So Gad came to David, and said unto him, Thus saith the LORD, Choose thee, 12 Either three years' famine; or three months to be destroyed before thy foes, while that the sword of thine enemies overtaketh *thee;* or else three days the sword of the LORD, even the pestilence, in the land, and the angel of the LORD destroying throughout all the coasts of Israel. Now therefore advise thyself what word I shall bring again to him that sent me. 13 And David said unto Gad, I am in a great strait: let me fall now into the hand of the LORD; for very great *are* his mercies: but let me not fall into the hand of man. 14 So the LORD sent pestilence upon Israel: and there fell of Israel seventy thousand men. 15 And God sent an angel unto Jerusalem to destroy it: and as he was destroying, the LORD beheld, and he repented him of the evil, and said to the angel that destroyed, It is enough, stay now thine hand. And the angel of the LORD stood by the threshing-floor of Ornan the Jebusite. 16 And David lifted up his eyes, and saw the angel of the LORD stand between the earth and the heaven, having a drawn sword in his hand stretched out over Jerusalem. Then David and the elders *of Israel, who were* clothed in sackcloth, fell upon their faces. 17 And David said unto God, *Is it* not I *that* commanded the people to be numbered? even I it is that have sinned and done evil indeed; but *as for* these sheep, what have they done? let thine hand, I pray thee, O LORD my God, be on me, and on my father's house; but not on thy people, that they should be plagued.

David is here under the rod for numbering the people, that rod of correction which drives out the foolishness that is bound up in the heart, the foolishness of pride. Let us briefly observe,

I. How he was corrected. If God's dearest children do amiss, they must expect to smart for it. 1. He is given to understand that God is displeased; and that is no small uneasiness to so good a man as David, *v.* 7. God takes notice of, and is displeased with, the sins of his people; and no sin is more displeasing to him than pride of heart: nor is any thing more humbling, and grieving, and mortifying to a gracious soul, than to see itself under God's displeasure. 2. He is put to his choice whether he will be punished by war, famine, or pestilence; for punished he must be, and by one of these. Thus, for his further humiliation, he is put into a strait, a great strait, and has the terror of all the three judgments impressed upon his mind, no doubt to his great amazement, while he is considering which he shall choose. 3. He hears of 70,000 of his subjects who in a few hours were struck dead by the pestilence, *v.* 14. He was proud of the multitude of his people, but divine Justice took a course to make them fewer. Justly is that taken from us, weakened, or embittered to us, which we are proud of. David must have the people numbered: *Bring me the number of them,* says he, *that I may know it.* But now God numbers them after another manner, *numbers to the sword,* Isa. lxv. 12. And David had another number of them brought, more to his confusion than that was to his satisfaction, namely, the number of the slain—a black bill of mortality, which is a drawback to his muster-roll. 4. He sees the destroying angel, with his sword drawn against Jerusalem, *v.* 16. This could not but be very terrible to him, as it was a visible indication of the anger of Heaven, and threatened the utter destruction of that beloved city. Pestilences make the greatest devastations in the most populous places. The sight of an angel, though coming peaceably and on a friendly errand, has made even mighty men to tremble; how dreadful then must this sight be of an angel with a drawn sword in his hand, a flaming sword, like that of the cherubim, which turned every way to keep the way of the tree of life! While we lie under the wrath of God the holy angels are armed against us, though we see them not as David did.

II. How he bore the correction. 1. He made a very penitent confession of his sin, and prayed earnestly for the pardon of it, *v.* 8. Now he owned that he had sinned, had sinned greatly, had done foolishly, very foolishly; and he entreated that, however he might be corrected for it, the iniquity of it might be done away. 2. He accepted the punishment of his iniquity: "Let thy hand be *on me, and on my father's house, v.* 17. I submit to the rod, only let me be the sufferer, for I am the sinner; mine is the guilty head at which the sword should be pointed." 3. He cast himself upon the mercy of God (though he knew he was angry with him) and did not entertain any hard thoughts of him. However it be, *Let us fall into the hands of the Lord, for his mercies are great, v.* 13. Good men, even when God frowns upon them, think well of him. *Though he slay me, yet will I trust in him.* 4. He expressed a very tender concern for the people, and it went to his heart to see them plagued for his transgression: *These sheep, what have they done?*

18 Then the angel of the LORD commanded Gad to say to David, that David should go up, and set up an altar unto the LORD in the threshingfloor of Ornan the Jebusite. 19 And David went up at the saying of Gad, which he spake in the name of the LORD. 20 And Ornan turned back, and saw the angel; and his four sons with him hid themselves. Now Ornan was threshing wheat. 21 And as David came to Ornan, Ornan looked and saw David, and went out of the threshingfloor, and bowed himself to David with *his* face to the ground. 22 Then David said to Ornan, Grant me the place of *this* threshingfloor, that I may build an altar therein unto the LORD: thou shalt grant it me for the full price: that the plague may be stayed from the people. 23 And Ornan said unto David, Take *it* to thee, and let my lord the king do *that which is* good in his eyes: lo, I give *thee* the oxen *also* for burnt offerings, and the threshing instruments for wood, and the wheat for the meat offering; I give it all. 24 And king David said to Ornan, Nay; but I will verily buy it for the full price: for I will not take *that* which *is* thine for the LORD, nor offer burnt offerings without cost. 25 So David gave to Ornan for the place six hundred shekels of gold by weight. 26 And David built there an altar unto the LORD, and offered burnt offerings and peace offerings, and called upon the LORD; and he answered him from heaven by fire upon the altar of burnt offering. 27 And the LORD commanded the angel; and he put up his sword again into the sheath thereof. 28 At that time when David saw that the LORD had

answered him in the threshingfloor of Ornan the Jebusite, then he sacrificed there. 29 For the tabernacle of the LORD, which Moses made in the wilderness, and the altar of the burnt offering, *were* at that season in the high place at Gibeon. 30 But David could not go before it to enquire of God: for he was afraid because of the sword of the angel of the LORD.

We have here the controversy concluded, and, upon David's repentance, his peace made with God. *Though thou wast angry with me, thy anger is turned away.* 1. A stop was put to the progress of the execution, *v.* 15. When David repented of the sin God repented of the judgment, and ordered the destroying angel to *stay his hand* and *sheath his sword, v.* 27. 2. Direction was given to David to rear an altar in the threshing-floor of Ornan, *v.* 18. The angel commanded the prophet Gad to bring David this direction. The same angel that had, in God's name, carried on the war, is here forward to set on foot the treaty of peace; for angels do not desire the woeful day. The angel could have given this order to David himself; but he chose to do it by his seer, that he might put an honour upon the prophetic office. Thus the revelation of Jesus Christ was notified by the angel to John, and by him to the churches. The commanding of David to build an altar was a blessed token of reconciliation; for, if God had been pleased to kill him, he would not have appointed, because he would not have accepted, a sacrifice at his hands. 3. David immediately made a bargain with Ornan for the threshing-floor; for he would not serve God at other people's charge. Ornan generously offered it to him gratis, not only in complaisance to the king, but because he had himself *seen the angel* (*v.* 20), which so terrified him that he and his four sons hid themselves, as unable to bear the brightness of his glory and afraid of his drawn sword. Under these apprehensions he was willing to do any thing towards making the atonement. Those that are duly sensible of the terrors of the Lord will do all they can, in their places, to promote religion, and encourage all the methods of reconciliation for the turning away of God's wrath. 4. God testified his acceptance of David's offerings on this altar: He *answered him from heaven by fire, v.* 26. To signify that God's anger was turned away from him, the fire that might justly have fastened upon the sinner fastened upon the sacrifice and consumed that; and, upon this, the destroying sword was returned into its sheath. Thus Christ was made sin and a curse for us, and it pleased the Lord to bruise him, that through him God might be to us, not a consuming fire, but a reconciled Father. 5. He continued to offer his sacrifices upon this altar. The brazen altar which Moses made was at Gibeon (*v.* 29), and there all the sacrifices of Israel were offered: but David was so terrified at the sight of the sword of the angel that he *could not go thither, v.* 30. The business required haste, when the plague was begun. Aaron must go quickly, nay, he must *run,* to make atonement, Num. xvi. 46, 47. And the case here was no less urgent; so that David had not time to go to Gibeon: nor durst he leave the angel with his sword drawn over Jerusalem, lest the fatal stroke should be given before he came back. And therefore God, in tenderness to him, bade him build an altar in that place, dispensing with his own law concerning one altar because of the present distress, and accepting the sacrifices offered on this new altar, which was not set up in opposition to that, but in concurrence with it. The symbols of unity were not so much insisted on as unity itself. Nay, when the present distress was over (as it should seem), David, as long as he lived, sacrificed there, though the altar at Gibeon was still kept up; for God had owned the sacrifices that were here offered and had testified his acceptance of them, *v.* 28. On those administrations in which we have experienced the tokens of God's presence, and have found that he is with us of a truth, it is good to continue our attendance. "Here God has graciously met me, and therefore I will still expect to meet with him."

CHAP. XXII.

"Out of the eater comes forth meat." It was upon occasion of the terrible judgment inflicted on Israel for the sin of David that God gave intimation of the setting up of another altar, and of the place where he would have the temple to be built, upon which David was excited with great vigour to make preparation for that great work, wherein, though he had long since designed it, it should seem, he had, of late, grown remiss, till awakened by the alarm of that judgment. The tokens of God's favour he received after those of his displeasure, I. Directed him to the place, ver. 1. II. Encouraged and quickened him to the work. 1. He set himself to prepare for the building, ver. 2—5. 2. He instructed Solomon, and gave him a charge concerning this work, ver. 6—16. 3. He commanded the princes to assist him in it, ver. 17—19. There is a great deal of difference between the frame of David's spirit in the beginning of the former chapter and in the beginning of this. There, in the pride of his heart, he was numbering the people; here, in his humility, preparing for the service of God. There corruption was uppermost (but the well of living water in the soul, though it may be muddied, will work itself clear again); grace here has recovered the upper hand

THEN David said, This *is* the house of the LORD God, and this *is* the altar of the burnt offering for Israel. 2 And David commanded to gather together the strangers that *were* in the land of Israel; and he set masons to hew wrought stones to build the house of God. 3 And David prepared iron in abundance for the nails for the doors of the gates, and for the joinings; and brass in abundance without weight; 4 Also cedar trees in abundance: for the Zidonians and they of Tyre brought much cedar wood to David. 5 And David said, Solomon my son *is* young and tender, and the house *that is* to be builded for the LORD *must be* exceeding magnifical, of fame and of glory throughout all countries: I will *therefore* now make preparation for it. So David prepared abundantly before his death.

Here is, I. The place fixed for the building of the temple (*v.* 1): *Then David said,* by inspiration of God, and as a declaration of his mind, *This is the house of the Lord God.* If a temple must be built for God, it is fit that it be left to him to choose the ground, for all the earth is his; and this is the ground he makes choice of—ground that pertained to a Jebusite, and perhaps there was not a spot of ground besides, in or about Jerusalem, that did so—a happy presage of the setting up of the gospel temple among the Gentiles. See Acts xv. 16, 17. The ground was a threshing-floor; for the church of the living God is his floor, his threshing, and *the corn of his floor,* Isa. xxi. 10. Christ's fan is in his hand, thoroughly to purge his floor. This is to be the house because this is the altar. The temple was built for the sake of the altar. There were altars long before there were temples.

II. Preparation made for that building. David must not build it, but he would do all he could towards it: He *prepared abundantly before his death, v.* 5. This intimates that the consideration of his age and growing infirmities, which showed him his death approaching, quickened him, towards his latter end, to be very diligent in making this preparation. What our hands find to do for God, and our souls, and our generation, let us do it with all our might before our death, because, after death, there is no device nor working. Now we are here told,

1. What induced him to make such preparation. Two things he considered:—(1.) That Solomon was young and tender, and not likely to apply with any great vigour to this business at first; so that, unless he found the wheels set a-going, he would be in danger of losing a great deal of time at first, the rather because, being young, he would be tempted to put it off; whereas, if he found the materials got ready to his hand, the most difficult part of the work would be over, and this would excite and encourage him to go about it in the beginning of his reign. Note, Those that are aged and experienced should consider those that are young and tender, and provide them what help they can, that they may make the work of God as easy to them as possible. (2.) That the house must be exceedingly magnificent, very stately and sumptuous, strong and beautiful, every thing about it the best in its kind, and for a good reason, since it was intended for the honour of the great God, the Lord of the whole earth, and was to be a type of Christ, in whom all fulness dwells and in whom are hid all treasures. Men were then to be taught by sensible methods. The grandeur of the house would help to affect the worshippers with a holy awe and reverence of God, and would invite strangers to come to see it, as the wonder of the world, who thereby would be brought acquainted with the true God. Therefore it is here designed to be of fame and glory throughout all countries. David foretold this good effect of its being magnificent, Ps. lxviii. 29. *Because of thy temple at Jerusalem shall kings bring presents unto thee.*

2. What preparation he made. In general, he prepared abundantly, as we shall find afterwards; cedar and stones, iron and brass, are here specified, *v.* 2—4. Cedar he had from the Tyrians and the Zidonians. *The daughter of Tyre shall be there with a gift,* Ps. xlv. 12. He also got workmen together, *the strangers that were in the land of Israel.* Some think that he employed them because they were generally better artists, and more ingenious in manual operations, than the Israelites; or, rather, because he would not employ the free-born Israelites in any thing that looked mean and servile. They were delivered from the bondage of making bricks in Egypt, and must not return to hew stone. These strangers were proselytes to the Jewish religion, but, though not enslaved, they were not of equal dignity with Israelites.

6 Then he called for Solomon his son, and charged him to build a house for the LORD God of Israel. 7 And David said to Solomon, My son, as for me, it was in my mind to build a house unto the name of the LORD my God: 8 But the word of the LORD came to me, saying, Thou hast shed blood abundantly, and hast made great wars: thou shalt not build a house unto my name, because thou hast shed much blood upon the earth in my sight. 9 Behold, a son shall be born to thee, who shall be a man of rest; and I will give him rest from all his enemies round about: for his name shall be Solomon, and I will give peace and quietness unto Israel in his days. 10 He shall build a house for my name; and he shall be my son, and I *will be* his father; and I will establish the throne of his kingdom over Israel for ever. 11 Now, my son, the LORD be with thee; and prosper thou, and build the house of

the LORD thy God, as he hath said of thee. 12 Only the LORD give thee wisdom and understanding, and give thee charge concerning Israel. that thou mayest keep the law of the LORD thy God. 13 Then shalt thou prosper, if thou takest heed to fulfil the statutes and judgments which the LORD charged Moses with concerning Israel: be strong, and of good courage; dread not, nor be dismayed. 14 Now, behold, in my trouble I have prepared for the house of the LORD a hundred thousand talents of gold, and a thousand thousand talents of silver; and of brass and iron without weight; for it is in abundance: timber also and stone have I prepared; and thou mayest add thereto. 15 Moreover *there are* workmen with thee in abundance, hewers and workers of stone and timber, and all manner of cunning men for every manner of work. 16 Of the gold, the silver, and the brass, and the iron, *there is* no number. Arise *therefore*, and be doing, and the LORD be with thee.

Though Solomon was young and tender, he was capable of receiving instructions, which his father accordingly gave him, concerning the work for which he was designed. When David came to the throne he had many things to do, for the foundations were all out of course; but Solomon had only one thing in charge, and that was *to build a house for the Lord God of Israel, v.* 6. Now,

I. David tells him why he did not do it himself. It was in his mind to do it (*v.* 7), but God forbade him, because *he had shed much blood, v.* 8. Some think this refers to the blood of Uriah, which fastened such a reproach upon him as rendered him unworthy the honour of building the temple: but that honour was forbidden him before he had shed that blood; therefore it must be meant, as it is here explained, of the blood he shed in his wars (for he had been a man of war from his youth), which, though shed very justly and honourably in the service of God and Israel, yet made him unfit to be employed in this service, or rather less fit than another that had never been called to such bloody work. God, by assigning this as the reason of laying David aside from this work, showed how precious human life is to him, and intended a type of him who should build the gospel temple, not by *destroying men's lives,* but *saving them,* Luke ix. 56.

II. He gives him the reason why he imposed this task upon him. 1. Because God had designed him for it, nominated him as the man that should do it: *A son shall be born to thee,* that shall be called *Solomon,* and *he shall build a house for my name, v.* 9, 10. Nothing is more powerful to engage us to any service for God, and encourage us in it, than to know that hereunto we are appointed. 2. Because he would have leisure and opportunity to do it. He should be a man of rest, and therefore should not have his time, or thoughts, or wealth, diverted from this business. He should have rest from his enemies abroad (none of them should invade or threaten him, or give him provocation), and he should have peace and quietness at home; and therefore let him build the house. Note, Where God gives rest he expects work. 3. Because God had promised to establish his kingdom. Let this encourage him to honour God, that God had honour in store for him; let him build up God's house, and God will build up his throne. Note, God's gracious promises should quicken and invigorate our religious service.

III. He delivers him an account of the vast preparations he had made for this building (*v.* 14), not in a way of pride and vain glory (he speaks of it as a poor thing—*I have, in my poverty, prepared,* margin), but as an encouragement to Solomon to engage cheerfully in the work, for which so solid a foundation was laid. The treasure here mentioned of 100,000 talents of gold, and 1,000,000 talents of silver, amounts to such an incredible sum that most interpreters either allow an error in the copy or think the talent here signifies no more than a plate or piece: *ingots* we call them. I am inclined to suppose that a certain number is here put for an uncertain, because it is said (*v.* 16) that of the gold and silver, as well as of the brass and iron, there was no number, and that David here includes all the dedicated things (*ch.* xviii. 11) which he designed *for the house of the Lord,* that is, not only for the building of it, but for the treasure of it; and, putting all together, it might come pretty near what is here spoken of. Hundreds and thousands are numbers which we often use to express that which is very much, when yet we would not be understood strictly.

IV. He charges him to keep God's commandments and to take heed to his duty in every thing, *v.* 13. He must not think by building the temple to purchase a dispensation to sin; no, on the contrary, his doing that would not be accepted, nor accounted of, if he did not *take heed to fulfil the statutes which the Lord charged Moses with, v.* 13. Though he was to be king of Israel, he must always remember that he was a subject to the God of Israel.

V. He encourages him to go about this great work, and to go on in it (*v.* 13): "*Be strong, and of good courage.* Though it is a vast undertaking, thou needest not fear coming under the reproach of the foolish builder, who began to build and was not able to finish; it is God's work, and it shall come to perfection. *Dread not, nor be dismayed.*" In our spiritual work, as well as in our spiritual warfare, we have need of courage and resolution.

VI. He quickens him not to rest in the preparations he had made, but to add thereto, *v.* 14. Those that enter into the labours of others, and build upon their advantages, must still be improving.

VII. He prays for him: *The Lord give thee wisdom and understanding, and give thee charge concerning Israel, v.* 12. Whatever charge we have, if we see God giving us the charge and calling us to it, we may hope he will give us wisdom for the discharge of it. Perhaps Solomon had an eye to this prayer of his father for him, in the prayer he offered for himself: Lord, *give me a wise and understanding heart.* He concludes (*v.* 16), *Up, and be doing, and the Lord be with thee.* Hope of God's presence must not slacken our endeavours. Though the Lord be with us, we must *rise and be doing,* and, if we do this, we have reason to believe he is and will be with us. Work out your salvation, and God will work in you.

17 David also commanded all the princes of Israel to help Solomon his son, *saying,* 18 *Is* not the LORD your God with you? and hath he *not* given you rest on every side? for he hath given the inhabitants of the land into mine hand; and the land is subdued before the LORD, and before his people. 19 Now set your heart and your soul to seek the LORD your God; arise therefore, and build ye the sanctuary of the LORD God, to bring the ark of the covenant of the LORD, and the holy vessels of God, into the house that is to be built to the name of the LORD.

David here engages the princes of Israel to assist Solomon in the great work he had to do, and every one to lend him a hand towards the carrying of it on. Those that are in the throne cannot do the good they would, unless those about the throne set in with them. David would therefore have the princes to advise Solomon and quicken him, and make the work as easy to him as they could, by promoting it every one in his place. 1. He shows them what obligations they lay under to be zealous in this matter, in gratitude to God for the great things he had done for them. He had given them victory, and rest, and a good land for an inheritance, *v.* 18. The more God has done for us the more we should study to do for him 2. He presses that upon them which should make them zealous in it (*v.* 19): " *Set your heart and soul to seek God,* place your happiness in his favour, and keep your eye upon his glory. Seek him as your chief good and highest end, and this *with your heart and soul.* Make religion your choice and business; and then you will grudge no pains nor cost to promote the building of his sanctuary." Let but the heart be sincerely engaged for God, and the head and hand, the estate and interest, and all, will be cheerfully employed for him.

CHAP. XXIII.

David, having given charge concerning the building of the temple, in this and the following chapters settles the method of the temple-service and puts into order the offices and officers of it. In the late irregular times, and during the wars in the beginning of his reign, we may suppose that, though the Levitical ordinances were kept up, yet it was not in the order, nor with the beauty and exactness, that were desirable. Now David, being a prophet, as well as a prince, by divine warrant and direction, "set in order the things that were wanting." In this chapter we are informed, I. He declared Solomon to be his successor, ver. 1. II. He numbered the Levites, and appointed them to their respective offices, ver. 2—5. III. He took an account of the several families of the Levites, ver. 6—23. IV. He made a new reckoning of them from twenty years old, and appointed them their work, ver. 24—32. And in this he prepared for the temple as truly as when he laid up gold and silver for it; for the place is of small account in comparison with the work.

SO when David was old and full of days, he made Solomon his son king over Israel. 2 And he gathered together all the princes of Israel, with the priests and the Levites. 3 Now the Levites were numbered from the age of thirty years and upward: and their number by their polls, man by man, was thirty and eight thousand. 4 Of which, twenty and four thousand *were* to set forward the work of the house of the LORD; and six thousand *were* officers and judges: 5 Moreover four thousand *were* porters; and four thousand praised the LORD with the instruments which I made, *said David,* to praise *therewith.* 6 And David divided them into courses among the sons of Levi, *namely,* Gershon, Kohath, and Merari. 7 Of the Gershonites *were,* Laadan, and Shimei. 8 The sons of Laadan; the chief *was* Jehiel, and Zetham, and Joel, three. 9 The sons of Shimei; Shelomith, and Haziel, and Haran, three. These *were* the chief of the fathers of Laadan. 10 And the sons of Shimei *were,* Jahath, Zina, and Jeush, and Beriah. These four *were* the sons of Shimei. 11 And Jahath was the chief, and Zizah the second: but Jeush and Beriah had not many sons; therefore they were in one reckoning, according to *their* father's house. 12 The sons of Kohath; Amram, Izhar, Hebron, and Uzziel, four. 13 The sons of Amram; Aaron and Moses: and Aaron was separated, that he should sanctify the most holy things, he and his sons for ever, to burn incense before the LORD, to minister unto him, and to bless in his name for ever. 14 Now *concerning* Moses the man of God, his sons were named of the tribe of Levi. 15 The sons of Moses *were*, Gershom, and Eliezer. 16 Of the sons of Gershom, Shebuel *was* the chief. 17 And the sons of Eliezer *were*, Rehabiah the chief. And Eliezer had none other sons; but the sons of Rehabiah were very many. 18 Of the sons of Izhar; Shelomith the chief. 19 Of the sons of Hebron; Jeriah the first, Amariah the second, Jehaziel the third, and Jekameam the fourth. 20 Of the sons of Uzziel; Micah the first, and Jesiah the second. 21 The sons of Merari; Mahli, and Mushi. The sons of Mahli; Eleazar, and Kish. 22 And Eleazar died, and had no sons, but daughters: and their brethren the sons of Kish took them. 23 The sons of Mushi; Mahli, and Eder, and Jeremoth, three.

Here we have, I. The crown entailed, according to the divine appointment, *v.* 1. David made Solomon king, not to reign with him, or reign under him, but only to reign after him. This he did, 1. When he was old and full of days. He was but seventy years old when he died, and yet he was full of days, *satur dierum—satisfied with living* in this world. When he found himself going off, he made provision for the welfare of the kingdom after his decease, and pleased himself with the hopeful prospect of a happy settlement both in church and state. 2. He did it in parliament, in a solemn assembly of all the princes of Israel, which made Adonijah's attempt to break in upon Solomon's title and set it aside, notwithstanding this public recognition and establishment of it, the more impudent, impious, and ridiculous. Note, The settling or securing of the crown in the interests of the temple is a great blessing to a people and a great satisfaction to those who are themselves leaving the world.

II. The Levites numbered, according to the rule in Moses's time, from thirty years old to fifty, Num. iv. 2, 3. Their number in Moses's time, by this rule, was 8580 (Num iv. 47, 48), but now it had increased above four-fold, much more in proportion than the rest of the tribes; for the serviceable men of Levi's tribe were now 38,000, unless we suppose that here those were reckoned who were above fifty, which was not the case there. Joab had not numbered the Levites (*ch.* xxi. 6), but David now did, not in pride, but for a good purpose, and then he needed not fear wrath for it.

III. The Levites distributed to their respective posts (*v.* 4, 5), that every hand might be employed (for, of all men, an idle Levite makes the worst figure), and that every part of the work might be carefully done. Now it was for the honour of God that so great a number of servants attended his house and the business of it. Much of the state of great men consists in the greatness of their retinue. When God kept house in Israel see what a great household he had, and all well fed and well taught. But what were these to the attendants of his throne above, and the innumerable company of angels? It was the happiness of Israel that they had among them such a considerable body of men who were obliged by their office to promote and keep up religion among them. If the worship of God go to decay in Israel, let it not be said that it was for want of due provision for the support of it, but that those who should have done it were careless and false. The work assigned the Levites was four-fold:—1. Some, and indeed far the greater number, were to set forward the work of the house of the Lord: 24,000, almost two-thirds, were appointed for this service, to attend the priests in killing the sacrifices, flaying them, washing them, cutting them up, burning them, to have the meat-offerings and drink-offerings ready, to carry out dirt, and keep all the vessels and utensils of the temple clean, and every thing in its place, that the service might be performed both with expedition and with exactness. These served 1000 a-week, and so went round in twenty-four courses. Perhaps while the temple was in building some of these were employed to set forward that work, to assist the builders, at least to quicken them, and keep good order among them, and the decorum which became temple-work. 2. Others were officers and judges, not in the affairs of the temple, and in controversies that arose there (for there, we may suppose, the priests presided), but in the country. They were magistrates, to give the laws of God in charge, to resolve difficulties, and to determine controversies that arose upon them. Of these there were 6000, in the several parts of the kingdom, that assisted the princes and elders of every tribe in the administration of justice. 3. Others were porters, to guard all the avenues of the house of God, to examine those that desired entrance, and to resist those that would force an entrance. These were the life-guards of the temple, and probably were armed accordingly. 4. Others were singers and players on instruments, whose business it was to keep up that part of the service; this was a new-erected office.

IV. The Levites mustered, and disposed of into their respective families and kindreds, that an account of them might the better be kept, and those that neglected their duty might the more easily be discovered, by calling over the roll, and obliging them to answer to their names, which each family might do for itself. When those of the same family were employed together it would engage them to love and assist one another. When Christ sent forth his disciples two and two he put together those that were brethren. Two families were here joined in one (*v.* 11) because they had not many sons. Those that are weak and little, separately, may be put together and appear considerable. That which is most observable in this account of the families of the Levites is that the posterity of Moses (that great man) stood upon the level with common Levites, and had no dignities or privileges at all peculiar to them; whilst the posterity of Aaron were advanced to the priest's office, to *sanctify the most holy things, v.* 13. It is said indeed of the grandson of Moses, Rehabiah, that *his sons were highly multiplied, v.* 17, *margin.* When God proposed to him that, if he would let fall his intercession for Israel, he would make of him a great nation, he generously refused it, in recompence for which his family is here greatly increased, and makes up in number what it wants in figure, in the tribe of Levi. Now, 1. The levelling of Moses' family with the rest is an evidence of his self-denial. Such an interest had he both with God and man that if he had aimed to raise his own family, to dignify and enrich that, he might easily have done so; but he was no self-seeking man, as appears from his leaving to his children no marks of distinction, which was a sign that he had the spirit of God and not the spirit of the world. 2. The elevation of Aaron's family above the rest was a recompence for his self-denial. When Moses (his younger brother) was made a god to Pharaoh, and he only his prophet or spokesman, to observe his orders and do as he was bidden, Aaron never disputed it, nor insisted upon his seniority, but readily took the inferior post God put him in, submitted to Moses, and, upon occasion, called him *his lord;* and because he thus submitted himself, in his own person, to his junior, in compliance with the will of God, God highly exalted his family, even above that of Moses himself. Those that are content to stoop are in the fairest way to rise. Before honour is humility.

24 These *were* the sons of Levi after the house of their fathers; *even* the chief of the fathers, as they were counted by number of names by their polls, that did the work for the service of the house of the LORD, from the age of twenty years and upward. 25 For David said, The LORD God of Israel hath given rest unto his people, that they may dwell in Jerusalem for ever: 26 And also unto the Levites; they shall no *more* carry the tabernacle, nor any vessels of it for the service thereof. 27 For by the last words of David the Levites *were* numbered from twenty years old and above: 28 Because their office *was* to wait on the sons of Aaron for the service of the house of the LORD, in the courts, and in the chambers, and in the purifying of all holy things, and the work of the service of the house of God; 29 Both for the showbread, and for the fine flour for meat offering, and for the unleavened cakes, and for *that which is baked in* the pan, and for that which is fried, and for all manner of measure and size; 30 And to stand every morning to thank and praise the LORD, and likewise at even; 31 And to offer all burnt sacrifices unto the LORD in the sabbaths, in the new moons, and on the set feasts, by number, according to the order commanded unto them, continually before the LORD: 32 And that they should keep the charge of the tabernacle of the congregation, and the charge of the holy *place,* and the charge of the sons of Aaron their brethren, in the service of the house of the LORD.

Here is, I. An alteration made in the computation of the effective men of the Levites—that whereas, in Moses's time, they were not enlisted, or taken into service, till they were thirty-years old, nor admitted as probationers till twenty-five (Num. viii. 24), David ordered, by direction from God, that they should be numbered *for the service of the house of the Lord,* from the age of twenty years and upwards, *v.* 24. This order he confirmed by his last words, *v.* 27. When he put his last hand to the draught of this establishment he expressly appointed this to be done for ever after; yet not he, but the Lord. 1. Perhaps the young Levites, having no work appointed them till twenty-five years old, had many of them got a habit of idleness, or grew addicted to their pleasures, which proved both a blemish to their reputation and a hindrance to their usefulness afterwards, to prevent which inconvenience they are set to work, and brought under discipline, at twenty-years old. Those that will be eminent must learn to take care and take pains betimes. 2. When the work of the Levites was to carry burdens, heavy burdens, the tabernacle and the furniture of it, God would not call any to it till they had come to their full strength; for he considers our frame, and, in service as well as sufferings, will lay no more upon us than we are able to bear. But now God had given rest to his people, and made Jerusalem his dwelling-place for ever, so that there was no more occasion to carry the tabernacle and the vessels thereof, the service was much easier, and what would not over-work them nor over-load them if they entered upon it at twenty-years old. 3. Now the people of Israel were multiplied, and there was a more general resort to Jerusalem, and would be when the temple was built, than had ever been at Shiloh, or Nob, or Gibeon; it was therefore requisite there should be more hands employed in the temple-service, that every Israelite who brought an offering might find a Levite ready to assist him. When more work is to be done it is a pity but there should be more workmen fetched in for the doing of it. When the harvest is plenteous why should the labourers be few?

II. A further account of the Levites' work. What the work of the priests was we are told (*v.* 13): To *sanctify the most holy things, to burn incense before the Lord,* and to *bless in his name;* that work the Levites were not to meddle with, and yet they had work enough, and good work, according to that to which they were appointed, *v.* 4, 5. 1. Those of them that were to *set forward the work of the house of God* (*v.* 4) were therein to *wait on the sons of Aaron* (*v.* 28), were to do the drudgery-work (if any work for God is to be called *drudgery)* of the house of God, to keep the courts and chambers clean, set things in their places, and have them ready when there was occasion to use them. They were to prepare the show-bread which the priests were to set on the table, to provide the flour and cakes for the meat-offerings, that the priests might have every thing ready to their hands. 2. Those of them that were judges and officers had an eye particularly upon all *measure and size, v.* 29. The standards of all weights and measures were kept in the sanctuary; and the Levites had the care of them, to see that they were exact, and to try other weights and measures by them when they were appealed to. 3. The work of the singers was to *thank and praise the Lord* (*v.* 30), at the offering of the morning and evening sacrifices, and other oblations on the sabbaths, new moons, &c., *v.* 31. Moses appointed that they should blow with trumpets over their burnt offerings and other sacrifices, and on their solemn days, Num. x. 10. The sound of the trumpet was awful, and might be affecting to the worshippers, but was not articulate, nor such a reasonable service as this which David appointed, of singing psalms on those occasions. As the Jewish church grew up from its infancy, it grew more and more intelligent in its devotions, till it came at length, in the gospel, to *put away childish things,* 1 Cor. xiii. 11; Gal. iv. 3, 9. 4. The work of the porters (*v.* 5) was to keep *the charge of the tabernacle and of the holy place,* that none might come nigh but such as were allowed, and those no nearer than was allowed them, *v.* 32. They were likewise to keep the charge of the sons of Aaron, to be at their beck and go on their errands, who yet are called *their brethren,* to be a memorandum to the priests that, though they were advanced to a high station, yet they were *hewn out of the same rock* with common Levites, and therefore must not lord it over them, but in all instances treat them as brethren.

CHAP. XXIV.

This chapter gives us a more particular account of the distribution of the priests and Levites into their respective classes, for the more regular discharge of the duties of their offices, according to their families. I. Of the priests, ver. 1—19. II. Of the Levites, ver. 20—31.

NOW *these are* the divisions of the sons of Aaron. The sons of Aaron; Nadab, and Abihu, Eleazar, and Ithamar. 2 But Nadab and Abihu died before their father, and had no children: therefore Eleazar and Ithamar executed the priest's office. 3 And David distributed them, both Zadok of the sons of Eleazar, and Ahimelech of the sons of Ithamar, according to their offices in their service. 4 And there were more chief men found of the sons of Eleazar than of the sons of Ithamar; and *thus* were they divided. Among the sons of Eleazar *there were* sixteen chief men of the house of *their* fathers, and eight among the sons of Ithamar according to the house of their fathers. 5 Thus were they divided by lot, one sort with another; for the governors of the sanctuary, and governors *of the house* of God, were of the sons of Eleazar, and of the sons of Ithamar. 6 And Shemaiah the son of Nethaneel the scribe, *one* of the Levites, wrote them before the king, and the princes, and Zadok the priest, and Ahimelech the son of Abiathar, and *before* the chief of the fathers of the priests and Levites: one principal household being taken for Eleazar, and *one* taken for Ithamar. 7 Now the first lot came forth to Jehoiarib, the second to Jedaiah, 8 The third to Harim, the fourth to Seorim, 9

The fifth to Malchijah, the sixth to Mijamin, 10 The seventh to Hakkoz, the eighth to Abijah, 11 The ninth to Jeshuah, the tenth to Shecaniah, 12 The eleventh to Eliashib, the twelfth to Jakim, 13 The thirteenth to Huppah, the fourteenth to Jeshebeab, 14 The fifteenth to Bilgah, the sixteenth to Immer, 15 The seventeenth to Hezir, the eighteenth to Aphses, 16 The nineteenth to Pethahiah, the twentieth to Jehezekel, 17 The one and twentieth to Jachin, the two and twentieth to Gamul, 18 The three and twentieth to Delaiah, the four and twentieth to Maaziah. 19 These *were* the orderings of them in their service to come into the house of the LORD, according to their manner, under Aaron their father, as the LORD God of Israel had commanded him.

The particular account of these establishments is of little use to us now; but, when Ezra published it, it was of great use to direct their church affairs after their return from captivity into the old channel again. The title of this record we have *v.* 1—*These are the divisions of the sons of Aaron,* not by which they divided one from another, or were at variance one with another (it is a pity there should ever be any such divisions among the sons of Israel, but especially among the sons of Aaron), but the distribution of them in order to the dividing of their work among themselves; it was a division which God made, and was made for him. 1. This distribution was made for the more regular discharge of the duties of their office. God was, and still is, the God of order, and not of confusion, particularly in the things of his worship. Number without order is but a clog and an occasion of tumult; but when every one has, and knows, and keeps, his place and work, the more the better. In the mystical body, every member has its use, for the good of the whole, Rom. xii. 4, 5; 1 Cor. xii. 12. 2. It was made by lot, that the disposal thereof might be of the Lord, and so all quarrels and contentions might be prevented, and no man could be charged with partiality, nor could any say that they had wrong done them. As God is the God of order, so he is the God of peace. Solomon says of the lot that it *causeth contention to cease.* 3. The lot was cast publicly, and with great solemnity, in the presence of the king, princes, and priests, that there might be no room for any fraudulent practices or the suspicion of them. The lot is an appeal to God, and ought to be managed with corresponding reverence and sincerity. Matthias was chosen to the apostleship by lot, with prayer (Acts i. 24, 26), and I know not but it might be still used in faith in parallel cases, as an instituted ordinance. We have here the name of the public notary that was employed in writing the names, and drawing the lots (*v.* 6): *Shemaiah, one of the Levites.* 4. What those priests were chosen to was to preside in the affairs of the sanctuary (*v.* 5), in their several courses and turns. That which was to be determined by the lot was only the precedency, not who should serve (for they chose all the chief men), but who should serve first, and who next, that every one might know his course, and attend in it. Of the twenty-four chief men of the priests sixteen were of the house of Eleazar and eight of Ithamar; for the house of Ithamar may well be supposed to have dwindled since the sentence passed on the family of Eli, who was of that house. The method of drawing the lots is intimated (*v.* 6), one chief household being taken for Eleazar, and one for Ithamar. The sixteen chief names of Eleazar were put in one urn, the eight for Ithamar in another, and they drew out of them alternately, as long as those for Ithamar lasted, and then out of those only for Eleazar, or two for Eleazar, and then one for Ithamar, throughout. 5. Among these twenty-four courses the eighth is that of Abijah or Abia (*v.* 10), which is mentioned (Luke i. 5) as the course which Zechariah was of, the father of John Baptist, by which it appears that these courses which David now settled, though interrupted perhaps in the bad reigns and long broken off by the captivity, yet continued in succession till the destruction of the second temple by the Romans. And each course was called by the name of him in whom it was first founded, as the high priest is here called *Aaron* (*v.* 19), because succeeding in his dignity and power, though we read not of any of them that bore that name. Whoever was high priest must be reverenced and observed by the inferior priests as their father, as Aaron their father. Christ is high priest over the house of God, to whom all believers, being made priests, are to be in subjection.

20 And the rest of the sons of Levi *were these:* Of the sons of Amram; Shubael: of the sons of Shubael; Jehdeiah. 21 Concerning Rehabiah: of the sons of Rehabiah, the first *was* Isshiah. 22 Of the Izharites; Shelomoth: of the sons of Shelomoth; Jahath. 23 And the sons *of Hebron;* Jeriah *the first,* Amariah the second, Jahaziel the third, Jekameam the fourth. 24 *Of* the sons of Uzziel; Micah: of the sons of Micah; Shamir. 25 The brother of Micah *was*

Isshiah: of the sons of Isshiah; Zechariah. 26 The sons of Merari *were* Mahli and Mushi: the sons of Jaaziah; Beno. 27 The sons of Merari by Jaaziah; Beno, and Shoham, and Zaccur, and Ibri. 28 Of Mahli *came* Eleazar, who had no sons. 29 Concerning Kish: the son of Kish *was* Jerahmeel. 30 The sons also of Mushi; Mahli, and Eder, and Jerimoth. These *were* the sons of the Levites after the house of their fathers. 31 These likewise cast lots over against their brethren the sons of Aaron in the presence of David the king, and Zadok, and Ahimelech, and the chief of the fathers of the priests and Levites, even the principal fathers over against their younger brethren.

Most of the Levites here named were mentioned before, *ch.* xxiii. 16, &c. They were of those who were to attend the priests in the service of the house of God. But they are here mentioned again as heads of the twenty-four courses of Levites (and about so many are here named), who were to attend the twenty-four courses of the priests: they are therefore said to *cast lots over against their brethren* (so they are called, not their *lords), the sons of Aaron,* who were not to lord it over God's *clergy,* as the original word is, 1 Pet. v. 3. And, that the whole disposal of the affair might be of the Lord, the principal fathers cast losts over against their younger brethren; that is, those that were of the elder house came upon the level with those of the younger families, and took their place, not by seniority, but as God by the lot directed. Note, In Christ no difference is made between bond and free, elder and younger. The younger brethren, if they be faithful and sincere, shall be no less acceptable to Christ than the principal fathers.

CHAP. XXV.

David, having settled the courses of these Levites that were to attend the priests in their ministrations, proceeds, in this chapter, to put those into a method that were appointed to be singers and musicians in the temple. Here is, I. The persons that were to be employed, Asaph, Heman, and Jeduthun (ver. 1), their sons (ver. 2—6), and other skilful persons, ver. 7. II. The order in which they were to attend determined by lot, ver. 8—31.

MOREOVER David and the captains of the host separated to the service of the sons of Asaph, and of Heman, and of Jeduthun, who should prophesy with harps, with psalteries, and with cymbals: and the number of the workmen according to their service was; 2 Of the sons of Asaph; Zaccur, and Joseph, and Nethaniah, and Asarelah, the sons of Asaph under the hands of Asaph, which prophesied according to the order of the king. 3 Of Jeduthun: the sons of Jeduthun; Gedaliah, and Zeri, and Jeshaiah, Hashabiah, and Mattithiah, six, under the hands of their father Jeduthun, who prophesied with a harp, to give thanks and to praise the LORD. 4 Of Heman: the sons of Heman; Bukkiah, Mattaniah, Uzziel, Shebuel, and Jerimoth, Hananiah, Hanani, Eliathah, Giddalti, and Romamti-ezer, Joshbekashah, Mallothi, Hothir, *and* Mahazioth: 5 All these *were* the sons of Heman the king's seer in the words of God, to lift up the horn. And God gave to Heman fourteen sons and three daughters. 6 All these *were* under the hands of their father for song *in* the house of the LORD, with cymbals, psalteries, and harps, for the service of the house of God, according to the king's order to Asaph, Jeduthun, and Heman. 7 So the number of them, with their brethren that were instructed in the songs of the LORD, *even* all that were cunning, was two hundred fourscore and eight.

Observe, I. Singing the praises of God is here called *prophesying* (*v.* 1—3), not that all those who were employed in this service were honoured with the visions of God, or could foretel things to come. Heman indeed is said to be the *king's seer in the words of God* (*v.* 5); but the psalms they sang were composed by prophets, and many of them were prophetical; and the edification of the church was intended in it, as well as the glory of God. In Samuel's time singing the praises of God went by the name of *prophesying* (1 Sam. x. 5; xix. 20), and perhaps that is intended in what St. Paul calls *prophesying,* 1 Cor. xi. 4; xiv. 24.

II. This is here called a *service,* and the persons employed in it *workmen, v.* 1. Not but that it is the greatest liberty and pleasure to be employed in praising God: what is heaven but that? But it intimates that it is our duty to make a business of it, and stir up all that is within us to it; and that, in our present state of corruption and infirmity, it will not be done as it should be done without labour and struggle. We must take pains with our hearts to bring them, and keep them, to this work, and to engage all that is within us.

III. Here were, in compliance with the temper of that dispensation, a great variety of musical instruments used, *harps, psalteries, cymbals* (*v.* 1, 6), and here was one that *lifted up the horn* (*v.* 5), that is, used wind-music. The bringing of such concerts of music into the worship of God now is what none pretend to. But those who use such concerts for their own entertainment should feel themselves obliged to preserve them always free from any thing that savours of immorality or profaneness, by this consideration, that time was when they were sacred; and then *those* were justly condemned who brought them into common use, Amos vi. 5. *They invented to themselves instruments of music like David.*

IV. The glory and honour of God were principally intended in all this temple-music, whether vocal or instrumental. It was *to give thanks, and praise the Lord,* that the singers were employed, *v.* 3. It was *in the songs of the Lord that they were instructed* (*v.* 7), that is, *for songs in the house of the Lord, v.* 6. This agrees with the intention of the perpetuating of psalmody in the gospel-church, which is *to make melody with the heart,* in conjunction with the voice, *unto the Lord,* Eph. v. 19.

V. The order of the king is likewise taken notice of, *v.* 2 and again *v.* 6. In those matters indeed David acted as a prophet; but his taking care for the due and regular observance of divine institutions, both ancient and modern, is an example to all in authority to use their power for the promoting of religion, and the enforcing of the laws of Christ. Let them thus be *ministers of God for good.*

VI. The fathers presided in this service, Asaph, Heman, and Jeduthun (*v.* 1), and the children were *under the hands of their father, v.* 2, 3, 6. This gives a good example to parents to train up their children, and indeed to all seniors to instruct their juniors in the service of God, and particularly in praising him, than which there is no part of our work more necessary or more worthy to be transmitted to the succeeding generations. It gives also an example to the younger to *submit themselves to the elder* (whose experience and observation fit them for direction), and, as far as may be, to do what they do *under their hand.* It is probable that Heman, Asaph, and Jeduthun, were bred up under Samuel, and had their education in the schools of the prophets which he was the founder and president of; then they were pupils, now they came to be masters. Those that would be eminent must begin early, and take time to prepare themselves. This good work of singing God's praises Samuel revived, and set on foot, but lived not to see it brought to the perfection it appears in here. Solomon perfects what David began, so David perfects what Samuel began. Let all, in their day, do what they can for God and his church, though they cannot carry it so far as they would; when they are gone God can out of stones raise up others who shall build upon their foundation and bring forth the top-stone.

VII. There were others also, besides the sons of these three great men, who are called their *brethren* (probably because they had been wont to join with them in their private concerts), who were *instructed in the songs of the Lord,* and were cunning or well skilled therein, *v.* 7. They were all Levites and were in number 288. Now, 1. These were a good number, and a competent number to keep up the service in the house of God; for they were all skilful in the work to which they were called. When David the king was so much addicted to divine poesy and music many others, all that had a genius for it, applied their studies and endeavours that way. Those do religion a great deal of good service that bring the exercises of devotion into reputation. 2. Yet these were but a small number in comparison with the 4000 whom David appointed thus to *praise the Lord, ch.* xxiii. 5. Where were all the rest when only 288, and those but by twelve in a course, were separated to this service? It is probable that all the rest were divided into as many courses, and were to follow as these led. Or, perhaps, these were *for song in the house of the Lord* (*v.* 6), with whom any that worshipped in the courts of that house might join; and the rest were disposed of, all the kingdom over, to preside in the country congregations, in this good work: for, though the sacrifices instituted by the hand of Moses might be offered but at one place, the psalms penned by David might be sung every where, 1 Tim. ii. 8.

8 And they cast lots, ward against *ward,* as well the small as the great, the teacher as the scholar. 9 Now the first lot came forth for Asaph to Joseph: the second to Gedaliah, who with his brethren and sons *were* twelve: 10 The third to Zaccur, *he,* his sons, and his brethren, *were* twelve: 11 The fourth to Izri, *he,* his sons, and his brethren, *were* twelve: 12 The fifth to Nethaniah, *he,* his sons, and his brethren, *were* twelve: 13 The sixth to Bukkiah, *he,* his sons, and his brethren, *were* twelve: 14 The seventh to Jesharelah, *he,* his sons, and his brethren, *were* twelve: 15 The eighth to Jeshaiah, *he,* his sons, and his brethren, *were* twelve: 16 The ninth to Mattaniah, *he,* his sons, and his brethren, *were* twelve: 17 The tenth to Shimei, *he,* his sons, and his brethren, *were* twelve: 18 The eleventh to Azareel, *he,* his sons, and his brethren, *were* twelve: 19 The twelfth to Hashabiah, *he,* his sons, and his brethren, *were* twelve: 20 The thirteenth

to Shubael, *he*, his sons, and his brethren, *were* twelve: 21 The fourteenth to Mattithiah, *he*, his sons, and his brethren, *were* twelve: 22 The fifteenth to Jeremoth, *he*, his sons, and his brethren, *were* twelve: 23 The sixteenth to Hananiah, *he*, his sons, and his brethren, *were* twelve: 24 The seventeenth to Joshbekashah, *he*, his sons, and his brethren, *were* twelve: 25 The eighteenth to Hanani, *he*, his sons, and his brethren, *were* twelve: 26 The nineteenth to Mallothi, *he*, his sons, and his brethren, *were* twelve: 27 The twentieth to Eliathah, *he*, his sons, and his brethren, *were* twelve: 28 The one and twentieth to Hothir, *he*, his sons, and his brethren, *were* twelve: 29 The two and twentieth to Giddalti, *he*, his sons, and his brethren, *were* twelve: 30 The three and twentieth to Mahazioth, *he*, his sons, and his brethren, *were* twelve: 31 The four and twentieth to Romamti-ezer, *he*, his sons, and his brethren, *were* twelve.

Twenty-four persons are named in the beginning of this chapter as sons of those three great men, Asaph, Heman, and Jeduthun. Ethan was the third (*ch.* vi. 44), but probably he was dead before the establishment was perfected and Jeduthun came in his room. [Or perhaps Ethan and Jeduthun were two names for the same person.] Of these three Providence so ordered it that Asaph had four sons, Jeduthun six [only five are mentioned *v.* 3; Shimei, mentioned *v.* 17, is supposed to have been the sixth], and Heman fourteen, in all twenty-four (who were named, *v.* 2—4), who were all qualified for the service and called to it. But the question was, In what order must they serve? This was determined by lot, to prevent strife for precedency, a sin which most easily besets many that otherwise are good people.

I. The lot was thrown impartially. They were placed in twenty-four companies, twelve in a company, in two rows, twelve companies in a row, and so they cast lots, *ward against ward*, putting them all upon a level, small and great, teacher and scholar. They did not go according to their age, or according to their standing, or the degrees they had taken in the music-schools; but it was referred to God, *v.* 8. Small and great, teachers and scholars, stand alike before God, who goes not according to our rules of distinction and precedency. See Matt. xx. 23.

II. God determined it as he pleased, taking account, it is probable, of the respective merits of the persons, which are of much more importance than seniority of age or priority of birth. Let us compare them with the preceding catalogue and we shall find that, 1. Joseph was the second son of Asaph. 2. Gedaliah the eldest son of Jeduthun. 3. Zaccur the eldest of Asaph. 4. Izri the second of Jeduthun. 5. Nethaniah the third of Asaph. 6. Bukkiah the eldest of Heman. 7. Jesharelah the youngest of Asaph. 8. Jeshaiah the third of Jeduthun. 9. Mattaniah the second of Heman. 10. Shimei the youngest of Jeduthun. 11. Azareel the third of Heman. 12. Hashabiah the fourth of Jeduthun. 13. Shubael the fourth of Heman. 14. Mattithiah the fifth of Jeduthun. 15. Jeremoth the fifth of Heman. 16. Hananiah the sixth of Heman. 17. Joshbekashah the eleventh of Heman. 18. Hanani the seventh of Heman. 19. Mallothi the twelfth of Heman. 20. Eliathah the eighth of Heman. 21 Hothir the thirteenth of Heman. 22. Giddalti the ninth of Heman. 23. Mahazioth the fourteenth of Heman. And, *lastly*, Romamti-ezer, the tenth of Heman. See how God increased some and preferred the younger before the elder.

III. Each of these had in his chorus the number of twelve, called *their sons and their brethren*, because they observed them as sons, and concurred with them as brethren. Probably twelve, some for the voice and others for the instrument, made up the concert. Let us learn with one mind and one mouth to glorify God, and that will be the best concert.

CHAP. XXVI.

We have here an account of the business of the Levites. That tribe had made but a very small figure all the time of the judges, till Eli and Samuel appeared. But when David revived religion the Levites were, of all men, in the greatest reputation. And happy it was that they had Levites who were men of sense, fit to support the honour of their tribe. We have here an account, I. Of the Levites that were appointed to be porters, ver. 1—19. II. Of those that were appointed to be treasurers and storekeepers, ver. 20—28. III. Of those that were officers and judges in the country, and were entrusted with the administration of public affairs, ver. 29—32.

CONCERNING the divisions of the porters: Of the Korhites *was* Meshelemiah the son of Kore, of the sons of Asaph. 2 And the sons of Meshelemiah *were*, Zechariah the firstborn, Jediael the second, Zebadiah the third, Jathniel the fourth, 3 Elam the fifth, Jehohanan the sixth, Elioenai the seventh. 4 Moreover the sons of Obed-edom *were*, Shemaiah the firstborn, Jehozabad the second, Joah the third, and Sacar the fourth, and Nethaneel the fifth, 5 Ammiel the sixth, Issachar the seventh, Peulthai the eighth: for God blessed him. 6 Also unto Shemaiah his son were sons born, that ruled throughout the house of their father: for they *were* mighty men of valour. 7 The sons of Shemaiah; Othni, and Rephael, and Obed, Elzabad, whose brethren *were* strong men, Elihu, and Semachiah. 8 All these of the sons of Obed-edom: they and their sons and their brethren, able men for strength for the service, *were* threescore and two of Obed-edom. 9 And Meshelemiah had sons and brethren, strong men, eighteen. 10 Also Hosah, of the children of Merari, had sons; Simri the chief, (for *though* he was not the firstborn, yet his father made him the chief;) 11 Hilkiah the second, Tebaliah the third, Zechariah the fourth: all the sons and brethren of Hosah *were* thirteen. 12 Among these *were* the divisions of the porters, *even* among the chief men, *having* wards one against another, to minister in the house of the LORD. 13 And they cast lots, as well the small as the great, according to the house of their fathers, for every gate. 14 And the lot eastward fell to Shelemiah. Then for Zechariah his son, a wise counsellor, they cast lots; and his lot came out northward. 15 To Obed-edom southward; and to his sons the house of Asuppim. 16 To Shuppim and Hosah *the lot came forth* westward, with the gate Shallecheth, by the causeway of the going up, ward against ward. 17 Eastward *were* six Levites, northward four a day, southward four a day, and toward Asuppim two *and* two. 18 At Parbar westward, four at the causeway, *and* two at Parbar. 19 These *are* the divisions of the porters among the sons of Kore, and among the sons of Merari.

Observe, I. There were porters appointed to attend the temple, who guarded all the avenues that led to it, opened and shut all the outer gates and attended at them, not only for state, but for service, to direct and instruct those who were going to worship in the courts of the sanctuary in the decorum they were to observe, to encourage those that were timorous, to send back the strangers and unclean, and to guard against thieves and others that were enemies to the house of God. In allusion to this office, ministers are said to have *the keys of the kingdom of heaven* committed to them (Matt. xvi. 19), that they may admit, and exclude, according to the law of Christ.

II. Of several of those that were called to this service, it is taken notice of that they were *mighty men of valour* (*v.* 6), *strong men* (*v.* 7), *able men* (*v.* 8), and one of them that he was *a wise counsellor* (*v.* 14), who probably, when he had *used this office of a deacon well* and given proofs of more than ordinary wisdom, *purchased to himself a good degree,* and was preferred from the gate to the council-board, 1 Tim. iii. 13. As for those that excelled in strength of body, and courage and resolution of mind, they were thereby qualified for the post assigned them; for whatever service God calls men to he either finds them fit or makes them so.

III. The sons of Obed-edom were employed in this office, sixty-two of that family. This was he that entertained the ark with reverence and cheerfulness; and see how he was rewarded for it. 1. He had eight *sons* (*v.* 5), *for God blessed him.* The increase and building up of families are owing to the divine blessing; and a great blessing it is to a family to have many children, when like these they are able for, and eminent in, the service of God. 2. His sons were preferred to places of trust in the sanctuary. They had faithfully attended the ark in their own house, and now were called to attend it in God's house. He that is trusty in little shall be trusted with more. He that keeps God's ordinances in his own tent is fit to have the custody of them in God's tabernacle, 1 Tim. iii. 4, 5. *I have kept thy law,* says David, and *this I had because I kept thy precepts,* Ps. cxix. 55, 56.

IV. It is said of one here that *though he was not the first-born his father made him the chief* (*v.* 10), either because he was very excellent, or because the elder son was very weak. He was made chief, perhaps not in inheriting the estate (for that was forbidden by the law, Deut. xxi. 16, 17), but in this service, which required personal qualifications.

V. The porters, as the singers, had their post assigned them by lot, so many at such a gate, and so many at such a one, that every one might know his post and make it good, *v.* 13. It is not said that they were cast into twenty-four courses, as before; but here are the names of about twenty-four (*v.* 1—11), and the posts assigned are twenty-four, *v.* 17, 18. We have therefore reason to think they were distributed into as many companies. Happy are those who dwell in God's house: for, as they are well fed, well taught, and well employed, so they are well guarded. Men attended at the gates of the temple, but angels attend at the gates of the New Jerusalem, Rev. xxi. 12.

20 And of the Levites, Ahijah *was* over the treasures of the house of God, and over the treasures of the dedicated things. 21 *As concerning*

the sons of Laadan; the sons of the Gershonite Laadan, chief fathers, *even* of Laadan the Gershonite, *were* Jehieli. 22 The sons of Jehieli; Zetham, and Joel his brother, *which were* over the treasures of the house of the LORD. 23 Of the Amramites, *and* the Izharites, the Hebronites, *and* the Uzzielites: 24 And Shebuel the son of Gershom, the son of Moses, *was* ruler of the treasures. 25 And his brethren by Eliezer; Rehabiah his son, and Jeshaiah his son, and Joram his son, and Zichri his son, and Shelomith his son. 26 Which Shelomith and his brethren *were* over all the treasures of the dedicated things, which David the king, and the chief fathers, the captains over thousands and hundreds, and the captains of the host, had dedicated. 27 Out of the spoils won in battles did they dedicate to maintain the house of the LORD. 28 And all that Samuel the seer, and Saul the son of Kish, and Abner the son of Ner, and Joab the son of Zeruiah, had dedicated; *and* whosoever had dedicated *any thing, it was* under the hand of Shelomith, and of his brethren.

Observe, 1. There were *treasures of the house of God.* A great house cannot be well kept without stores of all manner of provisions. Much was expended daily upon the altar—flour, wine, oil, salt, fuel, besides the lamps; quantities of these were to be kept beforehand, besides the sacred vestments and utensils. These were the *treasures of the house of God.* And, because money answers all things, doubtless they had an abundance of it, which was received from the people's offerings, wherewith they bought in what they had occasion for. And perhaps much was laid up for an exigence. These treasures typified the plenty there is in our heavenly Father's house, enough and to spare. In Christ, the true temple, are hid *treasures of wisdom and knowledge*, and *unsearchable riches.* 2. There were *treasures of dedicated things,* dedicated mostly *out of the spoils won in battle* (*v.* 27), as a grateful acknowledgment of the divine protection. Abraham gave Melchisedec the *tenth of the spoils,* Heb. vii. 4. In Moses's time the officers of the army, when they returned victorious, brought of their spoils an *oblation to the Lord,* Num. xxxi. 50. Of late this pious custom had been revived; and not only Samuel and David, but Saul, and Abner, and Joab, had dedicated of their spoils to the honour and support of the house of God, *v.* 28. Note, The more God bestows upon us the more he expects from us in works of piety and charity. Great successes call for proportionable returns. When we look over our estates we should consider, "Here are convenient things, rich things, it may be, and fine things; but where are the dedicated things?" Men of war must honour God with their spoils. 3. These treasures had treasurers, those that were over them (*v.* 20, 26), whose business it was to keep them, that neither *moth nor rust* might *corrupt them,* nor *thieves break through and steal,* to give out as there was occasion and to see they were not wasted, embezzled, or alienated to any common use; and it is probable that they kept accounts of all that was brought in and how it was laid out.

29 Of the Izharites, Chenaniah and his sons *were* for the outward business over Israel, for officers and judges. 30 *And* of the Hebronites, Hashabiah and his brethren, men of valour, a thousand and seven hundred, *were* officers among them of Israel on this side Jordan westward in all the business of the LORD, and in the service of the king. 31 Among the Hebronites *was* Jerijah the chief, *even* among the Hebronites, according to the generations of his fathers. In the fortieth year of the reign of David they were sought for, and there were found among them mighty men of valour at Jazer of Gilead. 32 And his brethren, men of valour, *were* two thousand and seven hundred chief fathers, whom king David made rulers over the Reubenites, the Gadites, and the half tribe of Manasseh, for every matter pertaining to God, and affairs of the king.

All the offices of the house of God being well provided with Levites, we have here an account of those that were employed as officers and judges in the outward business, which must not be neglected, no, not for the temple itself. The magistracy is an ordinance of God for the good of the church as truly as the ministry is. And here we are told, 1. That the Levites were employed in the administration of justice in concurrence with the princes and elders of the several tribes, who could not be supposed to understand the law so well as the Levites, who made it their business to study it. None of those Levites who were employed in the service of the sanctuary, none of the singers or porters, were concerned in this outward business; either one was enough to engage the whole man or it was presumption to undertake both. 2. Their charge was both *in all business of the Lord*, and *in the service of the kings*, *v.* 30 and again *v.* 32. They managed the affairs of the country, as well ecclesiastical as civil, took care both of God's tithes and the king's taxes, punished offences committed immediately against God and his honour and those against the government and the public peace, guarded both against idolatry and against injustice, and took care to put the laws in execution against both. Some, it is likely, applied themselves to the affairs of religion, others to secular affairs; and so, between both, God and the king were well served. It is happy with a kingdom when its civil and sacred interests are thus interwoven and jointly minded and advanced. 3. There were more Levites employed as judges with the two tribes and a half on the other side Jordan than with all the rest of the tribes; there were 2700; whereas on the west side of Jordan there were 1700, *v.* 30, 32. Either those remote tribes were not so well furnished as the rest with judges of their own, or because they, lying furthest from Jerusalem and on the borders of the neighbouring nations, were most in danger of being infected with idolatry, and most needed the help of Levites to prevent it. The frontiers must be well guarded. 4. This is said to be done (as were all the foregoing settlements) in the fortieth year of the reign of David (*v.* 31), that is, the last year of his reign. We should be so much the more industrious to do good *as we see the day approaching*. If we live not to enjoy the fruit of our labours, grudge it not to those that shall come after us.

CHAP. XXVII.

In this chapter we have the civil list, including the military. I. The twelve captains for every separate month of the year, ver. 1—15. II. The princes of the several tribes, ver. 16—24. III The officers of the court, ver. 25—34.

NOW the children of Israel after their number, *to wit*, the chief fathers and captains of thousands and hundreds, and their officers that served the king in any matter of the courses, which came in and went out month by month throughout all the months of the year, of every course *were* twenty and four thousand. 2 Over the first course for the first month *was* Jashobeam the son of Zabdiel: and in his course *were* twenty and four thousand. 3 Of the children of Perez *was* the chief of all the captains of the host for the first month. 4 And over the course of the second month *was* Dodai an Ahohite, and of his course *was* Mikloth also the ruler: in his course likewise *were* twenty and four thousand. 5 The third captain of the host for the third month *was* Benaiah the son of Jehoiada, a chief priest: and in his course *were* twenty and four thousand. 6 This *is that* Benaiah, *who was* mighty *among* the thirty, and above the thirty: and in his course *was* Ammizabad his son. 7 The fourth *captain* for the fourth month *was* Asahel the brother of Joab, and Zebadiah his son after him: and in his course *were* twenty and four thousand. 8 The fifth captain for the fifth month *was* Shamhuth the Izrahite: and in his course *were* twenty and four thousand. 9 The sixth *captain* for the sixth month *was* Ira the son of Ikkesh the Tekoite: and in his course *were* twenty and four thousand. 10 The seventh *captain* for the seventh month *was* Helez the Pelonite, of the children of Ephraim: and in his course *were* twenty and four thousand. 11 The eighth *captain* for the eighth month *was* Sibbecai the Hushathite, of the Zarhites: and in his course *were* twenty and four thousand. 12 The ninth *captain* for the ninth month *was* Abiezer the Anetothite, of the Benjamites: and in his course *were* twenty and four thousand. 13 The tenth *captain* for the tenth month *was* Maharai the Netophathite, of the Zarhites: and in his course *were* twenty and four thousand. 14 The eleventh *captain* for the eleventh month *was* Benaiah the Pirathonite, of the children of Ephraim: and in his course *were* twenty and four thousand. 15 The twelfth *captain* for the twelfth month *was* Heldai the Netophathite, of Othniel: and in his course *were* twenty and four thousand.

We have here an account of the regulation of the militia of the kingdom. David was himself a man of war, and had done great things with the sword; he had brought into the field great armies. Now here we are told how he marshalled them when God had given him rest from all his enemies. He did not keep them all together, for that would have been a hardship on them and the country; yet he did not disband and disperse them all, for then he would have left his kingdom naked, and his people would have forgotten the arts of war, wherein they had been instructed. He therefore contrived to keep up a constant force, and yet not a standing army. The model is very prudent. 1. He kept up 24,000 constantly in arms, I suppose in a body, and disciplined, in one part or other of the kingdom, the freeholders carrying their own arms and bearing their own charges while they were up. This was a sufficient strength for the securing of the public peace and safety. Those that are Israelites indeed must learn war; for we have enemies to grapple with, whom we are concerned constantly to stand upon our guard against. 2. He changed them every month; so that the whole number of the militia amounted to 288,000, perhaps about a fifth part of the able men of the kingdom. By being thus distributed into twelve courses, they were all instructed in, and accustomed to, military exercises; and yet none were compelled to be in service, and at expenses, above one month in the year (which they might very well afford), unless upon extraordinary occasions, and then they might all be got together quickly. It is the wisdom of governors, and much their praise, while they provide for the public safety, to contrive how to make it effectual and yet easy, and as little as possible burdensome to the people. 3. Every course had a commander in chief over it. Besides the subaltern officers that were rulers over thousands, and hundreds, and fifties, there was one general officer to each course or legion. All these twelve great commanders are mentioned among David's worthies and champions, 2 Sam. xxiii. and 1 Chron. xi. They had first signalized themselves by their great actions and then they were advanced to those great preferments. It is well with a kingdom when honour thus attends merit. Benaiah is here called *a chief priest, v.* 5. But, *cohen* signifying both a *priest* and a *prince*, it might better be translated here *a chief ruler*, or (as in the margin) *a principal officer*. Doda had Mikloth (*v.* 4) either for his substitute when he was absent or infirm, or for his successor when he was dead. Benaiah had his son under him, *v.* 6. Asahel had his son after him (*v.* 7), and by this it seems that this plan of the militia was laid in the beginning of David's reign; for Asahel was killed by Abner while David reigned in Hebron. When his wars were over he revived this method, and left the military affairs in this posture, for the peaceable reign of his son Solomon. When we think ourselves most safe, yet, while we are here in the body, we must keep in a readiness for spiritual conflicts. *Let not him that girdeth on the harness boast as he that puts it off.*

16 Furthermore over the tribes of Israel: the ruler of the Reubenites *was* Eliezer the son of Zichri: of the Simeonites, Shephatiah the son of Maachah: 17 Of the Levites, Hashabiah the son of Kemuel: of the Aaronites, Zadok: 18 Of Judah, Elihu, *one* of the brethren of David: of Issachar, Omri the son of Michael: 19 Of Zebulun, Ishmaiah the son of Obadiah: of Naphtali, Jerimoth the son of Azriel: 20 Of the children of Ephraim, Hoshea the son of Azaziah: of the half tribe of Manasseh, Joel the son of Pedaiah: 21 Of the half *tribe* of Manasseh in Gilead, Iddo the son of Zechariah: of Benjamin, Jaasiel the son of Abner: 22 Of Dan, Azareel the son of Jeroham. These *were* the princes of the tribes of Israel. 23 But David took not the number of them from twenty years old and under: because the LORD had said he would increase Israel like to the stars of the heavens. 24 Joab the son of Zeruiah began to number, but he finished not, because there fell wrath for it against Israel; neither was the number put in the account of the chronicles of king David. 25 And over the king's treasures *was* Azmaveth the son of Adiel: and over the storehouses in the fields, in the cities, and in the villages, and in the castles, *was* Jehonathan the son of Uzziah: 26 And over them that did the work of the field for tillage of the ground *was* Ezri the son of Chelub: 27 And over the vineyards *was* Shimei the Ramathite: over the increase of the vineyards for the wine cellars *was* Zabdi the Shiphmite: 28 And over the olive trees and the sycamore trees that *were* in the low plains *was* Baal-hanan the Gederite: and over the cellars of oil *was* Joash: 29 And over the herds that fed in Sharon *was* Shitrai the Sharonite: and over the herds *that were* in the valleys *was* Shaphat the son of Adlai: 30 Over the camels also *was* Obil the Ishmaelite: and over the asses *was* Jehdeiah the Meronothite: 31 And over the flocks *was* Jaziz the Hagerite. All these *were* the rulers of the substance which *was* king David's. 32 Also Jonathan David's uncle was a counsellor, a wise man, and a scribe: and Jehiel the son of Hachmoni *was* with the king's sons: 33 And Ahithophel *was* the king's counsellor: and Hushai the Archite *was* the king's companion: 34 And after Ahithophel *was* Jehoiada the son of Benaiah, and

Abiathar: and the general of the king's army *was* Joab.

We have here an account,

I. Of the princes of the tribes. Something of the ancient order instituted by Moses in the wilderness was still kept up, that every tribe should have its prince or chief. It is probable that it was kept up all along, either by election or by succession, in the same family; and those are here named who were found in that office when this account was taken. Elihu, or Eliab, who was prince of Judah, was the eldest son of Jesse, and descended in a right line from Nahshon and Salmon, the princes of this tribe in Moses's time. Whether these princes were of the nature of lord-lieutenants that guided them in their military affairs, or chief-justices that presided in their courts of judgment, does not appear. Their power, we may suppose, was much less now that all the tribes were united under one king than it had been when, for the most part, they acted separately. Our religion obliges us to be subject, not only to *the king as supreme, but unto governors under him* (1 Pet. ii. 13, 14), the princes that decree justice. Of Benjamin was Jaaziel the son of Abner, *v.* 21. Though Abner was David's enemy, and opposed his coming to the throne, yet David would not oppose the preferment of his son, but perhaps nominated him to this post of honour, which teaches us to render good for evil.

II. Of the numbering of the people, *v.* 23, 24. It is here said, 1. That when David ordered the people to be numbered he forbade the numbering of those under twenty years old, thinking thereby to save the reflection which what he did might otherwise cast upon the promise that they should be innumerable; yet it was but a poor salvo, for it had never been customary to number those under twenty, and the promise of their numbers chiefly respected the effective men. 2. That that account which David took of the people, in the pride of his heart, turned to no good account; for it was never perfected, nor done with exactness, nor was it ever recorded as an authentic account. Joab was disgusted with it, and did it by halves; David was ashamed of it, and willing it should be forgotten, because there fell wrath for it against Israel. A good man cannot, in the reflection, please himself with that which he knows God is displeased with, cannot make use of that, nor take comfort in that, which is obtained by sin.

III. Of the officers of the court. 1. The *rulers of the* king's *substance* (as they are called, *v.* 31), such as had the oversight and charge of the king's tillage, his vineyards, his olive-yards, his herds, his camels, his asses, his flocks. Here are no officers for state, none for sport, no master of the wardrobe, no master of the ceremonies, no master of the horse, no master of the hounds, but all for service, agreeable to the simplicity and plainness of those times. David was a great soldier, a great scholar, and a great prince, and yet a great husband of his estate, kept a great deal of ground in his own hand, and stocked it, not for pleasure, but for profit; for the king himself is *served of the field,* Eccl. v. 9. Those magistrates that would have their subjects industrious must themselves be examples of industry and application to business. We find, however, that afterwards the poor of the land were thought good enough to be vine-dressers and husbandmen, 2 Kings xxv. 12. Now David put his great men to preside in these employments. 2. The attendants on the king's person. They were such as were eminent for wisdom, being designed for conversation. His uncle, who was a wise man and a scribe, not only well skilled in politics, but well read in the scriptures, was his counsellor, *v.* 32. Another, who no doubt excelled in learning and prudence, was tutor to his children. Ahithophel, a very cunning man, was his counsellor: but Hushai, an honest man, was his companion and confidant. It does not appear that he had many counsellors; but those he had were men of great abilities. Much of the wisdom of princes is seen in the choice of their ministry. But David, though he had all these trusty and well-beloved cousins and counsellors about him, preferred his Bible before them all. Ps. cxix. 24, *Thy testimonies are my delight and my counsellors.*

CHAP. XXVIII.

The account we have of David's exit, in the beginning of the first book of Kings, does not make his sun nearly so bright as that given in this and the following chapter, where we have his solemn farewell both to his son and his subjects, and must own that he finished well. In this chapter we have, I. A general convention of the states summoned to meet, ver. 1. II. A solemn declaration of the divine entail both of the crown and of the honour of building the temple upon Solomon, ver. 2—7. III. An exhortation both to the people and to Solomon to make religion their business, ver. 8—10. IV. The model and materials delivered to Solomon for the building of the temple, ver. 11—19. V. Encouragement given him to undertake it and proceed in it, ver. 20, 21.

AND David assembled all the princes of Israel, the princes of the tribes, and the captains of the companies that ministered to the king by course, and the captains over the thousands, and captains over the hundreds, and the stewards over all the substance and possession of the king, and of his sons, with the officers, and with the mighty men, and with all the valiant men, unto Jerusalem. 2 Then David the king stood up upon his feet, and said, Hear me, my brethren, and my people: *As for me,* I *had* in mine heart to build a house of rest for the ark of the covenant of the LORD, and for the footstool of our God, and had made ready for the building: 3 But God said unto me, Thou shalt not build a house for my name, because thou *hast been* a man of war, and hast shed blood. 4 Howbeit the LORD God of Israel chose me before all the house of my father to be king over Israel for ever: for he hath chosen Judah *to be* the ruler; and of the house of Judah, the house of my father; and among the sons of my father he liked me to make *me* king over all Israel: 5 And of all my sons, (for the LORD hath given me many sons,) he hath chosen Solomon my son to sit upon the throne of the kingdom of the LORD over Israel. 6 And he said unto me, Solomon thy son, he shall build my house and my courts: for I have chosen him *to be* my son, and I will be his father. 7 Moreover I will establish his kingdom for ever, if he be constant to do my commandments and my judgments, as at this day. 8 Now therefore in the sight of all Israel the congregation of the LORD, and in the audience of our God, keep and seek for all the commandments of the LORD your God: that ye may possess this good land, and leave *it* for an inheritance for your children after you for ever. 9 And thou, Solomon my son, know thou the God of thy father, and serve him with a perfect heart and with a willing mind: for the LORD searcheth all hearts, and understandeth all the imaginations of the thoughts: if thou seek him, he will be found of thee; but if thou forsake him, he will cast thee off for ever. 10 Take heed now; for the LORD hath chosen thee to build a house for the sanctuary: be strong, and do *it*.

A great deal of service David had done in his day, had *served his generation according to the will of God,* Acts xiii. 36. But now the time draws nigh that he must die, and, as a type of the Son of David, the nearer he comes to his end the more busy he is, and does his work with all his might. He is now a little recovered from the indisposition mentioned 1 Kings i. 1, when they covered him with clothes, and he got no heat: but what cure is there for old age? He therefore improves his recovery, as giving him an opportunity of doing God and his country a little more service.

I. He summoned all the great men to attend him, that he might take leave of them all together, *v.* 1. Thus Moses did (Deut. xxxi. 28), and Joshua, *ch.* xxiii. 2; xxiv. 1. David would not declare the settlement of the crown but in the presence, and to the satisfaction, of those that were the representatives of the people.

II. He addressed them with a great deal of respect and tenderness. He not only exerted himself to rise from his bed, to give them the meeting (the occasion putting new spirits into him), but he rose out of his chair, and *stood up upon his feet* (*v.* 2), in reverence to God whose will he was to declare, and in reverence to this solemn assembly of the Israel of God, as if he looked upon himself, though *major singulis—greater than any individual among them,* yet *minor universis—less than the whole of them together.* His age and infirmities, as well as his dignity, might well have allowed him to keep his seat; but he would show that he was indeed humbled for the pride of his heart both in the numbers of his people and his dominion over them. It had been too much his pleasure that they were all his *servants* (*ch.* xxi. 3), but now he calls them his *brethren,* whom he loved, his people, whom he took care of, not his servants, whom he had the command of: *Hear me, my brethren, and my people.* It becomes superiors thus to speak with affection and condescension even to their inferiors; they will not be the less honoured for it, but the more beloved. Thus he engages their attention to what he was about to say.

III. He declared the purpose he had formed to build a temple for God, and God's disallowing that purpose, *v.* 2, 3. This he had signified to Solomon before, *ch.* xxii. 7, 8. *A house of rest for the ark* is here said to be *a house of rest for the footstool of our God;* for heaven is his throne of glory; the earth, and the most magnificent temples that can be built upon it, are but his footstool: so much difference is there between the manifestations of the divine glory in the upper and the lower world. Angels surround his throne, Isa. vi. 1. We poor worms do but *worship at his footstool,* Ps. xcix. 5; cxxxii. 7. As an evidence of the sincerity of his purpose to build the temple, he tells them that he had made ready for it, but that God would not suffer him to proceed because he had appointed other work for him to do, which was enough for one man, namely, the managing of the wars of Israel. He must serve the public with the sword; another must do it with the line and plummet. Times of rest are building times, Acts ix. 31.

IV. He produced his own title first, and then Solomon's, to the crown; both were undoubtedly *jure divino—divine.* They could make out such a title as no monarch on earth can; the Lord God of Israel chose them both immediately, by prophecy, not providence, *v.* 4, 5. No right of primogeniture is pretended. *Detur digniori, non seniori—It went by worth, not by age.* 1. Judah was not the eldest son of Jacob, yet God chose that tribe to be the ruling tribe; Jacob entailed the sceptre upon it, Gen. xlix. 10. 2. It does not appear that the family of Jesse was the senior house of that tribe; from Judah it is certain that it was not, for Shelah was before Pharez; whether from Nahshon and Salmon is not certain. Ram, the father of Nahshon, had an elder brother, 1 Chron. ii. 9. Perhaps so had Boaz, Obed, and Jesse. Yet "*God chose the house of my father.*" 3. David was the youngest son of Jesse, yet God liked him to make him king; so it seemed good unto him. God takes whom he likes, and likes whom he makes like himself, as he did David, a man after his own heart. 4. Solomon was one of the youngest sons of David, and yet God chose him to sit upon the throne, because he was the likeliest of them all to build the temple, the wisest and best inclined.

V. He opened to them God's gracious purposes concerning Solomon (*v.* 6, 7): *I have chosen him to be my son.* Thus he declares the decree, that the Lord had said to Solomon, as a type of Christ, *Thou art my son* (Ps. ii. 7), the son of my love; for he was called *Jedidiah,* because the Lord loved him, and Christ is his beloved Son. Of him God said, as a figure of him that was to come, 1. *He shall build my house.* Christ is both the founder and the foundation of the gospel temple. 2. *I will establish his kingdom for ever.* This must have its accomplishment in the kingdom of the Messiah, which shall continue in his hands through all the ages of time (Isa. ix. 7; Luke i. 33) and shall then be delivered up to God, even the Father, yet perhaps to be delivered back to the Redeemer for ever. As to Solomon, this promise of the establishment of his kingdom is here made conditional: *If he be constant to do my commandments, as at this day.* Solomon was now very towardly and good: "If he continue so, his kingdom shall continue, otherwise not." Note, If we be constant to our duty, then, and not otherwise, we may expect the continuance of God's favour. Let those that are well taught, and begin well, take notice of this—if they be constant, they are happy; perseverance wears the crown, though it wins it not.

VI. He charged them to adhere stedfastly to God and their duty, *v.* 8. Observe, 1. The matter of this charge: *Keep, and seek for all the commandments of the Lord your God.* The Lord was their God; his commandments must be their rule; they must have respect to them all, must make conscience of keeping them, and, in order thereunto, must seek for them, that is, must be inquisitive concerning their duty, search the scriptures, take advice, seek the law at the mouth of those whose lips were to keep this knowledge, and pray to God to teach and direct them. God's commandments will not be kept without great care. 2. The solemnity of it. He charged them in the sight of all Israel, who would all have notice of this public charge, and in the audience of their God. "God is witness, and this congregation is witness, that they have good counsel given them, and fair warning; if they do not take it, it is their fault, and God and man will be witnesses against them." See 1 Tim. v. 21; 2 Tim. iv. 1. Those that profess religion, as they tender the favour of God and their reputation with men, must be faithful to their profession. 3. The motive to observe this charge. It was the way to be happy, to have the peaceable possession of this good land themselves and to preserve the entail of it upon their children.

VII. He concluded with a charge to Solomon himself, *v.* 9, 10. He was much concerned that Solomon should be religious. He was to be a great man, but he must not think religion below him—a wise man, and this would be his wisdom. Observe,

1. The charge he gives him. He must look upon God as the God of his father, his good father, who had devoted him to God and educated him for God. He was born in God's house and therefore bound in duty to be his, brought up in his house and therefore bound in gratitude. *Thy own friend, and thy father's friend, forsake not.* He must know God and serve him. We cannot serve God aright if we do not know him; and in vain do we know him if we do not serve him, serve him with heart and mind. We make nothing of religion if we do not mind it, and make heart-work of it. Serve him with a perfect, that is, an upright heart (for sincerity is our gospel perfection), and with a willing mind, from a principle of love, and as a willing people, cheerfully and with pleasure.

2. The arguments to enforce this charge.

(1.) Two arguments of general inducement:—[1.] That the secrets of our souls are open before God; he searches all hearts, even the hearts of kings, which to men are unsearchable, Prov. xxv. 3. We must *therefore* be sincere, because, if we deal deceitfully, God sees it, and cannot be imposed upon; we must *therefore* employ our thoughts, and engage them in God's service, because he fully understands all the imaginations of them, both good and bad. [2.] That we are happy or miserable here, and for ever, according as we do, or do not, serve God. *If we seek him diligently, he will be found of us,* and that is enough to make us happy, Heb. xi. 6. If we forsake him, desert his service and turn from following him, he will cast us off for ever, and that is enough to make us miserable. Note, God never casts any off till they have first cast him off. Here is,

(2.) One argument peculiar to Solomon (*v.* 10): "*Thou art to build a house for the sanctuary;* therefore seek and serve God, that

that work may be done from a good principle, in a right manner, and may be accepted."

3. The means prescribed in order hereunto, and they are prescribed to us all. (1.) Caution: *Take heed;* beware of every thing that looks like, or leads to, that which is evil. (2.) Courage: *Be strong, and do it.* We cannot do our work as we should unless we put on resolution, and fetch in strength from divine grace.

11 Then David gave to Solomon his son the pattern of the porch, and of the houses thereof, and of the treasuries thereof, and of the upper chambers thereof, and of the inner parlours thereof, and of the place of the mercy seat, 12 And the pattern of all that he had by the spirit, of the courts of the house of the LORD, and of all the chambers round about, of the treasuries of the house of God, and of the treasuries of the dedicated things: 13 Also for the courses of the priests and the Levites, and for all the work of the service of the house of the LORD, and for all the vessels of service in the house of the LORD. 14 *He gave* of gold by weight for *things* of gold, for all instruments of all manner of service; *silver also* for all instruments of silver by weight, for all instruments of every kind of service: 15 Even the weight for the candlesticks of gold, and for their lamps of gold, by weight for every candlestick, and for the lamps thereof: and for the candlesticks of silver by weight, *both* for the candlestick, and *also* for the lamps thereof, according to the use of every candlestick. 16 And by weight *he gave* gold for the tables of showbread, for every table; and *likewise* silver for the tables of silver: 17 Also pure gold for the fleshhooks, and the bowls, and the cups: and for the golden basons *he gave gold* by weight for every bason; and *likewise silver* by weight for every bason of silver: 18 And for the altar of incense refined gold by weight; and gold for the pattern of the chariot of the cherubims, that spread out *their wings*, and covered the ark of the covenant of the LORD. 19 All *this, said David,* the LORD made me understand in writing by *his* hand upon me, *even* all the works of this pattern. 20 And David said to Solomon his son, Be strong and of good courage, and do *it*: fear not, nor be dismayed: for the LORD God, *even* my God, *will be* with thee; he will not fail thee, nor forsake thee, until thou hast finished all the work for the service of the house of the LORD. 21 And, behold, the courses of the priests and the Levites, *even they shall be with thee* for all the service of the house of God: and *there shall be* with thee for all manner of workmanship every willing skilful man, for any manner of service: also the princes and all the people *will be* wholly at thy commandment.

As for the general charge that David gave his son to seek God and serve him, the book of the law was, in that, his only rule, and there needed no other; but, in building the temple, David was now to give him three things:—1. A model of the building, because it was to be such a building as neither he nor his architects ever saw. Moses had a pattern of the tabernacle shown him in the mount (Heb. viii. 5), so had David of the temple, by the immediate hand of God upon him, *v.* 19. It was given him in writing, probably by the ministry of an angel, or as clearly and exactly represented to his mind as if it had been in writing. But it is said (*v.* 12), *He had this pattern by the Spirit.* The contrivance either of David's devotion or of Solomon's wisdom must not be trusted to in an affair of this nature. The temple must be a sacred thing and a type of Christ; there must be in it not only convenience and decency, but significancy: it was a kind of sacrament, and therefore it must not be left to man's art or invention to contrive it, but must be framed by divine institution. Christ the true temple, the church the gospel temple, and heaven the everlasting temple, are all framed according to the divine councils, and the plan laid in the divine wisdom, ordained before the world for God's glory and ours. This pattern David gave to Solomon, that he might know what to provide and might go by a certain rule. When Christ left with his disciples a charge to build his gospel church he gave them an exact model of it, ordering them to observe that, and that only, which he commanded. The particular models are here mentioned, of the porch, which was higher than the rest, like a steeple,—then the houses, both the holy place and the most holy, with the rooms adjoining, which were for treasuries, chambers, and parlours,—especially *the place of the mercy-seat* (*v.* 11),—of the courts likewise, and the chambers about them, in which the dedicated things were laid up. Bishop Patrick supposes that, among other things, the tabernacle which Moses reared and all the utensils of it, which there was now no further occasion for, were laid up here, signifying that in the fulness of time all the Mosaic economy, all the rites and ceremonies of that dispensation, should be respectfully laid aside, and something better come in their room. He gave him a table of the courses of the priests, patterns of the vessels of service (*v.* 13), and a pattern of the chariot of the cherubim, *v.* 18. Besides the two cherubim over the mercy-seat, there were two much larger, whose wings reached from wall to wall (1 Kings vi. 23, &c.), and of these David here gave Solomon the pattern, called a *chariot;* for the angels are the chariots of God, Ps. lxviii. 17. 2. Materials for the most costly of the utensils of the temple. That they might not be made any less than the patterns, he weighed out the exact quantity for each vessel both of gold and silver, *v.* 14. In the tabernacle there was but one golden candlestick; in the temple there were ten (1 Kings vii. 49), besides silver ones, which, it is supposed, were hand-candlesticks, *v.* 15. In the tabernacle there was but one table; but in the temple, besides that on which the show-bread was set, there were ten others for other uses (2 Chron. iv. 8), besides silver tables; for, this house being much larger than that, it would look bare if it had not furniture proportionable. The gold for the altar of incense is particularly said to be *refined gold* (*v.* 18), purer than any of the rest; for that was typical of the intercession of Christ, than which nothing is more pure and perfect. 3. Directions which way to look for help in this great undertaking. "Fear not opposition; fear not the charge, care, and trouble; fear not miscarrying in it, as in the case of Uzza; fear not the reproach of the foolish builder, that began to build and was not able to finish. Be not dismayed (1.) God will help thee, and thou must look up to him in the first place (*v.* 20): *The Lord God, even my God,* whom I have chosen and served, who has all along been present with me and prospered me, and to whom, from my own experience of his power and goodness, I recommend thee, he will be with thee, to direct, strengthen, and prosper thee; he will not fail thee nor forsake thee." Note, We may be sure that God, who owned our fathers and carried them through the services of their day, will, in like manner, if we be faithful to him, go along with us in our day, and will never leave us, while he has any work to do in us or by us. The same that was Joshua's encouragement (Josh. i. 5), and Solomon's, is given to all believers, Heb. xiii. 5. *He will never leave thee, nor forsake thee.* God never leaves any unless they first leave him. (2.) "Good men will help thee, *v.* 21. The priests and Levites will advise thee, and thou mayest consult them. Thou hast good workmen, who are both willing and skilful;" and these are two very good properties in a workman, especially in those that work at the temple. And, *lastly,* "The princes and the people will be so far from opposing or retarding the work that they will be wholly at thy command, every one in his place ready to further it." Then good work is likely to go on when all parties concerned are hearty in it, and none secretly clog it, but all drive on heartily in it.

CHAP. XXIX.

David had said what he had to say to Solomon. But he had something more to say to the congregation before he parted with them. I. He pressed them to contribute, according to their ability, towards the building and furnishing of the temple, ver. 1—5. II. They made their presents accordingly with great generosity, ver. 6—9. III. David offered up solemn prayers and praises to God upon that occasion (ver. 10—20), with sacrifices, ver. 21, 22. IV. Solomon was hereupon enthroned, with great joy and magnificence, ver. 23—25. V. David, soon after this, finished his course, ver. 26—30. And it is hard to say which shines brighter here, the setting sun or the rising sun.

FURTHERMORE David the king said unto all the congregation, Solomon my son, whom alone God hath chosen, *is yet* young and tender, and the work *is* great: for the palace *is* not for man, but for the LORD God. 2 Now I have prepared with all my might for the house of my God the gold for *things to be made* of gold, and the silver for *things* of silver, and the brass for *things* of brass, the iron for *things* of iron, and wood for *things* of wood; onyx stones, and *stones* to be set, glistering stones, and of divers colours, and all manner of precious stones, and marble stones in abundance. 3 Moreover, because I have set my affection to the house of my God, I have of mine own proper good, of gold and silver, *which* I have given to the house of my God, over and above all that I have prepared for the holy house, 4 *Even* three thousand talents of gold, of the gold of Ophir, and seven thousand talents of refined silver, to overlay the walls of the houses *withal:* 5 The gold for *things* of gold, and the silver for *things* of silver, and for all manner of work *to be made* by the hands of artificers. And who *then* is willing to consecrate his service this day unto the LORD? 6 Then the chief of the fathers and princes of the tribes of Israel, and the captains of thousands and of hundreds, with the rulers of the king's work, offered willingly, 7 And gave for the service of the house of God of gold five thousand talents and ten thousand drams, and of silver ten thousand talents, and of brass eighteen thousand talents, and one hundred thousand talents of iron. 8 And they with whom *precious* stones were found gave *them* to the treasure of the house of the LORD, by the hand of Jehiel the Gershonite. 9 Then the people rejoiced, for that they offered willingly, because with perfect heart they offered willingly to the LORD: and David the king also rejoiced with great joy.

We may here observe,

I. How handsomely David spoke to the great men of Israel, to engage them to contribute towards the building of the temple. It is our duty to *provoke one another to love and to good works,* not only to do good ourselves, but to draw in others to do good too as much as we can. There were many very rich men in Israel; they were all to share in the benefit of the temple, and of those peaceable days which were to befriend the building of it; and therefore, though David would not impose on them, as a tax, what they should give towards it, he would recommend the present as a fair occasion for a free-will offering, because what is done in works of piety and charity should be done willingly and not by constraint; for God loves a cheerful giver. 1. He would have them consider that Solomon was young and tender, and needed help; but that he was the person whom God had chosen to do this work, and therefore was well worthy their assistance. It is good service to encourage those in the work of God that are as yet young and tender. 2. That the work was great, and all hands should contribute to the carrying of it on. The palace to be built was not for man, but for the Lord God; and the more was contributed towards the building the more magnificent it would be, and therefore the better would it answer the intention. 3. He tells them what great preparations had been made for this work. He did not intend to throw all the burden upon them, nor that it should be built wholly by contributions, but that they should show their good will, by adding to what was done (*v.* 2): *I have prepared with all my might,* that is, "I have made it my business." Work for God must be done with all our might, or we shall bring nothing to pass in it. 4. He sets them a good example. Besides what was dedicated to this service out of the spoils and presents of the neighbouring nations, which was for the building of the house (of which before, *ch.* xxii. 14), he had, out of his own share, offered largely for the beautifying and enriching of it, 3000 talents of gold and 7000 talents of silver (*v.* 4, 5), and this because he had set his affection on the house of his God. He gave all this, not as Papists build churches, in commutation of penance, or to make atonement for sin, nor as Pharisees give alms, to be seen of men; but purely because he loved the habitation of God's house; so he professed (Ps. xxvi. 8) and here he proved it. Those who set their affection upon the service of God will think no pains nor cost too much to bestow upon it; and then our offerings are pleasing to God when they come from love. Those that set their affection on things above will set their affection on the house of God, through which our way to heaven lies. Now this he gives them an account of, to stir them up to do likewise. Note, Those who would draw others to do that which is good must themselves lead. Those especially who are advanced above others in place and dignity should particularly contrive how to make their light shine before men, because the influence of their example is more powerful and extensive than that of other people. 5. He stirs them up to do as he had done (*v.* 5): *And who then is willing to consecrate his service this day unto the Lord?* (1.) We must each of us, in our several places, serve the Lord, and consecrate our service to him, separate it from other things that are foreign and interfere with it, and direct and design it for the honour and glory of God. (2.) We must make the service of God our business, must *fill our hands to the Lord,* so the Hebrew phrase is. Those who engage themselves in the service of God will have their hands full; there is work enough for the whole man in that service. The filling of our hands with the service of God intimates that we must serve him only, serve him liberally, and serve him in the strength of grace derived from him. (3.) We must be free herein, do it willingly and speedily, do it this day, when we are in a good mind. *Who is willing?* Now let him show it.

II. How handsomely they all contributed towards the building of the temple when they were thus stirred up to it. Though they were persuaded to it, yet it is said, *They offered willingly, v.* 6. So he said who knew their hearts. Nay, they offered *with a perfect heart,* from a good principle and with a sincere respect to the glory of God, *v.* 9. How generous they were appears by the sum total of the contributions, *v.* 7, 8. They gave like themselves, like princes, like princes of Israel. And a pleasant day's work it was; for, 1. *The people rejoiced,* which may be meant of the people themselves that offered: they were glad of the opportunity of honouring God thus with their substance, and glad of the prospect of bringing this good work to perfection. Or the common people rejoiced in the generosity of their princes, that they had such rulers over them as were forward to this good work. Every Israelite is glad to see temple work carried on with vigour. 2. *David rejoiced with great joy* to see the good effect of his psalms and the other helps of devotion he had furnished them with, rejoiced that his son and successor would have those about him that were so well affected to the house of God, and that this work, upon which his heart was so much set, was likely to go on. Note, It is a great reviving to good men, when they are leaving the world, to see those they leave behind zealous for religion and likely to keep it up. *Lord, now let thou thy servant depart in peace.*

10 Wherefore David blessed the LORD before all the congregation: and David said, Blessed *be* thou, LORD God of Israel our father, for ever and ever. 11 Thine, O LORD, *is* the greatness, and the power, and the glory, and the victory, and the majesty: for all *that is* in the heaven and in the earth *is thine;* thine *is* the kingdom, O LORD, and thou art exalted as head above all. 12 Both riches and honour *come* of thee, and thou reignest over all; and in thine hand *is* power and might; and in thine hand *it is* to make great, and to give strength unto all. 13 Now therefore, our God, we thank thee, and praise thy glorious name. 14 But who *am* I, and what *is* my people, that we should be able to offer so willingly after this sort? for all things *come* of thee, and of thine own have we given thee. 15 For we *are* strangers before thee, and sojourners, as *were* all our fathers: our days on the earth *are* as a shadow, and *there is* none abiding. 16 O LORD our God, all this store that we have prepared to build thee a house for thine holy name *cometh* of thine hand, and *is* all thine own. 17 I know also, my God, that thou triest the heart, and hast pleasure in uprightness. As for me, in the uprightness of mine heart I have willingly offered all these things: and now have I seen with joy thy people, which are present here, to offer willingly unto thee. 18 O LORD God of Abraham, Isaac, and of Israel, our fathers, keep this for ever in the imagination of the thoughts of the heart of thy people, and prepare their heart unto thee: 19 And give unto Solomon my son a perfect heart, to keep thy commandments, thy testimonies, and thy statutes, and to do all *these things,* and to build the palace, *for* the which I have made provision. 20 And David said to all the congregation, Now bless the LORD your God. And all the congregation blessed the LORD God of their fathers, and bowed down their heads, and worshipped the LORD, and the king. 21 And they sacrificed sacrifices unto the LORD, and offered burnt offerings unto the LORD, on the morrow after that day, *even* a thousand bullocks, a thousand rams, *and* a thousand lambs, with their drink offerings, and sacrifices in abundance for all Israel: 22 And did eat and drink before the LORD on that day with great gladness. And they made Solomon the son of David king the second time, and anointed *him* unto the LORD, *to be* the chief governor, and Zadok *to be* priest.

We have here,

I. The solemn address which David made to God upon occasion of the noble subscriptions of the princes towards the building of the temple (*v.* 10): *Wherefore David blessed the Lord,* not only alone in his closet, but *before all the congregation.* This I expected when we read (*v.* 9) that *David rejoiced with great joy;* for such a devout man as he would no doubt make that the matter of his thanksgiving which was so much the matter of his rejoicing. He that looked round with comfort would certainly look up with praise. David was now old and looked upon himself as near his end; and it well becomes aged saints, and dying saints, to have their hearts much enlarged in praise and thanksgiving. This will silence their complaints of their bodily infirmities, and help to make the prospect of death itself less gloomy. David's psalms, towards the latter end of the book, are most of them psalms of praise. The nearer we come to the world of everlasting praise the more we should speak the language and do the work of that world. In this address,

1. He adores God, and ascribes glory to him as the God of Israel, *blessed for ever and ever.* Our Lord's prayer ends with a doxology much like this which David here begins with—*for thine is the kingdom, the power, and the glory.* This is properly praising God—with holy awe and reverence, and agreeable affection, acknowledging, (1.) His infinite perfections; not only that he is great, powerful, glorious, &c., but that his is the greatness, power, and glory, that is, he has them in and of himself, *v.* 11. He is the fountain and centre of every thing that is bright and blessed. All that we can, in our most exalted praises, attribute to him he has an unquestionable title to. His is the *greatness;*

his greatness is immense and incomprehensible; and all others are little, are nothing, in comparison of him. His is the *power*, and it is almighty and irresistible; power belongs to him, and all the power of all the creatures is derived from him and depends upon him. His is the *glory;* for his glory is his own end and the end of the whole creation. All the glory we can give him with our hearts, lips, and lives, comes infinitely short of what is his due. His is the *victory;* he transcends and surpasses all, and is able to conquer and subdue all things to himself; and his victories are incontestable and uncontrollable. And his is the *majesty*, real and personal; with him is terrible majesty, inexpressible and inconceivable. (2.) His sovereign dominion, as rightful owner and possessor of all: "*All that is in the heaven, and in the earth, is thine*, and at thy disposal, by the indisputable right of creation, and as supreme ruler and commander of all: *thine is the kingdom*, and all kings are thy subjects; for thou art head, and art to be exalted and worshipped as head above all. (3.) His universal influence and agency. All that are rich and honourable among the children of men have their riches and honours from God. This acknowledgment he would have the princes take notice of and join in, that they might not think they had merited any thing of God by their generosity; for from God they had their riches and honour, and what they had returned to him was but a small part of what they had received from him. Whoever are great among men, it is God's hand that makes them so; and, whatever strength we have, it is God that gives it to us, as the *God of Israel our father*, *v.* 10. Ps. lxviii. 35.

2. He acknowledges with thankfulness the grace of God enabling them to contribute so cheerfully towards the building of the temple (*v.* 13, 14): *Now therefore, our God, we thank thee.* Note, The more we do for God the more we are indebted to him for the honour of being employed in his service, and for grace enabling us, in any measure, to serve him. *Does he* therefore *thank that servant?* Luke xvii. 9. No: but that servant has a great deal of reason to thank him. He thanks God that they were *able to offer so willingly*. Note, (1.) It is a great instance of the power of God's grace in us to be able to do the work of God willingly. He works *both to will and to do;* and it is in the day of his power that his people are made willing, Ps. cx. 3. (2.) We must give God all the glory of all the good that is at any time done by ourselves or others. Our own good works must not be the matter of our pride, nor the good works of others the matter of our flattery, but both the matter of our praise; for certainly it is the greatest honour and pleasure in the world faithfully to serve God.

3. He speaks very humbly of himself, and his people, and the offerings they had now presented to God. (1.) For himself, and those that joined with him, though they were princes, he wondered that God should take such notice of them and do so much for them (*v.* 14): *Who am I, and what is my people?* David was the most honourable person, and Israel the most honourable people, then in the world; yet thus does he speak of himself and them, as unworthy the divine cognizance and favour. David now looks very great, presiding in an august assembly, appointing his successor, and making a noble present to the honour of God; and yet he is little and low in his own eyes: *Who am I, O Lord?* for (*v.* 15) *we are strangers before thee, and sojourners*, poor despicable creatures. Angels in heaven are at home there; saints on earth are but strangers here: *Our days on the earth are as a shadow.* David's days had as much of substance in them as most men's; for he was a great man, a good man, a useful man, and now an old man, one that lived long and lived to good purpose: and yet he puts himself not only into the number, but in the front, of those who must acknowledge that their *days on the earth are as a shadow*, which intimates that our life is a vain life, a dark life, a transient life, and a life that will have its period either in perfect light or perfect darkness. The next words explain it: *There is no abiding*, Heb. *no expectation.* We cannot expect any great matters from it, nor can we expect any long continuance of it. This is mentioned here as that which forbids us to boast of the service we do to God. Alas! it is confined to a scantling of time, it is the service of a frail and short life, and therefore what can we pretend to merit by it? (2.) As to their offerings, *Lord*, says he, *of thy own have we given thee* (*v.* 14), and again (*v.* 16), *It cometh of thy hand, and is all thy own.* "We have it from thee as a free gift, and therefore are bound to use it for thee; and what we present to thee is but rent or interest from thy own." "In like manner" (says bishop Patrick) "we ought to acknowledge God in all spiritual things, referring every good thought, good purpose, good work, to his grace, from whom we receive it." *Let him that glories* therefore *glory in the Lord.*

4. He appeals to God concerning his own sincerity in what he did, *v.* 17. It is a great satisfaction to a good man to think that God *tries the heart* and *has pleasure in uprightness*, that, whoever may misinterpret or contemn it, he is acquainted with and approves of the *way of the righteous*. It was David's comfort that God knew with what pleasure he both offered his own and saw the people's offering. He was neither proud of his own good work nor envious of the good works of others.

5. He prays to God both for the people and for Solomon, that both might hold on as they began. In this prayer he addresses God as *the God of Abraham, Isaac, and Jacob*, a God in covenant with them and with us for their

sakes. Lord, give us grace to make good our part of the covenant, that we may not forfeit the benefit of it. Or thus: they were kept in their integrity by the grace of God establishing their way; let the same grace that was sufficient for them be so for us. (1.) For the people he prays (*v.* 18) that what good God had put into their minds he would always keep there, that they might never be worse than they were now, might never lose the convictions they were now under, nor cool in their affections to the house of God, but always have the same thoughts of things as they now seemed to have. Great consequences depend upon what is innermost, and what uppermost, in the imagination of the thoughts of our heart, what we aim at and what we love to think of. If any good have got possession of our hearts, or the hearts of our friends, it is good by prayer to commit the custody of it to the grace of God: "Lord, keep it there, keep it for ever there. David has prepared materials for the temple; but, Lord, do thou prepare their hearts for such a privilege;" *establish* their hearts, so the *margin.* "Confirm their resolutions. They are in a good mind; keep them so when I am gone, them and theirs for ever." (2.) For Solomon he prays (*v.* 19), *Give him a perfect heart.* He had charged him (*ch.* xxviii. 9) to serve God *with a perfect heart;* now here he prays to God to give him such a heart. He does not pray, "Lord, make him a rich man, a great man, a learned man;" but, "Lord, make him an honest man;" for that is better than all. "Lord, *give him a perfect heart,* not only in general *to keep thy commandments,* but in particular *to build the palace,* that he may do that service with a single eye." Yet his building the house would not prove him to have a perfect heart unless he made conscience of keeping God's commandments. It is not helping to build churches that will save us if we live in disobedience to God's law.

II. The cheerful concurrence of this great assembly in this great solemnity. 1. They joined with David in the adoration of God. When he had done his prayer he called to them to testify their concurrence (*Now bless the Lord your God, v.* 20), which accordingly they did, by *bowing down their heads,* a gesture of adoration. Whoever is the mouth of the congregation, those only have the benefit who join with him, not by *bowing down the head* so much as by *lifting up the soul.* 2. They paid their respects to the king, looking upon him as an instrument in God's hand of much good to them; and, in honouring him, they honoured God. 3. The next day they offered abundance of sacrifices to God (*v.* 21), both burnt-offerings, which were wholly consumed, and peace-offerings, which the offerer had the greatest part of to himself. Hereby they testified a generous gratitude to God for the good posture their public affairs were in, though David was going the way of all the earth. 4. They feasted and rejoiced before God, *v.* 22. In token of their joy in God, and communion with him, they feasted upon their peace-offerings in a religious manner before the Lord. What had been offered to God they feasted upon, by which was intimated to them that they should be never the poorer for their late liberal contributions to the service of the temple; they themselves should feast upon the comfort of it. 5. They made Solomon king the second time. He having been before anointed in haste, upon occasion of Adonijah's rebellion, it was thought fit to repeat the ceremony, for the greater satisfaction of the people. They *anointed him to the Lord.* Magistrates must look upon themselves as set apart for God, to be his ministers, and must rule accordingly in the fear of God. Zadok also was anointed to be priest in the room of Abiathar, who had lately forfeited his honour. Happy art thou, O Israel! under such a prince and such a pontiff.

23 Then Solomon sat on the throne of the LORD as king instead of David his father, and prospered; and all Israel obeyed him. 24 And all the princes, and the mighty men, and all the sons likewise of king David, submitted themselves unto Solomon the king. 25 And the LORD magnified Solomon exceedingly in the sight of all Israel, and bestowed upon him *such* royal majesty as had not been on any king before him in Israel. 26 Thus David the son of Jesse reigned over all Israel. 27 And the time that he reigned over Israel *was* forty years; seven years reigned he in Hebron, and thirty and three *years* reigned he in Jerusalem. 28 And he died in a good old age, full of days, riches, and honour: and Solomon his son reigned in his stead. 29 Now the acts of David the king, first and last, behold, they *are* written in the book of Samuel the seer, and in the book of Nathan the prophet, and in the book of Gad the seer, 30 With all his reign and his might, and the times that went over him, and over Israel, and over all the kingdoms of the countries.

These verses bring king Solomon to his throne and king David to his grave. Thus the rising generation thrusts out that which went before, and says, "Make room for us." Every one has his day.

I. Here is Solomon rising (*v.* 23): *Solomon sat on the throne of the Lord.* Not his throne which he prepared in the heavens, but the throne of Israel is called *the throne of the Lord* because not only is he King of all nations, and all kings rule under him, but he was in a peculiar manner King of Israel, 1 Sam. xii. 12. He had the founding, he had the filling, of their throne, by immediate direction. The municipal laws of their kingdom were divine. Urim and prophets were the privy counsellors of their princes; therefore is their throne called *the throne of the Lord.* Solomon's kingdom typified the kingdom of the Messiah, and his is indeed *the throne of the Lord;* for the Father judgeth no man, but hath committed all judgment to him; hence he calls him *his King,* Ps. ii. 6. Being set on the *throne of the Lord,* the throne to which God called him, he prospered. Those that follow the divine guidance may expect success by the divine blessing. Solomon prospered; for, 1. His people paid honour to him, as one to whom honour is due: *All Israel obeyed him,* that is, were ready to swear allegiance to him (*v.* 23), the *princes and mighty men,* and even *the sons of David,* though by seniority their title to the crown was prior to his, and they might think themselves wronged by his advancement. God thought fit to make him king, and made him fit to be so, and therefore they all *submitted themselves to him.* God inclined their hearts to do so, that his reign might, from the first, be peaceable. His father was a better man than he, and yet came to the crown with much difficulty, after long delay, and by many and slow steps. David had more faith, and therefore had it more tried. *They submitted themselves* (Heb. *They gave the hand under Solomon),* that is, bound themselves by oath to be true to him (putting the hand under the thigh was a ceremony anciently used in swearing); or they were so entirely devoted that they would put their hand under his feet to serve him. 2. God put honour upon him; for those that honour him he will honour: *The Lord magnified Solomon exceedingly, v.* 25. His very countenance and presence, I am apt to think, had something in them very great and awful. All he said and all he did commanded respect. None of all the judges or kings of Israel, his predecessors, made such a figure as he did nor lived in such splendour.

II. Here is David's setting, that great man going off the stage. The historian here brings him to the end of his day, leaves him asleep, and draws the curtains about him.

1. He gives a summary account of the years of his reign, *v.* 26, 27. He reigned forty years, as did Moses, Othniel, Deborah, Gideon, Eli, Samuel, and Saul, who were before him, and Solomon after him.

2. He gives a short account of his death (*v.* 28), that he died *full of days, riches, and honour;* that is, (1.) Loaded with them. He was very old, and very rich, and very much honoured both of God and man. He had been a man of war from his youth, and, as such, had his soul continually in his hand; yet he was not cut off in the midst of his days, but was preserved through all the dangers of a military life, lived to a good old age, and died in peace, died in his bed, and yet in the bed of honour. (2.) Satiated with them. He was *full of days, riches, and honour;* that is, he had enough of this world and of the riches and honours of it, and knew when he had enough, for he was very willing to die and leave it, having said (Ps. xlix. 15), *God shall receive me,* and (Ps. xxiii. 4), *Thou art with me.* A good man will soon be full of days, riches, and honour, but will never be satisfied with them; no satisfaction but in God's loving kindness.

3. For a fuller account of David's life and reign he refers to the histories or records of those times, which were written by Samuel while he lived, and continued, after his death, by Nathan and Gad, *v.* 29. *There* was related what was observable in his government at home and his wars abroad, *the times,* that is, the events of *the times, that went over him, v.* 29, 30. These registers were then in being, but are now lost. Note, Good use may be made of those histories of the church which are authentic though not sacred or of divine inspiration.

AN

EXPOSITION,

WITH PRACTICAL OBSERVATIONS,

OF THE SECOND BOOK OF,

CHRONICLES.

THIS book begins with the reign of Solomon and the building of the temple, and continues the history of the kings of Judah thenceforward to the captivity and so concludes with the fall of that illustrious monarchy and the destruction of the temple. That monarchy of the house of David, as it was prior in time, so it was superior in worth and dignity to all those four celebrated ones of which Nebuchadnezzar dreamed. The Babylonian monarchy I reckon to begin in Nebuchadnezzar himself—*Thou art that head of gold*, and that lasted but about seventy years; the Persian monarchy, in several families, about 130; the Grecian, in their several branches, about 300; and 300 more went far with the Roman. But as I reckon David a greater hero than any of the founders of those monarchies, and Solomon a more magnificent prince than any of those that were the glories of them, so the succession was kept up in a lineal descent throughout the whole monarchy, which continued considerable between 400 and 500 years, and, after a long eclipse, shone forth again in the kingdom of the Messiah, *of the increase of whose government and peace there shall be no end.* This history of the Jewish monarchy, as it is more authentic, so it is more entertaining and more instructive, than the histories of any of those monarchies. We had the story of the house of David before, in the first and second books of Kings, intermixed with that of the kings of Israel, which *there* took more room than that of Judah; but here we have it entire. Much is repeated here which we had before, yet many of the passages of the story are enlarged upon, and divers added, which we had not before, especially relating to the affairs of religion; for it is a church-history, and it is written for our learning, to let nations and families know that then, and then only, they can expect to prosper, when they keep in the way of their duty to God: for all along the good kings prospered and the wicked kings suffered. The peaceable reign of Solomon we have (*ch.* i.—ix.), the blemished reign of Rehoboam (*ch.* x.—xii.), the short but busy reign of Abijah (*ch.* xiii.), the long and happy reign of Asa (*ch.* xiv.—xvi.), the pious and prosperous reign of Jehoshaphat (*ch.* xvii.—xx.), the impious and infamous reigns of Jehoram and Ahaziah (*ch.* xxi.—xxii.), the unsteady reigns of Joash and Amaziah (*ch.* xxiv., xxv.), the long and prosperous reign of Uzziah (*ch.* xxvi.), the regular reign of Jotham (*ch.* xxvii.), the profane and wicked reign of Ahaz (*ch.* xxviii.), the gracious glorious reign of Hezekiah (*ch.* xxix.—xxxii.), the wicked reigns of Manasseh and Amon (*ch.* xxxiii.), the reforming reign of Josiah (*ch.* xxxiv., xxxv.), the ruining reigns of his sons, *ch.* xxxvi. Put all these together, and the truth of that word of God will appear, *Those that honour me I will honour, but those that despise me shall be lightly esteemed.* The learned Mr. Whiston, in his chronology, suggests that the historical books which were written after the captivity (namely, the two books of Chronicles, Ezra, and Nehemiah) have more mistakes in names and numbers than all the books of the Old Testament besides, through the carelessness of transcribers: but, though that should be allowed, the things are so very minute that we may be confident *the foundation of God stands sure* notwithstanding.

CHAP. I.

In the close of the foregoing book we read how God magnified Solomon and Israel obeyed him; God and Israel concurred to honour him. Now here we have an account, I. How he honoured God by sacrifice (ver. 1—6) and by prayer, ver. 7—12. II. How he honoured Israel by increasing their strength, wealth, and trade, ver. 13—17.

AND Solomon the son of David was strengthened in his kingdom, and the LORD his God *was* with him, and magnified him exceedingly. 2 Then Solomon spake unto all Israel, to the captains of thousands and of hundreds, and to the judges, and to every governor in all Israel, the chief of the fathers. 3 So Solomon, and all the congregation with him, went to the high place that *was* at Gibeon; for there was the tabernacle of the congregation of God, which Moses the servant of the LORD had made in the wilderness. 4 But the ark of God had David brought up from Kirjath-jearim to *the place which* David had prepared for it: for he had pitched a tent for it at Jerusalem. 5 Moreover the brasen altar, that Bezaleel the son of Uri, the son of Hur, had made, he put before the tabernacle of the LORD: and Solomon and the congregation sought unto it. 6 And Solomon went up thither to the brasen altar before the LORD, which *was* at the tabernacle of the congregation, and offered a thousand burnt offerings upon it. 7 In that night did God appear unto Solomon, and said unto him, Ask what I shall give thee. 8 And Solomon said unto God, Thou hast showed great mercy unto David my father, and hast made me to reign in his stead. 9 Now, O LORD God, let thy promise unto David my father be established: for thou hast made me king over a people like the dust of the earth in multitude. 10 Give me now wisdom and knowledge, that I may go out and come in before this people: for who can judge this thy people, *that is so* great? 11 And God said to Solomon, Because this was in thine heart, and thou hast not asked riches, wealth, or honour, nor the life of thine enemies, neither yet hast asked long life; but hast asked wisdom and knowledge for thyself, that thou mayest judge my people, over whom I have made thee king: 12 Wisdom and knowledge *is* granted unto thee; and I will give thee riches, and wealth, and honour, such as none of the kings have had that *have been* before thee, neither shall there any after thee have the like.

Here is, I. Solomon's great prosperity, *v.* 1. Though he had a contested title, yet, God being with him, he was *strengthened in his kingdom;* his heart and hands were strengthened, and his interest in the people. God's presence will be our strength.

II. His great piety and devotion. His father was a prophet, a psalmist, and kept mostly to the ark; but Solomon, having read much in his Bible concerning the tabernacle which Moses built and the altars there, paid more respect to them than, it should seem, David had done. Both did well, and let neither be censured. If the zeal of one be carried out most to one instance of religion, and of another to some other instance, let them not judge nor despise each other.

1. All his great men must thus far be good men that they must join with him in worshipping God. He spoke to the captains and judges, the governors and chief of the fathers, to go with him to Gibeon, *v.* 2, 3. Authority and interest are well bestowed on those that will thus use them for the glory of God, and the promoting of religion. It is our duty to engage all with whom we have influence in the solemnities of religion, and it is very desirable to have many join with us in those solemnities—the more the better; it is the more like heaven. Solomon began his reign with this public pious visit to God's altar, and it was a very good omen. Magistrates are then likely to do well for themselves and their people when they thus take God along with them at their setting out.

2. He offered abundance of sacrifices to God there (*v.* 6): 1000 *burnt-offerings,* and perhaps a greater number of peace-offerings, on which he and his company *feasted before the Lord.* Where God sows plentifully he expects to reap accordingly. His father David had left him flocks and herds in abundance (1 Chron. xxvii. 29, 31), and thus he gave God his dues out of them. The ark was at Jerusalem (*v.* 4), but the altar was at Gibeon (*v.* 5), and thither he brought his sacrifices; for *it is the altar that sanctifieth every gift.*

3. He prayed a good prayer to God: this, with the answer to it, we had before, 1 Kings iii. 5, &c. (1.) God bade him ask what he would; not only that he might put him in the right way of obtaining the favours that were intended him *(Ask, and you shall receive, that your joy may be full),* but that he might try him, how he stood affected, and might discover what was in his heart. Men's characters appear in their choices and desires. What wouldst thou *have?* tries a man as much as, What wouldst thou *do?* Thus God tried whether Solomon was one of the *children of this world,* that say, *Who will show us any good,* or of the children of light, that say, *Lord, lift up the light of thy countenance upon us.* As we choose we shall have, and that is likely to be our portion to which we give the preference, whether the wealth and pleasure of this world or spiritual riches and delights. (2.) Like a genuine son of David, he chose spiritual blessings rather than temporal. His petition here is, *Give me wisdom and knowledge.* He owns those to be desirable gifts, and God to be the giver of them, Prov. ii. 6. God gave the faculty of understanding, and to him we must apply for the furniture of it. Two things are here pleaded which we had not in Kings:—[1.] *Thou hast made me reign in my father's stead,* *v.* 8. "Lord, thou hast put me into this place, and therefore I can in faith ask of thee grace to enable me to do the duty of it." What service we have reason to believe God calls us to we have reason to hope he will qualify us for. But that is not all "Lord, thou hast put me into this place in the stead

of David, the great and good man that filled it up so well; therefore give me wisdom, that Israel may not suffer damage by the change. Must I reign in my father's stead? Lord, give me my father's spirit." Note, The eminency of those that went before us, and the obligation that lies upon us to keep up and carry on the good work they were engaged in, should provoke us to a gracious emulation, and quicken our prayers to God for wisdom and grace, that we may do the work of God in our day as faithfully and well as they did in theirs. [2.] *Let thy promise to David my father be established, v.* 9. He means the promise concerning his successor. "In performance of that promise, *Lord, give me wisdom.*" We do not find that wisdom was any of the things promised, but it was necessary in order to the accomplishment of what was promised, 2 Sam. vii. 13—15. The promise was, *He shall build a house for my name, I will establish his throne, he shall be my son,* and *my mercy shall not depart from him.* "Now, Lord, unless thou give me wisdom, thy house will not be built, nor my throne established; I shall behave in a manner unbecoming my relation to thee as a Father, shall forfeit thy mercy, and fool it away; therefore, *Lord, give me wisdom.*" Note, *First,* God's promises are our best pleas in prayer. *Remember thy word unto thy servant. Secondly,* Children may take the comfort of the promises of that covenant which their parents, in their baptism, laid claim to, and took hold of, for them. *Thirdly,* The best way to obtain the benefit of the promises and privileges of the covenant is to be earnest in prayer with God for wisdom and grace to do the duties of it.

4. He received a gracious answer to this prayer, *v.* 11, 12. (1.) God gave him the wisdom that he asked for because he asked for it. Wisdom is a gift that God gives as freely and liberally as any gift to those that value it, and wrestle for it; and will resolve to make use of it; and he upbraids not the poor petitioners with their folly, James i. 5. God's grace shall never be wanting to those who sincerely desire to know and do their duty. (2.) God gave him the wealth and honour which he did not ask for because he asked not for them. Those that pursue present things most earnestly are most likely to miss of them; while those that refer themselves to the providence of God, if they have not the most of those things, have the most comfort in them. Those that make this world their end come short of the other and are disappointed in this too; but those that make the other world their end shall not only obtain that, and full satisfaction in it, but shall enjoy as much as is convenient of this world in their way.

13 Then Solomon came *from his journey* to the high place that *was* at Gibeon to Jerusalem, from before the tabernacle of the congregation, and reigned over Israel. 14 And Solomon gathered chariots and horsemen: and he had a thousand and four hundred chariots, and twelve thousand horsemen, which he placed in the chariot cities, and with the king at Jerusalem. 15 And the king made silver and gold at Jerusalem *as plenteous* as stones, and cedar trees made he as the sycamore trees that *are* in the vale for abundance. 16 And Solomon had horses brought out of Egypt, and linen yarn: the king's merchants received the linen yarn at a price. 17 And they fetched up, and brought forth out of Egypt a chariot for six hundred *shekels* of silver, and a horse for a hundred and fifty: and so brought they out *horses* for all the kings of the Hittites, and for the kings of Syria, by their means.

Here is, 1. Solomon's entrance upon the government (*v.* 13): He came *from before the tabernacle, and reigned over Israel.* He would not do any acts of government till he had done his acts of devotion, would not take honour to himself till he had given honour to God—first the tabernacle, and then the throne. But, when he had obtained wisdom from God, he did not bury his talent, but as he received the gift ministered the same, did not give up himself to ease and pleasure, but minded business: he reigned over Israel. 2. The magnificence of his court (*v.* 14): *He gathered chariots and horsemen.* Shall we praise him for this? We praise him not; for the king was forbidden to multiply horses, Deut. xvii. 16. I do not remember that ever we find his good father in a chariot or on horseback; a mule was the highest he mounted. We should endeavour to excel those that went before us in goodness rather than in grandeur. 3. The wealth and trade of his kingdom. He made silver and gold very cheap and common, *v.* 15. The increase of gold lowers the value of it; but the increase of grace advances its price; the more men have of that the more they value it. *How much better* therefore *is it to get wisdom than gold!* He opened also a trade with Egypt, whence he imported horses and linen-yarn, which he exported again to the kings of Syria, with great advantage no doubt, *v.* 16, 17. This we had before, 1 Kings x. 28, 29. It is the wisdom of princes to promote industry and encourage trade in their dominions. Perhaps Solomon took the hint of setting up the linen-manufacture, bringing linen-yarn out of Egypt, working it into cloth, and then sending that to other nations, from what his mother taught when she specified this as one of the characteristics of the virtuous woman, *She maketh fine linen, and selleth it, and delivereth girdles* of it *to the merchant,* Prov. xxxi. 24. *In all labour there is profit.*

CHAP. II.

Solomon's trading, which we read of in the close of the foregoing chapter, and the encouragement he gave both to merchandise and manufactures, were very commendable. But building was the work he was designed for, and to that business he is here applying himself. Here is, I. Solomon's determination to build the temple and a royal palace, and his appointing labourers to be employed herein, ver. 1, 2, 17, 18. II. His request to Huram king of Tyre to furnish him both with artists and materials, ver. 3—10. III. Huram's obliging answer to, and compliance with, his request, ver. 11—16.

AND Solomon determined to build a house for the name of the LORD, and a house for his kingdom. 2 And Solomon told out threescore and ten thousand men to bear burdens, and fourscore thousand to hew in the mountain, and three thousand and six hundred to oversee them. 3 And Solomon sent to Huram the king of Tyre, saying, As thou didst deal with David my father, and didst send him cedars to build him a house to dwell therein, *even so deal with me.* 4 Behold, I build a house to the name of the LORD my God, to dedicate *it* to him, *and* to burn before him sweet incense, and for the continual showbread, and for the burnt offerings, morning and evening, on the sabbaths, and on the new moons, and on the solemn feasts of the LORD our God. This *is an ordinance* for ever to Israel. 5 And the house which I build *is* great: for great *is* our God above all gods. 6 But who is able to build him a house, seeing the heaven and heaven of heavens cannot contain him? who *am* I then, that I should build him a house, save only to burn sacrifice before him? 7 Send me now therefore a man cunning to work in gold, and in silver, and in brass, and in iron, and in purple, and crimson, and blue, and that can skill to grave with the cunning men that *are* with me in Judah and in Jerusalem, whom David my father did provide. 8 Send me also cedar trees, fir trees, and algum trees, out of Lebanon: for I know that thy servants can skill to cut timber in Lebanon; and, behold, my servants *shall be* with thy servants, 9 Even to prepare me timber in abundance: for the house which I am about to build *shall be* wonderful great. 10 And, behold, I will give to thy servants, the hewers that cut timber, twenty thousand measures of beaten wheat, and twenty thousand measures of barley, and twenty thousand baths of wine, and twenty thousand baths of oil.

Solomon's wisdom was given him, not merely for speculation, to entertain himself (though it is indeed a princely entertainment), nor merely for conversation, to entertain his friends, but for action; and therefore to action he immediately applies himself. Observe,

I. His resolution within himself concerning his business (*v.* 1): *He determined to build,* in the first place, a *house for the name of the Lord.* It is fit that he who is the first should be first served—first a temple and then a palace, a house not so much for himself, or his own convenience and magnitude, as for the kingdom, for the honour of it among its neighbours and for the decent reception of the people whenever they had occasion to apply to their prince; so that in both he aimed at the public good. Those are the wisest men that lay out themselves most for the honour of the name of the Lord and the welfare of communities. We are not born for ourselves, but for God and our country.

II. His embassy to Huram, king of Tyre, to engage his assistance in the prosecution of his designs. The purport of his errand to him is much the same here as we had it 1 Kings v. 2, &c., only here it is more largely set forth.

1. The reasons why he makes this application to Huram are here more fully represented, for information to Huram as well as for inducement. (1.) He pleads his father's interest in Huram, and the kindness he had received from him (*v.* 3): *As thou didst deal with David, so deal with me.* As we must show kindness to, so we may expect kindness from, our fathers' friends, and with them should cultivate a correspondence. (2.) He represents his design in building the temple: he intended it for a place of religious worship (*v.* 4), that all the offerings which God had appointed for the honour of his name might be offered up there. The house was built that it might be dedicated to God and used in his service. This we should aim at in all our business, that our havings and doings may be all to the glory of God. He mentions various particular services that were there to be performed, for the instruction of Huram. The mysteries of the true religion, unlike those of the Gentile superstition, coveted not concealment. (3.) He endeavours to inspire Huram with very great and high thoughts of the God of Israel, by expressing the mighty veneration he had for his holy name: *Great is our God above all gods,* above all idols, above all princes. Idols are nothing, princes are little, and both under

the control of the God of Israel; and therefore, [1.] "The house must be great; not in proportion to the greatness of that God to whom it is to be dedicated (for between finite and infinite there can be no proportion), but in some proportion to the great value and esteem we have for this God." [2.] "Yet, be it ever so great, it cannot be a habitation for the great God. Let not Huram think that the God of Israel, like the gods of the nations, *dwells in temples made with hands,* Acts xvii. 24. No, the *heaven of heavens cannot contain him.* It is intended only for the convenience of his priests and worshippers, that they may have a fit place wherein to burn sacrifice before him." [3.] He looked upon himself, though a mighty prince, as unworthy the honour of being employed in this great work: *Who am I that I should build him a house?* It becomes us to go about every work for God with a due sense of our utter insufficiency for it and our incapacity to do any thing adequate to the divine perfections. It is part of the wisdom wherein we ought to walk towards those that are without carefully to guard against all misapprehension which any thing we say or do may occasion concerning God; so Solomon does here in his treaty with Huram.

2. The requests he makes to him are more particularly set down here. (1.) He desired Huram would furnish him with a good hand to work (*v.* 7): *Send me a man.* He had *cunning men* with him in Jerusalem and Judah, whom David provided, 1 Chron. xxii. 15. Let them not think but that the Jews had some among them that were artists. But "*send me a man* to direct them. There are ingenious men in Jerusalem, but not such engravers as are in Tyre; and therefore, since temple-work must be the best in its kind, let me have the best workmen that can be got." (2.) With good materials to work on (*v.* 8), cedar and other timber in abundance (*v.* 8, 9); for the house must be *wonderfully great,* that is, very stately and magnificent, no cost must be spared, nor any contrivance wanting in it.

3. Here is Solomon's engagement to maintain the workmen (*v.* 10), to give them so much wheat and barley, so much wine and oil. He did not feed his workmen with bread and water, but with plenty, and every thing of the best. Those that employ labourers ought to take care they be not only well paid, but well provided for with sufficient of that which is wholesome and fit for them. Let the rich masters do for their poor workmen as they would be done by if the tables were turned.

11 Then Huram the king of Tyre answered in writing, which he sent to Solomon, Because the LORD hath loved his people, he hath made thee king over them. 12 Huram said moreover, Blessed *be* the LORD God of Israel, that made heaven and earth, who hath given to David the king a wise son, endued with prudence and understanding, that might build a house for the LORD, and a house for his kingdom. 13 And now I have sent a cunning man, endued with understanding, of Huram, my father's, 14 The son of a woman of the daughters of Dan, and his father *was* a man of Tyre, skilful to work in gold, and in silver, in brass, in iron, in stone, and in timber, in purple, in blue, and in fine linen, and in crimson; also to grave any manner of graving, and to find out every device which shall be put to him, with thy cunning men, and with the cunning men of my lord David thy father. 15 Now therefore the wheat, and the barley, the oil, and the wine, which my lord hath spoken of, let him send unto his servants: 16 And we will cut wood out of Lebanon, as much as thou shalt need: and we will bring it to thee in flotes by sea to Joppa; and thou shalt carry it up to Jerusalem. 17 And Solomon numbered all the strangers that *were* in the land of Israel, after the numbering wherewith David his father had numbered them; and they were found a hundred and fifty thousand and three thousand and six hundred. 18 And he set threescore and ten thousand of them *to be* bearers of burdens, and fourscore thousand *to be* hewers in the mountain, and three thousand and six hundred overseers to set the people a work.

Here we have, I. The return which Huram made to Solomon's embassy, in which he shows a great respect for Solomon and a readiness to serve him. Meaner people may learn of these great ones to be neighbourly and complaisant. 1. He congratulates Israel on having such a king as Solomon was (*v.* 11): *Because the Lord loved his people, he has made thee king.* Note, A wise and good government is a great blessing to a people, and may well be accounted a singular token of God's favour. He does not say, *Because he loved* thee (though that was true, 2 Sam. xii. 24) *he made thee king,* but because he *loved his people.* Princes must look upon themselves as preferred for the public good, not for their own personal satisfaction, and should rule so as to prove that they were given in love and not in anger. 2. He blesses God for raising up such a successor to David, *v.* 12. It should seem that Huram was not only very well affected to the Jewish nation, and well pleased with their prosperity, but that he was proselyted to the Jewish religion, and worshipped Jehovah, *the God of Israel* (who was now known by that name to the neighbouring nations), as *the God that made heaven and earth,* and as the fountain of power as well as being; for he sets up kings. Now that the people of Israel kept close to the law and worship of God, and so preserved their honour, the neighbouring nations were as willing to be instructed by them in the true religion as Israel had been, in the days of their apostasy, to be infected with the idolatries and superstitions of their neighbours. This made them high, that they lent to many nations and did not borrow, lent truth to them, and did not borrow error from them; as when they did the contrary it was their shame. 3. He sent him a very ingenious curious workman, that would not fail to answer his expectations in every thing, one that had both Jewish and Gentile blood meeting in him; for his mother was an Israelite (Huram thought she was of the tribe of Dan, and therefore says so here (*v.* 14), but it seems she was of the tribe of Naphtali, 1 Kings vii. 14), but his father was a Tyrian—a good omen of uniting Jew and Gentile in the gospel temple, as it was afterwards when the building of the second temple was greatly furthered by Darius (Ezra vi.), who is supposed to have been the son of Esther—an Israelite by the mother's side. 4. He engaged for the timber, as much as he would have occasion for, and undertook to deliver it at Joppa, and withal signified his dependence upon Solomon for the maintenance of the workmen as he had promised, *v.* 15, 16. This agreement we had, 1 Kings v. 8, 9.

II. The orders which Solomon gave about the workmen. He would not employ the free-born Israelites in the drudgery work of the temple itself, not so much as to be overseers of it. In this he employed the strangers who were proselyted to the Jewish religion, who had not lands of inheritance in Canaan as the Israelites had, and therefore applied to trades, and got their living by their ingenuity and industry. There were, at this time, vast numbers of them in the land (*v.* 17), who, if they were of any of the devoted nations, perhaps fell within the case, and therefore fell under the law, of the Gibeonites, to be hewers of wood for the congregation: if not, yet being in many respects well provided for by the law of Moses, and put upon an equal footing with the native Israelites, they were bound in gratitude to do what they could for the service of the temple. Yet, no doubt, they were well paid in money or money's worth: the law was, *Thou shalt not oppress a stranger.* The distribution of them we have here (*v.* 2, and again *v.* 18), in all 150,000. Canaan was a fruitful land, that found meat for so many mouths more than the numerous natives; and the temple was a vast building, that found work for so many hands. Mr. Fuller suggests that the expedient peculiar to this structure, of framing all beforehand, must needs increase the work. I think it rather left so much the more room for this vast multitude of hands to be employed in it; for in the forest of Lebanon they might all be at work together, without crowding one another, which they could not have been upon Mount Sion. And, if there had not been such vast numbers employed, so large and curious a fabric, which was begun and ended in seven years, might, for aught I know, have been as long in building as St. Paul's.

CHAP. III.

It was a much larger and more particular account of the building of the temple which we had in the book of Kings than is here in this book of Chronicles. In this chapter we have, I. The place and time of building the temple, ver. 1, 2. II. The dimensions and rich ornaments of it, ver. 3—9. III. The cherubim in the most holy place, ver. 10—13. IV. The veil, ver. 14. V. The two pillars, ver. 15—17. Of all this we have already had an account, 1 Kings vi. vii.

THEN Solomon began to build the house of the LORD at Jerusalem in mount Moriah, where *the LORD* appeared unto David his father, in the place that David had prepared in the threshingfloor of Ornan the Jebusite. 2 And he began to build in the second *day* of the second month, in the fourth year of his reign. 3 Now these *are the things wherein* Solomon was instructed for the building of the house of God. The length by cubits after the first measure *was* threescore cubits, and the breadth twenty cubits. 4 And the porch that *was* in the front *of the house,* the length *of it was* according to the breadth of the house, twenty cubits, and the height *was* a hundred and twenty: and he overlaid it within with pure gold. 5 And the greater house he ceiled with fir tree, which he overlaid with fine gold, and set thereon palm trees and chains. 6 And he garnished the house with precious stones for beauty: and the gold *was* gold of Parvaim. 7 He overlaid also the house, the beams, the posts, and the walls thereof, and the doors thereof, with gold; and graved cherubims on the walls. 8 And he made the most holy house, the length whereof *was* according to the breadth of the house, twenty cubits, and the breadth thereof twenty cubits: and he overlaid it with fine gold, *amounting* to six hundred talents. 9 And the weight of the nails *was* fifty shekels of gold. And he overlaid the upper chambers with gold.

Here is, I. The place where the temple was built. Solomon was neither at liberty to choose nor at a loss to fix the place. It was before determined (1 Chron. xxii. 1), which was an ease to his mind. 1. It must be at Jerusalem; for that was the place where God had chosen to put his name there. The royal city must be the holy city. *There* must be *the testimony of Israel; for there are set the thrones of judgment,* Ps. cxxii. 4, 5. 2. It must be on Mount Moriah, which, some think, was that very place in the land of Moriah where Abraham offered Isaac, Gen. xxii. 2. So the Targum says expressly, adding, *But he was delivered by the word of the Lord, and a ram provided in his place.* That was typical of Christ's sacrifice of himself; therefore fitly was the temple, which was likewise a type of him, built there. 3. It must be *where the Lord appeared to David,* and *answered him by fire,* 1 Chron. xxi. 18, 26. There atonement was made once; and therefore, in remembrance of that, there atonement must still be made. Where God has met with me it is to be hoped that he will still manifest himself. 4. It must be in the place which David had prepared, not only which he had purchased with his money, but which he had pitched upon by divine direction. It was Solomon's wisdom not to enquire out a more convenient place, but to acquiesce in the appointment of God, whatever might be objected against it. 5. It must be in the threshing-floor of Ornan, which, if (as a Jebusite) it gives encouragement to the Gentiles, obliges us to look upon temple-work as that which requires the labour of the mind, no less than threshing-work does that of the body.

II. The time when it was begun; not till the fourth year of Solomon's reign, *v.* 2. Not that the first three years were trifled away, or spent in deliberating whether they should build the temple or no; but they were employed in the necessary preparations for it, wherein three years would be soon gone, considering how many hands were to be got together and set to work. Some conjecture that this was a sabbatical year, or year of release and rest to the land, when the people, being discharged from their husbandry, might more easily lend a hand to the beginning of this work; and then the year in which it was finished would fall out to be another sabbatical year, when they would likewise have leisure to attend the solemnity of the dedication of it.

III. The dimensions of it, in which Solomon was instructed (*v.* 3), as he was in other things, by his father. *This was the foundation* (so it may be read) *which Solomon laid for the building of the house.* This was the rule he went by, so many cubits the length and breadth, *after the first measure,* that is, according to the measure first fixed, which there was no reason to make any alteration of when the work came to be done; for the dimensions were given by divine wisdom, and *what God does shall be for ever; nothing can be put to it, or taken from it,* Eccl. iii. 14. His first measure will be the last.

IV. The ornaments of the temple. The timber-work was very fine, and yet, within, it was *overlaid with pure gold* (*v.* 4), with *fine gold* (*v.* 5), and that embossed with *palm-trees and chains.* It was gold of *Parvaim* (*v.* 6), the best gold. The *beams* and *posts,* the *walls* and *doors,* were *overlaid with gold, v.* 7. The most holy place, which was ten yards square, was all *overlaid with fine gold* (*v.* 8), even the *upper chambers,* or rather the *upper floor or roof*—top, bottom, and sides, were all overlaid with gold. Every nail, or screw, or pin, with which the golden plates were fastened to the walls that were overlaid with them, weighed fifty shekels, or was worth so much, workmanship and all. A great many precious stones were dedicated to God (1 Chron. xxix. 2, 8), and these were set here and there, where they would show to the best advantage. The finest houses now pretend to no better garnishing than good paint on the roof and walls; but the ornaments of the temple were most substantially rich. It was set with *precious stones,* because it was a type of the new Jerusalem, which has no temple in it because it is all temple, and the walls, gates, and foundations of which are said to be of *precious stones and pearls,* Rev. xxi. 18, 19, 21.

10 And in the most holy house he made two cherubims of image work, and overlaid them with gold. 11 And the wings of the cherubims *were* twenty cubits long: one wing *of the one cherub was* five cubits, reaching to the wall of the house: and the other wing *was likewise* five cubits, reaching to the wing of the other cherub. 12 And *one* wing of the other cherub *was* five cubits, reaching to the wall of the house: and the other wing *was* five cubits *also,* joining to the wing of the other cherub. 13 The wings of these cherubims spread themselves forth twenty cubits: and they stood on their feet, and their faces *were* inward. 14 And he made the vail *of* blue, and purple, and crimson, and fine linen, and wrought cherubims thereon. 15 Also he made before the house two pillars of thirty and five cubits high, and the chapiter that *was* on the top of each of them *was*

five cubits. 16 And he made chains, *as* in the oracle, and put *them* on the heads of the pillars; and made a hundred pomegranates, and put *them* on the chains. 17 And he reared up the pillars before the temple, one on the right hand, and the other on the left; and called the name of that on the right hand Jachin, and the name of that on the left Boaz.

Here is an account of, 1. The two cherubim, which were set up in the holy of holies. There were two already over the ark, which covered the mercy-seat with their wings; these were small ones. Now that the most holy place was enlarged, though these were continued (being appurtenances to the ark, which was not to be made new, as all the other utensils of the tabernacle were), yet those two large ones were added, doubtless by divine appointment, to fill up the holy place, which otherwise would have looked bare, like a room unfurnished. These cherubim are said to be of *image-work* (*v.* 10), designed, it is likely, to represent the angels who attend the divine Majesty. Each wing extended five cubits, so that the whole was twenty cubits (*v.* 12, 13), which was just the breadth of the most holy place, *v.* 8. They stood on their feet, as servants, their faces inward towards the ark (*v.* 13), that it might appear they were not set there to be adored (for then they would have been made sitting, as on a throne, and their faces towards their worshippers), but rather as themselves attendants on the invisible God. We must not worship angels, but we must worship *with* angels; for we have come into communion with them (Heb. xii. 22), and must do the will of God as the angels do it. The thought that we are worshipping him before whom the angels cover their faces will help to inspire us with reverence in all our approaches to God. Compare 1 Cor. xi. 10 with Isa. vi. 2. 2. The veil that parted between the temple and the most holy place, *v.* 14. This denoted the darkness of that dispensation, and the distance which the worshippers were kept at; but, at the death of Christ, this veil was rent; for through him we are made nigh, and have boldness not only to look, but to enter, into the holiest. On this he wrought cherubim. Heb. *he caused them to ascend,* that is, they were made in raised work, embossed. Or he made them on the wing in an ascending posture, as the other two that stood on their feet in an attending posture, to remind the worshippers to lift up their hearts, and to soar upwards in their devotions. 3. The two pillars which were set up before the temple. Both together were somewhat above thirty-five cubits in length (*v.* 15), about eighteen cubits high a-piece. See 1 Kings vii. 15, &c., where we took a view of those pillars, *Jachin* and *Boaz*, *establishment* and *strength* in temple-work and by it.

CHAP. IV.

We have here a further account of the furniture of God's house. I. Those things that were of brass. The altar for burnt-offerings (ver. 1), the sea and lavers to hold water (ver. 2–6), the plates with which the doors of the court were overlaid (ver. 9), the vessels of the altar, and other things, ver. 10—18. II. Those that were of gold. The candlesticks and tables (ver. 7, 8), the altar of incense (ver. 19), and the appurtenances of each of these, ver. 20—22. All these, except the brazen altar (ver. 1), were accounted for more largely, 1 Kings vii. 23, &c.

MOREOVER he made an altar of brass, twenty cubits the length thereof, and twenty cubits the breadth thereof, and ten cubits the height thereof. 2 Also he made a molten sea of ten cubits from brim to brim, round in compass, and five cubits the height thereof; and a line of thirty cubits did compass it round about. 3 And under it *was* the similitude of oxen, which did compass it round about: ten in a cubit, compassing the sea round about. Two rows of oxen *were* cast, when it was cast. 4 It stood upon twelve oxen, three looking toward the north, and three looking toward the west, and three looking toward the south, and three looking toward the east: and the sea *was set* above upon them, and all their hinder parts *were* inward. 5 And the thickness of it *was* a hand breadth, and the brim of it like the work of the brim of a cup, with flowers of lilies; *and* it received and held three thousand baths. 6 He made also ten lavers, and put five on the right hand, and five on the left, to wash in them: such things as they offered for the burnt offering they washed in them; but the sea *was* for the priests to wash in. 7 And he made ten candlesticks of gold according to their form, and set *them* in the temple, five on the right hand, and five on the left. 8 He made also ten tables, and placed *them* in the temple, five on the right side, and five on the left. And he made a hundred basons of gold. 9 Furthermore he made the court of the priests, and the great court, and doors for the court, and overlaid the doors of them with brass. 10 And he set the sea on the right side of the east end, over against the south.

David often speaks with much affection both of the *house of the Lord* and of the *courts of our God.* Both without doors and within there was that which typified the grace of the gospel and *shadowed* out *good things to come,* of which the substance is Christ.

I. There were those things in the open court, in the view of all the people, which were very significant.

1. There was the *brazen altar, v.* 1. The making of this was not mentioned in the Kings. On this all the sacrifices were offered, and it sanctified the gift. This altar was much larger than that which Moses made in the tabernacle; that was five cubits square, this was twenty cubits square. Now that Israel had become both more numerous and more rich, and it was to be hoped more devout (for every age should aim to be wiser and better than that which went before it), it was expected that there would be a greater abundance of offerings brought to God's altar than had been. It was therefore made such a capacious scaffold that it might hold them all, and none might excuse themselves from bringing those testimonies of their devotion by alleging that there was not room to receive them. God had greatly enlarged their borders; it was therefore fit that they should enlarge his altars. Our returns should bear some proportion to our receivings. It was ten cubits high, so that the people who worshipped in the courts might see the sacrifices burnt, and their eye might affect their heart with sorrow for sin: "It is of the Lord's mercies that I am not thus consumed, and that this is accepted as an expiation of my guilt." They might thus be led to consider the great sacrifice which should be offered in the fulness of time to take away sin and abolish death, which the blood of bulls and goats could not possibly do. And with the smoke of the sacrifices their hearts might ascend to heaven in holy desires towards God and his favour. In all our devotions we must keep the eye of faith fixed upon Christ, the great propitiation. How they went up to this altar, and carried the sacrifices up to it, we are not told; some think by a plain ascent like a hill: if by steps, doubtless they were so contrived as that the end of the law (mentioned Exod. xx. 26) might be answered.

2. There was the molten sea, a very large brass pan, in which they put water for the priests to wash in, *v.* 2, 6. It was put just at the entrance into the court of the priests, like the font at the church door. If it were filled to the brim, it would hold 3000 baths (as here, *v.* 5), but ordinarily there were only 2000 baths in it, 1 Kings vii. 26. The Holy Ghost by this signified, (1.) Our great gospel privilege, that *the blood of Christ cleanseth from all sin,* 1 John i. 7. To us there is a *fountain opened* for all believers (who are spiritual priests, Rev. i. 5, 6), nay, for *all the inhabitants of Jerusalem to wash in,* from sin, which is uncleanness. There is a fulness of merit in Jesus Christ for all those that by faith apply to him for the purifying of their consciences, that they may serve the *living God,* Heb. ix. 14. (2.) Our great gospel duty, which is to cleanse ourselves by true repentance from all the pollutions of the flesh and the corruption that is in the world. Our hearts must be sanctified, or we cannot sanctify the name of God. Those that draw nigh to God must *cleanse their hands, and purify their hearts,* Jam. iv. 8. *If I wash thee not, thou hast no part with me;* and he that *is washed* still needs *to wash his feet,* to renew his repentance, whenever he *goes in to minister,* John xiii. 10.

3. There were *ten lavers* of brass, in which *they washed such things as they offered for the burnt-offerings, v.* 6. As the priests must be washed, so must the sacrifices. We must not only purify ourselves in preparation for our religious performances, but carefully put away all those vain thoughts and corrupt aims which cleave to our performances themselves and pollute them.

4. The doors of the court were overlaid with brass (*v.* 9), both for strength and beauty, and that they might not be rotted with the weather, to which they were exposed. *Gates of brass* we read of, Ps. cvii. 16.

II. There were those things in *the house of the Lord* (into which the priests alone went to minister) that were very significant. All was of gold there. The nearer we come to God the purer we must be, the purer we shall be. 1. There were ten *golden candlesticks,* according to the form of that one which was in the tabernacle, *v.* 7. The written word is a lamp and a light, shining in a dark place. In Moses's time they had but one candlestick, the Pentateuch; but the additions which, in process of time, were to be made of other books of scripture might be signified by this increase of the number of the candlesticks. Light was growing. The candlesticks are the churches, Rev. i. 20. Moses set up but one, the church of the Jews; but, in the gospel temple, not only believers, but churches, are multiplied. 2. There were ten *golden tables* (*v.* 8), *tables whereon the show-bread was set, v.* 19. Perhaps every one of the tables had twelve loaves of show-bread on it. As the house was enlarged, the house-keeping was. *In my father's house there is bread enough for the whole family.* To those tables belonged 100 golden basins, or dishes; for God's table is well furnished. 3. There was a *golden altar* (*v.* 19), on which they burnt incense. It is probable that this was enlarged in proportion to the brazen altar. Christ, who once for all made atonement for sin, ever lives, making intercession, in virtue of that atonement.

11 And Huram made the pots, and the shovels, and the basons. And Huram finished the work that he was

to make for king Solomon for the house of God; 12 *To wit*, the two pillars, and the pommels, and the chapiters *which were* on the top of the two pillars, and the two wreaths to cover the two pommels of the chapiters which *were* on the top of the pillars; 13 And four hundred pomegranates on the two wreaths; two rows of pomegranates on each wreath, to cover the two pommels of the chapiters which *were* upon the pillars. 14 He made also bases, and lavers made he upon the bases; 15 One sea, and twelve oxen under it. 16 The pots also, and the shovels, and the fleshhooks, and all their instruments, did Huram his father make to king Solomon for the house of the LORD of bright brass. 17 In the plain of Jordan did the king cast them, in the clay ground between Succoth and Zeredathah. 18 Thus Solomon made all these vessels in great abundance: for the weight of the brass could not be found out. 19 And Solomon made all the vessels that *were for* the house of God, the golden altar also, and the tables whereon the showbread *was set;* 20 Moreover the candlesticks with their lamps, that they should burn after the manner before the oracle, of pure gold; 21 And the flowers, and the lamps, and the tongs, *made he of* gold, *and* that perfect gold; 22 And the snuffers, and the basons, and the spoons, and the censers, *of* pure gold: and the entry of the house, the inner doors thereof for the most holy *place*, and the doors of the house of the temple, *were of* gold.

We have here such a summary both of the brass-work and the gold-work of the temple as we had before (1 Kings vii. 13, &c.), in which we have nothing more to observe than, 1. That Huram the workman was very punctual: *He finished all that he was to make* (v 11), and left no part of his work undone. *Huram his father*, he is called, *v.* 16. Probably it was a sort of a nickname by which he was commonly known, *Father Huram;* for the king of Tyre called him *Huram Abi, my father*, in compliance with whom Solomon called him his, he being a great artist and *father of the artificers* in brass and iron. He acquitted himself well both for ingenuity and industry. 2. Solomon was very generous. He made *all the vessels in great abundance* (*v.* 18), many of a sort, that many hands might be employed, and so the work might go on with expedition, or that some might be laid up for use when others were worn out. Freely he has received, and he will freely give. When he had made vessels enough for the present he would not convert the remainder of the brass to his own use; it is devoted to God, and it shall be used for him.

CHAP. V.

The temple being built and furnished for God, we have here, I. Possession given to him, by bringing in the dedicated things (ver. 1), but especially the ark, the token of his presence, ver. 2—10. II. Possession taken by him, in a cloud, ver. 11—14. For if any man open the door of his heart to God he will come in, Rev. iii. 20.

THUS all the work that Solomon made for the house of the LORD was finished: and Solomon brought in *all* the things that David his father had dedicated; and the silver, and the gold, and all the instruments, put he among the treasures of the house of God. 2 Then Solomon assembled the elders of Israel, and all the heads of the tribes, the chief of the fathers of the children of Israel, unto Jerusalem, to bring up the ark of the covenant of the LORD out of the city of David, which *is* Zion. 3 Wherefore all the men of Israel assembled themselves unto the king in the feast which *was* in the seventh month. 4 And all the elders of Israel came; and the Levites took up the ark. 5 And they brought up the ark, and the tabernacle of the congregation, and all the holy vessels that *were* in the tabernacle, these did the priests *and* the Levites bring up. 6 Also king Solomon, and all the congregation of Israel that were assembled unto him before the ark, sacrificed sheep and oxen, which could not be told nor numbered for multitude. 7 And the priests brought in the ark of the covenant of the LORD unto his place, to the oracle of the house, into the most holy *place, even* under the wings of the cherubims: 8 For the cherubims spread forth *their* wings over the place of the ark, and the cherubims covered the ark and the staves thereof above. 9 And they drew out the staves *of the ark*, that the ends of the staves were seen from the ark before the oracle; but they were not seen without. And there it is unto this day. 10 *There was* nothing in the ark save the two tables which Moses put *therein* at Horeb, when the LORD made *a covenant* with the children of Israel, when they came out of Egypt.

This agrees with what we had 1 Kings viii. 2, &c., where an account was given of the solemn introduction of the ark into the new-erected temple. 1. There needed no great solemnity for the bringing in of the dedicated things, *v.* 1. They added to the wealth, and perhaps were so disposed as to add to the beauty of it; but they could not add to the holiness, for it was the *temple that sanctified the gold,* Matt. xxiii. 17. See how just Solomon was both to God and to his father. Whatever David had dedicated to God, however much he might have liked it himself, he would by no means alienate it, but put it among the treasures of the temple. Those children that would inherit their godly parents' blessing must religiously pursue their pious intentions and not defeat them. When Solomon had made all the vessels of the temple in abundance (*ch.* iv. 18), many of the materials were left, which he would not convert to any other use, but laid up in the treasury for a time of need. Dedicated things must not be alienated. It is sacrilege to do it. 2. But it was fit that the ark should be brought in with great solemnity; and so it was. All the other vessels were made new, and larger, in proportion to the house, than they had been in the tabernacle. But the ark, with the mercy-seat and the cherubim, was the same; for the presence and the grace of God are the same in little assemblies that they are in large ones, in the poor condition of the church that they are in its prosperous estate. Wherever two or three are gathered together in Christ's name there is he as truly present with them as if there were 2000 or 3000. The ark was brought in attended by a very great assembly of the elders of Israel, who came to grace the solemnity; and a very sumptuous appearance no doubt they made, *v.* 2—4. It was carried by the priests (*v.* 7), brought into the most holy place, and put under the wings of the great cherubim which Solomon had set up there, *v.* 7, 8. *There they are unto this day* (*v.* 9), not the day when this book was written after the captivity, but when that was written out of which this story was transcribed. Or they were there (so it might better be read) unto this day, the day of Jerusalem's desolations, that fatal day, Ps. cxxxvii. 7. The ark was a type of Christ, and, as such, a token of the presence of God. That gracious promise, *Lo, I am with you always, even unto the end of the world,* does in effect bring the ark into our religious assemblies if we by faith and prayer put that promise in suit; and this we should be most solicitous and earnest for. *Lord, if thy presence go not up with us,* wherefore should we go up? The temple itself, if Christ leave it, is a desolate place, Matt. xxiii. 38. 3. With the ark they brought up the tabernacle and all the *holy vessels that were in the tabernacle, v.* 5. Those were not alienated, because they had been dedicated to God, were not altered or melted down for the new work, though there was no need of them; but they were carefully laid up as monuments of antiquity, and probably as many of the vessels as were fit for use were still used. 4. This was done with great joy. They kept a holy feast upon the occasion (*v.* 3), and *sacrificed sheep and oxen without number, v.* 6. Note, (1.) The establishment of the public worship of God according to his institution, and with the tokens of his presence, is, and ought to be, matter of great joy to any people. (2.) When Christ is formed in a soul, the law written in the heart, the ark of the covenant settled there, so that it becomes the temple of the Holy Ghost, there is true satisfaction in that soul. (3.) Whatever we have the comfort of we must, by the sacrifices of praise, give God the glory of, and not be straitened therein; for *with such sacrifices God is well pleased.* If God favour us with his presence, we must honour him with our services, the best we have.

11 And it came to pass, when the priests were come out of the holy *place:* (for all the priests *that were* present were sanctified, *and* did not *then* wait by course: 12 Also the Levites *which were* the singers, all of them of Asaph, of Heman, of Jeduthun, with their sons and their brethren, *being* arrayed in white linen, having cymbals and psalteries and harps, stood at the east end of the altar, and with them a hundred and twenty priests sounding with trumpets:) 13 It came even to pass, as the trumpeters and singers *were* as one, to make one sound to be heard in praising and thanking the LORD; and when they lifted up *their* voice with the trumpets and cymbals and instruments of music, and praised the LORD, *saying,* For *he is* good; for his mercy *endureth* for ever: that *then* the house was filled with a cloud, *even* the house of the LORD; 14 So that the priests could not stand to minister by reason of the cloud: for the glory of the LORD had filled the house of God.

Solomon, and the elders of Israel, had done what they could to grace the solemnity of the introduction of the ark; but God, by testifying his acceptance of what they did, put the greatest honour upon it. The cloud of glory that filled the house beautified it more than all the gold with which it was overlaid or the precious stones with which it was garnished; and yet that was no glory in comparison with the glory of the gospel dispensation, 2 Cor. iii. 8—10. Observe,

I. How God took possession of the temple: He *filled it with a cloud, v.* 13. 1. Thus he signified his acceptance of this temple to be the same to him that the tabernacle of Moses was, and assured them that he would be the same in it; for it was by a cloud that he made his public entry into that, Exod. xl. 34. 2. Thus he considered the weakness and infirmity of those to whom he manifested himself, who could not bear the dazzling lustre of the divine light: it would have overpowered them; he therefore *spread his cloud upon it,* Job xxvi. 9. Christ revealed things unto his disciples as they were able to bear them, and in parables, which wrapped up divine things as in a cloud. 3. Thus he would affect all that worshipped in his courts with holy reverence and fear. Christ's disciples were afraid when they entered into a cloud, Luke ix. 34. 4. Thus he would intimate the darkness of that dispensation, by reason of which they could not stedfastly look to the end of those things which were now abolished, 2 Cor. iii. 13.

II. When he took possession of it. 1. *When the priests had come out of the holy place, v.* 11. This is the way of giving possession. All must come out, that the rightful owner may come in. Would we have God dwell in our hearts? We must leave room for him; let every thing else give way. We are here told that upon this occasion the whole family of the priests attended, and not any one particular course: *All the priests that were present were sanctified* (*v.* 11), because there was work enough for them all, when such a multitude of sacrifices were to be offered, and because it was fit that they should all be eye-witnesses of this solemnity and receive the impressions of it. 2. When the singers and musicians praised God, then the house was filled with a cloud. This is very observable; it was not when they *offered sacrifices,* but when they *sang the praises of God,* that God gave them this token of his favour; for the sacrifice of praise *pleaseth the Lord* better than that of *an ox or bullock,* Ps. lxix. 31. All the singers and musicians were employed, those of all the three families; and, to complete the concert, 120 priests, with their trumpets, joined with them, all standing at the east end of the altar, on that side of the court which lay outmost towards the people, *v.* 12. And, when this part of the service began, the glory of God appeared. Observe, (1.) It was when they were unanimous, when they were as one, to make one sound. The Holy Ghost descended on the apostles when they met with one accord, Acts ii. 1—4. Where unity is the Lord commands the blessing. (2.) It was when they were lively and hearty, and *lifted up their voice to praise the Lord.* Then we serve God acceptably when we are fervent in spirit serving him. (3.) It was when they were, in their praises, celebrating the everlasting mercy and goodness of God. As there is no one saying oftener repeated in scripture than this, *his mercy endureth for ever* (twenty-six times in one psalm, Ps. cxxxvi., and often elsewhere), so there is none more signally owned from heaven; for it was not the expression of some rapturous flights that the priests were singing when the glory of God appeared, but this plain song, *He is good, and his mercy endureth for ever.* This should endear those words to us. God's goodness is his glory, and he is pleased when we give him the glory of it.

III. What was the effect of it. The *priests themselves could not stand to minister, by reason of the cloud* (*v.* 14), which, as it was an evidence that the law made men priests that had infirmity, so (as bishop Patrick observes) it was a plain intimation that the Levitical priesthood should cease, and stand no longer to minister, when the Messiah should come, in whom *the fulness of the godhead should dwell bodily.* In him the glory of God dwelt among us, but covered with a cloud. The Word was made flesh; and when he comes to his temple, like a refiner's fire, *who may abide the day of his coming?* And *who shall stand when he appeareth?* Mal. iii. 1, 2.

CHAP. VI.

The glory of the Lord, in the vehicle of a thick cloud, having filled the house which Solomon built, by which God manifested his presence there, he immediately improves the opportunity, and addresses God, as a God now, in a peculiar manner, nigh at hand. I. He makes a solemn declaration of his intention in building this house, to the satisfaction of the people and the honour of God, both of whom he blessed, ver. 1—11. II. He makes a solemn prayer to God that he would please graciously to accept and answer all the prayers that should be made in, or towards, that house, ver. 12—42. This whole chapter we had before, with very little variation (1 Kings viii. 12—53), to which it may not be amiss here to look back.

THEN said Solomon, The LORD hath said that he would dwell in the thick darkness. 2 But I have built a house of habitation for thee, and a place for thy dwelling for ever. 3 And the king turned his face, and blessed the whole congregation of Israel: and all the congregation of Israel stood. 4 And he said, Blessed *be* the LORD God of Israel, who hath with his hands fulfilled *that* which he spake with his mouth to my father David, saying, 5 Since the day that I brought forth my people out of the land of Egypt I chose no city among all the tribes of Israel to build a house in, that my name might be there; neither chose I any man to be a ruler over my people Israel: 6 But I have chosen Jerusalem, that my name might be there; and have chosen David to be over my people Israel. 7 Now it was in the heart of David my father to build a house for the name of the LORD God of Israel. 8 But the LORD said to David my father, Forasmuch as it was in thine heart to build a house for my name, thou didst well in that it was in thine heart: 9 Notwithstanding thou shalt not build the house; but thy son which shall come forth out of thy loins, he shall build the house for my name. 10 The LORD therefore hath performed his word that he hath spoken: for I am risen up in the room of David my father, and am set on the throne of Israel, as the LORD promised, and have built the house for the name of the LORD God of Israel. 11 And in it have I put the ark, wherein *is* the covenant of the LORD, that he made with the children of Israel.

It is of great consequence, in all our religious actions, that we design well, and that our eye be single. If Solomon had built this temple in the pride of his heart, as Ahasuerus made his feast, only to *show the riches of his kingdom and the honour of his majesty*, it would not have turned at all to his account. But he here declares upon what inducements he undertook it, and they are such as not only justify, but magnify, the undertaking. 1. He did it for the glory and honour of God; this was his highest and ultimate end in it. It was *for the name of the Lord God of Israel* (*v.* 10), to be *a house of habitation for him, v.* 2. He has indeed, as to us, *made darkness his pavilion* (*v.* 1), but let this house be the residence of that darkness; for it is in the upper world that he dwells in light, such as no eye can approach. 2. He did it in compliance with the choice God had been pleased to make of Jerusalem, to be the city in which he would record his name (*v.* 6): *I have chosen Jerusalem.* A great many stately buildings there were in Jerusalem for the king, his princes, and the royal family. If God choose that place, it is fit that there be a building for him which may excel all the rest. If men were thus honoured there, let God be thus honoured. 3. He did it in pursuance of his father's good intentions, which he never had an opportunity to put in execution: "*It was in the heart of David my father to build a house for God;*" the project was his, be it known, to his honour (*v.* 7), and God approved of it, though he permitted him not to put it in execution (*v.* 8), *Thou didst well that it was in thy heart.* Temple-work is often thus done; one sows and another reaps (John iv. 37, 38), one age begins that which the next brings to perfection. And let not the wisest of men think it any disparagement to them to pursue the good designs which those that went before them have laid, and to build upon their foundation. Every good piece is not an original. 4. He did it in performance of the word which God had spoken. God had said, *Thy son shall build the house for my name;* and now he had done it, *v.* 9, 10. The service was appointed him, and the honour of it designed him, by the divine promise; so that he did not do it of his own head, but was called of God to do it. It is fit that he who appoints the work should have the appointing of the workmen; and those may go on in their work with great satisfaction who see their call to it clear.

12 And he stood before the altar of the LORD in the presence of all the congregation of Israel, and spread forth his hands: 13 For Solomon had made a brasen scaffold, of five cubits long, and five cubits broad, and three cubits high, and had set it in the midst of the court: and upon it he stood, and kneeled down upon his knees before all the congregation of Israel, and spread forth his hands toward heaven, 14 And said, O LORD God of Israel, *there is* no God like thee in the heaven, nor in the earth; which keepest covenant, and *showest* mercy unto thy servants, that walk before thee with all their hearts: 15 Thou which hast kept with thy servant David my father that which thou hast promised him; and spakest with thy mouth, and hast fulfilled *it* with thine hand, as *it is* this day. 16 Now therefore, O LORD God of Israel, keep with thy servant David my father that which thou hast promised him, saying, There shall not fail thee a man in my sight to sit upon the throne of Israel; yet so that thy children take heed to their way to walk in my law, as thou hast walked before me. 17 Now then, O LORD God of Israel, let thy word be verified, which thou hast spoken unto thy servant David. 18 But will God in very deed dwell with men on the earth? behold, heaven and the heaven of heavens cannot contain thee; how much less this

house which I have built! 19 Have respect therefore to the prayer of thy servant, and to his supplication, O LORD my God, to hearken unto the cry and the prayer which thy servant prayeth before thee: 20 That thine eyes may be open upon this house day and night, upon the place whereof thou hast said that thou wouldest put thy name there; to hearken unto the prayer which thy servant prayeth toward this place. 21 Hearken therefore unto the supplications of thy servant, and of thy people Israel, which they shall make toward this place: hear thou from thy dwelling place, *even* from heaven; and when thou hearest, forgive. 22 If a man sin against his neighbour, and an oath be laid upon him to make him swear, and the oath come before thine altar in this house; 23 Then hear thou from heaven, and do, and judge thy servants, by requiting the wicked, by recompensing his way upon his own head; and by justifying the righteous, by giving him according to his righteousness. 24 And if thy people Israel be put to the worse before the enemy, because they have sinned against thee; and shall return and confess thy name, and pray and make supplication before thee in this house; 25 Then hear thou from the heavens, and forgive the sin of thy people Israel, and bring them again unto the land which thou gavest to them and to their fathers. 26 When the heaven is shut up, and there is no rain, because they have sinned against thee; *yet* if they pray toward this place, and confess thy name, and turn from their sin, when thou dost afflict them; 27 Then hear thou from heaven, and forgive the sin of thy servants, and of thy people Israel, when thou hast taught them the good way, wherein they should walk; and send rain upon thy land, which thou hast given unto thy people for an inheritance. 28 If there be dearth in the land, if there be pestilence, if there be blasting, or mildew, locusts, or caterpillars; if their enemies besiege them in the cities of their land; whatsoever sore or whatsoever sickness *there be:* 29 *Then* what prayer *or* what supplication soever shall be made of any man, or of all thy people Israel, when every one shall know his own sore and his own grief, and shall spread forth his hands in this house: 30 Then hear thou from heaven thy dwelling place, and forgive, and render unto every man according unto all his ways, whose heart thou knowest; (for thou only knowest the hearts of the children of men:) 31 That they may fear thee, to walk in thy ways, so long as they live in the land which thou gavest unto our fathers. 32 Moreover concerning the stranger, which is not of thy people Israel, but is come from a far country for thy great name's sake, and thy mighty hand, and thy stretched out arm; if they come and pray in this house; 33 Then hear thou from the heavens, *even* from thy dwelling place, and do according to all that the stranger calleth to thee for; that all people of the earth may know thy name, and fear thee, as *doth* thy people Israel, and may know that this house which I have built is called by thy name. 34 If thy people go out to war against their enemies by the way that thou shalt send them, and they pray unto thee toward this city which thou hast chosen, and the house which I have built for thy name; 35 Then hear thou from the heavens their prayer and their supplication, and maintain their cause. 36 If they sin against thee, (for *there is* no man which sinneth not,) and thou be angry with them, and deliver them over before *their* enemies, and they carry them away captives unto a land far off or near; 37 Yet *if* they bethink themselves in the land whither they are carried captive, and turn and pray unto thee in the land of their captivity, saying, We have sinned, we have done amiss, and have dealt wickedly; 38 If they return to thee with all their heart and with all their soul in the land of their captivity, whither they have carried them captives, and pray toward their land, which thou gavest unto their fathers, and *toward* the city which thou hast chosen, and toward the house which I have built for thy name: 39 Then hear thou from the heavens, *even* from thy dwelling place, their prayer and their supplications, and maintain their cause, and forgive thy people which have sinned against thee. 40 Now, my God, let, I beseech thee, thine eyes be open, and *let* thine ears *be* attent unto the prayer *that is made* in this place. 41 Now therefore arise, O LORD God, into thy resting place, thou, and the ark of thy strength: let thy priests, O LORD God, be clothed with salvation, and let thy saints rejoice in goodness. 42 O LORD God, turn not away the face of thine anointed: remember the mercies of David thy servant.

Solomon had, in the foregoing verses, signed and sealed, as it were, the deed of dedication, by which the temple was appropriated to the honour and service of God. Now here he prays the consecration-prayer, by which it was made a figure of Christ, the great Mediator, through whom we are to offer all our prayers, and to expect all God's favours, and to whom we are to have an eye in every thing wherein we have to do with God. We have opened the particulars of this prayer (1 Kings viii.) and therefore shall now only glean up some few passages in it which may be the proper subjects of our meditation.

I. Here are some doctrinal truths occasionally laid down. As, 1. That the God of Israel is a being of incomparable perfection. We cannot describe him; but this we know, there is *none like him in heaven or in earth, v.* 14. All the creatures have their fellow-creatures, but the Creator has not his peer. He is infinitely above all, and *over all, God blessed for ever.* 2. That he is, and will be, true to every word that he has spoken; and all that serve him in sincerity shall certainly find him both faithful and kind. Those that set God always before them, and *walk before him with all their hearts,* shall find him as good as his word and better; he will both keep covenant with them and show mercy to them, *v.* 14. 3. That he is a being infinite and immense, whom the heaven, and heaven of heavens, cannot contain, and to whose felicity nothing is added by the utmost we can do in his service, *v.* 18. He is infinitely beyond the bounds of the creation and infinitely above the praises of all intelligent creatures. 4. That he, and *he only, knows the hearts of the children of men, v.* 30. All men's thoughts, aims, and affections, are naked and open before him; and, however the imaginations and intents of our hearts may be concealed from men, angels, and devils, they cannot be hidden from God, who knows not only what is in the heart, but the heart itself and all the beatings of it. 5. That there is no such thing as a sinless perfection to be found in this life (*v.* 36): *There is no man who sinneth not;* nay, who *doeth good and sinneth not;* so he writes, agreeable to what he here says, Eccl. vii. 20.

II. Here are some suppositions or cases put which are to be taken notice of. 1. He supposed that if doubts and controversies arose between man and man both sides would agree to appeal to God, and lay an oath upon the person whose testimony must decide the matter, *v.* 22. The religious reverence of an oath, as it was ancient, so, it may be presumed, it will continue as long as there are any remains of conscience and right reason among men. 2. He supposed that, though Israel enjoyed a profound peace and tranquillity, yet troublesome times would come. He did not think the mountain of their prosperity stood so strong but that it might be moved; nay, he expected sin would move it. 3. He supposed that those who had not called upon God at other times, yet, in their affliction, would seek him early and earnestly. "When they are in distress they will confess their sins, and confess thy name, and make supplication to thee." Trouble will drive those to God who have said to him, Depart, *v.* 24, 26, 28. 4. He supposed that strangers would come from afar to worship the God of Israel and to pay homage to him; and this also might reasonably be expected, considering what worthless things the gods of the nations were, and what proofs the God of Israel had given of his being Lord of the whole earth.

III. Here are petitions very pertinent. 1. That God would own this house, and have an eye to it, as the place of which he had said that he would put his name there, *v.* 20. He could not, in faith, have asked God to show such peculiar favour to this house above any other if he himself had not said that it should be his rest for ever. The prayer that will speed must be warranted by the word. We may with humble confidence pray to God to be well pleased with us in Jesus Christ, because he has declared himself well pleased in him—*This is my beloved Son;* but he says not now of any house, "This is my beloved place." 2. That God would hear and accept the prayers which should be made in or towards that place, *v.* 21. He asked not that God should help them whether they prayed for themselves or no, but that God would help them in answer to their prayers. Even Christ's intercessions do not supersede but encourage our supplications. He prayed that God would hear from his dwelling-place, even from heaven. Heaven is his dwelling-place still, not this temple; and thence help must come. *When thou hearest forgive.* Note, The forgiveness of our sins is that which makes way for all the other answers to our prayers, *Removendo prohibens—The evil which it drives away it keeps away.* 3. That God would give judgment according to equity upon all the appeals that should be made to him, *v.* 23, 30. This we may, in faith, pray for, for we are sure it shall be done. God sitteth on the throne judging right. 4. That God would return in mercy to his people when they repented, and reformed, and sought unto him, *v.* 25, 27, 38, 39. This we also may, in faith, pray for, building upon the repeated declarations God has made of his readiness to accept penitents. 5. That God would bid the strangers welcome to this house, and answer their prayers (*v.* 33); for, if there be in duty, why should there not be in privilege one law for the stranger and for one born in the land? Lev. xxiv. 22. 6. That God would, upon all occasions, own and plead the cause of his people Israel, against all the opposers of it (*v.* 35): *Maintain their cause;* and again, *v.* 39. If they be the Israel of God, their cause is the cause of God, and he will espouse it. 7. He concludes this prayer with some expressions which he had learned of his good father, and borrowed from one of his psalms. We had them not in the Kings, but here we have them, *v.* 41, 42. The whole word of God is of use to direct us in prayer; and how can we express ourselves in better language to God than that of his own Spirit? But these words were of use, in a special manner, to direct Solomon, because they had reference to this very work that he was now doing. We have them, Ps. cxxxii. 8—10. He prayed (*v.* 41), (1.) That God would take possession of the temple, and keep possession, that he would make it his resting-place: *Thou and the ark;* what will the ark do without the God of the ark—ordinances without the God of the ordinances? (2.) That he would make the ministers of the temple public blessings: *Clothe them with salvation,* that is, not only save them, but make them instrumental to save others, by offering the sacrifices of righteousness. (3.) That the service of the temple might turn abundantly to the joy and satisfaction of all the Lord's people: *Let thy saints rejoice in goodness,* that is, in the *goodness of thy house,* Ps. lxv. 4. "Let all that come hither to worship, like the eunuch, go away rejoicing." He pleads two things, *v.* 42. [1.] His own relation to God: "*Turn not away the face of thy anointed.* Lord, thou hast appointed me to be king, and wilt not thou own me?" [2.] God's covenant with his father: *Remember the mercies of David thy servant*—the *piety* of David towards God (so some understand it and so the word sometimes signifies), his pious care of the ark, and concern for it (see Ps. cxxxii. 1, 2, &c.), or the *promises* of God to David, which were mercies to him, his great support and comforts in all his troubles. We may plead, as Solomon does here, with an eye to Christ:—"We deserve that God should turn away our face, that he should reject us and our prayers; but we come in the name of the Lord Jesus, *thy anointed, thy Messiah* (so the word is), *thy Christ,* so the LXX. Him thou hearest always, and wilt never *turn away his face.* We have no righteousness of our own to plead, but, Lord, *remember the mercies of David thy servant.*" Christ is God's servant (Isa. xlii. 1), and is called *David,* Hos. iii. 5. "Lord, remember his mercies, and accept us on the account of them. Remember his tender concern for his Father's honour and man's salvation, and what he did and suffered from that principle. Remember the promises of the everlasting covenant, which free grace has made to us in Christ, and which are called *the sure mercies of David,*" Isa. lv. 3 and Acts xiii. 34. This must be all our desire and all our hope, all our prayer and all our plea; for it is all our salvation.

CHAP. VII.

In this chapter we have God's answer to Solomon's prayer. I. His public answer by fire from heaven, which consumed the sacrifices (ver. 1), with which the priests and people were much affected, ver. 2, 3. By that token of God's acceptance they were encouraged to continue the solemnities of the feast for fourteen days, and Solomon was encouraged to pursue all his designs for the honour of God, ver. 4—11. II. His private answer by word of mouth, in a dream or vision of the night, ver. 12—22. Most of these things we had before, 1 Kings viii. and ix.

NOW when Solomon had made an end of praying, the fire came down from heaven, and consumed the burnt offering and the sacrifices; and the glory of the LORD filled the house. 2 And the priests could not enter into the house of the LORD, because the glory of the LORD had filled the LORD's house. 3 And when all the children of Israel saw how the fire came down, and the glory of the LORD upon the house, they bowed themselves with their faces to the ground upon the pavement, and worshipped, and praised the LORD, *saying,* For *he is* good; for his mercy *endureth* for ever. 4 Then the king and all the people offered sacrifices before the LORD. 5 And king Solomon offered a sacrifice of twenty and two thousand oxen, and a hundred and twenty thousand sheep: so the king and all the people dedicated the house of God. 6 And the priests waited on their offices: the Levites also with instruments of music of the LORD, which David the king had made to praise the LORD, because his mercy *endureth* for ever, when David praised by their ministry; and the priests sounded trumpets before them, and all Israel stood. 7 Moreover Solomon hallowed the middle of the court that *was* before the house of the LORD: for there he offered burnt offerings, and the fat of the peace offerings, because the brasen altar which Solomon had made was not able to receive the burnt offerings, and the meat offerings, and the fat. 8 Also at the same time Solomon kept the feast seven days, and all Israel with him, a very great congregation, from the entering in of Hamath unto the river of Egypt. 9 And in the eighth day they made a solemn assembly: for they kept the dedication of the altar seven days, and the feast seven days. 10 And on the three and twentieth day of the seventh month he sent the people away into their tents, glad and merry in heart for the goodness that the LORD had showed unto David, and to Solomon, and to Israel his people. 11 Thus Solomon finished the house of the LORD, and the king's house: and all that came into Solomon's heart to make in the house of the LORD, and in his own house, he prosperously effected.

Here is, I. The gracious answer which God immediately made to Solomon's prayer: The *fire came down from heaven and consumed the sacrifice, v.* 1. In this way God testified his acceptance of Moses (Lev. ix. 24), of Gideon (Judg. vi. 21), of David (1 Chron. xxi. 26), of Elijah (1 Kings xviii. 38); and, in general, to accept the burnt-sacrifice is, in the Hebrew phrase, to turn it to ashes, Ps. xx. 3. The fire came down here, not upon the killing of the sacrifices, but the praying of the prayer.

1. This fire intimated that God was, (1.) Glorious in himself; for *our God is a consuming fire,* terrible even in his holy places. This fire, breaking forth (as it is probable) out of the thick darkness, made it the more terrible, as on Mount Sinai, Exod. xxiv. 16, 17. *The sinners in Sion* had reason to be *afraid* at this sight, and to say, *Who among us shall dwell near this devouring fire?* Isa. xxxiii. 14. And yet, (2.) Gracious to Israel; for this fire, which might justly have consumed them, fastened upon the sacrifice which was offered in their stead, and consumed that, by which God signified to them that he accepted their offerings and that his anger was turned away from them.

2. Let us apply this, (1.) To the sufferings of Christ. When it pleased the Lord to bruise him, and put him to grief, in that he showed his good-will to men, having laid on him the iniquity of us all. His death was our life, and he was made sin and a curse that we might inherit righteousness and a blessing. That sacrifice was consumed that we might escape. *Here am I, let these go their way.* (2.) To the sanctification of the Spirit, who descends like fire, burning up our lusts and corruptions, those beasts that must be sacrificed or we are undone, and kindling in our souls a holy fire of pious and devout affections, always to be kept burning on the altar of the heart. The surest evidence of God's acceptance of our prayers is the descent of this holy fire upon us. *Did not our hearts burn within us?* Luke xxiv. 32. As a further evidence that God accepted Solomon's prayer, still *the glory of the Lord filled the house.* The heart that is thus filled with a holy awe and reverence of the divine glory, the heart to which God manifests himself in his greatness, and (which is no less his glory) in his goodness, is thereby owned as a living temple.

II. The grateful return made to God for this gracious token of his favour.

1. The people *worshipped and praised God, v.* 3. When they saw the fire of God come down from heaven thus they did not run away affrighted, but kept their ground in the courts of the Lord, and took occasion from it, (1.) With reverence to adore the glory of God: *They bowed their faces to the ground and worshipped,* thus expressing their awful dread of the divine majesty, their cheerful submission to the divine authority, and the sense they had of their unworthiness to come into God's presence and their inability to stand before the power of his wrath. (2.) With thankfulness to acknowledge the goodness of God; even when the fire of the Lord came down they praised him, saying, *He is good, for his mercy endureth for ever.* This is a song never out of season, and for which our hearts and tongues should be never out of tune. However it be, yet God is good. When he manifests himself as a consuming fire to sinners his people can rejoice in him as their light. Nay, they had reason to say that in this God was good. "*It is of the Lord's mercies that we are not consumed,* but the sacrifice in our stead, for which we are bound to be very thankful."

2. The king and all the people offered sacrifices in abundance, *v.* 4, 5. With these they feasted this holy fire, and bade it welcome to the altar. They had offered sacrifices before, but now they increased them. Note, The tokens of God's favour to us should enlarge our hearts in his service, and make us to abound therein more and more. The king's example stirred up the people. Good work is then likely to go on when the leaders of a people lead in it. The sacrifices were so numerous that the altar could not contain them all; but, rather than any of them should be turned back (though we may

suppose the blood of them all was sprinkled upon the altar), the flesh of the burnt-offerings and the fat of the peace-offerings were burnt *in the midst of the court* (*v.* 7), which Solomon either hallowed for that service or hallowed by it. In case of necessity the pavement might be an altar.

3. The priests did their part; they waited on their offices, and the singers and musicians on theirs (*v.* 6), with the instruments that David made, and the *hymn that David had put into their hand,* as some think it may be read (meaning that 1 Chron. xvi. 7), or, as we read it, *when David praised by their ministry.* He employed, directed, and encouraged them in this work of praising God; and therefore their performances were accepted as his act, and he is said *to praise by their ministry.*

4. The whole congregation expressed the greatest joy and satisfaction imaginable. They kept the feast of the dedication of the altar seven days, from the second to the ninth; the tenth day was the day of atonement, when they were to afflict their souls for sin, and that was not unseasonable in the midst of their rejoicings; on the fifteenth day began the feast of tabernacles, which continued to the twenty-second, and they did not separate till the twenty-third. We must never grudge the time that we spend in the worship of God and communion with him, nor think it long, or grow weary of it.

5. Solomon went on in his work, and prosperously effected all he designed for the adorning both of God's house and his own, *v.* 11. Those that begin with the service of God are likely to go on successfully in their own affairs. It was Solomon's praise that what he undertook he went through with, and it was by the grace of God that he prospered in it.

12 And the LORD appeared to Solomon by night, and said unto him, I have heard thy prayer, and have chosen this place to myself for a house of sacrifice. 13 If I shut up heaven that there be no rain, or if I command the locusts to devour the land, or if I send pestilence among my people; 14 If my people, which are called by my name, shall humble themselves, and pray, and seek my face, and turn from their wicked ways; then will I hear from heaven, and will forgive their sin, and will heal their land. 15 Now mine eyes shall be open, and mine ears attent unto the prayer *that is made* in this place. 16 For now have I chosen and sanctified this house, that my name may be there for ever: and mine eyes and mine heart shall be there perpetually. 17 And as for thee, if thou wilt walk before me, as David thy father walked, and do according to all that I have commanded thee, and shalt observe my statutes and my judgments; 18 Then will I stablish the throne of thy kingdom, according as I have covenanted with David thy father, saying, There shall not fail thee a man *to be* ruler in Israel. 19 But if ye turn away, and forsake my statutes and my commandments, which I have set before you, and shall go and serve other gods, and worship them; 20 Then will I pluck them up by the roots out of my land which I have given them; and this house, which I have sanctified for my name, will I cast out of my sight, and will make it *to be* a proverb and a byword among all nations. 21 And this house, which is high, shall be an astonishment to every one that passeth by it; so that he shall say, Why hath the LORD done thus unto this land, and unto this house? 22 And it shall be answered, Because they forsook the LORD God of their fathers, which brought them forth out of the land of Egypt, and laid hold on other gods, and worshipped them, and served them: therefore hath he brought all this evil upon them.

That God accepted Solomon's prayer appeared by the fire from heaven. But a prayer may be accepted and yet not answered in the letter of it; and therefore God appeared to him in the night, as he did once before (*ch.* i. 7), and after a day of sacrifice too, as then, and gave him a particular answer to his prayer. We had the substance of it before, 1 Kings ix. 2—9.

I. He promised to own this house for *a house of sacrifice to Israel* and a *house of prayer for all people* (Isa. lvi. 7): *My name shall be there for ever* (*v.* 12, 16), that is, "There will I make myself known, and there will I be called upon."

II. He promised to answer the prayers of his people that should at any time be made in that place, *v.* 13—15. 1. National judgments are here supposed (*v.* 13), famine, and pestilence, and perhaps war, for by the locusts devouring the land may be meant enemies as greedy as locusts, and laying all waste. 2. National repentance, prayer, and reformation, are required, *v.* 14. God expects that his people who are called by his name, if they have dishonoured his name by their iniquity, should honour it by accepting the punishment of their iniquity. They must humble themselves under his hand, must pray for the removal of the judgment, must seek the face and favour of God; and yet all this will not do unless they turn from their wicked ways, and return to the God from whom they have revolted. 3. National mercy is then promised, that God will forgive their sin, which brought the judgment upon them, and then heal their land, redress all their grievances. Pardoning mercy makes way for healing mercy, Ps. ciii. 3; Matt. ix. 2.

III. He promised to perpetuate Solomon's kingdom, upon condition that he persevered in his duty, *v.* 17, 18. If he hoped for the benefit of God's covenant with David, he must imitate the example of David. But he set before him death as well as life, the curse as well as the blessing. 1. He supposed it possible that though they had this temple built to the honour of God, yet they might be drawn aside to worship other gods, *v.* 19. He knew their proneness to backslide into that sin. 2. He threatened it as certain that, if they did so, it would certainly be the ruin of both church and state. (1.) It would be the ruin of their state, *v.* 20. "Though they have taken deep root, and taken root long, in this good land, yet I will pluck them up by the roots, extirpate the whole nation, pluck them up as men pluck up weeds out of their garden, which are thrown to the dunghill." (2.) It would be the ruin of their church. This sanctuary would be no sanctuary to them, to protect them from the judgments of God, as they imagined, saying, *The temple of the Lord are we*, Jer. vii. 4. "This house which is high, not only for the magnificence of its structure, but for the designed ends and uses of it, shall be an astonishment, it shall come down wonderfully (Lam. i. 9), to the amazement of all the neighbours."

CHAP. VIII.

In this chapter we are told, I. What cities Solomon built, ver. 1—6. II. What workmen Solomon employed, ver. 7—10. III. What care he took about a proper settlement for his wife, ver. 11. IV. What a good method he put the temple-service into, ver. 12—16. V. What trading he had with foreign countries, ver. 17, 18.

AND it came to pass at the end of twenty years, wherein Solomon had built the house of the LORD, and his own house, 2 That the cities which Huram had restored to Solomon, Solomon built them, and caused the children of Israel to dwell there. 3 And Solomon went to Hamath-zobah, and prevailed against it. 4 And he built Tadmor in the wilderness, and all the store cities, which he built in Hamath. 5 Also he built Beth-horon the upper, and Beth-horon the nether, fenced cities, with walls, gates, and bars; 6 And Baalath, and all the store cities that Solomon had, and all the chariot cities, and the cities of the horsemen, and all that Solomon desired to build in Jerusalem, and in Lebanon, and throughout all the land of his dominion. 7 *As for* all the people *that were* left of the Hittites, and the Amorites, and the Perizzites, and the Hivites, and the Jebusites, which *were* not of Israel, 8 *But* of their children, who were left after them in the land, whom the children of Israel consumed not, them did Solomon make to pay tribute until this day. 9 But of the children of Israel did Solomon make no servants for his work; but they *were* men of war, and chief of his captains, and captains of his chariots and horsemen. 10 And these *were* the chief of king Solomon's officers, *even* two hundred and fifty, that bare rule over the people. 11 And Solomon brought up the daughter of Pharaoh out of the city of David unto the house that he had built for her: for he said, My wife shall not dwell in the house of David king of Israel, because *the places are* holy, whereunto the ark of the LORD hath come.

This we had 1 Kings ix. 10—24, and therefore shall only observe here,

I. Though Solomon was a man of great learning and knowledge, yet he spent his days, not in contemplation, but in action, not in his study, but in his country, in building cities and fortifying them, in a time of peace preparing for a time of war, which is as much a man's business as it is in summer to provide food for winter.

II. As he was a man of business himself, and did not consult his own ease, so he employed a great many hands, kept abundance of people to work. It is the interest of a state by all means possible to promote and encourage industry, and to keep its subjects from idleness. A great many strangers there were in Israel, many that remained of the Canaanites; and they were welcome to live there, but not to live and do nothing. The men of Laish, who had no business, were an easy prey to the invaders, Judg. xviii. 7.

III. When Solomon had begun with building the house of God, and made good work and quick work of that, he prospered in all his undertakings, so that *he built all that he desired to build, v.* 6. Those who have a genius for building find that one project draws on another, and the latter must amend and improve the former. Now observe, 1. How the divine providence gratified even Solomon's humour, and gave him success, not only in all that he needed to build and that it was for his advantage to build, but in all that he had a mind to build. So indulgent a Father God is sometimes to the innocent desires of his children that serve him. Thus he pleased Jacob with that promise, *Joseph shall put his hand on thy eyes.* 2. Solomon knew how to set bounds to his desires. He was not one of those that enlarge them endlessly, and can never be satisfied, but knew when to draw in; for he finished all he desired, and then he desired no more. He did not sit down and fret that he had not more cities to build, as Alexander did that he had not more worlds to conquer, Hab. ii. 5.

IV. That one reason why Solomon built a palace on purpose for the queen, and removed her and her court to it, was because he thought it by no means proper that she should *dwell in the house of David* (*v.* 11), considering that that had been a place of great piety, and perhaps her house was a place of great vanity. She was proselyted, it is likely, to the Jewish religion; but it is a question whether all her servants were. Perhaps they had among them the idols of Egypt, and a great deal of profaneness and debauchery. Now, though Solomon had not zeal and courage enough to suppress and punish what was amiss there, yet he so far consulted the honour of his father's memory that he would not suffer that place to be thus profaned where the ark of God had been and where holy David had prayed many a good prayer and sung many a sweet psalm. Not that all the places where the ark had been were so holy as never to be put to a common use; for then the houses of Abinadab and Obed-edom must have been so. But the place where it had been so long, and had been so publicly attended on, was so venerable that it was not fit to be the place of so much gaiety, not to say iniquity, as was to be found, I fear, in the court that Pharaoh's daughter kept. Note, Between things sacred and things common the ancient landmarks ought to be kept up. It was an outer-court of the temple that was the *court of the women.*

12 Then Solomon offered burnt offerings unto the LORD on the altar of the LORD, which he had built before the porch, 13 Even after a certain rate every day, offering according to the commandment of Moses, on the sabbaths, and on the new moons, and on the solemn feasts, three times in the year, *even* in the feast of unleavened bread, and in the feast of weeks, and in the feast of tabernacles. 14 And he appointed, according to the order of David his father, the courses of the priests to their service, and the Levites to their charges, to praise and minister before the priests, as the duty of every day required: the porters also by their courses at every gate: for so had David the man of God commanded. 15 And they departed not from the commandment of the king unto the priests and Levites concerning any matter, or concerning the treasures. 16 Now all the work of Solomon was prepared unto the day of the foundation of the house of the LORD, and until it was finished. *So* the house of the LORD was perfected. 17 Then went Solomon to Ezion-geber, and to Eloth, at the sea side in the land of Edom. 18 And Huram sent him by the hands of his servants ships, and servants that had knowledge of the sea; and they went with the servants of Solomon to Ophir, and took thence four hundred and fifty talents of gold, and brought *them* to king Solomon.

Here is, I. Solomon's devotion. The building of the temple was in order to the service of the temple. Whatever cost he was at in rearing the structure, if he had neglected the worship that was to be performed there, it would all have been to no purpose. Assisting the devotion of others will not atone for our own neglects. When Solomon had built the temple, 1. He kept up the holy sacrifices there, according to the law of Moses, *v.* 12, 13. In vain had the altar been built, and in vain had fire come down from heaven, if sacrifices had not been constantly brought as the food of that altar and the fuel of that fire. There were daily sacrifices, *a certain rate every day*, as duly as the day came, weekly sacrifices on the sabbath, double to what was offered on other days, monthly sacrifices *on the new moons,* and yearly sacrifices at the three solemn feasts. Those are spiritual sacrifices that are now required of us, which we are to bring daily and weekly; and it is good to be in a settled method of devotion. 2. He kept up the holy songs there, according to the *law of David,* who is here called *the man of God,* as Moses was, because he was both instructed and authorised of God to make these establishments; and Solomon took care to see them observed *as the duty of every day required, v.* 14. Solomon, though a wise and great man and the builder of the temple, did not attempt to amend, alter, or add to what the man of God had, in God's name, commanded, but closely adhered to that, and used his authority to have that duly observed; and then *none departed from the commandment of the king concerning any matter*, *v.* 15. He observed God's laws, and then all obeyed his orders. When the service of the temple was put into this good order, then it is said, *The house of the Lord was perfected*, *v.* 16. The work was the main matter, not the place; the temple was unfinished till all this was done.

II. Solomon's merchandise. He did himself in person visit the sea-port towns of Eloth and Ezion-geber; for those that deal much in the world will find it their interest, as far as they can, to inspect their affairs themselves and to see with their own eyes, *v.* 17. Canaan was a rich country, and yet must send to Ophir for gold; the Israelites were a wise and understanding people, and yet must be beholden to the king of Tyre for *men that had knowledge of the seas*, *v.* 18. Yet Canaan was God's peculiar land, and Israel God's peculiar people. This teaches us that grace, and not gold, is the best riches, and acquaintance with God and his law, not with arts and sciences, the best knowledge.

CHAP. IX.

Solomon here continues to appear great both at home and abroad. We had this account of his grandeur, 1 Kings x. Nothing is here added; but his defection towards his latter end, which we have there (ch. xi.), is here omitted, and the close of this chapter brings him to the grave with an unstained reputation. Perhaps none of the chapters in the Chronicles agree so much with a chapter in the Kings as this does with 1 Kings x. verse for verse, only that the first two verses there are put into one here, and verse 25 here is taken from 1 Kings iv. 26, and the last three verses here from 1 Kings xi. 41—43. Here is, I. The honour which the queen of Sheba did to Solomon, in the visit she made him to hear his wisdom, ver. 1—12. II. Many instances given of the riches and splendour of Solomon's court, ver. 13—28. III. The conclusion of his reign, ver. 29—31.

AND when the queen of Sheba heard of the fame of Solomon, she came to prove Solomon with hard questions at Jerusalem, with a very great company, and camels that bare spices, and gold in abundance, and precious stones: and when she was come to Solomon, she communed with him of all that was in her heart. 2 And Solomon told her all her questions: and there was nothing hid from Solomon which he told her not. 3 And when the queen of Sheba had seen the wisdom of Solomon, and the house that he had built, 4 And the meat of his table, and the sitting of his servants, and the attendance of his ministers, and their apparel; his cupbearers also, and their apparel; and his ascent by which he went up into the house of the LORD; there was no more spirit in her. 5 And she said to the king, *It was* a true report which I heard in mine own land of thine acts, and of thy wisdom: 6 Howbeit I believed not their words, until I came, and mine eyes had seen *it*: and, behold, the one half of the greatness of thy wisdom was not told me: *for* thou exceedest the fame that I heard. 7 Happy *are* thy men, and happy *are* these thy servants, which stand continually before thee, and hear thy wisdom. 8 Blessed be the LORD thy God, which delighted in thee to set thee on his throne, *to be* king for the LORD thy God: because thy God loved Israel, to establish them for ever, therefore made he thee king over them, to do judgment and justice. 9 And she gave the king a hundred and twenty talents of gold, and of spices great abundance, and precious stones: neither was there any such spice as the queen of Sheba gave king Solomon. 10 And the servants also of Huram, and the servants of Solomon, which brought gold from Ophir, brought algum trees and precious stones. 11 And the king made *of* the algum trees terraces to the house of the LORD, and to the king's palace, and harps and psalteries for singers: and there were none such seen before in the land of Judah. 12 And king Solomon gave to the queen of Sheba all her desire, whatsoever she asked, beside *that* which she had brought unto the king. So she turned, and went away to her own land, she and her servants.

This passage of story has been largely considered in the Kings; yet, because our Saviour has proposed it as an example to us in our enquiries after him (Matt. xii. 42), we must not pass it over without observing briefly, 1. *Those who honour God he will honour*, 1 Sam. ii. 30. Solomon had greatly honoured God, in building, beautifying, and dedicating the temple; all his wisdom and all his wealth were employed for the making of that a consummate piece: and now God made his wisdom and wealth to redound greatly to his reputation. The way to have both the credit and comfort of all our endowments and all our enjoyments is to consecrate them to God and use them for him. 2. Those who know the worth of true wisdom will grudge no pains nor cost to obtain it. The queen of Sheba put herself to a great deal of trouble and expense to hear the wisdom of Solomon; and yet, learning from him to serve God and do her duty, she thought herself well paid for her pains. Heavenly wisdom is that *pearl of great price* which it is a good bargain to purchase by parting with all that we have. 3. As every man has received the gift so he ought to minister the same for the edification of others, as he has opportunity. Solomon was communicative of his wisdom and willing to teach others what he knew himself. Being taught of God, freely he had received, and freely he gave. Let those that are rich in wisdom, as well as wealth, learn *to do good* and *be ready to distribute. Give to every one that asketh.* 4. Good order in a family, a great family, especially in the things of God, and a regular discharge of the duties of religious worship, are highly expedient, and to be much admired wherever found. The queen of Sheba was exceedingly affected to see the propriety with which Solomon's servants attended him and with which both he and they attended in the house of God. David's ascent to the house of the Lord was also pleasant and interesting, Ps. xlii. 4. 5. Those are happy who have the opportunity of a constant converse with such as are knowing, wise, and good. The queen of Sheba thought Solomon's servants happy who continually *heard his wisdom;* for, it seems, even to them he was communicative. And it is observable that the posterity of those who had places in his court were willing to have the names of their ancestors forgotten, and thought themselves sufficiently distinguished and dignified when they were called the *children of Solomon's servants* (Ezra. ii. 55; Neh. vii. 57); so eminent were they that it was honour enough to be named from them. 6. We ought to rejoice and give God thanks for the gifts, graces, and usefulness, of others. The queen of Sheba blessed God for the honour he put upon Solomon, and the favour he did to Israel, in advancing him to the throne, *v.* 8. By giving God the praise of the prosperity of others, we share in the comfort of it; whereas, by envying the prosperity of others, we lose the comfort even of our own. The happiness both of king and kingdom she traces up to the fountain of all bliss, the divine favour: it was because *thy God delighted in thee* and because he *loved Israel.* Those mercies are doubly sweet in which we can taste the kindness and good will of God as our God. 7. It becomes those that are wise and good to be generous according to their place and power. The queen of Sheba was so to Solomon, Solomon was so to her, *v.* 9, 12. They both knew how to value wisdom, and therefore were neither of them covetous of their money, but cultivated the acquaintance and confirmed the friendship they had contracted by mutual presents. Our Lord Jesus has promised to give us all our desire: *Ask, and it shall be given you.* Let us study what we shall render to him, and not think any thing too much to do, or suffer, or part with, for him.

13 Now the weight of gold that came to Solomon in one year was six hundred and threescore and six talents of gold; 14 Beside *that which* chapmen and merchants brought. And all the kings of Arabia and governors of the country brought gold and silver to Solomon. 15 And king Solomon made two hundred targets *of* beaten gold: six hundred *shekels* of beaten gold went to one target. 16 And three hundred shields *made he of* beaten gold: three hundred *shekels* of gold went to one shield. And the king put them in the house of the forest of Lebanon. 17 Moreover the king made a great throne of ivory, and overlaid it with pure gold. 18 And *there were* six steps to the throne, with a footstool of gold, *which were* fastened to the throne, and stays on each side of the sitting place, and two lions standing by the stays: 19 And twelve lions stood there on the one side and on the other upon the six steps. There was not the like made in any kingdom. 20 And all the drinking vessels of king Solomon *were of* gold, and all the vessels of the house of the forest of Lebanon *were of* pure gold: none *were of* silver; it was *not* any thing accounted of in the days of Solomon. 21 For the king's ships went to Tarshish with the servants of Huram: every three years once came the ships of Tarshish bringing gold, and silver, ivory, and apes, and peacocks. 22 And king Solomon passed all the kings of the earth in riches and wisdom. 23 And all the kings of the earth sought the presence of Solomon, to hear his wisdom, that God had put in his heart. 24 And they brought every man his present, vessels of silver, and vessels of gold, and raiment, harness, and spices, horses, and mules, a rate year by year. 25 And Solomon had four thousand stalls for horses and chariots, and twelve thousand horsemen; whom he bestowed in the chariot cities, and with the king at Jerusalem. 26 And he reigned over all the kings from the river even unto the land of the Philistines, and to the border of Egypt.

27 And the king made silver in Jerusalem as stones, and cedar trees made he as the sycamore trees that *are* in the low plains in abundance. 28 And they brought unto Solomon horses out of Egypt, and out of all lands. 29 Now the rest of the acts of Solomon, first and last, *are* they not written in the book of Nathan the prophet, and in the prophecy of Ahijah the Shilonite, and in the visions of Iddo the seer against Jeroboam the son of Nebat? 30 And Solomon reigned in Jerusalem over all Israel forty years. 31 And Solomon slept with his fathers, and he was buried in the city of David his father: and Rehoboam his son reigned in his stead.

We have here Solomon in his throne, and Solomon in his grave; for the throne would not secure him from the grave. *Mors sceptra ligonibus æquat—Death wrenches from the hand the sceptre as well as the spade.*

I. Here is Solomon reigning in wealth and power, in ease and fulness, such as, for aught I know, could never since be paralleled by any king whatsoever. I cannot pretend to be critical in comparing the grandeur of Solomon with that of some of the great princes of the earth. But I may observe that the most illustrious of them were famed for their wars, whereas Solomon reigned forty years in profound peace. Some of those that might be thought to vie with Solomon affected retirement, kept people in awe by keeping them at a great distance; nobody must see them, or come near them, upon pain of death: but Solomon went much abroad, and appeared in public business. So that, all things considered, the promise was fulfilled, that God would give him riches, and wealth, and honour, such as no kings *have had, or shall have, ch.* i. 12. 1. Never any prince appeared in public with greater splendour than Solomon did, which to those that judge by the sight of the eye, as most people do, would very much recommend him. He had 200 targets and 300 shields, all of beaten gold, carried before him (*v.* 15, 16), and sat upon a most stately throne, *v.* 17—19. *There was not the like in any kingdom.* The lustre wherein he appeared was typical of the spiritual glory of the kingdom of the Messiah and but a faint representation of his throne, which is above every throne. Solomon's pomp was all artificial; and therefore our Saviour prefers the natural beauty of the *lilies of the field* before it. Matt. vi. 29, *Solomon, in all his glory, was not arrayed like one of these.* 2. Never any prince had greater plenty of gold and silver, though there were no gold or silver mines in his own kingdom. Either he made himself master of the mines in other countries, and, having a populous country, sent hands to dig out those rich metals, or, having a fruitful country, he exported the commodities of it and with them fetched home all this gold that is here spoken of, *v.* 13 14—21. 3. Never any prince had such presents brought him by all his neighbours as Solomon had: *All the kings of Arabia, and governors of the country, brought him gold and silver* (*v.* 14), not as tribute which he extorted from them, but as freewill offerings to procure his favour, or in a way of exchange for some of the productions of his husbandry, corn or cattle. All the kings of the earth brought him presents, that is, all in those parts of the world (*v.* 24, 28), because they coveted his acquaintance and friendship. Herein he was a type of Christ, to whom, as soon as he was born, the wise men of the east brought presents, *gold, frankincense, and myrrh* (Matt. ii. 11), and to whom all that are about him must bring presents, Ps. lxxvi. 11; Rom. xii. 1. 4. Never any prince was so renowned for wisdom, so courted, so consulted, so admired (*v.* 23): *The kings of the earth* (for it was too great a favour for common persons to pretend to) *sought to hear his wisdom*—his natural philosophy, or his skill in physic, or his state policy, or his rules of prudence for the conduct of human life, or perhaps the principles of his religion, and the reasons of it. The application which they then made to Solomon to hear his wisdom will aggravate, shame, and condemn, men's general contempt of Christ and his gospel. Though in them are *hidden all the treasures of wisdom and knowledge, yet none of the princes of this world* desire to know them, for they are foolishness to them, 1 Cor. ii. 8, 14.

II. Here is Solomon dying, stripped of his pomp, and leaving all his wealth and power, not to one concerning whom he knew not *whether he would be a wise man or a fool* (Eccl. ii. 19), but who he knew would be a fool. This was not only vanity but vexation of spirit, *v.* 29—31. It is very observable that no mention is here made of Solomon's departure from God in his latter days, not the least hint given of it, 1. Because the Holy Ghost would teach us not to take delight in repeating the faults and follies of others. If those that have been in reputation for wisdom and honour misbehave, though it may be of use to take notice of their misconduct for warning to ourselves and others, yet we must not be forward to mention it, once speaking of it is enough; why should that unpleasing string be again struck upon? Why can we not do as the sacred historian here does, speak largely of that in others which is praise-worthy, without saying any thing of their blemishes, yea, though they have been gross and obvious? This is but doing as we would be done by. 2. Because, though he fell, yet he was not utterly cast down. His sin is not again recorded, because it was repented of, and pardoned, and so became as if it had never been. Scripture-silence sometimes speaks. I am willing to believe that its silence here concerning the sin of Solomon is an intimation that none of the sins he committed were mentioned against him, Ezek. xxxiii. 16. When God pardons sin he *casts it behind his back and remembers it no more.*

CHAP. X.

This chapter is copied almost verbatim from 1 Kings xii. 1—19, where it was opened at large. Solomon's defection from God was not repeated, but the defection of the ten tribes from his family is, in this chapter, where we find, I. How foolish Rehoboam was in his treating with them, ver. 1, 5—14. II. How wicked the people were in complaining of Solomon (ver. 2—4) and forsaking Rehoboam, ver. 16—19. III. How just and righteous God was in all this, ver. 15. His counsel was thereby fulfilled. With him are strength and wisdom; both the deceived and the deceiver (the fool and the knave) are his (Job xii. 16), that is, are made use of by him to suit his purposes.

AND Rehoboam went to Shechem: for to Shechem were all Israel come to make him king. 2 And it came to pass, when Jeroboam the son of Nebat, who *was* in Egypt, whither he had fled from the presence of Solomon the king, heard *it*, that Jeroboam returned out of Egypt. 3 And they sent and called him. So Jeroboam and all Israel came and spake to Rehoboam, saying, 4 Thy father made our yoke grievous: now therefore ease thou somewhat the grievous servitude of thy father, and his heavy yoke that he put upon us, and we will serve thee. 5 And he said unto them, Come again unto me after three days. And the people departed. 6 And king Rehoboam took counsel with the old men that had stood before Solomon his father while he yet lived, saying, What counsel give ye *me* to return answer to this people? 7 And they spake unto him, saying, If thou be kind to this people, and please them, and speak good words to them, they will be thy servants for ever. 8 But he forsook the counsel which the old men gave him, and took counsel with the young men that were brought up with him, that stood before him. 9 And he said unto them, What advice give ye that we may return answer to this people, which have spoken to me, saying, Ease somewhat the yoke that thy father did put upon us? 10 And the young men that were brought up with him spake unto him, saying, Thus shalt thou answer the people that spake unto thee, saying, Thy father made our yoke heavy, but make thou *it* somewhat lighter for us; thus shalt thou say unto them, My little *finger* shall be thicker than my father's loins. 11 For whereas my father put a heavy yoke upon you, I will put more to your yoke: my father chastised you with whips, but I *will chastise you* with scorpions.

We may observe here, 1. The wisest and best cannot give every body content. Solomon enriched and advanced his kingdom, did all (one would think) that could be done to make them happy and easy; and yet either he was indiscreet in burdening them with the imposition of taxes and services, or at least there was some colour of reason to think him so. No man is perfectly wise. It is probable that it was when Solomon had declined from God and his duty that his wisdom failed him, and God left him to himself to act in this impolitic manner. Even Solomon's treasures were exhausted by his love of women; and probably it was to maintain them, and their pride, luxury, and idolatry, that he burdened his subjects. 2. Turbulent and ungrateful spirits will find fault with the government, and complain of grievances, when they have very little reason to do so. Had they not peace in Solomon's time? They were never plundered by invaders, as formerly, never put in fear by the alarms of war, nor obliged to hazard their lives in the high places of the field. Had they not plenty—meat enough, and money enough? What would they more? *O fortunatos nimium, sua si bona norint!—O happy, if they knew their happy state!* And yet they complain that Solomon made their yoke grievous. If any complain thus of the yoke of Christ, that they may have a pretence to break his bands in sunder and cast away his cords from them, we are sure that he never gave them any cause at all for the complaint, whatever Solomon did. *His yoke is easy, and his burden light.* He never *made us serve with an offering, nor wearied us with incense.* 3. Many ruin themselves and their interests by trampling upon and provoking their inferiors. Rehoboam thought that because he was king he might assume as much authority as his father had done, might have what he would, and do what he would, and carry all before him. But, though he wore his father's crown, he wanted his father's brains, and ought to have considered that, being quite a different man from what his father was, he ought to take other measures. Such a wise man as Solomon may do as he will, but such a fool as Rehoboam must do as he can. The high-mettled horse may be kicked and spurred by him that has the art of managing him; but, if an unskilful horseman do it, it is at his peril. Rehoboam paid dearly for threatening, and talking big, and thinking to carry matters with a high hand. It was

Job's wisdom, as well as his virtue, that he *despised not the cause of his man-servant or maid-servant,* when they argued with him (Job xxxi. 13), but heard them patiently, considered their reasons, and gave them a soft answer. And a similar tender consideration of those in subjection, and a forwardness to make them easy, will be the comfort and praise of all in authority, in the church, in the state, and in families. 4. Moderate counsels are generally wisest and best. Gentleness will do what violence will not do. Most people love to be accosted mildly. Rehoboam's old experienced counsellors directed him to this method (*v.* 7): "*Be kind to this people, and please them, and speak good words to them,* and thou art sure of them for ever." Good words cost nothing but a little self-denial, and yet they purchase great things. 5. God often fulfils the counsels of his own wisdom by infatuating men, and giving them up to the counsels of their own folly. No more needs be done to ruin men than to leave them to themselves, and their own pride and passion.

12 So Jeroboam and all the people came to Rehoboam on the third day, as the king bade, saying, Come again to me on the third day. 13 And the king answered them roughly; and king Rehoboam forsook the counsel of the old men, 14 And answered them after the advice of the young men, saying, My father made your yoke heavy, but I will add thereto: my father chastised you with whips, but I *will chastise you* with scorpions. 15 So the king hearkened not unto the people: for the cause was of God, that the LORD might perform his word, which he spake by the hand of Ahijah the Shilonite to Jeroboam the son of Nebat. 16 And when all Israel *saw* that the king would not hearken unto them, the people answered the king, saying, What portion have we in David? and *we have* none inheritance in the son of Jesse: every man to your tents, O Israel: *and* now, David, see to thine own house. So all Israel went to their tents. 17 But *as for* the children of Israel that dwelt in the cities of Judah, Rehoboam reigned over them. 18 Then king Rehoboam sent Hadoram that *was* over the tribute; and the children of Israel stoned him with stones, that he died. But king Rehoboam made speed to get him up to *his* chariot, to flee to Jerusalem. 19 And Israel rebelled against the house of David unto this day.

We may learn here, 1. That when public affairs are in a ferment violent proceedings do but make bad worse. Rough answers (such as Rehoboam here gave) do but stir up anger and bring oil to the flames. The pilot has need to steer steadily in a storm. Many have been driven to the mischief they did not intend by being too severely dealt with for what they did intend. 2. That, whatever the devices and designs of men are, God is, by all, doing his own work, and fulfilling the word which he has spoken, no iota or tittle of which shall fall to the ground. The cause of the king's obstinacy and thoughtlessness was *of God, that he might perform the word which he spoke by Ahijah, v.* 15. This does not at all excuse Rehoboam's folly, nor lessen the guilt of his haughtiness and passion, that God was pleased to serve his own ends by them. 3. That worldly wealth, honour, and dominion, are very uncertain things. *Solomon reigned over all Israel,* and, one would think, had done enough to secure the monarchy entire to his family for many ages; and yet he is scarcely cold in his grave before ten of the twelve tribes finally revolt from his son. All the good services he had done for Israel were now forgotten: *What portion have we in David?* Thus is the government of Christ cast off by many, notwithstanding all he has done to bind the children of men for ever to himself; they say, *We will not have this man to reign over us.* But this rebellion will certainly be their ruin. 4. That God often visits the iniquities of the fathers upon the children. Solomon forsakes God, and therefore not he, but his son after him, is forsaken by the greatest part of his people. Thus God, by making the penal consequences of sin to last long and visibly to continue after the sinner's death, would give an indication of its malignity, and perhaps some intimation of the perpetuity of its punishment. He that sins against God not only wrongs his soul, but perhaps wrongs his seed more than he thinks of. 5. That, when God is fulfilling his threatenings, he will take care that, at the same time, promises do not fall to the ground. When Solomon's iniquity is remembered, and for it his son loses ten tribes, David's piety is not forgotten, nor the promise made to him; but for the sake of that his grandson had two tribes preserved to him. The failings of the saints shall not frustrate any promise made to Christ their Head. They shall be chastised, but the covenant not broken, Ps. lxxxix. 31—34.

CHAP. XI.

We are here going on with the history of Rehoboam. I. His attempt to recover the ten tribes he had lost, and the letting fall of that attempt in obedience to the divine command, ver. 1—4. II. His successful endeavours to preserve the two tribes that remained, ver. 5—12. III. The resort of the priests and Levites to him, ver. 13—17. IV. An account of his wives and children, ver. 18—23.

AND when Rehoboam was come to Jerusalem, he gathered of the house of Judah and Benjamin a hundred and fourscore thousand chosen *men*, which were warriors, to fight against Israel, that he might bring the kingdom again to Rehoboam. 2 But the word of the LORD came to Shemaiah the man of God, saying, 3 Speak unto Rehoboam the son of Solomon, king of Judah, and to all Israel in Judah and Benjamin, saying, 4 Thus saith the LORD, Ye shall not go up, nor fight against your brethren: return every man to his house: for this thing is done of me. And they obeyed the words of the LORD, and returned from going against Jeroboam. 5 And Rehoboam dwelt in Jerusalem, and built cities for defence in Judah. 6 He built even Beth-lehem, and Etam, and Tekoa, 7 And Beth-zur, and Shoco, and Adullam, 8 And Gath, and Mareshah, and Ziph, 9 And Adoraim, and Lachish, and Azekah, 10 And Zorah, and Aijalon, and Hebron, which *are* in Judah and Benjamin fenced cities. 11 And he fortified the strong holds, and put captains in them, and store of victual, and of oil and wine. 12 And in every several city *he put* shields and spears, and made them exceeding strong, having Judah and Benjamin on his side.

How the ten tribes deserted the house of David we read in the foregoing chapter. They had formerly sat loose to that family (2 Sam. xx. 1, 2), and now they quite threw it off, not considering how much it would weaken the common interest and take Israel down from that pitch of glory at which it had arrived in the last reign. But thus the *kingdom* must be corrected as well as the *house* of David. 1. Rehoboam at length, like a bold man, raises an army, with a design to reduce the revolters, *v.* 1. Judah and Benjamin were not only resolved to continue their allegiance to him, but ready to give him the best assistance they could for the recovery of his right. Judah was his own tribe, that owned him some years before the rest did; Benjamin was the tribe in which Jerusalem, or the greatest part of it, stood, which perhaps was one reason why that tribe clave to him. 2. Yet, like a conscientious man, when God forbade him to prosecute this design, in obedience to him he let it fall, either because he reverenced the divine authority or because he knew that he should not prosper if he should go contrary to God's command, but instead of retrieving what was lost would be in danger of losing what he had. It is dangerous undertaking any thing, but especially undertaking a war, contrary to the will of God. God calls him (*v.* 3), *Rehoboam the son of Solomon*, to intimate that this was determined for the sin of Solomon, and it would be to no purpose to oppose a decree that had gone forth. They *obeyed the words of the Lord;* and though it looked mean, and would turn to their reproach among their neighbours, yet, because God would have it so, they laid down their arms. 3. Like a discreet man, he fortified his own country. He saw it was to no purpose to think of reducing those that had revolted. A few good words might have prevented their defection, but now all the forces of his kingdom cannot bring them back. The thing is done, and so it must rest; it is his wisdom to make the best of it. Perhaps the same young counsellors that had advised him to answer them roughly urged him to fight them, notwithstanding the divine inhibition; but he had paid dearly enough for being advised by them, and therefore now, we may suppose, his aged and experienced counsellors were hearkened to, and they advised him to submit to the will of God concerning what was lost, and to make it his business to keep what he had. It was probably by their advice that, (1.) He fortified his frontiers, and many of the principal cities of his kingdom, which, in Solomon's peaceable reign, no care had been taken for the defence of. (2.) He furnished them with good store of victuals and arms, *v.* 11, 12. Because God forbade him to fight, he did not therefore sit down sullenly, and say that he would do nothing for the public safety if he might not do that, but prudently provided against an attack. Those that may not be conquerors, yet may be builders.

13 And the priests and the Levites that *were* in all Israel resorted to him out of all their coasts. 14 For the Levites left their suburbs and their possession, and came to Judah and Jerusalem: for Jeroboam and his sons had cast them off from executing the priest's office unto the LORD: 15 And he ordained him priests for the high places, and for the devils, and for the calves which he had made. 16 And after them out of all the tribes of Israel such as set their hearts to seek the LORD God of Israel came to Jerusalem, to sacrifice unto the LORD God of their fathers. 17 So they strengthened the kingdom of Judah, and made Rehoboam the son of So-

lomon strong, three years: for three years they walked in the way of David and Solomon. 18 And Rehoboam took him Mahalath the daughter of Jerimoth the son of David to wife, *and* Abihail the daughter of Eliab the son of Jesse; 19 Which bare him children; Jeush, and Shamariah, and Zaham. 20 And after her he took Maachah the daughter of Absalom; which bare him Abijah, and Attai, and Ziza, and Shelomith. 21 And Rehoboam loved Maachah the daughter of Absalom above all his wives and his concubines: (for he took eighteen wives, and threescore concubines; and begat twenty and eight sons, and threescore daughters.) 22 And Rehoboam made Abijah the son of Maachah the chief, *to be* ruler among his brethren: for *he thought* to make him king. 23 And he dealt wisely, and dispersed of all his children throughout all the countries of Judah and Benjamin, unto every fenced city: and he gave them victual in abundance. And he desired many wives.

See here,

I. How Rehoboam was strengthened by the accession of the priests and Levites, and all the devout and pious Israelites, to him, even all that were true to their God and their religion.

1. Jeroboam cast them off, that is, he set up such a way of worship as he knew they could not in conscience comply with, which obliged them to withdraw from his altar, and at the same time he would not allow them to go up to Jerusalem to worship at the altar there; so that he totally *cast them off from executing the priest's office, v.* 14. And very willing he was that they should turn themselves out of their places, that room might be made for those mean and scandalous persons whom he *ordained priests for the high places, v.* 15. Compare 1 Kings xii. 31. No marvel if he that cast off God cast off his ministers; they were not for his purpose, would not do whatever he might bid them do, would not *serve his gods, nor worship the golden image which he had set up.*

2. They thereupon *left their suburbs and possessions, v.* 14. Out of the lot of each tribe the Levites had cities allowed them, where they were comfortably provided for and had opportunity of doing much good. But now they were driven out of all their cities except those in Judah and Benjamin. One would think their maintenance well settled, and yet they lost it. It was a comfort to them that the law so often reminded them that the *Lord was their inheritance,* and so they should find him when they were turned out of their house and possessions. But why did they leave their possessions? (1.) Because they saw they could do no good among their neighbours, in whom (now that Jeroboam set up his calves) the old proneness to idolatry revived. (2.) Because they themselves would be in continual temptation to some base compliances, and in danger of being drawn insensibly to that which was evil. If we pray, in sincerity, not to be led into temptation, we shall get and keep as far as we can out of the way of it. (3.) Because, if they retained their integrity, they had reason to expect persecution from Jeroboam and his sons. The priests they made for the devils would not let the Lord's priests be long among them. No secular advantages whatsoever should draw us thither, or detain us there, where we are in danger of making shipwreck of faith and a good conscience.

3. They *came to Judah and Jerusalem* (*v.* 14) and *presented themselves to Rehoboam, v.* 13, *margin.* Where should God's priests and Levites be, but where his altar was? Thither they came because it was their business to attend at the times appointed. (1.) It was a mercy to them that they had a place of refuge to flee to, and that when Jeroboam cast them off there were those so near that would entertain them, and bid them welcome, and they were not forced into the lands of the heathen. (2.) It was an evidence that they loved their work better than their maintenance, in that they *left their suburbs and possessions in the country* (where they might have lived at ease upon their own), because they were restrained from serving God there, and cast themselves upon God's providence and the charity of their brethren in coming to a place where they might have the free enjoyment of God's ordinances, according to his institution. Poverty in the way of duty is to be chosen rather than plenty in the way of sin. Better live upon alms, or die in a prison, with a good conscience, than roll in wealth and pleasure with a prostituted one. (3.) It was the wisdom and praise of Rehoboam and his people that they bade them welcome, though they crowded themselves perhaps to make room for them. Conscientious refugees will bring a blessing along with them to the countries that entertain them, as they leave a curse behind them with those that expel them. *Open the gates, that the righteous nation, which keepeth truth, may enter in;* it will be good policy. See Isa. xxvi. 1, 2.

4. When the priests and Levites came to Jerusalem all the devout pious Israelites of every tribe followed them. Such as *set their hearts to seek the Lord God of Israel,* that made conscience of their duty to God and were sincere and resolute in it, left the inheritance of their fathers and went and took

houses in Jerusalem, that they might have free access to the altar of God and be out of the temptation to worship the calves, *v.* 16. Note, (1.) That is best for us which is best for our souls; and, in all our choices, advantages for religion must take place of all outward conveniences. (2.) Where God's faithful priests are his faithful people should be. If Jeroboam cast off God's ministers, every true-born Israelite will think himself obliged to own them and stand by them. *Forsake not the Levite,* the out-cast Levite, *as long as thou livest.* When *the ark removes do you remove and go after it,* Josh. iii. 3.

5. They *strengthened the kingdom of Judah* (*v.* 17), not only by the addition of so many persons to it, who, it is likely, brought what they could of their effects with them, but by their piety and their prayers they procured a blessing upon the kingdom which was a sanctuary to them. See Zech. xii. 5. It is the interest of a nation to protect and encourage religion and religious people, and adds more than any thing to its strength. They made him and his people *strong three years;* for so long they *walked in the way of David and Solomon,* their *good* way. But when they forsook that, and so threw themselves out of God's favour and protection, the best friends they had could no longer help to strengthen them. We retain our strength while we cleave to God and our duty, and no longer.

II. How Rehoboam was weakened by indulging himself in his pleasures. He *desired many wives,* as his father did (*v.* 23), yet, 1. In *this* he was more wise than his father, that he does not appear to have married strange wives. The wives mentioned here were not only daughters of Israel, but of the family of David; one was a descendant from Eliab, David's brother (*v.* 18), another from Absalom, probably that Absalom who was David's son (*v.* 20), another from Jerimoth, David's son. 2. In *this* he was more happy than his father, that he had many sons and daughters; whereas we read not of more than one son that his father had. One can scarcely imagine that he had no more; but, if he had, they were not worth mentioning; whereas several of Rehoboam's sons are here named (*v.* 19, 20) as men of note, and such active men that he thought it his wisdom to *disperse them throughout the countries of Judah and Benjamin* (*v.* 23), either, (1.) That they might not be rivals with his son Abijah, whom he designed for his successor, or rather, (2.) Because he could repose a confidence in them for the preserving of the public peace and safety, could trust them with fenced cities, which he took care to have well victualled, that they might stand him in stead in case of an invasion. Thus he that acted foolishly at first acted wisely afterwards in his affairs. After-wisdom is better than none at all; nay, they say, "Wit is never good till it is bought;" though his was dearly bought with the loss of a kingdom.

CHAP. XII.

This chapter gives us a more full account of the reign of Rehoboam than we had before in Kings and it is a very melancholy account. Methinks we are in the book of Judges again; for, I. Rehoboam and his people did evil in the sight of the Lord, ver. 1. II. God thereupon sold them into the hands of Shishak, king of Egypt, who greatly oppressed them, ver. 2—4. III. God sent a prophet to them, to expound to them the judgment and to call them to repentance, ver. 5. IV. They thereupon humbled themselves, ver. 6. V. God, upon their repentance, turned from his anger (ver. 7, 12) and yet left them under the marks of his displeasure, ver. 8—11. Lastly, Here is a general character of Rehoboam and his reign, with the conclusion of it, ver. 13—16.

AND it came to pass, when Rehoboam had established the kingdom, and had strengthened himself, he forsook the law of the LORD, and all Israel with him. 2 And it came to pass, *that* in the fifth year of king Rehoboam Shishak king of Egypt came up against Jerusalem, because they had transgressed against the LORD, 3 With twelve hundred chariots, and threescore thousand horsemen: and the people *were* without number that came with him out of Egypt; the Lubims, the Sukkiims, and the Ethiopians. 4 And he took the fenced cities which *pertained* to Judah, and came to Jerusalem. 5 Then came Shemaiah the prophet to Rehoboam, and *to* the princes of Judah, that were gathered together to Jerusalem because of Shishak, and said unto them, Thus saith the LORD, Ye have forsaken me, and therefore have I also left you in the hand of Shishak. 6 Whereupon the princes of Israel and the king humbled themselves; and they said, The LORD *is* righteous. 7 And when the LORD saw that they humbled themselves, the word of the LORD came to Shemaiah, saying, They have humbled themselves; *therefore* I will not destroy them, but I will grant them some deliverance; and my wrath shall not be poured out upon Jerusalem by the hand of Shishak. 8 Nevertheless they shall be his servants; that they may know my service, and the service of the kingdoms of the countries. 9 So Shishak king of Egypt came up against Jerusalem, and took away the treasures of the house of the LORD, and the treasures of the king's house; he took all: he carried away also the shields of gold which Solomon had made. 10 Instead of which king Rehoboam made shields of brass, and committed *them* to the hands of the chief of the guard, that kept the entrance of the king's house. 11 And when the king entered into the house of the LORD, the guard came and fetched them, and brought them again into the guard-chamber. 12 And when he humbled himself, the wrath of the LORD turned from him, that he would not destroy *him* altogether: and also in Judah things went well.

Israel was very much disgraced and weakened by being divided into two kingdoms; yet the kingdom of Judah, having both the temple and the royal city, both the house of David and the house of Aaron, might have done very well if they had continued in the way of their duty; but here we have all out of order there.

I. Rehoboam and his people left God: He *forsook the law of the Lord,* and so in effect forsook God, and *all Israel with him,* *v.* 1. He had his happy triennium, when he walked in the way of David and Solomon (*ch.* xi. 17), but it expired, and he grew remiss in the worship of God; in what instances we are not told, but he fell off, and Judah with him, here called *Israel,* because they walked in the evil ways into which Jeroboam had drawn the kingdom of Israel. Thus he did *when he had established the kingdom and strengthened himself.* As long as he thought his throne tottered he kept to his duty, that he might make God his friend; but, when he found it stood pretty firmly, he thought he had no more occasion for religion; he was safe enough without it. Thus *the prosperity of fools destroys them. Jeshurun waxed fat and kicked.* When men prosper, and are in no apprehension of troubles, they are ready to say to God, *Depart from us.*

II. God quickly brought troubles upon them, to awaken them, and recover them to repentance, before their hearts were hardened. It was but in the fourth year of Rehoboam that they began to corrupt themselves, and in the fifth year the king of Egypt came up against them with a vast army, took *the fenced cities of Judah, and came against Jerusalem, v.* 2, 3, 4. This great calamity coming upon them so soon after they began to desert the worship of God, by a hand they had little reason to suspect (having had a great deal of friendly correspondence with Egypt in the last reign), and coming with so much violence that all the *fenced cities of Judah,* which Rehoboam had lately fortified and garrisoned and on which he relied much for the safety of his kingdom, fell immediately into the hands of the enemy, without making any resistance, plainly showed that it was from the Lord, because they had transgressed against him.

III. Lest they should not readily or not rightly understand the meaning of this providence, God by the word explains the rod, *v.* 5. When the princes of Judah had all met at Jerusalem, probably in a great council of war, to concert measures for their own safety in this critical juncture, he sent a prophet to them, the same that had brought them an injunction from God not to fight against the ten tribes (*ch.* xi. 2), Shemaiah by name; he told them plainly that the reason why Shishak prevailed against them was not because they had been impolitic in the management of their affairs (which perhaps the princes in this congress were at this time scrutinizing), but because they had forsaken God. God never leaves any till they first leave him.

IV. The rebukes both of the word and of the rod being thus joined, the king and princes humbled themselves before God for their iniquity, penitently acknowledged the sin, and patiently accepted the punishment of it, saying, *The Lord is righteous, v.* 6. "We have none to blame but ourselves; let God be clear when he judgeth." Thus it becomes us, when we are under the rebukes of Providence, to justify God and judge ourselves. Even kings and princes must either bend or break before God, either be humbled or be ruined.

V. Upon the profession they made of repentance God showed them some favour, saved them from ruin, and yet left them under some remaining fears of the judgment, to prevent their revolt again.

1. God, in mercy, prevented the destruction they were now upon the brink of. Such a vast and now victorious army as Shishak had, having made themselves masters of all the fenced cities, what could be expected but that the whole country, and even Jerusalem itself, would in a little time be theirs? But when God saith, *Here shall the proud waves be stayed,* the most threatening force strangely dwindles and becomes impotent. Here again the destroying angel, when he comes to Jerusalem, is forbidden to destroy it: "*My wrath shall not be poured out upon Jerusalem*; not at this time, not by this hand, not utterly to destroy it," *v.* 7, 12. Note, Those that acknowledge God righteous in afflicting them shall find him gracious. Those that humble themselves before him shall find favour with him. So ready is the God of mercy to take the first occasion to show mercy. If we have humbled hearts under humbling providences, the affliction has done its work, and it shall either be removed or the property of it altered.

2. He granted them some deliverance, not complete, but in part; he gave them some advantages against the enemy, so that they recruited a little; he *gave them deliverance for a little while,* so some. They reformed but partially, and for a little while, soon relapsing again; and, as their reformation was, so was their deliverance. Yet it is said (*v.* 12), *in Judah things went well,* and began to

look with a better face. (1.) In respect of piety. *There were good things in Judah* (so it is in the margin), good ministers, good people, good families, who were made better by the calamities of their country. Note, In times of great corruption and degeneracy it is some comfort if there be a remnant among whom good things are found; this is a ground of hope in Israel. (2.) In respect of prosperity. In Judah things went ill when all the fenced cities were taken (*v.* 4), but when they repented the posture of their affairs altered, and things went well. Note, If things do not go so well as we could wish, yet we have reason to take notice of it with thankfulness if they go better than was to have been expected, better than formerly, and better than we deserved. We should own God's goodness if he do but grant us some deliverance.

3. Yet he left them to smart sorely by the hand of Shishak, both in their liberty and in their wealth.

(1.) In their liberty (*v.* 8): *They shall be his servants* (that is, they shall lie much at his mercy and be put under contribution by him, and some of them perhaps be taken prisoners and held in captivity by him), *that they may know my service, and the service of the kingdoms of the countries.* They complained, it may be, of the strictness of their religion, and *forsook the law of the Lord* (*v.* 1) because they thought it a yoke too hard, too heavy, upon them. "Well," saith God, "let them better themselves if they can; let the neighbouring princes rule them awhile, since they are not willing that I should rule them, and let them try how they like that. They might have *served God with joyfulness and gladness of heart,* and would not; let them *serve their enemies then in hunger and thirst* (Deut. xxviii. 47, 48), till they think of returning to *their first Master, for then it was better with them,*" Hos. ii. 7. This, some think, is the meaning of Ezek. xx. 24, 25: *Because they despised my statutes, I gave them statutes that were not good.* Note, [1.] The more God's service is compared with other services the more reasonable and easy it will appear. [2.] Whatever difficulties or hardships we may imagine there are in the way of obedience, it is better a thousand times to go through them than to expose ourselves to the punishment of disobedience. Are the laws of temperance thought hard? The effects of intemperance will be much harder. The service of virtue is perfect liberty; the service of lust is perfect slavery.

(2.) In their wealth. The king of Egypt plundered both the temple and the exchequer, the treasuries of both which Solomon left very full; but he *took them away;* yea, he *took all,* all he could lay his hands on, *v.* 9. This was what he came for. David and Solomon, who walked in the way of God, filled the treasuries, one by war and the other by merchandise; but Rehoboam, who forsook the law of God, emptied them. The taking away of the golden shields, and the substituting of brazen ones in their place (*v.* 9—11), we had an account of before, 1 Kings xiv. 25—28.

13 So king Rehoboam strengthened himself in Jerusalem, and reigned: for Rehoboam *was* one and forty years old when he began to reign, and he reigned seventeen years in Jerusalem, the city which the LORD had chosen out of all the tribes of Israel, to put his name there. And his mother's name *was* Naamah an Ammonitess. 14 And he did evil, because he prepared not his heart to seek the LORD. 15 Now the acts of Rehoboam, first and last, *are* they not written in the book of Shemaiah the prophet, and of Iddo the seer concerning genealogies? And *there were* wars between Rehoboam and Jeroboam continually. 16 And Rehoboam slept with his fathers, and was buried in the city of David: and Abijah his son reigned in his stead.

The story of Rehoboam's reign is here concluded, much as the story of the other reigns concludes. Two things especially are observable here:—1. That he was at length pretty well *fixed in his kingdom, v.* 13. His fenced cities in Judah did not answer his expectation, so he now *strengthened himself in Jerusalem,* which he made it his business to fortify, and there he reigned seventeen years, in *the city which the Lord had chosen to put his name there.* This intimates his honour and privilege, that he had his royal seat in the holy city, which yet was but an aggravation of his impiety—near the temple, but far from God. Frequent skirmishes there were between his subjects and Jeroboam's, such as amounted to *continual wars,* (*v.* 15), but he held his own, and reigned, and, as it should seem, did not so grossly *forsake the law of God* as he had done (*v.* 1) in his fourth year. 2. That he was never rightly fixed in his religion, *v.* 14. He never quite cast off God; and yet in this he did evil, that he *prepared not, he engaged not, his heart to seek the Lord.* See what the fault is laid upon. (1.) He did not serve the Lord because he did not seek the Lord. He did not pray, as Solomon did, for wisdom and grace. If we prayed better, we should be every way better. Or he did not consult the word of God, did not seek to that as his oracle, nor take directions from it. (2.) He made nothing of his religion because he did not set his heart to it, never minded it with any closeness of application, and never any hearty disposition to it, nor ever came up to a steady resolution in it. What little goodness he had was transient and passed away like the morning cloud. He did evil because he was never determined for that which is good. Those are easily drawn by Satan to any evil who are wavering and inconstant in that which is good and are never persuaded to make religion their business.

CHAP. XIII.

We have here a much fuller account of the reign of Abijah, the son of Rehoboam, than we had in the Kings. There we found that his character was no better than his father's: he "walked in the sins of his father, and his heart was not right with God," 1 Kings xv. 2, 3. But here we find him more brave and successful in war than his father was. He reigned but three years, and was chiefly famous for a glorious victory he obtained over the forces of Jeroboam. Here we have, I. The armies brought into the field on both sides, ver. 3. The remonstrance which Abijah made before the battle, setting forth the justice of his cause, ver. 4—12. III. The distress which Judah was brought into by the policy of Jeroboam, ver. 13, 14. IV. The victory they obtained notwithstanding, by the power of God, ver. 15—20. V. The conclusion of Abijah's reign, ver. 21, 22.

NOW in the eighteenth year of king Jeroboam began Abijah to reign over Judah. 2 He reigned three years in Jerusalem. His mother's name also *was* Michaiah the daughter of Uriel of Gibeah. And there was war between Abijah and Jeroboam. 3 And Abijah set the battle in array with an army of valiant men of war, *even* four hundred thousand chosen men: Jeroboam also set the battle in array against him with eight hundred thousand chosen men, *being* mighty men of valour. 4 And Abijah stood up upon mount Zemaraim, which *is* in mount Ephraim, and said, Hear me, thou Jeroboam, and all Israel; 5 Ought ye not to know that the LORD God of Israel gave the kingdom over Israel to David for ever, *even* to him and to his sons by a covenant of salt? 6 Yet Jeroboam the son of Nebat, the servant of Solomon the son of David, is risen up, and hath rebelled against his lord. 7 And there are gathered unto him vain men, the children of Belial, and have strengthened themselves against Rehoboam the son of Solomon, when Rehoboam was young and tenderhearted, and could not withstand them. 8 And now ye think to withstand the kingdom of the LORD in the hand of the sons of David; and ye *be* a great multitude, and *there are* with you golden calves, which Jeroboam made you for gods. 9 Have ye not cast out the priests of the LORD, the sons of Aaron, and the Levites, and have made you priests after the manner of the nations of *other* lands? so that whosoever cometh to consecrate himself with a young bullock and seven rams, *the same* may be a priest of *them that are* no gods. 10 But as for us, the LORD *is* our God, and we have not forsaken him; and the priests, which minister unto the LORD, *are* the sons of Aaron, and the Levites *wait* upon *their* business: 11 And they burn unto the LORD every morning and every evening burnt sacrifices and sweet incense: the showbread also *set they in order* upon the pure table; and the candlestick of gold with the lamps thereof, to burn every evening: for we keep the charge of the LORD our God; but ye have forsaken him. 12 And, behold, God himself *is* with us for *our* captain, and his priests with sounding trumpets to cry alarm against you. O children of Israel, fight ye not against the LORD God of your fathers; for ye shall not prosper.

Abijah's mother was called *Maachah,* the daughter of Absalom, *ch.* xi. 20; here she is called *Michaiah,* the daughter of Uriel. It is most probable that she was a granddaughter of Absalom, by his daughter Tamar (2 Sam. xiv. 27), and that her immediate father was this Uriel. But we are here to attend Abijah into the field of battle with Jeroboam king of Israel.

I. God gave him leave to engage with Jeroboam, and owned him in the conflict, though he would not permit Rehoboam to do it, *ch.* xi. 4. 1. Jeroboam, it is probable, was now the aggressor, and what Abijah did was in his own necessary defence. Jeroboam, it may be, happening to survive Rehoboam, claimed the crown of Judah be survivorship, at least hoped to get it from this young king, upon his accession to the throne. Against these impudent pretensions it was brave in Abijah to take up arms, and God stood by him. 2. When Rehoboam attempted to recover his ten tribes Jeroboam was upon his good behaviour, and there must be some trial of him; but now that he had discovered what manner of man he was, by setting up the calves and casting off the priests, Abijah is allowed to chastise him, and it does not appear that he intended any more; whereas Rehoboam aimed at no less than the utter reduction of the ten tribes, which was contrary to the counsel of God.

II. Jeroboam's army was double in number to that of Abijah (*v.* 3), for he had ten tribes to raise an army out of, while Abijah had but two. Of the army on both sides it is said, they were *mighty men, chosen men,* and *valiant;* but the army of Judah consisted only of 400,000, while Jeroboam's army amounted to 800,000. The inferior number however proved victorious; for the battle is not always to the strong nor the cause to the majority.

III. Abijah, before he fought them, reasoned with them, to persuade them, though not to return to the house of David (that matter was settled by the divine determination and he acquiesced), yet to desist from fighting against the house of David. He would not have them *withstand the kingdom of the Lord in the hands of the sons of David* (*v.* 8), but at least to be content with what they had. Note, It is good to try reason before we use force. If the point may be gained by dint of argument, better so than by dint of sword. We must never fly to violent methods till all the arts of persuasion have been tried in vain. War must be the *ultima ratio regum—the last resort of kings.* Fair reasoning may do a great deal of good and prevent a great deal of mischief. *How forcible are right words!* Abijah had got with his army into the heart of their country; for he made this speech upon a hill in Mount Ephraim, where he might be heard by Jeroboam and the principal officers, with whom it is probable he desired to have a treaty, to which they consented. It has been usual for great generals to make speeches to their soldiers to animate them, and this speech of Abijah had some tendency to do this, but was directed to Jeroboam and all Israel. Two things Abijah undertakes to make out, for the satisfaction of his own men and the conviction of the enemy:—

1. That he had right on his side, a *jus divinum—a divine right:* "You know, or ought to know, that *God gave the kingdom to David and his sons for ever*" (*v.* 5), not by common providence, his usual way of disposing of kingdoms, but by a covenant of salt, a lasting covenant, a covenant made by sacrifice, which was always salted; so bishop Patrick. All Israel had owned that David was a king of God's making, and that God had entailed the crown upon his family; so that Jeroboam's taking the crown of Israel at first was not justifiable: yet it is not certain that Abijah referred chiefly to that, for he knew that Jeroboam had a grant from God of the ten tribes. His attempt, however, to disturb the peace and possession of the king of Judah was by no means excusable; for when the ten tribes were given to him two were reserved for the house of David. Abijah shows, (1.) That there was a great deal of dishonesty and disingenuousness in Jeroboam's first setting himself up: He *rebelled against his lord* (*v.* 6) who had preferred him (1 Kings xi. 28), and basely took advantage of Rehoboam's weakness in a critical juncture, when, in gratitude to his old master and in justice to his title, he ought rather to have stood by him, and helped to secure the people in their allegiance to him, than to head a party against him and make a prey of him, which was unworthily done and what he could not expect to prosper in. Those that supported him are here called *vain men* (a character perhaps borrowed from Judg. xi. 3), men that did not act from any steady principle, but were given to change, and men of Belial, that were for shaking off the yoke of government and setting those over them that would do just as they would have them do. (2.) That there was a great deal of impiety in his present attempt; for, in fighting against the house of David, he fought *against the kingdom of the Lord.* Those who oppose right oppose the righteous God who sits in the throne judging right, and cannot promise themselves success in so doing. Right may indeed go by the worst for a time, but it will prevail at last.

2. That he had God on his side. This he insisted much upon, that the religion of Jeroboam and his army was false and idolatrous, but that he and his people, the men of Judah, had the pure worship of the true and living God among them. It appears from the character given of Abijah (1 Kings xv. 3) that he was not himself truly religious, and yet here he encouraged himself in this war chiefly from the religion of his kingdom. For, (1.) Whatever he was otherwise, it should seem that he was no idolater, or, if he connived at the high places and images (*ch.* xiv. 3, 5), yet he constantly kept up the temple-service. (2.) Whatever corruptions there were in the kingdom of Judah, the state of religion among them was better than in the kingdom of Israel, with which they were now contending. (3.) It is common for those that deny the power of godliness to boast of the form of it. (4.) It was the cause of his kingdom that he was pleading; and, though he was not himself so good as he should have been, yet he hoped that, for the sake of the good men and good things that were in Judah, God would now appear for them. Many that have little religion themselves yet have so much sense and grace as to value it in others. See how he describes, [1.] The apostasy of Israel from God. "*You are a great multitude,*" said he, "far superior to us in numbers; but we need not fear you, for you have that among yourselves which is enough to ruin you. For," *First,* "You have calves for your gods (*v.* 8), that are unable to protect and help you and will certainly cause the true and living God to oppose you. Those will be Achans, troublers of your camp." *Secondly,* "You have base men for your priests, *v.* 9. You have cast off the tribe of Levi, and the house of Aaron, whom God appointed to minister in holy things; and, in conformity to the custom of the idolatrous nations, make any man a priest that has a

mind to the office and will be at the charge of the consecration, though ever so much a scandal to the office." Yet such, though very unfit to be priests, were fittest of all to be *their* priests; for what more agreeable to gods that were no gods than priests that were no priests? Like to like, both pretenders and usurpers. [2.] The adherence of Judah to God: "*But as for us* (*v.* 10) *we have not forsaken God.* Jehovah is our God, the God of our fathers, the God of Israel, who is able to protect us, and give us success. He is with us, for we are with him." *First,* "At home in his temple: We *keep his charge, v.* 10, 11. We worship no images, have no priests but what he has ordained, no rites of worship but what he has prescribed. Both the temple service and the temple furniture are of his appointing. His appointment we abide by, and neither add nor diminish. These we have the comfort of, these we now stand up in the defence of: so that upon a religious as well as a civil account we have the better cause. *Secondly,* Here in the camp; he is our captain, and we may therefore be sure that he is with us, because we are with him, *v.* 12. And, as a token of his presence, we have here with us his priests, sounding his trumpets according to the law, as a testimony against you, and an assurance to us that in the day of battle we shall be *remembered before the Lord our God* and *saved from our enemies;*" for so this sacred signal is explained, Num. x. 9. Nothing is more effectual to embolden men, and put spirit into them, than to be sure that God is with them and fights for them. He concludes with fair warning to his enemies. "*Fight not against the God of your fathers.* It is folly to fight against the God of almighty power; but it is treachery and base ingratitude to fight against your fathers' God, and you cannot expect to prosper."

13 But Jeroboam caused an ambushment to come about behind them: so they were before Judah, and the ambushment *was* behind them. 14 And when Judah looked back, behold, the battle *was* before and behind: and they cried unto the LORD, and the priests sounded with the trumpets. 15 Then the men of Judah gave a shout: and as the men of Judah shouted, it came to pass, that God smote Jeroboam and all Israel before Abijah and Judah. 16 And the children of Israel fled before Judah: and God delivered them into their hand. 17 And Abijah and his people slew them with a great slaughter: so there fell down slain of Israel five hundred thousand chosen men. 18 Thus the children of Israel were brought under at that time, and the children of Judah prevailed, because they relied upon the LORD God of their fathers. 19 And Abijah pursued after Jeroboam, and took cities from him, Beth-el with the towns thereof, and Jeshanah with the towns thereof, and Ephrain with the towns thereof. 20 Neither did Jeroboam recover strength again in the days of Abijah: and the LORD struck him, and he died. 21 But Abijah waxed mighty, and married fourteen wives, and begat twenty and two sons, and sixteen daughters. 22 And the rest of the acts of Abijah, and his ways, and his sayings, *are* written in the story of the prophet Iddo.

We do not find that Jeroboam offered to make any answer at all to Abijah's speech. Though it was much to the purpose, he resolved not to heed it, and therefore heard it as though he heard it not. He came to fight, not to dispute. The longest sword, he thought, would determine the matter, not the better cause. Let us therefore see the issue, whether right and religion carried the day or no.

I. Jeroboam, who trusted to his politics, was beaten. He was so far from fair reasoning that he was not for fair fighting. We may suppose that he felt a sovereign contempt for Abijah's harangue. "One stratagem," thinks he, "is worth twenty such speeches; we will soon give him an answer to all his arguments; he shall soon find himself overpowered with numbers, surrounded on every side with the instruments of death, and then let him boast of his religion and his title to the crown." A parley, it is probable, was agreed on, yet Jeroboam basely takes the advantage of it, and, while he was treating, *laid his ambushment behind Judah,* against all the laws of arms. What honour could be expected in a *servant when he reigned?* Abijah was *for peace,* but, *when he spoke, they were for war,* Ps. cxx. 7.

II. Abijah and his people, who trusted in their God, came off conquerors, notwithstanding the disproportion of their strength and numbers.

1. They were brought into a great strait, put into a great fright, for *the battle was before and behind.* A good cause, and one which is designed to be victorious, may for a season be involved in embarrassment and distress. It was David's case. *They compassed me about like bees,* Ps. cxviii. 10—12.

2. In their distress, when danger was on every side, which way should they look but upwards for deliverance? It is an unspeak-

able comfort that no enemy (not the most powerful or politic), no stratagem or ambushment, can cut off our communication with heaven; our way thitherward is always open. (1.) *They cried unto the Lord, v.* 14. We hope they did this before they engaged in this war, but the distress they were in made them renew their prayers and quickened them to be importunate. God brings his people into straits, that he may teach them to *cry unto him.* Earnest praying is crying. (2.) They *relied on the God of their fathers,* depended upon his power to help them and committed themselves to him, *v.* 18. The prayer of faith is the prevailing prayer, and this is that by which we overcome the world, *even our faith,* 1 John v. 4. (3.) The *priests sounded the trumpets* to animate them by giving them an assurance of God's presence with them. It was not only a martial but a sacred sound, and put life into their faith. (4.) They shouted in confidence of victory: "The day is our own, for God is with us." To the cry of prayer they added the shout of faith, and so became more than conquerors.

3. Thus they obtained a complete victory: *As the men of Judah shouted* for joy in God's salvation, *God smote Jeroboam* and his army with such terror and amazement that they could not strike a stroke, but fled with the greatest precipitation imaginable, and the conquerors gave no quarter, so that they put to the sword 500,000 chosen men (*v.* 17), more, it is said, than ever we read of in any history to have been killed in one battle; but the battle was the Lord's, who would thus chastise the idolatry of Israel and own the house of David. But see the sad effect of division: it was the blood of Israelites that was thus shed like water by Israelites, while the heathen, their neighbours, to whom the name of Israel had formerly been a terror, cried, *Aha! so would we have it.*

4. The consequence of this was that the children of Israel, though they were not brought back to the house of David (which by so great a blow surely they would have been had not the determinate counsel of God been otherwise), yet, for that time, were *brought under, v.* 18. Many cities were taken, and remained in the possession of the kings of Judah; as Bethel particularly, *v.* 19. What became of the golden calf there, when it came into the hands of the king of Judah, we are not told; perhaps it was removed to some place of greater safety, and at length to Samaria (Hos. viii. 5); yet in Jehu's time we find it at Bethel, 2 Kings x. 29. Perhaps Abijah, when it was in his power to demolish it, suffered it to stand, for *his heart was not perfect* with God; and, not improving what he had got for the honour of God, he soon lost it all again.

Lastly, The death both of the conquered and of the conqueror, not long after. 1. Jeroboam never looked up after this defeat, though he survived it two or three years. He could not recover *strength again, v.* 20. The Lord struck him either with some bodily disease, of which he languished, or with melancholy and trouble of mind; his heart was broken, and vexation at his loss brought his head, probably by this time a hoary head, with sorrow to the grave. He escaped the sword of Abijah, but God struck him: and there is no escaping his sword. 2. Abijah waxed mighty upon it. What number of wives and children he had before does not appear; but now he multiplied his wives to fourteen in all, by whom he had thirty-eight children, *v.* 21. Happy is the man that hath his quiver full of those arrows. It seems, he had ways peculiar to himself, and sayings of his own, which were recorded with his acts in the history of those times, *v.* 22. But the number of his months was cut off in the midst, and, soon after his triumphs, death conquered the conqueror. Perhaps he was too much lifted up with his victories, and therefore God would not let him live long to enjoy the honour of them.

CHAP. XIV.

In this and the two following chapters we have the history of the reign of Asa, a good reign and a long one. In this chapter we have, I. His piety, ver. 1—5. II. His policy, ver. 6—8. III. His prosperity, and particularly a glorious victory he obtained over a great army of Ethiopians that came out against him, ver. 9—15.

SO Abijah slept with his fathers, and they buried him in the city of David: and Asa his son reigned in his stead. In his days the land was quiet ten years. 2 And Asa did *that which was* good and right in the eyes of the LORD his God: 3 For he took away the altars of the strange *gods,* and the high places, and brake down the images, and cut down the groves: 4 And commanded Judah to seek the LORD God of their fathers, and to do the law and the commandment. 5 Also he took away out of all the cities of Judah the high places and the images: and the kingdom was quiet before him. 6 And he built fenced cities in Judah: for the land had rest, and he had no war in those years; because the LORD had given him rest. 7 Therefore he said unto Judah, Let us build these cities, and make about *them* walls, and towers, gates, and bars, *while* the land *is* yet before us; because we have sought the LORD our God, we have sought *him,* and he hath given us rest on every side. So they built and prospered. 8 And Asa had an army *of men* that bare targets and spears, out of Judah three hundred thousand;

and out of Benjamin, that bare shields and drew bows, two hundred and fourscore thousand: all these *were* mighty men of valour.

Here is, I. Asa's general character (*v.* 2): He did *that which was good and right in the eyes of the Lord his God.* 1. He aimed at pleasing God, studied to approve himself to him. Happy are those that walk by this rule, to do that which is right, not in their own eyes, or in the eye of the world, but in the eyes of God. 2. He saw God's eye always upon him, and that helped much to keep him to what was good and right. 3. God graciously accepted him in what he did, and approved his conduct as good and right.

II. A blessed work of reformation which he set on foot immediately upon his accession to the crown. 1. He removed and abolished idolatry. Since Solomon admitted idolatry, in the latter end of his reign, nothing had been done to suppress it, and so, we presume, it had got ground. Strange gods were worshipped and had their altars, images, and groves; and the temple service, though kept up by the priests (*ch.* xiii. 10), was neglected by many of the people. Asa, as soon as he had power in his hands, made it his business to destroy all those idolatrous altars and images (*v.* 3, 5), they being a great provocation to a jealous God and a great temptation to a careless unthinking people. He hoped by destroying the idols to reform the idolaters, which he aimed at, rather than to ruin them. 2. He revived and established the pure worship of God; and, since the priests did their part in attending God's altars, he obliged the people to do theirs (*v.* 4): *He commanded Judah to seek the Lord God of their fathers,* and not the gods of the heathen, and *to do the law and the commandments,* that is, to observe all divine institutions, which many had utterly neglected. In doing this, *the land was quiet before him, v.* 5. Though they were much in love with their idols, and very loth to leave them, yet the convictions of their consciences sided with the commands of Asa, and they could not, for shame, refuse to comply with them. Note, Those that have power in their hands, and will use it vigorously for the suppression of profaneness and the reformation of manners, will not meet with so much difficulty and opposition therein as perhaps they feared. Vice is a sneaking thing, and virtue has reason enough on its side to make *all iniquity stop her mouth,* Ps. cvii. 42.

III. The tranquillity of his kingdom, after constant alarms of war during the last two reigns: *In his days the land was quiet ten years* (*v.* 1), no war with the kingdom of Israel, who did not recover the blow given them in the last reign for a great while. Abijah's victory, which was owing, under God, to his courage and bravery, laid a foundation for Asa's peace, which was the reward of his piety and reformation. Though Abijah had little religion himself, he was instrumental to prepare the way for one that had much. If Abijah had not done what he did to quiet the land, Asa could not have done what he did to reform it; for *inter arma silent leges—amidst the din of arms the voice of law is unheard.*

IV. The prudent improvement he made of that tranquillity: *The land had rest, for the Lord had given him rest.* Note, *If God give quietness, who then can make trouble?* Job xxxiv. 29. Those have rest indeed to whom God gives rest, peace indeed to whom Christ gives peace, *not as the world giveth,* John xiv. 27. Now, 1. Asa takes notice of the rest they had as the gift of God (*He hath given us rest on every side.* Note, God must be acknowledged with thankfulness in the rest we are blessed with, of body and mind, family and country), and as the reward of the reformation begun: *Because we have sought the Lord our God, he has given us rest.* Note, As the frowns and rebukes of Providence should be observed for a check to us in an evil way, so the smiles of Providence should be taken notice of for our encouragement in that which is good. See Hag. ii. 18, 19; Mal. iii. 10. We find by experience that it is good to *seek the Lord;* it *gives us rest.* While we pursue the world we meet with nothing but vexation. 2. He consults with his people, by their representatives, how to make a good use of the present gleams of peace they enjoyed, and concludes with them, (1.) That they must not be idle, but busy. Times of rest from war should be employed in work, for we must always find ourselves something to do, In the years when he had no war he said, "Let us build; still let us be doing." When the *churches had rest* they were *built up,* Acts ix. 31. When the sword is sheathed take up the trowel. (2.) That they must not be secure, but prepare for wars. In times of peace we must be getting ready for trouble, expect it and lay up in store for it. [1.] He fortified his principal cities with *walls, towers, gates, and bars, v.* 7. "This let us do," says he, "*while the land is yet before us,*" that is, "while we have opportunity and advantage for it and have nothing to hinder us." He speaks as if he expected that, some way or other, trouble would arise, when it would be too late to fortify, and when they would wish they had done it. *So they built and prospered.* [2.] He had a good army ready to bring into the field (*v.* 8), not a standing army, but the militia or trained-bands of the country. Judah and Benjamin were mustered severally; and Benjamin (which not long ago was called *little Benjamin,* Ps. lxviii. 27) had almost as many soldiers as Judah, came as near as 28 to 30, so strangely had that tribe increased of late. The blessing of God can make *a little one to become a thousand.* It should seem, these two tribes were differently armed, both offensively and defensively. The men of Judah guarded themselves with targets, the men of Benjamin with shields, the former of which were much larger than the latter, 1 Kings x. 16, 17. The men of Judah fought with spears when they closed in with the enemy; the men of Benjamin drew bows, to reach the enemy at a distance. Both did good service, and neither could say to the other, I have *no need of thee.* Different gifts and employments are for the common good.

9 And there came out against them Zerah the Ethiopian with a host of a thousand thousand, and three hundred chariots; and came unto Mareshah. 10 Then Asa went out against him, and they set the battle in array in the valley of Zephathah at Mareshah. 11 And Asa cried unto the LORD his God, and said, LORD, *it is* nothing with thee to help, whether with many, or with them that have no power: help us, O LORD our God; for we rest on thee, and in thy name we go against this multitude. O LORD, thou *art* our God; let not man prevail against thee. 12 So the LORD smote the Ethiopians before Asa, and before Judah; and the Ethiopians fled. 13 And Asa and the people that *were* with him pursued them unto Gerar: and the Ethiopians were overthrown, that they could not recover themselves; for they were destroyed before the LORD, and before his host; and they carried away very much spoil. 14 And they smote all the cities round about Gerar; for the fear of the LORD came upon them: and they spoiled all the cities; for there was exceeding much spoil in them. 15 They smote also the tents of cattle, and carried away sheep and camels in abundance, and returned to Jerusalem.

Here is, I. Disturbance given to the peace of Asa's kingdom by a formidable army of Ethiopians that invaded them, *v.* 9, 10. Though still they sought God, yet this fear came upon them, that their faith in God might be tried, and that God might have an opportunity of doing great things for them. It was a vast number that the Ethiopians brought against him: 1,000,000 *men;* and now he found the benefit of having an army ready raised against such a time of need. That provision which we thought needless may soon appear to be of great advantage.

II. The application Asa made to God on occasion of the threatening cloud which now hung over his head. *v.* 11. He that sought God in the day of his peace and prosperity could with holy boldness cry to God in the day of his trouble, and call him *his God.* His prayer is short, but has much in it. 1. He gives to God the glory of his infinite power and sovereignty: *It is nothing with thee to help* and save by many or few, by those that are mighty or by *those that have no power.* See 1 Sam. xiv. 6. God works in his own strength, not in the strength of instruments (Ps. xxi. 13), nay, it is his glory to *help the weakest* and to *perfect strength out of the mouth of babes and sucklings.* "We do not say, Lord, take our part, for we have a good army for thee to work by; but, take our part, for without thee we have no power." 2. He takes hold of their covenant-relation to God as theirs. *O Lord our God!* and again, "*Thou art our God,* whom we have chosen and cleave to as ours, and who hast promised to be ours." 3. He pleads their dependence upon God, and the eye they had to him in this expedition. He was well prepared for it, yet trusted not to his preparations; but, "Lord, *we rest on thee, and in thy name we go against this multitude,* by warrant from thee, aiming at thy glory, and trusting to thy strength." 4. He interests God in their cause: "*Let not man" (mortal man,* so the word is) "*prevail against thee.* If he prevail against us, it will be said that he prevails against thee, because thou art our God, and we rest on thee and go forth in thy name, which thou hast encouraged us to do. The enemy is a mortal man; make it to appear what an unequal match he is for an immortal God. Lord, maintain thy own honour; *hallowed be thy name.*"

III. The glorious victory God gave him over his enemies. 1. God defeated the enemy, and put their forces into disorder (*v.* 12): *The Lord smote the Ethiopians,* smote them with terror, and an unaccountable consternation, so that they fled, and knew neither why nor whither. 2. Asa and his soldiers took the advantage God gave them against the enemy. (1.) They destroyed them. They fell *before the Lord* (for who can stand before him?) and before his host, either an invisible host of angels that were employed to destroy them or the host of Israel, called *God's host* because owned by him. (2.) They took the plunder of their camp, *carried away very much spoil* from the slain and from the baggage. (3.) They *smote the cities* that were in league with them, to which they fled for shelter, and carried off the spoil of them (*v.* 14); andthey were not able to make any resistance, *for the fear of the Lord came upon them,* that is, a fear which God struck them with, to such a degree that they had no heart to withstand the conquerors. (4.) They fetched away the cattle out of the enemy's country, in vast numbers, *v.* 15. Thus the wealth of the sinner is laid up for the just.

CHAP. XV.

Asa and his army were now returning in triumph from the battle, laden with spoils and adorned with the trophies of victory, the pious prince, we may now suppose, studying what he should render to God for this great favour. He knew that the work of reformation, which he had begun in his kingdom, was not perfected; his enemies abroad were subdued, but there were more dangerous enemies at home that were yet unconquered—idols in Judah and Benjamin: his victory over the former emboldened him vigorously to renew his attack upon the latter. Now here we have, I. The message which God sent to him, by a prophet, to engage him to, and encourage him in, the prosecution of his reformation, ver. 1—7. II. The life which this message put into that good cause, and their proceedings in pursuance of it. Idols removed, ver. 8. The spoil dedicated to God, ver. 9—11. A covenant made with God, and a law for the punishing of idolaters, ver. 12—15. A reformation at court, ver. 16. Dedicated things brought into the house of God, ver. 18. All well, but that the high places were permitted, ver. 17. And the effect of this was great peace, ver 19.

AND the Spirit of God came upon Azariah the son of Oded: 2 And he went out to meet Asa, and said unto him, Hear ye me, Asa, and all Judah and Benjamin; The LORD *is* with you, while ye be with him; and if ye seek him, he will be found of you; but if ye forsake him, he will forsake you. 3 Now for a long season Israel *hath been* without the true God, and without a teaching priest, and without law. 4 But when they in their trouble did turn unto the LORD God of Israel, and sought him, he was found of them. 5 And in those times *there was* no peace to him that went out, nor to him that came in, but great vexations *were* upon all the inhabitants of the countries. 6 And nation was destroyed of nation, and city of city: for God did vex them with all adversity. 7 Be ye strong therefore, and let not your hands be weak: for your work shall be rewarded.

It was a great happiness to Israel that they had prophets among them; yet, while they were thus blessed, they were strangely addicted to idolatry, whereas, when the spirit of prophecy had ceased under the second temple, and the canon of the Old Testament was completed (which was constantly read in their synagogues), they were pure from idolatry; for the scriptures are of all other the *most sure word of prophecy*, and most effectual, and the church could not be so easily imposed upon by a counterfeit Bible as by a counterfeit prophet. Here was a prophet sent to Asa and his army, when they returned victorious from the war with the Ethiopians, not to compliment them and congratulate them on their success, but to quicken them to their duty; this is the proper business of God's ministers, even with princes and the greatest of men. The *Spirit of God came* upon the prophet (*v.* 1), both to instruct him what he should say and to enable him to say it with clearness and boldness.

I. He told them plainly upon what terms they stood with God. Let them not think that, having obtained this victory, all was their own for ever; no, he must let them know they were upon their good behaviour. Let them do well, and it will be well with them, otherwise not. 1. *The Lord is with you while you are with him.* This is both a word of comfort, that those who keep close to God shall always have his presence with them, and also a word of caution: "He is *with you, while you are with him*, but no longer; you have now a signal token of his favourable presence with you, but the continuance of it depends upon your perseverance in the way of your duty." 2. "*If you seek him, he will be found of you.* Sincerely desire his favour, and aim at it, and you shall obtain it. Pray, and you shall prevail. He never said, nor ever will, *Seek you me in vain.*" See Heb. xi. 6. But, 3. "If you forsake him and his ordinances, he is not tied to you, but will certainly forsake you, and then you are undone, your present triumphs will be no security to you; woe to you when God departs."

II. He set before them the dangerous consequence of forsaking God and his ordinances, and that there was no way of having grievances redressed, but by repenting, and returning unto God. When Israel forsook their duty they were over-run with a deluge of atheism, impiety, irreligion, and all irregularity (*v.* 3), and were continually embarrassed with vexatious and destroying wars, foreign and domestic, *v.* 5, 6. But when their troubles drove them to God they found it not in vain to seek him, *v.* 4. But the question is, What time does this refer to? 1. Some think it looks as far back as the days of the Judges. A *long season* ago Israel was *without the true God*, for they worshipped false gods; it was a time of ignorance, for, though they had priests, they had no teaching priests, though they had elders, yet no law to any purpose, *v.* 3. These were sad times, when they were frequently oppressed by one enemy or other and grievously harassed by Moabites, Midianites, Ammonites, and other nations. They were *vexed with all adversity* (*v.* 6), yet when, in their perplexity, they turned to God by repentance, prayer, and reformation, he raised up deliverers for them. Then was that maxim often verified, that God is with us while we are with him. Whatsoever things of this kind were written aforetime were written for our admonition. 2. Others think it describes the state of the ten tribes (who were now properly called *Israel)* in the days of Asa. "*Now*, since Jeroboam set up the calves, though he pretended to honour the God that brought them out of Egypt, yet his idolatry has brought them to downright infidelity; they are *without the true God*," and no marvel when they were without teaching priests. Jeroboam's priests were not teachers, and thus they came to be without law. It is next to impossible that any thing of religion should be kept up without a preaching ministry. In those times there was no peace, *v.* 5. Their war with Judah gave them frequent alarms; so did the late insurrection of Baasha and other occasions not mentioned. They provoked God with all iniquity, and then he *vexed them with all adversity;* yet, *when they turned to God,* he was entreated for them. Let Judah take notice of this; let their neighbours' harms be their warnings. Give no countenance to graven images, for you see what mischiefs they produce. 3. Others think the whole passage may be read in the future tense, and that it looks forward: Hereafter *Israel will be without the true God and a teaching priest,* and they will be destroyed by one judgment after another till they *return to God* and *seek him.* See Hos. iii. 4.

III. Upon this he grounded his exhortation to prosecute the work of reformation with vigour (*v.* 7): *Be strong, for your work shall be rewarded.* Note, 1. God's work should be done with diligence and cheerfulness, but will not be done without resolution. 2. This should quicken us to the work of religion, that we shall be sure not to lose by it ultimately. It will not go unrewarded. How should it, when the work is its own reward?

8 And when Asa heard these words, and the prophecy of Oded the prophet, he took courage, and put away the abominable idols out of all the land of Judah and Benjamin, and out of the cities which he had taken from mount Ephraim, and renewed the altar of the LORD, that *was* before the porch of the LORD. 9 And he gathered all Judah and Benjamin, and the strangers with them out of Ephraim and Manasseh, and out of Simeon: for they fell to him out of Israel in abundance, when they saw that the LORD his God *was* with him. 10 So they gathered themselves together at Jerusalem in the third month, in the fifteenth year of the reign of Asa. 11 And they offered unto the LORD the same time, of the spoil *which* they had brought, seven hundred oxen and seven thousand sheep. 12 And they entered into a covenant to seek the LORD God of their fathers with all their heart and with all their soul; 13 That whosoever would not seek the LORD God of Israel should be put to death, whether small or great, whether man or woman. 14 And they sware unto the LORD with a loud voice, and with shouting, and with trumpets, and with cornets. 15 And all Judah rejoiced at the oath: for they had sworn with all their heart, and sought him with their whole desire; and he was found of them: and the LORD gave them rest round about. 16 And also *concerning* Maachah the mother of Asa the king, he removed her from *being* queen, because she had made an idol in a grove: and Asa cut down her idol, and stamped *it,* and burnt *it* at the brook Kidron. 17 But the high places were not taken away out of Israel: nevertheless the heart of Asa was perfect all his days. 18 And he brought into the house of God the things that his father had dedicated, and that he himself had dedicated, silver, and gold, and vessels. 19 And there was no *more* war unto the five and thirtieth year of the reign of Asa.

We are here told what good effect the foregoing sermon had upon Asa.

I. He grew more bold for God than he had been. His victory would inspire him with some new degrees of resolution, but this message from God with much more. Now he took courage. He saw how necessary a further reformation was, and what assurance he had of God's presence with him in it; and this made him daring, and helped him over the difficulties which had before deterred him and driven him off from the undertaking. Now he ventured to destroy all the abominable idols (and all idolatries are abominable, 1 Pet. iv. 3) as far as ever his power went. Away with them all. He also *renewed the altar of the Lord,* which, it seems, had gone out of repair, though it was not above thirty-five years since Solomon's head was laid, who erected it. So soon did these ceremonial institutions begin to wax old, as things which, in the fulness of time, must *vanish away,* Heb. viii. 13.

II. He extended his influence further than before, *v.* 9. He summoned a solemn assembly, and particularly brought the strangers to it, who had come over to him from the ten tribes. 1. Their coming was a great encouragement to him; for the reason of their coming was because *they saw that the Lord his God was with him.* It is good to be with those that have God with them, to come into relation to, and contract acquaintance and friendship with, those that live in the fear and favour of God. *We will go with you, for we have heard that God is with you,* Zech. viii. 23. 2. The cognizance he took of them, and the invitation he gave them to the general assembly, were a great encouragement to them. All strangers are to be helped, but those that cast themselves upon God's good providence, purely to keep a good conscience, are worthy of double honour. Asa gave orders for the gathering of them together (*v.* 9), yet it is said (*v.* 10) that they *gathered themselves together*, made it their own act, so forward were they to obey the king's orders. This meeting was held in the third month, probably at the feast of Pentecost, which was in that month.

III. He and his people offered sacrifices to God, as his share of the spoil they had got, *v.* 11. Their offering here was nothing to Solomon's (*ch.* vii. 5), which was owing to the diminution either of their zeal or of their wealth, or of both. These sacrifices were intended by way of thanksgiving for the favours they had received, and supplication for further favours. Prayers and praises are now our spiritual sacrifices. And, as he took care that the altar should have its gift, so he took care that the temple should have its gold: *He brought into the house of God all the dedicated things, v.* 18. It is honesty to render to God the things that are his. What has been long designed for him, and long laid by for him, as it should seem these dedicated things had been, should at length be laid out for him. Will a man rob God, or make slow payment to him, who is always ready to do us good?

IV. *They entered into covenant with God*, repenting that they had violated their engagements to him and resolving to do better for the future. It is proper for penitents, for converts, to renew their covenants. It should seem, the motion came not from Asa, but from the people themselves. Let every man be a volunteer that covenants with God. *Thy people shall be willing*, Ps. cx. 3. Observe,

1. What was the matter of this covenant. Nothing but what they were before obliged to; and, though no vow or promise of theirs could lay any higher obligation upon them than they were already under from the divine precept, yet it would help to increase their sense of the obligation, to arm them against temptations, and would be a testimony to the equity and goodness of the precept. And, by joining all together in this covenant, they strengthened the hands one of another. Two things they engaged themselves to:—(1.) That they would diligently seek God themselves, seek his precepts, seek his favour. What is religion but seeking God, enquiring after him, applying to him, upon all occasions? We shall not enjoy him till we come to heaven; while we are here we must continue seeking. They would seek God as the *God of their fathers*, in the way that their fathers sought him and in dependence upon the promise made to their fathers; and they would do it *with all their heart* and *with all their soul*, for those only seek God acceptably and successfully that are inward with him, intent upon him, and entire for him, in their seeking him. We make nothing of our religion if we do not make heart-work of it. God will have all the heart or none; and, when a jewel of such inestimable value as the divine favour is to be found, it is worth while to seek it *with all our soul.* (2.) That they would, to the utmost of their power, oblige others to seek him, *v.* 13. They agreed that *whosoever would not seek the Lord God of Israel* (that is, would either worship other gods or refuse to join with them in the worship of the true God, that was either an obstinate idolater or an obstinate atheist) he should be put to death. This was no new law of their own making, but an order to put in execution that law of God to this purport, Deut. xvii. 2, &c. If this law had been duly executed, there would not have been so many abominable idols found in Judah and Benjamin, *v.* 8. Whether men may now, under the gospel, be compelled by such methods as these to seek the Lord is justly questioned; for the weapons of our warfare are not carnal, and yet mighty.

2. In what manner they made this covenant. (1.) With great cheerfulness, and all possible expressions of joy: *They swore unto the Lord;* not secretly, as if they were either ashamed of what they did or afraid of binding themselves too fast to him, but with a loud voice, to express their own zeal and to animate one another; and they all rejoiced at the oath, *v.* 14, 15. They did not swear to God with reluctancy (as the poor debtor confesses a judgment to his creditor), but with all the pleasure and satisfaction imaginable, as the bridegroom plights his troth to the bride in the marriage covenant. Every honest Israelite was pleased with his own engagements to God, and they were all pleased with one another's. They rejoiced in it as a hopeful expedient to prevent their apostasy from God and a happy indication of God's presence with them. Note, The times of renewing our covenant with God should be times of rejoicing, and national reformation cannot but give general satisfaction to all that are good. It is an honour and happiness to be in bonds to God. (2.) They did it with great sincerity, zeal, and resolution: *They swore to God with all their hearts,* and *sought him with their whole desire.* The Israelites were now in an extraordinarily good frame. O that there had always been such a heart in them! This comes in as the reason why they rejoiced so much in what they did: it was because they were hearty in it. Note, Those only experience the pleasure and comfort of religion that are sincere and upright in it. What is done in hypocrisy is a mere drudgery. But, if God has the heart, we have the joy.

V. We are told what was the effect of this their solemn covenanting with God. 1. God did well for them: *He was found of them, and gave them rest round about* (*v.* 15), so that there was no war for a long time after (*v.* 19), no open general war, though there were constant bickerings between Judah and Israel upon the frontiers, 1 Kings xv. 16. National piety procures national blessings. 2. They did, on the whole, well for him. They carried on the reformation so far that Maachah the queen-mother was deposed for idolatry and her idol destroyed, *v.* 16. This was bravely done of Asa, that he would not connive at idolatry in those that were nearest to him, like Levi, that *said to his father and mother, I have not seen him,* Deut. xxxiii. 9. Asa knows he must honour God more than his grandmother, and dares not leave an idol in an apartment of his palace while he is destroying idols in the cities of his kingdom. We may suppose this Maachah was so far convinced of her sin that she was willing to subscribe the association mentioned (*v.* 12, 13), binding herself to seek the Lord, and therefore was not put to death as those were that refused to sign it, great as well as small, women as well as men: probably it was with an eye to her that *women* were specified. But because she had been an idolater Asa thought fit to divest her of the dignity and authority she had, and probably he banished her the court and confined her to privacy, lest she should influence and infect others. But the reformation was not complete; the high places were not all taken away, though many of them were, *ch.* xiv. 3, 5. Those in the cities were removed, but not those in the country villages; or those in the cities of Judah, but not those in the cities of Israel which were reduced to the house of David; or those that were used in the service of false gods, but not those that were used in the service of the God of Israel. These he connived at, and yet his heart was perfect. There may be defects in some particular duties where yet the heart, in the main, is upright with God. Sincerity is something less than sinless perfection.

CHAP. XVI.

This chapter concludes the history of the reign of Asa, but does not furnish so pleasing an account of his latter end as we had of his beginning. I. Here is a foolish treaty with Benhadad king of Syria, ver. 1—6. II. The reproof which God sent him for it by a prophet, ver. 7—9. III. Asa's displeasure against the prophet for his faithfulness, ver. 10. IV. The sickness, death, and burial of Asa, ver. 11—14.

IN the six and thirtieth year of the reign of Asa Baasha king of Israel came up against Judah, and built Ramah, to the intent that he might let none go out or come in to Asa king of Judah. 2 Then Asa brought out silver and gold out of the treasures of the house of the LORD and of the king's house, and sent to Benhadad king of Syria, that dwelt at Damascus, saying, 3 *There is* a league between me and thee, as *there was* between my father and thy father: behold, I have sent thee silver and gold; go, break thy league with Baasha king of Israel, that he may depart from me. 4 And Ben-hadad hearkened unto king Asa, and sent the captains of his armies against the cities of Israel; and they smote Ijon, and Dan, and Abel-maim, and all the store cities of Naphtali. 5 And it came to pass, when Baasha heard *it,* that he left off building of Ramah, and let his work cease. 6 Then Asa the king took all Judah; and they carried away the stones of Ramah, and the timber thereof, wherewith Baasha was building; and he built therewith Geba and Mizpah.

How to reconcile the date of this event with the history of the kings I am quite at a loss. Baasha died in the twenty-sixth year of Asa, 1 Kings xvi. 8. How then could this be done in his thirty-sixth year, when Baasha's family was quite cut off, and Omri was upon the throne? It is generally said to be meant of the thirty-sixth year of the kingdom of Asa, namely, that of Judah, beginning from the first of Rehoboam, and so it coincides with the sixteenth of Asa's reign; but then *ch.* xv. 19 must be so understood; and how could it be spoken of as a great thing that there was no more war till the fifteenth year of Asa, when that passage immediately before was in his fifteenth year? (*ch.* xv. 10), and after this miscarriage of his, here recorded, he had wars, *v.* 9. Josephus places it in his twenty-sixth year, and then we must suppose a mistake in the transcriber here and *ch.* xv. 19, the admission of which renders the computation easy. This passage we had before (1 Kings xv. 17, &c.) and Asa was in several ways faulty in it. 1. He did not do well to make a league with Benhadad, a heathen king, and to value himself so much upon it as he seems to have done, *v.* 3. Had he relied more upon his covenant, and his father's, with God, he would not have boasted so much of his league, and his father's, with the royal family of Syria. 2. If he had had a due regard to the honour of Israel in general, he would have found some other expedient to give Baasha a diversion than by calling in a foreign force, and inviting into the country a common enemy, who, in process of time, might be a plague to Judah too. 3. It was doubtless a sin in Benhadad to break his league with Baasha upon no provocation, but merely through the influence of a bribe; and, if so, certainly it was a sin in Asa to move him to it, especially to hire him to do it. The public faith of kings and kingdoms must not be made so cheap a thing. 4. To take silver and gold out of the house of the Lord for this purpose was a great aggravation of the sin, *v.* 2. Must the temple be plundered to serve his carnal politics? He had better have brought gifts and offerings, with prayers and supplications, to the house of the Lord, that he might have engaged God on his side and made him his friend; then he would not have needed to be at this expense to make Benhadad his friend. 5. It was well if Asa had not to answer for all the mischief that the army of Benhadad did unjustly to the cities of Israel, all the blood they shed and all the spoil they made, *v.* 4. Perhaps Asa intended not that they should carry the matter so far. But those that draw others to sin know not what they do, nor where it will end. The beginning of sin is as the letting forth of water. However the project succeeded. Benhadad gave Baasha a powerful diversion, obliged him to leave off building Ramah and betake himself to the defence of his own country northward, which gave Asa an opportunity, not only to demolish his fortifications, but to seize the materials and convert them to his own use.

7 And at that time Hanani the seer came to Asa king of Judah, and said unto him, Because thou hast relied on the king of Syria, and not relied on the LORD thy God, therefore is the host of the king of Syria escaped out of thine hand. 8 Were not the Ethiopians and the Lubims a huge host, with very many chariots and horsemen? yet, because thou didst rely on the LORD, he delivered them into thine hand. 9 For the eyes of the LORD run to and fro throughout the whole earth, to show himself strong in the behalf of *them* whose heart *is* perfect toward him. Herein thou hast done foolishly: therefore from henceforth thou shalt have wars. 10 Then Asa was wroth with the seer, and put him in a prison house; for *he was* in a rage with him because of this *thing*. And Asa oppressed *some* of the people the same time. 11 And, behold, the acts of Asa, first and last, lo, they *are* written in the book of the kings of Judah and Israel. 12 And Asa in the thirty and ninth year of his reign was diseased in his feet, until his disease *was* exceeding *great:* yet in his disease he sought not to the LORD, but to the physicians. 13 And Asa slept with his fathers, and died in the one and fortieth year of his reign. 14 And they buried him in his own sepulchres, which he had made for himself in the city of David, and laid him in the bed which was filled with sweet odours and divers kinds *of spices* prepared by the apothecaries' art: and they made a very great burning for him.

Here is, I. A plain and faithful reproof given to Asa by a prophet of the Lord, for making this league with Baasha. The reprover was Hanani the seer, the father of Jehu, another prophet, whom we read of 1 Kings xvi. 1; 2 Chron. xix. 2. We observed several things amiss in Asa's treaty with Benhadad. But that which the prophet here charges upon him as the greatest fault he was guilty of in that matter is his *relying on the king of Syria and not on the Lord his God, v.* 7. He thought that, though God was on his side, this would not stand him in stead unless he had Benhadad on his side, that God either could not or would not help him, but he must take this indirect course to help himself. Note, God is much displeased when he is distrusted and when an arm of flesh is relied on more than his power and goodness. By putting our confidence in God we give honour to him, and therefore he thinks himself affronted if we give that honour to another. He plainly tells the king that herein he had done foolishly, *v.* 9. It is a foolish thing to lean on a broken reed, when we have the rock of ages to rely upon. To convince him of his folly he shows him,

1. That he acted against his experience, *v.* 8. He, of all men, had no reason to distrust God, who had found him such a present powerful helper, by whom he had been made to triumph over a threatening enemy, as his father before him, *because he relied upon the Lord his God, ch.* xiii. 18; xiv. 11. "*What!*" said the prophet, "*Were not the Ethiopians and the Lubim a huge host*, enough to swallow up a kingdom? And yet, *because thou didst rely on the Lord, he delivered them into thy hand;* and was not he sufficient to help thee against Baasha?" Note, The many experiences we have had of the goodness of God to us aggravate our distrust of him. Has he not helped us in six troubles? And have we any reason to suspect him in the seventh? But see how deceitful our hearts are! We trust in God when we have nothing else to trust to, when need drives us to him; but, when we have other things to stay on, we are apt to stay too much on them and to lean to our own understanding as long as that has any thing to offer; but a believing confidence will be in God only, when a smiling world courts it most.

2. That he acted against his knowledge of God and his providence, *v.* 9. Asa could not be ignorant that *the eyes of the Lord run to and fro through the earth, strongly to hold with those* (so it may be read) *whose heart is*

perfect towards him; that is, (1.) That God governs the world in infinite wisdom, and the creatures, and all their actions, are continually under his eye. The eye of Providence is quick-sighted—it *runs;* it is intent—it runs *to and fro;* it reaches far—*through the whole earth,* no corner of which is from under it, not the most dark or distant; and his eye directs his hand, and the arm of his power; for he shows himself strong. Does Satan walk to and fro in the earth? Providence *runs* to and fro, is never out of the way, never to seek, never at a loss. (2.) That God governs the world for the good of his people, does all in pursuance of the counsels of his love concerning their salvation, all *for Jacob his servant's sake, and Israel his elect,* Isa. xlv. 4. *Christ is head over all things to his church,* Eph. i. 22. (3.) That those whose hearts are upright with him may be sure of his protection and have all the reason in the world to depend upon it. He is able to protect them in the way of their duty (for wisdom and might are his), and he actually intends their protection A practical disbelief of this is at the bottom of all our departures from God and double-dealing with him. Asa could not trust God and therefore made court to Benhadad.

3. That he acted against his interest. (1.) He had lost an opportunity of checking the growing greatness of the king of Syria, (*v.* 7): His *host has escaped out of thy hand,* which otherwise would have joined with Baasha's and fallen with it. (2.) He had incurred God's displeasure and henceforth must expect no peace, but the constant alarms of war, *v.* 9. Those that cannot find in their hearts to trust God forfeit his protection and throw themselves out of it.

II. Asa's displeasure at this reproof. Though it came from God by one that was known to be his messenger, though the reproof was just and the reasoning fair, and all intended for his good, yet he was wroth with the seer for telling him of his folly; nay, *he was in a rage with him, v.* 10. Is this Asa? Is this he whose heart was perfect with the Lord his God all his days? Well, let him that thinks he stands take heed lest he fall. A wise man, and yet in a rage! An Israelite, and yet in a rage with a prophet! A good man, and yet impatient of reproof, and that cannot bear to be told of his faults! Lord, what is man, when God leaves him to himself? Those that idolize their own conduct cannot bear contradiction; and those that indulge a peevish passionate temper may be transported by it into impieties as well as into indecencies, and will, some time or other, fly in the face of God himself. See what gall and wormwood this root of bitterness bore. 1. In his rage he committed the prophet to the jail, *put him in a prison-house,* as a malefactor, *in the stocks* (so some read it,) or into *little-ease.* God's prophets meet with many that cannot bear reproof, but take it much amiss, yet they must do their duty. 2. Having proceeded thus far, *he oppressed some of the people,* probably such as owned the prophet in his sufferings, or were known to be his particular friends. He that abused his power for the persecuting of God's prophet was left to himself further to abuse it for the crushing of his own subjects, whereby he weakened himself and lost his interest. Most persecutors have been tyrants.

III. His sickness. Two years before he died *he was diseased in his feet* (*v.* 12), afflicted with the gout in a high degree. He had put the prophet in the stocks, and now God put him in the stocks; so his punishment answered his sin. *His disease was exceedingly great;* it came to the height (so some); it flew up to his head (so others), and then it was mortal. This was his affliction; but his sin was that in his disease, instead of seeking to the Lord for relief, he *sought to the physicians.* His making use of physicians was his duty; but trusting to them, and expecting that from them which was to be had from God only, were his sin and folly. The help of creatures must always be used with an eye to the Creator, and in dependence upon him, who makes every creature that to us which it is, and without whom the most skilful and faithful are physicians of no value. Some think that these physicians were strangers to the commonwealth of Israel, and were a sort of conjurers, to whom he applied as if there were not a God in Israel.

IV. His death and burial. His funeral had something of extraordinary solemnity in it, *v.* 14. They made a very magnificent *burying for him.* I am loth to think (as some do) that he himself ordered this funeral pomp, and that it was an instance of his vanity, that he would be buried like the Gentiles, and not after the way of the Jews. It is said indeed, *He digged the sepulchre for himself,* as one mindful of his grave; but I am willing to believe that this funeral pomp was rather an expression of the great respect his people retained for him, notwithstanding the failings and infirmities of his latter days. It was agreed to do him honour at his death. Note, The eminent piety and usefulness of good men ought to be remembered to their praise, though they have had their blemishes. Let their faults be buried in their graves, while their services are remembered over their graves. He that said, *There is not a just man that doeth good and sinneth not, yet* said also, *The memory of the just is blessed;* and let it be so.

CHAP. XVII.

Here begin the life and reign of Jehoshaphat, who was one of the first three among the royal worthies, one of the best that ever swayed the sceptre of Judah since David's head was laid. He was the good son of a good father, so that, at this time, grace ran in the blood, even in the blood-royal. Happy the son that had such a father, to lay a good foundation in him and for him. Happy the father that had such a son, to build so well upon the foundation he had laid! Happy the kingdom that was blessed with two such kings, two such reigns, together! In this chapter

we have, I. His accession to and establishment in the throne, ver. 1, 2, 5. II. His personal piety, ver. 3, 4, 6. III. The course he took to promote religion in his kingdom, ver. 7—9. IV. The mighty sway he bore among the neighbours, ver. 10, 11. V. The great strength of his kingdom, both in garrisons and standing forces, ver. 12—19. Thus was his prosperity the reward of his piety and his piety the brightest grace and ornament of his prosperity.

AND Jehoshaphat his son reigned in his stead, and strengthened himself against Israel. 2 And he placed forces in all the fenced cities of Judah, and set garrisons in the land of Judah, and in the cities of Ephraim, which Asa his father had taken. 3 And the LORD was with Jehoshaphat, because he walked in the first ways of his father David, and sought not unto Baalim; 4 But sought to the *LORD* God of his father, and walked in his commandments, and not after the doings of Israel. 5 Therefore the LORD stablished the kingdom in his hand; and all Judah brought to Jehoshaphat presents; and he had riches and honour in abundance. 6 And his heart was lifted up in the ways of the LORD: moreover he took away the high places and groves out of Judah. 7 Also in the third year of his reign he sent to his princes, *even* to Ben-hail, and to Obadiah, and to Zechariah, and to Nethaneel, and to Michaiah, to teach in the cities of Judah. 8 And with them *he sent* Levites, *even* Shemaiah, and Nethaniah, and Zebadiah, and Asahel, and Shemiramoth, and Jehonathan, and Adonijah, and Tobijah, and Tob-adonijah, Levites; and with them Eli-shama and Jehoram, priests. 9 And they taught in Judah, and *had* the book of the law of the LORD with them, and went about throughout all the cities of Judah, and taught the people.

Here we find concerning Jehoshaphat,

I. What a wise man he was. As soon as he came to the crown he *strengthened himself against Israel, v.* 1. Ahab, an active warlike prince, had now been three years upon the throne of Israel, the vigour of his beginning falling in with the decay of Asa's conclusion. It is probable that the kingdom of Israel had, of late, got ground of the kingdom of Judah and began to grow formidable to it; so that the first thing Jehoshaphat had to do was to make his part good on that side, and to check the growing greatness of the king of Israel, which he did so effectually, and without bloodshed, that Ahab soon courted his alliance, so far was he from giving him any disturbance, and proved more dangerous as a friend than he could have been as an enemy. Jehoshaphat strengthened himself not to act offensively against Israel or invade them, but only to maintain his own, which he did by fortifying the cities that were on his frontiers, and putting garrisons, stronger than had been, in the cities of Ephraim, which he was master of, *v.* 2. He did not strengthen himself, as his father did, by a league with the king of Syria, but by fair and regular methods, on which he might expect the blessing of God and in which he trusted God.

II. What a good man he was. It is an excellent character that is here given him. 1. He *walked in the ways of his father David.* In the characters of the kings, David's ways are often made the standard, as 1 Kings xv. 3, 11; 2 Kings xiv. 3; xvi. 2; xviii. 3. But the distinction is nowhere so strongly marked as here between his first ways and his last ways; for the last were not so good as the first. His ways, before he fell so foully in the matter of Uriah (which is mentioned long afterwards as the bar in his escutcheon, 1 Kings xv. 5), were good ways, and, though he happily recovered from that fall, yet perhaps he never, while he lived, fully retrieved the spiritual strength and comfort he lost by it. Jehoshaphat followed David as far as he followed God and no further. Paul himself thus limits our imitation of him (1 Cor. xi. 1): *Follow me, as I follow Christ,* and not otherwise. Many good people have had their first ways, which were their best ways, their first love, which was their strongest love; and in every copy we propose to write after, as we must single out that only which is good, so that chiefly which is best. The words here will admit another reading; they run thus: *He walked in the ways of David his father (Hareshonim), those first ways,* or those *ancient ways.* He proposed to himself, for his example, the primitive times of the royal family, those purest times, before the corruptions of the late reigns came in. See Jer. vi. 16. The LXX. leave out David, and so refer it to Asa: *He walked in the first ways of his father,* and did not imitate him in what was amiss in him, towards the latter end of his time. It is good to be cautious in following the best men, lest we step aside after them. 2. He *sought not to Baalim, but sought to the Lord God of his father, v.* 3, 4. The neighbouring nations had their Baalim, one had one Baal and another had another; but he abhorred them all, had nothing to do with them. He *worshipped the Lord God of his father* and him only, prayed to him only and enquired of him only; both are included in seeking him. 3. That he *walked in God's commandments,* not only worshipped the true God, but worshipped him according to his own institution, *and not after the doings of*

Israel, *v.* 4. Though the king of Israel was his neighbour and ally, yet he did not learn his way. Whatever dealings he had with him in civil matters, he would not have communion with him, nor comply with him in his religion. In this he kept close to the rule. 4. *His heart was lifted up in the ways of the Lord* (*v.* 6), or *he lifted up his heart.* He brought his heart to his work, and lifted up his heart in it; that is, he had a sincere regard to God in it. *Unto thee, O Lord! do I lift up my soul.* His heart was enlarged in that which is good, Ps. cxix. 32. He never thought he could do enough for God. He was lively and affectionate in his religion, *fervent in spirit, serving the Lord,* cheerful and pleasant in it; he went on in his work with alacrity, as Jacob, who, after his vision of God at Bethel, *lifted up his feet,* Gen. xxix. 1, *margin.* He was bold and resolute in the ways of God and went on with courage. His heart was lifted up above the consideration of the difficulties that were in the way of his duty; he easily got over them all, and was not frightened with *winds and clouds* from *sowing and reaping*, Eccl. xi. 4. Let us walk in the same spirit.

III. What a useful man he was, not only a good man, but a good king. He not only was good himself, but did good in his generation, did a great deal of good. 1. He took away the teachers of lies, so images are called (Hab. ii. 18), the *high places* and *the groves*, *v.* 6. It is meant of those in which idols were worshipped; for those that were dedicated to the true God only were not taken away, *ch.* xx. 33. It was only idolatry that he abolished. Nothing debauched the nation more than those idolatrous groves or images which he took away. 2. He sent forth teachers of truth. When he enquired into the state of religion in his kingdom he found his people generally very ignorant: they *knew not that they did evil.* Even in the last good reign there had been little care taken to instruct them in their duty; and therefore Jehoshaphat resolves to begin his work at the right end, deals with them as reasonable creatures, will not lead them blindfold, no, not into a reformation, but endeavours to have them well taught, knowing that that was the way to have them well cured. In this good work he employed, (1.) His princes. Those about him he sent forth; those in the country he sent *to teach in the cities of Judah*, *v.* 7. He ordered them, in the administration of justice, not only to correct the people when they did ill, but to teach them how to do better, and to give a reason for what they did, that the people might be informed of the difference between good and evil. The princes or judges upon the bench have a great opportunity of teaching people their duty to God and man, and it is not out of their province, for the laws of God are to be looked upon as laws of the land. (2.) The *Levites* and *priests* went *with the princes*, and *taught in Judah, having the book of the law with them*, *v.* 8, 9. They were teachers by office, Deut. xxxiii. 10. Teaching was part of the work for which they had their maintenance. The priests and the Levites had little else to do. But, it seems, they had neglected it, pretending perhaps that they could not get the people to hear them. "Well," says Jehoshaphat, "you shall go along with the princes, and they with their authority shall oblige the people to come and hear you; and then, if they be not well instructed, it is your fault." What an abundance of good may be done when Moses and Aaron thus go hand in hand in the doing of it, when princes with their power, and priests and Levites with their scripture learning, agree to teach the people the good knowledge of God and their duty! These itinerant judges and itinerant preachers together were instrumental to diffuse a blessed light throughout the cities of Judah. But it is said, *They had the book of the law of the Lord with them.* [1.] For their own direction, that thence they might fetch all the instructions they gave to the people, and not *teach for doctrines the commandments of men.* [2.] For the conviction of the people, that they might see that they had a divine warrant for what they said and delivered to them that only which they received from the Lord. Note, Ministers, when they go to teach the people, should have their Bibles with them.

IV. What a happy man he was. 1. How happy he was in the favour of his God, who signally owned and blessed him: *The Lord was with him* (*v.* 3); *the word of the Lord was his helper* (so the Chaldee paraphrase); *the Lord established the kingdom in his hand*, *v.* 5. Those stand firmly that have the presence of God with them. If the *beauty of the Lord our God be upon us*, that will *establish the work of our hands* and establish us in our integrity. 2. How happy he was in the affections of his people (*v.* 5): *All Judah brought him presents*, in acknowledgment of his kindness in sending preachers among them. The more there is of true religion among a people the more there will be of conscientious loyalty. A government that answers the end of government will be supported. The effect of the favour both of God and his kingdom was that he had *riches and honour in abundance.* It is undoubtedly true, though few will believe it, that religion and piety are the best friends to outward prosperity. And, observe, it follows immediately, *His heart was lifted up in the ways of the Lord.* Riches and honour in abundance prove to many a clog and a hindrance in the ways of the Lord, an occasion of pride, security, and sensuality; but they had a quite contrary effect upon Jehoshaphat: his abundance was oil to the wheels of his obedience, and the more he had of the wealth of this world the more was his heart *lifted up in the ways of the Lord.*

10 And the fear of the LORD fell upon all the kingdoms of the lands that *were* round about Judah, so that they made no war against Jehoshaphat. 11 Also *some* of the Philistines brought Jehoshaphat presents, and tribute silver; and the Arabians brought him flocks, seven thousand and seven hundred rams, and seven thousand and seven hundred he goats. 12 And Jehoshaphat waxed great exceedingly; and he built in Judah castles, and cities of store. 13 And he had much business in the cities of Judah: and the men of war, mighty men of valour, *were* in Jerusalem. 14 And these *are* the numbers of them according to the house of their fathers: Of Judah, the captains of thousands; Adnah the chief, and with him mighty men of valour three hundred thousand. 15 And next to him *was* Jehohanan the captain, and with him two hundred and fourscore thousand. 16 And next him *was* Amasiah the son of Zichri, who willingly offered himself unto the LORD; and with him two hundred thousand mighty men of valour. 17. And of Benjamin Eliada, a mighty man of bow and shield two hundred thousand. 18 And next him *was* Jehozabad, and with him a hundred and fourscore thousand ready prepared for the war. 19 These waited on the king, beside *those* whom the king put in the fenced cities throughout all Judah.

We have here a further account of Jehoshaphat's great prosperity and the flourishing state of his kingdom.

I. He had good interest in the neighbouring princes and nations. Though he was not perhaps so great a soldier as David (which might have made him their terror), nor so great a scholar as Solomon (which might have made him their oracle), yet *the fear of the Lord fell so upon them* (that is, God so influenced and governed their spirits) that they had all a reverence for him, *v.* 10. And, 1. *None of them made war against him.* God's good providence so ordered it that, while the princes and priests were instructing and reforming the country, none of his neighbours gave him any molestation, to take him off from that good work. Thus when Jacob and his sons were going to worship at Bethel the terror of God was upon the neighbouring cities, that they *did not pursue after them,* Gen. xxxv. 5, and see Exod. xxxiv. 24. 2. Many of them brought presents to him (*v.* 11), to secure his friendship. Perhaps these were a tribute imposed upon them by Asa, who made himself master of the cities of the Philistines and the tents of the Arabians, *ch.* xiv. 14, 15. With the 7700 rams, and the same number of he-goats, which the Arabians brought, there was probably a proportionable number of ewes and lambs, she-goats and kids.

II. He had very considerable stores laid up in the cities of Judah. He pulled down his barns, and built larger (*v.* 12), *castles and cities of store,* for arms and victuals. He was a man of business, and aimed at the public good in all his undertakings, either to preserve the peace or prepare for war.

III. He had the militia in good order. It was never in better since David modelled it. Five *lord-lieutenants* (if I may so call them) are here named, with the numbers of those under their command (the serviceable men, that were fit for war in their respective districts), three in Judah, and two in Benjamin. It is said of one of these great commanders, *Amasiah,* that *he willingly offered himself unto the Lord* (*v.* 16), not only to the king, to serve him in this post, but to the Lord, to glorify him in it. He was the most eminent among them for religion; he accepted the place, not for the honour, or power, or profit of it, but for conscience' sake towards God, that he might serve his country. It was usual for great generals then to offer of their spoils to the Lord, 1 Chron. xxvi. 26. But this good man offered himself first to the Lord, and then his dedicated things. The number of the soldiers under these five generals amounts to 1,160,000 men, a vast number for so small a compass of ground as Judah's and Benjamin's lot to furnish out and maintain. Abijah could bring into the field but 400,000 (*ch.* xiii. 3), Asa not 600,000 (*ch.* xiv. 8), yet Jehoshaphat has at command almost 1,200,000. But it must be considered, 1. That God had promised to make the seed of Abraham like the sand of the sea for number. 2. There had now been a long peace. 3. We may suppose that the city of Jerusalem was very much enlarged. 4. Many had come over to them from the kingdom of Israel (*ch.* xv. 19), which would increase the numbers of the people. 5. Jehoshaphat was under a special blessing of God, which made his affairs to prosper greatly. The armies, we may suppose, were dispersed all the country over, and each man resided for the most part on his own estate; but they appeared often, to be mustered and trained, and were ready at call whenever there was occasion. The commanders waited on the king (*v.* 19) as officers of his court, privy-counsellors, and ministers of state.

But, *lastly*, observe, It was not this formidable army that struck a terror upon the neighbouring nations, that restrained them from attempting any thing against Israel, or obliged them to pay tribute, but the fear of God which fell upon them when Jehoshaphat reformed his country and set up a preaching ministry in it, *v.* 10. The ordinances of God are more the strength and safety of a kingdom than its military force—its men of God more than its men of war.

CHAP. XVIII.

The story of this chapter we had just as it is here related in the story of the reign of Ahab king of Israel, 1 Kings xxii. There it looks more creditable to Ahab than any thing else recorded of him that he was in league with so good a man as Jehoshaphat; here it is a great blemish in the reign of Jehoshaphat that he thus connected himself with so bad a man as Ahab. Here is, I. The alliance he contracted with Ahab, ver. 1. II. His consent to join with him in his expedition for the recovery of Ramoth-Gilead out of the hands of the Syrians, ver. 2, 3. III. Their consulting with the prophets, false and true, before they went, ver. 4—27. IV. The success of their expedition. Jehoshaphat hardly escaped (ver. 28–32) and Ahab received his death's wound, ver. 33, 34.

NOW Jehoshaphat had riches and honour in abundance, and joined affinity with Ahab. 2 And after *certain* years he went down to Ahab to Samaria. And Ahab killed sheep and oxen for him in abundance, and for the people that *he had* with him, and persuaded him to go up *with him* to Ramoth-gilead. 3 And Ahab king of Israel said unto Jehoshaphat king of Judah, Wilt thou go with me to Ramoth-gilead? And he answered him, I *am* as thou *art*, and my people as thy people; and *we will be* with thee in the war.

Here is, I. Jehoshaphat growing greater. It was said before (*ch.* xvii. 5) that he had *riches and honour in abundance;* and here it is said again that his wealth and honour increased upon him by piety and good management.

II. Not growing wiser, else he would not have joined with Ahab, that degenerate Israelite, who had sold himself to work wickedness. What good could he get by a man that was so bad? What good could he do to a man that was so obstinately wicked—an idolater, a persecutor? With him he joined in affinity, that is, married his son Jehoram to Ahab's daughter Athaliah.

1. This was the worst match that ever was made by any of the house of David. I wonder what Jehoshaphat could promise himself by it. (1.) Perhaps pride made the match, as it does many a one, which speeds accordingly. His religion forbade him to marry his son to a daughter of any of the heathen princes that were about him—*Thou shalt not take their daughters to thy sons;* and, having riches and honour in abundance, he thought it a disparagement to marry him to a subject. A king's daughter it must be, and therefore Ahab's, little considering that Jezebel was her mother. (2.) Some think he did it in policy, hoping by this expedient to unite the kingdoms in his son, Ahab perhaps flattering him with hopes that he would make him his heir, when he intended no such thing.

2. This match drew Jehoshaphat, (1.) Into an intimate familiarity with Ahab. He paid him a visit at Samaria, and Ahab, proud of the honour which Jehoshaphat did him, gave him a very splendid entertainment, according to the splendour of those times: He *killed sheep and oxen for him,* plain meat, *in abundance, v.* 2. In this Jehoshaphat did not walk so closely as he should have done in the ways of his father David, who *hated the congregation of evil-doers and would not sit with the wicked* (Ps. xxvi. 5), nor desired to *eat of their dainties,* Ps. cxli. 4. (2.) Into a league with Ahab against the Syrians. Ahab persuaded him to join forces with him in an expedition for the recovery of Ramoth-Gilead, a city in the tribe of Gad, on the other side Jordan. Did not Ahab know that that, and all the other cities of Israel, did of right belong to Jehoshaphat, as heir of the house of David? With what face then could he ask Jehoshaphat to assist him in recovering it for himself, whose title to the crown was usurped and precarious? Yet Jehoshaphat, an easy man, yields to go with him: *I am as thou art, v.* 3. Some men's kindnesses are dangerous, as well as their society infectious. The feast Ahab made for Jehoshaphat was designed only to wheedle him into this expedition. The *kisses of an enemy are deceitful.*

4 And Jehoshaphat said unto the king of Israel, Enquire, I pray thee, at the word of the LORD to day. 5 Therefore the king of Israel gathered together of prophets four hundred men, and said unto them, Shall we go to Ramoth-gilead to battle, or shall I forbear? And they said, Go up; for God will deliver *it* into the king's hand. 6 But Jehoshaphat said, *Is there* not here a prophet of the LORD besides, that we might enquire of him? 7 And the king of Israel said unto Jehoshaphat, *There is* yet one man, by whom we may enquire of the LORD: but I hate him; for he never prophesied good unto me, but always evil: the same *is* Micaiah the son of Imla. And Jehoshaphat said, Let not the king say so. 8 And the king of Israel called for one *of his* officers, and said, Fetch quickly Micaiah the son of Imla. 9 And the king of Israel and Jehoshaphat king of Judah sat either of them on his throne,

clothed in *their* robes, and they sat in a void place at the entering in of the gate of Samaria; and all the prophets prophesied before them. 10 And Zedekiah the son of Chenaanah had made him horns of iron, and said, Thus saith the LORD, With these thou shalt push Syria until they be consumed. 11 And all the prophets prophesied so, saying, Go up to Ramoth-gilead, and prosper: for the LORD shall deliver *it* into the hand of the king. 12 And the messenger that went to call Micaiah spake to him, saying, Behold, the words of the prophets *declare* good to the king with one assent; let thy word therefore, I pray thee, be like one of their's, and speak thou good. 13 And Micaiah said, *As* the LORD liveth, even what my God saith, that will I speak. 14 And when he was come to the king, the king said unto him, Micaiah, shall we go to Ramoth-gilead to battle, or shall I forbear? And he said, Go ye up, and prosper, and they shall be delivered into your hand. 15 And the king said to him, How many times shall I adjure thee that thou say nothing but the truth to me in the name of the LORD? 16 Then he said, I did see all Israel scattered upon the mountains, as sheep that have no shepherd: and the LORD said, These have no master; let them return *therefore* every man to his house in peace. 17 And the king of Israel said to Jehoshaphat, Did I not tell thee *that* he would not prophesy good unto me, but evil? 18 Again he said, Therefore hear the word of the LORD; I saw the LORD sitting upon his throne, and all the host of heaven standing on his right hand and *on* his left. 19 And the LORD said, Who shall entice Ahab king of Israel, that he may go up and fall at Ramoth-gilead? And one spake saying after this manner, and another saying after that manner. 20 Then there came out a spirit, and stood before the LORD, and said, I will entice him. And the LORD said unto him, Wherewith? 21 And he said, I will go out, and be a lying spirit in the mouth of all his prophets. And *the* LORD said, Thou shalt entice *him*, and thou shalt also prevail: go out, and do *even* so. 22 Now therefore, behold, the LORD hath put a lying spirit in the mouth of these thy prophets, and the LORD hath spoken evil against thee. 23 Then Zedekiah the son of Chenaanah came near, and smote Micaiah upon the cheek, and said, Which way went the Spirit of the LORD from me to speak unto thee? 24 And Micaiah said, Behold, thou shalt see on that day when thou shalt go into an inner chamber to hide thyself. 25 Then the king of Israel said, Take ye Micaiah, and carry him back to Amon the governor of the city, and to Joash the king's son; 26 And say, Thus saith the king, Put this *fellow* in the prison, and feed him with bread of affliction and with water of affliction, until I return in peace. 27 And Micaiah said, If thou certainly return in peace, *then* hath not the LORD spoken by me. And he said, Hearken, all ye people.

This is almost word for word the same with what we had, 1 Kings xxii. We will not repeat what was there said, nor have we much to add, but may take occasion to think, 1. Of the great duty of acknowledging God in all our ways *and enquiring at his word,* whatever we undertake. Jehoshaphat was not willing to proceed till he had done this, *v.* 4. By particular believing prayer, by an unbiassed consultation of the scripture and our own consciences, and by an observant regard to the hints of providence, we may make such enquiries and very much to our satisfaction. 2. Of the great danger of bad company even to good men. Those that have most wisdom, grace, and resolution, cannot be sure that they can converse familiarly with wicked people and get no hurt by them. Jehoshaphat here, in complaisance to Ahab, sits in his robes, patiently hearing the false prophets speaking lies in the name of the Lord (*v.* 9), can scarcely find in his heart to give him a too mild and gentle reproof for hating a prophet of the Lord (*v.* 7), and dares not rebuke that false prophet who basely abused the faithful seer nor oppose Ahab who committed him to prison. Those who venture among the seats of the scornful cannot come off without a great deal of the guilt attaching to at least the omission of their duty, unless they have such measures of wisdom and courage as few can pretend to. 3. Of the unhappiness of those who are surrounded with flatterers, especially flattering prophets, who cry peace to them and prophesy nothing but smooth things. Thus was Ahab cheated into his ruin, and justly; for he hearkened to such, and preferred those that humoured him before a good prophet that gave him fair warning of his danger. Those do best for themselves that give their friends leave, and particularly their ministers, to deal plainly and faithfully with them, and take their reproofs not only patiently, but kindly. That counsel is not always best for us that is most pleasing to us. 4. Of the power of Satan, by the divine permission, *in the children of disobedience.* One lying spirit can make 400 lying prophets and make use of them to deceive Ahab, *v.* 21. The devil becomes a murderer by being a liar and destroys men by deceiving them. 5. Of the justice of God in giving those up to strong delusions, to believe a lie, who will not receive the love of the truth, but rebel against it, *v.* 21. Let the *lying spirit prevail* to entice those to their ruin that will not be persuaded to their duty and happiness. 6. Of the hard case of faithful ministers, whose lot it has often been to be hated, and persecuted, and ill-treated, for being true to their God and just and kind to the souls of men. Micaiah, for discharging a good conscience, was buffeted, imprisoned, and condemned to the bread and water of affliction. But he could with assurance appeal to the issue, as all those may do who are persecuted for their faithfulness, *v.* 27. The day will declare who is in the right and who in the wrong, when Christ will appear, to the unspeakable consolation of his persecuted people and the everlasting confusion of their persecutors, who will be made *to see in that day* (*v.* 24) what they will not now believe.

28 So the king of Israel and Jehoshaphat the king of Judah went up to Ramoth-gilead. 29 And the king of Israel said unto Jehoshaphat, I will disguise myself, and will go to the battle; but put thou on thy robes. So the king of Israel disguised himself; and they went to the battle. 30 Now the king of Syria had commanded the captains of the chariots that *were* with him, saying, Fight ye not with small or great, save only with the king of Israel. 31 And it came to pass, when the captains of the chariots saw Jehoshaphat, that they said, It *is* the king of Israel. Therefore they compassed about him to fight: but Jehoshaphat cried out, and the LORD helped him; and God moved them *to depart* from him. 32 For it came to pass, that, when the captains of the chariots perceived that it was not the king of Israel, they turned back again from pursuing him. 33 And a *certain* man drew a bow at a venture, and smote the king of Israel between the joints of the harness: therefore he said to his chariot man, Turn thine hand, that thou mayest carry me out of the host; for I am wounded. 34 And the battle increased that day: howbeit the king of Israel stayed *himself* up in *his* chariot against the Syrians until the even: and about the time of the sun going down he died.

We have here, 1. Good Jehoshaphat exposing himself in his robes, thereby endangered, and yet delivered. We have reason to think that Ahab, while he pretended friendship, really aimed at Jehoshaphat's life, to take him off, that he might have the management of his successor, who was his son-in-law, else he would never have advised him to enter into the battle with his robes on, which was but to make himself an easy mark to the enemy: and, if really he intended that, it was as unprincipled a piece of treachery as ever man was guilty of, and justly was he himself taken in the pit he digged for his friend. The enemy had soon an eye upon the robes, and vigorously attacked the unwary prince who now, when it was too late, wished himself in the habit of the poorest soldier, rather than in his princely raiment. He cried out, either to his friends to relieve him (but Ahab took no care of that), or to his enemies, to rectify their mistake, and let them know that he was not the king of Israel. Or perhaps he cried to God for succour and deliverance (to whom else should he cry?) and he found it was not in vain: *The Lord helped him out* of his distress, by *moving the captains to depart from him, v.* 31. God has all men's hearts in his hand, and turns them as he pleases, contrary to their own first intentions, to serve his purposes. Many are moved unaccountably both to themselves and others, but an invisible power moves them. 2. Wicked Ahab disguising himself, arming himself, thereby as he thought securing himself, and yet slain, *v.* 33. No art, no arms, can save those whom God has appointed to ruin. What can hurt those whom God will protect? And what can shelter those whom God will destroy? Jehoshaphat is safe in his robes, Ahab killed in his armour; for the race is not to the swift nor the battle to the strong.

CHAP. XIX.

We have here a further account of the good reign of Jehoshaphat, I. His return in peace to Jerusalem, ver. 1. II. The reproof given him for his league with Ahab, and his acting in conjunction with him, ver. 2, 3. III. The great care he took thereupon to reform his kingdom, ver. 4. IV. The instructions he gave to his judges, both those in the country towns that kept the inferior courts (ver. 5—7), and those in Jerusalem that sat in the supreme judicature of the kingdom, ver. 8—11.

AND Jehoshaphat the king of Judah returned to his house in peace to Jerusalem. 2 And Jehu the son of Hanani the seer went out to meet him, and said to king Jehoshaphat, Shouldest thou help the ungodly, and love them that hate the LORD? therefore *is* wrath upon thee from before the LORD. 3 Nevertheless there are good things found in thee, in that thou hast taken away the groves out of the land, and hast prepared thine heart to seek God. 4 And Jehoshaphat dwelt at Jerusalem: and he went out again through the people from Beer-sheba to mount Ephraim, and brought them back unto the LORD God of their fathers.

Here is, I. The great favour God showed to Jehoshaphat,

1. In bringing him back in safety from his dangerous expedition with Ahab, which had like to have cost him dearly (*v.* 1): *He returned to his house in peace.* Notice is taken of this to intimate, (1.) That he fared better than he had expected. He had been in imminent peril, and yet came home in peace. Whenever we return in peace to our houses we ought to acknowledge God's providence in preserving our going out and our coming in. But, if we have been kept through more than ordinary dangers, we are in a special manner bound to be thankful. There was but a step perhaps between us and death, and yet we are alive. (2.) That he fared better than he deserved. He was out of the way of his duty, had been out upon an expedition which he could not well account for to God and his conscience, and yet he returned in peace; for God is not extreme to mark what we do amiss, nor does he withdraw his protection every time we forfeit it. (3.) That he fared better than Ahab king of Israel did, who was brought home slain. Though Jehoshaphat had said to Ahab, *I am as thou art*, God distinguished him; for he knows and owns *the way of the righteous*, but *the way of the ungodly shall perish.* Distinguishing mercies are very obliging. Here were two kings in the field together, *one taken and the other left*, one brought home in blood, the other in peace.

2. In sending him a reproof for his affinity with Ahab. It is a great mercy to be made sensible of our faults, and to be told in time wherein we have erred, that we may repent and amend the error before it be too late. The prophet by whom the reproof is sent is Jehu the son of Hanani. The father was an eminent prophet in the last reign, as appeared by Asa's putting him in the stocks for his plain dealing; yet the son was not afraid to reprove another king. Paul would have his son Timothy not only not discouraged, but animated by his sufferings, 2 Tim. iii. 11, 14. (1.) The prophet told him plainly that he had done very ill in joining with Ahab: "*Shouldst thou,* a godly man, *help the ungodly,* give them a hand of fellowship, and lend them a hand of assistance?" Or, "*Shouldst thou love those that hate the Lord;* wilt thou lay those in thy bosom whom God beholds afar off?" It is the black character of wicked people that they are *haters of God,* Rom. i. 30. Idolaters are so reputed in the second commandment; and therefore it is not for those that love God to take delight in them or contract an intimacy with them. *Do I not hate those,* says David, *that hate thee?* Ps. cxxxix. 21, 22. Those whom the grace of God has dignified ought not to debase themselves. Let God's people be of God's mind. (2.) That God was displeased with him for doing this: "*There is wrath upon thee from before the Lord,* and thou must, by repentance, make thy peace with him, or it will be the worse for thee." He did so, and God's anger was turned away. Yet his trouble, as recorded in the next chapter, was a rebuke to him for meddling with strife that belonged not to him. If he be so fond of war, he shall have enough of it. And the great mischief which his seed after him fell into by the house of Ahab was the just punishment of his affinity with that house. (3.) Yet he took notice of that which was praiseworthy, as it is proper for us to do when we give a reproof (*v.* 3): "*There are good things found in thee;* and therefore, though God be displeased with thee, he does not, he will not, cast thee off." His abolishing idolatry with a heart fixed for God and engaged to seek him was a good thing, which God accepted and would have him go on with, notwithstanding the displeasure he had now incurred.

II. The return of duty which Jehoshaphat made to God for this favour. He took the reproof well, was not wroth with the seer as his father was, but submitted. *Let the righteous smite me, it shall be a kindness.* See what effect the reproof had upon him. 1. He *dwelt at Jerusalem* (*v.* 4), minded his own business at home, and would not expose himself by paying any more such visits to Ahab. *Rebuke a wise man, and he will be yet wiser,* and will take warning, Prov. ix. 8, 9. 2. To atone (as I may say) for the visit he had paid to Ahab, he made a pious profitable visitation of his own kingdom: He *went out through the people* in his own person from Beersheba in the south to Mount Ephriam in the north, and *brought them back to the Lord God of their fathers,* that is, did all he could towards recovering them. (1.) By what the prophet said he perceived that his former attempts for reformation were well pleasing to God, and therefore he revived them, and did what was then left undone. It is good when commendations thus quicken us to our duty, and when the more we are praised for doing well the more vigorous we are in well-doing. (2.) Perhaps he found that his late affinity with the idolatrous house of Ahab and kingdom of Israel had had a bad influence upon his own kingdom. Many, we may suppose, were emboldened to revolt to idolatry when they saw even their reforming king so intimate with idolaters; and therefore he thought himself doubly obliged to do all he could to restore them. If we truly repent of our sin, we shall do our utmost to repair the damage we have any way done by it to religion or the souls of others. We are particularly concerned to recover those that have fallen into sin, or been hardened in it, by our example.

5 And he set judges in the land throughout all the fenced cities of Judah, city by city, 6 And said to the judges, Take heed what ye do: for ye judge not for man, but for the LORD, who *is* with you in the judgment. 7 Wherefore now let the fear of the LORD be upon you: take heed and do *it:* for *there is* no iniquity with the LORD our God, nor respect of persons, nor taking of gifts. 8 Moreover in Jerusalem did Jehoshaphat set of the Levites, and *of* the priests, and of the chief of the fathers of Israel, for the judgment of the LORD, and for controversies, when they returned to Jerusalem. 9 And he charged them, saying, Thus shall ye do in the fear of the LORD, faithfully, and with a perfect heart. 10 And what cause soever shall come to you of your brethren that dwell in their cities, between blood and blood, between law and commandment, statutes and judgments, ye shall even warn them that they trespass not against the LORD, and *so* wrath come upon you, and upon your brethren: this do, and ye shall not trespass. 11 And, behold, Amariah the chief priest *is* over you in all matters of the LORD; and Zebadiah the son of Ishmael, the ruler of the house of Judah, for all the king's matters: also the Levites *shall be* officers before you. Deal courageously, and the LORD shall be with the good.

Jehoshaphat, having done what he could to make his people good, is here providing, if possible, to keep them so by the influence of a settled magistracy. He had sent preachers among them, to instruct them (*ch.* xvii. 7—9), and that provision did well; but now he saw it further requisite to send judges among them, to see the laws put in execution, and to be a terror to evil-doers. It is probable that there were judges up and down the country before, but either they neglected their business or the people slighted them, so that the end of the institution was not answered; and therefore it was necessary it should be new-modelled, new men employed, and a new charge given them. That is it which is here done.

I. He erected inferior courts of justice in the several cities of the kingdom, *v.* 5. The judges of these courts were to keep the people in the worship of God, to punish the violations of the law, and to decide controversies between man and man. Here is the charge he gave them (*v.* 6), in which we have,

1. The means he prescribes to them for the keeping of them closely to their duty; and these are two:—(1.) Great caution and circumspection: *Take heed what you do, v.* 6. And again, "*Take heed and do it, v.* 7. Mind your business; take heed of making any mistakes; be afraid of misunderstanding any point of law, or the matter of fact." Judges, of all men, have need to be cautious, because so much depends upon the correctness of their judgment. (2.) Great piety and religion: "*Let the fear of God be upon you,* and that will be a restraint upon you to keep you from doing wrong (Neh. v. 15; Gen. xlii. 18) and an engagement to you to be active in doing the duty of your place." Let destruction from God be a terror to them, as Job speaks (Job xxxi. 23), and then they will be a terror to none but evil-doers.

2. The motives he would have them consider, to engage them to faithfulness. These are three, all taken from God:—(1.) That from him they had their commission; his ministers they were. The powers that be are ordained by him and for him: "*You judge not for man, but for the Lord;* your business is to glorify him, and serve the interests of his kingdom among men." (2.) That his eye was upon them: "He is *with you in the judgment,* to take notice what you do and call you to an account if you do amiss." (3.) That he is the great example of justice to all magistrates: *There is no iniquity with him,* no bribery, nor respect of persons. Magistrates are called gods, and therefore must endeavour to resemble him.

II. He erected a supreme court at Jerusalem, which was advised with, and appealed to, in all the difficult causes that occurred in the inferior courts, and which gave judgment upon demurrers (to speak in the language of our own law), special verdicts, and writs of error. This court sat in Jerusalem; for *there were set the thrones of judgment:* there they would be under the inspection of the king himself. Observe,

1. The causes cognizable in this court; and they were of two kinds, as with us:—(1.) Pleas of the crown, called here *the judgment of the Lord,* because the law of God was the law of the realm. All criminals were charged with the breach of some part of his law and were said to offend against his peace, his crown and dignity. (2.) Common pleas, between party and party, called here *controversies* (*v.* 8) and *causes of their brethren* (*v.* 10), differences *between blood and blood* (this refers to Deut. xvii. 8), between the blood of the person slain and the blood of the man-slayer. Since the revolt of the ten tribes all the cities of refuge, except Hebron, belonged to the kingdom of Israel; and therefore, we may suppose, the courts of the temple, or the horns of the altar, were chiefly used as sanctuaries in that case, and hence the trial of homicides was reserved for the court at Jerusalem. If the inferior judges did not agree about the sense of any law or commandment, any statute or judgment, this court must determine the controversy.

2. The judges of this court were some of *the Levites and priests* that were most learned in the law, eminent for wisdom, and of approved integrity, and some of *the chief of the fathers of Israel, peers of the realm,* as I may call them, or persons of age and experience, that had been men of business, who would be the most competent judges of matters of fact, as the priests and Levites were of the sense of the law.

3. The two chiefs, or presidents, of this court. Amariah, the high priest, was to preside in ecclesiastical causes, to direct the court and be the mouth of it, or perhaps to be last consulted in cases which the judges themselves doubted of. Zebadiah, the prime-minister of that state, was to preside in all civil causes, *v.* 11. Thus there are diversities of gifts and operations, but all from the same Spirit, and for the good of the body. Some best understand *the matters of the Lord,* others *the king's matters;* neither can say to the other, *I have no need of thee,* for God's Israel has need of both; and, as every one has received the gift, so let him minister the same. Blessed be God both for magistrates and ministers, scribes and statesmen, men of books and men of business.

4. The inferior officers of the court. "Some of *the Levites* (such as had not abilities to qualify them for judges) *shall be officers before you,*" *v.* 11. They were to bring causes into the court, and to see the sentence of the judges executed. And these hands and feet were as necessary in their places as the eyes and heads (the judges) in theirs.

5. The charge which the king gave them. (1.) They must see to it that they acted from a good principle; they must do all in the *fear of the Lord,* setting him always before them, and then they would act faithfully, conscientiously, and *with a perfect upright heart, v.* 9. (2.) They must make it their great and constant care to prevent sin, *to warn the people that they trespass not against the Lord,* inspire them with a dread of sin, not only as hurtful to themselves and the public peace, but as an offence to God, and that which would bring wrath upon the people if they committed it and upon the magistrates if they did not punish it. "*This do, and you shall not trespass;*" this implies that those who have power in their hands contract the guilt of sin themselves if they do not use their power for the preventing and restraining of sin in others. "You trespass if you do not keep them from trespassing." (3.) They must act with resolution. "Deal courageously, and fear not the face of man; be bold and daring in the discharge of your duty, and, whoever is against you, God will protect you: *The Lord shall be with the good.*" Wherever he finds a good man, a good magistrate, he will be found a good God.

CHAP. XX.

We have here, I. The great danger and distress that Jehoshaphat and his kingdom were in from a foreign invasion, ver. 1, 2. II. The pious course he took for their safety, by fasting, and praying, and seeking God, ver. 3—13. III. The assurance which God, by a prophet, immediately gave them of victory, ver. 14—17. IV. Their thankful believing reception of those assurances, ver. 18—21. V. The defeat which God gave to their enemies thereupon, ver. 22—25. VI. A solemn thanksgiving which they kept for their victory, and for the happy consequences of it, ver. 26—30. VII. The conclusion of the reign of Jehoshaphat, not without some blemishes, ver. 31—37.

IT came to pass after this also, *that* the children of Moab, and the children of Ammon, and with them *other* beside the Ammonites, came against Jehoshaphat to battle. 2 Then there came some that told Jehoshaphat, saying, There cometh a great multitude against thee from beyond the sea on this side Syria; and, behold, they *be* in Hazazon-tamar, which *is* En-gedi. 3 And Jehoshaphat feared, and set himself to seek the LORD, and proclaimed a fast throughout all Judah. 4 And Judah gathered themselves together, to ask *help* of the LORD: even out of all the cities of Judah they came to seek the LORD. 5 And Jehoshaphat stood in the congregation of Judah and Jerusalem, in the house of the LORD, before the new court, 6 And said, O LORD God of our fathers, *art* not thou God in heaven? and rulest *not* thou over all the kingdoms of the heathen? and in thine hand *is there not* power and might, so that none is able to withstand thee? 7 *Art* not thou our God, *who* didst drive out the inhabitants of this land before thy people Israel, and gavest it to the seed of Abraham thy friend for ever? 8 And they dwelt therein, and have built thee a sanctuary therein for thy name, saying, 9 If, *when* evil cometh upon us, *as* the sword, judgment, or pestilence, or famine, we stand before this house, and in thy presence, (for thy name *is* in this house,) and cry unto thee in our affliction, then thou wilt hear and help. 10 And now, behold, the children of Ammon and Moab and mount Seir, whom thou wouldest not let Israel invade, when they came out of the land of Egypt, but they turned from them, and destroyed them not; 11 Behold, *I say, how* they reward us, to come to cast us out of thy possession, which thou hast given us to inherit. 12 O our God, wilt thou not judge them? for we have no might against this great company that cometh against us; neither know we what to do: but our eyes *are* upon thee. 13 And all Judah stood before the LORD, with their little ones, their wives, and their children.

We left Jehoshaphat, in the foregoing chapter, well employed in reforming his kingdom and providing for the due administration of justice and support of religion in it, and expected nothing but to hear of the peace and prosperity of his reign; but here we have him in distress, which distress, however, was followed by such a glorious deliverance as was an abundant recompence for his piety. If we meet with trouble in the way of duty, we may believe it is that God may have an opportunity of showing us so much the more of his marvellous loving-kindness. We have here,

I. A formidable invasion of Jehoshaphat's kingdom by the Moabites, and Ammonites, and their auxiliaries, *v.* 1. Jehoshaphat was surprised with the intelligence of it when the enemy had already entered his country, *v.* 2. What pretence they had to quarrel with Jehoshaphat does not appear; they are said to come *from beyond the sea,* meaning *the Dead Sea,* where Sodom had stood. It should seem, they marched through those of the ten tribes that lay beyond Jordan, and they gave them passage through their borders; so ungrateful were they to Jehoshaphat, who had lately put his hand to help them in recovering Ramoth-Gilead. Several nations joined in this confederacy, but especially *the children of Lot,* whom the rest helped, Ps. lxxxiii. 6—8. The neighbouring nations had feared Jehoshaphat (*ch.* xvii. 10), but perhaps his affinity with Ahab had lessened him in their esteem, and they had some intimation that his God was displeased with him for it, which they fancied would give them an opportunity to make a prey of his kingdom.

II. The preparation Jehoshaphat made against the invaders. No mention is made of his mustering his forces, which yet it is most probable he did, for God must be trusted in the use of means. But his great care was to obtain the favour of God, and secure him on his side, which perhaps he was the more solicitous about because he had been lately told that there was *wrath upon him from before the Lord, ch.* xix. 2. But he is of the mind of his father David. If we must be corrected, yet *let us not fall into the hands of man.* 1. He feared. Consciousness of guilt made him fear. Those that have least sin are most sensible of it. The surprise added to the fright. Holy fear is a spur to prayer and preparation, Heb. xi. 7. 2 *He set himself to seek the Lord,* and, in the first place, to make him his friend. Those that would seek the Lord so as to find him, and to find favour with him, must *set* themselves to seek him, must do it with fixedness of thought, with sincerity of intention, and with the utmost vigour and resolution to continue seeking him. 3. He *proclaimed a fast throughout all Judah,* appointed a day of humiliation and prayer, that they might join together in confessing their sins and *asking help of the Lord.* Fasting from bodily refreshments, upon such extraordinary occasions, is a token of self-judging for the sins we have committed (we own ourselves unworthy of the bread we eat, and that God might justly withhold it from us), and of self-denial for the future; fasting *for* sin implies a resolution to fast *from* it, though it has been to us as a sweet morsel. Magistrates are to call their people to the duty of fasting and prayer upon such occasions, that it may be a national act, and so may obtain national mercies. 4. The people readily assembled out of all the cities of Judah in the court of the temple to join in prayer (*v.* 4), and they *stood before the Lord,* as beggars at his door, with their wives and children; they and their families were in danger, and therefore they bring their families with them to seek the Lord. "Lord, we are indeed a provoking people, that deserve to be abandoned to ruin; but here are little ones that are innocent, let not them perish in the storm. Nineveh was spared for the sake of the little ones, Jonah iv. 11. The place they met in was the *house of the Lord,* before *the new court,* which was perhaps lately added to the former courts (that, as some think, which was called the *court of the women);* thus they came within reach of that gracious promise which God had made, in answer to Solomon's prayer, *ch.* vii. 15. *My ears shall be attentive to the prayer that is made in this place.* 5. Jehoshaphat himself was the mouth of the congregation to God, and did not devolve the work upon his chaplains. Though the kings were forbidden to burn incense, they were allowed to pray and preach; as Solomon and Jehoshaphat here. The prayer Jehoshaphat prayed, upon this occasion, is here recorded, or part of it; and an excellent prayer it is. (1.) He acknowledges the sovereign dominion of the divine Providence, gives to God the glory of it and takes to himself the comfort of it (*v.* 6): "*Art not thou God in heaven?* No doubt thou art, which none of the gods of the heathen are; make it to appear then. Is not thy dominion, supreme over kingdoms themselves, and universal, over all kingdoms, even those of the heathen that know thee not? Control these heathen then; set bounds to their daring threatening insults. Is there not *in thy hand* the *power and might* which *none is able to withstand?* Lord, exert it on our behalf. Glorify thy own omnipotence." (2.) He lays hold on their covenant-relation to God and interest in him. "Thou that art *God in heaven* art the *God of our fathers* (*v.* 6) and *our God, v.* 7. Whom should we seek to, whom should we trust to, for relief, but to the God we have chosen and served?" (3.) He shows the title they had to this good land they were now in possession of; an indisputable title it was: "*Thou gavest it to the seed of Abraham thy friend.* He was thy friend (this is referred to, James ii. 23, to show the honour of Abraham, that *he was called the friend of God); we* are *his seed,* and hope to be *beloved for the father's sake,*" Rom. xi. 28; Deut. vii. 8, 9. "We hold this land by grant from thee. Lord, maintain thy own grant, and warrant it against all unjust claims. Suffer us not to be *cast out of thy possession.* We are tenants; thou art our landlord; wilt thou not hold thy own?" *v.* 11. Those that use what they have for God may comfortably hope that he will secure it to them. (4.) He makes mention of the sanctuary, the temple they had built for God's name (*v.* 8), not as if that merited any thing at God's hand, for *of his own they gave him,* but it was such a token of God's favourable presence with them that they had promised themselves he would hear and help them when, in their distress, they cried to him before that house, *v.* 8, 9. "Lord, when it was built it was intended for the encouragement of our faith at such a time as this. Here thy name is; here we are. Lord, help us, for the glory of thy name." (5.) He pleads the ingratitude and injustice of his enemies: "We are such as it will be thy glory to appear *for;* they are such as it will be thy glory to appear *against;* for, [1.] They ill requite our ancient kindnesses. Thou *wouldst not let Israel invade them,* nor give them any disturbance." Deut. ii. 5, 9, 19, *Meddle not with the Edomites, distress not the Moabites, come not nigh the children of Ammon,* no, not though they provoke you. "Yet now see how they invade us." We may comfortably appeal to God against those that render us evil for good. [2.] "They break in upon our ancient rights. They come *to cast us out of our possessions,* and seize our land for themselves. *O! our God, wilt thou not judge them? v.* 12. Wilt thou not give sentence against them, and execute it upon them?" The justice of God is the refuge of those that are wronged. (6.) He professes his entire dependence upon God for deliverance. Though he had a great army on foot, and well disciplined; yet he said, "*We have no might against this great company,* none without thee, none that we can expect any thing from without thy special presence and blessing, none to boast of, none to trust to; but *our eyes are upon thee.* We rely upon thee, and from thee is all our expectation. The disease seems desperate: *we know not what to do,* are quite at a loss, in a great strait. But this is a sovereign remedy, *our eyes are upon thee,* an eye of acknowledgment and humble submission, an eye of faith and entire dependence, an eye of desire and hearty prayer, an eye of hope and patient expectation. *In thee, O God! do we put our trust; our souls wait on thee.*"

14 Then upon Jahaziel the son of Zechariah, the son of Benaiah, the son of Jeiel, the son of Mattaniah, a Levite of the sons of Asaph, came the Spirit of the LORD in the midst of the congregation; 15 And he said, Hearken ye, all Judah, and ye inhabitants of Jerusalem, and thou king Jehoshaphat, Thus saith the LORD unto you, Be not afraid nor dismayed by reason of this great multitude; for the battle *is* not your's, but God's. 16 To morrow go ye down against them: behold, they come up by the cliff of Ziz; and ye shall find them at the end of the brook, before the wilderness of Jeruel. 17 Ye shall not *need* to fight in this *battle:* set yourselves, stand ye *still,* and see the salvation of the LORD with you, O Judah and Jerusalem: fear not, nor be dismayed; to morrow go out against them: for the LORD *will be* with you. 18 And Jehoshaphat bowed his head with *his* face to the ground: and all Judah and the inhabitants of Jerusalem fell before the LORD, worshipping the LORD. 19 And the Levites, of the children of the Kohathites, and of the children of the

Korhites, stood up to praise the LORD God of Israel with a loud voice on high.

We have here God's gracious answer to Jehoshaphat's prayer; and it was a speedy answer. *While he was yet speaking God heard:* before the congregation was dismissed they had assurance given them that they should be victorious; for it is never in vain to seek God. 1. The spirit of prophecy came upon a Levite that was present, not in any place of eminency, but *in the midst of the congregation, v.* 14. The Spirit, like the wind, *blows where* and on whom *he listeth.* He was of the sons of Asaph, and therefore one of the singers; on that office God would put an honour. Whether he was a prophet before this or no is uncertain, most probably he was, which would make him the more regarded. There needed no sign, the thing itself was to be performed the very next day, and that would be confirmation enough to his prophecy. 2. He encouraged them to trust in God, though the danger was very threatening (*v.* 15): "*Be not afraid;* you have admitted fear enough to bring you to God, do not now admit that which will drive you from him again. *The battle is not yours;* it is not in your own strength, not for your own cause, that you engage; the *battle is God's:* he does and will, as you have desired, interest himself in the cause." 3. He gives them intelligence of the motions of the enemy, and orders them to march towards them, with particular directions where they should find them. *To-morrow* (the day after the fast) *go you down against them, v.* 16, 17. It is fit that he who commands the deliverance should command those for whom the deliverance is to be wrought, and give the necessary orders, both for time and place. 4. He assures them that they should be, not the glorious instruments, but the joyful spectators, of the total defeat of the enemy: "You shall not need to strike a stroke; the work shall be done to your hands; only stand still and see it," *v.* 17. As Moses said to Israel at the Red Sea (Exod. xiv. 13), "*God is with you,* who is able to do his work himself, and will do it. If the battle be his, the victory shall be his too." Let but the Christian soldier go out against his spiritual enemies, and the God of peace will *tread them under his feet* and make *him more than a conqueror.* 5. Jehoshaphat and his people received these assurances with faith, reverence, and thankfulness. (1.) They *bowed their heads,* Jehoshaphat first, and then all the people, *fell before the Lord, and worshipped,* receiving with a holy awe and fear of God this token of his favour, and saying with faith, *Be it unto us according to thy word.* (2.) They lifted up their voices in praise to God, *v.* 19. An active faith can give thanks for a promise though it be not yet performed, knowing that God's bonds are as good as ready money. *God hath spoken in his holiness; I will rejoice,* Ps. lx. 5.

20 And they rose early in the morning, and went forth into the wilderness of Tekoa: and as they went forth, Jehoshaphat stood and said, Hear me, O Judah, and ye inhabitants of Jerusalem; Believe in the LORD your God, so shall ye be established; believe his prophets, so shall ye prosper. 21 And when he had consulted with the people, he appointed singers unto the LORD, and that should praise the beauty of holiness, as they went out before the army, and to say, Praise the LORD; for his mercy *endureth* for ever. 22 And when they began to sing and to praise, the LORD set ambushments against the children of Ammon, Moab, and mount Seir, which were come against Judah; and they were smitten. 23 For the children of Ammon and Moab stood up against the inhabitants of mount Seir, utterly to slay and destroy *them:* and when they had made an end of the inhabitants of Seir, every one helped to destroy another. 24 And when Judah came toward the watch tower in the wilderness, they looked unto the multitude, and, behold, they *were* dead bodies fallen to the earth, and none escaped. 25 And when Jehoshaphat and his people came to take away the spoil of them, they found among them in abundance both riches with the dead bodies, and precious jewels, which they stripped off for themselves, more than they could carry away: and they were three days in gathering of the spoil, it was so much. 26 And on the fourth day they assembled themselves in the valley of Berachah; for there they blessed the LORD: therefore the name of the same place was called, The valley of Berachah, unto this day. 27 Then they returned, every man of Judah and Jerusalem, and Jehoshaphat in the forefront of them, to go again to Jerusalem with joy; for the LORD had made them to rejoice over their enemies. 28 And they came to Jerusalem with psalteries and harps and trumpets unto the house of the LORD. 29 And the

fear of God was on all the kingdoms of *those* countries, when they had heard that the LORD fought against the enemies of Israel. 30 So the realm of Jehoshaphat was quiet: for his God gave him rest round about.

We have here the foregoing prayer answered and the foregoing promise performed, in the total overthrow of the enemies' forces and the triumph (for so it was rather than a victory) of Jehoshaphat's forces over them.

I. Never was army drawn out to the field of battle as Jehoshaphat's army was. He had soldiers *ready prepared for war* (*ch.* xvii. 18), but here is no notice taken of their military equipment, their swords or spears, their shields or bows. But Jehoshaphat took care, 1. That faith should be their armour. As they went forth, instead of calling them to handle their arms, and stand to them, to keep ranks, observe orders, and fight valiantly, he bade them *believe in the Lord God* and give credit to his word in the mouth of his prophets, and assured them that then they should *prosper* and *be established*, *v.* 20. That is true courage which faith inspires a man with; nor will any thing contribute more to the establishing of the heart in shaking times than a firm belief of the power, and mercy, and promise of God. The heart is *fixed* that thus *trusteth in the Lord*, and is kept in perfect peace. In our spiritual conflicts, this is the victory, this is the prosperity, even our faith. 2. That praise and thanksgiving should be their vanguard, *v.* 21. Jehoshaphat called a council of war, and it was resolved to appoint *singers to go out before the army*, to charge in the front, who had nothing else to do but to praise God, to praise his holiness, which is his beauty, to praise him as they did in the temple (that beauty of holiness) with that ancient and good doxology which eternity itself will not wear thread-bare, *Praise the Lord; for his mercy endureth for ever*. By this strange advance towards the field of battle, Jehoshaphat intended to express his firm reliance upon the word of God (which enabled him to triumph before the battle), to animate his own soldiers, to confound the enemy, and to engage God on their side; for praise pleases God better than all *burnt-offering and sacrifice*.

II. Never was army so unaccountably destroyed as that of the enemy; not by thunder, or hail, or the sword of an angel, not by dint of sword, or strength of arm, or any surprising alarm, like that which Gideon gave the Midianites; but the Lord set ambushments against them, either hosts of angels, or, as bishop Patrick thinks, their own ambushments, whom God struck with such confusion that they fell upon their own friends as if they had been enemies, and *every one helped to destroy another*, so that *none escaped*. This God did *when his people began to sing and to praise* (*v.* 22), for he delights to furnish those with *matter* for praise that have *hearts* for it. We read of his being *angry at the prayers of his people* (Ps. lxxx. 4), but never at their *praises*. When they did but begin the work of praise God perfected the work of their deliverance. What ground there was for their jealousies one of another does not appear, perhaps there was none; but so it was that the Ammonites and the Moabites fell foul upon the Edomites and cut them off, and then they fell out with one another and cut one another off, *v.* 23. Thus God often makes wicked people instruments of destruction to one another; and what alliances can be so firm as to keep those together whom God designs to dash in pieces one against another? See the mischievous consequences of divisions which neither of the contending parties can give any good account of the reason of. Those are wretchedly infatuated, to their ruin, that fall foul upon their friends as if they were enemies.

III. Never was spoil so cheerfully divided, for Jehoshaphat's army had nothing to do besides; the rest was done for them. When they came to the view of this vast army, instead of finding living men to fight with, they found them all dead men, and their carcases spread as dung upon the face of the earth, *v.* 24. See how rich God is in mercy to those that call upon him in truth, and how often he out-does the prayers and expectations of his people. Jehoshaphat and his people prayed to be delivered from being spoiled by the enemy; and God not only delivered them, but enriched them with the spoil of the enemy. The plunder of the field was very great and very rich. They found precious jewels with the dead bodies, which yet could not save them from being loathsome carcases. The spoil *was more than they could carry away* at once, and they were *three days in gathering it*, *v.* 25. Now it appeared what was God's end in bringing this great army against Judah; it was to humble them and prove them, that he might *do them good in their latter end*. It seemed at first a disturbance to their reformation, but it proved a recompence of it.

IV. Never was victory celebrated with more solemn and enlarged thanksgivings. 1. They kept a day of praise in the camp, before they drew their forces out of the field. Many thanksgivings, no doubt, were offered up to God immediately; but on the fourth day they assembled in a valley, where they blessed God with so much zeal and fervency that that day's work gave a name to the place, the valley of *Berachah*, that is, *of blessing*, *v.* 26. The remembrance of this work of wonder was hereby perpetuated, for the encouragement of succeeding generations to trust in God. 2. Yet they did not think this enough, but came in solemn procession, all in a body, and Jehoshaphat at the head of them, to Jerusalem, that the country, as they passed along, might join with them in their praises, and that they might give thanks for the mercy where they had by prayer obtained it, *in the house of the Lord*, *v.* 27, 28. Praising God must not be the work of a day only; but our praises, when we have received mercy, must be often repeated, as our prayers were when we were in the pursuit of it. Every day we must bless God; as long as we live, and while we have any being, we must praise him, spending our time in that work in which we hope to spend our eternity. Public mercies call for public acknowledgments *in the courts of the Lord's house*, Ps. cxvi. 19.

V. Never did victory turn to a better account than this; for, 1. Jehoshaphat's kingdom was hereby made to look very great and considerable abroad, *v.* 29. When they heard that God fought thus for Israel, they could not but say, *There is none like unto the God of Jeshurun*, and *Happy art thou, O Israel!* It begat in the neighbours a reverence of God and a cautious fear of doing any injury to his people. It is dangerous fighting against those who have God with them. 2. It was made very easy and quiet at home, *v.* 30. (1.) They were quiet among themselves. Those that were displeased at the destroying of the images and groves were now satisfied, and obliged to own that since the God of Israel could deliver after this sort he only is to be worshipped, and in that way only which he himself has appointed. (2.) They were quiet from the fear of insults from their neighbours, God having given them rest round about. And, if he give rest, who can give disturbance?

31 And Jehoshaphat reigned over Judah: *he was* thirty and five years old when he began to reign, and he reigned twenty and five years in Jerusalem. And his mother's name *was* Azubah the daughter of Shilhi. 32 And he walked in the way of Asa his father, and departed not from it, doing *that which was* right in the sight of the LORD. 33 Howbeit the high places were not taken away: for as yet the people had not prepared their hearts unto the God of their fathers. 34 Now the rest of the acts of Jehoshaphat, first and last, behold, they *are* written in the book of Jehu the son of Hanani, who *is* mentioned in the book of the kings of Israel. 35 And after this did Jehoshaphat king of Judah join himself with Ahaziah king of Israel, who did very wickedly: 36 And he joined himself with him to make ships to go to Tarshish: and they made the ships in Ezion-gaber. 37 Then Eliezer the son of Dodavah of Mareshah prophesied against Jehoshaphat, saying, Because thou hast joined thyself with Ahaziah, the LORD hath broken thy works. And the ships were broken, that they were not able to go to Tarshish.

We are now drawing towards the close of the history of Jehoshaphat's reign, for a further account of which those who lived when this book was published were referred to an authentic history of it, written by Jehu the prophet (*ch.* xix. 2), which was then extant, *v.* 34. This was the general character of his reign, that he did that which was right in the sight of the Lord, kept close to the worship of God himself and did what he could to keep his people close to it. But two things are here to be lamented:—1. The people still retained a partiality for the high places, *v.* 33. Those that were erected to the honour of strange gods were taken away (*ch.* xvii. 6); but those where the true God was worshipped, being less culpable, were thought allowable, and Jehoshaphat was loth to disoblige the people so far as to take them away, for as yet they had not prepared their hearts to serve the God of their fathers. They complied with Jehoshaphat's reformation because they could not for shame do otherwise, but they were not hearty in it, did not direct their hearts to God in it, did not act in it from any good principle nor with any zeal or resolution: and the best magistrates cannot bring to pass what they would, in reformation, when the people are cool in it. 2. Jehoshaphat himself still retained a partiality for the house of Ahab, because he had married his son to a daughter of that family, though he had been plainly reproved for it and had like to have smarted for it. He saw and knew that Ahaziah, the son of Ahab, did very wickedly, and therefore could not expect to prosper; yet he joined himself with him, not in war, as with his father, but in trade, became his partner in an East India fleet bound for Ophir, *v.* 35, 36. There is an emphasis laid upon the time—*after this*, after God had done such great things for him, without any such scandalous and pernicious confederacies, given him not only victory, but wealth, yet after this to go and join himself with a wicked king was very ungrateful. *After God had given him such a deliverance as this should he again break God's commandments, and join in affinity with the people of these abominations?* What could he expect but that *God should be angry with him?* Ezra ix. 13, 14. Yet he sends to him, to show him his error and bring him to repentance, (1.) By a prophet, who foretold the blasting of his project, *v.* 37. And, (2.) By a storm, which broke the ships in the port before they set sail, by which he was warned to break off his alliance with Ahaziah; and it seems he took the warning, for, when Ahaziah afterwards pressed him to join with him, he *would not*, 1 Kings xxii. 49. See how pernicious a thing it is to join in friendship and society with evil-doers. It is a hard matter to break off from it. A man may much better keep himself from being taken in the snare than recover himself out of it.

CHAP. XXI.

Never surely did any kingdom change its king so much for the worse as Judah did, when Jehoram, one of the vilest, succeeded Jehoshaphat, one of the best. Thus were they punished for not making a better use of Jehoshaphat's good government, and their disaffectedness (or coldness at least) to his reformation, ch. xx. 33. Those that knew not how to value a good king are justly plagued with a bad one. Here is, I. Jehoram's elevation to the throne, ver. 1—3. II. The wicked course he took to establish himself in it, by the murder of his brethren, ver. 4. III. The idolatries and other wickedness he was guilty of, ver. 5, 6, 11. IV. The prophecy of Elijah against him, ver. 12—15. V. The judgments of God upon him, in the revolt of his subjects from him (ver. 8—10) and the success of his enemies against him, ver. 16, 17. VI. His miserable sickness and inglorious exit, ver. 18—20. VII. The preservation of the house of David notwithstanding, ver. 7.

NOW Jehoshaphat slept with his fathers, and was buried with his fathers in the city of David. And Jehoram his son reigned in his stead. 2 And he had brethren the sons of Jehoshaphat, Azariah, and Jehiel, and Zechariah, and Azariah, and Michael, and Shephatiah: all these *were* the sons of Jehoshaphat king of Israel. 3 And their father gave them great gifts of silver, and of gold, and of precious things, with fenced cities in Judah: but the kingdom gave he to Jehoram; because he *was* the first-born. 4 Now when Jehoram was risen up to the kingdom of his father, he strengthened himself, and slew all his brethren with the sword, and *divers* also of the princes of Israel. 5 Jehoram *was* thirty and two years old when he began to reign, and he reigned eight years in Jerusalem. 6 And he walked in the way of the kings of Israel, like as did the house of Ahab: for he had the daughter of Ahab to wife: and he wrought *that which was* evil in the eyes of the LORD. 7 Howbeit the LORD would not destroy the house of David, because of the covenant that he had made with David, and as he promised to give a light to him and to his sons for ever. 8 In his days the Edomites revolted from under the dominion of Judah, and made themselves a king. 9 Then Jehoram went forth with his princes, and all his chariots with him: and he rose up by night, and smote the Edomites which compassed him in, and the captains of the chariots. 10 So the Edomites revolted from under the hand of Judah unto this day. The same time *also* did Libnah revolt from under his hand; because he had forsaken the LORD God of his fathers. 11 Moreover he made high places in the mountains of Judah, and caused the inhabitants of Jerusalem to commit fornication, and compelled Judah *thereto*.

We find here,

I. That Jehoshaphat was a very careful indulgent father to Jehoram. He had many sons, who are here named (*v.* 2), and it is said (*v.* 13) that they were better than Jehoram, had a great deal more wisdom and virtue, and lived up to their education, which he went counter to. They were very hopeful, and any of them more fit for the crown than he; and yet, because he was the first-born (*v.* 3), his father secured the kingdom to him, and portioned his brethren and disposed of them so as that they would be easy and give him no disturbance; as Abraham, when he made Isaac his heir, dismissed his other children with gifts. Herein Jehoshaphat was very kind and fair to his son, which might have obliged him to be respectful to him, and tread in the steps of so good a father. But it is no new thing for the children that have been most indulged by their parents to be least dutiful to them. Whether in doing this he acted wisely and well for his people, and was just to them, I cannot say. His birthright entitled him to a double portion of his father's estate, Deut. xxi. 17. But if he appeared utterly unfit for government (the end of which is the good of the people), and likely to undo all that his father had done, it would have been better perhaps to have set him aside, and taken the next that was hopeful, and not inclined as he was to idolatry. Power is a sacred thing, with which men may either do much good or much hurt; and therefore *Detur digniori—Let him that deserves it have it. Salus populi suprema lex—The security of the people is the first consideration.*

II. That Jehoram was a most barbarous brother to his father's sons. As soon as he had settled himself in the throne he slew all his brethren with the sword, either by false accusation, under colour of law, or rather by assassination. By some wicked hand or other he got them all murdered, pretending (it is likely) that he could not think himself safe in the government till they were taken out of the way. Those that mean ill themselves are commonly, without cause, jealous of those about them. The wicked fear where no fear is, or pretend to do so, in order to conceal their malice. Jehoram, it is likely, hated his brethren and slew them for the same reason that Cain hated Abel and slew him, because their piety condemned his impiety and won them that esteem with the people which he had lost. With them he slew divers of the princes of Israel, who adhered to them, or were likely to avenge their death. The princes of Judah, those who had taught the good knowledge of the Lord (*ch.* xvii. 7), are here called princes of Israel, as before *fathers of Israel* (*ch.* xix. 8), because they were Israelites indeed, men of integrity. The sword which the good father had put into their hands this wicked son sheathed in their bowels. Woe unto him that thus *foundeth a kingdom in blood* (Hab. ii. 12); it will prove a foundation that will sink the superstructure.

III. That Jehoram was a most wicked king, who corrupted and debauched his kingdom, and ruined the reformation that his good father and grandfather had carried on: He *walked in the way of the house of Ahab* (*v.* 6), made high places, which the people were of themselves too forward to make, and did his utmost to set up idolatry again, *v.* 11. 1. As for the inhabitants of Jerusalem, where he kept his court, he easily drew them into his spiritual whoredom: He *caused them to commit fornication*, seducing them *to eat things sacrificed to idols*, Rev. ii. 20. 2. The country people seem to have been brought to it with more difficulty; but those that would not be corrupted by flatteries were driven by force to partake in his abominable idolatries: He *compelled Judah thereto.* He used that power for the destruction of the church which was given him for the edification of it.

IV. That when he forsook God and his worship his subjects withdrew from their allegiance to him. 1. Some of the provinces abroad that were tributaries to him did so. The Edomites revolted (*v.* 8), and, though he chastised them (*v.* 9), yet he could not reduce them, *v.* 10. 2. One of the cities of his own kingdom did so. Libnah revolted (*v.* 10) and set up for a free state, as of old it had a king of its own, Josh. xii. 15. And the reason is here given, not only why God permitted it, but why they did it; they shook off his government because he had forsaken the Lord God of his fathers, had become an idolater and a worshipper of false gods, and they could not continue subject to him without some danger of being themselves also drawn away from God and their duty. While he adhered to God they adhered to him; but, when he cast God off, they cast him off. Whether this reason will justify them in their revolt or no, it will justify God's providence which ordered it so.

V. That yet God was tender of his covenant with the house of David, and therefore would not destroy the royal family, though it was so wretchedly corrupted and degenerated, *v.* 7. These things we had before, 2 Kings viii. 19—22. The tenour of the covenant was that David's seed should be visited for their transgressions, but the covenant should never be broken, Ps. lxxxix. 30, &c.

12 And there came a writing to him from Elijah the prophet, saying, Thus saith the LORD God of David thy father, Because thou hast not walked in the ways of Jehoshaphat thy father, nor in the ways of Asa king of Judah, 13 But hast walked in the way of the kings of Israel, and hast made Judah and the inhabitants of Jerusalem to go a whoring, like to the whoredoms of the house of Ahab, and also hast slain thy brethren of thy father's house, *which were* better than thyself: 14 Behold, with a great plague will the LORD smite thy people, and thy children, and thy wives, and all thy goods: 15 And thou *shalt have* great sickness by disease of thy bowels, until thy bowels fall out by reason of the sickness day by day. 16 Moreover the LORD stirred up against Jehoram the spirit of the Philistines, and of the Arabians, that *were* near the Ethiopians: 17 And they came up into Judah, and brake into it, and carried away all the substance that was found in the king's house, and his sons also, and his wives; so that there was never a son left him, save Jehoahaz, the youngest of his sons. 18 And after all this the LORD smote him in his bowels with an incurable disease. 19 And it came to pass, that in process of time, after the end of two years, his bowels fell out by reason of his sickness: so he died of sore diseases. And his people made no burning for him, like the burning of his fathers. 20 Thirty and two years old was he when he began to reign, and he reigned in Jerusalem eight years, and departed without being desired. Howbeit they buried him in the city of David, but not in the sepulchres of the kings.

Here we have, I. A warning from God sent to Jehoram by a writing from Elijah the prophet. By this it appears that Jehoram came to the throne, and showed himself what he was, before Elijah's translation. It is true we find Elisha attending Jehoshaphat, and described as pouring water on the hands of Elijah, after the story of Elijah's translation (2 Kings iii. 11); but that might be, and that description might be given of him, while Elijah was yet on earth: and it is certain that that history is put out of its proper place, for we read of Jehoshaphat's death, and Jehoram's coming to the crown, before we read of Elijah's translation, 1 Kings xxii. 50. We will suppose that the time of his departure was at hand, so that he could not go in person to Jehoram; but that, hearing of his great wickedness in murdering his brethren, he left this writing it is probable with Elisha, to be sent him by the first opportunity, that it might either be a means to reclaim him or a witness against him that he was fairly told what would be in the end hereof. The message is sent him in the name of *the Lord God of David his father* (*v.* 12), upbraiding him with his relation to David as that which, though it was his honour, was an aggravation of his degeneracy. 1. His crimes are plainly charged upon him—his departure from the good ways of God, in which he had been educated, and which he had been directed and encouraged to walk in by the example of his good father and grandfather, who lived and died in peace and honour (*v.* 12)—his conformity to the ways of the house of Ahab, that impious scandalous family—his setting up and enforcing idolatry in his kingdom—and his murdering his brethren because they were better than himself, *v.* 13. These are the heads of the indictment against him. 2. Judgment is given against him for these crimes; he is plainly told that his sin should certainly be the ruin, (1.) Of his kingdom and family (*v.* 14): "With a heavy stroke, even that of war and captivity, *will the Lord smite thy people and thy children,*" &c. Bad men bring God's judgments upon all about them. His people justly suffer because they had complied with his idolatry, and his wives because they had drawn him to it. (2.) Of his health and life: "Thou shalt have great sickness, very painful and tedious, and at last mortal," *v.* 15. This he is warned of before, that his blood might be upon his own head, the watchman having delivered his soul; and that when these things, so particularly foretold, came to pass, it might appear that they did not come by chance, but as the punishment of his sins, and were so intended. And now if, as he had learned of Ahab to do wickedly, he had but learned even of Ahab to humble himself upon the receipt of this threatening message from Elijah—if, like him (1 Kings xxi. 27), he had *rent his clothes, put on sackcloth, and fasted*—who knows but, like him, he might have obtained at least a reprieve? But it does not appear that he took any notice of it; he threw it by as waste-paper; Elijah seemed to him *as one that mocked.* But those that will not believe shall feel.

II. The threatened judgments brought upon him because he slighted the warning. No marvel that hardened sinners are not frightened from sin and to repentance by the threatenings of misery in another world, which is future and out of sight, when the certain prospect of misery in this world, the sinking of their estates and the ruin of their healths, will not restrain them from vicious courses.

1. See Jehoram here stripped of all his comforts. God *stirred up the spirit of his neighbours* against him, who had loved and feared Jehoshaphat, but hated and despised him, looking upon it as a scandalous thing for a nation to change their gods. Some occasion or other they took to quarrel with him, invaded his country, but, as it should seem, fought neither against small nor great, but the king's house only; they made directly to that, and *carried away all the substance that was found in it.* No mention is made of their carrying any away captive but the *king's wives* and *his sons, v.* 17. Thus God made it evident that the controversy was with him and his house. Here it is only said, They *carried away* his sons; but we find (*ch.* xxii. 1) that they *slew them all.* Blood for blood. He had slain all his brethren, to strengthen himself; and now all his sons are slain but one, and so he is weakened. If he had not been of the house of David, that one would not have escaped. When Jeroboam's house, and Baasha's, and Ahab's, were destroyed, there was none left; but David's house must not be wholly extirpated, though sometimes wretchedly degenerated, because a blessing was in it, no less a blessing than that of the Messiah.

2. See him tormented with *sore diseases and of long continuance,* such as were threatened in the law against those that would not *fear the Lord their God,* Deut. xxviii. 58, 59. His disease was very grievous. It lay in his bowels, producing a continual griping, and with this there was a complication of other sore diseases. The affliction was moreover very tedious. Two years he continued ill, and could get no relief; for the disease was incurable, though he was in the prime of life, not forty years old. Asa, whose heart was perfect with God though in some instances he stepped aside, was diseased only in his feet; but Jehoram, whose heart was wicked, was struck in his inwards, and he that had no bowels of compassion towards his brethren was so plagued in his bowels that they fell out. Even good men, and those who are very dear to God, may be afflicted with diseases of this kind; but to them they are fatherly chastisements, and by the support of divine consolations the soul may dwell at ease even then when the body lies in pain. These sore diseases seized him just after his house was plundered and his wives and children were carried away. (1.) Perhaps his grief and anguish of mind for that calamity might occasion his sickness, or at least contribute to the heightening of it. (2.) By this sickness he was disabled to do any thing for the recovery of them or the re-

venge of the injury done him. (3.) It added, no doubt, very much to his grief, in his sickness, that he was deprived of the society of his wives and children and that all the substance of his house was carried away. To be sick and poor, sick and solitary, but especially to be sick and in sin, sick and under the curse of God, sick and destitute of grace to bear the affliction, and of comfort to counterbalance it—is a most deplorable case.

3. See him buried in disgrace. He reigned but eight years, and then *departed without being desired, v.* 20. Nobody valued him while he lived, none lamented him when he died, but all wished that no greater loss might ever come to Jerusalem. To show what little affection or respect they had for him, they would not *bury him in the sepulchres of the kings,* as thinking him unworthy to be numbered among them who had governed so ill. The excluding of his body from the sepulchres of his fathers might be ordered by Providence as an intimation of the everlasting separation of the souls of the wicked, after death, from the spirits of just men. This further disgrace they put upon him, that they *made no burning for him, like the burning of his fathers, v.* 19. His memory was far from being sweet and precious to them, and therefore they did not honour it with any sweet odours or precious spices, though we may suppose that his dead body, after so long and loathsome a disease, needed something to perfume it. The generality of the people, though prone enough to idolatry, yet had no true kindness for their idolatrous kings. Wickedness and profaneness make men despicable even in the eyes of those who have but little religion themselves, while natural conscience itself often gives honour to those who are truly pious. Those that *despise God shall be lightly esteemed,* as Jehoram was.

CHAP. XXII.

We read, in the foregoing chapter, of the carrying away of Jehoram's sons and his wives; but here we find one of his sons and one of his wives left, his son Ahaziah and his wife Athaliah, both reserved to be the shame and plague of his family. I. Ahaziah was the shame of it as a partaker, 1. In the sin, and, 2. In the destruction, of the house of Ahab, ver. 1—9. II. Athaliah was the plague of it, for she destroyed all the seed-royal, and usurped the throne, ver. 10—12.

AND the inhabitants of Jerusalem made Ahaziah his youngest son king in his stead: for the band of men that came with the Arabians to the camp had slain all the eldest. So Ahaziah the son of Jehoram king of Judah reigned. 2 Forty and two years old *was* Ahaziah when he began to reign, and he reigned one year in Jerusalem. His mother's name also *was* Athaliah the daughter of Omri. 3 He also walked in the ways of the house of Ahab: for his mother was his counsellor to do wickedly. 4 Wherefore he did evil in the sight of the LORD like the house of Ahab: for they were his counsellors after the death of his father to his destruction. 5 He walked also after their counsel, and went with Jehoram the son of Ahab king of Israel to war against Hazael king of Syria at Ramoth-gilead: and the Syrians smote Joram. 6 And he returned to be healed in Jezreel because of the wounds which were given him at Ramah, when he fought with Hazael king of Syria. And Azariah the son of Jehoram king of Judah went down to see Jehoram the son of Ahab at Jezreel, because he was sick. 7 And the destruction of Ahaziah was of God by coming to Joram: for when he was come, he went out with Jehoram against Jehu the son of Nimshi, whom the LORD had anointed to cut off the house of Ahab. 8 And it came to pass, that, when Jehu was executing judgment upon the house of Ahab, and found the princes of Judah, and the sons of the brethren of Ahaziah, that ministered to Ahaziah, he slew them. 9 And he sought Ahaziah: and they caught him, (for he was hid in Samaria,) and brought him to Jehu: and when they had slain him, they buried him: Because, said they, he *is* the son of Jehoshaphat, who sought the LORD with all his heart. So the house of Ahaziah had no power to keep still the kingdom.

We have here an account of the reign of Ahaziah, a short reign (of one year only), yet long enough, unless it had been better. He was called *Jeho-ahaz* (*ch.* xxi. 17); here he is called *Ahaz-iah,* which is the same name and of the same signification, only the words of which it is compounded are transposed. He is here said to be forty-two years old when he began to reign (*v.* 2), which could not be, for his father, his immediate predecessor, was but forty when he died, and it is said (2 Kings viii. 26) that he was twenty-two years old when *he began to reign.* Some make this forty-two to be the age of his mother Athaliah, for in the original it is, *he was the son of forty-two years,* that is, the son of a mother that was of that age; and justly is her age put for his, in reproach to him, because she managed him, and did what she would—she, in effect, reigned, and he had little more than the title of king. Many good expositors are ready to allow that this, with some few more such difficulties, arises from the mistake of some transcriber, who put forty-two for twenty-two, and the copies by which the error should have been corrected might be lost. Many ancient translations read it here twenty-two. Few books are now printed without some *errata*, yet the authors do not therefore disown them, nor are the errors of the press imputed to the author, but the candid reader amends them by the sense, or by comparing them with some other part of the work, as we may easily do this.

The history of Ahaziah's reign is briefly summed up in two clauses, *v.* 3, 4. His mother and her relations were his counsellors to do wickedly, and it was to his destruction.

I. He did wickedly. Though by a special providence of God he was preserved alive, when all his brethren were slain, and reserved for the crown, notwithstanding he was the youngest of them—though *the inhabitants of Jerusalem,* when they had buried his father ingloriously, made him king, in hopes he would take warning by that not to tread in his steps, but would do better for himself and his kingdom—yet he was not influenced by the favours either of God or man, but *walked in the way of the house of Ahab, did evil in the sight of the Lord* like them (*v.* 3, 4), that is, he worshipped the same false gods that they worshipped, Baalim and Ashtaroth, supposing (as the learned bishop Patrick thinks) that by these demons, as mediators, they might have easier access to the supreme *Numen,* the God of Israel, or that *these they might resort* to *at all times* and *for all matters,* as being *nearer at hand,* and *not of so high a dignity,* but of a *middle nature* between the immortal God and mortal men—deified heroes; so they worshipped them as the church of Rome does saints and angels. That was sufficiently bad; but I wish there was no reason to suspect worse. I am apprehensive that they looked upon Jehovah, the God of their fathers, to be altogether such a one as these Baalim, and them to be as great and as good as he, nay, upon one account, more eligible, inasmuch as these Baalim encouraged in their worshippers all manner of lewdness and sensuality, which the God of Israel strictly forbade.

II. He was counselled by his mother and her relations to do so. *She was his counsellor* (*v.* 3) and so were *they, after the death of his father, v.* 4. While his father lived *he* took care to keep him to idolatry; but, when he was dead, the house of Ahab feared lest his father's miserable end should deter him from it, and therefore they were very industrious to keep him closely to it, and to make him *seven times* more a *child of hell than themselves.* The counsel of the ungodly is the ruin of many young persons when they are setting out in the world. This young prince might have had better advice if he had pleased from the princes and the judges, the priests and the Levites, that had been famous in his good grandfather's time for teaching the knowledge of God; but the house of Ahab humoured him, and *he walked after their counsel,* gave himself up to be led by them, and did just as they would have him. Thus do those debase and destroy themselves that forsake the divine guidance.

III. He was counselled by them to his destruction. So it proved. Those that counsel us to do wickedly counsel us to our destruction; while they fawn, and flatter, and pretend friendship, they are really our worst enemies. Those that debauch young men destroy them. It was bad enough that they exposed him to the sword of the Syrians, drawing him in to join with Joram king of Israel in an expedition to Ramoth-Gilead, where Joram was wounded, an expedition that was not for his honour. Those that give us bad counsel in the affairs of religion, if regarded by us, may justly be made of God our counsellors to do foolishly in our own affairs. But that was not all: by engaging him in an intimacy with Joram king of Israel, they involved him in the common ruin of the house of Ahab. He came on a visit to Joram (*v.* 6) just at the time that Jehu was executing the judgment of God upon that idolatrous family, and so was cut off with them, *v.* 7—9. Here, 1. See and dread the mischief of bad company—of joining in with sinners. If not the infection, yet let the destruction be feared. *Come out from Babylon,* that falling house, Rev. xviii. 4. 2. See and acknowledge the justice of God. His providence brought Ahaziah, just at this fatal juncture, to see Joram, that he might fall with him and be taken as in a snare. This we had an account of before, 2 Kings ix. 27, 28. It is here added that he was decently buried (not as Jehoram, whose dead body was cast into Naboth's vineyard, 2 Kings ix. 26), and the reason given is because he was the son (that is, the grandson) of good Jehoshaphat, *who sought the Lord with his heart.* Thus is *he* remembered with honour long after his death, and some respect shown even to his degenerate unworthy seed for his sake. *The memory of the just is blessed, but the name of the wicked shall rot.*

10 But when Athaliah the mother of Ahaziah saw that her son was dead, she arose and destroyed all the seed royal of the house of Judah. 11 But Jehoshabeath, the daughter of the king, took Joash the son of Ahaziah, and stole him from among the king's sons that were slain, and put him and his nurse in a bedchamber. So Jehoshabeath, the daughter of king

Jehoram, the wife of Jehoiada the priest, (for she was the sister of Ahaziah,) hid him from Athaliah, so that she slew him not. 12 And he was with them hid in the house of God six years: and Athaliah reigned over the land.

We have here what we had before, 2 Kings xi. 1, &c. 1. A wicked woman endeavouring to destroy the house of David, that she might set up a throne for herself upon the ruins of it. Athaliah barbarously cut off all the seed-royal (*v.* 10), perhaps intending to transmit the crown of Judah after herself to some of her own relations, that though her family was cut off in Israel by Jehu it might be planted in Judah. 2. A good woman effectually preserving it from being wholly extirpated. One of the late king's sons, a child of a year old, was rescued from among the dead, and saved alive by the care of Jehoiada's wife (*v.* 11, 12), that a *lamp might be ordained for God's anointed;* for no word of God shall fall to the ground.

CHAP. XXIII.

Six years bloody Athaliah had tyrannised; in this chapter we have her deposed and slain, and Joash, the rightful heir, enthroned. We had the story before nearly as it is here related, 2 Kings xi. 4, &c. I. Jehoiada prepared the people for the king, acquainted them with his design, armed them, and appointed them their posts, ver. 1—10. II. He produced the king to the people, crowned him, and anointed him, ver. 11. III. He slew the usurper, ver. 12—15. IV. He reformed the kingdom, re-established religion, and restored the civil government, ver. 16—21.

AND in the seventh year Jehoiada strengthened himself, and took the captains of hundreds, Azariah the son of Jeroham, and Ishmael the son of Jehohanan, and Azariah the son of Obed, and Maaseiah the son of Adaiah, and Elishaphat the son of Zichri, into covenant with him. 2 And they went about in Judah, and gathered the Levites out of all the cities of Judah, and the chief of the fathers of Israel, and they came to Jerusalem. 3 And all the congregation made a covenant with the king in the house of God. And he said unto them, Behold, the king's son shall reign, as the LORD hath said of the sons of David. 4 This *is* the thing that ye shall do; A third part of you entering on the sabbath, of the priests and of the Levites, *shall be* porters of the doors; 5 And a third part *shall be* at the king's house; and a third part at the gate of the foundation: and all the people *shall be* in the courts of the house of the LORD. 6 But let none come into the house of the LORD, save the priests, and they that minister of the Levites; they shall go in, for they *are* holy: but all the people shall keep the watch of the LORD. 7 And the Levites shall compass the king round about, every man with his weapons in his hand; and whosoever *else* cometh into the house, he shall be put to death: but be ye with the king when he cometh in, and when he goeth out. 8 So the Levites and all Judah did according to all things that Jehoiada the priest had commanded, and took every man his men that were to come in on the sabbath, with them that were to go *out* on the sabbath: for Jehoiada the priest dismissed not the courses. 9 Moreover Jehoiada the priest delivered to the captains of hundreds spears, and bucklers, and shields, that *had been* king David's, which *were* in the house of God. 10 And he set all the people, every man having his weapon in his hand, from the right side of the temple to the left side of the temple, along by the altar and the temple, by the king round about. 11 Then they brought out the king's son, and put upon him the crown, and *gave him* the testimony, and made him king. And Jehoiada and his sons anointed him, and said, God save the king.

We may well imagine the bad posture of affairs in Jerusalem during Athaliah's six years' usurpation, and may wonder that God permitted it and his people bore it so long; but after such a dark and tedious night the returning day in this revolution was the brighter and the more welcome. The continuance of David's seed and throne was what God had sworn by his holiness (Ps. lxxxix. 35), and an interruption was no defeasance; the stream of government here runs again in the right channel. The instrument and chief manager of the restoration is Jehoiada, who appears to have been, 1. A man of great prudence, who reserved the young prince for so many years till he was fit to appear in public, and till the nation had grown weary of the usurper, who prepared his work beforehand, and then effected it with admirable secresy and expedition. When God has work to do he will qualify and animate men for it. 2. A man of great interest. The captains joined with him, *v.* 1. The Levites and the chief of the fathers of Israel came at his call to Jerusalem (*v.* 2) and were there ready to receive his orders. See what a command wisdom and virtue will give men. *The Levites and all Judah did as Jehoiada commanded* (*v.* 8), and, which is strange, all that were entrusted with the secret kept their own counsel till it was executed. Thus *the words of the wise are heard in quiet*, Eccl. ix. 17. 3. A man of great faith. It was not only common equity (much less his wife's relation to the royal family) that put him upon this undertaking, but a regard to the word of God, and the divine entail of the crown (*v.* 3): *The king's son shall reign*, must reign, *as the Lord hath said.* His eye to the promise, and dependence upon that, added a great deal of glory to this undertaking. 4. A man of great religion. This matter was to be done in the temple, which might occasion some breach of rule, and the necessity of the case might be thought to excuse it; but he gave special order that none of the people should come into the house of the Lord, but the priests and Levites only, who were holy, upon pain of death, *v.* 6, 7. Never let sacred things be profaned, no, not for the support of civil rights. 5. A man of great resolution. When he had undertaken this business he went through with it, *brought out the king, crowned him, and gave him the testimony*, *v.* 11. He ventured his head, but it was in a good cause, and therefore he went on boldly. It is here said that his sons joined with him in anointing the young king. One of them, it is likely, was that Zechariah whom Joash afterwards put to death for reproving him (*ch.* xxiv. 20), which was so much the more ungrateful because he bore a willing part in anointing him.

12 Now when Athaliah heard the noise of the people running and praising the king, she came to the people into the house of the LORD: 13 And she looked, and, behold, the king stood at his pillar at the entering in, and the princes and the trumpets by the king: and all the people of the land rejoiced, and sounded with trumpets, also the singers with instruments of music, and such as taught to sing praise. Then Athaliah rent her clothes, and said, Treason, Treason. 14 Then Jehoiada the priest brought out the captains of hundreds that were set over the host, and said unto them, Have her forth of the ranges: and whoso followeth her, let him be slain with the sword. For the priest said, Slay her not in the house of the LORD. 15 So they laid hands on her; and when she was come to the entering of the horse gate by the king's house, they slew her there. 16 And Jehoiada made a covenant between him, and between all the people, and between the king, that they should be the LORD's people. 17 Then all the people went to the house of Baal, and brake it down, and brake his altars and his images in pieces, and slew Mattan the priest of Baal before the altars. 18 Also Jehoiada appointed the offices of the house of the LORD by the hand of the priests the Levites, whom David had distributed in the house of the LORD, to offer the burnt offerings of the LORD, as *it is* written in the law of Moses, with rejoicing and with singing, *as it was ordained* by David. 19 And he set the porters at the gates of the house of the LORD, that none *which was* unclean in any thing should enter in. 20 And he took the captains of hundreds, and the nobles, and the governors of the people, and all the people of the land, and brought down the king from the house of the LORD: and they came through the high gate into the king's house, and set the king upon the throne of the kingdom. 21 And all the people of the land rejoiced: and the city was quiet, after that they had slain Athaliah with the sword.

Here we have, I. The people pleased, *v.* 12, 13. When the king stood at his pillar, whose right it was to stand there, *all the people of the land rejoiced to see a rod sprung out of the stem of Jesse*, Isa. xi. 1. When it seemed a withered root in a dry ground, to see what they despaired of ever seeing—a king of the house of David, what a pleasing surprise was it to them! They ran in transports of joy to see this sight, praised the king, and praised God, for they had with them such as *taught to sing praise*

II. Athaliah slain. She ran upon the point of the sword of justice; for, imagining her interest much better than it was, she ventured *into the house of the Lord* at that time, and cried, *Treason, treason!* But nobody seconded her, or sided with her. The pride of her heart deceived her. She thought all her own, whereas none were cordially so. Jehoiada, as protector in the king's minority, ordered her to be slain (*v.* 14), which was done immediately (*v.* 15), only care was taken that she should not be *slain in the house of the Lord*, that sacred place must not be so far disgraced, nor that wicked woman so far honoured.

III. The original contract agreed to, *v.* 16. In the *Kings* it is said that Jehoiada made a covenant between the *Lord*, the people, and the king, 2 Kings xi. 17. Here it is said to be between *himself*, the people, and the king; for he, as God's priest, was his representative in this transaction, or a sort of mediator, as Moses was. The indenture was tripartite, but the true intent and meaning of the whole was that *they should be the Lord's people.* God covenanted by Jehoiada to take them for his people; the king and people covenanted with him to be his; and then the king covenanted with the people to govern them *as the people of God,* and the people with the king to be subject to him *as the Lord's people,* in his fear and for his sake. Let us look upon ourselves and one another as *the Lord's people,* and this will have a powerful influence upon us in the discharge of all our duty both to God and man.

IV. Baal destroyed, *v.* 17. They would not have done half their work if they had only destroyed the usurper of the *king's* right, and not the usurper of *God's* right—if they had asserted the honour of the throne, and not that of the altar. The greatest grievance of Athaliah's reign was the bringing in of the worship of Baal, and supporting of that; therefore that must be abolished in the first place. Down with Baal's house, his altars, his images; down with them all, and let the blood of his priests be mingled with his sacrifices; for God had commanded that seducers to idolatry should be put to death, Deut. xiii. 5, 6.

V. The temple service revived, *v.* 18, 19. This had been neglected in the last reigns, the priest and people wanting either power or zeal to keep it up when they had princes that were disaffected to it. But Jehoiada restored *the offices of the house of the Lord,* which in the late times had been disturbed and invaded, to the proper course and proper hands. 1. He appointed the priests to their courses, for the due offering of sacrifices, according to the law of Moses. 2. The singers to theirs, according to the appointment of David. The sacrifices (it should seem) were *offered with rejoicing and singing,* and with good reason. We *joy in God* when we *receive the atonement,* Rom. v. 11. 3. The porters were put in their respective posts as David ordered (*v.* 19), and their office was to take care that none who were upon any account ceremonially unclean should be admitted into the courts of the temple.

VI. The civil government re-established, *v.* 20. They brought the king in state to his own palace, and set him *upon the throne of the kingdom,* to give law, and give judgment, either in his own person or by Jehoiada his tutor. Thus was this happy revolution perfected. The generality of the people rejoiced in it, and the rest were quiet and made no opposition, *v.* 21. When the Son of David is enthroned in the soul all is quiet and springs of joy are opened.

CHAP. XXIV.

We have here the history of the reign of Joash, the progress of which, and especially its termination, were not of a piece with its beginning, nor shone with so much lustre. How wonderfully he was preserved for the throne, and placed in it, we read before; now here we are told how he began in the spirit, but ended in the flesh. I. In the beginning of his time, while Jehoiada lived, he did well; particularly, he took care to put the temple in good repair, ver. 1—14. II. In the latter end of his time, after Jehoiada's death, he apostatized from God, and his apostasy was his ruin. 1. He set up the worship of Baal again (ver. 15—18), though warned to the contrary, ver. 19. 2. He put Zechariah the prophet to death because he reproved him for what he had done, ver. 20—22. 3. The judgments of God came upon him for it. The Syrians invaded him, ver. 23, 24. He was struck with sore diseases; his own servants conspired against him and slew him; and, as a mark of infamy upon him, he was not buried in the burying-place of the kings, ver. 25—27.

JOASH *was* seven years old when he began to reign, and he reigned forty years in Jerusalem. His mother's name also *was* Zibiah of Beer-sheba. 2 And Joash did *that which was* right in the sight of the LORD all the days of Jehoiada the priest. 3 And Jehoiada took for him two wives; and he begat sons and daughters. 4 And it came to pass after this, *that* Joash was minded to repair the house of the LORD. 5 And he gathered together the priests and the Levites, and said to them, Go out unto the cities of Judah, and gather of all Israel money to repair the house of your God from year to year, and see that ye hasten the matter. Howbeit the Levites hastened *it* not. 6 And the king called for Jehoiada the chief, and said unto him, Why hast thou not required of the Levites to bring in out of Judah and out of Jerusalem the collection, *according to the commandment* of Moses the servant of the LORD, and of the congregation of Israel, for the tabernacle of witness? 7 For the sons of Athaliah, that wicked woman, had broken up the house of God; and also all the dedicated things of the house of the LORD did they bestow upon Baalim. 8 And at the king's commandment they made a chest, and set it without at the gate of the house of the LORD. 9 And they made a proclamation through Judah and Jerusalem, to bring in to the LORD the collection *that* Moses the servant of God *laid* upon Israel in the wilderness. 10 And all the princes and all the people rejoiced, and brought in, and cast into the chest, until they had made an end. 11 Now it came to pass, that at what time the chest was brought unto the king's office by the hand of the Levites, and when they saw that *there was* much money, the king's scribe and the high priest's officer came and emptied the chest, and took it, and carried it to his place again. Thus they did day by day, and gathered money in abundance. 12 And the king and Jehoiada gave it to such as did the work of the service of the house of the LORD, and hired masons and carpenters to repair the house of the LORD, and also such as wrought iron and brass to mend the house of the LORD. 13 So the workmen wrought, and the work was perfected by them, and they set the house of God in his state, and strengthened it. 14 And when they had finished *it*, they brought the rest of the money before the king and Jehoiada, whereof were made vessels for the house of the LORD, *even* vessels to minister, and to offer *withal*, and spoons, and vessels of gold and silver. And they offered burnt offerings in the house of the LORD continually all the days of Jehoiada.

This account of Joash's good beginnings we had as it stands here 2 Kings xii. 1, &c., though the latter part of this chapter, concerning his apostasy, we had little of there. What is good in men we should take all occasions to speak of and often repeat it; what is evil we should make mention of but sparingly, and no more than is needful. We shall here only observe, 1. That it is a happy thing for young people, when they are setting out in the world, to be under the direction of those that are wise and good and faithful to them, as Joash was under the influence of Jehoiada, during whose time he *did that which was right*. Let those that are young reckon it a blessing to them, and not a burden and check upon them, to have those with them that will caution them against that which is evil and advise and quicken them to that which is good; and let them reckon it not a mark of weakness and subjection, but of wisdom and discretion, to hearken to such. He that will not be counselled cannot be helped. It is especially prudent for young people to take advice in their marriages, as Joash did, who left it to his guardian to choose him his wives, because Jezebel and Athaliah had been such plagues, *v.* 3. This is a turn of life which often proves either the making or marring of young people, and therefore should be attended to with great care. 2. Men may go far in the external performances of religion, and keep long to them, merely by the power of their education and the influence of their friends, who yet have no hearty affection for divine things nor any inward relish of them. Foreign inducements may push men on to that which is good who are not actuated by a living principle of grace in their hearts. 3. In the outward expressions of devotion it is possible that those who have only the form of godliness may out-strip those who have the power of it. Joash is more solicitous and more zealous about the repair of the temple than Jehoiada himself, whom he reproves for his remissness in that matter, *v.* 6. It is easier to build temples than to be temples to God. 4. The repairing of churches is a good work, which all in their places should promote, for the decency and conveniency of religious assemblies. The learned tell us that in the Christian church, anciently, part of the tithes were applied that way. 5. Many a good work would be done that now lies undone if there were but a few active men to stir in it and to put it forward. When Joash found that money did not come in as he expected in one way he tried another way, and that answered the intention. Many have honesty enough to follow that have not zeal enough to lead in that which is good. The throwing of money into a chest, through a hole in the lid of it, was a way that had not been used before, and perhaps the very novelty of the thing made it a successful expedient for the raising of money; a great deal was thrown in and with a great deal of cheerfulness: they all rejoiced, *v.* 10. An invention to please people's humour may sometimes bring them to their duty. Wisdom herein is profitable to direct. 6. Faithfulness is the greatest praise and will be the greatest comfort of those that are entrusted with public treasure or employed in public business. The king and Jehoiada faithfully paid the money to the workmen, who faithfully did the work, *v.* 12, 13.

15 But Jehoiada waxed old, and was full of days when he died; a hundred and thirty years old *was he* when he died. 16 And they buried him in the city of David among the kings, because he had done good in Israel, both toward God, and toward his house. 17 Now after the death of Jehoiada came the princes of Judah, and made obeisance to the king. Then the king hearkened unto them. 18 And they left the house of the LORD God of their fathers, and served groves and idols: and wrath came upon Judah and Jerusalem for this their trespass. 19 Yet he sent prophets to them, to bring them again unto the LORD; and they testified against them: but they would not give ear. 20 And the Spirit of God came upon Zechariah the son of Jehoiada the priest, which stood above the people,

and said unto them, Thus saith God, Why transgress ye the commandments of the LORD, that ye cannot prosper? because ye have forsaken the LORD, he hath also forsaken you. 21 And they conspired against him, and stoned him with stones at the commandment of the king in the court of the house of the LORD. 22 Thus Joash the king remembered not the kindness which Jehoiada his father had done to him, but slew his son. And when he died, he said, The LORD look upon *it*, and require *it*. 23 And it came to pass at the end of the year, *that* the host of Syria came up against him: and they came to Judah and Jerusalem, and destroyed all the princes of the people from among the people, and sent all the spoil of them unto the king of Damascus. 24 For the army of the Syrians came with a small company of men, and the LORD delivered a very great host into their hand, because they had forsaken the LORD God of their fathers. So they executed judgment against Joash. 25 And when they were departed from him, (for they left him in great diseases,) his own servants conspired against him for the blood of the sons of Jehoiada the priest, and slew him on his bed, and he died: and they buried him in the city of David, but they buried him not in the sepulchres of the kings. 26 And these are they that conspired against him; Zabad the son of Shimeath an Ammonitess, and Jehozabad the son of Shimrith a Moabitess. 27 Now *concerning* his sons, and the greatness of the burdens *laid* upon him, and the repairing of the house of God, behold, they *are* written in the story of the book of the kings. And Amaziah his son reigned in his stead.

We have here a sad account of the degeneracy and apostasy of Joash. God had done great things for him; he had done something for God; but now he proved ungrateful to his God and false to the engagements he had laid himself under to him. *How has the gold become dim, and the most fine gold changed!* Here we find,

I. The occasions of his apostasy. When he did that which was right it was *not with a perfect heart*. He never was sincere, never acted from principle, but in compliance to Jehoiada, who had helped him to the crown, and because he had been protected in the temple and rose upon the ruins of idolatry; and therefore, when the wind turned, he turned with it. 1. His good counsellor left him, and was by death removed from him. It was a mercy to him and his kingdom that Jehoiada lived so long—130 *years* (*v.* 15), by which it appears that he was born in Solomon's time, and had lived six entire reigns before this. It was an encouragement to him to go on in that good way which Jehoiada had trained him up in to see what honour was done to Jehoiada at his death: *They buried him among the kings,* with this honourable encomium (perhaps it was part of the inscription on his grave-stone), that *he had done good in Israel.* Judah is called *Israel* because, the other tribes having revolted from God, they only were Israelites indeed. Note, It is the greatest honour to do good in our generations, and those who *do that which is good shall have praise of the same.* He had done good towards God; not that any man's goodness can extend unto him, but he had done good towards his house, in reviving the temple service, *ch.* xxiii. 8. Note, Those do the greatest good to their country that lay out themselves in their places to promote religion. Well, Jehoiada finished his course with honour; but the little religion that Joash had was all buried in his grave, and, after his death, both king and kingdom miserably degenerated. See how much one head may sustain, and what a great judgment to any prince or people the death of godly, zealous, useful men is. See how necessary it is that, as our Saviour speaks, we *have salt in ourselves,* that we act in religion from an inward principle, which will carry us on through all changes. Then the loss of a parent, a minister, a friend, will not involve the loss of our religion. 2. Bad counsellors got about him, insinuated themselves into his affections, wheedled him, flattered him, *made obeisance* to him, and, instead of condoling, congratulated him upon the death of his old tutor, as his release from the discipline he had been so long under, unworthy a man, a king. They tell him he must be priest-ridden no longer, he is now discharged from *grave lessons and restraints,* he may do as he pleases: and (would you think it?) the princes of Judah were the men that were so industrious to debauch him, *v.* 17. His father and grandfather were corrupted by the house of *Ahab,* from whom no better could be expected. But that the princes of Judah should be seducers to their king was very sad. But those that incline to the *counsels of the ungodly* will never want ungodly counsellors. They *made obeisance to the king,* flattered him into an opinion of his absolute power, promised to stand by him in making his royal will and pleasure pass for a law, any divine precept or institution to the contrary in any wise notwithstanding. And he hearkened to them: their discourse pleased him, and was more agreeable than Jehoiada's dictates used to be. Princes and inferior people have been many a time thus flattered into their ruin by those who have promised them liberty and dignity, but who have really brought them into the greatest servitude and disgrace.

II. The apostasy itself: *They left the house of God, and served groves and idols, v.* 18. The princes, it is likely, had a request to the king, which they tell him they durst not offer while Jehoiada lived; but now they hope it will give no offence: it is that they may set up the groves and idols again which were thrown down in the beginning of his reign, for they hate to be always confined to the dull old-fashioned service of the temple. And he not only gave them leave to do it themselves, but he joined with them. The king and princes, who, a little while ago, were repairing the temple, now forsook the temple; those who had pulled down groves and idols now themselves served them. So inconstant a thing is man and so little confidence is to be put in him!

III. The aggravations of this apostasy and the additions of guilt to it. God *sent prophets to them* (*v.* 19) to reprove them for their wickedness, and to tell them what would be in the end thereof, and so *to bring them again unto the Lord.* It is the work of ministers to bring people, not to themselves, but to God—to bring those again to him who have gone a whoring from him. In the most degenerate times God *left not himself without witness;* though they had dealt very disingenuously with God, yet he sent prophets to them to convince and instruct them, and to assure them that they should find favour with him if yet they would return; for he would rather sinners should *turn and live* than *go on and die,* and those that perish shall be left inexcusable. The prophets did their part: *they testified against them;* but, few or none *received their testimony.*

1. They slighted all the prophets; they would not give ear, were so strangely wedded to their idols that no reproofs, warnings, threatenings, nor any of the various methods which the prophets took to convince them would reclaim them. Few would hear them, fewer would heed them, but fewest of all would believe them or be governed by them.

2. They slew one of the most eminent, *Zechariah the son of Jehoiada,* and perhaps others. Concerning him observe,

(1.) The message which he delivered to them in the name of God, *v.* 20. The people were assembled in the court of the temple (for they had not quite left it), probably on occasion of some solemn feast, when this Zechariah, being filled with the spirit of prophecy, and known (it is likely) to be a prophet, stood up in some of the desks that were in the court of the priests, and very plainly, but without any provoking language, told the people of their sin and what would be the consequences of it. He did not impeach any particular persons, nor predict any particular judgments, as sometimes the prophets did, but as inoffensively as possible reminded them of what was written in the law. Let them but look into their Bibles, and there they would find, [1.] The precept they broke: "*You transgress the commandments of the Lord,* you know you do so, in serving groves and idols: and why will you so offend God and wrong yourselves?" [2.] The penalty they incurred: "You know, if the word of God be true, you cannot prosper in this evil way; never expect to do ill and fare well. Nay, you find already that *because you have forsaken the Lord he hath forsaken you,* as he told you he would," Deut. xxix. 25; xxxi. 16, 17. This is the work of ministers, by the word of God, as a lamp and a light, to expose the sin of men and expound the providences of God.

(2.) The barbarous treatment they gave him for his kindness and faithfulness in delivering this message to them, *v.* 21. By the conspiracy of the princes, or some of their party, and *by the commandment of the king,* who thought himself affronted by this fair warning, they stoned him to death immediately, not under colour of law, accusing him as a blasphemer, a traitor, or a false prophet, but in a popular tumult, *in the court of the house of the Lord*—as horrid a piece of wickedness as perhaps any we read of in all the history of the kings. The *person* was sacred—a priest, the *place* sacred—the court of the temple (the inner court, *between the porch and the altar*), the *message* yet more sacred, and we have reason to think that they knew it came from the spirit of prophecy. The reproof was just, the warning fair, both backed with scripture, and the delivery very gentle and tender; and yet so impudently and daringly do they defy God himself that nothing less than the blood of the prophet can satisfy their indignation at the prophecy. *Be astonished, O heavens! at this,* and *tremble, O earth!* that ever such villany should be committed by men, by Israelites, in contempt and violation of every thing that is just, honourable, and sacred—that a king, a king in covenant with God, should command the murder of one whom it was his office to protect and countenance! The Jews say there were seven transgressions in this; for they killed a priest, a prophet, a judge, they shed innocent blood, and polluted the court of the temple, the sabbath, and the day of expiation: for on that day, their tradition says, this happened.

(3.) The aggravation of this sin, that this Zechariah, who suffered martyrdom for his faithfulness to God and his country, was the son of Jehoiada, who had done so much good in Israel, and particularly had been as a father to Joash, *v.* 22. The affront done by it to God, and the contempt put on religion, are not so particularly taken notice of as the ingratitude there was in it to the memory of Jehoiada. He remembered not the kindness of the father, but slew the son for doing his duty, and what the father would have done if he had been there. Call a man ungrateful, and you can call him no worse.

(4.) The dying martyr's prophetic imprecation of vengeance upon his murderers: *The Lord look upon it, and require it!* This came not from a spirit of revenge, but a spirit of prophecy: *He will require it.* This would be the continual cry of the blood they shed, as Abel's blood cried against Cain: "Let the God to whom vengeance belongs demand blood for blood. He will do it, for he is righteous." This precious blood was quickly reckoned for in the judgments that came upon this apostate prince; it came into the account afterwards in the destruction of Jerusalem by the Chaldeans—their misusing the prophets was that which brought upon them ruin without remedy (*ch.* xxxvi. 16); nay, our Saviour makes the persecutors of him and his gospel answerable for the blood of this Zechariah; so loud, so long, does the blood of the martyrs cry. See Matt. xxiii. 35. Such as this is the cry of the souls under the altar (Rev. vi. 10), *How long ere thou avenge our blood?* For it shall not always go unrevenged.

IV. The judgments of God which came upon Joash for this aggravated wickedness of his. 1. A small army of Syrians made themselves masters of Jerusalem, destroyed the princes, plundered the city, and sent the spoil of it to Damascus, *v.* 23, 24. God's people, while they kept in with God, had often been conquerors when the enemy had the advantage of the greater number; but now, on the contrary, an inconsiderable handful of Syrians routed a *very great host of Israelites, because they had forsaken the Lord God of their fathers,* and then they were not only put upon the level with their enemies, but opposed them with the utmost disadvantage; for their God not only departed from them, but *turned to be their enemy and fought against them.* The Syrians were employed as instruments in God's hand to *execute judgments against Joash,* though they little thought so, Isa. x. 6, 7, and see Deut. xxxii. 30. 2. God smote him with great diseases, of body, or mind, or both, either like his grandfather (*ch.* xxi. 18), or, like Saul, an evil spirit from God troubling him. While he was plagued with the Syrians he thought that, if he could but get clear of them, he should do well enough. But, before they departed from him, God smote him with diseases. If vengeance pursue men, the end of one trouble will but be the beginning of another. 3. His own servants conspired against him. Perhaps he began to hope his disease would be cured—he was but a middle-aged man and might recover it; but *he that cometh up out of the pit shall fall into the snare.* When he thought he should escape death by sickness he met it by the sword. They slew him in his bed *for the blood of the sons of Jehoiada,* by which it should seem that he did not only slay Zechariah, but others of the sons of Jehoiada for his sake. Perhaps those that slew him *intended* to take vengeance for that blood; but, whether they did or not, this was what God intended in permitting them to slay him. Those that drink the blood of the saints shall have their own blood given them to drink, for they are worthy. The regicides are here named (*v.* 26), and it is observable that the mothers of them both were foreigners, one an Ammonitess and the other a Moabitess. The idolatrous kings, it is likely, countenanced those marriages which the law prohibited for the prevention of idolatry; and see how they resulted in their own destruction. 4. His people would not bury him in the sepulchres of the kings because he had stained his honour by his mal-administration. *Let him not be written with the righteous,* Ps. lxix. 28. These judgments are called the *burdens laid upon him* (*v.* 27), for the wrath of God is a heavy burden, too heavy for any man to bear. Or it may be meant of the threatenings denounced against him by the prophets, for those are called *burdens.* Usually God sets some special marks of his displeasure upon apostates in this life, for warning to all to *remember Lot's wife.*

CHAP. XXV.

Amaziah's reign, recorded in this chapter, was not one of the wors and yet far from good. Most of the passages in this chapter we had before more briefly related, 2 Kings xiv. Here we find Amaziah, I. A just revenger of his father's death, ver. 1—4. II. An obedient observer of the command of God, ver. 5—10. III. A cruel conqueror of the Edomites, ver. 11—13. IV. A foolish worshipper of the gods of Edom and impatient of reproof for it, ver. 14—16. V. Rashly challenging the king of Israel, and smarting for his rashness, ver. 17—24. And, lastly, ending his days ingloriously, ver. 25—28.

AMAZIAH *was* twenty and five years old *when* he began to reign, and he reigned twenty and nine years in Jerusalem. And his mother's name *was* Jehoaddan of Jerusalem. 2 And he did *that which was* right in the sight of the LORD, but not with a perfect heart. 3 Now it came to pass, when the kingdom was established to him, that he slew his servants that had killed the king his father. 4 But he slew not their children, but *did* as *it is* written in the law in the book of Moses, where the LORD commanded, saying, The fathers shall not die for the children, neither shall the children die for the fathers, but every man shall die for his own sin. 5 Moreover Amaziah gathered Judah together, and made them captains over thousands, and captains over hundreds, according to the houses of *their* fathers, throughout all Judah and Benjamin: and he numbered them from twenty years old and above, and found them three hundred thousand choice *men, able* to go forth to war, that could handle spear and shield. 6 He hired also a hundred thousand mighty men of valour out of Israel for a hundred talents of silver. 7 But there came a man of God to him, saying, O king, let not the army of Israel go with thee; for the LORD *is* not with Israel, *to wit, with* all the children of Ephraim. 8 But if thou wilt go, do *it*, be strong for the battle: God shall make thee fall before the enemy: for God hath power to help, and to cast down. 9 And Amaziah said to the man of God, But what shall we do for the hundred talents which I have given to the army of Israel? And the man of God answered, The LORD is able to give thee much more than this. 10 Then Amaziah separated them, *to wit*, the army that was come to him out of Ephraim, to go home again: wherefore their anger was greatly kindled against Judah, and they returned home in great anger. 11 And Amaziah strengthened himself, and led forth his people, and went to the valley of salt, and smote of the children of Seir ten thousand. 12 And *other* ten thousand *left* alive did the children of Judah carry away captive, and brought them unto the top of the rock, and cast them down from the top of the rock, that they all were broken in pieces. 13 But the soldiers of the army which Amaziah sent back, that they should not go with him to battle, fell upon the cities of Judah, from Samaria even unto Beth-horon, and smote three thousand of them, and took much spoil.

Here is, I. The general character of Amaziah: *He did that which was right in the eyes of the Lord,* worshipped the true God, kept the temple service a going, and countenanced religion in his kingdom; but he did not do it *with a perfect heart* (*v.* 2), that is, he was not a man of serious piety or devotion himself, nor had he any zeal for the exercises of religion. He was no enemy to it, but a cool and indifferent friend. Such is the character of too many in this Laodicean age: they do that which is good, but not with the heart, not with a perfect heart.

II. A necessary piece of justice which he did upon the traitors that murdered his father: he put them to death, *v.* 3. Though we should suppose they intended to avenge on their king the death of the prophet (as was intimated, *ch.* xxiv. 25), yet this would by no means justify their wickedness; for *they* were not the avengers, but presumptuously took God's work out of his hands: and therefore Amaziah did what became him in calling them to an account for it, but kept within the rule of that law which forbade the putting of the children to death for the parents' sin, *v.* 4.

III. An expedition of his against the Edomites, who, some time ago, had revolted from under the dominion of Judah, to which he attempted to reduce them. Observe,

1. The great preparation he made for this expedition. (1.) He mustered his own forces, and marshalled them (*v.* 5), and found Judah and Benjamin in all but 300,000 men that were fit for war, whereas, in Jehoshaphat's time, fifty or sixty years before, they were four times as many. Sin weakens a people, diminishes them, dispirits them, and lessens their number and figure. (2.) He hired auxiliary troops out of the kingdom of Israel, *v.* 6. Finding his own kingdom defective in men, he thought to make up the deficiency with his money, and therefore took into his pay 100,000 Israelites. If he had advised with any of his prophets before he did this, or had but considered how little any of his ancestors got by their alliances with Israel, he would not have had this to undo again. But rashness makes work for repentance.

2. The command which God sent him by a prophet to dismiss out of his service the forces of Israel, *v.* 7, 8. He would not have him call in any assistance at all: it looked like distrust of God. If he made sure of God's presence, the army he had of his own was sufficient. But particularly he must not take in *their* assistance: *For the Lord is not with the children of Ephraim, because they are not with him,* but worship the calves. This was a good reason why he should not make use of them, because he could not depend upon them to do him any service. What good could be expected from those that had not God with them, nor his blessing upon their undertakings? It is comfortable to employ those who, we have reason to hope, have an interest in heaven, and dangerous to associate with those from whom the Lord has departed. The prophet assured him that if he persisted in his resolution to take these idolatrous apostate Israelites with him, in hopes thereby to make himself strong for the battle, it was at his peril;

they would prove a dead weight to his army, would sink and betray it: "*God shall make thee fall before the enemy*, and these Israelites will be the ruin of thy cause; for God has power to help thee without them, and to cast thee down though thou hast them with thee."

3. The objection which Amaziah made against this command, and the satisfactory answer which the prophet gave to that objection, *v.* 9. The king had remitted 100 talents to the men of Israel for advance-money. "Now," says he, "if I send them back, I shall lose that: *But what shall we do for the* 100 *talents?*" This is an objection men often make against their duty: they are afraid of losing by it. "Regard not that," says the prophet: "*The Lord is able to give thee much more than this;* and, thou mayest depend upon it, he will not see thee lose by him. What are 100 talents between thee and him? He has ways enough to make up the loss to thee; it is below thee to speak of it." Note, A firm belief of God's all-sufficiency to bear us out in our duty, and to make up all the loss and damage we sustain in his service abundantly to our advantage, will make his yoke very easy and his burden very light. What is it to trust in God, but to be willing to venture the loss of any thing for him, in confidence of the goodness of the security he gives us that we shall not lose by him, but that whatever we part with for his sake shall be made up to us in kind or kindness. When we grudge to part with any thing for God and our religion, this should satisfy us, that God is able to give us much more than this. He is just, and he is good, and he is solvent. The king lost 100 talents by his obedience; and we find just that sum given to his grandson Jotham as a present (*ch.* xxvii. 5); then the principal was repaid, and, for interest, 10,000 measures of wheat and as many of barley.

4. His obedience to the command of God, which is upon record to his honour. He would rather lose his money, disoblige his allies, and dismiss a fourth part of his army just as they were going to take the field, than offend God: *He separated the army of Ephraim, to go home again, v.* 10. And they went home in great anger, taking it as a great affront thus to be made fools of, and to be cashiered as men not fit to be employed, and being perhaps disappointed of the advantages they promised themselves in spoil and plunder by joining with Judah against Edom. Men are apt to resent that which touches them in their profit or reputation, though it frees them from trouble.

5. His triumphs over the Edomites, *v.* 11, 12. He left dead upon the spot, in the field of battle, 10,000 men; 10,000 more he took prisoners, and barbarously killed them all by throwing them down some steep and craggy precipice. What provocation he had to exercise this cruelty towards them we are not told; but it was certainly very severe.

6. The mischief which the disbanded soldiers of Israel did to the cities of Judah, either in their return or soon after, *v.* 13. They were so enraged at being sent home that, if they might not go to share with Judah in the spoil of Edom, they would make a prey of Judah. Several cities that lay upon the borders they plundered, killing 3000 men that made resistance. But why should God suffer this to be done? Was it not in obedience to him that they were sent home, and yet shall the country thus suffer by it? Surely God's way is in the sea! Did not the prophet say that God was not with the children of Ephraim, and yet they are suffered to prevail against Judah? Doubtless God intended hereby to chastise those cities of Judah for their idolatries, which were found most in those parts that lay next to Israel. The men of Israel had corrupted them, and now they were made a plague to them. Satan both tempts and torments.

14 Now it came to pass, after that Amaziah was come from the slaughter of the Edomites, that he brought the gods of the children of Seir, and set them up *to be* his gods, and bowed down himself before them, and burned incense unto them. 15 Wherefore the anger of the LORD was kindled against Amaziah, and he sent unto him a prophet, which said unto him, Why hast thou sought after the gods of the people, which could not deliver their own people out of thine hand? 16 And it came to pass, as he talked with him, that *the king* said unto him, Art thou made of the king's counsel? forbear; why shouldest thou be smitten? Then the prophet forbare, and said, I know that God hath determined to destroy thee, because thou hast done this, and hast not hearkened unto my counsel.

Here is, I. The revolt of Amaziah from the God of Israel to the gods of the Edomites. Egregious folly! Ahaz worshipped the gods of those that had conquered him, for which he had some little colour, *ch.* xxviii. 23. But to worship the gods of those whom he had conquered, who could not protect their own worshippers, was the greatest absurdity that could be. What did he see in the gods of the children of Seir that could tempt him to set them up for *his gods* and *bow himself down before them? v.* 14. If he had cast the idols down from the rock and broken them to pieces, instead of the prisoners, he would have manifested more of the piety as well as more of the pity of an Israelite; but perhaps for that barbarous inhumanity he was given up to this ridiculous idolatry.

II. The reproof which God sent to him, by a prophet, for this sin. *The anger of the Lord was kindled against him,* and justly; yet, before he sent to destroy him, he sent to convince and reclaim him, and so to prevent his destruction. The prophet reasoned with him very fairly and very mildly: *Why hast thou sought* the favour of those gods *which could not deliver their own people? v.* 15. If men would but duly consider the inability of all those things to help them to which they have recourse when they forsake God, they would not be such enemies to themselves.

III. The check he gave to the reprover, *v.* 16. He could say nothing in excuse of his own folly; the reproof was too just to be answered. But he fell into a passion with the reprover. 1. He taunted him as saucy and impertinent, and meddling with that which did not belong to him: *Art thou made of the king's counsel?* Could not a man speak reasonably to him, but he must be upbraided as usurping the place of a privy-counsellor? But, as a prophet, he really was made of the king's counsel by the King of kings, in duty to whom the king was bound not only to hear, but to ask and take his counsel. 2. He silenced him, bade him forbear and say not a word more to him. He *said to the seer, See not,* Isa. xxx. 10. Men would gladly have their prophets thus under their girdles, as we say, to speak just when and what they would have them speak, and not otherwise. 3. He threatened him: "*Why shouldst thou be smitten?* It is at thy peril if thou sayest a word more of this matter." He seems to remind him of Zechariah's fate in the last reign, who was put to death for making bold with the king; and bids him take warning by him. Thus he justifies the killing of that prophet by menacing this, and so, in effect, makes himself guilty of the blood of both. He had hearkened to the prophet who ordered him to send back the army of Israel, and was ruled by him, though he contradicted his politics and lost him 100 talents, *v.* 10. But this prophet, who dissuaded him from worshipping the gods of the Edomites, he ran upon with an unaccountable rage, which must be attributed to the witchcraft of idolatry. He was easily persuaded to part with his talents of silver, but by no means with his gods of silver.

IV. The doom which the prophet passed upon him for this. He had more to say to him by way of instruction and advice; but, finding him obstinate in his iniquity, he forbore. He is *joined to idols; let him alone,* Hos. iv. 17. Miserable is the condition of that man with whom the blessed Spirit, by ministers and conscience, *forbears to strive,* Gen. vi. 3. And both the reprovers in the gate and that in the bosom, if long browbeaten and baffled, will at length forbear. So I *gave them up to their own hearts' lusts.* The secure sinner perhaps values himself upon it as a noble and happy achievement to have silenced his reprovers and monitors, and to get clear of them; but what comes of it? "*I know that God has determined to destroy thee;* it is a plain indication that thou art marked for ruin *that thou hast done this, and hast not hearkened to my counsel.*" Those that are deaf to reproof are ripening apace for destruction, Prov. xxix. 1.

17 Then Amaziah king of Judah took advice, and sent to Joash, the son of Jehoahaz, the son of Jehu, king of Israel, saying, Come, let us see one another in the face. 18 And Joash king of Israel sent to Amaziah king of Judah, saying, The thistle that *was* in Lebanon sent to the cedar that *was* in Lebanon, saying, Give thy daughter to my son to wife: and there passed by a wild beast that *was* in Lebanon, and trode down the thistle. 19 Thou sayest, Lo, thou hast smitten the Edomites; and thine heart lifteth thee up to boast: abide now at home; why shouldest thou meddle to *thine* hurt, that thou shouldest fall, *even* thou, and Judah with thee? 20 But Amaziah would not hear; for it *came* of God, that he might deliver them into the hand *of their enemies,* because they sought after the gods of Edom. 21 So Joash the king of Israel went up; and they saw one another in the face, *both* he and Amaziah king of Judah, at Beth-shemesh, which *belongeth* to Judah. 22 And Judah was put to the worse before Israel, and they fled every man to his tent. 23 And Joash the king of Israel took Amaziah king of Judah, the son of Joash, the son of Jehoahaz, at Beth-shemesh, and brought him to Jerusalem, and brake down the wall of Jerusalem from the gate of Ephraim to the corner gate, four hundred cubits. 24 And *he took* all the gold and the silver, and all the vessels that were found in the house of God with Obed-edom, and the treasures of the king's house, the hostages also, and returned to Samaria. 25 And Amaziah the son of Joash king of Judah lived after the death of Joash son of Jehoahaz king of Israel fifteen years. 26 Now the rest of the acts of Amaziah, first and

last, behold, *are* they not written in the book of the kings of Judah and Israel? 27 Now after the time that Amaziah did turn away from following the LORD they made a conspiracy against him in Jerusalem; and he fled to Lachish: but they sent to Lachish after him, and slew him there. 28 And they brought him upon horses, and buried him with his fathers in the city of Judah.

We have here this degenerate prince mortified by his neighbour and murdered by his own subjects.

I. Never was proud prince more thoroughly mortified than Amaziah was by Joash king of Israel.

1. This part of the story (which was as fully related 2 Kings xiv. 8, &c., as it is here)—embracing the foolish challenge which Amaziah sent to Joash (*v.* 17), his haughty scornful answer to it (*v.* 18), with the friendly advice he gave him to sit still and know when he was well off, (*v.* 19),—his wilfully persisting in his challenge (*v.* 20, 21), the defeat that was given him (*v.* 22), and the calamity he brought upon himself and his city thereby (*v.* 23, 24),—verifies two of Solomon's proverbs:—(1.) That *a man's pride will bring him low,* Prov. xxix. 23. It goes before his destruction; not only procures it meritoriously, but is often the immediate occasion of it. *He that exalteth himself shall be abased.* (2.) That he that *goes forth hastily to strive* will probably not know what to do in the end thereof, *when his neighbour has put him to shame,* Prov. xxv. 8. He that is fond of contention may have enough of it sooner than he thinks of.

2. But there are two passages in this story which we had not before in the *Kings.* (1.) That *Amaziah took advice* before he challenged the king of Israel, *v.* 17. But of whom? Not of the prophet—he was *not made of the king's counsel;* but of his statesmen that would flatter him and bid him go up and prosper. It is good to take advice, but then it must be of those that are fit to advise us. Those that will not take advice from the word of God, which would guide them aright, will justly be left to the bad advice of those that will counsel them to their destruction. Let those be made fools that will not be made wise. (2.) Amaziah's imprudence is here made the punishment of his impiety (*v.* 20): *It was of the Lord;* he left him to himself to act thus foolishly, that he and his people might be *delivered into the hands of their enemies, because* they had forsaken God and *sought after the gods of Edom.* Those that will not be persuaded to do well for their souls will justly be given up to their own counsels to do ill for themselves even in their outward affairs.

II. Never was poor prince more violently pursued by his own subjects. *From the time* that he departed from the Lord (so it may be read, *v.* 27) the hearts of his subjects departed from him, and they began to form a design against him in Jerusalem. It is probable they were exasperated against him more for his rashly engaging in a war against Israel than for his worshipping the gods of Edom. But at length the ferment grew so high, and he perceived the plot to be laid so deeply, that he thought fit to quit his royal city and flee to Lachish, either as a private place where he might be hid or as a strong place where he might be guarded; but they sent after him thither, and slew him there. By this the putting of him to death seems to have been done deliberately, and to have been the act, not of a disgusted servant or two, but of a considerable body that durst avow it. How unrighteous soever they were herein, God was righteous.

CHAP. XXVI.

This chapter gives us an account of the reign of Uzziah (Azariah he was called in the Kings) more fully than we had it before, though it was long, and in some respects illustrious, yet it was very briefly related, 2 Kings xiv. 21; xv. 1, &c. Here is, I. His good character in general, ver. 1—5. II. His great prosperity in his wars, his buildings, and all the affairs of his kingdom, ver. 6—15. III. His presumption in invading the priests' office, for which he was struck with a leprosy, and confined by it (ver. 16—21) even to his death, ver. 22, 23.

THEN all the people of Judah took Uzziah, who *was* sixteen years old, and made him king in the room of his father Amaziah. 2 He built Eloth, and restored it to Judah, after that the king slept with his fathers. 3 Sixteen years old *was* Uzziah when he began to reign, and he reigned fifty and two years in Jerusalem. His mother's name also *was* Jecoliah of Jerusalem. 4 And he did *that which was* right in the sight of the LORD, according to all that his father Amaziah did. 5 And he sought God in the days of Zechariah, who had understanding in the visions of God: and as long as he sought the LORD, God made him to prosper. 6 And he went forth and warred against the Philistines, and brake down the wall of Gath, and the wall of Jabneh, and the wall of Ashdod, and built cities about Ashdod, and among the Philistines. 7 And God helped him against the Philistines, and against the Arabians that dwelt in Gur-baal, and the Mehunims. 8 And the Ammonites gave gifts to Uzziah: and his name spread abroad *even* to the entering in of Egypt; for he strengthened *himself* exceedingly. 9 Moreover Uzziah built towers in Jerusalem at the corner gate, and at the valley gate, and at the turning *of the wall,* and fortified them. 10 Also he built towers in the desert, and digged many wells: for he had much cattle, both in the low country, and in the plains: husbandmen *also,* and vine dressers in the mountains, and in Carmel: for he loved husbandry. 11 Moreover Uzziah had a host of fighting men, that went out to war by bands, according to the number of their account by the hand of Jeiel the scribe and Maaseiah the ruler, under the hand of Hananiah, *one* of the king's captains. 12 The whole number of the chief of the fathers of the mighty men of valour *were* two thousand and six hundred. 13 And under their hand *was* an army, three hundred thousand and seven thousand and five hundred, that made war with mighty power, to help the king against the enemy. 14 And Uzziah prepared for them throughout all the host shields, and spears, and helmets, and habergeons, and bows, and slings *to cast* stones. 15 And he made in Jerusalem engines, invented by cunning men, to be on the towers and upon the bulwarks, to shoot arrows and great stones withal. And his name spread far abroad; for he was marvellously helped, till he was strong.

We have here an account of two things concerning Uzziah:—

I. His piety. In this he was not very eminent or zealous; yet *he did that which was right in the sight of the Lord.* He kept up the pure worship of the true God *as his father* did, and was better than his father, inasmuch as we have no reason to think he ever worshipped idols as his father did, no, not in his latter days, when *his heart was lifted up.* It is said (*v.* 5), He *sought God in the days of Zechariah,* who, some think, was the son of that Zechariah whom his grandfather Joash slew. This Zechariah was one that *had understanding in the visions of God,* either the visions which he himself was favoured with or the visions of the preceding prophets. He was well versed in prophecy, and conversed much with the upper world, was an intelligent, devout, good man; and, it seems, had great influence with Uzziah. Happy are the great men who have such about them and are willing to be advised by them; but unhappy those who seek God only while they have such with them and have not a principle in themselves to bear them out to the end.

II. His prosperity.

1. In general, *as long as he sought the Lord,* and minded religion, *God made him to prosper.* Note, (1.) Those only prosper whom *God makes to prosper;* for prosperity is his gift. (2.) Religion and piety are very friendly to outward prosperity. Many have found and owned this, that as long as they sought the Lord and kept close to their duty they prospered; but since they forsook God every thing has gone cross.

2. Here are several particular instances of his prosperity:—(1.) His success in his wars: *God helped him* (*v.* 7), and then he triumphed over the Philistines (those old enemies of God's people), demolished the fortifications of their cities, and put garrisons of his own among them, *v.* 6. He obliged the Ammonites to pay him tribute, *v.* 8. He made all quiet about him, and kept them in awe. (2.) The greatness of his fame and reputation. His name was celebrated throughout all the neighbouring countries (*v.* 8) and it was a good name, a name for good things with God and good people. This is true fame, and makes a man truly honourable. (3.) His buildings. While he acted offensively abroad, he did not neglect the defence of his kingdom at home, but *built towers in Jerusalem* and fortified them, *v.* 9. Much of the wall of Jerusalem was in his father's time broken down, particularly at *the corner gate* (*ch.* xxv. 23); probably his father had repaired it, but he, to prevent the like mischief for the future, fortified it, and *built a tower at the corner gate.* But his best fortification of Jerusalem was his close adherence to the worship of God: if his father had not forsaken this the wall of Jerusalem would not have been broken down. While he fortified the city, he did not forget the country, but *built towers in the desert* too (*v.* 10), to protect the country people from the inroads of the plunderers, bands of whom sometimes alarmed them and plundered them, as *ch.* xxi. 16. (4.) His husbandry. He dealt much in cattle and corn, employed many hands, and got much wealth by his dealing; for he took a pleasure in it: he *loved husbandry* (*v.* 10), and probably did himself inspect his affairs in the country, which was no disparagement to him, but an advantage, as it encouraged industry among his subjects. It is an honour to the husbandman's calling that one of the most illustrious princes of the house of David followed it and loved it. He was not one of those that delight in war, nor did he addict himself to sport and pleasure, but delighted in the innocent and quiet employments of the husbandman. (5.) His standing armies. He had, as it should seem, two military establishments. [1.] A *host of fighting men* that were to make excursions abroad. These *went out to war by bands, v.* 11. They fetched in spoil from the neighbouring countries by way of reprisal for the depredations they

had so often made upon Judah, [2.] Another army for *guards and garrisons*, that were ready to defend the country in case it should be invaded, *v.* 12, 13. So great were their number and valour that they *made war with mighty power;* no enemy durst face them, or, at least, could stand before them. Men unarmed can do little in war. Uzziah therefore furnished himself with a great armoury, whence his soldiers were supplied with arms offensive and defensive (*v.* 14), spears, bows, and slings, shields, helmets, and habergeons: swords are not mentioned, because it is probable that every man had a sword of his own, which he wore constantly. Engines were invented, in his time, for annoying besiegers with darts and stones shot from the towers and bulwarks, *v.* 15. What a pity it is that the wars and fightings which come from men's lusts have made it necessary for cunning men to employ their skill in inventing instruments of death.

16 But when he was strong, his heart was lifted up to *his* destruction: for he transgressed against the LORD his God, and went into the temple of the LORD to burn incense upon the altar of incense. 17 And Azariah the priest went in after him, and with him fourscore priests of the LORD, *that were* valiant men: 18 And they withstood Uzziah the king, and said unto him, *It appertaineth* not unto thee, Uzziah, to burn incense unto the LORD, but to the priests the sons of Aaron, that are consecrated to burn incense: go out of the sanctuary; for thou hast trespassed; neither *shall it be* for thine honour from the LORD God. 19 Then Uzziah was wroth, and *had* a censer in his hand to burn incense: and while he was wroth with the priests, the leprosy even rose up in his forehead before the priests in the house of the LORD, from beside the incense altar. 20 And Azariah the chief priest, and all the priests, looked upon him, and, behold, he *was* leprous in his forehead, and they thrust him out from thence; yea, himself hasted also to go out, because the LORD had smitten him. 21 And Uzziah the king was a leper unto the day of his death, and dwelt in a several house, *being* a leper; for he was cut off from the house of the LORD: and Jotham his son *was* over the king's house, judging the people of the land. 22 Now the rest of the acts of Uzziah, first and last, did Isaiah the prophet, the son of Amoz, write. 23 So Uzziah slept with his fathers, and they buried him with his fathers in the field of the burial which *belonged* to the kings; for they said, He *is* a leper: and Jotham his son reigned in his stead.

Here is the only blot we find on the name of king Uzziah, and it is such a one as lies not on any other of the kings. Whoredom, murder, oppression, persecution, and especially idolatry, gave characters to the bad kings and some of them blemishes to the good ones, David himself not excepted, witness the matter of Uriah. But we find not Uzziah charged with any of these; and yet he *transgressed against the Lord his God*, and fell under the marks of his displeasure in consequence, not, as other kings, in vexatious wars or rebellions, but an incurable disease.

I. His sin was invading the priest's office. The good way is one; by-paths are many. The transgression of his predecessors was forsaking the temple of the Lord, flying off from it (*ch.* xxiv. 18), and burning incense upon idolatrous altars, *ch.* xxv. 14. *His* was intruding *into the temple of the Lord* further than was allowed him, and attempting himself to *burn incense upon the altar* of God, for which, it is likely, he pretended an extraordinary zeal and affection. See how hard it is to avoid one extreme and not run into another.

1. That which was at the bottom of his sin was pride of heart, a lust that ruins more than any other whatsoever (*v.* 16): *When he was strong* (and he was marvellously helped by the good providence of God *till he was so, v.* 15), when he had grown very great and considerable in wealth, interest, and power, instead of lifting up the name of God in gratitude to him who had done so much for him, his *heart was lifted up to his destruction.* Thus the prosperity of fools, by puffing them up with pride, destroys them. Now that he had done so much business, and won so much honour, he began to think no business, no honour, too great or too good for him, no, not that of the priesthood. Men's pretending to forbidden knowledge, and exercising themselves in things too high for them, are owing to the pride of their heart, and the fleshly mind they are *vainly puffed up with.*

2. His sin was *going into the temple of the Lord to burn incense,* probably on some solemn feast day, or when he himself had some special occasion for supplicating the divine favour. What could move him to this piece of presumption, or put it into his head, I cannot conjecture. None of all his predecessors, not the best, not the worst, attempted it. The law, he knew, was ex-

press against him, and there was no usage or precedent for him. He could not pretend any necessity, as there was for David's eating the show-bread. (1.) Perhaps he fancied the priests did not do their office so dexterously, decently, and devoutly, as they ought, and he could do it better. Or, (2.) He observed that the idolatrous kings did themselves burn incense at the altars of their gods; his father did so, and Jeroboam (1 Kings xiii. 1), an ambition of which honour was perhaps one thing that tempted them from the house of God, where it was not permitted them; and he, being resolved to cleave to God's altar, would try to break through this restraint and come as near it as the idolatrous kings did to their altars. But it is called a *transgression against the Lord his God.* He was not content with the honours God had put upon him, but would usurp those that were forbidden him, like our first parents.

3. He was opposed in this attempt by the chief priest and other priests that attended and assisted him, *v.* 17, 18. They were ready to burn incense for the king, according to the duty of their place; but, when he offered to do it himself, they plainly let him know that he meddled with that which did not belong to him, and that it was at his peril. They did not resist him by laying violent hands on him, though they were valiant men, but by reasoning with him and showing him, (1.) That it was not lawful for him to burn incense: "*It appertaineth not to thee, O Uzziah!* but *to the priests,* whose birthright it is, as sons of Aaron, and who are consecrated to the service." Aaron and his sons were appointed by the law to burn incense, Exod. xxx. 7. See Deut. xxxiii. 10; 1 Chron. xxiii. 13. David had blessed the people and Solomon and Jehoshaphat had prayed with them and preached to them. Uzziah might have done this, and it would have been to his praise; but, as for burning incense, that service was to be performed by the priests only. The kingly and priestly offices were separated by the law of Moses, not to be united again but in the person of the Messiah. If Uzziah did intend to honour God, and gain acceptance with him, in what he did, he was quite out in his aim; for, being a service purely of divine institution, he could not expect it should be accepted unless it were done in the way and by the hands that God had appointed. (2.) That it was not safe. It shall not be *for thy honour from the Lord God.* More is implied: "It will be thy disgrace, and it is at thy peril." The law runs expressly against all strangers that came nigh (Num. iii. 10; xviii. 7), that is, all that were not priests. Korah and his accomplices, though Levites, paid dearly for offering to burn incense, which was the work of the priests only, Num. xvi. 35. The incense of our prayers must be by faith put into the hands of our Lord Jesus, the great high priest of our profession, else we cannot expect it should be accepted by God, Rev. viii. 3.

4. He fell into a passion with the priests that reproved him, and would push forward to do what he intended notwithstanding (*v.* 19): *Uzziah was wroth,* and would not part with the censer out of his hand. He took it ill to be checked, and would not bear interference. *Nitimur in vetitum—We are prone to do what is forbidden.*

II. His punishment was an incurable leprosy, which rose up in his forehead while he was contending with the priests. If he had submitted to the priests' admonition, acknowledged his error, and gone back, all would have been well; but *when he was wroth with the priests,* and fell foul upon them, then God was wroth with him and smote him with a plague of leprosy. Josephus says that he threatened the priests with death if they opposed him, and that then the earth shook, the roof of the temple opened, and through the cleft a beam of the sun darted directly upon the king's face, wherein immediately the leprosy appeared. And some conjecture that that was the earthquake in the days of Uzziah which we read of Amos i. 1 and Zech. xiv. 5. Now this sudden stroke, 1. Ended the controversy between him and the priests; for, when the leprosy appeared, they were emboldened to thrust him out of the temple; nay, he himself *hasted to go out, because the Lord had smitten him* with a disease which was in a particular manner a token of his displeasure, and which he knew secluded him from common converse with men, much more from the altar of God. He would not be convinced by what the priests said, but God took an effectual course to convince him. If presumptuous men will not be made to see their error by the judgments of God's mouth, they shall be made to see it by the judgments of his hand. It evinced some religious fear of God in the heart of this king, even in the midst of his transgression, that, as soon as he found God was angry with him, he not only let fall his attempt, but retired with the utmost precipitation. Though he strove with the priests, he would not strive with his Maker. 2. It remained a lasting punishment of his transgression; for he continued a *leper to the day of his death,* shut up in confinement, and shut out from society, and forced to leave it to his son to manage all his business, *v.* 21. Thus God gave an instance of his resisting the proud and of his jealousy for the purity and honour of his own institutions; thus he gave fair warning even to great and good men to know and keep their distance, and not to intrude into those things which they have not seen; and thus he gave Uzziah a loud and constant call to repentance, and a long space to repent, which we have reason to hope he improved. He had been a man of much business in the world; but being taken off from that, and confined to a *separate house*, he had leisure to think of another world and prepare for it. By this judgment upon the king God intended to possess the people with a great veneration for the temple, the priesthood, and other sacred things, which they had been apt to think meanly of. While the king was a leper, he was as good as dead, dead while he lived, and buried alive; and so the law was, in effect, answered, that the stranger who cometh nigh shall be put to death. The disgrace survived him; for, when he was dead, they would not bury him in the *sepulchres of the kings* because he was a leper, which stained all his other glory. 3. It was a punishment that answered the sin as face does face in a glass. (1.) Pride was at the bottom of his transgression, and thus God humbled him and put dishonour upon him. (2.) He invaded the office of the priests in contempt of them, and God struck him with a disease which in a particular manner made him subject to the inspection and sentence of the priests; for to them pertained the *judgment of the leprosy*, Deut. xxiv. 8. (3.) He thrust himself into the temple of God, whither the priests only had admission, and for that was thrust out of the very courts of the temple, into which the meanest of his subjects that was ceremonially clean had free access. (4.) He confronted the priests that faced him and opposed his presumption, and for that the leprosy *rose in his forehead*, which, in Miriam's case, is compared to her father's *spitting in her face*, Num. xii. 14. (5.) He invaded the dignity of the priesthood, which he had no right to, and for that he was deprived even of his royal dignity, which he had a right to. Those that covet forbidden honours forfeit allowed ones. Adam, by catching at the tree of knowledge of which he might not eat, debarred himself from the tree of life, of which he might have eaten. Let all that read it say, *The Lord is righteous.*

CHAP. XXVII.

Here is a very short account of the reign of Jotham, a pious prosperous prince, of whom one would wish to have known more; but we may better dispense with the brevity of his story because that which lengthened the history of the last three kings was their degeneracy in their latter end, of which we have had a faithful account; but there was no occasion for such a melancholy conclusion of the history of this reign, which is only an account, I. Of the date and continuance of this reign, ver. 1, 8. II. The general good character of it, ver. 2, 6. III The prosperity of it, ver. 3—5. IV. The period of it, ver. 7, 9.

JOTHAM *was* twenty and five years old when he began to reign, and he reigned sixteen years in Jerusalem. His mother's name also *was* Jerushah, the daughter of Zadok. 2 And he did *that which was* right in the sight of the LORD, according to all that his father Uzziah did: howbeit he entered not into the temple of the LORD. And the people did yet corruptly. 3 He built the high gate of the house of the LORD, and on the wall of Ophel he built much. 4 Moreover he built cities in the mountains of Judah, and in the forests he built castles and towers. 5 He fought also with the king of the Ammonites, and prevailed against them. And the children of Ammon gave him the same year a hundred talents of silver, and ten thousand measures of wheat, and ten thousand of barley. So much did the children of Ammon pay unto him, both the second year, and the third. 6 So Jotham became mighty, because he prepared his ways before the LORD his God. 7 Now the rest of the acts of Jotham, and all his wars, and his ways, lo, they *are* written in the book of the kings of Israel and Judah. 8 He was five and twenty years old when he began to reign, and reigned sixteen years in Jerusalen 9 And Jotham slept with his fathers, and they buried him in the city of David: and Ahaz his son reigned in his stead.

There is not much more related here concerning Jotham than we had before, 2 Kings xv. 32, &c.

I. He reigned well He *did that which was right in the sight of the Lord;* the course of his reign was good, and pleasing to God, whose favour he made his end, and his word his rule, and (which shows that he acted from a good principle) he *prepared his ways before the Lord his God* (*v.* 6), that is, he walked circumspectly and with much caution, contrived how to shun that which was evil and compass that which was good. He looked before him, and cast his affairs into such a posture and method as made the regular management of them the more easy. Or he established or fixed his ways before the Lord, that is, he walked steadily and constantly in the way of his duty, was uniform and resolute in it: not like some of those that went before him, who, though they had some good in them, lost their credit by their inconstancy and inconsistency with themselves. They had run well, but something hindered them. It was not so with Jotham. Two things are observed here in his character:—1. What was amiss in his father he amended in himself (*v.* 2): He did *according to all that his father did* well and wisely; howbeit he would not imitate him in what he did amiss; for he *entered not into the temple of the Lord* to burn incense as his father did, but took warning by his fate not to dare so presumptuous a thing. Note, We must not imitate the best men, and those we have the greatest veneration for, any further than they did well; but, on the contrary, their falls, and the injurious consequences of them, must be warnings to us to walk the more circumspectly, that we stumble not at the same stone that they stumbled at. 2. What was amiss in his people he could not prevail to amend: *The people did yet corruptly.* Perhaps it reflects some blame upon him, that he was wanting in his part towards the reformation of the land. Men may be very good themselves, and yet not have courage and zeal to do what they might do towards the reforming of others. However it certainly reflects a great deal of blame upon the people, that they did not do what they might have done to improve the advantages of so good a reign: they had good instructions given them and a good example set before them, but they would not be reformed; so that even in the reign of their good kings, as well as in that of the bad ones, they were *treasuring up wrath against the day of wrath;* for they still did corruptly, and the founder melted in vain.

II. He prospered, and became truly reputable. 1. He built. He began with *the gate of the house of the Lord,* which he repaired, beautified, and raised. He then *fortified the wall of Ophel, and built cities in the mountains of Judah* (*v.* 3, 4), took all possible care for the fortifying of his country and the replenishing of it. 2. He conquered. He prevailed against the Ammonites, who had invaded Judah in Jehoshaphat's time, *ch.* xx. 1. He triumphed over them, and exacted great contributions from them, *v.* 5. 3. He *became mighty* (*v.* 6) in wealth and power, and influence upon the neighbouring nations, who courted his friendship and feared his displeasure; and this he got by *preparing his ways before the Lord his God.* The more stedfast we are in religion the more mighty we are both for the resistance of that which is evil and for the performance of that which is good.

III. He finished his course too soon, but finished it with honour. He had the unhappiness to die in the midst of his days; but, to balance that, the happiness not to out-live his reputation, as the last three of his predecessors did. He died when he was but forty-one years of age (*v.* 8); but *his wars and his ways,* his wars abroad and his ways at home, were so glorious that they were recorded in the book of the kings of Israel, as well as of the kings of Judah, *v.* 7. The last words of the chapter are the most melancholy, as they inform us that *Ahaz his son,* whose character, in all respects, was the reverse of his, *reigned in his stead.* When the wealth and power with which wise men have done good devolve upon fools, that will do hurt with them, it is a lamentation, and shall be for a lamentation.

CHAP. XXVIII.

This chapter is the history of the reign of Ahaz the son of Jotham; a bad reign it was, and which helped to augment the fierce anger of the Lord. We have here, I. His great wickedness, ver. 1—4. II. The trouble he brought himself into by it, ver. 5—8. III. The reproof which God sent by a prophet to the army of Israel for trampling upon their brethren of Judah, and the obedient ear they gave to that reproof, ver. 9—15. IV. The many calamities that followed to Ahaz and his people, ver. 16—21. V. The continuance of his idolatry notwithstanding (ver. 22—25), and so his story ends, ver. 26, 27.

AHAZ *was* twenty years old when he began to reign, and he reigned sixteen years in Jerusalem: but he did not *that which was* right in the sight of the LORD, like David his father: 2 For he walked in the ways of the kings of Israel, and made also molten images for Baalim. 3 Moreover he burnt incense in the valley of the son of Hinnom, and burnt his children in the fire, after the abominations of the heathen whom the LORD had cast out before the children of Israel. 4 He sacrificed also and burnt incense in the high places, and on the hills, and under every green tree. 5 Wherefore the LORD his God delivered him into the hand of the king of Syria; and they smote him, and carried away a great multitude of them captives, and brought *them* to Damascus. And he was also delivered into the hand of the king of Israel, who smote him with a great slaughter.

Never surely had a man greater opportunity of doing well than Ahaz had, finding things in a good posture, the kingdom rich and strong and religion established; and yet here we have him in these few verses, 1. Wretchedly corrupted and debauched. He had had a good education given him and a good example set him: but parents cannot give grace to their children. All the instructions he had were lost upon him: *He did not that which was right in the sight of the Lord* (*v.* 1), nay, he did a great deal that was wrong, a wrong to God, to his own soul, and to his people; he walked in the way of the revolted Israelites and the devoted Canaanites, made molten images and worshipped them, contrary to the second commandment; nay, he made them for Baalim, contrary to the first commandment. He forsook the temple of the Lord and sacrificed and burnt incense on the hills, as if they would place him nearer heaven, and under every green tree, as if they would signify the protection and influence of heaven by their shade and dropping. To complete his wickedness, as one perfectly divested of all natural affection as well as religion and perfectly devoted to the service and interest of the great enemy of mankind, he *burnt his children in the fire to Moloch* (*v.* 3), not thinking it enough to dedicate them to that infernal fiend by causing them to pass through the fire. See what an absolute sway the prince of the power of the air bears among the children of disobedience. 2. Wretchedly spoiled and made a prey of. When he forsook God, and at a vast expense put himself under the protection of false gods, God, who of right was his God, delivered him into the hands of his enemies, *v.* 5. (1.) The Syrians insulted him and triumphed over him, beat him in the field and carried away a great many of his people into captivity. (2.) The king of Israel, though an idolater too, was made a scourge to him, and *smote him with a great slaughter.* The people suffered by these judgments: their blood was shed, their country wasted, their families ruined; for when they had a good king, though *they did corruptly* (*ch.* xxvii. 2), yet then his goodness sheltered them; but now that they had a bad one all their defence had departed from them and an inundation of judgments broke in upon them. Those that knew not their happiness in the foregoing reign were taught to value it by the miseries of this reign.

6 For Pekah the son of Remaliah slew in Judah a hundred and twenty thousand in one day, *which were* all valiant men; because they had forsaken the LORD God of their fathers. 7 And Zichri, a mighty man of Ephraim, slew Maaseiah the king's son, and Azrikam the governor of the house, and Elkanah *that was* next to the king. 8 And the children of Israel carried away captive of their brethren two hundred thousand, women, sons, and daughters, and took also away much spoil from them, and brought the spoil to Samaria. 9 But a prophet of the LORD was there, whose name *was* Oded: and he went out before the host that came to Samaria, and said unto them, Behold, because the LORD God of your fathers was wroth with Judah, he hath delivered them into your hand, and ye have slain them in a rage *that* reacheth up unto heaven. 10 And now ye purpose to keep under the children of Judah and Jerusalem for bondmen and bondwomen unto you: *but are there* not with you, even with you, sins against the LORD your God? 11 Now hear me therefore, and deliver the captives again, which ye have taken captive of your brethren: for the fierce wrath of the LORD *is* upon you. 12 Then certain of the heads of the children of Ephraim, Azariah the son of Johanan, Berechiah the son of Meshillemoth, and Jehizkiah the son of Shallum, and Amasa the son of Hadlai, stood up against them that came from the war, 13 And said unto them, Ye shall not bring in the captives hither: for whereas we have offended against the LORD *already,* ye intend to add *more* to our sins and to our trespass: for our trespass is great, and *there is* fierce wrath against Israel. 14 So the armed men left the captives and the spoil before the princes and all the congregation. 15 And the men which were expressed by name rose up, and took the captives, and with the spoil clothed all that were naked among them, and arrayed them, and shod them, and gave them to eat and to drink, and anointed them, and carried all the feeble of them upon asses, and brought them to Jericho, the city of palm trees, to their brethren: then they returned to Samaria.

We have here,

I. Treacherous Judah under the rebukes of God's providence, and they are very severe. Never was such bloody work made among them since they were a kingdom, and by Israelites too. Ahaz walked in the ways of the kings of Israel, and the king of Israel was the instrument God made use of for his punishment. It is just with God to make those our plagues whom we make our patterns or make ourselves partners with in sin. A war broke out between Judah and Israel, in which Judah was worsted. For, 1. There was a great slaughter of men in the field of battle. Vast numbers (120,000 men, and valiant men too at other times) were slain (*v.* 6) and some of the first rank, the king's son for one. He had sacrificed some of his sons to Moloch; justly therefore is this sacrificed to the divine vengeance. Here is another that was *next the king,* his friend, the prime-minister of state, or perhaps next him in the battle, so that the king himself had a narrow escape, *v.* 7. The kingdom of Israel was not strong at this time, and yet strong enough to bring this great destruction upon Judah. But certainly so many men, great men, stout men, could not have been cut off in one day if they had not been strangely dispirited both by the consciousness of their own guilt and by the righteous hand of God upon them. Even valiant men were numbered *as sheep for the slaughter,* and became an easy prey to the enemy *because they had forsaken the Lord God of their fathers,* and he had therefore forsaken them. 2. There was a great captivity of *women and children*, *v*. 8. When the army in the field was routed, the cities, and towns, and country villages, were all easily stripped, the inhabitants taken for slaves, and their wealth for a prey.

II. Even victorious Israel under the rebuke of God's word for the bad principle they had gone upon in making war with Judah and the bad use they had made of their success, and the good effect of this rebuke. Here is,

1. The message which God sent them by a prophet, who went out to meet them, not to applaud their valour or congratulate them on their victory, though they returned laden with spoils and triumphs, but in God's name to tell them of their faults and warn them of the judgments of God.

(1.) He told them how they came by this victory of which they were so proud. It was not because God favoured them, or that they had merited it at his hand, but *because he was wroth with Judah*, and made them the rod of his indignation. *Not for your righteousness*, be it known to you, but *for their wickedness* (Deut. ix. 5) *they are broken off; therefore be not you high-minded, but fear, lest God also spare not you*, Rom. xi. 20, 21.

(2.) He charged them with the abuse of the power God had given them over their brethren. Those understand not what victory is who think it gives them authority to do what they will, and that the longest sword is the clearest claim to lives and estates *(Jusque datum sceleri—might is right)*; no, as it is impolitic not to use a victory, so it is impious to abuse it. The conquerors are here reproved, [1.] For the cruelty of the slaughter they had made in the field. They had indeed *shed the blood of war in war;* we suppose that to be lawful, but it turned into sin to them, because they did it from a bad principle of enmity to their brethren and after a bad manner, with a barbarous fury, *a rage reaching up to heaven*, that is, that cried to God for vengeance against such bloody men, that delighted in military execution. Those that serve God's justice, if they do it with rage and a spirit of revenge, make themselves obnoxious to it, and forfeit the honour of acting for him; *for the wrath of man worketh not the righteousness of God.* [2.] For the imperious treatment they gave their prisoners. "*You now purpose to keep them under*, to use them or sell them as slaves, though they are your brethren and free-born Israelites." God takes notice of what men purpose, as well as of what they say and do.

(3.) He reminded them of their own sins, by which they also were obnoxious to the wrath of God: *Are there not with you, even with you, sins against the Lord your God? v*. 10. He appeals to their own consciences, and to the notorious evidence of the thing. "Though you are now made the instruments of correcting Judah for sin, yet do not think that you are therefore innocent yourselves; no, you also are guilty before God." This is intended as a check, [1.] To their triumph in their success. "You are sinners, and it ill becomes sinners to be proud; you have carried the day now, but be not secure, the wheel may ere long return upon yourselves, for, if judgment begin thus with those that have *the house of God* among them, what shall be the end of such as worship the calves?" [2.] To their severity towards their brethren. "You have now got them under, but you ought to show mercy to them, for you yourselves are undone if you do not find mercy with God. It ill becomes sinners to be cruel. You have transgressions enough to answer for already, and need not add this to the rest."

(4.) He commanded them to release the prisoners, and to send them home again carefully (*v.* 11); "for you having sinned, *the fierce wrath of God is upon you*, and there is no other way of escaping it than by showing mercy."

2. The resolution of the princes thereupon not to detain the prisoners. They *stood up against those that came from the war*, though flushed with victory, and told them plainly that they should not bring their captives into Samaria, *v.* 12, 13. They had sin enough already to answer for, and would have nothing done to add to their trespass. In this they discovered an obedient regard to the word of God by his prophet and a tender compassion towards their brethren, which was wrought in them by the tender mercy of God; for he regarded the affliction of this poor people, and heard their cry, and *made them to be pitied of all those that carried them captive*, Ps. cvi. 44, 46.

3. The compliance of the soldiers with the resolutions of the princes in this matter, and the dismission of the captives thereupon. (1.) The armed men, though being armed they might by force have maintained their title to what they got by the sword, acquiesced, and left their captives and the spoil to the disposal of *the princes* (*v.* 14), and herein they showed more truly heroic bravery than they did in taking them. It is a great honour for any man to yield to the authority of reason and religion against his interest. (2.) The princes very generously sent home the poor captives well accommodated, *v.* 15. Those that hope to find mercy with God must learn hence with what tenderness to carry themselves towards those that lie at their mercy. It is strange that these princes, who in this instance discovered such a deference to the word of God, and such an influence upon the people, had not so much grace as, in obedience to the calls of God by so many prophets, to root idolatry out of their kingdom, which, soon after this, was the ruin of it.

16 At that time did king Ahaz send unto the kings of Assyria to help him.

17 For again the Edomites had come and smitten Judah, and carried away captives. 18 The Philistines also had invaded the cities of the low country, and of the south of Judah, and had taken Beth-shemesh, and Ajalon, and Gederoth, and Shocho with the villages thereof, and Timnah with the villages thereof, Gimzo also and the villages thereof: and they dwelt there. 19 For the LORD brought Judah low because of Ahaz king of Israel; for he made Judah naked, and transgressed sore against the LORD. 20 And Tilgath-pilneser king of Assyria came unto him, and distressed him, but strengthened him not. 21 For Ahaz took away a portion *out* of the house of the LORD, and *out* of the house of the king, and of the princes, and gave *it* unto the king of Assyria: but he helped him not. 22 And in the time of his distress did he trespass yet more against the LORD: this *is that* king Ahaz. 23 For he sacrificed unto the gods of Damascus, which smote him: and he said, Because the gods of the kings of Syria help them, *therefore* will I sacrifice to them, that they may help me. But they were the ruin of him, and of all Israel. 24 And Ahaz gathered together the vessels of the house of God, and cut in pieces the vessels of the house of God, and shut up the doors of the house of the LORD, and he made him altars in every corner of Jerusalem. 25 And in every several city of Judah he made high places to burn incense unto other gods, and provoked to anger the LORD God of his fathers. 26 Now the rest of his acts and of all his ways, first and last, behold, they *are* written in the book of the kings of Judah and Israel. 27 And Ahaz slept with his fathers, and they buried him in the city, *even* in Jerusalem: but they brought him not into the sepulchres of the kings of Israel: and Hezekiah his son reigned in his stead.

Here is, I. The great distress which the kingdom of Ahaz was reduced to for his sin. In general, 1. *The Lord brought Judah low,* *v.* 19. They had lately been very high in wealth and power; but God found means to bring them down, and make them as despicable as they had been formidable. Those that will not humble themselves under the word of God will justly be humbled by his judgments. Iniquity *brings men low,* Ps. cvi. 43. 2. Ahaz made Judah naked. As his sin debased them, so it exposed them. It made them naked to their shame; for it exposed them to contempt, as a man unclothed. It made them naked to their danger; for it exposed them to assaults, as a man unarmed, Exod. xxxii. 25. Sin strips men. In particular, the Edomites, to be revenged for Amaziah's cruel treatment of them (*ch.* xxv. 12), smote Judah, and carried off many captives, *v.* 17. The Philistines also insulted them, took and kept possession of several cities and villages that lay near them (*v.* 18), and so they were revenged for the incursions which Uzziah had made upon them, *ch.* xxvi. 6. And, to show that it was purely the sin of Ahaz that brought the Philistines upon his country, in the very year that he died the prophet Isaiah foretold the destruction of the Philistines by his son, Isa. xiv. 28, 29.

II. The addition which Ahaz made both to the national distress and the national guilt.

1. He added to the distress, by making court to strange kings, in hopes they would relieve him. When the Edomites and Philistines were vexatious to him, *he sent to the kings of Assyria to help him* (*v.* 16); for he found his own kingdom weakened and made naked, and he could not put any confidence in God, and therefore was at a vast expense to get an interest in the king of Assyria. He pillaged the house of God, and the king's house, and squeezed the princes for money to hire these foreign forces into his service, *v.* 21. Though he had conformed to the idolatry of the heathen nations, his neighbours, they did not value him for that, nor love him the better, nor did his compliance, by which he lost God, gain them, nor could he make any interest in them but with his money. It is often found that wicked men themselves have no real affection for those that revolt to them, nor do they care to do them a kindness. A degenerate branch is looked upon, on all sides, as *an abominable branch,* Isa. xiv. 19. But what did Ahaz get by the king of Assyria? Why, he *came to him,* but he *distressed him,* and *strengthened him not* (*v.* 20), *helped him not,* *v.* 21. The forces of the Assyrian quartered upon his country, and so impoverished and weakened it; they grew insolent and imperious, and created him a great deal of vexation, like a broken reed, which not only fails, but pierces the hand.

2. He added to the guilt, by making court to strange gods, in hopes they would relieve him. In his distress, instead of repenting of his idolatry, which he had reason enough to see the folly of, *he trespassed yet*

more (*v.* 22), was more mad than ever upon his idols. A brand of infamy is here set upon him for it: *This is that king Ahaz,* that wretched man, who was the scandal of the house of David and the curse and plague of his generation. Note, Those are wicked and vile indeed that are made worse by their afflictions, instead of being made better by them, who *in their distress trespass yet more,* have their corruptions exasperated by that which should mollify them, and their hearts more *fully set in them to do evil.* Let us see what his trespass was. (1.) He abused the house of God; for he *cut in pieces the vessels* of it, that the priests might not perform the service of the temple, or not as it should be performed, for want of vessels; and, at length, he *shut up the doors,* that the people might not attend it, *v.* 24. This was worse than the worst of the kings before him had done. (2.) He confronted the altar of God, for he *made himself altars in every corner of Jerusalem;* so that, as the prophet speaks, they were like *heaps in the furrows of the fields,* Hos. xii. 11. And in the cities of Judah, either by his power or by his purse, perhaps by both, he erected high places for the people to burn incense to what idols they pleased, as if on purpose to *provoke the God of his fathers, v.* 25. (3.) He cast off God himself; for he *sacrificed to the gods of Damascus* (*v.* 23), not because he loved them, for he thought they smote him; but because he feared them, thinking that they helped his enemies, and that, if he could bring them into his interest, they would help him. Foolish man! It was his own God that smote him and strengthened the Syrians against him, not the gods of Damascus; had he sacrificed to him, and to him only, he would have helped him. But no marvel that men's affections and devotions are misplaced when they mistake the author of their trouble and their help. And what comes of it? The gods of Syria befriend Ahaz no more than the kings of Assyria did; they were *the ruin of him and of all Israel.* This sin provoked God to bring judgments upon them, to cut him off in the midst of his days, when he was but thirty-six years old; and it debauched the people so that the reformation of the next reign could not prevail to cure them of their inclination to idolatry, but they retained that root of bitterness till the captivity in Babylon plucked it up.

The chapter concludes with the conclusion of the reign of Ahaz, *v.* 26, 27. For aught that appears, he died impenitent, and therefore died inglorious; for he was not buried *in the sepulchres of the kings.* Justly was he thought unworthy to be laid among them who was so unlike them—to be buried with kings who had used his kingly power for the destruction of the church and not for its protection or edification.

CHAP. XXIX.

We are here entering upon a pleasant scene, the good and glorious reign of Hezekiah, in which we shall find more of God and religion than perhaps in any of the good reigns we have yet met with; for he was a very zealous, devout, good man, none like him. In this chapter we have an account of the work of reformation which he set about with vigour immediately after his accession to the crown. Here is, I. His exhortation to the priests and Levites, when he put them in possession of the house of God again, ver. 1—11. II. The care and pains which the Levites took to cleanse the temple, and put things in order there, ver. 12—19. III. A solemn revival of God's ordinances that had been neglected, in which atonement was made for the sins of the last reign, and the wheels were set a-going again, to the great satisfaction of king and people, ver. 20—36.

HEZEKIAH began to reign *when he was* five and twenty years old, and he reigned nine and twenty years in Jerusalem. And his mother's name *was* Abijah, the daughter of Zechariah. 2 And he did *that which was* right in the sight of the LORD, according to all that David his father had done. 3 He in the first year of his reign, in the first month, opened the doors of the house of the LORD, and repaired them. 4 And he brought in the priests and the Levites, and gathered them together into the east street, 5 And said unto them, Hear me, ye Levites, sanctify now yourselves, and sanctify the house of the LORD God of your fathers, and carry forth the filthiness out of the holy *place.* 6 For our fathers have trespassed, and done *that which was* evil in the eyes of the LORD our God, and have forsaken him, and have turned away their faces from the habitation of the LORD, and turned *their* backs. 7 Also they have shut up the doors of the porch, and put out the lamps, and have not burned incense nor offered burnt offerings in the holy *place* unto the God of Israel. 8 Wherefore the wrath of the LORD was upon Judah and Jerusalem, and he hath delivered them to trouble, to astonishment, and to hissing, as ye see with your eyes. 9 For, lo, our fathers have fallen by the sword, and our sons and our daughters and our wives *are* in captivity for this. 10 Now *it is* in mine heart to make a covenant with the LORD God of Israel, that his fierce wrath may turn away from us. 11 My sons, be not now negligent: for the LORD hath chosen you to stand before him, to serve him, and that ye should minister unto him, and burn incense.

Here is, I. Hezekiah's age when he came to the crown. He was *twenty-five years old.* Joash, who came to the crown after two bad reigns, was but seven years old; Josiah, who came after two bad reigns, was but eight, which occasioned the delay of the reformation; but Hezekiah had come to years, and so applied himself immediately to it. We may well think with what a sorrowful heart he beheld his father's idolatry and profanenesss, how it troubled him to see the doors of the temple shut, though, while his father lived, he durst not open them. His soul no doubt wept in secret for it, and he vowed that when he should receive the congregation he would redress these grievances, which made him do it with more readiness and resolution.

II. His general character. He *did that which was right like David, v.* 2. Of several of his predecessors it had been said that they did that which was right, *but not like David*, not with David's integrity and zeal. But here was one that had as hearty an affection for the ark and law of God as ever David had.

III. His speedy application to the great work of restoring religion. The first thing he did was to *open the doors of the house of the Lord, v.* 3. We are willing to hope his father had not quite suppressed the temple service; for then the holy fire on the altar must have gone out, and we do not read of the re-kindling of it; but he had hindered the people from attending it, and the priests, except such of them as were of his own party, 2 Kings xvi. 15. But Hezekiah immediately threw the church doors open, and *brought in the priests and Levites.* He found Judah low and naked, yet did not make it his first business to revive the civil interests of his kingdom, but to restore religion to its good posture again. Those that begin with God begin at the right end of their work, and it will prosper accordingly.

IV. His speech to the priests and Levites. It was well known, no doubt, that he had a real kindness for religion and was disaffected to the corruptions of the last reign; yet we do not find the priests and Levites making application to him for the restoration of the temple service, but he calls upon them, which, I doubt, bespeaks their coldness as much as his zeal; and perhaps, if they had done their part with vigour, things would not have been brought into so very bad a posture as Hezekiah found them in. Hezekiah's exhortation to the Levites is very pathetic.

1. He laid before them the desolations of religion and the deplorable state to which it was brought among them (*v.* 6, 7): *Our fathers have trespassed.* He said not "*My* father," because it became him, as a son, to be as tender as might be of his father's name, and because his father would not have done all this if their fathers had not neglected their duty. Urijah the priest had joined with Ahaz in setting up an idolatrous altar. He complained, (1.) That the house of God had been deserted: *They have forsaken God, and turned their backs upon his habitation.* Note, Those that turn their backs upon God's ordinances may truly be said to forsake God himself. (2.) That the instituted worship of God there had been let fall. The lamps were not lighted, and incense was not burnt. There are still such neglects as these, and they are no less culpable, when the word is not duly read and opened (for that was signified by the *lighting of the lamps*) and when prayers and praises are not duly offered up, for that was signified by *the burning of incense.*

2. He showed the sad consequences of the neglect and decay of religion among them, *v.* 8, 9. This was the cause of all the calamities they had lain under. God had in anger delivered them to trouble, to the sword, and to captivity. When we are under the rebukes of God's providence it is good for us to enquire whether we have not neglected God's ordinances and whether the controversy he has with us may not be traced to this neglect.

3. He declared his own full purpose and resolution to revive religion and make it his business to promote it (*v.* 10): "*It is in my heart* (that is, I am fully resolved) *to make a covenant with the Lord God of Israel* (that is, to worship him only, and in that way which he has appointed); for I am sure that, otherwise, his fierce anger will not turn away from us." This covenant he would not only make himself, but bring his people into the bond of.

4. He engaged and excited the Levites and priests to do their duty on this occasion. This he begins with (*v.* 5); this he ends with, *v.* 11. He called them *Levites* to remind them of their obligation to God, called them his *sons* to remind them of their relation to himself, that he expected that, *as a son with the father, they should serve with him* in the reformation of the land. (1.) He told them what was their duty, to sanctify *themselves* first (by repenting of their neglects, reforming their own hearts and lives, and renewing their covenants with God to do their duty better for the time to come), and then to *sanctify the house of God,* as his servants, to make it clean from every thing that was disagreeable, either through the disuse or the profanation of it, and to set it up for the purposes for which it was made. (2.) He stirred them up to do it (*v.* 11): "*Be not now negligent*, or remiss, in your duty. Let not this good work be retarded through your carelessness." *Be not deceived,* so the *margin.* Note, Those that by their negligence in the service of God think to mock God, and put a cheat upon him, do but deceive themselves, and put a damning cheat upon their own souls. *Be not secure* (so some), as if there were no urgent call to do it or no danger in not doing it. Note, Men's negligence in religion is owing to their carnal security. The consideration he quickens them with is derived from their office. God had herein put honour upon them: He has

chosen you to stand before him. God therefore expected work from them. They were not chosen to be idle, to enjoy the dignity and leave the duty to be done by others, but to serve him and to minister to him. They must therefore be ashamed of their late remissness, and, now that the doors of the temple were opened again, must set about their work with double diligence.

12 Then the Levites arose, Mahath the son of Amasai, and Joel the son of Azariah, of the sons of the Kohathites: and of the sons of Merari, Kish the son of Abdi, and Azariah the son of Jehalelel: and of the Gershonites; Joah the son of Zimmah, and Eden the son of Joah: 13 And of the sons of Elizaphan; Shimri, and Jeiel: and of the sons of Asaph; Zechariah, and Mattaniah: 14 And of the sons of Heman; Jehiel, and Shimei: and of the sons of Jeduthun; Shemaiah, and Uzziel. 15 And they gathered their brethren, and sanctified themselves, and came, according to the commandment of the king, by the words of the LORD, to cleanse the house of the LORD. 16 And the priests went into the inner part of the house of the LORD, to cleanse *it*, and brought out all the uncleanness that they found in the temple of the LORD into the court of the house of the LORD. And the Levites took *it*, to carry *it* out abroad into the brook Kidron. 17 Now they began on the first *day* of the first month to sanctify, and on the eighth day of the month came they to the porch of the LORD: so they sanctified the house of the LORD in eight days; and in the sixteenth day of the first month they made an end. 18 Then they went in to Hezekiah the king, and said, We have cleansed all the house of the LORD, and the altar of burnt offering, with all the vessels thereof, and the showbread table, with all the vessels thereof. 19 Moreover all the vessels, which king Ahaz in his reign did cast away in his transgression, have we prepared and sanctified, and, behold, they *are* before the altar of the LORD.

We have here busy work, good work, and needful work, the cleansing of the house of the Lord.

I. The persons employed in this work were the priests and Levites, who should have kept the temple clean, but, not having done that, were concerned to make it clean. Several of the Levites are here named, two of each of the three principal houses, Kohath, Gershon, and Merari (*v.* 12), and two of each of the three families of singers, Asaph, Heman, and Jeduthun, *v.* 13, 14. We cannot think these are named merely because they were chief in place (for then surely the high priest, or some of the heads of the courses of the priests, would have been mentioned), but because they were more zealous and active than the rest. When God has work to do he will raise up leading men to preside in it. And it is not always that the first in place and rank are most fit for service or most forward to it. These Levites not only bestirred themselves, but *gathered their brethren,* and quickened them to do *according to the commandment of the king by the word of the Lord.* Observe, They did according to the king's command, but with an eye to God's word. The king commanded them what was already their duty by the word of God, and, in doing it, they regarded God's word as a rule to them and the king's commandment as a spur to them.

II. The work was *cleansing the house of God,* 1. From the common dirt it had contracted while it was shut up—dust, and cobwebs, and the rust of the vessels. 2. From the idols and idolatrous altars that were set up in it, which, though kept ever so neat, were a greater pollution to it than if it had been made the common sewer of the city. The priests were none of them mentioned as leading men in this work, yet none but they durst go *into the inner part of the house, no, not to cleanse it,* which they did, and perhaps the high priest into the holy of holies, to cleanse that. And, though the Levites had the honour to be the leaders in the work, they did not disdain to be servitors to the priests according to their office; for what filth the priests brought into the court the Levites carried to the brook Kidron. Let not men's usefulness, be it ever so eminent, make them forget their place.

III. The expedition with which they did this work was very remarkable. They began on the first day of the first month, a happy beginning of the new-year, and one that promised a good year. Thus should every year begin with the reformation of what is amiss, and the purging away, by true repentance, of all the defilements contracted the foregoing year. In eight days they cleared and cleansed the temple, and in eight days more the *courts* of the temple, *v.* 17. Let those that do good work learn to rid work and get it done. Let what is amiss be amended quickly.

IV. The report they made of it to Hezekiah was very agreeable, *v.* 18, 19. They gave him an account of what they had done, because it was he that set them on work, boasted not of their own care and pains, nor did they come to him to be paid, but to let him know that all the things that had been profaned were now sanctified according to law, and were ready to be used again whenever he pleased. They knew the good king had set his heart upon God's altar, and longed to be attending that, and therefore they insisted most upon the readiness they had put that into—that the vessels of the altar were scoured and brightened. Those vessels which Ahaz, in his *transgression, had cast away* as vessels in which there was no pleasure, they gathered together, sanctified them, and laid them in their place *before the altar*. Though the vessels of the sanctuary may be profaned for a while, God will find a time and a way to sanctify them. Neither his ordinances nor his people shall be suffered to fail for ever.

20 Then Hezekiah the king rose early, and gathered the rulers of the city, and went up to the house of the LORD. 21 And they brought seven bullocks, and seven rams, and seven lambs, and seven he goats, for a sin offering for the kingdom, and for the sanctuary, and for Judah. And he commanded the priests the sons of Aaron to offer *them* on the altar of the LORD. 22 So they killed the bullocks, and the priests received the blood, and sprinkled *it* on the altar: likewise, when they had killed the rams, they sprinkled the blood upon the altar: they killed also the lambs, and they sprinkled the blood upon the altar. 23 And they brought forth the he goats *for* the sin offering before the king and the congregation; and they laid their hands upon them: 24 And the priests killed them, and they made reconciliation with their blood upon the altar, to make an atonement for all Israel: for the king commanded *that* the burnt offering and the sin offering *should be made* for all Israel. 25 And he set the Levites in the house of the LORD with cymbals, with psalteries, and with harps, according to the commandment of David, and of Gad the king's seer, and Nathan the prophet: for *so was* the commandment of the LORD by his prophets. 26 And the Levites stood with the instruments of David, and the priests with the trumpets. 27 And Hezekiah commanded to offer the burnt offering upon the altar. And when the burnt offering began, the song of the LORD began *also* with the trumpets, and with the instruments *ordained* by David king of Israel. 28 And all the congregation worshipped, and the singers sang, and the trumpeters sounded: *and* all *this continued* until the burnt offering was finished. 29 And when they had made an end of offering, the king and all that were present with him bowed themselves, and worshipped. 30 Moreover Hezekiah the king and the princes commanded the Levites to sing praise unto the LORD with the words of David, and of Asaph the seer. And they sang praises with gladness, and they bowed their heads and worshipped. 31 Then Hezekiah answered and said, Now ye have consecrated yourselves unto the LORD, come near and bring sacrifices and thank offerings into the house of the LORD. And the congregation brought in sacrifices and thank offerings; and as many as were of a free heart burnt offerings. 32 And the number of the burnt offerings, which the congregation brought, was threescore and ten bullocks, a hundred rams, *and* two hundred lambs: all these *were* for a burnt offering to the LORD. 33 And the consecrated things *were* six hundred oxen and three thousand sheep. 34 But the priests were too few, so that they could not flay all the burnt offerings: wherefore their brethren the Levites did help them, till the work was ended, and until the *other* priests had sanctified themselves: for the Levites *were* more upright in heart to sanctify themselves than the priests. 35 And also the burnt offerings *were* in abundance, with the fat of the peace offerings, and the drink offerings for *every* burnt offering. So the service of the house of the LORD was set in order. 36 And Hezekiah rejoiced, and all the people, that God had prepared the people: for the thing was *done* suddenly.

The temple being cleansed, we have here an account of the good use that was immediately made of it. A solemn assembly was called to meet the king at the temple, the very next day (*v.* 20); and very glad, no doubt, all the good people in Jerusalem were, when it was said, *Let us go up to the house of the Lord*, Ps. cxxii. 1. As soon as Hezekiah heard that the temple was ready for him he lost no time, but made it appear that he was ready for it. He rose early to go up to the house of the Lord, earlier on that day than on other days, to show that his heart was upon his work there. Now this day's work was to look two ways:—

I. Atonement must be made for the sins of the last reign. They thought it not enough to lament and forsake those sins, but they brought a sin-offering. Even our repentance and reformation will not obtain pardon but in and through Christ, who was made *sin* (that is, a sin-offering) for us. No peace but through his blood, no, not for penitents. Observe, 1. The sin-offering was *for the kingdom, for the sanctuary*, and *for Judah* (*v.* 21), that is, to make atonement for the sins of princes, priests, and people, for they had all corrupted their way. The law of Moses appointed sacrifices to make atonement for the sins of the whole congregation (Lev. iv. 13, 14; Num. xv. 24, 25), that the national judgments which their national sins deserved might be turned away. For this purpose we must now have an eye to Christ the great propitiation, as well as for the remission and salvation of particular persons. 2. The law appointed only one goat for a sin-offering, as on the day of atonement (Lev. xvi. 15) and on such extraordinary occasions as this, Num. xv. 24. But they here offered seven (*v.* 21), because the sins of the congregation had been very great and long continued in. Seven is a number of perfection. Our great sin-offering is but one, yet that one *perfects* for ever *those that are sanctified.* 3. The king and the *congregation* (that is, the representatives of the congregation) *laid their hands on the heads of the goats* that were for the *sin-offering* (*v.* 23), thereby owning themselves guilty before God and expressing their desire that the guilt of the sinner might be transferred to the sacrifice. By faith we lay our hands on the Lord Jesus, and so *receive the atonement*, Rom. v. 11. 4. Burnt-offerings were offered with the sin-offerings, *seven bullocks, seven rams*, and *seven lambs.* The intention of the burnt-offerings was to give glory to the God of Israel, whom they owned as the only true God, which it was proper to do at the same time that they were by the sin-offering making atonement for their offences. The blood of those, as well as of the sin-offering, was *sprinkled upon the altar* (*v.* 22), to make reconciliation *for all Israel* (*v.* 24), and not for Judah only. Christ is a propitiation, not for the sins of Israel only, but *of the whole world*, 1 John ii. 1, 2. 5. While the offerings were burning upon the altar the *Levites* sang *the song of the Lord* (*v.* 27), the Psalms composed by David and Asaph (*v.* 30), accompanied by the musical instruments which God by his prophets had commanded the use of (*v.* 25), and which had been long neglected. Even sorrow for sin must not put us out of tune for praising God. By faith we must rejoice in Christ Jesus as our righteousness; and our prayers and praises must ascend with his offering, to be accepted only in virtue of it. 6. The king and all the congregation testified their consent to and concurrence in all that was done, by *bowing their heads* and *worshipping*, expressing an awful veneration of the divine Majesty, by postures of adoration. This is taken notice of, *v.* 28—30. It is not enough for us to be where God is worshipped, if we do not ourselves worship him, and that not with bodily exercise only, which profits little, but with the heart.

II. The solemnities of this day did likewise look forward. The temple service was to be set up again, that it might be continually kept up; and this Hezekiah calls them to, *v.* 31. "Now that you have *consecrated yourselves to the Lord*—have both made an atonement and made a covenant by sacrifice, are solemnly reconciled and engaged to him—now *come near, and bring sacrifices.*" Note, Our covenant with God must be pursued and improved in communion with him. Having consecrated ourselves, in the first place, to the Lord, we must bring the sacrifices of prayer, and praise, and alms, to his house. Now, in this work, it was found.

1. That the people were free. Being called to it by the king, they brought in their offerings, though not in such abundance as in the glorious days of Solomon (for Judah was now diminished, impoverished, and brought low), but according to what they had, and as much as one could expect considering their poverty and the great decay of piety among them. (1.) Some were so generous as to bring burnt-offerings, which were wholly consumed to the honour of God, and of which the offerer had no part. Of this sort there were seventy bullocks, 100 rams, and 200 lambs, *v.* 32. (2.) Others brought peace-offerings and thank-offerings, the fat of which was burnt upon the altar, and the flesh divided between the priests and the offerers, *v.* 35. Of this sort there were 600 oxen and 3000 sheep, *v.* 33. Perhaps the remembrance of their sin in sacrificing on the high places made them more willing to bring their sacrifices now to God's altar.

2. That *the priests were few*, too few for the service, *v.* 34. Many of them, it is likely, were suspended and laid aside as polluted and uncanonical, for having sacrificed to idols in the last reign, and the rest had not the zeal that one might have expected upon such an occasion. They thought that the king needed not to be so forward, that there was no necessity for such haste in opening the doors of the temple, and therefore they took no care to sanctify themselves, and being unsanctified, and so unqualified, they made that

their excuse for being absent from the service; as if their offence would be their defence. It is recorded here, to the perpetual shame of the priests, that, though they were so well provided for out of the offerings of the Lord made by fire, yet they did not mind their business. Here was work to do, and there wanted proper hands to do it.

3. That the Levites were forward. They had been *more upright in heart to sanctify themselves than the priests* (*v.* 34), were better affected to the work and better prepared and qualified for it. This was their praise, and, in recompence for it, they had the honour to be employed in that which was the priests' work: they *helped them to flay the offerings.* This was not according to the law (Lev. i. 5, 6), but the irregularity was dispensed with in cases of necessity, and thus encouragement was given to the faithful zealous Levites and a just disgrace put upon the careless priests. What the Levites wanted in the ceremonial advantages of their birth and consecration was abundantly made up in their eminent qualifications of skill and will to do the work.

4. That all were pleased. The king and all the people rejoiced in this blessed turn of affairs and the new face of religion which the kingdom had put on, *v.* 36. Two things in this matter pleased them:—(1.) That it was soon brought about: *The thing was done suddenly,* in a little time, with a great deal of ease, and without any opposition. Those that go about the work of God in faith and with resolution will find that there is not that difficulty in it which they sometimes imagine, but it will be a pleasing surprise to them to see how soon it is done. (2.) That the hand of God was plainly in it: *God had prepared the people* by the secret influences of his grace, so that many of those who had in the last reign doted on the idolatrous altars were now as much in love with God's altar. This change, which God wrought on their minds, did very much expedite and facilitate the work. Let magistrates and ministers do their part towards the reforming of a land, and then let them trust God to do his, and ascribe to him the glory of what is done, especially when it is done suddenly and is a pleasing surprise. *This is the Lord's doing, and it is marvellous.*

CHAP. XXX.

In this chapter we have an account of the solemn passover which Hezekiah kept in the first year of his reign. I. The consultation about it, and the resolution he and his people came to for the observance of it, ver. 2—5. II. The invitation he sent to Judah and Israel to come and keep it, ver. 1, 6—12. III. The joyful celebration of it, ver. 13—27. By this the reformation, set on foot in the foregoing chapter, was greatly advanced and established, and that nail in God's holy place clenched.

AND Hezekiah sent to all Israel and Judah, and wrote letters also to Ephraim and Manasseh, that they should come to the house of the LORD at Jerusalem, to keep the passover unto the LORD God of Israel. 2 For the king had taken counsel, and his princes, and all the congregation in Jerusalem, to keep the passover in the second month. 3 For they could not keep it at that time, because the priests had not sanctified themselves sufficiently, neither had the people gathered themselves together to Jerusalem. 4 And the thing pleased the king and all the congregation. 5 So they established a decree to make proclamation throughout all Israel, from Beer-sheba even to Dan, that they should come to keep the passover unto the LORD God of Israel at Jerusalem: for they had not done *it* of a long *time in such sort* as it was written. 6 So the posts went with the letters from the king and his princes throughout all Israel and Judah, and according to the commandment of the king, saying, Ye children of Israel, turn again unto the LORD God of Abraham, Isaac, and Israel, and he will return to the remnant of you, that are escaped out of the hand of the kings of Assyria. 7 And be not ye like your fathers, and like your brethren, which trespassed against the LORD God of their fathers, *who* therefore gave them up to desolation, as ye see. 8 Now be ye not stiffnecked, as your fathers *were, but* yield yourselves unto the LORD, and enter into his sanctuary, which he hath sanctified for ever: and serve the LORD your God, that the fierceness of his wrath may turn away from you. 9 For if ye turn again unto the LORD, your brethren and your children *shall find* compassion before them that lead them captive, so that they shall come again into this land: for the LORD your God *is* gracious and merciful, and will not turn away *his* face from you, if ye return unto him. 10 So the posts passed from city to city through the country of Ephraim and Manasseh even unto Zebulun: but they laughed them to scorn, and mocked them. 11 Nevertheless divers of Asher and Manasseh and of Zebulun humbled themselves, and came to Jerusalem. 12 Also in Judah the hand of God was to give them one heart to do the commandment of the king and of the princes, by the word of the LORD.

Here is, I. A passover resolved upon. That annual feast was instituted as a memorial of the bringing of the children of Israel out of Egypt. It happened that the reviving of the temple service fell within the appointed days of that feast, the seventeenth day of the first month: this brought that forgotten solemnity to mind. "What shall we do," says Hezekiah, "about the passover? It is a very comfortable ordinance, and has been long neglected. How shall we revive it? The time has elapsed for this year; we cannot go about it immediately; the congregation is thin, the people have not notice, the priests are not prepared, *v.* 3. Must we defer it till another year?" Many, it is likely, were for deferring it; but Hezekiah considered that by that time twelve-month the good affections of the people would cool, and it would be too long to want the benefit of the ordinance; and therefore, finding a proviso in the law of Moses that particular persons who were unclean in the first month might keep the passover the fourteenth day of the second month and be accepted (Num. ix. 11), he doubted not but that it might be extended to the congregation. Whereupon they resolved to keep the passover *in the second month.* Let the circumstance give way to the substance, and let not the thing itself be lost upon a nicety about the time. It is good striking while the iron is hot, and taking people when they are in a good mind. Delays are dangerous.

II. A proclamation issued out to give notice of this passover and to summon the people to it.

1. An invitation was sent to the ten revolted tribes to stir them up to come and attend this solemnity. Letters were written to Ephraim and Manasseh to invite them to Jerusalem to keep this passover (*v.* 1), not with any political design, to bring them back to the house of David, but with a pious design to bring them back to the Lord God of Israel. "Let them take whom they will for their king," says Hezekiah, "so they will but take him for their God." The matters in difference between Judah and Israel, either upon a civil or sacred account, shall not hinder but that if the people of Israel will sincerely return to the Lord their God Hezekiah will bid them as welcome to the passover as any of his own subjects. Expresses are sent post throughout all the tribes of Israel with memorials earnestly pressing the people to take this opportunity of returning to the God from whom they had revolted. Now here we have,

(1.) The contents of the circular letters that were despatched upon this occasion, in which Hezekiah discovers a great concern both for the honour of God and for the welfare of the neighbouring kingdom, the prosperity of which he seems passionately desirous of, though he not only received no toll, tribute, or custom, from it, but it had often, and not long since, been vexatious to his kingdom. This is rendering good for evil. Observe,

[1.] What it is which he presses them to (*v.* 8): "*Yield yourselves unto the Lord.* Before you can come into communion with him you must come into covenant with him." *Give the hand to the Lord* (so the word is), that is, "Consent to take him for your God." A bargain is confirmed by giving the hand. "Strike this bargain. Join yourselves to him in an everlasting covenant. *Subscribe with the hand* to be his, Isa. xliv. 5. Give him your hand, in token of giving him your heart. Lay your hand to his plough. Devote yourselves to his service, to work for him. *Yield to him,*" that is, "Come up to his terms, come under his government, stand it not out any longer against him." "*Yield to him,* to be absolutely and universally at his command, at his disposal, to be, and do, and have, and suffer, whatever he pleases. In order to this, be not *stiff-necked as your fathers were;* let not your corrupt and wicked wills rise up in resistance of and rebellion against the will of God. Say not that you will do what you please, but resolve to do what he pleases." There is in the carnal mind a stiffness, an obstinacy, an unaptness to comply with God. We have it from our fathers; it is bred in the bone with us. This must be conquered; and the will that had in it a spirit of contradiction must be melted into the will of God; and to his yoke the neck that was an iron sinew must be bowed and fitted. In pursuance of this resignation to God, he presses them *to enter into his sanctuary,* that is, to attend upon him in that place which he had chosen, to put his name there, and serve him in the ordinances which he had appointed. "The doors of the sanctuary are now opened, and you have liberty to enter; the temple service is now revived, and you are welcome to join in it." The king says, *Come;* the princes and priests say, *Come; whosoever will, let him come.* This he calls (*v.* 6) *turning to the Lord God;* for they had forsaken him, and worshipped other gods. *Repent now, and be converted.* Thus those who through grace have turned to God themselves should do all they can to bring others back to him.

[2.] What arguments he uses to persuade them to do this. *First,* "You are children of Israel, and therefore stand related, stand obliged, to the God of Israel, from whom you have revolted." *Secondly,* "The God you are called to return to is the God of Abraham, Isaac, and Jacob, a God in covenant with your first fathers, who served him and yielded themselves to him; and it was their honour and happiness that they did so." *Thirdly,* "Your late fathers that forsook him and trespassed against him have been given up to desolation; their apostasy and idolatry have been their ruin, as you see (*v.* 7); let their harms be your warnings." *Fourthly,* "You yourselves are but a *remnant* narrowly *escaped out of the hands of the kings of Assyria* (*v.* 6), and therefore are concerned to put yourselves under the protection of the God of your fathers, that you be not quite swallowed up." *Fifthly,* "This is the only way of *turning away the fierceness of God's anger from you* (*v.* 8), which will certainly consume you if you continue stiff-necked." *Lastly,* "If you return to God in a way of duty, he will return to you in a way of mercy." This he begins with (*v.* 6) and concludes with, *v.* 9. In general, "You will find him *gracious and merciful,* and one that *will not turn away his face from you,* if you seek him, notwithstanding the provocations you have given him." Particularly, "You may hope that he will turn again the captivity of your brethren that are carried away, and bring them back to their own land." Could any thing be expressed more pathetically, more movingly? Could there be a better cause, or could it be better pleaded?

(2.) The entertainment which Hezekiah's messengers and message met with. It does not appear that Hoshea, who was now king of Israel, took any umbrage from, or gave any opposition to, the dispersing of these proclamations through his kingdom, nor that he forbade his subjects to accept the invitation. He seems to have left them entirely to their liberty. They might go to Jerusalem to worship if they pleased; for, though he did evil, yet *not like the kings of Israel that were before him,* 2 Kings xvii. 2. He saw ruin coming upon his kingdom, and, if any of his subjects would try this expedient to prevent it, they had his full permission. But, for the people, [1.] The generality of them slighted the call and turned a deaf ear to it. The messengers went from city to city, some to one and some to another, and used pressing entreaties with the people to come up to Jerusalem to keep the passover; but they were so far from complying with the message that they abused those that brought it, *laughed them to scorn, and mocked them* (*v.* 10), not only refused, but refused with disdain. Tell them of the God of Abraham! they knew him not, they had other gods to serve, Baal and Ashtaroth. Tell them of the sanctuary! their high places were as good. Tell them of God's mercy and wrath! they neither dreaded the one nor desired the other. No marvel that the king's messengers were thus despitefully used by this apostate race when God's messengers were so, his servants the prophets, who produced credentials from him. The destruction of the kingdom of the ten tribes was now at hand. It was but two or three years after this that the king of Assyria laid siege to Samaria, which ended in the captivity of those tribes. Just before this they had not only a king of their own that permitted them to return to God's sanctuary, but a king of Judah that earnestly invited them to do it. Had they generally accepted this invitation, it might have prevented their ruin; but their contempt of it hastened and aggravated it, and left them inexcusable. [2.] Yet there were some few that accepted the invitation. The message, though to some it was a *savour of death unto death,* was to others a *savour of life unto life, v.* 11. In the worst of times God has had a remnant; so he had here, many of Asher, Manasseh, and Zebulun (here is no mention of any out of Ephraim, though some of that tribe are mentioned, *v.* 18), *humbled themselves, and came to Jerusalem,* that is, were sorry for their sins and submitted to God. Pride keeps men from yielding themselves to the Lord; when that is brought down, the work is done.

2. A command was given to the men of Judah to attend this solemnity; and they universally obeyed it, *v.* 12. They did it with one heart, were all of a mind in it, and *the hand of God gave* them that *one heart;* for it is in the day of power that Christ's subjects are made willing. It is God that works both *to will* and *to do.* When people, at any time, manifest an unexpected forwardness to do that which is good, we must acknowledge the hand of God in it.

13 And there assembled at Jerusalem much people to keep the feast of unleavened bread in the second month, a very great congregation. 14 And they arose and took away the altars that *were* in Jerusalem, and all the altars for incense took they away, and cast *them* into the brook Kidron. 15 Then they killed the passover on the fourteenth *day* of the second month: and the priests and the Levites were ashamed, and sanctified themselves, and brought in the burnt offerings into the house of the LORD. 16 And they stood in their place after their manner, according to the law of Moses the man of God: the priests sprinkled the blood, *which they received* of the hand of the Levites. 17 For *there were* many in the congregation that were not sanctified: therefore the Levites had the charge of the killing of the passovers for every one *that was* not clean, to sanctify *them* unto the LORD. 18 For a multitude of the people, *even* many of Ephraim, and Manasseh, Issachar, and Zebulun, had not cleansed themselves, yet did they eat the passover otherwise than it was written. But Hezekiah prayed for

them, saying, The good LORD pardon every one 19 *That* prepareth his heart to seek God, the LORD God of his fathers, though *he be* not *cleansed* according to the purification of the sanctuary. 20 And the LORD hearkened to Hezekiah, and healed the people.

The time appointed for the passover having arrived, a very great congregation came together upon the occasion, *v.* 13. Now here we have,

I. The preparation they made for the passover, and good preparation it was: *They took away* all *the* idolatrous *altars* that were found, not only in the temple, but *in Jerusalem, v.* 14. Before they kept the feast, they cast out this old leaven. The best preparation we can make for the gospel passover is to cast away our iniquities, our spiritual idolatries.

II. The celebration of the passover. In this the people were so forward and zealous that the priests and Levites blushed to see themselves out-done by the commonalty, to see them more ready to bring sacrifices than they were to offer them. This put them upon sanctifying themselves (*v.* 15), that the work might not stand still for want of hands to carry it on. The notice we take of the zeal of others should make us ashamed of our own coldness, and quicken us not only to do our duty, but to do it well, and to sanctify ourselves to it. They did according to the duty of their place (*v.* 16), sprinkling *the blood upon the altar,* which was a type of Christ our passover sacrificed for us.

III. The irregularities they were guilty of in this solemnity. The substance was well managed, and with a great deal of devotion; but, besides that it was a month out of time, 1. The *Levites killed the passover,* which should have been done by the priests only, *v.* 17. They also assisted more than the law ordinarily allowed in offering the other sacrifices, particularly those that were for the purifying of the unclean, many of which there was now occasion for. Some think that it was the offerers' work, not the priests', that the Levites had here the charge of. Ordinarily every man killed his lamb, but now for those that were under any ceremonial pollution the Levites killed it. 2. Many were permitted to eat the passover who were not purified according to the strictness of the law, *v.* 18. This was the second month, and there was no warrant to put them off further to the third month, as, if it had been the first month, the law would have permitted them to eat it the second. And they were loth to forbid them communicating at all, lest they should discourage new converts, and send those away complaining whom they desired to send away rejoicing. Grotius observes from this that ritual institutions must give way, not only to a public necessity, but to a public benefit and advantage.

IV. Hezekiah's prayer to God for the forgiveness of this irregularity. It was his zeal that had called them together in such haste, and he would not that any should fare the worse for being straitened of time in their preparation. He therefore thought himself concerned to be an intercessor for those that *ate the passover otherwise than it was written,* that there might not be wrath upon them from the Lord. His prayer was,

1. A short prayer, but to the purpose: *The good Lord pardon every one* in the congregation that has fixed, engaged, or *prepared, his heart* to those services, though the ceremonial preparation be wanting. Note, (1.) The great thing required in our attendance upon God in solemn ordinances is that we *prepare our hearts to seek him,* that we be sincere and upright in all we do, that the inward man be engaged and employed in it, and that we make heart-work of it; it is all nothing without this. *Behold, thou desirest truth in the inward part.* Hezekiah does not pray that this might be dispensed with, nor that the want of other things might be pardoned where there was not this. For *this* is the *one thing needful,* that we *seek God,* his favour, his honour, and that we set our hearts to do it. (2.) Where this sincerity and fixedness of heart are there may still be many defects and infirmities, both the frame of the spirit and the performance of the service may be short of *the purification of the sanctuary.* Corruptions may not be so fully conquered, thoughts not so closely fixed, affections not so lively, faith not so operative, as they should be. Here is a defect in sanctuary purification. There is nothing perfect under the sun, nor *a just man that doeth good, and sinneth not.* (3.) These defects need pardoning healing grace; for omissions in duty are sins as well as omissions of duty. If God should deal with us in strict justice according to the best of our performances, we should be undone. (4.) The way to obtain pardon for our deficiencies in duty, and all the iniquities of our holy things, is to seek it of God by prayer; it is not so a pardon of course but that it must be obtained by petition through the blood of Christ. (5.) In this prayer we must take encouragement from the goodness of God: *The good Lord pardon;* for, when he proclaimed his goodness, he insisted most upon this branch of it, *forgiving iniquity, transgression, and sin.* (6.) It is the duty of those that have the charge of others, not only to look to themselves, but to those also that are under their charge, to see wherein they are wanting, and to pray for them, as Hezekiah here. See Job i. 5.

2. A successful prayer: *The Lord hearkened to Hezekiah,* was well pleased with his pious concern for the congregation, and, in answer to his prayer, *healed the people* (*v.* 20), not only did not lay their sin to their charge, but graciously accepted their services notwithstanding; for healing denotes not only

forgiveness (Isa. vi. 10; Ps. ciii. 3), but comfort and peace, Isa. lvii. 18; Mal. iv. 2.

21 And the children of Israel that were present at Jerusalem kept the feast of unleavened bread seven days with great gladness: and the Levites and the priests praised the LORD day by day, *singing* with loud instruments unto the LORD. 22 And Hezekiah spake comfortably unto all the Levites that taught the good knowledge of the LORD: and they did eat throughout the feast seven days, offering peace offerings, and making confession to the LORD God of their fathers. 23 And the whole assembly took counsel to keep other seven days: and they kept *other* seven days with gladness. 24 For Hezekiah king of Judah did give to the congregation a thousand bullocks and seven thousand sheep; and the princes gave to the congregation a thousand bullocks and ten thousand sheep: and a great number of priests sanctified themselves. 25 And all the congregation of Judah, with the priests and the Levites, and all the congregation that came out of Israel, and the strangers that came out of the land of Israel, and that dwelt in Judah, rejoiced. 26 So there was great joy in Jerusalem: for since the time of Solomon the son of David king of Israel *there was* not the like in Jerusalem. 27 Then the priests the Levites arose and blessed the people: and their voice was heard, and their prayer came *up* to his holy dwelling place, *even* unto heaven.

After the passover followed the feast of unleavened bread, which continued seven days. How that was observed we are here told, and every thing in this account looks pleasant and lively. 1. Abundance of sacrifices were offered to God in peace-offerings, by which they both acknowledged and implored the favour of God, and on part of which the offerers feasted with their friends during these seven days (*v.* 22), in token of their communion with God and the comfort they took in his favour and their reconciliation to him. To keep up this part of the service, that God's altar might be abundantly regaled with the fat and blood and his priests and people with the flesh of the peace-offerings, Hezekiah gave out of his own stock 1000 bullocks and 7000 sheep, and the princes, excited by his pious example, gave the same number of bullocks and a greater number of sheep, and all for peace-offerings, *v.* 24. By this God was honoured, the joy of the festival was kept up, and the strangers were encouraged to come again to Jerusalem. It was generously done of the king and the princes thus plentifully to entertain the whole congregation; but what is a great estate good for but that it puts men into a capacity of doing so much the more good? Christ feasted those that followed him. I believe neither Hezekiah nor his princes were the poorer at the year's end for this their pious liberality. 2. Many good prayers were put up to God with the peace-offerings, *v.* 22. They *made confession to the Lord God of their fathers,* in which the intent and meaning of the peace-offerings were directed and explained. When the priests sprinkled the blood and burnt the fat they made confession, so did the people when they feasted on their part. They made a religious confession of their relation to God and dependence upon him, a penitent confession of their sins and infirmities, a thankful confession of God's mercies to them, and a supplicatory confession of their wants and desires; and, in all these, they had an eye to God as *the God of their fathers,* a God in covenant with them. 3. There was a great deal of good preaching. The Levites (whose office it was, Deut. xxxiii. 10) *taught the people the good knowledge of the Lord,* read and opened the scriptures, and instructed the congregation concerning God and their duty to him; and great need there was of this, after so long a famine of the word as there had been in the last reign. Hezekiah did not himself preach, but he *spoke comfortably to the Levites* that did, attended their preaching, commended their diligence, and assured them of his protection and countenance. Hereby he encouraged them to study hard and take pains, and put a reputation upon them, that the people might respect and regard them the more. Princes and magistrates, by owning and encouraging faithful and laborious preachers, greatly serve the interest of God's kingdom among men. 4. They sang psalms every day (*v.* 21): *The Levites and priests praised the Lord day by day,* both with songs and musical instruments, thus expressing their own and exciting one another's joy in God and thankfulness to him. Praising God should be much of our work in our religious assemblies. 5. Having kept the seven days of the feast in this religious manner, they had so much comfort in the service that they *kept other seven days, v.* 23. They did not institute any new modes of worship, but repeated and continued the old. The case was extraordinary: they had been long without the ordinance; guilt had been contracted by the neglect of it; they had now got a very great congregation together, and were in a devout serious frame; they knew not when they might have such another opportunity, and therefore could not now find in their hearts to separate till they had doubled the time. Many of them were a great way from home, and had business in the country to look after, for, this being the second month, they were in the midst of their harvest; yet they were in no haste to return: the zeal of God's house made them forget their secular affairs. How unlike those who snuffed at God's service, and said, *What a weariness is it!* Or those who asked, *When will the sabbath be gone?* The servants of God should abound in his work. 6. All this they did *with gladness* (*v.* 23); they all rejoiced, and particularly *the strangers, v.* 25. *So there was great joy in Jerusalem, v.* 26. Never was the like since the dedication of the temple in Solomon's time. Note, Holy duties should be performed with holy gladness; we should be forward to them, and take pleasure in them, relish the sweetness of communion with God, and look upon it as matter of unspeakable joy and comfort that we are thus favoured and have such earnests of everlasting joy. 7. The congregation was at length dismissed with a solemn blessing, *v.* 27. (1.) The priests pronounced it; for it was part of their office to *bless the people* (Num. vi. 22, 23), in which they were both the people's mouth to God by way of prayer and God's mouth to the people by way of promise; for their blessing included both. In it they testified both their desire of the people's welfare and their dependence upon God and that word of his grace to which they commended them. What a comfort is it to a congregation to be sent home thus crowned! (2.) God said *Amen* to it. The voice of the priests, when they *blessed the people, was heard in heaven* and came up to the *habitation of God's holiness.* When they pronounced the blessing God commanded it, and perhaps gave some sensible token of the ratification of it. The prayer that comes up to heaven in a cloud of incense will come down again to this earth in showers of blessings.

CHAP. XXXI.

We have here a further account of that blessed reformation of which Hezekiah was a glorious instrument, and of the happy advances he made in it. I. All the remnants of idolatry were destroyed and abolished, ver. 1. II. The priests and Levites were set to work again, every man in his place, ver. 2. III. Care was taken for their maintenance. 1. The royal bounty to the clergy, and for the support of the temple service, was duly paid, ver. 3. 2. Orders were given for the raising of the people's quota, ver. 4. 3. The people, thereupon, brought in their dues abundantly, ver. 5—10. 4. Commissioners were appointed for the due distribution of what was brought in, ver. 11—19. Lastly, Here is the general praise of Hezekiah's sincerity in all his undertakings, ver. 20, 21.

NOW when all this was finished, all Israel that were present went out to the cities of Judah, and brake the images in pieces, and cut down the groves, and threw down the high places and the altars out of all Judah and Benjamin, in Ephraim also and Manasseh, until they had utterly destroyed them all. Then all the children of Israel returned, every man to his possession, into their own cities. 2 And Hezekiah appointed the courses of the priests and the Levites after their courses, every man according to his service, the priests and Levites for burnt offerings and for peace offerings, to minister, and to give thanks, and to praise in the gates of the tents of the LORD. 3 *He appointed* also the king's portion of his substance for the burnt offerings, *to wit*, for the morning and evening burnt offerings, and the burnt offerings for the sabbaths, and for the new moons, and for the set feasts, as *it is* written in the law of the LORD. 4 Moreover he commanded the people that dwelt in Jerusalem to give the portion of the priests and the Levites, that they might be encouraged in the law of the LORD. 5 And as soon as the commandment came abroad, the children of Israel brought in abundance the firstfruits of corn, wine, and oil, and honey, and of all the increase of the field; and the tithe of all *things* brought they in abundantly. 6 And *concerning* the children of Israel and Judah, that dwelt in the cities of Judah, they also brought in the tithe of oxen and sheep, and the tithe of holy things which were consecrated unto the LORD their God, and laid *them* by heaps. 7 In the third month they began to lay the foundation of the heaps, and finished *them* in the seventh month. 8 And when Hezekiah and the princes came and saw the heaps, they blessed the LORD, and his people Israel. 9 Then Hezekiah questioned with the priests and the Levites concerning the heaps. 10 And Azariah the chief priest of the house of Zadok answered him, and said, Since *the people* began to bring the offerings into the house of the LORD, we have had enough to eat, and have left plenty: for the LORD hath blessed his people; and that which is left *is* this great store.

We have here an account of what was done after the passover. What was wanting in the solemnities of preparation for it before was made up in that which is better, a due improvement of it after. When the religious exercises of a Lord's day or a communion are finished we must not think that then the work is done. No, then the hardest part of our work begins, which is to exemplify the impressions of the ordinance upon our minds in all the instances of a holy conversation. So it was here; when all this was finished there was more to be done.

I. They applied themselves with vigour to destroy all the monuments of idolatry, *v.* 1. The king had done what he could of this kind (2 Kings xviii. 4), but the people could discover those profane relics which escaped the eye of the king's officers, and therefore they went out to see what they could do, *v.* 1. This was done immediately after the passover. Note, The comfort of communion with God should kindle in us a holy zeal and indignation against sin, against every thing that is offensive to God. If our hearts have been made to burn within us at an ordinance, that spirit of burning will consume the dross of corruption. *What have I now to do any more with idols?* Their zeal here in destroying the *images and groves, the high places and altars*, appeared, 1. In that they did this, not only in the cities of Judah and Benjamin, but in those of Ephraim and Manasseh. Some think that those cities are meant which had come under the protection and the jurisdiction of the kings of Judah. Others think that, Hoshea king of Israel not forbidding it, their zeal carried them out to the destruction of idolatry even in many parts of his kingdom. At least those that came out of Ephraim and Manasseh to keep the passover (as many did, *ch.* xxx. 18) destroyed all their own images and groves, and did the like for as many more as they had influence upon or could make interest in for leave to do it. We should not only reform ourselves, but do all we can to reform others too. 2. They destroyed all: they *utterly destroyed all;* they spared none through favour or affection either to the images or to their worshippers; though ever so ancient, ever so costly, ever so beautiful, and ever so well patronised, yet they must all be destroyed. Note, Those that sincerely set themselves against sin will set themselves against all sin. 3. They would not return to their houses, though they had been long absent, till this was done. They could not be easy, nor think themselves safe, in their cities, as long as the images and groves, those betrayers and destroyers of their country, were left standing. Perhaps the prophet Isaiah pointed to this when, a little before, he spoke of a day in which men should cast away the very idols that they themselves had made. So surprising was this blessed change, Isa. ii. 20; xxxi. 6, 7.

II. Hezekiah revived and restored the courses of the priests and Levites, which David had appointed and which had of late been put out of course, *v.* 2. The temple service was put into its proper method again, to run in the old channel. Every man was made to know his work, his place, his time, and what was expected from him. Note, Good order contributes much to the carrying on of a good work. The priests were appointed in their courses for *burnt-offerings and peace-offerings;* the Levites in their courses were some to minister to the priests, others to *give thanks and praise.* See 1 Chron. xxiii. 4, 5. And all this in the *gates* or *courts* of *the tents of the Lord.* The temple is here called a tent because the temple privileges are movable things and this temple was shortly to be removed.

III. He appropriated a branch of the revenue of his crown to the maintenance and support of the altar. Though the people were to be at the charge of the daily offerings, and those on the sabbaths, new moons, and feasts, yet, rather than they should be burdened with the expense, he allowed out of his own estate, or out of his exchequer, for all those offerings, *v.* 3. It was a generous act of piety, wherein he consulted both God's honour and his people's ease, as a faithful servant to him and a tender father to them. Let princes and great men reckon that well bestowed, and set out to the best interest, which they give for the support and encouragement of religion in their country.

IV. He issued out an order to the inhabitants of Jerusalem first, *v.* 4 (that those who were nearest the temple, and both saved and got by being so, might give a good example to others), but which was afterwards extended to, or at least admitted by, the *cities of Judah*, that they should carefully pay in their dues, according to the law, to the priests and Levites. This had been long neglected, which made the work to be neglected (for a scandalous maintenance makes a scandalous ministry); but Hezekiah, having himself been liberal, might with a good grace require his subjects to be just to the temple service. And observe the end he aims at in recovering and restoring to the priests and Levites their portion, that they *might be encouraged in the law of the Lord*, in the study of it, and in doing their duty according to it. Observe here, 1. It is fit that ministers should be not only maintained, but encouraged, that they should not only be kept to do their work, but that they should also have wherewith to live comfortably, that they may do it with cheerfulness. 2. Yet they are to be maintained, not in idleness, pride, and luxury, but in *the law of the Lord*, in their observance of it themselves and in teaching others the good knowledge of it.

V. The people thereupon brought in their tithes very readily. They wanted nothing but to be called upon; and therefore, *as soon as the commandment came abroad*, the first-fruits and all the holy things were duly brought in, *v.* 5, 6. What the priests had occasion for, for themselves and their families, they made use of, and the overplus was *laid in heaps, v.* 6. All harvest-time they were increasing these heaps, as the fruits of the earth were gathered in; for God was to have his dues out of them all. Though a prescription may be pleaded for a *modus decimandi—tenth proportion,* yet it cannot be pleaded *pro non decimando—for the omission of the tenth.* When harvest ended they finished their heaps, *v.* 7. Now here we have, 1. The account given to Hezekiah concerning those heaps. He *questioned the priests and Levites* concerning them, why they did not use what was paid in, but hoarded it up thus, (*v.* 9), to which it was answered that they had made use of all they had occasion for, for the maintenance of themselves and their families and for their winter store, and that this was that which was left over and above, *v.* 10. They did not hoard these heaps for covetousness, but to show what plentiful provision God by his law had made for them, if they could but have it collected and brought in, and that those who conscientiously give God his dues out of their estates bring a blessing upon all they have: *Since they began to bring in the offerings the Lord has blessed his people.* See for this Hag. ii. 19. "Try me," says God, "if you will not otherwise trust me, whether, upon your bringing the tithes into the store-house, you have not a blessing poured out upon you," Mal. iii. 10, 11; Ezek. xliv. 30. 2 The acknowledgment which the king and princes made of it, *v* 8. They gave thanks to God for his good providence, which gave them something to bring, and his good grace, which gave them hearts to bring it. And they also *blessed the people,* that is, commended them for their doing well now, without reproaching them for their former neglects. It is observable that after they had tasted the sweetness of God's ordinance, in the late comfortable passover, they were thus free in maintaining the temple service. Those that experience the benefit of a settled ministry will not grudge the expense of it.

11 Then Hezekiah commanded to prepare chambers in the house of the LORD; and they prepared *them,* 12 And brought in the offerings and the tithes and the dedicated *things* faithfully: over which Cononiah the Levite *was* ruler, and Shimei his brother *was* the next. 13 And Jehiel, and Azaziah, and Nahath, and Asahel, and Jerimoth, and Jozabad, and Eliel, and Ismachiah, and Mahath, and Benaiah, *were* overseers under the hand of Cononiah and Shimei his brother, at the commandment of Hezekiah the king, and Azariah the ruler of the house of God. 14 And Kore the son of Imnah the Levite, the porter toward the east, *was* over the freewill offerings of God, to distribute the oblátions of the LORD, and the most holy things. 15 And next him *were* Eden, and Miniamin, and Jeshua, and Shemaiah, Amariah, and Shecaniah, in the cities of the priests, in *their* set office, to give to their brethren by courses, as well to the great as to the small: 16 Beside their genealogy of males, from three years old and upward, *even* unto every one that entereth into the house of the LORD, his daily portion for their service in their charges according to their courses; 17 Both to the genealogy of the priests by the house of their fathers, and the Levites from twenty years old and upward, in their charges by their courses; 18 And to the genealogy of all their little ones, their wives, and their sons, and their daughters, through all the congregation: for in their set office they sanctified themselves in holiness: 19 Also of the sons of Aaron the priests, *which were* in the fields of the suburbs of their cities, in every several city, the men that were expressed by name, to give portions to all the males among the priests, and to all that were reckoned by genealogies among the Levites. 20 And thus did Hezekiah throughout all Judah, and wrought *that which was* good and right and truth before the LORD his God. 21 And in every work that he began in the service of the house of God, and in the law, and in the commandments, to seek his God, he did *it* with all his heart, and prospered.

Here we have,

I. Two particular instances of the care of Hezekiah concerning church matters, having put them into good order, to keep them so. The tithes and other holy things being brought in, he provided, 1. That they should be carefully laid up, and not left exposed in loose heaps, liable to be wasted and embezzled. He ordered chambers to be made ready in some of the courts of the temple for store-chambers (*v.* 11), and into them the offerings were brought and there kept under lock and key, *v.* 12, 13. Treasurers or store-keepers were appointed, who had the oversight of them, to see that *moth and rust* did not *corrupt* them nor *thieves break through to steal.* This wisdom of laying up the surplus in days of plenty we may learn from the ant, who *provideth meat in summer.* The laying up in store what was brought in was an encouragement to people to pay in their contributions. That will be given cheerfully by the public which appears to be well husbanded. 2. That they should be faithfully laid out, according to the uses they were intended for. Church treasures are not to be hoarded any longer than till there is occasion for them, lest even the rust should be a witness against those who hoard them. Officers were appointed, men (no doubt) of approved wisdom and faithfulness, to *distribute the oblations of the Lord and the most holy things* among the priests (*v.* 14), and to see that they all had a competent maintenance for themselves and their families. The law provided sufficient for them all, and therefore, if some had too little, it must be because others had too much; to prevent such inequality these officers were to go by some certain rule of proportion in the disposal of the incomes of the temple. It is said of the priests here (*v.* 18) *that in their set office they sanctified themselves; in faith* they sanctified themselves (so the word is), that is, as bishop Patrick explains it, they attended their ministry at the house of God, not doubting but they should be provided with all things necessary. Now, because they served God in that confidence, care was taken that they should not be made ashamed of their hope. Note, Those that sanctify themselves to God and his service in faith, believing that he will see them want for nothing that is good for them, *shall* certainly *be fed.* Out of the offerings of the Lord distribution was made, (1.) To the priests in the cities (*v.* 15), who staid at home while their brethren went to Jerusalem, and did good there in *teaching the good knowledge of the Lord.* The preaching priests were maintained as well as the sacrificing priests, and those that abode by the stuff as well as those that warred the warfare. (2.) To those that *entered into the house of the Lord,* all the *males from three years old and upwards;* for the male children even at that tender age, it seems, were allowed to come into the temple with their parents, and shared with them in this distribution, *v.* 16. (3.) Even the Levites from twenty years old and upwards had their share, *v.* 17. (4.) The wives and children of the priests and Levites had a comfortable maintenance out of those offerings, *v.* 18. In maintaining ministers, regard must be had to their families, that not they only, but theirs, may have food convenient. In some countries where ministers have their salary paid them by the state an addition is made to it upon the birth of a child. (5.) The priests in the country, that lived *in the fields of the suburbs,* were not overlooked in this ministration, *v.* 19. Those also had their share who were *inhabitants of the villages,* though they might be supposed to live at a less expense.

II. A general character of Hezekiah's services for the support of religion, *v.* 20, 21. 1. His pious zeal reached to all the parts of his kingdom: *Thus he did throughout all Judah;* every part of the country, and not those only that lay next him, shared in the good fruits of his government. 2. He sincerely designed to please God, and approved himself to him in all he did: He *wrought that which was good before the Lord his God;* all his care was to do that which should be accepted of God, which was *right* (that is, agreeable to natural equity), *and truth* (that is, agreeable to divine revelation and his covenant with God), *before the Lord;* to do according to that law which is holy, just, and good. 3. What he began he went through with, prosecuted it with vigour, and *did it with all his heart.* 4. All his good intentions were brought to a good issue; whatever he did in the service of the house of God, and in the government of his kingdom, he prospered in it. Note, What is undertaken with a sincere regard to the glory of God will succeed to our own honour and comfort at last.

CHAP. XXXII.

This chapter continues and concludes the history of the reign of Hezekiah. I. The descent which Sennacherib made upon him, and the care he took to fortify himself, his city, and the minds of his people, against that enemy, ver. 1—8. II. The insolent blasphemous letters and messages which Sennacherib sent him, ver. 9—19. III. The real answer God gave to Sennacherib's blasphemies, and to Hezekiah's prayers, in the total rout of the Assyrian army, to the shame of Sennacherib and the honour of Hezekiah, ver. 20—23. IV. Hezekiah's sickness and his recovery from that, his sin and his recovery from that, with the honours that attended him living and dead, ver. 24—33.

AFTER these things, and the establishment thereof, Sennacherib king of Assyria came, and entered into Judah, and encamped against the fenced cities, and thought to win them for himself. 2 And when Hezekiah saw that Sennacherib was come, and that he was purposed to fight against Jerusalem, 3 He took counsel with his princes and his mighty men to stop the waters of the fountains which *were* without the city: and they did help him. 4 So there was gathered much people together, who stopped all the fountains, and the brook that ran through the midst of the land, saying, Why should the kings of Assyria come, and find much water? 5 Also he strengthened himself, and built up all the wall that was broken, and raised *it* up to the towers, and another wall without, and repaired Millo *in* the city of David, and made darts and shields in abundance. 6 And he set captains of war over the people, and gathered them together to him in the street of the gate of the city, and spake comfortably to them, saying, 7 Be strong and courageous, be not afraid nor dismayed for the king of Assyria, nor for all the multitude that *is* with him: for *there be* more with us than with him: 8 With him *is* an arm of flesh; but with us *is* the LORD our God to help us, and to fight our battles. And the people rested themselves upon the words of Hezekiah king of Judah.

Here is, I. The formidable design of Sennacherib against Hezekiah's kingdom, and the vigorous attempt he made upon it. This Sennacherib was now, as Nebuchadnezzar was afterwards, the terror and scourge and great oppressor of that part of the world. He aimed to raise a boundless monarchy for himself upon the ruins of all his neighbours. His predecessor Shalmaneser had lately made himself master of the kingdom of Israel, and carried the ten tribes captives. Sennacherib thought, in like manner, to win Judah for himself. Pride and ambition put men upon grasping at universal dominion. It is observable that, just about this time, Rome, a city which afterwards came to reign more than any other had done *over the kings of the earth*, was built by Romulus. Sennacherib invaded Judah immediately after the reformation of it and the re-establishment of religion in it: *After these things he entered into Judah, v.* 1. 1. It was well ordered by the divine Providence that he did not give them this disturbance before the reformation was finished and established, as it might then have put a stop to it. 2. Perhaps he intended to chastise Hezekiah for destroying that idolatry to which he himself was devoted. He looked upon Hezekiah as profane in what he had done, and as having thrown himself out of the divine protection. He accordingly considered him as one who might easily be made a prey of. 3. God ordered it at this time that he might have an opportunity of showing himself strong on the behalf of this returning reforming people. He brought this trouble upon them that he might have the honour, and might put on them the honour, of their deliverance. *After these things, and the establishment thereof*, one would have expected to hear of nothing but perfect peace, and that none durst meddle with a people thus qualified for the divine favour; yet the next news we hear is that a threatening destroying army enters the country, and is ready to lay all waste. We may be in the way of our duty and yet meet with trouble and danger. God orders it so for the trial of our confidence in him and the manifestation of his care concerning us. The little opposition which Sennacherib met with in entering Judah induced him to imagine that all was his own. He thought to *win all the fenced cities* (*v.* 1), and purposed to *fight against Jerusalem, v.* 2. See 2 Kings xviii. 7, 13.

II. The preparation which Hezekiah prudently made against this storm that threatened him: *He took counsel with his princes* what he should do, what measures he should take, *v.* 3. With their advice he provided, 1. That the country should give him a cold reception, for he took care that he should find no water in it (and then his army must perish for thirst), or at least that there should be a scarcity of water, by which his army would be weakened and unfitted for service. A powerful army, if it want water but a few days, will be but a heap of dry dust. All hands were set immediately to work to *stop up the fountains*, and *the brook that ran through the midst of the land*, turning that (it is probable) into the city by pipes under-ground. Such as this is the policy commonly practised now-a-days of destroying the forage before an invading army. 2. That the city should give him a warm reception. In order to this he repaired the wall, raised towers, and made darts (or, as it is in the margin, *swords* or *weapons*) and shields in abundance (*v.* 5), and appointed captains, *v.* 6. Note, Those that trust God with their safety must yet use proper means for their safety, otherwise they tempt him, and do not trust him. *God will provide*, but so must we also.

III. The encouragement which he gave to his people to depend upon God in this distress. He gathered them together in a broad open street, and *spoke comfortably to them, v.* 6. He was himself undaunted, being confident the invasion would issue well. He was not like his father, who had much guilt to terrify him and no faith to encourage him, so that, in a time of public danger, *his heart was moved, as the trees of the wood are moved with the wind*, and then no marvel that *the heart of his people was so too*, Isa. vii. 2. With what he said he put life into his people, his captains especially, and *spoke to their heart*, as the word is. 1. He endeavoured to keep down their fears: "*Be strong and courageous;* do not think of surrendering the city or capitulating, but resolve to hold it out to the last man; do not think of losing the city, nor of falling into the enemy's hand; there is no danger. Let the soldiers be bold and brave, make good their posts, stand to their arms, and fight manfully, and let the citizens encourage them to do so: *Be not afraid nor dismayed for the king of Assyria.*" The prophet had thus encouraged them from God (Isa. x. 24): *Be not afraid of the Assyrians;* and here the king from him. Now it was that *the sinners in Zion were afraid* (Isa. xxxiii. 14), but the righteous *dwelt on high* (Isa. xxxiii. 15, 16) and *meditated on terror* so as to conquer it. See Isa. xxxiii. 18, which refers to what is recorded here. 2. He endeavoured to keep up their faith, in order to the silencing and suppressing of their fears. "Sennacherib has a *multitude with him,* and yet there are *more with us than with him;* for we have God with us, and how many do you reckon him for? With our enemy is an arm of flesh, which he trusts to; but *with us is the Lord,* whose power is irresistible, our God, whose promise is inviolable, a God in covenant with us, *to help us, and to fight our battles,* not only to help us to fight them, but to fight them for us if he please:" and so he did here. Note, A believing confidence in God will raise us above the prevailing fear of man. He that *feareth the fury of the oppressor forgetteth the Lord his Maker,* Isa. li. 12, 13. It is probable that Hezekiah said more to this purport, and that the people rested themselves upon what he said, not merely upon his word, but on the things he said concerning the presence of God with them and his power to relieve them, the belief of which made them easy. Let the good subjects and soldiers of Jesus Christ rest thus upon his word, and boldly say, *Since God is for us, who can be against us?*

9 After this did Sennacherib king of Assyria send his servants to Jerusalem, (but he *himself laid siege* against Lachish, and all his power with him,) unto Hezekiah king of Judah, and unto all Judah that *were* at Jerusalem, saying, 10 Thus saith Sennacherib king of Assyria, Whereon do ye trust, that ye abide in the siege in Jerusalem? 11 Doth not Hezekiah persuade you to give over yourselves to die by famine and by thirst, saying, The LORD our God shall deliver us out of the hand of the king of Assyria? 12 Hath not the same Hezekiah taken away his high places and his altars, and commanded Judah and Jerusalem, saying, Ye shall worship before one altar, and burn incense upon it? 13 Know ye not what I and my fathers have done unto all the people of *other* lands? were the gods of the nations of those lands any ways able to deliver their lands out of mine hand? 14 Who *was there* among all the gods of those nations that my fathers utterly destroyed, that could deliver his people out of mine hand, that your God should be able to deliver you out of mine hand? 15 Now therefore let not Hezekiah deceive you, nor persuade you on this manner, neither yet believe him: for no god of any nation or kingdom was able to deliver his people out of mine hand, and out of the hand of my fathers: how much less shall your God deliver you out of mine hand? 16 And his servants spake yet *more* against the LORD God, and against his servant Hezekiah. 17 He wrote also letters to rail on the LORD God of Israel, and to speak against him, saying, As the gods of the nations of *other* lands have not delivered their people out of mine hand, so shall not the God of Hezekiah deliver his people out of mine hand. 18 Then they cried with a loud voice in the Jews' speech unto the people of Jerusalem that *were* on the wall, to affright them, and to trouble them; that they might take the city. 19 And they spake against the God of Jerusalem, as against the gods of the people of the earth, *which were* the work of the hands of man. 20 And for this *cause* Hezekiah the king, and the prophet Isaiah the son of Amoz, prayed and cried to heaven. 21 And the LORD sent an angel, which cut off all the mighty men of valour, and the leaders and captains in the camp of the king of Assyria. So he returned with shame of face to his own land. And when he was come into the house of his god, they that came forth of his own bowels slew him there with the sword. 22 Thus the LORD saved Hezekiah and the inhabitants of Jerusalem from the hand of Sennacherib the king of Assyria, and from the hand of all *other,* and guided them on every side. 23 And many brought gifts unto the LORD to Jerusalem, and presents to Hezekiah king of Judah: so that he was magnified in the sight of all nations from thenceforth.

This story of the rage and blasphemy of Sennacherib, Hezekiah's prayer, and the deliverance of Jerusalem by the destruction of the Assyrian army, we had more at large in the book of Kings, 2 Kings xviii. and xix. It is contracted here, yet large enough to show these three things:—

I. The impiety and malice of the church's enemies. Sennacherib has his hands full in besieging Lachish (*v.* 9), but hears that Hezekiah is fortifying Jerusalem and encouraging his people to stand it out; and therefore, before he come in person to besiege it, he sends messengers to make speeches, and he himself writes letters to frighten Hezekiah and his people into a surrender of the city. See, 1. His great malice against the king of Judah, in endeavouring to withdraw his subjects from their allegiance to him. He did not treat with Hezekiah as a man of honour would have done, nor propose fair terms to him, but used mean and base artifices, unbecoming a crowned head, to terrify the common people and persuade them to desert him. He represented Hezekiah as one who designed to deceive his subjects into their ruin and betray them *to famine and thirst* (*v.* 11), as one who had done them great wrong and exposed them already to the divine displeasure by taking away the high places and altars (*v.* 12), and who, against the common interest of his people, held out against a force that would certainly be their ruin, *v.* 15. 2. His great impiety against the God of Israel, *the God of Jerusalem* he is called (*v.* 19), because that was the place he had chosen to put his name there, and because that was the place which was now threatened by the enemy and which the divine Providence had under its special protection. This proud blasphemer compared the great Jehovah, the Maker of heaven and earth, with the dunghill gods of the nations, the work of men's hands, and thought him no more able to deliver his worshippers than they were to deliver theirs (*v.* 19), as if an infinite and eternal Spirit had no more wisdom and power than a stone or the stock of a tree. He boasted of his triumphs over the gods of the nations, that they could none of them protect their people (*v.* 13—15), and thence inferred not only, *How shall your God deliver you?* (*v.* 14), but, as if he were inferior to them all, *How much less shall your God deliver you?* as if he were less able to help than any of them. Thus did they rail, rail in writing (which, being more deliberate, is so much the worse), *on the Lord God of Israel,* as if he were a cipher and an empty name, like all the rest, *v.* 17. Sennacherib, in the instructions he gave, said more than enough; but, as if his blasphemies had been too little, his servants, who learned insolence from their master, spoke yet more than he bade them *against the Lord God and his servant Hezekiah, v.* 16. And God resents what is said against his servants, and will reckon for it, as well as what is said against himself. All this was intended to frighten the people from their hope in God, which David's enemies sought to take him off from (Ps. xi. 1; xlii. 10), saying, *There is no help for him in God,* Ps. iii. 2; lxxi. 11. Thus they hoped to take the city by weakening the hands of those that should defend it. Satan, in his temptations, aims to destroy our faith in God's all-sufficiency, knowing that he shall gain his point if he can do that; as we keep our ground if our *faith fail not,* Luke xxii. 32.

II. The duty as well as the interest of the church's friends, and that is in the day of distress to pray and cry to Heaven. So Hezekiah did, and the prophet Isaiah, *v.* 20. It was a happy time when the king and the prophet joined thus in prayer. Is any troubled? Is any terrified? Let him pray. So we engage God for us; so we encourage ourselves in him. Praying to God is here called *crying to Heaven,* because we are, in prayer, to eye him as our Father in heaven, whence he beholds the children of men, and where he has prepared his throne.

III. The power and goodness of the church's God. He is able both to control his enemies, be they ever so high, and to relieve his friends, be they ever so low.

1. As the blasphemies of his enemies engage him against them (Deut. xxxii. 27), so the prayers of his people engage him for them. They did so here. (1.) The army of the Assyrians was cut off by the sword of an angel, which triumphed particularly in the slaughter of the mighty men of valour, and the leaders and captains, who defied the sword of any man. God delights to abase the proud and secure. The Targum says, The Word of the Lord (the eternal Word) sent Gabriel to do this execution, and that it was done with lightning, and in the passover night: that was the night in which the angel destroyed the first-born of Egypt. But that was not all. (2.) The king of the Assyrians, having received this disgrace, was cut off by the sword of his own sons. Those that *came forth of his own bowels slew him, v.* 21. Thus was he mortified first, and then murdered—shamed first, and then slain. Evil pursues sinners; and, when they escape one mischief, they run upon another unseen.

2. By this work of wonder, (1.) God was glorified, as the protector of his people. Thus he saved Jerusalem, not only from the hand of Sennacherib, but from the hand *of all others, v.* 22; for such a deliverance as this was an earnest of much mercy in store; and he *guided them,* that is, he guarded them, on every side. God defends his people by directing them, shows them what they should do, and so saves them from what is designed or done against them. For this *many brought gifts unto the Lord,* when they saw the great power of God in the defence of his people. Strangers were thereby induced to supplicate his favour and enemies to deprecate his wrath, and both brought gifts to his temple, in token of their care and desire. (2.) Hezekiah was magnified as the favourite and particular care of Heaven. Many *brought presents to him* (*v.* 22, 23), in token of the honour they had for him, and to make an interest in him. By the favour of God enemies are lost and friends gained.

24 In those days Hezekiah was sick to the death, and prayed unto the LORD: and he spake unto him, and he gave him a sign. 25 But Heze-

kiah rendered not again according to the benefit *done* unto him; for his heart was lifted up: therefore there was wrath upon him, and upon Judah and Jerusalem. 26 Notwithstanding Hezekiah humbled himself for the pride of his heart, *both* he and the inhabitants of Jerusalem, so that the wrath of the LORD came not upon them in the days of Hezekiah. 27 And Hezekiah had exceeding much riches and honour: and he made himself treasuries for silver, and for gold, and for precious stones, and for spices, and for shields, and for all manner of pleasant jewels; 28 Storehouses also for the increase of corn, and wine, and oil; and stalls for all manner of beasts, and cotes for flocks. 29 Moreover he provided him cities, and possessions of flocks and herds in abundance: for God had given him substance very much. 30 This same Hezekiah also stopped the upper watercourse of Gihon, and brought it straight down to the west side of the city of David. And Hezekiah prospered in all his works. 31 Howbeit in *the business of* the ambassadors of the princes of Babylon, who sent unto him to enquire of the wonder that was *done* in the land, God left him, to try him, that he might know all *that was* in his heart. 32 Now the rest of the acts of Hezekiah, and his goodness, behold, they *are* written in the vision of Isaiah the prophet, the son of Amoz, *and* in the book of the kings of Judah and Israel. 33 And Hezekiah slept with his fathers, and they buried him in the chiefest of the sepulchres of the sons of David: and all Judah and the inhabitants of Jerusalem did him honour at his death. And Manasseh his son reigned in his stead.

Here we conclude the story of Hezekiah with an account of three things concerning him:—

I. His sickness and his recovery from it, *v.* 24. The account of his sickness is but briefly mentioned here; we had a large narrative of it, 2 Kings xx. His disease seemed likely to be mortal. In the extremity of it he prayed. God answered him, and gave him a sign that he should recover, the going back of the sun ten degrees.

II. His sin and his repentance for it, which were also more largely related, 2 Kings xx. 12, &c. Yet several things are here observed concerning his sin which we had not there. 1. The occasion of it was the king of Babylon's sending an honourable embassy to him to congratulate him on his recovery. But here it is added that they came to enquire of *the wonder that was done in the land* (*v.* 31), either the destruction of the Assyrian army or the going back of the sun. The Assyrians were their enemies; they came to enquire concerning their fall, that they might triumph in it. The sun was their god; they came to enquire concerning the favour he had shown to Hezekiah, that they might honour him whom their god honoured, *v.* 31. These miracles were wrought to alarm and awaken a stupid careless world, and turn them from dumb and lame idols to the living God; and men were startled by them, but not converted till a greater wonder was done in that land, in the appearing of Jesus Christ, Matt. ii. 1, 2. 2. God left him to himself in it, to try him, *v.* 31. God, by the power of his almighty grace, could have prevented the sin; but he permitted it for wise and holy ends, that, by this trial and his weakness in it, he might know, that is, it might be known (a usual Hebraism), what was in his heart, that he was not so perfect in grace as he thought he was, but had his follies and infirmities as other men. God left him to himself to be proud of his wealth, to keep him from being proud of his holiness. It is good for us to know ourselves, and our own weakness and sinfulness, that we may not be conceited or self-confident, but may always think meanly of ourselves and live in a dependence upon divine grace. We know not the corruption of our own hearts, nor what we shall do if God leave us to ourselves. *Lord, lead us not into temptation.* 3. His sin was that *his heart was lifted up*, *v.* 25. He was proud of the honour God had put upon him in so many instances, the honour his neighbours did him in bringing him presents, and now that the king of Babylon should send an embassy to him to caress and court him: this exalted him above measure. When Hezekiah had destroyed other idolatries he began to idolize himself. O what need have great men, and good men, and useful men, to study their own infirmities and follies, and their obligations to free grace, that they may never think highly of themselves, and to beg earnestly of God that he will hide pride from them and always keep them humble! 4. The aggravation of his sin was that he made so bad a return to God for his favours to him, making even those favours the food and fuel of his pride (*v* 25): *He rendered not again according to the benefit done unto him.* Note, It is justly expected that those who have received mercy from God should study to make some suitable returns for the mercies they have received; and, if they do not, their ingratitude will certainly be charged upon them.

Though we cannot render an equivalent, or the payment of a debt, we must render the acknowledgment of a favour. *What shall I render* that may be so accepted? Ps. cxvi. 12. 5. The divine displeasure he was under for this sin; though it was but a heart-sin, and the overt-act seemed not only innocent but civil (the showing of his treasures to a friend), yet wrath came upon him and his kingdom for it, *v.* 25. Note, Pride is a sin that God hates as much as any, and particularly in his own people. Those that exalt themselves must expect to be abased, and put under humbling providences. Wrath came on David for his pride in numbering the people. 6. His repentance for this sin: *He humbled himself for the pride of his heart.* Note, (1.) Though God may, for wise and holy ends, suffer his people to fall into sin, yet he will not suffer them to lie still in it; they *shall not be utterly cast down.* (2.) Heart-sins are to be repented of, though they go no further. (3.) Self-humiliation is a necessary branch of repentance. (4.) Pride of heart, by which we have lifted up ourselves, is a sin for which we ought in a special manner to humble ourselves. (5.) People ought to mourn for the sins of their rulers. The inhabitants of Jerusalem humbled themselves with Hezekiah, because they either knew that they also had been guilty of the same sin, or at least feared that they might share in the punishment. When David, in his pride, numbered the people, they all smarted for his sin. 7. The reprieve granted thereupon. The wrath came not in his days. While he lived the country had peace and truth prevailed; so much does repentance avail to put by, or at least to put off, the tokens of God's anger.

III. Here is the honour done to Hezekiah, 1. By the providence of God while he lived. He had *exceeding much riches and honour* (*v.* 27), replenished his stores, victualled his camps, fortified his city, and did all he wished to do; for God *had given him very much substance, v.* 29. Among his great performances, his turning the water-course of Gihon is mentioned (*v.* 30), which was done upon occasion of Sennacherib's invasion, *v.* 3, 4. The water had come into that which is called the *old pool* (Isa. xxii. 11) and the *upper pool* (Isa. vii. 3); but he gathered the waters into a new place, for the greater convenience of the city, called the *lower pool,* Isa. xxii. 9. And, in general, he *prospered in all his works,* for they were good works. 2. By the respect paid to his memory when he was dead. (1.) The prophet Isaiah wrote his life and reign (*v.* 32), his acts and his goodness or piety, of which it is part of the honour to be recorded and remembered, for example to others. (2.) The people *did him honour at his death* (*v.* 33), buried him in the chief of the sepulchres, made as great a burning for him as for Asa, or, which is a much greater honour, made great lamentation for him, as for Josiah. See how the honour of serious godliness is manifested in the consciences of men. Though it is to be feared that the generality of the people did not heartily comply with the reforming kings, yet they could not but praise their endeavours for reformation, and the memory of those kings was blessed among them. It is a debt we owe to those who have been eminently useful in their day to do them honour at their death, when they are out of the reach of flattery and we have seen the end of their conversation. The due payment of this debt will be an encouragement to others to do likewise.

CHAP. XXXIII.

In this chapter we have the history of the reign, I. Of Manasseh, who reigned long. 1. His wretched apostasy from God, and revolt to idolatry and all wickedness, ver. 1—10. 2. His happy return to God in his affliction; his repentance (ver. 11—13), his reformation (ver. 15—17), and prosperity (ver. 14), with the conclusion of his reign, ver. 18—20. II. Of Amon, who reigned very wickedly (ver. 21—23), and soon ended his days unhappily, ver. 24, 25.

MANASSEH *was* twelve years old when he began to reign, and he reigned fifty and five years in Jerusalem: 2 But did *that which was* evil in the sight of the LORD, like unto the abominations of the heathen, whom the LORD had cast out before the children of Israel. 3 For he built again the high places which Hezekiah his father had broken down, and he reared up altars for Baalim, and made groves, and worshipped all the host of heaven, and served them. 4 Also he built altars in the house of the LORD, whereof the LORD had said, In Jerusalem shall my name be for ever. 5 And he built altars for all the host of heaven in the two courts of the house of the LORD. 6 And he caused his children to pass through the fire in the valley of the son of Hinnom: also he observed times, and used enchantments, and used witchcraft, and dealt with a familiar spirit, and with wizards: he wrought much evil in the sight of the LORD, to provoke him to anger. 7 And he set a carved image, the idol which he had made, in the house of God, of which God had said to David and to Solomon his son, In this house, and in Jerusalem, which I have chosen before all the tribes of Israel, will I put my name for ever: 8 Neither will I any more remove the foot of Israel from out of the land which I have appointed for your fathers; so that they will take heed to do all that I have commanded them, according to the whole law and the statutes and the ordinances by the hand of Moses. 9 So Manasseh made Judah and the inhabitants of Jerusalem to err, *and* to do worse than the heathen, whom the LORD had destroyed before the children of Israel. 10 And the LORD spake to Manasseh, and to his people: but they would not hearken.

We have here an account of the great wickedness of Manasseh. It is the same almost word for word with that which we had 2 Kings xxi. 1—9, and took a melancholy view of. It is no such pleasing subject that we should delight to dwell upon it again. This foolish young prince, in contradiction to the good example and good education his father gave him, abandoned himself to all impiety, transcribed the abominations of the heathen (*v.* 2), ruined the established religion, unravelled his father's glorious reformation (*v.* 3), profaned the house of God with his idolatry (*v.* 4, 5), dedicated his children to Moloch, and made the devil's lying oracles his guides and his counsellors, *v.* 6. In contempt of the choice God had made of Sion to be his rest for ever and Israel to be his covenant-people (*v.* 8), and the fair terms he stood upon with God, he embraced other gods, profaned God's chosen temple, and debauched his chosen people. He *made them to err,* and *do worse than the heathen* (*v.* 9); for, if the unclean spirit returns, he brings with him *seven other spirits more wicked than himself.* That which aggravated the sin of Manasseh was that God *spoke to him and his people* by the prophets, *but they would not hearken, v.* 10. We may here admire the grace of God in speaking to them, and their obstinacy in turning a deaf ear to him, that either their badness did not quite turn away his goodness, but still he waited to be gracious, or that his goodness did not turn them from their badness, but still they hated to be reformed. Now from this let us learn, 1. That it is no new thing, but a very sad thing, for the children of godly parents to turn aside from that good way of God in which they have been trained. Parents may give many good things to their children, but they cannot give them grace. 2. Corruptions in worship are such diseases of the church as it is very apt to relapse into again even when they seem to be cured. 3. The god of this world has strangely blinded men's minds, and has a wonderful power over those that are led captive by him; else he could not draw them from God, their best friend, to depend upon their sworn enemy.

11 Wherefore the LORD brought upon them the captains of the host of the king of Assyria, which took Manasseh among the thorns, and bound him with fetters, and carried him to Babylon. 12 And when he was in affliction, he besought the LORD his God, and humbled himself greatly before the God of his fathers, 13 And prayed unto him: and he was intreated of him, and heard his supplication, and brought him again to Jerusalem into his kingdom. Then Manasseh knew that the LORD he *was* God. 14 Now after this he built a wall without the city of David, on the west side of Gihon, in the valley, even to the entering in at the fish gate, and compassed about Ophel, and raised it up a very great height, and put captains of war in all the fenced cities of Judah. 15 And he took away the strange gods, and the idol out of the house of the LORD, and all the altars that he had built in the mount of the house of the LORD, and in Jerusalem, and cast *them* out of the city. 16 And he repaired the altar of the LORD, and sacrificed thereon peace offerings and thank offerings, and commanded Judah to serve the LORD God of Israel. 17 Nevertheless the people did sacrifice still in the high places, *yet* unto the LORD their God only. 18 Now the rest of the acts of Manasseh, and his prayer unto his God, and the words of the seers that spake to him in the name of the LORD God of Israel, behold, they *are written* in the book of the kings of Israel. 19 His prayer also, and *how God* was intreated of him, and all his sins, and his trespass, and the places wherein he built high places, and set up groves and graven images, before he was humbled: behold, they *are* written among the sayings of the seers. 20 So Manasseh slept with his fathers, and they buried him in his own house: and Amon his son reigned in his stead.

We have seen Manasseh by his wickedness undoing the good that his father had done; here we have him by repentance undoing the evil that he himself had done. It is strange that this was not so much as mentioned in the book of *Kings,* nor does any thing appear there to the contrary but that he persisted and perished in his sin. But perhaps the reason was because the design of that history was to show the wickedness of the nation which brought destruction upon them; and this repentance of Manasseh and the benefit of it, being personal only and not national, is overlooked there; yet here it is fully related, and a memorable instance it is of the riches of God's pardoning mercy and the power of his renewing grace. Here is,

I. The occasion of Manasseh's repentance, and that was his affliction. In his distress he did not (like king Ahaz) *trespass yet more against God,* but humbled himself and returned to God. Sanctified afflictions often prove happy means of conversion. What his distress was we are told, *v.* 11. God brought a foreign enemy upon him; the king of Babylon, that courted his father who faithfully served God, invaded him now that he had treacherously departed from God. He is here called *king of Assyria,* because he had made himself master of Assyria, which he would the more easily do for the defeat of Sennacherib's army, and its destruction before Jerusalem. He aimed at the treasures which the ambassadors had seen, and all those precious things; but God sent him to chastise a sinful people, and subdue a straying prince. The captain took *Manasseh among the thorns,* in some bush or other, perhaps in his garden, where he had hid himself. Or it is spoken figuratively: he was perplexed in his counsels and embarrassed in his affairs. He was, as we say, in the briers, and knew not which way to extricate himself, and so became an easy prey to the Assyrian captains, who no doubt plundered his house and took away what they pleased, as Isaiah had foretold, 2 Kings xx. 17, 18. What was Hezekiah's pride was their prey. They bound Manasseh, who had been held before with the cords of his own iniquity, and carried him prisoner to Babylon. About what time of his reign this was we are not told; the Jews say it was in his twenty-second year.

II. The expressions of his repentance (*v.* 12, 13): *When he was in affliction* he had time to bethink himself and reason enough too. He saw what he had brought himself to by his sin. He found the gods he had served unable to help him. He knew that repentance was the only way of restoring his affairs; and therefore to him he returned from whom he had revolted. 1. He was convinced that Jehovah is the only living and true God: *Then he knew* (that is, he believed and considered) that the *Lord he was God.* He might have known it at a less expense if he would have given due attention and credit to the word written and preached: but it was better to pay thus dearly for the knowledge of God than to perish in ignorance and unbelief. Had he been a prince in the palace of Babylon, it is probable he would have been confirmed in his idolatry; but, being a captive in the prisons of Babylon, he was convinced of it and reclaimed from it. 2. He applied to him as *his* God now, renouncing all others, and resolving to cleave to him only, the God of his fathers, and a God in covenant with him. 3. He humbled himself greatly before him, was truly sorry for his sins, ashamed of them, and afraid of the wrath of God. It becomes sinners to humble themselves before the face of that God whom they have offended. It becomes sufferers to humble themselves under the hand of that God who corrects them, and to accept the punishment of their iniquity Our hearts should be humbled under humbling providences; then we accommodate ourselves to them, and answer God's end in them. 4. He prayed to him for the pardon of sin and the return of his favour. Prayer is the relief of penitents, the relief of the afflicted. That is a good prayer, and very pertinent in this case, which we find among the apocryphal books, entitled, *The prayer of Manasses, king of Judah, when he was holden captive in Babylon.* Whether it was his or no is uncertain; if it was, in it he *gives glory to God* as the *God of their fathers* and *their righteous seed,* as the Creator of the world, a God whose *anger is insupportable,* and yet *his merciful promise unmeasurable.* He pleads that God has *promised repentance and forgiveness to those that have sinned,* and has *appointed repentance unto sinners, that they may be saved,* not *unto the just,* as to *Abraham, Isaac, and Jacob,* but *to me* (says he) *that am a sinner; for I have sinned above the number of the sands of the sea:* so he confesses his sin largely, and aggravates it. He prays, *Forgive me, O Lord! forgive me, and destroy me not;* he pleads, *Thou art the God of those that repent,* &c., and concludes, *Therefore I will praise thee for ever,* &c.

III. God's gracious acceptance of his repentance: *God was entreated of him, and heard his supplication.* Though affliction drive us to God, he will not therefore reject us if in sincerity we seek him, for afflictions are sent on purpose to bring us to him. As a token of God's favour to him, he made a way for his escape. Afflictions are continued no longer than till they have done their work. When Manasseh is brought back to his God and to his duty he shall soon be *brought back to his kingdom.* See how ready God is to accept and welcome returning sinners, and how *swift to show mercy.* Let not great sinners despair, when Manasseh himself, upon his repentance, found favour with God; in him God *showed forth a pattern of long-suffering,* as 1 Tim. i. 16; Isa. i. 18.

IV. The *fruits meet for repentance* which he brought forth after his return to his own land, *v.* 15, 16. 1. He turned from his sins. He *took away the strange gods,* the images of them, and that idol (whatever it was) which he had set up with so much solemnity *in the house of the Lord,* as if it had been master of that house. He cast out all the idolatrous altars that were *in the mount of the house* and in Jerusalem, as detestable things. Now (we hope) he loathed them as much as ever he had loved them, and said to them, *Get you hence*, Isa. xxx. 22. "*What have I to do any more with idols?* I have had enough of them." 2. He returned to his duty; for he *repaired the altar of the Lord*, which had either been abused and broken down by some of the idolatrous priests, or, at least, neglected and gone out of repair. He sacrificed thereon peace-offerings to implore God's favour, and thank-offerings to praise him for his deliverance. Nay, he now used his power to reform his people, as before he had abused it to corrupt them: *He commanded Judah to serve the Lord God of Israel.* Note, Those that truly repent of their sins will not only return to God themselves, but will do all they can to recover those that have by their example been seduced and drawn away from God; else they do not thoroughly (as they ought) undo what they have done amiss, nor make the plaster as wide as the wound. We find that he prevailed to bring them off from their *false gods*, but not from their *high places, v.* 17. They still sacrificed in them, *yet to the Lord their God only;* Manasseh could not carry the reformation so far as he had carried the corruption. It is an easy thing to debauch men's manners, but not so easy to reform them again.

V. His prosperity, in some measure, after his repentance. He might plainly see it was sin that ruined him; for, when he returned to God in a way of duty, God returned to him in a way of mercy: and then he *built a wall about the city of David* (*v.* 14), for by sin he had unwalled it and exposed it to the enemy. He also put captains of war in the fenced cities for the security of his country. Josephus says that all the rest of his time he was so changed for the better that he was looked upon as a very happy man.

Lastly, Here is the conclusion of his history. The heads of those things for a full narrative of which we are referred to the other writings that were then extant are more than of any of the kings, *v.* 18, 19. A particular account, it seems, was kept, 1. Of *all his sin, and his trespass,* the *high places* he built, *the groves and images he set up, before he was humbled.* Probably this was taken from his own confession which he made of his sin when God gave him repentance, and which he left upon record, in a book entitled, *The words of the seers.* To those seers that *spoke to him* (*v.* 18) to reprove him for his sin he sent his confession when he repented, to be inserted in their memoirs, as a token of his gratitude to them for their kindness in reproving him. Thus it becomes penitents to take shame to themselves, to give thanks to their reprovers, and warning to others. 2. Of *the words of the seers that spoke to him in the name of the Lord* (*v.* 10, 18), the reproofs they gave him for his sin and their exhortations to repentance. Note, Sinners ought to consider that, how little notice soever they take of them, an account is kept of the words of the seers that speak to them from God to admonish them of their sins, warn them of their danger, and call them to their duty, which will be produced against them in the great day. 3. Of his *prayer to God* (this is twice mentioned as a remarkable thing) *and how God was entreated of him.* This was *written for the generations to come, that the people that should be created might praise the Lord* for his readiness to receive returning prodigals. Notice is taken of the place of his burial, not in *the sepulchres of the kings,* but *in his own house;* he was buried privately, and nothing of that honour was done him at his death that was done to his father. Penitents may recover their comfort sooner than their credit.

21 Amon *was* two and twenty years old when he began to reign, and reigned two years in Jerusalem. 22 But he did *that which was* evil in the sight of the LORD, as did Manasseh his father: for Amon sacrificed unto all the carved images which Manasseh his father had made, and served them; 23 And humbled not himself before the LORD, as Manasseh his father had humbled himself; but Amon trespassed more and more. 24 And his servants conspired against him, and slew him in his own house. 25 But the people of the land slew all them that had conspired against king Amon; and the people of the land made Josiah his son king in his stead.

We have little recorded concerning Amon, but enough unless it were better. Here is,

I. His great wickedness. He did as *Manasseh had done* in the days of his apostasy, *v.* 22. Those who think this an evidence that Manasseh did not truly repent forget how many good kings had wicked sons. Only it should seem that Manasseh was in *this* defective, that, when he *cast out the images,* he did not utterly deface and destroy them, according to the law which required Israel to *burn the images with fire,* Deut. vii. 5. How necessary that law was this instance shows; for the *carved images* being only thrown by, and not burnt, Amon knew where to find them, soon set them up, and sacrificed to them. It is added, to represent him exceedingly sinful and to justify God in cutting him off so soon, 1. That he out-did his father in sinning: *He trespassed more and more, v.* 23. His father did ill, but he did worse. Those that were joined to idols grew more and more mad upon them. 2. That he came short of his father in repenting: He *humbled not himself before the Lord, as his father had humbled himself.* He fell like him, but did not get up again like him. It is not so much sin as impenitence in sin that ruins men, not so much that they offend as that they do not humble themselves for their offences, not the disease, but the neglect of the remedy.

II. His speedy destruction. He reigned but two years and then his servants *conspired against him* and *slew him, v.* 24. Perhaps when Amon sinned as his father did in the beginning of his days he promised himself that he should repent as his father did in the latter end of his days. But his case shows what a madness it is to presume upon that. If he hoped to repent when he was old, he was wretchedly disappointed; for he was cut off when he was young. He rebelled against God, and his own servants rebelled against him. Herein God was righteous, but they were wicked, and justly did the *people of the land* put them to death as traitors. The lives of kings are particularly under the protection of Providence and the laws both of God and man.

CHAP. XXXIV.

Before we see Judah and Jerusalem ruined we shall yet see some glorious years, while good Josiah sits at the helm. By his pious endeavours for reformation God tried them yet once more; if they had known in this their day, the day of their visitation, the things that belonged to their peace and improved them, their ruin might have been prevented. But after this reign they were hidden from their eyes, and the next reigns brought an utter desolation upon them. In this chapter we have, I. A general account of Josiah's character, ver. 1, 2. II. His zeal to root out idolatry, ver. 3—7. III. His care to repair the temple, ver. 8—13. IV. The finding of the book of the law and the good use made of it, ver. 14—28. V. The public reading of the law to the people and their renewing their covenant with God thereupon, ver. 29—33. Much of this we had 2 Kings xxii.

JOSIAH *was* eight years old when he began to reign, and he reigned in Jerusalem one and thirty years. 2 And he did *that which was* right in the sight of the LORD, and walked in the ways of David his father, and declined *neither* to the right hand, nor to the left. 3 For in the eighth year of his reign, while he was yet young, he began to seek after the God of David his father: and in the twelfth year he began to purge Judah and Jerusalem from the high places, and the groves, and the carved images, and the molten images. 4 And they brake down the altars of Baalim in his presence; and the images, that *were* on high above them, he cut down; and the groves, and the carved images, and the molten images, he brake in pieces, and made dust *of them,* and strowed *it* upon the graves of them that had sacrificed unto them. 5 And he burnt the bones of the priests upon their altars, and cleansed Judah and Jerusalem. 6 And *so did he* in the cities of Manasseh, and Ephraim, and Simeon, even unto Naphtali, with their mattocks round about. 7 And when he had broken down the altars and the groves, and had beaten the graven images into powder, and cut down all the idols throughout all the land of Israel, he returned to Jerusalem.

Concerning Josiah we are here told, 1. That he came to the crown when he was very young, only eight years old (yet his infancy did not debar him from his right), and he reigned *thirty-one years* (*v.* 1), a considerable time. I fear, however, that in the beginning of his reign things went much as they had done in his father's time, because, being a child, he must have left the management of them to others; so that it was not till his twelfth year, which goes far in the number of his years, that the reformation began, *v.* 3. He could not, as Hezekiah did, fall about it immediately. 2. That he reigned very well (*v.* 2), approved himself to God, trod in the steps of David, and did not decline either *to the right hand or to the left:* for there are errors on both hands. 3. That while he was young, about sixteen years old, he *began to seek after God, v.* 3. We have reason to think he had not so good an education as Manasseh had (it is well if those about him did not endeavour to corrupt and debauch him); yet he thus sought God when he was young. It is the duty and interest of young people, and will particularly be the honour of young gentlemen, as soon as they come to years of understanding, to *begin to seek God;* for those that seek him early shall find him. 4. That in the twelfth year of his reign, when it is probable he took the administration of the government entirely into his own hands, he *began to purge his kingdom from the remains of idolatry;* he destroyed the high places, groves, images, altars, all the utensils of idolatry, *v.* 3, 4. He not only cast them out as Manasseh did, but broke them to pieces, and made dust of them. This destruction of idolatry is here said to be in his twelfth year, but it was said (2 Kings xxiii. 23) to be in his eighteenth year. Something was probably done towards it in his twelfth year; then he began to purge out idolatry, but that good work met with opposition, so that it was not thoroughly done till they had found the book of the law six years afterwards. But here the whole work is laid together briefly which was much more largely and particularly related in the *Kings.* His zeal carried him out to do this, not only in Judah and Jerusalem, but in the cities of Israel too, as far as he had any influence upon them.

8 Now in the eighteenth year of his reign, when he had purged the land, and the house, he sent Shaphan the son of Azaliah, and Maaseiah the go-

vernor of the city, and Joah the son of Joahaz the recorder, to repair the house of the LORD his God. 9 And when they came to Hilkiah the high priest, they delivered the money that was brought into the house of God, which the Levites that kept the doors had gathered of the hand of Manasseh and Ephraim, and of all the remnant of Israel, and of all Judah and Benjamin; and they returned to Jerusalem. 10 And they put *it* in the hand of the workmen that had the oversight of the house of the LORD, and they gave it to the workmen that wrought in the house of the LORD, to repair and amend the house: 11 Even to the artificers and builders gave they *it*, to buy hewn stone, and timber for couplings, and to floor the houses which the kings of Judah had destroyed. 12 And the men did the work faithfully: and the overseers of them *were* Jahath and Obadiah, the Levites, of the sons of Merari; and Zechariah and Meshullam, of the sons of the Kohathites, to set *it* forward; and *other of* the Levites, all that could skill of instruments of music. 13 Also *they were* over the bearers of burdens, and *were* overseers of all that wrought the work in any manner of service: and of the Levites *there were* scribes, and officers, and porters.

Here, 1. Orders are given by the king for the repair of the temple, *v.* 8. When he had purged the house of the corruptions of it he began to fit it up for the services that were to be performed in it. Thus we must do by the spiritual temple of the heart, get it cleansed from the pollutions of sin, and then renewed, so as to be transformed into the image of God. Josiah, in this order, calls God *the Lord his God.* Those that truly love God will *love the habitation of his house.* 2. Care is taken about it, effectual care. The Levites went about the country and gathered money towards it, which was returned to the three trustees mentioned, *v.* 8. They brought it to Hilkiah the high priest (*v.* 9), and he and they put it into the hands of workmen, both overseers and labourers, who undertook to do it by the great, as we say, or *in the gross, v.* 10, 11. It is observed that the workmen were industrious and honest: They *did the work faithfully* (*v.* 12); and workmen are not completely faithful if they are not both careful and diligent, for a confidence is reposed in them that they will be so. It is also intimated that the overseers were ingenious; for it is said that all those were employed to inspect this work who were skilful in *instruments of music;* not that their skill in music could be of any use in architecture, but it was an evidence that they were men of sense and ingenuity, and particularly that their genius lay towards the mathematics, which qualified them very much for this trust. Witty men are then wise men when they employ their wit in doing good, in helping their friends, and, as they have opportunity, in serving the public. Observe, in this work, how God dispenses his gifts variously; here were some that were *bearers of burdens,* cut out for bodily labour and fit to work. Here were others (made *meliori luto—of finer materials*) that had skill in music, and they were *overseers of those that laboured,* and scribes and officers. The former were the hands: these were the heads. They had need of one another, and the work needed both. Let not the overseers of the work despise the bearers of burdens, nor let those that work in the service grudge at those whose office it is to direct; but let each esteem and serve the other in love, and let God have the glory and the church the benefit of the different gifts and dispositions of both.

14 And when they brought out the money that was brought into the house of the LORD, Hilkiah the priest found a book of the law of the LORD *given* by Moses. 15 And Hilkiah answered and said to Shaphan the scribe, I have found the book of the law in the house of the LORD. And Hilkiah delivered the book to Shaphan. 16 And Shaphan carried the book to the king, and brought the king word back again, saying, All that was committed to thy servants, they do *it*. 17 And they have gathered together the money that was found in the house of the LORD, and have delivered it into the hand of the overseers, and to the hand of the workmen. 18 Then Shaphan the scribe told the king, saying, Hilkiah the priest hath given me a book. And Shaphan read it before the king. 19 And it came to pass, when the king had heard the words of the law, that he rent his clothes. 20 And the king commanded Hilkiah, and Ahikam the son of Shaphan, and Abdon the son of Micah, and Shaphan the scribe, and Asaiah a servant of the king's, saying, 21 Go, enquire of the LORD for me, and for them that are left in Israel and in Judah, concerning the words of the

book that is found: for great *is* the wrath of the LORD that is poured out upon us, because our fathers have not kept the word of the LORD, to do after all that is written in this book. 22 And Hilkiah, and *they* that the king *had appointed*, went to Huldah the prophetess, the wife of Shallum the son of Tikvath, the son of Hasrah, keeper of the wardrobe; (now she dwelt in Jerusalem in the college:) and they spake to her to that *effect*. 23 And she answered them, Thus saith the LORD God of Israel, Tell ye the man that sent you to me, 24 Thus saith the LORD, Behold, I will bring evil upon this place, and upon the inhabitants thereof, *even* all the curses that are written in the book which they have read before the king of Judah: 25 Because they have forsaken me, and have burned incense unto other gods, that they might provoke me to anger with all the works of their hands; therefore my wrath shall be poured out upon this place, and shall not be quenched. 26 And as for the king of Judah, who sent you to enquire of the LORD, so shall ye say unto him, Thus saith the LORD God of Israel *concerning* the words which thou hast heard; 27 Because thine heart was tender, and thou didst humble thyself before God, when thou heardest his words against this place, and against the inhabitants thereof, and humbledst thyself before me, and didst rend thy clothes, and weep before me; I have even heard *thee* also, saith the LORD. 28 Behold, I will gather thee to thy fathers, and thou shalt be gathered to thy grave in peace, neither shall thine eyes see all the evil that I will bring upon this place, and upon the inhabitants of the same. So they brought the king word again.

This whole paragraph we had, just as it is here related, 2 Kings xxii. 8—20, and have nothing to add here to what was there observed. But, 1. We may hence take occasion to bless God that we have plenty of Bibles, and that they are, or may be, in all hands,—that the book of the law and gospel is not lost, is not scarce,—that, in this sense, the *word of the Lord* is not *precious*. Bibles are jewels, but, thanks be to God, they are not rarities. The fountain of the waters of life is not a spring shut up or a fountain sealed, but the streams of it, in all places, *make glad the city of our God. Usus communis aquarum—These waters flow for general use.* What a great deal shall we have to answer for if the great things of God's law, being thus made common, should be accounted by us as strange things! 2. We may hence learn, whenever we read or hear the word of God, to affect our hearts with it, and to get them possessed with a holy fear of that wrath of God which is there revealed against all ungodliness and unrighteousness of men, as Josiah's tender heart was. When he heard the words of the law he *rent his clothes* (*v.* 19), and God was well pleased with his doing so, *v.* 27. Were the things contained in the scripture new to us, as they were here to Josiah, surely they would make deeper impressions upon us than commonly they do; but they are not the less weighty, and therefore should not be the less considered by us, for their being well known. Rend the heart therefore, not the garments. 3. We are here directed when we are under convictions of sin, and apprehensions of divine wrath, to enquire of the Lord; so Josiah did, *v.* 21. It concerns us to ask (as they did, Acts ii. 37), *Men and brethren, what shall we do?* and more particularly (as the jailor), *What must I do to be saved?* Acts xvi. 30. *If you will* thus *enquire, enquire* (Isa. xxi. 12); and, blessed be God, we have the lively oracles to which to apply with these enquiries. 4. We are here warned of the ruin that sin brings upon nations and kingdoms. Those that forsake God bring evil upon themselves (*v.* 24, 25), and kindle a fire *which shall not be quenched.* Such will the fire of God's wrath be when the decree has gone forth against those that obstinately and impenitently persist in their wicked ways. 5. We are here encouraged to humble ourselves before God and seek unto him, as Josiah did. If we cannot prevail thereby to turn away God's wrath from our land, yet we shall deliver our own souls, *v.* 27, 28. And good people are here taught to be so far from fearing death as to welcome it rather when it *takes them away from the evil to come.* See how the property of it is altered by making it the matter of a promise: *Thou shalt be gathered to thy grave in peace,* housed in that ark, as Noah, when a deluge is coming.

29 Then the king sent and gathered together all the elders of Judah and Jerusalem. 30 And the king went up into the house of the LORD, and all the men of Judah, and the inhabitants of Jerusalem, and the priests, and the Levites, and all the people, great and small: and he read in their ears all the words of the book of the

covenant that was found in the house of the LORD. 31 And the king stood in his place, and made a covenant before the LORD, to walk after the LORD, and to keep his commandments, and his testimonies, and his statutes, with all his heart, and with all his soul, to perform the words of the covenant which are written in this book. 32 And he caused all that were present in Jerusalem and Benjamin to stand *to it*. And the inhabitants of Jerusalem did according to the covenant of God, the God of their fathers. 33 And Josiah took away all the abominations out of all the countries that *pertained* to the children of Israel, and made all that were present in Israel to serve, *even* to serve the LORD their God. *And* all his days they departed not from following the LORD, the God of their fathers.

We have here an account of the further advances which Josiah made towards the reformation of his kingdom upon the hearing of the law read and the receipt of the message God sent him by the prophetess. Happy the people that had such a king; for here we find that, 1. They were well taught. He did not go about to force them to do their duty, till he had first instructed them in it. He called all the people together, great and small, young and old, rich and poor, high and low. *He that hath ears to hear, let him hear* the words of *the book of the covenant;* for they are all concerned in those words. To put an honour upon the service, and to engage attention the more, though there were priests and Levites present, the king himself read the book to the people (*v.* 30), and he read it, no doubt, in such a manner as to show that he was himself affected with it, which would be a means of affecting the hearers. 2. They were well fixed. The articles of agreement between God and Israel being read, that they might intelligently covenant with God, both king and people with great solemnity did as it were subscribe the articles. The king in his place covenanted to keep God's commandments with all his heart and soul, according to what was *written in the book* (*v.* 31), and urged the people to declare their consent likewise to this covenant, and solemnly to promise that they would faithfully perform, fulfil, and keep, all and every thing that was on their part to be done, according to this covenant: this they did; they could not for shame do otherwise. He caused *all that were present* to *stand to it* (*v* 32), and made them all *to serve, even to serve the Lord their God* (*v.* 33), to do it and to *make a business* of it. He did all he could to bring them to it—*to serve, even to serve;* the repetition denotes that this was the only thing his heart was set on; he aimed at nothing else in what he did but to engage them to God and their duty. 3. They were well tended, were honest with good looking to. *All his days they departed not from following the Lord;* he kept them, with much ado, from running into idolatry again. *All his days* were days of restraint upon them; but this intimated that there was in them a *bent to backslide*, a strong inclination to idolatry. Many of them wanted nothing but to have him out of the way, and then they would have their high places and their images up again. And therefore we find that *in the days of Josiah* (Jer. iii. 6) God charged it upon treacherous Judah that she *had not returned to him with all her heart, but feignedly* (*v.* 10), nay, had *played the harlot* (*v.* 8) and thereby had even *justified backsliding Israel*, *v.* 11. In the twenty-third year of this reign, four or five years after this, they had *gone on to provoke God to anger with the works of their hands* (Jer. xxv. 3—7); and, which is very observable, it is from the beginning of Josiah's reformation, his twelfth or thirteenth year, that *the iniquity of the house of Judah*, which brought ruin upon them, and which the prophet was to bear lying on his right side, was dated (Ezek. iv. 6), for thence to the destruction of Jerusalem was just forty years. Josiah was sincere in what he did, but the generality of the people were averse to it and hankered after their idols still; so that the reformation, though well designed and well prosecuted by the prince, had little or no effect upon the people. It was with reluctancy that they parted with their idols; still they were in heart joined to them, and wished for them again. This God saw, and therefore from that time, when one would have thought the foundations had been laid for a perpetual security and peace, from that very time did the decree go forth for their destruction. Nothing hastens the ruin of a people nor ripens them for it more than the baffling of hopeful attempts for reformation and a hypocritical return to God. *Be not deceived, God is not mocked.*

CHAP. XXXV.

We are here to attend Josiah, I. To the temple, where we see his religious care for the due observance of the ordinance of the passover, according to the law, ver. 1—19. II. To the field of battle, where we see his rashness in engaging with the king of Egypt, and how dearly it cost him, ver. 20—23. III. To the grave, where we see him bitterly lamented, ver. 24—27. And so we must take our leave of Josiah.

MOREOVER Josiah kept a passover unto the LORD in Jerusalem: and they killed the passover on the fourteenth *day* of the first month. 2 And he set the priests in their charges, and encouraged them to the service of the house of the LORD, 3 And said unto the Levites that taught all Israel, which were holy unto the LORD, Put the holy ark in the house which

Solomon the son of David king of Israel did build; *it shall* not *be* a burden upon *your* shoulders: serve now the LORD your God, and his people Israel, 4 And prepare *yourselves* by the houses of your fathers, after your courses, according to the writing of David king of Israel, and according to the writing of Solomon his son. 5 And stand in the holy *place* according to the divisions of the families of the fathers of your brethren the people, and *after* the division of the families of the Levites. 6 So kill the passover, and sanctify yourselves, and prepare your brethren, that *they* may do according to the word of the LORD by the hand of Moses. 7 And Josiah gave to the people, of the flock, lambs and kids, all for the passover offerings, for all that were present, to the number of thirty thousand, and three thousand bullocks: these *were* of the king's substance. 8 And his princes gave willingly unto the people, to the priests, and to the Levites: Hilkiah and Zechariah and Jehiel, rulers of the house of God, gave unto the priests for the passover offerings two thousand and six hundred *small cattle*, and three hundred oxen. 9 Conaniah also, and Shemaiah and Nethaneel, his brethren, and Hashabiah, and Jeiel and Jozabad, chief of the Levites, gave unto the Levites for passover offerings five thousand *small cattle*, and five hundred oxen. 10 So the service was prepared, and the priests stood in their place, and the Levites in their courses, according to the king's commandment. 11 And they killed the passover, and the priests sprinkled *the blood* from their hands, and the Levites flayed *them*. 12 And they removed the burnt offerings, that they might give according to the divisions of the families of the people, to offer unto the LORD, as *it is* written in the book of Moses. And so *did they* with the oxen. 13 And they roasted the passover with fire according to the ordinance: but the *other* holy *offerings* sod they in pots, and in caldrons, and in pans, and divided *them* speedily among all the people. 14 And afterward they made ready for themselves, and for the priests: because the priests the sons of Aaron *were busied* in offering of burnt offerings and the fat until night; therefore the Levites prepared for themselves, and for the priests the sons of Aaron. 15 And the singers the sons of Asaph *were* in their place, according to the commandment of David, and Asaph, and Heman, and Jeduthun the king's seer; and the porters *waited* at every gate; they might not depart from their service; for their brethren the Levites prepared for them. 16 So all the service of the LORD was prepared the same day, to keep the passover, and to offer burnt offerings upon the altar of the LORD, according to the commandment of king Josiah. 17 And the children of Israel that were present kept the passover at that time, and the feast of unleavened bread seven days. 18 And there was no passover like to that kept in Israel from the days of Samuel the prophet; neither did all the kings of Israel keep such a passover as Josiah kept, and the priests, and the Levites, and all Judah and Israel that were present, and the inhabitants of Jerusalem. 19 In the eighteenth year of the reign of Josiah was this passover kept.

The destruction which Josiah made of idols and idolatry was more largely related in the *Kings*, and but just mentioned here in the foregoing chapter (*v.* 33); but his solemnizing the passover, which was touched upon there (2 Kings xxiii. 21), is very particularly related here. Many were the feasts of the Lord, appointed by the ceremonial law, but the passover was the chief. It *began them all* in the night wherein Israel came out of Egypt; it *concluded them all* in the night wherein Christ was betrayed; and in the celebration of it Hezekiah and Josiah, those two great reformers, revived religion in their day. The ordinance of the Lord's supper resembles the passover more than it does any of the Jewish festivals; and the due observance of that ordinance, according to the rule, is an instance and means both of the growing purity and beauty of churches and of the growing piety and devotion of particular Christians. Religion cannot flourish where that passover is either wholly neglected or not duly observed; return to that, revive that, make a solemn business of that affecting binding ordinance, and then, it is to be hoped, there will be a reformation in other instances also.

In the account we had of Hezekiah's passover the great zeal of the people was observable, and the transport of devout affection that they were in; but little of the same spirit appears here. It was more in compliance with the king that they all kept the passover (*v.* 17, 18) than from any great inclination they had to it themselves. Some pride they took in this form of godliness, but little pleasure in the power of it. But, whatever defect there was among the people in the spirit of the duty, both the magistrates and the ministers did their part and took care that the external part of the service should be performed with due solemnity.

I. The king exhorted and directed, quickened and encouraged, the priests and Levites to do their office in this solemnity. Perhaps he saw them remiss and indifferent, unwilling to go out of their road or mend their pace. If ministers are so, it is not amiss for any, but most proper for magistrates, to stir them up to their business. Say to Archippus, *Take heed to thy ministry,* Col. iv. 17. Let us see how this good king managed his clergy upon this occasion. 1. He reduced them to the office they were appointed to by the law of Moses (*v.* 6) and the order they were put into by David and Solomon, *v.* 4. *He set them in their charge, v.* 2. He did not cut them out new work, nor put them into any new method, but called them back to their institution. Their courses were settled in writing; let them have recourse to that writing, and marshal themselves according to the *divisions of their families, v.* 5. Our rule is settled in the written word; let magistrates take care that ministers walk according to that rule and they do their duty. 2. He ordered the ark to be put in its place. It should seem, it had of late been displaced, either by the wicked kings, to make room for their idols in the most holy place, or by Hezekiah, to make room for the workmen that repaired the temple. However it was, Josiah bids the *Levites put the ark in the house* (*v.* 3), and not carry it about from place to place, as perhaps of late they had done, justifying themselves therein by the practice before the temple was built. Now that the priests were discharged from this burden of the ark they must be careful in other services about it. 3. He charged them to *serve God and his people Israel, v.* 3. Ministers must look upon themselves as servants both to Christ and to his church for his sake, 2 Cor. iv. 5. They must take care, and take pains, and lay out themselves to the utmost, (1.) For the glory and honour of God, and to advance the interests of his kingdom among men. Paul, *a servant of God,* Tit. i. 1. (2.) For the welfare and benefit of his people, not as having dominion over their faith, but as helpers of their holiness and joy; and there will be no difficulty, in the strength of God, in honestly serving these two masters. 4. He charged them to *sanctify themselves,* and *prepare their brethren, v.* 6. Ministers' work must begin at home, and they must sanctify themselves in the first place, purify themselves from sin, sequester themselves from the world, and devote themselves to God. But it must not end there; they must do what they can to *prepare their brethren* by admonishing, instructing, exhorting, quickening, and comforting, them. *The preparation of the heart* is indeed *from the Lord;* but ministers must be instruments in his hand. 5. He *encouraged them to the service, v.* 2. He spoke comfortably to them, as Hezekiah did, *ch.* xxx. 22. He promised them his countenance. Note, Those whom we charge we should encourage. Most people love to be commended, and will be wrought upon by encouragements more than by threats.

II. The king and the princes, influenced by his example, gave liberally for the bearing of the charges of this passover. The ceremonial services were expensive, which perhaps was one reason why they had been neglected. People had not zeal enough to be at the charge of them; nor were they now very fond of them, for that reason, and therefore, 1. Josiah, at his own proper cost, furnished the congregation with paschal lambs, and other sacrifices, to be offered during the seven days of the feast. He allowed out of his own estate 30,000 *lambs* for *passover offerings,* which the offerers were to feast upon, and 3000 bullocks (*v.* 7) to be offered during the following seven days. Note, Those who are serious in religion should, when they persuade others to do that which is good, make it as cheap and easy to them as may be. And where God sows plentifully he expects to reap accordingly. It is to be feared that the congregation generally had not come provided; so that, if Josiah had not furnished them, the work of God must have stood still. 2. The chief of the priests, who were men of great estates, contributed towards the priests' charges, as Josiah did towards the people's. *The princes* (*v.* 8), that is, the chief of the priests, the princes of the holy tribe, *rulers of the house of God,* bore the priests' charges. And some of the rich and great men of the Levites furnished them also with cattle, both great and small, for offerings, *v.* 9. For, as to those that sincerely desire to be found in the way of their duty, Providence sometimes raises up friends to bear them out in it, beyond what they could have expected.

III. The priests and Levites performed their office very readily, *v.* 10. They killed the paschal lambs in the court of the temple, the priests sprinkled the blood upon the altar, the Levites flayed them, and then gave the flesh to the people according to their families (*v.* 11, 12), not fewer than ten, nor more than twenty, to a lamb. They took it to their several apartments, roasted it, and ate it *according to the ordinance, v.* 13. As for the other sacrifices that were eucharistical, the flesh of them was boiled according to the law of the peace-offerings and was *divided speedily among the people,* that they might feast upon it as a token of their joy in the atonement made and their reconciliation to God thereby. And, *lastly,* The priests and Levites took care to honour God by *eating of the passover* themselves, *v.* 14. Let not ministers think that the care they take for the souls of others will excuse their neglect of their own, or that being employed so much in public worship will supersede the religious exercises of their closets and families. The Levites here made ready for themselves and for the priests, because the priests were wholly taken up all day in the service of the altar; therefore, that they might not have their lamb to dress when they should eat it, the Levites got it ready for them against supper time. Let ministers learn hence to help one another, and to forward one another's work, as brethren, and fellow-servants of the same Master.

IV. The singers and porters attended in their places, and did their office, *v.* 15. The singers with their sacred songs and music expressed and excited the joy of the congregation, and made the service very pleasant to them; and the porters at the gates took care that there should be no breaking in of any thing to defile or disquiet the assembly, nor going out of any from it, that none should steal away till the service was done. While they were thus employed their brethren the Levites prepared paschal lambs for them.

V. The whole solemnity was performed with great exactness, according to the law (*v.* 16, 17), and, upon that account, there was none like it since Samuel's time (*v.* 18), for in Hezekiah's passover there were several irregularities. And bishop Patrick observes that in this also it exceeded the other passovers which the preceding kings had kept, that though Josiah was by no means so rich as David, and Solomon, and Jehoshaphat, yet he furnished the whole congregation with beasts for sacrifice, both paschal and eucharistical, at his own proper cost and charge, which was more than any king ever did before him.

20 After all this, when Josiah had prepared the temple, Necho king of Egypt came up to fight against Charchemish by Euphrates: and Josiah went out against him. 21 But he sent ambassadors to him, saying, What have I to do with thee, thou king of Judah? *I come* not against thee this day, but against the house wherewith I have war: for God commanded me to make haste: forbear thee from *meddling with* God, who *is* with me, that he destroy thee not. 22 Nevertheless Josiah would not turn his face from him, but disguised himself, that he might fight with him, and hearkened not unto the words of Necho from the mouth of God, and came to fight in the valley of Megiddo. 23 And the archers shot at king Josiah; and the king said to his servants, Have me away; for I am sore wounded. 24 His servants therefore took him out of that chariot, and put him in the second chariot that he had; and they brought him to Jerusalem, and he died, and was buried in *one of* the sepulchres of his fathers. And all Judah and Jerusalem mourned for Josiah. 25 And Jeremiah lamented for Josiah: and all the singing men and the singing women spake of Josiah in their lamentations to this day, and made them an ordinance in Israel: and, behold, they *are* written in the lamentations. 26 Now the rest of the acts of Josiah, and his goodness, according to *that which was* written in the law of the LORD, 27 And his deeds, first and last, behold, they *are* written in the book of the kings of Israel and Judah.

It was thirteen years from Josiah's famous passover to his death. During this time, we may hope, things went well in his kingdom, that he prospered, and religion flourished; yet we are not entertained with the pleasing account of those years, but they are passed over in silence, because the people, for all this, were not turned from the love of their sins nor God from the fierceness of his anger The next news therefore we hear of Josiah is that he is cut off in the midst of his days and usefulness, before he is full forty years old. We had this sad story, 2 Kings xxiii. 29, 30. Here it is somewhat more largely related. That appears here, more than did there, which reflects such blame on Josiah and such praise on the people as one would not have expected.

I. Josiah was a very good prince, yet he was much to be blamed for his rashness and presumption in going out to war against the king of Egypt without cause or call. It was bad enough, as it appeared in the *Kings,* that he meddled with strife which belonged not to him. But here it looks worse; for, it seems, the king of Egypt sent ambassadors to him, to warn him against this enterprise, *v.* 21.

1. The king of Egypt argued with Josiah, (1.) From principles of justice He professed that he had no desire to do him any hurt, and therefore it was unfair, against common equity and the law of nations, for Josiah to take up arms against him. If even a *righteous man* engage in an *unrighteous*

cause, let him not expect to prosper. *God is no respecter of persons.* See Prov. iii. 30; xxv. 8. (2.) From principles of religion: "*God is with me;* nay, *He commanded me to make haste*, and therefore, if thou retard my motions, thou meddlest with God." It cannot be that the king of Egypt only pretended this (as Sennacherib did in a like case, 2 Kings xviii. 25), hoping thereby to make Josiah desist, because he knew he had a veneration for the word of God; for it is said here (*v.* 22) that the words of Necho were from the mouth of God. We must therefore suppose that either by a dream, or by a strong impulse upon his spirit which he had reason to think was from God, or by Jeremiah or some other prophet, he had ordered him to make war upon the king of Assyria. (3.) From principles of policy: "*That he destroy thee not;* it is at thy peril if thou engage against one that has not only a better army and a better cause, but God on his side."

2. It was not in wrath to Josiah, whose heart was upright with the Lord his God, but in wrath to a hypocritical nation, who were unworthy of so good a king, that he was so far infatuated as not to hearken to these fair reasonings and desist from his enterprise. He *would not turn his face from him,* but went in person and fought the Egyptian army in the *valley of Megiddo, v.* 22. If perhaps he could not believe that the king of Egypt had a command from God to do what he did, yet, upon his pleading such a command, he ought to have consulted the oracles of God before he went out against him. His not doing that was his great fault, and of fatal consequence. In this matter he walked not in the ways of David his father; for, had it been his case, he would have enquired of the Lord, *Shall I go up? Wilt thou deliver them into my hands?* How can we think to prosper in our ways if we do not acknowledge God in them?

II. The people were a very wicked people, yet they were much to be commended for lamenting the death of Josiah as they did. That Jeremiah lamented him I do not wonder; he was the weeping prophet, and plainly foresaw the utter ruin of his country following upon the death of this good king. But it is strange to find that all Judah and Jerusalem, that stupid senseless people, *mourned for him* (*v.* 24), contrived how to have their mourning excited by singing men and singing women, how to have it spread through the kingdom (they made an ordinance in Israel that the mournful ditties penned on this sad occasion should be learned and sung by all sorts of people), and also how to have the remembrance of it perpetuated: these elegies were inserted in the collections of state poems; they are written in the Lamentations. Hereby it appeared, 1. That they had some respect to their good prince, and that, though they did not cordially comply with him in all his good designs, they could not but greatly honour him. Pious useful men will be manifested in the consciences even of those that will not be influenced by their example; and many that will not submit to the rules of serious godliness themselves yet cannot but give it their good word and esteem it in others. Perhaps those lamented Josiah when he was dead that were not thankful to God for him while he lived. The Israelites murmured at Moses and Aaron while they were with them and spoke sometimes of stoning them, and yet, when they died, they mourned for them many days. We are often taught to value mercies by the loss of them which, when we enjoyed them, we did not prize as we ought. 2. That they had some sense of their own danger now that he was gone. Jeremiah told them, it is likely, of the evil they might now expect to come upon them, from which he was taken away; and so far they credited what he said that they lamented the death of him that was their defence. Note, Many will more easily be persuaded to lament the miseries that are coming upon them than to take the proper way by universal reformation to prevent them, will shed tears for their troubles, but will not be prevailed upon to part with their sins. But godly sorrow worketh repentance and that repentance will be to salvation.

CHAP. XXXVI.

We have here, I. A short but sad account of the utter ruin of Judah and Jerusalem within a few years after Josiah's death. 1. The history of it in the unhappy reigns of Jehoahaz for three months (ver. 1—4), Jehoiakim (ver. 5—8) for eleven years, Jehoiachin three months (ver. 9, 10), and Zedekiah eleven years, ver. 11. Additions were made to the national guilt, and advances towards the national destruction, in each of those reigns. The destruction was, at length, completed in the slaughter of multitudes (ver. 17), the plundering and burning of the temple and all the palaces, the desolation of the city (ver. 18, 19), and the captivity of the people that remained, ver. 20. 2. Some remarks upon it—that herein sin was punished, Zedekiah's wickedness (ver. 12, 13), the idolatry the people were guilty of (ver. 14), and their abuse of God's prophets, ver. 15, 16. The word of God was herein fulfilled, ver. 21. II. The dawning of the day of their deliverance in Cyrus's proclamation, ver. 22, 23.

THEN the people of the land took Jehoahaz the son of Josiah, and made him king in his father's stead in Jerusalem. 2 Jehoahaz *was* twenty and three years old when he began to reign, and he reigned three months in Jerusalem. 3 And the king of Egypt put him down at Jerusalem, and condemned the land in a hundred talents of silver and a talent of gold. 4 And the king of Egypt made Eliakim his brother king over Judah and Jerusalem, and turned his name to Jehoiakim. And Necho took Jehoahaz his brother, and carried him to Egypt. 5 Jehoiakim *was* twenty and five years old when he began to reign, and he reigned eleven years in Jerusalem:

and he did *that which was* evil in the sight of the LORD his God. 6 Against him came up Nebuchadnezzar king of Babylon, and bound him in fetters, to carry him to Babylon. 7 Nebuchadnezzar also carried of the vessels of the house of the LORD to Babylon, and put them in his temple at Babylon. 8 Now the rest of the acts of Jehoiakim, and his abominations which he did, and that which was found in him, behold, they *are* written in the book of the kings of Israel and Judah: and Jehoiachin his son reigned in his stead. 9 Jehoiachin *was* eight years old when he began to reign, and he reigned three months and ten days in Jerusalem: and he did *that which was* evil in the sight of the LORD. 10 And when the year was expired, king Nebuchadnezzar sent, and brought him to Babylon, with the goodly vessels of the house of the LORD, and made Zedekiah his brother king over Judah and Jerusalem.

The destruction of Judah and Jerusalem is here coming on by degrees. God so ordered it to show that he has no pleasure in the ruin of sinners, but had rather they would turn and live, and therefore gives them both time and inducement to repent and waits to be gracious. The history of these reigns was more largely recorded in the last three chapters of the second of *Kings*. 1. Jehoahaz was set up by the people (*v.* 1), but in one quarter of a year was deposed by Pharaoh-necho, and carried a prisoner to Egypt, and the land fined for setting him up, *v.* 2—4. Of this young prince we hear no more. Had he trodden in the steps of his father's piety he might have reigned long and prospered; but we are told in the *Kings* that *he did evil in the sight of the Lord,* and therefore his triumphing was short and his joy but for a moment. 2. Jehoiakim was set up by the king of Egypt, and reigned eleven years. How low was Judah brought when the king of Egypt, an old enemy to their land, gave what king he pleased to the kingdom and what name he pleased to the king! *v.* 4. He made Eliakim king, and called him *Jehoiakim,* in token of his authority over him. *Jehoiakim did that which was evil* (*v.* 5), nay, we read of the *abominations which he did* (*v.* 8); he was very wild and wicked. Idolatries generally go under the name of abominations. We hear no more of the king of Egypt, but the king of Babylon came up against him (*v.* 6), seized him, and bound him with a design to carry him to Babylon; but, it seems, he either changed his mind, and suffered him to reign as his vassal, or death released the prisoner before he was carried away. However the best and most valuable vessels of the temple were now carried away and made use of in Nebuchadnezzar's temple in Babylon (*v.* 7); for, we may suppose, no temple in the world was so richly furnished as that of Jerusalem. The sin of Judah was that they had brought the idols of the heathen into God's temple; and now their punishment was that the vessels of the temple were carried away to the service of the gods of the nations. If men will profane God's institutions by their sins, it is just with God to suffer them to be profaned by their enemies. These were the vessels which the false prophets flattered the people with hopes of the return of, Jer. xxvii. 16. But Jeremiah told them that the rest should go after them (Jer. xxvii. 21, 22), and they did so. But, as the carrying away of these vessels to Babylon began the calamity of Jerusalem, so Belshazzar's daring profanation of them there filled the measure of the iniquity of Babylon; for, when he drank wine in them to the honour of his gods, the handwriting on the wall presented him with his doom, Dan. v. 3, &c. In the reference to the book of the *Kings* concerning this Jehoiakim mention is made of *that which was found in him* (*v.* 8), which seems to be meant of the treachery that was found in him towards the king of Babylon; but some of the Jewish writers understand it of certain private marks or signatures found in his dead body, in honour of his idol, such cuttings as God had forbidden, Lev. xix. 28. 3. Jehoiachin, or Jeconiah, the son of Jehoiakim, attempted to reign in his stead, and reigned long enough to show his evil inclination; but, after three months and ten days, the king of Babylon sent and fetched him away captive, with more of the goodly vessels of the temple. He is here said to be eight years old, but in *Kings* he is said to be eighteen when he began to reign, so that this seems to be a mistake of the transcriber, unless we suppose that his father took him at eight years old to join with him in the government, as some think.

11 Zedekiah *was* one and twenty years old when he began to reign, and reigned eleven years in Jerusalem. 12 And he did *that which was* evil in the sight of the LORD his God, *and* humbled not himself before Jeremiah the prophet *speaking* from the mouth of the LORD. 13 And he also rebelled against king Nebuchadnezzar, who had made him swear by God: but he stiffened his neck, and hardened his heart from turning unto the LORD God of Israel. 14 Moreover all the

chief of the priests, and the people, transgressed very much after all the abominations of the heathen; and polluted the house of the LORD which he had hallowed in Jerusalem. 15 And the LORD God of their fathers sent to them by his messengers, rising up betimes, and sending; because he had compassion on his people, and on his dwelling place: 16 But they mocked the messengers of God, and despised his words, and misused his prophets, until the wrath of the LORD arose against his people, till *there was* no remedy. 17 Therefore he brought upon them the king of the Chaldees, who slew their young men with the sword in the house of their sanctuary, and had no compassion upon young man or maiden, old man, or him that stooped for age: he gave *them* all into his hand. 18 And all the vessels of the house of God, great and small, and the treasures of the house of the LORD, and the treasures of the king, and of his princes; all *these* he brought to Babylon. 19 And they burnt the house of God, and brake down the wall of Jerusalem, and burnt all the palaces thereof with fire, and destroyed all the goodly vessels thereof. 20 And them that had escaped from the sword carried he away to Babylon; where they were servants to him and his sons until the reign of the kingdom of Persia: 21 To fulfil the word of the LORD by the mouth of Jeremiah, until the land had enjoyed her sabbaths: *for* as long as she lay desolate she kept sabbath, to fulfil threescore and ten years.

We have here an account of the destruction of the kingdom of Judah and the city of Jerusalem by the Chaldeans. Abraham, God's friend, was called out of that country, from Ur of the Chaldees, when God took him into covenant and communion with himself; and now his degenerate seed were carried into that country again, to signify that they had forfeited all that kindness wherewith they had been regarded for the father's sake, and the benefit of that covenant into which he was called; all was now undone again. Here we have,

I. The sins that brought this desolation.

1. Zedekiah, the king in whose days it came, brought it upon himself by his own folly; for he conducted himself very ill both towards God and towards the king of Babylon. (1.) If he had but made God his friend, that would have prevented the ruin. Jeremiah brought him messages from God, which, if he had given due regard to them, might have secured a lengthening of his tranquillity; but it is here charged upon him that he *humbled not himself before Jeremiah, v.* 12. It was expected that this mighty prince, high as he was, should humble himself before a poor prophet, when *he spoke from the mouth of the Lord,* should submit to his admonitions and be amended by them, to his counsels and be ruled by them, should lay himself under the commanding power of the word of God in his mouth; and, because he would not thus make himself a servant to God, he was made a slave to his enemies. God will find some way or other to humble those that will not humble themselves. Jeremiah, as a prophet, was set *over the nations and kingdoms* (Jer. i. 10), and, as mean a figure as he made, whoever would not humble themselves before him found that it was at their peril. (2.) If he had but been true to his covenant with the king of Babylon, that would have prevented his ruin; but he *rebelled against him,* though he had sworn to be his faithful tributary, and perfidiously violated his engagements to him, *v.* 13. It was this that provoked the king of Babylon to deal so severely with him as he did. All nations looked upon an oath as a sacred thing, and on those that durst break through the obligations of it as the worst of men, abandoned of God and to be abhorred by all mankind. If therefore Zedekiah falsify his oath, *when, lo, he has given his hand,* he *shall not escape,* Ezek. xvii. 18. Though Nebuchadnezzar was a heathen, an enemy, yet if, having sworn to him, he be false to him, he shall know *there is a God to whom vengeance belongs.* The thing that ruined Zedekiah was not only that he *turned not to the Lord God of Israel,* but that he *stiffened his neck and hardened his heart from turning to him,* that is, he was obstinately resolved not to return to him, would not lay his neck under God's yoke nor his heart under the impressions of his word, and so, in effect, he *would not be healed,* he *would not live.*

2. The great sin that brought this destruction was idolatry. The priests and people went after *the abominations of the heathen,* forsook the pure worship of God for the lewd and filthy rites of the Pagan superstition, and so *polluted the house of the Lord, v.* 14. The priests, the chief of the priests, who should have opposed idolatry, were ring-leaders in it. That place is not far from ruin in which religion is already ruined.

3. The great aggravation of their sin, and that which filled the measure of it, was the abuse they gave to God's prophets, who were sent to call them to repentance, *v.* 15, 16. Here we have, (1.) God's tender compassion towards them in sending prophets

to them. Because he was the *God of their fathers,* in covenant with them, and whom they worshipped (though this degenerate race forsook him), therefore he *sent to them by his messengers,* to convince them of their sin and warn them of the ruin they would bring upon themselves by it, *rising up betimes and sending,* which denotes not only that he did it with the greatest care and concern imaginable, as men rise betimes to set their servants to work when their heart is upon their business, but that, upon their first deviation from God to idols, if they took but one step that way, God immediately sent to them by his messengers to reprove them for it. He gave them early timely notice both of their duty and danger. Let this quicken us to seek God early, that he rises betimes to send to us. The prophets that were sent rose betimes to speak to them, were diligent and faithful in their office, lost no time, slipped no opportunity of dealing with them; and therefore God is said to rise betimes. The more pains ministers take in their work the more will the people have to answer for if it be all in vain. The reason given why God by his prophets did thus strive with them is because *he had compassion on his people and on his dwelling-place,* and would by these means have prevented their ruin. Note, The methods God takes to reclaim sinners by his word, by ministers, by conscience, by providences, are all instances of his compassion towards them and his unwillingness *that any should perish.* (2.) Their base and disingenuous carriage towards God (*v.* 16): *They mocked the messengers of God* (which was a high affront to him that sent them), *despised his word* in their mouths, and not only so, but *misused the prophets,* treating them as their enemies. The ill usage they gave Jeremiah who lived at this time, and which we read much of in the book of his prophecy, is an instance of this. This was an evidence of an implacable enmity to God, and an invincible resolution to go on in their sins. This brought wrath upon them without remedy, for it was sinning against the remedy. Nothing is more provoking to God than abuses given to his faithful ministers; for what is done against them he takes as done against himself. *Saul, Saul, why persecutest thou me?* Persecution was the sin that brought upon Jerusalem its final destruction by the Romans. See Matt. xxiii. 34—37. Those that mock at God's faithful ministers, and do all they can to render them despicable or odious, that vex and misuse them, to discourage them and to keep others from hearkening to them, should be reminded that a wrong done to an ambassador is construed as done to the prince that sends him, and that the day is coming when they will find it would have been better for them if they had been thrown *into the sea* with a mill-stone about their necks; for hell is deeper and more dreadful.

II. The desolation itself, and some few of the particulars of it, which we had more largely 2 Kings xxv. 1. Multitudes were put to the sword, even *in the house of their sanctuary* (*v.* 17), whither they fled for refuge, hoping that the holiness of the place would be their protection. But how could they expect to find it so when they themselves had polluted it with their abominations? *v.* 14. Those that cast off the dominion of their religion forfeit all the benefit and comfort of it. The Chaldeans not only paid no reverence to the sanctuary, but showed no natural pity either to the tender sex or to venerable age. They forsook God, who had compassion on them (*v.* 15), and would have none of him; justly therefore are they given up into the hands of cruel men, for they *had no compassion on young man or maiden.* 2. All the remaining vessels of the temple, great and small, and all the treasures, sacred and secular, the treasures of God's house and of the king and his princes, were seized, and brought to Babylon, *v.* 18. 3. The temple was burnt, the walls of Jerusalem were demolished, the houses (called here the *palaces,* as Ps. xlviii. 3, so stately, rich, and sumptuous were they) laid in ashes, and all the furniture, called here *the goodly vessels thereof,* destroyed, *v.* 19. Let us see here what woeful havock sin makes, and, as we value the comfort and continuance of our estates, keep that worm from the root of them. 4. The remainder of the people that escaped the sword were carried captives to Babylon (*v.* 20), impoverished, enslaved, insulted, and exposed to all the miseries, not only of a strange and barbarous land, but of an enemy's land, where those that hated them bore rule over them. They were servants to those monarchs, and no doubt were ruled with rigour so long as that monarchy lasted. Now they sat down by the rivers of Babylon, with the streams of which they mingled their tears, Ps. cxxxvii. 1. And though there, it should seem, they were cured of idolatry, yet, as appears by the prophet Ezekiel, they were not cured of mocking the prophets. 5. The land lay desolate while they were captives in Babylon, *v.* 21. That fruitful land, the glory of all lands, was now turned into a desert, not tilled, nor husbanded. The pastures were not clothed as they used to be with flocks, nor the valleys with corn, but all lay neglected. Now this may be considered, (1.) As the just punishment of their former abuse of it. They had served Baal with its fruits; *cursed* therefore *is the ground for their sakes.* Now the land *enjoyed her sabbaths;* (*v.* 21), as God had threatened by Moses, Lev. xxvi. 34, and the reason there given (*v.* 35) is, "Because *it did not rest on your sabbaths;* you profaned the sabbath-day, did not observe the sabbatical year." They many a time ploughed and sowed their land in the seventh year, when it should have rested, and now it lay unploughed and unsown for ten times seven years. Note, God will be no loser in his glory at last by the disobedience of men: if the tribute be not paid, he will distrain and recover it, as he speaks, Hos. ii. 9. If they would not let the land rest, God would make it rest whether they would or no. Some think they had neglected the observance of seventy sabbatical years in all, and just so many, by way of reprisal, the land now enjoyed; or, if those that had been neglected were fewer, it was fit that the law should be satisfied with interest. We find that one of the quarrels God had with them at this time was for not observing another law which related to the seventh year, and that was the release of servants; see Jer. xxxiv. 13, &c. (2.) Yet we may consider it as giving some encouragement to their hopes that they should, in due time, return to it again. Had others come and taken possession of it, they might have despaired of ever recovering it; but, while it lay desolate, it did, as it were, lie waiting for them again, and refuse to acknowledge any other owners.

22 Now in the first year of Cyrus king of Persia, that the word of the LORD *spoken* by the mouth of Jeremiah might be accomplished, the LORD stirred up the spirit of Cyrus king of Persia, that he made a proclamation throughout all his kingdom, and *put it* also in writing, saying, 23 Thus saith Cyrus king of Persia, All the kingdoms of the earth hath the LORD God of heaven given me; and he hath charged me to build him a house in Jerusalem, which *is* in Judah. Who *is there* among you of all his people? The LORD his God *be* with him, and let him go up.

These last two verses of this book have a double aspect. 1. They look back to the prophecy of Jeremiah, and show how that was accomplished, *v.* 22. God had, by him, promised the restoring of the captives and the rebuilding of Jerusalem, at the end of seventy years; and that time to favour Sion, that set time, came at last. After a long and dark night the day-spring from on high visited them. God will be found true to every word he has spoken. 2. They look forward to the history of Ezra, which begins with the repetition of these last two verses. They are there the introduction to a pleasant story; here they are the conclusion of a very melancholy one; and so we learn from them that, though God's church be cast down, it is not cast off, though his people be corrected, they are not abandoned, though thrown into the furnace, yet not lost there, nor left there any longer than till the dross be separated. Though God contend long, he will not contend always. The Israel of God shall be fetched out of Babylon in due time, and even the dry bones made to live. It may be long first; but the vision is for an appointed time, and at the end it shall speak and not lie; therefore, though it tarry, wait for it.

AN EXPOSITION,

WITH PRACTICAL OBSERVATIONS,

OF THE BOOK OF

EZRA.

THE Jewish church puts on quite another face in this book from what it had appeared with; its state much better, and more pleasant, than it was of late in Babylon, and yet far inferior to what it had been formerly. The dry bones here live again, but *in the form of a servant;* the yoke of their captivity is taken off, but the marks of it in their galled necks remain. Kings we hear no more of; *the crown has fallen from their heads.* Prophets they are blessed with, to direct them in their re-establishment, but, after a while, prophecy ceases among them, till the great prophet appears, and his fore-runner. The history of this book is the accomplishment of Jeremiah's prophecy concerning the return of the Jews out of Babylon at the end of seventy years, and a type of the accomplishment of the prophecies of the Apocalypse concerning the deliverance of the gospel church out of the New-Testament Babylon. Ezra preserved the records of that great revolution and transmitted them to the church in this book. His name signifies a helper; and

so he was to that people. A particular account concerning him we shall meet with, *ch.* vii., where he himself enters upon the stage of action. The book gives us an account, I. Of the Jews' return out of their captivity, *ch.* i. ii. II. Of the building of the temple, the opposition it met with, and yet the perfecting of it at last, *ch.* iii.—vi. III. Of Ezra's coming to Jerusalem, *ch.* vii. viii. IV. Of the good service he did there, in obliging those that had married strange wives to put them away, *ch.* ix. x. This beginning again of the Jewish nation was small, yet its latter end greatly increased.

CHAP. I.

In this chapter we have, I. The proclamation which Cyrus, king of Persia, issued out for the release of all the Jews that he found captives in Babylon, and the building of their temple in Jerusalem, ver. 1—4. II. The return of many thereupon, ver. 5, 6. III. Orders given for the restoring of the vessels of the temple, ver. 7—11. And this is the dawning of the day of their deliverance.

NOW in the first year of Cyrus king of Persia, that the word of the LORD by the mouth of Jeremiah might be fulfilled, the LORD stirred up the spirit of Cyrus king of Persia, that he made a proclamation throughout all his kingdom, and *put it* also in writing, saying, 2 Thus saith Cyrus king of Persia, The LORD God of heaven hath given me all the kingdoms of the earth; and he hath charged me to build him a house at Jerusalem, which *is* in Judah. 3 Who *is there* among you of all his people? his God be with him, and let him go up to Jerusalem, which *is* in Judah, and build the house of the LORD God of Israel, (he *is* the God,) which *is* in Jerusalem. 4 And whosoever remaineth in any place where he sojourneth, let the men of his place help him with silver, and with gold, and with goods, and with beasts, beside the freewill offering for the house of God that *is* in Jerusalem.

It will be proper for us here to consider, 1. What was the state of the captive Jews in Babylon. It was upon many accounts very deplorable; they were under the power of those that hated them, had nothing they could call their own; they had no temple, no altar; if they sang psalms, their enemies ridiculed them; and yet they had prophets among them. Ezekiel and Daniel were kept distinct from the heathen. Some of them were preferred at court, others had comfortable settlements in the country, and they were all borne up with hope that, in due time, they should return to their own land again, in expectation of which they preserved among them the distinction of their families, the knowledge of their religion, and an aversion to idolatry 2. What was the state of the government under which they were. Nebuchadnezzar carried many of them into captivity in the first year of his reign, which was the fourth of Jehoiakim; he reigned forty-five years, his son Evil-merodach twenty-three, and his grandson Belshazzar three years, which make up the seventy years. So Dr. Lightfoot. It is charged upon Nebuchadnezzar that he *opened not the house of his prisoners,* Isa. xiv. 17. And, if he had shown mercy to the poor Jews, Daniel told him it would have been the *lengthening of his tranquillity,* Dan. iv. 27. But the measure of the sins of Babylon was at length full, and then destruction was brought upon them by Darius the Mede and Cyrus the Persian, which we read of, Dan. v. Darius, being old, left the government to Cyrus, and he was employed as the instrument of the Jews' deliverance, which he gave orders for as soon as ever he was master of the kingdom of Babylon, perhaps in contradiction to Nebuchadnezzar, whose family he had cut off, and because he took a pleasure in undoing what he had done, or in policy, to recommend his newly-acquired dominion as merciful and gentle, or (as some think) in a pious regard to the prophecy of Isaiah, which had been published, and well known, above 150 years before, where he was expressly named as the man that should do this for God, and for whom God would do great things (Isa. xliv. 28; xlv. 1, &c.), and which perhaps was shown to him by those about him. His name (some say) in the Persian language signifies the *sun,* for he brought light and healing to the church of God, and was an eminent type of Christ the *Sun of righteousness.* Some say that his name signifies a *father,* and Christ is the everlasting Father. Now here we are told,

I. Whence this proclamation took its rise. *The Lord stirred up the spirit of Cyrus.* Note, The hearts of kings are in the hand of the Lord, and, like the rivulets of water, he turneth them which way soever he will. It is said of Cyrus that he knew not God, nor how to serve him; but God knew him, and how to serve himself by him, Isa. xlv. 4. God governs the world by his influence on the spirits of men, and, whatever good is done at any time, it is God that stirs up the spirit to do it, puts thoughts into the mind, gives to the understanding to form a right judgment, and directs the will which way he pleases. Whatever good offices therefore are, at any time, done for the church of God, he must have the glory of them.

II. The reference it had to the prophecy of Jeremiah, by whom God had not only promised that they should return, but had fixed the time, which set time to favour Sion had now come. Seventy years were determined (Jer. xxv. 12; xxix. 10); and he that kept the promise made concerning Israel's deliverance out of *Egypt to a day* (Exod. xii. 41) was doubtless as punctual to this. What Cyrus now did was long since said to be the *confirming of the word of God's servants,* Isa. xliv. 26. Jeremiah, while he lived, was hated and despised; yet thus did Providence honour him long after, that a mighty monarch was influenced to act in pursuance of the word of the Lord by his mouth.

III. The date of this proclamation. It was in his first year, not the first of his reign over Persia, the kingdom he was born to, but the first of his reign over Babylon, the kingdom he had conquered. Those are much honoured whose spirits are stirred up to begin with God and to serve him in their first years.

IV. The publication of it, both by word of mouth (he *caused a voice to pass throughout all his kingdom,* like a jubilee-trumpet, a joyful sabbatical year after many melancholy ones, proclaiming liberty to the captives), and also in black and white: he put it in writing, that it might be the more satisfactory, and might be sent to those distant provinces where the ten tribes were scattered in Assyria and Media, 2 Kings xvii. 6.

V. The purport of this proclamation of liberty.

1. The preamble shows the causes and considerations by which he was influenced, *v.* 2. It should seem, his mind was enlightened with the knowledge of *Jehovah* (for so he calls him), the God of Israel, as the only *living and true God,* the *God of heaven,* who is the sovereign Lord and disposer of all *the kingdoms of the earth;* of him he says (*v.* 3), *He is the God,* God alone, God above all. Though he had not known God by education, God made him so far to know him now as that he did this service with an eye to him. He professes that he does it, (1.) In gratitude to God for the favours he had bestowed upon him: *The God of heaven has given me all the kingdoms of the earth.* This sounds a little vain-glorious, for there were *many kingdoms of the earth* which he had nothing to do with; but he means that God had given him all that was given to Nebuchadnezzar, whose dominion, Daniel says, was *to the end of the earth,* Dan. iv. 22; v. 19. Note, God is the fountain of power; the kingdoms of the earth are at his disposal; whatever share any have of them they have from him: and those whom God has entrusted with great power and large possessions should look upon themselves as obliged thereby to do much for him. (2.) In obedience to God. He hath *charged me to build him a house at Jerusalem;* probably by a dream or vision of the night, confirmed by comparing it with the prophecy of Isaiah, where his doing it was foretold. Israel's disobedience to God's charge, which they were often told of, is aggravated by the obedience of this heathen king.

2. He gives free leave to all the Jews that were in his dominions to go up to Jerusalem, and to *build the temple of the Lord* there, *v.* 3. His regard to God made him overlook, (1.) The secular interest of his government. It would have been his policy to keep so great a number of serviceable men in his dominions, and seemed impolitic to let them go and take root again in their own land; but piety is the best policy. (2.) The honour of the religion of his country. Why did he not order them to build a temple to the gods of Babylon or Persia? He believed the God of Israel to be the *God of heaven,* and therefore obliged his Israel to worship him only. Let them *walk in the name of the Lord their God.*

3. He subjoins a brief for a collection to bear the charges of such as were poor and not able to bear their own, *v.* 4. "Whosoever remaineth, because he has not the means to bear his charges to Jerusalem, *let the men of his place help him.*" Some take it as an order to the king's officers to supply them out of his revenue, as *ch.* vi. 8. But it may mean a warrant to the captives to ask and receive the alms and charitable contributions of all the king's loving subjects. And we may suppose the Jews had conducted themselves so well among their neighbours that they would be as forward to accommodate them because they loved them as the Egyptians were because they were weary of them. At least many would be kind to them because they saw the government would take it well. Cyrus not only gave his good wishes with those that went (*Their God be with them, v.* 3), but took care also to furnish them with such things as they needed. He took it for granted that those among them who were of ability would offer their *free-will offerings for the house of God,* to promote the rebuilding of it. But, besides that, he would have them supplied out of his kingdom. Well-wishers to the temple should be well-doers for it.

5 Then rose up the chief of the fathers of Judah and Benjamin, and the priests, and the Levites, with all *them* whose spirit God had raised, to go up to build the house of the LORD which *is* in Jerusalem. 6 And all they that *were* about them strengthened their hands with vessels of silver, with gold, with goods, and with beasts, and with precious things, beside all *that* was willingly offered. 7 Also Cyrus the king brought forth the vessels of the house of the LORD, which Nebuchadnezzar had brought forth out of Jerusalem, and had put them in the

house of his gods; 8 Even those did Cyrus king of Persia bring forth by the hand of Mithredath the treasurer, and numbered them unto Sheshbazzar, the prince of Judah. 9 And this *is* the number of them: thirty chargers of gold, a thousand chargers of silver, nine and twenty knives, 10 Thirty basons of gold, silver basons of a second *sort* four hundred and ten, *and* other vessels a thousand. 11 All the vessels of gold and of silver *were* five thousand and four hundred. All *these* did Sheshbazzar bring up with *them of* the captivity that were brought up from Babylon unto Jerusalem.

We are here told,

I. How Cyrus's proclamation succeeded with others. 1. He having given leave to the Jews to go up to Jerusalem, many of them went up accordingly, *v.* 5. The leaders herein were the *chief of the fathers* of Judah and Benjamin, eminent and experienced men, from whom it might justly be expected that, as they were above their brethren in dignity, so they should go before them in duty. The priests and Levites were (as became them) with the first that set their faces again towards Zion. If any good work is to be done, let ministers lead in it. Those that accompanied them were such as God had inclined to go up. The same God that had raised up the spirit of Cyrus to proclaim this liberty raised up their spirits to take the benefit of it; for it was done, *not by might, nor by power, but by the Spirit of the Lord of hosts,* Zech. iv. 6. The temptation perhaps was strong to some of them to stay in Babylon. They had convenient settlements there, had contracted an agreeable acquaintance with the neighbours, and were ready to say, *It is good to be here.* The discouragements of their return were many and great, the journey long, their wives and children unfit for travelling, their own land was to them a strange land, the road to it an unknown road. Go up to Jerusalem! And what should they do there? It was all in ruins, and in the midst of enemies to whom they would be an easy prey. Many were wrought upon by these considerations to stay in Babylon, at least not to go with the first. But there were some that got over these difficulties, that ventured to break the ice, and feared not the lion in the way, the lion in the streets; and they were those whose spirits God raised. He, by his Spirit and grace, filled them with a generous ambition of liberty, a gracious affection to their own land, and a desire of the free and public exercise of their religion. Had God left them to themselves, and to the counsels of flesh and blood, they would have staid in Babylon; but he put it into their hearts to set their faces Zionward, and, as strangers, to ask the way thither (Jer. l. 5); for they, being a new generation, went out like their father Abraham from this land of the Chaldees, not knowing whither they went, Heb. xi. 8. Note, Whatever good we do, it is owing purely to the grace of God, and he raises up our spirits to the doing of it, *works in us both to will and to do.* Our spirits naturally incline to this earth and to the things of it. If they move upwards, in any good affections or good actions, it is God that raises them. The call and offer of the gospel are like Cyrus's proclamation. *Deliverance is preached to the captives,* Luke iv. 18. Those that are bound under the unrighteous dominion of sin, and bound over to the righteous judgment of God, may be made free by Jesus Christ. Whoever will, by repentance and faith, return to God, his duty to God, his happiness in God, Jesus Christ has opened the way for him, and let him go up out of the slavery of sin into the *glorious liberty of the children of God.* The offer is general to all. Christ makes it, in pursuance of the grant which the Father has made him of *all power both in heaven and in earth* (a much greater dominion than that given to Cyrus, *v.* 2) and of the charge given him to *build God a house,* to set him up a church in the world, a kingdom among men, Many that hear this joyful sound choose to sit still in Babylon, are in love with their sins and will not venture upon the difficulties of a holy life; but some there are that break through the discouragements, and resolve to *build the house of God,* to make heaven of their religion, whatever it cost them, and they are those *whose spirit God has raised* above the world and the flesh and whom he has made *willing in the day of his power,* Ps. cx. 3. Thus will the heavenly Canaan be replenished, though many perish in Babylon; and the gospel-offer will not be made in vain. 2. Cyrus having given order that their neighbours should help them, they did so, *v.* 6. All those that were about them furnished them with plate and goods to bear the charges of their journey, and to help them in building and furnishing both their own houses and God's temple. As the tabernacle was made of the spoils of Egypt, and the first temple built by the labours of the strangers, so the second by the contributions of the Chaldeans, all intimating the admission of the Gentiles into the church in due time. God can, where he pleases, incline the hearts of strangers to be kind to his people, and make those to strengthen their hands that have weakened them. *The earth helped the woman. Besides what was willingly offered* by the Jews themselves who staid behind, from a principle of love to God and his house, much was offered, as one may say, unwillingly by the Babylonians, who were influenced to do it by a divine power on their minds of which they themselves could give no account.

II. How this proclamation was seconded by Cyrus himself. To give proof of the sincerity of his affection to the house of God, he not only released the people of God, but restored the vessels of the temple, *v.* 7, 8. Observe here, 1. How careful Providence was of the vessels of the temple, that they were not lost, melted down, or so mixed with other vessels that they could not be known, but that they were all now forthcoming. Such care God has of the living *vessels of mercy, vessels of honour,* of whom it is said (2 Tim. ii. 19, 20), *The Lord knows those that are his,* and they shall *none of them perish.* 2. Though they had been put into an idol's temple, and probably used in the service of idols, yet they were given back, to be used for God. God will recover his own; and the spoil of the strong man armed shall be converted to the use of the conqueror. 3. Judah had a prince, even in captivity. Sheshbazzar, supposed to be the same with Zerubbabel, is here called *prince of Judah;* the Chaldeans called him *Sheshbazzar,* which signifies *joy in tribulation;* but among his own people he went by the name of *Zerubbabel—a stranger in Babylon;* so he looked upon himself, and considered Jerusalem his home, though, as Josephus says, he was captain of the life-guard to the king of Babylon. He took care of the affairs of the Jews, and had some authority over them, probably from the death of Jehoiachin, or Jeconiah, who made him his heir, he being of the house of David. 4. To him the sacred vessels were numbered out (*v.* 8), and he took care for their safe conveyance to Jerusalem, *v.* 11. It would encourage them to build the temple that they had so much rich furniture ready to put into it when it was built. Though God's ordinances, like the vessels of the sanctuary, may be corrupted and profaned by the New-Testament Babylon, they shall, in due time, be restored to their primitive use and intention; for not one jot or tittle of divine institution shall fall to the ground.

CHAP. II.

That many returned out of Babylon upon Cyrus's proclamation we were told in the foregoing chapter; we have here a catalogue of the several families that returned, ver. 1. I. The leaders, ver. 2. II. The people, ver. 3—35. III. The priests, Levites, and retainers to the temple, ver. 36—63. IV. The sum total, with an account of their retinue, ver. 64—67. V. Their offerings to the service of the temple, ver. 68—70.

NOW these *are* the children of the province that went up out of the captivity, of those which had been carried away, whom Nebuchadnezzar the king of Babylon had carried away unto Babylon, and came again unto Jerusalem and Judah, every one unto his city; 2 Which came with Zerubbabel: Jeshua, Nehemiah, Seraiah, Reelaiah, Mordecai, Bilshan, Mizpar, Bigvai, Rehum, Baanah. The number of the men of the people of Israel: 3 The children of Parosh, two thousand a hundred seventy and two. 4 The children of Shephatiah, three hundred seventy and two. 5 The children of Arah, seven hundred seventy and five. 6 The children of Pahath-moab, of the children of Jeshua *and* Joab, two thousand eight hundred and twelve. 7 The children of Elam, a thousand two hundred fifty and four. 8 The children of Zattu, nine hundred forty and five. 9 The children of Zaccai, seven hundred and threescore. 10 The children of Bani, six hundred forty and two. 11 The children of Bebai, six hundred twenty and three. 12 The children of Azgad, a thousand two hundred twenty and two. 13 The children of Adonikam, six hundred sixty and six. 14 The children of Bigvai, two thousand fifty and six. 15 The children of Adin, four hundred fifty and four. 16 The children of Ater of Hezekiah, ninety and eight. 17 The children of Bezai, three hundred twenty and three. 18 The children of Jorah, a hundred and twelve. 19 The children of Hashum, two hundred twenty and three. 20 The children of Gibbar, ninety and five. 21 The children of Beth-lehem, a hundred twenty and three. 22 The men of Netophah, fifty and six. 23 The men of Anathoth, a hundred twenty and eight. 24 The children of Azmaveth, forty and two. 25 The children of Kirjath-arim, Chephirah, and Beeroth, seven hundred and forty and three. 26 The children of Ramah and Gaba, six hundred twenty and one. 27 The men of Michmas, a hundred twenty and two. 28 The men of Beth-el and Ai, two hundred twenty and three. 29 The children of Nebo, fifty and two. 30 The children of Magbish, a hundred fifty and six. 31 The children of the other Elam, a thousand two hundred fifty and four. 32 The children of Harim, three hundred and twenty. 33 The children of Lod, Hadid, and Ono, seven hundred twenty and five. 34 The children of Jericho, three hundred forty and five,

35 The children of Senaah, three thousand and six hundred and thirty.

We may observe here, 1. That an account was kept in writing of the families that came up out of captivity, and the numbers of each family. This was done for their honour, as part of their recompence for their faith and courage, their confidence in God and their affection to their own land, and to stir up others to follow their good example. Those that honour God he will thus honour. The names of all those Israelites indeed that accept the offer of deliverance by Christ shall be found, to their honour, in a more sacred record than this, even in *the Lamb's book of life.* The account that was kept of the families that came up from the captivity was intended also for the benefit of posterity, that they might know from whom they descended and to whom they were allied. 2. That they are called *children of the province.* Judah, which had been an illustrious kingdom, to which other kingdoms had been made provinces, subject to it and dependent on it, was now itself made a province, to receive laws and commissions from the king of Persia and to be accountable to him. See how sin diminishes and debases a nation, which righteousness would exalt. But by thus being made servants (as the patriarchs by being sojourners in a country which was theirs by promise) they were reminded of the *better country, that is, the heavenly* (Heb. xi. 16), a *kingdom which cannot be moved,* or changed into a province. 3. That they are said to come *every one to his city,* that is, the city appointed them, in which appointment an eye, no doubt, was had to their former settlement by Joshua; and to that, as near as might be, they returned: for it does not appear that any others, at least any that were able to oppose them, had possessed them in their absence. 4. That the leaders are first mentioned, *v.* 2. Zerubbabel and Jeshua were their Moses and Aaron, the former their chief prince, the latter their chief priest. Nehemiah and Mordecai are mentioned here; some think not the same with the famous men we afterwards meet with of those names: probably they were the same, but afterwards returned to court for the service of their country. 5. Some of these several families are named from the persons that were their ancestors, others from the places in which they had formerly resided; as with us many surnames are the proper names of persons, others of places. 6. Some little difference there is between the numbers of some of the families here and in Neh. vii., where this catalogue is repeated, which might arise from this, that some who had given in their names at first to come afterwards drew back—said, *I go, Sir, but went not,* which would lessen the number of the families they belonged to; others that declined, at first, *afterwards repented and went,* and so increased the number. 7. Here are two families that are called *the children of Elam* (one *v.* 7, another *v.* 31), and, which is strange, the number of both is the same, 1254. 8. The children of Adonikam, which signifies *a high lord,* were 666, just the *number of the beast* (Rev. xiii. 18), which is there said to be *the number of a man,* which, Mr. Hugh Broughton thinks, has reference to this man. 9. The children of Bethlehem (*v.* 21) were but 123, though it was David's city; for Bethlehem was *little among the thousands of Judah,* yet there must the Messiah arise, Mic. v. 2. 10. Anathoth had been a famous place in the tribe of Benjamin and yet here it numbered but 128 (*v.* 23), which is to be imputed to the divine curse which the men of Anathoth brought upon themselves by persecuting Jeremiah, who was of their city. Jer. xi. 21, 23, *There shall be no remnant of them, for I will bring evil upon the men of Anathoth.* And see Isa. x. 30, *O poor Anathoth!* Nothing brings ruin on a people sooner than persecution.

36 The priests: the children of Jedaiah, of the house of Jeshua, nine hundred seventy and three. 37 The children of Immer, a thousand fifty and two. 38 The children of Pashur, a thousand two hundred forty and seven. 39 The children of Harim, a thousand and seventeen. 40 The Levites: the children of Jeshua and Kadmiel, of the children of Hodaviah, seventy and four. 41 The singers: the children of Asaph, a hundred twenty and eight. 42 The children of the porters: the children of Shallum, the children of Ater, the children of Talmon, the children of Akkub, the children of Hatita, the children of Shobai, *in* all a hundred thirty and nine. 43 The Nethinims: the children of Ziha, the children of Hasupha, the children of Tabbaoth, 44 The children of Keros, the children of Siaha, the children of Padon, 45 The children of Lebanah, the children of Hagabah, the children of Akkub, 46 The children of Hagab, the children of Shalmai, the children of Hanan, 47 The children of Giddel, the children of Gahar, the children of Reaiah, 48 The children of Rezin, the children of Nekoda, the children of Gazzam, 49 The children of Uzza, the children of Paseah, the children of Besai, 50 The children of Asnah, the children of Mehunim, the children of Nephusim, 51 The children of Bakbuk, the child-

ren of Hakupha, the children of Harhur, 52 The children of Bazluth, the children of Mehida, the children of Harsha, 53 The children of Barkos, the children of Sisera, the children of Thamah, 54 The children of Neziah, the children of Hatipha. 55 The children of Solomon's servants: the children of Sotai, the children of Sophereth, the children of Peruda, 56 The children of Jaalah, the children of Darkon, the children of Giddel, 57 The children of Shephatiah, the children of Hattil, the children of Pochereth of Zebaim, the children of Ami. 58 All the Nethinims, and the children of Solomon's servants, *were* three hundred ninety and two. 59 And these *were* they which went up from Tel-melah, Tel-harsa, Cherub, Addan, *and* Immer: but they could not show their father's house, and their seed, whether they *were* of Israel: 60 The children of Delaiah, the children of Tobiah, the children of Nekoda, six hundred fifty and two. 61 And of the children of the priests: the children of Habaiah, the children of Koz, the children of Barzillai: which took a wife of the daughters of Barzillai the Gileadite, and was called after their name: 62 These sought their register *among* those that were reckoned by genealogy, but they were not found: therefore were they, as polluted, put from the priesthood. 63 And the Tirshatha said unto them, that they should not eat of the most holy things, till there stood up a priest with Urim and with Thummim.

Here is an account, I. Of the priests that returned, and they were a considerable number, about a tenth part of the whole company: for the whole were above 42,000 *v.* 64), and four families of priests made up above 4200 (*v.* 36—39); thus was the tenth God's part—a blessed decimation. Three of the fathers of the priests here named were heads of courses, 1 Chron. xxiv. 7, 8, 14. The fourth was Pashur, *v.* 38. If these were of the posterity of that Pashur that abused Jeremiah (Jer. xx. 1), it is strange that so bad a man should have so good a seed, and so numerous.

II. Of the Levites. I cannot but wonder at the small number of them, for, taking in both the singers and the porters (*v.* 40—42), they did not make 350. Time was when the Levites were more forward to their duty than the priests (2 Chron. xxix. 34), but they were not so now. If one place, one family, has the reputation for pious zeal now, another may have it another time. *The wind blows where it listeth,* and shifts its points.

III. Of the Nethinim, who, it is supposed, were the Gibeonites, *given* (so their name signifies) by Joshua first (Josh. ix. 27), and again by David (Ezra viii. 20), when Saul had expelled them, to be employed by the Levites in the work of God's house as hewers of wood and drawers of water; and, with them, of the children of Solomon's servants, whom he gave for the like use (whether they were Jews or Gentiles does not appear) and who are here taken notice of among the retainers of the temple and numbered with the Nethinim, *v.* 55, 58. Note, It is an honour to belong to God's house, though in the meanest office there.

IV. Of some that were looked upon as Israelites by birth, and others as priests, and yet could not make out a clear title to the honour. 1. There were some that could not prove themselves Israelites (*v.* 59, 60), a considerable number, who presumed they were of the seed of Jacob, but could not produce their pedigrees, and yet would go up to Jerusalem, having an affection to the house and people of God. These shamed those who were true-born Israelites, and yet were not called Israelites indeed, *who came out of the waters of Judah* (Isa. xlviii. 1), but had lost the relish of those waters. 2. There were others that could not prove themselves priests, and yet were supposed to be of the seed of Aaron. What is not preserved in black and white will, in all likelihood, be forgotten in a little time. Now we are here told, (1.) How they lost their evidence. One of their ancestors married a daughter of Barzillai, that great man whom we read of in David's time; he gloried in an alliance to that honourable family, and, preferring that before the dignity of his priesthood, would have his children called after Barzillai's family, and their pedigree preserved in the registers of that house, not of the house of Aaron, and so they lost it. In Babylon there was nothing to be got by the priesthood, and therefore they cared not for being akin to it. Those who think their ministry, or their relation to ministers, a diminution or disparagement to them, forget who it was that said, *I magnify my office.* (2.) What they lost with it. It could not be taken for granted that they were priests when they could not produce their proofs, but they were, *as polluted, put from the priesthood.* Now that the priests had recovered their rights, and had the altar to live upon again, they would gladly be looked upon as priests. But they had sold their birthright for the honour of being gentlemen, and therefore were justly degraded, and forbidden to *eat of the most holy things.* Note, Christ will be ashamed of those that are ashamed of him and his service. It was the tirshatha, or governor, that put them under this sequestration, which some understand of Zerubbabel the present governor, others of Nehemiah (who is so called, Neh. viii. 9, x. 1, and who gave this order when he came some years after); but the prohibition was not absolute, it was only a suspension, till there should be a high priest *with Urim and Thummim,* by whom they might know God's mind in this matter. This, it seems, was expected and desired, but it does not appear that ever they were blessed with it under the second temple. They had the canon of the Old Testament complete, which was better than Urim; and, by the want of that oracle, they were taught to expect the Messiah the great Oracle, which the Urim and Thummim was but a type of. Nor does it appear that the second temple had the ark in it, either the old one or a new one. Those shadows by degrees vanished, as the substance approached; and God, by the prophet, intimates to his people that they should sustain no damage by the want of the ark, Jer. iii. 16, 17. *In those days,* when *they shall call Jerusalem the throne of the Lord,* and *all the nations shall be gathered* to it, they shall *say no more, The ark of the covenant of the Lord, neither shall it come to mind,* for they shall do very well without it.

64 The whole congregation together *was* forty and two thousand three hundred *and* threescore, 65 Beside their servants and their maids, of whom *there were* seven thousand three hundred thirty and seven: and *there were* among them two hundred singing men and singing women. 66 Their horses *were* seven hundred thirty and six; their mules, two hundred forty and five; 67 Their camels, four hundred thirty and five; *their* asses, six thousand seven hundred and twenty. 68 And *some* of the chief of the fathers, when they came to the house of the LORD which *is* at Jerusalem, offered freely for the house of God to set it up in his place: 69 They gave after their ability unto the treasure of the work threescore and one thousand drams of gold, and five thousand pound of silver, and one hundred priests' garments. 70 So the priests, and the Levites, and *some* of the people, and the singers, and the porters, and the Nethinims, dwelt in their cities, and all Israel in their cities.

Here is, I. The sum total of the company that returned out of Babylon. The particular sums before mentioned amount not quite to 30,000 (29,818), so that there were above 12,000 that come not into any of those accounts, who, it is probable, were of the rest of the tribes of Israel, besides Judah and Benjamin, that could not tell of what particular family or city they were, but that they were Israelites, and of what tribe. Now, 1. This was more than double the number that were carried captive into Babylon by Nebuchadnezzar, so that, as in Egypt, the time of their affliction was the time of their increase. 2. These were but few to begin a nation with, and yet, by virtue of the old promise made to their fathers, they multiplied so as before their last destruction by the Romans, about 500 years after, to be a very numerous people. When God says, "Increase and multiply," *a little one shall become a thousand.*

II. Their retinue. They were themselves little better than servants, and therefore no wonder that their servants were comparatively but few (*v.* 65) and their beasts of burden about as many, *v.* 66, 67. It was not with them now as in days past. But notice is taken of 200 *singing-men and women* whom they had among them, who, we will suppose, were intended (as those 2 Chron. xxxv. 25) to excite *their mourning,* for it was foretold that they should, upon this occasion, *go weeping* (Jer. l. 4), with ditties of lamentation.

III. Their oblations. It is said (*v.* 68, 69), 1. That they *came to the house of the Lord at Jerusalem;* and yet that house, that holy and beautiful house, was now in ruins, a heap of rubbish. But, like their father Abraham, when the altar was gone they came with devotion to *the place of the altar* (Gen. xiii. 4); and it is the character of the genuine sons of Zion that they favour even *the dust thereof,* Ps. cii. 14. 2. That they offered freely towards the *setting of it up in its place.* That, it seems, was the first house they talked of setting up; and though they came off a journey, and were beginning the world (two chargeable things), yet they offered, and offered freely, towards the building of the temple. Let none complain of the necessary expenses of their religion, but believe that when they come to balance the account they will find that it clears the cost. Their offering was nothing in comparison with the offerings of the princes in David's time; then they offered by talents (1 Chron. xxix. 7), now by drams, yet these drams, being after their ability, were as acceptable to God as those talents, like the widow's two mites. The 61,000 drams of gold amount, by Cumberland's calculation, to so many pounds of our money and so many groats. Every maneh, or pound of silver, he reckons to be sixty shekels (that is, thirty ounces), which we may reckon 7*l.* 10*s.* of our money, so that this 5000 pounds of silver will be above 37,000*l.* of our money. It seems, God had blessed them with an increase of their wealth, as well as of their numbers, in Babylon; and, as God had prospered them, they gave cheerfully to the service of his house. 3. That they *dwelt in their cities, v.* 70. Though their cities were out of repair, yet, because they were their cities, such as God had assigned them, they were content to dwell in them, and were thankful for liberty and property, though they had little of pomp, plenty, or power. Their poverty was a bad cause, but their unity and unanimity were a good effect of it. Here was room enough for them all and all their substance, so that there was no strife among them, but perfect harmony, a blessed presage of their settlement, as their discords in the latter times of that state were of their ruin.

CHAP. III.

In the close of the foregoing chapter we left Israel in their cities, but we may well imagine what a bad posture their affairs were in, the ground untilled, the cities in ruins, all out of order; but here we have an account of the early care they took about the re-establishment of religion among them. Thus did they lay the foundation well, and begin their work at the right end. I. They set up an altar, and offered sacrifices upon it, kept the feasts, and contributed towards the rebuilding of the temple, ver. 1—7. II. They laid the foundation of the temple with a mixture of joy and sorrow, ver. 8—13. This was the day of small things, which was not to be despised, Zech. iv. 10.

AND when the seventh month was come, and the children of Israel *were* in the cities, the people gathered themselves together as one man to Jerusalem. 2 Then stood up Jeshua the son of Jozadak, and his brethren the priests, and Zerubbabel the son of Shealtiel, and his brethren, and builded the altar of the God of Israel, to offer burnt offerings thereon, as *it is* written in the law of Moses the man of God. 3 And they set the altar upon his bases; for fear *was* upon them because of the people of those countries: and they offered burnt offerings thereon unto the LORD, *even* burnt offerings morning and evening. 4 They kept also the feast of tabernacles, as *it is* written, and *offered* the daily burnt offerings by number, according to the custom, as the duty of every day required; 5 And afterward *offered* the continual burnt offering, both of the new moons, and of all the set feasts of the LORD that were consecrated, and of every one that willingly offered a freewill offering unto the LORD. 6 From the first day of the seventh month began they to offer burnt offerings unto the LORD. But the foundation of the temple of the LORD was not *yet* laid. 7 They gave money also unto the masons, and to the carpenters; and meat, and drink, and oil, unto them of Zidon, and to them of Tyre, to bring cedar trees from Lebanon to the sea of Joppa, according to the grant that they had of Cyrus king of Persia.

Here is, I. A general assembly of the returned Israelites at Jerusalem, in the *seventh month, v.* 1. We may suppose that they came from Babylon in the spring, and must allow at least four months for the journey, for so long Ezra and his company were in coming, *ch.* vii. 9. The seventh month therefore soon came, in which many of the feasts of the Lord were to be solemnized; and then they gathered themselves together by agreement among themselves, rather than by the command of authority, to Jerusalem. Though they had newly come to their cities, and had their hands full of business there, to provide necessaries for themselves and their families, which might have excused them from attending on God's altar till the hurry was a little over, as many foolishly put off their coming to the communion till they are settled in the world, yet such was their zeal for religion, now that they had newly come from under correction for their irreligion, that they left all their business in the country, to attend God's altar; and (which is strange) in this pious zeal they were all of a mind, they came *as one man*. Let worldly business be postponed to the business of religion and it will prosper the better.

II. The care which their leading men took to have an altar ready for them to attend upon.

1. Joshua and his brethren the priests, Zerubbabel and his brethren the princes, built *the altar of the God of Israel* (*v.* 2), in the same place (it is likely) where it had stood, upon the same bases, *v.* 3. Bishop Patrick, observing that before the temple was built there seems to have been a tabernacle pitched for the divine service, as was in David's time, not on Mount Moriah, but Mount Sion (1 Chron. ix. 23), supposes that this altar was erected there, to be used while the temple was in building. Let us learn hence, (1.) To *begin with God*. The more difficult and necessitous our case is the more concerned we are to take him along with us in all our ways. If we expect to be directed by his oracles, let him be honoured by our offerings. (2.) To *do what we can* in the worship of God when *we cannot do what we would*. They could not immediately have a temple, but they would not be without an altar. Abraham, wherever he came, *built an altar;* and wherever we come, though we may perhaps want the benefit of the candlestick of preaching, and the showbread of the eucharist, yet, if we bring not the sacrifices of prayer and praise, we are wanting in our duty, for we have an altar that sanctifies the gift ever ready.

2. Observe the reason here given why they hastened to set up the altar: *Fear was upon them, because of the people of the land*. They were in the midst of enemies that bore ill

will to them and their religion, for whom they were an unequal match. And, (1.) *Though* they were so, yet they built the altar (so some read it); they would not be frightened from their religion by the opposition they were likely to meet with in it. Never let the fear of man bring us into this snare. (2.) *Because* they were so, therefore they set up the altar. Apprehension of danger should stir us up to our duty. Have we many enemies? Then it is good to have God our friend and to keep up our correspondence with him. This good use we should make of our fears, we should be driven by them to our knees. Even Saul would think himself undone if the enemy should come upon him before he had made his supplication to God, 1 Sam. xiii. 12.

III. The sacrifices they offered upon the altar. The altar was reared to be used, and they used it accordingly. Let not those that have an altar starve it.

1. They began *on the first day of the seventh month, v.* 6. It does not appear that they had any fire from heaven to begin with, as Moses and Solomon had, but common fire served them, as it did the patriarchs.

2. Having begun, they kept up the *continual burnt-offering* (*v.* 5), *morning and evening, v.* 3. They had known by sad experience what it was to want the comfort of the daily sacrifice to plead in their daily prayers, and now that it was revived they resolved not to let it fall again. The daily lamb typified the Lamb of God, whose righteousness must be our confidence in all our prayers.

3. They observed all the *set feasts of the Lord,* and offered the sacrifices appointed for each, and particularly *the feast of tabernacles, v.* 4, 5. Now that they had received such great mercy from God that joyful feast was in a special manner seasonable. And now that they were beginning to settle in their cities it might serve well to remind them of their fathers dwelling in tents in the wilderness. That feast also which had a peculiar reference to gospel times (as appears, Zech. xiv. 18) was brought, in a special manner, into reputation, now that those times drew on. Of the services of this feast, which continued seven days and had peculiar sacrifices appointed, it is said that they did *as the duty of every day required* (see Num. xxix. 13, 17, &c.), *Verbum diei in die suo—the word, or matter, of the day in its day* (so it is in the original)—a phrase that has become proverbial with those that have used themselves to scripture-language. If the feast of tabernacles was a figure of a gospel conversation, in respect of continual weanedness from the world and joy in God, we may infer that it concerns us all to do the *work of the day in its day, according as the duty of the day requires,* that is, (1.) We must improve time, by finding some business to do every day that will turn to a good account. (2.) We must improve opportunity, by accommodating ourselves to that which is the proper business of the present day. Every thing is beautiful in its season. The tenth day of this month was the day of atonement, a solemn day, and very seasonable now: it is very probable that they observed it, yet it is not mentioned, nor indeed in all the Old Testament do I remember the least mention of the observance of that day; as if it were enough that we have the law of it in Lev. xvi., and the gospel of it, which was the chief intention of it, in the New Testament.

4. They offered *every man's free-will offering, v.* 5. The law required much, but they brought more; for, though they had little wealth to support the expense of their sacrifices, they had much zeal, and, we may suppose, spared at their own tables that they might plentifully supply God's altar. Happy are those that bring with them out of the furnace of affliction such a holy heat as this.

IV. The preparation they made for the building of the temple, *v.* 7. This they applied themselves immediately to; for, while we do what we can, we must still be aiming to do more and better. Tyre and Sidon must now, as of old, furnish them with workmen, and Lebanon with timber, orders for both which they had from Cyrus. What God calls us to we may depend upon his providence to furnish us for.

8 Now in the second year of their coming unto the house of God at Jerusalem, in the second month, began Zerubbabel the son of Shealtiel, and Jeshua the son of Jozadak, and the remnant of their brethren the priests and the Levites, and all they that were come out of the captivity unto Jerusalem; and appointed the Levites, from twenty years old and upward, to set forward the work of the house of the LORD. 9 Then stood Jeshua *with* his sons and his brethren, Kadmiel and his sons, the sons of Judah, together, to set forward the workmen in the house of God: the sons of Henadad, *with* their sons and their brethren the Levites. 10 And when the builders laid the foundation of the temple of the LORD, they set the priests in their apparel with trumpets, and the Levites the sons of Asaph with cymbals, to praise the LORD, after the ordinance of David king of Israel. 11 And they sang together by course in praising and giving thanks unto the LORD; because *he is* good, for his mercy *endureth* for ever toward Israel. And all the people shouted with a great

shout, when they praised the LORD, because the foundation of the house of the LORD was laid. 12 But many of the priests and Levites and chief of the fathers, *who were* ancient men, that had seen the first house, when the foundation of this house was laid before their eyes, wept with a loud voice; and many shouted aloud for joy: 13 So that the people could not discern the noise of the shout of joy from the noise of the weeping of the people: for the people shouted with a loud shout, and the noise was heard afar off.

There was no dispute among the returned Jews whether they should build the temple or no; that was immediately resolved on, and that it should be done with all speed; what comfort could they take in their own land if they had not that token of God's presence with them and the record of his name among them? We have here therefore an account of the beginning of that good work. Observe,

I. When it was begun—in the second month of the second year, as soon as ever the season of the year would permit (*v.* 8), and when they had ended the solemnities of the passover. They took little more than half a year for making preparation of the ground and materials; so much were their hearts upon it. Note, When any good work is to be done it will be our wisdom to set about it quickly, and not to lose time, yea, though we foresee difficulty and opposition in it. Thus we engage ourselves to it, and engage God for us. Well begun (we say) is half ended.

II. Who began it—Zerubbabel, and Jeshua, and their brethren. Then the work of God is likely to go on well when magistrates, ministers, and people, are hearty for it, and agree in their places to promote it. It was God that gave them one heart for this service, and it boded well.

III. Who were employed to further it. They appointed the *Levites to set forward the work* (*v.* 8), and they did it by *setting forward the workmen* (*v.* 9), and strengthening their hands with good and comfortable words. Note, Those that do not work themselves may yet do good service by quickening and encouraging those that do work.

IV. How God was praised at the laying of the foundation of the temple (*v.* 10, 11); the priests with the trumpets appointed by Moses, and the Levites with the cymbals appointed by David, made up a concert of music, not to please the ear, but to assist the singing of that everlasting hymn which will never be out of date, and to which our tongues should never be out of tune, *God is good, and his mercy endureth for ever,* the burden of Ps. cxxxvi. Let all the streams of mercy be traced up to the fountain. Whatever our condition is, how many soever our griefs and fears, let it be owned that God is good; and, whatever fails, that his mercy fails not. Let this be sung with application, as here; not only his mercy endures for ever, but it endures for ever towards Israel, Israel when captives in a strange land and strangers in their own land. However it be, yet *God is good to Israel* (Ps. lxxiii. 1), good to us. Let the reviving of the church's interests, when they seemed dead, be ascribed to the continuance of God's mercy for ever, for therefore the church continues.

V. How the people were affected. A remarkable mixture of various affections there was upon this occasion. Different sentiments there were among the people of God, and each expressed himself according to his sentiments, and yet there was no disagreement among them, their minds were not alienated from each other nor the common concern retarded by it. 1. Those that only knew the misery of having no temple at all praised the Lord with shouts of joy when they saw but the foundation of one laid, *v.* 11. To them even this foundation seemed great, and was as life from the dead; to their hungry souls even this was sweet. They shouted, so that *the noise was heard afar off.* Note, We ought to be thankful for the beginnings of mercy, though we have not yet come to the perfection of it; and the foundations of a temple, after long desolations, cannot but be fountains of joy to every faithful Israelite. 2. Those that remembered the glory of the first temple which Solomon built, and considered how far this was likely to be inferior to that, perhaps in dimensions, certainly in magnificence and sumptuousness, *wept with a loud voice, v.* 12. If we date the captivity with the first, from the fourth of Jehoiakim, it was about fifty-two years since the temple was burnt; if from Jeconiah's captivity, it was but fifty-nine. So that many now alive might remember it standing; and a great mercy it was to the captives that they had the lives of so many of their priests and Levites lengthened out, who could tell them what they themselves remembered of the glory of Jerusalem, to quicken them in their return. These lamented the disproportion between this temple and the former. And, (1.) There was some reason for it; and if they turned their tears into the right channel, and bewailed the sin that was the cause of this melancholy change, they did well. Sin sullies the glory of any church or people, and, when they find themselves diminished and brought low, that must bear the blame. (2.) Yet it was their infirmity to mingle those tears with the common joys and so to cast a damp upon them. They *despised the day of small things,* and were unthankful for the good they enjoyed, because it was not so much as their ancestors had, though it was much more than they deserved. In the harmony of public joys, let not us be jarring strings. It was an aggravation of the discouragement they hereby gave to the people that they were priests and Levites, who should have known and taught others how to be duly affected under various providences, and not to let the remembrance of former afflictions drown the sense of present mercies. This mixture of sorrow and joy here is a representation of this world. Some are bathing in rivers of joy, while others are drowned in floods of tears. In heaven all are singing, and none sighing; in hell all are weeping and wailing, and none rejoicing; but here on earth we can scarcely *discern the shouts of joy from the noise of the weeping.* Let us learn to *rejoice with those that do rejoice* and *weep with those that weep*, and ourselves to rejoice as though we rejoiced not, and weep as though we wept not.

CHAP. IV

The good work of rebuilding the temple was no sooner begun than it met with opposition from those that bore ill will to it; the Samaritans were enemies to the Jews and their religion, and they set themselves to obstruct it. I. They offered to be partners in the building of it, that they might have it in their power to retard it; but they were refused, ver. 1—3. II. They discouraged them in it, and dissuaded them from it, ver. 4, 5. III. They basely misrepresented the undertaking, and the undertakers, to the king of Persia, by a memorial they sent him, ver. 6—16. IV. They obtained from him an order to stop the building (ver. 17—22), which they immediately put in execution, ver. 23, 24.

NOW when the adversaries of Judah and Benjamin heard that the children of the captivity builded the temple unto the LORD God of Israel; 2 Then they came to Zerubbabel, and to the chief of the fathers, and said unto them, Let us build with you; for we seek your God, as ye *do;* and we do sacrifice unto him since the days of Esar-haddon king of Assur, which brought us up hither. 3 But Zerubbabel, and Jeshua, and the rest of the chief of the fathers of Israel, said unto them, Ye have nothing to do with us to build a house unto our God: but we ourselves together will build unto the LORD God of Israel, as king Cyrus the king of Persia hath commanded us. 4 Then the people of the land weakened the hands of the people of Judah, and troubled them in building, 5 And hired counsellors against them, to frustrate their purpose, all the days of Cyrus king of Persia, even until the reign of Darius king of Persia.

We have here an instance of the old enmity that was put between the seed of the woman and the seed of the serpent. God's temple cannot be built, but Satan will rage, and the *gates of hell* will *fight against it*. The gospel kingdom was, in like manner, to be set up with much struggling and contention. In this respect the glory of the latter house was greater than the glory of the former, and it was more a figure of the temple of Christ's church, in that Solomon built his temple when there was *no adversary nor evil occurrent*, (1 Kings v. 4); but this second temple was built notwithstanding great opposition, in the removing and conquering of which, and the bringing of the work to perfection at last in spite of it, the wisdom, power, and goodness of God were much glorified, and the church was encouraged to trust in him.

I. The undertakers are here called the *children of the captivity* (v. 1), which makes them look very little. They had newly come out of captivity, were born in captivity, had still the marks of their captivity upon them; though they were not now captives, they were under the control of those whose captives they had lately been. Israel was God's son, his first-born; but by their iniquity the people sold and enslaved themselves, and so became children of the captivity. But, it should seem, the thought of their being so quickened them to this work, for it was by their neglect of the temple that they lost their freedom.

II. The opposers of the undertaking are here said to be *the adversaries of Judah and Benjamin,* not the Chaldeans or Persians (they gave them no disturbance—"let them build and welcome"), but the relics of the ten tribes, and the foreigners that had joined themselves to them, and patched up that mongrel religion we had an account of, 2 Kings xvii. 33. *They feared the Lord, and served their own gods too.* They are called *the people of the land, v.* 4. The worst enemies Judah and Benjamin had were those that *said they were Jews and were not,* Rev. iii. 9.

III. The opposition they gave had in it much of the subtlety of the old serpent. When they heard that the temple was in building they were immediately aware that it would be a fatal blow to their superstition, and set themselves to oppose it. They had not power to do it forcibly, but they tried all the ways they could to do it effectually.

1. They offered their service to build with the Israelites only that thereby they might get an opportunity to retard the work, while they pretended to further it. Now, (1.) Their offer was plausible enough, and looked kind: "*We will build with you,* will help you to contrive, and will contribute towards the expense; *for we seek your God as you do,*" *v.* 2. This was false, for, though they sought the same God, they did not seek him only, nor seek him in the way he appointed, and therefore did not seek him as they did. Herein they designed, if it were possible, to hinder the building of it, at least to hinder their comfortable enjoyment of it; as good almost not have it as not have it to them-

selves, for the pure worship of the true God and him only. Thus are the *kisses of an enemy deceitful;* his words are smoother than butter when war is in his heart. But, (2.) The refusal of their proffered service was very just, *v.* 3. *The chief of the fathers of Israel* were soon aware that they meant them no kindness, whatever they pretended, but really designed to do them a mischief, and therefore (though they had need enough of help if it had been such as they could confide in) told them plainly, "*You have nothing to do with us,* have no part nor lot in this matter, are not true-born Israelites nor faithful worshippers of God; *you worship you know not what,* John iv. 22. You are none of those with whom we dare hold communion, and therefore we ourselves will build it." They plead not to them the law of their God, which forbade them to mingle with strangers (though that especially they had an eye to), but that which they would take more notice of, the king's commission, which was directed to them only: "The king of Persia has commanded us to build this house, and we shall distrust and affront him if we call in foreign aid." Note, In doing good there is need of the *wisdom of the serpent,* as well as the *innocency of the dove,* and we have need, as it follows there, to *beware of men,* Matt. x. 16, 17. We should carefully consider with whom we are associated and on whose hand we lean. While we trust God with a pious confidence we must trust men with a prudent jealousy and caution.

2. When this plot failed they did what they could to divert them from the work and discourage them in it. They weakened their hands by telling them it was in vain to attempt it, calling them *foolish builders,* who began what they were not able to finish, and by their insinuations troubled them, and made them drive heavily in the work. All were not alike zealous in it. Those that were cool and indifferent were by these artifices drawn off from the work, which wanted their help, *v.* 4. And because what they themselves said the Jews would suspect to be ill meant, and not be influenced by, they, underhand, *hired counsellors against them,* who, pretending to advise them for the best, should dissuade them from proceeding, and so *frustrate their purpose* (*v.* 5), or dissuade the men of Tyre and Sidon from furnishing them with the timber they had bargained for (*ch.* iii. 7); or whatever business they had at the Persian court, to solicit for any particular grants or favours, pursuant to the general edict for their liberty, there were those that were hired and lay ready to appear of counsel against them. Wonder not at the restlessness of the church's enemies in their attempts against the building of God's temple. He whom they serve, and whose work they are doing, is *unwearied* in *walking to and fro through the earth* to do mischief. And let those who discourage a good work, and weaken the hands of those that are employed in it, see whose pattern they follow.

6 And in the reign of Ahasuerus, in the beginning of his reign, wrote they *unto him* an accusation against the inhabitants of Judah and Jerusalem. 7 And in the days of Artaxerxes wrote Bishlam, Mithredath, Tabeel, and the rest of their companions, unto Artaxerxes king of Persia; and the writing of the letter *was* written in the Syrian tongue, and interpreted in the Syrian tongue. 8 Rehum the chancellor and Shimshai the scribe wrote a letter against Jerusalem to Artaxerxes the king in this sort: 9 Then *wrote* Rehum the chancellor, and Shimshai the scribe, and the rest of their companions; the Dinaites, the Apharsathchites, the Tarpelites, the Apharsites, the Archevites, the Babylonians, the Susanchites, the Dehavites, *and* the Elamites, 10 And the rest of the nations whom the great and noble Asnapper brought over, and set in the cities of Samaria, and the rest *that are* on this side the river, and at such a time. 11 This *is* the copy of the letter that they sent unto him, *even* unto Artaxerxes the king; Thy servants the men on this side the river, and at such a time. 12 Be it known unto the king, that the Jews which came up from thee to us are come unto Jerusalem, building the rebellious and the bad city, and have set up the walls *thereof,* and joined the foundations. 13 Be it known now unto the king, that, if this city be builded, and the walls set up *again, then* will they not pay toll, tribute, and custom, and *so* thou shalt endamage the revenue of the kings. 14 Now because we have maintenance from *the king's* palace, and it was not meet for us to see the king's dishonour, therefore have we sent and certified the king; 15 That search may be made in the book of the records of thy fathers: so shalt thou find in the book of the records, and know that this city *is* a rebellious city, and hurtful unto kings and provinces, and that they have moved sedition within the

same of old time: for which cause was this city destroyed. 16 We certify the king that, if this city be builded *again,* and the walls thereof set up, by this means thou shalt have no portion on this side the river.

Cyrus stedfastly adhered to the Jews' interest, and supported his own grant. It was to no purpose to offer any thing to him in prejudice of it. What he did was from a good principle, and in the fear of God, and therefore he adhered to it. But, though his reign in all was thirty years, yet after the conquest of Babylon, and his decree for the release of the Jews, some think that he reigned but three years, others seven, and then either died or gave up that part of his government, in which his successor was Ahasuerus (*v.* 6), called also *Artaxerxes* (*v.* 7), supposed to be the same that in heathen authors is called *Cambyses,* who had never taken such cognizance of the despised Jews as to concern himself for them, nor had he that knowledge of the God of Israel which his predecessor had. To him these Samaritans applied by letter for an order to stop the building of the temple; and they did it in the beginning of his reign, being resolved to lose no time when they thought they had a king for their purpose. See how watchful the church's enemies are to take the first opportunity of doing it a mischief; let not its friends be less careful to do it a kindness. Here is,

I. The general purport of the letter which they sent to the king, to inform him of this matter. It is called (*v.* 6) *an accusation against the inhabitants of Judah and Jerusalem.* The devil is the *accuser of the brethren* (Rev. xii. 10), and he carries on his malicious designs against them, not only by accusing them himself before God, as he did Job, but by acting as a lying spirit in the mouths of his instruments, whom he employs to accuse them before magistrates and kings and to make them odious to the many and obnoxious to the mighty. Marvel not if the same arts be still used to depreciate serious godliness.

II. The persons concerned in writing this letter. The contrivers are named (*v.* 7) that plotted the thing, the writers (*v.* 8) that put it into form, and the subscribers (*v.* 9) that concurred in it and joined with them in this representation, this misrepresentation I should call it. Now see here, 1. How the *rulers take counsel together against the Lord* and his temple, with their companions. The building of the temple would do them no harm, yet they appear against it with the utmost concern and virulence, perhaps because the prophets of the God of Israel had foretold the *famishing* and *perishing* of all the *gods of the heathen,* Zeph. ii. 11; Jer. x. 11. 2. How the people concurred with them in imagining this vain thing. They followed the cry, though ignorant of the merits of the cause. All the several colonies of that plantation (nine are here mentioned), who had their denomination from the cities or countries of Assyria, Chaldea, Persia, &c., whence they came, set their hands, by their representatives, to this letter. Perhaps they were incensed against these returned Jews because many of the ten tribes were among them, whose estates they had got into their possession, and of whom they were therefore jealous, lest they should attempt the recovery of them hereafter.

III. A copy of the letter itself, which Ezra inserts here out of the records of the kingdom of Persia, into which it had been entered; and it is well we have it, that we may see whence the like methods, still taken to expose good people and baffle good designs, are copied.

1. They represent themselves as very loyal to the government, and greatly concerned for the honour and interest of it, and would have it thought that the king had no such loving faithful subjects in all his dominions as they were, none so sensible of their obligations to him, *v.* 14. *Because we are salted with the salt of the palace* (so it is in the *margin*), "we have our salary from the court, and could no more live without it than flesh could be preserved without salt; or, as some think, their pay or pension was sent them in salt; or "Because we had our education in the palace, and were brought up at the king's table," as we find, Dan. i. 5. These were those whom he intended to prefer; they did *eat their portion of the king's meat.* "Now, in consideration of this, *it is not meet for us to see the king's dishonour;*" and therefore they urge him to stop the building of the temple, which would certainly be the king's dishonour more than any thing else. Note, A secret enmity to Christ and his gospel is often gilded over with a pretended affection to Cæsar and his power. The Jews hated the Roman government, and yet, to serve a turn, could cry, *We have no king but Cæsar.* But (to allude to this), if those that lived upon the crown thought themselves bound in gratitude thus to support the interest of it, much more reason have we thus to argue ourselves into a pious concern for God's honour; *we have our maintenance from the God of heaven* and are *salted with his salt,* live upon his bounty and are the care of his providence; and therefore it is not *meet for us to see his dishonour* without resenting it and doing what we can to prevent it.

2. They represent the Jews as disloyal, and dangerous to the government, that Jerusalem was *the rebellious and bad city* (*v.* 12), *hurtful to kings and provinces, v.* 15. See how Jerusalem, *the joy of the whole earth* (Ps. xlviii. 2), is here reproached as the scandal of the whole earth. The enemies of the church could not do the bad things they design against it if they did not first give it a bad name. Jerusalem had been a loyal city to its rightful princes, and its present inha-

bitants were as well affected to the king and his government as any of his provinces whatsoever. Daniel, who was a Jew, had lately approved himself so faithful to his prince that his worst enemies could find no fault in his management, Dan. vi. 4. But thus was Elijah most unjustly charged with troubling Israel, the apostles with *turning the world upside down*, and Christ himself with *perverting the nation* and *forbidding to give tribute to Cæsar;* and we must not think it strange if the same game be still played. Now here,

(1.) Their history of what was past was invidious, that *within this city sedition had been moved of old time,* and, for *that cause, it was destroyed, v.* 15. It cannot be denied but that there was some colour given for this suggestion by the attempts of Jehoiakim and Zedekiah to shake off the yoke of the king of Babylon, which, if they had kept close to their religion and the temple they were now rebuilding, they would never have come under. But it must be considered, [1.] That they were themselves, and their ancestors, sovereign princes, and their efforts to recover their rights, if there had not been in them the violation of an oath, for aught I know, would have been justifiable, and successful too, had they taken the right method and made their peace with God first. [2.] Though these Jews, and their princes, had been guilty of rebellion, yet it was unjust therefore to fasten this as an indelible brand upon this city, as if that must for ever after go under the name of *the rebellious and bad city.* The Jews, in their captivity, had given such specimens of good behaviour as were sufficient, with any reasonable men, to roll away that one reproach; for they were instructed (and we have reason to hope that they observed their instructions) to *seek the peace of the city where* they were *captives* and *pray to the Lord for it,* Jer. xxix. 7. It was therefore very unfair, though not uncommon, thus to impute the iniquity of the fathers to the children.

(2.) Their information concerning what was now doing was grossly false in matter of fact. Very careful they were to inform the king that the Jews had *set up the walls of this city,* nay, had *finished* them (so it is in the *margin*) and *joined the foundations* (*v.* 12), when this was far from being the case. They had only begun to build the temple, which Cyrus commanded them to do, but, as for the walls, there was nothing done nor designed towards the repair of them, as appears by the condition they were in many years after (Neh. i. 3), all in ruins. *What shall be given,* and what *done, to these false tongues,* nay, which is worse, these false pens? *sharp arrows,* doubtless, *of the mighty,* and *coals of juniper,* Ps. cxx. 3, 4. If they had not been perfectly lost to all virtue and honour they would not, and if they had not been very secure of the king's countenance they durst not, have written that to the king which all their neighbours knew to be a notorious lie. See Prov. xxix. 12.

(3.) Their prognostics of the consequences were altogether groundless and absurd. They were very confident, and would have the king believe it upon their word, that if this city should be built, not only the Jews would *pay no toll, tribute, or custom* (*v.* 13), but (since a great lie is as soon spoken as a little one) that the king would have no portion at all on this side the river (*v.* 16), that all the countries on this side Euphrates would instantly revolt, drawn in to do so by their example; and, if the prince in possession should connive at this, he would wrong, not only himself, but his successors: *Thou shalt endamage the revenue of the kings.* See how every line in this letter breathes both the subtlety and malice of the old serpent.

17 *Then* sent the king an answer unto Rehum the chancellor, and *to* Shimshai the scribe, and *to* the rest of their companions that dwell in Samaria, and *unto* the rest beyond the river, Peace, and at such a time. 18 The letter which ye sent unto us hath been plainly read before me. 19 And I commanded, and search hath been made, and it is found that this city of old time hath made insurrection against kings, and *that* rebellion and sedition have been made therein. 20 There have been mighty kings also over Jerusalem, which have ruled over all *countries* beyond the river; and toll, tribute, and custom, was paid unto them. 21 Give ye now commandment to cause these men to cease, and that this city be not builded, until *another* commandment shall be given from me. 22 Take heed now that ye fail not to do this: why should damage grow to the hurt of the kings? 23 Now when the copy of king Artaxerxes' letter *was* read before Rehum, and Shimshai the scribe, and their companions, they went up in haste to Jerusalem unto the Jews, and made them to cease by force and power. 24 Then ceased the work of the house of God which *is* at Jerusalem. So it ceased unto the second year of the reign of Darius king of Persia.

Here we have,

I. The orders which the king of Persia gave, in answer to the information sent him by the Samaritans against the Jews. He suffered himself to be imposed upon by their fraud and falsehood, took no care to examine the allegations of their petition concerning that which the Jews were now doing, but took it for granted that the charge was true, and was very willing to gratify them with an order of council to stay proceedings. 1. He consulted the records concerning Jerusalem, and found that it had indeed rebelled against the king of Babylon, and therefore that it was, as they called it, a *bad city* (*v.* 19), and withal that in times past kings had reigned there, to whom all the countries on that side the river had been tributaries (*v.* 20), and that therefore there was danger that if ever they were able (which they were never likely to be) they would claim them again. Thus he says as they said, and pretends to give a reason for so doing. See the hard fate of princes, who must see and hear with other men's eyes and ears, and give judgment upon things as they are represented to them, though often represented falsely. God's judgment is always just because he sees things as they are, and it is according to truth. 2. He appointed these Samaritans to stop the building of the city immediately, till further orders should be given about it, *v.* 21, 22. Neither they, in their letter, nor he, in his order, make any mention of the temple, and the building of that, because both they and he knew that they had not only a permission, but a command, from Cyrus to rebuild that, which even these Samaritans had not the confidence to move for the repeal of. They spoke only of the *city:* "Let not *that* be built," that is, as a city with walls and gates; "whatever you do, prevent *that, lest damage grow to the hurt of the kings:*" he would not that the crown should lose by his wearing it.

II. The use which the enemies of the Jews made of these orders, so fraudulently obtained; upon the receipt of them they went up *in haste to Jerusalem, v.* 23. *Their feet ran to evil*, Prov. i. 16. They were impatient till the builders were served with this prohibition, which they produced as their warrant to *make them cease by force and power*. As they abused the king in obtaining this order by their mis-informations, so they abused him in the execution of it; for the order was only to prevent the walling of the *city*, but, having force and power on their side, they construed it as relating to the *temple,* for it was that to which they had an ill will, and which they only wanted some colour to hinder the building of. There was indeed a general clause in the order, to *cause these men to cease*, which had reference to their complaint about building the walls; but they applied it to the building of the temple. See what need we have to pray, not only for kings, but for all in authority under them, and *the governors sent by them,* because the *quietness* and *peaceableness* of our lives, *in all godliness and honesty*, depend very much upon the integrity and wisdom of inferior magistrates, as well as the supreme. The consequence was that *the work of the house of God ceased* for a time, through the power and insolence of its enemies; and so, through the coldness and indifference of its friends, it stood still till the second year of Darius Hystaspes, for to me it seems clear by the thread of this sacred history that it was that Darius, *v.* 24. Though now a stop was put to it by the violence of the Samaritans, yet that they might soon after have gone on by connivance, if they had had a due affection to the work, appears by this, that before they had that express warrant from the king for doing it (*ch.* vi.) they were reproved by the prophets for not doing it, *ch.* v. 1, compared with Hag. i. 1, &c. If they had taken due care to inform Cambyses of the truth of this case, perhaps he would have recalled his order; but, for aught I know, some of the builders were almost as willing it should cease as the adversaries themselves were. At some periods the church has suffered more by the coldness of its friends than by the heat of its enemies; but both together commonly make church-work slow work.

CHAP. V.

We left the temple-work at a full stop; but, being God's work, it shall be revived, and here we have an account of the reviving of it. It was hindered by might and power, but it was set a-going again "by the Spirit of the Lord of hosts." Now here we are told how that blessed Spirit, I. Warmed its cool-hearted friends, and excited them to build, ver. 1, 2. II. Cooled its hot-headed enemies, and brought them to better tempers; for, though they secretly disliked the work as much as those in the foregoing chapter, yet, 1. They were more mild towards the builders, ver. 3—5. 2. They were more fair in their representation of the matter to the king, of which we have here an account, ver. 6—17.

THEN the prophets, Haggai the prophet, and Zechariah the son of Iddo, prophesied unto the Jews that *were* in Judah and Jerusalem in the name of the God of Israel, *even* unto them. 2 Then rose up Zerubbabel the son of Shealtiel, and Jeshua the son of Jozadak, and began to build the house of God which *is* at Jerusalem: and with them *were* the prophets of God helping them.

Some reckon that the building of the temple was suspended for only nine years; I am willing to believe that fifteen years were the utmost. During this time they had an altar and a tabernacle, which no doubt they made use of. When we cannot do what we would we must do what we can in the service of God, and be sorry we can do no better. But the counsellors that were hired to hinder the work (*ch.* iv. 5) told them, and perhaps with a pretence to inspiration, that the time had not come for the building of the temple (Hag. i. 2); urging that it was long ere the time came for the building of Solomon's temple; and thus the people were made easy in their own *ceiled houses,* while *God's house lay waste.* Now here we are told how life was put into that good cause which seemed to lie dead.

I. They had two good ministers, who, in God's name, earnestly persuaded them to put the wheel of business in motion again. Observe,

1. Who these ministers were, namely, the prophets Haggai and Zechariah, who both began to prophesy in the second year of Darius, as appears, Hag. i. 1; Zech. i. 1. Note, (1.) The temple of God among men is to be built by prophecy, not by secular force (that often hinders it, but seldom furthers it), but by *the word of God.* As the *weapons of our warfare,* so the instruments of our building, *are not carnal,* but *spiritual,* and they are the ministers of the gospel that are the master-builders. (2.) It is the business of God's prophets to stir up God's people to that which is good, and to help them in it, to strengthen their hands, and, by suitable considerations fetched from the word of God, to quicken them to their duty and encourage them in it. (3.) It is a sign that God has mercy in store for a people when he raises up prophets among them to be their helpers in the way and work of God, their guides, overseers, and rulers.

2. To whom they were sent. They prophesied unto the *Jews* (for, as to them pertained the giving of the law, so also the gift of prophecy, and therefore they are called *the children of the prophets,* Acts iii. 25, because they were educated under their tuition and instruction), *even unto them, upon them,* even *upon them* (so it is in the original), as Ezekiel prophesied *upon the dry bones,* that they might live, Ezek. xxxvii. 4. They prophesied *against* them (so bishop Patrick), for they reproved them because they did not build the temple. The word of God, if it be not received now as a testimony to us, will be received another day as a testimony against us, and will judge us.

3. Who sent them. They prophesied in the name, or (as some read it) *in the cause,* or for the sake, *of the God of Israel;* they spoke by commission from him, and argued from his authority over them, his interest in them, and the concern of his glory among them.

II. They had two good magistrates, who were forward and active in this work. Zerubbabel their chief prince, and Jeshua their chief priest, *v.* 2. Those that are in places of dignity and power ought with their dignity to put honour upon and with their power to put life into every good work: thus it becomes those that precede, and those that preside, with an exemplary care and zeal to *fulfil all righteousness* and to *go before in a good work.* These great men thought it no disparagement to them, but a happiness, to be taught and prescribed to by the prophets of the Lord, and were glad of their help in reviving this good work. Read the first chapter of the prophecy of Haggai here (for that is the best comment on these two verses) and see what great things God does by his word, which he magnifies above all his name, and by his Spirit working with it.

3 At the same time came to them Tatnai, governor on this side the river, and Shethar-boznai, and their companions, and said thus unto them, Who hath commanded you to build this house, and to make up this wall? 4 Then said we unto them after this manner, What are the names of the men that make this building? 5 But the eye of their God was upon the elders of the Jews, that they could not cause them to cease, till the matter came to Darius: and then they returned answer by letter concerning this *matter.* 6 The copy of the letter that Tatnai, governor on this side the river, and Shethar-boznai, and his companions the Apharsachites, which *were* on this side the river, sent unto Darius the king: 7 They sent a letter unto him, wherein was written thus; Unto Darius the king, all peace. 8 Be it known unto the king, that we went into the province of Judea, to the house of the great God, which is builded with great stones, and timber is laid in the walls, and this work goeth fast on, and prospereth in their hands. 9 Then asked we those elders, *and* said unto them thus, Who commanded you to build this house, and to make up these walls? 10 We asked their names also, to certify thee, that we might write the names of the men that *were* the chief of them. 11 And thus they returned us answer, saying, We are the servants of the God of heaven and earth, and build the house that was builded these many years ago, which a great king of Israel builded and set up. 12 But after that our fathers had provoked the God of heaven unto wrath, he gave them into the hand of Nebuchadnezzar the king of Babylon, the Chaldean, who destroyed this house, and carried the people away into Babylon. 13 But in the first year of Cyrus the king of Babylon *the same* king Cyrus made a decree to build this house of God. 14 And the vessels also of gold and silver of the house of God, which Nebuchadnezzar took out of the temple that *was* in Jerusalem, and brought them into the

temple of Babylon, those did Cyrus the king take out of the temple of Babylon, and they were delivered unto *one,* whose name *was* Sheshbazzar, whom he had made governor; 15 And said unto him, Take these vessels, go, carry them into the temple that *is* in Jerusalem, and let the house of God be builded in his place. 16 Then came the same Sheshbazzar, *and* laid the foundation of the house of God which *is* in Jerusalem: and since that time even until now hath it been in building, and *yet* it is not finished. 17 Now therefore, if *it seem* good to the king, let there be search made in the king's treasure house, which *is* there at Babylon, whether it be *so,* that a decree was made of Cyrus the king to build this house of God at Jerusalem, and let the king send his pleasure to us concerning this matter.

We have here, I. The cognizance which their neighbours soon took of the reviving of this good work. A jealous eye, it seems, they had upon them, and no sooner did the Spirit of God stir up the friends of the temple to appear for it than the evil spirit stirred up its enemies to appear against it. While the people built and ceiled their own houses their enemies gave them no molestation (Hag. i. 4), though the king's order was to put a stop to the building of the city (*ch.* iv. 21); but when they fell to work again at the temple then the alarm was taken, and all heads were at work to hinder them, *v.* 3, 4. The adversaries are here named: *Tatnai* and *Shethar-boznai.* The governors we read of (*ch.* iv.) were, it is probable, displaced at the beginning of this reign, as is usual. It is the policy of princes often to change their deputies, proconsuls, and rulers of provinces. These, though real enemies to the building of the temple, were men of better temper than the other, and made some conscience of telling truth. If *all men have not faith* (2 Thess. iii. 2), it is well some have, and a sense of honour. The church's enemies are not all equally wicked and unreasonable. The historian begins to relate what passed between the builders and those inquisitors (*v.* 3, 4), but breaks off his account, and refers to the ensuing copy of the letter they sent to the king, where the same appears more fully and at large, which he began to abridge (*v.* 4), or make an extract out of, though, upon second thoughts, he inserted the whole.

II. The care which the divine Providence took of this good work (*v.* 5): *The eye of their God was upon the elders of the Jews,* who were active in the work, so that their enemies could not cause them to cease, as they would have done, till the matter came to Darius. They desired they would only cease till they had instructions from the king about it. But they would not so much as yield them that, for *the eye of God was upon them,* even their God. And, 1. That baffled their enemies, infatuated and enfeebled them, and protected the builders from their malicious designs. While we are employed in God's work we are taken under his special protection; his eye is upon us for good, seven eyes upon one stone in his temple; see Zech. iii. 9; iv. 10. 2. That quickened them. The elders of the Jews saw *the eye of God upon them,* to observe what they did and own them in what they did well, and then they had courage enough to face their enemies and to go on vigorously with their work, notwithstanding all the opposition they met with. Our eye upon God, observing his eye upon us, will keep us to our duty and encourage us in it when the difficulties are ever so discouraging.

III. The account they sent to the king of this matter, in which we may observe,

1. How fully the elders of the Jews gave the Samaritans an account of their proceedings. They, finding them both busy and prosperous, that all hands were at work to run up this building and that it went on rapidly, put these questions to them:—"By what authority do you do these things, and who gave you that authority? Who set you to work? Have you that which will bear you out?" To this they answered that they had sufficient warrant to do what they did; for, (1.) "*We are the servants of the God of heaven and earth.* The God we worship is not a local deity, and therefore we cannot be charged with making a faction, or setting up a sect, in building this temple to his honour: but we pay our homage to a God on whom the whole creation depends, and therefore ought to be protected and assisted by all and hindered by none." It is the wisdom as well as duty of kings to countenance the servants of the *God of heaven.* (2.) "We have a prescription to this house; it was built for the honour of our God by Solomon many ages ago. It is no novel invention of our own; we are but *raising the foundations of many generations,*" Isa. lviii. 12. (3.) "It was to punish us for our sins that we were, for a time, put out of the possession of this house; not because the gods of the nations had prevailed against our God, but because we had provoked him (*v.* 12), for which he delivered us and our temple into the hands of the king of Babylon, but never intended thereby to put a final period to our religion. We were only suspended for a time, not deprived for ever." (4.) "We have the royal decree of Cyrus to justify us and bear us out in what we do. He not only permitted and allowed us, but charged and commanded us to build this house (*v.* 13), and to build it in its place (*v.* 15), the same place where it had

stood before." He ordered this, not only in compassion to the Jews, but in veneration of their God, saying, *He is the God.* He also delivered the vessels of the temple to one whom he entrusted to see them restored to their ancient place and use, *v.* 14. And they had these to show in confirmation of what they alleged. (5.) "The building was begun according to this order as soon as ever we had returned, so that we have not forfeited the benefit of the order for want of pursuing it in time; still it has been in building, but, because we have met with opposition, it is not finished." But, observe, they mention not the falsehood and malice of the former governors, nor make any complaint of them, though they had cause enough, to teach us not to render bitterness for bitterness, nor the most just reproach for that which is most unjust, but to think it enough if we can obtain fair treatment for the future, without an invidious reference to former injuries, *v.* 16. This is the account they give of their proceedings, not asking what authority they had to examine them, nor upbraiding them with their idolatry, and superstitions, and medley religion. Let us learn hence with meekness and fear to *give a reason of the hope that is in us* (1 Pet. iii. 15), rightly to understand, and then readily to declare, what we do in God's service and why we do it.

2. How fairly the Samaritans represented this to the king. (1.) They called the temple at Jerusalem the *house of the great God* (*v.* 8); for though the Samaritans, as it should seem, had yet gods many and lords many, they owned the God of Israel to be the *great God,* who is above all gods. "It is the house of the *great God,* and therefore we dare not oppose the building of it without orders from thee." (2.) They told him truly what was done, not stating, as their predecessors did, that they were fortifying the city as if they intended war, but only that they were rearing the temple as those that intended worship, *v.* 8. (3.) They fully represented their plea, told him what they had to say for themselves, and were willing that the cause should be set in a true light. (4.) They left it to the king to consult the records whether Cyrus had indeed made such a decree, and then to give directions as he should think fit, *v.* 17. We have reason to think that if Artaxerxes, in the foregoing chapter, had had the Jews' cause as fairly represented to him as it was here to Darius, he would not have ordered the work to be hindered. God's people could not be persecuted if they were not belied, could not be baited if they were not dressed up in bears' skins. Let but the cause of God and truth be fairly stated, and fairly heard, and it will keep its ground.

CHAP. VI.

How solemnly the foundation of the temple was laid we read ch. iii. How slowly the building went on, and with how much difficulty, we found ch. iv. and v. But how gloriously the top-stone was at length brought forth with shoutings we find in this chapter; and even we, at this distance of time, when we read of it, may cry, "Grace, grace to it." As for God, his work is perfect; it may be slow work, but it will be sure work. We have here, I. A recital of the decree of Cyrus for the building of the temple, ver. 1—5. II. The enforcing of that decree by a new order from Darius for the perfecting of that work, ver. 6—12. III. The finishing of it thereupon, ver. 13—15. IV. The solemn dedication of it when it was built (ver. 16—18), and the handselling of it (as I may say) with the celebration of the passover, ver 19—22. And now we may say that in Judah and Jerusalem things went well, very well.

THEN Darius the king made a decree, and search was made in the house of the rolls, where the treasures were laid up in Babylon. 2 And there was found at Achmetha, in the palace that *is* in the province of the Medes, a roll, and therein *was* a record thus written: 3 In the first year of Cyrus the king *the same* Cyrus the king made a decree *concerning* the house of God at Jerusalem, Let the house be builded, the place where they offered sacrifices, and let the foundations thereof be strongly laid; the height thereof threescore cubits, *and* the breadth thereof threescore cubits; 4 *With* three rows of great stones, and a row of new timber: and let the expences be given out of the king's house: 5 And also let the golden and silver vessels of the house of God, which Nebuchadnezzar took forth out of the temple which *is* at Jerusalem, and brought unto Babylon, be restored, and brought again unto the temple which *is* at Jerusalem, *every one* to his place, and place *them* in the house of God. 6 Now *therefore,* Tatnai, governor beyond the river, Shethar-boznai, and your companions the Apharsachites, which *are* beyond the river, be ye far from thence: 7 Let the work of this house of God alone; let the governor of the Jews and the elders of the Jews build this house of God in his place. 8 Moreover I make a decree what ye shall do to the elders of these Jews for the building of this house of God: that of the king's goods, *even* of the tribute beyond the river, forthwith expences be given unto these men, that they be not hindered. 9 And that which they have need of, both young bullocks, and rams, and lambs, for the burnt offerings of the God of heaven, wheat, salt, wine, and oil, according to the appointment of the priests which *are* at

Jerusalem, let it be given them day by day without fail: 10 That they may offer sacrifices of sweet savours unto the God of heaven, and pray for the life of the king, and of his sons. 11 Also I have made a decree, that whosoever shall alter this word, let timber be pulled down from his house, and being set up, let him be hanged thereon; and let his house be made a dunghill for this. 12 And the God that hath caused his name to dwell there destroy all kings and people, that shall put to their hand to alter *and* to destroy this house of God which *is* at Jerusalem. I Darius have made a decree; let it be done with speed.

We have here, I. The decree of Cyrus for the building of the temple repeated. To this the Samaritans referred because the Jews pleaded it, and perhaps hoped it would not be found, and then their plea would be overruled and a stop put to their work. Search was ordered to be made for it among the records; for, it seems, the tribes had not taken care to provide themselves with an authentic copy of it, which might have stood them in good stead, but they must appeal to the original. It was looked for in Babylon (*v.* 1), where Cyrus was when he signed it. But, when it was not found there, Darius did not make that a pretence to conclude that therefore there was no such decree, and thereupon to give judgment against the Jews; but it is probable, having himself heard that such a decree was certainly made, he ordered the rolls in other places to be searched, and at length it was found at Achmetha, in the province of the Medes, *v.* 2. Perhaps some that durst not destroy it, yet hid it there, out of ill will to the Jews, that they might lose the benefit of it. But Providence so ordered that it came to light; and it is here inserted, *v.* 3—5. 1. Here is a warrant for the building of the temple: *Let the house of God at Jerusalem,* yea, *let that house be built* (so it may be read), within such and such dimensions, and with such and such materials. 2. A warrant for the taking of the expenses of the building out of the king's revenue, *v.* 4. We do not find that they had received what was here ordered them, the face of things at court being soon changed. 3. A warrant for the restoring of the vessels and utensils of the temple, which Nebuchadnezzar had taken away (*v.* 5), with an order that the priests, the Lord's ministers, should return them all to their places in the house of God.

II. The confirmation of it by a decree of Darius, grounded upon it and in pursuance of it.

1. The decree of Darius is very explicit and satisfactory.

(1.) He forbids his officers to do any thing in opposition to the building of the temple. The manner of expression intimates that he knew they had a mind to hinder it: *Be you far hence* (*v.* 6); *let the work of this house of God alone, v.* 7. Thus was the wrath of the enemy *made to praise God* and the remainder thereof did he restrain.

(2.) He orders them out of his own revenue to assist the builders with money, [1.] For carrying on the building, *v.* 8. Herein he pursues the example of Cyrus, *v.* 4. [2.] For maintaining the sacrifices there when it was built, *v.* 9. He ordered that they should be supplied with every thing they wanted both for burnt-offerings and meat-offerings. He was content it should be a rent-charge upon his revenue, and ordered it to be paid every day, and this without fail, that they might offer sacrifices and prayers with them (for the patriarchs, when they offered sacrifice, *called on the name of the Lord,* so did Samuel, Elijah, and others) for the life (that is, the happiness and prosperity) of the king and his sons, *v.* 10. See here how he gives honour, *First,* To Israel's God, whom he calls once and again the *God of heaven. Secondly,* To his ministers, in ordering his commissioners to give out supplies for the temple service at the appointment of the priests. Those that thought to control them must now be, in this matter, at their command. It was a new thing for God's priests to have such an interest in the public money. *Thirdly,* To prayer: *That they may pray for the life of the king.* He knew they were a praying people, and had heard that God was nigh to them in all that which they called upon him for. He was sensible he needed their prayers and might receive benefit by them, and was kind to them in order that he might have an interest in their prayers. It is the duty of God's people to pray for those that are in authority over them, not only for the good and gentle, but also for the froward; but they are particularly bound in gratitude to pray for their protectors and benefactors; and it is the wisdom of princes to desire their prayers, and to engage them. Let not the greatest princes despise the prayers of the meanest saints; it is desirable to have them for us, and dreadful to have them against us.

(3.) He enforces his decree with a penalty (*v.* 11): "Let none either oppose the work and service of the temple or withhold the supports granted to it by the crown upon pain of death. If any alter this decree, let him be (*hanged before his own door* as we say), hanged upon a beam of his own house, and, as an execrable man, *let his house be made a dunghill.*"

(4.) He entails a divine curse upon all those kings and people that should ever have any hand in the destruction of this house, *v.* 12. What he could not do himself for the protection of the temple he desired that God, *to whom vengeance belongs,* would do. This bespeaks him zealous in the cause; and though this temple was, at length, most justly destroyed by the righteous hand of God, yet perhaps the Romans, who were the instruments of that destruction, felt the effects of this curse, for that empire sensibly declined ever after.

2. From all this we learn, (1.) That the heart of kings is in the hand of God, and he turns it which way soever he pleases; what they are he makes them to be, for he is *King of kings.* (2.) That when God's time has come for the accomplishing of his gracious purposes concerning his church he will raise up instruments to promote them from whom such good service was not expected. *The earth sometimes helps the woman* (Rev. xii. 16), and those are made use of for the defence of religion who have little religion themselves. (3.) That what is intended for the prejudice of the church has often, by the overruling providence of God, been made serviceable to it, Phil. i. 12. The enemies of the Jews, in appealing to Darius, hoped to get an order to suppress them, but, instead of that, they got an order to supply them. Thus *out of the eater comes forth meat.* The apocryphal Esdras (or Ezra), Book I. *ch.* iii. and iv., gives another account of this decree in favour of the Jews, that Darius had vowed that if ever he came to the kingdom he would build the temple at Jerusalem, and that Zerubbabel, who was one of his attendants (whereas it is plain here that he was now at Jerusalem), for making an ingenious discourse before him on that subject (*Great is the truth and will prevail*), was told to ask what recompence he would, and asked only for this order, in pursuance of the king's vow.

13 Then Tatnai, governor on this side the river, Shethar-boznai, and their companions, according to that which Darius the king had sent, so they did speedily. 14 And the elders of the Jews builded, and they prospered through the prophesying of Haggai the prophet and Zechariah the son of Iddo. And they builded, and finished *it,* according to the commandment of the God of Israel, and according to the commandment of Cyrus, and Darius, and Artaxerxes king of Persia. 15 And this house was finished on the third day of the month Adar, which was in the sixth year of the reign of Darius the king. 16 And the children of Israel, the priests, and the Levites, and the rest of the children of the captivity, kept the dedication of this house of God with joy, 17 And offered at the dedication of this house of God a hundred bullocks, two hundred rams, four hundred lambs; and for a sin offering for all Israel, twelve he goats, according to the number of the tribes of Israel. 18 And they set the priests in their divisions, and the Levites in their courses, for the service of God, which *is* at Jerusalem; as it is written in the book of Moses. 19 And the children of the captivity kept the passover upon the fourteenth *day* of the first month. 20 For the priests and the Levites were purified together, all of them *were* pure, and killed the passover for all the children of the captivity, and for their brethren the priests, and for themselves. 21 And the children of Israel, which were come again out of captivity, and all such as had separated themselves unto them from the filthiness of the heathen of the land, to seek the LORD God of Israel, did eat, 22 And kept the feast of unleavened bread seven days with joy: for the LORD had made them joyful, and turned the heart of the king of Assyria unto them, to strengthen their hands in the work of the house of God, the God of Israel.

Here we have, I. The Jews' enemies made their friends. When they received this order from the king they came with as much haste to encourage and assist the work as their predecessors had done to put a stop to it, *ch.* iv. 23. What the king ordered they did, and, because they would not be thought to do it with reluctance, they *did it speedily, v.* 13. The king's moderation made them, contrary to their own inclination, moderate too.

II. The building of the temple carried on, and finished in a little time, *v.* 14, 15. Now the *elders of the Jews built* with cheerfulness. For aught I know, the elders themselves laboured at it *with their own hands;* and, if they did, it was no disparagement to their eldership, but an encouragement to the other workmen. 1. They found themselves bound to it *by the commandment of the God of Israel,* who had given them power that they might use it in his service. 2. They found themselves shamed into it by the commandment of the heathen kings, Cyrus formerly, Darius now, and Artaxerxes some time after. Can the elders of the Jews be remiss in this good work when these foreign princes appear so warm in it? Shall native Israelites grudge their pains and care about this building when strangers grudge not to be at the expense of it? 3. They found themselves encouraged in it by the prophesying of Haggai and Zechariah, who, it is likely, represented to them (as bishop Patrick suggests) the wonderful goodness of God in inclining the heart of the king of Persia to favour them thus. And now the work went on so prosperously that, in four years' time, it was brought to perfection. *As for God, his work is perfect.* The gospel church, that spiritual temple, is long in the building, but it will be finished at last, when the mystical body is completed. Every believer is a *living temple, building up himself in his most holy faith.* Much opposition is given to this work by Satan and our own corruptions. We trifle, and proceed in it with many stops and pauses; but he that has *begun the good work* will see it performed, and will *bring forth judgment unto victory. Spirits of just men* will be *made perfect.*

III. The dedication of the temple. When it was built, being designed only for sacred uses, *they showed by an example how it should be used,* which (says bishop Patrick) is the proper sense of the word *dedicate.* They entered upon it with solemnity and probably with a public declaration of the separating of it from common uses and the surrender of it to the honour of God, to be employed in his worship. 1. The persons employed in this service were not only *the priests and Levites* who officiated, but *the children of Israel,* some of each of the *twelve tribes,* though Judah and Benjamin were the chief, and *the rest of the children of the captivity* or *transportation,* which intimates that there were many besides the children of Israel, of other nations, who transported themselves with them, and became proselytes to their religion, unless we read it, *even the remnant of the children of the captivity,* and then, we may suppose, notice is hereby taken of their mean and afflicted condition, because the consideration of that helped to make them devout and serious in this and other religious exercises. A sad change! The *children of Israel* have become *children of the captivity,* and there appears but a remnant of *them,* according to that prediction (Isa. vii. 3), *Shear-jashub—The remnant shall return.* 2. The sacrifices that were offered upon this occasion were *bullocks, rams, and lambs* (*v.* 17), for burnt-offerings and peace-offerings; not to be compared, in number, with what had been offered at the dedication of Solomon's temple, but, being according to their present ability, they were accepted, for, *after a great trial of affliction, the abundance of their joy, and their deep poverty, abounded to the riches of their liberality,* 2 Cor. viii. 2. These hundreds were more to them than Solomon's thousands were to him. But, besides these, they offered twelve he-goats for sin-offerings, one for every tribe, to make atonement for their sins, which they looked upon as necessary in order to the acceptance of their services. Thus, by getting iniquity taken away, they would free themselves from that which had been the sting of their late troubles, and which, if not removed, would be a worm at the root of their present comforts. 3. This service was performed with joy. They were all glad to see the temple built and the concerns of it in so good a posture. Let us learn to welcome holy ordinances with joy and attend on them with pleasure. Let us serve the Lord with gladness. Whatever we dedicate to God, let it be done with joy that he will please to accept of it. 4. When they dedicated the house they settled the household. Small comfort could they have in the temple without the temple service, and therefore they *set the priests in their divisions* and *the Levites in their courses, v.* 18. Having set up the worship of God in this dedication, they took care to keep it up, and made *the book of Moses* their rule, to which they had an eye in this establishment. Though the temple service could not now be performed with so much pomp and plenty as formerly, because of their poverty, yet perhaps it was performed with as much purity and close adherence to the divine institution as ever, which was the true glory of it. No beauty like the beauty of holiness.

IV. The celebration of the passover in the newly-erected temple. Now that they were newly delivered out of their bondage in Babylon it was seasonable to commemorate their deliverance out of their bondage in Egypt. Fresh mercies should put us in mind of former mercies. We may suppose that they had kept the passover, after a sort, every year since their return, for they had an altar and a tabernacle. But they were liable to frequent disturbances from their enemies, were straitened for room, and had not conveniencies about them, so that they could not do it with due solemnity till the temple was built; and now they made a joyful festival of it, it falling out in the next month after the temple was finished and dedicated, *v.* 19. Notice is here taken, 1. Of the purity of the priests and Levites that *killed the passover, v.* 20. In Hezekiah's time the priests were many of them under blame for not purifying themselves. But now it is observed, to their praise, that *they were purified together, as one man* (so the word is); they were unanimous both in their resolutions and in their endeavours to make and keep themselves ceremonially clean for this solemnity; they joined together in their preparations, that they might help one another, so that all of them were pure, to a man. The purity of ministers adds much to the beauty of their ministrations; so does their unity. 2. Of the proselytes that communicated with them in this ordinance: *All such as had separated themselves unto them,* had left their country and the superstitions of it and cast in their lot with the Israel of God, and had *turned from the filthiness of the heathen of the land,* both their idolatries and immoralities, *to seek the Lord God of Israel* as their God, did eat the passover. See how the proselytes, the converts, are described. They separated themselves from the filthiness of sin and fellowship with sinners, joined themselves with the Israel of God in conformity and communion, and set themselves to seek the God of Israel; and those that do so in sincerity, though strangers and foreigners, are welcome to eat of the gospel feast, as *fellow-citizens with the saints and of the household of God.* 3. Of the great pleasure and satisfaction wherewith they *kept the feast of unleavened bread, v.* 22. *The Lord had made them joyful,* had given them both cause to rejoice and hearts to rejoice. It was now about twenty years since the foundation of this temple was laid, and we may suppose the old men that then wept at the remembrance of the first temple were most of them dead by this time, so that now there were no tears mingled with their joys. Those that are, upon good grounds, joyful, have therefore reason to be thankful, because it is God that *makes them to rejoice.* He is the fountain whence all the streams of our joy flow. God has promised to all those who take hold of his covenant that *he will make them joyful in his house of prayer.* The particular occasion they had for joy at this time was that God had *turned the heart* of the emperor to them, to *strengthen their hands.* If those that have been, or who we feared would have been, against us, prove to be for us, we may rejoice in it as a token for good, that *our ways please the Lord* (Prov. xvi. 7), and he must have the glory of it.

CHAP. VII.

Ezra's precious name saluted us, at first, in the title of the book, but in the history we have not met with it till this chapter introduces him into public action in another reign, that of Artaxerxes. Zerubbabel and Jeshua we will suppose, by this time, to have grown old, if not gone off; nor do we hear any more of Haggai and Zechariah; they have finished their testimony. What shall become of the cause of God and Israel when these useful instruments are laid aside? Trust God, who has the residue of the Spirit, to raise up others in their room. Ezra here, and Nehemiah in the next book, are as serviceable in their days as those were in theirs. Here is, I. An account, in general, of Ezra himself, and of his expedition to Jerusalem for the public good, ver. 1—10. II. A copy of the commission which Artaxerxes gave him, ver. 11—26. III. His thankfulness to God for it, ver. 27, 28. The next chapter will give us a more particular narrative of his associates, his journey, and his arrival at Jerusalem.

NOW after these things, in the reign of Artaxerxes king of Persia, Ezra the son of Seraiah, the son of Azariah, the son of Hilkiah, 2 The son of Shallum, the son of Zadok, the son of Ahitub, 3 The son of Amariah, the son of Azariah, the son of Meraioth, 4 The son of Zerahiah, the son of Uzzi, the son of Bukki, 5 The son of Abishua, the son of Phinehas, the son of Eleazar, the son of Aaron the chief priest: 6 This Ezra went up from Babylon; and he *was* a ready scribe in the law of Moses, which the LORD God of Israel had given: and the king granted him all his request, according to the hand of the LORD his God upon him. 7 And there went up *some* of the children of Israel, and of the priests, and the Levites, and the singers, and the porters, and the Nethinims, unto Jerusalem, in the seventh year of Artaxerxes the king. 8 And he came to Jerusalem in the fifth month, which *was* in the seventh year of the king. 9 For upon the first *day* of the first month began he to go up from Babylon, and on the first *day* of the fifth month came he to Jerusalem, according to the good hand of his God upon him. 10 For Ezra had prepared his heart to seek the law of the LORD, and to do *it,* and to teach in Israel statutes and judgments.

Here is, I. Ezra's pedigree. He was one of the sons of Aaron, a priest. Him God chose to be an instrument of good to Israel, that he might put honour upon the priesthood, the glory of which had been much eclipsed by the captivity. He is said to be *the son of Seraiah,* that Seraiah, as is supposed, whom the king of Babylon put to death when he sacked Jerusalem, 2 Kings xxv. 18, 21. If we take the shortest computation, it was seventy-five years since Seraiah died; many reckon it much longer, and, because they suppose Ezra called out in the prime of his time to public service, do therefore think that Seraiah was not his immediate parent, but his grandfather or great-grandfather, but that he was the first eminent person that occurred in his genealogy upwards, which is carried up here as high as Aaron, yet leaving out many for brevity-sake, which may be supplied from 1 Chron. vi. 4, &c. He was a younger brother, or his father was Jozadak, the father of Jeshua, so that he was not high priest, but nearly allied to the high priest.

II. His character. Though of the younger house, his personal qualifications made him very eminent. 1. He was a man of great learning, a scribe, a *ready scribe, in the law of Moses, v.* 6. He was very much conversant with the scriptures, especially the writings of Moses, had the words ready and was well acquainted with the sense and meaning of them. It is to be feared that learning ran low among the Jews in Babylon; but Ezra was instrumental to revive it. The Jews say that he collected and collated all the copies of the law he could find out, and published an accurate edition of it, with all the prophetical books, historical and poetical, that were given by divine inspiration, and so made up the canon of the Old Testament, with the addition of the prophecies and histories of his own time. If he was raised up of God, and qualified and inclined to do this, all generations have reason to call him blessed, and to bless God for him. God sent to the Jews *prophets and scribes*, Matt. xxiii. 34. Ezra went under the latter denomination. Now that prophecy was about to cease it was time to promote scripture-knowledge, pursuant to the counsel of God by the last of the prophets, Mal. iv. 4. *Remember the law of Moses*. Gospel ministers are called *scribes instructed to the kingdom of heaven* (Matt. xiii. 52), New-Testament scribes. It was a pity that such a worthy name as this should be worn, as it was in the degenerate ages of the Jewish church, by men who were professed enemies to Christ and his gospel *(Woe unto you, scribes and Pharisees*), who were learned in the letter of the law, but strangers to the spirit of it. 2. He was a man of great piety and holy zeal (*v.* 10): *He had prepared his heart to seek the law of the Lord*, &c. (1.) That which he chose for his study was *the law of the Lord.* The Chaldeans, among whom he was born and bred, were famed for literature, especially the study of the stars, to which, being a studious man, we may suppose that Ezra was tempted to apply himself. But he got over the temptation; the law of his God was more to him than all the writings of their magicians and astrologers, which he knew enough of with good reason to despise them. (2.) He *sought the law of the Lord,* that is, he made it his business to enquire into it, searched the scriptures, and sought the knowledge of God, of his mind and will, in the scriptures, which is to be found there, but not without seeking. (3.) He made conscience of doing according to it; he set it before him as his rule, formed his sentiments and temper by it, and managed himself in his whole conversation according to it. This use we must make of our knowledge of the scriptures; for happy are we if we do what we know of the will of God. (4.) He set himself *to teach Israel the statutes and judgments* of that law. What he knew he was willing to communicate for the good of others; for *the ministration of the Spirit is given to every man to profit withal.* But observe the method: he first learned and then taught, sought the law of the Lord and so laid up a good treasure, and then instructed others and laid out what he had laid up. He also first did and then taught, practised the commandments himself and then directed others in the practice of them; thus his example confirmed his doctrine. (5.) He *prepared his heart* to do all this, or he fixed his heart. He took pains in his studies, and thoroughly furnished himself for what he designed, and then put on resolution to proceed and persevere in them, and thus he became a ready scribe. Moses in Egypt, Ezra in Babylon, and both in captivity, were wonderfully fitted for eminent services to the church.

III. His expedition to Jerusalem for the good of his country: *He went up from Babylon* (*v.* 6), and, in four months' time, came to Jerusalem, *v.* 8. It was strange that such a man as he staid so long in Babylon after his brethren had gone up; but God sent him not thither till he had work for him to do there; and none went but those *whose spirits God raised* to go up. Some think that this Artaxerxes was the same with that Darius whose decree we had (*ch.* vi.), and that Ezra came the very year after the temple was finished: that was the sixth year, this the seventh (*v.* 8), so Dr. Lightfoot. My worthy and learned friend, lately deceased, Mr. Tallents, in his chronological tables, places it about fifty-seven years after the finishing of the temple; others further on. I have only to observe, 1. How kind the king was to him. He *granted him all his request,* whatever he desired to put him into a capacity to serve his country. 2. How kind his people were to him. When he went many more went with him, because they desired not to stay in Babylon when he had gone thence, and because they would venture to dwell in Jerusalem when he had gone thither. 3. How kind his God was to him. He obtained this favour from his king and country by *the good hand of the Lord that was upon him, v.* 6, 9. Note, Every creature is that to us which God makes it to be, and from him our judgment proceeds. As we must see the events that *shall* occur in the hand of God, so we must see the hand of God in the events that *do* occur, and acknowledge him with thankfulness when we have reason to call it his *good hand.*

11 Now this *is* the copy of the letter that the king Artaxerxes gave unto Ezra the priest, the scribe, *even* a scribe of the words of the commandments of the LORD, and of his statutes to Israel. 12 Artaxerxes, king of kings, unto Ezra the priest, a scribe of the law of the God of heaven, perfect *peace,* and at such a time. 13 I make a decree, that all they of the people of Israel, and *of* his priests and Levites, in my realm, which are minded of their own free will to go up to Jerusalem, go with thee. 14 Forasmuch as thou art sent of the king, and of his seven counsellors, to enquire concerning Judah and Jerusalem, according to the law of thy God which *is* in thine hand: 15 And to carry the silver and gold, which the king and his counsellors have freely offered unto the God of Israel, whose habi-

tation *is* in Jerusalem, 16 And all the silver and gold that thou canst find in all the province of Babylon, with the freewill offering of the people, and of the priests, offering willingly for the house of their God which *is* in Jerusalem: 17 That thou mayest buy speedily with this money bullocks, rams, lambs, with their meat offerings and their drink offerings, and offer them upon the altar of the house of your God which *is* in Jerusalem. 18 And whatsoever shall seem good to thee, and to thy brethren, to do with the rest of the silver and the gold, that do after the will of your God. 19 The vessels also that are given thee for the service of the house of thy God, *those* deliver thou before the God of Jerusalem. 20 And whatsoever more shall be needful for the house of thy God, which thou shalt have occasion to bestow, bestow *it* out of the king's treasure house. 21 And I, *even* I Artaxerxes the king, do make a decree to all the treasurers which *are* beyond the river, that whatsoever Ezra the priest, the scribe of the law of the God of heaven, shall require of you, it be done speedily, 22 Unto a hundred talents of silver, and to a hundred measures of wheat, and to a hundred baths of wine, and to a hundred baths of oil, and salt without prescribing *how much*. 23 Whatsoever is commanded by the God of heaven, let it be diligently done for the house of the God of heaven: for why should there be wrath against the realm of the king and his sons? 24 Also we certify you, that touching any of the priests and Levites, singers, porters, Nethinims, or ministers of this house of God, it shall not be lawful to impose toll, tribute, or custom, upon them. 25 And thou, Ezra, after the wisdom of thy God, that *is* in thine hand, set magistrates and judges, which may judge all the people that *are* beyond the river, all such as know the laws of thy God; and teach ye them that know *them* not. 26 And whosoever will not do the law of thy God, and the law of the king, let judgment be executed speedily upon him, whether *it be* unto death, or to banishment, or to confiscation of goods, or to imprisonment.

We have here the commission which the Persian emperor granted to Ezra, giving him authority to act for the good of the Jews; and it is very ample and full, and beyond what could have been expected. The commission runs, we suppose, in the usual form: *Artaxerxes, King of kings.* This however is too high a title for any mortal man to assume; he was indeed king of some kings, but to speak as if he were king of all kings was to usurp *his* prerogative who hath *all power both in heaven and in earth.* He sends greeting to his trusty and well-beloved Ezra, whom he calls a *scribe of the law of the God of heaven* (*v.* 12), a title which (it seems by this) Ezra valued himself by, and desired no other, no, not when he was advanced to the proconsular dignity. He reckoned it more his honour to be a *scribe of God's law* than to be a peer or prince of the empire. Let us observe the articles of this commission.

I. He gives Ezra leave to go up to Jerusalem, and as many of his countrymen as pleased to go up with him, *v.* 13. He and they were captives, and therefore they would not quit his dominions without his royal license.

II. He gives him authority to enquire into the affairs of Judah and Jerusalem, *v.* 14. The rule of his enquiry was to be *the law of his God, which was in his hand.* He must enquire whether the Jews, in their religion, had and did according to that law—whether the temple was built, the priesthood was settled, and the sacrifices were offered conformably to the divine appointment. If, upon enquiry, he found any thing amiss, he must see to get it amended, and, like Titus in Crete, must *set in order the things that were wanting,* Tit. i. 5. Thus is God's law magnified and made honourable, and thus are the Jews restored to their ancient privilege of governing themselves by that law, and are no longer under *the statutes that were not good,* the statutes of their oppressors, Ezek. xx. 25.

III. He entrusts him with the money that was freely given by the king himself and his counsellors, and collected among his subjects, for the service of the house of God, *v.* 15, 16.

1. Let this be taken notice of, (1.) To the honour of God, as the one only living and true God; for even those that worshipped other gods were so convinced of the sovereignty of the God of Israel that they were willing to incur expenses in order to recommend themselves to his favour. See Ps. xlv. 12; lxviii. 29. (2.) To the praise of this heathen king, that he honoured the God of Israel though his worshippers were a despicable handful of poor men, who were not able to bear the charges of their own religion and were now his vassals, and that, though

he was not wrought upon to quit his own superstitions, yet he protected and encouraged the Jews in their religion, and did not only say, *Be you warmed, and be you filled,* but gave them such things as they needed. (3.) To the reproach of the memory of the wicked kings of Judah. Those that had been trained up in the knowledge and worship of the *God of Israel,* and had his law and his prophets, often plundered and impoverished the temple; but here a heathen prince enriched it. Thus afterwards the gospel was rejected by the Jews, but welcomed by the Gentiles. See Rom. xi. 11, *Through their fall salvation has come to the Gentiles.* Acts xiii. 46.

2. We are here told that Ezra was entrusted, (1.) To receive this money and to carry it to Jerusalem; for he was a man of known integrity, whom they could confide in, that he would not convert to his own use the least part of that which was given to the public. We find Paul going to Jerusalem upon such an errand, *to bring alms to his nation and offerings,* Acts xxiv. 17. (2.) To lay out this money in the best manner, in sacrifices to be offered upon the altar of God (*v.* 17), and in whatever else he or his brethren thought fit (*v.* 18), with this limitation only that it should be *after the will of their God,* which they were better acquainted with than the king was. Let the *will of our God* be always our rule in our expenses, and particularly in what we lay out for his service. God's work must always be done according to his will. Besides money, he had vessels also given him for the service of the temple, *v.* 19. Cyrus restored what of right belonged to the temple, but these were given over and above: thus it *receiveth its own with usury.* These he must *deliver before the God of Jerusalem,* as intended for his honour, there where he had *put his name.*

IV. He draws him a bill, or warrant rather, upon the *treasurers on that side the river,* requiring them to furnish him with what he had occasion for out of the king's revenues, and to place it to the king's account, *v.* 20, 22. This was considerately done; for Ezra, having yet to enquire into the state of things, knew not what he should have occasion for and was modest in his demand. It was also kindly done, and evinced a great affection to the temple and a great confidence in Ezra. It is the interest of princes and great men to use their wealth and power for the support and encouragement of religion. What else are great revenues good for but that they enable men to do much good of this kind if they have but hearts to do it?

V. He charges him to let nothing be wanting that was requisite to be done in or about the temple for the honour of the God of Israel. Observe, in this charge (*v.* 23), 1. How honourably he speaks of God. He had called him before *the God of Jerusalem;* but here, lest it should be thought that he looked upon him as a local deity, he calls him twice, with great veneration, the *God of heaven.* 2. How strictly he eyes the word and law of God, which, it is likely, he had read and admired: "Whatsoever is *commanded by your God*" (whose institutions, though he wrote himself *King of kings,* he would not presume in the least iota or tittle to alter or add to) "let it be done, let it be diligently done, with care and speed." And, 3. How solicitously he deprecates the wrath of God: *Why should there be wrath against the realm?* The neglect and contempt of religion bring the judgments of God upon kings and kingdoms; and the likeliest expedient to turn away his wrath, when it is ready to break out against a people, is to support and encourage religion. Would we secure our peace and prosperity? Let us take care that the cause of God be not starved.

VI. He exempts all the ministers of the temple from paying taxes to the government. From the greatest of the priests to the least of the Nethinim, *it shall not be lawful* for the king's officers *to impose* that *toll, tribute, or custom upon them,* which the rest of the king's subjects paid, *v.* 24. This put a great honour upon them as free denizens of the empire, and would gain them respect as favourites of the crown; and it gave them liberty to attend their ministry with more cheerfulness and freedom. We suppose it was only what they needed for themselves and their families, and the maintenance of their ministry, that was hereby allowed to come to them custom-free. If any of them should take occasion from this privilege to meddle in trade and merchandise, they justly lost the benefit of it.

VII. He empowers Ezra to nominate and appoint judges and magistrates for all the Jews on that side the river, *v.* 25, 26. It was a great favour to the Jews to have such nobles of themselves, and especially to have them of Ezra's nomination. 1. All that *knew the laws of Ezra's God* (that is, all that professed the Jewish religion) were to be under the jurisdiction of these judges, which intimates that they were exempted from the jurisdiction of the heathen magistrates. 2. These judges were allowed and encouraged to make proselytes: Let them *teach the laws of God* to *those that do not know them.* Though he would not turn Jew himself, he cared not how many of his subjects did. 3. They were authorized to enforce the judgments they gave, and the orders they made, conformable to *the law of God* (which was hereby made *the law of the king*), with severe penalties—imprisonment, banishment, fine, or death, according as their law directed. They were not allowed to make new laws, but must see the laws of God duly executed; and they were entrusted with the sword in order that they might be *a terror to evil doers.* What could Jehoshaphat, or Hezekiah, or David himself, as king, have done more for the honour of God and the furtherance of religion?

27 Blessed *be* the LORD God of our fathers, which hath put *such a thing* as this in the king's heart, to beautify the house of the LORD which *is* in Jerusalem: 28 And hath extended mercy unto me before the king, and his counsellors, and before all the king's mighty princes. And I was strengthened as the hand of the LORD my God *was* upon me, and I gathered together out of Israel chief men to go up with me.

Ezra cannot proceed in his story without inserting his thankful acknowledgment of the goodness of God to him and his people in this matter. As soon as he has concluded the king's commission, instead of subjoining, *God save the king* (though that would have been proper enough), he adds, *Blessed be the Lord;* for we must *in every thing give thanks,* and, whatever occurrences please us, we must own God's hand in them, and praise his name. Two things Ezra blessed God for:—1. For his commission. We suppose he kissed the king's hand for it, but that was not all: *Blessed be God* (says he) *that put such a thing as this into the king's heart.* God can put things into men's hearts which would not arise there of themselves, and into their heads too, both by his providence and by his grace, in things *pertaining both to life and godliness.* If any good appear to be in our own hearts, or in the hearts of others, we must own it was God that put it there, and bless him for it; for it is he that *worketh in us both to will and to do* that which is good. When princes and magistrates act for the suppression of vice, and the encouragement of religion, we must thank God that *put it into their hearts* to do so, as much as if they had granted us some particular favour. When God's house was built Ezra rejoiced in what was done to beautify it. We read not of any orders given to paint or gild it, or to garnish it with precious stones, but to be sure that the ordinances of God were administered there constantly, and carefully, and exactly according to the institution; and that was indeed the beautifying of the temple. 2. For the encouragement he had to act in pursuance of his commission (*v.* 28): *He has extended mercy to me.* The king, in the honour he did him, we may suppose, had an eye to his merit, and preferred him because he looked upon him to be a very sensible ingenious man; but he himself ascribes his preferment purely to God's mercy. It was this that recommended him to the favour of his prince. Ezra himself was a man of courage, yet he attributed his encouragement not to his own heart, but to God's hand: "I was strengthened to undertake the services, *as the hand of the Lord my God was upon me* to direct and support me." If God gives us his hand, we are bold and cheerful; if he withdraws it, we are weak as water. Whatever service we are enabled to do for God and our generation, God must have all the glory of it. Strength for it is derived from him, and therefore the praise of it must be given to him.

CHAP. VIII.

This chapter gives us a more particular narrative of Ezra's journey to Jerusalem, of which we had a general account in the foregoing chapter. I. The company that went up with him, ver. 1—20. II. The solemn fast which he kept with his company, to implore God's presence with them in this journey, ver. 21—23. III. The care he took of the treasure he had with him, and the charge he gave concerning it to the priests, to whose custody he committed it, ver. 24—30. IV. The care God took of him and his company in the way, ver. 31. V. Their safe arrival at Jerusalem, where they delivered their treasure to the priests (ver. 32—34), their commissions to the king's lieutenants (ver. 36), offered sacrifices to God (ver. 35), and then applied to their business.

THESE *are* now the chief of their fathers, and *this is* the genealogy of them that went up with me from Babylon, in the reign of Artaxerxes the king. 2 Of the sons of Phinehas; Gershom: of the sons of Ithamar; Daniel: of the sons of David; Hattush. 3 Of the sons of Shechaniah, of the sons of Pharosh; Zechariah: and with him were reckoned by genealogy of the males a hundred and fifty. 4 Of the sons of Pahath-moab; Elihoenai the son of Zerahiah, and with him two hundred males. 5 Of the sons of Shechaniah; the son of Jahaziel, and with him three hundred males. 6 Of the sons also of Adin; Ebed the son of Jonathan, and with him fifty males. 7 And of the sons of Elam; Jeshaiah the son of Athaliah, and with him seventy males. 8 And of the sons of Shephatiah; Zebadiah the son of Michael, and with him fourscore males. 9 Of the sons of Joab; Obadiah the son of Jehiel, and with him two hundred and eighteen males. 10 And of the sons of Shelomith; the son of Josiphiah, and with him a hundred and threescore males. 11 And of the sons of Bebai; Zechariah the son of Bebai, and with him twenty and eight males. 12 And of the sons of Azgad; Johanan the son of Hakkatan, and with him a hundred and ten males. 13 And of the last sons of Adonikam, whose names *are* these, Eliphelet, Jeiel, and Shemaiah, and with them threescore males. 14 Of the sons also of Bigvai; Uthai, and Zabbud, and with them seventy males. 15 And I gathered them together to the river that runneth to Ahava; and there abode we in tents three days: and I viewed the people, and the priests, and found there none of the sons of Levi. 16 Then sent I for Eliezer, for Ariel, for Shemaiah, and for Elnathan, and for Jarib, and for Elnathan, and for Nathan, and for Zechariah, and for Meshullam, chief men; also for Joiarib, and for Elnathan, men of understanding. 17 And I sent them with commandment unto Iddo the chief at the place Casiphia, and I told them what they should say unto Iddo, *and* to his brethren the Nethinims, at the place Casiphia, that they should bring unto us ministers for the house of our God. 18 And by the good hand of our God upon us they brought us a man of understanding, of the sons of Mahli, the son of Levi, the son of Israel; and Sherebiah, with his sons and his brethren, eighteen; 19 And Hashabiah, and with him Jeshaiah of the sons of Merari, his brethren and their sons, twenty; 20 Also of the Nethinims, whom David and the princes had appointed for the service of the Levites, two hundred and twenty Nethinims: all of them were expressed by name.

Ezra, having received his commission from the king, beats up for volunteers, as it were, sets up an ensign to assemble the outcasts of Israel and the dispersed of Judah, Isa. xi. 12. "Whoever of the sons of Sion, that *dwell with the daughters of Babylon,* is disposed to go to Jerusalem, now that the temple there is finished and the temple-service set a-going, now is their time." Now one would think that under such a leader, with such encouragements, all the Jews should at length have *shaken themselves from their dust,* and *loosed the bands of their neck,* according to that call, Isa. lii. 1, 2, &c. I wonder how any of them could read that chapter and yet stay behind. But multitudes did. They loved their ease better than their religion, thought themselves well off where they were, and either believed not that Jerusalem would better their condition or durst not go thither through any difficulties. But here we are told,

I. That some offered themselves willingly to go with Ezra. The heads of the several families are here named, for their honour, and the numbers of the males that each brought in, amounting in all to 1496. Two priests are named (*v.* 2) and one of the sons of David; but, it should seem, they came without their families, probably intending to see how they liked Jerusalem and then either to send for their families or return to them as they saw cause. Several of their families, or clans, here named, we had before, *ch.* ii. Some went up from them at that time, more went up now, as God inclined their hearts; some were called into the vineyard at the third hour, others not till the eleventh, yet even those were not rejected. But here we read of *the last sons of Adonikam* (*v.* 13), which some understand to their dispraise, that they were the last that enlisted themselves under Ezra; I rather understand it to their honour, that now all the sons of that family returned and none staid behind.

II. That the Levites who went in this company were in a manner pressed into the service. Ezra appointed a general rendezvous of all his company at a certain place upon new-year's day, the first day of the first month, *ch.* vii. 9. Then and there he took a view of them, and mustered them, and (which was strange) *found there none of the sons of Levi, v.* 15. Some priests there were, but no others that were Levites. Where was the spirit of that sacred tribe? Ezra, a priest, like Moses proclaims, *Who is on the Lord's side?* They, unlike to Levi, shrink, and desire to *abide among the sheep-folds to hear the bleatings of the flock.* Synagogues we suppose they had in Babylon, in which they prayed, and preached, and kept sabbaths (and, when they could not have better, they had reason to be thankful for them); but now that the temple at Jerusalem was opened, to the service of which they were ordained, they ought to have preferred the gates of Zion before all those synagogues. It is upon record here, to their reproach; but *tell it not in Gath.* Ezra, when he observed that he had no Levites in his retinue, was much at a loss. He had money enough for the service of the temple, but wanted men. The king and princes had more than done their part, but the sons of Levi had not half done theirs. Eleven men, chief men, and men of understanding, he chooses out of his company, to be employed for the filling up of this lamentable vacancy; and here we are informed, 1. Of their being sent. Ezra sent them to a proper place, where there was a college of Levites, *the place Casiphia,* probably a street or square in Babylon allowed for that purpose—*Silver Street* one may call it, for *ceseph* signifies *silver.* He sent them to a proper person, to Iddo, the chief president of the college, not to urge him to come himself (we will suppose him to be old and unfit for such a remove), but to send some of the juniors, *ministers for the house of our God, v.* 17. The furnishing of God's house with good ministers is a good work, which will redound to the comfort and credit of all that have a hand in it. 2. Of their success. They did not return without their errand, but, though the warning was short, they brought about forty Levites to attend Ezra, Sherebiah, noted as a very intelligent man, and eighteen with him (*v.* 18), Hashabiah, and Jeshaiah, and twenty with them, *v.* 19. By this it appears that they were not averse to go, but were slothful and inattentive, and only wanted to be called upon and excited to go. What a pity it is that good men should omit a good work, merely for want of being spoken to! What a pity that they should need it, but, if they do, what a pity that they should be left without it! Of the Nethinim, the servitors of the sacred college, the *species infima—the lowest order* of the temple ministers, more appeared forward to go than of the Levites themselves. Of them 220, upon this hasty summons, enlisted themselves, and had the honour to be expressed by name in Ezra's muster-roll, *v.* 20. "Thus," says Ezra, "were we furnished with Levites, *by the good hand of our God upon us.*" If, where ministers have been wanting, the vacancies are well supplied, let God have the glory, and his good hand be acknowledged as qualifying them for the service, inclining them to it, and then opening a door of opportunity for them.

21 Then I proclaimed a fast there, at the river of Ahava, that we might afflict ourselves before our God, to seek of him a right way for us, and for our little ones, and for all our substance. 22 For I was ashamed to require of the king a band of soldiers and horsemen to help us against the enemy in the way: because we had spoken unto the king, saying, The hand of our God *is* upon all them for good that seek him; but his power and his wrath *is* against all them that forsake him. 23 So we fasted and besought our God for this: and he was intreated of us.

Ezra has procured Levites to go along with him; but what will that avail, unless he have God with him? That is therefore his chief care. In all our ways we must acknowledge God, and in those particularly wherein we are endeavouring to serve the interest of his kingdom among men. Ezra does so here. Observe,

I. The stedfast confidence he had in God and in his gracious protection. He told the king (*v.* 22) what principles he went upon, that those who seek God are safe under the shadow of his wings, even in their greatest dangers, but that those who forsake him are continually exposed, even when they are most secure. God's servants have his power engaged for them; his enemies have it engaged against them. This Ezra believed with his heart, and with his mouth made confession of it before the king; and therefore he was ashamed to ask of the king a convoy, lest thereby he should give occasion to the king, and those about him, to suspect either God's power to help his people or Ezra's confidence in that power. Those that trust in God, and triumph in him, will be ashamed of seeking to the creature for protection, especially of using any sorry shifts for their own safety, because thereby they contradict themselves and their own confidence. Not but that those who depend upon God must use proper means for their preservation, and they need not be ashamed to do so; but, when the honour of God is concerned, one would rather expose one's-self than do any thing to the prejudice of that, which ought to be dearer to us than our lives.

II. The solemn application he made to God in that confidence: He *proclaimed a fast, v.* 21. No doubt he had himself begged of God direction in this affair from the first time he had it in his thoughts; but for public mercies public prayers must be made, that all who are to share in the comfort of them may join in the request for them. Their fasting was, 1. To express their humiliation. This he declares to be the intent and meaning of it, "*that we might afflict ourselves before our God* for our sins, and so be qualified for the pardon of them." When we are entering upon any new condition of life our care should be to bring none of the guilt of the sins of our former condition into it. When we are in any imminent peril let us be sure to make our peace with God, and then we are safe: nothing can do us any real hurt. 2. To excite their supplications. Prayer was always joined with religious fasting. Their errand to the throne of grace was *to seek of God the right way*, that is, to commit themselves to the guidance of the divine Providence, to put themselves under the divine protection, and to beg of God to guide and keep them in their journey and bring them safely to their journey's end. They were strangers in the road, were to march through their enemies' countries, and had not a pillar of cloud and fire to lead them, as their fathers had; but they believed that the power and favour of God, and the ministration of his angels, would be to them instead of that, and hoped by prayer to obtain divine assistance. Note, All our concerns about ourselves, our families, and our estates, it is our wisdom and duty by prayer to commit to God, and leave the care of with him, Phil. iv. 6.

III. The good success of their doing so (*v.* 23): *We besought our God* by joint-prayer, *and he was entreated of us.* They had some comfortable assurance in their own minds that their prayers were answered, and the event declared it; for never any that sought God in earnest sought him in vain.

24 Then I separated twelve of the chief of the priests, Sherebiah, Hashabiah, and ten of their brethren with them, 25 And weighed unto them

the silver, and the gold, and the vessels, *even* the offering of the house of our God, which the king, and his counsellors, and his lords, and all Israel *there* present, had offered: 26 I even weighed unto their hand six hundred and fifty talents of silver, and silver vessels a hundred talents, *and* of gold a hundred talents; 27 Also twenty basons of gold, of a thousand drams; and two vessels of fine copper, precious as gold. 28 And I said unto them, Ye *are* holy unto the LORD; the vessels *are* holy also; and the silver and the gold *are* a freewill offering unto the LORD God of your fathers. 29 Watch ye, and keep *them*, until ye weigh *them* before the chief of the priests and the Levites, and chief of the fathers of Israel, at Jerusalem, in the chambers of the house of the LORD. 30 So took the priests and the Levites the weight of the silver, and the gold, and the vessels, to bring *them* to Jerusalem unto the house of our God.

We have here an account of the particular care which Ezra took of the treasure he had with him, that belonged to God's sanctuary, Observe, 1. Having committed the keeping of it to God, he committed the keeping of it to proper men, whose business it was to watch it, though without God they would have waked in vain. Note, Our prayers must always be seconded with our endeavours; the care of Christ's gospel, his church, and ordinances, must not be so left with him but that it must also be *committed to faithful men*, 2 Tim. ii. 2. 2. Having prayed to God to preserve all the substance they had with them, he shows himself especially solicitous for that part of it which belonged to the house of God and was an offering to him. Do we expect that God should, by his providence, keep that which belongs to us? Let us, by his grace, keep that which belongs to him. Let God's honour and interest be our care; and then we may expect that our lives and comforts will be his. Observe, (1.) The persons to whom he delivered the offerings of the house of God. Twelve chief priests, and as many Levites, he appointed to this trust (*v.* 24, 30), who were bound by their office to take care of the things of God, and were in a particular manner to have the benefit of these sacred treasures. Ezra tells them why he put those things into their hands (*v.* 28): *You are holy unto the Lord, the vessels are holy also;* and who so fit to take care of holy things as holy persons? Those that have the dignity and honour of the priesthood must take along with them the trust and duty of it. The prophet is foretelling the return of God's people and ministers out of Babylon, when he gives the solemn charge (Isa. lii 11), *Be you clean that bear the vessels of the Lord.* (2.) The great exactness with which he lodged this trust in their hands: He *weighed to them the silver, the gold, and the vessels* (*v.* 25), because he expected to have it from them again by weight. In all trusts, but especially sacred ones, we ought to be punctual, and preserve a right understanding on both sides. In Zerubbabel's time the vessels were delivered by number, here by weight, that all might be forth-coming and it might easily appear if any were missing, to intimate that such as are entrusted with holy things (as all the stewards of the mysteries of God are) are concerned to remember, both in receiving their trust and in discharging it, that they must shortly give a very particular account of it, that they may be faithful to it and so give up their account with joy. (3.) The charge he gave them with these treasures (*v.* 29): "*Watch you, and keep them,* that they be not lost, nor embezzled, nor mingled with the other articles. Keep them together; keep them by themselves; keep them safely, till you weigh them in the temple, before the great men there," hereby intimating how much it was their concern to be careful and faithful and how much it would be their honour to be found so. Thus when Paul charges Timothy with the gospel treasure he bids him keep it *until the appearing of Jesus Christ*, and his appearing before him to give account of his trust, when his fidelity would be his crown.

31 Then we departed from the river of Ahava on the twelfth *day* of the first month, to go unto Jerusalem: and the hand of our God was upon us, and he delivered us from the hand of the enemy, and of such as lay in wait by the way. 32 And we came to Jerusalem, and abode there three days. 33 Now on the fourth day was the silver and the gold and the vessels weighed in the house of our God by the hand of Meremoth the son of Uriah the priest; and with him *was* Eleazar the son of Phinehas; and with them *was* Jozabad the son of Jeshua, and Noadiah the son of Binnui, Levites; 34 By number *and* by weight of every one: and all the weight was written at that time. 35 *Also* the children of those that had been carried away, which were come out of the captivity, offered burnt offerings unto the God of Israel, twelve bullocks for all

Israel, ninety and six rams, seventy and seven lambs, twelve he goats *for* a sin offering: all *this was* a burnt offering unto the LORD. 36 And they delivered the king's commissions unto the king's lieutenants, and to the governors on this side the river: and they furthered the people, and the house of God.

We are now to attend Ezra to Jerusalem, a journey of about four months in all; but his multitude made his marches slow and his stages short. Now here we are told,

I. That his God was good, and he acknowledged his goodness: *The hand of our God was upon us,* to animate us for our undertaking. To him they owed it, 1. That they were preserved in their journey, and not all cut off; for there were enemies that *laid wait for them by the way* to do them a mischief, or at least, like Amalek, to *smite the hindmost of them,* but God protected them, *v.* 31. Even the common perils of journeys are such as oblige us to sanctify our going out with prayer and our returns in peace with praise and thanksgiving; much more ought God to be thus eyed in such a dangerous expedition as this was. 2. That they were brought in safety to their journey's end, *v.* 32. Let those that have stedfastly set their faces towards the new Jerusalem proceed and persevere to the end *till they appear before God in Zion,* and they shall find that he *who has begun the good work will perform it.*

II. That his treasurers were faithful. When they had come to Jerusalem they were impatient to be discharged of their trust, and therefore applied to the great men of the temple, who received it from them and gave them an acquittance in full, *v.* 33, 34. It is a great ease to one's mind to be discharged from a trust, and a great honour to one's name to be able to make it appear that it has been faithfully discharged.

III. That his companions were devout. As soon as they came to be near the altar they thought themselves obliged to offer sacrifice, whatever they had done in Babylon, *v.* 35. That will be dispensed with when we want opportunity which when the door is opened again will be expected from us. It is observable, 1. That among their sacrifices they had a sin-offering; for it is the atonement that sweetens and secures every mercy to us, which will not be truly comfortable unless *iniquity be taken away* and our peace made with God. 2. That the number of their offerings related to the number of the tribes, twelve bullocks, twelve he-goats, and ninety-six rams (that is, eight times twelve), intimating the union of the two kingdoms, according to what was foretold, Ezek. xxxvii. 22. They did not any longer go two tribes one way and ten another, but all the twelve met by their representatives at the same altar.

IV. That even the enemies of the Jews became their friends, bowed to Ezra's commission, and, instead of hindering the people of God, furthered them (*v.* 36), purely in complaisance to the king: when he appeared moderate they all coveted to appear so too. *Then had the churches rest.*

CHAP. IX.

The affairs of the church were in a very good posture, we may well suppose, now that Ezra presided in them. Look without; the government was kind to them. We hear no complaints of persecution and oppression; their enemies had either their hearts turned or at least their hands tied; their neighbours were civil, and we hear of no wars nor rumours of wars; there were none to make them afraid; all was as well as could be, considering that they were few, and poor, and subjects to a foreign prince. Look at home; we hear nothing of Baal, nor Ashtaroth, nor Moloch, no images, nor groves, nor golden calves, no, nor so much as high places (not only no idolatrous altars, but no separate ones), but the temple was duly respected and the temple service carefully kept up. Yet all was not well either. The purest ages of the church have had some corruptions, and it will never be presented "without spot or wrinkle" till it is "a glorious church," a church "triumphant," Eph. v. 27. We have here, I. A complaint brought to Ezra of the many marriages that had been made with strange wives, ver. 1, 2. II. The great trouble which he, and others influenced by his example, were in upon this information, ver. 3, 4. III. The solemn confession which he made of this sin to God, with godly sorrow and shame, ver. 5—15.

NOW when these things were done, the princes came to me, saying, The people of Israel, and the priests, and the Levites, have not separated themselves from the people of the lands, *doing* according to their abominations, *even* of the Canaanites, the Hittites, the Perizzites, the Jebusites, the Ammonites, the Moabites, the Egyptians, and the Amorites. 2 For they have taken of their daughters for themselves, and for their sons: so that the holy seed have mingled themselves with the people of *those* lands: yea, the hand of the princes and rulers hath been chief in this trespass. 3 And when I heard this thing, I rent my garment and my mantle, and plucked off the hair of my head and of my beard, and sat down astonied. 4 Then were assembled unto me every one that trembled at the words of the God of Israel, because of the transgression of those that had been carried away; and I sat astonied until the evening sacrifice.

Ezra, like Barnabas when he came to Jerusalem and *saw the grace of God* to his brethren there, no doubt *was glad, and exhorted them all that with purpose of heart they would cleave to the Lord,* Acts xi. 23. He saw nothing amiss (many corruptions lurk out of the view of the most vigilant rulers); but here is a damp upon his joys: information is brought him that many of the people, yea, and some of the rulers, had married wives out of heathen families, and joined themselves in affinity with strangers. Observe,

I. What the sin was that they were guilty

of: it was *mingling with the people of those lands* (*v.* 2), associating with them both in trade and in conversation, making themselves familiar with them, and, to complete the affinity, taking *their daughters in marriages* to their sons. We are willing to hope that they did not worship their gods, but that their captivity had cured them of their idolatry: it is said indeed that they *did according to their abominations;* but that (says bishop Patrick) signifies here only the imitation of the heathen in promiscuous marriages with any nation whatsoever, which by degrees would lead them to idolatry. Herein, 1. They disobeyed the express command of God, which forbade all intimacy with the heathen, and particularly in matrimonial contracts, Deut. vii. 3. 2. They profaned the crown of their peculiarity, and set themselves upon a level with those above whom God had by singular marks of his favour, of late as well as formerly, dignified them. 3. They distrusted the power of God to protect and advance them, and were led by carnal policy, hoping to strengthen themselves and make an interest among their neighbours by these alliances. A practical disbelief of God's all-sufficiency is at the bottom of all the sorry shifts we make to help ourselves. 4. They exposed themselves, and much more their children, to the peril of idolatry, the very sin, and introduced by this very way, that had once been the ruin of their church and nation.

II. Who were the persons that were guilty of this sin, not only some of the unthinking people of Israel, that knew no better, but *many of the priests and Levites,* whose office it was to teach the law, and this law among the rest, and in whom, by reason of their elevation above common Israelites, it was a greater crime. It was a diminution to the sons of that tribe to match into any other tribe, and they seldom did except into the royal tribe; but for them to match with heathen, with Canaanites, and Hittites, and I know not whom, was such a disparagement as, if they had had any sense, though not of duty, yet of honour, one would think, they would never have been guilty of. Yet this was not the worst: *The hand of the princes and rulers,* who by their power should have prevented or reformed this high misdemeanour, *was chief in this trespass.* If princes be in a trespass, they will be charged as chief in it, because of the influence their example will have upon others. *Many will follow their pernicious ways.* But miserable is the case of that people whose leaders debauch them and cause them to err.

III. The information that was given of this to Ezra. It was given by the persons that were most proper to complain, the princes, those of them that had kept their integrity and with it their dignity; they could not have accused others if they themselves had not been free from blame. It was given to the person who had power to mend the matter, who, as a *ready scribe in the law of God,* could argue with them, and, as king's commissioner, could awe them. It is probable that these princes had often endeavoured to redress this grievance and could not; but now they applied to Ezra, hoping that his wisdom, authority, and interest, would prevail to do it. Those that cannot of themselves reform public abuses may yet do good service by giving information to those that can.

IV. The impression this made upon Ezra (*v.* 3): *He rent his clothes, plucked off his hair,* and *sat down astonished.* Thus he expressed the deep sense he had, 1. Of the dishonour hereby done to God. It grieved him to the heart to think that a people called by his name should so grossly violate his law, should be so little benefited by his correction, and make such bad returns for his favours. 2. Of the mischief the people had hereby done to themselves and the danger they were in of the wrath of God breaking out against them. Note, (1.) The sins of others should be our sorrow, and the injury done by them to God's honour and the souls of men is what we should lay to heart. (2.) Sorrow for sin must be great sorrow; such Ezra's was, *as for an only son or a first-born.* (3.) The scandalous sins of professors are what we have reason to be astonished at. We may stand amazed to see men contradict, disparage, prejudice, ruin, themselves. Strange that men should act so inconsiderately and so inconsistently with themselves! Upright men are astonished at it.

V. The influence which Ezra's grief for this had upon others. We may suppose that he *went up to the house of the Lord,* there to humble himself, because he had an eye to God in his grief and that was the proper place for deprecating his displeasure. Public notice was soon taken of it, and all the devout serious people that were at hand assembled themselves to him, it should seem of their own accord, for nothing is said of their being sent to, *v.* 4. Note, 1. It is the character of good people that they *tremble at God's word;* they stand in awe of the authority of its precepts and the severity and justice of its threatenings, and to those that do so *will God look,* Isa. lxvi. 2. 2. Those that tremble *at the word of God* cannot but tremble *at the sins of men,* by which the law of God is broken and his wrath and curse are incurred. 3. The pious zeal of one against sin may perhaps provoke very many to the like, as the apostle speaks in another case, 2 Cor. ix. 2. Many will follow who have not consideration, talent, and courage, enough to lead in a good work. 4. All good people ought to own those that appear and act in the cause of God against vice and profaneness, to stand by them, and do what they can to strengthen their hands.

5 And at the evening sacrifice I

arose up from my heaviness; and having rent my garment and my mantle, I fell upon my knees, and spread out my hands unto the LORD my God, 6 And said, O my God, I am ashamed and blush to lift up my face to thee, my God: for our iniquities are increased over *our* head, and our trespass is grown up unto the heavens. 7 Since the days of our fathers *have* we *been* in a great trespass unto this day; and for our iniquities have we, our kings, *and* our priests, been delivered into the hand of the kings of the lands, to the sword, to captivity, and to a spoil, and to confusion of face, as *it is* this day. 8 And now for a little space grace hath been *showed* from the LORD our God, to leave us a remnant to escape, and to give us a nail in his holy place, that our God may lighten our eyes, and give us a little reviving in our bondage. 9 For we *were* bondmen; yet our God hath not forsaken us in our bondage, but hath extended mercy unto us in the sight of the kings of Persia, to give us a reviving, to set up the house of our God, and to repair the desolations thereof, and to give us a wall in Judah and in Jerusalem. 10 And now, O our God, what shall we say after this? for we have forsaken thy commandments, 11 Which thou hast commanded by thy servants the prophets, saying, The land, unto which ye go to possess it, is an unclean land with the filthiness of the people of the lands, with their abominations, which have filled it from one end to another with their uncleanness. 12 Now therefore give not your daughters unto their sons, neither take their daughters unto your sons, nor seek their peace or their wealth for ever: that ye may be strong, and eat the good of the land, and leave *it* for an inheritance to your children for ever. 13 And after all that is come upon us for our evil deeds, and for our great trespass, seeing that thou our God hast punished us less than our iniquities *deserve*, and hast given us *such* deliverance as this; 14 Should we again break thy commandments, and join in affinity with the people of these abominations? wouldest not thou be angry with us till thou hadst consumed *us*, so that *there should be* no remnant nor escaping? 15 O LORD God of Israel, thou *art* righteous: for we remain yet escaped, as *it is* this day: behold, we *are* before thee in our trespasses: for we cannot stand before thee because of this.

What the meditations of Ezra's heart were, while for some hours he sat down astonished, we may guess by the words of his mouth when at length he *spoke with his tongue;* and a most pathetic address he here makes to Heaven upon this occasion. Observe,

I. The time when he made this address—*at the evening sacrifice, v.* 5. Then (it is likely) devout people used to come into the courts of the temple, to grace the solemnity of the sacrifice and to offer up their own prayers to God in concurrence with it. In their hearing Ezra chose to make this confession, that they might be made duly sensible of the sins of their people, which hitherto they had either not taken notice of or had made light of. Prayer may preach. The sacrifice, and especially the evening sacrifice, was a type of the great propitiation, that *blessed Lamb of God* which in the evening of the world was to *take away sin by the sacrifice of himself,* to which we may suppose Ezra had an eye of faith in this penitential address to God; he makes confession with his hand, as it were, upon the head of that great sacrifice, through which *we receive the atonement.* Certainly Ezra was no stranger to the message which the angel Gabriel had some years ago delivered to Daniel, at the time of the evening sacrifice, and as it were in explication of it, concerning Messiah the Prince (Dan. ix. 21, 24); and perhaps he had regard to that in choosing this time.

II. His preparation for this address. 1. He *rose up from his heaviness,* and so far shook off the burden of his grief as was necessary to the lifting up of his heart to God. He recovered from his astonishment, got the tumult of his troubled spirits somewhat stilled and his spirit composed for communion with God. 2. He *fell upon his knees,* put himself into the posture of a penitent humbling himself and a petitioner suing for mercy, in both representing the people for whom he was now an intercessor. 3. He *spread out his hands,* as one affected with what he was going to say, offering it up unto God, waiting, and reaching out, as it were, with an earnest expectation, to receive a gracious answer. In this he had an eye to God as the Lord, and as his God, a God of power, but a God of grace.

III. The address itself. It is not properly to be called a prayer, for there is not a word of petition in it; but, if we give prayer its full latitude, it is the offering up of pious and devout affections to God, and very devout, very pious, are the affections which Ezra here expresses. His address is a penitent confession of sin, not his own (from a conscience burdened with its own guilt and apprehensive of his own danger), but the sin of his people, from a gracious concern for the honour of God and the welfare of Israel. Here is a lively picture of ingenuous repentance. Observe in this address,

1. The confession he makes of the sin and the aggravations of it, which he insists upon, to affect his own heart and theirs that joined with him with holy sorrow and shame and fear, in the consideration of it, that they might be deeply humbled for it. And it is observable that, though he himself was wholly clear from this guilt, yet he puts himself into the number of the sinners, because he was a member of the same community—*our sins and our trespass*. Perhaps he now remembered it against himself, as his fault, that he had staid so long after his brethren in Babylon, and had not separated himself so soon as he might have done from the people of those lands. When we are lamenting the wickedness of the wicked, it may be, if we duly reflect upon ourselves and give our own hearts leave to deal faithfully with us, we may find something of the same nature, though in a lower degree, that we also have been guilty of. However, he speaks that which was, or should have been, the general complaint.

(1.) He owns their sins to have been very great: "*Our iniquities are increased over our heads* (*v.* 6); we are ready to perish in them as in deep waters;" so general was the prevalency of them, so violent the power of them, and so threatening were they of the most pernicious consequences. "Iniquity has grown up to such a height among us that it reaches to the heavens, so very impudent that it dares heaven, so very provoking that, like the sin of Sodom, it cries to heaven for vengeance." But let this be the comfort of true penitents that though their sins reach to the heavens God's mercy is *in the heavens*, Ps. xxxvi. 5. *Where sin abounds grace will much more abound.*

(2.) Their sin had been long persisted in (*v.* 7): *Since the days of our fathers have we been in a great trespass.* The example of those that had gone before them he thought so far from excusing their fault that it aggravated it. "We should have taken warning not to stumble at the same stone. The corruption is so much the worse that it has taken deep root and begins to plead prescription, but by this means we have reason to fear that the measure of the iniquity is nearly full."

(3.) The great and sore judgments which God had brought upon them for their sins did very much aggravate them: "*For our iniquities we have been delivered to the sword and to captivity* (*v.* 7), and yet not reformed, yet not reclaimed—brayed in the mortar, and yet the *folly not gone* (Prov. xxvii. 22)—corrected, but not reclaimed."

(4.) The late mercies God had bestowed upon them did likewise very much aggravate their sins. This he insists largely upon, *v.* 8, 9. Observe, [1.] The time of mercy: *Now for a little space*, that is, "It is but a little while since we had our liberty, and it is not likely to continue long." This greatly aggravated their sin, that they were so lately in the furnace and that they knew not how soon they might return to it again; and could they yet be secure? [2.] The fountain of mercy: *Grace has been shown us from the Lord.* The kings of Persia were the instruments of their enlargement; but he ascribes it to God and to his grace, his free grace, without any merit of theirs. [3.] The streams of mercy,—that they were *not forsaken in their bondage*, but even in Babylon had the tokens of God's presence,—that they were a remnant of Israelites left, a few out of many, and those narrowly escaped out of the hands of their enemies, by the favour of the kings of Persia,—and especially that they had *a nail in his holy place*, that is (as it is explained, *v.* 9), that they had set up the *house of God.* They had their religion settled and the service of the temple in a constant method. We are to reckon it a great comfort and advantage to have stated opportunities of worshipping God. *Blessed are those that dwell in God's house,* like Anna that departed not from the temple. *This is my rest for ever,* says the gracious soul. [4.] The effects of all this. It enlightened their eyes, and it revived their hearts; that is, it was very comfortable to them, and the more sensibly so because it was in their bondage: it was life from the dead to them. Though but *a little reviving*, it was a great favour, considering that they deserved none and the day of small things was an earnest of greater. "Now," says Ezra, "how ungrateful are we to offend a God that has been so kind to us! how disingenuous to mingle in sin with those nations from whom we have been, in wonderful mercy, delivered! how unwise to expose ourselves to God's displeasure when we are tried with the returns of his favour and are upon our good behaviour for the continuance of it!"

(5.) It was a great aggravation of the sin that it was against an express command: *We have forsaken thy commandments, v.* 10. It seems to have been an ancient law of the house of Jacob not to match with the families of the uncircumcised, Gen. xxxiv. 14. But, besides that, God had strictly forbidden it. He recites the command, *v.* 11, 12. For sin appears sin, appears exceedingly sinful, when we compare it with the law which is broken by it. Nothing could be more express: *Give not your daughters to their sons, nor take their daughters to your sons.* The reason given is because, if they mingled with those nations, they would pollute themselves. It was an unclean land, and they were a holy people; but if they kept themselves distinct from them it would be their honour and safety, and the perpetuating of their prosperity. Now to violate a command so express, backed with such reasons, and a fundamental law of their constitution, was very provoking to the God of heaven.

(6.) That in the judgments by which they had already smarted for their sins God had *punished them less than their iniquities deserved,* so that he looked upon them to be still in debt upon the old account. "What! and yet shall we run up a new score? Has God dealt so gently with us in correcting us, and shall we thus abuse his favour and turn his grace into wantonness?" God, in his grace and mercy, had said concerning Sion's captivity, *She hath received of the Lord's hand double for all her sins* (Isa. xl. 2); but Ezra, in a penitential sense of the great malignity that was in their sin, acknowledged that, though the punishment was very great, it was less than they deserved.

2. The devout affections that were working in him, in making this confession. Speaking of sin,

(1.) He speaks as one much ashamed. With this he begins (*v.* 6), *O my God! I am ashamed and blush, O my God!* (so the words are placed) *to lift up my face unto thee.* Note, [1.] Sin is a shameful thing; as soon as ever our first parents had eaten forbidden fruit they were ashamed of themselves. [2.] Holy shame is as necessary an ingredient in true and ingenuous repentance as holy sorrow. [3.] The sins of others should be our shame, and we should blush for those who do not blush for themselves. We may well be ashamed that we are any thing akin to those who are so ungrateful to God and unwise for themselves. This is *clearing ourselves,* 2 Cor. vii. 11. [4.] Penitent sinners never see so much reason to blush and be ashamed as when they come to *lift up their faces before God.* A natural sense of our own honour which we have injured will make us ashamed, when we have done a wrong thing, to look men in the face; but a gracious concern for God's honour will make us much more ashamed to look him in the face. The publican, when he went to the temple to pray, hung down his head more than ever, as one ashamed, Luke xviii. 13. [5.] An eye to God as our God will be of great use to us in the exercise of repentance. Ezra begins, *O my God!* and again in the same breath, *My God.* The consideration of our covenant-relation to God as ours will help to humble us, and break our hearts for sin, that we should violate both his precepts to us and our promises to him; it will also encourage us to hope for pardon upon repentance. "He is my God, notwithstanding this;" and every transgression in the covenant does not throw us out of covenant.

(2.) He speaks as one much amazed (*v.* 10) "*What shall we say after this?* For my part I know not what to say: if God do not help us, we are undone." The discoveries of guilt excite amazement: the more we think of sin the worse it looks. The difficulty of the case excites amazement. How shall we recover ourselves? Which way shall we make our peace with God? [1.] True penitents are at a loss what to say. Shall we say, We have *not sinned,* or, *God will not require it?* If we do, *we deceive ourselves, and the truth is not in us.* Shall we say, Have patience with us and we will pay thee all, with *thousands of rams, or our first-born for our transgression?* God will not thus be mocked: he knows we are insolvent. Shall we say, *There is no hope,* and *let come on us what will?* That is but to make bad worse. [2.] True penitents will consider what to say, and should, as Ezra, beg of God to teach them. What shall we say? Say, "I have sinned; I have done foolishly; God be merciful to me a sinner;" and the like. See Hos. xiv. 2.

(3.) He speaks as one much afraid, *v.* 13, 14. "After all the judgments that have come upon us to reclaim us from sin, and all the deliverances that have been wrought for us to engage us to God and duty, *if we should again break God's commandments, by joining in affinity with the children of disobedience* and learning their ways, what else could we expect but that God should be *angry with us till he had consumed us,* and there should not be so much as a remnant left, nor any to escape the destruction? There is not a surer nor sadder presage of ruin to any people than revolting to sin, to the same sins again, after great judgments and great deliverances. Those that will be wrought upon neither by the one nor by the other are fit to be rejected, as reprobate silver, for the *founder melteth in vain.*

(4.) He speaks as one much assured of the righteousness of God, and resolved to acquiesce in that and to leave the matter with him whose judgment is *according to truth* (*v.* 15): "*Thou art righteous,* wise, just, and good; thou wilt neither do us wrong nor be hard upon us; and therefore behold *we are before thee,* we lie at thy feet, waiting our doom; *we cannot stand before thee,* insisting upon any righteousness of our own, having no plea to support us or bring us off, and therefore we fall down before thee, in our trespass, and cast ourselves on thy mercy. *Do unto us whatsoever seemeth good unto thee,* Judg. x. 15. We have nothing to say, nothing to do, but to *make supplication to our Judge,*" Job ix. 15. Thus does this good man lay his grief before God and then leave it with him.

CHAP. X.

In this chapter we have that grievance redressed which was complained of and lamented in the foregoing chapter. Observe, I. How the people's hearts were prepared for the redress of it by their deep humiliation for the sin, ver. 1. II. How it was proposed to Ezra by Shechaniah, ver. 2—4. III. How the proposa was put in execution. 1. The great men were sworn to stand to it, ver. 5. 2. Ezra appeared first in it, ver. 6. 3. A general assembly was called, ver. 7—9. 4. They all, in compliance with Ezra's exhortation, agreed to the reformation, ver. 10—14. 5. Commissioners were appointed to sit "de die in diem"—day after day, to enquire who had married strange wives and to oblige them to put them away, which was done accordingly (ver. 15—17), and a list of the names of those that were found guilty given in, ver. 18—44.

NOW when Ezra had prayed, and when he had confessed, weeping and casting himself down before the house of God, there assembled unto him out of Israel a very great congregation of men and women and children: for the people wept very sore. 2 And Shechaniah the son of Jehiel, *one* of the sons of Elam, answered and said unto Ezra, We have trespassed against our God, and have taken strange wives of the people of the land: yet now there is hope in Israel concerning this thing. 3 Now therefore let us make a covenant with our God to put away all the wives, and such as are born of them, according to the counsel of my lord, and of those that tremble at the commandment of our God; and let it be done according to the law. 4 Arise; for *this* matter *belongeth* unto thee: we also *will be* with thee: be of good courage, and do *it*. 5 Then arose Ezra, and made the chief priests, the Levites, and all Israel, to swear that they should do according to this word. And they sware.

We are here told,

I. What good impressions were made upon the people by Ezra's humiliation and confession of sin. No sooner was it noised in the city that their new governor, in whom they rejoiced, was himself in grief, and to so great a degree, for them and their sin, than presently there *assembled to him a very great congregation*, to see what the matter was and to mingle their tears with his, *v.* 1. Our weeping for other people's sins may perhaps set those a weeping for them themselves who otherwise would continue senseless and remorseless. See what a happy influence the good examples of great ones may have upon their inferiors. When Ezra, a scribe, a scholar, a man in authority under the king, so deeply lamented the public corruptions, they concluded that they were indeed very grievous, else he would not thus have grieved for them; and this drew tears from every eye: *men, women, and children, wept very sore*, when he wept thus.

II. What a good motion Shechaniah made upon this occasion. The place was *Bochim*—a place of *weepers;* but, for aught that appears, there was a profound silence among them, as among Job's friends, who *spoke not a word to him, because they saw that his grief was very great*, till Shechaniah (one of Ezra's companions from Babylon, *ch.* viii. 3, 5) stood up, and made a speech addressed to Ezra, in which,

1. He owns the national guilt, sums up all Ezra's confession in one word, and sets to his seal that it is true: "*We have trespassed against our God, and have taken strange wives, v.* 2. The matter is too plain to be denied and too bad to be excused." It does not appear that Shechaniah was himself culpable in this matter (if he had had the beam in his own eye, he could not have seen so clearly to pluck it out of his brother's eye), but his father was guilty, and several of his father's house (as appears *v.* 26), and therefore he reckons himself among the trespassers; nor does he seek to excuse or palliate the sin, though some of his own relations were guilty of it, but, in the cause of God, *says to his father, I have not known him*, as Levi, Deut. xxxiii. 9. Perhaps the strange wife that his father had married had been an unjust unkind step-mother to him, and had made mischief in the family, and he supposed that others had done the like, which made him the more forward to appear against this corruption; if so, this was not the only time that private resentments have been over ruled by the providence of God to serve the public good.

2. He encourages himself and others to hope that though the matter was bad it might be amended: *Yet now there is hope in Israel* (where else should there be hope but in Israel? those that are strangers to that commonwealth are said to have *no hope*, Eph. ii. 12) even *concerning this thing*. The case is sad, but it is not desperate; the disease is threatening, but not incurable. There is hope that the people may be reformed, the guilty reclaimed, a stop put to the spreading of the contagion; and so the judgments which the sin deserves may be prevented and all will be well. *Now there is hope;* now that the disease is discovered it is half-cured. Now that the alarm is taken the people begin to be sensible of the mischief, and to lament it, a spirit of repentance seems to be poured out upon them, and they are all thus humbling themselves before God for it, *now there is hope* that God will forgive, and have mercy. The *valley of Achor* (that is, of *trouble*) is the *door of hope* (Hos. ii. 15); for the sin that truly troubles us shall not ruin us. There is hope now that Israel has such a prudent, pious, zealous governor as Ezra to manage this affair. Note, (1.) In melancholy times we must see and observe what makes for us, as well as what makes against us. (2.) There may be good hopes through grace, even when there is the sense of great guilt before God. (3.) Where sin is seen and lamented, and good steps are taken towards a reformation, even sinners ought to be encouraged. (4.) Even great saints must thankfully receive seasonable counsel and comfort from

those that are much their inferiors, as Ezra from Shechaniah.

3. He advises that a speedy and effectual course should be taken for the divorcing of the strange wives. The case is plain; what has been done amiss must be undone again as far as possible; nothing less than this is true repentance. *Let us put away all the wives, and such as are born of them, v.* 3. Ezra, though he knew this was the only way of redressing the grievance, yet perhaps did not think it feasible, and despaired of ever bringing the people to it, which put him into that confusion in which we left him in the foregoing chapter; but Shechaniah, who conversed more with the people than he did, assured him the thing was practicable if they went wisely to work. As to us now, it is certain that sin must be put away, a bill of divorce must be given it, with a resolution never to have any thing more to do with it, though it be dear as the wife of thy bosom, nay, as a right eye or a right hand, otherwise there is no pardon, no peace. What has been unjustly got cannot be justly kept, but must be restored; but, as to the case of being *unequally yoked with unbelievers,* Shechaniah's counsel, which he was then so clear in, will not hold now; such marriages, it is certain, are sinful, and ought not to be made, but they are not null. *Quod fieri non debuit, factum valet—That which ought not to have been done must, when done, abide.* Our rule, under the gospel, is, *If a brother has a wife that believeth not,* and *she be pleased to dwell with him, let him not put her away,* 1 Cor. vii. 12, 13.

4. He puts them in a good method for the effecting of this reformation, and shows them not only that it must be done, but how. (1.) "Let Ezra, and all those that are present in this assembly, agree in a resolution that this must be done (pass a vote immediately to this effect: it will now pass *nemine contradicente—unanimously),* that it may be said to be done *according to the counsel of my lord,* the president of the assembly, with the unanimous concurrence of those that *tremble at the commandment of our God,* which is the description of those that were gathered to him, *ch.* ix. 4. Declare it to be the sense of all the sober serious people among us, which cannot but have a great sway among Israelites." (2.) "Let the command of God in this matter, which Ezra recited in his prayer, be laid before the people, and let them see that it is *done according to the law;* we have that to warrant us, nay, that binds us to what we do; it is not an addition of our own to the divine law, but the necessary execution of it." (3.) "While we are in a good mind, let us bind ourselves by a solemn vow and covenant that we will do it, lest, when the present impressions are worn off, the thing be left undone. Let us covenant, not only that, if we have strange wives ourselves, we will put them away, but that, if we have not, we will do what we can in our places to oblige others to put away theirs." (4.) "Let Ezra himself preside in this matter, who is authorized by the king's commission to enquire whether the law of God be duly observed in Judah and Jerusalem (*ch.* vii. 14), and let us all resolve to stand by him in it (*v.* 4): *Arise, be of good courage.* Weeping, in this case, is good, but reforming is better." See what God said to Joshua in a like case, Josh. vii. 10, 11.

III. What a good resolution they came to upon this good motion, *v.* 5. They not only agreed that it should be done, but bound themselves with an oath that they would do according to this word. Fast bind, fast find.

6 Then Ezra rose up from before the house of God, and went into the chamber of Johanan the son of Eliashib: and *when* he came thither, he did eat no bread, nor drink water: for he mourned because of the transgression of them that had been carried away. 7 And they made proclamation throughout Judah and Jerusalem unto all the children of the captivity, that they should gather themselves together unto Jerusalem; 8 And that whosoever would not come within three days, according to the counsel of the princes and the elders, all his substance should be forfeited, and himself separated from the congregation of those that had been carried away. 9 Then all the men of Judah and Benjamin gathered themselves together unto Jerusalem within three days. It *was* the ninth month, on the twentieth *day* of the month; and all the people sat in the street of the house of God, trembling because of *this* matter, and for the great rain. 10 And Ezra the priest stood up, and said unto them, Ye have transgressed, and have taken strange wives, to increase the trespass of Israel. 11 Now therefore make confession unto the LORD God of your fathers, and do his pleasure: and separate yourselves from the people of the land, and from the strange wives. 12 Then all the congregation answered and said with a loud voice, As thou hast said, so must we do. 13 But the people *are* many, and *it is* a time of much rain, and we are not able to stand without, neither *is this* a work of one day or two: for we are many that have trans-

gressed in this thing. 14 Let now our rulers of all the congregation stand, and let all them which have taken strange wives in our cities come at appointed times, and with them the elders of every city, and the judges thereof, until the fierce wrath of our God for this matter be turned from us.

We have here an account of the proceedings upon the resolutions lately taken up concerning the strange wives; no time was lost; they struck when the iron was hot, and soon set the wheels of reformation a-going. 1. Ezra went to the council-chamber, where, it is probable, the priests used to meet upon public business; *and till he came thither* (so bishop Patrick thinks it should be read), till he saw something done, and more likely to be done, for the redress of this grievance, *he did neither eat nor drink*, but continued mourning. Sorrow for sin should be abiding sorrow; be sure to let it continue till the sin be put away. 2. He sent orders to all the children of the captivity to attend him at Jerusalem *within three days* (*v.* 7, 8); and, being authorized by the king to enforce his orders with penalties annexed (*ch.* vii. 26), he threatened that whosoever refused to obey the summons should forfeit his estate and be outlawed. The doom of him that would not attend on this religious occasion should be that his substance should, in his stead, be for ever after appropriated to the service of their religion, and he himself, for his contempt, should for ever after be excluded from the honours and privileges of their religion; he should be excommunicated. 3. Within the time limited the generality of the people met at Jerusalem and made their appearance *in the street of the house of God*, *v.* 9. Those that had no zeal for the work they were called to, nay, perhaps had a dislike to it, being themselves delinquents, yet paid such a deference to Ezra's authority, and were so awed by the penalty, that they durst not stay away. 4. God gave them a token of his displeasure in the great rain that happened at that time (*v.* 9 and again *v.* 13), which perhaps kept some away, and was very grievous to those that met in the open street. When they wept the heavens wept too, signifying that, though God was angry with them for their sin, yet he was well pleased with their repentance, and (as it is said, Judg. x. 16) *his soul was grieved for the misery of Israel;* it was also an indication of the good fruits of their repentance, for the rain makes the earth fruitful. 5. Ezra gave the charge at this great assize. He told them upon what account he called them together now, that it was because he found that since their return out of captivity they had *increased the trespass of Israel* by *marrying strange wives,* had added to their former sins this new transgression, which would certainly be a means of again introducing idolatry, the very sin they had smarted for and which he hoped they had been cured of in their captivity; and he called them together that they might *confess their sin to God,* and, having done that, might declare themselves ready and willing to do his pleasure, as it should be made known to them (which all those will do that truly repent of what they have done to incur his displeasure), and particularly that they might separate themselves from all idolaters, especially idolatrous wives, *v.* 10, 11. On these heads, we may suppose, he enlarged, and probably made such another confession of the sin now as he made *ch.* ix., to which he required them to say *Amen.* 6. The people submitted not only to Ezra's jurisdiction in general, but to his inquisition and determination in this matter: "*As thou hast said, so must we do, v.* 12. We have sinned in mingling with the heathen, and have thereby been in danger, not only of being corrupted by them, for we are frail, but of being lost among them, for we are few; we are therefore convinced that there is an absolute necessity of our separating from them again." There is hope concerning people when they are convinced, not only that it is good to part with their sins, but that it is indispensably necessary: we must do it, or we are undone. 7. It was agreed that this affair should be carried on, not in a popular assembly, nor that they should think to go through with it all on a sudden, but that a court of delegates should be appointed to receive complaints and to hear and determine upon them. It could not be done at this time, for it was not put into a method, nor could the people stand out because of the rain. The delinquents were many, and it would require time to discover and examine them. Nice cases would arise, which could not be adjudged without debate and deliberation, *v.* 13. "And therefore let the crowd be dismissed, and the rulers stand to receive informations; let them proceed city by city, and let the offenders be convicted before them in the presence of the judges and elders of their own city; and let them be entrusted to see the orders executed. Thus *take time and we shall have done the sooner;* whereas, if we do it in a hurry, we shall do it by halves, *v.* 14. If, in this method, a thorough reformation be made, the *fierce wrath of God* will be *turned from us,* which, we are sensible, is ready to break forth against us for this transgression." Ezra was willing that his zeal should be guided by the people's prudence, and put the matter into this method; he was not ashamed to own that the advice came from them, any more than he was to comply with it.

15 Only Jonathan the son of Asahel and Jahaziah the son of Tikvah were employed about this *matter:* and Meshullam and Shabbethai the Le-

vite helped them. 16 And the children of the captivity did so. And Ezra the priest, *with* certain chief of the fathers, after the house of their fathers, and all of them by *their* names, were separated, and sat down in the first day of the tenth month to examine the matter. 17 And they made an end with all the men that had taken strange wives by the first day of the first month. 18 And among the sons of the priests there were found that had taken strange wives: *namely*, of the sons of Jeshua the son of Jozadak, and his brethren; Maaseiah, and Eliezer, and Jarib, and Gedaliah. 19 And they gave their hands that they would put away their wives; and *being* guilty, *they offered* a ram of the flock for their trespass. 20 And of the sons of Immer; Hanani, and Zebadiah. 21 And of the sons of Harim; Maaseiah, and Elijah, and Shemaiah, and Jehiel, and Uzziah. 22 And of the sons of Pashur; Elioenai, Maaseiah, Ishmael, Nethaneel, Jozabad, and Elasah. 23 Also of the Levites; Jozabad, and Shimei, and Kelaiah, (the same *is* Kelita,) Pethahiah, Judah, and Eliezer. 24 Of the singers also; Eliashib: and of the porters; Shallum, and Telem, and Uri. 25 Moreover of Israel: of the sons of Parosh; Ramiah, and Jeziah, and Malchiah, and Miamin, and Eleazar, and Malchijah, and Benaiah. 26 And of the sons of Elam; Mattaniah, Zechariah, and Jehiel, and Abdi, and Jeremoth, and Eliah. 27 And of the sons of Zattu; Elioenai, Eliashib, Mattaniah, and Jeremoth, and Zabad, and Aziza. 28 Of the sons also of Bebai; Jehohanan, Hananiah, Zabbai, *and* Athlai. 29 And of the sons of Bani; Meshullam, Malluch, and Adaiah, Jashub, and Sheal, and Ramoth. 30 And of the sons of Pahath-moab; Adna, and Chelal, Benaiah, Maaseiah, Mattaniah, Bezaleel, and Binnui, and Manasseh. 31 And *of* the sons of Harim; Eliezer, Ishijah, Malchiah, Shemaiah, Shimeon, 32 Benjamin, Malluch, *and* Shemariah. 33 Of the sons of Hashum; Mattenai, Mattathah, Zabad, Eliphelet, Jeremai, Manasseh, *and* Shimei. 34 Of the sons of Bani; Maadai, Amram, and Uel, 35 Benaiah, Bedeiah, Chelluh, 36 Vaniah, Meremoth, Eliashib, 37 Mattaniah, Mattenai, and Jaasau, 38 And Bani, and Binnui, Shimei, 39 And Shelemiah, and Nathan, and Adaiah, 40 Machnadebai, Shashai, Sharai, 41 Azareel, and Shelemiah, Shemariah, 42 Shallum, Amariah, *and* Joseph. 43 Of the sons of Nebo; Jeiel, Mattithiah, Zabad, Zebina, Jadau, and Joel, Benaiah. 44 All these had taken strange wives: and *some* of them had wives by whom they had children.

The method of proceeding in this matter being concluded on, and the congregation dismissed, that each in his respective place might gain and give intelligence to facilitate the matter, we are here told, 1. Who were the persons that undertook to manage the matter and bring the causes regularly before the commissioners—*Jonathan* and *Jahaziah*, two active men, whether of the priests or of the people does not appear; probably they were the men that made that proposal (*v.* 13, 14) and were therefore the fittest to see it pursued; two honest Levites were joined with them, and *helped them*, *v.* 15. Dr. Lightfoot gives a contrary sense of this: *only* (or *nevertheless) Jonathan and Jahaziah stood against this matter* (which reading the original will very well bear), and these two *Levites helped them* in opposing it, either the thing itself or this method of proceeding. It was strange if a work of this kind was carried on and met with no opposition. 2. Who were the commissioners that sat upon this matter. Ezra was president, and with him *certain chief* men *of the fathers* who were qualified with wisdom and zeal above others for this service, *v.* 16. It was happy for them that they had such a man as Ezra to head them; they could not have done it well without his direction, yet he would not do it without their concurrence. 3. How long they were about it. They began *the first day of the tenth month to examine the matter* (*v.* 16), which was but ten days after this method was proposed (*v.* 9), and they finished in three months, *v.* 17. They sat closely and minded their business, otherwise they could not have despatched so many causes as they had before them in so little time; for we may suppose that all who were impeached were fairly asked what cause they could show why they should not be parted, and, if we may judge by other cases, provided the wife were proselyted to the Jewish religion she was not to be put away, the trial of which would require great care. 4. Who the persons were that were found guilty of this crime. Their names are here recorded to their perpetual reproach; many of the priests, nay, of the family of Jeshua, the high priest, were found guilty (*v.* 18), though the law had particularly provided, for the preserving of their honour in their marriages, that being holy themselves they should not marry such as were profane. Lev. xxi. 7. Those that should have taught others the law broke it themselves and by their example emboldened others to do likewise. But, having lost their innocency in this matter, they did well to recant and give an example of repentance; for they promised *under their hand* to put away their strange wives (some think that they made oath to do so with their *hands lifted up)*, and they took the appointed way of obtaining pardon, bringing the ram which was appointed by the law *for a trespass offering* (Lev. vi. 6), so owning their guilt and the desert of it, and humbly suing for forgiveness. About 113 in all are here named who had married strange wives, and some of them, it is said (*v.* 44), had children by them, which implies that not many of them had, God not crowning those marriages with the blessing of increase. Whether the children were turned off with the mothers, as Shechaniah proposed, does not appear; it should seem not: however it is probable that the wives which were put away were well provided for, according to their rank. One would think this grievance was now thoroughly redressed, yet we meet with it again (Neh. xiii. 23 and Mal. ii. 11), for such corruptions are easily and insensibly brought in, but not without great difficulty purged out again. The best reformers can but do their endeavour, but, when the Redeemer himself shall *come to Sion,* he shall effectually *turn away ungodliness from Jacob.*

AN

EXPOSITION,

WITH PRACTICAL OBSERVATIONS,

OF THE BOOK OF

NEHEMIAH.

THIS book continues the history of the *children of the captivity*, the poor Jews, that had lately returned out of Babylon to their own land. At this time not only the Persian monarchy flourished in great pomp and power, but Greece and Rome began to be very great and to make a figure. Of the affairs of those high and mighty states we have authentic accounts extant; but the sacred and inspired history takes cognizance only of the state of the Jews, and makes no mention of other nations but as the Israel of God had dealings with them: for the Lord's portion is his people; they are his peculiar treasure, and, in comparison with them, the rest of the world is but as lumber. In my esteem, Ezra the scribe and Nehemiah the tirshatha, though neither of them ever wore a crown, commanded an army, conquered any country, or was famed for philosophy or oratory, yet both of them, being pious praying men, and very serviceable in their day to the church of God and the interests of religion, were really greater men and more honourable, not only than any of the Roman consuls or dictators, but than Xenophon, or Demosthenes, or Plato himself, who lived at the same time, the bright ornaments of Greece. Nehemiah's agency for the advancing of the settlement of Israel we have a full account of in this book of his own commentaries or memoirs, wherein he records not only the works of his hands, but the workings of his heart, in the management of public affairs, inserting in the story many devout reflections and ejaculations, which discover in his mind a very deep tincture of serious piety and are peculiar to his writing. Twelve years, from his twentieth year (*ch.* i. 1) to his thirty-second year (*ch.* xiii. 6), he was governor of Judea, under Artaxerxes king of Persia, whom Dr. Lightfoot supposes to be the same Artaxerxes as Ezra had his commission from. This book relates, I. Nehemiah's concern for Jerusalem and the commission he obtained from the king to go thither, *ch.* i. ii. II. His building the wall of Jerusalem notwithstanding the opposition he met with, *ch.* iii. iv. III. His redressing the grievances of the people, *ch.* v. IV. His finishing the wall, *ch.* vi. V. The account he took of the people, *ch.* vii. VI. The religious solemnities of reading the law, fasting, and praying, and renewing their covenants, to which he called the people, *ch.* viii.—x. VII. The care he took for the replenishing of the holy city and the settling of the holy tribe, *ch.* xi., xii. VIII. His zeal in reforming various abuses, *ch.* xiii. Some call this *the second book of Ezra*, not because he was the penman of it, but because it is a continuation of the history of the foregoing book, with which it is connected, *v.* 1. This was the last *historical* book that was written, as Malachi was the last *prophetical* book, of the Old Testament.

CHAP. I.

Here we first meet with Nehemiah at the Persian court, where we find him, I. Inquisitive concerning the state of the Jews and Jerusalem, ver. 1, 2. II. Informed of their deplorable condition, ver. 3. III. Fasting and praying thereupon (ver. 4), with a particular account of his prayer, ver. 5--11. Such is the rise of this great man, by piety, not by policy.

THE words of Nehemiah the son of Hachaliah. And it came to pass in the month Chisleu, in the twentieth year, as I was in Shushan the palace, 2 That Hanani, one of my brethren, came, he and *certain* men of Judah; and I asked them concerning the Jews that had escaped, which were left of the captivity, and concerning Jerusalem. 3 And they said unto me, The remnant that are left of the captivity there in the province *are* in great affliction and reproach: the wall of Jerusalem also *is* broken down, and the gates thereof are burned with fire. 4 And it came to pass, when I heard these words, that I sat down and wept, and mourned *certain* days, and fasted, and prayed before the God of heaven,

What tribe Nehemiah was of does nowhere appear; but, if it be true (which we are told by the author of the Maccabees, 2 Mac. i. 18) that he offered sacrifice, we must conclude him to have been a priest. Observe,

I. Nehemiah's station at the court of Persia. We are here told that he was *in Shushan the palace,* or royal city, of the king of Persia, where the court was ordinarily kept (*v.* 1), and (*v.* 11) that he was *the king's cup-bearer.* Kings and great men probably looked upon it as a piece of state to be attended by those of other nations. By this place at court he would be the better qualified for the service of his country in that post for which God had designed him, as Moses was the fitter to govern for being bred up in Pharaoh's court, and David in Saul's. He would also have the fairer opportunity of serving his country by his interest in the king and those about him. Observe, He is not forward to tell us what great preferment he had at court; it is not till the end of the chapter that he tells us he was *the king's cup-bearer* (a place of great trust, as well as of honour and profit), when he could not avoid the mentioning of it because of the following story; but at first he only says, *I was in Shushan the palace.* We may hence learn to be humble and modest, and slow to speak of our own advancements. But in the providences of God concerning him we may observe, to our comfort, 1. That when God has work to do he will never want instruments to do it with. 2. That those whom God designs to employ in his service he will find out proper ways both to fit for it and to call to it. 3. That God has his remnant in all places; we read of Obadiah in the house of Ahab, saints in Cæsar's household, and a devout Nehemiah in Shushan the palace. 4. That God can make the courts of princes sometimes nurseries and sometimes sanctuaries to the friends and patrons of the church's cause.

II. Nehemiah's tender and compassionate enquiry concerning the state of the Jews in their own land, *v.* 2. It happened that a friend and relation of his came to the court, with some other company, by whom he had an opportunity of informing himself fully how it went with the children of the captivity and what posture Jerusalem, the beloved city, was in. Nehemiah lived at ease, in honour and fulness, himself, but could not forget that he was an Israelite, nor shake off the thoughts of his brethren in distress, but in spirit (like Moses, Acts vii. 23) he *visited them and looked upon their burdens.* As distance of place did not alienate his affections from them (though they were out of sight, yet not out of mind), so neither did, 1. The dignity to which he was advanced. Though he was a great man, and probably rising higher, yet he did not think it below him to take cognizance of his brethren that were low and despised, nor was he ashamed to own his relation to them and concern for them. 2. The diversity of their sentiments from his, and the difference of their practice accordingly. Though he did not go to settle at Jerusalem himself (as we think he ought to have done now that liberty was proclaimed), but conformed to the court, and staid there, yet he did not therefore judge nor despise those that had returned, nor upbraid them as impolitic, but kindly concerned himself for them, was ready to do them all the good offices he could, and, that he might know which way to do them a kindness, *asked concerning them.* Note, It is lawful and good to enquire, "What news?" We should enquire especially concerning the state of the church and religion, and how it fares with the people of God; and the design of our enquiry must be, not that, like the Athenians, we may have something to talk of, but that we may know how to direct our prayers and our praises.

III. The melancholy account which is here given him of the present state of the Jews and Jerusalem, *v.* 3. Hanani, the person he enquired of, has this character given of him (*ch.* vii. 2), that he *feared God above many,* and therefore would not only speak truly, but, when he spoke of the desolations of Jerusalem, would speak tenderly. It is probable that his errand to court at this time was to solicit some favour, some relief or other, that they stood in need of. Now the account he gives is, 1. That the holy seed was miserably trampled on and abused, *in great affliction and reproach,* insulted upon all occasions by their neighbours, and *filled with the scorning of those that were at ease.*

2. That the holy city was exposed and in ruins. *The wall of Jerusalem was* still *broken down, and the gates* were, as the Chaldeans left them, in ruins. This made the condition of the inhabitants both very despicable under the abiding marks of poverty and slavery, and very dangerous, for their enemies might when they pleased make an easy prey of them. The temple was built, the government settled, and a work of reformation brought to some head, but here was one good work yet undone; this was still wanting. Every Jerusalem, on this side the heavenly one, will have some defect or other in it, for the making up of which it will require the help and service of its friends.

IV. The great affliction this gave to Nehemiah and the deep concern it put him into, *v.* 4. 1. He *wept and mourned.* It was not only just when he heard the news that he fell into a passion of weeping, but his sorrow continued *certain days.* Note, The desolations and distresses of the church ought to be the matter of our grief, how much soever we live at ease. 2. He *fasted and prayed;* not in public (he had no opportunity of doing that), but *before the God of heaven,* who sees in secret, and will reward openly. By his fasting and praying, (1.) He consecrated his sorrows, and directed his tears aright, *sorrowed after a godly sort,* with an eye to God, because his name was reproached in the contempt cast on his people, whose cause therefore he thus commits to him. (2.) He eased his sorrows, and unburdened his spirit, by pouring out his complaint before God and leaving it with him. (3.) He took the right method of fetching in relief for his people and direction for himself in what way to serve them. Let those who are forming any good designs for the service of the public take God along with them for the first conception of them, and utter all their projects before him; this is the way to prosper in them.

5 And said, I beseech thee, O LORD God of heaven, the great and terrible God, that keepeth covenant and mercy for them that love him and observe his commandments: 6 Let thine ear now be attentive, and thine eyes open, that thou mayest hear the prayer of thy servant, which I pray before thee now, day and night, for the children of Israel thy servants, and confess the sins of the children of Israel, which we have sinned against thee: both I and my father's house have sinned. 7 We have dealt very corruptly against thee, and have not kept the commandments, nor the statutes, nor the judgments, which thou commandedst thy servant Moses. 8 Remember, I beseech thee, the word that thou commandedst thy servant Moses, saying, *If* ye transgress, I will scatter you abroad among the nations: 9 But *if* ye turn unto me, and keep my commandments, and do them; though there were of you cast out unto the uttermost part of the heaven, *yet* will I gather them from thence, and will bring them unto the place that I have chosen to set my name there. 10 Now these *are* thy servants and thy people, whom thou hast redeemed by thy great power, and by thy strong hand. 11 O Lord, I beseech thee, let now thine ear be attentive to the prayer of thy servant, and to the prayer of thy servants, who desire to fear thy name: and prosper, I pray thee, thy servant this day, and grant him mercy in the sight of this man. For I was the king's cupbearer.

We have here Nehemiah's prayer, a prayer that has reference to all the prayers which he had for some time before been putting up to God day and night, while he continued his sorrows for the desolations of Jerusalem, and withal to the petition he was now intending to present to the king his master for his favour to Jerusalem. We may observe in this prayer,

I. His humble and reverent address to God, in which he prostrates himself before him, and gives unto him the glory due unto his name, *v.* 5. It is much the same with that of Daniel, *ch.* ix. 4. It teaches us to draw near to God, 1. With a holy awe of his majesty and glory, remembering that he is the God of heaven, infinitely above us, and sovereign Lord over us, and that he is *the great and terrible God,* infinitely excelling all the principalities and powers both of the upper and of the lower world, angels and kings; and he is a God to be worshipped with fear by all his people, and whose powerful wrath all his enemies have reason to be afraid of. Even the terrors of the Lord are improvable for the comfort and encouragement of those that trust in him. 2. With a holy confidence in his grace and truth, for he *keepeth covenant and mercy for those that love him,* not only the mercy that is promised, but even more than he promised: nothing shall be thought too much to be done for those that *love him and keep his commandments.*

II. His general request for the audience and acceptance of all the prayers and confessions he now made to God (*v.* 6): "*Let thy ear be attentive to the prayer,* not which I *say* (barely *saying* prayer will not serve), but which I *pray* before thee (then we are likely to speed in praying when we pray in pray ing), and let *thy eyes be open* upon the heart from which the prayer comes, and the case which is in prayer laid before thee." God *formed the eye* and *planted the ear;* and therefore shall he not see clearly? shall not he hear attentively?

III. His penitent confession of sin; not only Israel has sinned (it was no great mortification to him to own that), but *I and my father's house have sinned, v.* 6. Thus does he humble himself, and take shame to himself, in this confession. *We have* (I and my family among the rest) *dealt very corruptly against thee, v.* 7. In the confession of sin, let these two things be owned as the malignity of it—that it is a corruption of ourselves and an affront to God; it is *dealing corruptly against God,* setting up the corruptions of our own hearts in opposition to the commands of God.

IV. The pleas he urges for mercy for his people Israel.

1. He pleads what God had of old said to them, the rule he had settled of his proceedings towards them, which might be the rule of their expectations from him, *v.* 8, 9. He had said indeed that, if they broke covenant with him, he would *scatter them among the nations,* and that threatening was fulfilled in their captivity: never was people so widely dispersed as Israel was at this time, though at first so closely incorporated; but he had said withal that if they *turned to him* (as now they began to do, having renounced idolatry and kept to the temple service) he would *gather them again.* This he quotes from Deut. xxx. 1—5, and begs leave to put God in mind of it (though the Eternal Mind needs no remembrancer) as that which he guided his desires by, and grounded his faith and hope upon, in praying this prayer: *Remember, I beseech thee, that word;* for thou hast said, *Put me in remembrance.* He had owned (*v.* 7), *We have not kept the judgments which thou commandedst thy servant Moses;* yet he begs (*v.* 8), Lord, *remember the word which thou commandedst thy servant Moses;* for the covenant is often said to be commanded. If God were not more mindful of his promises than we are of his precepts we should be undone. Our best pleas therefore in prayer are those that are taken from the promise of God, the *word on which he has caused us to hope,* Ps. cxix. 49.

2. He pleads the relation wherein of old they stood to God: "These are *thy servants and thy people* (*v.* 10), whom thou hast set apart for thyself, and taken into covenant with thee. Wilt thou suffer thy sworn enemies to trample upon and oppress thy sworn servants? If thou wilt not appear for thy people, whom wilt thou appear for?" See Isa. lxiii. 19. As an evidence of their being God's servants he gives them this character (*v.* 11): "*They desire to fear thy name;* they are not only called by thy name, but really have a reverence for thy name; they now worship thee, and thee only, according to thy will, and have an awe of all the discoveries thou art pleased to make of thyself; this they have a desire to do," which denotes, (1.) Their good will to it. "It is their constant care and endeavour to be found in the way of their duty, and they aim at it, though in many instances they come short." (2.) Their complacency in it. "They take pleasure to fear thy name (so it may be read), not only do their duty, but do it with delight." Those shall graciously be accepted of God that truly desire to fear his name; for such a desire is his own work.

3. He pleads the great things God had formerly done for them (*v.* 10): "*Whom thou hast redeemed by thy great power,* in the days of old. Thy power is still the same; wilt thou not therefore still redeem them and perfect their redemption? Let not those be overpowered by the enemy that have a God of infinite power on their side."

Lastly, He concludes with a particular petition, that God would prosper him in his undertaking, and give him favour with the king: *this man* he calls him, for the greatest of men are but men before God; they must know themselves to be so (Ps. ix. 20), and others must know them to be so. *Who art thou that thou shouldst be afraid of a man? Mercy in the sight of this man* is what he prays for, meaning not the king's mercy, but mercy from God in his address to the king. Favour with men is then comfortable when we can see it springing from the mercy of God.

CHAP. II.

How Nehemiah wrestled with God and prevailed we read in the foregoing chapter; now here we are told how, like Jacob, he prevailed with men also, and so found that his prayers were heard and answered. I. He prevailed with the king to send him to Jerusalem with a commission to build a wall about it, and grant him what was necessary for it, ver. 1—8. II. He prevailed against the enemies that would have obstructed him in his journey (ver. 9—11) and laughed him out of his undertaking, ver. 19, 20. III. He prevailed upon his own people to join with him in this good work, viewing the desolations of the walls (ver. 12—16) and then gaining them to lend every one a hand towards the rebuilding of them, ver. 17, 18. Thus did God own him in the work to which he called him.

AND it came to pass in the month Nisan, in the twentieth year of Artaxerxes the king, *that* wine *was* before him: and I took up the wine, and gave *it* unto the king. Now I had not been *beforetime* sad in his presence. 2 Wherefore the king said unto me, Why *is* thy countenance sad, seeing thou *art* not sick? this *is* nothing *else* but sorrow of heart. Then I was very sore afraid, 3 And said unto the king, Let the king live for ever: why should not my countenance be sad, when the city, the place of my fathers' sepulchres, *lieth* waste, and the gates thereof are consumed with fire? 4 Then the king said unto me, For what dost thou make request? So I prayed to the God of heaven. 5 And I said unto the king, If it please the king, and if thy servant have found favour in thy sight, that thou wouldest send me unto Judah, unto the city of my fathers' sepulchres, that I may build it. 6 And the king said unto me, (the queen also sitting by him,) For how long shall thy journey be? and when wilt thou return? So it pleased the king to send me; and I set him a time. 7 Moreover I said unto the king, If it please the king, let letters be given me to the governors beyond the river, that they may convey me over till I come into Judah; 8 And a letter unto Asaph the keeper of the king's forest, that he may give me timber to make beams for the gates of the palace which *appertained* to the house, and for the wall of the city, and for the house that I shall enter into. And the king granted me, according to the good hand of my God upon me.

When Nehemiah had prayed for the relief of his countrymen, and perhaps in David's words (Ps. li. 18, *Build thou the walls of Jerusalem),* he did not sit still and say, "Let God now do his own work, for I have no more to do," but set himself to forecast what he could do towards it. Our prayers must be seconded with our serious endeavours, else we mock God. Nearly four months passed, from Chisleu to Nisan (from November to March), before Nehemiah made his application to the king for leave to go to Jerusalem, either because the winter was not a proper time for such a journey, and he would not make the motion till he could pursue it, or because it was so long before his month of waiting came, and there was no coming into the king's presence uncalled, Esth. iv. 11. Now that he attended the king's table he hoped to have his ear. We are not thus limited to certain moments in our addresses to the King of kings, but have liberty of access to him at all times; to the throne of grace we never come unseasonably. Now here is,

I. The occasion which he gave the king to enquire into his cares and griefs, by appearing sad in his presence. Those that speak to such great men must not fall abruptly upon their business, but fetch a compass. Nehemiah would try whether he was in a good humour before he ventured to tell him his errand, and this method he took to try him. He took up the wine and gave it to the king when he called for it, expecting that then he would look him in the face. He had not used to be sad in the king's presence, but conformed to the rules of the court (as courtiers must do), which would admit no sorrows, Esth. iv. 2. Though he was a stranger, a captive, he was easy and pleasant. Good men should do what they can by their cheerfulness to convince the world of the pleasantness of religious ways and to roll away the reproach cast upon them as melancholy; but there is a time for all things, Eccl. iii. 4. Nehemiah now saw cause both to be sad and to appear so. The miseries of Jerusalem gave him cause to be sad, and his showing his grief would give occasion to the king to enquire into the cause. He did not dissemble sadness, for he was really in grief for the afflictions of Joseph, and was not like the hypocrites who *disfigure their faces;* yet he could have concealed his grief if it had been necessary (the heart knows its own bitterness, and in the midst of laughter is often sad), but it would now serve his purpose to discover his sadness. Though he had wine before him, and probably, according to the office of the cup-bearer, did himself drink of it before he gave it to the king, yet it would not *make his heart glad,* while God's Israel was in distress.

II. The kind notice which the king took of his sadness and the enquiry he made into the cause of it (*v.* 2): *Why is thy countenance sad, seeing thou art not sick?* Note, 1. We ought, from a principle of Christian sympathy, to concern ourselves in the sorrows and sadnesses of others, even of our inferiors, and not say, What is it to us? Let not masters despise their servants' griefs, but desire to make them easy. The great God is not pleased with the dejections and disquietments of his people, but would have them both *serve him with gladness* and *eat their bread with joy.* 2. It is not strange if those that are sick have sad countenances, because of what is felt and what is feared; sickness will make those grave that were most airy and gay: yet a good man, even in sickness, may be of good cheer if he knows that his sins are forgiven. 3. Freedom from sickness is so great a mercy that while we have that we ought not to be inordinately dejected under any outward burden; yet sorrow for our own sins, the sins of others, and the calamities of God's church, may well sadden the countenance, without sickness.

III. The account which Nehemiah gave the king of the cause of his sadness, which he gave with meekness and fear. 1. With fear. He owned that now (though it appears by the following story that he was a man of courage) *he was sorely afraid,* perhaps of the king's wrath (for those eastern monarchs assumed an absolute power of life and death, Dan. ii. 12, 13; v. 19) or of misplacing a word, and losing his request by the mismanagement of it. Though he was a wise man, he was jealous of himself, lest he should say any thing imprudently; it becomes us to be so. A good assurance is indeed a good accomplishment, yet a humble self-diffidence is no man's dispraise. 2. With meekness. Without reflection upon any man, and with all the respect, deference, and good-will, imaginable to the king his master, he says, "*Let the king live for ever;* he is wise and good, and the fittest man in the world to rule." He modestly asked, "*Why should not my countenance be sad* as it is *when* (though I myself am well and at ease) *the city*" (the king knew what city he meant), "*the place of my fathers' sepulchres, lieth waste?*" Many are melancholy and sad but can give no reason for being so, cannot tell why nor wherefore; such should chide themselves for, and chide themselves out of, their unjust and unreasonable griefs and fears. But Nehemiah could give so good a reason for his sadness as to appeal to the king himself concerning it. Observe, (1.) He calls Jerusalem *the place of his fathers' sepulchres*, the place where his ancestors were buried. It is good for us to think often of our fathers' sepulchres; we are apt to dwell in our thoughts upon their honours and titles, their houses and estates, but let us think also of their sepulchres, and consider that those who have gone before us in the world have also gone before us out of the world, and their monuments are mementos to us. There is also a great respect owing to the memory of our fathers, which we should not be willing to see injured. All nations, even those that have had no expectation of the resurrection of the dead, have looked upon the sepulchres of their ancestors as in some degree sacred and not to be violated. (2.) He justifies himself in his grief: "I do well to be sad. Why should I not be so?" There is a time even for pious and prosperous men to be sad and to show their grief. The best men must not think to antedate heaven by banishing all sorrowful thoughts; it is a vale of tears we pass through, and we must submit to the temper of the climate. (3.) He assigns the ruins of Jerusalem as the true cause of his grief. Note, All the grievances of the church, but especially its desolations, are, and ought to be, matter of grief and sadness to all good people, to all that have a concern for God's honour and that are living members of Christ's mystical body, and are of a public spirit; they favour even Zion's dust, Ps. cii. 14.

IV. The encouragement which the king gave him to tell his mind, and the application he thereupon made in his heart to God, *v.* 4. The king had an affection for him, and was not pleased to see him melancholy. It is also probable that he had a kindness for the Jews' religion; he had discovered it before in the commission he gave to Ezra, who was a churchman, and now again in the power he put Nehemiah into, who was a statesman. Wanting therefore only to know how he might be serviceable to Jerusalem, he asks this its anxious friend, "*For what dost thou make request?* Something thou wouldst have; what is it?" He was afraid to speak (*v.* 2), but this gave him boldness; much more may the invitation Christ has given us to pray, and the promise that we shall speed, enable us to come boldly to the throne of grace. Nehemiah immediately *prayed to the God of heaven* that he would give him wisdom to ask properly and incline the king's heart to grant him his request. Those that would find favour with kings must secure the favour of the King of kings. He prayed to the God of heaven as infinitely above even this mighty monarch. It was not a solemn prayer (he had not opportunity for that), but a secret sudden ejaculation; he lifted up his heart to that God who understands the language of his heart: *Lord, give me a mouth and wisdom; Lord, give me favour in the sight of this man.* Note, It is good to be much in pious ejaculations, especially upon particular occasions. Wherever we are we have a way open heaven-ward. This will not hinder any business, but further it rather; therefore let no business hinder this, but give rise to it rather. Nehemiah had prayed very solemnly with reference to this very occasion (*ch.* i. 11), yet, when it comes to the push, he prays again. Ejaculations and solemn prayers must not jostle out one another, but each have its place.

V. His humble petition to the king. When he had this encouragement he presented his petition very modestly and with submission to the king's wisdom (*v.* 5), but very explicitly. He asked for a commission to go as governor to Judah, to build the wall of Jerusalem, and to stay there for a certain time, so many months, we may suppose; and then either he had his commission renewed or went back and was sent again, so that he presided there twelve years at least, *ch.* v. 14. He also asked for a convoy (*v.* 7), and an order upon the governors, not only to permit and suffer him to pass through their respective provinces, but to supply him with what he had occasion for, with another order upon the keeper of the forest of Lebanon to give him timber for the work that he designed.

VI. The king's great favour to him in asking him *when he would return*, *v.* 6. He intimated that he was unwilling to lose him, or to be long without him, yet to gratify him, and do a real office of kindness to his people, he would spare him awhile, and let him have what clauses he pleased inserted in his commission, *v.* 8. Here was an immediate answer to his prayer; for the seed of Jacob never sought the God of Jacob in vain. In the account he gives of the success of his petition he takes notice, 1. Of the presence of the queen; she sat by (*v.* 6), which (they say) was not usual in the Persian court, Esth. i. 11. Whether the queen was his back friend, that would have hindered him, and he observes it to the praise of

God's powerful providence that though she was by yet he succeeded, or whether she was his true friend, and it is observed to the praise of God's kind providence that she was present to help forward his request, is not certain. 2. Of the power and grace of God. He gained his point, not according to his merit, his interest in the king, or his good management, but *according to the good hand of his God upon him.* Gracious souls take notice of God's hand, his good hand, in all events which turn in favour of them. *This is the Lord's doing,* and therefore doubly acceptable.

9 Then I came to the governors beyond the river, and gave them the king's letters. Now the king had sent captains of the army and horsemen with me. 10 When Sanballat the Horonite, and Tobiah the servant, the Ammonite, heard *of it,* it grieved them exceedingly that there was come a man to seek the welfare of the children of Israel. 11 So I came to Jerusalem, and was there three days. 12 And I arose in the night, I and some few men with me; neither told I *any* man what my God had put in my heart to do at Jerusalem: neither *was there any* beast with me, save the beast that I rode upon. 13 And I went out by night by the gate of the valley, even before the dragon well, and to the dung port, and viewed the walls of Jerusalem, which were broken down, and the gates thereof were consumed with fire. 14 Then I went on to the gate of the fountain, and to the king's pool: but *there was* no place for the beast *that was* under me to pass. 15 Then went I up in the night by the brook, and viewed the wall, and turned back, and entered by the gate of the valley, and *so* returned. 16 And the rulers knew not whither I went, or what I did; neither had I as yet told *it* to the Jews, nor to the priests, nor to the nobles, nor to the rulers, nor to the rest that did the work. 17 Then said I unto them, Ye see the distress that we *are* in, how Jerusalem *lieth* waste, and the gates thereof are burned with fire: come, let us build up the wall of Jerusalem, that we be no more a reproach. 18 Then I told them of the hand of my God which was good upon me; as also the king's words that he had spoken unto me. And they said, Let us rise up and build. So they strengthened their hands for *this* good *work.* 19 But when Sanballat the Horonite, and Tobiah the servant, the Ammonite, and Geshem the Arabian, heard *it,* they laughed us to scorn, and despised us, and said, What *is* this thing that ye do? will ye rebel against the king? 20 Then answered I them, and said unto them, The God of heaven, he will prosper us; therefore we his servants will arise and build: but ye have no portion, nor right, nor memorial, in Jerusalem.

We are here told,

I. How Nehemiah was dismissed by the court he was sent from. The king appointed *captains of the army* and *horsemen* to go *with him* (*v.* 9), both for his guard and to show that he was a man whom *the king did delight to honour,* that all the king's servants might respect him accordingly. Those whom the King of kings sends he thus protects, he thus dignifies with a host of angels to attend them.

II. How he was received by the country he was sent to.

1. By the Jews and their friends at Jerusalem. We are told,

(1.) That while he concealed his errand they took little notice of him. He was at *Jerusalem three days* (*v.* 11), and it does not appear that any of the great men of the city waited on him to congratulate him on his arrival, but he remained unknown. The king sent horsemen to attend him, but the Jews sent none to meet him; he had no beast with him, but that which he himself rode on, *v.* 12. Wise men, and those who are worthy of double honour, yet covet not to come with observation, to make a show, or make a noise, no, not when they come with the greatest blessings. Those that shortly are to have *the dominion in the morning* the world now knows not, but they lie hid, 1 John iii. 1.

(2.) That though they took little notice of him he took great notice of them and their state. He arose in the night, and viewed the ruins of the walls, probably by moon-light (*v.* 13), that he might see what was to be done and in what method they must go about it, whether the old foundation would serve, and what there was of the old materials that would be of use. Note, [1.] Good work is likely to be well done when it is first well considered. [2.] It is the wisdom of those who are engaged in public business, as much as may be, to *see with their own eyes,* and not to proceed altogether upon the reports and representations of others, and yet to do this without noise, and if possible unobserved. [3.] Those that would build up the church's walls must first take notice of the ruins of those walls. Those that would know how to amend must enquire what is amiss, what needs reformation, and what may serve as it is.

(3.) That when he disclosed his design to the rulers and people they cheerfully concurred with him in it. He did not tell them, at first, what he came about (*v.* 16), because he would not seem to do it for ostentation, and because, if he found it impracticable, he might retreat the more honourably. Upright humble men will not sound a trumpet before their alms or any other of their good offices. But when he had viewed and considered the thing, and probably felt the pulse of the rulers and people, he told them *what God had put into his heart* (*v.* 12), even to *build up the wall of Jerusalem, v.* 17. Observe, [1.] How fairly he proposed the undertaking to them: "*You see the distress we are in,* how we lie exposed to the enemies that are round about us, how justly they reproach us as foolish and despicable, how easily they may make a prey of us whenever they have a mind; *come, therefore, and let us build up the wall.*" He did not undertake to do the work without them (it could not be the work of one man), nor did he charge or command imperiously, though he had the king's commission; but in a friendly brotherly way he exhorted and excited them to join with him in this work. To encourage them hereto, he speaks of the design, *First,* As that which owed its origin to the special grace of God. He takes not the praise of it to himself, as a good thought of his own, but acknowledges that God *put it into his heart,* and therefore they all ought to countenance it (whatever is of God must be promoted), and might hope to prosper in it, for what God puts men upon he will own them in. *Secondly,* As that which owed its progress hitherto to the special providence of God. He produced the king's commission, told them how readily it was granted and how forward the king was to favour his design, in which he saw the hand of his God *good upon him.* It would encourage both him and them to proceed in an undertaking which God had so remarkably smiled upon. Thus he proposed it to them; and, [2.] They presently came to a resolution, one and all, to concur with him: *Let us rise up and build.* They are ashamed that they have sat still so long without so much as attempting this needful work, and now resolve to rise up out of their slothfulness, to bestir themselves, and to stir up one another. "*Let us rise up,*" that is, "let us do it with vigour, and diligence, and resolution, as those that are determined to go through with it." *So they strengthened their hands,* their own and one another's, *for this good work.* Note, *First,* Many a good work would find hands enough to be laid to it if there were but one good head to lead in it. They all saw the desolations of Jerusalem, yet none proposed the repair of them; but, when Nehemiah proposed it, they all consented to it. It is a pity that a good motion should be lost purely for want of one to move it and to break the ice in it. *Secondly,* By stirring up ourselves and one another to that which is good, we strengthen ourselves and one another for it; for the great reason why we are weak in our duty is because we are cold to it, indifferent and unresolved. Let us now see how Nehemiah was received,

2. By those that wished ill to the Jews. Those whom God and his Israel blessed they cursed. (1.) When he did but show his face it vexed them, *v.* 10. Sanballat and Tobiah, two of the Samaritans, but by birth the former a Moabite, the latter an Ammonite, when they saw one come armed with a commission from the king to do service to Israel, *were exceedingly grieved* that all their little paltry arts to weaken Israel were thus baffled and frustrated by a fair, and noble, and generous project to strengthen them. Nothing is a greater vexation to the enemies of good people, who have misrepresented them to princes as turbulent, and factious, and not fit to live, than to see them stand right in the opinion of their rulers, their innocency cleared and their reproach rolled away, and that they are thought not only fit to live, but fit to be trusted. When they saw a man come in that manner, who professedly *sought the welfare of the children of Israel,* it vexed them to the heart. *The wicked shall see it, and be grieved.* (2.) When he began to act they set themselves to hinder him, but in vain, *v.* 19, 20. [1.] See here with what little reason the enemies attempted to discourage him. They represented the undertaking as a silly thing: *They laughed us to scorn and despised us* as foolish builders, that could not finish what we began. They represented the undertaking also as a wicked thing, no better than treason: *Will you rebel against the king?* Because this was the old invidious charge, though now they had a commission from the king and were taken under his protection, yet still they must be called rebels. [2.] See also with what good reason the Jews slighted these discouragements. They bore up themselves with this that they were the *servants of the God of heaven,* the only true and living God, that they were acting for him in what they did, and that therefore he would bear them out and prosper them, though the heathen raged, Ps. ii. 1. They considered also that the reason why these enemies did so malign them was because they had no right in Jerusalem, but envied them their right in it. Thus may the impotent menaces of the church's enemies be easily despised by the church's friends.

CHAP. III.

Saying and doing are often two things: many are ready to say, "Let us rise up and build," who sit still and do nothing, like that fair-spoken son who said, "I go, Sir, but went not." The undertakers here were none of those. As soon as they had resolved to build the wall about Jerusalem they lost no time, but set about it presently, as we find in this chapter. Let it never be said that we left that good work to be done to-morrow which we might as well have done to-day. This chapter gives an account of two things:—I. The names of the builders, which are recorded here to their honour, for they were such as herein discovered a great zeal for God and their country, both a pious and a public spirit, a great degree both of industry and courage; and what they did was fit to be thus largely registered, both for their praise and for the encouragement of others to follow their example. II. The order of the building; they took it before them, and ended where they began. They repaired, 1. From the sheep-gate to the fish-gate, ver. 1, 2. 2. Thence to the old-gate, ver. 3—5. 3. Thence to the valley-gate, ver. 6—12. 4. Thence to the dung-gate, ver. 13, 14. 5. Thence to the gate of the fountain, ver. 15. 6. Thence to the water-gate, ver. 16—26. 7. Thence by the horse-gate to the sheep-gate again, where they began (ver. 27—32), and so they brought their work quite round the city.

THEN Eliashib the high priest rose up with his brethren the priests, and they builded the sheep gate; they sanctified it, and set up the doors of it; even unto the tower of Meah they sanctified it, unto the tower of Hananeel. 2 And next unto him builded the men of Jericho. And next to them builded Zaccur the son of Imri. 3 But the fish gate did the sons of Hassenaah build, who *also* laid the beams thereof, and set up the doors thereof, the locks thereof, and the bars thereof. 4 And next unto them repaired Meremoth the son of Urijah, the son of Koz. And next unto them repaired Meshullam the son of Berechiah, the son of Meshezabeel. And next unto them repaired Zadok the son of Baana. 5 And next unto them the Tekoites repaired; but their nobles put not their necks to the work of their Lord. 6 Moreover the old gate repaired Jehoiada the son of Paseah, and Meshullam the son of Besodeiah; they laid the beams thereof, and set up the doors thereof, and the locks thereof, and the bars thereof. 7 And next unto them repaired Melatiah the Gibeonite, and Jadon the Meronothite, the men of Gibeon, and of Mizpah, unto the throne of the governor on this side the river. 8 Next unto him repaired Uzziel the son of Harhaiah, of the goldsmiths. Next unto him also repaired Hananiah the son of *one of* the apothecaries, and they fortified Jerusalem unto the broad wall. 9 And next unto them repaired Rephaiah the son of Hur, the ruler of the half part of Jerusalem. 10 And next unto them repaired Jedaiah the son of Harumaph, even over against his house. And next unto him repaired Hattush the son of Hashabniah. 11 Malchijah the son of Harim, and Hashub the son of Pahath-moab, repaired the other piece, and the tower of the furnaces. 12 And next unto him repaired Shallum the son of Halohesh, the ruler of the half part of Jerusalem, he and his daughters. 13 The valley gate repaired Hanun, and the inhabitants of Zanoah; they built it, and set up the doors thereof, the locks thereof, and the bars thereof, and a thousand cubits on the wall unto the dung gate. 14 But the dung gate repaired Malchiah the son of Rechab, the ruler of part of Beth-haccerem; he built it, and set up the doors thereof, the locks thereof, and the bars thereof. 15 But the gate of the fountain repaired Shallun the son of Col-hozeh, the ruler of part of Mizpah; he built it, and covered it, and set up the doors thereof, the locks thereof, and the bars thereof, and the wall of the pool of Siloah by the king's garden, and unto the stairs that go down from the city of David. 16 After him repaired Nehemiah the son of Azbuk, the ruler of the half part of Beth-zur, unto *the place* over against the sepulchres of David, and to the pool that was made, and unto the house of the mighty. 17 After him repaired the Levites, Rehum the son of Bani. Next unto him repaired Hashabiah, the ruler of the half part of Keilah, in his part. 18 After him repaired their brethren, Bavai the son of Henadad, the ruler of the half part of Keilah. 19 And next to him repaired Ezer the son of Jeshua, the ruler of Mizpah, another piece over against the going up to the armoury at the turning *of the wall.* 20 After him Baruch the son of Zabbai earnestly repaired the other piece, from the turning *of the wall* unto the door of the house of Eliashib the high priest. 21 After him repaired Meremoth the son of Urijah the son of Koz another piece, from the door of the house of Eliashib even to the end of the house of Eliashib. 22 And after him repaired the priests, the men of the plain. 23 After him repaired Benjamin and Hashub over against their house. After him repaired Azariah the son of Maaseiah the son of Ananiah by his house. 24 After him repaired Binnui the son of Henadad another piece, from the house of Azariah unto the turning *of the wall*, even unto the corner. 25 Palal the son of Uzai, over against the turning *of the wall*, and the tower which lieth out from the king's high house, that *was* by the court of the prison. After him Pedaiah the son of Parosh. 26 Moreover the Nethinims dwelt in Ophel, unto *the place* over against the water gate toward the east, and the tower that lieth out. 27 After them the Tekoites repaired another piece, over against the great tower that lieth out, even unto the wall of Ophel. 28 From above the horse gate repaired the priests, every one over against his house. 29 After them repaired Zadok the son of Immer over against his house. After him repaired also Shemaiah the son of Shechaniah, the keeper of the east gate. 30 After him repaired Hananiah the son of Shelemiah, and Hanun the sixth son of Zalaph, another piece. After him repaired Meshullam the son of Berechiah over against his chamber. 31 After him repaired Malchiah the goldsmith's son unto the place of the Nethinims, and of the merchants, over against the gate Miphkad, and to the going up of the corner. 32 And between the going up of the corner unto the sheep gate repaired the goldsmiths and the merchants.

The best way to know how to divide this chapter is to observe how the work was divided among the undertakers, that every one might know what he had to do, and mind it accordingly with a holy emulation, and desire to excel, yet without any contention, animosity, or separate interest. No strife appears among them but which should do most for the public good. Several things are observable in the account here given of the building of the wall about Jerusalem :—

I. That Eliashib the high priest, with his brethren the priests, led the van in this troop of builders, *v.* 1. Ministers should be foremost in every good work; for their office obliges them to teach and quicken by their example, as well as by their doctrine. If there be labour in it, who so fit as they to work? if danger, who so fit as they to venture? The dignity of the high priest was very great, and obliged him to signalize himself in this service. The priests repaired the *sheep-gate*, so called because through it were brought the sheep that were to be sacrificed in the temple; and therefore the priests undertook the repair of it because *the offerings of the Lord made by fire were* their inheritance. And of this gate only it is said that *they sanctified it* with the word and prayer, and perhaps with sacrifices perhaps, 1. Because it led to the temple; or, 2. Because with this the building of the wall began, and it is probable (though they were at work in all parts of the wall at the same time) that this was first finished, and therefore at this gate they solemnly committed their city and the walls of it to the divine protection; or, 3. Because the priests were the builders of it; and it becomes ministers above others, being themselves in a peculiar manner sanctified to God, to sanctify to him all their performances, and to do even their common actions *after a godly sort.*

II. That the undertakers were very many, who each took his share, some more and some less, in this work, according as their ability was. Note, What is to be done for the public good every one should assist in, and further, to the utmost of his place and power. United force will conquer that which no individual dares venture on. Many hands will make light work.

III. That many were active in this work who were not themselves inhabitants of Jerusalem, and therefore consulted purely the public welfare and not any private interest or advantage of their own. Here are the men of Jericho with the first (*v.* 2), the men of Gibeon and Mizpah (*v.* 7), and Zanoah, *v.* 13. Every Israelite should lend a hand towards the building up of Jerusalem.

IV. That several rulers, both of Jerusalem and of other cities, were active in this work, thinking themselves bound in honour to do the utmost that their wealth and power enabled them to do for the furtherance of this good work. But it is observable that they are called rulers of *part*, or the *half part*, of their respective cities. One was *ruler of the half part of Jerusalem* (*v.* 12), another of part of Beth-haccerem (*v.* 14), another of part of Mizpah (*v.* 15), another of *the half part of Beth-zur* (*v.* 16), one was ruler of *one half part*, and another of *the other half part*, of *Keilah*, *v.* 17, 18. Perhaps the Persian government would not entrust any one with a strong city, but appointed two to be a watch upon each other. Rome had two consuls.

V. Here is a just reproach fastened upon the nobles of Tekoa, that they *put not their necks to the work of their Lord* (*v.* 5), that is, they would not come under the yoke of an obligation to this service; as if the dignity and liberty of their peerage were their discharge from serving God and doing good, which are indeed the highest honour and the truest freedom. Let not nobles think any thing below them by which they may advance the interests of their country; for what else is their nobility good for but that it puts them in a higher and larger sphere of usefulness than that in which inferior persons move?

VI. Two persons joined in repairing *the old gate* (*v.* 6), and so were co-founders, and shared the honour of it between them. The good work which we cannot compass ourselves we must be thankful to those that will go partners with us in. Some think that this is called the *old gate* because it belonged to the ancient Salem, which was said to be first built by Melchizedek.

VII. Several good honest tradesmen, as well as priests and rulers, were active in this work—*goldsmiths, apothecaries, merchants*, *v.* 8, 32. They did not think their callings excused them, nor plead that they could not leave their shops to attend the public business, knowing that what they lost would certainly be made up to them by the blessing of God upon their callings.

VIII. Some ladies are spoken of as helping forward this work—*Shallum and his daughters* (*v.* 12), who, though not capable of personal service, yet having their portions in their own hands, or being rich widows, contributed money for buying materials and paying workmen. St. Paul speaks of some good women that *laboured with him in the gospel*, Phil. iv. 3.

IX. Of some it is said that they repaired *over against their houses* (*v.* 10, 23, 28, 29), and of one (who, it is likely, was only a lodger) that he repaired *over against his chamber*, *v.* 30. When a general good work is to be done each should apply himself to that part of it that falls nearest to him and is within his reach. If every one will sweep before his own door, the street will be clean; if every one will mend one, we shall be all mended. If he that has but a chamber will repair before that, he does his part.

X. Of one it is said that he *earnestly* repaired that which fell to his share (*v.* 20)—he did it with an inflamed zeal; not that others were cold or indifferent, but he was the most vigorous of any of them and consequently made himself remarkable. It is good to be thus *zealously affected in a good thing;* and it is probable that this good man's zeal provoked very many to take the more pains and make the more haste.

XI. Of one of these builders it is observed that he was *the sixth son* of his father, *v.* 30. His five elder brethren, it seems, laid not their hand to this work, but he did. In doing that which is good we need not stay to see our elders go before us; if they decline it, it does not therefore follow that we must. Thus the younger brother, if he be the better man, and does God and his generation better service, is indeed the better gentleman; those are most honourable that are most useful.

XII. Some of those that had *first done helped their fellows*, and undertook another share where they saw there was most need. Meremoth repaired, *v.* 4 and again, *v.* 21. And the Tekoites, besides the piece they repaired (*v.* 5), undertook another piece (*v.* 27), which is the more remarkable because their nobles set them a bad example by withdrawing from the service, which, instead of serving them for an excuse to sit still, perhaps made them the more forward to do double work, that by their zeal they might either shame or atone for the covetousness and carelessness of their nobles.

Lastly, Here is no mention of any particular share that Nehemiah himself had in this work. A name-sake of his is mentioned, *v.* 16. But did he do nothing? Yes, though he undertook not any particular piece of the wall, yet he did more than any of them, for he had the oversight of them all; half of his servants worked where there was most need, and the other half stood sentinel, as we find afterwards (*ch.* iv. 16), while he himself in his own person walked the rounds, directed and encouraged the builders, set his hand to the work where he saw occasion, and kept a watchful eye upon the motions of the enemy, as we shall find in the next chapter. The pilot needs not haul at a rope: it is enough for him to steer.

CHAP. IV.

We left all hands at work for the building of the wall about Jerusalem. But such good work is not wont to be carried on without opposition; now here we are told what opposition was given to it, and what methods Nehemiah took to forward the work, notwithstanding that opposition. I. Their enemies reproached and ridiculed their undertaking, but their scoffs they answered with prayers: they heeded them not, but went on with their work notwithstanding, ver. 1—6. II. They formed a bloody design against them, to hinder them by force of arms, ver. 7, 8, 10—12. To guard against this Nehemiah prayed (ver. 9), set guards (ver. 13), and encouraged them to fight (ver. 14), by which the design was broken (ver. 15), and so the work was carried on with all needful precaution against a surprise, ver. 16—23. In all this Nehemiah approved himself a man of great wisdom and courage, as well as great piety.

BUT it came to pass, that when Sanballat heard that we builded the wall, he was wroth, and took great indignation, and mocked the Jews. 2 And he spake before his brethren and the army of Samaria, and said, What do these feeble Jews? will they fortify themselves? will they sacrifice? will they make an end in a day? will they revive the stones out of the heaps of the rubbish which are burned? 3 Now Tobiah the Ammonite *was* by him, and he said, Even that which they build, if a fox go up, he shall even break down their stone wall. 4 Hear, O our God; for we are despised: and turn their reproach upon their own head, and give them for a prey in the land of captivity: 5 And cover not their iniquity, and let not their sin be blotted out from before thee: for they have provoked *thee* to anger before the builders. 6 So built we the wall; and all the wall was joined together unto the half thereof: for the people had a mind to work.

Here is, I. The spiteful scornful reflection which Sanballat and Tobiah cast upon the Jews for their attempt to build the wall about Jerusalem. The country rang of it presently; intelligence was brought of it to Samaria, that nest of enemies to the Jews and their prosperity; and here we are told how they received the tidings. 1. In heart. They were very angry at the undertaking, and had *great indignation*, *v.* 1. It vexed them that Nehemiah came to seek the welfare of the children of Israel (*ch.* ii. 10); but, when they heard of this great undertaking for their good, they were out of all patience. They had hitherto pleased themselves with the thought that while Jerusalem was unwalled they could swallow it up and make themselves masters of it when they pleased; but, if it be walled, it will not only be fenced against them, but by degrees become formidable to them. The strength and safety of the church are the grief and vexation of its enemies. 2. In word. They despised it, and made it the subject of their ridicule. In this they sufficiently displayed their malice; but good was brought out of it; for, looking upon it as a foolish undertaking that would sink under its own weight, they did not go about to obstruct it till it was too late. Let us see with what pride and malice they set themselves publicly to banter it. (1.) Sanballat speaks with scorn of the workmen: "*These feeble Jews*" (*v.* 2), "what will they do for materials? *Will they revive the stones out of the rubbish?* And what mean they by being so hasty? Do they think to make the walling of a city but one day's work, and to keep the feast of dedication with sacrifice the next day? Poor silly people! See how ridiculous they make themselves!" (2.) Tobiah speaks with no less scorn of the work itself. He has his jest too, and must show his wit, *v.* 3. Profane scoffers sharpen one another. "Sorry work," says he, "they are likely to make of it; they themselves will be ashamed of it: *If a fox go up*, not with his subtlety, but with his weight, he *will break down their stone wall.*" Many a good work has been thus looked upon with contempt by the *proud and haughty scorners*.

II. Nehemiah's humble and devout address to God when he heard of these reflections. He had notice brought him of what they said. It is probable that they themselves sent him a message to this purport, to discourage him, hoping to jeer him out of his attempt; but he did not answer these fools according to their folly; he did not upbraid them with their weakness, but looked up to God by prayer.

1. He begs of God to take notice of the indignities that were done them (*v.* 4), and in this we are to imitate him: *Hear, O our God! for we are despised.* Note, (1.) God's people have often been a despised people, and loaded with contempt. (2.) God does, and will, hear all the slights that are put upon his people, and it is their comfort that he does so and a good reason why they should be as though they were deaf, Ps. xxxviii. 13, 15. "Thou art our God to whom we appeal; our cause needs no more than a fair hearing."

2. He begs of God to avenge their cause and turn the reproach upon the enemies themselves (*v.* 4, 5); and this was spoken rather by a spirit of prophecy than by a spirit of prayer, and is not to be imitated by us who are taught of Christ to *pray for* those that *despitefully use and persecute us.* Christ himself prayed for those that reproached him: *Father, forgive them.* Nehemiah here prays, *Cover not their iniquity.* Note, (1.) Those that cast contempt on God's people do but prepare everlasting shame for themselves. (2.) It is a sin from which sinners are seldom recovered. Doubtless Nehemiah had reason to think the hearts of those sinners were desperately hardened, so that they would never repent of it, else he would not have prayed that it might *never be blotted out.* The reason he gives is not, *They have abused us*, but, *They have provoked thee*, and that *before the builders*, to whom, it is likely, they sent a spiteful message. Note, We should be angry at the malice of persecutors, not because it is abusive to us, but because it is offensive to God; and on that we may ground an expectation that God will appear against it, Ps. lxxiv. 18, 22.

III. The vigour of the builders, notwithstanding these reflections, *v.* 6. They made such good speed that in a little time they had run up the wall to half its height, for *the people had a mind to work;* their hearts were upon it, and they would have it forwarded. Note, 1. Good work goes on well when people have a mind to it. 2. The reproaches of enemies should rather quicken us to our duty than drive us from it.

7 But it came to pass, *that* when Sanballat, and Tobiah, and the Arabians, and the Ammonites, and the Ashdodites, heard that the walls of Jerusalem were made up, *and* that the breaches began to be stopped, then they were very wroth, 8 And conspired all of them together to come *and* to fight against Jerusalem, and to hinder it. 9 Nevertheless we made our prayer unto our God, and set a watch against them day and night, because of them. 10 And Judah said, The strength of the bearers of burdens is decayed, and *there is* much rubbish; so that we are not able to build the wall. 11 And our adversaries said, They shall not know, nei-

ther see, till we come in the midst among them, and slay them, and cause the work to cease. 12 And it came to pass, that when the Jews which dwelt by them came, they said unto us ten times, From all places whence ye shall return unto us *they will be upon you.* 13 Therefore set I in the lower places behind the wall, *and* on the higher places, I even set the people after their families with their swords, their spears, and their bows. 14 And I looked, and rose up, and said unto the nobles, and to the rulers, and to the rest of the people, Be not ye afraid of them: remember the Lord, *which is* great and terrible, and fight for your brethren, your sons, and your daughters, your wives, and your houses. 15 And it came to pass, when our enemies heard that it was known unto us, and God had brought their counsel to nought, that we returned all of us to the wall, every one unto his work.

We have here,

I. The conspiracy which the Jews' enemies formed against them, to stay the building by slaying the builders. The conspirators were not only Sanballat and Tobiah, but other neighbouring people whom they had drawn into the plot. They flattered themselves with a fancy that the work would soon stand still of itself; but, when they heard that it went on and prospered, they were angry at the Jews for being so hasty to push the work forward and angry at themselves for being so slow in opposing it (*v.* 7): *They were very wroth. Cursed be their anger, for it was fierce, and their wrath, for it was cruel.* Nothing would serve but they would *fight against Jerusalem, v.* 8. Why, what quarrel had they with the Jews? Had they done them any wrong? Or did they design them any? No, they lived peaceably by them; but it was merely out of envy and malice; they hated the Jews' piety, and were therefore vexed at their prosperity and sought their ruin. Observe, 1. How unanimous they were: *They conspired all of them together,* though of different interests among themselves, yet one in their opposition to the work of God. 2. How close they were; they said, "*They shall not know, neither see,* till we have them at our mercy." Thus they took crafty counsel, and digged deep to hide it from the Lord, and promised themselves security and success from the secresy of their management. 3. How cruel they were: *We will come and slay them.* If nothing less than the murder of the workmen will put a stop to the work, they will not stick at that; nay, it is their blood they thirst for, and they are glad of any pretence to glut themselves with it. 4. What the design was and how confident they were of success: it was to *cause the work to cease* (*v.* 11), and this they were confident that they should effect. The hindering of good work is that which bad men aim at and promise themselves; but good work is God's work, and it shall prosper.

II. The discouragements which the builders themselves laboured under. At the very time when the adversaries said, Let us *cause the work to cease,* Judah said, "Let us even let it fall, for we are not able to go forward with it," *v.* 10. They represent the labourers as tired, and the remaining difficulties, even of that first part of their work, the removing of the rubbish, as insuperable, and therefore they think it advisable to desist for the present. Can Judah, that warlike valiant tribe, sneak thus? Active leading men have many times as much ado to grapple with the fears of their friends as with the terrors of their enemies.

III. The information that was brought to Nehemiah of the enemies' designs, *v.* 12. There were *Jews that dwelt by them,* in the country, who, though they had not zeal enough to bring them to Jerusalem to help their brethren in building the wall, yet, having by their situation opportunity to discover the enemies' motions, had so much honesty and affection to the cause as to give intelligence of them; nay, that their intelligence might be the more credited, they came themselves to give it, and they said it ten times, repeating it as men in earnest, and under a concern, and the report was confirmed by many witnesses. The intelligence they gave is expressed abruptly, and finds work for the critics to make out the sense of it, which perhaps is designed to intimate that they gave this intelligence as men out of breath and in confusion, whose very looks would make up the deficiencies of their words. I think it may be read, without supplying any thing: "*Whatever place you turn to, they are against us,* so that you have need to be upon your guard on all sides." Note, God has many ways of bringing to light, and so bringing to nought, the devices and designs of his and his church's enemies. Even the cold and feeble Jews that contentedly dwell by them shall be made to serve as spies upon them; nay, rather than fail, *a bird of the air shall carry their voice.*

IV. The pious and prudent methods which Nehemiah, hereupon, took to baffle the design, and to secure his work and workmen.

1. It is said (*v.* 14) he *looked.* (1.) He looked up, engaged God for him, and put himself and his cause under the divine protection (*v.* 9): *We made our prayer unto our God.* That was the way of this good man, and should be our way; all his cares, all his griefs, all his fears, he spread before God, and thereby made himself easy. This was

the first thing he did; before he used any means, he made his prayer to God, for with him we must always begin. (2.) He looked about him. Having prayed, he *set a watch against them.* The instructions Christ has given us in our spiritual warfare agree with this example, Matt. xxvi. 41. *Watch and pray.* If we think to secure ourselves by prayer only, without watchfulness, we are slothful and tempt God; if by watchfulness, without prayer, we are proud and slight God; and, either way, we forfeit his protection.

2. Observe, (1.) How he posted the guards, *v.* 13. *In the lower places* he set them *behind the wall,* that they might annoy the enemy over it, as a breast-work; but *in the higher places,* where the wall was raised to its full height, he set them upon it, that from the top of it they might throw down stones or darts upon the heads of the assailants: he set them *after their families,* that mutual relation might engage them to mutual assistance. (2.) How he animated and encouraged the people, *v.* 14. He observed even the nobles and rulers themselves, as well as the rest of the people, to be in a great consternation upon the intelligence that was brought them, and ready to conclude that they were all undone, by which their hands were weakened both for work and war, and therefore he endeavours to silence their fears. "Come," says he, "*be not afraid of them,* but behave yourselves valiantly, considering, [1.] Whom you fight under. You cannot have a better captain: *Remember the Lord, who is great and terrible;* you think your enemies *great and terrible,* but what are they in comparison with God, especially in opposition to him? He is great above them to control them, and will be terrible to them when he comes to reckon with them." Those that with an eye of faith see the church's God to be great and terrible will see the church's enemies to be mean and despicable. The reigning fear of God is the best antidote against the ensnaring fear of man. He that is afraid of *a man that shall die forgets the Lord his Maker,* Isa. li. 12, 13. [2.] "Whom you fight for. You cannot have a better cause; you fight for *your brethren* (Ps. cxxii. 8), *your sons, and your daughters.* All that is dear to you in this world lies at stake; therefore *behave yourselves valiantly.*"

V. The happy disappointment which this gave to the enemies, *v.* 15. When they found that their design was discovered, and that the Jews were upon their guard, they concluded that it was to no purpose to attempt any thing, but that *God had brought their counsel to nought.* They knew they could not gain their point but by surprise, and, if their plot was known, it was quashed. The Jews hereupon *returned every one to his work,* with so much the more cheerfulness because they saw plainly that God owned it and owned them in the doing of it. Note, God's care of our safety should engage and encourage us to go on with vigour in our duty. As soon as ever a danger is over let us *return to our work,* and trust God another time.

16 And it came to pass from that time forth, *that* the half of my servants wrought in the work, and the other half of them held both the spears, the shields, and the bows, and the habergeons; and the rulers *were* behind all the house of Judah. 17 They which builded on the wall, and they that bare burdens, with those that laded, *every one* with one of his hands wrought in the work, and with the other *hand* held a weapon. 18 For the builders, every one had his sword girded by his side, and *so* builded. And he that sounded the trumpet *was* by me. 19 And I said unto the nobles, and to the rulers, and to the rest of the people, The work *is* great and large, and we are separated upon the wall, one far from another. 20 In what place *therefore* ye hear the sound of the trumpet, resort ye thither unto us: our God shall fight for us. 21 So we laboured in the work: and half of them held the spears from the rising of the morning till the stars appeared. 22 Likewise at the same time said I unto the people, Let every one with his servant lodge within Jerusalem, that in the night they may be a guard to us, and labour on the day. 23 So neither I, nor my brethren, nor my servants, nor the men of the guard which followed me, none of us put off our clothes, *saving that* every one put them off for washing.

When the builders had so far reason to think the design of the enemies broken *as to return to their work,* yet they were not so secure as to lay down their arms, knowing how restless and unwearied they were in their attempts, and that, if one design failed, they would be hatching another. Thus must we watch always against our spiritual enemies, and not expect that our warfare will be accomplished till our work is. See what course Nehemiah took, that the people might hold themselves in a readiness, in case there should be an attack. 1. While one half were at work, the other half were under their arms, holding *spears, and shields, and bows,* not only for themselves but for the labourers too, who would immediately quit their work, and betake themselves to their weapons, upon the first alarm, *v.* 16. It is probable that they changed services at stated hours, which would relieve the fatigue of both, and particularly would be an ease to the *bearers of burdens,* whose *strength* had *decayed* (*v.* 10); while they held the weapons, they were eased and yet not idle. Thus dividing their time between the trowels and the spears, they are said to *work with one hand* and hold their weapons *with the other* (*v.* 17), which cannot be understood literally, for the work would require both hands; but it intimates that they were equally employed in both. Thus must we work out our salvation with the weapons of our warfare in our hand; for in every duty we must expect to meet with opposition from our spiritual enemies, against whom we must still be *fighting the good fight of faith.* 2. Every builder had a sword by his side (*v.* 18), which he could carry without hindering his labour. The word of God is the sword of the Spirit, which we ought to have always at hand and never to seek, both in our labours and in our conflicts as Christians. 3. Care was taken both to get and give early notice of the approach of the enemy, in case they should endeavour to surprise them. Nehemiah kept a trumpeter always by him to sound an alarm upon the first intimation of danger. The work was large, and the builders were dispersed; for in all parts of the wall they were labouring at the same time. Nehemiah continually walked round to oversee the work and encourage the workmen, and so would have speedy intelligence if the enemy made an attack, of which, by sound of trumpet, he would soon give notice to all, and they must immediately repair to him with a full assurance that their *God* would *fight for them, v.* 18—20. When they acted as workmen, it was requisite they should be dispersed wherever there was work to do; but when as soldiers it was requisite they should come into close order, and be found in a body. Thus should the labourers in Christ's building be ready to unite against a common foe. 4. The inhabitants of the villages were ordered to lodge within Jerusalem, with their servants, not only that they might be the nearer to their work in the morning, but that they might be ready to help in case of an attack in the night, *v.* 22. The strength of a city lies more in its hands than in its walls; secure them, and God's blessing upon them, and be secure. 5. Nehemiah himself, and all his men, kept closely to their business. The spears were held up, with the sight of them to terrify the enemy, not only from sun to sun, but from twilight to twilight every day, *v.* 21. Thus ought we to be always upon our guard against our spiritual enemies, not only (as here) while *it is light,* but when *it is dark,* for they are the *rulers of the darkness of this world.* Nay, so very intent was Nehemiah upon his work, and so fast did he hold his servants to it, that while the heat of the business lasted neither he himself nor his attendants went into bed, but every night lay and slept in their cloth s (*v.* 23), except that they shifted them now and then, either for cleanliness or in a case of ceremonial pollution. It was a sign that their heart was upon their work when they could not find time to dress and undress, but resolved they would be at all times ready for service. Good work is likely to go on successfully when those that labour in it thus make a business of it.

CHAP. V.

How bravely Nehemiah, as a wise and faithful governor, stood upon his guard against the attacks of enemies abroad, we read in the foregoing chapter. Here we have him no less bold and active to redress grievances at home, and, having kept them from being destroyed by their enemies, to keep them from destroying one another. Here is, I. The complaint which the poor made to him of the great hardships which the rich (of whom they were forced to borrow money) put upon them, ver. 1—5. II. The effectual course which Nehemiah took both to reform the oppressors and to relieve the oppressed, ver. 6—13. III. The good example which he himself, as governor, set them of compassion and tenderness, ver. 14—19.

AND there was a great cry of the people and of their wives against their brethren the Jews. 2 For there were that said, We, our sons, and our daughters, *are* many: therefore we take up corn *for them,* that we may eat, and live. 3 *Some* also there were that said, We have mortgaged our lands, vineyards, and houses, that we might buy corn, because of the dearth. 4 There were also that said, We have borrowed money for the king's tribute, *and that upon* our lands and vineyards. 5 Yet now our flesh *is* as the flesh of our brethren, our children as their children: and, lo, we bring into bondage our sons and our daughters to be servants, and *some* of our daughters are brought unto bondage *already:* neither *is it* in our power *to redeem them;* for other men have our lands and vineyards.

We have here the tears of the oppressed, which Solomon considered, Eccl. iv. 1. Let us consider them as here they are dropped before Nehemiah, whose office it was, as governor, to *deliver the poor and needy, and rid them out of the hand of the wicked* oppressors, Ps. lxxxii. 4. Hard times and hard hearts made the poor miserable.

I. The times they lived in were hard. There was a dearth of corn (*v.* 3), probably for want of rain, with which God had chastised their neglect of his house (Hag. i. 9—11) and the non-payment of their church-dues, Mal. iii. 9, 10. Thus foolish sinful men bring God's judgments upon themselves, and then fret and complain of them. When the markets are high, and provisions scarce and dear, the poor soon feel from it, and are pinched by it. Blessed be God for the mercy, and God deliver us from the sin, of *fulness of bread,* Ezek. xvi. 49. That which made the scarcity here complained of the more grievous was that their *sons and their daughters were many, v.* 2. The families that were most necessitous were most numerous; here were the mouths, but where was the meat? Some have estates and no children to inherit them; others have children and no estates to leave them. Those who have both have reason to be thankful; those who have neither may the more easily be content. Those who have great families and little substance must learn to live by faith in God's providence and promise; and those who have little families and great substance must *make their abundance a supply for the wants of others.* But this was not all: as corn was dear, so the taxes were high; the king's tribute must be paid, *v.* 4. This mark of their captivity still remained upon them. Perhaps it was a poll-money that was required, and then, their sons and their daughters being many, it rose the higher. The more they had to maintain (a hard case!) the more they had to pay. Now, it seems, they had not wherewithal of their own to buy corn and pay taxes, but were necessitated to borrow. Their families came poor out of Babylon; they had been at great expense in building them houses, and had not yet got up their strength when these new burdens came upon them. The straits of poor housekeepers who make hard shift to get an honest livelihood, and sometimes want what is fitting for them and their families, are well worthy the compassionate consideration of those who either with their wealth or with their power are in a capacity to help them.

II. The persons they dealt with were hard. Money must be had, but it must be borrowed; and those that lent them money, taking advantage of their necessity, were very hard upon them and made a prey of them. 1. They exacted interest from them at twelve per cent., the hundredth part every month, *v.* 11. If men borrow large sums to trade with, to increase their stocks, or to purchase land, there is no reason why the lender should not share with the borrower in his profit; or if to spend upon their lusts, or repair what they have so spent, why should they not pay for their extravagances? But if the poor borrow to maintain their families, and we be able to help them, it is certain we ought either to lend freely what they have occasion for, or (if they be not likely to repay it) to give freely something towards it. Nay, 2. They forced them to mortgage to them their lands and houses for the securing of the money (*v.* 3), and not only so, but took the profits of them for interest (*v.* 5, compare *v.* 11), that by degrees they might make themselves masters of all they had. Yet this was not the worst. 3. They took their children for bond-servants, to be enslaved or sold at pleasure, *v.* 5. This they complain of most sensibly, as that which touched them in a tender part, and they aggravate it with this: "*Our children are as their children,* as dear to us as theirs are to them; not only of the same human nature, and entitled to the honours and liberties of that (Mal. ii. 10; Job xxxi. 15), but of the same holy nation, free-born Israelites, and dignified with the same privileges. Our flesh carries in it the sacred seal of the covenant of circumcision, as well *as the flesh of our brethren;* yet our heirs must be their slaves, and *it is not in our power to redeem them.*" This they made a humble remonstrance of to Nehemiah, not only because they saw he was a great man that could relieve them, but a good man that would. Whither should the injured poor flee for succour but *to the shields of the earth?* Whither but to the chancery, to the charity, in the royal breast, and those deputed by it for relief against the *summum jus—the extremity of the law?*

Lastly, We will leave Nehemiah hearing the complaint, and enquiring into the truth of the complainants' allegations (for the clamours of the poor are not always just), while we sit down and look, (1.) With a gracious compassion upon the oppressed, and lament the hardships which many in the world are groaning under; putting our souls into their souls' stead, and remembering in our prayers and succours those that are burdened, as burdened with them. (2.) With a gracious indignation at the oppressors, and abhorrence of their pride and cruelty, who drink the tears, the blood, of those they have under their feet. But let those who show no mercy expect *judgment without mercy.* It was an aggravation of the sin of these oppressing Jews that they were themselves so lately delivered out of the house of bondage, which obliged them in gratitude to *undo the heavy burdens,* Isa. lviii. 6.

6 And I was very angry when I heard their cry and these words. 7 Then I consulted with myself, and I rebuked the nobles, and the rulers, and said unto them, Ye exact usury, every one of his brother. And I set a great assembly against them. 8 And I said unto them, We after our ability have redeemed our brethren the Jews, which were sold unto the heathen; and will ye even sell your brethren? or shall they be sold unto us? Then held they their peace, and found nothing *to answer.* 9 Also I said, It *is* not good that ye do: ought ye not to walk in the fear of our God because of the reproach of the heathen our enemies? 10 I likewise, *and* my brethren, and my servants, might exact of them money and corn: I pray you, let us leave off this usury. 11 Restore, I pray you, to them, even

this day, their lands, their vineyards, their oliveyards, and their houses, also the hundredth *part* of the money, and of the corn, the wine, and the oil, that ye exact of them. 12 Then said they, We will restore *them*, and will require nothing of them; so will we do as thou sayest. Then I called the priests, and took an oath of them, that they should do according to this promise. 13 Also I shook my lap, and said, So God shake out every man from his house, and from his labour, that performeth not this promise, even thus be he shaken out, and emptied. And all the congregation said, Amen, and praised the LORD. And the people did according to this promise.

It should seem the foregoing complaint was made to Nehemiah at the time when he had his head and hands as full as possible of the public business about building the wall; yet, perceiving it to be just, he did not reject it because it was unseasonable; he did not chide the petitioners, nor fall into a passion with them, for disturbing him when they saw how much he had to do, a fault which men of business are too often guilty of; nor did he so much as adjourn the hearing of the cause or proceedings upon it till he had more leisure. The case called for speedy interposition, and therefore he applied himself immediately to the consideration of it, knowing that, let him build Jerusalem's walls ever so high, so thick, so strong, the city could not be safe while such abuses as these were tolerated. Now observe, What method he took for the redress of this grievance which was so threatening to the public.

I. He *was very angry* (*v.* 6); he expressed a great displeasure at it, as a very bad thing. Note, It well becomes rulers to show themselves angry at sin, that by the anger itself they may be excited to their duty, and by the expressions of it others may be deterred from evil.

II. He *consulted with himself*, *v.* 7. By this it appears that his anger was not excessive, but kept within bounds, that, though his spirit was provoked, he did not say or do any thing unadvisedly. Before he rebuked the nobles, he consulted with himself what to say, and when, and how. Note, Reproofs must be given with great consideration, that what is well meant may not come short of its end for want of being well managed. It is the *reproof of instruction* that *giveth life*. Even wise men lose the benefit of their wisdom sometimes for want of consulting with themselves and taking time to deliberate.

III. He *rebuked the nobles and rulers*, who were the monied men, and whose power perhaps made them the more bold to oppress. Note, Even nobles and rulers, if they do that which is evil, ought to be told of it by proper persons. Let no man imagine that his dignity sets him above reproof.

IV He set a great assembly against them. He called the people together to be witnesses of what he said, and to bear their testimony (which the people will generally be forward to do) against the oppressions and extortions their rulers were guilty of, *v.* 12. Ezra and Nehemiah were both of them very wise, good, useful men, yet, in cases not unlike, there was a great deal of difference between their management: when Ezra was told of the sin of the rulers in marrying strange wives he rent his clothes, and wept, and prayed, and was hardly persuaded to attempt a reformation, fearing it to be impracticable, for he was a man of a mild tender spirit; when Nehemiah was told of as bad a thing he kindled immediately, reproached the delinquents, incensed the people against them, and never rested till, by all the rough methods he could use, he forced them to reform; for he was a man of a hot and eager spirit. Note, 1. Very holy men may differ much from each other in their natural temper and in other things that result from it. 2. God's work may be done, well done, and successfully, and yet different methods taken in the doing of it, which is a good reason why we should neither arraign the management of others nor make our own a standard. There are diversities of operation, but the same Spirit.

V. He fairly reasoned the case with them, and showed them the evil of what they did. The regular way of reforming men's lives is to endeavour, in the first place, to convince their consciences. Several things he offered to their consideration, which are so pertinent and just that it appeared he had consulted with himself. He lays it before them, 1. That those whom they oppressed were their brethren: *You exact every one of his brother*. It was bad enough to oppress strangers, but much worse to oppress their poor brethren, from whom the divine law did not allow them to *take any usury*, Deut. xxiii. 19, 20. 2. That they were but lately redeemed *out of the hand of the heathen*. The body of the people were so by the wonderful providence of God; some particular persons among them were so, who, besides their share in the general captivity, were in servitude to heathen masters, and ransomed at the charge of Nehemiah and other pious and well-disposed persons. "Now," says he, "have we taken all this pains to get their liberty out of the hands of the heathen, and shall their own rulers enslave them? What an absurd thing is this! Must we be at the same trouble and expense to redeem them from you as we were to redeem them from Babylon?" *v.* 8. Those whom God by his grace has made free ought not to be again brought under *a yoke of bondage*, Gal. v. 1; 1 Cor. vii. 23. 3. That it was a great sin thus to oppress the poor (*v.* 9): "*It is not good that you do;* though you get money by it, you contract guilt by it, and *ought you not to walk in the fear of God?* Certainly you ought, for you profess religion, and relation to him; and, if you do walk in the fear of God, you will not be either covetous of worldly gain or cruel towards your brethren." Those that walk in the fear of God will not dare to do a wicked thing, Job xxxi. 13, 14, 23. 4. That it was a great scandal, and a reproach to their profession. "Consider *the reproach of the heathen our enemies,* enemies to us, to our God, and to our holy religion. They will be glad of any occasion to speak against us, and this will give them great occasion; they will say, These Jews, that profess so much devotion to God, see how barbarous they are one to another." Note, (1.) All that profess religion should be very careful that they do nothing to expose themselves to the reproach of those that are without, lest religion be wounded through their sides. (2.) Nothing exposes religion more to the reproach of its enemies than the worldliness and hard-heartedness of the professors of it. 5. That he himself had set them a better example (*v.* 10), which he enlarges upon afterwards, *v.* 14, &c. Those that rigorously insist upon their right themselves will with a very ill grace persuade others to recede from theirs.

VI. He earnestly pressed them not only not to make their poor neighbours any more such hard bargains, but to restore that which they had got into their hands, *v.* 11. See how familiarly he speaks to them: *Let us leave off this usury,* putting himself in, as becomes reprovers, though far from being any way guilty of the crime. See how earnestly, and yet humbly, he persuades them: *I pray you* leave off; and, *I pray you* restore. Though he had authority to command, yet, *for love's sake, he rather beseeches.* See how particularly he presses them to be kind to the poor, to give them up their mortgages, put them again in possession of their estates, remit the interest, and give them time to pay in the principal. He urged them to their loss, yet, urging them to their duty, it would be, at length, to their advantage. What we charitably forgive will be remembered and recompensed, as well as what we charitably give.

VII. He laid them under all the obligations possible to do what he pressed them to. 1. He got a promise from them (*v.* 12): *We will restore them.* 2. He sent for the priests to give them their oath that they would perform this promise; now that their convictions were strong, and they seemed resolved, he would keep them to it. 3. He bound them by a solemn curse or execration, hoping that would strike some awe upon them: *So let God shake out every man that performeth not this promise, v.* 13. This was a threatening that he would certainly do so, to which the people said *Amen,* as to those curses at Mount Ebal (Deut. xxvii.), that their throats might be cut with their own tongues if they should falsify their engagement, and that by the dread of that they might be kept to their promise. With this *Amen* the people *praised the Lord;* so far were they from promising with regret that they promised with all possible expressions of joy and thankfulness. Thus David, when he took God's vows upon him, *sang and gave praise,* Ps. lvi. 12. This cheerfulness in promising was well, but that which follows was better: *They did according to this promise,* and adhered to what they had done, not as their ancestors in a like case, who re-enslaved those whom a little before they had released, Jer. xxxiv. 10, 11. Good promises are good things, but good performances are all in all.

14 Moreover from the time that I was appointed to be their governor in the land of Judah, from the twentieth year even unto the two and thirtieth year of Artaxerxes the king, *that is,* twelve years, I and my brethren have not eaten the bread of the governor. 15 But the former governors that *had been* before me were chargeable unto the people, and had taken of them bread and wine, beside forty shekels of silver; yea, even their servants bare rule over the people: but so did not I, because of the fear of God. 16 Yea, also I continued in the work of this wall, neither bought we any land: and all my servants *were* gathered thither unto the work. 17 Moreover *there were* at my table a hundred and fifty of the Jews and rulers, beside those that came unto us from among the heathen that *are* about us. 18 Now *that* which was prepared *for me* daily *was* one ox *and* six choice sheep; also fowls were prepared for me, and once in ten days store of all sorts of wine: yet for all this required not I the bread of the governor, because the bondage was heavy upon this people. 19 Think upon me, my God, for good, *according* to all that I have done for this people.

Nehemiah had mentioned his own practice, as an inducement to the nobles not to burden the poor, no, not with just demands; here he relates more particularly what his practice was, not in pride or vain-glory, nor to pass a compliment upon himself, but as an inducement both to his successors and to the inferior magistrates to be as tender as might be of the people's ease.

I. He intimates what had been the way of his predecessors, *v.* 15. He does not name them, because what he had to say of them was not to their honour, and in such a case it is good to spare names; but the people knew how chargeable they had been, and how dearly the country paid for all the benefit of their government. The government allowed them *forty shekels of silver,* which was nearly five pounds (so much a day, it is probable); but, besides that, they obliged the people to furnish them with *bread and wine,* which they claimed as perquisites of their office; and not only so, but they suffered their servants to squeeze the people, and to get all they could out of them. Note, 1. It is no new thing for those who are in public places to seek themselves more than the public welfare, nay, and to serve themselves by the public loss. 2. Masters must be accountable for all the acts of fraud and injustice, violence and oppression, which they connive at in their servants.

II. He tells us what had been his own way.

1. In general, he had not done as the former governors did; he would not, he durst not, *because of the fear of God.* He had an awe of God's majesty and a dread of his wrath. And, (1.) The fear of God restrained him from oppressing the people. Those that truly fear God will not dare to do any thing cruel or unjust. (2.) It was purely that which restrained him. He was thus generous, not that he might have praise of men, or serve a turn by his interest in the people, but purely for conscience' sake, because of the fear of God. This will not only be a powerful, but an acceptable principle both of justice and charity. What a good hand his predecessors made of their place appeared by the estates they raised; but Nehemiah, for his part, got nothing, except the satisfaction of doing good: *Neither bought we any land, v.* 16. Say not then that he was a bad husband, but that he was a good governor, who aimed not to feather his own nest. Let us *remember the words of the Lord,* how he said, *It is more blessed to give than to receive,* Acts xx. 35.

2. More particularly, observe here, (1.) How little Nehemiah received of what he might have required. He did the work of the governor, but he did not *eat the bread of the governor* (*v.* 14), did not require it, *v.* 18. So far was he from extorting more than his due that he never demanded that, but lived upon what he had got in the king of Persia's court and his own estate in Judea: the reason he gives for this piece of self-denial is, *Because the bondage was heavy upon the people.* He might have used the common excuse for rigour in such cases, that it would be a wrong to his successors not to demand his dues; but let them look to themselves: he considered the afflicted state of the Jews, and, while they groaned under so much hardship, he could not find it in his heart to add to their burden, but would rather lessen his own estate than ruin them. Note, In our demands we must consider not only the justice of them, but the ability of those on whom we make them; where there is nothing to be had we know who loses his right. (2.) How much he gave which he might have withheld. [1.] His servants' work, *v.* 16. The servants of princes think themselves excused from labour; but Nehemiah's servants, by his order no doubt, were *all gathered to the work.* Those that have many servants should contrive how they may do good with them and keep them well employed. [2.] His own meat, *v.* 17, 18. He kept a very good table, not on certain days, but constantly; he had many honourable guests, at least 150 of his own countrymen, persons of the first rank, besides strangers that came to him upon business; and he had plentiful provisions for his guests, beef, and mutton, and fowl, and all sorts of wine. Let those in public places remember that they were preferred to do good, not to enrich themselves; and let people in humbler stations learn to *use hospitality one to another without grudging,* 1 Pet. iv. 9.

III. He concludes with a prayer (*v.* 19): *Think upon me, my God, for good.* 1. Nehemiah here mentions what he had *done for this people,* not in pride, as boasting of himself, nor in passion, as upbraiding them, nor does it appear that he had occasion to do it in his own vindication, as Paul had to relate his like self-denying tenderness towards the Corinthians, but to shame the rulers out of their oppressions; let them learn of him to be neither greedy in their demands nor paltry in their expenses, and then they would have the credit and comfort of their liberality, as he had. 2. He mentions it to God in prayer, not as if he thought he had hereby merited any favour from God, as a debt, but to show that he looked not for any recompence of his generosity from men, but depended upon God only to make up to him what he had lost and laid out for his honour; and he reckoned the favour of God reward enough. "If God do but *think upon me for good,* I have enough." His thoughts to us-ward are our happiness, Ps. xl. 5. He refers it to God to recompense him in such a manner as he pleased. "If men forget me, let my God think on me, and I desire no more."

CHAP. VI.

The cries of oppressed poverty being stilled, we are now to enquire how the building of the wall goes forward, and in this chapter we find it carried on with vigour and finished with joy, notwithstanding the restless attempts of the gates of hell to hinder it. How the Jews' enemies were baffled in their design to put a stop to it by force we read before, ch. iv. Here we find how their endeavours to drive Nehemiah off from it were frustrated. I. When they courted him to an interview, with design to do him a mischief, he would not stir, ver 1—4. II. When they would have made him believe his undertaking was represented as seditious and treasonable, he regarded not the insinuation, ver. 5—9. III. When they hired pretended prophets to advise him to retire into the emple for his own safety, still he kept his ground, ver. 10—14. IV. Notwithstanding the secret correspondence that was kept up between them and some false and treacherous Jews, the work was finished in a short time, ver. 15—19. Such as these were the struggles between the church and its enemies · but great is God's cause and will be prosperous and victorious.

NOW it came to pass, when Sanballat, and Tobiah, and Geshem the Arabian, and the rest of our enemies, heard that I had builded the wall, and *that* there was no breach left therein; (though at that time I had not set up the doors upon the gates;) 2 That Sanballat and Geshem sent unto me, saying, Come, let us meet together in *some one of* the villages in the plain of Ono. But they thought to do me mischief. 3 And I sent messengers unto them, saying, I *am* doing a great work, so that I cannot come down: why should the work cease, whilst I leave it, and come down to you? 4 Yet they sent unto me four times after this sort; and I answered them after the same manner. 5 Then sent Sanballat his servant unto me in like manner the fifth time with an open letter in his hand; 6 Wherein *was* written, It is reported among the heathen, and Gashmu saith *it*, *that* thou and the Jews think to rebel: for which cause thou buildest the wall, that thou mayest be their king, according to these words. 7 And thou hast also appointed prophets to preach of thee at Jerusalem, saying, *There is* a king in Judah: and now shall it be reported to the king according to these words. Come now therefore, and let us take counsel together. 8 Then I sent unto him, saying, There are no such things done as thou sayest, but thou feignest them out of thine own heart. 9 For they all made us afraid, saying, Their hands shall be weakened from the work, that it be not done. Now therefore, *O God*, strengthen my hands.

Two plots upon Nehemiah we have here an account of, how cunningly they were laid by his enemies and how happily frustrated by God's good providence and his prudence.

I. A plot to trepan him into a snare. The enemies had an account of the good forwardness the work was in, that all the breaches of the wall were made up, so that they considered it as good as done, though at that time the *doors of the gates* were off the hinges (*v.* 1); they must therefore now or never, by one bold stroke, take off Nehemiah. They heard how well guarded he was, so that there was no attacking him upon the spot; they will therefore try by all the arts of wheedling to get him among them. Observe, 1. With what hellish subtlety they courted him to meet them, not in any city, lest that should excite a suspicion that they intended to secure him, but in a village in the lot of Benjamin: "*Come, let us meet together* to consult about the common interests of our provinces." Or they would have him think that they coveted his friendship, and would be glad to be better acquainted with him, in order to a good understanding between them and the settling of a good correspondence. *But they thought to do him a mischief.* It is probable that he had some secret intelligence given him that they designed to imprison or murder him; or he knew them so well that, without breach of charity, he concluded they aimed at his life, and therefore, when they *spoke fair, he believed them not.* 2. See with what heavenly wisdom he declined the motion. His *God did instruct him* to give them that prudent answer by messengers of his own: "*I am doing a great work*, am very busy, and am loth to let the work stand still while I leave it to *come down to you*," *v.* 3. His care was that the work might not cease; he knew it would if he left it ever so little; and *why should it cease while I come down to you?* He says nothing of his jealousies, nor reproaches them for their treacherous design, but gives them a good reason and one of the true reasons why he would not come. Compliment must always give way to business. Let those that are tempted to idle merry meetings by their vain companions thus answer the temptation, "We have work to do, and must not neglect it." Four times they attacked him with the same solicitation, and he as often returned the same answer, which, we may suppose, was very vexatious to them; for really it was the ceasing of the work that they aimed at, and it would make them despair of breaking the undertaking to see the undertaker so intent upon it. *I answered them* (says he) *after the same manner*, *v.* 4. Note, We must never suffer ourselves to be overcome by the greatest importunity to do any thing sinful or imprudent; but, when we are attacked with the same temptation, must still resist it with the same reason and resolution.

II. A plot to terrify him from his work. Could they but drive him off, the work would cease of course. This therefore Sanballat attempts, but in vain. 1. He endeavours to possess Nehemiah with an apprehension that his undertaking to build the walls of Jerusalem was generally represented as factious and seditious, and would be resented accordingly at court, *v.* 5—7. The best men, even in their most innocent and excellent performances, have lain under this imputation. This is written to him in *an open letter*, as a thing generally known and talked of, that it was reported among the nations, and Gashmu will aver it for truth, that Nehemiah was aiming to make himself king and to shake off the Persian yoke. Note, It is common for that which is the sense only of the malicious to be falsely represented by them as the sense of the many. Now Sanballat pretends to inform Nehemiah of this as a friend, that he might hasten to court to clear himself, or stay his proceedings, for fear they should be thus misconstrued; at least, upon this surmise, he urges him to give him the meeting—"*Let us take counsel together* how to quell the report," hoping by this means either to take him off, or at least to take him off from his business. Thus were his words *softer than oil,* and yet *war was in his heart,* and he hoped, like Judas, to kiss and kill. But surely in vain is the net spread in the sight of any bird. Nehemiah was soon aware what they aimed at, to *weaken their hands from the work* (*v.* 9), and therefore not only denied that such things were true, but that they were reported; he was better known than to be thus suspected. 2. Thus he escaped the snare and kept his ground, nor would he be frightened by winds and clouds from sowing and reaping. Suppose it was thus reported, we must never omit known duty merely for fear it should be misconstrued; but, while we keep a good conscience, let us trust God with our good name. But indeed it was not thus reported. God's people, though sufficiently loaded with reproach, yet are not really so low in reputation as some would have them thought to be.

In the midst of his complaint of their malice, in endeavouring to frighten him, and so weaken his hands, he lifts up his heart to Heaven in this short prayer: *Now therefore, O God! strengthen my hands.* It is the great support and relief of good people that in all their straits and difficulties they have a good God to go to, from whom, by faith and prayer, they may fetch in grace to silence their fears and *strengthen their hands* when their enemies are endeavouring to fill them with fears and weaken their hands. When, in our Christian work and warfare, we are entering upon any particular services or conflicts, this is a good prayer for us to put up: "I have such a duty to do, such a temptation to grapple with; *now therefore, O God! strengthen my hands.*" Some read it, not as a prayer, but as a holy resolution (for *O God* is supplied in our translation): *Now therefore I will strengthen my hands.* Note, Christian fortitude will be sharpened by opposition. Every temptation to draw us from duty should quicken us so much the more to duty.

10 Afterward I came unto the house of Shemaiah the son of Delaiah the son of Mehetabeel, who *was* shut up; and he said, Let us meet together in the house of God, within the temple, and let us shut the doors of the temple: for they will come to slay thee; yea, in the night will they come to slay thee. 11 And I said, Should such a man as I flee? and who *is there*, that, *being* as I *am*, would go into the temple to save his life? I will not go in. 12 And, lo, I perceived that God had not sent him; but that he pronounced this prophecy against me: for Tobiah and Sanballat had hired him. 13 Therefore *was* he hired, that I should be afraid, and do so, and sin, and *that* they might have *matter* for an evil report, that they might reproach me. 14 My God, think thou upon Tobiah and Sanballat according to these their works, and on the prophetess Noadiah, and the rest of the prophets, that would have put me in fear.

The Jews' enemies leave no stone unturned, no way untried, to take Nehemiah off from building the wall about Jerusalem. In order to this they had tried to fetch him into the country to them, but in vain; now they try to drive him into the temple for his own safety; let him be any where but at his work. Observing him to be a cautious man, they will endeavour to gain their point by making him cowardly. Observe,

I. How basely the enemies managed this temptation.

1. That which they designed was to bring Nehemiah to do a foolish thing, that they might laugh at him, and insult over him for doing it, and so lessen his interest and influence (*v.* 13): *That I should be afraid,* and so they might have *matter for an evil report,* and *might reproach me.* This was indeed doing the devil's work, who is men's tempter that he may be their accuser, draws men to sin that he may glory in their shame. The greatest mischief our enemies can do us is to frighten us from our duty and bring us to do what is sinful.

2. The tools they made use of were a pretended prophet and prophetess, whom they hired to persuade Nehemiah to quit his work and retire for his own safety. The pretended prophet was Shemaiah, of whom it is said that he was *shut up* in his own house, either under pretence of retirement for meditation and to consult the mind of God or to give Nehemiah a sign in like manner to make himself a recluse. It should seem, Nehemiah had a value for him, for he went to his house to consult him, *v.* 10. Other prophets there were, and one prophetess, Noadiah (*v.* 14), that were in the interest of the Jews' enemies, pensioners to them and traitors to their country. Whether they pretended to inspiration does not appear; they do not say, *Thus saith the Lord,* as the false prophets of old did; if not so, yet they would be thought to excel in divine knowledge, and human prudence, and

to have uncommon measures of insight and foresight, and were therefore consulted in difficult cases, as prophets had been. These the enemies feed to be of counsel for them. Let us hence take occasion to lament, (1.) The wickedness of such bad men as these prophets, that ever any should be so perfidious as to betray the cause of God and their country even under the pretence of communion with God and concern for their country. (2.) The unhappiness of such good men as Nehemiah, who are in danger of being imposed upon by such cheats, and to whom no temptation comes with more force than that which comes under a colour of religion, of revelation and devotion, and is brought by the hand of prophets.

3. The pretence was plausible. These prophets suggested to Nehemiah that the enemies would come and slay him, *in the night* they would slay him, which he had reason enough to believe was true; they would, if they could, if they durst. They pretended to be much concerned for his safety. The people would be all undone if any harm should come to him; and therefore they very gravely advised him to hide himself in the temple till the danger was over; that was a strong and sacred place, where he would be under the special protection of Heaven, Ps. xxvii. 5. If Nehemiah had been prevailed upon to do this, immediately the people would both have left off their work and thrown down their arms, and every one would have shifted for his own safety; and then the enemies might easily, and without opposition, have demolished the works, broken down the wall again, and so gained their point. Though self-preservation is a fundamental principle of the law of nature, yet that is not always the best and wisest counsel which pretends to go upon that principle

II. See how bravely Nehemiah vanquished this temptation, and came off a conqueror.

1. He immediately resolved not to yield to it, *v.* 11. See here, (1.) What his reasonings are: "*Should such a man as I flee?* Shall I desert God's work, or discourage my own workmen whom I have employed and encouraged? Shall I be over-credulous of report, and over-solicitous about my own life? I that am the governor, on whom so many eyes are, both of friends and foes? Another might flee, but not I. *Who is there that being as I am*, in my post of honour, and power, and trust, would go into the temple, and lurk there, when business is to be done, yea, though it were to save his life?" Note, When we are tempted to sin we should remember who and what we are, that we may not do any thing unbecoming us, and the profession we make. *It is not for kings, O Lemuel!* Prov. xxxi. 4. (2.) What was the result of his reasonings. He is at a point: "I will not go in. I will rather die at my work than live in an inglorious retreat from it." Note, Holy courage and magnanimity will engage us, whatever it cost us, never to *decline a good work*, nor ever to *do a bad one*.

2. He was immediately aware of what was the rise of it (*v.* 12): "*I perceived that God had not sent him*, that he gave this advice, not by any divine direction, ordinary or extraordinary, but with a design against me." The wickedness of such mercenary wretches will sooner or later be brought to light. Two things Nehemiah says he dreaded in that which he was advised to:—(1.) Offending God: *That I should be afraid, and do so, and sin.* Note, Sin is that which above any thing we should dread; and a good preservative it is against sin to be afraid of nothing but sin. (2.) Shaming himself: *That they might reproach me.* Note, Next to the sinfulness of sin we should dread the scandalousness of it.

3. He humbly begs of God to reckon with them for their base designs upon him (*v.* 14): *My God, think thou upon Tobiah,* and the rest of them, *according to their works.* As, when he had mentioned his own good services, he did not covetously or ambitiously prescribe to God what reward he should give him, but modestly prayed, *Think upon me, my God* (*ch.* v. 19), so here he does not revengefully imprecate any particular judgment upon his enemies, but refers the matter to God. "Thou knowest their hearts, and art the avenger of falsehood and wrong; take cognizance of this cause; judge between me and them, and take what way and time thou mayest please to call them to an account for it." Note, Whatever injuries are done us we must not avenge ourselves, but commit our cause to him that judgeth righteously.

15 So the wall was finished in the twenty and fifth *day* of *the month* Elul, in fifty and two days. 16 And it came to pass, that when all our enemies heard *thereof*, and all the heathen that *were* about us saw *these things*, they were much cast down in their own eyes: for they perceived that this work was wrought of our God. 17 Moreover in those days the nobles of Judah sent many letters unto Tobiah, and *the letters* of Tobiah came unto them. 18 For *there were* many in Judah sworn unto him, because he *was* the son in law of Shechaniah the son of Arah; and his son Johanan had taken the daughter of Meshullam the son of Berechiah. 19 Also they reported his good deeds before me, and uttered my words to him. *And* Tobiah sent letters to put me in fear.

Nehemiah is here finishing the wall of Jerusalem, and yet still has trouble created him by his enemies.

I. Tobiah, and the other adversaries of the

Jews, had the mortification to see the wall built up, notwithstanding all their attempts to hinder it. The wall was begun and finished *in fifty-two days*, and yet we have reason to believe they rested on the sabbaths, *v.* 15. Many were employed, and there was room for them; what they did they did cheerfully, and minded their business because they loved it. The threats of their enemies, which were intended to weaken them, it is likely, quickened them to go on with their work the more vigorously, that they might get it done before the enemy came. Thus *out of the eater came forth meat*. See what a great deal of work may be done in a little time if we would set about it in earnest and keep close to it. When the enemies heard that the wall was finished before they thought it was well begun, and, when they doubted not but to put a stop to it, they were *much cast down in their own eyes, v.* 16. 1. They were ashamed of their own confidence that they should *cause the work to cease;* they were crest-fallen upon the disappointment. 2. They envied the prosperity and success of the Jews, grieved to see the walls of Jerusalem built, while, it may be, the kings of Persia had not permitted them thus to fortify the cities of Samaria. When Cain envied his brother his *countenance fell*, Gen. iv. 5. 3. They despaired of ever doing them the mischief they designed them, of bringing them down and making a prey of them; and well they might, for they perceived, by the wonderful success, *that the work was wrought of God*. Even these heathens had so much sense as, [1.] To see a special providence of God conversant about the affairs of the church when they did remarkably prosper. They *said among the heathen, The Lord has done great things for them;* it is his doing, Ps. cxxvi. 2. God fighteth for Israel and worketh with them. [2.] To believe that God's work would be perfect. When they perceived that the *work was of God* they expected no other than that it would go on and prosper. [3.] To conclude that, if it were of God, it was to no purpose to think of opposing it; it would certainly prevail and be victorious.

II. Nehemiah had the vexation, notwithstanding this, to see some of his own people treacherously corresponding with Tobiah and serving his interest; and a great grief and discouragement, no doubt, it was to him. 1. Even of the nobles of Judah there were those who had so little sense of honour and their country's good as to communicate with Tobiah by letter, *v.* 17. They wrote with all the freedom and familiarity of friends to him, and welcomed his letters to them. Could nobles do a thing so mean? Nobles of Judah so wicked a thing? It seems great men are not always wise, not always honest. 2. Many in Judah were in a strict but secret confederacy with him to advance the interest of his country, though it would certainly be the ruin of their own. They were *sworn unto him*, not as their prince, but as their friend and ally, because both he and his son had married daughters of Israel, *v.* 18. See the mischief of marrying with strangers; for one heathen that was converted by it ten Jews were perverted. When once they became akin to Tobiah they soon became sworn to him. A sinful love leads to a sinful league. 3. They had the impudence to court Nehemiah himself into a friendship with him: "*They reported his good deeds before me*, represented him as an intelligent gentleman and well worthy my acquaintance, an honest gentleman and one that I might confide in." We are indeed required to *speak ill of no man*, but never to speak well of bad men. *Those that forsake the law praise the wicked*, Prov. xxviii. 4. 4. They were so false as to betray Nehemiah's counsels to him; they uttered Nehemiah's words to him, perverting them, no doubt, and putting false constructions upon them, which furnished Tobiah with matter for letters to put him in fear and so drive him from his work and discourage him in it. Thus were all their thoughts against him for evil, yet God thought upon him for good.

CHAP. VII.

The success of one good design for God and our generation should encourage us to proceed and form some other; Nehemiah did so, having fortified Jerusalem with gates and walls, his next care is, I. To see the city well kept, ver. 1—4. II. To see it well peopled, in order to which he here reviews and calls over the register of the children of the captivity, the families that returned at first, and records it, ver. 5—73. It is the same, in effect, with that which we had, Ezra ii. What use he made of it we shall find afterwards, when he brought one of ten to live in Jerusalem, ch. xi. 1.

NOW it came to pass, when the wall was built, and I had set up the doors, and the porters and the singers and the Levites were appointed, 2 That I gave my brother Hanani, and Hananiah the ruler of the palace, charge over Jerusalem: for he *was* a faithful man, and feared God above many. 3 And I said unto them, Let not the gates of Jerusalem be opened until the sun be hot; and while they stand by, let them shut the doors, and bar *them:* and appoint watches of the inhabitants of Jerusalem, every one in his watch, and every one *to be* over against his house. 4 Now the city *was* large and great: but the people *were* few therein, and the houses *were* not builded.

God saith concerning his church (Isa. lxii. 6), *I have set watchmen upon thy walls, O Jerusalem!* This is Nehemiah's care here; for dead walls, without living watchmen, are but a poor defence to a city.

I. He appointed *the porters, singers, and Levites,* in their places to their work. This is meant of their work in general, which was to attend the temple service; it had been neglected in some degree, but now was revived. God's worship is the defence of a place, and his ministers, when they mind their duty, are watchmen on the walls. Or, in particular, he ordered them to be ready against the wall was to be dedicated, that they might perform that service in an orderly and solemn manner; and the dedication of it was its strength. That is likely to be beneficial to us which is devoted to God.

II. He appointed two governors or consuls, to whom he committed the care of the city, and gave them in charge to provide for the public peace and safety. Hanani, his brother, who came to him with the tidings of the desolations of Jerusalem, was one, a man of approved integrity and affection to his country; the other was Hananiah, who had been ruler of the palace: for he that has approved himself faithful in less shall be entrusted with more. Of this Hananiah it is said that he was a *faithful man and one that feared God above many, v.* 2. Note, 1. Among those who fear God truly there are some who fear him greatly, and excel others in the expressions and instances of that fear; and they are worthy a double portion of that honour which is due to those that *fear the Lord,* Ps. xv. 4. There were many in Jerusalem that feared God, but this good man was more eminent for religion and serious godliness than any. 2. Those that fear God must evidence it by their being faithful to all men and universally conscientious. 3. God's Jerusalem is then likely to flourish when those rule in it, and have charge of it, who excel in virtue, and are eminent both for godliness and honesty. It is supposed, by some, that Nehemiah was now about to return to the Persian court to have his commission renewed, and that he left these two worthy men in charge with the affairs of the city in his absence. Good governors, when and where they cannot act themselves, must be very careful whom they depute.

III. He gave orders about the shutting of the gates and the guarding of the walls, *v.* 3, 4. See here, 1. What the present state of Jerusalem was. The city, in compass, was large and great. The walls enclosed the same ground as formerly; but much of it lay waste, for the houses were not built, few at least in comparison with what had been; so that Nehemiah walled the city in faith, and with an eye to that promise of the replenishing of it which God had lately made by the prophet, Zech. viii. 3, &c. Though the people were now few, he believed they would be multiplied, and therefore built the walls so as to make room for them; had he not depended upon this he might have thought walls without a city as great a reproach as a city without walls. 2. What was the care of Nehemiah for it. He ordered the rulers of the city themselves, (1.) To stand by, and see the city-gates shut up and barred every night; for in vain had they a wall if they were careless of their gates. (2.) To take care that they should not be opened in the morning till they could see that all was clear and quiet. (3.) To set sentinels upon the walls, or elsewhere, at convenient distances, who should, in case of the approach of the enemy, give timely notice to the city of the danger; and, as it came to their turn to watch, they must post themselves *over against their own houses,* because of them, it might be presumed, they would be in a particular manner careful. The public safety depends upon every one's particular care to guard himself and his own family against sin, that common enemy. It is every one's interest to watch, but many understand not their own interest; it is therefore incumbent upon magistrates to appoint watches. And as this people had lately found God with them in their building (else they would have built in vain), so now that the wall was built, no doubt, they were made sensible that *except the Lord kept the city the watchman waked but in vain,* Ps. cxxvii. 1.

5 And my God put into mine heart to gather together the nobles, and the rulers, and the people, that they might be reckoned by genealogy. And I found a register of the genealogy of them which came up at the first, and found written therein, 6 These *are* the children of the province, that went up out of the captivity, of those that had been carried away, whom Nebuchadnezzar the king of Babylon had carried away, and came again to Jerusalem and to Judah, every one unto his city; 7 Who came with Zerubbabel, Jeshua, Nehemiah, Azariah, Raamiah, Nahamani, Mordecai, Bilshan, Mispereth, Bigvai, Nehum, Baanah. The number, *I say,* of the men of the people of Israel *was this;* 8 The children of Parosh, two thousand a hundred seventy and two. 9 The children of Shephatiah, three hundred seventy and two. 10 The children of Arah, six hundred fifty and two. 11 The children of Pahath-moab, of the children of Jeshua and Joab, two thousand and eight hundred *and* eighteen. 12 The children of Elam, a thousand two hundred fifty and four. 13 The children of Zattu, eight hundred forty and five. 14 The children of Zaccai, seven hundred and threescore. 15 The children of Binnui, six hundred forty and eight. 16 The

children of Bebai, six hundred twenty and eight. 17 The children of Azgad, two thousand three hundred twenty and two. 18 The children of Adonikam, six hundred threescore and seven. 19 The children of Bigvai, two thousand threescore and seven. 20 The children of Adin, six hundred fifty and five. 21 The children of Ater of Hezekiah, ninety and eight. 22 The children of Hashum, three hundred twenty and eight. 23 The children of Bezai, three hundred twenty and four. 24 The children of Hariph, a hundred and twelve. 25 The children of Gibeon, ninety and five. 26 The men of Beth-lehem and Netophah, a hundred fourscore and eight. 27 The men of Anathoth, a hundred twenty and eight. 28 The men of Beth-azmaveth, forty and two. 29 The men of Kirjath-jearim, Chephirah, and Beeroth, seven hundred forty and three. 30 The men of Ramah and Gaba, six hundred twenty and one. 31 The men of Michmas, a hundred and twenty and two. 32 The men of Beth-el and Ai, a hundred twenty and three. 33 The men of the other Nebo, fifty and two. 34 The children of the other Elam, a thousand two hundred fifty and four. 35 The children of Harim, three hundred and twenty. 36 The children of Jericho, three hundred forty and five. 37 The children of Lod, Hadid, and Ono, seven hundred twenty and one. 38 The children of Senaah, three thousand nine hundred and thirty. 39 The priests: the children of Jedaiah, of the house of Jeshua, nine hundred seventy and three. 40 The children of Immer, a thousand fifty and two. 41 The children of Pashur, a thousand two hundred forty and seven. 42 The children of Harim, a thousand and seventeen. 43 The Levites: the children of Jeshua, of Kadmiel, *and* of the children of Hodevah, seventy and four. 44 The singers: the children of Asaph, a hundred forty and eight. 45 The porters: the children of Shallum, the children of Ater, the children of Talmon, the children of Akkub, the children of Hatita, the children of Shobai, a hundred thirty and eight. 46 The Nethinims: the children of Ziha, the children of Hashupha, the children of Tabbaoth, 47 The children of Keros, the children of Sia, the children of Padon, 48 The children of Lebana, the children of Hagaba, the children of Shalmai, 49 The children of Hanan, the children of Giddel, the children of Gahar, 50 The children of Reaiah, the children of Rezin, the children of Nekoda, 51 The children of Gazzam, the children of Uzza, the children of Phaseah, 52 The children of Besai, the children of Meunim, the children of Nephishesim, 53 The children of Bakbuk, the children of Hakupha, the children of Harhur, 54 The children of Bazlith, the children of Mehida, the children of Harsha, 55 The children of Barkos, the children of Sisera, the children of Tamah. 56 The children of Neziah, the children of Hatipha. 57 The children of Solomon's servants: the children of Sotai, the children of Sophereth, the children of Perida, 58 The children of Jaala, the children of Darkon, the children of Giddel, 59 The children of Shephatiah, the children of Hattil, the children of Pochereth of Zebaim, the children of Amon. 60 All the Nethinims, and the children of Solomon's servants, *were* three hundred ninety and two. 61 And these *were* they which went up *also* from Tel-melah, Tel-haresha, Cherub, Addon, and Immer: but they could not show their father's house, nor their seed, whether they *were* of Israel. 62 The children of Delaiah, the children of Tobiah, the children of Nekoda, six hundred forty and two. 63 And of the priests: the children of Habaiah, the children of Koz, the children of Barzillai, which took *one* of the daughters of Barzillai the Gileadite to wife, and was called after their name. 64 These sought their register *among* those that were reckoned by genealogy, but it was not found: therefore were they, as polluted, put from the priesthood. 65 And the Tirshatha said unto them, that they should not eat of the most holy things, till there stood *up* a priest with Urim and Thummim. 66 The whole congregation together *was* forty and two thousand three hundred and threescore. 67 Beside their manservants and their maidservants, of whom *there were* seven thousand three hundred thirty and seven: and they had two hundred forty and five singing men and singing women. 68 Their horses, seven hundred thirty and six: their mules, two hundred forty and five: 69 *Their* camels four hundred thirty and five: six thousand seven hundred and twenty asses. 70 And some of the chief of the fathers gave unto the work. The Tirshatha gave to the treasure a thousand drams of gold, fifty basons, five hundred and thirty priests' garments. 71 And *some* of the chief of the fathers gave to the treasure of the work twenty thousand drams of gold, and two thousand and two hundred pound of silver. 72 And *that* which the rest of the people gave *was* twenty thousand drams of gold, and two thousand pound of silver, and threescore and seven priests' garments. 73 So the priests, and the Levites, and the porters, and the singers, and *some* of the people, and the Nethinims, and all Israel, dwelt in their cities; and when the seventh month came, the children of Israel *were* in their cities.

We have here another good project of Nehemiah's; for wise and zealous men will be always contriving something or other for the glory of God and the edification of his church. He knew very well that the safety of a city, under God, depends more upon the number and valour of the inhabitants than upon the height or strength of its walls; and therefore, observing that the people were few that dwelt in it, he thought fit to take an account of the people, that he might find what families had formerly had their settlement in Jerusalem, but were now removed into the country, that he might bring them back, and what families could in any other way be influenced by their religion, or by their business, to come and rebuild the houses in Jerusalem and dwell in them. So little reason have we to wish that we may be placed alone in the earth, or in Jerusalem itself, that much of our safety and comfort depends upon our neighbours and friends; the more the stronger, the more the merrier. It is the wisdom of the governors of a nation to keep the balance even between the city and country, that the metropolis be not so extravagantly large as to drain and impoverish the country, nor yet so weak as not to be able to protect it. Now observe,

I. Whence this good design of Nehemiah's came. He owns, *My God put it into my heart, v.* 5. Note, Whatever good motion is in our minds, either prudent or pious, we must acknowledge it to come from God. It was he that *put it into our hearts;* for every good gift and every good work are from above. He gives knowledge; he gives grace; all is of him, and therefore all must be to him. What is done by human prudence must be ascribed to the direction of divine Providence; he that teaches the husbandman his discretion (Isa. xxviii. 26) teaches the statesman his.

II. What method he took in prosecution of it.

1. He called the rulers together, and the people, that he might have an account of the present state of their families—their number and strength, and where they were settled. It is probable that when he summoned them to come together he ordered them to bring such an account along with them out of their several districts. And I doubt they were not so many but that it might be soon done.

2. He reviewed the old *register of the genealogy of those who came up at the first,* and compared the present accounts with that; and here we have the repetition of that out of Ezra ii. The title is the same here (*v.* 6, 7) as there (*v.* 1, 2): *These are the children of the province,* &c. Two things are here repeated and recorded a second time from thence—the names and numbers of their several families, and their oblations to the service of the temple. The repetition of these accounts may intimate to us the delight which the great God is pleased to take in the persons, families, and services of his spiritual Israel, and the particular notice he takes of them. He knows those that are his, knows them all, knows them by name, has his eye on the register of those children of the captivity, and does all according to the ancient counsel of his will concerning them.

(1.) Here is an account of the heads of the several families that first came up, *v.* 6—69. As to this, [1.] Though it seem of little use to us now, yet then it was of great use, to compare what they had been with what they now were. We may suppose they were much increased by this time; but it would do well for them to remember their small beginnings, that they might acknowledge God in multiplying their families and building them up. By this means likewise their genealogies would be preserved, and the distinction of their families kept up, till the Messiah should come, and then an end be put to all their genealogies, which were preserved for his sake, but afterwards were endless. But, [2.] There are many differences in the numbers between this catalogue and that in Ezra. Most of them indeed are exactly the same, and some others within a very few under or over (one or two perhaps); and therefore I cannot think, as some do, that that was the number of these families at their first coming and this as they were now, which was at least forty years after (some make it much more); for we cannot suppose so many families to be not at all, or but little, altered in their numbers in all that time; therefore what differences there are we may suppose to arise either from the mistakes of transcribers, which easily happen in numbers, or from the diversity of the copies from which they were taken. Or perhaps one was the account of them when they set out from Babylon with Zerubbabel, the other when they came to Jerusalem. The sum totals are all just the same there and here, except of the singing-men and singing-women, which there are 200, here 245. These were not of such importance as that they should keep any strict account of them.

(2.) Here is an account of the offerings which were given towards the work of God, *v.* 70, &c. This differs much from that in Ezra ii. 68, 69, and it may be questioned whether it refers to the same contribution; here the tirshatha, or chief governor, who there was not mentioned, begins the offering; and the single sum mentioned there exceeds all those here put together; yet it is probable that it was the same, but that followed one copy of the lists, this another; for the last verse is the same here that it was Ezra ii. 70, adding *ch.* iii. 1. Blessed be God that our faith and hope are not built upon the niceties of names and numbers, genealogy and chronology, but on the great things of the law and gospel. Whatever is given to the work of God, he is not unrighteous to forget it; nor shall even a cup of cold water, wherewith he is honoured, go without its reward.

CHAP. VIII.

Ezra came up out of Babylon thirteen years before Nehemiah came, yet we have here a piece of good work which he did, that might have been done before, but was not done till Nehemiah came, who, though he was not such a scholar nor such a divine as Ezra, nor such a scribe in the law of his God, yet was a man of a more lively active spirit. His zeal set Ezra's learning on work, and then great things were done, as we find here, where we have, I. The public and solemn reading and expounding of the law, ver. 1—8. II. The joy which the people were ordered to express upon that occasion, ver. 9—12. III. The solemn keeping of the feast of tabernacles according to the law, ver. 13—18.

AND all the people gathered themselves together as one man into the street that *was* before the water gate; and they spake unto Ezra the scribe to bring the book of the law of Moses, which the LORD had commanded to Israel. 2 And Ezra the priest brought the law before the congregation both of men and women, and all that could hear with understanding, upon the first day of the seventh month. 3 And he read therein before the street that *was* before the water gate from the morning until midday, before the men and the women, and those that could understand; and the ears of all the people *were attentive* unto the book of the law. 4 And Ezra the scribe stood upon a pulpit of wood, which they had made for the purpose; and beside him stood Mattithiah, and Shema, and Anaiah, and Urijah, and Hilkiah, and Maaseiah, on his right hand; and on his left hand, Pedaiah, and Mishael, and Malchiah, and Hashum, and Hashbadana, Zechariah, *and* Meshullam. 5 And Ezra opened the book in the sight of all the people; (for he was above all the people;) and when he opened it, all the people stood up: 6 And Ezra blessed the LORD, the great God. And all the people answered, Amen, Amen, with lifting up their hands: and they bowed their heads, and worshipped the LORD with *their* faces to the ground. 7 Also Jeshua, and Bani, and Sherebiah, Jamin, Akkub, Shabbethai, Hodijah, Maaseiah, Kelita, Azariah, Jozabad, Hanan, Pelaiah, and the Levites, caused the people to understand the law: and the people *stood* in their place. 8 So they read in the book in the law of God distinctly, and gave the sense, and caused *them* to understand the reading.

We have here an account of a solemn religious assembly, and the good work that was done in that assembly, to the honour of God and the edification of the church.

I. The time of it was the *first day of the seventh month, v.* 2. That was the day of the *feast of trumpets*, which is called a *sabbath*, and on which they were to have a *holy convocation*, Lev. xxiii. 24; Num. xxix. 1. But that was not all: it was on that day that the altar was set up, and they began to offer their burnt-offerings after their return out of captivity, a recent mercy in the memory of many then living; in a thankful remembrance of that, it is likely, they had kept this feast ever since with more than ordinary solemnity. Divine favours which are fresh in mind, and which we ourselves have been witnesses of, should be, and usually are, most affecting.

II. The place was in the *street that was before the water-gate* (*v.* 1), a spacious broad street, able to contain so great a multitude, which the court of the temple was not; for probably it was not now built nearly so large as it had been in Solomon's time. Sacrifices were to be offered only at the door of the temple, but praying, and praising, and preaching, were, and are, services of religion as acceptably performed in one place as in another. When this congregation thus met in the street of the city no doubt God was with them.

III. The persons that met were all the people, who were not compelled to come, but voluntarily gathered themselves together by common agreement, as one man: not only men came, but women and children, even as many as were capable of understanding what they heard. Masters of families should bring their families with them to the public worship of God. Women and children have souls to save, and are therefore concerned to acquaint themselves with the word of God and attend on the means of knowledge and grace. Little ones, as they come to the exercise of reason, must be trained up in the exercises of religion.

IV. The master of this assembly was Ezra the priest; he presided in this service. None so fit to expound and preach as he who was such a ready scribe in the law of his God. 1. His call to the service was very clear; for being in office as a priest, and qualified as a scribe, the *people spoke to him to bring the book of the law* and read it to them, *v.* 1. God gave him ability and authority, and then the people gave him opportunity and invitation. Knowledge is spiritual alms, which those that are able should give to every one that needs, to every one that asks. 2. His post was very convenient. He stood in a pulpit or tower of wood, *which they made for the word* (so it is in the original), *for the preaching of the word*, that what he said might be the more gracefully delivered and the better heard, and that the eyes of the hearers might be upon him, which would engage their attention, as Luke iv. 20. 3. He had several assistants. Some of these stood with him (*v.* 4), six on his right hand and seven on his left: either his pulpit was so contrived as to hold them all in a row, as in a gallery (but then it would scarcely have been called a *tower)*, or they had desks a degree lower. Some think that he appointed them to read when he was weary; at least his taking them as assessors with him put an honour upon them before the people, in order to their being employed in the same service another time. Others who are mentioned (*v.* 7) seem to have been employed at the same time in other places near at hand, to read and expound to those who could not come within hearing of Ezra. Of these also there were thirteen priests, whose lips were to keep knowledge, Mal. ii. 7. It is a great mercy to a people thus to be furnished with ministers that are apt to teach. Happy was Ezra in having such assistants as these, and happy were they in having such a guide as Ezra.

V. The religious exercises performed in this assembly were not ceremonial, but moral, praying and preaching. Ezra, as president of the assembly, was, 1. The people's mouth to God, and they affectionately joined with him, *v.* 6. He blessed the Lord as the great God, gave honour to him by praising his perfections and praying for his favour; and the people, in token of their concurrence with him both in prayers and praises, said, *Amen, Amen, lifted up their hands* in token of their desire being towards God and all their expectations from him, and *bowed their heads* in token of their reverence of him and subjection to him. Thus must we adore God, and address ourselves to him, when we are going to read and hear the word of God, as those that see God in his word very great and very good. 2. God's mouth to the people, and they attentively hearkened to him. This was the chief business of the solemnity, and observe, (1.) *Ezra brought the law before the congregation, v.* 2. He had taken care to provide himself with the best and most correct copies of the law; and what he had laid up for his own use and satisfaction he here brought forth, as a good householder out of his treasury, for the benefit of the church. Observe, [1.] The book of the law is not to be confined to the scribes' studies, but to be brought before the congregation and read to them in their own language. [2.] Ministers, when they go to the pulpit, should take their Bibles with them; Ezra did so; thence they must fetch their knowledge, and according to that rule they must speak and must show that they do so. See 2 Chron. xvii. 9. (2.) He opened the book with great reverence and solemnity, *in the sight of all the people, v.* 5. He brought it forth with a sense of the great mercy of God to them in giving them that book; he opened it with a sense of his mercy to them in giving them leave to read it, that it was not a spring shut up and a fountain sealed. The *taking of the book, and the opening of the seals,* we find celebrated with joy and praise, Rev. v. 9. Let us learn to address ourselves to the services of religion with solemn stops and pauses, and not to go about them rashly; let us consider what we are doing when we take God's book into our hands, and open it, and so also when we bow our knees in prayer; and what we do let us do deliberately, Eccl. v. 1. (3.) He and others read in the book of the law, *from morning till noon* (*v.* 3), and they read *distinctly, v.* 8. Reading the scriptures in religious assemblies is an ordinance of God, whereby he is honoured and his church edified. And, upon special occasions, we must be willing to attend for many hours together on the reading and expounding of the word of God: those mentioned here were thus employed for six hours. Let those that read and preach the word learn also to deliver themselves distinctly, as those who understand what they say and are affected with it themselves, and who desire that those they speak to may understand it, retain it, and be affected with it likewise. *It is a snare for a man to devour that which is holy.* (4.) What they read they expounded, showed the intent and meaning of it, and what use was to be made of it; they gave the sense in other words, that they might *cause the people to understand the reading, v.* 7, 8. Note, [1.] It is requisite that those who hear the word should understand it, else it is to them but an empty sound of words, Matt. xxiv. 15. [2.] It is therefore required of those who are teachers by office that they explain the word and give the sense of it. *Understandest thou what thou readest?* and, *Have you understood all these things?* are good questions to be put to the hearers; but, *How should we except some one guide us?* is as proper a question for them to put to their teachers, Acts viii. 30, 31. Reading is good, and preaching good, but expounding brings the reading and the preaching together, and thus makes the reading the more intelligible and the preaching the more convincing. (5.) The people conducted themselves very properly when the word was read and opened to them. [1.] With great reverence. When Ezra opened the book *all the people stood up* (*v.* 5), thereby showing respect both to Ezra and to the word he was about to read. It becomes servants to stand when their master speaks to them, in honour to their master and to show a readiness to do as they are bidden. [2.] With great fixedness and composedness. They *stood in their place* (*v.* 7); several ministers were reading and expounding at some distance from each other, and every one of the people kept his post, did not go to hear first one and then another, to make remarks upon them, but stood in his place, that he might neither give disturbance to another nor receive any disturbance himself. [3.] With great attention and a close application of mind: *The ears of all the people were unto the book of the law* (*v.* 3), were even chained to it; they heard readily, and minded every word. The word of God commands attention and deserves it. If through carelessness we let much slip in hearing, there is danger that through forgetfulness we shall let all slip after hearing.

9 And Nehemiah, which *is* the Tirshatha, and Ezra the priest the scribe, and the Levites that taught the people, said unto all the people, This day *is* holy unto the LORD your God; mourn not, nor weep. For all the people wept, when they heard the words of the law. 10 Then he said unto them, Go your way, eat the fat, and drink the sweet, and send portions unto them for whom nothing is prepared: for *this* day *is* holy unto our Lord; neither be ye sorry; for the joy of the LORD is your strength. 11 So the Levites stilled all the people, saying, Hold your peace, for the day *is* holy; neither be ye grieved. 12 And all the people went their way to eat, and to drink, and to send portions, and to make great mirth, because they had understood the words that were declared unto them.

We may here observe,

I. How the people were wounded with the words of the law that were read to them. The law works death, and speaks terror, shows men their sins, and their misery and danger because of sin, and thunders a curse against every one that continues not in every part of his duty. Therefore when they heard it they *all wept* (*v.* 9): it was a good sign that their hearts were tender, like Josiah's when he heard the words of the law. They wept to think how they had offended God, and exposed themselves, by their many violations of the law; when some wept all wept, for they all saw themselves guilty before God.

II. How they were healed and comforted with the words of peace that were spoken to them. It was well that they were so much affected with the word of God, and received the impressions of it; but they must not yield unduly to their mourning, especially at this time, because the day was holy to the Lord; it was one of the solemn feasts, on which it was their duty to rejoice; and even sorrow for sin must not hinder our joy in God, but rather lead us to it and prepare us for it.

1. The masters of the assembly endeavoured to pacify them and encourage them. Now Nehemiah is brought in, and not before, in this chapter; he took notice of the people's weeping. Ezra was pleased to see them so affected with the word, but Nehemiah observed to him, and Ezra concurred in the thought, that it was now unseasonable. This day was holy (it is called *a sabbath,* Lev. xxiii. 24), and therefore was to be celebrated with joy and praise, not as if it were *a day to afflict their souls.* (1.) They forbade the people to *mourn and weep* (*v.* 9): *Be not sorry* (*v.* 10); *hold your peace, neither be you grieved, v.* 11. Every thing is beautiful in its season; as we must not be merry when *God calls to mourning,* so we must not frighten and afflict ourselves when God gives us occasion to rejoice. Even sorrow for sin must not grow so excessive as to hinder our joy in God and our cheerfulness in his service. (2.) They commanded them to testify their joy, to put *on the garments of praise instead of the spirit of heaviness.* They allowed them, in token of their joy, to feast themselves, to eat and drink better than on other days, *to eat the fat and drink the sweet;* but then it must be, [1.] With charity to the poor: "*Send portions to those for whom nothing is prepared* that your abundance may supply

their want, that they may rejoice with you and their loins may bless you." Christ directs those that make feasts to invite their poor neighbours, Luke xiv. 13. But it is especially the duty of a religious feast, as well as of a religious fast, to *draw out the soul to the hungry*, Isa. lviii. 7, 10. God's bounty should make us bountiful. Many will eat the fat and drink the sweet themselves, even to excess, that will never allow portions, nor scarcely crumbs, to the poor, who may read their own doom in the parable of the rich man, Luke xvi. 19, &c. But such know not, or consider not, what God gave them their estates for. Observe, We must not only give to those that offer themselves, but send to those that are out of sight. *The liberal devises liberal things*, and seeks objects of charity. [2.] It must be with piety and devotion: *The joy of the Lord is your strength.* Let it not be a carnal sensual joy, but holy and spiritual, the *joy of the Lord*, joy in the goodness of God, under the direction and government of the grace of God, joy arising from our interest in the love and favour of God and the tokens of his favour. "This joy will be your strength, therefore encourage it; it will be your strength, *First*, For the performance of the other duties of the feast." The more cheerful we are in our religious exercises the more we shall abound in them. *Secondly*, "For all that which you have to do in conformity to the law of God which has been read to you." Holy joy will be oil to the wheels of our obedience. *Thirdly*, "For the resisting of your enemies that are plotting against you." The joy of the Lord will arm us against the assaults of our spiritual enemies, and put our mouths out of taste for those pleasures with which the tempter baits his hooks.

2. The assembly complied with the directions that were given them. Their weeping was *stilled* (*v.* 11) and they *made great mirth*, *v.* 12. Note, We ought always to have such a command of every passion as that, however it may break out, it may soon be restrained and called in again when we are convinced that it is either unreasonable or unseasonable. *He that has such a rule as this over his own spirit is better than the mighty.* Observe, (1.) After they had wept they rejoiced. Holy mourning makes way for holy mirth; those that *sow in tears shall reap in joy;* those that tremble at the convictions of the word may triumph in the consolations of it. (2.) The ground of their joy was very good. They made mirth, not because they had the fat to eat and the sweet to drink, and a great deal of good company, but because they had *understood the words that were declared to them.* Note, [1.] To have the holy scriptures with us, and helps to understand them, is a very great mercy, which we have abundant reason to rejoice in. Bibles and ministers are the joy of God's Israel. [2.] The better we understand the word of God the more comfort we shall find in it; for the darkness of trouble arises from the darkness of ignorance and mistake. When the words were first declared to them they wept; but, when they understood them, they rejoiced, finding at length precious promises made to those who repented and reformed and that therefore there was hope in Israel.

13 And on the second day were gathered together the chief of the fathers of all the people, the priests, and the Levites, unto Ezra the scribe, even to understand the words of the law. 14 And they found written in the law which the LORD had commanded by Moses that the children of Israel should dwell in booths in the feast of the seventh month: 15 And that they should publish and proclaim in all their cities, and in Jerusalem, saying, Go forth unto the mount, and fetch olive branches, and pine branches, and myrtle branches, and palm branches, and branches of thick trees, to make booths, as *it is* written. 16 So the people went forth, and brought *them*, and made themselves booths, every one upon the roof of his house, and in their courts, and in the courts of the house of God, and in the street of the water gate, and in the street of the gate of Ephraim. 17 And all the congregation of them that were come again out of the captivity made booths, and sat under the booths: for since the days of Jeshua the son of Nun unto that day had not the children of Israel done so. And there was very great gladness. 18 Also day by day, from the first day unto the last day, he read in the book of the law of God. And they kept the feast seven days; and on the eighth day *was* a solemn assembly, according unto the manner.

We have here,

I. The people's renewed attendance upon the word. They had spent the greatest part of one day in praying and hearing, and yet were so far from being weary of that new moon and sabbath that the next day after, though it was no festival, the chief of them came together again to hear Ezra expound (*v.* 13), which they found more delightful and gainful than any worldly pleasure or profit whatsoever. Note, The more we converse with the word of God, if we rightly understand it and be affected with it, the more we shall covet to converse with it, and to increase in our acquaintance with it, saying, *How sweet are thy words unto my mouth!* Those that understand the scriptures well will still be desirous to understand them better. Now the priests and the Levites themselves came with *the chief of the people to Ezra*, that prince of expositors, *to understand the words of the law*, or, as it is in the margin, *that they might instruct in the words of the law;* they came to be taught themselves, that they might be qualified to teach others. Observe, 1. Though, on the first day, Ezra's humility had set them *on his right hand and on his left, as teachers with him* (*v.* 4, 7), yet now, they being by trial made more sensible than ever of their own deficiencies and his excellencies, on the second day their humility set them at Ezra's feet, as learners of him. 2. Those that would teach others must themselves receive instruction. Priests and Levites must be taught first and then teach.

II. The people's ready obedience to the word, in one particular instance, as soon as they were made sensible of their duty therein. It is probable that Ezra, *after the wisdom of his God that was in his hand* (Ezra vii. 25), when they applied to him for instruction out of the law on the second day of the seventh month, read to them those laws which concerned the feasts of that month, and, among the rest, that of the feast of tabernacles, Lev. xxiii. 34; Deut. xvi. 13. Ministers should preach not only that which is true and good, but that which is seasonable, directing to the *work of the day in its day.* Here is, 1. The divine appointment of the feast of tabernacles reviewed, *v.* 14, 15. *They found written in the law* a commandment concerning it. Those that diligently search the scriptures will find those things written there which they had forgotten or not duly considered. This feast of tabernacles was a memorial of their dwelling in tents in the wilderness, a representation of our tabernacle state in this world, and a type of the holy joy of the gospel church. The conversion of the nations to the faith of Christ is foretold under the figure of this feast (Zech. xiv. 16); they shall come to *keep the feast of tabernacles*, as having here no continuing city. This feast was to be proclaimed in all their cities. The people were themselves to fetch boughs of trees (they of Jerusalem fetched them from the mount of Olives) and to make booths, or arbours, of them, in which they were to lodge (as much as the weather would permit) and to make merry during the feast. 2. This appointment religiously observed, *v.* 16, 17. Then we read and hear the word acceptably and profitably when we do according to what is written therein, when what appears to be our duty is revived after it has been neglected. (1.) They observed the ceremony: *They sat in booths*, which the priests and Levites set up in the courts of the temple; those that had houses of their own set up booths on the roofs of them, or in their courts; and those that had not such conveniences set them up in the streets. This feast had usually been observed (2 Chron. v. 3; Ezra iii. 4), but never with such solemnity as now since Joshua's time, when they were newly settled, as they were now newly re-settled in Canaan. That man loves his house too well that cannot find in his heart to quit it, awhile, in compliance either with an ordinance or with a providence of God. (2.) They minded the substance, else the ceremony, how significant soever, would have been insignificant. [1.] They did it with gladness, with *very great gladness*, rejoicing in God and his goodness to them. All their holy feasts, but this especially, were to be celebrated with joy, which would be much for the honour of God, and their own encouragement in his service. [2.] They attended the reading and expounding of the word of God during all the days of the feast, *v.* 18. They improved their leisure for this good work. Spare hours cannot be better spent than in studying the scriptures and conversing with them. At this feast of tabernacles God appointed the law to be read once in seven years. Whether this was that year of release in which that service was to be performed (Deut. xxxi. 10, 11) does not appear; however they spent all the days of the feast in that good work, and on the eighth day was a solemn assembly, as God had appointed, in which they finished the solemnity the twenty-second day of the month, yet did not separate, for the twenty-fourth day was appointed to be spent in fasting and prayer. Holy joy must not indispose us for godly sorrow any more than godly sorrow for holy joy.

CHAP. IX.

The tenth day of the seventh month between the feast of trumpets (ch. viii. 2) and the feast of tabernacles (ver. 14) was appointed to be the day of atonement; we have no reason to think but that it was religiously observed, though it is not mentioned. But here we have an account of an occasional fast that was kept a fortnight after that, with reference to the present posture of their affairs, and it was, as that, a day of humiliation. There is a time to weep as well as a time to laugh. We have here an account, I. How this fast was observed, ver. 1—3. II. What were the heads of the prayer that was made to God on that occasion, wherein they made a thankful acknowledgment of God's mercies, a penitent confession of sin, and a humble submission to the righteous hand of God in the judgments that were brought upon them, concluding with a solemn resolution of new obedience, ver. 4—38.

NOW in the twenty and fourth day of this month the children of Israel were assembled with fasting, and with sackclothes, and earth upon them. 2 And the seed of Israel separated themselves from all strangers, and stood and confessed their sins, and the iniquities of their fathers. 3 And they stood up in their place, and read in the book of the law of the LORD their God *one* fourth part of the day; and *another* fourth part they confessed, and worshipped the LORD their God.

We have here a general account of a public fast which the children of Israel kept, probably by order from Nehemiah, by and with the advice and consent of the chief of the fathers. It was a fast that men appointed, but such *a fast as God had chosen;* for, 1. It was a day *to afflict the soul,* Isa. lviii. 5. Probably they assembled in the courts of the temple, and they there appeared in sackcloth and in the posture of mourners, with earth on their heads, *v.* 1. By these outward expressions of sorrow and humiliation they gave glory to God, took shame to themselves, and stirred up one another to repentance. They were restrained from *weeping, ch.* viii. 9, but now they were directed to weep. The joy of our holy feasts must give way to the sorrow of our solemn fasts when they come. Every thing is beautiful in its season. 2. It was a day *to loose the bands of wickedness,* and that is the fast that God has chosen, Isa. lviii. 6. Without this, spreading sackcloth and ashes under us is but a jest. The seed of Israel, because they were a holy seed, appropriated to God and more excellent than their neighbours, *separated themselves from all strangers* with whom they had mingled and joined in affinity, *v.* 2. Ezra had separated them from their strange wives some years before, but they had relapsed into the same sin, and had either made marriages or at least made friendships with them, and contracted such an intimacy as was a snare to them. But now they separated themselves from the strange children as well as from the strange wives. Those that intend by prayers and covenants to join themselves to God must separate themselves from sin and sinners; for *what communion hath light with darkness?* 3. It was a day of communion with God. *They fasted to him, even to him* (Zech. vii. 5); for, (1.) They spoke to him in prayer, offered their pious and devout affections to him in the confession of sin and the adoration of him as the Lord and their God. Fasting without prayer is a body without a soul, a worthless carcase. (2.) They heard him speaking to them by his word; for they read in the book of the law, which is very proper on fasting days, that, in the glass of the law, we may see our deformities and defilements, and know what to acknowledge and what to amend. The word will direct and quicken prayer, for by it the Spirit helps our praying infirmities. Observe how the time was equally divided between these two. Three hours (for that is the fourth part of a day) they spent in reading, expounding, and applying the scriptures, and three hours in confessing sin and praying; so that they staid together six hours, and spent all the time in the solemn acts of religion, without saying, *Behold, what a weariness is it!* The varying of the exercises made it the less tedious, and, as the word they read would furnish them with matter for prayer, so prayer would make the word the more profitable. Bishop Patrick thinks that they spent the whole twelve hours of the day in devotion, that from six o'clock in the morning till nine they read, and then from nine to twelve they prayed, from twelve to three they read again, and from three till six at night they prayed again. The work of a fast day is good work, and therefore we should endeavour to make a day's work, a good day's work, of it.

4 Then stood up upon the stairs, of the Levites, Jeshua, and Bani, Kadmiel, Shebaniah, Bunni, Sherebiah, Bani, *and* Chenani, and cried with a loud voice unto the LORD their God. 5 Then the Levites, Jeshua, and Kadmiel, Bani, Hashabniah, Sherebiah, Hodijah, Shebaniah, *and* Pethahiah, said, Stand up *and* bless the LORD your God for ever and ever: and blessed be thy glorious name, which is exalted above all blessing and praise. 6 Thou, *even* thou, *art* LORD alone; thou hast made heaven, the heaven of heavens, with all their host, the earth, and all *things* that *are* therein, the seas, and all that *is* therein, and thou preservest them all; and the host of heaven worshippeth thee. 7 Thou *art* the LORD the God, who didst choose Abram, and broughtest him forth out of Ur of the Chaldees, and gavest him the name of Abraham; 8 And foundest his heart faithful before thee, and madest a covenant with him to give the land of the Canaanites, the Hittites, the Amorites, and the Perizzites, and the Jebusites, and the Girgashites, to give *it, I say,* to his seed, and hast performed thy words; for thou *art* righteous: 9 And didst see the affliction of our fathers in Egypt, and heardest their cry by the Red sea; 10 And showedst signs and wonders upon Pharaoh, and on all his servants, and on all the people of his land: for thou knewest that they dealt proudly against them. So didst thou get thee a name, as *it is* this day. 11 And thou didst divide the sea before them, so that they went through the midst of the sea on the dry land; and their persecutors thou threwest into the deeps, as a stone into the mighty waters. 12

Moreover thou leddest them in the day by a cloudy pillar; and in the night by a pillar of fire, to give them light in the way wherein they should go. 13 Thou camest down also upon mount Sinai, and spakest with them from heaven, and gavest them right judgments, and true laws, good statutes and commandments: 14 And madest known unto them thy holy sabbath, and commandedst them precepts, statutes, and laws, by the hand of Moses thy servant: 15 And gavest them bread from heaven for their hunger, and broughtest forth water for them out of the rock for their thirst, and promisedst them that they should go in to possess the land which thou hadst sworn to give them. 16 But they and our fathers dealt proudly, and hardened their necks, and hearkened not to thy commandments, 17 And refused to obey, neither were mindful of thy wonders that thou didst among them; but hardened their necks, and in their rebellion appointed a captain to return to their bondage: but thou *art* a God ready to pardon, gracious and merciful, slow to anger, and of great kindness, and forsookest them not. 18 Yea, when they had made them a molten calf, and said, This *is* thy God that brought thee up out of Egypt, and had wrought great provocations; 19 Yet thou in thy manifold mercies forsookest them not in the wilderness: the pillar of the cloud departed not from them by day, to lead them in the way; neither the pillar of fire by night, to show them light, and the way wherein they should go. 20 Thou gavest also thy good spirit to instruct them, and withheldest not thy manna from their mouth, and gavest them water for their thirst. 21 Yea, forty years didst thou sustain them in the wilderness, *so that* they lacked nothing; their clothes waxed not old, and their feet swelled not. 22 Moreover thou gavest them kingdoms and nations, and didst divide them into corners: so they possessed the land of Sihon, and the land of the king of Heshbon, and the land of Og king of Bashan. 23 Their children also multipliedst thou as the stars of heaven, and broughtest them into the land, concerning which thou hadst promised to their fathers, that they should go in to possess *it*. 24 So the children went in and possessed the land, and thou subduedst before them the inhabitants of the land, the Canaanites, and gavest them into their hands, with their kings, and the people of the land, that they might do with them as they would. 25 And they took strong cities, and a fat land, and possessed houses full of all goods, wells digged, vineyards, and oliveyards, and fruit trees in abundance: so they did eat, and were filled, and became fat, and delighted themselves in thy great goodness. 26 Nevertheless they were disobedient, and rebelled against thee, and cast thy law behind their backs, and slew thy prophets which testified against them to turn them to thee, and they wrought great provocations. 27 Therefore thou deliveredst them into the hand of their enemies, who vexed them: and in the time of their trouble, when they cried unto thee, thou heardest *them* from heaven; and according to thy manifold mercies thou gavest them saviours, who saved them out of the hand of their enemies. 28 But after they had rest, they did evil again before thee: therefore leftest thou them in the hand of their enemies, so that they had the dominion over them: yet when they returned, and cried unto thee, thou heardest *them* from heaven; and many times didst thou deliver them according to thy mercies; 29 And testifiedst against them, that thou mightest bring them again unto thy law: yet they dealt proudly, and hearkened not unto thy commandments, but sinned against thy judgments, (which if a man do, he shall live in them;) and withdrew the shoulder, and hardened their neck, and would not hear. 30 Yet many years didst thou forbear them, and testifiedst against them by thy spirit in thy prophets: yet would they not give ear: therefore gavest thou them into the hand of the people of the lands. 31 Nevertheless for thy great mercies' sake thou didst not utterly consume them, nor forsake them; for thou *art* a gracious and merciful God. 32 Now therefore, our God, the great, the mighty, and the terrible God, who keepest covenant and mercy, let not all the trouble seem little before thee, that hath come upon us, on our kings, on our princes, and on our priests, and on our prophets, and on our fathers, and on all thy people, since the time of the kings of Assyria unto this day. 33 Howbeit thou *art* just in all that is brought upon us; for thou hast done right, but we have done wickedly: 34 Neither have our kings, our princes, our priests, nor our fathers, kept thy law, nor hearkened unto thy commandments and thy testimonies, wherewith thou didst testify against them. 35 For they have not served thee in their kingdom, and in thy great goodness that thou gavest them, and in the large and fat land which thou gavest before them, neither turned they from their wicked works. 36 Behold, we *are* servants this day, and *for* the land that thou gavest unto our fathers to eat the fruit thereof and the good thereof, behold, we *are* servants in it: 37 And it yieldeth much increase unto the kings whom thou hast set over us because of our sins: also they have dominion over our bodies, and over our cattle, at their pleasure, and we *are* in great distress. 38 And because of all this we make a sure *covenant*, and write *it;* and our princes, Levites, *and* priests, seal *unto it*.

We have here an account how the work of this fast-day was carried on. 1. The names of the ministers that were employed. They are twice named (*v.* 4, 5), only with some variation of the names. Either they prayed successively, according to that rule which the apostle gives (1 Cor. xiv. 31, *You may all prophesy one by one*), or, as some think, there were eight several congregations at some distance from each other, and each had a Levite to preside in it. 2. The work itself in which they employed themselves. (1.) They prayed to God, cried to him with a loud voice (*v.* 4), for the pardon of the sins of Israel and God's favour to them. They cried aloud, not that God might the better hear them, as Baal's worshippers, but that the people might, and to excite their fervency. (2.) They praised God; for the work of praise is not unseasonable on a fast-day; in all acts of devotion we must aim at this, *to give unto God the glory due to his name.* The summary of their prayers we have here upon record; whether drawn up before, as a directory to the Levites what to enlarge on, or recollected after, as the heads of what they had in prayer enlarged upon, is uncertain. Much more no doubt was said than is here recorded, else confessing and worshipping God would not have taken up a fourth part of the day, much less two-fourths.

In this solemn address to God we have,

I. An awful adoration of God, as a perfect and glorious Being, and the fountain of all beings, *v.* 5, 6. The congregation is called upon to signify their concurrence herewith by standing up; and so the minister directs himself to God, *Blessed be thy glorious name.* God is here adored, 1. As the only living and true God: *Thou art Jehovah alone,* self-existent and independent; there is no God besides thee. 2. As the Creator of all things: *Thou hast made heaven, earth, and seas,* and all that is in them. The first article of our creed is fitly made the first article of our praises. 3. As the great Protector of the whole creation: "Thou preservest in being all the creatures thou hast given being to." God's providence extends itself to the highest beings, for they need it, and to the meanest, for they are not slighted by it. What God has made he will preserve; what he does is done effectually, Eccl. iii. 14. 4. As the object of the creatures' praises: "*The host of heaven,* the world of holy angels, *worshippeth thee, v.* 6. But thy *name is exalted above all blessing and praise;* it needs not the praises of the creatures, nor is any addition made to its glory by those praises." The best performances in the praising of God's name, even those of the angels themselves, fall infinitely short of what it deserves. It is not only exalted above our blessing, but above all blessing. Put all the praises of heaven and earth together, and the thousandth part is not said of what might and should be said of the glory of God. *Our goodness extendeth not to him.*

II. A thankful acknowledgment of God's favours to Israel.

1. Many of these are here reckoned up in order before him, and very much to the purpose, for, (1.) We must take all occasions to mention the loving kindness of the Lord, and *in every prayer give thanks.* (2.) When we are confessing our sins it is good to take notice of the mercies of God as the aggravations of our sins, that we may be the more humbled and ashamed, and call ourselves by the scandalous name of ungrateful. (3.) When we are seeking to God for mercy and relief in the time of distress it is an encouragement to our faith and hope to look back upon our own and our fathers' experiences: "Lord, thou hast done well for us formerly;

shall it be all undone again? Art not thou the same God still?"

2. Let us briefly observe the particular instances of God's goodness to Israel here recounted. (1.) The call of Abraham, *v.* 7. God's favour to him was distinguishing: "Thou didst choose him." His grace in him was powerful to bring him out of Ur of the Chaldees, and, in giving him the name of Abraham, he put honour upon him as his own and assured him that he should be the *father of many nations. Look unto Abraham your father* (Isa. li. 2) and see free grace glorified in him. (2.) The covenant God made with him to give the land of Canaan to him and his seed, a type of the better country, *v.* 8. And this covenant was sure, for God found Abraham's heart faithful before God, and found it so because he made it so (for faith is not of ourselves, it is the gift of God), and therefore performed his words; *for with the upright he will show himself upright*, and wherever he finds a faithful heart he will be found a faithful God. (3.) The deliverance of Israel out of Egypt, *v.*, 9—11. It was seasonable to remember this now that they were interceding for the perfecting of their deliverance out of Babylon. They were then delivered, in compassion to their affliction, in answer to their cry, and in resistance of the pride and insolence of their persecutors. Wherein they dealt proudly, God showed himself *above them* (Exod. xviii. 11), and so got himself *a name;* for he said, *I will get me honour upon Pharaoh.* Even to this day the name of God is glorified for that wonderful work. It was done miraculously: signs and wonders were shown for the effecting of it; their deliverance was the destruction of their enemies; they were *thrown into the deeps*, as irrecoverably *as a stone into the mighty waters.* (4.) The conducting of them through the wilderness, by the pillar of cloud and fire, which showed them which way they should go, when they should remove, and when and where they should rest, directed all their stages and all their steps, *v.* 12. It was also a visible token of God's presence with them, to guide and guard them. They mention this again (*v.* 19), observing that though they had by their sins provoked God to withdraw from them, and leave them to wander and perish in the by-paths of the wilderness, yet in his manifold mercy he continued to lead them, and took not away the *pillar of cloud and fire*, *v.* 19. When mercies, though forfeited, are continued, we are bound to be doubly thankful. (5.) The plentiful provision made for them in the wilderness, that they might not perish for hunger: Thou *gavest them bread from heaven*, and *water out of the rock* (*v.* 15), and, to hold up their hearts, a promise that they should go in and possess the land of Canaan. They had meat and drink, food convenient in the way, and the good land at their journey's end; what would they more? This also is repeated (*v.* 20, 21) as that which was continued, notwithstanding their provocations: *Forty years didst thou sustain them.* Never was people so long nursed and so tenderly; they were wonderfully provided for, and, in so long a time, *their clothes waxed not old*, and, though the way was rough and tedious, *their feet swelled not;* for they were *carried as upon eagles' wings.* (6.) The giving of the law upon Mount Sinai. This was the greatest favour of all that was done them and the greatest honour that was put upon them. The Lawgiver was very glorious, *v.* 13. "Thou didst not only send, but camest down thyself, and *didst speak with them*," Deut. iv. 33. The law given was very good. No nation under the sun had such *right judgments, true laws*, and *good statutes*, Deut. iv. 8. The moral and judicial precepts were true and right, founded upon natural equity and the eternal reasons of good and evil; and even the ceremonial institutions were good, tokens of God's goodness to them and types of gospel grace. Particular notice is taken of the law of the fourth commandment as a great favour to them: *Thou madest known unto them thy holy sabbath*, which was a token of God's particular favour to them, distinguishing them from the nations who had revolted from God and quite lost that ancient part of revealed religion, and was likewise a means of keeping up their communion with him. And, with *the law* and *the sabbath*, he *gave his good Spirit to instruct them*, *v.* 20. Besides the law given on Mount Sinai, the five books of Moses, which he wrote *as he was moved by the Holy Ghost*, were constant instructions to them, particularly the book of Deuteronomy, in which God's Spirit by Moses instructed them fully. Bezaleel was filled *with the Spirit of God* (Exod. xxxi. 3), so was Joshua (Num. xxvii. 18), and Caleb had another spirit. (7.) The putting of them in possession of Canaan, that good land, *kingdoms and nations*, *v.* 22. They were made so numerous as to replenish it (*v.* 23) and so victorious as to be masters of it (*v.* 24); the natives were given into their hands, *that they might do with them as they would*, set their feet, if they pleased, on the necks of their kings. Thus they gained a happy *settlement*, *v.* 25. Look upon their cities, and you see them strong and well fortified. Look into their houses, and you find them fine and well furnished, filled with all sorts of rich goods. Take a view of the country, and you will say that you never saw such a fat land, so well stored with *vineyards and oliveyards.* All these they found made ready to their hands; so they delighted themselves in the gifts of God's great goodness. They could not wish to be more easy or happy than they were, or might have been, in Canaan, had it not been their own fault. (8.) God's great readiness to pardon their sins, and work deliverance for them, when they had by their provocations brought his judgments upon themselves. When they were in the wilderness they found him *a God ready*

to pardon (*v.* 17), a *God of pardons* (so the margin reads it), who had proclaimed his name as a God *forgiving iniquity, transgression, and sin,* who has power to forgive sin, is willing to forgive, and glories in forgiving. Though they forsook him, he did not forsake them, as justly he might have done, but continued his care of them and favour to them. Afterwards, when they were settled in Canaan and sold themselves by their sins into the hands of their enemies, upon their submission and humble request he *gave them saviours* (*v.* 27), the judges, by whom God wrought many a great deliverance for them when they were on the brink of ruin. This he did, not for any merit of theirs, for they deserved nothing but ill, but according to his mercies, his manifold mercies. (9.) The admonitions and fair warnings he gave them by his servants the prophets. When he delivered them from their troubles he *testified against their sins* (*v.* 28, 29), that they might not misconstrue their deliverances as connivances at their wickedness. That which was designed in all the testimonies which the prophets bore against them was to bring them again to God's law, to lay their necks under its yoke, and walk by its rule. The end of our ministry is to bring people to God by bringing them to his law, not to bring them to ourselves by bringing them under any law of ours. This we have again (*v.* 30): *Thou testifiedst against them by thy Spirit in thy prophets.* The testimony of the prophets was the testimony of the Spirit in the prophets, and it was the Spirit of Christ in them, 1 Pet. i. 10, 11. They *spoke as they were moved by the Holy Ghost,* and what they said is to be received accordingly. God gave them *his Spirit to instruct them* (*v.* 20), but, they not receiving that instruction, he did by his Spirit testify against them. If we will not suffer God's word to teach and rule us, it will accuse and judge us. God sends prophets, in compassion to his people (2 Chron. xxxvi. 15), that he may not send judgments. (10.) The lengthening out of his patience and the moderating of his rebukes: *Many years did he forbear them* (*v.* 30), as loth to punish them, and waiting to see if they would repent; and, when he did punish them, he did not *utterly consume them nor forsake them, v.* 31. Had he forsaken them they would have been utterly consumed; but he did not stir up all his wrath, for he designed their reformation, not their destruction. Thus do they multiply, thus do they magnify, the instances of God's goodness to Israel, and we should do in like manner, that the goodness of God, duly considered by us, may lead us to repentance, and over ome our badness. The more thankful we are for God's mercies the more humbled we shall be for our own sins.

III. Here is a penitent confession of sin, their own sins, and the sins of their fathers. The mention of these is interwoven with the memorials of God's favours, that God's goodness, notwithstanding their provocations, might appear the more illustrious, and their sins, notwithstanding his favours, might appear the more heinous. Many passages in this acknowledgment of sins and mercies are taken from Ezek. xx. 5—26, as will appear by comparing those verses with these; for the word of God is of use to direct us in prayer, and by what he says to us we may learn what to say to him.

1. They begin with the sins of Israel in the wilderness: *They, even our fathers* (so it might better be read), *dealt proudly* (though, considering what they were, and how lately they had come out of slavery, they had no reason to be proud), *and hardened their necks, v.* 16. Pride is at the bottom of men's obstinacy and disobedience; they think it below them to bow their necks to God's yoke, and a piece of state to set up their own will in opposition to the will of God himself. (1.) There were two things which they did not duly give heed to, else they would not have done as they did:—The word of God they heard, but they did not hearken to God's commandments; and the works of God they saw, but they were not mindful of his wonders: had they duly considered them as miracles, they would have obeyed from a principle of faith and holy fear; had they duly considered them as mercies, they would have obeyed from a principle of gratitude and holy love. But, when men make no right use either of God's ordinances or of his providences, what can be expected from them? (2.) Two great sins are here specified, which they were guilty of in the wilderness—meditating a return, [1.] To Egyptian slavery, which, for the sake of the garlick and onions, they preferred before the glorious liberty of the Israel of God attended with some difficulty and inconvenience. *In their rebellion they appointed a captain to return to their bondage,* in distrust of God's power and contempt of his good promise, *v.* 17. [2.] To Egyptian idolatry: *They made a molten calf,* and were so sottish as to say, *This is thy God.*

2. They next bewail the provocations of their fathers after they were put in possession of Canaan. Though there they *delighted themselves in God's great goodness,* yet that would not prevail to keep them closely to him; for, *nevertheless, they were disobedient* (*v.* 26) *and wrought great provocations.* For, (1.) They abused God's prophets, *slew them* because they *testified against them* to *turn them to God* (*v.* 26), so returning the greatest injury for the greatest kindness. (2.) They abused his favours: *After they had rest,* they *did evil again, v.* 28. They were not wrought upon either by their troubles or their deliverances out of trouble. Neither fear nor love would hold them to their duty.

3. They at length come nearer to their own day, and lament the sins which had brought those judgments upon them which they had long been groaning under and were now but

in part delivered from: *We have done wickedly* (*v.* 33): *our kings, our princes, our priests, and our fathers,* have all been guilty, and we in them, *v.* 34. Two things they charge upon themselves and their fathers, as the cause of their troubles:—(1.) A contempt of the good law God had given them: They *sinned against thy judgments,* the dictates of divine wisdom, and the demands of divine sovereignty. Though they were told how much it would be for their own advantage to govern themselves by them, for, *if a man do them, he shall live in them* (*v.* 29), yet they would not do them, and so, in effect, said that they *would not live.* They *forsook their own mercies.* This abridgment of the covenant, *Do this and live,* is taken from Ezek. xx. 13, and is quoted, Gal. iii. 12, to prove that *the law is not of faith;* it was not then as it is now, *Believe and live,* yet *they gave a withdrawing shoulder,* so it is in the margin. They pretended to lay their shoulders under the burden of God's law, and put their shoulders to the work, but they proved withdrawing shoulders; they soon flew off, would not keep to it, would not abide by it. When it came, as we say, to the setting to, they shrunk back, and would not hear. They had a backsliding heart; and, though God by his prophets called them to return, they *would not give ear, v.* 30. He *stretched out his hands, but no man regarded.* (2.) A contempt of the good land God had given them (*v.* 35): "Our kings have *not served thee in their kingdom,* have not used their power for the support of religion; our people have not served thee in the use of the gifts of thy great goodness, and in that large and fat land which thou not only gavest them by thy grant, but gavest before them by the expulsion of the natives and the complete victories they obtained over them." Those that would not serve God in their own land were made to serve their enemies in a strange land, as was threatened, Deut. xxviii. 47, 48. It is a pity that a good land should have bad inhabitants, but so it was with Sodom. Fatness and fulness often make men proud and sensual.

IV. Here is a humble representation of the judgments of God, which they had been and were now under.

1. Former judgments are remembered as aggravations of their sins, that they had not taken warning. In the days of the judges their *enemies vexed them* (*v.* 27); and, when they did evil again, God did again *leave them in the hand of their enemies,* who could not have touched them if God had not given them up; but, when God left them, they got and kept dominion over them.

2. Their present calamitous state is laid before the Lord (*v.* 36, 37): *We are servants this day.* Free-born Israelites are enslaved, and the land which they had long held by a much more honourable tenure than grand sergeantry itself, even by immediate grant from the crown of heaven to them as a peculiar people above all people of the earth, they now held by as base a tenure as villanage itself, by, from, and under, the kings of Persia, whose vassals they were. A sad change! But see what work sin makes! They were bound to personal service: They have *dominion over our bodies;* they held all they had precariously, were tenants at will, and the land-tax that they paid was so great that it amounted even to a rack-rent; so that all the rents, issues, and profits, of their land did in effect accrue to the king, and it was as much as they could do to get a bare subsistence for themselves and their families out of it. This, they honestly own, was for their sins. Poverty and slavery are the fruits of sin; it is sin that brings us into all our distresses.

V. Here is their address to God under these calamities. 1. By way of request, that their trouble might not *seem little, v.* 32. It is the only petition in all this prayer. The trouble was universal; it had come on their *kings, princes, priests, prophets, fathers, and all their people;* they had all shared in the sin (*v.* 34), and now all shared in the judgment. It was of long continuance: *From the time of the kings of Assyria,* who carried the ten tribes captive, *unto this day.* "Lord, let it not all seem little and not worthy to be regarded, or not needing to be relieved." They do not prescribe to God what he shall do for them, but leave it to him, only desiring he would please to take cognizance of it, remembering that when he saw the affliction of his people in Egypt to be great he came down to deliver them, Exod. iii. 7, 8. In this request they have an eye to God as one that is to be feared (for he is *the great, the mighty, and the terrible, God),* and as one that is to be trusted, for he is *our God* in covenant, and a God that *keeps covenant and mercy.* 2. By way of acknowledgment, notwithstanding, that really it was less than they deserved, *v.* 33. They own the justice of God in all their troubles, that he had done them no wrong. "We have done wickedly in breaking thy laws, and therefore thou hast done right in bringing all these miseries upon us." Note, It becomes us, when we are under the rebukes of divine Providence, though ever so sharp and ever so long, to justify God and to judge ourselves; for he will be *clear when he judgeth.* Ps. li. 4.

VI. Here is the result and conclusion of this whole matter. After this long remonstrance of their case was made they came at last to this resolution, that they would return to God and to their duty, and oblige themselves never to forsake God, but always to continue in their duty. "Because of all this, we make a sure covenant with God; in consideration of our frequent departures from God, we will now more firmly than ever bind ourselves to him. Because we have smarted so much for sin, we will now stedfastly resolve against it, that we may not any more withdraw the shoulder." Observe, 1. This covenant was made with serious consideration. It is the result of a chain of suitable thoughts, and so is a reasonable service. 2. With great solemnity. It was written, *in perpetuam rei memoriam—that it might remain a memorial for all ages;* it was sealed and left upon record, that it might be a witness against them if they dealt deceitfully. 3. With joint consent: "*We make* it; we are all agreed in making it, and do it unanimously, that we may strengthen the hands one of another. 4. With fixed resolution: "It is *a sure covenant,* without reserving a power of revocation. It is what we will live and die by, and never go back from." A certain number of the princes, priests, and Levites, were chosen as the representatives of the congregation, to subscribe and seal it for and in the name of the rest. Now was fulfilled that promise concerning the Jews, that, when they returned out of captivity, they should *join themselves to the Lord in a perpetual covenant* (Jer. l. 5), and that in Isa. xliv. 5, that they should *subscribe with their hand unto the Lord.* He that bears an honest mind will not startle at assurances; nor will those that know the deceitfulness of their own hearts think them needless.

CHAP. X.

We have in this chapter a particular account of the covenant which in the close of the foregoing chapter was resolved upon; they struck while the iron was hot, and immediately put that good resolve in execution, when they were in a good frame, lest, if it should be delayed, it might be dropped. Here we have, I. The names of those that set their hands and seals to it, ver. 1—27. II. An account of those who signified their consent and concurrence, ver. 28, 29. III. The covenant itself, and the articles of it in general, that they would "keep God's commandments" (ver. 29); in particular, that they would not marry with the heathen (ver. 30), nor profane the sabbath, nor be rigorous with their debtors (ver. 31), and that they would carefully pay their church-dues, for the maintenance of the temple service, which they promise faithfully to adhere to, ver. 32—39.

NOW those that sealed *were,* Nehemiah, the Tirshatha, the son of Hachaliah, and Zidkijah, 2 Seraiah, Azariah, Jeremiah, 3 Pashur, Amariah, Malchijah, 4 Hattush, Shebaniah, Malluch, 5 Harim, Meremoth, Obadiah, 6 Daniel, Ginnethon, Baruch, 7 Meshullam, Abijah, Mijamin, 8 Maaziah, Bilgai, Shemaiah: these *were* the priests. 9 And the Levites: both Jeshua the son of Azaniah, Binnui of the sons of Henadad, Kadmiel; 10 And their brethren, Shebaniah, Hodijah, Kelita, Pelaiah, Hanan, 11 Micha, Rehob, Hashabiah, 12 Zaccur, Sherebiah, Shebaniah, 13 Hodijah, Bani, Beninu. 14 The chief of the people; Parosh, Pahath-moab, Elam, Zatthu, Bani, 15 Bunni, Azgad, Bebai, 16 Adonijah, Bigvai, Adin, 17 Ater, Hizkijah, Azzur, 18 Hodijah, Hashum, Bezai, 19 Hariph, Anathoth, Nebai, 20 Magpiash, Meshullam, Hezir, 21 Meshezabeel, Zadok, Jaddua, 22 Pelatiah, Hanan, Anaiah, 23 Hoshea, Hananiah, Hashub, 24 Hallohesh, Pileha, Shobek, 25 Rehum, Hashabnah, Maaseiah, 26 And Ahijah, Hanan, Anan, 27 Malluch, Harim, Baanah. 28 And the rest of the people, the priests, the Levites, the porters, the singers, the Nethinims, and all they that had separated themselves from the people of the lands unto the law of God, their wives, their sons, and their daughters, every one having knowledge, and having understanding; 29 They clave to their brethren, their nobles, and entered into a curse, and into an oath, to walk in God's law, which was given by Moses the servant of God, and to observe and do all the commandments of the LORD our Lord, and his judgments and his statutes; 30 And that we would not give our daughters unto the people of the land, nor take their daughters for our sons: 31 And *if* the people of the land bring ware or any victuals on the sabbath day to sell, *that* we would not buy it of them on the sabbath, or on the holy day: and *that* we would leave the seventh year, and the exaction of every debt.

When Israel was first brought into covenant with God it was done by sacrifice and the sprinkling of blood, Exod. xxiv. But here it was done by the more natural and common way of sealing and subscribing the written articles of the covenant, which bound them to no more than was already their duty. Now here we have,

I. The names of those public persons who, as the representatives and heads of the congregation, set their hands and seals to this covenant, because it would have been an endless piece of work for every particular person to do it; and, if these leading men did their part in pursuance of this covenant, their example would have a good influence upon all the people. Now observe, 1. Nehemiah, who was the governor, signed first, to show his forwardness in this work and to set others a good example, *v.* 1. Those that are above others in dignity and power should go before them in the way of God. 2. Next to him subscribed twenty-two priests, among whom I wonder we do not find Ezra, who was an active man in the solemnity (*ch.* viii. 2) which was but the first day of the same month, and therefore we cannot think he was absent; but he, having before done his part as a scribe, now left it to others to do theirs. 3. Next to the priests, seventeen Levites subscribed this covenant, among whom we find all or most of those who were the mouth of the congregation in prayer, *ch.* ix. 4, 5. This showed that they themselves were affected with what they had said, and would not bind those burdens on others which they themselves declined to touch. Those that lead in prayer should lead in every other good work. 4. Next to the Levites, forty-four of the chief of the people gave it under their hands for themselves and all the rest, chiefly those whom they had influence upon, that they would keep God's commandments. Their names are left upon record here, to their honour, as men that were forward and active in reviving and endeavouring to perpetuate religion in their country. The memory of such shall be blessed. It is observable that most of those who were mentioned, *ch.* vii. 8, &c., as heads of houses or clans, are here mentioned among the first of the chief of the people that subscribed, whoever was the present head bearing the name of him that was head when they came out of Babylon, and these were fittest to subscribe for all those of their father's house. Here are *Parosh, Pahath-moab, Elam, Zatthu, Bani* (*v.* 14), *Azgad, Bebai, Bigvai, Adin, Ater, Hashum, Bezai, Harip, Anathoth,* and some others in the following verses, that are all found in that catalogue. Those that have interest must use it for God.

II. The concurrence of the rest of the people with them, and the rest of the priests and Levites, who signified their consent to what their chiefs did. With them joined, 1. Their wives and children; for they had transgressed, and they must reform. Every one that had knowledge and understanding must covenant with God. As soon as young people grow up to be capable of distinguishing between good and evil, and of acting intelligently, they ought to make it their own act and deed to *join themselves to the Lord.* 2. The proselytes of other nations, *all that had separated themselves from the people of the lands,* their gods and their worship, *unto the law of God,* and the observance of that law. See what conversion is; it is separating ourselves from the course and custom of this world, and devoting ourselves to the conduct of the word of God. And, as there is one law, so there is one covenant, one baptism, for the stranger and for him that is born in the land. Observe how the concurrence of the people is expressed, *v.* 29. (1.) *They clave to their brethren* one and all. Here those whom the court blessed the country blessed too! The commonalty agreed with their nobles in this good work. Great men never look so great as when they encourage religion, and are examples of it; and they would by that, as much as any thing, secure an interest in the most valuable of their inferiors. Let but the nobles cordially espouse religious causes, and perhaps they will find people cleave to them therein closer than they can imagine. Observe, Their nobles are called their *brethren;* for, in the things of God, rich and poor, high and low, meet together. (2.) They *entered into a curse and an oath.* As the nobles confirmed the covenant with their hands and seals, so the people with a curse and an oath, solemnly appealing to God concerning their sincerity, and imprecating his just revenge if they dealt deceitfully. Every oath has in it a conditional curse upon the soul, which makes it a strong bond upon the soul; for our own tongues, if false and lying tongues, will fall, and fall heavily, upon ourselves.

III. The general purport of this covenant. They laid upon themselves no other burden than this necessary thing, which they were already obliged to by all other engagements of duty, interest, and gratitude—*to walk in God's law, and to do all his commandments, v.* 29. Thus David swore that he would *keep God's righteous judgments,* Ps. cxix. 106. Our own covenant binds us to this, if not more strongly, yet more sensibly, than we were before bound, and therefore we must not think it needless thus to bind ourselves. Observe, When we bind ourselves to do the commandments of God we bind ourselves to do *all* his commandments, and therein to have an eye to him as the Lord and our Lord.

IV. Some of the particular articles of this covenant, such as were adapted to their present temptations. 1. That they would not intermarry with the heathen, *v.* 30. Many of them had been guilty of this, Ezra ix. 1. In our covenants with God we should engage particularly against those sins that we have been most frequently overtaken in and damaged by. Those that resolve to *keep the commandments of God must say to evil doers, Depart,* Ps. cxix. 115. 2. That they would keep no markets on the sabbath day, or any other day of which the law had said, *You shall do no work therein.* They would not only not sell goods themselves for gain on that day, but they would not encourage the heathen to sell on that day by buying of them, no not victuals, under pretence of necessity; but would buy in their provisions for their families the day before, *v.* 31. Note, Those that covenant to keep all God's commandments must particularly covenant to keep sabbaths well; for the profanation of them is an inlet to other instances of profaneness. The sabbath is a market day for our souls, but not for our bodies. 3. That they would not be severe in exacting their debts, but would observe the seventh year as a year of release, according to the law, *v.* 31. In this matter they had been faulty (*ch.* v.), and here therefore they promise to reform. This was the acceptable fast, to *undo the heavy burden,* and to *let the oppressed go free,* Isa. lviii. 6. It was in the close of the day of expiation that the jubilee trumpet sounded. It was for the neglect of observing the seventh year as a year of rest for the land that God had made it enjoy its sabbaths seventy years (Lev. xxvi. 35), and therefore they covenanted to observe that law. Those are stubborn children indeed that will not amend the fault for which they have been particularly corrected.

32 Also we made ordinances for us, to charge ourselves yearly with the third part of a shekel for the service of the house of our God; 33 For the showbread, and for the continual meat offering, and for the continual burnt offering, of the sabbaths, of the new moons, for the set feasts, and for the holy *things*, and for the sin offerings to make an atonement for Israel, and *for* all the work of the house of our God. 34 And we cast the lots among the priests, the Levites, and the people, for the wood offering, to bring *it* into the house of our God, after the houses of our fathers, at times appointed year by year, to burn upon the altar of the LORD our God, as *it is* written in the law: 35 And to bring the firstfruits of our ground, and the firstfruits of all fruit of all trees, year by year, unto the house of the LORD: 36 Also the firstborn of our sons, and of our cattle, as *it is* written in the law, and the firstlings of our herds and of our flocks, to bring to the house of our God, unto the priests that minister in the house of our God: 37 And *that* we should bring the firstfruits of our dough, and our offerings, and the fruit of all manner of trees, of wine and of oil, unto the priests, to the chambers of the house of our God; and the tithes of our ground unto the Levites, that the same Levites might have the tithes in all the cities of our tillage. 38 And the priest the son of Aaron shall be with the Levites, when the Levites take tithes: and the Levites shall bring up the tithe of the tithes unto the house of our God, to the chambers, into the treasure house. 39 For the children of Israel and the children of Levi shall bring the offering of the corn, of the new wine, and the oil, unto the chambers, where *are* the vessels of the sanctuary, and the priests that minister, and the porters, and the singers: and we will not forsake the house of our God.

Having covenanted against the sins they had been guilty of, they proceed in obliging themselves to revive and observe the duties they had neglected. We must not only *cease to do evil*, but *learn to do well*.

I. It was resolved, in general, that the temple service should be carefully kept up, that the work of the house of their God should be done in its season, according to the law, *v.* 33. Let not any people expect the blessing of God unless they make conscience of observing his ordinances and keeping up the public worship of him. Then it is likely to go well with our houses when care is taken that the work of God's house go on well. It was likewise resolved that they would never *forsake the house of their God* (*v.* 39), as they and their fathers had done, would not forsake it for the house of any other god, or for the high places, as idolaters did, nor forsake it for their farms and merchandises, as those did that were atheistical and profane. Those that forsake the worship of God forsake God.

II. It was resolved, in pursuance of this, that they would liberally maintain the temple service, and not starve it. The priests were ready to do their part in all the work of God's house, if the people would do theirs, which was to find them with materials to work upon. Now here it was agreed and concluded, 1. That a stock should be raised for the furnishing of God's table and altar plentifully. Formerly there were treasures in the house of the Lord for this purpose, but these were gone, and there was no settled fund to supply the want of them. It was a constant charge to provide show-bread for the table, two lambs for the daily offerings, four for the sabbaths, and more, and more costly, sacrifices for other festivals, occasional sin-offerings, and meat-offerings, and drink-offerings for them all. They had no rich king to provide these, as Hezekiah did; the priests could not afford to provide them, their maintenance was so small; the people therefore agreed to contribute yearly, every one of them, the third part of a shekel, about ten pence a-piece for the bearing of this expense. When every one will act, and every one will give, though but little, towards a good work, the whole amount will be considerable. The tirshatha did not impose this tax, but the people made it an ordinance for themselves, and charged themselves with it, *v.* 32, 33. 2. That particular care should be taken to provide wood for the altar, to keep the fire always burning upon it, and wherewith to boil the peace-offerings. All of them, priests and Levites as well as people, agreed to bring in their quota, and cast lots in what order they should bring it in, which family first and which next, that there might be a constant supply, and not a scarcity at one time and an overplus at another, *v.* 34. Thus they provided the fire and the wood, as well as the lambs for the burnt-offerings. 3. That all those things which the divine law had appointed for the maintenance of the priests and Levites should be duly paid in, for their encouragement to mind their business, and that they might not be under any temptation to neglect it for the making of necessary provision for their families. Then the work of the house of God is likely to go on when those that serve at the altar live, and live comfortably, upon the altar. First-fruits and tenths were then the principal branches of the ministers' revenues; and they here resolve, (1.) To bring in the first-fruits justly, the first-fruits of their ground and trees (Exod. xxiii. 19; Lev. xix. 23), the first-born of their children (even the money wherewith they were to be redeemed) and of their cattle, Exod. xiii. 2, 11, 12 (this was given to the priests, Num. xviii. 15, 16), also the first-fruits of their dough (Num. xv. 21), concerning which there is a particular order given in the prophecy concerning the second temple, Ezek. xliv. 30. (2.) To bring in their tenths likewise, which were due to the Levites (*v.* 37), and a tenth out of those tenths to the priest, *v.* 38. This was the law (Num. xviii. 21—28); but these dues had been withheld, in consequence of which God, by the prophet, charges them with *robbing him* (Mal. iii. 8, 9), at the same time encouraging them to be more just to him and his receivers, with a promise that, if they brought the *tithes into the store-house,* he would *pour out blessings upon them, v.* 10. This therefore they resolved to do, that there might be meat in God's house, and plenty in the store-chambers of the temple, where the vessels of the sanctuary were, *v.* 39. "We will do it (say they) *in all the cities of our tillage," v.* 37. *In all the cities of our servitude,* so the LXX., for they were servants in their own land, *ch.* ix. 36. But (as Mr. Poole well observes), though they paid great taxes to the kings of Persia, and had much hardship put upon them, they would not make that an excuse for not paying their tithes, but would render to God the things that were his, as well as to Cæsar the things that were his. We must do what we can in works of piety and charity notwithstanding the taxes we pay to the government, and cheerfully perform our duty to God in our servitude, which will be the surest way to ease and liberty in God's due time.

CHAP. XI.

Jerusalem was walled round, but it was not as yet fully inhabited, and therefore was weak and despicable. Nehemiah's next care is to bring people into it; of that we have here an account. I. The methods taken to replenish it, ver. 1, 2. II. The principal persons that resided there, of Judah and Benjamin (ver. 3—9), of the priests and Levites, ver. 10—19. III. The several cities and villages of Judah and Benjamin that were peopled by the rest of their families, ver. 20—36.

AND the rulers of the people dwelt at Jerusalem: the rest of the people also cast lots, to bring one of ten to dwell in Jerusalem the holy city, and nine parts *to dwell* in *other* cities. 2 And the people blessed all the men, that willingly offered themselves to dwell at Jerusalem. 3 Now these *are* the chief of the province that dwelt in Jerusalem: but in the cities of Judah dwelt every one in his possession in their cities, *to wit,* Israel, the priests, and the Levites, and the Nethinims, and the children of Solomon's servants. 4 And at Jerusalem dwelt *certain* of the children of Judah, and of the children of Benjamin. Of the children of Judah; Athaiah the son of Uzziah, the son of Zechariah, the son of Amariah, the son of Shephatiah, the son of Mahalaleel, of the children of Perez; 5 And Maaseiah the son of Baruch, the son of Col-hozeh, the son of Hazaiah, the son of Adaiah, the son of Joiarib, the son of Zechariah, the son of Shiloni. 6 All the sons of Perez that dwelt at Jerusalem *were* four hundred threescore and eight valiant men. 7 And these *are* the sons of Benjamin; Sallu the son of Meshullam, the son of Joed, the son of Pedaiah, the son of Kolaiah, the son of Maaseiah, the son of Ithiel, the son of Jesaiah. 8 And after him Gabbai, Sallai, nine hundred twenty and eight. 9 And Joel the son of Zichri *was* their overseer: and Judah the son of Senuah *was* second over the city. 10 Of the priests: Jedaiah the son of Joiarib, Jachin. 11 Seraiah the son of Hilkiah, the son of Meshullam, the son of Zadok, the son of Meraioth, the son of Ahitub, *was* the ruler of the house of God. 12 And their brethren that did the work of the house *were* eight hundred twenty and two: and Adaiah the son of Jeroham, the son of Pelaliah, the son of Amzi, the son of Zechariah, the son of Pashur, the son of Malchiah, 13 And his brethren, chief of the fathers, two hundred forty and two: and Amashai the son of Azareel, the son of Ahasai, the son of Meshillemoth, the son of Immer, 14 And their brethren, mighty men of valour, a hundred twenty and eight: and their overseer *was* Zabdiel, the son of *one of* the great men. 15 Also of the Levites: Shemaiah the son of Hashub, the son of Azrikam, the son of Hashabiah, the son of Bunni; 16 And Shabbethai and Jozabad, of the chief of the Levites, *had* the oversight of the outward business of the house of God. 17 And Mattaniah the son of Micha, the son of Zabdi, the son of Asaph, *was* the principal to begin the thanksgiving in prayer: and Bakbukiah the second among his brethren, and Abda the son of Shammua, the son of Galal, the son of Jeduthun. 18 All the Levites in the holy city *were* two hundred fourscore and four. 19 Moreover the porters, Akkub, Talmon, and their brethren that kept the gates, *were* a hundred seventy and two.

Jerusalem is called here *the holy city* (*v.* 1), because there the temple was, and that was the place God had chosen to put his name there; upon this account, one would think, the holy seed should all have chosen to dwell there and have striven for a habitation there; but, on the contrary, it seems they declined dwelling there, 1. Because a greater strictness of conversation was expected from the inhabitants of Jerusalem than from others, which they were not willing to come up to. Those who care not for being holy themselves are shy of dwelling in a holy city; they would not dwell in the *New Jerusalem* itself for that reason, but would wish to have a continuing city here upon earth. Or, 2. Because Jerusalem, of all places, was most hated by the heathen their neighbours, and against it their malicious designs were levelled, which made that the post of danger (as the post of honour usually is) and therefore they were not willing to expose themselves there. Fear of persecution and reproach, and of running themselves into trouble, keeps many out of the holy city, and makes them backward to appear for God and religion, not considering that, as Jerusalem is with a special malice threatened and insulted by its enemies, so it is with a special care protected by its God and made a *quiet habitation*, Isa. xxxiii. 20; Ps. xlvi. 4, 5. Or, 3. Because it was more for their worldly advantage to dwell in the country. Jerusalem was no trading city, and therefore there was no money to be got there by merchandise, as there was in the country by corn and cattle. Note, *All seek their own, not the things that are Jesus Christ's*, Phil. ii. 21. It is a general and just complaint that most people prefer their own wealth, credit, pleasure, ease, and safety, before the glory of God and the public good. People being thus backward to dwell at Jerusalem, now that it was poor, we are here told,

I. By what means it was replenished. 1. The rulers dwelt there, *v.* 1. That was the proper place for them to reside in, because *there were set the thrones of judgment* (Ps. cxxii. 5), and thither, in all difficult matters, the people resorted with their last appeals. And if it were an instance of eminent affection to the house of God, zeal for the public good, and of faith, and holy courage, and self-denial, to dwell there at this time, the rulers would be examples of these to their inferiors. Their dwelling there would invite and encourage others to dwell there too. *Magnates magnetes—the mighty are magnetic.* When great men choose the holy city for their habitation their example brings holiness into reputation, and their zeal will provoke very many. 2. There were some that willingly offered themselves to dwell at Jerusalem, nobly foregoing their own secular interest for the public welfare, *v.* 2. It is upon record, to their honour, that when others were shy of venturing upon difficulty, loss, and danger, they *sought the good of Jerusalem, because of the house of the Lord their God. Those shall prosper that thus love Zion*, Ps. cxxii. 6, 9. It is said, *The people blessed them.* They praised them; they prayed for them; they praised God for them. Many that do not appear forward themselves for the public good will yet give a good word to those that do. God and man will bless those that are public blessings, which should encourage us to be zealous in doing good. 3. They, finding that *yet there was room*, concluded upon a review of their whole body to bring one in ten to dwell in Jerusalem; who they should be was determined by lot, the disposal whereof, all knew, was of the Lord. This would prevent strife, and would be a great satisfaction to those on whom the lot fell to dwell at Jerusalem, that they plainly saw God appointing the bounds of their habitation. They observed the proportion of one in ten, as we may suppose, to bring the balance between the city and country to a just and equal poise; so it seems to refer to the ancient rule of giving the tenth to God; and what is given to the holy city he reckons given to himself.

II. By what persons it was replenished. A general account is here given of the inhabitants of Jerusalem because the *governors of Judah* looked upon them as *their strength in the Lord of hosts their God*, and valued them accordingly, Zech. xii. 5. 1. Many of the children of Judah and Benjamin dwelt there; for, originally, part of the city lay in the lot of one of those tribes and part in that of the other; but the greater part was in the lot of Benjamin, and therefore here we find of the children of Judah only 468 families in Jerusalem (*v.* 6), but of Benjamin 928, *v.* 7, 8. Thus small were its beginnings, but afterwards, before our Saviour's time, it grew much more populous. Those of Judah all descended from Perez, or Pharez, that son of Judah of whom, as concerning the flesh, Christ came. And, though the Benjamites were more in number, yet of the men of Judah it is said (*v.* 6) that they were valiant men, fit for service, and able to defend the city in case of an attack. Judah has not lost its ancient character of a lion's whelp, bold and daring. Of the Benjamites that dwelt in Jerusalem we are here told who was *overseer*, and who was second, *v.* 9. For it is as necessary for a people to have good order kept up among themselves as to be fortified against the attacks of their enemies from abroad, to have good magistrates as to have good soldiers. 2. The priests and Levites did many of them settle at Jerusalem; where else should men that were holy to God dwell, but in the holy city? (1.) Most of the priests, we may suppose, dwelt there, for their business lay where the temple was. Of those that did the work of the house in their courses here were 822 of one family, 242 of another, and 128 of another, *v.* 12—14. It was well that those labourers were not few. It is said of some of them that they were *mighty men of valour* (*v.* 14): it was necessary that they should be so, for the priesthood was not only a work, which required might, but a warfare, which required valour, especially now. Of one of these priests it is said that he was *the son of one of the great men.* It was no disparagement to the greatest man they had to have his son in the priesthood; he might magnify his office, for his office did not in the least diminish him. (2.) Some of the Levites also came and dwelt at Jerusalem, yet but few in comparison, 284 in all (*v.* 18), with 172 porters (*v.* 19), for much of their work was to *teach the good knowledge of God* up and down the country, for which purpose they were to be scattered in Israel. As many as there was occasion for attended at Jerusalem; the rest were doing good elsewhere. [1.] It is said of one of the Levites that he had *the oversight of the outward business of the house of God, v.* 16. The priests were chief managers of the business within the temple gates; but this Levite was entrusted with the secular concerns of God's house, that were *in ordine ad spiritualia—subservient to its spiritual concerns,* the collecting of the contributions, the providing of materials for the temple service, and the like, which it was necessary to oversee, else the inward business would have been starved and have stood still. Those who take care of the τὰ ἔξω—*the outward concerns* of the church, the serving of its tables, are as necessary in their place as those who take care of its τὰ ἔσω—*its inward concerns,* who give themselves to the word and prayer. [2.] It is said of another that he was *the principal to begin the thanksgiving in prayer.* Probably he had a good ear and a good voice, and was a scientific singer, and therefore was chosen to lead the psalm. He was precentor in the temple. Observe, Thanksgiving is necessary in prayer; they should go together; giving thanks for former mercies is a becoming way of begging further mercies. And care should be taken in public service that every thing be done in the best manner, *decently and in good order*—in prayer, that one speak and the rest join—in singing, that one begin and the rest follow.

20 And the residue of Israel, of the priests, *and* the Levites, *were* in all the cities of Judah, every one in his inheritance. 21 But the Nethinims dwelt in Ophel: and Ziha and Gispa *were* over the Nethinims. 22 The overseer also of the Levites at Jerusalem *was* Uzzi the son of Bani, the son of Hashabiah, the son of Mattaniah, the son of Micha. Of the sons of Asaph, the singers *were* over the business of the house of God. 23 For *it was* the king's commandment concerning them, that a certain portion should be for the singers, due for every day. 24 And Pethahiah the son of Meshezabeel, of the children of Zerah the son of Judah, *was* at the king's hand in all matters concerning the people. 25 And for the villages, with their fields, *some* of the children of Judah dwelt at Kirjath-arba, and *in* the villages thereof, and at Dibon, and *in* the villages thereof, and at Jekabzeel, and *in* the villages thereof, 26 And at Jeshua, and at Moladah, and at Beth-phelet, 27 And at Hazar-shual, and at Beer-sheba, and *in* the villages thereof, 28 And at Ziklag, and at Mekonah, and in the villages thereof, 29 And at En-rimmon, and at Zareah, and at Jarmuth, 30 Zanoah, Adullam, and *in* their villages, at Lachish, and the fields thereof, at Azekah, and *in* the villages thereof. And they dwelt from Beer-sheba unto the valley of Hinnom. 31 The children also of Benjamin from Geba *dwelt* at Michmash, and Aija, and Beth-el, and *in* their villages, 32 *And* at Anathoth, Nob, Ananiah, 33 Hazor, Ramah, Gittaim, 34 Hadid, Zeboim, Neballat, 35 Lod, and Ono, the valley of craftsmen. 36 And of the Levites *were* divisions *in* Judah, *and* in Benjamin.

Having given an account of the principal persons that dwelt in Jerusalem (a larger account of whom we had before, 1 Chron. ix. 2, &c.), Nehemiah, in these verses, gives us some account of the other cities, in which dwelt *the residue of Israel*, *v.* 20. It was requisite that Jerusalem should be replenished, yet not so as to drain the country. *The king himself is served of the field*, which will do little service if there be not hands to manage it. Let there therefore be no strife, no envy, no contempt, no ill will, between the inhabitants of the cities and those of the villages; both are needful, both useful, and neither can be spared. 1. The Nethinims, the posterity of the Gibeonites, dwelt in Ophel, which was upon the wall of Jerusalem (*ch.* iii. 26), because they were to do the servile work of the temple, which therefore they must be posted near to, that they might be ready to attend, *v.* 21. 2. Though the Levites were dispersed through the cities of Judah, yet they had an overseer who resided in Jerusalem, superior of their order and their provincial, to whom they applied for direction, who took care of their affairs and took cognizance of their conduct, whether they did their duty, *v.* 22. 3. Some of the singers were appointed to look after the necessary repairs of the temple, being ingenious men, and having leisure between their hours of service; they were *over the business of the house of God*, *v.* 22. And, it seems, the king of Persia had such a kindness for their office that he allotted a particular maintenance for them, besides what belonged to them as Levites, *v.* 23. 4. Here is one that was the king's commissioner at Jerusalem. He was of the posterity of Zerah (*v.* 24); for of *that* family of Judah there were some now settled in Jerusalem, and not all of Pharez, as appears by that other catalogue, 1 Chron. ix. 6. He is said to be *at the king's hand*, or *on the king's part*, in *all matters concerning the people*, to determine controversies that arose between the king's officers and his subjects, to see that what was due to the king from the people was duly paid in and what was allowed by the king for the temple service was duly paid out, and happy it was for the Jews that one of themselves was in this post. 5. Here is an account of the villages, or country towns, which were inhabited by the residue of Israel—the towns in which the children of Judah dwelt (*v.* 25—30), those that were inhabited by the children of Benjamin (*v.* 31—35), and divisions for the Levites among both, *v.* 36. We will now suppose them safe and easy, though few and poor, but by the blessing of God they were likely to increase in wealth and power, and they would have been more likely if there had not been that general profaneness among them, and lukewarmness in religion, with which they were charged in God's name by the prophet Malachi, who, it is supposed, prophesied about this time, and in whom prophecy ceased for some ages, till it revived in the great prophet and his forerunner.

CHAP. XII.

In this chapter are preserved upon record, I. The names of the chief of the priests and the Levites that came up with Zerubbabel, v. 1.—9. II. The succession of the high priests, ver. 10, 11. III. The names of the next generation of the other chief priests, ver. 12—21. IV. The eminent Levites that were in Nehemiah's time, ver. 22—26. V. The solemnity of dedicating the wall of Jerusalem, ver. 27—43. VI. The settling of the offices of the priests and Levites in the temple, ver. 44—47.

NOW these *are* the priests and the Levites that went up with Zerubbabel the son of Shealtiel, and Jeshua: Seraiah, Jeremiah, Ezra, 2 Amariah, Malluch, Hattush, 3 Shechaniah, Rehum, Meremoth, 4 Iddo, Ginnetho, Abijah, 5 Miamin, Maadiah, Bilgah, 6 Shemaiah, and Joiarib, Jedaiah, 7 Sallu, Amok, Hilkiah, Jedaiah. These *were* the chief of the priests and of their brethren in the days of Jeshua. 8 Moreover the Levites: Jeshua, Binnui, Kadmiel, Sherebiah, Judah, *and* Mattaniah, *which was* over the thanksgiving, he and his brethren. 9 Also Bakbukiah and Unni, their brethren, *were* over against them in the watches. 10 And Jeshua begat Joiakim, Joiakim also begat Eliashib, and Eliashib begat Joiada, 11 And Joiada begat Jonathan, and Jonathan begat Jaddua. 12 And in the days of Joiakim were priests, the chief of the fathers: of Seraiah, Meraiah; of Jeremiah, Hananiah; 13 Of Ezra, Meshullam; of Amariah, Jehohanan; 14 Of Melicu, Jonathan; of Shebaniah, Joseph; 15 Of Harim, Adna; of Meraioth, Helkai; 16 Of Iddo, Zechariah; of Ginnethon, Meshullam; 17 Of Abijah, Zichri; of Miniamin, of Moadiah, Piltai; 18 Of Bilgah, Shammua; of Shemaiah, Jehonathan; 19 And of Joiarib, Mattenai; of Jedaiah, Uzzi; 20 Of Sallai, Kallai; of Amok, Eber; 21 Of Hilkiah, Hashabiah; of Jedaiah, Nethaneel. 22 The Levites in the days of Eliashib, Joiada, and Johanan, and Jaddua, *were* recorded chief of the fathers: also the priests, to the reign of Darius the Persian. 23 The sons of Levi, the chief of the fathers, *were* written in the book of the chronicles, even until the days of Johanan the son of Eliashib. 14 And the chief of the Levites: Hashabiah, Sherebiah, and Jeshua the son of Kadmiel, with their brethren over against them, to praise *and* to give thanks, according to the commandment of David the man of God, ward over against ward. 25 Mattaniah, and Bakbukiah, Obadiah, Meshullam, Talmon, Akkub, *were* porters keeping the ward at the thresholds of the gates. 26 These *were* in the days of Joiakim the son of Jeshua, the son of Jozadak, and in the days of Nehemiah the governor, and of Ezra the priest, the scribe.

We have here the names, and little more than the names, of a great many priests and Levites, that were eminent in their day among the returned Jews. Why this register should be here inserted by Nehemiah does not appear, perhaps to keep in remembrance those good men, that posterity might know to whom they were beholden, under God, for the happy revival and re-establishment of their religion among them. Thus must we contribute towards the performance of that promise, Ps. cxii. 6, *The righteous shall be in everlasting remembrance.* Let the memory of the just be blessed, be perpetuated. It is a debt we still owe to faithful ministers to *remember our guides,* who have *spoken to us the word of God,* Heb. xiii. 7. Perhaps it is intended to stir up their posterity, who succeeded them in the priest's office and inherited their dignities and preferments, to imitate their courage and fidelity. It is good to know what our godly ancestors and predecessors were, that we may learn thereby what we should be. We have here, 1. The names of the priests and Levites that came up with the first out of Babylon, when Jeshua was high priest. Jeremiah and Ezra are mentioned with the first (*v.* 1), but, it is supposed, not Jeremiah the prophet nor Ezra the scribe; the fame of the one was long before and that of the other some time after, though both of them were priests. Of one of the Levites it is said (*v.* 8) that he was *over the thanksgiving,* that is, he was entrusted to see that the psalms, the thanksgiving psalms, were constantly sung in the temple in due time and manner. The Levites kept their turns in their watches, relieving one another as becomes brethren, fellow-labourers, and fellow-soldiers. 2. The succession of high priests during the Persian monarchy, from Jeshua (or Jesus), who was high priest at the time of the restoration, to Jaddua (or Jaddus), who was high priest when Alexander the Great, after the conquest of Tyre, came to Jerusalem, and paid great respect to this Jaddus, who met him in his pontifical habit, and showed him the prophecy of Daniel, which foretold his conquests. 3. The next generation of priests, who were chief men, and active in the days of Joiakim, sons of the first set. Note, We have reason to acknowledge God's favour to his church, and care of it, in that, as one generation of ministers passes away, another comes. All those who are mentioned *v.* 1, &c., as eminent in their generation, are again mentioned, though with some variation in several of the names, *v.* 12, &c., except two, as having sons that were likewise eminent in their generation—a rare instance, that twenty good fathers should leave behind them twenty good sons (for so many here are) that filled up their places. 4. The next generation of Levites, or rather a latter generation; for those priests who are mentioned flourished in the days of Joiakim the high priest, these Levites in the days of Eliashib, *v.* 22. Perhaps *then* the forementioned families of the priests began to degenerate, and the third generation of them came short of the first two; but the work of God shall never fail for want of instruments. Then a generation of Levites was *raised up,* who were *recorded chief of the fathers* (*v.* 22), and were eminently serviceable to the interests of the church, and their service not the less acceptable either to God or to his people for their being Levites only, of the lower rank of ministers. Eliashib the high priest being allied to Tobiah (*ch.* xiii. 4), the other priests grew remiss; but then the Levites appeared the more zealous, as appears by this, that those who were now employed in expounding (*ch.* viii. 7) and in praying (*ch.* ix. 4, 5) were all Levites, not priests, regard being had to their personal qualifications more than to their order. These Levites were some of them singers (*v.* 24), *to praise and give thanks,* others of them porters (*v.* 25), *keeping the ward at the thresholds of the gates, and both according to the command of David.*

27 And at the dedication of the wall of Jerusalem they sought the Levites out of all their places, to bring them to Jerusalem, to keep the dedication with gladness, both with thanksgivings, and with singing, *with* cymbals, psalteries, and with harps. 28 And the sons of the singers gathered themselves together, both out of the plain country round about Jerusalem, and from the villages of Netophathi; 29 Also from the house of Gilgal, and out of the fields of Geba and Azmaveth: for the singers had builded them villages round about Jerusalem. 30 And the priests and the Levites purified themselves, and purified the people, and the gates, and the wall. 31 Then I brought up the princes of Judah upon the wall, and appointed two great *companies of them that gave* thanks, *whereof one* went on the right hand upon the wall toward the dung

gate: 32 And after them went Hoshaiah, and half of the princes of Judah, 33 And Azariah, Ezra, and Meshullam, 34 Judah, and Benjamin, and Shemaiah, and Jeremiah, 35 And *certain* of the priests' sons with trumpets; *namely*, Zechariah the son of Jonathan, the son of Shemaiah, the son of Mattaniah, the son of Michaiah, the son of Zaccur, the son of Asaph: 36 And his brethren, Shemaiah, and Azarael, Milalai, Gilalai, Maai, Nethaneel, and Judah, Hanani, with the musical instruments of David the man of God, and Ezra the scribe before them. 37 And at the fountain gate, which was over against them, they went up by the stairs of the city of David, at the going up of the wall, above the house of David, even unto the water gate eastward. 38 And the other *company of them that gave* thanks went over against *them*, and I after them, and the half of the people upon the wall, from beyond the tower of the furnaces even unto the broad wall; 39 And from above the gate of Ephraim, and above the old gate, and above the fish gate, and the tower of Hananeel, and the tower of Meah, even unto the sheep gate: and they stood still in the prison gate. 40 So stood the two *companies of them that gave* thanks in the house of God, and I, and the half of the rulers with me: 41 And the priests; Eliakim, Maaseiah, Miniamin, Michaiah, Elioenai, Zechariah, *and* Hananiah, with trumpets; 42 And Maaseiah, and Shemaiah, and Eleazar, and Uzzi, and Jehohanan, and Malchijah, and Elam, and Ezer. And the singers sang loud, with Jezrahiah *their* overseer. 43 Also that day they offered great sacrifices, and rejoiced: for God had made them rejoice with great joy: the wives also and the children rejoiced: so that the joy of Jerusalem was heard even afar off.

We have read of the building of the wall of Jerusalem with a great deal of fear and trembling; we have here an account of the dedicating of it with a great deal of joy and triumph. *Those that sow in tears shall* thus *reap.*

I. We must enquire what was the meaning of this dedication of the wall; we will suppose it to include the dedication of the city too *(continens pro contento—the thing containing for the thing contained)*, and therefore it was not done till the city was pretty well replenished, *ch.* xi. 1. It was a solemn thanksgiving to God for his great mercy to them in the perfecting of this undertaking, of which they were the more sensible because of the difficulty and opposition they had met with in it. 2. They hereby devoted the city in a peculiar manner to God and to his honour, and took possession of it for him and in his name. All our cities, all our houses, must have holiness to the Lord written upon them; but this city was (so as never any other was) a *holy city*, the *city of the great King* (Ps. xlviii. 2 and Matt. v. 35): it had been so ever since God chose it to put his name there, and as such, it being now refitted, it was afresh dedicated to God by the builders and inhabitants, in token of their acknowledgment that they were his tenants, and their desire that it might still be his and that the property of it might never be altered. Whatever is done for their safety, ease, and comfort, must be designed for God's honour and glory. 3. They hereby put the city and its walls under the divine protection, owning that *unless the Lord kept the city* the walls were *built in vain*. When this city was in possession of the Jebusites, they committed the guardianship of it to their gods, though they were blind and lame ones, 2 Sam. v. 6. With much more reason do the people of God commit it to his keeping who is all-wise and almighty. The superstitious founders of cities had an eye to the lucky position of the heavens (see Mr. Gregory's works, *p.* 29, &c.); but these pious founders had an eye to God only, to his providence, and not to fortune.

II. We must observe with what solemnity it was performed, under the direction of Nehemiah. 1. The Levites from all parts of the country were summoned to attend. The city must be dedicated to God, and therefore his ministers must be employed in the dedicating of it, and the surrender must pass through their hands. When those solemn feasts were over (*ch.* viii. and ix.) they went home to their respective posts, to mind their cures in the country; but now their presence and assistance were again called for. 2. Pursuant to this summons, there was a general rendezvous of all the Levites, *v.* 28, 29. Observe in what method they proceeded. (1.) They *purified themselves*, *v.* 30. We are concerned to *cleanse our hands*, and *purify our hearts*, when any work for God is to pass through them. They purified themselves and then the people. Those that would be instrumental to sanctify others must sanctify themselves, and set themselves apart for God, with purity of mind and sincerity of intention. Then they purified *the gates and the wall.* Then may we expect comfort when we are prepared to receive it. *To the pure all things are pure* (Tit. i. 15); and, to those who are sanctified, houses and tables, and all their creature comforts and enjoyments, are sanctified, 1 Tim. iv. 4, 5. This purification was performed, it is probable, by sprinkling the *water of purifying* (or of *separation*, as it is called, Num. xix. 9) on *themselves* and the *people*, the walls and the gates—a type of the blood of Christ, with which our consciences being *purged from dead works*, we become fit to *serve the living God* (Heb. ix. 14) and to be his care. (2.) The princes, priests, and Levites, walked round upon the wall in two companies, with musical instruments, to signify the dedication of it all to God, the whole circuit of it (*v.* 36); so that it is likely they sung psalms as they went along, to the praise and glory of God. This procession is here largely described. They had a rendezvous at one certain place, where they divided themselves into two companies. Half of the princes, with several priests and Levites, went on the right hand, Ezra leading their van, *v.* 36. The other half of the princes and priests, who gave thanks likewise, went to the left hand, Nehemiah bringing up the rear, *v.* 38. At length both companies met in the temple, where they joined their thanksgivings, *v.* 40. The crowd of people, it is likely, walked on the ground, some within the wall and others without, one end of this ceremony being to affect them with the mercy they were giving thanks for, and to perpetuate the remembrance of it among them. Processions, for such purposes, have their use. (3.) The people *greatly rejoiced*, *v.* 43. While the princes, priests, and Levites, testified their joy and thankfulness by *great sacrifices, sound of trumpet, musical instruments, and songs of praise*, the common people testified theirs by loud shouts, which were heard afar off, further than the more harmonious sound of their songs and music: and these shouts, coming from a sincere and hearty joy, are here taken notice of; for God overlooks not, but graciously accepts, the honest zealous services of mean people, though there is in them little of art and they are far from being fine. It is observed that *the women and children rejoiced;* and their hosannas were not despised, but recorded to their praise. All that share in public mercies ought to join in public thanksgivings. The reason given is that *God had made them rejoice with great joy*. He had given them both matter for joy and hearts to rejoice; his providence had made them safe and easy, and then his grace made them cheerful and thankful. The baffled opposition of their enemies, no doubt, added to their joy and mixed triumph with it. Great mercies call for the most solemn returns of praise, *in the courts of the Lord's house, in the midst of thee, O Jerusalem!*

44 And at that time were some appointed over the chambers for the treasures, for the offerings, for the first-fruits, and for the tithes, to gather into them out of the fields of the cities the portions of the law for the priests and Levites: for Judah rejoiced for the priests and for the Levites that waited. 45 And both the singers and the porters kept the ward of their God, and the ward of the purification, according to the commandment of David, *and* of Solomon his son. 46 For in the days of David and Asaph of old *there were* chief of the singers, and songs of praise and thanksgiving unto God. 47 And all Israel in the days of Zerubbabel, and in the days of Nehemiah, gave the portions of the singers and the porters, every day his portion: and they sanctified *holy things* unto the Levites; and the Levites sanctified *them* unto the children of Aaron.

We have here an account of the remaining good effects of the universal joy that was at the dedication of the wall. When the solemnities of a thanksgiving day leave such impressions on ministers and people as that both are more careful and cheerful in doing their duty afterwards, then they are indeed acceptable to God and turn to a good account. So it was here. 1. The ministers were more careful than they had been of their work; the respect the people paid them upon this occasion encouraged them to diligence and watchfulness, *v.* 45. *The singers kept the ward of their God*, attending in due time to the duty of their office; the *porters*, too, *kept the ward of the purification*, that is, they took care to preserve the purity of the temple by denying admission to those that were ceremonially unclean. When the joy of the Lord thus engages us to our duty, and enlarges us in it, it is then an earnest of that joy which, in concurrence with the perfection of holiness, will be our everlasting bliss. 2. The people were more careful than they had been of the maintenance of their ministers. The people, at the dedication of the wall, among other things which they made matter of their joy, rejoiced *for the priests and for the Levites that waited*, *v.* 44. They had a great deal of comfort in their ministers, and were glad of them. When they observed how diligently they waited, and what pains they took in their work, they rejoiced in them. Note, The surest way for ministers to recommend themselves to their people, and gain an interest in their affections, is *to wait on their ministry* (Rom. xii. 7), to be humble and industrious, and to mind their business. When these did so the people thought nothing too much to do for them, to encourage them. The law had provided them *their portions* (*v.* 44), but what the better were they for that provision if what the law appointed them either was not duly collected or not justly paid to them? Now, (1.) Care is here taken for the collecting of their dues. They were modest, and would rather lose their right than call for it themselves. The people were many of them careless and would not bring their dues unless they were called upon; and therefore *some were appointed* whose office it should be to gather into the treasuries, *out of the fields of the cities, the portions of the law for the priests and Levites* (*v.* 44), that their portion might not be lost for want of being demanded. This is a piece of good service both to ministers and people, that the one may not come short of their maintenance nor the other of their duty. (2.) Care is taken that, being *gathered in,* they might be duly *paid out, v.* 47. They gave the singers and porters their daily portion, over and above what was due to them as Levites; for we may suppose that when David and Solomon appointed them their work (*v.* 45, 46), above what was required from them as Levites, they settled a fund for their further encouragement. Let those that labour more abundantly in the word and doctrine be counted worthy of this double honour. As for the other Levites, the tithes, here called *the holy things,* were duly set apart for them, out of which they paid the priests their tithe according to the law. Both are said to be *sanctified;* when what is contributed, either voluntarily or by law, for the support of religion and the maintenance of the ministry, is given with an eye to God and his honour, it is sanctified, and shall be accepted of him accordingly, and it will *cause the blessing to rest on the house* and all that is in it, Ezek. xliv. 30.

CHAP. XIII.

Nehemiah, having finished what he undertook for the fencing and filling of the holy city, returned to the king his master, who was not willing to be long without him, as appears, ver. 6. But, after some time, he obtained leave to come back again to Jerusalem, to redress grievances, and purge out some corruptions which had crept in in his absence; and very active he was in reforming several abuses, which here we have an account of. I. He turned out from Israel the mixed multitude, the Moabites and Ammonites especially, ver. 1—3. With a particular indignation, he expelled Tobiah out of the lodgings he had got in the court of the temple, ver. 4—9. II. He secured the maintenance of the priests and Levites to them more firmly than it had been, ver. 10—14. III. He restrained the profanation of the sabbath day, and provided for the due sanctification of it, v. 15—22. IV. He checked the growing mischief of marrying strange wives, ver. 23—31.

ON that day they read in the book of Moses in the audience of the people; and therein was found written, that the Ammonite and the Moabite should not come into the congregation of God for ever; 2 Because they met not the children of Israel with bread and with water, but hired Balaam against them, that he should curse them: howbeit our God turned the curse into a blessing. 3 Now it came to pass, when they had heard the law, that they separated from Israel all the mixed multitude. 4 And before this, Eliashib the priest, having the oversight of the chamber of the house of our God, *was* allied unto Tobiah: 5 And he had prepared for him a great chamber, where aforetime they laid the meat offerings, the frankincense, and the vessels, and the tithes of the corn, the new wine, and the oil, which was commanded *to be given* to the Levites, and the singers, and the porters; and the offerings of the priests. 6 But in all this *time* was not I at Jerusalem: for in the two and thirtieth year of Artaxerxes king of Babylon came I unto the king, and after certain days obtained I leave of the king: 7 And I came to Jerusalem, and understood of the evil that Eliashib did for Tobiah, in preparing him a chamber in the courts of the house of God. 8 And it grieved me sore: therefore I cast forth all the household stuff of Tobiah out of the chamber. 9 Then I commanded, and they cleansed the chambers: and thither brought I again the vessels of the house of God, with the meat offering and the frankincense.

It was the honour of Israel, and the greatest preservation of their holiness, that they were a peculiar people, and were so to keep themselves, and not to mingle with the nations, nor suffer any of them to incorporate with them. Now here we have,

I. The law to this purport, which happened to be read *on that day, in the audience of the people* (*v.* 1), on the day of the dedication of the wall, as it should seem, for with their prayers and praises they joined the reading of the word; and though it was long after that the other grievances, here mentioned, were redressed by Nehemiah's power, yet this of the mixed multitude might be redressed then by the people's own act, for so it seems to be, *v.* 3. Or, perhaps, it was on the anniversary commemoration of that day, some years after, and therefore said to be *on that day.* They found a law, that the Ammonites and Moabites should not be naturalized, should not settle among them, nor unite with them, *v.* 1. The reason given is because they had been injurious and ill-natured to the Israel of God (*v.* 2), had not shown them common civility, but sought their ruin, though they not only did them no harm, but were expressly forbidden to do them any. This law we have, with this reason, Deut. xxiii. 3—5.

II. The people's ready compliance with

this law, *v.* 3. See the benefit of the public reading of the word of God; when it is duly attended to it discovers to us sin and duty, good and evil, and shows us wherein we have erred. Then we profit by the discovery when by it we are wrought upon to separate ourselves from all that evil to which we had addicted ourselves. They *separated from Israel all the mixed multitude,* which had of old been a snare to them, for the *mixed multitude fell a lusting,* Num. xi. 4. These inmates they expelled, as usurpers and dangerous.

III. The particular case of Tobiah, who was an Ammonite, and to whom, it is likely, the historian had an eye in the recital of that law (*v.* 1), and the reason of it, *v.* 2. For he had the same enmity to Israel that his ancestors had, the spirit of an Ammonite, witness his indignation at Nehemiah (*ch.* ii. 10) and the opposition he had given to his undertakings, *ch.* iv. 7, 8. Observe,

1. How basely Eliashib the chief priest took this Tobiah in to be a lodger even in the courts of the temple. (1.) He was allied to Tobiah (*v.* 4), by marriage first and then by friendship. His grandson had married Sanballat's daughter, *v.* 28. Probably some other of his family had married Tobiah's, and (would you think it?) the high priest thought the alliance an honour to his family, and was very proud of it, though really it was his greatest disgrace, and what he had reason to be ashamed of. It was expressly provided by the law that the high priest should marry *one of his own people,* else he *profanes his seed among his people,* Lev. xxi. 14, 15. And for Eliashib to contract an alliance with an Ammonite, a *servant* (for so he is called) and to value himself upon it, probably because he was a wit and a beau, and cried up for a fine gentleman (*ch.* vi. 19), was such a contempt of the crown of his consecration as one would not wish should be told in Gath or published in the streets of Ashkelon. (2.) Being allied to him, he must be acquainted with him. Tobiah, being a man of business, has often occasion to be at Jerusalem, I doubt upon no good design. Eliashib is fond of his new kinsman, pleased with his company, and must have him as near him as he can. He has not a room for him stately enough in his own apartment, in the courts of the temple; therefore, out of several little chambers which had been used for store-chambers, by taking down the partitions, he contrived to make one great chamber, a state-room for Tobiah, *v.* 5. A wretched thing it was, [1.] That Tobiah the Ammonite should be entertained with respect in Israel, and have a magnificent reception. [2.] That the high priest, who should have taught the people the law and set them a good example, should, contrary to the law, give him entertainment, and make use of the power he had, as overseer of the chambers of the temple, for that purpose. [3.] That he should lodge him in the courts of God's house, as if to confront God himself; this was next to setting up an idol there, as the wicked kings of old had done. An Ammonite must not *come into the congregation;* and shall one of the worst and vilest of the Ammonites be courted into the temple itself, and caressed there? [4.] That he should throw out the stores of the temple, to make room for him, and so expose them to be lost, wasted, and embezzled, though they were the *portions of the priests,* merely to gratify Tobiah. Thus did he *corrupt the covenant of Levi,* as Malachi complained at this time, *ch.* ii. 8. Well might Nehemiah add (*v.* 6), *But all this time was not I at Jerusalem.* If he had been there, the high priest durst not have done such a thing. The envious one, who sows tares in God's field, knows how to take an opportunity to do it when the *servants sleep* or are absent, Matt. xiii. 25. The golden calf was made when Moses was in the mount.

2. How bravely Nehemiah, the chief governor, threw him out, and all that belonged to him, and restored the chambers to their proper use. When he came to Jerusalem, and was informed by the good people who were troubled at it what an intimacy had grown between their chief priest and their chief enemy, it *grieved him sorely* (*v.* 7, 8) that God's house should be so profaned, his enemies so caressed and trusted, and his cause betrayed by him that should have been its protector and patron. Nothing grieves a good man, a good magistrate, more than to see the ministers of God's house do any wicked thing. Nehemiah has power and he will use it for God. (1.) Tobiah shall be expelled. He fears not disobliging him, fears not his resentments, or Eliashib's, nor excuses himself from interposing in an affair that lay within the jurisdiction of the high priest; but, like one zealously affected in a good thing, he expels the intruder, by casting forth all his household stuff. He did not seize it for his own use, but cast it out, that Tobiah, who it is probable was now absent, when he came again, might have no conveniences for his reception there. Our Saviour thus *cleansed the temple,* that the *house of prayer* might not be a *den of thieves.* And thus those that would expel sin out of their hearts, those living temples, must throw out its household stuff and all the provision made for it, strip it, starve it, and take away all those things that are the food and fuel of lust; this is, in effect, to mortify it. (2.) The temple stores shall be brought in again, and the *vessels of the house of God put in their places;* but the chambers must first be sprinkled with the water of purification, and so cleansed, because they had been profaned. Thus, when sin is cast out of the heart by repentance, let the blood of Christ be applied to it by faith, and then let it be furnished with the graces of God's Spirit for every good work.

10 And I perceived that the portions of the Levites had not been given *them:* for the Levites and the singers, that did the work, were fled every one to his field. 11 Then contended I with the rulers, and said, Why is the house of God forsaken? And I gathered them together, and set them in their place. 12 Then brought all Judah the tithe of the corn and the new wine and the oil unto the treasuries. 13 And I made treasurers over the treasuries, Shelemiah the priest, and Zadok the scribe, and of the Levites, Pedaiah: and next to them *was* Hanan the son of Zaccur, the son of Mattaniah: for they were counted faithful, and their office *was* to distribute unto their brethren. 14 Remember me, O my God, concerning this, and wipe not out my good deeds that I have done for the house of my God, and for the offices thereof.

Here is another grievance redressed by Nehemiah.

I. The Levites had been wronged. This was the grievance their *portions had not been given them, v.* 10. Perhaps Tobiah, when he took possession of the store-chambers, seized the stores too, and, by the connivance of Eliashib, converted them to his own use. The complaint is not that they were not collected from the people, but that they were not given to the Levites, and the Levites were so modest as not to sue for them; *for the Levites and singers fled every one to his field.* This comes in as a reason either, (1.) Why their payments were withheld. The Levites were non-residents: when they should have been doing their work about the temple, they were at their farms in the country; and therefore the people were little inclined to give them their maintenance. If ministers have not the encouragement they should have, let them consider whether they themselves be not accessory to the contempt they are under, by the neglect of their business. Or rather, (2.) It is the reason why Nehemiah soon perceived that their dues had been denied them, because he missed them from their posts. "Where are the singers" (said Nehemiah); "why do not they attend according to their office, to praise God?" "Why, truly, they have gone every one to his country seat, to get a livelihood for themselves and their families out of their grounds; for their profession would not maintain them." A scandalous maintenance makes a scandalous ministry. The work is neglected because the workmen are. It was not long since the payment of the salaries appointed for the singers was put into a very good method (*ch.* xii. 47); and yet how soon did it fail for want of being looked after!

II. Nehemiah laid the fault upon the rulers, who should have taken care that the Levites minded their business and had all due encouragement therein. This is required from Christian magistrates, that they use their power to oblige ministers to do their duty, and people to do theirs. Nehemiah began with the rulers, and called them to an account: "*Why is the house of God forsaken? v.* 11. Why are the Levites starved out of it? Why did not you take notice of this and prevent it?" The people *forsook the Levites,* which was expressly forbidden (Deut. xii 19; xiv. 27); and then the Levites forsook their post in the house of God. Both ministers and people who forsake religion and the services of it, and magistrates too who do not what they can to keep them to it, will have a great deal to answer for.

III. He delayed not to bring the dispersed Levites to *their places* again, and set them in *their stations* (as the word is), *v.* 11. A Levite in his field *(clericus in foro—a minister keeping the market)* is out of his station. God's house is his place, and there let him be found. Many that are careless would do much better than they do if they were but called upon. *Say to Archippus, Take heed to thy ministry.*

IV. He obliged the people to bring in their tithes, *v.* 12. His zeal provoked theirs; and, when they saw the Levites at their work, they could not for shame withhold their wages any longer, but honestly and cheerfully brought them in. The better church-work is done the better will church-dues be paid.

V. He provided that just and prompt payment should be made of the Levites' stipends. Commissioners were appointed to see to this (*v.* 13), and they were such as *were accounted faithful,* that is, had approved themselves so in other trusts committed to them, and so had *purchased to themselves this good degree,* 1 Tim. iii. 13. Let men be tried first and then trusted, tried in the less and then trusted with more. Their office was to receive and pay, to distribute to their brethren in due season and due proportions.

VI. Having no recompence (it is a question whether he had thanks) from those for whom he did these good services, he looks up to God as his paymaster (*v.* 14): *Remember me, O my God! concerning this.* Nehemiah was a man much in pious ejaculations; on every occasion he looked up to God, and committed himself and his affairs to him. 1. He here reflects with comfort and much satisfaction upon what he had done for the house of God and the offices thereof; it pleased him to think that he had been any way instrumental to revive and support religion in his country and to reform what was amiss. What kindness any show to God's ministers, thus shall it be returned into their own bosoms, in the secret joy they shall have there, not only in having done well, but in having done good, good to many, good to souls. 2. He here refers it to God to consider him for it, not in pride, or as boasting of what he had done, much less depending upon it as his righteousness, or as if he thought he had made God a debtor to him, but in a humble appeal to him concerning his integrity and honest intention in what he had done, and a believing expectation that he would not be unrighteous to *forget his work and labour of love*, Heb. vi. 10. Observe how modest he is in his requests. He only prays, *Remember me*, not *Reward me*—*Wipe not out my good deeds*, not *Publish them, Record them*. Yet he was rewarded and his good deeds were recorded; for God does more than we are able to ask. Note, Deeds done *for the house of God and the offices of it*, for the support of religion and the encouragement of it, are good deeds. There is both righteousness and godliness in them, and God will certainly remember them, and not wipe them out; they shall in no wise lose their reward.

15 In those days saw I in Judah *some* treading wine presses on the sabbath, and bringing in sheaves, and lading asses; as also wine, grapes, and figs, and all *manner of* burdens, which they brought into Jerusalem on the sabbath day: and I testified *against them* in the day wherein they sold victuals. 16 There dwelt men of Tyre also therein, which brought fish, and all manner of ware, and sold on the sabbath unto the children of Judah, and in Jerusalem. 17 Then I contended with the nobles of Judah, and said unto them, What evil thing *is* this that ye do, and profane the sabbath day? 18 Did not your fathers thus, and did not our God bring all this evil upon us, and upon this city? yet ye bring more wrath upon Israel by profaning the sabbath. 19 And it came to pass, that when the gates of Jerusalem began to be dark before the sabbath, I commanded that the gates should be shut, and charged that they should not be opened till after the sabbath: and *some* of my servants set I at the gates, *that* there should no burden be brought in on the sabbath day. 20 So the merchants and sellers of all kind of ware lodged without Jerusalem once or twice. 21 Then I testified against them, and said unto them, Why lodge ye about the wall? if ye do *so* again, I will lay hands on you. From that time forth came they no *more* on the sabbath. 22 And I commanded the Levites that they should cleanse themselves, and *that* they should come *and* keep the gates, to sanctify the sabbath day. Remember me, O my God, *concerning* this also, and spare me according to the greatness of thy mercy.

Here is another instance of that blessed reformation in which Nehemiah was so active. He revived sabbath-sanctification, and maintained the authority of the fourth commandment; and a very good deed this was for the house of God and the offices thereof, for, where holy time is over-looked and made nothing of, it is not strange if all holy duties be neglected. Here is,

I. A remonstrance of the abuse. The law of the sabbath was very strict and much insisted on, and with good reason, for religion is never in the throne while sabbaths are trodden under foot. But Nehemiah discovered even in Judah, among those to whom sabbaths were given for a sign, this law wretchedly violated. His own eyes were his informers. Magistrates who are in care to discharge their duty aright will as much as may be *see with their own eyes*, and *accomplish a diligent search* to find out that which is evil. To his great grief it appeared that there was a general profanation of the sabbath, that holy day, even in Jerusalem, that holy city, which was so lately dedicated to God. 1. The husbandmen trod their winepresses and brought home their corn on that day (*v.* 15), though there was an express command that *in earing-time, and in harvest-time, they should rest* on the sabbaths (Exod. xxxiv. 21), because then they might be tempted to take a greater liberty, and to fancy that God would indulge them in it. 2. The carriers *loaded their asses with all manner of burdens*, and made no scruple of it, though there was a particular proviso in the law for the cattle resting (Deut. v. 14) and that they should *bear no burden on the sabbath day*, Jer. xvii. 21. 3. The hawkers, and pedlars, and petty chapmen, that were men of Tyre, that famous trading city, *sold all manner of wares* on the sabbath day (*v.* 16); and the children of Judah and Jerusalem had so little grace as to buy of them, and so encourage them in making our Father's day a day of merchandise, contrary to the law of the fourth commandment, which forbids the *doing any manner of work*. No wonder there was a general decay of religion and corruption of manners among this people when they *forsook the sanctuary* and *profaned the sabbath*.

II. The reformation of it. Those that are jealous for the honour of God cannot bear to see his sabbath profaned. Observe in what method this good man proceeded in his zeal for the sabbath.

1. *He testified against those* who profaned it, *v.* 15, and again *v.* 21. He not only expressed his own dislike of it, but endeavoured to convince them that it was a great sin, and showed them the testimony of the word of God against it. He would not punish it till he had laid open the evil of it.

2. He reasoned with the rulers concerning it, took the nobles of Judah to task, and contended with them, *v.* 17. The greatest of men are not too high to be told of their faults by those whose proper office it is to reprove them; nay, great men should be, as here, contended with in the first place, because of the influence they have upon others.

(1.) He charges them with it: *You do it.* They did not carry corn, nor sell fish, but, [1.] They connived at those that did, and did not use their power to restrain them, and so made themselves guilty, as those magistrates do who bear the sword in vain. [2.] They set a bad example in other things. If the nobles allowed themselves in sports and recreations, in idle visits and idle talk, on the sabbath day, the men of business, both in city and country, would profane it by their worldly employments, as more justifiable. We must be responsible for the sins which others are led to commit by our example.

(2.) He charges it upon them as an evil thing, for so it is, proceeding from a great contempt of God and our own souls.

(3.) He reasons the case with them (*v* 18), and shows them that sabbath breaking was one of the sins for which God had brought judgments upon them, and that if they did not take warning, but returned to the same sins again, they had reason to expect further judgments: *You bring more wrath upon Israel by profaning the sabbath.* Thus Ezra concluded, *If we again break thy commandments, wilt not thou be angry with us till thou hast consumed us?* Ezra ix. 14.

3. He took care to prevent the profanation of the sabbath, as one that aimed only at reformation. If he could reform them, he would not punish them, and, if he should punish them, it was but that he might reform them. This is an example to magistrates to be heirs of restraint, and prudently to use the bit and bridle, that there may be no occasion for the lash. (1.) He ordered the gates of Jerusalem to be kept shut from the evening before the sabbath to the morning after, and set his own servants (whose care, courage, and honesty, he could confide in) to watch them, that no burdens should be brought in on the sabbath day, nor late the night before, nor early in the morning after, lest sabbath time should be encroached upon, *v.* 19. Those that came in to worship in the courts of the temple were no doubt admitted to pass and repass, but none that came to sell goods; *they* were forced to *lodge without the city* (*v.* 20), where no doubt they wished the sabbath were gone, that they might sell corn. (2.) He threatened those who came with goods to the gates, who pressed hard for entrance, telling them that, if they came again, he would certainly lay hands on them (*v.* 21), and this deterred them from coming any more. Note, If reformers will but put on resolution, more may be done towards the breaking of bad customs than they can imagine. Vice connived at is indeed a daring thing, and will bid defiance to counsel and reproof; but it may be made cowardly, and will be so when magistrates make themselves a terror to it. *The king that sits on the throne of judgment scatters away all evil with his eyes.* (3.) He charged the Levites to take care about the due sanctifying of the sabbath, that they should cleanse themselves in the first place, and so give a good example to the people, and *that they should* some of them *come and keep the gates, v.* 22. Because he and his servants must shortly return to court, he would leave this charge with some that might abide by it, that not only when he was present, but in his absence, the sabbath might be sanctified. Then there is likely to be a reformation, in this and other respects, when magistrates and ministers join their forces. The courage, zeal, and prudence of Nehemiah in this matter, are here recorded for our imitation; and we have reason to think that the cure he wrought was lasting; for, in our Saviour's time, we find the Jews in the other extreme, over-scrupulous in the ceremonial part of sabbath-sanctification.

4. He concludes this passage with a prayer (*v.* 22), in which observe, (1.) The petitions: *Remember me* (as the thief on the cross, *Lord, remember me); that* is enough. God's thoughts to us-ward are very precious, Ps. xl. 5. He adds, *Spare me.* So far is he from thinking that what he had done did properly merit a reward in strict justice that he cries earnestly to God to *spare him,* as Jeremiah (*ch.* xv. 15), *Take me not away in thy long-suffering* (*ch.* x. 24), *Correct me not in anger*, and (*ch.* xvii. 17), *Be not a terror to me.* Note, The best saints, even when they do the best actions, stand in need of *sparing mercy; for there is not a just man that doeth good and sinneth not.* (2.) The plea: *According to the greatness* (or multitude) *of thy mercies.* Note, God's mercy is what we must depend upon, and not any merit of our own, when we appear before God.

23 In those days also saw I Jews *that* had married wives of Ashdod, of Ammon, *and* of Moab: 24 And their children spake half in the speech of Ashdod, and could not speak in the Jews' language, but according to the language of each people. 25 And I contended with them, and cursed them, and smote certain of them, and plucked off their hair, and made them

swear by God, *saying,* Ye shall not give your daughters unto their sons, nor take their daughters unto your sons, or for yourselves. 26 Did not Solomon king of Israel sin by these things? yet among many nations was there no king like him, who was beloved of his God, and God made him king over all Israel: nevertheless even him did outlandish women cause to sin. 27 Shall we then hearken unto you to do all this great evil, to transgress against our God in marrying strange wives? 28 And *one* of the sons of Joiada, the son of Eliashib the high priest, *was* son in law to Sanballat the Horonite: therefore I chased him from me. 29 Remember them, O my God, because they have defiled the priesthood, and the covenant of the priesthood, and of the Levites. 30 Thus cleansed I them from all strangers, and appointed the wards of the priests and the Levites, every one in his business; 31 And for the wood offering, at times appointed, and for the firstfruits. Remember me, O my God, for good.

We have here one instance more of Nehemiah's pious zeal for the purifying of his countrymen as a peculiar people to God; that was the thing he aimed at in the use of his power, not the enriching of himself. See here,

I. How they had corrupted themselves by marrying strange wives. This was complained of in Ezra's time, and much done towards a reformation, Ezra. ix. and x. But, when the unclean spirit is cast out, if a watchful eye be not kept upon him, he will reenter; so he did here. Though in Ezra's time those that had married strange wives were forced to put them away, which could not but occasion trouble and confusion in families, yet others would not take warning. *Nitimur in vetitum—we still lean towards what is forbidden.* Nehemiah, like a good governor, enquired into the state of the families of those that were under his charge, that he might reform what was amiss in them, and so heal the streams by healing the springs. 1. He enquired whence they had their wives, and found that many of the Jews had *married wives of Ashdod, of Ammon, and of Moab* (*v.* 23), either because they were fond of what was far-fetched or because they hoped by these alliances to strengthen and enrich themselves. See how God by the prophet reproves this, Mal. ii. 11. *Judah has dealt treacherously,* and broken covenant with God, the covenant made in Ezra's time with reference to this very thing; he has *profaned the holiness of the Lord* by *marrying the daughter* (that is, the worshipper) *of a strange god.* 2 He talked with the children, and found they were *children of strangers,* for their *speech betrayed them.* The children were bred up with their mothers, and learned of them and their nurses and servants to speak, so that they could not speak the Jews' language, could not speak it at all, or not readily, or not purely, but *half in the speech of Ashdod,* or Ammon, or Moab, according as the country was which the mother was a native of. Observe, (1.) Children, in their childhood, learn much of their mothers. *Partus sequitur ventrem—they are prone to imitate their mothers.* (2.) If either side be bad, the corrupt nature will incline the children to take after that, which is a good reason why Christians should not be unequally yoked. (3.) In the education of children great care should be taken about the government of their tongues, that they learn not the language of Ashdod, any impious or impure talk, any corrupt communication.

II. What course Nehemiah took to purge out this corruption, when he discovered how much it had prevailed.

1. He showed them the evil of it, and the obligation he lay under to witness against it. He did not seek an occasion against them, but this was an iniquity to be punished by the judge, and which he must by no means connive at (*v.* 27): "*Shall we hearken to you,* who endeavour to palliate and excuse it? No, it is an evil, a great evil, it is a *transgression against our God, to marry strange wives,* and we must do our utmost to put a stop to it. You beg that they may not be divorced from you, but we cannot hearken to you, for there is no other remedy to clear us from the guilt and prevent the infection." (1.) He quotes a precept, to prove that it was in itself a great sin; and makes them swear to that precept: *You shall not give your daughters unto their sons,* &c., which is taken from Deut. vii. 3. When we would reclaim people from sin we must show them the sinfulness of it in the glass of the commandment. (2.) He quotes a precedent, to show the pernicious consequences of it, which made it necessary to be animadverted upon by the government (*v.* 26): *Did not Solomon king of Israel sin by these things?* The falls of great and good men are recorded in order that we may take warning by them to shun the temptations which they were overcome by. Solomon was famous for wisdom; there was no king like him for it; yet, when he married strange wives, his wisdom could not secure him from their snares, nay, it departed from him, and he did very foolishly. He was beloved of God, but his marrying strange wives threw him out of God's favour, and went near to extinguish the holy fire of grace in his soul: he was king over all Israel;

but his doing this occasioned the loss of ten of his twelve tribes. You plead that you can marry strange wives and yet retain the purity of Israelites; but Solomon himself could not; even *him did outlandish women cause to sin.* Therefore let him that *thinks he stands take heed lest he fall* when he runs upon such a precipice.

2. He showed himself highly displeased at it, that he might awaken them to a due sense of the evil of it: *He contended with them, v.* 25. They offered to justify themselves in what they did, but he showed them how frivolous their excuses were, and argued it warmly with them. When he had silenced them he *cursed them,* that is, he denounced the judgments of God against them, and showed them what their sin deserved. He then picked out some of them that were more obstinate than the rest, and fit to be made examples, and *smote them* (that is, ordered them to be beaten by the proper officers according to the law, Deut. xxv. 2, 3), to which he added this further mark of infamy that he *plucked off their hair,* or cut or shaved it off; for it may so be understood Perhaps they had prided themselves in their hair, and therefore he took it off to deform and humble them, and put them to shame; it was, in effect, to stigmatize them, at least for a time. Ezra, in this case, had plucked off his own hair, in holy sorrow for the sin; Nehemiah plucked off their hair, in a holy indignation at the sinners. See the different tempers of wise, and good, and useful men, and the divers graces, as well as divers gifts, of the same Spirit.

3. He obliged them not to take any more such wives, and separated those whom they had taken: *He cleansed them from all strangers,* both men and women (*v.* 30), and made them promise with an oath that they would never do so again, *v.* 25. Thus did he try all ways and means to put a stop to this mischief and to prevent another relapse into this disease.

4. He took particular care of the priests' families, that they might not lie under this stain, this guilt. He found, upon enquiry, that a branch of the high priest's own family, one of his grandsons, had married a daughter of Sanballat, that notorious enemy of the Jews (*ch.* ii. 10; iv. 1), and so had, in effect, twisted interests with the Samaritans, *v.* 28. How little love had that man either to God or his country who could make himself in duty and interest a friend to him that was a sworn enemy to both. It seems this young priest would not put away his wife, and therefore Nehemiah *chased him from him,* deprived him, degraded him, and made him for ever incapable of the priesthood. Josephus says that this expelled priest was Manasseh, and that when Nehemiah drove him away he went to his father-in-law Sanballat, who built him a temple upon Mount Gerizim, like that at Jerusalem, and promised him he should be high priest in it, and that then was laid the foundation of the Samaritans' pretensions, which continued warm to our Saviour's time. John iv. 20, *Our fathers worshipped in this mountain.* When Nehemiah had thus expelled one that had forfeited the honour of the priesthood he again posted the *priests and Levites every one in his business, v.* 30. It was no loss to them to part with one that was the scandal of their cloth; the work would be done better without him. When Judas had gone out Christ said, *Now is the Son of Man glorified,* John xiii. 30, 31. Here are Nehemiah's prayers on this occasion. (1.) He prays, *Remember them, O my God! v.* 29. "Lord, convince and convert them; put them in mind of what they should be and do, that they may come to themselves." Or, "Remember them to reckon with them for their sin; remember it against them." If we take it so, this prayer is a prophecy that God would remember it against them. Those that defile the priesthood despise God, and shall be lightly esteemed. Perhaps they were too many and too great for him to deal with. "Lord" (says he), "deal thou with them; take the work into thy own hands." (2.) He prays, *Remember me, O my God! v.* 31. The best services done to the public have sometimes been forgotten by those for whom they were done (Eccl. ix. 15); therefore Nehemiah refers it to God to recompense him, takes him for his paymaster, and then doubts not but he shall be well paid. This may well be the summary of our petitions; we need no more to make us happy than this: *Remember me, O my God! for good.*

AN

EXPOSITION,

WITH PRACTICAL OBSERVATIONS,

OF THE BOOK OF

ESTHER.

How the providence of God watched over the Jews that had returned out of captivity to their own land, and what great and kind things were done for them, we read in the two foregoing books; but there were many who staid behind, having not zeal enough for God's house, and the holy land and city, to carry them through the difficulties of a removal thither. These, one would think, should have been excluded the special protection of Providence, as unworthy the name of Israelites; but our God deals not with us according to our folly and weakness. We find in this book that even those Jews who were scattered in the provinces of the heathen were taken care of, as well as those who were gathered in the land of Judea, and were wonderfully preserved, when doomed to destruction and appointed as sheep for the slaughter. Who drew up this story is uncertain. Mordecai was as able as any man to relate, on his own knowledge, the several passages of it; *quorum pars magna fuit—for he bore a conspicuous part in it;* and that he wrote such an account of them as was necessary to inform his people of the grounds of their observing the feast of Purim we are told (*ch.* ix. 20, *Mordecai wrote these things*, and sent them enclosed in letters to all the Jews), and therefore we have reason to think he was the penman of the whole book. It is the narrative of a plot laid against the Jews to cut them all off, and which was wonderfully disappointed by a concurrence of providences. The most compendious exposition of it will be to read it deliberately all together at one time, for the latter events expound the former and show what Providence intended in them. The name of God is not found in this book; but the apocryphal addition to it (which is not in the Hebrew, nor was ever received by the Jews into the canon), containing six chapters, begins thus, *Then Mordecai said, God has done these things.* But, though the name of God be not in it, the finger of God is, directing many minute events for the bringing about of his people's deliverance. The particulars are not only surprising and very entertaining, but edifying and very encouraging to the faith and hope of God's people in the most difficult and dangerous times. We cannot now expect such miracles to be wrought for us as were for Israel when they were brought out of Egypt, but we may expect that in such ways as God here took to defeat Haman's plot he will still protect his people. We are told, I. How Esther came to be queen and Mordecai to be great at court, who were to be the instruments of the intended deliverance, *ch.* i. ii. II. Upon what provocation, and by what arts, Haman the Amalekite obtained an order for the destruction of all the Jews, *ch.* iii. III. The great distress the Jews, and their patriots especially, were in thereupon, *ch.* iv. IV. The defeating of Haman's particular plot against Mordecai's life, *ch.* v.—vii. V. The defeating of his general plot against the Jews, *ch.* viii. VI. The care that was taken to perpetuate the remembrance of this, *ch.* ix. x. The whole story confirms the Psalmist's observation (Ps. xxxvii. 12, 13), *The wicked plotteth against the just, and gnasheth upon him with his teeth. The Lord shall laugh at him; he sees that his day is coming.*

CHAP. I.

Several things in this chapter itself are very instructive and of great use; but the design of recording the story of it is to show how way was made for Esther to the crown, in order to her being instrumental to defeat Haman's plot, and this long before the plot was laid, that we may observe and admire the foresight and vast reaches of Providence. "Known unto God are all his works" before-hand. Ahasuerus the king, I. In his height feasts all his great men, ver. 1—9. II. In his heat he divorces his queen, because she would not come to him when he sent for her, ver. 10—22. This shows how God serves his own purposes even by the sins and follies of men, which he would not permit if he knew not how to bring good out of them.

NOW it came to pass in the days of Ahasuerus, (this *is* Ahasuerus which reigned, from India even unto Ethiopia, *over* a hundred and seven and twenty provinces:) 2 *That* in those days, when the king Ahasuerus sat on the throne of his kingdom, which *was* in Shushan the palace, 3 In the third year of his reign, he made a feast unto all his princes and his servants; the power of Persia and Media, the nobles and princes of the provinces *being* before him: 4 When he showed the riches of his glorious kingdom and the honour of his excellent majesty many days, *even* a hundred and fourscore days. 5 And when these days were expired, the king made a feast unto all the people that were present in Shushan the palace, both unto great and small, seven days, in the court of the garden of the king's palace; 6 *Where were* white, green, and blue, *hangings*, fastened with cords of fine linen and purple to silver rings and pillars of marble: the beds *were of* gold and silver, upon a pavement of red, and blue, and white, and black, marble. 7 And they gave *them* drink in vessels of gold, (the vessels being diverse one from another,) and royal wine in abundance, according to the state of the king. 8 And the drinking *was* according to the law; none did compel: for so the king had appointed to all the officers of his house, that they should do according to every man's pleasure. 9 Also Vashti the queen made a feast for the women *in* the royal house which *belonged* to king Ahasuerus.

Which of the kings of Persia this Ahasuerus was the learned are not agreed. Mordecai is said to have been one of those that were *carried* captive from *Jerusalem* (*ch.* ii. 5, 6), whence it should seem that this Ahasuerus was one of the first kings of that empire. Dr. Lightfoot thinks that he was that Artaxerxes who hindered the building of the temple, who is called also *Ahasuerus* (Ezra iv. 6, 7), after his great-grandfather of the Medes, Dan. ix. 1. We have here an account,

I. Of the vast extent of his dominion. In the time of Darius and Cyrus there were but 120 provinces (Dan. vi. 1); now there were 127, *from India to Ethiopia*, *v.* 1. It had become an over-grown kingdom, which in time would sink with its own weight, and, as usual, would lose its provinces as fast as it got them. If such vast power be put into a bad hand, it is able to do so much the more mischief; but, if into a good hand, it is able to do so much the more good. Christ's kingdom is, or shall be, far larger than this, when the kingdoms of the world shall all become his; and it shall be everlasting.

II. Of the great pomp and magnificence of his court. When he found himself fixed in his throne, the pride of his heart rising with the grandeur of his kingdom, he made a most extravagant feast, wherein he put himself to vast expense and trouble only *to show the riches of his glorious kingdom and the honour of his excellent majesty*, *v.* 4. This was vain glory, an affectation of pomp to no purpose at all; for none questioned the riches of his kingdom, nor offered to vie with him for honour. If he had shown the riches of his kingdom and he honour of his majesty, as some of his successors did, in contributing largely towards the building of the temple and the maintaining of the temple service (Ezra vi. 8, vii. 22), it would have turned to a much better account. Two feasts Ahasuerus made:—1. One for his nobles and princes, which lasted *a hundred and eighty days*, *v.* 3, 4. Not that he feasted the same persons every day for all that time, but perhaps the nobles and princes of one province one day, of another province another day, while thus he and his constant attendants fared sumptuously every day. The Chaldee paraphrast (who is very bold in his additions to the story of this book) says that there had been a rebellion among his subjects and that this feast was kept for joy of the quashing of it. 2. Another was made for *all the people, both great and small*, which lasted *seven days*, some one day and some another; and, because no house would hold them, they were entertained *in the court of the garden*, *v.* 5. The hangings with which the several apartments were divided, or the tents which were there pitched for the company, were very fine and rich; so were the beds or benches on which they sat, and the pavement under their feet, *v.* 6. Better is a dinner of herbs with quietness, and the enjoyment of one's self and a friend, than this banquet of wine with all the noise and tumult that must needs attend it

III. Of the good order which in some respects was kept there notwithstanding. We do not find this like Belshazzar's feast, in which dunghill-gods were praised and the vessels of the sanctuary profaned, Dan. v. 3, 4. Yet the Chaldee paraphrase says that the vessels of the sanctuary were used in this feast, to the great grief of the pious Jews. It was not like Herod's feast, which reserved a prophet's head for the last dish. Two things which are laudable we may gather from the account here given of this feast:—1. That there was no forcing of healths, nor urging of them: *The drinking was according to the law*, probably some law lately made; *none did compel*, no, not by a continual proposing of it (as Josephus explains it); they did not send the glass about, but every man drank as he pleased (*v.* 8), so that if there were any that drank to excess it was their own fault, a fault which few would commit when the king's order put an honour upon sobriety. This caution of a heathen prince, even when he would show his generosity, may shame many who are called Christians, who think they do not sufficiently show their good housekeeping, nor bid their friends welcome, unless they make them drunk, and, under pretence of sending the health round, send the sin round, and death with it. There is a woe to those that do so; let them read it and tremble, Hab. ii. 15, 16. It is robbing men of their reason, their richest jewel, and making them fools, the greatest wrong that can be. 2. That there was no mixed dancing; for the gentlemen and ladies were entertained asunder, not as in the feast of Belshazzar, whose wives and concubines drank with him (Dan. v. 2), or that of Herod, whose daughter *danced before him*. Vashti feasted the women in her own apartment; not openly in the court of the garden, but *in the royal house*, *v.* 9. Thus, while the king showed the honour of his majesty, she and her ladies showed the honour of their modesty, which is truly the majesty of the fair sex.

10 On the seventh day, when the heart of the king was merry with wine, he commanded Mehuman, Biztha, Harbona, Bigtha, and Abagtha, Zethar, and Carcas, the seven chamberlains that served in the presence of Ahasuerus the king, 11 To bring Vashti the queen before the king with the crown royal, to show the people and the princes her beauty: for she *was* fair to look on. 12 But the queen Vashti refused to come at the king's commandment by *his* chamberlains: therefore was the king very wroth, and his anger burned in him. 13 Then the king said to the wise men, which knew the times, (for so *was* the king's manner toward all that knew law and judgment: 14 And the next unto him *was* Carshena, Shethar, Admatha, Tarshish, Meres, Marsena, *and* Memucan, the seven princes of Persia and Media, which saw the king's face, *and* which sat the first in the kingdom;) 15 What shall we do unto the queen Vashti according to law, because she hath not performed the commandment of the king Ahasuerus by the chamberlains? 16 And Memucan answered before the king and the princes, Vashti the queen hath not done wrong to the king only, but also to all the princes, and to all the people that *are* in all the provinces of the king Ahasuerus. 17 For *this* deed of the queen shall come abroad unto all women, so that they shall despise their husbands in their eyes, when it shall be reported, The king Ahasuerus commanded Vashti the queen to be brought in before him, but she came not. 18 *Likewise* shall the ladies of Persia and Media say this day unto all the king's princes, which have heard of the deed of the queen. Thus *shall there arise* too much contempt and wrath. 19 If it please the king, let there go a royal commandment from him, and let it be written among the laws of the Persians and the Medes, that it be not altered, That Vashti come no more before king Ahasuerus; and let the king give her royal estate unto another that is better than she. 20 And when the king's decree which he shall make shall be published throughout all his empire, (for it is great,) all the wives shall give to their husbands honour, both to great and small. 21 And the saying pleased the king and the princes; and the king did according to the word of Memucan: 22 For he sent letters into all the king's provinces, into every province according to the writing thereof, and to every people after their language, that every man should bear rule in his own house, and that *it* should be published according to the language of every people.

We have here a damp to all the mirth of Ahasuerus's feast; it ended in heaviness, not as Job's children's feast by a wind from the wilderness, not as Belshazzar's by a handwriting on the wall, but by his own folly. An unhappy falling out there was, at the end of the feast, between the king and queen, which broke off the feast abruptly, and sent the guests away silent and ashamed.

I. It was certainly the king's weakness to send for Vashti into his presence when he was drunk, and in company with abundance of gentlemen, many of whom, it is likely, were in the same condition. *When his heart was merry with wine* nothing would serve him but Vashti must come, well dressed as she was, with *the crown on her head*, that the princes and people might see what a handsome woman she was, *v.* 10, 11. Hereby, 1. He dishonoured himself as a husband, who ought to protect, but by no means to expose, the modesty of his wife, who ought to be to her *a covering of the eyes* (Gen. xx. 16), not to uncover them. 2. He diminished himself as a king, in commanding that from his wife which she might refuse, much to the honour of her virtue. It was against the custom of the Persians for the women to appear in public, and he put a great hardship upon her when he did not court, but command her to do so uncouth a thing, and make her a show. If he had not been put out of the possession of himself by drinking to excess, he would not have done such a thing, but would have been angry at any one that should have mentioned it. When the wine is in the wit is out, and men's reason departs from them.

II. However, perhaps it was not her wisdom to deny him. *She refused to come* (*v.* 12); though he sent his command by seven honourable messengers, and publicly, and Josephus says sent again and again, yet she persisted in her denial. Had she come, while it was evident that she did it in pure obedience, it would have been no reflection upon her modesty, nor a bad example. The thing was not in itself sinful, and therefore to obey would have been more her honour than to be so precise. Perhaps she refused in a haughty manner, and then it was certainly evil; she *scorned to come at the king's commandment*. What a mortification was this to him! While he was showing the glory of his kingdom he showed the reproach of his family, that he had a wife that would do as she pleased. Strifes between yoke-fellows are bad enough at any time, but before company they are very scandalous, and occasion blushing and uneasiness.

III. The king thereupon grew outrageous. He that had rule over 127 provinces had no rule over his own spirit, but his *anger burned in him*, *v.* 12. He would have consulted his own comfort and credit more if he had stifled his resentment, had passed by the affront his wife gave him, and turned it off with a jest.

IV. Though he was very angry, he would not do any thing in this matter till he advised with his privy-counsellors; as he had seven chamberlains to execute his orders, who are named (*v.* 10), so he had seven counsellors to direct his orders. The greater power a man has the greater need he has of advice, that he may not abuse his power. Of these counsellors it is said that they were learned men, for they *knew law* and *judgment*,—that they were wise men, for they *knew the times*,—and that the king put great confidence in them and honour upon them, for they *saw the king's face and sat first in the kingdom*, *v.* 13, 14. In the multitude of such counsellors there is safety. Now here is,

1. The question proposed to this cabinet-council (*v.* 15): *What shall we do to the queen Vashti according to the law?* Observe, (1.) Though it was the queen that was guilty, the law must have its course. (2.) Though the king was very angry, yet he would do nothing but what he was advised was according to law.

2. The proposal which Memucan made, that Vashti should be divorced for her disobedience. Some suggest that he gave this severe advice, and the rest agreed to it, because they knew it would please the king, would gratify both his passion now and his appetite afterwards. But Josephus says that, on the contrary, he had a strong affection for Vashti, and would not have put her away for this offence if he could legally have passed it by; and then we must suppose Memucan, in his advice, to have had a sincere regard to justice and the public good. (1.) He shows what would be the bad consequences of the queen's disobedience to her husband, if it were passed by and not animadverted upon, that it would embolden other wives both to disobey their husbands and to domineer over them. Had this unhappy falling out between the king and his wife, wherein she was conqueror, been private, the error would have remained with themselves and the quarrel might have been settled privately between themselves; but it happening to be public, and perhaps the ladies that were now feasting with the queen having shown themselves pleased with her refusal, her bad example would be likely to have a bad influence upon all the families of the kingdom. If the queen must have her humour, and the king must submit to it (since the houses of private persons commonly take their measures from the courts of princes), the wives would be haughty and imperious and would scorn to obey their husbands, and the poor despised husbands might fret at it, but could not help themselves; for the *contentions of a wife are a continual dropping*, Prov. xix. 13; xxvii. 15; and see Prov. xxi. 9; xxv. 24. When wives *despise their husbands*, whom they ought to *reverence* (Eph. v. 33), and contend for *dominion* over those to whom they ought to be in *subjection* (1 Pet. iii. 1), there cannot but be continual guilt and grief, confusion and every evil work. And great ones must take heed of setting copies of this kind, *v.* 16—18. (2.) He shows what would be the good consequence of a decree against Vashti that she should be divorced. We may suppose that before they proceeded to this extremity they sent to Vashti to know if she would yet submit, cry *Peccavi—I have done wrong*, and ask the king's pardon, and that, if she had done so, the mischief of her example would have been effectually prevented, and process would have been stayed; but it is likely she continued obstinate, and insisted upon it as her prerogative to do as she pleased, whether it pleased the king or no, and therefore they gave this judgment against her, that she *come no more before the king*, and this judgment so ratified as never to be reversed, *v.* 19. The consequence of this, it was hoped, would be that *the wives would give to their husbands honour*, even the wives of the *great*, notwithstanding their own greatness, and the wives of the *small*, notwithstanding the husband's meanness (*v.* 20); and thus every man would bear rule in his own house, as he ought to do, and, the wives being subject, the children and servants would be so too. It is the interest of states

and kingdoms to provide that good order be kept in private families.

3. The edict that passed according to this proposal, signifying that the queen was divorced for contumacy, according to the law, and that, if other wives were in like manner undutiful to their husbands, they must expect to be in like manner disgraced (*v.* 21, 22): were they better than the queen? Whether it was the passion or the policy of the king that was served by this edict, God's providence served its own purpose by it, which was to make way for Esther to the crown.

CHAP. II.

Two things are recorded in this chapter, which were working towards the deliverance of the Jews from Haman's conspiracy:—I. The advancement of Esther to be queen instead of Vashti. Many others were candidates for the honour (ver. 1—4); but Esther, an orphan, a captive-Jewess (ver. 5—7), recommended herself to the king's chamberlain first (ver. 8—11) and then to the king (ver. 12—17), who made her queen, ver. 18—20. II. The good service that Mordecai did to the king in discovering a plot against his life, ver. 21—23.

AFTER these things, when the wrath of king Ahasuerus was appeased, he remembered Vashti, and what she had done, and what was decreed against her. 2 Then said the king's servants that ministered unto him, Let there be fair young virgins sought for the king: 3 And let the king appoint officers in all the provinces of his kingdom, that they may gather together all the fair young virgins unto Shushan the palace, to the house of the women, unto the custody of Hege the king's chamberlain, keeper of the women; and let their things for purification be given *them:* 4 And let the maiden which pleaseth the king be queen instead of Vashti. And the thing pleased the king; and he did so. 5 *Now* in Shushan the palace there was a certain Jew, whose name *was* Mordecai, the son of Jair, the son of Shimei, the son of Kish, a Benjamite; 6 Who had been carried away from Jerusalem with the captivity which had been carried away with Jeconiah king of Judah, whom Nebuchadnezzar the king of Babylon had carried away. 7 And he brought up Hadassah, that *is,* Esther, his uncle's daughter: for she had neither father nor mother, and the maid *was* fair and beautiful; whom Mordecai, when her father and mother were dead, took for his own daughter. 8 So it came to pass, when the king's commandment and his decree was heard, and when many maidens were gathered together unto Shushan the palace, to the custody of Hegai, that Esther was brought also unto the king's house, to the custody of Hegai, keeper of the women. 9 And the maiden pleased him, and she obtained kindness of him; and he speedily gave her her things for purification, with such things as belonged to her, and seven maidens, *which were* meet to be given her, out of the king's house: and he preferred her and her maids unto the best *place* of the house of the women. 10 Esther had not showed her people nor her kindred: for Mordecai had charged her that she should not show *it.* 11 And Mordecai walked every day before the court of the women's house, to know how Esther did, and what should become of her. 12 Now when every maid's turn was come to go in to king Ahasuerus, after that she had been twelve months, according to the manner of the women, (for so were the days of their purifications accomplished, *to wit,* six months with oil of myrrh, and six months with sweet odours, and with *other* things for the purifying of the women;) 13 Then thus came *every* maiden unto the king; whatsoever she desired was given her to go with her out of the house of the women unto the king's house. 14 In the evening she went, and on the morrow she returned into the second house of the women, to the custody of Shaashgaz, the king's chamberlain, which kept the concubines: she came in unto the king no more, except the king delighted in her, and that she were called by name. 15 Now when the turn of Esther, the daughter of Abihail the uncle of Mordecai, who had taken her for his daughter, was come to go in unto the king, she required nothing but what Hegai the king's chamberlain, the keeper of the women, appointed. And Esther obtained favour in the sight of all them that looked upon her. 16 So Esther was taken unto king Ahasuerus into his house royal in the tenth month, which *is* the month Tebeth, in the seventh year of his reign. 17 And the king loved Esther above all the women, and she obtained grace and favour in his sight more than all the virgins; so that he set the royal crown upon her head, and made her queen instead of Vashti. 18 Then the king made a great feast unto all his princes and his servants, *even* Esther's feast; and he made a release to the provinces, and gave gifts, according to the state of the king. 19 And when the virgins were gathered together the second time, then Mordecai sat in the king's gate. 20 Esther had not *yet* showed her kindred nor her people; as Mordecai had charged her: for Esther did the commandment of Mordecai, like as when she was brought up with him.

How God put down one that was high and mighty from her seat we read in the chapter before, and are now to be told how he exalted one of low degree, as the virgin Mary observes in her song (Luke i. 52) and Hannah before her, 1 Sam. ii. 4—8. Vashti being humbled for her height, Esther is advanced for her humility. Observe,

I. The extravagant course that was taken to please the king with another wife instead of Vashti. Josephus says that when his anger was over he was exceedingly grieved that the matter was carried so far, and would have been reconciled to Vashti but that, by the constitution of the government, the judgment was irrevocable—that therefore, to make him forget her, they contrived how to entertain him first with a great variety of concubines, and then to fix him to the most agreeable of them all for a wife instead of Vashti. The marriages of princes are commonly made by policy and interest, for the enlarging of their dominions and the strengthening of their alliances; but this must be made partly by the agreeableness of the person to the king's fancy, whether she were rich or poor, noble or ignoble. What pains were taken to humour the king! As if his power and wealth were given him for no other end than that he might have all the delights of sense wound up to the height of pleasureableness, and exquisitely refined, though at the best they are but dross and dregs in comparison with divine and spiritual pleasures. 1. All the provinces of his kingdom must be searched for fair young virgins, and officers appointed to choose them, *v.* 3. 2. A house (a seraglio) was prepared on purpose for them, and a person appointed to have the charge of them, to see that they were well provided for. 3. No less than twelve months was allowed them for their purification, some of them at least who were brought out of the country, that they might be very clean, and perfumed, *v.* 12. Even those who were the master-pieces of nature must yet have all this help from art to recommend them to a vain and carnal mind. 4. After the king had once taken them to his bed, they were made recluses ever after, except the king pleased at any time to send for them (*v.* 14); they were looked upon as secondary wives, were maintained by the king accordingly, and might not marry. We may see, by this instance, to what absurd practices those came who were destitute of divine revelation, and who, as a punishment for their idolatry, were given up to vile affections. Having broken through that law of creation which resulted from God's making man, they broke through another law, which was founded upon his making one man and one woman. See what need there was of the gospel of Christ to purify men from the lusts of the flesh and to reduce them to the original institution. Those that have *learned Christ* will think it *a shame even to speak of such things as* these which *were done of them,* not only *in secret,* but avowedly, Eph. v. 12.

II. The overruling providence of God thus bringing Esther to be queen. Had she been recommended to Ahasuerus for a wife, he would have rejected the motion with disdain; but when she came in her turn, after several others, and it was found that though many of them were ingenious and discreet, graceful and agreeable, yet Esther excelled them all, way was made for her, even by her rivals, into the king's affections and the honours consequent thereupon. It is certain, as bishop Patrick says, that those who suggest that she committed a great sin to come at this dignity do not consider the custom of those times and countries. Every one that the king took to his bed was married to him, and was his wife of a lower rank, as Hagar was Abraham's; so that, if Esther had not been made queen, the sons of Jacob need not say that he *dealt with their sister as with a harlot.* Concerning Esther we must observe,

1. Her original and character. (1.) She was one of the *children of the captivity,* a Jewess and a sharer with her people in their bondage. Daniel and his fellows were advanced in the land where they were captives; for they were of those whom God sent thither *for their good,* Jer. xxiv. 5. (2.) She was an orphan; her father and mother were both dead (*v.* 7), but, when they had forsaken her, then the Lord took her up, Ps. xxvii. 10. When those whose unhappiness it is to be thus deprived of their parents in their childhood yet afterwards come to be eminently pious and prosperous, we ought to take notice of it to the glory of that God, and his grace and providence, who has taken it among the titles of his honour to be a *Father of the fatherless.* (3.) She was a beauty, *fair of form, good of countenance;* so it is in the margin, *v.* 7. Her wisdom and virtue were her greatest beauty, but it is an advantage to a diamond to be well set. (4.) Mordecai, her cousin-german, was her guardian, ***brought***

her up, and took her for his own daughter. The LXX. say that he designed to make her his wife; if that were so, he was to be praised that he opposed not her better preferment. Let God be acknowledged in raising up friends for the fatherless and motherless; let it be an encouragement to that pious instance of charity that many who have taken care of the education of orphans have lived to see the good fruit of their care and pains, abundantly to their comfort. Dr. Lightfoot thinks that this Mordecai is the same with that mentioned Ezra ii. 2, who went up to Jerusalem with the first, and helped forward the settlement of his people until the building of the temple was stopped, and then went back to the Persian court, to see what service he could do them there. Mordecai being Esther's guardian or pro-parent, we are told, [1.] How tender he was of her, as if she had been his own child (*v.* 11): he walked before her door every day, to know how she did, and what interest she had. Let those whose relations are thus cast upon them by divine Providence be thus kindly affectioned to them and solicitous for them. [2.] How respectful she was to him. Though in relation she was his equal, yet, being in age and dependence his inferior, she honoured him as her father—*did his commandment, v.* 20. This is an example to orphans; if they fall into the hands of those who love them and take care of them, let them make suitable returns of duty and affection. The less obliged their guardians were in duty to provide for them the more obliged they are in gratitude to honour and obey their guardians. Here is an instance of Esther's obsequiousness to Mordecai, that she did not *show her people or her kindred,* because Mordecai had charged her that she should not, *v.* 10. He did not bid her deny her country, nor tell a lie to conceal her parentage; if he had told her to do so, she must not have done it. But he only told her not to proclaim her country. All truths are not to be spoken at all times, though an untruth is not to be spoken at any time. She being born in Shushan, and her parents being dead, all took her to be of Persian extraction, and she was not bound to undeceive them.

2. Her preferment. Who would have thought that a Jewess, a captive, an orphan, was born to be a queen, an empress! Yet so it proved. Providence sometimes *raiseth up the poor out of the dust, to set them among princes,* 1 Sam. ii. 8. (1.) The king's chamberlain honoured her (*v.* 9), and was ready to serve her. Wisdom and virtue will gain respect. Those that make sure of God's favour shall find favour with man too as far as it is good for them. All that looked upon Esther admired her (*v.* 15) and concluded that she was the lady that would win the prize, and she did win it. (2.) The king himself fell in love with her. She was not solicitous, as the rest of the maidens were, to set herself off with artificial beauty; she *required nothing* but just what was *appointed* for her (*v.* 15) and yet she was most acceptable. The more natural beauty is the more agreeable. *The king loved Esther above all the women, v.* 17. Now he needed not to make any further trials, or take time to deliberate; he is soon determined to *set the royal crown upon her head, and make her queen, v.* 17. This was done in his seventh year (*v.* 16) and Vashti was divorced in his third year (*ch.* i. 3); so that he was four years without a queen. Notice is taken, [1.] Of the honours the king put upon Esther. He graced the solemnity of her coronation with a *royal feast* (*v.* 18), at which perhaps Esther, in compliance with the king, made a public appearance, which Vashti had refused to do, that she might have the praise of obedience in the same instance in which the other incurred the blot of disobedience. He also granted a *release to the provinces,* either a remittance of the taxes in arrear or an act of grace for criminals; as Pilate, at the feast, released a prisoner. This was to add to the joy. [2.] Of the deference Esther continued to pay to her former guardian. She still *did the commandment of Mordecai, as when she was brought up with him, v.* 20. Mordecai sat *in the king's gate;* that was the height of his preferment: he was one of the porters or door-keepers of the court. Whether he had this place before, or whether Esther obtained it for him, we are not told; but there he sat contentedly, and aimed no higher; and yet Esther who was advanced to the throne was observant of him. This was an evidence of a humble and grateful disposition, that she had a sense of his former kindnesses and his continued wisdom. It is a great ornament to those that are advanced, and much to their praise, to remember their benefactors, to retain the impressions of their good education, to be diffident of themselves, willing to take advice, and thankful for it.

21 In those days, while Mordecai sat in the king's gate, two of the king's chamberlains, Bigthan and Teresh, of those which kept the door, were wroth, and sought to lay hand on the king Ahasuerus. 22 And the thing was known to Mordecai, who told *it* unto Esther the queen; and Esther certified the king *thereof* in Mordecai's name. 23 And when inquisition was made of the matter, it was found out; therefore they were both hanged on a tree: and it was written in the book of the chronicles before the king.

This good service which Mordecai did to the government, in discovering a plot against the life of the king, is here recorded, because the mention of it will again occur to his advantage. No step is yet taken towards Haman's design of the Jews' destruction, but several steps are taken towards God's design of their deliverance, and this for one. God now gives Mordecai an opportunity of doing the king a good turn, that he might have the fairer opportunity afterwards of doing the Jews a good turn. 1. A design was laid against the king by two of his own servants, who sought *to lay hands on him,* not only to make him a prisoner, but to take away his life, *v.* 21. Probably they resented some affront which they thought he had given them, or some injury which he had done them. Who would be great, to be so much the object of envy? Who would be arbitrary, to be so much the object of ill-will? Princes, above any mortals, have their souls continually in their hands, and often go down *slain to the pit,* especially those who *caused terror in the land of the living.* 2. Mordecai got notice of their treason, and, by Esther's means, discovered it to the king, hereby confirming her in and recommending himself to the king's favour. How he came to the knowledge of it does not appear. Whether he overheard their discourse, or whether they offered to draw him in with them, so it was that *the thing was known* to him. This ought to be a warning against all traitorous and seditious practices: though men presume upon secresy, *a bird of the air shall carry the voice..* Mordecai, as soon as he knew it, caused it to be made known to the king, which ought to be an instruction and example to all that would be found good subjects not to conceal any bad design they know of against the prince or the public peace, for it is making a confederacy with public enemies. 3. The traitors were hanged, as they deserved, but not till their treason was, upon search, fully proved against them (*v.* 23), and the whole matter was recorded in the king's journals, with a particular remark that Mordecai was the man who discovered the treason. He was not rewarded presently, but a book of remembrance was written. Thus with respect to those who serve Christ, though their recompence is adjourned till the resurrection of the just, yet an account is kept of their *work of faith and labour of love,* which *God is not unrighteous to forget,* Heb. vi. 10.

CHAP. III.

A very black and mournful scene here opens, and which threatens the ruin of all the people of God. Were there not some such dark nights, the light of the morning would not be so welcome. I. Haman is made the king's favourite, ver. 1. II. Mordecai refuses to give him the honour he demands, ver. 2—4. III. Haman, for his sake, vows to be revenged upon all the Jews, ver. 5, 6. IV. He, upon a malicious suggestion, obtains an order from the king to have them all massacred upon a certain day, ver. 7—13. V. This order is dispersed through the kingdom, ver. 14, 15.

AFTER these things did king Ahasuerus promote Haman the son of Hammedatha the Agagite, and advanced him, and set his seat above all the princes that *were* with him. 2 And all the king's servants, that *were* in the king's gate, bowed, and reverenced Haman: for the king had so commanded concerning him. But Mordecai bowed not, nor did *him* reverence. 3 Then the king's servants, which *were* in the king's gate, said unto Mordecai, Why transgressest thou the king's commandment? 4 Now it came to pass, when they spake daily unto him, and he hearkened not unto them, that they told Haman, to see whether Mordecai's matters would stand: for he had told them that he *was* a Jew. 5 And when Haman saw that Mordecai bowed not, nor did him reverence, then was Haman full of wrath. 6 And he thought scorn to lay hands on Mordecai alone; for they had showed him the people of Mordecai: wherefore Haman sought to destroy all the Jews that *were* throughout the whole kingdom of Ahasuerus, *even* the people of Mordecai.

Here we have,

I. Haman advanced by the prince, and adored thereupon by the people. Ahasuerus had lately laid Esther in his bosom, but she had no such interest in him as to get her friends preferred, or to prevent the preferring of one who she knew was an enemy to her people. When those that are good become great they still find that they cannot do good, nor prevent mischief, as they would. This Haman was an Agagite (an Amalekite, says Josephus), probably of the descendants of Agag, a common name of the princes of Amalek, as appears, Num. xxiv. 7. Some think that he was by birth a prince, as Jehoiakim was, whose seat was set above the rest of the captive kings (2 Kings xxv. 28), as Haman's here was, *v.* 1. The king took a fancy to him (princes are not bound to give reasons for their favours), made him his favourite, his confidant, his prime-minister of state. Such a commanding influence the court then had that (contrary to the proverb) those whom it blessed the country blessed too; for all men adored this rising sun, and the king's servants were particularly commanded *to bow before him and to do him reverence* (*v.* 2), and they did so. I wonder what the king saw in Haman that was commendable or meritorious; it is plain that he was not a man of honour or justice, of any true courage or steady conduct, but proud, and passionate, and revengeful; yet was he promoted, and caressed, and there was none so great as he. Princes' darlings are not always worthies.

II. Mordecai adhering to his principles with a bold and daring resolution, and therefore refusing to reverence Haman as the rest of the king's servants did, *v.* 2. He was urged to it by his friends, who reminded him of the king's commandment, and consequently of the danger he incurred if he refused to comply with it; it was as much as his life was worth, especially considering Haman's insolence, *v.* 3. They *spoke daily to him* (*v.* 4), to persuade him to conform, but all in vain: he hearkened not to them, but told them plainly that he was a Jew, and could not in conscience do it. Doubtless his refusal, when it came to be taken notice of and made the subject of discourse, was commonly attributed to pride and envy, that he would not pay respect to Haman because, on the score of his alliance to Esther, he was not himself as much promoted, or to a factious seditious spirit and a disaffection to the king and his government; those that would make the best of it looked upon it as his weakness, or his want of breeding, called it a humour, and a piece of affected singularity. It does not appear that any one scrupled at conforming to it except Mordecai; and yet his refusal was pious, conscientious, and pleasing to God, for the religion of a Jew forbade him, 1. To give such extravagant honours as were required to any mortal man, especially so wicked a man as Haman was. In the apocryphal chapters of this book (*ch.* xiii. 12—14) Mordecai is brought in thus appealing to God in this matter: *Thou knowest, Lord, that it was neither in contempt nor pride, nor for any desire of glory, that I did not bow down to proud Haman, for I could have been content with good will, for the salvation of Israel, to kiss the soles of his feet; but I did this that I might not prefer the glory of man above the glory of God, neither will I worship any but thee.* 2. He especially thought it a piece of injustice to his nation to give such honour to an Amalekite, one of that devoted nation with which God had sworn that he would have perpetual war (Exod. xvii. 16) and concerning which he had given that solemn charge (Deut. xxv. 17), *Remember what Amalek did.* Though religion does by no means destroy good manners, but teaches us to render *honour to whom honour* is due, yet it is the character of a citizen of Zion that not only in his heart, but *in his eyes*, such a *vile person as Haman was is contemned*, Ps. xv. 4. Let those who are governed by principles of conscience be steady and resolute, however censured or threatened, as Mordecai was.

III. Haman meditating revenge. Some that hoped thereby to curry favour with Haman took notice to him of Mordecai's rudeness, waiting to see whether he would bend or break, *v.* 4. Haman then observed it himself, and was *full of wrath*, *v.* 5. A meek and humble man would have slighted the affront, and have said, "Let him have his humour; what am I the worse for it?" But it makes Haman's proud spirit rage, and fret, and boil, within him, so that he becomes uneasy to himself and all about him. It is soon resolved that Mordecai must die. The head must come off that will not bow to Haman; if he cannot have his honours, he will have his blood. It is as penal in this court not to worship Haman as it was in Nebuchadnezzar's not to worship the golden image which he had set up. Mordecai is a person of quality, in a post of honour, and own cousin to the queen; and yet Haman thinks his life nothing towards a satisfaction for the affront: thousands of innocent and valuable lives must be sacrificed to his indignation; and therefore he vows the destruction of all the people of Mordecai, for his sake, because his being a Jew was the reason he gave why he did not reverence Haman. Herein appear Haman's intolerable pride, insatiable cruelty, and the ancient antipathy of an Amalekite to the Israel of God. Saul the son of Kish, a Benjamite, spared Agag, but Mordecai the son of Kish, a Benjamite (*ch.* ii. 5), shall find no mercy with this Agagite, whose design is to *destroy all the Jews throughout the whole kingdom of Ahasuerus* (*v.* 6), which, I suppose, would include those that had returned to their own land, for that was now a province of his kingdom. *Come and let us cut them off from being a nation*, Ps. lxxxiii. 4. Nero's barbarous wish is his, that they had all but one neck.

7 In the first month, that *is*, the month Nisan, in the twelfth year of king Ahasuerus, they cast Pur, that *is*, the lot, before Haman from day to day, and from month to month, *to* the twelfth *month*, that *is*, the month Adar. 8 And Haman said unto king Ahasuerus, There is a certain people scattered abroad and dispersed among the people in all the provinces of thy kingdom; and their laws *are* diverse from all people; neither keep they the king's laws: therefore it *is* not for the king's profit to suffer them. 9 If it please the king, let it be written that they may be destroyed: and I will pay ten thousand talents of silver to the hands of those that have the charge of the business, to bring *it* into the king's treasuries. 10 And the king took his ring from his hand, and gave it unto Haman the son of Hammedatha the Agagite, the Jews' enemy. 11 And the king said unto Haman, The silver *is* given to thee, the people also, to do with them as it seemeth good to thee. 12 Then were the king's scribes called on the thirteenth day of the first month, and there was written according to all that Haman had commanded unto the king's lieutenants, and to the governors

that *were* over every province, and to the rulers of every people of every province according to the writing thereof, and *to* every people after their language; in the name of king Ahasuerus was it written, and sealed with the king's ring. 13 And the letters were sent by posts into all the king's provinces, to destroy, to kill, and to cause to perish, all Jews, both young and old, little children and women, in one day, *even* upon the thirteenth *day* of the twelfth month, which *is* the month Adar, and *to take* the spoil of them for a prey. 14 The copy of the writing for a commandment to be given in every province, was published unto all people, that they should be ready against that day. 15 The posts went out, being hastened by the king's commandment, and the decree was given in Shushan the palace. And the king and Haman sat down to drink; but the city Shushan was perplexed.

Haman values himself upon that bold and daring thought, which he fancied well became his great spirit, of destroying all the Jews—an undertaking worthy of its author, and which he promised himself would perpetuate his memory. He doubts not but to find desperate and bloody hands enough to cut all their throats if the king will but give him leave. How he obtained leave, and commission to do it, we are here told. He had the king's ear, let him alone to manage him.

I. He makes a false and malicious representation of the Jews, and their character, to the king, *v.* 8. The enemies of God's people could not give them such bad treatment as they do if they did not first give them a bad name. He would have the king believe, 1. That the Jews were a despicable people, and that it was not for his credit to harbour them: "*A certain people there is,*" without name, as if nobody knew whence they came and what they were; "they are not incorporated, *but scattered abroad and dispersed in all the provinces* as fugitives and vagabonds on the earth, and inmates in all countries, the burden and scandal of the places where they live." 2. That they were a dangerous people, and that it was not safe to harbour them. "They have laws and usages of their own, and conform not to the statutes of the kingdom and the customs of the country; and therefore they may be looked upon as disaffected to the government and likely to infect others with their singularities, which may end in a rebellion." It is no new thing for the best of men to have such invidious characters as these given of them; if it be no sin to kill them, it is no sin to belie them.

II. He bids high for leave to destroy them all, *v.* 9. He knew there were many that hated the Jews, and would willingly fall upon them if they might but have a commission: *Let it be written* therefore *that they may be destroyed.* Give but orders for a general massacre of all the Jews, and Haman will undertake it shall be easily done. If the king will gratify him in this matter, he will make him a present of *ten thousand talents,* which shall be *paid into the king's treasuries.* This, he thought, would be a powerful inducement to the king to consent, and would obviate the strongest objection against him, which was that the government must needs sustain loss in its revenues by the destruction of so many of its subjects; so great a sum, he hoped, would be equivalent for that. Proud and malicious men will not stick at the expenses of their revenge, nor spare any cost to gratify it. Yet no doubt Haman knew how to re-imburse himself out of the spoil of the Jews, which his janizaries were to seize for him (*v.* 13), and so to make them bear the charges of their own ruin; while he himself hoped to be not only a saver but a gainer by the bargain.

III. He obtains what he desired, a full commission to do what he would with the Jews, *v.* 10, 11. The king was so inattentive to business, and so bewitched with Haman, that he took no time to examine the truth of his allegations, but was as willing as Haman could wish to believe the worst concerning the Jews, and therefore he gave them up into his hands, as lambs to the lion: *The people are thine, do with them as it seemeth good unto thee.* He does not say, "Kill them, slay them" (hoping Haman's own cooler thoughts would abate the rigour of that sentence and induce him to sell them for slaves); but "Do what thou wilt with them." And so little did he consider how much he should lose in his tribute, and how much Haman would gain in the spoil, that he gave him withal the ten thousand talents: *The silver is thine.* Such an implicit confidence likewise he had in Haman, and so perfectly had he abandoned all care of his kingdom, that he gave Haman his ring, his privy-seal, or sign-manual, wherewith to confirm whatever edict he pleased to draw up for this purpose. Miserable is the kingdom that is at the disposal of such a head as this, which has one ear only, and a nose to be led by, but neither eyes nor brains, nor scarcely a tongue of its own.

IV. He then consults with his soothsayers to find out a lucky day for the designed massacre, *v.* 7. The resolve was taken up in the first month, in the twelfth year of the king, when Esther had been his wife about five years. Some day or other in that year must be pitched upon; and, as if he doubted not but that Heaven would favour his design and further it, he refers it to *the lot,* that is, to the divine Providence, to choose the day for him; but that, in the decision, proved a better friend to the Jews than to him, for the lot fell upon *the twelfth month,* so that Mordecai and Esther had eleven months to turn themselves in for the defeating of the design, or, if they could not defeat it, space would be left for the Jews to make their escape and shift for their safety. Haman, though eager to have the Jews cut off, yet will submit to the laws of his superstition, and not anticipate the supposed fortunate day, no, not to gratify his impatient revenge. Probably he was in some fear lest the Jews should prove too hard for their enemies, and therefore durst not venture on such a hazardous enterprise but under the smiles of a good omen. This may shame us, who often acquiesce not in the directions and disposals of Providence when they cross our desires and intentions. He that believeth the lot, much more that believeth the promise, will not make haste. But see how God's wisdom serves its own purposes by men's folly. Haman has appealed to the lot, and to the lot he shall go, which, by adjourning the execution, gives judgment against him and breaks the neck of the plot.

V. The bloody edict is hereupon drawn up, signed, and published, giving orders to the militia of every province to be ready against *the thirteenth day of the twelfth month,* and, on that day, to murder all the Jews, men, women, and children, and seize their effects, *v.* 12—14. Had the decree been to banish all the Jews and expel them out of the king's dominions, it would have been severe enough; but surely never any act of cruelty appeared so barefaced as this, to *destroy, to kill, and to cause to perish, all the Jews,* appointing them *as sheep for the slaughter* without showing any cause for so doing. No crime is laid to their charge; it is not pretended that they were obnoxious to the public justice, nor is any condition offered, upon performance of which they might have their lives spared; but die they must, without mercy. Thus have the church's enemies thirsted after blood, the *blood of the saints and the martyrs of* Jesus, and drunk of it till they have been perfectly intoxicated (Rev. xvii. 6); yet still, like *the horse-leech,* they cry, *Give, give.* This cruel offer is ratified with the king's seal, directed to the king's lieutenants, and drawn up in the king's name, and yet the king knows not what he does. Posts are sent out, with all expedition, to carry copies of the decree to the respective provinces, *v.* 15. See how restless the malice of the church's enemies is: it will spare no pains; it will lose no time.

VI. The different temper of the court and city hereupon. 1. The court was very merry upon it: *The king and Haman sat down to drink,* perhaps to drink "Confusion to all the Jews." Haman was afraid lest the king's conscience should smite him for what he had done and he should begin to wish it undone again, to prevent which he engrossed him to himself, and kept him drinking. This cursed method many take to drown their convictions, and harden their own hearts and the hearts of others in sin. 2. The city was very sad upon it (and the other cities of the kingdom, no doubt, when they had notice of it): *The city Shushan was perplexed,* not only the Jews themselves, but all their neighbours that had any principles of justice and compassion. It grieved them to see their king so abused, to see *wickedness in the place of judgment* (Eccl. iii. 16), to see men that lived peaceably treated so barbarously; and what would be the consequences of it to themselves they knew not. But the king and Haman cared for none of these things. Note, It is an absurd and impious thing to indulge ourselves in mirth and pleasure when the church is in distress and the public are perplexed.

CHAP. IV.

We left God's Isaac bound upon the altar and ready to be sacrificed, and the enemies triumphing in the prospect of it; but things here begin to work towards a deliverance, and they begin at the right end. I. The Jews' friends lay to heart the danger and lament it, ver. 1—4. II. Matters are concerted between Mordecai and Esther for the preventing of it. 1. Esther enquires into this case, and receives a particular account of it, ver. 5—7. 2. Mordecai urges her to intercede with the king for a revocation of the edict, ver. 8, 9. III. Esther objects the danger of addressing the king uncalled, ver. 10—12. IV. Mordecai presses her to venture, ver. 13, 14. V. Esther, after a religious fast of three days, promises to do so (ver. 15—17), and we shall find that she sped well.

WHEN Mordecai perceived all that was done, Mordecai rent his clothes, and put on sackcloth with ashes, and went out into the midst of the city, and cried with a loud and a bitter cry; 2 And came even before the king's gate: for none *might* enter into the king's gate clothed with sackcloth. 3 And in every province, whithersoever the king's commandment and his decree came, *there was* great mourning among the Jews, and fasting, and weeping, and wailing; and many lay in sackcloth and ashes. 4 So Esther's maids and her chamberlains came and told *it* her. Then was the queen exceedingly grieved; and she sent raiment to clothe Mordecai, and to take away his sackcloth from him: but he received *it* not.

Here we have an account of the general sorrow that there was among the Jews upon the publishing of Haman's bloody edict against them. It was a sad time with the church. 1. Mordecai cried bitterly, *rent his clothes, and put on sackcloth, v.* 1, 2. He not only thus vented his grief, but proclaimed it, that all might take notice of it that he was not ashamed to own himself a friend to the Jews, and a fellow-sufferer with them, their brother and companion in tribulation, how despicable and how odious soever they were now represented by Haman's faction. It was nobly done thus publicly to espouse what he knew to be a righteous cause, and the cause of God, even when it seemed a desperate and a sinking cause. Mordecai laid the danger to heart more than any because he knew that Haman's spite was against him primarily, and that it was for his sake that the rest of the Jews were struck at; and therefore, though he did not repent of what some would call his obstinacy, for he persisted in it (*ch.* v. 9), yet it troubled him greatly that his people should suffer for his scruples, which perhaps occasioned some of them to reflect upon him as too precise. But, being able to appeal to God that what he did he did from a principle of conscience, he could with comfort commit his own cause and that of his people to him that judgeth righteously. God will keep those that are exposed by the tenderness of their consciences. Notice is here taken of a law that *none might enter into the king's gate clothed with sackcloth;* though the arbitrary power of their kings often, as now, set many a mourning, yet none must come near the king in a mourning dress, because he was not willing to hear the complaints of such. Nothing but what was gay and pleasant must appear at court, and every thing that was melancholy must be banished thence; all in king's palaces *wear soft clothing* (Matt. xi. 8), not sackcloth. But thus to keep out the badges of sorrow, unless they could withal have kept out the causes of sorrow—to forbid sackcloth to enter, unless they could have forbidden sickness, and trouble, and death to enter—was jest. However this obliged Mordecai to keep his distance, and only to come before the gate, not to take his place in the gate. 2. All the Jews in every province laid it much to heart, *v.* 3. They denied themselves the comfort of their tables (for they fasted and mingled tears with their meat and drink), and the comfort of their beds at night, for *they lay in sackcloth and ashes.* Those who for want of confidence in God, and affection to their own land, had staid in the land of their captivity, when Cyrus gave them liberty to be gone, now perhaps repented of their folly, and wished, when it was too late, that they had complied with the call of God. 3. Esther the queen, upon a general intimation of the trouble Mordecai was in, *was exceedingly grieved, v.* 4. Mordecai's grief was hers, such a respect did she still retain for him; and the Jews' danger was her distress; for, though a queen, she forgot not her relation to them. Let not the greatest think it below them to *grieve for the affliction of Joseph,* though they themselves be *anointed with the chief ointments,* Amos vi. 6. Esther sent change of raiment to Mordecai, the *oil of joy for mourning and the garments of praise for the spirit of heaviness;* but because he would make her sensible of the greatness of his grief, and consequently of the cause of it, *he received it not,* but was as one that refused to be comforted.

5 Then called Esther for Hatach, *one* of the king's chamberlains, whom he had appointed to attend upon her, and gave him a commandment to Mordecai, to know what it *was,* and why it *was.* 6 So Hatach went forth to Mordecai unto the street of the city, which *was* before the king's gate. 7 And Mordecai told him of all that had happened unto him, and of the sum of the money that Haman had promised to pay to the king's treasuries for the Jews, to destroy them. 8 Also he gave him the copy of the writing of the decree that was given at Shushan to destroy them, to show *it* unto Esther, and to declare *it* unto her, and to charge her that she should go in unto the king, to make supplication unto him, and to make request before him for her people. 9 And Hatach came and told Esther the words of Mordecai. 10 Again Esther spake unto Hatach, and gave him commandment unto Mordecai; 11 All the king's servants, and the people of the king's provinces, do know, that whosoever, whether man or woman, shall come unto the king into the inner court, who is not called, *there is* one law of his to put *him* to death, except such to whom the king shall hold out the golden sceptre, that he may live: but I have not been called to come in unto the king these thirty days. 12 And they told to Mordecai Esther's words. 13 Then Mordecai commanded to answer Esther, Think not with thyself that thou shalt escape in the king's house, more than all the Jews. 14 For if thou altogether holdest thy peace at this time, *then* shall there enlargement and deliverance arise to the Jews from another place; but thou and thy father's house shall be destroyed: and who knoweth whether thou art come to the kingdom for *such* a time as this? 15 Then Esther bade *them* return Mordecai *this answer,* 16 Go, gather together all the Jews that are present in Shushan, and fast ye for me, and neither eat nor drink three days, night or day: I also and my maidens will fast likewise; and so

will I go in unto the king, which *is* not according to the law: and if I perish, I perish. 17 So Mordecai went his way, and did according to all that Esther had commanded him.

So strictly did the laws of Persia confine the wives, especially the king's wives, that it was not possible for Mordecai to have a conference with Esther about this important affair, but divers messages are here carried between them by Hatach, whom the king had appointed to attend her, and it seems he was one she could confide in.

I. She sent to Mordecai to know more particularly and fully what the trouble was which he was now lamenting (*v.* 5) and why it was that he would not put off his sackcloth. To enquire thus after news, that we may know the better how to direct our griefs and joys, our prayers and praises, well becomes all that love Sion. If we must weep with those that weep, we must know why they weep.

II. Mordecai sent her an authentic account of the whole matter, with a charge to her to intercede with the king in this matter: *Mordecai told him all that had happened unto him* (*v.* 7), what a pique Haman had against him for not bowing to him, and by what arts he had procured this edict; he sent her also a true copy of the edict, that she might see what imminent danger she and her people were in, and charged her, if she had any respect for him or any kindness for the Jewish nation, that she should appear now on their behalf, rectify the misinformations with which the king was imposed upon, and set the matter in a true light, not doubting but that then he would vacate the decree.

III. She sent her case to Mordecai, that she could not, without peril of her life, address the king, and that therefore he put a great hardship upon her in urging her to it. Gladly would she wait, gladly would she stoop, to do the Jews a kindness; but, if she must run the hazard of being put to death as a malefactor, she might well say, *I pray thee have me excused,* and find out some other intercessor.

1. The law was express, and all knew it, that whosoever came to the king uncalled should be put to death, unless he was pleased to *hold out the golden sceptre to them,* and it was extremely doubtful whether she should find him in so good a humour, *v.* 11. This law was made, not so much in prudence, for the greater safety of the king's person, as in pride, that being seldom seen, and not without great difficulty, he might be adored as a little god. A foolish law it was; for, (1.) It made the kings themselves unhappy, confining them to their retirements for fear they should be seen. This made the royal palace little better than a royal prison, and the kings themselves could not but become morose, and perhaps melancholy, and so a terror to others and a burden to themselves. Many have their lives made miserable by their own haughtiness and ill nature. (2.) It was bad for their subjects; for what good had they of a king that they might never have liberty to apply to for the redress of grievances and appeal to from the inferior judges? It is not thus in the court of the King of kings; to the footstool of his throne of grace we may at any time *come boldly,* and may be sure of an answer of peace to the prayer of faith. We are welcome, not only into the inner court, but even into the holiest, through the blood of Jesus. (3.) It was particularly very uncomfortable for their wives (for there was not a proviso in the law to except them), who were *bone of their bone* and *flesh of their flesh.* But perhaps it was wickedly intended as much against them as any other, that the kings might the more freely enjoy their concubines, and Esther knew it. Miserable was the kingdom when the princes framed their laws to serve their lusts.

2. Her case was at present very discouraging. Providence so ordered it that, just at this juncture, she was under a cloud, and the king's affections cooled towards her, for she had been *kept from his presence thirty days,* that her faith and courage might be the more tried, and that God's goodness in the favour she now found with the king notwithstanding might shine the brighter. It is probable that Haman endeavoured by women, as well as wine, to divert the king from thinking of what he had done, and then Esther was neglected, from whom no doubt he did what he could to alienate the king, knowing her to be averse to him.

IV. Mordecai still insisted upon it that, whatever hazard she might run, she must apply to the king in this great affair, *v.* 13, 14. No excuse will serve, but she must appear an advocate in this cause; he suggested to her, 1. That it was her own cause, for that the decree to *destroy all the Jews* did not except her: "*Think not* therefore that *thou shalt escape in the king's house,* that the palace will be thy protection, and the crown save thy head: no, thou art a Jewess, and, if the rest be cut off, thou wilt be cut off too." It was certainly her wisdom rather to expose herself to a conditional death from her husband than to a certain death from her enemy. 2. That it was a cause which, one way or other, would certainly be carried, and which therefore she might safely venture in. "If thou shouldst decline the service, *enlargement and deliverance will arise to the Jews from another place.*" This was the language of a strong faith, which *staggered not at the promise* when the danger was most threatening, but *against hope believed in hope.* Instruments may fail, but God's covenant will not. 3. That if she deserted her friends now, through cowardice and unbelief, she would have reason to fear that some judgment from heaven would be the ruin of her and her family: "*Thou and thy father's house shall be destroyed*, when the rest of the families of the Jews shall be preserved." He that by sinful shifts will save his life, and cannot find in his heart to trust God with it in the way of duty, shall lose it in the way of sin. 4. That divine Providence had an eye to this in bringing her to be queen: "*Who knows whether thou hast come to the kingdom for such a time as this?*" and therefore, (1.) "Thou art bound in gratitude to do this service for God and his church, else thou dost not answer the end of thy elevation." (2.) "Thou needest not fear miscarrying in the enterprise; if God designed thee for it, he will bear thee out and give thee success." Now, [1.] It appeared, by the event, that she did come to the kingdom that she might be an instrument of the Jews' deliverance, so that Mordecai was right in the conjecture. *Because the Lord loved his people,* therefore he made Esther queen. There is a wise counsel and design in all the providences of God, which is unknown to us till it is accomplished, but it will prove, in the issue, that they are all intended for, and centre in, the good of the church. [2.] The probability of this was a good reason why she should now bestir herself, and do her utmost for her people. We should every one of us consider for what end God has put us in the place where we are, and study to answer that end; and, when any particular opportunity of serving God and our generation offers itself, we must take care that we do not let it slip; for we were entrusted with it that we might improve it. These things Mordecai urges to Esther; and some of the Jewish writers, who are fruitful in invention, add another thing which had *happened to him* (*v.* 7) which he desired she might be told, "that going home, the night before, in great heaviness, upon the notice of Haman's plot, he met three Jewish children coming from school, of whom he enquired what they had learned that day; one of them told him his lesson was, Prov. iii. 25, 26, *Be not afraid of sudden fear;* the second told him his was, Isa. viii. 10, *Take counsel together, and it shall come to nought;* the third told him his was Isa. xlvi. 4, *I have made, and I will bear, even I will carry and will deliver you.* 'O the goodness of God,' says Mordecai, 'who out of the mouth of babes and sucklings ordains strength!'"

V. Esther hereupon resolved, whatever it might cost her, to apply to the king, but not till she and her friends had first applied to God. Let them first by fasting and prayer obtain God's favour, and then she should hope to find favour with the king, *v.* 15, 16. She speaks here,

1. With the piety and devotion that became an Israelite. She had her eye up unto God, in whose hands the hearts of kings are, and on whom she depended to incline this king's heart towards her. She went in peril of her life, but would think herself safe, and would be easy, when she had committed the keeping of her soul to God and had put herself under his protection. She believed that God's favour was to be obtained by prayer, that his people are a praying people, and he a prayer-hearing God. She knew it was the practice of good people, in extraordinary cases, to join fasting with prayer, and many of them to join together in both. She therefore, (1.) Desired that Mordecai would direct the Jews that were in Shushan to *sanctify a fast* and *call a solemn assembly*, to meet in the respective synagogues to which they belonged, and to pray for her, and to keep a solemn fast, abstaining from all set meals and all pleasant food for three days, and as much as possible from all food, in token of their humiliation for sin and in a sense of their unworthiness of God's mercy. Those know not how to value the divine favours who grudge thus much labour and self-denial in the pursuit of it. (2.) She promised that she and her family would sanctify this fast in her apartment of the palace, for she might not come to their assemblies; her maids were either Jewesses or so far proselytes that they joined with her in her fasting and praying. Here is a good example of a mistress praying with her maids, and it is worthy to be imitated. Observe also, Those who are confined to privacy may join their prayers with those of the solemn assemblies of God's people; those that are absent in body may be present in spirit. Those who desire, and have, the prayers of others for them, must not think that this will excuse them from praying for themselves.

2. With the courage and resolution that became a queen. "When we have sought God in this matter, *I will go in unto the king* to intercede for my people. *I know it is not according to the king's law,* but it is according to God's law; and therefore, whatever comes of it, I will venture, and not count my life dear to me, so that I may serve God and his church, and, *if I perish, I perish.* I cannot lose my life in a better cause. Better do my duty and die for my people than shrink from my duty and die with them." She reasons as the lepers (2 Kings vii. 4): "*If I sit still, I die;* if I venture, I may live, and be the life of my people: if the worst come to the worst," as we say, "*I shall but die.*" Nothing venture, nothing win. She said not this in despair or passion, but in a holy resolution to do her duty and trust God with the issue; welcome his holy will. In the apocryphal part of this book (*ch.* xiii. and xiv.) we have Mordecai's prayer and Esther's upon this occasion, and both of them very particular and pertinent. In the sequel of the story we shall find that God said not to this seed of Jacob, *Seek you me in vain.*

CHAP. V.

The last news we had of Haman left him in his cups, ch. iii. 15. Our last news of queen Esther left her in tears, fasting and praying. Now this chapter brings in, I. Esther in her joys, smiled upon by the king and honoured with his company at her ban-

quet of wine, ver. 1—8. II. Haman upon the fret, because he had not Mordecai's cap and knee, and with great indignation setting up a gallows for him, ver. 9—14. Thus those that sow in tears shall reap in joy, but the triumphing of the wicked is short.

NOW it came to pass on the third day, that Esther put on *her* royal *apparel*, and stood in the inner court of the king's house, over against the king's house: and the king sat upon his royal throne in the royal house, over against the gate of the house. 2 And it was so, when the king saw Esther the queen standing in the court, *that* she obtained favour in his sight: and the king held out to Esther the golden sceptre that *was* in his hand. So Esther drew near, and touched the top of the sceptre. 3 Then said the king unto her, What wilt thou, queen Esther? and what *is* thy request? it shall be even given thee to the half of the kingdom. 4 And Esther answered, If *it seem* good unto the king, let the king and Haman come this day unto the banquet that I have prepared for him. 5 Then the king said, Cause Haman to make haste, that he may do as Esther hath said. So the king and Haman came to the banquet that Esther had prepared. 6 And the king said unto Esther at the banquet of wine, What *is* thy petition? and it shall be granted thee: and what *is* thy request? even to the half of the kingdom it shall be performed. 7 Then answered Esther, and said, My petition and my request *is;* 8 If I have found favour in the sight of the king, and if it please the king to grant my petition, and to perform my request, let the king and Haman come to the banquet that I shall prepare for them, and I will do to morrow as the king hath said.

Here is, I. Esther's bold approach to the king, *v.* 1. When the time appointed for their fast was finished she lost no time, but on the third day, when the impressions of her devotions were fresh upon her spirit, she addressed the king. When the heart is enlarged in communion with God it will be emboldened in doing and suffering for him. Some think that the three days' fast was only one whole day and two whole nights, in all which time they did not take any food at all, and that this is called *three days*, as Christ's lying in the grave so long is. This exposition is favoured by the consideration that on the third day the queen made her appearance at court. Resolutions which have difficulties and dangers to break through should be pursued without delay, lest they cool and slacken. *What thou doest*, which must be done boldly, *do it quickly.* Now she *put on her royal apparel*, that she might the better recommend herself to the king, and laid aside her fast-day clothes. She put on her fine clothes, not to please herself, but her husband; in her prayer, as we find in the Apocrypha (Esther xiv. 16), she thus appeals to God: *Thou knowest, Lord, I abhor the sign of my high estate which is upon my head, in the days wherein I show myself, &c.* Let those whose rank obliges them to wear rich clothes learn hence to be dead to them, and not make them their adorning. She stood *in the inner court over against the king*, expecting her doom, between hope and fear.

II. The favourable reception which the king gave her. When he *saw her* she *obtained favour in his sight.* The apocryphal author and Josephus say that she took two maids with her, on one of whom she leaned, while the other bore up her train,—that her countenance was cheerful and very amiable, but her heart was in anguish,—that the king, lifting up his countenance that shone with majesty, at first looked very fiercely upon her, whereupon she grew pale, and fainted, and bowed herself on the head of the maid that went by her; but then God changed the spirit of the king, and, in a fear, he leaped from his throne, took her in his arms till she came to herself, and comforted her with loving words. Here we are only told,

1. That he protected her from the law, and assured her of safety, by *holding out to her the golden sceptre* (*v.* 2), which she thankfully *touched the top of*, thereby presenting herself to him as a humble petitioner. Thus having had power with God and prevailed, like Jacob, she had power with men too. *He that will lose his life* for God shall *save it*, or find it in a better life.

2. That he encouraged her address (*v.* 3): *What wilt thou, queen Esther, and what is thy request?* So far was he from counting her an offender that he seemed glad to see her, and desirous to oblige her. He that had divorced one wife for not coming when she was sent for would not be severe to another for coming when she was not sent for. God can turn the hearts of men, of great men, of those that act most arbitrarily, which way he pleases towards us. Esther feared that she should perish, but was promised that she should have what she might ask for, though it were *the half of the kingdom.* Note, God in his providence often prevents the fears, and outdoes the hopes, of his people, especially when they venture in his cause. Let us from this story infer, as our Saviour does from the parable of the unjust judge, an encouragement to *pray always* to our God, *and not faint*, Luke xviii. 6—8. Hear what this

haughty king says *(What is thy petition, and what is thy request? It shall be granted thee)*, and say *shall not God* hear and answer the prayers of *his own elect, that cry day and night to him?* Esther came to a proud imperious man; we come to the God of love and grace. She was not called; we are: the Spirit says, *Come*, and the bride says, *Come*. She had a law against her; we have a promise, many a promise, in favour of us: *Ask, and it shall be given you.* She had no friend to introduce her, or intercede for her, while on the contrary he that was then the king's favourite was her enemy; but we have an advocate with the Father, in whom he is well pleased. *Let us therefore come boldly to the throne of grace.*

3. That all the request she had to make to him, at this time, was that he would please to come to a banquet which she had prepared for him, and bring Haman along with him, *v.* 4, 5. Hereby, (1.) She would intimate to him how much she valued his favour and company. Whatever she had to ask, she desired his favour above any thing, and would purchase it at any rate. (2.) She would try how he stood affected to her; for, if he should refuse this, it would be to no purpose as yet to present her other request. (3.) She would endeavour to bring him into a pleasant humour, and soften his spirit, that he might with the more tenderness receive the impressions of the complaint she had to make to him. (4.) She would please him, by making court to Haman his favourite, and inviting him to come whose company she knew he loved and whom she desired to have present when she made her complaint; for she would say nothing of him but what she durst say to his face. (5.) She hoped at the banquet of wine to have a fairer and more favourable opportunity of presenting her petition. Wisdom is profitable to direct how to manage some men that are hard to deal with, and to take them by the right handle.

4. That he readily came, and ordered Haman to come along with him (*v.* 5), which was an indication of the kindness he still retained for her; if he really designed the destruction of her and her people, he would not have accepted her banquet. There he renewed his kind enquiry *(What is thy petition?)* and his generous promise, that it should be granted, *even to the half of the kingdom* (*v.* 6), a proverbial expression, by which he assured her that he would deny her nothing in reason. Herod used it, Mark vi. 23.

5. That then Esther thought fit to ask no more than a promise that he would please to accept of another treat, the next day, in her apartment, and Haman with him (*v.* 7, 8), intimating to him that then she would let him know what her business was. This adjourning of the main petition may be attributed, (1.) To Esther's prudence; thus she hoped yet further to win upon him and ingratiate herself with him. Perhaps her heart failed her now when she was going to make her request, and she desired to take some further time for prayer, that God would give her *a mouth and wisdom.* The putting of it off thus, it is likely, she knew would be well taken as an expression of the great reverence she had for the king, and her unwillingness to be too pressing upon him. What is hastily asked is often as hastily denied; but what is asked with a pause deserves to be considered. (2.) To God's providence putting it into Esther's heart to delay her petition a day longer, she knew not why, but God did, that what was to happen in the night intervening between this and to-morrow might further her design and make way for her success, that Haman might arrive at the highest pitch of malice against Mordecai and might begin to *fall before him.* The Jews perhaps blamed Esther as dilatory, and some of them began to suspect her sincerity, or at least her zeal; but the event disproved their jealousy, and all was for the best.

9 Then went Haman forth that day joyful and with a glad heart: but when Haman saw Mordecai in the king's gate, that he stood not up, nor moved for him, he was full of indignation against Mordecai. 10 Nevertheless Haman refrained himself: and when he came home, he sent and called for his friends, and Zeresh his wife. 11 And Haman told them of the glory of his riches, and the multitude of his children, and all *the things* wherein the king had promoted him, and how he had advanced him above the princes and servants of the king. 12 Haman said moreover, Yea, Esther the queen did let no man come in with the king unto the banquet that she had prepared but myself; and to morrow am I invited unto her also with the king. 13 Yet all this availeth me nothing, so long as I see Mordecai the Jew sitting at the king's gate. 14 Then said Zeresh his wife and all his friends unto him, Let a gallows be made of fifty cubits high, and to morrow speak thou unto the king that Mordecai may be hanged thereon: then go thou in merrily with the king unto the banquet. And the thing pleased Haman; and he caused the gallows to be made.

This account here given of Haman is a comment upon that of Solomon, Prov. xxi. 24. *Proud and haughty scorner is his name that deals in proud wrath.* Never did any man more answer that name than Haman, in whom pride and wrath had so much the ascendant. See him,

I. Puffed up with the honour of being invited to Esther's feast. He was *joyful and glad of heart* at it, *v.* 9. Observe with what a high gust he speaks of it (*v.* 12), how he values himself upon it, and how near he thinks it brings him to the perfection of felicity, that Esther the queen did let no man come with the king to the banquet but his mighty self, and he thought it was because she was exceedingly charmed with his conversation that the next day she had invited him also to come with the king; none so fit as he to bear the king company. Note, Self-admirers and self-flatterers are really self-deceivers. Haman pleased himself with the fancy that the queen, by this repeated invitation, designed to honour him, whereas really she designed to accuse him, and, in calling him to the banquet, did but call him to the bar. What magnifying glasses do proud men look at their faces in! And how does the *pride of their heart deceive them!* Obad. 3.

II. Vexing and fretting at the slight that Mordecai put upon him, and thereby made uneasy to himself and to all about him. 1. Mordecai was as determined as ever: *He stood not up, nor moved for him, v.* 9. What he did was from a principle of conscience, and therefore he persevered in it, and would not cringe to Haman, no, not when he had reason to fear him and Esther herself complimented him. He knew God could and would deliver him and his people from the rage of Haman, without any such mean and sneaking expedients to mollify him. Those that walk in holy sincerity may walk in holy security, and go on in their work, not fearing what man can do unto them. *He that walks uprightly walks surely.* 2. Haman can as ill bear it as ever; nay, the higher he is lifted up, the more impatient is he of contempt and the more enraged at it. (1.) It made his own spirit restless, and put him into a grievous agitation. He was *full of indignation* (*v.* 9) and yet *refrained himself, v.* 10. Gladly would he have drawn his sword and run Mordecai through for affronting him thus; but he hoped shortly to see him fall with all the Jews, and therefore with much ado prevailed with himself to forbear stabbing him. What a struggle had he in his own bosom between his anger, which required Mordecai's death immediately (*O that I had of his flesh! I cannot be satisfied!* Job xxxi. 31), and his malice, which had determined to wait for the general massacre! Thus *thorns and snares are in the way of the froward.* (2.) It made all his enjoyments sapless. This little affront which he received from Mordecai was the dead fly which spoiled all his pot of precious ointment; he himself owned in the presence of his wife and friends, to the everlasting reproach of a proud and discontented mind, that he had no comfort in his estate, preferment, and family, as long as Mordecai lived and had a place *in the king's gate, v.* 10—13. He took notice of his own riches and honours, the numerousness of his family, and the high posts to which he was advanced, that he was the darling of the prince and the idol of the court; and *yet all this avails him nothing* as long as Mordecai is unhanged. Those that are disposed to be uneasy will never want something or other to be uneasy at; and proud men, though they have *much* to their mind, yet, if they have not *all* to their mind, it is as nothing to them. The thousandth part of what Haman had would serve to make a humble modest man as much of a happiness as he expects from this world; and yet Haman complained as passionately as if he had been sunk into the lowest degree of poverty and disgrace.

III. Meditating revenge, and assisted therein by his wife and his friends, *v.* 14. They saw how gladly he would dispense with his own resolution of deferring the slaughter till the time determined by the lot, and therefore advised him to take an earnest and foretaste of the satisfaction he then expected in the speedy execution of Mordecai; let him have that to please him at the moment; and having, as he thought, made sure the destruction of all the Jews, at the time appointed, he will not think scorn, for the present, to lay hands on Mordecai alone. 1. For the pleasing of his fancy they advise him to get *a gallows ready,* and have it set up before his own door, that, as soon as ever he could get the warrant signed, there might be no delay of the execution; he would not need so much as to stay the making of the gallows. This is very agreeable to Haman, who has the gallows made and fixed immediately; it must be fifty cubits high, or as near that as might be, for the greater disgrace of Mordecai and to make him a spectacle to every one that passed by; and it must be before Haman's door, that all men might take notice it was to the idol of his revenge that Mordecai was sacrificed and that he might feed his eyes with the sight. 2. For the gaining of his point they advise him to go early in the morning to the king, and get an order from him for the hanging of Mordecai, which, they doubted not, would be readily granted to one who was so much the king's favourite and who had so easily obtained an edict for the destruction of the whole nation of the Jews. There needed no feigned suggestion; it was enough if he let the king know that Mordecai, in contempt of the king's command, refused to reverence him. And now we leave Haman to go to bed, pleased with the thoughts of seeing Mordecai hanged the next day, and then going merrily to the banquet, and not dreaming of handselling his own gallows.

CHAP. VI.

It is a very surprising scene that opens in this chapter. Haman, when he hoped to be Mordecai's judge, was made his page, to

his great confusion and mortification; and thus way was made for the defeat of Haman's plot and the deliverance of the Jews. I. The providence of God recommends Mordecai in the night to the king's favour, ver. 1–3. II. Haman, who came to incense the king against him, is employed as an instrument of the king's favour to him, ver. 4—11. III. From this his friends read him his doom, which is executed in the next chapter, ver. 12–14. And now it appears that Esther's intercession for her people was happily adjourned, "De die in diem"—from day to day.

ON that night could not the king sleep, and he commanded to bring the book of records of the chronicles; and they were read before the king. 2 And it was found written, that Mordecai had told of Bigthana and Teresh, two of the king's chamberlains, the keepers of the door, who sought to lay hand on the king Ahasuerus. 3 And the king said, What honour and dignity hath been done to Mordecai for this? Then said the king's servants that ministered unto him, There is nothing done for him.

How Satan put it into the heart of Haman to contrive Mordecai's death we read in the foregoing chapter; how God put it into the heart of the king to contrive Mordecai's honour we are here told. Now, if the king's word will prevail above Haman's (for, though Haman be a great man, the king in the throne must be above him), much more will the *counsel of God stand,* whatever *devices there are in men's hearts.* It is to no purpose therefore for Haman to oppose it, when both God and the king will have Mordecai honoured, and in this juncture too, when his preferment, and Haman's disappointment, would help to ripen the great affair of the Jewish deliverance for the effort that Esther was to make towards it the next day. Sometimes delay may prove to have been good conduct. Stay awhile, and we may have done the sooner. *Cunctando restituit rem—He conquered by delay.* Let us trace the steps which Providence took towards the advancement of Mordecai.

I. *On that night could not the king sleep.* His *sleep fled away* (so the word is); and perhaps, like a shadow, the more carefully he pursued it the further it went from him. Sometimes we cannot sleep because we fain would sleep. Even after a banquet of wine he could not sleep when Providence had a design to serve in keeping him waking. We read of no bodily indisposition he was under, that might break his sleep; but God, *whose gift sleep is,* withheld it from him. Those that are ever so much resolved to cast away care cannot always do it; they find it in their pillows when they neither expect nor welcome it. He that commanded 127 provinces could not command one hour's sleep. Perhaps the charms of Esther's conversation the day before gave occasion to his heart to reproach him for neglecting her, and banishing her from his presence, though she was the wife of his bosom, for above thirty days; and that might keep him waking. An offended conscience can find a time to speak when it will be heard.

II. When he could not sleep he called to have the book of records, the Journals of his reign, read to him, *v.* 1. Surely he did not design that that should lull him asleep; it would rather fill his head with cares, and drive away sleep. But God put it into his heart to call for it, rather than for music or songs, which the Persian kings used to be attended with (Dan. vi. 18) and which would have been more likely to compose him to rest. When men do that which is unaccountable we know not what God intends by it. Perhaps he would have this book of business read to him that he might improve time and be forming some useful projects. Had it been king David's case, he would have found some other entertainment for his thoughts; when he could not sleep he would have remembered God and meditated upon him (Ps. lxiv. 6), and, if he would have had any book read to him, it would have been his Bible; for *in that law did he meditate day and night.*

III. The servant that read to him either lighted first on that article which concerned Mordecai, or, reading long, came to it at length. Among other things it was found written that Mordecai had discovered a plot against the life of the king which prevented the execution of it, *v.* 2. Mordecai was not in such favour at court that the reader should designedly pitch upon that place; but Providence directed him to it; nay, if we may believe the Jews' tradition (as bishop Patrick relates it), opening the book at this place he turned over the leaves, and would have read another part of the book, but the leaves flew back again to the same place where he opened it; so that he was forced to read that paragraph. How Mordecai's good service was recorded we read *ch.* ii. 23, and here it is found upon record.

IV. The king enquired *what honour and dignity had been done to Mordecai* for this, suspecting that this good service had gone unrewarded, and, like Pharaoh's butler, remembering it as *his fault this day,* Gen. xli. 9. Note, The law of gratitude is a law of nature. We ought particularly to be grateful to our inferiors, and not to think all their services such debts to us but that they make us indebted to them. Two rules of gratitude may be gathered from the king's enquiry here:—1. Better honour than nothing. If we cannot, or need not, make a recompence to those who have been kind to us, yet let us do them honour by acknowledging their kindnesses and owning our obligations to them. 2. Better late than never. If we have long neglected to make grateful returns for good offices done us, let us at length bethink ourselves of our debts.

V. The servants informed him that nothing

had been done to Mordecai for that eminent service; in the king's gate he sat before, and there he still sat. Note, 1. It is common for great men to take little notice of their inferiors. The king knew not whether Mordecai was preferred or no till his servants informed him. High spirits take a pride in being careless and unconcerned about those that are below them and ignorant of their state. The great God takes cognizance of the meanest of his servants, knows what dignity is done them and what disgrace. 2. Humility, modesty, and self-denial, though in God's account of great price, yet commonly hinder men's preferment in the world. Mordecai rises no higher than the king's gate, while proud ambitious Haman gets the king's ear and heart; but, though the aspiring rise fast, the humble stand fast. Honour makes proud men giddy, but *upholds the humble in spirit,* Prov. xxix. 23. 3. Honour and dignity are rated high in the king's books. He does not ask, What reward has been given Mordecai? what money? what estate? but only, What honour?—a poor thing, and which, if he had not wherewith to support it, would be but a burden. 4. The greatest merits and the best services are often overlooked and go unrewarded among men. Little honour is done to those who best deserve it, are fittest for it, and would do most good with it. See Eccl. ix. 14—16. The acquisition of wealth and honour is usually a perfect lottery, in which those that venture least commonly carry off the best prize. Nay, 5. Good services are sometimes so far from being a man's preferment that they will not be his protection. Mordecai is at this time, by the king's edict, doomed to destruction, with all the Jews, though it is owned that he deserved dignity. Those that faithfully serve God need not fear being thus ill paid.

4 And the king said, Who *is* in the court? Now Haman was come into the outward court of the king's house, to speak unto the king to hang Mordecai on the gallows that he had prepared for him. 5 And the king's servants said unto him, Behold, Haman standeth in the court. And the king said, Let him come in. 6 So Haman came in. And the king said unto him, What shall be done unto the man whom the king delighteth to honour? Now Haman thought in his heart, To whom would the king delight to do honour more than to myself? 7 And Haman answered the king, For the man whom the king delighteth to honour, 8 Let the royal apparel be brought which the king *useth* to wear, and the horse that the king rideth upon, and the crown royal which is set upon his head: 9 And let this apparel and horse be delivered to the hand of one of the king's most noble princes, that they may array the man *withal* whom the king delighteth to honour, and bring him on horseback through the street of the city, and proclaim before him, Thus shall it be done to the man whom the king delighteth to honour. 10 Then the king said to Haman, Make haste, *and* take the apparel and the horse, as thou hast said, and do even so to Mordecai the Jew, that sitteth at the king's gate: let nothing fail of all that thou hast spoken. 11 Then took Haman the apparel and the horse, and arrayed Mordecai, and brought him on horseback through the street of the city, and proclaimed before him, Thus shall it be done unto the man whom the king delighteth to honour.

It is now morning, and people begin to stir.

I. Haman is so impatient to get Mordecai hanged that he comes early to court, to be ready at the king's levee, before any other business is brought before him, to get a warrant for his execution (*v.* 4), which he makes sure that he shall have at the first word. The king would gratify him in a greater thing than that; and he could tell the king that he was so confident of the justice of his request, and the king's favour to him in it, that he had got the gallows ready: one word from the king would complete his satisfaction.

II. The king is so impatient to have Mordecai honoured that he sends to know who is in the court that is fit to be employed in it. Word is brought him that Haman is in the court, *v.* 5. *Let him come in,* says the king, the fittest man to be made use of both in directing and in dispensing the king's favour; and the king knew nothing of any quarrel he had with Mordecai. Haman is brought in immediately, proud of the honour done him in being admitted into the king's bed-chamber, as it should seem, *before he was up;* for let the king but give orders for the dignifying of Mordecai, and he will be easy in his mind and try to sleep. Now Haman thinks he has the fairest opportunity he can wish for to solicit against Mordecai; but the king's heart is as full as his, and it is fit he should speak first.

III. The king asks Haman how he should express his favour to one whom he had marked for a favourite: *What shall be done to the man whom the king delights to honour?* *v.* 6. Note, It is a good property in kings, and other superiors, to delight in bestowing rewards and not to delight in punishing. Parents and masters should take a pleasure in commending and encouraging that which is good in those under their charge.

IV. Haman concludes that he himself is the favourite intended, and therefore prescribes the highest expressions of honour that could, for once, be bestowed upon a subject. His proud heart presently suggested, "To whom will the king delight to do honour more than to myself? No one deserves it so well as I," thinks Haman, "nor stands so fair for it." See how men's pride deceives them. 1. Haman had a better opinion of his merits than there was cause for: he thought none so worthy of honour as himself. It is a foolish thing for us thus to think ourselves the only deserving persons, or more deserving than any other. The deceitfulness of our own hearts appears in nothing so much as in the good conceit we have of ourselves and our own performances, against which we should therefore constantly watch and pray. 2. He had a better opinion of his interest than there was reason for. He thought the king loved and valued no one but himself, but he was deceived. We should suspect that the esteem which others profess for us is not so great as it seems to be or as we are sometimes willing to believe it is, that we may not think too well of ourselves nor place too much confidence in others. Now Haman thinks he is carving out honour for himself, and therefore does it very liberally, *v.* 8, 9. Nay, he does it presumptuously, prescribing honours too great to be conferred upon any subject, that he must be dressed in the royal robes, wear the royal crown, and ride on the king's own horse; in short, he must appear in all the pomp and grandeur of the king himself, only he must not carry the sceptre, the emblem of power. He must be attended by one of *the king's most noble princes,* who must be his lacquey, and all the people must be made to take notice of him and do him reverence; for he must ride in state through the streets, and it must be *proclaimed before him,* for his honour, and the encouragement of all to seek the ruler's favour, *Thus shall it be done to the man whom the king delights to honour,* which had the same intention with that which was proclaimed before Joseph, *Bow the knee;* for every good subject will honour those whom the king delights to honour. And shall not every good Christian then honour those whom the King of kings delights to honour and call the *saints that are on the earth the excellent ones?*

V. The king confounds him with a positive order that he should immediately go himself and put all this honour upon Mordecai the Jew, *v.* 10. If the king had but said, as Haman expected, *Thou art the man,* what a fair opportunity would he have had to do the errand he came on, and to desire that, to grace the solemnity of his triumphs, Mordecai, his sworn enemy, might be hanged at the same time! But how is he thunderstruck when the king bids him not to order all this to be done, but to do it himself to Mordecai the Jew, the very man he hated above all men and whose ruin he was now designing! Now, it is to no purpose to think of moving any thing to the king against Mordecai when he is *the man whom the king delights to honour.* Solomon says, *The heart of the king is unsearchable* (Prov. xxv. 3), but it is not unchangeable.

VI. Haman dares not dispute nor so much as seem to dislike the king's order, but, with the greatest regret and reluctance imaginable, brings it to Mordecai, who I suppose did no more cringe to Haman now than he had done, valuing his counterfeit respect no more than he had valued his concealed malice. The apparel is brought, Mordecai is dressed up, and rides in state through the city, recognized as the king's favourite, *v.* 11. It is hard to say which of the two put a greater force upon himself, proud Haman in putting this honour upon Mordecai, or humble Mordecai in accepting it: the king would have it so, and both must submit. Upon *this* account it was agreeable to Mordecai as it was an indication of the king's favour, and gave hope that Esther would prevail for the reversing of the edict against the Jews.

12 And Mordecai came again to the king's gate. But Haman hasted to his house mourning, and having his head covered. 13 And Haman told Zeresh his wife and all his friends every *thing* that had befallen him. Then said his wise men and Zeresh his wife unto him, If Mordecai *be* of the seed of the Jews, before whom thou hast begun to fall, thou shalt not prevail against him, but shalt surely fall before him. 14 And while they *were* yet talking with him, came the king's chamberlains, and hasted to bring Haman unto the banquet that Esther had prepared.

We may here observe,

I. How little Mordecai was puffed up with his advancement. He *came again to the king's gate* (*v.* 12); he returned to his place and the duty of it immediately, and minded his business as closely as he had done before. Honour is well bestowed on those that are not made proud and idle by it, and will not think themselves above their business.

II. How much Haman was cast down with his disappointment. He could not bear it. To wait upon any man, especially Mordecai, and at this time, when he hoped to have seen him hanged, was enough to break such a proud heart as he had. He *hasted to his house mourning, and having his head covered,* as one that looked upon himself as sunk and in a manner condemned. What harm had it done him to stoop thus to Mordecai? Was he ever the worse for it? Was it not what he himself proposed to be done by *one of the king's most noble princes?* Why then should he grudge to do it himself? But that will break a proud man's heart which would not break a humble man's sleep.

III. How his doom was, out of this event, read to him by his wife and his friends: "If Mordecai be, as they say he is, *of the seed of the Jews, before whom thou hast begun to fall,* though but in a point of honour, never expect to *prevail against him;* for thou *shalt surely fall before him,*" *v.* 13. Miserable comforters were they all; they did not advise him to repent, and ask Mordecai's pardon for his bad design against him, but foretold his destiny as fatal and unavoidable. Two things they foresaw:—1. That Haman would be disappointed in his enterprise against the Jews: "*Thou shalt not prevail* to root out that people. Heaven plainly fights against thee." 2. That he himself would be destroyed: *Thou shalt surely fall before him.* The contest between Michael and the dragon will not be a drawn battle; no, Haman must fall before Mordecai. Two things they grounded their prognostications upon:—(1.) This Mordecai was *of the seed of the Jews; feeble Jews* their enemies sometimes called them, but formidable Jews they sometimes found them. They are a holy seed, a praying seed, in covenant with God, and a seed that the Lord hath all along blessed, and therefore let not their enemies expect to triumph over them. (2.) Haman had begun to fall, and therefore he was certainly a gone man. It has been observed of great court-favourites that when once they have been frowned upon they have fallen utterly, as fast as they rose; it is true of the church's enemies that when God begins with them he will make an end. As for God his work is perfect.

IV. How seasonably he was now sent for to the banquet that Esther had prepared, *v.* 14. He thought it seasonable, in hopes it would revive his drooping spirits and save his sinking honour. But really it was seasonable because, his spirits being broken by this sore disappointment, he might the more easily be run down by Esther's complaints against him. The wisdom of God is seen in timing the means of his church's deliverance so as to manifest his own glory.

CHAP. VII.

We are now to attend the second banquet to which the king and Haman were invited: and there, I. Esther presents her petition to the king for her life and the life of her people, ver. 1—4. II. She plainly tells the king that Haman is the man who designed her ruin and the ruin of all her friends, ver. 5, 6. III. The king thereupon gave orders for the hanging of Haman upon the gallows that he had prepared for Mordecai, which was done accordingly, ver. 7—10. And thus, by the destruction of the plotter, a good step was taken towards the defeating of the plot.

SO the king and Haman came to banquet with Esther the queen. 2 And the king said again unto Esther on the second day at the banquet of wine, What *is* thy petition, queen Esther? and it shall be granted thee: and what *is* thy request? and it shall be performed, *even* to the half of the kingdom. 3 Then Esther the queen answered and said, If I have found favour in thy sight, O king, and if it please the king, let my life be given me at my petition, and my people at my request: 4 For we are sold, I and my people, to be destroyed, to be slain, and to perish. But if we had been sold for bondmen and bondwomen, I had held my tongue, although the enemy could not countervail the king's damage. 5 Then the king Ahasuerus answered and said unto Esther the queen, Who is he, and where is he, that durst presume in his heart to do so? 6 And Esther said, The adversary and enemy *is* this wicked Haman. Then Haman was afraid before the king and the queen.

The king in humour, and Haman out of humour, meet at Esther's table. Now,

I. The king urged Esther, a third time, to tell him what her request was, for he longed to know, and repeated his promise that it should be granted, *v.* 2. If the king had now forgotten that Esther had an errand to him, and had not again asked what it was, she could scarcely have known how to renew it herself; but he was mindful of it, and now was bound with the threefold cord of a promise thrice made to favour her.

II. Esther, at length, surprises the king with a petition, not for wealth or honour, or the preferment of some of her friends to some high post, which the king expected, but for the preservation of herself and her countrymen from death and destruction, *v.* 3, 4.

1. Even a stranger, a criminal, shall be permitted to petition for his life; but that a friend, a wife, should have occasion to present such a petition was very affecting: *Let my life be given me at my petition, and my people at my request.* Two things bespeak lives to be very precious, and fit to be saved, if innocent, at any expense:—(1.) Majesty. If it be a crowned head that is struck at, it is time to stir. Esther's was such: "*Let my life be given me.* If thou hast any affection for the wife of thy bosom, now is the time to show it; for that is the life that lies at stake." (2.) Multitude. If they be many lives, very many, and those no way forfeited, that are aimed at, no time should be lost nor pains

spared to prevent the mischief. "It is not a friend or two, but *my people*, a whole nation, and a nation dear to me, for the saving of which I now intercede."

2. To move the king the more she suggests, (1.) That she and her people were bought and sold. They had not sold themselves by any offence against the government, but were sold to gratify the pride and revenge of one man. (2.) That it was not their liberty only, but their lives that were sold. "Had we been sold" (says she) "into slavery, I would not have complained; for in time we might have recovered our liberty, though the king would have made but a bad bargain of it, and not have increased his wealth by our price. Whatever had been paid for us, the loss of so many industrious hands out of his kingdom would have been more damage to the treasury than the price would countervail." To persecute good people is as impolitic as it is impious, and a manifest wrong to the interests of princes and states; they are weakened and impoverished by it. But this was not the case. *We are sold* (says she) *to be destroyed, to be slain, and to perish;* and then it is time to speak. She refers to the words of the decree (*ch.* iii. 13), which aimed at nothing short of their destruction; this would touch in a tender part if there were any such in the king's heart, and would bring him to relent.

III. The king stands amazed at the remonstrance, and asks (*v.* 5), "*Who is he, and where is he, that durst presume in his heart to do so?* What! contrive the murder of the queen and all her friends? Is there such a man, such a monster rather, in nature? *Who is he, and where is he, whose heart has filled him to do so?*" Or, Who hath *filled his heart.* He wonders, 1. That any one should be so bad as to think such a thing; Satan certainly filled his heart. 2. That any one should be so bold as to do such a thing, should have his heart so fully set in him to do wickedly, should be so very daring. Note, (1.) It is hard to imagine that there should be such horrid wickedness committed in the world as really there is. Who, where is he, that dares, presumes, to question the being of God and his providence, to banter his oracles, profane his name, persecute his people, and yet bid defiance to his wrath? Such there are, to think of whom is enough to make *horror take hold of us,* Ps. cxix. 53. (2.) We sometimes startle at the mention of that evil which yet we ourselves are chargeable with. Ahasuerus is amazed at that wickedness which he himself was guilty of; for he consented to that bloody edict against the Jews. *Thou art the man,* might Esther too truly have said.

IV. Esther plainly charges Haman with it before his face: "Here he is, let him speak for himself, for therefore he is invited: *The adversary and enemy is this wicked Haman* (*v.* 6); it is he that has designed our murder, and, which is worse, has basely drawn the king in to be *particeps criminis—a partaker of his crime,* ignorantly agreeing to it."

V. Haman is soon apprehensive of his danger: *He was afraid before the king and queen;* and it was time for him to fear when the queen was his prosecutor, the king his judge, and his own conscience a witness against him; and the surprising operations of Providence against him that same morning could not but increase his fear. Now he has little joy of his being invited to the banquet of wine, but finds himself in straits when he thought himself *in the fulness of his sufficiency. He is cast into a net by his own feet.*

7 And the king arising from the banquet of wine in his wrath *went* into the palace garden: and Haman stood up to make request for his life to Esther the queen; for he saw that there was evil determined against him by the king. 8 Then the king returned out of the palace garden into the place of the banquet of wine; and Haman was fallen upon the bed whereon Esther *was.* Then said the king, Will he force the queen also before me in the house? As the word went out of the king's mouth, they covered Haman's face. 9 And Harbonah, one of the chamberlains, said before the king, Behold also, the gallows fifty cubits high, which Haman had made for Mordecai, who had spoken good for the king, standeth in the house of Haman. Then the king said, Hang him thereon. 10 So they hanged Haman on the gallows that he had prepared for Mordecai. Then was the king's wrath pacified.

Here, I. The king retires in anger. He rose from table in a great passion, and *went into the palace garden* to cool himself and to consider what was to be done, *v.* 7. He sent not for his *seven wise counsellors who knew the times,* being ashamed to consult them about the undoing of that which he had rashly done without their knowledge or advice; but he went to walk in the garden awhile, to compare in his thoughts what Esther had now informed him of with what had formerly passed between him and Haman. And we may suppose him, 1. Vexed at himself, that he should be such a fool as to doom a guiltless nation to destruction, and his own queen among the rest, upon the base suggestions of a self-seeking man, without examining the truth of his allegations. Those that do things with self-will reflect upon them afterwards with self-reproach. 2. Vexed at Haman whom he had laid in his bosom, that he should be such a villain as to abuse his interest in him to draw him to consent to so wicked a measure. When he saw himself betrayed by one he had caressed he was full of indignation at him; yet he would say nothing till he had taken time for second thoughts, to see whether they would make the matter better or worse than it first appeared, that he might proceed accordingly. When we are angry we should pause awhile before we come to any resolution, as those that have a *rule over our own spirits* and are governed by reason.

II. Haman becomes a humble petitioner to the queen for his life. He might easily perceive by the king's hastily flying out of the room that *there was evil determined against him.* For *the wrath of a king*, such a king, *is as the roaring of a lion* and as *messengers of death;* and now see, 1. How mean Haman looks, when he stands up first and then falls down at Esther's feet, to beg she would save his life and take all he had. Those that are most haughty, insolent, and imperious, when they are in power and prosperity, are commonly the most abject and poor-spirited when the wheel turns upon them. Cowards, they say, are most cruel, and then consciousness of their cruelty makes them the more cowardly. 2. How great Esther looks, who of late had been neglected and doomed to the slaughter *tanquam ovis—as a sheep;* now her sworn enemy owns that he lies at her mercy, and begs his life at her hand. Thus did God *regard the low estate of his handmaiden* and *scatter the proud in the imagination of their hearts,* Luke i. 48, 51. Compare with this that promise made to the Philadelphian church (Rev. iii. 9), *I will make those of the synagogue of Satan to come and to worship before thy feet and to know that I have loved thee.* The day is coming when those that hate and persecute God's chosen ones would gladly be beholden to them. *Give us of your oil. Father Abraham, send Lazarus. The upright shall have dominion in the morning.*

III. The king returns yet more exasperated against Haman. The more he thinks of him the worse he thinks of him and of what he had done. It was but lately that every thing Haman said and did, even that which was most criminal, was taken well and construed to his advantage; now, on the contrary, what Haman did that was not only innocent, but a sign of repentance, is ill taken, and, without colour of reason, construed to his disadvantage. He lay in terror at Esther's feet, to beg for his life. What! (says the king) *will he force the queen also before me in the house?* Not that he thought he had any such intention, but having been musing on Haman's design to slay the queen, and finding him in this posture, he takes occasion from it thus to vent his passion against Haman, as a man that would not scruple at the greatest and most impudent piece of wickedness. "He designed to slay the queen, and to slay her *with me in the house;* will he in like manner force her? What! ravish her first and then murder her? He that had a design upon her life may well be suspected to have a design upon her chastity.'

IV. Those about him were ready to be the instruments of his wrath. The courtiers that adored Haman when he was the rising sun set themselves as much against him now that he is a falling star, and are even glad of an occasion to run him down: so little sure can proud men be of the interest they think they have. 1. As soon as the king spoke an angry word *they covered Haman's face,* as a condemned man, not worthy any more either to see the king or to be seen by him; they marked him for execution. Those that are hanged commonly have their faces covered. See how ready the servants were to take the first hint of the king's mind in this matter. *Turba Romæ sequitur fortunam, ut semper et odit damnatos—The Roman populace change as the aspects of fortune do, and always oppress the fallen.* If Haman be going down, they all cry, "Down with him." 2. One of those that had been lately sent to Haman's house, to fetch him to the banquet, informed the king of the gallows which Haman had prepared for Mordecai, *v.* 9. Now that Mordecai is the favourite the chamberlain applauds him—he *spoke good for the king;* and, Haman being in disgrace, every thing is taken notice of that might make against him, incense the king against him, and fill up the measure of his iniquity.

V. The king gave orders that he should be hanged upon his own gallows, which was done accordingly, nor was he so much as asked what he had to say why this judgment should not be passed upon him and execution awarded. The sentence is short—*Hang him thereon;* and the execution speedy—*So they hanged Haman on the gallows, v.* 10. See here, 1. Pride brought down. He that expected every one to do him homage is now made an ignominious spectacle to the world, and he himself sacrificed to justice who disdained that less than a whole nation should be sacrificed to his revenge. God resists the proud; and those whom he resists will find him irresistible. 2. Persecution punished. Haman was upon many accounts a wicked man, but his enmity to God's church was his most provoking crime, and for *that* the God to whom vengeance belongs here reckons with him, and, though his plot was defeated, gives him *according to the wickedness of his endeavours,* Ps. xxviii. 4. 3. Mischief returned upon the person himself that contrived it, the *wicked snared in the work of his own hands,* Ps. vii. 15, 16; ix. 15, 16. Haman was justly hanged on the very gallows he had unjustly prepared for Mordecai. If he had not set up that gallows, perhaps the king would not have thought of ordering him to be hanged; but, if he rear a gallows for *the man whom the king delights to honour,* the thought is very natural that he should be ordered to try it himself, and see how it fits him, see how he likes it. The enemies of God's church have often been thus taken in their own craftiness. In the morning Haman was designing himself for the robes and Mordecai for the gallows; but the tables are turned: Mordecai has the crown, Haman the cross. *The Lord is known by such judgments.* See Prov. xi. 8; xxi. 18.

Lastly, The satisfaction which the king had in this execution. *Then was the king's wrath pacified,* and not till then. He was as well pleased in ordering Haman to be hanged as in ordering Mordecai to be honoured. Thus shall it be done to the man whom the king delights to take vengeance on. God saith of wicked men (Ezek. v. 13), *I will cause my fury to rest upon them, and I will be comforted.*

CHAP. VIII.

We left the plotter hanging, and are now to see what becomes of his plot. I. His plot was to raise an estate for himself; and all his estate, being confiscated for treason, is given to Esther and Mordecai, ver. 1, 2. II. His plot was to ruin the Jews; and as to that, 1. Esther earnestly intercedes for the reversing of the edict against them, ver. 3–6. 2. It is in effect done by another edict, here published, empowering the Jews to stand up in their own defence against their enemies, ver. 7–14. III. This occasions great joy to the Jews and all their friends, ver. 15–17.

ON that day did the king Ahasuerus give the house of Haman the Jews' enemy unto Esther the queen. And Mordecai came before the king; for Esther had told what he *was* unto her. 2 And the king took off his ring, which he had taken from Haman, and gave it unto Mordecai. And Esther set Mordecai over the house of Haman.

It was but lately that we had Esther and Mordecai in tears and in fears, but fasting and praying; now let us see how to them there arose light in darkness. Here is, 1. Esther enriched. Haman was hanged as a traitor, therefore his estate was forfeited to the crown, and the king gave it all to Esther, in recompence for the fright that wicked man had put her into and the vexation he had created her, *v.* 1. His houses and lands, goods and chattels, and all the money he had heaped up while he was prime-minister of state (which, we may suppose, was no little), are given to Esther; they are all her own, added to the allowance she already had. Thus is *the wealth of the sinner laid up for the just,* and the *innocent divides the silver,* Prov. xiii. 22; Job xxvii. 17, 18. What Haman would have done mischief with Esther will do good with; and estate are to be valued as they are used. 2. Mordecai advanced. His pompous procession, this morning, through the streets of the city, was but a sudden flash or blaze of honour; but here we have the more durable and gainful preferments to which he was raised, which yet the other happily made way for. (1.) He is now owned as the queen's cousin, which till now, though Esther had been four years queen, for aught that appears, the king did not know. So humble, so modest, a man was Mordecai, and so far from being ambitious of a place at court, that he concealed his relation to the queen and her obligations to him as her guardian, and never made use of her interest for any advantage of his own. Who but Mordecai could have taken so little notice of so great an honour? But now he was brought *before the king,* introduced, as we say, to kiss his hand; for now, at length, *Esther had told what he was to her,* not only near a-kin to her, but the best friend she had in the world, who took care of her when she was an orphan, and one whom she still respected as a father. Now the king finds himself, for his wife's sake, more obliged than he thought he had been to delight in doing honour to Mordecai. How great were the merits of that man to whom both king and queen did in effect owe their lives! Being brought before the king, to him no doubt he bowed, and did reverence, though he would not to Haman an Amalekite. (2.) The king makes him lord privy-seal in the room of Haman. All the trust he had reposed in Haman, and all the power he had given him, are here transferred to Mordecai; for the ring which he had taken from Haman he gave to Mordecai, and made this trusty humble man as much his favourite, his confidant, and his agent, as ever that proud perfidious wretch was; a happy change he made of his bosom-friends, and so, no doubt, he and his people soon found it. (3.) The queen makes him her steward, for the management of Haman's estate, and for getting and keeping possession of it: *She set Mordecai over the house of Haman.* See the vanity of laying up treasure upon earth; he that *heapeth up riches knoweth not who shall gather them* (Ps. xxxix. 6), not only *whether he shall be a wise man or a fool* (Eccl. ii. 19), but whether he shall be a friend or an enemy. With what little pleasure, nay, with what constant vexation, would Haman have looked upon his estate if he could have foreseen that Mordecai, the man he hated above all men in the world, should have *rule over all that wherein he had laboured,* and thought that he showed himself wise! It is our interest, therefore, to make sure those riches which will not be left behind, but will go with us to another world.

3 And Esther spake yet again before the king, and fell down at his feet, and besought him with tears to put away the mischief of Haman the Agagite, and his device that he had devised against the Jews. 4 Then the king held out the golden sceptre toward Esther. So Esther arose, and stood before the king, 5 And said, If it please the king, and if I have

found favour in his sight, and the thing *seem* right before the king, and I *be* pleasing in his eyes, let it be written to reverse the letters devised by Haman the son of Hammedatha the Agagite, which he wrote to destroy the Jews which *are* in all the king's provinces: 6 For how can I endure to see the evil that shall come unto my people? or how can I endure to see the destruction of my kindred? 7 Then the king Ahasuerus said unto Esther the queen and to Mordecai the Jew, Behold, I have given Esther the house of Haman, and him they have hanged upon the gallows, because he laid his hand upon the Jews. 8 Write ye also for the Jews, as it liketh you, in the king's name, and seal *it* with the king's ring: for the writing which is written in the king's name, and sealed with the king's ring, may no man reverse. 9 Then were the king's scribes called at that time in the third month, that *is*, the month Sivan, on the three and twentieth *day* thereof; and it was written according to all that Mordecai commanded unto the Jews, and to the lieutenants, and the deputies and rulers of the provinces which *are* from India unto Ethiopia, a hundred twenty and seven provinces, unto every province according to the writing thereof, and unto every people after their language, and to the Jews according to their writing, and according to their language. 10 And he wrote in the king Ahasuerus' name, and sealed *it* with the king's ring, and sent letters by posts on horseback, *and* riders on mules, camels, *and* young dromedaries: 11 Wherein the king granted the Jews which *were* in every city to gather themselves together, and to stand for their life, to destroy, to slay, and to cause to perish, all the power of the people and province that would assault them, *both* little ones and women, and *to take* the spoil of them for a prey, 12 Upon one day in all the provinces of king Ahasuerus, *namely*, upon the thirteenth *day* of the twelfth month, which *is* the month Adar. 13 The copy of the writing for a commandment to be given in every province *was* published unto all people, and that the Jews should be ready against that day to avenge themselves on their enemies. 14 So the posts that rode upon mules *and* camels went out, being hastened and pressed on by the king's commandment. And the decree was given at Shushan the palace.

Haman, the chief enemy of the Jews, was hanged, Mordecai and Esther, their chief friends, were sufficiently protected; but many others there were in the king's dominions that hated the Jews and desired their ruin, and to their rage and malice all the rest of that people lay exposed; for the edict against them was still in force, and, in pursuance of it, their enemies would on the day appointed fall upon them, and they would be deemed as rebels against the king and his government if they should offer to resist and take up arms in their own defence. For the preventing of this,

I. The queen here makes intercession with much affection and importunity. She came, a second time, uncalled into the king's presence (*v.* 3), and was as before encouraged to present her petition, by the king's holding out the golden sceptre to her, *v.* 4. Her petition is that the king, having put away Haman, would put away the mischief of Haman and his device against the Jews, that that might not take place now that he was taken off. Many a man's mischief survives him, and the wickedness he devised operates when he is gone. What men project and write may, after their death, be either very profitable or very pernicious. It was therefore requisite in this case that, for the defeating of Haman's plot, they should apply to the king for a further act of grace, that by another edict he would reverse the letters devised by Haman, and which he wrote (she does not say which the king *consented to and confirmed with his own seal;* she leaves it to his own conscience to say that), by which he took an effectual course to *destroy the Jews in all the king's provinces, v.* 5. If the king were indeed, as he seemed to be, troubled that such a decree was made, he could not do less than revoke it; for what is repentance, but undoing, to the utmost of our power, what we have done amiss? 1. This petition Esther presents with much affection: She *fell down at the king's feet and besought him with tears* (*v.* 3), every tear as precious as any of the pearls with which she was adorned. It was time to be earnest when the church of God lay at stake. Let none be so great as to be unwilling to stoop, none so merry as to be unwilling to weep, when thereby they may do any service to God's church and people. Esther, though safe herself, fell down, and begged with tears for the deliverance of her people. 2. She expresses it with great submission, and a profound deference to the king and his wisdom and will (*v.* 5): *If it please the king and if I have found favour in his sight*—and again, "If the thing itself seem right and reasonable before the king, and if I that ask it *be pleasing in his eyes,* let the decree be reversed." Even when we have the utmost reason and justice on our side, and have the clearest cause to plead, yet it becomes us to speak to our superiors with humility and modesty, and all possible expressions of respect, and not to talk like demandants when we are supplicants. There is nothing lost by decency and good breeding. As *soft answers turn away wrath,* so soft askings obtain favour. 3. She enforces her petition with a pathetic plea: "*For how can I endure to see the evil that shall come upon my people?* Little comfort can I have of my own life if I cannot prevail for theirs: as good share in the evil myself as see it come upon them; for *how can I endure to see the destruction of my kindred,* that are dear to me?" Esther, a queen, owns her poor kindred, and speaks of them with a very tender concern. Now it was that she mingled her tears with her words, that *she wept and made supplication;* we read of no tears when she begged for her own life, but, now that she was sure of that, she wept for her people. Tears of pity and tenderness are the most Christ-like. Those that are truly concerned for the public would rather die in the last ditch than live to see the desolations of the church of God and the ruin of their country. Tender spirits cannot bear to think of the destruction of their people and kindred, and therefore dare not omit any opportunity of giving them relief.

II. The king here takes a course for the preventing of the mischief that Haman had designed. 1. The king knew, and informed the queen, that, according to the constitution of the Persian government, the former edict could not be revoked (*v.* 8): What is *written in the king's name, and sealed with the king's ring,* may not, under any pretence whatsoever, be reversed. This was a fundamental article of their *magna charta,* that no law or decree, when once it had passed the royal assent, could be repealed or recalled, no judgment vacated, no attainder reversed, Dan. vi. 15. This is so far from bespeaking the wisdom and honour of the Medes and Persians that really it bespeaks their pride and folly, and consequently their shame. It is ridiculous in itself for any man, or company of men, to pretend to such an infallibility of wisdom as to foresee all the consequences of what they decree; and therefore it is unjust, and injurious to mankind, to claim such a supremacy of power as to make their decrees irrevocable, whether the consequences prove good or bad. This savours of that old presumption which ruined us all: *We will be as gods.* Much more prudent is that proviso of our constitution, that no law can, by any words or sanctions whatsoever, be made unrepealable, any more than any estate unalienable. *Cujus est instruere, ejus est destruere—the right to enact implies the right to repeal.* It is God's prerogative not to repent, and to say what can never be altered or unsaid. 2. Yet he found an expedient to undo the devices of Haman, and defeat his design, by signing and publishing another decree to authorize the Jews to stand upon their defence, *vim vi repellere, et invasorem occidere—to oppose force to force, and destroy the assailant.* This would be their effectual security. The king shows them that he had done enough already to convince them that he had a concern for the Jewish nation, for he had ordered his favourite to be hanged *because he laid his hand upon the Jews* (*v.* 7), and he therefore would do the utmost he could to protect them; and he leaves it as fully with Esther and Mordecai to use his name and power for their deliverance as before he had left it with Haman to use his name and power for their destruction: "*Write for the Jews as it liketh you* (*v.* 8), saving only the honour of our constitution. Let the mischief be put away as effectually as may be without reversing the letters." The secretaries of state were ordered to attend to draw up this edict on the twenty-third day of the third month (*v.* 9), about two months after the promulgation of the former, but nine months before the time set for its execution: it was to be drawn up and published in the respective languages of all the provinces. Shall the subjects of an earthly prince have his decrees in a language they understand? and shall God's oracles and laws be locked up from his servants in an unknown tongue? It was to be directed to the proper officers of every province, both to the justices of peace and to the deputy-lieutenants. It was to be carefully dispersed throughout all the king's dominions, and true copies sent by expresses to all the provinces. The purport of this decree was to commission the Jews, upon the day which was appointed for their destruction, to draw together in a body for their own defence. And, (1.) To stand for their life, that, whoever assaulted them, it might be at their peril. (2.) They might not only act defensively, but might *destroy, and slay, and cause to perish, all the power of the people that would assault them, men, women, and children* (*v.* 11), and thus *to avenge themselves on their enemies* (*v.* 13), and, if they pleased, to enrich themselves by their enemies, for they were empowered to take the spoil of them for a prey. Now, [1.] This showed his kindness to the Jews, and sufficiently provided for their safety; for the latter decree would be looked upon as a tacit revocation of the former, though not in expression. But, [2.] It shows the absurdity of that branch of their constitution that none of the king's edicts might be repealed; for it laid the king here under a necessity of enacting a civil war in his own dominions, between the Jews and their enemies, so that both sides took up arms *by* his authority, and yet *against* his authority. No better could come of men's pretending to be wise above what is given them. Great expedition was used in dispersing this decree, the king himself being in pain lest it should come too late and any mischief should be done to the Jews by virtue of the former decree before the notice of this arrived. It was therefore *by the king's commandment,* as well as Mordecai's, that the messengers were *hastened and pressed on* (*v.* 14), and had swift beasts provided them, *v.* 10. It was not a time to trifle when so many lives were in danger.

15 And Mordecai went out from the presence of the king in royal apparel of blue and white, and with a great crown of gold, and with a garment of fine linen and purple: and the city of Shushan rejoiced and was glad. 16 The Jews had light, and gladness, and joy, and honour. 17 And in every province, and in every city, whithersoever the king's commandment and his decree came, the Jews had joy and gladness, a feast and a good day. And many of the people of the land became Jews; for the fear of the Jews fell upon them.

It was but a few days ago that we had Mordecai in sackcloth and all the Jews in sorrow; but here is a blessed change, Mordecai in purple and all the Jews in joy. See Ps. xxx. 5, 11, 12. 1. Mordecai in purple, *v.* 15. Having obtained an order for the relief of all the Jews, he was easy, he parted with his mourning weeds, and put on the *royal apparel,* which either belonged to his place or which the king appointed him as a favourite. His robes were rich, *blue and white, of fine linen and purple;* so was his coronet: it was *of gold.* These are things not worth taking notice of, but as they were marks of the king's favour, and *that* the fruit of God's favour to his church. It is well with a land when the ensigns of dignity are made the ornaments of serious piety. The *city Shushan* was sensible of its advantage in the preferment of Mordecai, and therefore *rejoiced and was glad,* not only pleased in general with the advancement of virtue, but promising itself, in particular, better times, now that so good a man was entrusted with power. Haman was hanged; *and, when the wicked perish, there is shouting,* Prov. xi. 10. Mordecai was preferred; and, *when the righteous are in authority, the people rejoice.* 2. The Jews in joy, *v.* 16, 17. The Jews, who awhile ago were under a dark cloud, dejected and disgraced, now had *light and gladness, joy and honour, a feast and a good day.* If they had not been threatened and in distress they would not have had occasion for this extraordinary joy. Thus are God's people sometimes made *to sow in tears* that they may *reap in* so much the more *joy.* The suddenness and strangeness of the turn of affairs in their favour added much to their joy. They were *like those that dream; then was their mouth filled with laughter,* Ps. cxxvi. 1, 2. One good effect of this deliverance was that *many of the people of the land,* that were considerate, sober, and well inclined, became Jews, were proselyted to the Jewish religion, renounced idolatry, and worshipped the true God only. Haman thought to extirpate the Jews, but it proves, in the issue, that their numbers are greatly increased and many added to the church. Observe, When *the Jews had joy and gladness* then *many of the people of the land became Jews.* The holy cheerfulness of those that profess religion is a great ornament to their profession, and will invite and encourage others to be religious. The reason here given why so many became Jews at this time is because *the fear of the Jews fell upon them.* When they observed how wonderfully divine Providence had owned them and wrought for them in this critical juncture, (1.) They thought them great, and considered those happy that were among them; and therefore they came over to them, as was foretold, Zech. viii. 23. *We will go with you, for we have heard,* we have seen, *that God is with you, the shield of your help, and the sword of your excellency,* Deut. xxxiii. 29. When the church prospers, and is smiled upon, many will come into it that will be shy of it when it is in trouble. (2.) They thought them formidable, and considered those miserable that were against them. They plainly saw in Haman's fate that, if any offered injury to the Jews, it was at their peril; and therefore, for their own security, they joined themselves to them. It is folly to think of contending with the God of Israel, and therefore it is wisdom to think of submitting to him.

CHAP. IX.

We left two royal edicts in force, both given at the court of Shushan, one bearing date the thirteenth day of the first month, appointing that on the thirteenth day of the twelfth month then next ensuing all the Jews should be killed; another bearing date the twenty-third day of the third month, empowering the Jews, on the day appointed for their slaughter, to draw the sword in their own defence and make their part good against their enemies as well as they could. Great expectation there was, no doubt, of this day, and the issue of it. The Jews' cause was to be tried by battle and the day was fixed for the combat by authority. Their enemies resolved not to lose the advantages given them by the first edict, in hope to overpower them by numbers; the Jews relied on the goodness of their God and the justice of their cause, and resolved to make their utmost efforts against their enemies. The day comes at length; and here we are told, I. What a glorious day it was, that year, to the Jews, and the two days following—a day of victory and triumph, both in the city Shushan and in all the rest of the king's provinces, ver. 1—19. II. What a memorable day it was made to posterity, by an annual feast, in commemoration of this great deliverance, called "the feast of Purim," ver. 20—32.

NOW in the twelfth month, that *is,* the month Adar, on the thirteenth day of the same, when the king's commandment and his decree drew near to be put in execution, in the day that the enemies of the Jews hoped to have power over them, (though it was turned to the contrary, that the Jews had rule over them that hated them;) 2 The Jews gathered themselves together in their cities throughout all the provinces of the king Ahasuerus, to lay hand on such as sought their hurt: and no man could withstand them; for the fear of them fell upon all people. 3 And all the rulers of the provinces, and the lieutenants, and the deputies, and officers of the king, helped the Jews; because the fear of Mordecai fell upon them. 4 For Mordecai *was* great in the king's house, and his fame went out throughout all the provinces: for this man Mordecai waxed greater and greater. 5 Thus the Jews smote all their enemies with the stroke of the sword, and slaughter, and destruction, and did what they would unto those that hated them. 6 And in Shushan the palace the Jews slew and destroyed five hundred men. 7 And Parshandatha, and Dalphon, and Aspatha, 8 And Poratha, and Adalia, and Aridatha, 9 And Parmashta, and Arisai, and Aridai, and Vajezatha, 10 The ten sons of Haman the son of Hammedatha, the enemy of the Jews, slew they; but on the spoil laid they not their hand. 11 On that day the number of those that were slain in Shushan the palace was brought before the king. 12 And the king said unto Esther the queen, The Jews have slain and destroyed five hundred men in Shushan the palace, and the ten sons of Haman; what have they done in the rest of the king's provinces? now what *is* thy petition? and it shall be granted thee: or what *is* thy request further? and it shall be done. 13 Then said Esther, If it please the king, let it be granted to the Jews which *are* in Shushan to do to morrow also according unto this day's decree, and let Haman's ten sons be hanged upon the gallows. 14 And the king commanded it so to be done: and the decree was given at Shushan; and they hanged Haman's ten sons. 15 For the Jews that *were* in Shushan gathered themselves together on the fourteenth day also of the month Adar, and slew three hundred men at Shushan; but on the prey they laid not their hand. 16 But the other Jews that *were* in the king's provinces gathered themselves together, and stood for their lives, and had rest from their enemies, and slew of their foes seventy and five thousand, but they laid not their hands on the prey, 17 On the thirteenth day of the month Adar; and on the fourteenth day of the same rested they, and made it a day of feasting and gladness. 18 But the Jews that *were* at Shushan assembled together on the thirteenth *day* thereof, and on the fourteenth thereof; and on the fifteenth *day* of the same they rested, and made it a day of feasting and gladness. 19 Therefore the Jews of the villages, that dwelt in the unwalled towns, made the fourteenth day of the month Adar *a day of* gladness and feasting, and a good day, and of sending portions one to another.

We have here a decisive battle fought between the Jews and their enemies, in which the Jews were victorious. Neither side was surprised; for both had notice of it long enough before, so that it was a fair trial of skill between them. Nor could either side call the other *rebels*, for they were both supported by the royal authority.

I. The enemies of the Jews were the aggressors. They hoped, notwithstanding the latter edict, *to have power over them*, by virtue of the former (*v.* 1), and made assaults upon them accordingly; they formed themselves into bodies, and joined in confederacy against them, to *seek their hurt*, *v.* 2. The Chaldee paraphrase says that none appeared against the Jews but Amalekites only, who were infatuated, and had their hearts hardened, as Pharaoh's against Israel, to take up arms to their own destruction. Some had such an inveterate implacable malice against the Jews that Haman's fall and Mordecai's advancement, instead of convincing them, did but exasperate them, and make them the more outrageous and resolute to cut all their throats. The sons of Haman, particularly, vowed to avenge their father's death, and pursue his designs, which they call *noble and brave*, whatever hazards they run; and a strong party they had formed both in Shushan and in the provinces in order hereunto. Fight they would, though they plainly saw Providence fight against them; and thus they were infatuated to their own destruction. If they would have sat still, and attempted nothing against the people of God, not a hair of their head would have fallen to the ground: but they cannot persuade themselves to do that; they must be meddling, though it prove to their own ruin, and roll a burdensome stone, which will return upon them.

II. But the Jews were the conquerors. That very day when the king's decree for their destruction was to be put in execution, and which the enemies thought would have been *their* day, proved *God's* day, Ps. xxxvii. 13. It was *turned to the contrary* of what was expected, and *the Jews had rule over those that hated them, v.* 1. We are here told,

1. What the Jews did for themselves (*v.* 2): *They gathered themselves together in their cities,* embodied, and stood upon their defence, offering violence to none, but bidding defiance to all. If they had not had an edict to warrant them, they durst not have done it, but, being so supported, they strove lawfully. Had they acted separately, each family apart, they would have been an easy prey to their enemies; but acting in concert, and gathering together in their cities, they strengthened one another, and durst face their enemies. *Vis unita fortior—forces act most powerfully when combined.* Those that write of the state of the Jews at this day give this as a reason why, though they are very numerous in many parts, and very rich, they are yet so despicable, because they are generally so selfish that they cannot incorporate, and, being under the curse of dispersion, they cannot unite, nor (as here) *gather together*, for, if they could, they might with their numbers and wealth threaten the most potent states.

2. What the rulers of the provinces did for them, under the influence of Mordecai. All the officers of the king, who, by the bloody edict, were ordered to help forward their destruction (*ch.* iii. 12, 13), conformed to the latter edict (which, being an estopel against an estopel, had set the matter at large, and left them at liberty to observe which they pleased) and *helped the Jews,* which turned the scale on their side, *v.* 3. The provinces would generally do as the rulers of the provinces inclined, and therefore their favouring the Jews would greatly further them. But why did they help them? Not because they had any kindness for them, but because *the fear of Mordecai fell upon them,* he having manifestly the countenance both of God and the king. They all saw it their interest to help Mordecai's friends because he was not only great in the king's house, and caressed by the courtiers (as many are who have no intrinsic worth to support their reputation), but *his fame* for wisdom and virtue *went out* thence *throughout all the provinces:* in all places he was extolled as a great man. He was looked upon also as a thriving man, and one that *waxed greater and greater* (*v.* 4), and therefore for fear of him all the king's officers helped the Jews. Great men may, by their influence, do a great deal of good; many that fear not God will stand in awe of them.

3. What God did for them: he struck *all people* with a *fear of them* (*v.* 2), as the Canaanites were made afraid of Israel (Josh. ii. 9, v. 1), so that, though they had so much hardiness as to assault them, yet they had not courage to prosecute the assault. Their hearts failed them when they came to engage, and *none of the men of might could find their hands.*

4. What execution they did hereupon: *No man could withstand them* (*v.* 2), but *they did what they would to those that hated them, v.* 5. So strangely were the Jews strengthened and animated, and their enemies weakened and dispirited, that none of those who had marked themselves for their destruction escaped, but they *smote them with the stroke of the sword.* Particularly, (1.) On the thirteenth day of the month Adar they slew in the city Shushan 500 men (*v.* 6) and the ten sons of *Haman, v.* 10. The Jews, when on the feast of Purim they read this book of Esther, oblige themselves to read the names of Haman's ten sons all in one breath, without any pause, because they say that they were all killed together, and all gave up the ghost just in the same moment. —*Buxt. Synag. Jud. c.* 24. The Chaldee paraphrase says that, when these ten were slain, Zeresh, with seventy more of his children, escaped, and afterwards begged their bread from door to door. (2.) On the fourteenth day they slew in Shushan 300 more, who had escaped the sword on the former day of execution, *v.* 15. This Esther obtained leave of the king for them to do, for the greater terror of their enemies, and the utter crushing of that malignant party of men. The king had taken account of the numbers that were put to the sword the first day (*v.* 11), and told Esther (*v.* 12), and asked her what more she desired. "Nothing," says she, "but commission to do such another day's work." Esther surely was none of the blood-thirsty, none of those that delight in slaughter, but she had some very good reasons that moved her to make this request. She also desired that the dead bodies of Haman's ten sons might be hanged up on the gallows on which their father was hanged, for the greater disgrace of the family and terror of the party (*v.* 13), and it was done accordingly, *v.* 14. It is supposed that they were hanged in chains and left hanging for some time. (3.) The Jews in the country kept to their orders, and slew no more of their enemies than what were slain the thirteenth day, which were in all, among all the provinces, 75,000, *v.* 16. If all these were Amalekites (as the Jews say), surely now it was that the remembrance of Amalek was *utterly put out,* Exod. xvii. 14. However, that which justifies them in the execution of so many is that they did it in their own just and necessary defence; they

stood for their lives, authorized to do so by the law of self-preservation, as well as by the king's decree. (4.) In these several executions it is taken notice of that on the prey they laid not their hand, *v.* 10, 15, 16. The king's commission had warranted them to *take the spoil* of their enemies *for a prey* (*ch.* viii. 11), and a fair opportunity they had of enriching themselves with it; if Haman's party had prevailed, no doubt, they would have made use of their authority to seize the goods and estates of the Jews, *ch.* iii. 13. But the Jews would not do so by them, [1.] That they might, to the honour of their religion, evidence a holy and generous contempt of worldly wealth, in imitation of their father Abraham, who scorned to enrich himself with the spoils of Sodom. [2.] That they might make it to appear that they aimed at nothing but their own preservation, and used their interest at court for the saving of their lives, not for the raising of their estates. [3.] Their commission empowered them to destroy the families of their enemies, even the *little ones* and *the women, ch.* viii. 11. But their humanity forbade them to do that, though that was designed against them. They slew none but those they found in arms; and therefore they did not take the spoil, but left it to the women and little ones, whom they spared, for their subsistence; otherwise as good slay them as starve them, take away their lives as take away their livelihoods. Herein they acted with a consideration and compassion well worthy imitation.

5. What a satisfaction they had in their deliverance. The Jews in the country cleared themselves of their enemies on the thirteenth day of the month, and they rested on the fourteenth day (*v.* 17), and made that a thanksgiving day, *v.* 19. The Jews in Shushan, the royal city, took two days for their military execution, so that they rested on the fifteenth day, and made that their thanksgiving-day, *v.* 18. Both of them celebrated their festival the very day after they had finished their work and gained their point. When we have received signal mercies from God we ought to be quick and speedy in making our thankful returns to him, while the mercy is fresh and the impressions of it are most sensible.

20 And Mordecai wrote these things, and sent letters unto all the Jews that *were* in all the provinces of the king Ahasuerus, *both* nigh and far, 21 To stablish *this* among them, that they should keep the fourteenth day of the month Adar, and the fifteenth day of the same, yearly, 22 As the days wherein the Jews rested from their enemies, and the month which was turned unto them from sorrow to joy, and from mourning into a good day: that they should make them days of feasting and joy, and of sending portions one to another, and gifts to the poor. 23 And the Jews undertook to do as they had begun, and as Mordecai had written unto them; 24 Because Haman the son of Hammedatha, the Agagite, the enemy of all the Jews, had devised against the Jews to destroy them, and had cast Pur, that *is*, the lot, to consume them, and to destroy them; 25 But when *Esther* came before the king, he commanded by letters that his wicked device, which he devised against the Jews, should return upon his own head, and that he and his sons should be hanged on the gallows. 26 Wherefore they called these days Purim after the name of Pur. Therefore for all the words of this letter, and *of that* which they had seen concerning this matter, and which had come unto them, 27 The Jews ordained, and took upon them, and upon their seed, and upon all such as joined themselves unto them, so as it should not fail, that they would keep these two days according to their writing, and according to their *appointed* time every year; 28 And *that* these days *should be* remembered and kept throughout every generation, every family, every province, and every city; and *that* these days of Purim should not fail from among the Jews, nor the memorial of them perish from their seed. 29 Then Esther the queen, the daughter of Abihail, and Mordecai the Jew, wrote with all authority, to confirm this second letter of Purim. 30 And he sent the letters unto all the Jews, to the hundred twenty and seven provinces of the kingdom of Ahasuerus, *with* words of peace and truth, 31 To confirm these days of Purim in their times *appointed*, according as Mordecai the Jew and Esther the queen had enjoined them, and as they had decreed for themselves and for their seed, the matters of the fastings and their cry. 32 And the decree of Esther confirmed these matters of Purim; and it was written in the book.

We may well imagine how much affected

Mordecai and Esther were with the triumphs of the Jews over their enemies, and how they saw the issue of that decisive day with a satisfaction proportionable to the care and concern with which they expected it. How were their hearts enlarged with joy in God and his salvation, and what new songs of praise were put into their mouths! But here we are told what course they took to spread the knowledge of it among their people, and to perpetuate the remembrance of it to posterity, for the honour of God and the encouragement of his people to trust in him at all times.

I. The history was written, and copies of it were dispersed among all the Jews in all the provinces of the empire, *both nigh and far*, *v.* 20. They all knew something of the story, being nearly concerned in it—were by the first edict made sensible of their danger and by the second of their deliverance; but how this amazing turn was given they could not tell. Mordecai therefore *wrote all these things*. And if this book be the same that he wrote, as many think it is, I cannot but observe what a difference there is between Mordecai's style and Nehemiah's. Nehemiah, at every turn, takes notice of divine Providence and the *good hand of his God* upon him, which is very proper to stir up devout affections in the minds of his readers; but Mordecai never so much as mentions the name of God in the whole story. Nehemiah wrote his book at Jerusalem, where religion was in fashion and an air of it appeared in men's common conversation; Mordecai wrote his at Shushan the palace, where policy reigned more than piety, and he wrote according to the genius of the place. Even those that have the root of the matter in them are apt to lose the savour of religion, and let their leaf wither, when they converse wholly with those that have little religion. Commend me to Nehemiah's way of writing; *that* I would imitate, and yet learn from Mordecai's that men may be truly devout though they do not abound in the shows and expressions of devotion, and therefore that we must not judge nor despise our brethren. But, because there is so little of the language of Canaan in this book, many think it was not written by Mordecai, but was an extract out of the journals of the kings of Persia, giving an account of the matter of fact, which the Jews themselves knew how to comment upon.

II. A festival was instituted, to be observed yearly from generation to generation by the Jews, in remembrance of this wonderful work which God wrought for them, that *the children who should be born* might know it, and *declare it to their children, that they might set their hope in God*, Ps. lxxviii. 6, 7. It would be for the honour of God as the protector of his people, and the honour of Israel as the care of Heaven, a confirmation of the fidelity of God's covenant, an invitation to strangers to come into the bonds of it, and an encouragement to God's own people cheerfully to depend upon his wisdom, power, and goodness, in the greatest straits. Posterity would reap the benefit of this deliverance, and therefore ought to celebrate the memorial of it. Now concerning this festival we are here told,

1. When it was observed—every year on *the fourteenth and fifteenth days of the twelfth month*, just a month before the passover, *v.* 21. Thus the first month and the last month of the year kept in remembrance the months that were past, even *the days when God preserved them*. They kept two days together as thanksgiving days, and did not think them too much to spend in praising God. Let us not be niggardly in our returns of praise to him who bestows his favours so liberally upon us. Observe, They did not keep the day when they fought, but the days when they rested. On the fourteenth day country-Jews rested, and on the fifteenth those in Shushan, and both those days they kept. The sabbath was appointed not on the day that God finished his work, but on the day that he *rested from it*. The modern Jews observe the thirteenth day, the day appointed for their destruction, as a fasting-day, grounding the practice on *v.* 31, *the matters of their fastings and cry*. But that refers to what was in the day of their distress (*ch.* iv. 3, 16), which was not to be continued when God had turned their fasts into *joy and gladness*, Zech. viii. 19.

2. How it was called—*The feast of Purim* (*v.* 26), from *Pur*, a Persian word which signifies *a lot*, because Haman had by lot determined this to be the time of the Jews' destruction, but the Lord, at whose disposal the lot is, had determined it to be the time of their triumph. The name of this festival would remind them of the sovereign dominion of the God of Israel, who served his own purposes by the foolish superstitions of the heathen, and outwitted the *monthly prognosticators* in their own craft (Isa. xlvii. 13), *frustrating the tokens of the liars and making the diviners mad*, Isa. xliv. 25, 26.

3. By whom it was instituted and enacted. It was not a divine institution, and therefore it is not called a *holy day*, but a human appointment, by which it was made a *good day*, *v.* 19, 22. (1.) The Jews ordained it, and took it upon themselves (*v.* 27), voluntarily *undertook to do as they had begun*, *v.* 23. They bound themselves to this by common consent. (2.) Mordecai and Esther confirmed their resolve, that it might be the more binding on posterity, and might come well recommended by those great names. They *wrote*, [1.] *With all authority* (*v.* 29), as well they might, Esther being queen and Mordecai prime-minister of state. It is well when those who are in authority use their authority to authorize that which is good. [2.] *With words of peace and truth*. Though they wrote with authority, they wrote with tenderness,

not imperious, not imposing, but in such language as the council at Jerusalem use in their decree (Acts xv. 29): "If you do so and so, *you shall do well. Fare you well.*" Such was the style of these letters, or such the salutation or valediction of them: *Peace and truth be with you.*

4. By whom it was to be observed—by *all the Jews,* and by *their seed,* and by all such as *joined themselves to them, v.* 27. The observance of this feast was to be both universal and perpetual; the proselytes must observe it, in token of their sincere affection to the Jewish nation and their having united interests with them. A concurrence in joys and praises is one branch of the communion of saints.

5. Why it was to be observed—that the memorial of the great things God had done for his church might never *perish from their seed, v.* 28. God does not work wonders for a day, but to be had in everlasting remembrance. *What he does shall be for ever,* and therefore should for ever be had in mind, Eccl. iii. 14. In this affair they would remember, (1.) Haman's bad practices against the church, to his perpetual reproach (*v.* 24): *Because he had devised against the Jews to destroy them.* Let this be kept in mind, that God's people may never be secure, while they have such malicious enemies, on whom they ought to have a jealous eye. Their enemies aim at no less than their destruction; on God therefore let them depend for salvation. (2.) Esther's good services to the church, to her immortal honour. When Esther, in peril of her life, *came before the king,* he repealed the edict, *v.* 25. This also must be remembered, that wherever this feast should be kept, and this history read in explication of it, this which she did might be *told for a memorial of her.* Good deeds done for the Israel of God ought to be remembered, for the encouragement of others to do the like. God will not forget them, and therefore we must not. (3.) Their own prayers, and the answers given to them (*v.* 31): *The matters of their fastings and their cry.* The more cries we have offered up in our trouble, and the more prayers for deliverance, the more we are obliged to be thankful to God for deliverance. *Call upon me in the time of trouble,* and then *offer to God thanksgiving.*

6. How it was to be observed. And of this let us see,

(1.) What was here enjoined, which was very good, that they should make it, [1.] A day of cheerfulness, *a day of feasting and joy* (*v.* 22), and *a feast was made for laughter,* Eccl. x. 19. When God gives us cause to rejoice why should we not express our joy? [2.] A day of generosity, *sending portions one to another,* in token of their pleasantness and mutual respect, and their being knit by this and other public common dangers and deliverances so much the closer to each other in love. Friends have their goods in common. [3.] A day of charity, sending *gifts to the poor.* It is not to our kinsmen and rich neighbours only that we are to send tokens, but to *the poor and the maimed,* Luke xiv. 12, 13. Those that have received mercy must, in token of their gratitude, show mercy; and there never wants occasion, for the poor we have always with us. Thanksgiving and almsgiving should go together, that, when we are rejoicing and blessing God, the heart of the poor may rejoice with us and their loins may bless us.

(2.) What was added to this, which was much better. They always, at the feast, read the whole story over in the synagogue each day, and put up three prayers to God, in the first of which they praise God for counting them worthy to attend this divine service; in the second they thank him for the miraculous preservation of their ancestors; in the third they praise him that they have lived to observe another festival in memory of it. So bishop Patrick.

(3.) What it has since degenerated to, which is much worse. Their own writers acknowledge that this feast is commonly celebrated among them with gluttony, and drunkenness, and excess of riot. Their Talmud says expressly that, in the feast of Purim, a man should drink till he knows not the difference between *Cursed be Haman,* and *Blessed be Mordecai.* See what the corrupt and wicked nature of man often brings that to which was at first well intended: here is a religious feast turned into a carnival, a perfect revel, as wakes are among us. Nothing more purifies the heart and adorns religion than holy joy; nothing more pollutes the heart and reproaches religion than carnal mirth and sensual pleasure. *Corruptio optimi est pessima—What is best becomes when corrupted the worst.*

CHAP. X.

This is but a part of a chapter; the rest of it, beginning at ver. 4, with six chapters more, being found only in the Greek, is rejected as apocryphal. In these three verses we have only some short hints, I. Concerning Ahasuerus in the throne, what a mighty prince he was, ver. 1, 2. II. Concerning Mordecai his favourite, what a distinguished blessing he was to his people, ver. 2, 3.

AND the king Ahasuerus laid a tribute upon the land, and *upon* the isles of the sea. 2 And all the acts of his power and of his might, and the declaration of the greatness of Mordecai, whereunto the king advanced him, *are* they not written in the book of the chronicles of the kings of Media and Persia? 3 For Mordecai the Jew *was* next unto king Ahasuerus, and great among the Jews, and accepted of the multitude of his brethren, seeking the wealth of his people, and speaking peace to all his seed.

We are here told,

I. How great and powerful king Ahasuerus was. He had a vast dominion, both in the continent and among the islands, from which he raised a vast revenue. Besides the usual customs which the kings of Persia exacted (Ezra iv. 13), he laid an additional tribute upon his subjects, to serve for some great occasion he had for money (*v.* 1): *The king laid a tribute.* Happy is our island, that pays no tribute but what is laid upon it by its representatives, and those of its own choosing, and is not squeezed or oppressed by an arbitrary power, as some of the neighbouring nations are. Besides this instance of the grandeur of Ahasuerus, many more might be given, that were *acts of his power and of his might.* These however are not thought fit to be recorded here in the sacred story, which is confined to the Jews, and relates the affairs of other nations only as they fell in with their affairs; but they are *written in the Persian chronicles* (*v.* 2), which are long since lost and buried in oblivion, while the sacred writings live, live in honour, and will live till time shall be no more. When the *kingdoms of men,* monarchs and monarchies, are destroyed, and *their memorial has perished with them* (Ps. ix. 6), the kingdom of God among men, and the records of that kingdom, shall remain and be *as the days of heaven,* Dan. ii. 44.

II. How great and good Mordecai was.

1. He was great; and it does one od to see virtue and piety thus in honour. (1.) He was great with the king, next to him, as one he most delighted and confided in. Long had Mordecai sat contentedly in the king's gate, and now at length he is advanced to the head of his council-board. Men of merit may for a time seem buried alive; but often, by some means or other, they are discovered and preferred at last. The declaration of the greatness to which the king advanced Mordecai was *written in the chronicles of the kingdom,* as very memorable, and contributing to the great achievements of the king. He never did such acts of power as he did when Mordecai was his right hand. (2.) He was *great among the Jews* (*v.* 3), not only great above them, more honourable than any of them, but great with them, dear to them, familiar with them, and much respected by them. So far were they from envying his preferment that they rejoiced in it, and added to it by giving him a commanding interest among them and submitting all their affairs to his direction.

2. He was good, very good, for he di good. This goodness made him truly great, and then his greatness gave him an opportunity of doing so much the more good. When the king advanced him, (1.) He did not disown his people the Jews, nor was he ashamed of his relation to them, though they were strangers and captives, dispersed and despised. Still he wrote himself *Mordecai the Jew,* and therefore no doubt adhered to the Jews' religion, by the observances of which he distinguished himself, and yet it was no hindrance to his preferment, nor looked upon as a blemish to him. (2.) He did not seek his own wealth, or the raising of an estate for himself and his family, which is the chief thing most aim at when they get into great places at court; but he consulted the welfare of his people, and made it his business to advance that. His power, his wealth, and all his interest in the king and queen, he improved for the public good. (3.) He not only did good, but he did it in a humble condescending way, was easy of access, courteous and affable in his behaviour, and spoke peace to all that made their application to him. Doing good works is the best and chief thing expected from those that have wealth and power; but giving good words is also commendable, and makes the good deed the more acceptable. (4.) He did not side with any one party of his people against another, nor make some his favourites, while the rest were neglected and crushed; but, whatever differences there were among them, he was a common father to them all, recommended himself to *the multitude of his brethren,* not despising the crowd, and spoke peace *to all their seed,* without distinction. Thus making himself acceptable by humility and beneficence, he was universally accepted, and gained the good word of all his brethren. Thanks be to God, such a government as this we are blessed with, which *seeks the welfare of our people, speaking peace to all their seed.* God continue it long, very long, and grant us, under the happy protection and influence of it, to *live quiet and peaceable lives, in godliness, honesty,* and charity!